THE DICTIONARY

OF

STATISTICS

THE DICTIONARY

OF

STATISTICS

BY

MICHAEL G. MULHALL

FELLOW OF THE ROYAL STATISTICAL SOCIETY

MEMBER OF THE COMMITTEE OF THE BRITISH ASSOCIATION

HONORARY CORRESPONDING MEMBER OF THE ROYAL SCOTTISH GEOGRAPHICAL SOCIETY

AUTHOR OF "THE PROGRESS OF THE WORLD," "THE HISTORY OF PRICES,"

"INDUSTRIES AND WEALTH OF NATIONS," ETC.

"Je n'impose rien ; je ne propose même rien ; j'expose."—DUNOYER

FOURTH EDITION, REVISED TO NOVEMBER 1898

LONDON

GEORGE ROUTLEDGE AND SONS, LIMITED

1899

REPUBLISHED BY GALE RESEARCH COMPANY, BOOK TOWER, DETROIT, 1969

Library Congress Catalog Card Number 68–18013

TO

THE MOST IMPARTIAL OF CRITICS

AND THE BEST OF COUNSELLORS,

MY WIFE,

I Dedicate this Book.

PREFACE

TO THE FOURTH EDITION.

THE Dictionary in its present form is one of the largest statistical works ever published, and as regards its utility, there is strong proof in the fact that since the first edition was published, in 1884, no fewer than 6000 copies have been disposed of, chiefly among the libraries of Europe, United States, and the British Colonies. The volume is now greatly enlarged, and will be found to consist of two distinct parts, the first comprising all known statistical data from the time of the Emperor Diocletian down to the year 1890, the second embracing so far the final decade of the century.

All civilised nations now devote so much attention to statistics that the field of research becomes vaster year by year, and the work of condensation easier. But when a task of such magnitude devolves, as in the present case, upon a single individual, it cannot be accomplished with the same efficiency as if it were confided to an international bureau under a competent head. The nations of Europe have already seen the convenience of establishing at Berne an International Department of Telegraphs, and another for the Postal Union. It is not, therefore, chimerical to hope that an International Statistical Bureau may be one of the earliest institutions of the twentieth century, publishing every year (in English, French, and German) a Conspectus of the World, with comparative tables for each decade since 1850. I seize this opportunity to thank the various foreign Governments that send me their blue-books, showing thereby the interest which they take in my labours, and their readiness to promote the development of this branch of science.

It is to be deplored that the British Government is indifferent to a matter of this kind, as if international statistics were unimportant. The growth of banking business in Great Britain led to the establishment of Clearing-houses, the advantage of which is unquestionable. What we require is a Statistical Clearing-house, in combination with the rest of mankind: the expense would be a mere trifle, while the benefits to be derived would be immeasurable.

Meantime the Dictionary of Statistics is a step in the right direction, and the success which has attended it is a good omen.

MICHAEL G. MULHALL.

HOTEL BEAU SITE, ROME,
Feb. 2, 1899.

Opinions on the Author's Works.

"This admirable dictionary."—*Emile de Laveleye.*

"The quintessence of statistics."—*Leroy Beaulieu.*

"We want an edition in French."—*Yves Guyot.*

"His statistics are most reliable."—*Baron Malortie.*

"Mulhall's history of prices is accurate."—*Neumann Spallart.*

"His figures are remarkably correct."—*Report of the U. S. Secretary of State.*

"A German edition of the Dictionary would be useful."—*Tech. Blatt. Berlin.*

"As useful as the Census report."—*Graphic.*

"No books of reference have higher claims."—*Globe.*

"Display a vast amount of research."—*Times.*

"Remarkably well arranged and clear."—*Economist.*

"Inexhaustible treasury of facts."—*Economiste Français.*

"This wonderful work stands alone."—*Boston Beacon.*

"An unrivalled arrangement of statistics."—*Academy.*

"Books of reference as trustworthy as they are unique."—*Scotsman.*

"A boon to the student or public writer."—*Irish Times.*

"The result of laborious and skilled research."—*Contemporary Review.*

"Compiled in a convenient and intelligible form."—*Spectator.*

"Written with great care and intelligence."—*N. Y. Nation.*

"His works are well known to our readers."—*Revue des Deux Mondes.*

"Clear, accurate, and comprehensive."—*Toronto Globe.*

"They are a mine of facts."—*Weekly Register.*

"No library should be without them."—*Colonial Register.*

"Bring a vast number of facts within small compass."—*Daily News.*

"The model of a statistical work."—*Mark Lane Gazette.*

NOTE.

PART I., down to page 606, comprehends all statistics from the earliest times to 1890; Part II. since
1890.

Money, weights, and measures are in all cases
English.

Scandinavia includes Sweden, Norway, and Denmark ; Austria the whole Austrian monarchy ;
Acadia all the maritime provinces of Canada,
except Quebec.

DIAGRAMS.

DICTIONARY OF STATISTICS.

A

AEROLITES

Date	Locality	Weight (lbs.)	Remarks
1748	Yenisey . . .	1,600	...
1783	Gran Chaco . .	32,000	Near Tucuman.
1784	Bendego, Brazil	17,000	...
1793	Graf Reinet . .	300	South Africa.
1803	Normandy . .	...	2000 red-hot stones.
1812	Prague . . .	...	200 hot stones.
1829	Bohnmelitz . .	103	Bohemia.
1866	Kuyahinza . .	670	With 1000 smaller.
1870	Greenland . .	49,000	Now at Copenhagen.
1871	Greenland . .	20,000	Now at St. Petersburg.

The last two were found in the years expressed, but may have fallen centuries ago. That of Gran Chaco is 95 per cent. iron. The British Museum has an aerolite weighing five tons.

AGE

The age of various nations in ratios of 1000 was stated by Wappaeus in 1850 thus :—

Age	France	Belgium	Holland	Denmark	Norway	Sweden	Italy	Canada
Under 5	93	116	113	125	135	126	119	183
5–10	92	109	111	108	114	107	114	144
10–15	88	98	108	95	100	96	107	122
15–20	88	90	93	95	86	98	101	116
20–30	163	166	174	181	174	177	168	169
30–40	148	135	134	130	136	135	134	106
40–50	125	118	106	109	88	100	105	74
50–60	102	78	82	75	78	83	78	47
60–70	65	55	49	53	57	51	51	24
Over 70	36	35	30	29	32	27	23	15
Total	1,000	1,000	1,000	1,000	1,000	1,000	1,000	1,000

The classification by the Bureau of Statistics in 1864 was as follows :—

Age	England	France	Belgium	Portugal	Spain	Italy	Medium
Under 10	251	186	206	241	249	244	229
10–20	201	169	191	185	193	192	189
20–30	169	164	165	168	171	170	168
30–40	130	144	140	142	151	143	142
40–50	103	125	116	115	107	107	112
50–60	71	101	94	78	72	79	82
60–70	47	72	55	49	42	44	52
Over 70	28	39	33	22	15	21	26
Total	1,000	1,000	1,000	1,000	1,000	1,000	1,000

According to the Bulletin Statistique the ratios in 1876 stood thus :—

Age	France	Belgium	Holland	Prussia	Sweden	Italy	Spain	Switzerland	Hungary
Under 15	272	302	329	353	323	323	348	315	372
15–60	610	610	591	577	597	595	590	595	579
Over 60	118	88	80	70	80	82	62	90	49
Total	1,000	1,000	1,000	1,000	1,000	1,000	1,000	1,000	1,000

The following table of age ratios in 1000 of population is from Census reports of the various nations :—

Country	Date	Under 5 Yrs.	5–20	20–40	40–60	Over 60
England . . .	1881	136	326	297	169	72
Scotland . . .	1881	137	331	290	165	77
Ireland . . .	1881	111	348	263	172	106
United Kingdom	1881	131	331	292	169	77
France . . .	1881	92	261	295	226	126
Prussia . . .	1880	139	315	290	180	76
Germany . . .	1871	127	308	298	190	77
Austria . . .	1880	132	304	298	195	71
Russia	1875	138	318	318	180	46
Finland . . .	1870	144	299	296	186	75
Italy	1871	123	293	306	196	82
Spain	1866	142	278	343	179	58
Portugal . . .	1864	137	289	310	193	71
Sweden . . .	1870	118	313	312	183	78
Norway . . .	1870	135	299	310	166	90
Denmark . . .	1870	125	297	310	184	84
Belgium . . .	1880	124	304	282	195	95
Holland . . .	1870	113	314	309	187	77
Switzerland . .	1880	117	296	289	209	89
Greece	1870	144	332	320	148	56
Brazil	1870	108	353	306	146	87
United States .	1880	137	342	310	155	56
Average . .	...	128	308	306	182	76

In the above table it will be observed that the lowest ratios of children are in France, Brazil, and Ireland. This is explained in the case of Ireland by the fact that the marriage rate is the lowest in the world. Moreover, the highest ratios for people over 60 years are in France and Ireland. The countries in which children form the largest ratios are Finland, Greece, and Spain, although the birth-rates in those countries are by no means the highest ; it is explained in the case of Greece and Spain by the short span of life, the proportion of persons passing their sixtieth year, as shown above, being very low.

Another distribution is as follows :—

Age.	France	Prussia	Austria Proper	Russia	Italy	Sweden	Belgium	Switzer-land	United States	Average
Under 10	183	254	240	253	226	234	236	222	262	234
10–20	170	200	196	203	190	197	192	191	217	195
20–30	158	162	159	188	167	152	155	153	183	164
30–40	137	128	139	130	139	130	127	136	127	133
40–50	123	101	109	99	111	119	108	116	93	109
50–60	103	79	86	81	85	90	87	93	62	85
Over 60	126	76	71	46	82	78	95	89	56	80
Total	1,000	1,000	1,000	1,000	1,000	1,000	1,000	1,000	1,000	1,000

AVERAGE AGE OF ALL LIVING IN EACH COUNTRY
Years

England 26.0 | Prussia 27.1 | Sweden . 28.3 | Portugal 27.6
Scotland 26.0 | Austria 27.6 | Belgium . 28.8 | Norway 28.0
Ireland 27.5 | Russia 25.6 | Switzerland 29.2 | Denmark 28.0
France . 32.6 | Italy . 28.5 | U. States . 25.0 | Greece . 25.2
Holland 28.0 | Spain 26.9 | Brazil . . 27.0 | Average 27.5

MALES OF WORKING AGE

If we assume the working age to be from 20 to 60 years, and count only male workers, the number of population dependent on the earnings of every 100 male adults would be as follows :—

France . . 387 | Belgium . . 418 | U. States . . 440
Spain . . . 388 | Sweden . . 420 | U. Kingdom 448
Austria . . 413 | Italy . . . 424 | Scotland . . 463
Germany . . 417 | England . . 438 | Ireland . . 476

The burden on the working population in Ireland is 10 per cent. heavier than in England, 23 per cent. heavier than in France.

VARIOUS CITIES

Age	London	Paris	St. Peters-burg	Prague	Liverpool	Man-chester	Birming-ham
Under 5	130	71	69	83	134	135	139
5–20	297	216	233	265	268	312	327
20–40	334	398	301	365	337	330	310
40–60	177	242	283	202	174	171	168
Over 60	62	73	114	85	87	52	56
Total	1,000	1,000	1,000	1,000	1,000	1,000	1,000

UNITED KINGDOM

The ratios for the three kingdoms by Census reports were :—

Age	England 1841	England 1881	Scotland 1841	Scotland 1881	Ireland 1841	Ireland 1881
Under 5 . . .	132	136	130	137	126	111
5–10	120	121	118	121	132	120
10–15	108	108	112	108	124	119
15–20	100	98	104	101	108	108
20–25	97	90	100	92	96	92
25–35	154	146	153	141	145	122
35–45	112	112	110	109	106	108
45–55	80	84	76	82	75	86
55–65	53	59	52	59	54	70
Over 65 . . .	44	46	45	50	34	64
Total . .	1,000	1,000	1,000	1,000	1,000	1,000

The composition of the population of England and Wales as regards sex and age in 1881 compares with 1841 thus :—

Age	Per 1000 Inhabitants 1841			1881		
	Males	Females	Total	Males	Females	Total
Under 5	66	66	132	68	68	136
5–15	115	113	228	114	115	229
15–25	94	103	197	92	96	188
25–35	74	80	154	70	76	146
35–45	55	57	112	54	58	112
45–55	39	41	80	40	44	84
Over 55	46	51	97	49	56	105
Total	489	511	1,000	487	513	1,000

The composition of Scotland in the same year was as follows :—

Age	1841			1881		
	Males	Females	Total	Males	Females	Total
Under 5	66	64	130	69	68	137
5–15	117	113	230	116	113	229
15–25	97	107	204	96	97	193
25–35	72	81	153	67	74	141
35–45	51	59	110	50	59	109
45–55	35	41	76	37	45	82
Over 55	42	55	97	46	63	109
Total	480	520	1,000	481	519	1,000

The population of Ireland was composed as follows :—

Age	Per 1000 Inhabitants 1841			1881		
	Males	Females	Total	Males	Females	Total
Under 5	64	62	126	56	55	111
5–15	130	126	256	122	117	239
15–25	99	105	204	98	102	200
25–35	69	76	145	57	65	122
35–45	51	55	106	51	57	108
45–55	36	39	75	41	45	86
Over 55	43	45	88	65	69	134
Total	492	508	1,000	490	510	1,000

The composition of the United Kingdom was as follows :—

Age	1841			1881		
	Males	Females	Total	Males	Females	Total
0–15	186	182	368	182	181	363
15–45	221	238	459	214	229	443
45–55	38	40	78	40	44	84
Over 55	46	49	95	51	59	110
Total	491	509	1,000	487	513	1,000

FRANCE

The effects of the Franco-Prussian War (1870–71) are visible in the diminished ratio of population of the age 15 to 60 in the Census returns of 1872.

The following table includes males and females :—

Age	1851	1861	1866	1872	1876	1881
Under 15 . .	282	275	272	279	272	266
15–60 . . .	618	619	617	606	610	608
Over 60. . .	100	106	111	115	118	126
Total . .	1,000	1,000	1,000	1,000	1,000	1,000

The composition of the population of France as regards sex and age in 1881 compared with 1851 as follows :—

Age	Per 1000 Inhabitants					
	1851			1881		
	Males	Females	Total	Males	Females	Total
Under 5	47	46	93	46	46	92
5–15	92	88	180	88	86	174
15–25	85	86	171	88	90	178
25–35	78	78	156	70	68	138
35–45	69	68	137	67	65	132
45–55	59	58	117	56	58	114
Over 55	67	79	146	84	88	172
Total	497	503	1,000	499	501	1,000

There is a marked decline in men and women of the best age, as shown thus :—

	Ratio per 1000 Inhabitants	
	1851	1881
Men between 15 and 55 . . .	291	281
Women between 15 and 45 . .	232	223

GERMANY (1885)

Years	Prussia	Bavaria	Saxony	All Germany
0–5	134	124	135	131
5–10	119	115	117	118
10–15	106	105	105	106
15–20	95	92	96	94
20–30	163	148	171	161
30–40	127	125	133	126
40–50	103	111	100	106
50–60	75	86	73	77
60–70	53	62	49	55
Over 70	25	32	21	26
	1,000	1,000	1,000	1,000

In Prussia in 1867 the average age of the inhabitants was as follows :—

	Years	
	Males	*Females*
Unmarried	14.9	14.7
Married	44.2	40.8
Widowed	61.5	58.2

The composition of the population of Prussia as to sex and age in 1880 compared with 1843 thus :—

Age	Per 1000 Inhabitants					
	1843			1880		
	Males	Females	Total	Males	Females	Total
Under 5	76	74	150	70	69	139
5–15	99	97	196	110	109	219
15–45	242	242	484	216	225	441
45–60	54	58	112	60	65	125
Over 60	28	30	58	36	40	76
Total	499	501	1,000	492	508	1,000

Males (1885)

Age	Prussia	Bavaria	Saxony	Wurtemberg	Minor States	Total
0–5	1,880,000	330,000	210,000	125,000	475,000	3,020,000
5–10	1,700,000	310,000	185,000	120,000	455,000	2,770,000
10–15	1,520,000	280,000	165,000	110,000	420,000	2,495,000
15–20	1,350,000	250,000	150,000	90,000	365,000	2,205,000
20–30	2,260,000	390,000	260,000	130,000	645,000	3,685,000
30–40	1,760,000	330,000	210,000	115,000	485,000	2,900,000
40–50	1,410,000	290,000	150,000	110,000	430,000	2,390,000
50–60	1,005,000	220,000	110,000	75,000	300,000	1,710,000
60–70	700,000	160,000	70,000	55,000	205,000	1,190,000
70–80	270,000	70,000	25,000	25,000	90,000	480,000
Over 80	40,000	10,000	5,000	5,000	30,000	90,000
Total	13,895,000	2,640,000	1,540,000	960,000	3,900,000	22,935,000

Females

Age	Prussia	Bavaria	Saxony	Wurtemberg	Minor States	Total
0–5	1,850,000	335,000	210,000	125,000	490,000	3,010,000
5–10	1,690,000	315,000	190,000	125,000	450,000	2,770,000
10–15	1,505,000	290,000	170,000	115,000	415,000	2,495,000
15–20	1,355,000	255,000	155,000	95,000	375,000	2,235,000
20–30	2,370,000	410,000	280,000	145,000	630,000	3,835,000
30–40	1,840,000	350,000	215,000	125,000	515,000	3,045,000
40–50	1,510,000	310,000	165,000	120,000	450,000	2,555,000
50–60	1,120,000	240,000	125,000	85,000	340,000	1,910,000
60–70	805,000	180,000	85,000	60,000	245,000	1,375,000
70–80	320,000	80,000	35,000	30,000	105,000	570,000
Over 80	55,000	15,000	10,000	5,000	35,000	120,000
Total	14,420,000	2,780,000	1,640,000	1,030,000	4,050,000	23,920,000

RUSSIA

The ratios of age, with distinction of sex, were in 1875 as follows :—

Age	Urban		Rural	
	Males	Females	Males	Females
Under 5	108	114	146	138
5–10	89	96	120	115
10–20	228	206	208	194
20–40	358	337	305	322
40–60	166	182	176	186
Over 60	51	65	45	45
Total	1,000	1,000	1,000	1,000

AUSTRIA

The population of Austria (without Hungary) was composed as to age and sex in the Census of 1880 thus :—

Age	Per 1000 Inhabitants		
	Males	Females	Total
Under 5	65	66	131
5–15	103	104	207
15–30	125	131	256
30–45	94	101	195
45–60	63	70	133
Over 60	39	39	78
Total	489	511	1,000

The following table shows the actual number of persons of either sex at the different ages.

Age	Males	Females	Total
0–5	1,450,000	1,465,000	2,915,000
5–10	1,210,000	1,210,000	2,420,000
10–15	1,090,000	1,105,000	2,195,000
15–20	1,020,000	1,065,000	2,085,000
20–30	1,750,000	1,835,000	3,585,000
30–40	1,440,000	1,530,000	2,970,000
40–50	1,180,000	1,270,000	2,450,000
50–60	865,000	975,000	1,840,000
60–70	570,000	610,000	1,180,000
70–80	210,000	220,000	430,000
Over 80	35,000	45,000	80,000
Total	10,820,000	11,325,000	22,145,000

The following table, likewise taken from the Census of 1880, shows the age of married, single, and widowed persons.

Age	Married	Single	Widowed	Total
0–20	50,000	9,560,000	...	9,610,000
20–25	405,000	1,535,000	5,000	1,945,000
25–30	905,000	720,000	15,000	1,640,000
30–40	2,260,000	625,000	85,000	2,970,000
40–50	1,935,000	330,000	185,000	2,450,000
50–60	1,305,000	220,000	315,000	1,840,000
60–70	670,000	140,000	370,000	1,180,000
70–80	165,000	50,000	215,000	430,000
Over 80	20,000	10,000	50,000	80,000
Total	7,715,000	13,190,000	1,240,000	22,145,000

ITALY

In 1871 the population was composed as follows :—

Age	Per 1000 Inhabitants		
	Males	Females	Total
Under 5	62	61	123
5–15	101	99	200
15–25	90	90	180
25–35	76	76	152
35–45	64	61	125
45–55	50	49	99
Over 55	59	62	121
Total	502	498	1,000

In 1879 the urban population was 8,824,000, in a total of 28,437,000, say, 31 per cent.

SWITZERLAND

In 1880 the population as to age and sex was composed as follows :—

Age	Per 1000 Inhabitants		
	Males	Females	Total
Under 5	58	58	116
5–15	101	101	202
15–30	122	126	248
30–45	96	102	198
45–60	71	77	148
Over 60	42	46	88
Total	490	510	1,000

BELGIUM

The composition of the population according to age and sex was as follows :—

Year	1846			1880		
	Males	Females	Total	Males	Females	Total
Under 1	22	22	22	27	27	27
1–5	95	93	94	98	96	97
5–10	110	108	109	112	110	111
10–15	100	96	98	101	99	100
15–20	91	89	90	93	91	92
21–30	167	165	166	154	154	154
31–40	137	133	135	127	127	127
41–50	121	115	118	108	106	107
51–60	72	84	78	86	86	86
61–70	51	59	55	57	61	59
Over 70	34	36	35	37	43	40
Total	1,000	1,000	1,000	1,000	1,000	1,000

SWEDEN

The ratios in this country were as follows :—

Age	1750	1785	1810	1835	1860	1875
Under 15 . .	336	313	318	352	335	323
15–60 . . .	564	600	597	569	583	597
Over 60 . . .	100	87	85	79	82	80
Total . .	1,000	1,000	1,000	1,000	1,000	1,000

NORWAY

Age	Urban	Rural	Rich	Poor	All Norway
Under 5	140	135	137	133	136
5–15	207	228	242	220	225
15–30	278	239	211	256	245
30–45	206	183	172	190	186
45–60	110	120	130	114	118
Over 60	59	95	108	87	90
Total	1,000	1,000	1,000	1,000	1,000

GREECE

The population in 1879 was composed as follows :—

Age	Per 1000 Inhabitants		
	Males	Females	Total
Under 5 . . .	78	70	148
5–15	129	111	240
15–20	46	51	97
20–40	160	149	309
40–60	82	69	151
Over 60 . . .	30	25	55
Total . . .	525	475	1,000

UNITED STATES

The ratios in the United States since 1830 have been :—

Age	1830	1840	1850	1860	1870	1880
Under 5 . . .	180	174	151	154	143	137
5–20 . . .	381	373	373	358	354	342
20–40 . . .	287	297	306	309	304	310
40–60 . . .	112	116	128	134	149	155
Over 60 . . .	40	40	42	45	50	56
Total . .	1,000	1,000	1,000	1,000	1,000	1,000

The composition of the sections of the Union as to age and sex in 1880 was as follows :—

Age	New England			Middle States		
	Males	Females	Total	Males	Females	Total
0–15	156	154	310	181	179	360
15–60	288	309	597	281	292	573
Over 60	44	49	93	33	34	67
Total	488	512	1,000	495	505	1,000

Age	South			West		
	Males	Females	Total	Males	Females	Total
0–15	233	225	458	201	195	396
15–60	245	252	497	299	255	554
Over 60	23	22	45	27	23	50
Total	501	499	1,000	527	473	1,000

The highest ratio for able-bodied men is in the West, and for women between 15 and 60 is in New England.

The great number of German, Irish, and Scandinavian settlers in the Western States explains the high ratio there of able-bodied men.

The composition of the population as regards sex and age was as follows :—

Age	1800			1810			1820		
	Males	Females	Total	Males	Females	Total	Males	Females	Total
0–16	260	242	502	257	242	499	249	240	489
16–45	192	188	380	191	189	380	196	193	389
Over 45	60	58	118	63	58	121	63	59	122
Total	512	488	1,000	511	489	1,000	508	492	1,000

After 1820 the classification according to age was altered by the Census officials: since 1830 the ratios show as follows :—

Age	1830			1840			1850		
	Males	Females	Total	Males	Females	Total	Males	Females	Total
0–5	92	88	180	90	84	174	76	74	150
5–15	138	132	270	134	129	263	135	131	266
15–50	236	231	467	245	234	479	254	240	494
Over 50	42	41	83	42	42	84	46	44	90
Total	508	492	1,000	511	489	1,000	511	489	1,000

Age	1860			1870			1880		
	Males	Females	Total	Males	Females	Total	Males	Females	Total
0–5	78	76	154	73	70	143	68	66	134
5–15	125	120	245	124	120	244	120	117	237
15–50	261	244	505	252	250	502	259	248	507
Over 50	50	46	96	58	53	111	63	59	122
Total	514	486	1,000	507	493	1,000	510	490	1,000

Men in the prime of life (15–50) held the highest ratio in 1860 ; women of child-bearing age (15–50) in 1870. It appears that the preponderance of males is due to immigration, the total number of settlers arrived in 42 years down to 1860 showing thus :—

				No.	Ratio
Males .	.	.	.	2,951,000	594
Females .	.	.	.	2,009,000	406
	Total	.	.	4,960,000	1,000

As regards the coloured population, the sexes are almost even, viz. : —

	Number		Ratio	
Year	Males	Females	Males	Females
1830	1,166,000	1,162,000	501	499
1850	1,811,000	1,828,000	498	502

The white population, owing to immigration, had a much higher ratio of persons of working age than the coloured, as shown in the tables for 1850, viz. :—

Age	Per 1000 Whites			Per 1000 Coloured		
	Males	Females	Total	Males	Females	Total
0–15	208	201	409	223	223	446
15–50	258	242	500	234	235	469
Over 50	47	44	91	41	44	85
Total	513	487	1,000	498	502	1,000

AGRICULTURE

This is the most important industry of mankind, for (without counting India, China, &c.) it occupies 80,000,000 peasants, represents a capital of 23,000 millions sterling, and has annual products to the value of almost 4000 millions. Capital and product have more than doubled since 1840, but the number of hands engaged has not risen 50 per cent., viz. :—

| Year | Millions, £ Sterling | | Agricultural Peasants |
	Capital	Product	
1840 . . .	9,036	1,824	55,080,000
1860 . . .	14,923	2,483	66,000,000
1887 . . .	23,006	3,948	80,050,000

The following tables show approximately how agricultural capital was made up at the above dates :—

| Year 1840. Value in Millions, £ Sterling | | | | |
	Land	Cattle	Sundries	Total
Europe	6,471	875	820	8,166
United States . .	400	96	100	596
Colonies, &c. . .	224	23	27	274
Total . . .	7,095	994	947	9,036

| Year 1860. Value in Millions, £ Sterling | | | | |
	Land	Cattle	Sundries	Total
Europe	9,957	1,260	1,227	12,444
United States . .	1,382	226	237	1,845
Colonies, &c. . .	523	76	35	634
Total . . .	11,862	1,562	1,499	14,923

| Year 1887. Value in Millions, £ Sterling | | | | |
	Land	Cattle	Sundries	Total
Europe	13,776	1,940	1,737	17,453
United States . .	2,560	501	635	3,696
Colonies, &c. . .	1,440	260	157	1,857
Total . . .	17,776	2,701	2,529	23,006

The agricultural capital of Europe has doubled since 1840; that of the United States has increased sixfold. The average increase has been 197 millions sterling per annum in Europe, and 67 millions in the United States.

The value of agricultural products at the above periods was approximately as follows :—

| Millions, £ Sterling | | | | |
Year	Grain	Other Crops	Pastoral Products	Total
1840	702	538	584	1,824
1860	1,130	575	778	2,483
1887	1,091	1,445	1,412	3,948

The value of grain crops has diminished since 1860, while that of pastoral products has nearly doubled, the price of grain having declined very notably, while that of meat, as also of dairy products, has risen. The relative importance of the three great branches of agricultural industry at the said dates is shown as follows, judged by money values :—

	1840	1860	1887
Grain	38.5	45.5	27.5
Other crops	29.8	23.2	36.8
Pastoral produce . .	31.7	31.3	35.7
Total	100.0	100.0	100.0

TILLAGE

The area under crops has risen from 492 million acres in 1840 to 807 millions in 1888, an increase of 315 millions, viz. :—

In Europe	.	. .	131 million acres.
„ United States	.	.	151 „ „
„ Colonies, &c.	.	.	33 „ „
Total	.	. .	315 „ „

In 48 years the area of tillage and planting has risen 65 per cent., but the grain crops have risen 120 per cent., viz. :—

| Millions of Bushels | | | | |
Year	Europe	U. States	Colonies	Total
1840	3,212	616	291	4,119
1860	4,046	1,240	464	5,750
1887	5,588	2,586	948	9,122

Improved implements and machinery have made tillage more productive and grain cheaper. In 1840 each peasant produced about 73 bushels of grain; in 1860 the average was 87, and in 1887 it had risen to 114; that is, two men now produce more grain than three did in 1840. The following table shows the distribution of grain-growing in 1887 :—

| | Millions of Acres | | | | | Crops, Millions of Bushels | | | | |
	Wheat	Oats	Barley	Various	Total	Wheat	Oats	Barley	Various	Total
Europe	90	72	38	148	348	1,336	1,628	694	1,930	5,588
United States . . .	38	26	3	75	142	442	640	58	1,446	2,586
Colonies, &c. . . .	46	3	7	13	69	465	97	82	304	948
Total . . .	174	101	48	236	559	2,243	2,365	834	3,680	9,122

In the United States 9,000,000 hands raise nearly half as much grain as 66 millions in Europe. Thus it appears that for want of implements or proper machinery there is a waste of labour in Europe equal to 48 millions of peasants. In other words, one farm labourer in the United States is worth more than three in Europe.

PLATE I.

AGRICULTURE.

Value of all agricultural products, in milions £ sterling.

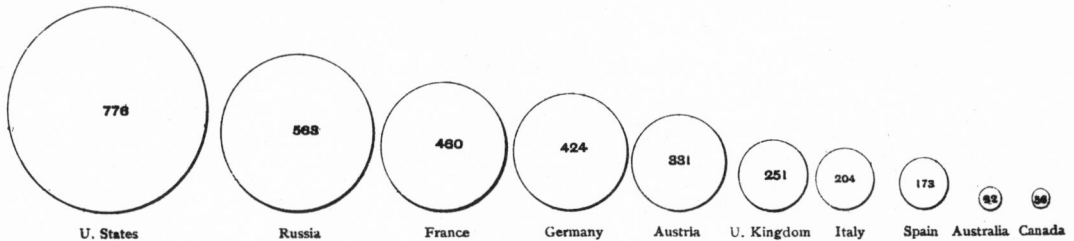

Pounds of grain produced per inhabitant.

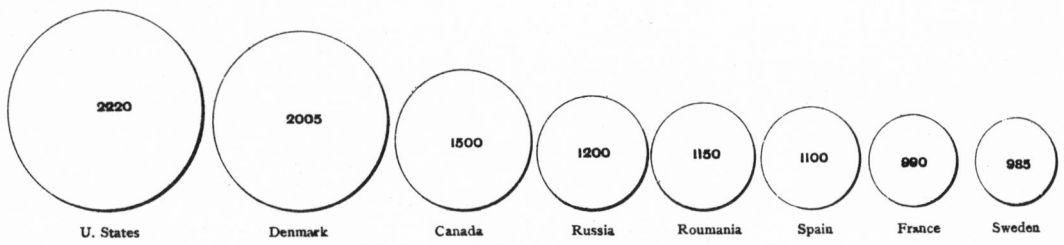

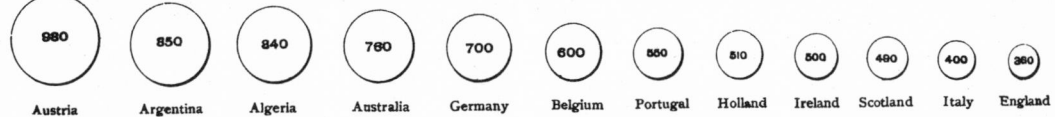

Acres under grain per 100 inhabitants

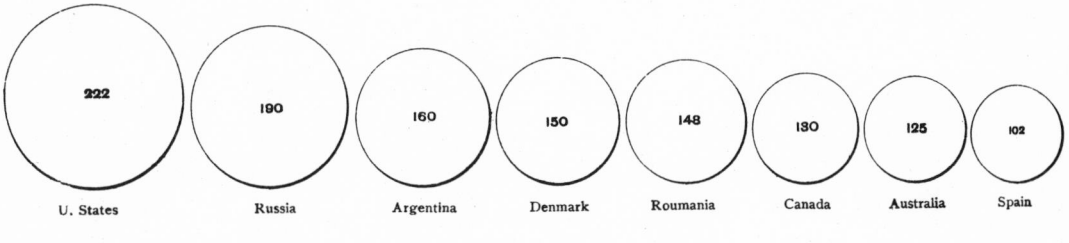

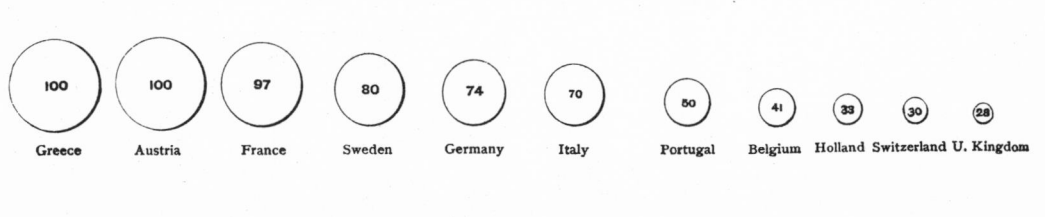

PASTORAL INDUSTRY.

The production of meat at the same periods was approximately as follows :—

Year	Tons			
	Europe	United States	Colonies, &c.	Total
1840	6,800,000	2,120,000	200,000	9,120,000
1860	7,630,000	2,970,000	400,000	11,000,000
1887	8,633,000	4,750,000	920,000	14,303,000

The production of meat has risen 57 per cent. since 1840, while that of grain, as we have already seen, has increased 120 per cent. In aliquot parts production of meat showed thus :—

	1840	1860	1887
Europe	74.5	69.3	60.4
United States . . .	23.3	27.0	33.2
Colonies, &c. . . .	2.2	3.7	6.4
Total	100.0	100.0	100.0

See *Cattle* and *Food*.

AGRICULTURAL AREA

The area under crops in the various countries was approximately as follows :—

	Millions of Acres				
	1820	1840	1860	1880	1888
U. Kingdom . . .	19	22	22	23	21
France	48	55	57	60	61
Germany	37	45	50	58	59
Russia	120	135	145	183	190
Austria	50	53	58	60	65
Italy	20	22	26	35	35
Spain	25	30	30	32	32
Portugal	3	4	5	5	5
Sweden	2	5	8	12	12
Norway	1	3	4	4	4
Denmark	2	5	6	8	8
Holland	4	4	5	5	5
Belgium	3	4	5	5	5
Other countries . .	30	40	50	56	56
Europe	364	427	471	546	558
U. States	30	50	90	166	201
Canada	2	4	8	10	13
Australia	1	2	3	10	14
Argentina	...	...	1	3	6
Brazil	...	1	1	2	2
Algeria	4	5	6	7	8
Egypt	2	4	4	5	5
Total . .	402	492	583	749	807

The area has doubled since 1820, the increase during the various periods having been as follows :—

Period	Millions of Acres	Acres per Annum
1820–40	90	4,500,000
1841–60	91	4,550,000
1861–80	166	8,300,000
1881–88	58	7,200,000

It is especially since 1860 that improvements in agricultural machinery have been attended with a notable extension of cultivated area.

AGRICULTURAL POPULATION

Hands engaged in tillage and pastoral industries were approximately as follows :—

	1840	1860	1887
Europe . . .	50,430,000	58,160,000	66,320,000
United States .	2,550,000	4,340,000	9,000,000
Colonies, &c. .	2,100,000	3,500,000	4,730,000
Total . .	55,080,000	66,000,000	80,050,000

The ratios of capital and products that corresponded to the agricultural population, that is, to each adult peasant, were :—

	Capital		Product	
	1840	1887	1840	1887
	£	£	£	£
Europe	162	263	31	43
United States . .	235	410	72	85
Colonies, &c. . . .	134	390	46	61
General average . .	164	287	33	50

Each hand in the United States produces double the annual value that prevails in Europe.

CROPS

The production of grain (excluding rice) was approximately as follows :—

	Millions of Bushels				Bushels per Inhabitant		
	1831–40	1851–60	1874–84	1887	1831–40	1851–60	1887
U. Kingdom .	408	390	334	311	16	15	8
France . . .	510	550	687	729	15	15	19
Germany . .	290	450	685	706	10	13	15
Russia . . .	1,040	1,270	1,461	1,854	20	20	20
Austria . . .	364	500	578	687	13	16	17
Italy	110	200	277	225	6	10	7
Spain	180	215	326	300	15	14	18
Portugal . . .	25	30	19	40	8	8	9
Sweden . . .	14	35	93	104	5	10	23
Finland . . .	10	15	22	20	10	10	10
Norway . . .	6	15	17	17	6	10	9
Denmark . .	40	65	78	84	36	43	42
Holland . . .	16	20	37	40	6	6	9
Belgium . . .	33	70	66	75	9	15	14
Switzerland . .	12	15	17	18	6	6	6
Greece . . .	6	9	11	18	6	7	10
Servia . . .	8	11	14	20	10	10	10
Roumania . .	70	90	109	120	22	23	24
Turkey, &c. .	170	196	209	220	12	14	15
Europe . . .	3,312	4,146	5,040	5,588	14	15	16
United States .	540	1,053	2,325	2,586	36	38	42
Canada . . .	22	45	128	148	14	15	30
Chili	5	12	18	18	5	8	8
Argentina . .	2	5	25	50	2	3	13
Australia . . .	1	10	36	51	3	10	15
Other countries	260	390	587	681	...	...	...
Total . .	4,042	5,661	8,159	9,122	...	...	...

The production of grain per inhabitant in Europe is higher now than fifty years ago.

The production of wheat was approximately as follows :—

	Millions of Bushels				
	1831-40	1851-60	1871-80	1881-87	1888
United Kingdom . .	120	121	85	78	76
France	190	223	275	290	275
Germany	50	70	94	98	103
Russia.	110	130	224	250	258
Austria	65	85	109	151	138
Italy	60	75	115	105	141
Spain	58	70	114	133	170
Portugal	4	5	8	10	10
Sweden and Norway .	1	2	4	4	6
Denmark	3	4	5	6	5
Holland	3	4	5	6	6
Belgium	8	13	16	17	16
Switzerland . . .	1	1	2	2	2
Greece	2	2	3	4	6
Servia	2	2	3	4	4
Roumania . . .	15	20	24	26	30
Turkey, &c . . .	20	30	40	47	50
Europe	712	857	1,126	1,231	1,296
United States . . .	78	137	338	440	415
Canada	6	9	24	36	37
Australia	2	8	24	38	45
India, &c. . . .	108	187	282	375	478
Total . . .	906	1,198	1,794	2,120	2,271

Mr. Spallart's estimate of the crops of the world down to 1884 compares with the official returns and latest estimates for 1887 as follows :—

	Millions of Bushels Yearly						
	Wheat	Rye	Barley	Oats	Maize	Sundry	Total
1871-80	1,944	1,256	774	1,870	1,528	312	7,684
1875-84	1,962	1,165	788	1,936	1,829	293	7,973
1883-84	2,115	1,196	803	2,189	2,035	324	8,662
1887	2,243	1,418	834	2,365	1,979	283	9,122

Newmann Spallart's statement of the ordinary production of grain (1874-84) is as follows :—

	Millions of Bushels						
	Wheat	Rye	Barley	Oats	Maize	Sundries	Total
U. Kingdom	88	2	82	162	...	...	334
France . .	277	70	50	220	26	44	687
Germany . .	102	220	95	260	...	8	685
Russia. . .	176	556	113	446	17	130	1,438
Poland . .	15	47	25	36	...	...	123
Austria . .	120	110	84	138	104	22	578
Italy . . .	140	9	9	18	85	16	277
Spain . . .	168	32	77	13	36	...	326
Portugal . .	9	7	2	1	...	...	19
Sweden . .	3	19	15	50	...	6	93
Norway . .	...	1	5	9	...	2	17
Denmark . .	5	16	26	30	...	1	78
Holland . .	6	9	5	11	...	6	37
Belgium . .	20	16	4	24	...	2	66
Finland . .	...	10	5	7	...	...	22
Switzerland .	2	8	2	5	...	...	17
Greece. . .	4	...	2	...	3	2	11
Servia . .	4	1	3	1	5	...	14
Roumania . .	26	3	14	3	61	2	109
Bosnia . .	2	...	2	.1	3	...	8
Bulgaria . .	23	1	11	2	7	...	44
Eur. Turkey .	22	13	12	2	8	...	57
Europe . .	1,212	1,150	643	1,439	355	241	5,040
United States	400	23	42	420	1,430	10	2,325
Canada . .	30	2	17	66	9	4	128
Chile . .	13	...	4	...	1	...	18
Argentina .	10	...	1	...	14	...	25
Australia . .	20	...	2	9	5	...	36
Japan . . .	11	...	50	...	...	33	94
India . .	250	...	...	...	...	...	250
Egypt . . .	18	...	7	...	12	...	37
Algeria . .	10	...	34	2	...	2	48
AsiaMinor,&c.	86	...	...	...	60	...	146
Cape Colony	8	...	...	...	...	4	...	12
*Total .	2,068	1,175	800	1,936	1,890	290	8,159

* The figures for the Argentine Republic, Asia Minor, and Cape Colony are not Mr. Spallart's.

The acreage of grain-crops (not including rice) in 1887-88 was as follows :—

	Acres					Acres per 100 Inhabitants
	Wheat	Oats	Barley	Other Grain	Total	
United Kingdom	2,670,000	4,180,000	2,260,000	680,000	9,790,000	28
France	17,180,000	9,230,000	2,340,000	7,850,000	36,600,000	97
Germany	4,740,000	9,410,000	4,280,000	15,870,000	34,300,000	74
Russia	28,950,000	34,890,000	12,450,000	83,510,000	159,800,000	190
Poland	1,500,000	3,000,000	1,000,000	5,600,000	11,100,000	140
Finland	10,000	300,000	300,000	710,000	1,320,000	66
Austria	9,760,000	7,190,000	5,240,000	15,360,000	37,550,000	100
Italy	11,700,000	1,100,000	860,000	6,690,000	20,350,000	70
Spain	8,000,000	1,000,000	4,000,000	5,000,000	18,000,000	102
Portugal	600,000	100,000	200,000	1,300,000	2,200,000	50
Sweden	200,000	2,000,000	600,000	1,060,000	3,860,000	80
Norway	10,000	220,000	140,000	100,000	470,000	25
Denmark	140,000	990,000	780,000	1,010,000	2,920,000	150
Holland	210,000	280,000	120,000	850,000	1,460,000	33
Belgium	680,000	620,000	100,000	990,000	2,390,000	41
Switzerland	150,000	200,000	130,000	420,000	900,000	30
Greece	900,000	...	400,000	700,000	2,000,000	100
Roumania, Turkey, &c. . .	6,900,000	...	3,600,000	10,760,000	21,260,000	140
Europe	94,300,000	74,710,000	38,800,000	158,460,000	366,270,000	110
United States	37,640,000	25,920,000	2,650,000	75,430,000	141,640,000	222
Colonies, &c.	45,240,000	3,460,000	5,650,000	7,840,000	62,190,000	...
Total	177,180,000	104,090,000	47,100,000	241,730,000	570,100,000	...

The crops in 1887–88 were approximately as follows (not counting rice) :—

	Millions of Bushels						Bushels	
	Wheat	Oats	Barley	Maize	Rye, &c.	Total	Per Acre	Per Inhab.
U. Kingdom	76	151	70	...	14	311	32	8
France	295	246	49	26	113	729	20	19
Germany	104	243	97	...	262	706	21	15
Russia	269	600	162	13	810	1,854	11	22
Poland	15	36	20	...	52	123	11	15
Finland	...	7	5	...	11	23	17	12
Austria	185	169	106	90	137	687	18	18
Italy	110	14	9	75	17	225	11	8
Spain	136	20	74	40	30	300	16	18
Portugal	10	1	2	15	12	40	15	9
Sweden	4	55	15	...	30	104	27	22
Norway	...	9	4	...	4	17	35	9
Denmark	6	30	22	...	26	84	28	42
Holland	6	13	5	...	16	40	14	9
Belgium	17	28	4	...	26	75	31	13
Switzerland	2	5	2	...	8	17	20	6
Greece	8	...	3	4	1	16	8	8
Roumania	25	...	14	64	9	112	15	22
Servia	4	1	3	5	3	16	14	8
Bulgaria	32	...	16	11	4	63	11	20
Turkey	32	...	12	20	16	80	11	20
Europe	1,336	1,628	694	363	1,601	5,622	15	17
United States	442	640	58	1,412	34	2,586	18	40
Canada	36	80	22	10	...	148	22	30
Australia	25	15	3	8	...	51	11	15
India	250	...	...	...	...	250	9	1
Egypt	18	...	7	12	36	73	16	12
Algeria	23	2	40	1	...	66	10	16
Japan	65	...	...	13	22	100	17	3
Mexico	10	...	6	130	8	154	...	15
Argentina	22	...	2	26	...	50	11	16
Chili	16	...	2	4	...	22	10	8
Total	2,243	2,365	834	1,979	1,701	9,122	...	...

The cultivation of wheat and barley requires as follows :—

	Days of Cultivation		Mean Temperature, Fahr.	
At	Wheat	Barley	Wheat	Barley
Alsace	131	122	60	57
Kingston, Canada	106	92	68	66
Cincinnati	137	...	60	...

According to Broch (1885), the average product per acre of different kinds of grain, taken from five years' results in the various countries, was as follows :—

	Bushels					
	Wheat	Rye	Barley	Oats	Maize	Potatoes
U. Kingdom	35	33	38	33	...	...
France	16	16	20	25	16	102
Germany	19	16	24	27	...	121
Russia	9	11	9	18	...	111
Austria	16	14	17	20	...	130
Hungary	12	...	16	18	17	107
Italy	12	...	15	20	21	164
Sweden	20	20	34	34	...	121
Norway	25	27	31	39	...	127
Denmark	25	25	27	30	...	95
Holland	23	18	37	42	...	177
Belgium	24	22	35	40	...	164
U. States	12	13	22	26	24	76
Australia	10	...	21	28	33	141

He estimates the crops in Europe as follows :—

	Millions of Bushels		
	Crop	Deduct Seed	For Consumption
Wheat	1,236	176	1,060
Rye	1,230	175	1,055
Barley	630	90	540
Oats	1,528	218	1,310
Maize	210	30	180
Total	4,834	689	4,145

He says that 2227 million bushels are used for human food, and 1918 for cattle, alcohol, &c. ; the average consumption of grain per head of population in Europe being 410 lbs., or almost 7 bushels, yearly. His estimates, however, appear altogether too low, being 100 million bushels short in wheat, and the same in oats, while his crop of maize is but little over half the reality. It is to be observed in his favour that the crops are now heavier than when he wrote, in 1885.

The production and consumption of grain in the various countries are approximately as follows :—

	Production. Million Bushels	Consumption, Millions of Bushels				
		Food	Sowing	Liquor	Cattle, &c.	Total
U. Kingdom	311	240	31	45	286	602
France	729	330	100	15	338	783
Germany	706	430	100	50	200	780
Russia	1,854	920	280	52	388	1,640
Austria	687	320	100	20	230	670
Italy	225	200	30	4	26	260
Spain	300	140	40	2	123	305
Portugal	40	32	6	1	6	45
Sweden	104	44	21	6	39	110
Norway	17	16	4	3	7	30
Denmark	84	20	10	3	41	74
Holland	40	40	3	6	14	63
Belgium	75	60	9	10	28	107
Switzerland	20	24	3	2	6	35
Greece	20	20	3	1	3	27
Servia	15	10	2	1	2	15
Roumania	120	30	18	2	10	60
Turkey, &c.	275	86	30	2	127	245
Europe	5,622	2,962	790	225	1,874	5,851
United States	2,586	360	400	50	1,590	2,400
Canada	148	32	25	5	56	118
Australia	51	24	10	3	3	40
Argentina	50	15	10	...	...	25
India	250	183	40	...	...	223
Other countries	415	271	40	...	154	465
Total	9,122	3,847	1,315	283	3,677	9,122

The average yield of crops per 100 lbs. of seed is approximately as follows :—

	Wheat	Oats	Barley	Rye
France	800	750	800	700
Germany	780	700	900	600
Russia	600	750	700	600
Denmark	900	800	800	800
Sweden	600	400	400	500
Holland	1,400	1,400	1,400	1,400
Belgium	1,200	880	1,310	1,210

The following is a summary of the crops and value since 1874 :—

	Million of Bushels, per Annum			Value, Millions £	
	1874–84	1884	1887	1874–84	1887
Wheat	2,068	2,348	2,243	543	412
Rye	1,175	1,226	1,418	235	227
Barley	800	795	834	153	108
Oats	1,936	2,152	2,365	202	185
Maize	1,890	2,148	1,979	204	186
Sundry	290	289	283	30	25
Total . . .	8,159	8,958	9,122	1,367	1,143

The values of these crops in 1887 were thus made up :—

	Millions, £ Sterling					
	Wheat	Oats	Barley	Maize	Rye, &c.	Total
Europe . . .	261	142	89	36	236	764
United States .	71	36	7	124	5	243
India and Japan	52	...	...	...	...	52
Colonies, &c. .	28	7	12	26	11	84
Total . . .	412	185	108	186	252	1,143

(Deducting India and Japan, the value will be 1091 millions, as in the table of nations at p. 11.)

If the average prices of 1874–84 had been maintained, mankind would have had to pay 1577 millions sterling for the crops of 1887, a sum nearly 40 per cent. in excess of the above value. The following table shows the countries (1886–87) that had surplus grain to export, and those that imported to cover deficits :—

Exporters	Bushels	Importers	Bushels
Russia .	215,000,000	United Kingdom .	286,000,000
Austria .	13,000,000	France	54,000,000
Roumania .	56,000,000	Germany . . .	72,000,000
U. States .	168,000,000	Scandinavia . . .	18,000,000
Argentina	24,000,000	Holland & Belgium	55,000,000
India . .	27,000,000	Switzerland . .	15,000,000
Australia .	12,000,000	Spain and Portugal	11,000,000
Canada .	30,000,000	Italy	36,000,000
Total .	545,000,000	Total . . .	547,000,000

Mr. Spallart sums up the value of all grain crops in 1884 thus :—

	Millions, £ Sterling						
	Wheat	Rye	Barley	Oats	Maize	Sundries	Total
United States .	69.5	3.2	6.3	34.0	134.6	1.4	249.0
Russia	35.2	75.0	11.5	28.9	1.3	5.7	157.6
France . . .	69.0	13.3	9.1	31.6	5.8	7.9	136.7
Germany . . .	23.7	38.2	15.4	27.5	...	0.9	105.7
Italy	35.1	1.5	1.5	1.7	16.0	11.0	66.8
Austria proper .	5.3	7.5	4.4	6 2	1.5	0.8	25.7
Hungary . . .	10.9	3.6	3.6	2.4	8.5	...	29.0
Spain	53.8	7.5	18.2	1.8	9.0	0.9	91.2
Denmark . . .	0.9	2.7	3.3	3.4	...	0.1	10.4
Holland . . .	1.4	1.8	0.7	1.2	...	0.5	5.6
Other countries .	135.7	11.7	33.6	29.8	11.3	4.8	226.9*
Total . .	440.5	166.0	107.6	168.5	188.0	34.0	1104.6

* He only gives the total for "Other countries ; " the distribution is mine.

According to Mr. Spallart the average values of grain in 1878–81 throughout the world were as in the following table, and if these prices were applied to the average crops for ten years ending 1884, the results would be as follows :—

	Price, Pence per Bushel	Crop, Million Bushels	Value, Million £
Wheat	63	2,068	543
Rye	48	1,175	235
Barley	46	800	153
Oats	25	1,936	202
Maize	26	1,890	204
Sundry	25	290	30
Total . .		8,159	1,367

As near as we can ascertain, the crops and aggregate value were :—

Period	Million Bushels	Value, Millions £	Average Price, Pence per Bushel
1831–40	4,043	624	37
1851–60	5,563	1,130	48
1874–84	8,159	1,367	40
1887	9,122	1,143	30

The value of agricultural and pastoral products in 1887 is shown approximately as follows :—

	Millions, £ Sterling			Per Agricultural Labourer
	Agricultural	Pastoral	Total	£
U. Kingdom .	141	110	251	98
France . . .	322	138	460	71
Germany . .	262	162	424	52
Russia . . .	373	190	563	25
Poland . . .	34	21	55	34
Finland . . .	9	6	15	37
Austria . . .	225	106	331	31
Italy	153	51	204	37
Spain . . .	126	47	173	63*
Portugal . .	23	8	31	35
Sweden . . .	31	18	49	58
Norway . . .	9	8	17	48
Denmark . .	20	15	35	85
Holland . .	20	19	39	46
Belgium . .	41	14	55	56
Switzerland .	9	10	19	43
Roumania . .	27	20	47	60
Servia . . .	6	8	14	47
Greece . . .	14	5	19	60
Bulgaria . .	14	5	19	40
Turkey . . .	16	9	25	45
Europe . . .	1,875	970	2,845	43
United States	467	309	776	85
Canada . .	35	21	56	70
Mexico . . .	25	8	33	...
Australia . .	27	35	62	98
Cape Colony .	2	6	8	40
Argentina . .	18	24	42	70
Uruguay . .	2	8	10	100
Chili	9	6	15	50
Brazil . . .	32	8	40	20
Algeria . . .	14	12	26	35
Egypt . . .	30	5	35	45
Total . .	2,536	1,412	3,948	50

* The above table includes timber as an agricultural product, although forestry is properly a distinct industry. See Part II., where timber is excluded.

The value of the principal items in 1887 was approximately as follows :—

Millions, £ Sterling

	Grain	Green Crops	Garden Products	Dairy	Wine	Meat	Sundries	Total
U. Kingdom	41	86	10	31	...	55	28	251
France	129	103	30	47	49	60	42	460
Germany	93	117	30	55	5	69	55	424
Russia	181	110	32	48	4	63	125	563
Poland	19	7	3	5	...	5	16	55
Finland	4	2	1	1	...	3	4	15
Austria	102	61	22	35	17	44	50	331
Italy	40	37	23	14	43	18	29	204
Spain	55	15	9	9	44	26	15	173
Portugal	7	3	2	2	10	5	2	31
Sweden	14	7	2	7	...	7	12	49
Norway	2	2	1	3	...	3	6	17
Denmark	13	6	1	6	...	6	3	35
Holland	6	11	3	10	...	6	3	39
Belgium	12	24	5	5	...	6	3	55
Switzerland	3	3	2	5	1	4	1	19
Greece	3	2	4	1	3	3	3	19
Roumania	17	7	3	5	3	11	1	47
Servia	3	1	1	2	1	4	2	14
Bulgaria	9	1	1	3	...	4	1	19
Turkey	11	2	1	3	1	5	2	25
Europe	764	607	186	297	181	407	403	2,845
United States	243	165	57	79	2	156	74	776
Canada	15	10	3	8	...	8	12	56
Mexico	20	4	1	2	...	4	2	33
Australia	9	15	3	4	...	9	22	62
Argentina	8	7	2	4	1	6	14	42
Uruguay	1	1	1	1	...	3	3	10
Cape Colony	2	...	1	1	...	2	2	8
Algeria	11	1	1	1	2	6	4	26
Egypt	13	17	...	1	...	2	2	35
Brazil	1	30	2	1	...	2	4	40
Chile	4	2	2	2	1	3	1	15
Total	1,091	859	259	401	187	608	543	3,948

The following table shows approximately the agricultural capital in 1888 :—

	Millions, £ Sterling				£ per Inhab.
	Land	Cattle	Sundries	Total	
U. Kingdom	1,873	185	229	2,287	60
France	2,688	218	323	3,229	84
Germany	1,815	262	230	2,307	50
Russia	...	...	...	...	...
Poland	150	30	20	200	25
Finland	52	11	7	70	35
Austria	706	106	90	902	38
Hungary	651	96	83	830	52
Bosnia	14	9	2	25	18
Italy	1,182	83	140	1,405	47
Spain	984	95	120	1,199	66
Portugal	132	13	16	161	36
Sweden	240	36	30	306	62
Norway	100	15	12	127	63
Denmark	217	30	27	274	137
Holland	314	28	38	380	85
Belgium	377	24	44	445	74
Switzerland	120	10	14	144	48
Greece	138	24	18	180	90
Roumania	254	37	32	323	64
Servia	94	16	12	122	61
Bulgaria	90	10	10	110	33
Turkey	280	26	31	337	67
Europe	...	...	...	...	...
United States	2,560	501	635	3,696	57
Canada	282	44	36	362	72
Mexico	103	15	13	131	13
Chile	50	8	6	64	21
Argentina	111	49	17	177	44
Uruguay	34	14	5	53	80
Brazil	105	7	12	124	10
Cape Colony	25	13	4	42	40
Australia	533	67	37	637	160
Algeria	87	28	13	128	32
Egypt	110	15	14	139	20
Total	...	...	...	...	..

The following table shows approximately the principal features of agricultural industry in 1840 and 1887 :—

	Capital, Million £		Product, Million £		Hands		Production per Hand	
	1840	1887	1840	1887	1840	1887	1840	1887
							£	£
United Kingdom	1,968	2,287	218	251	3,400,000	2,560,000	65	97
France	1,743	3,229	269	460	6,950,000	6,450,000	39	71
Germany	630	2,307	170	424	6,400,000	8,120,000	27	52
Russia	517	2,090	248	563	15,000,000	22,700,000	16	25
Austria	702	1,732	205	331	7,500,000	10,680,000	27	31
Italy	452	1,405	114	204	3,600,000	5,390,000	32	37
Spain	724	1,199	102	173	2,000,000	2,720,000	50	63
Portugal	100	161	18	31	700,000	870,000	26	35
Sweden	51	306	16	49	550,000	850,000	30	58
Norway	30	127	8	17	250,000	380,000	32	48
Denmark	46	274	16	35	280,000	420,000	56	85
Holland	245	380	20	39	600,000	840,000	33	46
Belgium	235	445	30	55	900,000	980,000	33	56
Switzerland	100	144	12	19	300,000	440,000	40	43
Turkey, &c.	623	1,367	98	194	2,000,000	2,900,000	40	58
Europe	8,166	17,453	1,544	2,845	50,430,000	66.320,000	31	43
United States	596	3,696	184	776	2,550,000	9,000,000	72	85
Canada	80	362	12	56	300,000	800,000	40	70
Australia	18	637	6	62	100,000	630,000	60	98
Cape Colony	8	42	2	8	50,000	200,000	40	40
Argentina	22	177	5	42	200,000	600.000	25	70
Uruguay	6	53	1	10	50,000	100,000	20	100
Various	140	586	70	149	140,000	2,400,000	50	62
Total	9,036	23,006	1,824	3,948	53,820,000	80,050,000	33	50

EUROPE

Area under crops was approximately as follows :—

Year	Million Acres	Year	Million Acres
1820	364	1860	471
1840	427	1888	558

The production of grain, wine, potatoes, and meat may be set down thus—

Year	Grain, Million Bushels	Wine, Million Gallons	Potatoes, Million Tons	Meat, Tons
1820	2,800	2,050	20	5,400,000
1840	3,300	2,150	40	6,800,000
1860	4,200	2,300	50	7,600,000
1880	5,040	2,500	60	8,300,000
1887	5,600	2,600	70	8,630,000

The ratio of the above products to population was as follows :—

Year	Per Inhabitant			
	Grain, Bushels	Wine, Gallons	Potatoes, lbs.	Meat, lbs.
1820	14	10	224	60
1840	14	9	370	64
1860	15	8	400	61
1880	15	8	430	56
1887	15	8	445	57

The following table shows the rank that European products hold in those of the world, as regards value (1888) :—

	Millions, £ Sterling			
	Europe	United States	Colonies, &c.	Total
Grain	764	243	84	1,091
Green crops . .	607	165	87	859
Garden crops . .	186	57	18	261
Wine	181	2	4	187
Dairy	297	79	25	401
Meat	407	156	45	608
Sundries . . .	403	74	64	541
Total . . .	2,845	776	327	3,948

	Grain	Green Crops	Garden Crops	Wine	Dairy	Meat	Sundries	Total
Europe . .	70.0	70.5	71.2	96.8	74.0	67.0	74.5	72.1
United States	22.3	19.2	21.9	1.1	19.8	25.6	13.7	19.6
Colonies, &c.	7.7	10.3	6.9	2.1	6.2	7.4	11.8	8.3
Total . .	100.0	100.0	100.0	100.0	100.0	100.0	100.0	100.0

It appears from the foregoing general summary that Europe stands for nearly three-fourths of the value of all the farm products of the world.

The weight and value of European grain crops in 1887–88 were approximately as follows :—

	Weight in Tons					Lbs. per Inhabitant
	Wheat	Oats	Barley	Rye, &c.	Total	
United Kingdom . .	2,100,000	2,510,000	1,600,000	350,000	6,560,000	400
France	8,200,000	4,200,000	1,200,000	3,300,000	16,900,000	990
Germany	2,800,000	4,300,000	2,200,000	5,800,000	15,100,000	700
Russia	7,500,000	10,400,000	3,800,000	22,600,000	44,300,000	1,200
Poland	400,000	600,000	300,000	1,500,000	2,800,000	800
Austria	5,100,000	2,830,000	2,600,000	6,570,000	17,100,000	980
Italy	3,000,000	340,000	170,000	1,790,000	5,300,000	400
Spain	3,700,000	350,000	1,700,000	1,950,000	7,700,000	1,000
Portugal . . .	270,000	...	...	780,000	1,050,000	550
Sweden and Norway .	110,000	1,100,000	450,000	840,000	2,500,000	900
Denmark . . .	140,000	560,000	520,000	600,000	1,820,000	2,000
Holland . . .	140,000	250,000	100,000	410,000	900,000	510
Belgium . . .	450,000	490,000	100,000	580,000	1,620,000	600
Roumania . . .	700,000	...	330,000	1,820,000	2,850,000	1,150
Various . . .	2,410,000	130,000	1,030,000	210,000	3,780,000	800
Europe . . .	37,020,000	28,060,000	16,100,000	49,100,000	130,280,000	820

The following is a summary of products approximately in 1888 :—

	Tons	£	Sundries	£
Wheat	37,020,000	261,000,000	Vegetables	186,000,000
Oats	28,060,000	142,000,000	Wine	181,000,000
Barley	16,100,000	89,000,000	Timber	108,000,000
Rye, &c.	49,100,000	272,000,000	Dairy	297,000,000
All grain . . .	130,280,000	764,000,000	Meat	404,000,000
Green crops .	...	607,000,000	Hides, wool, &c. . .	298,000,000
Principal crops . . .	...	1,371,000,000	Sundries	1,474,000,000

Making a total of 2845 millions sterling. It is not pretended that the foregoing table of values is mathematically correct. It is the result of the investigations, and in some cases the official valuations, bearing upon each country, as given hereafter in detail. The value of the various grain-crops of Europe, taking the average for 1887–88, is shown approximately in the following table :—

	Value, Millions £ Sterling					Shillings per Inhabitant
	Wheat	Oats	Barley	Rye, &c.	Total	
U. Kingdom .	16	15	8	2	41	22
France . . .	71	29	7	22	129	65
Germany. . .	19	25	15	34	93	40
Russia . . .	37	35	15	94	181	45
Poland . . .	3	4	2	10	19	50
Austria . . .	37	14	16	35	102	52
Italy	20	2	1	17	40	27
Spain	30	2	10	13	55	63
Portugal . . .	2	...	...	5	7	35
Sweden and Norway	1	6	3	6	16	50
Denmark . .	1	4	3	5	13	130
Holland . . .	1	2	1	2	6	30
Belgium . . .	4	3	1	4	12	40
Roumania . .	5	...	2	10	17	70
Various . . .	14	1	5	13	33	50
Total . .	261	142	89	272	764	47

M. Block drew up, in 1850, a statement of the agricultural products of various countries, thus :—

	Product Yearly, Tons		Value, Millions £			
	Grain	Meat	Grain	Meat	Various	Total
U. Kingdom .	7,650,000	450,000	82	28	154	264
France . . .	12,600,000	605,000	123	22	211	356
Prussia . . .	12,200,000	310,000	27	8	102	137
Bavaria . . .	950,000	105,000	8	3	8	19
Saxony . . .	400,000	25,000	3	1	5	9
Austria . . .	10,200,000	740,000	67	19	88	174
Spain	2,100,000	220,000	21	10	57	88
Belgium . . .	1,300,000	52,000	9	3	9	21
Holland . . .	800,000	55,000	6	2	13	21
Sweden and Norway .	1,100,000	130,000	4	2	7	13
Denmark . .	2,000,000	93,000	7	1	3	11
Total . .	51,300,000	2,785,000	357	99	647	1,113

The above table omitted Russia, Poland, Italy, Portugal, Switzerland, Roumania, Greece, and other countries. The values under the item "Various" were, moreover, too low.

The following table shows approximately the value of all agricultural products in Europe at different dates :—

Year	Millions, £ Sterling		
	Agricultural	Pastoral	Total
1830	914	341	1,255
1840	1,114	430	1,544
1850	1,328	542	1,870
1860	1,444	620	2,064
1870	1,552	818	2,370
1888	1,875	970	2,845

The various classes of live-stock were approximately as follows :—

Year	Horses	Cattle	Sheep	Pigs	Value, Mill. £
1830	25,020,000	67,370,000	169,040,000	44,460,000	730
1850	28,950,000	80,120,000	183,950,000	38,430,000	1,018
1870	32,080,000	89,820,000	209,370,000	43,950,000	1,496
1887	37,610,000	101,855,000	197,740,000	48,350,000	1,940

The agricultural capital of Europe was made up as follows :—

Year	Millions, £ Sterling			
	Land	Cattle	Sundries	Total
1840 . . .	6,471	875	820	8,166
1860 . . .	9,957	1,260	1,227	12,444
1887 . . .	13,776	1,940	1,737	17,453

The increase of agricultural capital was as follows :—

Period	Millions, £	Millions, £ per Annum
1840–60	4,278	214
1860–87	5,009	185

Notwithstanding the fact that the agricultural capital of Europe has more than doubled since 1840, further increase promises to be very questionable, or at least very slow.

UNITED KINGDOM

In the 17th century agriculture was the principal occupation of the people, and made great progress after the expulsion of the Stuarts, but its golden epoch was the reign of George II. (1727–60). We have no reliable statistics till the present century, viz. :—

ACRES UNDER CROPS

Year	England	Scotland	Ireland	United Kingdom	Authority
1827	11,140,000	2,550,000	5,450,000	19,140,000	Porter
1846	13,300,000	3,390,000	5,240,000	21,930,000	M'Culloch
1866	13,340,000	3,170,000	5,250,000	21,760,000	Official
1876	13,920,000	3,510,000	5,210,000	22,640,000	,,
1888	13,350,000	3,690,000	4,145,000	21,185,000	,,

In the last sixty years the area under crops has increased by 2,200,000 in England and 1,140,000 in Scotland, but in Ireland it has diminished by 1,300,000 acres.

PRINCIPAL CROPS OF ENGLAND, ACREAGE

	1812, Comber	1820, Middleton	1831, M'Culloch	1846, M'Culloch
Wheat . .	3,160,000	3,300,000	3,800,000	3,800,000
Oats . . .	2,870,000	3,000,000	3,000,000	2,500,000
Barley, &c. .	860,000	900,000	900,000	1,500,000
Roots . .	1,250,000	1,200,000	2,650,000	2,700,000
Clover . .	1,150,000	1,200,000		1,300,000
Fallow . .	2,310,000	2,400,000	1,650,000	1,500,000
Total .	11,600,000	12,000,000	12,000,000	13,300,000

In recent years there has been a marked decline in the area under grain, viz. :—

ACREAGE, UNITED KINGDOM

	1871–75	1881–85	1888
Wheat . . .	3,740,000	2,830,000	2,670,000
Oats	4,230,000	4,300,000	4,180,000
Barley, &c. . .	3,570,000	3,210,000	2,940,000
Potatoes . . .	1,510,000	1,380,000	1,410,000
Turnips, &c. . .	3,564,000	3,367,000	3,356,000
Flax	136,000	115,000	116,000
Hops	64,000	68,000	58,000
Clover and grass	29,530,000	31,710,000	32,680,000
Fallow . . .	640,000	760,000	470,000
Total . .	46,984,000	47,740,000	47,880,000

According to M'Culloch, the tillage of the United Kingdom in 1851 stood thus :—

	Grain		Other Crops, Acres	Total Acres	Value of Crops
	Acres	Mill. Bush.			
					£
England	7,200,000	200	5,500,000	12,700,000	80,500,000
Scotland	1,480,000	46	1,110,000	2,590,000	14,900,000
Ireland .	2,920,000	89	1,880,000	4,800,000	26,400,000
United Kingdom }	11,600,000	335	8,490,000	20,090,000	121,800,000

The average value of crops to the acre in 1851 was 110 shillings in Ireland, 114 in Scotland, 127 in England. At present the gross product of the United Kingdom averages 110 shillings per acre.

The distribution of crops in the three kingdoms in 1888 was thus :—

ACREAGE

	England	Scotland	Ireland	United Kingdom
Wheat . .	2,510,000	70,000	90,000	2,670,000
Oats . . .	1,885,000	1,015,000	1,280,000	4,180,000
Barley, &c. .	2,485,000	255,000	200,000	2,940,000
All grain .	6,880,000	1,340,000	1,570,000	9,790,000
Potatoes .	445,000	160,000	805,000	1,410,000
Turnips . .	1,480,000	480,000	290,000	2,250,000
Vetches, &c.	905,000	20,000	145,000	1,070,000
All green crops . }	2,830,000	660,000	1,240,000	4,730,000
Gardens, &c.	535,000	20,000	125,000	680,000
Clover, &c. .	3,105,000	1,670,000	1,205,000	5,980,000
Total crops	13,350,000	3,690,000	4,140,000	21,180,000
Pasture . .	14,590,000	1,190,000	10,920,000	26,700,000
Total . .	27,940,000	4,880,000	15,060,000	47,880,000

The yield per acre has much increased since the last century, when Arthur Young showed the wheat average for a number of years to be 23 bushels. The following estimates have been made :—

	Yield per Acre, Bushels		
	Wheat	Oats	Barley
Comber, 1810–15 . . .	22	36	32
M'Culloch, 1840–46 . .	31	37	37
Caird, 1857–77 . . .	28	46	37

The production of grain in the United Kingdom compared with population is now less than half what it was in 1830, having steadily declined since then, viz.:—

	Production, Millions of Bushels			Bushels per Inhabitant
	Wheat	Oats, Barley, &c.	Total	
1830	104	304	408	17
1846	143	258	401	15
1866	98	290	388	14
1876	84	270	354	11
1887	76	235	301	8

The consumption has nevertheless risen in quantity 40 per cent., nearly one-half now being imported, viz. :—

Consumption of Grain, Millions of Bushels Yearly

Period	Home-Grown	Imported	Total	Ratio Imported
1831–40	408	8	416	2 per cent.
1841–50	400	31	431	7 ,,
1851–60	390	78	468	17 ,,
1861–70	388	126	514	24 ,,
1871–80	340	226	566	40 ,,
1881–89	320	272	592	45 ,,

The production and consumption of wheat show as follows :—

Wheat, Millions of Bushels, Yearly Consumption

	Home-Grown	Imported	Total	Lbs. per Inhabitant	Ratio Imported
1811–30	97	4	101	300	4 per cent.
1831–50	113	14	127	280	11 ,,
1851–70	109	58	167	345	35 ,,
1871–80	90	116	206	370	57 ,,
1881–89	80	144	224	384	65 ,,

Consumption includes not only food, but also seed, say 8,000,000 bushels, or 12 lbs. per inhabitant.

The average yield of the principal crops in 1884–87 was as follows :—

	Average Crops, 1884–87		
	Great Britain	Ireland	United Kingdom
Wheat, bushels .	73,200,000	1,900,000	75,100,000
Barley, ,, .	72,500,000	5,800,000	78,300,000
Oats, ,, .	110,000,000	50,000,000	160,000,000
Beans, &c. ,, .	15,000,000	150,000	15,150,000
Potatoes, tons .	3,400,000	3,100,000	6,500,000
Turnips, ,, .	24,500,000	3,500,000	28,000,000
Mangold, ,, .	5,900,000	500,000	6,400,000
Hops, ,, .	30,000	...	30,000
Hay, ,, .	8,500,000	4,000,000	12,500,000

	Yield per Acre, 1884–87		
	Great Britain	Ireland	United Kingdom
Wheat, bushels . . .	30	28	30
Barley, ,, . . .	33	34	33
Oats, ,, . . .	37	38	37½
Beans, &c. ,, . . .	24	28	24
Potatoes, cwts. . . .	121	78	96
Turnips, ,, . . .	240	224	236
Hay, ,, . . .	26	34	29

Lawes and Gilbert's experiments of the yield of ground manured and unmanured showed as follows :—

BUSHELS PER ACRE

Period	Unmanured	Dung	Bone-Ash, &c.
1852–69	14.8	35.7	36.7
1870–79	10.2	29.5	31.7

The seed used for wheat-growing is usually 2½ bushels per acre, and the yield about eleven-fold for the United Kingdom.

According to Mr. Hermann Voss, the United Kingdom consumes annually 290,000 tons of mineral phosphates (93 per cent. imported) and 110,000 of bones (45 per cent. imported), in all, 400,000 tons, from which are produced 800,000 tons of artificial manure, as compared with 200,000 tons in 1860.

The consumption of dung is 79 million tons (see *Manure*) per annum, that is, about 1½ tons per acre.

The crops of 1889 were as follows :—

	England	Scotland	Ireland	United Kingdom	Acreage	Per Acre
Wheat, bushels	71,000,000	2,200,000	2,700,000	75,900,000	2,540,000	30
Oats, ,, ...	76,200,000	37,200,000	50,600,000	164,000,000	4,130,000	40
Barley, ,, ...	59,600,000	7,800,000	7,300,000	74,700,000	2,310,000	32
Beans, &c. ,, ...	14,500,000	500,000	200,000	15,200,000	540,000	28
Potatoes, tons	2,570,000	1,010,000	2,850,000	6,430,000	1,370,000	4.7
Turnips, ,, ...	20,300,000	7,800,000	3,900,000	32,000,000	2,220,000	14.4
Mangolds, ,, ...	6,100,000	...	600,000	6,700,000	370,000	18.0
Hay, ,, ...	10,400,000	1,000,000	4,900,000	16,300,000	9,660,000	1.7

Ensilage or the use of " silos " is increasing, the returns for 1889 showing 2820 in the United Kingdom.

Statistics of live-stock are as follows :—

Year	Horses	Cattle	Sheep	Pigs	Authority
1688	...	...	12,000,000	...	King
1774	...	2,850,000	12,000,000	...	Campbell
1812	1,500,000	5,500,000	25,000,000	3,000,000	Colquhoun
1831	1,500,000	5,220,000	...	4,000,000	M'Culloch
1855	2,050,000	7,955,000	27,972,000	3,686,000	,,
1867	...	8,730,000	33,820,000	4,220,000	Official
1877	1,890,000	9,730,000	32,220,000	3,730,000	,,
1888	1,940,000	10,270,000	28,940,000	3,820,000	,,

The figures before 1812 are for England and Wales, the rest for the United Kingdom. Horses used in towns are not included above.

In 1855, according to M'Culloch, the live-stock stood thus :—

	England	Scotland	Ireland	United Kingdom
Horses . .	1,309,000	185,000	556,000	2,050,000
Cattle . .	3,420,000	975,000	3,560,000	7,955,000
Sheep . .	18,690,000	5,680,000	3,602,000	27,972,000
Pigs . . .	2,360,000	146,000	1,180,000	3,686,000

The returns of the three kingdoms for 1888 are as follows :—

	England	Scotland	Ireland	United Kingdom
Horses . .	1,240,000	190,000	510,000	1,940,000
Cattle . .	5,060,000	1,110,000	4,100,000	10,270,000
Sheep . .	18,580,000	6,730,000	3,630,000	28,940,000
Pigs . . .	2,265,000	155,000	1,400,000	3,820,000

The proportion of cattle in England to size of farms in 1885 was :—

NUMBER TO 100 ACRES

Acres	Horses	Cows	Sheep	Pigs	Total
Under 5	7	30	30	50	117
5–50	5	29	38	17	89
50–100	5	23	51	9	88
100–500	4	17	74	6	101
Over 500	3	10	105	4	122

The production of meat is computed on an annual slaughter of 20 per cent. of all horned cattle, 40 per cent. of sheep, and 100 per cent. of pigs, the average carcase being taken at 600 lbs. beef, 70 lbs. mutton, and 100 lbs.* pig. The following table shows the production and consumption :—

Period	Tons of Meat Consumed Yearly			Lbs. Meat per Inhabitant
	Home-Grown	Imported	Total	
1831–40	940,000	...	940,000	80
1841–50	980,000	...	980,000	80
1851–60	1,000,000	44,000	1,044,000	81
1861–70	1,020,000	131,000	1,151,000	87
1871–80	1,050,000	288,000	1,338,000	87
1881–87	1,030,000	540,000	1,570,000	98

Machinery has introduced great changes in the mode of cultivation since the Waterloo epoch. The Census of 1821 showed 33 per cent. of the classified population of England was engaged in agriculture, that of 1881 only 12 per cent. The following table shows the number engaged in agriculture at various dates, and the approximate gross value of all farming products :—

AGRICULTURAL HANDS AND PRODUCT, UNITED KINGDOM

Year	Numbers Engaged	Product, Millions £	Product per Hand
			£
1821	2,930,000	190	65
1831	3,050,000	195	65
1841	3,401,000	200	59
1851	3,519,000	220	63
1861	3,149,000	240	76
1871	2,808,000	250	89
1881	2,561,000	251	98

The numbers engaged before 1841 are estimates as concerns Ireland and Scotland, the rest are from Booth's reports.

The earliest estimate of the value of agricultural products in England was by Gregory King, in 1698, as follows :—

	Bushels	Value, £	Pence per Bushel
Wheat	14,000,000	2,450,000	42
Barley	27,000,000	2,700,000	·24
Rye	10,000,000	1,250,000	30
Oats	16,000,000	1,200,000	18
Pease and beans .	11,000,000	1,375,000	30
Vetches	1,000,000	100,000	24
Total . .	79,000,000	9,075,000	27

* Major Craigie computes that 1000 cattle give 67 tons of beef, and 1000 sheep 12½ tons mutton yearly ; my estimate is 54 tons of beef, and 12½ tons of mutton.

He computed that 16 per cent. was required for seed, leaving the balance for consumption 66 million bushels, equal to 10 bushels per inhabitant. The following estimates have since been recorded of the total value of agricultural and pastoral products yearly :—

England and Wales			United Kingdom		
Date	Author	Mills. £	Date	Author	Mills. £
1812	Stevenson	131	1812	Colquhoun, &c.	260
1820	Middleton	127	1834	Spackmann	250
1846	M'Culloch	142	1846	M'Culloch	218
1889	Mulhall	158	1889	Mulhall	251

Colquhoun's estimate in 1812 was 194 millions sterling for tillage, omitting pastoral products, which were after-wards valued at 66 millions, thus making a total of 260 millions. This was only 34 millions over Arthur Young's estimate in 1790, which did not include Ireland. We may, therefore, conclude that the value of farm products has been almost stationary for 100 years, except the effects of a passing season of war or scarcity. Colquhoun's table showed thus in 1812 :—

	Quantity	Value, £
Wheat, tons . . .	1,800,000	32,300,000
Other grain, tons . .	5,200,000	41,300,000
Potatoes . . .	...	14,200,000
Turnips . . .	...	14,200,000
Fruit and vegetables . .	...	2,800,000
Hay, grass, &c. . .	...	89,200,000
Total . .	...	194,000,000

VALUE OF CROPS, &C., IN 1889

	England £	Scotland £	Ireland £	United Kingdom £	Price per Ton £
Wheat	13,100,000	400,000	500,000	14,000,000	6.5
Oats	7,200,000	3,600,000	4,800,000	15,600,000	5.7
Barley	9,600,000	1,300,000	1,200,000	12,100,000	6.6
All grain	29,900,000	5,300,000	6,500,000	41,700,000	...
Straw	5,300,000	900,000	1,100,000	7,300,000	1.1
Beans, &c.	1,800,000	100,000	...	1,900,000	5.0
Potatoes	7,000,000	2,700,000	8,000,000	17,700,000	2.7
Hay	17,700,000	1,700,000	8,000,000	27,400,000	1.7
Turnips, &c. . . .	21,100,000	6,200,000	3,600,000	30,900,000	0.8
Hops	2,200,000	...	...	2,200,000	75.0
Flax	...	...	850,000	850,000	45.0
Sundries	2,100,000	100,000	650,000	2,750,000	...
Total	87,100,000	17,000,000	28,700,000	132,800,000	...
Animal products . . .	64,400,000	16,000,000	29,600,000	110,000,000	...
Sundries	6,700,000	900,000	800,000	8,400,000	...
Total	158,200,000	33,900,000	59,100,000	251,200,000	...

M'Culloch also made tables for each of the three kingdoms in 1846, which compare with the results in 1889 as follows :—

ALL FARM PRODUCTS, MILLIONS £

	1846			1889		
	Agricultural	Pastoral	Total	Agricultural	Pastoral	Total
England .	80	62	142	94	64	158
Scotland .	19	9	28	18	16	34
Ireland . .	28	20	48	29	30	59
U. Kingdom	127	91	218	141	110	251

The following table shows the profits of farming, out of which the tenant-farmer has to pay his rent and maintain his family :—

	Cost per Acre			Number of Acres	Amount
	£	s.	d.		£
Labour	2	5	0	48,000,000	108,000,000
Team	1	0	0	,,	48,000,000
Taxes and Tithes .	0	8	4	,,	20,000,000
Seed	0	10	0	21,200,000	10,600,000
Manure	0	12	0	,,	12,700,000
Balance for rent, &c.	1	1	3	48,000,000	51,900,000
Total value of farm products . . .					251,200,000

Allowing the tenant one-half of the profits to support his family, the landlord's share would be 10½ shillings per acre.

Comparing M'Culloch's tables with the value of products in 1889, we find as follows :—

VALUE OF ALL FARM PRODUCTS

	1831	1846	1889
	England	England	United Kingdom
	£	£	£
Grain	53,300,000	51,500,000	41,700,000
Green crops . .	15,300,000	28,500,000	53,600,000
Hay and straw . .		13,000,000	34,700,000
Meat		26,200,000	55,200,000
Dairy		12,000,000	31,200,000
Poultry and eggs .	59,430,000	1,400,000	9,100,000
Foals		3,000,000	5,800,000
Hides, wool, &c. .		4,300,000	9,200,000
Timber.		1,800,000	1,400,000
Vegetables, fruit, &c.		...	9,300,000
Total . . .	128,030,000	141,700,000	251,200,000

IRELAND

According to Sir W. Petty, the war of Cromwell reduced Ireland to a wilderness, three-fourths of the cattle being destroyed : the value of live-stock fell from four millions sterling in 1641 to £500,000 in 1652, and such was the scarcity of grain, that a barrel of wheat rose in that interval from 12 to 50 shillings. The areas cultivated and uncultivated at various dates show thus :—

ACREAGE

Year	Cultivated	Uncultivated	Total	Authority
1726	11,043,000	9,777,000	20,820,000	Browne
1805	13,440,000	7,380,000	,,	Newenham
1812	13,454,000	7,366,000	,,	,,
1837	14,604,000	4,216,000	,,	Official
1874	15,720,000	3,100,000	,,	,,
1888	15,060,000	3,760,000	,,	,,

Secretary Larcom's statement of the crops in 1847 (excluding hay) compares with the returns for 1887 thus :—

	Crop		Value	
	1847	1887	1847	1887
Wheat, bushels	24,000,000	1,900,000	£ 6,700,000	£ 320,000
Oats, ,, .	92,000,000	43,500,000	11,500,000	3,630,000
Barley, &c. ,, .	13,000,000	4,800,000	2,300,000	600,000
Potatoes, tons .	2,000,000	3,570,000	8,200,000	10,800,000
Turnips, ,, .	5,800,000	3,170,000	3,500,000	1,200,000
Total . .	...	...	32,200,000	16,550,000

The acreage of crops, according to Larcom and other official returns, was :—

ACREAGE

	1847	1852	1859	1867	1876	1888
Wheat	744,000	354,000	466,000	281,000	120,000	90,000
Oats	2,201,000	2,283,000	1,981,000	1,680,000	1,487,000	1,280,000
Barley, &c. . .	333,000	340,000	205,000	163,000	242,000	200,000
Potatoes . . .	284,000	877,000	1,203,000	1,026,000	881,000	805,000
Turnips . . .	384,000	357,000	322,000	326,000	345,000	290,000
Flax	58,000	137,000	...	218,000	133,000	114,000
Sundries . . .	95,000	122,000	114,000	130,000	138,000	156,900
Clover, &c. . .	1,140,000	1,270,000	...	1,660,000	1,860,000	1,205,000
Total . . .	5,239,000	5,740,000	...	5,484,000	5,206,000	4,140,000

The Registrar-General for Ireland published recently his estimate of the agricultural products in cycles of five years thus :—

	Average Annual Value		
	1851-55	1866-70	1884-88
Crops	£ 43,660,000	£ 27,935,000	£ 16,470,000
Cattle, &c. . .	28,330,000	44,280,000	37,550,000
Total . .	71,990,000	72,215,000	54,020,000

Since 1870 the annual product of farming has declined 18 millions sterling. The landlords have voluntarily or judicially had their rents reduced about 30 per cent.—say, 3 millions sterling on a rental of 10 millions ; the tenants have suffered the rest of the loss, 15 millions sterling.

This loss of 18 millions sterling per annum, recorded by the Registrar-General, is, as he shows, 25 per cent. of the total farm product of Ireland.

In 1843-45 Sir Richard Griffith valued the crops, exclusive of grass and hay, at £43,000,000. In 1861 Hancock valued all crops at £34,900,000 ; and Fisher at £36,800,000. It would appear that in the preceding table hay is counted not with crops, but in the item of cattle products.

The decline of agriculture in Ireland has been mainly due to the cause stated by John Stuart Mill :—

"Alone among mankind the Irish peasant cannot be better or worse off by any act of his. If industrious or prudent, nobody but the landlord gains, if lazy or intemperate, it is at the landlord's expense."

Nevertheless, the value of live-stock has almost trebled since 1841.

VALUE OF LIVE-STOCK

					£
1841	.	.	.	.	21,100,000
1855	.	.	.	.	33,100,000
1888	.	.	.	.	55,200,000

The numbers of live-stock in 1855 compare with those of 1888 thus :—

	Number		Value	
	1855	1888	1855	1888
Horses . .	556,000	507,000	£ 4,500,000	£ 15,200,000
Cattle. . .	3,560,000	4,100,000	23,200,000	32,800,000
Sheep . . .	3,602,000	3,627,000	3,900,000	4,900,000
Pigs . . .	1,180,000	1,398,000	1,500,000	2,300,000
Total . .	...	...	33,100,000	55,200,000

The increase has been rather in value than in number, viz. :—

			In Value	In Number
Horses .	.	.	227 per cent.	0 ...
Cattle	.	.	41 ,,	15 per cent.
Sheep	.	.	26 ,,	0 ...
Pigs	.	.	54 ,,	20 per cent.

During the eighteenth century 60 per cent. of the Irish exports were meat, the price of which rose from twenty shillings per cwt. in 1776 to fifty shillings in 1800. After the Waterloo epoch almost down to the famine of 1846, England drew twenty million bushels of wheat yearly from Ireland.

Of late years the exportation of live-stock to Great Britain has declined, viz. :—

EXPORTS TO ENGLAND AND SCOTLAND.

				1877	1887
Cattle .	.	.	.	649,000	669,000
Sheep .	.	.	.	630,000	548,000
Pigs .	.	.	.	585,000	480,000

Emigration has drained the country so largely of men in the vigour of life that pauperism increased 46 per cent. between 1877 and 1887 (see *Paupers*). For rental, value, and tenure, see *Land*.

SCOTLAND

M'Culloch's tables for 1814 and 1846, with subsequent official returns, are as follows :—

ACREAGE

	1814	1846	1857	1867	1878	1888
Wheat	140,000	350,000	243,000	110,000	75,000	70,000
Oats	1,260,000	1,300,000	930,000	1,000,000	1,030,000	1,015,000
Barley, &c.	398,000	500,000	182,000	215,000	290,000	255,000
Turnips	410,000	450,000	470,000	480,000	500,000	480,000
Potatoes	80,000	200,000	145,000	150,000	165,000	160,000
Sundries	48,000	40,000	...	...	25,000	40,000
Clover, &c.	220,000	550,000	...	...	...	1,670,000
Total	2,556,000	3,390,000	...	...	...	3,690,000

M'Culloch estimated the farming products of 1846 as follows :—

	£
Grain	8,100,000
Green crops . . .	10,600,000
Pastoral products . .	9,000,000
Total . . .	27,700,000

He estimated the grain produced at 48 million bushels, against Larcom's estimate same year for Ireland, 129 millions.

The numbers of live-stock were :—

	1857	1867	1878	1888
Horses . .	...	...	191,000	190,000
Cattle . .	970,000	960,000	1,095,000	1,110,000
Sheep . .	5,750,000	6,070,000	7,036,000	6,730,000
Pigs . . .	137,000	204,000	140,000	155,000

For tenure and rental, see *Lands*.

ISLANDS

Isle of Man.—Area 145,000 acres, of which 98,000 cultivated, 24,000 under grain, 12,000 green crops, and the rest clover, &c.

Jersey.—Area 29,000 acres, of which 20,000 cultivated, half green crops, half clover.

Guernsey, &c.—Area 20,000 acres, of which 12,000 cultivated ; same mode as Jersey.

The products of these islands are included with those of England.

UNITED KINGDOM

AGRICULTURAL CAPITAL

Year	Millions, £ Sterling				£ per Inhabitant
	Land	Cattle	Sundries	Total	
1750	498	25	58	581	55
1780	702	35	81	812	65
1814	1,470	74	172	1,716	95
1843	1,677	94	197	1,968	72
1850	1,705	104	201	2,010	72
1860	1,748	140	210	2,098	72
1868	1,925	170	233	2,328	75
1880	2,086	209	255	2,550	72
1887*	1,873	185	229	2,287	61

In the above table land is capitalised at 30 years' rental. As for cattle, it was valued by King in 1688 at 25 millions ; the figures for 1814 and subsequent years are according to the numbers of live-stock at the several dates specified in table. Sundries are estimated at 10

* The actual value of land is supposed to be 1560 millions, the official valuation being 20 per cent. too high. In a paper read at the Surveyors' Institution in January 1890, Mr. H. H. Smith showed a decline of 523 millions sterling since 1880.

per cent. of the total, in preference to 14 per cent., adopted by Chaptal and other French economists.

There was a steady increase down to 1880, from which date agricultural capital has been declining, viz. :—

Period	Millions, £	£ per Annum
1750–1780	Increase, 231	7,450,000
1781–1814	,, 904	26,600,000
1815–1843	,, 252	8,700,000
1844–1860	,, 130	8,100,000
1861–1880	,, 452	22,600,000
1881–1889	Decline, 263	29,200,000

Notwithstanding the recent decline, agricultural capital still forms one-fourth of the wealth of the nation (see *Wealth*), and is almost three times as great as it was 100 years ago.

The distribution of this capital among the three kingdoms in 1887 was :—

AGRICULTURAL CAPITAL, MILLIONS £

	Land	Cattle	Sundries	Total	£ per Inhabitant
England . . .	1,362	104	163	1,629	57
Scotland . . .	213	26	27	266	61
Ireland . . .	298	55	39	392	80
United Kingdom	1,873	185	229	2,287	61

The relation between capital and product in 1887 was as follows :—

MILLION £

	Capital	Gross Product	Ratio to Capital
England	1,629	158	9.7 per cent.
Scotland	266	34	12.8 ,,
Ireland	392	59	15.0 ,,
United Kingdom	2,287	251	11.1 ,,

Further details will be found under the items *Cattle* and *Land*.

The value of tillage and pastoral products compares in the three kingdoms with the number of hands employed as follows :—

	Hands	Product, Million £	£ per Head
England . . .	1,341,000	158	118
Scotland . . .	234,000	34	145
Ireland	986,000	59	60
United Kingdom	2,561,000	251	97

FRANCE

This is the best cultivated country in Europe. The earliest statistics do not give us the total area under grain, being confined to wheat-growing in the last century, but the estimates of Chaptal, Rubichon, and Moreau, with the official reports of later times, afford some guide for the last ninety years, and may be summed up thus :—

Year	Acres under Grain	Crop, Millions of Bushels		
		Wheat	Oats, Rye, &c.	Total
1801–20	30,000,000	140	250	390
1825–35	32,000,000	170	310	480
1840–50	34,300,000	220	360	580
1860–76	36,000,000	265	450	715
1883–86	37,100,000	301	439	740

Official returns of wheat-growing, coupled with Moreau's tables since 1700, give the following :—

Year	Acres	Million Bushels	Bushels per Acre	Value of Crop, £
1700	12,400,000	83	6.7	12,000,000
1760	11,200,000	90	8.0	29,600,000
1764	12,400,000	97	7.8	28,100,000
1784	14,800,000	110	7.2	28,800,000
1791	11,500,000	130	11.2	37,800,000
1818	12,800,000	142	11.2	49,100,000
1839	13,900,000	195	14.0	60,800,000
1841	13,900,000	198	14.1	53,200,000
1851	15,000,000	238	15.9	49,800,000
1861	16,900,000	207	12.2	73,600,000
1871–80	17,100,000	270	15.7	90,800,000
1881–86	17,400,000	303	17.3	81,800,000
1889	17,600,000	309	17.5	74,200,000

Moreau states that 33 per cent. of the population were fed on wheat in the last century, and 60 per cent. in 1839.

The average yield of grain was officially stated thus (Spallart) :—

BUSHELS, PER ACRE

Year	Wheat	Oats	Barley	Rye
1815	9.4	16.0	13.2	8.4
1835	14.7	19.1	15.4	13.7
1855	12.5	26.2	20.7	11.0
1875	16.0	24.0	19.1	15.6
1880	16.0	26.4	20.7	15.1
1884	17.8	26.2	20.2	16.7

Notwithstanding the increase of grain-growing, France has paid large sums for imported grain. From 1801 to 1849, her net imports of wheat alone cost her 26 millions sterling, and the imports of grain from 1860 to 1886 (over exports) cost 211 millions sterling. The trade returns show :—

Year	Net Imports of Grain		Annual Average	
	Millions of Bushels	Value, Million £	Millions of Bushels	Value, £
1861–70	92	32	9	3,200,000
1871–80	384	101	38	10,100,000
1881–86	346	78	58	13,000,000
Total	822	211	32	8,100,000

The importation of grain would have been still greater but for the rapid increase of potatoes, which have multiplied fivefold since 1820.

CROP OF POTATOES, TONS PER ANNUM

1815–20 . . 1,950,000		1861–80 . . . 6,500,000		
1831–40 . . 4,900,000		1883–86 . . . 10,400,000		

The official returns of wine-growing since 1810 may be condensed as follows :—

VINEYARDS.

Period	Acres	Millions of Gallons	Value of Wine, £	Gallons per Acre
1810–12	4,064,000	455	26,600,000	112
1830–32	5,015,000	502	35,600,000	100
1840–42	5,230,000	790	52,700,000	151
1850–52	5,450,000	920	80,500,000	166
1860–62	5,510,000	703	68,900,000	126
1870–72	6,560,000	1,010	84,200,000	155
1880–82	5,150,000	720	59,200,000	139
1883–86	5,110,000	790	56,200,000	155
1889	4,550,000	525	44,000,000	112

Down to 1880 there was always a surplus of wine for exportation, but since that year the imports exceed the exports : the net importation in 1886 was 190 million gallons. The phylloxera completely destroyed 2,900,000 acres of vines, one-half of which have been newly planted with American and other vines, besides injuring 1,600,000 acres, which still yield crops. Only 2,100,000 acres of the vineyards of 1872 have escaped the pest.

Beet-root is another valuable crop, having been introduced by Bonaparte : the area and production have been approximately as follows :—

Year	Beet-Growing	
	Acres	Crop, Tons
1840	200,000	800,000
1860	490,000	3,000,000
1879	1,100,000	10,600,000
1886	1,310,000	14,800,000

In 1842 it was proposed in the Legislature to pull up the plantations and pay the owners £1,500,000 indemnity, but the bill was thrown out. The production of beet-sugar (see *Sugar*) at present exceeds 400,000 tons yearly against 35,000 in 1840.

Oil, flax, tobacco, chestnuts, &c., are crops of less note (see each under its own title).

M. Lavergne in 1859 compared the agricultural condition with that of 1789 as follows :—

ACRES

	1789	1859
Arable	61,720,000	64,190,000
Meadow	7,410,000	9,880,000
Gardens and vineyards . .	7,400,000	9,870,000
Woods and waste . . .	46,810,000	39,400,000
Total	123,340,000	123,340,000

Since 1848 no less than nine million acres of waste land have been reclaimed, the principal areas being approximately shown thus :—

ACRES

	1848	1884	Increase
Grain	34,500,000	37,500,000	3,000,000
Various crops .	23,000,000	24,500,000	1,500,000
Forest	16,200,000	20,700,000	4,500,000
Total . . .	73,700,000	82,700,000	9,000,000

Machinery was not much in use till after the reign of Louis Philippe ; it was common in 1840 to see horses treading out grain, but in 1862 an official report showed 101,000 threshing-machines, of which 2850 were worked by steam. Improved methods led to a better yield per acre, viz. :—

Yield, Bushels per Acre

	1821-30	1866-75
Wheat	13	16
Oats	17	27
Barley	14	22

The yield of wheat in the first period was 550 to 100 lbs. seed, and in the second period 750.

The principal crops for 1888 compare with those of 1880 thus :—

	Acreage		Product	
	1880	1888	1880	1888
Wheat	16,990,000	17,180,000	274,000,000 bushels	273,000,000
Oats	8,580,000	9,230,000	230,000,000 ,,	225,000,000
Rye	4,560,000	4,040,000	70,000,000 ,,	62,000,000
Barley	2,600,000	2,240,000	54,000,000 ,,	44,000,000
Maize	1,660,000	1,420,000	28,000,000 ,,	30,000,000
Mixed	2,620,000	2,330,000	46,000,000 ,,	40,000,000
All grain	37,010,000	36,440,000	702,000,000 bushels	674,000,000
Potatoes	3,220,000	3,570,000	9,500,000 tons	10,400,000
Beet-root	1,110,000	1,310,000	14,800,000 ,,	12,200,000
Vines	5,450,000	4,550,000	653,000,000 gallons	525,000,000
Colza	340,000	180,000	4,660,000 bushels	2,710,000
Flax and hemp	380,000	250,000	2,400,000 ,, seed	1,660,000
Olives	280,000	270,000	... bushels	6,620,000
Clover	2,580,000	2,250,000	... tons	3,790,000
Total . . .	50,370,000	48,820,000	...	...

The above is exclusive of 3,620,000 acres under other artificial grasses than clover, producing 6,100,000 tons grass yearly.

The statistics of live-stock at various dates have been as follows :—

Year	Horses	Cattle	Sheep	Pigs	Goats	Authority
1812	1,835,000	6,080,000	30,310,000	...	...	Smith
1830	2,500,000	7,130,000	29,130,000	4,500,000	1,210,000	M'Gregor
1840	1,870,000	9,930,000	32,150,000	4,500,000	900,000	Scknabel
1852	3,280,000	12,150,000	33,300,000	5,250,000	1,340,000	Official
1862	3,340,000	12,810,000	29,500,000	6,040,000	1,730,000	,,
1873	3,140,000	11,720,000	25,900,000	5,760,000	1,790,000	,,
1883	3,220,000	11,790,000	21,600,000	5,850,000	1,460,000	,,
1888	3,250,000	13,380,000	22,600,000	5,850,000	1,550,000	,,

The official valuation of live-stock in 1882 was :—

	No.	Value, £	£ per Head
Horses . . .	2,840,000	54,400,000	19.4
Mules . . .	250,000	4,300,000	17.2
Asses . . .	400,000	1,900,000	4.8
Cattle . . .	11,800,000	123,500,000	10.5
Sheep . . .	23,000,000	22,900,000	1.0
Goats . . .	1,500,000	1,200,000	0.8
Pigs	5,800,000	22,900,000	3.9
Total . .	...	231,100,000	...

The production of meat at various times, according to French writers, was :—

Years	Tons, Meat	Lbs. per Inhabitant
1840	671,000	43
1860	942,000	57
1880	1,155,000	67
1888	1,200,000	67

The above does not include horse-flesh, of which some 2000 tons are used at Paris alone.

In 1882 the annual slaughter was estimated thus :—

	Number	Tons, Meat	Lbs. per Carcase
25 per cent. of cattle .	3,300,000	640,000	430
33 per cent. of sheep .	7,700,000	210,000	60
70 per cent. of pigs . .	4,000,000	305,000	170

According to M. Lavergne, the production of meat was 39 lbs. per inhabitant in 1790, and 61 lbs. in 1859. (See *Food.*) The value of agricultural and pastoral products has been estimated at various dates as follows :—

Year	Value of Products, Millions £			Authorities
	Agricul-tural	Pas-toral	Total	
1815	134	88	222	Chaptal
1835	170	99	269	Schoen, Moreau
1843	212	101	313	Royer, Dupin
1862	307	...	...	Official
1882	322	182	504*	
1886	322	138	460	Mulhall

The number of persons engaged in agriculture was approximately as follows :—

Year	Principals	Retainers, &c.	Total
1851 . . .	7,310,000	14,620,000	21,930,000
1861 . . .	6,630,000	13,250,000	19,880,000
1872 . . .	6,170,000	12,340,000	18,510,000
1881 . . .	6,455,000	11,794,000	18,249,000

The number has declined 17 per cent. since 1851, while the value of products has increased, the ratio being about £49 per head in the former year, and £71 in 1886.

* The official table sums up a total of 538 millions sterling, but this includes £34,000,000 for 84 million tons of animal manure, which I am compelled to deduct, as other nations take no account of manure among agricultural products.

The official statement of crops for 1886 was as follows :—

	Tons	Value, £	Per Ton, £
Wheat	8,230,000	71,000,000	8.6
Oats.	4,220,000	29,200,000	7.0
Rye	1,620,000	10,300,000	6.4
Barley	1,150,000	7,200,000	6.3
Maize, &c. . .	1,720,000	11,600,000	6.7
All grain . . .	16,940,000	129,300,000	7.6
Potatoes . . .	11,290,000	22,500,000	2.0
Beetroot . . .	15,040,000	12,100,000	0.8
Hay.	25,600,000	57,600,000	2.2
Apples	1,100,000	3,200,000	3.0
Chestnuts . . .	760,000	1,800,000	2.4
Mulberry leaves .	210,000	400,000	2.0
Olives	170,000	1,200,000	7.0
Colza, &c.. . .	94,000	1,100,000	12.0
Hemp	43,000	1,500,000	35.0
Flax.	30,000	1,200,000	40.0
Tobacco . . .	22,000	800,000	36.0
Wine, gallons .	670,000,000	49,000,000	Per gal. 18d.
All crops . . .		281,700,000	
Milk, gallons . . 1,620,000,000		46,800,000	Per gal. 7d.
Poultry and eggs		12,000,000	
Vegetables and fruit		30,000,000	
Timber, 1000 million cubic feet		10,000,000	Not official
Foals		8,000,000	
Meat, 1,200,000 tons		60,000,000	
Hides, wool, tallow, wax, &c. .		11,500,000	
Total		460,000,000	

The value of crops for 1888 was returned at 254 millions sterling, being 28 millions less than in 1886, of which 15 millions stood for loss in the vintage.

AGRICULTURAL CAPITAL

MILLIONS, £ STERLING

Year	Land	Cattle	Sundries	Total	Product	Ratio to Capital
						Per cent.
1815	1,293	53	149	1,495	222	15.0
1835	1,473	96	174	1,743	269	15.5
1852	2,106	166	252	2,524	356	14.1
1881	2,986	231	357	3,574	504	14.1
1886	2,688	218	323	3,229	460	14.4

The value of land is stated above, as given by Chaptal and Dutens for 1815 and 1835, by Government reports for 1852 and 1881, the figures for 1886 being an estimated reduction of 10 per cent. from 1881, the prevalent opinion in France being that the fall is 15 per cent. As regards cattle, Chaptal gives the value for 1815, and the subsequent estimates are according to the number of cattle at the respective dates. Sundries are estimated at 10 per cent., although Chaptal and Dutens made them 14 per cent. of the total.

The increase of agricultural wealth was rapid down to 1881, viz. :—

Period	Millions, £	Per Annum, £
1815–35 . . .	248 increase	12,400,000
1836–52 . . .	781 ,,	46,000,000
1853–81 . . .	1,050 ,,	36,200,000
1882–86 . . .	345 decrease	69,000,000

The capital represented by agriculture is at present double what it was in the year 1815, and nearly 40 per cent. of the wealth of the nation.

See *Wealth*. For land-tenure, see *Land*.

GERMANY

Official returns give the area under tillage since 1837, thus :—

Year	Acres under Tillage	Grain, Million Bushels	Authority
1816	23,100,000	296	Fisher
1837	30,010,000	...	Official
1858	35,330,000	...	,,
1879	43,310,000	580	,,
1887	44,050,000	640	,,

The above area under tillage includes all crops except hay, which at present covers nearly 15 million acres. Since 1816 the area of tillage has almost doubled, and the production of grain more than doubled.

The area of tillage was distributed in this manner :—

ACRES OF TILLAGE

	1816	1837	1858	1887
Prussia . .	10,430,000	14,160,000	17,740,000	27,600,000
Hanover. .	1,310,000	1,690,000	1,840,000	
Bavaria . .	3,560,000	4,320,000	4,620,000	5,500,000
Wurtemburg	1,390,000	1,610,000	1,690,000	1,800,000
Saxony . .	1,200,000	1,650,000	2,120,000	1,900,000
Duchies, &c.	5,210,000	6,580,000	7,320,000	7,250,000
Total . .	23,100,000	30,010,000	35,330,000	44,050,000

According to a statement published in 1834, the kingdom of Prussia showed as follows :—

	Acres	*An. Profit £*
Arable and meadow . .	28,510,000	8,400,000
Pasture	13,620,000	3,300,000
Woods	17,300,000	1,100,000
Various	12,600,000	800,000
Total	72,030,000	13,600,000

The following table shows the tilled and untilled area of the several States, 1887 :—

AREA

	Prussia	Bavaria	Saxony	Wurtemburg	Small States	Total
Arable	27,600,000	5,500,000	1,900,000	1,800,000	7,250,000	44,050,000
Meadow	8,150,000	3,200,000	420,000	720,000	2,160,000	14,650,000
Forest	18,100,000	5,900,000	600,000	1,200,000	4,300,000	30,100,000
Pasture, &c . . .	26,450,000	2,800,000	580,000	480,000	7,290,000	37,600,000
Total . .	80,300,000	17,400,000	3,500,000	4,200,000	21,000,000	126,400,000

The area under principal crops in 1887 was as follows :—

ACRES

	Prussia	Bavaria	Saxony	Wurtemburg	Baden	Small States	Total
Wheat	2,700,000	800,000	120,000	75,000	100,000	955,000	4,750,000
Rye	10,950,000	1,550,000	520,000	550,000	300,000	1,470,000	15,340,000
Barley	2,300,000	850,000	100,000	220,000	150,000	680,000	4,300,000
Oats.	6,200,000	1,100,000	450,000	350,000	150,000	550,000	8,800,000
All grain	22,150,000	4,300,000	1,190,000	1,195,000	700,000	3,655,000	33,190,000
Meadow	8,150,000	3,200,000	420,000	720,000	500,000	1,660,000	14,650,000
Potatoes	4,980,000	740,000	300,000	200,000	210,000	820,000	7,250,000
Total . .	35,280,000	8,240,000	1,910,000	2,115,000	1,410,000	6,135,000	55,090,000

The crops were as follows :—

TONS IN 1887

	Prussia	Bavaria	Saxony	Wurtemburg	Baden	Small States	Total
Wheat	1,470,000	420,000	85,000	40,000	50,000	605,000	2,670,000
Rye, &c.	4,220,000	790,000	285,000	235,000	140,000	860,000	6,530,000
Barley	1,145,000	485,000	60,000	130,000	90,000	430,000	2,340,000
Oats	2,890,000	590,000	295,000	180,000	80,000	825,000	4,860,000
All grain	9,725,000	2,285,000	725,000	585,000	360,000	2,720,000	16,400,000
Hay	6,650,000	6,130,000	520,000	1,260,000	920,000	2,420,000	17,900,000
Potatoes	16,250,000	2,730,000	1,230,000	680,000	730,000	3,520,000	25,140,000

The crops of recent years compared thus :—

	1880	1881–85	1886	1887	1888	1889
	Tons	Tons	Tons	Tons	Tons	Tons
Wheat	2,345,000	2,410,000	2,600,000	2,670,000	2,830,000	2,530,000
Rye	5,440,000	6,200,000	5,940,000	6,530,000	6,480,000	5,630,000
Barley	2,145,000	2,180,000	2,260,000	2,340,000	2,205,000	2,260,000
Oats	4,230,000	4,120,000	4,340,000	4,860,000	4,300,000	4,650,000
All grain	14,160,000	14,910,000	15,140,000	16,400,000	15,815,000	15,070,000
Hay	19,560,000	17,100,000	15,880,000	17,900,000	16,360,000	17,895,000
Potatoes	19,470,000	25,020,000	27,950,000	25,140,000	25,270,000	21,910,000
Beetroot	11,300,000	...	13,970,000	15,500,000	12,650,000	...
Turnips, &c. . . .	3,300,000	...	3,850,000	2,640,000	...	...
Tobacco	52,000	...	38,000	39,000	41,000	26,000
Hops	...	...	33,000	30,000	24,000	22,000
Wine, gallons . . .	...	...	82,000,000	33,000,000	53,000,000	64,000,000

If we take the average for 1888–89 and compare same with that of the years 1881–85, we find an increase of 10 per cent. in wheat and oats, a falling-off in rye, and altogether an increase of 3 per cent. in the weight of grain produced. There is a decline of 6 per cent. in potatoes, while hay and beetroot remain stationary. Wine shows violent fluctuations, the yield in 1889 being almost double that of 1887. There is a remarkable decline in tobacco, the crop of 1889 being only half that of 1880, and also in hops, which have fallen off by one-third.

A table published in 1886 showed the production of grain in the previous year compared with population as follows :—

	Bushels, Grain	Population	Bushels per Head
Prussia . . .	347,000,000	28,300,000	12.3
Bavaria . . .	85,000,000	5,420,000	15.6
Saxony . . .	27,000,000	3,180,000	8.5
Wurtemburg .	16,000,000	1,990,000	8.0
Baden . . .	11,000,000	1,600,000	7.0
Mecklenburg .	22,000,000	680,000	32.5
Alsace . . .	18,000,000	1,560,000	11.5
Hesse . . .	11,000,000	960,000	11.4
Brunswick . .	8,000,000	370,000	21.5
Small States .	35,000,000	2,790,000	12.5
Total . .	580,000,000	46,850,000	12.3

The average yield per acre, according to observations in the several States spreading over a term of eight years ending 1885, was as follows :—

	Bushels per Acre					
	Prussia	Bavaria	Saxony	Wurtemburg	Baden	All Germany
Wheat . . .	18	20	23	18	17	19
Rye	14	18	20	18	15	15
Barley	21	23	25	25	23	22
Oats	24	28	35	29	27	27
Potatoes, cwts. .	58	76	80	68	70	64
Hay, cwts. . . .	18	39	25	34	44	26

The following table of live stock is made up of the statements of Malchus, Schnabel, and Brachelli in 1828 and 1850, and official returns since the latter date :—

	1828	1850	1867	1873	1883
Horses	2,500,000	2,500,000	3,190,000	3,350,000	3,520,000
Cows	9,770,000	11,270,000	14,900,000	15,780,000	15,790,000
Sheep	17,300,000	21,330,000	28,020,000	25,000,000	19,200,000
Pigs	4,500,000	3,920,000	6,460,000	7,120,000	9,210,000
Goats	700,000	1,300,000	1,820,000	2,320,000	2,640,000

German writers compute the amount of seed to the acre, and the average product as follows :—

	Seed, lbs.	Product, lbs.	Equiv. in Bushels
Wheat . . .	157	1,260	20.4
Rye	150	900	15.2
Oats	140	980	25.7
Barley . . .	133	1,200	23.0

The quantity of grain retained for seed is usually 82 million bushels, or one-seventh of the whole crop. It is found that 100 lbs. wheat gave 82 lbs. flour, and 100 lbs. barley 78 lbs. malt.

The following table shows the live stock of Prussia at various dates :—

	1816	1837	1873	1883
Horses . .	1,240,000	1,470,000	2,280,000	2,420,000
Cattle . .	4,010,000	4,850,000	8,610,000	8,740,000
Sheep . .	8,260,000	15,010,000	19,630,000	14,750,000
Pigs . . .	1,490,000	1,940,000	4,280,000	5,820,000

The returns for 1873 and 1883, include Hanover and other territories annexed to Prussia in 1867.

The distribution of live stock in 1883 was as follows :—

	Prussia	Bavaria	Saxony	Wurtemburg	Small States	All Germany
Horses	2,420,000	355,000	125,000	95,000	525,000	3,520,000
Cows	8,740,000	3,040,000	650,000	905,000	2,455,000	15,790,000
Sheep	14,750,000	1,180,000	150,000	550,000	2,560,000	19,190,000
Pigs	5,820,000	1,040,000	350,000	290,000	1,710,000	9,210,000
Goats	1,680,000	220,000	120,000	50,000	570,000	2,640,000

Per 100 Inhabitants

	Prussia	Bavaria	Saxony	Wurtemburg	Small States	All Germany
Horses	6.9	4.7	8.5	5.0	6.6	6.5
Cows	25.1	40.0	43.4	46.4	30.7	29.2
Sheep	42.3	15.5	9.9	28.2	32.0	35.5
Pigs	16.7	13.7	23.7	15.0	21.4	17.0
Goats	4.8	2.9	7.8	2.8	7.1	4.9

Prussia is above the average in horses and sheep, Bavaria in cows, Saxony in horses, cows, and pigs, Wurtemburg in cows only. The ratios of sheep in Bavaria and Saxony are very low.

The value of all kinds of live-stock in 1883 was officially given as follows :—

	Number	Value, £	£ per Head
Horses .	3,532,000	84,000,000	23.7
Cattle .	15,787,000	153,700,000	9.7
Sheep .	19,190,000	15,300,000	0.8
Pigs . .	9,206,000	23,800,000	2.6
Goats .	2,645,000	2,000,000	0.7
Total . .	...	278,800,000	...

Prices of live stock have since declined about 6 per cent. ; the value in 1887 would be approximately £262,000,000 sterling.

The production of meat, calculating 500 lbs. per carcase of beef, 56 lbs. per sheep, 100 lbs. per pig, and 28 lbs. per goat, was as follows :—

Year	Meat, Tons	Lbs. per Inhabitant
1828	760,000	60
1850	890,000	60
1867	1,150,000	67
1885 . . . . : .	1,375,000	64

The value of products in 1886 was approximately as follows :—

	Tons	£	Sundries	£
Wheat . .	2,600,000	18,700,000	Wine . .	5,000,000
Rye . . .	5,940,000	33,900,000	Vegetables	
Barley . .	2,260,000	14,700,000	&c. .	30,000,000
Oats . . .	4,340,000	25,200,000	Timber . .	13,000,000
			Dairy .	55,300,000
All grain .	15,140,000	92,500,000	Meat . .	68,700,000
Straw . .	15,100,000	15,100,000	Poultry . .	14,100,000
Hay . . .	15,900,000	31,800,000	Tobacco,	
Potatoes .	28,000,000	56,000,000	flax .	4,000,000
Beet, &c. .	17,800,000	14,400,000	Hides,	9,000,000
Principal crops	...	209,800,000	wool, &c.	15,100,000
			Sundries .	214,200,000

	£
Agricultural products	262,000,000
Animal products	162,000,000
Total . .	424,000,000

The value of products at different dates was approximately thus :—

Year	Millions, £ Sterling			
	Agricultural	Pastoral	Total	Authority
1840	105	...	...	Journ. des Econ.
1856	151	80	231	Block, Viebahn
1886	262	162	424	...

The products in 1886 were distributed as follows :—

	Agriculture	Animal	Total	£ per Inhab.
	£	£	£	
Prussia . . .	149,000,000	99,800,000	248,800,000	9.0
Bavaria . . .	43,700,000	24,100,000	67,800,000	12.9
Saxony . . .	12,300,000	5,900,000	18,200,000	6.0
Wurtemburg .	10,500,000	7,700,000	18,200,000	9.4
Small States .	46,400,000	24,600,000	71,000,000	9.2
Total .	261,900,000	162,100,000	424,000,000	9.4

The number of hands employed was approximately thus :—

Year	Hands	Product, £	£ per Head
1840 . . .	6,400,000	170,000,000	27
1856 . . .	7,400,000	231,000,000	31
1886 . . .	8,120,000	424,000,000	52

The introduction of machinery has increased production in a striking manner, one man now producing more than two did in 1840.

LAND VALUE

In 1837 the valuation of land in Prussia was 305 millions sterling. In 1856 Viebahn valued German lands at 1304 millions, a rise of 170 per cent. in twenty years. Wurtemburg averaged per acre 50 per cent. more value than the rest of Germany. Guided by Wurtemburg values in 1880 (that is, 50 per cent. over the rest), the value of Germany may be put down thus :—

	Acres	Price per Acre	Amount, Millions £
		£	
Arable	44,000,000	19	836
Meadow . . .	14,600,000	28	409
Garden, &c. . .	2,300,000	40	92
Pasture	35,400,000	5	177
Forest	30,100,000	10	301
Total . . .	126,400,000	...	1,815

The values of the principal States show thus :—

	Millions, £ Sterling					
	Prussia	Bavaria	Wurtemburg	Saxony	Duchies, &c.	Total
Arable . . .	513	103	49	35	136	836
Meadow . . .	227	89	25	12	56	409
Gardens . . .	24	12	8	4	44	92
Pasture . . .	127	13	3	3	30	176
Forest . . .	176	58	20	6	42	302
Total . .	1,067	275	105	60	308	1,815

AGRICULTURAL CAPITAL

The amount of capital and product may be put down approximately as follows :—

Year	Capital, Millions £				Product, Millions £	Ratio to Capital, per Cent.
	Land	Cattle	Sundries	Total		
1837	480	88	63	631	170	27.0
1856	1,304	138	160	1,602	231	14.4
1886	1,815	262	230	2,307	424	18.4

In 1886 the agricultural capital stood approximately thus :—

	Millions, £ Sterling					
	Prussia	Bavaria	Saxony	Wurtemburg	Duchies	Total
Land	1,067	275	60	105	308	1,815
Cattle	162	40	9	12	39	262
Sundries . . .	135	35	8	13	39	230
Total . .	1,364	350	77	130	386	2,307

Capital and product in the above States compare thus :—

	Millions, £ Sterling		
	Capital	Product	Ratio to Cap.
Prussia . . .	1,364	249	18.0
Bavaria . . .	350	68	19.0
Saxony . . .	77	18	23.2
Wurtemburg .	130	18	13.8
Duchies . . .	386	71	18.0
Total . .	2,307	424	18.4

The increase of agricultural capital in Germany was as follows :—

Interval	£	Average per Annum
1837–56	971,000,000	51,000,000
1856–86	705,000,000	23,500,000

The most rapid increase occurred between 1848 and 1858, consequent on the breaking up of large estates among the peasantry. See *Lands*.

RUSSIA

The area under grain previously to 1870 is not known, but may be estimated from the table of production, as below, published officially.

Period	Grain, Millions of Bushels Yearly			Approximate Area, Millions of Acres
	Crop	Exported	Home Consumption	
1800–13	890	10	880	100
1834–40	1,040	27	1,013	110
1841–47	1,210	32	1,178	120
1857–63	1,270	34	1,236	130
1871–80	1,730	146	1,584	167

The emancipation of serfs in 1861 was followed by a great increase of grain production,

These statistics refer to Russia proper, exclusive of Poland, Finland, Caucasus, or Siberia. The distribution of area is shown as follows :—

	Area, Acres		Product in 1887
	1872	1881	
			Tons
Grain	154,800,000	159,800,000	44,250,000
Potatoes . . .	3,170,000	3,710,000	7,500,000
Flax and hemp .	3,060,000	5,170,000	540,000
Meadow and pasture . . .	144,000	176,000,000	...
Forest	500,000	485,000,000	120,000,000
Waste	439,000	414,000,000	...
Total . .	1,244,000,000	1,244,000,000	...

The grain-crops of 1887 compare with those of 1872 as follows :—

	Millions of Bushels		Area under Grain	
	1872	1887	1872	1881
Wheat . .	158	269	28,700,000	28,900,000
Rye . . .	547	721	66,400,000	64,600,000
Oats . . .	544	599	32,800,000	34,900,000
Barley . .	125	162	15,500,000	12,500,000
Maize, &c. .	86	152	11,400,000	18,900,000
Total . .	1,460	1,903	154,800,000	159,800,000

Kaufmann gives the average crops of Russia and Poland in the years 1870–78, and the average value in the years 1878–81, as follows :—

	Millions of Bushels			Value, £
	Russia	Poland	Total	
Wheat	176	15	191	44,800,000
Rye	556	47	603	98,800,000
Oats	446	36	482	50,500,000
Barley, &c. . .	260	25	285	38,900,000
Total . . .	1,438	123	1,561	233,000,000

He shows, moreover, that the crops during the ensuing years 1883–84–85 gave an average (for Russia and Poland) as follows :—

	Million Bushels	Tons
Wheat	231	6,350,000
Rye	675	17,700,000
Oats	503	8,700,000
Barley, &c.	285	6,450,000
Total	1,694	39,200,000

So great, however, was the fall in prices that the grain crops of 1884 were valued at only £156,400,000.
A moujik's farm averages 35 acres, which requires three men to cultivate ; the product is estimated thus :—

	Acres	Bushels			
		Crop	Food	Seed	For Sale
Rye	10	100	70	17	13
Wheat	4	30	5	5	20
Oats, &c.	10	120	30	15	75
All grain . . .	24	250	105	37	108

The earliest official returns of live-stock are those of 1850, but we have also Schnabel's and Malchus's estimates for 1828 :—

	1828	1850	1870	1889
Horses . .	12,000,000	13,500,000	15,600,000	20,020,000
Cattle . .	19,000,000	20,960,000	21,400,000	23,840,000
Sheep . .	36,000,000	37,530,000	45,300,000	47,510,000
Pigs . .	15,800,000	8,890,000	9,100,000	9,200,000
Goats . .	...	1,600,000	1,200,000	1,370,000

The production of meat, at 500 lbs. per beef carcase, 50 lbs. per sheep, and 100 lbs. per pig, was as follows :—

Year	Tons, Meat	Lbs. per Inhabitant
1828	1,430,000	66
1850	1,670,000	67
1870	1,760,000	60
1889	1,885,000	51

The value of live-stock was approximately as follows :—

	No.	Price, £	Value, £
Horses	20,020,000		
Cattle	23,840,000		
Sheep	47,510,000	See Part II.	
Pigs	9,200,000	p. 619	
Goats	1,370,000		
Total . . .	...	...	...

The value of products in 1887 was as follows :—

	Tons	£	Sundries	£
Wheat . .	7,500,000	37,100,000	Wine . .	3,800,000
Rye . .	18,900,000	79,200,000	Beetroot .	4,000,000
Barley . .	3,750,000	14,800,000	Vegetables	32,000,000
Oats . . .	10,350,000	35,000,000	Poultry .	12,000,000
Buckwheat &c.	3,750,000	15,000,000	Tobacco .	3,200,000
			Dairy . .	47,700,000
			Timber . .	40,000,000
All grain .	44,250,000	181,100,000	Meat . .	63,000,000
Straw . .	44,000,000	22,000,000	Foals . .	38,000,000
Hay . .	60,000,000	60,000,000	Hides, wool, &c.	28,000,000
Potatoes .	7,500,000	11,200,000		
Flax, &c. .	540,000	16,200,000		
			Sundries .	272,500,000
Principal crops .	...	290,500,000		

	£
Agricultural products . . .	373,200,000
Animal products . . .	189,800,000
Total . . .	563,000,000

The values at the following dates were approximately :—

Year	Millions, £ Sterling		
	Agricultural	Animal	Total
1834	188	60	248
1850	213	82	295
1872	287	135	422
1887	373	190	563

The agricultural population in 1884 was approximately 56,815,000, but the number of adults engaged in tillage and pasture was not over 22,700,000, which gives an average product yearly of £25 per head.

LAND VALUE

Before the Crimean war the ordinary price of land was about £1 per acre, but when the emancipation of the serfs was decreed in 1861, the Government paid an indemnity to the nobles averaging 29 shillings per acre. According to the British Ambassador, Sir A. Buchanan, the value in 1869 was doubled by the emancipation, and this is confirmed by Strebinsky, whose estimate in 1879 was £3 per acre. This applies only to cultivated land, the value of waste and forest being about one-tenth. The following table shows the values :—

Year	Area, Millions of Acres			Value, Millions £ Sterling		
	Cultivated	Forest, &c.	Total	Cultivated	Forest	Total
1834	183	1,061	1,244	183	106	289
1850	200	1,044	1,244	200	104	304
1870	305	939	1,244	610	188	798

AGRICULTURAL CAPITAL

Year	Millions £ Sterling			
	Land	Cattle	Sundries	Total
1834	289	176	52	517
1850	304	223	59	586
1870	798	409	134	1,341

The increase of agricultural capital was as follows :—

Period	Millions £ Sterling	Per Annum, £
1834–50 . . .	69	4,060,000
1851–70 . . .	755	37,750,000

The emancipation of the serfs added about 1200 millions sterling to the rural wealth in 26 years, from 1860 to 1886. See *Lands*.

POLAND

Poland has an area of 32 million acres, of which nearly one-half is cultivated. In 1864 feudalism was abolished, the nobles receiving £24,000,000 for 21 million acres, distributed in ten-acre lots among 2,064,000 male serfs of all ages, three-fourths of the amount being advanced by Government and the rest made good by the serfs. The number of serfs is one-tenth of those who were emancipated in Russia; the area of the land given them (21 million acres) is one-ninth of the land so expropriated in Russia.

According to Kaufmann the average crops of Poland in the years 1870–78 were as follows :—

	Million Bushels	Value, £
Wheat	15	3,600,000
Rye	47	8,100,000
Oats	36	3,600,000
Barley, &c.	25	4,000,000
Total	123	19,300,000

According to Fisher (Food-Supply, 1860) the products of Poland increased as follows :—

	Tons Produced	
	1822	1857
Grain	800,000	2,300,000
Potatoes	280,000	1,750,000
Meat	85,000	157,000

The total value of farm products may be set down approximately thus :—

	£
Grain crops . . .	19,300,000
Other products . . .	14,700,000
Cattle farming . . .	21,000,000
Total .	55,000,000

The value of farms varies from £2 to £8 per acre, and the total agricultural capital is more or less £200 millions sterling, of which three-fourths are represented by land.

The number of agricultural male peasants was 1,240,000 in 1867, and is now about 1,600,000; the ratio of agricultural products is about £34 per head.

FINLAND

This territory is distinct from Russia, and has an area or 92 million acres, viz. :—

Estates Class					*Acres*
Nobles .	.	.	.	.	5,800,000
Peasants	.	.	.	.	50,200,000
Crown .	.	.	.	.	30,600,000
Waste, &c.	.	.	.	.	5,600,000
Total	.				92,200,000

Nobles' estates average 3000 acres, peasants 250 acres. Cultivated lands cover 7 million acres, of which 6 millions are meadow, forest comprising 50 million acres, and the remaining 35 millions being waste land or lakes. Grain crop averages 12 million bushels; not enough for home consumption.

Neumann Spallart gives the following agricultural statistics for the average of 1875–81 :—

	Acres	Crop, Bushels	Value, £
Wheat	7,000	100,000	20,000
Rye	700,000	10,000,000	1,700,000
Barley	300,000	5,000,000	900,000
Oats	300,000	7,000,000	900,000
Various	15,000	500,000	40,000
Total . .	1,322,000	22,600,000	3,560,000

Cattle comprised 1,030,000 horned cattle, 1,030,000 sheep, and 150,000 pigs, which would produce yearly 70,000 tons of meat, worth £3,500,000. The total products would be approximately worth 15 millions sterling, and the capital about 70 millions. Agricultural population about 400,000 male adults.

AUSTRIA-HUNGARY

Not more than 43 per cent. of the Empire is cultivated, 31 per cent. being forest, and 26 per cent. pasture plains or waste lands. The area under crops, other than meadow, has increased only 120,000 acres per annum in the last fifty years.

Year	Acres under Crops	Grain Crop, Mill. Bush.	Wine, Mill. Gall.	Authority
1828	...	367	590	Malchus
1836	38,400,000	364	470	Becker
1846	...	480	...	Fisher
1850	...	550	500	Brachelli
1862	...	560	500	Official
1876	37,500,000	480	160	,,
1880	39,600,000	601	92	,,
1885	44,500,000	676	207	.,

Becker's and other tables for 1836 (excluding the Italian provinces) compare with those of 1887 as follows, the latter not including Bosnia or Herzegovina :—

	Crop, Million Bushels, 1836.			Million Bushels, 1887		
	Austria	Hungary	Total	Austria	Hungary	Total
Wheat	17	48	65	51	141	192
Oats	68	48	116	102	60	162
Rye	52	48	100	88	50	138
Barley, &c.	35	48	83	90	136	226
All grain	172	192	364	331	387	718
Wine, million gallons	75	392	467	103	109	212

Grain has increased 90 per cent. since 1836, although the area under crops has barely risen 20 per cent. ; this is due to improved methods and machinery since the expropriation of the lands in 1848, when they were distributed among the peasantry (see *Serfs*).

Wine has declined more than one-half.

The production of potatoes has increased as follows :—

Year				Tons	Authority
1846	.	.	.	2,300,000	Fisher
1859	.	.	.	5,100,000	,,
1885	.	.	.	11,000,000	Official

The acreage of the two kingdoms in 1887 was thus :—

	Austria	Hungary	Total
Wheat	2,875,000	6,860,000	9,735,000
Barley	2,795,000	2,480,000	5,275,000
Oats	4,630,000	2,580,000	7,210,000
Rye	4,985,000	2,770,000	7,755,000
Maize	890,000	4,520,000	5,410,000
Buckwheat, &c.	1,490,000	605,000	2,095,000
All grain	17,665,000	19,815,000	37,480,000
Potatoes	2,760,000	1,020,000	3,780,000
Beetroot	760,000	340,000	1,100,000
Vineyards	580,000	870,000	1,450,000
Hops	35,000	...	35,000
Tobacco	5,000	135,000	140,000
Clover	2,010,000	...	2,010,000
Gardens	920,000	130,000	1,050,000
Meadow	7,700,000	6,360,000	14,060,000
Pasture	13,015,000	32,015,000	45,030,000
Forest	24,150,000	22,515,000	46,665,000
Total	69,600,000	83,200,000	152,800,000

The value of grain crops is stated by Spallart thus :—

MILLIONS £ PER ANNUM

Years	Austria	Hungary	Total
1850	...	...	60
1870	...	...	83
1877–80	40	50	90
1881–84	41	57	98

The ordinary yield of grain is only fivefold ; 130 million bushels are required for seed.

Becker's and Schnabel's tables of live-stock and subsequent official returns show :—

	1836	1850	1870	1880
Horses	2,060,000	3,240,000	3,540,000	3,560,000
Cattle	10,010,000	10,460,000	12,630,000	13,890,000
Sheep	15,990,000	17,080,010	20,100,000	13,680,000
Pigs	5,500,000	7,410,000	6,990,000	6,880,000
Goats	850,000	...	1,550,000	1,280,000

The numbers respectively for Austria and Hungary in 1880 were :—

	Austria	Hungary	Total	Percentage		
				Austria	Hungary	Total
Horses	1,480,000	2,080,000	3,560,000	42	58	100
Cattle	8,580,000	5,310,000	13,890,000	61	39	100
Sheep	3,840,000	9,840,000	13,680,000	28	72	100
Pigs	2,720,000	4,160,000	6,880,800	39	61	100
Goats	1,010,008	330,000	1,340,000	75	25	100

The production of meat, taking the carcase of beef at 500 lbs., sheep 56 lbs., and pig 100 lbs., was as follows :—

Year	Meat, Tons	Lbs. per Inhabitant
1836	840,000	67
1850	880,000	66
1870	970,000	62
1880	980,000	57

Assuming the values of the various kinds of stock to be 20 per cent. per head less than in Germany, we find :—

	No.	Price, £	Value, £
Horses	3,560,000	19	67,600,000
Cattle	13,890,000	8	111,200,000
Sheep	13,680,000	0.6	8,300,000
Pigs	6,880,000	2	13,800,000
Goats	1,340,000	0.6	800,000
Total	...	...	201,700,000

The value of products in 1887 was approximately thus :—

	Tons	£	Sundries	£
Wheat	5,300,000	37,100,000	Wine	17,300,000
Oats	2,800,000	14,000,000	Vegetables	22,000,000
Rye	3,600,000	19,800,000	Timber	18,000,000
Barley	2,600,000	15,600,000	Tobacco	1,800,000
Maize	2,200,000	12,100,000	Flax, &c.	2,200,000
Buckwheat &c.	600,000	3,600,000	Dairy	34,500,000
			Poultry	7,800,000
			Meat	44,100,000
All grain	17,100,000	102,200,000	Foals	10,000,000
Straw	17,000,000	12,800,000	Hides, wool, &c.	10,100,000
Hay	14,000,000	21,000,000		
Potatoes	11,000,000	22,000,000		
Beetroot	6,500,000	5,000,000	Sundries	167,800,000
Principal crops	...	163,000,000		

	£
Agricultural products . . .	224,700,000
Animal products . . .	106,100,000
Total .	330,800,000

Becker's estimate of products in 1840 compares with later years as follows :—

Year	Millions, £ Sterling		
	Agricultural	Pastoral	Total
1840	160	45	205
1863	194	87	281
1887	225	106	331

The shares corresponding to the two kingdoms in 1887 were as follows :—

	Millions, £ Sterling		
	Austria	Hungary	Total
Agricultural	120	105	225
Pastoral	55	51	106
Total . .	175	156	331

The number of hands engaged in agriculture in 1870 and 1880 showed thus :—

Year	Austria	Hungary	Total
1870	5,520,000	5,010,000	10,530,000
1880	6,160,000	4,520,000	10,680,000

The result in 1887 shows an average product of £29 per head in Austria and £35 in Hungary, or £31 for the whole.

LAND VALUE

The emancipation of Austrian serfs in 1849 had such effect that Austrian economists say the value of land doubled between 1846 and 1866. In the latter year, according to the Embassy report, it was £15 per acre for cultivated, and £3 for forest or waste land. In 1884 another valuation was made, respecting which Professor Sternegg made investigations, and found the real value was 66 per cent. higher, viz.:—

	£
Nominal annual value . . .	16,500,000
Real rental	27,500,000

Capitalising the rental at twenty-five-fold, we find the value of lands in Austria proper (excluding Crown-lands and forests) was 688 millions sterling.

The values of land would, therefore, appear to have been as follows :—

MILLIONS, £ STERLING

Year	Cultivated	Forest and Pasture	Total
1840	396	147	543
1866	885	276	1,161
1885	1,073	284	1,357

The proportions in 1885 were as follows :—

	Austria	Hungary	Total, Million £
Cultivated . . .	594	479	1,073
Forest, &c. . . .	112	172	284
Total . . .	706	651	1,357

AGRICULTURAL CAPITAL

Year	Millions, £ Sterling			
	Land	Cattle	Sundries	Total
1840	543	89	70	702
1866	1,161	150	146	1,457
1885	1,357	202	173	1,732

The distribution of capital in the two kingdoms in 1887 was approximately thus :—

	Millions, £ Sterling		
	Austria	Hungary	Total
Land	706	651	1,357
Cattle	106	96	202
Sundries . . .	90	83	173
Total . . .	902	830	1,732

The ratio between capital and product was as follows :—

	Millions, £ Sterling		Ratio to Capital
	Capital	Product	
Austria	902	175	19.3
Hungary . . .	830	156	18.8
Total . . .	1,732	331	19.1

The ratios of the whole monarchy between capital and product at various dates are shown approximately as follows :—

Year	Millions, £ Sterling		Ratio to Capital
	Capital	Product	
1840	702	205	29.2
1866	1,457	281	19.3
1887	1,732	331	19.1

The increase of capital has been as follows :—

Period	Millions, £ Sterling	£ per Annum
1840–66	755	27,700,000
1867–85	284	14,900,000
46 years	1,039	22,600,000

BOSNIA

The provinces of Bosnia and Herzegovina, recently annexed to Austria, produce 8 million bushels of grain, viz. :—

Grain Crop, Bushels		Live Stock	
Wheat . . .	1,500,000	Horses. . . .	210,000
Maize . . .	3,300,000	Cows	505,000
Oats, barley, &c.	3,000,000	Sheep	1,315,000
Total . .	7,800,000		

MONTENEGRO

This little principality has an area of 2,100,000 acres, or 9 to each inhabitant. Some maize, oats, and potatoes are grown. The live-stock comprises 3000 horses, 60,000 cows, and 350,000 sheep and goats.

ITALY

The area of the kingdom has been distributed as follows :—

	Acres		
	1868	1874	1880
Wheat . . .	9,500,000	11,700,000	11,700,000
Maize, &c. . .	6,200,000	8,200,000	8,600,000
Meadow . .	2,900,000	6,000,000	6,000,000
Olives . .	1,400,000	2,200,000	2,200,000
Chestnuts . .	1,500,000	1,200,000	1,200,990
Vineyards . .	4,000,000	4,500,000	4,800,000
Forest . .	10,200,000	9,000,000	10,300,000
Pasture and waste .	35,100,000	28,000,000	26,000,000
Total .	70,800,000	70,800,000	70,800,000

The above are official returns, except as regards vineyards in 1868, and meadow 1874 and 1880, the latter being estimated on basis of the hay-crop officially stated

(at one ton per acre). It appears from the foregoing that 9 million acres have been brought into cultivation in twelve years.

We have statistics in 1840 for Naples, Sicily, Austrian Italy, and Papal States, viz. :—

	Acreage (1840)				
	Naples	Sicily	Austrian Prov.	Papal States	Total
Arable	7,700,000	3,100,000	2,200,000	1,200,000	14,200,000
Vineyards	500,000	1,000,000	2,500,000	100,000	4,100,000
Forest	1,900,000	1,100,000	1,600,000	900,000	5,500,000
Pasture, &c.	8,600,000	1,000,000	6,400,000	8,700,000	24,700,000
Total . . .	18,700,000	6,200,000	12,700,000	10,900,000	48,500,000

The kingdom of Sardinia, which is not included above, was found in 1870 to produce 16 per cent. of the grain, and 18 per cent. of the wine of Italy. Taking this into account, the total figures for Italy in 1840 as compared with 1888 would stand thus :—

Acreage

	1840	1888
Arable . . .	16,900,000	21,440,000
Vineyards . .	5,000,000	7,700,000

There have been various estimates of the production of grain and wine since 1828, from which it would appear that both have doubled in sixty years. A notable improvement of agriculture followed the expulsion of the Austrians in 1859, the returns for Lombardy showing as follows :—

	Lombardy, Annual Crops		Increase
	1848–58	1870–74	Per Cent.
Wheat, bushels . .	4,100,000	7,300,000	80
Maize, ,, . .	6,300,000	12,300,000	95
Rice, ,, . .	1,000,000	4,400,000	340
Potatoes, cwts. . .	220,000	1,120,000	410
Oil, gallons . . .	66,000	138,000	110
Wine, ,, . . .	31,000,000	42,000,000	35

The production of grain and wine was approximately for all Italy as follows :—

Year	Grain, Million Bushels	Wine, Million Gallons
1828	116	...
1840	130	360
1870	203	480
1888	223	715

The detailed official report for 1888 shows as follows :—

	Acres	Tons	Value, £	Cwts, per Acre	Value per Ton, £
Wheat . .	11,010,000	2,530,000	32,100,000	4.6	12.7
Maize . .	4,720,000	1,610,000	15,300,000	6.9	9.5
Oats . . .	1,100,000	340,000	1,900,000	6.2	5.5
Barley . .	860,000	165,000	1,900,000	4.0	11.0
Rye and pulse	2,200,000	370,000	4,800,000	3.3	13.0
Rice . . .	500,000	290,000	5,400,000	11.6	18.6
Chestnuts .	1,050,000	320,000	3,300,000	6.0	10.2
Potatoes . .	370,000	620,000	1,600,000	33.5	2.6
Hemp . .	300,000	65,000	2,900,000	4.3	45.0
Flax . . .	170,000	13,000	800,000	1.5	62.0
Wine . . .	7,700,000	715,000,000g	42,600,000	93g	...
Oil . . .	2,250,000	50,000,000	13,400,000	23g	...
Tobacco . .	9,000	2,000	160,000	4.4	80.0
Silk cocoons	...	44,000	6,200,000	...	141.0
Oranges . .	...	225,000	3,000,000	...	13.3
Total .	...	...	135,360,000	...	...

The above values are, however, in many cases too high, and such important items as hay, straw, &c., are omitted. The following table is more in harmony with European prices :—

	Tons	£	Sundries	£
Wheat . .	2,530,000	21,500,000	Oranges . .	3,000,000
Maize . .	1,610,000	10,700,000	Vegetables .	22,500,000
Oats. . .	340,000	1,900,000	Hemp and } flax . }	2,800,000
Barley . .	165,000	1,150,000		
Rye, &c. .	370,000	2,600,000	Chestnuts .	800,000
Rice. . .	290,000	2,200,000	Tobacco . .	70,000
			Cocoons . .	6,200,000
All grain .	5,305,000	40,050,000	Timber . .	4,000,000
Potatoes .	620,000	1,250,000	Dairy . . .	14,400,000
Straw . .	5,000,000	4,000,000	Poultry . .	6,000,000
Hay. . .	12,000,000	18,000,000	Meat . . .	18,000,000
Wine . .	...	42,600,000	Foals . . .	3,000,000
Oil . . .	...	13,400,000	Hides, } wool, &c. }	4,130,000
Principal } crops }	...	119,300,000	Sundries . .	84,900,000

Agricultural products	153,000,000
Animal products	51,200,000
Total . .	204,200,000

The distribution of crops in 1870 was said to be as follows :—

	Grain	Wine	Chestnuts	Hay
Venetia	6	5	...	32
Lombardy	9	5	2	18
Piedmont	16	18	30	20
Tuscany, Romagna, &c. .	21	22	34	30
Naples	32	28	34	...
Sicily	16	22	...	...
Total . .	100	100	100	100

The official returns of live-stock are of recent date, besides which we have the estimates of Schnabel and Malchus for 1828, and of Spallart for 1852 :—

	1828	1852	1874	1882
Horses . .	800,000	800,000	1,070,000	1,120,000
Cattle . .	3,500,000	3,660,000	3,490,000	4,780,000
Sheep . .	6,500,000	7,000,000	6,980,000	8,595,000
Pigs . . .	2,500,000	2,000,000	1,550,000	1,160,000
Goats . . .	800,000	...	1,690,000	2,020,000

The production of meat at 500 lbs. per carcase of beef, 56 lbs. per sheep, and 100 lbs. per pig, was as follows :—

Year	Meat, Tons	Lbs. per Inhabitant
1828	335,000	...	44
1874	300,000	...	24
1882	360,000	...	28

The value of all kinds of live-stock may be set down approximately thus :—

	Number	Value, £	£ per Head
Horses	1,120,000	23,500,000	21.0
Cattle	4,780,000	47,800,000	10.0
Sheep	8,600,000	6,900,000	0.8
Pigs	1,160,000	2,900,000	2.5
Goats	2,020,000	1,400,000	0.7
Total . . .	...	82,500,000	...

The value of products at different dates was approximately as follows :—

Year	Millions, £ Sterling			Hands	Product per Hand, £
	Agricultural	Pastoral	Total		
1840	92	22	114	3,600,000	32
1874	146	34	180	5,100,000	35
1888	153	51	204	5,400,000	38

The relation between capital and product was approximately as follows :—

Year	Millions, £ Sterling		Ratio to Capital
	Capital	Product	
1840.	452	114	25.3
1874.	801	180	22.5
1888.	1,405	204	14.6

LAND VALUE

According to Dr. Bodio's estimate, the value of land is 34 times the assessed rental ; taking the same ratio for 1863 and 1871, and accepting the Foreign Office reports of 1844, which gave £11 per acre cultivated and £5 for pasture and woodland, the result is as follows :—

Year	Assessed Rental, £	Land Value, Million Sterling
1840	...	...	377
1863	16,000,000	...	544
1871	19,000,000	...	661
1885	34,700,000	...	1,182

The accuracy of Dr. Bodio's estimate for 1885 is borne out by the fact that the prices obtained for Church-lands sold by Government in 1870-77 in all parts of Italy gave a medium of £16 per acre, ranging from £8 in Romagna to £36 in Piedmont.

This average of £16 for 70 million acres would show a total value of 1120 millions. See *Lands.*

AGRICULTURAL CAPITAL

Year	Millions, £ Sterling			
	Land	Cattle	Sundries	Total
1840	377	30	45	452
1863	544	45	66	655
1871	661	60	80	801
1885	1,182	83	140	1,405

The increase of capital was as follows :—

Period	Millions, £ Sterling		£ per Annum
1840-63	203	...	8,500,000
1864-71	146	...	18,300,000
1872-85	604	...	43,100,000
46 years	953	...	20,700,000

It may be observed that the assessed rentals of 1863 and 1871 were probably below the reality, in which case the increase of landed values and agricultural capital would be less than appears above.

SPAIN

About 37 per cent. of Spain is cultivated, 26 per cent. being pasture or forest, and 37 per cent. barren mountains. In former times the cultivated area was said to be much greater.

Year	Millions of Acres			Authority
	Cultivated	Uncultivated	Total	
1660	43	78	121	Ozorio
1803	60	61	121	Registro
1828	23	98	121	Malchus
1876	32	89	121	Spallart

The production of grain and wine has been as follows :—

Year	Grain, Million Bushels	Wine, Million Gallons	Authority
1803	98	...	Registro
1828	136	170	Malchus
1876	326	550	N. Spallart *
1888	300	550	Moniteur Agricole

The distribution of area in 1876 and 1888 was variously stated, as follows :—

	Acres	
	1876	1888
Tillage	28,000,000	40,800,000
Vineyards	3,000,000	4,400,000
Olives	1,000,000	1,900,000
Pasture, &c.	28,000,000	24,000,000
Forest	7,000,000	7,000,000
Waste	55,000,000	42,900,000
Total	121,000,000	121,000,000

The following statistics of live-stock are official, except Brachelli's for 1841 :—

	1826	1841	1860	1880
Horses . .	900,000	1,000,000	1,080,000	1,830,000
Cattle . . .	2,950,000	3,000,000	1,870,000	3,090,000
Sheep . . .	13,000,000	14,000,000	17,600,000	22,800,000
Pigs . . .	2,730,000	1,000,000	1,610,000	4,465,000
Goats . . .	5,200,000	2,600,000	3,150,000	4,530,000

In the foregoing table horses include also mules and asses, one mule or four asses being equivalent to a horse : thus in 1880 the actual numbers were—horses, 670,000 ; mules, 940,000 ; and asses, 890,000.

The production of meat at an average of 450 lbs. per beef carcase, 50 lbs. per sheep, 25 lbs. per goat, and 90 lbs. per pig, was as follows :—

Year	Meat, Tons		Lbs. per Inhabitant
1826	405,000	...	77
1841	300,000	...	55
1860	310,000	...	45
1880	525,000	...	71

* N. Spallart's estimate was as follows :—Wheat, 168 ; barley, 77 ; maize, 36 ; rye, 33 ; oats, 12 million bushels.

The fluctuations of live-stock were doubtless the result of civil wars.

The value of the stock was approximately as follows :—

	No.	Value, £	£ per Head
Horses . . .	1,830,000	36,600,000	20.0
Cattle . . .	3,090,000	30,900,000	10.0
Sheep . . .	22,800,000	18,200,000	0.8
Pigs	4,465,000	6,700,000	1.5
Goats . . .	4,530,000	2,300,000	0.5
Total . .	...	94,700,000	...

The value of products in 1886 was approximately thus :—

	Tons	£	Sundries	£
Wheat . .	3,800,000	30,400,000	Wine . . .	44,000,000
Barley . .	1,700,000	10,200,000	Vegetables, &c. . . }	9,000,000
Maize . .	1,050,000	6,900,000		
Oats . . .	350,000	2,400,000	Cork oil . .	3,000,000
Rye, &c. .	800,000	5,200,000	Dairy . .	9,300,000
			Poultry . .	4,500,000
All grain .	7,700,000	55,100,000	Meat . . .	26,200,000
Straw . .	8,000,000	6,000,000	Foals . . .	3,000,000
Hay . . .	6,000,000	9,000,000	Hides, wool, &c. }	4,200,000
Principal crops .. }	...	70,100,000	Sundries .	103,200,000

	£
Agricultural products	126,100,000
Animal products	47,200,000
Total	173,300,000

The value of products at various dates was as follows :—

Year	Millions, £ Sterling			Authority
	Agricultural	Pastoral	Total	
1808	54	19	73	Official
1826	56	21	77	Miñano
1832	86	16	102	Argüelles
1886	126	47	173	...

The Census of 1871 showed 2,723,000 persons engaged in agriculture ; the product therefore averages £64 per head.

LAND VALUE

According to the report of the Junta de Medios, the total farming capital in 1832 was 724 millions sterling, between land, cattle, and sundries. The Embassy report of 1869 classified the land under three heads, with the respective rental values. If we capitalise the rental at thirty years, we find the values thus :—

	Acres	Rent, Shillings per Acre	Value, Million £
Irrigated . . .	2,000,000	80	240
Ordinary arable .	30,000,000	12	540
Pasture, &c. . .	34,000,000	4	204
Waste	55,000,000	...	...
Total . .	121,000,000	...	984

AGRICULTURAL CAPITAL
MILLIONS, £ STERLING

	Land	Cattle	Sundries	Total
1832 . .	614	38	72	724
1888 . .	984	95	120	1,199

Spanish statistics are doubtful, being often official exaggerations.

PORTUGAL

The estimates of Malchus, Brachelli, Tisserand, and the Statistique Agricole give the following :—

Year	Grain, Million Bushels		Wine, Million Gallons
1827	21	...	75
1850	30	...	...
1868	31	...	132
1886	40	...	125

The cultivated area is less than 5 million acres, that of waste land 17,600,000, the former being barely 21 per cent. of the kingdom.

The crops in 1868 (latest complete returns) were as follows :—

	Acres	Bushels	Value of Crops, £
Wheat	620,000	5,500,000	1,600,000
Maize	750,000	15,400,000	2,800,000
Barley	170,000	2,000,000	260,000
Rye	980,000	7,000,000	770,000
Oats	30,000	500,000	70,000
Rice	10,000	400,000	80,000
All grain . . .	2,560,000	30,800,000	5,580,000
Vines	480,000	132,000,000	8,000,000
Gardens . . .	200,000	...	1,800,000
Olives	100,000	...	500,000
Meadow . . .	500,000	...	2,120,000
Fallow	750,000	...	...
Forest	250,000	...	...
Total . .	4,840,000	...	18,000,000

Neumann Spallart gives the following for 1877 :—

	Acres	Bushels
Wheat	650,000	8,200,000
Rye	650,000	6,100,000
Maize	1,300,000	20,000,000
Barley, &c.	200,000	2,700,000
Total	2,800,000	37,000,000

The statistics of Portuguese live-stock were as follows :—

	1828	1850	1868	1883	Value in 1883
					£
Horses	...	120,000	130,000	140,000	2,800,000
Cattle	650,000	750,000	520,000	625,000	6,200,000
Sheep	1,200,000	1,980,000	2,420,000	2,980,000	2,400,000
Pigs	700,000	750,000	860,000	970,000	1,500,000
Goats	600,000	1,500,000	...	940,000	400,000
	...	...	...	...	
	...	...	...	...	13,300,000

The production of meat at the same weight of carcase as in Spain was :—

Year	Meat, Tons	Lbs. per Inhab.
1828	70,000	46
1868	77,000	41
1883	95,000	49

The value of products in 1886 was approximately thus :—

	Tons	£	Sundries	£
Wheat . .	270,000	2,200,000	Cork . . .	600,000
Maize . .	400,000	2,400,000	Vegetables, }	
Rye, &c. .	380,000	2,400,000	&c. . . }	2,200,000
			Poultry . .	1,100,000
All grain .	1,050,000	7,000,000	Dairy . .	1,900,000
Hay and }	2,000,000	3,000,000	Meat . . .	4,700,000
straw . }			Hides, &c. .	700,000
Wine. . .	...	10,000,000		
			Sundries .	11,200,000
Principal }	...	20,000,000		
crops . }				

	£
Agricultural products	23,000,000
Animal products	8,200,000
Total	31,200,000

According to the Census of 1861, the number of persons engaged was 870,000, of whom 310,000 in pasture. Ratio of product £35 per head.

The landed value is approximately as follows :—

	Area	Value, Million £	Per Acre, £
Cultivated . . .	5,000,000	90	18
Pasture	7,000,000	42.	6
Waste	10,450,000	...	...
Total . . .	22,450,000	132	...

Agricultural capital is only about £36 per head of the total population, being made up thus :—

	Millions £
Land	132
Cattle	13
Sundries	16
Total	161

The value of products is 19 per cent. on the capital.

SWEDEN

Agriculture was in its infancy till 1818, when the nobles (whose estates were heavily encumbered) began to sell their lands to the peasants ; by the year 1840 they had sold 16 million acres. As a consequence, we find that the cultivated area increased by 140,000 acres per annum between 1812 and 1837, and by 165,000 per annum between the latter year and 1884, as official returns show :—

Year	Acres Cultivated	Million Bushels	
		Grain	Potatoes
1812 . . .	1,360,000	1	...
1837 . . .	4,830,000	28	16
1859 . . .	...	39	21
1876 . . .	11,590,000	80	39
1887 . . .	12,200,000	106	59

Only 12 per cent. of the kingdom is cultivated, the area in 1886 showing :—

	Acres
Cultivated	12,200,000
Forest	44,900,000
Waste	43,200,000
Total . . .	100,300,000

The principal crops of recent years compare with those of 1837 thus :—

	1837	1880	1886
Wheat, bushels .	500,000	3,100,000	3,700,000
Rye, ,, .	4,500,000	18,300,000	19,600,000
Barley, ,, .	3,600,000	14,300,000	15,600,000
Oats, &c., ,, .	5,200,000	54,700,000	63,600,000
Potatoes, ,, .	8,200,000	55,400,000	49,100,000
Total .	22,000,000	145,800,000	151,600,000

The production of meat, at 500 lbs. per beef carcase, 56 lbs. per sheep, and 100 lbs. per pig, was as follows :—

Year	Meat, Tons	Lbs. per Inhabitant
1837 . . .	106,000	78
1870 . . .	120,000	63
1886 . . .	140,000	62

The yield of grain is poor. Oats and barley, fourfold; rye, fivefold; and wheat, in good years, sixfold; potatoes give sevenfold.

The value of products in 1886 was as follows :—

	Tons	£	Sundries	£
Wheat . .	100,000	800,000	Vegetables .	2,300,000
Oats . .	950,000	5,700,000	Timber . .	8,000,000
Barley . .	350,000	2,200,000	Poultry . .	1,200,000
Rye, &c. .	750,000	5,000,000	Dairy . .	7,000,000
			Meat . . .	7,000,000
All grain .	2,150,000	13,700,000	Foals. . .	1,200,000
Straw . .	2,000,000	1,500,000	Tallow . .	600,000
Hay . .	2,000,000	3,000,000	Hides, }	
Potatoes. .	1,200,000	2,400,000	wool, &c. }	1,200,000
Principal }	...	20,600,000	Sundries .	28,500,000
crops . }				

The following are the returns of live-stock :—

	1836	1860	1870	1880	1886	Approximate Value in 1886, £
Horses	385,000	400,000	430,000	460,000	485,000	9,700,000
Cattle	1,660,000	1,920,000	1,970,000	2,230,000	2,380,000	23,800,000
Sheep	1,410,000	1,640,000	1,600,000	1,460,000	1,440,000	1,200,000
Pigs	500,000	460,000	350,000	420,000	550,000	1,100,000
Goats	100,000	130,000	120,000	110,000	90,000	50,000
						35,850,000

Besides the foregoing, there are 220,000 reindeer.

	£
Agricultural products . . .	31,100,000
Pastoral products . . .	18,000,000
Total . .	49,100,000

The number of hands engaged in agriculture is 853,000, which gives an average product of £57 per head.

LANDED VALUE

Two official valuations exist—that of 1836, amounting to 33 millions sterling, and that of 1880, which reached millions sterling. We can also determine the value in 1818–20, the average price then obtained by the nobles being 18d. per acre — say £8,000,000 for the whole kingdom.

Year	Agricultural Capital, Millions £			
	Land	Cattle	Sundries	Total
1818 . . .	8	10	2	20
1837 . . .	33	13	5	51

See Part II., page 622.

NORWAY

Agriculture has not made so much progress as in Sweden. We have no statistics earlier than 1835, since which date the area under grain and potatoes and the yield have been as follows :—

Year	Acres	Million Bushels
1835	360,000	13
1855	...	31
1865	530,000	32
1875	560,000	36

Not more than 5 per cent. of the country is cultivated, viz. (1880) :—

	Acres
Cultivated	4,060,000
Forest	15,800,000
Waste	58,840,000
Total	78,700,000

The yield per acre has notably improved since 1835, viz. :—

	Bushels per Acre	
	1835	1875
Wheat	13	20
Oats	26	40

Nevertheless the climate is so little suited to cereals that we notice hardly any increase in the quantity produced, except in potatoes, viz. :—

	1855	1865	1875	Acreage in 1875
	Bushels	Bushels	Bushels	
Wheat . .	200,000	270,000	280,000	11,000
Barley . .	3,500,000	3,400,000	4,300,000	138,000
Oats . . .	8,100,000	7,900,000	8,900,000	224,000
Rye, &c. .	3,000,000	2,630,000	3,120,000	99,000
Potatoes .	16,500,000	18,000,000	19,600,000	86,000
Total	31,300,000	32,200,000	36,200,000	558,000

The following are the official returns of live-stock :—

	1835	1845	1855	1865	1875	Approximate Value in 1875, £
Horses	110,000	130,000	150,000	150,000	150,000	3,000,000
Cattle	640,000	840,000	950,000	950,000	1,020,000	10,200,000
Sheep	1,030,000	1,450,000	1,600,000	1,700,000	1,690,000	1,400,000
Pigs	80,000	90,000	110,000	100,000	100,000	200,000
Goats	180,000	290,0000	360,000	290,000	320,000	200,000
Reindeer	80,000	90,000	120,000	100,000	100,000	150,000
Total	...	...	...	...	...	15,150,000

The production of meat at the same weight of carcase as in Sweden was :—

Year	Meat, Tons	Lbs. per Inhabitant
1835 . . .	44,000	80
1855 . . .	64,000	95
1875 . . .	67,000	78

The value of products in 1886 was approximately thus :—

	Tons	£	Sundries	£
Wheat . . .	7,000	60,000	Vegetables .	1,000,000
Barley . . .	100,000	640,000	Timber . .	4,000,000
Oats	150,000	900,000	Dairy . . .	3,000,000
Rye, &c. . .	73,000	500,000	Poultry . .	500,000
			Meat . . .	3,300,000
All grain . .	330,000	2,100,000	Foals . . .	400,000
Potatoes . .	490,000	1,000,000	Hides, &c. .	800,000
Hay and straw	700,000	900,000		
			Sundries . .	13,000,000
Principal crops	...	4,000,000		

	£
Agricultural products . . .	9,000,000
Animal products . . .	8,000,000
Total . . .	17,000,000

The number of hands employed is about 380,000.

See Part II., page 622.

DENMARK

Malchus estimated the grain product in 1828 at 40 million bushels; Brachelli, in 1850, at 65 millions.

The agricultural area of Denmark and the duchies of Schleswig-Holstein in 1834 was stated thus:—

		Acres
Arable .	. . . . .	8,630,000
Meadow	. . . . .	605,000
Forest .	. . . . .	538,000
Waste, &c. .	. . . .	637,000
	Total . . .	10,410,000

	Acreage			Million Bushels	
	1866	1876	1881	1878	1886
Wheat . . .	120,000	150,000	140,000	5	5
Barley . . .	680,000	760,000	780,000	23	23
Oats . . .	830,000	940,000	990,000	31	33
Rye, &c. . .	750,000	950,000	1,010,000	24	25
Potatoes . .	85,000	100,000	110,000	10	14
Turnips, &c. .	42,000	40,000	85,000	15	29
Garden . . .	...	50,000	60,000	...	...
Fallow . . .	440,000	610,000	640,000	...	...
Grass . . .	2,670,000	3,070,000	3,560,000	...	...
Forest . . .	400,000	400,000	400,000	...	...
Waste . . .	2,553,000	1,500,000	795,000	...	...
Total . .	8,570,000	8,570,000	8,570,000	...	...

From 1866 to 1876 the reclamation of waste lands averaged 100,000 acres yearly, and from 1876 to 1881 no less than 140,000 yearly. Most of it went into meadow and pasture. Wheat averages 28 bushels an acre, and yields ninefold; other grain, eightfold; clover, two tons per acre. Statistics of live-stock (those for 1830 including Schleswig-Holstein) show as follows:—

	1830	1866	1876	1881	Approximate Value in 1881, £
Horses .	550,000	350,000	350,000	350,000	11,000,000
Cattle .	1,610,000	1,190,000	1,350,000	1,470,000	16,100,000
Sheep .	1,900,000	1,880,000	1,720,000	1,550,000	1,500,000
Pigs . .	450,000	380,000	500,000	530,000	1,200,000
					29,800,000

The conquest of Schleswig-Holstein by Germany in 1864 caused a great diminution in the live-stock of Denmark. The production of meat, at 560 lbs. per beef carcase, 56 lbs. per sheep, and 112 lbs. per pig, was:—

Year	Meat, Tons	Lbs. per Inhabitant
1850	76,000	130
1866	92,000	120
1881	108,000	120

Official returns regarding Denmark proper show as follows:—

	Tons	£	Sundries	£
Wheat . . .	140,000	1,200,000	Roots . .	1,100,000
Barley . . .	520,000	3,500,000	Vegetables	1,000,000
Oats . . .	560,000	3,900,000	Timber .	200,000
Rye, &c. . .	600,000	4,000,000	Poultry .	500,000
			Dairy . .	6,400,000
All grain . .	1,820,000	12,600,000	Meat . .	5,400,000
Straw . . .	2,000,000	1,800,000	Foals . .	1,100,000
Hay . . .	900,000	1,800,000	Hides, &c.	1,500,000
Potatoes . .	700,000	1,400,000		
			Sundries .	17,200,000
Principal crops	...	17,600,000		

	£
Agricultural products . . .	19,800,000
Animal products . . .	15,000,000
	34,800,000

The values, approximately, of products in 1850 compare with those of 1886 thus:—

Year	Millions, £ Sterling		
	Agricultural	Pastoral	Total
1850	13	9	22
1886	20	15	35

Agricultural hands 420,000, showing an average of £84 per head.

LANDED VALUE

The valuation of 1830 for landed estates amounted to £25,600,000. The Embassy report of 1869 gives average prices which would sum up thus:—

	Acre	Per Acre, £	Value, Million £
Arable	2,950,000	35	103
Grass	3,070,000	23	70
Waste	2,550,000	...	...
Total . . .	8,570,000	...	173

At the same valuation per acre as in 1869 the landed value would now stand as follows:—

	Acres	Value, £	Per Acre, £
Arable	3,815,000	133,500,000	35
Grass	3,560,000	81,900,000	23
Forest	400,000	2,000,000	5
Waste	795,000	...	...
Total . . .	8,570,000	217,400,000	...

The Government valuation for 1884 gives real estate 257 millions sterling, but this includes urban house property as well as lands.

Year	Agricultural Capital, Millions £			
	Land	Cattle	Sundries	Total
1840	26	16	4	46
1869	173	19	21	213
1889	217	30	27	274

The product in 1889 was 13 per cent. on capital. The increase of capital was as follows:—

Interval	Millions, £		Per Annum, £
1830–69	167	...	4,200,000
1870–89	61	...	3,050,000

For Tenure, &c., see *Land.*

HOLLAND

Tillage forms a secondary industry in Dutch agriculture. The production of grain, according to Brachelli and others, was as follows:—

Year	Bushels
1828	16,000,000
1861	34,000,000
1885	40,000,000

The reports of 1879 and 1885 compare as follows :—

	Acres				Average for 1871–80	
	1879	1885			Acres	Bushels
Grain	1,570,000	1,460,000	Wheat		210,000	5,200,000
Potatoes	350,000	350,000	Rye		500,000	9,500,000
Beetroot	40,000	60,000	Oats		270,000	10,500,000
Sundries	130,000	280,000	Barley		120,000	5,000,000
Grass	2,940,000	2,950,000	Buckwheat, &c.. . .		280,000	5,800,000
Forest	530,000	560,000				
Waste	2,240,000	2,140,000	Total . .		1,380,000	36,000,000
Total . .	7,800,000	7,800,000				

The statistics of live-stock showed as follows :—

	1840	1860	1870	1884
Horses . .	210,000	240,000	250,000	270,000
Cattle . .	1,050,000	1,250,000	1,410,000	1,480,000
Sheep . .	720,000	870,000	900,000	750,000
Pigs . . .	...	270,000	330,000	430,000
Goats . .	...	110,000	140,000	160,000

The production of meat, at 700 lbs. per beef carcase, 70 lbs. per sheep, and 120 lbs. per pig, was as follows :—

Year	Meat, Tons	Lbs. per Inhabitant
1860	104,000	62
1870	118,000	67
1884	125,000	69

The value of products in Holland in 1886 was approximately as follows :—

	Tons	£	Sundries	£
Wheat . .	140,000	1,200,000	Beetroot .	300,000
Rye . . .	270,000	1,900,000	Vegetables	3,000,000
Oats . . .	250,000	1,700,000	Poultry . .	1,200,000
Barley . .	100,000	700,000	Flax . .	300,000
Buckwheat, &c. }	140,000	900,000	Meat . .	6,200,000
			Tallow . .	400,000
			Dairy . .	9,500,000
All grain .	900,000	6,400,000	Foals . .	900,000
Potatoes . .	1,600,000	3,200,000	Hides, &c.. .	1,000,000
Straw . .	900,000	900,000		
Hay . . .	3,000,000	6,000,000	Sundries .	22,800,000
Principal crops . }	...	16,500,000		

	£
Agricultural products	20,100,000
Animal products.	19,200,000
Products of Holland .	39,300,000

The value of products in 1850 compares with the above thus :—

Year	Millions, £ Sterling		
	Agricultural	Pastoral	Total
1850	12	10	22
1886	20	19	39

Agricultural hands, 840,000, showing £46 per head.

LAND VALUE

In 1836 the value of the kingdom (excluding waste land) was estimated thus :—

	Acres	Per Acre, £	Value, Million £
Good . . .	2,000,000	54	108
Inferior . .	3,300,000	30	99
Total . .	5,300,000	...	207

The Bulletin Statistique for 1886 states the value at 314 millions sterling, an increase of 107 millions in 50 years :—

Year	Agricultural Capital, Million £			
	Land	Cattle	Sundries	Total
1836 . . .	207	14	24	245
1886 . . .	314	28	38	380

The increase averaged £2,700,000 per annum. The product in 1885 was only 10 per cent. on capital.

BELGIUM

The production of grain and potatoes has been, according to Malchus and the official returns, as follows :—

Year	Acres	Grain, Million Bushels	Potatoes, Tons
1828	...	33	...
1846	...	52	1,800,000
1856	2,840,000	69	1,800,000
1866	2,900,000	70	1,700,000
1880	2,880,000	75	2,800,000
1886	...	74	3,000,000

The distribution of area in Belgium is shown officially as follows :—

	Acreage					Average Product for Years 1871–80	Official Valuation
	1856	1866	1880			Tons	£
Grain	2,480,000	2,480,000	2,390,000	Wheat . . .		430,000	5,400,000
Potatoes . . .	370,000	420,000	490,000	Rye . . .		420,000	3,600,000
Beetroot . . .	20,000	90,000	150,000	Oats . . .		390,000	3,300,000
Flax	80,000	140,000	100,000	Barley . . .		80,000	700,000
Grass	1,170,000	1,340,000	1,420,000	Buckwheat, &c. .		130,000	1,200,000
Sundries . . .	400,000	640,000	420,000				
Forest . . . }	2,760,000	1,070,000	1,210,000	All grain . .		1,450,000	14,200,000
Waste . . . }		1,100,000	1,100,000	Potatoes . .		2,490,000	9,200,000
				Beetroot . .		2,050,000	1,600,000
Total . .	7,280,000	7,280,000	7,280,000	Hay . . .		5,220,000	10,200,000

The average of ten years to 1880 gave the weight of seed and the crop to the acre as follows :—

	Seed, lbs. per Acre	Crop, lbs. per Acre	Yield to 1 lb. Seed
Wheat	113	1,360	12.0
Rye	107	1,300	12.1
Oats	173	1,520	8.8
Barley . . .	123	1,610	13.1

The acreage of the principal kinds of grain at various dates was as follows :—

	1846	1856	1866	1880
Wheat . .	580,000	660,000	700,000	690,000
Rye . . .	700,000	720,000	710,000	690,000
Oats . . .	500,000	550,000	570,000	620,000
Barley . .	100,000	110,000	110,000	100,000
Total .	1,880,000	2,040,000	2,090,000	2,100,000

Returns of live-stock are as follows :—

	1840	1866	1880	Approximate Value in 1880
				£
Horses .	246,000	280,000	270,000	5,400,000
Cattle . .	910,000	1,240,000	1,380,000	16,600,000
Sheep . .	750,000	600,000	370,000	300,000
Pigs . .	420,000	630,000	650,000	1,300,000
Goats . .	80,000	200,000	250,000	100,000

The production of meat, at 600 lbs. per beef carcase, 70 lbs. per sheep, and 112 lbs. per pig, was :—

Year		Meat, Tons	Lbs. per Inhabitant
1840	. . . .	77,000	43
1866	. . . .	106,000	54
1880	. . . .	110,000	43

The official valuation of products gave the following average for ten years ending 1880 :—

			£
Grain .	. . . . .	.	21,700,000
Green crops	. . .	.	6,400,000
Hay .	. . . . .	.	10,200,000
Sundries	. . . .	.	18,200,000
All crops	. .	.	56,500,000
Cattle products .	. .	.	9,500,000
Total	.	.	66,000,000

The actual values at present are much lower. The value of all products in 1886 was approximately as follows :—

	Tons	£	Sundries	£
Wheat . .	450,000	4,050,000	Vegetables .	4,500,000
Spelt . . .	150,000	1,200,000	Timber . .	800,000
Barley . .	80,000	500,000	Beetroot .	1,600,000
Oats . . .	490,000	3,400,000	Flax . . .	2,700,000
Rye, &c. .	450,000	3,050,000	Turnips .	1,800,000
			Poultry . .	1,600,000
All grain .	1,620,000	12,200,000	Dairy . .	5,000,000
Straw . .	1,600,000	1,600,000	Meat . .	5,500,000
Hay . . .	5,000,000	10,000,000	Hides and }	
Potatoes .	3,000,000	6,000,000	foals . }	2,000,000
Principal crops . }	...	29,800,000	Sundries .	25,500,000

		£
Agricultural products .	. .	41,200,000
Animal products .	. . .	14,100,000
Total	. .	55,300,000

The number of adults engaged in 1880 was 980,000. This gives an average of £56 per head.

LANDED VALUE

An official report, dated 1886, gives the rental and the selling price of land (under cultivation) at various dates as follows :—

Year	Rent, Shillings per Acre	Price, £ per Acre
1846	22.2	42
1856	26.4	54
1866 . . .	32.5	66
1880 . . .	36.6	67

The value of lands in 1880 was officially set down as follows :—

	Acres	£	£ per Acre
Arable	3,960,000	271,800,000	67
Meadow . . .	970,000	64,500,000	67
Forest	1,210,000	39,200,000	33
Waste	1,140,000	1,800,000	1.5
Total . . .	7,280,000	377,300,000	...

According to the preceding scale the value at various dates was as follows :—

	Acres				Value, Millions, £			
	1846	1856	1866	1880	1846	1856	1866	1880
Cultivated . . .	3,930,000	4,520,000	5,110,000	4,970,000	165	243	337	336
Forest	1,400,000	1,300,000	1,070,000	1,210,000	29	35	35	39
Waste	1,950,000	1,460,000	1,100,000	1,100,000	2	2	2	2
Total	7,280,000	7,280,000	7,280,000	7,280,000	196	280	374	377

Year	Agricultural Capital, Millions, £			
	Land	Cattle	Sundries	Total
1846 . . .	196	16	23	235
1856 . . .	280	18	33	331
1866 . . .	374	20	44	438
1880 . . .	377	24	44	445

The increase of capital was as follows :—

Interval	Millions, £	£ per Annum
1846–56	96	9,600,000
1856–66	107	10,700,000
1866–80	7	500,000
34 years	210	6,200,000

Mr. Block estimated the value of all products in 1850 at 21 millions sterling, being about 7 per cent. on capital. In 1886 it was, as already shown, 55 millions, say 12½ per cent. on capital.

SWITZERLAND

Official returns are as follows :—

		Acres
Tillage	. . . .	1,450,000
Meadow	. . . .	1,600,000
Vineyards	. . . .	70,000
Pasture	. . . .	1,960,000
Forest	. . . .	1,760,000
Waste	. . . .	2,550,000
	Total area . .	9,390,000

Live-stock, according to Schnabel and later authorities, showed thus :—

	1830	1842	1852	1861	1886
Horses . .	...	...	...	94,000	98,000
Cattle . .	800,000	815,000	950,000	940,000	1,210,000
Sheep . .	500,000	465,000	550,000	430,000	340,000
Pigs . . .	250,000	310,000	280,000	330,000	395,000
Goats . .	...	346,000	...	370,000	420,000

The production of meat is about 82,000 tons yearly. The value of all products in 1886 was approximately thus :—

	Tons	£	Sundries	£
Wheat . . .	55,000	500,000	Vegetables, &c. . .	1,500,000
Barley . . .	45,000	300,000		
Oats	80,000	500,000	Poultry . .	900,000
Rye	210,000	1,300,000	Dairy . .	4,800,000
			Timber . .	1,200,000
All grain . .	390,000	2,600,000	Meat . . .	4,100,000
Hay and straw	1,700,000	2,000,000	Foals . .	300,000
Wine . . .	...	1,400,000	Hides, &c. .	500,000
Principal crops	...	6,000,000	Sundries .	13,300,000

	£
Agricultural products . . .	9,000,000
Animal products . . .	10,300,000
Total . .	19,300,000

Agricultural capital is approximately as follows :—

	£
Land, cultivated	93,000,000
Forest, &c.	27,000,000
Cattle	10,000,000
Sundries	14,000,000
Total . .	144,000,000

The annual product is about 13½ per cent. on capital.

GREECE

The official report for 1885 gives the following :—

	Acres	Sundries	Acres
Grain	2,000,000	Fallow . . .	1,000,000
Olives	325,000	Gardens . . .	40,000
Currants . . .	125,000	Meadows . .	1,000,000
Grapes	250,000	Pasture . .	5,000,000
Tobacco . . }	250,000	Forest . . .	1,500,000
Cotton . . . }		Waste . . .	4,510,000
Principal crops .	2,950,000	Sundries . . .	13,050,000

Live-stock comprised 160,000 horses, 164,000 cattle, 3,460,000 sheep, 45,000 pigs, and 2,510,000 goats, re-

presenting an aggregate value of 24 millions sterling. The value of products in 1885 was approximately as follows :—

	Tons	£	Sundries	£
Wheat . .	190,000	1,600,000	Wine . .	2,500,000
Barley . .	70,000	500,000	Timber . .	800,000
Rye . .	20,000	130,000	Olives . .	900,000
Maize . .	100,000	670,000	Vegetables .	1,100,000
			Dairy and } poultry }	1,400,000
All grain .	380,000	2,900,000		
Hay and } straw . }	1,200,000	2,000,000	Meat . . .	2,500,000
Currants	120,000	3,100,000	Foals, hides } &c. . }	1,700,000
Principal } crops . }	...	8,000,000	Sundries .	10,900,000

	£
Agricultural products . . .	13,700,000
Animal products . . .	5,200,000
Total . . .	18,900,000

In 1836 the Government sold the productive land at £3 an acre—say, in all, 15 millions sterling.

In 1869 the Embassy report makes the arable land worth about £22 an acre, the rest £5, viz. :—

	Acres	Per Acre, £	Value, Millions £
Arable	1,800,000	22	40
Pasture	3,200,000	5	16
Total . .	5,000,000	11	56

The acquisition of Thessaly, in 1881, added 5000 square miles to the area of Greece, and the present landed value, at the prices of the Embassy report of 1869, would be as follows :—

	Acres	Value, £
Cultivated	5,000,000	110,000,000
Pasture	5,000,000	25,000,000
Forest	1,500,000	3,000,000
Waste	4,500,000	...
Total . . .	16,000,000	138,000,000

See Part II., page 624.

ROUMANIA

The latest returns give the acreage as follows :—

	Acres		Acres
Grain . .	7,500,000	Pasture . .	6,500,000
Meadow . .	1,400,000	Forest . . .	5,200,000
Vines . . .	300,000	Waste . .	10,000,000
Cultivated . .	9,200,000	Uncultivated	21,700,000

Spallart says that the production of grain in 1876 was 20 per cent. greater than ten years before. The weight ot crops is variously estimated from 100 to 110 million bushels. The latest returns of live-stock show 600,000 horses, 2,380,000 cattle, 4,650,000 sheep, 2,310,000 pigs, and 190,000 goats, representing an aggregate value of about 37 millions sterling. The production of meat is approximately as follows :—

	Tons	Value, £
Beef	106,000	4,500,000
Mutton . . .	41,000	1,800,000
Pork	100,000	4,500,000
Total .	247,000	10,800,000

The value of all products may be put down approximately thus :—

	Tons	£	Sundries	£
Wheat . .	700,000	5,000,000	Vegetables	2,500,000
Barley . .	330,000	2,000,000	Meat . .	10,800,000
Maize . .	1,600,000	9,000,000	Dairy . .	4,800,000
Rye, &c. .	220,000	1,300,000	Poultry . .	1,100,000
			Timber . .	900,000
All grain .	2,850,000	17,300,000	Foals . .	1,200,000
Straw . .	3,000,000	1,500,000	Tallow . .	700,000
Hay . . .	1,400,000	2,100,000	Hides, }	1,200,000
Wine, gallons	40,000,000	3,100,000	wool, &c. }	
Principal crops }		24,000,000	Sundries .	23,200,000

		£
Agricultural products .	. .	27,400,000
Animal products	. .	19,800,000
Total	. . .	47,200,000

The value of the land appears to be approximately as follows :—

	Acres	Value, £
Cultivated	9,200,000	184,000,000
Forest and pasture .	11,700,000	70,000,000
Waste	10,000,000	...
Total . . .	30,900,000	254,000,000

See Part II., page 624.

SERVIA

The total area of this little kingdom is thus distributed :—

	Acres		Acres
Grain	1,160,000	Forest . . .	2,200,000
Vines	440,000	Pasture . . .	6,170,000
Meadow . . .	600,000	Waste . . .	1,430,000
Cultivated . .	2,200,000	Uncultivated .	9,800,000

An official report for 1887, not trustworthy, gives as follows :—

		Acres
Grain and wine .	. . .	7,030,000
Forest .	. . .	2,200,000
Waste, &c. .	. . .	2,770,000
Total	. . .	12,000,000

The apparent error in this report is including pasture-land as grain-bearing. The crops have been sometimes said to reach 20 million bushels, but Spallart says 14 millions, and the average weight seems to be 16 millions bushels. The value of product is approximately thus :—

	Tons	£	Sundries	£
Wheat . .	100,000	700,000	Vegetables	1,000,000
Barley . .	70,000	400,000	Timber . .	400,000
Maize . .	130,000	700,000	Poultry . .	400,000
Oats, rye, } &c. . . }	100,000	600,000	Dairy . .	2,000,000
			Meat . .	4,000,000
			Foals . .	400,000
All grain .	400,000	2,400,000	Tallow . .	300,000
Straw . .	400,000	200,000	Hides, }	
Hay . . .	600,000	1,000,000	wool, &c. }	500,000
Wine, galls.	16,000,000	1,200,000		
Principal crops . }	...	4,800,000	Sundries .	9,000,000

		£
Agricultural products .	. . .	6,200,000
Animal products	. . .	7,600,000
Total	. .	13,800,000

Statistics of live-stock in 1882 were :—Horses, 160,000; cattle, 960,000; sheep, 3,600,000; pigs, 1,700,000; and goats, 100,000—representing a total value of nearly 16 millions sterling. The production of meat was about 90,000 tons. The value of land was approximately thus :—

	Acres	£
Cultivated	2,200,000	44,000,000
Pasture	6,200,000	37,000,000
Forest	2,200,000	13,000,000
Waste	1,400,000	...
Total . . .	12,000,000	94,000,000

Agricultural capital is approximately as follows :—

	Millions, £
Land	94
Cattle	16
Sundries	12
Total . . .	122

The product is about 11½ per cent. on capital, and £28 per head of adults engaged.

BULGARIA

The area, including Eastern Roumelia, is somewhat larger than that of Ireland, viz. :—

	Acres
Bulgaria proper	16,000,000
Eastern Roumelia	8,300,000
Total .	24,300,000

The extent under grain in Eastern Roumelia is 1,660,000 acres, and in Bulgaria proper close on 4,000,000 acres. The crops of Bulgaria proper average 44 million bushels, of which 23 millions are wheat. The total grain crop of the Principality must be over 60 million bushels, or approximately 1,500,000 tons, representing a value of 10 millions sterling.

TURKEY

Agriculture is very backward, owing to the despotism of the Pashas and the exactions of money-lenders. Every province, meantime, has its own features and modes of agriculture. If we include the territories taken from Turkey by the Treaty of Berlin in 1878, we find as follows :—

	Acres	Population	Acre per Inhabitant
Bosnia-Herzegovina	15,000,000	1,500,000	10
Bulgaria	24,300,000	3,150,000	8
Turkey proper . .	41,000,000	4,350,000	9½
Turkey in Europe	80,300,000	9,000,000	9

Mr. Spallart compares the average grain crops of 1881–85 with those of 1868 thus :—

	1881–85, Millions of Bushels				1868
	Bosnia	Bulgaria	Eur. Turkey	Total	
Wheat . .	2	23	22	47	39
Maize . .	3	7	8	18	30
Barley . .	2	11	12	25	25
Rye, &c. .	1	3	15	19	13
Total .	8	44	57	109	107

Bosnia and Bulgaria have been already described. One of the most productive provinces in Turkey was Bessarabia, which was transferred to Russia by the Berlin Treaty of 1878 : it is rich in corn and wine. The vineyards often yield per acre 300 gallons of wine, worth £18 ; and the grain farms 60 bushels of maize per acre. The serfs were emancipated in 1870, the Boyars or nobles being compelled to either give the tenant half his farm gratis or sell the whole for 26s. per acre. Four hundred Boyars preferred the former, and let the remainder of their lands at 5s. an acre. In 1874 there were 350,000 small landowners whose farms averaged 30 acres each, maize being the chief product.

Turkey proper is held partly by Pashas, who let the lands in small farms of 20 acres to Murabàs, on the "metayer" system, the tenant giving half the crops in lieu of rent ; partly by peasant proprietors in 50-acre farm-lots, viz. :—

	Number of Farms	Acres
Murabàs	650,000	13,000,000
Peasant landowners .	600,000	29,700,000
Total . . .	1,250,000	42,700,000

The price of arable land ranges from £20 to £60 per acre, and it may be rented from 20s. to 40s. per annum. Waste land sells at £3 per acre. Live-stock is supposed to comprise 600,000 horses, 1,000,000 cattle, and 10,000,000 sheep, besides numbers of goats, pigs, and poultry.

Epirus is backward, the labours of the field devolving mostly on women, and large tracts of good land lying waste for want of hands to cultivate it. The country about Adrianople, on the other hand, is progressive, the use of steam-threshers being general. Oxen and buffaloes are employed for ploughing ; wheat and maize are the chief crops. The area under crops is not known ; probably about 8 or 10 million acres. The grain crops may be put down roughly at 80 million bushels.

ASIA MINOR

This portion of the Turkish Empire is sometimes called Anatolia, with an area of 220,000 square miles or 141 million acres, and a population of about 5,000,000 souls

About one-third of the area is actually farmed, either as Murabàs on the "metayer" system, or by the tenant proprietors, viz. :—

	Number of Farms	Acres	Average Farm, Acres
Murabàs . .	1,395,000	28,000,000	20
Proprietors . .	1,284,000	22,000,000	18
Total . .	2,679,000	50,000,000	19

Such is the want of roads, that the freight of a ton of grain 100 miles would be £9, or about the value of the grain. Tithes are oppressive, as well as transit custom-dues on products going from one province to another. Most of the lands, moreover, belong to the State or to the Vacouf institutions ; and although the soil is fertile, no progress is made.

Smyrna or Ardin is the best part of Asiatic Turkey, with an area of 35,500 square miles or 22 million acres, and a population of 1,000,000, nine-tenths Moslems. Most of the territory consists of Chiftliks or large estates, worked by the peasants on the Murabà system. Some small proprietors have bought their farms at 40s. per acre, the lowness of price being the result of heavy taxation, viz. :—1st, one-tenth of all crops and fruit to the State ; 2nd, four per mil, equal to one penny yearly for each £ of selling value of land and houses, or about 4 per cent. on the rental value ; 3rd, a charge of 5 per cent. on every transfer ; 4th, a cattle-tax of 32d. per sheep, and 21d. per pig or goat yearly. Land is allowed to lie fallow every third year. The ordinary yield of crops is wheat or barley twelve-fold, beans twenty-fold, maize thirty-fold. Vallonia is an important crop, Smyrna exporting 100,000 tons yearly.

EGYPT

The area under tillage has almost trebled in fifty years, the official report published in 1888 containing the following table :—

Year	Acres under Crops	Year	Acres under Crops
1833	1,930,000	1875	4,890,000
1840	4,020,000	1880	4,960,000
1863	4,570,000	1888	5,080,000

A statement of the crops in 1834 was as follows :—18 million bushels grain, 22 million lbs. raw cotton, 5000 tons tobacco, 3000 tons flax, and 1600 tons sugar, representing a total value of £4,000,000 sterling.

When Mehemet Ali was dying, in 1848, he could boast that in his reign Egypt had more than doubled the area under crops. Progress was also made under his grandson, Abbas, and still more under Ismail Pacha, from 1863 to 1879, in which period were made 8400 miles of canals, irrigating 1,370,000 acres, the cultivation of cotton being specially stimulated by high prices consequent on the American war.

The cotton crop is shown for the last sixty-seven years as follows :—

Period	Million lbs. Yearly	Value	Price per Lb.
		£	
1821–30 . . .	14	392,000	6.7
1831–40 . . .	18	677,000	9.0
1841–50 . . .	24	504,000	5.0
1851–60 . . .	51	1,120,000	5.3
1861–70 . . .	127	6,860,000	13.0
1871–80 . . .	237	7,580,000	7.7
1881–87 . . .	288	7,490,000	6.2

The distribution of tillage in 1888 was as follows :—

	Acres	Crop, Tons
Wheat	1,290,000	500,000
Maize	710,000	300,000
Barley	540,000	160,000
Peas, &c.	1,955,000	900,000
All grain	4,495,000	1,860,000
Cotton	900,000	130,000
Clover	980,000	2,000,000
Total . . .	6,375,000	...

Some of the land bears double crops, which accounts for the discrepancy between this and the previous table. There are 3,450,000 date-palms, producing annually 300,000 tons of fruit. There is room for further development, since there are still idle 2,200,000 acres suitable for tillage. More than three-fourths of the lands are State property, the Khedive holding 3,800,000 acres, which he lets to the Fellahs at a yearly rent of 8s. per acre in Upper Egypt and 30s. in the Nile Valley.

A statement of tenure in 1879 was as follows :—

Farmed by	Title	Acres	Tax, £	Shillings per Acre
Gentry . .	Ouchour	1,329,000	470,000	7
Fellahs . .	Karadji	3,514,000	3,850,000	22
Do. . .	Abadich	620,000	500,000	16
Total .	...	5,463,000	4,828,000	18

An official return of the value of crops in 1884 was :—

	£	Sundries	£
Grain	13,300,000	Clover . . .	2,500,000
Cotton	7,900,000	Dates and sugar	1,700,000
Cotton-seed . .	1,400,000	Lentils, flax, &c.	3,200,000
Principal crops .	22,600,000	Sundries . . .	7,400,000

Making a total of 30 millions sterling. The crop, however, depends so much on the Nile, that a difference

of one foot in flood-level is worth £2,000,000, the average Nile rising 24 feet. In ordinary years the cost of irrigation is 4s. an acre per annum. The agricultural condition of the country is shown thus :—

	Lower Egypt	Upper Egypt	Total
Villages . .	2,359	1,420	3,779
Inhabitants .	3,180,000	2,630,000	5,810,000
Acres cultivated .	2,880,000	2,330,000	5,210,000
Horses and cattle	466,000	284,000	750,000
Sheep and goats	380,000	555,000	935,000
Date-palms .	1,100,000	2,350,000	3,450,000

In Lower Egypt the soil gives four crops in three years; in Upper Egypt seven crops in six years.

CYPRUS

Area 2,300,000 acres, being 13 acres per inhabitant. The island is held partly by nobles, who have eighty Tchifliks or large estates, the rest being cut up in 70-acre farms belonging to peasant proprietors. The chief products are :—

	Value, £
Grain, 3 million bushels . . .	500,000
Wine, 450,000 gallons	40,000
Oil, 50,000 gallons	18,000
Sundries	82,000
Total	640,000

The farmers have 750,000 sheep, besides cows and horses. There are 600,000 carob or algarroba trees, covering an area of 20,000 acres, yielding 25,000 tons of locust-beans worth £75,000, most of which goes to Scotland to be made into whisky.

ALGERIA

The cultivated portion is about 16 per cent. of the total, viz. :—

	Acres
Under crops	7,720,000
Pasture	4,800,000
Forest and waste	63,920,000
Total	76,440,000

The returns for 1886 were as follows :—

	Acreage			Crop, Tons		
	European	Arab	Total	European	Arab	Total
Wheat	620,000	2,500,000	3,120,000	127,000	505,000	632,000
Barley	300,000	3,300,000	3,600,000	100,000	850,000	950,000
Oats	100,000	...	100,000	50,000	...	50,000
Maize, &c.	40,000	100,000	140,000	13,000	15,000	28,000
All grain . . .	1,060,000	5,900,000	6,960,000	290,000	1,370,000	1,660,000

The European settlers had also 190,000 acres under vines, which produced 36 million gallons of wine in 1886, the yield in 1890 being expected to reach 60 million gallons. The tenure of land in 1886 was as follows :—

Province	Acres held by				
	Arabs	Jews	French	Settlers	Total
Algiers . .	2,900,000	40,000	230,000	170,000	3,340,000
Oran . .	1,540,000	40,000	160,000	230,000	1,970,000
Constantine	3,570,000	30,000	150,000	100,000	3,850,000
Total .	8,010,000	110,000	540,000	500,000	9,160,000

The returns of live-stock were :—

	Owned by		
	Europeans	Arabs	Total
Horses	51,000	260,000	311,000
Asses	13,000	270,000	283,000
Camels	300	275,500	275,800
Cattle	137,000	1,060,000	1,197,000
Sheep	321,000	9,036,000	9,357,000
Goats	74,000	4,592,000	4,666,000
Pigs	85,000	...	85,000

The value of all live-stock was about 28 millions sterling ; the production of meat about 160,000 tons yearly. The grain crop has increased 50 per cent. in the last twenty years. The value of products in 1886 was approximately thus :—

	Tons	£	Sundries	£
Wheat . .	630,000	5,000,000	Meat . . .	6,400,000
Barley, &c. .	1,030,000	6,200,000	Dairy and }	2,600,000
Wine . . .	...	2,200,000	poultry }	
			Wool, }	
Principal } crops }	...	13,400,000	hides, &c. }	3,300,000
			Sundries .	12,300,000

UNITED STATES

Tillage was a chief occupation of the first settlers. In 1602 Captain Gosnold grew peas and beans in Massachusetts, and in 1611 wheat was grown in Virginia. The Dutch of Manhattan (New York) sent home some wheat to Holland in 1626. Potatoes, previously unknown in North America, were introduced from England in 1629 and successfully grown in Massachusetts. Stebbins relates that in 1637 there were 100 ploughs at work in Virginia, and 37 in Massachusetts. In 1640 Mr. Endicott of Salem sold 500 fruit-trees for 250 acres of land, and in the preceding year Manhattan apples were sent to Holland. South Carolina exported 700 bushels of potatoes in 1749. New York 70,000 barrels of flour in 1750. The production of grain in the eighteenth century can only be roughly estimated on the basis of population ; exact returns begin with the year 1840.

Year	Grain Product, Million of Bushels			Value of Crop, Million £
	Production	Home Consumption	Exported	
1700	5	5	...	1
1750	20	20	...	3
1775	60	60	...	8
1790	120	120	...	14
1800	160	160	...	18
1820	343	336	7	34
1830	463	455	8	46
1840	616	601	15	62
1850	867	855	12	97
1860	1,240	1,220	20	173
1870	1,629	1,569	60	198
1880	2,718	2,425	293	276
1889	3,454	...	...	243

The production is at present 52 bushels per inhabitant, against 30 in the year 1800. It forms 33 per cent. of the whole grain-crop of the world, and the ratio per inhabitant is only approached by Denmark, which has 42 bushels per inhabitant.

The various crops since 1840 show as follows :—

Year	Millions of Bushels						Bushels per Inhabitant
	Maize	Oats	Wheat	Barley	Rye, &c.	Total	
1840	378	123	85	4	26	616	36
1850	592	147	101	5	23	868	38
1860	840	173	173	16	38	1,240	40
1870	1,094	248	236	26	25	1,629	42
1880	1,717	418	499	45	39	2,718	54
1889	2,110	750	490	64	40	3,454	53

The production of grain in various parts of the Union was as follows :—

Year	Millions of Bushels				
	New England	Middle States	Southern	Western	Total
1840	22	135	280	179	616
1850	20	170	360	318	868
1860	21	204	412	603	1,240
1870	16	216	301	1,096	1,629
1880	18	233	442	2,025	2,718
1887	20	244	605	1,797	2,666

The ratio of bushels produced per inhabitant was as follows :—

Year	New England	Middle States	Southern	Western	Union
1840	10	27	44	54	36
1850	7	25	43	57	38
1860	7	25	40	62	40
1870	5	22	27	61	42
1880	4	20	29	106	54
1887	5	18	36	78	44

The aggregate of crops of 1887 was 10 per cent. below the average of 1884–88.

The distribution of the various crops in 1887 compares with that of 1850 as follows :—

MILLIONS OF BUSHELS

States	1850				1887			
	Wheat	Maize	Oats, &c.	Total	Wheat	Maize	Oats, &c.	Total
New England	1	11	8	20	1	9	10	20
Middle . .	32	61	77	170	33	103	108	244
Southern . .	19	298	43	360	47	474	84	605
Western . .	49	222	47	318	375	870	552	1,797
Union . . .	101	592	175	868	456	1,456	754	2,666

The progress of grain-growing in twenty years is shown in the Agricultural Report for 1889 as follows :—

	Acreage				Increase of 20 Years	Per Cent.
	1869	1870–79	1880–88	1889		
Wheat	19,180,000	25,190,000	37,280,000	38,120,000	18,940,000	99
Maize	37,100,000	43,740,000	70,540,000	78,320,000	41,220,000	111
Oats	9,460,000	11,080,000	22,000,000	27,460,000	18,000,000	190
Barley	1,030,000	1,530,000	2,480,000	3,000,000	1,970,000	⁻91
Rye	1,660,000	1,310,000	2,120,000	2,360,000	700,000	42
Buckwheat . . .	1,030,000	550,000	880,000	910,000	...	...
All grain . . .	69,460,000	83,400,000	135,300,000	150,170,000	80,710,000	116

	Value, £ Sterling				Increase of 20 Years	Per Cent.
	1869	1870-79	1880-88	1889		
Wheat . . .	51,000,000	68,100,000	77,300,000	71,300,000	20,300,000	40
Maize	135,700,000	104,700,000	138,900,000	123,700,000	...	...
Oats . . .	28,500,000	23,100,000	37,600,000	36,100,000	7,600,000	27
Barley . . .	4,900,000	5,200,000	6,600,000	6,600,000	1,700,000	35
Rye . . .	4,600,000	2,700,000	3,300,000	3,500,000	...	...
Buckwheat . . .	3,300,000	1,500,000	1,500,000	1,600,000	...	...
All grain . . .	228,000,000	205,300,000	265,200,000	242,800,000	13,200,000	6

	Yield, Million Bushels				Increase of 20 Years	Per Cent.
	1869	1870-79	1880-88	1889		
Wheat . . .	260	310	450	490	230	88
Maize	870	1,180	1,700	2,110	1,240	142
Oats	290	310	580	750	460	158
Barley	29	34	54	64	35	121
Rye	23	18	25	28	5	22
Buckwheat . .	17	10	11	12	...	...
All grain . . .	1,489	1,862	2,820	3,454	1,965	131

	Average Bushels, per Acre				Pence per Bushel			
	1869	1870-79	1880-88	1889	1869	1870-79	1880-88	1889
Wheat . .	13.5	12.4	12.1	12.9	47	52	41	35
Maize . .	23.6	27.1	24.1	27.0	38	21	20	14
Oats . .	30.4	28.4	26.6	27.4	24	18	15	11
Barley . .	27.9	22.0	21.7	21.3	41	37	29	25
Rye . . .	13.5	14.1	11.9	12.0	48	35	31	29
Buckwheat	16.9	17.7	12.8	13.2	45	36	32	32
All grain .	21.4	22.3	20.9	23.0	36	27	23	17

COTTON PRODUCTION, MILLION LBS.

Year	Production	Home Use	Exported	Value of Crop, Million £
1800	36	16	20	2
1810	115	20	95	5
1820	160	32	128	6
1830	350	52	298	6
1840	878	134	744	15
1850	890	225	665	17
1860	1,880	434	1,446	40
1870	1,540	530	1,010	41
1880	2,593	771	1,822	59
1888	3,440	1,060	2,380	61

The average crop is 190 lbs. ginned cotton per acre. The crop of cotton-seed usually reaches 3,000,000 tons, worth 22s. per ton.

The production of cotton in 1840 and 1886 was as follows :—

	Millions of Lbs.		Ratio	
	1840	1888	1840	1888
Mississippi	193	524	21.9	15.2
Georgia	163	464	18.5	13.5
Louisiana	153	220	17.4	6.4
Alabama	117	457	13.3	13.3
South Carolina	62	267	7.1	7.8
North Carolina	52	177	5.9	5.2
Arkansas, Tennessee, &c.	138	1,331	15.9	38.6
Total . . .	878	3,440	100.0	100.0

TOBACCO PRODUCTION, MILLION LBS.

Year	Production	Home Use	Export	Value of Crop, £
1800	107	18	89	1,300,000
1810	117	25	92	1,200,000
1820	127	34	93	2,100,000
1830	142	46	96	2,600,000
1840	219	78	141	3,900,000
1850	250	82	168	5,300,900
1860	303	110	193	3,700,000
1870	426	238	188	9,400,000
1880	460	243	217	7,500,000
1888	566	224	342	9,100,000

The production of tobacco in 1840 and 1886 was as follows :—

	Millions of Lbs.		Ratio	
	1840	1886	1840	1886
Virginia	75	94	34.3	18.6
Kentucky	53	194	24.2	36.2
Tennessee	30	32	13.8	6.0
Maryland	25	25	11.4	4.7
North Carolina . .	17	32	7.7	6.0
Other States . . .	19	152	8.6	28.5
Total . . .	219	529	100.0	100.0

The production of butter and cheese in 1850 and 1880 was as follows :—

	Millions of Lbs.				Milk, Million Gallons
	Butter		Cheese		
	1850	1880	1850	1880	1880
New York . .	80	112	50	84	232
Pennsylvania .	40	79	3	10	37
Ohio . . .	34	67	21	22	47
Illinois . . .	13	54	1	10	45
Indiana . . .	13	37	1	4	7
Vermont . . .	12	25	9	15	7
Virginia . . .	11	21	1	1	2
Kentucky . . .	10	18	1	1	3
Iowa	2	55	...	11	16
Michigan . . .	7	39	1	4	8
Wisconsin . .	4	33	...	23	25
Missouri . . .	8	29	...	3	3
Kansas . . .	...	22	...	5	1
Tennessee . .	8	18	...	1	1
Maine . . .	9	14	2	12	4
California . .	...	14	...	26	12
Texas . . .	2	14	...	1	1
Other States . .	60	126	16	39	79
Total . .	313	777	106	272	530

The production of other articles was as follows :—

	1840	1850	1860	1870	1880	1886
Sugar, million lbs. . .	155	248	269	166	246	240
Rice, ,, ,, . .	81	215	187	74	110	...
Butter, ,, ,, . .	...	313	460	514	777	960
Cheese, ,, ,, . .	...	106	104	153	272	380
Wool, ,, ,, . .	36	52	112	162	233	320
Hay, tons	10	14	19	27	35	42
Potatoes, bushels . .	108	104	111	143	169	168

Sugar is grown almost exclusively in Louisiana, rice in South Carolina and Georgia.

The following table shows the area under farms :—

Year	Millions of Acres		
	Improved	Unimproved	Total
1810.	64	100	164
1850.	113	180	293
1870.	190	220	410
1880.	285	249	534
1888.	345	302	647

The above figures are official except as regards 1888: this last is an estimate, adding 21 per cent. to the figures for 1880, as the agricultural report shows similar rise in the area under crops, namely, from 165 million acres in 1880 to 200 millions in 1886 (see *Lands*).

The distribution of the wheat, maize, hay, and potato crops in 1888–89 was as follows :—

	Acres			
	Wheat	Maize	Hay	Potatoes
Illinois . .	2,380,000	8,020,000	3,300,000	140,000
Iowa . . .	1,605,000	8,860,000	3,640,000	190,000
Indiana . .	2,800,000	3,680,000	1,450,000	80,000
Kansas . .	1,680,000	6,810,000	1,550,000	140,000
Missouri . .	1,590,000	6,800,000	1,500,000	90,000
Ohio . . .	2,520,000	3,005,000	2,570,000	150,000
Michigan .	1,610,000	970,000	1,400,000	120,000
Wisconsin .	1,190,000	1,080,000	1,730,000	140,000
Pennsylvania	1,350,000	1,380,000	2,720,000	205,000
Tennessee .	1,210,000	3,670,000	...	40,000
California .	3,290,000	160,000	1,180,000	60,000
Kentucky .	980,000	2,840,000	...	50,000
New York .	650,000	700,000	4,930,000	370,000
Texas . .	600,000	4,570,000	150,000	...
Various . .	14,665,000	25,775,000	12,470,000	755,000
Total . .	38,120,000	78,320,000	38,590,000	2,530,000

The increase of farming area between 1850 and 1880 was as follows :—

States	Millions of Acres		Rate of Increase, per Cent.
	1850	1880	
New England .	18	22	22
Middle . . .	43	53	23
Southern . . .	165	227	38
Western . . .	67	232	248
Union	293	534	82

The area of improved lands increased in the same interval thus :—

States	Millions of Acres		Rate of Increase, per Cent.
	1850	1880	
New England .	11	13	28
Middle	26	37	42
Southern . . .	49	82	67
Western . . .	27	153	467
Union	113	285	152

The acreage, product, and value of the principal crops in 1889 were as follows :—

	Acres	Tons	Value, £	Value per Ton, £	Product per Acre, £
Wheat .	38,120,000	13,200,000	71,300,000	5.40	1.87
Maize .	78,320,000	52,700,000	123,700,000	2.35	1.58
Oats . .	27,460,000	10,700,000	36,100,000	3.37	1.31
Barley .	3,000,000	1,400,000	6,600,000	4.72	2.20
Rye . .	2,360,000	700,000	3,500,000	5.00	1.50
Buckwheat	910,000	250,000	1,600,000	6.40	1.76
All grain .	150,170,000	78,950,000	242,800,000	3.07	1.62
Potatoes .	2,530,000	5,060,000	17,000,000	3.35	6.70
Hay . .	38,590,000	46,600,000	85,000,000	1.82	2.22
Cotton .	19,060,000	1,540,000	60,800,000	39.50	3.20
Tobacco .	750,000	250,000	9,100,000	36.40	12.10
Total .	211,100,000	...	414,700,000	...	1.97

The acreage of the principal crops at various dates was approximately as follows :—

	Acres				
	1850	1860	1870	1880	1889
Wheat	8,000,000	14,500,000	18,990,000	37,990,000	38,120,000
Maize	21,000,000	30,500,000	38,640,000	62,320,000	78,330,000
Oats	5,200,000	6,200,000	8,790,000	16,190,000	27,460,000
Barley	200,000	600,000	1,110,000	1,840,000	3,000,000
Rye, &c.	1,800,000	2,500,000	1,720,000	2,590,000	3,280,000
All grain	36,200,000	54,300,000	69,250,000	120,930,000	150,190,000
Potatoes	1,200,000	1,300,000	1,700,000	1,840,000	2,530,000
Cotton	6,000,000	12,000,000	10,200,000	15,950,000	19,060,000
Tobacco	360,000	430,000	550,000	610,000	750,000
Sugar	250,000	270,000	170,000	230,000	230,000
Rice	330,000	290,000	110,000	170,000	170,000
Meadow	10,000,000	13,000,000	20,000,000	25,860,000	38,590,000
Total . .	54,340,000	81,590,000	101,980,000	165,590,000	211,520,000

There are no returns as to rice and sugar in 1889, but they are doubtless the same as in 1880. The maize crop covers an area as large as Great Britain and Ireland, and the total acreage under grain exceeds the dimensions of the German Empire. The cotton covers as much land as the kingdoms of Holland and Belgium in the aggregate. The area under hay is as large as England. The dimensions of the United States may be briefly expressed thus :—

	Millions of Acres	Ratio
Under crops	212	9.2
Under pasture. . . .	447	19.5
Under forest	176	7.6
Unsettled lands . . .	1,456	63.7
Total . .	2,291	100.0

The following statistics are official :—

Cattle were first introduced into Virginia in 1609, and into New England in 1624. They increased so rapidly that in 1639 the number in the colonies was estimated at 30,000. Dairy-farming prospered in the eighteenth century, one farmer of Rhode Island in 1750 counting 100 milch-cows, and another in the same year selling six tons of cheese.

Nevertheless cattle-farming at first contended with difficulties. It is recorded that the first hogs, goats, and sheep introduced were killed and eaten by the colonists for want of food. A second supply was brought from the West Indies, and it was made in Virginia punishable with death to kill any of these animals. The records of New York show that in 1627 the price of a cow was £30, of a yoke of oxen £40; those of Philadelphia, that the city market consumed twenty head of horned cattle weekly, besides sheep and hogs. Sheep were found to thrive in Virginia, but no use was made of the wool; the sheep were shorn to keep them cool.

	1810	1840	1850	1860	1870	1880	1890
Horses	300,000	4,300,000	4,900,000	6,200,000	7,100,000	10,400,000	14,200,000
Mules	...	...	...	1,200,000	1,100,000	1,800,000	2,300,000
Cattle	600,000	14,900,000	17,800,000	25,600,000	23,800,000	35,900,000	52,800,000
Sheep	600,000	19,300,000	21,700,000	22,500,000	28,500,000	35,200,000	44,300,000
Pigs	...	26,300,000	30,350,000	33,500,000	25,100,000	47,700,000	51,600,000

Meat supply may be taken at 500 lbs. per beef carcase, 50 lbs. per sheep, and 110 lbs. per pig. Tallow is as 14 to 100 lbs. of beef or mutton, and lard 20 to 100 lbs. of pig's meat.

The values of cattle in 1870 and 1890 were as follows :—

	1870			1890		
	Number	Value, £	Per Head, £	Number	Value, £	Per Head, £
Horses	8,250,000	121,000,000	14.9	14,210,000	201,900,000	14.2
Mules	1,180,000	23,400,000	20.0	2,330,000	38,100,000	16.3
Milch-cows . . .	10,100,000	71,000,000	7.0	15,950,000	73,400,000	4.6
Oxen	15,400,000	62,000,000	4.0	36,850,000	116,600,000	3.2
Sheep	40,850,000	16,800,000	0.4	44,340,000	20,900,000	0.5
Swine	26,750,000	34,000,000	1.3	51,600,000	50,700,000	1.0
Total . . .	...	328,200,000	...	...	501,600,000	...

The distribution of live-stock in the great divisions of the Union in 1890 was as follows :—

States	Number					Value, £ Sterling
	Horses	Mules	Cattle	Sheep	Pigs	
New England . . .	360,000	...	1,502,000	1,220,000	350,000	16,600,000
Middle	1,680,000	60,000	5,170,000	3,280,000	2,960,000	68,000,000
South	1,730,000	1,200,000	6,980,000	3,440,000	13,130,000	77,400,000
West	10,440,000	1,070,000	39,148,000	36,400,000	35,160,000	339,100,000
Total . . .	14,210,000	2,330,000	52,800,000	44,340,000	51,600,000	501,100,000

The average value in dollars was as follows :—

States	Horses	Mules	Cows	Oxen	Sheep	Pigs
New England	94	...	28	24	3.0	9.0
Middle . .	91	102	28	25	3.4	6.5
South . . .	71	85	18	12	2.0	3.5
West . . .	64	71	20	15	2.3	5.0
The Union .	68	78	22	16	2.3	4.8

These values, as shown above, are much lower than prevailed in 1870, which in the foregoing table are computed in gold, after allowing 13 per cent. discount on greenbacks. If prices had not fallen, the live-stock of 1890 would represent a total value of 591 millions £ sterling.

Although the prices in the Western States are lower than in other parts of the Union, the wealth which they possess in cattle is two-thirds of the total, amounting to 339 millions sterling. This sum far exceeds the value of live-stock in any European country except Russia, and is five times as great as that of the cattle of all kinds in Australasia. The increase numerically of stock in the Western States has been as follows :—

	1860	1880	1890
Horses	3,220,000	7,030,000	10,440,000
Cattle	12,900,000	22,700,000	39,148,000
Sheep	11,150,000	25,200,000	36,400,000
Pigs	15,200,000	32,050,000	35,160,000

The States richest in live-stock were as follows :—

NUMBER

	Horses and Mules	Milch-Cows	Oxen	Sheep	Pigs	Value, £ Sterling
Iowa	1,140,000	1,330,000	2,580,000	480,000	5,810,000	39,900,000
Illinois	1,230,000	1,070,000	1,710,000	690,000	5,430,000	37,400,000
Texas	1,560,000	840,000	7,170,000	4,750,000	2,320,000	30,400,000
New York	680,000	1,550,000	780,000	1,550,000	690,000	29,300,000
Ohio	790,000	790,000	990,000	3,940,000	2,610,000	27,600,000
Missouri	1,020,000	770,000	1,520,000	1,200,000	5,100,000	25,600,000
Pennsylvania . . .	630,000	940,000	850,000	950,000	1,190,000	24,300,000
Kansas	820,000	750,000	1,830,000	440,000	2,730,000	23,700,000
Indiana	720,000	600,000	960,000	1,280,000	2,850,000	22,300,000
Nebraska	590,000	420,000	1,310,000	240,000	2,310,000	17,900,000
Michigan	480,000	450,000	550,000	2,240,000	980,000	16,000,000
Wisconsin	440,000	670,000	810,000	810,000	1,090,000	15,000,000
Kentucky	550,000	320,000	520,000	810,000	2,260,000	13,900,000
Tennessee	530,000	380,000	480,000	510,000	2,240,000	12,300,000
California	420,000	270,000	700,000	4,040,000	650,000	11,900,000
Minnesota	410,000	490,000	620,000	330,000	530,000	11,700,000
Dakota	310,000	250,000	820,000	270,000	480,000	8,900,000
Arkansas	320,000	330,000	590,000	270,000	1,660,000	7,100,000
Colorado	150,000	70,000	1,050,000	1,780,000	30,000	6,600,000
Various	3,750,000	3,660,000	11,010,000	17,760,000	10,640,000	119,300,000
Total	16,540,000	15,950,000	36,850,000	44,340,000	51,600,000	501,100,000

PRODUCT OF MEAT AND TALLOW

Year	Tons		Value, Million £ Sterling			Exported Meat, Tons
	Meat	Tallow, &c.	Meat	Tallow	Total	
1840	2,120,000	370,000	23	6	29	30,000
1850	2,460,000	440,000	26	8	34	75,000
1860	2,970,000	530,000	52	16	68	40,000
1870	2,540,000	460,000	68	14	82	46,000
1880	4,240,000	760,000	99	15	114	550,000
1886	4,750,000	880,000	140	16	156	380,000

The value of all agricultural products since 1840 is shown as follows :—

	Million £ Sterling					
	1840	1850	1860	1870	1880	1886
Grain	62	97	173	194	276	243
Cotton	15	18	40	41	59	53
Hay	20	29	33	40	62	74
Potatoes	8	9	10	12	14	16
Tobacco	4	5	4	9	8	8
Vegetables and fruit .	16	22	29	36	47	57
Meat and tallow .	29	34	68	82	114	156
Dairy products . .	14	17	34	41	57	78
Eggs and poultry . .	7	8	17	20	29	39
Wool	2	3	5	8	12	16
Hides, &c.	7	8	16	19	25	36
Total	184	250	429	502	703	776
Official value .	129	208	398	435	461	776

The difference between my statement of values and the official tables (excepting 1886) can only be explained by supposing that meat, dairy products, poultry, vegetables, &c., were omitted by Census Commissioners. On the other hand, the Commissioner for Agriculture in 1886 has omitted nothing, and I adopt his figures in every item. There is no allowance for forestry, because the Americans do not regard it as an agricultural pursuit.

According to the Census of 1880 it appears that 76 per cent. of all farming hands were males between 16 and 60

years of age. If we suppose the same ratio for previous dates, we find the product per male adult has been as follows :—

Year	Agricultural Hands	Male Adults	Product, Million £	Product per Male Adult, £
1840	2,550,000	1,935,000	184	95
1850	3,311,000	2,515,000	250	99
1860	4,342,000	3,305,000	429	130
1870	5,923,000	4,500,000	502	111
1880	7,671,000	5,890,000	703	119
1886	9,000,000	6,840,000	776	113

The number of agricultural hands in the above table is based on the Census returns for each date and the Commissioner's estimate in his agricultural report for 1886; but as the Census returns for 1840–60 do not include slaves, I have added for those years 50 per cent. of the adult slaves. It will be seen that the highest product per head was in 1860, although improved machinery has rendered farm labour much more productive in later years. The explanation is that wheat, for example, has fallen 60 cents a bushel, and maize in the same ratio. If prices had remained the same, the average product per head in 1886 would have been £180.

It is not possible to ascertain how the 9,000,000 hands in 1886 were distributed, but if it were in the same ratio as in 1880, the agricultural power of the great divisions of the country would be thus :—

States	Agricultural Hands	Male Adults	Product, Millions £	Product per Male Adult, £
New England .	351,000	267,000	35	130
Middle . . .	981,000	745,000	123	164
Southern . .	4,220,000	3,200,000	206	64
Western . .	3,448,000	2,628,000	412	160
Union . .	9,000,000	6,840,000	776	113

In Massachusetts, according to the Agricultural Report for 1888, the gross product of land per cultivated acre was, in English money, as follows :—

Grain .	£5	Onions .	£29	Tobacco .	£37
Potatoes .	11	Cabbage .	36	Strawberries .	42

The value of products consumed at home and exported were :—

Year	Millions, £ Sterling			Value Home Consumption £ per Inhab.
	Home Consumption	Exported	Total	
1840	167	17	184	10
1850	224	26	250	10
1860	367	62	429	12
1870	420	82	502	11
1880	561	142	703	11
1886	675	101	776	13

The principal States in order of production in 1886 were :—

States	Value of Product, Million £ Sterling				Ratio	
	In 1886			Nominal, 1880	1880	1886
	Agricultural	Pastoral	Total			
New York .	28	31	59	37	8.0	7.6
Illinois . . .	36	22	58	42	9.1	7.5
Iowa . . .	30	22	52	28	6.1	6.8
Ohio . . .	27	23	50	33	7.2	6.4
Pennsylvania .	24	23	47	27	5.9	6.0
Indiana . .	24	17	41	24	5.3	5.2
Texas . .	27	12	39	13	2.8	5.0
Missouri . .	19	14	33	20	4.4	4.2
Kansas . .	15	13	28	11	2.4	3.6
Michigan . .	14	13	27	19	4.2	3.5
Wisconsin .	14	11	25	15	3.2	3.2
Kentucky . .	15	7	22	13	2.8	2.7
California . .	13	7	20	13	2.8	2.6
Tennessee .	14	6	20	13	2.8	2.6
Other States .	167	88	255	153	33.0	32.9
Total .	467	309	776	461	100.0	100.0

In the above table for 1886 the agricultural values for each State are as set down in the Agricultural Report with 15 per cent. added for unclassified articles, the total, 467 millions sterling, being as given in the report. The pastoral products for each State are based on a medium of the value of dairy products (1880) and the value of cattle (1886).

The values, according to the great divisions of the country, were :—

States	Million £ Sterling (1886)				Ratio	
	Agricultural	Pastoral	Total	Nominal, 1880	1880	1886
New England	18	17	35	23	5.0	4.5
Middle . . .	62	61	123	77	16.5	15.7
Southern . .	150	56	206	131	28.5	26.5
Western . .	237	175	412	230	50.0	53.3
Union .	467	309	776	461	100.0	100.0

The product compares with the area of improved lands (1880) thus :—

	Acres Improved	Product, £	Shillings per Acre
New England .	13,000,000	35,000,000	54
Middle	37,000,000	123,000,000	66
Southern . . .	82,000,000	206,000,000	50
Western . . .	153,000,000	412,000,000	54
Union . .	285,000,000	776,000,000	54

Year	Agricultural Capital, Million £ Sterling				£ per Inhabitant
	Land	Cattle	Sundries	Total	
1790	96	4	24	124	31
1810	200	10	40	250	47
1840	400	96	100	596	35
1850	662	114	161	937	41
1860	1,382	226	237	1,845	58
1870	1,673	274	294	2,241	58
1880	2,116	340	518	2,974	60
1887	2,560	501	635	3,696	60

The above figures are official except as regards 1810 and 1840, also excepting the value of land in 1887, which is put down at 21 per cent. over 1880, because the area of crops is shown by the Commissioner to have risen 21 per cent. between 1880 and 1886.

The value of farms and cattle (without sundries), according to Census reports, was :—

Year	Million, £ Sterling					£ per Inhabitant				
	New England	Middle	Southern	Western	Union	New England	Middle	Southern	Western	Union
1850	88	276	245	167	776	32	42	30	30	35
1860	113	423	538	534	1,608	36	51	52	55	52
1870	124	570	318	935	1,947	35	58	28	68	50
1880	136	560	426	1,334	2,456	34	44	28	70	49

The increase of agricultural capital was as follows :—

Period	Increase, Million £	£ per Annum	Mean Number of Agricultural Male Adults	Increase per Head, £	Annual Increase per Head £
1841–60	1,249	62,500,000	2,530,000	500	25
1861–70	396	39,600,000	3,880,000	102	10
1871–87	1,455	85,600,000	5,710,000	255	15
47 years	3,100	65,700,000	4,040,000	775	16

It appears from the foregoing statement that the individual gains of those engaged in agriculture were greatest in the period from 1841 to 1860, averaging £25 a year ; the war which ensued in 1861 had a depressing effect, the average accumulation falling to £10 a year in the decade ending 1870, but since the latter year there has been a great recovery, the average reaching £15 per head per annum. This was not the annual average of earnings, but of savings, a result unexampled elsewhere.

CANADA

The area in acres is as follows :—

Province	Population	Acres	Acres per Inhabitant
Quebec . . .	1,360,000	121,200,000	90
Ontario . . .	1,920,000	117,200,000	60
Nova Scotia .	440,000	13,400,000	30
New Brunswick .	320,000	17,300,000	54
Prince Edward Island	110,000	1,300,000	12
Manitoba . . .	65,000	38,400,000	580
British Columbia .	50,000	217,600,000	4,350
North-West Territory	55,000	1,696,000,000	30,600
Total . .	4,320,000	2,222,400,000	510

The above was the population in 1881, but it is now estimated at 5,200,000, showing an average of 430 acres per inhabitant.

Tillage statistics for 1887 were as follows :—

ACREAGE

	Wheat	Barley	Oats	Maize	Potatoes	Total
Ontario . . .	1,380,000	770,000	1,680,000	160,000	140,000	4,130,000
Quebec and Coast . .	380,000	90,000	800,000	20,000	280,000	1,570,000
Manitoba, &c. . . .	870,000	100,000	260,000	...	10,000	1,240,000
Total . . .	2,630,000	960,000	2,740,000	180,000	430,000	6,940,000

CROP, TONS

	Wheat	Barley	Oats	Maize	Potatoes	Total
Ontario . . .	550,000	400,000	800,000	220,000	260,000	2,230,000
Quebec and Coast . .	110,000	50,000	400,000	25,000	900,000	1,485,000
Manitoba, &c. . . .	330,000	50,000	120,000	...	60,000	560,000
Total . . .	990,000	500,000	1,320,000	245,000	1,220,000	4,275,000

The above figures for Quebec and Coast Provinces are estimates based on the crops of 1881.
The statistics of live-stock at various dates were —

	1834	1861	1871	1881	1888
Horses	192,000	710,000	860,000	1,070,000	1,100,000
Cattle	885,000	2,320,000	2,690,000	3,510,000	3,790,000
Sheep	1,320,000	2,550,000	3,300,000	3,050,000	2,602,000
Pigs	...	1,250,000	1,410,000	1,210,000	1,205,000
Total value, £ . .	...	24,000,000	33,000,000	...	44,300,000

The grain-crops of the Dominion, measured in bushels, were as follows :—

	1871	1881	1884
Wheat	17,000,000	30,000,000	42,000,000
Oats	46,000,000	64,000,000	88,000,000
Barley	12,000,000	15,000,000	22,000,000
Maize	4,000,000	9,000,000	14,000,000
Rye, &c. . . .	5,000,000	6,000,000	6,000,000
Total . . .	84,000,000	124,000,000	172,000,000

In 1852 the total grain crop was 45 million bushels, and potatoes 6 million bushels.
The value of products in 1887 was approximately :—

	Tons	£	Sundries	£
Wheat . .	990,000	6,400,000	Timber . .	8,200,000
Oats . . .	1,320,000	5,300,000	Vegetables	2,500,000
Barley . .	500,000	2,500,000	Poultry . .	2,000,000
Maize . .	245,000	1,000,000	Dairy . .	7,500,000
			Meat . .	7,800,000
All grain .	3,055,000	15,200,000	Foals . .	1,100,000
Straw . .	3,000,000	1,500,000	Tallow . .	1,200,000
Hay . . .	4,000,000	6,000,000	Hides, }	
Potatoes .	1,200,000	1,800,000	wool,&c. }	1,300,000
Principal } crops . }	...	24,500,000	Sundries .	31,600,00

	£
Agricultural products . . .	35,200,000
Animal products . . .	20,900,000
Total . . .	56,100,000

Ontario has 48 per cent. of the cattle, 48 per cent. of the area (of Canada proper), and produces 65 per cent. of the grain. It may be said to represent 60 per cent. of the agricultural value of the Dominion. Its farms in 1887 covered 11,100,000 acres of cleared land, of which 7,430,000 were under crops. The official valuation for 1887 is as follows, and enables us to give an estimate for the rest of the Dominion :—

	Ontario	Quebec and Other Provinces	All Canada
	£	£	£
Land . . .	130,870,000	87,230,000	218,100,000
Buildings . .	38,510,000	25,690,000	64,200,000
Cattle . . .	21,700,000	22,600,000	44,300,000
Implements .	9,320,000	6,180,000	15,500,000
Total	200,400,000	141,700,000	342,100,000

The official valuation of all land occupied as farms in Canada in 1861 amounted to 102 millions sterling. The agricultural capital was approximately as follows :—

	Millions, £ Sterling	
	1861	1887
Farms	102	282
Cattle	24	44
Sundries	14	36
Total	140	362

This shows an increase of 222 millions sterling in 26 years, equal to £8,500,000 per annum, or one-tenth of the annual average in the United States from 1871 to 1887, the ratio of population being likewise about one-tenth. The relation between agricultural capital and product in Canada in 1861 and 1887 was as follows :—

Year	Millions, £		Ratio to Capital
	Capital	Product	
1861	140	21	15.0
1887	362	56	15.4

In the products of Canada the preceding table includes timber, a considerable item, but the United States does not include it as an agricultural product.

NEWFOUNDLAND

There are 47,000 acres under potatoes, turnips, &c. The live-stock consists of 5000 horses, 20,000 cows, 40,000 sheep, and 20,000 pigs.

MEXICO

The Republic has the following area :—

	Acres
Arable	34,500,000
Pasture	298,000,000
Mountain and forest . .	129,500,000
Total . . .	462,000,000

The crops in 1888 were as follows :—

	Tons	Value, £	Sundries	£
Maize . .	3,200,000	16,000,000	Cotton . .	1,600,000
Barley . .	150,000	900,000	Sugar . .	1,300,000
Wheat .	280,000	1,800,000	Coffee . .	500,000
Beans . .	200,000	1,000,000	Tobacco, &c.	900,000
Grain . .	3,830,000	19,700,000	Sundries .	4,300,000

The live-stock is supposed to number 2,000,000 horses, 2,000,000 sheep, 5,000,000 goats, and 3,000,000 cattle. There are 20,570 cattle farms, valued at 103 millions £ sterling.

CENTRAL AMERICA

The five little Republics have the following area :—

	Acres	Population	Acres per Inhabitant
Costa Rica . .	12,800,000	200,000	64
Guatemala . .	30,300,000	1,400,000	21
Honduras . . .	30,100,000	430,000	70
Nicaragua . .	31,700,000	400,000	80
Salvador . . .	4,800,000	650,000	7
Total . . .	109,700,000	3,080,000	36

Guatemala is the most important of these Republics. The products and live-stock are approximately as follows :—

	Crops, Tons		Stock, Number	
	Guatemala	Five Republics	Guatemala	Five Republics
Coffee .	30,000	50,000	Horses 150,000	250,000
Sugar .	25,000	30,000	Cows . 490,000	1,200,000
Maize .	90,000	150,000	Sheep . 460,000	700,000
Wheat .	20,000	30,000	Pigs . 190,000	300,000

The value of live-stock in Guatemala is £3,600,000, and in all five Republics about £7,000,000. Costa Rica crops are valued at £2,400,000. Those of the five Republics may reach £12,000,000. The value of coffee exported is £2,400,000, say 40,000 tons.

VENEZUELA

The area of the Republic is as follows :—

	Acres		
	Public Lands	Private	Total
Agricultural . .	56,500,000	30,900,000	87,400,000
Pastoral . . .	37,900,000	63,400,000	101,300,000
Forest	196,400,000	3,100,000	199,500,000
Total . .	290,800,000	97,400,000	388,200,000

The only crop worth notice is coffee, say 60,000 tons, of which two-thirds are exported, to the value of £2,400,000. The live-stock in 1888 was as follows :—

Cattle	8,480,000	Pigs	1,930,000
Sheep and goats	5,730,000	Horses	750,000

The last item includes 1,160,000 mules and asses, counting two mules or four asses as one horse.

COLUMBIA

Formerly known as New Granada, has an area of 320 million acres, or 82 acres per inhabitant. Some coffee is grown.
The live-stock in 1883 was as follows :—

Cattle	950,000	Horses	140,000
Sheep	40,000	Mules and asses .	110,000
Goats	610,000	Pigs	340,000

The only agricultural product exported is coffee, say 3000 tons, valued at £180,000.

ECUADOR

The Republic has an area of 77 million acres, but the extent under cultivation is trifling. Agricultural exports are as follows :—

	Tons		Value, £
Cocoa . . .	10,000	...	700,000
Coffee . . .	10,000	...	600,000

Besides a small quantity of indiarubber and chinchona. No statistics of cattle.

PERU

The Republic has an area of 295 million acres, or 112 per inhabitant. There are no agricultural statistics. The only agricultural exports are :—

	Tons	Value, £
Sugar	20,000	360,000
Wool	3,000	220,000
Cotton	4,000	200,000

This shows how backward is the condition of the country.

BOLIVIA

Area 540 million acres, of which perhaps one million acres are under cultivation. Among agricultural products are chinchona and coca ; the latter is a famous drug for enabling travellers to suffer hunger and hardships in so desolate a region. The crop of coca is valued at £360,000. There are 5,000,000 chinchona trees, and the crop of bark averages 90 tons.

CHILE

In 1882 there were 7,010,000 acres under crops, of which 1,100,000 were irrigated. The area of the Republic is 170 million acres, the acreage under crops being only 4 per cent. of the total.
The production of grain has been almost stationary for 30 years, averaging 450,000 tons of wheat and 150,000 of other grain, mostly barley and maize. About two-thirds of the wheat is required for home consumption, and a balance of 150,000 tons is exported. The official statistics of stock are : horses, 450,000 ; cattle, 1,530,000 ; sheep, 2,500,000, representing a value of £7,800,000 sterling.
Some superior wines are grown, the vineyards counting 86 million vines in 1882, and producing 14 million gallons of wine. The official report gives the following :—

	£
Agricultural products . . .	6,200,000
Animal products . . .	3,600,000
Total	9,800,000

This is, however, much below the reality, which may be estimated thus :—

	Tons	£	Sundries	£
Wheat . .	450,000	3,200,000	Vegetables .	1,500,000
Barley, &c. .	150,000	900,000	Dairy and } poultry }	2,800,000
Hay and } straw . }	1,000,000	2,000,000	Meat. . .	2,600,000
Wine, galls.	14,000,000	1,400,000	Hides, wool } &c. . }	900,000
Principal } crops . }	...	7,500,000	Sundries .	7,800,000

	£
Agricultural products . . .	9,000,000
Animal products	6,300,000
Total	15,300,000

The value of lands under farming was stated in 1882 to be £50,200,000. The total agricultural capital is therefore thus :—

	£
Land	50,200,000
Cattle	7,800,000
Sundries	6,400,000
Total . . .	64,400,000

The product is equal to 24 per cent. on capital. The number of men engaged in agriculture was 114,000 in 1865, and 173,000 in 1875. This gives the average of £89 per head.

ARGENTINA

The area under crops, from official returns, was as follows :—

Year	Acres	Acres per Inhabitant
1854	375,000	0.4
1864	506,000	0.4
1874	825,000	0.4
1884	4,260,000	1.4
1889	7,430,000	2.2

The area under tillage was as follows :—

	Acres		
	1874	1884	1889
Wheat	271,000	1,717,000	2,820,000
Sundries . . .	554,000	2,543,000	4,510,000
Total . .	825,000	4,260,000	7,430,000

The official statements published in May and December 1889 gave the following :—

	Acres				
	Wheat	Maize	Lucerne	Flax, Sugar, &c.	Total
Buenos Ayres	1,120,000	1,750,000	250,000	300,000	3,420,000
Santa Fé .	1,005,000	150,000	75,000	240,000	1,470,000
Entre Rios .	370,000	210,000	18,000	10,000	608,000
Cordoba .	140,000	200,000	195,000	55,000	590,000
Santiago .	75,000	150,000	40,000	35,000	300,000
Mendoza .	17,000	8,000	175,000	24,000	224,000
San Juan .	30,000	8,000	140,000	22,000	200,000
Corrientes .	...	65,000	4,000	46,000	115,000
Catamarca .	3,000	8,000	25,000	79,000	115,000
Other pro- } vinces }	60,000	165,000	80,000	80,000	385,000
Total .	2,820,000	2,714,000	1,002,000	891,000	7,427,000

Tillage has increased rapidly with the influx of Italian and other immigrants. The surplus grain for exportation was as follows :—

Year	Tons
1878–80	40,000
1881–84	120,000
1889	400,000

The last is only an estimate by local writers.

CROP.

	Tons.				Value of all Crops, £
	Wheat	Maize	Lucerne	Sugar	
Buenos Ayres .	280,000	520,000	500,000	...	6,800,000
Santa Fé . . .	250,000	45,000	150,000	8,000	2,800,000
Entre Rios . .	90,000	60,000	40,000	...	1,200,000
Cordoba . . .	35,000	60,000	400,000	...	1,200,000
Other provinces	50,000	125,000	910,000	44,000	5,800,000
Total	705,000	810,000	2,000,000	52,000	17,800,000

The summary of estimated crops in 1889 was as follows :—

	Quantity	Value, £	Acreage
Wheat, tons . .	705,000	4,200,000	2,800,000
Maize ,, . .	810,000	3,200,000	2,700,000
Barley ,, . .	120,000	600,000	300,000
Oats ,, . .	40,000	200,000	100,000
Lucerne ,, . .	2,000,000	3,500,000	1,000,000
Linseed ,, . .	40,000	300,000	200,000
Tobacco ,, . .	10,000	300,000	20,000
Sugar ,, . .	80,000	1,200,000	90,000
Wine, galls. . .	6,500,000	700,000	70,000
Sundries . . .	...	3,600,000	147,000
Total .	...	17,800,000	7,427,000

The live-stock shows the following official returns :—

	1864	1884	1888
Horses	3,875,000	4,186,000	4,400,000
Cattle	10,215,000	14,171,000	22,870,000
Sheep	23,111,000	70,910,000	70,450,000

The pastoral returns for 1888 showed thus :—

	Cows	Horses	Sheep	Value, £
Buenos Ayres	9,600,000	1,860,000	55,400,000	25,700,000
Entre Rios .	4,100,000	720,000	4,900,000	7,200,000
Santa Fé . .	2,300,000	530,000	2,900,000	4,300,000
Cordoba . .	2,100,000	410,000	2,400,000	3,700,000
Corrientes .	1,800,000	260,000	610,000	2,900,000
Santiago .	590,000	110,000	780,020	1,060,000
San Luis . .	480,000	110,000	240,000	810,000
Pampas . .	470,000	110,000	1,670,000	1,080,000
Catamarca .	240,000	50,000	150,000	410,000
Tucuman .	200,000	40,000	40,000	320,000
Mendoza . .	180,000	45,000	120,000	320,000
Salta . . .	160,000	30,000	160,000	290,000
Jujuy . . .	90,000	20,000	600,000	270,000
Rioja . . .	160,000	25,000	60,000	180,000
Rio Negro .	80,000	20,000	300,000	180,000
San Juan .	50,000	25,000	60,000	110,000
Misiones, &c.	270,000	35,000	60,000	120,000
Total .	22,870,000	4,400,000	70,450,000	48,950,000

D

The sheep-farming industry since 1830 shows as follows :—

Year	Sheep, Millions	Wool Export, Million Lbs.	Price of Sheep
1830 . .	3	6	15 pence
1840 . .	5	13	25 ,,
1850 . .	7	21	35 ,,
1860 . .	14	45	55 ,,
1870 . .	41	137	60 ,,
1880 . .	61	215	70 ,,
1889 . .	70	300	60 ,,

River Plate wool loses 65 per cent. in the washing, the above being wool in the grease ; whereas Australian loses only 44, and Cape wool 30 per cent. In 1882 the live-stock held by Irish settlers was valued at £7,200,000, and that of Scotch at £2,000,000 ; the land and stock of Irish and Scotch combined was worth 33 millions sterling.

The value of all farm products was approximately :—

	Agricultural	Pastoral	Total	Per Inhabitant
	£	£	£	£
Buenos Ayres	6,800,000	12,400,000	19,200,000	17.4
Santa Fé .	2,800,000	2,100,000	4,900,000	22.3
Entre Rios .	1,200,000	3,500,000	4,700,000	26.0
Cordoba .	1,200,000	1,800,000	3,000,000	15.1
Corrientes .	200,000	1,400,000	1,600,000	8.5
Mendoza .	900,000	150,000	1,050,000	14.0
Tucuman .	1,500,000	150,000	1,650,000	9.7
San Juan .	600,000	100,000	700,000	8.8
Salta . . .	600,000	150,000	750,000	5.0
Catamarca .	200,000	200,000	400,000	4.4
San Luis .	200,000	400,000	600,000	8.0
Santiago .	200,000	500,000	700,000	4.7
Rioja . . .	400,000	100,000	500,000	6.1
Jujuy . . .	400,000	100,000	500,000	8.0
Territories .	600,000	1,150,000	1,750,000	11.0
Total .	17,800,000	24,200,000	42,000,000	14.0

The agricultural wealth of the Republic is distributed approximately as follows (1888) :—

	Land	Cattle	Sundries	Total	Per Inhabitant
	£	£	£	£	£
Buenos Ayres	60,200,000	25,700,000	9,500,000	95,400,000	87
Santa Fé	9,000,000	4,300,000	1,500,000	14,800,000	67
Entre Rios	7,800,000	7,200,000	1,700,000	16,700,000	92
Cordoba	5,200,000	3,700,000	1,000,000	9,900,000	32
Corrientes	5,200,000	2,900,000	900,000	9,000,000	47
Mendoza	3,800,000	300,000	400,000	4,500,000	60
Tucuman	2,800,000	300,000	300,000	3,400,000	20
San Juan	2,600,000	100,000	300,000	3,000,000	35
Salta	2,200,000	300,000	300,000	2,800,000	18
Catamarca	2,000,000	400,000	300,000	2,700,000	30
San Luis	1,800,000	800,000	300,000	2,900,000	39
Santiago	1,200,000	1,100,000	200,000	2,500,000	17
Rioja	1,000,000	200,000	100,000	1,300,000	16
Jujuy	600,000	300,000	100,000	1,000,000	15
Territories . . .	5,200,000	1,400,000	700,000	7,300,000	45
Total . . .	110,600,000	49,000,000	17,600,000	177,200,000	60

SUMMARY OF PRODUCTS

	£
Crops already enumerated . .	17,800,000
Wool, 300 million lbs. . .	7,500,000
Meat, 300,000 tons . .	6,000,000
Dairy and poultry . .	4,000,000
Hides, tallow, &c. . .	6,700,000
Total	42,000,000

Agricultural wealth has quadrupled since 1857, viz. :—

	Millions £ Sterling	
	1857	1888
Land	22	111
Cattle	18	49
Sundries	4	17
Total . . .	44	177

The product in 1889 was equal to 24 per cent. on capital. In the preceding valuation the unoccupied lands of Gran Chaco, Patagonia, &c., are not included.

URUGUAY

This country (sometimes called Banda Oriental) is chiefly pastoral, but tillage has increased notably in the last thirty years.

Year	Acres under Crop	Grain, Bushels		
		Wheat	Maize	Total
1855	150,000	700,000	400,000	1,100,000
1870	400,000	2,100,000	700,000	2,800,000
1883	750,000	3,500,000	1,200,000	4,700,000
1888	1,500,000	5,000,000	2,000,000	7,000,000

The above figures are official except for 1888, which is a rough estimate. The area is 45 million acres, and more than half the Republic is owned by Europeans. The Contribucion Directa returns give only the *value* of properties held by each nationality, but if we arrange the area on the same basis, we find that the tenure of land is as follows :—

Nationality	Landowners	Acres	Ratio
Natives	31,000	18,700,000	41.6
Spaniards	4,400	6,300,000	14.0
Italians	3,900	5,700,000	12.6
Brazilians	2,200	7,400,000	16.5
French	1,600	2,900,000	6.4
British	300	1,600,000	3.5
Various	4,200	2,400,000	5.4
Total . .	47,600	45,000,000	100.0

The number of landowners is unknown, but supposed to be one-tenth of the population, as in the above table.

The returns of live-stock were as follows :—

	1860	1887
Cattle	5,220,000	6,120,000
Horses . . .	740,000	410,000
Sheep	2,590,000	15,900,000
Value, £	6,100,000	16,800,000

Agricultural and pastoral products in 1887 may be summed up thus :—

	Agricultural			Pastoral
	Tons	£		£
Wheat . . .	140,000	900,000	Wool .	1,800,000
Maize . . .	50,000	200,000	Meat . .	2,700,000
Hay and straw	300,000	600,000	Dairy, &c.	700,000
Vegetables, &c.	...	500,000	Hides, &c.	2,800,000
Total . .	...	2,200,000	Total .	8,000,000

Agricultural capital is estimated at 53 millions sterling, of which land stands for 34, and cattle for 14 millions. The product is almost 20 per cent. on capital.

PARAGUAY

Tillage has constituted almost the sole industry from the time of the Jesuit Missions, founded in 1557. The area under plough at the date of the expulsion of the Jesuits in 1767 was about 200,000 acres. A census was taken by President Lopez in 1863, and another in 1881, the country having been in the interim desolated (and all males over ten years killed) by the Brazilian army in the war of 1865–70. The areas under crops were :—

	Acres	
	1863	1881
Maize	349,000	206,000
Mandioca	110,000	120,000
Tobacco	23,000	10,000
Sugar	25,000	20,000
Cotton, rice, &c.	43,000	46,000
Total	550,000	402,000

All field-work is done by women, who cultivate 7 acres each. The men collect yerba-maté or Jesuit's tea, mind cattle, and convey the products to market. The soil is so rich that maize yields one hundred-fold, rice two hundred-fold. The ordinary crops are 4 million bushels of maize, 360,000 tons of mandioca, 10,000 tons sugar, 6000 tons tobacco, 300 million oranges, and 24 million lbs. of yerba-maté. The value of products may be summed up thus :—

	£
Maize and mandioca	1,600,000
Tobacco and sugar	300,000
Oranges, timber, &c. . . .	200,000
Yerba-maté	400,000
Meat and sundries . . .	500,000
Total	3,000,000

The statistics of live-stock show 730,000 cattle, 62,000 horses, 32,000 sheep.

The exports consist of 6000 tons yerba-maté, 7000 tons tobacco, 50 million oranges, and 2,000,000 feet of lumber, the whole worth £200,000 sterling. The price of land is from 1s. to 5s. an acre. In 1870 the Government made a general survey of the Republic, the result of which was as follows :—

	Acres
State lands, arable	27,300,000
Mountain and forest . . .	17,500,000
Yerba-maté groves	3,200,000
All public lands	48,000,000
Private estates	9,600,000
Total area . .	57,600,000

The above is Paraguay proper, not including the Chaco territory on the western side of the Paraguay river.

BRAZIL

The total area is 2104 million acres, or almost the same as that of the United States. It is made up thus :—

	Millions of Acres
Under crops	20
Forest	134
Uncultivated	1,950
Total	2,104

The principal products are as follows :—

	Acres	Crop, Tons	Value of Crop	Value Exported
			£	£
Coffee . .	1,600,000	340,000	20,000,000	14,000,000
Sugar . .	300,000	330,000	5,000,000	2,600,000
Cotton . .	70,000	24,000	1,200,000	600,000
Tobacco . .	60,000	30,000	1,500,000	1,000,000
Yerba-maté .	10,000,000	40,000	1,100,000	600,000
Indiarubber	...	6,000	1,200,000	1,200,000
Total . .	12,030,000	...	30,000,000	22,000,000

There are no returns of live-stock. The climate is too hot for sheep, and the number of cows and horses is probably about two millions, judging by the export of hides. Official returns give 16 million cows, a gross exaggeration. In 1882 the coffee-fields had 550 million plants, yielding about 1 lb. each, the number of hands being over 300,000 : the crop has since risen to 340,000 tons ; sugar plantations employ 90,000 negroes, cotton 50,000. The above table takes no account of maize or mandioca, large quantities of which are produced to feed the negroes.

Wheat and rice are also grown on a smaller scale. About one million persons altogether are engaged in agriculture, including 90,000 Germans, mostly in Rio Grande do Sul, and an equal number of Italians in San Paulo, Santa Catherina, and other southern provinces. The gross value of all agricultural products is said to average 40 millions sterling per annum.

An able-bodied man can cultivate the following ; that is, any one of these items :—

	Acres	Crop	Value, £
Coffee	5	25	50
Sugar	5	100	70
Cotton	7	100	70
Mandioca	4	160	80

An acre of coffee has 400 trees ; of cotton, 2000 plants. Coffee was first introduced in 1754.

AUSTRALIA

The several colonies show as follows :—

	Population	Acres	Acres per Inhabitant
New South Wales .	1,086,000	198,400,000	182
Victoria	1,090,000	56,300,000	52
Queensland . . .	390,000	427,500,000	1,095
South Australia .	310,000	578,000,000	1,870
New Zealand . .	610,000	66,600,000	109
Tasmania . . .	150,000	16,600,000	111
Western Australia .	40,000	624,000,000	15,600 .
Total . . .	3,676,000	1,967,400,000	532

Mr. Coghlan's work on Australia shows the progress of tillage from 1861 to 1888 as follows :—

	Acres Cultivated				Acres per 100 Inhabitants			
	1861	1871	1881	1888	1861	1871	1881	1888
New South Wales . . .	295,000	420,000	645,000	1,000,000	86	84	85	92
Victoria	420,000	930,000	1,680,000	2,230,000	75	130	190	202
Queensland . . .	5,000	60,000	120,000	190,000	18	52	52	50
South Australia . . .	400,000	840,000	2,170,000	2,340,000	320	455	805	750
New Zealand	225,000	1,110,000	4,940,000	7,525,000	280	440	1,020	1,250
Tasmania	245,000	310,000	350,000	460,000	280	310	305	310
Western Australia . . .	24,000	50,000	55,000	65,000	150	200	180	155
Total . . .	1,614,000	3,720,000	9,960,000	13,810,000	130	186	360	375

	Acres Cultivated							
	1861				1888			
	Grain	Hay	Sundries	Total	Grain	Hay	Sundries	Total
New South Wales . . .	190,000	45,000	60,000	295,000	480,000	210,000	310,000	1,000,000
Victoria	290,000	75,000	55,000	420,000	1,505,000	410,000	315,000	2,230,000
Queensland	...	...	5,000	5,000	95,000	20,000	75,000	190,000
South Australia . . .	320,000	65,000	15,000	400,000	1,625,000	310,000	405,000	2,340,000
New Zealand . . .	50,000	...	175,000	225,000	780,000	50,000	6,695,000	7,525,000
Tasmania	95,000	30,000	120,000	245,000	80,000	50,000	330,000	460,000
Western Australia . . .	15,000	7,000	2,000	24,000	37,000	24,000	4,000	65,000
Total . .	960,000	222,000	432,000	1,614,000	4,602,000	1,074,000	8,134,000	13,810,000

The following table shows in detail the cultivation in 1888 :—

	Acres						
	N. S. Wales	Victoria	Queensland	S. Australia	N. Zealand	Tasmania	W. Australia
Wheat	305,000	1,220,000	10,000	1,605,000	360,000	40,000	30,000
Maize	165,000	5,000	85,000	...	5,000	...	...
Oats	7,000	200,000	...	5,000	370,000	35,000	2,000
Barley	3,000	80,000	...	15,000	45,000	5,000	5,000
Hay	210,000	410,000	20,000	310,000	50,000	50,000	24,000
Grasses	200,000	185,000	5,000	25,000	6,230,000	180,000	..
Sundries	110,000	130,000	70,000	380,000	465,000	150,000	4,000
Total . .	1,000,000	2,230,000	190,000	2,340,000	7,525,000	460,000	65,000

The area and crops of grain were as follows :—

	Acres				Tons			
	1861	1871	1881	1888	1861	1871	1881	1888
Wheat	730,000	1,380,000	3,360,000	3,570,000	300,000	400,000	810,000	710,000
Maize	60,000	140,000	170,000	260,000	50,000	130,000	170,000	200,000
Oats	145,000	360,000	440,000	620,000	60,000	130,000	200,000	250,000
Barley	30,000	60,000	105,000	160,000	15,000	30,000	50,000	80,000
Total . .	965,000	1,940,000	4,075,000	4,610,000	425,000	690,000	1,230,000	1,240,000

The yield of barley from 1861 to 1881 was not ascertained, but the crop averages half a ton per acre, the estimate given above. The following table shows the approximate area and crop of grain from 1830 compared with population, viz. :—

Year	Acres, Grain	Crop, Tons	Cwts. per Inhabitant
1830	50,000	20,000	4.0
1840	180,000	70,000	5.6
1850	300,000	120,000	6.7
1861	965,000	425,000	6.6
1871	1,940,000	690,000	7.0
1881	4,075,000	1,230,000	9.0
1888	4,610,000	1,240,000	6.6

The acreage of other crops since 1861 is shown thus :—

	Acres			
	1861	1871	1881	1888
Vineyards . .	6,500	16,300	14,600	26,800
Sugar . . .	...	14,000	40,000	62,600
Tobacco . .	400	900	3,200	6,600
Potatoes . .	57,000	81,000	99,000	112,000
Hay	220,000	315,000	835,000	1,074,000
Grasses . . .	170,000	870,000	4,360,000	6,820,000
Sundries . .	195,100	492,800	533,200	1,098,000
Total .	649,000	1,790,000	5,885,000	9,200,000

The production in 1888 as regards the several Colonies was as follows :—

	Tons							Total
	New South Wales	Victoria	Queens-land	South Australia	New Zealand	Tasmania	Western Australia	
Wheat	40,000	230,000	...	170,000	240,000	20,000	10,000	710,000
Maize	140,000	...	60,000	...	...	...	...	200,000
Oats	...	50,000	...	...	185,000	15,000	...	250,000
Barley	...	40,000	...	5,000	31,000	2,000	2,000	80,000
All grain	180,000	320,000	60,000	175,000	456,000	37,000	12,000	1,240,000
Potatoes	41,000	155,000	21,000	20,000	135,000	53,500	1,500	427,000
Hay	140,000	275,000	15,000	205,009	34,000	36,000	15,000	720,000
Sugar	5,000	...	35,000	...	...	...	...	40,000
Tobacco	2,800	700	70	...	...	...	...	3,570

The weight of miscellaneous crops to the acre in 1888 was as follows :—

	Crop	Per Acre
Wine, galls. . .	2,800,000	104
Sugar, cwts. . .	800,000	13
Tobacco, cwts. .	70,000	11
Potatoes ,, .	8,600,000	77
Hay ,, .	15,000,000	14

The value of live-stock at various dates was approximately :—

Year	£	Year	£
1821	1,500,000	1861	21,000,000
1842	7,600,000	1888	67,000,000

The pastoral wealth of Australia is of paramount importance, and has doubled since 1871. The following table is official :—

Year	Horses	Cows	Sheep	Pigs	Export of Wool, lbs.
1800	200	1,040	6,100	...	...
1810	1,130	12,440	25,900	9,540	...
1821	4,560	102,900	209,100	33,900	...
1842	70,600	1,015,000	6,310,000	66,000	14,000,000
1861	449,200	4,040,000	23,700,000	280,000	70,000,000
1871	782,000	4,710,000	49,800,000	740,000	190,000,000
1881	1,249,000	8,710,000	78,600,000	905,000	325,000,000
1888	1,504,000	9,280,000	96,600,000	1,140,000	553,000,000*

In 1888 the distribution of stock was as follows :—

	Horses	Cattle	Sheep	Pigs	Approximate Value, £
New South Wales	410,000	1,620,000	46,500,000	250,000	24,900,000
Victoria	320,000	1,370,000	10,820,000	245,000	12,000,000
Queensland	320,000	4,655,000	13,445,000	70,000	11,700,000
South Australia	170,000	430,000	7,150,000	170,000	4,800,000
New Zealand	204,000	960,000	15,120,000	340,000	11,200,000
Tasmania	30,000	140,000	1,430,000	40,000	1,200,000
Western Australia	40,000	95,000	2,115,000	25,000	1,200,000
Total . .	1,504,000	9,280,000	96,580,000	1,140,000	67,000,000

Mr. Coghlan's official estimates of the value of agricultural and pastoral products is as follows for 1888 :—

	Agricultural	Pastoral	Total	Per Inhabitant
	£	£	£	£
N. S. Wales .	4,150,000	13,060,000	17,210,000	15.8
Victoria . .	7,330,000	6,280,000	13,610,000	12.5
Queensland .	1,845,000	6,445,000	8,290,000	21.2
South Australia	5,200,000	2,500,000	7,700,000	24.8
New Zealand .	6,775,000	5,785,000	12,560,000	20.6
Tasmania . .	1,270,000	660,000	1,930,000	13.0
W. Australia .	260,000	660,000	920,000	23.0
Total . .	26,830,000	35,390,000	62,220,000	17.1

The values of all rural products at various dates were approximately as follows :—

Year	Wool	Sundries	Total
	£	£	£
1840	1,400,000	2,200,000	3,600,000
1850	4,500,000	3,800,000	8,300,000
1860	6,600,000	13,000,000	19,600,000
1870	10,200,000	19,000,000	29,200,000
1880	22,000,000	34,000,000	56,000,000
1888	17,200,000	45,000,000	62,200,000

The values of agricultural products are not classified, but seem to have been approximately as in the subjoined table :—

	Agricultural		Pastoral
	£		£
Grain . . .	8,700,000	Wool . . .	17,100,000
Hay and straw	2,400,000	Mutton . .	4,000,000
Potatoes . .	1,100,000	Beef . . .	4,000,000
Fruit and vegetables }	2,600,000	Pork . . .	1,200,000
		Poultry . .	1,000,000
Sugar . . .	500,000	Dairy . . .	4,090,000
Wine . . .	300,000	Foals . . .	2,000,000
Tobacco. . .	100,000	Hides, tallow, &c. }	2,000,000
Clover, &c. . .	11,130,000		
Total .	26,830,000	Total .	35,390,000

The total agricultural capital is estimated by Mr. Coghlan at 373 millions sterling. If we suppose it to be distributed in the same ratio as the value of products, the result would be as follows :—

* This is the equivalent of unwashed wool, but the actual weight exported was less, a portion being washed.

	Agricultural Capital				Ratio
	Land	Cattle	Sundries	Total	
New South Wales . . .	68,000,000	24,900,000	10,300,000	103,200,000	27.5
Victoria	61,500,000	12,000,000	8,200,000	81,700,000	22.0
Queensland . . .	33,100,000	11,700,000	5,000,000	49,800,000	13.4
South Australia . .	36,800,000	4,800,000	4,600,000	46,200,000	12.4
New Zealand . . .	56,700,000	11,200,000	7,500,000	75,400,000	20.2
Tasmania . . .	9,200,000	1,200,000	1,200,000	11,600,000	3.0
Western Australia .	3,800,000	1,200,000	500,000	5,500,000	1.5
Total . . .	269,100,000	67,000,000	37,300,000	373,400,000	100.0

It would appear, however, that the agricultural capital is much greater than Mr. Coghlan's estimate. In another chapter of his book he shows the wealth of Australia (not including railways or public works) amounted in 1889 to 1136 millions sterling, of which 410 millions belonged to New South Wales, which included 181 millions for land.

In fact, the value of land seems to be 533 millions sterling, and the total agricultural capital as follows :—

	Capital, Millions Sterling			Product, Millions, £	Ratio to Capital
	Land	Cattle, &c.	Total		
N. S. Wales . .	181	35	216	17.2	8.0
Victoria . . .	107	20	127	13.6	9.3
Queensland . .	58	17	75	8.3	9.0
S. Australia . .	64	9	73	7.7	10.6
New Zealand . .	100	19	119	12.6	10.6
Tasmania. . .	16	2	18	1.9	10.5
W. Australia . .	7	2	9	0.9	10.0
Total . .	533	104	637	62.2	9.8

CAPE COLONY

Tillage is a secondary industry, the latest returns for 1875 comparing with those for 1865 as follows :—

	1865	1875
Acres under grain . .	387,000	465,000
Crop, bushels . .	2,440,000	4,180,000
Vineyards, acres .	16,000	18,000
Yield, galls. wine . .	3,240,000	4,488,000

Farms cover an area of 89 million acres, or 67 per cent. of the total, viz. :—

		Acres
Tillage	. . . . .	800,000
Pasture	. . . . .	78,000,000
Timber	. . . . .	10,800,000
Area of farms	. . . .	89,600,000
Public lands	. . .	45,400,000
Total	. .	135,000,000

The value of all products in 1887 was approximately :—

	Tons	£	Sundries	£
Wheat . .	100,000	700,000	Wine . .	300,000
Barley . .	15,000	100,000	Fruit, &c. .	500,000
Oats . . .	25,000	150,000	Dairy and } poultry }	1,000,000
Maize, &c. .	100,000	550,000	Meat . .	2,000,000
All grain .	240,000	1,500,000	Wool . .	1,700,000
Straw . .	200,000	100,000	Feathers, } hides, &c. }	1,100,000
Grain crops	...	1,600,000	Sundries .	6,600,000

Returns of live-stock were as follows :—

Year	Horses	Cattle	Sheep	Pigs	Goats	Ostriches
1840	57,000	307,000	2,340,000	...	394,000	...
1865	227,000	690,000	9,840,000	79,000	...	...
1875	241,000	1,330,000	11,280,000	130,000	2,790,000	22,200
1889	295,000	1,505,000	14,410,000	140,000	5,140,000	149,500

	£
Agricultural products . . .	2,400,000
Animal products	5,800,000
Total . .	8,200,000

The value of the farms may be roughly estimated at 42 millions sterling ; product, 19 per cent. on capital.

NATAL

This colony comprises 12,780,000 acres, viz. :—

Held by		Acres
European settlers	. . .	8,000,000
Kaffirs	. . . .	2,000,000
British Crown .	. . .	2,780,000
Total . . .		12,780,000

The area under tillage (chiefly sugar) is as follows :—

Farms of		Acres
Europeans	. . . .	66,000
Kaffirs	. . . .	175,000
Total		241,000

The returns of live-stock show thus :—

	Owned by		
	Europeans	Kaffirs	Total
Horses	23,000	31,000	54,000
Cows	165,000	447,000	612,000
Sheep	448,000	36,000	484,000
Goats	56,000	251,000	307,000

ORANGE FREE STATE

Area, 26,600,000 acres—say, 450 per inhabitant. There are 6000 cattle-farms, occupying 23,600,000 acres—say, 4000 each. They have 130,000 horses, 460,000 cattle, 5,050,000 sheep, 670,000 goats, and 2200 ostriches. Tillage, 115,000 acres.

MAURITIUS

A small island, only 450,000 acres, sugar being the principal crop. The industry rose rapidly till 1877, and is now declining, viz. :—

Year		Acres under Sugar	Tons Exported
1814	. . . .	2,000	500
1836	. . .	57,000	30,000
1877	. . .	160,000	136,000
1887	. . .	...	95,000

Timber is also produced, especially ebony.

CEYLON

Official returns are as follows :—

	Acreage			Stock
Rice	740,000	Horses	. .	4,000
Cocoa-nuts	630,000	Cattle . . .		950,000
Tea	200,000	Sheep . . .		46,000
Coffee	100,000	Goats . . .		88,000
Sundries	444,000			
Area cultivated . .	2,114,000			

The cultivated area is about 13 per cent. of the total, which is 16,230,000 acres. Among the crops of minor extent are chinchona 3400, tobacco 16,000, cinnamon 36,000 acres. The coffee plantations have been ravaged by an insect called Hemileia. New products have therefore been called into requisition.

The exports of 1887 compare with those of 1873 thus :—

	1873	1887	Value in 1887
	Tons	Tons	£
Coffee	49,500	9,000	900,000
Chinchona	...	6,400	190,000
Tea	...	5,500	660,000
Cinnamon	10,500	18,400	80,000
Oil, cwts	110,000	310,000	320,000

Many of the farms are owned by English settlers, who number 4000 in the island.

INDIA

The area in acres and the population in 1881 were :—

	Acres	Population	Acres per Inhabitant
Bengal	100,200,000	66,700,000	1.5
Bombay . . .	70,400,000	16,500,000	4.9
Madras	90,850,000	31,300,000	2.9
Assam	28,650,000	4,900,000	6.4
Punjaub	95,600,000	18,900,000	3.6
Oudh	15,300,000	11,800,000	1.3
N. W. Provinces	57,100,000	32,300,000	1.6
Central Provinces	74,200,000	9,800,000	5.5
Berar, &c. . . .	12,400,000	3,300,000	4.4
Upper Burmah .	128,000,000	5,000,000	25.6
Lower Burmah .	57,500,000	3,700,000	18.0
British India . .	730,200,000	204,200,000	3.4
Hydrabad . . .	52,500,000	9,800,000	5.4
Rajpoot . . .	83,200,000	10,300,000	8.1
Baroda	5,500,000	2,200,000	2.5
Mysore	15,900,000	4,200,000	3.8
Various	168,900,000	28,700,000	6.0
Feudatories . .	326,000,000	55,200,000	5.9
All India . . .	1,056,200,000	259,400,000	3.9

There are no late statistics available for Bengal. The cultivated area of the other provinces was as follows in 1888 :—

	Acres					
	Rice	Wheat	Other Grain	Cotton	Sundries	Total
Bombay	2,170,000	2,410,000	17,130,000	2,870,000	1,990,000	26,570,000
Madras	6,290,000	20,000	13,970,000	1,460,000	2,140,000	23,880,000
Assam	1,240,000	...	50,000	...	380,000	1,670,000
Punjaub	730,000	6,640,000	12,160,000	640,000	1,340,000	21,510,000
Oudh	2,220,000	1,550,000	6,140,000	80,000	520,000	10,510,000
North-West Provinces	3,930,000	3,460,000	17,550,000	1,450,000	2,010,000	28,400,000
Central Provinces	3,710,000	4,740,000	4,060,000	590,000	1,490,000	14,590,000
Berar, &c.	100,000	1,070,000	2,920,000	1,940,000	640,000	6,670,000
Lower Burmah	3,850,000	...	10,000	10,000	50,000	3,920,000
Total . .	24,240,000	19,890,000	73,990,000	9,040,000	10,560,000	137,720,000

The wheat area of Bengal is supposed to be about 7,000,000 acres, bringing up the total to nearly 27 millions. The crops which are included above as " Sundries " are :—

	Acres					
	Oil-Seed	Sugar	Coffee	Tea	Indigo	Tobacco
Bombay	1,810,000	80,000	...	...	5,000	90,000
Madras	1,510,000	50,000	60,000	5,000	500,000	85,000
Assam	150,000	20,000	...	210,000	...	...
Punjaub	820,000	370,000	...	10,000	75,000	65,000
Oudh	260,000	230,000	...	...	20,000	10,000
North-West Provinces .	700,000	960,000	...	10,000	300,000	40,000
Central Provinces . .	1,420,000	50,000	...	...	...	20,000
Berar, &c. . .	610,000	...	290,000	...	...	20,000
Lower Burmah . .	20,000	10,000	...	...	...	20,000
Total . .	7,300,000	1,770,000	350,000	235,000	900,000	350,000

If we suppose the working agricultural population to be 20 per cent. of the total, the average product of each man's labour in British India will be found as follows :—25 bushels grain, 24 bushels rice, 23 lbs. cotton, 2½ lbs. tea, 34 lbs. jute, 2¼ lbs. coffee, 5 oz. opium, 6 lbs. sugar, 50 lbs. oil-seed, which, with indigo, tobacco, and other products, bring up the average value to £8 sterling per head. Adding animal products, the total will be £10 per head.

The following statement for 1888 gives a comprehensive view :—

	Acres				
	Under Crops	Available for Cultivation	Not Available	Forest	Total
Bombay	26,350,000	14,770,000	8,450,000	5,880,000	55,450,000
Madras	23,330,000	13,320,000	12,480,000	9,370,000	58,500,000
Assam	1,700,000	660,000	9,340,000	1,900,000	13,600,000
Punjaub	20,590,000	27,560,000	12,110,000	4,620,000	64,880,000
Oudh	8,830,000	3,850,000	2,250,000	570,000	15,500,000
North-West Provinces . .	25,240,000	10,290,000	6,700,000	5,220,000	47,450,000
Central Provinces . .	14,140,000	8,910,000	7,380,000	12,810,000	43,240,000
Berar, &c.	6,780,000	2,110,000	3,280,000	930,000	13,100,000
Lower Burmah . . .	4,270,000	23,750,000	24,530,000	3,260,000	55,810,000
Total . . .	131,230,000	105,220,000	86,520,000	44,560,000	367,530,000

The aggregate area of the above States is 502 million acres, from which it appears that 135 million acres have not yet been classified as suitable or not for cultivation. The above table is, moreover, irrespective of Bengal and Upper Burmah, the total area of British India, as already shown, being 730 million acres. The following table shows the area of lands irrigated, of lands cultivated without irrigation, of lands uncultivated, and the extent of each Province :—

	Acres				
	Irrigated	Not Irrigated	Crops and Fallow	Uncultivated	Total
Bombay	2,420,000	31,980,000	34,400,000	36,000,000	70,400,000
Madras	6,230,000	22,070,000	28,300,000	62,550,000	90,850,000
Assam	...	2,350,000	2,350,000	26,300,000	28,650,000
Punjaub	6,090,000	18,610,000	24,700,000	70,900,000	95,600,000
Oudh	2,470,000	6,830,000	9,300,000	6,000,000	15,300,000
North-West Provinces . .	6,210,000	21,290,000	27,500,000	29,600,000	57,100,000
Central Provinces . .	500,000	15,000,000	15,500,000	58,700,000	74,200,000
Berar, &c.	1,000,000	7,050,000	8,050,000	4,350,000	12,400,000
Lower Burmah . . .	...	4,700,000	4,700,000	52,800,000	57,500,000
Total . . .	24,920,000	129,880,000	154,800,000	347,200,000	502,000,000

Including Bengal, but not Upper Burmah, the products of British India may be estimated as follows (1888) :—

	Product, Tons	Value, £	Export, Tons	Value, £
Wheat .	6,800,000	54,400,000	700,000	5,600,000
Rice . .	24,200,000	145,000,000	1,400,000	9,300,000
Cotton .	410,000	21,000,000	270,000	14,400,000
Tea . .	45,000	5,800,000	40,000	5,300,000
Jute . .	630,000	8,000,000	480,000	6,100,000
Coffee . .	40,000	4,000,000	15,000	1,500,000
Opium .	6,000	12,000,000	5,000	10,000,000
Sugar . .	100,000	1,100,000	60,000	600,000
Oil-seeds .	900,000	10,500,000	800,000	9,400,000
Various grain	18,500,000	92,500,000	...	...
Total	...	354,300,000	...	62,200,000

The above values, being computed by the Custom-House in rupees at 24d., are nominal; from each item should be deducted 25 per cent. to get a fair value.

The exports of wheat and rice showed thus : —

Wheat, Annual Average			Rice, Annual Average		
Period	Tons	Official Value, £	Period	Tons	Official Value, £
1873–76	72,000	600,000	1851–60	420,000	1,800,000
1877–81	190,000	1,600,000	1861–64	990,000	3,500,000
1882–85	900,000	7,550,000	1873–80	1,010,000	6,400,000
1886–88	950,000	7,400,000	1881–88	1,380,000	8,600,000

There are statistics for live-stock for the following provinces, but not for Bengal, Assam, or Central Provinces :—

	Cows	Buffaloes	Horses	Mules, &c.	Sheep and Goats
Bombay .	6,480,000	1,770,000	140,000	...	3,220,000
Madras .	9,080,000	2,450,000	40,000	105,000	9,580,000
Punjaub .	9,120,000	2,550,000	210,000	460,000	6,160,000
Oudh . .	5,520,000	1,070,000	125,000	60,000	1,700,000
N. W. Prov	13,120,000	3,120,000	325,000	270,000	4,540,000
Berar, &c.	1,850,000	360,000	40,000	25,000	650,000
Lower Burmah	920,000	660,000	10,000	...	20,000
Total	46,090,000	11,980,000	890,000	920,000	25,870,000

Including the provinces for which we have no returns, it may be estimated that the total live-stock of India is as follows :—

Cows	.	.	57,600,000	Mules, &c.	.	1,150,000
Buffaloes .	.	15,000,000	Sheep	.	13,500,000
Horses	.	.	1,100,000	Goats	.	19,000,000

The value of all products may be roughly estimated as follows :—

			£
Agricultural products	.	.	320,000,000
Animal products	.	.	80,000,000
Total .	.	.	400,000,000

JAVA

This island is mostly in the hands of a company founded by the King of Holland in 1824 ; paid-up capital, £3,200,000. There are 18 million inhabitants, who are "exploited" by the Dutch, yielding a net tribute of 3 millions sterling per annum. Governor Vanden Bosch planted 50 million coffee-trees in 1834, and the industry has thrived.

The goods annually sold by the Java Company at Amsterdam are :—

	Value, £
Coffee, 100,000 tons	3,300,000
Sugar, 220,000 ,,	4,000,000
Spices, &c.	700,000
Total	8,000,000

No statistics are published of the area under crops. Tillage is compulsory in the various villages, the Dutch fixing the price that they pay for each product.

The area under tillage in 1887 compared with 1881 as follows :—

	Acres	
	1881	1887
Rice	4,100,000	5,100,000
Maize	800,000	1,600,000
Sugar	52,000	105,000
Tobacco	190,000	185,000
Cotton	25,000	42,000
Beans	280,000	390,000
Sundries	953,000	1,078,000
Total	6,400,000	8,500,000

The improvement is mainly due to the new agrarian law, giving settlers a squatter's tenure for seventy-five years. Besides the lands held by the Dutch Company, there were in 1886 the following estates :—

	No.	Acres	Average, Acres
Europeans	121	1,980,000	16,500
Chinese	229	710,000	3,100
Malays, &c.	55	42,000	730
Total	405	2,732,000	6,800

The area under sugar was as follows :—

	Acres		
Year	Company	Private Lands	Total
1879	70,000	8,000	78,000
1887	25,000	46,000	71,000

The production of chinchona was as follows :—

	Tons		
Year	Company	Private	Total
1882	126	48	174
1886	263	672	935

The crops of 1886 also comprised 80,000 tons coffee, 300,000 tons sugar, 12,000 tons tobacco, 700 tons indigo, and 3400 tons tea.

JAPAN

The area may be described as follows :—

	Acres				Acres
	Public	Private	Total		
Open	29,780,000	2,960,000	32,740,000	Rice	6,460,000
Cultivated	...	11,500,000	11,500,000	Grain, &c.	4,110,000
Forest	16,900,000	18,300,000	35,200,000	Pasture	33,630,000
Total	46,680,000	32,760,000	79,440,000	Total	44,200,000

In 1887 the statistics showed as follows :—

	Acres	Tons	Cwts. per Acre
Rice	6,460,000	5,000,000	16
Wheat	3,900,000	2,200,000	11
Buckwheat	390,000	140,000	7
Millet	590,000	300,000	10
Beans	1,140,000	400,000	7
Sorghum	70,000	35,000	10
Sugar	...	35,000	...
Tea	...	25,000	...

The rice crop averages 5 million tons, of which 400,000 are used for making Sâke beer, 150,000 for confectionery, and the rest for food. A bushel of rice produces 10 gallons of Sâke, the quantity produced being about 160 million gallons yearly. There are 266 great landlords, called Daimios, who have rent-rolls from £15,000 a year upwards. They own most of Japan, and have 893,000 tenants. The value of the crops is approximately as follows : rice, £30,000,000 ; wheat, £17,200,000 ; other grain, £6,700,000 ; tea, £2,700,000 ; sugar and sundries, £1,400,000 ; making a total of 58 millions sterling for 13 million acres under crops.

WEST INDIES, BRITISH

The islands and the colony of Guiana on the mainland show approximately as follows :—

ACRES

	Sugar	Sundries	Cultivated	Uncultivated	Area
Jamaica	35,000	565,000	600,000	2,100,000	2,700,000
Trinidad	50,000	680,000	730,000	370,000	1,100,000
Small islands	80,000	520,000	600,000	3,800,000	4,400,000
Guiana	80,000	80,000	160,000	69,840,000	70,000,000
Total	245,000	1,845,000	2,090,000	76,110,000	78,200,000

The sugar crop of the islands has fluctuated thus :—

Year	Tons	Year	Tons
1824	400,000	1877	160,000
1830	220,000	1887	220,000

Jamaica is capable of producing much more than it does, not quite one-fourth of the island being cultivated.

The area under all crops and the production of sugar compare thus with population :—

	Popula- tion	Tillage		Sugar	
		Acres	Per In- habitant	Tons	Lbs. per Inhabitant
Jamaica .	600,000	600,000	1.0	40,000	150
Trinidad .	180,000	730,000	5.1	70,000	800
Small islands }	510,000	600,000	1.2	110,000	500
Guiana .	280,000	160,000	0.6	140,000	1,100
Total .	1,570,000	2,090,000	1.3	360,000	500

SPANISH WEST INDIES

The possessions are now reduced to two islands, viz :—

	Acres	Population	Acres per Inhabitant	Sugar Crop, Tons
Cuba . . .	30,700,000	1,020,000	30	580,000
Porto Rico .	2,400,000	640,000	4	120,000
Total .	33,100,000	1,660,000	20	700,000

Cuba is naturally a productive island, one-half larger than Ireland, but ruined by misgovernment and taxation. A rebellion, which lasted ten years, was put down in 1878, after one-third of the sugar estates had been burnt, reducing the number from 1190 to 700. The Census of 1880 showed 192 coffee estates, 700 sugar plantations, 4500 vegas or tobacco-fields, 3200 potreros or cattle farms, and 17,000 small farms and plantations.

The export of sugar has been :—

Year						Tons
1833 .	.	.	.	.	.	90,000
1869–73 .	.	.	.	.	.	660,000
1874–78 .	.	.	.	.	.	580,000
1880–86 .	.	.	.	.	.	540,000

The tobacco crop averages 20,000 tons, value 5 millions sterling, sugar being worth about 10 millions. The total value of products is over 20 millions.

Porto Rico, about the size of Corsica, suffers in a less degree than Cuba from exorbitant export duties. The crops average :—

	Tons	Value, £
Sugar	120,000	1,500,000
Coffee	20,000	1,200,000
Tobacco . . .	10,000	500,000
Total . .	...	3,200,000

The area under crops is less than one-fourth of the island. Cattle-farms also cover a portion.

CANARY ISLANDS

Another Spanish colony, backward owing to misgovernment. The islands are :—

	Acres	Population	Acres per Inhabitant
Teneriffe . . .	680,000	94,000	7
Grand Canary .	580,000	69,000	8
Palma	160,000	31,000	5
Other islands . .	380,000	43,000	9
Total . .	1,700,000	237,000	7

Most of the soil is barren, official returns showing only 450,000 acres under cultivation. The value of the farms in 1860 was assessed at 13 millions sterling ; that of the wine and grain crops, £400,000. The crops averaged 6 million gallons of wine, 800,000 bushels of grain, 40,000 tons of potatoes, and 6 million lbs. cochineal.

PHILIPPINE ISLANDS

Also Spanish, and badly governed. There are 10 large and 970 small islands, with an aggregate area of 85 million acres, of which 5 per cent. is cultivated.

Luzon has 2,670,000 acres, the other islands 1,780,000, under tillage, viz. :—

	Acres	Crops
Rice	3,140,000	60,000,000 bush.
Sugar	640,000	450,000 tons
Hemp	260,000	...
Tobacco, coffee, &c. .	410,000	...
Total . .	4,450,000	...

About one-third of the sugar is exported, besides 10,000 tons of tobacco. Coffee was first planted in 1836, and the crop now reaches 60,000 tons. There are 160 sugar-estates with steam-mills. The canals made by the Jesuits have been suffered to fill up.

ALCOHOL

The degrees in wines and liquors are :—

Beer . . .	4.0	Gooseberry .	11.8	Ratafia . .	21.0
Porter . . .	4.5	Champagne .	12.2	Madeira . .	21.0
Ale . . .	7.4	Claret . . .	13.3	Port . . .	23.2
Cider . . .	8.6	Burgundy .	13.6	Curaçoa . .	27.0
Perry . . .	8.8	Malaga .	17.3	Aniseed . .	33.0
Elder . . .	9.3	Lisbon . .	18.5	Maraschino .	34.0
Moselle . .	9.6	Canary . .	18.8	Chartreuse .	43.0
Tokay . .	10.2	Sherry .	19.0	Gin	51.6
Rhine . .	11.0	Vermouth .	19.0	Brandy . .	53.4
Orange . .	11.2	Cape . .	19.2	Rum . . .	53.7
Bordeaux .	11.5	Malmsey . .	19.7	Irish whisky .	53.9
Hock . . .	11.6	Marsala . .	20.2	Scotch whisky	54.3

Spirits are said to be " proof " when they contain 57 per cent. The maximum amount of alcohol, says Parkes, that a man takes daily without injury to his health is that contained in 2 oz. brandy, ¼ pint of sherry, ½ pint claret, or 1 pint of beer.

ALCOHOLIC DRINKS

The consumption of all kinds of liquor is as follows :—

	Millions of Gallons				Gallons per Inhab.			
	Wine	Beer and Cider	Spirits	All Reduced to Alcohol	Wine	Beer and Cider	Spirits	Equivalent in Alcohol
U. Kingdom .	14	1,020	34	71	0.4	27.0	0.9	1.9
France . . .	750	410	40	131	19.0	11.0	1.9	3.5
Germany . .	120	880	60	86	2.5	18.0	1.3	2.2
Russia . . .	40	80	91	52	0.5	0.9	1.0	0.6
Austria . .	200	250	30	45	5.2	6.5	1.6	1.6
Italy	480	30	13	56	16.5	1.0	0.4	1.9
Spain . . .	260	5	5	29	15.0	0.3	0.3	1.7
Portugal . .	60	1	1	7	12.7	0.2	0.2	1.5
Sweden . . .	2	30	20	11	0.4	6.2	4.2	2.3
Norway . . .	1	10	7	4	0.4	5.0	3.5	2.0
Denmark . .	1	25	8	5	0.5	12.5	4.0	2.5
Holland . .	3	40	12	8	0.7	8.8	2.6	1.8
Belgium . .	4	170	10	14	0.7	28.5	1.6	2.0
Switzerland .	30	10	5	6	10.0	3.3	1.7	2.0
Roumania . .	16	10	4	5	3.0	1.8	1.0	1.0
Servia . . .	10	4	2	3	5.0	2.0	1.0	1.5
Europe . . .	1,991	2,975	342	523	6.0	9.0	1.1	1.6
United States .	21	630	76	73	0.4	10.5	1.3	1.2
Canada . . .	3	40	5	5	0.6	8.0	1.0	1.0
Australia . .	2	40	3	4	0.6	12.0	1.0	1.2
Total .	2,017	3,685	426	605	5.0	8.8	1.1	1.4

The value of liquor consumed may be summed up as follows :—

	Million £
2,007 million gallons wine (20d.) . . .	167
3,685 ,, ,, beer, &c. (16d.) .	240
426 ,, ,, spirits (48d.). . .	85
Total	492

LIQUOR CONSUMPTION IN UNITED KINGDOM PER ANNUM

Year	Millions of Gallons				Gallons per Inhabitant			
	Wine	Beer and Cider	Spirits	Equivalent in Alcohol	Wine	Beer and Cider	Spirits	Equivalent in Alcohol
1700–20	3	390	3	21	0.3	43	0.3	2.32
1720–50	3	530	6	30	0.3	53	0.6	3.00
1760–80	4	560	4	31	0.3	51	0.3	2.76
1790–1800	6	370	6	23	0.4	27	0.4	1.63
1810–20	5	490	10	31	0.3	26	0.5	1.61
1830–50	6	670	23	47	0.2	26	0.9	1.79
1850–70	11	810	28	57	0.3	27	1.0	1.91
1871–80	16	1,005	34	70	0.5	30	1.0	2.10
1886–88	14	1,020	34	71	0.4	27	0.9	1.88

On this subject G. R. Porter (1843) gives good reasons that the consumption of alcohol affords no evidence as to intemperance. This is confirmed by the fact that, although convictions for drunkenness per 1000 inhabitants are much higher in Ireland than in England, the consumption of alcohol is one-third less. The consumption of liquor in 1885 was as follows :—

	Gallons, Millions				Gallons per Inhabitant			
	England	Scotland	Ireland	United Kingdom	England	Scotland	Ireland	United Kingdom
Beer . . .	880	48	80	1,008	32	16	16	28
Cider . . .	12	...	...	12	0.4	...		0.3
Spirits . .	23	7	5	35	0.8	1.9	1.0	0.9
Wine . . .	12	1	1	14	0.5	0.5	0.2	0.4
Equivalent in alcohol }	59	6	7	72	2.13	1.60	1.40	2.00

See *Beer, Cider, Spirits, Wine*, under their proper titles.

UNITED STATES

The returns of the Excise Department show consumption as follows :—

Year	Million Gallons				Gallons per Inhabitant			
	Spirits	Wine	Beer	Equivalent in Alcohol	Spirits	Wine	Beer	Equivalent in Alcohol
1840	43	5	23	24	2.5	0.3	1.4	1.38
1850	52	6	37	29	2.2	0.3	1.6	1.24
1860	90	11	101	52	2.9	0.4	3.2	1.70
1870	80	12	204	50	2.1	0.3	5.3	1.38
1880	64	28	413	58	1.2	0.6	8.3	1.14
1889	81	34	780	87	1.3	0.5	13.0	1.31

The above does not include cider, the consumption of which may reach 20 million gallons yearly, or one-third of a gallon per head. This would make the total consumption of alcohol about 1.34 per inhabitant, against 1.88 in the United Kingdom.

FRANCE

The annual consumption of wine, beer, and spirits has been as follows :—

Year	Million Gallons				Gallons per Inhabitant			
	Wine	Beer	Spirits	Equivalent in Alcohol	Wine	Beer	Spirits	Equivalent in Alcohol
1810–12	447	56	7	52	16	2	0.3	1.80
1830–32	484	62	8	55	16	2	0.3	1.80
1840–42	766	96	11	88	23	3	0.4	2.50
1850–52	882	110	14	101	25	3	0.4	2.70
1860–62	655	140	19	83	18	4	0.5	2.10
1870–72	940	155	22	113	25	5	0.6	2.80
1880–82	805	190	34	107	21	6	0.9	2.60
1886–88	750	200	40	105	19	6	1.1	2.50

The above does not include cider, of which 200 million gallons are consumed yearly. See *Wine, Beer,* &c.

The French Government publishes the following table of the production and consumption of alcohol :—

Year	Gallons Produced	Value, £	Pence per Gallon	Gallons Consumed	Gallons per Inhabitant
1850	20,700,000	2,150,000	25	12,800,000	0.32
1860	19,100,000	2,870,000	36	18,700,000	0.50
1870	27,300,000	2,840,000	25	19,400,000	0.51
1880	34,800,000	4,480,000	31	28,800,000	0.80
1885	40,900,000	3,580,000	21	31,700,000	0.85

EXPENDITURE ON ALCOHOLIC LIQUORS

	Millions Sterling					Amount per Inhabitant
	Wine	Beer	Cider	Spirits	Total	
						£ s. d.
United Kingdom . .	3	68	1	7	79	2 2 0
France	63	13	8	8	92	2 8 0
Germany	10	59	...	12	81	1 14 0
Russia	4	5	...	14	23	0 5 6
Austria	17	17	...	6	40	1 1 0
Italy	37	2	...	2	41	1 8 0
Spain and Portugal .	37	...	...	1	38	1 15 0
Sweden and Norway .	1	3	...	6	10	1 9 0
Belgium	1	11	...	2	14	2 7 0
Holland	1	3	...	2	6	1 7 0
United States . .	3	42	1	19	65	1 1 0
Total . .	177	223	10	79	489	1 5 0

The foregoing values are "in bond," that is, in first hands, and exclusive of duties, which come under the head of taxation. See *Wine, Beer, Drunkenness.*

AMPHITHEATRES

The first, of stone, was built by Statilius for the Emperor Augustus, in the Campus Martius, Rome. The Colosseum, begun by Vespasian, was finished by Titus, A.D. 80, and held 100,000 spectators.

The dimensions of the principal amphitheatres were :—

Colosseum	. . .	615 × 510 feet
Verona .	. . .	513 × 410 ,,
Vienne .	. . .	508 × 436 ,,
Pozzuoli .	. . .	480 × 382 ,,
Arles .	. . .	460 × 338 ,,
Limoges .	. . .	450 × 378 ,,
Nismes .	. . .	437 × 332 ,,
Pompeii .	. . .	430 × 335 ,,

The height ranged from 60 to 100 feet, except the Colosseum, which was 164 feet high.

ANATOMY

Blood.—An adult has ordinarily 28 lbs. of blood, and at each pulsation the heart sends 10 lbs. through the veins and arteries. The pulsations are 120 per minute in infancy, 80 in manhood, 60 in old age, and rather more in women than in men.

The components of human blood are:—

	Man	Woman
Water	77.8	79.6
Albumen	6.2	6.4
Colour	14.1	12.2
Saline, &c.	1.9	1.8
	100.0	100.0

Human blood compares with that of the brute creation as follows:—

	Man	Ox	Sheep	Dog	Pig	Chicken
Chlor. of sod.	58.5	46.7	57.1	50.5	41.3	50.3
Soda	4.2	21.9	13.3	3.9	7.6	14.3
Potash	12.0	7.0	5.3	17.2	22.2	4.4
Lime	1.7	0.8	1.0	0.4	1.2	1.0
Magnesia	1.0	0.4	0.3	2.5	1.2	0.8
Oxide of iron	8.3	7.0	8.7	10.7	9.1	9.1
Phosph. acid	10.2	4.2	5.2	12.8	12.3	13.4
Sulph.	1.7	1.2	1.7	1.4	1.7	4.1
Carbon	1.2	6.0	7.0	0.5	0.7	...
Sundries	1.2	4.8	0.4	0.1	2.7	2.6
Total	100.0	100.0	100.0	100.0	100.0	100.0

The temperature of human blood averages as follows (Fahrenheit):—

Good health	98.6	Strong fever, morning	102.2
Fever	101.3	,, ,, afternoon	104.0

The following table shows the temperature of man compared with some of the brute creation: *—

Snail	76	Cat	102
Oyster	82	Ox	102
Man	98½	Monkey	104¼
Horse	99½	Sheep	104½
Porpoise	100	Hog	105
Rat	102	Chicken	111

The quantity of iron in blood is shown thus:—

	Grammes per Ton	Oz. per Cwt.		Grammes per Ton	Oz. per Cwt.
Man	510	0.91	Pig	590	1.06
Ox	560	1.00	Frog	420	0.75

According to the *Dic. Sci. Med.*, the dimensions of the globules of blood, in parts of a millimetre, are:—

Goat	.0043	Ape	.0071
Sheep	.0048	Duck	.0074
Horse	.0055	Man	.0077
Ox	.0058	Fish	.0084
Pig	.0063	Elephant	.0095
Hare	.0070	Tortoise	.0117
Goose	.0070	Frog	.0133
Dog	.0070	Snake	.0188

A human adult has half an ounce of sugar in his blood, which is proportionately more than a sheep and less than a cow.

Brain.—The latest classification of races, according to Bastian and other experts, shows weight of brain as follows:—

	Oz.		Oz.
Scotch	50.0	Pawnees	47.1
Germans	49.6	Italians	46.9
English	49.5	Hindoo	45.1
French	47.9	Gypsy	44.8
Zulus	47.5	Bushmen	44.6
Chinese	47.2	Esquimaux	43.9

* For a complete alphabetical list, see *Animals.*

Compared with size of body, the brain of the Esquimaux is as heavy as the Scotchman's.

The measurement of that part of the skull which holds the brain is stated in cubic inches thus:—

Anglo-Saxon	105	Ancient Egyptian	93
German	105	Hottentot	58
Negro	96	Australian native	58

In all races the male brain is about 10 per cent. heavier than the female. The highest class of apes has only 16 oz. of brain.

After the age of 50 the brain loses an ounce every 10 years. Cuvier's weighed 64, Byron's 79, and Cromwell's 90 ounces, but the last was diseased. Post-mortem examinations in France give an average of 55 to 60 ounces for the brains of the worst class of criminals.

Hair.—The number of hairs on an adult's head usually ranges from 129,000 to 150,000.

Nervous System

	Infants	Youths	Adults	Aged Persons	Idiots
Water	82.8	74.3	72.5	73.9	70.9
Albumen	7.0	10.2	9.4	8.6	8.4
Fat	3.5	5.3	6.1	4.3	5.0
Salts, &c.	5.9	8.6	10.2	12.2	14.8
Phosphorus	0.8	1.6	1.8	1.0	0.9
Total	100.0	100.0	100.0	100.0	100.0

Respiratory System.—The quantity of carbonic acid exhaled in twenty-four hours is as follows:—

Person	Age	Oz. Exhaled	Person	Age	Oz. Exhaled
Girl	10	9	Boy	16	16
Boy	10	10	Man	28	17
Woman	19	12			

The quantity varies according to exertion, viz.:—

	Oz. per Hour		Oz. per Hour
Sleeping	0.6	Riding	4.0
Walking 2 miles per hr.	2.1	Swimming	4.4
,, 3 ,, ,,	3.0	Treadmill	5.5

Sight.—Experiments for the British Association, in 1889, gave the following result:—

	Judgment of Eye in Dividing a Line into Halves		Judgment of Eye in Estimating an Angle of 90 Degrees	
	Males	Females	Males	Females
Correct	35.6	45.5	63.0	33.7
Incorrect	64.4	54.5	37.0	66.3
Total	100.0	100.0	100.0	100.0

The colour of the eyes was as follows:—

	Males	Females
Light	44.6	34.2
Medium	43.1	45.1
Dark	12.3	20.7
Total	100.0	100.0

Sleep.—The *Dic. Sci. Med.* mentions many cases of forty days and upwards.

Sweat.—It has been analysed by Funke and Schottin thus:—

	Funke	Schottin
Water	98.84	97.74
Salt	44	70
Other solids	72	1.56
Total	100.000	100.000

Krause says an adult perspires 800 grammes, that is, 28 oz. in twenty-four hours. Funke states the quantity of sweat thrown off by an adult as follows :—

Temperature, Shade (Fahr.)	Condition	Oz. per Hour	Percentage of Solid Matter
64	Walking in a room . .	1.2	2.56
68	Walking in a room . .	1.7	1.70
66	Walking quickly in a room	2.6	1.17
55	Walking out of doors . .	4.7	0.79
80	Walking in the sun . .	11.3	0.84
77	Running in the sun . .	13.7	0.82
88	Running in the sun . .	18.0	0.86

Urine.—Harley says that the urine of males and females, age 25, weight 154 lbs., will be found to average thus, in grammes :—

	Men	*Women*
Organic matter . . .	36.6	31.5
Inorganic matter . . .	16.4	13.5

The temperature is the same as that of the blood. The composition varies with race, viz. :—

	Grammes	
French	39.5	of solid matter
English . . .	53.0	,, ,,
German . . .	67.8	,, ,,

A man in good health, weight 140 lbs., secretes 49 oz. in twenty-four hours ; a woman 35 oz. Children emit 50 per cent. more for their weight than adults. Food has a direct influence. Lehmann says that 100 oz. of animal food, such as eggs, give 97 oz. of urine, and 100 oz. of vegetable food only 74 of urine.

Weight.—Banting gives the following scale of normal weights for height :—

Inches	Lbs.	Inches	Lbs.	Inches	Lbs.	Inches	Lbs.
61	... 120	64	... 136	67	... 148	70	... 169
62	... 126	65	... 142	68	... 155	71	... 174
63	... 133	66	... 145	69	... 162	72	... 178

Detailed tables on this subject will be found under *Anthropometry.*

ANIMALS

The temperature of the animal creation, in Fahrenheit, is as follows :—

Ape	104	Guinea-pig .	100	Porpoise . .	100		
Bat . . .	100	Hare . . .	100	Rabbit . .	100		
Cat . . .	102	Hen. . .	108	Rat . . .	102		
Chicken . .	111	Hog . . .	105	Serpent . .	88		
Crow . .	109	Horse . . .	99	Shark . .	77		
Dog . . .	102	Jackal . .	101	Sheep . .	104		
Donkey . .	98	Jackdaw . .	107	Snail . .	76		
Duck . .	111	Man . . .	99	Sparrow . .	108		
Elephant .	100	Monkey . .	104	Squirrel . .	102		
Elk . . .	103	Ox . . .	102	Tiger . .	99		
Fox . . .	102	Oyster . . .	82	Turkey . .	109		
Glow-worm .	74	Panther . .	102	Woodcock .	108		
Goat . .	104	Parrot . .	106	Wolf . . .	105		
Goose . .	107	Petrel . . .	104	...			
Guinea-fowl .	111	Pigeon . . .	109	...			

A draught horse usually weighs 1100 lbs.

The period of gestation among animals is as follows :—

	Days		Days		Days		Days
Rabbit .	30	Pig . .	120	Bear. .	180	Mare .	342
Cat . .	55	Lion .	150	Monkey	210	Camel .	365
Dog . .	63	Sheep .	150	Cow . .	282	Ass . .	385
Wolf . .	90	Goat .	153	Buffalo .	308	Elephant	730

The longest span of life belongs to whales, say 500 years ; eagles, say 200; alligators about 300, and elephants from 100 upwards. The age of toads is said often to exceed any of the foregoing.

	Weight (Lbs.)	Years of Life		Weight (Lbs.)	Years of Life
Rabbit .	5	5	Cow . .	750	25
Dog . .	40	15	Ox . .	900	25
Sheep .	70	12	Horse .	1,000	27
Pig . .	160	10	Camel .	1,200	40
Lion . .	500	40	Elephant	6,000	100

The limits of animal life are not precisely fixed. Hooker found animal life in thermal springs of 208 Fahr., that is, 4 degrees below boiling-point ; and again at minus 70° centigrade, equal to 92 degrees below zero Fahrenheit.

Ape.—The cranium compares with that of man in dimensions as follows (man 100) :—

Male gorilla . 35	Male ourang . 29	Male chimpanze . 28
Female gorilla 31	Female ourang 28	Female chimpanze 27

Camel.—A camel has twice the carrying power of an ox ; with a load of 400 lbs. he can travel twelve or fourteen days without water, going forty miles a day. They are fit to work at five years old, but their strength begins to decline at twenty-five, and they live till forty. The Tartars have herds of 1000 or more. The patriarch Job had 3000. The Timbuctoo or Mehari breed is used only for couriers, going 800 miles in eight days, with a meal of dates or grain at nightfall. Napoleon conveyed 1500 infantry on camels across the desert from Cairo to St. Jean d'Acre. The caravans from Berber to Suakim use camels carrying 600 lbs., which travel three miles an hour, and earn one penny (English) per mile. These camels are sold from £5 to £20 each ; very fine ones fetch up to £40 sterling.

Cat.—The number of cats in the United Kingdom is fully seven millions, although a remarkable decrease has been noticed in seaports, owing to exportation. They came into England before the Conquest, for the tariff of indemnity, in the 10th century, valued them at twopence, being equal to two hens or two gallons of beer. Southey mentions that the first settlers in Brazil paid £300 for a cat, and for kittens, their weight in gold-dust. An offer of £500 for a Persian cat at the Sydenham Cat Show in 1869 was refused.

Dogs

	Number Licensed	Per 1000 Inhabitants
Great Britain . . .	1,128,000	38
Ireland . . .	368,000	73
France . . .	2,864,000	75
Germany . . .	1,432,000	31
Sweden . . .	513,000	11

The largest known is a St. Bernard dog, Plinlimmon, exhibited at Birmingham 1886 : weight, 214 lbs. ; height, 35 inches at shoulder.

Sheep-dogs are not taxed in the United Kingdom, and the total number of dogs in the kingdom is at least 2,000,000, say 55 per 1000 inhabitants, worth £800,000. It is found that 100 male dogs go mad as compared with 14 female. A dog accidentally locked up at Metz passed thirty-nine days without food, and recovered.

The number of hunting dogs in the United Kingdom is as follows :—

	England	Ireland	Scotland	United Kingdom
Stag-hounds .	604	246	...	850
Fox-hounds .	12,865	1,522	660	15,048
Harriers .	3,258	1,516	...	4,774
Beagles . .	448	...	74	522
Total .	17,176	3,284	734	21,194

The weight of brain in drachms is as follows :—

Sheep-dog .	29.5	Retriever . .	25.7	Greyhound.	23.4
Fox-hound .	29.2	Collie . . .	25.4	Terrier . .	20.0
Setter . . .	26.1	Bulldog . .	24.0	Spaniel . .	18.1
Mastiff . .	26.1	Newfoundland	24.0	Lapdog. .	18.0

As compared with the above, the wolf has 42, the jackal 15, the fox 13, and some classes of apes 120 drachms.

Elephant.—The ivory found on an ordinary elephant is 120 lbs., worth £60, and it is necessary to kill 12,000 yearly to supply 650 tons of ivory to the English market, of which Sheffield consumes one-third. A tusk weighing 162 lbs. was shown at London in 1851, but Gordon Cumming since got one of 173 lbs. Tame elephants have risen in price in India, from £45 in 1835, ranging at present between £150 and £800.

The demand for ivory threatens to exterminate elephants in Africa. Stanley calculates the consumption of ivory at 75,000 lbs. a year in Europe, 13,000 in India, and 7000 in United States ; that is, 95,000 lbs. a year.

Kangaroo.—In 1888 the total number in Australia was 1,170,000, having diminished notably in the last ten years. A kangaroo consumes as much grass as six sheep; for this reason the farmers destroy them.

Llamas.—There are four millions in Peru, mostly employed as beasts of burden. The skin weighs 6 lbs., gives 18 feet of leather, and is worth 20s.

Reindeer.—Official returns are :—

	Herds	Head of Deer	Average
Finland . . .	2,822	44,400	15
Norway . . .	2,400	101,800	43
Sweden . . .	3,200	220,800	65
Total . .	8,422	367,000	44

They can travel with a sleigh 130 miles a day, and are worth usually 30s. a head.

Squirrels.—There are 25 millions killed annually in Russia for their skins. See *Hunting*.

Turtle.—A good-sized one gives 80 lbs. of tortoise-shell.

ANTHROPOMETRY

The average height of male adults, according to Topinard, is as follows :—

	Inches		Inches		Inche
Laplanders .	60.7	Caucasians .	65.0	Danes . .	66.2
Bushmen .	62.0	Hindoos . .	65.0	Irish . . .	67.0
Malays . .	63.1	Esquimaux .	65.0	English . .	67.4
Peruvians .	63.1	Berbers . .	65.0	Scotch . .	67.4
Burmese . .	63.4	Russians . .	65.4	Swedes . .	67.4
Fins . . .	63.8	Kirghese .	65.4	Kaffirs . .	67.8
Araucans .	63.8	Fuegians .	65.4	Iroquois . .	68.2
Chinese . .	64.2	Germans . .	66.2	Polynesians .	69.5
Magyars . .	64.2	Arabs. . .	66.2	Patagonians	70.3
Jews . . .	64.6	Charruas .	66.2	Average . .	65.6
French . .	65.0	Belgians .	66.2		

HEIGHT AND WEIGHT OF ENGLISH, BELGIANS, AND AMERICANS

Age	A.—Height in Inches				B.—Weight in Lbs.			
	English Male	American Male	Belgian Male	Belgian Female	English Male	American Male	Belgian Male	Belgian Female
10	51.8	51.7	50.1	49.2	67	66	56	51
15	62.2	62.3	59.6	58.6	103	105	91	88
20	67.5	67.4	65.8	62.0	143	147	131	117
24	67.7	67.9	66.2	62.1	148	147	146	123
30	67.9	68.1	66.4	62.2	156	150	146	122

Height is without shoes, but weight includes clothing.

Dr. Gould's measurement of men in the United States army (1863) gave the following table of average :—

Age	Natives of									
	United States	Canada	Eng'and	Ireland	Scotland	France	Germany	Scandinavia	Spain	Average
18–20 . . .	67.0	66.2	66.0	66.1	66.3	65.7	65.9	66.7	65.5	66.1
20–22 . .	67.9	67.0	66.5	66.7	67.0	66.2	66.6	67.3	66.1	66.8
22–24 . .	68.2	67.4	66.8	67.0	67.2	66.7	66.9	67.5	66.2	67.1
24–26 . .	68.2	67.5	66.9	67.1	67.4	66.6	66.8	67.8	66.3	67.2
26–28 . .	68.3	67.5	67.0	67.2	67.3	66.7	66.8	67.6	66.4	67.2
28–30 . .	68.4	67.5	67.0	67.2	67.5	66.7	66.8	67.4	66.0	67.2
Over 30 . .	68.4	67.5	66.9	67.1	67.6	66.7	66.8	67.4	66.3	67.2
Average . .	67.8	67.1	66.7	67.0	67.3	66.5	66.7	67.3	66.1	67.0

The above measurement comprised great numbers of men ; Irish alone 83,000.

AVERAGE HEIGHT OF MEN IN EUROPEAN ARMIES (1860)

	Inches		Inches		Inches
Italian . .	65.0	Austrian . .	66.5	Irish . . .	68.0
Spaniard . .	65.5	Belgian . .	66.9	Scotch . .	68.5
French . .	66.0	Russian . .	67.0	Swede . .	68.9
Hungarian .	66.1	English . .	67.5	Norwegian .	69.0

HEIGHT OF CHILDREN IN VARIOUS COUNTRIES (INCHES)

Age	Manchester Cowell, 1860		Brussels Quetelet, 1870		Boston Bowditch, 1877		Turin Pagliani, 1876		Bordeaux Leyet, 1882		Average	
	Boys	Girls	Boys	Girls	Boys	Girls	Boys	Girls	Boys	Girls	Boys	Girls
5	...	...	39.0	38.2	41.8	41.4	38.2	38.2	41.4	...	40.1	39.3
6	...	...	41.4	40.6	43.9	43.5	41.0	40.2	42.6	...	42.2	41.4
7	...	...	43.3	42.9	45.7	45.7	44.5	42.9	45.0	...	44.6	43.8
8	...	...	45.7	44.8	47.4	47.4	46.5	45.7	47.4	47.8	46.7	46.4
9	48.5	48.1	47.8	46.9	49.6	49.2	48.9	47.7	48.9	49.4	48.7	48.3
10	50.5	49.5	50.0	49.2	51.7	51.3	49.7	50.1	50.9	50.9	50.5	50.2
11	51.3	51.7	52.5	51.3	53.2	53.6	51.3	52.1	52.1	52.9	52.1	52.3
12	53.2	53.6	54.4	53.2	55.2	56.0	53.6	54.0	54.8	55.2	54.2	54.4
13	54.8	55.6	56.0	55.2	57.6	58.8	55.2	56.4	56.4	58.0	56.0	56.8
14	56.7	57.9	58.0	57.2	59.9	60.3	57.2	59.2	58.0	60.4	58.0	59.0
15	59.1	58.7	59.5	58.7	62.2	61.0	59.9	60.3	...	...	60.2	59.7
16	62.2	59.5	61.1	59.9	65.0	61.4	62.2	60.6	...	...	62.6	60.3
17	63.8	60.7	62.6	61.1	66.2	61.8	63.0	61.0	...	...	63.9	61.2

LENGTH AND WEIGHT OF NEW-BORN INFANTS (DUNCAN)

Mother's Age	Length, Inches			Weight, Lbs.		
	Boys	Girls	General	Boys	Girls	General
Under 20 .	19.9	19.7	19.8	7.1	6.8	7.0
20 to 30 . .	20.1	19.9	20.0	7.3	7.0	7.2
30 to 40 . .	20.2	20.0	20.1	7.4	7.2	7.3
40 to 45 . .	20.3	20.1	20.2	7.3	7.3	7.3
Over 45 . .	19.7	19.8	19.8	6.6	7.0	6.8

An infant weighing 7 lbs. at birth will weigh 7½ lbs. on the tenth day, and 11 lbs. on the 30th day.

HEIGHT AND WEIGHT OF BELGIAN INFANTS AND ADULTS (QUETELET)

Age	Height, Ins.			Weight, Lbs.		
	Males	Females	General	Males	Females	General
Under 1 year .	27.6	27.2	27.4	19.8	18.0	18.9
1–2	31.1	30.7	30.9	24.2	24.2	24.2
2–3	33.9	33.5	33.7	27.5	27.3	27.4
3–4	36.7	36.3	36.5	30.8	30.6	30.7
4–5	38.6	38.2	38.4	35.0	33.6	34.3
5–6	41.4	40.6	41.0	39.2	37.0	38.1
6–8	45.8	45.0	45.4	47.5	41.8	44.7
8–10	50.2	49.4	49.8	55.4	50.8	53.1
10–12	54.4	53.2	53.8	63.8	63.8	63.8
12–14	58.0	57.2	57.6	81.6	79.8	80.7
14–16	61.2	60.0	60.6	99.9	95.7	97.8
16–18	64.4	61.6	63.0	118.6	109.6	114.1
18–20	66.0	62.0	64.0	130.9	117.0	124.0
20–22	66.0	62.0	64.0	138.4	119.6	129.0
22–25	66.4	62.4	64.4	145.6	119.6	132.6
25–30	66.8	62.4	64.6	145.4	121.6	133.5

DISTINCTION OF CLASSES (ENGLAND)

Age	Height, Ins.				Weight, Lbs.			
	Affluent	Artisan	Farm Labourer	Male Pop.	Affluent	Artisan	Farm Labourer	Male Pop.
10 . . .	52.9	50.7	50.9	51.8	69	64	67	67
15 . . .	62.9	61.4	61.8	62.2	107	96	101	103
20 . . .	68.3	66.5	66.9	67.5	146	136	144	143
24 . . .	68.4	66.6	67.5	67.7	148	143	152	148
30 . . .	68.5	66.8	67.6	67.9	160	149	158	156
40 . . .	68.7	67.1	67.6	68.0	170	154	161	164
50 . . .	68.1	66.6	67.8	67.9	172	149	166	164
60 . . .	68.1	66.5	68.0	67.7	170	138	171	162

Age	Height, Ins.				Weight, Lbs.			
	Artisan	Criminal	Farm Labourer	Male Pop.	Artisan	Criminal	Farm Labourer	Male Pop.
20–25 . .	66.5	65.2	67.2	67.6	139	137	150	146
25–35 . .	66.8	65.7	67.5	67.8	147	140	157	152
35–45 . .	67.0	65.7	67.5	68.0	154	141	161	164
45–55 . .	66.6	65.8	67.8	67.9	149	143	166	164
General average }	66.6	65.6	67.5	67.7	147	140	158	158

Rural population is usually taller and heavier than that of towns. In Scotland agricultural males are 4 inches and 36 lbs. over the average of Glasgow and Edinburgh. The fishing population of Yorkshire exceeds the Sheffield artisans by 3 inches and 24 lbs. On the other hand, London is 1½ inch and 8 lbs. over the population of Hertfordshire; and Quetelet observed the same in Belgium, which he ascribed to better food in the towns.

GROWTH OF MALE CONVICTS IN ENGLISH JAILS (DANSON)

Age	Height, Inches		Weight, Lbs.	
	1858	1878	1858	1878
18 . . .	64.3	64.1	122	125
20 . . .	65.2	65.1	133	137
22 . . .	66.2	65.7	139	142
24 . . .	65.9	65.4	142	141
26 . . .	66.2	65.6	142	143
28 . . .	66.7	65.7	143	144
30 . . .	66.4	65.5	142	144

GROWTH OF BOYS AND MEN (ENGLAND)

The following table is from the Anthropometric Report, British Association, 1883, the result of measurement of 10,000 males :—

Age	Height, Ins.	Weight, Lbs.	Chest, Ins.	Strength of Arm, Lbs.	Average Ann. Increase			
					Height, Ins.	Weight, Lbs.	Chest, Ins.	Strength, Lbs.
11	55	79	27	38	1.5	4.8	0.2	...
12	57	85	27	39	2.1	6.2	0.2	1.8
13	59	92	28	46	1.8	6.7	0.7	6.3
14	61	102	29	53	2.2	10.6	1.0	7.1
15	64	114	30	60	2.3	12.2	1.2	7.6
16	66	129	32	69	2.6	15.2	2.0	8.9
17	68	142	34	80	1.6	12.2	1.5	11.0
18	68	146	34	86	0.4	4.8	0.5	6.0
19	68	148	35	90	0.3	2.0	0.2	2.0
20	69	152	35	94	0.5	3.9	0.6	3.9
21	69	153	35	88	...	0.4	0.1	...
22	69	153	35	93	0.1	...	...	4.5
23–50	69	155	36	97	0.1	1.8	0.5	4.7

GROWTH OF MALES IN TOWNS AND RURAL DISTRICTS (ENGLAND)

Age	Height, Ins.		Weight, Lbs.		Rural Excess	
	Town	Rural	Town	Rural	Ins.	Lbs.
10–13	56	57	73	76	1	3
13–16	63	64	101	106	1	5
16–19	67	67	131	134	...	3
19–22	68	69	143	147	1	4
22–25	67	69	139	153	2	14

GROWTH OF TELEGRAPH GIRLS (ENGLAND)

The following results were obtained by the Committee from 3700 girls :—

Age	Height, Ins.	Weight, Lbs.	Chest, Ins.	Lifting Power, Lbs.	Average Annual Increase			
					Height, Ins.	Weight, Lbs.	Chest, Ins.	Lifting, Lbs.
13	56	79	25	182	...	...	...	...
14	58	85	26	192	2	6	1	10
15	60	90	27	218	2	5	1	26
16	62	108	28	278	2	18	1	60
17	64	116	30	308	2	8	2	30
18	65	127	30	316	1	11	0	8
19	66	130	30	329	1	3	0	13

ITALIAN BOYS AND GIRLS (PAGLIONI)

Age	Weight, Lbs.		Height, Ins.		Drawing Power, Lbs.	
	Boys	Girls	Boys	Girls	Boys	Girls
10	54	60	50	52	146	80
11	57	62	51	53	151	85
12	63	70	53	56	174	115
13	70	82	55	58	209	129
14	73	95	56	61	231	131
15	87	100	59	61	261	152
16	91	101	60	62	266	152
17	95	107	60	62	299	154
18	98	105	61	62	312	155
19	103	...	62	...	330	...

MEN AND WOMEN OF UNITED STATES

The average weight of 20,000 men and women at Boston in 1864, and of 22,000 weighed at Cincinnati in 1882, was as follows :—

	Men	Women
Boston . . .	142 lbs.	125 lbs.
Cincinnati . .	154 ,,	131 ,,

There was no account taken of age. The people of the Western States are evidently much heavier than those of New England, properly known as Yankees.

It is, moreover, to be observed that the above averages for Boston closely coincide with those of Belgium (p. 62), where Quetelet gives 146 lbs. for men, and 122 for women, aged 30 ; but the British Association found an average in England of 155 lbs. for men over 23 years.

ENGLISH MEN AND WOMEN (ROBERTS)

The comparison of weight, strength, &c., with stature, shows :—

Height, Ins.	Weight, Lbs.		Chest, Ins.		Drawing-Bow, Lbs.	
	Men	Women	Men	Women	Men	Women
58	133	114	31	26	68	41
60	138	118	32	27	71	43
62	143	122	33	28	73	44
64	147	125	35	29	76	45
66	152	129	36	30	78	47
68	156	133	37	31	80	48
70	161	137	38	32	83	50
72	166	141	39	33	85	51

BRITISH AND IRISH MALES, STATURE AND WEIGHT

The Anthropometric Committee in 1883 measured 8600 men, of ages from 23 to 50 years, and found as follows :—

Height					Weight				
Inches	English	Irish	Scotch	U. Kingdom	Pounds	English	Irish	Scotch	U. Kingdom
Under 60	0.9	0.3	0.2	0.7	Under 100	0.5	2.0	0.1	0.4
60–62	3.2	1.1	0.9	2.9	100–120	8.5	3.3	2.4	7.0
62–64	13.7	6.4	5.0	12.4	120–140	34.8	40.1	19.5	32.2
64–66	26.1	26.3	19.1	25.8	140–160	35.2	35.2	43.8	37.2
66–68	29.1	39.0	32.2	29.8	160–180	14.4	15.4	24.2	16.3
68–70	19.8	18.8	25.5	19.9	180–200	4.4	3.6	7.5	4.8
Over 70	7.2	8.1	17.1	8.5	Over 200	2.2	0.4	2.5	2.1
Total	100.0	100.0	100.0	100.0	Total	100.0	100.0	100.0	100.0

The following summary shows that the Irish are a much lighter race than the English, Welsh, or Scotch, and also that they weigh less per inch of stature :—

	Average Height, Ins.	Average Weight, Lbs.	Average, Lbs. per Inch
English . .	67.4	155	2.30
Welsh . .	66.7	158	2.38
Irish . . .	67.9	154	2.27
Scotch . .	68.7	165	2.41
U. Kingdom	67.7	158	2.33

HEIGHT ACCORDING TO CLASSES

Boys 11 to 12 Years	Ins.	Adults 25 to 30 Years	Ins.
Eton and Harrow .	55.0	Professional class . .	69.1
Middle schools . . .	53.8	Commercial class . .	68.0
Agricultural peasants .	53.0	Farmers	67.5
Artisans' sons . .	52.6	Artisans	66.6
Factory boys . . .	51.6	Criminals	66.0
Military orphans .	51.2	Tailors	65.9
Industrial schools .	50.0	Insane	65.7

The height and weight of factory children of ten to twelve years in England, have increased in the last half century :—

Year	Height, Inches		Weight, Lbs.	
	Boys	Girls	Boys	Girls
1833	50.5	50.4	59	57
1873	50.7	50.8	64	63
Increase	0.2	0.4	5	6

	Ins.	Lbs.
Fellows of the Royal Society average . .	69.5	161
Members of Athletic Associations	68.4	144
Policemen and Fire-brigade	70.1	185
Burglars and other convicts	65.6	140

The low physical type of criminals and insane is remarkable.

HEIGHT OF MALE ADULTS IN VARIOUS COUNTRIES

Inches	Jews	Saxons		Italians	Belgians	Swedes	Dutch	United Kingdom		
	Bavaria	Town	Rural	Conscripts	Militia	Conscripts	Conscripts	English	Irish	Scotch
Under 62	6.4	15.0	14.6	14.0	13.6	1.8	5.2	4.1	1.4	1.1
62–64	20.9	17.8	17.6	20.3	12.1	11.3	10.5	13.7	6.4	5.0
64–66	34.3	29.2	28.4	26.2	26.7	14.0	27.0	26.1	26.3	19.1
66–68	22.8	22.9	23.9	21.2	26.8	37.1	26.1	29.1	39.1	32.2
Over 68	15.6	15.1	16.5	18.3	20.8	35.8	31.2	27.0	26.9	42.6
Total . .	100.0	100.0	100.0	100.0	100.0	100.0	100.0	100.0	100.0	100.0

The Scotch are by far the tallest in the above table, but are surpassed by the Iroquois Indians, measured by Gould, of whom 54 per cent. exceeded 68 inches.

HEIGHT AND CHEST MEASUREMENT OF BRITISH ARMY (1882)

| Inches | Height | | | Inches | Chest |
	Eng-lish	Scotch	Irish		English,Scotch, Irish
Under 66	47.3	45.0	55.3	Under 36	33.5
66–70	41.1	42.6	36.1	36–38	41.8
Over 70	11.6	12.4	8.6	Over 38	24.7
	100.0	100.0	100.0		100.0

| Inches | Height of French Conscripts | | |
	1837–47	1848–57	1858–68
Under 62 . . .	14.0	13.6	11.5
62–64	24.1	25.3	26.6
64–66	33.2	32.6	32.2
66–68	21.9	21.8	22.7
Over 68 . . .	6.8	6.7	7.0
Total . .	100.0	100.0	100.0

| Inches | Height of Dutch Conscripts | | |
	1866–71	1872–77	1878–83
Under 62 . . .	9.3	7.6	5.7
62–64 . . .	13.9	12.9	11.6
64–68 . . .	52.0	53.5	53.9
Over 68 . . .	24.8	26.0	28.8
Total . .	100.0	100.0	100.0

The improvement of stature in Holland is ascribed to better food, resulting from the abolition of the Grist-tax, and to sanitation of cities. It is further observed that in swampy provinces 8½ per cent. of the young men drawn for military service are rejected for being under 62 inches, and in the rest of the kingdom only 5 per cent.

HEIGHT OF SWEDISH CONSCRIPTS

Period	Average Ins.	Period	Average Ins.
1841–50 . . .	66.0	1861–70 . . .	66.6
1851–60 . . .	66.2	1871–75 . . .	66.7

The improvement in Sweden is likewise ascribed to better food.

COMPLEXION OF PERSONS (UNITED KINGDOM)

| Hair | England | | | Scotland | | | Ireland | | |
	Gen. Pop.	Criminals	Insane	Gen. Pop.	Criminals	Insane	Gen. Pop.	Criminals	Insane
Light . . .	43	42	44	47	45	49	52	47	52
Red	6	5	4	7	5	3	6	4	7
Dark . . .	51	53	52	46	50	48	42	49	41
Total .	100	100	100	100	100	100	100	100	100
Eyes									
Light . . .	66	60	65	76	67	80	72	67	83
Dark . . .	34	40	35	24	33	20	28	33	17
Total .	100	100	100	100	100	100	100	100	100

DIFFERENCE OF SEXES (EUROPE)

	Male	Female		Male	Female
Height . .	100	94	Skull . . .	100	88
Size . . .	100	93	Brain . . .	100	91
Weight . .	100	84	Strength . .	100	67

ARMS

Artillery.—The first piece of cannon was invented by Friar Schwartz in 1330, and the Moors used artillery at Cordoba in 1343. The English had four pieces at Crecy in 1346; the Venetian fleet used artillery against the Genoese in 1377. Mortars for bombs were cast in England in 1543, having been invented at Naples in 1435. Petards were first used by the Huguenots in 1579. The most famous pieces of cannon have been :—

Date	Name	Place	Tons	Feet	Bore, Ins.
1430	Dulle Griete .	Holland .	14	...	...
1450	Mons Meg .	Edinburgh	6	13	20
1464	Mahomet . .	Turkey .	20	...	...
1540	Carlos Quinto	Dover .	...	24	...
1548	Malik Mydan	India . .	40	...	23
1550	Simon . . .	Cologne .	...	19	18
1586	Pooshka .	Moscow .	39	...	...
1856	Horsfall . .	Liverpool	22	16	...
1874	Infant . . .	Woolwich	80	27	...
1880	Armstrong .	Newcastle	100	...	12
1889	Krupp . . .	Essen . .	130	44	16

The cannon of the Middle Ages was as follows :—

Name	Shot, Lbs.	Powder, Lbs.	Gun, Cwts.	Length, Feet
Cannon	64	32	72	12
Serpentine . . .	52	26	62	12
Culverin	19	15	40	12
Demi-culverin . .	10 .	8	20	10
Falcon	2	2	6	7

The cannon used at Trafalgar (1805) were :—

Pounder	Inch	Gun, Cwts.	Powder, Lbs.
3	3.9	7	1.0
6	3.7	22	1.3
12	4.6	34	4.0
18	5.3	42	6.0
24	5.8	50	8.0
32	6.4	52	10.0

None of the above carried over 2000 yards.
The artillery now in use (1889) may be classified thus :—

Inches Bore	Gun, Tons	Shot, Lbs.	Powder, Lbs.	Initial Velocity, Feet per Second	Muzzle Energy, Foot-Tons	Penetration, Ins. at Muzzle
7	4½	112	22	1,325	1,400	7
8	9	175	35	1,384	2,300	9
9	12	253	50	1,440	3,600	11
10	18	406	70	1,379	5,400	13
11	25	543	85	1,360	7,000	14
12	35	706	140	1,390	9,500	16
16	80	1,700	450	1,590	29,000	25
16	100	2,000	550	1,700	40,000	27
16	111	1,800	960	2,104	...	36
16	119	2,028	846	2,000	...	...
16	130	2,600	700	...	...	...

The progress of artillery science since 1837 has been as follows :—

1859. Armstrong's breech-loading rifle-gun, charge only 5 lbs., sent a shot 5 miles.

1861. Richard Gatling, of North Carolina, patented his gun, firing 200 shots a minute; it now fires 400.

E

1862. Armstrong's smooth-bore, charge 40 lbs., sent a
300-lbs. shot through a 5-inch wrought-iron
plate.
1866. Woolwich 9-inch rifle, charge 43 lbs., sent a 250-lbs.
Palliser shot through an 8-inch plate.
1872. First Woolwich Infant, 35 tons, shot 700 lbs.,
powder 120 lbs.. It sent a Palliser shot through
18½ inches iron and 12 of teak.
1874. Second Woolwich Infant, 80 tons, shot 1650 lbs.,
powder 300 lbs.
1876. Third Woolwich Infant, 81 tons, shot 1250 lbs.,
went through 50 feet of sand.
1876. Armstrong 100-ton guns, broke 22-inch Creusot
steel plates.
1879. Shot from 9-inch gun, 75 lbs. powder, unable to
pierce a 12-inch plate of iron and steel, alternate
layers.
1880. Result of Krupp's experiments at Meppen :—

Gun	Inch	Shot, Lbs.	Penetration	Foot-Tons
Krupp . .	9¼	348	18.1	8,630
British . .	11½	812	17.9	12,260

Krupp's shot penetrated 18-inch plates; the British
did not.
1889. Krupp's cast steel 130-ton gun has a range of 12
miles, and fires two shots per minute ; each shot
costs £300 sterling, and weighs 2600 lbs., going
through 19 inches of armour ; charge of powder,
700 lbs.
Down to 1876, Mr. Krupp had delivered 15,000 cannons
from his factory to different nations. Great Britain sometimes manufactures two million shot and shell in a year,
weighing 20,000 tons of iron. The cost of heavy guns
is as follows (1882), per ton :—

Cast iron .	.	£21	Krupp	.	. £170
Armstrong	.	100	Whitworth	.	175

During the siege of Sebastopol, 1855, the Allies threw
30,000 tons of shot and shell into that place.
The cannon in various countries may be summed up thus
(those in fortifications, &c., being approximately) :—

	Army	Navy	Forts, &c.	Total
Great Britain . . .	702	3,087	2,000	5,789
France	2,060	2,834	2,800	7,694
Germany	1,486	570	3,324	5,380
Russia	1,540	836	2,048	4,424
Austria	850	320	1,000	2,170
Italy	700	480	500	1,680
Spain	416	525	300	1,241
Portugal	132	178	110	420
Holland	220	560	120	900
Belgium	204	...	120	324
Denmark	120	245	170	535
Sweden and Norway	300	672	100	1,072
Greece	120	70	110	300
Roumania	312	36	94	442
Turkey	1,188	200	2,374	3,762
Europe	10,350	10,613	15,170	36,133
United States . . .	100	1,055	3,000	4,155
Brazil	50	166	200	416
Japan	120	149	100	369
The World	10,620	11,983	18,470	41,073

RIFLES

	Maker	Weight, Lbs.	Calibre	Rounds
England . . .	Lee-Mitford	9.4	.303	8
France . .	Lebel	9.2	.315	8
Germany .	Mauser	9.5	.310	5
Austria . .	Mannlicher	10.2	.315	5
Italy . . .	Vetterli	10.6	.409	5
United States	Lee	...	.433	5
Belgium . .	Mauser	9.5	.310	5
Turkey . .	Mauser	...	.433	8
China . .	Lee	...	.433	5

The competition for the Elcho Shield in twenty-four
years shows the following score :—

	Average	Highest
England . . .	1,345	1,642
Ireland . .	1,540	1,652
Scotland . . .	1,280	1,510

ARMY

	Peace Footing (1889)					Artillery Guns	War Footing
	Cavalry	Infantry	Artillery	Engineers, &c.	Total		
Great Britain . . .	17,000	140,000	34,000	19,000	210,000	702	606,000
France . . .	77,000	327,000	77,000	74,000	555,000	2,060	1,315,000
Germany . . .	67,000	341,000	62,000	22,000	492,000	1,486	1,492,000
Russia . . .	109,000	579,000	62,000	50,000	800,000	1,540	1,720,000
Austria . . .	48,000	193,000	30,000	52,000	323,000	850	1,150,000
Italy . . .	26,000	107,000	33,000	89,000	255,000	700	940,000
Spain . . .	14,000	116,000	11,000	4,000	145,000	416	400,000
Portugal . . .	4,000	17,000	3,000	2,000	26,000	132	150,000
Belgium . . .	6,000	31,000	6,000	5,000	48,000	200	148,000
Holland . . .	2,000	21,000	5,000	1,000	29,000	220	55,000
Denmark . . .	2,000	12,000	2,000	1,000	17,000	120	60,000
Sweden and Norway .	6,000	43,000	6,000	2,000	57,000	300	230,000
Switzerland . .	3,000	96,000	18,000	9,000	126,000	42	207,000
Greece . . .	3,000	16,000	4,000	3,000	26,000	120	105,000
Roumania . . .	4,000	23,000	6,000	3,000	36,000	312	118,000
Servia . . .	1,000	14,000	2,000	1,000	18,000	144	100,000
Bulgaria . . .	2,000	23,000	2,000	2,000	29,000	96	100,000
Turkey . . .	20,000	98,000	30,000	12,000	160,000	1,190	470,000
Europe . . .	411,000	2,197,000	393,000	351,000	3,352,000	10,630	9,366,000
United States . .	8,000	15,000	2,000	1,000	26,000	100	...
South America .	17,000	59,000	6,000	7,000	89,000	200	...
Japan . . .	3,000	47,000	5,000	5,000	60,000	160	...
India . . .	23,000	114,000	4,000	4,000	145,000	...	...
Persia . . .	6,000	17,000	1,000	1,000	25,000	...	...
Total . .	468,000	2,449,000	411,000	369,000	3,697,000	11,110	...

In the war footing of European armies as given above only the first line of reserves is included. If all reserves were included the above numbers might be safely doubled.

According to Napoleon Bonaparte, the proportions of an army should be 70 per cent. infantry, 17 per cent. cavalry, and 13 per cent. between artillery, engineers, and train. The proportions of European armies in the above statement are 66 per cent. infantry, 12 per cent. cavalry, and 22 per cent. between artillery, engineers, and train.

The standing armies of twelve principal countries of Europe have been as follows :—

	Army			War Footing	Soldiers per 10,000 Inhabitants in 1888	
	1810	1851	1888–89	1888–89	Peace	War
Great Britain	307,000	129,000	210,000	606,000	56	160
France	570,000	365,000	555,000	1,315,000	138	370
Germany	160,000	346,000	492,000	1,492,000	102	310
Russia	558,000	644,000	800,000	1,720,000	100	210
Austria	347,000	282,000	323,000	1,150,000	80	280
Italy	75,000	142,000	255,000	940,000	85	310
Spain	54,000	87,000	145,000	400,000	76	230
Portugal	10,000	28,000	26,000	150,000	60	350
Belgium	...	40,000	48,000	148,000	85	240
Holland	22,000	50,000	29,000	55,000	70	140
Denmark	75,000	25,000	17,000	60,000	90	300
Sweden	43,000	57,000	57,000	230,000	90	330
Europe	2,221,000	2,195,000	2,957,000	8,266,000	91	270

The minimum height in the principal armies is as follows :

	Ins.			Ins.
British . .	63.0	Belgian . .	61.9
French . .	60.7	Swedish . .	63.3
German . .	61.9	American . .	63.0
Austrian . .	61.2	Prussian Guard .	67.0
Italian . .	61.5	Uhlans . .	65.9
Spanish . .	61.5	Infantry . .	61.9

For average height, see p. 62.

The proportion of men drafted to the ranks out of 1000 recruits or conscripts was :—

Nation	Rejected for		Good for Service	Date
	Under Height	Infirmity		
British . . .	...	...	670	1844–52
French . . .	61	327	612	1860–62
Prussian . .	95	380	525	1831–63
Bavarian . .	16	233	751	1822–53
Saxon . . .	220	380	400	1826–54
Wurtemburger	120	410	470	1834–57
Austrian . .	113	343	544	1857–64
Russian . .	...	...	780	1860–61
Swede . . .	101	180	719	1847–48
Dane . . .	150	320	530	1852–56
Spaniard . .	101	75	824	1857–66
Belgian . . .	121	107	772	1841–60
Hollander . .	160	71	769	1851–61
United States .	...	...	720	1863–65

The following table shows the death-rate and ratio invalided :—

Army	Per 10,000 Soldiers Yearly		Date
	Died	Invalided	
British	95	340	1860–68
French	101	70	1862–69
Prussian . .	64	140	1860–63
Belgian . . .	129	90	1868–69
Austrian . . .	116	210	1869
Portuguese . .	127	170	1861–67
Russian . . .	165	...	1858–68
United States .	140	250	1859
Do. Blacks	180	...	1859

The dietary of the various armies is as follows :—

Army	Daily Rations, Oz.					Weekly Rations, Oz.		Extras Weekly
	Bread	Meat	Rice	Dried Vegetables	Potatoes	Salt	Coffee	
British . .	16	12	2	8	16	2	4	9 oz. sugar
French . .	22	9	4	11	11	6	3	...
Russian . .	16	16	...	35	...	6	...	2 galls. beer
Austrian .	32	8	1	11	9	...	...	8 oz. grease
Italian . .	27	11	4	...	...	4	4	½ gall. wine
Spanish . .	18	8	6	...	16	...	3	3 lbs. fish
Belgian . .	27	9	...	...	35	8	3	5 oz. butter
Turkish . .	32	9	3	1	...	...	...	3 oz. grease
American .	22	20	2	...	16	5	10	22 oz. beans
German .	28	8	3	...	...	...	4	7 oz. sugar

The years of service under the colours and in the reserve are :—

	Colours	First Reserve	Second Reserve	Age at Enrolment
France . .	5	4	11	20
Germany .	3	4	15	20
Austria . .	3	7	12	20
Italy . . .	3	5	12	21

The equipment of infantry and cavalry weighs as follows :—

	Infantry	Cavalry
British	60 lbs.	125 lbs.
German	60 ,,	122 ,,
French	72 ,,	155 ,,
Russian	68 ,,	...

The rate of marching per hour is as follows :—

	English Miles		
	Ordinary	Quick	Double Quick
British . . .	3.0	3.3	5.0
German . . .	...	3.0	5.0
French . . .	2.7	3.3	5.0

BRITISH ARMY

The strength of the regular standing army at various periods has been thus :—

Year	Men	Per 10,000 Inhabitants	Year	Men	Per 10,000 Inhabitants	Year	Expenditure, £
1661 . . .	5,200	9	1810 . . .	306,700	171	1780	7,800,000
1688 . . .	28,000	51	1830 . . .	108,700	46	1810	26,700,000
1730 . . .	17,000	30	1850 . . .	138,800	52	1830	8,600,000
1764 . . .	40,000	53	1860 . . .	229,500	79	1860	18,000,000
1792 . . .	57,300	60	1889 . . .	212,000	58	1888	18,400,000

The forces of the United Kingdom, regular or irregular, were :—

	1850	1870	1888
Army	139,000	193,000	210,000
Reserves and militia .	20,000	122,000	174,000
Volunteers . . .	...	193,000	222,000
Total . .	159,000	508,000	606,000

If Yeomanry and Royal Irish Constabulary be added, the total for 1888 will reach 630,000 men. The several Arms in 1888 were :—

	Army	Reserves and Militia	Volunteers	Indian Army	Total
Infantry . .	140,000	122,000	174,000	114,000	550,000
Cavalry . .	17,000	18,000	1,000	23,000	59,000
Artillery . .	34,000	22,000	38,000	4,000	98,000
Engineers, &c.	19,000	12,000	9,000	4,000	44,000
Total. .	210,000	174,000	222,000	145,000	751,000

The total land force of the British Empire is as follows :—

British regular army . . .	212,000
Reserve and militia . . .	205,000
Volunteers	222,000
Yeomanry	14,000
Irish constabulary . . .	13,000
Anglo-Indian army . . .	145,000
Indian police . . .	190,000
Colonial forces . . .	15,000
Total . .	1,016,000

The regular army has 9,400 officers, and 16,100 petty officers.

The following table shows the garrison of the United Kingdom since 1800, exclusive of the auxiliary forces :—

Year	Horse	Foot	Artillery, &c.	Total
1800	14,000	49,000	8,000	71,000
1810	20,000	74,000	19,000	113,000
1820	10,000	47,000	4,000	61,000
1830	8,000	35,000	5,000	48,000
1840	7,000	39,000	4,000	50,000
1850	8,000	50,000	9,000	67,000
1860	11,000	62,000	17,000	90,000
1870	11,000	56,000	17,000	84,000
1880	13,000	72,000	22,000	107,000
1889	13,000	70,000	22,000	105,000

The equipment and distribution of the regular army were as follows :—

	1889		1888				
	Officers and Men	Horses	Infantry	Cavalry	Artillery	Engineers, &c.	Total
England	74,000	9,600	43,000	9,000	15,000	16,000	83,000
Scotland	4,000	340	3,000	1,000	...	1,000	5,000
Ireland	28,000	3,300	21,000	3,000	3,000	3,000	30,000
United Kingdom . .	106,000	13,240	67,000	13,000	18,000	20,000	118,000
India	73,000	11,100	53,000	6,000	13,000	...	72,000
Egypt	3,400	300	5,000	...	1,000	...	6,000
Colonies . . .	29,400	710	15,000	...	4,000	6,000	25,000
Total . .	211,800	25,350	140,000	19,000	36,000	26,000	221,000

The Indian establishment * is as follows :—

	European Army	Indian Army	Total Force		European Army
Horse .	6,000	23,000	29,000	Bengal . .	45,000
Foot .	54,000	114,000	168,000	Bombay .	13,000
Artillery .	13,000	8,000	21,000	Madras, &c.	15,000
Total	73,000	145,000	218,000		73,000

* The feudatory States of India have also armies of their own, viz. :—

		Men	Guns
Hindoo States	. .	275,000	3,372
Mahometan .	. .	75,000	865
Total	. .	350,000	4,237

The Volunteer force, created in 1860, showed as follows :—

Year			Roll	Efficient
1860 .	.	.	160,300	106,400
1865 .	.	.	226,700	133,800
1870 .	.	.	245,000	170,700
1875 .	.	.	238,300	168,700
1880 .	.	.	243,500	196,900
1888 .	.	.	258,000	222,000

The composition of the regular army is as follows :—

Nationality (1883)		Age (1883)		Religion (1889)	
English . .	70	Under 18 .	2	Church of England	67
Irish . .	20	18–30 . .	74	Roman Catholics .	19
Scotch . .	8	30–40 . .	20	Presbyterians . .	8
Colonial .	2	Over 40 . .	4	Dissenters . . .	6
Total .	100	Total .	100	Total . .	100

In 1881 there were 93 per cent. of the men able to read and write, against 68 per cent. in 1860.

The health of the army has been greatly improved since Dr. Farr's barrack reform begun in 1860, on a basis of 600 cubic feet of air per man in Europe, and 1000 in India, with an allowance of 1600 cubic feet for each horse. In many barracks of Great Britain, down to 1861, the average accommodation only allowed 300 to 400 cubic feet per man. The new barracks at Chelsea are considered a model, the cost being £245 per man, including cost of site.

The death-rate of the garrisons under the old and new systems (exclusive of deaths in war) showed thus :—

	Per 1000 Men Yearly	
	1830–40	1876–80
Great Britain . .	16	7
India . . .	68	10
Jamaica . .	143	22
Ceylon . . .	57	22
Canada . . .	21	18
Sierra Leone . .	483	...

The following table shows, moreover, what an improvement has taken place in the health of the army, both at home and abroad, since 1861 :—

	Per 1000 Men			
	Hospital Admissions		Deaths	
	1861	1871–80	1861	1871–80
India . . .	1,768	1,454	37	19
China . . .	1,492	1,196	28	14
Ceylon . . .	1,440	971	20	15
Bermuda . . .	461	632	14	9
West Indies . .	1,002	913	14	11
Mauritius . . .	608	1,834	12	17
Malta . . .	772	857	11	10
Canada . . .	644	667	8	7
Gibraltar . . .	927	675	9	7
United Kingdom .	1,025	817	9	8

Death-rate in the United Kingdom ranges from 5½ per 1000 in cavalry to 7½ in the engineers, the general average being under 7 per 1000. The saving of life consequent on the barrack reforms is equal to 4200 men yearly in India, and 2500 in the rest of the army.

In active service the death-rate among officers is heavier than among the rank and file.

The Duke of Wellington's army roll from 1811 to 1814 showed :—

	Officers	Men
Killed . .	14.5 per cent.	10.2 per cent.
Wounded . .	81.0 ,,	49.0 ,,
Died of disease .	13.0 ,,	38.0 ,,

FRENCH ARMY

The strength has been at various periods as follows :—

Date	Men	Horses	Expenditure, £
1783	127,000	30,000	...
1812	743,000	180,000	...
1836	280,000	54,000	8,700,000
1848	445,000	90,000	16,800,000
1869	426,000	90,000	18,400,000
1880	498,000	124,000	33,000,000
1888	525,000	122,000	22,200,000

The army list for 1890 shows as follows :—

	France	Algeria	Tunis, &c.	Total
Horse	67,000	8,000	2,000	77,000
Foot	291,000	29,000	7,000	327,000
Artillery	73,000	3,000	1,000	77,000
Gendarmes . . .	22,000	1,000	...	23,000
Engineers, &c. . .	40,000	9,000	2,000	51,000
Total . .	493,000	50,000	12,000	555,000
Horses	119,000	15,000	4,000	138,000

Deducting sick and absent, the effective force in January 1890 was 511,000 between officers and men, the officers numbering 26,600, reserve 860,000, militia 1,022,000, total 2,337,000. The artillery consists of 2060 field-guns and 99 fortress batteries. Napoleon's army in 1805 consisted of 380,000 infantry, 76,000 cavalry, and 35,000 artillery.

The army roll shows that from June 1791 to November 1813 the number enrolled was 4,556,000 men, but the Minister of War in 1814 was of opinion that only 2,022,000 had actually passed under the colours.

The following table shows the nominal and actual levies, the numbers rejected by the army doctors, and those drafted to the colours.

Years	Nominal Levy	Actual Levy	Rejected for			Drafted to Colours	Percentage Rejected
			Under Height	Other Causes	Total		
1813	1,140,000	...	...	...	...	...	...
1816–20 . . .	297,000	...	...	...	...	40,000	...
1821–30 . . .	283,000	...	...	...	...	60,000	...
1831–40 . . .	300,000	...	...	...	...	80,000	...
1841–50 . . .	305,000	143,000	12,000	51,000	63,000	80,000	37.7
1851–60 . . .	306,000	179,000	14,000	57,000	71,000	108,000	34.4
1861–70 . . .	316,000	164,000	10,000	54,000	64,000	100,000	35.1
1887	316,000	...	7,000	91,000	98,000	218,000	31.0

The minimum height at various periods was fixed thus :—

Year	Ins.	Year	Ins.	Year	Ins.
1691 . . .	66.1	1813 . . .	60.0	1832 . . .	61.5
1776 . . .	65.0	1818 . . .	61.8	1868 . . .	61.0
1792 . . .	64.0	1830 . . .	60.7	1872 . . .	60.7

For the average height of conscripts at various dates, see 65, Anthropometry.

The number of volunteers who joined the colours was as follows :—

1845 . .	6,800	1860 . . .	12,900
1850 . .	8,700	1865 . . .	10,100
1855 . .	21,900	1869 . . .	6,100

The average age of officers in 1866 was 37 years 8 months, and of men 26 years 3 months.

The annual death-rate for ten years ending 1884 averaged 10 per thousand. In 1885 it was only 7.6, which is about the same as in the United Kingdom, the arms varying thus :—

| Engineers | . 5.1 | Artillery | . 6.7 | Train | . . 8.5 |
| Cavalry | . . 6.6 | Infantry | . . 7.5 | Zouaves | . . 9.7 |

There were in 1885 under the colours 452,000 men, whose aggregate of days in hospital was 6,300,000 ; this was equal to nearly 4 per cent. (3.8) of the men being constantly in hospital. The number of courts-martial in 1886 was as follows :—

	Tried	Condemned
Officers	16	10
Men	5,549	4,750
Total . .	5,565	4,760

The numbers condemned in 1886 compared with 1882 thus :—

	1882	1886
Shot	57	69
Galleys	136	114
Imprisonment	3,828	4,313
Reprimand	289	264
Total . .	4,310	4,760

GERMAN ARMY

The strength at various periods has been as follows :—

Year		Strength	Year		Strength
1810	. . .	160,000	1865	. . .	441,000
1831	. . .	331,000	1871	. . .	937,000
1851	. . .	346,000	1890	. . .	492,000

The army of Prussia at various dates was :—

1740	. . .	76,000	1830	. . .	162,000
1744	. . .	95,000	1865	. . .	239,000
1801	. . .	220,000	1871	. . .	750,000
1808	. . .	42,000	1886	. . .	377,000

The army in 1890 stands thus :—

	1890			1886			
	Officers	Men	Total	Prussia	Bavaria	Other States	Total
Horse	2,360	65,000	67,360	51,000	7,000	7,000	65,000
Foot	11,200	329,000	340,200	267,000	40,000	38,000	345,000
Artillery	2,720	59,000	61,720	43,000	6,000	6,000	55,000
Engineers, &c. .	3,220	19,500	22,720	16,000	3,000	3,000	22,000
Total	19,500	472,500	492,000	377,000	56,000	54,000	487,000
Horses	...	...	...	66,000	9,000	9,000	84,000

The strength of the principal garrisons in 1883 was as follows :—

Berlin	.	17,800	Mayence	.	7,700	Konigsberg	6,400
Metz	.	14,400	Cologne	.	7,700	Potsdam	. 6,600
Strasburg	.	9,000	Coblentz	.	6,400	Magdeburg	6,100

The expenditure for the German army in 1889 amounted to £18,840,000, equal to £38 per man, of which £5,500,000 was for pay, £4,300,000 for food, and £1,200,000 for clothing.

RUSSIAN ARMY

The strength at various periods was as follows :—

Year	Force	Year	Force	Year	Force
1712	. . 108,000	1800	. . 433,000	1855	. . 888,000
1725	. . 196,000	1812	. . 540,000	1869	. . 834,000
1756	. . 163,000	1827	. . 870,000	1874	. . 794,000
1765	. . 313,000	1846	. . 730,000	1888	. . 770,000

Official returns in 1801 showed that the army then consisted of 234,000 infantry, 180,000 cavalry and Cos-

In 1801 it consisted of 40,000 horse and 180,000 foot.

Before the dismemberment of the German Confederation in 1865, the army also included an Austrian contingent, which is not included above. For example, the confederate army in 1865 comprised :—

	Men	Horses
Prussia	239,000	54,000
Austria	222,000	31,000
Bavaria	67,000	8,000
Small States	135,000	17,000
Total . . .	663,000	111,000

The forces in campaign against France at the outbreak of the war in August 1870, and their maximum in February 1871, are shown thus :—

	August 1870	February 1871
Prussians	564,000	719,000
Bavarians	98,000	105,000
Saxons	43,000	44,000
Wurtemburgers . .	27,000	29,000
Various	49,000	40,000
Total . . .	781,000	937,000

The recruits annually enrolled, and the proportion unable to read and write, were as follows :—

Period	Recruits	Illiterate, per Cent.	Recruits for 1887	
1876–80	141,000	19	Prussia . .	104,000
1881–87	154,000	12	Bavaria . .	20,500
1876	140,000	24	Other States	44,500
1887	169,000	7	Total .	169,000

sacks, and 19,000 artillery, in all 433,000 men, but the actual fighting strength was believed hardly to reach 250,000. During the war with Turkey in 1827 the nominal strength was 650,000 infantry, 170,000 cavalry, and 50,000 artillery, in all 870,000, but the real force was probably under 500,000.

According to an official statement in 1890 the army is summed up thus :—

	Peace		War	
	Men	Guns	Men	Guns
Infantry . . .	386,000	...	810,000	...
Cavalry . . .	57,000	...	156,000	...
Artillery . . .	62,000	1,540	75,000	4,030
Engineers, &c. .	50,000	...	71,000	...
Cossacks . . .	52,000	...	138,000	240
Reserves . . .	193,000	...	470,000	1,020
Total . .	800,000	1,540	1,720,000	5,290

The peace footing has 170,000 horses. The above does not include the Siberian force of 131,000 men and 200 guns. The *Statesman's Year-Book* gives the following estimated war footing for the whole Empire:—

	Combatants	Non-Combatants	Horses	Guns
European Russia	1,770,000	85,000	340,000	3,380
Caucasia . . .	250,000	15,000	68,000	300
Siberia, &c. . .	130,000	8,000	36,000	196
Total . .	2,150,000	108,000	444,000	3,876

AUSTRO-HUNGARIAN ARMY

The strength at various dates showed thus:—

Year	Army	Year	Army	Year	Army
1740 . .	30,000	1809 . .	280,000	1866 . .	647,000
1805 . .	220,000	1830 . .	286,000	1889 . .	323,000

The establishment for 1889 stood thus:—

	Peace Footing	War Footing		
		Army	Reserves	Total
Horse	48,000	64,000	29,000	93,000
Foot	193,000	563,000	737,000	1,300,000
Artillery . . .	30,000	91,000	...	91,000
Engineers, &c.	52,000	110,000	37,000	147,000
Total . .	323,000	828,000	803,000	1,631,000

The reserves consist of 350,000 Landwehr and 453,000 Landsturm. The artillery has 850 guns in time of peace, and 2008 on a war footing. There are 49,000 horses in peace, and 217,000 on war footing. Of the standing army in time of peace, Austria contributes 60, Hungary 40 per cent.

The strength of the several arms compares thus:—

	1830	1889	Ratio	
			1830	1889
Infantry . . .	196,000	193,000	68.5	59.8
Cavalry .	45,000	48,000	15.8	14.8
Artillery . . .	31,000	30,000	10.8	9.3
Engineers .	14,000	52,000	4.9	16.1
Total .	286,000	323,000	100.0	100.0

The proportion of conscripts rejected by the army doctors was much greater in ten years ending 1872 than before, viz.:—

	Rejected per 1000	
	1857–64	1863–72
Under height . . .	113	197
Physical infirmity .	343	553
Total .	456	750

In the latter period the proportion of Austrians rejected as too short was relatively one-fourth greater than that of Hungarians.

ITALIAN ARMY

The strength at various dates of the military forces of the States now forming the kingdom of Italy was:—

Year	Army	Year	Army
1810 . .	75,000	1869 . .	190,000
1830 . .	85,000	1878 . .	215,000
1851 . .	142,000	1889 . .	255,000

The establishment in 1889 was composed as follows:—

	Army		Reserves		War Footing
	Under Arms	On Furlough	Mobile	Territorial	Total
Horse . .	26,000	10,000	...	31,000	67,000
Foot . . .	107,000	203,000	210,000	567,000	1,087,000
Artillery .	33,000	60,000	25,000	49,000	167,000
Rifles . .	13,000	29,000	22,000	36,000	100,000
Carbineers .	24,000	4,000	...	9,000	37,000
Engineers, &c. . .	52,000	81,000	42,000	63,000	238,000
Total .	255,000	387,000	299,000	755,000	1,696,000

There is still another line of reserves, 1,069,000 men, which would bring up the total to 2,765,000.

The ratio of conscripts rejected by the army doctors shows thus:—

From Rome .	18 per cent.	From Piedmont	31 per cent.
,, Naples .	23 ,,	,, Venetia	34 ,,
,, Sicily .	30 ,,	,, Lombardy	44 ,,

According to the *Annales de Demog.*, the above results were obtained from one million conscripts.

SPANISH ARMY

The strength at various dates was as follows:—

Year	Army	Year	Army
1810 . . .	54,000	1851 . . .	87,000
1831 . . .	46,000	1889 . . .	145,000

The actual establishment is as follows:—

	Peace	War
Horse . . .	14,000	21,000
Foot . . .	116,000	343,000
Artillery . . .	11,000	30,000
Engineers . . .	4,000	7,000
Total . .	145,000	401,000

There are 104,000 men in Spain, 30,000 in Cuba and Porto Rico, and 11,000 in the Philippine Islands.

PORTUGUESE ARMY

The strength at various dates was as follows:—

Year	Army	Year	Army
1810 . . .	28,000	1851 . . .	28,000
1830 . . .	26,000	1888 . . .	26,000

Including reserves, the peace and war footings show thus:—

	Peace	War
Men	33,000	150,000
Horses	4,000	13,000
Guns	132	264

The garrison of Portugal is 17,000; of the colonies, 9000 men.

SWEDISH ARMY

Before the annexation of Norway, the Swedish army in 1805 counted 11,000 horse, 24,000 foot, and 4000 artillery, in all 39,000 men. The combined strength of Sweden and Norway in 1830, on peace footing, was 42,000, and in 1851 it amounted to 57,000. The present establishment is as follows:—

	Peace			War		
	Sweden	Norway	Total	Sweden	Norway	Total
Horse . .	5,000	1,300	6,300	9,000	3,000	12,000
Foot . .	27,500	15,000	42,500	157,500	34,000	191,500
Artillery .	4,500	1,800	6,300	13,000	2,000	15,000
Engineers .	1,300	700	2,000	10,500	1,000	11,500
Total .	38,300	18,800	57,100	190,000	40,000	230,000

DANISH ARMY

In 1805 it comprised the forces of Denmark and Norway, viz. :—

	Denmark	Norway	Total
Infantry . . .	30,000	34,000	64,000
Cavalry . . .	7,100	3,200	10,300
Artillery . . .	3,100	...	3,100
Total . .	40,200	37,200	77,400

In 1830 the force was only 39,000, Norway having been united to Sweden, and even this must have included irregulars; the regular army in 1850 amounted only to 25,000 men. In 1889, the forces were approximately as follows :—

	Peace	Reserves	War Footing
Horse . . .	2,000	2,000	4,000
Foot . . .	12,000	33,600	45,600
Artillery, &c. .	2,600	6,400	9,000
Total .	16,600	42,000	58,600

The artillery has 120 field-guns in time of peace.

DUTCH ARMY

The establishment in 1888 was approximately as follows :—

	Peace	Reserves	War Footing
Horse . . .	2,000	1,000	3,000
Foot . . .	21,000	16,000	37,000
Artillery . .	5,000	9,000	14,000
Engineers, &c. .	1,000	...	1,000
Total .	29,000	26,000	55,000

There is also a militia, numbering 100,000 men; also a colonial army in Java, comprising 34,000 men, of whom 15,000 are Dutch and 19,000 natives.

BELGIAN ARMY

The establishment is as follows :—

	Peace		Peace	War
Horse . . .	6,000	Men . . .	47,500	148,000
Foot	31,000	Horses . . .	9,000	14,000
Artillery, &c. .	10,500	Guns . . .	200	240
Total .	47,500		...	...

In time of war the Civic Guard (42,000) could be added, making a total of 190,000 men.
The death-rate has been as follows per 1000 men yearly :—

Year	Rate	Year	Rate	Year	Rate
1835	. . . 80	1860	. . . 20	1880	. . . 20
1850	. . . 40	1870	. . . 40	1888	. . . 13

The military hospital returns were :—

Year	Entries	Deaths	Deaths per 1000 Admitted	Days per Bed
1870	21,380	310	15.0	21
1880	16,290	190	12.4	21
1886	17,660	184	10.5	22

The levy averages 20,100 men, of whom 13,300 are passed to the colours; those rejected average 34 per cent. of the number drawn, 3½ per cent. being rejected as short of the required height.

SWISS ARMY

In 1889 the force was as follows :—

	Line	Landwehr	Landsturm	War Footing
Horse . . .	3,000	3,000	...	6,000
Foot	96,000	65,000	260,000	421,000
Artillery . .	18,000	10,000	3,000	31,000
Engineers, &c. .	9,000	3,000	...	12,000
Total .	126,000	81,000	263,000	470,000

The artillery has 42 guns in peace, and 300 on a war footing.

GREEK ARMY

The strength in 1889 was as follows :—

Horse . . .	3,000	Men . . .	26,000
Foot . . .	16,000	Horses . . .	3,700
Artillery, &c. .	7,000	Guns . . .	120
Total .	26,000		

By calling out the militia, the war footing could be raised to 105,000 men.

ROUMANIAN ARMY

In 1889 the establishment was approximately as follows :—

	Army	Militia	War Footing
Horse . . .	4,000	4,000	8,000
Foot . . .	23,000	75,000	98,000
Artillery . .	6,000	3,000	9,000
Engineers, &c. .	3,000	...	3,000
Total .	36,000	82,000	118,000

SERVIAN ARMY

The strength in 1889 was as follows, approximately :—

Horse . . .	1,000	Men . . .	18,000
Foot . . .	14,000	Horses . . .	2,000
Artillery, &c. .	3,000	Guns . . .	144
Total .	18,000		

By calling out the reserves a war footing of 100,000 could be attained.

BULGARIAN ARMY

In 1888 the strength was approximately thus :—

Horse . . .	2,000	Men . . .	29,000
Foot . . .	23,000	Horses . . .	2,000
Artillery, &c. .	4,000	Guns . . .	96
Total .	29,000		

The war footing is estimated at 100,000.

TURKISH ARMY

The strength at various dates was as follows :—

Year	Army	Year	Army
1810	. . . 297,000	1869	. . . 220,000
1855	. . . 165,000	1889	. . . 160,000

The present establishment is as follows :—

Horse . . .	20,000	Men . . .	160,000
Foot . . .	98,000	Horses . . .	25,000
Artillery, &c. .	42,000	Guns . . .	1,190
Total .	160,000		

The reserves and Bashi-Bazouks are variously estimated. On paper, Turkey has a war footing of 800,000 men, but the total is generally supposed not to exceed 470,000.

UNITED STATES

The number of soldiers at various periods was :—
1775–83, War of Independence, enrolled 231,800 men.
1812, war with England, 68,000 men, of whom 32,400 regulars, the rest volunteers and militia.
1861–63, Federal Government enrolled 2,688,000 men ; Confederate, 300,000.
In 1889 the army counted 2200 officers and 26,000 men, viz. :—Horse, 8000 ; foot, 15,000 ; artillery, &c., 3000. Two regiments of horse and two of foot are composed of negro soldiers, with white officers.

ARMIES OF SOUTH AMERICA

The following table shows approximately the disciplined forces of Spanish America :—

	Horse	Foot	Artillery, &c.	Total
Mexico . . .	5,500	19,500	2,500	27,500
Central America	1,200	5,000	800	7,000
Columbia . . .	1,000	4,000	1,000	6,000
Venezuela . . .	1,000	2,500	500	4,000
Ecuador . . .	500	2,000	500	3,000
Peru	600	4,800	500	5,900
Chile	1,000	4,000	500	5,500
Bolivia	500	2,000	500	3,000
Paraguay . . .	100	400	100	600
Uruguay . . .	1,000	2,000	500	3,500
Argentina . . .	2,500	3,500	1,000	7,000
Brazil	2,500	9,500	4,000	16,000
Total . .	17,400	59,200	12,400	89,000

In time of war the numbers are doubled, or even quadrupled, by adding raw levies of peasants.

JAPANESE ARMY

The actual strength, according to the *Statesman's Year-Book*, is as follows :—

Horse	.	.	.	3,000	Men	60,500
Foot .	.	.	.	47,000	Horses . . .	7,200
Artillery, &c.	.	.	10,500	Guns . . .	160
Total	.	.	60,500		...

There are also two lines of reserves, together 247,000 men, making up a total war footing of 307,500 men.

PERSIAN ARMY

It may be stated approximately as follows :—

	Peace	Reserves	War Footing
Horse	6,000	19,200	25,200
Foot	17,000	58,300	75,300
Artillery, &c.	2,000	3,000	5,000
Total . . .	25,000	80,500	105,500

The real strength of the Empire on war footing is believed not to exceed 50,000 men.

ARMIES OF ANTIQUITY

Date	General	Number	Observation
B.C. 480	Xerxes	1,800,000	Invading Greece
B.C. 332	Darius	750,000	War with Alexander
A.D. 720	Abderahman	300,000	Battle of Tours
A.D. 1095	{ Godfrey de Bouillon }	300,000	First Crusade

ARMY TRANSPORT

Date	Army of	Number	From	To	Miles	Days
193	Sept. Severus	35,000	Pannonia	Rome	800	40
1235	Gelaleddin	..	Tiflis	Kerman	1,000	17
1805	Napoleon	150,000	Boulogne	Germany	450	25
1863	Federals	25,000	Kentucky	Vicksburg	1,000	4
1865	Federals	16,000	Eastport	New Orleans	1,330	13
1866	Austrians	123,000	Venice	Danube	500	10
1877	Americans	400	Atalanta	Idaho	4,302	15

ASTRONOMY

According to Dr. Gould, there are 6100 stars in the Northern, and 7200 in the Southern Hemisphere distinctly visible to the naked eye. Mr. Proctor estimated the number of stars as follows :—

Down to 10th magnitude	.	.	.	.	1,000,000
,, 11th ,,	.	.	.		3,000,000
,, 12th ,,	.	.	.		9,000,000
,, 13th ,,	.	.	.		27,000,000

According to the Paris Observatory, the number down to 14th magnitude is about 50 millions. Dr. Gould fixed the position of 85,000 stars in the Southern Hemisphere in his *Uranometria Argentina*.
It seems that the first catalogue of the stars was that by Tycho Brahe, which included 777 fixed stars, and was published about 1590. A second, embracing 2884 stars, was made in 1725 by the Astronomer Royal at Greenwich, Flamsteed. His successor, Bradley, noted the position of 60,000, and the two Herschels, father and son, made catalogues respectively of the northern and southern hemispheres. The second Herschel also made a catalogue of 4000 double stars.

The following table shows the number of observatories and the size of the principal telescopes in the world :—

Observatories		Telescopes	
United Kingdom . . 14			*Inches Aperture*
France 6			
Germany . . . 29		Lord Rosse . . 72	
Russia . . . 12		Lassell . . 48	
Italy 9		Herschell . . 48	
Austria 8		Polkova . . 30	
Switzerland . . 4		San José, California . 28	
Other countries . 12		Vienna . . 27	
—		Washington . . 26	
Europe . . . 94		Newcastle . . 25	
United States . . 19		Pultowa . . 16	
Canada 1		Cambridge, U.S. . 15	
Spanish America . 7		Paris . . . 13	
Asia . . . 2		Greenwich . . 12	
Africa . . . 2		Cincinnati . . 12	
Australia . . 3		Munich . . . 11	
—		Rome . . . 10	
The World . . 128		Berlin . . . 10	

Leyden Observatory was founded 1632, Copenhagen 1637, Greenwich 1675, Paris 1677.

PLANETS

	Miles Diameter	Millions of Miles			Ratios of Size, Weight, &c.			
		Mean Distance from Sun	Least Distance from Earth	Greatest Distance from Earth	Size	Weight	Density	Days in Year
Earth	7,901	91	...	...	100	100	100	365
Mercury	2,962	35	47	136	5	7	124	88
Venus	7,510	66	23	160	80	79	90	225
Mars	4,920	139	62	245	14	12	96	687
Jupiter	85,390	476	409	592	138,700	30,000	20	4,333
Saturn	71,904	872	831	1,014	74,600	9,000	12	10,759
Uranus	33,024	1,753	1,746	1,929	7,200	1,300	18	30,687
Neptune	36,620	2,746	2,629	2,863	9,400	1,700	17	60,127

COMETS

Name	Years of Revolution	Millions of Miles from Sun		Next Return
		Greatest Distance	Least Distance	
Halley . .	77	3,200	56	1910
Mechain .	14	...	...	1899
Faye . . .	8	603	192	1896
D'Arrest .	7	...	...	1890
Biela . . .	7	585	82	1893
Brorsen . .	6	537	64	1890
Winnecke .	6	...	...	1891
De Vico . .	6	475	110	1895
Encke . .	3	387	32	1890

STARS ACCORDING TO MAGNITUDE

Magnitude		No.		Years for Light to Reach the Earth
1st	. .	18	...	3
2nd	. .	55	...	6
3rd	. .	170	...	9
4th	. .	500	...	12
6th	. .	6,000	...	36
12th	. .	10,000,000	...	...

All down to the 36th magnitude inclusive, that is, over 8000 in number, are clearly visible to the naked eye. A 9-foot telescope reveals those of the 12th magnitude, an 18-foot one those of the 13th, whose light takes 2700 years reach to us. Down to the 13th inclusive comprises 27,000,000.

ATHLETICS

Distance	Bicycle					Tricycle				
	Rider	Hours	Minutes	Seconds	Date	Rider	Hours	Minutes	Seconds	Date
1 mile	W. C. Jones .	0	2	20	1890	G. Gatehouse .	0	2	42	1887
5 ,,	S. G. Whittaker .	0	13	46	1888	G. Gatehouse .	0	14	28	,,
10 ,,	H. G. Crocker .	0	27	8	,,	J. B. King . .	0	29	10	1888
20 ,,	S. G. Whittaker .	0	56	32	,,	G. Gatehouse .	0	59	10	1887
30 ,,	E. Oxborough .	1	28	29	,,	F. W. Allard .	1	34	25	,,
50 ,,	W. F. Knapp .	2	29	41	,,	F. W. Allard .	2	43	54	,,
100 ,,	F. R. Fry . .	5	50	5	1883	A. L. Bower .	6	9	26	,,

G. P. Mills rode from Land's End to John o' Groats, 861 miles, in 5 days 2 hours; another person, from Tunbridge to Liverpool, 234 miles, in 18½ hours. In 1879, G. Waller rode, at the Agricultural Hall, Islington, 1405 miles in 6 days of 18 hours; in 1880, at the same place, H. Higham, 230 miles in 17 hours, without dismounting. In June 1888, in a six-days' race at Islington, between horse and bicycle, the horse won by 2 miles. In 1882 there were 9800 bicycle riders in London, and 96,000 in England and Wales.

CRICKET

The highest individual score on record is 485, by A. E. Stoddart, in 1886, in a match of Hampstead v. Stoics. The largest gross score is 920, by the Orleans Club, 3rd August 1882.

The highest records of throwing the cricket-ball are :—

Date	Throw	Yards	Place
1873	W. H. Game	127	Oxford
1888	— Crane	128	Melbourne

Mr. Crane, the champion thrower, is an American.

JUMPS

Date	Jump	Athlete	Feet	Inches
1881	Long standing	E. A. Johnson	11	1
1883	Long running	P. Davin	23	2
1878	High standing	E. A. Johnson	5	3
1887	High running	W. Byrd Page	6	4
1886	Pole jump	Tom Ray	11	6

RUNNING AND WALKING

Date	Miles	Athlete	Hours	Minutes	Seconds	Place
1886	1	W. S. George	0	4	13	London
1863	2	W. Lang	0	9	11	Manchester
1863	5	G. White	0	24	40	...
1885	10	W. Cummings	0	51	7	London
1880	20	J. E. Warburton	1	56	38	...
1881	30	G. Mason	3	15	9	...
1881	40	G. Bailey	4	34	27	...
1887	50	G. Cartwright	5	55	5	...
1882	100	C. Rowell	13	26	30	New York

The greatest distance walked in one hour was 8 miles 172 yards by W. Griffin in 1881, and in four hours was 27¼ miles by W. Franks in 1882. The greatest distance run in one hour was 11 miles 970 yards by Louis Bennett in 1863.

The following pedestrian feats in six days are recorded:—

Date	Miles	Athlete	Place
1880	550	Brown	London
1888	621	Albert	,,
1888	623	Littlewood	New York
1882	660	Hazel	,,

Mr. Hazel was an Englishman, and won £4000. In 1874, at Bristol, Miss Richards gained £50 for her aged parents by walking 1000 miles in 1000 consecutive hours. Mr. Weston has walked 5000 miles in 100 days.

SKATING

Date	Miles	Athlete	Hours	Minutes	Seconds	Place
1889	1	A. Paschin	0	2	57	Vienna
1889	1	O'Donoghue	0	2	57	,,
1890	2	Norseng	0	6	25	Amsterdam
1884	3	A. Paulsen	0	10	34	New York
1890	5	Norseng	0	16	48	Amsterdam
1884	10	A. Paulsen	0	36	37	New York
1884	20	,,	1	14	7	,,
1882	30	S. Montgomery	2	31	12	,,
1882	40	,,	3	21	22	,,
1882	50	,,	4	13	36	,,

SWIMMING

Captain Webb swam from Dover to Calais, August 24, 1875, in 21 hours 45 minutes, but was beaten by William Beckwith in a swimming match for 90 miles in 60 hours. Lord Byron swam across the Dardanelles.

Swimmer	Distance	Miles	Time
Miss Beckwith .	London to Greenwich	...	...
Miss Parker . .	London to Blackwall	7	95 min.
Miss Dicks . .	Shoreham to Brighton	6	...
Miss Saigeman .	,, ,,	6	...
Fr. Cavil . . .	Putney to Blackwall	16	4 hrs.
,, . . .	Calais to Dover	23	13 hrs.

Miss Beckwith was only 14 years of age when she swam from London to Greenwich (1875).

Date	Distance	Swimmer	Hrs.	Min.	Sec.
1884	1 mile	J. Collier	0	28	20
1881	500 yards	J. Finney	0	7	7

BOAT RACES

The quickest runs from Putney to Mortlake were :—

Year	Winner	Minutes	Seconds
1869 . . .	Oxford	20	4
1873 . . .	Cambridge	19	35

In 45 years Oxford won 23, Cambridge 21, and one was a dead heat.

B.

BALLOON

The most remarkable ascents on record are :—

Date	Aeronaut	Place of Ascent	Height, Yards	Distance, Miles
1783	Montgolfier .	Lyons . . .	2,000	...
1804	Gay-Lussac .	Paris . . .	7,700	...
1836	Holland . .	London . .	...	500
1859	Wise . . .	New York .	...	1,150
1862	Glaisher . .	Wolverton .	12,000	...

During the siege of Paris, September 1870 to February 1871, there were 64 balloons sent up, containing 91 passengers, 354 pigeons, and 3 million letters (weighing 9 tons). Mr. Glaisher states that in 3500 balloon ascents only fifteen deaths have occurred, that is, about four per thousand.

Mr. Godard, who died in November 1890, made over 2000 ascents. Charles Green, who died in 1870, had made 600; and Mr. Coxwell, who is still living, over 700, having attained with Mr. Glaisher a height of seven miles.

The results of Professor Glaisher's observations during nine ascents in 1863–64 were as follows :—

Elevation, Feet	Decrease of Temperature, Fahr.		Humidity	
	Cloudy Sky	Clear	Cloudy Sky (74)	Clear (59)
1,000	4	6	76	61
2,000	8	11	76	70
5,000	18	21	74	69
10,000	31	34	48	46
15,000	42	44	59	44
20,000	49	52	29	33
23,000	52	56	40	16
30,000	...	62	...	...

BANKS

The banking power of the world has increased in a surprising degree in the last fifty years, viz. :—

	1840	1870	1888–90
	Millions £	Millions £	Millions £
United Kingdom	132	720	910
United States .	90	440	1,030
France	16	64	268
Germany . . .	12	49	231
Australia . . .	5	38	134
Canada. . . .	3	12	40
River Plate . .	2	9	37
Other countries .	48	270	547
Total . .	308	1,602	3,197

The issues of State banks in England, France, Austria, Germany, Russia, and United States, compared with specie reserve at the subjoined dates as follows :—

	Issue, Millions £			Specie Reserve, Millions £		
	1870	1880	1890	1870	1880	1890
Bank of England	24	27	25	21	28	21
Bank of France	58	92	120	50	79	103
Bank of Austria	30	33	42	11	17	22
German banks .	43	50	49	20	31	42
Bank of Russia .	100	140	123	24	28	33
U. States banks	96	73	27	} 28	68	229
,, Treasury	63	72	181			
Total . .	414	487	567	154	251	450

In twenty years the specie reserve was trebled, while the paper issue only rose 33 per cent. The ratio of specie to paper money in general was 38 per cent. in 1870, and 79 per cent. in 1890.

It appears that the amount of capital employed in banking has almost doubled since 1870, and multiplied nearly tenfold since 1840. Banking power consists of capital, right of issue, and deposits in all banks, viz. :—

	Millions, £ Sterling			£ per Inhabitant
	Capital, &c.	Deposits	Total	
United Kingdom .	284	626	910	24.0
France	140	128	268	7.0
Germany	85	146	231	5.0
Russia	42	64	106	1.2
Austria	45	102	147	3.8
Italy	25	83	108	3.6
Spain	31	16	47	2.8
Portugal	6	4	10	2.2
Sweden	9	15	24	5.3
Norway	5	1	6	3.0
Denmark	2	21	23	11.6
Belgium	11	19	30	5.0
Holland	14	6	20	4.5
Switzerland . . .	5	12	17	6.0
Europe	704	1,243	1,947	5.5
United States . .	270	760	1,030	16.1
Australia	26	108	134	37.0
Canada	13	27	40	8.0
Cape Colony . .	2	7	9	6.0
Argentina . . .	12	17	29	8.0
Uruguay	3	5	8	12.0
Total . .	1,030	2,167	3,197	7.5

The issue and specie reserves of the banks of all nations in 1889 were as follows :—

	£ Sterling		Specie Ratio
	Issue	Specie in Safe	
			Per cent.
United Kingdom	39,000,000	28,000,000	70
France	121,400,000	101,000,000	84
Germany . . .	64,000,000	59,000,000	91
Russia	123,000,000	33,000,000	26
Austria	43,500,000	21,500,000	50
Italy	43,000,000	14,000,000	33
Spain	29,500,000	9,500,000	32
Sweden	6,300,000	2,700,000	44
Norway	2,400,000	2,500,000	104
Denmark . . .	4,400,000	3,100,000	70
Belgium . . .	15,200,000	4,400,000	29
Holland . . .	17,200,000	10,600,000	60
Switzerland . .	6,200,000	3,900,000	63
Greece	3,000,000	1,000,000	33
Europe	518,100,000	294,200,006	47
United States .	26,700,000	34,300,000	128
Canada	6,300,000	1,400,000	22
Australia . . .	5,400,000	19,300,000	357
Cape Colony . .	700,000	1,600,000	230
Argentina . . .	44,000,000	4,500,000	10
Uruguay . . .	3,100,000	600,000	20
India	12,000,000	12,000,000	100
Total . .	616,300,000	367,900,000	60

The above does not include Government issues (for which see *Money*. The specie reserve in Argentina and Uruguay is full of doubt.

The statements of the twelve great banks of Europe in December 1889 was as follows :—

Bank of	Issue, £	Specie, £	Deposits, £	Discount, £	Capital, £
England	24,400,000	17,800,000	28,600,000	36,900,000	14,500,000
France	121,400,000	100,900,000	27,800,000	51,600,000	7,300,000
Germany	50,000,000	38,900,000	17,600,000	33,100,000	6,000,000
Austria	43,500,000	21,500,000	10,700,000	17,900,000	9,000,000
Russia	123,500,000	33,100,000	5,400,000	11,500,000	4,000,000
Italy	23,400,000	9,300,000	6,500,000	7,700,000	8,100,000
Spain	29,500,000	10,500,000	16,100,000	42,200,000	6,000,000
Netherlands	17,200,000	10,600,000	1,200,000	9,500,000	2,000,000
Belgium	14,800,000	4,000,000	2,200,000	12,100,000	3,000,000
Denmark	4,400,000	3,100,000	...	2,000,000	1,000,000
Sweden	2,500,000	1,100,000	800,000	3,400,000	2,200,000
Norway	2,400,000	2,500,000	500,000	1,200,000	700,000
Total . . .	457,000,000	253,300,000	117,400,000	229,100,000	63,700,000

The figures for Spain and Netherlands are those of March 1890, the deposits for Austria of 1887, and the Scandinavian banks 1888.

The rates of interest * since 1851 have been as follows :—

	1851-60	1861-70	1871-80	1881-85	Average, 35 Years	1889
Great Britain .	4.17	4.23	3.28	3.30	3.81	3.55
France . . .	4.30	3.55	3.94	3.34	3.84	3.18
Germany . . .	4.05	4.56	4.30	4.20	4.28	3.70
Austria . . .	5.26	4.77	4.79	4.71	4.91	4.12
Italy	5.35	5.69	4.85	4.74	5.22	...
Holland . . .	3.60	3.98	3.40	3.56	3.64	2.50
Belgium . . .	3.62	3.59	3.60	3.66	3.62	3.62
Europe . . .	4.27	4.30	3.71	3.93	4.12	3.44

* In the Middle Ages 10 per cent. was the ordinary rate. Philip Augustus promulgated a law in France in 1222 limiting the maximum to 10 per cent.

The discounts of the principal banks (according to Spallart, down to 1880), were :—

Bank of—	1868	1880	1889-90
	£	£	£
England . . .	18,500,000	24,000,000	36,900,000
France . . .	19,700,000	41,000,000	51,600,000
Germany . .	22,800,000	32,400,000	33,100,000
Austria . . .	8,200,000	13,900,000	17,900,000
Belgium . . .	5,800,000	10,100,000	12,100,000
Holland . . .	3,200,000	4,600,000	9,500,000
U. States banks .	131,100,000	217,700,000	378,000,000
Total . .	209,300,000	343,700,000	539,100,000

It has been already shown that the banking power doubled between 1870 and 1888. The above table like-

PLATE II.

BANKING.

Banking Capital, millions £.

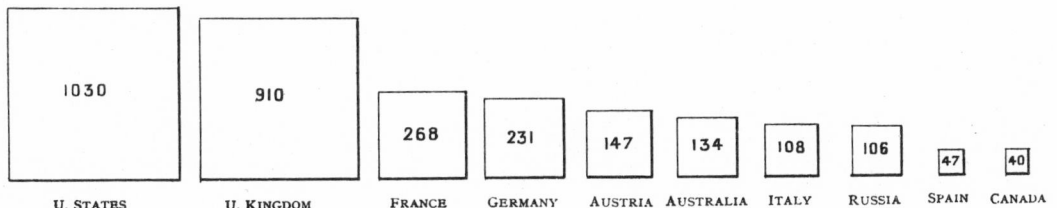

Savings-Banks Deposits, Shillings per Inhabitant.

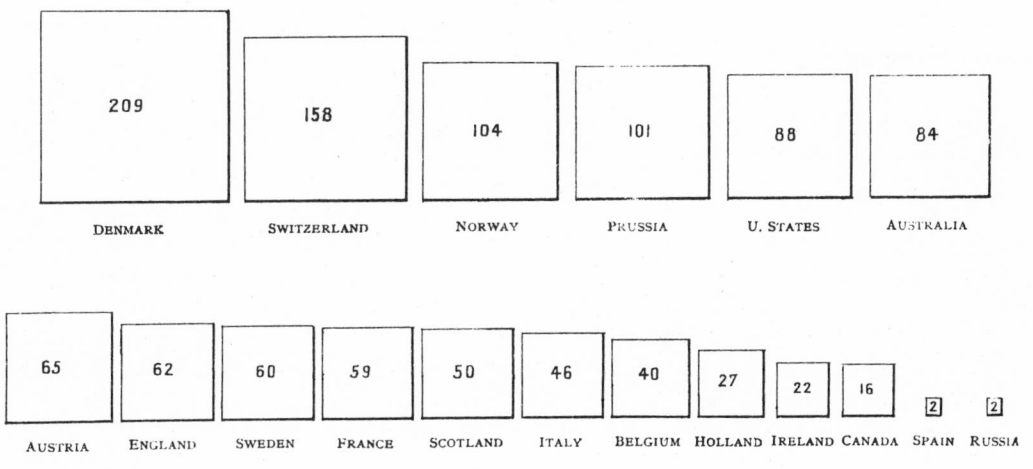

Depositors per 1000 Inhabitants.

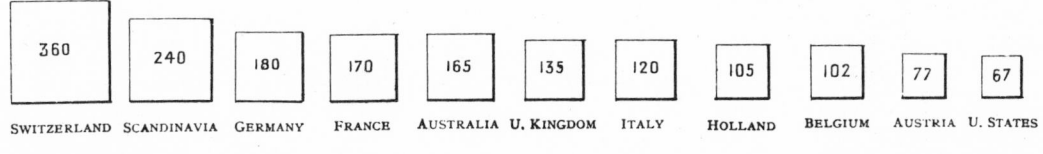

wise shows that discounts more than doubled between 1868 and 1890.

The rates of exchange in London on the principal markets for forty-two years were :—

| Period | London on | | | Calcutta on London | Price of Silver per Oz., Pence |
	Paris	Hamburg	Amster- dam		
1841–50	25.76	13.12	12.1	23.1	59.8
1851–60	25.44	13.08	11.4	25.1	61.6
1861–70	25.46	13.09	11.6	24.3	60.5
1871–80	25.55	20.62	12.3	21.6	56.1
1881–82	25.53	20.67	12.5	19.9	51.7
1885–89	...	...	...	...	45.0

London rates on Paris from 1800 to 1880 were :—

Period	Highest	Lowest	Average	Date of Highest	Date of Lowest
1800–10 . .	25.2	19.6	22.4	1805	1809
1811–20 . .	26.1	17.6	22.0	1816	1811
1821–30 . .	25.9	25.2	25.6	1829	1824
1831–40 . .	25.9	25.2	25.5	1832	1831
1841–50 . .	26.7	24.9	25.8	1848	1850
1851–60 . .	25.5	24.9	25.4	1856	1851
1861–70 . .	25.5	25.0	25.4	1869	1869
1871–80 . .	26.9	25.2	25.6	1872	1874

The rates of interest in the United States, according to the New England Mutual Insurance Company, have steadily declined in the last twenty-one years, viz. :—

Years	Per Cent.
1869–73	6.1
1874–78	5.9
1879–83	5.0
1884–89	4.7

Berlin rates on the other great cities were as follows :—

	1875	1880	1887	1888
London	20.60	20.44	20.35	20.48
Paris	81.60	80.95	80.70	81.00
Amsterdam	174.90	169.10	168.65	...
Vienna	183.50	170.70	160.60	172.60
St. Petersburg . . .	281.25	213.80	202.80	193.80

The use of cheques compared with money at various dates and places shows thus :—

| Date | Place | Per Cent. | |
		Cheques	Notes and Coin
1839 . . .	London	93.2	6.8
1859 . . .	,, ...	96.8	3.2
1881 . . .	,, ...	98.9	1.1
1859 . . .	Provinces	47.3	52.7
1872 . . .	,, ...	68.2	31.8
1881 . . .	England and Wales	97.0	3.0
1881 . . .	New York . . .	98.7	1.3
1881 . . .	Western States . .	81.7	18.3
1881 . . .	United States . .	91.6	8.4
1881 . . .	United States Banks	94.4	5.6

The cheques paid in London and New York in one month aggregate 1270 millions sterling, which is much in excess of all the gold and silver coin in existence.

The business of the principal clearing-houses shows thus :—

| LONDON | | | NEW YORK | | |
Year	Millions, £	Per Day, £	Year	Millions, £	Per Day, £
1817	880	2,900,000	1853	261	800,000
1839	980	3,200,000	1863	3,486	11,000,009
1867–70	3,540	12,000,000	1873	5,665	18,000,000
1871–80	5,210	17,000,000	1881	7,723	25,000,000
1881	6,383	20,500,000	1886	6,750	21,500,000
1889	7,620	25,400,000	...	...	...

The clearing-houses of thirty-six cities in the United States show the following aggregate returns :—

| 1886 . . . . | 10,240 millions sterling |
| 1889 . . . . | 11,580 ,, ,, |

The latest annual returns for Continental cities are, in millions sterling, thus : Berlin, 3780 ; Paris, 2200 ; Vienna, 498.

UNITED KINGDOM

The banking power has multiplied more than tenfold since 1825, viz. :—

Year	Million £	£ per Inhabitant
1825	89	4.1
1835	101	4.0
1840	132	5.0
1850	260	9.3
1874	782	24.4
1890	910	24.0

The figures from 1825 to 1840 are taken from the *British Almanac*, those since 1850 from the *Banker's Magazine*, viz. :—

| Banks | Million £ | | |
| | Capital and Deposit | | |
	1850	1874	1890
English	207	628	871
Scotch	36	106	111
Irish	17	48	56
Total	260	782	1,038

In the interval of twenty-four years from 1850 to 1874 the increase of banking power averaged 22 millions sterling per annum, and in that of sixteen years down to 1890 it averaged 16 millions per annum. In the whole period of forty years, about £18,500,000 per annum.

In the above table capital stands for the market value of the stock. English includes foreign and colonial banks domiciled in London, as appears from the following statement for 1890 :—

	Paid Capital	Reserve	Value of Stock	Deposits	Discounts	Assets
	£	£	£	£	£	£
England	53,800,000	27,800,000	165,500,000	387,700,000	289,800,000	517,100,000
Scotland	9,100,000	5,600,000	22,900,000	88,300,000	58,000,000	113,400,000
Ireland	7,000,000	3,100,000	17,700,000	37,800,000	27,600,000	54,800,000
Colonial	43,000,000	19,100,000	77,600,000	240,700,000	303,100,000	387,000,000
Total . . .	112,900,000	55,600,000	283,700,000	754,500,000	678,500,000	1,072,300,000

The value of stock or share capital along with the deposits makes up a total banking power of 1038 millions sterling; but this includes 128 millions of deposits belonging to the Colonies, deducting which, we find the banking power of the United Kingdom is 910 millions sterling. There are in the United Kingdom 4460 banking offices, representing 175 joint-stock banks, whose stock is held among 90,000 shareholders.

The Bank of England was founded in 1694 by Rev. W. Patterson, a Scotchman, who died in poverty. The principal features of its business are indicated below.

The capital of the Bank has risen as follows :—

Year	£	Year	£
1694 . . .	1,200,000	1782 . . .	11,600,000
1708 . . .	4,400,000	1816 . . .	14,500,000
1746 . . .	10,800,000	1882 . . .	14,500,000

Year	Yearly Average			
	Issue	Deposits	Securities	Bullion
	£	£	£	£
1780	8,400,000	4,700,000	10,900,000	3,600,000
1790	10,000,000	6,200,000	10,300,000	8,600,000
1800	16,800,000	7,100,000	21,400,000	6,100,000
1810	21,000,000	12,500,000	35,400,000	3,500,000
1820	23,500,000	4,100,000	26,200,000	4,900,000
1830	20,100,000	10,800,000	24,200,000	9,200,000
1840	16,500,000	6,600,000	21,600,000	4,300,000
1850	20,400,000	18,400,000	26,000,000	16,000,000
1860	21,500,000	18,800,000	29,400,000	14,000,000
1870	24,500,000	24,200,000	29,500,000	22,300,000
1880	27,100,000	33,100,000	34,800,000	27,900,000
1882	25,700,000	28,800,000	37,100,000	20,400,000
1886	24,400,000	29,400,000	34,100,000	21,900,000
1890	24,600,000	32,300,000	36,600,000	20,800,000

The Bank first issued £10 notes in 1759, and £5 notes in 1793.* Specie payments were suspended in 1797, consequent on the war with France, and one-pound notes issued. The notes steadily depreciated till 1813, when a £5 note was worth 73s., a loss of 27 per cent., that is to say, gold was at 37 per cent. premium. From 1814 a progressive improvement took place, until specie payments were resumed in 1821. The rate of interest was as follows :—

Period	Per Cent.		
	Highest	Lowest	Average
1694–1800	6.0	3.0	4.5
1801–1850	8.0	2.5	4.5
1851–1860	10.0	2.0	4.1
1861–1870	10.0	2.0	4.2
1871–1880	9.0	2.0	3.3
1881–1888	5.8	2.0	3.3

The year which had the highest average was 1864, namely, 7½ per cent., although the rate never exceeded 9 in that year; the year with lowest average was 1852, namely, 2¼ per cent. The rate has only twice reached 10 per cent.—in the crises of 1857 and 1866. The maximum issue of notes was in March 1879, namely, 31 millions sterling, and the highest bullion reserve in September of same year, namely, £35,500,000. In the crisis of 1857 the bullion reserve fell to £6,400,000. Deposits reached a maximum in June 1879, namely, 37 millions.

* There had been, nevertheless, issued at earlier dates, as the records show, viz. :—

Year	£	Year	£
1700 . . .	860,000	1740 . . .	4,500,000
1710 . . .	600,000	1750 . . .	4,200,000
1720 . . .	2,500,000	1760 . . .	4,900,000
1730 . . .	4,200,000	1770 . . .	5,500,000

The note issue of the United Kingdom was as follows :—

	1844	1854	1864	1874	1889
	£	£	£	£	£
England	28,400,000	27,900,000	26,700,000	31,500,000	27,200,000
Scotland	3,000,000	4,100,000	4,300,000	6,000,000	5,700,000
Ireland	5,900,000	6,400,000	5,600,000	6,800,000	5,800,000
Total . . .	37,300,000	38,400,000	36,600,000	44,300,000	38,700,000

The issue and specie reserves in 1849 and 1887 were as follows :—

	1849			1887		
	Issue, £	Specie, £	Ratio of Specie	Issue, £	Specie, £	Ratio of Specie
			Per Cent.			Per Cent.
Bank of England . .	18,300,000	14,300,000	79	24,400,000	21,200,000	87
All other banks . .	13,900,000	2,600,000	19	14,200,000	6,800,000	48
Total, United Kingdom	32,200,000	16,900,000	53	38,600,000	28,000,000	73

FRANCE.

Banking power seems to have increased seventeen-fold since 1839, viz. :—

Year	Millions, £ Sterling		£ per Inhabitant
1839	16	...	0.5
1869	64	...	1.7
1881	268	...	7.3

According to the *Journal des Economistes*, the increase of banking power between 1869 and 1881 was fourfold, viz. :—

	1869, Millions, £	1881, Millions, £
Capital . . .	32	140
Deposits . . .	32	128
Total . .	64	268

The number of joint-stock banks was 20 in 1869, and 192 in 1881. There is no statement of capital and deposits in 1839, but as the turnover of the Bank of France for that year was one-fourth of the same in 1869, it is reasonable to infer that banking business had increased in the same degree. In 1881, on the authority above stated, there were in Paris 51 banks with a paid-up capital of £48,200,000.* In 1889 were published the balance-sheets of 46 banks in France with an aggregate paid-up capital of £59,000,000. The market value of the stock being £96,000,000, that is, an average premium of 63 per cent. ; the aggregate dividend was £4,600,000, or almost 8 per cent. on capital. The Bank of France was founded in 1803, capital £3,650,000 in shares of £40, with sole right of issue ; no notes to be under £4. In 1857 the capital was doubled, the Bank lending the Government 40 millions sterling and receiving permission to issue £2 notes, the limit of issue being raised to 72 millions sterling. During the Franco-German war of 1870–71 the Government demands reached 260 millions sterling, the Bank being authorised to suspend specie payments and issue small notes down to five francs. The limit of issue was ultimately raised in 1872 to 128 millions sterling, at which it now stands. The Bank has 90 branches in the Departments. Official returns show as follows :—

Year	Issue, £	Gold, Reserve, £	Gold and Silver, £	Year's Discounts, £	Bank Rate
1800	640,000	300,000	300,000	3,800,000	6.0
1810	4,000,000	800,000	1,700,000	31,700,000	4.0
1820	6,200,000	...	7,800,000	12,200,000	4.7
1830	9,000,000	100,000	5,800,000	24,700,000	4.0
1840	9,000,000	800,000	9,900,000	44,200,000	4.0
1850	19,800,000	700,000	18,300,000	46,800,000	4.0
1860	29,400,000	...	20,600,000	198,600,000	3.6
1870	62,600,000	23,400,000	45,200,000	265,000,000	4.0
1880	92,400,000	27,200,000	81,000,000	348,000,000	2.8
1889	114,800,000	53,300,000	103,800,000	340,000,000	3.2

The share of discounts done at Paris was as follows :—

	1840	1850	1860	1870	1880	1887
Paris	84.3	29.2	32.7	43.2	47.0	47.2
Branches	15.7	70.8	67.3	56.8	53.0	52.8
Total	100.0	100.0	100.0	100.0	100.0	100.0

In 1887 the average amount per bill was £30 sterling ; 1,600,000 were for sums under £4.

GERMANY

If we take the annual turn-over of the Bank of Prussia as a measure of the banking power of Germany, the latter may be set down thus :—

Year	Banking Power, Millions £ Sterling
1840	7
1850	11
1860	31
1870	125
1888	231

In 1876 Germany had 195 joint-stock banks with an aggregate capital of £85,000,000. Deposits in 1888 reached £146,000,000. This gives a total banking power of 231 millions, but the official return for 1887 gives the total of current discounts at only 164 millions sterling. The discount business is distributed thus :—

	£
Imperial Bank	25,700,000
Other banks of issue	14,500,000
Joint-stock, &c.	123,800,000
Total	164,000,000

The *Almanach de Gotha* (1888) compares the aggregate banking returns as follows :—

	1875	1880	1885	1888
	£	£	£	£
Issue	52,500,000	49,200,000	53,000,000	64,400,000
Specie reserve	33,800,000	37,000,000	38,200,000	59,400,000
Current discounts	179,000,000	157,000,000	165,000,000	164,000,000

In 1875 there were thirty-three banks of issue, but the number soon after fell to nineteen, the Reichsbank or Imperial German Bank having bought up several of them. Besides the above banking issue the Government had £6,700,000 of Treasury notes in circulation.

The average rate of discount at Berlin for eight years ending 1889 was 3.9 per cent.

The Bank of Prussia (now the Imperial Bank) was founded in 1765, capital two millions sterling ; this was doubled in 1856, the Government taking one-fourth of the stock, and giving it a charter to issue notes up to three times the amount of bullion at any time on hand. In 1875 it was reconstructed as the Imperial Bank, capital £6,000,000 in shares of £150 each ; the Government drew out its capital, and the bank agreed to pay £100,000 per annum as royalty to the Imperial Treasury. The books of the old bank down to 1870 showed the turn-over thus :—

£		£
1820 11,400,000	1850	77,100,000
1830 35,500,000	1860	208,000,000
1840 45,200,000	1870	830,000,000

The turn-over of the Imperial Bank in 1877 was 2377 millions sterling.

The Bank of Munich, capital £1,700,000, has an issue

of about one million sterling ; those of Dresden and Stuttgart less. The aggregate issue of the minor banks in December 1887 amounted to £17,100,000 ; that of the Imperial Bank to £43,300,000.

RUSSIA

It appears that the banking capital is as follows :—

	£
Imperial Bank	4,000,000
29 great banks	15,000,000
347 small banks	23,000,000
Total	42,000,000

The latest complete returns are those of 1878, which showed an aggregate of deposits reaching 64 millions sterling. This makes the total banking power 106 millions. The aggregate of discounts was 82 millions sterling. The Imperial Bank was founded in 1859, with sole right of issue. It materially serves the Government by printing inconvertible paper money, the amount of which in circulation is 123 millions sterling, and has twenty-six branches in various parts of the Empire. The balance-sheet for December 1889 was as follows :—

Liabilities, £		Assets, £	
Issue	123,000,000	Bullion	33,100,000
Capital	4,000,000	Discounts	11,500,000
Deposits	5,400,000	Government bonds	90,500,000
Sundries	27,600,000	Sundries	24,900,000
Total	160,000,000	Total	160,000,000

For Land banks and Mortgage banks, see farther on.

---

* Deposits in 1881 were made up thus :—

	£
Bank of France	34,100,000
22 large banks	81,200,000
170 small banks	12,700,000
Total	128,000,000

AUSTRIA

Official returns of all banks for 1887 were as follows :—

	Austria	Hungary	Total
	£	£	£
Paid capital . .	24,200,000	14,000,009	38,200,000
Reserve fund . .	4,000,000	3,200,000	7,200,000
Deposits . . .	65,000,000	36,600,000	101,600,000
Banking power .	93,200,000	53,800,000	147,000,000

The Austro-Hungarian Bank has the exclusive right of issue until December 1897. It was founded in 1861 ; capital £3,000,000 in shares of £60 each, with authority to issue uncovered notes up to 20 millions sterling, in notes from two shillings upwards. It was remodelled in 1880, the capital being raised to £9,000,000 sterling. The balance-sheet for 1887 showed :—

	Liabilities, £		Assets, £
Capital . . .	9,000,000	Cash . . .	22,400,000
Issue	39,100,000	Discounts .	16,000,000
Mortgages, &c.	12,900,000	Sundries .	22,600,000
Total . .	61,000,000	Total .	61,000,000

The issue and reserve have been :—

Year	Issue	Reserve	Ratio of Reserve	Premium on Gold
	£	£	Per Cent.	Per Cent.
1848 . . .	27,600,000	3,100,000	11.2	...
1870 . . .	29,700,000	11,200,000	37.0	...
1875 . . .	28,600,000	13,400,000	47.0	17
1880 . . .	32,900,000	17,300,000	52.5	21
1890 . . .	42,500,000	21,400,000	50.1	25

The discounts of this bank during eight years ending 1885 averaged £5,900,000 in Vienna, £2,600,000 in Buda-Pesth, and £5,900,000 in the provinces; total, £14,400,000. The specie reserve in July 1890 was composed of £5,000,000 gold and £16,400,000 silver. There are 52 Austrian and 144 Hungarian joint-stock banks, besides 836 People's Banks in Hungary, and 1178 in Austria.

ITALY

Banking power in 1881 amounted to 87 millions sterling, viz. :—

	Capital and Reserve Fund	Deposits	Total
Bank of Italy . .	6,900,000 }	8,700,000	19,500,000
5 chartered banks .	3,900,000 }		
113 joint-stock banks	8,200,000	17,500,000	25,700,000
362 other banks . .	4,200,000	37,300,000	41,500,000
Total . . .	23,200,000	63,500,000	86,700,000

In 1889 the capital and deposits of all banks (exclusive of Post-Office savings banks) were approximately as follows :—

	Capital, £	Deposits, £	Banking-Power, £
Chartered banks .	12,600,000	28,500,000	41,100,000
Joint-stock, &c. . .	12,400,000	54,100,000	66,500,000
Total . .	25,000,000	82,600,000	107,600,000

The current discounts of the six great banks in 1889 amounted to 31 millions sterling, or three-fourths of their banking power.

The oldest chartered bank is that of Naples, founded in 1816, which now occupies the second rank, coming next after the Bank of Italy, founded in 1850. There are four other chartered banks with right of issue.

The returns of the chartered banks in 1876 were as follows :—

Founded	Name	Capital and Reserve, £	Number of Branches	Issue, £
1850	Bank of Italy .	6,900,000	68	16,300,000
1816	,, ,, Naples	1,700,000	12	5,800,000
1857	,, ,, Tuscany	900,000	8	2,000,000
1850	,, ,, Rome .	700,000	1	1,600,000
1843	,, ,, Sicily .	400,000	8	1,500,000
1860	Tuscan Credit .	200,000	1	600,000
	Total . .	10,800,000	98	27,800,000

The Bank of Italy has a nominal capital of 10 millions sterling, of which 8 millions are paid-up, and a reserve fund of £1,600,000. It has right of issue up to 40 millions sterling, its actual issue in 1889 being £23,200,000, and its specie reserve £9,400,000, equal to 40 per cent. Taking the aggregate of discount business of the six chartered banks, the Bank of Italy stands for 40 per cent. of the total, according to returns published for 1875 and 1876, viz. :—

	Number of Bills Discounted		Amount for Twelve Months	
	1875	1876	1875	1876
			£	£
Bank of Italy .	546,000	555,000	51,600,000	46,100,000
Other 5 chartered banks }	792,000	785,000	84,100,000	72,500,000
Total .	1,338,000	1,340,000	135,700,000	118,600,000

The bills in the Bank of Italy averaged 60, those in the other banks, 36 days. The amount of each bill was £90 in the five chartered banks, £81 in the Bank of Italy, and £44 in the joint-stock banks.

In December 1889 the Bank of Italy showed :—

	£		£
Capital and reserve fund . . }	9,600,000	Issue	23,400,000
Deposits . . .	6,500,000	Specie	9,300,000

SPAIN

In June 1890 the Bank of Spain had notes in circulation to the amount of £30,000,000, against a specie reserve of £11,500,000. The deposits reached £16,200,000, and discounts £43,500,000. The Bank of Madrid has likewise issue up to £1,000,000.

PORTUGAL

Banking power is much greater than might be expected, a statement published in 1878 giving the aggregate of banks as follows :—

	£
Capital	6,000,000
Deposits	3,500,000
Banking power	9,500,000

Nevertheless usurers do a large business. In 1861 they held mortgages for six millions sterling on real estate, interest 15 to 20 per cent.

SWITZERLAND

Banking power 17 millions sterling, the returns of all Swiss banks in 1880 showing thus :—

	£
Capital	4,500,000
Deposits	12,200,000
Banking power . . .	16,700,000

Free banking is the rule, and there are thirty-four banks of issue, which show :—

Year	Issue £	Specie Reserve £
1871 . . .	1,000,000	...
1877 . . .	2,900,000	1,400,000
1885 . . .	5,000,000	3,100,000
1890 . . .	6,200,000	3,900,000

The aggregate of discounts or bills in portfolio in 1877 was £6,900,000. The paid-up capital of the thirty-four banks is £4,900,000.

HOLLAND

The Netherlands Bank was founded in 1814, with sole right of issue up to 25 millions sterling, provided the specie reserve never fell below 40 per cent., the notes to have forced currency side by side with Government Treasury notes up to £1,200,000. The capital was at first £1,280,000 in £80 shares, but it has since been raised to two millions sterling. There are fifteen branches through Holland, and the notes are from £2 upwards. The statements for 1877 and 1890 showed thus :—

	1877 £	1890 £
Issue . . .	15,800,000	17,200,000
Specie reserve .	12,800,000	10,600,000

Discounts average £9,600,000 (or 86 millions yearly), the average term of bills being under forty days. There are 287 other banks and branches, holding deposits to the sum of £4,800,000. Total banking power about 20 millions sterling.

BELGIUM

The Bank of Belgium was founded in 1850, capital two millions sterling, which has since been raised to three millions in £40 shares, with sole right of issue. It has forty branches, and circulates notes from 16s. to £40. The balance-sheets showed as follows :—

Year	Issue, £	Bullion, £	Deposits, £	Discounts, £	Rate
1851	2,000,000	1,200,000	1,000,000	1,800,000	4.0
1860	4,800,000	2,500,000	3,300,000	6,200,000	3.2
1870	8,100,000	3,800,000	3,300,000	7,800,000	3.4
1880	13,600,000	4,000,000	2,900,000	11,400,000	3.4
1890	15,200,000	4,400,000	2,700,000	12,800,000	3.6

There are fifty-two other banks, the oldest, that of Flanders, founded at Ghent in 1836. The aggregate balance-sheets for 1888 showed :—

	£		£
Paid capital . .	7,600,000	Discounts . . .	16,600,000
Reserve fund . .	3,200,000	Loans & advances	8,200,000
Deposits, &c. .	16,400,000	Sundries . . .	2,400,000
Liabilities .	27,200,000	Assets .	27,200,000

The total banking power is just 30 millions £.

SWEDEN

The Riks-bank or State Bank of Sweden was founded in 1656 by John Palmstruck, having obtained right of issue. It stopped payment four times, viz., in 1745, 1776, 1808, and 1813. The creditors received 70 per cent. in 1776, and 37 per cent. in 1813.

In 1839 the first of the Enskilda or private banks of issue was established, of which there are now 28, with 153 branches all over Sweden. They issue notes from £5 upwards, their specie reserve never falling below 35 per cent. The shareholders must be Swedes, each bank with a minimum capital of £55,000, and each shareholder individually liable up to the whole of that sum. The stock of the 28 banks in 1876 was held by 9100 persons.

The other fifteen joint-stock banks have no right of issue, and the shareholders are liable for no more than the amount of their shares.

Returns of all banks in 1889 showed as follows :—

	State Bank £	Joint-Stock, &c. £	Total £
Capital	2,200,000	4,600,000	6,800,000
Reserve fund . .	300,000	900,000	1,200,000
Issue	2,500,000	3,800,000	6,300,000
Deposits . . .	800,000	14,100,000	14,900,000
Sundries . . .	1,700,000	10,400,000	12,100,000
Liabilities .	7,500,000	33,800,000	41,300,000
Bullion	1,100,000	1,600,000	2,700,000
Treasury bills .	1,100,000	2,200,000	3,300,000
Discounts . .	3,400,000	17,400,000	20,800,000
Cash, &c. . . .	1,900,000	12,600,000	14,500,000
Assets . .	7,500,000	33,800,000	41,300,000

NORWAY

The balance-sheets for 1888 summed up thus :—

	Norges £	Joint-Stock, &c. £	Total £
Paid capital . .	700,000	800,000	1,500,000
Reserve fund . .	230,000	170,000	400,000
Deposits . . .	500,000	10,200,000	10,700,000
Banking power .	1,430,000	11,170,000	12,600,000

The discounts of the Norges or State bank average £1,200,000, that is, £9,600,000 in a year, the average term being forty-five days. The Norges was founded in 1816 with sole right of issue, capital £450,000, since raised to £700,000, with a reserve fund of £230,000. It can issue up to £3,000,000 : the actual issue in 1888 was only £2,400,000, and the bullion reserve was £2,500,000.

DENMARK

The capital and deposits of all banks in Denmark in 1886 were as follows :—

	£
Capital	2,200,000
Deposits	20,800,000
Total . . .	23,000,000

In 1813 the currency was on a bad footing, gold being at 300 per cent. premium, and the notes only worth one-fourth of their written value.

In 1814 the Bank of Copenhagen was converted into a Riks-bank, with sole right of issue up to £2,250,000, provided the specie reserve never fell below 50 per cent.; it fell to 40 per cent. in 1865, but the notes remained at par. The charter was enlarged in 1860. The balance-sheet for 1888 showed thus : issue, £4,400,000 ; bullion, £3,100,000 ; discounts about £2,000,000. The first joint-stock bank was established at Copenhagen in 1857, with a paid-up capital of £700,000 ; in 1876 its discounts averaged £1,000,000.

F

SERVIA

There are 37 banks, the principal being the National, with sole right of issue, and a paid-up capital of £800,000 sterling; the issue in 1889 was £1,200,000, specie reserve, £180,000. The others are 16 ordinary and 22 savings-banks.

AUSTRALIA

The increase of banking power is shown by the following statement of discounts and deposits :—

Year	Discounts, £	Deposits, £
1872	31,500,000	32,000,000
1881	58,400,000	59,000,000
1890	134,200,000	108,300,000

The balance-sheets for 1881 and 1890 compare as follows :—

	Deposits, £		Discounts, £	
	1881	1890	1881	1890
New South Wales .	18,800,000	34,600,000	17,200,000	39,800,000
Victoria .	20,400,000	39,300,000	18,200,000	48,900,000
Queensland .	3,400,000	9,900,000	4,000,000	17,100,000
South Australia .	4,500,000	7,300,000	5,500,000	9,000,000
New Zealand .	9,300,000	12,200,000	11,500,000	14,500,000
Tasmania .	2,300,000	4,100,000	1,600,000	3,500,000
Western Australia .	300,000	900,000	400,000	1,400,000
Total .	59,000,000	108,300,000	58,400,000	134,200,000

	1890		
	Issue	Bullion	Deposits per Inhabitant
	£	£	£ s. d.
New South Wales	1,520,000	5,200,000	38 0 0
Victoria . .	1,670,000	6,900,000	43 0 0
Queensland . .	670,000	2,200,000	25 0 0
South Australia .	450,000	1,700,000	22 0 0
New Zealand . .	880,000	2,400,000	18 10 0
Tasmania . . .	160,000	600,000	27 10 0
West Australia .	50,000	300,000	22 10 0
Total . .	5,400,000	19,300,000	29 0 0

CANADA

In 1888 there were 41 banks, an increase of 14 since 1868; the balance-sheets summed up as follows :—

	1868	1878	1888
	£	£	£
Paid capital . .	6,300,000	13,100,000	12,500,000
Deposits . . .	6,900,000	15,000,000	26,800,000
Banking power .	13,200,000	28,100,000	39,300,000
Issue	1,800,000	4,100,000	6,300,000
Discounts . . .	...	...	31,200,000

The percentages of banking business in the principal provinces were in 1881 as follows :—

Quebec	. . . . .	55.4
Ontario	. . . . .	35.1
Nova Scotia, &c. .	. . . .	9.5
Total	. . . .	100.0

Bullion reserve in 1888 was only £1,400,000, or 22 per cent. of issue. Liabilities of all the banks, £34,400,000; assets, £50,800,000, being 48 per cent. over liabilities.

SOUTH AFRICA

Banking power is about nine millions sterling, capital two millions, deposits £7,000,000. The returns of 1887 for the two colonies were :—

	Cape	Natal	Total
	£	£	£
Issue	460,000	150,000	610,000
Deposits . . .	5,950,000	1,200,000	7,150,000
Specie reserve .	1,300,000	300,000	1,600,000
Discounts . . .	6,600,000	1,200,000	7,800,000

In 1888 the issue of Cape Colony reached £660,000, and the eleven banks had an aggregate of £2,350,000 in paid-up capital and reserve fund. Assets, £10,600,000.

UNITED STATES

In 1783 the total banking capital was only £600,000; it appears to have multiplied twelve-fold in the ensuing eighteen years. We have regular statistics from 1801, as follows :—

Year	Number of Banks	Capital, £	Deposits, £	Issue, £	Specie Reserve, £	Ratio of Reserve
						Per Cent.
1801 . . .	33	7,000,000	...	...	...	...
1811 . . .	89	11,000,000	...	...	...	...
1815 . . .	208	17,100,000	...	5,800,000	3,100,000	53
1820 . . .	308	28,400,000	...	9,600,000	3,500,000	36
1830 . . .	330	30,200,000	7,500,000	9,400,000	4,200,000	45
1836 . . .	689	48,000,000	11,600,000	12,700,000	4,600,000	36
1840 . . .	901	74,400,000	10,100,000	27,600,000	8,200,000	30
1845 . . .	707	42,800,000	15,800,000	24,400,000	6,900,000	28
1850 . . .	872	47,200,000	18,400,000	18,700,000	9,200,000	49
1860 . . .	1,562	87,600,000	27,100,000	32,200,000	10,200,000	31
1870 . . .	...	130,000,000	52,800,000	43,000,000	17,500,000	41
1876 . . .	6,611	149,600,000	420,000,000	62,800,000	...	...
1882 . . .	7,448	149,200,000	432,000,000	69,400,000	...	...
1887 . . .	6,666	167,600,000	604,200,000	65,600,000	21,400,000	33
1889 . . .	6,721	180,100,000	684,100,000	34,800,000	34,300,000	99
			759,400,000	26,700,000	34,300,000	128

In the above table it is well to remember that the figures for 1870 are depreciated paper-money at 13 per cent. discount, and 10 per cent. in 1876. Discounts in 1879 comprised 3,200,000 bills for 700 millions sterling, say £220 each.

The first bank was that of Massachusetts, founded in 1740, the second that of North America in 1781, the third that of New York in 1784. The United States Bank was established at Philadelphia in 1790 with a capital of $10,000,000, having several branches, and col-lapsed in the "Wild Cat" crisis of 1837. There were 901 banks in the year 1840, but the land speculation that ensued smashed more than 200, the number falling to 691 in 1843. From the latter year steady progress was made till 1861, when the war for the Union brought a suspension of specie payments. Nevertheless rapid advance was made till 1876, when a new tax on banks caused a contraction of about 10 per cent. in the capital employed in banking, without, however, causing any decline in the amount of deposits or discounts.

From information contained in the *Statesman's Year-Book* and the official Abstract for 1890, the banking of the Union may be summed up thus :—

Banks	No.	Capital	Reserve Fund	Deposits	Discounts
		£	£	£	£
National	3,194	125,000,000	41,000,000	317,000,000	378,000,000
State	1,403	32,200,000	11,800,000	85,400,000	...
Private	1,323	19,600,000	10,700,000	73,100,000	...
Savings	801	3,300,000	27,500,000	283,900,000	...
Total . .	6,721	180,100,000	91,000,000	759,400,000	...

The above shows a total banking power of 1030 millions sterling.
The National banks showed the following balance-sheets :—

	Liabilities				Assets	
	1880	1889			1880	1889
	£	£			£	£
Capital	130,000,000	166,000,000	Discounts		216,000,000	378,000,000
Issue	66,000,000	26,700,000	Bullion		20,800,000	34,000,000
Deposits	185,000,000	317,000,000	Bonds		75,000,000	30,400,000
Sundries	57,000,000	114,300,000	Sundries		126,200,000	181,600,000
Total . .	438,000,000	624,000,000	Total . .		438,000,000	624,000,000

In the above table capital includes also reserve fund.

The ratio of banking power to population was as follows :—

Year	Banking Power	Population	Banking Power per Head
	£	£	£
1801 . .	7,000,000	5,300,000	1.3
1820 . .	35,900,000	9,600,000	3.8
1840 . .	90,200,000	17,100,000	5.3
1860 . .	140,400,000	31,400,000	4.4
1876 . .	581,600,000	44,400,000	13.1
1889 . .	1,030,500,000	64,000,000	16.1

The distribution of banking power, according to official returns, was :—

States	Million, £ Sterling		
	1850	1860	1880
New England . .	18	34	162
Middle . . .	33	63	274
Southern . .	19	33	35
Western . .	4	10	125
Total .	74	140	596

No other than National banks have right of issue, and they compare with the earlier *chartered* banks of issue in 1811-30 as follows :—

Year	Capital	Issue	Deposit
	£	£	£
1811	5,100,000	2,700,000	...
1820	13,000,000	5,500,000	4,100,000
1830	19,800,000	8,100,000	6,800,000
1889	125,000,000	26,700,000	317,000,000

In 1880 the shares of the National Banks were held by 208,000 persons, showing an average banking capital of £700 per shareholder, against £800 in Great Britain. Of 7 million shares, only 26,000 were held in Europe, of which 7000 in Great Britain.

MEXICO

The Banco Nacional, founded in 1881, has a nominal capital of 20 million dollars or £3,000,000 sterling, of which only 40 per cent. is paid up. Its issue in December 1888 was 14 millions, say £2,100,000 sterling, and balance-sheet 48 millions, say £7,200,000. The Bank of London and Mexico has a capital of £300,000, and no issue ; balance-sheet, £1,500,000. There are various land-banks.

CHILE

There are nineteen banks of issue, aggregate capital 23 million dollars, say £2,500,000 ; issue, 17 millions, or £1,800,000. The balance-sheets of these banks in December 1886 showed :—

Bank of	Dollars	£ Sterling
Valparaiso . . .	83,000,000	9,100,000
Chile . . .	66,000,000	7,200,000
Guarantees . . .	50,000,000	5,500,000
Edwards . . .	16,500,000	1,800,000
Fifteen others . . .	68,500,000	7,500,000
Total . .	284,000,000	31,100,000

BRAZIL

In December 1886 there were sixteen banks, whose balance-sheets showed as follows :—

Bank	£	Bank	£
Brazil .	26,900,000	London and Brazil	3,100,000
Rural .	7,400,000	English .	2,200,000
Commercial	5,500,000	International	2,000,000
Industrial .	3,300,000	Nine others .	11,600,000

Summing up a total of 62 millions sterling. The Bank of Brazil was remodelled in 1872, with a paid-up capital of £3,600,000 in shares of £22 each; it has a reserve fund of £500,000, and a right of issue until December 1900 of £3,000,000 sterling; it must always lend up to 70 per cent. of its capital to planters, at 6 per cent. annual interest.

JAPAN

In December 1889 were published the accounts of 100 National Banks, with an aggregate capital of £7,100,000, the Tokio Bank standing for £3,500,000. Of the total number, 69 paid dividends ranging from 10 to 20 per cent., and 31 paid less than 10 per cent.

ARGENTINA

In 1884 there were six banks at Buenos Ayres, with an aggregate banking power of 35 millions sterling, viz, :—

	Capital, £	Deposits, £	Total, £
B. of Buenos Ayres	6,600,000	13,400,000	20,000,000
National	4,100,000	2,800,000	6,900,000
Four foreign banks	4,400,000	3,600,000	8,000,000
Total . .	15,100,000	19,800,000	34,900,000

In 1885 specie payments were suspended, and a number of banks sprung up issuing forced currency notes. In September 1889 there were 52 banks in Buenos Ayres and the other provinces of Argentina, with an aggregate capital of 185 million dollars, nominally 37 millions sterling, but the currency dollar having lost 67 cents of its value, the capital (in July 1890) is only equal to 12 millions sterling. Deposits in like manner were nominally close on 50 millions sterling, equivalent to 17 millions in gold. Banking power is therefore about 29 millions. In September 1889 the aggregate balance-sheets of 24 banks (nothing being stated of the other 28) showed as follows :—

	Gold, $	Paper, $	Nominal Value in £ Sterling	Approximate Real Value in 1890, £
Capital . .	8,500,000	149,600,000	31,600,000	10,500,000
Reserve fund	1,600,000	2,200,000	700,000	200,000
Deposits . .	66,300,000	166,000,000	46,400,000	15,500,000
Discounts .	85,200,000	253,700,000	68,000,000	22,700,000
Cash . . .	28,700,000	28,300,000	10,400,000	3,500,000

Paper issue has risen as follows :—

Year	Million $	Real Value Reduced to Gold, £
1836	15,000,000	360,000
1840	51,000,000	300,000
1852	125,000,000	1,250,000
1877	711,000,000	4,500,000
1884	56,000,000	11,200,000
1890	270,000,000	18,000,000

In 1881 the old currency was called in and converted, one new dollar being given for 25 old ones. Another

issue called Cedulas is described under *Land Banks*, p. 85.

URUGUAY

Banking power is about 8 millions sterling, discounts in June 1889 showing more or less as follows :—

	£
National Bank	3,800,000
Four foreign banks . . .	4,300,000
Total	8,100,000

Issue and reserve of specie were as follows :—

	Issue, £		Reserve of Specie, £
	1882	1889	1889
National Bank .	...	1,700,000	1,100,000
All other banks .	1,100,000	1,400,000	1,900,000
Total . .	1,100,000	3,100,000	3,000,000

The National Bank suspended specie payments in June 1890.

LAND BANKS

In many countries there are institutions called Land Banks or Mortgage Banks for lending money or debentures on real estate.

France.—The Credit Foncier, founded in 1852, capital £3,600,000, has the power to issue debentures up to £72,000,000. The issue was as follows :—

Year	Issue, £	No. of Mortgages	Average, £
1856	3,050,000	1,390	2,100
1866	31,170,000	12,180	2,500
1873	46,480,000	20,116	2,300

Deducting the amount redeemed, the actual issue in 1873 was £34,700,000. The Credit Agricole, founded in 1860, has a paid-up capital of £800,000; issue outstanding in 1873 about 15 millions sterling.

Germany.—The Bank of Munich has a Mortgage branch, being compelled by law to keep £1,200,000 always lent out to agriculturists at 4 per cent. per annum, the mortgage never to exceed 50 per cent. of the value of the farm. In 1864 it commenced to issue debentures bearing 4½ per cent. interest, the borrower having also to pay ½ per cent. sinking-fund. The borrower in selling these debentures gets barely 90 per cent. cash. In 1871 the issue had reached £5,000,000. The Bank of Nuremberg also grants loans on mortgage. Saxony has four Land Banks of this description, the borrower paying 5 per cent. for forty-one years, when the loan is extinct. The Ritter's Bank of Leipzig is a mutual landowner's bank, making advances only to its members, interest 4 per cent. The Wurtemburg Land Bank makes advances to small proprietors at 6 per cent., including sinking-fund, the loan becoming extinct in twenty-five years. The Mortgage Bank of Prussia, founded in 1810, issues 4 per cent. debentures; the issue and the market price were as follows :—

Year	Issue, £	Maximum	Minimum	Average Price
1815	9,500,000	103	64	84
1835	14,100,000	107	101	104
1845	16,500,000	105	94	100
1868	28,800,000	84	78	81

The above was mainly for impoverished noblemen. The Rent-charge Bank, founded in 1811, had issued to peasant proprietors debentures up to 13 millions sterling prior to 1870; these bore 4 per cent. interest, and sold in the market at 87 per cent. of nominal value; outstanding £11,500,000. The amount advanced on mortgage by banks and private individuals in 1870 was officially stated thus :—

	£
Prussia	190,000,000
Bavaria	25,000,000
Saxony	26,000,000
Wurtemburg	10,000,000
Small States . . .	22,000,000
Total . .	273,000,000

In 1837 it was found that many of the nobles had mortgaged their estates beyond their value, in some cases up to 114 per cent. From 1858 to 1867 the authorities sold off 34,000 bankrupt estates, which reduced the sum due by Prussian noblemen to the Land-banks to 25 millions sterling. The Mortgage Bank of Bavaria, distinct from the Munich Bank, was founded in 1848, to enable the peasants to buy their lands. In twenty-two years, down to 1870, the debentures issued by it reached 18½ millions sterling, the amount outstanding being £15,300,000. In 1880 the Land-banks of Germany had an aggregate capital of 18 millions sterling, and the debentures in circulation summed up 80 millions sterling.

Russia.—The Imperial Bank as early as 1859 had advanced 30 millions sterling on mortgage to the nobles, who owed altogether 60 millions sterling. Subsequently a separate office or bank was started as a Mortgage-bank, and in December 1889 the amount of existing loans on mortgage was 196 million roubles, nominally £31,000,000, but at the present exchange only £19,600,000. Moreover, a Land-bank was founded about 1861 to help the peasants to buy their lands from the nobles. According to Sir A. Buchanan, the peasants owed 85 millions sterling in 1875; this was perhaps an error, as the *Statesman's Year-Book* gives the following :—" Up to December 1889, the Land-bank lent 58 million roubles (say £5,800,000) to 234,000 peasants towards purchasing 4,240,000 acres, valued at £7,300,000, the peasants finding the remaining £1,500,000. The peasants did not buy individually, but in 7240 villages or associations. The above purchases only refer to Beggar's Lots (see *Land*), as the peasants in ten years, ending 1870, became masters of 35,000,000 acres.

Norway.—The Hypothek Bank was founded in 1852 to lend on mortgage; it belongs to the State, and has a capital of £600,000. The outstanding loans in December 1888 reached £4,600,000, and the bonds in circulation £4,200,000.

Austria.—The Bank of Vienna in 1878 held mortgages on real estate for £10,300,000, of which £7,900,000 was on lands. In 1886 the various banks held mortgages to the amount of £65,000,000.

Italy.—The Credito Fondiaro was founded in 1866 at Naples, with branches at Milan, &c., to make advances in 5 per cent. debentures on real estate, no loan to exceed £20,000, nor to be for more than 50 per cent. of the value of the property. The borrower pays also 1 per cent. sinking-fund; the debentures usually sell about 80 per cent. of nominal value. Issue averages £500,000 per annum. In 1870 two other Land-banks were founded, the Agricola Italiana and Agricola Nazionale. The amount of all mortgages held by these Land-banks in 1887 was £28,000,000 sterling.

Spain and Portugal.—There are no Land-banks in Spain; usurers have a free field. Murcia is mortgaged up to 65 per cent. of its value, and the usurers get 10 per cent. of the crops. The Credito Portuguez was founded in 1866 to rescue Portuguese landowners from usurers; it lends money at 6 per cent. in debentures, the advances down to 1869 reaching £1,100,000 on 1630 estates of distressed noblemen. In 1861 the mortgages then held in Portugal were :—

Loans by	Amount, £	Interest
Usurers . . .	6,300,000	15 per cent.
Religious houses .	1,600,000	5 ,,
Total . .	7,900,000	...

Sweden.—The General Mortgage Bank, founded in 1861, has 47,000 shareholders, the qualification being the possession of property worth £50, or upwards. In 1877, debentures had been issued to the amount of 13½ millions sterling, of which 2 millions had been redeemed. Borrowers pay 6 per cent. per annum, which cancels the loan in sixty years, the bank reserving ¼ per cent. for expenses, which, however, do not exceed 15d. per £100. The debentures rarely fall below 100; the reserve fund is £900,000, one-half in Government stock. The House-Mortgage Bank is on similar principles, applicable to house property.

Denmark.—The Landman's Bank advances on mortgages of land in 4 per cent. debentures, which sell in the market at 85 or 90 per cent. of their nominal value. Sinking-fund 1 per cent.; borrowers pay altogether 5 per cent.

Switzerland.—There are no distinct Land-banks; mortgages on land amount to one-fourth the estimated value.

Brazil.—The Rural Mortgage Bank was established in 1853 to make loans to planters; capital £900,000, reserve fund £400,000 sterling. The Bank of Brazil is, moreover, by its charter obliged to have always £2,600,000 in similar loans at 6 per cent. annual interest.

Chile.—There are several Mortgage-banks which issue Cedulas on houses and lands. The amount of these Cedulas in 1888 was 76 millions, say £8,300,000 sterling.

Argentina.—The Mortgage Bank of Buenos Ayres was founded in 1873, to make advances in 6 per cent. debentures up to half the value of the houses or lands mortgaged, the Bank charging 1 per cent. commission, its debentures being, moreover, guaranteed by the State. The National Mortgage Bank was established on like principles in 1886. Similar banks have been founded in Santa Fé and other provinces.

The balance-sheets for December 1888 showed as follows :—

	Issued	Redeemed	Balance Outstanding
	£	£	£
Mortgage Bank of Buenos Ayres .	47,000,000	11,300,000	35,700,000
National Mortgage Bank	15,000,000	600,000	14,400,000
Total . .	62,000,000	11,900,000	50,100,000

The above was the nominal amount, but the currency was at 33 per cent. discount. The real value of debentures in circulation was about £33,500,000.

In December 1889 the actual Cedulas in circulation were approximately :—

	Millions	Nominal Value	At Current Exchange
	$	£	£
National Mortgage Bank	120	24,000,000	10,000,000
Buenos Ayres Mortgage Bank	280	56,000,000	23,000,000
Total . .	400	80,000,000	33,000,000

SAVINGS-BANKS

The first was established at Brunswick in 1765, the second at Hamburg in 1778. Mrs. Wakefield founded one in England in 1803. The first in France was in 1818 at Paris. In 1835 we find the following returns of France, Vienna, and Prague :—

	Depositors	Amount, £
France	122,000	2,500,000
Vienna . . .	57,000	1,400,000
Prague . . .	18,000	520,000

From this time they began to grow rapidly in many countries. In the following table, 1889 includes latest information as regards some countries for which we have no particulars for that year :—

	1840	1850	1860	1870	1889
	£	£	£	£	£
United Kingdom	23,400,000	30,100,000	41,300,000	53,100,000	107,200,000
France	7,600,000	5,400,000	15,100,000	27,400,000	111,800,000
Prussia	4,000,000	5,500,000	14,500,000	76,600,000	144,600,000
Russia	...	...	1,100,000	2,400,000	7,200,000
Austria	3,000,000	4,500,000	28,000,000	40,300,000	122,600,000
Italy	700,000	1,600,000	12,400,000	14,800,000	69,200,000
Switzerland	...	700,000	5,100,000	11,600,000	23,700,000
Spain	...	...	200,000	1,000,000	2,000,000
Belgium and Holland . . .	...	1,800,000	2,200,000	4,500,000	16,400,000
Scandinavia	...	3,100,000	7,200,000	14,600,000	44,100,000
Europe . . .	38,700,000	52,700,000	127,100,000	246,300,000	648,800,000

	Number of Depositors			Number per 1000 Inhabitants		
	1850	1870	1882	1850	1872	1882
United Kingdom . .	1,060,000	2,620,000	3,715,000	40	85	95
France . . .	586,000	2,050,000	4,150,000	16	57	110
Germany . . .	530,000	2,200,000	5,000,000	16	55	111
Russia . . .	...	150,000	200,000	...	2	2
Austria . . .	160,000	1,300,000	1,850,000	5	37	48
Italy . . .	170,000	570,000	1,970,000	3	23	66
Belgium and Holland .	40,000	180,000	310,000	5	20	31
Switzerland . .	52,000	512,000	1,080,000	20	195	360
Scandinavia . .	150,000	900,000	1,600,000	25	110	180
Europe . . .	2,748,000	10,482,000	19,875,000	12	40	67

United Kingdom.—The savings-banks of the United Kingdom have shown as follows :—

Year	Amount of Deposits, £			Shillings per Inhabitant		
	England	Scotland	Ireland	England	Scotland	Ireland
	£	£	£			
1830	12,600,000	...	910,000	18	...	2
1840	20,700,000	520,000	2,200,000	25	4	5
1850	27,680,000	1,080,000	1,360,000	30	7	4
1860	36,700,000	2,410,000	2,140,000	37	16	7
1870	46,230,000	4,130,000	2,690,000	40	25	10
1880	66,900,000	7,200,000	3,700,000	52	39	15
1888	88,600,000	10,400,000	5,300,000	62	50	22

France.—The official returns show as follows :—

Year	Depositors	Amount, £
1835	80,000	1,700,000
1840	311,000	6,800,000
1850	586,000	3,000,000
1860	1,126,000	13,600,000
1870	2,050,000	27,400,000
1880	3,508,000	46,200,000
1886	4,937,000	88,400,000
1888	6,492,000	111,800,000

In 1888 the Post-Office savings-banks showed £12,000,000 in deposits, the average to each depositor

being £9, 4s. ; the private savings-banks £99,800,000, average £18, 6s.

Russia.—In 1888 the Government savings-banks showed £820,000 at St. Petersburg, £640,000 at Moscow, and £7,200,000 for the whole Empire.

Italy.—The number of depositors and amount showed :—

Year	Depositors	Amount, £
1850	170,000	2,200,000
1870	571,000	14,800,000
1881	1,970,000	33,600,000
1888	3,510,000	69,200,000

The returns for 1887 make up as follows :—

	Offices	Depositors	Deposits, £
Post-office . . .	4,237	1,571,000	9,600,000
Ordinary . . .	395	1,295,000	40,300,000
Co-operative . .	619	390,000	13,800,000
Total . .	5,251	3,256,000	63,700,000

Austria.—Depositors and amount are shown approximately as follows :—

Year	Depositors	Amount, £
1850	160,000	19,600,000
1870	1,300,000	40,300,000
1881	1,850,000	85,100,000
1887	3,017,000	122,600,000

The returns for 1887 give the following aggregates (taking the florin at 20 pence) :—

	Depositors	Amount, £		Depositors	Amount, £
Austria . . .	2,629,000	91,300,000	Post-office . . .	722,000	5,200,000
Hungary . . .	584,000	31,300,000	Ordinary . . .	2,491,000	117,400,000
Total . .	3,213,000	122,600,000	Total . .	3,213,000	122,600,000

Belgium.—The first was opened in 1835, in which year the deposits reached £720,000. Subsequent returns are as follows :—

Year		Depositors	Amount, £
1840	. . .	38,500	2,060,000
1850	. . .	29,500	1,100,000
1860	. . .	32,400	1,050,000
1870	. . .	52,000	800,000
1880	. . .	200,600	5,040,000
1888	. . .	599,000	10,400,000

The above does not include People's Banks, which showed as follows :—

Year	Capital, £	Discounts, £	Deposits, £
1861 . . .	1,400,000	300,000	200,000
1870 . . .	2,700,000	600,000	900,000
1880 . . .	3,200,000	800,000	1,200,000
1888 . . .	2,800,000	900,000	1,300,000

Holland.—The returns of 1888 for State savings-banks, and of 1885 for private ones, sum up thus :—

	Depositors	Amount, £
State	202,000	1,100,000
Private . . .	270,000	3,900,000
Total .	472,000	5,000,000

In 1888 there were 499,000 depositors, holding a total of £5,980,000.

Scandinavia.—The returns for 1886–88 were as follows :—

	Depositors	Amount, £
Denmark . . .	697,000	20,900,000
Sweden . . .	1,010,000	13,700,000
Norway . . .	452,000	10,400,000
Total .	2,159,000	44,100,000

United States.—No distinct returns were kept before 1873 ; the returns since then show as follows :—

Year		Depositors	Amount, £
1873	. . .	2,190,000	135,200,000
1880	. . .	2,528,000	185,400,000
1884	. . .	3,071,000	227,800,000
1889	. . .	4,022,000	283,900,000

The following table shows the States where savings banks are most in use (1889) :—

	Depositors	Amount, £	Depositors per 100 Inhab.	Amount per Inhabitant, £
New York . .	1,363,000	109,000,000	20	16.4
Massachusetts	983,000	65,500,000	42	26.5
Connecticut .	288,000	22,000,000	35	27.0
California . .	114,000	18,100,000	10	15.6
Pennsylvania .	213,000	13,500,000	4	2.4
N. Hampshire	145,000	12,000,000	31	25.5
Rhode Island .	123,000	12,100,000	34	33.0
Maine . . .	125,000	8,600,000	15	10.1
Maryland . .	123,000	7,100,000	10	5.8
New Jersey .	115,000	6,400,000	8	4.2
Various . . .	430,000	9,600,000	...	...
Total . .	4,022,000	283,900,000	6	4.4

Canada.—The deposits were as follow :—

Year	Sum		1887
	£		£
1867	300,000	Ontario	3,200,000
1879	1,900,000	Quebec	730,000
1887	4,060,000	Nova Scotia, &c.	130,000

Australia.—In 1888 the returns were as follows :—

	Depositors	Amount, £	Depositors per 100 Inhab.	Amount per Inhabitant, £
New South Wales	128,000	4,040,000	12	3.7
Victoria . . .	248,000	4,880,000	23	4.5
Queensland . .	43,000	1,610,000	11	4.2
South Australia .	62,000	1,760,000	20	5.6
New Zealand . .	103,000	2,690,000	17	4.4
Tasmania . . .	23,000	470,000	16	3.2
Western Australia	3,000	30,000	7	0.7
Total . .	610,000	15,480,000	17	4.2

The aggregate of the seven colonies was as follows :—

Year	Depositors	Amount, £	Depositors per 100 Inhabitants	Amount per Inhabitant, £
1861	28,800	1,360,000	2	1.1
1871	114,000	3,660,000	6	1.9
1881	308,000	9,420,000	11	3.3
1888	610,000	15,480,000	17	4.2

India.—The official returns for 1884 and 1888 (taking the rupee at 18 pence) were :—

	1884	1888	1888		
				No.	Amount
					£
Depositors	204,000	332,000	Europeans	65,000	1,100,000
Amount, £	3,010,000	4,940,000	Natives	267,000	3,840,000

There are 6150 savings-banks, of which 5960 belong to the Post-Office.

BANKRUPTCY

The averages for the years 1879–81 in five principal countries were :—

	No. of Failures	Amount	Ratio to Commerce
		£	Per Cent.
United Kingdom .	13,720	31,300,000	5½
France	5,580	10,200,000	3
Austria	1,414	1,820,000	1½
United States . .	5,715	16,300,000	5½
Canada	920	2,730,000	8

UNITED KINGDOM

Wholesale failures in the years 1880–89 were as follows :—

Year	London	Provinces	Scotland	Ireland	Total
1880	385	972	99	22	1,478
1882	399	823	78	14	1,314
1883	377	885	83	16	1,361
1889	193	563	51	11	818

Wholesale and retail for nineteen years in England and Wales showed thus :—

Years	Annual Average		Average per Failure, £	Assets, Annual Average, £	Percentage of Assets
	Number	Sum, £			
1870–72	6,039	15,300,000	2,500	4,600,000	30
1873–75	7,766	21,600,000	2,800	6,300,000	29
1876–78	10,077	23,500,000	2,300	7,100,000	30
1879–81	11,052	21,200,000	1,930	6,500,000	31
1882–84	7,263	18,100,000	2,500	5,200,000	29
1885–88	4,587	8,300,000	1,800	2,800,000	33

The ratio of assets for the years 1870 and 1881 in England and Wales were :—

Assets	Number		Percentage	
	1870	1881	1870	1881
Under 5 per cent. .	123	963	7	25
5–25 ,, .	833	2,256	44	58
25–40 ,, .	316	349	17	9
Over 40 ,, .	616	322	32	8
Total . .	1,888	3,890	100	100

From a judicial report in 1881 are taken the following :—

Year	No. of Cases	Amount	Assets	Ratio of Assets
		£	£	Per Cent.
1870 . . .	5,002	17,400,000	5,300,000	30
1880 . . .	10,298	16,200,000	4,600,000	28
Average 10 years	9,515	20,300,000	6,200,000	31

In eight years ending 1888 the bankruptcies averaged thus : liabilities, £13,100,000 ; assets, £3,300,000.

The cases liquidated in court showed that law-costs absorbed 40 per cent. of assets.

In the eighteenth century the number of bankruptcies in England averaged 177 yearly down to 1750, and 460 in the fifty years following.

In Scotland the bankruptcies were :—

Period	Annual Average		Average per Failure, £	Percentage of Assets
	No.	Amount, £		
1874–80	603	1,360,000	2,270	46
1881–84	412	6,300,000	15,200	11
1885–88	425	1,450,000	3,400	46
15 years	505	2,690,000	5,300	25

Some of the above were for bankruptcies of previous years, liquidated as above.

The aggregate of business in Ireland that passed through the Court of Bankruptcy in five years ending 1880 was as follows :—

Liabilities . . 2,750,000 | Law-costs . . . 245,000
Assets . . . . 805,000 | To creditors . . 560,000

The average dividend, therefore, was 20 per cent. on the liabilities. Law-costs absorbed 30 per cent. of the assets.

Irish bankruptcy business from 1880 to 1887 showed :—

		Per Annum
Number of bankruptcies	4,124	516
Liabilities, £ . .	9,700,000	1,210,000

This gives an average of £2300 per failure.

France.—Official returns give the following :—

Years	Annual Average	
	No. of Failures	Ratio of Assets
		Per Cent.
1840–50 . . .	3,480	31
1860–70 . . .	5,120	21
1878–81 . . .	5,580	17
1881–84 . . .	7,135	...
1885	8,024	25

The following table shows the number of failures compared with that of merchants and traders :—

Year	No. of Merchants	Failed	Ratio to Merchants	Failures over £2000
			Per Cent.	Per Cent.
1844 . . .	1,414,000	3,011	2.1	52
1854 . . .	1,420,000	3,691	2.6	48
1864 . . .	1,410,000	4,642	3.3	43
1874 . . .	1,606,000	5,508	3.4	54

Not only has the ratio of failures risen, but also the average amount per failure.

The following table is for fourteen years ending 1885 :—

Period	Annual Average		
	No. of Failures	Amount, £	Amount per Failure, £
1872–75 . . .	5,442	9,200,000	1,700
1876–80 . . .	5,832	10,600,000	1,800
1881–84 . . .	7,135	10,700,000	1,500
1885	8,024	14,200,000	1,750

Austria.—The annual number of bankruptcies was as follows :—

1871–75	. . . . . .	909
1876–80	. . . . . .	1,304
1881–83	. . . . . .	1,017

No returns as to liabilities or assets.

Germany.—The number of bankruptcies in 1886 was 5912, against 5905 in 1882; amount not stated.

Australia.—There are no returns for Western Australia. The aggregate for the other six colonies showed as follows :—

Year	Failures	Liabilities	Assets	Ratio of Assets
		£	£	Per Cent.
1861 . . .	2,037	2,000,000	1,095,000	55
1871 . . .	2,257	1,490,000	695,000	47
1881 . . .	3,632	1,720,000	1,230,000	72
1888 . . .	2,769	2,260,000	1,510,000	67

The returns for 1888 were as follows :—

	Failures	Liabilities	Assets	Ratio of Assets
		£	£	PerCent.
N. S. Wales . .	851	660,000	460,000	70
Victoria . . .	479	350,000	185,000	53
Queensland . .	249	260,000	120,000	46
South Australia .	219	80,000	60,000	75
New Zealand . .	881	865,000	670,000	77
Tasmania . . .	90	45,000	15,000	33
Total . .	2,769	2,260,000	1,510,000	67

UNITED STATES

The annual averages have been as follows since 1857 :—

Period	Number of Failures	Amount, £	Amount per Failure, £
1857–60 . . .	3,262	23,500,000	7,100
1861–65 . . .	1,830	10,600,000	5,800
1866–69 . . .	2,425	15,100,000	6,200
1870–75 . . .	4,882	30,500,000	6,100
1876–80 . , .	7,970	32,400,000	4,100
1881–86 . . .	8,823	28,300,000	3,200
1889 . . .	11,719	29,200,000	2,400

CANADA

Years	Number	Amount, £	Average, £
1879–80 . . .	1,060	3,080,000	3,000
1881–82 . . .	625	1,450,000	2,300
1885	1,246	1,920,000	1,600
1886	1,186	2,320,000	2,000

REMARKABLE CRISES

1763. Amsterdam, originating with the house of De Neufville. Failures—20 in Holland, 20 in England, 37 in Hamburg
1773. Failures in Holland exceeding 10 millions
1799. Hamburg, 82 failures, 2 millions.
1814. England, 240 banks suspended
1825. Manchester, failures 2 millions
1831. Calcutta, failures 15 millions.
1837. United States "Wild Cat" crisis; all banks closed.
1839. Bank of England saved by Bank of France. Severe also in France, where 93 companies failed for 6 millions.
1844. England. State loans to merchants.
1847. England, failures 20 millions; discount 13 per cent.
1857. United States, 7200 houses failed for 111 millions.
1866. London, Overend-Gurney; failures 100 millions.

BANQUET

One of the greatest on record was that given at Paris by President Carnot, 19th July 1889, to 15,000 mayors, senators, deputies, and other officials. There were 195 cooks, 1050 waiters, 80,000 plates, 30,000 loaves, 23,000 bottles of wine, 600 gallons soup, 3 tons fish, 32 cwts. beef, and 7200 poultry, with 6 tons ice.

BATHS

Baths.—The use of baths among the working-classes in London is shown by the receipts thus: 1850, £9,800; 1860, £25,000; 1880, £41,000.

BATTLES

	Men Engaged	Hors de Combat	Per Cent.
Agincourt . .	62,000	11,400	18
Alma	103,000	8,400	8
Bannockburn .	135,000	38,000	28
Borodino . . .	250,000	78,000	31
Cannæ	146,000	52,000	34
Cressy	117,000	31,200	27
Gravelotte . .	396,000	62,000	16
Sadowa . . .	291,000	33,000	11
Thrasymene . .	65,000	17,000	27
Waterloo . . .	221,000	51,000	23

Date	Battle	Won by	Lost by	Went into Action		Losses of		Per Cent. of Loss	
				Victors	Van-quished	Victors	Van-quished	Victors	Van-quished
1862 . . .	Antietam	Federals	Confederates	87,000	97,000	11,000	20,000	13	20
1805 . . .	Austerlitz	French	Austrians	70,000	84,000	12,000	26,000	17	31
1813 . . .	Bautzen	French	Prussians	150,000	110,000	28,000	24,000	18	21
1863 . . .	Gettysburg	Federals	Confederates	117,000	68,000	17,000	27,000	14	40
1870 . . .	Gravelotte	Germans	French	270,000	126,000	35,000	27,000	13	22
1806 . . .	Jena	French	Prussians	40,000	70,000	4,000	27,000	10	39
1813 . . .	Leipzig	Germans	French	300,000	171,000	47,000	60,000	16	36
1859 . . .	Magenta	French	Austrians	47,000	61,000	5,000	10,000	11	17
1800 . . .	Marengo	French	Austrians	28,000	40,000	7,000	12,000	25	30
1812 . . .	Moscow	French	Russians	120,000	125,000	23,000	51,000	19	40
1866 . . .	Sadowa	Prussians	Austrians	141,000	150,000	9,000	24,000	7	17
1870 . . .	Sedan	Prussians	French	190,000	124,000	9,000	38,000	5	31
1859 . . .	Solferino	French	Austrians	124,000	163,000	15,000	22,000	12	14
1809 . . .	Wagram	French	Austrians	140,000	90,000	32,000	25,000	22	28
1815 . . .	Waterloo	British	French	101,000	120,000	22,000	29,000	22	24

BEER

Table of yearly production and consumption (1886–89) :—

	Number of Breweries	Millions of Gallons		Value of Beer Produced, £
		Produced	Consumed	
U. Kingdom .	16,114	1,040	1,022	69,000,000
France . . .	2,722	186	193	12,000,000
Germany . .	26,458	930	910	62,000,000
Russia . . .	1,592	92	92	6,200,000
Austria . . .	1,962	290	280	19,000,000
Italy	135	4	5	300,000
Switzerland .	417	20	21	1,300,000
Belgium . .	1,248	204	206	14,000,000
Holland . .	560	32	32	2,100,000
Denmark . .	441	25	25	1,600,000
Sweden . . .	253	21	21	1,400,000
Norway . . .	56	13	13	900,000
Europe . . .	51,958	2,857	2,820	189,800,000
United States .	3,293	753	780	40,000,000
Australia . .	187	18	22	1,200,000
India . . .	24	3	5	200,000
Total . .	55,462	3,631	3,627	231,200,000

The breweries of the world consume yearly 4 million tons of barley (say 160 million bushels), and 70,000 tons of hops. Germany has an annual surplus of 8000 tons of hops, Austria 3000, but England and France have to import some. British breweries consume 56 million bushels barley, and 70,000 tons sugar.

RETROSPECT OF PRODUCTION

	Millions of Gallons						
	United Kingdom	France	Germany	Austria	Belgium	United States	Total
1840	650	92	500	160	100	23	1,525
1850	710	106	600	180	120	36	1,752
1860	770	140	700	200	140	100	2,050
1870	980	150	800	220	153	204	2,507
1880	1,020	180	815	240	200	413	2,868
1887	1,040	186	930	290	204	612	3,262

The figures for Germany, Austria, and Belgium previous to 1870 are conjectural.

ENGLAND AND WALES

The annual consumption in England and Wales has been :—

Period	Million Gallons	Per Inhab.	Period	Million Gallons	Per Inhab.
1660-1700	255	44	1801-1830	335	30
1701-1750	215	35	1831-1860	560	33
1751-1800	252	32	1861-1880	835	36

The price per gallon during 680 years has ruled thus :—

Period	Pence	Period	Pence
1201-1300	3	1701-1800	11
1301-1600	5	1801-1880	17
1601-1700	6	1882	20

The above are according to weight of silver, but the nominal price was, for example, in the thirteenth century one penny.

The strength varies as follows :—

	Alcohol		Bushels of Malt per Barrel
Burton ale	8.2	...	4.5
Bass's ale	8.4	...	4.2
Edinburgh ale	4.4	...	1.8
Guinness's ale	6.8	...	2.9
London porter	4.1	...	1.9
London beer	3.9	...	1.7
Lager beer	3.2	...	1.5

The annual consumption of malt in England has been as follows :—

Period	Bushels	Duty, Pence	Bushels per Inhabitant
1700-20	19.2	6	3.4
1720-50	26.7	6	4.2
1760-80	27.6	9	3.6
1790-1800	18.0	16	2.1
1810-20	23.7	50	2.2
1830-50	32.7	31	2.1
1850-70	39.8	31	1.9

In 1888 the consumption was about 48 million bushels in England, 3 millions in Scotland, and 5 millions in Ireland, total 56 millions, or two bushels per barrel of beer.

GERMANY (1885)

	Number of Breweries	Product, Gallons Beer	Gallons per Inhabitant
Prussia	7,691	540,000,000	19.2
Bavaria	5,395	277,000,000	50.5
Wurtemburg	7,381	66,000,000	33.0
Other States	4,539	47,000,000	4.3
Total	25,006	930,000,000	...

The statistics of German breweries showed as follows :—

Year	Beer, Gallons	Tons Grain Consumed	Beer per Inhabitant, Gallons	Lbs. Grain per Inhabitant
1873	830,000,000	780,000	20	40
1880	820,000,000	770,000	18	37
1887	990,000,000	930,000	21	43
15 years' average	880,000,000	830,000	19½	39

In the above years nearly 99 per cent. of the beer produced was consumed in Germany, exports ranging from 10 to 18 million gallons.

AUSTRIA

Year	Millions of Gallons			Number of Breweries
	Austria	Hungary	Total	
1870	204	16	220	2,743
1880	231	9	240	2,247
1887	275	15	290	1,962

UNITED STATES

Year	Number of Breweries	Capital, £	Gallons
1863	1,269	3,100,000	53,000,000
1870	2,785	13,500,000	204,000,000
1882	2,557	31,800,000	525,000,000
1889	1,964	...	777,000,000

Statistics of production and consumption were as follows :—

Year	Product, Gallons	Consumption, Galls.	Consumption per Inhab.
1875	293,000,000	295,000,000	6.5
1880	413,000,000	414,000,000	8.3
1885	594,000,000	596,000,000	9.5
1889	777,000,000	780,000,000	12.0

The principal beer-producing States were as follows :—

	1878	1884	1889
	Gallons	Gallons	Gallons
New York	109,000,000	204,000,000	250,000,000
Pennsylvania	31,000,000	62,000,000	71,000,000
Ohio	30,000,000	53,000,000	65,000,000
Illinois	18,000,000	35,000,000	62,000,000
Wisconsin	16,000,000	45,000,000	55,000,000
Missouri	17,000,000	35,000,000	52,000,000
New Jersey	16,000,000	28,000,000	42,000,000
Massachusetts	19,000,000	27,000,000	31,000,000
Various	60,000,000	99,000,000	149,000,000
Total	316,000,000	588,000,000	777,000,000

BEES

A hive of 5000 bees produces about 50 lbs. of honey yearly, and multiplies tenfold in five years. The ordinary value of a hive in Europe is £1 sterling.

Bees eat 20 lbs. honey in making 1 lb. of wax.

	Hives			Hives
France	950,000	Belgium	200,000
Germany	1,910,000	Holland	240,000
Russia	110,000	Denmark	90,000
Austria	1,550,000	Greece	30,000
Spain	1,690,000	United States	2,800,000

The largest bee-owner in the world is Mr. Harbison of California, who has 6000 hives, producing 200,000 lbs. honey yearly, worth £8000. There are in the United States 70,000 bee-growers, but the average which they get from their hives is only 22 lbs., whereas the average in England is 50 lbs. In 1888 there were in Ireland 28,600 hives, of which 9100 in movable frames; annual product 210 tons of honey, worth £12,000. The average is only 16 lbs. honey per hive, but in Kildare it reached 37 lbs. In 1889 the product in France was :—

	Tons	Value, £
Honey	6,600	370,000
Wax	2,000	180,000

The ordinary value is 10d. per lb. for wax and 6d. for honey.

In Austria the production of wax averages 2000 tons. The total annual yield of bees in Europe may be estimated thus :—

	Tons	Value, £
Honey . . .	40,000	2,200,000
Wax . . .	15,000	1,350,000
Total . .	55,000	3,550,000

One hundred bees weigh an ounce. The wing of a bee makes 190 movements a second, of a wasp 110, of a fly 330.

BEETROOT

This is grown both as cattle food and for making sugar.
The crop ranges from 5 tons of roots per acre in Russia, to 9 tons in Germany. In England it has given 12 tons per acre, equivalent for cattle food to 4 tons of hay, and worth 16 shillings per ton; but it has been found too costly in cultivation. Experimental growing in Canada has proved most successful. It takes about 11 tons of roots in Europe generally per ton of beet sugar, the average of saccharine matter being 9 per cent. as compared with 4 per cent. twenty years ago. In Germany 8 tons of roots give a ton of sugar.
The acreage and crop of all kinds of beetroot are approximately as follows :—

	Acres	Tons, Beet	Sugar, Beet
France . .	1,310,000	13,300,000	5,100,000
Germany . .	1,700,000	12,400,000	8,300,000
Russia . .	1,000,000	5,200,000	5,200,000
Austria . .	1,100,000	6,500,000	6,500,000
Belgium . .	145,000	2,100,000	2,100,000
Holland . .	60,000	600,000	400,000
Denmark . .	30,000	300,000	300,000
Europe . .	5,345,000	40,400,000	27,900,000

The *Journal de la Société Stat.* of Paris mentions that the production of beet sugar in the United States during five years ending 1884 averaged 337,000 tons per annum, from which must be inferred that the Union grows about 3 million tons of beetroot. The following table shows approximately the growth of all kinds of beetroot at different dates :—

	1836	1850	1870	1880	1888
	Tons	Tons	Tons	Tons	Tons
France .	700,000	1,500,000	6,600,000	14,800,000	13,300,000
Germany	40,000	550,000	2,700,000	11,200,000	12,400,000
Russia .	...	100,000	2,200,000	4,800,000	5,200,000
Austria .	10,000	200,000	1,500,000	5,500,000	6,500,000
Belgium .	...	150,000	800,000	1,800,000	2,100,000
Holland .	...	...	100,000	440,000	400,000
Denmark	...	...	200,000	300,000	300,000
Europe	750,000	2,500,000	14,100,000	38,840,000	40,200,000

It appears that two-thirds of the total crop is used for making sugar, the product of which now reaches 2,800,000 tons yearly in all the world.

BELLS

The largest are the following :—

	Tons		Tons		Tons
Moscow . .	202	Rouen . . .	18	Montreal . .	12
Burmah . .	117	Olmutz . .	18	Cologne . .	11
Pekin. . .	53	Vienna . .	18	Oxford . .	8
Novgorod .	31	St. Paul's . .	16	St. Peter's .	8
Notre Dame	18	Westminster .	14		...

Bell-metal should have 77 parts copper and 23 tin.

BIRDS

In hatching, the number of days that birds sit are :—

	Days		Days
Pigeon . . .	14	Duck . . .	30
Canary . .	14	Goose . .	30
Hen . . .	21	Parrot . .	40
Turkey . .	28	Swan . .	42

The ages to which birds attain are :—

	Years		Years		Years
Wren . .	3	Lark . .	18	Sparrow .	40
Thrush . .	10	Nightingale .	18	Goose . .	50
Hen . . .	10	Pigeon . .	20	Pelican . .	50
Robin . .	12	Linnet . .	23	Parrot . .	60
Blackbird .	12	Canary . .	24	Heron . .	60
Goldfinch .	15	Crane . .	24	Crow . .	100
Partridge .	15	Peacock . .	24	Swan . . .	100
Pheasant .	15	Skylark . .	30	Eagle . .	100

The flight of the following birds per hour is :—

Hawk . .	150 miles	Rook . . .	60 miles
Eider-duck .	90 „	Pigeon . .	40 „

Carrier-pigeons from Paris to Versailles, ten miles, usually take twenty minutes. In November 1882 some flew from Canton Vaud to Paris, 160 miles, in 6½ hours.
The departure and return of birds of passage from England (*Brit. Assoc. Report*) are usually on the following dates :—

	Leave England	Return	Days Absent
Cuckoo . . .	August 25th	April 14th	232
Blackcap . .	October 10th	„ 22nd	194
Martin . .	„ 12th	„ 14th	184
Swallow . .	„ 15th	„ 10th	177

Birds' nests are used in China for making soup; 9,000,000 are imported yearly into Canton, valued at 10s. per oz., fifty weighing about 1 lb.

BIRTHS

The birth-rate per 1000 of population was as follows :—

	1821–40	1841–60	1861–80	1881–85		1841–60	1861–80	1881–85
France . . .	29.7	26.7	25.8	24.7	Belgium . .	30.2	32.0	31.0
Prussia . . .	41.0	38.6	39.1	37.2	Denmark . .	32.8	31.4	32.5
Sweden . .	33.1	32.0	31.4	29.4	England . .	33.4	35.1	33.3
Norway . . .	31.3	32.4	30.8	30.9	Scotland . .	...	35.1	33.0
Russia . . .	44.6	45.5	49.6	48.7	Ireland . .	...	26.2	24.0
Saxony . .	38.1	39.3	41.5	41.9	Switzerland . .	...	31.0	28.2
Wurtemburg . .	...	...	41.8	37.7	Italy . . .	...	37.2	37.8
Austria . . .	39.5	40.3	39.0	38.3	Spain . . .	...	37.1	...
Bavaria . .	30.7	33.2	39.2	38.7	Hungary . .	...	...	45.0
Paris . . .	33.9	31.8	28.8	26.7	Roumania . .	...	...	37.4
Holland . . .	...	34.9	36.3	34.8	Australia . .	...	...	35.5

The following table of birth-rate for various cities is not for any uniform date or period :—

Alexandria	45.0	Dresden	35.4	Munich	39.5
Amsterdam	36.7	Dublin	29.1	Naples	32.0
Barcelona	29.2	Edinburgh	32.2	New York	39.4
Berlin	37.5	Geneva	24.3	Nottingham	36.7
Birmingham	37.6	Glasgow	37.4	Paris	30.5
Bombay	25.6	Hague	39.7	Philadelphia	36.0
Boston	30.0	Hamburg	37.5	Rio Janeiro	35.5
Breslau	37.7	Havana	25.4	Rome	27.2
Brighton	30.6	Hull	36.4	Rotterdam	38.8
Bristol	34.5	Leeds	36.8	St. Louis	30.0
Brussels	34.7	Liverpool	37.6	St. Petersburg	37.8
Bucharest	29.5	London	34.7	Sheffield	38.0
Buda-Pesth	35.8	Lyons	26.0	Stockholm	33.0
Buenos Ayres	31.7	Madras	39.0	Turin	31.5
Christiania	34.5	Madrid	37.5	Venice	30.2
Copenhagen	39.1	Manchester	36.9	Vienna	39.2

The sexes of children born average as follows :—

	Per 1000			Per 1000	
	Males	Females		Males	Females
England	511	489	Portugal	515	485
Scotland	514	486	Holland	513	487
Ireland	515	485	Belgium	514	486
U. Kingdom	512	488	Denmark	513	487
France	513	487	Sweden	512	488
Prussia	514	486	Norway	514	486
Russia	508	492	Switzerland	512	488
Austria	516	484	Greece	519	481
Italy	517	483	Roumania	521	479
Spain	516	484	Europe	513	487

Births occur according to months as follows :—

	Scotland	France	Germany	Italy	Greece	Spain	Holland
January	100	105	103	107	122	114	106
February	93	110	105	114	119	108	115
March	103	109	103	110	98	112	112
April	104	106	100	106	97	102	104
May	106	99	97	95	88	100	94
June	104	95	95	89	85	89	86
July	102	96	96	91	88	88	86
August	96	96	98	93	88	91	96
September	96	97	104	99	94	98	103
October	101	95	100	98	110	100	99
November	96	97	100	98	113	97	99
December	99	95	99	99	98	101	100
Total	1,200	1,200	1,200	1,200	1,200	1,200	1,200

	Sweden	Norway	Denmark	Geneva	Algeria	Hungary	Belgium	Average
January	106	108	104	105	95	108	105	107
February	106	108	99	106	136	99	103	107
March	107	107	110	112	64	105	112	107
April	102	102	107	111	124	98	104	103
May	98	100	104	107	107	99	101	99
June	94	97	98	96	109	95	95	94
July	92	94	96	98	110	98	96	93
August	91	96	98	98	92	104	98	95
September	108	111	102	94	83	102	96	101
October	99	96	97	99	90	103	97	99
November	96	83	91	90	90	97	95	97
December	101	98	94	97	100	92	98	98
Total	1,200	1,200	1,200	1,200	1,200	1,200	1,200	1,200

The number of births to 100 marriages was as follows :—

	1861–80	1881–85		1881–85
England	407	420	Germany	439
Scotland	447	439	Russia	500
Ireland	520	540	Norway	430
France	304	305	Switzerland	398
Belgium	408	418	Italy	440
Holland	422	470	Austria	419
Denmark	360	376	Hungary	404
Sweden	414	408		

BIRTHS ACCORDING TO HOURS

Between	French Towns	French Rural	Belgium, Quetelet	Dresden, Mayr	Medium
Midnight and 6 a.m.	30.3	29.4	29.6	28.5	29.5
6 a.m. and noon	25.6	25.4	23.2	23.8	24.5
Noon and 6 p.m.	21.4	23.4	21.5	21.7	22.0
6 p.m. and midnight	22.7	21.8	25.7	26.0	24.0
Total	100.0	100.0	100.0	100.0	100.0

From observations made (1855–74) in various countries, it appears that 1000 maids or widows between the ages of 15 and 50 have the following number of children yearly :—

Ireland	4	France	18	Scotland	24
Holland	10	Prussia	20	Denmark	31
Switzerland	11	Norway	21	Saxony	33
Belgium	17	Italy	21	Bavaria	42
England	17	Sweden	23	Average	21

The ratio of illegitimate children in various countries is shown as follows from observations in 1865–78 :—

ILLEGITIMATES IN 1000 BIRTHS

Greece	16	Spain	55	Norway	85
Ireland	23	Portugal	56	Germany	87
Russia	31	Italy	65	Scotland	93
Holland	35	United States	70	Sweden	102
Switzerland	48	Belgium	71	Denmark	111
Canada	50	Hungary	71	Austria	135
England	54	France	74		

The ratio of still-births in various countries is as follows :—

PER 1000 BIRTHS

France	45	Holland	52	Switzerland	46
Prussia	41	Belgium	45	Denmark	30
Austria	22	Sweden	32	Bavaria	34
Italy	25	Norway	35	Average	37

The occurrence of still-births according to months, 1861–70, was as follows :—

	France	Norway	Sweden	Leipzig	Frankfort	Hamburg
January	109	104	104	129	115	96
February	105	104	109	84	120	134
March	102	105	103	115	88	111
April	100	103	97	109	93	103
May	99	104	91	109	104	109
June	99	102	95	84	104	76
July	97	91	93	100	102	76
August	96	99	103	90	110	90
September	94	85	81	102	95	85
October	96	102	107	87	72	90
November	98	99	108	100	104	136
December	105	102	109	100	93	94
Total	1,200	1,200	1,200	1 200	1,200	1,200

Still-births are more frequent in towns than in rural districts, viz. :—

	Per 1000 Births			Per 1000 Births	
	Urban	Rural		Urban	Rural
Italy . .	31	22	France	53	39
Sweden .	41	31	Belgium	50	41
Prussia .	45	40	Holland	54	51

Males are oftener still-born than females, because, as Bertillon thinks, the former have larger heads. The following table shows the number of males to females :—

Still-Born Males to 100 Females

Holland . .	127	Austria . .	131	Belgium . .	135
Prussia . .	129	Sweden . .	133	Italy . . .	141
Norway . .	121	Denmark .	125	France . .	144

Multiple births, from observations in 1851–73, average thus :—

	Twins in 10,000 Births	Triplets in a Million Births		Twins in 10,000 Births	Triplets in a Million Births
England . .	112	23	Denmark . .	142	160
Scotland . .	117	...	Belgium . .	97	100
Ireland . . .	176	...	Holland . .	131	170
France . . .	108	120	Sweden . .	145	180
Prussia . . .	125	150	Norway . .	125	160
Russia . . .	121	...	Iceland . .	142	330
Austria . . .	134	180	Switzerland .	120	...
Italy . . .	118	150	Spain . . .	84	120
Bavaria . . .	174	310	Wurtemburg .	128	120

In France, Italy, and Bavaria twins are most numerous in those Departments which furnish the tallest conscripts. The age of the mother has also some influence, as the tables of Lebel and Puech show :—

Mother's Age	Lebel	Puech	Medium
Under 25 . . .	35	17	26
25–30 . . .	35	41	38
30–35 . . .	20	30	25
Over 35 . . .	10	12	11
Total .	100	100	100

According to Dubois, the mean ratio of multiple births in England, France, and Germany is 13 twins per 1000 births, and 160 triplets and 8 quadruplets per million births. Aristotle mentions a woman who had 5 children at a birth four times successively; Menage one who had 21 children in seven years. The Belgian official returns for 1851–60 give a case of 5 children at a birth, viz., 2 boys and 3 girls, and another case of 4, all boys. The Empress Catherine received a Russian peasant woman in 1757 who had 57 children, all living, having been born thus :—

```
        16 in   4 confinements
        21 in   7       ,,
        20 in  10       ,,
        ──  ──
        57   21
```

This woman's husband married again, and his second wife had 15 children in 7 confinements.

A similar case is that of Fedor Vassileff, of Moscow, 1782, who had 83 children living when pensioned by the Czar. He had 69 children by his first wife at 27 births, and after her death had 18 more by his second in 8 births.

The records of Florence also show that Signora Frescobaldi, who died in 1570, had 52 children, never less than 3 at a birth. Madrid newspapers in 1883 stated that Lucas Saez returned to Spain from the United States with 37 children, 79 grandchildren, and 81 great-grandchildren, in all 107 males and 90 females, his eldest son being aged 70.

The *Daily Telegraph* of London, November 1888, published the confinement of Mrs. George Hirsch, of Dallas, Texas, of 6 children, 4 being boys and 2 girls. This surpasses all records.

Twins give 108 males to 100 females, and triplets show a medium result for France, Germany, and Austria as follows :—

Birth of three boys	.	.	.	26.0
Birth of three girls	.	.	.	22.7
Two boys and a girl	.	.	.	27.0
Two girls and a boy	.	.	.	24.3
				100.0

This gives 156 boys and 144 girls, that is, precisely the same ratio as in the case of twins.

The child-bearing age of women rarely passes 50 ; one mother in 3300 occurs after that age. If a woman has been married 18 years without children, the probabilities are 6000 to 1 against her having any. The Dublin *Evening Post* of July 16, 1801, announces that Sarah, wife of Thomas Davis, was confined the previous week of a son, her first child, after 11 years of marriage, being in her 53rd year. Men of very advanced age have begotten children. Schneider mentions a case at 86, Meade at 89, Ruttell at 92, Plater (his own grandfather) at 100. We know also that Thomas Parr was sued for adultery at 118.

There are opposing estimates as to the period of gestation :—

	Days		Days		Days
Depaul . . .	268	Schwegel . .	270	Rann . .	272
Wallichs . .	269	Schoeder . .	271	Reid . .	276

Reid's table is as follows :—

Days					Ratio
260–266 .	.	.	.	.	12.5
267–273 .	.	.	.	.	17.5
274–280 .	.	.	.	.	45.0
281–287 .	.	.	.	.	15.0
288–294 .	.	.	.	.	10.0
					100.0

Reid and Tourdes agree in fixing 294 days as the maximum, but French law allows 300 as the limit for legitimacy. The number of children born yearly to 1000 wives is as follows :—

France .	.	.	180	Ireland .	298
Norway .	.	284	England	.	312
Prussia .	.	286	Belgium	.	317
Saxony .	.	295	Scotland	.	339

According to Bertillon and other authorities, the European averages show that 100 married women will have in their life 420 children, 100 unmarried 21 ; furthermore, that as regards prostitutes 100 will give birth in their life to 60 children. The poorer classes have more children than the rich. Bertillon's observations during ten years, 1851–60, in Norway, show as follows :—

```
100 rich families have 313 children
100 middle-class families have 360 children
100 poor families have 370 children
```

Drysdale found, in 1888, that 100 women of Montmartre, the work-people of Paris, have 175 children, while 100 women of the fashionable Champs Elysées quarter have only 86.

As regards the sexes of infants, it is observed that young couples are most likely to have boys, middle-aged ones girls. Bertillon says that observations in Denmark, Norway, and Austria give this average :—

Males Born to 100 Females

	First-Born		Subsequent Births
Lawful . . .	110	...	105
Illegitimate . . .	104	...	106

Salder's table, published in 1830, was as follows :—

	Children to 100 Couples	Male Infants to 100 Females
Husband younger . .	487	87
Even age with wife .	617	95
Husband 4 years older	571	104
,, 8 ,, ,,	547	127
,, 14 ,, ,,	558	146
,, 20 ,, ,,	455	163

UNITED KINGDOM

The surplus of births over deaths, per 1000 of the population, of late years is greater in England than in Scotland :—

	Births and Deaths per 1000 Population in England				
	1841–50	1851–60	1861–70	1871–80	40 Years
Births . . .	32.6	34.1	35.3	35.5	34.4
Deaths . .	22.4	22.2	22.6	21.5	22.2
Surplus births	10.2	11.9	12.7	14.0	12.2

SCOTLAND

	1855–60	1861–70	1871–80	26 Years
Births	33.9	35.0	35.2	34.8
Deaths	20.8	22.0	21.8	21.6
Surplus births . . .	13.1	13.0	13.4	13.2

IRELAND

	1864–70	1871–80	17 Years
Births	26.3	26.2	26.2
Deaths	16.7	18.1	17.5
Surplus births .	9.6	8.1	8.7

The percentage of births, according to Quarter, compares in England with other countries thus :—

Quarter Ending	England	Scotland	France	Germany
March . . .	26.2	24.7	27.0	25.9
June	26.0	26.2	25.0	24.2
September . .	24.0	24.4	24.1	24.9
December . .	23.8	24.7	23.9	25.0
Total .	100.0	100.0	100.0	100.0

According to the *Dic. Medicale*, the forceps is less used in lying-in hospitals of London or Dublin than elsewhere, viz. :—

In	Per 10,000 Births	In	Per 10,000 Births
Dublin . . .	15	Vienna . . .	37
London . . .	18	Paris . . .	39

Illegitimacy is declining in England, as appears thus :- -

Period	Per 1000 Births	Period	Per 1000 Births
1841–50 . . .	67	1861–70 . . .	61
1851–60 . . .	65	1871–80 . . .	51

FRANCE

The birth-rate is declining since 1801, viz. :—

Period	France	Paris	Period	France	Paris
1801–10	33.0	...	1841–50	27.3	31.4
1811–20	31.8	...	1851–60	26.1	31.5
1821–30	30.6	35.9	1861–70	26.0	30.1
1831–40	28.8	35.1	1871–80	25.6	27.4

In 1886 there were 10,425,341 families with children thus :—

Children	Number of Families	Ratio
None . . .	2,073,205	19.9
1 . . .	2,542,611	24.4
2 . . .	2,265,337	21.7
3 . . .	1,512,054	14.5
4 . . .	936,853	9.0
5 . . .	540,693	5.2
Over 5 . . .	554,588	5.3
	10,425,341	100.0

According to a return by the Minister of Finance, there are 148,808 families, each with seven children or more, which have claimed the exemption from certain taxes recently voted by the French Parliament. These families have 1,157,547 children, or as nearly as possible eight each.

In 1856 the ratio of married couples that had no children was much lower, only 15.5 per cent. If we compare the number of lawful births with that of marriages, we see, moreover, a constant decline since 1830, viz. :—

Period		Per Marriage
1800–30	. . . . . .	3.82
1831–60	. . . . . .	3.20
1861–70	. . . . . .	3.09
1871–80	. . . . . .	2.98

The ratio of illegitimacy has varied little in forty years, viz. :—

Period		Per 100 Births
1841–50	. . . . .	7.2
1851–60	. . . . .	7.4
1861–70	. . . . .	7.5
1871–80	. . . . .	7.3

It is a custom common in France for fathers to declare lawful their illegitimate children. The proportion thus recognised in the years 1870–74 was 25 per cent., against 21 per cent. in the fifteen years preceding. In ordinary births there are 105 males to 100 females, but in twins only 102 to 100. Births of twins average thus per 1000 :—

335 of boys
315 of girls
350 mixed
___
1000

The increase of still-births is an alarming feature, viz. :—

	Per 1000 Births					
	Male	Female	Total	Lawful	Illegitimate	Total
1841–50	39	29	34	32	66	34
1853–62	49	35	42	40	71	42
1863–70	51	38	45	41	81	45

GERMANY

The annual birth and death rates of all Germany for forty-six years ending 1886 were as follows :—

Period	Per 1000 Inhabitants			Of 100 Births	
	Births	Deaths	Surplus Births	Still-born	Illegiti-mate
1841–50 . . .	37.5	28.2	9.3	3.9	10.8
1851–60 . . .	36.8	27.8	9.0	4.0	11.4
1861–70 . . .	38.7	28.4	10.3	4.1	11.5
1871–80 . . .	40.7	28.7	12.0	4.0	8.9
1881–86 . . .	38.5	27.3	11.2	3.8	9.3

Birth-rates have been as follows :—

Prussia			Saxony		
Period	Per 1000 Population	Per Marriage	Period	Per 1000 Population	Per Marriage
1748–90 . .	40.6	...	1831–40 . .	38.1	4.2
1816–40 . .	40.8	4.3	1841–50 . .	39.2	4.1
1841–60 . .	38.6	...	1851–60 . .	39.4	4.1
1861–70 . .	39.5	4.6	1861–70 . .	40.4	4.0
1871–80 . .	38.7	4.5	1871–80 . .	42.7	4.5
1881–85 . .	37.4	4.7	1881–85 . .	41.9	4.7

Bavaria			Wurtemburg		
1830–50 . .	30.7	4.6	1815–29 . .	36.4	5.1
1851–70 . .	35.5	4.7	1861–68 . .	40.8	5.2
1871–80 . .	40.6	4.8	1876–80 . .	42.7	5.9
1881–85 . .	38.7	5.5	1881–85 . .	37.7	5.9

In Saxony the proportion of still-births was as follows :—

Per 1000 Births

Period	Lawful	Illegitimate	Total
1801–20 . . .	53	75	57
1821–40 . . .	47	75	51
1841–60 . . .	43	71	48
1861–70 . . .	40	74	47
1871–75 . . .	44	91	52

The proportion of still-births in Prussia was thus :—

	Per 1000 Jew Births (1820–64)	Per 1000 Christian Births (1865–74)
Male	22	... 44
Female . . .	19	... 36
General average .	21	... 41

The surplus of births over deaths in Prussia from 1822 to 1866 showed more favourably among Jews than in the Christian population, viz. :—

	Among 1000 Jews		Among 1000 Christians	
	1822–40	1841–66	1822–40	1841–66
Births	35.5	34.7	40.0	39.5
Deaths . . .	21.4	18.9	29.6	29.1
Surplus births .	14.1	15.8	10.4	10.4

In sixty years ending 1875 the average number of births yearly was :—

To 1000 married women . . . 285
To 1000 unmarried women . . . 25

In a period of forty-six years ending 1886 the proportion of illegitimate births was as follows :—

In 1000 Jewish births 24
In 1000 Roman Catholic births . . 58
In 1000 Protestant births 85

The proportion was 98 per 1000 in town births, and 72 in rural. The average during fifty-eight years in the large cities was as follows :—

	Per 1000		Per 1000
Cologne . . .	105	Breslau . . .	180
Berlin . . .	157	Königsberg . .	189

The illegitimate ratios in Bavaria and Saxony were :—

Bavaria		Saxony	
Period	Per 1000 Births	Period	Per 1000 Births
1850–59	240	1821–40	128
1862–70	210	1841–50	151
1871–78	130	1861–75	143

Twins appear to be increasing in Prussia, viz. :—

1821–57 . . . . 115 in 10,000 births
1858–74 . . . . 126 ,, ,,

In Saxony. the proportion in 1834–49 was 127 in 10,000. Sexes of twins in Prussia were: 327 of boys, 303 of girls, and 370 mixed, in 1000 cases, being as 105 boys to 100 girls.

HOLLAND

Birth-rate from 1840 showed as follows :—

Period	Per 1000 Inhab.		Per Marriage
1841–60 . . .	34.9	...	4.6
1861–80 . . .	36.3	...	4.5
1881–85 . . .	34.8	...	4.8

SWEDEN

The birth-rate from 1751 was as follows :—

Period	Per 1000 Pop.		Per Marriage
1751–70 . .	35.2	...	4.0
1771–90 . .	32.5	...	4.0
1791–1810 .	32.1	...	3.8
1811–30 . .	34.1	...	4.0
1831–50 . .	31.4	...	4.3
1851–70 . .	32.4	...	4.6
1871–80 . .	30.8	...	4.5
1881–85 . .	29.4	...	4.6

The number of births yearly to 1000 women of 15 to 50 years of age was as follows :—

1776–1820 . . 122 | 1841–60 . . . 127
1821–40 . . 130 | 1861–75 . . . 123

In 1875 of 10,000 births the ages of the mothers were :—

Age	Rural	City	Total
Under 18 . . .	21	25	22
18–20 . . .	115	185	125
21–25 . . .	1,378	1,555	1,404
26–35 . . .	4,988	5,326	5,041
36–45 . . .	3,315	2,818	3,238
46–50 . . .	180	88	167
Over 50 . . .	3	3	3
Total . .	10,000	10,000	10,000

The records of 100 years down to 1885 showed the average ages of every 10,000 women confined to be thus :—

Under 20 194
20–30 4,059
31–40 4,593
41–45 988
46 and upwards 166
            ——
Total . . 10,000

The number of children born yearly to 1000 women at various ages, married and unmarried, is as follows :—

Age	Per 1000		
	Wives	Unmarried	All Women
16–20	477	3	9
20–25	464	30	106
25–35	342	46	220
35–40	251	32	203
40–45	142	14	121
45–50	22	1	18

From observations during the years 1871–75 it appears that the mothers of every 1000 children born were as follows :—

Mothers	Urban	Rural	All Sweden
Wives	773	908	890
Spinsters	218	85	104
Widows	9	7	6
All births . .	1,000	1,000	1,000

Birth-rate was higher in the towns, with reference to population, than in rural districts, viz. :—

Period	Per 1000 of Population		
	Towns	Rural	All Sweden
1861–70	33.2	31.2	31.5
1871–75	31.9	30.5	30.7

In the same periods 1000 married women produced the following number of children :—

Period	Town	Rural	All Sweden
1861–70	197	172	174
1871–75	184	168	170

The ratio of women who had midwives in their confinement was as follows, per cent. :—

Period	Town	Rural	All Sweden
1861–70	93	37	45
1871–75	92	43	50

The number of boys born to 1000 girls was as follows :—

Period	Town	Rural	All Sweden
1861–70	1,046	1,052	1,050
1871–75	1,042	1,055	1,052

Bertillon found that the clergy had 108 boys, the nobles only 98 to 100 girls ; the common people 105. The ratio of births to 100 deaths was as follows :—

Period	Town	Rural	All Sweden
1861–70	126	162	157
1871–75	124	178	168

Illegitimate births have increased very rapidly : –

Period	Per 1000 Births	Period	Per 1000 Births
1771–90	41	1841–60	97
1791–1815	59	1861–70	105
1816–40	72	1871–75	115

In the last period the ratio was 90 per 1000 in the rural districts and 220 in the towns. Still-births were as follows :—

Period	Per 1000 Births	Period	Per 1000 Births
1816–40	27	1861–70	33
1841–60	32	1871–75	32

Still-births occur more frequently in town than in country : —

Period	Per 1000 Births		
	Urban	Rural	All Sweden
1861–70 . . .	40	32	33
1871–75 . . .	39	31	32

Twins and triplets occurred as follows :—

Period	Twins per 10,000 Births	Triplets per Million Births	Period	Twins per 10,000 Births	Triplets per Million Births
1776–95 . .	174	310	1831–50	140	200
1796–1810 .	165	260	1851–70	141	195
1811–30 . .	155	250	1871–75	146	160

In the years 1871–75 the rate for twins was 150 in towns and 144 in rural districts among 10,000 births.

NORWAY

Birth-rate from the beginning of the century was thus :—

Period	Per 1000 Inhab.	Per Marriage	Period	Per 1000 Inhab.	Per Marriage
1801–25	30.6	3.7	1861–70	30.8	4.7
1826–45	31.3	4.2	1871–80	30.8	4.3
1846–60	32.4	4.2	1881–85	31.1	4.7

The number of children born yearly to 1000 women between 20 and 45 years of age was as follows :—

Period	Per 1000 Wives	Per 1000 Unmarried
1836–45	286	25
1846–55	305	32
1856–65	311	32
1866–70	284	32

Wives and unmarried women had more children in town than in the country, the returns for ten years down to 1870 showing that 1000 women between the ages of 15 and 45 gave birth as follows :—

	Per 1000	
	Wives	Unmarried
Town	311	33
Rural	301	20
All Norway	303	21

The ratio of illegitimates in the same period was 80 per 1000 births rural, 95 for urban, and 83 per 1000 for all Norway. Still-births were 38 per 1000, against 42 in the decade ending 1860. Twins occurred as follows :—

Period	Per 10,000 Births		
	Urban	Rural	All Norway
1851–60	109	124	121
1861–70	117	120	119

The average of triplets in the above twenty years was 160 per million births. The number of boys born to 100 girls was as follows :—

	Urban	Rural	All Norway
Lawful	1,040	1,058	1,053
Illegitimate . . .	1,090	1,070	1,060
Total . .	1,045	1,060	1,055

The preponderance of males varies with the length of time the parents may be married, thus :—

Married under 7 years . . 116 boys to 100 girls.
,,   7-12   ,,   . . 107   ,,   ,,
,,   over 12   ,,   . . 94   ,,   ,,

The sex of the first-born likewise varies thus :—

Both parents under 25   . . 208 boys to 100 girls.
Father over 35 92   ,,   ,,
Both parents over 35 . . . 87   ,,   ,,

FINLAND

Birth-rate for fifteen years ending 1865 averaged 36.2, against 34.3 in the twenty years preceding; still-births, 29 in 1000 births; twins, 149 in 10,000; illegitimate, 72 per 1000.

ITALY

In the period from 1862 to 1885 the birth-rate showed :—

	Per 1000 Inhabitans		Per Marriage
1862–70	37.5	...	5.0
1871–80	36.9	...	4.9
1881–85	38.0	...	4.7

The ratio of still-births was found in 1872–74 to vary from 15 to 41 per 1000 in various parts of the kingdom, viz. :—

Sicily . . . 15 | Rome . . . 41 | Piedmont . . 34
Naples . . 18 | Lombardy . 38 | Tuscany . . 35

The ratio for the whole kingdom was only 29 per 1000. From a census taken in Turin it was found that of 1000 children born in a given year, the ratios were as follows :—

1st born   . . . 231 | 5th born . . . 88
2nd ,,   . . . 188 | 6th ,, . . . 67
3rd ,,   . . . 152 | 7th ,, . . . 50
4th ,,   . . . 118 | 8th, &c. born . . 106

RUSSIA

The birth-rate has been as follows per 1000 population :—

Years		Years		Years	
1801–20 . .	39.6	1846–58 . .	45.5	1876–80 . .	48.4
1826–45 . .	44.6	1861–65 . .	50.7	1881–83 . .	48.7

From 1861 to 1883 the number of births averaged 520 to 100 marriages. The sexes of children born were :—

1801 to 1830 . . . 110 males to 100 females
1831 to 1860 . . . 105   ,,   100   ,,

At St. Petersburg 1000 births occurred as follows :—

Quarter Ending
March 31st 256
June 30th 260
September 30th 247
December 31st 237

Total 1000

AUSTRIA-HUNGARY

Birth-rates in Austria and Hungary were as follows :—

Period	Austria		Hungary	
	Per 1000 Inhabitants	Per Marriage	Per 1000 Inhabitants	Per Marriage
1830–47	39.7	...	...	...
1853–60	40.6	4.9	...	...
1861–70	38.2	4.4	42.2	4.6
1871–80	39.7	4.6	43.0	4.5
1881–85	38.0	4.8	45.2	4.0

Illegitimacy has a high ratio in the cities, viz. :—

Vienna . . . . . 402 per 1000
Prague 470   ,,

In Prague in 1880 it was found that 1000 married women gave birth to 155 children yearly, and 1000 unmarried to 75. The birth-rate of Prague per 1000 inhabitants is 44, that of Vienna 42. Still-births in Vienna are 43 in 1000. The ratio of sexes in Vienna shows that 106 boys are born for 100 girls.

Returns for Austria proper during ten years to 1886 gave the following ratios of births :—

Male . . . 515 | Legitimate . 856 | Live-born . . 973
Female . . 485 | Illegitimate . 144 | Still-born . . 27

Total . 1000   1000   1000

Returns for Hungary for six years ending 1886 give the following average :—

	Live-Born	Illegitimate		Still-Births
Males .	295,200	26,300	Lawful . .	9,510
Females	281,700	25,200	Illegitimate	1,620
Total	576,900	51,000	Total .	11,130

This gives a ratio of nearly 9 per cent. for illegitimates; still-births 19 per 1000. The proportion of still-born among bastards was very high, 32 per 1000. In the said interval of six years there were in Hungary the following multiple births :—

	Number of Births	Male	Female	Total
Twins	8,485	8,620	8,350	16,970
Triplets	104	150	162	312
Quadruplets . . .	2	3	5	8

BELGIUM

The annual average of births was as follows :—

Period	Births	Excess over Deaths	Birth-rate per 1000 Population	Births to 100 Marriages
1831–40	140,000	32,000	33.4	4.57
1841–50	130,000	26,000	30.3	4.50
1851–60	137,000	35 000	30.0	4.08
1861–70	155,000	40,000	31.6	4.26
1871–80	172,000	52,000	32.1	4.42
1881–87	175,000	57,000	30.7	4.43

The above being the total number of births, legitimate and illegitimate, it follows that the number of children

G

born to each marriage was really less than shown above. The official tables show as follows :—

Period	Males Born to 100 Female Births	Births to 100 Deaths	Births to 100 Women of 15 to 45 Years of Age
1841–50	105.3	125	13.4
1851–60	105.2	134	13.1
1861–70	105.2	136	14.4
1871–80	104.7	143	14.5
1887	106.0	152	13.7

The following is an official table of ratios :—

Period	Percentage of Illegitimate Births	Illegitimate Births to 100 Single Women (15–45)	Male Births to 100 Female — Legitimate	Male Births to 100 Female — Illegitimate	Still-births, Percentage
1841–50	7.4	1.62	105.5	102.5	4.37
1851–60	7.9	1.67	105.4	102.5	4.73
1861–70	7.1	1.76	105.4	103.0	4.81
1871–80	7.2	1.84	104.9	102.4	4.54
1887	8.8	2.14	105.3	100.9	4.97

In Brussels the ratio of illegitimacy rises to 285 per 1000 births.

DENMARK

Since 1840 the birth-rate has been as follows :—

Period	Per 1000 Population	Per Marriage
1840–60 . . .	32.8	4.0
1861–70 . . .	31.0	4.1
1871–80 . . .	31.5	4.0
1881–85 . . .	32.5	4.2

The number of male children born to 100 females shows thus :—

Mother's Age	Male Births
Under 30	108
30 to 35	107
Over 35	106

The ages of 1000 women in their confinement in the years 1861–70 were :—

Under 20	14
20 to 30	414
30 to 40	461
Over 40	111
	1000

GREECE

During ten years ending 1878 the birth-rate averaged 120 per 1000 women between 15 and 50 years, and 27.6 per 1000 of the general population. The number of lawful births per 1000 married women was 178 yearly.

SWITZERLAND

Birth-rate during twenty years showed as follows :—

Period	Per 1000 Population	Per Marriage
1867–74 . .	29.8	…
1876–80	32.2	4.3
1881–85 . .	28.2	4.0
1886 . . .	27.4	4.0

The ratio of illegitimacy is high at Geneva, especially among the foreign population, viz. :—

Period	Illegitimacy in 100 Births — Swiss	Illegitimacy in 100 Births — Foreign
1847–56 . . .	6.8	11.4
1857–66 . . .	5.8	14.8
1867–76 . . .	6.7	18.1

ALGERIA

The birth-rate among various classes of the population showed :—

Race	1853–56	1873–76
French . . .	41.0	38.0
Spanish . . .	47.5	39.5
Italian . . .	38.5	39.0
Maltese . . .	44.0	38.4
Germans . . .	31.0	28.8
Jews	56.5	49.0

The number of children to 100 marriages, and the ratio of twins were as follows :—

Race	Children per 100 Marriages	Twins in 10,000 Births
French . . .	370	102
German . . .	480	160
Italian . . .	570	120
Spanish . . .	630	40

The average of children to marriages and the ratio of male births have been as follows :—

Period	Children to 100 Marriages	Boys to 100 Girls
1836–53 . . .	390	117
1854–77 . . .	440	107

AUSTRALIA

The annual birth and death rates of the seven colonies during thirteen years down to 1888 were as follows :—

	Per 1000 Population — Births	Per 1000 Population — Deaths	Per 1000 Population — Surplus Births	Percentage of Illegitimates
N. S. Wales . .	37.8	15.5	22.3	4.4
Victoria . . .	31.6	16.5	15.1	4.5
Queensland . .	36.9	17.3	19.6	4.0
South Australia .	36.9	14.1	22.8	2.2
New Zealand . .	37.2	11.1	26.1	2.7
Tasmania . . .	33.1	15.8	17.3	4.2
W. Australia . .	34.7	16.3	18.4	4.2
All Australia . .	35.5	15.0	20.5	4.3

ARGENTINA

The birth-rate of Buenos Ayres is 31 per 1000 of population. Of 1000 children born the parents were :—

Argentines	168
Italians	434
Various	398
	1000

There were 35 still-births in 1000 births.

BOTANY

The growth of various trees and products stops at the following heights above sea-level :—

	Feet		Feet		Feet
Vine	2,300	Oak	3,350	Pine	6,200
Maize	2,800	Walnut	3,600	Fir	6,700

The number of leguminous plants in various parts of the world is as follows :—

Europe	184	S. America	605	Levant	250
Mediterranean	468	Australia	229	N. Africa	108
United States	183	China	77	Central Africa	130
Mexico	152	East Indies	452	S. Africa	395
West Indies	221	Siberia	129	Islands	42

The number of seeds in a bushel is 556,000 of wheat, 888,000 of rye, 16,400,000 of clover.

The quantity of seed to the acre is usually, in bushels, thus :—

Wheat	1.6	Rye	1.5	Hemp	1.2
Barley	2.0	Rice	2.0	Flax	0.5
Oats	3.0	Beans	1.5	Potatoes	8.0

Batata.—Better known as the sweet potato, gives a crop of 5 tons per acre.

Carob.—Also called algarroba or locust tree; it flourishes in Cyprus, where there are 600,000 trees, covering 20,000 acres. The yield of beans varies from 10 to 100 lbs. Average crop 25,000 tons, value £75,000, the bulk being exported to Scotland to make whiskey. The bean has 66 per cent. sugar and gum.

Castor-oil Plant.—Flourishes in Algeria; average crop 10 cwts. per acre, which gives from 50 to 60 gallons oil, worth 10s. per gallon.

Mulberry.—An ordinary tree produces from 50 to 200 lbs. of leaves yearly, according to age, viz. :—

Age, Years	Lbs., Leaves	Age, Years	Lbs., Leaves
4	25	12	148
9	106	21	218

At the age of 45 the production begins to decline, and the tree dies at 70. Lombardy has 10 millions of these trees, and all Italy probably 40 millions ; France has 6 millions. It is found that 10 lbs. of leaves suffice to yield one ounce of raw silk.

BRIDGES AND VIADUCTS

One of the most remarkable bridges of the Middle Ages is that built over the Adda in Italy in 1377, which is of stone, and has a single span of 237 feet. Among those of historical interest may be mentioned :—

Name	Length (Feet)	Date	Over
Ratisbon	994	1135	Danube
St. Esprit	2,690	1285	Rhone
Cordoba	460	1301	Guadalquivir
Verona	365	1354	Po
Rialto	99	1588	At Venice
Prague	1,706	1650	Moldau
Schaffhausen	364	1758	Rhine
Neuilly	740	1768	Seine

Those of the greatest height appear to be the following :—

	Height (Feet)	Span (Feet)
Brooklyn	210	1,620
Annecy	656	636
Clifton	257	703
Forth	...	5,330

Brooklyn bridge has four cables, each of 5000 wires of ⅛ inch. Forth is by far the greatest ever constructed (see *Engineering*); the heaviest train deflection is 4 inches. The first iron bridge in the United Kingdom was at Coalbrookdale in 1779 ; the following table shows the most notable in all parts of the world since then :—

Date	Bridge	Over	Length (Feet)	Iron (Tons)	Cost £	Builder
1779	Coalbrookdale	Severn	100	378	...	Darby
1796	Sunderland	Wear	236	250	27,000	Wilson
1819	Southwark	Thames	800	5,780	800,000	Rennie
1825	Menai	Menai Straits	1,050	2,187	212,000	Telford
1849	Newcastle	Tyne	900	5,050	243,000	Stephenson
1850	Britannia	Menai Straits	1,511	9,600	602,000	Stephenson
1855	Niagara	Niagara	850	400	83,000	Roebling
1859	Victoria	St. Lawrence	7,200	8,230	1,700,000	Stephenson
1860	Pesth-Buda	Danube	1,900	7,000	...	...
1862	Freyburg	Sarine	1,095	3,100	100,000	...
1867	Cincinnati	Ohio	2,252	...	...	Roebling
1868	Clifton	Niagara	1,270	...	40,000	...
1874	St. Louis	Mississippi	2,200	4,200	400,000	Eads
1875	Wuzerabad	Punjaub	9,300	...	650,000	...
1877	Oporto	Douro	1,160	...	...	Eiffel
1878	Annan	Solway	5,120	1,600	...	...
1879	Empress	Sutlej	6,000	6,650	550,000	...
1880	Moerdyk	Maas	4,850	...	...	...
1880	Pultowa	Dnieper	3,550	...	...	...
1881	Saratov	Volga	4,872	5,150	695,000	Beleloubski
1882	Benares	Ganges	3,000	...	425,000	...
1883	Brooklyn	Hudson	4,500	30,000	3,100,000	Roebling
1889	Forth	Forth	5,330	48,000	2,550,000	Fowler

The Chinese had suspension bridges of iron chains during many centuries. Ogilvy saw one over the Yunnan in 1669, erected by the Emperor Ming, who was contemporary with Tiberius Cæsar.

In 1816 Captain Brown built an iron bridge of 112 feet, only for foot-passengers, at Galashiels, for the sum of £40, the cheapest bridge on record.

The quickest bridge ever built was by Mr. Dredge, in 1846, who in eight days placed an iron bridge, 74 feet span, across the Blackwater, co. Tyrone, Ireland. The greatest number of bridges built by one man was by Mr. Telford, surnamed Pontifex, who erected 1200 bridges in Scotland, between the years 1800 and 1820.

London has spent 5½ millions sterling on bridges since 1816, viz. :—

Name	Length, Feet	Cost	Per Foot	Date
		£	£	
London . . .	900	2,000,000	2,200	1831
Southwark . .	800	800,000	1,000	1819
Waterloo . . .	1,326	1,060,000	800	1817
Blackfriars . .	1,000	270,000	270	1869
Charing Cross .	1,365	180,000	130	...
Westminster . .	1,220	480,000	390	1862
Vauxhall . . .	806	412,000	500	1816
Hammersmith .	480	80,000	170	1827
Total .	7,897	5,412,000	680	...

The French Government in 56 years spent 76 millions sterling on bridges, thus :—

Years	Cost	Per Annum
	£	£
1814–30 . . .	13,500,000	800,000
1831–47 . . .	22,500,000	1,330,000
1848–70 . . .	40,200,000	1,800,000
56 years . . .	76,200,000	1,350,000

The most remarkable viaducts hitherto made are the following :—

	Length, Feet	No. of Arches	Span, Feet	Height, Feet	Width, Feet	Cost, Pence per Cubic Yd.
Weaver . .	1,484	20	60	84	30	92
Stockport .	1,792	26	63	90	32	91
Dane . . .	1,717	23	63	88	31	75
Rugby . . .	720	13	50	51	30	88
Tamworth .	710	20	30	45	...	99
Llangollen .	1,800	19	85	150	...	90
Wharncliffe .	895	11	70	83	35	144
Trent . . .	1,286	56	20	33	29	86
Kinzua (N.Y.)	2,050	20	60	301	...	...
Cantal (Fr.) .	1,880	...	...	413	...	...

The Kinzua, built by Mr. Barnes, consists of 2000 tons iron and 7000 tons masonry, supported by twenty iron piers, and costing altogether £62,000. The Cantal, by M. Eiffel, is the highest in the world, being nearly the same height as the top of the great Pyramid.

BURIALS

The minimum time between death and burial was among the Egyptians 4 days, Romans 6, and Greeks 11 days. At present it is 48 hours in England, Germany, and Austria, 36 in Holland, 24 in France.

The cemeteries in England and France in 1882 were :—

	No.	Per 100,000 Inhabitants
England . . .	11,304	45
Wales	958	71
France . .	38,041	101

London has 22 cemeteries, with an aggregate of 2210 acres, that is, an acre for 1700 inhabitants. Besides those above stated for England and Wales, there are 1411 cemeteries that have been closed by Order of Council.

The practice of cremation has been recently introduced. A body weighing 140 lbs. produces 3 lbs. ashes ; time for burning, 55 minutes.

Mr. Chadwick estimates the cost of funerals in England thus :—

Paupers . . .	13s.	Gentry . . . £100
Working-class . .	£5	Nobility . . £1000
Middle-class . .	£40	

Average—£10 for each interment, or 5 millions per annum.

The French official classification was as follows :—

Funerals of	Annual Percentage	
	1872–74	1878–79
Rich persons . . .	3.2	3.5
Middle-class . . .	13.6	14.3
Working-class . . .	83.2	82.2
Total . . .	100.0	100.0

BUTTER

The various kinds of butter give the following analyses :—

	Fat	Water	Various	Total	Ratio of Caseine
Devonshire . .	82.7	16.2	1.1	100.0	16.2
Norman . . .	82.4	12.6	5.0	100.0	10.6
London . . .	47.1	42.4	10.5	100.0	7.8
" . .	67.5	24.0	8.5	100.0	6.9
Isle of Wight .	86.3	3.8	9.9	100.0	3.3
Jersey	78.5	10.4	11.1	100.0	2.5
Oleomargarine .	86.0	10.0	4.0	100.0	0.6

An English cow giving 1800 quarts milk per annum produces 140 lbs. butter, consuming 4 tons hay, which contain 168 lbs. fat.

The price of butter in London since 1730 has been :—

	Pence		Pence
1730–1790 . . .	5¾	1841–1860 . .	12¼
1791–1815 . . .	13	1861–1880 . .	16
1816–1840 . .	9½	1881–1883 . .	18

See *Dairy.*

C.

CABS

There are 11,000 in London, and 6000 in Paris ; the former average 80,000, the latter 50,000 passengers daily. The medium fare earned per passenger is 15 pence in Paris, 18 pence in London. The earnings in London per cab are 19 shillings a day in "the season," 9 the rest of the year, or 12 shillings all the year round. In 1888 the Société Générale of Paris averaged 16½ francs receipts and 14 francs expenditure daily per cab, being a net profit of 2½ francs or 2 shillings ; the expenses included

2 francs a day in taxes per cab. The average earnings of this Company all the year round were 15 pence a day per cab over the average earnings in London. The cost of food per horse in Paris in 1888 was 13½ pence, against 18 pence in 1881 daily. The ratio of horses dead or disabled during the year in the Société Générale stables was :—

1858–60	20 per cent.
1867–69	18 ,,
1878–88	14 ,,

A statement published in 1844 showed that Paris had then 3100 cabs, earning on an average 14 francs (say 11 shillings) each daily, and 340 omnibuses, averaging 60 francs (48 shillings) daily.

Cabs kill or disable many thousands of persons yearly in the United Kingdom.

Of all males who die in England, one in 260 is killed by a cab or other vehicle, and of all females one in 2550. The ratio of these deaths to the general mortality is as follows :—

	Per 10,000 Deaths		Per 10,000 Deaths
Birmingham . . .	12	Manchester . . .	24
Sheffield	17	Dublin	33
Glasgow . . .	19	London	37
Liverpool	21	Leeds	79

The value of articles left in cabs in London, and handed over to the police at Scotland Yard, averages £21,000 per annum.

CALENDAR

1. Jewish, 383 days; the Jewish year 5650 began on September 26, 1889.

2. Julius Cæsar's, 365 days, B.C. 46, commenced in March.

3. Mahometan, 355 days, A.D. 622; the Mahometan year 1300 began March 1, 1883.

4. Charles IX., A.D. 1564, commenced 1st January.

5. Pope Gregory XIII., A.D. 1582; now used, except in Russia.

6. The Russian year begins on January 13 of our calendar. The Gregorian calendar was adopted in England in 1752, before which date the year began on March 25, which would now be April 5.

For the purpose of finding the day of the week of any event, the student will be facilitated by knowing the day on which the year began. The following table shows since 1601 the day of the week on which the 1st of January fell :—

Sunday	Monday	Tuesday	Wednesday	Thursday	Friday	Saturday
...	...	...	...	1601	1602	1603
1604	...	1605	1606	1607	1608	...
1609	1610	1611	1612	...	1613	1614
1615	1616	...	1617	1618	1619	1620
...	1621	1622	1623	1624	...	1625
1626	1627	1628	...	1629	1630	1631
1632	...	1633	1634	1635	1636	...
1637	1638	1639	1640	...	1641	1642
1643	1644	...	1645	1646	1647	1648
...	1649	1650	1651	1652	...	1653
1654	1655	1656	...	1657	1658	1659
1660	...	1661	1662	1663	1664	...
1665	1666	1667	1668	...	1669	1670
1671	1672	...	1673	1674	1675	1676
...	1677	1678	1679	1680	...	1681
1682	1683	1684	...	1685	1686	1687
1688	...	1689	1690	1691	1692	...
1693	1694	1695	1696	...	1697	1698
1699	1700	...	1701	1702	1703	1704
...	1705	1706	1707	1708	...	1709
1710	1711	1712	...	1713	1714	1715
1716	...	1717	1718	1719	1720	...
1721	1722	1723	1724	...	1725	1726
1727	1728	...	1729	1730	1731	1732
...	1733	1734	1735	1736	...	1737
1738	1739	1740	...	1741	1742	1743
1744	...	1745	1746	1747	1748	...
1749	1750	1751	1752	...	...	...

Sunday	Monday	Tuesday	Wednesday	Thursday	Friday	Saturday
...	1753*	1754	1755	1756	...	1757
1758	1759	1760	...	1761	1762	1763
1764	...	1765	1766	1767	1768	...
1769	1770	1771	1772	...	1773	1774
1775	1776	...	1777	1778	1779	1780
...	1781	1782	1783	1784	...	1785
1786	1787	1788	...	1789	1790	1791
1792	...	1793	1794	1795	1796	...
1797	1798	1799	1800	1801	1802	1803
1804	...	1805	1806	1807	1808	...
1809	1810	1811	1812	...	1813	1814
1815	1816	...	1817	1818	1819	1820
...	1821	1822	1823	1824	...	1825
1826	1827	1828	...	1829	1830	1831
1832	...	1833	1834	1835	1836	...
1837	1838	1839	1840	...	1841	1842
1843	1844	1845	1846	1847	1848	
...	1849	1850	1851	1852	...	1853
1854	1855	1856	...	1857	1858	1859
1860	...	1861	1862	1863	1864	...
1865	1866	1867	1868	...	1869	1870
1871	1872	...	1873	1874	1875	1876
...	1877	1878	1879	1880	...	1881
1882	1883	1884	...	1885	1886	1887
1888	...	1889	1890	1891	1892	...
1893	1894	1895	1896	...	1897	1898

In connection with the preceding calendar, it will be easy by means of the following table to find the day of the week of any event :—

January	.	.	1	8	15	22	29
February	.	.	5	12	19	26	...
March .	.	.	5	12	19	26	...
April .	.	.	2	9	16	23	30
May	.	.	7	14	21	28	...
June	.	.	4	11	18	25	...
July	.	.	2	9	16	23	30
August	.	.	6	13	20	27	...
September	.	.	3	10	17	24	...
October	.	.	1	8	15	22	29
November	.	.	5	12	19	26	...
December	.	.	3	10	17	24	31

Allowance must be made for February 29 in leap-years, which were those preceding the blank spaces in the previous calendar.

CANALS

The most remarkable canals are :—

Date	Name	Miles	Cost £	Per Mile £	Country
1668	Languedoc	160	680,000	4,250	France
1776	Bridgewater	38	360,000	9,050	England
1785	Eyder . .	26	510,000	19,500	Denmark
1822	Caledonian	60	1,140,000	19,000	Scotland
1825	Helder . .	60	900,000	15,000	Holland
1825	Erie . . .	363	1,820,000	5,000	U. States
1830	Cincinnati .	306	610,000	2,000	,,
...	Rideau . .	132	800,000	6,060	Canada
...	Welland .	41	1,400,000	34,150	,,
1832	Burgundy .	158	2,220,000	14,050	France
1854	Bengal . .	900	2,000,000	2,200	India
1869	Suez . .	92	17,030,000	185,000	Egypt
1874	North Sea .	14	2,030,000	145,000	Holland

* First year of new style, which began September 2, 1752.

The following table shows the mileage of canals and navigable rivers :—

	Miles		
	Canals	Rivers	Total
United Kingdom . . .	2,794	1,020	3,814
France	2,910	4,820	7,730
Germany	1,320	15,760	17,080
Russia	870	33,046	33,916
Austria	1,710	5,490	7,200
Italy	664	626	1,290
Spain and Portugal . .	270	1,285	1,555
Belgium	535	540	1,075
Holland	1,830	870	2,700
Scandinavia	390	300	690
Europe	13,293	63,757	77,050
United States	4,479	47,355	51,834
Canada	535	2,820	3,355
Brazil	...	22,200	22,200
Argentina	...	2,200	2,200
India	2,240	2,600	4,840
China	5,270	3,800	9,070
Total . .	25,817	144,732	170,549

The average cost of making canals has been £9600 in the United Kingdom, £7000 in France, £9800 in the United States, and £15,500 in Canada, per mile.

Among those projected or in construction are the following :—

Locality	Miles	Estimated Cost	Per Mile
		£	£
Panama	46	26,500,000	576,000
Alexandria and Suez . .	150	...	...
Manchester and Liverpool	44	5,200,000	120,000
Malacca	66	4,000,000	60,000
Bordeaux and Narbonne .	255	22,000,000	87,000
Corinth	4	1,200,000	300,000
Dniester and Vistula . .	460	21,000,000	45,000
Black Sea and Caspian .	310	4,000,000	13,000

The Panama Canal was begun in September 1884, the plans showing excavations of 160 million cubic yards; this included a tunnel of 4 miles or 7000 yards, 100 feet wide and 160 in height, to cost £800 per lineal yard. The whole was to be finished in 1892, at an estimated cost of 26½ millions sterling. In December 1885, Baron Lesseps had at work 10,000 men, 169 locomotives, 12,000 waggons and 7 dredges. Each of the dredges was capable of excavating 100,000 cubic yards monthly. In March 1888, after 42 months of work, the total excavations reached only 53 million cubic yards, or one-third of the total, and had cost 40 millions sterling—say 15 shillings per cubic yard, or five times the estimates. The work remaining to be excavated was 36 million tons of stone and 54 million of clay, in all 82 million cubic yards. The works were suspended in January 1889, the company having expended 60 millions sterling, but this was the nominal amount of stock. It is thought the actual works cost less than 40 millions. Death-rate among the men varied from 3 to 10 per cent. yearly.

The Suez Canal is the most remarkable and useful engineering work of ancient or modern times. It shortens the voyage between England and the East by one-third; that is, it enables two vessels to do the same work that would require three by the Cape of Good Hope, the distance in nautical miles being as follows :—

London to	By Canal	By Cape	Saving Miles
Bombay . . .	6,330	10,595	4,265
Madras . . .	7,330	10,830	3,500
Calcutta . . .	7,950	11,450	3,500
Singapore . . .	8,345	11,670	3,325

It was begun by Lesseps in 1856, and completed in 1869 at a cost of £17,000,000 sterling, viz.:—

	£
Preliminary expenses	3,800,000
Machinery	2,200,000
Excavation	7,700,000
Docks and harbours	1,400,000
Transport, buildings, &c. . .	1,936,000
Total . . .	17,036,000

Length, 92 miles; depth, 26 feet. Tolls average £800 per vessel, or 8 shillings per ton of net tonnage. Tugs are provided for sailing vessels at a charge of £200. The saving to commerce by reason of the canal is above five millions sterling per annum, that is, 2½ millions after payment of the fees. The flags of vessels passing through since 1870 have been 77 per cent. British, 8 French, 4 Dutch, and 11 per cent. of other nations.

The traffic returns show as follows :—

Year	Ships	Tons	Average Tonnage	Fees, £
1870	486	436,000	900	206,000
1875	1,494	2,940,000	1,960	1,156,000
1880	2,026	4,345,000	2,150	1,630,000
1886	3,100	8,180,000	2,640	2,260,000
1889	3,425	9,606,000	2,800	2,640,000

The above is the gross tonnage, the net being 70 per cent. of same, the tonnage ratio of the various flags in late years showed thus :—

	1886	1889
British	76.4	77.9
French	8.5	5.7
Italian	2.3	2.9
German	3.9	4.8
Dutch	3.8	3.8
Various	5.1	4.9
Total . .	100.0	100.0

Electric light is now used for passage by night. The mean duration of passage was 48 hours in 1883, and only 27 hours in 1889. Expenses in 1889 were £1,300,000, leaving a profit of £1,340,000.

The ordinary share capital of the company is only 8 millions sterling, and the dividend ranges from 15 per cent. per annum upwards. The sum due on debentures is £8,867,000. The nominal capital called up for making the canal and the exact sum realised are shown thus :—

Year	Issue	At	Realised
	£		£
1860	9,360,000	100	9,360,000
1868	6,667,000	60	4,000,000
1871	600,000	80	480,000
1880	240,000	67	160,000
Total . .	16,867,000	83	14,000,000

It appears, therefore, that the real cost was only 14 millions sterling, or £150,000 per mile. The British Government owns nearly half the ordinary share capital, having bought 176,602 shares, nominal value £3,530,0co, from the Khedive in 1876, at a premium of 12½ per cent., the price paid being £3,976,600. The coupons had been cut off till 1892, but the Khedive pays interest until then. The proportions of Eastern and Southern trade passing to and from Great Britain through the Suez Canal appear as follows :—

British Trade with	By Canal	By Cape	Total
	£	£	£
Australia . . .	12,000,000	43,000,000	65,000,000
China and Japan	23,000,000	2,000,000	25,000,000
India, &c. . . .	69,000,000	15,000,000	84,000,000
Total . .	104,000,000	60,000,000	164,000,000

The value of what passes through the canal is equal to one-seventh of the total foreign commerce of Great Britain.

Comparing the traffic on canals in the various parts of the world, we find the average of tons per mile as follows :—

Germany . 6,000 | England . 8,800 | U. States 10,000
France . . 8,000 | Russia . . 9,000 | Suez . . 102,000

UNITED KINGDOM

It is stated by Haydn that the first canal in England was made by Henry I. to connect the Trent with the Witham in the year 1134. The first, however, of any note was that made by the Duke of Bridgewater, James Brindley being engineer ; it was begun in 1759, completed in 1776 between Manchester and Liverpool at a cost of £360,000, length 38 miles. A canal from the Severn to the Thames was completed in 1789. The first in Scotland was that from the Forth to the Clyde, completed in 1790, after twenty-two years of labour. The Caledonian was begun in 1803 and completed in 1822, being known as Neptune's Staircase, with 28 locks, and so arduous in making that the cost exceeded £19,000 a mile. The Grand Canal of Ireland, connecting Dublin with the Shannon, was begun in 1765 and completed in 1788.

In 1889 the canals of the United Kingdom were :—

	Miles			Worked by	
	Canals	Canalised Rivers	Total	Railways	Canal Cos.
England .	2,500	550	3,050	1,025	2,025
Scotland .	150	...	150	75	75
Ireland . .	144	470	614	96	518
U. Kingdom	2,794	1,020	3,814	1,196	2,618

The annual traffic was estimated as follows :—

Worked by	Miles	Tons Carried	Tons per Mile
Railways	1,196	6,600,000	5,500
Companies . . .	2,618	27,700,000	10,600
Total . .	3,814	34,300,000	9,000

They represent a capital of 36 millions sterling, or £9500 per mile ; annual dividends ranging from 2 to 5 per cent. Some allow vessels of 6 feet draught, others only 3 feet.

The canals of the United Kingdom in actual use in 1887 were as follows :—

		Miles
Owned by railways	. . .	1,421
Independent of railways	. .	1,537
Total	. .	2,958

Nothing is known as to freight charges, but the net earnings do not seem to reach one shilling per ton carried.

FRANCE

The French statistics of canals are as follows :—

Date	Miles	Capital Cost	Per Mile
		£	£
1800 . . .	766	4,600,000	6,100
1813 . . .	890	7,700,000	8,600
1830 . . .	1,450	15,100,000	10,400
1847 . . .	2,690	27,800,000	10,300
1870 . . .	3,150	31,400,000	10,000

In the interval from 1770 to 1844 the following were constructed :—

Date of Works	Canal	Cost, £	Cost, £ Per Mile	Length, Miles	Fall, Feet
1770-1837	Somme	520,000	5,200	98	220
1775-1832	Burgundy	2,200,000	14,500	158	1,650
1784-1843	Nivernais	1,300,000	12,000	110	800
1785-1834	Rhone & Rhine	1,100,000	5,000	220	1,230
1806-1841	Nantes & Brest	1,800,000	8,000	230	1,810
1808-1841	Berry	1,100,000	5,500	200	810
1821-1838	Ardennes	600,000	9,000	65	440
1822-1838	Loire	1,200,000	9,600	124	350
...	Various	1,580,000	7,500	205	...
	Total	11,400,000	8,000	1,410	...

A statement published in 1870 of French canals showed :—

Date of Works	Miles	Cost, £	Cost, £ per Mile
1600-1820 . . .	710		
1821-1840 . . .	1,860	} 17,300,000	5,600
1841-1870 . . .	560		
Total . .	3,130	...	...

The following table shows the length and traffic of canals and canalised rivers at various dates :—

Year	Miles			Tons Carried 60 Miles		
	Canals	Rivers	Total	Canals	Rivers	Total
1850	2,425	4,200	6,625	7,300,000	9,400,000	16,700,000
1860	2,750	4,200	6,950	10,400,000	8,600,000	19,000,000
1870	2,850	4,200	7,050	9,000,000	5,500,000	14,500,000
1880	2,720	4,140	6,860	11,000,000	9,100,000	20,100,000
1885	2,910	4,820	7,730	13,300,000	11,200,000	24,500,000

It will be observed that there is only a seeming discrepancy in the above statements, the first referring merely to canals, the second including canalised rivers.

The first constructed in France was the Briare, connecting the Loire and Seine, 124 miles, begun in 1605 and finished in 1642 at a cost of £1,300,000 sterling. The Languedoc, one of the finest works of the kind, was made by Riquet under Louis XIV., being opened for traffic in 1668 ; it is 60 feet wide, 6½ deep, and is carried up to a height of 600 feet by means of 114 locks, affording transit for small vessels between the Mediterranean and the Bay of Biscay : length, 160 miles ; cost £680,000. The Central Canal connects the Loire and Saone, length 72 miles ; it was completed in 1791 at a cost of £6300 per mile, being carried to a height of 240 feet by means of 81 locks, and navigable for vessels of 5 feet draught. The Burgundy, connecting the Rhone and Seine, was 57 years in construction, length 158 miles, and the most costly in France, averaging £14,500 a mile, or three times as much as the Languedoc, being carried to a height of 1650 feet. France has altogether 74 canals, with an aggregate length of 2900 miles, the average cost having been £7000 a mile, and the traffic yearly 8000 tons per mile.

GERMANY

The German Empire by latest accounts has 1320 miles of canal and 15,760 of navigable rivers, which differs but slightly from a statement published in 1878, viz.:—

	Mileage of Canals and Rivers
Prussia	8,140
Bavaria	1,160
Other States	7,690
Total . .	16,990

The canals of Prussia in 1869 had a length of 430 miles, and the total of navigable waters 3800 miles, perhaps only for vessels of large size. The traffic in 1878 in all internal waters of Germany occupied 20,900 canal-boats and 463 steamers, with an aggregate of 1,550,000 tonnage; the goods carried on canals was about 8 million tons; the principal canal is the Altmuhl, connecting the Rhine and Danube, 107 miles long, 54 feet wide; vessels drawing 5 feet can go from the German Ocean to the Black Sea. The Elbe and Oder Canal is next in importance. By far the greatest inland water traffic is done by the Rhine, which carried 5,500,000 tons in 1866 and 6,100,000 in 1871 : the Prussian Government, between 1831 and 1871, spent 5 millions sterling on improving its course, reducing the length by one-fourth in point of time : the above traffic included 3 million tons of coal. The Elbe in 1872 was navigated by 11,760 vessels of all kinds, manned by 43,600 men; the Weser by 3080 vessels, manned by 10,400 men; the tonnage on the Elbe was 760,000, two-thirds up-stream.

RUSSIA

Official returns for 1886 show as follows :—

	Tons	System	Miles Open
Grain . . .	2,660,000	Caspian . .	8,880
Timber . . .	710,000	Black Sea. .	3,820
Fuel	2,220,000	Baltic . . .	5,050
Naphtha . .	540,000	Azof . . .	2,100
Sundries . .	2,480,000	Various . .	14,066
Total .	8,610,000	Total .	33,916

The total value of goods carried was £19,400,000. There were 1507 steamers, with an aggregate of 86,000 horse-power, 61,000 vessels without steam-power, and 74,000 rafts. In 1886 the Volga traffic stood for 86 per cent. of the total. It was completed in 1825 by the opening of the Vishney Canal, forming a direct highway of 1434 miles from St. Petersburg to the Caspian Sea. In 1889 a sum of £1,300,000 was set apart to make this route navigable for larger vessels up to 220 feet long. The Volga throws off another canal to Archangel in the North, by which goods are conveyed direct from the White Sea to the Caspian. The Tikwina, opened in 1822, is for empty boats returning from the Baltic to the Volga. The Kubinsko is mostly used for carrying timber ; it was opened in 1828 and has 300 vessels. The great centres of the Volga trade are Astrakan, Saratov, Nijni Novgorod, Moscow, and St. Petersburg, the whole system from Astrakan on the Caspian to Archangel on the White Sea being about 2500 miles in length, the Volga running

1900 miles without a rapid, whirlpool, or sandbank ; it is navigated by four steamboat companies with first-class steamers, and such is the traffic by boats and rafts that Nijni Novgorod employs 70,000 Bourlaki or raftsmen, going up or down to Moscow and Astrakan. Boats ascending the Volga usually take ninety days from the Caspian Sea to St. Petersburg. The proposed Dniester-Vistula canal, 460 miles, would connect the Black Sea with Dantzic on the German Ocean. The canal in construction from the Caspian to the Black Sea, 310 miles, is to cost £4,000,000. The inland waters of Russia employ 300,000 boatmen. Canals are open about 200 days of the year in the north, and 270 in the south. One of the earliest constructed was that by the Empress Marie at her own expense in 1808.

AUSTRIA-HUNGARY

A statement published in 1850 gave the Empire 5450 miles of internal navigation. In 1887 the total length of navigable rivers and canals was 7200 miles, including 1700 of canals. There are, however, only two canals of much traffic, that which connects the Theiss and Danube, 80 miles, and that from Vienna to Neustadt, 33 miles. There is continuous water communication from Vienna downward by the Danube to the Black Sea, and upward by the Altmuhl Canal and the Rhine to the German Ocean, in all 1800 miles, of which more than 1000 is by the Danube. Steamboats were introduced on this river in 1850, and it was thrown open to vessels of all flags in 1856. The traffic returns of the Danubian Company in 1880 and 1887 were as follows :—

	1880	1887
Steamers of Company . .	193	190
Tugs	700	729
Passengers	2,600,000	1,650,000
Goods, tons	1,350,000	1,710,000

In summer the part above Vienna is only navigable for vessels of two feet draught.

According to a Government report in 1887 Austria proper had :—

	Miles		Miles
Navigable rivers .	2,440	Vessels and rafts	2,450
Canals	1,710	Rafts only . .	1,700
Total . .	4,150	Total . .	4,150

A sum of £230,000, say £50 a mile, is spent annually on their maintenance. Hungary has 3050 navigable miles.

ITALY

The navigable mileage of Italy is as follows :—

	Miles		Miles
Po	340	Tiber . . .	90
Adige . . .	130	Arno . . .	66

to which add 664 miles of navigable canals, making in all 1290 miles. Lombardy has twelve canals, but only two are navigable, the rest being for irrigation, as are likewise those of Pavia, Padua, and Pisa. The Cavour Canal is the most important, pouring 400,000 tons of water hourly from the Po into the Ticino. Duke Torlonia made a canal recently at Lake Fucino. It is proposed to make a canal from Rome to Ostia, 16 miles long, 72 feet wide, 26 feet deep, cost £7,400,000.

SPAIN AND PORTUGAL

Spain has 1085 miles, Portugal 470, of inland navigation. The Imperial Canal of Arragon, begun in the last century, is far from completion. In combination with the Canal of Castile it will connect the Mediterranean with the Bay of Biscay, a length of 405 miles, of which only 175 are now made; it is 60 feet wide and 10 in depth. The other canals are of trifling importance, and sum up 95 miles. The principal watercourses of the Peninsula are :—

	Miles		Miles
Tagus	570	Ebro	470
Douro	490	Guadalquiver	300

Not more than half the above mileage is navigable.

HOLLAND

Without counting rivers, this country has 9 miles of canal for every 100 square miles of area, a proportion not equalled elsewhere, and four times as great as in the United Kingdom. The Dutch canals have an aggregate length of 1830 miles, the traffic occupying 5600 Trekshuits for conveying passengers, and 15,000 flat boats for cargo; for the maintenance of these canals the State expends £500,000 yearly. The Helder, begun in 1819 and completed six years later, is 60 miles long, 120 feet wide, and 20 deep, allowing two merchantmen to pass abreast, and navigable for the largest vessels; the traffic in 1877 exceeded 1,500,000 tons. The Y, or North Sea canal, made in 1863-74, is 240 feet wide and 23 deep, and brings Amsterdam within 15 miles of the sea: length, 14 miles, cost £2,000,000. The Maestricht is navigable for vessels up to 800 tons.

The water-ways of Holland sum up 2700 miles, irrespective of canals for irrigation.

BELGIUM

This country with relation to area possesses double the mileage of internal navigation that Holland can boast, and six times the European average. There are 29 canals, summing up 535 miles, and 540 miles of navigable rivers. The chief canal is from Brussels to Charleroi, 46 miles, the toll amounting to £1,020,000 yearly; working expenses, £460,000. The amount of tonnage carried on all the canals is 7,700,000 tons.

Traffic returns show as follows :—

| | Tons Carried 60 Miles ||
	1880	1886
Coal	1,600,000	1,700,000
Other minerals	2,100,000	2,100,000
Agricultural products	1,300,000	1,200,000
General merchandise	2,200,000	2,700,000
Total	7,200,000	7,700,000

SCANDINAVIA

Sweden has 365 miles of canal, which are open to traffic 210 days in the year, being frozen the rest. Over £200,000 was spent on canals between 1840 and 1860. The Gotha Canal is the most remarkable; it was attempted by various kings without success, and finally commenced by a joint-stock company in 1793, and completed in 1800, at a cost of £72,000, being only three miles long, but cut through a rock 150 feet high; it has eight locks, and is navigable for vessels of 6 feet draught, paying a usual dividend of 12 per cent. In later years a canal has been made from Lake Meler, near Stockholm, to the German Ocean. In 1886 there were 69,300 vessels paid canal tolls.

Denmark has the Eyder Canal connecting the Baltic and the German Ocean, 26 miles long and 10 feet deep, begun in 1777, and completed in 1784 at a cost of £510,000.

UNITED STATES

The water-ways of the great Republic were stated in 1880 thus :—

	Miles
Navigable rivers	47,355
Canals in use	2,515
Canals abandoned	1,964
Shore line of lakes	3,620
Total	55,454

In 1860 there were 118 canals, with an aggregate of 5460 miles, supposed to have cost 48 millions sterling. This is, however, in excess of an official return published in 1880, viz. :—

| | Miles ||| Tons Carried | Earnings per Mile | Cost of Construction |
	In Use	Abandoned	Total			
					£	£
New York	608	357	965	7,770,000	430	16,000,000
Pennsylvania	629	477	1,106	6,100,000	515	11,000,000
Ohio	674	205	879	840,000	60	4,000,000
Maryland	194	...	194	1,310,000	370	2,000,000
New Jersey	171	...	171	1,860,000	750	2,000,000
Illinois	102	...	102	750,000	220	1,500,000
Virginia	43	197	240	4,045,000	490	2,000,000
Other States	94	728	822	2,368,000	424	5,500,000
Total	2,515	1,964	4,479	25,043,000	355	44,000,000

The earnings per mile are computed on the canals in use. The first canal was that of Middlesex, from Boston to Concord, 27 miles, completed in 1789 at a cost of £110,000 sterling. The famous Hudson and Erie, 363 miles long and 40 feet wide, was opened in 1825, after eight years of labour, being carried over a range of hills 690 feet high by means of 83 locks and 18 aqueducts, at a cost of £1,800,000. The Delaware and Chesapeake, 14 miles long and 10 feet deep, was opened in 1826, having taken three years to make, and cost £400,000. A canal from Lake Champlain to the Hudson, 63 miles, cost £175,000. In 1830 was opened the great Cincinnati and Erie Canal, 306 miles, cost £600,000; also the Cincinnati and Miami, 70 miles, and a canal connecting the Dismal Swamp and the Ohio. Another grand work was the Chesapeake and Ohio, opened in 1834 after six years of construction, 360 miles long, 60 feet wide, including a tunnel four miles long through the Alleghanies. Various canals were at the same time opened in Pennsylvania, in the aggregate 730 miles.

The navigable rivers are officially stated thus :—

	Miles		Miles
Mississippi and tributaries	11,108	Arkansas	3,250
Missouri ,, ,,	7,830	Texas	1,210
Ohio ,, ,,	7,342	Big Black	1,190
Red River ,, ,,	4,924	Atlantic rivers	10,501

The traffic of these rivers and the great lakes is enormous. In 1880 the Mississippi and tributaries had 1100 steamboats and 850 flats, with a capacity of 415,000 tons, carrying merchandise worth 400 millions sterling per annum. The tug-boat *Ajax*, for example, has been known to tow at once 32 flats carrying 21,000 tons, which would have filled 2100 railway waggons. The great lakes have 900 steamers and 1800 sailing vessels, and flats with an aggregate of 590,000 tons, carrying over 9 million tons yearly, of which 2 million tons grain. The ordinary cost of freight in the inland waters of the Republic is 4s. per ton per 100 miles (one cent. per mile), or one-half of what is usual in Europe.

CANADA

There are 7 canals, and these with the navigable rivers make up a total of 3355 miles of water-way. The Rideau, from Kingston to Ottawa, 132 miles, has 47 locks, and was constructed by Great Britain at a cost of £800,000. The Grenville, from Rideau to Montreal, gives a complete system of navigation up to Niagara, 460 miles. The Welland, from Erie to Ontario, 41 miles, cost £1,400,000, width 80 feet, depth 56 feet. The construction of 7 canals cost £6,500,000, being an average of £12,000 per mile; aggregate length 535 miles. Moreover, the St. Lawrence has been canalised at a cost of 6 millions sterling, so that vessels of 4000 tons can ascend to Montreal, which is 1000 miles from the sea, and those of 500 tons, drawing 14 feet, can proceed from Montreal up to Lake Erie and Chicago: before the canalization no vessels exceeding 400 tons could get up to Montreal from the sea. The traffic showed as follows as regards vessels passing through Canadian canals:—

	1876	1887
Vessels	27,400	22,870
Tonnage	3,500,000	3,410,000
Passengers . . .	92,000	83,000

Tolls paid in 1876 reached £84,000. Freight of merchandise in 1887 showed 2,820,000 tons.

INDIA

Canals for navigation were begun in 1854, and the construction proceeded so rapidly that in 1862 the following were in traffic:—

Name	Miles	Cost, £
Bengal	900	2,000,000
Jumna	600	500,000
Punjaub	450	4,000,000
Total .	1,950	6,500,000

Irrigation canals have since been made at an outlay of 17 millions sterling. The maintenance of all canals in India costs 3 millions sterling per annum. The Bengal Canal connects with the Ganges, and has a depth of 10 feet. Navigable rivers have an aggregate length of about 2600 miles.

CHINA

The Imperial Canal of China is the longest in the world, and the greatest in point of traffic: its length is 2100 miles, including river sections (or 825 miles the canal proper), and it connects 41 cities situated on its banks. It was completed A.D. 1350, after 600 years spent in its construction. China has 400 minor canals, of a supposed aggregate of 4450 miles, besides 3800 miles of river navigation.

CANOE

The *Rob Roy*, which navigated 3000 miles of European rivers, was 13 feet long, 26 inches wide, and 12 inches deep.

CAPITAL

In 1882 the following table was published of stocks quoted on the London Exchange:—

	Millions £		
	Amount Quoted on Stock Exchange	Amount Held in Great Britain	Interest Earned in Great Britain
National debt .	762	700	21
Colonial debts .	220	200	10
Foreign ,, .	2,016	400	22
British railways .	730	700	30
Foreign and colonial . . }	825	275	14
Banks	272	260	15
Docks, gas, &c. .	125	120	10
Total . .	4,950	2,655	122

The amount of new capital called up in twelve years down to 1882 was:—

Years	Millions £			
	Loans	Companies	Total	Annual Average
1871–74 . .	930	1,230	2,160	540
1875–78 . .	520	420	940	235
1879–82 . .	430	820	1,250	312
Total .	1,880	2,470	4,350	362

Great Britain provided about one-fourth of the total; some estimates say one-third.

The aggregate amount called up in four years, 1879–82, was as follows:—

	Amount in Millions £		Amount in Millions £
Great Britain .	182	Spain . . .	25
France . . .	301	Portugal . .	11
Germany . .	38	Switzerland .	17
Russia . . .	107	Belgium . .	27
Austria . . .	75	Holland . .	14
Italy . . .	40	United States .	210

Mr. Neumann Spallart sums up the new capital called up in England, France, Germany, and Austria during fifteen years thus:—

Period	Millions £ Sterling		
	Public Loans	Railways and Companies	Total
1871–75 . . .	942	863	1,805
1876–80 . . .	702	539	1,241
1881–85 . . .	368	605	973
15 years . . .	2,012	2,007	4,019

This is an average of 270 millions sterling per annum, or about 40 per cent. of the wealth annually accumulated in the above four countries. One-half of the above went in public loans. If we consider only joint-stock companies Mr. Spallart's figures give an annual average of 135 millions sterling for the four countries, which is in harmony with a statement published in 1882 regarding the money invested in new companies of Europe, America, &c., in twelve years, viz. :—

Years	Millions £	
	Amount, Capital	Annual Average
1871–74 . . .	1,230	308
1875–78 . . .	420	105
1879–82 . . .	820	205
Total . .	2,470	206

It may be assumed that, irrespective of public loans, the amount of new capital absorbed by joint-stock companies all over the world reaches 200 millions sterling per annum. The average annual outlay of new capital in the years 1881–85 was approximately as follows :—

	£			£
Railways . . .	102,000,000		Mines	7,000,000
Banks . . .	22,000,000		Electricity . . .	6,000,000
Building . . .	15,000,000		Newspapers . .	5,000,000

The new companies formed in 1889 were said to represent 203 millions sterling in the United Kingdom.

United Kingdom.—According to the *Investor's Manual*, the new capital called up in London in eleven years was as follows :—

Years	Million £	Per Annum
1879–82 . . .	335	84
1883–85 . . .	246	82
1886–89 . . .	507	127
11 years . . .	1,088	99

The number and capital of joint-stock companies registered in the United Kingdom in twenty-four years down to 1885 were as follows :—

Period	Number	Capital, Million £	New Capital per Annum, Million £
1862–70	6,179	1,010	112
1871–80	10,862	970	97
1881–85	8,002	890	178
Total . . .	25,043	2,870	120

The amount of new capital in 1881–85, if all these companies had been successfully carried out, would have been in excess of the annual accumulation of wealth.

The new capital called up at Berlin in 1888–89 was :—

The result of the above companies down to 1885 was as follows :—

	Number	Capital, Million £
Burst or wound up . .	15,699	2,375
Existing in 1885 . . .	9,344	495
Total . .	25,043	2,870

The actual number of companies existing in the United Kingdom was :—

Year	Number	Capital, £
1877	...	307,200,000
1887	10,894	591,500,000

A return published down to March 1889 showed that in twenty-seven years 30,372 companies had been registered, with an aggregate capital of 3443 millions sterling ; of these, 1684 had been wound up judicially. The actual number may be taken as 11,000, with a capital of 600 millions.

The *Investor's Guardian* published the following list of new companies registered in the United Kingdom during the year 1889 :—

New Companies	Capital, £	New Companies	Capital, £
Banks	57,200,000	Railways. . .	10,100,000
Mines	37,000,000	Shipping. . .	5,300,000
Manufactures .	21,800,000	Electric . . .	5,300,000
Breweries . .	17,600,000	Gas and Water	2,700,000
Land	12,900,000	Various . . .	52,100,000

making a total of 222 millions sterling ; but nearly half of these companies died still-born, Messrs. Spackmann showing that the total subscribed was only £125,400,000, and the amount actually paid on calls £39,300,000.

France.—New capital called up at Paris in 1889 was :—

	£
Public loans	123,500,000
Railways	8,100,000
Banks, mines, &c. . .	19,800,000
Total . .	151,400,000

Prussia.—Engel gives the joint-stock companies established in seventy-five years thus :—

Period	Number	Capital, Millions £
1801–70	418	171
1871–75	857	238
75 years . . .	1,275	409
Liquidated . .	143	30
Existing in 1875 . .	1,132	379

Wenzel adds that from 1875 to 1883 there were established 567 new companies, with an aggregate capital of 28 millions sterling.

	1888	1889	1889	
			Foreign	German
	£	£	£	£
Public loans	55,500,000	20,800,000	10,000,000	10,800,000
Bonds, debentures, &c.	26,300,000	36,400,000	22,500,000	13,900,000
New companies	10,300,000	20,300,000	5,000,000	15,300,000
Total . . .	92,100,000	77,500,000	37,500,000	40,000,000

New companies were as follows :—

Year	Capital, £	No.	Average Capital, £
1888 . . .	9,700,000	184	52,500
1889 . . .	20,100,000	360	55,000

Austria.—The number of joint-stock companies existing at Vienna was as follows :—

Year	No.	Year	No.
1840	23	1867	154
1850	35	1873	1,159

In the last-mentioned year the aggregate capital was 400 millions sterling. The new companies formed from 1871 to 1880 in Austria-Hungary had an aggregate capital of 393 millions sterling.

An official return in 1887 showed the average profits on capital in Austria as follows :—

	Per Cent.			Per Cent.
Gas .	. 12.4	Foundries	.	. 6.5
Insurance .	. 10.5	Banks .	.	. 6.4
Sugar .	. 8.8	Paper-mills	.	. 5.6
Breweries .	. 8.3	Mines .	.	. 4.8
Textile mills .	. 6.6	Steamboats	.	. 2.0

The general average on all companies was as follows :—

1878–83 . . 7.1 | 1885–87 . . 6.5

The average was only 6.2 for the year 1887.

Italy.—Official returns of the existing joint-stock companies showed :—

Year	Number	Capital, Millions £
1870	413	68
1880	644	80
1884	1,037	110

India.—In 1888 there were 910 joint-stock companies, with an aggregate paid-up capital of 22 millions sterling ; this included 97 started during the year with a capital of £1,800,000 in the aggregate. The existing companies were :—

				£
Cotton-mills .	.	.	.	8,700,000
Banks .	.	.	.	3,500,000
Tea and coffee plantations	.	.	.	3,600,000
Sundries	.	.	.	6,200,000
Total	.	.	.	22,000,000

CARRIAGES

The number used in Great Britain has increased since 1812 faster than wealth, as appears on comparing the licenses with the number of persons paying income-tax on more than £200 a year :—

Year	Carriages	Over £200 Income	Ratio of Carriages	Carriages per 1000 Inhabitants
1812	63,130	39,765	158–100	5
1830	85,060	...	...	5
1860	245,000	85,530	287–100	11
1870	325,000	130,375	250–100	12
1880	463,000	210,430	221–100	15

CATTLE

In the last 60 years there has been a very great increase of the various kinds of live-stock : thus horses have increased 104 per cent., cattle 127, sheep 139, pigs 55 per cent. This is much greater (except as regards pigs) than the increase of population in Europe, United States, and Colonies, which has been just 70 per cent.

The following table shows approximately the numbers of each class of live-stock in all countries at various dates :—

HORSES

	1830	1850	1870	1837
United Kingdom	1,500,000	2,000,000	1,900,000	1,940,000
Continent	24,020,000	27,450,000	31,080,000	36,710,000
United States	2,500,000	4,900,000	9,400,000	15,400,000
British Colonies	300,000	800,000	1,900,000	2,900,000
River Plate	2,400,000	3,400,000	4,600,000	5,100,000
Total	30,720,000	38,550,000	48,880,000	62,050,000

CATTLE

	1830	1850	1870	1887
United Kingdom	5,200,000	7,950,000	8,700,000	10,300,000
Continent	62,170,000	72,170,000	81,100,000	91,550,000
United States	8,100,000	17,800,000	25,500,000	49,200,000
British Colonies	1,400,000	3,800,000	8,400,000	14,400,000
River Plate	9,200,000	14,400,000	18,300,000	29,700,000
Total	86,070,000	116,120,000	142,000,000	195,150,000

SHEEP

	1830	1850	1870	1887
United Kingdom	25,000,000	27,970,000	33,800,000	28,900,000
Continent	144,040,000	155,980,000	175,600,000	168,800,000
United States	6,500,000	21,700,000	40,850,000	43,500,000
British Colonies	4,400,000	17,200,000	64,300,000	112,300,000
River Plate	3,400,000	7,300,000	47,500,000	81,000,000
Total	183,340,000	230,150,000	362,050,000	434,500,000

PIGS

	1830	1850	1870	1887
United Kingdom	4,000,000	3,680,000	4,200,000	3,800,000
Continent	40,460,000	34,750,000	39,700,000	44,500,000
United States	16,000,000	30,400,000	26,700,000	44,400,000
British Colonies	1,100,000	1,400,000	2,200,000	2,400,000
River Plate	200,000	200,000	300,000	400,000
Total	61,760,000	70,430,000	73,100,000	95,500,000

VALUE OF ALL LIVE-STOCK, MILLIONS STERLING.

Year	Europe	U. States	Colonies, &c.	Total
1830	730	70	23	823
1850	1,018	114	48	1,180
1870	1,496	274	130	1,900
1887	1,900	501	215	2,616

The number of live-stock, as we have seen, has a little more than doubled in sixty years : the value, meantime, has more than trebled. It must be borne in mind that the foregoing tables include only Europe, the United States, British colonies (without India), and the River Plate, and in these the value of all descriptions of cattle has risen more than 700 millions sterling since 1870. In that interval the value in the United States and Colonies has almost doubled.

Mr. Simmonds has taken great pains to ascertain the number of each class of live stock in the several parts of the world in 1890, and sums up the result as follows :—

	Horses	Asses and Mules	Cattle	Sheep	Pigs	Goats
Europe	34,865,000	4,900,000	104,166,000	214,499,000	46,152,000	21,546,000
Asia	4,443,000	1,061,000	70,850,000	71,669,000	840,000	24,055,000
Africa	721,000	1,068,000	8,203,000	60,820,000	417,000	9,220,000
America	21,920,000	3,286,000	117,249,000	143,581,000	53,974,000	4,851,000
Australasia . . .	1,520,000	3,000	9,339,000	98,366,000	1,143,000	299,000
Total . .	63,469,000	10,318,000	309,807,000	588,935,000	102,526,000	59,971,000

In 1830 the live-stock of various countries in Europe was estimated approximately as follows :—

	Horses	Cattle	Sheep	Pigs	Value, Million £
United Kingdom	1,500,000	5,200,000	25,000,000	4,000,000	84
France	2,600,000	6,700,000	35,200,000	4,500,000	96
Germany	2,500,000	9,770,000	17,300,000	4,500,000	88
Russia	12,000,000	19,000,000	36,000,000	15,800,000	...
Austria	2,500,000	10,500,000	12,000,000	5,500,000	80
Italy	800,000	3,500,000	6,500,000	2,500,000	30
Spain	1,400,000	2,950,000	18,700,000	2,730,000	38
Portugal	100,000	650,000	1,200,000	700,000	8
Sweden and Norway . . .	490,000	2,300,000	2,440,000	580,000	19
Denmark	250,000	800,000	1,000,000	200,000	16
Holland and Belgium . . .	500,000	2,000,000	1,200,000	1,200,000	26
Switzerland	80,000	800,000	500,000	250,000	6
Turkey, &c.	800,000	3,200,000	12,000,000	2,000,000	63
Europe . .	25,520,000	67,370,000	169,040,000	44,460,000	...

In 1850 the numbers were approximately as follows :—

	Horses	Cattle	Sheep	Pigs	Value, Million £
United Kingdom	2,000,000	7,950,000	27,970,000	3,680,000	104
France	3,130,000	12,150,000	33,300,000	5,250,000	166
Germany	2,500,000	11,270,000	21,330,000	3,920,000	138
Russia	13,500,000	20,960,000	37,530,000	8,890,000	...
Austria	3,240,000	10,460,000	17,080,000	7,410,000	120
Italy	800,000	3,660,000	7,000,000	2,000,000	36
Spain	1,500,000	1,400,000	13,800,000	1,300,000	40
Portugal	120,000	750,000	1,980,000	750,000	10
Sweden	400,000	1,630,000	1,470,000	500,000	20
Norway	140,000	900,000	1,500,000	100,000	10
Denmark	300,000	880,000	1,160,000	200,000	17
Holland	270,000	1,260,000	620,000	500,000	20
Belgium	260,000	1,100,000	660,000	650,000	16
Switzerland	90,000	950,000	550,000	280,000	8
Turkey, &c.	1,200,000	4,800,000	18,000,000	3,000,000	90
Europe . .	29,450,000	80,120,000	183,950,000	38,430,000	...

In 1870 the numbers were approximately :—

	Horses	Cattle	Sheep	Pigs	Value, Million £
United Kingdom	1,900,000	8,700,000	33,800,000	4,200,000	170
France	2,990,000	11,720,000	25,900,000	5,760,000	205
Germany	3,200,000	15,400,000	26,500,000	6,800,000	212
Russia	15,600,000	21,400,000	45,300,000	9,100,000	...
Austria	3,540,000	12,630,000	20,100,000	6,990,000	178
Italy	1,020,000	3,490,000	6,980,000	1,550,000	45
Spain	1,610,000	2,450,000	20,200,000	3,000,000	64
Portugal	130,000	520,000	2,420,000	860,000	10
Sweden	430,000	1,970,000	1,600,000	350,000	25
Norway	150,000	980,000	1,700,000	100,000	14
Denmark	350,000	1,300,000	1,800,000	440,000	20
Holland	250,000	1,410,000	900,000	330,000	24
Belgium	280,000	1,240,000	600,000	630,000	20
Switzerland	100,000	1,010,000	570,000	340,000	10
Turkey, &c.	1,430,000	5,600,000	21,000,000	3,500,000	90
Europe	32,980,000	89,820,000	209,370,000	43,950,000	...

The returns for 1887 for the various countries show :—

	Horses	Cattle	Sheep	Pigs	Goats	Value, Million £
England	1,240,000	5,060,000	18,580,000	2,270,000	} 305,000	{ 104
Scotland	190,000	1,110,000	6,730,000	150,000	}	{ 26
Ireland	510,000	4,100,000	3,630,000	1,400,000	295,000	{ 55
United Kingdom	1,940,000	10,270,000	28,940,000	3,820,000	600,000	185
France	3,200,000	13,380,000	22,600,000	5,850,000	1,550,000	218
Germany	3,520,000	15,790,000	19,200,000	9,210,000	2,640,000	262
Russia	20,020,000	23,840,000	47,510,000	9,200,000	1,370,000	...
Austria	1,480,000	8,580,000	3,840,000	2,720,000	1,010,000	106
Hungary	2,080,000	5,310,000	9,840,000	4,160,000	330,000	96
Italy	1,120,000	4,780,000	8,590,000	1,160,000	2,020,000	83
Spain	1,840,000	3,090,000	22,800,000	4,470,000	4,530,000	...
Portugal	140,000	630,000	3,000,000	970,000	940,000	13
Sweden	490,000	2,380,000	1,440,000	550,000	90,000	36
Norway	150,000	1,020,000	1,690,000	100,000	320,000	15
Denmark	350,000	1,470,000	1,550,000	530,000	140,000	30
Holland	270,000	1,480,000	750,000	430,000	160,000	28
Belgium	270,000	1,380,000	370,000	650,000	250,000	24
Switzerland	110,000	1,100,000	700,000	340,000	370,000	...
Finland	...	1,030,000	1,030,000	150,000	...	11
Greece	100,000	260,000	2,300,000	30,000	1,860,000	...
Bosnia	210,000	505,000	1,310,000	...	...	9
Roumania	600,000	3,600,000	6,180,000	2,310,000	190,000	37
Servia	160,000	960,000	3,600,000	1,700,000	...	16
Turkey	600,000	1,000,000	10,500,000	...	720,000	26
Europe	38,650,000	101,855,000	197,740,000	48,350,000	19,090,000	...
United States	15,400,000	49,200,000	43,540,000	44,350,000	...	501
Canada	1,160,000	4,005,000	2,600,000	1,220,000	...	44
Australia	1,480,000	9,140,000	96,600,000	1,100,000	...	67
Cape Colony	260,000	1,270,000	13,070,000	140,000	2,790,000	13
Algeria	350,000	1,210,000	8,790,000	300,000	...	28
Argentina	4,400,000	22,870,000	70,450,000	300,000	...	49
Uruguay	670,000	6,830,000	10,540,000	100,000	...	14
Total	62,370,000	196,380,000	443,330,000	95,860,000	21,880,000	...

If we compare the various kinds of cattle with population in Europe at various dates, we find as follows :—

Year	Numbers				Per 1000 Inhabitants			
	Horses	Cattle	Sheep	Pigs	Horses	Cattle	Sheep	Pigs
1830	25,520,000	67,370,000	169,000,000	44,460,000	11	31	77	20
1850	29,450,000	80,100,000	183,900,000	38,400,000	11	32	72	15
1870	32,980,000	89,800,000	209,400,000	43,900,000	11	30	70	15
1880	36,100,000	96,200,000	200,000,000	47,000,000	11	30	63	15
1887	38,600,000	101,800,000	197,700,000	48,400,000	11	30	58	15

The following table shows the relative figures in Europe for population, horses, cattle, sheep, and pigs at various dates, taking 1830 at 100 :—

	1830	1850	1870	1880	1887
Population	100	118	134	142	150
Horses	100	116	130	144	151
Cattle	100	120	135	144	152
Sheep	100	108	123	118	117
Pigs..	100	86	99	107	109

It appears, therefore, that the increase of horses and cattle kept pace with that of population. The value of all kinds of cattle at different dates compared with population thus, in Europe :—

Year	Population	Value of Cattle, Millions £	Ratio per Inhabitant
			£ s. d.
1840 . . .	236,200,000	875	3 14 0
1860 . . .	275,900,000	1,260	4 9 0
1887 . . .	333,000,000	1,900	5 14 0

The following table shows the number of each kind of cattle to every 100 inhabitants in each country in 1850 and in 1887 :—

PER 100 INHABITANTS

	Horses		Cattle		Sheep		Pigs	
	1850	1887	1850	1887	1850	1887	1850	1887
U. Kingdom	6	5	28	28	135	76	15	10
France . .	9	8	40	36	94	60	15	15
Germany . .	7	8	48	35	70	42	16	20
Russia. . .	22	20	35	28	62	55	15	11
Austria . .	11	9	35	37	57	36	25	18
Italy . . .	4	4	17	16	33	28	10	4
Spain . . .	10	11	16	18	110	140	9	28
Portugal . .	3	3	19	14	50	70	19	22
Sweden . .	11	10	50	52	45	31	11	12
Norway . .	10	8	60	50	110	84	7	5
Denmark . .	40	18	112	74	135	80	33	27
Holland . .	8	7	36	35	25	17	7	10
Belgium . .	6	5	27	25	15	7	11	12
Switzerland .	4	4	38	40	18	25	13	12
Greece . .	5	6	20	15	170	130	14	3
Roumania . .	...	12	40	70	80	115	19	40
Servia . . .	...	8	60	50	215	185	102	90
Europe . .	11	11	34	30	78	58	16	15
United States	20	25	75	75	97	68	130	69
Canada . .	25	23	90	80	100	54	50	25
Australia . .	10	40	160	250	1,100	2,600	30	30
Cape Colony	33	25	140	120	1,800	1,300	20	14
Arg. Republic	280	120	820	605	1,200	1,860	10	11
Uruguay . .	210	110	1,340	1,140	680	1,800	5	5

The countries relatively richest in horses and horned cattle are the Argentine Republic and Uruguay, while Australia leads in sheep, and pigs are most numerous in Servia and Roumania. Those poorest in horses are Italy and Spain ; in cattle, Portugal ; in sheep, Belgium ; and in pigs, Greece. The highest prices for animals have been recorded in England, a cow called Ouida fetching £6200 in 1880, and a horse called Ormond £14,000 in 1889.

CEMENT

The exportation from the United Kingdom showed thus :—

Year	Tons	Value, £	Per Ton, £
1853	21,000	64,000	3.0
1860	79,000	215,000	2.9
1870	150,000	366,000	2.4
1880	277,000	690,000	2.5
1888	613,000	1,160,000	1.9

CHARITIES

The approximate value of property held for charitable purposes in 1880 was :—

	£	Per Inhabitant
		£ s. d.
England . . .	51,300,000	2 1 0
France . . .	70,000,000	1 17 0
Italy . . .	65,300,000	2 8 0

The supposed expenditure for charitable purposes and sources of income are shown thus :—

	United Kingdom	France	Italy
	£	£	£
Endowment . .	2,490,000	2,400,000	1,880,000
Annual bequests .	650,000	1,194,000 }	400,000
Subscription . .	6,900,000	1,500,000 }	
State subsidy . .	...	460,000	...
Total . . .	10,040,000	5,554,000	2,280,000

In 1889 charitable bequests of the United Kingdom amounted to one million sterling, of which £250,000 fell to London, irrespective of donations by living persons.

Hospitals constitute the principal element of charitable institutions.

Continental hospitals usually receive large municipal subsidies, viz. :—

City	Subsidy	Pence per Inhab.	City	Subsidy	Pence per Inhab.
	£			£	
Paris . . .	358,000	42	Nantes . .	15,000	30
Berlin . . .	70,000	16	Florence . .	14,000	21
New York .	34,000	7	Venice . .	14,000	25
Copenhagen .	32,000	36	Stockholm .	11,000	16
Leipsic . .	31,000	55	Toulouse .	10,000	18
Marseilles . .	24,000	16	Turin . . .	10,000	13
Vienna . . .	23,000	5	Buda . . .	9,000	6
Genoa . . .	23,000	27	Christiania .	8,000	22
San Francisco	20,000	21	Rennes . .	8,000	21
Rouen . . .	19,000	44	Havre . .	5,000	11
Bordeaux . .	17,000	18	Frankfort .	4,000	8

The following table shows the number of beds in various cities and countries :—

Year	Place	Beds	Beds per 10,000 Inhabitants	Year	Country	Beds	Beds per 10,000 Inhabitants
1889	London . . .	7,100	18	1882	U. Kingdom .	16,400	5
,,	Dublin . . .	800	21	1885	France . . .	73,900	19
1880	Paris	9,000	41	1886	Austria proper .	32,500	16
,,	New York . .	1,100	9	,,	Wurtemburg .	8,800	47
1876	Rome.	1,500	50	1880	Spain	18,200	10
1872	Rio Janeiro . .	1,100	48	1849	Prussia . . .	8,800	4

In the hospitals of the United Kingdom, New York, and France the average of days to each patient are :—

Dublin .	.	. 27	New York .	. 40
Paris .	.	. 28	All England .	. 31
Glasgow	.	. 30	All France .	. 35

The death-rate of hospitals in various countries is shown thus :—

	Per Cent.			Per Cent.
England .	. . 8.0	Austria .	. . 8.0
Scotland .	. . 9.5	Rome .	. . 7.1
Ireland .	. . 6.5	Lisbon .	. . 13.4
France .	. . 9.5	Norway .	. . 12.0

Next in importance after hospitals are asylums for the aged and infirm or for orphans. Those of the United Kingdom and France are shown thus :—

	United Kingdom	France
Number of beds . . .	104,000	120,300
Cost yearly	£2,600,000	2,760,000

In New York the Children's Aid Society picks up 10,000 yearly, and gives them trades. The orphan asylums of France in 1882 had 61,000 children under training. There are foundling hospitals in France (of which later on), that of Paris receiving 3000 infants yearly, of whom 60 per cent. die under 12 months. At Moscow a similar institute receives 12,000 per annum, the boys being brought up for the navy.

For founders of hospitals and asylums see *Munificence.*

UNITED KINGDOM

The expenditure for charities is estimated thus :—

	£
Charity schools	4,200,000
Asylums and homes , . .	2,600,000
Bible societies	2,040,000
Hospitals	1,200,000
Total . . .	10,040,000

London charities stand for 46 per cent. of the total. They were :—

	Number		Expenditure, £	
	1859	1889	1859	1889
Asylums for old, blind, &c.	135	205	113,000	641,000
Orphanages and homes .	181	318	409,000	835,000
Hospitals and dispensaries	92	209	301,000	655,000
Bible missions	14	112	460,000	1,980,000
Sundry institutions . . .	60	180	400,000	570,000
Total	482	1,024	1,683,000	4,681,000

London charities averaged 12s. per inhabitant in 1859, and 22s. in 1889. It is to be observed, however, that in 1889 almost half the total was devoted to Bible missions, most of which had no connection with London charities. The collections on Hospital Sunday in 1889 reached £38,700, those of Hospital Saturday average £5000 a year. These collections were distributed in 1889 among 86 hospitals and 35 dispensaries (the total number in London being 93 and 116 respectively), and the report published showed that in the year 1888 the said 121 institutions received and treated 76,900 indoor and 1,470,000 outdoor patients, at an outlay of £723,000, being £27,000 over income. The London hospitals had altogether nominally 9700 beds, but only 7100 in use, the remaining 2600 being kept vacant for want of funds.*

footnote: * There were also 27 poor-law infirmaries with 11,900 beds, which cost in the year £336,000, say £28 each. London has in the aggregate 239 institutions for sick relief, which in the year 1887 treated 122,050 indoor and 1,855,000 outdoor patients.

The cost per bed varied from £19 in larger to £42 in smaller hospitals.

The principal hospitals of the United Kingdom in 1882 were :—

Hospitals	Founded A.D.	Beds	Annual Patients	Death-Rate
St. Bartholomew's	1547	600	5,500	6.0
St. Thomas's . .	1548	360	3,200	12.0
Guy's	1722	620	5,600	9.7
Bristol	1735	270	2,600	7.0
Leicester . .	...	220	2,000	5.0
Edinburgh . .	1736	500	4,500	10.5
Aberdeen . . .	1739	240	2,100	6.5
Manchester . .	1753	330	3,000	10.8
Liverpool . . .	...	330	3,000	7.2
Leeds	1767	330	3,000	7.0
Birmingham . .	1778	300	2,700	8.0
Glasgow . . .	1794	630	5,700	10.7
Misericordia (Dublin) . }	1855	230	2,100	6.5
London (Whitechapel) . . }	...	790	7,170	...

There are in the United Kingdom 496 hospitals, with 16,400 beds, relieving 145,000 sick yearly, who are attended by 820 physicians. Total expenditure, £1,200,000, or £8 per patient, equal to 5s. a day for each bed occupied. Death-rate is lowest in small hospitals, viz. :—

Less than 100 beds	.	.	.	.	6.5
100 to 200 beds	.	.	.	.	7.1
Over 200 beds	.	.	.	.	8.0

In the year 1800 there were but 51 hospitals in Great Britain and Ireland.

Charitable endowments have not increased much in the last fifty years. The amounts in 1837 and 1876 compare as follows :—

Year	Endowments	Wealth of U. Kingdom in Millions £	Endowed Sums, per £1000 of Wealth
			£ s. d.
1837 . .	42,600,000	4,100	10 8 0
1876 . .	51,300,000	8,050	6 8 0

The income of endowed charities has actually declined since 1876, viz. :—

					£
1837	.	.	.	.	1,940,000
1876	.	.	.	.	2,198,000
1888	.	.	.	.	2,052,000

The endowments on which income-tax was refunded in 1888 were :—

				£
Hospitals	.	.	.	535,000
Almshouses, &c.	.	.	.	588,000
Schools	.	.	.	779,000
Religious purposes	.	.	.	150,000
Total	.	.		2,052,000

The investment and income of endowments in 1876 showed :—

	Capital, £	Income, £
Real estate	31,100,000	1,558,000
Stocks	20,200,000	640,000
Total . . .	51,300,000	2,198,000

The real estate comprises 154,000 acres of land and some house property.

The above does not include Irish endowed charities, which had in 1876 an income of £270,000 per annum.

FRANCE

Hospital returns for 1864 and 1885 compare as follows:—

	Admitted		Average Days		Died		Deaths Per 100	
	1864	1885	1864	1885	1864	1885	1864	1885
Men . .	203,100	236,200	30	32	16,480	22,700	8.1	8.7
Women	81,300	124,400	35	38	10,430	14,700	12.8	10.5
Children	26,800	44,500	42	58	2,780	5,500	10.4	10.8
Total	311,200	405,100	32	36	29,690	42,900	9.5	9.5

The above hospitals in 1864 had a staff as follows:—

Physicians	2,348
Sisters of Charity . . .	8,854
Servants, &c.	9,561
Total . . .	20,763

The expenditure was £2,320,000, say £7, 10s. per patient; the income was £2,480,000, leaving a surplus of £160,000.

In 1845 France had 9244 charitable institutions, with a gross annual outlay of £4,620,000, viz.:—

		£
1,138	hospitals	2,140,000
7,600	soup-kitchens . .	540,000
506	asylums	1,940,000
Total, 9,244	Total . . .	4,620,000

The summary of such institutions in 1881 and 1885 was as follows:—

	Beds		Finances	
	1881	1885	1881	1885
			£	£
Hospitals .	71,900	73,900	Receipts 4,320,000	4,320,000
Orphanages	17,200	16,700		
Asylums, &c.	77,300	79,400	Expenses 4,120,000	4,360,000
Total .	166,400	170,000		

Asylums and orphanages in 1885 showed as follows:—

	Asylums				Orphanages		
	Men	Women	Children	Total	Boys	Girls	Total
Admitted	28,200	30,100	7,200	65,500	34,900	31,700	66,600
Died . .	3,900	3,900	410	8,210	1,390	1,350	2,740
Death-rate	13.8	13.0	5.7	12.5	4.0	4.5	4.2

The expenses of the orphanages were £680,000, being a little over £10 per child.

The statistics of soup-kitchens or relief offices showed thus:—

	1840	1881	1885
Number . . .	7,600	14,033	14,574
Persons assisted .	696,000	1,449,000	1,778,000
Expenditure, £ .	540,000	1,240,000	1,360,000

The sums received for soup-kitchens were £1,920,000 in 1881, and £2,080,000 in 1885. In the latter year £840,000 was distributed in food, £320,000 in money, and the management cost £200,000, or 15 per cent. of the annual outlay.

The number of hospitals and asylums in 1791 was 1224, and rose in 1869 to 1557, viz:—

For sick	415
For aged . . .	291
For sick and aged . . .	851
Total . . .	1,557

In 1876 the above institutions admitted 438,000 persons. A statement published in 1845 showed the amount of charitable bequests as follows:—

Period	To Hospitals	To Clergy	To Convents, &c.	Total
	£	£	£	£
1801–14	600,000	7,000	8,000	615,000
1815–29	2,040,000	72,000	780,000	2,892,000
1830–45	2,260,000	112,000	232,000	2,604,000
45 years	4,900,000	191,000	1,020,000	6,111,000

In 1881 it was stated that the average number of charitable bequests yearly of all descriptions was 4200, averaging £290 each, say £1,220,000. Foundling hospitals were established at Paris by St. Vincent de Paul in 1642, the Government giving a subsidy of £120, which was raised in 1657 to 40,000 livres, or £1600 per annum. There was, however, a foundling hospital established at Lyons in 1526, which received in the eighteenth century about 1700 infants yearly. The statistics of the Paris Foundling House were:—

Admitted	1760	1860
Legitimate infants . .	735	594
Illegitimate infants . .	4,297	3,205
Total . . .	5,032	3,799

The statistics of Night Refuges and Foundling Asylums at Paris from 1876 to 1883 showed thus:—

Period	Annual Average	
	Night Refuge	Foundlings
1876–79	3,965	2,545
1880–83	6,660	2,865

Among the French charities are lying-in hospitals, where 68,000 confinements took place in 1876, at a cost to the State of only £17,000; besides dispensaries, which gave medicine the same year to 660,000 persons, at a cost of £224,000 for the year.

The hospitals of Paris, which admitted in 1813 only 32,000 patients, now admit 110,000 sick yearly, the deaths averaging 11,600 per annum, or 10½ per cent., against 12½ per cent. in the years 1861–62. Paris has at present:—

21 hospitals with 9,000 beds
13 asylums ,, 10,000 ,,

This is, of course, exclusive of lunatic asylums. The principal hospital is the Hotel Dieu, with 514 beds, which cost for building £1,600,000, say £3000 per bed, or ten times the ordinary cost.

ITALY

The endowed capital of charitable institutions in 1878 amounted to £65,040,000, belonging to 17,870 institutions, and yielding a gross revenue of £3,640,000, but a net income of only £1,880,000, distributed as follows:—

	£
Orphanages	229,000
Marriage-portions	192,000
Alms to indigent	440,000
Alms to sick poor	120,000
Hospitals, prisons, &c. . . .	899,000
Total . .	1,880,000

H

Charitable bequests average £124,000 per annum. The principal hospital at Rome is Santo Spirito, which admitted in 1871–76 an average of 22,600 patients yearly, of whom only 6 per cent. died. The death-rate from July to October was only 3½ per cent. of patients admitted, but in the rest of the year over 9 per cent. The annual death-rate from 1861–70 averaged 8½ per cent. In 1878 there were 102 foundling asylums, with endowed property yielding £65,000 yearly; they admit 40,000 infants yearly.

AUSTRIA

The hospitals of Austria proper in 1886 were as follows :—

	No.	Beds	Admitted	Died	Death-Rate	Average Days
Public .	176	21,830	220,000	21,980	10.0	26
Private	381	10,660	75,000	7,370	9.8	25
Total	557	32,490	295,000	29,350	9.9	26

The public charitable institutions in 1886 summed up thus :—

	Admitted	Cost, £	Per Patient, £
Hospitals	220,000	360,000	1.6
Lying-in hospitals .	16,000	32,000	2.0
Foundling houses . .	43,000	160,000	3.9
Asylums for old .	37,690	205,000	5.2
Soup-kitchens . . .	228,950	360,000	1.6
Orphanages . . .	124,030	...	...

The following table shows the number of these institutions, and the numbers admitted according to sex :—

	Institutes	Males	Females	Total Entries
Orphanages .	1,024	64,850	59,180	124,030
Aged persons .	1,579	16,460	21,230	37,690
Soup-kitchens .	10,645	111,940	117,010	228,950

The lying-in hospitals had 1557 beds, and admitted 16,605 women for confinement, who gave birth to 15,015 infants ; average of days for each woman under treatment, 18 ; average number of beds occupied, 820 ; average cost, 27 pence daily per mother. The number of deaths was :—

					Per 100
Mothers	.	.	.	155	0.9
Infants .	.	.	.	911	6.1

The foundling houses admitted during the year 42,870 children, three-fourths being at once put out to nurse. The year's returns showed :—

	Infants	Died	Death-Rate
In-door . . .	9,740	653	6.7
Out-door . .	33,130	4,962	15.0
Total .	42,870	5,615	13.5

The asylums for aged and infirm showed an average expenditure of sevenpence per head daily.

The only returns published for Hungary are those of orphanages and asylums for 1886, viz. :—

	Males	Females	Total	Cost, £	Per Head, £
Orphanages	1,015	1,581	2,596	23,000	9.0
Asylums .	1,443	2,060	3,503	31,000	9.0
Total .	2,458	3,641	6,099	54,000	9.0

VARIOUS COUNTRIES

Belgium in 1889 had 190,000 acres of land belonging to hospitals and similar institutions. Charitable bequests were as follows :—

Year					No.	Amount, £
1882	.	.	.	.	603	188,000
1887	.	.	.	.	926	105,000

The orphanages in 1887 contained 490 boys, 1213 girls—in all 1703, against 3473 in 1875, a decline of 50 per cent.

Norway has 44 hospitals, admitting yearly 8400 sick, of whom 12 per cent. die.

Brazil possesses the Misericordia Hospital of Rio Janeiro, one of the largest in the world. The returns for 1861–72 showed per annum :—

					Admitted	Died	Per Cent.
Sick .	.	.	.		12,698	2,090	16.7
Insane .	.	.	.		425	53	12.7
Foundlings .	.	.			601	296	48.5
Total	.	.			13,724	2,439	17.8

The New York hospitals in 1882 showed thus :—

	Revenues			Patients
Subsidies .	£34,000	Free . . .		6,945
Pay patients .	16,000	Pay . . .		2,220
Donations . .	38,000			
		Total .		9,165
Receipts .	£88,000			
		Days free .		262,000
Expenditure .	£92,000	Total days .		368,000

The average was 37 days to each free, and 48 to each paying, patient, and the cost in general £10 per patient, or 5s. per day.

CHEESE

Two analyses are given of the various kinds :—

	Chester	Parma	Brie	Dutch	Gruyère
Water . .	30.4	30.3	34.0	41.4	32.1
Nitrogen .	8.0	7.9	5.1	7.0	8.0
Fat . . .	36.6	31.1	53.3	42.8	41.8
Various . .	25.0	30.7	7.6	8.8	18.1
Total .	100.0	100.0	100.0	100.0	100.0

	Chester	Parma	Brie	Dutch	Gruyère	Camembert	Roquefort	Neufchâtel
Water . .	35.9	27.6	45.3	36.1	40.0	51.9	35.6	36.6
Azote . .	4.1	7.0	2.9	4.8	5.0	3.0	4.2	1.3
Fat . .	26.3	16.0	25.7	27.5	24.0	21.1	30.1	40.7
Salt . .	4.2	5.7	5.6	6.9	3.0	4.7	5.1	0.5
Sundry . .	29.5	43.7	20.5	24.7	28.0	19.3	25.0	20.9
Total .	100.0	100.0	100.0	100.0	100.0	100.0	100.0	100.0

The value of cheese produced yearly by a good cow is estimated in Canada at £7, in Parma at £10, in Neufchatel at £14, and at Camembert (France) at £36 sterling. The quantity produced annually in the United Kingdom is probably about 40,000 tons, or one-third of the consumption, the importation reaching 82,000 tons yearly. See *Dairy*.

CHURCH

The following table shows the number of churches and clergy in various countries (1880–82) :—

	Churches	Clergy	Number of Inhabitants to each Clergyman
England . . .	35,916	41,320	610
Ireland . . .	4,540	4,110	1,270
France . . .	39,314	42,543	900
Germany . . .	37,720	31,910	1,420
Austria . . .	36,180	55,240	700
Russia . . .	42,670	49,330	1,700
Italy . . .	22,260	40,150	750
Spain . . .	18,600	42,765	400
United States .	92,167	77,230	630
Australia . .	6,013	2,155	1,300

There are 126 Protestant bishops in the British Empire, viz. :—

	Archbishops	Bishops	Total
England . . .	2	32	34
Scotland . . .	...	7	7
Ireland . . .	2	10	12
Colonies . . .	...	73	73
Total .	4	122	126

The income of English bishops ranges from £3000 upwards, the Archbishop of Canterbury having £15,000 a year.

Since the report published in 1835, the English bishops have been increased from 27 to 34, the Irish reduced from 16 to 12.

There are 1263 bishops of the Roman Catholic Church, of whom 130 hold sees in the British Empire :—

	Archbishops	Bishops	Total
United Kingdom . .	7	42	49
France . . .	17	69	86
Germany . . .	5	23	28
Russia . . .	2	13	15
Austria . . .	19	51	70
Italy . . .	50	218	268
Spain . . .	9	45	54
Portugal . . .	3	15	18
Belgium and Holland .	2	10	12
Switzerland . .	...	6	6
Greece . . .	3	6	9
Turkey . . .	3	12	15
Europe . . .	120	510	630
United States .	12	52	64
Spanish America .	16	79	95
British America .	5	25	30
Australia . .	2	16	18
India . . .	2	22	24
Armenia, Persia, &c. .	27	47	74
Various missions .	...	328	328
Total .	184	1,079	1,263

There are 901 bishops holding Sees in communion with Rome, besides 362 acting as vicars-apostolic on missions.

Rite	Archbishops	Bishops	Total
Latin . . .	151	674	825
Greek, Armenian, &c.	33	43	76
Total . .	184	717	901

UNITED KINGDOM

The report of 1835 regarding the Established Church was as follows :—

	Clergy, Number			Net Tithes, £		
	England	Ireland	Total	England	Ireland	Total
Rectors	10,718	1,395	12,113	3,055,000	520,000	3,575,000
Vicars	4,813	833	5,646			
Canons	733	426	1,159	435,000	214,000	649,000
Bishops	27	16	43			
Total . . .	16,291	2,670	18,961	3,490,000	734,000	4,224,000

The patronage of the various livings was as follows :—

Nominated by	England	Ireland	Total
Crown	952	131	1,083
Noblemen . . .	5,096	340	5,436
Bishops, &c. . .	4,694	924	5,618
Total . .	10,742	1,395	12,137

In 1850 the income of the Established Church of England and Wales was as follows :—

	Number	Income	Average
		£	£
Clergy	10,478	3,005,000	285
Bishops . . .	27	160,000	6,000
Chapters . . .	...	253,000	...
Total . .	...	3,418,000	...

Income					Clergy, No.
Under £100 .	.	.	.	.	1,926
100–200 .	.	.	.	.	2,956
200–500 .	.	.	.	.	4,135
Over 500 .	.	.	.	.	1,461
Total	.	.	.	.	10,478

A report published in 1880 upon the income of the Established Church in England and Wales, was as follows :—

	£
Tithes	4,054,000
Committee grants . . .	776,000
Other sources . . .	973,000
Total . . .	5,803,000

The above, however, includes £962,000 of tithes that go to laymen, which leaves the real church income at £4,841,000, distributed as follows :—

Clergy	Number	Income	Per Head
		£	£
Bishops . . .	33	168,000	5,100
Canons . . .	166	240,000	1,440
Rectors . . .	11,780	3,830,000	330
Curates . . .	5,050	565,000	120
Total . .	17,029	4,803,000	...

Besides the above there is an offertory which has been found to range from £100 to £240 a year, and is supposed to average £120, that is £2,220,000.

At the same time the patronage of livings was as follows :—

Proprietor	No.
Crown	967
Noblemen	5,357
Bishops	2,088
Various	4,476
Total	12,888

The Ecclesiastical Report for 1880 shows that in 40 years the Commissioners expended 22½ millions in creating new endowments to an annual value of £746,000 in aid of 4700 distressed parishes, say £160 each. The Commissioners distribute about £700,000 a year in creating new benefices, to an average amount of £23,000 per annum. Balance still in hand, £8,200,000. The above tables do not include collegiate endowments, worth £550,000 a year. Total clergy of Church of England, 19,000, including 2000 schoolmasters. The Church of England has, moreover, 232 clergymen in Scotland, 820 in Ireland, and 2700 in colonies and foreign countries, making a grand total of 22,752.

The official statement of the Anglican Church in Ireland in 1880 was :—

Number of clergy . .	820	Donations . .	£118,000
Number of laity . .	635,100	Total income .	£248,000
Endowment . .	£130,000	Endowed capital	£3,260,000

There are 12 bishops who receive £41,500 per annum, average £3600 each.

In November 1880 the residue of property formerly belonging to the Protestant Church in Ireland was valued at 12 millions, producing a revenue of £574,000, to be devoted to purposes of general utility or beneficence. In 1889 all had been disposed of, except a surplus of £27,000 per annum.

The Presbyterian Church in Ireland comprises 553 chapels, with an income of £168,000, of which £102,000 goes to the pastors.

In a report on the Established Church of Scotland in 1890, the annual income was shown as follows :—

Period	£	Period	£
1851-60 . . .	208,000	1871-80 . . .	515,000
1861-70 . . .	371,000	1881-90 . . .	607,000

The number of churches in England and Wales in 1883 was :—

Church of England .	14,573	Quaker	375
Methodist	11,514	Presbyterian . . .	201
Independent . . .	2,603	Jewish	60
Baptist	2,243	Various	2,628
Calvinist	895		
Roman Catholic . .	824	Total . .	35,916

In the above are not included 364 Roman Catholic chapels attached to religious houses, possessing no marriage licence.

In 1882 the Roman Catholic Church in the British Empire stood thus :—

	Bishops	Priests	Churches	Laity
England . . .	15	2,112	1,188	1,066,000
Scotland . . .	6	306	295	318,000
Ireland	28	3,290	2,760	3,952,000
Canada . . .	24	1,210	1,050	2,150,000
Australia . . .	16	376	787	584,000
India	22	1,179	...	1,318,000
Other colonies .	20	315	240	466,000
Total . .	131	8,788	6,520	9,854,000

The average income in the United Kingdom is £400 for a bishop, and £80 for a priest. In India it is £260 per bishop, and £36 per priest. In Canada and Australia it is higher than in England.

UNITED STATES

The Census of 1880, and the estimates of numbers of congregations from that of pews, showed as follows :—

	Churches	Ministers	Laity	Property, 1870
				£
Baptist	24,794	15,401	8,532,000	8,400,000
Methodist . . .	28,281	16,759	10,944,000	14,100,000
Presbyterian . .	10,474	8,026	3,564,000	10,600,000
Roman Catholic .	5,975	6,366	6,371,000	12,200,000
Lutheran . . .	5,556	3,102	2,740,000	1,200,000
Christian Discip.	4,681	3,658	2,268,000	1,200,000
Congregational .	3,689	3,589	1,334,000	5,100,000
Episcopal . . .	3,104	3,564	1,412,000	7,200,000
United Brethren .	2,573	2,563	1,196,000	400,000
Unitarians . .	342	394	172,000	1,200,000
Quakers . . .	621	876	272,000	800,000
Jews	269	202	70,000	1,000,000
Mormons . . .	654	3,906	440,000	200,000
Various . . .	1,154	8,824	10,841,000	7,200,000
Total . .	92,167	77,230	50,156,000	70,800,000

At the opening of the Washington Catholic University in October 1889, Cardinal Gibbons stated that in 1789 (when Dr. O'Carroll was consecrated first bishop) the total number of Catholics was only 40,000, and that they are now about 9,000,000, with 84 bishops, 8000 priests, 10,500 churches, 520 hospitals and orphan asylums, 677 colleges, and 3100 schools.

FRANCE

The official statistics in 1880 were as follows :—

Clergy of all ranks	55,400
Sisters of charity, &c. . .	125,400
Church endowed incomes . .	£190,000
Schools, convents, asylums . .	£800,000

The capital value of endowments for churches, schools, convents, and asylums amounted in 1880 to £23,300,000. The annual State subsidy is £1,740,000, equal to 1s. per inhabitant, or £40 a year for each priest. The ordinary income of a curé is £80.

Official returns show the number of clergy and of young men ordained priests yearly as follows :—

Year	Clergy	Ordained during Year
1861 . . .	54,400	1,206
1880 . . .	55,400	1,541
1885 . . .	54,500	1,527

This would show that a priest's life averages 36 years from ordination, or a life span of about 63 years.

ITALY

The Italian Government confiscated properties worth 55 millions sterling, of which nearly half has been sold, viz. :—

	Capital, £	Income, £
Sold (1868–80) . . .	21,200,000	1,450,000
Held by State . . .	33,900,000	1,240,000
Total . .	55,100,000	2,690,000

Out of the above income the Italian Government pays £428,000 per annum to 32,590 monks and nuns, say £13 each. The Pope has always refused the allowance of £120,000 a year offered him, and is maintained by Peter's pence from all nations.

The amount of Peter's pence in 1889 was said to be as follows :—

	£			£
Austria . . .	16,000	Ireland . . .		6,000
Italy . . .	14,200	Portugal . . .		6,000
France . . .	12,800	Asia . . .		4,000
South America .	12,400	Roumania . .		4,000
Spain . . .	8,000	England . .		3,800
North America .	7,400	Africa . . .		3,800
Germany . .	7,200	Poland . . .		3,400
Belgium . . .	6,200	Switzerland . .		2,200

Besides other countries, the whole amounting to £120,000 sterling.

The Vatican records show that there have been 257 Popes, the longest reign being that of Pius IX., who sat for 32 years, the average being 7½ years. The table of duration shows thus :—

Over 20 years	. .	11	5–10 years . . .	57
10–20 ,, . . .		69	Under 5 years . .	120

The nationality of the various Popes has been as follows :—

English . . .	.	1	Spanish . . .	.	5
Dutch . . .	.	1	German . .	.	6
Swiss . . .	.	1	Syrian . . .	.	8
Portuguese . .	.	1	Greek . . .	.	14
African . . .	.	2	French . . .	.	15
Austrian . . .	.	2	Italian . . .	.	201

The number of parochial clergy in Italy is 20,067, of whom 2236 have less than £30 a year income.

AUSTRIA.

There are 98 Roman Catholic bishops, and the Church forests and other properties are valued at 19 millions sterling. Total Church revenue, £1,890,100, the highest income being £30,000 per annum to the Archbishop of Olmutz. Priests average £30 a year.

The latest returns of the clergy show thus :—

	Austria	Hungary	Total
Latin priests	15,026	4,206	19,232
Roman Catholic Greek priests	2,110	2,128	4,238
Russian Greek priests .	446	2,900	3,346
Protestant clergy . .	232	3,602	3,834
Jewish pastors . .	...	740	...
Total	17,814	13,576	31,390

GERMANY.

In 1849 the churches and pastors in Prussia were :—

	Churches	Pastors
Protestant	9,001	6,139
Roman Catholic . . .	7,238	5,605
Jewish	901	...
Total . . .	17,140	11,744

In 1880 the Census showed for all Germany as follows :—

Churches	. . . .	37,720
Clergy .	. . .	31,910

The Protestant Church will probably stand for about 18,000 clergy and 20,000 churches, the Roman Catholic about 12,000 clergy and 15,000 churches : there are 28 Catholic bishops, including 5 archbishops.

RUSSIA

According to Government reports published in 1880, we find :—

Bishops	40	Convents	550
Parish priests . .	49,200	Churches	35,400

The State subsidy is £800,000 per annum, besides which the Church lands give a revenue of £17 to each priest.

In 1801 Russia had 18,300 parish churches, 67,700 clergy, and 554 convents and monasteries, containing 7300 monks and 1300 nuns.

In 1839 there were 29,500 churches of all denominations, with :—

				Clergy
Greek	.	.	.	52,300
Roman Catholic .	.	.	.	10,330
Protestant .	.	.	.	1,050
Total			.	63,680

Besides 63,000 deacons and assistants of the Greek Church.

BELGIUM

Church properties cover 60,000 acres ; there are 6 bishops, and 5428 churches, being a church for 1100 inhabitants, besides 1560 convents.

HOLLAND

The latest returns show as follows :—

	Churches	Clergy
Protestant . , .	2,001	2,125
Roman Catholic . . .	1,022	2,371
Jews	182	137
Total . . .	3,205	4,633

SPAIN.

There are 54 bishops, 32,400 priests, 1680 monks, 14,600 nuns, 18,600 churches, including 65 cathedrals.

AUSTRALIA

The condition of the various creeds in 1881 was as follows :—

	Churches	Ministers	Laity	Churches per 100,000 Inhabitants
Church of England .	1,398	659	1,070,000	142
Roman Catholics . .	791	378	615,000	136
Methodists	1,608	359	301,000	402
Presbyterians . . .	1,046	370	374,000	285
Various	1,170	389	382,000	218
Total . .	6,013	2,155	2,742,000	210

	Churches	Ministers	Sunday Schools
New South Wales . .	1,330	706	1,285
Victoria	2,843	759	1,557
South Australia . . .	725	165	570
New Zealand	553	277	360
Queensland	172	76	100
Tasmania	319	139	112
West Australia . . .	71	33	40
Total . .	6,013	2,155	4,024

CITIES

	Population (1000)	Per 1000 Inhabitants			Mean Annual Temperature		Population (1000)	Per 1000 Inhabitants			Mean Annual Temperature
		Births	Deaths	Increase				Births	Deaths	Increase	
Alexandria . . .	232	45.0	34.2	10.8	69.0	Lisbon	244	...	...	...	60.4
Algiers	62	...	30.1	...	64.3	Liverpool . . .	600	37.6	26.7	10.9	50.8
Amsterdam . . .	372	36.7	23.7	13.0	49.9	London	4,280	34.7	21.2	13.5	50.8
Antwerp	205	...	24.7	...	...	Lyons	402	26.0	24.7	1.3	53.0
Baltimore	332	...	21.1	...	54.9	Madras	398	39.0	38.8	0.2	81.9
Barcelona	260	29.2	...	...	61.0	Madrid	396	37.5	37.4	0.1	56.2
Belfast	185	...	28.2	...	52.1	Manchester . . .	604	36.9	25.5	11.4	48.8
Berlin	1,438	37.5	27.6	9.9	48.2	Manilla	270	...	...	...	78.4
Birmingham . . .	448	37.6	19.8	17.8	48.2	Marseilles . . .	360	...	28.0	...	57.3
Bombay	773	25.6	33.7	...	80.3	Melbourne . . .	458	...	...	...	58.0
Bordeaux	241	...	26.7	...	57.0	Mexico	212	...	30.9	...	60.9
Boston	363	30.0	23.5	6.5	48.4	Milan	321	...	30.6	...	55.1
Boulogne	123	...	...	...	54 4	Montreal . . .	177	...	37.0	...	44.6
Bradford	184	33.1	21.1	12.0	...	Moscow	753	...	...	...	41.0
Breslau	273	37.7	32.5	5.2	46.7	Munich	280	39.5	32.8	6.7	48.4
Brighton	108	30.6	19.0	11.6	...	Naples	491	32.0	33.1	...	60.3
Bristol	207	34.5	19.6	14.9	51.7	Newcastle . . .	145	36.8	21.8	15.0	...
Brussels	463	34.7	23.9	10.8	50.7	New Orleans . .	216	...	22.7	...	69.1
Bucharest	222	29.5	24.5	5.0	46.4	New York . . .	1,443	34.6	26.2	8.4	51.8
Buda-Pesth . . .	443	35.8	35.2	0.6	51.0	Nottingham . .	187	36.7	22.4	14.3	...
Buenos Ayres . .	455	31.7	30.1	1.6	62.8	Oldham	115	35.4	22.8	12.6	...
Cairo	375	...	...	...	71.2	Palermo	245	...	28.5	...	63.1
Calcutta	429	...	31.1	...	78.4	Paris	2,269	30.5	28.6	1.9	51.3
Chicago	503	...	20.2	...	45.9	Philadelphia . .	1,017	30.0	20.5	9.5	52.1
Christiania . . .	136	34.5	18.8	15.7	41.5	Portsmouth . . .	128	34.4	19.7	14.7	...
Cincinnati . . .	256	...	20.2	...	54.7	Quebec	70	...	22.9	...	40.3
Constantinople . .	819	...	...	...	56.5	Quito	84	...	...	...	60.9
Copenhagen . . .	235	39.1	22.1	17.0	46.6	Rio Janeiro . . .	356	35.5	39.4	...	74.2
Dresden	259	35.4	25.4	10.0	49.1	Rome	388	27.2	26.8	0.4	60.5
Dublin	350	29.1	27.1	2.0	50.1	Rotterdam . . .	194	38.8	23.3	15.5	51.0
Edinburgh . . .	263	32.2	20.2	12.0	47.1	Rouen	106	...	31.3	...	...
Florence	168	...	...	...	59.2	St. Louis	351	30.0	19.3	10.7	55.0
Frankfort	138	...	...	...	49.6	St. Petersburg . .	843	37.8	51.4	...	39.6
Geneva	69	24.3	21.2	3.1	47.7	San Francisco . .	234	...	18.1	...	55.2
Genoa	179	...	...	...	61.1	Sheffield	284	38.0	21.6	16.4	...
Glasgow	512	37.4	25.3	12.1	49.8	Stockholm . . .	222	33.0	24.7	8.3	42.3
Hague	118	39.7	23.3	16.4	52.0	Sunderland . . .	117	39.3	20.9	18.4	...
Hamburg	454	37.5	24.5	13.0	47.0	Sydney	382	...	...	...	62.8
Havanna	230	25.4	45.7	...	78.1	Tunis	210	...	...	...	68.8
Hull	155	36.4	23.8	12.6	...	Turin	241	31.5	25.6	5.9	53.1
Jerusalem	28	...	...	...	62.6	Valparaiso . . .	101	...	64.6	...	58.0
Leeds	310	36.8	21.6	15.2	...	Venice	152	30.2	22.7	7.5	55.4
Leicester	123	38.4	21.8	16.6	...	Vienna	801	39.2	29.0	...	51.0
Leipsic	169	...	26.1	...	46.4	Warsaw	432	...	...	...	44.2
Lima	130	...	...	...	73.3	Washington . .	147	...	22.9	...	56.2

The density of population of some cities is shown in the following table :—

	Acres, Area	Inhabitants per Acre
London . . .	76,600	51
Paris	19,500	115
Berlin	16,200	70
Vienna . . .	13,700	55
Florence . . .	10,500	16
Genoa	7,900	22
Dresden . . .	7,200	31
Buda-Pesth . .	6,500	55
Milan	5,500	60
Turin	4,200	58

CIVIL SERVICE

In the United Kingdom there are 29,000 persons, with an aggregate salary of £4,000,000, say £130 each.

CLANS

For the Pretender in 1715 :—

Appin . . .	300		Marshall . . .	500
Breadalbane . .	2,000		Marr . . .	1,000
Caithness . . .	500		Montrose . . .	2,000
Cameron . . .	1,000		Murray . . .	300
Carnworth . . .	300		Nairn . . .	1,000
Clanronald . .	1,000		Nithsdale . . .	300
Glencoe . . .	300		Ogilvy . . .	500
Glengary . . .	500		Panmure . . .	500
Glenmoristan . .	100		Perth . . .	1,500
Gordon . . .	300		Robertson . . .	500
Hume . . .	500		Seaforth . . .	3,000
Kenmore . . .	300		Southesk . . .	300
Keppoch . . .	300		Stormont . . .	300
Linlithgow . . .	300		Straglas . . .	100
Lovat . . .	800		Strathmore . . .	300
M'Donald . . .	1,000		Tullibardine . .	6,000
M'Gregor . . .	500		Wigtown . . .	300
M'Intosh . . .	1,000		Wintoun . . .	300
M'Lean . . .	1,000			
M'Pherson . . .	500		Total . . .	31,700

For King George :—

Annandale	.	.	500	Dundonald	. .	300	Kilmarnock	. .	300	Ross	. . .	500
Argyle	.	.	4,000	Eglinton .	. .	300	Lauderdale	. .	300	Rothes	. . .	500
Buccleuch	.	.	1,000	Forbes .	. .	500	M'Leod .	. .	1,000	Roxburgh	. .	500
Cassils	.	.	500	Glencairn .	. .	300	M'Neil .	. .	120	Sutherland	. .	1,000
Douglas .	.	.	500	Grant .	. .	1,000	Morton .	. .	300	Weems .	. .	300
Dumfries .	.	.	200	Hamilton .	. .	1,000	Rae .	. .	500		

Total . 15,420

COAL

The total production of coal in the nineteenth century has been approximately as follows :—

Period	Great Britain	France	Germany	Russia	Belgium	Austria	United States	Spain	Canada	Australia	India	Japan	Various	Total
	Millions of Tons												
1801–20 . . .	210	18	25	...	8	3	5	...	...	...	...	...	8	277
1821–40 . . .	390	41	48	...	47	8	13	...	...	...	...	...	19	566
1841–50 . . .	420	41	47	...	51	14	44	...	...	...	...	...	20	637
1851–60 . . .	650	69	122	...	82	24	110	1	...	2	3	...	30	1,093
1861–70 . . .	970	117	277	3	120	70	260	3	5	7	5	1	35	1,873
1871–80 . . .	1,305	170	481	19	153	135	510	6	10	14	8	7	37	2,855
1881–89 . . .	1,461	190	662	37	160	184	970	10	17	30	12	12	40	3,785
89 years . . .	5,406	646	1,662	59	621	438	1,912	20	32	53	28	20	189	11,086

Period	Great Britain	France	Germany	Russia	Belgium	Austria	United States	Spain	Canada	Australia	India	Japan	Various	Total
	Value, Million £ Sterling												
1801–20 . . .	105	11	10	...	4	1	2	...	...	...	...	...	3	136
1821–40 . . .	175	23	18	...	19	3	5	...	...	...	...	...	7	250
1841–50 . . .	168	21	16	...	18	5	18	...	...	...	...	...	7	253
1851–60 . . .	228	31	34	...	33	7	40	...	...	1	1	...	10	385
1861–70 . . .	370	53	75	1	53	18	91	1	2	3	2	...	12	681
1871–80 . . .	600	89	121	6	64	27	167	2	3	8	3	2	12	1,104
1881–89 . . .	482	85	165	12	59	31	333	3	6	13	4	4	12	1,209
89 years . . .	2,128	313	439	19	250	92	656	6	11	25	10	6	63	4,018

The following table shows approximately the production and consumption in several countries at various dates :—

Year	Production, Tons							
	Great Britain	France	Germany	United States	Belgium	Austria	Various	The World
1800 . . .	10,100,000	800,000	300,000	200,000	...	...	200,000	11,600,000
1820 . . .	12,500,000	1,200,000	1,500,000	500,000	1,000,000	...	500,000	17,200,000
1840 . . .	30,000,000	3,300,000	3,400,000	1,800,000	3,900,000	400,000	2,000,000	44,800,000
1850 . . .	49,000,000	4,400,000	6,700,000	8,000,000	5,800,000	2,000,000	5,500,000	81,400,000
1860 . . .	82,000,000	8,300,000	16,700,000	15,200,000	9,600,000	3,500,000	7,000,000	142,300,000
1870 . . .	110,000,000	13,300,000	34,000,000	32,900,000	13,700,000	9,500,000	9,000,000	213,400,000
1880 . . .	147,000,000	19,400,000	59,100,000	70,500,000	16,900,000	16,100,000	11,000,000	340,000,000
1889 , . .	177,000,000	24,600,000	84,900,000	142,000,000	19,800,000	24,000,000	12,700,000	485,000,000

Year	Consumption, Tons					
	Great Britain	France	Germany	United States	Belgium	Austria
1830	15,500,000	2,700,000	2,500,000	1,300,000	2,000,000	300,000
1840	29,000,000	4,800,000	3,400,000	1,800,000	3,500,000	400,000
1850	46,000,000	9,300,000	6,000,000	8,000,000	4,500,000	2,000,000
1860	75,000,000	14,300,000	15,000,000	15,500,000	6,100,000	3,700,000
1870	98,000,000	18,800,000	30,000,000	33,000,000	10,500,000	10,000,000
1880	128,000,000	28,800,000	52,000,000	72,000,000	11,500,000	14,500,000
1889	148,000,000	34,600,000	75,000,000	143,000,000	14,300,000	22,000,000

The average consumption yearly per inhabitant was approximately as follows :—

	Cwts. per Inhabitant		
	1830	1850	1888
United Kingdom . .	13	33	72
United States . .	2	7	40
Germany . . .	1	4	28
France . . .	2	5	16
Belgium . . .	10	18	48
Russia . . .	...	...	2
Austria . . .	...	2	11
Holland . . .	...	5	16
Spain . . .	...	1	2
Italy . . .	...	1	2
Sweden . . .	...	1	6
Norway . . .	...	1	6
Denmark . . .	...	1	6
Switzerland . .	...	1	5
Europe . . .	2	5	18

Since 1830 the consumption in Europe of coal per inhabitant has multiplied ninefold.

This is caused partly by manufactures, partly by railways and steamboats, but it is expected that the use of electric power will in future supersede in some manner that of coal. Meantime the consumption of coal increases year by year.

The following table shows the extent and estimated contents of some of the coalfields of the world :—

	Square Miles	Tons
Great Britain . . .	9,000	90,000,000,000
France	1,800	...
Germany	3,600	39,000,000,000
Russia	27,000	10,000,000,000
Belgium, Spain, &c. .	1,400	...
United States . . .	194,000	...
India	35,000	14,000,000,000
China and Japan . .	200,000	150,000,000,000
Total . .	471,800	303,000,000,000

The contents, as estimated above, include nothing beyond a depth of 4000 feet, the deepest colliery at present working being that of Lambert in Belgium, 3500 feet. The deepest in the United Kingdom is the Rosebridge, 2500 feet. The above five coalfields contain apparently 303,000 millions of tons, which is enough for 700 years, at the present rate of consumption. If to the above be added the contents of coalfields in the United States, Canada, Australia, France, Spain, and Belgium, the supply will be found ample for 1000 years. Improved machinery has greatly increased the yield per miner, and thus produced a fall in price, to the advantage of all industries. The official returns of Great Britain, Belgium, and Austria show as follows :—

	1874			1885		
	Miners	Tons Raised	Tons per Miner	Miners	Tons Raised	Tons per Miner
Great Britain . .	539,000	125,000,000	232	485,000	160,000,000	330
Belgium . . .	110,000	15,000,000	136	101,000	17,000,000	168
Austria . . .	67,000	9,000,000	135	73,000	18,000,000	247

In 1889 the coal used for making iron was approximately as follows :—

	Tons
Great Britain	17,400,000
United States	16,600,000
Germany	10,000,000
France, &c.	10,300,000
Total . . .	54,300,000

In 1885 the coal-mining industry of the world stood approximately as follows :—

	Million Tons Coal	Number of Miners	Tons per Miner	Value of Coal, £	Product per Miner, £
Great Britain .	160	485,000	330	53,700,000	111
United States .	104	300,000	347	41,600,000	139
Germany . .	74	220,000	336	17,200,000	78
France . . .	20	102,000	196	9,000,000	88
Belgium . . .	17	101,000	168	6,400,000	63
Austria . . .	20	73,000	270	4,200,000	57
Other countries	20	100,000	200	5,000,000	50
Total ? .	415	1,381,000	300	137,100,000	99

The number of tons raised per miner is greater in United States and Germany than in Great Britain. Three English miners, nevertheless, raise as much as five French, and the price of coal in France is always much higher than in England.

Current prices at pit's mouth were :—

Period	Pence per Ton					
	England	France	Belgium	Austria	Germany	United States
1871–75 . . .	87	190	168	78	108	114
1876–80 . . .	88	120	102	66	66	80
1881–85 . . .	72	108	90	60	63	100

It appears that 9 tons of Massachusetts have as much carbon as 10 tons of Newcastle (English) coal. The percentage of coke obtained is as follows :—

Westphalia . .	36 per cent.	Pennsylvania .	89 per cent.
Marseilles . .	41 ,,	Mayenne . . .	90 ,,
Lancashire . .	58 ,,	Wales	91 ,,

The specific gravity and percentage of carbon in different kinds of coal are shown thus :—

	Weight, Lbs. per Cubic Yd.	Percentage Carbon		Weight, Lbs. per Cubic Yd.	Percentage Carbon
Rhode Island . . .	3,054	86	Newcastle . . .	2,160	87
Massachusetts . . .	2,882	97	Peat	2,160	57
Pennsylvania . . .	2,715	89	Marseilles . . .	2,080	63
Mayenne (France) . .	2,293	91	Greek . . .	2,020	60
Swansea . . .	2,266	89	Westphalia . . .	1,840	63
Lancashire . . .	2,240	83	Wood . . .	1,100	50

UNITED KINGDOM

The production, consumption, and export since 1820 were as follows :—

Year	Tons			Year	Tons		
	Production	Consumption	Export		Production	Consumption	Export
1820	12,500,000	12,250,000	250,000	1860 . . .	82,000,000	75,000,000	7,000,000
1830	15,000,000	15,500,000	500,000	1870 . . .	110,000,000	98,000,000	12,000,000
1840	30,000,000	29,000,000	1,000,000	1880 . . .	147,000,000	128,000,000	19,000,000
1850	49,000,000	46,000,000	3,000,000	1889 . . .	177,000,000	148,000,000	29,000,000

Chisholm's tables of British coal exported in 35 years, ending 1889, show as follows :—

Period	Tons Exported to							
	France	Germany	Russia	Italy	Spain	Egypt	Various	Total
1855–60 . .	7,500,000	7,800,000	1,600,000	...	2,500,000	500,000	19,100,000	39,000,000
1861–70 . .	17,200,000	17,400,000	5,500,000	2,700,000	6,600,000	3,300,000	43,300,000	96,000,000
1871–80 . .	28,000,000	25,500,000	10,200,000	10,900,000	9,400,000	5,500,000	59,500,000	149,000,000
1881–89 . .	37,300,000	27,800,000	13,800,000	24,000,000	14,700,000	10,100,000	86,300,000	214,000,000
35 years . .	90,000,000	78,500,000	31,100,000	37,600,000	33,200,000	19,400,000	208,200,000	498,000,000

In the above table Holland is included with Germany, and Portugal with Spain. About one-sixth of the coal raised in Great Britain is exported.

The existing coal-fields of Great Britain in 1880 were as follows :—

	Million Tons	Contents of Field, Million Tons	Years of Supply
South Wales . .	15	32,000	2,150
Midland . . .	15	18,000	1,200
Northumberland .	16	10,000	620
Stafford . . .	15	6,000	400
Lancashire . .	22	5,000	230
Yorkshire, &c. .	46	9,000	196
Scotland . . .	18	10,000	550
Total . .	147	90,000	612

The output in the seventeenth century averaged 2,400,000 tons per annum ; in the eighteenth nearly 5,000,000.

The production in 1889 was 177 million tons, and the uses to which the coal was devoted were more or less thus :—

	Tons
Factories	55,000,000
Domestic use	40,000,000
Railways and steamers . .	20,000,000
Gas and water works . . .	20,000,000
Mines	13,000,000
Export	29,000,000
Total .	177,000,000

The price of coal in London since 1730 has averaged as follows :—

Period	Per Ton	Period	Per Ton
1730–50	£1 7 2	1841–50	£0 19 0
1751–99	1 14 9	1851–60	0 18 6
1800–20	2 13 3	1861–70	0 18 5
1820–30	1 12 0	1871–80	0 18 4
1831–40	1 4 0		

The price in England since 1782, at port of shipment, has averaged as follows : —

Period	Pence	Period	Pence
1782–1800	180	1861–1870	122
1801–1820	156	1871–1875	184
1821–1850	120	1876–1880	116
1851–1860	115	1881–1889	108

Loss of life by colliery explosions since 1851 shows thus :—

Period	Explosions	Killed	Annual Average		
			Killed	Tons, Output	Tons, per Killed
1851–71	1,437	4,977	238	82,000,000	344,000
1872–80	353	2,387	265	131,000,000	495,000
1881–89	211	1,361	151	160,000,000	1,060,000

FRANCE

The following table shows the production and consumption, as officially stated :—

Period	Tons per Annum			Cwts. per Inhabitant
	Production	Net Imports	Consumption	
1787–89	227,000	233,000	460,000	0.4
1802	844,000	91,000	935,000	0.7
1811–20	895,000	183,000	1,078,000	0.7
1821–30	1,490,000	438,000	1,928,000	1.3
1831–40	2,570,000	894,000	3,464,000	2.0
1841–50	4,100,000	2,048,000	6,148,000	3.5
1851–60	6,900,000	4,550,000	11,450,000	6.5
1861–70	11,700,000	6,800,000	18,500,000	10.0
1871–80	17,000,000	7,700,000	24,700,000	13.5
1881–86	19,200,000	9,800,000	29,000,000	15.5
1889	24,600,000	10,000,000	34,600,000	18.0

The first colliery in France was opened in 1722 ; the number working in 1835 was 223, employing 19,000 miners, and steam-engines representing 6000 horse-power. The French collieries in 1879 gave :—

	Amount	Per Ton
	£	£ s. d.
Wages	4,040,000	0 4 8
Other expenses . . .	3,320,000	0 3 11
Net profit . . .	1,480,000	0 1 9
Value . .	8,840,000	0 10 4

The most productive mines in the returns of 1842 and 1864 were :—

Mines	Tons	
	1842	1864
Valenciennes	907,000	3,120,000
St. Etienne	1,290,000	2,950,000
Calais	290,000	1,170,000
Creuzot . .· . .	230,000	680,000
Others	483,000	2,880,000
Total . .	3,200,000	10,800,000

In 1888 there were 100,100 miners, average wages 3s. a day, who raised in twelve months 22,500,000 or 225 tons each, value 9s. a ton. There were 163 collieries that paid dividends, and 129 were worked at a loss. The Pas de Calais mines yielded 12,200,000 tons, or more than half the total.

GERMANY

The production of the last forty years may be summed up thus :—

Period	Millions of Tons		
	Coal	Lignite	Total
1850–59 . . .	88	27	115
1860–69 . . .	200	61	261
1870–79 . . .	356	100	456
1880–89 . . .	570	148	718
40 years . . .	1,214	336	1,550

According to "Engineering," Prussia has two coal-beds containing 100,000 millions of tons ; other estimates say 39,000 millions, but even the latter would suffice all Germany for 450 years.

RUSSIA

The production has grown tenfold in twenty years, viz. :—

Year						Tons
1866	.	.	.	.	.	390,000
1876	.	.	.	.	.	2,050,000
1887	.	.	.	.	.	4,450,000

The principal coalfields are :—

					Tons
Don	.	.	.	.	2,000,000
Kielo, Poland	.	.	.	2,000,000
Moscow.	.	.	.	.	450,000
Total	.	.	.	4,450,000

There are about 32,000 miners employed.

INDIA

The coalfields cover 35,000 square miles, or four times the area of those of the United Kingdom, but have less cubic capacity, as they are estimated to contain only 14,000 million of tons, or one-sixth of those of Great Britain. In fact, their contents would only last the British consumption for eighty years. The product of the Indian coalfields is increasing. In 1860 it was 390,000 tons, rising to 760,000 in 1880, and 1,800,000 in 1890.

CANADA

The official handbook gives the production thus :—

Year	Tons		
	Nova Scotia	British Columbia	Total
1874	980,000	80,000	1,060,000
1880	1,160,000	270,000	1,430,000
1886	1,680,000	330,000	2,010,000

Canada imports yearly 2,100,000 tons ; the consumption therefore reaches 4,100,000 tons, equal to 16 cwts. per inhabitant. Professor Dana says the Nova Scotia coal-bed has an area of 18,000 square miles.

AUSTRALIA

Coal was discovered in 1847, and the production has been :—

Year	New South Wales	New Zealand	Total
1860	370,000	...	370,000
1870	870,000	...	870,000
1880	1,450,000	300,000	1,750,000
1888	3,200,000	620,000	3,820,000

The total quantity raised has been approximately thus :—

Period	New South Wales	New Zealand	Total
1847–60 . . .	2,020,000	...	2,020,000
1861–70 . . .	6,700,000	...	6,700,000
1871–80 . . .	13,100,000	700,000	13,800,000
1881–88 . . .	21,330,000	3,900,000	25,230,000
42 years . . .	43,150,000	4,600,000	47,750,000

Small quantities have also been raised in Queensland and Tasmania. The total value of coal raised in forty-two years, according to Mr. Coghlan, was :—

					£
New South Wales	.	.	.	.	22,320,000
New Zealand	.	.	.	.	2,670,000
Queensland	.	.	.	.	900,000
Tasmania .	.	.	.	.	180,000
	Total	.	.	.	26,070,000

The returns for 1888 were as follows :—

	Miners	Tons Raised	Value, £	Tons per Miner
New South Wales	9,300	3,200,000	1,460,000	344
New Zealand . .	1,750	610,000	340,000	348
Queensland, &c. .	750	360,000	140,000	480
Total . .	11,800	4,170,000	1,940,000	355

The average pay per miner in New South Wales was £85 per annum, or 43 pence per ton of coal raised.

UNITED STATES

Coal was first discovered in 1768 in Rhode Island and Pennsylvania. Mining was commenced at Pittsburg in 1784, and in Rhode Island in 1808, both seams being anthracite. In the course of a few years the industry became of such importance that by 1850 Pennsylvania had already constructed 7 canals and 27 railways expressly for carrying coal. In 1840 the output was as follows :—

				Tons
Pennsylvania .	.	.	.	1,300,000
Virginia .	.	.	.	400,000
Rhode Island, &c.	.	.	.	100,000
	Total	.	.	1,800,000

In that year the number of miners engaged was 7000, showing an average of 260 tons per man. The production increased very rapidly, but was hardly sufficient for requirements, the Union always importing some coal from

Europe. The production, according to Census returns, compares thus with population :—

Year	Tons	Cwts. per Inhabitant
1840	1,800,000	2.1
1850	8,000,000	7.0
1860	15,200,000	9.5
1870	32,900,000	17.5
1880	70,500,000	28.0
1888	142,000,000	44.0

The production in 1888 was as follows :—

	Tons		
	Anthracite	Bituminous	Total
Pennsylvania . .	43,900,000	33,800,000	77,700,000
Illinois	...	14,700,000	14,700,000
Ohio	...	10,900,000	10,900,000
West Virginia .	...	5,500,000	5,500,000
Various . . .	...	33,200,000	33,200,000
Total . .	43,900,000	98,100,000	142,000,000

The estimated area of the principal fields is :—

Professor Dana		Census Report	
Bed	Sq. Miles	Bed	Sq. Miles
Alleghany . . .	59,000	Missouri . . .	27,000
Illinois	47,000	Illinois . . .	37,000
Missouri . . .	78,000	Kansas . . .	22,000
Michigan . . .	7,000	Various . . .	109,400
Total . .	191,000	Total . .	195,400

COCOA

Year	Consumption in United Kingdom			
	Lbs.	Duty, per Lb.	Price, per Lb.	Consumption, Oz. per Inhab.
		Pence	Pence	
1831 . .	440,000	6	9	$\frac{1}{4}$
1841 . .	1,220,000	2	7	$\frac{1}{4}$
1851 . .	5,310,000	2	5	3
1861 . .	4,520,000	1	6	$2\frac{1}{2}$
1871 . .	7,252,000	1	$5\frac{1}{2}$	4
1881 . .	10,885,000	1	8	5
1888 . .	18,200,000	1	$7\frac{1}{2}$	$\frac{5}{8}$

COFFEE

In a little over fifty years the crop has increased nearly eightfold, viz. :—

Year			Tons	Year			Tons
1832	.	.	95,000	1865	.	.	422,000
1844	.	.	255,000	1875	.	.	505,000
1855	.	.	321,000	1885	.	.	718,000

The production by countries is shown as follows :—

	1855	1880	1885
	Tons	Tons	Tons
Brazil	163,000	333,000	389,000
Java	70,000	90,000	92,000
Ceylon . . .	29,000	33,000	15,000
West Indies . .	28,000	42,000	54,000
Spanish America . .	16,000	70,000	123,000
Arabia . . .	5,000	5,000	5,000
India . . .	5,000	15,000	17,000
Manilla, &c. . .	5,000	20,000	23,000
Total .	321,000	608,000	718,000

It has been asserted that the total coffee crop of the world in 1820 did not exceed 50,000 tons.

Consumption for five years ending 1884 compares with five years ending 1864 as follows :—

	Tons, per Annum		Oz. yearly, per Inhabitant	
	1860–64	1880–84	1860–64	1880–84
United Kingdom .	16,000	15,000	19	14
France . . .	40,000	65,000	37	62
Germany . . .	70,000	105,000	69	81
Russia . . .	6,000	8,000	3	3
Austria . . .	21,000	36,000	19	32
Italy . . .	12,000	14,000	19	17
Spain and Portugal .	3,000	5,000	5	9
Scandinavia . .	12,000	25,000	80	110
Holland . . .	14,000	40,000	145	322
Belgium . . .	18,000	25,000	131	158
Switzerland . .	7,000	9,000	98	114
United States . .	90,000	215,000	90	140
Brazil, &c. . .	81,000	78,000	...	...
Total .	390,000	640,000	..	...

The coffee fields of Brazil cover 2,200,000 acres, with about 900 million trees—that is, 400 per acre, each tree averaging almost 1 lb. per annum, the industry employing 800,000 hands.

CONSUMPTION IN UNITED KINGDOM.

Year	Millions Lbs.	Oz. per Inhabitant	Duty, per Lb.	Price, per Cwt.
			Pence	Shillings
1801 . . .	1	1	6	87
1811 . . .	6	5	7	42
1821 . . .	7	5	12	102
1831 . . .	22	14	6	56
1841 . . .	27	16	6	98
1851 . . .	30	18	6	68
1861 . . .	35	21	3	69
1871 . . .	30	15	3	63
1881 . . .	31	14	2	78
1888 . . .	30	13	2	76

COLONIES

Those of the different European Powers show as follows :—

	Population	Square Miles	Commerce, £	Revenue, £	Railways, Miles
British	232,800,000	7,946,000	448,600,000	119,400,000	38,050
French	32,040,000	1,080,000	35,300,000	4,600,000	2,290
Spanish	8,200,000	170,000	42,500,000	10,000,000	400
Portuguese . . .	2,800,000	206,000	2,000,000	1,000,000	...
Dutch	24,000,000	660,000	32,000,000	12,000,000	...
Danish	130,000	75,000	1,000,000	...	...
German	385,000	99,000	...	...	...
Total . .	300,355,000	10,236,000	561,400,000	147,000,000	40,740

BRITISH

The British colonies are as follows :—

	Population	Commerce, £	Revenue, £	Debt, £	Railways, Miles	Area, Square Miles
Australia	3,550,000	107,800,000	24,800,000	157,500,000	9,620	3,160,000
Canada	5,020,000	43,900,000	7,600,000	47,300,000	11,780	3,450,000
South Africa . .	1,860,000	17,000,000	3,900,000	26,500,000	1,820	230,000
West Africa . .	1,560,000	2,500,000	250,000	100,000	...	33,000
Mauritius . . .	370,000	5,200,000	700,000	700,000	90	700
Ceylon	2,770,000	7,200,000	1,100,000	2,200,000	180	25,400
Singapore . . .	540,000	47,200,000	700,000	...	...	1,500
West Indies . .	1,570,000	14,900,000	2,100,000	3,100,000	160	127,000
Cyprus	220,000	500,000	200,000	...	...	3,600
Various . . .	740,000	39,400,000	700,000	500,000	20	45,400
Colonies . . .	18,200,000	285,600,000	42,050,000	237,900,000	23,670	7,076,600
India	214,600,000	163,000,000	77,300,000	185,700,000	14,380	870,000
Total . .	232,800,000	448,600,000	119,350,000	423,600,000	38,050	7,946,600

The above statement is to the end of 1887. Commerce includes merchandise and precious metals.

If we exclude Malta, Gibraltar, Cyprus, and Hong-Kong, for which the statistics are imperfect, we find the growth of the colonies (without India) as follows :—

Year	Population	Commerce, £	Revenue, £	Debt, £	Railways, Miles
1840	5,100,000	27,100,000	2,400,000	5,300,000	...
1860	9,100,000	116,600,000	12,500,000	64,700,000	2,330
1870	11,600,000	145,700,000	19,800,000	79,800,000	4,360
1880	14,700,000	214,700,000	30,100,000	143,400,000	13,080
1887	17,400,000	247,000,000	41,300,000	237,700,000	23,650

INDIA

The official returns show as follows :—

Year	Population	Commerce, £	Revenue, £	Debt, £	Railways, Miles
1814	40,000,000	10,500,000	13,100,000	18,000,000	...
1820	83,000,000	9,050,000	15,300,000	24,000,000	...
1830	91,000,000	9,800,000	17,000,000	30,400,000	...
1850	123,000,000	34,100,000	27,600,000	53,900,000	...
1860	143,000,000	69,500,000	39,700,000	98,100,000	840
1870	191,000,000	100,400,000	50,900,000	108,200,000	4,830
1880	199,000,000	122,100,000	68,400,000	160,400,000	9,310
1887	214,600,000	163,000,000	77,300,000	185,700,000	14,380

AUSTRALIA

This group of seven colonies has made great strides :—

Year	Population	Commerce, £	Revenue, £	Debt, £	Railways, Miles
1800	10,000	200,000	...	...	...
1820	90,000	800,000	70,000	...	...
1840	200,000	3,300,000	600,000	...	...
1850	240,000	6,100,000	...	...	...
1860	1,264,000	49,900,000	6,700,000	11,900,000	160
1870	1,980,000	57,300,000	11,600,000	36,200,000	950
1880	2,880,000	94,300,000	17,100,000	87,900,000	4,880
1888	3,680,000	121,800,000	27,600,000	166,000,000	10,430

In 1888 the several colonies stood thus :—

	Population	Commerce, £	Revenue, £	Debt, £	Railways, Miles
New South Wales	1,086,000	41,700,000	8,900,000	44,100,000	2,206
Victoria	1,091,000	37,800,000	7,600,000	34,600,000	2,191
South Australia . . .	313,000	12,400,000	2,500,000	19,200,000	1,500
New Zealand . . .	650,000	13,700,000	4,100,000	37,000,000	1,861
Queensland	387,000	11,800,000	3,500,000	25,900,000	1,931
Tasmania	146,000	2,900,000	600,000	4,500,000	485
Western Australia . . .	42,000	1,500,000	400,000	1,300,000	257
Total . .	3,715,000	121,800,000	27,600,000	166,600,000	10,431

In the above table commerce includes both merchandise and gold.

CANADA

The official returns of this colony, including Newfoundland, show thus :—

Year	Population	Commerce, £	Revenue, £	Debt, £	Railways, Miles
1820	840,000	1,000,000	240,000	...	...
1830	910,000	3,300,000	300,000	...	...
1840	1,690,000	6,200,000	500,000	1,200,000	...
1860	3,360,000	22,700,000	2,400,000	13,200,000	2,170
1870	3,830,000	33,600,000	3,600,000	17,000,000	3,200
1880	4,500,000	39,000,000	5,100,000	32,100,000	6,890
1887	5,020,000	43,900,000	7,600,000	47,300,000	11,788

SOUTH AFRICA

Official and other statements give us the following :—

Year	Population	Commerce, £	Revenue, £	Debt, £	Railways, Miles
1840	140,000	1,000,000	200,000	...	...
1860	420,000	5,200,000	800,000	600,000	...
1870	860,000	5,900,000	950,000	1,400,000	40
1880	1,120,000	19,200,000	3,100,000	13,000,000	1,005
1887	1,860,000	17,000,000	4,000,000	26,500,000	1,820

The statistics for the two colonies in 1887 were as follows :—

	Cape Colony	Natal	Total
Population . .	1,380,000	480,000	1,860,000
Commerce, £ .	13,700,000	3,300,000	17,000,000
Revenue, £ . .	3,200,000	800,000	4,000,000
Debt, £ . . .	22,500,000	4,000,000	26,500,000
Railways, miles .	1,600	220	1,820

The several colonies stood thus in 1887 :—

	Population	Commerce, £	Revenue, £	Debt, £
Gold Coast . .	1,405,000	700,000	120,000	...
Lagos	75,000	1,000,000	50,000	...
Sierra Leone . .	60,000	600,000	60,000	60,000
Gambia . . .	15,000	200,000	10,000	...
St. Helena . .	5,000	...	10,000	...
Total . .	1,560,000	2,500,000	250,000	60,000

WEST AFRICA

Official returns give the following respecting this group :—

Year	Population	Commerce, £	Revenue, £	Debt, £
1850	205,000	800,000	60,000	...
1860	...	1,000,000	80,000	...
1870	550,000	2,500,000	180,000	...
1880	...	3,100,000	280,000	90,000
1887	1,560,000	2,500,000	250,000	60,000

Excluding St. Helena, the West Coast colonies count only 520 whites, mostly Government officials or missionaries. The chief product is palm-oil.

MAURITIUS

We have statistics from 1827 as follows :—

Year	Population	Commerce, £	Revenue, £	Debt, £	Railway, Miles
1827	95,000	1,000,000	200,000	...	...
1850	180,000	2,300,000	300,000	...	...
1860	310,000	5,000,000	600,000	...	...
1870	320,000	4,200,000	600,000	1,100,000	70
1880	380,000	5,900,000	800,000	800,000	90
1887	370,000	5,200,000	700,000	700,000	90

The export of sugar, the chief product, rose from 30,000 tons in 1836 to 140,000 tons in 1877, but has now declined to 100,000 tons.

CEYLON

The principal items are shown as follows :—

Year	Population	Commerce, £	Revenue, £	Debt, £	Railway, Miles
1850	1,580,000	3,800,000	400,000	...	...
1860	1,890,000	6,100,000	800,000	...	...
1870	2,410,000	8,400,000	1,100,000	700,000	70
1880	2,760,000	8,700,000	1,200,000	1,400,000	140
1887	...	7,200,000	1,100,000	2,200,000	180

Coffee-planting began about 1840, the exportation reaching 32,000 tons in 1860, and rising to 50,000 tons in 1878, but now it barely reaches 9000 tons. Tea is, however, assuming importance, the shipment rising from £2000 worth in 1878, to a value of £700,000 in 1887. In like manner Chinchona* has risen from £90,000 in 1881 to £350,000 in 1886.

* This is often incorrectly called Cinchona. It takes its name from the Marquis of Chinchon, Viceroy of Peru, whose wife was cured by a Jesuit who prescribed this remedy.

SINGAPORE

Sometimes called the Straits Settlement. Statistics show thus :—

Year	Population	Commerce, £	Revenue, £
1860	280,000	14,500,000	100,000
1870	310,000	18,700,000	300,000
1880	420,000	25,700,000	400,000
1887	540,000	47,200,000	700,000

WEST INDIES

Under this heading may be comprised all the following colonies, for which the statistics are given for 1887 :—

	Population	Commerce, £	Revenue, £	Debt, £	Railway, Miles
Jamaica	600,000	2,800,000	600,000	1,600,000	70
Trinidad	180,000	3,800,000	500,000	600,000	50
Barbados	170,000	2,100,000	200,000	...	20
Bahamas	40,000	300,000	50,000	100,000	...
Honduras	30,000	400,000	50,000	...	...
British Guiana	280,000	3,800,000	500,000	600,000	20
Small islands	270,000	1,700,000	200,000	200,000	...
Total . .	1,570,000	14,900,000	2,100,000	3,100,000	160

The progress of the group is shown as follows :—

Year	Population	Commerce, £	Revenue, £	Debt, £	Railways, Miles
1850	900,000	9,100,000	700,000	900,000	...
1860	1,090,000	11,900,000	1,000,000	1,000,000	...
1870	1,280,000	14,600,000	1,400,000	1,600,000	30
1880	1,490,000	17,800,000	1,900,000	1,800,000	80
1887	1,570,000	14,900,000	2,100,000	3,100,000	160

OTHER BRITISH COLONIES

	Population	Commerce, £	Revenue, £	Debt, £	Square Miles
Malta . .	160,000	19,800,000	200,000	80,000	120
Gibraltar .	20,000	5,000,000	50,000	...	2
Aden . .	40,000	4,000,000	...	...	70
Cyprus . .	220,000	500,000	200,000	...	3,600
Bermudas .	15,000	400,000	30,000	10,000	20
Falklands .	2,000	200,000	10,000	...	6,500
Hong-Kong	210,000	9,000,000	300,000	200,000	30
Labuan .	6,000	200,000	5,000	...	30
N. Borneo .	150,000	300,000	50,000	...	31,000
Feegee . .	125,000	500,000	65,000	260,000	7,700
Total .	948,000	39,900,000	910,000	550,000	49,072

The above returns are for 1887, except as regards the commerce of Malta, Gibraltar, and Hong-Kong, the items for which are the latest published, over ten years old.

Hong-Kong is a thriving colony, with considerable trade, shipping entries in 1888 reaching 6,500,000 tons. Statistics show :—

	1879	1889
Saving-bank deposits, £ . . .	1,400,000	8,300,000
Joint-stock companies capital, £ .	8,000,000	20,000,000

FRENCH COLONIES

The protected countries are stated to be as follows :—

	Population	Square Miles
Tonquin . . .	12,000,000	34,700
Gambia . . .	850,000	268,000
Madagascar . .	1,500,000	228,000
Annam . . .	5,000,000	106,000
Cambodia . . .	1,500,000	32,400
Total . .	20,850,000	669,100

The following colonial statistics refer to 1885 :—

	Births	Deaths	Acres Tilled	Value of Farms, £
Reunion . . .	4,200	5,200	140,000	3,900,000
Cochin-China .	62,000	36,000	2,300,000	...
Martinique . .	5,570	4,020	90,000	3,600,000
Guadeloupe . .	4,300	4,720	100,000	5,900,000

An official statement in 1885 gives the following returns :—

	Population	Square Miles	Imports, £	Exports, £	Railway, Miles	Revenue, £
Algeria	3,820,000	257,400	9,400,000	7,900,000	1,580	1,700,000
Tunis	1,500,000	45,000	1,300,000	800,000	260	1,000,000
Cochin-China . . .	1,790,000	23,000	4,400,000	3,400,000	40	1,100,000
Pondicherry . . .	280,000	200	300,000	1,100,000	...	...
Nossi-Bè, &c. . .	30,000	2,400	200,000	200,000	...	...
Reunion	180,000	800	800,000	600,000	70	200,000
Senegal . . , .	140,000	138,400	1,000,000	700,000	250	100,000
Tahiti	10,000	450	200,000	100,000	...	...
New Caledonia . .	60,000	7,700	300,000	200,000	...	100,000
Guiana	30,000	46,800	300,000	200,000	...	...
Martinique . . .	170,000	380	900,000	800,000 }	120	400,000
Guadeloupe . . .	180,000	720	800,000	700,000 }		
Marquesas, &c. . .	50,000	500	300,000	300,000	...	...
Total . . .	8,240,000	523,750	20,200,000	17,000,000	2,320	4,600,000

ALGERIA

This is the best of the French colonies, and its progress is shown by the number of European settlers :—

	1833	1845	1856	1866	1876	1886
French	3,500	46,300	92,800	122,100	155,700	219,600*
Spaniards	1,300	25,300	42,200	58,500	92,500	120,100
Italians	1,100	7,700	9,500	16,700	25,800	
Maltese	1,200	8,100	7,100	10,600	14,200	} 86,200
Sundry	700	7,900	9,200	10,100	23,300	
Total . .	7,800	95,300	160,800	218,000	311,500	425,900

* This appears to include 70,000 children born in the colony.

The population of the territory was made up thus in 1876 :—

Arabs under military rule . .	1,408,000
Arabs under civil rule . . .	763,000
French settlers	156,000
Foreign settlers	155,000
Jewish population	33,000
Total . .	2,515,000

The territory under military law covered 110,000, that under civil law 16,000 square miles, total 126,000 square miles, or 78 million acres. The ordinary garrison is 50,000 men, not included above.

The work of colonisation from the time of the conquest (1830–36) was slow until 1848, when General Lamoricière obtained a grant of two millions sterling from the French Legislature for the purpose. In 1863 an agricultural census showed 102,000 Europeans living on farms that covered an area of 1,300,000 acres. Further grants of 240,000 acres were made in 1871 for Alsatian refugees, and in 1877 the area of farms held by settlers was 2,570,000 acres, distributed among 510 colonies or villages. The figures for 1863 and 1877 showed thus :—

	1863	1877
Men	42,300	57,600
Women	28,600	38,500
Children . . .	30,900	47,300
Farming population . .	101,800	143,300
Acres	1,300,000	2,570,000

Each colony or group of settlers averages 5000 acres, with 60 habitations and 300 inhabitants, the Government having expended £120 for each family, or £6000 per colony, in all £3,000,000 sterling. There are 2,100,000 Arabs, holding 39½ million acres. Forests and crown-lands cover 35 million acres. The Arabs have nearly 7 million acres under tillage ; their flocks and herds count 8,000,000 head. The French have spent over 20 millions sterling on roads and other public works : the roads over the Atlas and other ranges are excellent. The colony has suffered much from locusts. The first railway was begun in 1863, and there are now 1550 miles in traffic. In 1886 the imports were £9,700,000, exports £7,300,000. Revenue £1,800,000, which is much less than the annual expenditure. Entries of shipping 1,980,000 tons yearly, of which 1,170,000 are French.

TUNIS

This territory can hardly be called a colony : it was annexed by France in 1881, but has few French residents. There are 30,000 Christians and 30,000 Jews ; the former including 10,000 Italians, 8000 Maltese, and the rest a mixture of all nations. Revenue, £960,000 ; debt, £5,700,000. The shipping entries reach 1,600,000 tons yearly.

SPANISH COLONIES

Official and other documents give us the following :—

	Square Miles	Population	Commerce, £	Railway, Miles	Revenue, £
Cuba	46,000	1,520,000	28,000,000	930	5,100,000
Porto Rico . .	3,700	650,000	4,300,000	...	800,000
Canaries . . .	2,700	280,000	1,500,000	...	...
Philippines . .	114,400	5,600,000	9,300,000	...	2,000,000
Fernando Po .	1,500	50,000	...	...	...
Mariana Islands	400	10,000	...	...	...
Carolinas . .	1,500	40,000	...	...	...
Total . .	170,200	8,150,000	42,500,000	...	...

CUBA AND PORTO RICO

The principal products of these islands are as follows :—

	Value, £			Tons		
	Cuba	Porto Rico	Total	Cuba	Porto Rico	Total
Sugar	9,000,000	800,000	9,800,000	670,000	60,000	730,000
Tobacco . . .	5,000,000	130,000	5,130,000	20,000	2,000	22,000
Coffee	1,000,000	900,000	1,900,000	20,000	20,000	40,000
Sundries . . .	3,800,000	300,000	4,100,000	...	...	...
Total . . .	18,800,000	2,130,000	20,930,000	...	...	...

Cuba has 930 miles of railway and 2800 of telegraphs. The revenue averages £5,100,000, of which £2,400,000 are Customs-dues, the rest taxes. The consolidated debt consists of £25,000,000 in 6 per cents., largely held in Germany. Shipping entries at Havana and other ports sum up 1,350,000 tons yearly, 540,000 tons being Spanish, and the remainder 60 per cent. foreign flags. Havana has a population of 198,000.

The Philippine Islands have 120 miles of railway and 700 of telegraphs. Shipping entries at Manilla do not exceed yearly 300,000 tons. Imports, £4,100,000 ; exports, £5,200,000, viz. :—

	£
Sugar	1,800,000
Hemp	1,100,000
Tobacco	500,000
Coffee	300,000
Sundries	1,500,000
Total . . .	5,200,000

The revenue reaches £2,000,000, of which £400,000 are Customs-dues, the rest taxes. Population of Manilla 182,000.

Statistics of the Canary Islands and other colonies will be found under the head of *Agriculture*, p. 58.

PORTUGUESE COLONIES

Official and other documents give us the following :—

	Square Miles	Population	Revenue, £
Madeira	320	130,000	...
Azores	910	260,000	...
Cape Verd Islands .	1,860	105,000	50,000
St. Thomas and Prince .	420	20,000	25,000
Angola	115,000	900,000	130,000
Mozambique . . .	80,000	500,000	60,000
Goa	1,300	480,000	110,000
Timor	6,300	300,000	} 70,000
Macao	4	70,000	
Total . .	206,114	2,765,000	445,000

Madeira and the Azores are not treated as colonial possessions, but as two integral provinces of Portugal, with deputies sitting in the Lisbon Cortes.

DUTCH COLONIES

The latest information is to the following effect :—

	Square Miles	Population
Java	51,300	18,100,000
Sumatra . . .	46,200	940,000
Bencoolen . .	9,600	130,000
Borneo . . .	197,000	1,210,000
Celebes . . .	45,200	350,000
Moluccas . . .	42,400	330,000
New Guinea . .	67,400	200,000
Palembang . .	61,200	480,000
Other islands . .	95,200	2,160,000
East Indies . .	615,500	23,900,000
Dutch Guiana . .	46,100	60,000
Curaçoa, &c. . .	440	46,000
Total .	662,040	24,006,000

The East Indian possessions show an aggregate commerce of 14 millions sterling imports and 16 millions exports. The gross revenue is £11,800,000. The Dutch-India Company has a monopoly of Java, which gives a net profit of 3 millions sterling per annum. The population of the East Indian possessions is as follows :—

European settlers . . .	34,000
Garrison	14,000
Chinese	310,000
Natives	23,542,000
Total .	23,900,000

Most of the natives are Mahometans, except those of the Moluccas, who are Christians.
The revenue is obtained thus :—

Coffee plantations . .	£4,700,000
Opium plantations . .	1,500,000
Land-tax, &c. . .	5,600,000
Total .	11,800,000

DANISH COLONIES

Latest information may be summed up thus :—

	Square Miles	Population
Iceland	40,200	72,000
Greenland . . .	34,000	10,000
Faroe Islands . .	500	11,000
St. Thomas, &c. . .	140	33,000
Total . . .	74,840	126,000

Iceland is in reality a republic, under Danish protection. In 1804 the Census showed 4750 farms, with 47,000 inhabitants ; some grain was then cultivated. At present the island depends mainly on its fisheries. A vessel of 60 tons with twelve men can earn £440 in the cod-fishing season. Greenland also depends on fishing, the annual product averaging 12,000 barrels of blubber and 3000 of cod-liver. The West Indian possessions comprise the three islands of St. Thomas, Sainte Croix, and St. John, which produce yearly 7000 tons of sugar and one million barrels of rum. Denmark was the first of all countries to abolish slavery, by liberating her West Indian slaves in 1826.

GERMAN COLONIES

The extent and population of the new German possession of Cameroons in Africa are not known. The other possessions are :—

	Square Miles	Population
New Guinea . . .	70,000	107,000
Bismarck Archipelago	20,000	188,000
Solomon Islands . .	9,000	80,000
Marshall Islands . .	40	10,000
Total . . .	99,040	385,000

COMMERCE

International trade has increased fortyfold since the beginning of the eighteenth century. The following table shows approximately the aggregate value of imports and exports for each country :—

MILLIONS, £ STERLING

	1720	1750	1780	1800	1820	1830	1840	1850	1860	1870	1880	1889
Great Britain	13	21	23	67	74	88	114	169	375	547	698	740
France	7	13	22	31	33	41	66	95	167	227	339	311
Germany	8	15	20	36	40	46	52	70	130	212	294	367
Russia	8	14	17	30	22	28	33	40	48	103	131	118
Austria	2	4	6	8	10	15	22	29	47	83	107	92
Italy	3	5	7	10	15	20	30	38	52	66	91	94
Spain	10	14	18	12	10	7	10	11	25	41	50	59
Portugal	2	3	4	4	3	3	4	5	8	10	14	18
Scandinavia	2	3	5	5	.6	8	12	18	27	48	64	72
Holland and Belgium . .	4	6	8	15	24	30	45	61	86	136	237	310
Switzerland	1	2	3	5	6	8	10	20	30	45	60	60
Turkey, &c.	2	3	4	5	6	7	10	20	29	55	49	72
Europe	62	103	137	228	249	301	408	576	1,024	1,573	2,134	2,313
United States	...	...	3	17	23	22	41	62	136	165	308	320
Spanish America . . .	10	15	20	25	30	35	48	70	94	135	160	166
British Colonies . . .	2	3	1	2	3	9	21	44	103	128	203	298
India	9	9	10	10	11	10	20	30	52	85	108	131
Various	5	10	15	20	25	30	35	50	80	105	120	149
The World	88	140	186	302	341	407	573	832	1,489	2,191	3,033	3,377

The greatest relative increase was in the decade between 1850 and 1860, namely, 80 per cent., that period being contemporaneous with the introduction of free trade.

COMMERCE.

Aggregate of Imports and Exports, millions £.

Trade for Population, Shillings per Inhabitant.

Country	Aggregate (millions £)	Trade per Inhabitant (shillings)
G. BRITAIN	740	390
GERMANY	367	156
U. STATES	320	100
FRANCE	311	163
HOLLAND	199	900
RUSSIA	118	27
BELGIUM	111	370
ITALY	94	62
AUSTRIA	92	48
AUSTRALIA *	74	405
SWITZERLAND	60	400
SPAIN	59	70
CANADA	42	168
SWEDEN	30	126
DENMARK	26	260
PORTUGAL	18	80

* Exclusive of Inter-Colonial Trade.

The trade of all nations from 1861 to 1886 was as follows :—

MILLIONS £ STERLING

	Imports				Exports			
	1861–70	1871–80	1881–86	26 Years	1861–70	1871–80	1881–86	26 Years
United Kingdom . . .	2,701	3,714	2,348	8,763	2,129	2,778	1,745	6,652
France	1,090	1,560	1,086	3,736	1,100	1,390	806	3,296
Germany	950	1,740	921	3,611	680	1,270	925	2,875
Russia	270	490	306	1,066	286	480	339	1,099
Austria	302	570	302	1,174	350	505	360	1,215
Italy	361	472	319	1,152	263	444	262	969
Spain and Portugal . .	222	253	231	706	164	242	199	605
Belgium	305	562	355	1,222	246	441	307	994
Holland	319	630	517	1,466	258	432	399	1,089
Scandinavia	169	348	235	752	151	262	169	582
Other countries . . .	183	174	345	702	225	159	311	695
Europe	6,872	10,513	6,965	24,350	5,846	8,403	5,822	20,071
United States . . .	493	988	807	2,288	361	1,122	946	2,429
Canada	161	179	149	489	132	151	125	408
Australia	289	402	366	1,057	191	343	282	816
India	293	368	322	983	518	597	495	1,610
China and Japan . .	244	289	170	703	233	271	160	664
South America . . .	528	587	317	1,432	513	658	359	1,530
Egypt	73	52	49	174	184	136	74	394
Java	52	91	84	227	93	165	96	354
Other countries . . .	223	318	542	1,083	230	311	602	1,143
Total	9,228	13,787	9,771	32,786	8,301	12,157	8,961	29,419

Imports, of course, always sum up a higher value than exports, the former including freight, insurance, commission, and other charges, which make up about 6 per cent. on the original value of exports at port of shipment. The surplus thus represented by imports has been declining in ratio since 1880, probably owing to cheaper freights and the facilities afforded by telegraphs. The surplus was as follows :—

Period	Millions Sterling	Percentage over Exports
1861–70 . . .	927	11.7
1871–80 . . .	1,630	13.6
1881–86 . . .	810	9.0
1887–88 . . .	94	6.0

The surplus of imports has been chiefly among European nations as follows :—

	Millions £ Sterling				Percentage over Exports			
	1861–70	1871–80	1881–86	26 Years	1861–70	1871–80	1881–86	26 Years
United Kingdom . . .	572	936	603	2,111	27	33	35	32
France	...	170	280	440	...	12	35	14
Germany	270	470	...	736	40	38	...	26
Italy	98	28	57	183	37	6	22	19
Spain and Portugal . .	58	11	32	101	35	5	16	17
Belgium	59	121	48	228	24	27	16	23
Holland	61	198	118	377	23	46	30	35
Scandinavia	18	86	66	170	12	32	40	30

The following table shows the proportions of the world's commerce corresponding to various nations since 1830 :—

	1830	1850	1870	1881–86	1889
United Kingdom .	21.5	20.4	25.0	20.8	22.0
France	10.0	11.3	10.4	10.1	9.2
Germany	11.2	8.4	9.7	9.8	10.9
Russia	6.8	4.9	4.8	3.4	3.5
Austria	3.6	3.4	3.7	3.5	2.7
Italy	4.9	4.6	3.0	3.1	2.7
Spain and Portugal .	3.2	1.9	2.3	2.3	2.3
Belgium	3.5	2.5	2.8	3.6	3.3
Holland	3.8	4.9	3.2	4.8	5.9
Scandinavia . . .	2.0	2.1	2.2	2.1	2.1
Other countries . .	3.5	5.0	4.7	3.5	4.0
Europe	74.0	69.4	71.8	67.0	68.6
United States . .	5.4	7.5	7.5	9.3	9.5
South America . .	8.6	8.3	5.5	3.5	3.4
British colonies . .	4.6	8.9	9.5	10.7	9.0
China, &c. &c. . .	7.4	5.9	5.7	9.5	9.5
Total . .	100.0	100.0	100.0	100.0	100.0

The above comprises only merchandise ; specie, bullion and gold-dust are excluded. The item of British colonies includes also India.

The commerce of the principal nations compared with population thus :—

	1830			1870			1889		
	£	s.	d.	£	s.	d.	£	s.	d.
United Kingdom	3	12	0	17	7	0	19	10	0
France . . .	1	4	0	6	4	0	8	3	0
Germany . .	1	14	0	5	6	0	7	16	0
Russia . . .	0	12	6	1	7	0	1	7	0
Austria . . .	0	13	0	2	7	0	2	6	0
Italy	1	3	0	2	11	0	3	3	0
Spain & Portugal	0	16	8	2	12	0	3	5	0
Holland . .	5	14	0	19	8	0	45	0	0
Belgium . .	3	18	0	12	12	0	18	10	0
Scandinavia . .	1	12	0	6	5	0	8	1	0
Europe . . .	1	9	8	5	18	2	7	0	0
United States . .	2	0	0	4	9	3	5	0	0

The relative increase in the United States has been much less than in Europe.

I

The following table shows, in millions £ sterling, the average annual trade of each country in the years 1881 to 1886, and also for 1889, or the year last published :—

	1881–86			1889		
	Imports	Exports	Total	Imports	Exports	Total
United Kingdom	391	291	682	427	313	740
France . . .	181	134	315	167	144	311
Germany . . .	153	154	307	204	163	367
Russia . . .	51	56	107	39	79	118
Austria . . .	50	60	110	48	44	92
Italy	53	44	97	56	38	94
Spain	30	27	57	29	30	59
Portugal . . .	8	6	14	11	7	18
Sweden . . .	17	13	30	16	14	30
Norway . . .	9	6	15	9	7	16
Denmark . . .	13	9	22	15	11	26
Belgium . . .	59	51	110	61	50	111
Holland . . .	86	66	152	106	93	199
Switzerland . .	24	23	47	33	27	60
Greece . . .	5	3	8	4	3	7
Roumania . .	12	9	21	13	10	23
Servia	2	2	4	2	2	4
Bulgaria . . .	2	2	4	3	3	6
Turkey . . .	17	9	26	20	13	33
Europe . . .	1,163	965	2,128	1,263	1,051	2,314

	1881–86			1889		
	Imports	Exports	Total	Imports	Exports	Total
United States .	134	158	292	154	166	320
Canada . . .	25	21	46	23	19	42
Australia . . .	61	47	108	68	62	130
South Africa .	8	9	17	9	10	19
Mexico . . .	6	7	13	8	12	20
Central America	3	4	7	3	4	7
South America .	53	50	103	57	57	114
West Indies . .	8	8	16	7	8	15
India * . . .	43	66	109	54	77	131
China	22	19	41	26	23	49
Japan	6	8	14	11	11	22
Java	14	16	30	14	16	30
Persia	4	3	7	5	3	8
Egypt	8	12	20	7	12	19
Algeria . . .	10	7	17	9	8	17
Cuba	10	18	28	10	18	28
Other countries	40	48	88	40	52	92
The world . .	1,618	1,466	3,084	1,770	1,607	3,377

* In this table 20 per cent. is taken off the nominal value of Indian trade because the Government returns compute the rupee at 24 pence.

The following table shows approximately the weight of the principal articles of merchandise exchanged between nations :—

	Tons Merchandise Sea-borne Yearly				
	1840	1861–70	1871–80	1880	1887
Coal	1,400,000	20,300,000	30,900,000	39,200,000	49,300,000
Iron	1,100,000	4,200,000	6,000,000	8,500,000	11,800,000
Timber	4,100,000	6,300,000	8,000,000	9,000,000	12,100,000
Grain	1,900,000	4,400,000	11,200,000	16,800,000	19,200,000
Sugar	700,000	1,200,000	1,800,000	2,900,000	4,400,000
Petroleum . . .	...	240,000	1,400,000	2,100,000	2,700,000
Cotton	400,000	600,000	1,000,000	1,200,000	1,800,000
Wool	20,000	100,000	250,000	300,000	350,000
Jute	...	100,000	300,000	400,000	600,000
Meat	...	100,000	400,000	650,000	700,000
Coffee	200,000	300,000	400,000	500,000	600,000
Wine	200,000	500,000	900,000	1,200,000	1,400,000
Salt	800,000	1,000,000	1,200,000	1,300,000	1,300,000
Sundries . . .	9,180,000	16,660,000	24,250,000	28,950,000	33,750,000
Total . .	20,000,000	56,000,000	88,000,000	113,000,000	140,100,000

The total weight of sea-borne merchandise composing the commerce of 27 years, down to 1887, and the value approximately of same at shipment, are shown as follows :—

	Millions of Tons	Value, Millions	Ratio of	
			Weight	Value
Coal	830	410	36.0	1.3
Iron	170	480	7.4	1.6
Timber . . .	220	660	9.5	2.1
Grain	180	1,050	7.8	3.4
Sugar	55	1,130	2.4	3.7
Petroleum . .	32	180	1.4	0.6
Cotton	27	180	1.2	0.6
Salt	30	18	1.3	...
Wine	23	510	1.0	1.6
Coffee	11	840	0.5	2.7
Meat	10	560	0.4	1.8
Sundries . . .	712	24,982	31.1	80.6
Total .	2,300	31,000	100.0	100.0

If we compare the weight of sea-borne merchandise with the tonnage of shipping of all nations at various dates, we find as follows :—

Year	Tons Shipping	Tons Merchandise	Tons Carried per Ton of Shipping
1840	9,400,000	20,000,000	2.1
1865	17,000,000	56,000,000	3.3
1875	18,000,000	88,000,000	4.9
1880	20,300,000	113,000,000	5.6
1887	21,200,000	140,000,000	6.6

Each ton of shipping now carries more than three times as much as it did in 1840, which is, of course, due to the use of steam, one ton of steam-shipping being equivalent to four of sailing-ships. The traffic of 1887 was approximately as follows :—

	Tonnage Register	Tons Carried
Steamers . . .	8,600,000	102,000,000
Sailing . . .	12,600,000	38,000,000
Total . .	21,200,000	140,000,000

GREAT BRITAIN

There are non-continuous records of British commerce since the time of Edward III.

Year	Reign	Imports	Exports	Total	Per Inhabitant
		£	£	£	£ s. d.
1355	Edward III.	120,000	294,000	414,000	0 2 10
1573	Elizabeth	2,100,000	1,880,000	3,980,000	0 15 0
1614	James I.	2,140,000	2,090,000	4,230,000	0 16 6
1687	James II.	4,200,000	4,080,000	8,280,000	1 10 2
1697	William III.	3,500,000	3,500,000	7,000,000	1 5 6
1701	,, ...	5,900,000	6,900,000	12,800,000	2 2 0
1712	Anne	5,800,000	6,900,000	12,700,000	2 0 0
1726	George I.	6,700,000	7,700,000	14,400,000	1 18 0
1736	George II.	7,300,000	9,700,000	17,000,000	2 5 0
1750	,, ...	7,800,000	12,700,000	20,500,000	2 10 0
1760	George III.	10,700,000	15,800,000	26,500,000	3 3 0
1770	,, ...	13,400,000	16,000,000	29,400,000	3 6 0
1780	,, ...	10,800,000	12,600,000	23,400,000	2 10 0
1790	,, ...	19,100,000	20,100,000	39,200,000	3 18 0
1800	,, ...	24,100,000	43,200,000	67,300,000	6 8 0
1810	,, ...	30,200,000	58,800,000	89,000,000	5 0 0
1820	George IV.	29,700,000	44,200,000	73,900,000	3 10 0
1830	William IV.	42,300,000	45,800,000	88,100,000	3 14 0
1840	Victoria	51,600,000	62,000,000	113,600,000	4 4 0
1850	,, ...	99,000,000	70,000,000	169,000,000	6 4 0
1860	,, ...	210,500,000	164,500,000	375,000,000	12 17 0
1870	,, ...	303,300,000	244,100,000	547,400,000	17 7 0
1880	,, ...	411,200,000	286,400,000	697,600,000	20 5 0
1889	,, ...	427,200,000	313,000,000	740,200,000	19 10 0

The export trade of G. Britain in 1798 was as follows :—

British Products	£	Foreign and Colonial	£
Woollen goods .	6,200,000	Coffee	5,800,000
Cotton goods .	2,300,000	Indian textiles .	2,400,000
Linen goods . .	1,200,000	Sugar	1,300,000
Iron and steel .	900,000	Irish linen . .	500,000
Coal	500,000	Tea	400,000
Sugar	400,000	Sundries . . .	3,500,000
Silks	300,000		
Sundries . . .	7,900,000	Total . .	13,900,000
Total . .	19,700,000	Grand total . .	33,600,000

The trade for the years 1888 and 1889 was as follows :—

	Imports, Mill. £		Exports, Mill. £	
	1888	1889		1888	1889
Food	157	171	Textiles	109	110
Textile fibres . .	81	91	Metals	50	56
Hides, timber, &c.	37	44	Clothing . . .	11	11
Manufactures . .	58	64	Chemicals . . .	7	8
Metals	23	22	Sundries . . .	57	63
Chemicals . . .	15	16			
Sundries	16	19	British produce .	234	248
			Colonial	64	65
Total . .	387	427			
			Total . .	298	313

Commerce between France and the United Kingdom since 1831 shows thus :—

Period	Millions £			Annual Trade, £
	Exports to France	Imports from France	Total Exchanged	
1831–40	16	30	46	4,600,000
1841–50	31	55	86	8,600,000
1851–60	84	163	247	24,700,000
1861–70	230	298	528	52,800,000
1871–80	284	421	705	70,500,000
1881–89	209	349	558	62,000,000
59 years	854	1,316	2,170	36,800,000

The trade of 1889 was as follows :—

	Imports from, £	Exports to, £	Total Trade, £	Ratio
France	45,700,000	14,600,000	60,000,000	9.0
Germany . . .	27,100,000	18,400,000	45,500,000	6.8
Russia	27,200,000	5,300,000	32,500,000	4.9
Austria	2,300,000	1,000,000	3,300,000	0.5
Italy	3,200,000	7,100,000	10,300,000	1.5
Spain	11,500,000	4,200,000	15,700,000	2.2
Portugal . . .	3,100,000	2,500,000	5,600,000	0.8
Sweden and Norway . .	12,700,000	4,500,000	17,200,000	2.5
Denmark . . .	7,900,000	2,400,000	10,300,000	1.5
Holland . . .	26,700,000	9,700,000	36,400,000	5.4
Belgium . . .	17,700,000	7,100,000	24,800,000	3.7
Turkey	5,300,000	6,200,000	11,500,000	1.6
Europe	190,400,000	83,000,000	273,400,000	40.4
United States .	95,300,000	30,300,000	125,600,000	18.8
Spanish America	14,300,000	28,000,000	42,300,000	6.3
China	6,200,000	5,000,000	11,200,000	1.6
Japan	1,000,000	3,900,000	4,900,000	0.7
Egypt	8,500,000	2,900,000	11,400,000	1.6
Various . . .	14,300,000	12,100,000	26,400,000	3.9
Foreign countries	330,000,000	165,200,000	495,200,000	73.3
Australia . . .	26,800,000	22,800,000	49,600,000	7.4
Canada . . .	12,200,000	8,100,000	20,300,000	3.0
South Africa . .	6,100,000	8,900,000	15,000,000	2.2
East Indies . .	44,400,000	34,100,000	78,500,000	11.7
West Indies . .	2,200,000	2,200,000	4,400,000	0.6
Various . . .	5,500,000	6,700,000	12,200,000	1.8
British colonies .	97,200,000	82,800,000	180,000,000	26.7
Total . .	427,200,000	248,000,000	675,200,000	100.0

The above Board of Trade returns exclude exports of colonial and foreign merchandise from the United Kingdom, namely, £65,000,000, the total trade for the year having been £740,200,000. Our trade with the United States is much greater than with any other country, India coming second on the list, and France third.

*

The following table shows the value of merchandise imported from the several foreign countries and colonies since 1854, the earliest date supplied by statistical abstracts of the Board of Trade :—

	Millions £ Sterling					Percentage		
	1854–60	1861–70	1871–80	1881–87	34 Years	1854–60	1861–80	1881–87
France	89	298	421	264	1,072	7.3	11.2	9.7
Germany	88	162	217	171	638	7.3	5.9	6.3
Russia	71	169	200	120	560	5.8	5.8	4.4
Austria	6	10	12	12	40	0.5	0.3	0.4
Italy	17	33	39	22	111	1.4	1.1	0.8
Spain	25	54	94	71	244	2.0	2.3	2.6
Portugal	13	23	37	21	94	1.1	0.9	0.8
Belgium , . . .	23	71	131	102	327	1.9	3.1	3.8
Holland	48	110	175	174	507	4.0	4.5	6.4
Denmark . . .	18	20	40	36	114	1.5	0.9	1.3
Sweden and Norway .	24	56	97	76	253	2.0	2.4	2.8
Greece	5	11	18	13	47	0.4	0.4	0.5
Roumania	6	8	9	24	47	0.5	0.3	0.9
Turkey	17	54	57	33	161	1.4	1.7	1.3
Europe	450	1,079	1,547	1,139	4,215	37.1	40.8	42.0
United States . . .	239	360	773	627	1,999	19.7	17.7	23.1
Brazil	17	59	63	37	176	1.4	1.9	1.3
River Plate . . .	13	23	26	14	76	1.1	0.8	0.5
Chili	14	33	39	19	105	1.2	1.1	0.7
Peru	23	35	45	14	117	1.9	1.2	0.5
Central America . .	5	19	24	16	64	0.4	0.7	0.6
Mexico	2	11	5	4	22	0.2	0.2	0.1
Spanish Colonies . .	29	60	51	17	157	2.4	1.7	0.6
Java	1	1	14	22	38	0.1	0.2	0.8
China and Japan . .	63	113	132	69	377	5.2	3.8	2.5
Egypt	46	158	114	61	379	3.8	4.2	2.2
Various	32	46	57	35	170	2.5	1.7	1.3
Foreign countries . .	934	1,997	2,890	2,074	7,895.	77.0	76.0	76.2
India	105	345	299	241	990	8.7	10.1	8.9
Australia	38	103	201	173	515	3.1	4.8	6.4
Canada	42	75	108	75	300	3.5	2.9	2.8
West Indies . . .	45	69	67	32	213	3.7	2.1	1.3
Singapore . . .	5	21	29	31	86	0.4	0.8	1.2
Ceylon	11	33	36	15	95	0.9	1.1	0.6
South Africa . . .	10	23	42	38	113	0.8	1.0	1.4
Various	22	35	42	31	130	1.9	1.2	1.2
British colonies . .	278	704	824	636	2,442	23.0	24.0	23.8
Grand total . . .	1,212	2,701	3,714	2,710	10,337	100.0	100.0	100.0

The exports (including also colonial products) for the same period were :—

	Millions £ Sterling					Percentage		
	1854–60	1861–70	1871–80	1881–87	34 Years	1854–60	1861–80	1881–87
France	69	230	283	180	762	7.0	10.5	8.9
Germany	116	261	334	202	913	11.8	12.1	10.0
Russia	26	69	101	53	249	2.6	3.5	2.6
Austria	9	13	14	9	45	0.9	0.6	0.5
Italy	28	41	74	54	197	2.8	2.3	2.7
Spain	15	33	43	31	122	1.5	1.5	1.5
Portugal	12	22	27	17	78	1.2	1.0	0.8
Belgium	27	68	128	97	320	2.7	4.0	4.8
Holland	57	145	193	111	506	5.8	6.9	5.5
Denmark	7	14	23	17	61	0.7	0.8	0.8
Sweden and Norway .	9	22	53	35	119	0.9	1.5	1.7
Greece	2	8	10	8	28	0.2	0.4	0.4
Roumania	1	4	9	8	22	0.1	0.3	0.4
Turkey	31	67	70	48	216	3.1	2.8	2.4
Europe	409	997	1,362	870	3,638	41.3	48.2	43.0
United States . . .	146	233	299	254	932	14.9	10.8	12.6
Brazil	29	55	68	46	198	2.9	2.5	2.3
River Plate . . .	12	29	39	46	126	1.2	1.4	2.3
Chili	10	18	21	15	64	1.0	0.8	0.7
Peru	7	13	17	7	44	0.7	0.6	0.3

	Millions £ Sterling					Percentage		
	1854–60	1861–70	1871–80	1881–87	34 years	1854–60	1861–80	1881–87
Central America . . .	8	25	30	20	83	0.8	1.1	1.0
Mexico	4	13	10	9	36	0.4	0.5	0.4
Spanish colonies . . .	16	33	37	28	114	1.6	1.4	1.4
Java	6	10	15	13	44	0.6	0.5	0.6
China and Japan . .	12	54	78	57	201	1.2	2.7	2.8
Egypt	14	60	40	22	136	1.4	2.0	1.1
Various	24	65	50	32	171	2.4	2.4	1.6
Foreign countries . . .	697	1,605	2,066	1,419	5,787	70.4	74.9	70.1
India	99	197	241	223	760	10.2	8.9	11.0
Australia . . .	80	128	188	181	577	8.2	6.4	8.9
Canada . . .	29	60	87	66	242	3.0	3.0	3.3
West Indies . . .	16	32	32	22	102	1.6	1.3	1.1
Singapore . . .	7	16	23	18	64	0.7	0.8	0.9
Ceylon . . .	4	8	10	6	28	0.4	0.4	0.3
South Africa . . .	12	18	49	39	118	1.2	1.4	1.9
Various	36	65	82	51	234	4.3	2.9	2.5
British colonies . . .	283	524	712	606	2,125	29.6	25.1	29.9
Grand total . .	980	2,129	2,778	2,025	7,912	100.0	100.0	100.0

The total volume of trade with the various countries was :—

	Millions £ Sterling					Percentage		
	1854–60	1861–70	1871–80	1881–87	34 Years	1854–60	1861–80	1881–87
France	158	528	704	444	1,834	7.2	10.9	9.4
Germany . . .	204	423	551	373	1,551	9.3	8.6	7.9
Russia	97	238	301	173	809	4.4	4.7	3.6
Austria . . .	15	23	26	21	85	0.7	0.4	0.4
Italy	45	74	113	76	308	2.1	1.7	1.6
Spain . . .	40	87	137	102	366	1.8	2.0	2.2
Portugal . . .	25	45	64	38	172	1.1	1.0	0.8
Belgium . . .	50	139	259	199	647	2.3	3.5	4.2
Holland . . .	105	255	368	285	1,013	4.8	5.6	6.0
Denmark . . .	25	34	63	53	175	1.1	0.9	1.1
Sweden and Norway .	33	78	150	111	372	1.5	2.0	2.3
Greece . . .	7	19	28	21	75	0.3	0.4	0.4
Roumania . . .	7	12	18	32	69	0.3	0.3	0.6
Turkey	48	121	127	81	377	2.3	2.2	1.7
Europe . . .	859	2,076	2,909	2,009	7,853	39.2	44.2	42.2
United States . . .	385	593	1,072	881	2,931	17.6	14.8	18.6
Brazil	46	114	131	83	374	2.2	2.2	1.8
River Plate . . .	25	52	65	60	202	1.1	1.1	1.2
Chili	24	51	60	34	169	1.1	1.0	0.7
Peru	30	48	62	21	161	1.4	1.0	0.4
Central America . .	13	44	54	36	147	0.6	0.9	0.8
Mexico	6	24	15	13	58	0.3	0.3	0.3
Spanish colonies . .	45	93	88	45	271	2.1	1.6	1.0
Java	7	11	29	35	82	0.3	0.4	0.7
China and Japan . .	75	167	210	126	578	3.4	3.3	2.7
Egypt	60	218	154	83	515	2.7	3.3	1.8
Various	56	111	107	67	341	2.6	1.8	1.4
Foreign countries . . .	1,631	3,612	4,956	3,493	13,682	74.6	75.9	73.6
India	204	542	540	464	1,750	9.3	9.7	9.8
Australia . . .	118	231	389	354	1,092	5.4	5.6	7.5
Canada . . .	71	135	195	141	542	3.3	3.0	3.0
West Indies . . .	61	101	99	54	315	2.6	1.8	1.2
Singapore . . .	12	37	52	49	150	0.6	0.8	1.0
Ceylon . . .	15	41	46	21	123	0.7	0.8	0.4
South Africa . . .	22	41	91	77	231	1.0	1.2	1.6
Various	58	100	124	82	364	2.5	2.0	1.9
British colonies . . .	561	1,228	1,536	1,242	4,567	25.4	24.1	26.4
Grand total . .	2,192	4,830	6,492	4,735	18,249	100.0	100.0	100.0

The ratio of our trade with British colonies is increasing, and with European countries declining, except as regards Spain, Belgium, Holland, Scandinavia, and Roumania.

During the said period of 34 years there was a balance of trade against the United Kingdom, the value of imports exceeding that of exports by 2425 millions, or 72 millions sterling per annum. The countries from which we had the largest excess of imports are seen in the following table :—

From	Surplus Imports, Millions £		
	1854–80	1881–87	Total
United States	694	373	1,067
Russia	244	67	311
France	226	84	310
Egypt	204	39	243
India.	212	18	230
China and Japan . . .	164	12	176
Sweden and Norway .	93	41	134
Spain	82	40	122
West Indies	101	10	111
Other countries . . .	287	137	424
Total . .	2,307	821	3,128

At the same time there were twelve countries which showed a balance of trade in favour of Great Britain, the excess of our exports thither being as follows :—

To	Surplus Exports, Millions £		
	1854–80	1881–87	Total
Germany	244	31	275
Italy	54	32	86
Australia	54	8	62
Turkey	40	15	55
River Plate	18	32	50
Brazil	13	9	22
Other countries . . .	142	11	153
Total . .	565	138	703

The principal articles of merchandise that composed the import trade of the United Kingdom were as follows :—

	Millions Sterling *				
	1854	1860	1870	1880	1889
Grain	22.8	32.8	36.7	69.5	54.1
Cotton	20.2	35.8	53.5	42.8	45.3
Manufactures . .	4.1	6.4	26 5	33.7	64.3
Meat	3.8	3.9	7.7	26.5	31.7
Wool	6.5	11.0	15.8	26.4	29.7
Sugar	10.8	12.8	17.6	23.0	22.7
Dairy produce . . .	3.1	6.8	11.9	21.2	21.5
Tea and coffee . . .	7.2	9.7	15.4	19.3	14.4
Timber	11.5	10.7	13.2	16.8	19.8
Minerals	3.1	5.3	8.9	15.5	22.1
Wines	6.4	6.2	8.0	8.6	5.9
Flax and jute . . .	5.8	5.6	10.4	10.1	11.8
Silk	6.4	9.9	8.2	3.1	3.6
Sundries	40.7	53.6	69.5	94.7	80.3
Total . .	152.4	210.5	303.3	411.2	427.2

In the above table grain includes also rice and potatoes, wines likewise include spirits, and meat also live cattle and poultry. The above shows the total importation, not only for home use, but also what was re-shipped. The following table shows the value of what was retained for home consumption.

	Millions £ Sterling				
	1854	1860	1870	1880	1889
Grain	21.9	32.0	34.6	66.8	52.5
Cotton	17.9	30.4	45.4	37.3	39.4
Meat	3.8	3.9	7.7	25.7	31.0
Wool	5.0	8.7	10.2	12.0	14.3
Sugar	10.3	12.4	17.1	22.4	21.9
Tea and coffee . . .	5.9	7.5	9.2	10.9	10.1
Wines	4.6	4.7	7.1	7.4	7.0
Dairy produce . . .	3.1	6.8	11.9	21.2	21.5
Timber	11.5	10.7	13.2	16.8	19.8
Sundries	49.8	64.9	102.6	127.5	144.7
Total . .	133.8	182.0	259.0	348.0	362.2

* For example, 22.8 signifies £22,800,000.

The quantities of certain articles of imported merchandise retained for consumption were as follows :—

	1854	1860	1870	1880	1889
Grain, tons	1,460,000	2,630,000	3,760,000	6,700,000	7,380,000
Cotton ,, ...	360,000	530,000	510,000	625,000	735,000
Wool ,, ...	36,000	53,000	77,000	101,000	160,000
Sugar ,, ...	460,000	475,000	700,000	980,000	1,300,000
Butter ,, ...	24,000	42,000	58,000	114,000	155,000
Cheese ,, ...	19,000	29,000	52,000	87,000	92,000
Tea and coffee, tons	59,000	63,000	73,000	90,000	95,000
Meat, tons	84,000	87,000	140,000	590,000	790,000
Minerals ,, ...	120,000	190,000	290,000	3,070,000	5,150,000
Timber, ,, ...	2,650,000	2,850,000	4,500,000	6,400,000	7,870,000
Wine, gallons	11,900,000	12,200,000	23,500,000	24,300,000	23,800,000

Grain includes also potatoes and rice ; wine includes spirits ; meat includes also lard and live animals, and cocoa is comprised with tea and coffee ; sugar also includes molasses.
The quantities of the principal exports were as follows :—

	1854	1860	1870	1880	1889
Cotton cloth, million yards . . .	1,700	2,800	3,300	4,500	5,002
Woollen goods, ,,	150	190	290	260	274
Linen goods, ,,	112	144	226	165	181
Jute goods .	...	...	52	183	265
All textiles, statute miles .	1,120,000	1,790,000	2,220,000	2,910,000	3,220,000
Iron and steel, tons .	1,200,000	1,400,000	2,800,000	3,800,000	4,200,000
Other metals, ,, .	40,000	60,000	100,000	100,000	120,000
Coal, ,,	4,300,000	7,300,000	11,700,000	18,700,000	29,000,000
Chemicals, ,,	50,000	100,000	200,000	420,000	390,000
Cement, ,,	20,000	80,000	150,000	280,000	630,000
All yarns, million lbs.	184	259	276	274	345

The consumption per head of the population has been of various imported articles as follows :—

	1845	1850	1860	1870	1880	1889
Grain, bushels .	1.0	1.5	3.7	4.9	7.6	7.7
Sugar, lbs. . .	20	25	36	50	65	72
Meat ,, . .	0	6	6	10	38	43
Butter ,, . .	1	2	3	4	7	9
Cheese ,, . .	1	2	2	4	5	6
Tea, oz. . . .	25	31	43	60	75	78
Coffee, oz. . .	20	19	20	16	15	12
Wines, gallons .	0.4	0.4	0.4	0.7	0.7	0.6
Cotton, lbs. . .	20	20	40	35	40	43
Wool ,, . .	2	2	4	6	7	10

The principal exports from the United Kingdom * were in value thus :—

MILLIONS £ STERLING

	1854	1860	1870	1880	1889
Cotton goods . . .	31.7	52.0	71.4	75.6	70.5
Woollen goods . . .	10.7	16.0	26.6	20.6	25.7
Linen and jute . . .	5.1	6.6	10.4	9.3	9.8
Silken, &c.	1.2	2.4	2.6	2.7	4.2
Textiles	48.7	77.0	111.0	108.2	110.2
Iron	11.7	12.4	26.5	29.7	29.2
Machinery	2.2	3.8	5.3	9.2	15.3
Cutlery	4.1	5.3	6.4	5.5	3.0
Metals	3.8	5.6	4.7	4.8	8.7
Hardware	21.8	27.1	42.9	49.2	56.2
Coal	2.1	3.3	5.6	8.4	14.8
Sundries	24.6	28.5	40.1	57.3	66.9
Total . .	97.2	135.9	199.6	223.1	248.1

IRELAND

Dobbs gives returns for the 17th century ; the rest are from Blue-books :—

Date	Imports, £	Exports, £	Total, £
1665	336,000	358,000	694,000
1681	433,000	583,000	1,016,000
1695	392,000	296,000	688,000
1698	577,000	996,000	1,573,000
1725	1,000,000	1,400,000	2,400,000
1750–52 . . .	1,900,000	1,600,000	3,500,000
1760–62	2,300,000	1,700,000	4,000,000
1770–72	3,300,000	2,400,000	5,700,000
1780–82	3,100,000	2,700,000	5,800,000
1790–92	5,100,000	4,100,000	9,200,000
1800–2	4,100,000	5,600,000	9,700,000
1810	6,500,000	5,300,000	11,800,000
1820	6,000,000	6,300,000	12,300,000
1826	7,500,000	8,500,000	16,000,000

Since 1826 no separate tables of Irish trade have been kept. In 1725 the exports were as follows :—

	£
Meat	860,000
Linen	470,000
Grain &c.	70,000
	1,400,000

* This table is exclusive of colonial merchandise.

In the years 1796 to 1799 the annual average was as follows :—

From	Imports, £	To	Exports, £
Great Britain . .	4,010,000	Great Britain . .	4,970,000
Other countries .	1,270,000	Other countries .	810,000
Total .	5,280,000	Total .	5,780,000

The trade between Great Britain and Ireland in the same year was :—

	Imported from Great Britain		Exported to Great Britain
	£		£
Woollens . . .	690,000	Linen . .	2,490,000
Coal	160,000	Meat . . .	870,000
Cottons and silk	130,000	Butter . .	740,000
Iron and steel .	120,000	Wheat . .	440,000
Fish	100,000	Cattle . .	140,000
Sundries . . .	2,810,000	Sundries .	290,000
Total .	4,010,000	Total . . .	4,970,000

FRANCE

Official returns date continuously from 1716, yearly averages being as follows :—

Period	Imports	Exports	Total	Per Inhabitant
	£	£	£	£ s. d.
1716–20	2,600,000	4,200,000	6,800,000	0 7 0
1721–30	3,200,000	4,600,000	7,800,000	0 7 6
1731–40	3,600,000	5,200,000	8,800,000	0 8 0
1741–50	4,100,000	7,700,000	11,800,000	0 10 6
1751–60	5,800,000	9,200,000	15,000,000	0 12 6
1761–70	6,600,000	12,400,000	19,000,000	0 16 0
1771–80	8,300,000	10,400,000	18,700,000	0 15 0
1781–90	12,100,000	14,200,000	26,300,000	1 1 0
1791–1800	17,000,000	14,500,000	31,500,000	1 3 0
1801–10	16,300,000	14,400,000	30,700,000	1 1 0
1811–20	11,300,000	16,100,000	27,400,000	0 18 0
1821–30	20,600,000	20,900,000	41,500,000	1 6 0
1831–40	28,500,000	30,700,000	59,200,000	1 16 0
1841–50	33,000,000	40,500,000	73,500,000	2 2 0
1851–60	62,000,000	65,000,000	127,000,000	3 10 0
1861–70	110,000,000	110,000,000	220,000,000	6 0 0
1871–80	157,000,000	140,000,000	297,000,000	8 0 0
1881–86	181,000,000	134,000,000	315,000,000	8 6 0
1889	167,000,000	144,300,000	311,300,000	8 3 0

The trade returns of 1800 showed thus :—

	Imports, £		Exports, £
Coffee . . .	1,500,000	Wine . . .	2,000,000
Raw cotton .	1,400,000	Silks . . .	1,600,000
Sundries . .	10,100,000	Sundries . .	7,200,000
Total . .	13,000,000	Total . .	10,800,000

The weight of merchandise imported and exported yearly averaged thus :—

Period	Imports, Tons	Exports, Tons	Total, Tons
1857–66 . . .	9,200,000	2,400,000	11,600,000
1867–76 . . .	12,800,000	4,300,000	17,100,000
1877–89 . . .	20,400,000	4,600,000	25,000,000

The statement of French trade for ten years ending 1886 shows thus :—

	Millions £ Sterling			
	Imports from	Exports to	Gross Trade	Ratio
Great Britain . .	248	358	606	19.4
Belgium . . .	178	179	357	11.4
Germany . .	167	137	304	9.7
United States . .	171	114	285	9.1
Italy . . .	144	81	225	7.2
Spain . . .	118	62	180	5.8
Russia . . .	99	9	108	3.5
Argentina . . .	65	37	102	3.3
India . . .	74	3	77	2.5
Turkey . . .	53	19	72	2.3
Austria . . .	41	10	51	1.6
Switzerland . .	46	91	137	4.4
China and Japan .	49	...	49	1.5
Other countries .	241	158	399	12.8
Total foreign . .	1,694	1,258	2,952	94.5
French colonies .	91	80	171	5.5
Total . .	1,785	1,338	3,123	100.0

The imports according to quantity were as follows :—

	1876	1886	1877–86
Wine, million gallons	14	242	1,430
Wool, million lbs. .	270	426	3,300
Grain, million bushels	40	57	770
Silk, million lbs. . .	29	29	240
Hides, tons . . .	67,000	79,000	720,000
Cotton, million lbs. .	350	302	3,100
Coal, tons	7,900,000	9,300,000	92,000,000
Fruit and seeds, tons	420,000	760,000	6,600,000
Coffee, tons . . .	53,000	68,000	620,000
Flax, tons	41,000	56,000	710,000
Cheese and butter, tons	17,000	24,000	230,000
Copper, tons . . .	30,000	23,000	260,000

The principal exports were in value thus :—

	1876	1886	Average, 1877–86	1889
	£	£	£	£
Woollen fabrics }	12,700,000	15,100,000	14,100,000	13,400,000
Silk fabrics .	11,800,000	9,700,000	11,000,009	9,900,000
Wines . .	12,600,000	13,400,000	12,800,000	12,800,000
Raw silk .	6,900,000	5,900,000	6,100,000	5,400,000
Raw wool .	3,000,000	5,300,000	4,200,000	6,200,000
Sugar . .	6,400,000	2,200,000	4,100,000	4,200,000
Hides and leather . }	11,200,000	11,600,000	12,400,000	12,200,000
Cotton manufac. }	2,600,000	4,300,000	3,400,000	4,500,000
Clothing .	3,600,000	3,100,000	3,100,000	3,500,000
Grain . .	5,800,000	1,200,000	2,700,000	3,300,000
Cheese and butter . }	4,400,000	3,600,000	3,900,000	4,400,000
Raw cotton	3,200,000	1,200,000	2,100,000	1,100,000
Eggs . .	1,800,000	1,100,000	1,200,000	1,100,000
Jewellery .	2,200,000	2,000,000	2,400,000	2,400,000
Fruit . .	1,400,000	1,700,000	1,500,000	1,700,000
Metal wares	29,000,000	2,500,000	2,700,000	5,400,000
Haberdashery . }	6,900,000	5,000,000	6,000,000	5,700,000
Sundries .	43,600,000	41,100,000	40,100,000	47,200,000
Total . .	143,000,000	130,000,000	133,800,000	144,300,000

The principal imports were as follows :—

	1876	1886	Average, 1877–86	1889
	£	£	£	£
Wine . .	1,010,000	20,700,000	11,300,000	15,500,000
Wool . .	11,100,000	15,400,000	12,900,000	15,100,000
Grain . .	9,600,000	10,500,000	18,400,000	17,400,000
Silk . . .	21,800,000	11,700,000	12,100,000	10,800,000
Hides . .	6,800,000	7,000,000	6,900,000	6,500,000
Cotton . .	9,200,000	6,400,000	7,900,000	7,400,000
Timber .	8,100,000	5,800,000	8,400,000	6,200,000
Coal . .	6,900,000	5,000,000	6,300,000	5,400,000
Cattle and meat . }	7,400,000	6,400,000	8,600,000	4,800,000
Fruit and seeds . }	5,900,000	11,600,000	9,600,000	8,400,000
Coffee . .	4,300,000	4,100,000	3,800,000	5,100,000
Flax . .	2,000,000	2,200,000	2,600,000	2,400,000
Sundries .	65,390,000	61,500,000	69,700,000	62,100,000
Total .	159,500,000	168,300,000	178,500,000	167,000,000

The exports according to quantity were as follows :—

	1876	1886	1877–86
Wines, million gallons .	84	64	640
Wool, million lbs. .	46	108	730
Grain, million bushels .	23	7	120
Cheese and butter, tons .	43,000	34,000	370,000
Eggs, tons . . .	33,000	21,000	220,000
Fruit ,, . . .	44,000	64,000	520,000
Hides ,, . . .	24,000	35,000	340,000
Sugar ,, . . .	230,000	140,000	1,520,000
Raw cotton, million lbs. .	120	56	770

The net imports averaged for ten years, 1877–86, as follows :—

	Quantity	Value, £ Sterling
Wines, gallons . . .	79,000,000	6,400,000
Wool, lbs. . . .	257,000,000	8,700,000
Grain, bushels . . .	65,000,000	15,700,000
Silk, raw, lbs. . . .	13,000,000	6,000,000
Hides, tons . . .	38,000	4,000,000
Raw cotton, lbs. . .	233,000,000	5,800,000
Timber	...	7,200,000
Coal, tons . . .	9,200,000	6,300,000
Cattle and meat . .	...	7,400,000
Fruit and seeds, tons .	610,000	8,100,000
Coffee, tons . . .	62,000	3,800,000
Sundries . . .	...	72,300,000
Total . .	...	151,700,000

The French coasting trade in 1889 was 2,360,000 tons.

ALGERIA

Trade returns show as follows for 1888 :—

From	Imports, £	To	Exports, £	Total Trade, £
France . .	7,200,000	France . .	6,600,000	13.800,000
Other countries }	2,200,000	Other countries }	1,300,000	3,500,000
Total .	9,400,000	Total .	7,900,000	17,300.000

	Imports, £		Exports, £
Cotton goods .	1,100,000	Grain . . .	1,300,000
Leather. . .	600,000	Wine . . .	1,700,000
Hardware . .	300,000	Cattle . . .	1,400,000
Haberdashery	300,000	Wool . . .	800,000
Sundries . .	7,100,000	Sundries . .	2,700,000
Total .	9,400,000	Total .	7,900,000

The trade with Great Britain, imports and exports, reaches £900,000.

GERMANY

The *Répertoire Générale* gives the trade for 1822 as follows :—

	Imports, £	Exports, £	Total, £
Prussia	13,100,000	14,200,000	27,300,000
Other states . .	6,400,000	6,500,000	12,900,000
Total . .	19,500,000	20,700,000	40,200,000

In 1850, according to Levi's estimate, the total trade was :—

		£
Imports	. . . . .	22,000,000
Exports	. . . . .	20,000,000
	Total .	42,000,000

This was much below the reality. We know that the trade of the Zollverein in 1856 reached 106 millions sterling, and the increase of six years could hardly have exceeded 50 per cent. The trade seems to have been as follows :—

Year	Millions £ Sterling			Per Inhabitant
	Imports	Exports	Total	
				£ s. d.
1822 . . .	19	21	40	1 10 0
1840 . . .	25	27	52	1 14 0
1850 . . .	34	36	70	2 2 0
1872 . . .	163	116	279	7 0 0
1880 . . .	142	152	294	6 11 0
1888 . . .	172	168	340	7 4 0
1889 . . .	204	163	367	7 16 0

The statement for German trade for seven years ending 1886 was as follows :—

	Millions £ Sterling			Ratio
	Imports from	Exports to	Gross Trade	
Great Britain .	151	167	318	14.9
Austria . . .	151	107	258	12.1
Russia . . .	125	61	186	8.7
Belgium . . .	89	57	146	6.8
France . . .	84	101	185	8.7
Holland . . .	81	83	164	7.7
Switzerland .	55	58	113	5.3
United States .	48	61	109	5.1
Italy	25	26	51	2.5
Other countries	254	348	602	28.2
Total .	1,063	1,069	2,132	100.0

There is not much difference between the total value of imports and that of exports. The trade with Russia and Austria, however, shows a heavy excess of imports, which is counterbalanced by a surplus of exports to Great Britain, France, United States, and other countries.

The principal articles of import were as follows :—

	1876	1886	1877–86, Ten Years	Net Import
	£	£	Mill. £	Mill. £
Grain . .	29,800,000	10,300,000	222	133
Wool . .	10,400,000	10,900,000	104	78
Cotton . .	10,200,000	8,800,000	93	78
Coffee . .	9,600,000	6,900,000	73	73
Cattle . .	8,000,000	4,700,000	63	6
Hides . .	3,900,000	4,600,000	44	44
Horses . .	3,500,000	3,500,000	28	16
Petroleum	5,200,000	2,800,000	31	28
Silk, raw .	6,600,000	7,500,000	60	60
Tobacco .	4,100,000	3,200,000	33	29
Yarn . .	8,500,000	8,100,000	69	40
Wine . .	2,900,000	1,700,000	24	24
Sundries .	87,400,000	71,400,000	772	772
Total .	190,100,000	144,400,000	1,616	1,381

The principal exports were :—

	1876	1886	1877–86, Ten Years
	£	£	Mill. £
Woollen fabrics .	6,300,000	8,600,000	81
Silk fabrics . . .	2,800,000	9,000,000	71
Cotton fabrics . .	1,900,000	4,900,000	33
Sugar	1,900,000	7,100,000	64
Leather goods . .	3,400,000	7,600,000	56
Iron and machinery	5,500,000	7,500,000	80
Cattle	7,000,000	4,200,000	57
Yarn	2,700,000	3,100,000	29
Paper	800,000	2,500,000	18
Grain	11,100,000	3,100,000	89
Coal	1,600,000	4,000,000	28
Wool	3,300,000	2,000,000	26
Sundries . . .	79,100,000	85,700,000	859
Total . . .	127,400,000	149,300,000	1,491

The trade returns for 1888 were as follows :—

	Imports, £		Exports, £
Textiles . . .	51,300,000	Textiles . .	53,800,000
Food . . .	37,600,000	Food . . .	19,600,000
Cattle . . .	7,800,000	Metals . . .	24,300,000
Metals . . .	15,900,000	Chemicals .	11,800,000
Chemicals . .	12,100,000	Leather . .	11,800,000
Tallow, &c. .	10,800,000	Machinery .	6,800,000
Sundries . .	36,300,000	Sundries . .	39,500,000
Total . .	171,800,000	Total . .	167,600,000

RUSSIA

The principal imports of European Russia were as follows :—

	1876	1886	1877–86, Ten Years, Millions Sterling	Net Imports, Millions Sterling
	£	£	£	£
Cotton . .	5,200,000	7,200,000	74	74
Wool . . .	1,700,000	1,900,000	24	9
Tea . . .	5,200,000	3,600,000	46	46
Iron and steel	5,100,000	1,900,000	34	32
Machinery .	2,700,000	1,400,000	25	25
Coal . . .	1,600,000	1,300,000	17	17
Chemicals .	800,000	1,300,000	19	19
Sundries . .	36,800,000	18,800,000	282	282
Total .	59,100,000	37,400,000	521	504

The principal exports of European Russia were as follows :—

	1876	1886	1877–86, Ten Years, Millions Sterling
	£	£	£
Wheat . . .	14,000,000	9,700,000	162
Rye	7,600,000	4,800,000	74
Oats	3,300,000	2,600,000	45
Barley, &c. . .	2,200,000	4,600,000	42
All grain . .	27,100,000	21,700,000	323
Flax	5,100,000	4,300,000	70
Hemp . . .	1,200,000	1,200,000	18
Linseed . . .	3,200,000	1,500,000	31
Timber . . .	4,100,000	2,000,000	33
Wool	1,600,000	2,100,000	15
Cattle . . .	1,600,000	900,000	13
Sundries . . .	6,800,000	10,000,000	87
Total .	50,700,000	43,700,000	590

Exports of the whole Russian Empire at various dates were officially valued thus :—

Year	Grain, £	Sundries, £	Total, £
1830	3,000,000	9,400,000	12,400,000
1840	5,800,000	10,900,000	16,700,000
1860	10,400,000	15,800,000	26,200,000
1870	24,400,000	29,900,000	54,300,000
1880	26,600,000	31,600,000	58,200,000
1886	21,700,000	27,100,000	48,800,000

Official returns, allowing for discount on paper-money at various periods, may be summed up since 1742 thus :—

Date	Imports	Exports	Total	Per Inhabitant
	£	£	£	£ s. d.
1742	3,600,000	4,700,000	8,300,000	0 8 0
1750	6,900,000	7,200,000	14,100,000	0 13 0
1760	7,400,000	9,900,000	17,300,000	0 15 0
1770	11,400,000	15,000,000	26,400,000	1 2 0
1780	15,500,000	19,700,000	35,200,000	1 7 0
1790	20,800,000	21,800,000	42,600,000	1 10 0
1802	14,100,000	15,800,000	29,900,000	0 16 0
1820–39	10,500,000	12,000,000	22,500,000	0 10 0
1840	11,200,000	15,200,000	26,400,000	0 11 0
1841–49	15,000,000	18,000,000	33,000,000	0 12 0
1850–59	21,000,000	23,000,000	44,000,000	0 15 0
1860	21,500,000	26,200,000	47,700,000	0 15 0
1870	48,900,000	54,300,000	103,200,000	1 6 0
1880	72,600,000	58,200,000	130,800,000	1 11 0
1886	42,700,000	48,800,000	91,500,000	1 1 0
1888	39,100,000	79,400,000	118,500,000	1 7 0

The statement for ten years ending 1886 shows as follows :—

	Millions £ Sterling			Ratio
	Imports from	Exports to	Gross Trade	
Germany	201	165	366	36.2
Great Britain . . .	123	169	292	28.9
Austria	23	31	54	5.3
France	18	48	66	6.5
Turkey	14	10	24	2.4
Italy	9	12	21	2.1
Holland	6	36	42	4.1
Sweden and Norway	4	16	20	2.0
Other countries . .	79	49	128	12.5
Total . .	477	536	1,013	100.0

The exports of grain since 1867 averaged in quantity as follows :—

	Millions of Bushels			
	1867–76	1877–86	1887	1888
Wheat . . .	50	67	75	122
Oats . . .	20	46	59	85
Rye . . .	27	46	50	68
Barley . . .	6	20	34	58
Maize, &c. . .	7	16	28	34
Total .	110	195	246	367

The trade returns for European Russia in 1888 may be summed up thus :—

	Imports, £		Exports, £
Raw cotton .	6,800,000	Grain . . .	42,200,000
Wool . . .	2,500,000	Flax . . .	6,700,000
Tea	1,600,000	Seeds . . .	3,800,000
Machinery . .	1,600,000	Timber . .	3,800,000
Iron wares . .	1,500,000	Hemp . . .	1,700,000
Coal	1,300,000	Butter and eggs	1,500,000
Sundries . .	17,900,000	Sundries . .	13,000,000
Total . .	33,200,000	Total . .	72,700,000

AUSTRIA-HUNGARY

The following are the official returns :—

Year	Imports	Exports	Total	Per Inhab.
	£	£	£	£ s. d.
1831	6,800,000	7,900,000	14,700,000	0 12 0
1835	9,100,000	8,900,000	18,000,000	0 14 0
1840	11,000,000	10,800,000	21,800,000	0 15 6
1851	15,600,000	13,400,000	29,000,000	0 19 0
1860	20,900,000	26,500,000	47,400,000	1 10 0
1870	43,600,000	39,500,000	83,100,000	2 7 0
1880	51,100,000	56,300,000	107,400,000	2 16 0
1889	48,200,000	44,400,000	92,600,000	2 6 0

The principal exports of Austria-Hungary were :—

	1860	1870	1880	1886	Million £, 1877–86
	£	£	£	£	£
Timber	1,600,000	2,400,000	3,700,000	4,200,000	42
Grain	2,000,000	5,200,000	6,700,000	6,300,000	81
Fancy goods	1,800,000	4,400,000	4,300,000	5,200,000	56
Cattle	800,000	1,000,000	3,000,000	3,300,000	37
Leather goods	1,100,000	1,400,000	1,500,000	2,100,000	17
Textile goods	3,100,000	4,200,000	4,200,000	4,400,000	44
Sugar	...	...	4,900,000	4,000,000	47
Sundries	16,100,000	20,900,000	28,000,000	28,700,000	259
Total . .	26,500,000	39,500,000	56,300,000	58,200,000	583

Austro-Hungarian Imports	1860	1870	1880	1886	1877–86, Million £	Net Imports, Million £
	£	£	£	£	£	£
Raw cotton	2,900,000	3,800,000	3,600,000	3,800,000	37	34
Wool	1,100,000	1,400,000	3,100,000	2,700,000	30	14
Coffee	1,100,000	2,000,000	2,300,000	2,600,000	25	25
Tobacco	...	...	2,300,000	2,800,000	20	20
Hides	500,000	1,400,000	1,800,000	1,700,000	17	9
Silk, raw	500,000	1,100,000	1,300,000	1,600,000	13	13
Leather	500,000	1,400,000	1,600,000	1,300,000	16	16
Yarns	1,500,000	2,700,000	2,700,000	2,300,000	26	15
Flax and jute	...	...	1,000,000	1,500,000	12	12
Sundries	11,700,000	29,800,000	31,400,000	24,600,000	293	...
Total . .	20,900,000	43,600,000	51,100,000	44,900,000	491	...

Trade returns for 1887 may be summed up thus :—

	Imports, £		Exports, £
Cotton	4,700,000	Grain . .	7,800,000
Wool	3,600,000	Timber . .	4,600,000
Coffee	2,800,000	Sugar . .	3,700,000
Silk	1,600,000	Hardware .	3,000,000
Tobacco . . .	1,500,000	Woollens .	2,100,000
Yarn	2,600,000	Cattle . .	2,200,000
Hides and leather	2,700,000	Glass . .	1,700,000
Sundries . . .	27,900,000	Sundries .	31,000,000
Total . .	47,400,000	Total .	56,100,000

	Imports from	Exports to	Total Trade
	£	£	£
Germany . . .	30,200,000	33,300,000	63,500,000
Russia	2,100,000	1,500,000	3,600,000
Great Britain . .	1,600,000	900,000	2,500,000
Servia	1,200,000	1,000,000	2,200,000
Various	12,300,000	19,400,000	31,700,000
Total . .	47,400,000	56,100,000	103,500,000

The above includes the total foreign trade of both Austria and Hungary, in which only a small portion seems to fall to Hungary, since the returns for that kingdom for 1888, including trade with Austria, show :—

	Imports from	Exports to	Total Trade
	£	£	£
Austria	32,400,000	25,800,000	58,200,000
Foreign countries	6,300,000	11,400,000	17,700,000
Total . .	38,700,000	37,200,000	75,900,000

Hungary exported grain worth £14,000,000 and cattle £5,000,000 : her imports included textiles worth £16,600,000 sterling.

ITALY

The trade of Genoa increased 80 per cent. from 1835 to 1867.* If we suppose a similar increase for Italy, the trade of the kingdom would have been 35 millions sterling in the former year, but it was doubtless much below that figure. Levi's estimate for 1850 was only 11 millions for imports, and 8 millions for exports, which was certainly too low. We have regular statistics from 1861 :—

Year	Million £ Sterling			Per Inhabitant
	Imports	Exports	Total	
				£ s. d.
1835 . . .	13	11	24	1 7 0
1850 . . .	23	15	38	1 18 0
1861 . . .	33	19	52	2 7 0
1870 . . .	36	30	66	2 13 0
1880 . . .	47	44	91	3 3 0
1886 . . .	58	41	99	3 6 0
1889 . . .	56	38	94	3 3 0

The aggregate for ten years, 1877–86, was :—

	Millions £ Sterling			Ratio
	Imported from	Exported to	Gross Trade	
France	136	194	330	34.0
Great Britain .	116	36	152	15.6
Austria . . .	84	58	142	14.4
Germany . .	33	27	60	6.2
Switzerland .	21	44	65	6.7
Russia . . .	24	9	33	3.4
United States .	24	20	44	4.5
India . . .	27	8	35	3.6
Other countries	62	48	110	11.6
Total . .	527	444	971	100.0

This table includes bullion both ways.

* From £8,200,000 to £14,400,000.

Imports of Italy	1862	1870	1880	1886	1877–86, Millions Sterling	Net Imports, Millions Sterling
	£	£	£	£	£	£
Grain	3,000,000	3,200,000	3,600,000	8,100,000	49	18
Coal	700,000	1,500,000	2,300,000	2,700,000	23	23
Timber	800,000	1,000,000	1,200,000	2,400,000	15	15
Raw cotton . . .	300,000	1,400,000	3,300,000	3,000,000	30	22
Wool	500,000	500,000	1,200,000	1,300,000	13	13
Silk	5,000 000	2,200,000	2,100,000	2,000,000	18	...
Machinery . . .	...	200,000	1,600,000	1,700,000	19	19
Textile goods . .	...	4,800,000	4,400,000	4,900,000	52	47
Hides	500,000	700,000	1,100,000	1,400,000	14	14
Sundries	22,400,000	20,300,000	26,600,000	30,700,000	280	...
Total . .	33,200,000	35,800,000	47,400,000	58,200,000	505	...

The principal exports were : —

	1862	1870	1880	1886	1877–86, Millions Sterling
	£	£	£	£	£
Silk	8,200,000	9,200,000	11,600,000	12,600,000	114
Wine	400,000	400,000	2,600,000	3,300,000	20
Oil	2,600,000	3,400,000	3,400,000	3,100,000	37
Fruit	1,200,000	1,000,000	1,400,000	1,500,000	16
Eggs	60,000	160,000	1,400,000	1,200,000	13
Cattle	500,000	900,000	1,200,000	700,000	13
Hemp	400,000	800,000	900,000	1,000,000	11
Sulphur . . .	1,200,000	1,000,000	1,300,000	1,000,000	12
Sundries	8,540,000	13,340,000	20,300,000	16,400,000	190
Total . .	23,100,000	30,200,000	44,100,000	40,800,000	426

The trade of 1888 may be summed up thus : —

	Imports, £		Exports, £
Grain . . .	5,900,000	Silk . . .	11,600,000
Coal	3,600,000	Oil	2,500,000
Cotton . . .	3,400,000	Wine . . .	2,200,000
Textiles . . .	2,500,000	Fruit . . .	1,700,000
Machinery . .	1,600,000	Hemp . . .	1,100,000
Timber . . .	1,200,000	Sulphur . .	900,000
Sundries . .	28,800,000	Sundries . .	15,600,000
Total . .	47,000,000	Total . .	35,600,000

SPAIN

The official returns show as follows : —

Year	Imports	Exports	Total	Per Inhabitant
	£	£	£	£ s. d.
1795	8,800,000	4,800,000	13,600,000	1 7 0
1827	3,800,000	2,900,000	6,700,000	0 12 0
1850	5,900,000	4,800,000	10,700,000	0 15 0
1860	14,500,000	10,700,000	25,200,000	1 11 0
1872	21,100,000	20,100,000	41,200,000	2 11 0
1880	24,900,000	25,500,000	50,400,000	3 3 0
1885	29,500,000	27,500,000	57,000,000	3 7 0
1888	28,600,000	30,500,000	59,100,000	3 8 0

The imports were as follows : —

The exports of 1795 were as follows : —

		£
Wool		1,500,000
Wine		1,600,000
Sundries		1,700,000
Total . .		4,800,000

The statement for ten years ending December 1885 showed as follows : —

	Million £ Sterling			
	Imports from	Exports to	Gross Trade	Ratio
France	78	85	163	31.3
Great Britain . . .	61	77	138	26.6
Germany	20	3	23	4.4
United States . . .	33	7	40	7.7
Cuba	11	25	36	7.0
Other countries . .	72	47	119	23.0
Total . .	275	244	519	100.0

The above table includes bullion both ways. Notwithstanding heavy import duties, the imports surpassed exports. In 1888, however, there was a surplus of exports.

	1860	1872	1880	1885	1876–85, Millions Sterling	Net Imports, Millions Sterling
	£	£	£	£	£	£
Grain	...	200,000	300,000	900,000	10	4
Brandy	200,000	200,000	1,700,000	2,200,000	13	13
Cotton	1,300,000	2,600,000	3,200,000	2,600,000	29	29
Textiles	1,500,000	1,000,000	1,700,000	2,100,000	19	19
Sugar	1,100,000	1,100,000	900,000	1,200,000	11	11
Coal	300,000	700,000	800,000	1,000,000	9	9
Fish	500,000	700,000	700,000	1,200,000	8	8
Machinery . . .	300,000	700,000	2,000,000	1,400,000	18	18
Sundries	9,300,000	13,900,000	13,600,000	16,900,000	143	...
Total . .	14,500,000	21,100,000	24,900,000	29,500,000	260	...

The above is of merchandise only, excluding bullion. The exports were as follows : —

	1860	1872	1880	1885	1876–85, Millions Sterling
	£	£	£	£	£
Wine	3,200,000	6,800,000	10,000,000	12,600,000	92
Minerals	...	3,600,000	6,400,000	4,800,000	53
Fruit	...	2,100,000	1,600,000	1,900,000	19
Oil	200,000	600,000	500,000	1,600,000	7
Sundries	7,300,000	7,000,000	7,000,000	6,600,000	70
Total . .	10,700,000	20,100,000	25,500,000	27,500,000	241

The trade of 1888 may be summed up thus :—

	Imports, £		Exports, £
Cotton . . .	2,300,000	Wine . . .	12,100,000
Grain . . .	2,400,000	Metals and }	6,800,000
Coal	1,200,000	minerals }	
Textiles . . .	2,000,000	Fruit . . .	2,300,000
Machinery }	1,600,000	Cork . . .	800,000
and iron . }		Cattle . . .	700,000
Timber . . .	1,200,000	Wool . . .	600,000
Sugar . . .	1,200,000	Oil	400,000
Sundries . .	16,700,000	Sundries . .	6,800,000
Total . .	28,600,000	Total . .	30,500,000

PORTUGAL

Official returns are as follows :—

Year	Imports	Exports	Total	Per Inhabitant
	£	£	£	£ s. d.
1806	7,100,000	7,600,000	14,700,000	4 15 0
1842	2,400,000	1,700,000	4,100,000	1 4 0
1850	3,100,000	2,200,000	5,300,000	1 9 0
1870	5,700,000	4,600,000	10,300,000	2 11 0
1880	7,900,000	5,600,000	13,500,000	3 1 0
1886	10,500,000	5,700,000	16,200,000	3 10 0
1888	10,600,000	7,200,000	17,800,000	4 0 0

The trade of 1806 was probably abnormally high on account of the war with Spain. There has been a steady increase since 1842.

The returns for imports are as follows :—

	1872	1880	1886	1877–86, Average
	£	£	£	£
Grain . . .	400,000	1,200,000	1,100,000	1,200,000
Textile goods	1,500,000	1,200,000	1,400,000	1,300,000
Cotton and } wool . }	200,000	300,000	500,000	300,000
Fish . . .	300,000	300,000	400,000	300,000
Coal . . .	200,000	300,000	300,000	300,000
Sundries . .	3,900,000	6,800,000	6,800,000	4,700,000
Total .	6,500,000	7,900,000	10,500,000	8,100,000

The exports were as follows :—

	1872	1880	1886	1877–86
	£	£	£	£
Wine . . .	2,000,000	2,200,000	3,700,000	2,400,000
Copper . .	400,000	400,000	...	300,000
Cork . . .	200,000	600,000	500,000	500,000
Cattle . .	300,000	400,000	200,000	400,000
Fruit . . .	200,000	200,000	100,000	200,000
Sundries . .	2,100,000	1,800,000	1,200,000	1,400,000
Total .	5,200,000	5,600,000	5,700,000	5,200,000

The statement for ten years ending December 1882 was as follows :—

	Millions £ Sterling			Ratio
	Imports from	Exports to	Total	
Great Britain . . .	34	27	61	48.0
France	10	4	14	11.0
Brazil	5	10	15	11.8
United States . . .	7	1	8	6.3
Spain	5	3	8	6.3
Other countries . .	15	6	21	16.6
Total . . .	76	51	127	100.0

SWEDEN

Official returns of merchandise are as follows :—

Year	Imports	Exports	Total	Per Inhabitant
	£	£	£	£ s. d.
1801	1,400,000	1,000,000	2,400,000	1 1 0
1805	1,500,000	1,700,000	3,200,000	1 6 0
1831–40	1,300,000	1,600,000	2,900,000	1 1 0
1850	3,300,000	3,700,000	7,000,000	2 1 0
1860	4,400,000	4,800,000	9,200,000	2 8 0
1870	7,800,000	8,400,000	16,200,000	3 18 0
1880	15,100,000	13,100,000	28,200,000	6 5 0
1885	18,700,000	13,700,000	32,400,000	6 10 0
1887	16,300,000	13,500,000	29,800,000	6 0 0

A statement for ten years ending December 1885 shows thus :—

	Millions £ Sterling			Ratio
	Imports from	Exports to	Gross Trade	
Great Britain . . .	44	63	107	37.2
Germany	40	9	49	17.1
Denmark	28	13	41	14.3
Norway	9	4	13	4.5
France	4	15	19	6.6
Other countries . .	37	21	58	20.3
Total . .	162	125	287	100.0

The above table includes bullion both ways.
The imports were as follows of merchandise :—

	1875	1885	1876–85	Net Imports
	£	£	Mill. £	Mill. £
Textile goods .	1,500,000	2,000,000	16	15
Grain	1,100,000	2,000,000	16	...
Cotton, wool, } and yarns }	1,100,000	1,300,000	11	11
Coal	800,000	900,000	8	8
Sundries . . .	10,000,000	12,500,000	107	...
Total . .	14,500,000	18,700,000	158	...

The exports were as follows :—

	1875	1885	1876–85
	£	£	Million £
Timber	4,700,000	5,100,000	50
Iron	2,100,000	1,900,000	17
Grain	1,800,000	1,500,000	18
Butter	400,000	1,100,000	6
Sundries . . .	2,300,000	4,100,000	30
Total . .	11,300,000	13,700,000	121

The trade of 1887 may be summed up thus :—

	Imports, £		Exports, £
Textiles . . .	2,700,000	Timber . .	5,400,000
Grain . . .	1,700,000	Butter, &c. .	2,400,000
Fibre . . .	1,600,000	Metals . .	1,800,000
Coal . . .	1,200,000	Hardware . .	400,000
Sundries . .	9,100,000	Sundries . .	3,500,000
Total . .	16,300,000	Total . .	13,500,000

NORWAY

Previously to 1872 the value of exports was not recorded, but merely the quantities. The trade has been approximately as follows :—

Year	Imports	Exports	Total	Per Inhabitant
	£	£	£	£ s. d.
1830	700,000	800,000	1,500,000	1 8 0
1850	1,600,000	1,800,000	3,400,000	2 9 0
1860	2,400,000	2,200,000	4,600,000	3 0 0
1872	7,600,000	5,800,000	13,400,000	7 10 0
1880	8,400,000	6,100,000	14,500,000	7 3 0
1888	8,800,000	6,800,000	15,600,000	7 15 0

The imports were as follows :—

	1876	1886	1877–86
	£	£	Millions £
Grain	2,000,000	1,500,000	18
Textile goods .	800,000	800,000	8
Hardware . . .	700,000	500,000	5
Sundries . . .	5,800,000	4,700,000	54
Total . .	9,300,000	7,500,000	85

The exports were as follows :—

	1876	1886	1877–86
	£	£	Millions £
Timber . . .	2,400,000	1,600,000	19
Fish	2,400,000	1,800,000	19
Sundries . . .	1,800,000	2,300,000	22
Total . .	6,600,000	5,700,000	60

The statement for ten years ending December 1886 shows :—

	Millions £ Sterling			Ratio
	Imports from	Exports to	Gross Trade	
Great Britain .	22	20	42	29.0
Germany . .	25	8	33	22.7
Sweden . . .	9	7	16	11.0
Other countries	29	25	54	37.3
Total . .	85	60	145	100.0

The trade of 1888 may be summed up thus :—

	Imports, £		Exports, £
Grain . . .	1,700,000	Fish	2,300,000
Textiles . .	1,000,000	Timber	1,800,000
Hardware . .	700,000	Metals and minerals	500,000
Sundries . .	5,400,000	Sundries	2,200,000
Total . .	8,800,000	Total	6,800,000

DENMARK

Official returns show as follows :—

Year	Imports	Exports	Gross Trade	Per Inhab.
	£	£	£	£ s. d.
1789	950,000	1,020,000	1,970,000	...
1850	4,700,000	3,100,000	7,800,000	5 5 0
1872	10,800,000	8,100,000	18,900,000	10 8 0
1880	11,500,000	9,800,000	21,300,000	10 15 0
1888	15,200,000	10,700,000	25,900,000	13 0 0

The exports in 1836 were as follows :—

	Quantity		Value, £
Wheat, bushels . . .	800,000	...	150,000
Barley and rye, bushels .	2,300,000	...	250,000
Butter, barrels . . .	70,000	...	400,000
Cattle, No.	40,000	...	300,000
Sundries		...	...	860,000
Total .			1,960,000

The imports of merchandise in ten years ending 1885 were :—

	1875	1885	1876–85
Coal, tons . . .	500,000	900,000	7,000,000
Grain ,, . . .	65,000	145,000	1,150,000
Iron goods, tons . .	50,000	55,000	510,000
Oil	8,000	19,000	16,000
Salt	25,000	25,000	240,000
Sugar	26,000	20,000	270,000

The exports of Denmark were :—

	1875	1885	1876–85
Grain, tons . . .	240,000	150,000	2,100,000
Cattle, No. . .	340,000	350,000	4,200,000
Bacon, tons . .	5,000	16,000	75,000
Butter ,, . .	13,000	18,000	145,000

It will be observed that the exports of grain much exceeded the imports, the net export for ten years being one million tons, or 40 million bushels.

The countries trading with Denmark in the period of ten years ending December 1885 were :—

	Million £ Sterling			Ratio
	Imports from	Exports to	Total	
Germany . . .	49	31	80	34.8
Great Britain . .	30	37	67	29.1
Sweden	16	15	31	13.4
Other countries . .	38	15	53	22.7
Total . .	133	98	231	100.0

The trade of 1888 may be summed up thus :—

Imports	£	Exports	£
Textiles . .	2,200,000	Butter and eggs .	5,100,000
Grain	1,600,000	Cattle	1,600,000
Metals	1,300,000	Grain	900,000
Sundries . . .	10,100,000	Sundries . . .	3,100,000
Total .	15,200,000	Total .	10,700,000

HOLLAND

Official statements are as follows :—

Year	Imports	Exports	Total	Per Inhabitant
	£	£	£	£ s. d.
1843	15,200,000	11,400,000	26,600,000	8 10 0
1850	22,000,000	18,000,000	40,000,000	11 5 0
1860	25,300,000	20,200,000	45,500,000	12 10 0
1870	38,800,000	31,800,000	70,600,000	18 10 0
1880	69,000,000	52,100,000	121,100,000	30 5 0
1888	106,000,000	92,900,000	198,900,000	45 0 0

More than half the trade is in a manner goods in transit, since we see that the net imports are less than half the gross imports.

The imports of Holland were as follows :—

	1861	1870	1880	1886	1877–86	Net Import
	£	£	£	£	Millions £	Millions £
Chinchona . . .	600,000	500,000	2,500,000	8,800,000	46	4
Grain . . .	5,000,000	5,500,000	10,300,000	15,000,000	115	57
Iron	1,400,000	2,000,000	7,700,000	8,000,000	78	21
Coal . . .	1,400,000	1,500,000	2,500,000	3,000,000	26	26
Coffee . . .	2,700,000	3,500,000	3,500,000	3,100,000	37	12
Cotton and yarn . .	3,800,000	4,000,000	4,200,000	3,800,000	42	15
Wool and yarn . .	1,600,000	2,200,000	1,700,000	2,900,000	21	5
Timber . . .	800,000	900,000	1,800,000	1,800,000	19	19
Lard . . .	...	...	2,300,000	2,400,000	20	17
Sugar . . .	3,300,000	4,600,000	2,800,000	2,500,000	30	7
Petroleum . .	...	900,000	1,000,000	1,700,000	12	12
Sundries . . .	6,700,000	13,200,000	28,700,000	36,400,000	335	...
Total . .	27,300,000	38,800,000	69,000,000	89,400,000	781	...

The exports of Holland were as follows :—

	1861	1870	1880	1886	1877–86
	£	£	£	£	Million £
Chinchona	500,000	400,000	2,400,000	9,100,000	42
Iron	900,000	1,400,000	5,700,000	4,800,000	57
Butter	1,200,000	1,400,000	2,400,006	4,700,000	29
Coffee	2,300,000	2,900,000	2,400,000	2,700,000	25
Sugar	2,700,000	3,800,000	2,200,000	2,500,000	23
Cattle	700,000	800,000	1,100,000	1,100,000	11
Cotton and yarn . .	3,100,000	3,100,000	2,600,000	2,400,000	27
Wool and yarn . .	1,400,000	1,800,000	1,200,000	2,500,000	16
Grain	1,500,000	2,100,000	5,200,000	7,800,000	58
Sundries	7,200,000	14,500,000	29,300,000	50,400,000	300
Total . . .	21,000,000	31,800,000	52,100,000	78,900,000	588

The statement for ten years ending December 1886 showed :—

	Million £ Sterling			Ratio
	Imports from	Exports to	Total	
Germany . . .	227	267	494	35.5
Great Britain .	207	140	347	25.0
Belgium . .	107	92	199	14.3
Java . . .	58	37	95	6.8
United States .	48	17	65	4.7
Russia . .	57	6	63	4.5
Other countries .	92	34	126	9.2
Total . .	796	593	1,389	100.0

The above includes bullion both ways.

The summary for ten years shows that imports exceeded exports by 203 millions sterling. This excess is to be observed in the trade of Holland with all countries except Germany. The largest excess is in respect of Russia, the imports from which are ten times the exports thither. Trade with the United States is also very unequal.

The trade of 1888 may be summed up thus :—

	Imports, £		Exports, £
Grain . . .	16,300,600	Drugs	13,000,000
Drugs . . .	16,400,000	Textiles . . .	9,500,000
Iron and steel .	12,000,000	Grain	7,700,000
Textiles . .	9,000,000	Butter and cheese	4,900,000
Sundries . .	52,300,000	Sundries . . .	57,800,000
Total . .	106,000,000	Total . . .	92,900,000

BELGIUM

The values of the principal imports at various dates were as follows :—

	1840	1850	1860	1870	1880	1887
	£	£	£	£	£	£
Grain	400,000	200,000	2,400,000	2,900,000	7,400,000	6,600,000
Wool	500,000	700,000	2,100,000	3,500,000	7,400,000	3,100,000
Hides	100,000	200,000	1,900,000	2,400,000	2,600,000	2,900,000
Flax	...	200,000	600,000	2,200,000	2,800,000	2,000,000
Cattle	100,000	100,000	600,000	1,100,000	2,300,000	1,800,000
Coffee	1,000,000	900,000	1,300,000	1,200,000	1,800,000	1,600,000
Meat	...	...	...	700,000	3,600,000	2,000,000
Eggs	...	...	...	...	1,300,000	1,300,000
Cotton	600,000	700,000	800,000	1,400,000	1,700,000	1,000,000
Sundries	5,500,000	6,400,000	10,900,000	21,400,000	36,300,000	34,900,000
Total . .	8,200,000	9,400,000	20,600,000	36,800,000	67,200,000	57,200,000

The weight of certain imports was as follows :—

	Tons					
	1840	1850	1860	1870	1880	1887
Coal	21,000	9,000	97,000	229,000	937,000	1,025,000
Ores	...	...	1,000	569,000	922,000	1,452,000
Grain	92,000	53,000	243,000	315,000	786,000	1,001,000
Rice	4,000	6,000	27,000	35,000	62,000	76,000
Meat	3,000	3,000	22,000	52,000	133,000	95,000
Iron	...	...	2,000	91,000	251,000	175,000
Salt	26,000	32,000	40,000	49,000	100,000	115,000
Flax	1,000	4,000	10,000	41,000	41,000	50,000
Wool	3,000	4,000	14,000	42,000	49,000	44,000
Cotton	9,000	10,000	15,000	16,000	23,000	23,000
Sugar	25,000	25,000	21,000	24,000	23,000	14,000
Coffee	19,000	17,000	19,000	22,000	23,000	19,000
Wine, gallons	1,700,000	2,100,000	3,200,000	3,100,000	4,500,000	4,200,000

Official reports show as follows :—

Period	Imports	Exports	Gross Trade	Per Inhab.		
	Mill. £	Mill. £	Mill. £	£	s.	d.
1831–40	8	6	14	4	0	0
1841–50	13	12	25	5	15	0
1851–60	20	17	37	8	0	0
1861–70	30	24	54	10	10	0
1871–80	56	44	100	19	0	0
1881–86	59	51	110	20	0	0
1850	10	11	21	4	14	0
1860	21	19	40	8	10	0
1870	37	28	65	13	0	0
1880	67	49	116	21	10	0
1886	53	47	100	18	0	0
1888	61	50	111	18	10	0

The averages of imports and exports for ten years ending 1886 were :—

	Gross Imports, £	Net Imports, £		Exports, £
Grain	11,400,000	7,400,000	Yarn	4,600,000
Wool	5,000,000	5,000,000	Coal	2,800,000
Meat	3,600,000	3,600,000	Textiles	2,700,000
Timber	1,800,000	1,800,000	Flax	2,700,000
Flax	3,400,000	700,000	Iron wares	3,800,000
Cotton	1,400,000	1,400,000	Sugar	1,400,000
Minerals	2,900,000	2,900,000	Glass	1,900,000
Textile goods	1,900,000	...	Grain	4,000,000
Coffee	1,700,000	1,700,000	Hides	1,800,000
Hides	2,300,000	500,000	Stone	2,500,000
Sundries	24,700,000	...	Sundries	20,900,000
Total	60,100,000	...	Total	49,100,000

Exports	1860	1870	1880	1886
	£	£	£	£
Yarn	1,200,000	2,500,000	5,200,000	5,300,000
Coal	2,200,000	2,400,000	3,300,000	2,800,000
Textile goods	3,100,000	2,500,000	3,100,000	2,600,000
Flax	1,000,000	2,000,000	2,700,000	2,600,000
Iron goods	1,000,000	2,400,000	3,400,000	3,000,000
Sugar	...	900,000	1,300,000	1,000,000
Glass	500,000	600,000	2,000,000	2,000,000
Grain	...	...	4,800,000	2,200,000
Hides	1,200,000	1,400,000	1,500,000	2,200,000
Stone	...	...	2,300,000	2,300,000
Sundries	8,600,000	12,900,000	19,100,000	21,300,000
Total	18,800,000	27,600,000	48,700,000	47,300,000

The statement for ten years ending Dec. 1886 showed :—

	Millions £ Sterling			Ratio
	Imports from	Exports to	Gross Trade	
France	122	151	273	25.0
Great Britain	81	99	180	16.5
Holland	84	66	150	13.8
Germany	77	91	168	15.4
United States	72	13	85	7.7
Argentine Republic	19	4	23	2.2
Other countries	146	67	213	19.4
Total	601	491	1,092	100.0

The weight of exported goods was as follows :—

	1840	1850	1860	1870	1880	1887
Coal, tons	1,000,000	2,000,000	3,400,000	3,800,000	5,400,000	5,500,000
Iron ,,	17,000	109,000	104,000	251,000	314,000	416,000
Sugar ,,	65,000	66,000	35,000	54,000	88,000	130,000
Flax ,,	...	...	6,000	5,000	10,000	41,000
Wool ,,	6,000	11,000	17,000	23,000	28,000	2,000

The trade of 1888 may be summed up thus :—

	Imports, £		Exports, £
Grain	10,500,000	Yarn	5,400,000
Fibre	7,400,000	Fibre	3,200,000
Meat and cattle	3,500,000	Coal	3,200,000
Timber	2,800,000	Grain	2,800,000
Chemicals	2,700,000	Textiles	2,600,000
Sundries	34,500,000	Iron & machinery	4,400,000
		Sundries	28,200,000
Total	61,400,000	Total	49,800,000

SWITZERLAND

We have returns since 1855, viz. :—

Year	Imports	Exports	Total
	£	£	£
1855	14,400,000	19,600,000	34,000,000
1863	18,400,000	16,800,000	35,200,000
1888	33,100,000	26,900,000	60,000,000

	Imports, £				Exports, £	
	1855	1886			1855	1886
Raw silk	6,800,000	5,500,000	Clocks . . .	1,900,000	3,300,000
Grain	2,300,000	3,600,000	Lace . . . }		3,700,000
Textile goods . . .	1,000,000	1,300,000	Silks . . . } 12,100,000	{ 3,000,000
Cattle	600,000	1,700,000	Ribbons . . }		1,300,000
Raw cotton . . .	600,000	1,100,000	Cheese . . .	400,000	1,500,000
Sugar	400,000	1,000,000	Cotton goods . .	2,000,000	2,800,000
Sundries . . .	2,700,000	17,700,000	Sundries . . .	3,200,000	11,100,000
Total . . .	14,400,000	31,900,000	Total . . .	19,600,000	26,700,000

The returns for 1885 and 1886 show thus, two years aggregate :—

MILLIONS £

	Imports from	Exports to	Gross Trade	Ratio
France . . .	15	11	26	21.8
Italy	9	5	14	12.0
Great Britain . .	4	8	12	10.1
Austria . .	6	3	9	7.5
Germany . . .	20	13	33	27.7
United States .	2	7	9	7.5
Other countries .	6	10	16	13.4
Total .	62	57	119	100.0

GREECE

Official returns of merchandise show as follows :—

Year	Imports	Exports	Total	Per Inhabitant
	£	£	£	£ s. d.
1861	1,700,000	1,000,000	2,700,000	2 1 0
1870	3,100,000	1,400,000	4,500,000	3 1 0
1880	4,100,000	1,500,000	5,600,000	3 6 0
1888	4,000,000	3,400,000	7,400,000	3 15 0

The import trade was as follows :—

	1861	1870	1875	1888
	£	£	£	£
Grain . . .	220,000	650,000	1,100,000	1,400,000
Textile goods	360,000	540,000	600,000	800,000
Sundries . .	1,120,000	1,910,000	2,400,000	1,800,000
Total .	1,700,000	3,100,000	4,100,000	4,000,000

The exports were as follows :—

	1861	1870	1875	1888
	£	£	£	£
Fruit . . .	580,000	720,000	1,500,000	1,900,000
Oil. . . .	...	...	470,000	100,000
Sundries . .	420,000	680,000	730,000	1,400,000
Total .	1,000,000	1,400,000	2,700,000	3,400,000

The countries trading with Greece in 1888 showed thus :—

	Imports from	Exports to	Total Trade
	£	£	£
Great Britain . .	1,100,000	1,400,000	2,500,000
France	400,000	600,000	1,000,000
Austria	500,000	300,000	800,000
Various . . .	2,000,000	1,100,000	3,100,000
Total . .	4,000,000	3,400,000	7,400,000

TURKEY

Official returns are as follows :—

	Imports	Exports	Total
	£	£	£
1881	16,100,000	7,600,000	23,700,000
1889	19,500,000	13,500,000	33,000,000

Judging by the proportion of British trade with Turkey, the returns for the Ottoman Empire (excluding Egypt) should have been :—

Year	£ Sterling		
	Imports	Exports	Total
1854 . . .	8,000,000	7,000,000	15,000,000
1860 . . .	12,000,000	9,000,000	21,000,000
1870 . . .	19,000,000	20,000,000	39,000,000
1880 . . .	16,000,000	8,000,000	24,000,000
1879 . . .	19,500,000	13,500,000	33,000,000

The trade of 1888 may be summed up thus :—

	Imports, £		Exports, £
Cottons . . .	3,000,000	Fruit . . .	2,300,000
Linens . . .	800,000	Silk . . .	1,200,000
Woollens . .	700,000	Grain . . .	700,000
Sugar . . .	1,200,000	Wool . . .	600,000
Grain . . .	1,400,000	Mohair . .	500,000
Coffee . . .	700,000	Opium . .	400,000
Sundries . .	13,200,000	Sundries . .	7,800,000
Total .	21,000,000	Total .	13,500,000

The countries trading with Turkey were :—

	Imports from	Exports to	Total Trade
	£	£	£
Great Britain . .	8,500,000	3,600,000	12,100,000
Austria	3,800,000	1,000,000	4,800,000
France	2,400,000	4,200,000	6,600,000
Russia	2,200,000	200,000	2,400,000
Various . . .	4,100,000	4,500,000	8,600,000
Total . .	21,000,000	13,500,000	34,500,000

ROUMANIA

Official returns are as follows :—

Year	Imports	Exports	Total	Per Inhabitant
	£	£	£	£ s. d.
1872	4,400,000	6,700,000	11,100,000	2 4 0
1880	10,200,000	8,800,000	19,000,000	3 14 0
1887	12,600,000	10,600,000	23,200,000	3 12 0

K

The statement for ten years ending December 1885 showed thus :—

MILLIONS £ STERLING

	Imports from	Exports to	Total	Ratio
Austria . . .	54	30	84	42.4
Great Britain .	20	24	44	22.2
Germany . .	13	1	14	7.1
France . . .	9	8	17	8.6
Turkey . . .	5	7	12	6.1
Other countries	10	17	27	13.6
Total . .	111	87	198	100.0

The imports were as follows :—

	1880	1885	1880–85	1887
	£	£	£	£
Textile goods	1,600,000	1,800,000	1,700,000	5,500,000
Cotton yarn	1,000,000	400,000	700,000	...
Shoes and leather	500,000	800,000	700,000	700,000
Sundries . .	7,100,000	7,700,000	6,800,000	6,400,000
Total . .	10,200,000	10,700,000	9,900,000	12,600,000

The exports were as follows :—

	1880	1885	1880–85	1887
	£	£	£	£
Grain . .	6,000,000	6,800,000	6,200,000	8,600,000
Sundries .	2,800,000	3,100,000	2,700,000	2,000,000
Total . .	8,800,000	9,900,000	8,900,000	10,600,000

UNITED STATES
TRADE WITH ALL COUNTRIES, MILLIONS STERLING

	Gross Trade			Net Trade			Per Inhabitant
	Imports	Exports	Total	Imports	Exports	Total	
	£	£	£	£	£	£	£ s. d.
1791–1800	12	10	22	8	6	14	3 3 0
1801–10	19	16	35	12	8	20	3 9 0
1811–20	17	13	30	14	10	24	2 15 0
1821–30	15	15	30	12	11	23	2 2 0
1831–40	25	21	46	22	18	40	2 13 0
1841–50	25	25	50	23	23	46	2 6 0
1851–60	59	52	111	56	48	104	3 17 0
1861–70	69	53	122	66	50	116	3 6 0
1871–80	111	124	235	110	121	231	5 16 0
1881–86	137	161	298	135	156	291	5 10 0
1790	5	4	9	5	4	9	2 6 0
1800	19	15	34	11	6	17	3 5 0
1810	18	14	32	12	9	21	2 18 0
1820	15	14	29	12	11	23	2 8 0
1830	13	15	28	10	12	22	1 15 0
1840	20	26	46	18	23	41	2 6 0
1850	36	30	66	34	28	62	2 14 0
1860	74	70	144	70	66	136	4 8 0
1870	90	81	171	87	78	165	4 5 0
1880	138	174	312	136	172	308	6 3 0
1889	154	166	320	...	...	...	5 0 0

The above is of merchandise only, excluding bullion. Official records of gross trade, including re-shipments, and of the net trade of the Union, as well as of the Colonies with Great Britain before Independence, are shown as follows :—

Period	Imports from Great Britain	Exports to Great Britain	Total	Per Inhabitant
	£	£	£	£ s. d.
1700–10	267,000	266,000	533,000	1 16 0
1711–20	366,000	393,000	759,000	1 5 0
1721–30	471,000	579,000	1,050,000	1 2 0
1731–40	660,000	670,000	1,330,000	1 4 0
1741–50	813,000	709,000	1,522,000	1 7 0
1751–60	1,577,000	803,000	2,380,000	1 10 0
1761–70	1,763,000	1,045,000	1,808,000	0 15 0
1771–80	1,331,000	744,000	2,075,000	0 14 0
1785	2,308,000	894,000	3,202,000	1 0 0

The proportion of trade with Great Britain in the commerce of the United States since 1790 is shown as follows :—

Year	Millions £ Sterling			Ratio		
	Trade with Great Britain	With other Countries	Total	Great Britain	Other Countries	Total
1790	5	4	9	55	45	100
1800	15	19	34	44	56	100
1810	16	16	32	50	50	100
1820	15	14	29	52	48	100
1830	14	14	28	50	50	100
1840	23	23	46	50	50	100
1850	32	34	66	48	52	100
1860	68	76	144	47	53	100
1870	81	90	171	48	52	100
1880	145	167	312	46	54	100
1889	117	203	320	37	63	100

The statement for ten years ending 1886 was as follows :—

	Millions £ Sterling			Ratio
	Imports from	Exports to	Total	
Great Britain . . .	322	820	1,142	41.0
Germany	108	123	231	8.3
France	137	129	266	9.6
Cuba	154	27	181	6.5
Canada	75	73	148	5.3
China and Japan . .	66	21	87	3.1
Brazil	96	17	113	4.1
Italy	23	20	43	1.6
Other countries . .	263	309	572	20.5
Total . .	1,244	1,539	2,783	100.0

The values of exports in sixty years ending 1886 were :—

MILLIONS £ STERLING

	1827–36	1837–46	1847–56	1857–66	1867–76	1877–86	Sixty Years
Cotton	81	114	181	181	346	422	1,325
Grain	12	13	54	88	154	381	702
Meat	3	5	17	29	75	179	308
Petroleum	...	...	...	7	64	94	165
Tobacco	13	15	20	40	51	51	190
Butter and cheese .	...	1	2	11	20	33	67
Cotton manufacture	2	6	12	8	9	23	60
Iron ,,	...	2	5	9	27	33	76
Wooden ,,	5	6	12	18	34	43	118
Sundries . . .	29	40	59	89	90	280	587
Total . .	145	202	362	480	870	1,539	3,598

The values of imports for sixty years ending 1886 were as follows :—

MILLIONS £ STERLING

	1827–36	1837–46	1847–56	1857–66	1867–76	1877–86	60 Years
Sugar	15	18	29	69	153	179	463
Coffee	15	18	27	37	77	102	276
Woollens . . .	23	21	42	63	108	85	342
Cottons . . .	23	21	40	37	50	58	229
Silks	21	23	46	43	52	77	262
Linens	10	11	17	21	35	42	136
Iron manufactures . .	10	8	33	31	69	69	220
Tea	7	9	12	15	37	33	113
Sundries . . .	46	78	172	272	418	599	1,585
Total . . .	170	207	418	588	999	1,244	3,626

The imports were as follows :—

	1821	1840	1860	1880	1889
	£	£	£	£	£
Sugar	1,100,000	1,800,000	7,100,000	17,700,000	19,400,000
Coffee	900,000	1,800,000	4,500,000	12,500,000	15,600,000
Woollen goods	1,600,000	1,900,000	7,800,000	7,100,000	10,900,000
Cotton ,, ...	1,600,000	1,300,000	1,900,000	6,200,000	5,600,000
Silk ,, ...	900,000	2,000,000	6,200,000	9,200,000	7,300,000
Linen ,, ...	500,000	1,000,000	2,200,000	4,700,000	5,400,000
Iron ,, ...	400,000	600,000	3,800,000	11,200,000	8,800,000
Tea	200,000	1,100,000	1,800,000	4,100,000	2,600,000
Sundries	1,900,000	6,400,000	34,600,000	63,700,000	78,500,000
Total	9,100,000	17,900,000	69,900,000	136,400,000	154,100,000

The exports were as follows :—

	1821	1840	1860	1880	1889
	£	£	£	£	£
Cotton	4,200,000	13,300,000	39,900,000	44,000,000	49,600,000
Grain	1,100,000	2,500,000	4,600,000	58,200,000	25,800,000
Meat	300,000	400,000	2,100,000	22,900,000	21,600,000
Petroleum	...	...		7,500,000	9,400,000
Tobacco	1,100,000	2,100,000	3,900,000	3,800,000	4,700,000
Sundries	2,400,000	4,800,000	15,200,000	35,000,000	54,500,000
Total	9,100,000	23,100,000	65,700,000	171,400,000	165,600,000

The trade of the Colonies before independence was as follows :—

	1701		1750		1773	
	Imports, £	Exports, £	Imports, £	Exports, £	Imports, £	Exports, £
New England	33,000	86,000	48,000	344,000	125,000	527,000
New York	19,000	32,000	36,000	267,000	76,000	289,000
Pennsylvania	5,000	12,000	28,000	218,000	37,000	426,000
Carolina	17,000	14,000	192,000	133,000	457,000	345,000
Virginia, &c.	235,000	199,000	510,000	351,000	675,000	392,000
Total . .	309,000	343,000	814,000	1,313,000	1,370,000	1,979,000

The weight of the principal exports was approximately as follows :—

Period	Tons					
	Cotton	Grain	Meat	Tobacco	Butter and Cheese	Total
1827–36	1,600,000	1,800,000	60,000	450,000	...	3,910,000
1837–46	3,400,000	2,000,000	1,000,000	650,000	20,000	6,170,000
1847–56	4,800,000	6,000,000	350,000	750,000	40,000	11,940,000
1857–66	4,000,000	11,000,000	600,000	900,000	200,000	16,700,000
1867–76	4,200,000	18,500,000	1,500,000	900,000	400,000	25,500,000
1877–86	8,800,000	47,000,000	3,600,000	1,100,000	700,000	61,200,000
60 years	26,800,000	86,300,000	6,210,000	4,750,000	1,360,000	125,420,000

It appears that whereas the value of exports increased tenfold since the decade ending 1836 the weight increased 32-fold.

All the values in the above tables are in gold, allowance being made in each year from 1862 to 1878 for the difference between greenbacks and gold.

Bullion is not included in either imports or exports.

CANADA

Official returns show as follows :—

Year	Imports	Exports	Total	Per Inhabitant
	£	£	£	£ s. d.
1832	1,600,000	900,000	2,500,000	2 10 0
1834	2,490,000	1,100,000	3,590,000	2 15 0
1839	2,100,000	1,100,000	3,200,000	2 10 0
1851	7,600,000	5,200,000	12,800,000	5 2 0
1860	11,900,000	10,800,000	22,700,000	6 15 0
1870	16,100,000	15,000,000	31,100,000	8 1 0
1880	19,400,000	19,100,000	38,500,000	8 10 0
1887	24,200,000	19,600,000	43,800,000	8 18 2
1888	23,000,000	18,700,000	41,700,000	8 10 0

The statement for ten years ending 1886 showed as follows :—

The imports were as follows :—

	1851	1860	1876	1877–86	1888
	£	£	£	£	£
Textile goods .	1,900,000	2,400,000	3,700,000	3,900,000	3,800,000
Iron goods	500,000	500,000	2,200,000	2,500,000	2,200,000
Sugar	200,000	400,000	1,000,000	1,200,000	1,200,000
Coal	...	100,000	700,000	1,200,000	1,900,000
Sundries .	5,000,000	8,500,000	11,800,000	14,100,000	13,900,000
Total	7,600,000	11,900,000	19,400,000	22,900,000	23,000,000

The exports were as follows :—

	1851	1860	1876	1877–86	1888
	£	£	£	£	£
Grain	700,000	2,800,000	5,100,000	4,600,000	3,200,000
Meat	...	300,000	700,000	1,200,000	2,200,000
Cheese	...	...	800,000	1,200,000	1,900,000
Timber	1,000,000	1,800,000	3,700,000	3,700,000	4,500,000
Fish .	550,000	1,000,000	1,900,000	1,900,000	1,700,000
Sundries .	2,950,000	4,900,000	4,700,000	6,900,000	5,200,000
Total	5,200,000	10,800,000	16,900,000	19,500,000	18,700,000

In the foregoing tables the whole Canadian Dominion and Newfoundland are included. Meat includes live cattle.

MEXICO

Official reports are as follows :—

	Imports	Exports	Total	Per Inhabitant
	£	£	£	£ s. d.
1880	5,000,000	6,800,000	11,800,000	1 2 0
1889	8,100,000	12,500,000	20,600,000	2 2 0

The trade of ten years summed up thus :—

		£
Imports	. . . . .	71,000,000
Exports	. . . . .	87,000,000
Total	.	158,000,000

MILLIONS £ STERLING

	Imports from	Exports to	Total	Ratio
United States .	100	74	174	41.1
Great Britain .	91	95	186	44.0
Germany . .	3	...	3	0.7
France . .	4	1	5	1.2
Cuba . . .	3	2	5	1.2
Other countries	28	22	50	11.8
Total . .	229	194	423	100.0

The quantities of exported goods in thirty years showed approximately thus :—

	Tons			
	1857–66	1867–76	1877–86	30 Years
Grain . . .	3,600,000	3,900,000	7,500,000	15,000,000
Timber . .	12,400,000	17,900,000	19,200,000	49,500,000
Meat . . .	130,000	140,000	280,000	550,000
Cheese and butter .	25,000	80,000	320,000	425,000
Fish . . .	650,000	900,000	1,220,000	2,770,000
Coal . . .	...	2,500,000	4,300,000	6,800,000
Ores . . .	45,000	70,000	280,000	395,000
Total .	16,850,000	25,490,000	33,100,000	75,440,000

The returns for 1889 give only exports in detail, viz. :—

	Exports		Exported to
	£		£
Silver . . .	5,800,000	United States	6,100,000
Hemp . . .	1,000,000	Great Britain	1,900,000
Coffee . . .	600,000	France . .	500,000
Hides . . .	300,000	Germany. .	300,000
Sundries . .	4,800,000	Various . .	3,700,000
Total .	12,500,000	Total .	12,500,000

CENTRAL AMERICA

The aggregate trade of Guatemala, Salvador, Honduras, Costa Rica, and Nicaragua in 1888 summed up—imports, $19,600,000 ; exports, $23,100,000 ; but as these dollars are worth only three shillings, the amount is only £3,000,000 for imports, and £3,500,000 for exports.

SOUTH AMERICA

The latest returns for the various States show as follows:—

	Imports	Exports	Total
	£	£	£
Brazil	19,700,000	21,200,000	40,900,000
Argentina . . .	14,300,000	12,500,000	26,800,000
Chili	6,600,000	7,500,000	14,100,000
Uruguay	6,300,000	6,200,000	12,500,000
Venezuela . . .	2,500,000	3,300,000	5,800,000
Colombia . . .	2,800,000	1,600,000	4,400,000
Ecuador . . .	2,200,000	2,000,000	4,200,000
Peru	1,800,000	1,300,000	3,100,000
Bolivia	900,000	1,500,000	2,400,000
Paraguay . . .	300,000	200,000	500,000
Total . .	57,200,000	57,300,000	114,500,000

BRAZIL

Inconvertible paper money has so often been a disturbing element that values were at times obscured. Reduced to gold, the trade showed approximately thus:—

Period	Annual Average		
	Imports	Exports	Total
	£	£	£
1836–41	5,200,000	4,700,000	9,900,000
1852–61	12,000,000	10,800,000	22,800,000
1862–74	15,500,000	18,300,000	33,800,000
1882–88	17,200,000	18,000,000	35,200,000

The exports in 1888 were as follows:—

	£	To	£
Coffee . . .	15,100,000	United States	11,000,000
Sugar . . .	1,300,000	Great Britain	5,200,000
Cotton . . .	1,200,000	France . .	2,800,000
Sundries . .	3,600,000	Various . .	2,200,000
Total . .	21,200,000	Total .	21,200,000

The weight of exports in the years 1880–84 averaged thus:—

	Tons		Tons
Coffee . . .	230,000	Tobacco . .	22,000
Sugar . . .	217,000	India-rubber .	7,100

ARGENTINA

Official records of merchandise are as follows:—

Year	Imports	Exports	Total	Per Inhab.
	£	£	£	£ s. d.
1795	510,000	920,000	1,430,000	3 10 0
1825	1,600,000	1,200,000	2,800,000	4 0 0
1837	1,200,000	1,400,000	2,600,000	3 0 0
1842	1,300,000	1,400,000	2,700,000	3 3 0
1850	2,100,000	2,200,000	4,300,000	4 6 0
1865	5,400,000	4,400,000	9,800,000	6 0 0
1870	9,500,000	5,800,000	15,300,000	8 0 0
1880	8,800,000	11,300,000	20,100,000	8 0 0
1889	14,300,000	12,500,000	26,800,000	8 0 0

The trade of the country was stagnant from the period of Independence down to 1842, but after the latter date numbers of Irish sheep-farmers arrived (now numbering 20,000), to whom, in Consul Cowper's words, "the wealth and progress of Argentina are in a great measure due."

The statement for ten years ending December 1886 showed:—

	Millions £ Sterling			Ratio
	Imports from	Exports to	Total	
Great Britain . . .	38	11	49	21.8
France	22	31	53	23.4
Belgium	7	23	30	13.7
Germany	8	7	15	6.8
United States . . .	8	·6	14	6.4
Uruguay	6	4	10	4.4
Other countries . .	28	24	52	23.5
Total . . .	117	·106	223	100.0

The principal exports appear in the following table:—

	1873	1880	1888	1877–86
	£	£	£	£
Wool . . .	3,900,000	5,300,000	5,900,000	5,100,000
Hides and skins .	2,800,000	3,600,000	2,700,000	2,900,000
Meat . . .	700,000	900.000	700,000	700,000
Grain . . .	...	150,000	1,400,000	700,000
Sundries . .	1,800,000	1,350,000	2,600,000	1,200,000
Total .	9,200,000	11,300,000	13,300,000	10,600,000

Fuller details of exports will be found under *Agriculture*, p. 49.

URUGUAY

Official returns are as follows:—

Period	Annual Trade, £ Sterling			Per Inhabitant
	Imports	Exports	Total	
	£	£	£	£ s. d.
1841–50	1,300,000	1,200,000	2,500,000	20 10 0
1851–60	1,800,000	1,700,000	3,500,000	20 5 0
1861–70	2,700,000	2,400,000	5,100,000	18 10 0
1871–80	3,500,000	3,300,000	6,800,000	18 12 0
1881–87	4,500,000	4,600,000	9,100,000	16 10 0
1888	6,300,000	6,200,000	12,500,000	20 0 0

The statement for ten years ending 1886 was as follows:—

MILLIONS £ STERLING

	Imports from	Exports to	Total	Ratio
Great Britain . . .	12	10	22	26.2
France	7	7	14	16.7
United States . . .	3	5	8	9.5
Brazil	4	8	12	14.4
Belgium	1	6	7	8.3
Germany	3	1	4	4.8
Other countries . .	10	7	17	20.1
Total . .	40	44	84	100.0

The returns for 1887 were as follows:—

	Imports		Exports
	£		£
Wines . . .	700,000	Wool . . .	1,200,000
Raw material .	1,000,000	Meat . . .	1,200,000
Textile goods .	900,000	Hides . . .	700,000
Groceries . .	1,100,000	Sundries . .	1,400,000
Sundries . . .	1,500,000	Total . .	4,500,000
Total . .	5,200,000		

CHILE

Official reports give the following :—

Year	Imports	Exports	Total
	£	£	£
1844 . . .	1,500,000	1,400,000	2,900,000
1854 . . .	3,400,000	3,000,000	6,400,000
1865 . . .	4,800,000	4,400,000	9,200,000
1875 . . .	7,600,000	7,200,000	14,800,000
1888 . . .	6,600,000	7,500,000	14,100,000

The statement for ten years ending 1886 showed :—

	Millions £ Sterling			Ratio
	Imports from	Exports to	Total	
Great Britain . . .	18	45	63	54.6
Germany	7	3	10	9.0
France	7	4	11	10.0
Argentine Republic .	3	1	4	3.2
United States . . .	2	2	4	3.6
Other countries . .	11	12	23	19.6
Total . . .	48	67	115	100.0

The above amounts for 1888 are computed at the current rate for the year, 27 pence per dollar.

AUSTRALIA

Official reports show as follows :—

Year	Imports	Exports	Total	Per Inhab.
	£	£	£	£ s. d.
1824	420,000	120,000	540,000	5 2 0
1830	670,000	310,000	980,000	8 2 0
1838	2,970,000	1,530,000	4,500,000	17 10 0
1851	4,300,000	3,700,000	8,000,000	17 10 0
1861	25,100,000	24,500,000	49,600,000	31 10 0
1871	30,100,000	34,700,600	64,800,000	24 0 0
1881	50,200,000	48,600,090	98,800,090	33 0 0
1888	65,300,000	57,600,000	122,900,000	29 5 0
1889	68,300,000	61,500,000	129,800,000	35 0 0

The above exports include gold, the production of which has been as follows :—

Period	Millions £ Sterling		Per Annum £
1851–60 . . .	104	...	10,400,000
1861–70 . . .	82	...	8,200,000
1871–80 . . .	72	...	7,200,000
1881–88 . . .	42	...	5,200,000
38 years . . .	300		8,000,000

The export of wool during the same period has been as follows :—

Period	Million Lbs.	Value, Million £	Million Lbs. Yearly	Value, £ Yearly
1851–60	560	48	56	4,800,000
1861–70	1,350	102	135	10,200,000
1871–80	3,060	184	306	18,400,000
1881–88	3,100	142	390	17,800,000
38 years	8,070	476	212⁄	12,600,000

It appears that the wool exports of 38 years exceeded the product of the goldfields in the same term by 176 millions sterling. At present the clip averages a value of 21 millions sterling, or five times that of the gold product.

The statement for ten years ending 1886 showed, including bullion :—

	Millions £ Sterling		
	Imports from	Exports to	Total
Great Britain	274	243	517
United States	18	8	26
France	2	2	4
China	10	...	10
Other countries . . .	77	98	175
Foreign trade	381	351	732
Intercolonial	178	137	315
Total . .	559	488	1,047

The trade of the several colonies in the same period was :—

	Millions £ Sterling			Per Inhab. per Annum
	Imports	Exports	Total	
				£ s. d.
New South Wales	188	161	349	47 0 0
Victoria .	171	151	322	37 0 0
New Zealand .	76	64	140	28 0 0
South Australia .	55	52	107	38 0 0
Queensland . .	49	41	90	42 0 0
Tasmania .	15	14	29	25 0 0
Western Australia	5	5	10	33 0 0
Total . .	559	488	1,047	38 0 0

The following table shows the growth of trade since 1861 :—

From	Imports, £			
	1861	1871	1881	1888
Great Britain	13,500,000	12,000,000	25,700,000	30,100,000
Foreign nations	5,000,000	4,600,000	7,700,000	9,700,000
Intercolonial	6,600,000	13,500,000	16,800,000	25,500,000
Total . .	25,100,000	30,100,000	50,200,000	65,300,000

To	Exports, £			
	1861	1871	1881	1888
Great Britain	12,200,000	18,500,000	24,300,000	28,700,000
Foreign nations	4,400,000	4,600,000	6,800,000	5,600,000
Intercolonial	7,900,000	11,600,000	17,500,000	23,300,000
Total . .	24,500,000	34,700,000	48,600,000	57,600,000

With	Total Trade, £			
	1861	1871	1881	1888
Great Britain	25,700,000	30,500,000	50,000,000	58,800,000
Foreign nations	9,400,000	9,200,000	14,500,000	15,300,000
Intercolonial	14,500,000	25,100,000	34,300,000	48,800,000
Total .	49,600,000	64,800,000	98,800,000	122,900,000

In the above table foreign includes even British colonies outside of Australia, and intercolonial only the traffic between the seven Australasian colonies.

Excluding intercolonial traffic, the trade of Australia has risen from 40 millions sterling in 1871 to 74 millions in 1888, an increase of 85 per cent. The following table of ratios shows that trade with Great Britain is relatively on the decline, probably the result of Protection tariffs.

With	Ratio of Trade			
	1861	1871	1881	1888
Great Britain . . .	51.8	47.1	50.6	48.2
Foreign nations . .	19.0	14.2	14.7	12.4
Intercolonial . . .	29.2	38.7	34.7	39.4
Total . .	100.0	100.0	100.0	100.0

The trade returns of 1889 were as follows :—

	Imports, £	Exports, £	Total, £	£ per Inhab.
N. S. Wales	22,600,000	23,300,000	45,900,000	41.7
Victoria . .	24,200,000	12,500,000	36,700,000	33.4
Queensland .	6,000,000	6,900,000	12,900,000	32.5
S. Australia .	6,800,000	7,300,000	14,100,000	44.7
New Zealand	6,300,000	9,300,000	15,600,000	26.0
Tasmania .	1,600,000	1,500,000	3,100,000	21.0
W. Australia	800,000	700,000	1,500,000	36.0
Total .	68,300,000	61,500,000	129,800,000	35.5

The figures for Western Australia are those of 1888.

The foreign and intercolonial trade of the several colonies was distinguished in the returns for 1888 as follows :—

	Imports £	Exports £	Total £	Foreign £	Intercolonial £
New South Wales	20,900,000	20,900,000	41,800,000	23,400,000	18,400,000
Victoria	24,000,000	13,900,000	37,900,000	25,000,000	12,900,000
Queensland	6,700,000	6,100,000	12,800,000	5,600,000	7,200,000
South Australia	5,400,000	7,000,000	12,400,000	7,400,000	5,000,000
New Zealand	5,900,000	7,800,000	13,700,000	10,900,000	2,800,000
Tasmania	1,600,000	1,300,000	2,900,000	800,000	2,100,000
Western Australia	800,000	700,000	1,500,000	1,000,000	500,000
Total	65,300,000	57,700,000	123,000,000	74,100,000	48,900,000

The exports were as follows :—

SOUTH AFRICA

	1860	1870	1880	1888	1877–86
	£	£	£	£	£
Wool	1,400,000	1,800,000	2,900,000	2,900,000	2,500,000
Diamonds	...	200,000	3,400,000	4,000,000	3,000,000
Copper	100,000	150,000	300,000	900,000	400,000
Feathers	20,000	100,000	900,000	300,000	800,000
Sundries	680,000	750,000	1,100,000	2,200,000	1,100,000
Total . . .	2,200,000	3,000,000	8,600,000	10,300,000	7,800,000

The foregoing table shows that, although sheep-farming is prosperous, and wool continues to form a staple product of the colony, the first rank as regards value among the exports now belongs to diamonds, of which there seems to be no decline in number or quality. In twelve years ending 1889 the production of diamonds reached a value of nearly 40 millions sterling. At the same time the yield of copper has risen to importance. The only item which shows a decline is ostrich feathers, an industry which gave great promise ten years ago.

Official returns, comprising Cape Colony and Natal, show as follows :—

Year	Imports £	Exports £	Total £	Per Inhabitant £ s. d.
1851	1,800,000	700,000	2,500,000	8 0 0
1860	3,000,000	2,200,000	5,200,000	12 10 0
1870	2,800,000	3,000,000	5,800,000	7 0 0
1880	10,000,000	8,600,000	18,600,000	17 0 0
1888	8,400,000	10,300,000	18,700,000	15 0 0

Distinguishing Natal from Cape Colony, the trade stood thus :—

	Imports		Exports	
	1860	1888	1860	1888
	£	£	£	£
Cape Colony	2,600,000	5,500,000	2,100,000	8,900,000
Natal . .	400,000	2,900,000	100,000	1,400,000
Total . .	3,000,000	8,400,000	2,200,000	10,300,000

The statement for ten years ending 1886 showed :—

	Millions £ Sterling			Ratio
	Imports from	Exports to	Total	
Great Britain .	66	72	138	84.7
Other countries	19	6	25	15.3
Total . .	85	78	163	100.0

Exports for 1888 were as follows :—

	Cape, £	Natal, £	South Africa, £
Wool. . . .	2,200,000	700,000	2,900,000
Diamonds . .	4,000,000	...	4,000,000
Sundries . .	2,700,000	700,000	3,400,000
Total . .	8,900,000	1,400,000	10,300,000

WEST AFRICA

This group of colonies comprises Lagos, Gold Coast, Sierra Leone, and Gambia. Official records show the aggregate trade thus :—

Year	Imports	Exports	Total	Per Inhabitant
	£	£	£	£ s. d.
1851	300,000	300,000	600,000	3 0 0
1860	400,000	400,000	800,000	2 0 0
1870	1,000,000	1,300,000	2,300,000	4 10 0
1880	1,300,000	1,500,000	2,800,000	4 14 0
1888	1,200,000	1,200,000	2,400,000	1 12 0

The trade of the several colonies in 1887 was :—

	Imports, £	Exports, £
Lagos . . .	420,000	490,000
Gold Coast . .	360,000	270,000
Sierra Leone . .	310,000	310,000
Gambia . . .	80,000	90,000
Total .	1,170,000	1,160,000

The statement for ten years ending 1886 showed :—

MILLIONS £ STERLING

	Imports from	Exports to	Total	Ratio
Great Britain . . .	36	49	85	50.0
United States . . .	17	15	32	19.0
Canada	6	4	10	6.0
Other countries . .	25	17	42	24.0
Total . . .	84	85	169	100.0

INDIA

Imports of British merchandise in the early part of the eighteenth century averaged to India as follows per annum :—

The statement for ten years ending 1886 showed :—

	Millions £ Sterling			Ratio
	Imports from	Exports to	Total	
Great Britain .	9	7	16	58.5
Germany . .	2	2	4	14.6
Other countries	2	5	7	26.9
Total . .	13	14	27	100.0

WEST INDIES

Under this term may be comprised the various British possessions, Jamaica, Trinidad, Guiana, Barbadoes, and minor islands. Official records show :—

Year	Imports	Exports	Total	Per Inhab.
	£	£	£	£ s. d.
1851	4,600,000	4,500,000	9,100,000	10 2 0
1860	5,800,000	6,100,000	11,900,000	10 10 0
1870	6,800,000	7,500,000	14,300,000	11 0 0
1880	8,100,000	8,500,000	16,600,000	11 1 0
1887	6,900,000	8,000,000	14,900,000	9 10 0

The exports have been nearly stationary in value during the past twenty years, sugar having fallen greatly in price. Returns show as follows :—

	1851	1860	1870	1887	£ Mill. 1877-86
	£	£	£	£	
Sugar .	2,100,000	3,000,000	3,800,000	3,700,000	41
Rum .	300,000	600,000	600,000	400,000	5
Coffee .	100,000	100,000	200,000	200,000	2
Cocoa .	100,000	100,000	200,000	400,000	4
Sundries	1,900,000	2,300,000	2,700,000	3,300,000	33
Total .	4,500,000	6,100,000	7,500,000	8,000,000	85

The exports were from the West Indies in 1887 as follows :—

	Sugar	Rum	Coffee	Cocoa	Sundries	Total
	£	£	£	£	£	£
Jamaica	260,000	300,000	210,000	...	740,000	1,510,000
Barbadoes	800,000	...	...	...	260,000	1,060,000
Trinidad	850,000	...	...	...	...	...
Guiana	1,840,000	140,000	...	410,000	610,000	1,870,000
Small islands	...	...	...	...	210,000	2,190,000
						1,370,000
Total . . .	...	...	...	...	...	8,000,000

1709-18 .	.	.	.	.	£4,800,000
1719-28 .	.	.	.	.	4,400,000
1729-34 .	.	.	.	.	5,000,000

The trade, excluding bullion, has been :—

Year	Imports	Exports	Total	Per Inhabitant
	£	£	£	£ s. d.
1815	8,100,000	2,600,000	10,700,000	0 2 6
1830	5,700,000	4,100,000	9,800,000	0 2 0
1851	11,600,000	18,200,000	29,800,000	0 5 0
1860	24,200,000	28,000,000	52,200,000	0 7 0
1870	32,900,000	52,500,000	85,400,000	0 11 0
1880	41,200,000	67,200,000	108,400,000	0 12 0
*1889	66,600,000	97,000,000	163,600,000	0 16 0

* The Indian Customs still compute rupees at 24 pence, and hence the values here stated are 33 per cent. too much.

Imports of India were as follows :—

	1851	1870	1880	1889	1877–86
	£	£	£	£	£
Cotton manufactures . .	3,600,000	13,600,000	16,900,000	31,500,000	19,300,000
Woollen ,, . .	200,000	600,000	900,000	1,600,000	1,100,000
Silk ,, . .	100,000	500,000	800,000	1,500,000	1,000,000
Metals	1,800,000	3,400,000	3,300,000	5,200,000	4,000,000
Machinery . . .	...	1,800,000	1,600,000	2,300,000	2,200,000
Sugar	...	700,000	1,100,000	1,800,000	1,200,000
Cotton yarn . . .	1,000,000	2,700,000	2,700,000	3,500,000	3,000,000
Coal	...	500,000	1,100,000	1,900,000	1,100,000
Sundries . . .	4,900,000	9,100,000	12,800,000	17,300,000	15,100,000
Total . .	11,600,000	32,900,000	41,200,000	66,600,000	48,000,000

For importation of bullion see *Gold and Silver*.
The exports of India were as follows :—

	1851	1870	1880	1889	1877–86
	£	£	£	£	£
Cotton	3,500,000	19,100,000	11,100,000	15,100,000	12,200,000
Opium	5,500,000	11,700,000	14,300,000	10,500,000	12,300,000
Grain	700,000	3,000,000	9,500,000	15,500,000	12,800,000
Jute	200,000	2,200,000	5,600,000	7,900,000	5,400,000
Seeds	300,000	2,300,000	4,800,000	9,600,000	7,300,000
Tea	...	1,100,000	3,100,000	5,300,000	3,400,000
Cotton goods . . .	700,000	1,300,000	2,800,000	6,400,000	3,300,000
Dyes	2,100,000	3,600,000	3,600,000	4,700,000	4,500,000
Hides	300,000	1,700,000	3,700,000	4,800,000	4,100,000
Sundries	4,900,000	6,500,000	8,700,000	17,200,000	9,700,000
Total	18,200,000	52,500,000	67,200,000	97,000,000	75,000,000

The statement for ten years ending 1886 showed :—

MILLIONS £ STERLING

	Imports from	Exports to	Total	Ratio
Great Britain . . .	437	323	760	55.3
Hong-Kong . . .	33	103	136	10.0
Australia	10	6	16	1.2
Singapore	15	31	46	3.3
Mauritius	10	10	20	1.5
United States . . .	6	28	34	2.5
China	9	35	44	3.2
France	6	65	71	5.2
Other countries . .	·77	168	245	17.8
Total . .	603	769	1,372	100.0

The trade of India has almost doubled since 1870, imports having increased 102 per cent., exports 85 per cent., taking the rupee at 24d.

CEYLON

Official records are as follows :—

Year	Imports	Exports	Total	Per Inhabitant
	£	£	£	£ s. d.
1851	1,000,000	1,100,000	2,100,000	1 8 0
1860	2,400,000	2,300,000	4,700,000	2 7 0
1870	4,100,000	3,800,000	7,900,000	3 6 0
1880	4,000,000	4,200,000	8,200,000	3 2 0
1888	4,700,000	3,200,000	7,900,000	2 15 0

The imports of Ceylon were as follows :—

	1851	1860	1870	1877–86	1888
	£	£	£	£	£
Grain	500,000	700,000	1,600,000	1,800,000	2,000,000
Cotton	200,000	600,000	1,000,000	400,000	400,000
Coal	...	200,000	200,000	200,000	500,000
Sundries	300,000	900,000	1,300,000	1,400,000	1,800,000
Total . .	1,000,000	2,400,000	4,100,000	3,800,000	4,700,000

The exports were as follows :—

	1851	1860	1870	1877–86	1888
	£	£	£	£	£
Coffee	1,000,000	1,600,000	2,800,000	1,900,000	600,000
Chinchona . . .	...	...	...	200,600	150,000
Oil	...	200,000	200,000	300,000	550,000
Sundries	100,000	500,000	800,000	1,100,000	1,900,000
Total . .	1,100,000	2,300,000	3,800,000	3,500,000	3,200,000

Sundries for 1888 included £1,020,000 for tea, now the principal export of the island.

The statement for ten years ending 1886 showed—

	Millions £ Sterling			Ratio
	Imports from	Exports to	Total	
India . . .	28	5	33	42.3
Great Britain .	12	22	34	43.6
Other countries	3	8	11	14.1
Total . .	43	35	78	100.0

STRAITS SETTLEMENT

This colony, formerly known as Singapore, shows the following trade :—

	Imports, £	Exports, £	Total, £
1861	7,900,000	6,600,000	14,500,000
1870	9,700,000	7,100,000	16,800,000
1880	11,700,000	10,500,000	22,200,000
1887	21,500,000	18,800,000	40,300,000

Singapore is a great emporium for trade between Europe and the East, and hence its trade is out of all proportion to the population of the colony ; average, £80 per inhabitant.

The imports were as follows :—

	1851	1860	1870	1887	1877–86
	£	£	£	£	£
Grain	330,000	770,000	660,000	570,000	600,000
Textiles	110,000	170,000	280,000	170,000	200,000
Sundries	460,000	1,360,000	1,060,000	1,660,000	1,500,000
Total . .	900,000	2,300,000	2,000,000	2,400,000	2,300,000

The exports were as follows :—

	1851	1860	1870	1888	1877–86
	£	£	£	£	£
Sugar	1,000,000	2,100,000	1,900,000	2,300,000	3,300,000
Sundries	100,000	200,000	200,000	300,000	300,000
Total . .	1,100,000	2,300,000	2,100,000	2,600,000	3,600,000

CHINA

Official returns are as follows :—

Year	Imports, £	Exports, £	Total, £
1876	20,900,000	24,100,000	45,000,000
1880	23,000,000	22,500,000	45,500,000
1888	26,000,000	23,000,000	49,000,000

The statement for ten years ending 1886 showed :—

	Millions £ Sterling			Ratio
	Imports from	Exports to	Total	
Hong-Kong . . .	84	45	129	30.7
Great Britain . . .	45	63	108	25.6
India	52	1	53	12.5
Japan	11	4	15	3.6
Other countries . .	30	84	114	27.6
Total . .	222	197	419	100.0

The statement for ten years ending 1886 showed :—

	Millions £ Sterling			Ratio
	Imports from	Exports to	Total	
Great Britain .	36	28	64	21.5
India . . .	25	9	34	11.4
Hong-Kong .	18	11	29	9.8
Java . . .	27	36	63	21.2
Malacca .	17	13	30	10.1
Siam . . .	11	10	21	7.1
Other countries	22	34	56	18.9
Total .	156	141	297	100.0

The trade of 1888, merchandise and bullion, amounted to—imports, 32 ; exports, 27 millions sterling.

MAURITIUS

The trade returns show as follows :—

	Imports, £	Exports, £	Total, £
1851	900,000	1,200,000	2,100,000
1860	2,300,000	2,300,000	4,600,000
1870	2,000,000	2,100,000	4,100,000
1880	1,700,000	3,000,000	4,700,000
1888	1,200,000	2,600,000	3,800,000

The imports were as follows :—

	1876	1886	1877–86	1888
	£	£	£	£
Opium . .	8,400,000	6,200,000	7,500,000	7,600,000
Cotton goods	6,000,000	7,200,000	6,600,000	10,500,000
Sundries . .	6,500,000	8,500,000	8,200,000	7,900,000
Total .	20,900,000	21,900,000	22,300,000	26,000,000

The exports were as follows :—

	1876	1886	1877–86	1888
	£	£	£	£
Tea . . .	11,000,000	8,500,000	8,900,000	7,200,000
Silk . . .	10,800,000	7,200,000	6,900,000	7,500,000
Sundries . .	2,300,000	3,600,000	3,900,000	8,300,000
Total .	24,100,000	19,300,000	19,700,000	23,000,000

The quantities of tea exported were :—

1876	190 million lbs.
1880	222 ,, ,,
1888	290 ,, ,,

PERSIA

The total trade of the Empire in 1881 was said to reach £7,700,000, but the estimates of the *Times* correspondent for 1889 do not exceed £6,000,000, viz.:—

	Imports, £		Exports, £
Cottons . . .	1,800,000	Opium . . .	500,000
Silks . . .	600,000	Silk, raw . .	400,000
Woollens . .	400,000	Rice . . .	300,000
Sugar . . .	300,000	Fruit . . .	100,000
Sundries . .	700,000	Sundries . .	900,000
Total . .	3,800,000	Total .	2,200,000

PHILIPPINE ISLANDS

The exports of these islands were as follows :—

	1889		To	1888
	Tons	£		£
Sugar	220,000	2,200,000	Great Britain .	1,700,000
Hemp .	115,000	3,200,000	Spain	600,000
Coffee .	6,000	500,000	Other countries	4,300,000
Tobacco	10,000	700,000		
			Total .	6,600,000
Total	...	6,600,000		

Imports average about £2,000,000, English cotton goods representing £900,000.

JAPAN

Official returns are as follows :—

Year	Imports, £	Exports, £	Total, £
1876	5,000,000	5,700,000	10,700,000
1880	7,600,000	5,700,000	13,300,000
1888	10,900,000	10,800,000	21,700,000

The imports and exports in 1888 were :—

	Imports, £		Exports, £
Cotton yarn . .	2,300,000	Silk . . .	4,800,000
Cotton manu- ⎱ facture ⎰	500,000	Tea . . .	1,000,000
		Copper . .	600,000
Woollen . . .	1,100,000	Rice . . .	1,200,000
Sugar . . .	1,100,000	Sundries . .	3,200,000
Sundries . . .	5,900,000		
		Total .	10,800,000
Total . .	10,900,000		

The statement for seven years ending 1886 showed :—

	Millions £ Sterling			Ratio
	Imports from	Exports to	Total	
Great Britain . . .	20	5	25	25.8
China	8	8	16	16.5
United States . . .	4	20	24	24.7
Other countries . .	13	19	32	33.0
Total . .	45	52	97	100.0

EGYPT

Official returns are as follows :—

Year	Imports, £	Exports, £	Total, £
1824	1,100,000	2,100,000	3,200,000
1874	5,300,000	14,000,000	19,300,000
1880	6,800,000	13,500,000	20,300,000
1889	7,300,000	12,200,000	19,500,000

The imports of 1889 were as follows :—Textiles, £1,800,000; coal, £450,000; iron and machinery, £500,000; coffee, £300,000; and sundries, £4,250,000. The exports were as follows :—

	1876	1886	1877–86	1889
	£	£	£	£
Raw cotton .	9,200,000	7,500,000	7,800,000	8,800,000
Cotton seed .	1,500,000	1,300,000	1,400,000	1,500,000
Sugar . . .	500,000	500,000	600,000	500,000
Grain . . .	1,700,000	700,000	1,400,000	600,000
Sundries . .	1,200,000	900,000	1,200,000	800,000
Total .	14,100,000	10,900,000	12,400,000	12,200,000

Egyptian exports have been for some years declining in value, which is due rather to a fall in prices than to any decrease of quantities produced.

CONGRESS

The first United States Federal Congress met, 4th March 1789. and the fifty-first on 4th March 1889. The first actual Congress of American delegates took place in 1774, and another was held on July 4, 1776, at which the Act of Independence was signed. Congress now consists of 82 Senators and 330 Representatives, all of whom receive a salary of $5000 each per annum, besides 20 cents a mile travelling expenses, and $125 for stationery.

There have been nine Statistical Congresses, attended by members as follows :—

Date	Place	British	French	German	Russian	Austrian	Italian	Hungarian	Dutch	Various	Total
1853	Brussels	16	11	22	...	1	2	...	5	96	153
1855	Paris	22	203	29	...	5	9	...	2	41	311
1859	Vienna	4	11	37	3	430	8	24	4	16	537
1860	London	478	9	25	12	5	1	...	4	51	585
1863	Berlin	13	7	397	13	10	4	2	3	28	477
1867	Florence . . .	16	14	17	14	4	665	...	1	20	751
1869	Hague	20	15	18	10	5	9	3	372	36	488
1872	Petersburgh . .	17	5	23	512	15	10	7	4	45	638
1876	Pesth	10	12	33	32	42	8	282	3	33	455
	Total . .	596	287	601	596	517	716	318	398	366	4,395

Valuable statistical papers were read at the above meetings.

COPPER

The production of this metal has multiplied fivefold since 1850, shown thus :—

	Fine Copper, Tons				
	1850	1860	1870	1880	1888
Great Britain .	11,800	13,540	7,220	3,440	1,500
France . .	2,300	2,500	4,900	5,100	3,000
Germany . .	1,650	3,200	6,850	10,140	15,000
Russia . . .	6,000	5,500	5,500	6,100	5,000
Spain . . .	200	300	1,100	21,300	53,000
Sweden . . .	2,300	2,200	2,000	1,600	1,000
Austria, &c. .	1,600	1,900	2,000	2,200	2,700
Europe . . .	25,850	9,140	29,570	49,880	81,200
United States .	2,700	5,530	12,650	20,260	103,000
Chili . . .	14,300	25,100	30,200	36,800	31,000
Australia . .	2,400	7,600	9,700	13,100	8,000
Cape Colony .	...	...	1,000	5,000	8,000
Venezuela . .	2,000	2,000	3,000	4,000	4,000
Japan . . .	3,000	3,000	3,000	5,000	11,000
Other countries	2,000	3,000	5,000	8,000	15,800
Total . .	52,250	75,370	94,120	142,040	262,000

In 1889 the production in the United States was 107,000 tons fine copper, and the consumption 75,000 tons.

The ratio of copper to copper ore is as follows :—

Per Cent. of Pure Copper		Per Cent. of Pure Copper	
Germany .	. 3	England .	. 7
Austria .	. 4	Australia .	. 12
France .	. 5	United States	. 18

The British copper trade since 1850 has been as follows :—

Year	Tons		Value		Fine Copper per Ton
	Im- ported	Ex- ported	Imports	Exports	
			£	£	£
1850 .	51,000	11,000	1,412,000	1,080,000	102
1851–60 .	78,000	26,000	2,254,000	2,531,000	98
1860 .	109,000	31,000	3,404,000	3,153,000	107
1861–70 .	133,000	46,000	4,016,000	3,844,000	89
1870 .	137,000	52,000	4,039,000	3,772,000	76
1871–80 .	147,000	56,000	5,151,000	4,413,000	78
1881 .	182,000	65,000	4,593,200	4,284,000	68
1888 .	280,000	40,000	8,600,000	3,100,000	80

The imports include, besides copper, a quantity of "regulus," or half-smelted ore.

The following table shows the annual yield of copper-mines in Great Britain :—

Period	Tons	Value, £	Period	Tons	Value, £
1725–45 . .	560	84,000	1801–20 .	5,880	720,000
1746–65 . .	1,030	160,000	1821–40 .	13,220	1,360,000
1766–85 . .	2,020	290,000	1841–60 .	12,840	1,355,000
1786–1800 .	2,710	430,000	1861–80 .	8,070	686,000

The total value of the output for 100 years ending 1880 was 91 millions sterling. In 1888 the total product of copper in the world was valued at 20 millions sterling per annum. The prices of this metal, however, vary exceedingly ; in 1882 it was £67 per ton, falling in 1886 to £40 ; whereupon a French "ring" drove up the price to £80, but it fell afterwards to £50.

It is remarkable that, although copper-money is no longer in use, the consumption of this metal is more than five times as great as it was forty years ago. This is in great measure explained by the enormous development of telegraph wire, cartridges, and other things in which copper largely enters.

COTTON

According to Baines and other authorities, the production of raw cotton was as follows :—

	Million Lbs.					
	United States	South America	Egypt	India	Various	Total
1791	2	102	...	130	256	490
1801	48	102	...	160	210	520
1811	80	104	...	170	201	555
1821	180	86	6	175	183	630
1831	385	82	18	180	155	820
1840	878	90	30	212	100	1,310
1850	890	90	45	310	100	1,435
1860	1,880	90	51	420	100	2,551
1870	1,540	270	240	625	100	2,775
1880	2,593	86	282	540	100	3,601
1888	3,420	85	290	888	100	4,783

Ellison's table and others show the consumption to have been at various dates as follows :—

	Millions of Lbs.						
	1830	1840	1850	1860	1869	1880	1887–8
United Kingdom	250	454	588	1,140	1,101	1,404	1,530
France . . .	68	116	140	226	220	200	310
Germany . . .	16	26	46	140	147	286	378
Russia	4	14	48	87	97	201	369
Austria	20	34	58	94	96	140	235
Italy	4	8	16	26	26	64	152
Spain	6	14	34	52	50	88	105
Sweden . . .	1	2	8	16	16	25	28
Holland . . .	2	4	5	6	10	20	24
Belgium . . .	8	16	22	29	35	50	52
Switzerland . .	9	18	24	30	39	49	52
Europe . . .	388	707	988	1,847	1,837	2,546	3,235
United States .	77	135	288	390	400	768	1,010
India	...	...	...	26	35	172	283
Various . . .	5	10	10	10	20	60	100
Total .	470	852	1,286	2,273	2,292	3,546	4,628

The production and consumption of raw cotton in 67 years ending December 1887 were approximately as follows :—

Period	Production, Tons Aggregate				
	United States	India	Egypt	Brazil, &c.	Total
1821–30	1,050,000	310,000	100,000	120,000	1,580,000
1831–40	2,270,000	480,000	120,000	120,000	2,990,000
1841–50	3,950,000	950,000	170,000	150,000	5,220,000
1851–60	6,450,000	1,400,000	260,000	150,000	8,260,000
1861–70	3,750,000	2,900,000	870,000	670,000	8,190,000
1871–80	8,700,000	2,630,000	1,290,000	305,000	12,925,000
1881–87	8,680,000	2,240,000	910,000	230,000	12,060,000
67 years	34,850,000	10,910,000	3,720,000	1,685,000	51,165,000

It appears that the United States have produced two-thirds of the cotton which has been consumed by the factories of the world in the last 67 years, and that the cotton-crop of the world shows a steady increase, the decade ending 1890 showing 400,000 tons a year more than the preceding. Great Britain consumes one-third of all the cotton produced, the United States being the next largest consumer. In this industry France stood ahead of Germany until the war of 1870.

	Consumption, Tons Aggregate						
	1821–40	1841–50	1851–60	1861–70	1871–80	1881–87	Total
Great Britain . . .	2,310,000	2,320,000	3,830,000	3,540,000	5,650,000	4,550,000	22,200,000
France	660,000	610,000	830,000	760,000	950,000	940,000	4,750,000
Germany . . .	190,000	410,000	660,000	650,000	1,140,000	1,220,000	4,270,000
Russia . . .	180,000	240,000	360,000	320,000	820,000	890,000	2,810,000
Austria . . .	160,000	200,000	370,000	330,000	650,000	640,000	2,350,000
Italy	40,000	50,000	90,000	120,000	310,000	410,000	1,020,000
Spain	80,000	110,000	200,000	170,000	340,000	340,000	1,240,000
Sweden . . .	10,000	20,000	50,000	50,000	90,000	90,000	310,000
Holland . . .	10,000	20,000	25,000	20,000	•65,000	70,000	210,000
Belgium . . .	150,000	120,000	130,000	120,000	200,000	170,000	890,000
Switzerland . . .	80,000	90,000	120,000	100,000	200,000	160,000	750,000
Europe	3,870,000	4,190,000	•6,665,000	6,180,000	10,415,000	9,480,000	40,790,000
United States . .	650,000	990,000	1,550,000	1,970,000	2,320,000	2,780,000	10,260,000
India . . .	40,000	40,000	45,000	40,000	130,000	710,000	1,025,000
Total . .	4,560,000	5,220,000	8,260,000	8,190,000	12,865,000	12,970,000	52,075,000

There is an apparent discrepancy in the above table, the consumption of cotton in the period 1881–87 exceeding the production by 910,000 tons, which is explained by the circumstance that cotton yarn is often counted with raw cotton. In the said period the cotton-mills of Continental Europe figure above for 4,930,000 tons of raw cotton, but this included 910,000 tons of yarn, which was thus counted twice, having been already included as raw cotton in the mills of Great Britain and other countries, that produce more yarn than they require.

The following table shows approximately the output of cotton cloth in English statute miles :—

	1821–40	1841–60	1861–70	1871–80	1881–87	Total
Great Britain . . .	9,410,000	27,450,000	16,300,000	29,300,000	23,300,000	105,760,000
France	3,800,000	8,000,000	4,300,000	5,500,000	5,500,000	27,100,000
Germany . . .	1,100,000	5,800,000	3,500,000	6,500,000	7,000,000	23,900,000
Russia . . .	1,050,000	3,500,000	1,800,000	4,600,000	5,150,000	16,100,000
Austria . . .	900,000	3,200,000	1,900,000	3,600,000	3,500,000	13,100,000
Italy	200,000	750,000	650,000	1,700,000	2,300,000	5,600,000
Spain	400,000	1,700,000	900,000	1,900,000	1,900,000	6,800,000
Sweden . . .	50,000	350,000	250,000	500,000	500,000	1,650,000
Holland . . .	100,000	200,000	100,000	350,000	400,000	1,150,000
Belgium . . .	800,000	1,450,000	700,000	1,100,000	950,000	5,000,000
Switzerland . . .	450,000	1,150,000	550,000	1,100,000	900,000	4,150,000
Europe	18,260,000	53,550,000	30,950,000	56,150,000	51,400,000	210,310,000
United States . .	3,700,000	14,500,000	11,200,000	13,300,000	16,200,000	58,900,000
India, &c. . . .	240,000	600,000	250,000	650,000	3,550,000	5,290,000
Total . .	22,200,000	68,650,000	42,400,000	70,100,000	71,150,000	274,500,000

The following summary shows the business for 67 years approximately, viz., 1821–87 :—

	Value, Millions £		Tons Cotton Consumed	Miles Cloth Made
	Cotton	Manufactures	Net		
U. Kingdom	1,595	4,461	2,866	22,200,000	105,760,000
France . .	355	1,037	682	4,750,000	27,100,000
Germany .	317	801	484	4,270,000	23,900,000
Russia . .	206	530	324	2,810,000	16,100,000
Austria . .	173	443	270	2,350,000	13,100,000
Italy . . .	75	178	103	1,020,000	5,600,000
Spain . . .	93	232	139	1,240,000	6,800,000
Sweden . .	24	56	32	310,000	1,650,000
Holland . .	16	39	23	220,000	1,150,000
Belgium . .	69	193	124	870,000	5,000,000
Switzerland .	56	153	97	750,000	4,150,000
Europe . .	2,979	8,123	5,144	40,790,000	210,310,000
United States	705	1,563	858	10,260,000	58,900,000
India, &c. .	60	141	81	1,025,000	5,290,000
Total .	3,744	9,827	6,083	52,075,000	274,500,000

The following table shows the latest information of manufacturing industry as regards cotton ; the number of operatives in some countries is uncertain :—

	No. of Spindles	Cotton, Million Lbs.	Operatives	Output, £
Great Britain	42,740,000	1,530	504,000	101,400,000
United States	13,500,000	1,010	200,000	60,200,000
France . .	4,900,000	310	110,000	18,600,000
Germany .	5,150,000	378	290,000	23,000,000
Russia . .	4,000,000	369	180,000	22,200,000
Austria . .	2,100,000	235	150,000	14,100,000
Italy . . .	1,200,000	152	80,000	9,100,000
Spain and Portugal	2,200,000	120	53,000	7,200,000
Belgium . .	800,000	52	20,000	3,100,000
Holland . .	300,000	24	10,000	1,500,000
Scandinavia	300,000	28	10,000	1,700,000
Switzerland	1,900,000	52	30,000	3,100,000
India . . .	2,380,000	283	81,000	14,200,000
Japan . .	500,000	30	10,000	1,600,000
Total .	82,370,000	4,573	1,728,000	281,000,000

COTTON MANUFACTURES OF ALL NATIONS

	Tons Cotton	Miles Cloth	Value Millions £			
			Cotton	Manufactures	Net
1821–30	1,570,000	7,380,000	113	632	519
1831–40	2,990,000	14,820,000	220	874	654
1841–50	5,220,000	26,050,000	267	1,055	788
1851–60	8,260,000	42,600,000	500	1,440	940
1861–70	8,190,000	42,400,000	987	1,810	823
1871–80	12,865,000	70,100,000	915	2,234	1,319
1881–87	12,970,000	71,150,000	742	1,782	1,040
67 years	52,075,000	274,500,000	3,744	9,827	6,083

The world produces and consumes annually more than 10 million miles of cotton cloth. The cost of production was found in 1880 to be :—

Pence per 100 Yds.

					Calico	Prints
British	.	.	.	.	276	384
American	.	.	.	.	424	502
Greek	.	.	.	.	353	...
Chinese	.	.	.	.	310	510
German	.	.	.	.	298	408
French	.	.	.	.	312	425

The area under cotton in the principal countries is shown thus :—

	Acres	Crop, Million Lbs.	Lbs. per Acre
United States .	18,450,000	3,420	186
India . .	14,530,000	888	62
Egypt. .	1,060,000	290	275
Brazil . .	150,000	35	230
Other countries .	240,000	50	208
*Total . .	34,260,000	4,733	140

One man can cultivate 12 acres, or, with machinery, 30 acres. Seed-cotton weighs three times as much as ginned cotton or cotton-wool, the seed forming two-thirds. Thus, in the above table, in the United States a yield of 186 lbs. cotton means that before ginned the crop averaged 560 lbs. seed-cotton per acre.

The average length of fibre is as follows :—

			Inches				Inches
Sea Island	.	.	1.61	Brazilian	.	.	1.17
Egyptian .	.	.	1.41	New Orleans	.	.	1.02
Peruvian .	.	.	1.30	East Indian	.	.	0.89

The cotton manufacturing industry is shown as follows, according to Spencer's tables (to 1875) :—

			Spindles					
			1832	1845	1861	1875	1885	1888
Great Britain	.	.	9,000,000	17,500,000	30,300,000	37,500,000	44,300,000	42,740,000
United States	.	.	1,200,000	2,500,000	5,000,000	9,500,000	13,300,000	13,500,000
Continent .	.	.	2,800,000	7,500,000	10,000,000	19,500,000	22,350,000	23,780,000
India, &c. .	.	.	...	...	340,000	1,000,000	2,400,000	2,420,000
Total	.	.	13,000,000	27,500,000	45,640,000	67,500,000	82,350,000	82,640,000

The number of spindles has increased more than sixfold since 1832, the production of cotton more than sevenfold.

GREAT BRITAIN

The principal features of cotton manufacture are shown thus :—

Year	Raw Cotton, Million Lbs.	Yarn Spun, Million Lbs.	Cloth Produced, Million Yards	Value, Millions £		
				Manufactures	Yarn, &c., Exported	Total
1720	2	2	8	...	...	...
1785	11	10	40	...	...	...
1800	52	47	180	...	...	...
1814	95	86	340	28	2	30
1820	119	108	425	30	3	33
1830	245	223	795	34	5	39
1840	452	407	1,445	40	8	48
1850	588	529	2,025	43	6	49
1860	1,140	1,027	4,150	71	10	81
1870	1,101	991	4,647	76	15	91
1880	1,404	1,258	6,146	86	19	105
1887	1,499	1,346	6,534	82	19	101

According to Kennedy, Cowell, and others, 10 lbs. raw cotton produce 9 lbs. spun yarn.

The cotton manufactures of Great Britain are almost equal to the aggregate of all other European nations. They constitute, moreover, one of the most important elements of British industry, the output, as shown above, being valued at more than £300,000 a day. If we measure the production of cotton cloth not by yards, but by English statute miles, we find that the mills of Great Britain turn out daily more than 10,000 miles. The daily consumption of raw cotton averages 5,000,000 lbs., say 2200 tons. Each operative consumes yearly as much cotton as 20 acres can produce, and turns out about 7 miles of cotton cloth. This is irrespective of yarn produced for exportation. If all the yarn spun in Great Britain were made into cotton cloth, the output would be nearly one-fourth more.

The quantities of cotton cloth and yarn consumed in Great Britain and exported were approximately as follow :—

Year	Cotton Cloth, Million Yards			Yarn, Million Lbs.		
	Home Use	Exported	Total	Home Use	Exported	Total
1814	148	192	340	70	16	86
1820	176	249	425	85	23	108
1830	350	445	795	159	64	223
1840	654	791	1,445	289	118	407
1850	677	1,348	2,025	405	124	529
1860	1,385	2,765	4,150	830	197	1,027
1870	1,380	3,267	4,647	805	186	991
1880	1,650	4,496	6,146	1,042	216	1,258
1889	1,630	5,002	6,632	1,125	252	1,377

* Ellison estimates the total crop at 5330 million lbs., including 600 millions in China and 150 millions in Central Africa, which are consumed in those countries, and not counted in the above table.

The following table is a summary of British cotton manufacturing industry since 1820 :—

Period	Tons Cotton Consumed	Statute Miles of Cloth Made	Value, Millions £				Net Product
			Raw Cotton	Manufactured	Yarn Exported	Total Product	
1821–30	810,000	3,480,000	61	301	41	342	281
1831–40	1,505,000	5,930,000	109	322	71	393	284
1841–50	2,320,000	9,940,000	112	388	81	469	357
1851–60	3,830,000	17,510,000	241	597	80	677	436
1861–70	3,540,000	16,300,000	430	698	115	813	383
1871–80	5,650,000	29,300,000	390	933	138	1,071	681
1881–87	4,550,000	23,300,000	252	563	133	696	444
67 years	22,205,000	105,760,000	1,595	3,802	659	4,461	2,866

The quantities and values of cotton goods exported averaged as follows per annum :—

Period	Cotton Cloth, Million Yards			Yarn, Million Lbs.	Value, £ Sterling			Value of a Mile of Cloth
	Plain	Printed	Total		Cloth	Yarn, &c.	Total	
								£
1821–30 . . .	172	168	340	39	13,100,000	4,100,000	17,200,000	70
1831–40 . . .	314	275	589	90	14,300,000	7,100,000	21,400,000	43
1841–50 . . .	584	381	965	136	16,100,000	8,100,000	24,200,000	31
1851–60 . . .	1,252	736	1,988	171	30,100,000	7,950,000	38,050,000	27
1861–70 . . .	1,606	838	2,444	136	48,100,000	11,500,000	59,600,000	34
1871–80 . . .	2,592	1,101	3,693	222	58,100,000	13,800,000	71,900,000	28
1820 . . .	114	135	249	23	13,200,000	3,300,000	16,500,000	95
1830 . . .	245	200	445	64	14,200,000	5,200,000	19,400,000	57
1840 . . .	433	358	791	118	16,300,000	8,400,000	24,700,000	36
1850 . . .	758	590	1,348	124	21,900,000	6,400,000	28,300,000	29
1860 . . .	1,790	975	2,765	197	42,200,000	9,800,000	52,000,000	26
1870 . . .	2,294	973	3,267	186	56,700,000	14,700,000	71,400,000	31
1880 . . .	3,059	1,437	4,496	216	57,100,000	18,500,000	75,600,000	23
1887 . . .	3,473	1,431	4,904	251	51,700,000	19,300,000	71,000,000	19
1888 . . .	3,608	1,430	5,038	256	52,600,000	19,400,000	72,000,000	19

The birth of the cotton industry may be said to date from 1793, when Whitney's improved gin was invented in the United States. From that time, as shown above, there was a steady and rapid increase, until the American war of 1861 caused a cotton famine, which was estimated to have caused a loss of 66 millions sterling to Great Britain—more properly 98 millions. The cotton-factories of the United Kingdom advanced thus :—

Year	Number of Factories	Operatives	Spindles	Power-Looms	Cotton, Million Lbs.	Cotton, Lbs. per Operative
1838	1,815	259,000	13,000,000	109,000	410	1,574
1850	1,952	331,000	20,900,000	250,000	588	1,780
1860	2,887	...	30,400,000	400,000	1,140	...
1870	2,483	449,000	38,000,000	440,000	1,101	2,420
1880	2,674	487,000	41,900,000	513,000	1,404	2,860
1885	2,635	504,000	44,400,000	561,000	1,500	2,975

In 1889 Mr. Ellison published the following statement :—

	1859–61	1887
	£	£
Products exported . . .	49,030,000	70,960,000
Home consumption . . .	27,970,000	30,440,000
Total value of products .	77,000,000	101,400,000
Paid for cotton . . .	29,290,000	34,460,000
Wages	20,990,000	29,400,000
Expenses and profits .	26,720,000	37,540,000
Total as above . . .	77,000,000	101,400,000

In 1869 Mr. Forwood, of Liverpool, published the following comparative statement :—

	1860	1868
	Million Lbs.	Million Lbs.
Cotton consumed . .	1,079	996
Waste in spinning . .	113	120
Yarn produced . . .	966	876
Yarn exported . . .	197	169
Yarn manufactured . .	769	707
	£	£
Value of manufactures	70,000,000	76,600,000
Do. home use . . .	24,400,000	19,200,000
Do. exported . . .	46,300,000	57,400,000
Do. yarn exported . .	9,900,000	14,700,000
Total product . . .	80,600,000	91,300,000
Cost of cotton . . .	28,900,000	41,000,000
Wages, &c.	33,600,000	34,900,000
Net profit	18,100,000	15,400,000

The ratios of the four preceding tables may be shown thus :—

	Forwood			Ellison	
	1860	1868		1859–61	1887
Cost of cotton .	35.9	44.9	Cotton . .	38.0	34.0
Wages, &c. .	41.7	38.2	Wages . .	27.3	29.0
Net profit . .	22.4	16.9	Balance .	34.7	37.0
Total .	100.0	100.0	Total .	100.0	100.0

Although Mr. Forwood estimated the profits of mill-owners at £15,400,000 per annum, it is believed that this is above the reality.

The consumption of British cotton cloth was approximately as follows :—

	Millions of Yards				
	1820	1840	1860	1880	1889
United Kingdom . .	176	654	1,385	1,650	1,630
United States . . .	24	32	227	78	49
Spanish America . .	56	279	527	652	720
Europe.	128	200	201	365	370
Africa	10	75	358	589	630
East Indies	11	145	825	1,813	2,363
China	3	30	324	632	557
Various	17	30	303	367	313
Total . .	425	1,445	4,150	6,146	6,632

The customers who took British yarn were as follows :—

	Exported Yarn, Million Lbs.				
	1820	1840	1860	1880	1889
Europe . . .	22	92	116	95	133
East Indies . . .	...	16	31	47	49
China and Japan .	...	2	9	46	36
Various . . .	1	9	41	28	34
Total .	23	119	197	216	252

Ellison shows the progress of British cotton-mills as follows :—

Period	Spinners	Weavers	Yarn Produced, Million Lbs.	Yarn Consumed, Million Lbs.	Lbs. per Spinner	Lbs. per Weaver
1819–21	110,000	250,000	107	81	968	342
1829–31	140,000	275,000	217	142	1,546	521
1844–46	190,000	210,000	523	348	2,754	1,681
1859–61	248,000	203,000	910	651	3,671	3,206
1886–87	245,000	255,000	1,415	1,162	5,900	4,559

He estimates the capital employed in cotton-mills in 1887 at 105 millions sterling.

FRANCE

The earliest mention of cotton factories is in 1688, when the consumption of raw cotton reached 500,000 lbs. yearly. The next is in 1750, when it was 4 million pounds. The following table shows approximately the principal features of this industry.

Period	Tons, Cotton Consumed	Miles Cloth Made	Value, Millions Lbs.		
			Cotton	Manu-factures	Net
1821–30	230,000	1,300,000	17	106	89
1831–40	430,000	2,500,000	33	160	127
1841–50	610,000	3,300,000	33	136	103
1851–60	830,000	4,700,000	50	158	108
1861–70	760,000	4,300,000	95	180	85
1871–80	950,000	5,500,000	71	165	94
1881–87	940,000	5,500,000	56	132	76
67 years	4,750,000	27,100,000	355	1,037	682

The loss of Alsace in 1871 reduced the number of cotton-spindles in France from 6,120,000 to 4,620,000. In 1884 the number had risen to 5,111,000, but this included 227,000 that were idle. There are 1065 cotton-mills in France, with 108,000 operatives, 75,000 power-looms and 40,000 hand-looms. In ten years ending 1887 the imports of cotton manufactures averaged £2,600,000, the exports £3,600,000 per annum.

GERMANY

The consumption of raw cotton and imported yarn has grown sixfold in half a century, viz. :—

Period	Consumption Yearly, Million Lbs. Fibre	Number of Spindles	Output, £
1836–40 . . .	62	600,000	5,600,000
1861–70 . . .	147	2,260,000	14,700,000
1881–87 . . .	378	5,150,000	24,000,000

The business of sixty-seven years was approximately as follows :—

Period	Tons Cotton Consumed	Miles Cloth Made	Value Millions £		
			Cotton	Manu-factures	Net
1821–30	70,000	400,000	5	32	27
1831–40	120,000	700,000	9	42	33
1841–50	410,000	2,300,000	23	92	69
1851–60	660,000	3,500,000	40	125	85
1861–70	650,000	3,500,000	81	147	66
1871–80	1,140,000	6,500,000	86	195	109
1881–87	1,220,000	7,000,000	73	168	95
Total	4,270,000	23,900,000	317	801	484

Germany gained 1,450,000 spindles by the annexation of Alsace. The imports of cotton manufactures in ten years down to 1888 averaged £900,000, exports £3,600,000 per annum.

RUSSIA

In 1824, according to Schubert, the mills consumed 4 million pounds of cotton and yarn yearly. There were then 484 mills, against 129 in 1812.

The industry has grown rapidly of late years, viz. :—

Year	Million Lbs. Fibre	Spindles	Output, £
1840 . . .	44	700,000	4,300,000
1870 . . .	94	2,500,000	9,800,000
1887 . . .	369	4,400,000	21,000,000

The business of 67 years is summed up approximately thus :—

Period	Tons Cotton Consumed	Miles Cloth Made	Value, Millions £		
			Cotton	Manu-factures	Net
1821–30	50,000	300,000	4	24	20
1831–40	130,000	750,000	10	45	35
1841–50	240,000	1,400,000	14	56	42
1851–60	360,000	2,100,000	22	69	47
1861–70	320,000	1,800,000	40	75	35
1871–80	820,000	4,600,000	62	138	76
1881–87	890,000	5,150,000	54	123	69
67 years	2,810,000	16,100,000	206	530	324

In ten years ending 1887 Russia imported cotton goods worth £6,400,000 yearly.

AUSTRIA

In 1830 the consumption of raw cotton barely reached 20 million lbs. The following table sums up the business approximately :—

Period	Tons Cotton Consumed	Miles Cloth Made	Value, Millions £		
			Cotton	Manufactures	Net
1821–30	60,000	350,000	5	30	25
1831–40	100,000	550,000	7	31	24
1841–50	200,000	1,100,000	11	44	33
1851–60	370,000	2,100,000	22	69	47
1861–70	330,000	1,900,000	41	77	36
1871–80	650,000	3,600,000	49	108	59
1881–87	640,000	3,500,000	38	84	46
67 years	2,350,000	13,100,000	173	443	270

Imports and exports of cotton manufactures in the last ten years were even.

ITALY

The annual consumption of cotton in 1830 was only 4 million lbs. The business of 67 years sums up thus :—

Period	Tons Cotton Consumed	Miles Cloth Made	Value, Millions £		
			Cotton	Manufactures	Net
1821–30	10,000	50,000	1	6	5
1831–40	30,000	150,000	2	9	7
1841–50	50,000	250,000	3	12	9
1851–60	90,000	500,000	6	18	12
1861–70	120,000	650,000	15	27	12
1871–80	310,000	1,700,000	23	51	28
1881–87	410,000	2,300,000	25	55	30
67 years	1,020,000	5,600,000	75	178	103

A statement published in 1877 showed that the mills had 54,000 operatives, 14,000 looms, 880,000 spindles, steam-power 3000 horse, water-mills 10,000 horse. In ten years ending 1887 Italy imported cotton manufactures worth £2,100,000 yearly.

SPAIN

In 1769 the first cotton factory was built in Spain. A statement published in 1833 showed 2840 mills, with 810,000 spindles, 60,000 operatives, consuming 11 million lbs. cotton and yarn ; product, 55 million yards cloth. The business of 67 years was approximately as follows :—

Period	Tons Cotton Consumed	Miles Cloth Made	Value, Millions £		
			Cotton	Manufactures	Net
1821–30	30,000	150,000	3	15	12
1831–40	50,000	250,000	4	15	11
1841–50	110,000	600,000	6	24	18
1851–60	200,000	1,100,000	12	36	24
1861–70	170,000	900,000	21	39	18
1871–80	340,000	1,900,000	26	57	31
1881–87	340,000	1,900,000	21	46	25
67 years	1,240,000	6,800,000	93	232	139

A statement in 1886 gave 53,000 operatives, 33,000 looms, 1,800,000 spindles, and goods manufactured to the yearly value of £12,400,000, that is, at an average of sixpence per yard of calico. The value is absurd, a fictitious one, being the result of enormous import duties.

In ten years ending 1887 Spain imported £400,000 worth of cotton goods yearly, and Portugal £700,000.

As regards Portugal, the consumption is close on 10 million lbs. cotton and yarn yearly ; output, £600,000 ; spindles, 140,000.

SWEDEN

In 1830 the output of the mills was valued at £200,000 a year. The business may be summed up thus :—

Period	Tons Cotton Consumed	Miles Cloth Made	Value, Millions £		
			Cotton	Manufactures	Net
1821–50	30,000	150,000	2	8	6
1851–60	50,000	250,000	3	9	6
1861–70	50,000	250,000	6	11	5
1871–80	90,000	500,000	7	15	8
1881–87	90,000	500,000	6	13	7
67 years	310,000	1,650,000	24	56	32

Denmark and Norway have no cotton factories, but consume imported goods. In ten years ending 1887 the net imports of cotton manufactured goods averaged thus :—

		£
Denmark	. . . . .	2,200,000
Sweden and Norway	. . .	600,000
Total	. .	2,800,000

Thus the total consumption of cotton goods in Scandinavia approaches a value of 5 millions sterling per annum.

HOLLAND

The industry may be briefly summed up as follows :—

Period	Tons Cotton Consumed	Miles Cloth Made	Value, Millions £		
			Cotton	Manufactures	Net
1821–50	30,000	150,000	2	8	6
1851–60	25,000	150,000	2	6	4
1861–70	20,000	100,000	3	5	2
1871–80	65,000	350,000	5	11	6
1881–87	70,000	400,000	4	9	5
67 years	210,000	1,150,000	16	39	23

BELGIUM

The business of 67 years was approximately as follows :—

Period	Tons Cotton Consumed	Miles Cloth Made	Value, Millions £		
			Cotton	Manufactures	Net
1821–30	40,000	200,000	3	16	13
1831–40	110,000	600,000	8	36	28
1841–50	120,000	700,000	7	28	21
1851–60	130,000	750,000	8	25	17
1861–70	120,000	700,000	15	29	14
1871–80	200,000	1,100,000	15	33	18
1881–87	170,000	950,000	13	26	13
67 years	890,000	5,000,000	69	193	124

The report for 1835 showed that 60,000 operatives turned out goods to the value of £3,400,000 sterling. At present Belgium produces a little more cotton goods than she requires, the net exports for ten years ending 1887 averaging £200,000.

L

SWITZERLAND

The business since 1820 sums up approximately thus :—

Period	Tons Cotton Consumed	Miles Cloth Made	Value, Millions £		
			Cotton	Manufactures	Net
1821–40	80,000	450,000	6	33	27
1841–50	90,000	500,000	5	20	15
1851–60	120,000	650,000	7	21	14
1861–70	100,000	550,000	13	24	11
1871–80	200,000	1,100,000	15	33	18
1881–87	160,000	900,000	10	22	12
67 years	750,000	4,150,000	56	153	97

UNITED STATES

The first cotton-mill was founded at Providence, Rhode Island, in 1790, and power-looms were first used at Waltham in 1815. The consumption of raw cotton in 1810 was 5 million lbs.

Mr. Atkinson's report on the cotton-mills of Massachusetts shows, since 1830, as follows :—

Year	Average Wages per Operative	Yards Cloth per Operative	Cost of Work, Pence per 100 Yards
	£		
1830	34	8,300	98
1840	36	9,600	91
1850	40	12,200	78
1860	41	21,800	46
1870	49	19,900	59
1880	54	28,000	47
1884	60	28,000	54

The growth of this manufacture is shown as follows :—

Year	No. of Mills	Spindles	Looms	Operatives	Cotton, Million Lbs.	Capital, Mill.Stg.	Wages, Mill.Stg.	Cotton, Mill.Stg.	Product, Mill.Stg.
						£	£	£	£
1830	801	1,240,000	33,000	62,000	77	8	2	...	8
1840	...	2,200,000	...	72,000	135	...	...	...	10
1850	1,094	3,000,000	...	92,000	288	15	3	7	14
1860	1,091	5,240,000	126,000	122,000	390	21	5	12	24
1870	956	7,130,000	157,000	135,000	400	25	7	19	30
1880	756	10,650,000	226,000	173,000	768	43	9	21	44
1888	...	13,500,000	...	...	1,010	...	...	...	60

The industry in the United States may be summed up thus approximately :—

Period	Tons Cotton Consumed	Miles Cloth Made	Value, Millions £		
			Cotton	Manufactures	Net
1821–30	160,000	900,000	11	43	32
1831–40	490,000	2,800,000	31	109	78
1841–50	990,000	5,700,000	49	160	111
1851–60	1,550,000	8,800,000	84	218	134
1861–70	1,970,000	11,200,000	223	376	153
1871–80	2,320,000	13,300,000	157	337	180
1881–87	2,780,000	16,200,000	150	320	170
67 years	10,260,000	58,900,000	705	1,563	858

In ten years ending 1887, the imports of cotton manufactures averaged £5,800,000, the exports £2,500,000. The consumption between home-made and imported goods in 1887 amounted to £52,300,000 sterling.

The cotton crop proceeds from 11 States, and is given by Ellison as follows :—

	Million Lbs.						
	1800	1820	1840	1860	1870	1880	1888
North Carolina	4	10	52	58	58	175	177
South Carolina	16	44	62	141	90	235	267
Georgia . . .	10	40	163	281	190	366	463
Virginia . . .	5	8	10	22	1	26	6
Tennessee . .	1	18	27	119	73	149	176
Alabama . .	...	20	117	396	172	315	456
Mississippi . .	...	10	196	481	226	433	524
Louisiana . .	...	10	152	311	140	228	220
Texas . .	...	...	...	172	140	362	807
Arkansas . .	...	...	6	151	99	274	297
Florida . . .	...	...	12	26	16	25	30
Total crop . .	36	160	797	2,158	1,205	2,588	3,423
Exported . .	20	128	661	1,760	806	1,820	2,385
Consumption .	16	32	136	398	399	768	1,038

The above figures from 1840 to 1870 differ somewhat from those of the Agricultural Report, as on page 42.

INDIA

The first cotton-mill was established at Bombay in 1851 ; there were 51 mills in 1876, with 40,000 operatives and 1,240,000 spindles, since which year 46 mills have been built, besides 10 more now in course of construction. In June 1889 there were 124 mills, with 92,000 operatives, 19,000 looms, 2,760,000 spindles, consuming yearly 353 million lbs. The capital employed is about £8,800,000 sterling. Cotton-growing covers an area of 14,530,000 acres, of which 5½ millions in Bombay and Scinde : about 30 per cent. of the crop is exported, the rest consumed in India.

CRIME

The following table is from Professor Bodio's international records of crime, mostly for the years 1876-84 :—

	Number of Crimes, Annual Average				
	Murder	Wounding	Robbery	Various	Total
France .	701	21,404	36,140	3,610	61,855
Germany .	610	54,250	31,480	10,550	96,890
Italy . . .	2,902	48,620	49,860	1,420	102,802
Spain . .	1,330	7,310	9,513	245	18,398
Total .	5,543	131,584	126,993	15,825	279,945

	Number of Criminals Tried, Annual Average				
	Murder	Wounding	Robbery	Various	Total
England .	294	902	59,220	642	61,058
Scotland .	40	510	10,840	64	11,454
Ireland . .	96	506	5,260	64	5,926
U. Kingdom	430	1,918	75,320	770	78,438
France . .	816	25,780	45,940	4,340	76,876
Germany .	602	70,502	143,810	7,780	222,694
Hungary .	1,682	7,920	14,520	2,452	26,574
Italy . . .	3,712	59,210	62,910	1,540	127,372
Spain . .	1,807	8,985	12,430	280	23,502
Belgium . .	117	11,740	7,880	925	20,662
Total .	9,166	186,055	362,810	18,087	576,118

	Number of Criminals Condemned, Annual Average						Criminals Condemned Yearly per Million Inhabitants				
	Murder	Wound-ing	Robbery	Various	Total		Murder	Wound-ing	Robbery	Various	Total
England .	148	696	43,100	432	44,376	England .	6	27	1,665	17	1,715
Scotland .	19	434	10,020	53	10,526	Scotland .	5	116	2,680	14	2,815
Ireland . .	54	324	3,410	44	3,832	Ireland . .	11	62	662	9	744
						U. Kingdom	6	40	1,615	15	1,676
U. Kingdom	221	1,454	56,530	529	58,734	France . .	16	634	1,110	102	1,862
France . .	582	23,910	41,830	3,880	70,202	Germany .	11	1,265	2,260	141	3,677
Germany .	505	57,420	102,260	6,364	166,549	Austria . .	23	2,320	...	92	2,435
Austria . .	540	51,160	...	2,060	53,760	Hungary .	67	298	586	68	1,019
Hungary .	1,180	5,265	10,270	1,210	17,925	Italy . . .	95	1,540	1,662	41	3,338
Italy . . .	2,720	44,220	47,220	1,160	95,320	Spain . .	83	432	592	10	1,117
Spain . .	1,265	7,180	9,920	172	18,537	Belgium . .	14	1,760	1,110	136	3,020
Belgium . .	80	9,710	6,110	764	16,664						
Total .	7,093	200,319	274,140	16,139	497,691						

The ratios of criminals in the United Kingdom are over-stated by Professor Bodio : see official returns, p. 164.

The number of criminals and offenders in various countries in 1872 per million inhabitants, according to the *Bulletin Statistique*, was as follows :—

	Convictions per Million Inhabitants of each Sex			Detained in all Prisons, per Million Inhabitants of each Sex		
	Males	Females	Both Sexes	Males	Females	Both Sexes
England	800	108	450	2,020	460	1,220
Ireland	323	115	216	950	342	639
France	1,060	174	612	2,100	422	1,260
Prussia	1,600	292	952	...	...	...
Saxony	1,515	336	914	2,440	512	1,455
Austria	915	153	526	1,910	274	1,070
Italy	1,960	54	1,010	5,140	267	2,710
Sweden	1,634	372	983	2,180	470	1,296
Denmark	906	256	575	1,390	386	879
Holland	858	82	464	1,635	207	910
Belgium	394	...	...	1,207	...	...

The number of days of imprisonment suffered yearly (1872) by 10,000 inhabitants was as follows :—

	Males	Females	Both Sexes
England . . .	74	17	45
Ireland	36	13	24
France . . .	66	15	41
Saxony	80	20	54
Italy	72	20	47
Sweden	67	14	40
Denmark . . .	50	13	31
Holland . . .	31	3	17
Belgium . . .	41	6	23

The percentage of old offenders in the number of convicts is :—

	Per 100 Males	Per 100 Females	Both Sexes
England	41	63	44
Ireland	53	76	58
France	...	...	41
Wurtemburg	...	...	50
Russia	8	6	7
Austria	59	51	57
Italy	26	13	24
Spain	18	11	16
Sweden	43	32	40
Denmark	26	24	25
Holland	...	...	80
Belgium	...	...	46
Switzerland . . .	...	...	45

The latest returns of prison population (not including officials) show as follows :—

	Number	Per 100,000 Popula-tion	Of 1000 Criminals Males	Of 1000 Criminals Females	Year
England . . .	25,100	90	853	147	1887
Scotland . . .	2,074	52	848	152	1887
Ireland . . .	3,300	66	828	172	1881
United Kingdom	30,474	80	845	155	...
France	60,836	158	876	124	1885
Russia	108,840	120	907	93	1887
Austria proper .	11,224	50	870	130	1886
Hungary . . .	6,278	38	905	95	1886
Italy	68,828	230	920	80	1887
Belgium . . .	5,711	98	890	110	1887
Holland . . .	3,653	82	896	104	1882
Sweden and Norway .	2,794	40	843	157	1887
United States .	59,258	120	914	86	1880
Canada . . .	3,024	64	...	...	1887
India	76,510	38	966	34	1887
Japan	63,828	160	950	50	1887
Cape Colony .	2,232	150	910	90	1888
Jamaica . . .	749	150	...	...	1888
Singapore . .	1,276	228	...	...	1888

The percentage of criminals as regards sex in Germany is 826 males to 174 females, and in Denmark 754 to 246.

The prison population of Italy is relatively three times as great as in the United Kingdom. *

The percentage of criminals punished yearly for insubordination or misconduct in prison was (1871):—

	Per 100 Males	Per 100 Females		Per 100 Males	Per 100 Females
Great Britain .	51	31	Sweden . .	8	8
France . . .	46	34	Denmark . .	8	4
Prussia . . .	21	14	Holland . .	24	14
Austria . . .	44	13	Belgium . .	14	...
Italy . . .	38	30	Switzerland .	18	21

The classification of crime differs so much in countries that it is almost impossible to make comparisons. As regards murder, some countries include infanticide and all cases of criminal homicide. Statistics on this subject will be found under the various countries in the following pages. Dr. Lombroso found skulls of Italian criminals had 10 per cent. less than ordinary capacity. Dr. Bordier found the reverse in France. Dugdall considers crime in a manner hereditary, and cites the case of Jukes, an Englishman, who emigrated to North America in 1720, and whose descendants numbered 709 persons, including 76 criminals, 128 prostitutes, 142 vagabonds, and 131 blind, insane, and otherwise infirm.

UNITED KINGDOM

The annual average of committals from 1840 was as follows :—

Period	Annual Average of Committals				Number per 100,000 Inhabitants			
	England	Scotland	Ireland	United Kingdom	England	Scotland	Ireland	United Kingdom
1840–49 . . .	27,910	4,045	25,220	57,175	164	149	302	204
1850–59 . . .	23,924	3,860	13,640	41,424	126	130	227	151
1860–69 . . .	19,230	3,315	5,060	27,605	91	104	91	92
1870–79 . . .	15,290	3,110	4,412	22,812	64	89	84	69
1880–89 . . .	14,100	2,450	3,320	19,870	50	70	66	55

The annual average of convictions was :—

Period	Annual Average				Percentage of Convictions to Committals			
	England	Scotland	Ireland	United Kingdom	England	Scotland	Ireland	United Kingdom
1840–49 . . .	21,280	3,029	11,730	36,039	75	75	47	63
1850–59 . . .	18,291	2,902	7,705	28,898	76	74	58	70
1860–69 . . .	14,530	2,463	2,918	19,911	76	74	58	72
1870–79 . . .	11,720	2,190	2,492	16,402	78	71	56	72
1880–89 . . .	10,800	1,910	1,760	14,470	77	77	53	72

The number of criminal convictions has declined 37 per cent. in the last 22 years, viz. :—

Year	Number of Convictions				Per 100,000 Inhabitants			
	England	Scotland	Ireland	United Kingdom	England	Scotland	Ireland	United Kingdom
1867	14,207	2,510	2,733	19,450	64	75	50	63
1877	11,942	2,009	2,300	16,251	48	60	45	48
1889	9,348	1,723	1,225	12,296	32	43	25	33

The number of offenders of all descriptions in the three kingdoms in 1880 was as follows :—

Guilty of	England	Scotland	Ireland	United Kingdom	Per 10,000 Inhabitants			
					England	Scotland	Ireland	United Kingdom
Crimes and offences .	203,600	80,900	55,100	339,600	80	220	104	100
Drunkenness .	172,900	26,900	88,000	287,800	68	73	166	85
Misdemeanour .	301,400	26,700	101,400	429,500	118	72	191	126
Total . .	677,900	134,500	244,500	1,056,900	266	365	461	311

Similar returns for 1887 showed as follows :—

Guilty of	England	Scotland	Ireland	United Kingdom	Per 10,000 Inhabitants			
					England	Scotland	Ireland	United Kingdom
Crimes and offences .	163,359	73,650	34,978	271,987	58	185	70	73
Drunkenness .	162,772	17,621	79,476	259,869	58	45	160	70
Misdemeanour .	366,683	29,133	105,209	501,025	99	75	210	135
Total . .	692,814	120,404	219,663	1,032,881	215	305	440	278

In 1887 there were 237 persons tried for wilful murder, viz., 163 in England, 23 in Scotland, and 51 in Ireland, the last being for the most part connected with agrarian troubles.

The prison population in 1880 was as follows :—

	England	Scotland	Great Britain
Males . . .	23,791	2,063	25,854
Females . .	4,533	1,008	5,541
Total .	28,324	3,071	31,395

	Per 100,000 Inhabitants		
	England	Scotland	Great Britain
Males . . .	189	114	179
Females . .	34	52	36
General . .	109	83	105

In England there are 84 male to 16 female offenders ; in Scotland 67 of the former to 33 of the latter.

ENGLAND AND WALES

There are no records of the number of criminals before the present century. Henry VIII. put to death 71,400 persons as criminals during his reign, but most of them were either virtuous or unoffending persons. He hanged 300 beggars in one year for soliciting alms. In the first half of the present century 2734 persons were hanged in England.

For murder 616
For burglary 1235
For incendiarism 147
For forgery, &c. 736

Total . 2734

Hantute's table of convictions compared with the number of executions shows thus :—

Period	Convictions Yearly	Executed Yearly	Per 1000 Convictions
1801–20	9,600	85	9.0
1821–30	18,100	67	3.7
1831–50	25,000	18	0.7

In one year (1820) no fewer than 46 persons were hanged for forging Bank of England notes, some of which were afterwards asserted to be good. In twenty years ending 1880 there were 279 criminals executed for murder in the United Kingdom, say fourteen yearly.

The number of homicides in England and Wales in 1880 was as follows :—

	Number of Victims		
	Male	Female	Total
Wilful murder . . .	43	54	97
Manslaughter . . .	115	58	173
Infanticide . . .	48	56	104
Total . .	206	168	374

Judicial statistics for ten years ending December 1888 in England and Wales show thus :—

Murders committed 1766
No trace of criminal . . . 1094
Persons tried for murder . . 672
Acquitted 231
Found insane 142
Sentenced to death . . . 299
Executed 154

Of those sentenced to death, fifty were women, of whom only nine were executed.

The total number of offenders punished in 1887 was as follows :—

Criminals 163,359
Misdemeanants 529,455

Total . . 692,814

The nationality of the criminals was as follows :—

English . . . . 135,770 = 83.1
Welsh . . . . . 5,193 = 3.2
Scotch . . . . . 3,103 = 1.9
Irish . . . . . 15,928 = 9.7
Foreign . . . . 3,365 = 2.1

Total . . 163,359 100.0

The nationality of criminals in 1887 compares with similar returns for 25 years down to 1881 thus :—

	1857–71	1872–81	1887
English	78.2	78.7	83.1
Welsh	2.6	3.0	3.2
Scotch	2.1	2.3	1.9
Irish	14.4	13.6	9.7
Foreign	2.7	2.4	2.1
Total . .	100.0	100.0	100.0

The nature of the crimes for which they were punished in 1887 was :—

Murder 163   Grave crimes . . . 5,863
Shooting or stabbing . 970   Robbery 47,223
Burglary . . . 3,852   Assault 75,873
Attacks on women . 878   Sundry 34,400

Total . . . 5,863   Total . . 163,359

The sentences passed on the criminals were :—

Death 35
Penal servitude 948
Imprisonment 162,376

Total . . 163,359

In 1880 the ratio of ages in local prisons was as follows :—

Under 21 years 20.6
21 to 40 ,, ... 54.7
41 to 60 ,, ... 20.8
Over 60 ,, ... 3.9

Total . . 100.0

The sexes of all classes of offenders and misdemeanants in 1887 showed :—

Males . . . 568,280
Females . . . 124,534

Total . . 692,814

As regards criminals the classification was as follows :—

	Number	Ratio
Able to read	119,993	68.6
Unable to read . . .	43,366	31.4
Total . . .	163,359	100.0
Shopkeepers, &c. . . .	8,445	5.2
Mechanics . . .	23,310	14.3
Operatives . . .	48,353	29.6
Vagrants, &c. . . .	83,251	50.9
Total . . .	163,359	100.0

There are 60 local prisons which admitted in 1887 :—

	Number	Ratio
New offenders	96,112	55.6
Convicted up to ten times . .	62,024	36.0
Convicted over ten times . .	14,311	8.4
Total	172,447	100.0

The proportion of sexes showed as follows :—

	Number	Ratio
Males	131,812	76.7
Females	40,635	23.3
Total . . .	172,447	100.0

The record for 1887 showed thus :—

	Local Prisons	Convict Prisons
Served time . . .	156,406	2,038
Committed suicide . .	12	4
Died	117	73
Sent to lunatic asylums .	169	5
Sent to convict prisons .	1,347	...
Remaining, December 31st	14,396	6,413
Total . . .	172,447	8,533

Of those who served their time out in convict prisons and were liberated, only 617 really finished the term of sentences, 1421 being released on "ticket-of-leave."

The cost of maintenance and the proceeds of labour in the sixty local and ten convict prisons in 1887 showed :—

	Maintenance	Labour Proceeds
	£	£
Local prisons . . .	340,000	116,000
Convict prisons . .	245,000	145,000
Total . .	585,000	261,000

The mean prison population and the cost per criminal were :—

	Criminals, Number	Cost per Annum
		£ s. d.
Local prisons . . .	15,119	22 10 0
Convict prisons . .	6,800	36 14 0
Total . .	21,919	26 12 0

The cost in 1868 averaged £33 per criminal.

The criminal population of England and Wales is shown thus :—

In prison	21,919
In reformatories	3,230
Adult criminals at large . . .	28,730
Juvenile criminals at large . . .	4,870
Total . .	58,749

As regards the inmates of convict prisons, 11 per cent. of the men and 34 per cent. of the women have been convicted ten times or upwards. During the year 1889 there were 1512 juvenile convicts sent to reformatories.

SCOTLAND

The prison population has been as follows :—

Year	Males	Females	Total	Per 100,000 Inhabitants
1840	1,362	686	2,048	80
1850	2,042	1,017	3,059	108
1860	1,106	1,059	2,165	71
1870	1,726	1,099	2,825	83
1888	2,065	1,008	3,073	83
1887	...	...	2,074	52

The record for 1887 was composed thus :—

Murder	23
Burglary	948
Robbery	11,119
Assault, &c.	61,560
Total . . .	73,650

The classification of offences and misdemeanours being different from that used in England and Ireland, the number of crimes and offences appears unduly high. The local and convict prisons admitted in 1887 offenders of both sexes to the number of 46,108; the cost of prison maintenance reaching £127,000, or about £40 per inmate.

IRELAND

The record for 1887 showed as follows for persons tried :—

Murder	51	Crimes	1,213
Shooting, &c. . . .	171	Offences . . .	33,765
Burglary	135	Drunkenness . .	79,476
Assault, &c. . . .	856	Sundry	105,209
Crimes . .	1,213	Total . .	219,663

The following classifications are given :—

	Per Cent.	
	Men	Women
Able to read . . .	70	53
Unable to read . . .	30	47
Total . .	100	100

There are 4 convict and 26 local prisons, the admissions to which showed :—

	Per Cent.	
	Men	Women
New offenders . . .	47	24
Convicted up to 10 times .	37	23
Convicted over 10 times .	16	53
Total . .	100	100

The maintenance of the prisons in 1887 cost £124,000.

FRANCE

Official returns since 1826 are as follows :—

Period	Convictions Yearly for Crime	For Crimes and Offences
1831–40	5,486	55,100
1841–60	4,970	97,200
1861–70	3,572	119,500
1871–80	3,650	132,500
1883–87	3,105	206,400

The number of crimes and offences compared with population was as follows :—

Period	Per Million Inhabitants			Convicts in Penal Servitude	
	Crimes	Offences	Total	Number	Per Million Inhabitants
1830–40	230	2,080	2,310	16,820	511
1841–60	195	3,610	3,805	18,330	515
1861–70	110	3,870	3,980	18,210	489
1871–80	120	4,320	4,440	16,630	458
1883–87	81	5,390	5,471	13,380	352

The annual ratio of some of the graver crimes is shown as follows :—

Period	Arson	Infanti- cide	Assault on Girls	Murder
1826–30	87	120	136	10
1831–40	122	184	196	64
1841–50	194	247	383	80
1851–60	225	347	638	116
1861–70	202	343	744	116
1871–80	180	296	758	70

Before 1860 the law against criminal assaults regarded only girls under eleven, but since that year it was extended to the age of thirteen. The above return of murders only comprises those of the most aggravated character ; the real number is much greater. In 1880, for example, there were 645 murders and homicides, against 808 in the United Kingdom.

The classification of criminals since 1826 has been as follows :—

Period	Sexes per Cent.		Percentage of Age			Per Cent.		Per Cent.	
	Males	Females	Under 21	21–40	Over 40	Married	Unmarried	Able to Read	Unable
1826–30 . . .	81	19	18	58	24	...	...	39	61
1831–40 . . .	83	17	17	60	23	42	58	42	58
1841–50 . . .	83	17	17	57	26	45	55	48	52
1851–60 . . .	82	18	16	56	28	47	53	56	44
1861–70 . . .	84	16	16	54	30	46	54	61	39
1871–80 . . .	83	17	18	54	28	45	55	67	33

The proportion of " recidivistes " or old offenders has increased as follows :—

1826 . . .	10 per cent.	1870	41 per cent.
1850 . . .	28 ,,	1880	48 ,,

The number of criminals to each class in society was as follows :—

	Per Million Persons	
	Male	Female
Unmarried	400	90
Married	200	30
Widowed	240	40

In eight years ending 1868 the number to each class was as follows :—

Criminals per Million

Husband with child . .	186	Widower with child . .	237
Wife with child . . .	32	Widow with child . .	44
Husband without child .	287	Widower without child .	262
Wife without child . .	60	Widow without child .	35

The following table shows the total number of persons tried :—

Year	Tried			Con- demned	Per 1000 Population
	Law Courts	Police	Total		
1831	372,000	105,000	477,000	426,000	13.3
1840	373,000	228,000	601,000	549,000	16.1
1850	486,000	306,000	792,000	736,000	21.0
1860	431,000	509,000	940,000	894,000	24.2
1870	337,000	234,000	571,000	549,000	14.4
1880	598,000	424,000	1,022,000	995,000	26.5
1885	675,000	467,000	1,142,000	1,111,000	29.4

The prison population at various dates was thus :—

Year	Galleys	Prisons	Refor- matories	Total
1852	6,800	47,000	6,400	60,200
1860	3,600	42,100	8,600	54,300
1870	2,600	33,600	6,800	43,000
1880	11,700	40,600	9,000	61,300
1884	13,400	40,000	7,000	60,400

The prison population in 1885 was :—

Males .	.	. 53,299	Prisons . . .	47,456
Females .	.	. 7,537	Penal colonies .	13,380
Total	.	60,836	Total .	60,836

In December 1880 there were 13,927 at the galleys, viz. :—

First offenders . . .	2,891	=	20.9 per cent.
Up to 3 convictions .	4,733	=	34.0 ,,
Over 3 convictions . .	6,303	=	45.1 ,,
Total . .	13,927	=	100.0 ,,

	Per Million	
	Males	Females
Unmarried	590	100
Married	200	35
Widowed	270	50

Age	Per Million		
	Males	Females	Both Sexes
7–21	230	50	90
21–40	370	75	240
41–60	180	35	130
Over 60	100	10	60

The general ratio was 100 criminals in rural population and 220 in towns per million inhabitants.

The rank and position of French criminals was :—

Men of fortune .	.	.	.	6 per cent.
Servants	.	.	.	13 ,,
Tradesmen	.	.	.	14 ,,
Artisans, &c.	.	.	.	67 ,,
				100.0 ,,

Criminals under sixteen years of age in 1859 were :—

Guilty of	Boys	Girls	Total
Murder . . .	6	3	9
Wounding . . .	269	50	319
Robbery, &c. . .	6,887	1,706	8,593
Total .	7,162	1,759	8,921

The number of criminals of all ages tried annually in the term of five years ending 1880 was as follows :—

Males . . 3,682 = 200 per million of population
Females. . 692 = 40 ,, ,,

Total . 4,374 = 120 ,, ,,

In a period of 47 years ending 1880 sentence of death was passed on 1775 murderers, of whom 205 were women ; they were as follows :—

1833–40 . . . 326		1861–70 . . . 193		
1841–50 . . . 485		1871–80 . . . 272		
1851–60 . . . 499				
		48 years . . . 1,775		

The ratio of age of the above murderers was :—

	Number	Ratio
Under 21	106	6.2
21–40	1,182	66.2
41–60	420	24.1
Over 60	67	3.5
Total . .	1,775	100.0

Only 1067 were actually executed, 671 being commuted, and 37 dying in prison, for the most part of suicide.

In the year 1885 the number of prisoners sent to hospital was equal to 67 per cent. among the men and 60 per cent. among women.

Prison diet consists of 5 oz. of bread and 13 oz. vegetables and potatoes daily, with a meat ration of 4 oz. twice a week.

GERMANY

In 1886 the criminal records of the Empire were :—

	Accused	Condemned	Under 18 Years of Age	Condemned Men	Condemned Women
Murder . .	337	298	18	231	67
Assault . .	56,785	42,586	720	31,188	11,398
Burglary .	19,325	15,983	509	13,880	2,103
Robbery .	104,206	88,816	17,266	64,668	24,148
Fraud . .	17,628	13,609	1,195	10,825	2,784
Perjury . .	3,330	2,948	345	2,425	523
Embezzlement }	18,025	14,731	1,514	11,639	3,092
Various . .	213,171	174,029	9,946	156,578	17,451
Total .	432,807	353,000	31,513	291,434	61,566

It appears that women formed less than 18 per cent. of the total number of convicts, but as regards robbery their ratio was much higher, namely, 27 per cent. Convicts under 18 years of age were 9 per cent. of the total.

The condemned persons belonged to the following States :—

Against	Prussia	Bavaria	Saxony	Wurtemburg	Baden	Duchies	Total
Person	79,839	24,147	5,786	4,968	3,891	15,388	134,019
Property	97,864	20,433	10,675	5,636	5,170	18,745	158,523
Public order	39,011	5,084	3,976	3,013	1,435	7,939	60,458
Total .	216,714	49,664	20,437	13,617	10,496	42,072	353,000

Of the above offenders 102,800, say 29 per cent., had been previously convicted. The number of persons convicted compared with the population over twelve years of age gave the following ratios per 10,000 :—

Against	1882	1883	1884	1885	1886
Person . . .	34	35	39	39	41
Property . .	53	51	51	49	48
Order . . .	16	16	17	17	18
Total . .	103	102	107	105	107

The ratios in 1886 were as follows :—

	Offenders per 10,000 Population over 12 Years Old ; against— Person	Property	Order	Total
Prussia	40	49	20	109
Bavaria	62	53	13	128
Saxony	26	47	18	91
Wurtemburg . .	35	40	22	97
Baden	34	45	13	92
Hesse	39	32	12	83
Mecklenburg . . .	20	31	16	67
Oldenburg . . .	20	34	14	68
Brunswick	31	43	15	89
Hamburg	28	61	25	114
Bremen	35	72	36	143
Alsace	41	32	25	98

In a term of 14 years ending 1852 the number of criminals and offenders in Saxony averaged yearly as follows :—

Age	Per Million Persons Males	Per Million Persons Females
16–20 . . .	900	180
21–30 . . .	2,100	400
31–40 . . .	2,300	600
41–50 . . .	1,300	250
51–60 . . .	800	160
Over 60 . . .	300	60

The number of male criminals and offenders per million male inhabitants rose as follows in Saxony :—

Period	Per Million
1832–44	1,170
1845–54	1,280
1872	1,515

In a period of 10 years ending 1879, the number of criminals found guilty of wilful murder in Prussia, Bavaria, and Austria was :—

	Number	Per Annum
Prussia . . .	484	48
Bavaria . . .	245	25
Austria . . .	816	82
Total . .	1,945	195

Only 23 of the above assassins suffered death, namely, 16 in Austria and 7 in Bavaria.

In Prussia during a term of 14 years ending 1874 the number of murders yearly committed showed as compared with population thus :—

Committed by men . . 30 per million
Committed by women . . 10 ,, ,,

RUSSIA

Statistics for 1887 may be summed up thus :—

Before	Convictions	Sentence	
Senate	10,800	Exile	20,590
Supreme courts .	172,100	Penal servitude .	58,020
Divisional . . .	207,000	Hard labour, &c.	1,097,190
Police	785,900		
		Total . .	1,175,800
Total . .	1,175,800		

The prison population was made up thus :—

Convicts .	82,570	Males .	98,710	In Russia . .	75,350
Untried .	26,270	Females .	10,130	Siberia, &c.	33,490
Total .	108,840	Total .	108,840	Total .	108,840

AUSTRIA

The criminal records of Austria proper in 1886 showed :—

For	Supreme Court		For	Police and other Courts	
	Accused	Condemned		Accused	Condemned
Murder .	379	274	Fraud .	25,030	13,083
Assault .	5,702	4,787	Theft .	184,182	124,521
Fraud .	3,920	2,689	Assault .	148,186	98,843
Robbery .	17,383	15,054	Disorder	130,753	87,881
Various .	8,750	6,902	Sundry .	549,952	234,115
Total .	36,134	29,706	Total .	1,038,103	558,443

The sentences passed on the condemned persons were :—

Supreme Court		Lower Courts	
Death . . .	5	8 to 30 days .	83,663
Galleys for life .	27	Over 30 days .	13,254
5 to 20 years .	574	Fined . .	368,311
1 to 5 years .	4,147	Reprimanded .	980
Under 12 months .	24,953	...	...
Total .	29,706	Total . .	558,443

The age and condition of the greater criminals were :—

	Age		Males	Females	Total
Under 20	5,287	Single .	15,113	2,318	17,431
20 to 30 .	12,370	Married .	9,767	1,553	11,320
30 to 60 .	11,328	Widowed	572	383	955
Over 60 .	721	...	...	...	...
Total .	29,706	Total .	25,452	4,254	29,706

The reformatories contain 3046 boys and 279 girls. The ratios of sex among all persons condemned in 1886 were :—

	Supreme Court	Lower Courts
Males . . .	85.7	81.5
Females . . .	14.3	18.5
Total . .	100.0	100.0

Prison population was as follows :—

	1882	1886
Males . . .	10,139	9,785
Females . . .	1,598	1,439
Total . .	11,737	11,224

There are 21 penal establishments, of which six are for women.

HUNGARY

The records for 1886 show the number of persons condemned as follows :—

	Males	Females	Total
Supreme court .	17,817	2,393	20,210
Divisional . . .	44,113	14,891	59,004
Correctional . .	29,583	6,501	36,084
Police	220,026	35,032	255,058
Total . .	311,539	58,817	370,356

The crimes tried and sentences passed at the Supreme Court were : —

Crimes		Sentences	
Murder .	190	Death	20
Incendiarism	132	Imprisonment over 5 years	771
Assault .	2,502	,, 1 to 5 years	5,119
Robbery .	4,905	,, 6 to 12 months	5,505
Various .	12,481	,, under 6 months	8,795
Total	20,210	Total .	20,210

The convictions in the Divisional and Correctional Courts were as follows :—

	Divisional			Correctional		
	Males	Females	Total	Males	Females	Total
Theft . .	8,830	2,021	10,851	7,766	1,455	9,221
Assault . .	7,304	541	7,845	6,114	406	6,520
Disorder .	9,256	1,815	11,071	7,224	1,204	8,428
Fraud . .	2,552	580	3,132	1,156	224	1,380
Various .	16,171	9,934	26,105	7,323	3,212	10,535
Total	44,113	14,891	59,004	29,583	6,501	36,084

The sentences passed in the above courts and that of Police were :—

Imprisonment	Divisional	Correctional	Police	Total
Over 6 months	...	885	...	885
1 to 6 months .	3,340	2,650	2,230	8,226
14 to 30 days .	7,934	6,242	5,080	19,256
1 to 14 days .	24,505	26,301	44,850	95,656
Fined . . .	23,225	...	134,400	157,625
Reprimanded .	...	...	68,498	68,498
Total .	59,004	36,084	255,058	350,146

Criminals condemned at the Supreme Court and offenders at the Divisional Court were classified thus according to age :—

Age	Criminals			Offenders		
	Males	Females	Total	Males	Females	Total
Under 20	2,574	393	2,967	4,592	1,333	5,925
20–30	7,923	925	8,848	19,054	6,129	25,183
30–60	6,950	1,013	7,963	19,654	7,192	26,846
Over 60	370	62	432	813	237	1,050
Total	17,817	2,393	20,210	44,113	14,891	59,004

The condition of the criminals was :—

	Males	Females	Total	Prison Population	
Married .	9,412	1,228	10,640	Males .	5,678
Single. .	7,792	825	8,617	Females .	600
Widowed	613	340	953		
				Total	6,278
Total	17,817	2,393	20,210		

ITALY

Averages for nine years ending 1884 give as follows :—

	No. of Crimes	Criminals Tried	Convicted	Per 100,000 Population
Murder . .	2,902	3,712	2,720	10
Stabbing, &c.	48,620	59,210	44,220	154
Robbery . .	49,860	62,910	47,220	166
Sundry . .	1,420	1,540	1,160	4
Total	102,802	127,372	95,320	334

In 1887 the convictions and prison population were as follows :—

Convictions		Prison Population			
Assize court }	5,546	Males	63,365	In Prison	34,264
Minor courts }	309,813	Females	5,473	Penal servitude }	34,564
Total	315,359	Total	68,828	Total	68,828

Among those in prison are included 5477 children in reformatories, viz. :—

Boys	.	.	.	.	.	.	3,633
Girls	.	.	.	.	.	.	1,844
	Total	.	.	.	.	5,477	

Murder, or rather homicide in some form, constitutes a principal feature in Italian crime. The number of such crimes was :—

Year					Murders
1871 .	.	.	.	.	5,297
1872 .	.	.	.	.	4,524
1875 .	.	.	.	.	3,408

In 1875 the prisons of Italy admitted the following criminals :—

Age	Number			Ratio		
	Males	Females	Total	Males	Females	Both Sexes
Under 21	39,150	5,100	44,250	22.8	14.8	21.5
21–30. .	54,500	11,040	65,540	31.7	32.0	31.8
31–40. .	37,300	8,960	46,260	21.7	25.9	22.4
Over 40 .	41,250	9,400	50,650	23.8	27.3	24.3
Total .	172,200	34,500	206,700	100.0	100.0	100.0

The cities of Italy stand for 32 per cent. of the population, and 42 per cent. of the crime. The predominance of crime in towns is therefore notably less than in France. The nature of crimes in 1875 was as follows :—

	Number		Ratio
Against the person . . .	51,000	...	36.4
Against property . . .	88,000	...	63.6
Total . .	139,000		100.0

In December 1875 the prisons and reformatories held 53,500 criminals, having admitted 356,500 during the year. The classes of prisoners were :—

					Per Cent.
Agricultural	.	.	.	.	65
Operatives	.	.	.	.	30
Tradesmen, &c.	.	.	.	.	5
					100

In ten years ending 1876 there were 392 murderers sentenced to death, but only 34 were executed.

The proportion of convicts who die under sentence is as follows :—

5 years penal servitude	.	.	.	29 per cent.
10 ,, ,, ,,	.	.	.	42 ,,
15 ,, ,, ,,	or upwards .			80 ,,

In Italy the average number of crimes in the years 1874–76 was 7085, of which 2470 were murders or homicides.

BELGIUM

Judicial records give the following :—

Court	Cases Tried			
	1835	1850	1870	1887
Civil . . .	8,463	7,896	15,482	27,136
Correctional .	25,337	24,752	26,640	47,942
Police . .	19,209	49,890	70,179	132,011
Total .	53,009	82,538	112,301	207,089
Sentences				
Acquitted . .	9,877	10,083	12,662	23,285
Galleys . .	137	134	43	72
Imprisonment .	8,511	21,442	19,498	44,993
Fine . . .	34,484	50,879	80,098	138,739
Total .	53,009	82,538	112,301	207,089

The following tables show the convictions for crime and the prison population :—

Year	Number of Convicts		Per 10,000 Inhabitants
1840 . . .	9,012	...	23
1850 . . .	11,133	...	25
1860 . . .	10,810	...	23
1876 . . .	12,420	...	24

Year	Prison Population		
	Males	Females	Totals
1840	4,365	427	4,792
1860	5,104	838	5,942
1870	4,202	499	4,701
1887	4,162	509	4,671

The above prison population is exclusive of 1040 juvenile offenders detained in reformatories.

SERVIA

In 1887 were tried 7538 criminals, with this result :—

Imprisoned .	.	.	.	.	2,567
Fined .	.	.	.	.	3,130
Acquitted .	.	.	.	.	1,841
	Total	.	.	7,538	

Prison population at end of the year was 1725.

SCANDINAVIA

The convictions for 1881 and 1887 show as follows :—

Tried for	Sweden		Norway	
	1881	1887	1881	1887
Crimes . .	9,608	9,157	3,318	2,932
Offences . .	48,598	45,404	25,369	22,664
Total .	58,206	54,561	28,687	25,596
Males . .	54,792	51,491	26,684	23,639
Females . .	3,414	3,070	2,003	1,957
Total .	58,206	54,561	28,687	25,596

Denmark showed 3525 persons convicted of crime in 1885, including 872 women.

EGYPT

The records for five years are as follows :—

	1888		*Average Four Years*
Crimes . . .	1,144	...	530
Offences . .	32,236	...	17,710
Total .	33,380		18,240

The above does not include Upper Egypt.

AUSTRALIA

Official returns are as follows :—

Year	Arrests	Committals	Convictions	Per 10,000 Pop. Arrests	Committals	Convictions
1861. . . .	53,570	2,745	1,656	433	22	13
1871. . . .	68,800	2,617	1,557	362	14	8
1881. . . .	117,130	3,361	2,024	432	12	7
1888. . . .	130,250	3,630	2,212	365	10	6

Arrests include all manner of crimes and offences ; committals only crimes. The several colonies showed thus in 1888 :—

	Arrests	Committals	Convictions	Convictions per 10,000 Population
New South Wales	42,580	1,423	915	8.3
Victoria . . .	37,310	873	557	5.1
Queensland . .	18,430	538	275	7.0
South Australia .	6,600	190	91	2.9
New Zealand. .	19,170	499	308	5.1
Tasmania . . .	6,160	107	66	4.4
Total . .	130,250	3,630	2,212	6.2

CANADA

The records for 1888 may be summed up thus :—

Crimes			*Offences*		
Accused .	.	. 5,867	Fined .	.	. 31,276
Acquitted	.	. 2,120	Imprisoned	.	. 2,626
Convicted	.	3,747	Total	.	. 33,902

The prison population in December 1887 was 3024, say 64 per 100,000 inhabitants.

CAPE COLONY

The official returns for 1888 were as follows :—

Prison Population				Convictions in 1888	
Coloured .	2,012	Males . .	2,032	Crimes .	1,408
White . .	220	Females .	200	Offences .	39,172
Total .	2,232	Total .	2,232	Total .	40,580

The prison population was equal to 150 per 100,000 inhabitants.

INDIA

The returns for all classes of criminals and offenders in 1887 compare with those for 1881 as follows :—

	1881	1887
Tried	1,172,000	1,377,000
Acquitted . . .	527,000	703,000
Convicted . . .	645,000	674,000
Fined	468,000	500,000
Imprisoned . . .	177,000	174,000

The prison population in the same years was as follows :—

	1881	1887
Males	83,429	73,940
Females	3,888	2,570
Total . .	87,317	76,510

There were 15,259 criminals whipped in 1887, against 75,200 in 1878. The prison population is only 38 per 100,000 inhabitants, or less than half the ratio that prevails in the United Kingdom.

ALGERIA

In 1886 the records showed as follows :—

Convictions		Sentence	
Criminal courts . .	12,408	Imprisonment . .	17,502
Police courts . . .	59,981	Fine	54,887
Total . .	72,389	Total . .	72,389

MINOR COLONIES

	Crimes	Offences	Total	Per Million Inhab.	Year
Mauritius . .	129	13,707	13,836	381	1888
Jamaica . .	2,412	8,119	10,531	176	1887
Singapore . .	227	36,111	36,338	179	1888
Hong-Kong .	99	9,932	10,031	478	1888
Ceylon . . .	1,330	12,961	14,291	48	1886

UNITED STATES

The number of offenders in prison at the following dates, according to Census returns, was :—

Year	Number	Per Million Inhabitants
1850	6,737	292
1860	19,086	610
1870	32,901	875
1880	59,258	1,180

The Census of 1880 classified offenders as follows :—

Males . .	54,190	Americans	46,348	White .	42,280
Females .	5,068	Foreigners	12,910	Coloured	16,978
Total .	59,258	Total	59,258	Total .	59,258

The *Chicago Tribune* gives the following statistics of murders and executions in the United States since 1884 :—

Year	Murders	Legal Executions	Lynchings
1884 . . .	3,377	103	219
1885 . . .	1,808	108	181
1886 . . .	1,499	83	133
1887 . . .	2,335	79	123
1888 . . .	2,184	87	144
1889 . . .	3,567	98	175
Total .	14,770	558	975

There are four States in which capital punishment is not allowed : Maine, Rhode Island, Wisconsin, and Michigan.

CURIOSITIES

Prices paid in recent times have been for—
Books.—Mr. Quaritch paid £4900 for a Latin Psalter, and £3900 for a Mazarin Bible at Syston Hall sale.
Coins.—In 1889 a silver penny of William the Conqueror fetched £32, a half-crown of Elizabeth £44, and one of Charles I. £35 sterling.

Letters and Autographs.—In 1889 at public sale in London the following prices were paid :—

	£		£		£
Addison . .	5	Franklin . .	6	Pope . . .	16
Bolingbroke .	9	Gibbon . .	6	Quincey . .	7
Bruce (trav.) .	6	Hood . . .	6	Richelieu . .	5
Burke . .	8	Hume . .	5	Schiller . .	6
Burns . . .	18	Irving, W. .	2	Scott . . .	17
Byron . . .	7	Johnson, S. .	6	Shelley . . .	19
Carlyle . . .	4	Kean, E. . .	9	Smollett . .	8
Coleridge . .	3	Keats . . .	14	Sterne . . .	8
Dickens . .	9	Lamb, C. . .	6	Tennyson . .	7
Disraeli . .	5	Nelson . . .	11	Thackeray . .	6
Elizabeth, Q.	11	Newton . .	64	Washington .	10
Elliot, G. . .	11	Poe, E. . .	6		

Manuscripts.—That of Burns's poem "Scots Wha Hae" was sold in London in May 1890 for £70 ; that of Wilkie Collins's novel "The Woman in White," on the same occasion, for £320.
Postage Stamps.—A collection was sold in Paris in 1880 for £8000 sterling ; the purchaser was said to be the Duchess Galiera, otherwise known for her princely donations to the poor of Genoa.
Violins.—At a sale in Paris in 1887 the following prices were paid :—

					Date	£
Stradivarius	.	.	.	.	1689	760
"	.	.	.	.	1691	480
Ruggeri	.	.	.	.	1650	1,280

A violin bow by Tourte fetched £44 sterling.
Walking-Stick.—That of George IV. was sold at auction in July 1890 for £18 sterling.

CUSTOMS

The following table shows the customs revenue of nations :—

	Amount, £		Ratio to Total Commerce		Shillings per Inhabitant	
	1871–80	1887	1871–80	1887	1871–80	1887
			Per Cent	Per Cent.	Per Cent.	Per Cent.
United Kingdom . .	20,110,000	19,900,000	3.36	3.10	12.5	10.5
France	10,320,000	13,400,000	3.78	4.45	5.7	7.0
Germany	8,640,000	12,700,000	3.28	4.10	4.0	4.5
Russia	10,525,000	10,200,000	10.02	10.20	3.0	2.2
Austria	2,610,000	3,000,000	2.38	2.40	1.5	1.6
Italy	5,080,000	10,000,000	5.80	11.10	3.6	6.5
Spain	4,410,000	3,600,000	12.10	6.00	5.5	4.2
Portugal	1,790,000	3,400,000	15.22	41.00	8.5	18.0
Belgium	780,000	1,200,000	0.87	1.10	3.1	4.0
Holland	415,000	400,000	0.36	0.20	2.2	2.0
Denmark	950,000	1,200,000	5.42	5.70	10.0	12.0
Sweden and Norway .	2,390,000	2,600,000	7.05	6.10	7.6	8.0
Europe . . .	68,020,000	81,600,000	3.90	4.10	4.4	5.5
United States . . .	26,030,000	44,600,000	13.10	15.00	12.0	15.0
Canada	2,715,000	4,800,000	8.23	11.20	13.0	18.5
Australia	4,250,000	7,500,000	6.11	7.50	34.0	45.0
Brazil	6,680,000	9,200,000	20.32	21.00	13.1	15.0
India	2,220,000	3,200,000	2.33	2.20	0.2	0.3
Egypt	780,000	800,000	4.51	4.00	4.0	4.0
The world . . .	110,695,000	151,700,000	5.10	5.60	3.9	5.2

The British customs revenue is shown as follows :—

Year	£	Ratio to Commerce	Shillings per Inhabitant
1580 . .	14,000	0.42	0.1
1614 . .	178,000	4.22	0.8
1684 . .	530,000	6.70	2.0
1720 . .	1,555,000	10.40	5.1
1800 . .	6,788,000	10.02	13.0
1827 . .	21,009,000	23.10	18.1
1844 . .	24,277,000	20.05	18.0
1866 . .	21,276,000	4.95	14.2
1881 . .	19,184,000	3.36	11.4
1888 . .	20,100,000	2.93	10.5

In 1883 the incidence of British Customs was estimated :—

	Amount Paid by Classes			Total Amount
	Rich	Middle	Working	
	£	£	£	£
Spirits . .	170,000	1,350,000	2,703,000	4,223,000
Wine . . .	455,000	885,000	26,000	1,366,000
Tea . . .	160,000	1,288,000	2,526,000	3,974,000
Coffee . .	11,000	90,000	212,000	313,000
Fruits . .	35,000	285,000	190,000	510,000
Tobacco, &c.	370,000	2,890,000	5,620,000	8,890,000
Total .	1,201,000	6,808,000	11,267,090	19,276,000

The incidence per head on each class was as follows :—

	Rich			Middle			Working			Total		
	£	s.	d.	£	s.	d.	£	s.	d.	£	s.	d.
Spirits . .	0	2	11	0	2	10	0	2	3	0	2	5
Wine . . .	0	7	10	0	1	10		...		0	0	10
Tea . . .	0	2	9	0	2	9	0	2	1	0	2	3
Coffee . .	0	0	2	0	0	2	0	0	2	0	0	2
Fruits. . .	0	0	7	0	0	7	0	0	2	0	0	3
Tobacco, &c.	0	6	5	0	5	6	0	5	0	0	5	5
Total .	1	0	8	0	13	8	0	9	8	0	11	4

The working classes form 69 per cent., the middle class 28 per cent., and the upper class 3 per cent. of the population of the United Kingdom, as appears from the Probate returns (1877).

The duties *ad valorem* on English cotton goods in foreign countries in 1884 were :—

	Per Cent.		Per Cent.
China, Guiana . . .	5	Belgium, Greece . .	15
India, Queensland . .	5	Holland, New Zealand	15
Turkey	7	Austria	18
Cape, Feejee. . . .	10	Canada	20
Tasmania, S. Australia	10	Victoria, Chili . . .	25
Uruguay, W. Indies .	12	Brazil	30
Newfoundland . . .	13	Argentine Republic .	40

The following table shows the British tariff at various epochs :—

DUTIES EXPRESSED IN SHILLINGS

	1787	1819	1834	1888
Bacon, cwt. . . .	47	56	28	...
Books ,, . . .	20	100	100	...
Butter ,, . . .	2½	20	20	...
Cheese ,, . . .	1½	10	10	...
Cocoa ,, . . .	240	280	19	9
Coffee ,, . . .	224	280	140	14
Cotton ,, . . .	9	9	3	...
Eggs ,, . . .	3	6	6	...
Paper ,, . . .	?	94	28	...
Potatoes,, . . .	4	2	2	...
Rice ,, . . .	7	15	15	...
Soap ,, . . .	44	90	90	...
Spirits, gallon . . .	6	22	22	10
Sugar, cwt. . . .	27	63	63	...
Tallow ,, . . .	...	3	1	...
Tea ,, . . .	45	224	240	56
Tobacco ,, . . .	392	448	784	392
Wine, gallon . . .	5	14	5½	1
Wool, cwt. . . .	...	56	9	...

Blanks in the above table signify duty-free. Grain was subject to import-dues on a sliding scale, according to market prices in Great Britain, down to 1846.

The customs revenue of China in 1888 reached 6 millions sterling.

D.

DAIRY

The subjoined table shows approximately the number of milch cows and the dairy products of various countries. English cows average 400 gallons of milk yearly, and the butter produce of a good cow is about 140 lbs. In Holland each cow gives about 80 lbs. of butter, and 180 lbs. cheese. New York cows average 330 lbs. cheese, Canadian 280 lbs., and Parma 300 lbs. It takes a gallon of milk to make a pound of cheese.

	Milch Cows	Tons Butter and Cheese	Value of Butter, Cheese, and Milk
			£
United Kingdom	3,400,000	110,000	31,200,000
France	4,800,000	160,000	47,000,000
Germany . . .	6,800,000	200,000	55,300,000
Russia	7,900,000	220,000	47,700,000
Austria	4,600,000	130,000	34,500,000
Italy	1,600,000	50,000	14,400,000
Spain . . .	1,000,000	30,000	9,300,000
Portugal . . .	200,000	6,000	1,900,000
Sweden . . .	800,000	40,000	7,000,000
Norway . . .	400,000	10,000	3,000,000
Denmark . . .	900,000	60,000	6,400,000
Holland . . .	900,000	80,000	9,500,000
Belgium . . .	600,000	30,000	5,000,000
Switzerland . .	400,000	40,000	4,800,000
Roumania . . .	1,200,000	20,000	4,800,000
Servia	300,000	10,000	2,000,000
Turkey . . .	300,000	10,000	2,000,000
Europe	36,100,000	1,206,000	285,800,000
United States .	15,900,000	610,000	79,000,000
Canada . . .	1,300,000	100,000	7,500,000
Australia . . .	600,000	30,000	4,000,000
Total . .	53,900,000	1,946,000	376,300,000

The following table shows approximately the consumption of butter and cheese in various countries :—

	Consumption, Tons			Lbs. per Inhab.
	Native	Imported	Total	
U. Kingdom .	110,000	218,000	328,000	19
France . . .	145,000	...	145,000	8
Germany . .	185,000	...	185,000	8
Russia . . .	210,000	...	210,000	5
Austria . . .	130,000	...	130,000	7
Italy	50,000	10,000	60,000	4
Spain . . .	30,000	...	30,000	3
Portugal . .	6,000	1,000	7,000	3
Sweden . . .	25,000	...	25,000	11
Norway . .	10,000	3,000	13,000	14
Denmark . .	20,000	...	20,000	22
Holland . .	30,000	...	30,000	15
Belgium . .	30,000	10,000	40,000	15
Switzerland .	15,000	...	15,000	11
Roumania, &c.	40,000	...	40,000	9
Europe . . .	1,036,000	242,000	1,278,000	9
United States	560,000	...	560,000	20
Canada . . .	50,000	...	50,000	22
Australia . .	30,000	...	30,000	17
Total .	1,676,000	242,000	1,918,000	11

UNITED KINGDOM

The annual production of milk in the United Kingdom exceeds 400 gallons per cow, say 1400 million gallons, of which 400 millions are used for making butter and cheese, 600 millions as milk for the table at an average of 16 gallons per inhabitant, and 400 millions in fattening calves, &c. The consumption in London is only a little over 6 gallons per inhabitant. At the churning competition of England in 1889 the average production of butter was 4 per cent., that is 2½ gallons milk to one pound of butter.

The consumption of dairy products in the United Kingdom has been approximately as follows:—

Year	Native Butter and Cheese, Tons	Tons Imported			Total Con- sumption	Lbs. per Inhabitant
		Butter	Cheese	Total		
1850	90,000	15,000	15,000	30,000	120,000	10
1860	95,000	37,000	26,000	63,000	158,000	12
1870	100,000	52,000	46,000	98,000	198,000	14
1880	105,000	104,000	79,000	183,000	288,000	18
1889	110,000	136,000	82,000	218,000	328,000	19

The item of imported butter in 1889 was made up of 83,000 tons real butter and 53,000 tons margarine.

A farm in Cheshire of fifty milch cows has been found to produce 9½ tons of cheese, equal to 420 lbs. per cow, valued at £750 sterling. The farm covered 200 acres, of which 15 were under wheat, and the farmer's balance-sheet was as follows:—

	Payments, £		Receipts, £
Rent	400	Cheese . .	750
Taxes	60	Pigs . . .	150
Labour (7 hands)	296	Sheep . .	133
Sundries . . .	268	Wheat . .	180
Total . .	1,024	Total .	1,213

This left the farmer a balance of £189 to support his family.

FRANCE

In 1888 the production of milk reached 1660 million gallons, or about 350 per cow. French economists think that about 40 per cent., say 660 million gallons, is used for making butter and cheese, the product of which would be about 360 million lbs. or 160,000 tons. The value of milk is officially put down at 7d. per gallon.

UNITED STATES

The following table shows the official returns of butter and cheese for various years, and an estimate for 1890:—

Year	Milch Cows	Cheese, Tons	Butter, Tons	Total Product	Con- sumed	Lbs. per Inhab.
1850	6,400,000	47,000	138,000	185,000	178,000	16
1860	8,600,000	46,000	205,000	251,000	237,000	17
1870	10,100,000	68,000	228,000	296,000	268,000	15
1880	12,030,000	121,000	347,000	468,000	394,000	17
1890	15,950,000	160,000	450,000	610,000	560,000	20

DEATHS

The death-rates per 1000 inhabitants yearly were:—

	1861–70	1871–80
England	22.6	21.3
Scotland	22.1	21.8
Ireland	16.8	18.3
United Kingdom . .	21.4	21.0
France	22.9	24.3
Germany	...	27.1
Austria Proper . .	30.4	31.2
Hungary	38.7	40.1
Italy	30.1	29.7
Spain	...	29.7
Belgium	22.8	22.6
Holland	24.9	24.3
Denmark	20.1	19.3
Sweden	20.0	18.4
Switzerland . . .	24.0	24.0

The rates in the principal cities (1878–80) were:—

Alexandria .	34.2	Dublin . .	27.1	New York .	26.2
Amsterdam .	23.7	Edinburgh .	20.2	Nottingham .	24.4
Baltimore .	21.1	Geneva . .	21.2	Oldham . .	22.8
Belfast . .	28.2	Glasgow .	25.3	Palermo . .	28.5
Berlin . .	27.6	Hamburg .	24.5	Paris . .	28.6
Birmingham	19.8	Havanna .	45.7	Philadelphia .	20.3
Bombay .	33.7	Hull . . .	23.8	Portsmouth .	19.7
Bordeaux .	26.7	Leeds . .	21.6	Quebec . .	22.9
Boston . .	23.5	Leicester .	21.8	Rio Janeiro .	39.4
Bradford .	21.1	Leipsic . .	26.1	Rome . . .	26.8
Breslau . .	32.5	Liverpool .	26.7	Rotterdam .	23.3
Brighton .	19.0	London . .	21.1	Rouen . .	31.3
Bristol . .	19.6	Lyons . .	24.7	St. Louis .	19.3
Brooklyn .	25.6	Madras . .	38.8	St. Petersburg	51.4
Brussels .	23.9	Madrid . .	37.4	San Francisco	18.1
Bucharest .	24.5	Manchester	25.5	Sheffield . .	21.6
Buda-Pesth .	35.2	Marseilles .	28.0	Stockholm .	24.7
Buenos Ayres	30.1	Mexico . .	30.9	Sunderland .	20.9
Calcutta . .	31.1	Milan . .	30.6	Turin . . .	25.6
Chicago . .	27.2	Montreal .	37.2	Valparaiso .	64.6
Christiania .	18.8	Munich . .	32.8	Venice . .	22.7
Copenhagen	22.1	Naples . .	33.1	Vera Cruz .	70.5
Cork . . .	26.1	Newcastle .	21.8	Vienna . .	29.0
Dresden . .	25.4	New Orleans	22.7	Zurich . . .	25.6

The following table shows the death-rate for ages per 1000 inhabitants:—

	Under 5	5–10	10–25	25–45	45–55	55–65	65–75
England . .	63.6	6.6	5.5	10.2	17.4	31.8	64.3
United States	58.8	10.1	5.4	10.8	17.6	27.2	51.4
France . .	75.6	9.2	8.8	12.7	16.6	28.3	66.3
Prussia . .	...	9.2	6.4	11.5	18.6	33.0	64.5
Austria . .	111.7	9.8	6.6	11.3	21.1	41.5	92.8
Switzerland .	...	8.5	6.3	11.6	19.3	38.4	82.5
Italy . . .	110.6	11.6	7.8	11.7	17.3	33.1	70.1
Spain . . .	106.2	11.7	8.8	12.9	23.8	42.0	95.0
Belgium . .	68.1	12.7	8.1	12.9	19.0	32.3	74.5
Sweden . .	57.6	8.0	4.8	8.2	14.7	27.4	62.6
Medium . .	81.5	9.7	6.8	11.4	18.5	33.5	72.4

Under another classification of ages the *Demografia* (1877) gives as follows:—

	Under 1	1–5	5–15	15–30	30–60	Over 60	General	Period
Norway . .	116	29.1	7.2	6.5	11.0	58.9	18.4	1860–68
Sweden . .	150	31.1	6.9	5.9	12.6	70.0	20.5	1861–70
Denmark . .	150	23.4	7.4	6.8	13.0	71.4	21.6	1860–69
France . .	216	34.7	7.2	8.6	12.9	68.2	22.8	1856–65
England . .	191	36.7	6.7	8.2	15.7	67.9	22.8	1857–66
Belgium . .	186	36.1	7.7	8.5	13.4	79.1	23.3	1851–60
Holland . .	211	36.4	8.0	8.0	15.4	70.1	25.0	1860–68
Prussia . .	220	46.0	7.2	7.0	15.4	72.7	25.8	,,
Bavaria . .	372	39.8	7.4	8.8	17.3	81.5	29.5	,,
Spain . .	226	67.8	8.2	8.2	17.0	95.0	29.6	,,
Italy . .	254	53.7	8.2	8.1	17.4	88.2	30.1	,,
Austria . .	303	40.6	7.3	8.1	17.1	84.0	32.4	,,
Russia . .	312	54.7	9.7	8.6	19.4	78.1	36.8	,,
Scotland . .	157	34.4	7.1	9.3	16.4	67.9	22.3	,,
Portugal .	139	36.0	7.2	6.0	13.5	80.0	...	1860–62

According to the above table the countries which have the highest and the lowest death-rates at various ages are as follow:—

Age, Years	Highest	Lowest
Under 1 . . .	Bavaria	Norway
1–5 . . .	Spain	Denmark
5–15 . . .	Russia	England
15–30 . . .	Scotland	Sweden
30–60 . . .	Russia	Norway
Over 60 . .	Spain	Norway
All ages . .	Russia	Norway

Death-Rate at Certain Ages per 1000

Age	England	Scotland	France	Belgium	Spain	Switzer-land	Austria Proper	Prussia	Sweden	Italy
5	12.5	13.0	11.2	11.4	30.4	13.2	28.3	17.5	15.9	23.3
10	4.3	5.7	5.4	4.3	7.9	4.5	8.5	6.5	6.2	8.0
15	4.1	5.9	5.4	4.6	6.4	4.4	6.2	4.6	4.5	5.9
20	5.5	7.3	7.4	6.4	7.7	6.3	8.7	6.1	5.2	7.8
25	6.9	8.2	9.1	7.7	8.2	7.7	11.6	7.6	6.1	8.8
30	8.2	8.9	9.8	8.6	9.0	8.7	11.5	9.7	6.8	8.8
35	10.2	10.4	10.1	9.4	10.1	10.1	11.4	10.7	7.4	9.7
40	11.9	11.6	11.1	11.1	12.3	11.9	14.1	10.9	8.7	10.4
45	14.7	14.5	12.6	12.4	14.1	14.0	16.2	11.6	9.9	12.9
50	17.0	16.9	15.5	16.3	16.3	17.5	22.3	18.0	13.0	15.4
55	24.4	23.9	20.1	19.4	18.0	24.4	27.1	24.3	15.5	22.0
60	30.4	29.6	28.3	30.5	31.1	36.1	40.9	37.1	24.9	29.8
65	47.2	45.3	41.5	39.4	41.6	52.3	52.0	50.1	32.3	48.2
70	60.7	57.9	62.9	66.6	70.4	79.4	84.3	80.3	56.9	71.8
75	96.7	92.9	92.2	88.4	93.5	116.2	110.2	107.1	76.5	112.6
80	125.5	121.0	135.6	143.5	124.1	167.5	172.9	151.1	130.0	146.4

The percentage of death at various ages was as follows :—

Age	France	Prussia	Austria Pr.	Italy	Switzerland	Belgium	Holland	Sweden	Brussels
	1866–72	1868–73	1868–74	1872–74	1873–74	1865–74	1870–73	1865–73	...
Under 1 year .	18.5	21.1	32.4	26.4	26.3	20.2	29.1	21.3	21.3
1–5 . . .	11.0	24.5	16.1	21.3	7.7	16.7	15.7	13.6	18.1
5–10 . . .	3.2	4.1	4.2	4.5	2.5	4.7	3.9	4.7	3.7
10–15 . . .	1.8	1.9	1.9	2.1	1.6	2.1	2.2	2.1	1.9
15–20 . . .	2.6	2.3	2.1	2.2	2.1	2.4	2.3	2.2	2.0
20–30 . . .	7.7	5.7	5.4	5.6	5.8	6.3	5.6	5.3 }	17.1
30–40 . . .	6.5	6.1	5.7	5.2	6.5	6.1	5.9	5.9 }	
40–50 . . .	6.9	6.8	6.3	5.5	7.3	6.3	6.0	7.2	8.9
50–60 . . .	8.7	7.9	7.8	6.5	9.4	7.2	6.8	8.4	8.7
60–70 . . .	12.6	9.5	8.7	8.8	13.7	10.8	8.8	10.8	8.8
70–80 . . .	13.9	7.5	6.7	8.1	12.5	11.4	9.6	12.6 }	9.5
80–90 . . .	6.0	2.4	2.4	3.4	4.4	5.2	3.8	5.4 }	
Over 90 . .	0.6	0.2	0.3	0.4	0.3	0.6	0.3	0.5	...
Total .	100.0	100.0	100.0	100.0	100.0	100.0	100.0	100.0	100.0

The ratio of deaths in quarters of the year was :—

	March 31st	June 30th	Sept. 30th	Dec. 31st	Year
Amsterdam	298	235	223	244	1,000
Berlin	216	252	325	207	1,000
Birmingham	306	224	235	235	1,000
Bombay	288	257	233	222	1,000
Buda-Pesth	272	278	238	212	1,000
Calcutta	254	233	207	306	1,000
Christiania . . .	260	220	237	283	1,000
Dublin	318	224	200	258	1,000
Edinburgh	294	240	222	244	1,000
Florence	292	242	233	233	1,000
Glasgow	319	245	216	220	1,000
Hamburg	294	232	252	222	1,000
Liverpool	303	225	232	240	1,000
London	287	231	226	256	1,000
Manchester	297	237	224	242	1,000
Milan	308	295	231	166	1,000
Munich	282	261	231	225	1,000
Naples	306	245	228	221	1,000
New York	258	228	301	213	1,000
Paris	272	266	229	233	1,000
Philadelphia	262	253	270	215	1,000
Rome	286	182	246	286	1,000
Turin	322	250	205	223	1,000
Vienna	280	277	304	239	1,000

Deaths according to seasons * are as follows :—

	Spring	Summer	Autumn	Winter	Total
Algiers	142	235	353	270	1,000
Amsterdam	260	227	241	272	1,000
Austria	288	205	227	280	1,000
Bagdad	270	213	257	260	1,000
Belgium	279	218	220	283	1,000
Berlin	250	239	248	263	1,000
Biscay	223	206	238	333	1,000
Brussels	274	235	225	266	1,000
Constantinople . . .	263	238	231	268	1,000
Denmark	288	230	215	267	1,000
England	275	240	238	247	1,000
France	260	227	243	270	1,000
Geneva	265	218	240	277	1,000
Germany	277	230	237	256	1,000
Holland	220	227	315	238	1,000
Iceland	201	339	252	208	1,000
Italy	230	257	253	260	1,000
Lisbon	240	239	250	271	1,000
London	250	237	241	272	1,000
Norway	288	219	223	270	1,000
Paris	312	262	216	210	1,000
Rome	204	228	262	306	1,000
St. Petersburg . . .	294	264	216	226	1,000
Scotland	275	228	220	277	1,000
Sicily	194	312	257	237	1,000
Sweden	283	215	222	280	1,000
Switzerland	271	238	216	275	1,000

* In the following table Spring is supposed to begin March 1st, Summer June 1st, Autumn September 1st, and Winter December 1st.

The ratio according to months, taking the year as 1200, are :—

Month	London	France	Germany	Sweden	Denmark	Scotland	Belgium	Italy	Greece	Finland
January . . .	103	114	104	114	113	112	119	109	105	96
February . . .	99	112	100	115	106	114	122	106	102	105
March . . .	124	110	113	116	119	113	121	100	91	114
April . . .	91	107	109	115	114	111	112	94	90	129
May . . .	84	95	110	108	113	105	101	81	85	138
June . . .	99	88	94	92	96	96	93	85	97	115
July . . .	89	87	94	83	91	90	84	108	107	95
August . . .	95	97	89	82	88	87	85	115	105	85
September . . .	113	102	94	82	83	84	89	106	104	76
October . . .	84	96	92	87	86	85	86	99	106	78
November . . .	92	94	98	98	89	95	89	99	103	83
December . . .	127	98	103	108	102	108	99	98	105	86
Year	1,200	1,200	1,200	1,200	1,200	1,200	1,200	1,200	1,200	1,200

Month	Amster-dam	Lisbon	Berlin	St. Peters-burg	Dantzic	Paris Hospital	Geneva	Algiers	Rome	Brussels
January	111	113	117	90	98	82	113	118	113	107
February	109	101	114	97	103	90	112	78	101	113
March	114	99	100	104	96	125	112	77	91	114
April	105	100	101	122	116	135	111	50	76	108
May	93	90	100	127	111	114	94	43	77	106
June	93	91	95	115	101	118	89	61	81	99
July	94	99	93	102	93	107	84	101	99	96
August	85	97	99	99	91	90	89	121	94	87
September	96	100	100	91	94	102	98	126	90	85
October	96	101	94	82	98	81	94	151	107	90
November	97	99	103	86	103	76	96	146	118	95
December	107	110	84	85	96	80	108	128	153	100
Year	1,200	1,200	1,200	1,200	1,200	1,200	1,200	1,200	1,200	1,200

Wappaeus gives the following table on the subject :—

Month	Sardinia 1828–37	Bavaria 1844–51	Saxony 1847–59	Belgium 1841–50	Holland 1840–49	Denmark 1845–54	Norway 1845–55	Sweden 1851–55	France 1831–40
January . .	114	114	115	125	119	108	118	99	107
February . .	116	123	103	122	109	111	114	115	111
March . .	107	128	105	121	110	118	114	121	123
April . .	105	119	106	114	102	118	118	118	114
May . .	86	98	104	101	97	111	113	107	97
June . .	84	88	92	96	94	97	95	85	87
July . .	91	83	88	85	91	97	84	76	84
August . .	108	86	97	84	95	88	84	82	92
September . .	102	88	98	87	99	80	88	102	102
October . .	91	88	92	83	91	83	88	95	91
November . .	98	92	99	85	91	91	92	101	84
December . .	98	93	101	97	102	98	92	99	108
Year . . .	1,200	1,200	1,200	1,200	1,200	1,200	1,200	1,200	1,200

The death-rate distinguishing married and single shows thus :—

DEATHS YEARLY PER 10,000 OF EACH CLASS

Men

Age	France, 1856–65 Single	France, 1856–65 Married	Belgium, 1851–60 Single	Belgium, 1851–60 Married	Holland, 1850–59 Single	Holland, 1850–59 Married	Average Single	Average Married
15–20	69	513	64	119	64	121	66	251
20–30	117	75	88	82	106	76	104	78
31–40	124	71	96	80	144	102	121	84
41–50	180	105	144	118	220	150	181	124
51–60	288	186	225	197	365	258	293	214
61–70	515	385	430	406	605	465	517	418
71–80	990	902	840	870	1,110	940	980	903

Women

Age	France, 1856–65		Belgium, 1851–60		Holland, 1850–59		Average	
	Single	Married	Single	Married	Single	Married	Single	Married
15–20	75	119	84	132	67	140	75	130
20–30	86	95	83	126	78	126	82	115
31–40	104	94	91	117	115	143	103	118
41–50	145	104	122	119	160	141	142	121
51–60	240	167	212	175	280	200	244	181
61–70	490	380	440	355	525	415	485	383
71–80	1,150	905	920	750	1,030	870	1,033	842

The general rates for single and married of both sexes show thus :—

Age	Scotland		France		Belgium		Holland		Average	
	Single	Married	Single	Married	Single	Married	Single	Married	Single	Married
15–20	...	...	72	316	74	126	65	130	70	191
20–30 :	136	72	101	85	86	104	92	101	104	90
31–40	160	102	114	82	93	99	130	122	124	101
41–50	198	155	162	105	133	119	190	145	171	131
51–60	274	228	264	176	218	186	322	230	270	205
61–70	524	440	502	382	435	380	565	440	506	410
71–80	...	...	1,070	903	880	810	1,070	905	1,007	873

The above does not include widowed persons.

The deaths according to sex for ten years ending 1874 were :—

Deaths of Males to 100 Females

England . .	107	Austria . .	107	Hungary .	108
France . .	107	Sweden . .	107	Switzerland .	108
Prussia . .	107	Holland . .	104	Italy . . .	106
Bavaria . .	107	Belgium . .	106	Average . .	106

The following table shows the percentage of deaths according to condition for ten years ending 1874 :—

	France	Prussia	Belgium	Holland	Sweden	Italy
Single	505	641	594	628	552	652
Married . . .	305	231	250	232	267	216
Widowed . .	190	128	156	140	181	132
Total . .	1,000	1,000	1,000	1,000	1,000	1,000

According to Dr. Gairdner, overcrowding increases the death-rate notably, viz. :—

Population per Square Mile	Deaths per 1000 Inhabitants Yearly
100–150	16
150–300	20
Over 300	24

The following table shows death-rate with distinction of sex and age :—

Age	Per 10,000 of each Class					
	France, 1857–65		Belgium, 1856		Sweden, 1861–70	
	Males	Females	Males	Females	Males	Females
1–5	348	344	237	250	235	225
5–10	85	89	73	72	54	49
10–20	60	69	77	92	53	46
20–30	96	91	129	110	75	62
30–40	87	98	168	154	107	90
40–50	123	115	177	195	162	122
50–60	208	186	298	225	280	214
60–70	427	410	660	575	630	530
70–80	1,000	1,000	1,210	1,170	1,310	1,150

The following table was published about 1870, showing the death-rate of clergymen in various countries :—

	Age		
	25–45	45–65	25–65
Church of England	5.4	15.8	10.1
Catholic priests, English . .	9.7	26.9	15.7
German Protestant clergy . .	5.8	20.0	11.8
Population of Germany . . .	9.7	25.9	16.8
Austrian Catholic priests . .	8.0	21.8	15.2
Austrian Greek clergy . . .	8.7	22.1	15.1
English male population . .	11.5	25.2	18.4

It is observed in most countries that the death-rate among the poor is much heavier than in the classes of easy fortune. Professor Conrad's table is as follows :—

	Ratio of Deaths		
	Affluent	Middle	Working
Still-born	28	53	53
0–1 year	118	240	206
1–5 years	95	192	220
5–15 ,, ...	48	49	58
15–20 ,, ...	35	24	21
20–30 ,, ...	86	63	64
30–60 ,, ...	247	204	222
Over 60 years	343	175	156
Total . . .	1,000	1,000	1,000

Infant Mortality

The annual death-rate of infants under twelve months was in the years 1876–80 as follows :—

Per 1000 Living

England . .	145	Bavaria . .	298	Italy . . .	209
France . .	163	Wurtemburg	302	Switzerland .	189
Prussia . .	205	Austria . .	249	Sweden . .	126

M

The influence of season on the death-rate of infants is shown in the ratio of deaths thus :—

	Deaths under Two Years of Age							
	Holland	Belgium	Nice	Genoa	Naples	Palermo	Algiers	Bagdad
Spring	246	279	226	224	230	202	205	212
Summer	235	203	307	242	307	318	278	353
Autumn	254	216	222	244	209	241	285	222
Winter	265	302	245	290	254	239	232	213
Total . .	1,000	1,000	1,000	1,000	1,000	1,000	1,000	1,000

	Deaths under Thirty Days				
	Spring	Summer	Autumn	Winter	Year
Austria . .	250	246	255	249	1,000
Belgium . .	259	193	246	302	1,000
France . .	239	225	267	269	1,000
Florence .	253	183	182	382	1,000
Geneva . .	280	177	210	333	1,000
Genoa . .	253	169	214	364	1,000
Holland . .	246	212	248	294	1,000
Hungary .	231	216	271	282	1,000
Levant . .	285	162	178	375	1,000
Milan . .	231	214	225	330	1,000
Naples . .	263	202	187	348	1,000
Sicily . . .	228	205	240	328	1,000

According to Lombard and other authorities, deaths of children under five form the following proportions in 1000 deaths of all ages :—

France . . .	295	Prussia . . . 456
Switzerland . .	340	Italy 477
Sweden . .	349	Austria . . . 485
Belgium . .	369	Russia . . . 554
Holland . .	448	

The following table shows how many of 1000 infants born died in each of the first five years of life :—

Period	1st Year	2nd Year	3rd Year	4th Year	5th Year	Total	Number Surviving
England, 1866–75 . .	154	54	24	16	11	259	741
Italy, „ . .	223	91	38	26	19	397	603
Austria prop.„ . .	259	56	32	21	17	385	615
Belgium, „ . .	174	53	29	17	12	285	715
Prussia, „ . .	218	56	29	18	13	534	666
Sweden, „ . .	137	42	21	15	12	227	773
Scotland, 1876–80 . .	123	55	28	19	14	239	761
Switzerland, „ . .	190	32	14	9	7	252	748
Bavaria, 1860–69 . .	324	40	19	13	10	406	594

According to the latest tables published, the number of children of 1000 born who live to complete their fifth year is as follows :—*

In		In		In	
Russia . . .	425	Prussia . .	684	England . .	762
Spain . .	571	Switzerland .	748	Scotland . .	780
Austria . .	614	France. . .	751	Sweden . .	783
Bavaria . .	622	Denmark . .	755	Ireland . .	837
Italy . . .	632	Belgium . .	756	Norway . .	838

The death-rate of illegitimate children is 55 per cent. extra in Switzerland, and 100 per cent. in France over the normal rate. In Paris it is observed that for 100 children who die if suckled by the mother, 220 die if given out to nurse ; also that 230 spoon-fed children die for 100

* This table, except as regards Ireland and Russia, is for the years 1881-83. Brun makes the number of children in Russia who complete their fifth year 460 per thousand ; later writers only 425.

reared at the breast. The death-rate of foundlings in the first year was as follows : Marseilles, 38 ; St. Petersburg, 40 ; Lyons, 42 ; Paris, 57 per cent.

The following table from the archives of 1881 shows the deaths of infants at Rome and Berlin during the years 1877–80 :—

	Die per 1000 Born			
At	Under 30 Days		Under 12 Months	
	Lawful	Illegitimate	Lawful	Illegitimate
Rome . .	52	164	174	329
Berlin . .	57	262	133	452

The following table is from Sir Lyon Playfair and the Swedish returns, showing how many of 1000 infants born in each class will survive to complete their fifth year :—

Condition	England	Sweden	Medium
Rich	820	750	785
Middle class. . .	640	630	635
Poor	450	560	505

Dr. Bianco gives similar tables for Turin.

According to Drysdale, the death-rate of infants in 1889 was 11 per cent. in the wealthy parishes of London, and 38 per cent. among the poor of the East End.

DEATHS FROM VIOLENCE

The following table was published in 1840 :—

PER MILLION INHABITANTS YEARLY

Period	Country	Suicides	Accidents, &c.	Total Violent Deaths
1810–30	Sweden . .	51	626	677
1820–34	Prussia . .	90	396	486
1838–39	England .	64	682	746
1839	France . .	81	187	268

In or about the year 1880 the number of violent deaths in various countries was as follows :—

	Number	Ratio per 1000 Deaths
United Kingdom . .	23,822	33.1
France	16,373	19.7
Germany	24,592	21.4
Russia	18,500	7.4
Austria proper . .	10,150	16.0
Italy	6,656	8.3
Spain	4,700	9.6
Switzerland . . .	2,550	38.2
Belgium	2,577	22.0
Denmark	1,054	28.1
Sweden	2,740	31.6
Norway	1,290	37.7
Europe	115,004	16.2
United States . . .	22,740	41.1

The following table of violent deaths was published in 1865 :—

	Period	No. per Million Inhabitants per Annum	Per 1000 Deaths			Females to 100 Males
			Males	Females	General	
England	1850–64	692	28	10	19	36
Belgium	1840–49	332	22	7	14	33
Norway	1851–55	679	...	...	40	...
Sweden	1856–60	420	32	9	21	27
United States . . .	1860	575	60	30	46	50
France	1854–60	450	26	6	16	22
Bavaria	1857–61	236	12	4	8	32
Hanover	1852–57	396	27	7	17	26
Prussia	1851–60	407	22	7	15	29
Saxony	1852–58	298	13	3	8	25

The following table was published in 1875 :—

	Period	Annual Average				Per Million Inhabitants	Per 1000 Deaths
		Accidents	Murders	Suicides	Total		
England	1865–73	15,083	413	1,470	16,966	763	34.2
Italy	1865–74	6,704	2,165	801	9,670	370	12.3
Prussia	1865–73	10,430	414	3,211	14,055	601	21.4
Bavaria	1868–74	1,617	157	436	2,210	450	14.4
Austria proper . . .	1866–74	6,575	698	1,610	8,883	426	13.5
Belgium	1870–74	1,974	82	364	2,420	466	20.1
Sweden	1865–73	2,100	88	342	2,530	603	32.0

The ratio of violent deaths was stated to be :—

	England	Italy	Prussia	Bavaria	Austria	Belgium	Sweden	Seven Countries
Accidents	88.7	69.4	74.1	73.2	74.1	81.5	83.0	78.5
Murders	2.5	22.3	2.9	7.0	7.8	3.4	3.5	7.1
Suicides	8.8	8.3	23.0	19.8	18.1	15.1	13.5	14.4
Total .	100.0	100.0	100.0	100.0	100.0	100.0	100.0	100.0

If we take the returns of the United Kingdom for 1886 and the latest information regarding other countries, estimating the United States with its actual population at the latest ascertained ratios, we can have a conspectus of all the violent deaths approximately that occur every year. Hungary and Holland are missing, and the number of murders in Russia, Denmark, and Norway is unknown. The table stands thus :—

	Number Yearly				Per Million Inhabitants	Per 10,000 Deaths	Percentage of Males in 100 Violent Deaths
	Accidents	Suicides	Murders	Total			
England	14,830	2,254	311	17,414	622	324	72
Scotland	2,164	261	19	2,444	614	328	71
Ireland	1,611	116	131	1,860	380	207	70
United Kingdom . .	18,605	2,631	461	21,718	590	310	71
France	13,205	7,070	701	20,976	540	250	75
Germany	17,800	8,480	610	26,890	570	224	76
Austria proper . . .	6,433	3,543	663	10,639	450	163	74
Italy	5,430	1,397	2,902	9,729	324	120	75
Russia	16,800	2,520	...	19,320	220	70	...
Spain	3,670	255	1,330	5,255	280	115	80
Belgium	2,039	441	86	2,566	430	214	82
Sweden	2,210	347	105	2,662	602	356	73
Denmark	640	516	...	1,156	578	290	...
Norway	1,360	146	...	1,506	753	480	...
Switzerland . . .	1,400	650	88	2,138	713	356	...
Europe	89,592	27,996	6,946	124,555	410	168	...
United States . . .	36,000	2,100	2,462	40,562	620	370	...
Total . .	125,592	30,096	9,408	165,117	450	190	...

The ratio of accidental deaths yearly per million inhabitants in or about 1880 was as follows :—

	Number per Million Inhabitants	Ratio of Sexes		Percentage of Accidental Deaths		Accidental in 10,000 Deaths
		Male	Female	Drowned	Burnt	
England .	670	74	26	22	9	303
France . .	280	78	22	41	...	130
Prussia . .	407	76	24	...	...	150
Saxony . .	298	76	24	...	...	...
Bavaria .	236	75	25	...	...	108
Hanover .	396	79	21	...	...	...
Austria . .	258	73	27	...	...	98
Switzerland	605	...	...	40	4	280
Italy . .	181	75	25	...	...	85
Spain . .	202	80	20	24	3	70
Belgium .	330	82	18	27	...	163
Denmark .	232	...	...	60	2	116
Sweden .	479	73	27	54	5	260
Norway .	681	...	...	75	4	340
Finland .	589	...	...	54	...	...
Russia . .	201	...	....	53	6	65
U. States .	623	67	33	16	24	340
New York .	668	...	...	...	...	270
London .	665	...	...	...	...:	315
Paris . .	682	...	...	...	...	240

DEATHS FROM ALCOHOL

The following is a table of deaths from drink :—

	Per Annum	Per 1000 Deaths		Per Annum	Per 1000 Deaths
England . .	1,405	2.60	Italy . . .	709	0.85
Scotland . .	230	3.29	Switzerland .	244	3.81
Ireland . . .	280	2.78	Sweden . .	502	6.25
France . . .	448	0.54	Norway . .	72	2.36
Belgium . .	456	3.83	New York .	324	12.08

Lombard's table on deaths from drink will be found under *Diseases :*—

The returns of sickness and death from drink in armies is as follows :—

In the French army 33 men per million die yearly of drink. In the American war, 1861–63, deaths from drink were 350 per million, and 15 in 10,000 were sent to hospital for drink. In the British army the sick and deaths from this cause are :—

Station	*Sick* per 10,000		*Deaths* per 100,000
United Kingdom .	. 64	...	13
Mediterranean .	. 130	...	18
Halifax . . .	. 200	...	70
West Indies . .	. 400	...	138
Trinidad . .	. 530	...	290
Demerara . .	. 850	...	560

DEATH-RATES OF ARMIES

Army death-rates per 10,000 men yearly, not including killed in war, are shown as follows :—

Army	*Date*		*Per* 10,000
British . .	. 1879–80	...	67
French . .	. 1872–74	...	87
German . .	. 1878	...	58
Russian . .	. 1871–74	...	147
Austrian . .	. 1870–73	...	153
Italian . .	. 1870–76	...	116
Belgian . .	. 1870–74	...	107
Portuguese .	. 1861–67	...	127

The rates for the United Kingdom in later years compare with those of 1830–40 as follows :—

Deaths Yearly per 10,000

	1830–1840	1879–80	1887
Cavalry . . .	153	52	43
Infantry . . .	155	65	46

The death-rate among our troops before Dr. Farr's barrack reforms was enormous, the averages for the years 1818–40 being as follows per 10,000 men :—

Great Britain	. 159	Mauritius	. . . 305
Australia	. 141	Madras .	. . . 520
Cape .	. 155	Ceylon .	. . . 570
Canada .	. 212	Bengal .	. . . 630
Gibraltar	. 221	Jamaica	. . 1430
Corfu .	. 283	Sierra Leone	. 4830

The rates in the United Kingdom in 1879–80 were as follows per 10,000 :—

Station		*Arm*	
Ireland . . .	. 65	Cavalry . . .	. 52
England . . .	. 65	Engineers . .	. 63
Scotland . . .	. 78	Infantry . . .	. 65
United Kingdom .	. 67	Artillery . .	. 72

The improved condition of troops in England is shown by the returns for the foot-guards thus :—

Deaths per 10,000

	1858		1875
Fever . . .	. 25	...	4
Phthisis . .	. 125	...	17
Various . .	. 54	...	56
Total .	. 204		77

On foreign service the death-rates have declined per 10,000 thus :—

	1818–36		1875
Gibraltar . .	. 214	...	55
India . .	. 690	....	175

The death-rates of the French army in the years 1872–77 were :—

Per 10,000 *Men*

Engineers . .	60	Artillery . .	106	Under 20 . .	54
Infantry . .	95	Cavalry . .	114	20–26 . . .	103
Zouaves . .	106	Turcos . .	177	26–36 . . .	71

The French army, according to a report in 1867, showed the following ratios :—

Years of Service	Composition of Force	Ratio of Deaths	Annual Death-Rate per 1000 Men
Under 1 .	9.6	9.7	10.1
1–4 . . .	19.3	21.3	12.0
4–6 . . .	19.0	21.0	11.2
6–8 . . .	16.4	14.0	8.6
8–11 . .	12.5	9.8	7.8
11–14 . .	10.5	11.0	10.4
Over 14 .	12.7	13.2	10.4
	100.0	100.0	100.0

It appears the mortality is heaviest from the first to the end of the fifth year, and lightest from the sixth to the end of the tenth year. The death-rate has declined, viz. :—

1862–69 .	.	.	.	.	. 11.5
1872–77 .	.	.	.	.	. 9.5

The ratio in Algeria is usually double what it is in France. The Prussian army in 1872 had a death-rate of 7.2 per 1000, but in 1878 the rate for the whole German army had been brought down to 5.8. The Austrian, moreover, which averaged 15.3 in the years 1870–73, showed only 9 per thousand in 1878.

The Italian army likewise shows improvement, viz. :—

1860–70	13.8
1870–76	11.6

In Russia the army death-rate has been reduced by one-half, viz. :—

Arm	1841–52	1857–61
Infantry . . .	42.0	21.0
Cavalry . . .	23.0	14.0
Artillery . . .	27.0	15.0
General rate . .	38.0	19.0

ENGLAND AND WALES

The death-rate of England and Wales showed thus :—

Age	Death-Rate per 1000 Inhabitants per Annum			
	1841–50	1851–60	1861–70	1871–80
Under 5	66.2	68.0	68.6	63.5
5–20	7.3	7.2	6.3	5.3
20–35	9.8	9.3	9.0	8.1
35–55	15.1	14.6	15.2	15.3
55–65	30.1	29.1	30.5	32.0
65–75	64.0	62.0	63.0	65.0

Age	Males			Females		
	1841–60	1861–80	1881–85	1841–60	1861–80	1881–85
0–5	72.0	71.0	59.6	62.1	61.1	59.5
5–10	8.8	7.5	5.8	8.6	7.1	5.6
10–15	5.0	4.2	3.2	5.2	4.2	3.3
15–20	6.9	5.8	4.6	7.6	6.2	4.7
20–25	9.2	8.0	6.0	8.8	7.4	5.9
25–35	9.8	9.6	8.2	10.2	9.2	7.9
35–45	12.7	13.7	12.7	12.6	11.8	10.9
45–55	18.2	19.4	19.4	15.7	15.5	15.2
55–65	31.4	33.9	33.6	27.8	28.4	27.8
65–75	66.5	67.8	68.8	59.9	59.9	59.5
75–85	147.4	147.4	144.6	135.2	134.0	129.4

Period	Per 1000 Inhabitants per Annum		
	Male	Female	Total Pop.
1841–50 . . .	23.1	21.6	22.4
1851–60 . . .	23.1	21.4	22.3
1861–70 . . .	23.7	21.4	22.6
1871–80 . . .	22.6	20.1	21.3
1881–85 . . .	20.4	18.2	19.3

Neison gives the following death-rate per annum for 1000 persons between the ages of 25 and 65 :—

Ladies' maids . . .	8.0	Coachmen	18.4
Protestant clergy . .	10.6	Surgeons	19.1
Barristers	11.9	Apothecaries . . .	19.1
Grooms	12.6	Wine merchants . .	25.0
Physicians	12.9	Innkeepers	27.0
Valets	16.7	Cabdrivers	26.6
Attorneys	16.8	All England	18.0
Catholic priests . . .	18.3		

The total of deaths in 18 years ending 1830 was :—

Males .	.	.	1,996,200
Females .	.	.	1,942,300
Total	.	.	3,938,500

The annual death-rate from 1818 to 1824 was 20.3.

The ratio of all deaths in England for 18 years ending 1830 and that for 1886 were :—

	1813–1830				1886		
Age	Males	Females	Total Pop.	Age	Males	Females	Total Pop.
0–1	219	176	198	0–1	272	229	251
1–4	150	145	147	1–5	141	139	140
5–9	44	41	42	5–10	28	28	28
10–19	58	64	61	10–20	36	40	38
20–29	72	84	78	20–35	78	85	82
30–39	62	73	67	35–45	66	66	66
40–49	65	67	66	45–55	78	70	74
50–59	72	68	70	55–65	94	95	95
60–69	91	92	92	65–75	110	122	116
70–79	101	108	105	75–85	78	96	86
80	66	82	74	Over 85	19	30	24
Total	1,000	1,000	1,000	Total	1,000	1,000	1,000

In 1879 the death-rate of able-bodied males was as follows :—

	Death-rate per 1000		Death-rate per 1000
Civilians . . .	10.02	Royal navy . .	8.58
Soldiers . . .	6.66	Merchant navy .	19.10

Of 100 deaths in merchant shipping, 55 are from drowning, 35 from sickness, and 10 from various causes.

Dr. Farr shows the influence of town life on the death-rate of the working classes as follows :—

DEATHS PER 1000 YEARLY

Age	Rural	Urban
35–45	9	12
45–55	12	17
55–65	25	29
65–75	55	68
75–85	148	174
Over	324	418

The distribution of all deaths in the United Kingdom in quarters of the year is as follows :—

Quarter Ending	England	Scotland	Ireland
March 31st . . .	28.0	29.3	30.9
June 30th . . .	24.5	25.0	25.9
September 30th . .	22.4	21.8	20.0
December 31st . .	25.1	23.9	23.2
	100.0	100.0	100.0

The death-rate of London in the early part of the seventeenth century was 70 per thousand, or more than three times what it is at present ; the returns for the healthy years 1606–10 were :—

Quarter Ending	Deaths per 1000 Inhab. per Annum
31st March	56
30th June	60
30th September	84
31st December	80
Year's average	70

The following table shows the number of deaths in London from 1647 to 1829, and those that were violent :—

Period	Total Number of Deaths	Violent Deaths	Ratio per 10,000 Deaths	Number of Violent Deaths Yearly
1647–1700	1,054,000	10,700	102	200
1701–49	1,223,000	12,600	104	257
1750–99	1,044,000	13,600	130	272
1800–29	586,000	9,900	170	330

	1647–1700	1741–49	1750–99	1800–29
Suicide . .	85	162	150	186
Murder . .	65	34	21	17
Executed .	99	56	90	101
Drowned .	327	323	544	520
Burnt . .	40	31	71	96
Various . .	384	394	124	80
Total .	1,000	1,000	1,000	1,000

The following table shows the death-rate of London since 1725 :—

1725–50 . .	39.9	1800–30 . .	33.7	1874–78 . .	22.8
1751–99 . .	38.8	1840–45 . .	24.5	1879–81 . .	21.7

VIOLENT DEATHS IN ENGLAND (1886).

Cause	Males	Females	Total	Per 100,000 of all Deaths
Railways . . .	736	62	798	149
Mines	916	...	916	170
Fire	891	990	1,881	350
Drowned (accidentally) .	2,389	410	2,799	521
Poisoned . . .	213	116	329	61
Cabs, &c. . . .	1,259	213	1,472	273
Fall	1,867	829	2,696	502
Suffocation . .	975	779	1,754	325
Various . . .	1,566	619	2,185	407
Accidental . .	10,812	4,018	14,830	2,758
Suicide	1,694	560	2,254	420
Murder . . .	181	130	311	58
Executed . . .	18	1	19	4
Total . .	12,705	4,709	17,414	3,240

The ratio of sex in violent deaths in late years averaged thus :—

Per Cent.

	Male	Female
England	72.6	27.4
Scotland . . .	73.7	26.3
Ireland	69.7	30.3
United Kingom .	72.5	27.5

A return of accidental deaths in England and Wales for the year 1838 showed at follows :—

Ratio in 10,000 Deaths of each Class		Nature of Accident	
Educated classes . .	29	Fractures . . .	32.9
Tradesmen . . .	51	Drowned . . .	20.9
Servants . . .	95	Burnt . . .	19.2
Labourers . . .	150	Poisoned . . .	3.6
		Scalded . . .	4.0
		Various . . .	19.4
			100.0

The ratios of violent deaths according to age and sex in England were (1871–80) :—

PER MILLION PERSONS YEARLY

Age	Males	Females	General Population
Under 5 . . .	1,300	1,080	1,200
5–15 . . .	670	260	470
16–45 . . .	960	110	540
46–65 . . .	1,340	250	800
66–75 . . .	1,560	600	1,060
Over 75 . . .	2,270	1,740	2,000

The violent deaths of the United Kingdom from 1840 to 1880 were :—

Period	Per 1000 Deaths			
	England	Scotland	Ireland	United Kingdom
1840–60 . .	34.2	32.3	...	...
1861–70 . .	34.5	31.8	24.1	32.7
1871–80 . .	34.3	35.5	21.1	32.6

SCOTLAND

The death-rate per 1000 inhabitants yearly was :—

1855–60 .	. . .	20.8
1861–70 .	. . .	22.0
1871–80 .	. . .	21.8

The death-rate for various professions of persons between 45 and 55 years of age is stated thus :—

Per 1000		Per 1000		Per 1000	
Farmers . .	12	Carpenters . .	17	Beersellers . .	28
Shoemakers .	15	Miners . .	20	Scotchmen . .	19
Grocers . . .	16	Butchers . .	23	Scotchwomen .	16

The rates for age, distinguishing urban from rural, show thus :—

Age	Deaths Yearly per 1000 of each Class				
	Male	Female	General	Urban	Rural
0–1 . . .	154	126	140	159	96
1–5 . . .	31.9	30.7	31.3	37.9	15.6
0–5 . . .	58.9	51.8	55.3	65.5	31.9
5–15 . . .	6.2	6.2	6.2	7.2	3.9
15–30 . .	8.5	7.7	8.1	8.7	7.5
30–60 . .	17.5	14.3	15.9	18.2	10.9
Over 60 . .	208	210	209	167	256

The ratios of deaths at each age were as follows :—

Age	All Scotland				Scotch Cities, 1886	
	1876–85		1886			
	Males	Females	Males	Females	Males	Females
0–1 . .	223	176	226	176	242	193
1–2 . .	84	77	77	70	99	89
2–3 . .	37	36	33	31	42	41
3–4 . .	24	23	20	18	26	24
4–5 . .	17	17	14	14	17	15
Under 5 .	385	329	370	309	426	362
5–10 . .	45	43	41	38	44	44
10–15 . .	25	26	25	25	23	24
15–20 . .	34	33	31	33	31	31
20–30 . .	67	72	66	71	69	76
30–40 . .	59	66	60	66	70	73
40–50 . .	68	64	72	66	83	76
50–60 . .	79	76	84	81	87	90
60–70 . .	95	101	98	111	87	100
70–80 . .	91	112	96	116	60	82
Over 80 .	52	78	57	84	20	42
Total .	1,000	1,000	1,000	1,000	1,000	1,000

The death-rate in Scotch cities in 1886 was :—

PER 1000 INHABITANTS

Edinburgh .	. .	19.2	Aberdeen .	. .	19.4
Glasgow .	. .	25.1	Greenock .	. .	17.3
Dundee .	. .	18.2	Paisley .	. .	22.7

The death-rate at various dates per 1000 of population was :—

Year	Scotland		Cities		Small Towns		Rural	
	Males	Females	Males	Females	Males	Females	Males	Females
1855	21.6	20.0	29.3	25.8	21.6	19.9	...	...
1860	23.2	21.5	31.7	28.0	23.0	21.3	...	...
1871	22.9	21.5	30.4	27.9	21.4	20.6	16.7	16.0
1880	21.3	19.6	25.8	22.7	20.7	19.7	16.6	16.0
1886	19.1	18.3	21.9	20.2	18.3	17.9	15.9	14.9

The proportion of deaths in cities according to age and season were :—

Age	Spring	Summer	Autumn	Winter
0–5	42.6	42.3	43.1	41.4
5–20	10.6	11.7	10.6	9.1
20–60	29.5	28.9	29.2	30.2
Over 60	17.3	17.1	17.1	19.3
Total	100.0	100.0	100.0	100.0

The number of children of either sex who die in the first five years is as follows :—

	Of 1000 Born of each Class		
	Boys	Girls	Total
1st Year . . .	133	113	123
2nd Year . . .	56	55	55
3rd Year . . .	27	28	28
4th Year . . .	19	19	19
5th Year . . .	13	14	14
Total . .	248	229	239

Violent deaths in 1886 were as follows :—

Cause	Number			Per Million Inhab.	Per 10,000 Deaths
	Males	Females	Total		
Fire . . .	116	116	232	58	31
Drowned .	423	67	490	123	66
Suffocated .	168	140	308	77	41
Poison . .	34	20	54	14	7
Fracture . .	649	173	822	206	110
Various . .	180	78	258	65	35
Accidents .	1,570	594	2,164	543	290
Suicide . .	188	73	261	66	35
Murder . .	8	11	19	5	3
Total . .	1,766	678	2,444	614	328

IRELAND

Deaths at various ages in 1886 were as follows :—

Age	Number			Ratio		
	Males	Females	Total	Males	Females	Total
0–1	5,995	4,765	10,760	138	109	124
1–5	3,620	3,661	7,281	83	83	83
5–10	1,262	1,399	2,661	29	32	31
10–15	939	1,257	2,196	21	29	25
15–20	1,514	1,780	3,294	35	41	38
20–35	4,528	4,651	9,179	104	107	105
35–45	2,478	2,816	5,294	57	64	61
45–55	3,317	3,302	6,619	76	76	76
55–65	4,755	4,982	9,737	110	112	111
65–75	6,436	6,677	13,113	149	153	151
75–85	6,160	6,147	12,307	141	140	140
Over 85	2,489	2,362	4,851	57	54	55
Total	43,493	43,799	87,292	1,000	1,000	1,000

The death-rate is the lowest rate in Europe, viz. :—

1864–70 . . . 16.7 per 1000 population
1871–80 . . . 18.1 ,, ,,
1877–86 . . . 18.4 ,, ,,

This is the more remarkable as the cities have very high rates, viz., Dublin, 24 ; Cork, 26 ; Belfast, 28 per 1000.

In the year 1886 violent deaths formed the same ratio to population as for the ten years ending 1885, and were made up thus :—

	Number			Per Million Population	Per 10,000 Deaths
	Males	Females	Total		
Fire . .	160	184	344	70	38
Drowned .	296	62	358	73	39
Suffocated .	82	39	121	25	14
Poison .	26	7	33	7	4
Fracture .	431	171	602	123	68
Various .	113	40	153	30	17
Accidents .	1,108	503	1,611	328	180
Suicide .	92	24	116	25	13
Murder .	91	40	131	27	14
Executed .	2	...	2	...	...
Total	1,293	567	1,860	380	207

Under the above item of Murder are included deaths from aggravated assault, which in some countries are put down as deaths from fracture, also deaths resulting from riot. The Registrar-General classified the Dublin death-rate in 1887 thus :—

Affluent 15.9
Middle class 26.0
Poor 29.4

The general rate for the city in that year was 23.5 per 1000.

AUSTRALIA

The death-rate for thirteen years ending 1888 of the several colonies, and that of the four principal cities, for three years to 1889 was as follows :—

Per 1000 Population Yearly

N. S. Wales . 15.5 | Queensland . 17.3 | Sydney . . 16.9
Victoria . . 15.1 | Tasmania . 15.8 | Adelaide . . 16.4
S. Australia . 14.1 | W. Australia 16.3 | Brisbane . 17.7
N. Zealand . 11.1 | Melbourne . 21.7 | All Australia 15.0

There is no part of the world with so low a death-rate as Australia, which is partly explained by the preponderance of young people. The ratio of ages in New South Wales by the Census of 1881 compares with the United Kingdom thus :—

Years	U. Kingdom		N. S. Wales
Under 20	462	...	498
20–40 . . .	292	...	309
Over 40 . . .	246	...	193
Total . 1,000		...	1,000

CANADA

The returns for 1886 of deaths in the principal towns were as follow :—

Age	Montreal	Toronto	Quebec	Hamilton	Halifax	Ottawa	St. John, N.B.	Winnipeg
0–5	605	495	604	408	414	625	316	526
5–20	73	112	87	123	119	94	137	124
20–40	116	148	82	152	147	105	167	224
40–60	87	110	76	133	122	66	123	81
Over 60	119	135	151	184	198	110	257	45
Total .	1,000	1,000	1,000	1,000	1,000	1,000	1,000	1,000
Per 1000 population . .	28.0	21.5	33.6	20.7	20.5	28.8	21.2	19.8

VARIOUS COLONIES

The rates in some of the colonies for the years 1876–80 were :—

St. Helena . 13.2	Jamaica . . 21.9	Mauritius . . 28.3
Singapore . 20.1	Bermuda . . 24.1	Trinidad . . 34.1
Ceylon . . 21.6	Hong-Kong . 25.6	Demerara . 34.5

FRANCE

The death-rate per 1000 inhabitants yearly has been :—

1800–10 . . . 27.7	1841–50 . . . 23.3
1811–20 . . . 26.0	1851–60 . . . 23.9
1821–30 . . . 25.0	1861–70 . . . 23.6
1831–40 . . . 24.8	1871–80 . . . 24.3

The rate for various ages in France and at Paris in the years 1874–78 showed thus :—

Age	Per 1000 Persons	
	France	Paris
0–5 . . .	64.6	102.0
5–10 . . .	6.6	9.5
11–20 . . .	5.0	5.7
21–30 . . .	8.9	10.0
31–40 . . .	9.9	12.6
41–50 . . .	12.0	15.8
51–60 . . .	19.5	24.6
61–70 . . .	40.3	48.7

The span of life has lengthened much in the last 100 years, the ratio of deaths in France showing thus :—

Age	1770	1857–66
Under 1 . . .	27.9	20.4
1–3 . . .	13.7	8.6
3–5 . . .	5.0	3.4
5–10 . . .	5.2	3.4
10–20 . . .	4.1	4.7
20–30 . . .	6.2	6.5
30–40 . . .	7.2	5.8
40–50 . . .	7.0	6.5
50–60 . . .	7.2	8.5
60–70 . . .	7.5	12.7
Over 70 . . .	9.0	19.5
	100.0	100.0

French death-rate in the years 1872–75 showed as follows :—

Towns	25.1
Rural	21.1
France	22.4

Infant mortality has, nevertheless, increased of late, viz. :—

Period	Deaths under Twelve Months of 1000 Born		
	Boys	Girls	Total
1840–49 . . .	172	151	160
1850–59 . . .	185	158	172
1860–69 . . .	188	161	175
1874–76 . . .	...	...	180

In the last period, of 1000 children born, 50 died in the first month, 32 in the two following, 35 between three and six months, and 63 in the second half-year, making in all 180 before reaching the age of twelve months. The following table shows the difference of infant mortality according to conditions :—

General Rate 100

Males . . . 107	Rural . . 92	Legitimate . 93
Females . . 93	Urban . . 113	Illegitimate . 185

The following table shows the death-rate of Paris for sixty years :—

Deaths Yearly per 1000 Inhabitants

1821–30 . . . . . 32.0	1861–70 . . . . . 26.7
1831–40 . . . . . 31.9	1871–74 . . . . . 21.6
1841–50 . . . . . 29.6	1875–77 . . . . . 23.7
1851–60 . . . . . 30.0	1878–80 . . . . . 24.5

Deaths according to months, taking the year as 1200, were :—

	France, 1853		Rural Population		
	Urban	Rural	Under 5 Years	5–60	Over 60
January . .	101	104	96	112	113
February .	113	125	98	110	107
March . .	123	134	95	112	106
April . . .	113	122	96	109	109
May . . .	101	101	88	105	100
June . . .	91	91	89	96	92
July . . .	89	82	96	90	84
August . .	97	83	124	90	87
September .	97	88	140	96	96
October . .	86	84	106	97	102
November .	85	84	87	95	101
December .	104	102	85	88	103
Total .	1,200	1,200	1,200	1,200	1,200

Accidental deaths in France showed the following :—

Year	Number	Year	Number
1830 4,478	1870 . . . 10,418
1840 6,805	1880 . . . 12,787
1850 9,151	1885 . . . 13,205
1860 10,298		

The causes of violent deaths in ten years ending 1860 averaged thus .—

	Males	Females	Total
Drowned . . .	43.6	45.0	43.9
Run over . . .	11.7	6.8	10.8
Burnt	5.0	22.0	8.1
Hunger . . .	2.1	3.1	2.3
Drink	1.5	2.5	1.7
Machinery . . .	4.3	1.6	3.8
Fall	15.5	10.2	14.5
Various . . .	16.3	8.8	14.9
	100.0	100.0	100.0

Accidents in Paris in the years 1861–67 showed the following yearly average :—

PER MILLION PERSONS OF EACH CLASS

	Killed			Injured		
	Men	Women	Children	Men	Women	Children
Run over	118	16	32	1,180	317	237
Other accidents }	554	82	209	1,356	167	265
Total .	672	98	241	2,536	484	502

The general ratio for the whole population, per million inhabitants, was as follows :—

	Killed	Injured
Run over	62	648
Other accidents . .	300	666
Total per million	362	1,314

Accidents in French mines showed thus :—

Period	Number of Miners	Killed Yearly	Killed per 10,000
1851–54 . . .	72,000	115	16
1855–59 . . .	108,000	196	18
1860–63 . . .	117,000	228	20

Deaths at various ages according to season showed :—

	2–5	5–10	10–20	20–30	30–50	50–70
Spring . . .	29.0	32.5	29.7	28.9	29.3	29.4
Summer . . .	23.6	23.6	24.2	23.0	22.4	20.5
Autumn . . .	22.3	18.6	20.9	21.8	21.4	21.3
Winter . . .	25.1	25.3	25.2	26.3	26.9	28.8
Total .	100.0	100.0	100.0	100.0	100.0	100.0

The returns for the Institute of France during 75 years ending 1870 showed the following comparison of death-rate with the general population of France :—

Age	Death-Rate		Life-Expectation, Years	
	Institute	General Population	Institute	General Population
35–40	12	13	32	29
40–50	14	15	26	24
50–60	21	22	18	17
60–70	44	47	12	11
70–80	82	90	7	6½

Deaths from lightning in France in ten years ending 1863 averaged 64 men and 24 women yearly. The total

number of persons killed on railways in sixteen years was as follows :—

	No.	Per Annum
Travellers . . .	324	20
Servants . . .	2,154	135
Others	992	62
Total .	3,470	217

Deaths from drowning were in 1881 as follows :—

	Men	Women	Total
Accidental . . .	3,263	679	3,942
Suicidal . . .	1,295	639	1,934
Total . .	4,558	1,318	5,876

The distribution of deaths according to the hours of day or night is shown for France, compared with Quetetet's observations for Belgium, thus :—

	France		Quetetet, Belgium
	Towns	Rural	
Midnight to 6 A.M. . .	21.9	24.4	27.4
6 A.M. to noon . . .	26.3	27.5	26.4
Noon to 6 P.M. . . .	30.8	26.3	24.0
6 P.M. to midnight . .	21.0	21.8	22.2

GERMANY

The death-rate of all Germany during eleven years ending 1881 for 1000 persons of each age was as follows :—

Age	Males	Females	Age	Males	Females
1 . . '.	64.9	63.6	25 . . .	8.5	8.2
2 . . .	33.2	32.6	30 . . .	9.3	9.7
3 . . .	23.1	22.5	40 . . .	13.6	12.2
4 . . .	17.1	16.9	50 . . .	21.5	16.0
5 . . .	13.0	12.9	60 . . .	38.2	32.9
10 . . .	4.7	4.8	70 . . .	81.1	74.7
15 . . .	3.9	4.2	80 . . .	174.5	168.3
20 . . .	7.5	6.1			

The death-rate of Prussia in the years 1868–72 was :—

Age	Deaths per 1000		Expectations of Life, Years	
	Males	Females	Males	Females
4–5 . . .	19.0	19.3	51.9	53.7
5–10 . . .	10.1	10.2	51.5	53.3
10–15 . . .	4.8	5.2	48.1	49.8
15–20 . . .	6.2	6.0	44.1	45.5
20–30 . . .	9.5	8.8	38.0	39.5
30–40 . . .	11.2	11.6	30.3	31.3
40–50 . . .	18.0	15.0	23.0	23.7
50–60 . . .	27.0	25.0	16.2	16.2
60–70 . . .	49.0	50.0	10.0	9.9
70–80 . . .	90.0	94.0	5.7	5.4

The average age of all who died in ten years ending 1876 was :—

Males 25.8
Females 27.6

The death-rate among Jews was much lower than among Christians, as shown thus :—

Period	Deaths Yearly per 1000			
	Christians		Jews	
	Males	Females	Males	Females
1822–40 . .	28.7	27.0	22.1	19.1
1841–66 . .	30.2	28.2	19.8	17.9

The mean death-rate of five principal cities during sixty years down to 1875 was as follows :—

1816–40 . . . . 33.9	1867–71 . . . . 37.4
1841–66 . . . . 35.4	1872–75 . . . . 40.6

The mean rate during sixty years was as follows :—

	Males		Females
Berlin . . .	36.7	...	28.5
Breslau . . .	36.8	...	33.0
Cologne . .	30.6	...	28.8
Königsberg . .	38.2	...	31.9

The mean rate for all Prussia in sixty years was per 1000 inhabitants :—

Males 30.2	Urban population . 30.1
Females 27.7	Rural „ . 28.4

The general rate for all Prussia during sixty years averaged 29.0 per thousand.

The deaths of infants at Berlin show that of 1000 born 237 die in the first year, 80 the second, 36 the third, and 9 the fourth, leaving only 638 surviving to begin their fifth year. Of 100 accidental deaths in Prussia in ten years down to 1874, 78 were of males, 22 of females.

Hanoverian statistics show the death-rate of unhealthy trades as follows :—

Per 1000 Yearly

Painters 15.6	Glass-blowers . . 20.8
Varnishers . . . 18.8	Dyers 25.1

In Saxony the death-rates in 1845–47 were :—

Age	Per 1000 Yearly		
	Males	Females	General
1–14	17.5	15.8	16.6
14–30	6.6	6.6	6.6
30–60	16.2	16.3	16.2
Over 60	94.4	94.6	94.5

Distinguishing town-rates from rural, the rates in the year 1863 were :—

Age	Cities			Rural		
	Males	Females	General	Males	Females	General
Under 6	116.0	100.0	108.0	101.0	83.0	92.0
6–14	4.6	4.8	4.7	4.4	4.3	4.4
14–20	4.8	5.5	5.1	4.3	4.1	4.2
20–30	8.7	8.5	8.6	6.4	6.9	6.7
30–40	11.4	12.9	12.1	8.1	10.3	9.2
40–50	19.0	14.4	16.6	14.2	13.4	13.8
50–60	32.0	25.9	28.8	26.9	24.6	25.7
60–70	62.5	56.9	59.5	58.8	57.9	58.3
70–80	142.0	150.0	146.0	118.0	134.0	126.0

Distinguishing married from single at Leipzig, in ten years ending 1875 the rates were :—

Age	Males		Females		General
	Married	Single	Married	Single	
15–20	...	3.6	11.0	3.0	3.4
20–30	9.0	8.2	8.2	6.5	7.5
30–40	12.5	18.5	11.6	8.8	12.5
40–50	21.8	31.0	12.2	13.2	18.8
50–60	31.0	31.4	17.4	22.2	26.6
60–70	55.0	56.0	35.0	55.0	49.0
Over 70	117.0	111.0	85.0	111.0	123.0

The effect of over-crowding on death-rate is shown thus :—

Living in	Berlin, 1871	Leipzig, 1875
One room . . .	48.7	21.4
Two rooms . .	24.9	25.9
Three rooms . .	11.2	20.2
Over three rooms .	15.2	32.5
	100.0	100.0

It would appear from the foregoing that there is much over-crowding at Berlin and little at Leipzig, nearly half the deaths in the former city occurring in families living in one room, and at Leipzig less than one-fourth. The mortality of infants, however, is much higher at Leipzig in the crowded population than among the other quarters of the city, viz. :—

Inhabitants per Room	Death-Rate Yearly per 1000 Infants	
	Under Twelve Months	Twelve Months to Five Years
Over 3 . . .	419	49
2–3 . . .	338	45
1 . . .	255	37
Less than 1 . .	111	14

The death-rate in Leipzig for all persons over five years was 9.9 per 1000 where the population was less than one per room, and 18.4 in the rest. Infant mortality at Leipzig in ten years ending 1875 showed thus :—

Of 1000 born, die under twelve months

Males 233
Females 205
General rate 219

The death-rate of infants is increasing, the rates for all Saxony of 1000 born who die under twelve months showing thus :—

Period	Boys	Girls	General Rate
1845–55 . . .	277	235	257
1856–65 . . .	283	241	263
1866–75 . . .	293	252	272

Mortality is much higher with illegitimate than with lawful children, averages for six years ending 1870 being thus :—

Deaths per 1000 Born

	Saxony	Dresden
Legitimate . . .	256	250
Illegitimate . .	353	705

The general death-rate of Saxony was 30.1 in ten years ending 1849, and 30.3 in ten years ending 1876.

At Munich the death-rate of infants shows that of 1000 born, the Jews lose 170 in the first year, Protestants 320, and Roman Catholics 400, the last including all the working-classes, who suffer from overcrowding.

SWITZERLAND

The death-rate per 1000 inhabitants yearly for all Switzerland for ten years ending 1880 was 24.0. Rates, however, vary much with the cantons. For example, infant mortality at Berne is 101 per thousand, and at St. Gall 301. The statistics of Geneva for 25 years ending 1871 showed the annual average death-rate thus :—

Swiss 21.7
Foreign residents . . . 15.4

At Geneva there were 101 deaths to 100 births among natives, whereas among foreign residents there were 156 births to 100 deaths. Ladame gives the rates of infant mortality, distinguishing legitimate from illegitimate, thus :—

Of 1000 Born

	Die in 30 Days	Die in 12 Months
Legitimate . .	77	...	180
Illegitimate . .	136	...	280

Climatic changes have occurred at Geneva since the seventeenth century, August and September having much lower ratios of deaths than in 1633–1700, viz. : —

Of 1200 Deaths Yearly

	1633–1700	1838–55		1633–1700	1838–55
January . .	114	114	July . . .	84	86
February . .	106	117	August . .	108	83
March . . .	105	120	September .	105	90
April . . .	100	111	October . .	89	95
May . . .	100	95	November .	95	96
June . . .	86	92	December .	108	101

Accidental deaths in the years 1876–81 averaged 1697 per annum, equal to 605 per million inhabitants, or 280 in 10,000 deaths.

Sweden

Death-rates for age from 1751 to 1875 showed thus :—

Age	1751–90	1791–1830	1831–60	1861–70	1871–75
0–10 . .	55.4	45.4	36.5	35.1	30.0
10–20 . .	7.3	5.8	5.1	4.5	4.0
21–30 . .	9.5	8.5	7.3	6.4	7.0
31–40 . .	12.4	11.6	10.5	8.3	8.7
41–50 . .	17.2	16.6	15.1	12.0	11.4
51–60 . .	24.9	26.6	24.5	20.3	18.1
Over 60 .	76.5	81.0	74.0	68.8	64.0

The rates for the years 1871–75 were thus :—

	0–20	20–30	31–40	41–50	Over 50
Males . .	19.1	7.8	9.3	13.0	42.2
Females . .	16.8	6.3	8.1	10.0	38.9

Distinguishing the sexes, and also urban from rural, the rates for ten years ending 1870 were :—

	Males		Females	
Age	Town	Rural	Town	Rural
Under 1 . .	256.0	159.0	222.0	133.0
1–5 . . .	54.0	31.0	53.0	29.0
5–10 . . .	12.9	9.2	12.9	8.6
10–20 . . .	5.9	4.4	4.8	4.2
20–30 . . .	10.5	6.6	8.1	5.4
30–40 . . .	16.7	7.7	10.2	7.4
40–50 . . .	25.4	12.5	13.8	10.5
50–60 . . .	40.0	22.0	20.0	17.0
60–70 . . .	66.0	46.0	36.0	39.0
70–80 . . .	130.0	112.0	96.0	94.0
General rate	29.7	20.5	25.5	18.9

The average age at death was in years as follows :—

	Males			Females		
	1861–65	1866–70	1871–75	1861–65	1866–70	1871–75
Town	23.3	24.3	25.8	28.4	29.9	31.3
Rural	30.0	33.5	34.2	34.5	37.4	38.4
Gen.	29.0	32.0	32.6	33.6	36.2	37.3

Ratio of Deaths

	Males		Females	
	1861–70	1871–75	1861–70	1871–75
Unmarried .	59.7	57.5	54.3	51.3
Married . .	28.4	29.8	22.6	24.6
Widowed .	11.9	12.7	23.1	24.1
Total	100.0	100.0	100.0	100.0

The number of females dying to 100 males was :—

	1861–70	1871–75
Town . . .	95.4	92.2
Rural . . .	96.4	97.3
Sweden . . .	96.2	96.3

Ratios of deaths according to months showed thus :—

	1749–60	1851–55	1861–72		
	Sweden	Sweden	Urban	Rural	General
January . .	102	100	107	115	114
February .	104	116	108	117	116
March . .	113	121	107	119	117
April . . .	124	118	109	117	116
May . . .	120	107	103	108	108
June . . .	105	84	95	92	92
July . . .	94	76	96	81	83
August . .	90	82	95	79	81
September .	86	102	95	79	81
October . .	84	95	91	86	87
November .	87	100	92	99	98
December .	91	99	102	108	107
Total	1,200	1,200	1,200	1,200	1,200

Violent deaths were as follows :—

	Annual Average		Total Number in 15 years	Ratio
	1861–70	1871–75		1861–75
Drowned . .	1,132	1,202	17,268	45.7
Burnt . . .	152	150	2,267	6.0
Suffocated . .	146	102	1,974	5.2
Murdered . .	78	105	1,299	3.4
Crushed . .	461	573	7,482	19.7
Poisoned accidentally . }	20	21	310	0.8
Shot accidentally . }	29	38	489	1.3
Lightning . .	11	14	183	0.5
Frozen . . .	54	64	862	2.3
Various . . .	43	46	681	1.8
Suicide . . .	328	347	5,068	13.3
Total .	2,454	2,662	37,883	100.0

Accidental deaths (including also murders) in the above fifteen years, distinguishing urban from rural districts, were per million inhabitants yearly as follows :—

	Town	Rural		Town	Rural
Drowned . .	436	255	Crushed . .	174	112
Burnt . . .	31	37	Choked . .	6	2
Lightning . .	...	3	Shot . . .	8	8
Murdered . .	3	2	Poisoned . .	10	4

Norway

Death-rate per 1000 inhabitants yearly from 1801 to 1875 was as follows :—

1801–15 . . 25.0	1836–45 . . 18.9	1856–65 . . 17.7
1816–35 . . 19.2	1846–55 . . 18.1	1866–75 . . 17.5

Rates distinguishing age and sex showed as follows :—

Age	Males			Females		
	1816–40	1841–60	1861–65	1816–40	1841–60	1861–65
Under 10	32.2	27.4	31.2	28.0	24.2	28.8
10–20	4.7	4.7	5.5	4.2	4.2	5.1
21–30	8.2	8.2	8.4	6.5	6.0	6.3
31–40	9.5	9.0	8.0	9.0	8.6	8.3
41–50	13.2	12.8	11.1	11.6	10.8	9.9
51–60	21.7	20.0	17.0	17.3	15.8	14.0
61–70	40.0	38.0	35.0	35.0	33.0	30.0
71–80	81.0	84.0	81.0	77.0	77.5	72.0

Infant mortality has been as follows :—

Period	Deaths under 12 Months of 1000 Born	
	Males	Females
1836–55	130	109
1856–65	112	96
1866–73	115	98

FINLAND

Death-rate per 1000 inhabitants yearly was as follows :—

1751–70 . .29.6	1811–20 . .26.1	1841–50 . .23.6
1771–1800 .26.4	1821–30 . .24.7	1851–60 . .28.6
1801–10 . .32.3	1831–40 . .28.2	1861–65 . .26.2

In 1865 the span of life, in years, was as follows :—

Males 35.6
Females 38.4

The general span for the whole population was thirty-seven years.

Death-rate for age was as follows :—

Age	Age	Age
Under 1. .139.0	10–20 . . .4.0	40–50 . . . 11.5
1–5 . . . 25.0	20–30 . . .6.5	50–60 . . . 19.0
5–10 . . . 8.0	30–40 . . .7.5	60–70 . . . 44.0

RUSSIA

In 1867 the following table of death-rate was published :—

Per 1000 Yearly

Age	Age
5–15 . . . 7.3	30–60 . . . 21.5
15–30 . . . 8.0	Over 60 . . . 121.0

Of 1000 boys born, 254 die, and of girls 231, in their first year. At Nijni Novgorod infant mortality is 360, and in the government of Perm 446 per thousand births.

HOLLAND

Death-rate per 1000 inhabitants yearly was :—

1861–70. . . . . . . 24.9
1871–80. . . . . . . 24.3

The influence of season on death-rate at various ages is seen as follows :—

Age	Spring	Summer	Autumn	Winter	Year
Under 3 months	246	212	248	294	1,000
3–24 ,,	247	259	259	235	1,000
2–5 years . .	273	229	235	263	1,000
5–10 ,, . . .	269	259	231	241	1,000
11–20 ,, . . .	265	261	229	245	1,000
21–30 ,, . . .	261	253	232	254	1,000
31–50 ,, . . .	260	246	226	268	1,000
51–70 ,, . . .	253	223	228	296	1,000

GREECE

In ten years ending 1878 the death-rate for age was as follows :—

Age	Males	Females	General Population
Under 5 . . .	50.3	49.0	49.7
5–10	11.2	10.8	11.1
10–20	7.4	7.2	7.3
20–30	9.8	8.5	9.1
30–40	11.3	10.7	11.0
40–50	15.5	14.9	15.2
50–60	28.5	24.4	26.5
60–70	49.0	46.0	47.7
70–80	91.0	105.0	98.0

BELGIUM

The annual average of deaths since 1830 was :—

Year	Number	Per 1000 Population	Year	Number	Per 1000 Population
1831–40	108,000	26.7	1861–70	115,000	23.3
1841–50	104,000	24.2	1871–80	120,000	22.5
1851–60	102,000	22.2	1881–87	118,000	20.7

The percentage of deaths according to age was as follows :—

	1841–50	1851–60	1861–66	1878–82	1887
Under 5	34.1	35.9	37.4	36.4	33.9
5–10	4.9	4.1	4.7	2.9	2.7
10–20	6.1	5.7	4.7	4.0	3.9
20–30	7.1	6.6	6.4	5.4	5.6
30–40	6.3	6.1	6.2	5.6	5.3
40–50	7.2	6.4	6.4	6.0	6.3
50–60	7.6	8.3	7.7	7.9	7.9
60–70	10.1	10.1	10.9	11.1	11.9
70–80	10.7	11.1	10.2	13.6	14.1
Over 80	5.9	5.7	5.4	7.1	8.4
Total	100.0	100.0	100.0	100.0	100.0

Sanitary improvements have done much for public health. For instance, the percentage of deaths between 5 and 20 years of age is now little more than half what it was in the decade of 1841–50; that of deaths over 70 years is one-third higher.

The mean averages for 35 years, 1846–80, showed as follows :—

	Unmarried		Married		Total Population	
	Males	Females	Males	Females	Males	Females
0–15	73.8	71.3	...	...	43.4	40.8
15–20	4.1	5.2	...	0.2	2.4	3.1
20–30	6.3	7.4	3.6	9.4	6.6	6.5
30–40	4.2	3.1	11.4	19.1	5.6	6.5
40–50	3.0	2.3	17.6	19.3	6.9	6.4
50–60	2.7	2.6	21.4	17.9	8.5	7.3
60–70	2.7	3.2	23.6	18.8	10.7	10.5
70–80	2.3	3.3	17.6	12.5	10.8	12.1
Over 80	0.9	1.6	4.8	2.8	5.1	6.8
Total	100.0	100.0	100.0	100.0	100.0	100.0

Death-rate for age is stated as follows :—

Age	Per 1000	Age	Per 1000	Age	Per 1000
0–1 . . . 186.0		10–20 . . . 6.2		40–60 . . . 20.6	
1–10 . . . 20.1		20–40 . . . 13.4		Over 60 . . 79.1	

Violent deaths were as follows :—

By	Annual Average, 1871–80			1881–85
	Males	Females	Total	
Firearms .	21	3	24	23
Fire . . .	135	101	236	226
Fall	291	42	333	320
Railway . .	161	18	179	175
Machinery .	107	11	118	103
Drowning .	503	100	603	607
Vehicles . .	131	19	150	147
Various . .	328	68	396	384
All accidents	1,677	362	2,039	1,985
Murder . .	67	19	86	98
Suicide . .	373	68	441	602
Total .	2,117	449	2,566	2,685

Other tables will be found at page 179. The influence of season on death-rate is shown by the following ratios :—

		Death Ratios		
		Under 3 Months	3 to 24 Months	General Population
Spring .	. . .	264	293	279
Summer	. . .	200	206	218
Autumn	. . .	225	207	220
Winter .	. . .	311	294	283
		1,000	1,000	1,000

ITALY

The death-rate per 1000 inhabitants yearly has been :—

    1861–70 . . . . 30.1
    1871–80 . . . . 29.7

Deaths in Italian cities according to season showed thus :—

GENOA

	Under 5	5–10	10–30	30–50	50–70
Spring . .	21.3	21.7	22.5	20.4	22.1
Summer . .	26.0	25.7	27.0	26.8	23.9
Autumn . .	26.3	29.4	29.3	30.0	28.1
Winter . .	26.4	23.2	21.2	22.8	25.9
	100.0	100.0	100.0	100.0	100.1

NAPLES

	Under 5	5–10	10–30	30–50	50–70
Spring . .	23.8	28.6	24.2	24.6	25.3
Summer . .	29.5	26.1	25.3	25.6	20.8
Autumn . .	21.0	18.4	25.0	23.0	22.3
Winter . .	25.7	26.9	25.5	26.8	31.6
	100.0	100.0	100.0	100.0	100.0

SPAIN AND PORTUGAL

The ratios of ages in deaths for Spain and Lisbon were :—

Age	Spain	Lisbon
0–20	59.9	50.1
20–40	10.3	10.5
40–60	12.0	13.0
Over 60	17.8	26.4
Total . .	100.0	100.0

AUSTRIA-HUNGARY

The death-rates have been as follows :—

	1861–70	1871–80
Austria	30.4	31.2
Hungary	38.7	40.1

Death-rates for age were as follows :—

Age	Austria, 1860–68	Hungary, 1869–73	Age	Austria, 1860–68	Hungary, 1869–73
Under 1	303.0	...	15–30	8.1	9.3
1–5	40.6	34.3	30–60	17.1	20.0
5–15	7.3	10.2	Over 60	84.0	...

Deaths at Vienna, according to season, showed thus :—

	Under 5	5–15	15–40	40–60	Over 60
Spring	29.7	28.8	32.4	30.9	30.3
Summer	23.5	21.9	22.6	21.1	20.6
Autumn	21.9	22.7	19.0	22.0	21.2
Winter	24.9	26.6	26.0	26.0	27.9
	100.0	100.0	100.0	100.0	100.0

Statistics of Prague show the death-rate thus :—

Age	Per 1000	Age	Per 1000
Under 1 . . .	497	20–40	14
1–5	85	40–60	25
5–20	10	Over 60 . . .	71

The general rate for the population was 35 per 1000. Violent deaths in 1886 in Austria proper were as follows :—

	Number			In 100,000 Deaths		
	Males	Females	Total	Males	Females	Total
Accidents .	4,603	1,830	6,433	138	57	96
Murders .	493	170	663	15	5	10
Suicides .	3,013	824	3,837	90	25	57
Total .	8,109	2,824	10,933	243	87	163

In five years ending 1886 the average per 100,000 deaths showed there were 10 murders, 55 suicides, and 90 deaths by accident.

ALGERIA

There has been a notable decline of death-rate, as the following table shows :—

Nationality	Deaths per 1000 Persons Yearly	
	1853–56	1873–76
French	46.3	26.8
Spaniards	30.0	27.9
Italians	30.0	28.9
Maltese	28.2	26.7
Germans	54.8	36.9
Jews	27.9	24.4

Deaths in Algeria according to season were :—

    Spring 19.5
    Summer 29.3
    Autumn 28.5
    Winter 22.7
                  100.0

Algerian statistics show that of 1000 infants born the following numbers die in the first twelve months :—

Parents	Death per 1000		
	Boys	Girls	General
French	244	146	207
Spanish . . .	238	250	257
Italian	245	184	224
Jewish	236	182	213
Mahometan . . .	530	488	500
German	...	...	344

Deaths according to months in Algeria, taking the year as 1200, were :—

January	.	.	.	96	July	.	.	.	127
February	.	.	.	86	August	.	.	.	138
March.	.	.	.	91	September	.	.	.	102
First quarter		.	273		Third quarter		.	367	
April	.	.	.	71	October	.	.	.	127
May	.	.	.	72	November	.	.	.	113
June	.	.	.	86	December	.	.	.	91
Second quarter		.	229		Fourth quarter		.	331	

JAPAN

The returns for 1878–80 showed as follows :—

	Death-Rate per 1000	Ratio of Deaths
Under 10 . . .	25.8	28.0
10–20	5.4	4.9
20–30	8.6	7.7
30–40	9.2	8.6
40–50	8.9	8.7
50–60	11.5	11.4
60–70	13.9	13.8
70–80	12.1	11.6
Over 80 . . .	4.8	5.3
General rate . .	17.0	100.0

In 1000 deaths 527 were of males, 473 females.

BRAZIL

Death-rate at Rio Janeiro in 1867–69 averaged 24.4 per 1000, the ratio showing thus :—

Under 1	.	.	.	14.8	Quarter ending—		
1–7 .	.	.	.	11.6	March 31st	.	284
7–25 .	.	.	.	18.4	June 30th .	.	261
25–40	.	.	.	22.9	September 30th	.	228
Over 40	.	.	.	32.3	December 31st	.	227
				100.0	Year	.	1,000

In 1000 deaths, 546 were of males, 454 females ; 627 natives, and 373 foreigners.

The only death-rates published are these :—

Age	Annual Deaths per 1000 Inhabitants		
	Massachusetts	Maryland	United States
Under 5 .	65.8	51.7	58.8
5–10 . .	10.7	9.5	10.1
10–15 . .	5.1	5.4	5.3
15–25 . .	5.8	5.4	5.6
25–45 . .	11.9	10.1	10.8
45–55 . .	16.4	18.2	17.6
55–65 . .	26.3	28.1	27.2
65–75 . .	46.9	56.5	51.4

DEPOPULATION

The only European country which has suffered depopulation in the present century is Ireland. It is the result partly of famine, partly of evictions by the landowners. The official returns show the number of persons evicted thus :—

1849–51	.	.	.	.	.	263,000
1852–70	.	.	.	.	.	157,000
1871–87	.	.	.	.	.	113,000
	Total		.	.		533,000

This is, however, far short of the reality. The Census of 1861 showed the number of one-room cabins to be 89,400 against 491,300 in the Census of 1841, from which it appears that 402,000 cabins had been pulled down, the abodes of 2,000,000 inhabitants. The official number of emigrants from 1837 to 1888 was 4,338,000, but this did not include 600,000 who went to England or Scotland. The population has fallen from 8,275,000 in 1845 to 4,716,000 in 1889, a decline of 43 per cent. At present it is but 150 per square mile, against 190 in France, 240 in Germany, and 270 in Italy. The marriage-rate and birth-rate are the lowest in the world. The ratio of able-bodied population, male and female, between the ages of 20 and 55 is much less than in the sister kingdoms, as shown by the Census of 1881, viz. :—

England	.	.	.	.	432 per 1000
Scotland	.	.	.	.	424 ,,
Ireland	.	.	.	.	408 ,,

The drain upon persons of the able-bodied age has been attended by a remarkable increase of pauperism, as the official returns show :—

Year	No. of Paupers	Per 1000 Inhab.
1874. . . .	79,600	15
1880. . . .	100,900	19
1888. . . .	113,900	24

In the above interval of 14 years the population declined by 584,000 souls, and yet the number of paupers increased in the ratio of 43 per cent.

DIET

The principal components of animal food are as follows :—

	Fat	Nitrogen	Water		Fat	Nitrogen	Water
Lobster	1.2	19.2	76.6	Tripe	16.4	13.2	68.0
Oyster . . .	1.5	14.0	80.4	Beef	17.1	17.2	61.5
Turbot	2.9	18.1	78.0	Mutton . . .	18.1	15.3	62.5
Rabbit . . .	3.2	13.9	73.2	Cheese . . .	41.3	7.0	38.8
Salmon . . .	5.5	16.1	77.0	Pork	44.9	9.8	43.0
Milk	7.9	4.5	87.0	Bacon . . .	63.3	8.8	25.0
Eggs	10.5	14.0	74.0	Butter . . .	81.0	5.0	11.0

The components of vegetable food are :—

	Starch	Nitrogen	Water		Starch	Nitrogen	Water
Mushroom . . .	3.5	4.7	91.0	Bread . . .	49.0	10.0	33.6
Cabbage	4.0	1.8	92.0	Beans	52.6	22.0	12.8
Turnip	5.1	1.2	91.0	Peas	52.6	22.3	14.5
Carrot	5.5	0.7	87.3	Tea	55.2	28.8	12.0
Beer	9.2	0.9	89.7	Lentils . . .	56.0	25.2	11.5
Parsnip	9.6	1.1	82.0	Coffee . . .	59.4	26.2	12.0
Beet-root. . .	11.3	5.0	82.7	Wheat-flour . .	59.7	12.6	14.5
Asparagus . . .	11.8	1.2	86.0	Oatmeal . . .	63.8	12.6	15.0
Artichoke . . .	14.7	3.1	76.0	Cocoa . . .	71.0	24.0	4.0
Yam	16.0	2.0	74.0	Maize . . .	71.2	9.9	13.5
Truffles . . .	16.6	8.8	72.0	Rye . . .	73.2	8.0	15.0
Sugar-cane . . .	18.0	5.5	72.0	Barley . . .	74.3	6.3	15.0
Banana . . .	19.7	4.8	73.9	Rice . . .	79.5	6.3	13.0
Potato . . .	20.2	2.3	75.9	Buckwheat . . .	79.9	2.6	12.8

The percentage of carbon in food is as follows :—

Cabbage . .	3	Eggs. . . .	16	Biscuit . .	42
Beer	4	Beef . . .	27	Oatmeal. .	42
Carrots . .	5	Bread . .	27	Sugar . .	42
Milk . . .	7	Cheese . .	36	Flour . .	46
Parsnips . .	8	Peas . . .	36	Bacon . .	54
Fish . . .	9	Rice . . .	38	Cocoa . .	69
Potatoes. .	12	Maize . . .	38	Butter . .	79

The nutritive value of food (taking beef as 100) is expressed thus :—

Oysters . . .	22	Turbot . .	84	Beef. . .	100
Milk . . .	24	Mutton. .	87	Duck . . .	104
Lobsters .	50	Venison .	89	Salmon. .	108
Cream . .	56	Veal . .	92	Pork . .	116
Cod-fish . .	68	Fowl . .	94	Butter . .	124
Eggs . . .	72	Herring .	100	Cheese . .	155

The following table shows foot-tons of energy contained per ounce of food :—

	Foot-Tons		Foot-Tons		Foot-Tons
Cabbage .	16	Porter . .	42	Rice . .	145
Carrots .	20	Beef . .	55	Flour . .	148
Milk . .	24	Egg . .	57	Arrowroot	151
Apples . .	25	Ham . .	65	Oatmeal .	152
Fish . .	30	Bread . .	83	Cheese .	168
Ale . . .	30	Salt . .	120	Butter . .	281
Potatoes .	38	Sugar . .	130		

The loss of weight in meat in cooking is as follows :—

100 lbs. raw beef	= 67 lbs. roast
,, ., beef	= 74 ,, boiled
,, ,, mutton	= 75 ,, roast
,, ,, fowl	= 80 ,, roast
,, ,, fowl	= 87 ,, boiled
,, ,, fish	= 94 ,, boiled

Payn's table gives the following percentages in food :—

	Azote	Carbon	Fat	Water		Azote	Carbon	Fat	Water
Batata . . .	0.2	9.0	0.3	80.0	Kidneys . . .	2.7	12.2	2.1	78.2
Beans . . .	3.9	43.0	2.8	10.0	Lard . . .	1.2	71.0	71.0	20.0
Beef, raw . . .	3.0	11.0	2.3	78.0	Lentils . . .	3.9	43.0	2.6	11.5
Beef, roast . . .	3.5	11.8	5.2	70.0	Lobsters . . .	2.9	11.0	1.2	76.6
Beer . . .	0.1	4.5	...	90.0	Mackerel . . .	3.7	19.3	6.8	68.3
Bread . . .	1.1	29.5	1.2	35.0	Maize . . .	1.7	44.0	8.8	12.0
Butter . . .	0.6	83.0	82.0	14.0	Milk, cow's . . .	0.7	8.0	3.7	86.5
Carrots . . .	0.3	5.5	0.2	88.0	Milk, goat's . . .	0.7	8.6	4.1	83.6
Cheese, Brie . . .	2.9	35.0	25.8	45.3	Mushrooms . . .	0.7	4.5	0.4	91.0
Chestnuts . . .	0.6	35.0	4.1	26.0	Oil, olive . . .	...	98.0	96.0	2.0
Chestnuts, dry . . .	1.0	48.0	6.0	10.0	Oyster . . .	2.1	7.2	1.5	80.4
Cod, salt . . .	5.0	16.0	0.4	47.0	Potato . . .	0.3	11.0	0.1	74.0
Eel . . .	4.0	12.7	5.0	80.0	Rice . . .	1.8	41.0	0.8	13.0
Figs . . .	0.4	15.5	0.3	66.0	Rye-flour . . .	1.8	41.0	2.2	15.0
Figs, dry . . .	0.9	34.0	0.3	25.0	Salmon . . .	2.1	16.0	4.9	75.7
Flour . . .	1.6	39.0	1.8	14.0	Sole . . .	1.9	12.3	0.2	86.1
Herring . . .	1.8	21.0	10.0	70.0	Wheat . . .	3.0	41.0	2.1	12.0
Herring, salt . . .	3.1	23.0	12.7	49.0	Wine . . .	...	4.0	...	90.0

The analysis of bread gives conflicting results, the following being taken from respectable sources :—

	A.	B.	C.
Nitrogen . . .	6.8	8.1	12.6
Water . . .	43.0	37.0	14.6
Starch . . .	44.0	47.4	65.6
Sugar . . .	3.4	3.6	4.8
Fat . . .	1.3	1.5	1.4
Mineral . . .	1.5	2.4	1.0
	100.0	100.0	100.0

In 1862 the bread supplied to the French army was found superior in nitrogen to that of other Continental armies, as follows, French being 100 :—

Prussian . .	50	Austrian . .	70	Belgian . . .	91
Spanish . .	69	Dutch . . .	90	Italian . . .	96

A sack of flour containing 280 lbs. will make 368 lbs. of bread in England, and 420 lbs. in United States, that is, 7 lbs. of American are equal to 8 lbs. of English flour. The ingredients for 368 lbs. of English bread are :—280 lbs. flour, 3 gallons water, half-gallon yeast, half-gallon alum, and 4 lbs. salt.

The following comparison has been made between flour of Odessa wheat and that used at bakeries at Paris :—

	Odessa Flour	Paris Flour
Water	12.0	10.0
Dry gluten . . .	14.5	10.2
Starch . . .	66.5	72.8
Glucose, &c. . . .	7.0	7.0
	100.0	100.0

The nutritive value of various kinds of flour is stated thus :—

| English | . | 100 | Canadian | . | 117 | Scotch | . . . | 134 |
| German | . . | 115 | Essex | . . . | 121 | United States | | 145 |

An analysis of the different kinds of bread supplied to European armies in 1860 showed as follows :—

	French	Prussian	Bavarian	Belgian	Dutch
Starch . .	42	37	54	44	40
Water . .	34	35	30	31	32
Azote . .	9	5	6	9	9
Various . .	15	23	10	16	19
	100	100	100	100	100

The percentage of nitrogen digested in food is as follows :—

	Per Cent.		Per Cent.
Lentils . . .	60	Bread	81
Potatoes . . .	68	Cheese	96
Peas	72	Meat . . .	97
Rice	75	Eggs . . .	98

The time required for digestion is :—

	Hours	Min.		Hours	Min.
Rice . . .	1	0	Mutton, boiled .	3	0
Eggs, raw . .	1	30	Beef, roast .	3	0
Apples . .	1	30	Bread, fresh .	3	15
Trout, boiled .	1	30	Carrots, boiled .	3	15
Venison, broiled	1	35	Turnips, boiled .	3	30
Sago, boiled .	1	45	Potatoes, boiled	3	30
Milk, boiled .	2	0	Butter . .	3	30
Bread, stale .	2	0	Cheese . .	3	30
Milk, raw . .	2	15	Oysters, stewed .	3	30
Turkey, boiled .	2	25	Eggs, hard .	3	30
Goose, roast .	2	30	Pork, boiled .	3	30
Lamb, broiled .	2	30	Fowl, roast .	4	0
Potatoes, baked	2	30	Beef, fried .	4	0
Beans, boiled .	2	30	Cabbage . .	4	30
Parsnips, boiled	2	30	Wild-fowl . .	4	30
Oysters, raw .	2	55	Pork, roast .	5	15
Eggs, boiled .	3	0	Veal, roast .	5	30

According to Keleti, the average amount of food required per annum is as follows :—

	Lbs. Food	Containing Lbs. Albumen
Man	1,600	100
Woman	1,200	75
Child	900	50

The man's food to be made up thus :—

	Lbs. Food	Lbs. Albumen
Animal	290	28
Vegetable . . .	1,310	72
Total . .	1,600	100

According to the *Dict. Sciences Medic.*, a man's daily food should contain at least ¾ oz. of azote and 11 oz. of carbon, the proportions of which contained in the food of certain classes are as follows :—

	Per Week	
	Azote, Oz.	Carbon, Oz.
English peasant . . .	7.7	120
Irish peasant . . .	4.0	168
French peasant . . .	6.0	150
Lombard peasant . . .	7.0	175

Animal food constitutes, according to the same authority the following percentage in the weight of all food consumed :—

Irish peasant	.	.	.	.	1 per cent.
French peasant .	.	.	.	7	,,
French sailor	.	.	.	25	,,
English "navvy"	.	.	.	28	,,

The proportions of azote and carbon contained in bread and meat are as follows :—

In	Percentage of	
	Azote	Carbon
Bread	1	30
Meat	3	10

The weekly rations in different countries and classes are as follows :—

	Rations	Nitrogenous	Carbon
	Lbs.	Lbs.	Lbs.
British soldiers .	25.7	2.46	4.84
British soldiers in India .	20.0	2.33	4.52
French soldiers .	23.6	2.26	5.81
German soldiers .	28.8	1.56	5.25
Dutch soldiers .	25.0	1.67	4.82
Chelsea Hospital .	22.6	1.99	5.31
English convicts .	22.2	1.38	4.99
Farm labourer . .	22.1	1.82	5.11
Workhouse, aged .	17.8	1.50	3.96
Chelsea boys . .	16.7	0.88	3.93

Field-rations of the various armies are as follows :—

	Ounces Daily					
	Beef	Bread	Rice	Coffee	Sugar	Total
British . . .	16	24	2	¼	2	44¼
French . . .	7	26	3	½	1	37½
German . . .	8	28	3	½	1	40½
Russian . . .	16	16	...	...	...	32
Austrian . . .	5	26	1	...	...	32
American . . .	20	18	2	2	2	44

	Ounces Daily					Energy, Foot-Tons
	Nitrogen	Fat	Carbon	Salt	Total	
British . .	4.1	1.6	17.4	0.8	23.4	3,552
French . .	4.3	1.3	18.0	1.0	24.6	3,719
German .	4.0	1.1	19.6	1.5	26.2	3,834
Austrian .	3.7	1.6	17.0	1.0	23.4	3,590
Standard .	4.6	3.0	14.3	1.1	23.0	3,888

The rations in use in the United Kingdom are as follow :—

	Weight in Lbs. Weekly				
	Bread	Cooked Meat	Vegetables	Sugar	Sundries
Soldier . . .	7.0	3.5	7.0	0.7	7.5
Seaman . . .	8.8	5.2	3.5	0.9	...
Convict . . .	10.0	2.6	7.6	0.2	1.8
Pauper . . .	7.0	3.0	6.0	0.4	0.8
Female pauper	6.0	2.0	4.0	0.3	0.6
Lunatic . . .	5.4	2.0	5.4	0.2	1.0
Hospitals . .	6.0	3.0	3.5	0.5	2.0

The components of the British navy rations give the following analysis :—

	Ounces Daily	Components			Energy Foot-Tons
		Nitrogen	Fat	Carbon	
Biscuit . . .	20	2.0	0.2	8.4	1,720
Meat . . .	14	1.8	3.0	5.4	1,310
Peas, flour, &c.	7	1.0	...	3.0	560
Sugar . . .	2	...	...	0.8	240
Cocoa . . .	1	0.2	...	0.7	125
Total ,	44	5.0	3.2	18.3	3,955

Prison rations in the United Kingdom are as follows :—

	Ounces Daily		Energy, Foot-Tons	
	Hard Labour	Light Labour	Hard Labour	Light Labour
Bread . .	24.0	21.0	1,992	1,743
Meat . .	4.5	3.5	340	270
Milk . . .	2.0	2.0	48	48
Molasses .	1.0	1.0	100	100
Oatmeal . .	2.0	2.0	304	304
Cheese . .	0.6	0.6	98	98
Flour . . .	1.3	0.7	192	104
Salt . . .	0.5	0.5	60	60
Cocoa . .	0.5	0.5	62	62
Vegetables .	1.0	1.0	10	10
Potatoes . .	14.0	14.0	530	530
Total .	51.4	46.8	3,736	3,329

The French navy rations weekly are as follows :—

	Weight, Oz.	Azote, Oz.	Carbon, Oz.
Bread	190	2.0	55.5
Meat	77	2.3	8.0
Peas	30	1.2	12.0
Butter	5	...	3.5
Coffee	5	...	1.0
Sugar	6	...	2.5
Wine	120	...	5.0
Brandy	15	...	4.0
Salt	5	...	...
Total . .	453	5.5	91.5

The following table shows approximately the ordinary weekly consumption of food by a male adult between twenty and sixty years :—

	Bread, Lbs.	Meat, Oz,	Butter, &c., Oz.	Sugar, Oz.	Potatoes, Lbs.	Daily Energy, Foot-Tons
U. Kingdom .	9	50	10	36	9	4,030
France . . .	12	35	4	9	13	4,170
Germany . .	11	30	4	9	24	4,920
Russia . . .	11	25	3	5	4	2,960
Austria . .	10	30	4	9	13	3,730
Italy . . .	8	12	2	4	1	1,940
Spain . . .	10	32	2	3	...	2,330
Portugal . .	8	23	2	6	...	1,950
Sweden . .	8	30	6	10	12	3,390
Norway . .	8	35	7	6	12	3,350
Denmark . .	10	30	11	10	8	3,460
Holland . .	9	28	7	16	16	4,090
Belgium . .	11	30	7	13	25	5,050
Switzerland .	11	30	6	12	3	3,170
Europe . .	10½	30	4	11	10	3,600
U. States . .	9	75	10	25	3	3,390
Canada . .	8	43	11	20	14	3,950
Australia . .	10½	95	9	37	7	4,490

The above does not include fish, eggs, fruit, vegetables, chestnuts, rice, and other articles of much importance. The aggregate food for a man doing physical or mental work should be equal to at least 3300 foot-tons daily, for a woman 2200, and for a child 1100 foot-tons.

Meat is apparently the most important element of food. Dr. De Renzi states that 4 per cent. of the population of Naples die of impoverishment of the blood caused by want of meat. At the ironworks of Thorn the operatives fed on vegetables, &c., lost fifteen days a year by sickness until meat was introduced in 1833, when the average fell to three days per operative. See *Food*.

DISEASE

In 1883 the deaths per 100,000 inhabitants from certain diseases were as follows :—

	Small-pox	Typhoid	Whooping Cough	Diph-theria	Scarlatina	Measles	Infant Diarrhœa
London . .	3	24	40	40	50	61	64
Edinburgh .	...	25	48	45	39	57	43
Glasgow . .	2	46	557	162	90	139	250
Paris . . .	20	92	30	87	4	47	216
Marseilles .	38	139	19	102	6	139	315
Berlin . . .	1	18	29	224	68	96	412
Brussels . .	94	28	33	28	4	31	325
St. Petersburg	46	153	14	136	75	57	236
Vienna . .	10	21	30	35	17	31	76
Baltimore . .	155	91	15	194	82	31	22

The following table shows approximately the ratios of various diseases in 10,000 deaths :—

	England	France	Germany	Russia	Italy	Switzerland	Belgium	Holland	Scandinavia	United States	Canada
Apoplexy	270	400	390	210	360	370	310	280	350	140	110
Bronchitis . . .	1,150	310	400	1,500	30	600	480	220	620	...	130
Cancer	235	...	260	150	160	300	140	180	330	130	126
Diphtheria . . .	55	360	270	210	360	304	280	130	230	480	114
Erysipelas . . .	36	48	35	...	50	...	40	...	...	...	68
Heart	620	290	230	200	580	385	190	180	220	350	370
Measles	184	180	100	80	95	46	165	150	...	...	220
Phthisis	1,100	1,120	1,270	1,960	900	1,110	1,820	950	1,020	1,420	1,620
Pneumonia . . .	510	720	400	1,150	540	600	450	570	710	...	660
Puerperal	49	100	...	70	...	50	...	50	100	40	145
Rheumatism . . .	41	35	25	40	...	...	...	...	40	59	70
Scarlatina . . .	402	20	160	90	10	146	140	40	360	220	458
Scrofula	62	130	...	180	30	...	90	140	70	70	...
Small-pox . . .	130	80	8	40	60	54	150	100	120	...	55
Typhoid	210	720	450	480	240	184	460	460	280	310	364
Whooping-cough .	250	115	...	...	50	112	280	180	185	148	260

N

Ague.—In 10,000 deaths those from ague were :—

At		At			At		
London	. . 2	Amsterdam .	. 106	Finland	. 180		
Lisbon	. . 60	Naples .	. . 107	U. States	. 240		
Haarlem	. . 70	Portuguese army	120	Athens	. . 420		
Zeeland	. . 80	Genoa . .	. 133	Rome .	. 460		

Apoplexy.—In 10,000 deaths those from this disease were :—

At		At		At	
Amsterdam	. 380	Geneva . . 400		Naples . . 370	
Athens .	. 630	Gibraltar . . 150		New Orleans 91	
Bavaria	. 370	Hamburg . . 620		Nova Scotia . 55	
Belgium	. 410	Holland . . 280		Paris . . . 330	
Berlin .	. 410	Iceland . . 100		Quebec . . 105	
Berne .	. 420	Ireland . . 160		Rome . . . 530	
Bologna	. 420	Italian cities . 360		St. Helena . 430	
Bordeaux	. 780	Lima . . . 70		St. Petersburg 210	
Brussels	. 310	Lisbon . . . 685		Scotland . . 420	
Buda Pesth	. 140	Malaga . . 350		Shanghai . . 200	
Canada	. 98	Malta . . 600		Spain . . . 400	
Christiania	. 220	Mantua . . 590		Sweden . . 590	
Copenhagen	. 230	Mexico . . 340		Turin . . . 610	
England	. 280	Milan . . . 200		U. States,Nor. 184	
Frankfort	. 380	Montevideo . 430		,, South 96	
French cities	. 400	Munich . . 390		Zurich . . . 400	

The occurrence of apoplexy is most frequent in France, Russia, and Holland in winter, and in Canada in summer :—

Seasons	France	Russia	Holland	Canada
Spring . . .	27.0	24.0	25.8	25.3
Summer . . .	23.7	23.8	20.1	26.3
Autumn . . .	19.3	21.2	23.6	22.5
Winter . . .	30.0	31.0	30.5	25.9
Total .	100.0	100.0	100.0	100.0

Its occurrence according to months, taking the year as 1200, was as follows :—

	London (1840)	Den-mark	France	Calcutta	Italian Cities
January . .	123	122	139	108	143
February .	108	110	112	102	135
March . .	104	93	91	111	110
April . .	95	99	127	138	95
May . . .	96	97	106	97	94
June . . .	76	93	109	64	74
July . . .	89	98	109	75	78
August . .	88	77	67	83	74
September .	98	85	67	87	80
October . .	89	103	67	97	90
November .	120	110	97	120	110
December .	114	113	109	118	117
	1,200	1,200	1,200	1,200	1,200

The increase of this disease in England is remarkable, deaths yearly per million inhabitants being as follows :—

1850–66	. . . 457	1874–80	. . . 550
1867–70	. . . 504	1886	. . . 577
1871–73	. . . 517		

In Holland it is found that of 100 patients 46 are males, 54 females.

The distribution of this disease according to age in France was :—

Of 1000 Cases

Age		Age		Age	
Under 10	. . 22	30–40 . . . 110		61–70 . . . 229	
10–20	. . 30	41–50 . . . 153		Over 70 . . 192	
21–30	. . 62	51–60 . . . 202			

Asthma.—Of 10,000 deaths there are from this disease 66 in England, 48 in Scotland, and 33 in Ireland. Deaths according to season show :—

Spring	16.1
Summer	7.0
Autumn	23.2
Winter	53.7
	100.0

Bright's Disease.—In 10,000 deaths there were of this disease :—

At		At		At	
Amsterdam	. 120	Denmark . . 80		Lisbon . . 30	
Berne .	. . 100	Frankfort . . 130		Munich . . 30	
Brussels	. . 50	French cities . 14		Norway . . 60	
Budapesth	. 90	Holland . . 50		Shanghai . . 150	
Copenhagen	. 100	Italy . . . 40		United States 35	

Bronchitis.—In 10,000 deaths there were of this disease :—

At		At		At	
Amsterdam	. 220	Canada . 130		London . . 1,450	
Athens	. 391	England . 1,080		Rome . . 290	
Berlin .	. 420	Ireland . . 1,220		St. John's . 2,330	
Brussels	. 480	Lisbon . 420		Scotland . 1,310	

The death-rate among bronchitis patients in the Paris hospitals is 6 per cent. in the quarter ending March, 4 per cent. in that ending June, 2 per cent. in the September, and 6 per cent. in the December quarter, giving an average of 5 per cent. for the year. In Sweden and Norway the prevalence of bronchitis in the various months is (taking 1200 per annum as a total) thus :—

Month	Sweden	Norway	Month	Sweden	Norway
January . .	150	160	July . . .	49	53
February . .	160	152	August . .	46	48
March . .	143	132	September .	58	62
April . . .	130	112	October . .	82	82
May . . .	102	96	November .	104	110
June . . .	67	72	December .	109	121

The prevalence of bronchitis among British troops on foreign stations was as follows :—

Bronchitis Patients per 1000 Sick

St. Helena	. 61	Mauritius . . 84		Gibraltar . . 132	
Ceylon .	. . 70	Jamaica . . 85		Malta . . . 140	
Bengal	. . 71	Cape Colony 98		Canada . . 156	

The ratio among garrisons in the United Kingdom was 161.

Deaths occur in London according to season thus :—

Spring	20.2
Summer	12.5
Autumn	27.0
Winter	40.3
	100.0

Calculus or Stone.—In 10,000 deaths there were of this disease :—

At		At		At	
Belgium	. . 4	Geneva . . . 6		Riga 3	
Brussels	. . 4	Hamburg . . 2		Russia . . . 5	
Copenhagen	. 13	Holland . . 3		Turin . . . 2	
Denmark	. . 4	Iceland . . . 20		U. States N. . 1	
England	. . 6	Paris 2		U. States, S. . 2	

The ages at which this disease occur are as follows :—

Age	Males	Females
Under 30 . . .	4.5	18.2
30–40 . . .	14.8	28.0
41–50 . . .	34.3	20.6
51–60 . . .	21.5	22.0
Over 60 . . .	24.9	11.2
Total . .	100.0	100.0

In 100 cases 38 are males, 62 females.

Cataract.—Of 100 cases 54 are males, 46 females.
The ratio of age is shown thus :—

Per 1000 Cases

Age		Age		Age	
Under 10 . .	28	31–40 . . .	36	61–70 . . .	344
10–20 . . .	32	41–50 . . .	102	Over 70 . .	218
21–30 . . .	36	51–60 . . .	204		

Cancer.—In 10,000 deaths there were of this disease :—

At		At		At	
Amsterdam .	230	England, men	170	New York .	80
Bâle . . .	320	Do., women .	300	Norway . .	320
Belgium . .	140	Frankfort . .	370	Paris . . .	270
Berlin . . .	160	Geneva . .	530	Potsdam . .	250
Berne . . .	320	Glasgow . .	130	Rome . . .	170
Bordeaux . .	320	Hamburg . .	330	St. Petersburg	150
Breslau . .	360	Holland . .	180	Scotland . .	170
Brussels . .	420	Iceland . .	30	Shanghai . .	300
Carlsruhe . .	330	Ireland . .	190	Stettin . . .	210
Christiania .	290	Kiel . . .	340	Stockholm .	240
Copenhagen .	360	Königsberg .	180	Turin . . .	160
Dantzig . .	180	Lisbon . .	260	United States	130
Dresden . .	240	London . .	200	Do., North .	170
Edinburgh .	230	Milan . . .	220	Do., South .	90
England . .	230	Montevideo .	150		

Mental worry, says Dr. Herbert Snow, of the Cancer Hospital, is the chief exciting cause of cancer. In 1864 in England the proportion of cancer sufferers was 385 to the million; in 1888 it had risen to 610—the number of deaths in the latter year being 6284 males, and 11,222 females, or 17,506 in all.

Cholera.—The losses may be approximately set down in the principal visitations of this epidemic as follows :—

	1832	1849	1854	1865	1873	1884	Total
United Kingdom	53,000	55,000	22,000	18,000	...	...	148,000
France	115,000	110,000	144,000	15,000	63,000	10,000	457,000
Germany	67,000	80,000	119,000	33,000	52,000	...	351,000
Austria	99,000	145,000	218,000	220,000	436,000	...	1,118,000
Italy	...	...	...	13,000	...	14,300	?
Spain and Portugal . .	...	...	236,700	150,000	...	119,000	507,000
Other countries . . .	200,000	850,000	400,000	245,000	70,000	10,000	1,775,000
Total . .	534,000	1,240,000	1,139,700	694,000	621,000	153,900	4,382,600

According to Rosemberg, one million persons perished in the cholera of 1848–49. According to Kolb, in that visitation in Russia 1,687,000 persons were attacked, of whom 668,000 died. It was apparently the worst plague that visited Europe since the Middle Ages. The death-rate on that occasion was 22 per 100 sick in England, and 40 in Austria. In the previous visitation of 1832 the rate varied little in all countries, from 38 to 42 per cent. In the cholera of 1855 it was as follows :—

	Per 100 Cases			Per 100 Cases
Spain . . .	30	Sweden . . .	52
Austria . . .	42	Prussia . .	59
Russia . . .	50	Denmark . .	65

In that of 1866 the average was 50 per cent. in Belgium and 55 in Italy, being in the latter 56 for men and 54 for women.

The victims in various cities in 1865 were as follows :—

Deaths per 10,000 Inhabitants

London . .	18	Paris . . .	66	Madrid . .	102
Dublin . .	41	Berlin . . .	83	Brussels . .	184
Vienna . .	51	Naples . .	89	Palermo . .	197
Marseilles .	64	St. Petersburg	98	Constantinople	738

The greatest mortality was at Rome and Madrid on Sundays, at London and Berlin on Wednesdays, and at Paris on Saturdays.

The following table shows the deaths from cholera in various cities at different periods :—

City	Date	Deaths	In 100 Sick	In 10,000 Population	City	Date	Deaths	In 100 Sick	In 10,000 Population
Aleppo . . .	1865	12,000	...	1,020	Malaga . . .	1865	2,000	40	200
Antwerp . .	1865	2,300	50	205	Madrid . . .	1865	3,300	...	102
Berlin . . .	1865	5,600	...	83	Naples . . .	1884	7,100	...	144
Brussels . .	1865	3,100	75	184	Palermo . .	1867	4,000	...	197
Constantinople	1865	12,000	...	190	,, . . .	1884	3,000	53	125
Copenhagen .	1853	4,800	65	402	Paris . . .	1832	18,700	...	205
Dublin . .	1865	1,200	...	41	,, . . .	1848	19,200	...	190
Genoa . . .	1854	2,200	52	190	,, . . .	1854	9,100	...	76
Guadeloupe .	1856	1,900	...	1,480	,, . . .	1866	9,900	...	66
Liège . . .	1865	2,600	55	280	Riga . . .	1848	2,000	29	390
London . .	1832	6,700	48	40	St. Petersburg .	1848	28,000	54	510
,, . . .	1849	14,600	47	70	,, . . .	1865	6,000	...	98
,, . . .	1854	40,300	...	180	Smyrna . . .	1856	2,500	45	300
,, . . .	1865	5,500	...	20	Stockholm . .	1832	3,300	41	405
Marseilles . .	1884	1,800	...	49	Toulon . . .	1854	2,600	...	510

The ratios of age in the deaths at Paris were as follows :—

Age	1832 Ratio	Age	1854 Deaths per 10,000 Persons
Under 10 . .	9.2	Under 2 .	255
10–20 . . .	3.2	2–5 . . .	104
20–30 . . .	11.8	5–15 . .	33
30–40 . . .	15.2	15–20 . .	55
40–50 . . .	15.2	20–40 . .	66
50–60 . . .	15.4	40–60 . .	79
Over 60 . . .	30.0	Over 60 .	171
	100.0		

Its ravages in 1854 were especially among very young or very old persons. The ratio of sexes in 1832 was 100 males to 101 females, and in the same year the mortality according to the floors in houses occupied by the patients was distributed thus :—

Basement	.	.	.	.	.	.	13.5
1st floor .		.	.	.	.	.	25.8
2nd floor	.	.	.	.	.	.	20.4
Over 2nd floor		.	.	.	.	.	40.3
			Total	.	.	.	100.0

One of the most deadly outbreaks on record was at the Salpetrière lunatic asylum, near Paris, in 1849, when 45 per cent. of the inmates were attacked, and of the patients 76 per cent. died. In the Anglo-Indian army cholera makes more ravages among Europeans than natives, viz. :—

Soldiers attacked . . 250 Europeans to 100 natives
Deaths 230   ,,   ,,   ,,

The prevalence at Bombay according to months, taking the year as 1200, is as follows :—

January	.	.	.	122	July	.	.	.	135
February	.	.	.	113	August	.	.	49
March	.	.	.	130	September	.	.	31
	First quarter	.	365		Third quarter	.	215
April	.	.	.	151	October	.	.	40
May	.	.	.	151	November	.	.	50
June	.	.	.	143	December	.	.	85
	Second quarter	.	445		Fourth quarter	.	175

Convulsions (Infant).—In 10,000 deaths there were of this disease as follows :—

At		At		At	
Algiers . .	790	Christiania .	110	Mexico . .	630
Amsterdam .	600	Copenhagen .	560	Paris . . .	667
Athens . .	266	Dresden . .	2,110	Rio Janeiro .	320
Berlin . .	1,380	England . .	440	St. Petersburg	200
Brussels . .	450	Glasgow . .	300	Shanghai .	150
Buda Pesth .	730	Hamburg . .	1,070	Turin . . .	560
Cairo . .	2,030	Lisbon . .	190	U. States (N.)	320
Canada . .	180	London . .	360	U. States (S.)	170

Croup.—In England there are of 10,000 deaths 70 from croup, and in Bavaria 392. In Sweden and Norway 52 per cent. of cases are fatal. The prevalence of the disease according to months (taking the year as 1200) is shown thus :—

Month	Sweden	Norway	Month	Sweden	Norway
January	.	144	141	July	. .	45	47
February	.	136	132	August	.	48	50
March	.	130	134	September	76	89
April	. .	110	105	October	.	108	103
May	. .	88	84	November	128	125
June	. .	64	64	December	123	126

Cretinism.—According to a statement published in 1860, the number of cretins was as follows :—

Country				Number	Per Million Population
Switzerland	.	.	.	20,000	8,100
France	.	.	.	31,000	870
Italy	.	.	.	10,460	480
Germany .	.	.	.	20,200	550
Austria .	.	.	.	13,800	440
Ireland	.	.	.	4,900	740
Denmark	.	.	.	1,990	1,470
United States .	.	.	1,200	40

Diabetes.—Deaths from this disease are seven in 10,000 in the United Kingdom, and 150 at Shanghai. The ratio of sexes among patients is :—

				France		England
Males	.	.	.	74	...	67
Females	.	.	.	26	...	33
				100	...	100

The ratio of age and profession are in France as follows :—

Age	Males	Females	Profession	Per Cent.
Under 20	14.4	32.0	Capitalists . .	25
20–30	24.4	26.4	Lawyers . .	21
30–40	28.4	20.7	Merchants .	15
40–50	18.0	9.4	Clergy . . .	8
Over 50	14.8	11.5	Various . .	31
Total .	100.0	100.0	Total .	100

This disease was in 45 per cent. of cases accompanied by obesity, and in 38 per cent. by rheumatism.

Diarrhœa.—In 10,000 deaths there were of this disease :—

In		In		In	
London . .	460	Ireland . .	250	Mexico . .	950
England . .	212	Canada . .	110	Hong-Kong	1480
Scotland . .	210	United States	880		

The prevalence of this disease according to months (taking the year as 1200) was as follows :—

Month	Sweden	Norway	Bavaria	Belgium
January	.	.	41	98	52	83
February	.	.	41	89	56	77
March	.	.	31	72	53	102
April	.	.	33	61	53	93
May	.	.	30	65	52	98
June	.	.	55	60	70	109
July	.	.	150	113	110	138
August	.	.	292	190	210	132
September	.	.	227	143	238	112
October	.	.	149	95	160	96
November	.	.	94	109	89	79
December	.	.	54	105	57	81
Year	.	1200	1200	1200	1200

Digestive Disorders.—In 10,000 deaths there were of these diseases :—

In		In		In	
Brussels .	1,500	Genoa . .	1,580	Rome . .	1,100
Catania .	2,900	Milan . .	1,300	Turin . .	1,550
England .	990	Paris . .	1,050		

Diphtheria.—In 10,000 deaths there were of this disease :—

In		In		In	
Amsterdam	200	Dresden	130	Italian cities	360
Athens	219	England	55	London	180
Bavaria	248	Edinburgh	250	Munich	240
Berlin	320	France	360	New York	300
Brussels	440	Frankfort	130	Philadelphia	370
Canada	300	Glasgow	220	Roumania	360
Christiania	440	Hamburg	320	St. Petersburg	210
Copenhagen	160	Holland	130	United States	480

The prevalence of this disease according to months (taking the year as 1200) was in Sweden, Norway, Saxony, and the hospitals of Paris as follows :—

	Sweden	Norway	Saxony	Paris	Death-Rate at Paris
					Per Cent.
January	121	136	135	101	76
February	119	120	126	104	76
March	99	112	100	116	77
April	93	89	79	106	71
May	85	88	75	110	73
June	72	79	71	84	65
July	69	79	54	75	51
August	77	73	50	90	62
September	86	87	91	83	71
October	112	102	119	103	70
November	137	118	155	117	75
December	130	117	145	111	74
	1,200	1,200	1,200	1,200	72

Deaths in Paris from this disease were as follows :—

Period	Deaths Yearly	Per 10,000 Inhabitants
1865–69	816	43
1872–75	1,165	61
1876–80	2,020	95
1881–83	2,230	99

Dropsy.—Of 10,000 deaths there are from this disease in England 94, in Scotland 56, in Ireland 98, in Bavaria 650, and in Belgium 423. Deaths occur in England according to seasons thus :—

Spring	24.0
Summer	21.6
Autumn	26.4
Winter	28.0
	100.0

Drink.—Lombard states that in 10,000 deaths in various countries the ratio for deaths from drink stood thus :—

Italy	1	London	12	Brussels	40
Genoa	5	Berlin	13	Copenhagen	70
Turin	5	Bâle	20	New York	75
Amsterdam	5	Breslau	20	Oldenburg	87
Munich	6	Vienna	20	Kiel	90
Dublin	10	England	21	Stockholm	90
Edinburgh	10	Berne	35		

In nine years ending 1876 the annual deaths from drink in France averaged 448, of which 87 per cent. were men and 13 per cent. women.

Another table on this subject will be found under *Deaths*, p. 180.

Dysentery.—In 10,000 deaths there were of this disease :—

In		In		In	
Ceylon	2,300	Holland	290	Senegal	2,900
England	10	Italian cities	130	Valparaiso	1,060
Gold Coast	420	Lima	610	United States	160
Guinea	4,130	Montevideo	570	Zanzibar	420

On the Guinea Coast it attacks 50 per cent. of the garrison yearly, and 8 per cent. of cases prove fatal. At Bombay 9 per cent. of the troops are attacked, and 9 per cent. of cases prove fatal. Annesley gives the percentage of soldiers attacked at various stations thus :—

	Per Cent.		Per Cent.		Per Cent.
North India	12	South India	34	Hyderabad	36
Mysore	22	Middle India	38	Madras	47

According to Hirsch, there have been in various parts of Europe since 1719 no fewer than 546 epidemics of dysentery, of which 404 were in summer, 113 in autumn, and 29 in other seasons. In Saxony it is found that, supposing 1200 deaths occur in a year from this disease, the months will stand thus :—

January	6	July	101
February	20	August	367
March	14	September	352
First quarter	40	Third quarter	820
April	13	October	181
May	13	November	73
June	27	December	33
Second quarter	53	Fourth quarter	287

The ages of soldiers at Mauritius attacked by this disease were :—

Age	Cases per 1000 Men
18–24	6
25–33	11
34–40	19
41–50	36

Epilepsy.—The ratio of deaths from this disease among 10,000 deaths is as follows :—

England	51	Ireland	38
Scotland	33	Norway	13

In France the attacks of this disease, taking the year as 1200, occur thus :—

January	106	July	98
February	111	August	83
March	103	September	87
First quarter	320	Third quarter	268
April	104	October	94
May	107	November	95
June	112	December	100
Second quarter	323	Fourth quarter	289

Erysipelas.—In 10,000 deaths there were of this disease :—

In		In	
Belgium	40	Ireland	25
Canada	40	Italy	50
Cape Colony	25	Malta	14
England	36	Mexico	20
France	48	Montevideo	53
Germany	35	Paris	70
Gibraltar	15	Scotland	50
India	17	Switzerland	40

Fever.—The predisposition to fever varies with age in the following degrees :—

Age	Degree	Age	Degree
Under 5	10	25–30	102
5–10	94	30–40	44
10–15	182	40–50	16
15–20	269	50–55	6
20–25	197	Over 55	2

Napoleon lost 51,000 soldiers by fever in his campaign of 1812, and the French army 17,000 men in the Crimea in 1855.

Fractures.—Dr. Gurlt (Berlin, 1863), collected statistics of 17,300 cases ; results :—

Head	5 per cent.
Trunk	14 ,,
Arms	48 ,,
Legs	33 ,,
	100 ,,

The total showed 75 per cent. males, 25 per cent. females, the relation of cases according to age with regard to sexes being :—

Age	Males		Females
Under 12	72	to	28
13–20	86	,,	14
21–30	91	,,	9
31–40	96	,,	4
51–80	65	,,	35

Fractures are more frequent in winter than in summer.

Goitre.—This disease as well as cretinism is common in those parts of France and Italy more than 3000 feet over sea-level. There are 420,000 goitrous people in France, and 2 per cent. of conscripts are rejected for this cause. There are 3400 cases in Siberia.

Gout.—The ratio of deaths in England from this disease is usually 12 per 10,000 ; it is eighteen among men and six among women. Of 100 patients in France 94 are usually males, 6 females. The ratio of age at which first symptoms appear is shown thus :—

Age	
Under 20	2.4
20–30	27.6
30–40	37.6
40–50	23.0
Over 50	9.4
	100.0

Of 10,000 patients admitted to hospital at Munich, 24 suffered from gout ; in the same number 210 at St. George's Hospital, London, and at Paris only one.

Heart-Disease.—In 10,000 deaths there were of this disease :—

In		In		In	
Algiers . .	100	Germany .	230	Norway . .	170
Amsterdam .	290	German cities	270	Paris . . .	270
Athens . .	323	Holland . .	180	Rio Janeiro .	350
Belgium . .	190	Hungary .	170	St. Petersburg	200
Brussels . .	685	Ireland . .	510	Scotland . .	650
Canada . .	370	London . .	420	Shanghai .	1,510
Copenhagen	320	Mexico . .	95	Switzerland .	350
England . .	610	Milan . . .	640	Turin . . .	490
Edinburgh .	490	Montevideo .	470	United States	350
France . .	290				

The ages at which this disease prevails in France are shown by the ratio of deaths thus :—

Of 1000 Deaths

Age		Age		Age	
Under 10 .	2	31–40 . . .	388	61–70 . . .	50
10–20 . . .	10	41–50 . . .	254	Over 70 . .	28
21–30 . . .	140	51–60 . . .	128		

Hepatitis.—In 10,000 deaths there were of this disease :—

In		In		In	
Amsterdam .	81	Italy . . .	90	Portugal . .	94
Brussels . .	81	Malta . . .	250	St. Helena .	290
Buenos Ayres	350	Mexico . .	380	Senegal . .	500
Corfu . . .	150	Montevideo .	340	Shanghai .	740
Frankfort .	24	Paris . . .	130	Swatow . .	2,500
French cities	110				

The ratio of British soldiers on foreign service attacked in twelve months by this disease was as follows :—

In	Per 1000	In	Per 1000	In	Per 1000
Australia .	3	Cape . . .	27	Mauritius .	24
Bengal . .	54	Ceylon . .	48	N. Zealand .	6
Bombay . .	37	Hong-Kong	26	Shanghai .	14
Burmah . .	61	Madras . .	73	Yokohama .	14

Among Sepoy troops the ratio is only 3, and on the Abyssinian expedition it was 14 per 1000.

Hernia.—The number of conscripts per 1000 affected by this disease was in Italy 21, Sardinia 17, Corsica 17, Nice 28, France 33.

Hydrophobia.—The annual number of deaths from hydrophobia in one million deaths in various countries from this disease was as follows :—

Country	Period	Deaths Yearly, per Million	Country	Period	Deaths Yearly, per Million
England	1853–57	25	Prussia	1816–70	165
,,	1869–88	74	,,	1871–73	90
France	1851–60	24	Sweden	1786–90	282
,,	1861–72	42	,,	1856–60	40
Bavaria	1851–56	42	Belgium	1856–60	32

There has been an increase in France since the dog-tax was imposed in 1860. Tables for ten years in France down to 1872 showed that the disease declared itself in the following ratio of days after the person was bitten :—

Days		Per Cent.
Under 20		8.7
20–40		31.0
40–60		29.8
60–90		21.7
Over 90		8.8
Total	.	100.0

The term of incubation when animals were bitten varied as follows :—

Days	Horses	Cows	Sheep	Dogs
Under 20	4.4	...	16.5	16.8
20–30	13.2	30.0	45.2	26.6
30–40	8.8	35.0	33.0	21.7
40–50	26.4	25.0	3.4	14.0
Over 50	47.2	10.0	1.9	20.9
Total . .	100.0	100.0	100.0	100.0

Of 3000 cases collected in thirty years by eleven French physicians the bites were :—

In		
Spring		27.6
Summer		25.5
Autumn		22.5
Winter		24.4
Total	.	100.0

The average term of incubation was approximately influenced by the age of the person bitten, and also the relative mortality :—

Age	Days of Incubation	Death-Rate
Under 10	55	36 per cent.
10–20	52	39 ,,
21–30	64	60 ,,
31–60	60	61 ,,
Over 60	65	70 ,,
General average . . .	60	47 ,,

The above was for a period of ten years, but tables for 23 years down to 1872 reduced the death-rate in France to 42 per cent of persons bitten by mad dogs, &c., viz.:—

Bite in	Number Bitten	Died	Ratio of Deaths	Mean Days of Incubation
Hands, arms .	485	213	44 per cent.	74
Face	102	90	88 ,,	48
Legs	190	40	21 ,,	61
Body	80	12	15 ,,	...
Total .	857	355	42 ,,	...

Of 717 recorded cases in France in the above period, 655 persons were bitten by a dog, 38 by a wolf, 22 by a cat, 1 by a fox, and 1 by a cow.

Bouley's tables for 1863–68 showed that 31 per cent. of cauterised persons died, and 85 per cent. of non-cauterised. After the disease making its appearance death ensued usually on the third or fourth day, as the following table shows:—

First or second day	28.1
Third or fourth day . . .	53.7
Over fourth day	18.2
	100.0

Under Dr. Pasteur's treatment the following results have been obtained at Paris:—

Year	Cases Treated	Died	Recovered
1887 . . . 306	...	3 ...	303
1888 . . . 385	...	4 ...	381

The British Government in the above two years sent 85 patients to be treated by Dr. Pasteur, of whom 5 died and 80 recovered.

Influenza.—This epidemic is caused by sudden changes of temperature. On January 2, 1782, at St. Petersburg, the thermometer suddenly rose 40 degrees in one night, and 40,000 people were attacked next day. In 1827 it carried off thousands of horses all over Europe. In 1872 it killed 16,000 horses in New York city. In December 1889 it ravaged Europe, attacking over three million persons, but the mortality was probably under 2 per cent. of cases.

The duration of the attack varies with age, the French reports showing thus:—

Age	Days	Age	Days
20 to 30 . . .	7	50 to 60 . . .	12
30 to 50 . .	9'	Over 60 . . .	23

Leprosy.—The number of lepers in various countries is as follows:—

Canton . . . 10,000	Norway . . . 1,770
Crete . . . 900	Portugal . . . 3,000
Greece . . . 350	Reunion . . . 600
Iceland . . . 13	Rio Janeiro . . 120
India . . 131,600	Sandwich Islands . 1,800
Mauritius . . 3,300	Sweden . . . 100

The establishment at Molokai, Sandwich Islands, was several years under the charge of Father Damien, who died in 1889. The proportion of sexes in Greece is 64 males to 36 female lepers, and the ages at which the disease makes its first appearance give the following ratios:—

Age	Males	Females	General Average
Under 10 . . .	10.8	2.8	8.0
10–20 . . .	33.0	38.6	35.0
20–30 . . .	28.0	23.0	26.0
30–40 . . .	20.2	27.6	23.0
Over 40 . . .	8.0	8.0	8.0
Total .	100.0	100.0	100.0

In Russia leprosy is found in sixty-five districts, and the number of fresh victims registered in 1887 was 615. This would lead us to suppose that the existing number of lepers in the empire is about 6000.

Indian statistics for 1881 showed lepers thus:—

Males 98,982	Bengal 53,880
Females 32,636	Madras, &c. . . 77,738
Total . 131,618	Total . 131,618

Norway has five leper hospitals, containing altogether about 600 patients. The disease is on the decline, viz.:—

Year	Lepers	Per 100,000 Inhabitants
1856	2,612	191
1875	1,771	98

In Cyprus a leper-farm was established in 1830, one mile from Nicosia: area, 100 acres, tillage 11 acres; house of 26 rooms occupied by:—

Greeks 44	Males 33
Turks 2	Females 13
Total . . 46	Total . . 46

Death-rate, 16 per cent. per annum; new patients 14 in the year (1879). All very clean. Five married couples; two have children quite healthy, but rest are childless. All the lepers have lost fingers. One woman of 80 has been there fifty years.

Measles.—In 10,000 deaths there were of this disease— in England 184, London 265, Scotland 140, Ireland 110, and Holland 150.

The prevalence of this disease, as shown by the ratio of deaths in the various months, taking the year as 1200, was:—

	London	Saxony		London	Saxony
January .	85	119	July . .	117	94
February .	55	112	August .	108	120
March .	74	84	September	96	64
April . .	80	65	October .	100	64
May . .	82	90	November	119	119
June . .	125	93	December	159	176
Half year	501	563	Half year	699	637

Meningitis. — In 10,000 deaths there were of this disease:—

In	In	In
Amsterdam . 370	Buda-Pesth . 460	St. Petersburg 500
Belgium . . 280	France . . . 300	United States 190

Epidemics of this disease have occurred: we have no returns of the number attacked, but the death-rate per 100 patients is recorded thus:—

Versailles . . 41	Sweden and } 33	Metz . . . 70
Naples . . 46	Norway }	Aigues Mortes 75
Strasburg . . 51	Lille . . . 65	Rochefort . . 84
	Orleans . . 70	

The general relative mortality was 63 per cent., most of the above epidemics occurring among garrison troops. Swedish statistics give the following particulars:—

Age	Ratio of Cases	Death-Rate
Under 3 . . .	23.0	42 per cent.
3–10 . . .	33.6	25 ,,
10–20 . . .	31.2	35 ,,
Over 20 . . .	12.2	30 ,,
Total . .	100.0	33 ,,

Mumps.—Lombard gives the ratio of age of cases thus:—

In 1000 Patients

Age	Age	Age
Under 5 . . 95	10–15 . . . 256	30–40 . . . 108
5–10 . . . 243	15–30 . . . 230	Over 40 . . 68

The prevalence of cases according to months was as follows, according to Hirsch :—

January	.	.	.	292	July	55
February	.	.	.	97	August . . .	14
March .	.	.	.	124	September . .	27

First quarter .	.	513	Third quarter	.	96

April	.	.	.	124	October . . .	176
May	.	.	.	27	November . .	110
June	.	.	.	70	December . .	84

Second quarter	.	221	Fourth quarter	.	370

Neuralgia.—The prevalence of this disease according to sex is variously stated, viz. :—

	Anstie	Valleix	Eulenberg	Medium
Males . .	32	47	28	36
Females . .	68	53	72	64
Total .	100	100	100	100

The ratio according to age is stated thus :—

Age						Valleix	Eulenberg
Under 20 .	.	.	.	.	.	8.1	6.0
20–30	.	.	.	.	.	22.9	19.0
30–50	.	.	.	.	.	44.8	55.0
Over 50	.	.	.	.	.	24.2	20.0
	Total	.	.			100.0	100.0

Obesity.—Of 100 patients, 36 are men and 64 women. The disease is hereditary in 49 per cent. of cases. Remarkable instances of obesity are the following :—

Name	Weight, Lbs.	Age	Residence
James Mansfield .	476	82	Debden, Monmouth
Mr. Bright . .	596	29	Maldon, Essex
Dan. Lambert .	739	40	Stamford, Lincoln

Ophthalmia.—Of 1000 persons in hospitals in Sweden, 48 suffered from this disease.

Paralysis.—Of 100 cases of general paralysis 86 are male, 14 female. The ratio of age is thus :—

Age				Males	Females
Under 30 .	.	.	.	7.1	...
30–40	.	.	.	40.8	32.0
41–50	.	.	.	33.4	50.0
Over 50	.	.	.	18.7	18.0
	Total	.	.	100.0	100.0

Of 10,000 deaths there are from this disease 260 in England, 280 in Scotland, and 145 in Ireland. Deaths in England according to season :—

Spring .	.	.	.	.	24.2
Summer	.	.	.	.	19.0
Autumn	.	.	.	.	25.6
Winter .	.	.	.	.	31.2
		Total	.	.	100.0

The ratio of age in cases of spinal paralysis is as follows :—

Under 16	.	.	.	.	.	9.5
16–20	.	.	.	.	.	26.4
20–25	.	.	.	.	.	18.0
25–35	.	.	.	.	.	26.4
35–45	.	.	.	.	.	13.5
Over 45 .	.	.	.	.	.	6.2
		Total	.	.	.	100.0

In 100 patients 70 were males and 30 females.

Pellagra.—The number of cases yearly, per million inhabitants, is 150 at Lodi, 800 at Cremona, 2400 at Bergamo, and 2900 at Brescia. About 1000 persons die of pellagra yearly in Venetia.
In 1879 the sufferers from pellagra were :—

	Number	Per 1000 Inhabitants
Lombardy	40,800	31.7
Venetia	29,800	30.5
Emilia	18,700	23.7
Other provinces . .	8,600	...
Total .	97,900	...

Peritonitis.—The ratios of age of patients stand thus :—

Age						Per Cent.
Under 20	.	.	.	.	.	14.0
20–30 .	.	.	.	.	.	26.0
30–40 .	.	.	.	.	.	27.5
Over 40 .	.	.	.	.	.	32.5
			Total	.	.	100.0

Phthisis.—In 10,000 deaths there were of this disease as follows :—

Alabama	.	630	Flanders . .	2600	Norway . . 1288
Alexandria	.	250	Florida . .	570	Nuremberg . 1410
Amsterdam	.	870	France . .	1120	Paris . . . 1430
Antwerp .	.	1590	Frankfort .	1550	Pennsylvania 1420
Archangel	.	1960	Geneva . .	1250	Philadelphia 1320
Athens .	.	1076	Glasgow . .	1580	Riga . . . 300
Augsburg	.	1000	Holland . .	950	Rio Janeiro . 1880
Bavaria .	.	1010	Iceland . .	5	Rome . . 1140
Belgium .	.	1825	Ireland . .	1160	Russia . . 1960
Berlin .	.	990	Lima . . .	1770	St. Petersburg 1510
Bologna .	.	1340	Lisbon . .	1147	S. Francisco 1590
Bordeaux	.	1620	London . .	1280	Santa Cruz . 1400
Brussels .	.	1750	Louisiana .	970	Scotland . . 1050
Buda-Pesth.		1545	Lyons . .	1340	Shanghai . 600
Cairo . .	.	1010	Maine . .	2580	Stockholm . 1600
California .		1380	Maryland .	1720	Sweden . . 1340
Canada . .		1610	Massach'setts	2000	Switzerland . 770
Catania .	.	450	Melbourne .	740	Turin . . . 830
Christiania .		1720	Mexico . .	490	Ulm . . . 1130
Copenhagen		1270	Milan . .	1320	U. States . 1420
Corfu . .	.	2190	Missouri .	750	Vienna . . 2080
Drontheim .		1700	Montevideo .	1270	Vologda . . 2060
England .	.	1010	Munich . .	1320	Wisconsin . 1320
Finland .	.	840	New York .	1550	Zeeland . . 640

Height above sea-level has a marked effect on this disease, as shown by the following death-rates from phthisis in Baden and Switzerland :—

Feet over Sea	Per 10,000 Deaths		
	Baden	Switzerland	Medium
Less than 1,600 . .	1,040	860	950
1,600–2,700 . .	830	730	780
2,700–3,200 . .	750	390	570
Over 3,200 . .	860	500	680

Similar results are obtained in the Andes.
Some occupations predispose to phthisis ; the following table shows among 100 sick persons of each trade the ratio of those suffering from it :—

RATIO OF PHTHISIS TO ALL SICKNESS

	Per Cent.		Per Cent.		Per Cent.
Needle-makers	70	Hairdressers .	32	Masons . . .	13
File-makers .	63	Weavers . .	25	Millers . . .	11
Lithographers	48	Painters . .	25	Brewers . . .	11
Grinders . .	40	Printers . .	22	Tanners . . .	9
Tobacconists .	37	Shoemakers .	19	Bakers . . .	7
Watchmakers	37	Glaziers . .	18	Butchers . . .	7
Stonecutters .	36	Hatters . .	16	Charcoal-burners	2
Glassworkers .	35	Carpenters .	14	Miners . . .	1

The above table has reference only to the United Kingdom, the deaths from phthisis per million inhabitants showing as follows yearly :—

England	.	1850–59	2,730	Scotland	.	1876–85	2,183
,,	.	1860–69	2,547	Ireland.	.	1886	2,220
,,	.	1870–79	2,205	London	.	1879	2,476
,,	.	1886	1,718	,,	.	1886	2,010

In Scotland the deaths yearly from phthisis average thus :—

	Per Million Persons Living			Age	Age Ratio		
	Urban	Rural	Total		Males	Females	Total
Males . .	2,680	1,970	2,370	0–20 .	16.2	16.8	16.5
Females .	2,850	1,680	2,460	20–40 .	51.4	53.6	52.5
Gen. pop.	2,760	1,820	2,420	Over 40 .	32.4	29.6	31.0
				Total	100.0	100.0	100.0

During the years 1830–46, the mean mortality from phthisis in the British army on home service amounted to 7.8 per 1000 of strength, the highest mortality being among the Foot Guards, with whom it reached 11.3 per 1000 of strength. In the Equitable Assurance Company at that time, the average mortality between the ages of thirty and forty, from all diseases of the lungs, amounted to 3.4 per 1000. The army mortality from phthisis was, therefore, three times greater than necessary. The mortality of troops from the same cause appeared to be equally great at some foreign stations. Thus at Gibraltar 41 per cent. of the total deaths among the troops were caused by phthisis in the years 1837–46, while in the year 1875 only 23 per cent. of the deaths were due to this cause. At Jamaica the deaths from phthisis in the years 1817–36 amounted to 7.5 per 1000 of strength, while in 1859–66 the mortality from this cause had fallen to 1.4 per 1000 of strength. In Trinidad, lung disease killed on an average 11.5 per 1000 of strength between 1817 and 1836. Among the black troops at Sierra Leone phthisis appears to be the most fatal disorder. In ten years, 1861–70, the deaths were 22.5 per 1000 of strength, and of these phthisis caused one-third. In the twenty years 1817–36, the deaths in Canada from phthisis were 4.2 per 1000 of strength, whereas in 1859–65 they were but 1.6 per 1000. In India the annual ratio of deaths and invalided from phthisis were for the years 1863–70 as follows :—

					Died per 1000	Invalided per 1000
Bengal	.	.	.	.	1.7	3.2
Bombay .	.	.	.	.	1.4	3.4
Madras .	.	.	.	.	1.4	4.2

Deaths from phthisis in the Royal Navy average 2.6 per 1000 yearly, which is attributed to the foulness of the air.

The deaths and invalided from phthisis in the British army at home in the years 1864–70 were per 1000 men yearly thus :—

				Deaths	Invalided
Household cavalry .	.	.		3.8	8.2
Cavalry of line	.	.		1.4	4.0
Foot guards	.	.		2.3	9.5
Infantry of line	.	.		2.1	5.5

Among the causes of phthisis the most potent is overcrowding. At the ill-ventilated Leopoldstadt prison of Vienna in 1843–47 no fewer than 51 per 1000 deaths were from phthisis. At the well-ventilated House of

Correction in the same city, in the years 1850–54, the deaths from phthisis were only 8 per 1000.

Among British garrisons abroad 12 per 1000 in Ceylon are attacked yearly with phthisis, 12 in the Anglo-Indian army, 3 among Sepoys, 6 at Yokohama, and 15 at Hong-Kong. Among hospital patients in Tasmania 7 per cent. suffered from this disease, and in the French hospital at Senegal 8 per cent.

Plague.—Milroy gives a list of 196 of the most destructive plagues since the year 1500, viz. :—

				1501–1600	1601–1700	1701–1800	1801–1841
England	.	.	.	15	12	0	0
France .	.	.	.	14	11	1	0
Germany	.	.	.	12	19	4	1
Low Countries	.	.	.	2	14	0	0
Russia and Scandinavia .	.	.		2	7	4	2
Italy and Levant	.	.	.	26	15	12	11
Spain	.	.	.	.	5	3	3	1
Total	.	.	.	76	81	24	15

The most terrible, however, which is recorded was that commonly known as the Black Death, which came from Persia into Europe in 1346. It was preceded by myriads of locusts, which filled the wells and poisoned the water in the countries east of the Caspian Sea. At Bagdad 500,000 persons died in 90 days; at Cairo the mortality reached 10,000 in 24 hours. In Europe it lasted four years, and was supposed to have carried off 24,000,000 persons, more than 30,000 towns and villages being depopulated. So late as 1350 ships were met at sea with all dead on board. Among the cities which suffered most were :—

Avignon	.	.	60,000	Paris	.	.	.	50,000
Dublin .	.	.	14,000	Parma .	.	.	.	40,000
Florence	.	.	100,000	Siena	.	.	.	70,000
Genoa .	.	.	40,000	Strasburg	.	.	.	26,000
London.	.	.	100,000	Valencia	.	.	.	100,000
Marseilles	.	.	56,000	Venice .	.	.	.	70,000
Naples .	.	.	60,000	Vienna .	.	.	.	40,000
Norwich	.	.	50,000					

Since the beginning of the seventeenth century the worst plagues have been :—

Date	Place	Deaths	Weeks	Deaths per Week
1656	Naples . .	380,000	28	13,400
1665	London . .	68,800	33	2,100
1720	Marseilles . .	39,100	36	1,100
1771	Moscow . .	87,800	32	2,700
1778	Constantinople	170,000	18	9,500
1798	Cairo . . .	88,000	25	3,500
1812	Constantinople	144,000	13	11,100
1834	Cairo . . .	57,000	18	3,200
1835	Alexandria .	14,900	17	900
1871	Buenos Ayres	26,300	11	2,400

The relative mortality in certain plagues was as follows :—

Date	Place	Died, per Cent.	Recovered, per Cent.	Authority
1798	Cairo . . .	67	33	Genettes
1798	Aboukir . .	25	75	M'Grigor
1813	Malta . . .	50	50	Greaves
1815	Corfu . . .	91	9	White
1834	Cairo . . .	29	71	Gaetani
1835	Alexandria .	35	65	Clot Bey
1871	Buenos Ayres	40	60	Bosch

Pneumonia.—In 10,000 deaths there were of this disease :—

In		In		In	
Amsterdam	. 570	Buenos Ayres	400	Ireland	. . 220
Athens	. 856	Copenhagen	. 710	London	. . 530
Bombay	. 26	Edinburgh	. 270	Paris	. . 680
Bordeaux	. 400	England	. 450	Scotland	. 410
Brussels	. 430	Frankfort	. 400	Valparaiso	1,890
		Glasgow	. 490		

Puerperal Fever.—In 10,000 deaths there were of this disease :—

In		In		In	
Amsterdam	. 53	Copenhagen	. 160	London	. . 25
Athens	. 110	England	. 37	New York	. . 56
Austria	. 40	France	. 100	St. Petersburg	74
Bâle	. 90	Geneva	. 95	Scotland	. 50
Berne	. 80	Holland	. 50	Switzerland	. 77
Brussels	. 210	Iceland	. 70	United States	. 40
Canada	. 140	Ireland	. 52		

At the lying-in hospital of St. Petersburg in 32 years down to 1871 there were 39,200 accouchements, and 1960 mothers died—just 5 per cent. The death-rate per 1000 accouchements according to months was :—

January	. . 54	May	. . . 55	September	. 34
February	. . 56	June	. . . 68	October	. . 35
March	. . 60	July	. . . 52	November	. 40
April	. . 59	August	. . . 29	December	. 55

The quarter ending June showed the highest rate, 61, and that ending September only 38.

In Prussia during 25 years down to 1866 it was found that 33 per 1000 of married women died of puerperal fever. Lefort states that the average in lying-in hospitals in Europe is 34 per 1000, and only 5 per 1000 in women confined at home.

Rheumatism.—In 10,000 deaths there were of this disease :—

In		In		In	
Bordeaux	. 50	Germany	. 25	Paris	. . 29
Canada	. 70	Glasgow	. 21	Scotland	. 38
Copenhagen	. 35	Iceland	. 80	Switzerland	. 25
Denmark	. 70	Ireland	. 56	United States	. 59
Edinburgh	. 23	Italy	. 21	Upsala	. . 40
England	. 50	Lisbon	. 43	Valparaiso	. 44
Frankfort	. 46	London	. 55		

Of 1000 cases of sickness the ratio of rheumatism is as follows :—

In		In		In	
Algiers	. 12	Hong-Kong	. 30	New Zealand	. 32
Amoy	. 39	India	. 50	Riga	. . 84
Bombay	. 30	Lisbon	. 40	Sandwich Isds.	41
Buda-Pesth	. 65	London	. 60	Shanghai	. 92
Burmah	. 48	Lyons	. 98	Singapore	. 60
Cape	. 30	Madras	. 60	Sweden	. . 77
Corfu	. 35	Malaga	. 51	Switzerland	. 30
England	. 100	Mauritius	. 31	Tahiti	. . 41
Gibraltar	. 47	Melbourne	. 77	Yokohama	. 65
		Natal	. 30		

During the war of 1861–63 in the United States the Federals had 5,825,000 men under colours, and of these 254,700 were sent to hospital for rheumatism, being 44 per 1000. The French army at home has usually 30 rheumatic patients yearly per 1000 men, but in Algeria only 12; the garrison at Rome also averaged 12. In 1873 the deaths from this disease in the French army were 3 per 100,000 men.

In 14 years ending 1874 the ratio of British seamen on home and foreign stations attacked yearly with rheumatism was :—

Per 1000 Seamen

U. Kingdom	. 56	China	. . . 84	Australia	. . 89
West Indies	. 71	Mediterranean	85	Pacific	. . . 97
South America	75	East Indies	. 87	Cape	. . . 104

The general average for the said period was 84.

The following table shows the distribution of rheumatism according to months, taking the year as 1200 :—

	Cases		Deaths		Deaths to 1000 Cases	Relative Malignancy
	London	Paris	In France	At Paris		
January . .	96	83	107	109	25	150
February . .	115	92	105	79	12	72
March . .	85	92	105	95	30	180
April . .	114	109	105	102	7	40
May . .	90	104	97	103	21	128
June . .	118	112	92	94	6	37
July . .	102	120	92	121	22	130
August . .	77	102	100	97	15	90
September . .	91	92	109	110	23	135
October . .	115	97	100	107	16	94
November . .	95	97	95	85	16	94
December . .	102	100	93	98	8	50
Year . . .	1,200	1,200	1,200	1,200	17	100

The ratio of age in deaths from rheumatism at Paris (1865–74) was as follows :—

In 1000 Deaths from Rheumatism

Age		Age		Age	
Under 5	. . 11	15–25	. . . 115	40–60	. . . 331
5–15	. . . 58	25–40	. . . 279	Over 60	. . 206

There were 102 males to 100 female deaths.

Scarlatina.—In 10,000 deaths there were of this disease :—

In		In		In	
Amsterdam	. 50	England	. 350	Rome	. . . 10
Bavaria	. 236	Germany	. 160	Switzerland	. 430
Berlin	. 60	Holland	. 40	Scotland	. 180
Brussels	. 140	Ireland	. 290	St. Petersburg	90
Copenhagen	. 240	London	. 480	U. States	. 220
		Paris	. 60		

The prevalence of this disease in Sweden, Norway, and Saxony, according to months (taking the year as 1200), is shown thus :—

Month			Sweden	Norway	Saxony
January	.	.	106	122	116
February	.	.	99	110	102
March	.	.	93	103	78
April	.	.	95	92	63
May	.	.	91	90	59
June	.	.	90	85	59
July	.	.	81	80	68
August	.	.	80	76	84
September	.	.	91	72	113
October	.	.	118	100	155
November	.	.	136	137	151
December	.	.	120	133	152

Sciatica.—Arnoldi gives the age of 1000 patients of this disease :—

Under 10	. . 36	30–40	. . . 218	60–70	. . . 115
10–20	. . . 101	40–50	. . . 199	Over 70	. . 28
20–30	. . . 145	50–60	. . . 158		

Scrofula.—In 10,000 deaths there were of this disease :—

In		In		In	
Amsterdam	. 140	England	. 56	New York	. 83
Berlin	. 100	France	. 130	Norway	. 80
Bordeaux	. 67	Glasgow	. 60	Paris	. . 47
Brussels	. 90	Ireland	. 110	Russia	. . 180
Canada	. 15	Lisbon	. 110	St. Petersburg	260
Copenhagen	. 70	London	. 60	Scotland	. 150
Dresden	. 90	Lyons	. 60	Turin	. . 30
Edinburgh	. 95	Munich	. 33	United States	70

In German cities 50 per cent. of foundlings die of scrofula. In Buda-Pesth 2½ per cent. of hospital patients suffer from this disease. In Italy 7 per 1000 of conscripts are rejected for it.

Scurvy.—In the British navy the returns were :—

Period	Cases Yearly		Per 10,000 Seamen
1856–65	28	...	6
1866–75	4	...	1

In the year 1820 the garrison of St. Peters, Iowa, 1000 men, had 500 cases, of whom 168 died. The United States army in 20 years ending 1859 had 26 cases yearly per 1000 men, but only 1 per cent. of the cases proved fatal. The French army in the Crimea had 23,400 cases and 639 deaths, say 3 per cent. In the hospital at Constantinople, 1855–56, there were 25,200 cases and 2916 deaths, or nearly 12 per cent. In the Franco-German war the French prisoners at Ingolstadt had 16 cases per 1000. In Lord Anson's expedition, 1740, the *Centurion* lost 58 per cent. and the *Gloucester* 78 per cent. of her crew from scurvy. Admiral Martin lost 10 per cent. of his men in 1746.

Small-Pox. — In 10,000 deaths there were of this disease :—

In		In		In	
Amsterdam	100	Denmark	70	Marseilles	152
Austria	250	England	130	Paris	80
Baltimore	620	Finland	60	Rome	290
Berlin	4	Germany	8	St. Petersburg	40
Brussels	150	Glasgow	8	Scotland	14
Buda-Pesth	140	Ireland	41	Sweden	160
Canada	55	Italy	60	Switzerland	54
Copenhagen	70	London	106	Vienna	40

The months in which it is most prevalent are shown in the following table, taking the year as 1200 :—

Month	Sweden	Norway	Bavaria	London
January	120	144	120	50
February	130	161	152	23
March	129	157	162	45
April	156	142	165	38
May	152	172	142	65
June	128	133	110	57
July	91	78	70	68
August	52	46	52	80
September	41	34	46	93
October	43	27	45	153
November	68	40	58	225
December	90	66	78	303
Year	1,200	1,200	1,200	1,200

Deaths yearly from this disease in various European armies averaged thus :—

	Per 100,000 Men	
	1872–75	1876–81
British	8 ...	3
German	1 ...	0
French	8 ...	16
Austrian	99 ...	18

In Germany the deaths from this disease averaged in 10,000 deaths as follows :—

1816–70	101
1871–74	555
1875–82	8

In 1874 a law was passed making re-vaccination compulsory on all persons in Germany over twelve years of age. The ratio in 10,000 deaths for Berlin and London was as follows :—

	1870–79		1880–83
Berlin	324	...	4
London	230	...	106

In Austria the ratio per 10,000 deaths showed :—

1872–76	560
1877–81	250

French physicians have instituted a comparison between Paris and Rio Janeiro touching this disease at various seasons and temperatures, viz. :—

Quarter ending	Mean Temperature, Fahrenheit		Ratio of Year's Death	
	Paris	Rio Janeiro	Paris	Rio Janeiro
31st March	38	77	24.2	12.6
30th June	50	72	22.8	15.6
30th September	65	70	16.5	37.7
31st December	52	76	36.5	34.1
Year	51	74	100.0	100.0

In the hot season at both places the deaths are fewer. The ratio of ages showed thus :—

Age	Deaths	
	Paris	Rio Janeiro
Under 7	30.3	28.4
7–25	19.6	34.2
25–40	34.2	26.9
Over 40	15.9	10.5
	100.0	100.0

The deaths per million inhabitants in the United Kingdom yearly averaged thus :—

England		London		Scotland		Ireland	
Date	Deaths	Date	Deaths	Date	Deaths	Date	Deaths
...	...	1660–80	4,170	...	...	...	...
1760–1800	3,000	1760–90	2,260	...	...	...	...
1840–54	430	1840–60	408	...	...	1844	403
1871–73	178	1871–73	1,040	1864	305	1864–74	108
1881	100	1881	640	1874–82	28	1875–82	82

In the epidemic of 1861 the deaths in England were per million : army, 455 ; civilians, 928 ; London, 2420. In that of 1881 the returns showed deaths per million inhabitants as follows :—

	Vaccinated		Unvaccinated		Difference
London	90	...	3,350	...	35 to 1
England	98	...	4,380	...	44 to 1

In 10,000 deaths in London at the following periods those from small-pox were as follows :—

Period						Per 10,000
1622–1700						525
1701–1800						808
1801–30						480
1841–60						150
1861–70						105
1871–81						202

In the epidemic at Leipzig in 1871 the death-rate was 12,700 per million inhabitants, 70 per cent. of whom were unvaccinated. The following table shows the relative mortality as affected by vaccination :—

	Vaccinated, Per Cent.	Unvaccinated, Per Cent.
London	15	45
Montreal	16	54
Boston	15	50
Philadelphia	17	64

During the Franco-German war the Germans lost only 263 men from this disease, the French 23,499, the former having been re-vaccinated in barracks. In the war in Paraguay, the Brazilians lost 43,000 men from malignant or black small-pox, that is, 35 per cent. of their army, nine cases in ten proving fatal.

In ten years ending 1869 the average number of vaccinations in France was 587,000 per annum, leaving 405,000 children born yearly over that number unvaccinated.

The cases of small-pox averaged 18,100 yearly, and deaths 2490, or 14 per cent. Deaths in Paris from small-pox averaged yearly as follows :—

Period	Deaths Yearly	Per 10,000 Deaths
1821–30	585	180
1831–40	465	160
1841–50	319	90
1851–60	426	85
1861–70	1,512	310
1871–80	695	140

In the ratio of sexes, 130 males died of this disease to 100 females. Swedish statistics compare vaccinations and deaths from small-pox as follows :—

Period	Vaccinations per 1000 Births	Small-Pox, Deaths Yearly per Million Inhab.
1800–9	280	560
1810–19	520	190
1820–29	680	132
1830–39	730	270
1840–49	720	43
1850–55	810	160
1861–75	...	110

Between 1770 and 1799, when vaccination was not in use, the deaths in Sweden yearly from small-pox averaged 2100 per million inhabitants.

In Norway vaccination is not compulsory, but persons unvaccinated are not allowed to vote at elections. In Austria the number of vaccinations yearly shows :—

Year	Vaccinations	Per 1000 Births	
		Vaccinated	Not Vaccinated
1882	675,000	810	190
1884	686,000	799	201
1886	692,000	803	197

In Japan, in 1880, the number of vaccinations was 1,459,000, of which 3 per cent. were unsuccessful.

This disease was known in Ireland in 1241, and in Denmark in 1527.

Sunstroke.—In 10,000 deaths in England two are usually from this cause, the annual average of such deaths showing thus :—

	1863–70	1871–78
Men	57	88
Women	9	23
Total	66	111

This disease is most prevalent at Bassorah in the Persian Gulf, and also in the United States. In 1874 the steamer *Liverpool* in the Persian Gulf lost in one day 3 officers and 21 seamen by sunstroke.

Syphilis.—In 10,000 deaths there were of this disease—

In		In		In	
Amsterdam	18	London	68	Portugal	80
Bordeaux	42	Louisiana	23	Riga	36
Brussels	42	Lyons	9	St. Petersburg	20
Copenhagen	34	Massachusetts	12	Scotland	17
Edinburgh	55	Milan	5	Shanghai	50
England	40	New York	40	Strasburg	14
Genoa	20	Norway	8	Sweden	10
Ireland	20	Pennsylvania	9	Turin	30

This disease was unknown in Norway till 1710, in Italy till 1786, in Canada till 1790, and in Tasmania till 1821. The percentage of patients in various hospitals found to be suffering from it was :—

Hospital	Men, Per Cent.	Women, Per Cent.
Berlin	20	25
Vienna	15	...
Stettin	10	51
Brunswick	33	85

In Holland 10 per cent. of men in hospital, in Strasburg 38 per cent., in Malaga 18, in Gibraltar 8, in Amoy 43, in Dantzig 10, in Bremen 7 per cent. suffered from syphilis. In Hanover 20, and in Magdeburg 30 per cent. of the women in hospital. The prevalence of this disease in 1000 soldiers was as follows :—

Prussia	54	France	102	Canada	160
Austria	63	Holland	105	Bengal	167
Russia	65	Australia	110	Gibraltar	187
Italy	71	Mauritius	122	Cape	303
Malta	81	Jamaica	123	Algeria	309
Belgium	90	Spain	115	Java	333
Great Britain	101	Portugal	135		

In Paris 23 per cent. of foundlings, and in Moscow and St. Petersburg 25 per cent. are infected with this disease. In French military hospitals 19 per cent. are syphilitic cases, in Belgian 7, in British 29.

Tetanus.—The ratio of wounded soldiers who got tetanus in various campaigns was as follows :—

Date	Army	Per 1000 Wounded
1782	British in India	25
1811	,, Spain	13
1855	,, Crimea	2
1798	French in Egypt	35
1836	,, Algeria	57
1855	,, Crimea	3
1859	,, Italy	7
1870	,, Strasburg	5
1864	German in Denmark	7
1866	Hanoverian at Sadowa	12
1870	German at Strasburg	9
1871	,, Paris	10
1859	Spanish in Morocco	18
1862	War of United States, Northerns	2

Death-rate in cases of tetanus is stated thus :—

Date	Per Cent.	Observer
1793	100	Heurteloup
1834	96	Curling
1825–50	86	Guy's Hospital
1855	91	English in Crimea
1859	92	French in Italy
1861–63	90	Federals in United States
1870	70	Glasgow Hospital
1877	85	Richter

In the American War, 1863, the rate was 87 per cent. when the wound was in the arm, 90 in the leg, 91 in the body, and 95 in the head or neck.

The *Lancet* (1870) gives the following ratio of mortality as to the number of days elapsing before tetanus pronounced itself :—

Days	Ratio of Cases	Death-Rate	Recovered
		Per Cent.	Per Cent.
Before 10 . . .	47.5	78	22
10 to 22 . . .	45.0	52	48
Over 22 . . .	7.5	48	52

Typhoid Fever.—In 10,000 deaths there were of typhoid fever :—

In		In		In	
Algiers	. 340	England .	. 210	Naples	. 300
Amsterdam	. 460	France.	. 720	New York	. 350
Antwerp	. 290	Frankfort .	. 420	Norway	. 990
Astrakan	. 870	Geneva .	. 350	Palermo	. 890
Athens.	. 475	Germany .	. 450	Paris .	. 680
Belgium	. 460	Glasgow .	. 810	Rome .	. 230
Berlin .	. 320	Ireland .	. 210	Russia .	. 480
Brussels	. 220	Italy .	. 290	Scotland .	. 235
Catania	. 840	Liege .	. 270	Strasburg .	. 230
Christiania	. 630	London .	. 240	Sweden .	. 203
Copenhagen	. 700	Lubeck .	. 370	Turin .	. 460
Denmark .	. 400	Lyons .	. 270	Vienna .	. 560
Edinburgh	. 460	Milan .	. 320	United States	450
		Munich .	. 450		

In Paris hospitals 21 per cent. of typhoid cases prove fatal. In St. Petersburg of 10,000 males between 15 and 20 years of age 38 die yearly of typhoid, and of women of the same age 17.

Wolfshugal states the yearly deaths from typhoid per 100,000 inhabitants as follows :—

Amsterdam	.	39	Hamburg .	.	54	New York	.	35
Berlin .	.	96	Leipzig	.	300	Paris .	.	50
Birmingham	.	54	Lille .	.	40	Pesth .	.	96
Bristol .	.	5	Liverpool .	.	92	Rome .	.	91
Christiania	.	7	London .	.	37	Rotterdam	.	17
Dublin .	.	79	Manchester	.	58	Strasburg .	.	33
Frankfort .	.	42	Metz .	.	48	Turin .	.	143
Genoa .	.	63	Milan .	.	95	Venice .	.	70
Hague .	.	38	Munich .	.	118	Vienna	.	59
			Naples	.	128			

The ratio of sickness shows 22 typhoid patients in 1000 sick at Bremen, 30 at Stuttgart, 31 at Hamburg and Munich, 34 at Breslau, and 54 at Vienna, during ten years ending 1855.

Deaths from typhoid in the French army average 18 per 10,000 yearly, in the Bavarian 28, and in the garrison of Munich 84. The rate of deaths yearly from this disease in the French army, according to years of military service, was thus :—

Years of Service	Deaths per 10,000 Men	Years of Service	Deaths per 10,000 Men
1st . . .	44	6–7	12
2–3. . .	42	8–9	5
4–5. . .	19	10 or over	4

Deaths from typhoid and other fevers, according to months, taking the year as 1200, occurred thus :—

		Typhoid						Other Fevers		London	Ague
		London	Holland	Saxony	Switzerland	Norway	Belgium	W. Africa	Mauritius	Typhus	Algeria
January .	. .	87	60	102	106	150	62	118	20	135	119
February	. .	62	30	95	83	103	95	129	65	108	78
March .	. .	58	54	87	73	64	106	98	208	129	77
April .	. .	41	55	81	67	43	99	105	340	133	50
May .	. .	48	54	80	85	38	72	110	275	133	42
June .	. .	70	55	79	92	32	62	107	111	110	60
July .	. .	97	36	92	98	57	69	102	71	92	101
August .	. .	150	78	121	107	95	128	85	34	81	121
September	. .	171	158	131	131	117	128	83	25	68	126
October .	. .	165	240	126	126	116	167	78	15	72	152
November	. .	151	240	105	130	209	113	84	16	71	146
December	. .	100	140	101	102	176	99	101	20	68	128
Year .	.	1,200	1,200	1,200	1,200	1,200	1,200	1,200	1,200	1,200	1,200

Typhus.—In 10,000 deaths there were of this disease in England 30, Scotland 47, Holland 21, Amsterdam 23. The rate of mortality among persons attacked is 20 per cent. in England. An epidemic of typhus occurred in Ireland in 1817–19, when 800,000 persons were attacked, of whom 45,000 died ; a second was in 1847, caused by famine, and was still more fatal. Emigrants conveyed it to Quebec, where 8600 sick were at one time under treatment in 1847. The hospitals of Russia had 57,000 typhus patients in 1857. Deaths from typhus in Vienna averaged 734 per annum in the years 1865–71, but since the sanitary improvements of 1872 the average has been only 291 per annum.

Whooping-Cough.—In 10,000 deaths there were of this disease :—

In		In		In	
Belgium	. 280	Edinburgh	. 360	London .	. 370
Brussels	. 70	England .	. 250	Norway .	. 190
Christiania	. 100	Glasgow .	. 610	Scotland .	. 220
Copenhagen	. 160	Holland .	. 180	Sweden .	. 190
Denmark .	. 160	Ireland .	. 250	U. States .	. 148
		Italy .	. 50		

Of 100 cases in Belgium 64 occur under twelve months, 32 between that age and five years, and four over the age of five years.

Yellow Fever.—It made its first appearance at Rio Janeiro in December 1849. The official record of deaths from 1851 to 1860 averaged 910 per annum, and in 1870–74 they were 1245 per annum. This is supposed to represent one-fourth of the real number. An outbreak occurred at Buenos Ayres in January 1871, which carried off 26,200 persons, or nearly 10 per cent. of the population.

At Vera Cruz the deaths from this disease, according to months, taking the year as 1200, stand thus :—

January	.	. 26	July .	.	. 125
February	.	. 42	August .	.	. 109
March .	.	. 90	September	.	. 109
First quarter	. 158		Third quarter	. 343	
April .	.	. 125	October	.	. 34
May .	.	. 195	November	.	. 42
June .	.	. 212	December	.	. 41
Second quarter	. 532		Fourth quarter	167	

At Rio Janeiro, where the seasons are reversed, the distribution is :—

January	. . .	112	July . . .	52
February	. .	140	August . . .	36
March .	. .	214	September . .	24

First quarter	. 466		Third quarter	. 112
April	. . .	243	October . .	23
May	. . .	171	November . . .	26
June	. . .	110	December . .	49

Second quarter	. 524	Fourth quarter	. 98

ENGLAND AND WALES

The following table shows the deaths from various diseases in England and Wales since 1861 :—

	Deaths Yearly per Million Inhabitants				Ratio in 10,000 Deaths in 1886
	1861–70	1871–80	1881–85	1886	
Cancer . . .	386	455	545	583	302
Cholera . .	107	25.	16	19	10
Convulsions .	1,231	1,041	844	821	426
Croup . . .	248	169	162	132	69
Diabetes . .	30	38	51	59	30
Diarrhœa . .	968	916	652	888	461
Diphtheria . .	188	121	156	147	76
Erysipelas . .	85	93	83	55	28
Intemperance .	38	40	48	49	26
Liver . . .	417	425	370	335	175
Measles . .	443	379	410	431	224
Nervous system	1,575	1,760	1,800	1,835	955
Old age . .	1,315	1,140	1,009	1,021	530
Phthisis . .	2,487	2,130	1,820	1,718	891
Puerperal . .	56	74	92	75	39
Respiratory .	3,357	3,742	3,580	3,595	1,870
Rheumatism .	112	133	132	91	47
Scarlatina . .	971	720	434	215	112
Small-pox . .	156	244	78	10	5
Typhoid . .	885	485	272	213	111
Venereal . .	84	94	93	91	47
Violent . . .	771	735	663	626	324
Whoop.-cough .	530	513	457	464	241
Various. . .	6,063	5,906	5,533	5,805	3,001
Total . .	22,503	21,378	19,300	19,278	10,000

The returns may be summed up thus : —

Disease	Deaths per Million Inhabitants				No. of Deaths in 1886
	1871–80	1881–82	1883–85	1886	
Zymotic . .	3,724	2,874	2,747	2,648	73,747
Constitutional	3,594	3,627	3,362	3,330	92,751
Local . . .	9,920	9,470	9,780	9,915	276,302
Various . .	3,404	2,566	2,814	2,759	77,032
Violent . . .	736	683	650	626	17,444
Total .	21,378	19,220	19,353	19,278	537,276

The bills of mortality in London show as follows :—

Dr. Farr stated that if zymotic or preventible diseases were unknown in England the span of life would be six years longer. There is some improvement in this direction, as shown by zymotic deaths since 1838, viz.:—

Period	Annual Average	Per Cent. of Deaths
1838–40	61,807	17.7
1848–50	88,924	22.1
1858–60	79,930	17.6
1867–68	87,114	18.2
1871–80	90,620	17.4
1881–85	75,040	14.5
1886	73,747	13.7

The following table shows the ratio of deaths in 1886 according to sex :—

	Per Million Inhabitants			In 10,000 Deaths
	Male	Female	Total	
Apoplexy	561	592	577	300
Asthma	106	70	87	45
Brain	366	303	334	173
Bright's disease . .	273	219	245	128
Bronchitis	2,247	2,164	2,208	1,143
Cancer	424	733	583	302
Convulsions . . .	951	698	821	426
Croup	148	117	132	69
Diarrhœa	954	823	888	461
Diphtheria	141	152	147	76
Drink	65	35	49	26
Dropsy	10	14	12	6
Epilepsy	123	105	114	59
Erysipelas	59	50	55	29
Gout	31	7	19	10
Heart	277	289	283	147
Hydrophobia . . .	2	...	1	...
Liver	354	317	335	174
Measles	449	414	431	224
Old age	906	1,129	1,021	530
Phthisis	1,846	1,596	1,718	891
Pneumonia	1,187	839	1,008	523
Puerperal fever . .	...	145	75	39
Rheumatism . . .	28	34	31	16
Scarlatina	221	209	215	112
Small-pox	14	6	10	5
Syphilis	86	74	80	42
Typhoid	197	167	182	95
Typhus	10	7	9	5
Whooping-cough . .	435	492	464	241
Various	7,870	6,470	7,144	3,703
Total . .	20,341	18,270	19,278	10,000

It will be observed that phthisis and pneumonia are more fatal among males than females, but cancer and apoplexy are more frequent among females.

	Deaths per Million Inhabitants				Actual Number of Deaths in 1886		
	1859	1869	1879		Males	Females	Total
Bronchitis . .	2,310	2,995	3,622	Measles . .	1,088	1,003	2,091
Phthisis . .	2,850	2,756	2,476	Scarlatina . .	368	362	730
Diarrhœa . .	1,210	1,061	495	Typhoid . .	321	297	618
Fever . . .	657	558	249	Whooping-cough	1,289	1,582	2,871
Measles . . .	488	455	670	Diphtheria . .	427	424	851
Scarlatina . .	1,280	1,325	719	Diarrhœa . .	2,074	1,922	3,996
Small-pox . .	425	86	122	Phthisis . .	4,884	3,525	8,409
Violent deaths .	752	747	774	Cancer . .	967	1,721	2,688
Whooping-cough .	639	1,178	792	Various . .	30,739	29,551	60,291
Total .	...	...	...	...	42,157	40,388	82,545

SCOTLAND

The causes of death during ten years ending 1885 were :—

Age	Per Million Males of each Age							
	Phthisis	Bronchitis	Pneumonia	Diarrhœa	Bright's	Apoplexy	Cancer	Total from all Causes
0–5	957	8,263	3,108	2,713	134	362	27	49,170
5–10	615	289	293	74	108	74	8	6,090
10–15	856	93	133	31	67	41	7	4,100
15–20	2,552	104	276	31	95	47	25	5,650
20–30	3,624	150	463	42	119	65	53	7,460
30–40	3,308	417	794	69	202	209	144	9,760
40–50	2,741	1,316	1,346	113	308	488	554	14,980
50–60	2,415	3,286	1,935	262	481	1,278	1,401	24,370
60–70	1,925	6,258	2,817	720	756	3,031	2,624	43,930
70–80	1,060	11,418	3,387	1,867	1,022	6,243	3,745	90,770
80–90	445	19,011	4,080	3,413	1,190	9,305	3,835	192,420
90–100	177	24,113	4,078	5,142	887	7,447	3,901	407,350
General average . .	2,093	2,253	1,158	535	213	538	384	19,050

Age	Per Million Females of each Age							
	Phthisis	Bronchitis	Pneumonia	Diarrhœa	Bright's	Apoplexy	Cancer	Total from all Causes
0–5	958	7,118	2,567	2,361	92	285	19	43,270
5–10	764	335	282	72	72	66	9	6,100
10–15	1,459	114	132	37	67	41	13	4,360
15–20	3,434	115	203	28	73	42	21	6,170
20–30	3,928	175	254	48	127	66	64	7,650
30–40	3,592	431	433	81	190	146	381	9,780
40–50	2,559	1,121	564	128	233	457	1,158	11,980
50–60	1,694	2,873	874	289	319	1,182	2,162	20,030
60–70	1,192	6,119	1,484	771	388	2,312	3,098	38,760
70–80	707	12,366	2,489	1,977	531	4,462	3,844	79,150
80–90	317	20,072	2,878	3,649	447	6,948	3,959	176,410
90–100	171	26,199	3,425	5,479	171	6,678	2,911	354,760
General average . .	2,273	2,213	786	498	164	512	637	18,260

The following classification for 1886 distinguishes urban and rural :—

Disease	Deaths per 100,000 Persons Living							
	Cities		Towns		Rural		All Scotland	
	Males	Females	Males	Females	Males	Females	Males	Females
Zymotic	266	259	197	230	125	140	203	211
Constitutional	417	434	313	371	257	304	342	380
Nervous	284	244	246	214	193	185	248	220
Respiratory	495	440	363	291	287	239	393	342
Digestive	152	138	142	134	122	119	139	131
Violent deaths	100	39	92	32	87	30	93	34
Various	471	464	481	519	504	548	487	508
Total . .	2,185	2,018	1,834	1,791	1,575	1,565	1,905	1,826
Small-pox	1	1	1	1	1	1	1	1
Measles	25	22	22	22	9	8	18	17
Scarlatina	42	35	24	29	15	15	28	26
Whooping-cough	69	76	33	41	19	20	45	51
Diphtheria	18	15	15	15	13	12	16	14
Typhoid	15	16	22	25	18	24	18	20
Diarrhœa	61	54	53	59	28	25	49	46
Erysipelas	8	7	7	7	8	7	8	7
Puerperal	...	13	...	12	...	15	...	13
Rheumatism	10	13	10	14	9	12	10	13
Cancer	44	72	43	72	42	81	43	74
Phthisis	245	247	172	197	147	158	197	210
Scrofula	24	19	18	18	12	11	18	16
Old age	46	90	87	133	153	228	97	150
Apoplexy	55	60	56	59	51	57	53	59
Paralysis	54	53	53	50	55	51	53	51
Convulsions	44	32	27	21	18	15	32	24
Croup	19	18	19	15	17	10	19	15
Bronchitis	253	261	183	177	146	145	200	205
Pneumonia	169	122	109	65	78	52	123	85
Various	983	792	880	759	746	618	877	729
Total . .	2,185	2,018	1,834	1,791	1,575	1,565	1,905	1,826

The following table was published in 1840, showing the distribution of diseases according to months :—

LONDON IN '1840

	Small-pox	Measles	Scarlatina	Whoop-ing-Cough	Typhus	Apoplexy	Pneu-monia	Phthisis	General Mortality
January . .	50	85	112	134	113	123	115	104	108
February . .	23	55	103	95	95	108	72	93	89
March . . .	45	74	91	109	101	104	105	108	105
April . . .	38	8c	97	118	107	95	107	102	99
May . . .	65	82	97	99	113	96	94	100	92
June . . .	57	125	128	107	87	76	71	98	89
July . . .	68	117	79	82	87	89	70	105	96
August . . .	80	108	123	74	95	88	59	102	97
September .	93	96	109	65	102	98	62	91	93
October . .	153	100	116	76	96	89	107	93	97
November . .	225	119	86	81	100	120	140	92	103
December . .	303	159	59	160	104	114	198	112	132
Year .	1,200	1,200	1,200	1,200	1,200	1,200	1,200	1,200	1,200

IRELAND

Deaths in 1886 were as follows :—

Disease	Number of Deaths			Ratio in 10,000		
	Males	Females	Total	Males	Females	Total
Zymotic	3,079	3,579	6,658	708	817	763
Constitutional	7,883	8,900	16,783	1,811	2,033	1,922
Local	19,221	17,445	36,666	4,414	3,984	4,202
Violent deaths	1,293	567	1,860	297	130	213
Various	12,017	13,308	25,325	2,770	3,036	2,900
Total . .	43,493	43,799	87,292	10,000	10,000	10,000

The causes of death in 1886 were as follows :—

Disease	Number of Deaths			Ratio in 10,000 Deaths		
	Males	Females	Total	Males	Females	Total
Phthisis	4,903	5,791	10,694	1,127	1,323	1,225
Bronchitis	4,763	5,175	9,938	1,095	1,182	1,140
Pneumonia	1,793	1,014	2,807	412	232	322
Convulsions	1,775	1,416	3,191	408	323	365
Diarrhœa	734	747	1,481	169	170	170
Whooping-cough	541	678	1,219	124	155	140
Cancer	894	1,135	2,029	205	259	232
Old age	8,152	9,360	17,512	1,874	2,136	2,005
Small-pox	...	2	2	...	...	...
Measles	137	147	284	31	33	32
Scarlatina	401	449	850	92	102	97
Typhus	204	190	394	46	43	45
Typhoid	385	387	772	89	86	87
Diphtheria	156	180	336	34	41	38
Erysipelas	127	105	232	29	23	26
Puerperal	...	332	332	...	75	38
Rheumatism	216	282	498	50	64	57
Apoplexy	607	521	1,128	140	120	130
Croup	410	352	762	95	80	88
Various	17,295	15,536	32,831	3,980	3,553	3,763
Total . .	43,493	43,799	87,292	10,000	10,000	10,000

Deaths from violence were 1860, say 207 per 10,000 deaths, or 380 per million of population.

The average of deaths yearly from zymotic diseases for ten years, 1877–86, was as follows :—

Per 100,000 Inhabitants

Small-pox .	223	Diphtheria .	315	Erysipelas .	265
Measles .	1,055	Whooping-cough	} 1,360	Influenza .	58
Scarlatina .	1,404			Diarrhœa .	1,754
		Fever . .	2,374		

FRANCE

In 10,000 deaths in France the following ratios occur :—

Erysipelas .	. 48	Heart . .	. 290	Apoplexy .	400
Puerperal .	. 100	Meningitis .	300	Typhoid .	720
Scrofula .	. 130	Diphtheria .	360	Phthisis .	. 1,120

The returns of Paris hospitals in 1882 showed as follows :—

	Adults		Children		Death-Rate per Cent.	
	Admitted	Died	Admitted	Died	Adults	Children
Bronchitis	5,070	273	497	53	5.4	10.6
Croup	55	25	1,207	821	45.0	68.0
Diarrhœa and dysentery . . .	494	49	541	212	10.0	40.0
Erysipelas	1,175	109	76	32	9.1	42.0
Fractures, &c.	6,753	286	240	1	4.3	0.4
Heart disease	2,116	659	31	11	31.0	35.0
Measles	261	3	404	111	1.1	27.5
Paralysis	421	42	...	...	10.0	...
Phthisis	6,348	3,477	163	116	55.0	71.0
Pleurisy	1,407	176	85	6	12.6	7.0
Pneumonia	2,211	722	322	151	33.0	47.0
Rheumatism	4,416	39	67	1	0.9	1.5
Scarlatina	477	29	258	31	6.2	12.0
Small-pox	1,985	395	204	50	19.9	24.5
Syphilis	3,861	18	115	26	0.5	22.5
Typhoid	3,616	823	470	83	22.8	17.5
Various	33,944	2,212	3,174	292	6.5	9.1
Total	74,610	9,337	7,854	1,997	12.5	25.5

In 10,000 deaths the various diseases stood thus :—

Bronchitis	.	292	Measles . .	103	Rheumatism .	36
Croup . .	.	760	Paralysis .	. 38	Scarlatina .	54
Diarrhœa .	.	235	Phthisis .	3,233	Small-pox .	401
Erysipelas .		126	Pleurisy . .	164	Syphilis . .	40
Fractures .	.	258	Pneumonia .	786	Typhoid . .	815
Heart disease	603					

In 10,000 cases of sickness they stood thus :—

Bronchitis	.	682	Measles . .	81	Rheumatism .	550
Croup . .	.	155	Paralysis . .	51	Scarlatina .	90
Diarrhœa .		127	Phthisis . .	798	Small-pox .	268
Erysipelas .		153	Pleurisy . .	182	Syphilis . .	487
Fractures .	.	857	Pneumonia .	310	Typhoid . .	500
Heart disease	264					

Of 10,000 deaths in the city of Paris in 1883 the ratios were :—

	Male	Female	Total
Scarlatina . . .	15	20	17
Small-pox . . .	78	86	81
Whooping-cough . .	97	146	115
Measles . . .	170	212	185
Bronchitis . . .	310	320	314
Diphtheria and croup .	330	370	345
Typhoid . . .	368	366	367
Violent . . .	435	147	301
Pneumonia . . .	710	750	725
Phthisis . . .	2,110	1,710	1,890
Sundry . . .	5,877	5,874	5,660
Total .	10,000	10,000	10,000

The reports of reformatories for 1880 showed the ratio of inmates who were sick during the year as follows :—

Complaint	Per 1000			Deaths per 100 Cases
	Boys	Girls	General Average	
Digestive disorders .	73	65	71	3
Phthisis	12	26	15	40
Scrofula	11	84	25	3
Typhoid	6	4	5	33
Various	220	48	190	3
Total . .	322	227	306	5

The death-rate at various seasons of pulmonary patients in the Paris hospitals was as follows :—

Quarter Ending	Per 100 Patients				
	Phthisis	Pneumonia	Bronchitis	Pleurisy	Average
March . .	55	40	6	16	29
June . . .	53	27	4	13	29
September .	50	25	2	9	22
December .	56	39	6	13	33
Year . .	54	32	5	13	30

The ratio of age in the Paris hospitals in cases of certain diseases was in 1861–64 as follows :—

Age	Typhoid	Apoplexy	Aneurism	Cataract
Under 20 .	24.5	5.2	1.2	6.0
20–30 . .	54.2	6.2	14.0	3.6
30–40 . . .	14.8	11.0	38.8	3.6
Over 40 . .	6.5	77.6	46.0	86.8
	100.0	100.0	100.0	100.0

The convict settlement of Cayenne, French Guiana, in 1876–81 gave the following averages :—

	Sick per 1000 Convicts	Deaths in 100 Sick
Phthisis	14	22
Enteric fever . . .	170	4
Anæmia	180	10
Digestive disorders . .	35	15
Various	681	4
Total . .	1,080	6

The French garrison at Senegal in 22 years ending 1873 gave the following returns :—

	Per 1000 Men		Relative Mortality
	Hospital Admissions	Deaths	
Fever	920	25	2.7
Dysentery and cholera	301	22	7.3
Syphilis . . .	119	...	...
Sundry . . .	479	30	6.3
Total . .	1,819	77	4.2

O

The death-rate of the French army in the years 1872–77 showed thus :—

	Of 1000 Deaths	Deaths per 10,000 Men
Typhoid	307	33
Phthisis	290	31
Diarrhœa, &c. . . .	76	8
Suicide	33	4
Various	294	31
Total . .	1,000	107

The average number invalided yearly was 50 officers per 10,000, and 220 men in the same number, being over double the death-rate.

The military hospital report in 1865 showed among 1000 sick the following ratios :—

Phthisis	.	18	Rheumatism.	40	Fever .	. .	131
Small-pox	.	20	Dysentery, &c.	76	Syphilis	. .	137
Pneumonia	.	31	Bronchitis	. 115	Various	. .	432

The expeditionary troops in Tonquin showed deaths, excluding those killed or wounded in war, made up of the following ratios :—

Phthisis	.	.	. 3.8	Spring	.	.	. 20.7
Diarrhœa	.	.	. 4.8	Summer	.	.	. 42.1
Dysentery	.	.	. 30.2	Autumn	.	.	. 23.9
Fever .	.	.	. 45.6	Winter	.	.	. 13.3
Sundry	.	.	. 15.6				
Total	.	. 100.0		Total	.	. 100.0	

GERMANY

The following table of mortality includes the whole urban population of the Empire, that is, of all towns over 15,000 population :—

	Number of Deaths			Ratio		
	1877	1877–86	1886	1877	1877–86	1886
Small-pox	42	101	49	2	5	2
Measles	2,179	2,670	3,981	111	121	155
Scarlatina	4,452	4,052	3,187	227	184	124
Diphtheria and croup .	7,523	9,360	12,208	384	426	475
Typhoid	7,325	3,020	2,589	170	142	101
Puerperal	1,115	1,067	998	57	48	39
Phthisis	27,027	29,370	32,981	1,378	1,344	1,283
Respiratory	18,710	22,820	26,984	954	1,040	1,049
Enteritis	9,985	11,430	11,979	509	520	466
Diarrhœa . . . ,	8,259	10,210	17,197	421	460	669
Various	113,409	125,100	144,977	5,787	5,710	5,637
Total . .	196,026	219,200	257,130	10,000	10,000	10,000
Population . . .	7,260,000	8,370,000	9,820,000	...	...	...

The urban death-rate of the Empire was 26.2 per 1000 inhabitants during the period of ten years down to 1886.

In 10,000 deaths all over Germany the following ratios occur :—

Rheumatism.	25	Heart . .	. 230	Apoplexy	.	390
Erysipelas	. 35	Cancer .	. 260	Typhoid	.	450
Scarlatina	. 160	Diphtheria	. 270	Phthisis.	.	. 1,270

In 10,000 deaths in Prussia (1843) the ratios showed— small-pox 80, puerperal 110, apoplexy and paralysis 690, acute internal disorders 240, and chronic disease 388 ; besides suicide 35, and accidental deaths 140.

Deaths in Saxony in the years 1873–76 showed the following diseases thus :—

Per 100,000 Inhabitants Yearly

Small-pox .	. 28	Typhoid .	. 39	Diphtheria and }	81
Scarlatina .	. 55	Cancer .	. 61	croup . . . }	
				Phthisis . . . 232	

Of 10,000 deaths in Berlin, Munich, and Frankfort there were :—

	Berlin	Munich	Frankfort
Scrofula . . .	100	33	...
Cancer . . .	160	...	370
Diphtheria . . .	320	240	130
Typhoid . . .	320	450	420
Apoplexy . . .	410	390	380
Phthisis . . .	990	1,320	1,550

The distribution of deaths in Saxony from various diseases according to months, taking the year as 1200, was thus :—

	Measles	Scarlatina	Diphtheria and Croup	Whooping-Cough	Typhoid	Dysentery
January . .	119	116	135	88	102	6
February . .	112	102	126	85	95	20
March . .	84	78	100	99	87	14
April . . .	65	63	79	84	81	13
May . . .	90	59	75	88	80	13
June . . .	93	59	71	75	79	27
July . . .	93	68	54	95	92	101
August . .	120	84	50	107	121	367
September . .	64	113	91	118	131	352
October . .	64	155	119	124	126	181
November . .	119	151	155	126	105	73
December . .	176	152	145	111	101	33
	1,200	1,200	1,200	1,200	1,200	1,200

The ratios of various diseases in 10,000 deaths in Bavaria were as follows :—

Phthisis	.	.	. 1010	Apoplexy	.	.	. 372
Dropsy	.	.	. 650	Diphtheria	.	.	. 248
Croup	.	.	. 392	Scarlatina	.	.	. 236

In Hanover the prevalence of certain diseases among given trades is as follows :—

	Percentage of Causes of Death					
	Glass-Blowers	Dyers	Painters	Varnishers	Printers	Average
Phthisis . . .	18	25	24	25	22	23
Acute disease .	28	22	19	18	30	23
Heart disease .	4	9	5	5	3	5
Stomach disease	15	16	15	35	14	19
Rheumatism .	11	13	11	5	8	10
Various . . .	24	15	26	12	23	20
Total . .	100	100	100	100	100	100

In Bavaria the prevalence of typhoid fever according to age was as follows :—

Per Million Inhabitants of each Age

Age		Age		Age	
Under 10 .	300	21–30 . . .	850	41–50 . . .	690
10–20 . . .	480	31–40 . . .	650	Over 50 . .	980

And the death-rate according to age was :—

Age	Per 100 Patients	Age	Per 100 Patients
Under 5	24	41–60 . . .	29
5–15	10	61–70 . . .	46
16–40	20	Over 70 . . .	75

At page 197 will be found a table from an English medical work showing the predisposition to fever according to age, which is at variance with the above table for Bavaria.

The prevalence of certain diseases in the different seasons was as follows :—

CASES OF SICKNESS

Season	Diarrhœa		Cholera		Phthisis	Pneumonia	Liver
	Breslau	Dresden	Stuttgart	Breslau	Breslau	Breslau	Dresden
Spring	15.5	19.0	10.6	8.7	30.1	34.1	20.5
Summer	43.9	29.7	65.4	58.5	22.6	18.3	33.3
Autumn	27.1	29.1	15.0	26.5	22.8	20.8	17.3
Winter	13.5	22.2	9.0	6.3	25.5	26.8	28.9
	100.0	100.0	100.0	100.0	100.0	100.0	100.0

DEATHS FROM VARIOUS DISEASES

Season	Measles		Diarrhœa	Phthisis	Convulsions		Diarrhœa	Scarlatina
	Berlin	Dresden	Berlin	Berlin	Berlin	Frankfort	Frankfort	Berlin
Spring	9.9	61.0	9.5	27.6	26.2	27.8	15.7	21.6
Summer	55.6	24.0	68.5	22.6	27.2	21.4	49.6	25.4
Autumn	16.9	8.0	16.7	22.8	22.7	19.9	25.1	37.2
Winter	17.6	7.0	5.3	27.0	23.9	30.9	9.6	15.8
	100.0	100.0	100.0	100.0	100.0	100.0	100.0	100.0

DEATHS FROM APOPLEXY

Season	Berlin	Hamburg	Dresden	Breslau	Frankfort
Spring .	25.5	26.3	28.9	25.9	26.3
Summer	19.9	22.7	22.7	23.1	22.7
Autumn	22.5	22.7	20.0	22.9	22.7
Winter	32.1	28.3	28.4	28.1	28.3
	100.0	100.0	100.0	100.0	100.0

Season	Deaths from Pneumonia					From Typhoid
	Berlin	Hamburg	Frankfort	Dresden	Germany	Berlin
Spring . . .	30.0	41.4	37.5	39.9	18.2	19.7
Summer . .	18.4	15.4	17.3	17.7	22.9	25.2
Autumn . .	17.8	13.5	15.7	16.7	35.5	33.4
Winter . .	33.8	29.7	29.5	25.7	23.4	21.7
	100.0	100.0	100.0	100.0	100.0	100.0

It appears from the preceding tables that diarrhœa and cholera are most frequent in summer, phthisis and pneumonia in spring, apoplexy in winter, and typhoid in autumn. As regards measles and scarlatina, the seasons seem to have little effect.

RUSSIA

The death-rate from various diseases per 10,000 inhabitants of each age at St. Petersburg was as follows :—

Disease	5–10	11–20	21–30	31–40	41–50	51–60	61–70	Over 70
Typhoid . . .	12	23	27	18	17	23	23	30
Pneumonia . .	11	7	9	12	19	37	57	85
Phthisis . . .	10	27	61	71	72	72	53	50
Various . . .	110	55	86	97	145	248	452	1,155
Total . .	142	112	183	198	253	380	585	1,320
Males	146	131	203	227	306	475	702	1,660
Females . . .	133	79	147	159	193	297	510	1,160

The aggregate returns of the hospital at Astrakan for 25 years gave the ratio of sick thus :—

In 10,000 Patients

Cancer . . .	55	Rheumatism .	.	1,398
Cholera . . .	375	Scurvy .	. .	147
Dysentery . .	591	Small-pox .	.	93
Erysipelas . .	115	Syphilis . .	.	1,332
Fever . . .	2,021	Typhus . .	.	1,498
Leprosy . . .	173	Various . .	.	1,464
Phthisis . .	286			
Pleurisy . . .	187	Total .	.	10,000
Pneumonia . .	265			

The death-rate in the same hospital for various diseases was :—

In 100 Patients

Cancer . . . 30	Leprosy . . 41	Scurvy . . . 16
Cholera . . . 73	Phthisis . . . 60	Small-pox . . 42
Dysentery . . 41	Pleurisy . . . 15	Syphilis . . . 2
Erysipelas . . 10	Pneumonia . 35	Typhus . . . 37
Fever . . . 5	Rheumatism . 1	Various . . . 12

The annual death-rate in St. Petersburg of children under five years is 182 per 1000, made up as follows :—

Bowel complaints . . 60	Croup 9
Pneumonia . . . 36	Small-pox and scarlatina 8
Meningitis . . . 18	Bronchitis . . . 5
Convulsions . . . 13	Sundry 24
Scrofula . . . 9	

In 10,000 deaths at St. Petersburg the following ratios occurred :—

Small-pox . . 40	Heart . . . 200	Scrofula . 260
Puerperal . . 74	Convulsions . 200	Meningitis . 500
Scarlatina . . 90	Apoplexy . . 210	Phthisis . . 1,510
Cancer . . . 150	Diphtheria . 210	Bronchitis . 1,590

The occurrence of certain diseases according to season at St. Petersburg was shown by the ratio of deaths as follows :—

	Infant Cholera	Typhoid	Apoplexy	Puerperal Fever
Spring . . .	33.4	30.8	24.0	29.0
Summer . . .	20.6	21.8	23.8	25.2
Autumn . . .	18.3	16.8	21.2	18.2
Winter . . .	27.7	30.6	31.0	27.6
	100.0	100.0	100.0	100.0

The death-rate in St. Petersburg is so high that deaths exceed births. In 125 years, from 1764 to 1888, there were 1,539,000 births and 1,772,000 deaths, being an excess of 233,000 deaths.

AUSTRIA-HUNGARY

The returns of Austria proper for 1886 showed thus :—

	Number of Deaths			Ratio
	Males	Females	Total	
Small-pox . . .	4,340	4,454	8,794	133
Measles	7,228	6,981	14,209	214
Scarlatina . . .	6,258	5,889	12,147	183
Typhoid	8,008	7,882	15,890	240
Diarrhœa . . .	4,895	4,718	9,613	146
Whooping-cough .	10,409	10,568	20,977	316
Diphtheria . . .	16,231	15,435	31,666	477
Respiratory . . .	36,459	32,907	69,366	1,045
Phthisis	46,912	44,643	91,555	1,380
Enteritis	17,670	15,298	32,968	496
Apoplexy	8,710	7,069	15,779	237
Cancer	4,809	6,313	11,122	168
Various	166,850	161,320	328,170	4,965
Total . .	338,779	323,477	662,256	10,000

The returns of Hungary for 1886 showed as follows :—

	Number of Deaths		
	Males	Females	Total
Unmarried	36,800	31,800	68,600
Married	59,200	46,500	105,700
Widowed	18,300	36,200	54,500
Over five years . . .	114,300	114,500	228,800
Infants under five . .	134,700	116,800	251,500
Total . .	249,000	231,300	480,300

The municipal hospitals of Hungary showed the number of cases and deaths as follows :—

	Cases	Died	Death-Rate	Ratio Cases	Ratio Deaths
Small-pox . .	16,055	3,740	23.4	268	348
Measles . . .	24,801	1,752	7.0	413	163
Scarlatina . .	6,325	1,221	19.3	106	112
Diphtheria . .	4,189	2,292	54.6	70	214
Diarrhœa . . .	3,211	500	15.6	54	46
Typhoid . . .	771	102	13.2	13	9
Whooping-cough	1,890	147	7.7	32	14
Cholera . . .	1,871	989	53.0	32	92
Various . . .	710	19	2.7	12	2
Year 1886 . . .	59,823	10,762	17.9	1,000	1,000
Average 1880–85	52,200	9,905	19.1	...	...

The hospital returns of Vienna give the following percentages :—

	Cases of Sickness					Deaths	
	Measles	Diarrhœa	Liver	Pneumonia	Phthisis	From Phthisis	Scarlatina
Spring .	38.9	25.7	29.7	39.1	34.1	34.1	18.9
Summer .	33.7	31.6	25.9	17.9	24.5	24.7	26.9
Autumn .	8.7	21.7	20.4	17.3	17.7	17.5	25.8
Winter .	18.7	21.0	24.0	25.7	23.7	23.7	38.4
	100.0	100.0	100.0	100.0	100.0	100.0	100.0

In 10,000 deaths at Buda-Pesth 90 were of Bright's disease, 140 apoplexy, 460 meningitis, 730 convulsions, and 1545 phthisis. At Vienna the ratios were :—Puerperal 40, heart 170, small-pox 40, pneumonia 714, and phthisis 2080. The effects of overcrowding of population on the death-rate is shown in the returns at Buda-Pesth of deaths among the working classes for the years 1872–75.

	Deaths Yearly of Work-People, Living		
	Not more than Two in a Room	Over Two in a Room	Total
Small-pox . . .	52	415	467
Typhus . . .	45	155	200
Scarlatina . . .	31	141	172
Diphtheria . . .	11	63	74
Various . . .	19	180	199
Contagious diseases .	158	954	1,112
Pneumonia . . .	65	286	351
Phthisis . . .	194	704	898
Diarrhœa . . .	48	453	501
Various . . .	1,052	3,900	4,952
Total .	1,517	6,297	7,814

It appears that 80 per cent. of the mortality among working-classes was of people living more than two in a room.

ITALY

Of 10,000 deaths at Rome the ratio showed :—

Scarlatina . 10	Typhoid . . 230	Apoplexy . 530
Bronchitis . 29	Small-pox . 290	Digestive . 1,100
Cancer . . 170	Ague . . . 460	Phthisis . . 1,140

At Naples the ratios were in 10,000 :—Ague, 107 ; typhoid, 300 ; and apoplexy, 370 ; at Genoa, ague, 133 ; digestive disorders, 1580. The mean ratios in 10,000 deaths of all Italian cities were :—

Bright's	40	Measles	95	Apoplexy	360
Whoop.-cough	50	Dysentery	130	Diphtheria	360
Erysipelas	50	Small-pox	220	Pneumonia	540
Hepatitis	90	Typhoid	240	Heart	585

The ratios in Turin in 10,000 deaths were :—

Scrofula	30	Typhoid	460	Apoplexy	610
Syphilis	30	Heart	490	Phthisis	830
Cancer	160	Convulsions	560	Digestive	1,550

The prevalence of some diseases according to months, taking the year as 1200, is shown thus :—

	Deaths from Apoplexy			Admission to Fever Hospital	Deaths	
					Ague	Sciatica
	Turin	Milan	Bologna	Rome	Turin	Italy
January	147	132	149	38	30	265
February	107	128	169	44	30	78
March	107	108	114	56	48	126
April	90	99	95	63	78	78
May	99	93	91	62	78	76
June	77	79	67	65	30	76
July	81	78	76	122	48	46
August	80	73	69	299	156	110
September	83	84	72	211	270	92
October	90	93	85	113	204	76
November	120	112	97	80	114	110
December	119	121	116	47	114	67
Year	1,200	1,200	1,200	1,200	1,200	1,200

SPAIN

Madrid hospitals publish the following table of proportions of deaths from phthisis according to age :—

Under 20	.	.	.	.	.	13.4
20–30	.	.	.	.	.	28.9
30–40	.	.	.	.	.	23.8
40–50	.	.	.	.	.	18.1
Over 50	.	.	.	.	.	15.8
		Total	.	.	.	100.0

The prevalence of this disease according to months is shown in the number of deaths at Madrid, taking the year as 1200 :—

January	.	.	162	July	.	.	18
February	.	.	126	August	.	.	27
March	.	.	131	September	.	.	86
First quarter	.	419		Third quarter	.	131
April	.	.	113	October	.	.	92
May	.	.	74	November	.	.	129
June	.	.	40	December	.	.	202
Second quarter	.	227		Fourth quarter	.	423

PORTUGAL

Of 10,000 deaths in Lisbon the ratios showed :—

Bright's	30	Scrofula	110	Bronchitis	420
Rheumatism	43	Convulsions	190	Apoplexy	685
Ague	60	Cancer	260	Phthisis	1,147

SWEDEN

The deaths per million inhabitants were as follows :—

	1861–65	1866–70	1871–75
Diphtheria	2,873	1,497	1,579
Scarlatina	2,292	3,475	1,899
Small-pox	545	1,189	1,576
Typhoid	1,449	3,408	2,031

The deaths in hospital in 1878 were as follows :—

Diseases	Number	Per Cent.
Respiratory	4,353	31.4
Digestive	2,177	15.8
Contagious	2,123	15.3
Nervous	1,436	10.3
Various	3,785	27.2
Total	13,874	100.0

Hospital mortality in 1860 was 15 per cent. of the sick, and in the years 1870–76 only 12 per cent. The relative mortality of Sweden and Norway in different diseases was per 100 patients as follows :—Croup 52, diphtheria 20, scarlatina 18, pneumonia 15, small-pox 13, typhus 12, diarrhœa 11. The percentage of deaths under and over ten years of age in certain diseases was as follows :—

Age	Small-pox	Scarlatina	Diphtheria	Typhoid
Under 10	41.2	89.8	86.4	13.2
Over 10	58.8	10.2	13.6	86.8
Total	100.0	100.0	100.0	100.0

The hospital returns of sickness showed the following ratio :—

Per 10,000 Inhabitants

Diarrhœa	.	165	Ague	.	.	36
Small-pox	.	42	Scarlatina	.	.	15
Whooping-cough	.	40	Typhus	.	.	24
Diphtheria	.	38	Dysentery	.	.	7
Typhoid	.	37				

The death-rate of various diseases showed thus :—

Deaths per 1000 Patients of each Disease

Ague	2	Typhoid	110	Small-pox	171
Diarrhœa	10	Dysentery	134	Typhus	204
Whoop.-cough	70	Pneumonia	148	Diphtheria	251
Measles	83	Scarlatina	155	Croup	550

The effect of town-life on death-rate in Sweden is shown thus :—

	Deaths Yearly per 100,000 Persons of each Class			
	Under 10 Years Old		Over 10 Years	
	Rural	Town	Rural	Town
Typhoid	18	53	32	96
Diarrhœa, &c.	31	1,276	3	21
Small-pox	56	25	26	56
Whooping-cough	76	119	...	...
Measles	80	173	2	2
Diphtheria and croup	292	425	8	7
Scarlatina	376	460	11	11
Total, 7 diseases	929	2,531	82	193

Deaths of puerperal fever average 27 per 10,000 births in rural parts, and 74 in towns, the rate for all Sweden being 34. The prevalence of certain diseases according to season shows thus :—

				Pneumonia	Ague
Spring	.	.	.	37.9	31.1
Summer	.	.	.	21.2	18.6
Autumn	.	.	.	17.2	25.9
Winter	.	.	.	23.7	24.4
		Total	.	100.0	100.0

The prevalence of diseases according to months, taking the year as 1200, shows :—

	Bronchitis	Diarrhœa	Diphtheria	Scarlatina	Small-pox	Croup
January . . .	150	41	121	106	120	144
February . . .	160	41	119	99	130	136
March . . .	143	31	99	93	129	130
April	130	33	93	95	156	110
May	102	30	85	91	152	88
June	67	55	72	90	128	64
July	49	150	69	81	91	45
August . . .	46	292	77	80	52	48
September . .	58	227	86	91	41	76
October . . .	82	149	112	118	43	108
November . .	104	94	137	136	68	128
December . .	109	54	130	120	90	123
Year .	1,200	1,200	1,200	1,200	1,200	1,200

In 10,000 deaths these ratios occurred :—

Ague . . .	14	Diarrhœa . .	190	Small-pox .	158
Puerperal . .	38	Whoop.-cough	190	Scarlatina .	190
Rheumatism .	40	Cancer . .	240	Pneumonia .	850
Drink . . .	40	Apoplexy . .	590	Typhoid .	203
Liver . . .	90	Bronchitis .	630	Phthisis . .	1,340
Croup . . .	165	Diphtheria .	160		

FINLAND

Official returns for 1870-71 give the distribution of 10,000 deaths as follows :—

Measles . .	50	Dysentery .	170	Typhus . .	810
Small-pox. .	60	Croup . .	250	Phthisis . .	2,210
Scarlatina .	60	Whoop.-cough	510	Various . .	5,880

Deaths of puerperal fever were 96 in 10,000 births; the rate in towns was 18 per cent. higher than in rural departments.

NORWAY

In 1876 among 10,000 deaths the diseases stood thus :—

Typhoid . .	220	Diarrhœa .	280	Infant con-}	784
Apoplexy .	240	Cancer . .	415	vulsions }	
Heart. . .	260	Bronchitis .	608	Scarlatina .	1285
				Phthisis . .	1450

The prevalence of certain diseases according to months was as follows :—

	Bronchitis	Pneumonia	Diarrhœa	Typhoid	Diphtheria	Scarlatina	Small-pox	Croup
January	160	98	98	150	136	122	144	141
February	152	169	89	103	120	110	161	132
March	132	161	72	64	112	103	157	134
April	112	160	61	43	89	92	142	105
May	96	134	65	38	88	90	172	84
June	72	77	60	32	79	85	133	64
July	53	55	113	57	79	80	78	47
August	48	37	190	95	73	76	46	50
September . . .	62	55	143	117	87	72	34	89
October	82	76	95	116	102	100	27	103
November . . .	110	91	109	209	118	137	40	125
December . . .	121	87	105	176	117	133	66	126
Year . .	1,200	1,200	1,200	1,200	1,200	1,200	1,200	1,200

In 10,000 deaths at Christiania there were :—

Whooping .	100	Cancer . .	290	Scarlatina .	670
Convulsions.	110	Erysipelas .	270	Diarrhœa .	420
Heart. . .	130	Diphtheria .	440	Pneumonia .	680
Apoplexy .	220	Typhoid. .	630	Phthisis . .	1720

DENMARK

Of 10,000 deaths at Copenhagen the ratios were :—

Rheumatism.	35	Diphtheria .	160	Cancer . .	360
Scrofula . .	70	Whooping .	160	Convulsions.	560
Drink . . .	70	Puerperal .	160	Typhoid . .	700
Small-pox .	70	Apoplexy .	230	Pneumonia .	710
Bright's . .	100	Scarlatina .	240	Phthisis . .	1270
		Heart . .	320		

HOLLAND

In 10,000 deaths throughout Holland the principal diseases stood thus :—

Typhus . .	21	Diphtheria .	130	Apoplexy .	280
Scarlatina .	40	Cancer . .	180	Dysentery .	290
Bright's . .	50	Heart . . .	180	Phthisis. .	950
Puerperal . .	50	Whooping-} cough . }	180	Various . .	7,649

In 10,000 deaths at Amsterdam the ratios were :—

Syphilis . .	18	Bright's . .	120	Meningitis .	370
Typhus . .	23	Scrofula . .	140	Apoplexy .	380
Scarlatina. .	50	Measles . .	150	Typhoid .	460
Puerperal. .	53	Diphtheria .	200	Pneumonia .	570
Hepatitis . .	81	Bronchitis .	220	Convulsions .	600
Small-pox .	100	Cancer . .	230	Phthisis . .	870
Ague . . .	106	Heart . . .	290		

BELGIUM

The prevalence of certain diseases according to season is shown thus :—

	Deaths from					
	Phthisis	Apoplexy	Rheumatism	Bronchitis	Pneumonia	Diarrhœa
Spring . . .	27.7	26.9	33.4	26.4	32.6	24.4
Summer . . .	23.2	22.2	12.5	17.3	17.7	31.5
Autumn . . .	24.3	22.3	22.9	21.4	21.4	23.9
Winter . . .	24.8	28.6	31.2	34.9	28.3	20.2
Total .	100.0	100.0	100.0	100.0	100.0	100.0

The ages of phthisis and other diseases stand thus :—

Age	Deaths from					
	Phthisis	Typhoid	Apoplexy	Bronchitis	Diarrhœa, &c.	Pneumonia
Under 20 . .	25.7	43.3	5.6	60.4	70.0	29.0
20-30 . . .	19.2	18.0	2.6	2.0	3.0	5.4
31-40	15.4	11.2	4.2	1.9	3.0	6.2
41-50	12.2	9.6	8.1	2.8	4.0	8.1
51-60	11.3	8.9	17.0	5.3	6.0	14.0
Over 60 . . .	16.2	9.0	62.5	27.6	14.0	37.3
Total .	100.0	100.0	100.0	100.0	100.0	100.0

The causes of death were as follows :—

	Annual Averages			Ratio in 10,000 Deaths		
	1856–60	1871–80	1886–87	1856–60	1871–80	1886–87
Bronchitis, &c.	10,237	16,827	19,974	997	1,402	1,664
Phthisis	14,523	17,642	16,606	1,416	1,470	1,384
Diarrhœa, &c.	3,451	8,552	9,107	336	713	759
Whooping-cough	2,172	3,840	3,885	212	320	324
Croup	3,033	3,250	3,758	296	271	313
Measles	1,062	3,452	2,943	10	288	245
Typhoid	4,630	4,161	2,480	451	347	207
Puerperal	654	1,313	1,342	63	109	112
Scarlatina	1,204	1,963	1,146	117	164	95
Small-pox	1,116	5,080	911	108	423	76
Accidents	1,542	2,039	1,964	150	170	164
Various	59,033	52,279	55,982	5,844	4,323	4,657
Total . .	102,657	120,398	120,098	10,000	10,000	10,000

In 10,000 deaths throughout Belgium the ratios of some were :—

Erysipelas .	40	Meningitis . 280	Pneumonia 450
Cancer . .	140	Whooping- } 280	Typhoid . 460
Measles . .	165	cough . }	Convulsions 720
Heart . . .	190	Diphtheria . 280	Phthisis . . 1,825
		Diarrhœa . . 370	

The ratios at Brussels were as follows :—

Whooping-cough } 70 | Puerperal . . 210 | Convulsions 450
Hepatitis . . 81 | Typhoid . . 220 | Bronchitis . 480
Scrofula . . 90 | Apoplexy . . 310 | Heart . . 685
Scarlatina . 140 | Cancer . . 420 | Phthisis . . 1,750
Small-pox . 150 | Pneumonia . 430 | Digestive } 1,500
| | Diphtheria . 440 | disorders }

SWITZERLAND

In 10,000 deaths the various diseases stood thus :—

Measles . . 46 | Scarlatina . 146 | Heart . . 385
Puerperal . . 50 | Typhoid . . 184 | Phthisis . . 1,110
Small-pox . 54 | Diphtheria . 304 | Bronchitis } 1,180
Whoop.-cough 112 | Apoplexy . 370 | Pneumonia }

In Berne, of 10,000 deaths, there were of puerperal fever, 80 ; of Bright's disease, 100 ; of cancer, 320 ; of apoplexy, 420.

In Geneva the ratios in 10,000 deaths showed :—

Bright's . . 15 | Typhoid . . 350 | Cancer . . 530
Puerperal . . 95 | Apoplexy . . 400 | Phthisis . . 1,250

GREECE

At Athens the deaths from various diseases occurred in the following ratios according to season :—

Quarter Ending	Digestive	Phthisis	Pneumonia	Heart Disease	Typhoid	Diphtheria	Liver	Bronchitis	General Mortality
March . . .	10.6	25.4	34.5	31.4	6.0	22.8	22.2	36.0	23.6
June . . .	31.0	27.0	29.0	21.4	12.0	15.4	26.7	29.6	26.1
September . .	36.1	22.9	14.0	17.5	66.5	19.6	28.9	9.6	25.9
December . .	22.3	24.7	22.5	29.7	15.5	42.2	22.2	24.8	24.4
Year .	100.0	100.0	100.0	100.0	100.0	100.0	100.0	100.0	100.0

In 10,000 deaths the averages during the years 1876–82 were as follows :—

Liver . . . 124 | Heart disease 323 | Apoplexy . 630
Whoop.-cough 210 | Bronchitis . 391 | Pneumonia . 856
Diphtheria . 219 | Ague . . . 420 | Phthisis . . 1,076
Convulsions . 266 | Typhoid . . 475 | Digestive dis. 1,658

The returns for ague, apoplexy, convulsions, and whooping-cough are not for the whole period.

Fever cases occur mostly from July to September ; if we take the year as 1200, the various months will stand thus :—

	Cases		Cases		Cases
January . .	40	May . . .	69	September .	168
February . .	41	June . . .	101	October . .	103
March . . .	50	July . . .	240	November .	63
April . . .	53	August . . .	226	December . .	46

UNITED STATES

Of 10,000 deaths, according to the Census of 1880, the following ratios occurred :—

Calculus . .	1	Apoplexy . .	140	Convulsions	250
Bright's . .	35	Whooping .	148	Typhoid .	310
Puerperal . .	40	Dysentery .	160	Heart . .	350
Rheumatism .	59	Meningitis .	190	Diphtheria .	480
Scrofula . .	70	Scarlatina .	220	Diarrhœa .	880
Cancer . .	130	Ague . . .	240	Phthisis . .	1,420

The prevalence of diarrhœa at New York and of infant cholera at Philadelphia, according to seasons, was thus :—

Season	Diarrhœa, New York	Infant Cholera, Philadelphia
Spring	9.2	2.0
Summer	79.8	92.8
Autumn	7.0	4.5
Winter	4.0	0.7
	100.0	100.0

The ratios in New York of 10,000 deaths showed :—

Syphilis . . 40 | Scrofula . . 83 | Typhoid . 350
Puerperal . . 56 | Drink . . . 70 | Phthisis . . 1,550
Cancer . . 80 | Diphtheria . 300 |

CANADA

Rates for phthisis and typhoid in 10,000 deaths are :—

	Phthisis	Typhoid
Ontario	1,540	417
Quebec	1,380	374
Nova Scotia . . .	2,410	205

In 10,000 deaths the various diseases, according to the *Dict. Medicale*, stand thus :—

Ague . . .	43	Croup . . .	182	Hydrocephalus .	130	Puerperal . . .	145
Apoplexy . .	110	Diphtheria . .	114	Infant cholera .	110	Rheumatism . .	70
Bowel disease .	320	Diarrhœa . .	410	Liver disease .	140	Scarlatina . .	458
Brain disease .	420	Dysentery . .	107	Measles . .	220	Small-pox . .	55
Bronchitis . .	130	Epilepsy . .	30	Paralysis . .	210	Typhoid . .	364
Cancer . .	126	Erysipelas . .	68	Phthisis . .	1,620	Whooping-cough .	260
Convulsions .	180	Heart disease .	370	Pneumonia .	660		

Ague is almost confined to Ontario, showing only 10 in 10,000 deaths in the other provinces. The deaths in the principal cities in 1886 were as follows :—

Disease	Montreal	Toronto	Quebec	Hamilton	Halifax	Winnipeg	Ottawa	Seven Cities
Phthisis	486	236	182	96	95	30	62	1,187
Lung	465	351	164	98	102	51	83	1,314
Diarrhœa	687	177	257	79	57	65	248	1,570
Brain	341	127	244	51	47	21	30	861
Diphtheria	235	184	118	76	39	23	46	721
Throat	200	111	129	21	56	19	28	564
Heart	216	127	76	48	47	14	27	555
Debility	1,014	255	235	68	39	15	40	1,666
Various	1,570	978	738	318	337	162	351	4,454
Total . .	5,214	2,546	2,143	855	819	400	915	12,892

Disease	Ratio in 10,000 Deaths							
	Montreal	Toronto	Quebec	Hamilton	Halifax	Winnipeg	Ottawa	Seven Cities
Phthisis	930	924	847	1,123	1,158	750	677	920
Lung	891	1,378	766	1,147	1,244	1,275	905	1,020
Diarrhœa	1,317	697	1,200	922	695	1,625	2,707	1,218
Brain	652	497	1,140	597	573	525	328	668
Diphtheria	447	721	551	886	475	575	502	560
Throat	383	437	602	246	683	475	306	438
Heart	415	497	354	561	573	350	295	430
Debility	1,945	1,003	1,093	796	475	375	437	1,293
Various	3,020	3,846	3,447	3,722	4,124	4,050	3,843	3,453
Total . .	10,000	10,000	10,000	10,000	10,000	10,000	10,000	10,000

JAPAN

The prevalence of various diseases at certain ages is shown by the ratio of deaths according to age thus :—

Age	Small-pox	Diphtheria	Cholera	Age	Typhoid	Typhus	Dysentery
Under 3 . .	29.6	34.9	1.8	Under 10 . .	12.1	10.2	30.1
3-7 . . .	22.0	30.3	4.9	10-15 . . .	11.6	11.2	13.4
7-15 . . .	26.8	18.0	8.3	15-25 . . .	26.2	23.9	17.2
15-30 . . .	18.7	10.4	24.0	25-40 . . .	25.7	28.5	17.3
30-50 . . .	} 2.9	6.4	33.2	40-60 . . .	17.2	18.0	13.1
Over 50 . .			27.8	Over 60 . .	7.2	8.2	8.9
Total .	100.0	100.0	100.0	Total .	100.0	100.0	100.0

The death-rate among typhoid patients was 32 per cent. The classification of sickness and of deaths was as follows :—

Prevalent Diseases		*Causes of Death*		
Typhoid . . .	36.1	Contagious diseases .	13.7
Dysentery . . .	30.4	Nervous ,, .	15.7
Small-pox . .	19.1	Digestive ,, .	20.6
Typhus . . .	9.3	Respiratory ,, .	14.7
Diphtheria . .	5.1	Sundry ,, .	35.3
Total .	100.0	Total .	100.0

DISTANCES

The principal ocean routes are as follows in nautical miles, of which six are equal to seven statute miles :—

Aden—Mauritius	2,822
Alexandria—Southampton . . .	2,960
Amoor River—San Francisco . .	3,946

Ascension—Cape Horn . . .	3,800
Auckland—Panama . . .	6,490
Azores—Portsmouth . . .	1,390
Bahia—Southampton . . .	4,366
Batavia—Sydney . . .	3,870
Behring's Straits—San Francisco .	2,720
Bermuda—Southampton . . .	2,973
Bombay—Cape of Good Hope . .	4,527
,, Mauritius . . .	2,503
,, Melbourne . . .	5,530
,, London . . .	6,330
Boston—Galway . . .	2,385
Calcutta—London . . .	7,950
,, Melbourne . . .	5,230
,, Suez . . .	4,580
Cape of Good Hope—Calcutta .	5,381
,, Bombay .	4,527
,, Java . .	5,025
,, Liverpool .	5,998
Cape Horn—Ascension . . .	3,800
,, Liverpool . . .	7,325
,, Sydney . . .	5,470

Demerara—London	4,030
Fernando Po—Plymouth . . .	4,130
Galway—Boston	2,385
Gibraltar—Southampton . . .	1,160
Glasgow—New York	3,400
Halifax—Galway	2,165
Havanna—New York	1,190
,, Portsmouth . . .	4,029
Hong-Kong—Honolulu . . .	4,838
Honolulu—Callao	5,145
,, San Francisco . . .	2,081
,, Tahiti	2,378
,, Valparaiso . . .	5,902
Jamaica—Portsmouth . . .	4,050
Java—Cape of Good Hope . .	5,025
Liverpool—Cape of Good Hope .	5,998
,, Cape Horn . . .	7,325
,, Melbourne . . .	11,555
,, New York . . .	2,980
,, Portland . . .	2,770
,, Quebec . . .	2,634
Lisbon—Madeira	535
London—Bombay	6,330
,, Calcutta	7,950
,, Demerara . . .	4,030
,, Madras	7,330
,, Singapore . . .	8,345
Madeira—Plymouth . . .	1,200
Madras—London	7,330
Mauritius—Aden	2,822
,, Bombay	2,503
,, Cape of Good Hope .	2,400
,, Melbourne . . .	4,570
Melbourne—Calcutta . . .	5,230
,, Liverpool . . .	11,555
,, Mauritius . . .	4,570
Montevideo—Falmouth . . .	2,886
,, Valparaiso . . .	2,550
New York—Galway	2,731
,, Glasgow	3,400
,, Havanna	1,190
,, Liverpool . . .	2,980
,, Portsmouth . . .	3,075
,, Southampton . . .	3,080
Pernambuco—Teneriffe . . .	2,450
Plymouth—Fernando Po . . .	4,130
,, Madeira	1,200
Portsmouth—Azores . . .	1,390
,, Havanna	4,029
,, Jamaica	4,050
,, New York . . .	3,075
,, St. Helena . . .	4,330
,, Tahiti	11,530
Quebec—Galway	2,392
,, Liverpool	2,634
Rio Janeiro—Southampton . .	5,060
,, Valparaiso . . .	3,560
St. Helena—Portsmouth . . .	4,330
,, Cape of Good Hope .	1,800
St. Thomas—Southampton . .	3,570
St. Vincent—Pernambuco . .	1,608
,, Teneriffe . . .	850
San Francisco—Amoor River . .	3,946
,, Behring's Straits .	2,720
,, Honolulu . . .	2,081
,, Panama . . .	3,150
Shanghai—Sydney	4,640
Singapore—London	8,345
Suez—Calcutta	4,580
Sydney—Batavia	3,870
,, Cape Horn . . .	5,470
,, Shanghai	4,640
,, Valparaiso . . .	6,198
Tahiti—Honolulu	2,378
,, Portsmouth . . .	11,530
Teneriffe—Pernambuco . . .	2,450
Valparaiso—Honolulu . . .	5,902
,, Tahiti	4,233
,, Sydney	6,198
,, Panama	2,700

The following table shows distances from London as the bird flies, in English statute miles :—

Algiers . .	1,050	Jerusalem . .	2,100
Amsterdam .	210	Lima . .	6,900
Astrakan .	2,180	Lisbon . .	980
Azores .	1,680	Madeira . .	1,600
Barcelona .	680	Madras . .	5,170
Belgrade .	1,040	Madrid . .	780
Berlin . .	580	Malta . .	1,260
Bordeaux .	460	Manilla . .	6,700
Boston . .	3,190	Marseilles . .	620
Bremen .	390	Mauritius . .	6,010
Brussels .	190	Melbourne . .	9,990
Bucharest .	1,270	Mexico . .	5,800
Buda-Pesth .	900	Montevideo . .	7,150
Buenos Ayres .	7,260	Montreal . .	3,340
Cadiz . .	1,080	Moscow . .	1,580
Cairo . .	2,160	Naples . .	1,000
Calcutta .	4,870	Natal . .	5,850
Canton .	5,960	New Orleans .	4,820
Cape Town .	5,950	New York . .	3,620
Chicago . .	4,050	Palermo . .	1,150
Colombo .	5,370	Paris . .	200
Constantinople .	1,540	Pekin . .	5,400
Copenhagen .	600	Philadelphia .	3,700
Cyprus . .	1,980	Quebec . .	3,200
Dresden .	600	Quito . .	6,500
Dublin . .	280	Rio Janeiro .	6,000
Edinburgh . .	300	Rome . .	900
Falklands .	8,150	San Francisco .	6,000
Florence . .	730	St. Petersburg .	1,380
Frankfort .	400	Sierra Leone .	3,300
Geneva . .	460	Singapore . .	7,050
Genoa . .	650	Stockholm . .	910
Gibraltar .	1,100	Sydney . .	10,120
Halifax .	2,940	Teneriffe . .	2,080
Hamburg . .	450	Utah . .	5,500
Havanna .	4,700	Valparaiso . .	7,850
Hong-Kong .	6,040	Vienna . .	760
Honolulu . .	8,430	Warsaw . .	910
Iceland . .	1,060	Washington . .	3,800
Jamaica . .	4,800	Yeddo . .	6,600
Jersey .	170		

Distances by railway route from London are :—

	Miles		*Miles*
Antwerp . .	260	Munich . .	758
Berlin . .	733	Paris . .	283
Constantinople .	2,260	Rome . .	1,195
Copenhagen .	854	St. Petersburg .	1,748
Hamburg .	849	Stockholm . .	1,195
Lisbon . .	1,603	Turin . .	781
Madrid . .	1,191	Vienna . .	963
Moscow . .	1,940	Warsaw . .	1,130

DIVORCE

Bertillon's and other tables show that the number of divorces compare with marriages in various countries as follows :—

	Per 10,000 Marriages			Per 10,000 Marriages	
	1867–76	1877–86		1867–76	1877–86
England .	9	19	Norway .	24	30
Scotland .	16	29	Sweden .	56	73
Ireland . .	1	2	Holland .	50	91
U. Kingdom	9	18	Belgium .	40	69
France . .	72	127	Roumania .	99	106
Germany .	107	152	Switzerland	...	468
Russia . .	18	22	Paris . .	297	322
Poland . .	49	55	Berlin . .	420	533
Austria . .	7	10	Vienna . .	210	290
Hungary .	...	64	Australia .	...	35
Italy . . .	31	24	U. States .	330	444
Denmark .	353	406	Canada . .	5	12

Kummer's table for five countries covers a period of 50 years :—

Period	Divorces per 10,000 Marriages						
	Sweden	Belgium	Saxony	Holland	Paris	Brussels	France
1831–40	49	12	256	...	70	53	17
1841–50	43	14	252	...	90	66	27
1851–60	43	24	255	33	156	99	44
1861–70	49	29	205	37	229	112	68
1871–80	65	51	256	48	249	124	78

The following table shows the number of divorces (including judicial separations) in the various countries during twenty years ending December 1886. The figures are mainly from Commissioner Carroll Wright's work (Washington, 1889), compiled from Bertillon's and other returns :—

	Actual Number of Divorces Granted				
	1867–71	1872–76	1877–81	1882–86	20 Years
England .	724	1,050	1,743	1,891	5,408
Scotland .	177	220	337	390	1,124
Ireland . .	4	13	21	17	55
U. Kingdom	905	1,283	2,101	2,298	6,587
France . .	9,850	11,384	13,132	22,750	57,116
Germany .	18,450	22,085	24,143	29,140	93,818
Russia . .	4,597	5,095	5,721	6,563	21,976
Poland . .	809	1,073	1,432	1,725	5,039
Austria . .	...	690	808	856	...
Hungary .	...	...	5,246	4,835	...
Italy . . .	3,136	...	3,195	2,828	...
Sweden . .	619	953	1,053	1,109	3,734
Norway . .	...	162	195	...	...
Denmark .	...	2,677	3,046	...	...
Holland . .	700	810	1,160	1,570	4,240
Switzerland .	...	...	4,811	4,588	...
Roumania .	...	1,787	1,900	...	...
Belgium . .	620	899	1,189	1,501	4,209
Europe, approximately	} 46,600	57,500	69,132	85,100	258,332
Canada . .	15	16	33	52	116
U. States .	53,574	68,547	89,284	117,311	328,716
Total	100,189	126,063	158,449	202,463	587,164

In the above table Germany is an estimate down to 1881 (see p. 221), and in some cases where the record of a year is missing, the average for the other four years of the period is added.

Kummer also gives the following table of the increase of divorce :—

	1851-55	1856-60	1861-65	1866-70	1871-75	1876-80
France . . .	100	128	150	190	163	225
Belgium . . .	100	140	160	190	280	420
Holland . . .	100	100	112	115	139	151
Saxony . . .	100	83	75	72	80	105
Sweden . . .	100	98	109	113	132	161

Classifying the nations according to creed, we find divorces per 10,000 marriages :—

Among Catholics 41
Among Protestants 123

In countries of mixed creeds the ratios were as follows :—

	Divorces per 10,000 Marriages			Date
	Protestant Provinces	Catholic Provinces	Mixed Provinces	
U. Kingdom .	15	1	...	1871–80
Bavaria . . .	61	57	223	1862–75
Holland . .	45	9	...	1850–64
Switzerland .	595	128	505	1876–80
Hungary . .	283	12	...	1878–79

As regards cities Kummer gives the following :—

Divorces per 10,000 Marriages

Antwerp	.	.	26	Liege .	.	.	115
Augsburg	.	.	15	London	.	.	40
Berlin	.	.	103	Munich	.	.	153
Breslau .	.	.	307	Nuremberg .	.	.	77
Brussels	.	.	124	Paris .	.	.	250
Bucharest	.	.	443	Prague	.	.	18
Christiania	.	.	17	Ratisbon .	.	.	63
Cologne	.	.	64	Rotterdam .	.	.	197
Copenhagen .	.	.	292	San Francisco	.	.	2233
Frankfort	.	.	171	Stockholm .	.	.	281
Ghent .	.	.	17	Vienna	.	.	233
Hague .	.	.	111				

The above results are for different periods between 1860 and 1875, usually averages of five years.

The proportions of divorces according to length of marriage were :—

Years Married	France	Saxony	Italy	Switzerland	Sweden	Roumania	Average
Under 5	21.5	35.7	40.9	36.0	11.2	50.9	32.4
5–10 . . .	29.6	29.3	22.9	34.1	24.8	37.4	29.0
Over 10 . . .	48.9	35.0	36.2	39.9	64.0	11.7	38.6
Total .	100.0	100.0	100.0	100.0	100.0	100.0	100.0
Date	1876–79	1875–77	1866–79	1876–80	1876–80	1875–77	...

The percentages of marriages dissolved at the petition of husband or of wife showed thus :—

Petition by	Scotland	Norway	Belgium	Saxony	Italy	Roumania	Massachusetts	Average
Husband	56	68	44	45	34	27	33	42
Wife	44	32	56	55	66	73	67	58
Total . .	100	100	100	100	100	100	100	100
Date	1878–81	1875–80	1880	1875 80	1866–79	1875–77	1860–78	...

The proportion of marriages dissolved, with or without children, shows thus :—

	France (1851-80)	Italy (1866-79)	Holland (1876-78)	Switzerland (1877-80)
With children	62	52	35	63
Without children	38	48	65	37
Total	100	100	100	100

In the term of five years ending 1880 the number of children corresponding to 100 divorce couples in Holland was 75, and in Sweden 130. Want of children in Holland seems a primary pretext for divorce ; not so much so elsewhere.

The ratio of persons divorced per million inhabitants yearly of each class was as follows :—

	France (1865-75)	Switzerland (1876-80)	Sweden (1876-80)
Learned class	125	470	130
Merchants	135	620	218
Farmers	20	190	20
Operatives	133	490	140
Gen. population	55	370	46

The number of divorced persons married in every 10,000 marriages, according to various returns down to 1880, averaged thus :—

	Men		Women
England	7	...	5
Holland	10	...	8
Hungary	12	...	10
Prussia	22	...	24
Denmark	32	...	32
Switzerland	60	...	42

There is apparently some relationship between divorce and suicide in the various countries, viz. :—

	Divorces per 10,000 Marriages	Suicides per Million Inhabitants		Divorces per 10,000 Marriages	Suicides per Million Inhabitants
Ireland	2	17	Germany	210	143
England	22	67	Denmark	410	282
Scotland	29	40	Switzerland	478	202
Italy	22	37	London	40	86
Sweden	75	81	Berlin	103	170
Belgium	74	71	Brussels	124	271
Holland	73	96	Vienna	233	287
France	91	156	Paris	250	422

UNITED KINGDOM

The official report of the working of the Divorce Act in Great Britain during 30 years showed thus :—

Period	Number of Petitions	Granted	Annual Average per Million Inhabitants
1858-67	2,724	1,492	6
1868-77	4,199	1,971	7
1878-87	5,991	3,832	13
30 Years	12,914	7,295	9

The total of divorces and marriages in 20 years was :—

	Number		Ratio of Divorces per 10,000 Marriages
	Divorces	Marriages	
England	5,408	3,881,000	14.0
Scotland	1,124	499,000	22.5
Ireland	55	492,000	1.1
U. Kingdom	6,587	4,872,000	...

The returns for England and Wales showed as follows :—

Period	Divorces	Annual Average	Per Million Population
1867-71	724	145	6.2
1872-76	1,050	210	9.0
1877-81	1,743	349	13.0
1882-86	1,891	378	14.0
20 Years	5,408	271	11.0

The returns for Scotland were as follows :—

Period	Divorces	Annual Average	Per Million Population
1867-71	177	35	11.0
1872-76	220	44	12.5
1877-81	337	67	15.3
1882-86	390	78	21.0
20 years	1,124	56	15.0

The returns for Ireland were as follows :—

Period	Divorces	Annual Average	Per Million Population
1867-71	4	1	0.2
1872-76	13	3	0.6
1877-81	21	4	0.8
1882-86	17	3	0.6
20 years	55	3	0.5

The number of divorces compared with marriages thus :—

Period	England and Wales		
	Marriages	Divorces	Divorces per 1000 Marriages
1867-71	905,000	724	0.8
1872-76	1,012,000	1,050	1.0
1877-81	955,000	1,743	1.8
1882-86	1,009,000	1,891	1.9
20 years	3,881,000	5,408	1.4

Period	Scotland		
	Marriages	Divorces	Divorces per 1000 Marriages
1867-71	115,000	177	1.5
1872-76	131,000	220	1.7
1877-81	125,000	337	2.7
1882-86	128,000	390	3.1
	490,000	1,124	2.2

| Period | Ireland | | |
	Marriages	Divorces	Divorces per 1000 Marriages
1867–71 . . .	142,000	4	0.03
1872–76 . . .	126,000	13	0.10
1877–81 . . .	116,000	21	0.18
1882–86 . . .	108,000	17	0.16
20 years . . .	492,000	55	0.11

UNITED KINGDOM

Period	Marriages	Divorces	Divorces per 1000 Marriages
1867–71	1,162,000	905	0.8
1872–76	1,269,000	1,283	1.0
1877–81	1,196,000	2,101	1.7
1882–86	1,245,000	2,298	1.8
20 years	4,872,000	6,587	1.3

FRANCE

The number of divorces and judicial separations, according to Bertillon, compares with marriages thus :—

Period	Divorces	Marriages	Per 10,000 Marriages	Divorce Yearly	Per Million Pop.
1802–10	4,853	2,029,000	23	539	20
1811–19	1,561	2,136,000	7	173	6
1820–29	2,730	2,411,000	11	273	9
1830–40	5,173	3,013,000	17	470	14
1841–50	7,687	2,800,000	27	769	22
1851–60	12,835	2,878,000	44	1,284	35
1861–70	19,884	2,942,000	66	1,988	52
1871–80	22,817	2,952,000	76	2,282	60
1881–86	20,608	1,704,000	121	3,435	90
85 years	98,148	22,865,000	43	1,154	38

The following table shows the number of petitions for divorce compared with the divorces granted from 1841 to 1880 :—

Period	Petitions	Granted	Ratio Granted per Cent.	Percentage of Application By Husband	By Wife
1841–50	10,620	7,687	72	7	93
1851–60	17,210	12,835	74	9	91
1861–70	26,140	19,884	76	11	89
1871–80	29,550	22,817	77	13	87

The various causes alleged in petitions for divorce were :—

	1841–50	1851–60	1861–70	1871–80	40 Years
Cruelty . .	9,720	15,690	24,840	28,500	78,750
Adultery .	655	1,170	1,005	735	3,565
Various . .	245	350	295	315	1,205
Total	10,620	17,210	26,140	29,550	83,520

In several cases there were double charges and cross-bills, which makes the above classification difficult.

Altogether the charges and cross-charges of adultery in forty years were as follows :—

| Period | Alleged Adultery Committed by | | | Yearly Average |
	Husband	Wife	Total	
1841–50 . .	565	525	1,090	109
1851–60 . .	910	1,135	2,045	204
1861–70 . .	870	1,485	2,355	236
1871–80 . .	870	1,530	2,400	240
40 years . .	3,215	4,675	7,890	197

The occupations of persons applying for divorce were :—

	1841–50	1851–60	1861–70	1871–80	40 Years
Professions .	3,245	4,280	4,900	4,890	17,315
Merchants .	2,195	3,490	5,385	5,110	16,180
Farmers . .	1,840	2,690	3,670	3,860	12,060
Labourers .	2,380	6,050	10,550	13,015	31,995
Various . .	960	700	1,635	2,675	5,970
Total .	10,620	17,210	26,140	29,550	83,520

The condition of the parents, as to with or without children, was as follows :—

Period	Had Children	Had None	Not Known	Total	Ratio with Children Per Cent.
1841–50 .	5,910	3,850	860	10,620	56
1851–60 .	10,150	6,660	400	17,210	59
1861–70 .	16,440	9,610	90	26,140	63
1871–80 .	18,750	10,800	...	29,550	64
40 years .	51,250	30,920	1,350	83,520	62

The number of marriages and that of divorces compared thus :—

Period	Marriages	Divorces	Divorces per 1000 Marriages
1867–71 . . .	1,391,000	9,850	7.1
1872–76 . . .	1,569,000	11,384	7.3
1877–81 . . .	1,403,000	13,132	9.4
1882–86 . . .	1,422,000	22,750	16.0
20 years . .	5,785,000	57,116	9.9

The French Government published a table of divorces granted in five years ending December 1889, in all 15,521, viz. :—

	Number	Annual Average
Paris	4,607	921
Towns	7,047	1,410
Rural districts	3,867	773
Total . .	15,521	3,104

The ages of the divorced persons in the said five years were :—

Age	Men	Women	Total	Ratio
Under 25	198	1,313	1,511	4.9
25–35	3,926	6,096	10,022	32.2
35–40	3,669	3,155	6,824	22.0
40–50	4,696	3,331	8,027	25.9
Over 50	3,032	1,626	4,658	15.0
Total . .	15,521	15,521	31,042	100.0

Petition by husband	8,621	For adultery . . .	6,980
Petition by wife . .	6,900	Other causes . . .	8,541
Total . .	15,521	Total . .	15,521

The returns for Paris in twenty years to December 1886 were :—

Period	Marriages	Divorces	Divorces per 1000 Marriages
1867–71 . . .	69,000	2,148	31.1
1872–76 . . .	96,000	2,733	28.4
1877–81 . . .	96,000	3,177	33.0
1882–86 . . .	103,000	3,228	31.3
20 years . . .	364,000	11,286	30.9

In 1889 there were in France 23 divorces in 10,000 couples, and at Paris 100. The mean duration of the dissolved marriages was 15 years in 1884, and fell to 13 years in 1889.

GERMANY

The returns are incomplete, and may be summed up thus :—

	1867–71	1872–76	1877–81	1882–86	20 Years
Prussia . .	...	...	...	17,450	...
Bavaria . .	1,400	1,170	...	1,189	...
Saxony . .	2,342	3,234	3,535	4,526	13,637
Wurtemburg	518	593	609	707	2,427
Baden . .	170	305	396	522	1,393
Hesse . .	159	189	225	321	894
Alsace . .	...	...	398	629	...
Hamburg .	...	...	...	1,115	...
Other States	...	...	...	2,681	...
Total .	...	...	...	29,140	...

If the ratio for Prussia be supposed to have been the same as regards the whole of Germany in previous periods as in the years 1882–86, namely, 60 per cent., and the minor States, for which we have no returns, in like manner, the whole number of divorces for Germany will stand thus :—

	1867–71	1872–76	1877–81	1882–86	20 Years
Prussia . .	11,070	13,251	14,486	17,450	56,257
Bavaria . .	1,400	1,170	1,253	1,189	5,012
Saxony . .	2,342	3,234	3,535	4,526	13,637
Wurtemburg	518	593	609	707	2,427
Baden . .	170	305	396	522	1,393
Small States	2,950	3,532	3,864	4,746	15,092
Total .	18,450	22,085	24,143	29,140	93,818

According to the Census of 1880, the number and ratio of divorced persons living in the various States was as follows :—

	Number	Per 100,000 Inhabitants		Number	Per 100,000 Inhabitants
Prussia . .	37,162	135	Baden . .	825	55
Saxony . .	8,121	270	Hesse . .	612	65
Wurtemburg	3,637	184	Brunswick .	558	160
Bavaria . .	3,108	60	Weimar . .	589	190
Hamburg .	2,883	634	Various . .	3,208	107
Alsace .	1,359	85	All Germany	62,062	136

The comparison between marriages and divorces in the various States during the five years ending 1886 showed thus :—

	Marriages	Divorces	Divorces per 1000 Marriages
Prussia	1,126,000	17,450	15.5
Bavaria	204,000	1,189	5.9
Saxony	142,000	4,526	32.0
Wurtemburg . .	64,000	707	11.0
Baden	53,000	522	9.8
Hesse	34,000	321	9.4
Alsace	52,000	629	12.1
Hamburg . . .	22,000	1,115	50.7
Various	109,000	2,681	24.5
Total . .	1,806,000	29,140	16.2

The following table compares marriages and divorces for all Germany :—

Period	Marriages	Divorces	Divorces per 1000 Marriages
1867–71	1,756,000	18,450	10.5
1872–76	1,994,000	22,085	11.0
1877–81	1,701,000	24,143	14.2
1882–86	1,805,000	29,140	16.2
20 years	7,256,000	93,818	13.0

At Berlin the number of marriages and of divorces in twenty years showed as follows :—

Period	Marriages	Divorces	Divorces per 1000 Marriages
1867–71	42,000	1,988	47.0
1872–76	64,000	2,360	36.8
1877–81	53,000	2,574	48.5
1882–86	66,000	3,830	58.1
20 years	225,000	10,752	47.7

Berlin divorces in the five years ending 1884 showed thus :—

Cause		Husband's Occupation		Religion	
Adultery .	1,071	Merchants .	688	Protestants	2,585
Desertion .	817	Artisans .	1,033	Catholics .	64
Mutual consent }	746	Labourers .	713	Jews . . .	97
Various . .	533	Various . .	733	Various . .	421
Total .	3,167	Total .	3,167	Total .	3,167

Of the above couples 45 per cent. had children, 55 per cent. had none.

Returns for Saxony, covering 14 years down to 1879, give the mean duration of marriages dissolved by divorce as follows :—

Years	Number	Ratio	Cause	13 Years
Under 5 . .	2,737	33.7	Adultery	2,571
5–10 . . .	2,454	30.2	Desertion	2,273
10–20 . .	2,289	28.2	Cruelty	1,807
Over 20 . .	636	7.9	Various	774
Total .	8,116	100.0	Total	7,425

ITALY

The returns for 14 years ending 1879 may be summed up thus :—

Petition by		Cause		Result	
Husband	. 1,269	Cruelty	. 4,462	Granted .	6,056
Wife .	. 4,945	Desertion .	1,835	Withdrawn	4,173
Both .	. 5,217	Adultery .	982	Disallowed	1,202
		Various .	4,152		
Total	. 11,431			Total .	11,431
		Total .	11,431		

Marriages and divorces compared as follows :—

Period	Marriages	Divorces	Divorces per 1000 Marriages
1869–73 . . .	1,004,000	3,141	3.1
1879–81 . . .	640,000	1,917	3.0
1882–85 . . .	929,000	1,632	1.7
12 years . . .	2,573,000	6,690	2.5

AUSTRIA

Marriages and divorces compared as follows :—

Period	Marriages	Divorces	Divorces per 1000 Marriages
1872–76 . . .	932,000	690	0.7
1877–81 . . .	839,000	808	1.0
1882–86 . . .	893,000	856	1.0
15 years . . .	2,664,000	2,354	0.9

The returns for Vienna showed as follows :—

Period	Marriages	Divorces	Divorces per 1000 Marriages
1872–76 . . .	33,000	689	21
1877–81 . . .	27,000	708	26
1882–86 . . .	33,000	1,069	32
15 years . . .	93,000	2,466	26

HUNGARY

Marriages and divorces compared as follows :—

Period	Marriages	Divorces	Divorces per 1000 Marriages
1877–81 . . .	754,000	5,246	7.0
1882–86 . . .	825,000	4,835	5.9
10 years . . .	1,579,000	10,081	6.4

The returns for Buda-Pesth showed thus :—

Period	Marriages	Divorces	Divorces per 1000 Marriages
1877–81 . . .	13,000	91	7.0
1882–86 . . .	19,000	129	6.8
10 years . . .	32,000	220	6.9

ROUMANIA

The returns are to the following effect :—

Period	Marriages	Divorces	Divorces per 1000 Marriages
1871–75	157,000	1,560	9.9
1876–80	182,000	1,932	10.6
10 years . . .	339,000	3,492	10.3

RUSSIA

The returns of marriages and divorces in the Greek Church were as follows :—

Period	Marriages	Divorces	Divorces per 1000 Marriages
1867–71	2,832,000	3,910	1.4
1872–76	3,031,000	4,322	1.4
1877–81	2,846,000	4,705	1.7
1882–86	3,111,000	5,474	1.8
20 years . . .	11,820,000	18,411	1.5

Those in the Protestant congregations were as follows :—

Period	Marriages	Divorces	Divorces per 1000 Marriages
1867–71	104,000	687	6.5
1872–76	116,000	773	6.7
1877–81	115,000	778	6.8
1882–86	129,000	870	6.7
20 years . . .	464,000	3,108	6.7

The returns for Poland showed as follows :—

Period	Marriages	Divorces	Divorces per 1000 Marriages
1867–71	176,000	809	4.6
1872–76	208,000	1,073	5.2
1877–81	262,000	1,432	5.5
1882–86	308,000	1,725	5.6
20 years . . .	954,000	5,039	5.3

The returns for Finland are as follows :—

Period	Marriages	Divorces	Divorces per 1000 Marriages
1877–81	76,000	238	3.2
1882–86	81,000	219	2.7

The gross total for European Russia was as follows :—

Period	Marriages	Divorces	Divorces per 1000 Marriages
1867–71	3,112,000	5,406	1.7
1872–76	3,355,000	6,168	1.8
1877–81	3,299,000	7,153	2.2
1882–86	3,629,000	8,288	2.3
20 years . . .	13,395,000	27,015	2.0

The causes for divorces granted in the Greek Church were :—

	1866–75	1876–85	20 Years	Ratio
Adultery . .	426	1,302	1,728	9.3
Exile	1,541	2,745	4,286	23.2
Disappearance	5,872	5,606	11,478	62.3
Sterility . . .	70	178	248	1.3
Consanguinity	100	85	185	1.0
Bigamy . . .	223	304	527	2.9
Total .	8,232	10,220	18,452	100.0

Marriages and divorces in Poland, according to creed, were :—

	Marriages			Divorces			Divorces per 1000 Marriages		
	1867–76	1877–86	Total	1867–76	1877–86	Total	1867–76	1877–86	Total
Roman Catholics .	343,000	501,000	844,000	330	340	670	1.0	0.7	0.8
Protestants . . .	30,000	37,000	67,000	170	205	375	5.7	5.5	5.6
Jews, &c. . . .	11,000	32,000	43,000	1,382	2,612	3,994	125.6	81.5	92.8
Total . .	384,000	570,000	954,000	1,882	3,157	5,039	4.9	5.5	5.3

DENMARK

The returns are as follows :—

Period	Marriages	Divorces	Divorces per 1000 Marriages
1871–76	89,000	3,156	35.3
1877–81	75,000	3,046	40.6
11 Years	164,000	6,202	37.5

NORWAY

The returns of marriages and divorces show thus :—

Period	Marriages	Divorces	Divorces per 1000 Marriages
1872–76	67,000	162	2.4
1877–81	65,000	195	3.0
1882–84	39,000	120	3.1
13 Years	171,000	477	2.8

SWEDEN

The number of marriages and of divorces was as follows :—

Period	Marriages	Divorces	Divorces per 1000 Marriages
1867–71	124,000	619	5.0
1872–76	154,000	953	6.2
1877–81	146,000	1,053	7.2
1882–86	149,000	1,109	7.4
20 years	573,000	3,734	6.5

The returns for Stockholm were as follows :—

Period	Marriages	Divorces	Divorces per 1000 Marriages
1867–71	4,810	146	30.2
1872–76	6,930	190	27.4
1877–81	7,512	285	38.0
1882–86	9,280	306	32.8
20 years	28,532	927	32.5

The causes of divor e in Sweden were as follows :—

Causes				Number	Ratio
Adultery	.	.	.	537	14.4
Desertion	.	.	.	2,195	58.6
Various	.	.	.	1,002	27.0
	Total	.	.	3,734	100.0

The above is the aggregate for twenty years ending 1886.

BELGIUM

The number of marriages and of divorces was as follows :—

Period	Marriages	Divorces	Divorces per 1000 Marriages
1831–40	302,000	135	0.4
1841–50	290,000	224	0.8
1851–60	335,000	412	1.2
1861–70	363,000	866	2.4
1871–80	389,000	1,923	4.9
1881–86	237,000	1,785	7.5
56 years	1,916,000	5,345	2.8

In order to compare Belgium with the other countries in the twenty years ending 1886, the following table will be useful :—

Period	Marriages	Divorces	Divorces per 1000 Marriages
1867–71	185,000	620	3.4
1872–76	198,000	899	4.5
1877–81	192,000	1,189	6.2
1882–86	197,000	1,501	7.6
20 years	772,000	4,209	5.5

By the Census of 1880 it appeared that 43 persons per 100,000 of the population were divorced, viz., 1028 men and 1347 women. The growth of divorce, especially in cities, appears as follows ; the Belgian cities included below are Brussels, Antwerp, Ghent, and Liege :—

Year	Cities			All Belgium		
	Marriages	Divorces	Divorces per 1000 Marriages	Marriages	Divorces	Divorces per 1000 Marriages
1870	4,735	41	8.9	35,300	81	2.3
1875	5,337	64	12.0	39,050	126	3.2
1880	5,219	102	19.6	38,900	214	5.5
1885	5,503	129	23.5	39,900	230	5.8

HOLLAND

Marriages and divorces during twenty years were thus :—

Period	Marriages	Divorces	Divorces per 1000 Marriages
1867–71	144,000	699	4.8
1872–76	157,000	811	5.2
1877–81	153,000	1,161	7.6
1882–86	150,000	1,571	10.5
20 years	604,000	4,242	7.0

SWITZERLAND

The marriages and divorces were as follows :—

Period	Marriages	Divorces	Divorces per 1000 Marriages
1877–81	101,000	4,811	47.6
1882–86	100,000	4,588	45.9
10 years	201,000	9,399	46.7

The returns of age were in 1880 as follows :—

Years	Husband	Wife	Total	Ratio
Under 30 . . .	144	217	361	21.1
30–40	302	287	589	34.5
40–50	211	178	389	22.7
Over 50	199	174	373	21.7
Total . .	856	856	1,712	100.0

The occupations of persons divorced are shown thus :—

Per Million Inhabitants

Agriculturists	190
Mechanics	510
Merchants	620

The duration of marriage was as follows :—

Years	Marriages	Ratio
Under 2	81	9.5
2–5	220	25.4
5–10	230	27.0
10–20	235	27.6
Over 20	90	10.5
Total . .	856	100.0

Youthful marriages seem most exposed to divorce, the ratios being as follows :—

Marrying Age	*Divorces per 10,000 Marriages*
Under 20	620
20–40	330
Over 40	320

UNITED STATES

The following table compares marriages with divorces in the only States in which the former are fully reported, viz. :—Connecticut, District of Columbia, Massachusetts, Ohio, Rhode Island, and Vermont :—

Period	Aggregate of Six States		
	Marriages	Divorces	Divorces per 1000 Marriages
1867–71 . . .	258,000	10,753	41
1872–76 . . .	261,000	12,577	48
1877–81 . . .	263,000	13,929	53
1882–86 . . .	296,000	16,308	55
20 years* . .	1,078,000	53,567	50

* The ratio of divorces to marriages in the United States may be estimated from the above six States, which, during twenty years, had a marriage-rate of 9 per 1000 inhabitants.

The several States in their aggregate returns for twenty years showed as follows :—

	Marriages	Divorces	Divorces per 1000 Marriages
Connecticut . .	97,000	8,542	88
District of Columbia	24,000	1,105	45
Massachusetts .	308,000	9,853	32
Ohio . . .	544,000	26,367	48
Rhode Island . .	50,000	4,462	89
Vermont . .	55,000	3,238	59
Total . .	1,078,000	53,567	50

The number of divorces yearly compared with the mean population of the great sections of the United States was approximately as follows :—

States·	Divorces Yearly per 100,000 Population				
	1867–71	1872–76	1877–81	1882–86	20 Years
N. England	52	54	53	52	53
Middle . .	17	15	16	19	17
South . .	13	17	24	31	24
West . . .	43	50	54	65	60
The Union .	30	32	35	42	36

The figures for twenty years will, therefore, stand thus :—

Period	Marriages	Divorces	Divorces per 1000 Marriages
1867–71	1,710,000	53,574	31.3
1872–76	1,980,000	68,547	34.6
1877–81	2,210,000	89,284	40.4
1882–86	2,430,000	117,311	48.3
20 years . . .	8,330,000	328,716	39.5

The causes for divorces granted were as follows :—

Cause	Summary of Divorces Granted			Ratio
	To Husband	To Wife	Total	
Adultery	38,184	29,502	67,686	20.6
Cruelty	6,122	45,473	51,595	15.7
Desertion . . .	51,485	75,191	126,676	38.5
Drunkenness . .	1,434	12,432	13,866	4.3
Neglect	7,426	40,374	47,800	14.5
Various	7,889	13,204	21,093	6.4
Total . .	112,540	216,176	328,716	100.0

The average duration of marriage before divorce was :—

Cause	Years of Marriage before Divorce Granted		
	To Husband	To Wife	Total
Adultery . . .	7.8	9.5	8.6
Cruelty . . .	9.8	9.2	9.3
Desertion . . .	9.8	9.2	9.4
Drunkenness . .	10.9	11.0	11.0
Neglect	8.7	9.3	9.2
Various	7.6	7.2	7.4
All causes . . .	9.0	9.3	9.2

The number of divorces compared with the medium population of each State in 1870–80 thus :—

		Number of Divorces				Yearly Average per 100,000 Pop.
		1867–71	1871–76	1877–81	1881–86	Twenty Years	
Maine		1,948	2,101	2,511	1,852	8,412	67
New Hampshire . .		781	1,173	1,392	1,633	4,979	75
Vermont		830	851	798	759	3,238	50
Rhode Island . . .		938	1,030	1,197	1,297	4,462	89
Connecticut . . .		2,314	2,319	1,923	1,986	8,542	74
Massachusetts . . .		1,781	2,448	2,624	3,000	9,853	30
New England . . .		8,592	9,922	10,445	10,527	39,486	53
New York		3,755	3,224	3,617	4,759	15,355	16
New Jersey . . .		390	528	652	1,072	2,642	13
Pennsylvania . . .		3,158	3,325	4,117	5,420	16,020	21
Delaware		69	43	83	94	289	10
District of Columbia .		161	318	294	332	1,105	37
Maryland		425	465	495	800	2,185	13
Middle		7,958	7,903	9,258	12,477	37,596	17
Virginia (2) . . .		758	932	1,435	2,065	5,190	14
North Carolina . .		130	266	364	578	1,338	5
South Carolina . .		6	92	65	...	163	1
Georgia		587	893	1,025	1,454	3,959	15
Florida		198	340	625	965	2,128	48
Alabama		479	752	1,502	2,471	5,204	23
Mississippi . . .		373	858	1,506	2,303	5,040	25
Louisiana		173	319	446	759	1,697	10
Texas		699	1,547	3,338	5,888	11,472	48
Arkansas		562	846	1,947	2,686	6,041	48
Kentucky		1,726	2,242	2,845	3,435	10,248	34
Tennessee		1,415	1,954	2,838	3,418	9,625	34
South		7,106	11,041	17,936	26,022	62,105	24
Ohio		4,729	5,611	7,093	8,934	26,367	46
Illinois		5,803	8,516	9,702	12,051	36,072	64
Missouri		2,281	3,220	4,073	5,704	15,278	38
Indiana		5,741	5,089	6,523	7,840	25,193	67
Iowa		2,838	3,509	4,614	5,603	16,564	59
Michigan		2,635	3,783	5,492	6,523	18,433	66
Wisconsin		2,006	2,146	2,484	3,352	9,988	42
Minnesota		403	659	918	1,643	3,623	30
Kansas		725	1,293	1,891	3,282	7,191	52
Nebraska		151	391	818	1,674	3,034	50
Colorado		80	338	1,005	2,264	3,687	152
California		1,288	2,553	3,400	4,877	12,118	87
Oregon		369	448	759	1,033	2,609	98
Utah		387	1,387	1,594	710	4,078	170
Nevada, Dakota, &c. . .		482	738	1,279	2,795	5,294	...
West		29,918	39,681	51,645	68,285	189,529	60
Total . .		53,574	68,547	89,284	117,311	328,716	36

The number of married couples and that of divorces in certain States and cities were as follows :—

States	Estimated Married Couples		Divorces		Divorces per 100,000 Couples	
	1870	1880	1870	1880	1870	1880
New York .	828,000	961,000	731	834	88	87
Pennsylvania .	666,000	809,000	623	951	93	114
Massachusetts	275,000	337,000	404	595	147	178
Illinois . . .	480,000	582,000	1,178	2,139	245	369
Ohio . .	504,000	601,000	992	1,553	197	259
Maryland .	148,000	177,000	84	128	56	72
Louisiana .	137,000	178,000	30	109	22	61
Missouri .	325,000	410,000	491	930	152	227
California . .	106,000	163,000	298	683	280	410
9 States	3,469,000	4,218,000	4,831	7,922	140	187

Cities	Estimated Married Couples		Divorces		Divorces per 100,000 Couples	
	1870	1880	1870	1880	1870	1880
New York .	178,000	228,000	265	227	150	100
Philadelphia .	127,000	160,000	124	194	97	121
Boston . . .	51,000	73,000	113	156	223	214
Baltimore . .	51,000	63,000	60	98	118	156
Washington .	25,000	34,000	39	66	156	194
New Orleans .	36,000	41,000	15	38	42	93
St. Louis . .	59,000	66,000	155	241	263	365
San Francisco .	28,000	44,000	87	242	311	550
Brooklyn . .	79,000	113,000	54	111	68	98
Cleveland . .	25,000	37,000	114	168	456	454
Memphis . .	14,000	15,000	26	61	186	406
Milwaukee .	17,000	26,000	57	104	335	400
12 cities	690,000	900,000	1,109	1,706	160	190

P

CANADA

The number of marriages is not known, but if we assume the medium rate of 8 per 1000 inhabitants (as compared with 7½ in Australia and 9 in the United States), the record will stand thus :—

Period	Marriages	Divorces	Divorces per 1000 Marriages
1867–71 . . .	31,000	15	0.5
1872–76 . . .	33,000	16	0.5
1877–81 . . .	35,000	33	0.9
1882–86 . . .	37,000	52	1.4
20 years . .	136,000	116	0.9

AUSTRALIA

The returns for five years ending 1888 were as follows :—

Colony	Marriages	Divorces	Divorces per 1000 Marriages
New South Wales .	38,400	135	3.5
Victoria . . .	34,000	93	2.7
Queensland .	12,500	8	0.6
South Australia .	12,400	115	9.3
New Zealand .	20,100	72	3.6
Tasmania .	5,500	12	2.2
West Australia .	1,500	2	1.4
Total .	124,400	437	3.5

DOCKS AND HARBOURS

The sums spent on docks and harbours in recent years are as follows :—

	£		£
Alexandria . .	2,550,000	Glasgow . . .	7,600,000
Amsterdam . .	2,600,000	Hamburg . . .	5,500,000
Antwerp . .	6,800,000	Havre . . .	6,400,000
Bordeaux . . .	1,700,000	Holyhead . . .	2,000,000
Boulogne . .	1,200,000	Hull	1,200,000
Bremen	1,800,000	Liverpool . . .	18,200,000
Bristol . . .	900,000	London . . .	20,100,000
Calais	1,500,000	Marseilles . .	3,400,000
Cette	1,800,000	Plymouth . . .	1,550,000
Cherbourg . .	3,500,000	Rotterdam . .	2,400,000
Dieppe	1,200,000	St. Nazaire . .	1,800,000
Dundee	800,000	Trieste	1,100,000
Dunkirk . . .	4,600,000		

The area under docks and average dues are :—

	Docks, Acres	Dock-Dues on Vessels of 1000 Tons
London	690	£125
Liverpool	560	133
Antwerp	105	93
Cardiff	113	...
Trieste	86	...

The largest lock in the world is that of Cardiff, 600 feet long by 80 feet in width; ordinary depth of water, 36 feet.

Dock-dues in Hamburg for a vessel of 1000 tons would be £110, in Amsterdam £81. As regards length of quay-wall, Marseilles has 8 miles, Amsterdam 7, Antwerp 7, Trieste 3, Rotterdam 3, Genoa 2.

As regards warehouses, Marseilles has 20 acres, Trieste 7, Genoa 4. Depth of water in docks, 60 feet at Antwerp, 36 at Cardiff, 30 at Trieste, 25 at Amsterdam. The new dock at Barry, in the Bristol Channel, covers 70 acres, depth of water 34 feet.

The following table shows the depth of water and mileage of quay-wall at the principal French ports :—

	Feet, Water	Quay, Miles		Feet, Water	Quay, Miles
Marseilles .	23	8.3	St. Nazaire	22	2.8
Havre .	26	8.0	Boulogne .	26	2.0
Cette . .	22	4.8	Bordeaux .	19	2.0
Dunkirk .	20	3.5	Dieppe . .	18	1.8
Rouen . .	17	3.0	Calais . .	25	1.5

The French Government has expended the following sums on the above ports :—

		£
Down to 1876		24,800,000
1876–90		22,600,000
Total .		47,400,000

The following are some of the finest breakwaters :—

Name	Date	Yards Long	Cost, £	Builder
Plymouth .	1812–41	1,720	1,550,000	Rennie
Cherbourg	1784–1857	4,100	3,200,000	...
Delaware .	...	1,200	...	...
Alexandria	1873–76	2,000	2,550,000	Greenway

The Plymouth breakwater has the same quantity of stone, 3,800,000 tons, as the great pyramid of Cheops, and encloses 1120 acres of harbour; Cherbourg, 1927 acres; and Delaware, 420 acres.

DRUGS AND CHEMICALS

The British trade returns show imports under this head thus :—

	Value, £			
	1860	1870	1880	1888
Bones . . .	300,000	630,000	530,000	390,000
Caoutchouc .	470,000	1,600,000	2,400,000	2,600,000
Chemicals, sundry .	...	530,000	1,140,000	1,300,000
Chinchona .	...	...	1,180,000	550,000
Cinnamon .	50,000	250,000	100,000	40,000
Cochineal .	410,000	580,000	430,000	50,000
Cutch . . .	220,000	470,000	660,000	710,000
Drugs, various	...	310,000	670,000	900,000
Dye-woods and extracts	240,000	280,000	2,030,000	2,120,000
Esparto . .	...	...	1,640,000	2,300,000
Guano . .	1,560,000	3,480,000	810,000	200,000
Gum . . .	...	...	1,120,000	1,140,000
Gutta-percha	160,000	500,000	530,000	180,000
Indigo . .	2,530,000	2,720,000	1,710,000	1,700,000
Madder . .	690,000	430,000	...	...
Nitre . . .	500,000	880,000	700,000	980,000
Opium . .	...	...	360,000	360,000
Paints . .	...	...	820,000	900,000
Pepper . .	240,000	420,000	400,000	920,000
Rosin . . .	180,000	370,000	340,000	270,000
Saltpetre . .	660,000	380,000	300,000	300,000
Shumach .	170,000	230,000	150,000	140,000
Sulphur . .	500,000	390,000	250,000	170,000
Turpentine .	220,000	130,000	380,000	520,000
Valonia . .	270,000	400,000	520,000	460,000
Yeast . . .	180,000	290,000	540,000	730,000
Total .	9,550,000	15,270,000	19,710,000	19,930,000

The exports show as follows :—

	Value, £			
	1860	1870	1880	1888
Alkali . . .	960,000	1,490,000	2,400,000	1,640,000
Bleaching materials }	...	...	440,000	620,000
Caoutchouc . .	140,000	550,000	1,060,000	1,340,000
Chemicals, sundries }	...	1,330,000	2,380,000	2,400,000
Chinchona . .	210,000	120,000	610,000	340,000
Cinnamon . .	50,000	170,000	80,000	40,000
Cochineal . . .	300,000	320,000	280,000	30,000
Cutch	...	...	210,000	250,000
Drugs, sundry .	590,000	170,000	510,000	370,000
Gum	...	...	630,000	640,000
Gunpowder . .	350,000	430,000	370,000	360,000
Indigo	1,900,000	1,600,000	1,300,000	1,100,000
Medicine . . .	...	...	810,000	930,000
Opium	...	200,000	190,000	330,000
Paints	...	880,000	1,160,000	1,450,000
Pepper	170,000	260,000	240,000	590,000
Total .	4,670,000	7,520,000	12,670,000	12,430,000

Alkali.—The annual production in 1882 was as follows :—

	Tons
Great Britain	432,000
France	127,000
Germany	101,000
Austria	40,000
Belgium, United States, &c. . . .	11,000
Total . . .	711,000

The production in Great Britain has quadrupled since 1850, when it was 104,000 tons. The exportation from Great Britain showed the following quantities and prices:—

Year	Tons	Value, £ per Ton
1853	53,000	9.0
1860	102,000	9.5
1870	193,000	8.0
1880	344,000	7.0
1888	317,000	5.1

Arsenic.—In Styria in 1875 two men were seen to eat 30 centigrammes of yellow arsenic without injury.

Blacking.—For boots. The consumption in England in 1880 amounted to a value of £560,000.

Chinchona or Peruvian Bark.—The annual production was in 1882 as follows :—

	Lbs.
Peru	8,900,000
India	2,200,000
Java	110,000
Jamaica	21,000
Total .	11,231,000

The Indian plantations showed as follows in 1880 :—

Planted A.D.	Locality	Trees	Crops, Lbs. Bark
1860 . .	Nilghiri	540,000	180,000
1861 . .	Darjeeling . . .	4,680,000	378,000
1869 . .	Ceylon	77,000,000	1,260,000
1875 . .	Burmah	2,000	200
	Total . .	82,222,000	1,818,200

The exports from Ceylon rose very rapidly, viz. :—

	Lbs.
1880	1,260,000
1884	11,000,000
1886	15,000,000
1888	11,000,000

Indian bark yields from 4 to 5 per cent. of sulphate of quinine, but the superior quality introduced into Java by Mr. Charles Ledger gives from 6 up to 15 per cent. The plantations in India and Ceylon are valued at 5 millions sterling. Some Germans have planted near La Paz, Bolivia, 600,000 trees of the Ledger or Caupolican species.

The quantities of bark imported into Great Britain have been as follows :—

Year	Tons	Value per Ton, £	Net Imports, Tons
1874 . . .	2,100	210	400
1880 . . .	4,000	300	1,600
1888 . . .	7,200	76	1,000

The manufacture of quinine in 1879 was, according to the Archivio, as follows :—

	Lbs.		Lbs.
East Indies . .	11,000	Germany . . .	55,000
England . .	26,000	Italy . . .	44,000
France . .	40,000	America . . .	60,000

Making a total of 236,000 lbs., which was only 2 per cent. on the crop of bark.

Cochineal.—Canary Islands exported in 1880 three million lbs., valued at £350,000.

Dynamite.—Messrs. Nobel of Glasgow make 1200 tons yearly.

Glycerine.—Production in 1880 :—

	Tons		Tons
England . . .	300	Russia . . .	900
France . . .	4,000	Belgium . . .	800
Germany . . .	1,500	Italy . . .	400
Holland . . .	900	Spain . . .	200

Guano.—The Peruvian Government exported from the Chincha Islands between 1850 and 1880 more than 12 million tons, worth 110 millions sterling. Great Britain paid 55 millions for 5,200,000 tons since 1855. The first quantity exported to Europe was in 1840. The supply is now almost exhausted. The analysis is as follows :—

Azote	52.5
Phosphate of lime . . .	19.3
Alkali	7.6
Water	15.8
Sundry	4.8
Total . . .	100.0

Gunpowder

	Saltpetre	Charcoal	Sulphur	Total
English . . .	75	15	10	100
French . . .	75	13	12	100
German . . .	75	11	14	100
Russian . . .	74	14	12	100
Austrian . . .	72	17	11	100
Spanish . . .	76	11	13	100
Swedish . . .	75	16	9	100
Chinese . . .	76	14	10	100
American . . .	75	13	12	100
Sporting . . .	77	13	10	100

*

The quantities exported from Great Britain, and the price per ton were :—

Year	Tons	Value, £ per Ton
1853	4,200	55
1860	5,000	70
1870	7,800	55
1880	6,700	55
1888	6,000	60

India-rubber.—This is mostly obtained from the Seringueros of the Amazon, who sell it for sixpence a pound to the merchants of Para, but its value on reaching England or United States is over two shillings a pound. The quantities imported into Great Britain and United States have been as follows :—

Into	Tons Imported			
	1860	1870	1880	1887
Great Britain . .	2,150	7,606	8,479	11,800
United States . .	1,610	4,316	7,529	12,900
Total . .	3,760	11,922	16,008	24,700
Value per ton . .	£224	£215	£277	£215

The best rubber-forests in Brazil will ultimately be exhausted, owing to the reckless mode followed by the Seringueros or tappers. The ordinary product of a tapper's work is from 10 to 16 lbs. daily. A tree 15 inches diameter bled 8 feet high will yield 3 pints of milk. There are 120 india-rubber manufacturers in the United States, employing 15,000 operatives, who produce 280,000 tons of goods, valued at 52 millions sterling per annum.

Madder.—The best is grown near Avignon, on irrigated lands, for which the tenants pay £5 an acre rent. Average crop, 2 tons per acre, worth £50, leaving small profit to the cultivator.

Official returns of this crop in France are as follows :—

Year	Acres	Tons
1840 . . .	36,000	25,000
1862 . . .	51,000	54,000
1874 . . .	12,500	17,300

It gives 9 per cent. of ashes, of which 4 per cent. soluble salts and 3½ per cent. carbonate of lime.

Maqui.—This berry is grown in Chili for colouring wine. Exports thus :—

	Tons
1887	26
1888	431

France takes 75 per cent. of the total.

Nitre.—Atacama (Chile) exports 350,000 tons per annum. The nitre is about 2 feet below the surface ; one bed covers 5000 acres, 4 feet in thickness, say 25 million tons, worth 300 millions sterling. The quantities imported into Great Britain and the value per ton were :—

Year	Tons	Value, £ per Ton
1853	17,000	20
1860	37,000	14
1870	57,000	15
1880	46,000	15
1888	103,000	10

It is also called nitrate of potash.

Chili, in 1889, exported 930,000 tons valued at £7,800,000, or £8 per ton.

Opium.—Annual shipments from India :—

Years	Chests	Tons	Value £	Per Ton £
1861–65	73,100	4,305	10,810,000	2,510
1866–70	82,800	4,870	11,240,000	2,290
1871–75	89,200	5,250	11,790,000	2,250
1876–80	102,100	6,005	12,640,000	2,106
1881–86	90,200	5,400	11,800,000	2,180
1887–88	93,000	5,600	10,600,000	1,900

The Chinese impose a duty of £5 per ton. It is retailed at 2s. per ounce, or double the price of native opium. The province of Hankow produces 5300 tons per annum. There are in China 3 million opium-smokers. The average importation yearly into Great Britain shows :—

Year	Imported Tons	Re-Shipped Tons	Home Use Tons
1875–80	220	115	105
1881–85	290	170	120
1886–88	270	185	85

The cultivation in India gives an average crop of 30 lbs. per acre, value £100.

DRUNKENNESS

The returns of insanity caused by drunkenness, and those of suicide from the same cause, in various countries show :—

Insanity			Suicide		
England . .	14 per cent.		England . .	12 per cent.
Ireland . . .	12 ,,		France . . .	12 ,,
France . . .	14 ,,		Prussia . . .	14 ,,
Prussia . . .	10 ,,		Oldenburg .	17 ,,
Denmark . .	11 ,,		Saxony . . .	9 ,,
Finland . . .	12 ,,		Belgium . .	8 ,,
Norway . . .	20 ,,		Russia . . .	38 ,,
Holland . .	16 ,,		Baden . . .	6 ,,
Austria . . .	14 ,,		Europe . . .	15 ,,

Kaspar considers that the official returns are much too low, and estimates that 25 per cent. of suicides in Germany are produced by drunkenness.

The increase of alcoholic insanity and suicide in France is remarkable, viz. :—

Period	Ratio of Dipsomaniacs (France)	
	Per 1000 Insane	Per 1000 Suicides
1840–49 . . .	78	67
1861–70 . . .	108	130
1871–80 . . .	148	113
1881–85 . . .	144	120

In France drunkenness and alcoholic insanity have progressed with the consumption of spirits, the average of which is now three times as much per head as in 1840–42. See *Alcohol*, p. 59.

Drunkenness as a cause of insanity and of suicide is much commoner among men than women, viz. :—

Males to Females			Males to Females	
England .	.	75–25	Austria . .	89–11
France .	.	74–26	Denmark . .	82–18
Prussia .	.	88–12	Oldenburg .	85–15
Belgium .	.	72–28	General average	80–20

Of insane males in Italy, 12 per cent. are caused by drink ; in United States, 26 per cent. ; and in Scotland, 28 per cent.

DEATHS FROM DRINK YEARLY

	Number	Per 1000 Deaths of Population	Per Million Inhabitants
England . . .	1,082	2.04	40
Scotland . . .	230	3.29	60
Ireland	280	2.78	56
United Kingdom	1,592	2.27	43
France	872	1.05	23
Germany . . .	3,240	2.70	70
Belgium . . .	456	3.83	80
Sweden	502	6.25	106
Norway . . .	72	2.36	40
Switzerland . .	244	3.81	85
Italy	709	0.85	24

Deaths from drink in New York are said to average 12 per 1000 of the total, that is, five times more numerous than in the United Kingdom.

YEARS OF INTEMPERANCE TO PRODUCE DEATH

Class		Liquor	
Women . . .	14	Beer	22
Gentlemen .	15	Spirits . . .	17
Working class .	18	Mixed . . .	16

This shows that the working class can stand drink longest, and that beer is the least deadly form of intemperance.

RATIO OF DRUNKENNESS TO POPULATION.

The number of drunkards fined yearly per 1000 inhabitants in some of the large towns of the United Kingdom is as follows (1880–84):—

Belfast . .	21	Glasgow . .	38	Dublin . . .	43
Manchester .	31	Liverpool . .	42	Cork . . .	56

The prevalence of drunkenness in the rural districts is much less than in towns, the general average of persons fined in England being about 6 per 1000 of the population,* viz. :—

Year				Persons Fined	Per 1000 Inhabitants
1860	.	.	.	88,400	4.4
1870	.	.	.	137,200	6.0
1881	.	.	.	174,500	6.7
1888	.	.	.	166,300	6.0

* As the same person will be fined probably ten times in the year, it may be assumed that drunkards are not 6 per 1000, but 6 in 10,000 of the population.

In 1880 there were 61,000 persons fined in France for drunkenness, say 1.7 per 1000 inhabitants, or one-fourth of the ratio in England.

DRUNKENNESS AND CRIME

According to the *Dict. des Sciences Medicales* the proportion of crime caused by habits of intemperance is as follows :—

			Per Cent.				Per Cent.
England	.	.	43	Germany	.	.	44
Belgium	.	.	80	Denmark	.	.	74
Sweden	.	.	31	General average		.	54

In Denmark 23 per cent. of divorces originate in habits of intemperance.

VALUE OF LIFE, DRUNK AND SOBER

Age	Expectancy of Years	
	Drunk	Sober
20	15	44
30	14	36
40	11	29

In a period of 35 years down to 1874, the United Kingdom Assurance Company issued 25,500 policies in two distinct sections, temperance and general. The number of insured persons who died, compared with those expected to die by the actuaries, were :—

Section			Expected to Die	Died
Temperance	.	.	2,644	1,861
General	.	.	4,408	4,339

This would seem to indicate that "teetotallers" and blue-ribbon men live 17 years longer than others.

DWARFS

Name	Height (Inches)	Date of Birth	Birthplace
Borowlaski	39	1739	Warsaw
Tom Thumb . . .	31	1838	New York
Mrs. T. Thumb . .	32	1842	,,
Che-Mah	25	1838	China
Lucia Zarate . . .	20	1863	Mexico
General Mite . . .	21	1864	New York

Count Borowlaski was a friend of George III., and one of the most accomplished men in London society. Tom Thumb's real name was Charles Stratton

E.

EARTH

The area and cubic contents, according to Murray (*Challenger* expedition), are shown thus :—

	Area, Square Miles	Cubic Miles
Land	51,410,700	21,923,200
Water	137,199,000	323,722,000
Total . .	188,609,700	345,645,200

The mean height of the land has been stated thus :—

FEET OVER SEA-LEVEL

	Humboldt	Lapparent	Murray	Tillo
Europe	672	958	939	1,046
Asia	1,151	2,884	3,189	3,160
North America .	748	1,952	1,888	2,052
South America . .	1,132	1,762	2,078	2,036
Africa	...	1,975	2,021	2,020
Australia	...	1,188	805	790
Mean	1,007	2,120	2,252	2,290

The elevation of the various continents is as follows :—

	Square Miles					Mean Height in Feet
	Under 600 Feet	600 to 1500 Feet	1500 to 3000 Feet	Over 3000 Feet	Total	
Europe	2,040,600	991,800	362,000	275,700	3,670,100	939
Asia	4,049,500	2,603,700	3,551,900	6,163,400	16,368,500	3,189
Africa	1,410,100	3,859,800	3,066,200	2,756,700	11,092,800	2,021
North America . . .	2,466,200	2,450,600	1,015,900	1,690,400	7,623,100	1,888
South America . . .	2,725,600	1,842,800	1,151,000	1,142,000	6,861,400	2,078
Australia	896,300	1,935,700	123,900	58,200	3,014,100	805
Islands	476,400	600,000	611,500	1,092,800	2,780,700	2,387
The world . .	14,064,700	14,284,400	9,882,400	13,179,200	51,410,700	2,252

The cubic contents and area of the various oceans and seas, according to Murray's measurement (*Challenger* expedition), are shown thus :—

	Depth, Feet		Cubic Miles	Square Miles	Ratio	
	Greatest	Mean			Cubic Measure	Area
North Atlantic . . .	27,366	12,810	34,804,000	14,343,000	10.8	10.4
South Atlantic . . .	18,600	14,250	27,510,000	10,193,000	8.5	7.4
Arctic Ocean . . .	9,000	3,780	3,418,000	4,781,000	1.1	3.5
Norwegian Sea . .	12,030	5,448	1,162,000	1,127,000	0.3	0.9
Caribbean Sea . . .	19,014	7,614	1,675,000	1,161,000	0.5	0.9
Gulf of Mexico . . .	12,714	4,632	628,000	716,000	0.2	0.6
Mediterranean . . .	12,900	4,608	710,000	813,000	0.2	0.6
Black Sea	6,420	2,472	65,000	139,000	...	0.1
Baltic	2,580	342	13,000	196,000	...	0.2
North Pacific . . .	30,000	15,420	77,994,000	26,705,000	24.1	19.4
South Pacific . . .	19,830	14,208	63,522,000	23,604,000	19.6	17.2
China Sea . . .	13,200	3,228	835,000	1,367,000	0.3	1.0
Behring Sea . . .	9,000	3,816	622,000	859,000	0.2	0.6
Indian Ocean . . .	18,582	13,716	44,377,000	17,084,000	13.7	12.4
Red Sea	7,200	2,250	68,000	159,000	...	0.1
Southern Ocean . .	25,200	12,020	64,875,000	30,592,000	20.1	22.3
Other seas . . .	25,200	4,800	1,434,000	3,360,000	0.4	2.4
	...	...	323,722,000	137,199,000	100.0	100.0

According to Tillo, the mean depth of the ocean is 12,550 feet.

The area and cubic contents of the continents show thus :—

	Sq. Miles	Cubic Miles	Superficial Ratio	Cubic Ratio
Europe . .	3,670,100	652,800	7.2	3.0
Asia . . .	16,368,500	9,887,000	31.8	45.2
Africa . .	11,092,800	4,246,400	21.6	19.3
N. America .	7,623,100	2,725,500	14.7	12.4
S. America .	6,861,400	2,699,900	13.4	12.3
Australia .	3,014,100	459,400	5.8	2.1
Islands . .	2,780,700	1,252,200	5.5	5.7
Total .	51,410,700	21,923,200	100.0	100.0

The following table shows the elevation of various places over sea-level, in feet :—

Bangalore	.	3,015	Mexico . . .	7,480
Berne	.	1,775	Milan . . .	420
Bogota	.	8,680	Moscow . . .	985
Darjeeling	.	7,460	Munich . . .	1,740
Erzeroum .	.	5,255	Quito . . .	9,545
Friburg	.	2,050	Rome . . .	150
Geneva	.	1,250	St. Gall . .	1,820
Gondar	.	7,260	St. Helena . .	1,775
Gratz	.	1,295	St. Remy . .	5,265
Guatemala	.	4,705	Salzburg . .	1,350
Innspruck	.	1,895	Seringapatam .	2,390
Jerusalem	.	2,515	Vevay . .	1,245
Kandy	.	1,695	Zurich . .	1,240
Madrid	.	2,090		

The depth of the minor seas is shown thus :—

		Average, Feet		Maximum, Feet
Irish Sea	. .	240	...	710
English Channel .	.	110	...	300
Levant .	. .	72	...	...
Adriatic	. .	45	...	...

EARTHQUAKES

Since the beginning of the eighteenth century the most destructive have been the following :—

Year	Place	Lives Lost
1703	Yeddo	190,000
1716	Algiers	18,000
1726	Palermo	6,000
1731	Pekin	95,000
1746	Lima	18,000
1754	Cairo	40,000
1755	Lisbon	35,000
1773	Guatemala . . .	33,000
1797	Quito	41,000
1822	Aleppo	22,000
1861	Mendoza, South America	12,000
1868	Arica	6,000
1880	Manilla	3,000
1883	Ischia	2,000

PLATE IV

EDUCATION.

Percentage of Adults able to write.

Percentage of population attending school ; average attendance.

EDUCATION

The following is a general view of the educational condition of the various countries according to latest information :—

Country	Year	Schools	Teachers	Pupils	Expenditure, £	School Children per 1000 Pop.
United Kingdom . .	1888	30,522	85,000	4,605,000	9,690,000	123
France	1887	85,545	136,800	6,308,000	6,000,000	170
Germany	1881	57,000	120,000	7,100,000	4,000,000	140
Russia	1889	43,100	...	2,510,000	3,800,000	25
Austria	1889	35,718	99,200	4,903,000	2.400,000	130
Italy	1887	70,507	86,400	3,071,000	3,100,000	90
Spain	1885	31,880	36,000	1,843,000	1,200,000	106
Portugal	1886	5,663	...	257,000	200,000	54
Switzerland . . .	1886	6,794	12,720	630,000	400,000	210
Belgium . . .	1887	8,257	10,800	808,000	1,100,000	135
Holland . . .	1888	5,448	19,870	758,000	1,300,000	145
Scandinavia . . .	1886	19,936	...	1,263,000	1,200,000	140
Roumania . . .	1883	2,807	...	134,000	...	27
Servia . . .	1888	702	1,650	60,000	200,000	30
Greece	1884	2,700	3,374	143,000	240,000	72
Europe . . .		406,579	...	34,393,000	34,830,000	105
United States . .	1888	171,200	272,700	7,850,000	25,500,000	130
Canada . . .	1887	15,607	18,942	487,000	1,100,000	100
Australia . . .	1888	9,104	13,200	510,000	1,900,000	140
India	1888	133,352	...	3,474,000	2,100,000	17
South Africa . .	1888	1,530	...	56,000	250,000	40
Ceylon . . .	1888	3,650	...	131,000	...	50
Algeria . . .	1888	1,214	...	110,000	...	30
Argentina . .	1888	3,227	7,300	255,000	500,000	70
Chile . . .	1888	1,450	...	86,000	...	34
Uruguay . . .	1888	780	1,530	54,000	120,000	90
Venezuela . . .	1888	2,042	...	105,000	30,000	45
Brazil	1889	7,500	...	300,000	...	30
Egypt	1887	6,640	7,240	170,000	...	25
Japan	1888	27,550	62,520	2,835,000	...	70
Total . . .	...	791,425	...	50,816,000	...	...

The following table shows approximately the spread of education in the last fifty years :—

	Average Attendance at School			Percentage of Adults able to Write	
	1840	1888	Increase per Cent.	1840	1889
U. Kingdom	2,100,000	4,600,000	118	59	90
France . .	2,900,000	6,300,000	117	47	85
Germany .	3,700,000	7,100,000	92	82	96
Russia . .	460,000	2,510,000	444	2	15
Austria . .	2,310,000	4,900,000	113	21	55
Italy . . .	550,000	3,070,000	458	16	47
Spain . . .	450,000	1,840,000	309	14	28
Portugal. .	50,000	260,000	420	...	...
Holland . .	300,000	760,000	153	70	86
Belgium . .	320,000	810,000	153	45	80
Scandinavia	550,000	1,260,000	130	80	97
Switzerland .	400,000	630,000	60	80	95
Greece, &c..	90,000	350,000	290	...	...
Europe . .	14,180,000	34,390,000	145	...	...
U. States .	1,260,000	7,850,000	520	80	92
India . . .	150,000	3,470,000	2,210	...	...
Colonies, &c.	650,000	5,100,000	680	...	...
Total .	16,240,000	50,810,000	217	...	...

The march of education in Europe has been remarkable, for whereas population has only increased 33 per cent. since 1840, the average number of children attending school has risen 145 per cent.

The percentage of conscripts who could read was as follows :—

	1868	1880	1884
Germany . . .	96	98	99
Holland . . .	82	88	90
France . . .	76	86	88
Belgium . . .	74	81	85
Austria . . .	34	61	69
Italy	32	52	53
Hungary . . .	22	49	55
Sweden . . .	...	...	100
Denmark . . .	...	...	100
Switzerland . .	...	...	98
Russia . . .	...	...	21
Servia . . .	...	...	21

The following table shows the proportions of men and women able to sign the marriage register, also of conscripts able to read, at various dates :—

Year	Able to Sign Register						Able to Read in 100 Conscripts	
	In 100 Men			In 100 Women				
	England	France	Italy	England	France	Italy	France	Italy
1841	67	...	...	51	...	...	...	...
1851	69	...	...	55	...	...	...	...
1861	75	71	...	65	55	...	70	...
1871	81	75	43	73	63	23	80	43
1883	88	86	55	84	78	33	87	52

As respects superior education, the universities of the world stand thus :—

	Universities	Professors	Students
United Kingdom . .	11	344	13,400
France	1	180	10,300
Germany	21	1,920	26,680
Russia	8	701	10,400
Austria	10	1,430	18,600
Italy	21	600	9,000
Spain.	10	380	16,200
Portugal	1	40	1,300
Belgium	4	120	5,900
Holland	4	150	2,300
Denmark	1	60	1,400
Sweden	2	173	2,710
Norway	1	46	1,700
Switzerland. . . .	4	90	2,000
Greece	2	40	1,800
Europe	101	6,274	123,690
United States . . .	360	4,240	60,100
Morocco.	1	40	700
Total . . .	462	10,554	184,490

There are also universities in Canada, Australia, and India, of which statistics are wanting.

The number of university students compared with population is much greater in Spain and Belgium than in other European countries.

Intermediate education embraces a great number of colleges, academies, lyceums, &c., of which details will be found in the various countries.

UNITED KINGDOM

In 1830 the Board of Education was established, with power to spend £30,000 on schools. The returns for Great Britain (excluding Ireland) have been as follows :—

Year	Sum Voted, £	Number of Schools Inspected	Accommodation for Pupils	Average Attendance
1850 . . .	180,000	2,613	...	225,400
1860 . . .	724,000	7,272	1,400,000	884,000
1870 . . .	912,000	10,949	2,215,000	1,454,000
1880 . . .	2,854,000	20,670	4,843,000	3,155,000
1888 . . .	4,168,000	22,326	6,043,000	4,111,000

The number of schools of all kinds, and the average attendance of school-children in the three kingdoms, showed thus :—

	Schools		Scholars	
	1846	1888	1846	1888
England . . .	22,200	19,221	1,500,000	3,615,000
Scotland . . .	5,042	3,105	220,000	496,000
Ireland. . . .	9,657	8,196	330,000	494,000
Total . .	36,899	30,522	2,050,000	4,605,000

The proportion of adults able to write is shown by those signing the marriage register, viz. :—

	Per Cent.		
	Men	Women	General
England . . .	92	90	91
Scotland . . .	96	92	94
Ireland. . .	78	76	77
United Kingdom .	91	89	90

If we compare the returns of the whole United Kingdom for 1888 with those of 1878 we find as follows :—

	1878	1888	Ratio of Increase
			Per Cent.
Number of schools	26,734	30,522	14
Accommodation .	5,543,000	7,105,000	29
Average attendance . . . }	3,219,000	4,605,000	44

The returns for the three kingdoms in 1888 were as follows :—

	Expenditure, £	Number of Schools	Accommodation	Average Attendance
England .	7,440,000	19,221	5,356,000	3,615,000
Scotland .	1,160,000	3,105	687,000	496,000
Ireland . .	1,090,000	8,196	1,062,000	494,000
U. Kingdom	9,690,000	30,522	7,105,000	4,605,000

The income of the schools in 1888 was made up thus :—

	England	Scotland	Ireland	United Kingdom
	£	£	£	£
State subsidy	3,600,000	570,000	900,000	5,070,000
Rates, &c. .	3,840,000	590,000	190,000	4,620,000
Total	7,440,000	1,160,000	1,090,000	9,690,000

From 1870 to 1888 the new schools built in England and Wales were :—

Schools	Number	Accommodation for Pupils
Board	4,562	1,809,000
Voluntary . . .	6,738	1,668,000
Total . .	11,300	3,477,000

In 1888 the schools of England and Wales had 68,683 certified teachers and 29,901 pupil teachers ; the average expenditure yearly was :—

	£	s.	d.	
Board schools . . .	2	4	8	per child
Voluntary schools . .	1	16	4	,, ,,

Local taxation supplied 18s. per child, fees 10s., and the subsidy from the State the rest. In London the expenditure was much higher, namely, 61s. in Board Schools, and 44s. in voluntary per child in average attendance. The working of both kinds of schools in England and Wales in 1881 is shown thus :—

	Schools		Average Attendance	
	1881	1888	1881	1888
Voluntary .	14,370	14,659	2,008,000	...
Board . .	3,692	4,562	856,000	...
Total .	18,062	19,221	2,864,000	3,615,000

In 1880 the religion of the school-children of the United Kingdom was as follows :—

	School Children	Percentage
Church of England . .	1,539,700	42.8
Presbyterian . . .	527,400	14.6
Roman Catholic . .	526,600	14.6
Various	1,030,300	28.0
Total .	3,624,000	100.0

The average attendance of children compared with population thus :—

	Numbers		Per 1000 Inhabitants	
	1881	1888	1881	1888
England . . .	2,864,000	3,615,000	110	127
Scotland . . .	410,000	496,000	108	123
Ireland . . .	454,000	494,000	88	104
United Kingdom .	3,728,000	4,605,000	106	123

The increase of schools has been accompanied by a decrease of crime. The returns for England, Wales, and Scotland show :—

Period	Children Attending School	Annual Convictions	School-Children per 1000 Population	Criminals per 100,000 Population
1841–50	220,000	24,300	11	122
1851–60	560,000	21,200	26	96
1861–70	1,170,000	17,010	47	68
1871–80	2,300,000	13,900	82	50
1887	4,019,000	12,150	125	38

In 1838 Judge Coleridge pointed attention in this direction, and soon afterwards the Committee Report of the House of Commons contained the following testimony :—"We find that the neglect of education causes much crime that might be avoided."

The growth of crime has been materially checked in late years by industrial schools and reformatories, which were begun in 1857, the first for vagrant or destitute children, the second for youthful criminals, the Police Report showing that in 1856 there were 100,000 children and youths under 17 living as vagabonds or thieves in England only. The returns published in 1888 for these institutions show :—

	Reformatories	Industrial Schools	Total
England . . .	4,225	14,585	18,810
Ireland . . .	923	7,991	8,914
Total . .	5,148	22,576	27,724
Expenditure, £ . .	96,000	433,000	529,000

The average expenditure is £19 per head in the above institutions. The entries in England in 1887 were as follows :—

	Reformatories	Industrial Schools	Total
Boys	1,048	4,952	6,000
Girls	184	1,113	1,297
Total . .	1,232	6,065	7,297

The summary of eleven years' working of reformatories, down to 1880, showed as follows :—

Admitted	36,232
Put to trades	23,550
Died or removed	5,547
Remaining under instruction . .	7,135

The good effect of reformatories, since their introduction in 1869, is shown thus :—

	1869	1881
Juvenile offenders . . .	10,314	5,579
Per million inhabitants . .	458	215

This gives a decline of 53 per cent. in juvenile crime.

The Universities of the United Kingdom in 1876 showed as follows :—

	Students	Annual Expenditure	Per Student
		£	£
Oxford . .	1,860	414,000	220
Cambridge . .	1,920	340,000	177
Dublin . .	810	62,000	78
Edinburgh . .	2,320	200,000	87
Glasgow . .	1,340	90,000	68
Aberdeen . .	650	30,000	45
St. Andrew's .	300	17,000	56

Besides the above, there are the Universities of London, Durham, Manchester, and the new Royal University of Ireland.

The salaries of the first three are as follows :—

	Fellows and Professors	Salaries, £	Average, £
Oxford . . .	424	159,000	373
Cambridge . .	483	132,000	274
Trinity, Dublin .	59	31,000	530

The incomes were derived thus :—

	Endowments, £	Fees, &c., £	Total, £
Oxford	280,000	134,000	414,000
Cambridge . .	235,000	115,000	340,000
Dublin	49,000	13,000	62,000

The register of Cambridge shows that the number of B.A. graduates admitted yearly averaged thus :—

16th century	70
17th ,, ...	235
19th ,, ...	326

The ratios of winners at Indian competition examinations in 1880 were :—

	Per Cent.
Oxford students . . .	28
Cambridge students . .	24
Dublin students . . .	17
Scotch Universities . . .	14
London, Cork, &c. . . .	17
	100

IRELAND

In his *Progress of the Nation* (1843) Mr. Porter says :—"The Commissioners for National Education in Ireland have met with a most determined hostility on the part of the Protestant clergy." In order to prevent Catholics from receiving instruction, it was felony for a Catholic (in the last century) to keep a school; and so late as 1801 the Protestant Bishop of Cork prosecuted a man for this offence, but the Lord Chancellor quashed the suit as contrary to the spirit of the age.

The first system of public schools was started in 1817 by the Kildare Street Society, but one of the statutes was to read a chapter daily from King James's version of the Bible. The National Schools were begun by Parliament in 1830. The register shows the children on the rolls; and, as the average attendance in Ireland has always been under 46 per cent. of the number on the rolls, we can estimate the latter for those early years :—

Year	Schools	Scholars Enrolled	Average Attendance	Average Attendance per 1000 Inhabitants
1820	241	16,800	7,600	1
1825	1,395	102,400	46,000	6
1835	1,106	145,500	65,000	8
1840	1,978	232,600	104,000	13
1861	...	803,400	262,800	45
1871	...	1,021,700	363,800	67
1881	7,590	1,066,000	453,600	88
1888	8,196	1,060,900	493,900	104

The annual expenditure is £1,090,000, of which £900,000 is a State subsidy, the rest made up of rates, fees, &c.

As in England, the increase of schools in Ireland has brought a decrease of crime, viz. :—

	Children Attending School	Annual Convictions	School Children per 1000 Pop.	Criminals per 100,000 Pop.
1851-60	220,000	7,705	35	124
1861-70	310,000	2,918	56	53
1871-80	405,000	2,492	77	47
1887	513,000	1,412	106	29

FRANCE

The best measure of educational progress is the ratio of male and female adults able to sign the marriage register, and of conscripts able to write when enrolled for service, viz. :—

Year	Conscripts Able to Write	Adults of Both Sexes
1830	45 per cent. ...	42
1855	66 ,, ...	60
1865	76 ,, ...	66
1876	84 ,, ...	75
1881	86 ., ...	82

In December 1887 the primary and secondary schools stood thus :—

	Number	Pupils
Primary	85,087	6,208,000
Lycées, &c.	346	89,400
Girls' colleges	112	10,400
Total	85,545	6,307,800

The above is exclusive of schools for adults, which were attended by 156,000 men and 28,000 women.

Although France has but one University, that of Paris, it has 16 University Colleges. The numbers who graduated in 1885 were :—

	Examined	Graduated		Examined	Graduated
Paris	3,540	1,500	Montpellier	644	266
Toulouse	1,218	443	Aix	519	207
Rennes	1,116	571	Clermont	540	173
Lyons	983	423	Dijon	430	155
Douai	848	305	Nancy	343	150
Poitiers	823	314	Grenoble	341	121
Bordeaux	782	278	Besançon	192	93
Caen	675	293	Algiers	118	48

Official returns of the Educational Department show as follows :—

Year	Schools	Average Attendance	Average Attendance per 1000 Inhabitants
1840	55,930	2,882,000	85
1864	64,978	3,414,000	90
1887	85,545	6,308,000	170

Public expenditure on education of all kinds and that on primary schools only are shown as follows :—

Education		Primary Schools	
Year	Amount, £	Year	Amount, £
1840	400,000	1830	12,000
1863	1,300,000	1855	240,000
1872	2,250,000	1870	350,000
1881	3,600,000	1888	5,800,000

In 1886 the primary schools showed as follows :—

	Lay	Clerical	Total
Schools	60,865	18,890	79,955
Teachers	88,668	46,548	135,216
Pupils	3,780,000	1,737,000	5,517,000

	Male	Female	Total
Teachers	62,796	72,420	135,216
Pupils	2,786,000	2,731,000	5,517,000

Of the total number of pupils, 58 per cent. were free, and 42 per cent. paid for their education.

In the boys' schools there is one teacher for 45 children ; in the girls' schools one for 38. Clerical schools average 93 pupils, lay 63.

	Primary Schools	
	Number	Teachers
Lay	67,133	90,300
Clerical	17,954	46,500
Total	85,087	136,800

Making a total of 13,112 candidates, of whom 5330 graduated. There are altogether 10,300 students, who are thus distributed :—

Law . . . 2,500 | Literature . . 3,500
Medicine . . . 2,800 | Science . . . 1,500

In the rank and file of the French army 15 per 1000 are university graduates.

ALGERIA

The system of education in 1888 was as follows :—

	No.	Pupils
Colleges	9	3,100
Primary schools	921	70,500
Arab schools	76	9,000
Infant schools	208	27,000
Total	1,214	109,600

Only 14 per cent. of children of school-age attend school; there are 535,000 Moslem children not at school.

GERMANY

In 1876 it was officially stated that the Empire counted 60,000 primary schools, the annual outlay by the State in maintaining them amounting to £3,400,000 sterling. In 1871 the report showed as follows:—

	Schools	Teachers	Pupils	Pupils to Population, per Cent.
Prussia . . .	34,988	57,936	4,008,000	16
Bavaria . . .	7,184	11,921	841,000	17
Saxony . . .	2,134	7,219	451,000	16
Baden . . .	1,957	3,603	245,000	16
Other States .	6,540	11,320	784,000	$15\frac{1}{2}$
Total .	52,803	91,999	6,329,000	16

In 1881 there were 57,000 schools, with 120,000 teachers and 7,100,000 pupils.
Superior education shows the following statistics:—

	Gymnasia	Grammar-Schools	Total
Prussia . . .	231	223	454
Other States . .	105	172	277
Total .	336	395	731

The gymnasia are maintained at a cost of £220,000 a year, of which one-half is defrayed by municipal rates. They have 6670 teachers and are as follows:—

	Gymnasia	Pupils
Protestants	173	192,500
Catholics	53	35,500
Mixed	110	28,000
Total . .	336	256,000

Official statistics for Prussia in 1843 compare with those in 1871 as follows:—

	1843	1871	Ratio of Increase
Schools	23,100	34,988	52 per cent.
Teachers	27,600	57,936	110 ,,
Pupils	2,271,000	4,008,000	75 ,,

Germany has 21 Universities, with 1920 professors and 26,700 students. The following table shows the percentage of students according to religious belief, as compared with the percentage of population according to creed:—

	General Population	University Students
Protestants . . .	64	70
Roman Catholics . .	34	20
Jews	12	10
Total . .	100	100

The Universities stand in this order:—

	Students			Students
Berlin . . .	5,700	Bonn . . .		1,200
Leipzig . . .	3,100	Göttingen .		1,100
Munich . .	2,300	Wurzburg .		1,100
Breslau . .	1,600	Heidelberg .		1,020
Halle . .	1,600	Königsberg .		910
Tübingen .	1,400	Ten others .		7,100

Of the total number of students 89 per cent. are Germans and 11 per cent. of other nations, Americans being 1 per cent. The oldest University is that of Heidelberg, which dates from 1386.

RUSSIA

The *Rousski Kalendar* and other semi-official documents give the following statistics:—

Year	Schools	Pupils	Pupils per 1000 Population
1804	627	109,000	3
1824	2,118	263,000	6
1838	3,956	461,000	9
1875	32,100	1,213,000	15
1889	43,100	2,270,000	25

The returns for 1875 and 1888 compare as follows:—

	School-Children		Increase per Cent.
	1875	1888	
Boys	985,000	1,726,000	73
Girls	228,000	544,000	138
Total . .	1,213,000	2,270,000	89

The ratios of children at school were approximately:—

	1875			1888		
	Boys	Girls	Total	Boys	Girls	Total
At school . .	11.5	2.6	6.9	16.7	5.4	11.0
Not at school .	88.5	97.4	93.1	83.3	94.6	89.0
Total .	100.0	100.0	100.0	100.0	100.0	100.0

In 1802 the Czar Alexander I. founded the Universities of St. Petersburg and Moscow. It was not, however, until after the emancipation of the serfs, in 1861, that great efforts were made to educate the masses, 20,000 new schools being opened in the ensuing ten years. Besides the above primary schools there are gymnasia and middle-schools, as follows:—

	No.	Pupils
For boys . . .	622	168,000
For girls . . .	324	62,300
Total .	946	230,300

These schools had 7100 teachers, and half their cost is defrayed by the State. The Russian Government expended £3,800,000 on schools in 1889.
There were eight Universities in 1884, viz.:—

	Professors	Students	State Subsidy, £
Moscow . . .	103	2,430	53,000
St. Petersburg . .	99	2,050	43,000
Kiev	105	1,470	46,000
Dorpat . . .	65	1,430	26,000
Warsaw . . .	79	1,000	29,000
Kharkov . . .	89	820	37,000
Kazan . . .	109	780	38,000
Odessa . . .	52	380	25,000
Total . .	701	10,360	297,000

In 1888 the number of University students reached 12,900.
The annual subsidy for primary schools is £900,000, equal to 8s. per pupil.

AUSTRIA-HUNGARY

Official returns for the whole Empire were as follows :—

Year	Schools	School-Children	Per 1000 Population
1837 . . .	16,754	2,313,000	83
1870 . . .	31,100	3,189,000	90
1878 . . .	31,740	3,663,000	99
1889 . . .	35,720	4,903,000	130

The amount spent yearly by Government on the above primary schools is £1,500,000, equal to 8s. per pupil. The returns for 1878 were as follows :—

	Austria	Hungary	Total
Number of schools .	15,166	16,574	31,740
Teachers . . .	31,200	22,300	53,500
Pupils, boys . .	1,093,000	833,000	1,926,000
Pupils, girls . .	1,042,000	695,000	1,737,000
Total pupils . .	2,135,000	1,528,000	3,663,000

The whole educational system of Austria proper in 1889 is shown thus :—

	Number	Professors	Scholars
Universities . . .	7	1,092	13,680
High schools . .	61	691	4,720
Middle schools .	318	5,850	79,450
Technical schools .	1,570	7,890	111,200
Free schools .	16,945	57,236	2,748,300
Total . . .	18,902	72,759	2,957,350

The statistics of seven Austrian Universities show as follows :—

	Professors	Students Theology	Law	Medicine	Philosophy	Total	State Grant, £
Vienna . .	361	217	1,998	2,598	643	5,456	83,000
Grätz . .	139	102	549	490	167	1,308	23,000
Innspruck .	86	251	261	202	104	818	21,000
Prague .	285	269	1,580	1,404	421	3,674	63.000
Lemberg .	69	361	598	...	125	1,084	15,000
Cracow .	110	89	484	392	129	1,094	29,000
Czernowitz	42	59	138	...	52	249	8,000
Total .	1,092	1,348	5,608	5,086	1,641	13,683	242,000

The religion of the students showed these ratios :—

	Percentage of Religion of Students							
	Vienna	Grätz	Innspruck	Prague	Lemberg	Cracow	Czernowitz	Total
Catholic . .	54.9	86.5	99.1	86.2	87.0	83.8	29.3	72.7
Protestant .	7.0	5.4	0.5	1.9	0.3	4.3	4.4	4.8
Jew . . .	33.2	3.8	0.3	11.6	12.7	11.9	21.7	19.6
Greek . . .	3.9	4.3	0.1	0.3	...	...	44.6	2.9
	100.0	100.0	100.0	100.0	100.0	100.0	100.0	100.0

In 1886 the ratios of children of school-age at school * were :—

	Austria	Hungary
Attending school . .	85.0	80.4
Not at school . . .	15.0	19.6
Total . . .	100.0	100.0

Hungary has three Universities, viz. :—

	Professors	Students
Buda-Pesth . . .	211	3,660
Klausenburg . . .	81	525
Agram . . .	48	415
Total . . .	340	4,600

The whole system of education in Hungary in 1886 stood thus :—

	Number	Teachers	Pupils	Males	Females
Universities . .	3	340	4,600	4,600	...
Middle schools .	405	3,140	73,700	69,200	4,500
Primary . . .	16,410	23,980	1,868,000	993,000	875,000
Total . . .	16,818	27,460	1,946,300	1,066,800	879,500

The sum paid yearly in salaries to teachers of primary schools is £880,000 sterling, or £36 each.
The following table shows the advance of education in Hungary in eight years :—

Year	Primary Schools		All Schools	
	Teachers	Pupils	Teachers	Pupils
1880 . . .	21,700	1,620,000	24,900	1,670,000
1884 . . .	23,100	1,790,000	27,100	1,850,200
1888 . . .	24,400	1,950,000	28,900	2,015,000

The languages taught in the primary schools are :—

Austria	Schools	Hungary	Schools
German . .	7,001	Magyar . .	7,938
Czech . .	4,246	Various . .	8,472
Various . .	5,698		
Total .	16,945	Total .	16,410

The advance of public instruction among the masses between the years 1868 and 1880 is shown by the ratio of conscripts able to read, viz. :—

	1868	1880
Austrian	34 per cent.	61 per cent.
Hungarian	22 ,,	49 ,,

In 1874 the ratios of conscripts able to read and write were :—

	Per Cent.		Per Cent.
Galitzia . . .	15.5	Moravia . . .	71.4
Croatia . . .	42.3	Styria . . .	73.7
Tyrol . . .	53.4	Bohemia . . .	84.7
Hungary . . .	60.0	Austria . . .	90.0

In 1880 the ratio of adults able to sign the marriage register were as follows :—

	Per Cent.		
	Males	Females	Both Sexes
Austria	61	53	57
Hungary . . .	49	30	39

* This shows the ratio of children on the school-rolls ; the average attendance was only 65 per cent. of children of school-age.

The ratios of children of school-age attending school were :—

	Per Cent.			Per Cent.
Galitzia . . .	27	Styria . . .		80
Illyria . . .	47	Moravia . . .		90
Hungary . . .	76	Austria . . .		90

The general average for the whole Empire was 70 per cent.

ITALY

Official returns show that the number of children at primary schools has doubled since 1862, viz. :—

Year	Boys	Girls	Total	Per 1000 Population
1862	627,000	483,000	1,110,000	50
1870	890,000	683,000	1,573,000	61
1877	...	...	2,082,000	75
1887	1,194,000	1,059,000	2,253,000	75

The returns for 1887 compare with 1877 thus :—

	1877		1887	
	Schools	Pupils	Schools	Pupils
Primary . .	44,050	2,082,000	53,630	2,253,000
Superior . .	13,910	555,000	16,877	818,000
Total	57,960	2,637,000	70,507	3,071,000

The returns for 1887 showed as follows :—

Primary Schools		All Schools, Teachers	
Boys . . .	1,194,000	Primary . . .	55,300
Girls . . .	1,059,000	Superior . . .	31,100
Total .	2,253,000	Total . .	86,400

The progress of instruction is shown in the following table :—

Year	Conscripts Able to Read	Percentage Signing Marriage Register	
	Per Cent.	Men	Women
1866	36.0	40.0	21.0
1871	43.3	42.3	23.3
1881	52.3	51.8	30.1
1887	55.0	57.2	37.2

The percentage of persons in Italy, at various ages, who could read was as follows :—

Age, Years	Towns Only.				All Italy			
	Males		Females		Males		Females	
	1871	1881	1871	1881	1871	1881	1871	1881
6–18	52	59	45	56	34	43	27	38
18–25	60	68	51	59	43	53	30	37
25–40	59	66	48	53	40	46	23	27
40–60	55	58	43	43	37	40	17	19

In 1871 the percentage of persons over seven years who could read, in the various provinces, stood thus :—

	Males	Females	Total Population
Sicily . . .	35	24	30
Naples . . .	34	22	28
Tuscany . . .	49	38	44
Romagna . . .	49	39	44
Venetia . . .	55	37	46
Lombardy . .	67	59	63
Piedmont . . .	73	59	66

The ratio was 35 at Messina, 76 at Florence and Genoa, and 83 per cent. at Turin.

There are twenty-one Universities, with 600 professors and 9000 students ; the principal Universities are :—

	Students			Students
Naples . . .	1,450	Padua . . .		970
Turin . . .	1,230	Rome . . .		560

The annual Government expenditure for education is £3,100,000 sterling.

SPAIN

The number of schools and scholars was as follows :—

Year	Public	Private	Total	Pupils	Per 1000 Population
1850	13,334	4,100	17,434	664,000	51
1870	22,711	5,406	28,117	1,426,000	94
1885	24,529	7,350	31,879	1,843,000	106

The sexes of pupils are said to be sixty males to forty females.

The percentage of persons able to read and write was as follows :—

	1860			1877		
	Men	Women	Total	Men	Women	Total
Read and write . }	31	9	20	34	15	25
Read only .	4	5	5	3	4	3
Ignorant .	65	86	75	63	81	72
Total .	100	100	100	100	100	100

The progress made in middle-class or superior schools has been :—

Year	Pupils
1858	15,000
1868	25,300
1878	33,500

The total expenditure for schools in 1879 was one million sterling,* besides £100,000 for Universities. There are 10 universities, with 380 professors and 16,200 students ; the number in 1865 was only 9700. The oldest University is Salamanca, founded in 1240 ; it has 40 professors and 1300 students. In Spain 35 per cent. of adults can sign the marriage register, against 18 per cent. in 1848. The Census of 1860 showed as follows :—

	Able to Read	Ratio to Population over 7 Years Old
Males	2,731,000	40 per cent.
Females	1,105,000	16 ,,
Total . .	3,836,000	28 ,,

PORTUGAL

The educational system is as follows :—

	Number	Pupils
University	1	1,300
Colleges . : . .	70	14,200
Private schools . : . .	1,935	65,100
Public schools . : . .	3,657	176,000
Total . .	5,663	256,600

* Of this sum the Government provides only £80,000, the rest being supplied by municipal rates. Teachers earn about £20 a year.

The increase of primary instruction is remarkable :—

Year	Schools	Scholars	Per 1000 Population
1854.	1,350	55,000	14
1870.	3,000	130,000	32
1878.	4,520	198,000	46
1886.	5,384	237,000	54

The annual outlay for education is £220,000 sterling.

HOLLAND

The scheme of instruction in 1888 was :—

	Number	Teachers	Pupils
Universities	4	180	2,600
Colleges	212	2,120	18,700
Private schools . . .	1,204	4,767	177,100
Public schools . . .	2,940	12,823	449,400
Infant schools . . .	1,088	...	110,000
Total . .	5,448	19,890	757,800

The returns of primary schools showed thus :—

Year	Schools	Scholars	Per 1000 Population
1835.	2,830	304,000	102
1870.	3,614	456,000	120
1877.	3,821	523,000	132
1888.	4,144	627,000	145

In 1887 the expenditure was :—

	£		£
Primary schools .	1,060,000	State grant . . .	580,000
Colleges . . .	240,000	Communal grant .	720,000
Total . .	1,300,000	Total . .	1,300,000

The ratio of conscripts able to read and write was as follows :—

Year	Able to Read	To Read and Write
1850	77.2	74.9
1860	80.2	78.0
1876	88.0	87.0

The sexes of children attending school were boys 54, girls 46.

BELGIUM

The whole educational system may be summed up as follows :—

	Number	Pupils
Universities	4	5,900
Colleges	171	33,100
Adult schools . . .	1,644	65,300
Primary schools . .	5,491	604,100
Infant schools . . .	947	99,300
Total . . .	8,257	807,700

The public primary schools of Belgium were as follows :—

Year	Number of Schools	Pupils			Free	Paying
		Male	Female	Total		
1845	3,431	182,900	143,700	326,600	174,400	152,200
1857	3,787	219,100	180,500	399,600	250,200	149,400
1869	4,260	267,400	226,000	493,400	339,200	154,200
1878	4,839	318,500	279,700	598,200	452,300	145,900
1887	5,491	331,400	272,600	604,000	516,700	87,400

The income and expenditure of the above schools were as follows :—

	1843	1860	1870	1880	1886
	£	£	£	£	£
Fees	28,000	34,000	46,000	44,000	72,000
Local grants	34,000	74,000	132,000	266,000	375,000
State grants	8,000	54,000	140,000	376,000	290,000
Sundries	34,000	108,000	289,000	714,000	343,000
Expenditure	104,000	270,000	607,000	1,400,000	1,080,000

There are four Universities, the returns of which show the number of students thus :—

	1840	1870	1888		1840	1870	1888
Ghent	396	459	838	Philosophy . . .	344	257	657
Liege	331	653	1,470	Science	293	350	1,351
Brussels	279	496	1,795	Law	359	605	1,392
Louvain	490	907	1,757	Medicine . . .	272	562	1,484
				Engineering, &c. . .	228	741	976
Total . .	1,496	2,515	5,860	Total . .	1,496	2,515	5,860

The number of persons able to read and write was as follows :—

	1866	1888
Males . . .	1,209,000	1,661,000
Females . . .	1,070,000	1,527,000
Total . .	2,279,000	3,188,000

The ratio of conscripts able to read and write was as follows :—

	1843	1860	1870	1889
Illiterate . . .	43.6	31.8	24.0	13.1
Read only . .	7.2	7.6	5.2	2.9
Read and write . .	49.2	60.6	70.8	84.0
	100.0	100.0	100.0	100.0

SWEDEN

Latest returns are to this effect :—

	Number	Pupils
Universities . . .	2	2,700
Colleges	146	16,700
Primary schools . .	10,338	708,000
Total . .	10,486	727,400

In 1859 the primary schools had 2950 teachers, and the ratio of children of school-age attending school was 71 per cent. In 1888 there were 12,880 teachers, and the ratio of children at school was 98 per cent. Only three recruits in 1000 cannot read and write. The outlay for schools is £600,000 a year, one-fourth from the Treasury, the rest municipal. The University of Upsal has 1800 students, that of Lund 900.

NORWAY

The scheme of instruction in 1886 was as follows :—

	Number	Pupils
University. . . .	1	1,700
Academies . . .	128	12,500
Primary schools . .	6,340	288,700
Total . .	6,469	302,900

The annual outlay is £260,000, mostly raised by municipal rates. The State gives £25,000 a year to the University of Christiania.

DENMARK

The returns for 1888 show as follows :—

	Number	Pupils
University. . . .	1	1,300
Colleges . . .	40	...
Primary schools . .	2,940	232,000
Total . .	2,981	233,300

The University of Copenhagen, founded in 1479, has sixty professors.

SWITZERLAND

The number of Swiss students (exclusive of 630 foreigners) was as follows at the four Universities :—

Geneva . . .	217	Medicine . . .	558
Berne	430	Law . . .	219
Zurich. . . .	335	Divinity . . .	200
Basel	293	Science . . .	298
Total .	1,275	Total . .	1,275

In 1886 the returns showed as follows :—

	Number	Teachers	Pupils
Universities . . .	4	351	1,900
Academies . . .	882	...	41,000
Girls' academies . .	1,600	3,543	136,500
Primary schools . .	4,308	8,826	461,600
Other schools . .	...	...	260,500
Total . .	...	...	901,500

In 1830 only 78 per cent. were able to sign the marriage register ; in 1871 the ratio was 88 per cent. The above school total includes 245,000 adults attending night-schools.

ROUMANIA

In 1883 the official returns were :—

	Number	Pupils
Universities . .	2	700
Academies. . .	62	8,800
Primary schools. .	2,743	124,100
Total . .	2,807	133,600

The Universities of Bucharest and Jassy had ninety-seven professors.

SERVIA

The educational system in 1888 was as follows :—

	Number	Teachers	Pupils
University . . .	1	31	300
Academies . . .	33	423	7,200
Primary schools . .	668	1,194	52,400
Total . .	702	1,648	59,900

The annual expenditure by the State is £100,000, besides municipal subsidies. In 1884 only 10 per cent. of the population could read and write, that is, about 15 per cent., excluding infants.

GREECE

The educational system in 1884 showed thus :—

	Number	Teachers	Pupils
University . . .	1	98	2,400
Academies . . .	418	776	22,300
Primary schools . .	2,281	2,500	118,000
Total . .	2,700	3,374	142,700

The annual expenditure is £240,000 sterling.

UNITED STATES

The first educational census was taken in 1840, and the official returns since then show thus :—

Year	Schools	Revenue, £ Sterling	Teachers	Scholars	Scholars per 1000 Pop.
1840	50,700	...	...	2,025,000	119
1850	87,300	3,400,000	...	3,642,000	160
1860	113,000	7,100,006	148,700	5,693,000	180
1870	141,600	19,400,000	221,040	6,596,000	171
1880	171,200	29,100,000	272,700	9,705,000	194
1888	...	...	347,300	11,950,000	196

The number of scholars is that on the rolls, but the average attendance is about 63 per cent. of same.

Year	On the Rolls	Average Attendance	Ratio
1880 . . .	9,705,000	6,049,000	62 per cent.
1885 . . .	11,170,000	7,020,000	63 ,,
1888 . . .	11,950,000	7,852,000	65 ,,

As the population in 1888 was 60 millions, the average attendance was equal to 131 per thousand of population, against 123 in the United Kingdom. Considering the vast extent and scattered population of the United States, this result is admirable.

School revenue seems largely to exceed expenditure, the latter in 1888 being stated at £25,510,000, whereas the school revenue of 1880 was said to reach £29,100,000 sterling.

The school-children in the various States were as follows :—

	1840	1860	1885	Average Attendance, 1885	Average Attendance per 1000 Population, 1880
Alabama	21,000	98,000	234,000	145,000	116
Arkansas	3,000	43,000	153,000	93,000 *	116
California	...	26,000	184,000	116,000	136
Colorado	...	...	34,000	25,000	130
Connecticut . . .	72,000	90,000	126,000	83,000	133
Delaware	8,000	19,000	31,000	21,000	140
Florida	2,000	9,000	62,000	46,000	170
Georgia	24,000	95,000	292,000	195,000	130
Illinois	37,000	338,000	739,000	491,000	160
Indiana	51,000	336,000	501,000	325,000	162
Iowa	2,000	185,000	473,000	284,000	175
Kansas	...	...	336,000	194,000	194
Kentucky	31,000	183,000	283,000	179,000	109
Louisiana	7,000	48,000	100,000	70,000	74
Maine	173,000	189,000	145,000	99,000	151
Maryland	22,000	80,000	176,000	93,000	100
Massachusetts . . .	178,000	249,000	340,000	254,000	140
Michigan	31,000	205,000	412,000	253,000	152
Minnesota	...	...	233,000	119,000	151
Mississippi . . .	11,000	67,000	279,000	184,000	162
Missouri	19,000	203,000	544,000	372,000	170
Nebraska	...	...	162,000	81,000	178
Nevada	...	...	8,000	5,000	166
New Hampshire . . .	90,000	83,000	64,000	45,000	133
New Jersey	59,000	119,000	217,000	123,000	110
New York	537,000	806,000	1,025,000	611,000	120
North Carolina . . .	19,000	117,000	298,000	186,000	133
Ohio	225,000	606,000	775,000	518,000	160
Oregon	...	...	46,000	31,000	170
Pennsylvania . . .	198,000	670,000	982,000	657,000	153
Rhode Island . . .	21,000	31,000	53,000	34,000	122
South Carolina . . .	17,000	47,000	178,000	122,000	122
Tennessee	31,000	163,000	374,000	192,000	128
Texas	...	63,000	245,000	154,000	97
Vermont	87,000	80,000	72,000	49,000	150
Virginia	47,000	155,000	475,000	286,000	134
Wisconsin	2,000	189,000	322,000	175,000	134
Territories	...	101,000	195,000	110,000	140
Total . .	2,025,000	5,693,000	11,170,000	7,020,000	140

In the preceding table the ratio of school children to population in 1885 is not correct, as the only basis for comparison is the Census of 1880, which figures are on an average 15 per cent. too low.

The two Virginias, be it noted, are put together as one State.

Taking the four great divisions of the Union, we find :—

States	Average Attendance		Ratio of Increase	Per 1000 Population in 1885
	1880	1885		
New England	541,000	564,000	4 per cent.	140
Middle . .	1,417,000	1,505,000	6 ,,	120
South . . .	1,509,000	1,852,000	22 ,,	120
West . . .	2,582,000	3,099,000	19 ,,	164
Total .	6,049,000	7,020,000	17 per cent.	140

The expenditure on primary schools in 1880 was :—

States	Amount	Ratio per Inhabitant	Per Pupil, Average Attending
	£	£ s. d.	£ s. d.
New England .	1,908,000	0 9 6	3 12 0
Middle	4,563,000	0 6 9	3 5 6
South	1,479,000	0 2 0	0 19 6
West	7,952,000	0 9 6	3 5 8
Pacific	683,000	0 10 9	5 3 0
The Union .	16,585,000	0 6 6	2 15 0

* Arkansas, Michigan, and Texas give no returns of "average attendance." For the sake of comparison, I assume the general ratio of the Union, that is, 63 per cent. of the children on the rolls.

The number of white population over twenty years of age who could not read was as follows :—

Year	Number	Percentage of Population
1840	550,000	7.8
1850	1,053,000	11.2
1860	1,218,000	9.2

The Census subsequently extended the inquiry to all persons, white or coloured, over ten years of age, with the result :—

Year	Unable to Read over Ten Years	Percentage of Population
1870	4,528,000	16.0
1880	3,019,000	8.1

This shows what progress education has made since 1870, the proportion of illiterate persons over ten years old having been reduced by one-half in a single decade. The greatest relative advancement is in the South, where (as shown above) the average attendance of school children rose 22 per cent. between 1880 and 1885. The number of children on the school rolls in 1860 and 1885 compared thus :—

States	Children on Rolls		Increase
	1860	1885	
New England .	722,000	801,000	11 per cent.
Middle . . .	1,694,000	2,431,000	44 ,,
South . . .	1,088,000	2,973,000	173 ,,
West	2,189,000	4,965,000	127 ,,
Total . .	5,693,000	11,170,000	96 per cent.

The intermediate and superior instruction in 1880 showed thus :—

	Number	Teachers	Students
University colleges .	364	4,240	60,000
Academies . . .	1,860	5,960	183,000
Total . .	2,224	10,200	243,000

The most celebrated University is Harvard, near Boston, founded in 1638. The number of universities and colleges in 1775 was ten, rising to 21 in 1791. The University students in 1880 were :—

Law	3,100	Medicine . .	12,000
Theology . . .	5,800	Arts . . .	30,200
Science . . .	8,900		
		Total .	60,000

In the preceding tables no account is taken of orphanages, &c., which in 1880 instructed 774,000 children, viz. :—

	Number	Children
Orphanages	411	751,000
Blind, &c.	83	8,600
Reformatories	67	14,200
Total . .	561	773,800

The grand total of 1888 therefore reaches 13,126,000 persons receiving instruction, or 22 per cent. of the population.

CANADA

In 1850 there were but 1700 schools, and in 1887 the number exceeded 15,600. The returns for 1887 compare with 1879 as follows :—

	1879		1887
Schools . . .	12,786	...	15,607
Teachers . . .	16,297	...	18,942
Pupils . . .	866,000	...	984,000

The returns for 1887 were as follows :—

Province	Teachers	Pupils on Roll	Average Attendance	Expenditure, £
Ontario	7,775	504,000	248,000	700,000
Quebec	6,121	253,000	130,000	70,000
Nova Scotia . .	2,119	105,000	51,000	130,000
New Brunswick .	1,644	69,000	34,000	80,000
P. Edward I. . .	518	22,000	12,000	30,000
Manitoba, &c. .	765	26,000	12,000	90,000
Total .	18,942	979,000	487,000	1,100,000

The Universities of Quebec, Montreal, and Toronto are ably conducted and largely attended.

MOROCCO

There is a Mahometan university at Fez, attended by 700 students, but the studies are mostly limited to the Koran.

INDIA

Public instruction may be said to date from 1858, when the East India Company possessions were annexed to the British Crown. The records show as follows : —

Year	Schools	Scholars	Expenditure
1857 . . .	...	200,000	200,000
1874 . . .	43,188	977,000	760,000
1878 . . .	82,561	2,196,000	1,660,000
1888 . . .	133,352	3,474,000	2,100,000

The records of Indian education for 1888 sum up thus :—

Schools	No.	Pupils	Schools	No.	Pupils	Schools	No.	Pupils
State	78,304	2,959,000	Males . . .	126,298	3,193,700	Primary . . .	89,400	2,557,000
Private . . .	55,048	515,000	Females . . .	7,054	280,300	Secondary . .	43,952	917,000
Total .	133,352	3,474,000	Total .	133,352	3,474,000	Total .	133,352	3,474,000

The above is the number of children on the rolls, the average attendance being 78 per cent., say 2,710,000 children.

The Government subsidy is £600,000, fees and local rates £1,500,000. The Universities of Calcutta, Madras. and Bombay have 6000 students.

AUSTRALIA

The returns for 1880 showed thus :—

	Schools	Teachers	Pupils		Expenditure, £
			En-rolled	Average Attendance	
N. S. Wales .	1,910	3,393	169,000	72,000	475,000
Victoria . .	2,430	4,950	269,000	120,000	553,000
New Zealand .	836	2,681	84,000	63,000	384,000
S. Australia .	370	837	36,000	20,000	87,000
Queensland .	338	924	43,000	24,000	124,000
Tasmania . .	171	323	12,000	8,000	24,000
W. Australia .	102	108	5,000	3,000	10,000
Total .	6,157	13,216	618,000	311,000	1,657,000

The progress of instruction in late years has been very rapid, as these figures show :—

Year	Schools	Pupils			Expenditure, £
		Boys	Girls	Total	
1861 . .	...	69,000	61,000	130,000	...
1871 . .	...	165,000	147,000	312,000	...
1881 . .	6,157	344,000	327,000	671,000	1,657,000
1888 . .	9,104	401,000	382,000	783,000	1,930,000

The returns for 1888 were as follows :—

	Pupils	Schools	Average
Public schools .	618,000	6,816	90
Private schools .	165,000	2,288	72
Total .	783,000	9,104	86

	Schools			Pupils on Roll	Average at Public Schools	Expenditure, £
	Public	Private	Total			
New South Wales	2,291	659	2,950	227,000	112,000	600,000
Victoria	1,930	752	2,682	280,000	129,000	620,000
New Zealand	1,208	300	1,508	130,000	96,000	380,000
South Australia	530	293	823	60,000	28,000	100,000
Queensland	544	134	678	59,000	39,000	180,000
Tasmania	220	150	370	22,000	9,000	40,000
Western Australia	93	...	93	5,000	4,000	10,000
Total . .	6,816	2,288	9,104	783,000	417,000	1,930,000

The number of persons who could read and write in the several colonies, according to Census returns, was as follows :—

	Census of 1861					
	Number			Percentage		
.	Read and Write	Read Only	Cannot Read	Read and Write	Read Only	Cannot Read
New South Wales	189,000	46,000	116,000	54	13	33
Victoria	328,000	57,000	156,000	60	11	29
Queensland	17,000	4,000	9,000	57	12	31
South Australia	72,000	19,000	36,000	57	14	29
New Zealand	68,000	9,000	22,000	68	9	23
Tasmania	48,000	13,000	29,000	53	15	32
Western Australia	8,000	2,000	6,000	56	10	34
Total . . .	730,000	150,000	374,000	58	12	30

	Census of 1881					
New South Wales	507,000	49,000	195,000	68	7	25
Victoria	652,000	50,000	161,000	76	6	18
Queensland	137,000	14,000	63,000	65	6	29
South Australia	200,000	15,000	65,000	72	5	23
New Zealand	346,000	27,000	116,000	71	6	23
Tasmania	75,000	10,000	31,000	65	8	27
Western Australia	20,000	2,000	8,000	67	7	26
Total . . .	1,937,000	167,000	639,000	70	7	23

From the preceding table it appears that in 1881 popular instruction was most general in Victoria, and that, on the other hand, Tasmania and Queensland stood lowest.

The percentage of persons able to sign the marriage register in Australasia was as follows :—

Year			Men	Women	Total
1861	.	.	81	69	75
1871	.	.	89	84	87
1881	.	.	96	93	95
1888	.	.	97	97	97

SOUTH AFRICA

The colonies of the Cape and Natal in 1888 showed :—

	Schools	Pupils	Average Attendance	Outlay, £
Cape . . .	1,407	88,000	47,000	220,000
Natal . . .	124	11,000	9,000	30,000
Total .	1,531	99,000	56,000	250,000

There is a University at Cape Town with 250 students.

CEYLON

The returns for 1872 and 1888 compare thus :—

	Schools		Pupils	
	1872	1888	1872	1888
Public . .	602	1,357	36,000	102,000
Private . .	365	2,292	9,000	29,000
Total .	967	3,649	45,000	131,000

The Government subsidy is £40,000 yearly. About 5 per cent. of the whole population attend school.

CYPRUS

In 1888 the returns were as follows :—

	Schools	Pupils
Christian	219	10,400
Mahometan . . .	86	3,100
Total . .	305	13,500

Annual expenditure, £9000, one-third being a State grant.

MINOR COLONIES

The latest returns show as follows :—

	Schools			Pupils		
	Public	Private	Total	Public	Private	Total
Hong-Kong	97	107	204	6,000	2,000	8,000
Singapore .	150	32	182	7,000	3,000	10,000
Mauritius .	144	...	144	16,000	...	16,000
Jamaica. .	771	...	771	72,000	...	72,000

There are many private schools at Jamaica, but no returns.

JAPAN

Education has lost ground of late years, viz. :—

	1882	1888
Schools	30,660	27,550
Teachers	89,600	62,600
Pupils	3,091,000	2,830,000

There are sixteen free libraries. The number of new works published was 9550 in the year 1888. There were 470 newspapers and magazines.

SOUTH AMERICA

The Argentine Republic has taken the foremost place in the South American continent. The official returns for 1876 and 1888 were :—

	1876	1888	Increase
Schools. . . .	1,946	3,227	65 per cent.
Teachers . . .	5,893	7,332	23 ,,
Pupils	116,200	254,600	119 ,,

The returns for 1888 show as follows :—

	Schools	Teachers	Scholars
State	2,263	4,744	175,200
Private	964	2,588	79,400
Total . .	3,227	7,332	254,600

The ratio of school-children was 70 per 1000 of the population. The above includes 2 universities and 34 colleges, with 13,000 students.

Brazil in 1880 had 4 universities, 26 colleges, and 5890 schools, the whole numbering 191,000 pupils, or 16 per 1000 of population.

Chile in 1880 had 1650 schools, attended by 98,000 children, equal to 50 per 1000 of population, and a university at Santiago.

ELECTORS

The numbers of electors and voters in various countries are :—

	Electors	Voters	Percentage who Vote	Per 1000 of Population		
				Electors	Voters	Year
United Kingdom	5,837,000	4,550,000	78	155	121	1889
United States	...	10,868,000	...	...	176	1888
France	9,948,000	8,012,000	81	266	220	1880
Germany	9,124,000	5,832,000	64	205	130	1880
Spain	942,000	610,000	63	57	36	1880
Austria	1,291,000	462,000	36	60	22	1880
Switzerland	639,000	256,000	40	230	92	1880
Portugal	217,000	145,000	67	54	36	...
Belgium	118,000	86,000	72	21	15	1880
Italy	627,000	370,000	59	21	13	1880
Sweden	43,000	17,000	40	10	4	1880

The returns for the United Kingdom show the electors for 1889, and the ratio of voters is assumed to be as at the election of 1885, that is, 78 per cent.

UNITED KINGDOM

	Percentage of Electors				Ratio to 100 Inhabitants			
	1835	1871	1881	1889	1835	1871	1881	1889
England	79.5	80.8	82.4	77.2	4.6	9.0	9.7	15.8
Ireland	11.7	9.0	7.5	13 0	1.2	4.2	4.4	16.0
Scotland . . .	8.8	10.2	10.1	9.8	3.0	7.6	8.4	14.2
United Kingdom . . .	100.0	100.0	100.0	100.0	3.3	8.1	8.9	15.5

Until 1885 Ireland had less than half her fair share of electors for population. The proportion of county and borough electors in the United Kingdom has been as follows :—

	Electors			Ratio		
	1846	1881	1885	1846	1881	1885
County	622,000	1,198,000	3,497,000	58.5	39.0	61.0
Borough	445,000	1,879,000	2,219,000	41.5	61.0	39.0
Total . .	1,067,000	3,077,000	5,716,000	100.0	100.0	100.0

The franchise has been extended at intervals, and now counts seven times as many electors as in 1835, viz. :—

Year	England	Scotland	Ireland	U. Kingdom
1835	668,000	73,000	98,000	839,000
1846	845,000	93,000	129,000	1,067,000
1871	2,066,000	260,000	227,000	2,553,000
1881	2,538,000	310,000	229,000	3,077,000
1889	4,502,000	572,000	763,000	5,837,000

The franchise of 1885 exactly reversed the ratios of 1881. The proportion of members of Parliament to electors in the three kingdoms is as follows :—

England . . . . . 1 to 9100
Scotland . . . . . 1 ,, 8000
Ireland . . . . . 1 ,, 7400
United Kingdom . . . . 1 ,, 8700

Of 100 electors, 80 vote in England, 79 in Scotland, 67 in Ireland, the ratio for the whole United Kingdom being 78—say 4,500,000 voters.

UNITED STATES

The presidential elections since 1824 have been as follows :—

Year	Electoral Votes			Popular Votes			Votes per 100 of Population
	Winner	Other Candidates	Total	Winner	Others	Total	
1824	99	162	261	156,000	196,000	352,000	3
1828	178	83	261	647,000	509,000	1,156,000	10
1832	219	67	286	688,000	562,000	1,250,000	10
1836	170	124	294	762,000	737,000	1,499,000	10
1840	234	60	294	1,275,000	1,136,000	2,411,000	14
1844	170	105	275	1,337,000	1,361,000	2,698,000	14
1848	163	127	290	1,360,000	1,511,000	2,871,000	13
1852	254	42	296	1,601,000	1,542,000	3,143,000	13
1856	174	122	296	1,838,000	2,217,000	4,055,000	15
1860	180	123	303	1,866,000	2,811,000	4,677,000	15
1864	212	102	314	2,216,000	1,809,000	4,025,000	12
1868	214	103	317	3,015,000	2,710,000	5,725,000	16
1872	286	80	366	3,597,000	2,870,000	6,467,000	16
1876	185	184	369	4,034,000	4,375,000	8,409,000	19
1880	214	155	369	4,449,000	4,761,000	9,210,000	18
1884	219	182	401	4,911,000	5,145,000	10,056,000	19
1888	...	...	...	5,186,000	5,682,000	10,868,000	18

FRANCE

The most important elections, known as plebiscites, were as follows :—

Year	For	Against	Total	Per 100 Inhabitants
1793	1,801,000	12,000	1,813,000	7
1803	3,568,000	9,000	3,577,000	12
1815	1,302,000	4,000	1,306,000	4
1852	7,828,000	253,000	8,081,000	23
1870	7,336,060	1,561,000	8,897,000	25

The general election of 1881 showed as follows :—

Class				Per Cent.
Republicans .	.	.	4,570,000	45.7
Orleanists .	.	.	1,103,000	11.1
Bonapartists .	.	.	538,000	5.4
Not voted .	.	.	3,740,000	37.8
Total	.	.	9,951,000	100.0

ITALY

The following elections resulted thus :—

Year	Electors on Roll	Voted	Voted, Per Cent.	Voters per 100 Inhabitants
1861	421,000	240,000	57	1.1
1865	504,000	272,000	54	1.1
1870	535,000	241,000	45	0.9
1876	607,000	358,000	59	1.3
1880	627,000	370,000	59	1.3

GERMANY

The members from the various States composing the Imperial Council are as follows :—

Prussia . . . 17 | Wurtemburg . 4 | Mecklenburg . 2
Bavaria . . . 6 | Baden . . . 3 | Brunswick . . 2
Saxony . . . 4 | Hesse . . . . 3 | Small States . 17

Making a total of 58 members of the Bundesrath.

The voters and electors of the Empire were as follows :—

Year	Electors	Voters	Percentage Voting	Electors per 1000 Inhab.
1874	8,523,000	5,292,000	62	200
1880	9,124,000	5,832,000	64	205

BELGIUM

The following table shows the registered electors and the numbers that voted :—

Year	Electors	Voted
1841	24,900	19,100
1859	61,900	45,100
1878	125,100	64,200
1884 . . .	195,700	146,800

ELECTRICITY

Lights.—The following are some of the largest lights in use :—

	Candle-Power		Candle-Power
Kensington Museum .	2,000	Marseilles, lighthouse	40,000
Crystal Palace . . .	3,000	Palais d'Industrie, ⎱	
British Museum . .	5,000	Paris . . . . ⎰	150,000
Liverpool Docks . .	6,000	Sydney, lighthouse .	180,000
San Josè, California	24,000		

The cost varies from 10d. an hour at Kensington, to 27d. at Marseilles, both Brush system.

The arc light at Liverpool costs 15d., the Siemens at the British Museum 24d. The San Josè electric moon stands on a tower 200 feet high, is worked by a 9-horse engine, and shows light for two miles around. The Sydney light is visible 50 miles, being the most powerful yet made. The Marseilles gives six times more light than the old system, at a saving of 9d. per hour. The Kensington Museum saves £235 a year by the change. The smallest lights are Swan and Edison's arc lights of 8 candle-power for domestic use. A contract with the Nottingham Municipality in May 1883 was for works and plant for supplying 60,000 Swan lamps of 20 candle-power. The cost of instalment was £220,000, and after allowing for all expenses and interest on capital, the electric light would cost 40 per cent. less than gas, and give 40 per cent. more light. In the United States, in 1890, there were 3,230,000 electric lights in use, 90 per cent. of the incandescent kind. Turin is lit with 73,000 candle-power (equal to 6000 gas lamps), at a cost of £5200 per annum. The gas only cost £3200.

In 1885 the *Journal of Arts* said :—" As regards the electric light, at the present time upwards of 600 dynamos and 20,000 lamps are in use, and the cost of their installation may be estimated at about one million sterling."

The Lane-Fox system may be described as follows :—

Horse-Power	Lights	Candle-Power	Aggregate Candle-Power
3	36	10	360
5	30	20	600
8	40	25	1,000
20	60	40	2,400

The Brush system, with an engine 40 horse-power, serves as follows :—

Number of Lights	Candle-Power	Aggregate Candle-Power
1	150,000	150,000
12	8,000	96,000
40	2,000	80,000
400	150	60,000

One engine of the above power feeds 400 lamps on a line of 30 miles, consuming 150 lbs. coal per hour, as compared with one ton per hour for gaslight over same length.

The Yablochkoff system is said to supply 100 candle-power at a cost of 1d. per hour, having reduced the cost from 6d. an hour in 1877.

The number of Edison lights, underground wires, in use in Europe on the 1st January 1889 was as follows :—

Berlin . .	73,400	Hamburg .	5,000	Schwerin .	3,000
Hanover .	20,000	Dresden .	4,000	Rotterdam .	2,500
Milan . .	20,000	Lübeck . .	3,000	Munich . .	2,500
London .	6,000	Turin . .	3,000	St. Etienne	4,000
Liverpool .	2,000	Elberfeld .	3,000	Strasbur .	2,500

besides Brunswick, Stuttgart, Halle, Crefeld, and Darmstadt, making a total of 170,000.

According to the *Magasin du Louvre* the relative cost of lighting is—gas 100, Edison 75, Yablochkoff 55 (in 1884).

MOTOR

1873. At the Vienna Exhibition a pump was worked at a distance of 1400 yards by means of an electric wire.

1879. At Sermaize, La Marne, a field of six acres was ploughed in six hours with a wire attached to a 12-horse engine a mile distant.

1881. At Oisiel a farmer named Meiner ploughed a large field by connecting an electric wire with a waterfall.

1882. Project to tap the force of Niagara by constructing turbines, the power of water being estimated at ten million cubic feet per second, or eight million horse-power, and to transmit this force through the United States. Estimated value, £300,000 a day, or 108 millions sterling per annum. A copper wire, half-inch diameter and 300 miles long, would suffice to convey 30,000 horse-power from Niagara to New York.

1883. Four electric locomotives constructed by the New York Railway Company to do the work of 160 ordinary locomotives. Tramcar at Kew, near London, running by electricity at six miles an hour, one accumulator of 80 lbs. sufficing for seven hours' work ; cost 6s. per day, against 26s. worked by horses. Electric railway from Portrush to Giant's Causeway, Ireland. Electric screw-boat on the Thames at Greenwich, 9 miles an hour.

1889. City of Buffalo contracts with Niagara Power Company for 10,000 horse-power at £30,000 per annum, to light the city and drive factories ; cable, 20 miles long.

1890. There are at present 645 miles of street railways operated by electricity in the United States and Canada. At present 45 electric roads are in course of construction, aggregating 512 miles of way, for which 167 cars are being built. In a short time the total number of electric roads will be 854, running 1927 motor and trailing cars, with a mileage of 1158. See *Telegraph, Telephones.*

EMIGRATION

Since the battle of Waterloo, no fewer than 27 millions of people in Europe have left their homes, broken up family ties, and sought their futures in new lands : *—

	1816–50	1851–88	Total
United Kingdom	2,369,000	7,491,000	9,860,000
France	320,000	1,220,000	1,540,000
Germany . . .	1,130,000	4,540,000	5,670,000
Russia	50,000	350,000	400,000
Austria	130,000	1,160,000	1,290,000
Italy	320,000	3,260,000	3,580,000
Switzerland . .	150,000	610,000	760,000
Spain	160,000	580,000	740,000
Portugal . . .	90,000	450,000	540,000
Sweden and Norway . ⎱	100,000	970,000	1,070,000
Denmark . . .	40,000	180,000	220,000
Holland . . .	25,000	320,000	345,000
Belgium . . .	90,000	880,000	970,000
Other countries .	20,000	200,000	220,000
Europe. . . .	4,994,000	22,211,000	27,205,000

* Besides the exodus of Europeans there has been an efflux of Coolies.

The emigration from India averages 22,000 yearly, the number registered abroad in 1880 being 335,000, viz. :—

Mauritius	.	. 141,000	Trinidad .	. 26,000
Demerara	.	. 54,000	Natal . .	. 18,000
Bourbon .	.	. 43,000	Jamaica, &c. .	. 53,000

Numbers of Chinese Coolies emigrate to Cuba and Peru, where they are ill-treated. Cuba imported 116,000 in the years 1866–73, and refused to let them return to China on the expiration of their contracts ; 67,000 died. The number imported into Peru in the year 1871 was 38,650, of whom many were put to death. In 1880 in one province 2000 were massacred.

The destinations of European emigrants were :—

	Down to 1850	1851–88	Total
United States .	2,633,000	12,330,000	14,963,000
Australia . . .	140,000	1,710,000	1,850,000
Canada. . . .	790,000	977,000	1,767,000
Argentina . . .	80,000	1,450,000	1,530,000
Brazil	90,000	790,000	880,000
Uruguay . . .	40,000	170,000	210,000
Algeria	140,000	420,000	560,000
Cape Colony . .	30,000	130,000	160,000
Various countries	1,051,000	4,234,000	5,285,000
Total . .	4,994,000	22,211,000	27,205,000

The exact proportions of sex and age cannot be given ; the following table is not of uniform importance, some of the countries being classed from observations of ten years, others for a single year.

	Emigrants from							
	United Kingdom	Germany	Holland	Austria	Sweden	Denmark	Italy	Switzerland
Men	46	50	52	32	45	51	70	55
Women . . .	32	25	23	28	35	26	18	22
Children . .	22	25	25	40	20	23	12	23
Total .	100	100	100	100	100	100	100	100

If the proportions for the unascertained countries be taken on the basis of the first six countries in the above table, the whole emigration from Europe over the seas for 74 years may be put down thus :—

Men .	.	.	.	.	11,550,000
Women	.	.	.	.	6,730,000
Children	.	.	.	.	5,120,000
			Total	.	23,400,000

The numbers of those who died on sea can never be arrived at even approximately. Kapp says that 20,000 Irish perished of ship-fever in 1846–47. Many vessels lost 20 per cent. If we were to adopt the death-rate on Government emigrant-ships to Australia and Cape Colony, namely, 5 per 1000 for men, 6 for women, and 52 for children, the number of the foregoing who died at sea would be as follows :—

Men	.	.	.	.	.	58,000
Women	.	.	.	.	.	40,000
Children	.	.	.	.	.	266,000
			Total	.		364,000

Births partly compensate for deaths, being about 1 in 200 women carried.

The professions of emigrants have not been uniformly classed ; the following conveys a general idea :—

	Emigrants from			
	United Kingdom	Germany	Italy	Sweden
Educated . .	7	17	6	} 35
Artisans, &c. .	55	47	43	
Farm labourers	18	24	39	32
Servants . .	20	12	12	33
Total .	100	100	100	100

The amount of money which the emigrants took to their new homes was found to average as follows :—

	Per Head
	£ s. d.
Germans, 1848–52	29 10 0
,, 1853–54	35 0 0
British in Canada, 1834 . . .	33 5 0
New York arrrivals, 1856 . .	14 0 0

A moderate estimate of £10 per able-bodied man would result as follows :—

To	£
United States	75,000,000
Australia	9,200,000
Canada	8,800,000
River Plate	8,700,000
Brazil	4,400,000
Various countries . .	9,400,000
Total . .	115,500,000

The great value of the emigrants, meantime, has been in their capacity for work. Dr. Farr valued a man of 20 at £234 sterling, Engel at £200, and other writers at £260.

In Australia it is found that each immigrant, big and little, increases the revenue by £4 yearly. In the Argentine Republic the influx of 800,000 immigrants in twenty years ending 1883 was accompanied by a rise of £4,800,000 in the revenue, say £6 per head. But it is in the United States where the value of immigration is most apparent ; for example, a group of 200 persons settled in 1858 on the territory now known as the State of Colorado, and in 1880 there were 1220 miles of railway, 14 daily papers, 190,000 inhabitants, real and personal estate valued at 9 millions sterling, agricultural products worth £700,000 a year ; in 1886 the value of property in Colorado had risen to 27 millions sterling.

In the Republic of Uruguay in 1884 an official report showed 166,000 European settlers, holding property worth 52 millions. In the city of Buenos Ayres 40,000 Europeans in 1883 held bank-deposits and real property worth £47,600,000, besides Irish and Scotch sheep-farms valued at 21 millions sterling. The Census report of the United States in 1880 showed an increase of wealth since 1850 of 7593 millions sterling, and as immigrants were 12½ per cent. of the population, it follows that they stand for 949 millions of the increase.

In Canada the agricultural capital rose from 140 millions in 1861 to 343 millions in 1887, and as immigrants formed 30 per cent. of the population, they are entitled to take credit for that share of the increase, say 61 millions. Agricultural constituting only 50 per cent. of the wealth of Canada, the total accumulation due to the immigrants will be 122 millions sterling.

There has been, moreover, a notable increase of wealth in the Brazilian provinces of Rio Grande do Sul, San Paulo, &c., where numerous German colonies have converted forests into productive lands. The following table is exclusive of Brazil and Cape Colony.

Country	Wealth Accumulated by Immigrants				
	Period	Arrivals	Mean European Population	Wealth, Million £	Yearly Average per Head
					£ s. d.
United States	1850–80	8,002,000	4,600,000	949	6 17 6
Australia	1850–88	1,710,000	1,200,000	714	15 12 0
Argentine Republic	1850 84	880,000	300,000	80	7 14 0
Uruguay	1850–84	305,000	166,000	52	8 18 6
Canada	1861–87	799,000	700,000	122	6 14 0

Except in Australia, the annual accumulations have been pretty much on a level, about £7 to £8 per annum, this ratio applying equally to men, women, and children. From the foregoing figures we can construct a table of the accumulations of emigrants between 1850 and 1888 as follows:—

Emigrants	Mean Number Abroad	Accumulation, Million £	Per Head, £
English . . .	1,200,000	410	342
Scotch . . .	250,000	95	380
Irish . . .	1,520,000	411	270
Germans . . .	1,700,000	452	266
Various nations .	2,296,000	460	200
Total .	6,966,000	1,828	261

It is a coincidence that each emigrant accumulated in the last 38 years about £260, and that this is the precise value set by some writers on each able-bodied adult. The strongest impulse to immigration was given by the Homestead Law of the United States and similar measures, giving lands to colonists at nominal or low prices. Down to 1886 the United States Government had thus disposed of 255 million acres, the Australian colonies 101 million acres. (See *Lands*.)

The total number of persons living out of their own country is approximately as follows (exclusive of Coolies):—

			Per 1000 Inhab.
In Europe *	.	2,537,000	10
,, United States	.	8,510,000	137
,, Australia	.	1,200,000	300
,, River Plate	.	1,086,000	240
,, Canada .	.	800,000	160
,, Brazil .	.	460,000	40
,, Algeria .	.	190,000	50
,, Egypt .	.	91,000	14
,, South Africa .	.	50,000	33
,, Chile .	.	40,000	15
,, China and Japan	.	6,000	...
,, Other countries	.	200,000	...
Total .	.	15,170,000	...

Foreign residents in the various countries of Europe are as follows:—

	Number		Number
U. Kingdom .	155,000	Sweden and Norway	26,000
France. . . .	1,115,000	Denmark . . .	61,000
Germany . .	276,000	Holland . . .	69,000
Russia . . .	148,000	Belgium . . .	143,000
Austria . . .	127,000	Switzerland . . .	211,000
Italy	60,000	Roumania . . .	89,000
Spain	37,000	Greece . . .	20,000

* The number of foreigners in the various European States being 2,537,000, as shown above, it is made up approximately as follows:—

Germans	.	540,000	Spaniards	. .	120,000
Belgians	.	460,000	Dutch .	. .	72,000
Austrians	.	360,000	British .	. .	70,000
Italians.	.	330,000	Russians	. .	70,000
French .	.	180,000	Swedes .	. .	60,000
Swiss .	.	140,000	Various	. .	135,000

Comparing the above figures with the emigration statistics the result is approximately as follows:—

Period	Emigrated	Now Living Abroad
1815–50	4,994,000	430,000
1851–80	15,868,000	8,640,000
1881–88	6,343,000	6,100,000
74 years	27,205,000	15,170,000

from which it appears that 12,035,000 either died abroad or returned to their own countries.

The following table shows European emigration in 1888, as compared with population:—

From	Number	Per Cent. of Population
England	171,000	0.60
Scotland	36,000	0.90
Ireland	73,000	1.60
United Kingdom . .	280,000	0.74
France	23,000	0.06
Germany	104,000	0.23
Austria	46,000	0.12
Italy	297,000	1.00
Spain	71,000	0.40
Portugal	13,000	0.30
Holland	18,000	0.40
Belgium	23,000	0.40
Scandinavia . . .	77,000	0.90
Switzerland . . .	8,000	0.27

Making a total of 960,000 souls. Their destination was approximately as follows:—

United States .	.	.	.	570,000
South America .	.	.	.	280,000
British colonies	.	.	.	105,000
Various parts .	.	.	.	5,000
				960,000

Emigrants from Northern Europe still go mostly to the United States; those from the Mediterranean to South America. The current of emigration to Canada and Australia is chiefly British.

UNITED KINGDOM

Official returns may be summed up as follows:—

			Per Annum
1815–29 .	.	314,000	21,000
1830–49 .	.	2,164,000	108,000
1850–69 .	.	4,278,000	214,000
1870–79 .	.	2,153,000	215,000
1880–88 .	.	3,228,000	359,000
74 years .	.	12,137,000	164,000

The above, however, includes foreign emigrants, who formed about 22 per cent. of the total. The number of British subjects was a little under ten millions, the following classification of natives of the three kingdoms being as close as can be ascertained, the figures before 1840, as Porter shows, being defective :—

Period	English	Scotch	Irish	Total	Per Annum
1815–34	110,000	30,000	420,000	560,000	28,000
1835–50	320,000	80,000	1,409,000	1,809,000	113,000
1851–60	640,000	183,000	1,231,000	2,054,000	205,000
1861–70	650,000	158,000	867,000	1,675,000	168,000
1871–80	970,000	166,000	542,000	1,678,000	168,000
1881–88	1,245,000	228,000	612,000	2,085,000	261,000
74 years	3,935,000	845,000	5,081,000	9,861,000	133,000

The destinations were as follows :—

To	1815–75	1876–88	Total
United States . .	4,425,000	1,807,000	6,232,000
Canada	1,260,000	317,000	1,577,000
Australia . . .	1,022,000	485,000	1,507,000
Cape, &c. . . .	317,000	228,000	545,000
Total . .	7,024,000	2,837,000	9,861,000

The United States took 140,000 a year in the 13 years ending 1888, Canada 25,000, and Australia 37,000 settlers.

The returns for the years 1888–89 were as follows :—

	Emigrants			Destination	
	1888	1889		1888	1889
English	170,000	164,000	United States . . .	196,000	169,000
Scotch	37,000	25,000	Canada	35,000	28,000
Irish	73,000	65,000	Australia	31,000	28,000
			Various	18,000	29,000
United Kingdom . .	280,000	254,000	Total . .	280,000	254,000

At all periods the United States attracted the bulk of the emigration.

	United States	British Colonies, &c.	Total	U. States Ratios
1815–50	1,308,000	1,061,000	2,369,000	55.2
1851–60	1,257,000	797,000	2,054,000	61.3
1861–70	1,185,000	490,000	1,675,000	70.7
1871–80	1,088,000	590,000	1,678,000	65.0
1881–88	1,394,000	691,000	2,085,000	66.9
74 years	6,232,000	3,629,000	9,861,000	63.2

The respective destinations of the people of the three kingdoms were approximately as follows :—

	United States	Canada	Australia	Cape, &c.	Total
English . .	1,893,000	872,000	820,000	350,000	3,935,000
Scotch . .	265,000	225,000	247,000	108,000	845,900
Irish . . .	4,074,000	480,000	440,000	87,000	5,081,000
Total . .	6,232,000	1,577,000	1,507,000	545,000	9,861,000

The number of colonists who survive and are still abroad, and the number of their children (estimated according to result of United States Census in 1880) may be set down approximately as follows :—

Settlers in	Now Living	Children	Population
United States .	3,180,000	4,310,000	7,490,000
Canada . . .	720,000	940,000	1,660,000
Australia . . .	1,080,000	1,400,000	2,480,000
Cape, &c. . . .	360,000	470,000	830,000
Total . .	5,340,000	7,120,000	12,460,000

In recent years there has been a steady influx of returned emigrants, averaging 78,000 for the years 1881-88, or about 30 per cent. of the number of emigrants in that period. The remittances by Irish settlers in the United States to their friends at home, from 1851 to 1887, amounted to £32,200,000. The accumulations of wealth by British and Irish emigrants since 1850, as already shown, amounted to 916 millions sterling.

The number of foreigners residing in the United Kingdom has been as follows :—

Year			Number		Per 1000 Inhab.
1841 .	.	.	36,000	...	1.3
1851	.	.	62,000	...	2.3
1861	.	.	102,000	...	3.5
1871	.	.	161,000	...	5.2
1881	.	.	155,000	...	4.4

FRANCE

In ten years ending 1887 the number of emigrants that left French ports was 460,000, but of these only 55,000 were French, say 5500 per annum.

In five years ending 1872 the number of French emigrants from Havre averaged 5100 yearly. The above figures do not include settlers going to Algeria (for which see *Colonies*, p. 126).

Approximately the emigration from France has been as follows :—

	1840–88	Per Annum
United States	320,000	6,600
Algeria	300,000	6,300
Argentina	190,000	4,000
Uruguay	50,000	1,000
Egypt	30,000	600
Europe	450,000	9,500
Total . .	1,340,000	28,000

The number of French living abroad in 1860 and 1885 compared as follows :—

In	1860	1885
Belgium	35,000	51,000
Switzerland	45,000	59,000
United Kingdom . . .	16,000	20,000
Spain	11,000	20,000
Italy	5,000	11,000
Egypt	14,000	16,000
Algeria	72,000	262,000
United States	110,000	107,000
South America . . .	59,000	167,000
Total . .	367,000	713,000

The chief currents of French emigration were :—

	Number	Period	Number now Living
United States . . .	314,000	1820–80	100,000
Argentine Republic .	156,000	1860–88	120,000
Algeria	300,000	1840–88	160,000
Uruguay	44,000	1860–88	30,000

The influx of foreigners is, meantime, greater than the outflow of emigration. According to Census returns we find :—

Year	Foreigners in France		Ratio to Pop. per 1000
1851 .	. .	379,000 ...	11
1861 .	, .	497,000 ...	13
1872 .	. .	731,000 ...	20
1886 .	. .	1,115,000 ...	29

Molinari says that in fifteen years France received (1872–87) able-bodied emigrants equal to an accession of 140 millions sterling to the national wealth. The foreigners living in France at various dates were as follows :—

	1851	1872	1881
Belgians . . .	128,000	348,000	432,000
Italians	63,000	113,000	241,000
Germans . . .	57,000	39,000	82,000
Swiss	26,000	43,000	66,000
Spaniards . . .	30,000	53,000	74,000
English . . .	20,000	26,000	37,000
Various	55,000	109,000	69,000
Total . .	379,000	731,000	1,001,000

Paris has 213,000 foreign residents, being 9 per cent. of the population.

In 1888 the Government expelled the following foreigners from France :—

	Men	Women	Total
Spaniards . . .	1,575	37	1,612
Belgians . . .	1,296	120	1,416
Germans . . .	504	69	573
Various	590	58	648
Total .	3,965	284	4,249

GERMANY

The Archivio figures are as follows :—

Period	Emigrated	Per Annum
1820–49 . . .	168,000 ...	5,600
1850–59 . . .	660,000 ...	66,000
1860–69 . . .	750,000 ...	75,000
1870–79 . . .	790,000 ...	79,000
1880–86 . . .	1,342,000 ...	192,000
66 years . .	4,710,000	72,000

The *Almanach de Gotha* says that 4,900,000 Germans emigrated between 1820 and December 1887, of which 3,700,000 to the United States. Duval, however, makes the efflux down to 1859 much greater, as follows :—

1820–29 .	.	.	.	.	49,600
1830–39 .	.	.	.	.	220,900
1840–49 .	.	.	.	.	661,200
1850–59 .	.	.	.	.	1,017,100
40 years	.	.	.	.	1,948,800

Gaebler is of the same opinion, making the number 1,800,000 from 1819 to 1855. It must be observed, meantime, that the Archivio gives only the departures by sea, whereas Gaebler includes the total outflow by sea and land. Official returns give much lower

figures. For example, the Prussian Blue-book makes the total for thirty years down to 1871 as 642,000, and the Board of Trade Abstract for eighteen years ending 1888 only 1,771,000, a total of 2,413,000, which is less than half the reality. If we consult the statistics of Germans in United States, Russia, Brazil, River Plate, and various countries in Europe, we may form an approximate table as follows :—

Period	Actual Emigration		Official Figures	
	Number	Per Annum	Number	Per Annum
1821–40	270,000	13,500	...	...
1841–70	2,880,000	96,000	642,000	21,400
1871–80	1,050,000	105,000	626,000	62,600
1881–88	1,470,000	184,000	1,365,000	170,000
68 years	5,670,000	84,000	2,633,000	39,000

	Actual Emigration 1821–88	Official 1871–87
United States . . .	4,316,000	1,880,000
Brazil	84,000	31,000
Spanish America . .	70,000	19,000
Australia	60,000	17,000
Other parts . . .	1,140,000	44,000
Total . .	5,670,000	1,991,000

In official returns only persons going out of Europe are considered emigrants.

Immigration into Germany is small, the number of resident foreigners being less than one-tenth of that of Germans abroad. The Census of 1880 showed a total of 276,000 resident foreigners, thus :—

Austrians	118,000	Dutch . .	18,000	English . 11,000
Swiss . .	28,000	French . .	17,000	Swedes . 10,000
Danes . .	24,000	Russians .	15,000	Various . 35,000

The total makes up less than 6 in 1000 of population.

RUSSIA

The United States Census of 1880 showed 49,000 Poles and 36,000 Russians, but since that year there has been a great influx. In 1888 no fewer than 37,300 Russian settlers arrived. In 1874–78 the severity of military service drove 40,000 Mennonites from the Empire, who made settlements at Manitoba, San Paulo, and Buenos Ayres, where they have prospered. Jews also in late years been expelled in large numbers.

In a period of 36 years down to 1886, according to police reports, there were 1,733,000 foreigners who settled in Russia, viz. :—

Germans .	.	.	.	.	952,000
Austrians	.	.	.	.	677,000
Various .	.	.	.	.	104,000
Total	.	.	1,733,000		

These figures are a mere fiction of the Russian police ; the actual number of foreigners in Russia at the Census of 1880 was only 148,000.

AUSTRIA-HUNGARY

In 1880 there were 135,000 Austrians and Hungarians in the United States. The official returns for ten years' emigration ending 1886 show as follows :—

United States .	.	.	.	.	227,000
Argentina	.	.	.	.	10,000
Various .	.	.	.	.	37,000
Total	.	.	274,000		

The number of Austrian immigrants who arrived in the United States in 1888 was 42,000. Before 1880 the annual emigration averaged only 7000 yearly. The total for ten years ending 1880 was 71,000, of whom 46,000 were Bohemians.

ITALY

Official returns of the Argentine Republic show that in 28 years ending 1888 there were landed at Buenos Ayres and Rosario 550,000 Italians. In the same period 80,000 landed at Montevideo. There were 73,000 who emigrated to the United States in sixty years, of whom 44,000 were living in 1880. Official returns, much below the reality, give the following for nine years down to December 1887 :—

River Plate	261,000
United States	153,000
Brazil	98,000
North Africa	37,000
Various	68,000
Total .	617,000

Carpi shows that the official returns are much less than the real number, because they fail to include Italians who go to the other parts of Europe. An official report published in 1883 showed the number of Italians living abroad as follows :—

	1873	1883
Argentina	88,000	254,000
Brazil and Peru . . .	28,000	115,000
Uruguay	32,000	40,000
France	118,000	241,000
Austria	27,000	44,000
Switzerland . . .	18,000	42,000
United States . . .	70,000	170,000
Levant, &c. . . .	95,000	127,000
Total .	476,000	1,033,000

The following table shows approximately the currents of emigration :—

	United States	South America	Other Countries	Total	Annual Average
1821–40	3,000	10,000	150,000	163,000	8,100
1841–60	11,000	30,000	400,000	441,000	22,000
1861–70	13,000	180,000	460,000	653,000	65,300
1871–80	46,000	430,000	700,000	1,176,000	117,600
1881–87	153,000	365,000	629,000	1,147,000	164,000
67 years	226,000	1,015,000	2,329,000	3,580,000	54,000

According to the Archivio the emigration in the years 1882–86 summed up 803,000, whereas the official figures for the same years do not exceed 363,000. In the preceding decade Professor Carpi made the average about 110,000 yearly, and estimated the number of returned emigrants at 60 per cent. of those who leave in any year. This is about double the proportion of the stream of emigration from Buenos Ayres to Italy, compared with the number of Italians arriving there. It may be therefore assumed that 33 per cent. of the above emigrants returned to Italy. The account may be put down thus :—

Settled in River Plate . . .	560,000
,, Brazil	70,000
,, United States . .	170,000
,, other countries . .	1,050,000
Died	540,000
Returned to Italy	1,190,000
Total emigrated .	3,580,000

The number of foreign residents in Italy is only 60,000, including 16,000 Austrians, 12,000 Swiss, 11,000 French, 7000 English, and 5000 Germans, the whole being as 2 per 1000 of the population.

SWITZERLAND

The returns for ten years ending 1887 are as follows :—

United States	70,000
South America	11,000
Total .	81,000

By the Census of 1880 it appears there were 89,000 Swiss in the United States. There are 15,000 in the Argentine Republic. A large number of foreigners reside in Switzerland, and the number steadily increases :—

	1870	1880
French	62,000	54,000
Germans	57,000	95,000
Italians	18,000	42,000
Various	14,000	20,000
Total .	151,000	211,000

This is more than 7 per cent. of the population. The principal centre of foreign residents is Geneva, viz. :—

	Number of Inhab.		Percentage	
	1850	1870	1850	1870
Swiss . . .	18,400	17,600	58	38
Foreign . .	13,300	28,800	42	62
Total .	31,700	46,400	100	100

SPAIN

Official returns at Buenos Ayres show that in 32 years down to 1888 there were landed in the Argentine Republic 172,000 Spaniards. In the same interval those landed at Montevideo were about 80,000. The United States report shows only 29,000 in 60 years down to 1880, the actual number of Spanish settlers in the said year being 5100, but in the ensuing years there was a notable increase, 9000 having arrived between 1880 and 1888. Spain also sends out numbers to Cuba and her other colonies. The currents of emigration have been approximately :—

Period	River Plate	Other Countries	Total	Per Annum
1861–80 . . .	160,000	180,000	340,000	17,000
1881–88 . . .	92,000	50,000	142,000	18,000
28 years . . .	252,000	230,000	482,000	17,200

The annual outflow at present is little over 1 per 1000 of the population. About 5 per cent. of those who emigrate return to Spain.

In 1888 there were Spaniards residing abroad as follows :—Algeria, 114,000 ; River Plate, 99,000 ; France, 74,000 ; and others in various countries, the total reaching 346,500.

The number of foreigners residing in Spain is only 37,000, including 18,000 French, 8000 Portuguese, and 5000 English, the total being barely as 2 per 1000 of the population in 1877.

PORTUGAL

Brazil is the principal destination of Portuguese emigrants, of whom more than 300,000 landed at Brazilian ports since 1855, viz. :—

1855–65	.	.	.	.	.	81,000
1866–75	.	.	.	.	.	62,000
1876–88	.	.	.	.	.	172,000
34 years	.	.	.	.	.	315,000

The Census of 1880 in the United States showed only 8000 Portuguese. A small number go to the Portuguese colonies in Africa, the average for the last ten years being under 400. The total yearly emigration is about 13,000, or 3 per 1000 of the population.

SWEDEN

Official returns for 1851 show as follows :—

Period	To United States	Other Countries	Total	Per Annum
1851–60 . .	15,000	2,000	17,000	1,700
1861–70 . .	88,000	34,000	122,000	12,200
1871–80 . .	98,000	51,000	149,000	14,900
1881–86 . .	174,000	34,000	208,000	34,700
36 years . .	375,000	121,000	496,000	13,700

It seems that in thirty years down to 1880 there were 201,000 Swedes who emigrated to the United States, and the American Census for that year showed 194,000 Swedish settlers then living. The number at present in the United States is doubtless near 300,000. There is also a current of emigration to Denmark, where the Census of 1880 showed 24,000 Swedish settlers. The number of foreigners residing in Sweden is only 18,000, of whom 5000 are Danes, 4000 Norwegians, and 3000 Germans. The total is equal to 4 per 1000 of the population.

NORWAY

Emigration has been almost exclusively to the United States. We have no returns before 1856.

			Emigrants		*Per Annum*
1856–65	.	.	54,000	...	5,400
1870–74	.	.	56,000	...	11,200
1876–87	.	.	182,000	...	15,200

The United States Census showed 182,000 Norwegian settlers, and since that year 142,000 have gone thither (to December 1887), so that the present number cannot fall short of 240,000. There are also 3000 Norwegians settled in Denmark. The number of foreigners residing in Norway is 8000, being 4 per 1000 of the population.

DENMARK

Official returns are to the following effect :—

Period	To United States	Other Countries	Total	Per Annum
1868–70	7,300	1,400	8,700	2,900
1871–80	32,800	5,800	38,600	3,900
1881–87	51,600	2,100	53,700	7,700
20 years	91,700	9,300	101,000	5,000

The United States Census of 1880 showed 64,000 Danish residents, and, with the influx of later years, the number must now reach 90,000. Since 1870 more than 3500 Danes have gone to Australia. The current of emigration at present averages 4 per 1000 of population.

Denmark has 61,000 foreign residents, including 33,000 Germans and 24,000 Swedes, the total being equal to 3 per cent. of population.

HOLLAND

Official returns show as follows :—

Period	To United States	Other Countries	Total	Per Annum
1875–80	84,200	1,100	85,300	14,200
1881–86	113,000	1,200	114,200	19,000
12 years	197,200	2,300	199,500	16,600

The United States Census of 1880 showed 71,000 Dutch settlers; the present number cannot fall short of 170,000. The numerous Dutch colonies seem to have no attraction for emigrants. The present rate of emigration is equal to 5 per 1000 of the population.

There are in Holland 69,000 foreigners, including 42.000 Germans, 19,000 Belgians, and 2000 English ; in all equal to 15 per 1000 of the population.

BELGIUM

The currents of immigration and emigration would appear to be about equal, according to official records from 1841 to 1886. Those of the year 1846 are lost, but allowing the average in that decade, we find as follows :—

Period				Immigrants	Emigrants
1841–50	.	.	.	37,000	51,000
1851–60	.	.	.	60,000	89,000
1861–70	.	.	.	94,000	110,000
1871–80	.	.	.	150,000	119,000
1881–86	.	.	.	108,000	90,000
46 years	.	.	.	449,000	459,000

These figures represent only the arrivals and departures at ports. The actual number of emigrants in 1841–86 must have reached a million, the Census of 1885 showing the following number of Belgians abroad :—

France	.	.	.	.	.	482,300
Holland	.	.	.	.	.	18,800
United States	.	.	.	.	.	15,500
Germany	.	.	.	.	.	9,200
United Kingdom	.	.	.	.	.	2,600
Various	.	.	.	.	.	1,300

making in all 530.000 souls. In 57 years ending 1887 there were 2553 foreigners naturalised as Belgians, viz. :—

Germans	.	933	French	.	.	622
Dutch .	.	640	Various	.	.	358

Notwithstanding the great influx of foreigners, the number of foreign residents at the last Census was only 143,000, including 49,000 Dutch, 51,000 French, 34,000 Germans, and 4000 English, in all 24 per thousand of the population.

UNITED STATES

The emigration to the United States before 1830 * can only be approximately estimated ; since that year minute returns have been kept.

Period				Immigrants	Per Annum
1654–1701 .	.	.	.	134,000	2,800
1702–1750 .	.	.	.	182,000	3,700
1751–1800 .	.	.	.	310,000	6,200
1801–20 .	.	.	.	178,000	8,900
1821–30 .	.	.	.	264,000	26,400
1831–40 .	.	.	.	599,000	59,900
1841–50 .	.	.	.	1,713,000	171,300
1851–60 .	.	.	.	2,590,000	259,000
1861–70 .	.	.	.	2,455,000	245,500
1871–80 .	.	.	.	3,042,000	304,200
1881–89 .	.	.	.	4,792,000	532,000
236 years .	.	.	.	16,259,000	...

* The official returns for 1820–30 are admittedly defective and valueless.

The official returns are as follows :—

	1821-40	1841-50	1851-60	1861-70	1871-80	1881-89	69 Years
English	95,000	263,000	388,000	615,000	449,000	602,000	2,412,000
Scotch	6,000	4,000	38,000	45,000	88,000	137,000	318,000
Irish	258,000	781,000	908,000	445,000	440,000	602,000	3,434,000
United Kingdom	359,000	1,048,000	1,334,000	1,105,000	977,000	1,341,000	6,164,000
French	54,000	77,000	74,000	38,000	73,000	44,000	360,000
Germans	159,000	435,000	947,000	817,000	755,000	1,362,000	4,475,000
Scandinavians	2,000	14,000	22,000	136,000	255,000	362,000	791,000
Various	168,000	139,000	213,000	359,000	982,000	1,683,000	3,544,000
Total . . .	742,000	1,713,000	2,590,000	2,455,000	3,042,000	4,792,000	15,334,000

In the above returns the number of English is made to appear 459,000 in excess of, and that of Irish fully 600,000 less than the reality, as shown on p. 248, which is accounted for by the fact that many of the Irish were in earlier years classified as English or British. Moreover, the Census of 1880 showed that Irish settlers were more than double the number of English and Scotch collectively (1,855,000 to 917,000), whereas the above classification down to 1880 would make the ratio as 140 to 100. The total immigration of 69 years may be correctly summed up as follows :—

	Number	Ratio
English	1,963,000	12.8
Scotch	318,000	2.8
Irish	4,140,000	27.0
United Kingdom . . .	6,421,000	41.8
Germans . . .	4,475,000	29.2
Scandinavians .	791,000	5.2
French	360,000	2.4
Various . . .	3,287,000	21.4
Total .	15,334,000	100.0

During 31 years the record of ages was kept; and if we suppose the ratios to apply to the whole 69 years, the ages of immigrants showed as follows :—

	Number	Ratio
Under 10	2,300,000	15.0
10-20	3,220,000	21.0
20-30	5,670,000	37.0
30-40	2,450,000	16.0
Over 40	1,694,000	11.0
Total .	15,334,000	100.0

The returns of the Census of 1880, and the estimates resulting from the immigration since then as to the actual number of foreigners, are :—

	Census, 1880	Arrivals, 1881-88	Estimated Residents, 1888
Germans . . .	1,967,000	1,104,000	2,450,000
Irish . . .	1,855,000	536,000	1,920,000
British . . .	917,000	658,000	1,260,000
Scandinavians .	376,000	412,000	630,000
Italians . .	44,000	201,000	190,000
French . . .	107,000	20,000	100,000
Dutch . . .	58,000	151,000	170,000
Swiss	89,000	68,000	130,000
Austrians & Hungarians	135,000	266,000	320,000
Russians and Poles .	85,000	160,000	190,000
Various . .	693,000	744,000	1,150,000
Total .	6,326,000	4,320,000	8,510,000

In the last fifty years the United States received nearly 15,000,000 settlers, and the Census of 1880 showed that every 100 settlers had the following number of children living :—German, 148; Irish, 144; British, 122; general average, 124. The foreign population in December 1888 stood approximately thus :—

	Immigrants	Children	Total
German . . .	2,450,000	3,650,000	6,100,000
Irish	1,920,000	2,760,000	4,680,000
British	1,260,000	1,550,000	2,810,000
Various . . .	2,880,000	2,670,000	5,550,000
Total foreign .	8,510,000	10,630,000	19,140,000

The numbers and proportion of resident foreigners in the whole population have been as follows :—

Year	Population	Foreign Residents	Percentage
1820 . . .	9,634,000	177,000	1.8
1840 . . .	17,069,000	859,000	5.0
1850 . . .	23,192,000	2,241,000	9.7
1860 . . .	31,443,000	4,136,000	13.1
1870 . . .	38,558,000	5,566,000	14.5
1880 . . .	50,410,000	6,326,000	12.5
1888 . . .	60,000,000	8,510,000	14.2

In the above table "foreign residents" of course include naturalised American citizens. Foreigners and their children, as shown in a previous table, constitute almost one-third of the population.

CANADA

The net increase of population by settlers may be estimated on comparing the several Census returns; and allowing for natural increase, the figures result approximately thus :—

Year	Population	Natural Increase of Decade	Net Immigration of Decade	Net Immigration per Annum
1831	1,158,000	...	...	...
1841	1,690,000	230,000	302,000	30,200
1851	2,482,000	305,000	487,000	48,700
1861	3,030,000	370,000	178,000	17,800
1871	3,833,000	420,000	383,000	38,300
1881	4,504,000	460,000	211,000	21,100
1887	5,019,000	310,000	205,000	34,200
56 years	...	2,095,000	1,766,000	31,500

The number of British and Irish emigrants who went to Canada from 1815 to 1888 amounted (see p. 248) to 1,577,000, or 90 per cent. of the above total.

Only a portion of the European emigrants who landed in the colony settled there, the rest proceeding to the

United States. An official statement published in 1877 showed as follows :—

Period	Arrived	Proceeded to United States	Remained
1851–71	1,051,000	595,000	456,000
1872–76	351,000	179,000	172,000
26 years	1,402,000	774,000	628,000

AUSTRALIA

The current of emigration since 1820 has been approximately thus :—

Period	Number	Per Annum
1821–40	40,000	2,000
1841–50	90,000	9,000
1851–60	710,000	71,000
1861–70	320,000	32,000
1871–80	340,000	34,000
1881–88	350,000	44,000
68 years	1,850,000	27,000

We have already seen (page 248) that 1,505,000 British subjects emigrated to Australia, or 81 per cent. of the above total. In 1871 there were 34,000 German residents.

The Australian colonies have expended 8½ millions in promoting immigration, viz. :—

	Expended	Immigrants	Per Head
	£		£
New Zealand . . .	1,950,000	101,000	19
Victoria	2,880,000	167,000	17
Queensland, &c., &c. .	3,600,000	202,000	18
Total . .	8,430,000	470,000	18

Assisted passages are still provided by some of the colonies.

CAPE COLONY

The white population in 27 years, ending 1875, rose from 87,000 to 237,000, and as the natural increase was 24 per cent. per decade, we find that the total immigration must have been 70,000, say 2600 per annum. This includes 15,000 Government immigrants introduced from 1847 to 1872. The discovery of diamonds in 1867, and construction of railways, have stimulated European immigration, which now may be estimated at 5000 yearly. There are also more than 10,000 settlers at Natal.

BRAZIL

The number of European settlers has been as follows:—

		Per Annum
1855–64 . . .	120,000	12,000
1866–74 . . .	116,000	11,600
1875–84 . . .	228,000	22,800
1885–88 . . .	266,000	66,000
Total .	730,000	21,500

In the year 1825 the Emperor Pedro I. founded the first German colony, 909 souls, at San Leopoldo, Rio Grande do Sul. In 1854 the little settlement counted 11,172 Germans, including 3680 born in the country. Each family had received on arrival a free land-grant of 130 acres. In 1866 the colonists numbered 25,000, including children, and in 1871 the product of the farms was valued officially at one million sterling, or nearly £200 per family. Meantime the influx of more Germans, and the increasing number of the San Leopoldo com-

munity, led to the establishment of 42 other German settlements in Rio Grande, for the most part between the years 1849 and 1860: the whole in 1871 counted 70,000 Germans, one half born in the country, their farms being valued at six millions sterling. German colonies were introduced into the neighbouring province of Santa Catharina in 1849, and about the same time into San Paulo; in later years into Minas Geraes, Paranà, and other provinces. In 1871 there were the following colonies :—

Rio Grande do Sul	43
San Paulo	12
Other provinces	21
Total . . .	76

The agricultural settlements had about 90,000 Europeans, more than half being Germans, the rest Swiss, Italians, &c. Since 1880 a great influx of Italians has taken place in San Paulo, and these settlers have begun planting vines on a large scale : in 1888 no fewer than 92,000 immigrants settled in that province, the total immigration that year reaching 131,000. The Government devotes £550,000 per annum to free passages. In 1872 the number of Europeans in Brazil was 243,000, at present it is probably about 460,000.

ARGENTINA

The official returns are as follows :—

		Per Annum
1861–70 . . .	185,000	18,500
1871–80 . . .	453,000	45,300
1881–88 . . .	766,000	96,000
28 years . . .	1,404,000	50,000

The number of immigrants in 1888 was 181,000, which shows that this country comes next after the United States as a field for European emigration. The returns from 1871 to 1888 show nationalities thus :—

Italians .	550,000	French .	100,000	Germans .	15,000
Spaniards	122,000	British .	20,000	Unascertained }	412,000

The bulk of those unascertained were Italians, who formed 65 per cent. of the whole number. Before the year 1860 the average immigration was 5000 yearly, one third being Italians.

Agricultural colonies were begun in Santa Fè in 1856, and in 1884 there were 78 of these settlements, counting in all 66,000 inhabitants, who cultivated 940,000 acres, and possessed properties to the value of £8,400,000. The first settlers were Swiss, but at present Italians, Swiss, Germans, and French are almost equal in numbers. The growth of the Santa Fè colonies is shown thus :—

Year	Acres	Population
1871	140,000	13,600
1879	404,000	40,700
1884	940,000	66,000

In 1884 there were also ten colonies in Entre Rios; in 1856 they had 9900 inhabitants, mostly Italians and Germans, who cultivated 170,000 acres. Two colonies in Cordoba had 3000 settlers. The Welsh settlement in Patagonia had 1300 souls, whose farms were valued at £122,000, having 17,000 acres under wheat, the crop averaging 200,000 bushels. It was founded in 1865.

The total area under crops in 1887 held by agricultural colonies was estimated at 2,200,000 acres, cultivated by 140,000 settlers, and producing 20 million bushels of grain. These colonies account for only 10 per cent. of the immigration since 1860, most of the Italians having preferred to settle about Buenos Ayres in every variety of calling. The official returns of money in bank and real estate, in the city of Buenos Ayres, in 1883, were as follows :—

	Number of Depositors	Deposits, in £ Sterling	Real Estate, £ Sterling
Italians . . .	10,090	. 2,800,000	6,600,000
Argentines . .	7,056	2,860,000	22,100,000
Spaniards . . .	3,008	1,100,000	1,800,000
French	2,022	620,000	2,200,000
English. . . .	801	450,000	1,200,000
Germans . . .	451	250,000	600,000
Various	1,291	1,200,000	3,800,000
Total . .	24,719	9,280,000	38,300.000

The above returns are only for the city, and have no reference to the thriving Irish and Scotch communities in the province of Buenos Ayres.

The Scotch made their first settlement at Monte Grande in 1826, the Irish at various places in 1840. Their numbers and possessions in 1884 stood thus :—

	Population	Area of Lands, Square Miles	Number of Sheep	Value of Property, £ Sterling
Irish . . .	22,000	4,900	9,200,000	15,200,000
Scotch . .	3,600	2,500	3,000,000	6,100,000
Total .	25,600	7,400	12,200,000	21,300,000

According to the census of 1869 there were 212,000 European residents, since which year 1,260,000 emigrants have arrived, of whom 29 per cent. returned. Allowing for deaths the number of foreign population would be as follows :—

	Number in 1869	Arrivals, 1870–88	Present Number	Population Including Children
Italians . . .	71,000	820,000	530,000	1,320,000
Spaniards . .	34,000	180,000	140,000	310,000
French . . .	32,000	150,000	120,000	250,000
British and Irish .	11,000	30,000	30,000	70,000
German and Swiss .	11,000	30,000	30,000	70,000
Various . . .	53,000	50,000	70,000	150,000
Total . .	212,000	1,260,000	920,000	2,170,000

The population of the Republic in January 1888 was estimated at 3,930,000, from which it appears that foreigners form 23 per cent., and with their children 55 per cent. of the total. Buenos Ayres is the chief centre of European settlers, 72 per cent. of the children born in that city being of foreign parents.

URUGUAY

Official returns as to immigrants landed at Monte Video are :—

Period	Number	Per Annum
1835–52 . . .	36,600	2,000
1853–62 . . .	28,000	2,800
1863–72 . . .	143,000	14,300
1873–87 . . .	156,000	10,400
53 years . . .	363.600	6,800

It is, however, beyond doubt that one-half proceeded to Buenos Ayres, the number of settlers remaining in the country averaging about 6000 yearly in the last twenty-five years. Taking the ratio of nationality as entered in

the records, the actual immigrants since 1863 may be set down as follows :—

Italians.	.	.	.	.	81,000
Spaniards	.	.	.	.	33,000
French .	.	.	.	.	8,000
British .	.	.	.	.	5,000
Various	.	.	.	.	23,000
Total	.	.	.		150,000

In 1884 there were eight agricultural colonies, Swiss and Italian, with 6200 settlers, who cultivated 110,000 acres, and raised 900,000 bushels of grain, valued at £140,000 sterling. The farms of these settlers were assessed at £780,000 sterling. An official report in 1884 showed the number of European settlers in the Republic, and the amount of property paying tax held by those of each nation.

	Number	Wealth, £ Sterling	£ per Head
Spaniards . . .	44,000	12,500,000	280
Italians . . .	39,000	11,200,000	286
Brazilians . . .	22,000	14,700,000	660
French	16,000	5,700,000	350
British	3,000	3,100,000	1,030
Various . . .	42,000	4,800,000	115
Foreign settlers .	166,000	52,000,000	315

Foreigners were 27 per cent. of the population, and held 58 per cent. of the assessed wealth of the Republic.

ALGERIA

Complete statistics of immigration from 1883 to 1886 will be found under the title *Colonies*, page 126.

ENGINEERING

Some of the most remarkable works carried out in ancient or modern times, as well as those projected, will be found in the following list :—

Aqueducts.—Those of Rome under the Cæsars supplied 320 million gallons water daily, and were 249 miles long in the aggregate. The Incas of Peru had one 360 miles long.

Blasting.—At Dover, in 1873, the South Eastern Railway Company removed at one blast 800,000 tons of the granite cliff, using eight tons of powder in three charges. At Loch Fyne, near Glasgow, 13th December 1888, Mr. Gardiner's electric battery displaced at a single blast 75,000 tons of granite.

Boring.—The greatest depth yet reached is 5200 feet, at Schladerbach, near Halle. The cost of boring with diamond-drill in the Barrow ironstone district, England, varies from 32 to 44 pence per foot.

Bridges.—That of Forth, Scotland, finished in 1889, employed 48,000 tons of steel, and 125,000 cubic yards of masonry, has three spans of 1700 feet each, total length 5330 feet. It rests on four cylindrical pillars of masonry, 70 feet diameter, built on rocks 90 feet under water : it can support safely a weight of 84,000 tons ; the cost was £2,000,000. In 1867 De Gamond proposed a metal tubular bridge, 30 by 24 feet, from Calais to Dover, to cost £7,200,000, and be completed in seven years.

This scheme was revived in 1889, at a proposed cost of 34½ millions sterling, the bridge to be 200 feet above water, and consist of 74 spans of 550 yards each, resting on masonry pillars, averaging 200 feet down into the sea, the superstructure to employ one million tons of steel, the whole to be completed in ten years ; masonry, £15,200,000; superstructure, £19,200,000. See *Bridges*.

Canal.—That of China, 2100 miles long, was completed in 1350, after 600 years of labour. That of Suez, opened in 1869 after thirteen years' work, is 92 miles long, and cost 17 millions sterling.

Earthworks

	Cost, Cubic Yd.		Cost, Cubic Yd.
England . . .	21 pence	Panama Canal .	15 pence
Suez Canal . . .	12 ,,	Cyprus	6 ,,

The work of the Thames Embankment, completed after eight years, in 1869, at a cost of £1,710,000, consisted as follows :—

	Cubic Yards		Cubic Yards
Brickwork. . . .	80,000	Granite. . . .	650,000
Concrete	140,000	Earthwork . . .	970,000

The Hercules Ditcher, Michigan, removes 700 tons of clay per hour.

Harbours.—That of Cherbourg, completed by Napoleon III. in 1857, was 74 years in construction, and cost £3,500,000. That of Holyhead, finished in 1880, has a pier consisting of seven million tons of granite, length 7860 feet, width varying from 250 to 400 feet. Plymouth breakwater, begun in 1812, finished in 1841, has 3,800,000 tons of stone, length 5300 feet, cost £1,550,000.

Pumps.—Those employed at Zegedin, Hungary, in 1879, pumped out 500,000 tons or 110,000,000 gallons water daily. Those of the Severn Tunnel in 1880 pumped out each 150,000 gallons an hour. The Haarlem Pumps lifted 109 tons of water 10 feet at each stroke; they drained Lake Haarlem, pumping out 1100 million tons water in eleven years, say 400,000 tons daily.

Pyramid.—That of Cheops, near Cairo, contains four million tons of stone, and cost 40 millions sterling. It would now cost only 4 millions.

Removal.—The Pelham Hotel, Boston, stone-built, 96 feet high, weight 10,000 tons, was moved by engineers, to widen the street, a distance of 14 feet in 70 hours.

Tower.—That of Babel, according to Herodotus, was 610 feet high. The Eiffel Tower, at Paris, built in six months, 1889, is 990 feet high, of iron.

Tunnel.—The longest yet made is the St. Gothard, 16,400 yards, begun in 1873, completed in 1881, at a cost of £152 per yard.

Wall.—That of China contains 6350 million cubic feet of material, or 160 times as much as the Great Pyramid of Egypt.

EXHIBITIONS

Date	Place	Area, Acres	Visitors	Days Open	Receipts	Exhibitors
1851	London . .	21	6,200,000	141	424,000	17,000
1855	Paris . .	24	4,500,000	200	128,000	24,000
1862	London . .	23	6,200,000	171	408,000	29,000
1867	Paris . .	37	9,300,000	217	420,000	50,000
1873	Vienna . .	48	7,300,000	186	206,000	43,000
1876	Philadelphia	55	10,200,000	...	800,000	...
1878	Paris . . .	60	16,100,000	194	974,000	60,000
1889	Paris . . .	...	25,000,000	180	1,980,000	55,000

The exhibitors and winners of prizes at the London Exhibition of 1851 were as follows :—

	Exhibitors	Prizes
British	9,970	2,089
French	1,750	1,050
German	1,450	482
Austrian	750	236
United States . . .	600	152
Various	2,880	1,177
Total . .	17,400	5,186

At the Paris Exhibition of 1889 the following prizes were given :—

Grand prizes	890
Gold medals	5,599
Silver medals	11,104
Bronze medals	10,980
Total . .	28,573

The London Exhibition of 1851 left a net profit of £104,000; that of Paris in 1878, a loss of £1,270,000; and that of Paris in 1889, a net profit of £320,000.

At the last-mentioned the police estimated 5 million French and 1,500,000 foreign visitors, the latter including 380,000 English, 225,000 Belgians, 160,000 Germans, 56,000 Spaniards, 52,000 Swiss, 38,000 Italians, 32,000 Austrians, 7000 Russians, 90,000 North Americans, and 25,000 South Americans.

The balance-sheet of the Exhibition of 1889 showed thus :—

	£
Tickets	980,000
Paris subsidy	320,000
State subsidy	680,000
Receipts	1,980,000
Expenses	1,660,000
Surplus	320,000

The largest number of visitors in one day was 400,000.

F.

FACTORIES

Some countries have precise statistics only touching textile factories, others include every industrial establishment in which more than a dozen hands are employed. The following table shows approximately the number of factory operatives of various nations :—

United Kingdom	1,703,000	Spain	200,000
France	1,783,000	Switzerland . .	300,000
Germany . . .	1,527,000	Belgium . . .	400,000
Russia	955,000	Sweden	53,000
Austria	499,000	United States . .	2,739,000
Italy	382,000	Canada . . .	255,000

The textile factories of the United Kingdom show as follows :—

Year	Number of Factories	Spindles	Power Looms	Steam, Horse-Power	Operatives
1835	3,160	...	117,000	...	355,000
1840	4,213	...	...	69,000	424,000
1850	4,601	31,000,000	302,000	108,000	596,000
1860	6,378	36,000,000	499,000	375,000	776,000
1870	6,258	42,000,000	606,000	473,000	907,000
1880	7,105	47,000,000	725,000	570,000	976,000
1885	7,465	47,800,000	774,000	...	1,034,000

The following table shows British textile factories at three dates :—

Factories	Hands			Horse-Power			Power Looms, Number		
	1838	1856	1885	1838	1856	1885	1838	1856	1885
Cotton . . .	259,000	379,000	504,000	60,000	97,000	356,000	109,000	299,000	560,000
Woollen . .	86,000	167,000	282,000	28,000	41,000	122,000	5,000	53,000	140,000
Linen, &c. . .	44,000	80,000	164,000	11,000	18,000	73,000	2,000	9,000	60,000
Silk . . .	34,000	56,000	43,000	3,000	5,000	10,000	...	8,000	12,000
Total .	423,000	682,000	993,000	102,000	161,000	561,000	116,000	369,000	772,000

Besides the foregoing there are factories of hosiery, lace, &c.
The hands employed in textile factories of the United Kingdom were made up thus :—

	1870			1885		
	Males	Females	Total	Males	Females	Total
England	304,000	414,000	718,000	338,000	476,000	814,000
Scotland	34,000	93,000	127,000	45,000	107,000	152,000
Ireland	21,000	41,000	62,000	22,000	46,000	68,000
Total	359,000	548,000	907,000	405,000	629,000	1,034,000

Factory legislation as to the minimum age for children being employed, and their hours of labour, is shown thus :—

	Minimum Age	Maximum of Hours Daily for					
		Children Under 11	Under 12	Under 13	Under 14	Under 15	Under 16
France . . .	10	6	6	12	12	12	12
Germany . .	12	...	...	6	6	10	10
Russia . . .	10	6	6	12	12	12	12
Austria . .	10	10	10	12	12	12	12
Italy . . .	9	8	10	10	10	10	...
Spain . . .	10	5	5	5	8	8	8
Switzerland .	10	6	6	12	12	12	12
Denmark .	10	4	4	4	4	12	12

The minimum in Belgium is 10 years, in Holland 12. In all cases the children are to have Sunday free.

At the Berlin Congress in 1890 it was recommended that children should not be admitted to work in any industry under 12 years of age, and then only for 6 hours per day till they were 14 ; that young persons from 14 to 16 years of age should not work more than 10 hours per day, and that women should in no case work more than 11 hours per day. In India, however, children of 7 years of age are employed in the cotton-mills for 9 hours a day.

The average of working hours and of wages weekly in 1840 and 1880 were as follows :—

	Hours Weekly		Wages, Shillings Weekly		Pence per Hour	
	1840	1880	1840	1880	1840	1880
Great Britain .	69	52	12	24	2.1	5.5
France . . .	78	60	6	19	0.9	3.8
Germany . . .	83	60	4	16	0.6	3.2
United States .	78	60	15	28	2.3	5.6
Belgium . . .	...	62	...	20	...	3.9
Italy	...	72	...	15	...	2.5

The working hours average 72 per week in Russia, 64 in Holland, 66 in Switzerland and Austria. Wages average 16s. in Spain.

The cost of erecting and equipping a factory was estimated by M'Culloch at £100 per operative. Port Dundas factory, near Glasgow, has a chimney 454 feet high, supposed to be the highest in the world.

FAIRS

In that of Leipzig the annual average of sales is four millions sterling, comprising 20,000 tons of merchandise, of which 8000 tons are books.

The fair of Nijni-Novgorod is the greatest in the world, the returns showing :—

Year	Goods Offered	Goods Sold
	£	£
1841	8,000,000	7,000,000
1857	13,000,000	12,000,000
1876	30,000,000	28,000,000

This fair is attended by 150,000 dealers from all parts of the world, and the goods sold in 1876 were :—

	£
Cottons, linens, &c.	8,000,000
Furs, leather, &c.	7,000,000
Ural metals	7,000,000
Flour, fish, brandy	3,000,000
Tea and luxuries	3,000,000
Total . . .	28,000,000

FAMINES

Walford mentions 160 since the eleventh century, viz. :—

England . .	57	Scotland . .	12	Germany . .	11
Ireland . .	34	France . . .	10	Italy, &c., .	36

The worst in modern times have been :—

In	Date	Victims
France	1770	48,000
Ireland	1816–17	737,000
Ireland	1846–47	1,009,000
India	1866	1,450,000
India	1877	500,000
China	1878	9,500,000

The number of victims in Ireland in 1816–17 was stated by Murchison and Kennedy as above.

The Commissioners' report for 1846–47 reduced the number of victims to 600,000 by supposing " that 500,000 Irish went into Great Britain, and that the ordinary death-rate of Irish population is 22 per thousand yearly." Neither supposition was correct, the Census of 1851 showing that only 314,000 Irish had removed to England and Scotland, and the Registrar-General's report for 16 years ending 1880 showing that the normal death-rate of Ireland is 17 per 1000. In 1851 the number of persons missing in Ireland was 3,157,000, accounted for in this manner :—

	Official Report	Real Figures
Emigrated . . .	1,079,000	1,079,000
Went to Great Britain . .	500,000	314,000
Natural deaths . . .	978,000	755,000
Died of famine . . .	600,000	1,009,000
Accounted for . . .	3,157,000	3,157,000

Deaths from hunger and destitution in the United Kingdom average more than 500 per annum, and are most frequent in London. In 1879 the deaths recorded from this cause were :—

	Number	Per 1000 Deaths
London	101	1.2
England	312	0.6
Ireland	3,789	37.6
France	260	0.3

In England there were 60 male to 40 female victims ; in France 85 to 15. In London the real number of victims was much greater, many of the suicides resulting from hunger. In 1880 Mr. Forster said the Irish death-rate was 10 per cent. over the average of five years. In 1879–80 there were 17,200 extra deaths, apparently caused by destitution, in Ireland.

FASTING

1684. Four men taken alive out of a mine in England, after 24 days without food.

1880. Dr. Tanner, New York, lived on water 40 days, losing 36 lbs. weight.

On December 14, 1810, a pig was buried alive by fall of a cliff at Dover, and on May 23, 1811, it was dug out alive, after 160 days.

In 1870, during the siege of Metz, a dog that was accidentally locked in a room passed 39 days without food and recovered.

FINANCE

The revenue of the principal countries was approximately as follows :—

	1680	1750	1810	1850	1889
	£	£	£	£	£
United Kingdom . . .	2,120,000	9,200,000	55,800,000	58,200,000	88,500,000
France	4,800,000	14,200,000	40,000,000	51,000,000	121,800,000
Germany	2,000,000	7,000,000	11,500,000	23,800,000	154,700,000
Russia	400,000	1,600,000	11,000,000	39,000,000	88,800,000
Austria	...	4,000,000	10,400,000	20,000,000	74,800,000
Italy	...	1,500,000	4,600,000	12,000,000	72,000,000
Spain	1,930,000	3,320,000	6,000,000	11,500,000	35,400,000
Portugal	...	...	1,200,000	3,200,000	8,400,000
Sweden	...	...	1,000,000	1,500,000	4,800,000
Norway	...	...	...	800,000	2,400,000
Denmark	...	...	1,100,000	1,500,000	3,000,000
Holland	...	2,200,000	4,800,000	5,800,000	10,100,000
Belgium	...	...	...	4,700,000	12,900,000
Switzerland	...	...	...	1,000,000	2,900,000
Greece	...	...	...	1,000,000	3,100,000
Turkey, &c.	...	...	3,000,000	9,000,000	23,200,000
Europe	15,000,000	35,000,000	150,400,000	244,000,000	706,800,000
United States	...	...	1,900,000	9,200,000	80,600,000
Australia	...	...	...	900,000	27,600,000
Canada	...	...	...	1,100,000	7,800,000
India	...	...	15,600,000	27,600,000	69,100,000
South Africa	...	...	...	500,000	4,000,000
Argentina	...	...	200,000	900,000	5,400,000
Brazil	...	...	1,800,000	4,000,000	14,100,000
Chile	...	...	...	1,000,000	5,000,000
Peru	...	...	...	2,000,000	1,500,000
Venezuela	...	...	...	500,000	1,000,000
Colombia	...	...	...	500,000	1,000,000
Mexico	...	...	...	3,000,000	5,400,000
Egypt	...	...	...	4,000,000	9,700,000
Persia	...	...	...	1,500,000	1,700,000
Japan	...	...	...	5,000,000	13,100,000
China	...	...	...	18,000,000	26,000,000
Cuba	...	...	...	1,500,000	2,500,000
The world .	18,000,000	40,000,000	180,000,000	325,200,000	982,200,000

The revenue of nations has trebled since 1850, multiplied 5½ times since 1810, and 55 times since 1680. The various blanks in the above table from 1680 to 1810 show that the revenue cannot be stated for those countries ; approximate totals are nevertheless given, for comparison.

R

The revenue of the various nations since 1820 is shown approximately in million £ annual averages, as follows :—

	1821-40	1841-50	1851-60	1861-70	1871-80	1881-88
U. Kingdom	64	61	68	71	77	88
France	40	50	60	78	105	140
Germany	16	21	34	40	73	110
Russia	22	33	38	46	60	74
Austria	13	18	28	44	61	68
Italy	9	11	20	43	53	63
Spain	8	10	12	20	30	33
Portugal	2	3	4	5	6	8
Sweden and Norway	2	2	3	4	7	7
Denmark	1	2	2	2	3	3
Holland	3	5	7	8	9	10
Belgium	3	4	5	7	9	13
Turkey	5	7	9	11	14	16
Other countries	1	2	3	5	8	11
Europe	189	229	293	384	515	644
United States	5	6	12	37	62	76
Egypt	3	4	5	7	8	9
India	19	24	33	46	56	73
British Colonies	1	2	7	15	23	36
Other countries	20	24	33	42	60	72
The world	237	289	383	531	724	910

If we take the year 1840 for point of departure, we find the expenditure per inhabitant in the principal countries has risen as follows :—

	1840	1850	1860	1870	1881	1881-88
U. Kingdom	100	100	125	113	118	120
France	100	103	135	147	200	247
Germany	100	113	120	167	267	360
Russia	100	130	150	190	200	180
Austria	100	130	140	170	200	215
Italy	100	155	190	170	200	240
Spain	100	121	150	242	242	230
United States	100	117	133	500	351	333
Australia	100	90	375	360	424	570
Canada	100	114	128	142	192	285

The average annual revenues from different sources in the decade 1871-80 were as follows :—

	Customs	Property-Tax	Various	Total
	£	£	£	£
U. Kingdom	20,100,000	6,600,000	50,600,000	77,300,000
France	10,300,000	8,700,000	85,500,000	104,500,000
Germany	8,600,000	10,500,000	53,500,000	72,600,000
Russia	8,500,000	10,300,000	41,500,000	60,300,000
Austria	2,600,000	9,400,000	44,000,000	56,000,000
Italy	5,000,000	13,000,000	35,400,000	53,400,000
Spain	4,400,000	9,600,000	15,800,000	29,800,000
Portugal	1,800,000	800,000	3,200,000	5,800,000
Holland	400,000	1,800,000	6,500,000	8,700,000
Belgium	800,000	1,500,000	7,000,000	9,300,000
Denmark	1,000,000	500,000	1,200,000	2,700,000
Sweden and Norway	2,400,000	500,000	4,000,000	6,900,000
Europe	65,900,000	73,200,000	348,200,000	487,300,000
U. States	26,000,000	...	36,200,000	62,200,000
Canada	2,700,000	...	2,200,000	4,900,000
Australia	4,100,000	...	10,100,000	14,200,000
Brazil	6,700,000	400,000	2,200,000	9,300,000
Egypt	800,000	5,000,000	2,300,000	8,100,000
India	2,200,000	21,100,000	31,800,000	55,100,000
The world	108,400,000	99,700,000	430,000,000	641,100,000

The expenditure of the principal nations in 1887 appeared under the principal heads as follows :—

	Government	Debt	Army and Navy	Total
	£	£	£	£
U.Kingdom	30,200,000	27,900,000	31,900,000	90,000,000
France	41,000,000	52,800,000	31,400,000	125,200,000
Germany	82,300,000	16,700,000	31,000,000	130,000,000
Russia	30,500,000	28,100,000	25,000,000	83,600,000
Austria	44,200,000	16,200,000	13,600,000	74,000,000
Italy	34,700,000	20,700,000	14,200,000	69,600,000
Spain	15,800,000	10,900,000	7,300,000	34,000,000
Portugal	4,000,000	3,600,000	1,400,000	9,000,000
Sweden and Norway	5,100,000	700,000	1,400,000	7,200,000
Denmark	1,300,000	500,000	1,200,000	3,000,000
Holland	5,500,000	3,100,000	2,800,000	11,400,000
Belgium	7,900,000	3,900,000	2,000,000	13,800,000
Switzerland	1,600,000	...	800,000	2,400,000
Greece	1,700,000	1,500,000	600,000	3,800,000
Roumania	1,200,000	2,700,000	1,300,000	5,200,000
Servia	700,000	500,000	600,000	1,800,000
Europe	307,700,000	189,800,000	166,500,000	664,000,000
U. States	34,700,000	9,900,000	11,200,000	55,800,000
Total	342,400,000	199,700,000	177,700,000	719,800,000

The above does not include Turkey, whose expenditure is about 16 millions sterling.

National expenditure at various dates since 1830 was as follows :—

Millions Sterling							
	1830	1840	1850	1860	1870	1881	1881-88
United Kingdom	55	52	55	73	70	83	88
France	41	57	60	83	90	121	160
Germany	16	22	28	32	51	90	127
Russia	23	30	42	56	69	80	95
Austria	18	28	39	45	59	75	82
Italy	12	19	31	37	41	56	72
Spain	9	11	14	21	33	33	36
Portugal	2	3	4	4	5	8	9
Holland	3	5	7	7	8	10	11
Belgium	3	5	6	7	7	11	14
Denmark	2	2	2	2	3	2	3
Sweden and Norway	2	2	2	3	5	7	8
Greece	1	1	1	1	2	5	3
Roumania	...	...	...	...	...	5	5
Turkey	4	6	8	13	21	13	16
Europe	191	243	299	383	464	598	729
United States	3	5	7	12	58	54	55
Mexico	3	3	4	6	5	4	5
S. American Republics	2	2	3	4	8	11	15
Brazil	2	3	5	6	8	11	15
Canada	1	1	2	3	4	6	10
Australia	1	1	1	8	12	20	33
Cape Colony	1	1	1	1	2	5	6
Egypt	2	2	3	5	14	8	9
India	22	25	28	52	35	76	77
Java	2	4	5	6	8	11	11
Japan	...	...	...	...	...	11	11
The world	230	290	358	486	638	815	976

In the above table the expenditure for Germany includes the budgets of Prussia, Bavaria, Saxony, and the minor States. It does not include State expenditure in the United States, nor local taxes in any country.

The following table shows approximately the chief sources of revenue in 1890 (or latest year), how much is raised by taxation, how much for public services :—

| | Amount, £ | | | | | Shillings per Inhabitant |
	Direct Taxes	Customs	Other Taxes	Public Services	Total	
United Kingdom	15,300,000	20,000,000	38,200,000	15,000,000	88,500,000	46
France	17,900,000	15,000,000	69,100,000	19,800,000	121,800,000	64
Germany	12,500,000	13,500,000	38,900,000	89,800,000	154,700,000	65
Russia	8,200,000	12,100,000	40,900,000	27,600,000	88,800,000	20
Austria	11,700,000	3,900,000	34,500,000	24,700,000	74,800,000	39
Italy	16,200,000	10,600,000	27,000,000	18,200,000	72,000,000	48
Spain	12,400,000	6,900,000	12,600,000	3,500,000	35,400,000	38
Portugal	1,000,000	3,100,000	2,500,000	1,800,000	8,400,000	38
Sweden	600,000	2,100,000	1,000,000	1,100,000	4,800,000	20
Norway	...	1,100,000	400,000	900,000	2,400,000	24
Denmark	500,000	1,400,000	600,000	500,000	3,000,000	30
Holland	2,300,000	400,000	5,600,000	1,800,000	10,100,000	44
Belgium	2,100,000	1,100,000	3,600,000	6,100,000	12,900,000	43
Switzerland	...	1,200,000	600,000	1,100,000	2,900,000	20
Greece	900,000	700,000	800,000	700,000	3,100,000	31
Europe	101,600,000	93,100,000	276,300,000	212,600,000	683,600,000	45
United States	...	46,600,000	27,200,000	6,800,000	80,600,000	26
Canada	...	4,500,000	1,300,000	2,000,000	7,800,000	31
Australia	...	8,200,000	2,500,000	16,900,000	27,600,000	150
India	19,500,000	1,200,000	26,800,000	21,600,000	69,100,000	7
Argentina	800,000	3,900,000	400,000	300,000	5,400,000	30
Total	121,900,000	157,500,000	334,500,000	260,200,000	874,100,000	...

Expenditure compared with population at the above date thus :—

| | Shillings per Inhabitant | | | | | | |
	1830	1840	1850	1860	1870	1881	1881-88
United Kingdom	46	40	40	50	45	47	48
France	25	34	35	46	50	68	84
Germany	12	15	17	18	25	40	54
Russia	9	10	13	15	19	20	18
Austria	15	20	26	28	34	40	43
Italy	15	20	31	38	34	40	48
Spain	16	18	20	27	40	40	42
Portugal	11	17	20	20	24	36	40
Holland	24	34	46	44	46	50	52
Belgium	18	25	27	25	28	42	50
Denmark	36	35	33	31	34	24	30
Sweden and Norway	10	10	10	12	17	22	25
Greece	20	20	20	16	34	45	40
Roumania	...	...	...	...	...	19	20
Turkey	7	10	13	18	27	60	70
Europe	16	20	22	28	31	39	45
United States	4	6	7	8	30	21	20
Brazil	7	9	12	15	18	23	26
Canada	10	14	16	18	20	27	40
Australia	40	33	30	125	120	141	188
Cape Colony	...	30	28	49	27	90	100
India	5	5	5	7	7	8	8
Java	7	10	10	10	10	12	12
Egypt	12	12	27	40	56	30	33
Argentine Republic	10	10	10	15	34	40	44
Chili	7	7	15	13	21	35	38
The world	11	13	14	18	22	25	28

It appears that since 1830 the annual public expenditure in Europe per head of population has trebled, but that in the United Kingdom there has been no sensible increase. The ratio per inhabitant has, meantime, risen more in the United States, Canada, Australia, and Argentina than in Europe.

The revenue and expenditure of the principal countries since 1870 have been as follows :—

| | 1871-88 | | |
| | Amount in Million £ | | |
	Revenue	Expenditure	Surplus Expenditure
United Kingdom	1,474	1,467	...
France	2,170	2,935	765
Germany	1,610	1,880	270
Russia	1,192	1,606	414
Austria	1,154	1,342	188
Italy	1,034	1,161	127
Spain	564	784	220
United States	1,228	964	...
Australia	333	464	131
Canada	109	139	30
India	1,152	1,230	78
Other countries	2,500	2,792	292
Total	14,520	16,764	2,244

The revenue and expenditure of Europe were approximately as follows :—

| | Millions Sterling £ | | |
	Revenue	Expenditure	Surplus Expenditure
1821-40	3,780	3,840	60
1841-50	2,290	2,320	30
1851-60	2,930	3,400	470
1861-70	3,840	4,760	920
1871-80	5,080	6,030	950
1881-88	5,150	6,110	960
68 years	23,070	26,460	3,390

In 38 years, from 1851 to 1888, the expenditure surpassed income by 3300 millions sterling, say 87 millions yearly, which went mostly in wars and armaments.

The public debt, stated in millions £ sterling, was as follows :—

	1713	1763	1793	1816	1848	1870	1889
Great Britain .	54	147	370	900	773	801	698
France . . .	48	110	32	140	260	504	1,269
Germany . .	...	...	...	39	69	148	435
Russia . . .	...	...	47	145	90	342	756
Austria . . .	10	15	42	99	125	340	580
Italy	...	...	...	25	36	333	460
Spain . . .	7	11	20	117	113	285	260
Portugal . . .	...	...	1	7	22	59	113
Holland . . .	...	...	70	110	114	76	89
Belgium . . .	...	...	...	...	25	28	77
Denmark . .	...	...	2	12	12	13	11
Sweden and } Norway . }	...	...	...	...	2	6	20
Greece . . .	...	...	...	...	10	18	23
Turkey . . .	...	...	...	...	...	92	180
Roumania . .	...	...	...	...	...	...	36
Servia . . .	...	...	...	...	...	...	13
Europe . . .	119	283	584	1,594	1,651	3,045	5,020
United States .	...	...	17	26	10	485	221
Spanish America	...	...	...	...	17	135	333
Canada . . .	...	...	...	...	5	17	49
Australia . .	...	...	...	...	...	37	171
India	...	..	9	29	51	108	186
Japan . . .	...	...	...	...	2	10	50
Egypt . . .	...	...	...	...	...	37	163
South Africa .	...	...	...	...	...	2	27
The world .	119	283	610	1,649	1,736	3,876	6,160

Debt has multiplied tenfold in ninety-six years. The annual increase since 1870 has averaged 118 millions sterling. The increase from the date of the Treaty of Utrecht, 1713, to the present is shown in successive stages thus :—

Period	Millions, £	Per Annum
		£
1713-63	164	3,300,000
1764-93	327	10,900,000
1794-1816	1,039	45,200,000
1817-1848	87	2,700,000
1849-70	2,140	97,300,000
1871-89	2,244	118,100,000
176 years . . , .	6,001	34,100,000

The origin of the debt may be approximately summed up thus :—

War and armaments . . . 3,610 millions
Railways and telegraph . . . 1,450 ,,
Roads and bridges . . . 780 ,,
Sundries . . . . . 161 ,,
                                    ─────
                                   6,001

In 1889 the interest which bondholders received, taking the various loans of nations at the prices current in the market, were as follows per £100 per annum.

	£		£
United Kingdom .	. 2.7	Austria . . .	. 4.3
United States .	. 3.1	Chile . . .	. 4.3
Belgium . .	. 3.2	Russia . .	. 4.6
Holland .	. 3.3	Brazil . .	. 4.8
New South Wales .	. 3.4	Spain . .	. 4.9
Canada . .	. 3.5	Portugal . .	. 5.0
Switzerland .	. 3.5	Argentina . .	. 5.1
France . .	. 3.6	Egypt . .	. 5.1
Victoria . .	. 3.5	China . .	. 5.4
Cape Colony .	. 3.6	Buenos Ayres .	. 5.9
Prussia . .	. 3.7	Hawaii . .	. 6.0
Norway . .	. 3.7	Santa Fé .	. 6.0
Sweden . .	. 3.8	Japan . .	. 6.3
New Zealand .	. 3.9	Uruguay .	. 6.6

The following table shows approximately the wealth and debt of the principal nations in 1888 :—

	Millions £ Sterling		
	Wealth	Debt	Ratio of Debt
United Kingdom . .	9,400	698	7.7
France . . .	8,598	1,269	14.7
Germany . . .	6,437	435	6.8
Russia . . .	5,089	756	14.8
Austria . . .	3,855	580	15.0
Italy . . .	2,963	460	15.5
Spain . . .	2,516	260	10.3
Portugal . . .	408	113	27.5
Sweden and Norway .	880	20	2.2
Denmark . . .	404	11	2.8
Holland . . .	980	89	9.1
Belgium . . .	1,007	77	7.6
Switzerland . .	494	17	3.5
Greece . . .	300	23	7.7
Roumania . . .	593	36	6.1
Servia . . .	217	13	6.0
Turkey . . .	593	180	30.3
Europe . . .	44,734	5,037	11.2
United States . .	12,824	221	1.7
Canada . . .	980	49	5.0
Australia . . .	1,373	171	12.5
South Africa . .	135	27	20.0
Argentina . .	509	110	21.6
Total . .	60,555	5,615	9.3

For local finances see *Local Taxation*.

UNITED KINGDOM

The financial year ends March 31. The various principal items of revenue and expenditure for 52 years to date are shown as follows :—

REVENUE IN MILLIONS £ STERLING

	1837-51	1852-61	1862-71	1872-81	1882-89	52 Years
Customs	324	237	221	199	159	1,140
Excise	216	181	204	268	210	1,079
Stamps . . .	101	78	94	110	95	478
Income-tax . .	55	102	78	71	103	409
Post-office . .	25	30	45	74	79	253
Sundries . . .	66	50	69	77	58	320
Total . .	787	678	711	799	704	3,679

EXPENDITURE IN MILLIONS £ STERLING

Years	Millions £.			
	Govern-ment	Debt	Army and Navy	Total
1837-51	139	395	219	753
1852-61	136	285	288	709
1862-71	164	265	263	692
1872-81	233	281	280	794
1882-89	238	222	247	707
52 years	910	1,448	1,297	3,655

Expenditure includes sums paid for redemption of national debt, and as this has been reduced 94 millions during the present reign, the net expenditure may be set down thus :—

	Millions £	Per Annum, £
Revenue of 52 years . . .	3,679	70,700,000
Reduction of debt . . .	94	1,800,000
Real expenditure	3,585	68,900,000

The following table shows approximately the revenue and expenditure from the accession of William III. to the present time :—

Reign	Date	Millions £		Annual Average, £		Public Debt, Millions £
		Revenue	Expenditure	Revenue	Expenditure	
William III.	1689–1702	59	72	4,500,000	5,500,000	13
Anne	1702–14	62	122	5,200,000	10,200,000	73
George I.	1714–27	77	80	5,900,000	6,100,000	76
George II.	1727–60	217	276	6,600,000	8,400,000	135
George III.	1760–1820	1,666	2,252*	27,800,000	37,500,000	900
George IV.	1820–30	648	608	64,800,000	60,800,000	800
William IV.	1830–37	439	431	62,400,000	61,300,000	792
Victoria	1837–51	787	753	60,500,000	57,900,000	787
,, ...	1852–61	678	709	67,800,000	70,900,000	819
,, ...	1862–71	711	692	71,100,000	69,200,000	798
,, ...	1872–81	799	794	79,900,000	79,400,000	772
,, ...	1882–89	704	707	88,000,000	88,400,000	698

The following table shows the revenue of England down to 1707, of Great Britain from 1713 to 1810, and of the United Kingdom from the last-mentioned year down to date. The groat, 4d., from William the Conqueror down to Edward III., had more than three times as much silver as our shilling of to-day ; hence the real amount in silver must be distinguished from the nominal. The purchasing power of £1 sterling has also varied, and in the following table this is likewise given :—

Date	Reign	Nominal	In Silver	Purchasing Value	Shillings per Inhab.
					In Silver
		£	£	£	
1080	William I.	400,000	1,320,000	4,010,000	12
1090	Rufus	350,000	1,150,000	3,520,000	10
1120	Henry I.	300,000	990,000	3,005,000	9
1150	Stephen	250,000	830,000	2,510,000	8
1180	Henry II.	200,000	660,000	2,005,000	6
1210	John	100,000	330,000	1,000,000	3
1250	Henry III.	80,000	264,000	800,000	2⅔
1300	Edward I.	150,000	495,000	1,502,000	4½
1350	Edward III.	154,000	460,000	1,360,000	4
1400	Henry IV.	100,000	264,000	900,000	2
1480	Edward IV.	100,000	162,000	530,000	1
1500	Henry VII.	400,000	650,000	2,100,000	3
1540	Henry VIII.	800,000	1,300,000	2,600,000	6
1600	Elizabeth	500,000	550,000	1,000,000	2
1620	James I.	600,000	640,000	1,000,000	2¼
1640	Charles I.	896,000	950,000	1,300,000	4¾
1662	Charles II.	1,800,000	1,910,000	2,300,000	7
1686	James II.	2,002,000	2,120,000	2,300,000	8
1700	William III.	3,895,000	4,135,000	...	15
1713	Anne	5,692,000	6,030,000	...	18
1716	George I.	6,763,000	7,160,000	...	21
1728	George II.	8,523,000	9,030,000	...	25
1780	George III.	8,880,000	9,420,000	...	20
1790	,,	13,745,000	14,540,000	...	29
1800	,,	37,520,000	39,700,000	...	76
1810	,,	52,672,000	55,810,000	...	93
1820	George IV.	61,634,000	61,634,000	...	62
1830	William IV.	59,365,000	59,365,000	...	50
1840	Victoria	52,916,000	52,916,000	...	40
1850	,,	58,205,000	58,205,000	...	43
1860	,,	71,090,000	71,090,000	...	49
1870	,,	75,434,000	75,434,000	...	49
1880	,,	81,265,000	81,265,000	...	47
1889	,,	88,470,000	88,470,000	...	49

The value of the £ sterling in gold and silver coin was unaltered from the time of James II. until the year 1817, when the currency was debased 5 per cent., the same quantity of metal serving for 21s. as previously for 20s.

The following table shows the incidence of revenue and expenditure per inhabitant during the present reign :—

SHILLINGS PER INHABITANT YEARLY

	Revenue				Expenditure			
	Customs	Excise	Sundries	Total	Army, &c.	Debt	Government	Total
1837–51	16.7	11.2	14.1	42.0	11.9	21.3	7.5	40.7
1852–61	16.9	12.8	18.5	48.2	20.5	20.3	9.7	50.5
1862–71	14.7	13.5	18.9	47.1	17.5	17.7	10.9	46.1
1872–81	12.2	16.2	20.2	48.6	16.9	17.0	14.2	48.1
1882–89	11.0	14.5	23.1	48.6	17.0	15.2	16.3	48.5

The following table shows the outlay compared with population over the whole period of 52 years, taking the mean population at 32 million souls :—

	Expenditure, Millions £	Average, £ Yearly	Shillings per Inhabitant Yearly
Army and navy .	1,297	24,940,000	15.7
Debt	1,354	26,040,000	16.3
Redemption of debt . . . }	94	1,810,000	1.1
Government . .	910	17,500,000	11.0
Total . .	3,655	70,290,000	44.1

The following table shows how the three kingdoms contribute to the national revenue (1888) :—

	"Economist" Estimates			
	England, £	Scotland, £	Ireland, £	U. Kingdom, £
Stamps . .	7,440,000	840,000	440,000	8,720,000
Customs .	16,130,000	1,640,000	2,020,000	19,790,000
Excise . .	16,680,000	4,680,000	4,260,000	25,620,000
Income-tax .	12,500,000	1,180,000	600,000	14,280,000
Land, &c. .	2,790,000	160,000	...	2,950,000
Total .	55,540,000	8,500,000	7,320,000	71,360,000

* Loans amounting nominally to 733 millions sterling were emitted, the net product of which was 526 millions, which helped to meet deficit, there being also 60 millions of floating debt, which brings up the total expenditure to 2252 millions.

The above compare with the Treasury estimates thus :—

	Economist, £	Treasury, £	Ratio Economist	Ratio Treasury
England . .	55,540,000	58,860,000	77.8	81.0
Scotland .	8,500,000	7,790,000	11.9	10.7
Ireland . .	7,320,000	6,080,000	10.3	8.3
Total .	71,360,000	72,730,000	100.0	100.0

If we compare the income-tax assessments with the share of revenue raised in each of the three kingdoms, we find, taking the latter at a medium between the "Economist" and the Treasury estimates, as follows :—

	Assessed Incomes	Revenue	Ratio of Latter to Income,
	£	£	£
England . .	542,500,000	57,200,000	10.6
Scotland . .	57,200,000	8,200,000	14.3
Ireland . . .	36,600,000	6,700,000	18.0
Total .	636,300,000	72,100,000	11.3

It would appear that England bears much less than her share, and the sister kingdoms a great deal too much.

Debt.—The National Debt began with William III., and reached its maximum in 1816, after the overthrow of Bonaparte, when the amount was variously estimated, viz. :—

	£
Doubleday	944,152,000
Porter	885,186,000
M'Culloch	840,850,000

The last mentioned appears to have regarded only the funded debt, the total, according to Whittaker, having stood thus in January 1816 :—

	£
Funded	816,312,000
Unfunded	44,727,000
Terminable annuities . .	39,397,000
Total . .	900,436,000

The estimated wealth of the nation, according to the best authorities, may be placed side by side with the debt to show the relative magnitude of the latter at different epochs :—

Date	Millions £ Stg. Wealth	Millions £ Stg. Debt	Ratio of Debt	£ per Inhab. Wealth	£ per Inhab. Debt	Obs.
1702	490	13	2.7	72	2	England
1763	1,100	147	13.4	156	21	G. Britain
1797	1,800	413	22.9	177	41	,,
1816	2,400	900	37.5	120	45	U. K.
1837	3,900	788	20.2	158	32	,,
1860	5,560	826	14.9	193	29	,,
1870	7,080	801	11.3	230	26	,,
1889	9,400	698	7.4	250	19	,,

The history of the National Debt may be briefly explained thus :—

	Millions £	Date
Wars of William and Anne .	73	1689–1712
Conquest of Canada . .	62	1759–61
American war	121	1775–80
Campaigns against Bonaparte .	581	1793–1815
Malversation in Ireland . .	63	1802–16
Total in 1816 .	900	

The war loans negotiated by George II. and George III. amounted to 794 millions sterling, but produced in reality only 585 millions, or 73 per cent. of the written value, viz. :—

Years	Nominal Amount	Realised	Annual Charge	Actual Interest
	£	£	£	
1756–63	60,670,000	59,500,000	2,315,000	3.90
1776–84	114,687,000	92,700,000	5,012,000	5.40
1785–1816	618,404,000	433,000,000	23,387,000	5.40
60 years	793,761,000	585,200,000	30,714,000	5.25

The principal conversions of debt were the following :—

Date	Minister	Sum, £	Annual Saving, £
1716	Walpole	32,500,000	325,000
1749	Pelham	56,500,000	565,000
1822	Vansittart	153,000,000	1,530,000
1824	Robinson	76,000,000	380,000
1830	Goulburn	153,000,000	760,000
1844	,,	248,000,000	1,240,000
1860–74	Gladstone	59,000,000	330,000
1884	,,	79,000,000	...
1888	Goschen	549,100,000	1,400,000

Walpole and Vansittart converted 5 into 4 per cents., Pelham 4 into 3 per cents., Robinson 4 into 3½ per cents. The conversions effected by Gladstone were connected with sums held in the Court of Chancery and Savingsbank funds. Goschen's conversion reduced the 3 per cents. into new stock bearing 2¾ per cent. for a number of years, after which to be reduced to 2½ per cents., which latter will lead to an annual saving of £2,800,000, as compared with the interest payable in 1887.

In March 1889 the debt was made up thus :—

	£
Funded	607,058,000
Terminable annuities . .	75,279,000
Unfunded debt	16,093,000
Total . . .	698,430,000

The following table shows the quotations of Consols :—

Period	Debt, Millions £	Quotations Maximum	Quotations Minimum	Quotations Average	Year of Highest	Year of Lowest
1740–60 . . .	78	104	82	93.5	1749	...
1761–80 . .	139	91	61	82.1	...	1780
1781–1800 . .	240	97	47	67.2	...	1798
1801–20 . . .	841	84	50	64.9	1817	1803
1821–40 . . .	781	97	69	85.8	1824	1821
1841–60 . . .	786	102	79	93.4	1852	1847
1861–81 . . .	776	103	84	93.1	1867	1866
1882–88 . . .	740	103	96	100.8	1883	1885

The following table shows the number of holders of Consols at various dates :—

Average, £	1830	1848	1880
100,000	172	177	283
50,000	1,810	1,550	1,892
10,000	22,189	20,561	19,140
3,000	124,014	120,487	112,077
500	132,960	141,352	103,122
Total	281,145	284,127	236,514

Unclaimed dividends in March 1882 amounted to £3,027,000.

When Mr. Goschen converted the debt in 1889, no fewer than 12,700 notices were returned by the Post-Office as "not known." After every inquiry, £7,850,000 was unclaimed, and credited to 10,900 accounts in the Bank of England ; most were probably dead or gone away.

SCOTLAND

Official returns of Scottish revenue show as follows :—

Period	Annual Average	Per Inhabitant
	£	£ s. d.
1804–09 . . .	3,500,000	2 1 0
1810–15 . . .	4,950,000	2 15 0

In the estimate already given for 1881 the revenue of Scotland appears as £9,990,000, or 54s. per inhabitant, almost the same as the ratio of 75 years ago.

IRELAND

Ware says that the revenue of the royal palace at Kincora was 5100 horned cattle, 100 horses, and 4800 swine, contributed yearly by the various chieftains. Noy states that Edward III. drew £30,000 from Ireland for the campaigns of the Black Prince. Henry VII. levied a duty of 5 per cent. *ad valorem* on all Irish imports and exports, which would probably produce £10,000 a year. Regular records were kept under William III. and subsequent monarchs, which show as follows :—

Period	Annual Average, £	Per Inhab.
		£ s. d.
1690–1700	640,000	0 7 6
1730–60	620,000	0 6 3
1761–70	890,000	0 6 8
1771–80	1,340,000	0 9 6
1790	2,162,000	0 11 0
1802–10	5,480,000	1 0 2
1811–16	7,400,000	1 5 0
1817–20	5,850,000	0 17 0
1821–30	4,930,000	0 14 0

In 1801 the Act of Union ordained the revenues and debt of Ireland to be kept distinct. The debt was :—

Year	£
1784	1,997,000
1793	2,220,000
1801	31,950,000
1809	77,445,000

The finances got into very bad hands after the Union. The Budgets of Ireland from 1802 to 1816 summed up as follows :—

Period	Revenue	Expenditure	Deficit
	£	£	£
1802–10 . . .	49,400,000	89,500,000	40,100,000
1811–16 . . .	44,200,000	90,300,000	46,100,000
15 years . . .	93,600,000	179,800,000	86,200,000

In 1817 Great Britain took over the Irish debt and amalgamated the finances of the two countries, but separate statements of revenue were published down to 1831, from which date none have been kept. The revenue from 1821 to 1830 was made up thus :—

	Annual Average, £
Customs	1,920,000
Excise	1,940,000
Sundries	1,070,000
Total . .	4,930,000

FRANCE

The revenue at various periods has been as follows :—

Date	Reign	Amount	Per Inhabitant	National Debt, Millions £
		£	£ s. d.	
1252	Louis IX. . .	140,000	0 0 4	...
1380	Charles V. .	120,000	0 0 4	...
1460	Charles VII. .	150,000	0 0 4	...
1546	Francis I. .	640,000	0 1 0	...
1607	Henry IV. .	1,300,000*	0 2 0	...
1661	Louis XIV. .	3,400,000	0 4 0	...
1683	,,	4,800,000	0 5 6	48
1742	Louis XV. .	13,700,000	0 13 0	110
1775	Louis XVI. .	14,800,000	0 12 0	129
1786	,,	20,800,000	0 16 0	200
1791	,,	27,800,000	1 2 0	468
1814	Napoleon I. .	40,000,000	1 7 0	50
1830	Charles X. .	36,500,000	1 2 6	187
1846	Louis Philippe	46,400,000	1 7 0	260
1850	Republic . .	51,000,000	1 9 0	248
1860	Napoleon III. .	68,500,000	1 16 0	410
1870	,,	87,600,000	2 6 0	504
1880	Republic . .	135,700,000	3 10 0	1,060
1889	,, . .	121,800,000	3 5 0	1,269

* The gross revenue, including tithes and local taxes, was £3,800,000 ; the royal revenue as here given.

The following is an official statement of national revenue and expenditure during 71 years to 1885 :—

Period	Millions £ Sterling		
	Revenue	Expenditure	Excess of Latter
1815–20 . . .	211	257	46
1821–30 . . .	384	402	18
1831–40 . . .	419	458	39
1841–50 . . .	504	610	106
1851–60 . . .	619	762	143
1861–70 . . .	781	926	145
1871–80 . . .	1,151	1,301	150
1881–85 . . .	687	814	127
71 years . . .	4,756	5,530	774

Some extraordinary items, such as the indemnity to Germany in 1872, are omitted. The above may be also stated according to the successive forms of government as follows :—

Reign	Date	Millions £		Annual Average, £		Debt, Millions £
		Revenue	Expenditure	Revenue	Expenditure	
Bourbons . . .	1815–30	595	659	36,800,000	41,100,000	177
Louis Philippe . .	1831–48	749	979	47,800,000	50,600,000	230
Republic . . .	1848–52	220	280	55,000,000	70,000,000	290
Empire . . .	1853–70	1,354	1,497	74,500,000	82,200,000	468
Republic . . .	1871–80	1,151	1,301	115,100,000	130,100,000	1,060
,, . . .	1881–88	1,118	1,280	139,700,000	160,000,000	1,269
74 years . . .	...	5,187	5,996	...	...	...

During the decade 1871–80 loans were emitted to the nominal sum of 410 millions sterling, producing 329 millions, besides which about 65 millions were added to floating debt. The following table shows the expenditure at different dates :—

	1830 £	1851 £	1869 £	1877 £	1885 £
Debt	14,500,000	16,600,000	21,400,000	47,600,000	52,800,000
Army	7,500,000	11,800,000	16,800,000	21,600,000	24,000,000
Navy	2,600,000	4,200,000	7,200,000	7,700,000	12,400,000
Public works . . .	1,600,000	4,900,000	5,200,000	9,200,000	16,800,000
Government . . .	10,300,000	13,500,000	35,200,000	38,900,000	51,700,000
Total .	36,500,000	51,000,000	85,800,000	125,000,000	157,700,000

The increase in items of revenue is as follows :—

	1869 £	1875 £	1885 £	Ratio of Increase 1869	Ratio of Increase 1875	Ratio of Increase 1885
Customs	5,800,000	10,700,000	16,800,000	100	184	290
Excise	25,100,000	42,300,000	42,600,000	100	169	170
Stamps	18,200,000	24,300,000	27,000,000	100	134	149
Taxes	23,000,000	27,400,000	30,300,000	100	119	132
Post-office . . .	3,800,000	4,800,000	6,600,000	100	126	173
Sundries	8,300,000	14,500,000	18,300,000	100	175	220
Total .	84,200,000	124,000,000	141,600,000	100	148	170

The total revenue and expenditure in the decade 1871–80 were as follows :—

MILLIONS £ STERLING

	Revenue		Expenditure
Customs . .	109	Franco-German war	304
Excise . .	386	Army and navy . .	305
Stamps . . .	240	Debt and pensions .	466
Direct taxes .	271	Justice and schools .	60
Post-office . .	44	Public works . .	90
Sundries . .	101	Gen. administration .	380
Total . .	1,151	Total . .	1,605

Mr. Yves Guyot compares the rise of revenue since the Bonaparte epoch * thus :—

	1800–10	1822	1840	1860	1870	1880
Customs . .	100	154	198	190	171	408
Stamps . .	100	92	130	203	223	400
Property-tax .	100	85	85	92	102	112
Value of land	100	140	...	370	400	366

Debt.—This began with Louis XIV., who spent great sums in war and in building Versailles. It increased with John Law's state-bank, and rose in the latter years of Louis XVI. to 468 millions sterling. It was repudiated by the Republic, some creditors getting 33 per cent., the rest nothing, and thus reduced to about 30 millions sterling. At the fall of Bonaparte it was only 50 millions. Of late years the accounts published are incomplete, but M. Leroy Beaulieu estimates it now at

* The Budget for 1802 was made up thus :—

	Revenue £		Expenditure £
Land-tax . .	8,800,000	Army . . .	9,700,000
Forests . . .	7,600,000	Navy . . .	5,100,000
Customs, &c. .	6,400,000	Government .	6,200,000
Total .	22,800,000	Total .	21,000,000

1269 millions sterling, exclusive of municipal debts. The official returns are as follows :—

Year	Millions £ Sterling Funded	Millions £ Sterling Floating	Millions £ Sterling Total
1814	50	...	...
1830	177	10	187
1848	238	22	260
1852	221	27	248
1869	468	36	504
1880	794	61	855
1886	789	40	829

These returns are misleading, as it would appear from them that the debt declined 26 millions between 1880 and 1886, whereas it increased. Even the Budget returns show a deficit of 93 millions sterling in those six years, the aggregate revenue being 834 millions, expenditure 927 millions. The floating debt in 1888 was officially stated at 118 millions sterling. The following table shows the funded debt at various dates :—

Year	5 per Cent.	4½ per Cent.	4 per Cent.	3 per Cent.	Total
1814	51	...	...	...	51
1830	131	1	3	42	177
1848	117	1	26	94	238
1852	146	1	2	72	221
1871	...	33	...	465	498
1880	276	33	...	485	794
1887	...	301	...	527	828

The floating debt at different dates was stated thus :—

Year	Exchequer Bills	Savings Banks	Sundries	Total
1860	5.7	9.2	17.5	32.4
1869	4.6	10.2	17.0	31.8
1880	6.2	23.5	31.5	61.2
1888	59.1	38.4	21.0	118.5

Taking the total debt at M. Leroy Beaulieu's estimate of 1269 millions, it may be said approximately to represent the following extraordinary outlay :—

	Millions £
Bonaparte's wars	51
Restoration indemnities . . .	60
Conquest of Algeria	38
Crimean war	93
Wars in Italy, Mexico, &c. . . .	33
Franco-German	316
Sundries	678
Total . .	1269

There was a loss of 200 millions on the issue of loans, and an expenditure of 260 millions on public works, which leaves a balance of 218 millions for sundries unaccounted for. The loans issued between 1816 and 1881 were as follows :—

Period	Number of Loans	Issue, £	Realised, £	Per Cent.
1816–30	11	80,000,000	57,500,000	72
1831–48	13	95,000,000	70,400,000	74
1849–69	14	200,000,000	134,600,000	67
1870–81	6	410,000,000	329,000,000	80
Total	44	785,000,000	591,500,000	75

The interest paid yearly on the above loans was as follows :—

Period	Sum Realised, £	Interest, £	Rate
1816–30 . .	57,500,000	3,970,000	6.9
1831–48 . .	70,400,000	3,850,000	5.5
1849–69 . .	134,600,000	6,240,000	4.6
1870–81 . .	329,000,000	18,140,000	5.5

The total issues of 65 years are summed up thus :—

	Millions £
6 per cent	10
5 ,, ...	400
4½ ,, ...	16
4 ,, ...	11
3 ,, ...	348
Total	785

If we compare the debt of France with the estimated wealth at various dates, we find thus :—

Year	Millions £ Sterling		Ratio of Debt
	Wealth	Debt	
1830	3,480	187	5.3
1848	5,000	260	5.2
1869	7,000	504	7.2
1889	8,600	1,269	14.7

The burden of debt is almost double what it is in the United Kingdom. See also *Local Taxation*.

GERMANY

The revenue and debt of Prussia singly, and also of Prussia and the other States now composing the German Empire, were at various dates approximately as follows :—

Year	Prussia		Germany	
	Revenue, £	Debt, £	Revenue, £	Debt, £
1752	1,800,000	...	...	...
1786	5,400,000	...	...	...
1801	4,700,000	4,500,000	10,000,000	8,000,000
1810	2,700,000	10,000,000	11,500,000	20,000,000
1822	7,000,000	14,000,000	14,400,000	39,000,000
1850	13,300,000	27,000,000	23,800,000	69,000,000
1865	21,800,000	42,200,000	36,000,000	128,300,000
1875	34,700,000	65,000,000	85,000,000	215,000,000
1890	79,300,000	207,300,000	154,700,000	434,800,000

The revenue and expenditure of Germany since 1850 may be stated approximately as follows :—

Period	Millions £		Yearly Average	
	Revenue	Expenditure	Revenue, £	Expenditure, £
1851–70	740	850	37,000,000	42,500,000
1871–80	725	840	72,500,000	84,000,000
1881–89	1,050	1,170	117,000,000	130,000,000
39 years	2,515	2,860	64,500,000	73,300,000

Revenue, £					
	1822	1850	1867	1882	1887
Prussia	7,000,000	13,300,000	25,300,000	39,000,000	64,400,000
Bavaria	2,500,000	4,000,000	5,900,000	11,100,000	12,000,000
Wurtemburg	1,000,000	1,100,000	1,300,000	2,500,000	2,700,000
Saxony	900,000	1,400,000	2,200,000	3,200,000	3,800,000
Other States . . .	3,000,000	4,000,000	5,800,000	10,700,000	11,200,000
Total . .	14,400,000	23,800,000	40,500,000	66,500,000	94,100,000

The total for 1882 and 1887 do not include the Imperial revenue.

The revenue of Prussia from 1822 to 1833 averaged thus :—

	£
Customs	3,200,000
Land-tax	2,700,000
Sundries	1,900,000
Total . . .	7,800,000

The total revenue of Germany is made up approximately as follows :—

	£
Customs	13,500,000
Income-tax	12,500,000
Excise	22,100,000
Stamps, &c.	16,800,000
Railways	55,000,000
Post-office, domains, &c. .	34,800,000
Total . .	154,700,000

It may also be classified thus :—

	£
Imperial taxes	27,700,000
Direct State taxes . . .	13,700,000
Indirect State taxes . . .	23,500,000
Railways	55,000,000
Post-office, domains, &c. . .	34,800,000
Total . .	154,700,000

Besides the Imperial taxes the Empire receives "matricular quotas" from the several States in this order (1890) :—

	£		£
Prussia . .	7,800,000	Baden . . .	500,000
Bavaria . .	1,900,000	Alsace . .	500,000
Saxony . .	900,000	Hesse . .	260,000
Wurtemburg .	700,000	Others . .	940,000

Making a total of £13,500,000 sterling. These matricular quotas are included in the revenue of the several States. The total Budgets for 1890 may be summed up thus :—

	£
Imperial revenue	60,400,000
Prussian budget	79,300,000
Bavaria, Saxony, &c. . . .	28,500,000
Total . . .	168,200,000
Deduct repetitions . . .	13,500,000
Total revenue .	154,700,000

The reason for deducting repetitions is that the "matricular quotas" are counted in the State Budgets and also in that of the Empire.

The civil list of the Emperor is defrayed solely by Prussia, and reaches £786,000, of which £386,000 arises from crown forests, the rest from ordinary revenue.

As near as we can ascertain the debts of the several States at different periods, they stood thus :—

	1820–22	1849–50	1889
	£	£	£
Prussia	14,000,000	27,000,000	222,500,000
Bavaria	9,200,000	10,700,000	67,100,000
Saxony	3,700,000	7,000,000	32,700,000
Wurtemburg . .	2,000,000	4,800,000	21,700,000
Baden	2,000,000	3,300,000	19,400,000
Hamburg . . .	1,200,000	1,600,000	11,800,000
Brunswick . . .	1,000,000	1,500,000	3,600,000
Small States . .	6,000,000	13,100,000	10,800,000
Total . .	39,100,000	69,000,000	389,600,000

The total for 1889 does not include the Imperial debt, which is £45,200,000, bringing up the whole debt of the nation to nearly 435 millions sterling.

The debt of Germany in 1887 stood as follows :—

Class	Amount, Million £	Interest, £
4 per cents. . . .	310	12,400,000
3½ per cents. . . .	50	1,750,000
Various	59	2,550,000
Total . .	419	16,700,000

There are 20,000 miles of State railways, representing a value of 410 millions sterling, that is, practically the whole sum of public debt. Hence it would be in a manner justifiable to say that Germany has no public debt.

RUSSIA

Revenue and debt have been so violently affected by the fluctuation of currency, that they can only be taken approximately at the various dates, thus :—

				Millions £	
Year	Reign		Revenue, £	Funded Debt	Total Debt
1620	Michael . .		160,000	...	...
1725	Peter I. . .		1,600,000	...	...
1799	Paul . . .		3,900,000	7	47
1806	Alexander I. .		9,500,000	7	95
1810	,,		11,200,000	7	146
1840	Nicholas . .		17,600,000	40	150
1861	Alexander II. .		54,000,000	90	200
1875	,,		74,400,000	240	370
1889	Alexander III.		89,900,000	624	756

In 1799 the revenue was made up thus :—

Customs	700,000
Serf-tax	1,500,000
Liquor-tax	700,000
Sundries	1,000,000
Total . .	3,900,000

The finances since 1850 may be summed up approximately thus :—

Period	Millions £		Annual Average	
	Revenue	Expenditure	Revenue	Expenditure
1851–70	840	1,050	42,000,000	52,500,000
1871–80	603	903	60,300,000	90,300,000
1881–87	518	668	74,000,000	95,400,000
37 years	1,961	2,621	53,000,000	70,800,000

The items of Russian revenue and expenditure have been as follows, reduced to gold values :—

	Revenue			Expenditure	
	1875	1889		1875	1889
	£	£		£	£
Customs	8,300,000	14,100,000	Debt	14,400,000	27,900,000
Excise	29,700,000	31,100,000	Army	23,300,000	21,200,000
Poll-tax	16,000,000	8,200,000	Navy	3,500,000	4,100,000
Post-office . . .	2,100,000	2,900,000	Interior . . .	7,000,000	7,200,000
Crown lands . .	3,200,000	3,300,000	Schools . . .	1,900,000	2,100,000
Sundries . . .	15,100,000	30,300,000	Sundries . . .	22,300,000	25,700,000
Total . .	74,400,000	89,900,000	Total . .	72,400,000	88,200,000

The above includes extraordinary expenditure. New railways, for example, took 19 millions sterling during the interval of 1884–87.

Debt.—It commenced with the issue of inconvertible notes, which rose as follows:—

Year	£ Sterling	Exchange per 100 Gold Roubles
1774	3,250,000	103
1796	25,600,000	190
1800	34,600,000	220
1810	93,800,000	300
1815	145,000,000	418
1823	96,800,000	360
1843	27,000,000	100
1850	49,000,000	100
1864	113,000,000	105
1873	130,000,000	116
1880	190,000,000	170
1888	174,500,000	170

In 1843 the Empire was declared bankrupt, the Treasury calling in the paper issue of 97 millions sterling, and giving the holders new notes of 2 roubles for 7 of the old currency. The new issue began to lose value in 1864, and has now depreciated 40 per cent., a paper rouble being worth only 60 kopecks silver, that is to say, a silver rouble is worth 170 kopecks of paper-money. The first foreign loan was in 1818, which was followed by another in 1820. The growth of debt since 1842 is shown as follows:—

Year	Millions £			
	Foreign	Internal	Paper-Money	Total
1842 . . .	6	23	8	37
1852 . . .	12	61	22	95
1862 . . .	41	99	61	202
1872 . . .	105	133	104	342
1882 . . .	189	273	161	623
1888 . . .	216	408	132	756

In the above table only "uncovered" paper-money is counted under that heading. Most of the debt being payable in paper-money worth 2s. per rouble, the debt may be properly put down thus: Foreign 216, internal 324, total 540 millions sterling. The origin of the debt may be approximately set down thus:—

	Millions £
Redemption of serfs	85
Railways and telegraphs	170
Crimean war	142
Turkish war	133
Sundries	226
Total . . 756	

In 1887 the existing railway loans amounted to 143 millions sterling.

AUSTRIA-HUNGARY

The revenue and expenditure since 1831 were approximately:—

Period	Millions £		Yearly Average, £	
	Revenue	Expenditure	Revenue	Expenditure
1831–50	340	440	17,000,000	22,000,000
1851–70	720	940	36,000,000	47,000,000
1871–80	560	630	56,000,000	63,000,000
1881–88	544	652	68,000,000	81,500,000
58 years	2,164	2,662	37,300,000	46,000,000

The revenue and debt are shown approximately thus:—

Year	Millions £		Year	Millions £	
	Revenue	Debt		Revenue	Debt
1740	4	12	1862	35	252
1793	8	42	1872	51	324
1815	12	83	1880	62	420
1840	16	125	1889	78	580

The general revenue and expenditure are made up thus (1889):—

	Revenue, £		Expenditure, £
Customs . . .	3,300,000	Army . .	9,500,000
Austrian quota .	5,800,000	Navy . .	900,000
Hungarian quota	2,700,000	Sundries .	600,000
Total . .	11,800,000	Total .	11,000,000

The special budgets of Austria and Hungary may be stated thus:—

	Revenue, £	Expenditure, £
Austria	45,300,000	45,000,000
Hungary	29,500,000	29,600,000
Total . .	74,800,000	74,600,000

These Budgets include the quotas previously mentioned for the joint or general revenue. The total outlay, therefore, of the whole monarchy is £78,100,000, at the current rate of exchange in 1889, that is, 20d. to the florin.

The finances of Austria proper in 1889 were:—

	Revenue, £		Expenditure, £
Customs . . .	3,100,000	Imperial quota .	5,800,000
Excise . . .	16,800,000	Debt	12,000,000
Property-tax . .	8,500,000	Army and navy .	8,500,000
Stamps. . . .	1,600,000	Schools . . .	1,000,000
Lottery . . .	1,800,000	Board of Trade .	4,700,000
Post-office and railways }	6,200,000	Justice . . .	1,700,000
		Government . .	11,400,000
Sundries . . .	7,300,000		
Total . .	45,300,000	Total . .	45,100,000

The Hungarian budget for 1889 was as follows:—

	Revenue, £		Expenditure, £
Trade items . .	5,300,000	Imperial quota .	2,700,000
Agricultural . .	1,000,000	Debt	11,000,000
Financial . . .	22,200,000	Army	900,000
Sundries . . .	1,200,000	Government, &c.	15,100,000
Total . .	29,700,000	Total . .	29,700,000

The whole debt of the Empire was as follows:—

	1875	1889
	£	£
General	300,800,000	320,000,000
Austrian	33,200,000	105,900,000
Hungarian . . .	72,000,000	154,500,000
Total . .	406,000,000	580,400,000

ITALY

Estimates were made in 1810, in 1830, and again in 1850 of the revenue and debt of the various States, excepting those provinces held by Austria. Since 1861 the kingdom of Italy publishes official returns :—

Year	Revenue, £	Funded Debt, £	Total Debt, £
1810	4,600,000	...	...
1830	8,300,000	...	48,300,000
1850	12,000,000	...	...
1861	38,000,000	85,000,000	97,000,000
1870	48,000,000	242,000,000	333,000,000
1880	55,000,000	322,000,000	393,000,000
1890	72,000,000	363,000,000	460,000,000

Revenue and expenditure since 1860 have been approximately as follows :—

	Millions £ Sterling	
	Revenue	Expenditure
1861–70 . . .	430	660
1871–80 . . .	534	594
1881–87 . . .	440	505
27 years . . .	1,404	1,759

The annual excess of expenditure over revenue since 1861 has been about 13 millions sterling.

The revenue and debt of the various States in 1830 showed as follows :—

	Population	Revenue, £	Debt, £	Per Head, £	
				Revenue	Debt
Naples	7,420,000	3,400,000	20,000,000	0.45	2.70
Sardinia	4,160,000	2,600,000	4,000,000	0.63	0.98
Church	2,590,000	1,200,000	24,000,000	0.45	9.20
Tuscany	1,280,000	700,000	...	0.55	...
Parma and Modena . .	790,000	400,000	300,000	0.50	0.40
Total . .	16,240,000	8,300,000	48,300,000	0.51	5.80

The items of ordinary revenue at various dates were :—

	1871	1880	1888	Ratio	
				1871	1888
Customs . .	3,200,000	5,000,000	9,800,000	100	306
Excise . . .	5,900,000	7,400,000	9,800,000	100	166
Property-tax .	13,400,000	14,400,000	15,800,000	100	118
Grist-tax . .	1,700,000	2,200,000	...	...	...
Lottery . .	3,400,000	2,900,000	3,400,000	100	100
Stamps . .	1,200,000	1,600,000	1,500,000	100	125
Post-office .	1,100,000	1,500,000	2,400,000	100	218
Sundries . .	11,400,000	17,300,000	20,900,000	100	183
Total .	41,300,000	52,300,000	63,600,000	100	154

The expenditure was made up as follows :—

	1871	1880	1888
Debt	15,200,000	17,400,000	20,700,000
Army	6,400,000	8,300,000	12,900,000
Navy	1,200,000	1,700,000	4,900,000
Public works . .	4,800,000	5,300,000	14,600,000
Schools	600,000	1,100,000	1,500,000
Government . .	22,900,000	21,600,000	26,000,000
Total . .	51,100,000	55,400,000	80,600,000

Debt.—This has grown very rapidly, the increase since 1861 being 363 millions sterling, say 14 millions per annum. It may be approximately accounted for as follows :—

	Millions £
Railways	80
War and military expenditure . .	270
Sundries	110
Total . .	460

Communal and provincial finances in 1885 showed :—

	£
Revenues	27,200,000
Debts	41,400,000

The incidence of debt and interest on population showed thus :—

Year	Debt, Millions £	Interest, £	Debt per Inhabitant, £	Interest per Inhabitant, Shillings
1850	40	2,000,000	2.0	2
1861	97	4,600,000	4.4	4
1870	333	16,600,000	13.0	13
1880	393	19,700,000	14.0	14
1887	460	20,700,000	15.0	14

SPAIN

From official and other statements we find as follows :—

Year	Reign	Revenue, £	Debt, £
1610	Philip III.	1,320,000	40,000,000
1670	Charles II.	1,930,000	...
1750	Ferdinand VI.	3,320,000	11,000,000
1780	Charles III.	6,400,000	20,000,000
1808	Ferdinand VII.	6,000,000	69,000,000
1817	,,	7,130,000	117,000,000
1836	Isabella II.	8,500,000	276,000,000
1850	,,	11,500,000	113,000,000
1868	,,	21,000,000	221,000,000
1878	Alfonso XII.	29,500,000	550,000,000
1888	Alfonso XIII.	35,400,000	260,000,000

Revenue and expenditure since 1831 have been approximately as follows :—

Period	Millions £		Annual Average, £	
	Revenue	Expenditure	Revenue	Expenditure
1831–50	210	320	10,500,000	16,000,000
1851–70	320	410	16,000,000	20,500,000
1871–80	298	450	29,800,000	45,000,000
1881–88	264	284	33,000,000	35,500,000
58 years	1,092	1,464	19,000,000	25,400,000

The finances of Spain for 1887 showed as follows :—

	Revenue, £		Expenditure, £
Customs . . .	6,900,000	Debt	10,900,000
Direct taxes . .	12,400,000	Army and navy	7,300,000
Indirect taxes .	12,600,000	Public works .	4,000,000
Sundries . . .	2,100,000	Sundries . .	11,800,000
Total . .	34,000,000	Total . .	34,000,000

Debt.—It amounted in 1556 to one million sterling, rising to 40 millions under Philip III., after whose reign it was repudiated. A new debt arose with the War of Succession, which reached eight millions sterling in 1713, and went on increasing till Ferdinand repudiated the most of it. A third debt was caused by the wars of Isabella II. and the Carlists, which reached 276 millions, and was likewise repudiated, holders getting new scrip for about 30 per cent. of the old stock. The fourth debt amounted to 550 millions, when Spain again compounded in 1882, giving bondholders about 40 per cent. in new scrip.

The actual debt stands thus :—

	Amount, £	Interest, £
4 per cent. foreign . . .	78,800,000	3,100,000
Home debt, 4 and 4½ per cent.	143,200,000	5,700,000
Floating, &c.	38,000,000	1,200,000
Total . .	260,000,000	10,000,000

PORTUGAL

Various statements since 1810 show revenue and debt as follows :—

Year	Revenue, £	Debt, £
1810 . . .	1,200,000	...
1825 . . .	2,200,000	7,000,000
1840 . . .	2,700,000	17,000,000
1850 . . .	3,200,000	22,000,000
1878 . . .	5,700,000	94,000,000
1888 . . .	8,400,000	113,000,000

The finances in 1887 were as follows :—

	Revenue, £		Expenditure, £
Customs . . .	4,000,000	Debt	3,600,000
Property-tax . .	700,000	Army and navy .	1,400,000
Sundries . . .	3,700,000	Government . .	4,000,000
Total . .	8,400,000	Total . .	9,000,000

Since 1850 expenditure has exceeded revenue by 80 millions, say two millions per annum.

Revenue and expenditure since 1831 were approximately as follows :—

Period	Millions £		Annual Average, £	
	Revenue	Expenditure	Revenue	Expenditure
1831–50	54	74	2,700,000	3,700,000
1851–70	80	120	4,000,000	6,000,000
1871–80	58	87	5,800,000	8,700,000
1881–88	60	72	7,500,000	9,000,000
58 years	252	353	4,300,000	6,000,000

Debt.—This dates from 1500, but was small in amount till the middle of the present century. It consists at present of 51 millions foreign 3 per cents., 58 millions home 3 per cents., and four millions of floating debt.

SWEDEN AND NORWAY

The revenue of these two kingdoms showed as follows :—

Year	Sweden, £	Norway, £	Total, £
1810	1,000,000	...	...
1822	1,300,000	300,000	1,600,000
1850	1,500,000	800,000	2,300,000
1878	4,100,000	2,400,000	6,500,000
1888	4,800,000	2,400,000	7,200,000

Before the annexation of Norway the finances of Sweden showed thus :—

	1772	1784
	£	£
Crown lands . . .	330,000	330,000
Sundries	730,000	920,000
Total . .	1,060,000	1,250,000

The Swedish debt in 1784 amounted to £8,800,000 sterling.

The items composing the revenue of the two kingdoms in 1887 were :—

	Sweden, £	Norway, £	Total, £
Customs . . .	2,000,000	1,100,000	3,100,000
Excise	840,000	230,000	1,070,000
Property-tax . .	440,000	...	440,000
Railways . . .	330,000	330,000	660,000
Post-office . . .	330,000	170,000	500,000
Sundries . . .	860,000	570,000	1,430,000
Total . .	4,800,000	2,400,000	7,200,000

The expenditure in 1887 showed as follows :—

	Sweden, £	Norway, £	Total, £
Debt	500,000	200,000	700,000
Army and navy .	1,100,000	350,000	1,450,000
Schools	600,000	240,000	840,000
Government . .	2,600,000	1,610,000	4,210,000
Total . .	4,800,000	2,400,000	7,200,000

Revenue and expenditure for the two kingdoms collectively may be stated approximately since 1831 as follows :—

	Millions £		Annual Average, £	
	Revenue	Expenditure	Revenue	Expenditure
1831–50	42	42	2,100,000	2,100,000
1851–70	66	74	3,300,000	3,700,000
1871–80	69	74	6,900,000	7,400,000
1881–88	56	61	7,000,000	7,600,000
58 years	233	251	3,800,000	4,200,000

Debt.—The amount at various dates is shown thus :—

Year	Sweden, £	Norway, £	Total, £
1784	8,800,000	...	8,800,000
1840	1,200,000	300,000	1,500,000
1876	9,800,000	3,900,000	13,700,000
1888	13,700,000	5,900,000	19,600,000

State railways represent an outlay of £19,800,000, so that it may be said that the public debt of Sweden and Norway is merely a nominal one.

DENMARK

Revenue and debt since 1771 are shown thus :—

Year	Revenue, £	Debt, £
1771 . . .	1,060,000	3,000,000
1786 . . .	1,580,000	5,800,000
1810 . . .	1,100,000	10,000,000
1835 . . .	1,560,000	14,100,000
1850 . . .	1,500,000	11,800,000
1866 . . .	2,000,000	14,800,000
1882 . . .	3,000,000	11,100,000
1889 . . .	3,040,000	10,800,000

Before the French revolution Denmark comprised not only that kingdom and the duchies of Schleswig-Holstein, but also Norway; and the Budget of 1786 showed as follows :—

Revenue, £		Expenditure, £	
From Denmark .	900,000	Army and navy .	600,000
,, Duchies. .	300,000	Debt	260,000
,, Norway. .	380,000	Civil service . .	670,000
Total .	1,580,000	Total .	1,530,000

The Budgets of 1872 and 1890 compare thus :—

The revenue of Denmark in the eighteenth century consisted partly of a land-tax, averaging 1s. per acre. The Budget of 1835 was made up as follows :—

Revenue, £		Expenditure, £	
Land and forests .	520,000	Army	300,000
Customs . .	390,000	Debt	530,000
Sundries . .	650,000	Government . .	750,000
Total . .	1,560,000	Total . .	1,580,000

Denmark contributed £1,060,000, the duchies £500,000 to the revenue.

The revenue and expenditure from 1831 were approximately as follows :—

	Millions £		Annual Average, £	
	Revenue	Expenditure	Revenue	Expenditure
1831–50	28	28	1,400,000	1,400,000
1851–70	36	40	1,800,000	2,000,000
1871–80	27	23	2,700,000	2,300,000
1881–87	21	21	3,000,000	3,000,000
57 years	112	112	1,900,000	1,900,000

	Revenue, £			Expenditure, £	
	1872	1890		1872	1890
Customs . . .	900,000	1,400,000	Debt	530,000	390,000
Property-tax . . .	400,000	500,000	Army and navy . .	710,000	920,000
Stamps . . .	100,000	150,000	Schools . . .	40,000	110,000
Railways . . .	60,000	210,000	Public works . .	100,000	170,000
Sundries . . .	610,000	780,000	Sundries . . .	650,000	1,610,000
Total . .	2,070,000	3,040,000	Total . .	2,030,000	3,200,000

In 1856 Denmark received £3,600,000 from the European Powers for abolition of the Sound Dues. In 1864 Schleswig-Holstein, on joining Prussia, took over £3,300,000 of the Danish debt.

HOLLAND

Revenue and debt at various dates stood thus :—

Year	Revenue, £	Debt, £
1770 . . .	2,200,000	...
1786 . . .	3,300,000	...
1810 . . .	4,800,000	...
1828 . . .	6,400,000	152,000,000
1850 . . .	5,800,000	98,000,000
1879 . . .	9,400,000	80,500,000
1888 . . .	10,000,000	89,200,000

The sources of revenue were as follows :—

	1879	1888
	£	£
Customs	380,000	400,000
Excise	3,220,000	2,000,000
Property-tax	1,700,000	1,900,000
Post-office	420,000	450,000
Sundries	3,680,000	5,250,000
Total . .	9,400,000	10,000,000

The expenditure was as follows :—

	1879	1888
	£	£
Debt	2,400,000	3,100,000
Army	1,800,000	1,700,000
Navy	1,100,000	1,100,000
Government	4,600,000	5,500,000
Total . .	9,900,000	11,400,000

Holland had no public debt till its conquest by the French in 1793, but when Louis Bonaparte was made king in 1806 the debt was 83 millions sterling, and it rapidly rose to 152 millions. At present there is a set-off to the amount of 21 millions for State railways, so that the debt may be properly stated at 68 millions sterling. When Belgium separated from Holland in 1830 it caused a decline of revenue, as shown above. The revenue and expenditure since 1830 were approximately as follows :—

Period	Millions £		Annual Average, £	
	Revenue	Expenditure	Revenue	Expenditure
1831–50	94	94	4,700,000	4,700,000
1851–80	240	220	8,000,000	7,300,000
1881–88	76	85	9,500,000	10,600,000
Total	410	399	...	...

BELGIUM

When Belgium formed part of the kingdom of the Netherlands, her contribution to the national exchequer averaged, says Kolb, £3,500,000 per annum, or half the total revenue. On attaining her independence she took over £8,800,000 of the Dutch debt, involving an annual burden of £440,000. The revenue and debt at various dates show thus :—

Year	Revenue, £	Debt, £
1832 . . .	3,500,000	8,800,000
1850 . . .	4,700,000	25,100,000
1870 . . .	7,600,000	27,300,000
1878 . . .	10,200,000	42,000,000
1890 . . .	12,900,000	77,400,000

The revenue and expenditure have been approximately as follows :—

Period	Millions £		Annual Average, £	
	Revenue	Expenditure	Revenue	Expenditure
1831–50	82	98	4,100,000	4,900,000
1851–70	124	126	6,200,000	6,300,000
1871–87	186	236	11,000,000	14,000,000
Total	392	460	...	...

The revenue was made up as follows :—

	1835	1850	1870	1890
	£	£	£	£
Customs . .	300,000	500,000	900,000	1,100,000
Income-tax .	1,000,000	1,100,000	1,200,000	1,800,000
Railways .	...	600,000	1,700,000	4,200,000
Sundries . .	2,300,000	2,500,000	3,800,000	5,800,000
Total .	3,600,000	4,700,000	7,600,000	12,900,000

The items of expenditure were :—

	1835	1850	1870	1890
	£	£	£	£
Army . . .	1,600,000	1,000,000	2,400,000	1,800,000
Debt . . .	400,000	1,400,000	1,700,000	4,000,000
Government	1,400,000	2,200,000	3,600,000	7,000,000
Total .	3,400,000	4,600,000	7,700,000	12,800,000

There are 2000 miles of State railways, which cost 29 millions sterling, representing nearly 40 per cent. of the public debt.

SWITZERLAND

The *Almanac de Gotha* for 1810 puts the revenue at only £100,000 for that year. The *Repertoire Economique* puts it for 1822 at £800,000, whereas a statement published in 1850 makes it for the last-mentioned year only £500,000.
Official figures give us the following for later years:—

Year			Revenue, £	Debt, £
1868	.	.	1,700,000	200,000
1877	.	.	1,700,000	1,300,000
1889	.	.	2,400,000	1,200,000

The above debt is that of the Confederation, besides which the various Cantons have their own, which Kauffmann says amounted in 1876 to 16 millions sterling. The sources of Federal revenue were :—

	1877	1888
	£	£
Customs . . .	650,000	1,200,000
Sundries . . .	1,050,000	1,200,000
Total . .	1,700,000	2,400,000

The expenditure was as follows :—

	1877	1888
	£	£
Army . . .	600,000	800,000
Government . .	1,100,000	1,600,000
Total . .	1,700,000	2,400,000

These tables do not include the Cantonal revenues or expenditure.

GREECE

The kingdom dates from 1832, but the finances for some years were obscure. The following shows approximately revenue and debt :—

Year			Revenue, £	Debt, £
1840	.	.	800,000	10,000,000
1879	.	.	1,600,000	19,400,000
1889	.	.	3,400,000	22,700,000

Revenue and expenditure were approximately as follows :—

Period	Millions £		Annual Average, £	
	Revenue	Expenditure	Revenue	Expenditure
1833–50	16	25	900,000	1,400,000
1851–70	24	30	1,200,000	1,500,000
1871–80	14	18	1,400,000	1,800,000
1881–87	18	22	2,600,000	3,100,000
55 years	72	95	1,300,000	1,700,000

The finances for 1887 showed as follows :—

	Revenue, £		Expenditure, £
Direct taxes .	900,000	Debt . .	1,500,000
Indirect taxes .	1,900,000	Army . .	600,000
Sundries . .	1,000,000	Government	1,700,000
Total .	3,800,000	Total .	3,800,000

The debt is mostly internal, and includes £3,200,000 of bank-notes.

ROUMANIA AND SERVIA

The finances of these two kingdoms in 1889 showed thus :—

	Roumania, £	Servia, £
Revenue—		
Customs . . .	900,000	200,000
Excise . . .	1,700,000	800,000
Taxes . . .	3,600,000	800,000
Total .	6,200,000	1,800,000
Expenditure—		
Debt	2,600,000	460,000
Army	1,400,000	640,000
Government .	2,500,000	700,000
Total .	6,500,000	1,800,000

The Roumanian debt is 36 millions sterling, that of Servia 13 millions, one-half of the amount in each case having its origin in State railways.

BULGARIA

Revenue, £2,900,000. A loan for £1,200,000 in 6 per cents. was effected at Vienna in January 1890. The estimates for 1890 were — Army, £1,200,000; debt, £250,000; public works, £400,000; government, £1,150,000, making a total of three millions sterling. Deficit, £100,000.

TURKEY

Revenue and debt are shown approximately thus :—

Year			Revenue, £	Debt, £
1810	.	.	3,000,000	...
1830	.	.	4,000,000	8,000,000
1854	.	.	9,000,000	12,000,000
1870	.	.	12,000,000	92,000,000
1878	.	.	13,000,000	245,000,000
1887	.	.	16,200,000	180,000,000

The debt has been reduced by compounding with the bond-holders. It now comprises 105 millions foreign consols, over 40 millions of internal debt, and 32 millions war indemnity due to Russia. Revenue and expenditure since 1851 were approximately as follows :—

Period	Millions £		Annual Average, £	
	Revenue	Expenditure	Revenue	Expenditure
1851–70	210	300	10,500,000	15,000,000
1871–80	140	240	14,000,000	24,000,000
1881–87	110	110	16,000,000	16,000,000
37 years	460	650	12,400,000	17,600,000

The Budget for 1889 showed—Revenue, £16,700,000 ; expenditure, £19,300,000. Since the composition of 1882 the bond-holders receive 1 per cent. annual interest. The taxes set apart for this purpose gave as follows in 1888 :—

	£		£
Tobacco	680,000	Excise	200,000
Salt	620,000	Sundries	480,000

These taxes also provide a sinking-fund.

EGYPT

The finances may be approximately set down thus ;—

Year	Revenue, £	Debt, £
1833	2,520,000	...
1863	6,000,000	3,300,000
1870	7,000,000	37,000,000
1878	7,400,000	85,000,000
1889	9,700,000	103,400,000

Revenue and expenditure were approximately as follows :—

Period	Millions £		Annual Average, £	
	Revenue	Expenditure	Revenue	Expenditure
1841–60	90	90	4,500,000	4,500,000
1861–70	65	100	6,500,000	10,000,000
1871–80	75	135	7,500,000	13,500,000
1881–88	68	68	8,500,000	8,500,000
48 years	298	393	6,200,000	8,200,000

Revenue and expenditure for 1889 showed as follows :—

Revenue, £		Expenditure, £	
Land-tax	4,890,000	Debt charge	4,090,000
Customs	1,030,000	Police	740,000
Railways	1,300,000	Khedive	270,000
Sundries	2,375,000	Government	4,300,000
Total	9,595,000	Total	9,400,000

The sources of American revenue have been as follows :—

Debt.—Before 1860 there was no debt, although large sums had been expended in irrigation works. The debt reached 120 millions sterling in 1880, and was thus accounted for :—

	£		£
Railways	13,360,000	*Loss on*	
Suez Canal	6,770,000	Goschen loans	1,900,000
Nile Canal	12,600,000	Oppenheim do.	18,900,000
Sugar-mills	6,100,000	Bischoffsheim do.	2,100,000
Alexandria harbour	2,540,000	Rothschild do.	2,500,000
Bridges,schools,&c.	4,890,000	Various do.	1,000,000
		Ballet-dancers,&c.	47,340,000
Public works	46,260,000	Unproductive	73,740,000

The nine loans effected between 1862 and 1880 represented nominally £77,000,000, but produced only £50,589,000, the difference being lost in discounts and other unavoidable drawbacks.

UNITED STATES

Official returns for 100 years show as follows :—

Year	Revenue, £	Expenditure, £	Debt, £
1790	900,000	600,000	15,700,000
1800	2,200,000	2,200,000	17,200,000
1810	1,900,000	1,800,000	11,000,000
1820	3,500,000	3,800,000	19,000,000
1830	5,100,000	3,100,000	9,000,000
1840	4,100,000	5,000,000	1,100,000
1850	9,200,000	8,600,000	13,200,000
1860	11,600,000	13,100,000	13,500,000
1870	71,500,000	53,700,000	485,000,000
1880	69,200,000	55,000,000	399,000,000
1889	80,600,000	68,600,000	221,000,000

The total revenue and expenditure of 100 years were :—

Period	Millions £ Sterling		Annual Average, £	
	Revenue	Expenditure	Revenue	Expenditure
1790–1809	40	31	2,000,000	1,550,000
1810–1829	85	82	4,250,000	4,100,000
1830–1849	115	112	5,750,000	5,600,000
1850–1859	123	120	12,300,000	12,000,000
1860–1869	370	713	37,000,000	71,300,000
1870–1879	596	517	59,600,000	51,700,000
1880–1889	757	545	75,700,000	54,500,000
100 years	2,086	2,120	20,860,000	21,200,000

If we compare revenue with population we find :—

Period	Shillings per Inhab.
1831–50	7
1851–60	8
1861–70	22
1871–80	26
1881–88	28

Period	Millions £ Sterling				Annual Average, £		
	Customs	Internal Revenue	Sundries	Total	Customs	Internal	Sundries
1790–1809	35	1	4	40	1,750,000	50,000	200,000
1810–29	73	3	9	85	3,650,000	150,000	450,000
1830–59	201	...	37	238	6,700,000	...	1,230,000
1860–69	165	183	22	370	16,500,000	18,300,000	2,200,000
1870–79	316	236	44	596	31,600,000	23,600,000	4,400,000
1880–89	426	266	65	757	42,600,000	26,600,000	6,500,000
100 years	1,216	689	181	2,086	12,160,000	6,890,000	1,810,000

The items of expenditure were as follows :—

Period	Millions £ Sterling					
	Government	Army and Navy	Indians	Pensions	Interest	Total
1790–1809 . .	6	12	...	...	13	31
1810–29 . . .	12	47	2	4	17	82
1830–49 . . .	25	68	8	8	3	112
1850–59 . . .	48	55	7	3	7	120
1860–69 . . .	57	527	5	17	107	713
1870–79 . . .	125	115	11	57	209	517
1880–89 . . .	151	117	14	136	127	545
100 years. . .	424	941	47	225	483	2,120

Debt.—There was hardly any (except local debts) previous to the war of 1861. It reached its maximum in August 1865, namely, 572 millions sterling (2756 million dollars), being £16 per inhabitant, and fell in 1889 to 221 millions sterling, or less than £4 per inhabitant. Debt and wealth compared thus :—

Year	Millions £ Sterling		Ratio of Debt
	Wealth	Debt	
1865 . . .	4,180	572	13.6 per cent.
1889 . . .	12,824	221	1.7 ,, ,,

AUSTRALIA

The aggregate revenue and debt of the seven colonies which form Australia are shown thus :—

Year	Revenue, £	Debt, £	Ratio per Inhabitant	
			Revenue, £	Debt, £
1825	72,000	...	0.8	...
1840	680,000	...	2.2	...
1850	930,000	...	2.0	...
1860	6,700,000	11,900,000	5.3	9.5
1870	11,600,000	36,200,000	5.8	18.1
1880	17,100,000	87,900,000	6.0	31.0
1888	27,600,000	166,500,000	7.5	45.0

The revenue and expenditure since 1850 may be summed up approximately as follows :—

Period	Millions £	
	Revenue	Expenditure
1851–60 . . .	38	50
1861–70 . . .	92	116
1871–80 . . .	147	199
1881–88 . . .	186	265
38 years . . .	463	630

The income and expenditure of the several colonies in the last eight years, 1881–88, were :—

	Millions £		
	Revenue	Expenditure	Surplus Expenditure
New South Wales .	60	89	29
Victoria . . .	50	64	14
Queensland .	22	36	14
South Australia .	17	26	9
West Australia .	2	3	1
Tasmania . .	4	6	2
New Zealand .	31	41	10
Total .	186	265	79

The aggregate of customs revenue in the last eight years compares with trade and population as follows :—

	Customs	Trade, Millions £	Population	Ratio of Customs	
				Per cent. of Trade	Per Inhabitant Yearly
	£				£ s. d.
N. S. Wales	13,760,000	309	900,000	4.5	1 19 0
Victoria . .	16,050,000	269	950,000	5.8	2 2 0
Queensland	7,270,000	87	290,000	8.4	3 3 0
S. Australia	4,330,000	88	300,000	5.0	1 16 0
W. Australia	1,110,000	9	35,000	12.1	4 0 0
Tasmania .	2,220,000	24	130,000	9.3	2 3 0
New Zealand	11,160,000	113	590,000	9.8	2 8 0
Total .	55,900,000	899	3,195,000	6.2	2 4 0

The revenue of New South Wales in 1889 reached £9,100,000.

The revenue of the several colonies in 1888 was made up thus :—

	Customs	Railways, &c.	Lands	Sundries	Total
	£	£	£	£	£
New South Wales	2,140,000	3,660,000	2,270,000	820,000	8,890,000
Victoria	2,350,000	3,230,000	660,000	1,370,000	7,610,000
Queensland	1,350,000	1,000,000	640,000	470,000	3,460,000
South Australia	530,000	1,170,000	320,000	470,000	2,490,000
West Australia	180,000	60,000	80,000	40,000	360,000
Tasmania	300,000	110,000	80,000	150,000	640,000
New Zealand	1,390,000	1,330,000	300,000	1,090,000	4,110,000
Total . .	8,240,000	10,560,000	4,350,000	4,410,000	27,560,000

Debt.—In June 1889 it amounted to 171 millions sterling, having risen almost 160 millions since 1860. The money has been expended thus :—

	£
Railways	99,300,000
Waterworks	13,000,000
Immigration	5,500,000
Sundries	48,700,000
Total . .	166,500,000

The railways in 1889 showed gross receipts £8,160,000, working expenses £5,110,000, leaving a net profit of £3,050,000, equal to 3 per cent. on cost of construction. The annual interest on debt is £7,000,000 ; hence the railways pay nearly half the annual charge on the country for debt. If we deduct the value of railways and waterworks, the public debt will be only 54 millions sterling, or 4 per cent. of the wealth of Australia, against 7½ per cent. in the United Kingdom.

The increase of public debt has been accompanied by an enormous increase of wealth, as we see by comparing the two items:—

Year	Millions £ Sterling		Ratio to Wealth
	Wealth	Debt	
1860 . . .	180	12	6.6 per cent.
1870 . . .	320	36	11.2 ,,
1888 . . .	1,373	166	12.1 ,,

The wealth and debt of the several colonies in 1888 were as follows:—

	Millions £		Debt Ratio
	Wealth	Debt	
New South Wales .	483	44	9.1
Victoria . . .	370	35	9.5
Queensland . .	132	26	19.5
South Australia . .	131	19	14.5
Western Australia .	13	1	7.7
Tasmania . . .	36	4	11.2
New Zealand . .	208	37	17.8
Total .	1,373	166	12.1

The increase of debt since 1870 has averaged in the aggregate 7 millions sterling per annum, that of wealth 58 millions. Debt is equal to six years of revenue, the same as in Canada.

The debt and annual charge in the several colonies in December 1889 stood as follows:—

	Debt, £	Interest, £	Debt per Inhab., £
New South Wales .	46,800,000	1,810,000	43
Victoria . . .	37,400,000	1,520,000	34
Queensland . .	25,800,000	1,035,000	65
South Australia .	20,500,000	820,000	63
New Zealand . .	37,000,000	1,530,000	60
Tasmania . .	5,300,000	210,000	36
Western Australia .	1,300,000	50,000	30
Total .	174,100,000	6,975,000	48

CANADA

Official returns show revenue and debt as follows:—

Year	Amount, £		Per Inhabitant	
	Revenue	Debt	Revenue, £	Debt, £
1840	500,000	1,200,000	0.3	0.7
1860	2,400,000	14,100,000	0.7	4.0
1870	3,600,000	16,700,000	1.0	4.6
1880	5,100,000	32,100,000	1.1	7.0
1889	7,760,000	49,200,000	1.5	9.9

The revenue and expenditure since 1840 may be approximately summed up as follows:—

Period	Millions £ Sterling		
	Revenue	Expenditure	Surplus Expenditure
1841–60	30	43	13
1861–70	33	36	3
1871–80	49	64	15
1881-89	66	83	17
49 years	178	226	48

Customs revenue averages 60 per cent. of total revenue, and is about 12 per cent. as compared with the value of trade. Debt has been largely caused by expenditure for railways. If we compare it with an approximate of public wealth, the account stands thus:—

Year	Millions £ Sterling		Debt Ratio	Per Inhabitant	
	Wealth	Debt		Wealth, £	Debt, £
1860	392	14	3.6	120	4.2
1888	980	49	5.0	196	9.9

The incidence of debt is less than £10 per inhabitant, against £48 in Australia; but, compared with revenue, it is equal, being six times the revenue in both cases.

In 1889 the debt consisted of £39,000,000 due in London and £10,000,000 internal debt. When the Dominion was constituted in 1867 the total debt was £15,600,000; the subsequent increase of £33,600,000 was caused thus:—

	£
Pacific Railway	13,000,000
Other railways	8,300,000
Canals	6,800,000
Other public works . . .	5,500,000
Total . .	33,600,000

The total cost of the Pacific Railway was £21,600,000. The annual interest on the public debt of Canada is £2,040,000.

INDIA

Revenue and debt according to official returns were:—

Year	Revenue, £	Debt, £
1810 . . .	15,600,000	31,900,000
1820 . . .	19,500,000	39,800,000
1830 . . .	19,600,000	36,400,000
1840 . . .	19,400,000	32,500,000
1850 . . .	27,600,000	53,900,000
1860 . . .	39,700,000	98,100,000
1870 . . .	50,900,000	108,200,000
1880 . . .	69,700,000	160,400,000
1890 . . .	82,900,000	191,900,000

Revenue and expenditure may be summed up approximately thus:—

Period	Millions £ Sterling	
	Revenue	Expenditure
1810–40	565	565
1841–60	572	638
1861–70	473	483
1871–80	564	616
1881–87	514	540
77 years	2,688	2,842

In the foregoing tables the rupee is taken at the official value of 2s. Revenue and expenditure in 1890 stood thus:—

	Revenue, £		Expenditure, £
Land-tax . .	23,400,000	Army . .	22,100,000
Railways . .	16,700,000	Railways .	18,700,000
Opium . . .	8,300,000	Post-office .	13,300,000
Salt-tax . . .	8,000,000	Roads . .	5,500,000
Post-office . .	2,300,000	Irrigation .	2,600,000
Irrigation . .	1,900,000	Debt . .	4,400,000
Sundries . .	22,300,000	Sundries .	16,200,000
Total .	82,900,000	Total .	82,800,000

SOUTH AFRICA

Revenue and debt were as follows :—

Year	Revenue, £	Debt, £
1840 . . .	200,000	...
1860 . . .	800,000	600,000
1870 . . .	950,000	1,400,000
1880 . . .	3,100,000	13,000,000
1887 . . .	4,000,000	26,500,000

Revenue and expenditure are approximately summed up thus :—

Period	Millions £	
	Revenue	Expenditure
1841–60	10	11
1861–70	9	10
1871–80	19	31
1881–87	27	40
47 years	65	92

WEST INDIES

Revenue and debt were as follows :—

Year	Revenue, £	Debt, £
1850 . . .	700,000	900,000
1860 . . .	1,000,000	1,000,000
1870 . . .	1,400,000	1,600,000
1880 . . .	1,900,000	1,800,000
1887 . . .	2,100,000	3,100,000

ARGENTINA

Official returns are to the following effect :—

Year	Revenue, £	Debt, £
1864 . . .	1,400,000	5,100,000
1870 . . .	3,000,000	10,100,000
1880 . . .	3,900,000	23,000,000
1888 . . .	5,440,000	46,500,000

Revenue and expenditure seem therefore to have been as follows :—

Period	Millions £ Sterling		
	Revenue	Expenditure	Surplus Expenditure
1864–70 . . .	15	20	5
1871–80 . . .	35	48	13
1881–88 . . .	38	62	24
25 years . . .	88	130	42

The Budgets for 1884 and 1889 compared as follows :—

	Revenue	
	1884	1889
	£	£
Import dues . . .	4,230,000	3,880,000
Railways . . .	410,000	80,000
Stamps . . .	420,000	350,000
Sundries . . .	1,440,000	1,130,000
Total . .	6,500,000	5,440,000

	Expenditure	
	1884	1889
	£	£
Exchequer . . .	2,720,000	2,470,000
Interior . . .	1,200,000	1,480,000
Army and navy . .	1,680,000	1,090,000
Schools, &c. . . .	900,000	960,000
Total . .	6,500,000	6,000.000

Interest on debt takes £2,400,000, or 40 per cent. of the total revenue.

The statement of debt omits inconvertible paper-money issued by Government banks, and Cedulas or mortgage debentures guaranteed by Government (see *Banks*). On the other hand, the Government claims to have assets worth 71 millions sterling, viz. :—

	£
Treasury department . . .	27,260,000
Interior	37,560,000
Schools	2,920,000
War and Marine	2,850,000
Sundries	220,000
Total .	70,810,000*

Real estate consisting of lands and public buildings stands for 41 millions, bank and railway shares and Treasury balances for 26 millions, and sundries four millions.

Each of the fourteen Argentine provinces, as well as the capital, Buenos Ayres, has its own revenue and debt, distinct from those of the Federal Government. Latest returns were as follows :—

Province	Revenue	Debt
	£	£
Capital	1,500,000	2,400,000
Buenos Ayres . . .	2,400,000	17,400,000
Santa Fé	600,000	9,400,000
Cordoba	300,000	4,000,000
Entre Rios . . .	300,000	4,000,000
Corrientes	160,000	1,100,000
Santiago	80,000	1,100,000
Mendoza	120,000	1,000,000
Salta	80,000	1,000,000
Rioja	40,000	1,000,000
Tucuman	100,000	600,000
Catamarca . . .	40,000	600,000
San Luis . . .	60,000	600,000
San Juan	50,000	400,000
Jujuy	20,000	...
Total . .	5,850,000	44,600,000

The consolidated debt, federal and provincial, may be summed up thus :—

	Foreign	Home Debt		Total
	£	$	£	£
Federal .	25,800,000	207,300,000 =	20,700,000	46,500,000
Provincial .	38,700,000	44,100,000 =	4,400,000	43,100,000
Total .	64,500,000	251,400,000 =	25,100,000	89,600,000

If we add 20 millions sterling for 300 million dollars of forced issue, it makes the total debt 110 millions sterling, without counting 400 millions of Cedulas worth about 30 millions sterling (see *Banks*). Wealth and debt at various dates were approximately as follows :—

Year	Millions £ Sterling		Debt Ratio
	Wealth	Debt	
1857	74	2	2.7
1864	139	5	3.6
1884	375	43	11.4
1890	509	110	21.6

* This valuation does not merit confidence, since it magnifies certain items exceedingly. No impartial person would put the total at more than 10 or 12 millions sterling.

URUGUAY

Official records since 1831 show thus :—

Period	Millions £ Sterling		
	Revenue	Expenditure	Debt
1831–50 . . .	4	5	1
1851–60 . . .	4	7	4
1861–70 . . .	6	10	8
1871–80 . . .	13	16	11
1881–88 . . .	20	24	15
58 years. . .	47	62	15

The value of real estate and cattle in 1886 amounted to 282 million gold dollars, or 59 millions sterling. The total wealth of the Republic is approximately 100 millions. The debt is therefore 15 per cent. against 22 per cent. in Argentina.

BRAZIL

Official returns give as follows :—

Year	Revenue, £	Debt, £
1864	6,100,000	18,700,000
1874	11,200,000	72,100,000
1888	14,100,000	107,200,000

The finances since 1850 may be summed up approximately thus :—

Period	Millions £	
	Revenue	Expenditure
1851–60 . . .	45	50
1861–70 . . .	65	130
1871–80 . . .	115	135
1881–88 . . .	105	122
Total . .	330	437

The origin of the debt is shown thus :—

	£
Paraguayan war , . .	48,000,000
Railways	29,000,000
Sundries	30,200,000
Total . . .	107,200,000

MEXICO

Official returns give the following :—

Debt, 1889		Revenue		1889	
	£		£		£
Foreign	12,700,000	1870	2,800,000	Customs	3,000,000
Home	18,500,000	1880	3,400,000	Sundries	2,000,000
		1889	5,000,000		
Total	31,200,000			Total	5,000,000

CHINA

In 1889 the revenue was stated thus :—

	£
Land-tax	4,800,000
Customs	5,500,000
Salt-tax	2,300,000
Sundries	6,400,000
Total . . .	19,000,000

JAPAN

The revenue in 1889 was £13,400,000, and the debt stood thus :—

	£
Funded	41,100,000
Forced currency . . .	9,000,000
Total . . .	50,100,000

FINES

The following were in force in the Middle Ages in France and England :—

Offence	£	s	d
Drawing a knife to any one . .	0	10	0
Wounding a person . . .	2	0	0
Calling a woman a prostitute .	2	0	0

FIRE

The *Journal des Economistes* (1883) published the following table of property annually destroyed by fire, except the countries in italics, the figures for which are doubtful :—

	£		£
United Kingdom	9,100,000	*Spain*	500,000
France	3,200,000	*Holland* . . .	400,000
Germany . . .	6,100,000	Belgium . . .	500,000
Russia	21,000,000	Scandinavia . .	1,000,000
Austria . . .	3,500,000	United States .	22,500,000
Italy	1,000,000	Canada . . .	4,100,000

The total reaches 73 millions sterling. In twelve years ending 1883 the average for Austria proper was £1,800,000 per annum, exclusive of Hungary.

Losses in the principal cities are shown thus :—

	Number of Fires	Number per 100,000 Inhabs.	Loss, £	Per Inhabitant, Pence
London . . .	2,338	56	1,100,000	66
Paris	...	...	270,000	34
New York . .	1,783	144	780,000	150
Manchester .	328	59	120,000	55
San Francisco .	...	...	112,000	122
Philadelphia .	655	76	460,000	130
Chicago . . .	490	98	360,000	180
Boston . . .	389	117	130,000	95
Baltimore . .	172	52	70,000	55
Cincinnati . .	213	85	144,000	144
St. Louis . .	197	49	160,000	98
Vienna . . .	365	36	100,000	24

The record of London fires since 1840 has been as follows :—

Years	Annual Average		
	Number of Fires	Houses to a Fire	Inhabitants to a Fire
1840–49 . . .	768	362	2,731
1850–59 . . .	977	331	2,570
1860–69 . . .	1,430	288	2,390
1870–80 . . .	1,795	264	2,150
1881–89 . . .	2,160	260	1,780

Fires on Saturday are 5 per cent. more numerous than on any other day in London ; but in Paris Friday has 20 per cent. over the average.

FRANCE

Official returns for the whole of France show thus :—

Years	Annual Average		
	Number of Fires	Houses to a Fire	Inhabitants to a Fire
1845–50 . . .	8,260	873	4,120
1851–60 . . .	10,556	715	3,435
1861–70 . . .	13,865	562	2,720

RUSSIA

The number of houses burnt yearly from 1860 to 1864 was only 10,600, representing a value of barely two millions sterling. Police estimates seem to have a cipher too much.

UNITED STATES.

Down to 1880 the annual losses from fire averaged only 17 millions sterling. Possibly the figure given above includes Canada, a large portion of Canadian property being insured at New York. The *Chronicle* (N.Y.) gives the losses in United States as follows :—

Period	£ Sterling per Annum
1875–80	14,800,000
1881–85	19,900,000

This was only 1 per cent. of the property insured, which exceeded 2100 millions sterling, or one-fifth of the total wealth of the United States.

Loss of Life.—The following table shows the deaths by fire per million inhabitants in various cities :—

Munich .	.	.	. 4	Naples .	.	.	. 41
Glasgow .	.	. 17		Hanover .	.	.	57
Berlin .	.	.	. 20	Cologne	.	.	. 71
Paris .	.	.	. 24	London .	.	.	. 83

The loss of life in England and Wales from fire averages 1490 persons yearly, of whom 42 per cent. are males and 58 per cent. females. The London firemen save 110 lives yearly. Three persons in England per 1000 die by fire.

Remarkable Fires.—The worst recorded in history have been :—

Year		Place			Loss
1570 .	.	Moscow	.	.	200,000 victims
1666 .	.	London	.	.	13,200 houses
1812 .	.	Moscow	.	.	15,500 houses
1824 .	.	Cairo .	.	.	4000 victims
1831 .	.	Constantinople	.	.	18,000 houses
1835 .	.	New York	.	.	£6,000,000
1842 .	.	Hamburg	.	.	£7,200,000
1851 .	.	San Francisco	.	.	2500 blocks
1863 .	.	Santiago	.	.	1800 victims
1871 .	.	Chicago	.	.	£33,000,000
1872 .	.	Boston .	.	.	£15,000,000

See also *Theatres*, in which some fires caused great loss of life.

Fire-Brigades.—The first in London was established in 1791. The various brigades in 1882 stood thus :—

	Fire-Engines	Fire-men	Cost of Brigade	Firemen per 100,000 Inhabitants	Cost of Brigade, Pence per Inhab.
London . .	38	536	£80,000	13	5
Paris . . .	203	1,500	98,000	68	11
St. Petersburg	37	1,150	...	127	...
Hamburg . .	53	790	...	305	...
New York . .	38	690	250,000	55	48
Philadelphia .	27	404	103,000	49	29
Chicago . .	27	200	94,000	40	48
Boston . .	26	472	110,000	138	79
Cincinnati . .	18	155	62,000	62	64
St. Louis . .	17	100	40,000	26	24
Baltimore . .	18	140	40,000	43	30
San Francisco	14	200	...	82	...
Berlin . . .	50	1,090	...	96	...
Lyons . . .	48	475	...	98	...

The expenditure on fire-brigades compared with the number of fires shows the following average per fire :—

	£		£		£
London . .	40	Philadelphia.	153	Baltimore . .	230
Sydney . .	88	Chicago . .	188	Boston . . .	280
New York .	138	St. Louis . .	201	Cincinnati .	295

The London fire-brigade uses 17 million gallons water yearly, that is, 4½ gallons per inhabitant, or 8500 gallons for each fire. The New York brigade consumes 32 million gallons, that is, 25 gallons per inhabitant, or 18,000 gallons per fire.

FISH

Anchovy.—The fishermen of Finisterre, France, take 700 tons yearly, value £10,000.

Cod.—The average take is as follows :—

	Million Fish	Tons	Value, £
Great Britain . .	8	13,000	200,000
France	21	34,000	340,000
Norway . . .	65	110,000	1,050,000
Canada . . .	28	45,000	520,000
Total . .	122	202,000	2,110,000

The production of cod-liver oil averages 900,000 gallons yearly, chiefly in Norway and Canada, 100 livers yielding one gallon of oil.

Herring

Fishers	Tons Herrings	Value, £
Scotch	140,000	1,700,000
English	80,000	950,000
Irish	20,000	240,000
French	42,000	550,000
Norwegian . . .	60,000	700,000
Canadian . . .	48,000	600,000
Total . .	390,000	4,740,000

About 10,000 herrings go to a ton, a British barrel containing 1000, a Norwegian 500 fish. The number of men engaged in herring-fishing is 180,000, who catch on an average 22,000 fish each.

Mussels.—In 1850 there were 300 mussel-beds, and now there are 3000, in the Bay of Aguillon, France, extending seven miles along the shore. The industry was introduced by an Irish settler, and these beds produce annually 350,000 bushels, valued at £55,000.

Oysters.—The ordinary production and consumption are :—

	Per Annum			
	Product, Millions		Consumption, Millions	Per Inhabitant
U. Kingdom	29	London .	500	120
France . .	300	Paris . .	57	26
United States	3,500	New York	810	660
Portugal . .	600	France .	260	7
Total .	4,429		...	...

Baltimore packs seven million bushels per annum. An oyster three months old is the size of a shilling, six months half-a-crown, but is not fit to eat before four years old. The oyster-beds established by advice of Abbé Bonnetard in France produced 97 million oysters in 1881. According to Mayhew, the consumption in London in 1864 was 310,000 barrels, containing 496 million oysters, being 1600 to the barrel, and representing a value of £2,100,000 ; this, however, seems a retail value, as they were valued the same year in France at £2 per thousand, which would be only one million sterling. The American oyster-fishing is valued at five millions sterling per annum, that of Canada (60,000 barrels) at £40,000 yearly.

Pilchards.—The Cornishmen take 150 millions yearly ; exportation, 12,000 hogsheads.

Salmon.—The annual fishery in the United Kingdom is as follows :—

				Tons	Value, £
England	.	.	.	360	40,000
Scotland	.	.	.	2,600	280,000
Ireland	.	.	.	2,900	320,000
	Total	.		5,860	640,000

London consumes nearly one-third, namely, 1840 tons yearly. England imports 50 tons per annum from Norway. Salmon have been caught in the Tay weighing 70 lbs., but the average weight of this fish is only 8 lbs. The exportation of tinned salmon from California exceeds 10 million lbs. yearly, of which one-half goes to England, one-fourth to the Continent, and the rest to New York, &c. The quantity has doubled since 1875. This is irrespective of six million lbs. annually consumed in California. There is a royal salmon-fishery at Ulea, in Finland, where 60,000 are taken yearly. The largest salmon caught in the United Kingdom in 1889 was one of 61 lbs., in the Severn. The fishermen of Colombia River, Canada, exported 415,000 cases of tinned salmon to England in 1889, containing 21,000,000 tins. The total consumption of British and imported salmon in London in 1883 was 5000 tons, or nearly 3 lbs. per inhabitant.

Sardines

	Annual Fishery	
	Million Fish	Tons Weight
Spain	1,260	52,000
France	980	41,000

The exportation from France averages 450 millions per annum, say 20,000 tons.

Seals

Fishery	Annual Slaughter	Tons Oil
Canadian . . .	460,000	9,200
Norwegian . .	80,000	1,600
Falkland Islands .	5,000	100
Montevideo . .	5,000	100
Total .	550,000	11,000

The skins vary in value ; the oil fetches £25 per ton. One fishing vessel sometimes kills as many as 50,000 in a season off Nova Scotia. The practice of slaughtering seals while suckling their young threatens to exterminate the breed. In 1889 the British seal-fishers of British Colombia killed 28,000, the American 7000, and the skins were valued at 35s. each.

FISHERIES

UNITED KINGDOM

The Report for 1888 gave the following :—

				Tons Fish	Value, £
England .	.	.	.	317,000	4,210,000
Scotland .	.	.	.	238,000	1,690,000
Ireland .	.	.	.	20,000	510,000
	Total	.		575,000	6,410,000

The above would seem to be the value of the fish when first caught. Some estimates place the value much higher : hence apparent discrepancies on this point.

According to a previous statement, the strength of the fishing marine and the take of herrings were :—

	Vessels	Men	Barrels Herrings
English	14,420	44,200	845,000
Scotch	14,650	47,100	1,580,000
Irish	5,830	21,300	210,000
Total . .	34,900	112,600	2,635,000

The above vessels take other fish besides herrings, but the latter form 70 per cent. of the total value of our sea-fishing. Including fresh-water fish, the value in 1885 was estimated at £5,100,000, viz.:—

Kind					Tons	Value, £
Salmon .	.	.	.	.	3,600	390,000
Cod .	.	.	.	.	13,000	200,000
Whale .	.	.	.	.	...	700,000
Herrings .	.	.	.	.	260,000	2,900,000
Pilchards .	.	.	.	.	3,000	30,000
Lobsters, &c. .	.	.	.	.	...	900,000
		Total	.		...	5,120,000

The take of salmon is 45 per cent. Scotch, 50 per cent. Irish, and 6 per cent. English. A barrel of herrings contains 1000 ; of pilchards, 3000 fish. About half of the herrings and two-thirds of the pilchards are exported.

The railways in 1887 carried 341,000 tons of fish, against 278,000 in 1882, viz.:—

					1882	1887
England .	.	.	.	.	215,000	250,000
Scotland .	.	.	.	.	57,000	84,000
Ireland .	.	.	.	.	6,000	7,000
		Total	.		278,000	341,000

The value of fish taken in England and Wales in 1888 was :—

Kind			Tons	Value, £	Value per Ton, £
Turbot .	.	.	2,700	170,000	63
Sole .	.	.	3,600	380,000	106
Haddock .	.	.	77,000	600,000	8
Herrings .	.	.	86,000	490,000	6
Cod .	.	.	12,000	160,000	13
Mackerel .	.	.	16,000	250,000	15
Pilchards .	.	.	8,000	40,000	5
Plaice .	.	.	35,000	610,000	18
Salmon .	.	.	360	40,000	110
Various .	.	.	76,340	1,200,000	16
	Total	.	317,000	3,940,000	12
Oysters (million) .			29	100,000	...
Lobsters, &c. (million) .			5½	170,000	...
	Total	.	...	4,210,000	...

In 1888 there were 298 fishermen drowned at sea, equal to 9 per 1000 of those constantly engaged in English and Welsh waters in fishing, or 6 per 1000 if casuals be included. In that year London took 180,000 tons, or nearly 60 per cent. of all fish caught in England, equal to 100 lbs. of fish per inhabitant for yearly consumption. The Scotch fisheries have multiplied fourteen-fold since the time of the Napoleon wars, viz. :—

1805-10.—Cured . . 90,000 barrels fish per annum
1881-83.—Cured . 1,250,000   ,,   ,,

The imports and exports of fish at various dates were :—

Year	Imports		Exports	
	Tons	Value, £	Tons	Value, £
1853 . . .	10,000	170,000	43,000	. 450,000
1860 . . .	22,000	370,000	42,000	580,000
1870 . . .	38,000	770,000	75,000	910,000
1880 . . .	67,000	1,670,000	134,000	1,780,000
1888 . . .	95,000	2,320,000	136,000	1,570,000

The quantities exported can only be given approximately, the weight only of herrings, the value of other kinds being stated in the Customs. Herrings are about three-fourths of the total of fish exports.

FRANCE

The product in 1880 was as follows :—

Kind	Tons	Value, £
Cod	34,000	310,000
Herring and mackerel	48,000	680,000
Sardines . . .	38,000	1,650,000
Various . . .	10,000	840,000
Total . .	130,000	3,480,000

The difference between deep-sea and coast fishing was as follows :—

	Deep-Sea	Coast	Total
Men . . .	13,000	72,000	85,000
Tons, fish . .	34,000	96,000	130,000
Value, £ . .	350,000	3,130,000	3,480,000

Being an average of £26 per deep-sea, and £44 per coast fisherman.
The following report was published in 1886 :—

Class	1874		1885	
	Fishermen	Tons Fish	Fishermen	Tons Fish
Cod . . .	11,700	31,000	12,300	40,000
Various . .	101,300	71,000	131,700	113,000
Total . .	113,000	102,000	144,000	153,000

The take of oysters and sardines was as follows :—

Year	Oysters, Million		Sardines, Million
1874	52	...	611
1885	127	...	494

The French oyster-beds showed the following product :—

Year	Millions					
	Arca-chon	Roche-fort	Auray	Gran-ville	Can-cale	Total
1862 . . .	8	1	...	13	18	40
1868 . . .	8	3	3	0	1	15
1872 . . .	10	1	7	1	4	23
1874 . . .	42	2	10	1	9	64
1876 . . .	197	30	22	1	9	259

The Cancale beds produced 70 millions in 1843, the Granville 46 millions in 1857. The total French product was valued at £34,000 in 1869, at £74,000 in 1874.

The value of all fish taken in 1885 was £3,700,000, against £2,900,000 in 1874. The exportation of sardines was as follows :—

Year				Tons	Million Fish
1880	.	.	.	10,300	260
1889	.	.	.	12,400	310

In 1888 France exported 19,000 tons of dried codfish ; the fish bounty paid that year by Government was £160,000 sterling. Nevertheless, the deep-sea fishery is not progressing ; the returns of sixty years ago (1830) showed 441 vessels of 67,000 tons burthen, manned by 12,100 fishermen, the same number as at present.

HOLLAND

Such was the importance of Dutch fisheries 300 years ago, that Amsterdam was said to be built of herring-bones. In the sixteenth century the Dutch had 1500 vessels in the Shetland herring-fisheries, and 260 Arctic whalers, manned by 14,000 seamen. Injudicious restrictions and heavy taxes brought down this industry, till, in 1854, Holland had only 80 busses.

The returns of herring-fishery in recent years show thus :—

Year	Busses			Value Taken, £		
	Deep-Sea	Coast	Total	Deep-Sea	Coast	Total
1874 . .	114	218	332	110,000	40,000	150,000
1880 . .	133	284	417	150,000	60,000	210,000
1882 . .	145	261	416	190,000	80,000	270,000

Deep-sea fishing showed annual averages as follows :—

Period	Busses	Tons Fish	Value, £
1858-67 .	86	4,000	50,000
1868-77 .	110	7,200	100,000
1878-82 .	134	15,000	150,000

Coast-fishing was as follows :—

Year	Busses	Barrels Fish	Value, £
1874 . .	218	27,600	35,000
1880 . .	284	56,700	60,000
1882 . .	261	51,100	80,000

The oyster-fishery produced as follows :—

Year				Number	Tons
1876	.	.	.	36,600,000	2,900
1880	.	.	.	16,500,000	1,200
1882	.	.	.	15,600,000	1,100

It appears that 14,000 oysters go to a ton. The consumption was as follows :—

					Tons
Holland	.	.	.	.	154
Germany	.	.	.	.	346
England, &c.	.	.	.	.	600
Total	.	.	.		1,100

RUSSIA

In 1800 Hermann valued the fisheries at £1,500,000 per annum. In 1880 the take was estimated at 220,000 tons, worth £2,200,000.

SWEDEN

In 1800 the annual take was 600 million fish, or 600,000 barrels, of which three-fourths were consumed at home. The exports have been as follows :—

Year				Tons	Value, £
1800	.	.	.	15,000	150,000
1830	.	.	.	30,000	300,000
1886	.	.	.	25,000	280,000

In 1880 there were 29,000 fishermen ; the annual take would probably exceed 60,000 tons.

NORWAY

In 1883 the returns showed as follows :—

Class	Fishermen	Fish, Millions	Value, £
Cod . . .	58,000	65	920,000
Herring . . .	53,000	410	640,000
Total .	111,000	475	1,560,000

Besides the above, the Norwegians take 350 whales, 80,000 seals, and in fresh waters a quantity of salmon.

UNITED STATES

In 1880 there were 131,400 fishermen, with 51,400 boats of all sizes, and the annual take was valued at £8,610,000.

CANADA

According to a statement in 1883 we find :—

Fish		Value, £
Cod, tons . . .	45,000	520,000
Herring, tons . .	48,000	580,000
Seals, number .	460,000	280,000
Whales, &c. . . .	...	1,070,000
Total . . .		2,450,000

In 1889 there were 31,600 vessels, manned by 59,800 fishermen, whose take was valued at £3,800,000 yearly.

The fisheries of the principal nations may be summed up thus, approximately :—

	Vessels	Men	Tons Fish	Value, £	Value per Man, £
England .	14,400	47,300	320,000	4,200,000	95
Scotland .	14,600	50,000	240,000	1,700,000	34
Ireland . .	5,800	21,800	25,000	500,000	23
U. Kingdom	34,800	129,100	585,000	6,400,000	50
France . .	23,900	144,000	153,000	3,700,000	26
Germany .	8,100	17,000	40,000	400,000	24
Russia . .	13,500	68,000	220,000	2,200,000	32
Austria . .	2,800	7,000	15,000	150,000	22
Italy . . .	18,200	61,000	100 000	1,000,000	17
Spain . .	10,200	38,000	50,000	500,060	13
Sweden . .	7,000	29,000	60,000	600,000	21
Norway . .	31,600	111,000	160,000	1,600,000	15
Holland . .	500	8,000	20,000	270,000	34
Europe . .	150,600	612,100	1,403,000	16,820,000	27
U. States .	51,400	131,400	600,000	8,600,000	65
Canada . .	31,600	59,800	300,000	3,800,000	63
Total .	233,600	803,300	2,303,000	29,220,000	36

FLAX AND LINEN.

Flax-growing received an abnormal impulse by the American War of 1861-64 and ensuing cotton-famine, but has been on the decline in most countries, except Russia, during the last ten years. The production in the United Kingdom was as follows :—

Year					Tons	Value of Crop, £
1830 .	.	.	.	.	15,500	1,240,000
1850 .	.	.	.	.	21,000	760,000
1870 .	.	.	.	.	32,500	1,700,000
1888 .	.	.	.	.	20,000	680,000

Neumann-Spallart's table for 1885 and some later figures show flax-growing as follows :—

	Acres	Tons Flax	Lbs. per Acre
United Kingdom . .	116,000	21,000	400
France	109,000	28,000	570
Germany	270,000	44,000	365
Russia	3,000,000	330,000	240
Austria	240,000	47,000	440
Italy	170,000	20,000	265
Belgium	98,000	21,000	470
Holland	38,000	8,000	460
Sweden	28,000	3,000	230
Other countries * . .	46,000	4,000	200
United States . . .	400,000	42,000	230
Total	4,515,000	568,000	320

Linen Manufacture.—The latest information may be summed up thus, the consumption of flax and value of product being given approximately :—

	Number of Spindles	Power-Looms	Tons Flax Consumed	Value of Manufacture £
U. Kingdom	1,160,000	47,600	85,000	8,500,000
France . .	500,000	23,000	90,000	9,000,000
Germany .	318,000	8,000	64,000	7,000,000
Russia . .	150,000	2,500	120,000	9,000,000
Austria . .	399,000	500	57,000	5,700,000
Italy . . .	59,000	800	27,000	2,700,000
Spain . .	...	1,000	10,000	1,000,000
Sweden . .	4,000	100	3,000	300,000
Holland . .	8,000	1,200	5,000	500,000
Belgium . .	289,000	4,800	50,000	5,000,000
Switzerland.	9,000	...	3,000	300,000
U. States .	13,000	7,000	42,000	4,200,000
Total . .	2,909,000	96,500	556,000	53,200,000

UNITED KINGDOM.

The production of linen from 1700 to 1830 was recorded for the purpose of bounties ; since the latter year it is estimated according to the consumption of flax. The production in the three kingdoms was approximately as follows :—

Period	Millions of Yards per Annum			
	England	Scotland	Ireland †	Total
1701–50 . . .	...	5	8	13
1751–99 . . .	8	14	31	53
1800–10 . . .	15	25	46	86
1811–20 . . .	20	33	60	113
1821–30 . . .	24	60	90	174
1831–40 . . .	35	90	125	250
1841–50 . . .	50	100	160	310
1851–60 . . .	50	100	150	300
1861–70 . . .	50	110	190	350
1871–80 . . .	50	100	150	300
1881–90 . . .	45	95	140	280

* New Zealand exports yearly 1500 tons of a fibre which yields 17 per cent. flax.

† The production and export of Irish linen in the 18th century were approximately as follows :—

Year	Yards Made	Yards Exported	Home Use
1710 . . .	4,500,000	2,000,000	2,500,000
1740 . . .	12,000,000	7,000,000	5,000,000
1800 . . .	44,000,000	36,000,000	8,000,000

The following table shows the consumption of flax and the domestic and foreign trade in linen since 1806 :—

Year	Flax, Tons	Millions of Yards Linen			Export Yarn, Million Lbs.	Value of Manu-facture, £
		Made	Exported	Home Use		
1806	22,000	86	40	46	...	3,800,000
1820	40,000	145	50	95	...	5,800,000
1830	62,000	223	62	161	...	7,600,000
1840	94,000	290	87	203	16	10,800,000
1850	110,000	340	105	235	18	12,600,000
1860	102,000	270	144	126	31	11,400,000
1870	130,000	360	226	134	37	13,500,000
1881	102,000	310	174	136	18	11,700,000
1888	85,000	260	177	83	15	8,500,000

The total value represented by the linen industry since 1821 is approximately as follows :—

Period	Millions £ Sterling			
	Home Use	Exported Linens	Exported Yarn	Total
1821–30 . .	52	21	...	73
1831–40 . .	60	25	3	88
1841–50 . .	63	34	6	103
1851–60 . .	56	44	13	113
1861–70 . .	52	71	24	147
1871–80 . .	50	66	16	132
1881–88 . .	36	44	8	88
68 years . .	369	305	70	744

The following table shows approximately the output of linen in English statute miles, the amount paid for flax in 68 years, and the product of this industry :—

Period	Miles of Linen	Amount in Millions £			Price of Linen per Mile, £
		Flax	Manu-factures	Net Product	
1821–30	990,000	41	73	32	70
1831–40	1,420,000	58	88	30	60
1841–50	1,760,000	54	103	49	55
1851–60	1,700,000	46	113	67	52
1861–70	2,000,000	59	147	88	60
1871–80	1,700,000	56	132	76	55
1881–88	1,300,000	29	88	59	45
68 years	10,870,000	343	744	401	55

The factory statistics of this industry are as follows :—

Year		Factories	Operatives	Spindles
1840	. .	392	43,000	...
1870	. .	502	125,000	1,480,000
1885	. .	388	112,000	1,160,000

In 1879 the industry stood thus :—

	No. of Factories	Spindles	Power-Looms	Operatives
England . .	101	191,000	4,100	15,000
Scotland . .	155	265,000	16,800	37,000
Ireland . . .	144	809,000	19,600	56,000
U. Kingdom .	400	1,265,000	40,500	108,000

FRANCE

In 1839 the linen manufactures were estimated by Berghus at £10,400,000, which would be equivalent to 280 million yards, and indicate a consumption of 70,000 tons of flax. They were valued by Tolosan in the previous century, 1788, at about five millions sterling. France consumes three times as much flax as she produces, the import of this fibre showing thus :—

Year		Tons
1872 .	. . . . .	56,000
1880 .	. . . . .	67,000
1887 .	. . . . .	60,000

In this branch of manufacture she is ahead of the United Kingdom, and turns out about 360 million yards per annum. In five years ending 1888 France exported £3,200,000 of linens yearly.

GERMANY

In 1805 Oddy valued the linen manufactures of Prussia at £1,800,000; and in 1843 the value had risen to £2,800,000. At the latter date Prussia stood for three-fourths of the linen manufactures of the Zollverein.

Germany in 1838 counted 13,000 spindles and 283,000 looms, showing an increase of 30 per cent. since 1822, but it was not until after the land-reform of 1848 and the introduction of railways that this industry notably expanded. In 1855 there were 74,000 flax-spindles, and 189,000 in 1865.

The home production of flax is 44,000 tons.

The net imports are as follows :—

Year		Tons
1873 .	. . . . .	24,000
1880 .	. . . . .	13,000
1887 .	. . . . .	20,000

The consumption, therefore, seems to average 64,000 tons yearly, which is equivalent to a make of 260 million yards of linen.

RUSSIA

In 1828 there were 214 linen-factories, which turned out 20 million yards, valued at £800,000; this was exclusive of Poland, which made two million yards yearly. In 1864 there were 599 factories, with 44,000 operatives, the production being estimated by Bushen at £5,300,000.

According to Mr. Spallart and the official report, an enormous increase took place recently in flax-growing, the area under this crop reaching 3,785,000 acres, and being supposed to yield 400,000 tons of flax; a pure delusion, for we see that the exports of flax have diminished. The area under flax in 1872 was 2,250,000 acres, the crop 242,000 tons ; the real figures are probably still the same. During ten years ending 1887 Russia imported linen manufactures worth £400,000 a year. The exports of flax were :—

Period		Tons Yearly
1861–63 .	. . . .	65,000
1870–71 .	. . . .	162,000
1885–87 .	. . . .	140,000

AUSTRIA

An official return published in 1828 showed that the production of linen since 1824 averaged 92 million yards per annum. In 1840 there were 869 factories, with

280,000 hands. Most of the industry is situate in Bohemia, where it has flourished since the fourteenth century.

The production of flax averages 5000 tons in Hungary, 8000 in Bohemia, and amounts altogether to 47,000 tons, besides which the Empire imports 10,000 tons. The factories may, therefore, be estimated to produce 230 million yards linen per annum. In ten years ending 1887 Austria exported £600,000 per annum of linen goods.

ITALY

The official report of 1877 showed linen-factories with an aggregate of 13,000 operatives, and 59,000 spindles worked by 3000 horse-power, of which 2500 water and 500 steam. About 20,000 tons of flax are grown, and linen yarn is imported, the imports showing thus:—

Period	Tons Yarn Yearly
1862–64	3000
1872–73	4000
1885–87	6600

The actual product of linen is about 120 million yards yearly.

SPAIN

A statement published about 1870 gives the linen-factories a total of 6000 operatives and 5000 looms, the annual product being valued at £1,100,000 sterling. This indicates a consumption of 10,000 tons flax and an output of 40 million yards. At that time the average importation of flax and linen yarn was 5000 tons yearly, from which it would appear that Spain produces 5000 tons of her own.

The import of linen yarn yearly was as follows:—

Period	Tons
1863–66	7500
1873–76	5500
1883–87	3800

This shows a very steady decline of the industry, notwithstanding the enormous import dues on foreign linen goods. In ten years ending 1887 the import of linens averaged £400,000 yearly.

BELGIUM

The industry has been almost stationary for 50 years. Thus in 1835 there were 101,000 acres under flax, producing 21,000 tons, and the factories turned out 90 million yards linen, valued at four millions sterling. At present the flax area is 98,000 acres, and the mills turn out about 120 million yards linen. The output has always been, as in the United Kingdom, largely in excess of the requirements for home consumption. The export of linen fabrics and yarn has been:—

Period	Annual Average, £
1860–62	1,700,000
1870–72	2,600,000
1885–87	4,100,000

This includes 13,000 tons of linen yarn. Belgium imports about 30,000 tons of flax, the mills consuming altogether about 50,000 tons. In ten years ending 1887 the export of linens averaged £800,000 yearly.

UNITED STATES

The industry is of no magnitude, counting only 13,000 spindles and 7000 looms, which appear to consume native flax only, the crop being estimated at 42,000 tons. The Americans, meantime, consume imported linens largely, the value averaging thus:—

Period	£
1841–43	800,000
1861–63	1,400,000
1871–73	3,800,000
1881–83	3,700,000

The consumption of linen is about 300 million yards, of which one-half is made in the country.

APPROXIMATE PRODUCTION OF LINEN

	Million Yards		Million Yards
United Kingdom .	300	Spain . . .	40
France . . .	320	Sweden . . .	10
Germany . . .	260	Holland . . .	20
Russia . . .	360	Belgium . . .	120
Austria . . .	230	United States . .	160
Italy . . .	120	Switzerland . .	10

The whole makes up nearly 2000 million yards, worth about 50 millions sterling.

FLOODS

Date	Place	Loss
1642 . .	China . . .	300,000 lives
1646 . .	Holland . . .	110,000 lives
1875 . .	Toulouse. . .	£15,000,000
1876 . .	Bengal . . .	200,000 lives
1879 . .	Zegedin . . .	£8,500,000
1883 . .	Rhine Valley . .	£6,000,000

In the last-mentioned the area of country under water was 260 square miles, equal to the extent of the Lake of Constance.

FODDER

In feeding animals it is found that 10 lbs. hay are equivalent to:—

	Lbs.		Lbs.		Lbs.
Oil-cake . .	3	Wheat . .	6	Mangel-wurzel	33
Beans . . .	4	Potatoes . .	22	Straw . . .	45
Oats . . .	5	Cabbage . .	25	Turnips . .	47
Maize . . .	6	Carrots . .	30	Clover . .	50

A horse will eat in a year nine times his own weight, a cow nine times, an ox six times, a sheep six times.

FOOD

The food supply of the civilised nations, that is, Europe, United States, British Colonies, &c., has increased (except as regards meat) during the nineteenth century much faster than population, which shows that the material welfare of mankind has advanced in its most important particular.

The following table shows approximately the quantities of food produced and the population subsisting thereon:—

Period	Tons Produced Yearly				Population
	Grain	Meat	Sugar	Coffee and Tea	
1831–40	101,000,000	8,700,000	530,000	210,000	251,000,000
1851–60	139,000,000	10,490,000	1,100,000	390,000	300,000,000
1875–84	204,000,000	13,260,000	3,670,000	745,000	370,000,000
1888	241,000,000	14,430,000	5,260,000	920,000	404,000,000

In the above table grain includes what is used both for man and beast. The averages per head of population were :—

Period	Lbs. per Inhabitant			
	Grain	Meat	Sugar	Coffee and Tea
1831–40	900	79	5	2
1851–60	1,040	79	8	3
1874–84	1,240	72	22	4½
1887	1,330	79	29	5

The production of wheat, as shown already when treating of Agriculture, has averaged as follows :—

Period	Tons Yearly			
	Europe	United States	Colonies, &c.	Total
1831–40	17,800,000	1,950,000	2,900,000	22,650,000
1851–80	21,420,000	3,430,000	5,120,000	29,970,000
1871–80	28,150,000	8,450,000	8,250,000	44,850,000
1881–87	30,770,000	11,000,000	11,230,000	53,000,000
1888	32,400,000	10,370,000	14,050,000	56,820,000

In the period ending 1840 Europe produced 80 per cent. of the wheat of the world, as compared with 56 per cent. at present. In the interval the production in the United States and in the Colonies has quintupled.

The production of other grain during the same period was approximately as follows :—

Period	Tons Yearly			
	Europe	United States	Colonies, &c.	Total
1831–40	62,500,000	11,550,000	4,300,000	78,350,000
1851–60	79,730,000	22,920,000	6,380,000	109,030,000
1871–80	86,850,000	49,500,000	7,150,000	143,500,000
1881–87	101,230,000	56,500,000	10,270,000	168,000,000
1888	105,800,000	68,710,000	9,450,000	183,960,000

The total grain production since 1830 has been approximately :—

Period	Tons Yearly			
	Europe	United States	Colonies, &c.	Total
1831–40	80,300,000	13,500,000	7,200,000	101,000,000
1851–60	101,150,000	26,350,000	11,500,000	139,000,000
1871–80	115,000,000	57,950,000	15,400,000	188,350,000
1881–87	132,000,000	67,500,000	21,500,000	221,000,000
1888	138,200,000	79,080,000	23,500,000	240,780,000

The ratio of increase in production of grain was thus :—

	1831–40	1851–60	1871–80	1888
Europe	100	126	144	172
United States . . .	100	195	430	585
Colonies, &c.	100	160	214	326
Total . . .	100	138	186	238

The weight and value of grain used for human food in 1887 are shown approximately in the following table :—

	Tons				Value, Millions £
	Wheat	Rye	Oats, &c.	Total	
United Kingdom . . .	6,200,000	...	200,000	6,400,000	46
France	8,200,000	900,000	...	9,100,000	77
Germany	3,000,000	6,000,000	2,200,000	11,200,000	68
Russia	4,200,000	14,500,000	4,300,000	23,000,000	97
Austria	4,300,000	3,300,000	800,000	8,400,000	52
Italy	3,000,000	400,000	1,900,000	5,300,000	39
Spain*	3,000,000	400,000	400,000	3,800,000	28
Portugal	300,000	300,000	300,000	900,000	6
Sweden	300,000	700,000	200,000	1,200,000	8
Norway	100,000	200,000	100,000	400,000	3
Denmark	200,000	300,000	...	500,000	4
Holland	500,000	400,000	200,000	1,100,000	8
Belgium	800,000	600,000	200,000	1,600,000	12
Switzerland	300,000	200,000	100,000	600,000	4
Roumania	300,000	200,000	300,000	800,000	4
Servia	100,000	100,000	100,000	300,000	2
Europe	34,800,000	28,500,000	11,300,000	74,600,000	458
United States . . .	7,300,000	600,000	2,100,000	10,000,000	48
Canada	800,000	...	100,000	900,000	6
Australia	700,000	...	...	700,000	5
Total . .	43,600,000	29,000,000	13,500,000	86,200,000	517

The different kinds of meat produced were as follows :—

Period	Tons Yearly			
	Beef	Mutton	Pork	Total
1831–40	3,821,000	2,050,000	2,830,000	8,701,000
1851–60	4,950,000	2,203,000	3,340,000	10,493,000
1874–84	6,303,000	2,470,000	4,490,000	13,263,000
1887	7,205,000	2,709,000	4,479,000	14,393,000

* Spanish statistics, as a rule, bear the impress of exaggeration, and hence the production and consumption of grian and the numbers of live-stock must be doubtful.

The consumption of meat in Europe at present averages 61 lbs. yearly per inhabitant, against 64 lbs. in the decade ending 1840, viz. :—

	Lbs. per Inhabitant	
	1840	1888
United Kingdom . .	87	109
France	43	77
Germany	60	64
Russia	67	51
Austria	76	61
Belgium	50	65

Meantime there has been an increased consumption per head in towns.

About 60,000 tons of frozen mutton are imported into Europe annually from Australia and the River Plate. An engine of 70-horse power serves to refrigerate a chamber containing 250 tons of meat, and consumes 50 tons of coal in a voyage of forty days.

The production of meat was approximately as follows :—

	Tons Yearly			
	1831–40	1851–60	1874–84	1887
U. Kingdom	980,000	1,047,000	1,100,000	1,105,000
France . .	670,000	940,000	1,155,000	1,200,000
Germany .	900,000	1,246,000	1,300,000	1,375,000
Russia . .	1,430,000	1,670,000	1,800,000	1,885,000
Austria . .	990,000	980,000	1,080,000	1,080,000
Italy . . .	300,000	300,000	330,000	360,000
Spain . .	405,000	350,000	470,000	525,000
Portugal . .	70,000	77,000	90,000	95,000
Sweden . .	106,000	120,000	135,000	140,000
Norway . .	44,000	64,000	67,000	67,000
Denmark .	100,000	115,000	110,000	115,000
Holland . .	96,000	104,000	120,000	125,000
Belgium . .	70,000	90,000	106,000	110,000
Other countries	310,000	360,000	440,000	451,000
Europe . .	6,471,000	7,463,000	8,303,000	8,633,000
U. States .	2,050,000	2,650,000	4,120,000	4,750,000
Canada . .	90,000	140,000	240,000	260,000
Australia .	40,000	140,000	300,000	450,000
Argentine Republic	50,000	100,000	300,000	300,000
Total .	8,701,000	10,493,000	13,263,000	14,393,000

The annual production in tons was as follows :—

Period	Beef				
	United Kingdom	Continent	United States	Colonies, &c.	Total
1831–40	300,000	2,790,000	630,000	100,000	3,820,000
1851–60	410,000	3,420,000	920,000	200,000	4,950,000
1874–84	520,000	3,843,000	1,540,000	400,000	6,303,000
1887	545,000	4,029,000	2,190,000	441,000	7,205,000

Period	Mutton.				
1831–40	480,000	1,320,000	170,000	80,000	2,050,000
1851–60	430,000	1,390,000	220,000	163,000	2,203,000
1874–84	390,000	1,420,000	310,000	350,000	2,470,000
1887	365,000	1,480,000	390,000	474,000	2,709,000

Period	Pork.				
1831–40	200,000	1,380,000	1,250,000	...	2,830,000
1851–60	210,000	1,600,000	1,510,000	20,000	3,340,000
1874–84	190,000	1,940,000	2,270,000	90,000	4,490,000
1887	195,000	2,019,000	2,170,000	95,000	4,479,000

Period	Total of Meat.				
1831–40	980,000	5,490,000	2,050,000	170,000	8,700,000
1851–60	1,050,000	6,410,000	2,650,000	340,000	10,493,000
1874–84	1,100,000	7,203,000	4,120,000	840,000	13,263,000
1887	1,105,000	7,528,000	4,750,000	920,000	14,393,000

The relative increase of each kind of meat since 1840 is shown in the following table :—

	1831–40	1851–60	1887
Beef	100	130	188
Mutton . . .	100	108	132
Pork	100	118	158
All meat . . .	100	120	166

The production in the various countries in 1887 was approximately as follows :—

	Tons Produced				Consumption
	Beef	Mutton	Pork	Total	
United Kingdom . . .	545,000	365,000	195,000	1,105,000	1,783,000
France	660,000	250,000	290,000	1,200,000	1,320,000
Germany	710,000	210,000	455,000	1,375,000	1,385,000
Russia	1,050,000	415,000	420,000	1,885,000	1,854,000
Austria	640,000	120,000	320,000	1,080,000	1,050,000
Italy	220,000	85,000	55,000	360,000	330,000
Spain	125,000	220,000	180,000	525,000	525,000
Portugal	25,000	25,000	45,000	95,000	94,000
Sweden	103,000	14,000	23,000	140,000	140,000
Norway	48,000	15,000	4,000	67,000	73,000
Denmark	74,000	15,000	26,000	115,000	57,000
Holland	93,000	9,000	23,000	125,000	105,000
Belgium	74 000	5,000	31,000	110,000	166,000
Switzerland	48,000	6,000	14,000	68,000	83,000
Roumania	120,000	40,000	80,000	240,000	210,000
Servia	27,000	23,000	50,000	100,000	75,000
Greece	12,000	28,000	3,000	43,000	47,000
Europe	4,574,000	1,845,000	2,214,000	8,633,000	9,297,000
United States	2,190,000	390,000	2,170,000	4,750,000	4,100,000
Canada	176,000	24,000	60,000	260,000	200,000
Australia	115,000	300,000	35,000	450,000	420,000
Argentina	150,000	150,000	...	300,000	250,000
Total . . .	7,205,000	2,709,000	4,479,000	14,393,000	14,267,000

There is a surplus production of 126,000 tons, which is consumed in the West Indies, Brazil, and other countries. At present Europe imports 660,000 tons yearly, and large supplies may in future be obtained from the United States, Australia, and the River Plate. Taking the slaughter as usual in Europe, viz., 20 per cent. yearly of horned cattle, 40 per cent. of sheep, and 100 per cent. of pigs, and the average carcase at 500 lbs. of beef, 50 lbs. of mutton, and 100 lbs. pork, the annual production and the available surplus for exportation would be :—

PLATE V.

FOOD-SUPPLY.

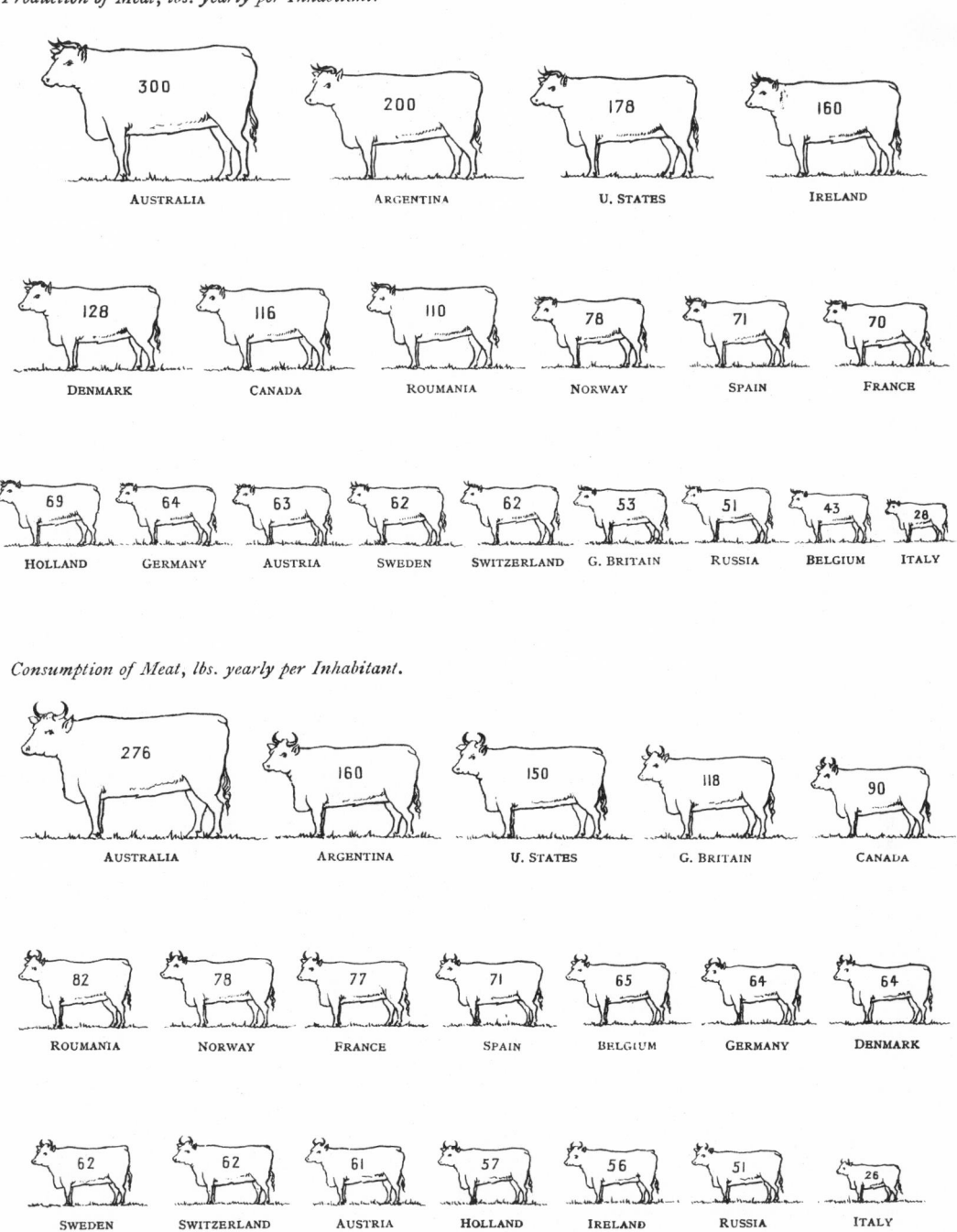

Production of Meat, lbs. yearly per Inhabitant.

300 AUSTRALIA · 200 ARGENTINA · 178 U. STATES · 160 IRELAND

128 DENMARK · 116 CANADA · 110 ROUMANIA · 78 NORWAY · 71 SPAIN · 70 FRANCE

69 HOLLAND · 64 GERMANY · 63 AUSTRIA · 62 SWEDEN · 62 SWITZERLAND · 53 G. BRITAIN · 51 RUSSIA · 43 BELGIUM · 28 ITALY

Consumption of Meat, lbs. yearly per Inhabitant.

276 AUSTRALIA · 160 ARGENTINA · 150 U. STATES · 118 G. BRITAIN · 90 CANADA

82 ROUMANIA · 78 NORWAY · 77 FRANCE · 71 SPAIN · 65 BELGIUM · 64 GERMANY · 64 DENMARK

62 SWEDEN · 62 SWITZERLAND · 61 AUSTRIA · 57 HOLLAND · 56 IRELAND · 51 RUSSIA · 26 ITALY

	Tons Production				Tons Consumption	Tons for Export
	Beef	Mutton	Pork	Total		
United States . . .	2,190,000	390,000	2,170,000	4,750,000	4,140,000	610,000
Australia . . .	400,000	870,000	30,000	1,300,000	420,000	880,000
River Plate . . .	1,120,000	900,000	10,000	2,030,000	260,000	1,770,000
Total . . .	3,710,000	2,160,000	2,210,000	8,080,000	4,820,000	3,260,000

The available surplus of the above three countries will be equal to 34 per cent. of the annual meat consumption of Europe, say four months' supply.

At present, however, the beef of the River Plate is out of the question, owing to the poor quality of the beasts. The importation of frozen mutton into England from the Southern Hemisphere has increased rapidly of late years. In 1889 the following quantities were received :—

From	Tons	Value, £	Per Ton, £
Australia . . .	30,600	1,290,000	43
Argentina . . .	19,700	750,000	38
Falklands, &c. .	7,100	360,000	50
Total . .	57,400	2,400,000	42

New Zealand sheep average 70 lbs., Argentine 40 lbs., and the approximate cost of the mutton delivered in London is as follows :—

	Pence per Lb.	£ per Ton
First cost of meat . .	2.5	23.3
Freezing process . .	0.5	4.7
Freight and charges .	1.0	9.4
Total .	4.0	37.4

The production of beef-extract has also increased, as the slaughter at Liebig's factory at Fray Bentos, Uruguay, rose from 200,000 head of cattle in 1881 to 580,000 in 1884.

Block gave the average annual consumption of meat in the following cities in ten years down to 1877 as follows :—

Pounds Meat per Inhabitant

Paris . . . 207	Milan . . . 106
Vienna . . 150	Berlin . . . 90
Dresden . . 140	Naples . . 75
Turin . . . 125	Boston . . 306

In London the apparent consumption is only 230,000 tons, or 128 lbs. per inhabitant, but this does not include tinned meats, such as corned beef.

In 1861 the consumption per head was estimated at 172 lbs. in London, 138 in Paris, 119 in Berlin, and 103 in Madrid.

The consumption of food is approximately :—

	Lbs. per Inhabitant						Tea and Coffee, Oz.
	Grain	Meat	Butter and Cheese	Sugar	Potatoes	Salt	
U. Kingdom . .	378	109	19	75	380	40	91
France	540	77	8	20	570	20	66
Germany . . .	550	64	8	18	1,020	17	78
Russia	635	51	5	11	180	19	6
Austria	460	61	7	18	560	14	28
Italy	400	26	4	8	50	18	20
Spain	480	71	3	6	20	17	6
Portugal . . .	500	49	3	12	40	17	18
Sweden	560	62	11	22	500	28	112
Norway	440	78	14	13	500	40	144
Denmark . . .	560	64	22	22	410	25	140
Holland . . .	560	57	15	35	820	20	240
Belgium . . .	590	65	15	27	1,050	...	142
Switzerland . .	440	62	11	26	140	...	110
Roumania . .	400	82	9	4	80	...	8
Servia . .	400	84	9	4	80	...	8
Europe	480	61	9	22	420	20	21
United States . .	370	150	20	53	170	39	162
Canada	400	90	22	45	600	40	72
Australia . . .	440	276	21	77	310	...	134
General average .	440	72	11	28	380	...	64

The quantities of food consumed by mankind in the various countries in 1887 were approximately as follows :—

	Tons					
	Grain	Meat	Butter and Cheese	Sugar	Potatoes	Coffee and Tea
United Kingdom	6,400,000	1,783,000	328,000	1,300,000	6,300,000	92,000
France	9,100,000	1,320,000	145,000	400,000	10,000,000	70,000
Germany	11,200,000	1,385,000	185,000	410,000	22,000,000	110,000
Russia	23,000,000	1,854,000	210,000	412,000	6,700,000	15,000
Austria	8,400,000	1,050,000	130,000	305,000	10,000,000	33,000
Italy	5,300,000	330,000	60,000	98,000	600,000	16,000
Spain	3,800,000	525,000	30,000	53,000	200,000	7,000
Portugal	900,000	94,000	7,000	24,000	100,000	3,000
Sweden	1,200,000	140,000	25,000	47,000	1,100,000	15,000
Norway	400,000	73,000	13,000	11,000	500,000	7,000
Denmark	500,000	57,000	20,000	21,000	300,000	9,000
Holland	1,100,000	105,000	30,000	63,000	1,400,000	27,000
Belgium	1,600,000	166,000	40,000	70,000	2,700,000	24,000
Switzerland	600,000	83,000	15,000	34,000	200,000	9,000
Roumania	800,000	210,000	20,000	10,000	300,000	1,000
Servia	300,000	75,000	10,000	4,000	100,000	...
Europe	74,600,000	9,250,000	1,268,000	3,262,000	62,500,000	438,000
United States	10,000,000	4,100,000	560,000	1,440,000	3,800,000	280,000
Canada	900,000	200,000	50,000	100,000	1,300,000	10,000
Australia	700,000	420,000	36,000	110,000	500,000	16,000
Total . .	86,200,000	13,970,000	1,914,000	4,912,000	68,100,000	744,000

The annual value of food consumed in various countries is approximately as follows :—

	Expenditure, Millions £ Sterling *									Per Inhabitant
	Grain	Meat	Sugar	Dairy and Poultry	Potatoes	Coffee, &c.	Liquor	Sundries	Total	
										£ s. d.
United Kingdom . .	46	87	23	61	19	9	79	48	372	9 12 6
France	77	66	6	59	22	7	92	32	361	9 8 0
Germany	68	69	6	69	56	11	81	40	400	8 8 0
Russia	97	60	6	60	11	2	42	82	360	4 12 0
Austria	52	44	5	41	22	3	40	28	235	6 1 0
Italy	39	17	2	19	1	2	41	23	144	4 16 0
Spain	28	26	1	14	...	1	30	12	112	6 10 0
Portugal	6	5	...	3	...	...	6	3	24	5 10 0
Sweden	8	7	1	7	...	...	7	3	37	7 13 0
Norway	3	3	...	3	1	1	3	1	15	7 10 0
Denmark	4	3	...	4	1	1	3	2	18	9 0 0
Holland	8	5	1	5	3	3	6	5	36	8 0 0
Belgium	12	8	1	7	6	3	14	5	56	9 7 0
Switzerland . . .	4	5	...	3	...	1	3	3	20	6 12 0
Roumania . . .	4	8	...	6	...	...	3	3	25	5 0 0
Servia	2	3	...	2	...	...	1	1	10	5 0 0
Europe . . .	458	416	53	363	146	47	481	261	2,225	6 10 0
United States . .	48	123	21	115	16	24	66	42	455	7 12 0
Canada . . .	6	6	2	7	4	1	3	3	32	6 10 0
Australia . . .	5	8	2	5	1	1	3	3	28	8 5 0
Total . .	517	553	78	490	167	73	553	309	2,740	7 0 0

The above represents the values in first hands, to which must be added 30 per cent. for distribution in retail. As regards liquor, the excise duties are not included, these being comprised under *Taxes.* Professor Keleti estimates the expenditure for food in Austria-Hungary at £9 per man, £7 per woman, and £5 per child, or £7 per inhabitant, which would be 266 millions sterling, being 20 per cent. over the estimate in the above table : his calculation is probably at retail prices.

* The blanks in the table stand for fractions, the amount of which is included at foot.

UNITED KINGDOM

The home production of wheat and meat is as follows :—

	Wheat, Bushels	Beef, Tons	Mutton, Tons	Pork, Tons	Total Meat, Tons
England	77,000,000	268,000	234,000	113,000	615,000
Scotland	2,000,000	58,000	88,000	8,000	154,000
Ireland	1,900,000	218,000	44,000	70,000	332,000
United Kingdom . . .	79,900,000	544,000	366,000	191,000	1,101,000

Food-supply has improved in late years, and the people of this country are the best fed in Europe. The consumption per inhabitant has been approximately as follows :—

	Wheat	Meat	Sugar	Tea	Salt	Beer	Rice	Eggs
	Lbs.	Lbs.	Lbs.	Oz.	Lbs.	Galls.	Lbs.	No.
1811–30	270	80	19	18	16	22	1	40
1831–50	255	87	20	23	25	24	1	48
1851–70	320	90	35	44	45	28	3	60
1871–80	354	93	60	67	72	29	11	65
1881–88	370	102	70	77	72	27	11	70
1889	354	109	75	78	72	27	11	76

The consumption of meat in Great Britain and Ireland differs considerably, viz. :—

	Tons Consumed		Lbs. Meat per Inhab.	
	Great Britain	Ireland	Great Britain	Ireland
British . .	769,000	...	53	...
Irish . . .	237,000	95,000	16	43
Foreign . .	712,000	30,000	49	13
Total .	1,718,000	125,000	118	56

The actual amount of salt consumed for food is probably no more than 36 lbs. per inhabitant, as one-half is supposed to be used in manufactures. The following table shows how our bread-supply and meat are provided :—

Period	Wheat, Million Bushels per Annum			Meat, Tons per Annum		
	Native	Imported	Total	Native	Imported	Total
1841–50	108	14	122	1,014,000	...	1,014,000
1851–60	103	47	150	1,047,000	44,000	1,091,000
1861–70	102	73	175	1,078,000	131,000	1,209,000
1871–80	77	114	191	1,091,000	288,000	1,379,000
1881–88	72	144	216	1,105,000	540,000	1,645,000
1889	70	154	224	1,100,000	742,000	1,842,000

In 1889 Ireland exported to Great Britain the following cattle :—

717,000 cows = 193,000 tons meat.
636,000 sheep = 20,000 ,,
545,000 pigs = 24,000 ,,

Total . . 237,000 ,,

The annual slaughter in the United Kingdom was approximately as follows :—

Period	Horned Cattle	Sheep	Pigs	Tons Meat		
				Beef	Mutton	Pork
1831–40 . . .	1,140,000	15,200,000	2,700,000	305,000	475,000	200,000
1841–50 . . .	1,350,000	14,400,000	2,700,000	364,000	450,000	200,000
1851–60 . . .	1,540,000	13,600,000	2,800,000	412,000	425,000	210,000
1861–70 . . .	1,730,000	13,000,000	2,800,000	462,000	406,000	210,000
1871–80 . . .	1,920,000	12,400,000	2,500,000	514,000	387,000	190,000
1881–88 . . .	2,040,000	11,800,000	2,600,000	544,000	366,000	195,000

The weight and value of all kinds of meat imported in 1889 were as follows :—

	Tons	Value, £	£ per Ton
Live cattle . .	300,000	10,400,000	35
Bacon	175,000	7,300,000	41
Beef	127,000	5,200,000	41
Mutton	61,000	2,600,000	42
Hams	50,000	2,500,000	50
Pork	19,000	700,000	36
Lard	60,000	2,200,000	36
Poultry	10,000	500,000	50
Rabbits . . .	6,000	300,000	50
Total . .	808,000	31,700,000	39

As regards live cattle, the above is an estimate of their equivalent in dead meat, on the assumption that £35 sterling stands for a ton of meat. Deducting lard, poultry, and rabbits, the importation of meat was 742,000 tons.

Full-grown animals in England average as follows :—

	Meat	Fat, &c.	Hide	Total, Lbs.
Cattle . .	680	356	84	1,120
Sheep . .	91	43	18	152

Cows give from 70 to 160 lbs. tallow.

The importation of articles of food is shown in the following tables, that is, the quantities and values of what were retained for consumption.

	1860	1870	1880	1889
Wheat, tons	1,270,000	1,550,000	2,760,000	3,850,000
Sugar, ,,	470,000	740,000	980,000	1,300,000
Meat, ,,	87,000	140,000	590,000	742,000
Butter, ,,	37,000	52,000	104,000	136,000
Cheese, ,,	26,000	46,000	79,000	82,000
Rice, ,,	18,000	90,000	290,000	180,000
Tea & coffee, tons }	63,000	73,000	90,000	96,000
Potatoes, tons }	28,000	39,000	490,000	90,000
Eggs, mill.	168	431	747	1,130
Fish, tons	22,000	38,000	67,000	95,000
Fruit, ,,	80,000	110,000	280,000	370,000
Spirits, gall.	7,000,000	13,800,000	7,000,000	9,600,000
Wine, ,,	10,200,000	16,100,000	16,000,000	14,200,000

VALUES OF FOOD IMPORTS.

	1860	1870	1880	1889
	£	£	£	£
Wheat .	20,900,000	19,700,000	39,300,000	31,100,000
Sugar . .	12,400,000	17,600,000	22,200,000	22,600,000
Meat . .	4,400,000	7,700,000	26,600,000	31,600,000
Butter. .	4,100,000	6,800,000	12,100,000	13,900,000
Cheese .	1,600,000	3,300,000	5,100,000	4,500,000
Tea . .	5,900,000	9,000,000	8,800,000	8,400,000
Coffee. .	1,200,000	800,000	1,300,000	1,100,000
Rice . .	400,000	900,000	2,100,000	1,500,000
Eggs . .	500,000	1,100,000	2,200,000	3,100,000
Potatoes .	140,000	250,000	2,800,000	700,000
Fish . .	400,000	800,000	1,700,000	2,600,000
Fruit . .	1,900,000	2,200,000	5,500,000	6,100,000
Spirits. .	1,300,000	2,800,000	1,500,000	1,700,000
Wine . .	3,400,000	4,300,000	5,900,000	5,000,000
Human food }	58,540,000	77,250,000	137,100,000	133,900,000
Oats,barley,&c. }	10,800,000	14,500,000	23,600,000	19,700,000
Total .	69,340,000	91,750,000	160,700,000	153,600,000

The weight of all food imports at the above dates was :—

	Human Food		All Food	
	Tons	Lbs. per Inhab.	Tons	Lbs. per Inhab.
1860 . . .	2,202,000	170	3,560,000	280
1870 . . .	3,062,000	218	5,270,000	380
1880 . . .	5,901,000	380	9,840,000	630
1889 . . .	7,160,000	420	10,910,000	640

The number of days in each year in which the population subsisted on native and on imported food was as follows :—

	Wheat				Meat			
	1860	1870	1880	1889	1860	1870	1880	1889
Native	244	210	142	114	340	323	236	223
Imported	122	155	224	251	26	42	130	142
Total . .	366	365	366	365	366	365	366	365

The number of people fed in those years on native and on imported food were :—

Year	Wheat		Meat		
	Native	Imported	Native	Imported	Total
1860	19,000,000	9,500,000	26,500,000	2,000,000	28,500,000
1870	17,900,000	13,300,000	27,600,000	3,600,000	31,200,000
1880	13,500,000	21,000,000	22,100,000	12,400,000	34,500,000
1889	11,800,000	26,000,000	23,100,000	14,700,000	37,800,000

The importation of food from foreign countries has greatly diminished the expenditure of the nation in this regard, and thus enabled the masses to procure more food than before. Hence we find that, while the people are better fed, the annual outlay for the principal articles of food, per inhabitant, is much less than it has been for 30 years back. The more largely we import food the cheaper and more abundant the supply, which, moreover, accounts partly for the increasing span of life.

The following table shows approximately the annual expenditure on certain articles of food since 1830 :—

| | Millions £ Sterling | | | | Per Inhabitant |
	Wheat	Meat	Tea and Sugar	Total	
					£ s. d.
1831–40	41	40	8	89	3 12 0
1841–50	40	42	9	91	3 7 0
1851–60	51	50	15	116	4 2 0
1861–70	57	59	26	142	4 15 0
1871–80	58	83	32	173	5 5 0
1881–85	55	102	30	187	5 4 0
1888	46	80	31	157	4 5 0

If we consider collectively all the food, of whatever kind, for man and beast (except wines, liquors, and tobacco), the annual outlay for ten years ending 1885 averaged thus :—

| | Millions £ Sterling | | |
	Home-Grown	Imported	Total
Grain	68	59	127
Meat	79	25	104
Dairy products . .	39	16	55
Sundries . . .	69	18	87
Tea, sugar, &c. . .	...	40	40
Total . .	255	158	413

The following table shows the net imports of grain for 130 years :—

Period	Tons per Annum	Lbs. per Inhabitant	Period	Tons per Annum	Lbs. per Inhabitant
1760–90	25,000	5	1851–60	1,950,000	154
1791–1810	110,000	16	1861–70	3,200,000	238
1811–30	115,000	12	1871–80	5,720,000	374
1831–50	480,000	45	1881–89	6,800,000	420

The meat consumption of London (exclusive of tinned meats) was estimated at 100,000 tons in 1842, and 210,000 tons in 1882, being as 112 and 128 lbs. respectively per inhabitant.

FRANCE

The production of wheat and meat has been as follows :—

| Year | Tons | | Lbs. per Inhabitant | |
	Wheat	Meat	Wheat	Meat
1840 . . .	4,900,000	670,000	326	45
1860 . . .	5,200,000	942,000	314	60
1880 . . .	7,200,000	1,200,000	440	73
1888 . . .	7,200,000	1,200,000	417	70

The percentage of people fed on wheat, comparing Moreau's tables with our own time, appears as follows :—

| Year | Percentage Fed on | | Year | Percentage Fed on | |
	Wheat	Rye, &c.		Wheat	Rye, &c.
1700	33	67	1818	45	55
1764	36	64	1839	60	40
1791	39	61	1888	86	14

The net annual importations of grain averaged approximately as follows :—

Period	Tons per Annum	Lbs. per Inhabitant
1801–40	14,000	1
1841–60	35,000	2
1861–70	79,000	4
1871–80	260,000	15
1881–87	1,460,000	84

The weight and value of grain used for food in 1887 were approximately as follows :—

	Tons	Value, £
Wheat	8,200,000	71,000,000
Rye	900,000	6,000,000
Total . .	9,100,000	77,000,000

Mr. Neumann-Spallart estimated the meat-supply as follows :—

| Year | Tons | | | Lbs. per Inhabitant |
	Native	Imported	Total	
1856 . . .	835,000	38,000	873,000	54
1867 . . .	1,053,000	85,000	1,138,000	67
1877 . . .	1,200,000	117,000	1,317,000	78

French economists seem to over-estimate the production of pork, which they put at 140 lbs. yearly per pig. Adopting their figures for the past, and putting pigs in 1888 at 112 lbs., the production of meat was as follows :—

| | Tons | | | | Per Inhabitant, Lbs. | | | |
	1840	1860	1880	1888	1840	1860	1880	1888
Beef	299,000	450,000	640,000	660,000	19	27	37	37
Mutton	82,000	114,000	210,000	250,000	5	7	12	14
Pork	290,000	378,000	305,000	290,000	19	23	18	16
Total . .	671,000	942,000	1,155,000	1,200,000	43	57	67	67

The average weight of animals in 1885 was nearly 50 per cent. greater than in 1847, viz. :—

	Weight in Lbs.	
	1847	1885
Oxen	700	1,030
Cows	500	740
Sheep . . .	50	80
Goats . . .	50	70
Pigs	200	224

In 1859 M. Lavergne compared the food consumption with what it was in 1789 thus :—

	Consumption Lbs. per Head	
	1789	1859
Meat . . .	39	61
Wheat . . .	210	330
Rye, &c. . .	280	160

The food consumption of Paris, according to a statement published in 1838, was as follows :—

Year	Population	Per Inhabitant			
		Meat, Lbs.	Wine, Bottles	Beer, Bottles	Brandy, Bottles
1789	600,000	179	120	9	4
1817	714,000	150	114	11	6
1827	802,000	146	126	20	5
1837	842,000	128	111	13	11

The consumption in Paris in 1880 was as follows :—

	Per Inhab. Lbs.		Per Inhab. Lbs.
Meat . . .	187	Butter and cheese .	18
Fish . . .	29	Vegetables and fruit .	660
Fowl . . .	24	Coal	960

Also 127 eggs, 48 gallons wine, and 1½ gallon spirits.

The consumption of bread per inhabitant in Paris has declined as follows :—

Year	Lbs.	Year	Lbs.
1833-35	392	1860-69	361
1856-59	345	1879	331

The consumption of game in Paris in 1888 was as follows :—

	Native	Imported	Total
Partridges . .	160,000	421,000	581,000
Pheasants . . .	8,000	85,000	93,000
Larks	153,000	110,000	263,000
Wild ducks . .	10,000	40,000	50,000
Pigeons, &c. . .	375,100	626,700	1,001,800
Deer	2,800	10,500	13,300
Wild boars . .	300	1,400	1,700
Total . .	709,200	1,294,600	2,003,800

The urban population is much better fed than the rural, notwithstanding the fact that food is dearest in towns. The consumption of meat in French cities averages three times as much per head as in the rural departments.

In 1885 the consumption of food in French cities was as follows :—

Cities	Population	Tons		Gallons, Millions		Lbs. per Head		Gallons per Head	
		Bread	Meat	Wine	Beer	Bread	Meat	Wine	Beer
Paris	2,260,000	355,000	171,000	97.0	6.0	343	167	43	2.4
Lyons	350,000	55,000	25,000	1.4	0.6	348	176	42	1.8
Marseilles . . .	270,000	58,000	18,000	1.1	0.6	464	143	43	2.0
Bordeaux . . .	220,000	38,000	17,000	1.0	0.4	380	170	46	1.5
Lille	150,000	32,000	7,100	0.9	9.0	480	106	6	60.0
Toulouse . . .	130,000	28,000	7,700	5.0	0.2	498	132	38	2.2
Nantes	120,000	34,000	5,600	4.0	...	627	104	33	0.7
St. Etienne . . .	110,000	18,000	5,700	4.0	0.4	348	110	41	1.3
Havre	110,000	20,000	5,500	0.9	0.4	411	114	8	4.0
Rouen	110,000	19,000	6,600	1.1	0.3	400	136	10	2.6
Nice	50,000	12,000	3,600	3.0	0.3	480	145	58	2.4
Total .	3,880,000	669,000	272,800	119.4	18.2	385	154	31	5.0

Meat in the above table does not include live cattle introduced for consumption. Thus Paris also consumed 300,000 horned cattle, 1,900,000 sheep, and 250,000 pigs, equal to 130,000 tons of meat, which would bring up the total to 301,000 tons, say 295 lbs. per head.

There was, moreover, the following consumption of cider in certain cities, per head :—

	Galls.			Galls.
Rouen . . .	33.0	Havre . . .	21.0
Paris . . .	3.5	Nantes . . .	3.5

The aggregate of 25 French cities, including those in the above table, showed as follows (pop. 4,780,000) :—

Bread, tons . . .	839,000	Bread, lbs. per head .	387
Meat, „ . .	331,400	Meat, „ „ .	154
Wine, gallons	178,000,000	Wine, gallons . . .	38
Beer, „	26,400,000	Beer, „	5½

The average in the same cities in 1880 was: bread 449 lbs., meat 127, wine 35, beer 5 gallons per head. There has been, therefore, a decrease in bread, but an increase of meat and wine.

The quantity of horse-flesh used for human food at Paris was only 400 tons in 1867, rising to 994 in 1872. The slaughter of horses for the city market was 4680 animals in 1874, and 9830 in 1883. The principal food imports into France since 1860 have been as follows :—

	Annual Average of Value		
	1861-70	1871-80	1881-87
	£	£	£
Grain	6,300,000	15,800,000	14,300,000
Cattle and meat .	3,800,000	6,600,000	7,300,000
Sugar	4,800,000	4,200,000	3,700,000
Wine	...	2,600,000	15,700,000

The meat-supply since 1850 has been approximately thus :—

| Period | Tons Yearly | | | Pounds Per Inhab. |
	Native	Imported	Total	
1851–60 . .	840,000	40,000	880,000	50
1861–70 . .	1,020,000	76,000	1,096,000	65
1871–80 . .	1,100,000	110,000	1,210,000	74
1881–87 . .	1,200,000	120,000	1,320,000	80

The consumption of coffee, sugar, wine, and beer per inhabitant was as follows, per annum :—

	1860–64	1870–74	1880–84	1887
Coffee, oz. .	37	40	62	64
Sugar, lbs. .	12	15	23	20
Wine, galls. .	18	25	21	19
Beer ,,	4	4	5	5

Professor Boch makes the consumption of sugar in 1860–64 only 8 lbs. per inhabitant yearly, but the French estimates of production and consumption make it 12 lbs.

GERMANY

The production of grain and meat, the former including what was used both for man and beast, has been approximately as follows :—

| Year | Tons | | Lbs. per Inhabitant | |
	Grain	Meat	Grain	Meat
1816	5,000,000	600,000	440	54
1837	7,500,000	760,000	560	60
1852	11,200,000	890,000	750	60
1875	14,300,000	1,280,000	740	67
1887	16,000,000	1,375,000	745	64

A statement published in Saxony in 1876 gave the meat consumption per head as follows :—

Period	Beef and Mutton	Pork	Total, Lbs.
1836–55	14	18	32
1856–65	18	26	44
1866–75	21	30	51
1875	26	34	60

The average in 1875 for all the towns of Saxony collectively was 68 lbs., for rural districts 47 lbs. per inhabitant. In 1870 the consumption in various cities was as follows :—

Pounds per Inhabitant

Berlin . . . 99 | Cologne . . 104 | Hamburg . . 92
Bremen . . 113 | Dresden . . 104 | Leipzig . . 164
Breslau . . 94 | Dusseldorf . 104 | Magdeburg . 102
Coblenz . . 104 | Frankfort . 171 | Munich . . 166

The net imports of grain and meat into Germany were :—

| Year | Tons | | Lbs. per Inhabitant | |
	Grain	Meat	Grain	Meat
1873	800,000	30,000	40	2
1880	700,000	...	35	...
1887	1,900,000	10,000	90	½

The weight and value of grain used for food were in 1887 approximately as follows :—

				Tons	Value, £
Wheat	.	.	.	3,000,000	21,000,000
Rye .	.	.	.	6,000,000	34,000,000
Oats, &c. .	.	.	.	1,200,000	7,000,000
	Total	.	.	10,200,000	62,000,000

The consumption of potatoes is large, averaging 1020 lbs. yearly per inhabitant.

The consumption of grain according to Spallart in the years 1881–84 averaged thus :—

| | Millions of Bushels | | | Lbs. per Inhabitant |
	Native	Imported	Total	
Wheat . .	81	21	102	132
Rye . . .	193	29	222	290
Barley . .	76	14	90	120
Oats . . .	138	11	149	200
Total .	488	75	563	742

The consumption of secondary articles was as follows :—

| Year | Consumption per Inhabitant | | | | |
	Sugar, Lbs.	Coffee, Lbs.	Foreign Fish, Lbs.	Tobacco, Oz.	Beer, Gallons
1873	14	5.0	4	72	18
1880	14	4.8	4	35	18
1887	18	4.6	7	56	18

The only articles of which Germany has a surplus for exportation are sugar and butter, viz. :—

| Year | Tons Exported | | Value, £ | |
	Butter	Sugar	Butter	Sugar
1873 . . .	12,000	13,000	1,200,000	440,000
1880 . . .	12,000	250,000	1,050,000	5,500,000
1887 . . .	15,000	620,000	1,100,000	9,050,000

The net importation of wine averages 10 million gallons, and the exportation of beer 30 million gallons yearly.

The following table shows the consumption of imported food since 1836 :—

| Period | Tons Yearly | | Barrels Fish | Lbs. per Inhabitant | | |
	Coffee	Rice		Coffee	Rice	Fish
1836–40	27,000	5,000	190,000	2.2	0.4	2.4
1841–50	37,000	11,000	265,000	2.8	0.8	3.1
1851–60	54,000	30,000	295,000	3.7	2.1	3.1
1861–70	74,000	36,000	460,000	4.4	2.2	4.2
1871–80	97,000	68,000	690,000	5.0	3.5	5.3
1881–85	111,000	83,000	915,000	5.4	4.0	6.6
1887	102,000	83,000	1,095,000	5.3	3.8	8.0

RUSSIA.

This is a great food-producing country, with a constant surplus for exportation. The production of all kinds of grain and of meat has been approximately as follows :—

| Year | Tons | | Lbs. per Inhab. | |
	Grain	Meat	Grain	Meat
1835	26,000,000	1,430,000	1,210	67
1850	31,000,000	1,670,000	1,270	67
1870	36,000,000	1,760,000	1,220	60
1887	47,500,000	1,885,000	1,260	51

Exports of grain and meat have been as follows, per annum :—

| Period | Tons | | Value, £ |
	Grain	Meat	
1810–13 . . .	250,000	...	2,000,000
1834–40 . . .	700,000	...	4,200,000
1841–47 . . .	800,000	...	4,800,000
1861.	1,400,000	4,000	9,200,000
1870.	3,050,000	16,000	20,800,000
1887.	6,100,000	31,000	31,700,000

The exports of grain, taken from official returns, were :—

| Period | Millions of Bushels Yearly | | | | | Value, £ |
	Wheat	Rye	Barley	Oats, &c.	Total	
1851–60 .	20	7	3	6	36	5,500,000
1861–70 .	36	10	4	9	59	10,100,000
1871–80 .	59	43	12	43	157	27,700,000
1881–87 .	70	40	24	60	194	29,000,000

It would seem that the home consumption has only kept pace with population. For human food, wheat and rye are mainly used. The consumption per head was as follows :—

| Year | Pounds per Head | | |
	Wheat	Rye, &c.	Total
1861 . . .	124	556	680
1870 . . .	118	552	670
1880 . . .	122	538	660
1887 . . .	110	530	640

The consumption of secondary articles was as follows :—

| Year | Tons | | | | Per Inhabitant | | | |
	Sugar	Coffee	Tea	Foreign Salt, Lbs.	Sugar, Lbs.	Coffee, Oz.	Tea, Oz.	Foreign Salt, Lbs.
1860	146,000	6,000	4,000	150,000	6	3	2	6
1870	200,000	7,000	9,000	170,000	7	4	5	6
1880	250,000	8,000	18,000	150,000	8	4	9	5
1887	410,000	5,000	10,000	150,000	11	2	4	4

Russia produces more sugar than she needs, and exports 60,000 tons. Her consumption of wine averages 30 million gallons, of which 25 millions are grown at home.

The quantity and value of grain used for food in 1887 were as follows :—

	Tons	Value, £
Wheat	4,200,000	21,000,000
Rye	14,500,000	61,000,000
Oats, &c. . .	4,300,000	15,000,000
Total . .	23,000,000	97,000,000

AUSTRIA-HUNGARY.

The production of grain and meat was as follows :—

| Year | Million Tons | | Lbs. per Inhab. | |
	Grain	Meat	Grain	Meat
1836	9,100,000	990,000	750	79
1850	13,700,000	980,000	840	73
1870	12,500,000	1,080,000	780	68
1887	18,000,000	1,080,000	1,040	63

The average consumption of grain and meat has steadily decreased per head, but that of potatoes has increased, the last crop reaching 7,500,000 tons, or 3½ bushels per inhabitant.

The production and consumption of grain has been as follows :—

| Year | Millions of Bushels | | | | | |
	Crop	Seed	Exported	Food	Cattle, &c.	Total
1835 .	1,040	160	28	670	182	1,040
1850 .	1,240	190	32	750	268	1,240
1870 .	1,450	220	122	800	308	1,450
1887 .	1,900	290	244	926	440	1,900

The production and consumption of wheat are shown approximately thus :—

| Year | Millions of Bushels | | | | |
	Crop	Seed	Exported	Food	Total
1861	180	30	29	121	180
1870	217	36	55	126	217
1880	220	37	35	148	220
1887	270	45	75	150	270

The quantities of wheat, rye, oats, &c., retained for home consumption have been approximately as follows :—

| Year | Millions of Bushels | | | | | Bushels per Inhabitant |
	Wheat	Rye	Oats	Maize, &c.	Total	
1861	121	454	442	43	1,060	18
1870	126	475	450	57	1,108	17
1880	148	505	475	112	1,240	16½
1887	150	550	460	206	1,366	16

The exports of grain, meat, and sugar were as follows :—

| Year | Tons | | | Value, £ |
	Grain	Meat	Sugar	
1860 . . .	400,000	15,000	...	3,400,000
1870 . . .	620,000	20,000	64,000	7,900,000
1880 . . .	900,000	72,000	240,000	20,100,000
1887 . . .	800,000	40,000	220,000	12,200,000

The disposal approximately of all grain was as follows :—

| Year | Millions of Bushels | | | | |
	Crop	Seed	Exported	Consumption	Total
1870 . . .	500	70	25	405	500
1880 . . .	600	85	36	479	600
1887 . . .	717	102	32	583	717

The weight and value of grain consumed for food in 1887 were approximately as follows :—

	Tons	Value, £
Wheat . . .	4,300,000	30,000,000
Rye . . .	3,300,000	18,000,000
Other grain .	800,000	4,000,000
Total . .	8,400,000	52,000,000

The production and consumption of wine were as follows :—

	Millions of Gallons Yearly			Gallons per Inhab.
	Vintage	Exported	Consumed	
1876–85 . .	198	8	190	5
1887 . . .	212	14	198	5

The consumption of sugar and coffee was approximately as follows :—

Year	Tons		Per Inhab.	
	Sugar	Coffee	Sugar, Lbs.	Coffee, Oz.
1860 . . .	60,000	20,000	4	20
1870 . . .	100,000	27,000	6	26
1880 . . .	230,000	31,000	14	29
1887 . . .	305,000	32,000	18	28

Austria consumes only 60 per cent. of the sugar she produces, exporting over 200,000 tons yearly.

The exports of food from Italy were as follows :—

	Per Annum			Value, £		
	1861–70	1871–80	1881–87	1861–70	1871–80	1881–87
Meat, tons . . .	16,000	38,000	30,000	800,000	1,900,000	1,520,000
Rice ,, . . .	61,000	68,000	73,000	960,000	840,000	1,020,000
Fruit ,, . . .	75,000	96,000	165,000	1,500,000	1,400,000	1,800,000
Eggs, millions . . .	71	320	480	110,000	680,000	1,300,000
Oil, million gallons . .	13	17	16	3,100,000	4,300,000	3,200,000
Wine ,, ,, . .	6	14	48	480,000	900,000	2,800,000
Total .	...	...	...	6,950,000	10,020,000	11,640,000

The consumption of wine, grain, and meat was :—

	Yearly per Inhabitant		
	1861–70	1871–80	1881–87
Wine, gallons	16	20	18
Grain, lbs.	420	424	455
Meat, ,, ...	23	24	26

The weight and value of grain consumed for food in 1887 were approximately as follows :—

	Tons	Value, £
Wheat . . .	3,000,000	24,000,000
Rye	400,000	3,000,000
Maize, &c. . .	1,900,000	12,000,000
Total .	5,300,000	39,000,000

SPAIN

The production of grain and meat was apparently thus :—

Year	Tons		Lbs. per Inhabitant	
	Grain	Meat	Grain	Meat
1826	3,400,000	405,000	560	77
1886	7,500,000	525,000	1,050	71

This is supposing official figures to be correct, but it is remarkable that in recent years Spain has largely imported grain, which would be apparently unnecessary if

ITALY

Notwithstanding her fertile soil, Italy produces an insufficient food-supply, except as regards wine and fruit. The production of grain and meat was approximately as follows :—

Year	Tons		Lbs. per Inhabitant	
	Grain	Meat	Grain	Meat
1828	2,900,000	330,000	380	44
1840	3,200,000	300,000	385	35
1874	5,100,000	300,000	403	24
1886	5,600,000	360,000	426	28

The net imports of sundry articles of food was as follows :—

	Per Annum, Tons			Lbs. per Inhabitant		
	1861–70	1871–80	1881–87	1861–70	1871–80	1881–87
Grain	252,000	160,000	390,000	22	14	30
Sugar	61,000	78,000	98,000	5	7	8
Fish .	25,000	39,000	43,000	2	$3\frac{1}{2}$	$3\frac{1}{2}$
Cheese	5,000	7,000	10,000	7 oz.	9 oz.	12 oz.
Coffee	11,000	13,000	16,000	15 oz.	17 oz.	20 oz.

each inhabitant produced half a ton, as above. The net imports of grain have averaged yearly as follows :—

Period		Tons	Lbs. per Inhab.
1880–82	. . .	73,000	10
1883–85	. . .	122,000	16
1886–87	. . .	208,000	28

Before 1880 there was always a surplus of grain for exportation, viz. :—

Period		Tons Yearly	Value, £
1863–68	. . .	72,000	900,000
1872–75	. . .	144,000	1,550,000
1876–79	. . .	26,000	300,000

The imports of minor articles were as follows :—

	1860	1872	1880	1887
Cocoa, tons	4,000	6,000	8,000	7,000
Sugar ,,	32,000	35,000	44,000	53,000
Fish ,,	20,000	34,000	28,000	46,000
Value, £	2,000,000	2,000,000	2,200,000	2,900,000

The imports and exports of live cattle in recent years were equal. The food exports were as follows :—

	1860	1872	1880	1887
Wine, mill. galls.	22	44	138	183
Oil ,,	1	5	4	3
Fruit, tons . .	...	120,000	150,000	160,000
Salt ,, . .	...	220,000	320,000	220,000
Aggreg. value, £	3,400,000	9,600,000	12,400,000	13,800,000

PORTUGAL

The production of grain and meat was as follows :—

Year	Tons		Lbs. per Inhabitant	
	Grain	Meat	Grain	Meat
1828	520,000	70,000	340	46
1868	770,000	77,000	410	41
1886	1,000,000	95,000	510	49

There is a constant deficit of grain, but a small surplus of meat for exportation. The imported food averaged thus :—

	Tons Yearly		Lbs. per Inhabitant	
	1872–75	1884–87	1872–75	1884–87
Grain . .	42,000	135,000	22	69
Rice . . .	8,500	14,000	4	7
Sugar . .	16,000	24,000	8	12
Coffee . .	2,000	2,500	15 oz.	18 oz.
Fish . . .	16,000	22,000	8 lbs.	11 lbs.

Exports of food averaged as follows :—

		Yearly	
		1872–75	1884–87
Wine, gallons . . .		11,200,000	31,400,000
Oil ,, . . .		900,000	230,000
Fruit, tons . . .		440,000	130,000
Meat ,, . . .		4,000	1,300
Salt ,, . . .		230,000	120,000

The consumption of food per inhabitant is about 500 lbs. grain, 48 lbs. meat, 11 lbs. fish, 12 lbs. sugar, and 14 gallons of wine.

The weight and value of grain consumed for food in 1887 were :—

		Tons	Value, £
Wheat	. . .	300,000	2,400,000
Rye	. . . .	300,000	1,800,000
Other grain	.	300,000	1,700,000
Total	.	900,000	5,900,000

SWEDEN

The production of grain and meat was as follows :—

Year	Tons		Lbs. per Inhabitant	
	Grain	Meat	Grain	Meat
1837	350,000	106,001	280	78
1886	2,510,000	140,000	1,100	62

There is a surplus of grain, the net exports averaging as follows per annum :—

Period					Tons
1860–64	.	.	.	.	205,000
1876–80	.	.	.	.	290,000
1882–86	.	.	.	.	140,000

The meat-supply is sufficient and no more, the export of live cattle being equivalent to 10,000 tons of meat yearly, which is just the quantity of pork ordinarily imported. There is a constant surplus of butter, the export of which has increased of late years, the annual average showing :—

Period					Tons
1876–80	.	.	.	.	4,000
1883–86	.	.	.	.	10,500

The consumption of imported articles shows thus :—

	Tons Yearly			Lbs. per Inhabitant		
	1860–62	1870–72	1884–86	1860–62	1870–72	1884–86
Coffee .	7,000	8,500	15,000	4	4	7
Rice . .	1,400	2,200	9,200	1	1	4
Sugar . .	18,000	21,000	47,000	10	11	22
Salt . .	40,000	55,000	64,000	22	30	28

The weight and value of grain used for food in 1887 were approximately as follows :—

				Tons	Value, £
Wheat	.	.	.	300,000	2,100,000
Rye .	.	.	.	700,000	4,600,000
Other grain	.	.	.	200,000	1,200,000
Total	.			1,200,000	7,900,000

NORWAY

The production of grain and meat was as follows :—

Year	Tons		Lbs. per Inhabitant	
	Grain	Meat	Grain	Meat
1835 . . .	170,000	44,000	320	80
1855 . . .	370,000	64,000	540	95
1875 . . .	400,000	67,000	470	78

The net importation of grain has been as follows :—

Period				Tons Yearly	Lbs. per Inhabitant
1861–70	.	.	.	145,000	200
1871–80	.	.	.	205,000	245
1881–87	.	.	.	220,000	240

The only food exported is fish, the average showing thus :—

Period			Tons Yearly	Value, £
1861–70	.	.	124,000	...
1871–80	.	.	123,000	1,900,000
1881–87	.	.	135,000	1,950,000

The consumption of some articles of importation was :—

	Tons Yearly		Lbs. per Inhabitant	
	1860–62	1885–87	1860–62	1885–87
Coffee . .	5,000	7,300	7	9
Sugar . .	5,500	11,000	7	13
Meat . . .	400	6,000	...	7
Salt . . .	69,000	80,000	84	92

Potatoes are much used, the consumption averaging 500 lbs. per inhabitant, all home-grown.

The weight and value of grain consumed in 1887 were approximately :—

				Tons	Value, £
Wheat .	.	.	100,000	800,000
Rye	.	.	.	200,000	1,300,000
Other grain .	.	100,000	600,000
Total	.		400,000	2,700,000

DENMARK.

The production of grain and meat was as follows :—

Year	Tons		Lbs. per Inhab.	
	Grain	Meat	Grain	Meat
1866 . . .	1,750,000	98,000	2,280	127
1886 . . .	2,150,000	115,000	2,400	128

The net exports of grain and meat averaged thus :—

Period	Tons Yearly	
	Grain	Meat
1865–70	263,000	17,000
1875–80	185,000	38,000
1883–87	...	58,000

In the last period of five years there was an average importation of 10,000 tons grain yearly over and above exports. Instead of growing more than her needs, Denmark has now to rely partly on imported grain. Butter is largely exported, viz. :—

Year	Tons
1874	13,000
1887	24,000

So far back as 1830 Denmark exported 5000 tons of butter and 9000 tons of cheese.

The consumption of imported articles was as follows :—

	Tons Yearly		Lbs. per Inhab.	
	1865–67	1885–87	1865–67	1885–87
Coffee . .	6,300	8,500	9	9
Sugar . .	16,400	21,000	22	22
Rice . . .	4,000	14,000	5	14
Salt . . .	14,500	25,000	19	25

The consumption of potatoes averages 410 lbs. per inhabitant.

The weight and value of grain used for food in 1887 were approximately thus :—

	Tons	Value, £
Wheat	200,000	1,600,000
Rye	400,000	2,400,000

HOLLAND

The production of grain and meat was approximately as follows :—

Year	Tons		Lbs. per Inhabitant	
	Grain	Meat	Grain	Meat
1828	400,000	96,000	290	70
1860	600,000	104,000	360	62
1884	1,000,000	125,000	550	69

Holland has never grown enough grain for her requirements, the net imports averaging yearly as follows :—

	Tons	Value, £
1861–70	180,000	2,400,000
1871–80 . . .	370,000	3,400,000
1881–87 . . .	460,000	4,400,000

The other food imports show as follows, net, per annum :—

	Tons		Lbs. per Inhabitant	
	1861–63	1885–87	1861–63	1885–87
Coffee . .	13,000	27,000	9	15
Sugar . . .	17,000	18,000	12	10
Rice . . .	24,000	75,000	17	40
Lard . . .	...	62,000	...	34

Holland produces about 45,000 tons of beet-sugar per annum, so that the consumption of sugar is about 63,000 tons, or 35 lbs. per inhabitant. The consumption of lard is supposed to be in great measure for making butter or oleo-margarine.

The exports of food are as follows :—

	Tons Yearly		Value, £	
	1861–63	1885–87	1861–63	1885–87
Meat . . .	14,000	20,000	700,000	1,050,000
Butter . .	16,000	71,000	1,050,000	4,500,000
Cheese . .	28,000	32,000	800,000	900,000

The consumption of potatoes is 820 lbs. per inhabitant yearly.

The weight and value of grain used for food in 1887 were approximately thus :—

	Tons	Value, £
Wheat	500,000	4,000,000
Rye	400,000	2,800,000
Other grain . . .	200,000	1,200,000
Total . .	1,100,000	8,000,000

BELGIUM

The production of grain and meat was approximately thus :—

Year	Tons		Lbs. per Inhabitant	
	Grain	Meat	Grain	Meat
1828	820,000	70,000	530	45
1856	1,720,000	90,000	970	51
1866	1,750,000	106,000	890	54
1886	1,850,000	110,000	750	43

The net imports of grain have averaged thus :—

Period	Tons Yearly		Lbs. per Inhabitant
1861–70 . .	270,000	...	140
1871–80 . .	860,000	...	380
1881–87 . .	1,230,000	...	505

It appears that 40 per cent. of the grain consumed is imported from other countries.

The imports of meat averaged thus :—

Period	Tons Yearly		Lbs. per Inhabitant
1861–70 . .	12,000	...	7
1871–80 . .	61,000	...	27
1881–87 . .	56,000	...	22

Minor articles of import are as follows :—

	Quantity Yearly		Per Inhabitant	
	1860–62	1885–87	1860–62	1885–87
Coffee, tons	20,000	24,000	12 lbs.	9 lbs.
Wine, galls.	2,600,000	8,700,000	0.6	1.5

Butter and sugar are exported, the averages showing thus :—

	1860–62	1870–72	1885–87
Butter, tons . .	...	4,500	4,200
Sugar ,, . .	1,700	56,000	62,000

The production of beet-sugar is 130,000 tons yearly, the consumption about 70,000 tons, or 27 lbs. per inhabitant. Potatoes are largely used, the average being 1050 lbs. yearly per inhabitant.

The weight and value of grain used for food in 1887 were approximately thus :—

	Tons	Value, £
Wheat	800,000	6,800,000
Rye	600,000	4,200,000
Other grain . . .	200,000	1,200,000
Total . .	1,600,000	12,200,000

SWITZERLAND

The consumption of grain and meat in the years 1883–87 averaged as follows :—

	Tons			Lbs. per Inhabitant		
	Native	Imported	Total	Native	Imported	Total
Grain .	450,000	390,000	840,000	330	300	630
Meat .	68,000	15,000	83,000	51	11	62

The importation of grain is more than treble what it was before 1855, viz. :—

Period	Tons per Annum	Lbs. per Inhabitant
1851–55 . . .	120,000	103
1876–80 . . .	320,000	231
1883–87 . . .	390,000	300

Three-fourths of the imported grain is wheat, the remainder maize and oats.

Other imported articles in the same years averaged :—

	Quantity	Lbs. per Inhab.
Coffee, tons .	9,200	7
Sugar, ,, . .	34,000	26
Rice ,, . .	6,800	5
Wine, gallons .	12,000,000	galls. 4

Cheese and condensed milk are exported, the average being :—

	Tons Yearly	Value, £
Cheese . . .	26,000	1,600,000
Milk . . .	13,000	480,000

The consumption of wine averaged 14 gallons yearly per inhabitant.

GREECE

The consumption of grain and meat averaged thus :—

	Tons			Lbs. per Inhabitant		
	Native	Imported	Total	Native	Imported	Total
Grain .	450,000	130,000	580,000	560	170	730
Meat .	43,000	4,000	47,000	50	5	55

The ordinary consumption of sugar is 4000 tons, and of coffee 800 tons yearly, being respectively as 5 lbs. and 1 lb. per inhabitant. The only food exports are :—

	Quantity	Value, £
Fruit, tons . .	140,000	1,520,000
Oil, gallons .	2,100,000	210,000
W ne, ,, .	1,500,000	50,000

The consumption of wine averages 18 gallons per inhabitant.

ROUMANIA

The production of grain and meat is approximately thus :—

	Tons	Lbs. per Inhabitant
Grain . . .	3,000,000	1,250
Meat . . .	280,000	110

The average export of grain in the years 1882–86 was :—

	Tons Yearly	Value, £
Wheat . . .	360,000	2,500,000
Barley . . .	240,000	850,000
Rye	85,000	400,000
Maize . . .	640,000	2,600,000
Total . .	1,325,000	6,350,000

The exportation of cattle is not known, but may be estimated as equal to one-fourth of the meat product, say 70,000 tons yearly. This would leave the consumption thus :—

	Tons	Lbs. per Inhabitant
Grain . . .	1,680,000	650
Meat . . .	210,000	82

These ratios seem very high, but they are based on the tables of the *Statistique Agricole*. The consumption of sugar is only 4 lbs., and of coffee 8 oz. yearly per inhabitant.

SERVIA

The production of grain and meat is approximately thus :—

	Tons	Lbs. per Inhabitant
Grain . . .	370,000	420
Meat . . .	100,000	112

The export of grain, says Spallart, averages 40,000 tons ; the meat surplus is probably 25,000 tons per annum.

EGYPT

The average food exports in the years 1883–87 were :—

	Value, £	Tons, Approximately
Grain . . .	1,010,000	200,000
Sugar . . .	460,000	33,000

The imports and exports of rice are about equal.

UNITED STATES

The production of the principal articles of food was :—

Year	Tons						
	Grain	Meat	Sugar	Rice	Potatoes	Butter	Cheese
1840	15,400,000	2,050,000	70,000	36,000	2,700,000	...	...
1850	21,700,000	2,390,000	110,000	96,000	2,600,000	140,000	74,000
1860	31,000,000	2,890,000	120,000	83,000	2,800,000	205,000	47,000
1870	34,700,000	2,480,000	74,000	33,000	3,600,000	230,000	68,000
1880	67,500,000	4,120,000	110,000	50,000	4,200,000	350,000	120,000
1886	71,100,000	4,750,000	110,000	50,000	4,200,000	430,000	170,000

Some of the above articles were produced in excess of requirements for home use, the quantities and values exported being thus :—

Period	Tons Yearly			Value, £		
	Grain	Meat	Butter and Cheese	Grain	Meat	Butter and Cheese
1821–30	150,000	10,000	1,000	1,200,000	300,000	40,000
1831–40	160,000	14,000	1,000	1,060,000	420,000	40,000
1841–50	370,000	40,000	6,000	3,120,000	1,040,000	210,000
1851–60	710,000	60,000	8,000	6,100,000	1,800,000	300,000
1861–70	1,200,000	100,000	40,000	9,400,000	3,300,000	1,550,000
1871–80	3,700,000	390,000	60,000	27,100,000	12,600,000	2,800,000
1881–87	5,020,000	510,000	72,000	38,100,000	20,200,000	3,900,000

The disposal of the grain crops since 1840 was approximately as follows :—

Period	Millions of Bushels Yearly				
	Crop	Seed	Exported	Home Use	Total
1841–50	740	74	15	652	740
1851–60	1,050	105	29	916	1,050
1861–70	1,210	121	48	1,041	1,210
1871–80	1,980	198	148	1,634	1,980
1881–87	2,700	270	200	2,230	2,700

The disposal of wheat crop was as follows approximately :—

Period	Millions of Bushels Yearly				
	Crop	Seed	Exported	Home Use	Total
1841–50	93	9	10	74	93
1851–60	137	14	24	99	137
1861–70	194	20	38	136	194
1871–80	338	34	85	219	338
1881–87	440	44	134	262	440

The disposal of the maize crop was approximately thus :—

Period	Millions of Bushels Yearly				
	Crop	Seed	Exported	Home Use	Total
1841–50	485	48	5	432	485
1851–60	715	72	5	638	715
1861–70	965	97	10	858	965
1871–80	1,400	140	54	1,206	1,400
1881–87	1,602	160	53	1,389	1,602

The disposal of oats, rye, barley, buckwheat, &c., was as follows :—

Period	Millions of Bushels Yearly				
	Crop	Seed	Exported	Home Use	Total
1841–50	162	16	...	146	162
1851–60	198	20	...	178	198
1861–70	51	5	...	46	51
1871–80	242	24	9	209	242
1881–87	658	66	13	579	658

The consumption of food compared with population was as follows :—

Year	Lbs. per Inhabitant					
	Wheat	Other Grain	Meat	Sugar	Potatoes	Butter and Cheese
1840 . .	240	1,400	260	19	360	...
1850 . .	220	1,510	224	20	265	20
1860 . .	260	1,540	202	34	200	18
1870 . .	244	1,620	140	41	202	14
1880 . .	320	1,870	157	40	190	18
1887 . .	250	1,610	155	53	170	20

Native sugar only forms 7 per cent. of what is consumed. The importation of coffee and tea has been as follows :—

	Tons Yearly			Lbs. per Inhabitant		
	1861–63	1871–73	1885–87	1861–63	1871–73	1885–87
Coffee	58,000	134,000	250,000	4.0	7.4	9.3
Tea .	11,000	27,000	36,000	0.8	1.5	1.4

The meat product of the United States was approximately as follows :—

Year	Tons				Lbs. per Inhabitant
	Beef	Mutton	Pork	Total	
1840	662,000	172,000	1,286,000	2,120,000	280
1850	790,000	193,000	1,477,000	2,460,000	240
1860	1,140,000	200,000	1,630,000	2,970,000	215
1870	1,060,000	253,000	1,230,000	2,540,000	150
1880	1,590,000	312,000	2,338,000	4,240,000	190
1888	2,190,000	390,000	2,190,000	4,750,000	178

It may be seen that the rapid increase of population causes the surplus of meat to diminish. As soon as the production falls to 120 lbs. per inhabitant, there will be no meat to export.

The Americans are the best fed people in the world, and contribute in a great measure to the abundance and cheapness of food in other countries, their share of production being shown thus :—

	Tons Grain Grown Yearly			Tons of Meat Produced Yearly		
	1841-50	1861–70	1881–87	1841–50	1861–70	1881–87
United States . . .	18,500,000	30,300,000	67,700,000	2,200,000	2,680,000	4,400,000
Europe . . .	90,500,000	111,000,000	132,000,000	6,380,000	6,950,000	7,740,000
Colonies, &c. . . .	9,200,000	15,700,000	22,500,000	220,000	390,000	920,000
Total . .	117,200,000	157,000,000	222,200,000	8,800,000	10,020,000	13,060,000

It appears, therefore, that the United States produce 30 per cent. of the grain, and 33 per cent. of the meat of the world.

CANADA

The production of grain and meat was approximately as follows :—

Year	Tons Yearly		Lbs. per Inhabitant	
	Grain	Meat	Grain	Meat
1852	1,120,000	140,000	1,020	128
1873	1,850,000	220,000	1,030	126
1887	3,720,000	260,000	1,680	116

There has been of late years a surplus of grain and other articles, the net exports averaging yearly as follows :—

	1875-78	1882-84	1885-87
Grain, tons . .	175,000	405,000	410,000
Meat ,, . .	21,000	42,000	57,000
Butter ,, . .	5,500	4,800	3,100
Cheese ,, . .	16,500	31,000	39,000
Fish ,, . .	64,000	77,000	71,000
Potatoes ,, . .	21,000	58,000	39,000
Eggs, millions .	53	142	152

The consumption of imported food was thus :—

	Tons Yearly		Lbs. per Inhabitant	
	1875-77	1885-87	1875-77	1885-87
Sugar . .	68,000	102,000	37.0	45.0
Tea . . .	6,000	9,000	3.4	4.1
Salt . . .	72,000	87,000	39.0	38.0

The ordinary consumption of wheat is 350 lbs. per inhabitant, and of meat 90 lbs., per annum.

AUSTRALIA

The production of grain and meat was approximately thus :—

Period	Tons Yearly		Lbs. per Inhabitant	
	Grain	Meat	Grain	Meat
1831-40 . .	60,000	40,000	440	300
1851-60 . .	250,000	140,000	500	300
1881-87 . .	1,550,000	450,000	1,100	300

Food exports have averaged yearly as follows :—

	1875-77	1885-87
Grain, tons . .	125,000	150,000
Meat, ,, . .	9,000	34,000

According to Mr. Coghlan, Government statist, the consumption of food averages as follows :—

	Wheat	Rice	Potatoes	Sugar	Tea	Meat	Tobacco
	Lbs. Yearly per Inhabitant						
New South Wales . .	405	12	215	94	8.2	249	3.4
Victoria . . .	384	15	282	100	7.2	265	2.7
New Zealand . .	...	9	412	78	6.7	...	2.0
Tasmania . .	371	9	389	86	6.4	...	1.8
South Australia . .	...	5	195	87	6.4	...	2.1
Queensland . .	366	24	250	59	8.7	370	3.5
Australasia . .	374	13	279	89	7.5	276	2.8

	Gallons Yearly per 100 Inhabitants			
	Wine	Beer	Spirits	Equivalent in Alcohol
New South Wales .	80	1,170	110	290
Victoria . .	110	1,940	120	410
New Zealand . .	20	770	80	180
Tasmania . . .	20	970	60	190
South Australia .	160	1,410	50	280
Queensland . . .	60	980	180	320
Australasia . . .	80	1,230	100	290

The consumption of imported articles was as follows :—

	Tons Yearly		Lbs. per Inhabitant	
	1875-77	1885-87	1875-77	1885-87
Tea . . .	8,200	11,500	7.5	8.1
Sugar . . .	82,000	110,000	75.0	77.0

The sugar was not imported wholly from abroad, Queensland supplying 5 per cent. in the first, and 36 per cent. in the second period.

ARGENTINA

The production of grain and meat was approximately thus :—

Period	Tons		Lbs. per Inhabitant	
	Grain	Meat	Grain	Meat
1831-40 . .	50,000	50,000	200	200
1851-60 . .	120,000	100,000	280	220
1881-87 . .	850,000	300,000	600	220
1889 . . .	1,510,000	320,000	910	200

The surplus food for exportation was as follows :—

Year	Tons	
	Grain	Meat
1873	2,300	35,000
1883	108,400	39,000
1889	350,000	60,000

The Republic grows 80,000 tons sugar and 6 million gallons of wine, which is about half the quantity consumed of the former and one-fifth of the latter.

FORESTS

Forests cover about 10 per cent. of the earth's landed area, and 25 per cent. of Europe. The highest yield is in the United Kingdom, namely, 60 cubic feet of timber per acre, whereas in Brazil it is about one cubic foot. The terms used in measurement are :—

Load, 50 cubic feet.	Klafter, 2 tons or 200 fagots.
Stère, 35 cubic feet.	Cord, 2½ tons or 125 cubic feet.

The ordinary cutting in Europe (except Russia) is 5 acres per 100 of forest. An acre of forest, if cut down, would produce about 1000 cubic feet of timber.

The annual felling of timber is hardly half what it might be, without reducing the forest resources of the world. The average shown above is only 17 cubic feet per acre, the ordinary yield available being from 30 to 40 cubic feet. It appears, however, that forests within easy reach are sufficiently developed, while those more remote of Canada, Brazil, and Gran Chaco have not yet been brought into much use.

The forests of the world may be summed up approximately thus :—

	Millions of Acres	Product, Million Cubic Feet	Cubic Feet per Acre	Value of Product, £
Russia	426	6,200	15	40,800,000
United States .	466	9,300	20	112,000,000
Brazil	135	150	1	1,000,000
Canada . . .	64	650	5	8,200,000
Sweden and Norway . . }	61	900	15	12,000,000
Austria-Hungary	46	2,000	45	18,000,000
Gran Chaco . .	37	40	1	500,000
Germany . . .	32	1,300	40	13,000,000
France	21	1,100	50	10,000,000
Italy	10	440	44	4,000,000
Algeria	6	120	20	1,000,000
Switzerland . .	2	140	70	1,200,000
United Kingdom	2	120	60	2,000,000
Total . .	1,308	22,460	17	223,700,000

The following table shows the average yield of firewood per acre of forest, according to the age of the trees :—

Age of Trees, Years	Cubic Feet	Age of Trees, Years	Cubic Feet	Age of Trees, Years	Cubic Feet
10	700	50	6,200	150	12,800
20	1,800	60	7,500	200	13,400
30	3,300	80	9,200	250	12,000
40	4,900	100	10,000	300	11,000

The following tables refer to the principal kinds of forest trees :—

	Density	Cohesion	Strength
Acacia	0.717	7.93	...
Alder	0.601	4.54	...
Ash	0.697	6.78	983
Aspen	0.602	7.20	...
Beech	0.823	3.57	...
Birch	0.812	4.30	672
Fir	0.493	4.18	585
Maple	0.674	3.58	...
Oak	0.808	6.49	1,000
Pine	0.559	2.48	565
Poplar	0.477	1.97	538
Sycamore . . .	0.692	6.16	744

The following scale serves to ascertain the age of trees :—

Age, Years	Inches Diameter				
	Oak	Larch	Elm	Spruce	Yew
10 . . .	5	4	1	4	1
20 . . .	10	9	5	8	2
30 . . .	14	14	10	12	3
50 . . .	23	24	23	19	4
70 . . .	32	33	36	24	6
100 . . .	41	40	50	27	9
150 . . .	54	50	61	36	14
200 . . .	64	58	71	44	20
250 . . .	74	67	83	52	25
300 . . .	84	75	94	60	30

Eucalyptus or Australian gum-tree sometimes grows 24 feet in three months; bamboo, 2 feet in twenty-four hours.

The maximum age to which trees of different kinds arrive is shown as follows :—

	Years		Years		Years
Palm . .	250	Lemon . .	640	Spruce . .	1,200
Elm . . .	355	Plane . .	720	Oak . .	1,600
Cypress . .	388	Cedar . .	800	Olive . .	2,000
Ivy . . .	448	Chestnut . .	860	Yew . .	2,880
Maple . .	516	Walnut . .	900	Baobab . .	5,100
Larch . .	576	Lime . . .	1,076	Dragon .	5,900

The Crown forests of various countries are as follows :—

	Area, Acres	Product, £	Pence per Acre
Russia . . .	180,000,000	10,000,000	13
India	35,500,000	...	...
Sweden and Norway	10,300,000	1,500,000	35
Germany . . .	9,400,000	3,700,000	95
Austria . . .	7,500,000	1,500,000	48
France . . .	2,110,000	1,700,000	180
Italy	500,000	200,000	96
Belgium . . .	100,000	40,000	96

Besides the foregoing, there are communal forests, the area of which is not easily ascertained.

The following table shows approximately the consumption of all kinds of timber and firewood in the various countries, and the quantities of timber imported or exported.

	Millions of Cubic Ft. Consumed Yearly			Cubic Ft. Consumed per Inhab.	Millions of Cubic Ft.	
	Firewood	Building, &c.	Total		Imported	Exported
U. Kingdom .	60	470	530	14	390	...
France . . .	800	500	1,300	35	200	...
Germany . . .	700	600	1,300	28	...	...
Russia . . .	4,500	1,600	6,100	70	...	120
Austria . . .	1,200	700	1,900	50	...	100
Italy	240	240	480	18	40	...
Spain and Portugal . }	110	150	260	13	60	...
Belgium and Holland . }	20	90	110	12	40	...
Sweden and Norway . }	320	300	620	92	...	200
United States .	3,000	6,000	9,000	150	...	160
Canada . . .	300	200	500	100	...	150
Total . .	11,250	10,850	22,100	40	730	730

UNITED KINGDOM

The consumption of timber has been as follows :—

Year	Millions of Cubic Ft.			Cubic Ft. per Inhabitant	Per Load (50 Cubic Ft.)	
	British	Imported	Total		Duty	Price
					s.	s.
1790	106	11	117	8	7	70
1803	110	12	122	8	25	90
1811	110	14	124	7	55	185
1820	115	22	137	7	65	160
1830	115	28	143	6	55	150
1840	115	41	156	6	55	150
1850	120	85	205	8	7	70
1860	120	145	265	9	4	68
1870	130	252	382	12	...	65
1880	140	290	430	12	...	50
1889	140	392	532	14	...	42

The most remarkable planters in the United Kingdom are :—

Planter	Locality	No. of Trees	Area, Acres
Duke of Athol .	Dunkeld	28,000,000	16,600
Earl of Seafield .	Inverness	60,000,000	40,000
Lord Powerscourt	Wicklow	3,000,000	1,000

The last-mentioned began in 1869, and his outlay has averaged 66s. per acre; he expects after 1894 to get a return of 8s. per acre, and that in 1915 the plantation will be worth £50 an acre.

The largest forests in England are New Forest, 67,000 acres, and Dean Forest, 23,000.

FRANCE

France has been steadily increasing her forests in the last forty years, their area being now 7 million acres more than in 1848. In that interval no less than 9 million acres of waste mountain lands have been planted, the increase of urban population causing a great demand for firewood, the consumption of which averages 23 cubic feet per inhabitant. In 1868 the area and product of forests was as follows :—

	Acres	Product, £
State	2,110,000	1,720,000
Private	15,950,000	8,580,000
Total .	18,060,000	10,300,000

The product was made up approximately thus :—

	£
800 million cubic feet firewood . .	4,000,000
300 ,, ,, ,, timber . . .	6,300,000

Paris requires one million acres for her supply of firewood, as she consumes the equivalent of 50,000 acres yearly, say 1000 acres each week. France is obliged to import 200 million cubic feet of timber yearly, her forests being insufficient for her requirements. The Government has planted largely in Algeria : at Lake Fetzara, on an area of 130,000 acres, 12,700,000 Australian gum-trees.

GERMANY

The forest area is as follows :—

	Acres
Prussia	17,800,000
Bavaria	5,900,000
Other States . . .	8,600,000
Total .	32,300,000

German forests produce 40 cubic feet per acre, those belonging to the Crown forming 30 per cent. of the total. In Prussia the average yield is only 30 cubic feet, but in Bavaria it rises to 45 feet per acre. The consumption of firewood for the whole of Germany averages 15 cubic feet per inhabitant. The value of product is :—

	£
700 million cubic feet firewood . .	3,000,000
600 ,, ,, ,, timber . . .	10,000,000

The forest area has been reduced by two million acres in Prussia since the breaking up of the nobles' estates in 1850–59.

RUSSIA

Forests are steadily diminishing with the increase of population, and especially since the emancipation of the serfs. No less than 101 million acres of forest have been cleared since 1872 according to official returns, being at the rate of 7 million acres yearly. In 1860 the Crown forests covered 333 million acres, and in 1878 according to Strebinski they comprised only 180 million acres ; but of course the emancipation transferred (see *Lands*) several millions to the serfs.

The Czar has 27,000 wood-police, who cut each 150 fagots, or 1½ ton of wood (mostly firewood) daily ; say 450 tons per policeman yearly, the product per man being valued at £45 sterling. These men, for example, felled 670 million cubic feet in 1872, and 540 million in 1878 ; we have no later dates. The foregoing applies merely to 30 million acres of forest, the personal property of the Czar, besides which the Crown or Exchequer owns 150 million acres, the yield of which may be estimated at 2000 million cubic feet. The product of Crown forests averages only 1s. per acre yearly, that of private or communal forests 30d., viz. :—

	Million Acres	Product, £.
Crown forests . . .	180	10,000,000
Private and communal .	246	30,800,000
	426	40,800,000

Bushen estimated the product of Russian forests in 1864 at £24,000,000 sterling.

The consumption of firewood is estimated at one ton or 50 cubic feet per inhabitant, a ton being composed of 100 fagots, and worth about a silver rouble or 3s. per ton. At St. Petersburg, according to Simmonds, the consumption is much greater, reaching 3,000,000 tons yearly, or nearly 200 cubic feet per inhabitant. In 1882 the value of all wood and timber was approximately :—

	Tons	Value, £
Firewood	90,000,000	13,600,000
Exported by land and water . ⎱	34,000,000	⎰ 5,600,000
Used for building, &c. . . . ⎰		⎱ 21,600,000
Total . . .	124,000,000	40,800,000

In 1878 the forests were held approximately thus :—

	Million Acres
Crown	180
Nobles, &c. . . .	284
Peasants . . .	21
Total . . .	485

In 1881 the total area was estimated at 426 million acres.

AUSTRIA-HUNGARY

In Austria-Hungary nearly one-fourth of the forests belongs either to the Crown or the Church, the clergy of Hungary holding 1,500,000 acres.

The yield varies from one to two stères; average 45 cubic feet per acre. Value of product approximately as follows :—

	£
1200 million cubic feet firewood . .	4,000,000
800 ,, ,, ,, timber . .	14,000,000

About one-eighth of the timber is exported.

The forest area of Austria is 46,100,000 acres, viz. :—

	Acres		Acres
Hungary . . .	13,420,000	Bohemia . . .	3,240,000
Transylvania .	6,550,000	Tyrol	2,200,000
Galitzia . . .	5,730,000	Other provinces	14,960 000

ITALY

Italian forests show an average product of 44 cubic feet per acre, more than half of which goes in firewood, the rest to the carpenters, viz. :—

	£
240 million cubic feet firewood . .	1,000,000
200 ,, ,, ,, timber . .	4,000,000

The price of forest land averages £13 per acre.

The consumption of firewood is 8 cubic feet per inhabitant. The supply of timber is short, Italy having to import 40 million cubic feet yearly.

SWEDEN AND NORWAY

Sweden and Norway produce about 900 million cubic feet, the felling of which employs 40,000 woodcutters. One-third is used for firewood, the rest made into timber for building, &c., of which 200 million cubic feet are exported. Of the total production, two-thirds correspond to Sweden, one-third to Norway.

BELGIUM

The total forest area is 1,220,000 acres, including 80,000 that belong to the State, and 340,000 to Communes, the rest being private estates. Annual product 70 millions cubic feet, which yields about 7s. an acre.

UNITED STATES

The value of timber and firewood consumed yearly is shown approximately as follows :—

	Value, £	
	1870	1880
Firewood	15,000,000	20,000,000
Fences	30,000,000	40,000,000
Sleepers, furniture, &c. .	28,000,000	48,000,000
Export	4,000,000	4,000,000
Total . .	77,000,000	112,000,000

About 30,000 acres of timber are felled daily, the sawmills of Maine consuming 50 million feet, those of Michigan 80 million feet monthly. In 1880 the Union counted 25,700 sawmills, with 141,600 hands, whose wages reached £6,700,000 yearly, turning out 18,000 million linear feet of boards, valued at £48,000,000 sterling. The consumption of wood for manufactures is enormous. Even trifling articles of use enter largely into the annual consumption. For example, the Harbour Springs factory turns out 8,000,000 wooden toothpicks daily. Minneapolis requires 2,000,000 barrels yearly for its flour-mills. The forest area is distributed as follows :—

States	Acres	States	Acres
New England	. 19,000,000	Southern . .	. 233,000,000
Middle	18,000,000	West	196,000,000

Making up a total of 466 million acres.

CANADA

The annual production averages 70 million logs, equal to 560 million cubic feet, and 190,000 masts. The total value is £8,200,000, home use £4,000,000, exportation £4,200,000.

INDIA

Excluding Bengal and Upper Burmah, there are 45 million acres of forest (see p. 56).

AUSTRALIA

According to Simmonds, the forest area is :—

		Acres
New South Wales .	. .	3,760,000
Tasmania . . .	. .	4,000,000
Western Australia .	. .	19,200,000
Victoria . . .	. .	25,600,000
New Zealand . .	. .	12,100,000
Total	.	64,660,000

He adds that in New Zealand it is being rapidly diminished.

FORTIFICATIONS

Louis Philippe spent 16 millions sterling on forts, especially the *enceinte* of Paris. Lord Palmerston spent 7½ millions on the coast fortifications begun by him in 1860. The German Government has spent 2½ millions in military works around Strasburg. The site occupied by the Paris fortifications is 3900 acres, and was valued in 1840 at £140 an acre ; it is now about to be sold for £700 an acre, on the levelling of the forts.

FREIGHT

The carrying trade of the world has been prodigiously developed since the introduction of railways and steamboats. Down to the year 1850, when the Continent of Europe had only 7600 miles of railway, the ordinary cost of land-carriage for goods was £3 a ton per 100 miles, or six times what it is at present. Freight by sea then averaged over 40s. a ton, or more than double what it is now. The following table shows approximately the tonnage borne by rail and shipping at various dates :—

Year	Millions of Tons		
	Rail	Shipping	Total
1830	3	24	27
1840	16	30	46
1850	97	37	134
1860	193	48	241
1870	602	64	666
1875	715	80	795
1880	893	112	1,005
1887	1,358	139	1,497

The saving to the people of Prussia alone, in having their merchandise carried by rail, was estimated in 1878 at 120 millions sterling per annum ; this would imply that the saving in 1887 for all nations (per annum) was as follows :—

		Tons		Millions £ Saved
Europe .	. .	752	...	1,128
United States	.	552	...	828
Colonies	. .	54	...	81
Total	.	1,358		2,037

This saving may be considered approximately correct, and is equal to 80 per cent. of the total annual expenditure for food (see *Food*) by the nations comprised above. Nevertheless, the cost of railway carriage for goods is by no means uniform ; the averages in 1885 showed thus :—

Cost per 100 Miles, Pence per Ton

U. States .	.	63	Italy . . .	108	G. Britain .	135
Belgium .	.	70	Austria . .	111	France . .	154
Germany .	.	84	Holland . .	118	Sweden . .	160

In 1888 the railways of the United Kingdom carried about 260 million tons of merchandise, the average haulage being supposed to be 30 miles : the freight charged was £38,800,000, equal to 120d. per 100 miles. This is precisely the rate charged on the London and North-Western line for carrying meat from Liverpool to London.

American railways have reduced their charges more than 50 per cent. in twenty years, viz. :—

Railways of United States, Charge per Ton 100 Miles

Year		£ s. d.	Year			£ s. d.
1865 .	..	0 17 2	1880 .	.	.	0 7 4
1870 .	.	0 11 9	1885 .	.	.	0 5 4

The cost of sending a ton of grain from Chicago to Liverpool *via* New York was as follows : —

Year	Chicago to New York		New York to Liverpool	Chicago to Liverpool, Water-Route
	By Water	By Rail		
	£ s. d.	£ s. d.	£ s. d.	£ s. d.
1868 . . .	2 2 0	3 10 0	1 3 0	3 5 0
1873 . . .	1 12 0	2 16 0	1 15 0	3 7 0
1880 . . .	1 1 0	1 12 0	1 0 0	2 1 0
1884 . . .	0 12 0	1 1 0	0 12 0	1 4 0

The above charge for 1884 was equal to 7d. per bushel, and even lower rates have prevailed since then. The charge from Chicago to Liverpool fell 63 per cent. in the above interval of sixteen years. In 1888 the charges from Chicago to European ports per ton were as follows :—

Chicago to	Shillings per Ton	
	Bacon	Flour
Liverpool	37	31
London	35	32
Hamburg	44	37
Antwerp	43	36

The freights current for ocean routes in 1888 were :—

Route	Shillings per Ton	Miles	Pence per 1000 Miles
London to Singapore . .	25	8,400	36
London to Australia . .	27	11,000	30
London to San Francisco .	30	14,000	26
London to Cape Town .	40	6,000	80
Newcastle to Bombay . .	22	6,500	40
Antwerp to Rio Janeiro .	36	5,400	80
China to New York . .	45	14,000	39

This gives a general average of 37d. per thousand miles of ocean freight, against 90s. by railway ; that is, the latter costs thirty times the former. The President of Civil Engineers in his inaugural speech for 1890 stated that in 1870 it cost £25 to send a ton of merchandise from London to Sydney, which now costs only 30s., a fall of 94 per cent. He added that in 1820 the conveyance of cotton bales from Liverpool to Manchester, thirty miles, cost 40s. a ton, which is now done at 7s., a fall of 82 per cent. With reference to the Manchester ship-canal, it was stated in 1889 that the railway charges between Manchester and Liverpool were still excessive, the freight on a ton of merchandise being as follows :—

Liverpool to Bombay . . . 10 shillings
Liverpool to Manchester . . 12 ,,

The countries which import fruit are the following :—

The ordinary expense of carrying goods in 1884 in all countries was estimated thus :—

Shillings per Ton, 1000 Miles·

By sea. . . . 5 | By railway. . . 100
,, canal . . 20 | ,, highroad . . 300

There is not much difference between the freight paid by waggon on highroads in France and that charged by caravans across Central Africa. Thus, a camel-load of 600 lbs. from Berber to Suakim (280 miles) costs 25s., which is equal to 33s. a ton per 100 miles, 10 per cent. over the ordinary charge by waggon in Europe. The effects of freight on prices are shown by the fact that Athens imports wheat from Odessa because land-carriage in the interior of Greece is £10 a ton per 100 miles, and consequently it is cheaper to consume Russian wheat.

Brazilian railways still charge enormous freights—coffee, for example, paying 550d. per 100 miles, or nine times as much as in the United States. Even freight by water in Brazil is dear, the Brazilian steamers charging £16 a ton from Montevideo to Matto Grosso, the distance being 2500 miles.

In Australia the construction of railways has been attended with the following reduction of freight charges :—

Haulage of One Ton Ten Miles

Year							Pence
1864	.	.	.	.	.	.	75
1872	.	.	.	.	.	.	36
1878	.	.	.	.	.	.	24
1887	.	.	.	.	.	.	18

During the gold fever extravagant sums were paid for freight, the ordinary charge in 1851 from Melbourne to Bendigo being £150 per ton.

FRUIT

The degrees of sugar in various fruits are :—

Peach . . . . 1.6 | Apple 7.9
Raspberry . . . 4.0 | Mulberry . . . 9.2
Strawberry . . . 5.7 | Pear 9.4
Currant . . . 6.1 | Cherry 10.8
Gooseberry . . . 7.2 | Grape 14.9

The countries which import fruit are the following :—

			Tons			Value, £		
			1860	1880	1887	1860	1880	1887
United Kingdom	.	.	79,000	107,000	320,000	1,800,000	3,300,000	6,200,000
France	.	.	...	32,000	195,000	...	3,900,000	3,000,000
United States .		.	13,000	40,000	67,000	800,000	2,700,000	4,300,000

The countries which export fruit are the following :—

			Tons			Value, £		
			1862	1875	1887	1862	1875	1887
Italy	.	.	.	48,000	99,000	240,000	1,200,000	1,600,000	2,200,000
Spain	.	.	.	34,000	72,000	160,000	700,000	1,500,000	2,200,000
Portugal .	.	.	.	...	24,000	17,000	...	160,000	140,000
Greece	.	.	.	42,000	87,000	107,000	540,000	1,470,000	1,900,000

The price of fruit in most countries has fallen notably in the last thirty years, which is due to the great increase of production, and to improved facilities for bringing fruit to ports for shipment.

Mr. Loring, ex-Commissioner of Agriculture, valued the fruit crop of the United States in 1880 at £42,000,000 sterling, and the annual consumption of fruit at 12s. English, per inhabitant of the Union, and 24s. in New York. The *Royal Agricultural Journal* of England states the acreage under fruit-trees in the United King-dom, and the importation of apples from abroad, to be thus :—

Fruit Acreage		Apples Imported	
Year	Acres	Year	Tons
1839	90,000	1839	1,800
1872	172,000	1869	12,300
1889	214,000	1888	95,000

The annual consumption of fruit and vegetables in London and Paris is stated by the *Farming World* thus :—

	Fruit, Lbs. per Inhab.			Vegetables, Lbs. per Inhab.	
	London	Paris		London	Paris
Apples . .	65	145	Carrots . .	7	37
Cherries . .	2	20	Celery . .	1	6
Pears . . .	40	170	Onions . .	34	5
Plums . .	17	183	Peas . . .	3	7
Raspberries.	1	2	Potatoes .	173	49
Strawberries	4	13	Tomatoes .	57	17

Almonds.—The exportation from Italy was as follows:—

Year	Tons	Value, £	Value per Ton, £
1862 . . .	2,500	190,000	76
1870 . . .	3,100	240,000	78
1887 . . .	11,100	600,000	54

And from Spain as follows :—

Year	Tons	Value, £	Value per Ton, £
1872 . . .	3,800	180,000	47
1882 . . .	4,100	180,000	44
1887 . . .	4,400	220,000	50

The almond flourishes between 27 and 45 N. lat., and requires a medium annual temperature of 58° F. In France the yield averages 12 lbs., in California 20 lbs. per tree. The fruit usually sells at £100 per ton. The crop in California averages a value of £100 sterling per acre.

Apple.—The apple crop in Great Britain averages 85,000 tons, valued at £10 per ton ; about 12 million gallons of cider are made yearly. The production of cider in France averages 230 million gallons. Apples in France are worth £5 per ton, ordinary crop 1,600,000 tons. The orchards of Great Britain cover 180,000 acres : a ton of ordinary good apples will produce from 100 to 200 gallons of cider. Great Britain imports 900,000 barrels of apples yearly from the United States and Canada. The imports show thus :—

							Tons
1839 .	.	.	.	.	.	.	1,800
1869 .	.	.	.	.	.	.	12,300
1888 .	.	.	.	.	.	.	95,000

The annual consumption in the United Kingdom averages 11 lbs. per inhabitant.

Banana.—The most prolific of all fruits of the earth, being 44 times more productive than potatoes, and 131 times more than wheat.

Chestnuts form an important item of food in France and Italy. Returns for 1886–88 were :—

	France	Italy
Acres . .	1,220,000	1,010,000
Bushels .	19,000,000	14,000,000

The yield of a good tree averages two bushels. The French crop is valued at £1,600,000, the Italian at £1,200,000 sterling ; the average yield in France is 15, in Italy 14 bushels per acre. Italy exports 500,000 bushels.

Currants.—The exportation from Greece shows :—

Period	Annual Average		Value per Ton, £
	Tons	Value, £	
1867–70	52,000	600,000	12
1871–75	67,000	1,200,000	18
1880	54,000	840,000	16
1889	56,000	900,000	16

Greece produces annually 100,000 tons, the home consumption averaging 40,000 tons.
Imports into the United Kingdom were as follows :—

Period	Annual Average		Value per Ton, £
	Tons	Value, £	
1866–70 . . .	45,000	910,000	20
1871–80 . . .	54,000	1,450,000	27
1881–88 . . .	53,000	1,420,000	27

Date-Palm

	Number of Trees	Yield of Sugar, Tons
India . .	13,000,000	26,000
Egypt .	4,500,000	...

Figs.—The exportation by Greece and Portugal is as follows :—

Greece			Portugal		
Year	Tons	Value, £	Year	Tons	Value, £
1867	7,000	65,000	1877	5,000	52,000
1888	8,000	90,000	1887	13,000	110,000

Oranges and Lemons flourish in Italy, Spain, and Portugal. The orange was introduced into Europe by the Moors in the eleventh century, and. first brought to England by Sir Walter Raleigh in the sixteenth. It was first planted in Australia, near Sydney, in 1788, and has thrived there. The cost of clearing and planting an orange-farm in New South Wales is £30 per acre, and the product begins in the fourth year, rising as follows :—

4th year . .	£10 per acre	6th year . .	£25 per acre
5th ,, . .	15 ,, ,,	7th ,, . .	40 ,, ,,

Sometimes the product reaches £100 per acre, a single tree often giving from 1500 to 2000 oranges, worth 4s. per hundred. In Italy the ordinary yield is 250 lemons and 300 oranges per tree, but a single tree will often give in Sicily as many as 3000, The average in Seville is 600, in Paraguay 700 oranges per tree.

The island of St. Michael, Azores, has 210 acres mostly under oranges, of which it exports 250 millions yearly.

The number of trees and fruit in Italy are :—

	Trees	Millions Fruit Yearly
Orange . . .	5,400,000	1,600
Lemon . . .	4,800,000	1,200

Italy exports about 2500 millions oranges and lemons yearly, Spain 1400 millions, Portugal 80 millions, worth £40,000 ; Paraguay 60 millions, worth £20,000. The Argentine provinces also grow largely, and export 7 millions yearly to Bolivia, value £2000. Dundee consumes yearly 6000 chests of bitter oranges, and exports 1500 tons of marmalade. In Sicily it is found that 1000 lemons give 17 gallons of juice.

The number approximately of oranges imported into the United Kingdom has been :—

Year	Millions	Per Inhabitant	Price, Shillings per 1000
1854	244	9	30
1861	390	13	36
1871	712	23	26
1881	1,152	33	23
1889	1,760	46	20

The consumption of oranges per inhabitant represents 1s. yearly or about 2s. by retail.

The weight, value, and approximate number of oranges and lemons exported in 1888 by Italy and Spain were :—

	Tons	Millions of Fruit	Value, £	£ per Ton
Italy .	165,000	2,470	1,200,000	7.3
Spain .	95,000	1,430	800,000	8.4

A box contains 226, a chest 340 oranges.

Raisins.—The exportation from Spain was as follows :—

Annual Average

Period	Tons	Value, £	Value per Ton, £
1872-80. . .	37,000	100,000	30
1881-87. . .	36,500	900,000	25

Imports into the United Kingdom have been yearly thus :—

Period	Tons	Value, £	Value per Ton, £
1866-70. . .	20,000	640,000	32
1871-80. . .	25,000	880,000	35

FUEL

The annual consumption is approximately as follows :—

	Millions		Per Inhabitant	
	Coal, Tons	Firewood, Cubic Feet	Coal, Cwts.	Firewood, Cubic Feet
United Kingdom . .	140	60,	74	2
France	27	800	14	21
Germany	55	700	24	15
Russia	9	4,000	2	45
Austria	16	1,200	9	32
Italy	3	240	2	8
Spain and Portugal .	2	110	2	6
Belgium	12	...	44	...
Holland	3	20	14	5
Sweden and Norway	2	320	5	45
Europe	269	7,450	17	20
United States . . .	155	3,000	28	50
Canada	2	140	9	28
Total . . .	426	10,590	18	24

Pounds of water evaporated by 1 lb. of fuel as follows :—

Straw .	.	.	.	1.9	Coke or charcoal	.	6.4
Wood .	.	.	.	3.1	Coal .	. .	7.9
Peat .	.	.	.	3.8	Petroleum	.	14.6

To make a ton of charcoal will be required of wood as follows :—

	Tons		Tons		Tons
Oak . . .	4.4	Beech . . .	5.1	Birch . . .	5.9
Chestnut . .	4.5	Elm . . .	5.2	Pine . . .	6.0

For heating power 12 lbs. charcoal are equal to 10 lbs. coal or 13 lbs. coke. It is much used in America, France, and Italy. The ironworks of the United States consume 600,000 tons charcoal yearly, the yield of 50,000 acres, the average being 12 tons per acre. At Noirmoutiers, in France, 200 furnaces are constantly at work making charcoal from seaweed, 20 tons of fresh weed or 4 tons of dry producing 1 ton of charcoal, value 10s. In Ireland

it is often made from peat. The heating power of peat varies as follows :—

Bog of Allen, Ireland .	100	Passy, France	.	.	52
Hartz Mountains .	61	Ham, ,,		.	49
Königsbrunn .	.	57	Troyes, ,,	.	32

The production in France is declining, not exceeding 300,000 tons per annum. Some years ago an estimate was made of the area and contents of peat bogs in the United Kingdom, and the value of the peat at 6d. per ton, viz. :—

	Acres	Millions of Tons	Value at 6d. per Ton, £
Ireland	2,831,000	33,972	850,000,000
Great Britain . .	3,505,000	42,060	1,050,000,000
United Kingdom	6,336,000	76,032	1,900,000,000

The average depth of peat is 12 feet, equal to a yield per acre of 12,000 tons of dried turf.

FURNITURE

Insurance agents say that furniture usually represents a value equal to half that of the house in which it is, including carriages, clothing, jewellery, and works of art. On this basis the value at various dates of furniture in the United Kingdom would be thus :—

Year	Millions £	Per House, £	Per Inhab., £
1802	190	70	12
1830	270	75	13
1850	440	95	16
1860	580	118	20
1870	740	131	24
1880	1,030	158	29
1888	1,320	186	34

In 1880 this value was approximately distributed among five classes of householders, as follows :—

Class	Houses, Thousands	Furniture, Millions £	Average, £	
			Per House	Per Inhab.
1st . .	23	136	5,900	1,080
2nd . .	261	274	1,050	190
3rd . .	563	172	307	55
4th . .	1,423	186	130	23
5th . .	4,175	262	...	6,211
Total	6,445	1,030	158	29

The above does not include churches and other public buildings.

In 1883 Professor Leone Levi found 79,000 cabinetmakers in the United Kingdom, whose wages reached £4,600,000. The output of furniture represents a value of nearly 40 millions sterling per annum, almost wholly for home use. The export of furniture has been :—

	£			£
1855	. . . 180,000	1875	. . .	390,000
1865	. . . 290,000	1888	. . .	750,000

The annual expenditure on furniture in the United Kingdom is about £1 sterling per inhabitant.

G.

GAMES

Billiards.—At billiards the greatest " break " on record is 2413, scored by W. J. Peall, November 5, 1886, at the Aquarium, London. The same player made the greatest number of spot hazards in succession, 633, in the year 1888.

Bull-Fighting.—In 1866 the balance-sheet of ninety-nine bull-rings then in Spain contained the following items :—

	No.	Cost, £	Average, £
Bulls killed . .	2,375	61,000	26
Horses killed . .	3,561	70,000	20
Bull-rings, rent .	99	130,000	1,310
Total .	...	261,000	...

The number of bull-rings in 1878 was still the same. The above does not include the pay of Matadores, Bandilleros, &c.

GAS

The following table shows the cost of street lighting in 1880 in various cities :—

	Cost per Annum, £	Price per 1000 Feet, Pence	Cost per Inhab., Pence	Candle-Power
London . . .	460,000	45	30	12
Paris	620,000	68	70	13
Rome . . .	24,000	...	20	...
Vienna . . .	43,000	45	10	15
Berlin . . .	53,000	51	13	16
New York . .	...	120	...	16
San Francisco .	59,000	...	67	...
Glasgow . .	...	48	...	28
Bucharest . .	20,000	...	24	...
Palermo . .	20,000	...	23	...
Liverpool . .	...	42	...	22
Turin . . .	18,000	...	20	...
Florence . .	14,000	...	22	...
Manchester .	...	36	...	22
Buda-Pesth .	16,000	...	12	...

The consumption in London and Paris was as follows :—

	London			Paris		
	1860	1880	1888	1860	1880	1889
Millions cubic ft.	8,200	18,100	24,700	2,660	8,470	11,010
Per inhab. ,, ,,	2,930	4,750	5,400	1,610	3,940	4,800

Paris has 49,000 street lamps, the other French towns 190,000. London has 71,100.

The following table shows various analyses of gas :—

	London	Paris	Bonn	Gas from Wood	From Peat	From Rock-Oil	From Petroleum
Hydrogen . . .	46.0	50.2	39.8	31.8	27.5	3.1	32.7
Gas de marais . . .	39.5	32.8	43.1	35.3	42.7	64.8	45.7
Oxide of carbon . .	7.5	12.9	4.7	25.6	20.3	6.7	...
Various . . .	7.0	4.1	12.4	7.3	9.5	25.4	21.6
Total . .	100.0	100.0	100.0	100.0	100.0	100.0	100.0

The consumption in the United Kingdom in 1880 was as follows :—

	London	Other Towns	Total
Millions cubic feet . . .	18,100	53,500	71,600
Per inhabitant, cubic feet	4,750	3,100	3,400

The average expenditure for gas is 21s. per inhabitant per annum in London, and 10s. in other towns. A ton of coal gives 9000 cubic feet of gas.

The London Gas Company showed in 1880 as follows :—Capital, £13,026,000 ; receipts, £3,993,000 ; expenses, £2,610,000 ; net earnings, £1,383,000.

In 1888 London consumed as follows :—

	Millions of Cubic Feet
Private lights	23,300
Public lights	1,400
Total . .	24,700

The paid-up capital of London gas companies in 1888 was £14,100,000, including £3,000,000 loan capital.

The statistics of gas companies in the United Kingdom, including those belonging to municipal bodies, are as follows :—

	1885	1888
Capital, £ . .	55,100,000	59,100,000
Tons coal used . .	8,400,000	9,300,000
Millions cubic feet gas	85,600	94,700
Number of consumers	2,100,000	2,200,000

The returns for 1888 of joint-stock companies and municipal ones were :—

	Joint-Stock	Municipal	Total
Capital, £ . . .	37,750,000	21,350,000	59,100,000
Tons coal used . .	6,100,000	3,200,000	9,300,000
Millions cubic feet gas	62,300,000	32,400,000	94,700,000
Number of consumers	1,100,000	1,100,000	2,200,000
Receipts, £ . .	10,500,000	4,800,000	15,300,000
Expenditure, £ . .	7,100,000	3,400,000	10,500,000
Net profit, £ . . .	3,400,000	1,400,000	4,800,000

The consumption in London on one day of thick fog, 14th January 1889, reached 105 million cubic feet, representing a cost of £18,000. The largest gasometer in England is that of Liverpool, which can hold 3,100,000 cubic feet.

The balance-sheet of the Paris Gas Company for 1889 showed thus :—

Consumption, cubic feet . . .	11,010,000
Paid for coal, £ . .	840,000
Total expenditure, £ .	2,600,000
Receipts, £ .	4,200,000
Net profit, £ .	1,600,000
Dividend	31 per cent.

GEOLOGY

Professor Philips in 1836 published the following table of strata, and number of organic forms to each stratum :—

			Feet Thick	Organic Forms per 100 Feet
Tertiary	.	. .	2,000	141
Cretaceous .	.	. .	1,100	71
Oolitic	.	. .	2,500	46
Saliferous .	.	. .	2,000	8
Carboniferous	.	. .	10,000	5
Primary	.	. .	20,000	2

FOSSIL REMAINS

Mammalia	. . .	144	Terrestrial plants . .	500
Reptiles .	. . .	71	,, animals .	330
Fishes .	. . . .	183	Marine plants . . .	40
Insects	. . . .	74	,, animals .	6,065
Conchifera	. . .	2,026	Fresh-water plants .	40
Gasteropoda	. . .	880	,, animals .	260
Kephalopoda	. . .	788		
Crustacea, &c. .	. .	1,970	Total . .	7,235
Total	. .	6,136		

The distribution of France is as follows :—

			Acres	Ratio
Tertiary	.	. .	38,900,000	30
Jurassic	.	. .	25,900,000	20
Primitive	.	. .	24,000,000	18
Cretaceous .	.	. .	15,400,000	11
Transitionary	.	. .	13,000,000	10
Triassic	.	. .	6,500,000	5
Porphyry and coal	.	.	1,300,000	1
Volcanic, &c.	.	.	4,600,000	5
Total	.	.	129,600,000	100

The experiments of Schubler and Schleiden give the power of absorbing water in an area of 50 square inches as follows, per 1000 grains of soil :—

	Grains Absorbed in			
	12 Hours	24 Hours	48 Hours	72 Hours
Gypsum . . .	1	1	1	1
Limestone sand .	2	3	3	3
Loam clay . .	21	26	28	28
Muddy	25	30	34	35
Calcareous clay .	26	31	35	35
Field	16	22	23	23
Slaty marl . . .	24	29	32	33
Garden mould .	35	45	50	52
Humus	80	97	110	120

GEOLOGICAL SURVEYS

Various geological surveys of countries have been made, viz. :—

Country	One in	Inches to 100 Miles	Country	One in	Inches to 100 Miles
U. Kingdom	63,000	100	Spain . .	50,000	127
France . .	80,000	79	Portugal .	100,000	63
Prussia . .	25,000	253	Sweden .	200,000	32
Austrian } Empire }	75,000	84	Holland .	200,000	32
			Belgium .	20,000	320
Russia . .	420,000	15	Finland .	200,000	32
Italy . . .	100,000	63			

GIANTS

Name	Place	Height, Feet	Period
Goliath	Palestine .	11.0	B.C. 1063
Galbara . . .	Rome . .	10.0	Claudius Cæsar
Funnam . . .	Scotland .	11.5	Eugene II.
De Vallemont .	Rouen . .	17.0	14th century
Count Bucart . .	Dauphiny .	22.6	16th ,,
Theutobochus .	,,	25.5	16th ,,
Unknown . . .	Palermo .	30.0	15th ,,
John Middleton .	England .	9.3	A.D. 1578
Frederic's Swede	Sweden .	8.4	...
Cujanus . . .	Finland . .	7.9	...
Gilly	Tyrol . .	8.1	...
Patrick Cotter .	Cork . .	8.7	1806
Chang Gow . .	Pekin . .	7.8	1880

GLASS

Consumption in United Kingdom as follows :—

	Tons
1801	16,300
1833	18,200

In 1834 M'Culloch estimated that the glass factories of the United Kingdom employed 50,000 men, and produced thus :—

England	1,850,000
Scotland	100,000
Ireland	50,000
Total . .	2,000,000

In 1880 the consumption of plate glass in Great Britain amounted to six million square feet, of which one-sixth was imported, the rest native manufacture. The imports and exports of all kinds of glass showed thus :—

Year	Imports, £	Exports, £
1874 . . .	1,600,000	1,200,000
1880 . . .	1,800,000	920,000
1888 . . .	1,900,000	1,100,000

The total glass manufactures of the United Kingdom may be estimated at about three millions sterling per annum.

GLOVES

Great Britain imports annually (1887–89) no less than 19 million pair, valued at £1,900,000. France makes 30 million, and exports about two-thirds, the industry representing a yearly value of £3,000,000. Austria exported 100 tons of gloves in 1885, being twenty times the quantity exported in 1860 ; there are numerous factories at Prague, which city turns out five million pair yearly, valued at £400,000. Italy exports approximately 20 million pair, the value being stated at £1,800,000 ; and, according to Mr. Simmonds, the factories in the United States produce gloves to the value of nearly £4,000,000 sterling, besides which the Americans in 1887 consumed £830,000 worth of European gloves.

GOATS

The numbers in the various countries mentioned under *Cattle* will be found at p. 110. There are also 720,000 in Turkey, 2,790,000 in South Africa, and 19,000,000 in India.

An ordinary goat gives a quart of milk daily, and lives ten years. The Turkish breed known as Angora produces a fine hair worth 2s. per lb., say 2 lbs. per goat per annum. One-third of the goats in South Africa are of Angora or mixed breed, the first having been introduced from Smyrna in 1860.

U

GOLD AND SILVER

The quantity of precious metals at remote dates of antiquity has been often discussed. The following facts are worthy of note :—

Date		£
B.C. 520.	Cyrus's booty from Asia . .	8,000,000
B.C. 323.	Alexander's from Persia was 351,000 talents, equal to	} 81,000,000
B.C. 44.	Julius Cæsar seized in the Roman treasury 520 tons gold and 700 tons silver, together worth . .	} 75,000,000

According to Jacob, the Roman Empire in time of Augustus, A.D. 14, possessed 358 millions sterling of gold and silver. Jacob, Tooke, Newmarch, &c., estimated the stock of precious metals in the world at various dates, the result of their views being contained in the following table, with later information added :—

A.D.	Tons		Millions £		
	Gold	Silver	Gold	Silver	Total
1600 . .	830	23,000	116	276	392
1700 . .	1,310	45,000	183	450	633
1800 . .	2,730	88,000	382	760	1,142
1850 . .	3,620	113,000	507	976	1,483
1880 . .	7,800	145,000	1,092	1,090	2,182
1888 . .	8,600	160,000	1,204	1,010	2,214
1890 . .	8,820	165,000	1,235	1,213	2,448

But for the sudden rise of 15 per cent. in the price of silver in 1890, the stock of that metal, at prices of 1889, would stand for no more than 1040 millions sterling.

Several eminent statists have published estimates of the production of precious metals since Columbus discovered the New World.

Soetbeer's table of the production of gold and silver is as follows :—

Period	Tons		Value, Million £			Annual Average of Total, £
	Gold	Silver	Gold	Silver	Total	
1493–1520	162	1,316	23	14	37	1,300,000
1521–1600	593	21,519	83	258	341	4,300,000
1601–1700	911	37,234	128	372	500	5,000,000
1701–40	638	15,736	90	140	230	5,700,000
1741–80	906	23,718	127	213	340	8,500,000
1781–1800	356	17,581	50	151	201	10,500,000
1801–20	292	14,350	41	125	166	8,300,000
1821–30	142	4,606	20	37	57	5,700,000
1831–40	203	5,965	28	52	80	8,000,000
1841–50	548	7,804	77	67	144	14,400,000
1851–60	2,018	8,956	282	78	360	36,000,000
1861–70	1,885	12,201	264	105	369	36,900,000
1871–80	1,715	22,347	241	178	419	41,900,000
1881–88	1,067	21,960	148	154	302	37,700,000
396 years	11,436	215,293	1,602	1,944	3,546	9,000,000

The values were as follows :—

Period	Tons Gold					
	United States	Spanish America	Russia	Australia	Various	Total
1493–1850	30	3,045	310	...	1,366	4,751
1851–60	830	50	256	772	110	2,018
1861–70	713	60	271	741	100	1,885
1871–80	620	105	380	525	85	1,715
1881–88	373	60	280	260	94	1,067
396 years	2,566	3,320	1,497	2,298	1,755	11,436

Period	Value, Millions £					
1493–1850	4	429	43	...	191	667
1851–60	116	7	36	108	15	282
1861–70	100	8	38	104	14	264
1871–80	87	15	53	74	12	241
1881–88	52	8	39	36	13	148
396 years	359	467	209	322	245	1,602

Period	Tons Silver					
	United States	Mexico	South America	Germany	Various	Total
1493–1850	...	63,480	61,500	5,800	19,049	149,829
1851–60	7	4,570	2,045	550	1,784	8,956
1861–70	2,375	4,970	2,105	790	1,961	12,201
1871–80	7,750	6,360	3,620	1,530	3,087	22,347
1881–88	8,860	5,800	2,800	2,100	2,400	21,960
396 years	18,992	85,180	72,070	10,770	28,281	215,293

Period	Value, Millions £					
1493–1850	...	606	586	55	182	1,429
1851–60	...	40	18	5	15	78
1861–70	20	43	18	7	17	105
1871–80	62	51	29	12	24	178
1881–88	62	41	20	15	16	154
396 years	144	781	671	94	254	1,944

The value of gold is taken at £140,000 per ton, that of silver at the current market price.

Jacob estimated the production of precious metals from 1492 (date of the discovery of America) to 1829 as follows:—

Period	America	Old World	Total	Annual Average
	£	£	£	£
1492–1545	17,200,000	5,400,000	22,600,000	420,000
1546–1600	111,400,000	7,600,000	119,000,000	2,200,000
1601–1700	307,000,000	30,000,000	337,000,000	3,370,000
1701–1809	786,000,000	94,000,000	880,000,000	8,150,000
1810–29	84,000,000	19,000,000	103,000,000	5,150,000
337 years	1,305,600,000	156,000,000	1,461,600,000	4,400,000

He estimated the total stock of gold and silver in Europe in 1492 at no more than £33,400,000, and accounted for the stock and production down to 1829 as follows :—

Period	Production, £	Consumption			Balance
		India and China	Manufactures	Mint	
1492–1600	141,600,000	14,000,000	28,000,000	5,000,000	94,600,000
1601–1700	337,000,000	33,000,000	60,000,000	77,000,000	167,000,000
1701–1809	880,000,000	352,000,000	352,000,000	93,000,000	83,000,000
1810–29	103,000,000	40,000,000	112,000,000	18,000,000	...
Total . .	1,461,600,000	439,000,000	552,000,000	193,000,000	...

The consumption in 337 years amounted to 1184 millions sterling, being 277 millions less than the production.

Messedaglia's table of precious metals for 383 years is as follows from 1493 to 1875 :—

	Tons Produced		Value, Mill. £ Stg.		
	Gold	Silver	Gold	Silver	Total
Russia	1,033	2,400	142	22	164
Germany	...	7,900	...	70	70
Austria	460	7,800	64	70	134
Europe	1,493	18,100	206	162	368
Africa	732	...	101	...	101
Australia	1,812	...	250	...	250
United States	2,026	5,300	280	47	327
Mexico	265	76,200	36	677	713
Peru	164	31,200	22	280	302
Chile	27	2,600	4	23	27
Brazil	1,037	...	143	...	143
Potosi	291	37,700	40	336	376
Columbia	1,214	...	168	...	168
Spanish America	2,998	147,700	413	1,316	1,729
Various	392	9,400	52	79	131
Total	9,453	180,500	1,302	1,604	2,906

Tooke's table comparing the production of precious metals in 1848 with 1800 was as follows :—

	Gold		Silver	
	1800	**1848**	**1800**	**1848**
	£	£	£	£
Russia	100,000	4,100,000	200,000	200,000
Rest of Europe	150,000	360,000	1,320,000	560,000
Africa	280,000	550,000	...	...
India, &c.	830,000	3,000,000	1,000,000	100,000
Old World	1,360,000	8,010,000	2,520,000	860,000
Mexico	220,000	500,000	4,080,000	4,800,000
N. Grenada	650,000	680,000	40,000	...
Peru	100,000	100,000	1,330,000	1,250,000
Bolivia	70,000	60,000	460,000	980,000
Chili	380,000	140,000	290,000	180,000
Brazil	510,000	340,000	...	...
U. States	...	240,000	...	...
America	1,930,000	2,060,000	6,200,000	7,210,000
The world	3,290,000	10,070,000	8,720,000	8,070,000

He estimated the production in Russia and Siberia as follows :—

Period	Gold	Silver	Total	Annual Product
	£	£	£	£
1704–1809	17,100,000	9,760,000	26,860,000	250,000
1810–24	2,200,000	1,680,000	3,880,000	260,000
1825–47	31,000,000	3,940,000	34,940,000	1,520,000
1848–50	10,100,000	480,000	10,580,000	3,530,000
1851–54	12,300,000	610,000	12,910,000	3,230,000
150 years	72,700,000	16,470,000	89,170,000	590,000

He estimated the production in the rest of Asia as follows :—

Period	Gold	Silver	Total	Annual Average
	£	£	£	£
1492–1809	127,000,000	16,900,000	143,900,000	460,000
1810–24	12,040,000	1,600,000	13,640,000	920,000
1825–47	37,000,000	8,200,000	45,200,000	1,970,000
1848–50	8,000,000	2,900,000	10,900,000	3,670,000
1851–54	14,400,000	3,920,000	18,320,000	4,580,000
362 years	198,440,000	33,520,000	231,960,000	640,000

It is worthy of remark, as shown in Soetbeer's table on the preceding page, that from 1851 to 1888 the annual production of precious metals averaged from 37 to 41 millions sterling. At present it is close on 40 millions, and there is no indication of any future decline.

The production of silver in the last ten years, according to the United States Mint Report, was as follows :—

Year	Ounces Fine Silver			Price, Average Pence per Oz.
	United States	Other Countries	The World	
1880	30,300,000	44,500,000	74,800,000	52
1881	33,300,000	45,600,000	78,900,000	52
1882	36,200,000	50,300,000	86,500,000	54
1883	35,700,000	53,400,000	89,100,000	51
1884	37,800,000	43,800,000	81,600,000	50½
1885	39,900,000	51,700,000	91,600,000	48½
1886	39,400,000	53,800,000	93,200,000	45½
1887	41,300,000	54,900,000	96,200,000	45
1888	45,800,000	64,200,000	110,000,000	43
1889	50,000,000	76,000,000	126,000,000	42½
10 years	389,700,000	538,200,000	927,900,000	48½

The production of gold in eight years ending December 1888 was as follows :—

Year	Ounces Fine Gold				Value of Product, £
	United States	Australia	Russia	Total	
1881	1,880,000	1,250,000	2,030,000	5,160,000	21,000,000
1882	1,600,000	1,150,000	1,820,000	4,570,000	17,600,000
1883	1,450,000	1,050,000	1,900,000	4,400,000	16,900,000
1884	1,490,000	1,000,000	1,900,000	4,390,000	16,900,000
1885	1,540,000	1,100,000	1,850,000	4,490,000	17,300,000
1886	1,880,000	1,040,000	1,840,000	4,760,000	18,300,000
1887	1,600,000	1,150,000	1,860,000	4,610,000	17,800,000
1888	1,600,000	1,500,000	1,850,000	4,950,000	19,200,000
8 years	13,040,000	9,240,000	15,050,000	37,330,000	145,000,000

The production of precious metals in the United States is officially estimated as follows :—

Period	Gold, Oz.	Silver, Oz.	Value, £
1845–50 . . .	5,200,000	300,000	21,000,000
1851–60 . . .	28,500,000	500,000	114,000,000
1861–70 . . .	24,700,000	80,000,000	120,000,000
1871–80 . . .	20,500,000	310,000,000	163,000,000
1881–88 . . .	13,100,000	310,000,000	129,000,000
44 years . . .	92,000,000	700,800,000	547,000,000

In the above table, however, silver is valued at 60d. per oz.—much above the market price. The gold produced from 1851 to 1888 amounts to 2486 tons, the silver to 20,300 tons, which latter is about 5 per cent. over Soetbeer's estimate. The relative quantities of the two metals, as shown above, and the price of silver per oz., as well as its value in exchange for gold, are given in the following table, which shows conclusively that it is a fallacy to suppose that the world is being flooded with silver. If the production were, as compared with gold, to be of the same magnitude as in the eighteenth century, we should require double the present quantity to be produced yearly. It appears, meantime, that silver is relatively much less used in manufactures than gold, the annual consumption under this head being 45 per cent. of the gold produced, and 27 per cent. of silver :—

Period	Tons of Silver to 1 of Gold	Price of Silver, Pence per Oz.	Ounces of Silver for 1 of Gold
1600–20 . . .	27.7	77.0	12.1
1700–20 . . .	34.3	62.0	15.1
1800–20 . . .	32.2	61.0	15.3
1821–40 . . .	33.1	60.0	15.6
1841–60 . . .	31.0	60.0	15.6
1861–70 . . .	22.6	60.0	15.6
1871–80 . . .	18.6	56.0	16.7
1881–82 . . .	18.4	53.0	17.6
1883–84 . . .	18.5	50.7	18.4
1885–86 . . .	18.6	47.0	19.9
1887–88 . . .	18.6	44.0	21.2
1890	18.7	51.0	18.3

The uses to which the precious metals were put in fifty years down to 1888 are stated by Soetbeer to be :—

Period	Gold, Tons				Silver, Tons			
	Coinage	Manufactures	The East	Total	Coinage	Manufactures	The East	Total
1831–40 . . .	50	180	10	240	2,700	2,000	2,200	6,900
1841–50 . . .	350	200	28	578	4,800	2,200	2,400	9,400
1851–60 . . .	1,633	280	100	2,013	...	2,700	11,300	14,000
1861–70 . . .	1,008	570	300	1,878	...	3,100	12,300	15,400
1871–80 . . .	849	840	120	1,809	1,200	4,500	10,800	16,500
50 years . . .	3,890	2,070	558	6,518	8,700	14,500	39,000	62,200

The stock of silver is relatively much lower now, as compared with gold, than in the early years of the present century, when there were 33 tons of silver in the world for 1 ton of gold. If the price of silver were ruled by ratio it would have been as follows :—

Period	Ratio of Silver to Stock of Gold		Pence per Oz.
1821–40	33.1	...	60
1881–88	18.6	...	107

If the foregoing estimates be correct, there has been a dearth of both gold and silver, the production falling short of the consumption, viz. :—

1831–80	Gold, Tons	Silver, Tons
Production . . .	6,358	57,273
Consumption . . .	6,518	62,200
Deficit . . .	160	4,927

The deficit was probably met by melting down old plate. The current of bullion (coined or uncoined) between nations since 1861 was as follows :—

Period	Gold, Millions £ Sterling Imported				
	Great Britain	France	United States	Various	Total
1861–70 . .	171	189	31	121	512
1871–80 . .	180	151	42	131	504
1881–88 . .	96	63	64	144	367
Total .	447	403 .	137	396	1,383

Period	Gold Exported, Millions £					
	Great Britain	France	United States	Australia	Various	Total
1861–70 . . .	112	119	113	108	60	512
1871–80 . . .	172	90	74	76	92	504
1881–88 . . .	96	67	35	34	135	367
Total . .	380	276	222	218	287	1,383

Period	Silver Imported, Millions £					
	Great Britain	France	United States	The East	Various	Total
1861–70 . . .	93	92	12	233	44	474
1871–80 . . .	132	111	18	126	40	427
1881–88 . . .	66	62	23	116	36	303
Total . .	291	265	53	475	120	1,204

Period	Silver Exported, Millions £					
	Great Britain	France	United States	Spanish America	Various	Total
1861–70 . . .	91	78	22	74	209	474
1871–80 . . .	119	48	73	68	119	427
1881–88 . . .	68	49	41	37	108	303
Total . .	278	175	136	179	436	1,204

Period	Gold and Silver, Millions £ Imported					
	Great Britain	France	United States	The East	Various	Total
1861–70 . . .	264	281	43	233	165	986
1871–80 . . .	312	262	60	126	171	931
1881–88 . . .	162	125	87	128	168	670
Total . .	738	668	190	487	504	2,587

Period	Gold and Silver Exported, Millions £						
	Great Britain	France	United States	Australia	Spanish America	Various	Total
1861–70	203	197	135	108	81	262	986
1871–80	291	138	147	76	75	204	931
1881–88	164	116	76	34	41	239	670
Total	658	451	358	218	197	705	2,587

The current of bullion in the last eight years is more clearly shown as follows :—

1881–88	Imports, Millions £			Exports, Millions £		
	Gold	Silver	Total	Gold	Silver	Total
U. Kingdom .	96	66	162	96	68	164
France . . .	63	62	125	67	49	116
United States .	64	23	87	35	41	76
Spanish America	20	...	20	4	37	41
The East. . .	12	116	128	2	19	21
Australia . . .	2	...	2	34	...	34
Various . . .	110	36	146	129	89	218
Total .	367	303	670	367	303	670

Since 1881 Great Britain appears to have neither increased nor diminished her stock of gold, but to have exported a small quantity of silver. France has lost gold and gained silver: the United States has done exactly the reverse. India has absorbed both gold and silver.

The total current to and from the United States for sixty-eight years is stated thus :—

Period	Millions £ Sterling	
	Imports	Exports
1821–40	36	3
1841–60	34	93
1861–88	190	358
68 years	260	454

According to Mr. O'Conor, India received in thirty years (1860–89) and retained no less than :—

	£
Gold	113,200,000
Silver	227,000,000
Total . .	340,200,000

To which he adds 102 millions for the preceding twenty-five years, making altogether 442 millions sterling in fifty-five years. He considers that the gold has been practically withdrawn from circulation, to be hoarded or converted into ornaments. Another writer says that in 280 years ending 1830 India absorbed 55,000 tons of

silver, worth 490 millions sterling. Official tables give the net imports as follows :—

Period	Millions £ Sterling		
	Gold	Silver	Total
1850–59 . . .	18	52	70
1860–69 . . .	59	101	160
1870–79 . . .	18	50	68
1880–86 . . .	28	50	78
37 years . . .	123	253	376

Mr. N. Spallart summed up the production and consumption of precious metals in fifty years down to 1880 as follows :—

	Value, Millions £ Sterling		
	Gold	Silver	Total
Coinage . . .	543	38	581
The East . . .	78	351	429
Manufactures .	294	131	425
Total . .	915	520	1,435
Production . .	915	520	1,435

In the above, "coinage" does not include what was minted in the East.

The weight of precious metals used in forty years in the various mints (including re-coinage) from 1850 to December 1889 was :—

	Tons		Aggregate Value, Millions £
	Gold	Silver	
Great Britain . . .	1,301	2,620	207
France	2,159	5,135	349
Germany	894	6,420	183
Russia	1,102	2,580	178
Austria	137	5,360	67
Italy	123	2,530	40
Spain and Portugal .	220	1,480	43
Scandinavia	35	230	7
Holland	48	3,290	37
Belgium	170	2,060	42
Europe	6,189	31,705	1,153
United States . . .	2,096	11,460	397
Australia	644	...	90
India	15	29,270	265
Japan	110	1,100	25
Spanish America . .	140	7,700	90
Total . .	9,194	81,235	2,020

The total is made up of 1227 millions sterling of gold, and 793 millions of silver money. The stocks of coined and uncoined bullion appear to have been at various dates approximately as follows :—

A.D.	Gold, Millions £			Silver, Millions £		
	Coined	Uncoined	Total	Coined	Uncoined	Total
1600	29	87	116	102	174	276
1700	75	108	183	225	225	450
1800	126	256	382	360	400	760
1848	157	343	500	388	580	968
1880	735	357	1,092	556	534	1,090
1890	790	445	1,235	642	571	1,213

The above table will be clearer if given in tons, viz.:—

A.D.	Gold, Tons			Coined, Ratio per Cent.	Silver, Tons			Coined, Ratio per Cent.
	Coined	Uncoined	Total		Coined	Uncoined	Total	
1600	208	622	830	25	8,500	14,500	23,000	37
1700	537	773	1,310	41	22,500	22,500	45,000	50
1800	908	1,822	2,730	33	42,000	46,000	88,000	48
1848	1,125	2,450	3,575	32	45,200	67,800	113,000	40
1880	5,250	2,550	7,800	67	73,700	71,300	145,000	51
1890	5,640	3,180	8,820	64	88,100	76,900	165,000	53

It appears that coinage now absorbs nearly two-thirds of the total stock of gold, and more than half the silver, whereas forty years ago it took only 32 per cent. of gold, and 40 per cent. of silver.

The actual bulk of gold and silver coin in various countries, according to Spallart, in 1885 was as follows :—

	Tons		Aggregate Value, Millions £ Sterling
	Gold Coin	Silver Coin	
Great Britain . . .	915	2,420	144
France	1,335	16,500	328
Germany.	915	4,950	167
Russia	293	1,540	53
Austria	60	2,100	27
Italy	165	1,210	33
Spain	143	2,640	43
Portugal	67	220	11
Scandinavia. . . .	52	220	9
Switzerland	22	330	6
Holland	37	1,430	18
Belgium	82	1,210	22
Roumania	8	330	4
Turkey, &c.. . . .	113	990	24
Europe	4,207	36,090	889
United States . . .	1,058	9,570	228
Australia.	165	220	24
Japan	143	990	28
China.	...	16,500	150
Java	...	1,980	18
India	...	17,600	160
Singapore	...	2,640	24
Cape Colony . . .	52	...	7
Cuba	30	...	4
Canada	23	110	4
Algeria	15	330	5
Spanish America, &c.	232	2,070	50
The world .	5,925	88,100	1,591

The total value is made up of 790 millions sterling in gold coin and silver money nominally representing 801 millions, but worth only 642 millions.

In 1886 Spallart estimated the annual consumption for manufactures as follows :—

	Gold, Oz.	Silver, Oz.	Per 1000 Population	
			Gold, Oz.	Silver, Oz.
U. States .	683,000	4,020,000	12	70
G. Britain .	600,000	2,520,000	16	66
France . .	595,000	2,600,000	15	65
Germany .	420,000	2,870,000	9	60
Switzerland.	370,000	840,000	125	285
Austria . .	84,000	1,120,000	2	28
Italy . . .	155,000	665,000	5	22
Russia . .	85,000	1,100,000	1	12
Holland & Belgium	102,000	840,000	10	84
Various . .	56,000	1,445,000	...	...
Total .	3,150,000	18,020,000	...	...

The total makes up 90 tons gold and 515 tons silver yearly, which is in harmony with Soetbeer's estimate.

Besides the consumption for manufactures, gold coin loses 1 per cent. of its weight in fifty years, silver 1 per cent. in ten years. This means a yearly loss of 1¼ tons of gold, and 88 tons of silver.

The following table shows the amount of gold and silver plate stamped yearly in the United Kingdom and France :—

Date	United Kingdom, Oz. Yearly		Date	France, Oz. Yearly	
	Gold	Silver		Gold	Silver
1801-20	6,080	1,072,000	1830	101,000	1,740,000
1821-40	6,640	1,130,000	1840	164,000	2,290,000
1841-50	7,333	1,007,000	1850	169,000	1,840,000
1851-60	38,415	930,000	1860	288,000	2,290,000
1861-70	29,204	875,000	1870	380,000	2,380,000
1871-80	42,190	790,000	1878	409,000	2,460,000

GRAIN

The average yield per acre in various countries, mostly from 1880 to 1887, was in bushels as follows :—

	Wheat	Barley	Oats	Rye	Maize	General Average
U. Kingdom	28	33	37	...	...	30
France . .	18	20	26	16	19	19
Germany. .	22	20	18	16	...	18
Russia . .	8	9	15	10	15	10
Austria . .	16	18	22	16	20	18
Hungary. .	18	19	22	15	18	18
Italy . . .	12	15	19	...	20	14
Spain . . .	12	18	20	...	18	15
Portugal . .	12	15	15	...	...	14
Sweden . .	22	26	30	25	...	30
Norway . .	21	27	36	24	...	33
Denmark .	36	30	33	25	...	30
Finland . .	15	17	23	15	...	17
Holland . .	27	40	42	21	...	28
Belgium . .	25	33	36	20	...	28
Switzerland .	16	...	12	12	...	15
Roumania .	16	...	20	...	30	18
Greece . .	10	12	...	...	15	12
Turkey . .	10	12	...	...	15	12
Europe . .	14	17	22	14	20	...
United States	12	22	26	11	23	21
Canada . .	16	27	48	...	63	22
Australia. .	12	20	28	...	30	15
Cape Colony	10	15	10	...	10	11
India . . .	10	...	...	...	...	10
Egypt . . .	13	14	...	...	18	16
Algeria . .	13	15	...	...	...	14
Argentina .	10	...	...	...	20	15

Tables showing the acreage and production of the various kinds of grain will be found under *Agriculture*, p. 8. For consumption, see *Food*.

In the manufacture of grain it is found that 100 lbs. of wheat produce 82 lbs. of flour, and 100 lbs. of barley 78 of malt.

GRAVITY, SPECIFIC

A.—COMPARED WITH WATER

Liquids		Timber		Metals	
Water . .	100	Cork . . .	24	Zinc . . .	719
Sea-water .	103	Poplar . .	38	Cast iron .	721
Dead Sea .	124	Fir . . .	55	Tin . . .	729
Alcohol . .	84	Cedar . .	61	Bar iron .	779
Olive-oil . .	92	Pear . . .	66	Steel . . .	783
Turpentine .	99	Walnut . .	67	Copper . . .	869
Wine . . .	100	Cherry . .	72	Brass . .	840
Urine . . .	101	Maple . .	75	Silver . .	1,051
Cider . . .	102	Apple . .	79	Lead . . .	1,135
Beer . . .	102	Ash . . .	84	Mercury .	1,357
Woman's milk	102	Beech . .	85	Gold . . .	1,926
Cow's ,,	103	Mahogany .	106	Platina . .	1,950
Goat's ,,	104	Oak . . .	117		
Porter . .	104	Ebony . .	133		

A gallon of wine or water weighs 10 lbs.

PRECIOUS STONES

Emerald . .	277	Diamond .	353	Garnet . .	406
Crystal . .	265	Topaz . .	401	Ruby . . .	428

SUNDRIES

Indigo . .	77	Peat . . .	133	Porcelain .	226
Ice . . .	92	Opium . .	134	Stone . . .	252
Gunpowder .	93	Honey . .	145	Marble . .	270
Butter . .	94	Ivory . .	183	Granite . .	278
Clay . . .	120	Brick . . .	200	Chalk . .	279
Coal . . .	130	Sulphur . .	203	Glass . . .	289

B.—WEIGHT IN CUBIC FEET

	Lbs. per Cubic Feet	Cubic Feet per Ton
Cork	15	150.0
Cedar	36	62.0
Beech	51	44.0
Butter	56	40.0
Ice	57	39.0
Water	62	36.0
Mahogany	66	34.0
Oak	70	32.0
Clay	72	31.0
Coal	80	28.0
Peat	80	28.0
Brick	120	19.0
Stone	150	15.0
Granite	166	13.5
Glass	172	13.0
Iron	470	4.8
Copper	520	4.3
Silver	630	3.6
Lead	680	3.3
Gold	1,155	2.0

GYPSIES

The number in Europe reaches 712,000, viz. :—

Great Britain .	18,000	Austria . . .	197,000
Russia . .	15,000	Roumania .	193,000
Scandinavia .	7,000	Turkey .	200,000
Spain . .	40,000	Germany, &c.	42,000

H.

HATS

In 1835 M'Culloch estimated the value of hats made yearly in the United Kingdom at £2,400,000. In 1882 there were 12,000,000 men's hats made, worth £4,000,000. The hat industry flourished in New England in the eighteenth century; more than 10,000 beaver hats were made in 1731, and some exported, but in 1732 Great Britain prohibited the exportation.

HAY AND STRAW

The production is approximately as follows :—

	Hay, Tons	Straw, Tons	Collective Value, £
Great Britain . .	8,500,000	6,500,000	25,600,000
Ireland	4,000,000	1,500,000	9,000,000
France	25,000,000	17,000,000	74,000,000
Germany . . .	16,000,000	15,000,000	47,000,000
Russia	60,000,000	45,000,000	82,000,000
Austria	14,000,000	17,000,000	33,800,000
Italy	12,000,000	5,000,000	22,000,000
Spain and Portugal	6,500,000	9,500,000	18,000,000
Sweden and Norway . .	2,000,000	3,000,000	5,400,000
Denmark . . .	1,000,000	2,000,000	3,600,000
Holland . . .	3,000,000	1,000,000	6,900,000
Belgium . . .	5,000,000	1,600,000	11,600,000
Roumania and Servia . .	2,000,000	3,400,000	4,800,000
Europe	159,000,000	127,500,000	343,700,000
United States .	42,000,000	60,000,000	104,000,000
Total . .	201,000,000	187,500,000	447,700,000

The production in the United States has been as follows :—

Year	Hay, Tons	Straw, Tons	Collective Value, £
1840 . . .	10,000,000	12,000,000	26,000,000
1850 . . .	14,000,000	17,000,000	37,000,000
1860 . . .	19,000,000	25,000,000	45,000,000
1870 . . .	27,000,000	28,000,000	54,000,000
1880 . . .	35,000,000	54,000,000	89,000,000
1886 . . .	42,000,000	60,000,000	104,000,000

Official returns give only the quantity of hay; that of straw is estimated above at 1 ton per 50 bushels of grain.

In the United Kingdom the hay crop averages 30 cwt. per acre, in Prussia 33, in France 30, in Italy 30 on irrigated and 16 on unirrigated land, in the United States 24. Italy has 3 millions irrigated and 10 millions unirrigated producing hay.

Three tons of grass usually give one ton of hay.

The weekly consumption of hay is—160 lbs. for a horse, 100 for a cow, 30 for a pig, 10 for a sheep, 8 for a goat.

HEMP

The world's crop is worth about 10 millions sterling, and the value of the manufactured goods is between 25 and 30 millions; the statistics are in many countries mixed with those of flax. The Factory Report for the United Kingdom gives the hemp industry thus :—

Year	Factories	Spindles	Hands
1870 . . .	35	32,000	3,100
1878 . . .	58	25,000	4,800
1885 . . .	107	39,000	9,900

The production and consumption of hemp, as given by N. Spallart in 1885 were :—

	Tons Produced	Tons Consumed
Russia . . .	120,000	56,000
Austria . . .	90,000	90,000
Italy . . .	96,000	56,000
France . . .	50,000	68,000
Germany . . .	10,000	30,000
United States .	13,000	16,000
Other countries* .	16,000	79,000
Total . .	395,000	395,000

The imports of hemp into the United Kingdom are the only guide to extent of manufacture, the value of which is approximately as below :—

Year	Consumed, Tons	Price per Ton, £	Value of Manufactures, £
1810 . . .	48,000	58	8,600,000
1830 . . .	26,000	25	2,000,000
1840 . . .	30,000	27	2,400,000
1850 . . .	54,000	30	4,900,000
1860 . . .	35,000	30	1,900,000
1870 . . .	71,000	38	7,100,000
1880 . . .	73,000	29	5,400,000
1888 . . .	58,000	31	4,500,000

HOLIDAY

On Bank-holiday, 5th August 1889, in London the number of visitors to museums, &c., was as follows :—

British Museum . .	5,200	Zoological Gardens .	21,000
National Gallery . .	8,400	Crystal Palace . .	40,000
Kensington Museum	18,100	Kew Gardens . . .	64,000

besides 11,000 to Tussaud's waxworks and 7000 to Windsor Castle.

HOPS

	Acres	Crop, Tons	Value, £
England . . .	65,000	26,000	3,120,000
Germany . . .	62,000	19,000	2,340,000
France . . .	9,000	4,500	550,000
United States . .	10,000	5,000	600,000

Germany consumes only three-fourths of her crop, but England has to import annually 7000 tons, her consumption averaging 33,000 tons. Returns for the United Kingdom show thus :—

Period	Acres Under Crop	Crop, Tons	Import, Tons	Annual Consumption, Tons
1869–75	63,000	24,600	8,400	33,000
1888–89	65,000	25,400	8,400	33,800

HORIZON

Objects at sea are visible at the following distances :—

Elevation, Feet	Miles	Elevation, Feet	Miles
5 . . .	3	200 . . .	18
10 . . .	4	300 . . .	23
20 . . .	6	500 . . .	30
50 . . .	9	800 . . .	37
100 . . .	13	1,000 . . .	42

* This table seems to omit Manilla, where there were 260,000 acres under hemp in 1880.

HORSES

The number in each country will be found under *Cattle*, p. 109. A horse lives 25 years, but a tramway horse lasts only five years : horse-flesh is eaten in France, the carcase yielding 450 lbs. meat. Napoleon in 1812 crossed the Niemen with 100,000 horses, of which 95,000 died before he reached Moscow.

HOTELS

On a given day in each year the number of guests in hotels at Paris was as follows :—

Year	Number of Hotels	French Guests	Foreign Guests	Total
1875	9,207	114,000	19,000	133,000
1879	10,189	140,000	41,000	181,000
1883	11,753	196,000	44,000	240,000

The hotels at Vienna admitted 240,000 guests during the whole year 1888. The hotels of Switzerland in 1889 were 1000 in number, making up 58,000 beds, employing 16,000 servants ; the invested capital was £1,600,000, receipts £1,680,000, expenditure £1,150,000, and profit £530,000.

HOUSES

The number of houses, inhabitants per house, and approximate value may be set down thus. We have no value as regards Portugal, which is estimated at the same ratio per inhabitant as in Spain :—

	Houses	Value, Millions £	Average per House, £	Average per Inhab, £	Inhab. per House
United Kingdom .	7,100,000	2,424	340	63	5.4
France . .	9,080,000	1,704	187	45	4.2
Germany . .	5,770,000	1,232	214	26	8.0
Russia . .	11,436,000	701	62	8	8.0
Austria . .	5,000,000	501	100	13	7.8
Italy . .	4,420,000	394	90	13	6.6
Spain and Portugal .	3,810,000	410	107	20	5.6
Belgium . .	1,060,000	106	100	18	5.8
Holland . .	729,000	132	180	29	6.2
Scandinavia .	1,200,000	137	114	16	7.0
Europe . .	49,605,000	7,741	154	26	6.0
United States .	11,400,000	2,850	250	46	5.5
Canada . .	...	127	...	25	...
Australia . .	...	239	...	67	...
Cape Colony .	...	17	...	13	...
Argentina . .	...	95	...	30	...
Uruguay . .	...	28	...	45	...

The value of house property in cities was as follows :—

	Millions £	£ per Inhab.
London	673	153
Paris	286	128
Berlin	158	108
Vienna	102	130
Buenos Ayres . .	85	153
New York . . .	271	180
Boston	117	234
Sydney	90	245
Melbourne . . .	92	209
Cape Town . . .	5	110

The annual increase of house property in various countries and cities is approximately as follows :—

	£			£
U. Kingdom .	33,000,000	Sydney . .		6,700,000
London . .	10,100,000	Buenos Ayres .		5,500,000
Scotland . .	2,400,000	United States .		69,000,000
France . .	26,000,000	New York . .		6,400,000
Paris . .	5,200,000	Philadelphia .		6,200,000
Hamburg . .	840,000	Toronto . .		320,000

Notable improvements in Paris and London have cost as follows :—

	Cost, £
Rue Rivoli, Paris	2,860,000
Boulevard Sebastopol . .	1,390,000
New Cannon Street, London	590,000
Victoria Street	330,000

Baron Haussman rebuilt a great portion of Paris in the years 1853 to 1869, at an outlay of 85 millions sterling.

UNITED KINGDOM

The number of houses, population per house, and approximate valuation for Great Britain down to 1811, and the United Kingdom afterwards, showed thus :—

Year	Houses	Pop. per House	Rental, £	Value, Millions £	Value per Inhab., £
1801	1,870,000	5.6	9,400,000	170	11
1811	2,102,000	5.7	14,000,000	252	14
1821	3,572,000	5.8	20,300,000	366	17
1831	4,101,000	5.9	24,500,000	441	18
1841	4,775,000	5.6	41,500,000	747	28
1851	4,694,000	5.8	50,000,000	900	33
1861	5,131,000	5.7	61,200,000	1,102	38
1871	5,632,000	5.6	86,400,000	1,555	48
1881	6,485,000	5.4	117,500,000	2,115	60
1888	7,100,000	5.4	134,700,000	2,424	63

In 1887 the valuation of houses in the principal cities was :—

	Rental, £	Value, Millions £	Per Inhabitant, £
London . . .	37,400,000	673	153
Liverpool . . .	3,300,000	60	100
Manchester. . .	3,200,000	58	100
Birmingham . .	1,800,000	32	80
Leeds	1,200,000	22	63
Sheffield . . .	1,100,000	20	63
Bristol	990,000	18	80
Bradford . . .	980,000	18	80
Nottingham . .	920,000	16	70
Newcastle . . .	860,000	15	105
Brighton . . .	670,000	12	110

The highest prices paid in London for building sites have been :—

Year	Street	Feet	Sq. Feet	Price, £	£ per Sq. Foot	£ per Acre
1880	Cannon . .	12 × 50	600	4,500	7.5	330,000
1880	Grace Church	...	...	...	18.9	820,000
1886	Old Broad .	42 × 30	1,285	37,000	28.8	1,260,000

In 1888 there were let on lease for eighty years six lots at Piccadilly and Charing Cross Road covering 19,000 square feet for £3600 per annum, being at the rate of £8300 per acre, the tenant erecting buildings worth £27,000. This would represent a selling value of £300,000 per acre for the land. House property has risen in value faster in London than throughout England. There is a house in Lombard Street, the rent of which was £25 a year in 1665, and the building on the same site is now rented for £2600 a year under lease from 1877. The value of land in the suburbs is also prodigious. An acre at Hampstead was recently leased for building at £1000 a year for eighty years.

The rental and value of London show as follows :—

Year	Houses	Rental, £	Value Million £	Miles of Streets	Value per Mile, £
1801	130,000	3,700,000	67	470	142,000
1811	155,000	4,500,000	82	560	146,000
1821	170,000	5,300,000	96	610	157,000
1831	197,000	6,900,000	124	700	177,000
1841	256,000	9,600,000	174	905	192,000
1851	301,000	12,600,000	229	1,050	218,000
1861	369,000	16,800,000	306	1,290	235,000
1871	445,000	23,900,000	434	1,550	280,000
1881	520,000	33,400,000	601	1,740	343,000
1888	600,000	37,400,000	673	2,010	335,000

Since 1861 the value of houses in London has risen 14 millions per annum, of which probably 30 per cent. was merely an enhancement of value, leaving about 10 millions a year as the cost of new buildings.

The number of new houses built within a radius of 15 miles from Charing Cross, London, and the length of new streets opened, were :—

Period	Houses Built	Streets, Miles Opened	Annual Average	
			Houses	Miles Street
1871–80	136,200	410	13,600	41
1881–88	142,100	278	17,800	35
18 years	278,300	688	15,400	38

Glasgow built £360,000 per annum in the years 1883–87, viz. :—

				£
Dwelling-houses .	.	.	.	130,000
Churches and schools	.	.	.	49,000
Warehouses .	.	.	.	121,000
Improvements, &c. .	.	.	.	60,000
Total	.	.	.	360,000

The above, however, does not include the value of sites, but only the structures. The cost of public buildings varies. Churches and schools may be built at £10 per head of the intended number of occupants. Hospitals sometimes cost £300 per bed. Chelsea barracks cost £245 a man.

Dwellings for the working classes are an urgent necessity, and could easily be constructed in all large towns. Those built in London have cost from 6d. to 8d. per cubic foot, the sites costing from 2s. to 5s. per square foot, the whole outlay being £36 per occupant, which involves an average rent of 2s. a week per room. The Peabody Buildings in 1889 showed an outlay of £900,000, including £500,000 given by the founder and £400,000 borrowed from Government ; they had 11,300 rooms, occupied by 20,400 persons, or 5070 families ; each family had weekly earnings that averaged 24s., and the average rent was 4s. 9d., or 26d. per room : gross rental £60,000, expenses and interest on loan £30,000, net profit £30,000. In 1882 Messrs. Guinness built in Dublin a block holding 540 rooms, to accommodate 180 families at 4s. a week. Sir Edward Guinness in 1889 gave £200,000 for a similar purpose in London.

The Town Council of Dublin also built a block for 1200 persons, on land which was bought at £6600 per acre : cost, £40,000 ; average rent, 4s. a week.

In a paper read by Mr. Hoey at the British Association,

1889, he stated that the population of Glasgow was lodged thus :—

Living in	Number of Souls	Death-rate per 1000
One room	133,000	35.0
Two rooms . .	235,000	27.7
Three to four rooms . }	158,000	19.5
Five or more rooms . }		11.2
Total . .	526,000	25.0

He further showed that the rents paid by the poor in London were exorbitant, a room 10 × 7 and 13 feet high, say 910 cubic feet, on a fifth floor, costing 18d. a week or £4 a year : often a whole family in a room 15 × 12 × 13, say 2300 cubic feet, paying 3s. or 4s. a week.

In 1887 the house property of the United Kingdom was as follows :—

	Rental, £	Value, Millions £	£ per Inhabitant
London	37,400,000	673	153
Ten large towns .	15,020,000	270	81
Rest of England .	64,780,000	1,166	55
England and Wales	117,200,000	2,109	73
Scotland	12,600,000	228	57
Ireland	3,500,000	63	13
United Kingdom .	133,300,000	2,400	63

There is no house-duty in Ireland. The houses subject to duty in Great Britain showed as follows :—

	1851	1871	1881
Subject to duty .	434,000	797,000	1,002,000
Exempt . . .	3,214,000	3,875,000	4,569,000
Total . .	3,648,000	4,672,000	5,571,000

This shows the great improvement in the class of houses ; in 1851 only 12 per cent. were subject to duty, the ratio being 18 per cent. in 1881. The average value of a house in the United Kingdom was as follows :—

Year	£	Year	£	Year	£
1801	90	1841	156	1871	278
1821	103	1851	190	1881	325
1831	108	1861	214	1888	340

The average value of a house is now more than double what it was in 1841.

ENGLAND AND WALES

In 1688 Gregory King estimated the house rental at two millions sterling. In 1798 it was put down at £6,500,000. The first official valuation was in 1812, viz., £8,490,000, and a later one in 1831 amounted to £12,350,000, but Porter showed that farmhouses and cottages were exempted. These would probably constitute one-third of the total. The rental would therefore be :—

Year	Rental, £	Value, Million £	£ per Inhabitant
1688	2,000,000	36	6
1798	6,500,000	117	14
1812	12,700,000	229	21
1831	18,500,000	333	24
1850	42,000,000	756	42
1860	52,000,000	936	47
1870	70,900,000	1,276	55
1880	100,100,000	1,802	69
1888	118,500,000	2,133	73

The number of houses and souls per house was as follows :—

Census	Houses.	Population per House
1801	1,576,000	5.6
1811	1,798,000	5.6
1821	2,088,000	5.8
1831	2,482,000	5.6
1841	2,944,000	5.4
1851	3,278,000	5.5
1861	3,740,000	5.4
1871	4,259,000	5.3
1881	4,832,000	5.4

Houses in England and Wales in 1862 :—

Annual Rental, £	Number	Aggregate Rental, £	Value, Millions £	Ratio
Over 1000 .	233	440,000	8	0.7
500–1000 . .	924	650,000	12	1.1
200–500 . .	8,633	2,860,000	51	4.5
100–200 . .	32,806	4,830,000	86	7.6
50–100 . .	101,948	7,120,000	128	11.3
30–50 . .	169,920	6,880,000	124	11.0
20–30 . .	205,528	5,110,000	92	8.3
Under 20 .	3,624,608	34,700,000	626	55.5
Total .	4,144,600	62,590,000	1,127	100.0

Official returns for 1875 and 1886 compare as follows :—

Rental	1875	1886	Increase per Cent.	Amount of Rent	
				1875	1886
£				£	£
Under 20	3,922,000	4,626,000	18	28,600,000	38,000,000
20–50	394,000	595,000	51	11,700,000	17,800,000
50–100	119,000	167,000	40	7,700,000	10,800,000
Over 100	56,000	77,000	37	11,100,000	14,700,000
Total	4,491,000	5,465,000	22	59,100,000	81,300,000

The above is exclusive of shops, which were as follows :—

	Number	Rental, £
1875 . . .	295,000	14,300,000
1886 . . .	366,000	18,900,000

The valuations for house-duty are about 10 per cent. lower than the income-tax assessments.

SCOTLAND.

The number and rental valuation showed thus :—

Year	Number	Rental, £	£ per House	Capital Value, Millions £
1801 .	295,000	...	...	...
1811 .	304,000	...	...	...
1821 .	341,000	...	...	...
1831 .	369,000	...	...	...
1841 .	503,000	...	...	...
1851 .	370,000	5,000,000	14	90
1861 .	393,000	5,500,000	14	100
1871 .	412,000	7,300,000	18	131
1881 .	739,000	11,800,000	16	212
1888 .	...	12,700,000	...	229

Before 1851 the Census collectors counted as houses each separate holding or flat.

GREAT BRITAIN.

The following table shows the number of houses and approximate rental at each Census :—

Census	Number	Rental, £	Value, Millions £
1801	1,870,000	9,400,000	170
1811	2,102,000	14,000,000	252
1821	2,429,000	17,300,000	311
1831	2,851,000	21,500,000	387
1841	3,447,000	38,500,000	693
1851	3,648,000	47,000,000	846
1861	4,139,000	58,200,000	1,048
1871	4,672,000	82,700,000	1,489
1881	5,571,000	114,200,000	2,056

Colquhoun's classification of houses in Great Britain, excluding Ireland, in 1812 was as follows :—

Rental, £	Number			Value, Millions £
	Urban	Rural	Total	
Over 100 . .	6,500	500	7,000	18
40–100 . . .	30,000	6,000	36,000	41
20–40 . . .	100,000	20,000	120,000	72
10–20 . . .	200,000	100,000	300,000	89
Under 10 . .	579,000	995,000	1,574,000	110
Total . .	915,500	1,121,500	2,037,000	330

A classification published in 1881 was as follows :—

Class	Houses	Rental, £	Average Rental, £	Ratio of Houses
1 . . .	21,000	14,000,000	665	0.4
2 . . .	238,000	28,500,000	120	4.3
3 . . .	512,000	17,900,000	35	9.3
4 . . .	1,294,000	19,400,000	15	23.4
5 . . .	3,410,000	34,400,000	10	62.6
Total .	5,475,000	114,200,000	21	100.0

The annual consumption of bricks was known down to 1850, when the tax was abolished. If the same ratio per house as in 1821–50 be supposed from 1850 to 1881, the consumption in sixty years will show thus :—

Annual Average

Period	Million Bricks	Houses Built	Bricks per Inhabitant
1821–30 . .	1,210	42,000	78
1831–40 . .	1,530	59,600	90
1841–50 . .	1,662	20,100	85
1851–60 . .	1,884	49,100	86
1861–70 . .	1,910	53,300	84
1871–80 . .	3,240	89,900	120

English bricks measure 9 × 4½ × 3 inches, and weigh 8 lbs., or 3 tons per 1000. An Adams or Liddell machine, 16-horse power, can make 30,000 daily, the average of hand-made bricks per moulder being 4000 a day. Fire-bricks will resist a crushing force varying from 600 up to 3000 lbs. per square inch.

IRELAND

The number of houses at each Census compared thus with population :—

Census	Number	Pop. per House	Census	Number	Pop. per House
1821	1,143,000	6.0	1861	992,000	5.8
1831	1,250,000	6.2	1871	960,000	5.6
1841	1,328,000	6.2	1881	914,000	5.7
1851	1,046,000	6.3	...	...	...

The Census of 1871 classified the houses the same as in 1841 thus :—

Houses of	1841	1871	Decrease, per Cent.
One room . . .	491,000	156,000	68
Two to four rooms	533,000	357,000	33
Five or more . .	304,000	449,000	...
Total . .	1,328,000	962,000	28

FRANCE

The number of houses and approximate value are shown thus :—

Year	Houses	Value, Millions £	Pop. per House	Windows per House	Value per House, £
1826	6,484,000	510	4.9	4.4	80
1836	6,805,000	720	5.0	4.5	106
1846	7,146,000	850	5.5	4.9	120
1856	7,633,000	985	4.8	5.0	130
1866	7,811,000	1,150	4.9	5.5	148
1882	8,813,000	1,550	4.3	5.6	175
1888	9,081,000	1,704	4.2	...	187

Lavoisier valued the houses in 1789 at 280 millions sterling ; Chaptal in 1815 at 462 millions. The next valuation was in 1835 by Moreau, only rural buildings, which he set down at 161 millions sterling, an advance of 19 millions in twenty years. In 1869 the Embassy Report gives a total of 1200 millions, and in 1884 the Minister of Finance makes it 1600 millions sterling. This gives an average building value increase of 26 millions per annum, say 1704 millions for 1888. If we compare the houses of 1835 with those of 1888 we find as follows :—

Windows	Houses		Ratio	
	1835	1888	1835	1888
One . . .	2,164,000	2,047,000	32.2	22.4
Two to four	2,747,000	3,658,000	40.8	40.2
Five or more	1,816,000	3,376,000	27.0	37.4
Total .	6,727,000	9,081,000	100.0	100.0

Cabins of one window form a much smaller ratio, while houses of the best class have nearly doubled in number.

In eight years ending December 1887 the official returns showed as follows :—

	Number	Per Annum
New houses . .	1,048,000	131,000
Pulled down . .	703,000	88,000
Net increase .	345,000	43,000

The classification of houses in 1868 was as follows :—

Class	Houses	Ratio
Gentry . . .	158,000	2.2
Commercial, &c. .	583,000	7.9
Tradesmen . .	2,167,000	29.4
Operatives, &c. .	4,453,000	60.5
Total .	7,361,600	100.0

The growth of house property in Paris was as follows :—

Year	Millions £	Per Inhabitant, £
1848	81	82
1860	188	109
1870	223	122
1882	286	128

The number of houses compared with population at two periods thus :—

Year	Houses	Population	Inhabitants per House
1817 . . .	28,800	714,000	25
1880 . . .	76,100	2,240,000	30

Each house represents nine *logements* or residences, owing to the custom of flats, and in 1882 these were 685,000 in number, and were let as follows :—

Rent, £	Number	Rental, £	Value, Millions £	Ratio
Over 500 .	1,920	1,100,000	17	6.0
160 to 500 .	13,100	4,200,000	63	22.0
40 to 160 .	65,250	6,300,000	94	32.7
15 to 40 . .	135,400	2,800,000	42	14.8
Under 15 .	469,000	4,700,000	70	24.5
Total .	684,670	19,100,000	286	100.0

In 1882 a sum of £1,100,000 was expended in buildings for the working-classes, to accommodate 3000 families or 10,000 souls, say £110 per head, each *logement* being supplied with gas and water, the rent 8s. a week: total rent £60,000 a year, or 5½ per cent. on first outlay. In 1879 the official estimated rental of all houses in France was 74 millions sterling, from which, for purposes of taxation, the Government allowed an abatement of 20 per cent. for repairs, &c., making the net rental 59 millions. In 1884 the Finance Minister estimated the gross rental at 88 millions sterling, which would represent a capital value of 1600 millions. The tax-collector's valuation the same year, after deducting one-fifth for repairs, was 1280 millions sterling, which confirms the Minister's estimate as above. Building sites in Paris, according to Yves Guyot, have quintupled in value in sixty years, the highest price in 1826 being £18 per square metre, and in 1883 ranging from £80 to £120: the maximum may therefore be taken as £10 per square foot, against £20 in London (even £30 having been paid in the latter city). In 1887 there were 250,000 persons in Paris living in furnished apartments, say 11 per cent. of the population :—

Ordinary Rent per Annum

Unfurnished	£	*Furnished (Boulevards)*	£
1 room, suburbs . . .	8	3 rooms, 5th flat . . .	160
2 rooms, suburbs . .	12	3 rooms, 4th flat . . .	200
2 rooms, Passy . . .	15	3 rooms, 3rd flat . . .	250
2 rooms, Madeleine . .	20	3 rooms, 2nd flat . .	300
2 rooms, Rue Rivoli .	30	4 rooms, Rue Rivoli . .	400
3 rooms, Rue Rivoli . .	50	5 rooms, Rue Rivoli . .	600

GERMANY

An official report for Prussia in 1869 gave the number and rental of houses. In the following table the value is capitalised at 18 times the rental :—

	Number	Rental, £	Value, Millions £
Urban	467,000	8,400,000	151
Rural	1,701,000	5,100,000	92
Total . .	2,168,000	13,500,000	243

In the same year the urban house property of Saxony was valued at 70 millions sterling, that of rural being apparently no more than 10 millions. These two kingdoms form exactly two-thirds of the German Empire as regards population, and we may conclude that the total house property of Germany in 1869 was of the value of 485 millions sterling. Official returns for Berlin show as

follows (except that the capitalisation at 18 years' rent is mine) :—

Year	Number of Houses	Rent, £	Value, £	Value per House, £
1867	14,100	3,390,000	61,100,000	4,400
1872	15,050	5,370,000	96,700,000	6,500
1882	19,700	8,800,000	158,400,000	8,000

The total value of house property in 1888 may be estimated thus :—

	Population	Houses, Millions £	£ per Head
Berlin	1,460,000	158	108
114 cities . . .	6,900,000	310	45
Rural districts .	38,200,000	764	20
Total . .	46,560,000	1,232	26

In four years ending 1886 Hamburg put up new suburbs and houses worth £3,350,000, say £840,000 per annum, the value of the sites being 60, and the buildings 40 per cent. of the total. Overcrowding in the large cities is as bad as in England, official returns showing the ratio of population living in one room as follows :—

City	Year	Per 1000 Inhab.	City	Year	Per 1000 Inhab.
Königsberg	1864	560	Leipzig .	1871	471
Chemnitz .	1871	702	Hamburg	1875	356
Frankfort .	1871	225	Leipzig .	1875	214

There was a marked improvement in Leipzig between 1871 and 1875; in the former year 108 per 1000 of the population lived in cellars.

In 1875 Leipzig had 3455 houses (comprising probably 18,000 flats or residences), which contained 140,000 souls, viz.:—

Class of House	Inhabitants per House	Number of Houses	Approximate Population
1st . . .	Up to 10	481	4,000
2nd . . .	11–20	661	10,000
3rd . . .	21–40	1,138	36,000
4th . . .	Over 40	1,175	90,000
Total .	...	3,455	140,000

RUSSIA

There are 11,436,000 houses, but no returns of valuation. Strebinsky estimated the poorest kind of rural dwellings at £27 sterling, and a general average of £40 may be taken. As regards the 787,000 houses in cities, they may be estimated at 10 per cent. per inhabitant less than in Germany. The account will stand thus :—

	Houses	Population	Per Inhabitant, £	Value, Mill. £
St Petersburg } 87 cities . . }	787,000	810,000 4,900,000	97 40	79 196
Rural . . .	10,649,000	78,200,000	5½	426
Total .	11,436,000	83,910,000	7½	701

Of the houses in St. Petersburg and 87 other cities there were 127,000 of stone and 660,000 of wood ; perhaps the term stone also includes brick.

In 1867 Buschen estimated the value of all buildings in Russia at 270 millions sterling, that is, dwelling-houses 150 millions, factories, &c., 120 millions.

AUSTRIA-HUNGARY

The last Census does not give the number of houses in Hungary, which may, however, be estimated at 2,000,000. The number in Austria has increased in the same ratio as population:—

	1840	1880
Austria	2,364,000	2,996,000
Hungary	1,732,000	2,000,000
Total	4,096,000	4,996,000

In Austria the houses in 1880 were as follows:—

	Number	Approximate Value, £	Per House, £
Vienna	183,900	102,000,000	545
Towns	388,100	77,600,000	200
Rural	2,424,000	121,200,000	50
Total . .	2,996,000	300,800,000	100

The house property of Hungary, at the same general ratio of £100 per house, would amount to 200 millions sterling, making a total of 501 millions for the whole Empire. In 1883 Roschmann valued the houses of Austria (without Hungary) at 256 millions sterling; but this seems 15 per cent. too low.

In 1886 the annual rental of Vienna showed as follows:—

Rent	Houses	Gross Rental, £	Ratio of Houses
Under £20 . .	89,192	1,200,000	48.5
20–50	68,993	2,200,000	37.5
50–100	17,736	1,200,000	9.7
Over 100 . . .	7,985	1,100,000	4.3
Total . .	183,906	5,700,000	100.0

ITALY

Neumann Spallart estimates the house property of Italy at 360 millions sterling, although the official value in 1881 was only 240 millions, but the latter was confessedly one-third too low. The *Archivio* gives the value in 1880 as 380 millions sterling. Approximately the house property may be estimated thus:—

	Houses	Population	Rental, £	Value, Millions £	£ per Inhab.
Urban .	650,000	5,100,000	8,400,000	153	30
Rural .	3,770,000	24,100,000	13,400,000	241	10
Total	4,420,000	29,200,000	21,800,000	394	13

The house property of Rome is estimated at 14 millions sterling, or about £45 per inhabitant.

HOLLAND

The official returns of house property show number and rental:—

Year	Houses Taxed	Rental, £	Value, £
1877 .	372,400	6,060,000	109,000,000
1883 .	398,900	6,660,000	120,000,000

This represents only the houses above a certain letting value, as the Census of 1879 showed 729,000 inhabited houses, of which 379,000 were subject to house-duty, and 350,000 were exempted. The assessment of 1880 showed as follows:—

Over £80 rental	.	.	.	.	13,673
£32 to £80	.	.	.	.	30,558
Under £32	.	.	.	.	313,218
Total	.	.	.	357,449

We may add 10 per cent. to the official valuation, say 12 millions sterling, as the value of the untaxed houses, which is equal to £34 per house. This makes the total house property of Holland worth 132 millions sterling.

SPAIN

In 1832 the *Junta de Medios* valued all buildings at 243 millions sterling, of which 68 millions were for public buildings and factories, the rest for dwelling-houses: the average was £20 per head of the population, and at the same rate Spain would now have 340 millions worth of house property distributed approximately as follows:—

	Houses	Population	Rental, £	Value, Millions £	£ per Inhab.
28 cities	380,000	2,100,000	5,000,000	90	45
Rural .	2,600,000	14,800,000	14,000,000	250	17
Total	2,980,000	16,900,000	19,000,000	340	20

SCANDINAVIA

Official valuations of house property in Sweden distinguish urban from rural; in Norway, give only urban, and in Denmark, confuse the same with landed property. The values are approximately as follows:—

	House Property, Millions £			£ per Inhabitant		
	Urban	Rural	Total	Urban	Rural	Total
Sweden . .	64	16	80	72	4	17
Norway . .	10	7	17	30	4	9
Denmark .	31	9	40	60	6	20
Total .	105	32	137	63	5	16

In Sweden 9 per cent. of house property stood for schools, &c.

BELGIUM

The Census returns of Belgium show:—

Year	Number of Inhabited Houses	Population per House
1846 . . .	799,000	5.42
1856 . . .	834,000	5.43
1866 . . .	930,000	5.19
1880 . . .	1,061,000	5.20

The official rental valuation in 1884 was £5,900,000, equal to a capital value of 106 millions sterling.

UNITED STATES

The Census of 1880 showed 8,956,000 houses. Compared with the numbers at previous Censuses, the existing houses in 1880 would appear approximately as follows:—

				Ratio
Built before 1840	.	.	2,430,000	27.4
,, 1840–1850 .	.	.	932,000	9.4
,, 1850–1860 .	.	.	1,608,000	18.2
,, 1860–1870 .	.	.	2,073,000	23.4
,, 1870–1880 .	.	.	1,913,000	21.6
Total	.	.	8,956,000	100.0

The first settlers lived in wooden houses, the ordinary cost of which, in 1684, was estimated at £5 sterling, a clergyman's house costing £35. Fires were frequent. The first brick-kiln was at Salem, Massachusetts, in 1629, and Mr. Coddington built the first brick house at Boston in 1638, the number reaching 1000 by the year 1700. The house which W. Penn built at Philadelphia was of bricks brought from England, and cost £5000.

The earliest estimate of house property was in 1790, when there was found to be 277,000 houses, valued at £29,200,000 sterling, being £105 per house. The number of houses at the following dates was:—

Year	Houses	Population	Inhabitant per House
1840	2,430,000	17,069,000	7.1
1850	3,362,000	23,192,000	6.9
1860	4,970,000	31,443,000	6.3
1870	7,043,000	38,558,000	5.5
1880	8,956,000	50,410,000	5.5

According to the Census of 1840, there were 54,100 houses built during the year, namely, 45,700 of wood, and 8400 of brick or stone, representing a total value of £8,800,000, say £160 per house, viz.:—

State	Houses Built	Value, £	Value per House, £
New York . . .	6,400	1,520,000	240
Pennsylvania . .	4,400	1,100,000	250
Illinois	4,400	440,000	100
Ohio . . .	3,800	790,000	210
Massachusetts .	1,600	580,000	360
Other States .	33,500	4,370,000	130
Total . .	54,100	8,800,000	160

The number of new houses built yearly in the Union since 1840 is shown officially as follows:—

1841–50	93,200
1851–60	161,000
1861–80	199,000
1887	303,000

In 1880 the Census showed 156,000 men engaged in building, the annual value of new houses being put down at 35 millions sterling, but in 1887 it was estimated at 86 millions sterling; the average cost of city houses was estimated at £940, and of rural at £210 each. The following annual returns of city buildings are given:—

City	New Houses	Value, £	Value per House, £	Years
New York .	1,950	6,400,000	3,240	1886–88
Philadelphia	8,202	6,240,000	760	1888
Kansas City	4,510	2,040,000	440	1886–88

The value of house property in some cities was as follows:—

Year	City	Value, Millions £	Population	£ per Head
1888	New York .	271	1,500,000	180
1888	Boston . . .	117	500,000	234
1880	Philadelphia .	119	850,000	140
1880	Brooklyn . .	45	570,000	80
1880	St. Louis . .	32	350,000	92
Total	...	584	3,770,000	155

The increase of value in New York from 1880 to 1888 was 49 millions sterling, that is, 7 millions per annum. There is no city in England equal in valuation per inhabitant to Boston or New York, but the Australian cities are higher, Melbourne being £29 higher than New York, and Sydney £11 over Boston.

The average value of each house built in 1840 was £160, and in 1887 it was £285. The total value of house property in the Union may be estimated for various dates thus:—

Year	Houses	Average Value, £	Millions, £	£ per Inhab.
1870	7,043,000	220	1,550	40
1880	8,956,000	240	2,160	43
1890	11,400,000	250	2,850	46

This shows an average value per head much below what it is in England, namely, £73.

CANADA

In Montreal the years 1887–88 averaged 1005 new houses, valued at £860,000, say £860 each, or £100 higher than in Philadelphia. The value of houses built at Toronto during the year 1880 was £320,000. In 1887 Upper Canada had, by official returns, a value of £38,500,000 in farm-buildings exclusive of towns. The total value of house property in the Dominion may be estimated thus:—

	Population	House, Value £ per Head	Millions £
Urban . .	460,000	60	27
Rural . .	4,560,000	22	100
Total .	5,020,000	25	127

AUSTRALIA

House property is much more valuable compared with population than it is in Europe. In 1888, for example, Sydney and Melbourne showed thus:—

	Population	Rental, £	Value, £	£ per Inhabitant
Sydney . .	367,000	5,220,000	78,300,000	211
Melbourne .	438,000	5,320,000	79,800,000	181

There is at Melbourne a block of houses valued at £494,000, the site of which was bought in 1838 for £45, and close to it is Menzies' Hotel, recently sold for £150,000, the site of which cost £10 in 1840. The following table shows approximately the value of all house property in the seven colonies:—

	Value, Millions £			£ per Inhabitant		
	Urban	Rural	Total	Urban	Rural	Total
N. S. Wales .	78	14	92	211	21	83
Victoria . . .	80	11	91	181	18	83
New Zealand .	20	5	25	100	10	40
South Australia	11	2	13	100	10	40
Queensland . .	9	3	12	100	10	30
Tasmania . .	4	1	5	100	10	33
W. Australia .	1	...	1	100	10	25
Total . . .	203	36	239	170	15	67

CAPE COLONY

In 1883 the house property of the principal towns was officially valued thus:—

	Population	Value, £	£ per Inhabitant
Cape Town . .	45,000	4,980,000	110
Port Elizabeth .	13,000	1,950,000	150
Kimberley . . .	14,000	1,710,000	122
Total . .	72,000	8,640,000	120

HONG-KONG

In 1889 the best building sites fetched £3 per square foot, or £130,000 per acre.

ARGENTINE REPUBLIC

The classification of houses at Buenos Ayres in 1889 was as follows :—

Yearly Rent	Houses	Approximate Value, £
Under £50 . . .	3,067	1,600,000
£50–£100	10,320	9,500,000
£100–£200 . . .	12,506	23,600,000
£200–£300 . . .	6,512	21,100,000
Over £300 . . .	4,835	28,700,000
Total . .	37,248	84,500,000

The increase in eight years was exceedingly rapid, the official returns for 1881 having shown 22,700 houses valued at £39,800,000 and owned as follows :—

	Value, £
By Argentines	22,800,000
Italians	6,800,000
Other foreigners	10,200,000
Total .	39,800,000

In eight years there were built 14,500 new houses, and the average annual increase of house property was £5,500,000 sterling. The average value of each house was £1700 in 1881 and £2,300 in 1889. The province of Buenos Ayres, outside the city, had 106,000 houses in 1881, valued at £12,300,000, say £120 per house or £22 per inhabitant. The houses in the other 13 provinces were estimated at 35 millions sterling, or £17 per inhabitant. The total for the Republic, including public buildings, was £94,500,000.

URUGUAY

In 1884 the value of house property was 28 millions sterling, about £45 per inhabitant. New houses at Monte-Video show an average of £230,000 per annum.

HUNTING

UNITED KINGDOM

The annual shooting is estimated thus :—

	Number	Value, £
Hares and rabbits . .	30,000,000	2,200,000
Grouse . . .	500,000	50,000
Partridges . .	400,000	30,000
Pheasants, &c. . .	900,000	90,000
Deer . . .	10,500	50,000
Total . .	...	2,420,000

BELGIUM

The number of shooting licenses issued was 12,900 in 1888, against 10,600 in 1860, and 6100 in 1840. The value of game killed yearly in the forests is 14 francs per hectare or 5s. an acre.

FRANCE

The State pays £3 for each wolf killed. The numbers killed were :—

1882	1,225	1886	760
1885	900	1887	701

Game licenses average 350,000 yearly. French writers estimate the number of rabbits killed yearly in France at 70 millions.

GERMANY

Game licenses, 146,000 ; slaughter, 20,000 foxes, 30,000 deer, 2,000,000 hares, 3,000,000 partridges. The annual fair at Leipzig shows a sale of several million skins. In 1880 there were sold :—

Bear . . .	6,000	Ermine . .	160,000
Sable . . .	54,000	Fox . .	180,000
Otter . . .	66,000	Skunk . . .	950,000
Beaver . . .	80,000	Squirrel, &c. .	4,850,000
Wild cat . .	125,000		

The forests of Prussia in 1869 contained 6000 wild boars and 151,000 deer.

RUSSIA

In Russia and Siberia the annual slaughter of fur-bearing animals is as follows : 50,000 martens, 3 million ermines, 15 million marmots, 25 million squirrels. The Russian forests contained in 1880 over 170,000 wolves, which devoured 200 children or travellers per annum. In 1889 Russian peasants killed or captured 318 boars, 85 wolves, 503 foxes, 14,834 hares, 71,960 squirrels, 539 martens, &c. On the other hand, bears and wolves destroyed between them 500 horses, more than 1000 oxen, and over 4000 other domestic animals.

AUSTRIA

The slaughter of large game in the whole Empire averages thus :—

Bears . . .	160	Wolves . . .	1,200
Lynxes . . .	200	Foxes . . .	8,000

Besides 3000 tiger-cats and various other kinds. The returns of game killed in Austria proper showed in 1885 thus :—

Bears . . .	22	Wild boars . .	3,000
Wolves . . .	113	Hares . .	1,430,000
Lynxes . .	24	Woodcock .	12,500
Foxes . . .	26,400	Pheasants .	103,000
Martens . .	9,700	Partridges .	1,336,000
Deer . .	72,500	Snipe . . .	99,000
Chamois . .	7,700	Wild duck . .	50,300

SWEDEN

The annual slaughter averaged as follows :—

	1827–36	1850–59	1867–76
Bears	135	118	110
Lynxes	243	140	91
Wolves	542	162	53
Foxes	7,882	5,396	...

About 5000 eagles and vultures are shot yearly in Sweden : in 1868 the number killed was 27,000. Laplanders sometimes follow a wolf 200 miles to kill him. Of foxes about 10,000 are killed yearly, 5000 skins being annually exported : in 1867 there were 18,000 killed. The annual killing of martens reaches 1000, and of ermines and otters 3000.

FINLAND

In Finland wolves destroy 5500 horned cattle yearly. The average of wild beasts killed in the decade ending 1870, per annum, was :—

Bears . .	104	Lynxes . .	42	Gluttons . .	35
Wolves . .	393	Foxes . .	2,046	Martens . .	5

EAST INDIES

In Java there are 270 persons killed by tigers, and 180 by crocodiles, yearly. In India 23,000 persons and 68,000 cattle are killed yearly by tigers, snakes, &c. The Indian Government pays £16,000 per annum for killing 20,000 wild beasts and 560,000 snakes. In Cochin-China the French killed in 1882 no fewer than 109 tigers and 25 panthers.

UNITED STATES

Between 1860 and 1882 more than 15 millions of bison were killed.

I.

ICE

The consumption in the United Kingdom exceeds 500,000 tons yearly, the quantity imported averaging 300,000 tons, mostly from Norway. The ice-crop of the United States, according to Simmonds, averages 12 million tons, of which the Hudson supplies 2,400,000. The capital employed in this trade in the United States has been estimated at 8 millions sterling: the ice, when cut, is valued at 4s. a ton, but is retailed at 12s. Some of the cities of the world consume as follows:—

	Tons	Lbs. per Inhab.
London	200,000	102
Paris	60,000	60
New York	700,000	1,300
Boston	100,000	700

Russia consumes enormous quantities, St. Petersburg alone counting 10,000 ice-houses.

INCOME

The subjoined table shows approximately the annual earnings or income of nations. It is compiled thus: 90 per cent. of agricultural values, 90 per cent. of mining, 60 per cent. of manufactures. Transport is computed at 10 per cent. on the gross value of agriculture, mining, and manufactures; house-rent, according to the assessed valuation or the nearest estimate; commerce, 10 per cent. on imports and exports; shipping, 30s. per ton yearly of carrying power; banking, 5 per cent. on banking power; and furthermore an allowance of 10 per cent. on the total of the preceding eight items, to cover the earnings of domestic servants, learned professions, army, police, civil service, &c. This is, of course, a conventional method for estimating the earnings of nations, but will answer fairly well for the sake of comparison.

NATIONAL EARNINGS FROM VARIOUS SOURCES

	MILLIONS £ STERLING										Per Inhab., £
	Agriculture	Mining	Manufactures	Internal Transport	House Rent	Commerce	Shipping	Banking	Professions	Total	
U. Kingdom	226	53	492	113	135	74	30	45	117	1,285	33.7
France	414	9	291	96	93	31	4	13	95	1,046	27.8
Germany	382	22	350	103	68	37	4	12	98	1,076	22.2
Russia	507	14	218	94	34	12	2	5	89	975	11.5
Austria	298	7	152	59	27	9	1	7	56	616	15.5
Italy	184	2	73	33	22	9	2	5	33	363	12.2
Spain	156	4	51	27	18	6	2	2	27	293	16.5
Portugal	28	1	10	5	4	2	...	...	5	55	12.1
Sweden	44	1	30	10	4	3	1	1	10	104	22.0
Norway	15	1	12	4	1	1	3	...	4	41	20.5
Denmark	31	...	16	6	2	3	1	1	6	66	32.5
Holland	35	...	21	8	7	20	1	1	9	102	22.6
Belgium	50	6	61	17	6	11	...	1	15	167	28.0
Switzerland	17	...	19	5	2	6	...	1	5	55	19.0
Europe	2,387	120	1,796	580	423	224	51	94	569	6,244	19.4
United States	698	96	856	231	157	32	12	52	214	2,358	39.0
Canada	50	2	39	12	7	4	2	2	12	130	26.0
Australia	56	7	25	10	13	12	1	7	13	144	40.2
Argentina	38	...	24	8	5	3	...	1	8	87	24.0
Total	3,229	225	2,750	841	605	275	66	156	816	8,963	20.8

UNITED KINGDOM

The income of the nation has been estimated thus:—

Year	Millions £	Per Inhabitant, £	Kingdom
1664	42	7.8	England and Wales
1688	45	8.2	,,
1770	122	16.3	,,
1800	230	26.0	,,
1822	280	19.8	Great Britain
1840	504	19.2	United Kingdom
1860	760	26.2	,,
1889	1,285	33.6	,,

King's classification in 1688 compares with later dates:—

A.D. 1688

Class	Families	Average Income, £	Amount, £
Gentry	16,500	360	6,000,000
Middle	114,000	105	12,000,000
Trades	310,000	50	15,500,000
Working	759,500	15	11,500,000
Total	1,200,000	37	45,000,000

A.D. 1800

Class	Families	Average Income, £	Amount, £
Gentry	36,000	770	28,000,000
Middle	181,000	315	57,000,000
Trades	446,000	150	67,000,000
Working	1,117,000	70	78,000,000
Total	1,780,000	127	230,000,000

A.D. 1889

Class	Families	Average Income, £	Amount, £
Gentry	222,000	1,500	333,000,000
Middle	604,000	400	241,000,000
Trades	1,220,000	200	244,000,000
Working	4,774,000	97	467,000,000
Total	6,820,000	188	1,285,000,000
England	5,200,000	208	1,084,000,000
Scotland	740,000	173	128,000,000
Ireland	880,000	84	73,000,000
United Kingdom	6,820,000	188	1,285,000,000

Professor Leone Levi in 1884 estimated the earnings of the people as follows :—

	Millions £ Sterling Yearly			
	England	Scotland	Ireland	U. Kingdom
Upper class . .	477	59	36	572
Middle class . .	98	14	8	120
Working class .	401	62	42	505
Total . .	976	135	86	1,197

He estimated the wage-earners in 1884 as follows :—

	Number	Millions £	£ per Head
Professional . .	300,000	16	53
Domestic . . .	2,400,000	86	36
Commercial . .	900,000	45	50
Agricultural . .	1,900,000	67	35
Industrial . . .	6,700,000	307	46
Total . .	12,200,000	521	43

	Workers	Millions £	£ per Head
England . . .	8,600,000	401	47
Scotland . . .	1,500,000	62	41
Ireland	1,800,000	42	23
Undefined . . .	300,000	16	53
Total . .	12,200,000	521	43

	Number	Millions £	£ per Head
Males under 20 .	1,650,000	29	18
,, 20–65 . .	6,530,000	363	56
Females under 20	1,300,000	30	23
,, 20–65 .	2,720,000	99	37
Total . .	12,200,000	521	43

According to income-tax assessments, the number of persons in the United Kingdom since 1860, and Great Britain before that date, having an income of £200 or upwards yearly, was as follows :—

Year				Number	Per Million Population
1812	.	.	.	39,765	3,314
1850	.	.	.	65,389	3,115
1860	.	.	.	85,530	2,949
1870	.	.	.	130,375	4,206
1880	.	.	.	210,430	6,313

The number of persons enjoying great wealth has by no means increased in the same ratio. Assessments over £5000 a year showed as follows :—

Year				Number	Per Million Population
1812	.	.	.	409	34
1850	.	.	.	1,181	56
1860	.	.	.	1,558	53
1870	.	.	.	2,080	67
1880	.	.	.	2,954	88

Taking the relative numbers of each class to the whole population, we find :—

Persons of	Per Million Inhabitants		Rate of Increase
	1860	1880	
Great wealth . .	53	88	66 per cent.
Easy fortune . .	2,949	6,313	112 ,,

This shows a greater diffusion of wealth, contrary to the common impression that "the rich are getting richer every day."

The classification of incomes in 1877 was as follows :—

	Over £10,000	£1000 to £10,000	£150 to £1000	Total
England . .	975	18,622	275,733	295,330
Scotland . .	147	2,191	27,642	29,980
Ireland . .	35	878	14,473	15,386
U. Kingdom	1,157	21,691	317,848	340,696

The earnings of the classes which pay income-tax are supposed to reach just one-half those of the nation. Levi made the earnings of the working-classes in 1883 amount to 521 millions, and Jeans in 1884 to 535 millions sterling. The assessments to income-tax have more than doubled since 1850, the following table including an estimate of 18 millions for Ireland in 1850 (in which year that country was exempt from this tax) :—

Year	Annual Income, Millions £			
	Houses	Lands	Profes-sions, &c.	Total
1850 . . .	47	56	171	274
1860 . . .	61	58	216	335
1870 . . .	77	65	303	445
1880 . . .	115	70	392	577
1888 . . .	135	61	440	636

Year	England	Scotland	Ireland	United Kingdom
1860 . . .	282	30	23	335
1870 . . .	379	40	26	445
1880 . . .	486	56	36	578
1888 . . .	543	57	36	636

The relative increase of the several items of income since 1850 showed thus :—

Year	Houses	Lands	Railways	Professions	Total
1850 . . .	100	100	100	100	100
1860 . . .	130	104	143	125	122
1870 . . .	164	116	228	174	162
1880 . . .	238	123	295	228	211
1888 . . .	280	107	351	252	232

The relative increase of each of the three kingdoms since 1860 was :—

Year	England	Scotland	Ireland	United Kingdom
1860 . . .	100	100	100	100
1870 . . .	134	133	113	133
1888 . . .	193	190	156	191

FRANCE

The income has been estimated as follows :—

Year			Millions £	£ per Inhab.	Population
1780 .	.	.	160	6.1	26,300,000
1800 .	.	.	216	7.7	27,400,000
1820 .	.	.	315	10.4	30,300,000
1840 .	.	.	480	14.1	34,000,000
1868 .	.	.	806	21.6	37,500,000
1888 .	.	.	1,046	27.8	38,500,000

X

The distribution of income, according to house valuation, seems to be approximately as follows:—

Class	Number of Families	Average Income, £	Amount, Millions £
Rich . . .	160,000	800	128
Middle . .	1,700,000	260	442
Working .	6,000,000	79	476
Total .	7,860,000	133	1,046

GERMANY

In 1885 Soetbeer and others estimated the earnings of the people of Prussia, Saxony, and Baden at 517 millions sterling, to which adding *pro rata* for the rest of Germany, the table stands thus:—

	Population	Earnings, £	Per Head, £
Prussia	28,300,000	438,000,000	15.5
Saxony	3,180,000	57,100,000	18.0
Baden	1,600,000	22,400,000	14.0
Bavaria, &c. . .	13,770,000	220,000,000	16.0
Total . .	46,850,000	737,500,000	15.8

The above, perhaps, has reference only to the classes liable to income-tax, the total being manifestly too low to include also the working-classes.

The income-tax assessments of Prussia in 1881 and 1886 were as follows:—

Income,	Families Assessed	
	1881	1886
£150 to £210 . . .	79,000	89,600
£210 to £480 . . .	71,700	82,400
Over £480 . . .	21,800	26,800
Total .	172,500	198,800

The above comprises only families with incomes over £150 a year. In 1883 there were 7,800,000 persons paying a poll-tax whose incomes were under £150. In Saxony the income assessments were:—

Year	Number	£
1875 . . .	972,000	50,900,000
1884 . . .	1,213,000	57,100,000

The annual earnings of the whole Empire would seem to be distributed approximately as follows:—

Class	Families	Average, £	Total, Millions £
Rich	150,000	1,230	185
Middle	1,200,000	240	288
Working . . .	8,050,000	75	603
Total . .	9,400,000	114	1,076

According to the scheme laid down in page 320, the

gross earnings of the German people in 1889 amounted to 1076 millions sterling, or £22 4s. per inhabitant, against £28 in France, and £34 in the United Kingdom.

AUSTRIA

Neumann Spallart estimated the national earnings at 600 millions sterling in 1874, as compared with 430 millions in 1868, and 336 millions in 1859, this last being Czernig's estimate. If we take the florin at its nominal value of 24d., the estimate of Roschmam for 1883 will be 650 millions sterling; but if we allow for the depreciation of the currency, it will not exceed 610 millions. My estimate for 1888 is 616 millions sterling, as shown in the table.

ITALY

Official returns published in 1881 give a very inadequate idea of the earnings of the nation; the first two columns are official, the last is the apparent result:—

Income,	Number Assessed	Gross Result, £
Under £40 . . .	559,000	8,400,000
£40 to £200 . .	71,000	7,100,000
£200 to £400 . .	5,300	1,600,000
Over £400 . . .	3,200	11,300,000
Total .	638,500	28,400,000

As already shown, the earnings of the Italian nation are about 364 millions sterling, or £12 per inhabitant, which is less than half the average per head in France.

UNITED STATES

In 1840 Tucker's estimate of the earnings of the American people was 1066 millions dollars, or 221 millions £ sterling, made up thus:—

	£
Product of farms . . .	137,200,000
Manufactures, &c. . . .	83,600,000
Total . .	220,800,000

The above estimate was too low, seeing that agricultural products were worth 184 millions sterling (as already shown).

The national earnings at various dates are shown approximately thus:—

	Millions £		
	1850	1870	1886-89
Agriculture . . .	225	452	698
Manufactures . . .	127	444	866
Mines . . .	40	60	96
Transport . . .	50	130	231
Commerce . . .	7	17	32
Shipping . . .	7	10	12
Banking . . .	5	19	52
Sundries . . .	109	218	371
Total .	570	1,350	2,358

AUSTRALIA

Mr. Coghlan, Government statist, estimates the fruits of all industries as follows:—

	Farming	Mining	Manufactures, &c.	Total	Per Inhabitant
	£	£	£	£	£
New South Wales . .	17,200,000	3,800,000	6,600,000	27,600,000	25.1
Victoria . . .	13,600,000	2,700,000	7,100,000	23,400,000	21.3
Queensland . .	8,300,000	2,100,000	2,300,000	12,700,000	32.0
South Australia . .	7,700,000	400,000	1,600,000	9,700,000	31.0
New Zealand . .	12,600,000	1,200,000	3,300,000	17,100,000	28.5
Tasmania . .	1,900,000	500,000	900,000	3,300,000	22.0
Western Australia . .	900,000	200,000	300,000	1,400,000	33.0
Total . .	62,200,000	10,900,000	22,100,000	95,200,000	26.4

The above takes no account of transport, shipping, banking, commerce, &c., which brings up the total earnings to 144 millions sterling.

INDIANS

The number in the United States in 1830 and in 1880 was :—

	1830	1880
East of Rocky Mountains .	213,100	188,400
West ,, ,, .	100,000	143,700
	313,100	332,100

In 1830 some of the States had the following Indian population :—

Mississippi . . .	23,400	Missouri	5,600
Alabama	19,200	New York	4,800
Michigan . . .	9,400	Indiana	4,100
Arkansas . . .	7,200	Florida	4,000
Illinois	5,900		

In 1837 the principal tribes were as follows :—

East of Mississippi

Cherokees . . .	22,000	Winnebagos . .	4,500
Chippewas . . .	6,500	Various	11,365
Seminoles . . .	5,000		
		Total . .	49,365

West of Mississippi

Blackfeet	30,000	Pawnees . . .	12,500
Sioux	21,600	Eutaws	19,200
Creeks	20,437	Crows	7,200
Apaches	20,280	Various	117,710
Camanches . . .	19,200		
Choctaws . . .	15,000	Total . .	283,127

In 1880 the principal tribes were :—

Cherokees, Choctaws	47,800
Esquimaux, &c.	62,400
Shoshones, Snakes	25,300
Dacotah, Sioux	28,100
Crow, Flathead	19,400
Pawnee, Fox	18,100
Apaches, Navajas	20,100
Oregon, Arizona, &c.	111,000
Total . .	332,100

	Civilised	Half-Civilised	Savage	Total
Population . .	104,800	144,300	83,000	332,100
Acres tilled . .	273,000	157,000	...	430,000
Grain, bushels .	2,780,000	1,070,000	...	3,850,000
Hay, tons . .	177,000	48,000	...	225,000
Vegetables, tons	8,500	9,800	...	18,300
Churches . .	117	...	...	117
Schools . . .	344		...	344
Pupils . . .	13,350		...	13,350
Horses . . .	301,000		...	301,000
Cows	311,000		...	311,000
Sheep . . .	447,000		...	447,000
Pigs	214,000		...	214,000

The number of Indians who vote as American citizens is 24,600. That of Indians paying tax was as follows :—

State	1870	1880	Increase
California . . .	7,241	16,277	9,036
New Mexico . .	1,309	9,772	8,463
Michigan . . .	4,926	7,249	2,323
Washington Territory .	1,319	4,405	3,086
Arizona . . .	31	3,493	3,462
Wisconsin . . .	1,206	3,161	1,955
Various . . .	9,699	22,050	12,351
Total .	25,731	66,407	40,676

In Canada a report on Indians in 1880 was as follows :—

	Number	Property, £	£ per Head
Ontario	16,000	1,968,000	123
Quebec	11,000	363,000	33
Manitoba, &c. . .	75,400	...	...
Total . .	102,400	...	...

INDUSTRIES

The following table shows approximately the value yearly of the chief occupations of mankind :—

	Millions £ Sterling *						£ per Inhabitant
	Agriculture	Manufactures	Mining	Transport	Commerce	Total	
U. Kingdom	251	820	60	113	740	1,984	52
France . .	460	485	10	96	310	1,361	36
Germany . .	424	583	25	103	370	1,505	32
Russia . .	563	363	15	94	120	1,155	13
Austria . .	331	253	6	59	95	744	19
Italy . . .	204	121	2	33	95	455	15
Spain . . .	173	85	4	27	60	349	20
Portugal . .	31	16	1	5	20	73	16
Sweden . .	49	50	1	10	30	140	30
Norway . .	17	19	1	4	10	51	25
Denmark . .	35	26	...	6	25	92	46
Holland . .	39	35	...	8	200	282	61
Belgium . .	55	102	7	17	110	291	48
Switzerland .	19	32	...	5	60	116	39
Various . .	194	40	...	23	72	329	22
Europe . .	2,845	3,030	132	603	2,317	8,927	27
United States	776	1,443	107	231	320	2,877	46
Canada . .	56	64	3	12	40	175	36
Australia . .	62	41	8	10	120	241	66
Argentina .	42	40	...	8	30	120	32
Total .	3,781	4,618	250	864	2,827	12,340	30

The value of the above industries in the above countries at various dates was approximately as follows in millions £ sterling :—

Year	Agriculture	Manufactures	Mining	Transport	Commerce	Total
1820	1,405	865	19	229	287	2,805
1840	1,750	1,314	35	310	485	3,894
1860	2,380	2,404	108	490	1,305	6,687
1888	3,781	4,618	250	864	2,827	12,340

The relative increase of the principal industries is shown approximately as follows :—

	1820	1840	1860	1888
Agriculture	100	124	170	270
Manufactures . . .	100	153	280	536
Mining	100	183	567	1,320
Transport	100	135	213	376
Commerce	100	166	450	990
Total . .	100	152	336	440

* The values here given represent the gross amounts without any deduction. For net values see *Income*, p. 320.

The ratios of the various industries in forming the aggregate were as follows :—

	1820	1840	1860	1888
Agriculture	50.1	44.8	35.6	30.5
Manufactures . . .	30.8	33.8	36.0	37.6
Mining	0.7	0.9	1.6	2.1
Transport	8.2	8.0	7.3	7.0
Commerce	10.2	12.5	19.5	22.8
Total . .	100.0	100.0	100.0	100.0

If we take the first four items as the direct fruits of human industry in the aggregate, and compare with population, we find as follows :—

Year	Population	Industries, Millions £	£ per Head
1820 . . .	208,000,000	2,518	12.1
1840 . . .	256,000,000	3,409	13.3
1860 . . .	313,000,000	5,382	17.2
1888 . . .	416,000,000	9,513	22.8

The population and industries are those of Europe, United States, Canada, Australia, and Argentina. It appears that, owing to improved machinery, the product of a man's labour represents at present double the value that it did in 1820. But as prices have fallen in the interval about 33 per cent., it follows that the average in 1888 was equal to £34 per head measured by prices of 1820. Thus one man now, in whatever industry, produces as much as 3 did in 1820, or 2½ in 1840, or 2 in 1860.

INFIRM

The principal classes of infirm of body are blind and deaf-mutes, whose numbers by latest returns were as follows :—

	Blind	Deaf-Mutes	Total	Per Million Population
England	22,800	13,300	36,100	1,390
Scotland	3,200	2,200	5,400	1,455
Ireland	6,100	4,000	10,100	1,940
United Kingdom .	32,100	19,500	51,600	1,475
France	32,060	21,100	53,160	1,390
Germany	39,000	45,000	84,000	1,830
Russia	178,500	53,500	232,000	2,730
Austria proper . .	15,800	26,800	42,600	1,940
Hungary	20,600	15,000	35,600	2,350
Italy	28,200	19,800	48,000	1,610
Spain	20,300	10,700	31,000	1,700
Scandinavia . . .	7,900	7,800	15,700	1,840
Belgium and Holland	6,700	4,200	10,900	1,050
Switzerland . . .	2,100	6,800	8,900	3,200
Europe	383,260	230,200	613,460	1,840
United States . .	48,900	33,900	82,800	1,650
Total . .	432,160	264,100	696,260	1,760

In 1881 Professor Haltkenhoff of Geneva said that there were 311,000 blind persons in Europe, mostly the result of fevers, and that 75 per cent. of them could have kept their sight if they had been properly treated.

The proportion of sexes shows thus :—

Females Blind to 100 Males

France . . 76 | Prussia . . 88 | Sweden . . 118
Belgium . . 89 | Norway . . 108 | United States 82

The following table is by Principal Campbell :—

Blind per Million Persons of Each Sex					
	Male	Female		Male	Female
England .	953	809	Austria . .	1,280	1,183
Scotland .	865	827	Italy . . .	1,106	925
Ireland . .	1,141	1,219	Spain . .	1,242	1,011
France . .	948	726	Norway . .	1,313	1,411
Germany .	884	881	Holland . .	499	394
Sweden .	767	843	Belgium .	982	641
Denmark .	776	793	Finland . .	1,514	2,938

The number of blind institutions and of pupils were :—

	Institutions	Inmates
United Kingdom	80	2,830
France	23	1,210
Germany	35	1,810
Austria	11	680
Italy	22	670
Spain	12	650
Russia	15	400
Scandinavia	10	330
Belgium and Holland . . .	14	500
United States	36	2,500
Canada	3	200
Total . .	261	11,780

The number of deaf-mutes in most countries increases faster than population, as the following table shows :—

	Number		Per Million Inhab.	
	1831	1871	1831	1871
United Kingdom .	14,328	19,237	597	611
France . . .	20,189	21,130	630	603
Germany . . .	20,470	30,900	724	770
Russia . . .	27,834	...	631	...
Austria . . .	21,684	34,450	802	980
Italy . . .	12,618	19,800	628	702
Spain . . .	7,255	10,700	633	655
Switzerland .	3,967	6,820	1,996	2,620
Denmark . .	1,260	...	1,114	...
Sweden and Norway	2,397	5,540	605	920
United States .	6,030	18,150	460	480

Sex ratio is in most countries 55 male deaf-mutes to 45 females, but in Italy 58 to 42.

Colour-blindness, which usually takes the form of inability to distinguish red from green, is found to prevail thus :—

	Per 1000 Persons		
	Male	Female	General Population
England . . .	47	40	44
Scotland . . .	30	...	...
France . . .	70	...	...
Sweden . . .	32	26	29
Switzerland . . .	47	9	28
United States . .	40	10	26
Boston . . .	40	17	30
Holland . . .	...	...	58
Belgium . . .	...	...	26
Russia . . .	...	...	80
London . . .	34	...	...

Of French marines 82 per 1000, of British sailors 45.

UNITED KINGDOM

The number and ratios of blind were as follows :—

Year	Number of Blind			U. Kingdom
	England	Scotland	Ireland	
1851 . . .	18,306	3,010	7,587	28,903
1861 . . .	19,352	2,820	6,879	29,051
1871 . . .	21,590	3,019	6,347	30,956
1881 . . .	22,832	3,158	6,111	32,101

Year	Number of Population to one Blind Person			
	England	Scotland	Ireland	U. Kingdom
1851 . . .	979	1,065	864	948
1861 . . .	1,037	1,090	843	1,002
1871 . . .	1,052	1,112	852	1,022
1881 . . .	1,138	1,182	847	1,094

The number of blind in England per million persons of each age was in 1881 as follows :—

Years	Per Million
0–5	166
5–15	288
15–20	388
20–25	422
25–45 . . . . . , .	641
45–65	1,625
Over 65 . . . . , .	6,915
General average	877

The number of deaf-mutes in the United Kingdom rose from 14,328 in 1831 to 19,237 in 1871. The number per million inhabitants was as follows :—

	1831	1861	1871
England	545	581	504
Scotland	552	753	633
Ireland	664	975	1,028
United Kingdom . . .	597	701	611

The number of short-sighted people is not known, but Ware found at Oxford, in 1813, that 26 per cent. of those in the University used glasses.

FRANCE

The returns for 1866 showed as follows :—

Cause	Blind	Deaf-Mutes	Total
From birth . . .	4,726	15,296	20,022
Accident or illness .	27,242	5,918	33,160
Total . .	31,968	21,214	53,182

The ratios of blind and deaf-mutes per million persons of each sex were :—

	Blind		Deaf-Mutes		Total	
	Male	Female	Male	Female	Male	Female
Under 15 .	270	210	470	380	740	590
Unmarried } adults	1,100	1,150	1,480	1,250	2,580	2,400
Married . .	900	520	185	120	1,085	640
Widowed .	3,810	2,180	386	223	4,196	2,403

The number of persons born blind was 65 in a million of male population, 35 in a million of the female.

In 1876 the number of afflicted persons was :—

	Blind	Deaf-Mutes	Total
Males . . .	15,526	11,460	26,986
Females . . .	12,965	9,935	22,900
Total . .	28,491	21,395	49,886

In 1883 there were 32,056 blind, of whom 2548 were under 21 years of age.

GERMANY

In 1843 the kingdom of Prussia showed as follows :—

	Male	Female	Total	Per Million Population
Blind . . .	5,222	4,930	10,152	680
Deaf-mutes .	6,460	5,037	11,497	770
Total .	11,682	9,967	21,649	1,450

In 1880 the German Empire had 37,800 blind, of whom 1810 were receiving instruction in Blind schools. In 1888 there were 28 Blind institutions, with 2139 pupils, the total number of blind in the Empire being estimated at 39,000. The numbers of deaf-mutes in Prussia in 1871 and 1880 were :—

	Number		Per Million Population	
	1871	1880	1871	1880
Males	13,118	15,168	1,080	1,130
Females . . .	11,197	12,026	900	910
Total . .	24,315	27,194	990	1,020

The rate was 990 per million among Protestants, 1040 among Catholics, and 1440 among Jews. There are in Prussia 96 schools for deaf-mutes, with 331 teachers and 3991 pupils.

RUSSIA

The total number of blind is estimated at about 180,000, the rate per million inhabitants varying in the different provinces for which there are returns, viz. :—

Kieff . . . 1,960	Livonia . . . 5,020
Pultowa . . . 1,780	Esthonia . . . 4,110
Kazan . . . 5,700	Finland . . . 2,140

In the city of St. Petersburg the rate is only 890 per million, the total number of blind being 771, namely, 320 males and 451 females; only 17 per cent. of the whole number were born blind. There are 21 Blind asylums in the Empire.

FINLAND

The ratio of blind in 1875 was : 214 per 100,000 males, 438 for females, and 328 for the general population ; this is nearly 2½ times as much as in Norway, four times as much as in France. Smoky huts are one of the causes. Finland has 233 deaf-mutes per million.

ALGERIA

There are 6666 blind persons, of whom 5330 are adult. The above number compared with population shows 1750 per million, which is 50 per cent. over the European average.

AUSTRIA

Official returns for 1886 showed as follows for Austria, without Hungary :—

	Males	Females	Total	Per Million Population
Blind . . .	8,480	7,282	15,762	710
Deaf-mutes .	15,041	11,752	26,793	1,220
Total .	23,521	19,034	42,555	1,930

The institutions contained the following :—

	Males	Females	Total
Blind	403	281	684
Deaf-mutes . .	807	621	1,428
Total . .	1,210	902	2,112

	Born so	Became so	Total
Blind	101	583	684
Deaf-mutes . .	469	959	1,428
Total . .	570	1,542	2,112

In 1884 there were 26,245 deaf-mutes, of whom 22,319, say 92 per cent., were born so.

HUNGARY

The number of blind was as follows :—

	Number		Per Million Population	
	1870	1880	1870	1880
Males	9,800	10,242	127	128
Females . . .	8,723	10,597	113	132
Total . .	18,523	20,639	120	130

The number of deaf-mutes in 1880 was 15,000, or 960 per million population.

ITALY

The ratios of blind and of deaf-mutes in 1872 showed : —

	Per Million Inhabitants		
	Blind	Deaf-Mutes	Total
Sicily . .	1,282	687	1,969
Central Italy . .	1,000	744	1,744
Lombardy. . .	795	1,153	1,948
Sardinia, &c. . .	1,929	719	2,648
Italy	1,050	738	1,788

The distribution according to sexes was as follows :—

	Males	Females	Total
Blind . . .	15,946	12,181	28,127
Deaf-mutes . .	11,615	8,164	19,779
Total . .	27,561	20,345	47,906

The Census of 1881 showed 21,718 blind and 15,300 deaf-mutes, but the authorities believe the real numbers to be much greater.

BELGIUM AND HOLLAND

In Belgium the asylums for the blind and for deaf-mutes contained in 1885 :—

Males .	.	.	.	.	.	729
Females .	.	.	.	.	.	540
			Total	.	.	1,269

The ratio of blind in Belgium was 874 per million inhabitants in 1860, and has now declined to 810. Deaf-mutes were 450 per million in 1835, and have declined to 404. As regards Holland, there are no returns since 1869, when there were 1593 blind, or 450 per million of population.

NORWAY

The ratios of blind and of deaf-mutes at various dates were :—

Year	Blind per 100,000 Inhab.			Deaf-Mutes per 100,000 Inhabitants	Total
	Town	Rural	Norway		
1835 . .	123	183	177	91	268
1845 . .	127	218	209	83	292
1855 . .	119	195	186	83	269
1865 . .	90	145	136	92	228
1875 . .	79	148	136	86	222

The actual numbers of deaf-mutes were as follows :—

Year	Males	Females	Total	Per 100,000 Population
1835	598	493	1,091	91
1855	650	592	1,242	83
1875	819	752	1,571	86

SWEDEN AND DENMARK

The numbers in these countries are :—

	Number		Per Million	
	Blind	Deaf-Mutes	Blind	Deaf-Mutes
Sweden . .	3,723	4,834	810	1,050
Denmark .	1,249	...	705	...

UNITED STATES

The classification in 1880 was as follows :—

	Males	Females	Total
Blind	26,748	22,180	48,928
Deaf-mutes . .	18,567	15,311	33,878
Total . .	45,315	37,491	82,806

	American	Foreign	Total
Blind	40,509	8,419	48,928
Deaf-mutes . .	30,507	3,371	33,878
Total . .	71,016	11,790	82,806

	White	Coloured	Total
Blind	41,278	7,650	48,928
Deaf-mutes . .	30,661	3,217	33,878
Total . .	71,939	10,867	82,806

The returns of deaf-mutes at various dates showed :—

Year	Number	Per Million Inhabitants	Ratio of Sex	
			Males	Females
1830 . . .	6,106	470	...	...
1840 . . .	7,706	453	...	...
1850 . . .	9,803	427	55	45
1860 . . .	12,820	413	55	45
1870 . . .	16,205	422	55	45
1880 . . .	33,880	678	56	44

Deaf-mutes and blind have risen in numbers much faster than population. The ratio per million inhabitants rises at each successive census, perhaps because the ratio of urban population is at each period higher.

The number and ratio of blind at various dates were :—

Year	Number	Per Million Population	Ratio of Sex	
			Males	Females
1830 . . .	5,444	420	...	...
1840 . . .	6,916	407	...	...
1850 . . .	9,790	426	55	45
1860 . . .	12,660	410	58	42
1870 . . .	20,320	530	56	44
1880 . . .	48,928	970	55	45

CANADA

The general ratios are not published. In 1886 Manitoba had per million inhabitants 147 blind and 735 deaf-mutes, being a very low ratio for blindness.

INQUESTS

In 1887 there were 30,030 held in England and Wales, viz. :—

Cause of Death.

Natural causes	11,231
Suicide	2,227
Drink	372
Murder	350
Hunger	250
Various causes	15,600
Total . . .	30,030

INSANE

The following table shows the number of insane, including idiots, in the various countries, about 1880-84 (except Italy, 1872) :—

	Number	Per 10,000 Inhab.	Ratio of Recovery	Annual Death-Rate	Asylums
			Per Cent.	Per Cent.	
England . . .	81,600	32	39	10 ⎫	
Scotland . . .	11,600	32	42	8 ⎬	81
Ireland . . .	19,500	37	48	8 ⎭	
France . . .	93,900	25	33	15	110
Germany . . .	108,100	24	31	8	130
Russia . . .	80,000	11	...	...	74
Austria . . .	44,500	20	...	12	28
Italy . . .	44,100	17	...	...	33
Spain and Portugal .	13,000	7	...	...	11
Belgium and Holland	10,400	12	32	14	68
Switzerland .	3,100	11	...	?...	42
Scandinavia . .	18,100	29	...	...	27
Europe . . .	518,400	16	33	12	604
United States .	168,900	33	47	10	...
Canada . . .	7,300	18	...	...	...
Australia . .	4,900	17	45	7	...
Total .	695,500	19	36	11	...

As regards the causes of insanity, not including idiots, the average returns for England, France, Denmark, and United States combined give this result :—

	Per Cent.		Per Cent.
Hereditary . .	24	Loss of friends .	11
Drink . . .	24	Sickness . .	10
Business . .	12	Various . .	19

The ratios of sex in various countries show thus :—

	Inmates of Asylums		
	Males	Females	Total
England . . .	47	53	100
Scotland . . .	48	52	100
Ireland . . .	52	48	100
France . . .	48	52	100
Italy . . .	56	44	100
United States . .	51	49	100

Even in countries where the number of insane females exceeds that of males, it is found that men are more liable than women to insanity, but die faster. Thus in France there are annually admitted 110 males to 100 females, though the existing number of the latter is greater.

The percentage of insanity caused by drink is stated thus :—Italy 2, Austria 15, France 20, England 32, Sweden 50.

The relative numbers of insane persons cured is :—

	Per 100 of each Class		
	Males	Females	Total
France . . .	35	32	33
England . . .	36	42	39
Scotland . . .	40	44	42

Taking the existing numbers of mad people in the following countries, the sexes stood thus :—

	Males to Females	
England and Wales . . .	100	118
France	100	110
Italy	100	73

UNITED KINGDOM

The returns for 1883 showed as follows :—

	England	Scotland	Ireland	United Kingdom
Pauper insane . .	65,400	8,000	12,200	85,600
Private insane . .	16,200	3,600	7,300	27,100
Total . .	81,600	11,600	19,500	112,700
Lunatics	39,600	6,800	9,800	56,200
Idiots	29,500	4,600	6,700	40,800
Unclassified . . .	12,500	200	3,000	15,700
Total . .	81,600	11,600	19,500	112,700

There has been a notable increase of insane paupers since 1861, viz. :—

Period	Paupers Insane per Million Inhab.	
	England and Wales	Scotland
1861-65 . . .	2,080	2,050
1871-75 . . .	2,581	2,290
1880 . . .	2,792	2,580

Insanity varies with locality, as shown thus :—

Pauper Insane per 100,000 Inhabitants

Shetland . .	96	Edinburgh .	172	Argyll . .	259
Orkney . .	107	Sheffield .	179	Manchester .	270
Bradford . .	121	Newcastle .	191	Birmingham .	301
Durham . .	129	Swansea . .	202	Oxford . .	312
Cornwall . .	158	Liverpool . .	219	Nottingham .	342
Leeds . . .	160	Perth . . .	233	London . .	361

FRANCE

Year	Number	Per 100,000 Inhabitants	Caused by Drink, per Cent.
1851	46,400	129	8
1856	59,800	166	9
1866	90,100	238	14
1869	94,800	247	15
1879	93,970	252	15

The returns of lunatic asylums showed as follows :—

Year	Males	Females	Total
1871	18,020	19,700	37,720
1880	22,100	22,960	45,060
1886	24,990	27,880	52,870

The returns for 1885 were as follows :—

	Males	Females	Total
Old patients . .	24,400	27,400	51,800
New patients .	8,100	7,300	15,400
Total .	32,500	34,700	67,200
Cured . . .	1,655	1,519	3,174
Died . . .	3,326	2,785	6,111

The death-rate was 10.2 for males, 8.2 for females, and 9.1 for all. The expenditure during the year was £780,000, of which the families defrayed only £56,000, the rest being borne by the State. The number of patients treated during the year was :—

Asylums	Males	Females	Total
Public . . .	20,100	21,400	41,500
Private . . .	12,400	13,300	25,700
Total .	32,500	34,700	67,200

The death-rate was much lower in private than in public asylums, viz. :—

Asylums	Deaths			Per Cent.
	Males	Females	Total	
Public . . .	2,263	1,802	4,065	9.7
Private . . .	1,063	983	2,046	7.9
Total .	3,326	2,785	6,111	9.1

The statistics published by the Prefecture of Police in Paris indicate a very rapid increase in the number of insane persons admitted into the special infirmary of the capital, viz. :—

Year	Males	Females	Total
1872	1,695	1,389	3,084
1880	1,932	1,552	3,484
1888	2,549	1,900	4,449

The form of insanity known as *folie alcoölique* is twice as frequent now as it was fifteen years ago, and the number of persons placed under restraint on account of it has increased by 25 per cent. in the last three years. This is ascribed to the increased consumption of alcohol.

The returns for 1866 were as follows :—

	Insane	Idiots	Total
In asylums . .	31,992	3,980	35,972
In families . . .	18,734	35,973	54,707
Total . .	50,726	39,953	90,679

Of lunatics there were 91 males to 100 females, and of idiots 132 males to 100 females : taken collectively, the proportion was 107 males to 100 females. According to Lunier (1856) the number of persons who go mad yearly in a million of each class is as follows :—

Peasants	. . . 52	Learned professions .	525
Tradesmen	. . . 180	Soldiers . . .	590
Capitalists	. . . 275	Officers . . .	1,300

GERMANY

The returns for Prussia showed as follows :—

Year	Males	Females	Total	Per 100,000 Inhabitants
1871 . .	28,002	27,041	55,043	221
1880 . .	34,309	32,036	66,345	243

Mayr's tables for Bavaria showed a stronger tendency to insanity among Jews than Christians, viz., 620 Protestants, 840 Catholics, and 1190 Jews per million. He also found that 30 per cent. of lunatics had hereditary taint, and that in 1877 there were 34 insane for every 1000 lawsuits.

RUSSIA

In 1860 there were 41 asylums, containing 3100 insane. In 1882 the number of asylums had risen to 74 ; that of inmates was not stated. It was roughly supposed that the total number of insane and idiots in asylums and their own houses might reach 80,000, but nothing is really known. In Finland the ratio of insane persons is 170 per 100,000 inhabitants.

AUSTRIA

The returns do not include Hungary, and show thus for 1886 :—

	Males	Females	Total
In asylums . .	4,394	3,715	8,109
In families . . .	10,991	8,958	19,949
Lunatics . . .	15,385	12,673	28,058
Idiots . . .	9,507	6,913	16,420
Total . .	24,892	19,586	44,478

The average cost was 16d. daily, or £24 a year, for each inmate of asylums.

BELGIUM

The number of insane at various dates was as follows :—

	1858	1868	1878	1888
Males . .	3,481	4,287	5,288	5,200
Females . .	2,994	3,953	4,732	5,080
Total .	6,475	8,240	10,020	10,280

The returns for 1888 comprise only those in asylums; the statistics for previous dates showed thus :—

In	1858	1868	1878
Asylums . . .	4,420	6,032	7,886
Families . . .	2,055	2,208	2,134
Total . .	6,475	8,240	10,020
Age			
Under 30 . . .	1,313	1,660	1,903
30–50	2,658	3,382	4,186
Over 50 . . .	2,504	3,198	3,931
Total . .	6,475	8,240	10,020
Married men . .	499	639	821
Married women .	468	685	813
Unmarried men .	2,809	3,453	4,244
Unmarried women .	2,184	2,806	3,394
Widowers . . .	173	195	223
Widows . . .	342	462	525
Total . .	6,475	8,240	10,020
Deaths . . .	503	557	882
Per cent. . .	7.7	6.7	8.8
Cured . . .	520	626	617

Of 100 persons who become insane, 16 will be under 20 years of age, 24 between 20 and 30 years, 22 in the ensuing decade, 16 between 40 and 50, and 22 over 50 years.

ITALY

Between 1872 and 1877 the number of pauper lunatics increased 24 per cent., namely, from 12,210 to 15,173, but the total number of insane in the latter year was unknown.

The returns for 1872 showed thus :—

	Males	Females	Total
In asylums . .	6,476	5,734	12,210
In families . . .	19,140	12,752	31,892
Total . .	25,616	18,486	44,102

Insane per 100,000 Inhabitants

Naples . . 111	Tuscany . . 185	Lombardy . 230
Rome . . . 157	Piedmont . . 222	Italy . . . 171
Venice . . . 174	Liguria . . 226	

The ratio of insanity according to condition, that is, married or unmarried, was as follows :—

100 unmarried males to 52 married
100 ,, females to 58 married

The ratio of population is 100 unmarried to 60 married ; it appears, therefore, that insanity is more prevalent among unmarried than married persons.

The returns for 1877 refer only to pauper lunatics, viz. :—

Males 8,010
Females 7,163
Total . . . 15,173

Pauper lunatics compared with population thus :—

Per 100,000 Inhabitants

Sardinia . . 18	Venice . . . 61	Lombardy . 76
Naples . . . 19	Piedmont . . 62	Rome . . . 85
Sicily . . . 23	Genoa . . . 68	

Insanity was most prevalent between forty and sixty years of age, the number per million of each class showing thus :—

Under 20 . . 93	41 to 60 . . 1,098
20–40 . . . 944	Over 60 . . 557

In 100,000 Christians there were 58 pauper lunatics; in 100,000 Jews there were 260. The prevalence of insanity among Jews has already been noted in Germany.

NORWAY

The ratios of idiots and insane persons showed thus :—

Year	Per 100,000 Inhabitants		
	Idiots	Insane	Total
1835 . . .	142	160	302
1845 . . .	153	168	321
1855 . . .	160	181	341
1865 . . .	120	185	305
1875 . . .	...	...	480

HOLLAND

The number of insane paupers per million inhabitants rose from 594 in 1856 to 754 in 1863.

UNITED STATES

Year	Lunatics	Idiots	Total	Per 100,000 Inhabitants	Sex Ratio (Percentage of Males)		
					Lunatics	Idiots	Total
1840	...	...	17,410	102	...	...	...
1850	15,610	15,790	31,400	136	51	60	55
1860	24,040	18,930	42,970	139	49	58	53
1870	37,430	24,530	61,960	161	47	60	53
1880	91,990	76,890	168,880	330	46	60	51

In 1880 the insane were classified thus :—

	Males	Females	Total
Idiots	45,309	31,586	76,895
Insane	44,388	47,571	91,959
Total . .	89,697	79,157	168,854

	White	Coloured	Total
Idiots	67,316	9,579	76,895
Insane	85,802	6,157	91,959
Total . .	153,118	15,736	168,854

	Americans	Foreigners	Total
Idiots	72,888	4,007	76,895
Insane	65,630	26,329	91,959
Total . .	138,518	30,331	168,854

AUSTRALIA

In December 1887 the seven colonies counted 10,130 insane persons, being 286 per 100,000 inhabitants. The ratios were :—

	Per 100,000		Per 100,000
New South Wales .	270	South Australia .	240
Victoria . . .	329	Tasmania . .	243
New Zealand .	281	Western Australia .	285
Queensland .	244	General average .	286

INSECTS

On an average, 15 tons of vegetable mould are annually thrown up by earth-worms on an acre of cultivable land, equal to a weight of 705 million tons in the United Kingdom. There are about 26,800 worms to each acre.

According to the *Edinburgh Review* (336), the annual value of agricultural products consumed by insects in the United States is 60 millions sterling. The value of 2,900,000 acres of vineyard devastated by phylloxera in France was 132 millions sterling.

Locusts inflict enormous damage in many countries. In Cyprus the peasants are paid £40 for every ton of locust eggs which they destroy, some years destroying 60 tons, which is equivalent to 680 million locusts. In Russia 600 soldiers can sweep a ton of locusts daily into ditches and destroy them.

INSURANCE

The *Bulletin Statistique* of 1886 has the following tables :—

	Amount of Life Insurances, Millions £ Sterling					
	1859	1864	1869	1874	1879	1883
Great Britain .	160	210	269	362	415	445
Continent . .	30	61	112	176	236	327
United States .	30	85	397	431	311	383
Total . .	220	356	778	969	962	1,155

	Average Amount of Insurance, £				
	Great Britain	France	Germany	Austria	United States
1859 . . .	580	420	168	152	616
1869 . . .	420	400	136	136	604
1879 . . .	460	440	172	112	520
1883 . . .	464	448	184	128	544

Besso considers that 8,500,000 persons in Europe have their lives insured, say 2½ per cent. of the population. The latest returns show as follows :—

Year			Country	Amount, £	Premiums, £
1889	.	.	U. Kingdom	545,000,000	17,400,000
1888	.	.	Germany .	170,300,000	14,680,000
1885	.	.	Austria . .	45,200,000	7,800,000
1885	.	.	Russia . .	10,000,000	...
1886	.	.	France . .	117,600,000	6,050,000
1885	.	.	Scandinavia	11,200,000	...
1885	.	.	Switzerland	8,100,000	...
1885	.	.	U. States .	420,000,000	21,900,000
1880	.	.	Canada . .	17,000,000	...

The above does not include the Industrial Life Assurances of Great Britain, of which later on.

According to the *Archivio*, the aggregate insurance business of Germany, Austria and Switzerland multiplied 15-fold in the period of 25 years down to 1877, viz. :—

Year			Existing Policies	Amount, £
1852	.	.	46,980	8,600,000
1865	.	.	280,500	41,600,000
1877	.	.	753,400	116,900,000

The following table shows how the aggregate for 1877 was made up, and also the new business for that year :—

	New Business, 1877		Total on Books, 1877	
	Policies	Amount, £	Policies	Amount, £
Germany .	78,030	15,100,000	552,200	92,400,000
Austria . .	21,800	2,900,000	178,900	19,300,000
Switzerland	2,300	550,000	22,200	5,100,000
Total .	102,130	18,550,000	753,300	116,800,000

In 1880 the new business done in various countries was :—

	New Policies	Amount, £	Policies Paid, £
Great Britain . .	44,900	20,900,000	11,200,000
United States. .	123,000	37,500,000	...
Germany . . .	47,600	13,800,000	1,900,000
France	47,800	17,700,000	1,200,000

The life insurance of the principal countries in 1880 compared with the returns for 1870 as follows :—

	Existing Policies		Amount	
	1870	1880	1870 £	1880 £
Great Britain	688,000	879,000	338,000,000	422,000,000
U. States .	748,000	725,000	405,000,000	312,000,000
Germany .	456,000	797,000	64,000,000	127,000,000
France . .	129,000	208,000	51,000,000	87,000,000
Austria . .	90,000	170,000	...	20,000,000
Canada . .	40,000	48,000	14,000,000	17,000,000

Besides the ordinary system in England of companies charging an annual premium for a policy payable only on death, there is another mode of insurance, whereby the insured person on reaching a certain age receives an annuity for life. In Denmark any person who pays in at the age of 21 a sum of £6 10s. will be entitled to an annuity of £13 on reaching the age of 65 ; if he die meantime, the sum is forfeit. In Germany, whoever pays 20d. a week during three years, beginning at the age of 18, will receive an annuity of £13 on arriving at that of 65. The German system of compulsory insurance divides the annual premium into three equal parts, one paid by the workman, one by his employer, one by the State. In England, by payment of £100 to any of the first-class insurance companies the following annuity may be secured, varying with the age of the person who buys the annuity :—

Age	Annuity for £100	
	Man	Woman
	£ s. d.	£ s. d.
50	7 7 0	6 13 0
60	9 0 0	8 0 0

UNITED KINGDOM

There are 95 principal companies, which showed the following aggregate of business for life insurance :—

	1877	1886	1889
Policies. . . .	779,000	902,000	...
Amount, £ . .	384,000,000	421,000,000	545,000,000
Premiums, £ . .	11,700,000	12,800,000	13,930,000
Assets, £ . . .	124,000,000	143,000,000	165,700,000

There are also industrial life insurances of the working classes, which showed thus :—

	1880	1885
Number of policies .	5,440,000	9,132,000
Amount, £ . .	49,000,000	83,000,000
Annual premiums, £. .	1,940,000	3,550,000

The average annual premium in British companies, per £100 of policy, varies with age thus :—

Age		£ s. d.	Age			£ s. d.
25	.	2 2 0	40	.	.	3 4 0
30	.	2 8 0	45	.	.	3 15 0
35	.	2 15 0	55	.	.	5 11 0

The business of 95 companies in 1889 compared with 1884 thus :—

	1884	1889
	£	£
Premiums	12,300,000	13,930,000
Other receipts . . .	6,600,000	7,710,000
Total income .	18,900,000	21,640,000
Paid claims . . .	10,600,000	11,000,000
Expenses	5,600,000	5,640,000
Total payments .	16,200,000	16,640,000

The assets amount to 166 millions sterling, and include £11,300,000 paid-up capital.

FRANCE

In 1886 there were life policies running to the amount of £117,600,000, the premiums reaching £6,050,000 per annum ; assets or reserve fund £35,800,000. The number and amount of policies for life insurance issued in twenty years down to 1880 were :—

Period	Number	Amount, £	Average, £
1861–70 . .	128,700	51,000,000	396
1871–80 . .	250,400	104,500,000	418
	379,100	155,500,000	410

There were 26,600 new policies issued during the year 1885. The foregoing are payable at the death of the insured person. As regards the purchase of annuities, the annuity fund in 1881 amounted to 16 millions sterling, and the new annuities purchased yearly average a capital value of £900,000. The annuities now running average as follows :—

	Per Annum £		Per Annum £
Military officers . .	95	Physicians . .	56
Naval officers . . .	90	Farmers . . .	40
Men of property . .	62	Workmen . . .	36
Civil service . . .	60	Servants . . .	26

There is, moreover, a special life insurance against accidental deaths, which showed in 1886 premiums received £440,000, payments for persons killed £240,000.

GERMANY

Year	Policies	Amount, £	Policies Paid, £
1850 . . .	40,900	7,400,000	150,000
1860 . . .	129,600	21,200,000	350,000
1870 . . .	456,200	64,000,000	1,020,000
1880 . . .	797,100	127,300,000	1,870,000
1888 . . .	816,300	170,300,000	...

The above table shows the total number of existing policies and the aggregate amounts at the various dates. The increase of business in ten years appears on comparing the figures for 1888 with those of 1878 :—

	1878 £	1888 £
Amount of policies .	97,700,000	170,300,000
Amount of assets . .	28,000,000	52,300,000

AUSTRIA

The returns of 1885 compare with those of previous years thus :—

Year	Amount of Policies, £	Amount of Premiums, £
1876 . . .	25,500,000	3,000,000
1880 . . .	31,200,000	6,500,000
1885 . . .	45,200,000	7,800,000

UNITED STATES

According to Bradstreet's, the income of American life companies rose from £1,300,000 in 1861 to £21,900,000 in 1885. The assets in 1880 amounted to 84 millions sterling. A statement in 1860 showed 47 life companies, 60,000 persons insured, aggregate amount 37 millions sterling.

Fire Insurance

In 1887 a statement was published in London that the insurance companies of the United Kingdom covered properties to the amount of 5500 millions sterling, the annual premiums on the policies amounting to £14,500,000. The *Journal des Economists* published in 1883 a table of fire insurance for other countries. The result is as follows :—

Country	Property Insured, Millions £	Annual Premium, £	Rate per 1000	Annual Loss by Fire, £	Loss per Inhabitant, Pence
U. Kingdom	5,500	14,500,000	2.5	9,100,000	60
France . .	4,056	3,760,000	1.0	3,200,000	20
Germany .	3,170	6,500,000	2.0	6,100,000	32
Russia . .	180	900,000	5.0	9,000,000	26
Belgium . .	400	400,000	1.0	500,000	22
Scandinavia	115	300,000	2.7	1,000,000	38
U. States .	2,180	19,600,000	9.0	21,400,000	78
Canada . .	140	1,550,000	11.0	4,100,000	220
Total .	15,741	47,510,000	3.0	54,400,000	...

The figures for the United States are taken from the *Journal of Commerce*, 1887.

UNITED KINGDOM

Official returns were published down to 1868, when the insurance duty was abolished ; they showed thus :—

Year	Amount, Millions £				Per Inhabitant, £
	England	Scotland	Ireland	United Kingdom	
1801	220	4	9	233	15
1810	325	12	17	354	20
1830	482	34	19	535	22
1850	680	43	34	757	28
1868	921	99	52	1,072	36

The assets of fire companies in 1881 amounted to 24 millions sterling.

FRANCE

The following table shows fire insurance :—

Year	Amount Insured		Premium, £	Losses Paid, £
	Millions £	£ per Inhabitant		
1851 . . .	1,318	41	1,140,000	560,000
1856 . . .	1,810	54	1,566,000	774,000
1868 . . .	3,092	88	2,440,000	1,460,000
1875 . . .	3,190	90	3,030,000	2,390,000
1881 . . .	4,056	112	3,855,000	2,430,000

The balance-sheet for 1886 showed as follows :—

Receipts, £		Payments, £	
Fire premiums .	3,650,000	Fire losses . . .	2,040,000
Investments . .	270,000	Expenses . . .	1,360,000
Total . .	3,920,000	Total . .	3,400,000

This left a profit of £520,000, say about 6 per cent. on a capital of £8,500,000 sterling. The following is an official record of all payments by insurance companies for losses by fire or other calamity :—

	1871	1885
	£	£
Fire	1,560,000	2,280,000
Hail	1,920,000	5,100,000
Frost	4,500,000	1,400,000
Cattle-plague . . .	1,800,000	1,500,000
Phylloxera . . .	...	6,640,000
Sundries	220,000	880,000
Total . .	10,000,000	17,800,000

The total payments in 1881 were £16,000,000, including £5,700,000 for phylloxera.

GERMANY

The returns of fire insurance show as follows :—

Year	Amount Insured		Premium, £	Losses Paid, £
	Millions £	£ per Inhabitant		
1850 . . .	815	27	1,650,000	1,200,000
1860 . . .	1,450	40	3,000,000	2,000,000
1870 . . .	2,030	50	4,160,000	2,900,000
1880 . . .	3,125	67	6,370,000	4,400,000

RUSSIA

Official estimates for 1884–85 show an average loss of property yearly amounting to £9,100,000 sterling, of which £3,300,000 covered by insurance. The loss compared with population is estimated at 4s. per head in towns, and 2s. in the rural population yearly.

AUSTRIA

Policies paid on losses caused on farms in 1886 amounted in Austria to £2,900,000, of which £1,800,000 by fire, the rest by hail. Losses paid on farms in Hungary for fire were £1,100,000, being 20 per cent. over the average of six preceding years.

UNITED STATES

The *Journal of Commerce* (New York) gives the following :—

Year	Insurances in Force, £	Loss by Fire, £
1875	1,260,000,000	16,200,000
1880	1,494,000,000	15,600,000
1885	2,180,000,000	21,400,000

The above table shows the total loss by fire, insured and uninsured. The latter shows the amounts paid by the companies for losses :—

Year	Amount Insured, £	Premium, £	Losses Paid, £
1856	175,000,000	1,440,000	880,000
1862	365,000,000	3,100,000	1,900,000
1876	1,310,000,000	11,800,000	8,800,000
1881	1,290,000,000	11,630,000	8,950,000

Marine Insurance

In 1880 the amount of marine insurance was estimated at 887 millions sterling, viz. :—

	Millions £
Lloyds	480
Hamburg	105
French, &c.	302

In 1888 the aggregate returns of seven Liverpool companies showed an average premium on all insurances during three years of only 7 per 1000, viz.: Average annual insurances, 137 millions sterling ; premium, £950,000 ; damages settled, £400,000 ; expenses of management, £100,000 ; annual dividend, 14 per cent. on a paid-up capital of £840,000. The losses, therefore, of ships and cargoes were only 3 per 1000 of value. The Hamburg Company showed as follows :—

Year	Insured, £	Rate per 1000
1803	400,000	...
1820	11,000,000	17
1840	20,000,000	15
1860	47,000,000	14
1878	105,000,000	12

The French marine insurance returns were :—

	1884	1886
	£	£
Policies issued . . .	200,100,000	175,100,000
Premiums . . .	740,000	710,000
Rate per £1000 . .	3.7	4.1
Losses paid . .	530,000	460,000

The losses, therefore, averaged 53s. per £1000.

IRON

The production of pig iron, which amounted to 60,000 tons in the year 1500, advanced very slowly until the nineteenth century. The following table shows the quantities approximately :—

Date	Tons					
	Great Britain	France	Germany	United States	Various	Total
1500	6,000	12000	5,000	...	37,000	60,000
1700	12,000	22,000	10,000	...	60,000	104,000
1740	20,000	26,000	18,000	1,000	92,000	157,000
1790	68,000	40,000	30,000	30,000	110,000	278,000
1800	190,000	60,000	40,000	40,000	130,000	460,000
1810	250,000	85,000	46,000	55,000	180,000	616,000
1820	400,000	140,000	90,000	110,000	270,000	1,010,000
1830	680,000	220,000	120,000	180,000	385,000	1,585,000
1840	1,390,000	350,000	170,000	290,000	480,000	2,680,000
1850	2,250,000	570,000	402,000	560,000	640,000	4,422,000
1860	3,830,000	900,000	530,000	820,000	1,100,000	7,180,000
1870	5,960,000	1,180,000	1,390,000	1,670,000	1,710,000	11,910,000
1880	7,750,000	1,730,000	2,730,000	3,840,000	2,090,000	18,140,000
1885	7,420,000	1,630,000	3,690,000	4,050,000	2,310,000	19,100,000
1889	8,250,000	1,720,000	4,530,000	7,600,000	3,060,000	25,160,000

The figures from 1500 to 1740 are those given by Seaman.

IRON AND COAL.

Consumption of Iron, lbs. per inhabitant.

In the year 1830.

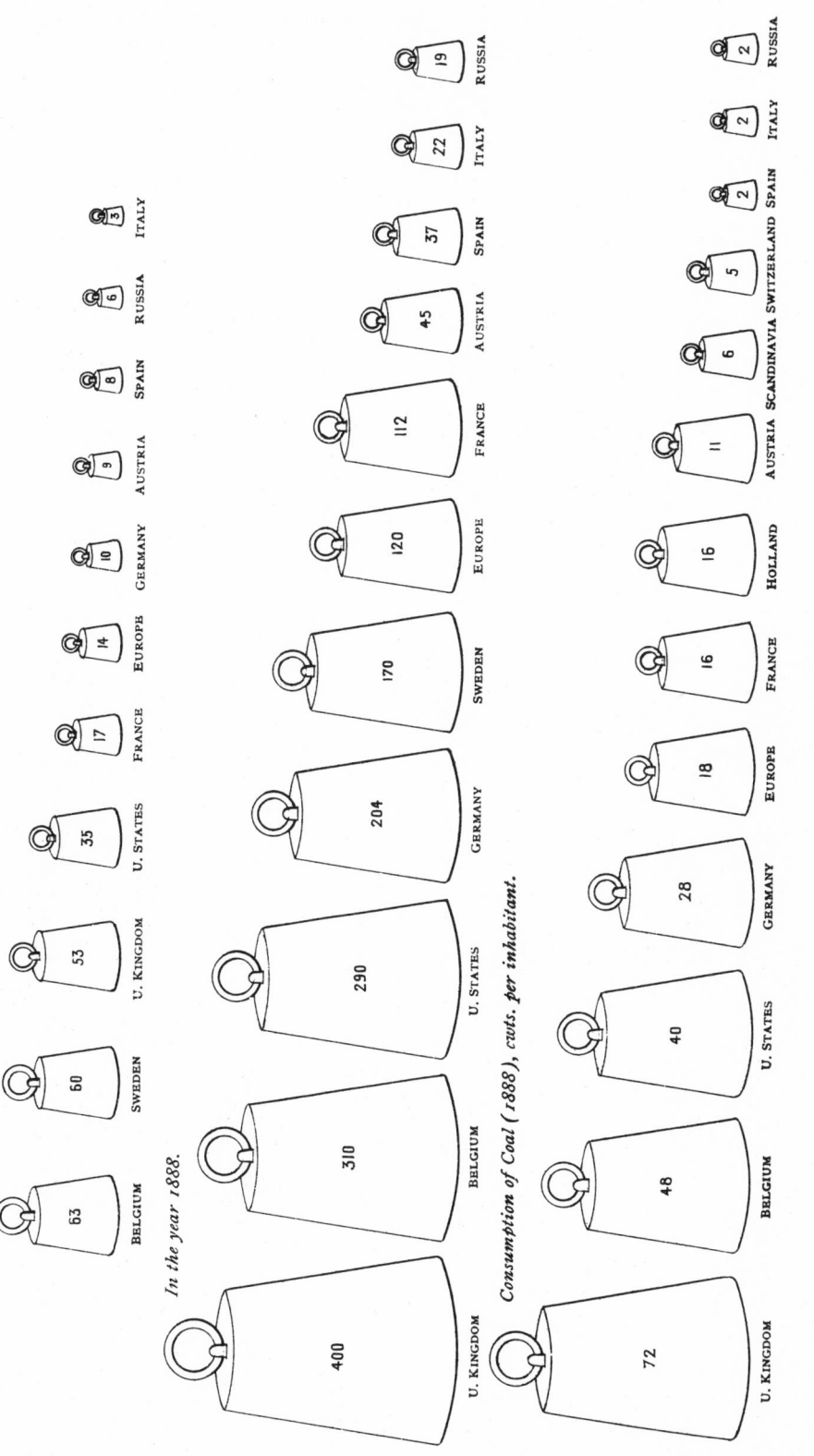

BELGIUM 63 — SWEDEN 60 — U. KINGDOM 53 — U. STATES 35 — FRANCE 17 — EUROPE 14 — GERMANY 10 — AUSTRIA 9 — SPAIN 8 — RUSSIA 6 — ITALY 3

In the year 1888.

BELGIUM 310 — U. STATES 290 — GERMANY 204 — SWEDEN 170 — EUROPE 120 — FRANCE 112 — AUSTRIA 45 — SPAIN 37 — ITALY 22 — RUSSIA 19

Consumption of Coal (1888), cwts. per inhabitant.

U. KINGDOM 72 — BELGIUM 48 — U. STATES 40 — GERMANY 28 — EUROPE 18 — FRANCE 16 — HOLLAND 16 — AUSTRIA 11 — SCANDINAVIA 6 — SWITZERLAND 5 — SPAIN 2 — ITALY 2 — RUSSIA 2

Ballantyne, Hanson & Cº Edinburgh & London.

The production among minor countries since 1830 has been approximately thus :—

	1830	1850	1860	1870	1880	1889
	Tons					
Belgium . . .	35,000	73,000	220,000	520,000	490,000	850,000
Austria	80,000	140,000	310,000	400,000	470,000	760,000
Russia . . .	120,000	220,000	290,000	350,000	450,000	600,000
Sweden . . .	105,000	130,000	180,000	290,000	400,000	460,000
Spain	20,000	40,000	50,000	70,000	160,000	230,000
Various . . .	25,000	37,000	50,000	80,000	120,000	160,000
Total . . .	385,000	640,000	1,100,000	1,710,000	2,090,000	3,060,000

The percentage of iron contained in ironstone is as follows :—

France. . . 31	United States 43	Canada . . 60
Germany . . 36	Australia . . 55	Russia. . . 44
England . . 41	Algeria . . 58	Sweden . . 52

The number of blast-furnaces was :—

	Total Number		Working in 1885	Average Product Tons Iron per Furnace
	1875	1885		
United Kingdom	959	891	429	17,400
United States .	713	591	276	14,700
France. . . .	...	...	270	7,000
Germany . . .	456	...	252	17,500
Russia. . . .	...	...	206	2,400
Austria . . .	180	137	80	8,900
Sweden . . .	...	...	224	1,800
Belgium . . .	...	61	32	22,000

The furnaces of Great Britain in 1885 had a productive capacity of 16,900,000 tons, the actual production having been only 7,510,000 : it would appear that the furnaces of Europe and America could produce at least 40 million tons of iron yearly.

The production in 1885 was as follows :—

	Pig	Wrought	Steel
	Tons		
Great Britain . . .	7,510,000	1,940,000	1,920,000
United States . . .	4,040,000	1,640,000	1,600,000
Germany.	3,700,000	1,460,000	1,140,000
France	1,600,000	770,000	530,000
Belgium	700,000	460,000	160,000
Austria	700,000	300,000	200,000
Russia	500,000	290,000	250,000
Sweden	400,000	50,000	40,000
Spain, &c.	290,000	190,000	310,000
Total . .	19,440,000	7,100,000	6,150,000

The following table shows approximately the consumption in the principal countries :—

	Tons				Lbs. per Inhabitant			
	1830	1850	1870	1888	1830	1850	1870	1888
United Kingdom . . .	560,000	1,970,000	4,260,000	6,700,000	53	170	310	400
France	250,000	600,000	1,350,000	1,900,000	17	37	80	112
Germany	120,000	420,000	1,340,000	4,340,000	10	27	74	204
Russia	120,000	300,000	655,000	730,000	6	11	20	17
Austria	100,000	160,000	430,000	770,000	9	12	28	45
Italy	20,000	50,000	100,000	290,000	3	6	9	22
Spain	40,000	80,000	150,000	300,000	8	13	23	37
Sweden	80,000	100,000	310,000	380,000	60	63	165	170
Belgium	95,000	170,000	550,000	830,000	63	90	242	310
Various	30,000	60,000	140,000	210,000	6	9	15	20
Europe	1,415,000	3,910,000	9,285,000	16,450,000	14	35	70	120
United States . . .	200,000	600,000	1,730,000	7,900,000	35	56	100	290
Colonies, &c. . . .	70,000	132,000	225,000	590,000	...	...	...	...
Total . .	1,685,000	4,642,000	11,240,000	24,940,000	...	...	...	...

The approximate value of goods manufactured from iron and steel in various countries is as follows :—

	Iron, £	Steel, £	Total £
United Kingdom	50,100,000	84,000,000	134,100,000
France	19,500,000	15,900,000	35,400,000
Germany . . .	40,500,000	37,800,000	78,300,000
Russia	5,400,000	7,000,000	12,400,000
Austria	6,200,000	7,600,000	13,800,000
Italy	3,500,000	600,000	4,100,000
Spain	2,800,000	900,000	3,700,000
Sweden	4,100,000	2,200,000	6,300,000
Belgium . . .	8,100,000	6,200,000	14,300,000
Europe	140,200,000	162,200,000	302,400,000
United States .	72,000,000	94,500,000	166,500,000
Total . .	212,200,000	256,700,000	368,900,000

The cost of producing a ton of iron or of steel in various countries was stated in 1883 in a report drawn up by the French Government as follows :—

	Shillings per Ton		
	Pig	Wrought Iron	Steel
England . . .	50	122	160
France	73	182	224
Germany . . .	59	144	192
Belgium . . .	47	130	131

A bar of iron, value 20s., may be manufactured into goods representing any of the following values :—

	£			£
Needles . . .	11	Buttons . .		6,100
Penknives . . .	650	Watch-springs .		51,000

The production of pig iron in ninety years from 1800 has been approximately as follows :—

Period	Tons				
	United Kingdom	United States	Germany	Other Countries	Total
1800–20	5,700,000	1,400,000	1,300,000	4,800,000	13,200,000
1821–40	16,400,000	3,800,000	2,500,000	10,100,000	32,800,000
1841–50	18,200,000	4,200,000	2,600,000	8,500,000	33,500,000
1851–60	32,500,000	6,600,000	4,400,000	13,600,000	57,100,000
1861–70	47,400,000	11,400,000	10,300,000	24,500,000	93,600,000
1871–80	65,600,000	24,200,000	20,600,000	31,700,000	142,100,000
1881–89	71,200,000	47,900,000	33,300,000	38,700,000	191,100,000
90 years	257,000,000	99,500,000	75,000,000	131,900,000	563,400,000

Period	Value, £ Sterling				
	United Kingdom	United States	Germany	Other Countries	Total
1800–20	40,100,000	12,600,000	10,400,000	38,400,000	101,500,000
1821–40	90,200,000	30,400,000	17,500,000	70,700,000	208,800,000
1841–50	72,800,000	23,100,000	13,000,000	42,500,000	151,400,000
1851–60	89,400,000	26,400,000	17,600,000	54,400,000	187,800,000
1861–70	128,000,000	51,300,000	36,400,000	88,200,000	303,900,000
1871–80	166,800,000	109,000,000	58,500,000	90,300,000	424,600,000
1881–89	148,000,000	196,500,000	73,200,000	92,000,000	509,700,000
90 years	735,300,000	449,300,000	226,600,000	476,500,000	1,887,700,000

	Tons	Value, £
Great Britain . . .	257,000,000	735,300,000
United States . . .	99,500,000	449,300,000
Germany	75,000,000	226,600,000
France	49,700,000	189,400,000
Belgium	22,200,000	77,500,000
Russia	18,600,000	65,300,000
Austria	17,200,000	58,600,000
Sweden	15,100,000	52,300,000
Spain, Italy, &c. . .	9,100,000	33,400,000
Total . .	563,400,000	1,887,700,000

	Tons		
	1870	1880	1889
Great Britain . .	215,000	1,440,000	3,670,000
France . .	84,000	385,000	530,000
Germany . .	126,000	660,000	1,860,000
Russia . .	5,000	295,000	250,000
Austria . .	22,000	100,000	300,000
Belgium . .	6,000	95,000	185,000
Sweden . .	12,000	30,000	70,000
United States .	70,000	1,250,000	3,385,000
Total .	540,000	4,255,000	10,250,000

Visiting cards are now sometimes made of very thin sheet-iron, viz. :—

	Per Inch Thick		Per Inch Thick
Belgian . . .	400	Baron Krupp's .	820
Count Harrach's .	640	Count Renard's .	1,000

The production of steel has been approximately as follows, in tons :—

	1850	1870	1881	1889
U. Kingdom .	49,000	215,000	1,440,000	3,670,000
Continent . .	17,000	255,000	1,565,000	3,195,000
United States .	5,000	70,000	1,250,000	3,385,000
Total .	71,000	540,000	4,255,000	10,250,000

According to Mr. Chisholm's tables and others, the production of steel in all countries has been as follows since 1870 :—

Steel rails were first used for railways at Chalk Farm, near London, in 1862. They bore an annual traffic of 96,000,000 tons, and after three years were found worn ¼ inch. The consumption of steel for railways in 1882 was as follows :—

	Consumption, Tons per Annum		
	New Lines	Renewal	Total
United States .	1,200,000	900,000	2,100,000
Great Britain . .	60,000	160,000	220,000
Continent, &c. .	680,000	655,000	1,335,000
Total . .	1,940,000	1,715,000	3,655,006

In twenty years ending 1889 it appears that railways have absorbed 43,500,000 tons of steel, or almost half the total product. The life of an iron rail is sixteen, that of a steel one forty, years.

The aggregate production of steel in forty years may be set down approximately as follows :—

Period	Tons					
	Great Britain	United States	Germany	France	Various	Total
1850–69	2,600,000	700,000	1,300,000	800,000	700,000	6,100,000
1870–79	8,300,000	3,800,000	3,100,000	2,200,000	2,100,000	19,500,000
1880–89	25,100,000	21,700,000	12,200,000	3,800,000	6,100,000	68,900,000
40 years . . .	36,000,000	26,200,000	16,600,000	6,800,000	8,900,000	94,500,000

Taking the strength of Swedish iron at 100, the tensile strength of steel compares thus :—

Swedish iron	.	. 100	Cannon steel .	. 173
Boiler steel .	.	. 118	Spring steel .	. 202

A bar of chrome steel, ½ inch square and 5 inches long, gives a strength of 141,000 lbs. per square inch, being 37 per cent. more than carbon steel. The nominal strength of steel is 30 tons per square inch, but Professor Siemens shows that it is really 36 tons. The tests used by the French Admiralty as minimum breaking load are as follows :—

Iron Plates	Lbs.	Steel Plates, Inch	Lbs.
Common	. . 52	0.16 ,, 0.24	101
Better	. . . 62	0.24 ,, 0.80	99
Best	. . . 64	0.80 ,, 1.20	97

The plates supplied by Messrs. Cammell of Sheffield for seven French ironclads were subjected to 36,000 foot-tons of energy, viz. :—Shot, 760 lbs.; charge, 150 lbs., fired from a 12-inch gun, with velocity 1425 feet per second; range, 264 feet.

The plates in question were 11 feet long and 7 feet wide by 18 inches thick.

In 1879 some vessels were built of steel on the Clyde, it being found that a steel ship could carry 20 per cent. more than one of iron. In 1882 the *Oregon*, 7400 tons, was built of steel ; the construction in this metal being as follows :—

						Tons
1879 .	.	.	.	.	.	18,000
1883 .	.	.	.	.	.	143,000

About three tons of steel are consumed daily in making pens, of which Birmingham consumes 1½ tons. The output of steel pens yearly in 1882 was as follows :—

				Pens	Per Inhab.
United Kingdom .	.	810,000,000			23
France .	.	.	.	420,000,000	11
United States	.	.	105,000,000		2

There are fourteen steel-pen factories at Birmingham, three in France, two in Germany, and one in the United States. A ton of steel produces 1,500,000 pens. The price when first made by Gillott, sixty years ago, was 12s. a dozen, 150 times the present price.

UNITED KINGDOM

The following is a summary of iron and steel exports in thirty-five years, from Mr. Chisholm's tables :—

Period	Tons to									Total
	U. States	France	Germany	Belgium	Italy	Russia	India	Australia	Canada	
1855–59	1,600,000	600,000	1,200,000	20,000	...	230,000	860,000	280,000	...	6,900,000
1860–69	3,300,000	1,400,000	2,400,000	310,000	220,000	1,020,000	2,010,000	800,000	170,000	18,100,000
1870–79	5,100,000	1,100,000	5,900,000	1,240,000	780,000	2,200,000	1,500,000	1,700,000	1,600,000	27,100,000
1880–89	8,600,000	1,200,000	5,300,000	800,000	1,600,000	1,520,000	3,900,000	3,700,000	2,400,000	38,300,000
35 years	18,600,000	4,300,000	14,800,000	2,370,000	2,600,000	4,970,000	8,270,000	6,480,000	4,170,000	90,400,000

In the above table Germany also includes Holland. The total includes many countries not above stated. The production of iron compares with the exports from the United Kingdom thus :—

Period	Tons Iron Made	Tons Exported	Home Use
1855–59 . .	18,500,000	6,900,000	11,600,000
1860–69 . .	46,000,000	18,100,000	27,900,000
1870–79 . .	64,000,000	27,100,000	36,900,000
1880–89 . .	74,200,000	38,300,000	35,900,000
35 years . .	202,700,000	90,400,000	112,300,000

The consumption of coal in making pig iron was as follows :—

Year	Tons		Tons of Coal to One Ton of Iron
	Iron	Coal	
1796 . . .	125,000	750,000	6.0
1806 . . .	243,000	1,220,000	5.0
1840 . . .	1,396,000	4,877,000	3.5
1870 . . .	5,230,000	16,220,000	3.1
1875 . . .	6,365,000	15,700,000	2.5
1881 . . .	8,326,000	18,300,000	2.2
1889 . . .	8,200,000	17,400,000	2.1

Neilson's invention in 1829 of the hot-blast, 600° Fahr., caused a saving of 33 per cent. in the quantity of coal required. Cowper's "Regenerator" of 1500° Fahr., in 1857, caused a further saving. Meantime the total consumption of coal in British ironworks is about 35 million tons. The estimate in 1881 was as follows :—

	Tons Coal Used
Making pig-iron	18,300,000
Finished iron	8,040,000
Steel	1,680,000
Engines and shipbuilding .	1,510,000
Sundries	5,230,000
Total . .	34,760,000

The furnaces of the United Kingdom in 1880 were :—

	In Blast	Idle	Total
England . . .	329	233	562
Wales	45	66	111
Scotland . . .	87	53	140
Total . .	461	352	813

FRANCE

In the eighteenth century, according to Seaman, France produced more iron than Great Britain until the French Revolution, when England took the foremost place. In that century France only doubled her output from 22,000 to 50,000 tons, while Great Britain increased hers ten-fold. The wars of Bonaparte considerably retarded this industry, for we find that in 1814 the production did not exceed 100,000 tons, whereas in Great Britain it reached 300,000 tons. A table published in 1840 was as follows :—

Year	Blast Furnaces	Tons Pig Iron
1825	...	160,000
1828 . . .	393	220,000
1839 . . .	569	350,000

In this latter year the number of hands employed was 44,000, giving an average of eight tons per man. The production and consumption of iron and steel were approximately as follows :—

Year	Iron, Tons		Lbs. Con-sumed per Inhabitant	Production of Steel, Tons
	Production	Consump-tion		
1700 . . .	22,000	22,000	2	...
1800 . . .	60,000	60,000	5	...
1850 . . .	570,000	600,000	37	8,000
1870 . . .	1,180,000	1,350,000	80	94,000
1889 . . .	1,720,000	1,900,000	112	530,000

In 1880 there were 600 blast-furnaces and 500 others. In 1885 the foundries employed 55,000 workmen, who turned out 780,000 tons of iron bars, &c., and 550,000 tons of steel, representing a value of £10,200,000, say £184 per man.

GERMANY

The production of iron has increased an hundred-fold since 1810, viz. :—

Year	Tons Iron	Tons Steel	Lbs. Iron per Inhabitant
1810	46,000	...	4
1850	402,000	6,000	27
1870	1,390,000	170,000	74
1889	4,530,000	1,400,000	204

In 1888 there were 1470 foundries, employing 170,000 men. The most remarkable in the world is that of Mr. Krupp, at Essen, Prussia, covering 1100 acres : the number of workmen never falls below 16,000, and there are 800 steam-engines, with an aggregate of 18,000 horse-power, and 82 steam-hammers, the heaviest weighing 50 tons : the daily consumption of iron and steel averages 500 tons. Down to 1876 Mr. Krupp had delivered 15,000 pieces of cannon to various nations.

Germany is now the third great producer of iron, her output being half that of Great Britain. In seven years ending 1887 the imports and exports of pig-iron were equal, but the exports of railway bars and other manufactured iron averaged 340,000 tons yearly.

RUSSIA

In 1828 there were 900 furnaces at work at Perm, Vialka, and Nijni, and 600 workshops for cutlery at Tula, with 7000 operatives : the production of iron was then estimated at 115,000 tons, but it was so dear that horses were unshod and farm implements were entirely of wood. In 1866 Tegebolski's report showed 1732 foundries, with 137,000 operatives, who consumed 300,000 tons of iron yearly, turning out manufactures valued at 10 millions sterling ; an excessive valuation, equal to £28 a ton, the real value being about 7 millions. The following table shows approximately the production and consumption :—

Year	Tons Iron		Lbs. per Inhabitant	Steel, Tons
	Production	Consumption		
1828 . .	115,000	120,000	6	...
1850 . .	220,000	300,000	11	...
1870 . .	350,000	655,000	20	9,000
1888 . .	600,000	730,000	19	260,000

There has been a remarkable increase in the manufacture of farming implements, namely, from £220,000 in 1867 to one million sterling in 1885.

AUSTRIA

In sixty years the production of iron has grown nearly tenfold, and Austria now holds sixth place. The production and consumption were approximately :—

Year	Tons		Lbs. per Inhabitant	Steel, Tons
	Production	Consumption		
1830 . .	80,000	100,000	9	...
1850 . .	140,000	160,000	12	...
1870 . .	400,000	430,000	28	22,000
1888 . .	760,000	770,000	45	280,000

Austria proper in 1888 produced 565,000, and Hungary 195,000, tons pig-iron.

ITALY

The production and consumption were approximately as follows :—

Year	Tons Iron		Lbs. per Inhabitant	Steel, Tons
	Production	Consumption		
1830 . .	10,000	20,000	3	...
1860 . .	40,000	75,000	8	...
1870 . .	50,000	100,000	9	...
1887 . .	70,000	290,000	22	20,000

A statement published in 1877 was as follows as to production :—

Year	Tons		Value, £		
	Bar Iron	Steel	Bar Iron	Steel	Total
1860 . . .	30,000	...	540,000	...	540,000
1870 . . .	38,000	1,000	660,000	25,000	685,000
1876 . . .	49,000	3,000	720,000	56,000	776,000

Italy pays £1,200,000 for imported pig and bar iron, which she converts into merchandise worth £3,200,000.

SPAIN

Although Spain possesses some of the best iron-fields in the world, her production is small, and she is forced to import 30 per cent. of what is used in her foundries. Meantime she exports 5 million tons yearly of iron ores. The production and consumption approximately were :—

Year	Tons		Lbs. per Inhabitant	Steel, Tons
	Production	Consumption		
1830 . .	20,000	40,000	8	...
1850 . .	40,000	80,000	13	...
1870 . .	70,000	150,000	23	...
1889 . .	230,000	300,000	37	30,000

Spain pays £700,000 a year for imported pig and bar iron : her manufactures of iron and steel are approximately worth £2,700,000.

SWEDEN

In the beginning of the nineteenth century Sweden produced as much iron as Germany, but her production now is only one-tenth of that of the latter country. She holds eighth rank, coming next after Russia. The production and consumption were approximately :—

Year	Tons Iron		Lbs. per Inhabitant	Steel, Tons
	Production	Consumption		
1812 . .	65,000	40,000	37	...
1830 . .	105,000	80,000	60	...
1850 . .	130,000	100,000	63	...
1870 . .	290,000	210,000	105	6,000
1889 . .	460,000	380,000	170	80,000

Sweden exports yearly 200,000 tons bar iron and 60,000 tons pig-iron. Her manufactures of iron and steel are about £4,200,000.

BELGIUM

In 1816 Mr. John Cockerill, from England, introduced the method of smelting with coke, and established at Seraing one of the finest ironworks in Europe. The industry advanced greatly after the separation from Holland in 1830, but its most striking progress has been in the last thirty years. Official returns since 1845 show as follows :—

Year	Blast Furnaces	Operatives	Output, Tons	
			Iron	Steel
1845 . . .	56	14,600	62,000	...
1850 . . .	65	11,600	73,000	...
1860 . . .	51	26,300	218,000	...
1870 . . .	48	41,200	523,000	4,000
1880 . . .	36	37,300	493,000	132,000
1887 . . .	29	34,100	534,000	216,000

The exports of bar and wrought iron were as follows :—

Year	Tons	Value, £	Year	Tons	Value, £
1860	63,000	440,000	1875	183,000	2,000,000
1865	118,000	800,000	1880	228,000	1,600,000
1870	220,000	1,400,000	1887	335,000	1,600,000

The iron and steel manufactures are worth about £10,600,000.

UNITED STATES

In 1620 a group of forty ironworkers arrived from Sussex, England, and commenced to make iron, but in 1662 a decree was issued to prohibit the importation of this metal, with the view to promote iron manufactures in the Colony. This prohibition was removed in 1682. The first regular foundry in North America was that established by Joseph Jenks in 1663, at Lynn, Massachusetts. There were six existing in the Colonies in 1750, when the British Parliament passed a law to close all mills, forges, or furnaces in the Colonies, the better to protect British manufactures. After the Independence this branch of industry made progress, but soon collapsed, owing to the influx of British merchandise. In 1833 Frederick Gersenhamer obtained a patent for using hot-blast with anthracite coal, and in 1835 produced the first iron so made.

The total output of iron, which was only 40,000 tons in 1796, rose to 287,000 in 1840, viz. :—

	Tons
Pennsylvania	98,000
Ohio	35,000
Other States	154,000
Total . . .	287,000

A table published in the latter year compared the production and the number of operatives with 1830 as follows :—

Year	Operatives	Tons Iron	Tons per Man
1830 . .	29,000	184,000	6.3
1840 . .	56,000	287,000	5.1

From this time the construction of railways, especially after the war of 1861–65, gave a great impetus to this industry, the production being as follows :—

Year	Tons
1850	564,000
1870	1,580,000

In 1873 there were 719 furnaces at work. In 1889 the output of pig-iron reached 7,600,000 tons, being second only to Great Britain.

The Census returns of foundries and ironworks showed thus :—

	1870	1880
Hands . . .	78,000	141,000
Wages, £ .	7,500,000	11,600,000
Manufactures, £ .	37,400,000	62,000,000

The production of pig-iron in 1888 and 1889 was as follows :—

	1888 Tons	1889 Tons
Pennsylvania .	3,200,000	3,730,000
Ohio . .	990,000	1,090,000
Other States .	2,300,000	2,780,000
Total .	6,490,000	7,600,000

The manufacture of steel dates from 1808, as follows :—

Year	Tons
1808	900
1850	2,000
1860	12,000
1870	64,000
1876	520,000
1889	3,390,000

At present the United States produce one-third the steel of the world. The make of steel in 1889 included 1,510,000 tons of rails.

The rivalry between Great Britain and the United States in iron and steel production is thus indicated by Mr. Swank :—

	Great Britain, Tons		United States, Tons	
	1882	1889	1882	1889
Pig-iron . .	8,580,000	8,250,000	4,620,000	7,605,000
Steel ingots .	1,670,000	2,140,000	1,510,000	2,930,000
Steel rails .	1,230,000	940,000	1,280,000	1,510,000

The production of steel of all descriptions in 1889 was 3,690,000 tons in Great Britain and 3,390,000 in the United States.

IRRIGATION

FRANCE

Only 260,000 acres irrigated, which yield crops worth £3 per acre more than ordinary.

ITALY

The canals in the Po valley irrigate 1,370,000 acres, which receive every day in summer 45 million tons of water, measured through a great number of little sluice-gates: the permanent right to an inch of water is worth from £500 to £800. The usual rent of these lands is £6 per acre per annum.

BELGIUM

Since 1859 an area of 160,000 acres of waste lands has been made valuable by irrigation, adjoining State canals.

SPAIN

Land unwatered may be rented at 5s. an acre, but the irrigated lands of Valencia, where the old canals and works of the Moors remain, readily rent at £5 per acre. The total area of irrigated lands is 2½ million acres.

ALGERIA

The most important work is the "barrage" at Habra, with a basin holding 30 million tons of water, the main wall being 110 feet high, 120 feet thick, and 1500 feet long. The distributory canals are 310 miles, irrigating 70,000 acres. It belongs to a French Company, and cost £160,000.

Y

EGYPT

During his reign of seventeen years, from 1863 to 1879, Ismael Pasha constructed 112 canals branching from the Nile, to irrigate 1,400,000 acres, with an aggregate length of 8400 miles, the cost amounting to about 12 millions sterling. The lands thus newly irrigated produce crops worth £10,600,000, or 22 per cent. of the total value of Egyptian crops. The actual length of Nile canals is 52,000 miles, the task of irrigation employing 476 steam-pumps, 107,000 Persian water-wheels, 150,000 men, and 60,000 animals, at an annual cost averaging 4s. per acre.

INDIA

The Ganges Canal irrigates 400,000 acres, is 880 miles long, having 902 bridges and 297 aqueducts, and cost £2,400,000. In the Madras Presidency irrigation is also carefully studied : there are 53,000 tank-reservoirs, 30,000 miles of dykes, the whole having cost 16 millions sterling, and producing a revenue of £1,500,000 per annum. The largest reservoir or artificial lake in the world is the great tank of Dhebar, Rajputana, which covers an area of 21 square miles. The masonry dam is 1000 feet long by 95 feet high, 50 feet wide at the base, and 15 feet at the top.

CYPRUS

The canals made by the Venetians had fallen to ruin under the Turks, but many of them have been restored by British engineer officers since 1878. Irrigated lands yield three times heavier crops than the rest of the island.

CALIFORNIA

Since 1870 there have been constructed 2000 miles of canals, irrigating more than 10 millions of acres.

SOUTH AMERICA

The Incas had a perfect network of canals irrigating the lands on the western slope of the Andes. Near Mendoza, at the eastern foot of the Andes, still exists the Zanjon or canal made by the Cacique Guaymallen, irrigating a tract of eighteen miles of country.

AUSTRALIA

The Melbourne Government has already spent £470,000, and proposes to spend two millions more on works of irrigation.

J.

JEWELLERY

Diamonds

Weight in Carats of Six Largest

Kohinoor	.	.	. 103	Austrian Kaiser	.	. 139
Star of Brazil	.	. 125	Russian Czar	.	. 193
Regent of France	.	. 136	Rajah of Borneo	.	. 367

The value of the above is not regulated by size, nor easy to estimate, but none of them is worth less than £100,000.

Scale of Value for Small Stones

	£		£
1 carat	. . . 8	5 carat	. . . 200
3 carat	. . . 72	10 carat	. . . 800

Cape diamonds are of inferior value ; one of the largest, the Stewart, found in November 1872, sold for £11,000, weighing 288 carats uncut. The Kimberley field, covering nine acres, has produced diamonds to the value of 15 millions sterling since 1871, the diggings being from 100 to 170 feet deep. The annual export of diamonds from the Cape is about 1400 lbs., worth over four millions, and the fields employ 2000 white and 22,000 coloured diggers. In 1889 the value of diamonds extracted was £4,300,000 sterling. The total product in eighteen years was approximately 46,000,000 carats, worth £56,000,000 sterling.

Emerald.—The ordinary value is as follows :—

Grains	£	Grains	£
5	. . . 5	15	. . . 50
10	. . . 20	24	. . . 100

Opal.—The Emperor of Austria has one for which he refused £50,000 : it weighs 17 oz.

Pearls.—The pearl-fishery of Ceylon in 1890 only lasted 22 days, and during that period 11,000,000 oysters were brought to the surface by fifty divers. They are paid by one-fourth of the number. This season the whole produce was sold at the rate of 24s. per 1000 shells. The Government received £20,000 as their share, and the divers £6400. The largest pearls are worth in Ceylon from £40 to £60, and in Europe they fetch three times the price or more.

JEWS

	1860	1880	Increase
Russia	2,025,000	2,621,000	596,000
Austria	1,048,000	1,375,000	327,000
Germany . . .	393,000	512,000	119,000
France	88,000	49,000	...
Holland . . .	63,000	78,000	15,000
Great Britain . .	45,000	51,000	6,000
Italy	33,000	35,000	2,000
Turkey, &c. . .	260,000	280,000	20,000
Europe	3,955,000	5,001,000	1,046,000
Morocco . . .	340,000	350,000	10,000
Tripoli . . .	160,000	170,000	10,000
Algeria	82,000	133,000	51,000
Egypt	7,000	8,000	1,000
America . . .	85,000	110,000	25,000
Asia	200,000	200,000	...
Total . .	4,829,000	5,972,000	1,143,000

The vital statistics of Jews in Germany compare with those of Christians as follows : —

Births		Jews per Cent.	Europeans per Cent.
Excess of male births	. .	16 ...	5
Illegitimate births	. .	2 ...	6
Still-births	. .	2½ ...	4½

	Marrying Age			
Age	Jews		Europeans	
	Males	Females	Males	Females
Under 20 .	2.2	23.5	1.8	12.1
20–30 . . .	66.4	58.5	62.6	65.6
30–40 . . .	17.4	9.8	25.3	16.2
40–50 . . .	7.4	5.4	6.2	4.6
Over 50 . .	6.6	2.8	4.1	1.5
Total .	100.0	100.0	100.0	100.0

RATIO OF DEATHS

Age	Jews		Christians, Both Sexes
	Males	Females	
Under 1 . . .	38.4	33.7	29.3
1–5	18.5	16.7	19.2
5–10 . . .	4.7	4.3	4.9
10–20 . . .	4.3	4.5	4.6
20–40 . . .	8.5	12.5	11.3
40–60 . . .	12.0	13.3	12.9
Over 60 . . .	13.6	15.0	17.8
Total . .	100.0	100.0	100.0

The life-value of Prussian Jews compares with that of Christians as follows :—

SURVIVAL OF 1000 PERSONS BORN

Age	Jews, Prussia	Christians	
		Prussia	England
5	593	639	751
10	535	620	727
15	514	610	714
20	482	602	699
30	432	562	650
40	364	506	587
50	305	438	506
60	237	345	398
70	153	206	253
80	62	80	108

JUTE

In 1828 India produced 18 tons of jute, valued at £62 sterling, say 70s. a ton; but it rapidly rose both in quality and price, the export from that country showing thus :—

Year	Tons	Value, £	Per Ton
			£ s. d.
1835	600	...	...
1850	19,500	89,000	4 10 0
1860	38,000	290,000	7 12 0
1870	120,000	1,520,000	12 13 0
1880	305,000	4,880,000	16 0 0
1890	501,000	6,500,000*	13 0 0

The cost of cultivation averages 16s. an acre, the yield half a ton per acre, worth £6.

There were in 1889 in India twenty-five factories, with 160,000 spindles, 8000 power-looms, and 61,000 operatives, consuming annually 190,000 tons of jute, and turning out 100 million sacks, of which California took 20 and China 15 millions.

Jute factories in the United Kingdom have increased as follows :—

		1870	1885
Number . . .		63	120
Spindles . .		115,000	264,000
Power-looms .		4,300	12,000
Operatives . .		18,000	42,000

* The nominal value was £8,600,000, taking the rupee at 24d.

The manufacture in the United Kingdom showed approximately thus :—

Year	Con-sumed, Tons	Make, Million Yards	Export, Million Yards	Export Yarn, Million Lbs.	Manu-factures, Value, £
1850	19,000	63	...	...	900,000
1860	38,000	126	...	...	1,900,000
1870	98,000	300	52	13	4,700,000
1880	178,000	560	183	17	7,200,000
1889	268,000	810	265	34	9,100,000

The output averages at present only £215 per operative yearly, against £260 in 1870, the price having fallen from 365d. to 216d. per 100 yards. The number of yards produced per operative is about 19,000 yards, or 11 miles yearly.

The jute manufacture since 1850 may be summed up approximately thus :—

Period	Great Britain	Other Coun-tries	Total	Value of Manufac-ture, Mil-lions £	Price of Cloth, £ per Mile
1851–60	500,000	100,000	600,000	17	29
1861–70	1,200,000	400,000	1,600,000	43	27
1871–80	2,500,000	1,500,000	4,000,000	96	24
1881–88	2,700,000	3,200,000	5,900,000	118	20
Total	6,900,000	5,200,000	12,100,000	274	23

The value of manufactured goods produced in thirty-eight years was shared approximately as follows :—

	Million £
Great Britain	160
India	21
Other countries	93
Total . . .	274

The profit of this industry to Great Britain appears thus :—

Period	Millions £ Sterling		
	Raw Jute	Manu-factured	Net Product
1851–60	2	14	12
1861–70	7	32	25
1871–80	20	60	40
1881–88	24	54	30
38 years	53	160	107

This industry enriched the United Kingdom by over three millions sterling per annum in the last thirty years, of which apparently about £1,500,000 a year went in wages. The above, moreover, does not include exported yarn, the total value of which in thirty-eight years amounted to five millions sterling, thus bringing up the total net product to 112 millions sterling.

K.

KANGAROO

These animals will soon be extinct, as the squatters kill them wholesale. The export of kangaroo skins from Melbourne was as follows :—

Year		No.	Value, £
1883	. . . .	20,000	1,500
1888	. . . .	260,000	54,000

Kangaroos can jump a fence 11 feet high.

KOUMISS

Extracted by the Tartars from mares' milk, a gallon of milk giving three ounces of Koumiss brandy.

KINGS

There are 22 kings or emperors. The number who have ruled in various countries since the battle of Hastings, A.D. 1066, has been as follows :—

	No.	Average Reign, Years		No.	Average Reign, Years
England . .	35	23	Spain . . .	32	26
France . . .	34	24	Denmark .	39	21
Germany . .	39	21	Sweden . .	53	15
Russia . . .	50	16	Turkey . .	35	17

The Turkish dynasty dates only from 1299. The average reign of the above 317 monarchs was just twenty years.

L.

LABOURER

Dr. Farr estimates the value of an agricultural labourer to the commonwealth as follows :—

Age	Value, £	Age	Value, £	Age	Value, £
10	. . . 117	30	. . . 241	55	. . . 138
15	. . . 192	35	. . . 228	60	. . . 97
20	. . . 234	40	. . . 212	65	. . . 46
25	. . . 246	50	. . . 168	70	. . . 0

These figures of Dr. Farr have been often called in question as being too high, but the best authorities in the United States and Australia set even a higher value on able-bodied immigrants.

LACE

This industry employs in Great Britain 9000 men and 41,000 women, who produce lace annually to the value of 6 millions sterling. It is stated that more than 500,000 women on the Continent make lace worth 30 millions yearly, or £60 each, but this seems a high average.

LAKES

The following table is merely intended as a comparison of some of the most remarkable lakes in the world :—

	Square Miles	Depth, Feet	Area Equal to
Superior . .	32,100	688	Ireland
Victoria Nyanza .	26,900	...	...
Aral . . .	23,300	731*	Holland
Huron . .	20,400	600	Greece
Baikal . .	14,800	580	Denmark
Michigan .	12,900	690	Belgium
Erie . .	9,600	84	Sardinia Island
Ontario . .	7,650	510	...
Ladoga . .	6,250	...	Wurtemburg
Onega . .	3,350	...	Corsica
Wenner . .	2,130	294*	Devonshire
Wetter . .	733	410	Oxfordshire
Constance . .	180	1,027*	Isle of Man
Neagh . .	153	42	Malta
Maggiore .	130	700	...
Zurich . .	40	600	St. Helena

* Maximum depth ; the rest show the average depth.

LAND

The following conspectus shows at a glance the distribution and tenure of land in various countries, the number of owners, the approximate value, the cultivated area, and other important features. The "data" do not correspond to any particular year, but represent the latest information :—

	Area, Millions of Acres			Number of Owners	Average Acres per Estate	Value of Land, Million £
	Cultivated	Uncultivated	Total			
U. Kingdom	48	30	78	180,000	390	1,544
France . .	90	41	131	3,226,000	32	2,688
Germany . .	65	68	133	2,436,000	37	1,815
Russia . .	345	899	1,244	11,336,000	31	1,507
Austria . .	73	80	153	6,150,000	20	1,371
Italy . . .	27	44	71	1,265,000	36	1,182
Spain . . .	22	99	121	596,000	95	984
Portugal . .	5	17	22	419,000	30	132
Sweden . .	12	89	101	194,000	300	240
Norway . .	3	74	77	75,000	200	100
Denmark .	7	2	9	71,000	115	217
Holland . .	5	3	8	154,000	45	314
Belgium . .	5	2	7	315,000	18	377
Greece . .	2	9	11	163,000	30	138
Europe . .	709	1,457	2,166	26,580,000	48	12,609
United States	205	2,086	2,291	4,005,000	134	2,560
Canada . .	16	1,902	1,918	408,000	120	282
Australia . .	12	1,846	1,858	168,000	380	535
Argentina .	7	770	777	...	...	111
Total .	949	8,061	9,010	31,161,000	70	16,097

Colbert in his letter to Louis XIV. estimated the value of land in France, England, and Holland in the seventeenth century (1660) as follows :—

	Value	Rental	Per Acre	
			Value	Rental
	£	£	s.	s.
France . .	122,000,000	15,000,000	24	3
England . .	135,000,000	8,500,000	90	6
Holland . .	46,000,000	4,000,000	180	15

UNITED KINGDOM

The rental of the three kingdoms has been at various dates as follows :—

A.D.	England	Scotland	Ireland	United Kingdom	Authority
	£	£	£	£	
1544	1,500,000	...	...	...	Haydn
1600	6,000,000	...	...	...	,,
1660	8,500,000	...	...	...	Colbert
1688	10,000,000	...	900,000	...	King, Petty
1729	...	...	2,025,000	...	Browne
1750	12,700,000	800,000	3,100,000	16,600,000	...
1776	16,000,000	1,100,000	5,340,000	22,440,000	Young
1800	22,500,000	2,100,000	8,000,000	32,600,000	{ M'Culloch, Newenham
1815	34,330,000	5,075,000	7,100,000	46,505,000	M'Culloch
1843	40,170,000	5,590,000	8,630,000	54,390,000	Official
1860	42,990,000	6,280,000	8,990,000	58,260,000	,,
1870	47,800,000	7,190,000	9,140,000	64,130,000	,,
1880	51,800,000	7,770,000	9,980,000	69,550,000	,,
1888	44,470,000	6,820,000	9,960,000	61,250,000	,,

Since 1880 the valuation of England has been reduced 14 per cent., that of Scotland 13 per cent., that of Ireland nothing. The Local Government Board estimated the real land rental of the three kingdoms in 1878 thus :—

	Rental, £	Extent, Acres	Number of Proprietors	Average Estate Acres	Average Estate Rental, £	Shillings per Acre
England	70,240,000	32,860,000	262,850	125	266	44
Scotland	12,900,000	18,920,000	19,225	980	670	14
Ireland	12,050,000	20,150,000	32,610	620	370	12
United Kingdom . .	95,190,000	71,930,000	314,685	230	310	26

If we exclude owners of less than ten acres, we find the landed property of the three kingdoms, according to the Local Government Report, is held thus :—

	10 to 100 Acres	Over 100	Total No. of Owners	Rental, £	Average, £
England . .	99,000	42,100	141,100	63,800,000	450
Scotland .	4,700	5,020	9,720	11,470,000	1,180
Ireland . .	11,200	14,500	25,700	11,550,000	450
U. Kingdom	114,900	61,620	176,520	86,820,000	495

ENGLAND

The estate-owners in England of more than one acre are as follows (Local Government Board Report) :—

Holding Acres	Number of Owners	Acres Owned	Annual Rental, £	Shillings per Acre	Percentage of Area
Under 50	194,620	2,230,000	12,950,000	116	7.0
50–100	25,840	1,790,000	4,300,000	48	5.4
100–500	32,320	6,830,000	13,680,000	40	20.8
Over 500	10,070	22,010,000	39,310,000	36	66.8
Total	262,850	32,860,000	70,240,000	44	100.0

SCOTLAND

Holding Acres	Number of Owners	Acres Owned	Annual Rental, £	Shillings per Acre	Percentage of Area
Under 50	12,940	110,000	2,270,000	413	0.6
50–100	1,210	90,000	380,000	84	0.5
100–500	2,370	560,000	1,680,000	60	2.9
Over 500	2,705	18,160,000	8,570,000	9	96.0
Total	19,225	18,920,000	12,900,000	14	100.0

IRELAND

Holding	Owners	Acres	Rental, £	s. p. Acre	Per Cent.
Under 50	14,600	224,000	980,000	88	1.1
50–100	3,500	250,000	310,000	25	1.2
100–500	8,010	1,956,000	1,770,000	18	9.7
Over 500	6,500	17,720,000	8,990,000	10	88.0
Total	32,610	20,150,000	12,050,000	12	100.0

UNITED KINGDOM

Holding	Owners	Acres	Rental, £	s. p. Acre	Per Cent.
Under 50	222,160	2,564,000	16,200,000	122	3.6
50–100	30,550	2,130,000	4,990,000	47	3.0
100–500	42,700	9,346,000	17,130,000	38	13.1
Over 500	19,275	57,890,000	56,870,000	20	80.3
Total	314,685	71,930,000	95,190,000	26	100.0

The number of farmers in the United Kingdom was :—

Holding Acres	England	Scotland	Ireland	United Kingdom	Percentage
Under 5 .	114,000	21,000	62,000	197,000	18.7
5–50 . .	200,000	33,000	365,000	598,000	57.2
50–100 .	55,000	10,000	56,000	121,000	11.5
100–500 .	79,000	15,000	31,000	125,000	11.9
Over 500 .	5,000	1,000	1,000	7,000	0.7
Total .	453,000	80,000	515,000	1,048,000	100.0

Acres	Area of Farms, Acres				Percentage
Under 50	4,100,000	700,000	7,800,000	12,600,000	26.5
50–100 .	3,900,000	700,000	4,400,000	9,000,000	18.8
Over 100	19,600,000	3,400,000	3,100,000	26,100,000	54.7
Total	27,600,000	4,800,000	15,300,000	47,700,000	100.0

The above refers only to the cultivated area. In all these tables properties or holdings of less than an acre are excluded.

In some parts of England rent has quadrupled in 120 years. For example, the farm of One Ash Grange, on the Duke of Devonshire's property, Derbyshire, has been let as follows :—

1769 at	.	.	. £190	1855 at	. . . £610
1788 ,,	.	.	. 242	1876 ,,	. . . 700
1810 ,,	.	.	. 440	1888 ,,	. . . 900

The average rental valuation of land in the three kingdoms was as follows :—

A.D.	Shillings per Acre				Cultivated Area, Acres
	England	Scotland	Ireland	United Kingdom	
1760	11	6	5	10	37,100,000
1776	14	8	9	11	38,600,000
1800	18	12	13	16	40,320,000
1815	28	25	15	24	42,500,000
1843	32	28	12	24	43,800,000
1860	34	30	12	25	44,000,000
1870	35	33	13	28	46,000,000
1880	36	34	14	28	47,600,000
1888	32	29	14	26	47,880,000

The official rental valuation in England in 1810 for various counties was :—

Shillings per Acre

Leicester	. . . 28		Lincoln	. . . 18
Somerset	. . . 27		Surrey	. . . 17
Worcester	. . . 24		Devonshire	. . . 16
Warwick	. . . 23		Cornwall	. . . 15
Lancashire	. . . 22		Monmouth	. . . 14
Stafford	. . . 21		Durham	. . . 9
Kent	. . . 20		Cardigan	. . . 6
Bedford	. . . 19			

In 120 years more than 10 million acres of waste land in the United Kingdom have been enclosed, viz. :—

Period	Acres	
	Quantity	Per Annum
1760–1800	3,221,000	81,000
1801–1829	3,380,000	116,000
1830–1869	2,217,000	55,000
1870–1879	1,687,000	169,000
Total . .	10,505,000	88,000

It is doubtful whether the reclaimed lands are now worth what they have cost.

IRELAND

According to a report quoted by Mr. Molinari in 1880 the estated property of Ireland was held thus :—

Proprietors	Number	Acres Owned	Assessed Rental £	Percentage of Area
Resident on estate	3,966	9,733,000	5,090,000	52.4
Resident in Dublin	4,465	4,362,000	2,130,000	23.2
Absentees . . .	1,623	4,514,000	2,140,000	24.4
Total . .	10,054	18,609,000	9,360,000	100.0

The above seems to exclude all estate-owners of less than 100 acres, the number of whom (as already shown) is 18,000. See preceding page.

As regards tenants, the number has been as follows :—

Holding Acres	1841	1851	1861	1871	1878
1–5 . . .	310,000	88,000	86,000	75,000	66,000
5–15 . . .	253,000	192,000	184,000	171,000	163,000
Over 15 . .	128,000	290,000	299,000	298,000	298,000
Total .	691,000	570,000	569,000	544,000	527,000

The amount of rental drawn by absentee landlords has been :—

Date	Rental of Ireland	Drawn by Absentees	Absentee Ratio	Authority
	£	£	Per Cent.	
1729	2,025,000	627,000	31	Browne, Prior
1776	5,340,000	1,610,000	30	Young
1880	9,360,000	2,140,000	23	Molinari

The progressive rise of rent in Ireland is shown in Dr. Todd's evidence (July 1890) at the House of Commons respecting a certain estate in that country :—

Year					Per Annum, £
1609 .	.	.	.	.	1,800
1635 .	.	.	.	.	2,200
1697 .	.	.	.	.	9,150
1758 .	.	.	.	.	20,000
1858 .	.	.	.	.	131,000
1882 .	.	.	.	.	160,000

The landed property of Ireland changed masters three times in 100 years,—first confiscation under Elizabeth, A.D. 1590–1600; second under Cromwell, 1650–52; third under William III., 1690–92. The following recent changes of tenure are remarkable :—

I. Encumbered Estates Court (established 1850).—Sold in thirty years down to 1880, estates covering 4,930,000 acres for £52,700,000, say £11 per acre, in 12,400 lots, averaging 400 acres each. The purchase-money represented 85 per cent. by Irish, 15 per cent. Scotch or English buyers.

II. Bright's Act.—From 1870 to 1880 the tenants bought 49,000 acres for £860,000, of which the Government advanced 60 per cent. (£516,000). Average price paid, £17 per acre.

III. Church Act.—From 1870 to 1885 about 6000 tenants bought their farms, covering —— acres, for £1,674,000, the Government advancing £1,200,000, say 75 per cent. Price paid was 22½ years' rental. Of the sums advanced by Government, only £6000 was due by the purchasers in 1888 (Official Report, November 1888).

IV. Gladstone's Act, August 1881.—In seven years ending August 1888 the Land Court altered the rents of 243,490 farms, viz. :—

					£
Old rent	.	.	.	.	3,852,000
New rent	.	.	.	.	3,094,000

This was a reduction of 20 per cent. There were also 61,300 cases pending inquiry.

V. The Ashbourne Act, passed in 1885, regarding which an official report in 1890 was as follows :—

Year	Farms Bought	Price, £	Sum Lent, £	Years of Rental	Net Rental, £
1886	2,426	1,095,000	1,065,000	18.0	61,000
1887	4,636	1,925,000	1,903,000	17.6	110,000
1888	4,384	1,776,000	1,750,000	17.0	104,000
1889	2,574	1,170,000	1,155,000	16.4	71,000
4 years	14,020	5,966,000	5,873,000	17.3	346,000

In four years the tenants were enabled to purchase nearly 3 per cent. of Ireland as measured by rental ; thus in 132 years the Ashbourne Act would settle the agrarian question.

FRANCE

The official valuation of lands (which appears high) gave the following summary in 1881 :—

Quality	Acres	Value per Acre, £	Value, Millions £
Orchards . . .	1,783,000	81	144
Vineyards . . .	5,445,000	44	239
Meadows . . .	6,170,000	55	340
Arable	41,319,000	36	1,488
Pasture, &c. . .	23,010,000	18	414
Forest	21,288,000	12	256
Waste	17,516,000	6	105
Total . .	116,531,000	26	2,986

The rise in the value of land from 1852 to 1881 appears in the official valuation thus :—

£ per Acre

	1852		1881
Arable . . .	24	...	36
Meadow . . .	36	...	55
Vineyards . .	32	...	44

According to the Government inquiry of 1815, France comprised 1,854,000 farms (exclusive of 1,952,000 under five acres), classified as follows :—

Average	Number	Area, Acres	Ratio of Area	Ratio of Holdings
10 . . .	930,000	8,750,000	8.1	50.2
20 . . .	259,000	5,900,000	5.5	14.1
30 . . .	259,000	7,450,000	7.0	13.9
55 . . .	218,000	11,920,000	11.1	11.7
150 . .	169,000	26,040,000	24.2	9.1
2200 . .	21,400	47,500,000	44.1	1.1
Total .	1,854,400	107,560,000	100.0	100.0

The number of Côtes Foncières and the probable number of owners above five acres was :—

Year	Côtes	Landowners
1826 . . .	10,300,000	1,300,000
1835 . . .	10,900,000	1,400,000
1851 . . .	12,400,000	1,500,000
1861 . . .	13,700,000	1,700,000
1871 . . .	13,800,000	1,700,000
1885 . . .	14,075,000	1,825,000

The returns for 1885 showed the owners of less than five acres to be 10,426,000 in number. Of the remainder, it is believed by French economists that the number of côtes is double that of actual owners, by reason of repetition, one person holding two or three properties. The real number of landowners, therefore, in 1885 was as follows :—

Acres	Côtes	Land Owners	Acres	Acres per Owner
5–15 . .	2,174,000	1,087,000	18,860,000	17
15–125. .	1,352,000	676,000	48,040,000	72
125–500 .	106,000	53,000	23,890,000	450
Over 500 .	18,000	9,000	20,050,000	2,200
Total .	3,650,000	1,825,000	110,840,000	60

The number of Côtes Foncières over 12 acres in 1862 was 1,411,000 by the Government returns, whereas the number over 15 acres in 1885 was 1,476,000, which shows a marked increase.

The tenure of land in 1862 and in 1873 was as follows:—

	Number		Acres Held in 1873	Ratio of Area in 1873	Ratio of Cultivation in 1873
	1862	1873			
Owners .	1,813,000	2,826,000	42,530,000	50.1	71.0
Tenants .	1,035,000	832,000	29,900,000	35.2	21.0
Metayers*	405,000	319,000	11,920,000	14.7	8.0
Total .	3,253,000	3,977,000	84,350,000	100.0	100.0

The farms cultivated by owners averaged 15 acres in extent, those of tenants and metayers 35 acres. In 1882 the area cultivated by metayer had declined, viz.:—

Acres

Tilled by owner	50,500,000
Tilled by tenant	22,800,000
Tilled by metayer . . .	11,100,000
Total . .	84,400,000

In eight years ending 1887 there were 39,300,000 acres sold in France, in lots averaging 4½ acres, that is, nearly five million acres yearly.

GERMANY

The German Empire comprises 5,276,000 farms, viz.:—

Cultivated by owner . . .	2,953,000
Cultivated by tenants . . .	829,000
Farms of mixed character . .	1,494,000
Total . .	5,276,000

It appears, therefore, that about 85 per cent. of the farms are cultivated wholly or in part by their owners, as compared with 71 per cent. in France.

* System by which landlord receives share of the crops instead of a fixed rent.

If we exclude all farms under 2½ acres,, we find the total in Germany reduced to 2,953,000, held as follows :—

Size, Acres	Number of Farms Held			Area, Acres			Ratio of Area
	By Owner	By Tenant	Total	Cultivated	Wood and Pasture	Total	
2½–12	1,613,000	107,000	1,720,000	10,600,000	2,100,000	12,700,000	12.9
12–50	911,000	16,000	927,000	22,900,000	5,800,000	28,700,000	29.3
50–125	234,000	6,000	240,000	17,900,000	4,800,000	22,700,000	23.2
Over 125	58,000	8,000	66,000	26,300,000	7,800,000	34,100,000	34.6
Total . .	2,816,000	137,000	2,953,000	77,700,000	20,500,000	98,200,000	100.0

The number of land-owners is of course less than that of farms, the returns for 1869 showing as follows :—

	Owners	Extent, Acres	Average, Acres
Prussia	1,033,000	49,000,000	48
Bavaria	456,000	11,000,000	25
Saxony	54,000	2,500,000	46
Wurtemburg . .	152,000	2,500,000	17
Baden	111,000	1,700,000	15
Darmstadt . . .	140,000	1,400,000	10
Small States . .	490,000	19,500,000	40
Total . .	2,436,000	87,600,000	36

PRUSSIA

The total area of Prussia is 86 million acres, but this includes 23 millions of mountain and forest. The tenure in 1869 was as follows :—

Held by	Number of Estates	Acres	Average, Acres
Crown . .	...	11,200,000	...
Nobles . .	22,470	21,200,000	950
Farmers . .	1,503,000	44,800,000	30
Cottiers . .	1,087,000	3,100,000	3
Total .	2,612,470	80,300,000	26

In 1859 the nobles held 37,900,000 acres, but in the ensuing ten years their possessions were reduced by 16,700,000 acres, broken up into farms for the peasantry. The farmers alluded to in the above table, excluding princes and cottiers, held their land thus :—

Estate of, Acres	Number	Acres	Average
5–20 . . .	1,100,000	11,000,000	10
20–200 . .	390,000	28,000,000	72
Over 200 . .	13,000	6,000,000	460
Total .	1,503,000	45,000,000	30

The owners, as already shown, numbering 1,033,000, it appears that for two owners there are three estates.

In Saxony the Crown owns 1,077,000 acres, and the rest is held thus :—

By	Number	Acres	Average
Nobles . .	440	490,000	1,100
Farmers . .	53,000	1,440,000	27
Cottiers . .	33,000	160,000	5
Total .	86,440	2,090,000	24

In Bavaria the Crown owns 3,430,000 acres, and the rest is held thus :—

By	Number	Acres	Average
Nobles . .	1,100	400,000	370
Farmers . .	226,000	11,700,000	50
Cottiers . .	290,000	1,500,000	5
Total .	517,100	13,600,000	26

In Wurtemburg the Crown owns 1,100,000 acres, and the rest is held as follows :—

By	Number	Acres	Average
Nobles . .	718	650,000	840
Farmers . .	85,000	1,900,000	22
Cottiers . .	246,000	750,000	3
Total .	331,718	3,300,000	10

The Stein law transferred nearly the half of Germany from the nobles to the peasantry. The nobles received Consols equal to eighteen years' rental of the lands taken from them. The peasants were compelled to pay a land-tax equal to 5 per cent. during forty-seven years, the land to be free to them after that period.

RUSSIA

Down to 1860 the land was almost equally held by the Crown and the nobles, the former possessing 26,200,000 serfs, the latter 21,800,000, by whom the soil was cultivated. Crown-serfs were in reality tenants, who paid 6d. an acre yearly rent, the farm of each family averaging 35 acres. They were emancipated in 1861, receiving their lands in fee on condition of paying 12s. a year for each male serf (three usually going to a family) during forty years. The other serfs were also tenants, although bought and sold like cattle, each family holding a farm of about 30 acres, subject to a rent of £6, or else the obligation to work two days each week for their masters. Lavish expenditure had so much encumbered the estates of nobles that in 1859 they had mortgaged 7,107,000 serfs and 102 million acres of land for sums in the aggregate reaching 60 millions sterling.

Between 1861 and 1870 the Government bought up from the nobles 40,954 estates, covering 35,000,000 acres, at an average cost of 35s. an acre, the Crown paying five-sixths, the serfs one-sixth of the amount, which was £61,100,000. The assessment, however, was made according to the number of serfs, the owners receiving £3 per head for 20,700,000 ; but the option was left to the serfs of receiving "beggar lots" of 10 acres free, in which case the noble received no indemnity. About 610,000 families preferred these lots, which they received free of conditions, the lands thus ceded to them covering 6,440,000 acres. The rest received farms of about 30 acres each, subject to a Crown-rent of 2s. an acre for forty-nine years.

In 1870 the arable land was held as follows :—

Owners					Acres
Nobles .	.	.	.	.	83,500,000
Peasants .	.	.	.	.	88,700,000
Crown, merchants, &c.	.	.		.	133,000,000
Total	.	305,000,000			

Strebinsky's report in 1879 showed that 19,700,000 male serfs (6,600,000 families) possessed 68 million dessiatines or 186 million acres, that is, an average of 27 acres per family. He made a catastral survey of eight provinces, viz., Koursk, Tula, Voroneja, Tambow, Penza, Oral, Riazan, and Kalonga, with an acreage of 142,600 square miles, say 91 million acres, and a population of 13 millions.

The tenure of the eight provinces was as follows :—

	Acres	Value, £	Average Farm, Acres
1,770,000 peasant families . . .	49,740,000	158,300,000	28
24,740 nobles . . .	25,100,000	59,200,000	1,020
10,870 citizens, &c. .	4,070,000	8,900,000	370
Crown-lands, &c. . .	12,090,000	...	...
Total . .	91,000,000	226,400,000	430

The aggregate value of 78 million acres was 226½ millions sterling, a fraction under £3 per acre ; the average was 45s. for lands held by citizens, 48s. for that of nobles, and 64s. an acre for what is held by peasants.

The proportions of land under crops in the estates of nobles and peasants were (1879) :—

| Owners | Acres | | | Percentage under Crops |
	Under Crops	Pasture and Forest	Total	
Peasants . .	38,400,000	11,040,000	49,440,000	77
Nobles and citizens	21,200,000	7,970,000	29,170,000	73
Total .	59,600,000	19,010,000	78,610,000	75

In the said eight provinces no less than 96 per cent. of the land held by peasants was in communes or villages. There were 26,456 villages, with 1,893,000 houses and 1,713,000 families, averaging 72 houses per village, with 447 inhabitants, the aggregate population being 11,840,000, of which 5,830,000 were males; the communal lands being

valued at 154 millions sterling, and covering an area of 47,800,000 acres, and the houses valued at £18,000,000, say £11 each. There were also 57,000 peasant proprietors, holding in their own right an aggregate area of 1,930,000 acres, an average of 35 acres each, valued at £4,300,000. Strebinsky also found that agriculture prevailed most where the population per square mile was highest, viz. :—

Section	Area, Square Miles	Population per Square Mile	Area under Crops, Acres	Cultivated Ratio
				Per Cent.
First . . .	54,000	112	27,600,000	80
Second . .	65,000	81	26,900,000	65
Third . . .	23,000	63	5,100,000	35
Total .	142,000	90	59,600,000	67

In 1878, according to Strebinsky, the tenure of all descriptions of land was as follows :—

| | Millions of Acres | | | | Ratio | | | |
	Arable	Pasture and Waste	Forest	Total	Arable	Pasture and Waste	Forest	Total
Crown	5	94	180	279	1.5	21.8	37.1	22.4
Peasants	115	50	21	186	35.2	11.6	4.3	15.0
Nobles, &c. . . .	206	289	284	779	63.3	66.6	58.6	62.6
Total . . .	326	433	485	1,244	100.0	100.0	100.0	100.0

The character of the land in possession of the three classes appears in the following table :—

	Crown	Peasants	Nobles,&c.	Total
Arable . .	1.7	61.5	26.4	26.3
Pasture, &c.	33.6	36.8	37.1	35.0
Forest . .	64.7	11.7	36.5	38.7
Total .	100.0	100.0	100.0	100.0

Of the area comprised under the item " pasture and waste " 201 million acres are considered worthless.

AUSTRIA

Down to 1849 the tenure of land was similar to that in Russia, the nobles of Bohemia and Hungary holding vast estates, with sometimes as many as 10,000 serfs. Each serf had to work two days a week for his master, besides giving him 11 per cent. of all products in lieu of rent. In 1819 the number of serfs was 7,000,000, of whom 1,427,000 were male adults. In 1832 the Bohemian nobles resident at Vienna possessed lands valued at 45 millions sterling.

The largest estates in Austria proper are the following:—

Of	Acres
Prince Schwarzenburg . . .	510,000
Prince Lichtenstein . . .	460,000
Archduke Albert . . .	305,000

There are in Bohemia 63 nobles holding estates, none of which is less than 12,000 acres. The Grand-Duchy of Austria counts 292 nobles and squires holding between them 2,900,000 acres. The proportions of land still held by this class in 1888 were :—

In	Acres	Of which under Forest
Bohemia . . .	4,300,000	2,800,000
Duchy of Austria .	1,600,000	1,100,000
Styria . . .	1,100,000	900,000
Galitzia . . .	7,500,000	4,200,000
Tyrol . . .	700,000	600,000
Moravia . . .	2,100,000	1,200,000
Other provinces .	3,300,000	2,500,000

The emancipation law of 1849 changed the ownership of one-half the Empire. According to an official return in 1869, the peasant properties in Austria proper covered 25 million acres, in farms averaging 17 acres, viz.:—

Province	Peasant Properties	Area of Same, Acres	Average Estate, Acres	Total Area of Province, Acres	Ratio held by Peasants, per Cent.
Gd.-Duchy of Austria	189,000	3,020,000	16	7,700,000	40
Styria . .	134,000	1,240,000	9	5,600,000	22
Bohemia .	199,000	5,470,000	27	12,800,000	43
Galitzia . .	496,000	8,440,000	17	19,200,000	44
Tyrol. . .	113,000	890,000	8	7,000,000	12
Moravia. .	98,000	2,720,000	28	5,500,000	49
Dalmatia .	47,000	1,450,000	31	5,000,000	29
Other provinces	231,000	1,950,000	8	13,200,000	15
Total .	1,507,000	25,180,000	17	76,000,000	33

The tenure of Hungary and Transylvania in 1880 was as follows :—

| Holding Acres | Number of Owners | |
	Hungary	Transylvania
7 to 42	1,815,700	532,900
42 to 280	91,100	27,900
Over 280	16,030	2,650
Total . .	1,922,830	563,450

The whole Empire counts 6,150,000 landowners, viz.:—

Class	Number	Land-Tax
Peasants . . .	4,673,000	Under £4
Farmers . . .	1,259,000	£4 to £20
Gentry . . .	162,200	£20 to £40
Nobles . . .	56,500	Over £40

ITALY

The tenure of land in the whole kingdom is as follows (1870) :—

Province	Number of Farms held by				Average Size of Farms, Acres
	Proprietors	Tenants	Metayer	Total	
Piedmont . .	608,000	25,000	81,000	714,000	14
Lombardy . .	160,000	53,000	236,000	449,000	11
Parma and Modena }	69,000	17,000	102,000	188,000	15
Tuscany . .	56,000	10,000	227,000	293,000	17
Papal States .	80,000	3,000	573,000	656,000	8
Naples . . .	224,000	194,000	24,000	442,000	42
Sicily . . .	52,000	8,000	5,000	65,000	90
Island of Sardinia . . }	16,000	...	...	16,000	360
Total .	1,265,000	310,000	1,248,000	2,823,000	25

The total is made up thus :—

Class	Number	Farms, Acres	Average, Acres
Proprietors . .	1,265,000	33,000,000	26
Metayers . . .	1,248,000	18,000,000	15
Tenants . . .	310,000	20,000,000	66
Total . .	2,823,000	71,000,000	25

The various quality and value of the land in different parts of Italy are shown in the following official table of 1882 :—

Province	Area, Acres	Rental Value, Shillings per Acre	Price per Acre, £	Value, Millions £
Sardinia . .	9,840,000	15	26.1	260
Lombardy . .	4,800,000	22	37.4	180
Parma . .	1,280,000	13	22.1	28
Modena . .	1,580,000	15	25.2	39
Papal States .	10,840,000	7	11.0	117
Tuscany . .	5,020,000	10	18.3	92
Naples . .	18,740,000	11	19.0	356
Sicily . . .	6,170,000	11	18.8	116
Total .	58,270,000	13	22.1	1,188

SWITZERLAND

The land rental in 1880 was 191 million francs, or £7,600,000 sterling per annum. This would indicate a selling value of 228 millions sterling, or nearly double my estimate at page 37, which was evidently too low.

SPAIN

The report of the Cortes in 1808 was as follows :—

Estates of		Acres
Crown, churches, and hospitals	. .	10,000,000
Nobles and grandees		30,500,000
Citizens and peasants		19,500,000
Mountain and waste		60,900,000
Total . . .		120,900,000

The *Registro Catastral* for 1877 gives the total number of landowners (exclusive of urban house-owners) as 596,000, whose estates covered 65 million acres, averaging 110 acres each. There were but 3900 whose rent-roll reached £400 a year.

PORTUGAL

The kingdom comprises 559,000 farms by official report, viz. :—

Class	Number	Area, Acres	Average Farm, Acres
Nobles . .	62,000	12,450,000	200
Proprietors . .	357,000	5,950,000	17
Tenants . .	140,000	2,800,000	20
Total .	559,000	21,200,000	38

SWEDEN

In 1810 the kingdom was held by 1200 noblemen, who owned 65,300 farms let to tenants ; each farm covered a quarter of a "mantal," or 400 acres. Between 1818 and 1840 the peasants bought from the nobles 16 million acres, at an average price of 1s. 5d. per acre. In 1876 the tenure was as follows :—

	Number	Millions of Acres			Average Farm, Acres
		Cultivated	Forest, &c.	Total	
Landowners	194,000	10	60	70	360
Tenants . .	40,000	2	14	16	400
Crown . .	...	...	9	9	...
Total .	234,000	12	83	95	370

Each farm averages 18 acres under crops, 32 meadow, and the remainder forest or waste. The uncultivated portion of the kingdom, as shown above, covers 83 million acres, of which (according to Government Report of 1885) the forests comprise 45 million acres, the remaining 38 millions being mountain waste. The landowners comprise two classes, viz. :—

Class	No.	Area, Acres	Average Area
Nobles . . .	2,650	38,000,000	14,000
Freeholders . .	191,000	48,000,000	250

The latter class includes 10,000 forest-owners, devoted to felling timber.

NORWAY

The number of farms in 1870 was 110,000, of which 75,000 were cultivated by their owners, 35,000 by tenants. An ordinary farm of 300 acres may be rented at £50 a year, or purchased for £1000 sterling, comprising about 30 acres cultivated, 180 of forest, and 90 acres pasture.

DENMARK

In 1801 the kingdom belonged to 614 nobles, who possessed until 1788 the right to buy and sell the tenantry the same as cattle. In 1840 the tenants had bought from the landlords 3,500,000 acres, that is, half the kingdom, at prices averaging £6 per acre, representing a gross value of 21 millions sterling. The tenure of land in 1870 was as follows :—

	Number	Acres	Average Farm, Acres
Nobles . .	550	1,380,000	2,500
Freeholders .	70,300	4,560,000	65
Huusmen . .	137,000	570,000	4
Total .	207,850	6,510,000	32

HOLLAND

There are 100,000 farms, of about 80 acres each, cultivated by their owners. The province of Grœningen has some tenant-farmers called *meejers*. The landlord can never raise the rent nor disturb the tenant.

BELGIUM

Excluding holdings of less than 2½ acres, the tenure of land has been :—

Acres	Number of Holdings			Holdings in 1880		
	1846	1866	1880	Cultivated by Owners	By Tenants	Total
2½–12	166,000	220,000	226,000	152,000	74,000	226,000
12–50	69,000	82,000	74,000	51,000	23,000	74,000
Over 50	19,000	22,000	15,000	8,000	7,000	15.000
Total . .	254,000	324,000	315,000	211,000	104,000	315,000

In 1866, according to Consul Grattan's report, only 34 per cent. of the land was cultivated by proprietors; in 1880, by the official returns, the proportion was 60 per cent.

GREECE

In 1836 the State sold farm-lots of 30 acres each to a large number of agricultural families at 47s. per acre, say £70 per farm. In 1862 there were 147,500 peasant proprietors, who held 5,600,000 acres, an average of 38 acres, one-third being under crops ; also 16,100 landed gentry with large farms, who usually let their lands to tenants at 22s. per acre. The area of the kingdom was as follows :—

	Acres
Under crops	1,920,000
Capable of cultivation . .	3,700,000
Woods	1,440,000
Mountain and pasture . .	4,700,000
Total . .	11,760,000

ALGERIA

The land grants ceded to settlers were :—

	Acres
1840–70	2,110,000
1871–80	1,120,000
Total .	3,230,000

The tenure is described at p. 40. Only 4 per cent. of the landed area is held by European settlers, the Arabs holding 52 per cent. in farms of 100 acres per family, and the remainder (44 per cent.) being under forest or Crown-lands.

UNITED STATES

The area of the United States and the portion under cultivation appear as follows :—

Date	Total Area, Millions of Acres	Under Farms, Millions Acres	Improved, Million Acres	Ratio under Farms, per Cent.	Ratio of Improved, per Cent.
1776	269	80	30	30	11
1810	1,018	164	64	16	6
1850	1,902	293	113	16	6
1860	2,291	407	163	18	7
1870	2,291	410	190	18	8
1880	2,291	534	285	23	12
1888	2,291	...	356	...	15

The above are official returns except for 1888 (see fourth paragraph on p. 43, *Agriculture*), and estimate of farms in 1776 based on Census of 1790.

Sales of public lands in United States were as follows :—

Period	Acres	Amount Received, £	Annual Average Acres Sold
1787–1810 . . .	4,700,000	1,800,000	200,000
1811–20 . . .	15,300,000	8,600,000	1,530,000
1821–30 . . .	10,100,000	2,800,000	1,010,000
1831–40 . . .	62,300,000	14,100,000	6,230,000
1841–60 . . .	68,500,000	12,700,000	3,430,000
1861–80 . . .	94,100,000	9,500,000	4,710,000
Total . .	255,000,000	49,500,000	2,700,000
1881–88 . . .	99,400,000	...	12,400,000
Grand total .	354,400,000	...	3,500,000

The sales of lands during ten years ending 1889 showed thus :—

	Acres		Acres
Dakota . . .	41,300,000	Minnesota . .	9,000,000
Kansas . . .	23,200,000	Florida . . .	7,300,000
Nebraska . .	21,000,000	Montana . . .	6,700,000
Washington .	12,900,000	Louisiana . . .	4,300,000
California . .	11,400,000	Various . . .	39,500,000
Colorado . .	10,900,000	Total .	187,500,000

The disposal of public lands in 102 years was approximately as follows :—

	Millions of Acres		
	1787–1860	1861–1888	Total
Sold	154	68	222
School grants. .	68	9	77
Railway grants .	26	166	192
Military grants .	44	18	62
Homestead grants	...	125	125
Sundry grants .	45	18	63
Total . .	337	404	741

In this last table Homestead grants are distinguished, but in the preceding one they are included among lands sold. In eight years ending 1887 the lands taken up by settlers comprised 124 million acres of Government lands and 18 millions belonging to railway companies, in all averaging 18 million acres yearly, say 120,000 farms of 150 acres each. The Homestead Law of 1862 has had a powerful influence in promoting agriculture, the area of improved lands being now apparently 356 million acres against 163 millions in 1860, an increase of 118 per cent., the area newly improved each year averaging 7,100,000 acres. By this law any immigrant family can obtain a farm-lot of 160 acres, on condition of five years occupation, without other cost than £3 for the title-deeds. From 1862 to 1886 no fewer than 690,000 families received farm-lots of this kind, covering 111 million acres, or one-fifth of the total area under farms.

According to the agricultural product of 1886 for the Union, the average for these Homestead farms would be products of an annual value of 155 millions sterling, or £220 per family, and the farms would represent a capital value of 816 millions sterling, or nearly £1200 per farm. Compared with the total earnings of the nation, these

Homestead farmers appear to earn almost 8 per cent., and the value of their farms and stock stands for 7 per cent. of the aggregate wealth of the United States.

The number and area of farms in the great divisions of the country, according to Census reports, were as follows :—

States	Number of Farms				Millions of Acres			
	1850	1860	1870	1880	1850	1860	1870	1880
New England	167,000	185,000	182,000	207,000	18	20	21	22
Middle	351,000	413,000	456,000	539,000	43	47	49	53
Southern	488,000	640,000	849,000	1,481,000	165	220	185	227
Western	444,000	716,000	1,167,000	1,778,000	67	120	155	232
Total	1,450,000	1,954,000	2,654,000	4,005,000	293	407	410	534

The proportion of farms over 100 acres is increasing :—

Acres	Number of Farms			Ratio		
	1860	1870	1880	1860	1870	1880
Under 20	306,000	467,000	390,000	15.0	17.6	9.8
20–50	617,000	848,000	781,000	30.1	32.0	19.5
50–100	609,000	754,000	1,033,000	29.8	28.4	25.7
100–500	487,000	565,000	1,696,000	23.9	21.3	42.4
Over 500	25,000	20,000	105,000	1.2	0.7	2.6
Total	2,844,000	2,654,000	4,005,000	100.0	100.0	100.0

The size of farms in the Union is, however, diminishing, as appears from the following Census reports, viz. :—

Census	Number of Farms	Area, Acres	Average Acres per Farm
1850	1,450,000	293,000,000	202
1860	2,044,000	407,000,000	200
1870	2,654,000	410,000,000	154
1880	4,005,000	534,000,000	134

It may be noted that farms over 100 acres constituted only 22 per cent. of the total in 1870, and rose to 45 per cent. in 1880.

Although most of the farms are cultivated by the owners, the three forms of tenure known in France and Italy exist in the United States, namely, owners, tenants, and "metayers," the last-mentioned giving the landlord half or other portion of the crops in lieu of rent. The Census of 1880 showed as follows :—

Farms Held by	New England	Middle States	Southern	Western	Total
Proprietors	190,000	510,000	690,000	1,594,000	2,984,000
Tenants	10,000	56,000	141,000	115,000	322,000
Metayers	7,000	88,000	306,000	302,000	703,000
Total	207,000	654,000	1,137,000	2,011,000	4,009,000

The proportion of these holdings is shown as follows :—

Held by	New England	Middle States	Southern	Western	Total
Proprietors	91.8	78.0	60.6	79.2	74.5
Tenants	4.8	8.5	12.4	5.7	8.0
Metayers	3.4	13.5	27.0	15.1	17.5
Total	100.0	100.0	100.0	100.0	100.0

It will be observed that the metayer or share system is twice as common as that of tenants paying rent in money. The above table refers merely to the number of farms.

The classification according to size of farms in 1880 was :—

Acres	Number of Farms held by			Total
	Owner	Tenant	Metayer	
Under 10	88,000	24,000	27,000	139,000
10–50	583,000	138,000	314,000	1,035,000
50–100	805,000	70,000	159,000	1,034,000
100–500	1,416,000	85,000	196,000	1,697,000
Over 500	92,000	5,000	7,000	104,000
Total	2,984,000	322,000	703,000	4,009,000

The value of land per acre is highest in New Jersey, the Agricultural Report for 1888 showing the following table of averages :—

State	Dollars per Acre	State	Dollars per Acre
New Jersey	65	Vermont	36
Massachusetts	50	Maryland	32
Ohio	46	Illinois	32
New York	44	Wisconsin	23

In some of the Western States it is less than five dollars or £1 sterling per acre.

The following table shows the areas of lands improved and unimproved, the number of hands engaged in agriculture, and the value of the farms :—

States	Millions of Acres							
	Improved				Unimproved			
	1850	1860	1870	1880	1850	1860	1870	1880
New England	11	12	12	13	7	8	8	8
Middle	26	30	33	37	16	16	16	15
Southern	49	65	58	82	117	155	126	147
Western	27	56	87	153	40	65	70	79
Total	113	163	190	285	180	244	220	249

States	Hands Employed			Value of Farms, Millions £			
	1860	1870	1880	1850	1860	1870	1880
New England . . .	293,000	316,000	301,000	77	99	107	121
Middle	721,000	793,000	847,000	248	380	508	506
Southern	860,000	2,669,000	3,626,000	198	445	253	347
Western	1,346,000	2,144,000	2,896,000	158	458	818	1,148
Total . .	3,220,000	5,922,000	7,670,000	681	1,382	1,686	2,122

In the above table of "hands employed" are omitted for 1860 the able-bodied slaves of the Southern States. Assuming that one-half of such slaves were engaged in agriculture (say 1,122,000), the number of persons so employed in 1860 would be 4,342,000 for the whole Union, and 1,982,000 for the Southern States. The value of farms (without live-stock, crops, or implements) was as follows to the number of hands engaged in agriculture :—

							Per Head
1860	.	.	.	.	.	.	£318
1870	.	.	.	.	.	.	286
1880	.	.	.	.	.	.	276

The ratio of improved acres to the number of hands engaged was :—

States	Acres Improved per Head		
	1860	1870	1880
New England . .	41	38	43
Middle	41	41	43
Southern . . .	33	22	23
Western . . .	42	41	53
Average . .	36	32	39

It appears that agricultural skill has made most progress in the Western States, where three men in 1880 cultivated as much land as four in 1870.

CANADA

At the beginning of the present century agriculture was in the hands of the old French "*habitans*," who had a chain of farms 400 miles long on the banks of the St. Lawrence. These farms comprised, besides pastures, about 500,000 acres under crops, the quantity of grain produced being over 5 million bushels. According to a statement published in 1830, the average annual export of wheat to England since 1805 had been a trifle over one million bushels. Free grants of 200-acre farms were given by the British Government to military and other settlers down to 1826, on condition of building a hut and barn (cost £72) and getting four acres under crops. In 1826 these land grants were abolished, and farm lots were sold by auction at prices payable in four annual instalments without interest, the average for backwood lands being 5s. an acre.

A rush of settlers ensued. In 1834 the area covered by farms in the colony was 12,640,000 acres, of which 4,910,000 were cultivated. In 1842 Upper Canada, now called Ontario, counted 100,000 agricultural families, who had under tillage an area of 1,928,000 acres, and in 1852 there were 190,000 families, with 3,698,000 acres under plough. The grain crop of Ontario and Quebec in 1852 exceeded 45 million bushels.

In 1870 the Government of Canada passed a Homestead Law similar to that of the United States, granting farm lots of 200 acres to each head of a family and 100 to each male adult free, on condition of building a log-hut not less than 16 × 20 feet, cultivating 15 acres in every 100, and residing six months in each year during five years on the farm : these grants to be limited to Manitoba. In all other parts of Canada public lands cost about 4s. an acre. The usual cost of felling timber to clear the land is £3 an acre.

In 1874 Canada proper, that is, Ontario and Quebec, had 368,000 farms covering an area of 34 million acres, the Government having still 167 million acres of public lands undisposed of. The tenure of the said farms was as follows :—

Acres	Number of Farms	Area, Acres
Under 10	40,300	250,000
10-100	220,700	12,000,000
Over 100	107,400	22,000,000
Total . .	368,400	34,250,000

Of the above farms, 322,400 were cultivated by their owners, and 44,000 by tenants. The average size of each farm was 93 acres. The returns for 1881 showed 588,970 farms, against 57,890 in 1831 ; the area under farms in 1881 was 67,650,000 acres, that is, an average of 115 acres, against 134 in the United States. The increase of grain from 1874 to 1886 was 102 per cent.; of cattle, 35 per cent.

AUSTRALIA

Farming land first came into use near Sydney about 1790. It was not until 1813 that two farmers crossed the Blue Mountains, from which time squatters began to settle on Government lands. Some obtained free grants, others a squatter's privilege for lots of 6400 acres at a nominal rent of £10 a year. In 1831 free grants were abolished, the British Government fixing the price at 5s. an acre, which was raised to 12s. in 1838, and to 20s. in 1842. Between 1831 and 1842 the Government sold two million acres, the half of the money so obtained being given as a bonus to shipowners to bring out settlers from England. In 1850 Mr. Palmer wrote, " There are men who landed here without a guinea who have farms of 20,000 acres or more, stocked with 4000 cattle or 40,000 sheep."

In 1887 the lands sold and those unalienated in the seven colonies were :—

Colony	Millions of Acres			Percentage of Lands Sold
	Sold	Undisposed of	Total Area	
New South Wales .	42	154	196	21
Victoria	15	42	57	26
South Australia .	9	234	243	4
Western Australia .	2	676	678	...
Queensland . . .	9	419	428	2
Tasmania . . .	5	11	16	30
New Zealand . .	19	48	67	29
Total . .	101	1,584	1,685	6

The sales in the several colonies were as follows :—

	Acres, Freehold			Price, £	Shillings per Acre
	1831–75	1876–87	Total		
New South Wales . . .	13,600,000	28,500,000	42,100,000	42,000,000	20
Victoria	10,400,000	4,800,000	15,200,000	23,300,000	31
South Australia . . .	5,600,000	3,800,000	9,400,000	10,000,000	23
Western Australia . . .	1,500,000	400,000	1,900,000	1,000,000	10
Queensland . . .	1,800,000	7,200,000	9,000,000	5,800,000	13
Tasmania	4,000,000	600,000	4,600,000	4,000,000	18
New Zealand . . .	13,600,000	5,300,000	18,900,000	12,000,000	12
Total .	50,500,000	50,600,000	101,100,000	98,100,000	19

The sums received for lands in New South Wales, South Australia, Western Australia, Tasmania, and New Zealand are not known precisely. The above are estimates based on the ordinary prices.

The number of landowners and of squatters in 1880, and the lands held by them, were as follows :—

	Number of		Acres		Acres to Average Farm	
	Landowners	Squatters	Freehold	Sheep Runs	Freehold	Sheep Run
New South Wales . .	39,900	4,330	25,500,000	133,200,000	634	30,700
Victoria . . .	49,600	612	14,800,000	14,300,000	321	23,300
South Australia . .	31,000	1,472	9,200,000	115,000,000	296	78,000
Western Australia . .	1,800	4,500	1,700,000	24,000,000	950	5,300
Queensland . . .	9,500	6,600	4,600,000	239,000,000	478	36,000
Tasmania . . .	12,000	500	4,200,000	1,800,000	353	3,500
New Zealand . . .	24,100	997	4,100,000	12,100,000	167	12,050
Total . .	167,900	19,011	64,100,000	539,400,000	384	28,300

The average freehold farm in 1880 was 384 acres, against 93 in Canada and 134 in the United States. The area of freehold farms in 1887, as shown in preceding table, was 101 million acres.
The sales of land were as follows :—

Period	Acres Sold	Acres per Annum
1831–42 . .	2,100,000	200,000
1843–75 . .	48,400,000	1,450,000
1876–87 . .	50,600,000	4,220,000

The number of freehold landowners in 1880 was equal to 5 per cent. of the population, against 8 per cent. in the United States and 9 per cent. in Canada.

CAPE COLONY

When this colony was taken from the Dutch in 1806, it comprised 10,000 families, mostly following pastoral pursuits. In 1826 a small Scotch colony was sent out by the British Government.
The area is 212,000 square miles, or 135 million acres, viz. :—

	Acres	Per Annum
Sold from 1806 to 1875 .	67,400,000	960,000
„ „ 1876 to 1887 .	22,200,000	1,850,000
Still unsold . . .	45,400,000	...
Total .	135,000,000	...

The nominal price was 1s. per acre, but the amount received has not averaged more than 6d. Sheep farms vary from 3000 to 10,000 acres, being much smaller than in Australia or the Argentine Republic. The number of farms is unknown, probably about 40,000, averaging 2200 acres each.

INDIA

The tenure of land is as follows :—

	Number	Annual Payment to Government, £
Nobles . .	130,000	13,000,000
Farmers . .	724,000	7,300,000
Ryots . .	9,750,000	970,000
Total .	10,604,000	21,270,000

OTHER COLONIAL CROWN-LANDS

Ceylon.—This island has an area of 16 million acres. The Government has sold down to December 1887 only 1,150,000, the public lands still undisposed of reaching 12,040,000 acres. Usual price, 30s. per acre. The estates of English settlers, mostly under coffee, chinchona, and tea, cover 300,000 acres, and were valued in 1880 at 9 millions sterling.

Natal.—This colony has an area of 12,100,000 acres, having been separated from Cape Colony in 1856 :—

	Acres	Per Annum
Lands sold from 1856 to 1875	8,000,000	400,000
Lands sold from 1876 to 1887	300,000	25,000
Lands still undisposed of . .	3,800,000	...
Total . .	12,100,000	...

The usual price is 3s. per acre. The Kaffirs own nine-tenths of the total area.

Jamaica.—This island has an area of 2,600,000 acres, which have been sold to planters at prices varying from 4s. to 20s. per acre. The Government has still 100,000 acres unsold.

Trinidad.—Area 1,100,000 acres. It was taken from the Spaniards in 1797, but two-thirds of the island are still in the hands of the British Government.
Sales of Crown-lands show :—

	Acres	Per Annum
Sold from 1797 to 1875 . .	290,000	3,500
Sold from 1876 to 1887 . .	90,000	8,000
Still undisposed of	740,000	...
Total . . .	1,120,000	...

The average price is 25s. per acre. The farms are mostly under cocoa and sugar.

ARGENTINA

The tenure and value of land vary exceedingly. In such provinces as Buenos Ayres and Santa Fè, where great numbers of the inhabitants are landowners, and the soil is subdivided. the prices are high; while in other provinces, where a few families possess great tracts of

land, the value is low. The following table is taken from the *River Plate Handbook* (1885) :—

	Acres			Value per Square Mile (640 Acres)	
	Pasture	Tillage	Total	Pasture, £	Tillage, £
Buenos Ayres	53,800,000	2,300,000	56,100,000	600	3,000
Santa Fè	20,100,000	1,500,000	21,600,000	300	1,200
Cordoba	44,000,000	200,000	44,200,000	150	1,000
San Luis	25,600,000	100,000	25,700,000	100	1,000
Mendoza	32,000,000	500,000	32,500,000	80	2,000
San Juan	28,800,000	300,000	29,100,000	80	1,500
Salta	30,700,000	200,000	30,900,000	50	1,000
Tucuman	10,200,000	200,000	10,400,000	150	4,000
Jujuy	14,100,000	100,000	14,200,000	50	1,000
Rioja	22,400,000	100,000	22,500,000	50	1,000
Catamarca	49,600,000	100,000	49,700,000	50	1,000
Santiago	22,300,000	100,000	22,400,000	50	1,000
Entre Rios	23,000,000	200,000	23,200,000	300	1,200
Corrientes. . . .	25,600,000	100,000	25,700,000	200	1,000
Total . .	402,200,000	6,000,000	408,200,000	130	1,800

The above refers merely to the inhabited portion of the Republic, besides which there are the following territories, for the most part public lands, with a scanty population, viz. :—

	Acres
Gran Chaco	102,400,000
Misiones	6,400,000
Pampas	96,000,000
Patagonia	192,000,000
Total : .	396,800,000

The unsettled portion covers nearly as much area as that which is inhabited; the total is 805 million acres, or one-third of the extent of the United States.

The number of landowners is about 100,000, mostly Argentines. There are in Buenos Ayres 4000 Irish and Scotch sheep-farmers, whose land and stock in 1882 was worth 33 millions sterling.

In Santa Fè 16,000 grain-growers, Italians, Swiss, French, and Germans, possess farms worth 12 millions sterling. There are also 10,000 grain-growers, mostly Italians, in the province of Buenos Ayres. At least 70,000 Argentines have sheep and cattle farms in Buenos Ayres and the upper provinces. Land usually carries 2000 sheep and 100 cattle to the square mile.

LAND-TAXES

The total burthens on agriculture in various countries, by latest accounts, were approximately as follows :—

	Taxes, £	Agricultural Product, £	Tax, Percentage
England . . .	16,200,000	157,000,000	10.3
Scotland . . .	1,900,000	40,000,000	4.8
Ireland	2,700,000	54,000,000	5.0
United Kingdom	20,800,000	251,000,000	8.3
France	21,800,000	460,000,000	4.8
Germany . . .	12,700,000	424,000,000	3.0
Austria proper .	8,600,000	175,000,000	4.9
Italy	14,200,000	204,000,000	7.0
Belgium . . .	1,530,000	55,000,000	2.8
Holland . . .	1,080,000	39,000,000	2.8
Egypt	4,890,090	35,000,000	14.0
India	23,400,000	400,000,000	5.8
Total . .	109,000,000	2,043,000,000	5.4

UNITED KINGDOM

The taxes on agrarian industry in the United Kingdom may be set down approximately thus :—

	England	Scotland	Ireland	United Kingdom
	£	£	£	£
Tithes . .	4,050,000	...	...	4,050,000
Rates . .	8,300,000	1,400,000	2,100,000	11,800,000
Income-tax .	1,200,000	200,000	250,000	1,650,000
Land-tax .	1,050,000	50,000	...	1,100,000
Duties and } stamps	1,600,000	250,000	350,000	2,200,000
Total .	16,200,000	1,900,000	2,700,000	20,800,000

FRANCE

Councillor Tisserand enumerates the agrarian taxes as follows :—

	£
National	4,800,000
Departmental . . .	4,800,000
Indirect	8,600,000
Roads, &c.	3,600,000
Total .	21,800,000

Mr. Yves Guyot published the following table of rental and land-tax down to 1874 :—

Year	*Land Rental,* £	*Land-Tax,* £	*Per Cent.*
1791 . .	57,600,000	9,600,000	17
1821 . .	63,200,000	6,200,000	10
1862 . .	124,000,000	6,400,000	5
1874 . .	158,000,000	6,700,000	4

The ratios of properties according to tax assessment were :—

Taxes		**1835**	**1858**
Under 5 francs . . .	47.8	51.0
5–10 ,, . . .	16.1	15.4
10–20 ,, . . .	13.9	13.3
20–50 ,, . . .	13.1	12.1
Over 50 ,, . . .	9.1	8.2
Total . .	100.0	100.0

Those under five francs may be considered pauper holdings, being mostly exempted from tax on the plea of extreme poverty.

AUSTRIA

In Austria (without Hungary) the agricultural taxes in 1882 were :—

	£
Land-tax	2,600,000
Local rates	2,400,000
Stamp-duties, &c.	3,600,000
Total . .	8,600,000

GERMANY

Professor Meitzen shows that the taxes on agriculture are as follows :—

Taxes	Per Cent. on Rental Valuation	Per Cent. on Real Rental
State . . .	17.4	7.0
Communal . .	17.1	6.8
Special . . .	9.3	3.7
Total . .	43.8	17.5

ITALY

The taxes levied on landed property in 1883 were as follows :—

	£
National	5,020,000
Provincial	2,060,000
Communal	3,130,000
Total . .	10,210,000

Farmers have also to pay a cattle-tax, legacy-duty, and other imposts, thus bringing up the total, as Professor Sbrojavacca shows, to £14,240,000 per annum. The land-tax proper was in 1882 as follows :—

	£	Pence per Acre	Percentage of Land Product
Sardinia . .	820,000	20	11
Lombardy . .	960,000	48	18
Parma . .	150,000	28	18
Modena . .	145,000	22	13
Papal States .	480,000	22	14
Tuscany . .	230,000	11	9
Naples . .	1,420,000	18	13
Sicily . . .	360,000	14	11
Total .	4,565,000	20	13

HOLLAND

In 1884 the agrarian imposts were :—

	£
Land-tax	560,000
Local rates	140,000
Stamp-duties, &c.	380,000
Total . .	1,080,000

BELGIUM

According to Professor Leemans the agricultural taxes in 1884 were :—

	£
Land-tax	790,000
Indirect taxes . . .	560,000
Roads, &c.	180,000
Total . .	1,530,000

EGYPT

The land-tax in 1833 was £1,120,000, and had risen in 1889 to £4,890,000 sterling.

CHINA

In 1889 the land-tax was £4,800,000.

LANGUAGE

The numbers of persons speaking the various languages in 1801 and in 1890 were as follows :—

	1801	1890	Ratio 1801	Ratio 1890
English . .	20,520,000	111,100,000	12.7	27.7
French . .	31,450,000	51,200,000	19.4	12.7
German . . .	30,320,000	75,200,000	18.7	18.7
Russian . .	30,770,000	75,000,000	19.0	18.7
Spanish . .	26,190,000	42,800,000	16.2	10.7
Italian . .	15,070,000	33,400,000	9.3	8.3
Portuguese .	7,480,000	13,000,000	4.7	3.2
Total .	161,800,000	401,700,000	100.0	100.0

It will be observed what a wonderful advance the English language has made in ninety years. The following table shows in detail the distribution of the various principal languages in 1801 and in 1890. In the United States many speak both English and German.

SPOKEN IN 1801

In	English	French	Italian	Spanish	German
Europe	14,540,000	30,155,000	14,840,000	10,265,000	30,005,000
United States	5,250,000	230,000	5,000	5,000	280,000
Other parts	730,000	1,065,000	225,000	15,920,000	35,000
Total	20,520,000	31,450,000	15,070,000	26,190,000	30,320,000

SPOKEN IN 1890

In	English	French	Italian	Spanish	German
Europe	38,600,000	45,200,000	31,100,000	17,300,000	67,600,000
United States	58,000,000	1,100,000	400,000	650,000	7,100,000
Other parts	14,500,000	4,900,000	1,900,000	24,850,000	500,000
Total	111,100,000	51,200,000	33,400,000	42,800,000	75,200,000

The number of persons speaking Gaelic in the United Kingdom is said to reach nearly 4 per cent. of the population, including 660,000 in Ireland, 350,000 in Wales, and 230,000 in Scotland.

The proportion of letters in the various languages in prose works is found to be as follows:—

	English	French	Italian	Spanish	Latin	German
A . . .	78	80	99	121	79	64
B . . .	23	8	2	11	14	20
C . . .	25	30	40	48	42	22
D . . .	39	35	42	55	29	71
E . . .	138	184	131	145	92	178
F . . .	18	8	12	6	13	14
G . . .	19	12	20	11	22	31
H . . .	46	2	11	20	2	40
I . . .	68	76	103	37	120	86
J . . .	2	2	4	8	4	6
K . . .	6	...	...	...	...	9
L . . .	47	47	71	61	29	29
M . . .	19	37	12	26	62	22
N . . .	78	73	71	55	44	110
O . . .	70	41	96	107	50	27
P . . .	21	33	28	24	32	11
Q . . .	3	8	9	15	11	...
R . . .	59	73	52	69	77	84
S . . .	64	99	74	69	79	55
T . . .	88	70	55	48	66	48
U . . .	37	58	47	46	106	40
V . . .	10	17	15	10	18	9
W . . .	19	...	...	...	...	20
X . . .	1	5	...	...	9	...
Y . . .	22	2	...	5	...	...
Z . . .	...	...	6	3	...	4
Total	1,000	1,000	1,000	1,000	1,000	1,000

Where blanks occur, it shows either that the letter is not used, or that the use does not reach 1 in 1000, such as "z" in English or "x" in Spanish. The Spanish N, of which 55 are used, includes three "ñ," equivalent to "gn" in Italian.

LATITUDE AND LONGITUDE

	Latitude	Longitude
Algiers	36.46 N.	3.6 E.
Amsterdam . . .	51.21 ,,	4.58 ,,
Antwerp	51.13 ,,	4.25 ,,
Archangel . . .	65.40 ,,	43.0 ,,
Azores . . .	28.0 ,,	26.0 W.
Bagdad	33.20 ,,	44.24 E.
Baltimore . . .	39.15 ,,	76.30 W.
Belfast . . .	54.36 ,,	5.55 ,,
Berlin . . .	52.33 ,,	13.25 E.
Bombay . . .	19.2 ,,	72.50 ,,
Bordeaux . . .	45.0 ,,	0.20 W.
Boston . . .	42.20 ,,	71.9 ,,
Brussels . . .	50.52 ,,	3.21 E.
Bucharest . . .	44.28 ,,	26.9 ,,
Buda-Pesth . .	47.31 ,,	19.1 ,,
Buenos Ayres . .	34.36 S.	58.22 W.
Cadiz . . .	36.32 N.	6.18 ,,
Cairo . . .	30.5 ,,	31.45 E.
Calcutta . . .	22.40 ,,	88.25 ,,
Canton . . .	23.10 ,,	113.9 ,,
Cape Town . . .	34.30 S.	18.0 ,,
Caracas . . .	10.30 N.	67.10 W.
Chicago . . .	42.0 ,,	83.31 ,,
Cincinnati . . .	39.0 ,,	84.15 ,,
Constantinople . .	41.1 ,,	28.58 E.
Copenhagen . .	55.42 ,,	12.34 ,,
Demerara . . .	5.30 ,,	58.20 W.
Dresden . . .	51.6 ,,	13.36 E.
Dublin . . .	53.21 ,,	6.17 W.
Edinburgh . . .	55.57 ,,	3.12 ,,
Falkland Islands . .	51.30 S.	59.0 ,,
Faroe Islands . .	62.0 N.	7.0 ,,
Florence . . .	43.45 ,,	11.16 E.
Frankfort . . .	50.8 ,,	8.33 ,,
Geneva . . .	46.2 ,,	6.9 ,,
Genoa . . .	44.30 ,,	9.0 ,,

	Latitude	Longitude
Gibraltar	36.8 N.	5.20 W.
Glasgow	55.52 ,,	4.8 ,,
Guatemala . . .	14.0 ,,	88.0 ,,
Halifax . . .	44.30 ,,	63.55 ,,
Hamburg . . .	53.34 ,,	10.3 E.
Havanna . . .	23.7 ,,	82.28 W.
Hobart . . .	42.54 S.	147.27 E.
Jersey . . .	49.15 N.	2.5 W.
Jerusalem . . .	31.48 ,,	35.10 E.
Lima . . .	12.0 S.	77.0 W.
Lisbon . . .	38.44 N.	9.6 ,,
Liverpool . . .	53.24 ,,	2.58 ,,
London . . .	51.31 ,,	0.5 ,,
Madeira . . .	33.0 ,,	18.0 ,,
Madras . . .	13.12 ,,	80.21 E.
Madrid . . .	40.28 ,,	3.40 W.
Malta . . .	35.54 ,,	14.27 E.
Manchester . . .	53.29 ,,	2.14 W.
Manilla . . .	14.35 ,,	120.48 E.
Marseilles . . .	43.18 ,,	5.28 ,,
Mauritius . . .	20.15 S.	57.0 ,,
Melbourne . . .	37.52 ,,	145.0 ,,
Mexico . . .	19.30 N.	99.2 W.
Milan . . .	45.40 ,,	9.10 E.
Montreal . . .	45.30 ,,	73.30 W.
Moscow . . .	55.40 ,,	37.28 E.
Munich . . .	48.7 ,,	11.35 ,,
Naples . . .	40.52 ,,	14.15 ,,
New Orleans . . .	30.7 ,,	90.0 W.
New York . . .	40.40 ,,	74.0 ,,
Palermo . . .	38.6 ,,	13.23 E.
Paris . . .	48.52 ,,	2.21 ,,
Pekin . . .	40.0 ,,	116.23 ,,
Philadelphia . . .	39.52 ,,	77.30 W.
Prague . . .	50.5 ,,	14.25 E.
Quebec . . .	46.50 ,,	72.0 W.
Quito . . .	0.7 S.	78.49 ,,
Rio Janeiro . . .	23.0 ,,	43.20 ,,
Rome . . .	41.53 N.	12.28 E.
Rotterdam . . .	51.55 ,,	4.29 ,,
St. Louis . . .	38.40 ,,	90.12 W.
St. Petersburg . . .	59.40 ,,	31.0 E.
San Francisco . . .	37.59 ,,	121.59 W.
Sierra Leone . . .	8.45 ,,	13.10 ,,
Singapore . . .	1.27 ,,	103.48 E.
Stockholm . . .	59.20 ,,	18.0 ,,
Sydney . . .	34.0 S.	151.12 ,,
Teneriffe . . .	28.30 N.	17.0 W.
Toronto . . .	43.47 ,,	79.25 ,,
Trinidad . . .	10.50 ,,	61.15 ,,
Tunis . . .	36.44 ,,	10.5 E.
Turin . . .	45.5 ,,	7.44 ,,
Valparaiso . . .	33.02 S.	71.45 W.
Venice . . .	45.27 N.	12.25 E.
Vera Cruz . . .	19.30 ,,	96.40 W.
Vienna . . .	48.9 ,,	16.24 E.
Warsaw . . .	52.15 ,,	21.0 ,,
Washington . . .	38.55 ,,	77.5 W.

The length of a degree of longitude varies with latitude as follows:—

Latitude	Miles	Latitude	Miles
10	68¼	40	54
15	67½	45	50
20	65¼	50	45
25	63¼	60	35
30	59¾	70	24
35	57	80	12

LAW

The ordinary number of civil lawsuits in a year is as follows:—

	Lawsuits	Per 1000 Inhabitants
England . . .	1,150,000	42
Scotland . . .	75,000	20
Germany . . .	3,239,000	70
Italy . . .	1,390,000	52
France . . .	708,000	19
Belgium . . .	94,000	18

The Queen's Bench in England in 1887 disposed of 80,000 suits; the upper courts in Scotland, 11,000. There is an arbitration tribunal between employers and workmen called "Prudhommes," which settles 52,000 cases yearly in France and 4000 in Belgium.

There are 14,000 solicitors or attorneys in England, 17,000 in France, without counting barristers. In 1866 the English law reports comprised 1308 volumes, containing 60,000 law and 28,000 equity cases; about 30 volumes are added yearly. In 1873 statute law comprised 18,000 statutes. The Russian edicts down to Alexander I. were 31,900 in number.

When Tribonian compiled the Pandects, A.D. 530, he condensed 3,000,000 sentences and 2000 volumes into 150 volumes.

LEAD

The production of metallic lead in tons has been approximately as follows :—

	1830	1850	1880	1888
Great Britain	48,000	55,000	51,000	36,000
France . .	1,100	7,000	32,000	30,000
Germany . .	9,500	16,000	58,600	92,000
Italy . . .	8,000	12,000	33,000	30,000
Spain . . .	23,000	27,000	92,300	84,000
Austria . .	7,000	11,000	8,900	10,000
Greece, Belgium, &c.	4,000	6,500	14,400	15,000
Europe . .	100,600	134,500	290,200	297,000
United States	3,700	36,000	89,000	160,000
Total .	104,000	170,500	379,200	457,000

Good lead ore gives 70 per cent. of lead, and in smelting it takes two tons of coal to produce three tons of lead. The Cordoba mines in Spain are said to be the richest in the world. The Missouri lead-field, near Chicago, is $1\frac{1}{2}$ miles in length, the ore giving 70 per cent. lead. The importation of lead into the United States fell from 42,000 tons in 1870 to 4000 in 1880.

The production in the United States has been as follows :—

	1880	1889
	Tons	Tons
Colorado	36,000	70,000
Missouri	28,000	34,000
Various	25,000	87,000
Total .	89,000	191,000

LEATHER

The annual consumption in the United Kingdom, and the value of manufactured articles, were approximately :—

Year	Millions Lbs. Leather			Manufactured Value		
	British Hides	Foreign Hides	Total	Home, £	Export, £	Total, £
1805	27	...	27	8,000,000	15,000	8,015,000
1820	36	12	48	10,000,000	40,000	10,040,000
1830	40	30	70	12,600,000	80,000	12,680,000
1840	45	37	82	14,200,000	170,000	14,370,000
1850	50	70	120	19,700,000	610,000	20,310,000
1860	55	87	142	22,300,000	2,130,000	24,430,000
1870	60	132	192	28,600,000	2,640,000	31,240,000
1881	65	144	209	30,100,000	3,930,000	34,030,000
1888	66	164	230	38,000,000	4,100,000	42,100,000

In 1835 M'Culloch estimated the manufactures thus :—

Boots and shoes	7,500,000
Saddlery, &c.	6,000,000
Total .	13,500,000

There was an estimate in the *Parliamentary Gazetteer* of 1806 which put down the leather manufactures at £10,000,000; this was less than Eden's valuation in 1803, namely, £12,000,000. That of M'Pherson in 1783 was £10,500,000 (see *Manufactures*).

LEGACY AND PROBATE

The following table shows the amount of property changing hands by death, the amount under the head of Succession before 1870 being an estimate as one-third of the amount paying legacy-duty :—

Period	Annual Average, £			Ratio to Pop. per Inhabitant
	Legacy	Succession	Total	
				£ s. d.
1811–20	25,500,000	8,500,000	34,000,000	1 18 0
1841–50	43,900,000	14,600,000	58,500,000	2 4 0
1861–70	73,600,000	24,500,000	98,100,000	3 6 0
1876–80	113,000,000	41,000,000	154,000,000	4 10 0
1885–89	143,200,000	44,800,000	188,000,000	5 2 0

The exact amount of all property passing through the Probate Court in 1840 was ascertained by Porter to be £54,700,000, and if we compare his statement with those fo subsequent years from the *Statistical Abstract*, we find :—

	Total Legacy and Succession Property			Ratio	
	1840	1875	1889	1840	1889
	£	£	£		
England .	47,100,000	119,900,000	161,700,000	86.0	85.2
Scotland .	3,100,000	14,500,000	17,200,000	5.7	9.1
Ireland .	4,500,000	10,000,000	10,900,000	8.3	5.7
United Kingdom	54,700,000	144,400,000	189,800,000	100.0	100.0

The returns for Scotland in 1840 did not include mortgages, and if these were added, the amount, it is thought, would have reached £4,000,000, or about $7\frac{1}{2}$ per cent. of the total. Even allowing for this, the increase of wealth in Scotland since 1840 has been prodigious, namely, 330 per cent. against 244 per cent. in England.

The estates proved in the United Kingdom for legacy-duty, exclusive of succession estates, were as follows :—

Estates	Number, Annual Average		Amount, Annual Average, £	
	1883–84	1888–89	1883–84	1888–89
Over £100,000 .	149	172	32,700,000	43,500,000
£50,000–£100,000	242	261	16,800,000	18,200,000
£10,000–£50,000	2,019	2,045	41,300,000	43,500,000
£1000–£10,000 .	10,771	11,285	34,700,000	36,000,000
Under £1000 .	27,594	31,047	8,800,000	10,600,000
Total . .	40,775	44,810	134,300,000	151,800,000

Ratio as to Value

Estates	1883–84	1888–89
Over £100,000	24.0	28.6
£10,000–£100,000 . . .	43.5	40.6
£1000–£10,000 . . .	26.0	23.8
Under £1000	6.5	7.0
Total . . .	100.0	100.0

The number of estates proved in the three kingdoms for legacy-duty only in 1877 was as follows :—

Amount	England	Scotland	Ireland	United Kingdom
Over £20,000 . .	945	125	59	1,129
£5000–£20,000 .	2,784	356	199	3,339
£1000–£5000 . .	7,625	1,262	800	9,687
Under £1000 . .	21,913	2,567	2,271	26,751
Total . .	33.267	4,310	3,329	40,906

Further details on this subject as regards the United Kingdom, France, Italy, and Belgium will be found under the title *Wealth*.

HOLLAND

The legacy and succession returns for the years 1880–83 gave the following averages :—

	Estates
Over £40,000	58
£4000–£40,000	356
£1000–£4000	2,722
Under £1000	6,280
Total . .	9,416

LIBRARIES

	Libraries		Volumes	
	1848	1880	1848	1880
United Kingdom . .	28	202	1,542,000	3,770,000
France	107	505	3,975,000	7,298,000
Germany	80	594	3,053,000	4,070,000
Russia	12	145	451,000	950,000
Austria	41	577	2,193,000	5,476,000
Italy	45	493	2,274,000	4,349,000
Spain and Portugal .	24	90	963,000	1,200,000
Switzerland	13	1,654	465,000	1,819,000
Belgium	10	105	400,000	610,000
Holland	10	220	330,000	800,000
Scandinavia . . .	13	94	968,000	1,250,000
Europe	383	4,679	16,614,000	31,592,000
United States . . .	20	59	600,000	2,263,000
Total . .	403	4,738	17,214,000	33,855,000

The above does not include any libraries with less than 10,000 volumes (except possibly those of Switzerland). The principal libraries of the world are :—

	Volumes	*MSS.*
British Museum . .	1,120,000	41,000
Imperial, Paris . .	2,078,000	86,000
St. Petersburg . .	1,045,000	34,000
Berlin	740,000	15,000
Munich	810,000	24,000
Vienna	420,000	21,000
Dresden	500,000	4,000
Vatican	340,000	32,000
Copenhagen . . .	410,000	5,000
Göttingen . . .	400,000	5,000
Oxford	300,000	22,000
Brussels	210,000	20,000
St. Geneviève, Paris .	250,000	30,000
Washington . . .	230,000	...
Boston	202,000	...
Astor, New York . .	160,000	...

The library of the British Museum has 32 miles of shelves filled with books, and is visited by 91,000 readers yearly. The Bibliothèque Impériale of Paris has 18 miles of books and 37,000 readers yearly.

The libraries in the United States were as follows :—

Year	Number	Volumes
1850	15,615	4,640,000
1860	19,581	8,550,000
1870	56,015	19,460,000

In 1880 there were 23,000 school libraries containing 45,000,000 volumes, and 314 large public libraries, exclusive of all containing less than 10,000 volumes.

LIFE

The following table shows the expectation of life in various countries at different ages :—

Age	Years to Live					
	England	United States	Belgium	Holland	Saxony	Sweden
10	49.2	48.7	44.3	46.5	47.0	48.0
20	41.0	42.2	37.1	38.9	39.3	40.1
30	33.6	35.3	31.2	32.1	32.1	33.2
40	26.7	28.2	25.5	26.2	25.0	25.9
50	20.2	20.9	19.6	20.0	18.0	19.1
60	13.9	14.1	13.2	13.3	11.7	12.9
70	8.9	8.5	8.2	8.0	6.9	8.0
80	5.5	4.4	5.3	4.6	3.9	4.1

The expectation of life is always longer with females than males, viz. :—

Age	Years to Live							
	England		Holland		Sweden		Belgium	
	Male	Female	Male	Female	Male	Female	Male	Female
Birth .	41.9	45.2	34.1	36.4	41.3	45.6	...	...
5 years	51.5	53.6	48.7	49.2	49.4	53.0	...	...
10 ,,	48.2	50.3	45.9	46.5	46.5	50.0	43.8	44.8
20 ,,	39.9	42.1	38.3	39.2	38.6	42.1	36.4	37.7
30 ,,	33.2	34.1	31.8	32.4	31.2	34.5	30.5	31.9
40 ,,	26.5	27.5	25.0	26.4	24.3	27.2	24.8	26.1
50 ,,	19.9	20.8	18.5	19.7	18.0	20.1	18.9	20.3
60 ,,	13.6	14.5	12.8	13.3	12.3	13.5	12.4	13.9
70 ,,	8.6	9.1	7.9	8.1	7.4	8.0	8.1	8.3
80 ,,	5.2	5.6	4.4	4.5	3.9	4.3	5.2	5.4
90 ,,	2.8	3.1	2.4	2.7	2.4	2.8	2.9	3.1

It will be observed that the mean expectation at five years of age is greater than at birth, but after five years it diminishes. Finlayson's table of expectation for English ladies of fortune coincides closely with the result of widows in France in receipt of pensions :—

Age	Years of Life		
	English Ladies	French Widows	French Male
40	29.9	29.3	...
50	23.0	22.8	18.7
60	16.2	16.0	14.3
70	10.1	10.1	8.7
80	5.7	5.9	4.4

Kasper gives the percentage of persons of various professions who reach 70 years thus :—

	Per Cent.		*Per Cent.*		*Per Cent.*
Physicians	24	Lawyers .	29	Merchants .	33
Teachers .	27	Clerks . .	32	Farmers .	40
Artists . .	28	Soldiers .	32	Clergy . .	42

Expectation of life varies as follows in England with condition:—

Age	Years to Live			
	Gentry	Farm Labourers	Sober	Intemperate
20 . . .	38	48	40	14
30 . . .	31	41	34	13
40 . . .	24	33	27	10
50 . . .	18	25	20	8
60 . . .	12	18	14	6

In the United States the span of life for various professions is as follows:—

	Years			Years
Shopmen .	41.8	Mechanics	.	47.3
Waggoners	43.6	Merchants	.	48.4
Labourers	44.6	Lawyers .		52.6
Seamen .	46.1	Farmers .	.	64.2

Madden's table of famous men, and Neuville's average for professions at Frankfort, give the following spans of life:—

Madden's Famous Men		Neuville's Frankfort		
	Years			Years
Clergymen .	67	Physicians .	.	52
Physicians .	68	Lawyers .	.	54
Lawyers .	69	Merchants .	.	57
Artists .	70	Teachers .	.	57
Naturalists .	71	Clergy .	.	66

Many remarkable cases of longevity are recorded in all countries and all ranks of life.

1. Countess of Desmond, killed by falling from a cherry-tree in her 146th year. 2. Thomas Parr, died after a dinner-party at Lord Arundel's, aged 152. 3. Cardinal de Salis, who recommended daily exercise in all weathers, aged 110. 4. John Riva, of Venice, who chewed citron bark daily, died aged 116, leaving a son of 14 years. 5. Henry Jenkins, died aged 116, at Bolton-on-Swale in 1670. 6. Mme. Roviro, aged 164, who died in 1741, leaving a son aged 116. 7. Peter Garden, died at Edinburgh in 1775, aged 131. Bertherand's death-roll of slaves at Carthage showed 5 per cent. over 80, and 1 per cent. over 100 years. The Third Legion of Augustus had a death-record which showed that 17 per cent. passed 70 years. Moreover, Pliny says—"The year of our Lord 76 is memorable, for in that year there was a Census from which it appears that in the part of Italy lying between the Apennines and the River Po, there were found fifty-four persons 103 years old; fifty-seven 110 years; two 120 years; four 130 years; four 135 years; and three 140 years each."

In the eighteenth century Sejoncourt published a list of 49 persons who had died between the ages of 130 and 175 years. Among centenarians of recent date were Mrs. Anne Butler, daughter of Admiral Winn, died at Portsmouth, January 1883, aged 103, and Mrs. Betty Lloyd, at Ruabon, Wales, March 1883, aged 107. According to Dr. Farr's tables, of one million male and female persons born, 77 males and 147 females will reach 100 years; but the newer tables of Dr. Ogle give only 41 males and 112 females.

A meeting of 2000 persons over 70 years of age is annually held at Leicester, and of these 400 die before the next anniversary.

Age	Table of Survivals of a Thousand Born									
	England	France	Prussia	Austria	Italy	Spain	Sweden	Norway	Belgium	Switzerland
	1881–82	1880–82	1881–83	1880–82	1881–83	1880–84	1881–82	1881–82	1881–83	1881–83
Number born . . .	1,000	1,000	1,000	1,000	1,000	1,000	1,000	1,000	1,000	1,000
5 years	762	751	684	614	632	571	783	838	756	747
10 ,, ...	736	724	648	569	591	530	746	803	732	721
15 ,, ...	723	706	632	551	572	514	727	783	718	707
20 ,, ...	706	685	616	532	554	496	711	760	699	689
25 ,, ...	685	657	596	506	531	476	691	733	675	665
30 ,, ...	660	627	571	477	508	457	669	704	648	639
40 ,, ...	597	566	514	423	462	412	621	644	589	578
50 ,, ...	516	499	452	357	407	358	560	585	517	502
60 ,, ...	405	408	351	267	328	292	473	494	419	393
70 ,, ...	255	268	205	150	203	184	330	338	271	231
80 ,, ...	96	104	65	44	65	69	139	161	101	69

The following table distinguishes the sexes in certain countries, but the figures are not so recent as those above:—

Age	France		Belgium		Italy		Denmark	
	Males	Females	Males	Females	Males	Females	Males	Females
Number born	1,000	1,000	1,000	1,000	1,000	1,000	1,000	1,000
5 years	716	744	720	741	590	608	741	769
10 ,, ...	693	719	684	699	552	567	711	737
20 ,, ...	660	680	640	650	518	528	676	698
30 ,, ...	602	626	566	576	466	478	624	650
40 ,, ...	543	567	484	499	418	424	569	590
50 ,, ...	476	507	403	415	357	368	488	522
60 ,, ...	383	425	319	337	279	294	376	429
70 ,, ...	245	291	179	221	170	180	238	289
80 ,, ...	86	113	60	76	58	62	84	114

Kasper's table of rich and poor shows survivals thus:—

Age	Rich	Poor
Number born . . .	1,000	1,000
5 years	943	655
20 ,, ...	886	566
40 ,, ...	695	396
70 ,, ...	235	65

Korösi shows that poverty and overcrowding shorten the span of life at Buda-Pesth: in healthy quarters it is 47 years, in the workmen's tenement dwellings only 32 to 37.

Evidence to the same effect will be found in other parts of this book; the reader has only to turn to the Index for the items *Infant-mortality* and *Overcrowding*.

UNITED KINGDOM

The Registrar-General's returns show the expectation of life is now about three years longer than for the period of 17 years ending 1854, which is probably due to abolishing the duty on soap and the window-tax, as well as to water supply, drainage, &c.

Ages	Persons 1838–54	Persons 1876–80	Male 1838–54	Male 1876–80	Female 1838–54	Female 1876–80
o years .	40.86	43.56	39.91	41.92	41.85	45.25
5 ,, .	50.02	52.56	49.71	51.47	50.33	53.65
10 ,, .	47.36	49.24	47.05	48.16	47.67	50.32
15 ,, .	43.54	45.05	43.18	43.94	43.90	46.15
20 ,, .	39.88	40.98	39.48	39.86	40.29	42.10
25 ,, .	36.57	37.21	36.12	36.05	37.04	38.36
35 ,, .	29.99	30.01	29.40	28.88	30.59	31.12
45 ,, .	23.41	23.29	22.76	22.34	24.06	24.21
55 ,, .	16.94	16.75	16.45	16.09	17.43	17.37
65 . ,, .	11.17	11.19	10.82	10.79	11.51	11.55
75 ,, .	6.72	6.81	6.49	6.52	6.93	7.04

Dr. Humphrey's table of survivals for England, for the periods ending 1854 and 1880, and a table compiled for Scotland in 1879–81, compare as follows, being in favour of Scotland :—

Age	England Males 1838–54	England Males 1876–80	England Females 1838–54	England Females 1876–80	England General Pop. 1838–54	England General Pop. 1876–80	Scotland 1879–81
No. born	1,000	1,000	1,000	1,000	1,000	1,000	1,000
5 years	724	736	751	766	737	751	780
10 ,,	690	712	716	742	703	727	748
15 ,,	673	700	697	729	685	715	729
20 ,,	652	685	674	714	663	699	706
25 ,,	624	664	644	692	634	678	679
35 ,,	564	608	580	639	572	623	620
45 ,,	496	531	510	571	503	551	550
55 ,,	410	435	433	490	421	462	460
65 ,,	295	304	324	364	309	333	335
75 ,,	148	152	175	196	161	173	176

FRANCE

There has been a steady improvement in the span of life, which Duvillard estimated in the last century at 26 years and 2 months, and Lombard at 40 years in 1868. The tables of survivals are as follows :—

Age	1750 St. Maur	1789 Duvillard	1817–32 Montferrand	1856–65 Bertillon	1880–82 Stat. Gen.
Number born	1,000	1,000	1,000	1,000	1,000
5 years . .	540	583	707	710	751
10 ,, . .	484	551	668	681	724
15 ,, . .	472	529	647	664	706
20 ,, . .	449	502	624	642	685
30 ,, . .	388	438	560	584	627
40 ,, . .	314	369	510	533	566
50 ,, . .	242	297	449	473	499
60 ,, . .	168	213	365	389	408
70 ,, . .	90	118	229	249	268
80 ,, . .	23	35	76	89	104

Levasseur gives a table of 1474 centenarians in 20 years ending 1885, from which it appears that 28 men and 46 women die yearly over 100 years of age.

RUSSIA

In 1867 the span of life was estimated thus :—

Among	Years Males	Years Females	Among	Years Males	Years Females
Greeks .	22.1	23.6	Jews . . .	29.4	31.1
Catholics	28.0	29.7	Mussulmen .	26.5	27.1
Protestants	32.9	36.2	General pop.	23.0	24.6

GERMANY

The German official returns for 11 years, 1871–81, give the following table of survivals :—

Of 1000 Born

Age	Males	Females	Age	Males	Females
1 . .	747	783	30 . . .	545	576
3 . . .	676	709	40 . . .	488	516
5 . . .	649	681	50 . . .	412	452
10 . . .	621	652	60 . . .	311	363
15 . . .	609	639	70 . . .	178	219
20 . . .	593	623	80 . . .	50	66

HOLLAND AND SWEDEN

Tables of survivals show a great improvement in both these countries, as compared with former periods :—

Age	Holland 1840–51 Baumhauer	Holland 1870–80 Von Pesch	Sweden 1757–63 Vargentin	Sweden 1861–70 Berg	Sweden 1881–82 Stat. Gen.
No. born .	1,000	1,000	1,000	1,000	1,000
10 years . .	644	654	611	737	746
20 ,, . .	630	620	570	703	711
30 ,, . .	568	566	519	656	669
40 ,, . .	502	515	459	593	621
50 ,, . .	434	494	385	511	560
60 ,, . .	310	357	293	401	473
70 ,, . .	182	224	175	246	330
80 ,, . .	58	76	56	78	139

Persons dying over eighty years of age in Sweden formed the following ratio of all deaths :—

Period	Per 1000
1811–30	47
1831–50	53
1851–60	46
1861–75	58

LIGHT

It requires 50 lbs. of tallow candles to produce as much light as 1000 cubic feet of gas. Dr. Frankland's table (1866) of the cost of light was as follows :—

	Cost for Ten Hours of Light
One gallon paraffin oil . . .	6 pence
Equivalent amount of gas . .	3 ,,
Thirty-three tallow candles . .	32 ,,
Sixteen paraffin ,, .	46 ,,
Twenty sperm ,, .	84 ,,
Twenty-four wax ,, .	87 ,,

A light of 100 candle-power, says Mr. Fischer, throws out the following degrees of heat :—

Electric, arc .	.	100	Petroleum, flat .	7,200
,, incandescent		410	100 wax candles .	7,960
Gas, Siemens .	.	1,500	100 stearine candles ..	8,940
Petroleum, round .	.	3,360	Paraffin lamps .	9,200
Gas, argand .	.	4,860	100 tallow candles .	9,700
Colza . .	.	6,800	Manchester gas-burner	12,150

Light travels 185,000 miles per second.

LIGHTHOUSES

The number in various countries at different dates was approximately :—

	1830	1860	1885
England . . .	...	244	396
Scotland . .	...	130	193
Ireland . . .	...	90	138
United Kingdom . .	260	464	727
France . . .	63	228	422
Germany . . .	20	40	183
Russia . . .	18	77	194
Austria . . .	5	10	63
Italy . . .	10	91	263
Spain . . .	11	50	178
Portugal . . .	4	15	30
Sweden and Norway	110	120	337
Denmark . . .	70	77	63
Holland . . .	10	58	102
Belgium . . .	4	8	25
Greece . . .	...	...	58
Turkey . . .	10	15	134
Europe . . .	595	1,253	2,779
United States .	130	379	1,991
Canada . . .	38	92	651
Australia . . .	10	47	343
India . . .	15	49	96
China . . .	2	5	68
Japan . . .	...	...	59
Brazil . . .	5	16	57
West Indies . .	40	74	110
Spanish America .	15	27	54
Total . .	850	1,942	6,208

See Sir James Douglas's report to the British Association in 1886. The cost of lighting Smeaton's Eddystone lighthouse in 1759, with a light of 67 candle-power, was 18d. per hour, a sum now sufficient to provide a light of 160,000 candle-power. Canada uses 100,000 gallons of petroleum for lighting yearly, at a cost of £4000. Dungeness first adopted the electric light in 1862, and the French lighthouses followed in 1863.

LIGHTNING

According to Mr. Preece, there are 500,000 lightning conductors in the United Kingdom. The number of houses burnt yearly by lightning in Bavaria was :—

1833–43	32
1880–82	134

The number of persons killed by lightning averages 23 in England, 92 in France, 165 in Germany, 908 in Russia.

LIVING, COST OF

The cost of a workman's food in various countries in 1880 was :—

	Shillings per Week		Percentage of Food Cost
	Food	Wages	
Great Britain . .	14	31	45
France . . .	12	21	57
Germany . . .	10	16	62
Belgium . . .	12	20	60
Italy . . .	9	15	60
Spain . . .	10	16	62
United States . .	16	48	33
Australia . . .	11	40	28

The following table shows approximately the expenditure of the principal nations in the ordinary items that make up the cost of living. Food is at wholesale price in first hands (retail price being 30 per cent. higher), and taxes include all duties, tolls, and rates, direct or indirect, that go towards national or local revenues :—

	Millions £ Yearly							
	Food	Clothing	House Rent	Taxes	Transport	Fodder, &c.	Sundries	Total
United Kingdom . .	372	66	135	119	113	89	242	1,136
France . . .	361	64	93	144	96	74	98	930
Germany . . .	400	53	68	109	103	87	160	980
Russia . . .	360	51	34	72	94	128	190	929
Austria . . .	235	30	27	55	59	44	121	571
Italy . . .	144	24	22	81	33	22	24	350
Spain . . .	112	16	18	37	27	15	50	275
Portugal . . .	24	3	4	8	5	1	8	53
Sweden . . .	37	6	4	7	10	4	30	98
Norway . . .	15	2	1	3	4	1	12	38
Denmark . . .	18	3	2	4	6	6	21	60
Holland . . .	36	6	7	15	8	7	17	96
Belgium . . .	56	12	6	11	17	12	41	155
Switzerland . .	20	3	2	3	5	2	19	54
Europe . . .	2,190	339	423	668	580	492	1,033	5,725
United States .	455	98	127	165	231	228	746	2,050
Canada . . .	32	8	7	10	12	8	40	117
Australia . . .	28	7	13	12	10	14	40	124
Argentina . . .	25	6	5	14	8	7	20	85
Total . .	2,730	458	575	869	841	749	1,879	8,101

It is hardly necessary to say that the foregoing table is merely intended to shew comprehensively in round numbers the annual outlay of each nation under the principal headings and in the aggregate. Nothing like mathematical accuracy is to be expected, for it would be impossible. The figures, however, are not set down at random, but are estimates based on the observations of well-known writers and whatever is available in the way of official or semi-official statements. It is true that the cost of food, and indeed the outlay under any of the above heads, is likely to vary remarkably from one year to another, from which some persons may feel disposed to think that the table is of no value whatever. But this is an objection that might be made to many tables of a similar kind, whether in the present work or in those of other writers.

A statement was published in Paris in 1882 of the cost of maintenance of an artisan's family, and another by Miss Octavia Hill of a similar family in London in 1888, viz. :—

	Weekly Expenditure, Pence	
	Paris	London
Rent	30	69
Clothing . . .	24	56
Coal and light . . .	10	16
Bread . . .	90	40
Meat	63	48
Vegetables and fruit . .	21	36
Milk, butter, &c. . .	39	23
Tea and coffee . .	14	16
Sugar	7	10
Wine and liquor . .	35	10
Total . .	£1 7 9	£1 7 0

The earnings in both cases are supposed to reach 30s. a week. The London artisan has to pay, moreover, 20d. a week to his insurance club : his surplus therefore is only 16d. a week.

The retail prices paid by workmen for food in 1880 were (pence) :—

	England	France	Germany	Italy	New York	Chicago
Beef, lb. . . .	10.0	9.5	9.0	8.0	6.0	4.0
Bread, ,, . . .	2.0	1.6	2.0	3.0	2.0	2.0
Butter, ,, . . .	17.0	13.0	11.0	14.0	14.0	12.0
Eggs, dozen . .	11.0	9.0	10.0	9.0	14.0	9.0
Milk, quart . .	4.0	...	2.0	4.0	5.0	3.0
Sugar, lb. . .	4.0	5.0	5.0	4.0	5.0	5.0
Coffee, ,, . .	15.0	15.0	17.0	16.0	13.0	14.0
Rice, ,, . .	3.0	...	4.0	3.0	5.0	5.0
Pork, ,, . .	7.0	7.0	8.0	7.0	5.0	3.0
Potatoes, cwt. .	6.0	4.0	4.0	8.0	11.0	6.0

GREAT BRITAIN

The cost of living at various epochs, from estimates at the respective dates, is shown thus :—

Gentleman's Family in London

	1792	1823	1845	1883
	£	£	£	£
Rent	60	90	100	120
Taxes . . .	18	40	30	40
Servants (2) . .	18	24	30	40
Clothing . . .	60	70	80	100
Bread . . .	25	26	25	20
Meat	25	30	50	80
Groceries . . .	22	35	40	60
Wines . . .	23	39	40	40
Dairy . . .	50	70	70	90
Coal and light . .	30	38	30	25
Washing . . .	16	22	30	40
Sundries . . .	58	81	95	110
Total . .	405	565	620	765

Family of five persons, besides two servants.

The period between 1792 and 1823 shows a rise of 40 per cent. in 31 years ; that from 1845 to 1883 one of 23 per cent. in 38 years.

Tradesman's Family (Bristol)

	1792	1823	1845	1883
	£	£	£	£
Rent . . .	10	15	18	20
Clothing . . .	10	12	12	15
Bread . . .	20	21	20	16
Meat	10	14	20	28
Groceries . . .	10	15	20	22
Sundries . . .	10	13	15	19
Total . .	70	90	105	120

English Labourer and Mechanic

	Labourer			Mechanic		
	1792	1823	1883	1792	1823	1883
	£	£	£	£	£	£
Bread, meat, &c.	16	17	20	18	20	22
Groceries . .	2	3	5	4	6	8
Rent	2	3	4	3	4	6
Clothing, &c. .	7	8	8	17	22	24
Total . .	27	31	37	42	52	60

In 1881 Professor Leone Levi estimated the annual expenditure of the people of the United Kingdom thus :—

	Quantity	£	Per Inhabitant
			£ s. d.
Meat, tons . . .	1,400,000	99,800,000	2 17 0
Fish, ,, . . .	300,000	14,500,000	0 8 2
Sugar, ,, . . .	1,000,000	27,000,000	0 15 4
Potatoes, tons . .	4,600,000	32,200,000	0 18 3
Bread, ,, . .	6,300,000	77,500,000	2 4 0
Butter and cheese, tons	350,000	36,000,000	1 0 6
Milk and eggs . .	...	42,000,000	1 4 0
Fruit and vegetables .	...	28,100,000	0 16 0
Tea and coffee . .	...	18,300,000	0 10 0
Wine and liquor .	...	124,000,000	3 11 0
Food . . .	...	499,400,000	14 4 9
House-rent . .	...	77,000,000	2 4 0
Coal and light . .	...	28,700,000	0 16 0
Taxes . . .	...	47,500,000	1 7 0
Textiles and clothing .	...	142,800,000	4 2 0
Science and books .	...	12,000,000	0 7 0
Amusements . .	...	12,600,000	0 7 4
Education . .	...	11,000,000	0 6 6
Tobacco . .	...	13,100,000	0 7 8
Furniture and plate .	...	16,000,000	0 9 0
Churches . .	...	12,000,000	0 7 0
Water-supply .	...	5,900,000	0 3 6
Total .	...	878,000,000	25 1 9

FRANCE

The cost of maintaining a small family of the middle class has been at various dates as follows :—

	Per Annum, £	
Year	France	Paris
1789	15	29
1840	19	48
1860	44	114
1880	51	135

In the seventeenth century the maintenance of a noble family cost £600 per annum, but 10 francs at that time contained as much silver as 19 at present, and £600 was therefore in reality £1100, irrespective of the superior purchasing power at that period. In 1679 Madame de Maintenon writes to her sister, whose family consisted of her husband, herself, seven male and three female servants, "You can live like a princess on £600 a year," viz. :—

	House Expenses		Per Annum
Meat	£44	Food, &c.	£240
Bread	20	Rent	40
Wine	20	Wages	40
Butter	36	Opera, &c.	120
Sundries	120	Dress, &c.	160
Total	240	Total	600

The expenditure of the population of Paris in 1826 was :—

	Per Inhabitant	Amount
	£ s. d.	£
Food	14 2 0	12,350,000
Taxes	5 9 0	4,760,000
Rent	4 11 3	4,000,000
Clothing	2 16 5	2,470,000
Furniture	2 14 6	2,400,000
Fuel and light	2 14 0	2,380,000
Servants	1 16 8	1,610,000
Cabs and horses	1 15 6	1,540,000
Instruction	1 11 3	1,370,000
Washing	1 8 9	1,260,000
Sundries	1 9 5	1,290,000
Total	40 8 9	35,430,000

The chief items of food were :—

	Per Inhabitant	£ s. d.
Bread, lbs.	400	2 12 5
Wine, gallons	25	3 2 0
Meat, lbs.	165	3 19 0
Dairy	...	1 0 6
Sugar, lbs.	26	1 0 0
Sundries	...	2 8 0
Total	...	14 2 0

The Industrial Committee of Mulhouse reported that of every 100 francs earned by a workman, 20 went for bread, 15 for groceries, 18 for milk, &c., 8 for meat, 15 for rent, and 16 for clothes, leaving 8 francs for sundries.

GERMANY

In 1850 the annual maintenance of a peasant family of five persons in Prussia cost as follows :—

	£ s. d.
Food	16 0 0
Clothing	5 8 0
Rent	2 14 0
Coal and light	2 14 0
Taxes	1 5 0
Sundries	3 9 0
Total	31 10 0

Engel estimates the annual cost of maintenance for a peasant family in Germany thus :—

	£
Man	19
Wife	16
Three children	21
Family of five persons	56

He considers that a child of 10 years represents an outlay of £80, a youth of 15 one of £140.

Roth estimates that a child of 10 has cost £132, and one of 13 no less than £186.

Engel's figures are preferable.

The students of Heidelberg University in 1871 were able to maintain themselves at an average outlay of £31 per annum, but this rose to £58 in 1875, and to £69 in 1878.

RUSSIA

The income and expenditure of a fisherman's family yearly is as follows :—

Income	£ s. d.	Expenditure	£ s. d.
Game, 200 lbs.	2 10 0	Rye, 1 ton	7 0 0
Caviar, 200 lbs.	2 10 0	Taxes	2 6 0
Fish	5 0 0	Clothing	2 10 0
Woodcutting	2 10 0	Sundries	0 14 0
Total	12 10 0	Total	12 10 0

As regards the income and expenditure of the ordinary Moujik or peasant, Strebinski writes as follows : "The surplus grain which he has for sale brings him in £10 sterling, which goes thus :—

	£ s. d.
Rent	3 12 0
Taxes	0 16 0
Clothing	2 10 0
Sundries	3 2 0
Total	10 0 0

"His agricultural capital is (exclusive of cattle) about £33 sterling, viz.:—

	£ s. d.
House	18 0 0
Barn	7 0 0
Carts and harness	3 0 0
Implements, &c.	5 8 0
Total	33 8 0

ITALY

The Piedmontese peasant, who earns 18s. a week, spends 13s. on food ; the labourer of the island of Sardinia earns only 9s., and spends 7s. on food, viz. :—

	Piedmont, Pence Weekly	Island of Sardinia, Pence Weekly
Bread	16	26
Meat	42	5
Wine	40	6
Sundries	58	47
Total	156	84

LOCAL TAXATION

The amount annually levied by local authorities in taxes, tolls, &c., was approximately in the various countries as follows, 1886–87 :—

	£		£
England	38,010,000	Russia	11,200,000
Scotland	4,440,000	Austria	5,300,000
Ireland	3,330,000	Italy	27,200,000
United Kingdom	45,780,000	Holland	2,100,000
France	40,800,000	Belgium	2,250,000
Germany	44,000,000	United States	84,200,000

Local taxation of the United Kingdom and France compare as follows :—

Year	United Kingdom, £	France, £	Shillings per Inhab.	
			United Kingdom	France
1830	10,820,000	7,100,000	9	4
1840	10,240,000	8,800,000	8	5
1850	11,050,000	11,700,000	8	7
1860	14,950,000	18,100,000	10	10
1870	24,300,000	21,300,000	16	12
1882	38,100,000	32,400,000	22	17
1887	45,800,000	40,800,000	24	21

The finances of various cities in 1880–81 showed thus :—

	Annual Expenditure, £	Debt, £	£ per Inhabitant	
			Expenditure	Debt
Antwerp . . .	376,000	...	2.1	...
Berlin	2,200,000	5,610,000	2.0	5.1
Birmingham . .	1,610,000	6,110,000	4.0	15.0
Boston	...	6,200,000	...	16.5
Bradford . . .	1,100,000	3,400,000	6.0	19.0
Breslau . . .	361,000	1,270,000	1.5	5.3
Brighton . . .	210,000	700,000	1.6	5.5
Bristol	405,000	600,000	2.0	2.9
Brooklyn . . .	...	7,900,000	...	14.9
Bucharest . . .	337,000	570,000	1.5	1.8
Buda-Pesth . .	672,000	1,280,000	2.2	4.3
Christiania . .	250,000	345,000	3.3	4.5
Copenhagen . .	325,000	850,000	1.6	4.1
Florence . . .	950,000	5,540,000	5.7	33.5
Frankfort . . .	422,000	1,460,000	3.5	12.1
Genoa	466,000	1,600,000	2.6	9.0
Leeds	1,300,000	3,500,000	4.2	11.3
Leipzig . . .	312,000	740,000	2.3	5.5
Liège	309,000	1,500,000	2.7	13.5
Liverpool . . .	3,200,000	21,600,000	5.9	39.6
London	11,300,000	20,600,000	2.9	5.3
Manchester . .	1,900,000	6,200,000	3.3	10.9
Milan	...	3,050,000	...	9.3
Munich . . .	395,000	1,500,000	1.8	7.0
Naples	...	4,860,000	...	9.9
Newcastle . .	400,000	700,000	2.7	4.8
New York . . .	...	23,100,000	...	19.1
Palermo . . .	320,000	540,000	1.3	2.2
Paris	10,440,000	85,300,000	4.7	34.2
Philadelphia . .	...	3,400,000	...	4.1
Rome	820,000	2,340,000	2.7	7.8
San Francisco .	970,000	750,000	4.1	3.2
St. Louis . . .	...	4,800,000	...	14.0
Sheffield . . .	410,000	500,000	1.4	1.8
Stockholm . .	360,000	480,000	2.3	3.0
Stuttgart . . .	120,000	400,000	1.1	3.7
Trieste	373,000	500,000	3.7	4.9
Turin	520,000	510,000	2.7	2.7
Venice	182,000	430,000	1.4	3.3
Vienna	2,700,000	8,470,000	2.5	7.8

The following is a synopsis of local revenues :—

ENGLAND

	1868	1880	1887
	£	£	£
Rates	16,400,000	25,700,000	32,800,000
Tolls	4,350,000	4,600,000	5,250,000
Loans	5,520,000	13,720,000	8,940,000
Government subsidy	950,000	2,700,000	3,980,000
Sundries . . .	3,220,000	6,290,000	3,940,000
Total .	30,440,000	53,010,000	54,910,000

SCOTLAND

	1868	1880	1887
Rates	1,500,000	2,600,000	3,400,000
Tolls	500,000	1,060,000	1,030,000
Loans	250,000	1,120,000	1,800,000
Government subsidy	200,000	550,000	710,000
Sundries . . .	550,000	740,000	370,000
Total .	3,000,000	6,070,000	7,310,000

IRELAND

	1868	1880	1887
Rates	2,280,000	2,650,000	2,840,000
Tolls	280,000	510,000	490,000
Loans	240,000	260,000	480,000
Government subsidy	80,000	100,000	120,000
Sundries . . .	180,000	350,000	285,000
Total .	3,060,000	3,870,000	4,215,000

UNITED KINGDOM

	1868	1880	1887
	£	£	£
Rates . . .	20,180,000	30,950,000	39,040,000
Tolls . . .	5,130,000	6,170,000	6,770,000
Loans . . .	6,010,000	15,100,000	11,220,000
Government subsidy	1,230,000	3,350,000	4,810,000
Sundries . .	3,950,000	7,380,000	4,595,000
Total .	36,500,000	62,950,000	66,435,000

Local expenditure was as follows :—

ENGLAND

	1868	1880	1887
	£	£	£
Poor relief . .	7,500,000	8,040,000	8,200,000
Police and works .	15,350,000	32,200,000	32,200,000
Schools . . .	...	3,650,000	5,400,000
Roads and bridges	2,600,000	2,200,000	2,100,000
Harbours and lights	2,700,000	3,200,000	3,800,000
Sundries . .	2,300,000	2,200,000	2,700,000
Total .	30,450,000	51,490,000	54,400,000

SCOTLAND

	1868	1880	1887
Poor relief . .	870,000	880,000	880,000
Police and works .	970,000	2,300,000	3,100,000
Schools . . .	...	1,200,000	1,400,000
Roads and bridges	320,000	350,000	690,000
Harbours and lights	240,000	1,000,000	1,060,000
Sundries . .	180,000	190,000	150,000
Total .	2,580,000	5,920,000	7,280,000

IRELAND

	1868	1880	1887
Poor relief .	840,000	1,000,000	1,100,000
Roads and bridges	1,120,000	1,140,000	1,180,000
Harbours and lights	460,000	530,000	520,000
Sundries . .	680,000	1,090,000	1,490,000
Total .	3,100,000	3,760,000	4,290,000

UNITED KINGDOM

	1868	1880	1887
Poor relief . .	9,210,000	9,920,000	10,180,000
Police and works .	16,320,000	34,500,000	35,300,000
Schools . . .	...	4,850,000	6,800,000
Roads and bridges	4,040,000	3,690,000	3,970,000
Harbours and lights	3,400,000	4,730,000	5,380,000
Sundries . .	3,160,000	3,480,000	4,340,000
Total .	36,130,000	61,170,000	65,970,000

Schools and police in Ireland, as well as other items, are defrayed out of the Imperial Treasury at a cost of £3,015,000, of which £1,600,000 are for police and £900,000 for schools, bringing up all local expenditure in Ireland to £7,100,000.

Local taxation in England and Wales was as follows :—

Year			£	Year			£
1688 .	.	.	780,000	1840	.	.	8,020,000
1730 .	.	.	1,380,000	1850	.	.	8,910,000
1770 .	.	.	1,690,000	1862	.	.	12,210,000
1790 .	.	.	2,420,000	1868	.	.	16,100,000
1803 .	.	.	5,350,000	1880	.	.	31,060,000
1813 .	.	.	8,650,000	1886	.	.	37,300,000

The expenditure in England and Wales for support of the poor was as follows :—

Period	Annual Average, £	Rental Valuation, £*	Poor-Rate per £, Pence	Poor-Rate per Inhab., Pence
1702–14 .	910,000	14,200,000	16	41
1760–75 .	1,520,000	24,900,000	15	58
1783–93 .	2,050,000	30,300,000	16	66
1803 . .	4,080,000	35,100,000	27	107
1815 . .	6,100,000	53,800,000	27	133
1816–20 .	7,310,000	58,200,000	30	152
1830–35 .	6,742,000	75,900,000	22	116
1842–50 .	5,290,000	90,400,000	14	74
1851–60 .	5,510,000	109,600,000	12	69
1861–70 .	6,740,000	134,300,000	12	77
1871–80 .	7,710,000	167,200,000	11	75
1880 . .	8,015,000	191,150,000	10	74

The above shows only the rates expended on the poor, but the poor-rate often rose 50 per cent. higher, as it included police and other items. The valuation included many items of real estate not liable to poor-rate, and in 1880 was made up thus :—

	£
Houses	96,500,000
Lands	51,700,000
Railways	24,500,000
Mines	10,300,000
Gasworks, &c.	8,150,000
Tota . . .	191,150,000

* This table must not be confused with poor-law assessment, which was always less; for instance, in 1880 the assessed gross rental was only £158,000,000, and the taxable rental £134,000,000.

Local debts in Great Britain in 1880 were as follows :—

	£
Sanitary	56,700,000
Docks	23,200,000
Sundry	57,000,000
Scotch	16,300,000
Total . . .	153,200,000

In 1888 the local debts were known to exceed 200 millions sterling. Those of England and Wales rose as follows :—

Year	London, £	Provinces, £	Total, £
1882 .	32,200,000	119,500,000	151,700,000
1885 .	35,900,000	137,300,000	173,200,000
1888 .	39,700,000	152,500,000	192,200,000

FRANCE

The local taxes at various dates stood thus :—

	1806 £	1837 £	1864 £	1882 £	1886 £
Paris	736,000	2,760,000	5,370,000	9,805,000	10,200,000
Thirty cities	490,000	1,490,000	2,460,000	4,230,000	} 30,600,000
Communes	800,000	4,030,000	12,300,000	18,405,000	
Total	2,026,000	8,290,000	20,130,000	32,440,000	40,800,000

The following statement of Octroi for all France was published in 1886 :—

Year	Towns Taxed	Liquor	Food	Fuel	Fodder	Sundries	Total
1831	1,467	880,000	700,000	300,000	120,000	200,000	2,200,000
1840	1,435	1,280,000	880,000	400,000	160,000	380,000	3,100,000
1850	1,436	1,680,000	1,150,000	450,000	200,000	320,000	3,800,000
1860	1,460	2,300,000	1,640,000	700,000	300,000	860,000	5,800,000
1870	1,516	3,200,000	1,800,000	650,000	300,000	750,000	6,700,000
1880	1,541	4,900,000	3,000,000	1,200,000	600,000	1,340,000	11,040,000
1885	1,529	4,900,000	3,100,000	1,300,000	600,000	1,150,000	11,050,000

Octroi is the principal municipal tax, and presses most heavily on the working-classes, as it augments the cost of food, fuel, and other necessaries. In sixty years this tax increased five-fold, while the population of the cities so taxed had only doubled, the ratio per inhabitant being now 20 shillings yearly as compared with 8 shillings in 1823. The following table shows the aggregate amount collected for Octroi in French towns at various dates :—

Year	Amount, £	Population Taxed	Per Inhab., Shillings
1823 . . .	2,470,000	5,998,000	8
1833 . . .	2,640,000	6,306,000	8
1843 . . .	3,302,000	7,297,000	9
1853 . . .	3,617,000	7,330,000	10
1863 . . .	6,298,000	9,582,000	13
1873 . . .	8,451,000	10,517,000	16
1880 .	11,040,000	11,255,000	20

The Octroi of Paris contributes one-half of the total, that is, it is equal to the aggregate of all other French cities. It was at various dates as follows :—

Year	Amount, £	Population	Per Head, Shillings
1801 . . .	441,000	553,000	16
1821 . . .	1,040,000	724,000	29
1845 . . .	1,370,000	986,000	28
1867 . . .	4,030,000	1,732,000	46
1880 . . .	5,640,000	2,180,000	52
1889 . . .	6,030,000	2,400,000	50

In all French cities this tax has grown faster than population. The figures of all four cities in 1880 compare with 1867 thus :—

	Octroi, £		Shillings per Inhab.	
	1867	1880	1867	1880
Paris . . .	4,030,000	5,640,000	46	52
Marseilles .	307,000	490,000	21	28
Lyons . .	244,000	480,000	16	25
Rouen . .	102,000	155,000	21	29

The aggregate population of the 1529 towns and cities was 12,000,000, and the amount paid in Octroi in 1885 showed thus:—

	Amount, £	Pence per Head
Wine	2,840,000	57
Alcohol, &c. . .	1,000,000	20
Oil	240,000	5
Food	3,100,000	62
Fuel	1,300,000	26
Fodder . . .	600,000	12
Bricks, &c. . .	1,000,000	20
Sundries . . .	970,000	20
Total . .	11,050,000	212

The above is for all, including Paris; but the Octroi of Paris was much above the average, namely, 60 francs or 48s. per head, the average for the other 1528 towns being 14 francs or 11s. per head.

GERMANY

Local expenditure in Prussia was as follows:—

	1869	1876
	£	£
Schools . . .	1,900,000	3,500,000
Streets . . .	1,700,000	3,000,000
Interest on debt .	2,500,000	4,800,000
Poor . . .	2,300,000	2,700,000
Police, &c. . .	3,400,000	5,900,000
Total .	11,800,000	19,900,000

Municipal expenditure in 1876 at Berlin, Breslau, and Cologne was as follows:—

	Berlin	Breslau	Cologne
	£	£	£
Schools . .	230,000	55,000	32,000
Streets . .	400,000	27,000	10,000
Interest on debt .	300,000	80,000	70,000
Poor . . .	270,000	13,000	25,000
Police, &c. .	420,000	65,000	23,000
Total .	1,620,000	240,000	· 160,000

The average municipal expenditure was as follows:—

Year	Shillings per Inhabitant			
	Berlin	Breslau	Cologne	Frankfort
1869 . .	15	11	12	18
1876 . .	27	18	21	20

All local taxation in Germany may be estimated at 18s. per inhabitant, say 44 millions sterling.

AUSTRIA-HUNGARY

The municipal finances of Prague in 1884 showed:—

Receipts, £		Expenses, £	
House-tax . .	47,000	Water supply . .	40,000
Tolls . . .	60,000	Schools and hospitals	41,000
Sundries . .	88,000	Sundries . . .	164,000
Total .	195,000	Total .	245,000

BELGIUM

The district finances in 1887 showed thus:—

Receipts, £		Expenditure, £	
Tobacco, &c. .	70,000	Schools . . .	100,000
Dog-tax . .	50,000	Roads . . .	110,000
Sundries . .	170,000	Sundries . .	240,000
State subsidy .	250,000		
		Total .	450,000
Total .	540,000		

The above does not include city finances. Those of Brussels in 1884 showed:—

Receipts, £		Expenses, £	
Gas and water rates	280,000	Schools . .	50,000
Municipal properties	190,000	Debt . .	40,000
Tolls . . .	160,000	Police, &c. .	560,000
Sundries . .	170,000	Sundries . .	120,000
Total .	800,000	Total .	770,000

ITALY

Local taxation, according to official returns, showed thus:—

Year	£	Shillings per Inhabitant
1867 . .	12,900,000	10.0
1877 . .	20,100,000	15.0
1885 . .	27,200,000	18.0

The average per inhabitant, distinguishing urban from rural communes, was as follows:—

Year	Shillings per Inhabitant	
	Urban	Rural
1867	18 ...	6
1877	27 ...	9

Urban taxes in 1877 comprised: Octroi, £5,100,000; legacy dues, £1,700,000; sundries, £5,200,000; making a total of £12,000,000.

The average Octroi per head in 1877 was:—

Shillings per Inhabitant

Naples . .	12	Milan . . .	14	Rome . . .	22
Turin . .	12	Palermo . .	16	Florence . .	24
Venice . .	14	Leghorn . .	16	Genoa . . .	26

Local debts in 1885 amounted to £41,500,000 sterling.

UNITED STATES

The taxes in the several States for local purposes (not municipal) were in 1889 as follows:—

	Tax, £	Population in 1890	Shillings per Head
New England .	1,660,000	4,690,000	7.0
Middle States .	4,060,000	14,110,000	5.9
Southern States .	3,640,000	18,280,000	4.0
Western States .	5,740,000	25,400,000	4.5
Total . .	15,200,000	62,480,000	4.9

In some of the principal States the taxes were in 1889 thus:—

	Tax, £	Population	Shillings per Head
New York . . .	1,900,000	5,980,000	6.2
Pennsylvania . .	1,740,000	5,250,000	6.7
Massachusetts .	1,050,000	2,230,000	9.6
Ohio	1,040,000	3,670,000	5.7
Illinois	780,000	3,820,000	4.1
Kentucky . . .	780,000	1,850,000	8.4
Various	7,910,000	39,680,000	4.0
Total . .	15,200,000	62,480,000	4.9

Municipal taxes ranged ordinarily from 2 to 3 per cent. on all assessed properties, making up a total of about 37 millions sterling, or £3 per inhabitant yearly. These added to state taxes made up altogether £52,200,000 of local taxation, or 17s. per head of the total population. Compared with 1860 we find:—

Year	Local Taxes, £	Population	Shillings per Head
1860 . . .	19,600,000	31,400,000	13
1889 . . .	52,200,000	62,480,000	17

The aggregate of state and municipal debts at various dates was as follows :—

	1850	1870	1880	£ per Inhabitant		
				1850	1870	1880
	£	£	£			
New York . . .	4,800,000	29,100,000	45,500,000	1.6	6.5	9.0
Pennsylvania . .	8,800,000	16,200,000	22,100,000	3.9	4.5	5.1
Massachusetts . .	1,200,000	12,700,000	19,000,000	1.2	8.0	10.5
Maryland . . .	3,100,000	5,400,000	2,300,000	5.3	7.0	2.4
Virginia . . .	2,900,000	10,200,000	9,000,000	2.1	6.0	4.3
Ohio	3,300,000	4,000,000	10,200,000	1.7	1.5	3.3
Various . . .	15,800,000	80,600,000	109,500,000	1.3	3.3	3.3
Total . .	39,900,000	158,200,000	217,600,000	1.8	4.1	4.3

The local debts of 1880 were made up thus :—

	State	City, &c.	Total
	£	£	£
New York . . .	1,600,000	43,900,000	45,500,000
Pennsylvania . .	2,600,000	19,500,000	22,100,000
Massachusetts .	4,200,000	14,800,000	19,000,000
Maryland . . .	1,600,000	700,000	2,300,000
Virginia . . .	6,100,000	2,900,000	9,000,000
Ohio	1,200,000	9,000,000	10,200,000
Missouri . . .	3,400,000	8,400,000	11,800,000
New Jersey . .	100,000	10,200,000	10,300,000
Louisiana . . .	4,900,000	4,100,000	9,000,000
Illinois	...	9,400,000	9,400,000
Tennessee . . .	5,700,000	2,100,000	7,800,000
Various	15,700,000	45,500,000	61,200,000
Total . .	47,100,000	170,500,000	217,600,000

The amount of state debt, exclusive of city and county debts, in 1888 was as follows :—

	Debt, £	Shillings per Inhabitant
New York	1,400,000	5.0
Pennsylvania . . .	3,100,000	12.0
Massachusetts . . .	6,500,000	3.1
Virginia	6,400,000	3.0
Tennessee . . .	3,600,000	2.0
Louisiana . . .	2,500,000	2.1
North Carolina . . .	3,000,000	1.8
Various	19,700,000	10.0
Total . .	46,200,000	15.0

In 1883 the public debt of 138 cities and towns summed up 99 millions sterling.

LONDON

In 1885 London had 555,000 houses, with 4,120,000 inhabitants, covering an area of 117 square miles or 75,000 acres, that is 56 persons per acre. There were 400,000 foot-passengers and 80,000 vehicles passing daily over the bridges, and 370,000 passengers in the Underground Railway. There were 1830 miles of streets, and 2300 miles of sewers, the latter ranging from 1 foot to 12 feet in diameter. The sewage reservoirs (12 miles below London) discharged 150 million gallons daily into the Thames at ebb-tide. Water supply was 140 million gallons daily, or 34 per inhabitant, for which the companies charged £1,500,000, or 1½d. (1.60) per ton. Gas consumption amounted to 20 milliards of cubic feet, at 3s. per 1000 feet, say £3,000,000 per annum, consuming 2 millions tons coal, and conveyed by 2500 miles of pipes some 4 feet in diameter. Fire-brigade had 58 engines, 124 escapes, 580 firemen, costing £100,000 per annum, and using 17 million gallons water. Police, 13,000 men, or 1 in 316 inhabitants. Parks, 42, covering 4490 acres. Markets, 14, covering 15 acres; the meat consumption including 330,000 oxen, 2,100,000 sheep, and amounting altogether to 210,000 tons per annum. There are 220 deaths and 360 births daily, being a natural increase of 140 persons, but the increase of population averages 200 daily, the difference being caused by immigration. Of all deaths, 21 per cent. occur in hospital, and almost 4 per cent. (3.7) are violent deaths, say ten daily. There are 5550 coroners' inquests yearly, and 3580 persons killed or wounded by cabs. About 120 adults are missing every year, and 50 dead bodies are not identified. The number of stray dogs taken up is 29,500 per annum. The foreign trade of London, that is, imports and exports, exceeds 200 millions sterling per annum. There are 11,000 cabs and 2000 omnibuses, which carry 78 million passengers yearly. The growth of the Metropolis has been as follows :—

Year	Population	Houses	Miles of Streets	Valuation, £
1801 . . .	959,000	130,000	470	3,700,000
1821 . . .	1,379,000	170,000	610	5,300,000
1841 . . .	1,948,000	256,000	905	9,600,000
1861 . . .	2,804,000	369,000	1,290	16,800,000
1885 . . .	4,120,000	555,000	1,830	35,600,000

Municipal expenditure in 1881 was £11,000,000, and debt £21,000,000. Paris, with half the population, spends the same amount yearly, and has a debt of £90,000,000 sterling. The rental valuation of London in 1888 was £38,100,000.

LOTTERIES

The Spanish lottery gave a net profit of £403,000 in 1882.
The Italian and Austrian lotteries produced as follows :—

	Italy		Austria	
	1868	1877	1868	1877
	£	£	£	£
Receipts . .	2,420,000	2,705,000	1,380,000	2,172,000
Expenses . .	1,670,000	1,713,000	850,000	1,160,000
Profit . .	750,000	992,000	530,000	1,012,000

M.

MACHINERY

The following examples show the economy of labour resulting from machinery :—

1. Arkwright's spinning-jenny enabled one operative in 1815 to produce as much yarn as 200 could a few years before.

2. The crane of Cologne Cathedral in 1870, with two men, did the same work in one hour, in lifting stone, as required 60 men to work 12 hours in the Middle Ages ; that is, one man now is equal to 180 of the olden time.

3. The American boot-making machine enables one man to turn out 300 pair of boots daily ; one factory near Boston makes as many boots as 32,000 bootmakers in Paris. In 1880 there were 3100 of these machines at work, producing 150 million pair of boots yearly.

4. Altmann's American reaper cuts and binds grain at 45 minutes per acre. D. Glynn of California cuts, threshes, winnows, and bags with each of his machines 60 acres of grain daily.

5. The United States in 1888 produced 600,000 sewing-machines, which could do the work of 7,200,000 women.

6. In the Western States of America one man can raise as much wheat as will feed 1000 persons for 12 months ; a second can thresh, winnow, and bag it, and a third convey it to market.

7. A girl 12 years of age in a Lancashire mill can turn out 35 yards of printed calico daily, her work in one year sufficing to clothe yearly 1200 persons in the East.

The export of machinery from Great Britain is large. In 1888 Russia took 300 steam-threshers and 250 portable steam-engines.

The Trade Returns show the value of British machinery exported thus :—

	£		£
1853	2,000,000	1870	5,300,000
1860	3,800,000	1888	13,000,000

MAIZE

The crop of 1887 was stated thus :—

	Acres	Bushels
France	1,480,000	26,000,000
Russia	1,360,000	13,000,000
Austria	5,410,000	90,000,000
Italy	4,680,000	75,000,000
Spain	2,000,000	40,000,000
Portugal	200,000	4,000,000
Roumania, &c.	2,000,000	40,000,000
Europe	27,130,000	288,000,000
United States	72,390,000	1,412,000,000
Canada	180,000	9,000,000
Australia	250,000	7,000,000
Egypt	680,000	10,000,000
Algeria	400,000	10,000,000
Argentina	1,700,000	17,000,000
Total	102,730,000	1,753,000,000

The United States crop in 1888 reached 1988 million bushels, or 49,700,000 tons. Spallart estimated the crop for the whole world thus :—

Year	Millions of Bushels
1871–80	1,528
1883–84	2,035
1887	1,979

MANUFACTURES

The following table shows approximately the value of all manufactures in 1888 :—

	Textiles	Hardware	Clothing	Beer and Spirits	Leather	Sundries	Total	Per Inhabitant, £
	Million £ Sterling Yearly							
U. Kingdom	170	155	66	75	42	312	820	21.5
France	108	42	64	21	52	198	485	12.7
Germany	82	91	53	71	53	233	583	12.3
Russia	52	14	51	20	51	175	363	4.3
Austria	36	15	30	23	39	110	253	5.1
Italy	21	4	24	4	17	51	121	4.1
Spain	16	4	16	1	12	36	85	5.0
Portugal	2	1	3	...	3	7	16	3.6
Sweden	2	6	6	6	8	22	50	10.5
Norway	1	1	2	3	4	8	19	9.5
Denmark	1	1	3	4	6	11	26	13.0
Holland	3	1	6	5	6	14	35	8.0
Belgium	16	17	12	13	6	38	102	17.0
Switzerland	11	2	3	2	2	12	32	11.0
Europe	521	354	339	248	301	1,227	2,990	9.0
U. States	112	194	98	61	104	874	1,443	24.0
Australia	7	15	4	3	6	6	41	11.5
Total	640	563	441	312	411	2,107	4,474	11.2

The latest official return of the manufactures of Canada gives a total of 64 millions sterling. The following table shows approximately the value of manufactures produced yearly in the several countries at various dates :—

	Millions £ Sterling					
	1780	1800	1820	1840	1860	1888
U. Kingdom	177	230	290	387	577	820
France	147	190	220	264	380	485
Germany	50	60	85	150	310	583
Russia	10	15	20	40	155	363
Austria	30	50	80	142	200	253
Italy	10	15	25	40	80	121
Spain	10	20	30	45	60	85
Belgium	...	...	...	60	90	102
U. States	15	25	55	96	392	1,443
Various	31	45	60	90	160	363
Total	480	650	865	1,314	2,404	4,618

Hardware.—The hardware manufactures of the world may be approximately summed up thus :—

	Millions £ Sterling					
	Iron	Steel	Copper	Lead	Tin	Zinc	Total
U. Kingdom	50	84	10	3	5	3	155
France	20	16	3	1	1	1	42
Germany	40	38	3	3	1	6	91
Russia	5	7	1	1	...	...	14
Austria	6	8	...	1	...	...	15
Italy	3	1	...	...	...	...	4
Spain	3	1	...	...	...	...	4
Sweden	4	2	...	...	...	...	6
Belgium	8	6	1	1	1	...	17
United States	72	95	14	7	4	2	194
Various	17	20	3	1	1	1	43
Total	228	278	35	18	13	13	585

For details regarding the above metals, see each under its own title. The total value of hardware manufactures at various dates was approximately as follows :—

Year	Millions £ Sterling											
	U. Kingdom	France	Germany	Russia	Austria	Italy	Spain	Sweden	Belgium	U. States	Various	Total
1780 . . .	15	8	3	2	2	1	1	1	...	2	2	37
1800 . . .	20	9	4	3	3	1	1	1	...	3	3	48
1820 . . .	30	10	6	4	4	2	2	2	...	7	5	72
1840 . . .	40	12	7	5	5	2	2	3	2	10	7	95
1860 . . .	85	30	40	11	12	3	3	4	9	29	17	243
1888 . . .	155	42	91	14	15	4	4	6	17	194	43	585

The production of the principal metals at various dates was approximately as follows :—

Year	Tons					
	Iron	Copper	Lead	Tin	Zinc	Total
1780 .	270,000	6,000	50,000	2,000	2,000	330,000
1800 .	460,000	8,000	60,000	3,000	3,000	534,000
1820 .	1,010,000	10,000	70,000	4,000	3,000	1,097,000
1840 .	2,680,000	25,000	120,000	6,000	12,000	2,843,000
1860 .	7,180,000	70,000	220,000	8,000	65,000	7,543,000
1888 .	24,800,000	190,000	410,000	35,000	240,000	25,675,000

It appears that the production of metals has multiplied fifty-fold since 1800.

Textile Manufactures.—The consumption of fibre by all nations has been approximately as follows :—

Year	Millions of Lbs.						
	Cotton	Wool	Flax	Hemp	Jute	Silk	Total
1780 .	220	440	500	350	...	30	1,540
1800 .	303	460	600	400	...	30	1,793
1820 .	402	520	700	450	...	33	2,105
1840 .	1,210	694	800	500	...	35	3,239
1850 .	1,335	886	900	600	60	37	3,818
1860 .	2,451	1,074	925	700	130	40	5,320
1870 .	2,675	1,579	1,200	750	410	42	6,656
1880 .	3,501	1,915	1,120	820	900	45	8,301
1887 .	4,433	2,242	1,230	880	1,310	50	10,145

Reducing to tons the total weight of fibre consumed in 100 years down to 1880, we find it was approximately as follows :—

	Tons Aggregate						
	Cotton	Wool	Flax	Hemp	Jute	Silk	Total
1781–1800	2,200,000	4,100,000	4,900,000	3,400,000	...	270,000	14,870,000
1801–20	2,500,000	4,400,000	5,800,000	3,800,000	...	270,000	16,770,000
1821–40	4,560,000	5,500,000	6,700,000	4,200,000	...	300,000	21,260,000
1841–50	5,220,000	3,600,000	3,700,000	2,500,000	200,000	160,000	15,380,000
1851–60	8,260,000	4,400,000	4,100,000	2,900,000	600,000	170,000	20,430,000
1861–70	8,190,000	5,900,000	4,800,000	3,200,000	2,000,000	170,000	24,260,000
1871 80	12,860,000	7,700,000	5,200,000	3,400,000	3,500,000	180,000	32,840,000
100 years	43,790,000	35,600,000	35,200,000	23,400,000	6,300,000	1,520,000	145,810,000

The total output of textile manufactures in 107 years was approximately as follows :—

Period	Millions £ Sterling										
	U. Kingdom	France	Germany	Russia	Austria	Italy	Spain	Belgium	Various	U. States	Total
1781–1800 . .	620	480	160	70	100	50	90	...	110	50	1,730
1801–20 . .	980	680	210	90	140	70	120	...	160	80	2,530
1821–40 . .	1,538	921	334	172	243	101	172	60	192	208	3,941
1841–50 . .	970	634	318	250	199	74	94	54	101	261	2,955
1851–60 . .	1,265	740	396	294	242	94	115	59	126	375	3,706
1861–70 . .	1,546	958	486	352	279	128	134	108	163	628	4,782
1871–80 . .	1,872	945	607	486	331	156	158	151	198	706	5,610
1881–87 . .	1,218	672	520	361	256	131	110	106	214	651	4,239
107 years . .	10,009	6,030	3,031	2,075	1,790	804	993	538	1,264	2,959	29,493

	1781 1800	1801–20	1821–40	1841–50	1851–60	1861–70	1871–80	1881–87	Total
Cottons . .	140	660	1,506	1,055	1,440	1,810	2,234	1,782	10,627
Woollens . .	1,040	1,100	1,280	1,064	1,243	1,661	1,921	1,366	10,675
Linens . .	255	370	550	372	431	544	575	397	3,494
Silks . .	265	340	480	311	406	522	559	475	3,358
Sundries . .	30	60	125	153	186	245	321	219	1,339
Total .	1,730	2,530	3,941	2,955	3,706	4,782	5,610	4,239	29,493

The value of all textile manufactures in each country at various dates from 1780 was as follows, approximately :—

	Millions £ Sterling								
	1780	1800	1820	1840	1850	1860	1870	1880	1887
U. Kingdom .	26	36	67	92	108	143	174	184	170
France . . .	21	27	42	52	70	88	109	110	108
Germany . .	7	9	12	22	30	39	53	72	82
Russia . . .	3	4	5	14	22	29	40	49	52
Austria . . .	4	6	9	18	20	24	29	34	36
Italy . . .	2	3	4	6	9	13	15	20	21
Spain . . .	4	5	7	11	12	14	15	17	16
Belgium . .	...	...	...	8	11	12	17	17	16
Switzerland,&c.	5	6	7	8	10	13	15	17	15
Europe . .	72	96	153	231	292	375	467	520	516
United States .	2	3	5	15	28	45	70	98	112
Total .	74	99	158	246	320	420	537	618	628

The value of fibre consumed by various nations since 1840 was approximately as follows :—

UNITED KINGDOM

Period	Millions £ Sterling				
	Cotton	Wool	Silk	Flax, Hemp, &c.	Total
1841–50 . .	112	91	65	73	341
1851–60 . .	241	119	68	66	494
1861–70 . .	430	140	55	91	716
1871–80 . .	390	156	32	108	686
1881–87 . .	252	97	16	60	425
47 years . .	1,425	603	236	398	2,662

FRANCE

1841–50 . .	33	86	86	63	268
1851–60 . .	50	96	120	53	319
1861–70 . .	95	111	166	62	434
1871–80 . .	71	113	125	70	379
1881–87 . .	56	72	72	40	240
47 years . .	305	478	569	288	1,640

GERMANY

1841–50 . .	23	53	13	31	120
1851–60 . .	40	65	18	29	152
1861–70 . .	81	73	23	33	210
1871–80 . .	86	81	40	40	247
1881–87 . .	73	57	38	25	193
47 years . .	303	329	132	158	922

RUSSIA

1841–50 . .	14	49	1	30	94
1851–60 . .	22	54	2	33	111
1861–70 . .	40	56	4	42	142
1871–80 . .	62	72	6	53	193
1881–87 . .	54	41	5	37	137
47 years . .	192	272	18	195	677

AUSTRIA

1841–50 . .	11	33	6	28	78
1851–60 . .	22	35	8	26	91
1861–70 . .	41	34	11	30	116
1871–80 . .	49	36	14	36	135
1881–87 . .	38	25	10	24	97
47 years . .	161	163	49	144	517

ITALY

Period	Millions £ Sterling				
	Cotton	Wool	Silk	Flax, Hemp, &c.	Total
1841–50 . .	3	13	6	10	32
1851–60 . .	6	15	7	11	39
1861–70 . .	15	17	11	14	57
1871–80 . .	23	20	9	17	69
1881–87 . .	25	12	5	12	54
47 years . .	72	77	38	64	251

SPAIN

1841–50 . .	6	17	2	9	34
1851–60 . .	12	22	3	7	44
1861–70 . .	21	24	3	7	55
1871–80 . .	26	26	4	7	63
1881–87 . .	21	14	3	5	43
47 years . .	86	103	15	35	239

BELGIUM

1841–50 . .	7	5	...	6	18
1851–60 . .	8	6	1	7	22
1861–70 . .	15	18	1	11	45
1871–80 . .	15	29	3	16	63
1881–87 . .	13	15	2	13	43
47 years . .	58	73	7	53	191

SCANDINAVIA, SWITZERLAND, &C.

1841–50 . .	9	19	7	7	42
1851–60 . .	15	23	9	7	54
1861–70 . .	26	29	3	10	68
1871–80 . .	36	29	6	10	81
1881–87 . .	60	18	4	7	89
47 years . .	146	118	29	41	334

UNITED STATES

1841–50 . .	49	30	2	7	88
1851–60 . .	84	38	4	12	138
1861–70 . .	223	62	14	17	316
1871–80 . .	157	101	15	24	297
1881–87 . .	150	83	20	16	269
47 years . .	663	314	55	76	1,108

THE WORLD

1841–50 . .	267	396	188	264	1,115
1851–60 . .	500	473	240	251	1,464
1861–70 . .	987	564	291	317	2,159
1871–80 . .	915	663	254	381	2,213
1881–87 . .	742	434	175	239	1,590
47 years . .	3,411	2,530	1,148	1,452	8,541

The value of goods manufactured from the above fibres in 47 years was approximately, in millions sterling :—

Period	Cottons	Woollens	Linens	Silks	Hemp, &c.	Total
1841–50 . .	1,055	1,064	372	311	153	2,955
1851–60 . .	1,440	1,243	431	406	186	3,706
1861–70 . .	1,810	1,661	544	522	245	4,782
1871–80 . .	2,234	1,921	575	559	321	5,610
1881–87 . .	1,782	1,366	397	475	219	4,239
47 years . .	8,321	7,255	2,319	2,273	1,124	21,292

	Cottons	Woollens	Linens	Silks	Hemp, &c.	Total
	Millions £ Aggregate					
U. Kingdom	3,726	1,768	572	435	370	6,871
France . .	771	1,368	505	1,132	173	3,949
Germany . .	727	948	290	280	82	2,327
Russia . .	461	780	260	37	205	1,743
Austria . .	382	484	217	99	125	1,307
Italy . .	163	195	90	72	63	583
Spain . .	202	293	58	32	26	611
Belgium . .	141	190	115	17	15	478
Scandinavia .	52	126	...	...	...	178
U. States . .	1,411	911	132	115	52	2,621
Various . .	285	192	80	54	13	624
Total .	8,321	7,255	2,319	2,273	1,124	21,292

The following table shows approximately the value of goods manufactured in each decade :—

UNITED KINGDOM

Period	Cottons	Woollens	Linens	Silks	Hemp, Jute, &c.	Total
	Millions £ Aggregate					
1841–50	469	249	103	108	41	970
1851–60	677	311	113	115	49	1,265
1861–70	813	412	147	96	78	1,546
1871–80	1,071	476	132	71	122	1,872
1881–87	696	320	77	45	80	1,218
47 years	3,726	1,768	572	435	370	6,871

FRANCE

1841–50	136	233	105	140	20	634
1851–60	158	252	105	200	25	740
1861–70	180	325	120	298	35	958
1871–80	165	328	110	288	54	945
1881–87	132	230	65	206	39	672
47 years	771	1,368	505	1,132	173	3,949

GERMANY

1841–50	92	142	50	22	12	318
1851–60	125	171	55	30	15	396
1861–70	147	215	65	41	18	486
1871–80	195	235	70	85	22	607
1881–87	168	185	50	102	15	520
47 years	727	948	290	280	82	2,327

RUSSIA

1841–50	56	132	25	2	35	250
1851–60	69	141	40	4	40	294
1861–70	75	166	60	6	45	352
1871–80	138	211	75	12	50	486
1881–87	123	130	60	13	35	361
47 years	461	780	260	37	205	1,743

AUSTRIA

1841–50	44	90	35	10	20	199
1851–60	69	93	40	15	25	242
1861–70	107	107	45	20	30	279
1871–80	108	110	55	28	30	331
1881–87	84	84	42	26	20	256
47 years	382	484	217	99	125	1,307

ITALY

Period	Cottons	Woollens	Linens	Silks	Hemp, Jute, &c.	Total
	Millions £ Aggregate					
1841–50	12	32	10	10	10	74
1851–60	18	34	15	15	12	94
1861–70	27	46	20	20	15	128
1871–80	51	49	25	16	15	156
1881–87	55	34	20	11	11	131
47 years	163	195	90	72	63	583

SPAIN

1841–50	24	47	14	4	5	94
1851–60	36	56	13	5	5	115
1861–70	39	71	12	6	6	134
1871–80	57	75	11	9	6	158
1881–87	46	44	8	8	4	110
47 years	202	293	58	32	26	611

BELGIUM

1841–50	28	11	10	3	2	54
1851–60	25	13	15	3	3	59
1861–70	29	47	25	4	3	108
1871–80	33	75	35	4	4	151
1881–87	26	44	30	3	3	106
47 years	141	190	115	17	15	478

UNITED STATES

1841–50	160	81	10	5	5	261
1851–60	218	117	20	10	10	375
1861–70	376	190	30	20	12	628
1871–80	337	282	42	30	15	706
1881–87	320	241	30	50	10	651
47 years	1,411	911	132	115	52	2,621

The net product of these manufactures in 47 years was approximately thus :—

	Fibre	Manufactures	Net Product
	Millions £ Sterling		
Cotton	3,411	8,321	4,910
Wool	2,530	7,255	4,725
Flax	963	2,319	1,356
Silk	1,148	2,273	1,125
Hemp and jute .	489	1,124	635
Total . .	8,541	21,292	12,751

The net product to the several countries was as follows :—

	Fibre	Manufactures	Net Product
	Millions £ Sterling		
United Kingdom	2,662	6,871	4,209
France	1,640	3,949	2,309
Germany . . .	922	2,327	1,405
Russia	677	1,743	1,066
Austria	517	1,307	790
Italy	251	583	332
Spain	239	611	372
Belgium . . .	191	478	287
United States . .	1,108	2,621	1,513
Various	334	802	468
Total . .	8,541	21,292	12,751

The weight of fibre consumed in 1888 was approximately as follows :—

	Millions of Lbs.						Lbs. per Inhabitant
	Cotton	Wool	Flax	Silk	Hemp and Jute	Total	
United Kingdom . .	1,530	412	191	3	690	2,826	75
France	310	421	203	15	246	1,195	41
Germany	378	349	143	7	90	967	20
Russia	369	145	240	1	140	895	11
Austria	235	90	127	2	130	584	16
Italy	152	52	60	1	120	385	13
Spain	120	60	22	1	20	223	13
Belgium . . .	52	100	112	...	20	284	48
Switzerland, &c. .	76	75	40	1	30	222	12
Europe . . .	3,222	1,704	1,138	31	1,486	7,581	24
United States . .	1,010	434	92	4	330	1,870	30
India, &c. . .	313	104	...	15	374	806	...
Total . .	4,545	2,242	1,230	50	2,190	10,257	...

The value of textiles produced in 1887 was approximately as follows :—

	Millions £ Sterling					
	Cottons	Woollens	Linens	Silks	Sundries	Total
U. Kingdom .	101	43	9	6	11	170
France . . .	19	46	9	29	5	108
Germany . . .	23	35	7	15	2	82
Russia . . .	22	14	9	2	5	52
Austria . . .	14	9	6	4	3	36
Italy	9	5	3	2	2	21
Spain	7	6	1	1	1	16
Scandinavia . .	2	2	...	...	1	5
Belgium . . .	3	6	5	1	1	16
Switzerland . .	3	1	...	6	...	10
Europe . . .	203	167	49	66	31	516
United States .	60	39	4	7	2	112
India, &c. . .	16	1	...	23	8	48
Total . .	279	207	53	96	41	676

The consumption of textile manufactures in 1888 was approximately as follows :—

	Millions £ Sterling					
	Cottons	Woollens	Silks	Linens	Hemp and Jute	Total
U. Kingdom .	30	27	15	3	9	84
France . . .	18	31	22	6	4	81
Germany . . .	20	25	6	7	2	60
Russia . . .	28	14	2	9	4	57
Austria . . .	14	9	4	5	2	34
Italy	11	7	2	3	2	25
Spain	7	7	2	1	1	18
Scandinavia . .	4	5	1	1	1	12
Holland . . .	2	1	1	1	1	6
Belgium . . .	3	6	1	1	1	12
Other countries .	3	5	1	2	5	16
Europe . . .	140	137	57	39	32	405
United States .	66	44	14	8	5	137
Other countries .	73	26	25	6	6	136
Total . .	279	207	96	53	43	678

UNITED KINGDOM

The value of British manufactures, that is, of the gross annual product, without deducting raw material or anything else, has been .estimated as follows at various epochs :—

Year	Millions £	Writers
1783 . . .	57	M'Pherson
1803–10 . .	105	Eden, Stevenson, &c.
1835 . . .	149	Lavergne
1850 . . .	180	Poole
1888 . . .	820	Mulhall

The earlier estimates were too low, as they omitted beer, flour, clothing, and other large items.

If we study the consumption of raw material, and the prices current at the several periods, we may construct the following approximate table :—

	Millions £ Sterling				
	1780	1810	1840	1860	1888
Woollens . . .	17	18	22	34	43
Cottons . . .	2	20	48	81	101
Linens, jute, &c. . .	4	13	13	16	20
Silks . . .	3	5	9	12	6
Leather . . .	11	14	18	30	42
Clothing . . .	20	30	40	55	66
Liquor and food . .	55	60	87	94	116
Hardware . . .	15	25	40	85	155
Furniture . . .	5	7	10	15	20
Printing . . .	1	2	3	9	16
Sundries . . .	44	66	97	146	235
Total . .	177	260	387	577	820

The textile manufactures have been greatly developed in the present century, the consumption of fibre in the United Kingdom showing thus :—

Year	Millions of Lbs. Weight					
	Cotton	Wool	Flax	Hemp	Jute	Total
1801 . . .	54	117	48	82	...	301
1810 . . .	114	123	60	107	...	404
1820 . . .	123	125	87	95	...	430
1830 . . .	246	138	59	59	...	593
1840 . . .	448	173	210	67	...	898
1850 . . .	565	185	249	122	42	1,163
1860 . . .	1,140	234	228	78	86	1,766
1870 . . .	1,101	309	291	160	324	2,185
1880 . . .	1,404	338	227	165	404	2,538
1887 . . .	1,499	378	190	196	494	2,757

2 A

The following table shows the approximate value of all British and Irish textile industries during the past 100 years at various dates :—

Year	Millions £ Sterling					
	Cottons	Woollens	Linens	Silks	Jute, &c.	Total
1780	2	17	2	3	2	26
1800	8	18	4	4	2	36
1810	20	18	5	5	8	56
1820	33	19	6	7	2	67
1830	39	20	8	8	2	77
1840	48	22	11	9	2	92
1850	49	28	13	12	6	108
1860	81	34	12	12	4	143
1870	91	48	14	9	12	174
1880	105	48	12	7	12	184
1887	101	43	9	6	11	170

The total consumption of fibre, excluding silk, in the factories during forty-five years, down to 1885, was as follows :—

	Tons		
	1841–70	1871–85	Total
Cotton	9,650,000	8,950,000	18,600,000
Wool	3,150,000	2,430,000	5,580,000
Flax and hemp .	4,600,000	2,700,000	7,300,000
Jute	1,300,000	2,700,000	4,000,000
Total . .	18,700,000	16,780,000	35,480,000

The output of stuffs and cloths in English statute miles was approximately as follows :—

	1841–70	1871–85	Total
Cottons	43,750,000	45,620,000	89,370,000
Woollens . . .	3,420,000	2,860,000	6,280,000
Linens	5,460,000	2,500,000	7,960,000
Jute	1,700,000	2,100,000	3,800,000
Total . .	54,330,000	53,080,000	107,410,000

The output of fifteen years ending 1885 was almost equal to that of thirty years ending 1870.
In the following table are shown the cost of fibre, and value of the manufactures :—

Period	Millions £ Sterling		
	Raw Fibre	Manufactures	Net Result
1841–50 . . .	341	970	629
1851–60 . . .	494	1,265	771
1861–70 . . .	716	1,546	830
1871–80 . . .	686	1,872	1,186
1881–87 . . .	425	1,218	793
47 years . . .	2,662	6,871	4,209

	Millions £ Sterling		
	Raw fibre	Manufactures	Net Result
Cotton	1,425	3,726	2,301
Wool	603	1,768	1,165
Silk	236	435	199
Flax	240	572	332
Hemp, jute . .	158	370	212
Total . .	2,662	6,871	4,209

The annual product of each operative, as well in the gross as the net result, after deducting cost of raw material, are shown as follows :—

			Gross, £	Net, £
Cotton	.	.	178	101
Woollen	.	.	155	108
Linen	.	.	95	60
Jute .	.	.	230	154
Silk .	.	.	161	99

In the preceding tables, the value of manufactures includes not only stuffs, but also yarns exported to other countries.
The export of yarn showed thus :—

Year	Millions of Lbs. Yarn				
	Cotton	Woollen	Linen	Jute	Total
1841 . . .	119	4	18	...	141
1851 . . .	144	14	19	...	177
1861 . . .	178	28	26	2	234
1871 . . .	194	44	36	14	288
1885 . . .	246	44	17	31	338
1889 . . .	252	45	14	34	345

	Aggregate in Tons Yarn				
	Cotton	Woollen	Linen	Jute	Total
1841–50	580,000	40,000	80,000	...	700,000
1851–60	710,000	90,000	100,000	...	900,000
1861–70	830,000	160,000	135,000	40,000	1,165,000
1871–80	990,000	180,000	120,000	70,000	1,360,000
1881–89	1,010,000	175,000	70,000	105,000	1,360,000
49 years	4,120,000	645,000	505,000	215,000	5,485,000

The following table shows the consumption of fibre in the United Kingdom, and in the whole world in 1840 and 1887.

	1840		1887	
	Millions of Lbs.		Millions of Lbs.	
	United Kingdom	The World	United Kingdom	The World
Cotton	448	1,210	1,499	4,433
Wool	173	694	378	2,242
Flax	210	800	190	1,230
Hemp	67	500	196	880
Jute	...	...	494	1,310
Total . .	898	3,204	2,757	10,095

In 1840 the United Kingdom consumed 28 per cent., and in 1883 27½ per cent. of all the fibre in the world. As regards iron, leather, timber, &c., details of these industries will be found under their respective titles.
The gross value of British manufactures has increased in far greater ratio than the number of hands employed, as we see by comparing the Factory Returns, and Booth's Digest of the Censuses, with the approximate values already stated, viz. :—

Year	Engaged in Manufactures			Manu- factures, Millions £	Value per Ope- rative, £
	In Mills	Artisans	Total		
1840 . .	424,000	2,713,000	3,137,000	400	127
1860 . .	776,000	3,388,000	4,164,000	583	140
1888 . .	1,034,000	3,501,000	4,535,000	820	181

Owing to machinery, two workpeople can now produce manufactures to the same value as three could in 1841 ; but if the volume, instead of the value of merchandise were considered, we should find that two now produce more than five did fifty years ago.

In 1835 the textile factories had 355,000 hands :—

	Cotton	Woollen	Silk	Flax, &c.	Total
England .	183,000	66,000	30,000	16,000	295,000
Scotland .	33,000	3,000	1,000	13,000	50,000
Ireland . .	4,000	2,000	...	4,000	10,000
U. Kingdom	220,000	71,000	31,000	33,000	355,000
Males . .	101,000	37,000	10,000	10,000	158,000
Females . .	119,000	34,000	21,000	23,000	197,000
Total .	220,000	71,000	31,000	33,000	355,000

In 1885 the factories had 1,034,000 hands, as follows :—

	Men	Women	Children	Total
England	301,000	437,000	76,000	814,000
Scotland	41,000	101,000	10,000	152,000
Ireland	19,000	44,000	5,000	68,000
United Kingdom .	361,000	582,000	91,000	1,034,000
Cotton	172,000	282,000	50,000	504,000
Woollen	113,000	146,000	23,000	282,000
Flax and hemp . .	33,000	80,000	9,000	122,000
Jute	11,000	26,000	5,000	42,000
Silk	12,000	28,000	3,000	43,000
Hosiery, &c. . .	20,000	20,000	1,000	41,000
Total . .	361,000	582,000	91,000	1,034,000

The value of hardware manufactures may be estimated approximately as follows :—

	Tons	Value, £
Pig iron exported . . .	1,200,000	3,000,000
Iron wares, home use .	1,800,000	27,000,000
Steel exported . . .	300,000	3,000,000
Steel, home manufactures .	2,700,000	81,000,000
Iron wares exported .	2,000,000	20,000,000
Lead manufactures . .	100,000	3,000,000
Copper	100,000	10,000,000
Tin	20,000	5,000,000
Zinc	70,000	2,800,000
Total . .	...	154,800,000

FRANCE

The value of manufactures produced annually has been estimated as follows :—

Year	Millions £ Sterling	Writer
1788	37	Tolosan
1819	73	Chaptal
1835	158	...
1878	390	Kolb
1888	485	Mulhall

Several items seem to have been omitted in the early estimates. The following is an approximate table :—

	Millions £ Sterling			
	1788	1835	1868	1888
Textiles . . .	21	47	96	108
Hardware . . .	8	10	31	42
Food . . .	52	82	112	114
Clothing . . .	22	44	56	64
Leather . . .	20	24	40	52
Sundries . . .	24	57	92	105
Total . .	147	264	427	485

The tables of Tolosan and Chaptal showed as follows :—

	1788	1819
	£	£
Textiles . . .	17,400,000	27,000,000
Hardware . . .	1,400,000	8,400,000
Jewellery . . .	4,500,000	5,000,000
Skins	2,600,000	5,700,000
Sundries . . .	11,300,000	26,700,000
Total . .	37,200,000	72,800,000

The following estimate of French manufactures was published in 1835 :—

	Number	Value, £
Mills	82,900	49,800,000
Factories . . .	38,300	76,600,000
Foundries . . .	4,425	10,600,000
Steam-engines .	1,448	2,900,000
Workshops and waggons . . }	...	17,700,000
Total . .	...	157,600,000

Product, £		Balance-sheet, £	
Silks . . .	9,600,000	Raw material .	56,100,000
Woollens . .	16,100,000	Wages . . .	60,800,000
Cottons . . .	16,600,000	Wear and tear .	20,900,000
Linens . . .	12,000,000	Interest on capital	13,100,000
Iron	14,000,000	Net profit . .	6,700,000
Sundries . . .	89,300,000		
Total . .	157,600,000	Total . .	157,600,000

An incomplete official report in 1854 showed the following averages for seven previous years :—

	Factories	Engines	Operatives	Manufactures, £
Textiles .	12,858	934	695,000	65,600,000
Food . .	41,762	429	136,000	62,800,000
Sundries .	4,687	426	118,000	9,800,000
Total .	59.307	1,789	949,000	138,200,000

Another report in 1866 gave the average for five preceding years thus :—

	Factories	Engines	Operatives	Manufactures, £
Textiles . .	12,480	777	685,000	93,300,000
Food . .	52,845	2,131	174,000	112,100,000
Sundries .	8,553	1,369	179,000	22,200,000
Total .	73,878	4,277	1,038,000	227,600,000

Kolb mentions a report in 1878 showing 123,000 factories employing 1,783,000 operatives, turning out products to the value of 390 millions sterling per annum, of which textiles stood for 105 millions sterling.

Respecting these factories we find :—

Worked by	Number	Horse-Power
Steam . . .	16,500	220,000
Water . . .	52,700	298,000
Wind . . .	11,300	40,000
Total . .	80,500	558,000

The *Statesman's Year-Book* for 1890 gives the following :—

	Factories	Operatives	Horse-Power	Spindles	Power-Looms	Hand-Looms
Cotton	1,000	119,000	62,400	5,100,000	72,000	30,000
Wool	1,926	115,000	42,800	3,300,000	46,000	28,000
Silk	1,172	110,000	...	1,100,000	51,000	56,000
Total . .	4,098	344,000	105,200	9,500,000	169,000	114,000

There are also 365 flax, hemp, and jute factories, consuming 310,000 tons fibre yearly.

In 1875 an estimate of French manufactures was published, differing but slightly from the figures given by Kolb ; it was as follows :—

	Hands	Product, £
Textiles . . .	770,000	137,000,000
Flour-mills . . .	120,000	80,000,000
Clothing . . .	156,000	52,000,000
Leather . . .	300,000	36,000,000
Metals and minerals .	330,000	36,000,000
Soap, candles, &c. .	100,000	30,000,000
Sugar, beer, &c. .	70,000	26,000,000
Fancy goods . .	90,000	19,000,000
Total . .	1,936,000	416,000,000

The value of textile manufactures was approximately as follows, in millions £ sterling :—

	1810	1840	1860	1880
Woollens . . .	16	17	31	45
Cottons . . .	4	12	16	16
Silks . . .	5	9	24	29
Linens, &c. . .	7	12	14	17
Total . .	32	50	85	107

The balance-sheet of textile industries for forty-seven years, ending 1887, may be summed up thus :—

	Millions £		
	Fibre	Manufactures	Net Product
Silk . . .	569	1,132	563
Cotton . .	305	771	466
Wool . . .	478	1,368	890
Flax, &c. . .	288	678	390
Total .	1,640	3,949	2,309
1841–50 . .	268	634	366
1851–60 . .	319	740	421
1861–70 . .	434	958	524
1871–80 . .	379	945	566
1881–87 . .	240	672	432
47 years . .	1,640	3,949	2,309

Production and consumption in 1887 compared thus :—

	Millions £	
	Production	Consumption
Cottons	19	18
Woollens . . .	46	31
Silks . . .	29	22
Linens . . .	9	6
Sundries . . .	5	4
Total . .	108	81

The metallic industries may be estimated approximately thus :—

	Tons Consumed	Value of Product, £
Steel . . .	530,000	15,900,000
Iron . . .	1,300,000	19,500,000
Copper . . .	35,000	3,500,000
Lead, &c. . .	...	3,100,000
Total .	...	42,000,000

GERMANY

In 1805 the manufactures of Prussia were estimated by Oddy as follows :—

	£			£
Woollens . .	1,700,000	Hardware . .		1,300,000
Linens . .	1,800,000	Furniture .		1,000,000
Silks . . .	700,000	Leather .		400,000
Cottons . .	500,000	Sundry .		200,000
All textiles . .	4,700,000	Miscellaneous .		2,900,000

This made a grand total of only £7,600,000, but it omitted beer, food, clothing, and other large items. In 1843 the following estimate, likewise for Prussia, was published :—

	£			£
Cottons . .	5,000,000	Linens .	.	2,800,000
Woollens . .	17,400,000	Tobacco .	.	2,400,000
Silks . .	3,600,000	Beer, &c. . .		4,800,000

This summed up 36 millions sterling, but was also defective.

The Census returns show the number of hands employed in manufactures in 1846 was 842,000, and in 1861 amounted to 1,093,000. That of 1869 for all Germany was as follows :—

	Factory Hands	Artisans	Total	Number of Factories
Prussia . .	680,000	1,794,000	2,474,000	79,529
Hanover . .	46,000	170,000	216,000	6,949
Bavaria . .	164,000	512,000	676,000	37,967
Saxony . .	214,000	413,000	627,000	11,357
Wurtemberg	86,000	235,000	321,000	19,231
Baden . .	63,000	156,000	219,000	6,764
Small States	168,000	500,000	668,000	28,803
Total .	1,421,000	3,780,000	5,201,000	190,600

The hands and horse-power in 1880 were as follows :—

	Hands	Horse-Power
Textiles	910,000	391,000
Clothing	1,260,000	21,000
Food	744,000	176,000
Wood	470,000	52,000
Machinery . . .	356,000	195,000
Metals	460,000	106,000
Building	534,000	22,000
Sundries	983,000	320,000
Total . .	5,717,000	1,283,000

The Census of 1880 gave the following tables :—

	Hands Engaged in Factories			Manufacturing Population	
	Males	Females	Total		
Textiles	195,000	190,000	385,000	Prussia	9,394,000
Hardware	312,000	15,000	327,000	Bavaria	1,492,000
Food	219,000	46,000	265,000	Saxony	1,696,000
Printing	29,000	7,000	36,000	Wurtemburg . . .	674,000
Various	444,000	70,000	514,000	Small States . . .	2,802,000
Total . . .	1,199,000	328,000	1,527,000	Total . .	16,058,000

In 1876 Engel found 28,985 factories had steam-power with an aggregate of 888,000 horse-power. The number of persons engaged in certain industries in 1880 was as follows :—

	Textiles	Iron	Machinery	Leather	Wood	Paper
Prussia	452,000	201,000	194,000	67,000	243,000	49,000
Bavaria	65,000	37,000	18,000	11,000	57,000	8,000
Saxony	166,000	27,000	42,000	9,000	41,000	18,000
Wurtemburg	36,000	18,000	17,000	7,000	26,000	6,000
Small States	191,000	101,000	83,000	28,000	103,000	20,000
Total	910,000	384 000	354,000	122,000	470,000	101,000

The production and consumption of textile goods in Germany in 1887 represented approximately the following values :—

	Millions £ Sterling		Spindles in Factories
	Manufacture	Consumption	
Cottons . . .	23	20	4,900,000
Woollens . . .	35	25	2,000,000
Linens	7		300,000
Silks	15	7	900,000
Sundries . . .	2	2	100,000
Total . .	82	60	8,200,000

The following table gives approximately the value of all textiles manufactured at various dates, in millions £ sterling :—

	1810	1840	1860	1880	1887
Woollens .	3	8	16	28	35
Cottons . .	1	5	9	20	23
Silks . . .	1	2	4	11	15
Linens, &c.	4	6	8	9	9
Total .	9	21	37	68	82

The balance-sheet of textile industries for 47 years to 1887 may be summed up thus :—

	Millions £ Sterling		
	Fibre	Manufactures	Net Product
Cotton	303	727	424
Wool	329	948	619
Silk	132	280	148
Flax, &c. . . .	158	372	214
Total . .	922	2,327	1,405
1841–50 . . .	120	318	198
1851–60 . . .	152	396	244
1861–70 . . .	210	486	276
1871–80 . . .	247	607	360
1881–87 . . .	193	520	327
47 years . . .	922	2,327	1,405

Hardware manufactures in 1888 were estimated thus :—

	Tons	Manufactures, Value, £
Steel . . .	1,400,000	37,800,000
Iron . . .	3,000,000	40,500,000
Copper . . .	32,000	3,200,000
Lead, zinc, &c. . .	250,000	9,500,000
Total . .	3,682,000	91,000,000

RUSSIA

The number of factories at various dates was :—

	1812	1824	1839	1864
Tanneries . . .	1,150	1,784	1,918	...
Tallow . . .	181	1,023	998	1,254
Cotton . . .	129	484	467	423
Woollen . . .	136	324	616	536
Linen . . .	170	214	267	599
Silk . . .	105	184	227	326
Iron . . .	33	170	486	...
Sundries . . .	423	1,103	1,876	12,315
Total . .	2,327	5,286	6,855	15,453

Year	Number of Factories	Operatives	Product, £
1812 . . .	2,327	69,000	...
1824 . . .	5,286	250,000	5,100,000
1839 . . .	6,855	413,000	12,400,000
1851 . . .	9,256	457,000	15,700,000
1864 . . .	15,453	465,000	52,000,000
1879 . . .	27,927	685,000	90,900,000
1882 . . .	56,905	955,000	112,600,000
1888 . . .	83,182	1,134,000	136,000,000

	1824	1835
	£	£
Woollens	2,600,000	3,800,000
Cottons	1,600,000	2,500,000
Linens	500,000	700,000
Silks	400,000	700,000
All textiles . . .	5,100,000	7,700,000

Schubert's tables for 1828 give the output of the factories thus :—

	Yards		Tons
Cottons . .	60,000,000	Tobacco . . .	28,000
Linens . .	20,000,000	Sugar	17,000
Woollens .	16,000,000	Soap and potash	22,000
Total .	96,000,000	Total . .	67,000

Moreover, the tanneries turned out 3,500,000 tanned hides. There were 100 steam-engines at work in the Empire.

In 1835 it was estimated that the factories contained 280,000 hands, and that 800,000 artisans worked on their own account, making a total manufacturing strength of 1,080,000 persons.

In 1839 the seats of factories were :—

	Factories	Operatives
Moscow	1,058	83,000
Vladimir	315	84,000
Perm	352	37,000
Kaluga	164	20,000
Tula	124	17,000
Various	4,842	172,000
Total . . .	6,855	413,000

In 1864 the following table was published :—

	Factories	Operatives	Output, £
Woollens . .	536	92,000	5,900,000
Cottons . .	423	58,000	6,100,000
Linens . .	599	44,000	5,300,000
Silks . .	326	9,000	900,000
All textiles . .	1,884	203,000	18,200,000
Sugar . .	432	55,000	4,900,000
Tallow . .	1,254	7,000	2,100,000
Liquor . .	1,446	31,000	8,300,000
Sawmills . .	2,508	12,000	2,600,000
Sundries . .	7,929	157,000	15,900,000
Total .	15,453	465,000	52,000,000

At the same time Buschen valued all the manufactures of Russia at 136 millions sterling, viz. :—

Textiles	£	Miscellaneous	£
Linens . . .	18,200,000	Hardware .	10,800,000
Cottons . . .	15,800,000	Liquor . .	52,000,000
Woollens . .	7,100,000	Leather . .	8,000,000
Hemp . . .	6,300,000	Tallow . .	3,200,000
Silks	2,300,000	Sundries . .	11,600,000
Total .	49,700,000	Total .	86,500,000

The above of course includes not only factories, but also the product of the labours of artisans.

An official statement in 1882 shows that the output of the mills had more than doubled since 1864, viz. :—

	1864	1882
	£	£
Textiles	18,200,000	31,300,000
Sugar	4,900,000	14,100,000
Liquor	8,300,000	19,500,000
Sundries	20,600,000	47,700,000
Total . . .	52,000,000	112,600,000

The manufacture of liquor stands officially thus :—

	Factories	Gallons	Value, £
Whisky . .	2,377	91,000,000	13,800,000
Beer . .	1,870	75,500,000	5,700,000
Total .	4,247	166,500,000	19,500,000

It is believed that the illicit distillation of whisky is large, and that in reality Russians consume 160 million gallons of whisky yearly. The above is irrespective of Poland, whose manufactures in 1882 reached £14,700,000, and Finland £1,500,000. If these were added, the grand total of factory products would be £128,800,000. The following table shows approximately the value of textile manufactures at stated periods, in millions sterling :—

	1820	1840	1860	1870	1880
Woollens . . .	3	5	8	10	14
Cottons . . .	1	4	7	12	14
Linens	1	2	5	7	8
Silks, &c. . . .	...	4	5	6	6
Total . .	5	15	25	35	42

The balance-sheet of textile industries for 47 years may be summed up thus :—

	Millions £ Sterling		
	Fibre	Manufactures	Net
Cotton	192	461	269
Wool	272	780	508
Silk	18	37	19
Flax, &c. . . .	195	465	270
Total . .	677	1,743	1,066
1841–50 . . .	94	250	156
1851–60 . . .	111	294	183
1861–70 . . .	142	352	210
1871–80 . . .	193	486	293
1881–87 . . .	137	361	224
47 years . .	677	1,743	1,066

The production and consumption of textiles in 1887 was approximately as follows, in millions sterling :—

	Production	Consumption
Cottons . . .	22	28
Woollens . . .	14	14
Linens . . .	9	9
Silks, &c. . . .	7	6
Total . .	52	57

The hardware industry may be estimated thus :—

	Tons	Manufactures, Value, £
Iron	400,000	5,400,000
Steel	260,000	7,000,000
Copper, lead, &c. .	26,000	1,100,000
Total . .	686,000	13,500,000

The above is 50 per cent. over the Government valuation for metallic manufactures in 1886, namely, 86 million roubles ; these industries employ 85,400 hands.

AUSTRIA

In 1805 the textile factories employed 170,000 hands. Becher's table in 1834 was as follows :—

Factories	No.	Factories	No.	Factories	No.
Leather	580	Chemicals	82	Iron	700
Flax and hemp	869	Spirits	250	Steel	210
Cotton	298	Glass	210	Copper	185
Wool	165	Pottery	165	Sundry	8,432

He summed up the whole manufacturing industry thus :—

Number of factories	11,064
Operatives	2,330,000
Product, £.	142,000,000

There was a rapid increase of textile industry after Becher's time, as shown by the number of looms in factories :—

Year	Steam-Looms		Hand-Looms
1850	1,140	...	100,000
1860	10,360	...	80,000
1870	16,650	...	70,000
1875	23,000	...	55,000

In the last-mentioned year there were in Austria proper, without Hungary, 6400 factories, using 11,400 steam-engines.

In 1887 the principal manufacturing companies in Vienna had the following capital :—

	£		£
Mining	7,200,000	Paper-mills	1,500,000
Textiles	2,300,000	Breweries	1,400,000
Sugar	2,300,000	Ironworks	1,200,000

In 1888 the principal textile industries showed thus :—

	Factories	Operatives	Spindles	Power-Looms
Cotton	1,900	96,000	2,350,000	42,000
Wool	2,707	59,000	650,000	17,500
Linen	348	60,000	400,000	5,000
Total	4,955	215,000	3,400,000	64,500

At the same time Hungary had 988 mills, with 90,000 operatives and 63,000 horse-power. The following table shows the production of textiles (excluding Lombardy) in the Empire at various dates, in millions £ sterling :—

	1830	1850	1860	1870	1880
Woollens	4	6	7	8	9
Cottons	3	5	6	8	10
Linens	3	4	4	5	6
Silks, &c.	3	3	5	5	6
Total	13	18	22	26	31

The balance-sheet of textile industries for 47 years may be summed up thus :—

	Millions £ Sterling		
	Fibre	Manufactures	Net
Cotton	161	382	221
Wool	163	484	321
Silk	49	99	50
Flax, &c.	144	342	198
Total	517	1,307	790
1841-50	78	199	121
1851-60	91	242	151
1861-70	116	279	163
1871-80	135	331	196
1881-87	97	256	159
47 years	517	1,307	790

The production and consumption in 1887 were approximately as follows :—

	Millions £ Sterling	
	Production	Consumption
Cottons	14	14
Woollens	9	9
Linens	6	5
Silks, &c.	7	6
Total	36	34

The number of hands engaged in manufactures in 1880, and that of the manufacturing population, are shown thus :—

	Principals	Dependents	Total
Austria	576,000	4,134,000	4,710,000
Hungary	381,000	408,000	789,000
Total	957,000	4,542,000	5,499,000

Hardware manufactures may be estimated thus :—

	Tons Consumed	Manufactures, Value £
Iron	460,000	6,200,000
Steel	280,000	7,600,000
Copper, &c.	...	1,200,000
Total	...	15,000,000

ITALY

In the 18th century the woollen factories of Florence had 30,000 operatives. After a long period of depression, industry began to revive, and in 1840 the kingdom of Sardinia had :—

	Factories	Workmen	Women	Total
Cottons	312	7,900	9,000	16,900
Silks	590	4,900	10,000	14,900
Woollens	62	3,400	2,000	5,400
Total	964	16,200	21,000	37,200

In 1877 the official report was as follows :—

	Men	Women and Children	All Hands	Spindles
Silk	16,000	184,000	200,000	2,083,000
Cotton	16,000	38,000	54,000	880,000
Woollen	12,000	13,000	25,000	305,000
Linen and hemp	11,000	11,000	22,000	60,000
Paper	7,000	10,000	17,000	...
Leather	10,000	1,000	11,000	...
Sundries	32,000	21,000	53,000	...
Total	104,000	278,000	382,000	...

	Number of Spindles				
	Cotton	Silk	Wool	Linen	Total
Piedmont	312,000	357,000	135,000	2,000	806,000
Lombardy	220,000	1,638,000	10,000	32,000	1,900,000
Liguria	104,000	13,000	12,000	3,000	132,000
Venice	39,000	54,000	69,000	4,000	166,000
Other provinces	205,000	21,000	79,000	18,000	323,000
Total	880,000	2,083,000	305,000	59,000	3,327,000

The distribution of power was as follows :—

	Horse-Power			Number of Power-Looms
	Steam	Water	Total	
Cotton . . .	3,000	10,000	13,000	42,000
Wool . . .	1,100	6,200	7,300	6,600
Linen . . .	500	2,500	3,000	800
Paper . . .	300	13,700	14,000	...
Silk, &c. . .	10,000	7,000	17,000	1,500
Total . .	14,900	39,400	54,300	50,900

The increase of steam-power since 1878 has been remarkable, the consumption of coal having trebled in nine years, viz. :—

Year						Tons
1862	.	.	.	.	.	446,000
1878	.	.	.	.	.	1,325,000
1887	.	.	.	.	.	3,580,000

The following table shows approximately the production of textile industries in millions £ sterling :—

	1850	1860	1870	1880
Woollens . . .	3	4	4	5
Cottons . . .	2	3	4	6
Silks, &c. . .	3	5	6	7
Total . .	8	12	14	18

The production and consumption in 1887 were approximately :—

	Millions £ Sterling	
	Production	Consumption
Cottons	9	11
Woollens . . .	5	7
Linens . . .	3	3
Silks, &c. . . .	4	4
Total . .	21	25

The balance-sheet of textile industries for 47 years may be summed up thus :—

	Millions £ Sterling		
	Fibre	Manufactures	Net
Cotton . .	72	163	91
Wool . .	77	195	118
Silk . .	38	72	34
Flax, &c. .	64	153	89
Total . .	251	583	332
1841-50 . .	32	74	42
1851-60 . .	39	94	55
1861-70 . .	57	128	71
1871-80 . .	69	156	87
1881-87 . .	54	131	77
47 years . .	251	583	332

Hardware manufactures may be summed up thus :—

	Tons Consumed	Manufactures, Value, £
Iron	260,000	3,500,000
Steel	20,000	600,000
Lead, &c. . . .	...	200,000
Total . .	...	4,300,000

Italy has a manufacturing population of 4,494,000 souls, the number of operatives and artisans being approximately 2,281,000.

SPAIN

Manufacturing industry has progressed but little, if it has not positively declined. Seville had 16,000 silk-looms in the sixteenth century; at present there are only 3000 in all Spain. Toledo, so famous for its swords, has still one small factory with 300 workmen. Cotton-mills were introduced so far back as 1769, yet the whole number of operatives in this industry does not exceed 53,000. According to a Government report, in 1826 the value of textile and other manufactures produced yearly was £14,700,000 sterling; much too low an estimate. A semi-official statement published in 1873 showed 563 textile factories in the kingdom, with an aggregate capital of £21,000,000 sterling, counting 48,000 looms, 1,220,000 spindles, 93,000 operatives, and 17,000 horse-power. By placing a fictitious value on the articles manufactured, the output of the mills was raised to £21,000,000 sterling, which was 50 per cent. over the reality.

The statement was as follows :—

	Operatives	Looms	Output, £
Cottons . .	53,000	33,000	12,400,000
Woollens . .	25,000	7,000	4,300,000
Silks . .	9,000	3,000	2,800,000
Linens . .	6,000	5,000	1,100,000
Total .	93,000	48,000	20,600,000

The production and consumption of textiles in 1887 were approximately as follows :—

	Millions £	
	Production	Consumption
Cottons	7	7
Woollens . . .	6	7
Linens, silks, &c. . .	3	4
Total . . .	16	18

The balance-sheet of textile industries for 47 years may be summed up thus :—

	Millions £ Sterling		
	Fibre	Manufactures	Net
Cotton . . .	86	202	116
Wool . . .	103	293	190
Silk	15	32	17
Flax, &c. . .	35	84	49
Total . .	239	611	372
1841-50 . . .	34	94	60.
1851-60 . . .	44	115	71
1861-70 . . .	55	134	79
1871-80 . . .	63	158	95
1881-87 . . .	43	110	67
47 years . . .	239	611	372

Hardware manufacture may be estimated thus :—

	Tons Consumed	Manufactures, Value, £
Iron	210,000	2,800,000
Steel	30,000	900,000
Copper, &c. . .	...	300,000
Total . .	...	4,000,000

In 1873 the Government estimated all Spanish manu-factures at £60,000,000 sterling : much too low a figure.

SCANDINAVIA

In 1765 the Government of Sweden, finding the nobles unable to keep up agriculture, passed a law to close most of the factories, which caused the skilled workmen in steel-works and silk-mills to migrate into Russia. The law was repealed in 1785, but the mischief was done. The factory statistics show thus :—

Year	Factories	Product, £
1772	886	...
1830	1,857	700,000
1840	2,176	1,200,000
1850	2,513	2,100,000
1865	2,315	4,200,000
1876	2,825	9,600,000

A statement published in 1837 was as follows :—

	Woollens	Cottons, &c.	All Textiles
Factories	109	1,940	2,049
Operatives	3,000	10,300	13,300
Output, £	300,000	760,000	1,060,000

The statement for 1865 was as follows :—

Textiles	£	Miscellaneous	£
Cottons	490,000	Sugar	730,000
Woollens	480,000	Tobacco	360,000
Silks, linens, &c.	470,000	Hardware,&c.	1,680,000
All textiles	1,440,000	Total	2,770,000

According to Knut Bonde, the factories represented about half the manufactures produced, the total value having been £1,400,000 in 1824, and £4,800,000 in 1850. The hands employed in factories were 13,300 in 1837, and 53,000 in 1876. In the latter year the factories were as follows :—

Worked by	Number	Horse-Power
Steam	684	28,000
Water	637	...
Animals	1,504	...
Total	2,825	...

In later years a valuable industry has sprung up at Jönköping in the manufacture of wooden matches, of which 450 millions are exported yearly, weighing 15,000 tons.

In 1880 Denmark had 720 factories, with 25,000 opera-tives and 10,000 horse-power. The textile products of all Scandinavia hardly reach four millions sterling per annum.

Hardware manufactures in Sweden may be estimated thus :—

	Tons Consumed	Manufactures, Value £
Iron	300,000	4,100,000
Steel	80,000	2,200,000
Total	380,000	6,300,000

Those of Norway are about £400,000, and of Denmark £600,000.

BELGIUM

In 1830, when Belgium threw off the Dutch yoke, her factories were already flourishing, for they counted 12,000 steam-engines, with an aggregate of 20,000 horse-power. Since then her steam-power in fixed engines for factories and mines has grown prodigiously, viz. :—

Year	Horse-Power
1830	20,000
1838	25,300
1860	162,000
1880	209,000

In 1838 the following table was published :—

	Textile Factories		
	Capital, £	Operatives	Product, £
Cotton	2,400,000	122,000	3,400,000
Woollen	3,000,000	40,000	1,000,000
Hosiery	...	50,000	...

Besides the foregoing, the linen factories turned out 750,000 pieces yearly, and the production of lace was valued at £350,000.

There were also 175 foundries, with 14,000 operatives, turning out 150,000 tons pig iron.

The production of textiles was approximately as fol-lows :—

Year	Millions £			
	Woollens	Cottons	Linens,&c.	Total
1840	2	3	1	6
1860	3	3	2	8
1880	6	3	8	17

Production and consumption in 1887 were approxi-mately :—

	Millions £	
	Production	Consumption
Cottons	3	3
Woollens	6	6
Linens	5	1
Silks, &c.	2	1
Total	16	11

The following table combines the official reports of 1846 and 1880 :—

	1846		1880		
	Opera-tives	Horse-Power	Opera-tives	Horse-Power	Product, Value, £
Coal-mines	46,200	22,500	97,700	87,400	6,200,000
Ironworks	42,300	5,700	70,000	38,500	14,100,000
Potteries	35,800	1,200	51,500	7,700	3,800,000
Cotton-mills	14,700	1,600	17,500	9,900	2,700,000
Woollen-mills	18,200	1,600	25,000	13,100	6,000,000
Flax, &c., mills	60,700	1,100	50,900	9,800	5,400,000
Food	29,900	2,000	57,600	54,700	31,600,000
Sundries	67,000	1,300	58,600	21,300	17,200,000
Total	314,800	37,000	428,800	242,400	87,000,000

Motive power in 1880 was as follows :—

By	Factories	Horse-Power
Steam	8,433	209,500
Water	2,436	19,600
Wind	2,158	13,300
Total	13,027	242,400

In 1880 the ratio of horse-power was 56 to every 100 operatives, whereas in 1846 it was less than 12. Horse-power grew seven-fold in thirty-four years.

The balance-sheet of textile industries for 47 years may be summed up thus:—

	Millions £ Sterling		
	Fibre	Manufactures	Net
Cotton	58	141	83
Wool	73	190	117
Silk	7	17	10
Flax, &c. . . .	53	130	77
Total . .	191	478	287
1841–50 . . .	18	54	36
1851–60 . . .	22	59	37
1861–70 . . .	45	108	63
1871–80 . . .	63	151	88
1881–87 . . .	43	106	63
47 years . . .	191	478	287

The hardware industries may be estimated thus:—

	Tons Consumed	Manufactures, Value, £
Iron	600,000	8,100,000
Steel	230,000	6,200,000
Zinc, copper, &c. . .	...	2,200,000
Total . .	...	16,500,000

According to the Census of 1880 there were 953,000 persons engaged in manufactures, and the gross value of their products was 87 millions sterling. The statement at page 365 gives 102 millions for 1888.

SWITZERLAND

In 1887 the Factory Report showed thus:—

	Factories	Operatives
Cotton	398	36,400
Silk	246	26,500
Wool, flax, &c. . .	77	4,200
Lace	1,240	23,300
Watches . . .	201	11,100
Sundries . . .	925	49,200

The total was 3087 factories with 151,000 operatives.

The manufactures, between the above factories and the work done outside, represented approximately the following values:—

Textiles	£	Miscellaneous	£
Silks	5,800,000	Hardware . . .	1,600,000
Cottons . . .	3,100,000	Watches . . .	3,800,000
Woollens, &c. .	1,400,000	Lace	4,200,000
		Sundries . . .	15,400,000
Total . .	10,300,000	Total . .	25,000,000

UNITED STATES

Reduced to English money, the principal manufactures may be summed up thus:—

	Census Values, Millions of £ Sterling					Approximate Value in 1888
	1810	1840	1860	1870	1880	
Textiles . .	10	14	38	55	80	112
Hardware .	4	10	29	92	129	194
Food . . .	8	18	64	110	168	202
Clothing . .	3	8	15	27	50	98
Leather . .	4	7	34	56	83	104
Lumber . .	1	3	20	42	49	63
Sundries . .	1	36	192	323	558	670
Total . .	31	96	392	705	1,117	1,443

The principal manufactures were as follows, in millions of dollars. The paper value of 1870 is reduced to its proper equivalent in gold:—

	Millions of Dollars					
	1810	1840	1850	1860	1870	1880
Flour . . .	21	71	136	224	356	505
Iron . . .	17	37	49	71	287	336
Leather . .	18	33	92	162	271	397
Lumber . .	6	15	59	96	202	233
Cottons . .	30	46	66	115	142	211
Machinery .	...	11	28	47	111	214
Clothing . .	...	36	48	70	130	242
Sugar . .	...	...	10	38	96	155
Woollens . .	17	21	48	69	121	161
Liquor . .	16	15	22	43	75	144
Cabinet-work .	...	18	18	24	55	83
Printing . .	...	...	12	42	46	91
Implements .	...	...	7	18	42	69
Paper . .	...	...	10	18	39	55
Soap and candles	...	...	10	17	18	27
Sundries . .	27	155	404	832	1,395	2,447
Total . .	152	458	1,019	1,886	3,386	5,370

There was no Census of manufactures in 1820; that of 1830 took only the number of hands engaged. The Census of 1810 gave the following; the values being reduced to English money:—

States	Textile Goods	Sundries	Total	Ratio
	£	£	£	
New England	2,600,000	4,900,000	7,500,000	23.8
Middle . .	3,500,000	12,300,000	15,800,000	50.0
South . . .	3,560,000	4,640,000	8,200,000	25.9
West . . .	40,000	60,000	100,000	3
Total .	9,700,000	21,900,000	31,600,000	100.0

The Census of 1840 gave the following:—

	Hands	Value, £	Product per Hand, £
Cottons . .	72,100	9,700,000	136
Woollens . .	21,300	4,300,000	206
Mixed . .	38,400	9,700,000	247
Hardware .	44,100	7,700,000	175
Machinery .	13,000	2,300,000	177
Flour . .	60,800	14,800,000	244
Houses . .	85,500	8,700,000	102
Carpentry .	39,900	3,900,000	98
Timber . .	22,100	3,200,000	145
Liquor . .	12,200	3,100,000	245
Leather . .	26,100	6,900,000	263
Sundries . .	160,000	20,900,000	130
Total . .	595,500	95,200,000	160

States	Manufactures	Capital
	£	£
New England . . .	31,800,000	18,000,000
Middle	41,600,000	22,400,000
South	11,900,000	8,600,000
West	9,900,000	6,600,000
Total . .	95,200,000	55,600,000

Since 1840 there has been a steady increase in the average product per operative, which was then only £160, and in 1880 exceeded £400. This is mainly due to improved machinery, enabling two men now to produce as much as five did in 1840.

The Census of 1850 showed as follows :—

States	Opera-tives	Millions £ Sterling			Product per Hand, £
		Capital	Wages	Product	
N. England	313,000	34	16	59	186
Middle . .	418,000	49	21	98	233
South . .	104,000	13	4	20	192
West . . .	122,000	14	8	35	288
Total .	957,000	110	49	212	220

The Census of 1860 showed as follows :—

States	Opera-tives	Millions £ Sterling			Product per Hand, £
		Capital	Wages	Product	
N. England	390,000	54	22	98	250
Middle . .	542,000	89	31	166	306
South . .	126,000	23	7	39	310
West . . .	253,000	42	20	91	360
Total .	1,311,000	208	80	394	301

That of 1870, reduced to gold values, showed :—

States	Opera-tives	Millions £ Sterling			Product per Hand, £
		Capital	Wages	Product	
N. England	526,000	85	37	167	317
Middle . .	801,000	156	56	295	370
South . .	187,000	24	8	47	250
West . . .	540,000	102	34	196	363
Total .	2,054,000	367	135	705	344

That of 1880 showed as follows :—

States	Opera-tives	Millions £ Sterling			Product per Hand, £
		Capital	Wages	Product	
N. England	645,000	130	48	231	358
Middle . .	1,102,000	243	83	462	420
South . .	228,000	40	11	70	307
West . . .	758,000	168	56	354	470
Total .	2,733,000	581	198	1,117	408

The value of manufactures was artificially heightened by protective customs duties. My estimate for 1888, at page 378, is 1443 millions sterling. The results of the last five Censuses may be summed up thus :—

Year	Opera-tives	Millions £ Sterling			Product per Hand, £
		Capital	Wages	Product	
1840 . .	596,000	...	...	95	160
1850 . .	957,000	110	49	212	220
1860 . .	1,311,000	208	80	394	301
1870 . .	2,054,000	367	135	705	344
1880 . .	2,733,000	581	198	1,117	408

The numbers for 1870 and 1880 seem to include only factory hands, as the Censuses for those years give the

numbers employed in manufactures throughout the Union as 2,707,000 and 3,837,000 respectively. See *Occupation.*

The production and consumption of textile goods in 1888 were approximately as follows :—

	Millions £ Sterling	
	Production	Consumption
Cottons	60	63
Woollens	39	44
Silks.	7	14
Linens, &c. . . .	6	13
Total . .	112	134

The value of all textile manufactures at various dates, was approximately :—

Year	Millions £ Sterling				
	Woollens	Cottons	Silks	Linens,&c.	Total
1810	4	6	...	...	10
1840	4	9	...	1	14
1850	10	13	...	1	24
1860	13	22	1	2	38
1870	23	26	2	4	55
1880	30	38	7	5	80
1888	39	60	8	5	112

The balance-sheet of textile industries for 47 years was approximately as follows :—

	Millions £ Sterling		
	Fibre	Manufactures	Net Product
Cotton . .	663	1,411	748
Wool . .	314	911	597
Silk . .	55	115	60
Flax, &c. .	76	184	108
Total .	1,108	2,621	1,513
1841–50 . .	88	261	173
1851–60 . .	138	375	237
1861–70 . .	316	628	312
1871–80 . .	297	706	409
1881–87 . .	269	651	382
47 years .	1,108	2,621	1,513

The value of hardware manufactures may be estimated for 1888 as follows :—

	Tons Consumed	Manufactures, Value, £
Iron	4,800,000	72,000,000
Steel	3,150,000	94,500,000
Copper . . .	110,000	14,000,000
Lead	180,000	6,700,000
Tin, zinc, &c. . .	70,000	6,300,000
Total .	8,310,000	193,500,000

The principal manufacturing States have been as follows :—

States	Operatives				Product, Millions £			
	1850	1860	1870	1880	1850	1860	1870	1880
New York	199,000	230,000	351,000	501,000	50	79	131	224
Pennsylvania . . .	147,000	222,000	319,000	387,000	32	60	119	155
Massachusetts . . .	178,000	217,000	279,000	352,000	33	53	93	131
Other States . . .	433,000	642,000	1,105,000	1,493,000	97	202	362	607
Total . .	957,000	1,311,000	2,054,000	2,733,000	212	394	705	1,117

States	Ratio per Operative							
	Wages, £				Product, £			
	1850	1860	1870	1880	1850	1860	1870	1880
New York .	51	59	68	83	250	340	373	448
Pennsylvania .	52	56	69	72	220	267	372	400
Massachusetts	49	54	73	76	180	240	332	370
Ohio . .	54	61	62	70	255	334	330	395
Illinois . .	50	70	64	80	250	500	409	593
New Jersey .	50	59	75	76	210	270	373	420
Connecticut .	49	61	75	81	196	270	300	344
Other States .	52	68	57	63	225	316	317	384
General average	51	61	66	72	220	300	344	408

The motive-power in 1880 compared with 1870 thus :—

Year	Factories			Horse-Power		
	Steam	Water	Total	Steam	Water	Total
1870	40,191	51,018	91,209	1,216,000	1,130,000	2,346,000
1880	56,483	55,400	111,883	2,186,000	1,225,000	3,411,000

The distribution of motive-power and that of operatives were as follows :—

Factories	Horse-Power		Hands	
	1870	1880	1870	1880
Cotton . .	146,000	276,000	136,000	186,000
Woollen . .	93,000	123,000	90,000	105,000
Flour . .	577,000	771,000	58,000	58,000
Lumber . .	642,000	822,000	150,000	148,000
Iron . .	171,000	397,000	78,000	141,000
Paper . .	53,000	124,000	18,000	24,000
Implements, &c.	664,000	898,000	2,177,000	2,175,000
Sundries . .	2,346,000	3,411,000	2,707,000	3,837,000

	Ratio of Power in 1880		
	Steam	Steam and Water	Hands
Pennsylvania .	18.4	15.0	13.8
New York . .	10.7	13.3	16.4
Ohio . .	10.2	7.7	6.3
Massachusetts .	7.8	9.1	9.6
Michigan .	6.0	4.8	3.4
Illinois .	5.8	4.2	5.4
Other States .	41.1	45.9	45.1
Total .	100.0	100.0	100.0

CANADA

The earliest record of manufactures was published in 1830, as follows :—Domestic looms 1300, turning out 4,000,000 yards of woollens and linens yearly ; saw-mills 1580, with an aggregate capital of £1,250,000 ; export of timber £1,000,000 sterling. There were also 1086 mills of various other kinds, and seven foundries.

The industrial Census of 1881 compared with 1871 as follows :—

Year	Capital, £	Product, £	Operatives	Average Wages, £
1871 .	16,200,000	46,000,000	188,000	45.2
1881 .	34,400,000	64,400,000	255,000	48.4

The average product per operative was £244 in 1871, and £253 in 1881.

AUSTRALIA

Only three of the Australian colonies publish detailed statistics of manufactures, which are given for 1886–89 in Mr. Coghlan's Official Report for New South Wales. These three Colonies, however, comprise three-fourths of the population, and if we suppose the others have manufactures in the same ratio, the account will stand thus :—

	Factories	Hands	Value of Machinery, £
New South Wales .	3,106	45,600	5,740,000
Victoria . . .	2,974	54,500	5,490,000
New Zealand . .	1,946	22,100	2,110,000
Four other Colonies .	2,680	40,700	4,450,000
Total . .	10,706	162,900	17,790,000

In New South Wales the value of land and buildings occupied by factories in 1888 was £9,350,000, making a total of £15,100,000 invested in this branch of industry. Supposing the ratio to be the same in the other Colonies as compared with value of machinery, the result is :—

	Manufactures, Capital, £	£ per Inhabitant
New South Wales . .	15,100,000	13.6
Victoria	14,400,000	13.0
New Zealand . .	5,500,000	9.0
Four other Colonies . .	11,500,000	12.7
Total . .	46,500,000	12.8

The principal industries of Australia as regards number of hands employed were :—

	Textiles	Hardware	Food	Sundries	Total
New South Wales . . .	5,700	16,700	7,400	15,800	45,600
Victoria	9,600	20,600	5,800	18,500	54,500
New Zealand	4,100	8,100	3,200	6,700	22,100
Total .	19,400	45,400	16,400	41,000	122,200

The average product per operative being £253 in Canada and £297 in the United States, we may fairly suppose £250 for Australia, in which case the result would be :—

	Value Produced, £			Value Produced, £
New South Wales	11,400,000	Textiles . .		6,500,000
Victoria . . .	13,600,000	Hardware . .		15,100,000
New Zealand .	5,500,000	Food . . .		5,500,000
Four other Colonies	10,200,000	Sundries . .		13,600,000
Total . .	40,700,000	Total . .		40,700,000

The above is the output of factories, the total value of manufactures being probably about 64 millions sterling, as already stated.

The growth of manufactures has been very rapid, the number of hands in New South Wales, for example, having risen thus :—

	1878	1888
Males	21,500	41,300
Females . . .	3,200	4,300
Total . .	24,700	45,600

This shows a rise of 80 per cent. in ten years.

MANURE

The following table gives the annual yield of animal manure according to the scale of French official estimates and its value approximately :—

	Tons	Value, £
United Kingdom	79,000,000	31,600,000
France	84,000,000	33,600,000
Germany	113,000,000	45,200,000
Russia	213,000,000	85,200,000
Austria	100,000,000	40,000,000
Italy	25,000,000	10,000,000
Spain and Portugal	39,000,000	15,600,000
Belgium and Holland	17,000,000	6,800,000
Scandinavia	30,000,000	12,000,000
Turkey, &c.	32,000,000	12,800,000
Europe	732,000,000	292,800,000
United States	385,000,000	154,000,000
Total	1,117,000,000	446,800,000

Animal manure forms the chief ingredient of farm-yard dung, mixed with straw, &c. In England about 13 tons of dung go to the acre ; in Belgium 45 ; in Russia 7 on the Moujiks' farms, and 14 on those of the nobility. In France fish is often used, as also in Norfolk ; it costs 16s. a ton, and is mixed with mould as 1 to 40, producing heavy turnip crops. Nitrate potash and bone-ash are also much used in England. The results obtained on a farm in Oxfordshire in 1888 were :—

Tons per Acre

	Grass	Hay
Unmanured	5.0	1.3
Manured	12.0	2.5

The manure consisted of 6 cwt. of nitrate and potash per acre. The production of animal manure yearly is 10 cwt. for a goat, 14 a sheep, 30 a pig, 5 tons for a horse, and 6 tons a cow ; but a portion of this is lost.
Artificial manures imported into Great Britain were :—

Year	Tons		Value, £	
	Guano	Nitrate	Guano	Nitrate
1860	140,000	37,000	1,560,000	500,000
1870	280,000	56,000	3,480,000	880,000
1880	80,000	46,000	810,000	700,000
1889	28,000	118,000	200,000	1,100,000

Great Britain also imported in 1889 the following :—

	Tons	Value, £
Phosphates	305,000	700,000
Bones	62,000	310,000
Various	90,000	125,000
Total	457,000	1,135,000

Making a total of 603,000 tons of artificial manure, worth £2,500,000.
In the United States the production of phosphates is 430,000 tons, of which 270,000 for home-use, 160,000 tons being exported. Canada exported 22,000 tons in 1887, against 3000 in 1877.

MARBLE

Is worth about £4 per ton, Italy exporting anually 105,000 tons, valued at £400,000. It is 7 per cent. heavier than stone, and 5 per cent. lighter than granite. One cubic foot weighs 160 lbs., that is, 14 cubic feet per ton.

MARRIAGE

The proper age for marriage, as laid down by the ancients, was as follows :—

According to	Years	
	Husband	Wife
Hesiod	30	15
Plato	30	20
Aristotle	37	18

The minimum age fixed by law was as follows :—

Law of	Years	
	Husband	Wife
Sparta	30	20
Roman Empire	25	20
Canon Law	14	12
England	16	15
France	18	15
Saxony	21	18
Prussia	18	14
Austria	14	14

The Emperor Tiberius made an edict against marriage by women over fifty or men over sixty, but it was soon repealed.
The medium marrying age in various nations is as follows :—

	Years				Years	
	Man	Woman			Man	Woman
England	27.7	25.5		Sweden	31.1	28.3
Scotland	28.6	25.7		Norway	31.1	27.1
Ireland	29.9	25.2		Belgium	31.3	28.5
France	30.2	24.9		Holland	30.9	28.0
Prussia	29.7	27.1		Jews	30.1	26.2
Russia	25.2	21.5		Vienna	32.0	27.0
Italy	30.2	25.4		Leipzig	28.9	26.2

The relative numbers in 1000 persons of either sex marrying at different ages are shown thus :—

Men

	Under 20	20–30	30–40	40–50	Over 50	Total
England	35	731	144	52	38	1,000
Scotland	32	684	189	62	33	1,000
Ireland	26	600	269	67	38	1,000
France	23	607	262	65	43	1,000
Italy	11	623	259	68	39	1,000
Prussia	8	663	231	64	34	1,000
Russia	373	428	122	56	21	1,000
Norway	8	572	291	83	46	1,000
Sweden	1	574	299	81	45	1,000
Belgium	9	548	307	91	45	1,000
Holland	23	562	281	87	47	1,000
Jews	22	664	174	74	66	1,000

Women

	Under 20	20–30	30–40	40–50	Over 50	Total
England	149	680	111	41	19	1,000
Scotland	134	686	134	37	9	1,000
Ireland	137	713	111	27	12	1,000
France	204	593	145	40	18	1,000
Italy	171	657	125	34	13	1,000
Prussia	111	686	152	41	10	1,000
Russia	573	334	64	23	6	1,000
Norway	93	657	185	53	12	1,000
Sweden	51	643	232	59	15	1,000
Belgium	63	625	222	66	24	1,000
Holland	99	607	212	61	21	1,000
Jews	235	585	98	54	28	1,000

The distribution of marriages according to months in the various countries is as follows :—

	Scotland	France	Russia	Austria	Belgium	Italy	Holland	Scandinavia	Greece	Vienna	Berlin	Hungary
January . .	160	126	232	167	105	110	67	61	148	78	69	165
February . .	70	125	270	205	114	167	90	57	121	237	71	267
March . . .	71	55	12	57	39	46	59	76	21	18	83	56
April . . .	78	127	43	87	130	119	136	108	135	78	168	36
May	49	91	90	80	149	84	254	102	98	143	112	114
June	174	112	62	70	107	86	101	115	63	94	82	81
July	124	89	62	62	95	64	76	96	87	77	91	37
August . . .	73	91	20	52	87	73	86	54	68	104	71	40
September . .	74	91	41	60	100	95	73	68	89	88	103	54
October . .	74	98	185	86	101	111	83	141	161	90	146	86
November . .	114	120	174	241	120	139	116	166	145	180	111	234
December . .	139	75	9	33	53	106	59	156	64	13	93	30
Year . .	1,200	1,200	1,200	1,200	1,200	1,200	1,200	1,200	1,200	1,200	1,200	1,200

From observations made in England and France (1858-67) and in Prussia (1844-61) the relation between the ages of husband and wife was ascertained to be as follows :—

When the Age of Husband is	That of the Wife will be		
	In England	In France	In Prussia
Under 20 . .	20.0	22.7	24.4
20-30 . .	23.2	23.3	25.4
30-40 . .	28.9	27.8	28.0
40-50 . .	36.8	35.5	33.6
Over 50 . .	44.3	39.8	42.3

The condition of persons marrying in the various countries is shown as follows :—

	Husband			Wife		
	Bachelor	Widower	Total	Maid	Widow	Total
England .	861	139	1,000	902	98	1,000
France .	881	119	1,000	922	78	1,000
Prussia .	847	153	1,000	902	98	1,000
Russia .	808	192	1,000	864	136	1,000
Austria .	819	181	1,000	886	114	1,000
Hungary .	811	189	1,000	864	136	1,000
Italy . .	863	137	1,000	924	76	1,000
Spain . .	851	149	1,000	912	88	1,000
Belgium .	878	122	1,000	913	87	1,000
Holland .	848	152	1,000	898	102	1,000
Denmark .	865	135	1,000	914	86	1,000
Sweden .	883	117	1,000	940	60	1,000
Norway .	883	117	1,000	941	59	1,000
Greece .	899	101	1,000	926	74	1,000
Roumania .	880	120	1,000	912	88	1,000

	Bachelor with		Widower with		Total	Children per Marriage
	Maid	Widow	Maid	Widow		
England .	816	45	86	53	1,000	4.16
France .	840	41	82	37	1,000	2.98
Prussia .	794	53	108	45	1,000	4.12
Bavaria .	823	54	106	17	1,000	...
Russia .	762	46	102	90	1,000	4.85
Austria .	755	64	131	50	1,000	4.04
Hungary .	771	40	93	96	1,000	...
Italy . .	825	38	99	38	1,000	4.49
Spain .	811	40	101	48	1,000	4.66
Belgium .	827	51	86	36	1,000	4.21
Holland .	794	54	104	48	1,000	4.34
Denmark .	813	52	101	34	1,000	3.55
Sweden .	847	36	93	24	1,000	4.01
Norway .	845	38	96	21	1,000	3.85
Greece .	858	41	68	33	1,000	...
Roumania .	850	30	62	58	1,000	...

The above tables are mostly from observations of 10 years down to 1875. Earlier observations are embodied in the following table :—

	Period of Observation	Bachelor with		Widower with		Total
		Maid	Widow	Maid	Widow	
France . .	1856-65	841	36	89	34	1,000
England .	1845-51	823	42	89	46	1,000
Bavaria . .	1851-60	777	64	141	18	1,000
Belgium .	1851-60	821	49	101	29	1,000
Denmark .	1843-49	765	86	127	22	1,000
Spain . .	1858-62	780	48	116	56	1,000
Scotland .	1846-50	836	37	97	34	1,000
Greece .	1861-65	868	26	66	40	1,000
Holland .	1850-59	786	49	120	43	1,000
Italy . .	1863-66	799	44	111	46	1,000
Norway .	1846-55	834	51	90	25	1,000
Sweden .	1861-60	847	41	90	22	1,000
Switzerland .	1856-60	834	46	96	24	1,000
Austria . .	1855-63	728	58	132	82	1,000
Hungary .	1852-59	665	56	140	139	1,000

The ratios of married, unmarried, and widowed persons in the various countries, as derived from Census returns, show :—

	Unmarried	Married	Widowed	Total
England . . .	602	345	53	1,000
France . . .	518	402	80	1,000
Prussia . . .	600	340	60	1,000
Wurtemburg . .	623	319	58	1,000
Austria . . .	596	348	56	1,000
Hungary . . .	532	407	61	1,000
Italy	582	352	66	1,000
Switzerland . .	609	319	72	1,000
Spain . . .	572	360	68	1,000
Portugal . . .	626	308	66	1,000
Holland . . .	611	328	61	1,000
Belgium . . .	624	317	59	1,000
Scandinavia . .	618	330	52	1,000
Chile	688	260	52	1,000

The above comprises the whole population.

Considering only the women of child-bearing age, which is usually counted from 15 to 45 years, the married ratio (per 1000) will be found as follows ;—

England . . 496 | Germany . . 463 | Denmark . . 450
Scotland . . 444 | Italy . . 520 | Belgium . . 409
Ireland . . 401 | Sweden . . 420 | Holland . . 439
France . . 531 | Norway . . 437 | Switzerland . 421

The lowest ratio is in Ireland ; this is the strongest proof of the wretched condition of the Irish people, and offers no hope of improvement.

The following table from the *Demografia* gives the distribution of adults (1879) :—

	Males over 18 Years				Females over 15 Years			
	Unmarried	Married	Widowers	Total	Unmarried	Married	Widows	Total
France . . .	322	603	75	1,000	326	542	132	1,000
England . .	319	617	64	1,000	361	522	117	1,000
Bavaria. . .	440	502	58	1,000	440	457	103	1,000
Belgium . .	426	503	71	1,000	427	463	110	1,000
Denmark .	356	585	59	1,000	375	507	118	1,000
Scotland . .	355	582	63	1,000	414	453	133	1,000
Norway . .	358	581	61	1,000	400	488	112	1,000
Holland . .	378	556	66	1,000	405	476	119	1,000
Portugal . .	440	502	58	1,000	437	435	128	1,000
Prussia . . .	361	583	56	1,000	368	512	120	1,000
Sweden . .	365	573	62	1,000	403	472	125	1,000
Switzerland .	413	512	75	1,000	426	449	125	1,000

The married population in various countries has been found to be made up as follows :—

	Not before Married		Was Married before		
	Husband	Wife	Husband	Wife	Total
England . .	432	452	68	48	1,000
France . . .	440	461	60	39	1,000
Prussia . . .	421	451	79	49	1,000
Austria . . .	411	442	89	58	1,000
Italy . . .	430	461	70	39	1,000
Holland . .	419	451	81	49	1,000
Sweden . .	443	472	57	28	1,000

The average age at which widowers and widows re-enter matrimony, and the ratio of second marriages, are as follows :—

	Marrying Age of		Second Marriages in 1000	
	Widowers	Widows	Husband	Wife
England . . .	42.2	39.0	139	98
France	42.4	38.0	119	78
Belgium . . .	42.5	40.0	122	87
Holland . . .	41.6	40.3	152	102

The average duration of marriages is as follows :—

	Years		Years		Years
England .	27	Russia . .	30	Holland . .	23
France . .	26	Norway . .	24	Belgium . .	23
Germany .	26	Sweden . .	23	Jews . . .	25

In England, if the mother die first, the father survives 9½ years, but if the father die first, the mother survives 11½ years. In the English Census of 1871, the married people living had an average age of 42 years, and had been married 15 years. An enumeration of the inhabitants of Aggerhus, Norway, in 1763, showed that 150 couples had been over eighty years married. There are at least two cases on record of persons married over a dozen times ; James Gay, who died at Bordeaux in 1772, aged 101, was married 16 times, having no children by any of his wives ; Margaret M'Dowal, Scotland, died in 1768, having survived 13 husbands, aged 106.

Consanguineous marriages, that is, of uncles, nieces, aunts, nephews, and cousins, appear to be of a deteriorat-ing tendency. Bertillon, indeed, says that they do not originate any new infirmity, while they multiply any hereditary defect, but most other writers show that they are a fertile source of new ills. Bemiss says 27 per cent. of such marriages prove barren ; Lent, that 35 per cent. of the children are deaf mutes ; Boudin, that 28 per cent. of deaf mutes in France are children of marriages within the fourth degree ; Darwin, that 35 per 1000 of blind deaf mutes and lunatics in England are children of cousins-german ; and Poucet, that 20 per cent. of such marriages in Mexico are childless. Boudin says that for one deaf mute of ordinary marriages there will be 18 if the parents are cousins, 37 if uncle and niece, and 70 if nephew and aunt. Marriages of cousins are commoner among Protestants than Catholics, and still more so among Jews : hence it is found at Berlin that there are—

3 deaf mutes among 10,000 Catholics
6   ,,   ,,   10,000 Protestants
27   ,,   ,,   10,000 Jews

Of 1549 marriages contracted in Prussia in 1889 between blood relations, 1422 were between cousins, 110 between uncles and nieces, and 16 between aunts and nephews.

The ratio of consanguineous among 10,000 marriages, in the various countries, is as follows :—

Prussia . . 67 | England . . 75 | France. . . 126
Italy . . . 69 | Alsace . . . 107 | Jews . . . 230

These marriages are increasing in France, but diminishing in Alsace and Italy, viz. :—

	Date	No. per 10,000	Date	No. per 10,000
France .	1853–60	97	1861–71	126
Alsace .	1858–65	143	1872–75	107
Italy . .	1868–71	84	1872 75	69

They are always more frequent in rural districts than in towns :—

	Per 10,000 Marriages		
	Rural	Urban	General
England . . .	79	71	75
France	130	115	126
Alsace	121	41	107

Darwin says that 450 per 10,000 marriages among the nobility of England are consanguineous, being six times the average of such marriages in England ; and it appears that 19 per cent. of the English nobility are childless, which is more than three times the averages for England. It appears, however, that in France the ratio of children to a marriage is highest where consanguineous marriages are most frequent ; and that the blind, deaf mutes, and insane are decidedly increased by such marriages. The returns of all France for five years ending 1865 show the eighty-nine departments thus :—

Departments	Consanguineous per 10,000 Marriages	Children to 100 Marriages	Blind, Insane, &c., per 100,000 Population
20	69	303	254
20	103	300	275
20	124	320	282
20	153	312	348
9	195	329	345
89	119	308	290

Furthermore, the increase in France of blind, deaf

mutes, and insane has been simultaneous with a rise in this kind of marriages :—

Period	Consanguineous per 10,000 Marriages	Blind,Insane,&c., per 100,000 Population
1853-55 . . .	93	224
1856-60 . . .	100	279
1861-65 . . .	119	290
1866-71 . . .	126	292

The above table seems to show that consanguineous marriages increase the number of blind, insane, &c.

The ratio of these marriages of 100,000 in France, during fifteen years ending 1875, was as follows :—

	Towns	Rural	All France
Nephew and aunt . .	16	24	21
Uncle and niece . .	60	56	58
Cousins. . . .	960	1,190	1,131
Total . .	1,036	1,270	1,212

The marriages with deceased wife's sister or husband's brother averaged 355 per 100,000 marriages.

In Italy in 1872-75 the ratio of consanguineous in 10,000 marriages was as follows :—

Venice. . . 24 | Lombardy . 100 | Piedmont . . 131
Naples . . 30 | Sicily . . . 117 | Liguria . . 183

The ratio of the whole kingdom was 69, as already shown. In seven years ending 1874, of all consanguineous marriages 92 per cent. were of cousins, and 8 per cent. of uncles or aunts with nieces or nephews.

Regarding barrenness in marriages, it is commonly believed that 5 per cent. of marriages in Great Britain are sterile, and that sterility among women is half again more frequent than among men. A census taken in Prussia on this subject in 1842 showed 11 per 1000 males, 29 per 1000 females, and 34 per 1000 marriages were sterile.

The marriage-rate per 1000 inhabitants yearly in various countries was as follows :—

Persons Married Yearly per 1000

	1841-50	1871-80		1841-50	1871-80
England	16.1	16.3	Sweden .	15.0	13.6
France .	15.8	15.9	Holland .	14.4	16.1
Germany	17.4	17.7	Belgium .	13.8	14.6
Austria .	...	17.1	Denmark .	15.8	15.6
Hungary	...	20.6	Spain . .	...	15.1
Italy . .	...	15.3	Switzerland	...	15.3

From the above it appears that notwithstanding the improved condition of the working-classes, and the reduced price of food in all countries since 1850, the marriage-rate has not risen perceptibly. In Sweden and Denmark it has fallen. The following table, from observations in 1857-66, shows the marriage-rate among adults at various ages :—

Age	Married Yearly among 1000 of Each Class					
	England		France		Belgium	
	Men	Women	Men	Women	Men	Women
20-25	121	131	58	108	34	63
25-30	143	104	114	110	83	89
30-35	104	64	114	80	84	78
35-40	81	45	88	49	71	59
40-45	55	27	47	21	46	31
45-50	32	3	25	2	19	2

The marriage-rate yearly per 1000 persons of either sex between the ages of 15 and 60 was as follows :—

	Men	Women		Men	Women
England . .	69	62	Belgium . .	41	44
France . . .	55	59	Denmark . .	60	61
Holland . .	54	51	Norway . .	56	52

Observations in 1866-72 showed that the annual marriage-rate of 1000 unmarried persons, male and female, between 15 and 60 years of age was as follows :—

England . . 65 | Prussia . . 71 | Belgium . . 51
France . . 64 | Italy . . . 58 | Switzerland . 52

UNITED KINGDOM

In 1871 the married and unmarried of the three kingdoms stood in the following ratios :—

	England		Scotland		Ireland		United Kingdom	
	Male	Female	Male	Female	Male	Female	Male	Female
Married	35.1	33.9	30.7	28.8	29.5	28.4	33.6	32.6
Unmarried	61.3	58.6	66.0	62.8	66.8	62.1	62.8	59.4
Widowed	3.6	7.5	3.3	8.4	3.7	9.5	3.6	8.0
Total . .	100.0	100.0	100.0	100.0	100.0	100.0	100.0	100.0

The married ratio in Ireland is remarkably low. The variations of condition in England since 1851 have been as follows :—

	Males			Females		
	1851	1861	1871	1851	1861	1871
Married . . .	33.7	35.0	35.1	32.9	33.9	33.9
Unmarried . .	62.6	61.3	61.3	59.8	58.8	58.6
Widowed . .	3.7	3.7	3.6	7.3	7.3	7.5
Total . .	100.0	100.0	100.0	100.0	100.0	100.0

The variations in Scotland showed an increase of married people from 1851 to 1871, viz.:—

	Males			Females		
	1851	1861	1871	1851	1861	1871
Married . . .	29.9	30.9	30.7	27.8	28.6	28.8
Unmarried . .	66.8	65.8	66.0	63.8	63.0	62.8
Widowed . .	3.3	3.3	3.3	8.4	8.4	8.4
Total . .	100.0	100.0	100.0	100.0	100.0	100.0

The figures for Ireland in 1881 show a rapid decline of the married ratio since 1871, viz. :—

	Males		Females	
	1871	1881	1871	1881
Married . .	29.5	27.6	28.4	27.0
Unmarried .	66.8	68.5	62.1	63.4
Widowed .	3.7	3.9	9.5	9.6
Total .	100.0	100.0	100.0	100.0

The marriage rate per 1000 population in the three kingdoms showed thus :—

England		Scotland		Ireland		U. Kingdom	
Year	Per 1000	Year	Per 1000	Year	Per 1000	Year	Per 1000
1841–50	16.1	...	...	...	...	...	...
1851–60	16.9	1855–60	13.7	...	...	...	...
1861–70	16.7	1861–70	14.1	1864–70	10.5	1861–70	15.3
1871–80	16.3	1871–80	14.5	1871–80	9.3	1871–80	15.2
1881–89	14.8	1881–89	13.2	1881–89	8.7	1881–89	13.8

The ratios of marrying age in England in 1871–80 compare with those of 1838 as follows :—

Age	1838		1871–80	
	Men	Women	Men	Women
Under 20 .	33	142	35	149
20–30 . .	758	697	731	680
30–40 . .	127	105	144	111
Over 40 . .	82	56	90	60
Total .	1,000	1,000	1,000	1,000

FRANCE

The ratios of married and unmarried in the whole population were at various dates as follows :—

Year	Males				Females			
	Unmarried	Married	Widowers	Total	Unmarried	Married	Widows	Total
1806	588	366	46	1,000	560	364	86	1,000
1836	578	377	45	1,000	542	363	95	1,000
1856	555	396	49	1,000	519	386	95	1,000
1866	545	403	52	1,000	498	404	98	1,000
1876	533	413	54	1,000	482	409	109	1,000

The marriage rate per 1000 population was as follows :—

Period		Period		Period	
1801–10 . .	15.6	1831–40 . .	15.9	1861–70 . .	15.8
1811–20 . .	15.8	1841–50 . .	15.9	1871–80 . .	15.9
1821–30 . .	15.5	1851–60 . .	15.8	80 years . .	15.8

The *Demografia* of 1880 gives a table of the ages in France at which men or women become widowed, in ratios thus :—

Age at Loss of Spouse	Town		Rural	
	Men	Women	Men	Women
Under 25 . . .	22	35	14	22
25–30 . . .	91	78	56	46
30–40 . . .	231	198	178	158
40–50 . . .	206	220	171	190
Over 50 . . .	450	469	581	584
Total . .	1,000	1,000	1,000	1,000

There is a notable difference between town and country population as to the distribution of marriages in months. Taking the year's total as 1200, we find thus for the years 1861–65 :—

	Town	Rural	France		Town	Rural	France
January . .	114	135	128	July . . .	99	91	94
February . .	135	164	152	August . .	88	63	72
March . . .	54	49	52	September .	99	85	90
April . . .	115	109	111	October . .	107	98	101
May . . .	99	95	97	November .	120	139	131
June . . .	110	120	116	December .	60	52	56
Half year . .	627	672	656	Half year .	573	528	544

GERMANY

The marriage rate of Prussia for sixty years down to 1876 averaged 18.1 per thousand. After the wars of 1815 and 1871 it rose 10 per cent. in the following year, and after the cholera visitations of 1831, 1848, 1856, 1866, and 1873, there was a rise of 1 per cent. Observations for eighteen years ending 1861 showed the marriage rate among the population over fourteen years of age was as follows :—

Among	Per 1000 Yearly	
	Males	Females
Christians	54.0	52.5
Jews	49.0	44.9

In the same period it was found that the adult male and female population of Prussia showed thus :—

Marrying Age	Men	Women
Under 20	8	87
20–30	487	556
30–40	178	128
40–50	51	34
Over 50	24	8
Never marry	252	187
Total . .	1,000	1,000

Of 1000 men who marry, it is found that—

332 marry younger women
579 ,, women of same age
89 ,, older women

Of 1000 Catholics who marry, the ratios show—

In	Married to		
	Catholics	Protestants	Total
Towns . .	863	137	1,000
Rural parts . .	965	35	1,000
All Prussia . .	935	65	1,000

In Bavaria, it appears that of 1000 marriages 681 are Roman Catholics, 254 Protestants, and 65 mixed. The duration of marriage in Leipzig, until death of husband and wife, shows the following ratios :—

Years					Ratio
Less than 5					186
5–10					163
10–20					243
20–30					198
30–40					143
Over 40					67
Total . .					1,000

2 B

The Census of 1885 gave the numbers of married and unmarried as follows :—

	Prussia			Germany		
	Males	Females	Total	Males	Females	Total
Unmarried . . .	8,670,000	8,355,000	17,025,000	14,250,000	13,895,000	28,145,000
Married . . .	4,775,000	4,795,000	9,570,000	7,910,000	7,945,000	15,855,000
Widowed . . .	450,000	1,270,000	1,720,000	775,000	2,080,000	2,855,000
Total .	13,895,000	14,420,000	28,315,000	22,935,000	23,920,000	46,855,000

AUSTRIA-HUNGARY

In Vienna the observations for 1872–76 showed :—

Husband older .	. 503	Catholics . .	. 873
Wife older . .	. 129	Jews . . .	. 77
Both same age .	. 368	Protestants .	. 50
Total	1,000	Total	1,000

The marrying age for men averaged 32, women 27 years ; and the mean duration of marriage was 16 years.
In Hungary, in 1874, the conditions of the people were :—

	Males	Females
Unmarried . . .	556	503
Married . . .	412	407
Widowed . . .	32	90
Total . .	1,000	1,000

The marrying age in Sweden was as follows :—

Years	Men			Women			Men and Women		
	Urban	Rural	Total	Urban	Rural	Total	Nobles	Citizens	Peasants
Under 26 . . .	169	216	208	289	385	370	95	143	289
26–35	601	564	570	529	471	480	529	599	556
36–50	199	173	177	171	129	136	308	220	126
Over 50	31	47	45	11	15	14	68	38	29
Total . .	1,000	1,000	1,000	1,000	1,000	1,000	1,000	1,000	1,000

NORWAY

The marriage-rate was per 1000 inhabitants as follows :—

Period		Period		Period	
1801–25 . .	16.2	1836–45 . .	14.5	1856–65 . .	14.4
1826–35 . .	15.0	1846–55 . .	15.5	1866–75 . .	13.7

The condition of the adult population, men and women, between the ages of 15 and 60 was in 1875 as follows :—

	Men			Women		
	Town	Rural	Total	Town	Rural	Total
Unmarried . .	480	470	472	474	446	451
Married . . .	492	506	504	456	507	498
Widowed . .	28	24	24	70	47	51
Total . .	1,000	1,000	1,000	1,000	1,000	1,000

The marrying age for men is rising, for women falling :—

Average Age at Marriage

Period	Men		Women
1841–50	30.4	...	28.1
1861–70	30.9	...	27.9

ITALY

Observations for 1875–77 showed the marriage rate as follows :—

Naples . .	18.4	Lombardy .	17.0	Tuscany .	15.8
Sicily . .	17.4	Piedmont .	16.6	Venice . .	15.4

The general rate for the kingdom was 16.2.

SWEDEN

In 1870 the male and female population over 15 years of age showed thus :—

	Men	Women
Unmarried . .	422	403
Married . .	521	472
Widowed . .	57	125
Total .	1,000	1,000

Taking the year as 1200, the marriages according to months were :—

January . .	50	May . . .	84	September .	66
February .	59	June . . .	102	October .	158
March . . .	80	July . . .	66	November .	173
April . . .	102	August . .	47	December.	213

Taking the year as 1200, the marriages according to months stood thus :—

January . .	75	May . . .	77	September .	72
February .	48	June . . .	158	October .	132
March . .	65	July . . .	146	November .	144
April . . .	110	August . .	54	December.	118

BELGIUM

In Belgium the different Censuses showed as follows :—

Males

	1846	1866	1880
Unmarried . .	1,417,000	1,546,000	1,761,000
Married . . .	662,000	766,000	879,000
Widowed . . .	85,000	108,000	118,000
Total . .	2,164,000	2,420,000	2,758,000

Females

	1846	1866	1880
Unmarried . .	1,355,000	1,466,000	1,681,000
Married . . .	661,000	763,000	876,000
Widowed . . .	158,000	180,000	205,000
Total . .	2,174,000	2,409,000	2,762,000

Both Sexes	1846	1866	1880
Unmarried	2,772,000	3,012,000	3,442,000
Married	1,323,000	1,529,000	1,755,000
Widowed	243,000	288,000	323,000
Total	4,338,000	4,829,000	5,520,000

Of males over 18 years of age the conditions were :—

	1846	1866	1880
Unmarried	582,000	646,000	672,000
Married	662,000	766,000	879,000
Widowed	85,000	108,000	118,000
Total	1,329,000	1,520,000	1,669,000

Of females over 18 the returns showed thus :—

	1846	1866	1880
Unmarried	545,000	576,000	611,000
Married	660,000	761,000	874,000
Widowed	158,000	180,000	205,000
Total	1,363,000	1,517,000	1,690,000

The condition of persons marrying showed these ratios :—

	1841–50	1851–60	1861–70	1871–80
Bachelor and maid	80.8	82.1	82.6	83.7
Bachelor and widow	5.0	4.9	4.9	5.1
Widower and maid	11.5	10.1	9.1	7.8
Widower and widow	2.7	2.9	3.4	3.4
Total	100.0	100.0	100.0	100.0

The ages of the parties marrying showed as follows :—

	Men		Women	
	1841–50	1871–80	1841–50	1871–80
Under 25	19.3	21.6	35.6	41.1
25–30	33.5	34.3	29.6	28.0
30–40	32.9	30.4	25.2	21.8
40–50	10.3	9.1	7.6	6.8
50–60	2.8	3.4	1.7	1.8
60–70	1.0	1.0	0.3	0.5
Over 70	0.2	0.2	0.0	0.0
Total	100.0	100.0	100.0	100.0

SWITZERLAND

Of 1000 men married at Geneva there were :—

	1847–51	1872–76
Genevans	641	305
Foreigners	359	695
Total	1,000	1,000

The children to 100 foreign fathers were 263 ; to Genevans, 242.

RUSSIA

The marrying rate per 1000 inhabitants in 1875 was 20.2 among Greeks, 16.2 among Roman Catholics, 18.0 among Armenians, and 14.6 among Protestants.

PORTUGAL

In 1860 the marriage rate was 12.2 per 1000, and in 1864 the population was composed thus :—

	Male	Female	Total
Unmarried	635	617	626
Married	321	296	308
Widowed	44	87	66
Total	1,000	1,000	1,000

ALGERIA

In 1872 the European population of the colony was :—

	Male	Female
Unmarried	621	504
Married	342	384
Widowed	37	112
Total	1,000	1,000

FINLAND

The marriage rate averaged 16.0 from 1812 to 1840, and only 15.5 from 1851 to 1865.

MATCHES

Sweden and Norway export 20,000 tons of wooden matches yearly, being nearly one-third of the quantity consumed in Europe per annum. The tax on matches in France averages 4d. per inhabitant.

MEDICINE

The number of physicians and surgeons in various countries is stated as follows :—

	Number	Per Million Population
England	15,090	550
Scotland	3,455	850
Ireland	3,560	630
United Kingdom	22,105	578
Russia	13,475	155
Spain	5,200	305
France	14,380	380
Germany	16,270	355
Austria	10,690	275
Italy	8,580	280
Holland	1,860	410
Belgium	2,160	390
Norway	502	275

The above is exclusive of army and navy doctors, of which there are these returns :—

French navy	666
Russian navy	413
German navy	50
United States navy	221

Dispensaries are maintained in the United Kingdom to give relief gratis to the poor. In England 972,000 persons received medical attendance and medicines gratis. In Ireland the cost of these institutions is £150,000 a year. In France 230,000 persons annually receive medicine free at a cost of £58,000. The number of medical students in London in October 1882 was 949. The Italian Universities turn out 630 physicians and surgeons yearly. The French Universities made 33,000 M.D.'s in eighty-two years, viz. :—

Years	No.	Years	No.
1801–14	3,178	1849–69	9,145
1815–30	6,423	1870–82	5,901
1831–48	8,468	82 years	33,115

The ratio of physicians in France is declining : in 1847 it was 510 per million, the progress of sanitary science causing this decline, or perhaps the heavy tax on doctors, which Leroy-Beaulieu says produces £500,000 a year.

The progress of medicine in Austria proper is shown thus :—

	1840	1886
Physicians, &c. . . .	9,440	13,228
Midwives . . .	14,100	16,940
Total . .	23,540	30,168

The returns for Belgium show thus :—

	1850	1880
Physicians, &c. . . .	2,786	3,189
Midwives . . .	1,128	2,176
Total . .	3,914	5,365

In the above returns apothecaries are counted with physicians.

In Holland there are 803 graduated M.D.'s, 950 surgeons, 106 pensioned army doctors, 66 dentists, 750 midwives, and 752 apothecaries.

The death-rate of physicians is very high. The French army in the Crimea lost 7 per cent. of officers and 18 per cent. of surgeons.

The death-rate in England of physicians and civilians differs as follows :—

	Age 20-54
Civilians	12 per 1000
Married doctors . . .	19 ,,
Unmarried doctors . . .	26 ,,

During the typhus plague in ·Ireland in 1843–47, no fewer than 66 per thousand of physicians died. Among the people 9 per cent. of deaths were from typhus, but among physicians 32 per cent.

MENSTRUATION

The medium age at which it commences is stated in the *Dic. des Sciences Médicale* as follows :—

	Years		Years
Marseilles . .	13.9	Manchester .	15.3
Corfu .	14.0	Lyons .	15.5
Hungary . .	14.1	Vienna .	15.7
London . .	15.1	Halle .	16.0
Paris . .	15.2	Copenhagen .	16.8

Despine and Boismont give the following results respecting 8600 girls in France as the average ages at which it begins :—

	Years	Months	Days
Under 5 feet . . .	14	7	14
Over 5 ,, . .	14	9	21
Dark eyes . .	14	5	8
Blue ,, . .	14	11	24

According to Guy and Murphy the average ages in England are :—

	Years	Months	Days
London . . .	14	11	6
Manchester . .	14	10	9
Rural population .	16	1	24
Urban . . .	15	4	9

In Calcutta and Bombay the averages are as follow :—

Years	Calcutta	Bombay
Under 12 . . .	29.4	15.2
12–14 . . .	47.8	48.2
14–16 . . .	18.9	24.9
Over 16 . .	3.9	11.7
Total . .	100.0	100.0

Dubois gives the age at which it stops as follows :—

	Years		Years
Java . . .	30.0	Poland . .	47.1
India . .	32.5	Norway . .	48.1
France . .	45.5	Portugal . .	50.0

METALS

The production is stated under *Mining*.

	Conductors of	
	Heat	Electricity
Gold	100	94
Platinum . . .	98	16
Silver . . .	97	74
Copper . . .	90	100
Iron . . .	37	16
Zinc . . .	36	29
Tin . . .	30	15
Lead . . .	18	8

A wire 0.84 of a line in diameter will sustain the following weights :—

Lead . .	28 lbs.	Silver . .	187 lbs.
Tin . .	35 ,,	Platinum .	274 ,,
Zinc . .	110 ,,	Copper . .	302 ,,
Gold . .	150 ,,	Iron . .	549 ,,

The fluid density is as follows :—

Zinc . .	6.48	Copper . .	8.22
Iron . .	6.88	Silver . .	9.51
Tin . .	7.03	Lead . .	10.37

METEOROLOGY

Air.—In its pure state it is composed thus :—

Nitrogen	77
Oxygen	21
Other compounds	2
	100

The percentage of oxygen varies as follows :—

Locality	Percentage	Locality	Percentage
Sea-shore . . .	21.00	Mines	20.50
Confined houses . .	20.75	When candles go out	18.50

The following table shows how oxygen varies with climate :—

Ben Lomond . . .	20.940	Berlin	20.953
Atlantic	20.942	Paris	20.956
Lyons	20.942	Geneva	20.956
Mediterranean . .	20.947	Andes	20.963
Madrid	20.949		

Air travels in England in healthy years about 4¼ miles an hour, and 3½ in unhealthy. The percentage of carbonic acid ranges thus :—

In country	.03	In fogs	.07
,, town	.04	,, crowded lanes .	.13
,, hospitals . . .	.05	,, theatres .	.30

Each adult inhales a gallon of air per minute, and consumes daily 30 oz. of oxygen. For the conversion of this oxygen a certain amount of food is required—say 13 oz. of carbon for a male, and 11 oz. for a female, equivalent to 3 lbs. bread and 2½ lbs. respectively. The proper allowance of air in barracks is 600 cubic feet per man in Europe, and 1000 in India : for hospitals, 1200 cubic feet per bed in Europe, and 1800 in India. Horses require in England 1600 cubic feet each, or nearly as much as three men.

The Scottish Meteorological Society report on the presence of ozone as follows :—May, 6.2 ; November, 5.3 ; annual average, 6.0.

The atmosphere of Paris shows the prevalence of ozone and bacteria in the various months as follows :—

	Ozone at Mont Souris per 1000 Cubic Metres Air	Bacteria per Cubic Metre Air	
		Mont Souris	Rue Rivoli
January . . .	3	380	2,200
February . .	9	255	1,850
March . . .	8	380	4,600
April	7	380	6,400
May	7	420	6,900
June	9	400	6,450
July	12	815	6,370
August . . .	8	670	6,350
September . .	8	630	6,400
October . . .	8	480	5,100
November . .	12	290	3,800
December . .	6	230	2,520
Average. . .	8	444	4,910

The foregoing is taken from the *Dic. des Sciences Medicales*, but M. Miguel gives other results for 1882–83 as follows :—

	Microbes per Cubic Metre	
	Mont Souris	Rue Rivoli
Spring	550	1,900
Summer	?	3,960
Autumn	115	2,060
Winter	115	2,040
Yearly average . . .	...	2,490

He adds that at a height of 6000 feet in the Swiss mountains no bacteria were found, and gives this table :—

Bacteria in Ten Cubic Metres of Air.

1. At a height of 2000 metres . . . 0
2. On the Lake of Thun (560 metres) . 8
3. Near the Hotel Bellevue, Thun . . 25
4. In a room of the hotel . . . 600
5. In the park at Mont Souris . . . 7,600
6. In the Rue de Rivoli, Paris . . . 55,000

M. Miguel's researches on the air of the wards of hospitals were carried out at the Hotel Dieu and the Hospital Notre Dame, and with the result that for the whole year the hospital air contained on an average 11,000 bacteria per cubic metre, as against 850 bacteria per cubic metre of the air of the Rue de Rivoli. The hospital bacteria reached their minimum at the time when the windows could be kept open, in June, July, and August—average, 5500—at a time when the bacteria in the street had attained a maximum of about 13,000, or 50 per cent. in excess of the average. The maximum of the hospital (28.000) was reached in January, when the weather was cold and the windows shut, and the average in the street had fallen to 160. Microbes multiply so fast that one may become 16 millions in twenty-four hours.

Barometer.—In London it usually ranges between 28.700 and 30.700, but it has exceeded the latter figure three times on record :—

In 1778 . . . . . 30.935
February 11, 1849 . . . . . 30.895
January 18, 1882 . . . . . 30.983

The lowest reading in London was on Christmas Day, 1821, namely, 28.016. The lowest reading known in the British Islands was at Ochtertyre, near Crieff, Jan. 26, 1884: 27.332. The highest reading known also occurred in Scotland, Jan. 8–9, 1820, near Leith, when the reading was 31.065. The highest reading recorded in England was at St. Leonards, Hastings, Jan. 18, 1882: 30.990.

Mr. Glaisher's barometer in his various balloon ascents marked as follows :—

Miles High			Inches	Miles High			Inches
1	.	.	24.7	4	.	.	13.7
2	.	.	20.3	5	.	.	11.3
3	.	.	16.7				

He therefore estimates for 10 miles 4.2 and for 15 miles 1.6 inches.

The mean height of barometer varies according to latitude, and in the northern hemisphere averages as follows :—

Degree of Latitude			Barometer	Degree of Latitude			Barometer
10	.	.	29.98	45	.	.	30.00
20	.	.	30.06	50	.	.	29.81
30	.	.	30.11	60	.	.	29.80
40	.	.	30.02	67	.	.	29.67

But in latitudes south of 25° S. the decrease is very much more rapid, the mean elevation in 55° S. being about 29.30. It also varies according to elevation, the reading diminishing approximately at the rate of 1 inch for 1000 feet. The actual mean readings at different places are as follows :—

Place	Feet over Sea	Mean Height of Barometer	Boiling-point (Fahrenheit).
Sea-level . .	0	30.00	212.0
Rome . .	151	29.76	211.6
Milan . .	420	29.45	211.1
Moscow . .	984	28.82	210.2
Geneva . .	1,221	28.54	209.5
Munich . .	1,765	27.95	208.6
Madrid . .	1,995	27.72	208.0
Briançon . .	4,285	25.39	203.9
St. Remo . .	5,265	24.45	202.1
St. Gothard . .	6,808	23.07	199.2
Mexico . .	7,471	22.52	198.1
Bogota . .	8,731	21.42	195.6
Quito . . .	9,541	20.75	194.2
Antisana . .	13,455	17.87	187.4

Atmospheric pressure, moreover, varies at the same place with the season. For example, at Ben Nevis, height 4300 feet, the mean pressure marks thus :—

January .	.	.	25.16	July .	.	.	25.43
February .	.	.	25.49	August .	.	.	25.42
March .	.	.	25.39	September .	.	.	25.36
April .	.	.	25.38	October .	.	.	25.45
May .	.	.	25.47	November .	.	.	25.09
June .	.	.	25.68	December .	.	.	25.09

The mean pressure for the year was 25.37, or nearly the same as that of Briançon, which is 4300 feet over sea-level.

Martin publishes the following table of the average number of monthly oscillations of the barometer at various towns in France :—

	Summer	Winter	Year
Bordeaux . . .	14	29	22
Dijon	11	26	19
Marseilles . . .	17	23	20
Metz	14	26	20
Montpellier . .	13	23	18
Mulhouse . . .	13	27	20
Nantes	15	29	22
Paris	17	31	24
Rochelle . . .	16	32	24
Strasburg . . .	15	29	22

Clouds.—The University of Upsala has (1884–85) determined the average height of clouds thus :—

			Yards				Yards
Stratus	.	.	685	Strato-cumulus .		.	2,560
Nimbus	.	.	1,680	Cirro-cumulus .		.	7,110
Cumulus	.	.	2,040	Cirrus	.	.	9,760

Evaporation.—Gasparim's table estimates 25 inches for the level parts of France, 27 for the western coast, 35 for the hilly country, and 90 for the Southern Departments. He also gives twelve cities thus:—

	Inches		Inches		Inches
Arles . .	90	Marseilles .	96	Rome . .	98
Bordeaux .	82	Paris . .	24	Rotterdam .	27
Geneva . .	48	Poitiers . .	32	Toulouse .	26
Lille . . .	36	Rochelle . .	25	Troyes . .	33

Hail.—1656, July 20th, Norwich, wrecked houses and killed many persons.

1697, May 4th, killed sheep in many parts of England.

1775, May 13th, Murcia, Spain, hailstones like oranges, weighing 20 oz.

1844, in Languedoc, pieces of ice fell weighing 11 lbs.

1874, New Jersey, U.S., hailstones like turkey eggs.

Damage to crops in France by hail since 1850 has averaged £1,420,000 per annum.

Magnetic Observations.—At Paris the magnetic declension was recorded thus:—

Year		Year		Year		
1580.	. 11.30 E.	1700	. 8.10 W.	1835 .	22.4	W.
1618.	. 8.0 ,,	1780	. 19.55 ,,	1851 .	20.25	,,
1663.	. 0	1805	. 25.5 ,,	1861 .	19.6	,,

The variations of the needle at Paris showed the following angle of inclination:—

Year		Year		Year	
1671	. . 75.0	1798	. . 69.51	1831	. . 67.40
1754	. . 72.15	1806	. . 69.12	1851	. . 66.35
1780	. . 71.48	1820	. . 68.20	1861	. . 66.7

The following table of magnetic intensity is chiefly from Humboldt:—

	North Latitude	Magnetic Intensity
Peruvian Andes . .	...	1,087
Carthegena . .	10.25	1,294
Naples . . .	40.50	1,274
Lyons . . .	45.46	1,333
Paris . . .	48.52	1,348
St. Petersburg . .	59.46	1,410
Berlin . . .	52.51	1,366
Christiania . .	59.55	1,419
Brussels . . .	50.52	1,374
Baffin's Bay . .	12.43	1,590
Spitzbergen . .	79.40	1,562
New York . .	40.43	1,803

Meteors.—November 27, 1885, the Greenwich Observatory counted 3000 between 6 and 11 P.M. : first hour at intervals 40 per minute ; at 9 P.M. about 20.

On November 14, 1868, the Observatory at Philadelphia counted 4800 between 12.20 and 5 A.M.

Mineral Heat.—The temperature of water being taken as 100, that of the various minerals is as follows:—

Lead .	.	.	. 29	Copper	.	.	. 95
Mercury	.	.	. 33	Iron .	.	.	. 110
Silver .	.	.	. 56	Glass .	.	.	. 117
Zinc .	.	.	. 93	Sulphur	.	.	. 188

The average rainfall is heaviest near the Equator, and diminishes as the latitude rises, viz. :—

Latitude							Inches Rainfall
0 .	.	.	.	.	.	.	100
20 .	.	.	.	.	.	.	80
30 .	.	.	.	.	.	.	60
40 .	.	.	.	.	.	.	40
50 .	.	.	.	.	.	.	30
60 .	.	.	.	.	.	.	20
70 .	.	.	.	.	.	.	10
80 .	.	.	.	.	.	.	5

Rainfall.—The rainfall according to seasons (Gasparim) is as follows, in inches :—

	Spring	Summer	Autumn	Winter	Year
England . .	6	8	10	8	32
Scandinavia .	3	7	6	3	19
Russia .	2	7	4	4	17
France .	6	9	7	5	27
Germany .	5	8	6	5	24
Italy . .	5	5	7	20	37
Europe .	4	7	7	5	23
United States .	11	11	12	11	45
Atlantic States .	11	11	11	3	36
Southern .	13	17	11	14	55
Western .	6	11	6	3	26
Pacific .	12	7	18	25	62
Australia .	8	9	12	6	35
West Indies .	31	22	27	8	88
Sierra Leone .	12	65	46	2	125
Patagonia . .	3	3	6	3	15

The heaviest rainfalls recorded in the United Kingdom have been :—

7 inches at Ardrishaig, Argyle, on 7th Dec. 1863.
4½ inches at London on 13th April 1878.

It is stated that 24 inches have fallen at Bombay in 24 hours, also 30 inches at the Khasi Hills, India, 30 at Genoa, and 33 at Gibraltar.

The wettest place in England is Seathwaite, 145 inches; and in the world Cherrapungi, in South-Western Assam, where the average for 15 years is 493 inches, reaching in 1861 up to 905 inches.

The rainfall of the United Kingdom (54 stations), European Continent (45 stations), and the United States (34 stations), from 1824 to 1867, was :—

Period	Inches per Annum		
	United Kingdom	European Continent	United States
1824–30 . .	29	25	44
1831–40 . .	29	29	40
1841–50 . .	31	29	42
1851–60 . .	33	26	40
1861–67 . .	38	25	...

The rainfall of various countries reduced to horse-power is valued as follows :—

	Horse-power		Horse-power
United Kingdom	9,300,000	Russia .	77,700,000
France .	12,000,000	Italy .	8,500,000
Germany .	11,800,000	United States	430,200,000

The average in inches is as follows, yearly :—

	Inches		Inches		Inches
Aberdeen .	30	Baltimore .	41	Bologna . .	22
Adelaide .	20	Barcelona .	17	Bombay .	85
Agen . .	27	Barbadoes .	58	Bordeaux .	29
Agra . .	23	Bath . .	30	Boston .	45
Alexandria .	10	Bayonne .	52	Bourbon .	47
Algiers .	32	Batavia .	78	Brescia .	50
Alicante .	71	Baton Rouge	61	Brest . .	36
Allahabad .	27	Belfast .	32	Brighton .	31
Ancona .	29	Beauvais .	22	Brisbane .	43
Apulia . .	22	Bergen .	89	Bristol . .	23
Arles . .	23	Berlin . .	24	Brussels .	29
Armagh .	36	Bermuda .	55	Buda-Pesth .	17
Asuncion .	82	Benares .	42	Buenos Ayres	33
Auckland .	44	Bengal .	36	Bushire .	13
Augsburg .	41	Berne . .	46	Cairo . .	1
Aurillac .	46	Besançon .	25	Calais . .	29
Auzerre .	26	Beziers .	17	Calcutta .	71
Azores . .	30	Birmingham .	24	Cambray .	17
Bag. Bigorre	54	Black Sea .	61	Cambridge .	24
Baku . .	14	Blois . .	25	Canary Islands	83

Inches		Inches		Inches		Inches		Inches		Inches
Cannes .. 36	Edinburgh . 31	Lisbon. ... 27	Naples. .. 31	Quetta... 8	Texas ... 12
Canton .. 39	Elgin ... 24	Liverpool. . 35	Nashville .. 51	Rangoon . 173	Ticino ... 67
Capetown . 23	Erfurth .. 14	London .. 25	Natchez .. 58	Ratisbon .. 23	Tiflis ... 20
Caracas . 155	Feejee Islands 50	Louisville .. 49	New Brunswick 51	Reikjavik . 30	Toronto .. 38
Carcasonne . 30	Fernando Po 102	Lucca ... 55	Newfoundland 58	Rheims .. 19	Toulon .. 24
Carlsruhe . 27	Florence .. 38	Lucknow .. 37	New Orleans. 51	Rio Janeiro . 53	Toulouse .. 25
Castille . 12	Friburg .. 48	Lyons ... 28	New York .. 43	Rhone Valley 38	Tours ... 22
Catania .. 28	Galveston. . 52	Macao. ... 71	New Zealand. 53	Rochelle .. 25	Trieste. .. 43
Cayenne .. 116	Geneva .. 33	Macori. .. 30	Nice .. 29	Rohilcund . 36	Trinidad .. 64
Chalons .. 25	Genoa ... 50	Madeira .. 25	Nismes .. 21	Rotterdam . 25	Truro .. 44
Chambery . 41	Ghauts Mtns. 173	Madras .. 46	Nilgherries . 65	Rome ... 30	Tübingen. . 26
Charleston . 54	Gibraltar .. 44	Madrid .. 12	Norfolk, U.S. 53	Rouen .. 27	Tucuman .. 42
Cincinnati . 46	Gironde .. 23	Magellan Straits 15	Norwich .. 24	St. Bernard . 60	Tunis ... 12
Clermont .. 21	Glasgow .. 44	Majorca .. 14	Nottingham . 26	St. Domingo. 108	Turin ... 32
Coblenz .. 22	Gondar .. 37	Malabar .. 82	Oporto. .. 54	St. Etienne . 53	Udine ... 68
Coimbra . 173	Goree ... 21	Malaga .. 20	Oran ... 17	St. Gothard . 73	Ulm ... 27
Colombo .. 73	Grahamstown 25	Malta ... 20	Orleans .. 25	St. John's. . 58	Upsal ... 19
Comorin, C. . 28	Grenada,W.I. 105	Manchester . 36	Oxford. .. 27	St. Petersburg 17	Utah .. 24
Constantinople 41	Grenoble .. 37	Manilla .. 87	Padua. .. 34	St. Helena . 45	Utrecht .. 29
Copenhagen . 22	Grimsel .. 93	Mannheim . 22	Palermo .. 23	St. Louis .. 42	Valdivia .. 106
Copiapo .. 1	Guadaloupe . 129	Mantua .. 31	Para ... 71	Salt Lake. . 18	Valence .. 37
Cordoba, S. America }31	Guatemala . 49	Maranham . 280	Paris ... 23	San Francisco 23	Valparaiso . 14
Corfu ... 54	Havana .. 77	Marseilles. . 21	Parana. .. 36	San Luis, Argentine Republic }22	Venice. .. 34
Cork ... 40	Hayti ... 56	Matamoros . 36	Parma .. 32		Vera Cruz . 183
Coromandel . 54	Himalaya, S. 622	Mauritius. . 36	Pau. ... 45	Santiago, Chile 11	Verona .. 38
Corrientes . 58	Hobart .. 22	Meerut. .. 32	Pekin ... 27	Savannah. . 55	Vevay .. 47
Cracow .. 13	Hong-Kong . 101	Melbourne . 27	Penzance .. 46	Seville ... 22	Vicenza .. 44
Crimea .. 15	Hyderabad . 8	Memphis,U.S. 42	Pernambuco . 109	Sienna... 38	Vienna. .. 20
Curaçoa .. 27	Iceland .. 30	Mendoza .. 6	Perpignan .. 21	Sierra Leone. 125	Viviers... 36
Cyprus .. 13	Isle of Man . 37	Messina .. 26	Perth, W.A. . 29	Simla .. 71	Vosges. .. 27
Darjeeling . 104	Isle of Wight 31	Metz ... 28	Peshawur .. 13	Simplon .. 41	Washington. 41
Delhi .. 24	Jamaica .. 66	Middleburg . 26	Philadelphia . 41	Singapore. . 150	Wellington . 52
Demerara. . 126	Jerusalem. . 16	Milan .. 38	Pisa .. 50	Sitka .. 91	Wilmington . 59
Detroit .. 30	Kandy. .. 85	Milwaukee . 30	Pittsburg .. 37	Smyrna .. 24	Windermere . 140
Dijon ... 29	Key West . 36	Mogador .. 50	Poitiers .. 23	Splugen .. 73	Würzburg . 14
Dover ... 48	Königsberg . 27	Montevideo . 44	Poona .. 19	Stockholm . 20	Yakutsk .. 11
Dovrefeld Mt. 90	Lausanne . 39	Montpelier . 34	Port Said .. 2	Strasburg. . 27	Yokohama . 71
Dublin .. 30	Leeds ... 27	Mooltan .. 7	Port Elizabeth 24	Stuttgart .. 25	York ... 24
Dumfries .. 37	Lille ... 27	Nagpoor .. 45	Potsdam .. 20	Sumatra .. 189	Zürich .. 34
Dunedin .. 29	Lima ... 9	Namur .. 21	Prague. .. 15	Sydney .. 43	Zambesi .. 61
Durban .. 42	Limerick .. 35	Nancy ... 28,	Provence .. 26		Zanzibar .. 58
	Limoges .. 35	Nantes. .. 52			

The rainfall according to months in various parts of the world is :—

	January	February	March	April	May	June	July	August	September	October	November	December	Year
Ben Nevis	17.8	13.3	5.9	7.5	4.0	7.5	11.5	8.7	11.0	12.2	9.0	17.6	126.0
Bourbon	8.8	11.2	5.3	4.8	3.0	0.6	0.3	1.7	0.8	1.7	3.2	5.3	46.7
Cannes	3.2	2.5	3.7	2.7	2.2	1.4	0.6	0.9	3.1	6.3	4.5	4.9	36.0
Canton	0.8	0.6	...	3.6	8.2	8.5	2.7	7.7	6.1	0.6	...	0.3	39.1
Chambery	3.0	2.4	3.6	2.8	3.3	3.2	2.9	4.3	4.0	4.2	3.9	3.4	41.0
Colombo	3.0	2.1	2.1	7.5	13.5	6.9	3.4	2.8	5.3	11.4	10.8	4.5	73.4
Copenhagen	1.4	1.2	1.3	1.2	1.5	2.2	2.6	2.4	2.7	2.2	2.0	1.7	22.4
Fernando Po	1.0	3.7	9.2	8.4	8.5	11.1	6.5	11.3	16.8	15.6	8.9	1.1	102.1
Hayti (P. Prince)	0.9	2.9	3.1	5.4	11.9	3.7	3.7	6.2	7.3	5.8	3.6	1.4	55.9
Hong-Kong	0.6	1.6	2.3	6.4	7.6	21.1	16.4	13.9	15.3	6.4	7.0	3.0	101.6
Macao	0.6	1.7	2.5	5.6	11.8	11.1	7.7	9.9	11.1	5.5	2.4	0.9	70.8
Magellan Straits	1.4	1.0	2.0	3.3	1.0	1.1	0.4	1.5	0.6	0.9	1.1	1.0	15.3
Natal	4.2	5.2	4.1	2.3	0.5	0.1	0.2	0.7	1.7	2.6	5.7	4.5	31.8
Paris	1.4	1.4	1.3	1.8	1.4	2.5	2.0	2.2	2.1	2.3	2.2	1.8	22.4
Pekin	3.4	5.6	4.4	0.4	1.1	2.4	4.2	5.8	7.7	1.3	0.3	4.8	41.4
Perpignan	1.8	1.6	1.6	1.8	2.6	1.4	0.8	1.3	2.1	2.0	2.2	1.9	21.1
Sebastopol	2.9	2.6	2.2	3.8	0.9	6.2	4.7	1.7	1.3	1.6	3.2	3.7	34.8
Senegal (St. Louis)	0.3	0.8	...	...	0.5	0.4	3.0	6.5	5.1	0.4	...	...	17.0
Sierra Leone	0.5	0.3	0.6	3.2	8.2	14.7	25.8	28.6	30.0	14.7	5.1	1.4	133.1

RAINFALL OF UNITED KINGDOM

The average annual rainfall of Great Britain since 1815 has been as follows:—

Years	Inches	Years	Inches
1815-24	29.0	1845-54	28.6
1825-34	28.5	1855-64	26.6
1835-44	28.3	1865-82	29.3

The average rainfall is equal to 630,000 gallons (almost 3000 tons) per acre per annum, of which 2000 tons are required to feed the rivers and crops, and 1000 tons per acre are lost, being allowed to run off. The above does not include Ireland, where the rainfall averages 35 inches. Scotland appears to have less rainfall than England or Ireland.

The rainfall of the United Kingdom is shown in months thus :—

	England (1815-48)	U. Kingdom (1850-59)	Scotland	Ireland
	Inches	Inches	Inches	Inches
January	1.7	3.4	3.3	4.0
February .	1.6	2.2	2.2	2.8
March	1.6	2.0	2.1	2.3
April .	1.7	2.1	1.9	2.8
May .	2.0	1.8	1.6	2.1
June .	1.8	2.5	2.2	2.7
July .	2.4	2.9	2.6	3.0
August	2.4	3.0	2.6	3.2
September .	2.4	2.7	2.5	2.5
October	2.7	3.5	3.1	3.0
November .	2.5	3.0	2.9	3.0
December .	2.0	3.0	3.0	3.6
Year .	24.8	32.1	30.0	35.0

The quantity of ammonia in rain differs greatly with locality, viz. :—

Valentia, Kerry .	1.00	Germany .	10.61
Scotland, West Coast .	2.69	London	19.17
,, mountains .	2.96	Scotland	21.22
,, East Coast .	5.51	Liverpool	29.89
England, East Coast .	5.94	Manchester	36.54
,, West Coast .	10.55	Glasgow	50.58

The average rainfall in London for seventy years has been :—

Summer, half-year 12.87
Winter ,, ... 12.03

Annual rainfall . . . 24.90

Taking the above figures as par, the variations of seventy years have been as follows :—

	Summer	Winter	Year		Summer	Winter	Year
1813–22	97	110	103	1853–62	105	85	95
1823–32	108	93	101	1863–72	93	107	100
1833–42	92	99	95	1873–82	110	106	108
1843–52	95	101	98				

RAINFALL OF FRANCE.

Raulins states the rainfall according to seasons in France and Geneva thus :—

	Spring	Summer	Autumn	Winter	Year
	\multicolumn{5}{c}{Inches}
Agen	7.6	6.4	7.4	6.2	27.6
Arles	5.4	3.2	8.0	5.5	22.1
Auxerre . . .	5.8	8.7	6.2	5.0	25.7
B. Bigorre . .	18.6	10.2	13.2	11.7	53.7
Bayonne . . .	12.5	10.4	16.1	12.7	51.7
Beauvais . . .	5.1	6.1	6.3	4.8	22.3
Besançon . . .	5.8	10.1	6.8	2.6	25.3
Blois	7.1	5.9	7.1	5.3	25.4
Bordeaux . . .	6.8	7.0	9.1	8.8	31.7
Calais	6.5	5.0	9.3	8.6	29.4
Cambray . . .	3.2	6.7	4.7	1.9	16.5
Carcassonne . .	9.2	5.2	7.6	7.4	29.4
Chalons, Saone .	5.1	7.4	7.8	4.6	24.9
Clermont . . .	5.2	6.5	5.9	3.6	21.2
Dijon	6.3	7.1	8.7	5.8	27.9
Geneva	7.4	9.2	10.5	6.5	33.6
Grenoble . . .	9.2	9.7	11.8	8.2	38.9
Lille	5.6	7.5	7.6	6.0	26.7
Limoges . . .	8.2	8.7	10.0	8.4	35.3
Lyons	6.9	7.8	8.5	4.1	27.3
Marseilles . .	4.2	2.0	8.2	4.7	19.1
Metz	6.1	8.2	7.0	5.6	26.9
Montpellier . .	8.0	4.3	13.2	9.3	34.8
Nancy	6.7	8.2	7.4	6.2	28.5
Nice	7.2	3.2	12.4	8.8	31.6

	Spring	Summer	Autumn	Winter	Year
	\multicolumn{5}{c}{Inches}
Nismes . . .	6.2	4.0	9.1	5.5	24.8
Orleans . . .	6.4	6.9	7.0	5.1	25.4
Pau	16.2	9.0	12.0	10.4	47.6
Poitiers . . .	5.3	5.0	7.0	5.8	23.1
Rheims . . .	4.0	5.9	5.4	3.5	18.8
Rochelle . . .	4.6	3.7	8.5	6.9	23.7
Rouen . . .	6.0	7.5	7.7	6.2	27.4
Strasburg . . .	7.0	9.5	6.7	4.3	27.5
Toulon . . .	6.4	1.8	12.2	8.5	28.9
Toulouse . . .	6.9	5.9	5.9	4.7	23.4
Tours	5.2	5.6	7.0	4.6	22.4
Valence . . .	8.7	7.4	14.9	6.0	37.0
Average . . .	7.0	6.6	8.7	6.4	28.7

The annual rainfall of Paris has been as follows :—

Period	Ins.	Period	Ins.	Period	Ins.
1689-1747 .	18	1789-1818 .	18	1849-1872 .	21
1748-1788 .	21	1819-1848 .	21	1873-1882 .	23

The total rainfall of France is as follows :—

	Million Tons per Annum	Tons per Second
Outflow by Rhone . . .	54,000	1,718
,, Gironde . .	37,000	1,178
,, Loire . . .	31,000	985
,, Seine . . .	22,000	694
Other rivers	36,000	1,146
Absorbed for crops, &c. .	195,000	6,180
Total . .	375,000	11,901

France loses nearly half her rainfall, England more than one-third.

Snow.—The average number of days on which snow falls in a year is as follows :—

Aberdeen . .	42	Macon . .	21	St. Petersburg	62
Brussels . .	24	Madrid . .	3	Saragossa .	5
Charleston .	2	Milan . . .	11	Sebastopol .	12
Copenhagen .	23	Moscow . .	71	Sienna . . .	6
Dublin . .	15	Newfoundland	78	Strasburg . .	16
Florence . .	2	Odessa . . .	19	Trieste . . .	6
Geneva . .	20	Ostend . . .	15	Turin . . .	9
Greenland .	80	Oxford . . .	18	Upsal . . .	61
Grenoble . .	18	Paris . . .	13	Vancouver .	7
Halifax . .	64	Quebec . .	66	Vienna . . .	33
Hamburg . .	18	Rome . . .	2	Warsaw . .	45
Iceland . .	46	St. Gothard .	116	Winnipeg . .	54
Lisbon . . .	1	St. Louis . .	11	Yakutsk . .	55

The most remarkable snowfalls in England have been in the following years :—

1141	1683	1784	1814
1606	1709	1799	1820
1674	1762	1812	1836

The earliest snow of the season was that of October 7th, 1829, in the present century. There was no snow from November 1862 till February 1864.

The line of perpetual snow varies with latitude, and is as follows in feet above sea-level :—

Lat.		Feet	Lat.			Feet
0 .	.	15,260	40 .	.	.	9,000
10 .	.	14,764	50 .	.	.	6,334
20 .	.	13,478	60 .	.	.	3,818
30 .	.	11,484	70 .	.	.	1,278

		Feet			Feet
Norway .	.	2,400	Himalayas, S. .	.	13,100
Iceland .	.	3,090	Abyssinia .	.	14,200
Straits of Magellan .	4,700	Ararat .	.	14,300
Siberia .	.	4,800	Mexico .	.	14,800
Alps .	.	8,400	Andes, E. .	.	15,800
Pyrenees .	.	9,000	Chilian do.	.	15,900
Caucasus .	.	11,100	Himalayas, N. .	.	16,700
S. Nevada	.	11,200	Andes, W.	.	18,600

Storms.—The most destructive in the United Kingdom have been :—

1703, November 27th.—Damage in London, £2,000,000. On the coast twelve war-ships sunk and 1800 men lost.

1775, October 29th.—Almost equal to the above. Houses blown down and ships sunk.

1839, January 6th.—Many houses blown down at Liverpool and Dublin, and 200 persons killed at Liverpool.

1859, October 25th.—Great loss of shipping, including the "Royal Charter" near Holyhead.

1879, December 28th.—Tay Bridge blown down ; loss of 90 lives. See *Wind-pressure.*

Submarine Temperature.—The decrease of temperature with depth varies according to latitude : thus 500 fathoms at the Equator make a difference of 39 degrees Fahr. from the surface, while abreast of Lisbon it would be only 23 degrees, and at the Farol Islands little over 10 degrees.

The following table shows the variations thus :—

	Degrees Fahrenheit	
	Equator	Off Lisbon
Surface	78	70
100 fathoms	56	64
500 ,, ...	39	47
1,000 ,, ...	37	38
1,500 ,, ...	36	37
2,700 ,, ...	35	35

The average depth of the Mediterranean is 800 fathoms, and the temperature at the bottom is found to average 54° Fahr. The Red Sea, with surface temperature of 90°, was found to have 70° Fahr. at the bottom—a depth of 400 fathoms—which is rather more than the difference quoted above at the Equator.

Subterranean Temperature.—Subterranean temperature seems the same in the southern as in the northern hemisphere, a well at Buenos Ayres showing (in winter) 97° Fahr. at a depth of 2000 ft.

The variations of a well in Yorkshire, 350 ft. deep, according to season, have been recorded thus :—

	At 100 Feet	At 350 Feet
April . . .	45	42
June . . .	65	46
December . .	41	43

The following table shows a variety of mines and borings, and the average increase of temperature per 1000 feet :—

	Depth, Feet	Increase, Fahr., per 1000 Feet
Flint	1,041	12.5
Kentish Town . . .	1,100	18.0
Whitehaven . . .	1,250	22.0
Grenelle	1,312	17.3
Schemnitz	1,368	13.3
Bootle	1,392	7.7
Monkwearmouth. . .	1,584	14.3
Seraing	1,657	20.0
Przibrau . . .	1,900	8.0
Lincoln	2,000	14.5
Rosebridge . . .	2,443	18.4
Ashton Moss . . .	2,790	13.0
Speremberg. . . .	3,500	19.4
Bohemian Mine . .	4,600	16.5
Mont Cenis . . .	5,280	12.6
St. Gothard . . .	5,578	12.2

The temperature at various depths in the Rosebridge, Speremberg, and the Bohemian mine above mentioned was as follows :—

Bohemian		Speremberg		Rosebridge	
Depth, Ft.	Fahr.	Depth, Ft.	Fahr.	Depth, Ft.	Fahr.
300	49	720	71	480	65
600	51	1,130	80	600	66
1,200	58	1,550	84	1,800	80
1,650	61	2,160	97	2,200	89
4,600	120	3,500	116	2,450	94

Sun Spots.—Wolf's table for sixty-six years showed as follows :—

Period	Maximum Year	Number of Spots	Minimum Year	Number of Spots
1811-20 . .	1816	47	1811	2
1821-30 . .	1829	67	1823	3
1831-40 . .	1837	136	1833	9
1841-50 . .	1848	125	1843	13
1851-60 . .	1860	95	1856	5
1861-70 . .	1870	132	1867	9
1871-77 . .	1871	114	1877	7

Thunder.—The average number of days of thunder yearly in France is :—

Marseilles .	11	Toulouse . .	16	Poitiers . .	20
Paris . . .	14	Strasburg . .	17	Nancy . . .	20
Rouen . . .	15	Metz . . .	18	Mulhouse . .	26

Thermometer.—The mean temperature of the various cities of the world in degrees Fahrenheit is :—

	January	February	March	April	May	June	July	August	September	October	November	December	Year	Range
Aberdeen . . .	37	38	41	45	52	56	59	58	55	48	42	40	48	12
Adelaide . . .	74	74	70	65	58	54	52	54	57	63	67	71	63	22
Agra . . .	60	65	76	88	94	95	87	86	84	80	70	62	79	35
Ajaccio . . .	50	52	54	58	62	70	76	78	72	64	56	51	62	28
Albany . . .	24	25	35	47	59	68	72	70	61	49	39	28	48	48
Alexandria . . .	56	58	61	66	72	76	78	81	78	75	69	61	69	25
Algiers . . .	54	55	57	61	66	72	76	77	74	68	60	55	65	23
Amsterdam . . .	33	37	41	48	55	62	65	63	61	51	42	37	50	32
Ancona . . .	42	46	50	57	67	73	80	78	73	62	53	46	61	38
Archangel . . .	6	9	21	31	40	55	61	57	47	35	23	12	33	55
Arica . . .	72	71	70	68	66	65	64	63	63	66	69	72	67	9
Astrakan . . .	20	21	31	49	64	73	78	74	64	51	37	26	49	58
Asuncion . . .	80	83	82	74	68	60	70	74	78	83	82	81	76	23
Athens . . .	47	48	52	59	68	76	81	80	74	66	57	50	63	34
Auckland . . .	68	68	66	62	57	53	52	52	55	58	61	66	60	16
Ava . . .	65	73	75	93	84	86	82	82	82	81	74	68	77	28

	January	February	March	April	May	June	July	August	September	October	November	December	Year	Range
Azores . . .	57	56	57	59	62	65	71	71	69	65	61	58	62	16
Bagdad . . .	52	53	64	72	87	91	95	94	86	76	62	53	74	43
Barcelona . . .	48	51	53	58	62	70	77	78	72	65	55	48	61	30
Batavia . . .	78	78	79	80	80	80	79	79	80	79	79	78	79	2
Benares . . .	61	66	77	88	91	90	84	84	83	79	68	60	78	31
Ben Nevis . .	25	27	24	26	32	45	41	40	37	28	26	23	31	22
Bergen . . .	34	36	37	44	52	55	61	59	54	48	41	37	47	27
Berlin . . .	31	34	38	47	56	64	66	65	58	50	39	33	48	35
Bermuda . . .	64	64	63	67	72	77	81	83	80	75	71	66	72	20
Berne . . .	26	32	38	46	54	59	62	61	55	47	37	31	46	36
Biskra . . .	50	54	57	66	76	84	90	88	80	68	58	51	69	40
Bogota . . .	60	61	59	59	59	59	57	62	61	59	59	59	60	5
Bombay . . .	74	75	79	83	85	83	81	80	80	81	79	76	80	11
Bordeaux . . .	41	45	51	56	61	67	73	73	67	58	48	43	57	32
Boston . . .	28	28	36	46	57	66	72	70	62	52	41	33	49	44
Brest . . .	44	45	46	52	56	60	64	64	61	54	47	43	53	21
Brisbane . . .	79	77	76	71	66	60	60	63	68	72	77	78	70	19
Brussels . . .	36	39	42	50	56	61	66	63	59	50	42	37	50	30
Buda-Pesth . .	28	33	39	50	64	68	71	71	62	51	40	32	51	43
Buenos Ayres .	76	74	70	62	57	52	50	53	57	62	68	73	63	26
Burlington, U.S. .	21	21	31	42	55	65	70	68	59	48	36	25	45	49
Bushire . . .	57	57	63	72	81	84	88	89	85	78	69	61	74	32
Cadiz . . .	52	55	55	60	64	70	70	73	70	67	59	54	63	21
Cagliari . .	48	52	51	58	66	71	76	78	71	67	59	53	62	30
Cairo . . .	56	56	65	71	80	83	85	84	79	74	65	59	71	29
Calcutta . . .	65	71	79	84	85	85	83	82	82	80	73	65	78	20
Canton . . .	53	58	63	70	77	81	83	82	80	73	65	57	71	30
Capetown . . .	70	70	67	63	58	56	55	56	58	61	64	68	62	15
Carlsruhe . . .	33	37	42	51	60	64	67	66	60	51	42	36	51	34
Cashmere . . .	17	20	31	41	47	56	62	60	52	40	30	23	40	39
Cawnpore . . .	64	70	72	89	97	91	87	88	85	80	75	68	80	33
Cayenne . . .	79	79	79	80	80	80	81	81	82	82	81	79	80	3
Charleston . .	51	53	58	65	73	81	83	82	76	68	58	51	66	32
Christiania . .	24	26	30	37	48	58	62	61	52	41	34	24	41	38
Cincinnati . .	33	34	44	54	63	72	77	74	66	55	44	34	54	44
Colombo . . .	80	81	82	83	83	82	81	81	81	81	80	80	81	3
Constantinople .	40	41	46	51	59	67	72	73	67	60	52	44	56	33
Copenhagen .	30	26	32	41	50	60	66	62	59	49	38	34	46	40
Copiapo . . .	70	71	69	64	60	57	57	56	61	65	67	71	64	15
Cordoba, Arg. Rep. .	73	70	65	58	53	50	47	54	60	62	68	73	61	26
Corfu . . .	50	51	53	60	67	74	79	79	73	68	59	53	64	29
Cyprus . . .	53	50	57	63	72	81	84	85	82	73	61	52	68	35
Darjeeling . .	39	41	48	54	56	60	61	61	59	55	48	42	52	22
Delhi . . .	58	62	74	85	90	94	87	87	85	79	68	60	77	36
Dieppe . . .	39	43	42	52	58	63	66	64	61	52	46	41	52	27
Drontheim . .	19	26	21	34	51	59	65	59	54	39	27	25	40	46
Dublin . . .	39	41	43	48	54	60	61	61	56	51	44	42	50	22
Dunedin . . .	58	58	55	52	47	44	43	43	47	51	53	56	51	15
Durban . . .	74	76	72	66	60	56	55	56	60	64	69	71	65	21
Edinburgh . .	37	38	41	44	50	56	58	57	54	48	41	40	47	21
Erfurt . . .	30	34	37	48	57	64	67	65	61	47	39	30	48	37
Erzeroum . . .	28	36	48	65	68	83	89	90	78	65	44	30	60	62
Etna Mountain .	16	15	22	23	34	38	46	47	39	30	23	18	29	31
Feejee Islands .	81	81	81	80	79	78	77	77	78	79	80	82	79	5
Fernando Po .	81	82	81	79	76	75	76	75	74	76	78	80	78	8
Florence . . .	41	45	51	60	65	71	77	76	69	60	50	46	59	36
Frankfort . . .	31	36	42	49	58	64	66	65	59	50	41	35	50	35
Friburg . . .	24	30	39	46	55	59	62	61	54	45	36	30	45	38
Galveston . . .	53	58	64	69	78	83	84	83	79	72	62	56	70	31
Geneva . . .	31	33	40	47	54	63	65	64	58	50	42	34	48	34
Gondar . . .	67	70	71	72	72	68	62	56	62	62	64	65	65	16
Grahamstown .	74	73	72	67	65	63	63	66	67	68	69	70	68	11
Grätz . . .	25	31	37	47	58	66	68	66	60	48	42	28	48	43
Grenoble . . .	31	39	47	51	57	64	68	67	60	51	41	32	51	37
Guatemala . .	61	62	67	68	69	68	66	66	66	65	65	62	65	8
Hague . . .	35	40	44	51	57	62	66	67	61	54	43	40	52	32
Hamburg . . .	31	34	37	45	54	59	64	64	58	50	40	33	47	33
Havana . . .	72	72	74	78	80	82	82	82	81	79	75	73	78	10
Havre . . .	41	44	43	53	59	64	68	66	62	54	46	43	54	27
Helsingfors . .	18	18	23	34	44	56	61	60	52	42	34	23	39	43
Hobart . . .	63	62	60	55	51	47	46	49	51	54	58	61	55	17
Hong-Kong . .	61	62	63	71	79	82	83	82	81	73	71	66	73	22
Honolulu . . .	72	72	72	74	76	78	80	79	78	76	74	74	75	8
Hydrabad . . .	63	66	78	86	91	91	88	85	86	83	71	63	79	28
Iceland . . .	30	28	30	37	44	52	55	51	47	38	30	28	39	27

	January	February	March	April	May	June	July	August	September	October	November	December	Year	Range
Innspruck	28	34	37	48	58	65	65	62	58	53	37	29	48	37
Isle of Man	42	41	43	47	52	57	60	59	56	51	46	43	50	19
Jamaica	76	76	76	78	78	80	82	81	82	79	77	77	78	6
Jersey	41	44	45	51	57	61	63	63	60	55	48	45	53	22
Jerusalem	47	49	58	60	68	73	75	76	72	72	61	50	63	29
Kandy	74	76	79	79	79	76	76	76	76	76	75	75	76	5
Kazan	6	9	20	38	53	62	67	62	51	42	24	8	37	61
Königsberg	25	27	31	41	52	57	62	61	54	44	36	27	44	37
Lausanne	33	36	40	48	57	64	63	66	60	50	40	32	49	34
Lille	37	37	41	48	55	61	64	64	60	52	42	38	50	27
Lisbon	51	52	54	58	62	67	70	71	68	62	56	50	60	21
London	37	40	42	47	53	58	62	62	57	51	44	40	50	25
Lucknow	61	66	77	87	92	92	86	86	85	79	69	61	78	31
Lyons	36	40	44	53	61	66	70	68	63	53	42	37	53	34
Macao	62	55	64	71	78	82	82	83	81	76	74	74	75	28
Maçon	31	40	47	49	56	63	65	68	60	48	42	34	50	37
Madeira	61	61	61	62	65	69	70	73	72	69	65	62	66	12
Madras	76	77	81	85	87	88	86	85	84	81	78	76	82	12
Madrid	41	42	47	55	61	69	76	75	66	56	47	41	56	35
Magellan Straits	55	52	52	45	39	36	35	39	43	47	49	52	45	20
Majorca	52	53	56	60	65	73	79	81	75	68	59	52	64	29
Malaga	55	57	59	64	68	76	81	81	76	69	61	55	67	26
Malta	56	55	57	61	67	73	78	79	76	71	63	58	66	24
Manilla	75	77	78	81	82	82	80	80	80	79	78	76	79	7
Mannheim	34	36	41	51	60	66	68	67	60	50	39	34	51	34
Marseilles	43	47	51	56	61	67	72	72	65	59	50	44	57	29
Mauritius	79	79	78	77	73	70	69	69	70	73	75	78	74	10
Melbourne	67	66	64	59	53	50	48	50	53	57	61	64	58	19
Messina	54	54	57	61	67	74	78	79	76	69	63	56	66	25
Mexico	55	57	61	68	68	66	64	62	62	60	58	54	60	14
Milan	33	38	46	55	64	71	75	74	66	57	47	37	55	42
Mogador	62	63	65	68	69	72	72	72	71	70	66	62	68	10
Montevideo	73	72	69	64	58	53	52	52	56	61	65	70	62	21
Montgomery, U.S.	49	53	58	65	76	81	83	80	75	66	55	50	66	34
Montpelier	39	42	49	57	65	72	76	73	67	57	48	40	57	37
Montreal	15	17	29	43	58	68	73	71	61	46	33	19	44	58
Mooltan	54	58	70	80	89	94	92	89	87	77	66	56	76	40
Moscow	11	15	23	37	53	62	67	65	54	40	27	17	41	56
Munich	29	31	38	48	58	64	65	65	59	48	37	29	48	36
Muscat	68	70	73	85	92	93	93	87	87	80	76	71	81	25
Nagasaki	41	43	49	58	65	71	79	81	76	65	55	45	61	40
Nagpoor	69	74	82	89	93	86	79	79	79	77	71	67	79	26
Naples	47	48	51	57	64	71	76	76	71	63	54	49	61	29
Nashville	39	44	50	56	74	78	82	79	69	62	48	41	60	43
New Caledonia	79	79	79	77	75	73	68	65	72	75	78	79	75	14
New Orleans	55	55	61	68	72	79	81	80	77	69	58	57	69	26
Nice	45	47	51	56	60	67	72	72	64	59	50	44	58	28
Norfolk, U.S.	40	43	48	57	69	76	80	77	71	62	50	42	59	40
North Cape	22	23	25	30	34	40	46	44	37	32	26	26	32	24
Odessa	25	28	33	46	57	66	73	70	59	52	40	29	48	48
Oporto	50	52	53	60	63	69	70	70	67	61	55	51	60	20
Oran	50	52	55	59	65	71	76	76	71	65	58	52	62	26
Orenburg	2	10	19	39	57	66	71	67	55	37	24	8	38	69
Palermo	51	51	54	58	65	71	76	76	73	67	59	55	63	25
Para	80	80	80	79	80	81	81	81	81	81	82	82	81	3
Paris	36	40	45	50	55	63	66	65	60	52	44	37	51	30
Pau	44	47	52	59	62	69	73	74	69	61	50	45	59	30
Pekin	24	29	41	57	68	76	79	76	68	55	39	28	53	55
Penzance	42	44	45	48	54	59	62	61	57	53	47	45	52	20
Perth, W. Australia	76	76	72	66	60	56	55	56	60	64	69	71	65	21
Peshawur	50	52	63	71	82	90	89	87	81	71	58	51	70	40
Port Darwin	83	82	84	84	80	77	76	79	82	84	86	89	82	13
Prague	28	32	38	50	60	66	69	69	62	50	41	30	50	41
Pultowa	15	18	28	42	54	63	68	66	55	43	33	22	42	53
Quetta	41	41	51	59	68	74	77	75	67	56	45	41	58	36
Quito	58	61	60	60	61	59	59	61	61	60	60	61	60	3
Ratisbon	28	32	39	50	58	63	65	65	59	48	37	30	48	37
Rio Janeiro	80	80	78	75	71	69	67	70	71	73	74	77	74	13
Rome	45	48	51	57	65	72	77	76	70	61	52	46	60	32
St. Bernard	15	18	21	26	35	42	43	43	38	31	23	19	30	28
St. Gall	29	34	40	49	56	61	65	68	58	49	39	34	48	39
St. Helena	64	66	67	66	63	60	58	57	57	58	60	62	62	10
St. Louis	33	35	44	58	66	74	78	77	68	55	41	34	55	45
St. Petersburg	15	18	26	36	48	58	62	61	51	40	30	22	39	47
Salta	69	70	65	62	55	59	55	58	64	65	68	70	63	15

	January	February	March	April	May	June	July	August	September	October	November	December	Year	Range
Salt Lake	29	32	40	48	57	69	77	75	64	52	40	30	52	48
Salzburg	29	31	35	48	53	61	62	61	57	49	41	33	46	33
San Francisco	51	53	54	55	57	59	58	58	60	60	57	52	56	9
Santiago, Chili	68	66	62	55	49	46	45	47	52	56	62	67	56	23
Saratov	14	16	25	41	57	66	72	68	58	43	32	21	42	58
Savannah	52	55	60	66	74	81	83	82	75	68	69	53	67	31
Sebastopol	35	36	41	50	59	68	72	72	64	55	47	26	53	46
Senegal	68	68	69	69	71	77	81	82	82	82	77	79	75	14
Seringapatam	71	77	80	84	85	79	77	73	77	77	74	72	77	14
Seville	52	56	60	64	70	77	86	82	80	69	60	52	67	34
Shanghai	38	40	47	55	65	73	83	81	73	63	51	42	59	45
Sierra Leone	82	82	84	84	82	80	79	79	78	80	82	81	80	6
Simla	40	41	49	59	64	67	64	63	61	56	49	45	55	27
Smyrna	51	51	57	62	71	78	83	82	77	69	60	54	60	32
Stockholm	24	25	28	38	48	59	64	62	53	43	34	28	42	40
Strasburg	32	37	42	48	59	61	65	64	58	50	41	35	50	33
Sumatra	80	80	80	81	81	81	80	80	80	79	79	79	80	2
Surinam	77	77	77	78	78	77	78	78	78	79	78	78	78	2
Sydney	71	71	69	65	58	55	52	54	59	63	66	69	63	19
Teneriffe	56	55	56	59	62	66	69	76	74	69	62	58	64	21
Tiflis	33	35	44	53	64	70	76	76	67	57	46	37	55	43
Tobolsk	12	18	23	32	41	49	52	48	42	33	23	15	32	40
Toulon	46	50	49	55	62	69	73	71	68	59	51	46	58	27
Trieste	38	39	44	53	62	69	72	72	65	57	48	50	55	34
Tucuman	74	74	71	68	58	53	54	61	66	67	74	77	66	24
Tunis	52	55	59	64	72	77	85	86	80	71	61	57	68	34
Turin	31	36	44	53	62	68	73	73	64	54	43	33	53	42
Upsal	27	28	30	36	41	47	49	48	43	38	32	28	37	22
Valdivia	62	61	57	53	50	46	45	46	49	52	56	59	52	17
Valparaiso	63	63	61	58	56	54	53	53	54	57	59	63	58	10
Venice	35	39	46	55	63	70	75	74	66	57	45	40	55	40
Vera Cruz	71	72	74	78	82	82	82	82	82	79	75	72	77	11
Vevay	33	36	43	50	58	64	68	64	59	53	40	38	51	35
Vienna	29	33	41	51	60	67	70	70	61	51	40	34	51	41
Vologda	21	20	25	31	42	48	51	49	42	34	27	23	35	31
Warsaw	22	26	32	44	55	62	65	64	60	45	35	26	44	43
Washington	34	36	45	55	66	74	78	76	68	56	44	37	56	44
Wilmington	47	50	55	61	70	76	80	78	73	65	55	48	63	33
Würzburg	33	34	41	52	62	68	69	67	62	51	38	33	51	36
Yakutsk	10	4	9	23	35	45	49	46	36	22	4	7	21	59
Yarkand	29	41	55	77	83	89	95	88	79	67	44	30	65	66
Yokohama	39	42	46	55	65	72	79	79	70	60	50	48	58	40
Zanzibar	83	83	83	82	80	79	77	77	78	79	81	82	80	6
Zürich	27	33	40	46	60	61	65	65	58	50	39	30	48	38

The mean temperature of the United States is as follows:—

State	Spring	Summer	Autumn	Winter	Year	Highest Month	Lowest Month
Alabama	67	79	66	52	66	82	42
Arkansas	61	78	60	40	60	84	25
California	61	72	64	52	62	76	46
Carolina, N.	64	80	67	51	66	83	40
Carolina, S.	66	81	68	52	66	84	40
Connecticut	46	69	53	30	50	76	20
Delaware	52	76	57	34	54	80	22
Florida	71	81	73	61	72	85	52
Georgia	64	80	63	48	64	85	39
Illinois	52	75	54	26	52	78	24
Indiana	59	77	55	38	57	79	34
Iowa	47	69	46	21	46	74	8
Kansas	54	81	54	29	53	83	10
Kentucky	54	75	56	34	55	80	18
Louisiana	69	82	70	55	68	87	40
Maine	41	64	46	20	43	68	14
Maryland	53	75	57	34	55	80	24
Massachusetts	45	68	50	26	47	74	20
Michigan	40	64	46	22	43	73	10
Minnesota	46	71	46	16	44	82	2
Mississippi	68	81	67	52	67	81	52

State	Spring	Summer	Autumn	Winter	Year	Highest Month	Lowest Month
Missouri	55	75	55	33	55	83	21
New Hampshire	43	65	48	24	45	67	23
New Jersey	49	71	52	32	51	73	31
New Mexico	49	70	50	30	50	75	24
New York	45	69	50	27	48	74	16
Ohio	50	72	53	31	51	74	28
Oregon	53	71	53	36	53	76	22
Pennsylvania	50	73	54	32	52	80	21
Rhode Island	46	69	53	30	50	73	24
Tennessee	58	74	59	41	58	77	36
Texas	75	82	73	63	74	86	52
Utah	52	76	53	32	53	...	...
Vermont	40	64	44	19	42	67	18
Virginia	56	76	59	39	58	80	31
Washington Terr.	49	63	51	42	50	67	35
Wisconsin	46	70	47	20	46	80	7

The States of highest and lowest mean annual temperature are:—

Highest		Fahr.	Lowest		Fahr.
Texas		74	Vermont		42
Florida		72	Maine		43
Louisiana		68	Michigan		43

The following table shows the greatest degrees of cold on record :—

Place	Year	Latitude	Degrees Fahr.	Maximum Recorded
Turin . . .	1864	45.50	0	In Italy
London . .	1796	51.31	16	In England
Paris . . .	1879	48.52	13	At Paris
Frankfort . .	1789	50.10	23	In Germany
Pontarlier . .	1846	...	25	In France
Stockholm .	...	59.20	27	By Nicander
Prague . . .	...	50.50	28	By Strandt
St. Petersburg	1733	59.56	34	...
Basle . . .	1789	...	36	In Switzerland
Sweden . .	1781	...	40	In Sweden
Moscow . .	1809	55.45	48	In Russia
Fort Enterprise	...	64.30	50	By Franklin *
Fort Elizabeth	...	70.00	51	By Ross
Fort Reliance	1835	62.46	57	By Back
Yakutsk . .	1829	...	73	In the World

Besides the foregoing we find 27° below zero at Washington, 37° at Montreal, and 51° by Captain Parry in his Arctic voyage.

Among the highest readings recorded are :—

	Degrees Fahrenheit in the Shade
London, July 15, 1881	95.5
Naples, July 25, 1881	96.2
Paris, August 26, 1765	104.0
Orange, July 1830	104.0
Rio Janeiro, December 1880 . .	103.0
Adelaide, South Australia, January 1881	114.0
Mourzuk, India	133.0

The mean temperature of Great Britain, as registered for each month at Greenwich during 107 years, seems to have risen very notably since 1841, viz. :—

Months	Greenwich			Scotland, 1855–64
	1771–1841	1842–79	Rise	
January . . .	35.5	38.7	3.2	37.2
February . . .	38.3	39.4	1.1	37.4
March. . . .	40.8	41.6	0.8	39.8
April	45.5	47.2	1.7	44.1
May . . . ,.	52.4	52.7	0.3	49.5
June	57.8	59.0	1.2	55.6
July.	61.3	62.2	0.9	57.6
August. . . .	60.6	61.5	0.9	57.3
September . .	56.2	57.1	0.9	52.8
October . .	49.3	50.2	0.9	47.2
November . .	41.6	43.5	1.9	40.2
December. . .	38.6	40.0	1.4	38.6
Annual mean .	48.1	49.4	1.3	46.7

This rise of temperature in England has been coincident with a diminution of frost in Canada and Labrador. The mean temperature of France is stated as follows :—

Authority	Spring	Summer	Autumn	Winter	Year
Cotte. . .	52	68	54	39	53
Fuster . .	51	67	53	38	52

The mean temperature of Paris has risen since the last century, viz. :—

Quarter Ending	1734–40	1806–70
March 31	40	40
June 30	56	57
September 30 . . .	65	64
December 31 . . .	43	45
Yearly average . .	51	51½

* Cold appears to diminish in Canada with the increase of population, the average number of days in each year that Hudson's Bay is closed by frost showing thus :—

1828–37 . . 184 days | 1871–80 . . 179 days

The greatest variations observed between days in the same month in 1866 were :—

	Paris	Lille	Bordeaux	Toulouse	Lyons	Perpignan	Marseilles	Nice
January	12	10	11	13	7	10	3	2
February	12	12	7	12	11	12	4	16
March.	12	9	5	17	12	15	4	4
April	16	18	16	21	14	13	4	6
May	14	11	16	19	14	15	15	19
June	15	14	18	18	17	15	14	17
July	14	13	17	18	17	13	29	9
August	14	13	14	14	16	15	13	23
September . . .	12	11	8	9	13	12	10	18
October	10	13	14	14	10	11	13	17
November . . .	11	11	15	16	11	16	12	9
December . . .	16	11	6	7	8	14	10	7
Maximum . . .	16	18	18	21	17	16	29	23

Thermometer

Centigrade	Reaumur	Fahrenheit	Centigrade	Reaumur	Fahrenheit
100	80	212	40	32.0	104.0
98	78.4	208.4	38	30.4	100.4
96	76.8	204.8	36	28.8	96.8
94	75.2	201.2	34	27.2	93.2
92	73.6	197.6	32	25.6	89.6
90	72.0	194.0	30	24.0	86.0
88	70.4	190.4	28	22.4	82.4
86	68.8	186.8	26	20.8	78.8
84	67.2	183.2	24	19.2	75.2
82	65.6	179.6	22	17.6	71.6
80	64.0	176.0	20	16.0	68.0
78	62.4	172.4	18	14.4	64.4
76	60.8	168.8	16	12.8	60.8
74	59.2	165.2	14	11.2	57.2
72	57.6	161.6	12	9.6	53.6
70	56.0	158.0	10	8.0	50.0
68	54.4	154.4	8	6.4	46.4
66	52.8	150.8	6	4.8	42.8
64	51.2	147.2	4	3.2	39.2
62	49.6	143.6	2	1.6	35.6
60	48.0	140.0	0	0.0	32.0
58	46.4	136.4	2	1.6	28.4
56	44.8	132.8	4	3.2	24.8
54	43.2	129.2	6	4.8	21.2
52	41.6	125.6	8	6.4	17.6
50	40.0	122.0	10	8.0	14.0
48	38.4	118.4	12	9.6	10.4
46	36.8	114.8	14	11.2	6.8
44	35.2	111.2	16	12.8	3.2
42	33.6	107.6	18	14.4	0.0

Range in Degrees Fahrenheit

	Degrees		Degrees
Ice melts . . .	32	Lead melts .	594
Temperature of globe	50	Heat of common fire	1,140
Blood-heat . .	98	Brass melts .	2,233
Alcohol boils . .	174	Iron melts .	3,479
Water boils . .	212		

Wind.—Velocity and pressure are shown as follows :—

Feet per Second	Miles per Hour	Pressure, Lbs. per Sq. Foot	Feet per Second	Miles per Hour	Pressure, Lbs. per Sq. Foot
10	7	4 oz.	80	54	16 lbs.
20	14	1 lb	100	68	25 ,,
40	27	4 lbs.	120	82	36 ,,
60	41	9 ,,	150	102	56 ,,

According to a register kept in London for 18 years, down to 1830, the prevalent winds were westerly, viz. :—

	Days			
	N. to E.	E. to S.	S. to W.	W. to N.
January . . .	6.0	5.6	7.1	10.0
February . . .	4.2	5.0	7.8	9.5
March . . .	5.8	4.9	8.3	10.5
April . . .	6.5	6.5	6.4	9.2
May . . .	7.9	6.8	6.8	7.9
June . . .	7.2	4.3	6.7	10.5
July . . .	4.4	3.6	8.8	12.6
August . . .	5.2	3.5	8.6	13.0
September . . .	6.3	5.5	8.8	8.3
October . . .	5.5	6.6	8.4	9.5
November . . .	4.5	4.4	9.3	10.7
December . . .	5.4	5.5	9.5	9.3
Total . .	68.9	62.2	106.5	121.0

At Plymouth in the years 1841-42, the mean velocity of wind in the several months, that is, feet per second, was as follows :—

Feet per Second

January . 12.76	May . . . 11.60	September . 15.42	
February . 13.97	June . . . 10.90	October . 15.29	
March . . 14.63	July . . . 9.00	November . 14.96	
April . . 13.00	August . . 12.87	December . 12.54	
1st Quarter . . 13.80	3rd Quarter . 12.40		
2nd ,, . . 11.80	4th ,, . . 14.30		

The mean amount of wind at Plymouth was :—

Wind	Spring	Summer	Autumn	Winter	Total
N.E . .	143	2	...	133	278
E.N.E . .	134	13	102	134	383
E. . .	321	124	130	25	600
S.E . .	...	...	...	6	6
S.S.E. .	19	...	3	7	29
S. . .	657	86	798	545	2,086
S.S.W. .	725	689	476	275	2,165
S.W. .	...	...	34	...	34
W.N.W. .	50	65	128	99	342
N.W. .	59	46	17	...	122
N.N.W. .	...	58	...	...	58
Total	2,108	1,083	1,688	1,224	6,103

In 1889 the Meteorological Council gave a summary of gales in the United Kingdom for 15 years.

	Gales		Gales		Gales
January .	171	May . . .	12	September .	55
February .	115	June . . .	10	October .	133
March .	117	July . . .	11	November .	158
April . .	40	August . .	32	December .	134

From N.E.	.	.	.	.	.	96
,, S.E.	.	.	.	.	.	165
,, N.W.	.	.	.	.	.	279
,, S.W.	.	.	.	.	.	448
						988

This gives an average of 66 gales a year.

The record at Athens for twelve years to 1870 showed as follows :—

	Spring	Summer	Autumn	Winter	Year
N. and N.E. .	28.3	42.5	41.0	40.2	38.0
E. and S.E. . .	4.8	3.9	4.7	6.4	4.9
S. and S.W. .	48.8	39.3	41.5	34.7	41.1
W. and N.W. .	18.1	14.3	12.8	18.7	16.0
Total .	100.0	100.0	100.0	100.0	100.0

Observations in the Crimea gave this result in quarters of the year :—

	N.-E.	E.-S.	S.-W.	W.-N.	Year
March 31 . . .	62	76	62	58	258
June 30 . . .	70	42	101	56	269
September 30 . .	86	15	74	66	241
December 31 . .	62	52	62	56	232
Total .	280	185	299	236	1,000

MILK

The analysis shows as follows :—

	Woman	Cow	Ass	Goat	Ewe
Fat . . .	2.5	4.0	1.1	3.3	4.2
Caseine . .	3.4	7.2	1.9	4.0	4.5
Sugar . . .	4.8	2.8	6.1	5.9	5.7
Water . . .	89.3	86.0	90.9	86.8	85.6
Total .	100.0	100.0	100.0	100.0	100.0

See *Dairy*.

MILLIONAIRES

Name	Profession	Estim. Wealth, £	Residence	Died
Seneca . .	Philosopher	3,400,000	Rome	65
Fugger . .	Banker	6,500,000	Augsburg	1506
Goldsmid .	,,	10,000,000	London	...
Astor . .	Furrier	6,000,000	New York	1848
Stewart . .	Haberdasher	16,000,000	,,	...
Vanderbilt .	Railroad director	36,000,000	,,	1877
Overstone .	Banker	4,000,000	London	1883
Rothschild .	,,	3,500,000	,,	1879
Brassey . .	Contractor	5,000,000	,,	1870
Krupp . .	Founder	3,000,000	Essen	...

MINING

In the early years of the present century the total output of the mines of the world was barely a million tons daily, and in the eight years ending 1888 it averaged over 12 million tons daily. In the former period minerals extracted stood for a value of 9 millions sterling per annum; at present the value at the pit's mouth is £210,000,000 yearly.

The mining products of the nineteenth century may be summed up approximately thus :—

		Tons							
	Gold	Silver	Copper Ore	Lead Ore	Zinc Ore	Tin Ore	Iron Ore	Coal
1801–20 . .	292	14,350	2,100,000	2,000,000	240,000	90,000	35,000,000	277,000,000
1821–40 . .	345	10,571	4,100,000	3,100,000	400,000	130,000	82,000,000	566,000,000
1841–50 . .	548	7,804	4,300,000	2,700,000	1,300,000	90,000	96,000,000	637,000,000
1851–60 . .	2,018	8,956	9,100,000	5,100,000	2,400,000	100,000	150,000,000	1,093,000,000
1861–70 . .	1,886	12,201	13,500,000	7,000,000	5,200,000	150,000	205,000,000	1,873,000,000
1871–80 . .	1,703	22,347	19,400,000	7,600,000	9,600,000	450,000	338,000,000	2,855,000,000
1881–88 . .	1,150	19,330	32,400,000	7,100,000	12,360,000	420,000	367,000,000	3,300,000,000
88 years . .	7,942	95,559	84,900,000	34,600,000	31,500,000	1,430,000	1,273,000,000	10,601,000,000

PLATE VII.

MINING.

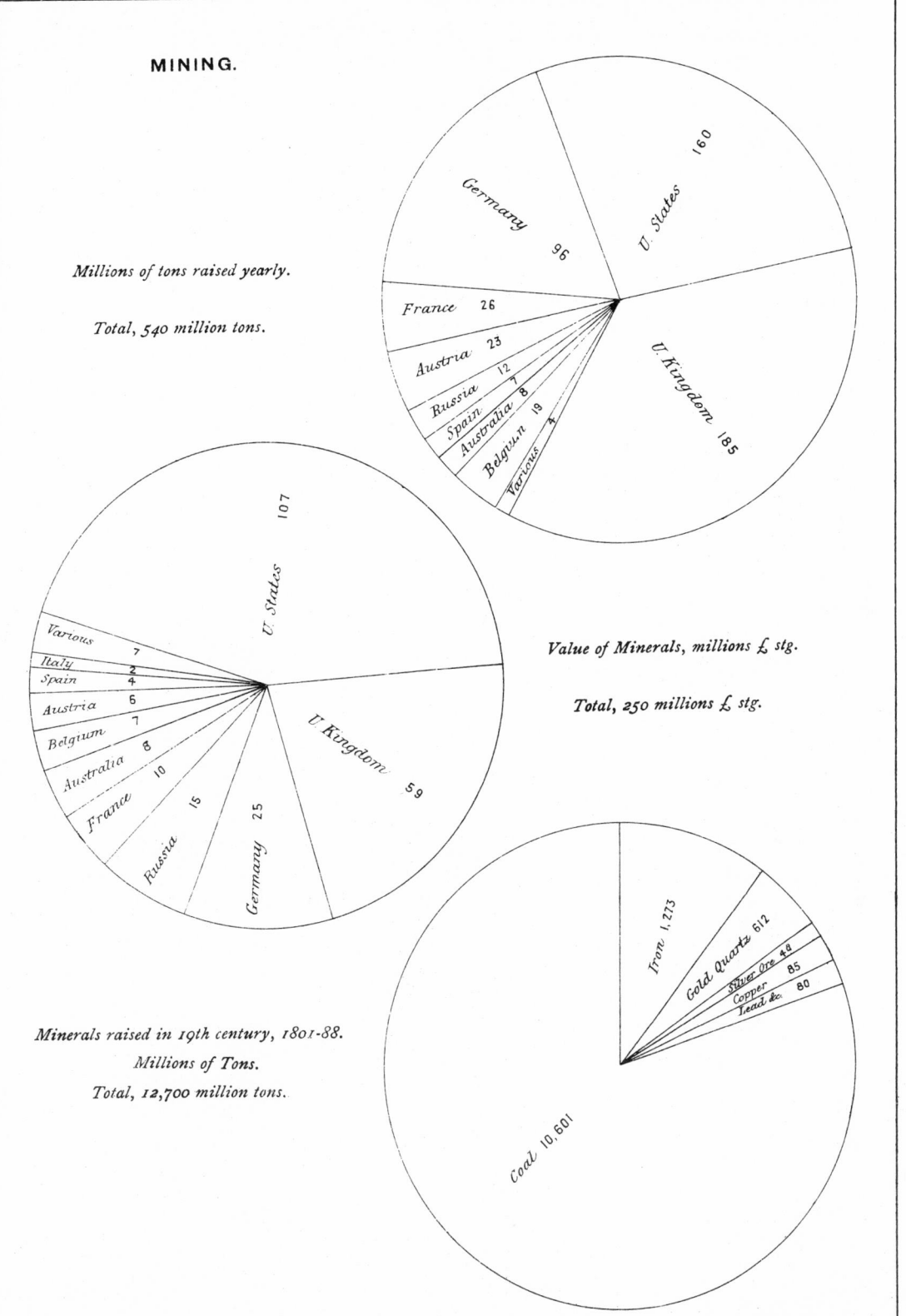

Millions of tons raised yearly.

Total, 540 million tons.

U. States 160

Germany 96

U. Kingdom 185

France 26

Austria 23

Russia 12

Spain 7

Australia 8

Belgium 19

Various 4

Value of Minerals, millions £ stg.

Total, 250 millions £ stg.

U. States 107

U. Kingdom 59

Germany 25

Russia 15

France 10

Australia 8

Belgium 7

Austria 6

Spain 4

Italy 2

Various 7

Minerals raised in 19th century, 1801-88.

Millions of Tons.

Total, 12,700 million tons.

Iron 1,273

Gold Quartz 612

Silver Ore 48

Copper 85

Lead &c. 80

Coal 10,601

Ballantyne, Hanson & Co. Edinburgh & London.

	Value Millions £ Sterling								
	Gold	Silver	Copper	Lead	Zinc	Tin	Iron	Coal	Total
1801–20	41	125	4	10	...	4	13	136	333
1821–40	48	89	8	15	...	5	26	250	441
1841–50	77	67	9	14	1	5	30	253	456
1851–60	282	78	18	25	2	5	48	385	843
1861–70	264	105	25	29	4	8	70	681	1,186
1871–80	241	178	35	30	11	23	110	1,104	1,732
1881–88	148	154	50	28	14	21	115	1,050	1,580
88 years	1,101	796	149	151	32	71	412	3,859	6,571

The foregoing table of tonnage gives only the metal of gold and silver, the quantities of ore being unknown. It has been, however, stated that the average was in California 70,000 tons for one ton of gold, and in Australia 94,000 tons for one.* As regards silver, the ordinary yield in Spanish America is 80 oz. to the ton. At these rates we can estimate the amount of ore raised. The account of all mining will then stand thus:—

	Millions of Tons Raised					
	Gold Quartz	Silver Ore	Iron Ore	Lead, &c.	Coal	Total
1801–20	23	7	35	4	277	346
1821–40	28	5	82	8	566	689
1841–50	44	4	96	8	637	789
1851–60	162	5	150	17	1,093	1,427
1861–70	142	7	205	26	1,873	2,253
1871–80	127	12	338	37	2,855	3,369
1881–88	86	9	367	52	3,300	3,814
88 years	612	49	1,273	152	10,601	12,687

As regards quantity, coal stood for nearly 85 per cent. of all minerals extracted.

The total mining product may be summed up thus:—

	Millions £ Sterling
Precious metals	1,897
Metallic ores	815
Coal	3,859
Total	6,571

The shares corresponding to the several countries were:—

	Millions £ Sterling						
	Precious Metals	Iron Ore	Lead Ore	Copper Ore	Zinc and Tin	Coal	Total
United Kingdom	...	168	33	24	36	2,072	2,333
France	...	37	7	4	...	303	351
Germany	40	51	31	11	15	419	567
Russia	222	5	...	6	...	17	250
Austria	60	11	2	1	...	89	163
Belgium	...	8	...	...	7	243	258
United States	508	67	42	44	6	612	1,279
Australia	322	...	...	13	...	23	358
Various	745	65	36	46	39	81	1,012
Total	1,897	412	151	149	103	3,859	6,571

Excluding precious metals, the values of mining products were, in order of time, as follows:—

	Millions £ Sterling							
Period	U. Kingdom	France	Germany	Austria	Belgium	U. States	Various	Total
1801–20	123	13	12	1	4	4	10	167
1821–40	204	27	23	4	19	7	20	304
1841–50	194	26	22	6	19	25	20	312
1851–60	267	37	45	8	36	54	36	483
1861–70	416	61	96	20	56	113	55	817
1871–80	658	101	151	31	68	205	99	1,313
1881–88	471	86	178	33	56	357	97	1,278
88 years	2,333	351	527	103	258	765	337	4,674

Iron-mining may be summed up approximately as follows:—

	Million Tons Ore						
Period	Great Britain	United States	Germany	France	Spain	Various	Total
1801–20	17	3	4	6	...	5	35
1821–40	44	9	6	12	1	10	82
1841–50	49	10	7	14	1	15	96
1851–60	90	15	11	12	2	20	150
1861–70	101	27	31	17	4	25	205
1871–80	160	58	54	26	10	30	338
1881–88	116	90	72	22	37	30	367
88 years	577	212	185	109	55	135	1,273

The extraction of other minerals in 88 years was approximately as follows:—

	Tons		
	Lead	Copper	Tin
Great Britain	6,800,000	11,200,000	800,000
France	1,600,000	1,600,000	...
Germany	6,000,000	9,700,000	...
Russia	...	5,100,000	...
Austria	1,400,000	600,000	...
Italy	1,300,000	...	...
Spain	7,500,000	11,400,000	...
United States	9,600,000	29,300,000	...
Australia	...	4,500,000	360,000
Various	400,000	11,500,000	270,000
Total	34,600,000	84,900,000	1,430,000

The number of persons employed in mining at various dates was approximately as follows:—

Year	Great Britain	United States	France	Germany	Various	Total
1820	165,000	10,000	20,000	30,000	25,000	250,000
1840	245,000	15,000	40,000	50,000	92,000	442,000
1860	497,000	70,000	70,000	159,000	220,000	1,016,000
1870	561,000	152,000	100,000	217,000	275,000	1,305,000
1880	654,000	234,000	120,000	300,000	450,000	1,758,000
1888	593,000	550,000	112,000	337,000	440,000	2,032,000

* The quartz raised by the gold mines of California and Australia would suffice to build 150 pyramids like that of Cheops. The gold extracted would fit in a room 40 by 20 feet, and 15 high.

The weight of minerals raised compares with miners approximately, thus :—

Year	No. of Miners	Tons Raised	Tons per Man
1820 . . .	250,000	27,000,000	108
1840 . . .	442,000	71,000,000	160
1860 . . .	1,016,000	198,000,000	194
1870 . . .	1,305,000	290,000,000	222
1888 . . .	2,032,000	565,000,000	270

The ratio for British miners in 1889 was 330 tons per man.

The superiority of English miners is stated by the Iron and Steel Institute to be shown in the proportion of iron ore extracted by each miner yearly as follows :—

	Tons			Tons
England . . .	923	Spain		292
France . . .	393	Germany . . .		283
Algeria . . .	323	Belgium . . .		127

This, however, appears to be exaggerated as regards English miners, for we find (see p. 401) that the annual product of all minerals in Great Britain in 1888 did not exceed 301 tons per miner.

In 1884 the deepest mines in the world were :—

Mine	Country	Mineral	Depth, Feet
Lambert	Belgium	Coal	3,490
Birkenberg	Austria	Silver	3,280
Zwickau	Saxony	Coal	2,637
St. Andre	Prussia	Silver	2,532
Rosebridge	England	Coal	2,510
Duckinfield	,,	,,	2,448
Magdala	Australia	Gold	1,990
Chaumont	France	Coal	1,876
Kongsberg	Norway	Silver	1,869
Schemnitz	Hungary	,,	1,771
La Huerta	Spain	,,	1,548

The production of metals in the present century has been approximately as follows :—

	Tons					
	Pig Iron	Copper	Lead	Tin	Zinc	Total
1801–20 . . .	13,200,000	170,000	1,400,000	60,000	40,000	14,870,000
1821–40 . . .	32,800,000	370,000	1,900,000	90,000	70,000	35,230,000
1841–50 . . .	33,500,000	335,000	1,600,000	60,000	210,000	35,555,000
1851–60 . . .	57,100,000	585,000	3,000,000	70,000	370,000	60,125,000
1861–70 . . .	93,600,000	780,000	4,000,000	100,000	950,000	97,880,000
1871–80 . . .	142,100,000	1,200,000	4,400,000	300,000	1,470,000	148,170,000
1881–88 . . .	176,000,000	1,540,000	4,100,000	280,000	1,910,000	183,030,000
88 years . . .	548,300,000	4,980,000	20,400,000	960,000	5,020,000	574,860,000

	Value, Millions £ Sterling					
	Pig Iron	Copper	Lead	Tin	Zinc	Total
1801–20 . .	97	17	42	5	1	162
1821–40 . .	209	37	38	6	1	291
1841–50 . .	151	34	29	6	4	224
1851–60 . .	188	58	43	8	7	304
1861–70 . .	301	70	49	12	18	450
1871–80 . .	425	94	62	33	24	638
1881–88 . .	446	105	50	25	28	654
88 years . .	1,817	415	313	95	83	2,723

	Value, Millions £ Sterling					
	Pig Iron	Copper	Lead	Tin	Zinc	Total
Great Britain	723	162	82	61	29	1,057
France . .	181	19	16	5	1	222
Germany .	245	36	65	5	36	387
Russia . .	70	20	5	2	2	99
Austria . .	66	10	15	2	1	94
Belgium . .	72	10	16	2	2	102
U. States . .	380	60	55	2	10	507
Various . .	80	98	59	16	2	255
Total .	1,817	415	313	95	83	2,723

UNITED KINGDOM

The progress of British mining may be approximately shown thus :—

	Tons Raised						
	Coal	Iron Ore	Copper Ore	Lead Ore	Zinc Ore	Tin Ore	Total
1780 . . .	8,500,000	200,000	30,000	40,000	5,000	5,000	8,780,000
1800 . . .	10,100,000	500,000	50,000	50,000	5,000	5,000	10,710,000
1820 . . .	14,000,000	1,000,000	100,000	60,000	5,000	5,000	15,170,000
1830 . . .	16,100,000	1,700,000	150,000	70,000	5,000	5,000	18,080,000
1840 . . .	35,000,000	3,500,000	150,000	80,000	10,000	5,000	38,795,000
1850 . . .	49,000,000	5,500,000	180,000	80,000	15,000	10,000	54,785,000
1860 . . .	80,000,000	8,000,000	240,000	100,000	15,000	10,000	88,285,000
1870 . . .	110,000,000	14,400,000	110,000	110,000	15,000	15,000	124,650,000
1880 . . .	147,000,000	18,000,000	55,000	90,000	30,000	15,000	165,190,000
1888 . . .	170,000,000	14,600,000	20,000	60,000	40,000	15,000	184,735,000

About 100 years ago the weight of minerals raised daily in Great Britain was 25,000 tons, and in 1888 it rose to 600,000. Improved machinery has effected a great economy of labour, one man in 1888 raising as much as four could do in 1800. This has caused a notable fall in the price of minerals. Thus it happens that although the weight of minerals raised has increased twenty-one-fold since 1780, the value of same has only risen ten-fold.

The total value of British mining in 88 years was approximately as follows :—

Period	Millions £ Sterling					
	Coal	Ironstone	Lead	Copper	Tin, &c.	Total
1801–20 .	105	6	5	3	4	123
1821–40 .	175	13	6	6	4	204
1841–50 .	168	14	4	4	4	194
1851–60 .	228	25	5	4	5	267
1861–70 .	370	31	5	4	6	416
1871–80 .	600	44	5	2	7	658
1881–88 .	426	35	3	1	6	471
88 years .	2,072	168	33	24	36	2,333

The weight of mineral raised compares with the number of miners approximately as follows :—

Year	Miners	Tons Raised	Tons per Man
1820 . . .	165,000	15,200,000	92
1840 . . .	245,000	38,800,000	160
1860 . . .	497,000	88,300,000	180
1870 . . .	561,000	122,300,000	218
1880 . . .	654,000	161,200,000	247
1888 . . .	593,000	184,600,000	301

The value of British mining per head of the population is shown in the following table :—

	Coal	Metallic Ores	Total	Per Inhabitant
	£	£	£	£ s. d.
1780	4,600,000	1,010,000	5,610,000	0 11 0
1800	5,500,000	1,210,000	6,710,000	0 9 0
1820	7,000,000	1,510,000	8,510,000	0 8 6
1830	6,500,000	2,010,000	8,510,000	0 7 6
1840	12,200,000	2,720,000	14,920,000	0 11 6
1850	16,500,000	3,430,000	19,930,000	0 15 0
1860	26,600,000	4,230,000	30,830,000	1 2 0
1870	45,000,000	6,630,000	51,630,000	1 14 0
1880	49,000,000	6,560,000	55,560,000	1 13 0
1888	53,600,000	5,180,000	58,780,000	1 10 6

In the above estimate of value, coal is taken at 25 per cent. under the price at port of shipment.

The value of metals produced from British ores at various dates was approximately as follows :—

	1780	1800	1820	1840	1860	1889
	£	£	£	£	£	£
Iron	400,000	700,000	1,000,000	3,500,000	7,500,000	12,700,000
Tin	500,000	400,000	400,000	400,000	700,000	900,000
Lead, &c.. . . .	800,000	1,200,000	2,000,000	3,100,000	3,000,000	800,000
Total . .	1,700,000	2,300,000	3,400,000	7,000,000	11,200,000	14,400,000

FRANCE

The products of mines may be approximately summed up thus :—

	Tons		Value, £
	Coal	Iron Ore	
1800 . . .	800,000	200,000	600,000
1830 . . .	1,800,000	700,000	1,000,000
1850 . . .	5,000,000	900,000	2,800,000
1870 . . .	13,300,000	2,600,000	6,600,000
1888 . . .	23,000,000	2,600,000	9,600,000

The official valuation for 1889 is as follows :—

	Tons	Value, £
Coal	176,900,000	56,200,000
Iron ore . . .	14,550,000	3,850,000
Tin ore . . .	14,000	730,000
Lead ore . . .	50,000	430,000
Copper ore . .	15,000	60,000
Zinc ore . . .	25,000	100,000
Salt	1,950,000	890,000
Oil shale . . .	2,010,000	500,000
Clays	3,040,000	830,000
Slate	460,000	1,050,000
Total .	199,014,000	64,640,000

The above is exclusive of stone, to the value of £8,700,000, say 11,000,000 tons, which brings up the total to 210 million tons, representing an aggregate value of 73½ millions sterling.

The quantity and value of metals extracted from the foregoing minerals may be summed up as follows :—

	Tons	Value, £
Iron	5,180,000	12,700,000
Lead	36,000	460,000
Tin	9,000	860,000
Copper . . .	1,500	120,000
Zinc	10,000	190,000
Silver	10	70,000
Total . .	5,236,510	14,400,000

The number of persons employed in mines in 1888 was as follows :—

Underground	465,000
Overground	127,700
Total . . .	592,700

Among those overground were 5700 women. The number of miners killed was as follows :—

Year	Killed	Per 10,000 Miners	One Killed in	Tons Raised per Miner Killed
1851–60	10,018	41	245	57,000
1861–70	10,626	33	300	104,000
1871–80	11,349	23	425	140,000
1888	960	21	484	198,000

The above is irrespective of salt and some minor items. An official return in 1883 of the coal-mines showed thus :—

Year	Miners	Tons Raised	Value, £
1860 . . .	59,000	8,300,000	2,400,000
1870 . . .	83,000	13,300,000	6,200,000
1880 . . .	107,000	19,400,000	9,900,000
1883 . . .	113,000	21,300,000	10,700,000

Detailed statistics of coal-mining in France will be found at pages 121 and 122.

The statement for all mining in 1886 showed thus :

	Miners	Tons Raised	Value, £
Coal	102,000	19,500,000	9,200,000
Iron ore . . .	6,000	2,300,000	400,000
Salt	4,000	640,000	500,000
Total . .	112,000	22,440,000	10,100,000

The quarries, moreover, employed 111,000 men, and their annual yield was about 8 million tons, valued at £6,600,000. The slate quarries of Ardenne, Bretagne, yield 120 million slates yearly. The total value of French mining in 88 years was approximately as follows :—

Period	Millions £ Sterling			
	Coal	Iron-stone	Lead and Copper	Total
1801–20 . .	11	2	...	13
1821–40 . .	23	4	...	27
1841–50 . .	21	4	1	26
1851–60 . .	31	5	1	37
1861–70 . .	53	6	2	61
1871–80 . .	89	9	3	101
1881–88 . .	75	7	4	86
88 years . .	303	37	11	351

Von Decken's and official tables of mining in Germany show as follows :—

Year	Tons							
	Coal	Lignite	Iron Ore	Lead Ore	Zinc Ore	Copper Ore	Salt	Total
1850 . .	5,100,000	1,500,000	800,000	170,000	150,000	50,000	300,000	8,070,000
1860	12,300,000	4,400,000	1,400,000	150,000	310,000	90,000	400,000	19,050,000
1870	26,400,000	7,600,000	3,800,000	100,000	370,000	200,000	500,000	38,970,000
1880	47,000,000	12,100,000	7,200,000	130,000	500,000	380,000	670,000	67,980,000
1888	65,400,000	16,600,000	10,700,000	160,000	670,000	530,000	950,000	95,010,000

	Value, £							
1850 . .	1,500,000	200,000	200,000	300,000	100,000	50,000	300,000	2,650,000
1860	4,000,000	700,000	400,000	600,000	200,000	150,000	400,000	6,350,000
1870	8,200,000	1,100,000	1,200,000	800,000	300,000	250,000	500,000	12,350,000
1880	12,100,000	2,000,000	1,700,000	600,000	400,000	300,000	600,000	17,700,000
1888	16,500,000	2,500,000	2,000,000	800,000	700,000	300,000	500,000	23,800,000

Year	Number of Miners				Tons Raised	Tons per Miner
	Coal	Iron	Lead, &c.	Total		
1850	47,300	16,000	25,500	88,800	8,100,000	91
1860	102,100	18,500	38,500	159,100	19,100,000	119
1870	145,800	27,300	44,200	217,300	39,000,000	180
1875	209,100	26,400	41,800	277,300	52,600,000	190
1886	247,000	32,000	58,000	337,000	85,200,000	253

The total value of German mining in 88 years was approximately as follows :—

Period	Millions £ Sterling					
	Coal	Ironstone	Lead	Copper	Zinc	Total
1801–20 .	10	1	1	...	...	12
1821–40 .	18	2	2	...	1	23
1841–50 .	16	2	3	...	1	22
1851–60 .	34	3	5	1	2	45
1861–70 .	75	9	7	2	3	96
1871–80 .	121	16	7	3	4	151
1881–88 .	145	18	6	5	4	178
88 years .	419	51	31	11	15	527

The production of metals was approximately as follows :—

Year	Tons			Total Value, £
	Iron	Lead	Copper	
1830 . . .	220,000	1,000	1,000	1,600,000
1850 . . .	570,000	7,000	2,000	3,700,000
1880 . . .	1,720,000	32,000	5,000	6,200,000

GERMANY

The mining industry is shown approximately thus :—

Year	Tons				Value, £
	Coal	Iron Ore	Sundries	Total	
1800	300,000	100,000	200,000	600,000	200,000
1830	2,000,000	300,000	500,000	2,800,000	900,000
1850	6,600,000	800,000	800,000	8,100,000	2,600,000
1870	33,600,000	3,800,000	1,400,000	38,800,000	12,400,000
1888	82,000,000	10,700,000	3,100,000	95,800,000	24,700,000

At the beginning of the 19th century the quantity of minerals raised averaged only 2000 tons daily, but in 1888 it rose to 300,000 daily.

Prussia has the lion's share of the mining industry, as appears from the returns for 1888, viz. :—

	Coal Raised, Tons	Value of all Minerals, £	Ratio	Pig Iron, Tons
Prussia . .	72,700,000	20,600,000	83.0	3,100,000
Saxony . .	5,200,000	2,200,000	9.0	300,000
Other States	4,100,000	1,900,000	8.0	940,000
Total .	82,000,000	24,700,000	100.0	4,340,000

There are 77 zinc mines in Prussia, which produce half the zinc of the world.
The production of metals was approximately as follows :—

Year	Tons				Total Value, £
	Iron	Lead	Copper	Zinc	
1850	400,000	16,000	2,000	30,000	4,400,000
1860	900,000	30,000	3,000	59,000	7,500,000
1870	1,340,000	54,000	5,000	65,000	12,000,000
1880	2,800,000	86,000	14,000	100,000	14,400,000
1888	4,400,000	92,000	18,000	130,000	18,500,000

Official statements of the production and consumption of the following metals show thus :—

	Production, Tons		Consumption, Tons	
	1871	1886	1871	1886
Lead . . .	54,000	92,000	39,000	56,000
Copper . .	4,600	18,200	15,500	23,500
Zinc . . .	65,000	130,000	29,000	70,000
Tin . . .	100	100	2,500	6,500
Total .	123,700	240,300	86,000	156,000

RUSSIA

The mining product is shown approximately thus :—

Year	Tons				
	Coal	Iron Ore	Copper Ore	Salt	Naphtha
1840	10,000	110,000	60,000	440,000	...
1850	50,000	160,000	80,000	400,000	...
1860	130,000	180,000	90,000	420,000	...
1870	700,000	250,000	100,000	450,000	...
1880	4,100,000	650,000	100,000	780,000	350,000
1888	5,000,000	800,000	100,000	1,200,000	2,000,000

All the above are, however, of minor value compared with the gold-fields, which are mostly situated in Siberia, the product of precious metals showing as follows :—

Period	Tons		Value, £		
	Gold	Silver	Gold	Silver	Total
1821–30	33	200	4,600,000	1,600,000	6,200,000
1831–40	69	250	9,800,000	2,200,000	12,000,000
1841–50	217	230	30,400,000	2,500,000	32,900,000
1851–60	256	170	35,800,000	1,500,000	37,300,000
1861–70	271	150	38,000,000	1,300,000	39,300,000
1871–80	380	130	53,200,000	1,000,000	54,200,000
1881–88	280	90	39,200,000	600,000	39,800,000
68 years	1,506	1,220	211,000,000	10,700,000	221,700,000

The regular mining of precious metals began in Siberia in 1704, silver being the first metal found. Gold was discovered in the Ural Mountains in 1745, near Eka-terinenberg, and in 1810 these mines were producing 10,000 oz., worth £40,000 per annum. From 1814 to 1880 the yield of the various gold mines was :—

	Tons	Value, £
Ural	330	46,200,000
East Siberia . . .	790	110,600,000
West Siberia . . .	80	11,200,000
Total . .	1,200	168,000,000

An official report of mining for Austria proper in 1887 showed :—

The total mining product of Russia in the nineteenth century may be summed up approximately thus :—

Period	Millions Sterling		
	Gold and Silver	Copper, Coal, &c.	Total
1801–20 . .	3	1	4
1821–40 . .	18	2	20
1841–50 . .	33	3	36
1851–60 . .	37	3	40
1861–70 . .	39	5	44
1871–80 . .	54	12	66
1881–88 . .	40	16	56
88 years . .	224	42	266

The production of base metals in 1886 was as follows :—

	Tons	Approximate Value, £
Iron	530,000	1,600,000
Copper	4,500	400,000
Zinc	4,100	60,000
Total . .	538,600	2,060,000

The annual value of all mining and metallic industries is about 15 millions sterling. They occupy 290,000 persons and 3450 steam-engines, with an aggregate of 100,000 horse-power.

AUSTRIA

Mining industry is summed up approximately thus :—

Year	Tons			
	Coal	Iron Ore	Copper Ore	Lead Ore
1840 . .	400,000	180,000	5,000	10,000
1860 . .	3,500,000	500,000	10,000	15,000
1880 . .	16,100,000	1,100,000	15,000	15,000
1888 . .	20,000,000	1,800,000	15,000	15,000

In 1834 the following report was published :—

	Mining Output, Tons		
	Austria	Hungary	Total
Coal . . .	170,000	20,000	190,000
Iron, pig . .	70,000	15,000	85,000
Salt . . .	160,000	100,000	260,000
Lead ore . .	4,000	1,000	5,000
Copper ore . .	200	2,000	2,200
Total . .	404,200	138,000	542,200

In 1850 the mines of the Empire were estimated to yield as follows :—

	Tons
Coal	2,000,000
Iron ore	280,000
Salt	600,000
Lead, &c.	24,000
	2,904,000

	Tons			Value, £		
	Bohemia	Other Provinces	Total	Bohemia	Other Provinces	Total
Coal . . .	3,500,000	4,300,000	7,800,000	800,000	1,000,000	1,800,000
Lignite . . .	8,900,000	2,700,000	11,600,000	900,000	600,000	1,500,000
Iron ore . . .	300,000	540,000	840,000	40,000	120,000	160,000
Salt . . .	...	280,000	280,000	...	280,000	280,000
Lead, &c. . . .	200,000	120,000	320,000	300,000	500,000	800,000
Total . .	12,900,000	7,940,000	20,840,000	2,040,000	2,500,000	4,540,000

The hands employed in the above mines in 1887 were :—

	Men	Women	Total
Coal	36,600	6,000	42,600
Lignite. . . .	30,000	2,500	32,500
Iron	4,000	100	4,100
Salt, &c. . . .	22,200	3,300	25,500
Total . .	92,800	11,990	104,700
Bohemia . . .	42,000	4,500	46,500
Silesia	13,600	2,800	16,400
Galitzia . . .	12,200	1,000	13,200
Styria, &c. . . .	25,000	3,600	28,600
Total .	92,800	11,900	104,700

A report on the production of minerals and metals in Hungary showed thus :—

	1864	1874	1883
	Tons	Tons	Tons
Coal . . .	350,000	620,000	900,000
Lignite . .	250,000	780,000	1,500,000
Pig iron . .	120,000	170,000	180,000
Copper . .	2,200	1,000	1,000
Lead . . .	1,500	1,500	2,000
Total .	723,700	1,572,500	2,583,000

There was also a yield of £200,000 worth of gold and £100,000 of silver.
The mining values in 1886 were stated thus :—

	Austria	Hungary	Total
	£	£	£
Coal . . .	1,800,000	400,000	2,200,000
Lignite . .	1,800,000	400,000	2,200,000
Pig iron . .	1,800,000	800,000	2,600,000
Lead, &c. . .	1,400,000	600,000	2,000,000
Total .	6,800,000	2,200,000	9,000,000

This table confuses the values of minerals and metals; the actual value was—minerals £5,400,000, metals £3,600,000.

ITALY

The production of iron ore is recorded as follows :—

Year	Tons	Value, £
1850	64,000	36,000
1860	71,000	40,000
1870	74,000	42,000
1887	230,000	100,000

The returns for 1877 and 1887 compare as follows :—

	Tons		Value, £	
	1877	1887	1877	1887
Sulphur . .	130,000	340,000	1,050,000	950,000
Iron ore . .	110,000	230,000	110,000	100,000
Zinc ore . .	45,000	90,000	180,000	250,000
Lead ore .	18,000	40,000	440,000	280,000
Sundries .	21,000	470,000	260,000	420,000
Total . .	324,000	1,170,000	2,040,000	2,000,000

In 1877 the number of miners was 41,000, and in 1887 it was 47,000. This is exclusive of marble quarries, which employ 20,000 men, and have an annual output of a million sterling.

SPAIN

An official report of mining products in 1780 was as follows :—

	Tons	Valve, £
Iron	9,000	70,000
Lead	1,600	30,000
Quicksilver . . .	900	180,000
Antimony, &c. . .	500	30,000
Total . . .	12,000	310,000

A report published in 1863 was as follows :—

	Tons			Tons
Coal . . .	320,000	Ironstone . .		170,000
Salt . . .	3,800,000	Zinc ore . .		110,000
Copper ore. .	140,000	Sulphur. .		23,000
Lead ore .	310,000	Quicksilver .		1,000

In 1887 the export of minerals showed :—

	Tons	Value, £
Iron Ore	5,200,000	1,800,000
Copper Ore . . .	800,000	1,200,000
Lead	63,000	900,000
Quicksilver . . .	1,300	300,000
Sundries	300,000	500,000
Total . .	6,364,000	4,700,000

The mines employed 57,000 hands in 1887.
There has been of late years a great increase in the production of coal, ironstone and copper, but a decline in lead.

The mining industry of Spain in the last 28 years may be summed up approximately as follows :—

Period	Coal	Ironstone	Copper Ore	Lead Ore	Zinc Ore	Quicksilver	Total
1861–70 . . .	3,000,000	2,000,000	1,500,000	2,500,000	1,000,000	10,000	10,010,000
1871–80 . . .	6,000,000	10,400,000	3,800,000	2,000,000	1,000,000	10,000	23,210,000
1881–88 . . .	8,600,000	37,100,000	5,300,000	1,500,000	800,000	10,000	53,310,000
28 years . . .	17,600,000	49,500,000	10,600,000	6,000,000	2,800,000	30,000	86,530,000
	Value, £						
1861–70 . . .	1,000,000	800,000	2,400,000	7,500,000	2,000,000	2,000,000	15,700,000
1871–80 . . .	2,000,000	4,200,000	6,000,000	6,000,000	2,000,000	2,000,000	22,200,000
1881–88 . . .	2,800,000	13,000,000	8,400,000	4,500,000	1,600,000	2,000,000	32,300,000
28 years . . .	5,800,000	18,000,000	16,800,000	18,000,000	5,600,000	6,000,000	70,200,000

BELGIUM

The official records for 48 years show as follows :—

Year	Tons Raised			Value, £			Miners	Tons Coal per Collier
	Coal	Iron	Total	Coal	Iron	Total		
1840 . . .	3,900,000	200,000	4,100,000	1,800,000	100,000	1,900,000	...	...
1850 . . .	5,800,000	300,000	6,100,000	1,800,000	100,000	1,900,000	42,100	121
1860 . . .	9,600,000	800,000	10,400,000	4,300,000	300,000	4,600,000	71,100	123
1870 . . .	13,700,000	700,000	14,400,000	6,000,000	200,000	6,200,000	79,800	149
1880 . . .	16,900,000	300,000	17,200,000	6,800,000	100,000	6,900,000	81,400	164
1887 . . .	18,400,000	200,000	18,600,000	5,950,000	50,000	6,000,000	77,000	182

There are, moreover, stone quarries, whose product is valued at £1,300,000 per annum.

SWEDEN AND NORWAY

The mining products of Sweden may be summed up as 900,000 tons of iron ore and 300,000 tons of coal ; the mines employ 29,000 persons. The production of iron ore has trebled since 1850. Norway has 28 mines, employing 2000 hands, the output averaging £180,000 per annum. The mining returns of Sweden for 1870 and 1887 compare thus :—

	Tons Ore	
	1870	1887
Iron	700,000	900,000
Copper	2,000	1,000
Zinc	33,000	50,000

Of precious metals Sweden raised in 1870 gold to the value of £150,000 and silver worth £10,000 ; in 1887 silver represented £40,000 sterling.

GREECE

The lead mines of Laurium have been worked for many years by a French company, producing 1,200,000 tons ore in twelve years ending 1888, one half of which was smelted near the mines. Small quantities of zinc ore are also raised in Greece. The total value of mineral products is about £600,000 yearly.

UNITED STATES

The following table shows the date of discovery and the commencement of mining of certain minerals :—

	Place	Discovered	Began Mining
Iron	Virginia	1610	1663
Copper . . .	Massachusetts	1632	1648
Coal . . .	Pennsylvania	1768	1784
Lead . . .	...	1823	1829
Petroleum . .	Pennsylvania	1826	1845
Gold . . .	California	1849	1849
Silver . . .	Nevada	1858	1859
Quicksilver . .	California	1860	1860

The first iron-foundry was at Lynn, Massachusetts, the first copper smelting-works at Salem in the same State. In 1660 the Dutch worked copper mines in New Jersey, and about the same time the French Jesuits at Lake Superior. A cargo of ninety tons of copper was shipped from New York in 1766, but little progress was made until 1843, when the United States Government bought the Lake Superior copper-fields from the Chippeway Indians. The production of lead in 1829 was 7200 tons. The first regular oil-wells were found near Pittsburg, Pennsylvania, in 1845 (see *Oil*). Gold was discovered at Sutor's Mill, California, in 1849, silver by J. H. Comstock and James Phinney at Storey Co., Nevada, in 1858 ; small quantities of gold had been found in the Southern States previously.

The following table shows approximately the principal mining products (except gold and silver) at various dates :—

Year	Tons				
	Coal	Iron Ore	Copper Ore	Lead Ore	Total
1830	1,300,000	400,000	...	7,000	1,707,000
1840	1,800,000	600,000	...	10,000	2,410,000
1850	8,000,000	1,200,000	5,000	50,000	9,255,000
1860	15,000,000	1,600,000	40,000	80,000	16,720,000
1870	33,000,000	3,200,000	80,000	100,000	36,380,000
1880	70,500,000	8,000,000	120,000	150,000	78,770,000
1889	142,000,000	13,300,000	600,000	250,000	156,150,000

The production of precious metals is shown as follows :—

Period	Tons		Value, Millions £ Sterling		
	Gold	Silver	Gold	Silver	Total
1851–60 . .	830	7	116	...	116
1861–70 . .	713	2,375	100	20	120
1871–80 . .	620	7,750	87	62	149
1881–88 . .	373	8,860	52	62	114
38 years . .	2,536	18,992	355	144	502

The total value of mining products in 88 years was approximately as follows :—

Period	Millions £ Sterling								
	Gold	Silver	Ironstone	Copper	Lead	Petroleum	Coal	Sundries	Total
1801–40 . .	1	...	3	...	1	...	7	...	12
1841–50 . .	8	...	3	1	3	...	18	...	33
1851–60 . .	116	...	5	3	6	3	40	...	173
1861–70 . .	100	20	9	5	8	17	91	2	252
1871–80 . .	87	62	18	9	11	33	167	4	391
1881–88 . .	52	62	29	26	13	37	289	5	513
88 years . .	364	144	67	44	42	90	612	11	1,374

The production of metallic copper and lead, according to Keller, was as follows :—

Copper			Lead		
Year		Tons	Year		Tons
1845 . . .		100	1832 . . .		9,100
1850 . . .		650	1842 . . .		21,800
1855 . . .		3,000	1852 . . .		14,300
1860 . . .		7,300	1862 . . .		12,900
1865 . . .		8,600	1872 . . .		23,500
1870 . . .		12,800	1875 . . .		54,100
1875 . . .		18,300	1878 . . .		82,600
1880 . . .		27,400	1880 . . .		88,700
1882 . . .		41,600	1882 . . .		120,000

About 60 per cent. of the copper comes from the Lake Superior fields above mentioned, which produced 190,000 tons of metallic copper in the ten years ending 1882.

Official returns for 1888 are as follows :—

	Metallic Products				Non-Metallic	
	Tons	Value, £			Tons	Value, £
Pig iron	6,500,000	22,200,000	Coal		142,040,000	47,100,000
Copper	105,000	7,100,000	Stone		...	5,300,000
Lead	160,000	3,300,000	Lime		4,500,000	5,100,000
Zinc	50,000	1,100,000	Cement		900,000	900,000
Gold, oz.	1,600,000	6,800,000	Salt		1,050,000	900,000
Silver, oz. . . .	45,800,000	12,300,000	Petroleum		5,500,000	5,100,000
Sundries	...	300,000	Sundries		...	7,000,000
Total . .	...	53,100,000	Total . .		...	71,400,000

Mining and metallic industries together represent 125 millions sterling, but this allows an excessive value for silver, from which a deduction of £2,000,000 should be made.

AUSTRALIA

The official report by Mr. Coghlan shows the total value of minerals extracted in thirty-eight years down to 1888 was as follows :—

	£ Sterling					
	Gold	Silver	Copper	Tin	Coal	Total
New South Wales . .	37,200,000	2,900,000	5,400,000	8,500,000	22,300,000	76,300,000
Victoria . . .	222,500,000	100,000	200,000	700,000	...	223,500,000
Queensland . .	21,300,000	400,000	1,700,000	5,100,000	900,000	29,400,000
South Australia . .	900,000	...	19,200,000	...	...	20,100,000
New Zealand . .	44,800,000	100,000	...	...	2,700,000	47,600,000
Tasmania . . .	2,000,000	...	...	4,400,000	200,000	6,600,000
Western Australia . .	200,000	300,000	500,000	...	...	1,000,000
Total .	328,900,000	3,800,000	26,000,000	18,700,000	26,100,000	404,500,000

The quantities of gold extracted were as follows :—

Colony	Gold Found	Ounces Extracted	Value, £
New South Wales .	1851	9,973,000	37,200,000
Victoria . . .	1851	55,636,000	222,500,000
South Australia . .	1852	248,000	900,000
Tasmania . . .	1852	533,000	2,000,000
Queensland . .	1858	6,089,000	21,300,000
New Zealand .	1858	11,422,000	44,800,000
Western Australia .	1886	55,000	200,000
Total . .	...	83,955,000	328,900,000

The values of gold produced and exported were as follows :—

Period	Produced, £	Exported, £
1851–60 . . .	118,000,000	97,500,000
1861–70 . . .	95,000,000	97,900,000
1871–80 . . .	81,000,000	65,200,000
1881–88 . . .	35,000,000	33,200,000
38 years . . .	329,000,000*	293,800,000

Copper was first found in South Australia in 1843, tin in New South Wales in 1872, and silver in the latter colony in 1881. The first coal was raised in New South Wales in 1847, namely, 40,000 tons, the product now reaching 4,200,000 tons.

* In the article on gold and silver (p. 306), it will be seen that the gold yield of Australia for the said thirty-eight years is put down at 322 millions sterling. Liversidge makes the yield of coal 44 million tons to 1888.

The yield of gold-fields in 1888 was as follows :—

	Gold, Oz.	Value, £	No. of Miners	Oz. per Man
New South Wales	88,000	320,000	8,300	10.6
Victoria . . .	625,000	2,500,000	25,100	25.0
Queensland . .	482,000	1,700,000	9,300	52.0
South Australia . .	17,000	70,000	400	39.0
Tasmania . . .	40,000	150,000	900	44.0
New Zealand . .	201,000	800,000	9,400	21.5
Western Australia	50,000	200,000	800	62.0
Total . .	1,502,000	5,740,000	54,200	27.5

The largest nuggets on record are :—

Name	Locality	Oz.	Value, £	Date
Welcome	Ballarat	2,020	8,380	9th June 1858
Stranger	...	2,280	9,460	9th Feb. 1869

The deepest mines are Magdala, Stawell, 2409 feet, and Lansell's, Sandhurst, 2640 feet.

SOUTH AFRICA

The Transvaal gold-fields, recently discovered, promise to be very productive, the value extracted in 1889 reaching £1,300,000 sterling.

BOLIVIA

In 1883 the extraction of silver was as follows :—

	Oz.	Value, £
Huanchaca . . .	5,600,000	900,000
Potosi . . .	1,200,000	200,000
Oruro . . .	1,200,000	200,000
Aullagas . . .	3,200,000	500,000
Guadelupe, &c. . .	4,800,000	800,000
Total . .	16,000,000	2,600,000

The Potosi mines yielded 600 millions sterling in 320 years.

CANADA

The mining products in 1887 were :—

	Tons	Value, £
Coal	2,100,000	1,000,000
Gold	...	200,000
Sundries	...	1,800,000
Total . . .	...	3,000,000

MEXICO

There are 350 mines, which are said to occupy 100,000 men. In sixty years ending 1880 were raised 180 millions sterling worth of silver, and nearly one million sterling of gold. The mines are supposed at present to stand for a capital of 6 millions sterling. According to Messdaglia, the mines yielded in 383 years, to 1875, as follows :—

	Tons	Value, £
Gold	265	36,000,000
Silver	76,200	677,000,000
Total . . .	76,465	713,000,000

ARGENTINA

Rickard's report in 1869 showed 2700 men employed in various mines. The product was 3000 oz. gold, 44,000 oz. silver, 700 tons copper, and 1000 tons lead ; total value £70,000 per annum, the capital employed being £300,000.

In 1885 the yield of the mines was estimated thus :—

		£
Catamarca	Copper	70,000
San Juan	Silver	40,000
Mendoza	,,	40,000
Cordoba and Rioja	,,	64,000
Total . . .		214,000

The actual yield is supposed at present to barely reach £150,000.

CHILE

Copper is the most important mineral, and the ores extracted since 1850 are supposed to be equivalent to the following quantities of fine copper :—

Period	Tons	Value, £
1851–60	190,000	15,200,000
1861–70	270,000	20,500,000
1871–80	330,000	20,300,000
1881–88	300,000	18,000,000
38 years . . .	1,090,000	74,000,000

In late years nitrate has obtained importance, shipments rising from 350,000 tons in 1885 to 800,000 in 1888. The coal-fields are supposed to yield 10 million tons yearly ; and the silver mines 5 million oz. of that metal, worth £800,000.

VENEZUELA

The latest reports show as follows :—

	Oz.	Value, £
Gold	250,000	900,000
Copper	...	150,000
Total . . .	...	1,050,000

MONEY

The amount of money in use among nations at various dates was (excluding copper and nickel, which are of trifling value) approximately as follows :—

	Millions £ Sterling			
	Gold	Silver	Paper	Total
1600 . . .	29	102	...	131
1700 . . .	75	225	1	301
1800 . . .	126	360	82	568
1848 . . .	157	388	260	805
1860 . . .	340	480	360	1,180
1890 . . .	830	801	771	2,402

The above includes the paper-money only of Europe, United States, the British Colonies, and the Colonies of France and Spain. No account is taken of the depreciated currency of South America, the value of which is merely conventional, and for the most part ideal.

The money now in use is approximately as follows :—

	Millions £ Sterling				£ per Inhabitant
	Gold	Silver	Paper	Total	
Great Britain . .	102	22	39	163	4.4
France . .	178	150	115	443	11.8
Germany . .	122	45	71	238	5.0
Russia . .	39	14	123	176	2.1
Austria . .	8	19	76	103	2.6
Italy . .	22	11	57	90	3.0
Spain . .	19	24	30	73	4.2
Portugal . .	9	2	1	12	2.7
Scandinavia . .	6	2	13	21	2.8
Holland . .	5	13	17	35	7.7
Belgium . .	11	11	15	37	6.1
Switzerland . .	3	3	6	12	4.0
Turkey, &c. . .	17	12	9	38	3.4
Europe . .	541	328	572	1,441	4.0
United States . .	141	87	208	436	7.0
Canada . .	3	1	6	10	2.0
Australia . .	22	2	6	30	8.2
Japan . .	19	9	26	54	1.4
China . .	...	150	...	150	0.5
India . .	10	170	12	192	1.0
Java . .	...	18	...	18	0.9
Cape Colony . .	7	...	1	8	6.0
Egypt . .	27	4	...	31	6.2
Algeria . .	2	3	3	8	2.0
Cuba . .	4	...	12	16	10.0
Various . .	14	29	...	43	...
Total . .	790	801	846	2,437	...

For the amounts of gold and silver coined between 1850 and 1890 see *Gold*.

The amount of uncovered paper-money, according to Spallart, was as follows :—

	Millions £ Sterling		
	1850	1870	1885
United Kingdom . .	15	12	12
France . . .	3	8	27
Germany . . .	2	22	25
Russia . . .	31	91	67
Austria . . .	18	58	40
Italy . . .	...	36	34
United States . .	15	130	65
Various . . .	4	32	72
Total . .	88	390	342

The following table shows approximately the amounts of paper-money at various dates :—

	Millions £ Sterling			
	1840	1860	1880	1890
United Kingdom .	35	39	45	39
France . . .	9	33	90	115
Germany . . .	8	25	57	71
Russia . . .	70	105	115	123
Austria . . .	43	60	65	76
Italy	2	6	65	57
Various . . .	18	36	64	91
Europe . . .	185	304	501	572
United States . .	20	41	144	133
Colonies, &c. . .	1	15	66	69
Total . .	206	360	711	771

The above is exclusive of the paper-money of South America, which has a very doubtful value.

Money was first coined by King Pheidon of Argos, 800 B.C., of silver only. Crœsus was the first, says Herodotus, to coin gold. Darius coined gold and silver at 13½ units of silver to one of gold.

The principal coins at present in use are :—

Gold

Country	Name	Weight	Fineness	Value
		Oz.		£ s. d.
Austria . . .	Ducat . .	0.112	986	0 9 6
,, . . .	Crown . .	0.357	900	1 7 8
Bolivia . . .	Doubloon .	0.867	870	3 5 0
Brazil . . .	20-Milrei .	0.575	917	2 5 6
Chili . . .	Condor . .	0.492	900	1 18 2
Denmark . .	10-Thaler .	0.427	895	1 13 0
France . . .	20-Francs .	0.207	899	0 16 0
Germany . .	10-Thaler .	0.427	903	1 13 4
Great Britain .	Sovereign .	0.257	916	1 0 0
Greece . . .	20-Drachms	0.185	900	0 14 4
Holland . .	10-Guilder .	0.215	899	0 16 8
India . . .	Mohur . .	0.374	916	1 9 6
Japan . . .	Cobang . .	0.362	568	0 18 6
Persia . . .	Toman . .	...	885	0 5 3
Russia . . .	5-Rouble .	0.210	916	0 16 8
Spain . . .	Alfonso . .	0.268	896	1 0 8
Sweden . . .	Ducat . .	0.111	975	0 9 4
Turkey . . .	100-Piastres	0.231	915	0 18 2

Silver

Country	Name	Weight	Fineness	Value
		Oz.		£ s. d.
Austria . . .	Florin . .	0.397	900	0 2 0
,, . . .	Dollar . .	0.596	900	0 3 0
Bolivia . . .	Half-dollar .	0.432	667	0 1 8
Brazil . . .	Milrei . .	0.410	918	0 2 2
Chili . . .	Dollar . .	0.801	900	0 4 1
China . . .	Tael . . .	...	...	0 6 0
Denmark . .	2-Rigsdaler	0.927	877	0 4 7
France . . .	5-Francs .	0.800	900	0 4 0
Germany . .	Thaler . .	0.595	900	0 3 0
Great Britain .	Shilling . .	0.182	925	0 1 0
Greece . . .	5-Drachms .	0.719	900	0 3 8
Holland . .	2½-Guilder .	0.804	944	0 4 2
India . . .	Rupee . .	0.374	916	0 1 10
Japan . . .	Itzebu . .	0.279	890	0 1 5
Persia . . .	Kran . .	...	...	0 0 6
Russia . . .	Rouble . .	0.667	875	0 3 4
Spain . . .	Peseta . .	0.166	899	0 0 10
Sweden . . .	Rixdaler .	1.092	750	0 4 8
Turkey . . .	20-Piastres .	0.770	830	0 3 7

Some African tribes use cowrie-shells, 200 being value for 1d.

According to the best economists, the amount of money at various dates was approximately as follows :—

	Millions £ Sterling				
	Gold	Silver	Paper	Total	£ per Inhabitant
1600 . . .	1	2	...	3	0.6
1700 . . .	12	4	1	17	3.0
1800 . . .	37	8	25	70	4.4
1848 . . .	55	11	34	100	3.7
1890 . . .	102	22	39	163	4.4

The following table shows the principal gold coins in use from the fourteenth century to date :—

Name	Date	Nominal Value	In Present Money
		£ s. d.	£ s. d.
Noble . . .	1345	0 6 8	1 1 10
Angel . . .	1465	0 6 8	0 11 9
Crown . . .	1530	0 5 0	0 7 6
Sovereign . .	1551	1 10 0	1 8 0
Noble . . .	1600	0 15 0	0 16 0
Sovereign . .	1626	1 0 0	1 1 4

The amount of gold and silver coined from Henry III. to December 1889 was as follows :—

Reign	Gold	Silver	Total	Per Annum
	£	£	£	£
Henry III..	...	3,898	3,898	...
Edward I..	...	38,603	38,603	1,100
Edward II.	...	45,751	45,751	2,300
Edward III.	11,344	85,703	97,047	1,960
Richard II.	3,988	2,228	6,216	300
Henry IV..	396	315	711	...
Henry V..	19,746	6,924	26,670	3,000
Henry VI..	318,444	579,225	897,669	22,000
Edward IV.	10,248	47,843	58,091	2,700
Henry VII.	8,399	116,100	124,499	5,000
Henry VIII.	675,400	642,810	1,318,210	34,500
Mary . .	...	6,500	6,500	...
Elizabeth .	795,135	4,836,802	5,631,937	125,000
James I. .	3,666,400	1,807,300	5,473,700	248,000
Charles I. .	3,319,700	8,776,545	12,096,245	502,000
Cromwell .	154,512	1,000,000	1,154,512	115,000
Charles II.	4,177,254	3,722,180	7,899,434	320,000
James II. .	2,113,639	2,115,600	4,229,239	1,410,000
William III.	3,418,060	7,094,080	10,512,140	820,000
Anne . .	2,485,100	618,200	3,103,300	255,000
George I. .	8,492,900	223,050	8,715,950	670,000
George II..	11,662,200	304,360	11,966,560	360,000
George III.	75,447,489	6,827,800	82,275,289	1,370,000
George IV.	36,395,100	2,216,168	38,611,268	3,860,000
William IV.	10,920,035	1,122,100	12,042,135	1,720,000
Victoria .	312,300,000	231,800,000	544,100,000	10,300,000
Total .	476,390,489	274,040,085	750,430,574	...

Henry III. coined at Canterbury, Edward III. at York and Calais, Edward IV. at Bristol, the rest mostly at London. The coinage, however, of the present reign has been as follows :—

At	Gold, £	Silver, £	Total, £
London .	207,000,000	25,800,000	232,800,000
Sydney .	61,300,000	...	61,300,000
Melbourne .	42,000,000	...	42,000,000
India . .	2,000,000	206,000,000	208,000,000
Total .	312,300,000	231,800,000	544,100,000

It appears that Queen Victoria has coined 65 per cent. of the gold and 84 per cent. of the silver struck by British monarchs in 600 years. Shillings were first coined by Henry VIII. in 1544; crowns, half-crowns, sixpences, and threepennies by Edward VI. The percentage of alloy in British coins was as follows:—

Reigns	Per Cent.
Henry III. to Henry VII. . . .	8
Henry VIII.	33
Edward VI.	25

Queen Elizabeth improved the character of the coinage, but reduced the size of all coins: thus 3s. of her money had only the same quality of silver as 1s. of Edward I. The following table shows how much money was coined out of 12 oz. troy weight of either metal in successive reigns:—

Date	Gold, 12 oz. (24 carats)	Silver, 12 oz.	Reign
	£ s. d.	£ s. d.	
1280 . . .	12 10 0	1 0 3	Edward I.
1370 . . .	15 0 0	1 5 0	Edward III.
1420 . . .	16 13 4	1 10 0	Henry V.
1470 . . .	22 10 0	1 17 6	Edward IV.
1540 . . .	30 0 0	2 8 0	Henry VIII.
1550 . . .	36 0 0	3 12 0	Edward VI.
1590 . . .	33 0 0	3 12 0	Elizabeth
1640 . . .	44 10 0	3 2 0	Charles I.

The total amount of currency called in by Queen Elizabeth and re-minted was:—

	Oz.	Value, £
Gold . . .	360,000	1,080,000
Silver . . .	4,800,000	1,200,000

No change was made in the weight or value of coins from 1640 until 1816, in which latter year the pound of silver (12 oz. troy) was ordered to be made into 66s. instead of 62s. as before. The Mint thus established a seignorage or profit of 4s. an ounce on silver, but no charge is made on gold; the expense of coining gold is 10s. per £100. Silver money is legal tender only up to 40s.; gold to any amount.

The paper-money of the United Kingdom has been stationary since 1830, viz.:—

	1830	1890
	£	£
Bank of England . .	20,100,000	24,600,000
Other English banks. .	10,100,000	3,000,000
Scotch banks . . .	4,000,000	5,700,000
Irish banks . . .	4,200,000	5,800,000
Total . .	38,400,000	39,100,000

For details of the Bank of England see *Banks*.

The suspension of specie payments caused by the war against Bonaparte began in 1797 and lasted till 1821, the value of a £5 Bank of England note varying as follows:—

Gold Value of Bank of England £5 Note

Years	Shillings	Years	Shillings
1797–99 . . .	100	1813 . . .	73
1800–1 . . .	92	1814 . . .	80
1802–3 . . .	96	1815 . . .	84
1804–8 . . .	97	1816 . . .	96
1809 . . .	91	1817 . . .	98
1810 . . .	87	1818–19 . . .	97
1811 . . .	83	1820 . . .	100
1812 . . .	79		

In 1878 the currency of the Bank of England was found to be composed as follows:—

Value of Note	Number	Amount	Ratio per Cent.
£5 . . .	2,208,000	£11,040,000	39
£10 . . .	507,000	5,070,000	18
£20–50–100 .	160,000	8,030,000	28
£200–300–500 .	7,000	2,120,000	8
£1000 . . .	2,000	2,000,000	7
Total . .	2,884,000	£28,260,000	100

The notes cost one halfpenny each. The life of a bank-note in 1880 was under seventy days, the number issued during the year having been 15,260,000 for an aggregate amount of 338 millions, say £22 each. The average in the above table for 1878 is only £10 each.

According to the Mint report for 1890, the gold currency of the United Kingdom consists of about 80 million sovereigns and 45 million half-sovereigns, together £102,500,000.

FRANCE

The following is a table of old French coins:—

Date	Name	Value	Date	Name	Value
		£ s. d.			£ s. d.
1226	Angel	0 11 3	1507	Porcupine	0 9 0
1258	Tournois	0 0 9	1539	Salamander	0 9 0
1289	Esterlin	0 0 3	1550	Henri	0 9 5
1294	Royal	0 19 0	1575	Franc	0 2 3
1346	Couronne	0 15 0	1640	Louis	0 16 8
1428	Mouton	0 5 6	1652	,, silver	0 4 8
1430	Royal	0 10 4	1655	Lily, gold	0 10 6
1435	Ecu	0 8 4	1656	,, silver	0 1 5

The average value of the mark of silver and that of the livre are shown as follows from the thirteenth century:—

Date	Livres in One Mark of Silver	Francs in One Livre
1280–1300 . . .	3	19.00
1301–50 . . .	4	14.00
1351–1400 . . .	6	9.50
1401–50 . . .	8	7.00
1451–1500 . . .	11	5.20
1501–50 . . .	13	4.50
1551–1600 . . .	18	3.20
1601–50 . . .	28	2.00
1651–1700 . . .	33	1.70
1701–20 . . .	40	1.50
1726–89 . . .	55	1.00

The output of the French Mint in ninety-five years has been as follows:—

Date	Gold, £	Silver, £	Total, £	Government
1795–1815 .	21,200,000	39,800,000	61,000,000	Bonaparte
1816–30 .	17,600,000	49,900,000	67,500,000	Bourbons
1831–48 .	8,600,000	70,300,000	78,900,000	Louis Philippe
1849–52 .	17,000,000	18,400,000	35,400,000	Republic
1853–70 .	246,000,000	25,200,000	271,200,000	Napoleon III.
1871–89 .	40,100,000	17,200,000	57,300,000	Republic
95 years .	350,500,000	220,800,000	571,300,000	...

The amount of currency at various dates was estimated as follows:—

Year	Gold, £	Silver, £	Paper, £	Total, £
1805	3,000,000	99,000,000	2,000,000	104,000,000
1840	4,000,000	111,000,000	9,000,000	124,000,000
1889	178,000,000	150,000,000	115,000,000	443,000,000

Paper-money was first issued by John Law: the amount of his notes in 1719 reached 3000 million livres, or about 120 millions sterling.

The issue of assignats under the first Republic reached its maximum in 1790. namely, 9000 millions, or about 360 millions sterling. They fell to less than one-hundredth part of their nominal value: thus, a pair of boots cost' 7500, and a pound of butter 750 of these notes.

The currency of the Bank of France in 1883 was as follows :—

Notes, Francs	Number	Amount, £
5	175,000	35,000
20	198,000	158,000
25	28,000	28,000
50	4,725,000	9,450,000
100	10,812,000	43,248,000
200	3,000	24,000
500	625,000	12,496,000
1,000	1,263,300	50,532,000
5,000	5	1,000
Total . .	17,829,305	115,972,000

GERMANY

On the reconstitution of the German Empire the currency was remodelled, and the following amounts of coin issued from the Mint :—

Period	Gold	Silver	Nickel, &c.	Total
	£	£	£	£
1872–80	87,400,000	21,600,000	2,300,000	111,300,000
1881–89	34,100,000	1,600,000	...	35,700,000
18 years	121,500,000	23,200,000	2,300,000	147,000,000

The total currency in 1889 was approximately thus :—

	£
Gold	122,000,000
Silver	45,000,000
Bank-notes . . .	64,300,000
Treasury notes . . .	6,500,000
Total . .	237,800,000

The above, however, includes 22 millions sterling of old silver money no longer in circulation.

SCANDINAVIA

The total currency may be summed up thus :—

	Sweden	Norway	Denmark	Total
	£	£	£	£
Gold . . .	2,800,000	900,000	1,900,000	5,600,000
Silver . . .	900,000	300,000	1,000,000	2,200,000
Bank-notes .	6,200,000	2,400,000	4,400,000	13,000,000
Total . .	9,900,000	3,600,000	7,300,000	20,800,000

RUSSIA

The Mint issued in forty years down to 1890 as follows :—

	Tons	Value, £
Gold	1,102	154,100,000
Silver	2,580	23,500,000
Total . .	3,682	177,600,000

Notwithstanding the Siberian gold mines, which have produced 1500 tons of gold, worth 210 millions sterling, since 1820, Russia has been a prey to inconvertible notes.

These are the result of unscrupulous finances, the Government printing millions of roubles at will. The following table shows the issue :—

Year	Issue, Millions	Value, Pence	Year	Issue, Millions	Value, Pence
1774	20	38	1843	600	12
1786	100	36	1844	180	35
1796	160	24	1850	310	33
1800	210	18	1860	690	30
1810	580	12	1870	720	28
1817	870	9	1880	1,180	24
1823	605	10	1888	1,046	22

The conversion of 1843 consisted in calling in the old notes, and giving 30 new roubles for 100 old ones. The currency rose in 1890 to 26d. the paper rouble.

AUSTRIA

This country, like Russia, although producing gold, has been afflicted with inconvertible currency owing to reckless issues of paper-money. The amounts and the rate of exchange were approximately as follows :—

Date	Currency, Million Florins	Exchange, Pence	Gold Premium per Cent.
1788	20	24	...
1802	237	10	140
1811	1,060	4	500
1812	212	24	...
1816	639	6	300
1838	200	10	140
1876	635	20	20
1889	762	20	20

In 1811, the Empire being bankrupt, the notes were "converted," the holders getting one new note for five old ones, that is, losing 80 per cent. In 1816 the new notes had fallen to 25 per cent. of their nominal value, and a second conversion was made, holders getting two new notes for seven old ones. Thus the holders of 100 florins of currency in 1810 found themselves with six florins in 1817.

The value of the currency in the last twenty-two years has been as follows :—

Period	Florin, Pence	Gold Premium per Cent.
1867–70 . . .	19.7	22
1871–75 . . .	21.2	13
1876–80 . . .	20.2	19
1881–89 . . .	19.5	23

The paper-money in 1889 was as follows :—

	Florins	£ Nominal
Bank issue . . .	435,000,000	43,500,000
Treasury notes . .	327,000,000	32,700,000
Total . .	762,000,000	76,200,000

The current of bullion during twenty-five years was as follows :—

Period	Imported, £	Exported, £
1863–70 . . .	23,500,000	27,000,000
1871–80 . . .	35,300,000	26,200,000
1881–87 . . .	10,300,000	6,500,000
25 years . . .	69,100,000	59,700,000

The Hungarian Mint turned out in twenty years as follows :—

Period	Gold, £	Silver, £	Total, £
1867–80 . . .	3,100,000	7,000,000	10,100,000
1881–86 . . .	1,500,000	2,900,000	4,400,000
20 years . . .	4,600,000	9,900,000	14,500,000

The total coinage of the Empire from 1850 to 1890 was as follows :—

	Tons	Value, £
Gold	137	19,200,000
Silver . . .	5,360	48,200,000
Total . . .	...	67,400,000

ITALY

In consequence of the war with Austria in 1866, forced currency was given by the Government to Treasury notes and those of six chartered banks, with the following results :—

Year	Aggregate Issue, £	Specie Reserve, £	Gold, Premium per Cent.
1870	22,000,000	...	...
1874	35,000,000	...	13
1877	37,600,000	3,000,000	10
1880	65,000,000	...	10
1885	51,000,000	25,000,000	0
1888	56,800,000	11,100,000	0

The currency in December 1884 was composed thus:—

Note, Lire	Number	Value, Lire	£ Sterling
½ . . .	7,600,000	3,800,000	152,000
1 . . .	33,300,000	33,300,000	1,332,000
2 . . .	27,300,000	54,600,000	2,184,000
5 . . .	35,400,000	177,000,000	7,080,000
10 . . .	23,500,000	235,000,000	9,400,000
20 . . .	2,160,000	43,200,000	1,700,000
100 . . .	525,000	52,500,000	2,100,000
250 . . .	266,000	66,500,000	2,660,000
1,000 . . .	127,000	127,000,000	5,080,000
Total .	130,178,000	792,900,000	31,688,000

In 1888 the total paper issue was :—

	£
Treasury notes	13,800,000
Bank-notes	43,000,000
Total . . .	56,800,000

Italy resumed specie payments on April 12, 1883, after a suspension of sixteen years. The total of gold and silver minted in forty years to 1890 was as follows :—

	Tons	Value, £
Gold	123	17,200,000
Silver	2,530	22,800,000
Total . .	...	40,000,000

BELGIUM

The Mint returns for fifty-eight years show as follows :—

Period	Gold, £	Silver, £	Total, £
1832–60 . .	600,000	6,400,000	7,000,000
1861–70 . .	7,000,000	8,100,000	15,100,000
1871–80 . .	16,000,000	7,400,000	23,400,000
1881–89 . .	400,000	300,000	700,000
58 years . .	24,000,000	22,200,000	46,200,000

Copper and nickel money were also issued to £640,000 worth.

HOLLAND

The total currency in 1889 was as follows :—

	£	In Bank, £
Gold	5,000,000	2,000,000
Silver	13,000,000	5,000,000
Bank-notes . . .	17,300,000	...
Treasury notes .	1,000,000	...
Total . .	36,300,000	...

The coinage of forty years down to 1890 was as follows :—

	Tons	Value, £
Gold	48	6,700,000
Silver	3,290	29,700,000
Total . .	...	36,400,000

SPAIN AND PORTUGAL

In 1888 the currency of these kingdoms was estimated thus :—

	Spain, £	Portugal, £	Total, £
Gold . .	19,000,000	9,000,000	28,000,000
Silver . .	24,000,000	2,000,000	26,000,000
Bank-notes .	29,000,000	1,300,000	30,300,000
Total .	72,000,000	12,300,000	84,300,000

The total coinage from 1850 to 1881 was :—

	Gold, £	Silver, £	Total, £
Spain . . .	17,000,000	10,000,000	27,000,000
Portugal . .	13,000,000	2,000,000	15,000,000
Total .	30,000,000	12,000,000	42,000,000

UNITED STATES

The currency, according to American writers, was estimated at various dates thus :—

Year	Coin, £	Paper, £	Total, £
1820 . .	7,400,000	9,400,000	16,800,000
1849 . .	29,300,000	25,000,000	54,300,000
1854 . .	50,900,000	37,500,000	88,400,000
1880 . .	104,000,000	153,000,000	257,000,000
1889 . .	228,000,000	208,000,000	436,000,000

The components in 1880 and 1889 were as follows in American currency :—

	Millions of Dollars					
	Treasury		Banks and Public		Total	
	1880	1889	1880	1889	1880	1889
Gold . .	126	304	226	376	352	680
Silver .	74	315	75	106	149	421
Bank-notes .	7	4	338	207	345	211
Treasury notes .	40	89	349	699	389	788
Total .	247	712	988	1,388	1,235	2,100

The above may be converted into English money at $4.80 per £. The output of the Mint, computed in £ sterling, was as follows :—

Period	Gold, £	Silver, £	Total, £
1792–1820	1,300,000	2,200,000	3,500,000
1821–40 .	1,900,000	8,900,000	10,800,000
1841–50 .	19,800,000	4,500,000	24,300,000
1851–60 .	66,000,000	9,300,000	75,300,000
1861–70 .	60,400,000	4,600,000	65,000,000
1871–80 .	85,200,000	35,600,000	120,800,000
1881–89 .	73,200,000	58,900,000	132,100,000
98 years .	307,800,000	124,000,000	431,800,000

The Silver Law, passed by Congress in July 1890, obliges Government to coin $4,500,000 of silver monthly, equal to £11,300,000 sterling per annum.

The war for the Union in 1861 caused a suspension of specie payments, which lasted nineteen years. The quotations of paper-money were as follows :—

Year	Value compared with Gold			
	Maximum	Minimum	Average	Value of $100
				£ s. d.
1862 . .	98	75	88	18 6 0
1863 . .	79	62	69	14 6 6
1864 . .	64	39	49	10 4 0
1865 . .	74	46	64	13 6 4
1866 . .	79	66	71	14 15 0
1867 . .	74	70	72	14 19 0
1868 . .	74	69	72	14 19 0
1869 . .	82	72	75	15 12 0
1870 . .	90	82	87	18 2 0
1871 . .	92	87	90	18 14 0
1872 . .	92	87	89	18 10 0
1873 . .	92	85	88	18 6 0
1874 . .	91	88	90	18 14 0
1875 . .	89	85	87	18 2 0
1876 . .	93	87	90	18 14 0
1877 . .	97	94	96	19 19 0
1878 . .	...	...	98	20 7 0
1879 . .	100	100	100	20 16 0

The average for ten years ending 1870 was 75, and for the following decade 93.

PERSIA

The currency has been depreciated since 1875 by increasing the alloy in gold and silver coins. The kran has now but 71 grains of silver, against 83 in the year 1875, and the alloy of gold has been raised from 109 to 115 per 1000. The kran has fallen from a value of 10d. to 6½d., and the gold is at 45 per cent. premium. Baron Reuter has a concession to issue bank-notes up to £800,000, with bullion reserve 50 per cent.

JAPAN

In 1888 the currency was as follows :—

	£
Gold	19,000,000
Silver	9,000,000
Bank-notes	15,500,000
Treasury notes . . .	10,500,000
Total .	54,000,000

Paper-money is at a discount, gold being 25 per cent. premium.

ARGENTINA

The currency consists wholly of paper-money notes, ranging from one halfpenny up to £20 sterling. The halfpenny notes are nominally for 5 cents, the dollar being worth about 12d. In December 1884 the paper dollar

was worth 48d., but specie payments were suspended in January 1885, and the quotations since then have been :—

	Value of Dollar, Pence					
	1885	1886	1887	1888	1889	1890
January . . .	39.5	33.2	38.5	33.0	31.8	21.3
February . . .	37.5	32.6	37.2	32.2	31.0	21.3
March . . .	36.2	31.5	36.3	31.8	30.2	19.0
April	32.8	31.0	35.6	33.0	30.2	17.8
May	35.8	31.0	35.0	32.8	30.4	20.4
June	36.8	32.2	36.1	32.0	29.2	17.0
July	36.5	35.0	36.5	31.1	28.1	16.5
August . . .	33.5	36.8	37.2	32.0	27.4	19.2
September . .	34.0	40.1	36.0	32.5	23.7	19.0
October . . .	33.2	41.0	33.6	32.3	22.7	18.0
November . .	32.4	37.5	33.0	33.2	21.8	17.0
December . .	33.5	37.0	32.9	33.6	20.4	15.5
Average . . .	35.0	34.2	36.0	32.5	27.0	18.5

MONUMENTS

According to Strabo, the Tower of Babel was 600 feet high. The following are remarkable monuments and obelisks :—

Name	Locality	Height, Feet	Weight, Tons
Wellington .	Dublin . . .	205	1,000
Monument .	London . .	202	1,800
Nelson . .	London . .	177	1,500
Nelson . .	Dublin . . .	125	1,000
*Lateran . .	Rome . . .	105	445
Alexander .	St. Petersburg	84	200
*Vatican . .	Rome . . .	83	220
*Luxor . . .	Paris . . .	76	240
*Cleopatra .	London . .	68	140
*Meidan . .	Constantinople	50	60
*Quirinal . .	Rome . . .	48	60

In the foregoing table those marked with an asterisk are Egyptian monoliths, or real obelisks, of extreme antiquity. There is also a fine obelisk at Heliopolis, still standing. The second of Cleopatra's Needles has been removed to the United States, for erection in New York.

The height of certain edifices is as follows :—

	Feet		Feet
Eiffel Tower, Paris .	990	Freyburg Cathedral .	412
Cologne Cathedral . .	528	Salisbury Cathedral .	406
St. Nicholas, Hamburg	475	Florence Cathedral .	393
St. Peter's, Rome . .	472	St. Paul's, London . .	366
Strasburg Cathedral .	468	Milan Cathedral . .	360
Pyramid of Cheops .	452	Brussels Townhall .	355
St. Stephen's, Vienna .	445	Invalides, Paris . . .	346
Amiens Cathedral . .	440		

The diameter of the following domes and arches is :—

	Feet		Feet
Milan Cathedral . . .	55	St. Paul's, London . .	112
Pantheon, Paris . . .	67	St. Sophia	115
Invalides, Paris . . .	80	Sta. Maria, Florence .	139
Achmet's Mosque . .	92	St. Peter's, Rome . .	139

The cost of certain buildings is stated to have been :—

Opera House, Paris . . .	£1,600,000
Law Courts, Brussels . . .	1,200,000
Cathedral, Cologne . . .	2,100,000
Parliament, Westminster . .	3,500,000
St. Peter's, Rome	3,500,000

The Great Pyramid of Cheops has 85 million cubic feet of material, the Wall of China 6350 millions. The Pyramids are supposed to have been built 1500 B.C., the Wall of China 202 B.C. Next in antiquity are the Round Towers of Ireland, probably of the 6th century or earlier: there are 45, the highest at Kilmacduagh, Galway, 108 ft., diameter 18½ ft.

MOORS

The Moors built in Cordoba 4437 mosques, 4300 towers, 900 public baths, 28 squares, 80,400 shops, 60,000 palaces and hotels, and 213,000 houses. At Granada they built 1030 towers and 70,000 houses.

MORTGAGES

United Kingdom.—Lord Reay estimates the mortgages at 58 per cent. in England of the value of real estate. In Ireland, according to Commissioner Greene, they amount to 40 per cent., say 120 millions sterling.

France.—New mortgages average 30 millions sterling per annum: on December 31, 1876, all existing mortgages were officially estimated at 575 millions sterling.

Germany.—In 1870 the mortgages in Prussia reached 190, and in all Germany 273, millions sterling. Professor Meitzen, however, considers that 41 per cent. of all real estate in the Empire is mortgaged. An official return for 1883 shows that the houses of Berlin were mortgaged for 105 millions sterling, being 67 per cent. of their assessed value.

Russia.—Mortgages on land are known to reach 148 millions sterling, but probably amount to much more.

Austria.—In 1860 the amount on mortgage was 165 millions sterling, average interest 5 per cent.: in 1884 the amount was 320 millions sterling. The new mortgages registered in the years 1876 and 1884 were:—

	1876	1884
	£	£
Austria . . .	4,400,000	2,400,000
Hungary . . .	5,600,000	6,400,000
Total .	10,000,000	8,800,000

Belgium.—The registration of mortgages was as follows:—

Year					Amount, £
1860	.	.	.	.	3,400,000
1870	.	.	.	.	4,400,000
1886	.	.	.	.	8,200,000

Holland.—In 1883 the existing mortgages were 77 millions sterling, as against £37,500,000 in 1869.

Spain.—Estimated amount, 172 millions sterling; annual average of new mortgages, £8,500,000.

Italy.—The total reaches 580 millions sterling, but of this sum only 288 millions bear interest.

Norway.—The amount of mortgage bonds is £4,600,000 sterling.

New Zealand.—New mortgages average £9,000,000 per annum; releases, one-third of that amount.

Australia.—The colony of New South Wales had new mortgages for 113 millions sterling between 1876 and 1888.

Argentina.—Cedulas or mortgage-bonds in 1890 amounted to 450 million dollars, nominally 90 millions sterling.

Egypt.—New mortgages average £1,300,000 per annum.

Canada.—Sir R. Cartwright ascertained in 1889 that Ontario had mortgages to the amount of 42 millions sterling.

United States.—Commissioner Loring summed up the mortgages during thirty-eight years in one of the Western States, and found:—

No. of mortgages	.	.	.	.	200,000
Amount	.	.	.	.	£36,000,000
Paid off	.	.	.	.	20,400,000
Still due	.	.	.	.	15,600,000

The name of the State is not given.

MOUNTAINS

Some of the most remarkable are:—

	Feet		Feet
Gibraltar . .	1,432	Morrison . .	12,847
Snowdon . .	3,571	Fuziyama . .	14,180
Vesuvius . .	3,978	Big Horn . .	14,430
Ben Nevis . .	4,358	Blanc . . .	15,781
Puy-Dome . .	4,750	Ararat . .	17,266
Olympus . .	6,500	Orizaba . .	17,371
Sinai . .	7,500	Kaa Mowna .	18,400
Kosciusko . .	7,176	Elburz . .	18,514
Ankaratra . .	8,887	Kilimanjaro .	18,800
Lebanon . .	9,520	Cotopaxi . .	19,620
Etna . .	10,963	Wrangel . .	20,000
St. Bernard . .	11,006	Schopenhauer .	20,073
Petermann . .	11,400	Chimborazo .	21,440
Egmont . .	11,433	Illimani . .	24,450
Teneriffe . .	12,036	Sorata . .	25,250
Cook . .	12,400	Everest . .	29,002

Everest is the highest of the Himalayas, Schopenhauer is in New Guinea, Wrangel in North America, Morrison in Formosa, Petermann in Greenland, Ankaratra in Madagascar, and Kosciusko in Australia. The greatest height attained by Humboldt was 19,510 feet, in the Andes, but Mr. Whymper, in 1880, ascended Cotopaxi to 19,620 feet, and Chimborazo to 20,545 feet, and W. Graham in 1883 the Kabru peak of the Himalayas to 23,500 feet, the greatest height yet attained by any individual. The passes of the Alps and the Andes are:—

Alps	Feet over Sea	Andes	Feet over Sea
St. Gothard .	6,848	Bariloche . .	2,770
Simplon . .	6,616	Antuco . .	6,930
St. Bernard .	8,158	Planchon . .	8,225
Little St. Bernard .	6,576	Uspallata . .	12,870
Mont Cenis .	6,818	Patos . .	13,200
Madelaine .	6,584	Humahuaca . .	14,060
Col di Tenda .	5,925	Portillo . .	13,860

There are carriage-roads over all the above Alpine passes except the St. Gothard and St. Bernard. There are none over the Andes, but a railway is in construction over the Uspallata Pass.

MUNIFICENCE

Donor	£	Locality	Object
Astor . .	100,000	New York	Library
Baird . .	500,000	Aberdeen	Church
Berridge . .	200,000	London	Schools
Cooper . .	160,000	New York	Schools
Crossley . .	100,000	Yorkshire	Orphanage
Day . .	100,000	London	Blind
Firth . .	100,000	Sheffield	Asylum
Galignani . .	100,000	Paris	Asylum
Galliera . .	400,000	Genoa	Hospitals
Gardner . .	300,000	London	Blind
Guinness . .	150,000	Dublin	Church
Guinness . .	200,000	London	Lodging-house
Guy . .	240,000	London	Hospital
Holloway . .	350,000	London	Hospital
Jeejeebhoy . .	500,000	Bombay	Schools
Lick . .	200,000	California	Observatory
Mason . .	430,000	Birmingham	Orphanage
M'Calmont . .	100,000	London	Hospital
M'Kellar . .	100,000	London	Schools
Peabody . .	500,000	London	Lodging-house
Quinn . .	200,000	Newry	Aged
Robinson . .	100,000	New York	Schools
Ross . .	200,000	Glasgow	Hospitals
Rossini . .	100,000	Paris	Asylum
Rowe . .	120,000	Dublin	Church
Rylands . .	200,000	Birmingham	Asylum
Salt . .	100,000	Yorkshire	Hospital
Stewart . .	150,000	New York	Hospital
Sturge . .	300,000	London	Asylum
Urquijo . .	180,000	Madrid	Orphanage
Vanderbilt . .	200,000	New York	Asylum
Whitworth . .	100,000	Manchester	Schools

MURDER

According to Professor Bodio (see p. 162), the number of criminals tried for murder in the years 1876–84 averaged as follows :—

	Number Yearly	Per Million Population
United Kingdom .	450	12
France . . .	816	23
Germany . .	602	14
Hungary . .	1,682	107
Italy . • • •	3,712	134
Spain . . .	1,807	105

MUSIC

In 1890, at an auction in London, the following prices were obtained for copyrights of songs :—

Song	Composer	Price, £
Wild Winds	Mattei	611
In the Gloaming . . .	Lady Hill	286
The Old Way . . .	Roeckel	253
Jolly Smiths	Leslie	265
Kathleen Mavourneen . .	Crouch	400

The price of "Wild Winds" (Odi tu) is the highest on record.

N.

NAMES

The ratio in England per 1000 shows :—

Mary . . . 68	Thomas . . . 39	James . . . 31	Joseph . . . 18
William . . . 66	George . . . 36	Charles . . . 23	Jane . . . 17
John . . . 62	Sarah . . . 36	Henry . . . 21	Ellen . . . 16
Eliza . . . 61	Anne . . . 33	Alice . . . 19	

NATIONS

	Square Miles	Population	Steam-Power	Millions £ Sterling		
				Revenue	Commerce	Wealth
United Kingdom . . .	121,000	38,000,000	9,200,000	89	740	9,400
France	201,000	38,500,000	4,520,000	122	311	8,598
Germany	212,000	48,000,000	6,200,000	155	367	6,437
Russia	2,262,000	92,000,000	2,240,000	89	118	5,089
Austria	269,000	40,000,000	2,150,000	75	92	3,855
Italy	114,000	30,000,000	830,000	72	94	2,963
Spain	183,000	18,000,000	740,000	35	59	2,516
Portugal	37,000	4,700,000	80,000	8	18	408
Sweden	171,000	4,800,000	300,000	5	30	637
Norway	122,000	2,000,000	180,000	2	16	243
Denmark	15,000	2,000,000	150,000	3	26	404
Holland	21,000	4,500,000	340,000	10	199	980
Belgium	11,000	6,100,000	810,000	13	111	1,007
Switzerland	16,000	3,000,000	290,000	3	60	494
Greece	20,000	2,000,000	} 600,000 {	3	7	300
Roumania	48,000	5,500,000		6	23	593
Servia	21,000	2,000,000		2	4	217
Bulgaria	39,000	3,000,000		3	6	205
Turkey	67,000	4,700,000		16	33	593
Europe	3,950,000	348,300,000	28,630,000	711	2,314	44,939
United States . .	3,604,000	62,500,000	14,400,000	81	320	12,824
Canada	3,372,000	5,100,000	...	8	42	980
Mexico	751,000	10,500,000	...	5	20	638
Central America . .	169,000	3,000,000	...	2	7	...
Venezuela	567,000	2,500,000	...	1	6	...
Peru	405,000	3,000,000	...	1	3	...
Ecuador	248,000	1,100,000	...	1	4	...
Columbia	331,000	4,000,000	...	3	4	...
Chili	257,000	2,600,000	...	5	14	...
Bolivia	472,000	2,300,000	...	1	2	...
Argentina	1,095,000	3,600,000	...	5	27	509
Uruguay	72,000	600,000	...	2	12	100
Brazil	3,288,000	12,400,000	...	14	41	...
Australia	3,104,000	3,700,000	...	28	130	1,373
South Africa . . .	230,000	1,900,000	...	4	19	135
Algeria	123,000	3,800,000	...	2	17	...
Egypt	494,000	6,800,000	...	10	19	...
India	870,000	215,000,000	...	83	131	...
Siberia	6,179,000	9,400,000	...	...	8	...
China	3,925,000	320,000,000	...	26	49	...
Persia	636,000	7,600,000	...	2	8	...
Java	51,000	18,000,000	...	10	30	...
Japan	148,000	38,000,000	...	13	22	...
Total . . .	34,341,000	1,085,700,000	50,150,000	1,018	3,249	...

NAVY

The following is a table of the principal navies :—

	1810		1840		1889	
	Ships	Guns	Ships	Guns	Ships	Guns
G. Britain .	450	24,800	392	16,310	373	1,460
France . .	212	6,000	146	7,600	348	1,450
Germany .	...	...	...	...	101	519
Russia . .	346	4,450	83	5,460	391	942
Austria . .	...	...	...	...	106	295
Italy . . .	36	200	...	...	140	318
Spain . .	301	8,000	57	1,200	135	492
Holland .	76	1,600	30	1,640	147	560
Turkey . .	42	1,700	33	2,440	90	200
U. States .	158	526	60	3,250	75	542
Various . .	60	1,300	57	2,779	385	1,605
Total .	1,681	48,576	858	40,679	2,291	8,383

The average of guns to a vessel was 29 in 1810, rising to 46 in 1840, and declining to less than 4 in 1889. Modern naval warfare has been changed by the invention of armour-plated ships, the first of which were built for the Crimean war, 4-inch plates perfectly shot-proof, in 1853. The *Merrimacs* and *Monitors* of the United States in 1862 marked a great advance. Finally, the Italians used plates 36 inches thick for the *Lepanto*. The ironclad fleets of the world stand at present approximately as follows :—

	Vessels	Tons	Max. Plating, Inches	Guns	Tonnage of Guns
Great Britain	66	460,000	24	610	9,100
France . .	52	310,000	22	470	6,500
Germany .	27	104,000	12	160	2,200
Russia . .	40	160,000	16	421	4,600
Austria . .	10	55,000	14	137	1,500
Italy . . .	14	82,000	36	110	2,200
Spain . .	13	35,000	20	254	900
Portugal .	1	2,000	8	3	30
Sweden . .	15	8,000	12	24	90
Norway . .	4	2,000	...	12	50
Denmark .	8	25,000	12	107	900
Holland . .	24	45,000	8	72	800
Greece . .	4	7,000	...	24	...
Turkey . .	15	61,000	12	134	1,340
United States	13	40,000	12	74	...
Brazil . .	12	15,000	12	60	...
Argentina .	3	8,000	9	15	...
Chili . . .	3	9,000	9	22	220
China . .	9	38,000	14	50	...
Japan . .	1	4,000	9	6	60
Total .	334	1,470,000	36	2,765	30,490

The average cost of building ironclads has been, per ton: British £48, French £55, Italian £57, German £60. Including guns and equipment, an ordinary ironclad now costs £80 per ton. The largest war-vessels now are :—

Name	Flag	Tons	Horse-Power
Italia	Italian . . .	13,900	18,000
Trafalgar . .	British . . .	12,000	12,000
Formidable . .	French . . .	11,400	8,300
Catherine . . .	Russian . .	10,200	9,000
Pelayo . . .	Spanish . .	10,000	8,000
Wilhelm . . .	German . .	9,800	8,000
Mesoudiyé . . .	Turkish . .	8,800	6,800
Tegethoff . . .	Austrian . .	7,400	5,000
Ting	Chinese . .	7,300	6,000
Maine	United States	6,600	8,600
Heligoland . .	Danish . .	5,400	4,000
Koenig	Holland . .	5,400	4,500

The following comparison of navies was published in the *Daily News*, 1890 :—

	Great Britain	France	Germany	Russia	Italy
Sea-going ironclads .	56	33	13	22	21
Cruisers (16 knots) . .	28	17	7	2	3
Coast ironclads . . .	6	21	12	13	...
Gunboats	95	45	12	36	15
Various	185	190	131	188	124
Total . . .	370	306	175	261	163

The same paper says: "In ships we are well ahead of any competitor. It is in the matter of guns that our weakness lies. We have afloat or ready to go afloat 1065 modern heavy guns; France has 1447, Russia has 423, Italy has 180, and Germany has 508. When all our war-ships are armed, we shall have afloat of guns that can pierce 15 in. of armour and upwards 104, while France will have 124, Russia 38, Italy 40, and Germany 61."

The torpedo fleets of the various flags are as follows :—

Great Britain	.	.	165	Austria .	. .	42
France	.	.	175	Holland	. .	31
Germany	.	.	135	Brazil .	. .	18
Russia	.	.	185	Chili	. .	25
Italy .	.	.	116	Turkey .	. .	52
Spain .	.	.	26	China .	. .	31
Sweden .	.	.	19	Portugal	. .	6
Denmark	.	.	42	Argentina	.	9

The number of seamen and annual cost of the navies are :—

	Men	Annual Expenditure, £	Per Man, £
Great Britain . .	65,000	13,700,000	211
France . . .	54,000	9,000,000	165
Germany . .	16,600	2,000,000	120
Russia . . .	29,000	4,000,000	140
Austria . . .	8,500	900,000	106
Italy . . .	13,000	5,000,000	386
Spain . . .	14,000	1,600,000	114
Holland . .	8,000	1,100,000	138
Turkey . . .	39,500	800,000	20
United States .	10,000	3,000,000	300
Total .	257,600	41,100,000	160

GREAT BRITAIN

The statistics of the Royal Navy may be summed up as follows :—

Year	Vessels	Tons	Guns	Men	Cost per Annum, £
1603 . .	42	17,000	...	...	180,000
1685 . .	179	104,000	6,930	10,000	390,000
1760 . .	325	321,000	10,600	51,000	5,611,000
1803 . .	450	461,000	24,800	180,000	12,037,000
1850 . .	585	570,000	17,200	48,000	6,438,000
1890 . .	373	680,000	1,460	65,000	13,700,000

When Philip II. sent the Armada in 1588 for the conquest of England it comprised :—

Ships	.	.	132	Seamen . . . 10,854
Cannon	.	.	3,165	Soldiers . . . 23,200

The British fleet under Lord Howard, supported by Drake and Hawkins, consisted of :—

	Royal Navy	Vessels Hired	Total
Ships . . .	41	135	176
Tonnage . .	16,000	18,500	34,500
Seamen . .	8,200	6,600	14,800

The Spaniards lost 35 ships and 13,600 men. During the wars with Bonaparte, according to Haydn, the British navy captured or destroyed the following :—

Ships of the line	.	207	French	.	.	.	683
Frigates	.	351	Spanish	.	.	.	213
Corvettes	.	552	Various	.	.	.	214
Total	.	1,110	Total	.	.	1,110

The above is exclusive of 1396 brigs and small vessels.

In 1888 the Channel Fleet consisted as follows :—

	Tons	Guns	Broadsides, Lbs.	Men
Inflexible . .	11,880	4	3,400	460
Northumberland .	10,780	27	2,630	710
Agincourt .	10,690	17	2,150	710
Benbow .	10,600	12	2,300	500
Rodney .	10,300	10	2,300	500
64 others .	185,750	354	32,720	12,120
Total .	240,000	424	45,500	15,100

The Channel Fleet represents nearly one-third of the strength of the British navy.

The strength of the navy in 1889 was as follows :—

	Number	In Commission	
		Number	Guns
Ironclads . . .	66	32	310
Steamers . . .	292	172	790
Sailing	212	63	380
Torpedo-boats . .	146	13	...
Total . .	716	280	1,480

The navy counts 65,000 seamen, including 14,000 marines and 5300 coastguards. In fifteen years ending 1880 the cost of vessels built was as follows :—

Built by	Tons			Cost, £		
	Iron	Wooden	Total	Iron	Wooden	Total
Government	123,000	85,000	208,000	5,466,000	3,964,000	9,430,000
Contractors	55,000	41,000	96,000	2,709,000	2,321,000	5,030,000
Total . .	178,000	126,000	304,000	8,175,000	6,285,000	14,460,000

The cost of construction per ton of displacement was less in Government yards, but less per ton of hull in contractors' yards, viz. :—

	Dockyard	Contractors'
	£ s. d.	£ s. d.
Per ton displacement .	45 7 0	52 8 0
Per ton of hull . . .	43 8 0	41 12 0

The cost of French ironclads built in State dockyards has been 30 per cent. more than those built by contractors. Lord Brassey gives the cost of vessels built for the British and French fighting navies since 1864 thus :—

Period	England, £	France, £
1864–70 . . .	9,900,000	5,700,000
1871–80 . . .	15,700,000	9,900,000
1881–90 . . .	24,200,000	16,100,000
27 years . . .	49,800,000	31,700,000

The cost of the effective ships afloat has been as follows :—

		Number	£
Ironclads		66	24,000,000
Torpedo-boats . . .		146	1,500,000
Steamers, &c. . . .		161	11,100,000
Total . .		373	36,600,000

There are in construction 11 ironclads and 128 other vessels, to be completed before 1894, at a cost of 22 millions sterling. In 1889 there were 26 war-vessels launched, besides 23 new torpedo-boats, and the most remarkable were :—

Name	Tons	Horse-Power	Cost, £	Speed, Knots per Hour
Blake . . .	9,000	20,000	440,000	22
Vulcan . . .	6,600	12,000	300,000	20
Barham . .	1,800	6,000	100,000	19
Blanche . .	1,600	3,000	100,000	16

The *Blake* is 400 ft. long, 65 ft. beam, and carries two 24-ton guns and 10 smaller : the hull cost £213,000, the engines £134,000, the guns £25,000 (£310 per ton), and the fittings £68,000. Lord Armstrong, comparing the new ship *Victoria* with Nelson's ship *Victory*, says :— "Nelson's heaviest shot was 68 lbs.; but the *Victoria's* weighs 1800 lbs.; his broadside consumed 325 lbs. of powder, that of the *Victoria* 3000 lbs. He required one man to every 4 tons, but now we can do with one man for 17 tons." A first-class ironclad, built of steel, has this weight :—

						Tons
Hull .	.	.	.	.	.	3,400
Plating	.	.	.	.	.	2,800
Machinery .	.	.	.	.	.	1,400
Guns, &c. .	.	.	.	.	.	1,100
Coal, &c. .	.	.	.	.	.	1,370
				Total	.	10,070

FRANCE

The strength at various dates has been as follows :—

Year	Vessels	Guns	Men
1780 . . .	266	13,300	78,000
1810 . .	212	6,000	94,000
1840 . . .	146	7,600	24,500
1868 . .	480	2,750	43,100
1889 . . .	348	1,450	54,000

The expenditure has averaged yearly approximately thus :—

Period					£
1831–50 .	.	.	.	.	3,400,000
1851–70 .	.	.	.	.	5,700,000
1871–88 .	.	.	.	.	9,400,000

In 1889 the navy comprised 52 ironclads and 296 smaller vessels, the total valued at £20,100,000, and carrying 29,000 blue-jackets, 25,000 marines, and 1450 guns. Some of the heaviest vessels are :—

	Tons	Armour, Inches	Guns	Horse-Power	Knots per Hour
Formidable .	11,400	22	15	8,300	15
Duperrè . .	10,500	22	19	8,000	15
Baudin . . .	11,200	22	15	8,000	15
Duquesne . .	5,700	...	21	8,000	17
Courbet . .	9,500	15	14	8,000	15

In 1882 the following comparative table of the French and British ironclad fleets was published :—

	Vessels	Tonnage of Guns	Per Ship
British . . .	51	7,030	138
French . . .	59	5,960	101

In 1869 the largest vessel in the French navy was the *Magenta*, 1000 horse-power, being one-eighth of that of the present first-class ironclads.

GERMANY

In 1888 the fleet was composed thus :—

	Number	Guns	Tons	Horse-Power	Men
Ironclads . .	27	160	104,000	84,000	7,300
Frigates . .	9	122	28,000	28,000	3,700
Corvettes, &c. .	65	237	50,000	56,000	5,600
Total .	101	519	182,000	168,000	16,600

The heaviest ships are the following :—

	Tons	Horse-Power	Guns	Armour, Inches
Wilhelm . .	9,800	8,000	29	12
Kaiser . .	7,700	8,000	15	10

The navy costs £2,000,000 per annum.

RUSSIA

The strength of the Russian navy at various dates was :—

Year					Ships	Guns
1779	.	.	.	.	56	3,400
1791	.	.	.	.	94	5,200
1810	.	.	.	.	346	4,450
1840	.	.	.	.	83	5,460
1868	.	.	.	.	292	3,690
1889	.	.	.	.	391	942

The navy in 1889 was as follows :—

Fleets	Ironclads	Other Vessels	Total
Baltic . . .	26	209	235
Black Sea . .	5	67	72
Caspian . . .	9	14	23
Siberian, &c. . .	...	61	61
Total .	40	351	391

	Guns	Tons	Horse-Power
Ironclads . .	421	160,000	17,000
Steamers, &c. .	521	126,000	32,000
Total .	942	286,000	49,000

The whole manned by 29,000 officers and men.

The heaviest ships are : —

Name	Tons	Horse-Power	Guns	Armour, Inches	Knots per Hour
Sinope . . .	10,200	9,000	13	16	16
Catherine . .	10,200	9,000	13	16	16

The navy costs £4,000,000 per annum.

HOLLAND

In 1888 the navy comprised 24 ironclads and 123 corvettes and smaller vessels, carrying 560 guns and 8000 men, the heaviest ship being the *King of Holland*, 5400 tons, 4500 horse-power, 8 guns, 8-inch armour, speed 12 knots. The navy costs £1,100,000 a year.

AUSTRIA

The actual strength is as follows :—

	Number	Tons	Horse-Power	Guns	Men
Ironclads . . .	10	55,000	11,000	137	4,000
Corvettes, &c. .	96	69,000	13,000	158	7,000
Total . .	106	124,000	24,000	295	11,000

The heaviest vessels are :—

	Tons	Horse-Power	Guns	Armour, Inches	Knots per Hour
Tegetthoff . .	7,400	5,000	6	14	14
Custozza . .	7,000	4,500	8	9	14

The navy costs £900,000 per annum, and is manned by 8500 men.

ITALY

The navy is composed as follows :—

	Vessels	Guns	Tons	Horse-Power	Men
Ironclads . . .	14	110	82,000	64,000	6,000
Corvettes, &c. .	23	117	34,000	41,000	4,000
Small vessels .	103	91	34,000	35,000	3,000
Total . .	140	318	150,000	140,000	13,000

The heaviest ships are :—

	Tons	Horse-Power	Guns	Armour, Inches	Knots per Hour
Italia . .	13,900	18,000	12	36	18
Lepanto .	13,600	18,000	12	36	18
Humberto .	13,300	15,200	12	36	18

There are 17,000 officers and seamen, the navy costing £5,000,000 sterling per annum.

SPAIN

In 1889 the naval strength was as follows :—

	Number	Guns	Horse-Power
Ironclads . . .	13	254	19,000
Other vessels . .	122	238	46,000
Total . .	135	492	65,000

The fleet is manned by 14,000 men. The largest ship is the *Pelayo*, 10,000 tons, 8000 horse-power, armour 20 inches, carrying 17 guns. The navy in 1708 was one of the greatest in Europe, manned by 16,400 seamen.

PORTUGAL

The actual strength is as follows :—

	Number	Guns	Horse-Power
Steam . . .	38	139	20,000
Sail	15	42	...
Total . .	53	181	20,000

There are 3000 seamen. The only ironclad is the *Vasco da Gama*, 2400 tons, 3200 horse-power, 8-inch armour, speed 13 knots. The navy costs £250,000 a year.

SWEDEN

The navy is composed thus :—

	Number	Horse-Power	Guns
Ironclads . . .	15	6,000	24
Corvettes, &c. . .	53	22,000	127
Total . .	68	28,000	151

The heaviest ship is the *Scea*, 12-inch armour, 2900 tons, 6 guns, and 3100 horse-power. The fleet has 4000 seamen, and costs £350,000 a year.

NORWAY

The fleet counts as follows :—

	Number	Horse-Power	Guns
Ironclads . . .	4	1,800	12
Corvettes, &c. . .	17	8,000	157
Small boats . .	27	4,200	23
Total .	48	14,000	192

They are manned by *1100* men ; naval reserve, 27,000. The cost of the navy is £110,000 a year.

DENMARK

The navy before its destruction by Nelson consisted in 1805 of 35 vessels, carrying 2350 guns. In 1850 it counted 25 vessels with 940 guns. The present strength is :—

	Number	Horse-Power	Guns
Ironclads . . .	8	19,000	107
Corvettes, &c. . .	31	18,000	122
Total . .	39	37,000	229

The heaviest vessel is the *Heligoland*, 12-inch armour, 5400 tons, 4000 horse-power, 5 guns, speed 14 knots. The navy costs £600,000 a year.

GREECE

The actual strength is :—

	Number	Tons	Guns
Ironclads . . .	4	7,000	24
Brigs, &c. . . .	31	...	176
Total . .	35	...	200

The whole is manned by 2900 men. The heaviest ship is the *Olga*, 2000 tons, 6 guns, 10 knots. The navy costs £160,000 a year.

TURKEY

The navy comprises 15 ironclads, 15 corvettes, 60 gunboats, &c., the whole carrying 200 guns, and supposed to be manned by 30,000 blue-jackets, and 9500 marines. The Turkish navy has been repeatedly almost annihilated. At Lepanto in 1571, Ali Pacha's fleet counted 372 vessels, manned by 120,000 men ; that of Don John of Austria, 208 vessels with 80,000 men. The Turks lost 175 captured and 129 sunk or burnt, only 68 escaping. Again, at Navarino in 1827, the English and French destroyed 30 Turkish war-vessels, and in 1853 the Russians at Sinope destroyed an Ottoman fleet of 11 vessels with 4000 men.

At present the heaviest ships are :—

	Tons	Horse-Power	Guns	Armour, Inches	Knots per Hour
Mesoudiyè. .	8,800	6,800	12	12	14
Hamidieh . .	6,500	4,500	9	9	13

The navy costs £800,000 a year.

BRAZIL

The fleet comprises 12 ironclads and 30 war-steamers, carrying 222 guns and 6000 men. The heaviest vessel is the *Jaoarè*, 3500 tons, 2200 horse-power, 4 guns, 12-inch armour. The navy costs £1,100,000 a year.

ARGENTINA

The actual strength is 3 ironclads and 16 gunboats, carrying 58 guns and 1500 men. The *Admiral Brown* is 4200 tons, 5400 horse-power, 8 guns, 9-inch armour. The navy costs £300,000 a year.

CHILI

There are 3 ironclads and 18 smaller vessels, carrying 55 guns and 2000 men. The *Cochrane* is 3500 tons, 2900 horse-power, 9-inch armour, 3 guns, speed 12 knots. A steel ironclad of 6000 tons is in construction.

UNITED STATES

The strength of the navy at various dates was :—

	Vessels	Guns
1812	158	526
1815	276	1,636
1840	60	3,250
1865	684	4,477
1888	75	542

Americans are fairly entitled to claim the invention of ironclad war-vessels. In 1811 Robert Stevens of New Jersey, a youth of twenty-two years, proposed iron-plating for ships, and in 1842 made a contract with the Navy Department for ironclad floating batteries. Ericcson invented turret-ships in 1860 with plates 8-inch thick, carrying a pair of 15-inch guns.

The actual fleet comprises 13 ironclads, 37 corvettes, and 25 small vessels, manned by 8000 blue-jackets. and 2000 marines. The sums spent on the navy have averaged yearly thus :—

Period	£
1801–40	700,000
1841–60	1,900,000
1861–70	7,500,000
1871–80	4,000,000
1881–88	3,100,000

Congress has recently ordered the construction of 1c ironclads and 18 other vessels. The *Puritan*, *Maine*, and *Texas* will be each over 6000 tons, 8000 horse-power, 12-inch armour, speed 17 knots. The new corvette *Baltimore*, 10,000 horse-power, goes 20 knots.

JAPAŃ.

The navy is as follows :—

	Number	Guns	Tons	Horse-Power	Knots
Ironclad . . .	1	6	3,700	3,500	13
Corvettes, &c. .	24	169	35,400	31,000	...
Total . .	25	175	39,100	34,500	...

The vessels are manned by 5000 blue-jackets, and cost £800,000 a year.

CHINA

In 1888 the navy comprised 9 ironclads and 121 small vessels. The heaviest vessels were the *Ting* and *Chen*, each 7300 tons, 6000 horse-power, 14-inch plating, with 4 Krupp guns of 12-inch bore.

NIGHT

The following table shows the longest and shortest nights, according to latitude :—

Latitude	Longest		Shortest	
	Hours	Minutes	Hours	Minutes
5 . . .	12	17	11	43
15 . . .	12	53	11	7
25 . . .	13	34	10	26
35 . . .	14	22	9	38
45 . . .	15	26	8	34
50 . . .	16	9	7	51
55 . . .	17	7	6	53
60 . . .	18	30	5	30
65 . . .	21	10	2	50

At 66½ north or south the midnight sun is visible in summer. The above table is equally true of the length of days.

NOBLES

In Austria-Hungary the number declines, viz. :—

	1840	1865
Austria	140,000	87,000
Hungary	260,000	163,400
Total . .	400,000	250,400

In Spain they are as follows :—

	Grandees	Only Titular	Total
Dukes . .	79	2	81
Marquises . .	60	615	675
Counts . .	60	480	540
Barons . .	4	156	160
Total .	203	1,253	1,456

The British House of Lords comprises 4 princes, **23** dukes, 19 marquises, 139 earls, 32 viscounts, 26 bishops, and 272 barons; in all, **515** members.

The total nobility of the United Kingdom is as follows :—

	Dukes	Marquises	Earls	Viscounts	Barons	Total
England . .	27	21	120	28	294	490
Scotland . .	8	4	43	5	25	85
Ireland . .	2	11	64	36	64	177
Total .	37	36	227	69	383	752

There are also 26 English bishops who rank as peers.

O.

OCCUPATION

The following table shows approximately the number of persons supported by the principal industries in the several countries :—

	Agriculture	Manufactures	Commerce, &c.	Total
England .	3,435,000	7,313,000	15,226,000	25,974,000
Scotland .	523,000	1,155,000	2,058,000	3,736,000
Ireland . .	2,562,000	640,000	1,898,000	5,100,000
U. Kingdom	6,520,000	9,108,000	19,182,000	34,810,000
France . .	18,249,000	8,194,000	10,035,000	36,478,000
Germany .	18,841,000	16,058,000	10,323,000	45,222,000
Russia . .	56,815,000	10,520,000	8,965,000	76,300,000
Austria . .	16,710,000	5,499,000	12,252,000	34,461,000
Italy . . .	9,169,000	4,494,000	12,007,000	25,670,000
Spain . .	8,170,000	3,490,000	5,040,000	16,700,000
Portugal .	3,200,000	700,000	300,000	4,200,000
Sweden . .	2,130,000	850,000	1,520,000	4,500,000
Norway . .	903,000	306,000	598,000	1,807,000
Denmark .	940,000	560,000	450,000	1,950,000
Belgium . .	1,200,000	1,910,000	2,390,000	5,500,000
Holland . .	2,600,000	900,000	800,000	4,300,000
Switzerland .	1,140,000	970,000	730,000	2,840,000
Greece . .	940,000	260,000	440,000	1,640,000
Europe . .	147,527,000	63,819,000	85,032,000	296,378,000
U. States .	23,010,000	11,520,000	15,620,000	50,150,000
Australia .	1,200,000	950,000	1,450,000	3,600,000
Total .	171,737,000	76,289,000	102,102,000	350,128,000

As the Census returns of different countries adopt no uniform classification, some including children and dependents, the tables cannot be followed unreservedly. The actual number of persons engaged in the various industries is approximately as follows :—

	Agriculture	Manufactures	Commerce, &c.	Total
England . .	1,341,000	4,161,000	6,210,000	11,712,000
Scotland . .	234,000	641,000	773,000	1,648,000
Ireland . .	986,000	387,000	1,002,000	2,375,000
U. Kingdom	2,561,000	5,189,000	7,985,000	15,735,000
France . .	6,455,000	4,443,000	5,210,000	16,108,000
Germany .	8,120,000	5,350,000	5,910,000	19,380,000
Russia . .	22,700,000	4,760,000	3,600,000	31,060,000
Austria . .	10,682,000	3,090,000	2,438,000	16,210,000
Italy . . .	5,397,000	2,281,000	2,200,000	9,878,000
Spain . . .	2,723,000	1,167,000	1,200,000	5,090,000
Portugal .	873,000	300,000	100,000	1,273,000
Sweden . .	853,000	400,000	350,000	1,603,000
Norway . .	380,000	170,000	150,000	700,000
Denmark .	420,000	250,000	160,000	830,000
Belgium . .	980,000	953,000	280,000	2,213,000
Holland . .	840,000	400,000	360,000	1,600,000
Switzerland .	440,000	370,000	290,000	1,100,000
Greece . .	187,000	52,000	91,000	330,000
Europe . .	63,611,000	29,175,000	30,324,000	123,110,000
U. States .	7,671,000	3,837,000	5,884,000	17,392,000
Australia .	398,000	327,000	563,000	1,288,000
Total .	71,680,000	33,339,000	36,771,000	141,790,000

The following table shows the number of persons in 1000 of the population dedicated to each industry :—

	Per 1000 of Population			
	Agricul- ture	Manu- factures	Commerce, &c.	Total
England	52	160	238	450
Scotland	61	168	202	431
Ireland	195	76	196	467
United Kingdom	73	148	229	450
France	170	117	137	424
Germany	178	118	130	426
Russia	298	65	47	410
Austria	280	81	64	425
Italy	190	80	77	347
Spain	160	70	72	302
Portugal	220	70	23	313
Sweden	190	90	80	360

	Per 1000 of Population			
	Agricul- ture	Manu- facture	Commerce, &c.	Total
Norway	190	85	75	350
Denmark	210	120	80	410
Holland	200	93	85	378
Belgium	166	160	46	372
Switzerland	150	125	100	375
Greece	115	32	55	202
Europe	187	80	90	357
United States	153	77	117	347
Australia	110	88	154	352

The number of persons occupied is no test of industry or the reverse. In some countries women and children are engaged in manufacture, which swells the ratio of workers; in others, the children are at school, the women prudently employed at home.

UNITED KINGDOM

In his *Resources of Nations* (1835) M'Gregor gives the following :—

	England, Families	Great Britain, Families			Ireland, Adults
	1811	1811	1821	1831	1823
Agriculture	697,000	896,000	979,000	961,000	1,138,000
Trade, manufactures, &c.	1,315,000	1,648,000	1,963,000	2,453,000	1,699,000
Total	2,012,000	2,544,000	2,942,000	3,414,000	2,837,000

Booth's digest of the Census returns 1841-81 shows the principal occupations of the United Kingdom as follows :—

	1841	1851	1861	1871	1881
Agriculture	3,401,000	3,519,000	3,149,000	2,808,000	2,561,000
Manufactures	3,137,000	3,922,000	4,164,000	4,377,000	4,535,000
Commerce	684,000	1,165,000	1,418,000	1,712,000	1,946,000
Mines	245,000	299,000	497,000	561,000	654,000
Building	485,000	588,000	687,000	817,000	964,000
Professions	223,000	320,000	363,000	422,000	524,000
Domestics	1,555,000	1,542,000	1,914,000	2,233,000	2,448,000
Various	1,632,000	1,406,000	1,368,000	1,754,000	2,103,000
Total	11,362,000	12,761,000	13,560,000	14,684,000	15,735,000

Agriculture

	1841	1851	1861	1871	1881
England	1,297,000	1,760,000	1,700,000	1,504,000	1,341,000
Scotland	260,000	299,000	276,000	258,000	234,000
Ireland	1,844,000	1,460,000	1,173,000	1,046,000	986,000
United Kingdom	3,401,000	3,519,000	3,149,000	2,808,000	2,561,000

Manufactures

	1841	1851	1861	1871	1881
England	1,798,000	2,755,000	3,117,000	3,359,000	3,599,000
Scotland	350,000	480,000	481,000	518,000	557,000
Ireland	989,000	687,000	566,000	500,000	379,000
United Kingdom	3,137,000	3,922,000	4,164,000	4,377,000	4,535,000

Commerce

	1841	1851	1861	1871	1881
England	499,000	892,000	1,110,000	1,362,000	1,578,000
Scotland	74,000	121,000	145,000	179,000	208,000
Ireland	111,000	152,000	163,000	171,000	160,000
United Kingdom	684,000	1,165,000	1,418,000	1,712,000	1,946,000

Mines

	1841	1851	1861	1871	1881
England	210,000	235,000	425,000	475,000	562,000
Scotland	26,000	52,000	62,000	77,000	84,000
Ireland	9,000	12,000	10,000	9,000	8,000
United Kingdom . . .	245,000	299,000	497,000	561,000	654,000

Building

	1841	1851	1861	1871	1881
England	353,000	461,000	539,000	664,000	797,000
Scotland	60,000	69,000	82,000	95,000	111,000
Ireland	72,000	58,000	66,000	58,000	56,000
United Kingdom . . .	485,000	588,000	687,000	817,000	964,000

Learned Professions

	1841	1851	1861	1871	1881
England	159,000	246,000	284,000	337,000	423,000
Scotland	24,000	30,000	34,000	36,000	49,000
Ireland	40,000	44,000	45,000	49,000	52,000
United Kingdom . . .	223,000	320,000	363,000	422,000	524,000

Domestic Servants

	1841	1851	1861	1871	1881
England	1,078,000	1,121,000	1,384,000	1,684,000	1,838,000
Scotland	135,000	138,000	165,000	160,000	183,000
Ireland	342,000	283,000	365,000	389,000	427,000
United Kingdom . . .	1,555,000	1,542,000	1,914,000	2,233,000	2,448,000

Total Employed Population

	1841	1851	1861	1871	1881
England	6,631,000	8,429,000	9,452,000	10,623,000	11,712,000
Scotland	1,107,000	1,317,000	1,374,000	1,494,000	1,648,000
Ireland	3,624,000	3,015,000	2,734,000	2,567,000	2,375,000
United Kingdom . . .	11,362,000	12,761,000	13,560,000	14,684,000	15,735,000

The useless classes in the three kingdoms were :—

	England			Scotland		
	1861	1871	1881	1861	1871	1881
Paupers	843,000	977,000	758,000	117,000	124,000	99,000
Insane	40,000	57,000	73,000	9,000	11,000	14,000
Prisoners	26,000	29,000	28,000	2,000	3,000	3,000
Total . .	909,000	1,063,000	859,000	128,000	138,000	116,000

	Ireland			United Kingdom		
Paupers	217,000	282,000	590,000	1,177,000	1,383,000	1,447,000
Insane	14,000	17,000	17,000	63,000	85,000	104,000
Prisoners	4,000	4,000	3,000	32,000	36,000	34,000
Total . .	235,000	303,000	610,000	1,272,000	1,504,000	1,585,000

The following table shows manufacturing industries :—

	1841	1851	1861	1871	1881
Chemicals	7,000	21,000	31,000	46,000	55,000
Paper . .	15,000	28,000	32,000	44,000	61,000
Leather .	44,000	63,000	65,000	70,000	72,000
Pottery .	34,000	51,000	61,000	73,000	78,000
Food . .	119,000	170,000	190,000	206,000	230,000
Carpentry	197,000	235,000	265,000	280,000	286,000
Metals .	250,000	362,000	451,000	522,000	572,000
Clothing .	795,000	1,150,000	1,230,000	1,210,000	1,223,000
Textiles .	1,481,000	1,605,000	1,457,000	1,400,000	1,283,000
Various .	195,000	237,000	382,000	526,000	675,000
Total .	3,137,000	3,922,000	4,164,000	4,377,000	4,535,000

The learned professions in the United Kingdom show almost twice as great a relative increase as the population in general. The numbers were :—

	1841	1851	1861	1871	1881
Divinity . .	30,000	44,000	56,000	64,000	78,000
Law . . .	39,000	45,000	45,000	50,000	56,000
Medicine .	56,000	75,000	76,000	87,000	102,000
Arts and science	22,000	33,000	38,000	52,000	64,000
Education .	76,000	123,000	148,000	169,000	224,000
Total .	223,000	320,000	363,000	422,000	524,000

	Ratio of Persons Employed in the United Kingdom				
	1841	1851	1861	1871	1881
Agriculture . . .	298	276	233	192	162
Manufactures . .	277	307	307	298	288
Commerce . . .	60	92	104	116	124
Mines	22	24	37	38	41
Building . . .	43	46	51	55	61
Professions . . .	19	25	26	28	33
Domestics . . .	137	120	141	153	156
Various . . .	144	110	101	120	135
Total . .	1,000	1,000	1,000	1,000	1,000

The occupations according to sexes were as follows :—

1841	Males	Females	Total	Ratio Males	Females	Total
Agriculture .	3,151,000	250,000	3,401,000	276	22	298
Manufactures	1,823,000	1,314,000	3,137,000	161	116	277
Commerce .	577,000	107,000	684,000	51	9	60
Professions .	162,000	61,000	223,000	14	5	19
Domestics .	325,000	1,230,000	1,555,000	29	108	137
Various . .	1,989,000	373,000	2,362,000	176	33	209
Total .	8,027,000	3,335,000	11,362,000	707	293	1,000

1851	Males	Females	Total	Ratio Males	Females	Total
Agriculture .	3,123,000	396,000	3,519,000	245	31	276
Manufactures	2,262,000	1,660,000	3,922,000	177	130	307
Commerce .	977,000	188,000	1,165,000	77	15	92
Professions .	207,000	113,000	320,000	16	9	25
Domestics .	197,000	1,345,000	1,542,000	15	105	120
Various . .	2,086,000	207,000	2,293,000	164	16	180
Total .	8,852,000	3,909,000	12,761,000	694	306	1,000

1861	Males	Females	Total	Ratio Males	Females	Total
Agriculture .	2,885,000	264,000	3,149,000	214	19	233
Manufactures	2,427,000	1,737,000	4,164,000	179	128	307
Commerce .	1,196,000	222,000	1,418,000	88	16	104
Professions .	224,000	139,000	363,000	16	10	26
Domestics .	229,000	1,685,000	1,914,000	16	125	141
Various . .	2,363,000	189,000	2,552,000	175	14	189
Total .	9,324,000	4,236,000	13,560,000	688	312	1,000

1871	Males	Females	Total	Ratio Males	Females	Total
Agriculture .	2,569,000	239,000	2,808,000	176	16	192
Manufactures	2,583,000	1 794,000	4,377,000	176	122	298
Commerce .	1,436,000	276,000	1,712,000	98	18	116
Professions .	253,000	169,000	422,000	17	11	28
Domestics .	248,000	1,985,000	2,233,000	17	135	152
Various . .	2,875,000	257,000	3,132,000	197	17	214
Total .	9,964,000	4,720,000	14,684,000	681	319	1,000

1881	Males	Females	Total	Ratio Males	Females	Total
Agriculture .	2,348,000	213,000	2,561,000	149	13	162
Manufactures	2,740,000	1,795,000	4,535,000	174	114	288
Commerce .	1,650,000	296,000	1,946,000	105	19	124
Professions .	299,000	225,000	524,000	19	14	33
Domestics .	359,000	2,089,000	2,448,000	23	133	156
Various . .	3,424,000	297,000	3,721,000	218	19	237
Total .	10,820,000	4,915,000	15,735,000	688	312	1,000

The number of adults and that of actual workers are shown as follows :—

Males

	Over 15 years of Age		Workers	
	1841	1881	1841	1881
England .	4,940,000	7,961,000	4,797,000	8,108,000
Scotland .	778,000	1,106,000	764,000	1,130,000
Ireland . .	2,444,000	1,609,000	2,466,000	1,582,000
U. Kingdom	8,162,000	10,676,000	8,027,000	10,820,000

Females

England .	5,325,000	8,613,000	1,834,000	3,604,000
Scotland .	898,000	1,263,000	343,000	518,000
Ireland . .	2,624,000	1,741,000	1,158,000	793,000
U. Kingdom	8,847,000	11,617,000	3,335,000	4,915,000

Total

England .	10,265,000	16,574,000	6,631,000	11,712,000
Scotland .	1,676,000	2,369,000	1,107,000	1,648,000
Ireland . .	5,068,000	3,350,000	3,624,000	2,375,000
U. Kingdom	17,009,000	22,293,000	11,362,000	15,735,000

It appears that the number of males employed in 1881 was greater than that of male adults in the population. Males are classified thus according to age :—

Age	Agriculture			Manufacture		
	1861	1871	1881	1861	1871	1881
0-15	177,000	158,000	95,000	178,000	166,000	126,000
15-65	2,458,000	2,141,000	2,008,000	2,131,000	2,289,000	2,496,000
Over 65 . . .	250,000	270,000	245,000	118,000	128,000	118,000
Total . .	2,885,000	2,569,000	2,348,000	2,427,000	2,583,000	2,740,000

Age	Various			Total		
	1861	1871	1881	1861	1871	1881
0-15	184,000	209,000	173,000	539,000	533,000	394,000
15-65	3,581,000	4,278,000	5,149,000	8,170,000	8,708,000	9,653,000
Over 65 . . .	247,000	325,000	410,000	615,000	723,000	773,000
Total . .	4,012,000	4,812,000	5,732,000	9,324,000	9,964,000	10,820,000

Agriculture	1851	1861	1871	1881
Men . . .	2,930,000	2,708,000	2,411,000	2,253,000
Women . .	396,000	264,000	239,000	213,000
Boys . . .	193,000	177,000	158,000	95,000
Total .	3,519,000	3,149,000	2,808,000	2,561,000

Various	1851	1861	1871	1881
Men . . .	3,318,000	3,828,000	4,603,000	5,559,000
Women . .	1,853,000	2,235,000	2,687,000	2,907,000
Boys . . .	149,000	184,000	209,000	173,000
Total .	5,320,000	6,247,000	7,499,000	8,639,000

Manufactures	1851	1861	1871	1881
Men . . .	2,083,000	2,249,000	2,417,000	2,614,000
Women . .	1,660,000	1,737,000	1,794,000	1,795,000
Boys . . .	179,000	178,000	166,000	126,000
Total .	3,922,000	4,164,000	4,377,000	4,535,000

All Occupations	1851	1861	1871	1881
Men . . .	8,331,000	8,785,000	9,431,000	10,426,000
Women . .	3,909,000	4,236,000	4,720,000	4,915,000
Boys . . .	521,000	539,000	533,000	394,000
Total .	12,761,000	13,560,000	14,684,000	15,735,000

If we compare the total number of persons of all occupations in 1881 with that in 1851, we find an increase of 25 per cent. in the men and 57 per cent. in the women, but a decrease of 25 per cent. in boys, which latter is doubtless due to the Board Schools.

The number of persons supported or making a living out of the several occupations is shown by Booth as follows :—

ENGLAND

	1841	1851	1861	1871	1881
Agriculture	3,875,000	4,247,000	4,194,000	3,746,000	3,435,000
Manufacture	4,006,000	5,263,000	5,940,000	6,553,000	7,313,000
Transport	474,000	868,000	1,177,000	1,406,000	1,799,000
Dealing	973,000	1,385,000	1,684,000	2,054,000	2,334,000
Mines	564,000	828,000	1,065,000	1,231,000	1,553,000
Building	1,126,000	1,381,000	1,633,000	1,984,000	2,464,000
Domestics	1,111,000	1,211,000	1,523,000	1,859,000	2,230,000
Sundry	3,783,000	2,745,000	2,850,000	3,879,000	4,846,000
Total . .	15,912,000	17,928,000	20,066,000	22,712,000	25,974,000

SCOTLAND

	1841	1851	1861	1871	1881
Agriculture	669,000	688,000	663,000	604,000	523,000
Manufacture	726,000	925,000	940,000	1,040,000	1,155,000
Transport	84,000	141,000	173,000	215,000	252,000
Dealing	129,000	180,000	214,000	248,000	287,000
Mines	74,000	142,000	176,000	217,000	239,000
Building	200,000	225,000	254,000	293,000	347,000
Domestics	146,000	147,000	184,000	190,000	242,000
Sundry	592,000	440,000	458,000	553,000	691,000
Total . .	2,620,000	2,888,000	3,062,000	3,360,000	3,736,000

IRELAND

	1841	1851	1861	1871	1881
Agriculture	5,074,000	3,650,000	3,020,000	2,635,000	2,562,000
Manufacture	1,498,000	1,059,000	879,000	777,000	640,000
Transport	60,000	122,000	137,000	154,000	148,000
Dealing	195,000	214,000	227,000	237,000	234,000
Mines	27,000	33,000	29,000	25,000	23,000
Building	229,000	171,000	192,000	172,000	176,000
Domestics	346,000	286,000	371,000	409,000	457,000
Sundry	746,000	1,017,000	944,000	1,004,000	935,000
Total . .	8,175,000	6,552,000	5,799,000	5,413,000	5,175,000

UNITED KINGDOM

	1841	1851	1861	1871	1881
Agriculture	9,618,000	8,585,000	7,877,000	6,985,000	6,520,000
Manufacture	6,230,000	7,247,000	7,759,000	8,370,000	9,108,000
Transport	618,000	1,131,000	1,487,000	1,775,000	2,199,000
Dealing	1,297,000	1,779,000	2,125,000	2,539,000	2,855,000
Mines	665,000	1,003,000	1,270,000	1,473,000	1,815,000
Building	1,555,000	1,777,000	2,079,000	2,449,000	2,987,000
Domestics	1,603,000	1,644,000	2,078,000	2,458,000	2,929,000
Sundry	5,121,000	4,202,000	4,252,000	5,436,000	6,472,000
Total . .	26,707,000	27,368,000	28,927,000	31,485,000	34,885,000

Ratios for the United Kingdom

	1841	1851	1861	1871	1881
Agriculture . . .	360	314	272	223	187
Manufactures . .	233	265	268	267	261
Domestics . . .	60	60	73	77	84
Building . . .	58	65	73	77	86
Dealing . . .	48	65	74	80	81
Mines . . .	25	36	44	47	52
Transport . . .	23	41	51	56	63
Sundry . . .	193	154	145	173	186
Total . .	1,000	1,000	1,000	1,000	1,000

ENGLAND AND WALES

The following are the official classifications :—

Year	Agriculture	Trade and Manufactures	Various	Total	Percentage of Total Population
1811	896,000	1,129,000	519,000	2,544,000	25.0
1821	979,000	1,350,000	612,000	2,941,000	24.3
1831	961,000	1,435,000	1,018,000	3,414,000	24.4
1841	1,499,000	3,111,000	2,180,000	3,990,000	24.9
1851	2,029,000	3,692,000	5,927,000	11,648,000	64.0
1861	2,011,000	4,829,000	6,234,000	13,074,000	64.7
1871	1,657,000	5,953,000	7,153,000	14,763,000	64.8
1881	1,383,000	7,353,000	...	...	...

Booth's digest of the Censuses from 1841 is as follows for England and Wales :—

	1841	1851	1861	1871	1881
Agriculture	1,297,000	1,760,000	1,700,000	1,504,000	1,341,000
Manufactures . . .	1,798,000	2,755,000	3,117,000	3,359,000	3,599,000
Commerce . . .	499,000	892,000	1,110,000	1,362,000	1,578,000
Professions . . .	159,000	246,000	284,000	337,000	423,000
Domestics . . .	1,078,000	1,121,000	1,384,000	1,684,000	1,838,000
Various	1,800,000	1,655,000	1,857,000	2,377,000	2,933,000
Total . . .	6,631,000	8,429,000	9,452,000	10,623,000	11,712,000

1841

	Males	Females	Total	Males	Females	Total
				Ratio per 1000		
Agriculture .	1,239,000	58,000	1,297,000	187	9	196
Manufactures	1,306,000	492,000	1,798,000	198	74	272
Commerce .	439,000	60,000	499,000	66	9	75
Professions .	112,000	47,000	159,000	17	7	24
Domestics .	234,000	843,000	1,077,000	35	127	162
Various . .	1,467,000	334,000	1,801,000	221	50	271
Total .	4,797,000	1,834,000	6,631,000	724	276	1,000

1851

	Males	Females	Total	Males	Females	Total
Agriculture .	1,591,000	169,000	1,760,000	189	20	209
Manufactures	1,720,000	1,035,000	2,755,000	205	122	327
Commerce .	772,000	120,000	892,000	92	14	106
Professions .	149,000	97,000	246,000	17	12	29
Domestics .	150,000	971,000	1,121,000	17	115	132
Various . .	1,494,000	161,000	1,655,000	178	19	197
Total .	5,876,000	2,553,000	8,429,000	698	302	1,000

1861

	Males	Females	Total	Males	Females	Total
Agriculture .	1,584,000	116,000	1,700,000	167	12	179
Manufactures	1,916,000	1,201,000	3,117,000	204	127	331
Commerce .	962,000	148,000	1,110,000	102	16	118
Professions .	167,000	117,000	284,000	18	12	30
Domestics .	169,000	1,215,000	1,384,000	18	128	146
Various . .	1,720,000	137,000	1,857,000	182	14	196
Total .	6,518,000	2,934,000	9,452,000	691	309	1,000

1871

	Males	Females	Total	Males	Females	Total
Agriculture .	1,419,000	85,000	1,504,000	133	8	141
Manufactures	2,079,000	1,280,000	3,359,000	196	120	316
Commerce .	1,169,000	193,000	1,362,000	110	18	128
Professions .	196,000	141,000	337,000	18	13	31
Domestics .	197,000	1,487,000	1,684,000	18	141	159
Various . .	2,190,000	187,000	2,377,000	207	18	225
Total .	7,250,000	3,373,000	10,623,000	682	318	1,000

1881

	Males	Females	Total	Males	Females	Total
Agriculture .	1,275,000	66,000	1,341,000	109	6	115
Manufactures	2,236,000	1,363,000	3,599,000	191	116	307
Commerce .	1,360,000	218,000	1,578,000	116	18	134
Professions .	234,000	189,000	423,000	20	15	35
Domestics .	292,000	1,546,000	1,838,000	25	132	157
Various . .	2,711,000	222,000	2,933,000	233	19	252
Total .	8,108,000	3,604,000	11,712,000	694	306	1,000

The following table shows the relative increase or decrease of the number of hands in each decade for each industry :—

Males

Year	Agriculture	Manufactures	Commerce	Professions	Domestics	Total
1841	100	100	100	100	100	100
1851	128	132	175	133	64	122
1861	128	147	219	149	72	135
1871	115	159	266	175	84	151
1881	103	171	309	209	125	167

Females

Year	Agriculture	Manufactures	Commerce	Professions	Domestics	Total
1841	100	100	100	100	100	100
1851	291	211	162	206	115	140
1861	200	245	247	248	144	160
1871	146	261	322	300	177	183
1881	114	278	363	402	184	196

Total

Year	Agriculture	Manufactures	Commerce	Professions	Domestics	Total
1841	100	100	100	100	100	100
1851	135	153	178	154	104	127
1861	130	173	222	179	127	142
1871	116	187	272	210	155	160
1881	103	201	316	264	170	176

Males are classified according to age :—

Agriculture

Age	1851	1861	1871	1881
0–15 . .	110,000	123,000	103,000	72,000
15–65. .	1,352,000	1,311,000	1,164,000	1,083,000
Over 65 .	129,000	150,000	152,000	120,000
Total .	1,591,000	1,584,000	1,419,000	1,275,000

Manufactures

	1851	1861	1871	1881
0–15 . .	139,000	147,000	137,000	107,000
15–65. .	1,498,000	1,678,000	1,840,000	2,035,000
Over 65 .	83,000	91,000	102,000	94,000
Total .	1,720,000	1,916,000	2,079,000	2,236,000

Commerce

	1851	1861	1871	1881
0–15 . .	57,000	54,000	69,000	74,000
15–65. .	675,000	858,000	1,036,000	1,228,000
Over 65 .	40,000	50,000	64,000	58,000
Total .	772,000	962,000	1,169,000	1,360,000

Domestics

	1851	1861	1871	1881
0–15 . .	8,000	10,000	10,000	10,000
15–65. .	138,000	153,000	180,000	269,000
Over 65 .	4,000	6,000	7,000	13,000
Total .	150,000	169,000	197,000	292,000

Various

	1851	1861	1871	1881
0–15 . .	60,000	80,000	85,000	58,000
15–65. .	1,463,000	1,681,000	2,136,000	2,636,000
Over 65 .	120,000	126,000	165,000	251,000
Total .	1,643,000	1,887,000	2,386,000	2,945,000

Total of Males

	1851	1861	1871	1881
0–15 . .	374,000	414,000	404,000	321,000
15–65. .	5,126,000	5,681,000	6,356,000	7,251,000
Over 65 .	376,000	423,000	490,000	536,000
Total .	5,876,000	6,518,000	7,250,000	8,108,000

Agriculture

	1851	1861	1871	1881
Men . . .	1,481,000	1,461,000	1,316,000	1,203,000
Women . .	169,000	116,000	85,000	66,000
Boys . . .	110,000	123,000	103,000	72,000
Total .	1,760,000	1,700,000	1,504,000	1,341,000

Manufactures

Men . . .	1,581,000	1,769,000	1,942,000	2,129,000
Women . .	1,035,000	1,201,000	1,280,000	1,363,000
Boys . . .	139,000	147,000	137,000	107,000
Total .	2,755,000	3,117,000	3,359,000	3,599,000

Commerce

Men . . .	715,000	908,000	1,100,000	1,286,000
Women . .	120,000	148,000	193,000	218,000
Boys . . .	57,000	54,000	69,000	74,000
Total .	892,000	1,110,000	1,362,000	1,578,000

Domestics

Men . . .	142,000	159,000	187,000	282,000
Women . .	971,000	1,215,000	1,487,000	1,546,000
Boys . . .	8,000	10,000	10,000	10,000
Total .	1,121,000	1,384,000	1,684,000	1,838,000

Various

Men . . .	1,583,000	1,807,000	2,301,000	2,887,000
Women . .	258,000	254,000	328,000	411,000
Boys . . .	60,000	80,000	85,000	58,000
Total .	1,901,000	2,141,000	2,714,000	3,356,000

Total

Men . . .	5,502,000	6,104,000	6,846,000	7,787,000
Women . .	2,553,000	2,934,000	3,373,000	3,604,000
Boys . . .	374,000	414,000	404,000	321,000
Total .	8,429,000	9,452,000	10,623,000	11,712,000

SCOTLAND

Booth's digest of the Censuses classifies as follows :—

	1841	1851	1861	1871	1881
Agriculture	260,000	299,000	276,000	258,000	234,000
Manufactures	350,000	480,000	481,000	518,000	557,000
Commerce	74,000	121,000	145,000	179,000	208,000
Professions	24,000	30,000	34,000	36,000	49,000
Domestics	135,000	138,000	165,000	160,000	183,000
Various	264,000	249,000	273,000	343,000	417,000
Total . .	1,107,000	1,317,000	1,374,000	1,494,000	1,648,000

	1841			Ratio per 1000				1851			Ratio per 1000		
	Males	Females	Total	Males	Females	Total		Males	Females	Total	Males	Females	Total
Agriculture .	213,000	47,000	260,000	192	43	235	Agriculture .	239,000	60,000	299,000	181	45	226
Manufactures	214,000	136,000	350,000	192	123	315	Manufactures	285,000	195,000	480,000	217	148	365
Commerce .	60,000	14,000	74,000	54	13	67	Commerce .	99,000	22,000	121,000	75	17	92
Professions .	20,000	4,000	24,000	18	4	22	Professions .	26,000	4,000	30,000	20	3	23
Domestics .	20,000	115,000	135,000	18	104	122	Domestics .	12,000	126,000	138,000	9	96	105
Various . .	237,000	27,000	264,000	214	25	239	Various . .	220,000	29,000	249,000	167	22	189
Total .	764,000	343,000	1,107,000	688	312	1,000	Total .	881,000	436,000	1,317,000	669	331	1,000

	1861			Ratio per 1000		
	Males	Females	Total	Males	Females	Total
Agriculture .	229,000	47,000	276,000	166	34	200
Manufactures	280,000	201,000	481,000	204	146	350
Commerce .	117,000	28,000	145,000	85	20	105
Professions .	26,000	8,000	34,000	19	6	25
Domestics .	15,000	150,000	165,000	11	109	120
Various . .	254,000	19,000	273,000	185	15	200
Total .	921,000	453,000	1,374,000	670	330	1,000

1871						
Agriculture .	207,000	51,000	258,000	138	34	172
Manufactures	310,000	208,000	518,000	207	139	346
Commerce .	142,000	37,000	179,000	95	25	120
Professions .	26,000	10,000	36,000	17	7	24
Domestics .	21,000	139,000	160,000	14	93	107
Various . .	310,000	33,000	343,000	206	25	231
Total .	1,016,000	478,000	1,494,000	677	323	1,000

1881						
Agriculture .	183,000	51,000	234,000	111	31	142
Manufactures	340,000	217,000	557,000	206	132	338
Commerce .	169,000	39,000	208,000	102	24	126
Professions .	34,000	15,000	49,000	20	9	29
Domestics .	31,000	152,000	183,000	19	92	111
Various . .	373,000	44,000	417,000	227	27	254
Total .	1,130,000	518,000	1,648,000	685	315	1,000

The following table shows the relative increase or decrease of hands in each decade for each industry:—

Year	Agriculture	Manufactures	Commerce	Professions	Domestics	Total
1841	100	100	100	100	100	100
1851	115	137	162	125	102	119
1861	106	137	196	141	122	124
1871	99	148	242	150	118	135
1881	90	159	281	204	135	149

Males are classified thus according to age:—

Agriculture

Age	1851	1861	1871	1881
0–15 . . .	11,000	11,000	9,000	6,000
15–65 . . .	208,000	196,000	177,000	159,000
Over 65 . .	20,000	22,000	21,000	18,000
Total .	239,000	229,000	207,000	183,000

Manufactures

Age	1851	1861	1871	1881
0–15 . . .	23,000	19,000	18,000	12,000
15–65 . . .	247,000	246,000	278,000	314,000
Over 65 . .	15,000	15,000	14,000	14,000
Total .	285,000	280,000	310,000	340,000

Commerce

Age	1851	1861	1871	1881
0–15 . . .	6,000	5,000	8,000	9,000
15–65 . . .	88,000	106,000	128,000	154,000
Over 65 . .	5,000	6,000	6,000	6,000
Total .	99,000	117,000	142,000	169,000

Various

Age	1851	1861	1871	1881
0–15 . . .	9,000	13,000	18,000	13,000
15–65 . . .	231,000	263,000	307,000	386,000
Over 65 . .	18,000	19,000	32,000	39,000
Total .	258,000	295,000	357,000	438,000

Total of Males

Age	1851	1861	1871	1881
0–15 . . .	49,000	48,000	53,000	40,000
15–65 . . .	774,000	811,000	890,000	1,013,000
Over 65 . .	58,000	62,000	73,000	77,000
Total .	881,000	921,000	1,016,000	1,130,000

Agriculture

	1851	1861	1871	1881
Men . . .	228,000	218,000	198,000	177,000
Women . .	60,000	47,000	51,000	51,000
Boys . . .	11,000	11,000	9,000	6,000
Total .	299,000	276,000	258,000	234,000

Manufactures

	1851	1861	1871	1881
Men . . .	262,000	261,000	292,000	328,000
Women . .	195,000	201,000	208,000	217,000
Boys . . .	23,000	19,000	18,000	12,000
Total .	480,000	481,000	518,000	557,000

Commerce

	1851	1861	1871	1881
Men . . .	93,000	112,000	134,000	163,000
Women . .	22,000	28,000	37,000	39,000
Boys . . .	6,000	5,000	8,000	6,000
Total .	121,000	145,000	179,000	208,000

Domestics

	1851	1861	1871	1881
Men . . .	12,000	15,000	21,000	31,000
Women . .	126,000	150,000	139,000	152,000
Total .	138,000	165,000	160,000	183,000

Various

	1851	1861	1871	1881
Men . . .	237,000	267,000	318,000	391,000
Women . .	33,000	27,000	43,000	59,000
Boys . . .	9,000	13,000	18,000	16,000
Total .	279,000	307,000	379,000	466,000

Total

	1851	1861	1871	1881
Men . . .	832,000	873,000	963,000	1,090,000
Women . .	436,000	453,000	478,000	518,000
Boys . . .	49,000	48,000	53,000	40,000
Total .	1,317,000	1,374,000	1,494,000	1,648,000

The number of men employed in Scotland in all occupations rose 30 per cent. in 30 years, that of women 18 per cent., while that of boys (as in England) shows a falling off.

IRELAND

Booth's digest of the Censuses is condensed as follows :—

	1841	1851	1861	1871	1881
Agriculture	1,844,000	1,460,000	1,173,000	1,046,000	986,000
Manufactures	989,000	687,000	566,000	500,000	379,000
Commerce	111,000	152,000	163,000	171,000	160,000
Professions	40,000	44,000	45,000	49,000	52,000
Domestics	342,000	283,000	365,000	389,000	427,000
Various	298,000	389,000	422,000	412,000	371,000
Total . . .	3,624,000	3,015,000	2,734,000	2,567,000	2,375,000

1841

	Males	Females	Total	Males	Females	Total
Agriculture .	1,699,000	145,000	1,844,000	467	40	507
Manufactures	303,000	686,000	989,000	84	190	274
Commerce .	78,000	33,000	111,000	22	9	31
Professions .	30,000	10,000	40,000	8	3	11
Domestics .	71,000	271,000	342,000	20	75	95
Various . .	285,000	13,000	298,000	79	3	82
Total .	2,466,000	1,158,000	3,624,000	680	320	1,000

1871

	Males	Females	Total	Males	Females	Total
Agriculture .	943,000	103,000	1,046,000	367	40	407
Manufactures	194,000	306,000	500,000	76	119	195
Commerce .	125,000	46,000	171,000	48	18	66
Professions .	31,000	18,000	49,000	12	7	19
Domestics .	30,000	359,000	389,000	12	140	152
Various . .	375,000	37,000	412,000	146	15	161
Total .	1,698,000	869,000	2,567,000	661	339	1,000

1851

	Males	Females	Total	Males	Females	Total
Agriculture .	1,293,000	167,000	1,460,000	428	56	484
Manufactures	257,000	430,000	687,000	86	142	228
Commerce .	106,000	46,000	152,000	35	15	50
Professions .	32,000	12,000	44,000	11	4	15
Domestics .	35,000	248,000	283,000	12	82	94
Various . .	372,000	17,000	389,000	123	6	129
Total .	2,095,000	920,000	3,015,000	695	305	1,000

1881

	Males	Females	Total	Males	Females	Total
Agriculture .	890,000	96,000	986,000	376	40	416
Manufactures	164,000	215,000	379,000	70	90	160
Commerce .	121,000	39,000	160,000	50	17	67
Professions .	31,000	21,000	52,000	12	8	20
Domestics .	36,000	391,000	427,000	15	164	179
Various . .	340,000	31,000	371,000	145	13	158
Total .	1,582,000	793,000	2,375,000	668	332	1,000

1861

	Males	Females	Total	Males	Females	Total
Agriculture .	1,072,000	101,000	1,173,000	393	37	430
Manufactures	231,000	335,000	566,000	84	123	207
Commerce .	117,000	46,000	163,000	42	17	59
Professions .	31,000	14,000	45,000	11	5	16
Domestics .	45,000	320,000	365,000	17	116	133
Various . .	389,000	33,000	422,000	143	12	155
Total .	1,885,000	849,000	2,734,000	690	310	1,000

The following table shows the relative increase or decrease of hands in each decade for each industry :—

Year	Agriculture	Manufactures	Commerce	Professions	Domestics	Total
1841	100	100	100	100	100	100
1851	79	70	138	110	82	83
1861	63	57	148	112	107	75
1871	57	51	155	122	114	71
1881	53	38	146	130	125	65

Males are classified thus according to age :—

Age	Agriculture			Manufactures		
	1861	1871	1881	1861	1871	1881
0–15	43,000	46,000	17,000	12,000	11,000	7,000
15–65	951,000	800,000	766,000	207,000	171,000	147,000
Over 65	78,000	97,000	107,000	12,000	12,000	10,000
Total . .	1,072,000	943,000	890,000	231,000	194,000	164,000

Age	Various			Total		
0–15	22,000	19,000	9,000	77,000	76,000	33,000
15–65	520,000	491,000	476,000	1,678,000	1,462,000	1,389,000
Over 65	40,000	51,000	43,000	130,000	160,000	160,000
Total . .	582,000	561,000	528,000	1,885,000	1,698,000	1,582,000

Agriculture	1851	1861	1871	1881
Men . . .	1,221,000	1,029,000	897,000	873,000
Women . .	167,000	101,000	103,000	96,000
Boys . . .	72,000	43,000	46,000	17,000
Total .	1,460,000	1,173,000	1,046,000	986,000

Various	1851	1861	1871	1881
Men . . .	536,000	560,000	542,000	519,000
Women . .	323,000	413,000	460,000	482,000
Boys . . .	9,000	22,000	19,000	9,000
Total .	868,000	995,000	1,021,000	1,010,000

Manufactures				
Men . . .	240,000	219,000	183,000	157,000
Women . .	430,000	335,000	306,000	215,000
Boys . . .	17,000	12,000	11,000	7,000
Total .	687,000	566,000	500,000	379,000

Total				
Men . . .	1,997,000	1,808,000	1,622,000	1,549,000
Women . .	920,000	849,000	869,000	793,000
Boys . . .	98,000	77,000	76,000	33,000
Total .	3,015,000	2,734,000	2,567,000	2,375,000

FRANCE

Successive Censuses have distinguished agricultural from other population as follows :—

	1851	1861	1872	1881
Agricultural	21,920,000	19,870,000	18,513,000	18,249,000
Various	13,863,000	17,876,000	18,500,000	19,157,000
Total . .	35,783,000	36,746,000	37,013,000	37,406,000

The Censuses of 1872 and 1881 compare as follows :—

	1872			1881		
	Principals	Dependents	Total	Principals	Dependents	Total
Agriculture . . .	5,970,000	12,543,000	18,513,000	6,456,000	11,793,000	18,249,000
Manufactures . . .	3,827,000	4,624,000	8,451,000	3,980,000	4,214,000	8,194,000
Commerce . . .	1,151,000	1,809,000	2,960,000	1,163,000	1,516,000	2,679,000
Various . . .	2,461,000	2,737,000	5,198,000	3,309,000	4,047,000	7,356,000
Total . .	13,409,000	21,713,000	35,122,000	14,908,000	21,570,000	36,478,000

	1881					
	Heads of Families			Principals, Family, and Servants		
	Males	Females	Total	Males	Females	Total
Agriculture . . .	4,757,000	1,698,000	6,455,000	9,157,000	9,092,000	18,249,000
Factories . . .	658,000	379,000	1,037,000	1,032,000	1,069,000	2,101,000
Artisans . . .	1,931,000	1,012,000	2,943,000	2,999,000	3,094,000	6,093,000
Mines . . .	387,000	76,000	463,000	616,000	513,000	1,129,000
Transport . . .	285,000	22,000	307,000	444,000	357,000	801,000
Commerce . . .	818,000	345,000	1,163,000	1,330,000	1,349,000	2,679,000
Innkeepers, &c. . .	306,000	137,000	443,000	562,000	603,000	1,165,000
Civil service . . .	265,000	49,000	314,000	418,000	388,000	806,000
Capitalists . . .	437,000	425,000	862,000	734,000	1,116,000	1,850,000
Professions . . .	240,000	135,000	375,000	353,000	426,000	779,000
Various . . .	523,000	23,000	546,000	609,000	217,000	826,000
Total . .	10,607,000	4,301,000	14,908,000	18,254,000	18,224,000	36,478,000

GERMANY

The Census of 1882 gave the following results :—

	Agriculture	Manufactures	Commerce	Sundry	Total
Prussia	11,678,000	9,394,000	2,725,000	3,491,000	27,288,000
Bavaria	2,644,000	1,492,000	436,000	697,000	5,269,000
Saxony	579,000	1,696,000	361,000	379,000	3,015,000
Wurtemburg	927,000	674,000	143,000	213,000	1,957,000
Baden	752,000	492,000	141,000	174,000	1,559,000
Small states	2,261,000	2,310,000	725,000	838,000	6,134,000
Total . .	18,841,000	16,058,000	4,531,000	5,792,000	45,222,000

The item of "Sundry" comprises 3,546,000 persons of various occupations, and 2,246,000 who have none.

The Prussian Census of 1867 was as follows :—

	Principals	Dependents	Males	Females	Total
			1867		
Agriculture	4,105,000	7,422,000	5,612,000	5,915,000	11,527,000
Manufactures	1,990,000	3,448,000	2,965,000	2,473,000	5,438,000
Mines	202,000	426,000	344,000	284,000	628,000
Commerce	290,000	540,000	430,000	400,000	830,000
Various	2,539,000	3,009,000	2,519,000	3,029,000	5,548,000
Total . .	9,126,000	14,845,000	11,870,000	12,101,000	23,971,000

The occupations of the people of Saxony were in the following ratio :—

	1849		1871		1882
	Males	Females	Males	Females	All
Agriculture . . .	209	228	158	166	193
Manufactures . .	486	443	532	506	563
Commerce . . .	61	55	99	103	120
Sundry	244	274	211	225	124
Total . .	1,000	1,000	1,000	1,000	1,000

RUSSIA

The Census of 1872 gave approximately as follows for Russia and Poland :—

	Males	Females	Total	Ratio
Nobles . . .	437,300	436,800	874,100	12
Merchants . .	232,600	216,100	448,700	6
Clergy	281,500	315,000	596,500	8
Artisans, &c. .	3,044,000	3,105,000	6,149,000	85
Peasants . . .	31,941,600	32,223,000	64,164,700	889
Total . .	35,937,000	36,296,100	72,233,000	1,000

The following table of ratios was published in 1867 :—

	Ratio	
	Russia	Poland
Clergy	10	2
Nobles	13	14
Soldiers	57	13
Citizens, &c. . . .	96	267
Peasants	824	704
Total . .	1,000	1,000

Lendheim gave the following table in 1873, apparently excluding Poland :—

		Ratio
Nobles	919,000	13
Clergy	633,000	9
Foreigners	148,000	2
Military	3,943,000	53
Merchants, artisans, &c.	6,907,000	99
Peasants . . .	56,815,000	824
Total . .	69,365,000	1,000

AUSTRIA-HUNGARY

The Census of 1870 showed as follows :—

	Austria	Hungary	Total
Agriculture . .	5,520,000	5,010,000	10,530,000
Manufactures . .	2,198,000	647,000	2,845,000
Commerce . .	303,000	105,000	408,000
Transport . .	139,000	29,000	168,000
Mines . . .	104,000	50,000	154,000
Capitalists . .	435,000	81,000	516,000
Servants, &c. . .	2,806,000	1,143,000	3,949,000
Various . . .	465,000	264,000	729,000
Total . .	11,970,000	7,329,000	19,299,000

That of 1880 was as follows :—

	Austria	Hungary	Total
Agriculture . .	6,161,000	4,521,000	10,682,000
Manufactures . .	2,157,000	789,000	2,946,000
Commerce . .	435,000	186,000	621,000
Mines . . .	118,000	26,000	144,000
Capitalists . .	278,000	53,000	331,000
Civil service . .	99,000	66,000	165,000
Domestics . . .	890,000	430,000	1,320,000
Various . . .	1,217,000	1,216,000	2,433,000
Total . .	11,355,000	7,287,000	18,642,000

	Austria		Hungary		All Empire	
	Males	Females	Males	Females	Males	Females
Agriculture . . .	3,432,000	2,729,000	3,548,000	973,000	6,980,000	3,702,000
Manufactures . . .	1,632,000	525,000	714,000	75,000	2,346,000	600,000
Commerce . . .	351,000	84,000	166,000	20,000	517,000	104,000
Servants . . .	245,000	645,000	46,000	384,000	291,000	1,029,000
Various . . .	1,101,000	611,000	734,000	628,000	1,835,000	1,239,000
Total . .	6,761,000	4,594,000	5,208,000	2,080,000	11,969,000	6,674,000

In 1880 the population of Austria was classified thus :—

	Principals	Family	Servants	Total	Ratio
Agriculture .	2,365,000	5,697,000	4,127,000	12,189,000	550
Manufactures	576,000	2,399,000	1,735,000	4,710,000	212
Commerce .	185,000	459,000	196,000	840,000	38
Transport .	18,000	227,000	114,000	359,000	16
Capitalists .	207,000	273,000	63,000	543,000	24
Various . .	518,000	1,691,000	1,294,000	3,503,000	160
Total .	3,869,000	10,746,000	7,529,000	22,144,000	1,000

The population of Hungary is classified thus :—

	Principals	Family, &c.	Total	Ratio
Agriculture .	1,475,000	3,046,000	4,521,000	367
Manufactures .	381,000	408,000	789,000	64
Commerce . .	97,000	89,000	186,000	15
Various . . .	264,000	6,557,000	6,821,000	554
Total . .	2,217,000	10,100,000	12,317,000	1,000

Besides the above, there were in Hungary 3,325,000 persons of no occupation.

Adding together the two foregoing tables, we find for the whole monarchy as follows :—

	Principals	Family,&c.	Total	Ratio
Agriculture .	3,840,000	12,870,000	16,710,000	484
Manufactures .	957,000	4,542,000	5,499,000	160
Commerce . .	282,000	744,000	1,026,000	30
Various. . .	1,007,000	10,219,000	11,226,000	326
Total . .	6,086,000	28,375,000	34,461,000	1,000

ITALY

The Census of 1861 gave the following classification :—

Agriculture	8,290,000
Manufactures . . .	3,230,000
Sundry and children . . .	10,250,000
Total population .	21,770,000

That of 1871 was as follows :—

Agriculture	8,566,000
Manufactures, &c. . . .	5,817,000
Sundry and children . . .	12,423,000
Total population .	26,801,000

That of 1881 was as follows :—

	Men	Women	Children	Total
Agriculture .	5,397,000	3,094,000	678,000	9,169,000
Manufactures	2,281,000	1,904,000	309,000	4,494,000
Commerce .	247,000	33,000	5,000	285,000
Transport .	310,000	3,000	9,000	322,000
Mines . .	60,000	...	5,000	65,000
Professions .	215,000	80,000	...	295,000
Domestics .	266,000	448,000	47,000	761,000
Various . .	1,102,000	675,000	42,000	1,819,000
Useful occupations }	9,878,000	6,237,000	1,095,000	17,210,000
Indefinite .	1,308,000	4,999,000	2,150,000	8,457,000
Prisoners and vagrants . }	73,000	56,000	5,000	134,000
Total . .	11,259,000	11,292,000	3,250,000	25,801,000

The total population was 28,460,000, including 2,659,000 infants under 9 years, of whom the Census took no cognisance. Children in the above table are all over 9 and under 14 years.

SPAIN

The Census of 1877 showed as follows :—

		Ratio
Agriculture . . .	2,723,000	475
Manufactures . . .	1,167,000	203
Commerce, &c. . .	213,000	37
Vagrants, smugglers, &c. .	1,630,000	285
Total .	5,736,000	1,000
Women and children .	11,018,000	
Total population .	16,754,000	

SWEDEN

The classification of the people down to 1855 was as follows :—

	1805	1830	1855	Families in 1855
Nobles . .	9,503	10,458	11,742	1,666
Clergy . .	15,145	14,153	15,362	2,232
Citizens . .	65,411	66,693	81,408	13,366
Peasants . .	1,759,000	2,169,000	2,378,000	394,610
Various . .	563,641	627,796	1,152,788	180,429
Total .	2,412,700	2,888,100	3,639,300	592,303

The Census of 1870 showed as follows :—

	Principals			Principals and Dependents, Ratio		
	Males	Females	Total	Males	Females	Total
Agriculture .	414,000	33,000	447,000	270	271	541
Manufactures	62,000	6,000	68,000	52	47	99
Commerce .	22,000	2,000	24,000	17	17	34
Various . .	190,000	214,000	404,000	145	181	326
Total .	688,000	255,000	943,000	484	516	1,000

The Census of Sweden for 1880 gave the following results :—

	Principals			Families		
	Males	Females	Total	Males	Females	Total
Agriculture . . .	641,000	212,000	853,000	434,000	840,000	1,274,000
Manufactures . . .	157,000	17,000	174,000	134,000	243,000	377,000
Commerce . . .	68,000	5,000	73,000	41,000	81,000	122,000
Various . . .	66,000	8,000	174,000	...	...	...
Total . . .	932,000	242,000	1,174,000	664,000	1,265,000	1,929,000
Unoccupied . . .	270,000	214,000	484,000	237,000	428,000	665,000
Total population .	1,202,000	456,000	1,658,000	901,000	1,693,000	2,594,000

	Total Population			Ratio		
Agriculture . . .	1,172,000	1,173,000	2,345,000	257	257	514
Manufactures . . .	297,000	280,000	577,000	64	62	126
Commerce . . .	113,000	109,000	222,000	25	24	49
Various . . .	125,000	128,000	253,000	27	27	54
Unoccupied . . .	509,000	660,000	1,109,000	112	145	257
Total . .	2,216,000	2,350,000	4,566,000	485	515	1,000

NORWAY

The Censuses of 1865 and 1875 gave these results :—

	Principals, 1875		Total Population, 1875			Total Popula-tion, 1865
	Males	Females	Males	Females	Total	
Agriculture . . .	106,000	9,000	437,000	466,000	903,000	1,035,000
Manufactures . . .	39,000	26,000	155,000	151,000	306,000	343,000
Commerce . . .	12,000	2,000	96,000	99,000	195,000	149,000
Various	75,000	4,000	189,000	214,000	403,000	175,000
Total . .	232,000	41,000	877,000	930,000	1,807,000	1,702,000

There was a further classification in 1875 as follows :—

	Principals	Families	Servants	Total
Agriculture . .	115,000	523,000	265,000	903,000
Manufactures .	65,000	91,000	150,000	306,000
Commerce . .	14,000	39,000	142,000	195,000
Various . . .	79,000	86,000	238,000	403,000
Total . .	273,000	739,000	795,000	1,807,000

DENMARK

The official tables give the occupations of the people thus :—

	1860	1880	No. in 1880
Agriculture . . .	395	469	931,000
Manufactures .	228	229 }	590,000
Commerce . . .	53	68 }	
Various . . .	324	234	459,000
Total . .	1,000	1,000	1,980,000

The numbers in 1880 include children, and are double the real numbers.

FINLAND

The Census of 1865 showed the following ratios :—

	Males	Females	Total Population
Agriculture . . .	834	755	793
Manufactures . .	55	43	49
Commerce . . .	20	12	16
Various . . .	91	190	142
Total . .	1,000	1,000	1,000

BELGIUM

The Census of 1856 was as follows :—

	Males	Females	Total
Agriculture . .	709,000	353,000	1,062,000
Manufactures .	466,000	326,000	792,000
Commerce . . .	80,000	49,000	129,000
Transport . . .	26,000	1,000	27,000
Domestics . . .	19,000	68,000	87,000
Mines	63,000	10,000	73,000
Capitalists . . .	22,000	28,000	50,000
Various . . .	88,000	19,000	107,000
Total . .	1,473,000	854,000	2,327,000
Children, &c.. .	799,000	1,404,000	2,203,000
Population . .	2,272,000	2,258,000	4,530,000

That of 1880 for Belgium was as follows :—

	Males	Females	Total
Mines	226,000	18,000	244,000
Manufactures .	467,000	242,000	709,000
Commerce . . .	143,000	101,000	244,000
Agriculture . .	530,000	452,000	982,000
Various . . .	433,000	148,000	581,000
Total . .	1,799,000	961,000	2,760,000
Children, &c.. .	1,010,000	1,825,000	2,835,000
Population . .	2,809,000	2,786,000	5,595,000

GREECE

The principal occupations in 1861 were :—

		Ratio
Agriculture	187,000	566
Manufactures . . .	52,000	158
Commerce, &c. . . .	91,000	276
Total . .	330,000	1,000

The above is exclusive of 1,003,000 women and children.

SWITZERLAND

The Census of 1880 gave as follows :—

		Ratio
Agriculture	1,139,000	401
Manufactures . . .	971,000	341
Commerce	206,000	72
Transport	112,000	39
Various	418,000	147
Total . .	2,846,000	1,000

That of 1870 was as follows :—

		Ratio
Agriculture	543,000	414
Manufactures . . .	492,000	374
Commerce	49,000	37
Various	233,000	175
Total . .	1,317,000	1,000

The latter is apparently only of adults, that of 1880 of the whole population. In 1860 the number of hands employed in manufactures was 330,000.

PORTUGAL

The Census of 1861 gave as follows :—

		Ratio
Agriculture	873,000	770
Manufactures . . .	210,000	185
Commerce	30,000	27
Various	20,000	18
Total . .	1,133,000	1,000

The above is exclusive of 2,650,000 women and children.

UNITED STATES

The first Census as to occupation was taken in 1820, the second in 1840, since which latter date they have been decennial, viz. :—

Year	Agriculture	Manufactures	Commerce, &c.	Total
1820	2,071,000	350,000	72,000	2,493,000
1840	3,718,000	792,000	287,000	4,797,000
1850	2,401,000	958,000	2,013,000	5,372,000
1860	3,220,000	1,311,000	3,756,000	8,287,000
1870	5,923,000	2,054,000	4,529,000	12,506,000
1880	7,671,000	2,707,000	7,014,000	17,392,000

The returns for 1820 and 1840 include all ages and colours, but those for 1850 and 1860 are only for free male adults. Assuming that in these years 50 per cent. of negro adults were engaged in agriculture, and 50 per cent. in commerce, &c., the real number of workers would be :—

Year	Agriculture	Manufactures	Commerce, &c.	Total
1820	2,071,000	350,000	72,000	2,493,000
1840	3,718,000	792,000	287,000	4,797,000
1850	3,329,000	958,000	2,950,000	7,237,000
1860	4,342,000	1,311,000	4,878,000	10,531,000
1870	5,923,000	2,054,000	4,529,000	12,506,000
1880	7,671,000	2,707,000	7,014,000	17,392,000

Adopting the second table as more correct, and comparing the numbers of persons occupied with that of all inhabitants, male and female, between 16 and 60 years of age, we find as follows :—

	Workers	Persons of Working Age	Ratio of Workers
1820	2,493,000	4,816,000	51.7
1840	4,797,000	8,887,000	53.9
1850	7,237,000	12,596,000	57.4
1860	10,531,000	17,301,000	60.7
1870	12,506,000	21,561,000	58.2
1880	17,392,000	27,307,000	63.6

The Census for 1820 showed as follows :—

States	Agriculture	Manufactures	Commerce, &c.	Total
New England	285,000	82,000	22,000	389,000
Middle . .	523,000	160,000	23,000	706,000
South . . .	1,064,000	83,000	22,000	1,169,000
West . . .	199,000	25,000	5,000	229,000
Total .	2,071,000	350,000	72,000	2,493,000

That of 1840 was as follows :—

States	Agriculture	Manufactures	Commerce, &c.	Total
New England	415,000	187,000	74,000	676,000
Middle . .	810,000	334,000	108,000	1,252,000
South . . .	1,790,000	149,000	63,000	2,002,000
West . . .	703,000	122,000	42,000	867,000
Total .	3,718,000	792,000	287,000	4,797,000

The minor industries of 1840 were in detail thus :—

States	Commerce	Navigation	Professions	Mining	Total
New England	18,000	44,000	11,000	1,000	74,000
Middle . .	50,000	27,000	24,000	7,000	108,000
South . .	31,000	11,000	17,000	4,000	63,000
West . . .	19,000	7,000	13,000	3,000	42,000
Total .	118,000	89,000	65,000	15,000	287,000

The Census of 1850 excluded the slave population, as already observed, and showed as follows :—

States	Agriculture	Manufactures	Commerce, &c.	Total
New England	269,000	313,000	230,000	812,000
Middle . .	592,000	418,000	780,000	1,790,000
South . . .	736,000	104,000	360,000	1,200,000
West . . .	804,000	123,000	643,000	1,570,000
Total .	2,401,000	958,000	2,013,000	5,372,000

The Census of 1860 also excluded the slave population, and showed thus :—

States	Occupied	Persons of Working Age (16–60)			Ratio of Workers
		Males	Females	Total	
New England	1,104,000	915,000	968,000	1,883,000	58.7
Middle . .	2,684,000	2,357,000	2,406,000	4,763,000	56.4
South . . .	1,645,000	2,548,000	2,463,000	5,011,000	33.0
West . . .	2,854,000	3,098,000	2,554,000	5,652,000	50.5
Total .	8,287,000	9,918,000	8,391,000	17,309,000	47.8

States	Agriculture	Manufactures	Commerce, &c.	Total
New England	293,000	390,000	421,000	1,104,000
Middle . .	721,000	542,000	1,421,000	2,684,000
South . .	860,000	126,000	659,000	1,645,000
West . . .	1,346,000	253,000	1,255,000	2,854,000
Total .	3,220,000	1,311,000	3,756,000	8,287,000

That of 1870 included the entire population, and gave the following results :—

States	Agriculture	Manufactures	Commerce, &c.	Total
New England	316,000	555,000	428,000	1,299,000
Middle . .	793,000	1,012,000	1,302,000	3,107,000
South . . .	2,669,000	283,000	792,000	3,744,000
West . . .	2,145,000	857,000	1,354,000	4,356,000
Total .	5,923,000	2,707,000	3,876,000	12,506,000
Males . .	5,526,000	2,353,000	2,790,000	10,670,000
Females . .	397,000	354,000	1,086,000	1,836,000
Total .	5,923,000	2,707,000	3,876,000	12,506,000

In 1870	Americans	Irish	Germans	British	Various	Total
Agriculture . . .	5,303,000	138,000	225,000	95,000	162,000	5,923,000
Manufactures . . .	1,778,000	265,000	308,000	176,000	180,000	2,707,000
Commerce, &c. . .	2,721,000	544,000	303,000	103,000	205,000	3,876,000
Total . .	9,802,000	947,000	836,000	374,000	547,000	12,506,000

That of 1880 gave the following :—

States	Agriculture	Manufactures	Commerce, &c.	Total
New England	301,000	709,000	562,000	1,572,000
Middle . .	847,000	1,425,000	1,912,000	4,184,000
South. . .	3,626,000	392,000	1,236,000	5,254,000
West . . .	2,897,000	1,311,000	2,174,000	6,382,000
Total .	7,671,000	3,837,000	5,884,000	17,392,000

States	Males	Females	Total	Ratio Males	Ratio Females	Ratio Total
New England	1,239,000	333,000	1,572,000	72	19	91
Middle . .	3,453,000	731,000	4,184,000	198	42	240
South . .	4,253,000	1,001,000	5,254,000	245	57	302
West . . .	5,800,000	582,000	6,382,000	333	34	367
Total .	14,745,000	2,647,000	17,392,000	848	152	1,000

Some of the principal States showed as follows :—

	Agriculture	Manufactures	Commerce, &c.	Total	Ratio of Workers
New York .	377,000	630,000	878,000	1,885,000	10.9
Pennsylvania	301,000	528,000	627,000	1,456,000	8.4
Illinois . .	436,000	206,000	357,000	999,000	5.8
Ohio . . .	397,000	242,000	355,000	994,000	5.8
Massachusetts	65,000	370,000	286,000	721,000	4.1
Missouri . .	355,000	110,000	228,000	693,000	4.0
Indiana . .	331,000	110,000	194,000	635,000	3.6
Georgia . .	432,000	36,000	130,000	598,000	3.5
Michigan .	240,000	131,000	198,000	569,000	3.3
Iowa . . .	304,000	70,000	154,000	528,000	3.0
Texas. . .	359,000	30,000	133,000	522,000	3.0
Kentucky .	321,000	61,000	138,000	520,000	3.0
Various . .	3,753,000	1,313,000	2,206,000	7,272,000	41.6
Total .	7,671,000	3,837,000	5,884,000	17,392,000	100.0

The classification of nationality (counting sons of foreigners as Americans) was in 1880 as follows :—

		Ratio
Americans . . .	13,897,000	802
Germans . . .	1,033,000	59
Irish	979,000	56
British	467,000	26
Various	1,016,000	57
Total . .	17,392,000	1,000

Age and sex are classified in the following manner :—

	Males			
	Under 16	16 to 60	Over 60	Total
Agriculture .	585,000	5,888,000	603,000	7,076,000
Manufactures	87,000	2,978,000	140,000	3,205,000
Commerce .	26,000	1,672,000	53,000	1,751,000
Various . .	128,000	2,447,000	138,000	2,713,000
Total .	826,000	12,985,000	934,000	14,745,000

	Females			
Agriculture .	136,000	436,000	23,000	595,000
Manufactures	47,000	577,000	8,000	632,000
Commerce .	3,000	54,000	2,000	59,000
Various . .	108,000	1,215,000	38,000	1,361,000
Total .	294,000	2,282,000	71,000	2,647,000

	Total			
Agriculture .	721,000	6,320,000	626,000	7,671,000
Manufactures	134,000	3,555,000	148,000	3,837,000
Commerce .	29,000	1,726,000	55,000	1,810,000
Various . .	236,000	3,666,000	176,000	4,074,000
Total .	1,120,000	15,267,000	1,005,000	17,392,000

Of the total number of workers 80 per cent. were men, 13 per cent. women, 5 per cent. boys, 2 per cent. girls.

AUSTRALIA

The Census of 1881 showed as follows :—

	Agriculture	Commerce	Mining	Various	Children and Servants	Total
New South Wales	113,000	28,000	18,000	165,000	427,000	751,000
Victoria	124,000	21,000	36,000	177,000	504,000	862,000
Queensland	33,000	6,000	11,000	42,000	122,000	214,000
South Australia	35,000	8,000	2,000	60,000	175,000	280,000
New Zealand	55,000	14,000	14,000	90,000	317,000	490,000
Tasmania	19,000	3,000	3,000	22,000	69,000	116,000
Western Australia	5,000	1,000	...	6,000	18,000	30,000
Total . . .	384,000	81,000	84,000	562,000	1,632,000	2,743,000

Under agriculture are included both tillage and pastoral pursuits. It is probable that the real number employed in such occupations in 1881 was larger than appears, say 50 per cent. more, as the numbers under "Servants" and "Various" are large. The ratios show :—

	N.S. Wales	Victoria	Queensland	South Australia	New Zealand	Tasmania	Western Australia
Agriculture	15.0	14.4	15.6	12.4	11.1	16.8	16.0
Mining . .	2.4	4.2	5.4	0.8	2.9	2.7	0.3
Sundries	82.6	81.4	79.0	86.8	86.0	80.5	83.7
Total .	100.0	100.0	100.0	100.0	100.0	100.0	100.0

OIL

There are three principal kinds of oil—vegetable, marine, and mineral. The annual product, in gallons, is approximately as follows : vegetable, 140 millions ; marine, 6 millions ; mineral, 1800 millions.

The yield of oil from vegetable products is as follows :—

Pounds of Oil from 100 Lbs. of

Horse-chestnuts .	. 6	Rape .	. .	. 33
Beech-mast .	. 16	Colza .	. .	. 40
Hempseed .	. 18	Almonds .	. .	. 48
European linseed .	. 25	Poppy .	. .	. 58
Indian linseed .	. 29	Walnuts .	. .	. 60
Olives . . .	. 33	Castor-oil seed	.	. 62

2 E

The ordinary product of olive-oil is approximately as follows :—

	Tons Olives	Gallons Oil	Value, £
France . .	170,000	12,000,000	3,300,000
Italy . . .	720,000	50,000,000	13,400,000
Spain . .	300,000	21,000,000	5,800,000
Portugal .	90,000	6,000,000	1,700,000
Greece . .	50,000	3,500,000	1,000,000

The production of colza in 1884 was as follows :—

	Acres	Bushels	Oil, Gallons
France . .	284,000	5,800,000	14,000,000
Belgium . .	17,000	380,000	1,000,000
Denmark . .	2,500	70,000	200,000

The imports into Great Britain of palm-oil and cocoa-nut-oil have been as follows :—

Year	Tons		
	Palm	Cocoa-nut	Total
1840 . . .	15,800	2,100	17,900
1850 . . .	22,400	4,900	27,300
1860 . . .	40,200	9,700	49,900
1870 . . .	43,400	9,900	53,300
1880 . . .	51,600	15,900	67,500
1889 . . .	54,600	10,700	65,300

These figures are by Mr. Simmonds, author of *Science and Commerce.*

The annual production of marine oil is approximately as follows :—

	Annual Slaughter	Gallons Oil	Gallons per Carcass
Whales . .	1,500	3,300,000	2,200
Seals . . .	550,000	2,600,000	5
Penguins . .	1,300,000	130,000	1-10th

About 300 gallons of oil will suffice in twenty minutes to smooth the roughest sea (Admiralty experiments, Aberdeen, December 3, 1882).

The production of mineral oil is shown as follows :—

UNITED STATES

Two men boring for salt, 25 miles from Pittsburg, in 1845, struck an oil spring, which gave 40 gallons in 24 hours. The first oil company was formed at New York in 1854. A well sunk at Oil Creek, Pennsylvania, in 1859, gave 1000 gallons daily, and in a week others were sunk 600 feet, which gave 3000 gallons each in 24 hours. An oil fever ensued, and in 1860 there were 2000 wells at Oil Creek, 74 of which gave collectively 50,000 gallons daily. Down to 1889 more than 53,000 wells had been dug, the depth varying from 400 to 1200 feet, each bore costing about £800. One well in five strikes oil, and the number now working is about 6000. The total product since their discovery in 1859 has been approximately :—

Period	Millions of Gallons			Price, Cents per Gallon		Value at Pit's Mouth, £
	Raised	Exported	Home Use	Pit's Mouth	Refined	
1859–63	240	24	168	10	44	5,000,000
1864–73	2,250	900	900	5	22	23,500,000
1874–80	4,760	2,400	1,400	2½	10	24,000,000
1881–88	8,630	3,740	3,160	2⅛	9	37,300,000
30 years	15,880	7,064	5,628	...	...	89,800,000

The cost of boring wells, good and bad, was 42 millions sterling, or about 46 per cent. of the value of crude oil extracted. The market value of the refined petroleum exported or consumed in the United States was 330 millions sterling. The ordinary yield of refined oil is 80 gallons to 100 of crude petroleum.

RUSSIA

The Baku oil springs began to yield in 1863, and 363 wells have been sunk, of which 207 are working. The average depth is 550 feet, but some are only 190, others 1000 feet deep. At first the yield averaged 35 gallons of refined to 100 of crude oil, but it has since fallen to 28 gallons.

The production has been approximately as follows :—

	Millions of Gallons		Value at Pit, £
	Crude	Refined	
1863–73 . . .	120	42	2,500,000
1874–80 . . .	550	165	5,500,000
1881–89 . . .	4,510	1,300	18,000,000
27 years . . .	5,180	1,507	26,000,000

AUSTRIA

Ozokerit is a mineral oil from layers of wax found at Borislav, Galitzia. The mines are about 250 feet deep.

Year	Mines	Miners	Tons Raised	Value, £
1883 . .	1,292	3,800	4,500	210,000
1887 . .	560	4,800	5,000	210,000

GERMANY

The consumption of petroleum has increased very notably, viz. :—

Year	Tons per Annum	Year	Tons per Annum
1861–70 . .	70,000	1881–85 . .	390,000
1871–80 . .	195,000	1887 . .	510,000

ORDERS

The principal religious Orders are the following :—

	Founded A.D.		Founded A.D.
Benedictines .	543	Dominicans . .	1215
Carthusians .	1084	Augustinians .	1256
Carmelites .	1156	Jesuits .	1534
Franciscans .	1209	Sisters of Charity	1634

Chambers's Encyclopædia (1891) has the following regarding the Jesuits : "In 1634 the Order comprised 13,112 members, distributed all over the world in 32 'provinces.' In 1773 it counted 22,589 members, who had 930 colleges and 610 residences or missionary stations."

The Jesuit Missions of Paraguay, in the territory now called Misiones, counted in 1732 an Indian population of 30,362 families, or 141,242 souls, possessing 788,000 cows, 225,000 sheep, and 111,400 horses. The annual tribute to the King of Spain was £3000 sterling. The value of exports, such as yerba-màte, hides and timber, averaged £25,000 yearly. For military service against the Portuguese, the Indians, whenever required, had to furnish the Viceroy with a force of 3000 men, 4000 horses, and 5000 draught oxen.

The Jesuit Order counted in 1882 the following members :—

Great Britain and United States . .	1,894
Spain and South America . . .	1,933
China, India, Africa, &c. . . .	7,222
Total . . .	11,049

Respecting the other Orders the *Catholic Times* says : " During the last 600 years the Order of St. Francis has given to the Church 247 saints, 1500 martyrs, 10 popes, and 4000 archbishops and bishops ; the Order of St. Dominic, 4 popes, 80 cardinals, and 2000 bishops ; the Order of St. Benedict, 43. popes, 200 cardinals, 256 patriarchs, 600 archbishops, and 40,000 bishops, besides 25 emperors, kings, and queens who left their thrones for the cloisters of the celebrated Order."

England

At the Dissolution Henry VIII. confiscated 608 abbeys, with an aggregate income of £141,000, equal to the rent of 720,000 acres. The number of religious houses in the United Kingdom in 1873 was :—

For men	86
For women	286
Total . . .	372

Of this total there were 256 in Ireland and 116 in Great Britain, mostly devoted to teaching the poor or caring the sick.

France

The numbers of religious of both sexes were as follows :—

1815	. . 12,200	1861	. . 108,120
1842	. . 25,000	1871	. . 97,400

The composition of the houses in 1861 was :—

	Men	Women	Total
Hospitals . . .	389	20,292	20,681
Schools. . . .	12,845	58,883	71,728
Contemplative .	4,542	11,169	15,711
Total . .	17,776	90,344	108,120

	Houses	Endowed Capital, £	Approximate Income, £
Friars	2,026	100,000	5,000
Nuns	12,004	4,100,000	205,000
Total . .	14,030	4,200,000	210,000

The estates of religious houses consist of £3,200,000 in house property and £1,000,000 in lands. The total number of religious in 1871 was 13,000 men and 84,300 women.

Russia

The religious houses of the Greek Church are :—

	Houses	Religious	Aspirants
Men.	484	6,800	3,470
Women . . .	198	6,037	16,018
Total . .	682	12,837	19,488

Austria

In 1880 the Orders stood thus :—

	Austria		Hungary	
	Houses	Religious	Houses	Religious
Men . . .	475	7,127	186	2,243
Women . .	429	8,727	64	915
Total .	904	15,854	250	3,158

The above communities possessed houses and lands valued at £4,680,000. The abbeys and convents suppressed in 1790 by Joseph II. were 359 in number.

Italy

In 1867 the Government suppressed 4254 religious houses, containing 31,000 men and 28,250 women, whose endowed estates gave an annual income of £970,000, equal to £16 per religious. The estates were sold for £17,510,000, averaging £13 per acre. In ten years ending 1876, the Government paid to friars and nuns pensions which made up an aggregate of £6,840,000 sterling. In 1840 Rome counted 1560 priests, 2140 friars, and 1500 nuns, besides 440 ecclesiastical students. In 1830 the kingdom of Naples had 8500 friars and 8200 nuns.

Spain

There are four military Orders :—

Name	Commanderies	Income, £
Calatrava . . .	56	64,000
Santiago . . .	87	73,000
Alcantara . . .	37	37,000
Montesa . . .	193	196,000
Total . .	373	370,000

In 1803 there were 2923 religious houses, but in 1884, after numerous suppressions, the number had fallen to 1188, including 161 of friars, and 1027 of nuns. The numbers of religious at various dates compared thus :—

	1788	1803	1884
Friars . . .	49,270	69,700	1,684
Nuns . . .	22,230	38,400	14,592
Total .	71,500	108,100	16,276

In 1820 the Government confiscated monastic properties to the value of £3,200,000.

Belgium

In 1789 there were 631 houses with 12,000 religious. The numbers in later times have been :—

	1846		1866	
	Houses	Religious	Houses	Religious
Men . . .	137	2,051	178	2,991
Women . .	642	9,917	1,144	15,205
Total .	779	11,968	1,322	18,196

The houses in 1866 were composed thus :—

Occupation	Men	Women	Total
Teaching . . .	975	7,249	8,224
Hospitals . . .	797	5,527	6,324
Various . . .	1,219	2,429	3,648
Total . .	2,991	15,205	18,196

Houses and lands held by the above communities represented a total value of £940,000, including £640,000 of charitable bequests by 2615 benefactors since 1838. According to the Census of 1880 there were :—

		Houses	Religious
Friars		213	4,027
Nuns . . .		1,346	20,645
	Total . .	1,559	24,672

GERMANY

The Orders in 1873 stood thus :—

				Houses	Religious
Prussia	.	.	.	958	9,048
Bavaria	.	.	.	620	6,148
Other states	.	.	450	4,238

| | | Total | . | . 2,028 | 19,434 |

	Prussia	Bavaria	Other States
Men	1,037	1,094	457
Women . . .	8,011	5,054	3,781
Total . .	9,048	6,148	4,238

HOLLAND

In 1862 the Orders stood thus :—

					Houses	Religious
Friars	.	.	.	.	38	820
Nuns	.	.	.	.	137	2,187

| | | Total | . | . 175 | 3,007 |

PORTUGAL

In 1834 the Government suppressed 750 religious houses, and seized the revenues.

SWITZERLAND

In 1871 there were :—

					Houses	Religious
Men	.	.	.	.	33	546
Women	.	.	.	.	55	2,020

| | | Total | . | . 88 | 2,566 |

These houses held real estate valued at £480,000, producing an income of about £10 a year for each religious. The Capuchins numbered 235, other friars 311. The most numerous Order of nuns was Theodosians, who were 417, the Sisters of St. Francis coming next.

GREECE

There are 161 religious houses of the Greek Church, containing 2620 monks and 485 nuns.

UNITED STATES

According to a Catholic paper there are in the United States 7000 nuns in charge of schools and orphans, 3000 Sisters of Charity tending the sick, and 3000 clergy of monastic Orders doing missionary work or in colleges.

ORGANS

	Benches of Keys	Stops	Pipes
Hamburg . . .	4	70	...
Lübeck	4	82	...
Cologne . . .	4	104	...
Ulm	4	100	6,564
Meresburg . . .	4	81	5,866
Frankfort . . .	3	75	...
Prague . . .	4	71	...
Stuttgart . . .	4	70	...
Seville . . .	...	110	5,300
Rotterdam . . .	4	75	5,700
Haarlem . . .	...	60	4,088
San Sulpice, Paris	5	100	6,700
Albert Hall, London	4	111	...
Alexandra Palace .	4	88	...
Town-Hall, Leeds .	...	100	6,500
St. George's Hall, Liverpool . .	4	100	...
Doncaster . . .	...	94	...
Glasgow . . .	4	64	...
Boston Music-Hall .	4	89	...
Riga	...	...	7,000

That of Haarlem, built in 1735, cost £12,000 ; that of Liverpool, £10,000. The proposed new organ for St. Peter's at Rome is to have 124 stops, some 32 ft. long.

OSTRICHES

The production of ostrich feathers averages as follows :—

	Lbs. Feathers	Value, £
Cape Colony . . .	260,000	1,040,000
Tripoli . . .	20,000	200,000
Egypt	4,000	40,000
Morocco . . .	2,000	20,000
Buenos Ayres . . .	160,000	32,000

About 35,000 birds are plucked annually at the Cape, averaging 3 lbs. per bird. In Buenos Ayres they are slaughtered, and the race is dying out.

According to Simmonds, the Buenos Ayres "rhea" is not really an ostrich at all, and the feathers are sold as "vulture feathers." He gives the exports of Cape feathers and the imports of ostrich feathers from all quarters into Great Britain thus :—

Year	Cape Export, Lbs.	Year	Great Britain Import, Lbs.	Value, £
1875 . .	50,000	1860 . .	25,000	80,000
1880 . .	160,000	1870 . .	65,000	175,000
1885 . .	250,000	1880 . .	190,000	1,010,000
1889 . .	230,000	1889 . .	150,000	400,000

P.

PALMS

The number of cocoa-nut palms given by Simmonds is :—

New Caledonia	.	.	.	45,000,000
Ceylon .	.	.	.	30,000,000
Madras	.	.	.	11,000,000
Feejee Islands	.	.	.	500,000

Brazil has probably 100 millions. The betel-nut palm is also cultivated in India ; the area under this tree in Ceylon is 50,000 acres. As for the date-palm, Tunis has 2,500,000, Egypt 4,500,000, and India 13,000,000. Even in the oases of Sahara there are 16,000. See *Fruit*.

PAPER

The consumption in 1882 was estimated as follows :—

				Tons
Printing .	.	.	.	455,000
Schools and offices .	.	.	160,000
Account-books	.	.	.	55,000
Letter-paper .	.	.	.	100,000
Wall-paper .	.	.	.	200,000
Sundry manufactures	.	.	80,000

| | Total | . | . 1,050,000 |

In 1881 there were 3960 paper-mills, employing 90,000 men and 180,000 women : there were 2780 mills worked by steam-power. The capital employed in the industry exceeded 62 millions sterling. The paper industry of the world sums up thus :—

Rag, jute, &c.	£14,000,000
Chemicals	8,500,000
Wages	9,000,000
Coal	3,400,000
Profit, interest on capital, &c.	3,600,000
Value of paper	£38,500,000

In 1882 the production and consumption in the several countries was stated as follows (the consumption in 1890 being probably one-fourth more) :—

	Millions Lbs.		Consumption, Lbs. per Inhab.
	Production	Consumption	
United Kingdom	470	430	12.1
France*	380	330	8.4
Germany	450	410	9.1
Russia	80	90	1.2
Austria	160	120	3.3
Italy	105	110	3.9
Spain	20	32	2.0
Portugal	10	10	2.2
Belgium	70	40	7.2
Holland	16	16	4.0
Scandinavia	38	30	3.5
Switzerland	20	18	6.8
Turkey and Greece	...	12	1.2
Europe	1,819	1,648	5.1
United States	530	540	10.2
Canada	14	18	4.1
Spanish America	2	44	1.3
Australia	...	17	6.1
Other countries	...	98	...
Total	2,365	2,365	...

The above total was equivalent to 1,050,000 tons, which were supposed to be produced from the following materials :—

Material	Tons Used	Tons, Paper	Ratio of Paper to Material, per Cent.
Woollen rags	670,000	390,000	59
Cotton rag	450,000	280,000	62
Linen, &c., rags	100,000	50,000	50
Jute and sparta	300,000	50,000	17
Wood and straw	400,000	40,000	10
Sundries	2,400,000	240,000	10
Total	4,320,000	1,050,000	25

In 1813 Stevenson estimated the value of paper made yearly in Great Britain at one million sterling; in 1835, M'Culloch at £1,300,000. The consumption has risen twelvefold since 1840, viz. :—

Year	Tons		
	Press	Sundries	Total
1840	3,000	13,000	16,000
1864	31,000	52,000	83,000
1885	95,000	100,000	195,000

* The quantity of paper which paid excise in France in 1885 was only 217,000 tons.

In 1880–85 the paper-mills in various countries were :—

	Number	Hands	Steam, Horse-Power	Water, Horse-Power	Product, Tons
Great Britain	354	28,000	27,000	8,000	200,000
France	512	31,000	7,000	13,000	170,000
Germany	446	54,000	24,000	30,000	200,000

The consumption of paper for books is relatively small, only 6 per cent. of the total ; the annual issue being supposed to reach 85 million volumes, which take 65,000 tons of paper, an average of 14 oz. per volume.

The first paper-mill in America was at Germantown, Pennsylvania, in 1693. There were 63 in 1787, which turned out 250 tons yearly. In 1870 one factory in Massachusetts produced 25,000 tons of writing-paper yearly, and another 100 miles a day of wall-paper.

PARIS

In 1887 this city had 82,500 houses and 2,261,000 population, including 180,000 foreigners. The streets had a length of exactly 600 miles. Total area, 18,700 acres, of which 14,500 are covered by houses, the rest being streets and squares. In the parish of the Temple there are 290 persons per acre, in that of Passy only 42 ; general average 116. There are 440 miles of sewers, the construction of which cost 4 millions sterling ; they vary from 5 ft. to 18 ft. diameter. Water-supply averages 90 million gallons daily, there being 66,000 subscribers who pay water-rate. Gas-supply in 1888 reached 8800 million cubic feet, of which 900 millions were used for streets and public buildings. Vital statistics showed 57,000 deaths and 60,000 births, 28 per cent. of the latter being illegitimate. The hospitals admitted 131,000 patients, of whom 13,900 died, say 10½ per cent. There are 6000 police, 500 steamboats, 8000 cabs, and 1200 busses or tramcars. Food consumption was 350,000 tons of bread, 175,000 tons of meat, 24,000 tons of poultry, 5500 tons of cheese, 400 million eggs, and 104 million gallons of wine and liquors.

PARKS

The area of park to the principal cities of the United Kingdom is shown in the following table :—

Cities	Area, Acres	Park, Acres	Inhabitants to an Acre	
			Municipal Area	Park Area
Birmingham	8,400	211	46	1,736
Bradford	7,200	215	26	889
Brighton	2,400	106	45	996
Bristol	4,500	442	47	475
Dublin	10,100	1,753	31	175
Edinburgh	4,200	407	54	410
Glasgow	6,100	447	96	1,293
Hull	3,600	26	40	4,721
Leeds	21,600	350	14	681
Leicester	3,200	65	39	1,256
Liverpool	5,200	525	103	1,025
London	75,400	1,790	48	1,114
Manchester	9,500	191	77	2,846
Newcastle	5,400	91	27	4,199
Norwich	7,500	7	11	12,175
Nottingham	9,900	150	17	1,129
Oldham	4,700	60	24	1,855
Plymouth	1,400	22	53	3,377
Portsmouth	4,500	31	29	8,239
Sheffield	19,700	49	15	3,761
Sunderland	2,800	24	41	4,774
Wolverhampton	3,400	50	22	1,510

The most remarkable are :—

Name	Place	Acres
Regent's . . .	London .	450
Hyde . . .	London .	400
Bois de Boulogne .	Paris . .	2,100
Phœnix . . .	Dublin . .	1,760
Prater . . .	Vienna . .	2,300
Royal . . .	Munich . .	1,300
Queen's . . .	Edinburgh .	407

PARLIAMENT

That of the United Kingdom made 27,010 laws in eighty-two years, as follows :—

Period	Acts of Parliament		
	Public	Private	Total
1801–10 . . .	1,322	2,514	3,836
1811–20 . . .	1,487	2,233	3,720
1821–30 . . .	986	1,979	2,965
1831–40 . . .	1,038	1,706	2,744
1841–50 . . .	1,129	2,140	3,269
1851–60 . . .	1,158	2,057	3,215
1861–68 . . .	1,010	2,140	3,150
1869–82 . . .	1,283	2,828	4,111
82 years . . .	9,413	17,597	27,010

The following Ministers have held power since 1801 :—

Period	Premier	Months
1801–4 . .	Addington . .	38
1804–6 . .	Pitt . . .	20
1806–7 . .	Grenville . .	14
1807–10 . .	Portland . .	39
1810–12 . .	Perceval . .	24
1812–27 . .	Liverpool . .	178
1827 . .	Canning . .	4
1827–28 . .	Goderich . .	5
1828–30 . .	Wellington . .	34
1830–34 . .	Grey . . .	44
1834 . .	Melbourne . .	5
1834–35 . .	Peel . . .	4
1835–41 . .	Melbourne . .	77
1841–46 . .	Peel . . .	58
1846–52 . .	Russell . . .	68
1852 . .	Derby . . .	10
1852–55 . .	Aberdeen . .	25
1855–58 . .	Palmerston . .	37
1858–59 . .	Derby . . .	16
1859–65 . .	Palmerston . .	76
1865–66 . .	Russell . . .	8
1866–68 . .	Derby . . .	20
1868 . .	Disraeli . .	9
1868–74 . .	Gladstone . .	62
1874–80 . .	Disraeli . .	74
1880–85 . .	Gladstone . .	62
1885–86 . .	Salisbury . .	7
1886 . .	Gladstone . .	6
1886 . .	Salisbury . .	...

Parliament consists of 515 Lords and 670 Commons. The composition of the latter House was greatly changed in 1885 under the new Reform Act, viz. :—

	County		Borough		University		Total	
	1884	1885	1884	1885	1884	1885	1884	1885
England . . .	172	234	282	226	5	5	459	465
Wales . . .	15	19	15	11	...	...	30	30
Scotland . . .	32	39	26	31	2	2	60	72
Ireland . . .	64	85	37	16	2	2	103	103
United Kingdom	283	377	360	284	9	9	652	670

The French Chamber contained 97 noblemen, 116 lawyers, 57 manufacturers, 92 farmers, 48 doctors, 40 journalists, 14 engineers, 23 soldiers, 12 bankers, and 123 of various occupations in 1888.

PASSENGERS

In 1885 it was computed that 80,000 vehicles and 400,000 foot-passengers crossed the bridges of London daily.

The number of persons who crossed Waterloo Bridge in a year was as follows :—

1820 . . .	1,821,000	1850 . . .	4,295,000
1830 . . .	2,423,000	1860 . . .	4,873,000
1840 . . .	2,486,000	1863 . . .	5,145,000

At present the number will probably reach 8,000,000. In 1875 there were 7,300,000 vehicles and 38,500,000 persons that crossed London Bridge. In 1882 the ferryboats between Liverpool and Birkenhead carried 22,000,000 passengers. London has 12,000 cabs, Paris 8000 ; the former carry 90,000, the latter 60,000 passengers daily, the average fare earned being 15d. per passenger in Paris, 18d. in London. The daily earnings of a cab in London are 19s. in the season, 9s. the rest, and 12s. all the year round.

The London Omnibus Company carried as follows :—

	1888	1889
Passengers . . .	61,200,000	69,300,000
Receipts, £ . . .	400,000	430,000
Expenses . . .	375,000	395,000

The local passenger traffic of London has grown as follows :—

	Millions of Passengers Yearly		
	1864	1874	1884
Underground . .	42	65	115
Omnibus . . .	11	48	75
Tramway . . .	...	42	119
Total . .	53	155	309

The Underground Railway now carries 150 million persons yearly.

As regards Paris, the traffic shows thus :—

Year	Passengers	Year	Passengers
1860 . .	72,000,000	1880 . .	234,000,000
1870 . .	108,000,000	1888 . .	279,000,000

The traffic of 1880 and of 1888 was computed thus :—

	1880	1888
Tramcars and busses . .	209,000,000	241,000,000
Steamboats, &c.	25,000,000	38,000,000
Total . . .	234,000,000	279,000,000

The above does not include about 22,000,000 persons carried in cabs in 1888. The average fare paid in 1880 was about three halfpence (1.6). The passenger traffic between the various ports of the United Kingdom is not ascertained, but it is found that between domestic and foreign traffic 10,000 persons leave the ports of the United Kingdom daily. The number of pilgrims yearly to Mecca is not known, but 35,000 pass through Suez.

PATENTS

The number applied for, and that of those granted, in the United Kingdom were as follows :—

Period	Applications	Granted
1860–69	34,870	21,910
1870–79	44,950	30,360
1880–87	91,940	53,040
28 years	171,760	105,310

FRANCE

The number granted in various years was as follows :—

Year			Patents	Year			Patents
1844	.	.	625	1870	.	.	3,029
1850	.	.	1,687	1880	.	.	6,057
1860	.	.	4,606	1885	.	.	7,060

AUSTRIA

The total number granted in the Empire was :—

Period						Patents
1852–69	.	.	.	.	.	10,480
1870–84	.	.	.	.	.	24,090
33 years	.	.	.	.	.	34,570

BELGIUM

The returns for forty-eight years showed as follows :—

Period	Inventions	Improvements	Total
1841–60 . . .	5,879	10,651	16,530
1861–70 . . .	7,572	10,355	17,927
1871–88 . . .	30,600	25,680	56,280
48 years . . .	44,051	46,686	90,737

UNITED STATES

The records show as follows :—

Year	Applications	Granted	Fees, £
1840 . . .	735	473	8,000
1850 . . .	2,193	993	18,000
1860 . . .	7,653	4,778	53,000
1870 . . .	19,171	13,333	120,000
1880 . . .	23,021	13,917	156,000
1889 . . .	40,575	24,158	266,000

PAUPERS

It is difficult to compare the numbers in different countries. England, for example, counts the number receiving relief on 1st January ; France the total of persons succoured during the year, the latter being a repetition of persons who needed relief. The following may be taken as an estimate of pauperism in 1888 :—

	Paupers	Per 100 Population	Annual Outlay, £
England . . .	810,000	2.8	8,400,000
Scotland . . .	96,000	2.4	900,000
Ireland	109,000	2.3	1,400,000
France	290,000	0.8	1,500,000
Germany . . .	320,000	0.7	4,600,000
Russia	350,000	0.4	...
Austria	290,000	0.7	400,000
Italy	270,000	0.9	1,900,000
Holland . . .	88,000	2.0	510,000

In 1884 the number of paupers relieved at various capitals was as follows :—

	Paupers	Outlay, £	Per Head, £
Paris	490,000	800,000	1.6
St. Petersburg .	215,000	140,000	0.7
Berlin	310,000	370,000	1.2
Vienna	286,600	530,000	1.8

For some years back the average number of paupers receiving relief in London has been 102,000, at an outlay of more than a million sterling per annum.

UNITED KINGDOM

Official returns show as follows :—

Year	England	Scotland	Ireland	U. Kingdom	Ratio to Population			
					England	Scotland	Ireland	U. Kingdom
1850	921,000	79,000	308,000	1,308,000	5.11	2.72	4.61	4.75
1860	851,000	77,000	45,000	973,000	4.26	2.50	0.77	3.35
1870	1,079,000	126,000	74,000	1,279,000	4.69	3.78	1.38	4.06
1880	803,000	99,000	115,000	1,016,000	3.09	2.66	2.21	2.90
1889	810,000	96,000	109,000	1,015,000	2.80	2.40	2.30	2.65

Expenditure :—	1850	1860	1870	1880	1888
	£	£	£	£	£
England	5,400,000	5,450,000	7,650,000	8,020,000	8,440,000
Scotland	580,000	660,000	910,000	850,000	890,000
Ireland	1,830,000	530,000	810,000	1,190,000	1,390,000
United Kingdom . . .	7,810,000	6,640,000	9,370,000	10,060,000	10,720,000

The average outlay yearly on each pauper, and the cost per inhabitant, as regards the three kingdoms, are shown as follows :—

Year	Outlay per Pauper, £			Cost per Inhabitant, Pence		
	England	Scotland	Ireland	England	Scotland	Ireland
1850 . .	5.9	7.3	6.0	72	48	65
1860 . .	6.4	8.6	11.6	66	52	22
1870 . .	7.1	7.4	11.0	60	66	36
1880 . .	10.0	8.5	10.4	74	55	54
1889 . .	10.4	9.3	12.7	72	54	70

The amount spent annually on poor-relief in England and Wales has been at various dates as follows :—

Period	Annual Expenditure, £	Per Inhabitant, Pence	National Income, Millions £	Percentage of Burden
1702–14 . .	910,000	41	65	1.40
1760–75 . .	1,520,000	58	122	1.24
1783–93 . .	2,050,000	66	145	1.41
1801–5 . .	5,100,000	78	180	2.80
1815–20 . .	7,106,000	152	220	3.23
1830 35 . .	6,742,000	114	385	1.75
1841–50 . .	5,250,000	74	490	1.07
1851–60 . .	5,510,000	69	580	0.95
1861–70 . .	6,740,000	77	720	0.94
1871–80 . .	7,710,000	75	935	0.82
1884–88 . .	8,400,000	73	1,084	0.78

*

In the period just after Waterloo the burden was five times as great as it has been in the past five years.

In 1886 the condition of the poor in the east part of London was found by school-agents to be thus:—

Class	Number	Weekly Wages, Shillings
Indigent . . .	314,000	10 to 21
Struggling . . .	498,000	22 to 50
Well to do . . .	80,000	...
Total . .	892,000	

The above is the estimated population of the poorer parishes of London.

FRANCE

In 1886 the number of persons who received relief during the year was 1,440,000, but as the same persons probably were relieved at least five times, the actual number of such paupers would not exceed 290,000. There was much distress in 1847, when 6,000,000 were relieved—that is to say, about 1,200,000 in reality; the sum so expended reaching 8 millions sterling, of which £4,600,000 passed through public officials and £3,400,000 was given by St. Vincent de Paul societies and other charitable associations. In 1884 the sum officially expended was as follows:—

In	£	In	£
Paris . . .	800,000	Food . . .	520,000
Departments .	660,000	Money, &c. .	940,000
Total .	1,460,000	Total .	1,460,000

There are 15,000 offices all over France for poor-relief, the funds being mainly derived from a tax of 10 per cent. on tickets for theatres, and averaging £2,100,000 per annum.

GERMANY

In 1885 the sum of £4,560,000 was expended in poor-relief, viz.:—

	Paupers	Outlay, £	Per Head, £
Prussia . .	953,000	2,670,000	2.8
Bavaria . .	152,000	550,000	3.5
Saxony . .	89,000	270,000	3.1
Alsace . .	73,000	220,000	3.0
Baden . .	68,000	170,000	2.5
Wurtemburg .	63,000	180,000	2.8
Various . .	194,000	500,000	2.6
Total .	1,592,000	4,560,000	2.9

The number of paupers relieved in cities per 1000 of the population was as follows:—

Strasburg . . .	102	Berlin . . .	61
Königsberg . . .	84	Leipzig . . .	59
Bremen . . .	76	Dresden . . .	56
Frankfort . . .	70	Stuttgart . . .	51

RUSSIA

In 1884 the number of registered mendicants was 350,000; that of persons relieved in St. Petersburg 215,000, at an average of 14s. each.

AUSTRIA

The system of poor-relief resembles that in France, for which purpose there are 10,650 offices. In 1886 were relieved 290,000 paupers at a cost of £400,000, say 27s. each.

ITALY

According to the *Statesman's Year-Book*, there are 21,800 offices for poor-relief, endowed with funds representing a capital value of 80 millions sterling, with an annual income of £3,500,000; expenses of management, &c., £1,600,000; balance for the poor, £1,900,000. In 1881 there were 1,365,000 persons relieved; the same remark applies as in France, and the actual number of paupers may be set down at about 270,000.

BELGIUM

The number of paupers receiving indoor relief is small, viz.:—

Year	Paupers	Outlay, £	Per Head, £
1835 . . .	2,260	11,000	4.9
1850 . . .	3,478	21,000	6.0
1870 . . .	1,925	20,000	10.4
1888 . . .	4,399	48,000	10.8

The above is the mean number in each year, the number of paupers passing through the depôts being four times as great.

HOLLAND

The number of persons relieved in the year 1881 was:—

Permanent paupers	88,300
Temporary ,, ...	128,300
Total . . .	216,600

The total expenditure was £510,000, or about £2, 8s. per pauper, religious communities provided £270,000, and the civil authorities £240,000.

SWEDEN

The number of paupers compared with population thus:—

Year	Paupers	Per 100 Pop.
1860	133,000	3.5
1870	204,000	4.8
1880	220,000	5.0
1887	230,000	4.8

There are 2300 workhouses, capable of admitting 40,000 persons.

PAWN-OFFICES

The number of these offices increases in Great Britain faster than population, viz.:—

Year	No.	Per Million Inhab.	Year	No.	Per Million Inhab.
1851 . .	1,873	89	1871 . .	3,450	132
1861 . .	2,578	111	1881 . .	4,372	146

The number of pledges is said to reach 190 millions per annum.

In 1882 the loans of similar institutions, called Monts de Piété, were:—

	Borrowers	Amount
France . . .	2,970,000	£2,300,000
Spain . . .	235,000	985,000
Holland . . .	602,000	260,000

The French returns for 1885 showed thus:—

Under 8s.	2,187,000
8s. to 40s.	715,000
£2 to £4	136,000
Over £4	71,000
Total . . .	3,109,000

PEPPER

The annual production averages:—

	Tons
Sumatra	13,000
Siam	3,500
Malacca, &c.	6,500
Total . . .	23,000

PICTURES

Raphael's " Holy Family," from the Blenheim Gallery, was sold to the National Gallery for £70,000. Millet's " Angelus " was sold at Paris for £24,000 in 1889, Millet having painted it for £72 sterling.

PINS

In 1888 the production was as follows :—

	Millions Weekly
England	280
France	120
Holland and Germany . . .	120
Total . . .	520

Birmingham stands for 180 millions of those made in England. In 1850 the annual output in England was 1250 tons, valued at £1,100,000.

PLACARDS

The largest use on record was prior to the Paris election of 27th January 1889. General Boulanger had 15,000 billstickers, who put up 45,000 daily, in all 900,000, at a cost of £8000 sterling. Jacques had 10,000 men, who put up 25,000 daily, in all 500,000, at a cost of £5000. In some places, when they were torn down after the election, there were found sixty layers alternating of the rival placards.

POLICE

In 1881 the maintenance of police in various cities cost as follows :—

	£	Per Inhab., Pence		£	Per Inhab., Pence
London .	1,060,000	68	Genoa . .	15,000	21
Paris . .	1,160,000	122	Florence .	14,000	20
Vienna .	390,000	99	Turin . .	13,000	18
Berlin. .	70,000	16	Antwerp .	13,000	19
S. Francisco	48,000	52	Trieste . .	12,000	27
Buda-Pesth	38,000	27	Christiania .	11,000	36
Rome . .	30,000	24	Frankfort .	7,000	14
Leipsic .	24,000	49	Liege . .	6,000	12
Bucharest	22,000	26	Venice . .	6,000	12
Stockholm	21,000	33	Palermo .	6,000	6
Copenhagen	20,000	24	Stuttgart .	14,000	28

The following comparison between the police of London and Paris was published in 1881 :—

	London	Paris	Per 10,000 Inhab. London	Per 10,000 Inhab. Paris
Number of men . .	10,940	8,250	29	39
Arrests made . . .	79,490	231,140	210	1,065

The London police cost £97 a year, the Paris £140, per man. The London man arrests seven persons ; the Paris, twenty-nine persons, per annum. For each offender (including drunkenness and misdemeanours), the police expenditure is £13 in London, and £5 in Paris. The number of London police in 1888 was 13,900.

In the United Kingdom the number of police was as follows :—

	Number 1878	Number 1888	Per 10,000 Pop. 1878	Per 10,000 Pop. 1888
England . . .	30,700	37,300	12	13
Scotland . . .	3,400	4,000	10	10
Ireland . . .	12,300	13,900	24	29
United Kingdom .	46,400	55,200	14	15

The expenditure in 1887 was as follows :—

	Amount, £	Per Policeman, £	Pence per Inhabitant
England . . .	3,700,000	98	31
Scotland . . .	380,000	92	23
Ireland	1,570,000	115	80
United Kingdom	5,650,000	102	36

In India the police number 144,000 men, of whom 46,000 carry swords, and 55,000 firearms.

POPULATION

The population of the Roman Empire at the death of Augustus, 14 B.C., was little more than that of the present German Empire, being estimated by Bodio thus :—

Italy	6,000,000
Spain	6,000,000
Greece	3,000,000
Gaul	3,400,000
Other countries . . .	4,600,000
Europe	23,000,000
Asia	19,500,000
Africa	11,500,000
Total . .	54,000,000

The population of Europe hardly exceeded 50 millions before the 15th century.

The growth of the great European Powers in the last 400 years is shown as follows :—

	1480	1580	1680	1780	1880
England	3,700,000	4,600,000	5,532,000	9,561,000	35,004,000
France	12,600,000	14,300,000	18,800,000	25,100,000	37,400,000
Prussia	800,000	1,000,000	1,400,000	5,460,000	45,260,000
Russia	2,100,000	4,300,000	12,600,000	26,800,000	84,440,000
Austria	9,500,000	16,500,000	14,000,000	20,200,000	37,830,000
Italy	9,200,000	10,400,000	11,500,000	12,800,000	28,910,000
Spain	8,800,000	8,150,000	9,200,000	9,960,000	16,290,000
Total . .	46,700,000	59,250,000	73,032,000	109,881,000	285,134,000

In the above, England at present stands for the United Kingdom, and Prussia for the German Empire.

The population of the world has been estimated as follows :—

Date	Author	Millions	Date	Author	Millions
1804	Malte-Brun .	640	1874	Behm-Wagner	1,391
1828	Balbi . . .	847	1878	Levasseur . .	1,439
1845	Michelot . .	1,009	1883	Behm-Wagner	1,433

The population of Europe, according to the best authorities, has been as follows :—

Date	Author	Population	Date	Author	Population
1762	Expilly .	130,000,000	1850	Confronti.	255,000,000
1778	Moheau .	150,000,000	1861	Hausner .	283,900,000
1800	Levasseur	175,000,000	1871	Berg-Loua	293,000,000
1828	Balbi . .	214,000,000	1882	B.-Wagner	327,800,000
1841	Berg-Loua	233,700,000	1886	Levasseur	345,700,000

The distribution of the population of the world was as follows :—

	Millions				
	1810	1828	1845	1874	1886
	Gotha	Balbi	Michelot	Behm-Wagner	Levasseur
Europe . .	180	214	245	301	347
America. .	21	40	50	85	112
Asia . . .	380	481	620	798	822
Africa . .	99	109	90	203	197
Australia .	2	3	4	4	5
Total .	682	847	1,009	1,391	1,483

Michelot's and Levasseur's estimates divide Asia and Australia differently from what is usual, including all the Malay Archipelago as Australian. Thus Levasseur would make Australia in 1886 have a population of 38,000,000 ; but if we follow the ordinary distribution, it will be as above.

The population per square mile in 1820 and 1880 stood thus :—

	1820	1880		1820	1880
U. Kingdom	172	290	Sweden . .	15	27
France . .	148	180	Norway . .	8	15
Germany . .	124	217	Denmark . .	71	127
Russia . .	20	40	Holland . .	195	312
Austria . .	99	158	Belgium . .	287	480
Italy . . .	138	247	Switzerland .	127	175
Spain . . .	58	82	Greece . .	40	84
Portugal . .	92	124	Europe . .	54	85

Levasseur's tables and the various estimates for 1890 show the population of Europe as follows :—

	1800	1830	1860	1880	1890
United Kingdom . . .	16,200,000	24,400,000	29,100,000	35,300,000	38,200,000
France	27,350,000	32,500,000	36,700,000	37,600,000	38,800,000
Germany	23,180,000	29,700,000	38,100,000	45,200,000	48,600,000
Russia	35,000,000	45,500,000	68,700,000	84,900,000	92,600,000
Austria	25,000,000	29,900,000	34,700,000	37,600,000	40,100,000
Italy	17,240,000	21,210,000	25,000,000	28,500,000	30,300,000
Spain	10,540,000	11,200,000	15,600,000	16,700,000	17,600,000
Portugal	2,930,000	3,100,000	3,600,000	4,200,000	4,700,000
Sweden	2,350,000	2,800,000	3,800,000	4,600,000	4,800,000
Norway	880,000	1,100,000	1,600,000	1,900,000	2,000,000
Denmark	930,000	1,200,000	1,600,000	2,000,000	2,100,000
Holland	2,100,000	2,600,000	3,300,000	4,000,000	4,600,000
Belgium	...	3,800,000	4,700,000	5,500,000	6,100,000
Switzerland	1,800,000	2,000,000	2,500,000	2,800,000	3,000,000
Turkey	9,500,000	9,500,000	15,500,000	8,600,000	4,500,000
Greece	...	600,000	1,100,000	1,600,000	2,200,000
Roumania	...	1,300,000	4,000,000	5,300,000	5,500,000
Servia	...	400,000	1,000,000	1,700,000	2,000,000
Bulgaria and E. R. . .	...	...	...	2,000,000	3,100,000
Total . .	175,000,000	222,810,000	290,600,000	330,000,000	350,200,000

In the eighty years that have elapsed since 1810 the ratio of increase in each decade, including estimates for 1890, in the various countries is shown as follows :—

	Increase per 1000 Inhabitants in Decade ending							
	1820	1830	1840	1850	1860	1870	1880	1890
United Kingdom .	171	150	113	25	56	88	108	109
France . . .	47	69	51	45	27	7	11	37
Germany . .	148	112	111	80	64	78	137	74
Russia . . .	...	70	72	50	40	105	130	140
Austria . . .	...	...	15	10	75	85	52	50
Italy . . .	50	95	72	74	44	72	60	60
Spain . . .	45	...	65	...	100	77	35	54
Sweden . . .	80	120	86	108	109	80	96	55
Norway . . .	90	155	118	112	130	100	88	70
Denmark . . .	...	90	80	93	140	111	101	65
Holland . . .	...	...	96	68	81	80	118	135
Belgium . . .	...	...	60	88	68	75	84	115
Switzerland . .	...	...	95	90	46	64	67	60

The increase would have been much greater but for the tide of emigration, which took 23,400,000 persons out of Europe between the years 1816 and 1888, viz. :—

To United States .	.	.	.	14,963,000
To British Colonies	.	.	.	3,767,000
To South America	.	.	.	2,620,000
To other parts	.	.	.	2,050,000
Total	.	.		23,400,000

The above emigration may be divided into two periods, thus :—

Period	Emigrants	Average Yearly
1816–50 . .	4,309,000	123,000
1851–88 . .	19,091,000	503,000

The above does not include about 4,800,000 persons who, without leaving Europe, migrated from their own to another country, as appears from the fact that in 1880–81 there were, according to Census returns, 3,429,000 foreigners then living in the various countries.

The relative loss or gain by emigration or immigration in recent years, as compared with the number of inhabitants, is shown as follows :—

Countries that Gained

	Increase Yearly per 10,000 Pop.			Period
	Natural	Actual	Gain by Immigration	
France . . .	21	32	11	1882–86
Russia . . .	133	146	13	1871–82
Finland . . .	149	155	6	1871–80
Greece . . .	83	159	76	1870–79
Roumania . .	68	73	5	1866–84
Servia . . .	184	222	38	1879–84
United States .	206	274	68	1871–80
Australia . .	207	430	223	1876–80
Canada . . .	120	180	60	1871–80
Argentina . .	130	450	320	1880–88

PLATE VIII.

POPULATION.

Inhabitants per square mile
1820—Left-hand box   1890—Right-hand box

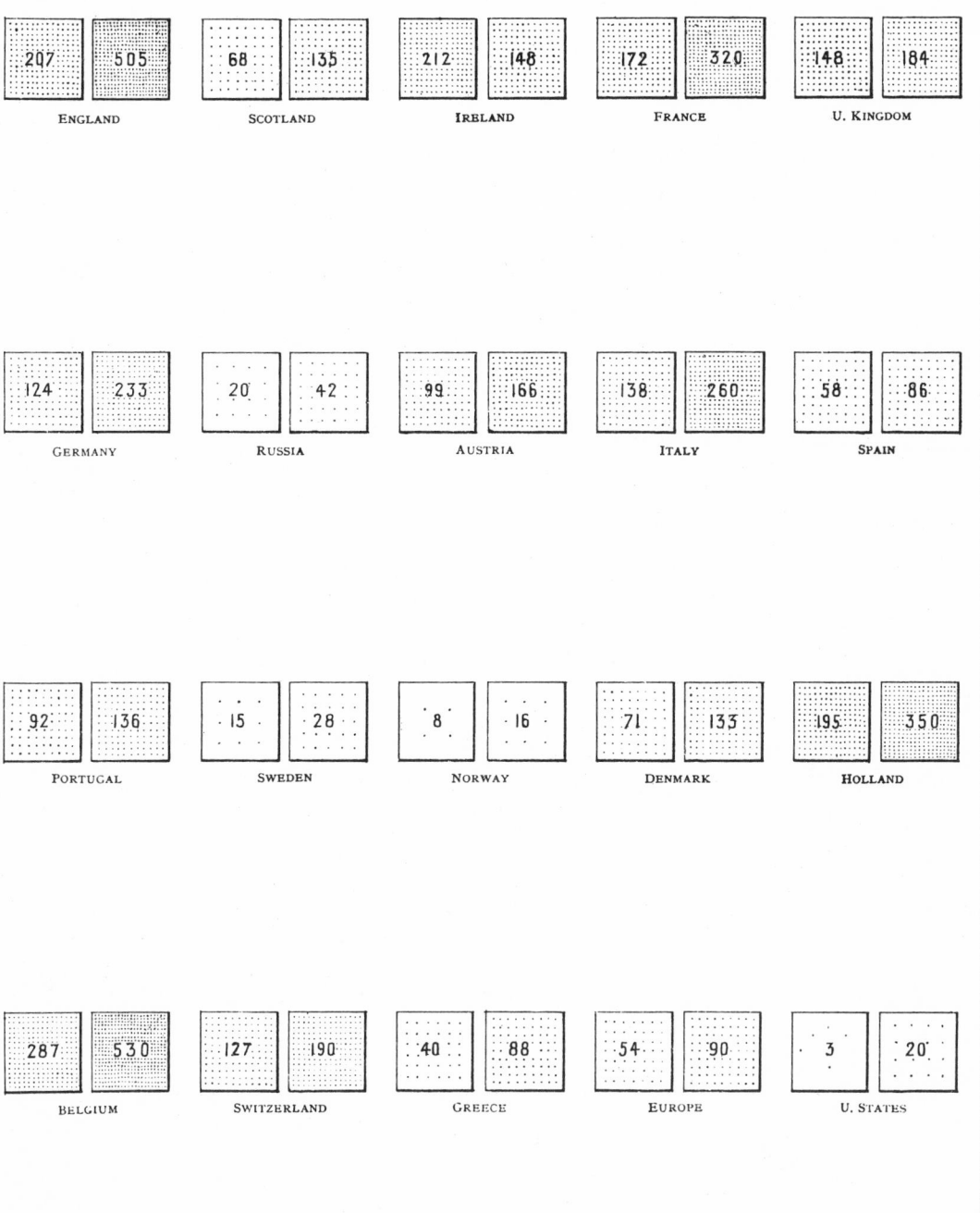

Ballantyne, Hanson & Cº Edinburgh & London.

Countries that Lost

	Increase per 10,000 Population		Loss by Emigration Yearly	Period
	Natural	Actual		
England . . .	140	132	8	1871–80
Scotland . . .	134	98	36	1871–80
Ireland . . .	81	...	128	1871–80
U. Kingdom .	131	108	23	1871–80
Germany . .	115	74	41	1881–85
Austria . . .	87	70	17	1870–80
Hungary. . .	29	16	13	1870–80
Italy	72	54	18	1871–81
Spain	75	34	41	1860–77
Portugal. . .	73	60	13	1864–77
Sweden . . .	119	87	32	1871–80
Norway . . .	122	80	42	1865–75
Denmark . .	119	92	27	1871–80
Holland . . .	119	106	13	1871–80
Belgium . . .	96	77	19	1871–80
Switzerland . .	73	61	12	1871–80

The number of men capable of bearing arms, say from 15–55, and that of women of child-bearing age, say 15–45 years of age, are shown for the various countries approximately as follows :—

	Men Capable of Bearing Arms		Women of Child-Bearing Age	
	1860	1890	1860	1890
U. Kingdom	7,530,000	9,730,000	6,960,000	8,766,000
France . .	10,890,000	10,844,000	8,700,000	8,586,000
Germany .	10,555,000	12,460,000	9,140,000	10,930,000
Russia . .	17,700,000	25,200,000	16,500,000	23,200,000
Austria . .	9,135,000	10,440,000	8,490,000	9,680,000
Italy . . .	7,020,000	8,480,000	5,670,000	6,850,000
Spain. . .	4,060,000	4,510,000	3,740,000	4,130,000
Portugal. .	860,000	1,120,000	830,000	1,080,000
Sweden . .	1,050,000	1,315,000	930,000	1,170,000
Norway . .	420,000	505,000	370,000	465,000
Denmark . .	420,000	530,000	370,000	490,000
Holland . .	880,000	1,220,000	770,000	1,070,000
Belgium . .	1,230,000	1,585,000	1,030,000	1,340,000
Switzerland .	670,000	805,000	580,000	690,000
Greece . .	300,000	590,000	250,000	490,000
Roumania .	1,040,000	1,430,000	920,000	1,260,000
Servia . .	260,000	510,000	230,000	450,000
Europe . .	74,020,000	91,274,000	65,480,000	80,647,000

It is worthy of notice that France is the only country which has fewer men and women than thirty years ago of the able-bodied ages. The following table shows the ratios of men and women of the above ages to population in the several countries :—

Per 1000 Population

	Men, 15–55	Women, 15–45		Men, 15–55	Women, 15–45
England .	256	230	Spain. . .	260	240
Scotland .	250	230	Portugal. .	240	230
Ireland . .	247	224	Sweden . .	274	245
U. Kingdom	254	228	Norway . .	252	233
France . .	281	223	Denmark .	260	232
Germany .	256	225	Holland. .	267	233
Russia . .	259	240	Belgium . .	260	220
Austria . .	261	242	Switzerland.	268	230
Italy . . .	280	227	Greece . .	270	225

Ireland and Portugal are lowest as regards the ratio of able-bodied men.

The *Almanach de Gotha* gives the ratio of sexes in 1884 in the various countries thus :—

Females to 1000 Males

U.Kingdom	1,047	Holland .	1,022	Canada. .	976
France . .	1,004	Belgium .	1,001	Brazil . .	938
Germany .	1,039	Switzerland	1,040	Argentina .	942
Russia . .	1,027	Servia . .	957	Chili. . .	1,004
Austria . .	1,034	Bulgaria .	952	Peru. . .	986
Italy . . .	995	Roumania .	937	Venezuela .	1,063
Spain . . .	1,045	Greece . .	906	Uruguay .	934
Portugal . .	1,084	Egypt . .	1,025	Colombia .	1,058
Sweden . .	1,064	Cape. . .	972	Greenland .	1,134
Norway . .	1,049	India . .	944	Europe . .	1,019
Denmark . .	1,035	Japan . .	973	America . .	970
Finland . .	1,042	U. States .	965	Australia .	843

The latest Census returns show the ratio of foreigners in various countries thus :—

Per 1000 of Population

U. Kingdom .	4	Spain . . .	3	Belgium .	26
France . . .	29	Sweden . . .	4	Switzerland .	74
Germany . .	6	Norway. . .	20	Servia . . .	21
Austria . .	16	Denmark . .	32	Greece . . .	19
Hungary . .	15	Holland . .	17	United States	133
Italy	2				

The ratio of foreigners to population is 21 per thousand in London, 90 in Paris, 13 in Berlin, 14 in Buda-Pesth, 210 in Monte Video, and 360 in Buenos Ayres.

The population of the great cities of the world is shown as follows :—

					1831	1888
Amsterdam	.	.	.		201,000	372,000
Antwerp .	.	.	.		65,000	205,000
Belfast .	.	.	.		53,000	230,000
Berlin .	.	.	.		220,000	1,438,000
Birmingham	.	.	.		142,000	448,000
Bombay .	.	.	.		229,000	773,000
Bordeaux .	.	.	.		94,000	241,000
Boston .	.	.	.		61,000	363,000
Brussels .	.	.	.		102,000	462,000
Buda-Pesth	.	.	.		67,000	443,000
Buenos Ayres	.	.	.		81,000	455,000
Cairo .	.	.	.		333,000	375,000
Calcutta .	.	.	.		280,000	433,000
Constantinople .	.	.			590,000	874,000
Copenhagen	.	.	.		109,000	300,000
Christiania	.	.	.		21,000	136,000
Dresden .	.	.	.		70,000	259,000
Dublin .	.	.	.		227,000	353,000
Edinburgh	.	.	.		130,000	263,000
Florence .	.	.	.		82,000	168,000
Genoa .	.	.	.		83,000	179,000
Glasgow .	.	.	.		164,000	526,000
Hamburg .	.	.	.		112,000	306,000
Havana .	.	.	.		111,000	230,000
Leipsic .	.	.	.		42,000	170,000
Lisbon .	.	.	.		202,000	243,000
Liverpool .	.	.	.		165,000	600,000
London .	.	.	.		1,655,000	4,283,000
Lyons .	.	.	.		146,000	402,000
Madrid .	.	.	.		205,000	387,000
Manchester	.	.	.		238,000	604,000
Manilla .	.	.	.		134,000	270,000
Marseilles .	.	.	.		116,000	376,000
Milan .	.	.	.		125,000	321,000
Moscow .	.	.	.		308,000	753,000
Munich .	.	.	.		65,000	275,000
Naples .	.	.	.		354,000	491,000
New Orleans	.	.	.		46,000	216,000
New York .	.	.	.		203,000	1,493,000
Palermo .	.	.	.		168,000	245,000
Philadelphia	.	.	.		167,000	1,017,000
Prague .	.	.	.		85,000	296,000
Rio Janeiro	.	.	.		145,000	356,000

	1831	1888
Rome	128,000	388,000
Rotterdam . . .	66,000	194,000
St. Petersburg . . .	324,000	843,000
Smyrna	115,000	187,000
Stockholm . . .	79,000	222,000
Stuttgart	32,000	126,000
Turin	114,000	241,000
Tunis	108,000	210,000
Venice	110,000	151,000
Vienna	280,000	801,000
Warsaw	151,000	432,000

Dr. Beloch gives the population of ancient cities thus:—

City	Date	Population	Area, Acres	Population per Acre
Rome . .	A.D. 14	900,000	2,950	306
Thebes . .	B.C. 335	50,000	500	100
Tyre . . .	,, 332	40,000	185	210
Palermo . .	,, 254	27,000	115	230
Athens . .	,, 350	150,000	145	103
Alexandria .	,, 60	500,000	230	218

The density of population in modern cities is shown thus, according to figures for 1881 :—

	Population	Acres	Population per Acre
London . . .	3,893,000	75,000	52
Paris . . .	2,240,000	14,500	154
Berlin . . .	1,192,000	4,500	264
Vienna . . .	724,000	2,800	258
Rome . . .	273,000	800	341

The city of greatest density in the United Kingdom is Liverpool, with 106 inhabitants to the acre.

The ratios of urban and rural population are not ascertained in all countries, nor determined alike in many. Some include in the former villages and small towns. If we consider only towns of 20,000 or more inhabitants, we find as follows (1881) :—

	Number of Towns	Aggregate Population	Percentage of Total Population	
			Urban	Rural
England . .	101	11,420,000	44	56
Scotland . .	10	1,310,000	35	65
Ireland . .	9	820,000	16	84
United Kingdom	120	13,550,000	39	61
France . .	91	6,810,000	18	82
Germany . .	114	7,420,000	16	84
Russia . .	128	8,220,000	10	90
Austria . .	37	2,550,000	7	93
Italy . . .	76	4,570,000	16	84
Spain . . .	28	1,940,000	12	88
Portugal . .	3	420,000	10	90
Belgium . .	24	1,510,000	27	73
Holland . .	19	1,140,000	28	72
Denmark . .	2	260,000	13	87
Sweden . .	6	350,000	8	92
Norway . .	5	210,000	11	89
Switzerland .	6	230,000	8	92
Greece . .	4	100,000	6	94
Roumania . .	12	620,000	11	89
Servia . .	1	270,000	6	94
Turkey . .	4	960,000	12	88
Europe . .	680	51,130,000	15	85
United States .	102	9,160,000	18	82
Canada . .	9	370,000	9	91
Australia . .	16	710,000	25	75
Total .	807	61,370,000	15	85

UNITED KINGDOM

The kingdoms now composing the United Kingdom, according to the most reliable estimates and official returns at various periods, had the following population :—

Year	England	Scotland	Ireland	Total	Inhabitants per Square Mile		
					England	Scotland	Ireland
1066	2,150,000	350,000	1,000,000	3,500,000	37	11	32
1381	2,360,000	400,000	1,100,000	3,860,000	41	13	35
1528	4,356,000	550,000	770,000	5,676,000	75	17	24
1672	5,500,000	900,000	1,320,000	7,720,000	96	29	41
1712	6,280,000	1,050,000	2,099,000	9,429,000	110	34	66
1754	7,020,000	1,265,000	2,373,000	10,658,000	120	40	74
1780	8,080,000	1,430,000	3,050,000	12,560,000	140	47	96
1801	8,893,000	1,608,000	5,216,000	15,717,000	155	53	165
1811	10,164,000	1,806,000	5,957,000	17,927,000	175	60	189
1821	12,090,000	2,092,000	6,802,000	20,984,000	207	68	212
1831	14,001,000	2,364,000	7,768,000	24,133,000	241	77	243
1841	16,038,000	2,620,000	8,197,000	26,855,000	275	86	256
1851	18,071,000	2,889,000	6,574,000	27,534,000	310	94	205
1861	20,209,000	3,062,000	5,799,000	29,070,000	347	100	181
1871	22,857,000	3,360,000	5,412,000	31,629,000	391	110	169
1881	26,109,000	3,734,000	5,160,000	35,003,000	443	122	161
1889	29,016,000	4,077,000	4,716,000	37,809,000	500	133	150

Meantime it must be observed that the estimates for Ireland in 1754 and 1780 were much too low, since it is impossible to suppose an increase of 70 per cent. between 1780 and 1801. It is clear that the above table should be amended thus :—

Year	England	Scotland	Ireland	Total
1754 . . .	7,020,000	1,265,000	3,200,000	11,485,000
1780 . . .	8,080,000	1,430,000	4,200,000	13,710,000

The ratio of sexes at each Census stood for the United Kingdom thus :—

	1821	1831	1841	1851	1861	1871	1881
Males .	487	486	488	489	485	486	485
Females.	513	514	512	511	515	514	515
Total .	1,000	1,000	1,000	1,000	1,000	1,000	1,000

This shows an increasing preponderance of females.

The population according to sexes since 1821 has been as follows :—

Year	Males			
	England	Scotland	Ireland	U. Kingdom
1821	5,850,000	980,000	3,340,000	10,170,000
1831	6,770,000	1,110,000	3,790,000	11,672,000
1841	7,770,000	1,240,000	4,010,000	13,020,000
1851	8,780,000	1,370,000	3,190,000	13,340,000
1861	9,801,000	1,453,000	2,832,000	14,086,000
1871	11,059,000	1,603,000	2,640,000	15,302,000
1881	12,625,000	1,798,000	2,523,000	16,946,000

	Females			
1821	6,140,000	1,100,000	3,450,000	10,690,000
1831	7,120,000	1,240,000	3,970,000	12,330,000
1841	8,130,000	1,370,000	4,150,000	13,650,000
1851	9,140,000	1,510,000	3,360,000	14,010,000
1861	10,318,000	1,616,000	2,957,000	14,891,000
1871	11,653,000	1,757,000	2,773,000	16,183,000
1881	13,343,000	1,937,000	2,637,000	17,917,000

The ratios of males of working age, 15 to 55, were as follows :—

	Per 1000 Inhabitants	
	1841	1881
England . . .	262	256
Scotland . . .	255	250
Ireland . . .	255	247

Women of child-bearing age, 15 to 45, were as follows :—

	Per 1000 Inhabitants	
	1841	1881
England . . .	240	230
Scotland . . .	247	230
Ireland . . .	236	224

Ireland stands lowest in men and women of the most useful and productive ages, which is the result of emigration.

The principal towns of England in the 14th century (1377) were supposed to have the following population :—

London .	35,200	Norwich .	6,300	Newcastle .	4,300
York . .	11,400	Lincoln .	5,500	Oxford . .	3,800
Bristol . .	9,200	Lynn . .	5,200	Gloucester .	3,400
Plymouth .	7,300	Canterbury	4,700	Leicester .	3,200
Coventry .	7,100	Colchester .	4,500	Shrewsbury	3,000

The twelve great towns of England have grown in this manner :—

	1801	1821	1841	1861	1887
London . .	959,000	1,379,000	1,948,000	2,804,000	4,215,000
Liverpool .	82,000	138,000	286,000	444,000	593,000
Manchester .	77,000	129,000	243,000	358,000	378,000
Birmingham	71,000	102,000	183,000	296,000	441,000
Leeds . .	53,000	84,000	152,000	207,000	345,000
Sheffield. .	46,000	65,000	111,000	185,000	316,000
Bristol . .	61,000	85,000	125,000	154,000	224,000
Nottingham	29,000	40,000	52,000	75,000	224,000
Bradford .	13,000	26,000	67,000	106,000	224,000
Hull . . .	30,000	45,000	67,000	97,000	199,000
Newcastle .	33,000	42,000	70,000	109,000	157,000
Brighton .	7,000	25,000	49,000	87,000	118,000
Total .	1,461,000	2,160,000	3,353,000	4,922,000	7,434,000

The urban and rural population have been as follows :—

	Rural	Urban	Total	Rural, Ratio per Cent.
1851 . . .	8,772,000	9,156,000	17,928,000	49.0
1861 . . .	9,133,000	10,933,000	20,066,000	45.5
1871 . . .	9,802,000	12,911,000	22,713,000	43.2
1881 . . .	10,523,000	15,445,000	25,968,000	40.4

According to the Census of 1881 the population showed :—

England and Wales		Ireland		Scotland	
Natives	24,856,000	Natives	5,064,000	Natives	3,398,000
Irish	562,000	English.	69,000	English.	92,000
Scotch	254,000	Scotch	22,000	Irish	219,000
Foreign.	303,000	Foreign.	20,000	Foreign.	27,000
Total	25,975,000	Total	5,175,000	Total	3,736,000

The density of towns in England (that is, the population per acre) is shown thus :—

Norwich . .	12	Bradford . .	28	Bristol . . .	49
Leeds . . .	15	Portsmouth .	31	London . .	49
Sheffield . .	16	Leicester . .	42	Plymouth . .	54
Nottingham .	18	Hull . . .	42	Manchester .	85
Oldham . .	26	Birmingham .	48	Liverpool . .	106

FRANCE

According to respectable authorities and Census returns, the population was at various dates as follows :—

Year	Population	Year	Population	Year	Population
1328 .	10,000,000	1791 .	26,303,000	1851 .	35,783,000
1515 .	14,000,000	1801 .	27,350,000	1861 .	36,746,000
1599 .	16,000,000	1811 .	29,090,000	1866 .	38,067,000
1698 .	19,670,000	1821 .	30,462,000	1872 .	37,013,000
1762 .	21,770,000	1831 .	32,569,000	1881 .	37,406,000
1778 .	23,665,000	1841 .	34,230,000	1886 .	38,219,000

The area varied often from the 14th century downwards; but comparing it with population, we find at different dates the inhabitants per square mile were as follows :—

Year	Per Sq. Mile	Year	Per Sq. Mile	Year	Per Sq. Mile
1515	. . . 80	1754	. . . 96	1800	. . . 135
1600	. . . 88	1778	. . . 112	1881	. . . 180

The ratio of sexes to population showed as follows :—

Males to 1000 Females

Year	Males	Year	Males	Year	Males
1801	. . . 950	1841	. . . 976	1866	. . . 1,005
1821	. . . 945	1851	. . . 982	1876	. . . 993

Urban and rural population stood in these ratios :—

	1846	1851	1861	1872
Urban . .	244	255	289	311
Rural . . .	756	745	711	689
Total .	1,000	1,000	1,000	1,000

The nine principal cities of France had the following population :—

	1801	1835	1881	1886
Paris . . .	553,000	881,000	2,226,000	2,345,000
Lyons . .	110,000	162,000	377,000	402,000
Marseilles .	111,000	125,000	360,000	376,000
Bordeaux .	91,000	110,000	212,000	241,000
Lille . . .	55,000	77,000	178,000	188,000
Toulouse .	50,000	62,000	140,000	148,000
Nantes . .	42,000	78,000	124,000	127,000
Rouen . .	48,000	91,000	106,000	107,000
Havre . .	16,000	24,000	106,000	112,000
Total .	1,076,000	1,610,000	3,829,000	4,046,000

The population of Paris has been as follows :—

Year	Population	Year	Population	Year	Population
1675 . .	540,000	1800 . .	547,000	1851 .	1,053,000
1700 . .	720,000	1811 . .	623,000	1861 .	1,697,000
1762 . .	600,000	1831 . .	786,000	1872 .	1,852,000
1789 . .	525,000	1841 . .	935,000	1886 .	2,345,000

GERMANY

Levasseur gives the following :—

Year	Population	Year	Population	Year	Population
1816 .	24,830,000	1840 .	32,786,000	1871 .	41,060,000
1822 .	27,040,000	1852 .	35,960,000	1880 .	45,234,000
1831 .	29,768,000	1861 .	38,140,000	1885 .	46,856,000

The German Confederation at various dates, down to its dissolution at the battle of Königgratz in 1866, showed as follows :—

States	Area, Sq. Miles		Population		
	1786	1866	1786	1815	1866
Austria . .	84,500	76,400	10,930,000	9,180,000	13,250,000
Prussia . .	46,500	72,000	4,110,000	7,920,000	14,720,000
Bavaria . .	22,600	29,600	2,100,000	3,560,000	4,810,000
Saxony . .	15,600	5,800	1,870,000	1,200,000	2,340,000
Brunswick .	2,000	1,400	185,000	210,000	290,000
Wurtemburg	4,300	7,500	585,000	1,400,000	1,750,000
Hanover. .	...	14,900	...	1,310,000	1,920,000
Baden . .	...	5,900	...	1,000,000	1,430,000
Various . .	92,200	30,100	6,485,000	4,380,000	5,900,000
Total .	267,700	243,600	26,265,000	30,160,000	46,410,000

Kolb gives the population according to sexes since 1855 as follows :—

	1855	1864	1871	1885
Males . .	16,185,000	17,785,000	20,250,000	22,934.000
Females. .	16,535,000	18,095,000	21,005,000	23,922,000
Total .	32,700,000	35,880,000	41,255,000	46,856,000

	Ratio			
Males . .	495	495	491	489
Females. .	505	505	509	511
Total .	1,000	1,000	1,000	1,000

The Census of 1885 may be condensed thus :—

	Males	Females	Total	No. per Sq. Mile
Prussia . .	13,894,000	14,425,000	28,319,000	216
Bavaria . .	2,639,000	2,781,000	5,420,000	192
Saxony . .	1,542,000	1,640,000	3,182,000	560
Wurtemburg	961,000	1,034,000	1,995,000	272
Baden . .	782,000	819,000	1,601,000	280
Alsace-Lorraine }	771,000	793,000	1,564,000	288
Small Duchies }	2,345,000	2,430,000	4,775,000	...
Total .	22,934,000	23,922,000	46,856,000	230

Official records of Prussia give the population thus :—

Year	Population	Year	Population	Year	Population
1801 .	8,020,000	1840 .	14,929,000	1875 .	25,742,000
1816 .	10,349,000	1850 .	16,608,000	1880 .	27,251,000
1831 .	13,039,000	1861 .	18,497,000	1885 .	28,319,000

The Census of 1843 for Prussia showed as follows :—

Married . . .	5,133,000	Urban . . .	4,263,000
Unmarried . .	10,388,000	Rural	11,208,000
Total . .	15,471,000	Total . .	15,471,000

The ratio of sexes in Prussia has been as follows :—

	1810	1820	1840	1880
Males . . .	495	495	499	492
Females . . .	505	505	501	508
Total .	1,000	1,000	1,000	1,000

The effects of the Franco-German war are visible in the increased preponderance of women in 1880. The composition of the population of Prussia as to sex and age in 1880 compared with 1843 thus :—

	Per 1000 Inhabitants					
Age	1843			1880		
	Males	Females	Total	Males	Females	Total
Under 5 .	76	74	150	70	69	139
5–15 . .	99	97	196	110	109	219
15–45 . .	242	242	484	216	225	441
45–60 . .	54	58	112	60	65	125
Over 60 . .	28	30	58	36	40	76
Total .	499	501	1,000	492	508	1,000

The records of Bavaria, Saxony, and Hanover show thus :—

Bavaria		Saxony		Hanover	
Year	Population	Year	Population	Year	Population
1818	3,708,000	1815	1,179,000	1822	1,464,000
1843	4,440,000	1841	1,687,000	1836	1,688,000
1861	4,690,000	1861	2,225,000	1852	1,819,000
1875	5,022,000	1875	2,761,000	1862	1,958,000
1885	5,420,000	1885	3,182,000	1880	2,118,000

Since 1866 Hanover has formed a province of Prussia. The ratio of sexes in Saxony has been as follows :—

In 1815 there were 1080 females to 1000 males
In 1832   ,,   1058   ,,   1000 ,,
In 1875   ,,   1041   ,,   1000 ,,

The Census of 1885 showed the chief cities of Germany thus :—

Berlin . .	1,315,000	Königsberg . .	151,000
Hamburg . .	306,000	Magdeburg . .	143,000
Breslau . .	300,000	Hanover . .	140,000
Munich . .	262,000	Stuttgart . .	126,000
Dresden . .	246,000	Bremen . .	118,000
Leipzig . .	170,000	Nuremberg . .	115,000
Cologne . .	161,000	Dantzig . .	115,000
Frankfort . .	155,000	Strasburg . .	112,000

The records of Berlin give the population as follows :—

Year	Population	Year	Population	Year	Population
1602 . .	8,000	1819 . .	185,000	1861 . .	548,000
1700 . .	55,000	1831 . .	249,000	1871 . .	826,000
1787 . .	147,000	1852 . .	433,000	1885 .	1,315,000

In 1875 the population of Berlin was made up thus :—

Males . . .	481,500	Born in Berlin .	399,100
Females . .	477,700	,, elsewhere .	560,100
Total .	959,200	Total .	959,200

There were 213,900 families, of whom 43,600 kept servants, the rest none.

The number of foreign residents in Germany was as follows :—

In	1871	1885
Prussia	87,000	157,000
Bavaria . . .	39,000	62,000
Saxony . . .	24,000	53,000
Other States . .	57,000	101,000
Total . .	207,000	373,000

RUSSIA

M'Gregor's tables for the 17th and 18th centuries, along with later estimates for Russia and Poland, show population thus :—

Year	Population	Year	Population	Year	Population
1689	. 15,000,000	1820	. 51,500,000	1871	. 72,233,000
1762	. 25,000,000	1840	. 59,134,000	1885	. 89,680,000
1801	. 40,170,000	1858	. 64,096,000		

Kolb, however, gives the following table :—

Year	Sq. Miles	Population	Year	Sq. Miles	Population
1722	5,953,000	14,000,000	1811	7,123,000	42,000,000
1742	6,889,000	16,000,000	1829	,,	50,500,000
1762	,,	19,000,000	1838	,,	59,000,000
1782	7,123,000	27,500,000	1851	,,	65,000,000
1803	,,	36,000,000	1870	7,867,000	78,000,000

The preponderance of females is not so great as it was forty years ago, the official returns showing :—

Year	Males	Females	Females to Males
1840	28,896,000	30,238,000	1,045 to 1,000
1882	42,289,000	43,007,000	1,016 to 1,000

In 1867, on the other hand, the males preponderated in all the large cities except Warsaw, viz. :—

Females to 100 Males

Moscow . . 56	Saratov . . 87	Kazan . . . 92
St. Petersburg 72	Riga . . . 88	Warsaw . . 112
Kiev . . . 76	Odessa . . 91	

The principal cities in 1882 showed the following population :—

St. Petersburg	. 843,000	Kazan . . . 141,000
Moscow	. 753,000	Kichinev . . 130,000
Warsaw	. 432,000	Kiev . . . 127,000
Odessa	. 240,000	Lodz . . . 113,000
Riga	. 169,000	Saratov . . 112,000
Kharkoff	. 167,000	Tiflis . . . 104,000

In 1882 the total urban population amounted' to 13,800,000 :—

4 first-class cities	 2,354,000
9 second-class	. . . 1,163,000
23 third-class .	. . . 1,610,000
93 fourth-class	. . . 3,100,000
164 fifth-class	. . . 2,190,000
690 villages	. . . 3,383,000
Total . .	. 13,800,000

The population in 1888 was made up thus :—

Russia proper	 81,700,000
Poland .	 7,980,000
Total . .	. 89,680,000

This gave for Poland an average of 170 per square mile against 125 in 1865, in which year there were 107 females to 100 males, and the urban population was 20 per cent. of the total.

Asiatic Russia in 1801 had 3,600,000 inhabitants, and in 1883 the number was 16,400,000.

Finland is not strictly a part of the Russian Empire : its population in 1885 was 2,200,000.

The ratio of sexes and of urban population in Finland was as follows :—

Males to 1000 Females		*Percentage of Urban Population*	
Year	*Males*	*Year*	*Urban*
1751	917	1815	47
1800	949	1840	59
1820	929	1850	64
1840	940	1860	63
1860	947	1870	77

The advance of population in the Russian Empire since 1858 is shown as follows :—

	1858	1870	1885
Russia	59,331,000	65,705,000	81,725,000
Poland	4,765,000	6,026,000	7,960,000
Finland	1,636,000	1,774,000	2,176,000
Caucasus . . .	4,309,000	4,763,000	7,285,000
Siberia	2,936,000	3,405,000	4,314,000
Tartary	1,295,000	3,357,000	5,327,000
Total . .	74,272,000	85,030,000	108,787,000

The distribution of sexes was in 1880 as follows :—

	Males	Females	Total	Females to 100 Males
Russia and Poland	40,925,000	42,051,000	82,976,000	103
Finland . .	1,019,000	1,063,000	2,082,000	104
Caucasus .	3,352,000	2,939,000	6,291,000	88
Siberia . .	2,044,000	1,904,000	3,948,000	93
Tartary . .	2,631,000	2,445,000	5,076,000	93
Total .	49,971,000	50,402,000	100,373,000	101

AUSTRIA

The population of the Empire, exclusive of the Italian provinces, was as follows :—

Year	*Population*	*Year*	*Population*
1789 . .	18,000,000	1857 . .	31,994,000
1810 . .	22,420,000	1869 . .	35,811,000
1840 . .	32,835,000	1880 . .	37,882,000

Year	Austria	Hungary	Total
1840 . . .	17,455,000	15,380,000	32,835,000
1857 . . .	18,225,000	13,769,000	31,994,000
1869 . . .	20,395,000	15,416,000	35,811,000
1880 . . .	22,144,000	15,738,000	37,882,000

As regards sex, the Census of 1880 compares with that of 1840 as follows :—

	1840					
	Population			Ratio		
	Austria	Hungary	Total	Austria	Hungary	Total
Males .	8,850,000	7,560,000	16,410,000	507	491	500
Females	8,605,000	7,820,000	16,425,000	493	509	500
Total	17,455,000	15,380,000	32,835,000	1,000	1,000	1,000

	1880					
Males .	10,820,000	7,703,000	18,523,000	489	491	490
Females	11,324,000	8,035,000	19,359,000	511	509	510
Total	22,144,000	15,738,000	37,882,000	1,000	1,000	1,000

In 1880 the various nationalities that made up the Empire were:—

Austria		Hungary	
Germans . . .	8,009,000	Magyars . . .	6,165,000
Bohemians . .	5,181,000	Germans . . .	1,798,000
Poles	3,239,000	Slovacs	1,790,000
Ruthenians . .	2,793,000	Wallacks . . .	2,324,000
Various . . .	2,922,000	Croats, &c. . .	3,661,000
Total . .	22,144,000		15,738,000

The principal cities in 1888 showed as follows:—

Vienna	801,000	Prague	296,000
Buda-Pesth . . .	443,000	Lemberg. . . .	110,000

The population of Vienna, including the suburbs, has been:—

Year	Population	Year	Population	Year	Population
1754 . .	175,000	1830 . .	333,000	1860 .	608,000
1800 . .	231,000	1840 . .	357,000	1880 .	1,104,000

ITALY

Estimates before 1860, and Census returns since then, gave:—

Year	Population	Year	Population	Year	Population
1800 .	13,380,000	1840 .	18,610,000	1871 .	26,801,000
1820 .	15,790,000	1858 .	24,860,000	1888 .	30,565,000

The principal cities in 1881 were as follows:—

Naples .	463,000	Turin .	230,000	Florence.	135,000
Milan .	320,000	Palermo .	206,000	Venice .	129,000
Rome .	273,000	Genoa .	138,000	Bologna .	104,000

The population and sexes of Rome were as follows:—

Period	Males	Females	Total	Males to 100 Females
1716 . .	79,900	58,100	138,000	138
1777 . .	89,800	73,300	163,200	123
1872 . .	105,200	139,200	244,400	76

The population of Italy, according to sexes, was as follows:—

	Number		Ratio	
	1871	1881	1871	1881
Males . .	13,472,000	14,265,000	502	501
Females . .	13,329,000	14,195,000	498	499
Total .	26,801,000	28,460,000	1,000	1,000

The population of Milan has grown as follows:—

1780	. . .	133,000	1871	. . .	261,000
1848	. . .	195,000	1884	. . .	349,000

Its great development has been since the expulsion of the Austrians in 1867.

SPAIN

Official reports gave the population as follows:—

Year	Population	Year	Population	Year	Population
1681 .	7,500,000	1797 .	10,514,000	1860 .	15,664,000
1723 .	7,625,000	1803 .	10,351,000	1870 .	16,799,000
1769 .	9,302,000	1821 .	11,248,000	1877 .	16,754,000
1788 .	10,140,000	1837 .	12,195,000	1887 .	17,550,000

The Census of 1788 showed as follows:—

	Male	Female	Total
Unmarried . .	2,926,000	2,754,000	5,680,000
Married . .	1,947,000	1,943,000	3,890,000
Widowed . .	282,000	470,000	752,000
Total . .	5,155,000	5,167,000	10,322,000

The Census of 1877 showed the sexes thus:—

						Ratio
Males .	.	.	.	.	8,253,000	492
Females	.	.	.	.	8,501,000	508
	Total	.	.	16,754,000		1,000

The principal cities were in 1885 as follows:—

Madrid.	.	.	387,000	Valencia	.	.	140,000
Barcelona	.	.	243,000	Seville .	.	.	131,000

PORTUGAL

Official returns are as follows:—

Year	Population	Year	Population	Year	Population
1732 .	1,770,000	1850 .	3,471,000	1878 .	4,551,000
1805 .	3,630,000	1860 .	3,608,000		

The population of Lisbon in 1878 was 243,000, and of Oporto 106,000.

The sexes stood thus:—

						Ratio
Males .	.	.	.	.	2,176,000	478
Females	.	.	.	.	2,375,000	522
	Total	.	.	4,551,000		1,000

SWEDEN

The Census reports show as follows:—

Year	Males	Females	Total	Males to 1000 Females
1751 . .	841,000	945,000	1,786,000	889
1772 . .	968,000	1,057,000	2,025,000	915
1790 . .	1,033,000	1,126,000	2,159,000	918
1810 . .	1,134,000	1,244,000	2,378,000	913
1830 . .	1,391,000	1,407,000	2,888,000	928
1850 . .	1,687,000	1,795,000	3,482,000	940
1860 . .	1,874,000	1,985,000	3,859,000	944
1870 . .	2,047,000	2,152,000	4,169,000	936
1888 . .	2,301,000	2,447,000	4,748,000	941

The ratios of urban and rural population were:—

	1810	1830	1850	1875	1888
Urban . .	94	97	101	140	181
Rural . .	906	903	899	860	819
Total .	1,000	1,000	1,000	1,000	1,000

The principal cities in 1888 showed thus:—

Stockholm . . . 235,000 | Gothenburg. . . 100,000

NORWAY

Official returns give the following population:—

Year	Population	Year	Population	Year	Population
1665 . .	460,000	1825 .	1,051,000	1865 .	1,702,000
1769 .	746,000	1845 .	1,328,000	1875 .	1,807,000
1801 . .	884,000	1855 .	1,490,000	1885 .	1,947,000

The ratio of sexes was at various dates as follows:—

	1801	1825	1845	1875
Males . .	482	485	491	488
Females . .	518	515	509	512
Total .	1,000	1,000	1,000	1,000

Urban and rural population had the following ratios:—

	1665	1801	1825	1845	1865	1875
Urban . . .	80	90	113	123	156	181
Rural. . . .	920	910	887	877	844	819
Total . .	1,000	1,000	1,000	1,000	1,000	1,000

The foreign population comprises 37,000, of whom 29,000 are Swedes. Christiania has 130,000 inhabitants.

DENMARK

The population of Denmark proper was as follows :—

Year	Population	Year	Population	Year	Population
1769 .	786,000	1834 .	1,226,000	1870 .	1,785,000
1787 .	840,000	1850 .	1,408,000	1880 .	1,969,000
1801 .	926,000	1860 .	1,608,000	1886 .	2,097,000

Previous to 1806 Norway was a province of the Danish monarchy, with 950,000 inhabitants.

In 1866 Denmark was stripped of Sleswig-Holstein, with 900,000 inhabitants. Iceland remains with 60,000 souls, but will soon be depopulated, the inhabitants going to Canada. The distribution of sexes in Denmark in 1880 was as follows :—

		Ratio
Males	967,000	492
Females . . .	1,002,000	508
	1,969,000	1,000

BELGIUM

Since the Independence the Census returns show :—

Year	Population	Year	Population
1830 . . .	3,780,000	1870 . . .	5,088,000
1860 . . .	4,732,000	1886 . .	5,910,000

In 1830 the population was distinguished thus :—

		Ratio
Urban	998,000	245
Rural	3,066,000	755
	4,064,000	1,000

In 1886 the languages spoken were :—

		Inhabitants
Only Flemish . . .		2,485,000
,, French . . .		2,230,000
French and Flemish . .		424,000
German and French . .		38,000
Walloon, &c. . . .		733,000
Total		5,910,000

The principal cities in 1886 were as follows :—

Brussels . .	430,000	Ghent . . .	145,000
Antwerp . .	205,000	Liege . . .	138,000

The population of Brussels has more than trebled since 1830, official returns showing :—

1830 . . .	121,000	1863 . . .	301,000
1850 . . .	222,000	1884 . . .	421,000

The sexes in Belgium compared as follows :—

	1846	1866	1887	Ratio 1846	1866	1887
Males .	2,164,000	2,420,000	2,983,000	499	501	499
Females .	2,173,000	2,408,000	2,992,000	501	499	501
Total .	4,337,000	4,828,000	5,975,000	1,000	1,000	1,000

The composition of the population of Belgium in 1880 was as follows :—

Age	Per 1000 Inhabitants		
	Males	Females	Total
Under 5 . . .	61	60	121
5–15 . . .	105	104	209
15–30 . . .	122	121	243
30–40 . . .	62	62	124
40–50 . . .	53	53	106
50–60 . . .	43	43	86
Over 60 . . .	53	58	111
Total . .	499	501	1,000

HOLLAND

Official returns show population as follows (the figure for 1785 apparently including Belgium) :—

Year	Population	Year	Population
1785 . . .	2,760,000	1859 . . .	3,309,000
1829 . . .	2,613,009	1869 . . .	3,580,000
1839 . . .	2,861,000	1879 . . .	4,013,000
1849 . . .	3,057,000	1886 . . .	4,391,000

Sexes compared as follows in 1879 and 1886 :—

	1879	1886	Ratio 1879	1886
Males . .	1,983,000	2,174,000	495	495
Females . .	2,030,000	2,217,000	505	505
Total .	4,013,000	4,391,000	1,000	1,000

In 1886 Amsterdam had 372,000 inhabitants, Rotterdam 174,000, and Hague 139,000.

SWITZERLAND

Census returns show as follows :—

1850 . . .	2,393,000	1880 . . .	2,846,000
1870 . . .	2,669,000	1888 . . .	2,934,000

In 1860 and 1880 the ratios of sexes were as follows :—

	Number 1860	1880	Ratio 1860	1880
Males . .	1,255,000	1,395,000	495	490
Females . .	1,280,000	1,451,000	505	510
Total .	2,535,000	2,846,000	1,000	1,000

The languages spoken in 1880 were as follows :—

		Ratio
German . . .	2,031,000	71.4
French . . .	608,000	21.3
Italian . . .	207,000	7.3
Total .	2,846,000	100.0

GREECE

According to Beloch, the population of Greece in the year 432 B.C. was as follows :—

	Free	Slaves	Total
Attica . .	235,000	100,000	335,000
Sparta . .	230,000	175,000	405,000
Thessaly . .	460,000	250,000	710,000
Macedon . .	400,000	25,000	425,000
Other States .	721,000	455,000	1,176,000
Total .	2,046,000	1,005,000	3,051,000

Since the Independence the population of modern Greece shows :—

Year	Population	Year	Population
1835 . . .	690,000	1870 . . .	1,458,000
1853 . . .	1,042,000	1879 . . .	1,980,000
1861 . . .	1,097,000	1889 . . .	2,187,000

The sexes in 1879 and 1889 stood thus :—

	1879	1889	Ratio 1879	1889
Males . .	881,000	1,133,000	525	515
Females . .	799,000	1,054,000	475	485
Total .	1,680,000	2,187,000	1,000	1,000

TURKEY

In 1840 the population and area of the component States were :—

	Square Miles	Population	Inhabitants per Square Mile
Turkey Proper .	130,000	7,100,000	55
Moldavia and Wallachia . }	44,000	1,420,000	32
Servia	12,000	380,000	32
European Turkey	186,000	8,900,000	48
Asia Minor . .	710,000	16,100,000	23
Tripoli	360,000	1,000,000	3
Egypt	480,000	3,100,000	6
Total . .	1,736,000	29,100,000	...

Since 1840 Turkey has lost Moldavia, Wallachia, Egypt, Servia, Bulgaria, Bosnia, Herzegovina, Roumelia, &c., and is at present reduced to :—

	Square Miles	Population
Turkey in Europe.	61,000	4,490,000
Asia Minor . .	710,000	16,133,000
Total .	771,000	20,623,000

In 1880 the principal cities were the following :—

Constantinople. . 874,000 | Damascus . . . 150,000
Smyrna . . . . 187,000 | Bagdad 100,000

In 1888 European Turkey was supposed to have only 4,500,000 inhabitants.

EGYPT

Without including the outlying dominions, the population of Egypt proper has been officially stated thus :—

1840	. . . . . .	3,100,000
1872	. . . . . .	5,210,000
1882	. . . . . .	6,818,000

The last Census showed 499 males to 501 females, viz. :—

	Number			Per 1000	
	Males	Females	Total	Males	Females
Egyptians .	3,222,000	3,258,000	6,480,000	497	503
Bedouins .	131,000	116,000	247,000	530	470
Foreigners .	49,000	42,000	91,000	538	462
Total .	3,402,000	3,416,000	6,818,000	499	501

The population of Cairo and of Alexandria was in 1882 as follows :—

	Cairo	Alexandria
Natives	353,000	178,000
Foreigners . . .	22,000	49,000
Total . .	375,000	227,000

UNITED STATES

The population of the country now known as the United States was estimated at various periods before Independence, and has been regularly taken in decennial Census since 1790.

Year	Population	Year	Population	Year	Population
1673 .	160,000	1800 .	5,308,000	1850 .	23,192,000
1701 .	297,000	1810 .	7,240,000	1860 .	31,443,000
1750 .	1,161,000	1820 .	9,655,000	1870 .	38,558,000
1775 .	2,803,000	1830 .	12,866,000	1880 .	50,156,000
1790 .	3,930,000	1840 .	17,063,000	1890 .	62,481,000

The earliest detailed records of population are as follows :—

	1701	1749	1775	1790
Massachusetts . . .	70,000	220,000	352,000	475,000
Connecticut	30,000	100,000	262,000	238,000
Rhode Island . . .	10,000	35,000	58,000	69,000
New Hampshire . .	10,000	30,000	102,000	228,000
New England . . .	120,000	385,000	774,000	1,010,000
New York	30,000	100,000	260,000	340,000
New Jersey	15,000	60,000	150,000	184,000
Pennsylvania and Delaware . . . }	20,000	250,000	401,000	494,000
Maryland	25,000	85,000	255,000	320,000
Virginia	75,000	200,000	516,000	748,000
Carolinas, &c. . . .	12,000	81,000	447,000	834,000
Middle and South . .	177,000	776,000	2,029,000	2,920,000
Total . .	297,000	1,161,000	2,803,000	3,930,000

Dr. Currie's tables published in 1798 are complete as regards the 18th century, and besides the above he gives figures for the New England States in the preceding century, showing a population of 24,100 souls in 1654, and of 68,400 in 1673. It is to be observed that in the above table the column for 1775 includes 500,000 slaves, and in 1795 likewise 698,000.

The population, according to Tucker and the Census returns, was composed as follows :—

Year	White, Native	Coloured	Foreigners	Total
1800	4,262,000	1,002,000	44,000	5,308,000
1810	5,770,000	1,377,000	93,000	7,240,000
1820	7,684,000	1,772,000	177,000	9,633,000
1830	10,178,000	2,328,000	360,000	12,866,000
1840	13,336,000	2,874,000	859,000	17,069,000
1850	17,308,000	3,639,000	2,245,000	23,192,000
1860	22,801,000	4,486,000	4,139,000	31,426,000
1870	28,085,000	4,906,000	5,567,000	38,558,000
1880	36,829,000	6,647,000	6,680,000	50,156,000

The increase of population chiefly arose from surplus of births over deaths, but was materially swelled by the number of European settlers. Tucker's tables down to 1820, and the Census returns since that year, show as follows :—

Period	Natural Increase	Immigration Increase	Total	Ratio of Increase per 1000 Pop.
1801–10	1,883,000	49,000	1,932,000	365
1811–20	2,309,000	84,000	2,393,000	330
1821–30	3,050,000	183,000	3,233,000	335
1831–40	3,602,000	595,000	4,197,000	327
1841–50	4,473,000	1,656,000	6,129,000	359
1851–60	5,624,000	2,627,000	8,251,000	356
1861–70	4,820,000	2,295,000	7,115,000	226
1871–80	8,783,000	2,815,000	11,598,000	301
1881–90	7,078,000	5,247,000	12,325,000	246
90 years	41,622,000	15,551,000	57,173,000	...

The Census Commissioner believes that the Census returns for 1870 were defective, especially in the Southern States, and that the real returns since 1860 should be read thus :—

Period	Natural Increase	Immigration	Total	Per 1000
1861–70	6,262,000	2,295,000	8,557,000	272
1871–80	7,341,000	2,815,000	10,156,000	254
1881–90	7,078,000	5,247,000	12,325,000	246

Allowing this amendment, as recommended by Commissioner Porter, the ratio of increase in each decade per 1000 inhabitants was as follows :—

	1801–10	1811–20	1821–30	1831–40	1841–50	1851–60	1861–70	1871–80	1881–90
Natural	356	318	316	280	262	242	200	181	141.
Immigration . .	9	12	19	47	97	114	72	73	105
Total . .	365	330	335	327	359	356	272	254	246

The various nationalities that composed nearly 15 millions of settlers from 1820 to 1888 stood thus :—

	1821–50	1851–60	1861–70	1871–80	1881–88	Total
Germans	682,000	951,000	820,000	759,000	1,104,000	4,316,000
Irish	1,352,000	1,013,000	723,000	450,000	536,000	4,074,000
British	49,000	325,000	385,000	542,000	658,000	1,959,000
Scandinavians .	5,000	25,000	136,000	261,000	412,000	839,000
Italians	...	9,000	13,000	61,000	201,000	284,000
French	125,000	76,000	38,000	75,000	36,000	350,000
Dutch	5,000	11,000	10,000	18,000	151,000	195,000
Swiss	4,000	25,000	24,000	31,000	68,000	152,000
Various	354,000	163,000	318,000	748,000	1,154,000	2,737,000
Total . .	2,576,000	2,598,000	2,467,000	2,945,000	4,320,000	14,906,000

There is a very marked decline of natural increase, which is now only two-thirds of the ratio that prevailed early in the century. The total immigration may be summed up thus :—

Period	Number	Per Annum
1654–1701	134,000	2,800
1702–1800	492,000	4,950
1801–20	178,000	8,900
1821–50	2,576,000	86,000
1851–80	8,010,000	267,000
1881–90	5,247,000	540,000
237 years	16,637,000	...

The number of foreign residents at each Census, and the number of those who died or left the country, are shown in the following table :—

Census Year	Number Enrolled	Immi- grants of Decade	Total	Number at End of Decade	Missing
1850	2,245,000	2,598,000	4,843,000	4,139,000	704,000
1860	4,139,000	2,467,000	6,606,000	5,567,000	1,039,000
1870	5,567,000	2,945,000	8,512,000	6,680,000	1,832,000
1880	6,680,000	...	...	...	...
	...	...	...	...	3,575,000

The number missing at the end of each decade ranged from 15 to 21 per cent.

The foreign residents found living in the United States at each Census since 1850 were as follows :—

	1850	1860	1870	1880
Germans . . .	584,000	1,276,000	1,691,000	1,967,000
Irish	962,000	1,611,000	1,856,000	1,855,000
British	380,000	588,000	766,000	916,000
Scandinavians .	18,000	73,000	242,000	440,000
Italians . . .	4,000	11,000	17,000	44,000
French	54,000	110,000	116,000	107,000
Dutch	10,000	28,000	47,000	58,000
Swiss	13,000	53,000	75,000	89,000
Various . . .	220,000	389,000	757,000	1,204,000
Total . .	2,245,000	4,139,000	5,567,000	6,680,000

The losses among Germans in the several decades were :—

Census	Resident	Immi- gration	Total	Number at End of Decade	Missing
1850	584,000	951,000	1,535,000	1,276,000	259,000
1860	1,276,000	820,000	2,096,000	1,691,000	405,000
1870	1,691,000	759,000	2,450,000	1,967,000	483,000
1880	1,967,000	...	...	...	...
	...	...	...	...	1,147,000

The percentage of loss was less than among Irish, as appears from the subjoined table of all nationalities.

The loss by death or leaving the country in thirty years ending 1880 is shown as follows :—

	Germans	Irish	British	Various	Total
Number in 1850 . . .	584,000	962,000	380,000	319,000	2,245,000
Arrived, 1851–80 . . .	2,530,000	2,186,000	1,252,000	2,042,000	8,010,000
Total . .	3,114,000	3,148,000	1,632,000	2,361,000	10,255,000
Number in 1880 . . .	1,967,000	1,855,000	916,000	1,942,000	6,680,000
Loss	1,147,000	1,293,000	716,000	419,000	3,575,000

In thirty years 35 per cent. of the total either died or left the country.

The loss in the first decade ending 1860 was 17 per cent., and in the subsequent decades almost 20 per cent.

The tables as regard Irish settlers show as follows :—

Census	Resident	Immigration	Total	Number at End of Decade	Missing
1850	962,000	1,013,000	1,975,000	1,611,000	364,000
1860	1,611,000	723,000	2,334,000	1,856,000	478,000
1870	1,856,000	450,000	2,306,000	1,855,000	451,000
1880	1,855,000	...	...	...	...
	...	...	...	...	1,293,000

The loss among Irish settlers in the first decade was 18 per cent., in the second 20, and in the third 19 per cent. The war of 1861-65 apparently cost the Union 53,000 German, and 48,000 Irish settlers. According to the Census of 1880, it appeared that for every 100 foreign settlers, of whatever age, there were 124 children born in the country of foreign parents, whereas in 1870 there were only 96. It appears, moreover, that foreign settlers comprise a larger ratio of people of working age than they do of the general population, viz. :—

	Population of all Ages					
	1830	1840	1850	1860	1870	1880
Americans . .	972	950	903	868	856	867
Foreigners . .	28	50	97	132	144	133
Total .	1,000	1,000	1,000	1,000	1,000	1,000

	Population between 15 and 60					
Americans . .	960	928	866	821	807	817
Foreigners . .	40	72	134	179	193	183
Total .	1,000	1,000	1,000	1,000	1,000	1,000

When the American native population would have 100 persons of working age, foreigners have 145.

The percentages of persons of working age in Ameri-can and in foreign population are shown at each decade thus :—

Year	Persons between 15 and 60 Years of Age		
	Of 1000 Americans	Of 1000 Settlers	Of 1000 General Pop.
1830 . . .	504	750	511
1840 . . .	509	751	521
1850 . . .	520	748	543
1860 . . .	520	748	551
1870 . . .	527	752	559
1880 . . .	513	750	544

There was a steady rise until 1870, notwithstanding the war of 1861-65, but the last decade showed a fall, which is explained by the greater number of persons over sixty years of age, who were 56 per 1000 in 1880, against 50 in 1870. It is, nevertheless, surprising to find that the able-bodied ratio among foreign settlers is precisely the same as it was fifty years ago, and has not sensibly varied in the whole period. It has improved remarkably among the American population. If we compare the growth of the three great elements of population between 1850 and 1880, counting the children born of foreign parents as foreigners, and assuming their ratio in 1850 to have been as in 1870—that is, 96 per 100 settlers—we find as follows :—

	1850	1880	Ratio of Increase, per Cent.
American whites .	15,152,000	28,553,000	88
Coloured population	3,639,000	6,647,000	83
Foreign	4,401,000	14,956,000	240
Total . .	23,192,000	50,156,000	116

The aliquot parts of the population, always counting children of foreign parents as foreign, show as follows :—

	1800	1820	1840	1860	1880
Americans.	794	781	733	602	570
Coloured population .	190	184	169	141	132
Foreign	16	35	98	257	298
Total . .	1,000	1,000	1,000	1,000	1,000

The growth of the white American and of the coloured population, in intervals of twenty years, is shown thus :—

Year	Number		Increase		Rate of Increase	
	American	Coloured	American	Coloured	American, per Cent.	Coloured, per Cent.
1800	4,220,000	1,002,000	...	...	...	...
1820	7,514,000	1,772,000	3,294,000	770,000	78	77
1840	12,511,000	2,874,000	4,997,000	1,102,000	67	62
1860	18,827,000	4,486,000	6,316,000	1,612,000	51	56
1880	28,553,000	6,647,000	9,726,000	2,161,000	52	48

The white American race increased faster than the coloured, except during the interval of 1841-60.

The total increase during eighty years was :—

    American whites   .   .   . 576 per cent.
    Coloured population   .   . 564 per cent.

The difference is small, but the figures show conclusively that the white American race has no tendency to die out, as often stated.

The rate of increase has, however, declined very notably since 1820, both among whites and blacks, especially the latter, that among whites having been nearly stationary since 1840.

In considering the ratios of the sexes, we find the preponderance of males was very great in 1860, the year before the war, and the lowest as in 1870. If the ratio in the latter year were the same as in 1860, there would have been 19,900,000 males, instead of 19,550,000. This shows a loss of 350,000 males, which may be set down as the blood-cost of the war.

It will be seen from the preceding tables that the white American population in 1880 was 28,553,000, or 57 per cent. of the total. This, however, supposes the grandchildren of European settlers to be of American race, which is not strictly true.

The Census returns give the sexes since 1790, but only for the white population down to 1810. The returns from 1820 are complete :—

Census	Males	Females	Per 1000 Population	
			Males	Females
1790	1,615,000	1,557,000	509	491
1800	2,204,000	2,100,000	512	488
1810	2,988,000	2,874,000	510	490
1820	4,896,000	4,738,000	508	492
1830	6,521,000	6,333,000	508	492
1840	8,693,000	8,381,000	509	491
1850	11,837,000	11,355,000	511	489
1860	16,061,000	15,365,000	511	489
1870	19,550,000	19,008,000	507	493
1880	25,519,000	24,637,000	510	490

It is remarkable that the relative numbers of the sexes have varied little since 1790. Meantime the ratio of females was highest in 1870, being the census year next following the war for the Union. If there had been no war, and the ratio of males in 1870 were the same as in 1860, the population for 1870 would have shown thus :—

Males 19,827,000
Females 19,008,000

Total   .   . 38,835,000

The actual number of males was 277,000 less, which is not surprising, since the Northern army lost 227,300 men killed or who died in hospital.

The preponderance of males has increased since 1870, due to immigration, but is still much less than in Australia, Argentina, Brazil, India or Greece (see p. 443). The sexes will probably be nearly even in 1920.

The distribution of the coloured population was at various dates thus :—

States	Number				Ratio			
	1850	1860	1870	1880	1850	1860	1870	1880
New England . .	24,000	25,000	31,000	40,000	7	5	6	6
Middle . . .	326,000	338,000	388,000	483,000	90	75	80	73
South . . .	3,153,000	3,890,000	4,173,000	5,658,000	866	868	850	851
West . . .	136,000	233,000	314,000	466,000	37	52	64	70
Total . .	3,639,000	4,486,000	4,906,000	6,647,000	1,000	1,000	1,000	1,000

This shows that the coloured population has not migrated to any extent since the emancipation of the slaves in 1861, but continues mostly in the Southern States.

The distribution of the foreign population is shown thus :—

Germans

States	Number				Ratio			
	1850	1860	1870	1880	1850	1860	1870	1880
New England . .	6,000	23,000	27,000	37,000	11	18	16	19
Middle . . .	236,000	476,000	584,000	640,000	404	373	344	325
South . . .	53,000	101,000	103,000	115,000	91	79	61	58
West . . .	289,000	676,000	977,000	1,175,000	494	530	579	598
Total . .	584,000	1,276,000	1,691,000	1,967,000	1,000	1,000	1,000	1,000

Irish

States	Number				Ratio			
	1850	1860	1870	1880	1850	1860	1870	1880
New England . .	197,000	306,000	361,000	371,000	205	190	194	200
Middle . . .	552,000	801,000	890,000	865,000	574	496	480	467
South . . .	65,000	107,000	81,000	74,000	67	66	44	40
West . . .	148,000	397,000	524,000	545,000	154	248	282	293
Total . .	962,000	1,611,000	1,856,000	1,855,000	1,000	1,000	1,000	1,000

All Foreigners

States	Number				Ratio			
	1850	1860	1870	1880	1850	1860	1870	1880
New England . .	299,000	469,000	648,000	793,000	133	113	116	118
Middle . . .	1,068,000	1,652,000	1,980,000	2,130,000	475	400	356	320
South . . .	176,000	292,000	290,000	341,000	78	71	52	51
West . . .	702,000	1,726,000	2,649,000	3,416,000	314	416	476	511
Total . .	2,245,000	4,139,000	5,567,000	6,680,000	1,000	1,000	1,000	1,000

This shows considerable and constant movement westward among all classes of foreigners. The percentages of native Americans and of foreigners (the children of these being counted as American) were :—

	1850				1880			
	New England	Middle	South	West	New England	Middle	South	West
Americans . .	890	838	979	874	802	820	978	820
Foreigners . .	110	162	21	126	198	180	22	180
Total . .	1,000	1,000	1,000	1,000	1,000	1,000	1,000	1,000

The following table shows the population of each State at three distinct periods:—

	1800	1840	1880	1890
New York . . .	589,000	2,429,000	5,083,000	5,982,000
Pennsylvania . .	602,000	1,724,000	4,283,000	5,249,000
Ohio	45,000	1,519,000	3,198,000	3,667,000
Illinois	...	476,000	3,078,000	3,819,000
Missouri . . .	...	384,000	2,168,000	2,677,000
Indiana	6,000	686,000	1,978,000	2,189,000
Massachusetts .	423,000	738,000	1,783,000	2,233,000
Kentucky . . .	221,000	780,000	1,649,000	1,855,000
Michigan . . .	...	212,000	1,637,000	2,090,000
Iowa	...	43,000	1,625,000	1,907,000
Texas	...	...	1,592,000	2,232,000
Tennessee . . .	106,000	829,000	1,542,000	1,764,000
Georgia	163,000	691,000	1,542,000	1,834,000
Virginia	880,000	1,240,000	1,513,000	1,649,000
North Carolina .	478,000	753,000	1,399,000	1,617,000
Wisconsin . . .	...	31,000	1,315,000	1,684,000
Alabama . . .	...	591,000	1,263,000	1,508,000
Mississippi . .	9,000	376,000	1,132,000	1,285,000
New Jersey . .	211,000	373,000	1,131,000	1,441,000
Kansas	...	...	996,000	1,423,000
South Carolina .	346,000	594,000	996,000	1,147,000
Louisiana . . .	...	352,000	940,000	1,117,000
Maryland . . .	342,000	470,000	935,000	1,040,000
California . . .	...	...	865,000	1,204,000
Arkansas . . .	...	98,000	803,000	1,125,000
Minnesota . . .	...	...	781,000	1,300,000
Maine	152,000	502,000	649,000	660,000
Connecticut . .	251,000	310,000	623,000	746,000
West Virginia . .	...	...	618,000	760,000
Nebraska . .	...	...	452,000	1,057,000
New Hampshire .	184,000	285,000	347,000	376,000
Vermont . . .	154,000	292,000	332,000	332,000
Rhode Island . .	69,000	109,000	277,000	345,000
Delaware . . .	64,000	78,000	147,000	168,000
Florida	...	54,000	269,000	390,000
Colorado . . .	...	...	194,000	411,000
Oregon . . .	...	...	175,000	312,000
Utah	...	...	144,000	206,000
Dakota	...	...	135,000	510,000
Territories . . .	13,000	50,000	564,000	1,169,000
The Union . . .	5,308,000	17,069,000	50,153,000	62,480,000

The principal cities showed at various dates thus:—

Year	New York	Philadelphia	Boston	Baltimore	New Orleans	Cincinnati	Chicago
1730	8,600	12,000	11,500	...	...	...	...
1750	10,000	18,000	14,000	....	...	...	...
1790	33,000	44,000	18,000	13,800	...	...	...
1800	60,000	69,000	25,000	26,000	...	...	...
1810	96,000	95,000	33,000	36,000	17,000	3,000	...
1820	124,000	113,000	43,000	63,000	27,000	10,000	...
1830	203,000	161,000	61,000	81,000	46,000	25,000	...
1840	313,000	220,000	93,000	102,000	102,000	46,000	4,500
1850	516,000	340,000	137,000	169,000	116,000	115,000	30,000
1860	814,000	568,000	178,000	214,000	171,000	160,000	109,000
1870	942,000	674,000	251,000	267,000	191,000	216,000	299,000
1880	1,207,000	847,000	363,000	332,000	216,000	256,000	503,000
1888	1,493,000	1,017,000	...	...	...	...	...

AUSTRALIA

The population was at various dates as follows:—

1800 . . .	6,500	1860 . . .	1,224,000
1820 . . .	35,600	1870 . . .	1,900,000
1840 . . .	257,000	1880 . . .	2,725,000
1850 . . .	510,000	1888 . . .	3,672,000

The ratio of increase was:—

1851–60	140 per cent.
1861–70	55 ,,
1871–80	43 ,,
1881–88	33 ,,

Dividing the Union into four great sections, the population stood thus at each Census:—

Year	New England	Middle States	South	West	Total
1790	1,010,000	1,342,000	1,580,000	...	3,932,000
1800	1,233,000	1,807,000	2,214,000	54,000	5,308,000
1810	1,472,000	2,479,000	2,997,000	292,000	7,240,000
1820	1,659,000	3,194,000	3,932,000	849,000	9,634,000
1830	1,954,000	4,138,000	5,164,000	1,610,000	12,866,000
1840	2,236,000	5,088,000	6,367,000	3,378,000	17,069,000
1850	2,724,000	6,593,000	8,288,000	5,587,000	23,192,000
1860	3,145,000	8,294,000	10,297,000	9,707,000	31,443,000
1870	3,506,000	9,770,000	11,330,000	13,952,000	38,558,000
1880	4,010,000	11,757,000	15,254,000	19,135,000	50,156,000
1890	4,691,000	14,110,000	18,283,000	25,396,000	62,480,000

At the beginning of the century there were only four towns that had more than 20,000 inhabitants: in 1880 there were 102, viz.:—

Population	1800	1820	1840	1860	1880
Over 100,000	0	2	4	9	20
50 to 100,000	2	1	1	9	16
20 to 50,000	2	2	16	25	66
Total . .	4	5	21	43	102

The aggregate of urban compared with total population in the United States was as follows:—

	Urban	Total	Ratio of Urban
1800	340,000	5,310,000	6.4
1820	460,000	9,640,000	4.8
1840	1,550,000	17,070,000	9.1
1860	4,240,000	31,440,000	13.5
1880	9,160,000	50,310,000	18.2

The urban class comprises only towns over 20,000 population.

The several Colonies since 1850 stood thus:—

	1850	1860	1870	1880	1888
N. S. Wales	189,000	349,000	499,000	742,000	1,086,000
Victoria. .	76,000	538,000	727,000	860,000	1,091,000
S. Australia	99,000	124,000	184,000	268,000	313,000
Tasmania .	70,000	88,000	101,000	115,000	146,000
New Zealand	63,000	79,000	248,000	485,000	607,000
Queensland	...	28,000	116,000	226,000	387,000
W. Australia	13,000	16,000	25,000	29,000	42,000
Total .	510,000	1,222,000	1,900,000	2,725,000	3,672,000

Mr. Coghlan compares 1860 and 1888, to show the natural increase from excess of births over deaths, and the net immigration into each Colony in that interval, viz. :—

	1860–1888		
	Natural Increase	Immigration	Total Increase
New South Wales . .	415,000	322,000	737,000
Victoria	431,000	122,000	553,000
South Australia . . .	150,000	39,000	189,000
Tasmania	53,000	5,000	58,000
New Zealand	262,000	266,000	528,000
Queensland	103,000	256,000	359,000
West Australia . . .	13,000	13,000	26,000
Total . .	1,427,000	1,023,000	2,450,000

The Census of 1881 showed the population to be compared thus :—

	Total	N. S. Wales	Victoria	South Australia	Tasmania	New Zealand	Queensland	Western Australia
Australian	60.8	62.2	57.9	59.8	69.1	45.6	40.4	59.8
English .	18.2	14.7	17.1	21.1	15.0	24.7	17.5	22.8
Irish . .	9.6	9.2	10.1	6.5	6.2	10.1	13.3	10.0
Scotch . .	5.5	3.3	5.6	3.8	3.2	10.8	4.6	2.5
Various .	5.9	10.6	9.3	8.8	6.5	8.8	24.2	4.9
Total .	100.0	100.0	100.0	100.0	100.0	100.0	100.0	100.0

The ratio of sexes since 1861 showed as follows :—

	Number			Ratio		
	1861	1871	1887	1861	1871	1887
Males .	731,000	1,094,000	1,929,000	576	552	543
Females .	536,000	885,000	1,622,000	424	448	457
Total .	1,267,000	1,979,000	3,551,000	1,000	1,000	1,000

The disparity of the sexes is diminishing year by year. It is nevertheless more remarkable in some of the Colonies than in others, the figures for 1887 being as follows :—

	Males	Females	Females to 100 Males
New South Wales	574,000	469,000	82
Victoria . .	550,000	486,000	88
South Australia .	165,000	152,000	92
Western Australia .	24,000	17,000	71
Tasmania . .	76,000	66,000	88
New Zealand . .	325,000	279,000	86
Queensland . .	215,000	153,000	74
Total .	1,929,000	1,622,000	84

Mr. Coghlan gives the male population of working age (20 to 60) in the seven Colonies as follows :—

		Ratio
Victoria . . .	211,000	29.2
New South Wales .	200,000	27.6
New Zealand .	135,000	18.6
South Australia .	74,000	10.2
Queensland .	69,000	9.5
Tasmania .	26,000	3.6
Western Australia .	9,000	1.3
Total .	724,000	100.0

The population of the cities has been as follows :—

	1841	1861	1871	1881	1889
Melbourne	4,000	140,000	207,000	283,000	458,000
Sydney .	39,000	94,000	135,000	224,000	382,000
Adelaide .	5,000	18,000	60,000	104,000	122,000
Brisbane .	...	6,000	15,000	31,000	87,000
Auckland .	...	10,000	30,000	50,000	62,000
Wellington	...	5,000	10,000	21,000	33,000
Hobart .	10,000	19,000	19,000	21,000	35,000
Perth . .	2,000	3,000	5,000	6,000	9,000
Total .	60,000	295,000	481,000	740,000	1,188,000

There are twenty minor towns, with an aggregate population of 355,000 souls, making a total urban population of 1,543,000, or 40 per cent. of the total.

CANADA

The population of Canada, including Nova Scotia, Newfoundland, &c., has been as follows :—

Year	Population	Year	Population	Year	Population
1665 . .	3,200	1800 .	476,000	1860 .	3,360,000
1695 . .	13,700	1820 .	840,000	1870 .	3,830,000
1726 . .	29,400	1830 .	910,000	1880 .	4,500,000
1736 . .	39,000	1840 .	1,690,000	1887 .	5,020,000

The Census of 1881 showed the population of Canada thus :—

	Number	Ratio
French Canadians .	1,299,000	30.0
Irish	957,000	22.2
English . . .	881,000	20.4
Scotch	700,000	16.2
Germans . . .	254,000	5.9
Indians . . .	109,000	2.5
Various . . .	125,000	3.0
Total .	4,325,000	100.0
Males	2,189,000	506
Females . . .	2,136,000	494
Total .	4,325,000	1,000

MEXICO

The Census of 1882 showed as follows :—

Sex		Ratio	Race		Ratio
Males .	5,070,000	485	White . .	1,980,000	18.9
Females .	5,375,000	515	Indian, &c.	8,465,000	81.1
Total	10,445,000	1,000	Total .	10,445,000	100.0

The city of Mexico has 350,000, Puebla 112,000 inhabitants. An official return in 1837 gave the population of Mexico as 7,557,000, and another in 1857 as 7,995,000.

CHILE

According to Census returns the population was :—

1865	.	.	.	.	.	1,811,000
1875	.	.	.	.	.	2,076,000
1885	.	.	.	.	.	2,548,000

The Census of 1885 was as follows :—

		Ratio
Males . . .	1,284,000	504
Females . .	1,264,000	496
Total .	2,548,000	1,000

Santiago had 189,000, Valparaiso 105,000 inhabitants. There were 87,000 foreign residents, including 35,000 Peruvians, 13,000 Bolivians, 7000 Germans, and 4000 Italians.

BRAZIL

The Census of 1883 compares with that of 1872 thus :—

	1872	1883
Free	8,420,000	10,684,000
Slaves	1,511,000	1,319,000
Total .	9,931,000	12,003,000

The sexes in 1872 stood as follows :—

	Free	Slaves	Total	Ratio Free	Ratio Slaves	Ratio Total
Males .	4,319,000	805,000	5,124,000	503	533	516
Females .	4,101,000	706,000	4,807,000	497	467	484
Total .	8,420,000	1,511,000	9,931,000	1,000	1,000	1,000

In 1872 there were 244,000 foreign residents, including 121,000 Portuguese, 46,000 Germans, besides Italians, French, &c.

The population was classified thus :—

		Ratio
Europeans . . .	244,000	2.5
White Brazilians . .	3,543,000	35.7
Mulattoes . . .	3,802,000	38.2
Negroes . . .	1,954,000	19.6
Indians . . .	388,000	4.0
Total . .	9,931,000	100.0

ARGENTINA

The population has trebled in thirty years, viz. :—

	1857	1869	1886
Buenos Ayres . .	277,000	495,000	1,085,000
Upper Provinces . .	883,000	1,342,000	2,009,000
Total .	1,160,000	1,837,000	3,094,000

Estimates for 1886 compare with the Census returns of 1869 as follows :—

	Number 1869	Number 1886	Ratio 1869	Ratio 1886
Italians	71,000	530,000	3.8	17.1
French	32,000	120,000	1.8	3.9
Spaniards	34,000	140,000	1.9	4.5
British and Irish . .	11,000	30,000	0.6	1.0
Germans, Swiss, &c. .	64,000	100,000	3.5	3.2
Argentines	1,625,000	2,174,000	88.4	70.3
Total . .	1,837,000	3,094,000	100.0	100.0

In 1869 the sexes stood thus :—

		Ratio
Males	898,000	515
Females	846,000	485
Total .	1,744,000	1,000

In 1886 the population appears to have been composed as follows :—

		Ratio
Europeans . . .	920,000	29.7
Children of settlers .	1,250,000	40.6
Argentines . . .	924,000	29.7
	3,094,000	100.0

A Census taken in the city of Buenos Ayres in 1887 showed 435,000 inhabitants, against 178,000 in 1869.

CHINA

According to different authorities we find as follows :—

Year	Population	Year	Population
1736 . .	125,046,000	1812 . .	360,280,000
1792 . .	307,467,000	1877 . .	381,600,000

Probably the figures for 1736 were much too low, or applied only to a part of the Empire. The population of eight cities in 1877 was stated thus :—

Pekin . .	1,600,000	Shanghai	. .	355,000
Canton .	1,600,000	Ningpo .	. .	240,000
Tientsin .	950,000	Takao .	. .	235,000
Hankow .	750,000	Tchinkiang .		135,000
Foochoo . .	630,000			

The number of foreign residents is only 6000, of whom 2500 are British, 800 Americans, 600 Germans, and 400 French.

The occupations of the natives are as follows :—

Per 1000 of the Population

Agriculture .	100	Bricklayers .	10	Blacksmiths .	7
Washing . .	10	Carpenters .	10	Sundry . .	863

JAPAN

The Census of 1888 showed as follows :—

		Ratio
Males	20,008,000	505
Females	19,599,000	495
	39,607,000	1,000

There were 7,803,000 houses, and 7,420,000 married couples.

The principal cities are as follows :—

	Population		Population
Tokio . .	903,000	Kioto . .	255,000
Osaka .	353,000	Nagoya .	127,000

There are 3000 foreign residents including 1400 British and 600 Americans.

POST-OFFICE

The total traffic in 1888 may be approximately summed up thus :—

	Millions Letters and Cards	Millions Papers, &c.	Millions Total	Postal Revenue, £
United Kingdom	1,759	542	2,363	11,200,000
Continent . . .	3,727	3,147	6,874	31,200,000
United States .	2,300	4,728	7,028	11,700,000
South America .	125	105	230	1,100,000
British Colonies .	570	210	780	3,200,000
Various . . .	146	27	173	700,000
Total . .	8,569	8,759	17,448	59,100,000

In the above postal revenue are included, moreover, the receipts for telegraphic service, except in the case of the United States and those other countries where the telegraphs are mostly owned by companies.

Postal traffic increased 95 per cent. in seven years, viz. :—

	Millions of Letters, Papers, &c. 1881	1888
United Kingdom . .	1,682	2,363
Continental	4,536	6,874
United States . . .	2,243	7,028
British Colonies . .	287	780
South America . . .	54	230
Various	86	173
Total . .	8,888	17,448

The following table gives a general view of the traffic in 1888, or latest year published:—

	Millions					Average per Inhabitant	Postal Revenue, £
	Letters	Cards	Papers	Sundries	Total		
U. Kingdom	1,558	201	152	452	2,363	60	11,200,000
France	672	41	402	408	1,523	39	6,500,000
Germany	956	296	725	511	2,488	53	11,400,000
Russia	153	18	106	49	326	4	2,600,000
Austria	611	122	147	80	960	24	4,000,000
Italy	178	48	181	69	476	16	2,300,000
Spain	102	1	21	...	124	7	...
Portugal	20	3	17	...	40	9	...
Sweden	60	...	46	...	106	22	340,000
Norway	18	1	16	3	38	19	190,000
Denmark	42	...	4	4	50	25	380,000
Holland	66	27	83	4	180	40	600,000
Belgium	107	27	96	60	290	49	750,000
Switzerland	105	17	80	19	221	74	...
Greece	6	...	6	...	12	6	30,000
Roumania	16	3	6	...	25	5	180,000
Servia	8	...	1	...	9	4	30,000
Bulgaria	3	...	2	1	6	2	20,000
Europe	4,681	805	2,091	1,660	9,237	25	...
U. States	2,300	...	1,500	3,228	7,028	110	11,700,000
Canada	93	19	66	21	199	40	620,000
Mexico	13	...	25	...	38	4	...
Venezuela	4	...	...	...	4	2	...
Peru	2	...	...	...	2	1	...
Chili	41	...	...	...	41	14	...
Argentina	40	...	37	...	77	20	...
Uruguay	6	...	14	...	20	30	...
Brazil	18	1	29	...	48	4	200,000
America	2,517	20	1,671	3,249	7,457	75	...
Australia	175	...	95	24	294	82	1,200,000
India	274	...	...	...	274	1	1,200,000
Japan	77	40	18	2	137	4	400,000
Java	5	...	3	...	8	...	...
Persia	2	...	...	...	2	...	...
Egypt	13	...	4	...	17	3	90,000
Algeria	10	...	...	...	10	3	...
Cape Colony	8	...	4	...	12	11	150,000
The World	7,762	865	3,886	4,935	17,448	25	...

In the preceding table post-cards are in many cases included with letters. As regards the United States, the official table gives no more than the total of letters, papers, and parcels, but the figures given above may be taken as a fair estimate, the returns for 1881 having shown 1155 million letters and cards and 761 million newspapers.

A summary of postal traffic in Europe in 1883 was published at Florence in 1885, which compares with the figures given above for 1888 as follows:—

Year	Millions					Postal Revenue, £
	Letters	Cards	Papers	Sundries	Total	
1883	3,683	546	1,672	1,046	6,947	38,150,000
1888	4,681	805	2,091	1,660	9,237	42,500,000

In 1883 there were in Europe 65,500 post-offices, 41,150 telegraph offices, and 225,000 letter-boxes. The postal service employed 356,000 men, and carried (Europe only) 800,000 tons of letters, papers, &c., according to the Florentine writer. In 1879 there were, says Fischer, 70 regular lines of mail-steamers, 26 British, 11 German, 11 French, 6 Dutch, 6 American, 5 Italian, and 5 Austrian. The amount represented by money orders transmitted through countries of the Postal Union in 1887 was 480

millions sterling; the value of goods sent through the parcel-post, 540 millions sterling.

Telegraphs have increased in late years with great rapidity, as shown thus:—

	Miles			Messages, Millions	
	1858	1870	1888	1870	1888
United Kingdom	10,000	24,000	30,700	10	58
France	8,000	25,600	58,500	6	28
Germany	9,500	20,400	57,700	9	24
Russia	5,000	29,200	92,700	3	11
Austria	6,500	22,000	38,200	5	13
Italy	2,500	11,100	21,100	2	9
Spain & Portugal	1,000	9,000	14,700	2	5
Scandinavia	2,400	9,000	14,500	2	5
Holland	700	1,700	3,100	2	4
Belgium	900	2,700	4,200	2	7
Switzerland	1,600	3,200	4,400	2	3
Roumania, &c.	300	8,400	28,200	1	3
Europe	48,400	166,300	368,000	46	170
United States	35,000	54,100	200,000	9	57
Canada	5,000	8,000	29,500	1	4
South America	5,000	17,000	61,500	3	11
Australia	1,600	15,000	39,200	2	11
India	4,800	14,500	31,900	1	3
Japan	...	...	6,200	...	3
Java	...	...	6,600	...	1
Persia	...	...	3,800	...	1
Egypt	...	3,100	6,500	...	1
Algeria	...	2,000	6,700	...	2
Cape Colony	...	600	4,400	...	1
Various	...	400	3,500	...	1
The World	99,800	281,000	767,800	62	266

The following is the summary of a report published in 1886 on the progress of telegraphs in Europe only, from 1860 to 1885:—

Year	Miles	Offices	Messages
1860	78,000	3,500	9,000,000
1865	110,000	7,800	21,000,000
1870	170,000	13,400	39,000,000
1875	210,000	26,100	79,000,000
1880	260,000	34,000	90,000,000
1885	315,000	45,000	118,000,000

The number of messages for 1870 is too low; perhaps official messages were not counted; but even this would not wholly explain the deficit. According to Mr. Preece, the telegraph system of the world in 1886 was summed up thus:—

	Miles	Cost, £
Land lines	714,000	51,700,000
Company cables	107,550	36,000,000
Government cables	12,520	3,700,000
Total	834,070	91,400,000

In 1888 the mileage was considerably higher, and at the value expressed above would stand thus:—

	Miles	Cost, £
Land lines	768,000	55,500,000
950 cables	132,000	44,000,000
Total	900,000	99,500,000

Mr. Preece shows that the maximum speed of transmission has been thus :—

Year	Words per Minute
1870	80
1880	200
1885	350
1887	600

Six messages can now go on one wire simultaneously.
The time occupied in sending a message from London to various parts of the world is as follows :—

To	Minutes	To	Minutes
Egypt . . .	20	China . . .	120
Bombay . .	50	Australia . .	160

The following table shows the number of post and telegraph offices, of employees, the average receipt on each telegram, and on every 100 letters or papers sent :—

	Post-Offices	Telegraph Offices	Employees	Telegrams	Per 100 Letters. &c.
	1888	1888	1881	Pence	Pence
U. Kingdom	17,800	7,030	74,000	8	88
France . .	6,930	8,000	49,000	9	88
Germany .	20,660	13,400	79,000	12	82
Russia . .	5,430	3,780	15,000	22	111
Austria . .	8,670	5,240	19,000	12	87
Italy . . .	5,300	4,060	16,000	16	86
Spain . . .	3,070	950	7,400	16	...
Portugal. .	1,640	275	1,300	10	...
Scandinavia	3,770	1,560	5,700	11	67
Holland . .	1,650	600	4,100	6	66
Belgium . .	820	1,530	4,400	4	52
Switzerland.	815	1,330	5,700	10	...
Greece . .	250	170	200	9	66
Roumania .	300	360	1,400	...	122
Bulgaria . .	110	106	400	...	80
Servia . .	90	118	400	...	77
Turkey . .	1,150	670	...	...	...
Europe . .	79,455	49,179	283,000	11	82
U. States .	59,000	19,700	...	19	40
Canada . .	7,840	2,230	...	...	72
Australia .	5,610	1,750	...	15	50
India . . .	16,970	750	...	7	110
Japan . .	4,800	230	...	12	55
Total .	173,675	73,839	...	...	...

UNITED KINGDOM

The importance of the post-office at successive dates may be judged by its receipts, viz. :—

Year	Receipts, £	Pence per Inhabitant
1663	22,000	1
1685	65,000	3
1707	111,000	5
1744	235,000	7
1790	480,000	12
1835	2,353,000	22
1889	10,340,000	66

The following were the charges on letters at three distinct epochs :—

London to	Pence		
	1645	1835	1889
York . . .	6	11	1
Edinburgh . .	8	13	1
Dublin . . .	...	16	1
Madrid . . .	...	26	$2\frac{1}{2}$
New York . .	...	26	$2\frac{1}{2}$
Rio Janeiro . .	...	42	4

The inland postal tariff from 1710 to 1840 was as follows :—

Miles	Pence		
	1710	1783	1812–40
Under 15 . . .	3	2	4
15–30 . . .	3	3	5
30–50 . . .	3	4	7
50–80 . . .	3	4	8
80–120 . . .	4	5	9
Over 120 . . .	4	6	10–16

The number of letters yearly passing through the United Kingdom was :—

Year	Millions Yearly Average			
	England	Scotland	Ireland	Total
1839	65	8	9	82
1841–45 . . .	179	24	24	227
1851–55 . . .	330	41	39	410
1861–65 . . .	534	61	53	648
1871–75 . . .	772	85	68	926
1881–85 . . .	1,082	116	85	1,283
1889	1,327	136	95	1,558

The annual number of letters was about 1,500,000 under Charles II., 8,000,000 under George II., and 20,000,000 at the beginning of the wars with Bonaparte.

In 1881 the number of letters, papers, &c., which passed through the British post-office was 1682 millions, viz. :—

	Millions of Letters, Papers, &c.			Ratio
	Received from	Sent to	Total	
United Kingdom .	1,526	1,526	1,526	90.7
America	22	22	44	2.6
European Continent	37	44	81	4.8
The East . . .	4	9	13	0.8
Australia	4	6	10	0.6
Africa	2	6	8	0.5
Total . .	1,595	1,613	1,682	100.0

The following table, comparing the number of letters in the United Kingdom and France, was published in 1882 :—

Period	Annual Average, Millions		Number per Inhabitant	
	U. Kingdom	France	U. Kingdom	France
1841–50 . .	277	122	10	4
1851–60 . .	466	210	17	6
1861–70 . .	724	340	24	9
1881	1,299	595	37	16

The letters and papers despatched from the United Kingdom in 1888 showed this ratio :—

To	
France	21.3
United States	19.4
Germany	16.7
Colonies	16.4
Various	26.2
Total	100.0

In nine years the postal traffic rose 50 per cent., viz. :—

	1880	1889
	Millions	Millions
Letters	1,128	1,558
Cards	114	201
Books, &c. . . .	214	452
Papers	131	152
Total .	1,587	2,363

In 1889 the British post-office left a net profit of £3,000,000, against £400,000 in 1855 and £1,800,000 in 1875.

The telegraphs showed as follows :—

Year	Miles of Wire	Stations	Messages
1851 . . .	7,303	198	48,000
1862 . . .	57,879	1,616	2,676,000
1872 . . .	87,719	5,179	15,502,000
1881 . . .	121,052	5,637	31,345,000
1889 . . .	183,500	7,030	58,000,000

The following table shows the increase, in ten years, in letters and telegrams for the three kingdoms :—

	Letters, Millions		Letters per Inhab.	
	1879	1889	1879	1889
England . . .	922	1,327	37	46
Scotland . . .	99	136	27	33
Ireland . .	76	95	14	20
United Kingdom .	1,097	1,558	32	41

	Telegrams		Per Inhab.	
	1879	1889	1879	1889
England . .	20,400,000	48,500,000	0.8	1.7
Scotland . .	2,500,000	6,000,000	0.7	1.5
Ireland . .	1,600,000	3,200,000	0.3	0.7
U. Kingdom .	24,500,000	57,700,000	0.7	1.5

The number and amount of postal and money orders issued in the United Kingdom were as follows :—

Year	Number	Amount, £
1880	17,300,000	26,400,000
1889	50,800,000	42,700,000

The parcel post, begun in 1883, showed as follows :—

Year	Number	Weight, Tons	Receipts, £	£ per Ton	Paid to Railways, £
1884 . .	22,100,000	19,700	490,000	25	250,000
1888 . .	38,800,000	40,900	860,000	21	425,000

Official returns of postal revenue and expenditure show as follows :—

Period	Revenue, £	Expenditure, £	Profit, £
1865–69 . .	22,200,000	15,400,000	6,800,000
1870–74 . .	28,000,000	21,000,000	7,000,000
1875–79 . .	36,400,000	25,400,000	11,000,000
1880–84 . .	43,200,000	29,100,000	14,100,000
1885–89 . .	51,700,000	38,800,000	12,900,000
25 years . .	181,500,000	129,700,000	51,800,000

In 1889 the accounts stood thus :—

	Receipts, £	Expenses, £	Profit, £
Post-office . . .	9,100,000	6,300,000	2,800,000
Telegraphs . .	2,100,000	1,950,000	150,000
Total . .	11,200,000	8,250,000	2,950,000

FRANCE

The official returns are as follows :—

Year	Millions			Receipts, £
	Letters	Papers, &c.	Total	
1830 . .	64	40	104	1,200,000
1840 . .	94	53	147	1,600,000
1850 . .	160	94	254	1,500,000
1860 . .	264	179	443	2,400,000
1870 . .	281	348	629	2,600,000
1880 . .	531	700	1,231	4,300,000
1887 . .	671	852	1,523	6,500,000

The receipts of course include the telegraph department, of which we have the following :—

Year	Miles	Messages	Receipts, £	Pence per Message
1851 . . .	1,200	9,000	3,000	80
1860 . . .	14,700	720,000	168,000	56
1870 . . .	25,600	5,660,000	380,000	16
1880 . . .	40,200	17,100,000	930,000	13
1887 . . .	58,500	27,900,000	1,060,000	9

The above does not include railway telegraphic service. In 1885 the railways had 21,000 miles of telegraphs, which carried 6,500,000 messages. This makes the total 80,000 miles, 34,500,000 messages.

The parcel-post was instituted in 1880, in which year 4,000,000 parcels were carried ; in 1888 more than 21 millions. In nine years the total carried was 131 million parcels, which paid £3,550,000, averaging 6d. each. Money orders in 1887 were issued to the number of 22,600,000, the aggregate amount being £28,500,000, being an average of 25s. each. France has 6932 post-offices and 58,500 letter-boxes.

GERMANY

Official returns give the number of letters thus :—

Year	Millions	Per Inhabitant
1871	339	85
1877	717	160
1888	956	200

The total traffic of 1888 compares with that of 1881 as follows :—

	1881	1888
	Millions	Millions
Letters and cards . .	721	1,252
Newspapers . . .	452	725
Sundries	126	511
Total . .	1,299	2,488

In 1888 the amount transmitted in 74 million money orders was £933,600,000, or about 3 millions sterling daily. The postal and telegraph services earned £11,350,000 ; expenditure £9,800,000 ; net profit

£1,550,000. Telegraphic service has grown as follows, viz. :—

	Miles	Messages	Receipts, £	Pence per Message
1870 . . .	20,400	8,600,000	390,000	11
1880 . . .	44,100	17,200,000	850,000	12
1888 . . .	57,700	24,100,000	1,200,000	12

The number of postal and telegraph servants in 1886 was 98,000, the weight of goods carried by parcel-post 404,000 tons.

RUSSIA

The returns for 1887 compare with those for 1881 thus :—

	1881	1887
Letters	110,000,000	152,600,000
Newspapers . .	75,000,000	106,200,000
Sundries . . .	7,000,000	66,900,000
Total .	192,000,000	325,700,000

Besides the railways and canals, there are 110,000 miles of mail-coach roads, on which the State maintains 47,000 horses at various posting-stations. The post-office in 1887 transmitted money orders to the number of 11,300,000, and value of 390 millions sterling, an average of £34 each. The growth of telegraphs has been as follows :—

Year	Miles	Messages	Receipts, £	Pence per Message
1870 . . .	29,200	2,700,000	300,000	26
1880 . . .	58,800	7,300,000	770,000	25
1887 . . .	92,700	10,500,000	950,000	22

There are 3780 telegraph offices. In the years 1884–87 the annual averages for postal and telegraph services were :—

	£
Receipts	2,550,000
Expenditure	2,470,000

Leaving a net profit of £80,000 a year.

AUSTRIA

Official returns are as follows :—

Year	Letters and Papers, Millions		
	Austria	Hungary	Total
1850 . . .	42	...	...
1860 . . .	60	...	...
1870 . . .	194	57	251
1880 . . .	399	135	534
1888 . . .	730	230	960

The figures for the whole Empire were made up thus in 1888 :—

	Austria	Hungary	Total
Letters . .	484,400,000	126,600,000	611,000,000
Cards . . .	91,200,000	30,800,000	122,000,000
Newspapers .	93,400,000	53,500,000	146,900,000
Books, &c. . .	59,900,000	20,500,000	80,400,000
Total .	728,900,000	231,400,000	960,300,000

In 1886 there were 29,200,000 postal orders transmitted, for a total value of £70,600,000, averaging 48s. each.

The progress of telegraphs is shown as follows :—

Year	Miles	Messages	Receipts, £	Pence per Message
1875 . . .	29,300	6,800,000	320,000	11
1880 . . .	30,800	8,300,000	410,000	12
1887 . . .	38,200	13,200,000	...	...

The returns for 1887 showed thus :—

	Austria	Hungary	Total
Miles . . .	26,700	11,500	38,200
Offices . .	3,690	1,550	5,240
Messages . .	9,520,000	3,720,000	13,240,000

The total postal and telegraph receipts and outlay were :—

	Receipts, £	Outlay, £
Austria . . .	2,800,000	2,410,000
Hungary . . .	1,230,000	860,000
Total .	4,030,000	3,270,000

ITALY

The post-office traffic at various dates showed thus :—

Year	Letters	Papers, &c.	Total	Per Inhab.
1862	72,000,000	40,000,000	112,000,000	5
1871	99,000,000	96,000,000	195,000,000	8
1881	169,000,000	107,000,000	276,000,000	10
1887	252,000,000	199,200,000	452,800,000	15

There are 5300 post-offices and 4060 telegraph offices. Receipts and expenses were in 1888 as follows :—

	Receipts, £	Expenses, £
Mails . . .	1,700,000	1,400,000
Telegraphs . .	600,000	520,000
Total .	2,300,000	1,920,000

In 1885 there were 4,300,000 postal orders transmitted, showing an aggregate of 22 millions sterling, say £5 each. Telegraph service has grown as follows :—

Year	Miles	Messages	Receipts, £	Pence per Message
1870 . . .	11,100	2,200,000	200,000	22
1880 . . .	16,200	6,100,000	420,000	16
1887 . . .	21,100	8,800,000	560,000	16

Government lines exceed 20,000 miles, the rest belonging to companies.

SPAIN

Official returns show the number of letters thus :—

Year	Letters	Per Inhabitant
1846	15,200,000	1.2
1880	71,400,000	4.4
1887	102,600,000	6.0

There are 3070 post-offices and 952 telegraph offices. There were 90,000 postal orders in 1887, representing a total of 7 millions sterling, averaging £78 each. Telegraph lines have grown as follows :—

Year	Miles	Messages	Receipts, £	Pence per Message
1855	440	3,000	5,000	400
1860	4,500	310,000	60,000	45
1870	7,200	1,040,000	60,000	14
1880	10,010	2,290,000	160,000	17
1887	11,510	3,550,000	240,000	16

Down to 1886 the construction of telegraphs had cost £700,000 sterling.

PORTUGAL

The number of letters carried was as follows :—

Year	Letters	Per Inhabitant
1878	12,200,000	3.0
1887	20,200,000	4.4

Telegraphs show as follows :—

Year	Miles	Messages	Receipts, £	Pence per Message
1875	2,200	1,300,000	45,000	8
1880	2,700	1,600,000	55,000	8
1885	3,200	1,730,000	70,000	10

There are 1640 post-offices and 275 for telegraphs.

SWEDEN AND NORWAY

The aggregate post-office traffic of the two kingdoms was as follows :—

Year	Letters and Papers	Per Inhabitant
1881	81,000,000	12
1887	142,000,000	21

The telegraph returns for 1888 showed thus :—

	Miles	Messages
Sweden	5,120	1,430,000
Norway	5,640	1,310,000
Total .	10,760	2,740,000

In 1886 the Norwegian post-office transmitted money orders worth 11 millions sterling. The postal finances showed thus for the two kingdoms :—

	Sweden	Norway	Total
	£	£	£
Receipts . . .	340,000	185,000	525,000
Expenses . . .	335,000	195,000	530,000

If we take collectively the whole telegraph system of the two countries, we find as follows :—

Year	Miles	Messages	Receipts, £	Pence per Message
1855	1,900	80,000	9,000	27
1860	4,700	290,000	40,000	34
1870	7,800	1,060,000	70,000	16
1880	9,800	1,770,000	120,000	16
1888	10,760	2,740,000	130,000	11

The above does not include Government telegrams.

DENMARK

The total business in 1887 comprised :—

Letters	42,000,000
Papers, &c.	45,000,000
Total . . .	87,000,000

Total post-office income £380,000, expenses £470,000. Telegraphic service shows as follows :—

	Miles	Messages
1870	1,210	520,000
1880	2,200	1,170,000
1887	3,670	1,500,000

No separate accounts of receipts are kept, being included in those of the post-office. There are 360 telegraph offices, of which 200 belong to the railway companies.

HOLLAND

Postal traffic was as follows :—

	1884	1888
Letters and cards . .	84,300,000	92,700,000
Papers, &c. . .	73,600,000	86,200,000
Total .	157,900,000	178,900,000

Telegraphic service has progressed as follows :—

Year	Miles	Messages	Receipts, £	Pence per Message
1855	620	140,000	13,000	23
1865	1,220	970,000	43,000	11
1875	2,140	2,200,000	62,000	7
1880	2,370	3,100,000	85,000	7
1888	3,100	4,100,000	100,000	6

The above comprises only the State lines, besides which there are twenty-nine companies, but their business is small. In 1888 the finances of the post-office and telegraph service were :—

	Receipts, £	Expenses, £
Post-office . . .	500,000	380,000
Telegraphs . . .	100,000	120,000
Total .	600,000	500,000

BELGIUM

The official tables show as follows :—

Year	Letters	Papers, &c.	Total	Per Inhab.	Receipts, £
1850	13,000,000	12,000,000	25,000,000	6	120,000
1860	28,000,000	33,000,000	61,000,000	13	200,000
1870	53,000,000	67,000,000	120,000,000	24	280,000
1880	85,000,000	131,000,000	216,000,000	39	480,000
1888	106,900,000	183,300,000	290,200,000	49	620,000

Telegraphic statistics are summed up thus :—

Year	Miles	Messages	Receipts, £	Pence per Message
1850 . . .	250	14,000	4,000	68
1860 . . .	920	330,000	20,000	15
1870 . . .	2,700	2,400,000	60,000	6
1880 . . .	3,500	6,200,000	100,000	4
1888 . . .	4,200	7,300,000	130,000	4

The aggregate income in 1888 from mails and telegraphs was £750,000; expenditure £505,000; leaving a net profit of £245,000.

SWITZERLAND

Postal traffic showed as follows :—

	1881	1888
Letters and cards . .	65,000,000	121,800,000
Papers, &c. . . .	65,000,000	99,400,000
Total . .	130,000,000	221,200,000

Postal orders in 1888 amounted to £13,200,000 sterling. The telegraphic service was as follows :—

Year	Miles	Messages	Receipts, £	Pence per Message
1855 . . .	1,350	160,000	12,000	18
1860 . . .	1,790	300,000	20,000	16
1870 . . .	3,200	1,600,000	50,000	8
1880 . . .	4,070	2,800,000	95,000	8
1887 . . .	4,400	3,200,000	140,000	10

Down to 1887 the cost of construction was £200,000 sterling.

UNITED STATES

Official returns for 100 years show as follows :—

Year	Routes, Miles	Post-Offices	Revenue, £	Expenditure, £
1790	1,875	75	8,000	7,000
1800	20,800	903	60,000	45,000
1810	36,400	2,300	110,000	100,000
1820	72,400	4,500	220,000	240,000
1830	115,200	8,450	390,000	395,000
1840	155,700	13,470	950,000	980,000
1850	178,700	18,420	1,150,000	1,120,000
1860	240,600	28,500	1,770,000	3,950,000
1870	231,200	28,500	3,680,000	4,400,000
1880	343,900	42,990	6,920,000	7,600,000
1889	416,200	59,000	11,700,000	12,800,000

The railroad postal service is shown as follows :—

Year	Miles of Railway	Miles Run with Mails	Cost, £
1844 . . .	4,380	5,750,000	110,000
1850 . . .	9,020	6,520,000	170,000
1860 . . .	30,640	27,600,000	700,000
1870 . . .	52,910	47,600,000	940,000
1880 . . .	93,350	96,500,000	2,240,000
1889 . . .	156,080	204,200,000	4,500,000

The number of letters and papers, &c., that passed through the post-office was :—

Year	Millions	Per Inhab.
1885	4,965	90
1889	7,028	110

In 1889 there were issued 17,760,000 money orders, to a value of £29,400,000, averaging 34s. each.

The postal traffic of the United States, as already shown (at p. 457), constitutes 40 per cent. of that of the world, and exceeds the aggregate of all the nations of Continental Europe. As compared with population, the ratio in the United States is almost double what it is in the United Kingdom, or three times that of France. Postal revenue in the above table does not include telegraph receipts, which belong to companies; but if these were added, the total would be £16,500,000, or a little over 5s. per head, against 6s. in the United Kingdom.

The Western Union Telegraph has most of the busi-ness of the United States, possessing in 1889 a mileage of 179,000 out of a total of 200,000 miles. The Western Company showed as follows :—

Year	Miles	Offices	Messages	Receipts, £	Pence per Message
1867	46,300	2,560	5,880,000	1,360,000	54
1870	54,100	3,970	9,200,000	1,400,000	36
1880	85,600	9,080	29,200,000	2,660,000	23
1889	178,800	18,470	54,100,000	4,320,000	19

If the other lines, which sum up 21,000 miles, be credited with half the mileage traffic of the Western Union, this would add 2,900,000 messages, bringing up the total to 57 millions and the receipts to £4,800,000 per annum.

CANADA

The Handbook gives the following statistics :—

Year	Post-Offices	Letters	Papers, &c.	Total	Per Inhab.	Postal Reve-nue, £
1870	3,820	24,500,000	20,200,000	44,700,000	12	210,000
1880	5,770	45,800,000	58,400,000	104,200,000	24	340,000
1888	7,840	92,700,000	106,400,000	199,100,000	40	620,000

The expenditure in 1888 was £160,000 over the receipts, caused by the fact that many post-offices are in remote, thinly-settled districts. In 1888 the mails were carried over 25,760,000 miles, against 10,600,000 miles in 1868. The "dead-letter" office in 1887 showed 830,000 letters and papers, say 5 per 1000 of total traffic, against 592,000, or 6 per 1000, in 1880.

The money order office showed as follows :—

Year	Orders	Amount, £	Average, £
1870 . . .	110,000	820,000	7.5
1880 . . .	306,000	1,500,000	4.9
1888 . . .	674,000	2,360,000	3.5

Telegraph lines mostly belong to companies. The traffic in 1887 was as follows :—

	Miles	Offices	Messages
Pacific Railroad Co. . .	5,000	550	500,000
North-Western Co. . .	17,660	1,502	3,100,000
Western	2,920	176	400,000
Total . . .	25,580	2,228	4,000,000

The returns for 1888 compare with 1880 as follows :—

	Miles	Messages
1880	11,300	1,200,000
1888	29,460	4,050,000

In 1888 the mileage included 2900 miles of Government lines.

AUSTRALIA

Coghlan's table shows as follows for Australasia :—

Year	Letters	Papers, &c.	Total	Per Inhab.
1851 . .	2,100,000	2,200,000	4,300,000	9
1861 . .	14,600,000	11,500,000	26,100,000	21
1871 . .	31,300,000	17,600,000	48,900,000	26
1881 . .	99,020,000	53,440,000	152,460,000	56
1888 . .	174,500,000	119,200,000	293,700,000	82

In 1888 the several Colonies stood thus :—

	Post-Offices	Letters	Papers, &c.	Total	Per Inhab.	Receipts, £	Expenses, £
New South Wales . .	1,203	49,000,000	40,400,000	89,400,000	81	370,000	420,000
Victoria	1,544	47,700,000	30,800,000	78,500,000	71	...	...
Queensland . . .	766	12,900,000	12,200,000	25,100,000	62	130,000	200,000
South Australia . .	594	17,000,000	8,700,000	25,700,000	82	110,000	180,000
New Zealand . . .	1,145	42,100,000	20,900,000	63,000,000	103	210,000	160,000
Tasmania . . .	278	4,700,000	4,800,000	9,500,000	64	35,000	40,000
Western Australia . .	78	1,100,000	1,400,000	2,500,000	60	15,000	...
Total . .	5,608	174,500,000	119,200,000	293,700,000	82	...	...

The telegraph service was introduced at Sydney in 1851, and a line was opened from that city to Melbourne and Adelaide in 1858. A cable from Melbourne to Tasmania was laid in 1869, and communication by cable with Europe commenced in 1872. Connection was established with New Zealand in 1876, and finally in 1877 Western Australia was joined to the other colonies. The line between London and Adelaide consists of 9146 miles of cable and 3424 of land line. The cable from Australia to New Zealand is 1191 miles long. The land lines of the Colonies had the following :—

Year	Miles	Messages
1861	2,385	...
1880	26,900	5,100,000
1888	39,200	10,580,000

In 1888 the telegraphs of the several Colonies showed :—

	Miles	Messages	Receipts, £	Pence per Message
N. S. Wales .	10,690	3,410,000	185,000	13
Victoria . . .	4,190	2,740,000	125,000	11
Queensland . .	9,170	1,440,000	105,000	17
South Australia	5,510	990,000	105,000	25
New Zealand .	4,790	1,550,000	90,000	14
Tasmania . .	1,900	270,000	20,000	18
W. Australia .	2,960	180,000	10,000	13
Total . .	39,210	10,580,000	640,000	15

INDIA

Postal development dates from the overthrow of the East India Company in 1856, when there were only 750 post-offices. The traffic in 1884 and 1888 showed :—

Year	Post-Offices	Letters and Papers	Revenue, £	Expenditure, £
1884 . .	14,305	203,300,000	1,100,000	1,010,000
1888 . .	16,970	274,400,000	1,200,000	1,370,000

The mileage of mails carried was as follows :—

By	1870	1888
Rail	4,200	14,040
Boat	40,600	48,900
Horse	5,500	4,000
Total . .	50,300	66,940

The telegraph service shows as follows :—

Year	Miles	Messages	Receipts, £	Pence per Message
1880 . . .	22,200	1,600,000	...	...
1888 . . .	31,900	2,800,000	76,000	7

The above does not include Government messages, nor those of the Indo-European cable.

ARGENTINA

Official returns give the following :—

Year	Letters and Papers	Per Inhabitant
1860	410,000	0.3
1865	990,000	0.6
1875	6,920,000	3.0
1880	9,880,000	3.6
1888	76,810,000	21.2

There are 14,700 miles of telegraph, of which 7300 belong to the State. In 1889 the number of messages was 3,510,000.

POTATOES

Spallart's table down to 1884 is included in the following :—

	Production, Tons 1880–84, Average	Value, £	Year 1887 Tons	Year 1887 Acres	Tons per Acre
G. Britain	3,300,000	9,900,000	3,560,000	560,000	6.4
Ireland .	3,590,000	9,700,000	3,570,000	800,000	4.5
France .	11,300,000	22,600,000	11,290,000	3,570,000	3.2
Germany	21,860,000	44,000,000	25,140,000	7,250,000	3.5
Russia .	12,110,000	18,200,000	7,500,000	3,700,000	2.0
Austria .	7,210,000	14,400,000	8,200,000	2,760,000	3.0
Hungary	2,390,000	4,800,000	2,200,000	1,020,000	2.2
Italy . .	700,000	1,400,000	620,000	370,000	1.7
Spain. .	1,590,000	3,200,000	1,590,000	800,000	2.0
Portugal	280,000	600,000	280,000	140,000	2.0
Sweden .	1,610,000	3,200,000	1,500,000	390,000	3.9
Norway .	630,000	1,300,000	500,000	90,000	5.5
Denmark	360,000	700,000	360,000	110,000	3.3
Finland .	380,000	750,000	380,000	100,000	3.8
Holland .	1,490,000	3,000,000	1,550,000	350,000	4.4
Belgium .	2,490,000	5,000,000	3,000,000	490,000	6.1
Switzer- land }	1,250,000	2,500,000	1,250,000	400,000	3.1
Roumania	500,000	1,000,000	500,000	200,000	2.5
Servia .	250,000	500,000	250,000	100,000	2.5
Greece .	250,000	500,000	250,000	100,000	2.5
Europe .	73,540,000	147,250,000	73,490,000	23,300,000	3.2
U. States	4,590,000	16,000,000	5,060,000	2,530,000	2.0
Canada .	1,200,000	2,400,000	1,200,000	430,000	2.8
Australia	400,000	800,000	430,000	110,000	3.9
Total .	79,730,000	166,450,000	80,180,000	26,370,000	3.1

We have nothing later than 1884 as regards Spain, Portugal, Switzerland, Roumania, Servia, and Greece. Four bushels of potatoes contain as much food as one bushel of wheat. They were first introduced into Germany in 1710, into Russia in 1769, and into Scotland about

1775: the man who sowed the first field of potatoes in Scotland died in 1850.

The production in various countries at different dates was approximately as follows :—

France		Germany		Russia	
Years	Tons	Year	Tons	Year	Tons
1815-20	1,950,000	1861	15,200,000	1849	2,550,000
1861-80	6,500,000	1879	18,900,000	1870	8,000,000
1887	11,300,000	1887	25,100,000	1887	7,500,000

Austria		Holland		Belgium	
1846	2,300,000	1851	700,000	1846	1,800,000
1859	5,020,000	1861	850,000	1856	2,000,000
1887	8,200,000	1887	1,550,000	1887	3,000,000

Sweden		United States			
1837	400,000	1840	2,700,000	1870	3,600,000
1859	510,000	1850	2,600,000	1880	4,200,000
1887	1,500,000	1860	2,800,000	1887	5,060,000

For consumption of potatoes see *Food*.

POULTRY.

The numbers are not known. The following is an approximate estimate :—

	Poultry, Number	Eggs Millions Yearly		Consumption per Inhabitant
		Production	Consumption	
United Kingdom	30,000,000	2,100	3,230	85
France	50,000,000	3,500	3,000	78
Germany	50,000,000	3,500	3,500	75
Belgium	4,500,000	320	420	70
Denmark	4,000,000	280	160	80
Italy	25,000,000	1,800	1,400	47
Canada	10,000,000	700	450	90
United States	80,000,000	5,600	5,600	85

In the United Kingdom it is believed that 5 per cent. of eggs are hatched, and the gross product yearly is set down thus :—

	£
160 million dozen eggs	5,300,000
80 million birds	4,000,000
Total	9,300,000

The countries which have a surplus for exportation, and the quantities exported, appear as follows :—

Year	Millions Eggs Exported				Value, £			
	France	Italy	Canada	Denmark	France	Italy	Canada	Denmark
1861	264	42	12	...	710,000	67,000	19,000	...
1870	499	129	31	...	1,250,000	206,000	65,000	...
1880	428	502	109	23	1,202,000	1,450,000	230,000	60,000
1888	500	420	220	111	1,100,000	1,000,000	450,000	260,000

Importation into the United Kingdom has been as follows :—

Year	Millions	Eggs per Inhabitant
1853	123	4
1865	364	12
1875	741	23
1889	1,131	30

The ordinary weight of hen-eggs is seven to 1 lb. in Spain, eight in England and France, nine in Poland, and ten in Germany. Frankland says that 100 oz. of eggs contain as much nutriment as 104 oz. of beef, but 100 oz. of the yolk of eggs contain as much as 230 oz. of beef.

Mr. Baker, of New York, the "chicken-king," hatches 250,000 chickens yearly by steam. France has 1,800,000 turkeys, the United Kingdom 1,500,000.

POWER

The working-power of an able-bodied adult is equal to 300 foot-tons daily, that of a horse 3000, and of steam horse-power 4000. In the following table the number of horses in Russia is supposed to be only half that recorded officially, as it is probable that not more than half are available for labour :—

	Millions of Foot-Tons Daily				Foot-Tons per Inhab.
	Hand	Horse	Steam	Total	
U. Kingdom	2,310	8,700	36,800	47,810	1,260
France	2,970	9,600	18,100	30,670	770
Germany	3,330	10,500	24,800	38,630	790
Russia	6,300	30,000	9,000	45,300	520
Austria	2,850	11,300	8,600	22,750	550
Italy	2,160	3,300	3,300	8,760	290
Spain	1,260	5,500	3,000	9,760	550
Portugal	360	400	300	1,060	280
Switzerland	210	330	1,200	1,740	580
Belgium	420	850	3,200	4,470	760
Holland	300	840	1,400	2,540	550
Scandinavia	630	2,900	2,500	6,030	660
Europe	23,100	84,220	112,200	219,520	700
United States	4,400	46,200	57,600	108,200	700
Total	27,500	130,420	169,800	327,720	900

In Spain and Italy mules are counted the same as horses. The above table excludes water-power, as it is impossible to make any comparison of how much is available in the various countries.

PRESS

The number of newspapers has multiplied nearly ten-fold since 1840, viz. :—

	1840	1890	Approximate Issue Monthly	Date of First Paper
United Kingdom	493	1,840	150,000,000	1622
France	776	4,100	120,000,000	1605
Germany	305	5,500	140,000,000	1524
Russia	204	667	12,000,000	1714
Austria	132	2,233	40,000,000	1560
Italy	210	1,606	36,000,000	1562
Spain	74	1,161	11,000,000	1704
Portugal	18	42	3,000,000	...
Belgium	52	872	13,000,000	1764
Holland	28	300	6,000,000	1757
Scandinavia	104	250	9,000,000	1644
Switzerland	54	450	6,000,000	...
Greece, &c.	10	100	1,000,000	...
Europe	2,460	19,121	547,000,000	...
United States	1,210	15,392	230,000,000	1704
Spanish America	99	1,170	14,000,000	1728
Australia	43	408	13,000,000	1803
Canada	88	565	9,000,000	1765
India	63	644	...	1781
Japan	1	470	...	...
Africa	14	200	...	...
West Indies, &c.	38	66	...	...
Total	4,016	38,036	813,000,000	...

This means an average circulation in the world of about 33,000,000 newspapers daily. The number of books printed yearly cannot be ascertained; a certain London publisher sells a million. Great Britain exports annually over 10 millions.

According to *Hubbard's American Newspaper Directory* for 1880, there were in :—

	Dailies	Periodicals	Total
Europe	2,403	10,730	13,133
North America .	1,136	9,656	10,792
South America .	208	427	635
Africa	25	125	150
Asia	154	337	491
Australasia . .	94	471	565
Total .	4,020	21,746	26,766

Mr. P. L. Simmonds, an old journalist, from a careful investigation, gives the following result, excluding the papers published at intervals longer than a week :—

Europe	17,000
North America	12,794
South America	1,260
Africa	210
Asia	692
Australasia.	568
West Indies	181
Total . .	32,705

Mr. Simmonds also gives the following as a rough

summary of the papers published in the English language :—

United Kingdom	2,100
North America	12,700
South America and the West Indies .	60
Australasia.	575
European Continent	20
Africa	114
Asia	203
	15,772

The average number of works published yearly has been as follows :—

	1828–32	1866–69	1878–80
Great Britain . .	1,060	3,220	5,771
France	4,640	7,350	7,000
Germany . . .	5,530	9,095	14,560
United States. .	1,013	2,165	2,500
Total . .	12,243	21,830	29,831

No book has been so often printed as the Bible. No fewer than 1326 editions of the Bible were published in the 16th century. In the 17th and 18th centuries it was translated and published in many languages by the polyglot press of the Propaganda Fide at Rome. Rev. Dr. Ginsburg, British Museum, has more than 4000 editions of the Bible, one of the most interesting being the polyglot version printed by Cardinal Ximenes at the University of Alcalà. Down to 1870 there were printed 55,000,000 copies of Webster's Spelling-book, and the sale of his Dictionary is said to average 300,000 yearly. There were two million copies of *Uncle Tom's Cabin* sold in ten years down to 1870.

UNITED KINGDOM

The advance of the newspaper press is shown thus :—

	Average Monthly Issue				Per 1000 Inhabitants	
	1801	1831	1864	1882	1831	1882
England.	1,330,000	2,750,000	40,200,000	112,500,000	190	4,270
Scotland. . . .	80,000	160,000	2,300,000	11,700,000	70	3,130
Ireland	160,000	330,000	3,000,000	10,800,000	43	2,120
United Kingdom . .	1,570,000	3,240,000	45,500,000	135,000,000	137	3,700

The new works issued in 1888 and 1889 were :—

	1888	1889
Economy	111	110
History and travels . .	601	513
Theology	743	630
Medicine	136	133
Poetry	163	133
Fiction	929	1,040
Sundries	2,277	2,135
New	4,960	4,694
Reprints	1,631	1,375
Total . .	6,591	6,069

In 1885 the newspapers of the United Kingdom were :—

	Dailies	Weeklies,&c.	Total
London . . .	15	360	375
Provinces . . .	116	987	1,103
Scotland . . .	22	161	183
Ireland . . .	16	140	156
United Kingdom	169	1,648	1,817

FRANCE

In 1811 the news in the Paris papers took the following number of days to reach Paris :—

From	Days	From	Days	From	Days
Strasburg . .	6	Brest . . .	6	Rome . . .	11
Lyons . . .	6	Antwerp . .	7	Madrid . .	21

The average speed was 70 miles a day.

In 1882 the French daily papers issued as follows :—

	Daily	Copies per 1000 Inhab.
Paris . . .	1,470,000	630
Lyons . . .	73,000	190
Marseilles . .	70,000	194
Bordeaux . .	40,000	188
Other towns . .	647,000	...
France . . .	2,300,000	60

In 1840 the daily issue of all the Paris journals summed up only 90,000 copies. The number of new works published yearly in France exceeds 7000.

GERMANY

The first steam printing-press was put up in 1848. At present about 11,000,000 books are printed yearly, of which 5,000,000 are exported. At the annual fair of Leipzig 8000 tons of books are sold, valued at £1,600,000 sterling. Germany had 2350 newspapers in 1882, the oldest being the *Allgemeine Zeitung* of Augsburg, dating from 1794. The new works published yearly average 17,500 on the following subjects :—

	Annual Average	
	1884-85	**1888-89**
Theology	1,425	1,605
Trade, economy, &c. . .	1,475	1,520
Romance and poetry . .	1,320	1,570
School-books	2,100	2,020
Medicine	915	1,180
Classics	1,190	1,185
History and geography .	1,270	1,390
Sundries	6,255	7,030
Total	15,950	17,500

RUSSIA

In 1882 this immense Empire had only 360 printing offices, and 1543 book-shops. The importation of books from France and elsewhere averages two million volumes yearly.

The press turned out in 1882 the following :—

	Newspapers	Books
St. Petersburg . . .	123	714
Moscow	31	525
Provinces . . .	164	853
Total . .	318	2,092

The total number of works published down to 1839 was :—

Period	Number
1750-1807	4,000
1808-21	9,250
1822-39	13,750
Total . .	27,000

In 1888 the following number of books was published :—

Language	Number	Copies
Russian . . .	5,318	17,400,000
Polish . . .	716	1,890,000
Hebrew . . .	343	1,005,000
German . . .	311	515,000
Various . . .	739	2,295,000
Total . .	7,427	23,105,000

The aggregate daily issue of newspapers in St. Petersburg in 1880 was 125,000 copies. There were in the Empire 318 newspapers—264 Russian, 29 German, 6 French, 19 in various provincial tongues. According to the *Statesman's Yearbook* there were in 1889 no fewer than 667 papers and magazines :—

Russian	493
Polish	76
German	49
Various	49
Total . .	667

AUSTRIA

The first paper was the *Wiener Blatt*, 1671. The number of newspapers (excluding Hungary) was as follows :—

1847	.	79	1873	. .	866
1862	. .	345	1886	. .	1,473

In twenty-five years down to 1873 there were 1931 papers started, of which—

Died under twelve months . . .	910
Between first and fifth year . . .	781
Survived fifth year	240
Total . .	1,931

The age of papers in 1873 was—

Over 20 years	51
3 to 20 years	409
Under 3 years	406
Total . .	866

In 1886 the press of Austria counted—

	Papers
German	965
Bohemian	263
Italian	54
Polish	84
Various	107
Total . .	1,473

There were 100 dailies, 450 weeklies, and 923 reviews, &c. In 1887 Hungary had 760 newspapers.

ITALY

The number of newspapers has been as follows :—

1840	210
1875	914
1887	1,606

In 1875 the press stood thus :—

Milan . . .	104	Dailies . .	127
Florence . .	82	Weeklies, &c. .	787
Turin . .	68		
Rome . . .	67	Total .	914
Naples . .	52	20 years old .	80
Various . .	541	5 to 20 . .	236
Total .	914	Under 5 . .	598
		Total .	914

In 1887 the papers were as follows :—

Dailies . .	135	Political . .	429
Weeklies . .	667	Agricultural .	198
Reviews, &c. .	804	Various . .	979
Total .	1,606	Total .	1,606

All were in Italian except twelve French and five English. The book-press issued in 1888 the following works :—

Religious	992
History and geography . .	1,141
Agriculture and industries . .	1,133
Various	7,597
Total . .	10,863

SPAIN

In 1889 there were 1161 papers and magazines, with an aggregate issue of 1,250,000, or about 1100 copies each, viz. :—

Madrid . . .	327	Political . .	496
Barcelona . .	117	Scientific . .	237
Seville . .	38	Religious . .	113
Various . .	679	Various . .	315
Total .	1,161	Total .	1,161

BELGIUM

In 1888 the press stood thus :—

Dailies . . .	81	Political . .	365
Weeklies . .	594	Scientific . .	90
Reviews, &c. .	197	Various . .	417
Total .	872		872

In 1878, excluding reviews, there were 180 papers, of which 124 were in French and 56 in Flemish.

UNITED STATES

The first printing-press was brought from Amsterdam with 49 lbs. of type, and set up at Cambridge, Massachusetts, A.D. 1639, where Harvard University now stands. Another was started by W. Penn at Philadelphia in 1686. The "Hoe" press was invented by Robert Hoe at New York in 1833, and improved by his sons, who have made 10-cylinder presses for many of the great journals of America and Great Britain. The first newspaper was at Boston in 1690, and was at once suppressed by the Governor. The *Boston Newsletter* was founded in 1704; the *Mercury* of Philadelphia in 1719. Franklin began the *New England Courant* in 1721. The *New York Gazette* appeared in 1725.

The number of papers at various dates, and the aggregate issue of copies monthly, were as follows :—

Year	Dailies	Weeklies	Reviews, &c.	Total	Issue Monthly
1788	...	...	...	37	330,000
1810	...	...	...	364	1,850,000
1828	....	...	...	892	6,100,000
1840	130	1,304	200	1,634	...
1850	254	1,902	370	2,526	34,400,000
1860	387	3,173	491	4,051	74,600,000
1870	574	4,296	1,001	5,871	119,600,000
1880	980	8,718	1,705	11,403	186,100,000
1890	...			15,392	230,000,000

The monthly issue for 1890 is only an estimate. The circulation was as follows :—

	1850	1860	1870	1880
Dailies . .	760,000	1,480,000	2,602,000	3,640,000
Weeklies .	2,940,000	7,580,000	10,594,000	19,460,000
Reviews, &c.	1,440,000	4,605,000	7,646,000	8,080,000
Total .	5,140,000	13,665,000	20,842,000	31,180,000

The aggregate number of copies issued monthly in the above years was approximately as follows :—

	1850	1860	1870	1880
Dailies . .	19,000,000	37,000,000	65,000,000	90,000,000
Weeklies .	14,000,000	33,000,000	47,000,000	88,000,000
Reviews, &c.	1,400,000	4,600,000	7,600,000	8,100,000
Total .	34,400,000	74,600,000	119,600,000	186,100,000

Census returns give the following *daily* issues :—

States	Number of Papers		Issue	
	1870	1880	1870	1880
New England .	60	84	310,000	403,000
Middle . . .	171	259	1,369,000	1,799,000
South	82	122	146,000	174,000
West	261	497	776,000	1,264,000
Total . .	574	962	2,601,000	3,640,000

In 1880 there were 10,515 papers in English, 641 in German, 49 in Swedish or Danish, 41 in French, and 26 in Spanish. No fewer than 57 were edited by women.

JAPAN

In 1888 there were 470 newspapers and magazines, the principal journal being the *Osoka-Nippo*, which issues 10,000 copies daily. The *Japan Mail* and *Hiogo Times* are in English. The aggregate issue of newspapers is about two millions monthly. The Life of Washington was published in 1880 in 42 quarto volumes.

CHINA

The *Pekin Court Gazette* celebrated in 1884 the completion of its 10th century : it was 640 years old when the first newspaper was printed in Europe in 1524. Secretary Ho has published a translation of Shakespeare, and a Pekin publisher has also issued Blackstone's Commentaries in Chinese.

AUSTRALIA

The first paper was printed at Sydney in 1803. There were 43 in Australasia in 1840, and the number rose to 270 in 1882. The returns at present are incomplete, but may be taken approximately thus :—

Dailies	156
Weeklies, &c.	252
Total . .	408

The number of newspapers sent through the post compared with population thus :—

Year	Number	Per Inhab.
1851	2,150,000	4.7
1871	17,580,000	9.3
1888	93,410,000	25.9

The above shows an average postal circulation of 300,000 copies daily : the total issue, therefore, can hardly fall short of half-a-million copies, say 13 millions monthly, or one-tenth of that of the United Kingdom in 1882.

CANADA

In 1765 the first paper was printed at Quebec. There were 88 in 1840, and the latest report showed 565. The number of newspapers sent through the post was :—

Year	Number	Per Inhab.
1870 . . .	20,200,000	5.5
1887 . . .	64,300,000	13.2

The total issue is approximately 350,000 copies daily.

SOUTH AMERICA

The first printing-press introduced into the New World was that established by the Jesuits at Cordoba, in the province of Tucuman, about 1610. Another was established at Misiones, in Paraguay, about 1680, and some books of this press are in the British Museum, dated 1705-24. General Auchmuty, after the capture of Monte Video, founded a paper called the *Southern Star* in 1806, which lasted only three months. In 1826 Mr. Love founded at Buenos Ayres a weekly called the *British Packet*, which died in 1858. A well-known weekly paper called the *Panama Star*, was founded by Archibald Boyd in 1849, which still flourishes. The first daily paper in the English language which appeared in Spanish America was the *Buenos Ayres Standard*, founded by the author of this Dictionary, 1st May 1861, which is now the best known journal of South America. The press of Argentina in 1886 was as follows :—

	Dailies	Weeklies,&c.	Total
Buenos Ayres . .	25	57	82
Provinces . . .	13	101	114
Total . .	38	158	196

There are 4 English, 3 French, 3 Italian, 2 German, and 184 Spanish newspapers, which issue 3,600,000 copies monthly.

INDIA

In 1880 there were 644 newspapers, of which forty were in English, the rest in Bengali, Marathi, and other native tongues. In 1886 there were published 8900 works, of which nine-tenths were in native languages.

PRICES

The earliest table of prices is that fixed by the Emperor Diocletian, A.D. 303, for the whole Roman Empire, viz. :—

Prices in English Pence and English Measure

Wines, &c.	Per Pint	Meat, &c.	Per Lb.	Game	Per Head
Falernian .	15	Beef . .	4	Grouse .	15
Sorrento .	15	Mutton .	4	Dove .	12
Sabine .	15	Lamb . .	6	Pigeon .	18
Ordinary .	10	Pork . .	6	Wood do.	15
Inferior .	8	Ham . .	10	Partridge	24
Rustic .	4	Sausages .	4	Duck . .	30
Vinegar .	3	Venison .	7	Rabbit .	30
Beer .	2	Boar .	9	Fowl . .	45
Small do. .	1	Sea-fish .	14	Goose .	75
Oil, 1st .	20	River-fish .	7	Fat do. .	150
,, 2nd .	12	Salted ,, .	4	Pheasant .	80
,, 3rd .	6	Snails, dozen.	1	Hare . .	110

Groceries	Per Lb.	Vegetables, &c.	Per 20	Clothing, &c.	Pence
Tallow. .	3	Apples .	2	Socks. .	3
Cheese. .	7	Cherries .	1	Tunic .	12
Butter .	9	Almonds .	½	Breeches.	15
Lard .	9	Walnuts .	1	Cloak. .	30
Honey. .	12	Chestnuts .	1	Boots. .	100
Beans .	5	Onions .	4	Shoes. .	120
Peas .	3	Turnips .	8	Slippers .	50
Lentils. .	5	Cucumbers .	8	Clogs. .	40
20 eggs .	15	Lettuce .	15	Saddle .	400
20 oysters .	15	Cauliflowers .	15	Bridle .	80
20 figs .	2	Melons .	30	Whip. .	12
20 roses .	1	Artichokes .	30	Bath . .	2

According to Landrin and Roswag, the quantity of wheat that could be bought at various epochs for an ounce of silver, say 4s. of present money, was as follows :—

Period	Lbs. of Wheat for 4s.	Price per Ton
		£ s. d.
B.C. 600 .	430	1 1 6
,, 300 .	360	1 5 0
,, 200 .	346	1 6 0
,, 50 .	330	1 7 0
A.D. 50–300 .	324	1 7 6
,, 301–500 .	320	1 8 0
,, 501–800 .	314	1 8 6
,, 801–1400 .	307	1 9 0
,, 1401–1500 .	314	1 8 6
,, 1501–1600 .	250	1 16 0
,, 1601–1650 .	200	2 4 6
,, 1651–1700 .	154	2 18 0
,, 1701–1750 .	124	3 12 0
,, 1751–1800 .	75	6 0 0
,, 1801–1850 .	37	12 0 0
,, 1851–1880 .	34	13 5 0

From the above it would appear that from the time of Alexander the Great down to that of Columbus the price of wheat averaged 28s. per ton; but the discovery of America, in 1492, was followed by such an influx of gold and silver into Europe that prices of all commodities rose in succeeding centuries, and the price of wheat from 1751 to 1800 averaged four times as much as in the time of Columbus.

The tables of Sir Morton Eden and Marquis Garnier from 1401 to 1756, with continuation to the present date, show the price of wheat reduced to English money as follows :—

Period	England, per Ton			Year of Price		France, per Ton			Year of Price	
	Highest	Lowest	Average	Highest	Lowest	Highest	Lowest	Average	Highest	Lowest
	£ s.	£ s.	£ s.			£ s.	£ s.	£ s.		
1401–10 . . .	2 15	0 13	1 8	1401	1404	3 18	2 7	3 2	1410	1406
1411–20 . . .	3 3	1 0	1 18	1416	1411	2 10	1 3	1 17	1411	1413
1421–30 . . .	2 2	1 0	1 10	1429	1427	9 1	1 0	4 1	1430	1428
1431–40 . . .	6 13	1 2	2 15	1434	1437	13 4	1 15	6 15	1437	1435
1441–50 . . .	1 13	1 0	1 7	1442	1450	5 14	0 14	2 1	1443	1448
1451–60 . . .	1 15	0 11	1 5	1451	1454	2 7	0 19	1 15	1457	1452
1461–70 . . .	1 13	0 18	1 6	1464	1463	2 12	0 12	1 4	1466	1464
1471–80 . . .	...	...	2 0	...	...	1 18	1 0	1 8	1478	1472
1481–90 . . .	4 2	0 18	1 12	1486	1489	3 18	1 7	2 7	1482	1489
1491–1500 . .	5 0	0 18	1 12	1497	1495	2 5	0 18	1 10	1499	1495
1501–10 . . .	1 15	0 18	1 9	1501	1509	2 12	0 15	1 15	1501	1510
1511–20 . . .	4 13	1 10	2 8	1512	1515	5 14	0 16	2 5	1515	1511
1521–30 . . .	5 17	1 7	3 10	1521	1530	6 17	1 10	3 19	1521	1526
1531–40 . . .	4 7	1 18	3 5	1538	1534	8 14	2 11	4 15	1539	1534
1541–50 . . .	6 7	1 13	4 5	1544	1548	4 12	2 15	3 16	1544	1541
1551–60 . . .	6 17	2 8	3 13	1556	1555	7 19	4 6	4 6	1556	1558
1561–70 . . .	5 3	3 7	4 4	1561	1568	11 3	4 19	7 15	1563	1564
1571–80 . . .	8 4	4 0	5 10	1573	1576	18 13	5 7	9 5	1574	1577
1581–90 . . .	8 0	3 11	5 7	1586	1588	12 12	5 12	7 17	1590	1581
1591–1600 . .	15 9	4 3	9 10	1597	1592	31 19	7 10	17 6	1591	1600
1601–10 . . .	12 13	6 1	8 0	1608	1604	10 15	5 14	7 6	1608	1602
1611–20 . . .	10 16	6 2	8 15	1617	1620	12 17	5 17	7 6	1618	1620
1621–30 . . .	13 1	6 5	9 15	1622	1628	14 19	6 15	9 11	1626	1624
1631–40 . . .	15 2	9 10	11 10	1631	1639	17 16	7 4	9 18	1631	1639
1641–50 . . .	18 18	7 16	13 5	1648	1644	19 18	7 0	11 10	1650	1646
1651–60 . . .	13 15	5 12	10 5	1651	1654	19 5	7 13	11 11	1651	1657
1661–70 . . .	16 5	6 7	10 10	1662	1666	20 2	5 19	11 17	1662	1668
1671–80 . . .	15 5	7 15	10 8	1674	1676	12 7	5 18	8 14	1679	1673
1681–90 . . .	10 1	5 15	8 5	1681	1688	12 1	5 5	8 7	1685	1688
1691–1700 . .	14 19	7 10	12 0	1698	1691	24 5	6 11	13 3	1694	1691
1701–10 . . .	17 0	5 12	9 5	1709	1706	22 0	4 7	9 19	1709	1707
1711–20 . . .	11 15	7 15	9 10	1711	1719	16 4	3 11	8 10	1714	1718
1721–30 . . .	12 5	7 6	9 2	1728	1723	14 8	5 1	7 15	1725	1728
1731–40 . . .	12 1	5 15	8 1	1740	1732	10 18	4 2	6 8	1740	1733
1741–50 . . .	8 5	5 9	7 5	1746	1743	10 1	4 8	7 2	1741	1744
1751–60 . . .	14 5	7 10	9 10	1757	1755	9 15	4 7	6 12	1752	1759

Period	England, per Ton			Years of Price		France, per Ton			Years of Price	
	Highest	Lowest	Average	Highest	Lowest	Highest	Lowest	Average	Highest	Lowest
	£ s.	£ s.	£ s.			£ s.	£ s.	£ s.		
1761–70 . . .	15 1	6 6	10 12	1767	1761	10 15	5 8	7 5	1770	1763
1771–80 . . .	13 11	8 13	11 9	1774	1779	10 12	7 6	8 13	1771	1780
1781–90 . . .	13 14	10 0	12 0	1790	1786	12 14	7 16	9 5	1789	1781
1791–1800 . .	28 9	10 15	15 18	1800	1792	11 16	9 8	10 12	1800	1799
1801–10 . . .	29 18	14 14	21 0	1801	1803	14 5	8 12	11 12	1803	1809
1811–20 . . .	31 13	16 8	21 18	1812	1815	21 0	10 5	14 7	1817	1814
1821–30 . . .	17 2	11 3	14 17	1825	1822	13 2	9 0	10 13	1829	1822
1831–40 . . .	17 13	9 17	14 4	1839	1835	12 17	8 17	11 1	1839	1834
1841–50 . . .	17 5	10 1	13 7	1847	1850	16 17	8 6	11 9	1847	1850
1851–60 . . .	18 14	9 13	13 17	1855	1851	17 0	8 13	13 0	1855	1851
1861–70 . . .	16 2	10 1	13 0	1867	1864	15 10	9 11	12 10	1868	1865
1871–80 . . .	14 14	11 0	11 17	1873	1879	14 18	11 5	13 3	1871	1875
1881–89 . . .	11 7	7 14	9 5	1881	1889	12 18	9 15	10 15	1881	1885

The average prices of wheat in periods in England, France, Italy, Russia, and United States were as follows, per ton :—

Period	England	France	Russia	Italy	United States	Average
	£ s.	£ s.	£ s.	£ s.	£ s.	£ s.
1771–80 . . .	11 10	8 15	...	8 5	...	9 10
1781–90 . . .	12 0	9 5	...	8 16	...	10 0
1791–1800 . .	16 0	10 10	...	11 5	...	12 12
1801–10 . . .	21 0	11 10	...	13 0	...	15 3
1811–15 . . .	23 10	14 0	...	14 0	...	17 3
1816–20 . . .	20 5	14 15	9 5	12 4	12 0	13 12
1821–25 . . .	14 5	9 10	4 10	5 8	7 12	8 5
1826–30 . . .	15 10	11 10	6 0	8 14	7 11	9 18
1831–35 . . .	13 5	10 0	6 5	7 14	8 8	9 4
1836–40 . . .	15 5	11 10	6 10	8 7	9 16	10 6
1841–45 . . .	13 15	11 5	7 10	8 3	7 4	9 12
1846–50 . . .	13 0	11 15	8 5	10 5	9 4	10 10
1851–55 . . .	14 0	13 5	11 0	12 6	9 12	12 1

In 1881 was published the following table of average prices of wheat in various countries during sixty years, per ton :—

Period	Great Britain	France	Germany	Russia	Austria	United States	General Average
	£ s.	£ s.	£ s.	£ s.	£ s.	£ s.	£ s.
1821–30	15 0	10 10	8 3	7 17	6 10	10 0	10 2
1831–40	14 6	11 0	7 14	7 7	5 17	11 7	9 12
1841–50*	13 7	11 10	9 7	7 0	7 10	9 14	9 15
1851–60	13 17	13 0	11 13	10 16	11 7	13 3	12 6
1861–70	13 0	12 10	11 7	11 7	13 0	12 10	12 6
1871–80	11 17	13 3	13 13	11 3	11 13	10 16	12 1

* The price of wheat in 1846, the year of the Irish famine, was as follows in various parts of the world, per ton :—

	£ s.		£ s.
Alexandria	5 16	Edinburgh	14 10
Amsterdam . . .	20 6	Genoa	13 18
Ancona	9 18	London	15 14
Bilbao	11 0	Malaga	13 7
Brussels	15 8	Milan	13 7
Christiania	15 2	New York	9 18
Copenhagen . . .	11 12	Odessa	8 2
Dantzic	13 7	St. Petersburg . .	10 8
Dublin	19 14	Trieste	11 0

Commendatore Bodio gives the following prices of wheat per ton in ten different markets, from 1869 to 1884 :—

Year	London	Paris	Berlin	Brussels	Amsterdam	Rome	Vienna	Buda-Pesth	Algiers	New York
	£ s.	£ s.	£ s.	£ s.	£ s.	£ s.	£ s.	£ s.	£ s.	£ s.
1869	11 8	10 18	10 0	11 8	11 10	9 18	8 6	...	10 2	10 8
1870	11 4	12 4	9 18	11 18	11 18	11 18	9 5	...	10 9	9 6
1871	12 16	14 15	10 15	15 0	13 4	11 18	10 18	10 0	11 18	12 6
1872	12 15	12 7	11 18	13 8	12 17	12 1	11 12	10 18	11 10	12 2
1873	13 6	14 4	12 10	14 7	14 1	13 1	13 0	13 5	12 16	12 12
1874	12 18	13 3	11 12	13 16	11 12	13 8	10 6	11 15	12 6	11 7
1875	10 10	9 18	9 12	10 18	10 17	10 8	7 12	8 14	9 14	9 14
1876	10 19	11 0	10 6	11 10	12 3	10 8	7 19	9 1	9 12	9 19
1877	12 12	12 16	11 7	13 4	14 16	12 10	8 16	10 0	12 6	11 18
1878	12 6	12 10	9 14	11 10	11 12	11 15	8 0	8 8	12 3	9 7
1879	11 10	11 12	9 12	11 0	10 11	11 0	8 8	9 6	10 2	9 6
1880	12 6	12 5	10 16	11 12	10 12	12 1	9 2	10 12	10 10	10 0
1881	10 18	12 1	10 15	11 11	10 15	10 12	9 3	10 18	11 16	10 4
1882	10 12	10 18	10 3	10 12	9 12	10 4	8 3	9 9	10 7	8 16
1883	10 1	10 6	8 16	9 18	9 8	9 10	7 8	8 10	10 4	9 1
1884	9 1	9 5	8 16	8 17	8 0	8 18	6 10	7 12	8 12	7 10
average 16 years . .	11 11	11 18	10 8	11 18	11 8	11 4	8 12	9 18	10 18	10 5
1889	6 18	9 6	9 6	...	6 12	...	...	...	...	6 12

The highest average of prices for sixteen years was at Paris, namely £11, 18s. ; the lowest at Vienna, namely £8, 12s. The highest price for a year was at Brussels, £15 in 1871 ; the lowest at Vienna, £6, 10s. in 1884. The greatest variation of price was at Vienna, falling from £13 in 1873 to half that sum in 1884 ; the least variation was at Berlin.

Mr. Newmarch gives the following table of prices at Melbourne during the gold fever :—

	1852	1853	1854	1855	1856	1852–56
	s. d.	s. d.	s. d.	s. d.	s. d.	s. d.
Barley, bushel .	4 0	12 0	9 6	6 0	...	8 0
Beef, lb. . .	0 5	0 6	0 7	0 6	0 5	0 6
Beer, hhd. . .	160 0	160 0	200 0	200 0	182 0	180 0
Brandy, gallon .	12 3	13 0	10 3	12 0	13 9	12 2
Bricks, 1000 .	120 0	235 0	175 0	80 0	65 0	135 0
Candles, lb. .	2 3	2 3	1 10	1 7	1 7	1 10
Coffee, cwt. .	70 0	76 0	56 0	51 0	90 0	69 0
Ducks, pair .	9 0	15 0	24 0	20 0	18 0	17 0
Flour, cwt. . .	33 0	30 0	33 0	41 0	27 0	33 0
Goose . . .	7 6	18 0	23 0	20 0	19 0	17 6
Hay, cwt. . .	16 0	29 0	30 0	15 0	8 0	19 6
Hens, pair . .	8 6	15 0	14 0	15 0	15 0	13 6
Oats, bushel .	5 9	8 6	10 3	8 6	...	8 3
Ox	120 0	165 0	220 0	220 0	195 0	184 0
Potatoes, cwt..	14 6	21 6	23 0	10 6	10 0	16 0
Rice, cwt. . .	9 0	11 6	16 0	15 6	14 6	13 6
Sheep . . .	5 6	13 0	22 6	18 6	18 6	15 6
Sugar, cwt. .	21 3	19 6	23 0	28 0	...	23 0
Tea, chest . .	63 0	96 0	102 0	83 0	82 0	85 0
Tobacco, lb. .	2 2	2 0	2 2	2 0	...	2 1
Wheat, bushel .	8 6	9 0	14 3	15 6	8 2	11 1
Wine, gallon .	3 4	3 4	3 9	4 2	3 4	3 7

He also gives the prices of food at San Francisco under similar circumstances in 1854 as follows :—

	s. d.		s. d.		s. d.
Beef, lb. .	1 7	Duck . .	4 2	Cauliflower .	2 0
Butter, lb. .	4 2	Hen . .	11 0	Milk, quart .	1 0
Eggs, doz. .	5 3	Cabbage .	1 0	Potatoes, cwt.	13 0

Neumann Spallart ascertained the prices of all kinds of grain in 1884 in the principal countries of the world to be as follows :—

	Per Ton				
	Wheat	Rye	Barley	Oats	Maize
	£ s.	£ s.	£ s.	£ s.	£ s.
England . .	8 2	...	8 1	7 5	5 14
Russia . .	4 16	4 6	3 19	3 8	...
France . .	7 16	7 0	7 3	7 10	7 12
Germany . .	7 16	7 0	7 0	6 1	...
Italy . .	8 11	5 17	6 13	4 17	6 7
Austria . .	4 10	3 19	3 15	3 8	3 10
Hungary . .	3 12	3 10	2 17	2 13	3 3
Denmark . .	7 7	6 14	7 0	6 15	...
Holland . .	8 11	6 14	6 9	6 6	...
United States .	5 2	4 10	5 0	4 8	3 3
Average . .	6 12	5 8	5 14	5 6	5 6

The prices of various commodities in different countries in 1888 were as follows :—

	G. Britain	France	Germany	Austria	Sweden	Norway	Belgium	Switzerland	U. States
	£ s.	£ s.	£ s.	£ s.	£ s.	£ s.	£ s.	£ s.	£ s.
Bacon, ton . . .	44 15	...	...	...	...	40 0	...	...	39 0
Barley	5 14	7 0	6 11	7 10	5 2	5 6	6 18	9 6	6 16
Butter	107 0	...	...	53 0	67 0	61 0	105 0	70 0	85 0
Cheese	47 0	...	...	55 0	56 0	63 0	61 0	70 0	47 0
Coffee	75 0	...	82 0	102 0	91 0	72 0	65 0	84 0	61 0
Fish	24 7	...	7 0	...	19 0	...	...	...	22 0
Lard	41 2	...	...	...	33 0	...	28 0	...	36 0
Maize	5 3	7 0	...	5 0	6 10	5 19	...	...	4 11
Oats	4 18	7 10	7 10	4 18	4 19	4 16	5 18	6 12	6 13
Pork	37 10	58 0	44 0	38 10	39 0	...	...	...	35 0
Potatoes . . .	6 14	2 16	1 14	3 15	2 16	...	3 11	3 2	3 14
Raisins	30 7	...	...	17 10	33 0	21 0	28 0	18 5	19 0
Rice	7 9	...	10 5	16 0	11 10	10 15	...	13 10	8 8
Spirits, 100 gals. .	8 3	...	...	...	...	...	11 13	8 11	15 0
Sugar, ton . . .	17 11	...	30 17	29 0	21 0	23 0	21 0	20 10	29 0
Tea	102 0	...	...	268 0	168 0	118 0	280 0	198 0	73 0
Tobacco . . .	70 0	...	56 0	90 0	...	59 0	65 0	47 0	39 0
Wheat	7 14	10 0	9 8	6 17	8 4	7 18	7 18	9 1	6 10
Wine, 100 gals. .	36 10	...	...	18 15	...	...	16 7	5 11	14 2

GREAT BRITAIN

The prices of various commodities during the last 690 years, according to Arthur Young, Shuckburgh, and other writers, were as follows :—

	Nominal Price						
	1201–99	1300–99	1400–99	1500–99	1600–99	1700–99	1800–85
	£ s. d.	£ s. d.	£ s. d.	£ s. d.	£ s. d.	£ s. d.	£ s. d.
Ox	0 13 0	0 16 0	1 0 0	1 11 0	5 0 0	8 0 0	14 0 0
Sheep	0 1 0	0 1 6	0 2 0	0 3 0	0 7 0	0 18 0	1 5 0
Pig	0 2 0	0 3 0	0 3 0	0 4 0	0 8 0	1 2 0	1 10 0
Goose	0 0 3	0 0 4	0 0 6	0 0 8	0 1 0	0 2 0	0 4 0
Rabbit	0 0 2	0 0 2	0 0 3	0 0 3	0 0 6	0 0 8	0 1 0
Hen	0 0 1	0 0 2	0 0 3	0 0 4	0 0 8	0 1 0	0 1 6
Horse	...	...	2 0 0	3 0 0	5 0 0	15 0 0	30 0 0
Pigeons, doz. . .	0 0 3	0 0 4	0 0 6	0 0 9	0 1 0	0 1 6	0 3 0
Eggs, ,, . .	0 0 1	0 0 2	0 0 3	0 0 3	0 0 4	0 0 8	0 1 0
Butter, lb. . .	...	0 0 1	0 0 1	0 0 2	0 0 4	0 0 5	0 1 0
Beef, 8 lbs. . .	0 0 2	0 0 4	0 0 5	0 0 6	0 2 0	0 3 0	0 7 0
Wheat, ton . .	...	1 10 0	1 10 0	4 0 0	10 10 0	12 10 0	14 0 0
Wine, gallon . .	0 1 0	0 1 0	0 1 0	0 3 0	0 5 0	0 16 0	0 16 0
Beer, ,, . .	0 0 1	0 0 2	0 0 2	0 0 3	0 0 4	0 0 8	0 1 6

	Prices According to Weight of Silver						
	1201–99	1300–99	1400–99	1500–99	1600–99	1700–99	1800–85
	£ s. d.	£ s. d.	£ s. d.	£ s. d.	£ s. d.	£ s. l.	£ s. d.
Ox	2 3 0	2 5 0	2 2 0	2 0 0	5 6 0	8 10 0	14 0 0
Sheep	0 3 0	0 4 6	0 4 0	0 4 0	0 8 0	0 19 0	1 5 0
Pig	0 6 0	0 9 0	0 6 0	0 6 0	0 9 0	1 3 0	1 10 0
Goose	0 0 9	0 1 0	0 1 0	0 0 11	0 1 0	0 2 1	0 4 0
Rabbit	0 0 6	0 0 6	0 0 6	0 0 4	0 0 6	0 0 8	0 1 0
Hen	0 0 3	0 0 6	0 0 6	0 0 5	0 0 9	0 1 0	0 1 6
Horse	...	...	4 4 0	4 0 0	5 6 0	15 15 0	30 0 0
Pigeons, doz. . .	0 0 9	0 1 0	0 1 0	0 1 0	0 1 1	0 1 6	0 3 0
Eggs, ,, . .	0 0 3	0 0 6	0 0 6	0 0 4	0 0 4	0 0 8	0 1 0
Butter, lb. . .	...	0 0 3	0 0 2	0 0 3	0 0 4	0 0 5	0 1 0
Beef, 8 lbs. . .	0 0 6	0 1 0	0 0 10	0 0 8	0 2 1	0 3 2	0 7 0
Wheat, ton . .	...	4 0 0	3 0 0	5 5 0	11 5 0	13 5 0	14 0 0
Wine, gallon . .	0 3 0	0 3 0	0 2 0	0 4 0	0 6 0	0 17 0	0 16 0
Beer ,, . .	0 0 3	0 0 5	0 0 4	0 0 4	0 0 4	0 0 8	0 1 6

The following tables of prices from 1782 to 1859 are from Tooke's *History of Prices*:—

	1782	1783	1784	1785	1786	1787	1788	1789	1790	1782–90
	s. d.	s. d.	s. d.	s. d.	s. d.	s. d.	s. d.	s. d.	s. d.	s. d.
Coffee, cwt.	70 0	66 0	65 0	69 0	78 0	91 0	92 0	95 0	78 0	78 0
Copper, ,, ...	85 0	85 0	85 0	80 0	82 0	81 0	80 0	82 0	84 0	83 0
Cotton, ,, ...	330 0	285 0	205 0	203 0	252 0	242 0	225 0	185 0	170 0	233 0
Flax, ,, ...	43 0	46 0	44 0	44 0	45 0	43 0	44 0	46 0	46 0	44 6
Hemp, ,, ...	34 0	32 0	28 0	23 0	25 0	36 0	36 0	28 0	27 0	30 0
Hops, ,, ...	85 0	150 0	95 0	98 0	75 0	140 0	260 0	140 0	90 0	126 0
Indigo, lb. . . .	5 0	5 6	4 0	4 0	3 6	4 6	4 0	6 0	3 0	4 4
Iron, cwt. . . .	6 9	5 9	4 9	4 9	4 9	4 6	5 0	5 0	5 0	5 1
Oil, gallon . . .	3 6	3 8	3 10	3 10	3 8	3 2	3 1	3 5	3 4	3 6
Pepper, cwt. . . .	205 0	195 0	170 0	140 0	122 0	130 0	121 0	130 0	140 0	150 2
Rice, ,, . . .	26 0	28 0	24 0	16 0	19 0	18 0	17 0	17 0	16 0	20 1
Rum, gallon . . .	4 7	3 1	3 5	2 11	2 6	2 9	3 4	2 9	3 4	3 3
Silk, lb. . . .	19 0	19 0	19 0	22 0	31 0	31 0	26 0	20 0	20 0	23 0
Sugar, cwt. . . .	45 0	34 0	32 0	32 0	38 0	36 0	38 0	39 0	42 0	37 6
Tea, lb. . . .	5 0	4 9	5 1	4 1	4 9	4 0	4 6	3 9	3 7	4 4
Timber, load . .	68 0	51 0	42 0	40 0	37 0	33 0	33 0	29 0	37 0	41 0
Tin, cwt. . . .	83 0	83 0	83 0	85 0	85 0	85 0	81 0	74 0	77 0	82 0
Tobacco, cwt. . . .	140 0	65 0	50 0	37 0	33 0	36 0	33 0	33 0	33 0	51 0
Wheat, quarter . .	54 0	54 0	54 0	48 0	42 0	46 0	49 0	56 0	56 0	51 0
Wool, lb. . . .	3 4	3 6	3 5	3 5	3 3	3 3	3 7	3 7	3 7	3 5

	1791	1792	1793	1794	1795	1796	1797	1798	1799	1800	1791–1800
	s. d.	s. d.	s. d.	s. d.	s. d.	s. d.	s. d.	s. d.	s. d.	s. d.	s. d.
Coffee, cwt. . .	78 0	90 0	83 0	80 0	95 0	110 0	118 0	139 0	141 0	117 0	105 0
Copper, ,, . .	87 0	96 0	110 0	109 0	109 0	115 0	120 0	120 0	130 0	150 0	114 0
Cotton, ,, . .	195 0	233 0	225 0	186 0	176 0	230 0	270 0	305 0	330 0	270 0	242 0
Flax, ,, . .	38 0	34 0	35 0	35 0	47 0	55 0	51 0	52 0	61 0	67 0	47 0
Hemp, ,, . .	23 0	25 0	26 0	28 0	39 0	55 0	45 0	37 0	41 0	64 0	38 4
Hops, ,, . .	110 0	78 0	143 0	151 0	95 0	80 0	135 0	135 0	295 0	297 0	152 0
Indigo, lb. . . .	6 6	7 9	5 9	5 6	5 9	5 6	4 1	6 10	7 0	6 3	6 1
Iron, cwt. . . .	6 3	6 3	6 3	6 6	6 6	6 6	6 6	6 6	6 6	7 0	6 6
Oil, gallon . . .	3 2	3 5	4 2	4 7	4 8	4 9	5 0	5 6	5 11	5 2	4 7
Pepper, cwt. . .	160 0	190 0	130 0	128 0	130 0	127 0	128 0	122 0	168 0	170 0	145 4
Rice, ,, . .	16 0	17 0	17 0	39 0	31 0	17 0	17 0	28 0	39 0	38 0	26 0
Rum, gallon . .	3 9	4 1	4 8	3 7	6 0	7 9	6 3	6 3	4 3	6 0	5 4
Silk, lb. . . .	21 0	22 0	18 0	17 0	18 0	20 0	20 0	24 0	25 0	24 0	21 0
Sugar, cwt. . . .	56 0	58 0	57 0	50 0	59 0	69 0	64 0	71 0	58 0	51 0	59 4
Tea, lb. . . .	3 10	4 0	3 9	3 4	3 9	3 8	3 4	3 5	3 1	3 3	3 8
Timber, load . .	52 0	46 0	46 0	51 0	58 0	56 0	62 0	58 0	84 0	115 0	63 0
Tin, cwt. . . .	82 0	98 0	104 0	102 0	100 0	102 0	103 0	100 0	103 0	107 0	100 1
Tobacco, cwt. . .	30 0	32 0	35 0	33 0	51 0	59 0	85 0	112 0	88 0	58 0	58 4
Wheat, quarter .	49 0	47 0	50 0	54 0	82 0	80 0	62 0	54 0	76 0	127 0	68 0
Wool, lb. . . .	3 9	4 2	4 2	3 9	3 9	4 0	4 1	4 1	4 6	4 8	4 1

	1801	1802	1803	1804	1805	1806	1807	1808	1809	1810	1801–10
	s. d.	s. d.	s. d.	s. d.	s. d.	s. d.	s. d.	s. d.	s. d.	s. d.	s. d.
Coffee, cwt. . .	95 0	78 0	108 0	133 0	145 0	115 0	100 0	88 0	93 0	93 0	105 0
Copper, ,, . .	160 0	145 0	135 0	153 0	182 0	191 0	155 0	174 0	160 0	160 0	161 6
Cotton, ,, . .	260 0	234 0	112 0	130 0	130 0	129 0	112 0	177 0	130 0	132 0	155 0
Flax, ,, . .	68 0	71 0	81 0	82 0	76 0	68 0	72 0	109 0	120 0	84 0	83 0
Hemp, ,, . .	65 0	41 0	53 0	50 0	53 0	55 0	62 0	93 0	95 0	66 0	63 6

	1801	1802	1803	1804	1805	1806	1807	1808	1809	1810	1801–10
	s. d.	s. d.	s. d.	s. d.	s. d.	s. d.	s. d.	s. d.	s. d.	s. d.	s. d.
Hops, cwt.	185 0	164 0	160 0	95 0	110 0	120 0	119 0	100 0	98 0	108 0	136 0
Indigo, lb.	6 10	7 6	8 0	7 9	8 3	9 6	7 0	6 3	6 4	7 0	7 6
Iron, cwt.	7 3	7 3	7 3	8 0	8 0	8 0	8 0	8 0	8 0	8 0	7 9
Oil, gallon	5 1	4 10	5 1	5 2	6 0	5 10	5 7	6 5	5 10	5 2	5 6
Pepper, cwt.	140 0	138 0	121 0	95 0	93 0	77 0	75 0	85 0	102 0	95 0	102 0
Rice, ,,	38 0	35 0	34 0	35 0	38 0	36 0	30 0	49 0	49 0	28 0	37 3
Rum, gallon	6 3	5 1	5 3	4 7	4 11	3 11	3 11	5 2	5 3	5 7	5 0
Silk, lb.	23 0	25 0	22 0	23 0	25 0	30 0	29 0	32 0	32 0	41 0	28 3
Sugar, cwt.	54 0	39 0	45 0	56 0	53 0	43 0	34 0	40 0	43 0	48 0	45 6
Tea, lb.	3 3	3 4	3 1	3 1	3 4	3 0	3 3	3 4	3 5	3 5	3 4
Timber, load	102 0	69 0	97 0	70 0	70 0	101 0	125 0	235 0	260 0	200 0	133 0
Tin, cwt.	111 0	114 0	116 0	116 0	118 0	126 0	128 0	119 0	124 0	151 0	122 0
Tobacco, cwt.	54 0	47 0	49 0	58 0	54 0	56 0	56 0	128 0	126 0	74 0	70 0
Wheat, quarter	128 0	67 0	60 0	69 6	88 0	88 0	78 0	85 0	106 0	112 0	88 0
Wool, lb.	5 6	6 0	6 2	6 8	6 8	6 8	6 8	8 6	19 0	10 6	8 3

The above prices were in Bank of England notes, but the values in gold were as follows :—

Gold	1801	1802	1803	1804	1805	1806	1807	1808	1809	1810	1801–10
	s. d.	s. d.	s. d.	s. d.	s. d.	s. d.	s. d.	s. d.	s. d.	s. d.	s. d.
Coffee, cwt.	87 0	73 0	105 0	129 0	140 0	112 0	97 0	85 6	85 0	81 0	99 6
Copper, ,,	147 0	135 0	131 0	148 0	176 0	185 0	150 0	169 0	145 0	140 0	152 6
Cotton, ,,	240 0	218 0	109 0	126 0	126 0	125 0	109 0	172 0	118 0	116 0	146 0
Flax, ,,	63 0	66 0	78 0	79 6	74 0	66 0	70 0	106 0	109 0	73 0	78 6
Hemp, ,,	60 0	38 0	51 0	48 6	51 6	53 6	60 0	90 0	86 0	58 0	59 9
Hops, ,,	170 0	153 0	155 0	92 0	107 0	116 0	115 0	97 0	89 0	94 0	119 0
Indigo, lb.	6 3	7 0	7 8	7 5	7 11	9 2	6 9	6 0	5 9	6 2	7 0
Iron, cwt.	6 8	6 9	7 0	7 8	7 8	7 8	7 8	7 8	7 4	7 0	7 4
Oil, gallon	4 8	4 6	4 10	5 0	5 9	5 8	5 5	6 2	5 4	4 6	5 3
Pepper, cwt.	129 0	128 0	117 0	92 0	90 0	75 0	73 0	82 6	93 0	83 0	96 4
Rice, ,,	35 0	32 0	33 0	34 0	37 0	35 0	29 0	47 6	44 6	25 0	35 3
Rum, gallon	5 9	4 9	5 1	4 5	4 9	3 9	3 9	5 0	4 10	5 0	4 9
Silk, lb.	21 0	23 0	21 6	22 3	24 3	29 0	28 0	31 0	29 0	36 0	26 6
Sugar, cwt.	50 0	36 0	43 6	54 6	51 6	41 6	33 0	38 6	39 0	42 0	43 2
Tea, lb.	3 0	3 1	3 0	3 0	3 2	2 11	3 2	3 3	3 2	3 0	3 1
Timber, load	94 0	64 0	94 0	68 0	68 0	98 0	121 0	228 0	237 0	175 0	124 6
Tin, cwt.	102 0	106 0	112 0	112 0	114 0	122 0	124 0	115 0	113 0	132 0	115 3
Tobacco, cwt.	50 0	44 0	47 6	55 4	52 6	54 6	54 6	124 0	115 0	65 0	66 4
Wheat, quarter	118 0	62 0	58 0	67 6	85 6	85 6	76 0	82 6	96 0	98 0	83 0
Wool, lb.	5 6	5 7	5 11	6 5	6 5	6 5	6 5	8 2	17 0	9 3	7 8

Notes	1811	1812	1813	1814	1815	1816	1817	1818	1819	1820	1811–20
	s. d.	s. d.	s. d.	s. d.	s. d.	s. d.	s. d.	s. d.	s. d.	s. d.	s. d.
Coffee, cwt.	50 0	45 0	75 0	87 0	78 0	65 0	75 0	115 0	113 0	109 0	81 3
Copper, ,,	148 0	138 0	133 0	130 0	130 0	108 0	119 0	123 0	133 0	115 0	128 0
Cotton, ,,	97 0	116 0	196 0	242 0	177 0	160 0	186 0	177 0	140 0	102 0	159 0
Flax, ,,	88 0	102 0	89 0	76 0	73 0	56 0	61 0	68 0	56 0	52 0	72 0
Hemp, ,,	77 0	92 0	80 0	57 0	42 0	33 0	33 0	38 0	35 0	33 0	52 0
Hops, ,,	146 0	200 0	310 0	170 0	220 0	240 0	490 0	370 0	128 0	91 0	236 6
Indigo, lb.	9 0	10 3	12 9	13 6	10 6	9 10	10 0	8 7	8 0	7 3	10 1
Iron, cwt.	8 0	8 0	8 0	8 0	8 0	8 0	8 0	8 0	8 11	8 5	8 2
Oil, gallon	5 5	7 2	7 6	6 2	6 2	6 0	6 11	6 6	6 2	5 0	6 4
Pepper, cwt.	71 0	77 0	112 0	154 0	97 0	77 0	79 0	85 0	70 0	61 0	88 4
Rice, ,,	32 0	61 0	66 0	43 0	34 0	39 0	43 0	47 0	32 0	37 0	43 6
Rum, gallon	5 3	5 4	6 9	6 3	4 9	3 10	4 1	4 5	3 3	3 10	4 10
Silk, lb.	43 0	31 0	25 0	21 0	20 1	17 0	22 0	24 0	23 0	22 0	24 10
Sugar, cwt.	40 0	45 0	63 0	76 0	67 0	52 0	49 0	51 0	43 0	36 0	52 3
Tea, lb.	3 4	3 4	3 4	3 7	3 3	3 3	3 2	2 11	2 11	3 0	3 3
Timber, load	225 0	185 0	145 0	122 0	88 0	60 0	63 0	70 0	60 0	55 0	107 4
Tin, cwt.	165 0	135 0	140 0	170 0	144 0	119 0	100 0	95 0	79 0	79 0	122 6
Tobacco, cwt.	56 0	48 0	140 0	305 0	177 0	117 0	88 0	93 0	74 0	65 0	116 4
Wheat, quarter	108 0	118 0	120 0	85 0	76 0	82 0	116 0	98 0	78 0	76 0	95 6
Wool, lb.	8 3	9 3	8 9	8 0	7 0	6 6	6 6	6 6	5 4	4 0	7 0

The prices in the above decade as above given were in paper-money ; the gold value was as follows :—

Gold	1811	1812	1813	1814	1815	1816	1817	1818	1819	1820	1811–20
	s. d.	s. d.	s. d.	s. d.	s. d.	s. d.	s. d.	s. d.	s. d.	s. d.	s. d.
Coffee, cwt.	42 0	36 0	56 0	70 0	65 0	62 0	73 6	112 0	109 0	109 0	73 6
Copper, ,,	123 0	110 0	100 0	104 0	108 0	104 0	116 6	119 0	128 0	115 0	118 0
Cotton, ,,	81 0	92 0	146 0	194 0	148 0	154 0	186 0	172 0	134 0	102 0	141 0

Gold	1811		1812		1813		1814		1815		1816		1817		1818		1819		1820		1811-20	
	s.	d.	s.	d.	s.	d.	s.	d.	s.	d.	s.	d.	s.	d.	s.	d.	s.	d.	s.	d.	s.	d.
Flax, cwt. . . .	73	0	82	0	67	0	61	0	61	0	54	0	59	6	66	0	54	0	52	0	63	0
Hemp, ,, . .	64	0	74	0	60	0	45	0	35	0	31	6	32	4	37	0	33	6	33	0	44	6
Hops, ,, . .	122	0	160	0	232	0	136	0	183	0	230	0	480	0	359	0	123	0	91	0	212	0
Indigo, lb. . . .	7	6	8	1	9	6	10	8	8	9	9	5	9	9	8	4	7	8	7	3	8	8
Iron, cwt. . . .	6	8	6	4	6	0	6	4	6	8	7	8	7	10	7	9	8	7	8	5	7	3
Oil, gallon . .	4	6	5	8	5	7	4	10	5	2	5	9	6	9	6	4	5	11	5	0	5	8
Pepper, cwt. . .	59	0	62	0	84	0	123	0	81	0	74	0	77	0	82	6	67	0	61	0	77	0
Rice, ,, . .	27	0	49	0	49	0	34	0	28	0	37	6	42	0	45	6	31	0	37	0	38	0
Rum, gallon . .	4	5	4	3	5	1	5	0	4	0	3	8	4	0	4	3	3	1	3	10	4	3
Silk, lb. . . .	36	0	25	0	18	6	17	0	16	8	16	3	21	6	23	3	22	0	22	0	22	0
Sugar, cwt. . .	33	0	36	0	47	0	61	0	56	0	50	0	48	0	49	6	41	0	36	0	45	8
Tea, lb. . . .	2	9	2	8	2	6	2	10	2	9	3	1	3	1	2	10	2	10	3	0	2	10
Timber, load . .	188	0	148	0	109	0	98	0	73	0	57	6	61	6	68	0	57	6	55	0	91	6
Tin, cwt. . . .	138	0	108	0	105	0	136	0	120	0	114	0	98	0	92	0	76	0	79	0	106	5
Tobacco, cwt. . .	47	0	38	0	105	0	244	0	147	0	112	0	86	0	90	0	71	0	65	0	100	6
Wheat, quarter .	90	0	94	0	90	0	68	0	63	0	78	6	113	6	95	0	75	0	76	0	84	4
Wool, lb. . . .	7	0	7	4	6	7	6	4	5	10	6	3	6	4	6	4	5	2	4	0	6	1

In 1820 gold and paper money were of equal value.

	1821		1822		1823		1824		1825		1826		1827		1828		1829		1830		1821-30	
	s.	d.	s.	d.	s.	d.	s.	d.	s.	d.	s.	d.	s.	d.	s.	d.	s.	d.	s.	d.	s.	d.
Coffee, cwt. . .	102	0	94	0	80	0	64	0	63	0	52	0	46	0	41	0	36	0	34	0	61	3
Copper, ,, . .	99	0	101	0	105	0	105	0	100	0	115	0	115	0	110	0	97	0	89	0	103	6
Cotton, ,, . .	84	0	83	0	80	0	75	0	120	0	77	0	58	0	57	0	57	0	60	0	75	0
Flax, ,, . .	50	0	48	0	54	0	46	0	46	0	37	0	37	0	35	0	36	0	42	0	43	0
Hemp, ,, . .	34	0	35	0	33	0	36	0	42	0	41	0	41	0	39	0	42	0	41	0	38	6
Hops, ,, . .	86	0	86	0	105	0	242	0	260	0	250	0	112	0	107	0	165	0	228	0	164	0
Indigo, lb. . . .	9	0	10	0	9	6	10	1	13	0	11	0	11	10	10	4	8	6	8	9	10	3
Iron, cwt. . . .	6	10	6	6	6	3	8	6	10	10	8	3	7	3	6	6	5	9	5	2	7	3
Oil, gallon . .	4	2	3	9	3	9	3	9	3	7	3	4	3	10	3	5	3	6	3	11	3	8
Pepper, cwt. . .	66	0	67	0	60	0	52	0	65	0	51	0	38	0	33	0	33	0	36	0	50	1
Rice, ,, . .	33	0	33	0	38	0	34	0	37	0	35	0	39	0	36	0	35	0	34	0	35	6
Rum, gallon . .	2	10	2	5	2	6	2	3	2	9	3	5	3	10	4	0	3	6	2	10	3	0
Silk, lb. . . .	20	0	21	0	19	0	18	0	22	0	16	0	20	0	21	0	15	0	14	0	18	6
Sugar, cwt. . .	32	0	31	0	32	0	32	0	37	0	35	0	34	0	35	0	28	0	23	0	32	0
Tea, lb. . . .	3	0	3	2	3	2	3	2	3	2	2	10	2	10	2	8	2	9	2	9	3	0
Timber, load . .	60	0	50	0	52	0	51	0	58	0	48	0	46	0	42	0	46	0	41	0	49	6
Tin, cwt. . . .	79	0	89	0	101	0	89	0	100	0	86	0	81	0	76	0	79	0	77	0	85	6
Tobacco, cwt. . .	48	0	55	0	50	0	47	0	56	0	56	0	48	0	38	0	47	0	48	0	49	4
Wheat, quarter .	71	0	53	0	57	0	72	0	84	0	73	0	58	6	60	6	66	0	64	0	66	0
Wool, lb. . . .	3	6	4	0	4	2	3	8	3	10	3	6	3	0	2	9	2	6	2	4	3	4

	1831		1832		1833		1834		1835		1836		1837		1838		1839		1840		1831-40	
	s.	d.	s.	d.	s.	d.	s.	d.	s.	d.	s.	d.	s.	d.	s.	d.	s.	d.	s.	d.	s.	d.
Coffee, cwt. . .	56	0	76	0	78	0	68	0	75	0	81	0	81	0	78	0	90	0	86	0	77	0
Copper, ,, . .	87	0	91	0	98	0	99	0	94	0	105	0	92	0	90	0	94	0	98	0	95	0
Cotton, ,, . .	58	0	58	0	80	0	79	0	95	0	93	0	84	0	63	0	70	0	56	0	73	6
Flax, ,, . .	48	0	47	0	39	0	48	0	55	0	46	0	40	0	37	0	41	0	39	0	44	0
Hemp, ,, . .	40	0	32	0	26	0	25	0	25	0	29	0	31	0	35	0	41	0	38	0	32	3
Hops, ,, . .	197	0	165	0	167	0	161	0	132	0	140	0	132	0	130	0	110	0	...		148	3
Indigo, lb. . . .	6	6	5	5	6	5	6	6	6	1	6	7	7	3	7	6	8	1	6	1	6	8
Iron, cwt. . . .	5	0	5	2	5	6	5	3	5	3	7	2	5	6	6	1	6	0	9	2	6	0
Oil, gallon . .	3	5	3	8	3	11	4	0	4	9	4	10	4	2	4	7	4	9	5	2	4	4
Pepper, cwt. . .	37	0	36	0	36	0	38	0	42	0	43	0	35	0	38	0	39	0	40	0	38	6
Rice, ,, . .	34	0	37	0	35	0	32	0	31	0	31	0	32	0	36	0	41	0	...		34	6
Rum, gallon . .	2	9	2	10	3	0	3	1	3	2	3	10	4	1	4	3	5	4	5	1	3	9
Silk, lb. . . .	15	0	14	0	18	0	18	0	20	0	23	0	19	0	21	0	24	0	25	0	19	8
Sugar, cwt. . .	24	0	27	0	28	0	32	0	34	0	42	0	35	0	37	0	38	0	47	0	34	6
Tea, lb. . . .	2	9	2	7	2	6	2	10	2	4	2	0	1	9	2	2	1	10	2	8	2	4
Timber, load . .	51	0	46	0	49	0	49	0	49	0	55	0	54	0	52	0	...		106	0	55	6
Tin, cwt. . . .	77	0	76	0	75	0	78	0	85	0	116	0	90	0	90	0	85	0	82	0	85	0
Tobacco, cwt. . .	37	0	37	0	41	0	47	0	51	0	61	0	52	0	55	0	78	0	65	0	52	6
Wheat, quarter .	66	0	59	0	53	0	46	0	39	0	49	6	56	0	65	0	71	0	66	0	57	0
Wool, lb. . . .	2	8	2	6	2	7	3	3	2	9	3	0	2	8	2	5	2	7	2	4	2	7

	1841		1842		1843		1844		1845		1846		1847		1848		1849		1850		1841-50	
	s.	d.	s.	d.	s.	d.	s.	d.	s.	d.	s.	d.	s.	d.	s.	d.	s.	d.	s.	d.	s.	d.
Coffee, cwt. . .	99	0	93	0	83	0	81	0	72	0	70	0	70	0	74	0	60	0	65	0	76	6
Copper, ,, . .	98	0	91	0	84	0	84	0	88	0	91	0	93	0	89	0	84	0	86	0	89	0
Cotton, ,, . .	60	0	47	0	45	0	47	0	38	0	43	0	61	0	47	0	48	0	65	0	50	3
Flax, ,, . .	39	0	...		...		34	0	...		...		...		43	0	37	0	40	0	39	0

	1841		1842		1843		1844		1845		1846		1847		1848		1849		1850		1841-50	
	s.	d.	s.	d.	s.	d.	s.	d.	s.	d.	s.	d.	s.	d.	s.	d.	s.	d.	s.	d.	s.	d.
Hemp, cwt. . .	38	0	34	0	30	0	30	0	29	0	33	0	39	0	32	0	30	0	31	0	32	6
Indigo, lb. . . .	5	6	4	9	5	0	4	0	4	2	3	10	3	10	3	0	3	4	4	2	4	3
Iron, cwt. . . .	7	6	6	2	4	10	5	6	8	9	9	6	9	10	7	9	6	5	5	9	7	3
Oil, gallon . . .	6	2	5	4	4	1	3	10	3	6	3	6	4	2	3	8	3	5	3	7	4	1
Pepper, cwt. . .	37	0	36	0	37	0	33	0	30	0	30	0	28	0	28	0	28	0	34	0	32	0
Rum, gallon . .	4	6	4	1		...	2	8	2	7	2	10	4	2	3	4	2	6	2	5	3	3
Silk, lb.	21	0	20	0	19	0	20	0	18	0	16	0	14	0	14	0	16	0	18	0	17	6
Sugar, cwt. . .	43	0	37	0	33	0	33	0	34	0	35	0	28	0	23	0	26	0	28	0	32	0
Tea, lb.	2	5	2	2	1	7	1	8	1	7	1	6	1	11	1	2	1	3	1	3	1	8
Timber, load . .	104	0	95	0	89	0	83	0	83	0	85	0	85	0	75	0	68	0	63	0	83	0
Tin, cwt. . . .	82	0	72	0	65	0	73	0	87	0	99	0	93	0	80	0	82	0	78	0	81	0
Tobacco, cwt. . .	47	0	38	0	36	0	34	0	32	0	36	0	37	0	38	0	42	0	65	0	40	6
Wheat, quarter .	64	0	57	0	50	0	51	0	51	0	55	0	70	0	51	0	44	0	40	0	53	3
Wool, lb. . . .	2	3	2	3	2	3	2	1	2	5	2	0	1	10	1	9	1	5	1	5	2	0

	1851		1852		1853		1854		1855		1856		1857		1858		1859		1851-59	
	s.	d.	s.	d.	s.	d.	s.	d.	s.	d.	s.	d.	s.	d.	s.	d.	s.	d.	s.	d.
Coffee, cwt. . . .	68	0	58	0	68	0	68	0	67	0	67	0	74	0	56	0	64	0	65	6
Copper, ,, . . .	86	0	95	0	112	0	126	0	126	0	117	0	117	0	107	0	107	0	110	6
Cotton, ,, . . .	61	0	54	0	53	0	52	0	52	0	58	0	75	0	57	0	65	0	58	6
Flax, ,, . . .	40	0	48	0	49	0	47	0	56	0	53	0	57	0	57	0	57	0	51	6
Hemp, ,, . . .	31	0	34	0	38	0	56	0	51	0	38	0	35	0	29	0	29	0	38	0
Indigo, lb. . . .	4	4	4	4	4	9	4	9	4	3	4	3	4	8	6	3	4	6	4	8
Iron, cwt. . . .	5	8	6	4	9	6	10	0	8	6	9	0	8	3	7	3	7	0	8	0
Oil, gallon . . .	3	2	4	0	5	2	4	7	4	6	4	2	4	7	4	0	3	11	4	3
Pepper, cwt. . .	28	0	32	0	37	0	42	0	42	0	50	0		...		...		...	38	6
Butter, ,, . . .	76	0	74	0	92	0	101	0	103	0	107	0	100	0	110	0	105	0	96	6
Rum, gallon . .	2	5	2	2	3	2	3	10	3	11	3	6	4	8	3	10	3	2	3	4
Silk, lb. . . .	18	0	17	0	19	0	14	0	14	0	17	0	23	0	18	0	16	0	17	4
Sugar, cwt. . .	27	0	24	0	25	0	25	0	35	0	36	0	42	0	25	0	24	0	29	3
Tea, lb. . . .	1	2	1	1	1	5	1	4	1	6	1	6	1	3	1	1	0	11	1	3
Timber, load . .	63	0	61	0	78	0	83	0	80	0	73	0	69	0	71	0	63	0	71	3
Tin, cwt. . . .	84	0	91	0	113	0	124	0	117	0	133	0	143	0	109	0	124	0	115	0
Tobacco, cwt. . .	102	0	56	0	65	0	65	0	70	0	71	0	90	0	82	0	70	0	74	6
Wheat, quarter .	39	0	41	0	53	0	72	0	75	0	69	0	56	0	44	0	44	0	55	0
Wool, lb. . . .	1	5	1	5	1	5	1	4	1	7	2	0	1	8	1	2	1	3	1	6

PRICES OF BRITISH IMPORTS AND EXPORTS, 1854-88.

There are ninety-five principal articles of British commerce, and these attained their highest and lowest prices in the years stated below :—

Years	Highest	Lowest	Years	Highest	Lowest
1854-55	12	11	Brought forward	75	25
1856-57	19	0	1874-75	6	0
1858-59	1	2	1876-77	2	0
1860-61	1	0	1878-79	2	7
1862-63	3	4	1880-81	1	0
1864-65	12	1	1882-83	3	1
1866-67	9	1	1884-85	2	7
1868-69	7	3	1886-87	2	30
1870-71	2	1	1888	0	16
1872-73	9	0	1889	2	9
Total . .	75	25	Total . .	95	95

The highest and lowest prices recorded, and the years in which these prices occurred, are given as follows :—

	Highest	Lowest	Year of Price Highest	Year of Price Lowest	Average Price for 36 Years
	£ s. d.	£ s. d.			£ s. d.
Bacon, cwt.	3 6 0	1 15 0	1869	1862	2 7 6
Barley, ,,	0 10 2	0 5 3	1868	1887	0 8 1
Beef, ,,	2 13 0	1 9 0	1883	1863	2 2 6
Brandy, gall	0 13 0	0 5 1	1857	1866	0 8 3
Butter, cwt.	5 17 0	3 8 0	1876	1854	4 17 6

	Highest	Lowest	Year of Price Highest	Year of Price Lowest	Average Price for 36 Years
	£ s. d.	£ s. d.			£ s. d.
Cheese, cwt.	3 4 0	2 3 0	1866	1879	2 13 0
Cigars, lb. .	0 14 3	0 6 4	1882	1869	0 11 9
Cochineal, lb.	0 4 1	0 1 0	1857	1884	0 2 7
Cocoa, cwt.	4 13 6	1 8 0	1879	1854	3 3 0
Coffee, ,,	5 1 0	2 3 0	1874	1858	3 8 0
Copper ore, cwt.	1 9 0	0 6 10	1856	1886	0 14 0
Cotton, cwt.	12 15 0	2 10 0	1864	1886	4 1 0
Eggs (120) .	0 8 7	0 4 7	1874	1854	0 6 7
Flax, cwt. .	3 0 0	1 14 0	1856	1888	2 7 6
Flour, ,,	1 4 0	0 11 1	1855	1887	0 16 2
Guano, cwt.	0 13 0	0 7 0	1857	1889	0 11 0
Hemp, ,,	2 14 0	1 8 0	1854	1879	1 14 0
Hides, ,,	4 3 0	2 7 0	1873	1854	3 8 0
Hops, ,,	9 5 0	2 5 0	1882	1859	5 0 6
Indigo, lb. .	0 6 10	0 3 6	1868	1889	0 5 2
Jute, cwt. .	1 5 0	0 11 3	1863	1886	0 16 4
Lard, ,, .	3 13 0	1 14 0	1869	1879	2 11 0
Maize, cwt.	0 11 0	0 4 9	1855	1889	0 7 2
Molasses, cwt.	0 18 0	0 6 4	1857	1888	0 10 6
Nitre, cwt. .	1 0 0	0 9 4	1857	1889	0 14 0
Oats, ,, .	0 9 6	0 4 10	1868	1888	0 7 7
Oil, olive, tun .	67 0 0	35 15 0	1868	1889	41 5 0
Oranges, bushel	0 13 3	0 5 11	1862	1889	0 9 6
Pepper, cwt.	76 0 0	33 0 0	1887	1864	48 0 0
Pork, ,,	3 2 0	1 11 4	1870	1879	2 2 0
Potatoes . .	0 8 0	0 3 0	1889	1854	0 5 0
Raisins . .	2 8 0	1 5 0	1856	1862	1 14 0
Rice . . .	0 14 8	0 7 6	1867	1886	0 10 6
Rum . . .	0 3 8	0 1 6	1857	1886	0 2 4

	Highest	Lowest	Year of Price Highest	Year of Price Lowest	Average Price for 36 Years
	£ s. d.	£ s. d.			£ s. d.
Saltpetre .	2 0 0	0 16 10	1860	1885	1 6 0
Seed, clover	3 17 0	2 0 10	1856	1886	2 13 0
Sheep, each	2 9 0	1 11 0	1878	1868	2 1 6
Silk, lb. . .	1 7 0	0 12 3	1866	1888	1 2 6
Sugar, cwt.	2 6 0	0 15 8	1857	1887	1 11 0
Tallow, ,,	3 3 0	1 4 0	1854	1887	2 3 0
Tea, ,,	9 6 0	4 18 0	1865	1887	7 8 0
Tobacco, cwt.	7 2 0	3 2 0	1863	1878	3 19 0
Wheat, ,,	0 16 10	0 7 6	1854	1886	0 11 3
Wine, gall.	0 14 9	0 3 10	1856	1864	0 7 9
Wood, load	3 16 0	1 18 0	1854	1887	2 17 6
Wool, cwt. .	10 4 0	4 5 0	1857	1886	7 8 0

The highest and lowest prices for exports, and the years in which they occurred, are shown as follows:—

	Highest	Lowest	Year of Price Highest	Year of Price Lowest	Average Price for 36 Years
	£ s. d.	£ s. d.			£ s. d.
Alkali, ton . .	12 7 0	5 3 0	1873	1888	8 5 0
Bags, gross .	9 0 0	2 6 0	1864	1886	4 18 0
Beer, barrel .	4 8 0	3 6 0	1874	1854	3 16 0
Books, cwt. . .	15 0 0	8 7 0	1855	1889	11 15 0
Boots, doz. pair	3 12 0	2 14 0	1864	1888	3 2 0
Brass, cwt. . .	6 11 0	3 15 0	1857	1886	5 3 6
Butter, ,, . .	7 0 0	4 12 0	1884	1854	5 12 0
Candles, cwt. .	8 13 0	2 1 0	1857	1888	4 2 6
Carpet, doz. yds.	2 0 0	1 4 0	1867	1887	1 11 6
Cement, ton, .	3 16 0	1 18 0	1856	1888	2 11 3
Cheese, cwt.. .	4 8 0	3 16 0	1870	1854	4 2 3
Cloth, doz. yds. .	2 1 0	1 4 0	1884	1854	1 14 6
Coal, ton. . .	1 1 0	0 8 4	1873	1887	0 9 10
Copper, cwt. .	6 0 0	2 4 0	1857	1886	4 4 6

	Highest	Lowest	Year of Price Highest	Year of Price Lowest	Average Price for 36 Years
	£ s. d.	£ s. d.			£ s. d.
Cordage, cwt. .	3 3 0	2 1 0	1854	1886	2 12 3
Cottons, 100 yds.	2 8 4	0 18 0	1864	1886	1 6 3
,, printed, 100 yds. . .	2 12 6	1 5 0	1864	1889	1 15 8
Firearms, each .	2 1 0	0 18 0	1875	1854	1 9 0
Flannel, doz. yds.	1 0 0	0 11 0	1864	1888	0 16 3
Glass, flint, cwt.	3 13 0	2 2 0	1855	1885	2 15 0
,, bottles, ton	11 10 0	9 5 0	1854	1883	10 4 0
Gunpowder, cwt.	3 12 0	2 14 0	1859	1868	3 1 0
Hats, dozen . .	1 19 0	0 19 0	1865	1886	1 9 9
Herrings, barrel	1 15 0	1 1 0	1881	1887	1 7 0
Horses . . .	81 0 0	35 0 0	1876	1870	58 0 0
Iron, pig, ton .	6 5 0	2 3 0	1873	1888	3 1 6
,, rail, ,, .	13 5 0	4 11 0	1873	1887	7 16 0
,, hoop, ton .	14 12 0	6 1 0	1873	1887	10 5 0
,, wire, ,, .	23 10 0	12 10 0	1873	1885	17 15 0
Jute, 100 yards .	2 10 0	0 17 0	1854	1886	1 12 0
Lead, ton . .	25 0 0	12 5 0	1856	1885	19 18 0
Leather, cwt. .	11 5 0	6 17 0	1866	1879	8 14 0
Linens, 100 yds.	3 11 0	2 6 0	1864	1888	2 18 9
,, printed, ,,	4 2 6	2 9 0	1866	1888	3 4 10
Oil-seed, ton. .	34 10 0	18 7 0	1866	1886	27 5 0
Paper, cwt. . .	4 16 0	1 13 0	1854	1888	3 2 0
Sailcloth, 100 yds.	5 17 0	4 8 0	1874	1888	5 4 0
Salt, ton . . .	0 19 0	0 9 0	1873	1863	0 11 9
Soap, cwt. . .	1 8 0	0 19 0	1869	1888	1 4 9
Silk, doz. yds. .	2 10 0	1 17 0	1887	1889	2 1 3
Spirits, gallon .	0 7 0	0 2 5	1889	1865	0 4 4
Steel bar, ton .	38 6 0	15 7 0	1874	1889	30 10 0
Sugar, cwt. . .	3 0 0	0 13 0	1857	1887	1 13 9
Tin, ,, . .	7 10 0	3 6 0	1872	1878	5 7 0
Wool, ,, . .	11 4 0	4 9 0	1865	1885	7 15 0
Yarn, cotton, cwt.	13 10 0	5 1 0	1864	1886	6 17 0
,, linen, ,,	8 8 0	5 12 0	1864	1855	6 17 2
,, woollen, ,,	19 10 0	10 12 0	1866	1888	14 11 0
Zinc, ton . . .	32 0 0	13 6 0	1857	1885	21 2 0

British Imports from 1854 to 1860:—

	1854	1855	1856	1857	1858	1859	1860	1854–60
	s. d.	s. d.	s. d.	s. d.	s. d.	s. d.	s. d.	s. d.
Bacon, cwt.	40 0	48 0	55 0	55 0	46 0	48 0	53 0	49 0
Barley, ,,	9 0	8 7	9 6	8 9	7 9	7 6	9 6	8 8
Beans, ,,	10 2	9 7	8 2	9 0	8 4	8 3	9 9	8 6
Beef, ,,	38 0	41 6	37 6	51 0	39 0	41 0	31 4	40 0
Brandy, gallon	8 4	9 9	10 2	12 10	7 7	7 0	9 6	9 4
Butter, cwt.	68 6	70 0	72 6	80 0	73 6	71 0	84 8	74 6
Cheese, ,,	51 9	52 10	53 0	47 3	45 3	51 0	56 10	51 6
Cigars, lb. .	10 6	11 6	11 0	11 5	11 1	11 0	11 7	11 3
Cochineal, lb.	4 0	3 11	3 10	4 1	3 10	3 8	3 4	3 10
Cocoa, cwt.	32 0	40 0	50 0	80 0	50 0	50 0	62 0	52 0
Coffee, ,,	45 6	46 0	46 9	48 8	42 6	50 9	58 6	48 6
Copper ore, cwt.	24 0	21 6	23 0	17 0	18 10	19 4	18 10	20 6
Cotton, ,,	53 7	55 5	60 8	73 9	67 0	65 10	60 4	62 4
Eggs (120)	4 6	5 8	5 8	6 0	5 5	5 5	7 0	5 8
Flax, cwt. .	51 3	51 0	44 0	35 8	46 3	52 4	50 3	47 0
Flour, cwt. .	21 6	24 0	20 0	17 0	15 0	14 0	16 4	18 6
Guano, ,,	11 0	11 4	11 6	13 0	12 6	12 0	12 0	11 10
Hams, ,,	60 0	66 0	69 6	68 9	59 0	56 7	68 9	64 0
Hemp, ,,	59 2	43 8	35 0	32 2	28 8	27 10	30 0	36 6
Hides, dry, cwt.	56 0	67 8	86 4	95 9	65 2	74 5	75 6	74 6
,, wet, ,,	49 0	56 0	74 8	80 6	63 0	75 3	72 6	67 6
Indigo, lb. .	4 2	5 0	5 6	6 0	6 5	5 8	6 0	5 6
Lard, cwt. .	51 6	52 6	62 3	66 9	55 0	56 7	59 3	57 6
Linseed, cwt.	15 6	16 0	12 6	14 0	12 8	11 0	12 1	13 6
Maize, ,,	10 3	11 0	8 0	8 10	7 10	7 0	8 4	8 8
Molasses, ,,	11 0	13 8	15 6	19 4	9 9	10 0	12 3	13 2
Nitre, ,,	17 3	16 6	17 0	20 0	16 0	15 0	13 6	16 6
Oats, ,,	8 6	8 10	8 6	8 3	7 8	7 4	8 0	8 2
Oil, olive, gallon	4 6	4 4	4 1	4 3	3 9	4 0	4 8	4 3
,, palm, cwt.	46 0	43 6	43 0	43 9	38 10	45 1	44 8	43 6
Oranges, bushel	9 3	10 10	13 0	12 10	11 5	11 9	10 6	11 6

	1854		1855		1856		1857		1858		1859		1860		1854–60	
	s.	d.	s.	d.	s.	d.	s.	d.	s.	d.	s.	d.	s.	d.	s.	d.
Peas, cwt.	11	8	12	0	10	8	9	7	10	2	9	4	10	0	10	6
Pepper, cwt.	47	0	49	0	47	0	46	0	45	0	42	0	42	0	45	6
Pork, ,,	45	0	44	6	45	6	47	6	41	4	41	4	43	5	44	0
Potatoes, ,,	3	0	3	6	3	6	3	8	3	10	3	2	4	6	3	7
Raisins, ,,	32	6	33	0	47	8	44	8	27	3	37	2	33	10	36	6
Rice, ,,	14	0	14	6	10	6	11	3	8	10	10	9	13	0	11	10
Rum, gallon	3	8	3	4	3	2	3	8	3	2	3	2	3	0	3	4
Saltpetre, cwt.	27	6	28	8	35	0	39	8	38	8	37	4	40	4	35	4
Seeds, clover, cwt.	52	3	68	0	77	4	71	6	57	8	67	10	62	3	65	3
Sheep, each	30	0	35	6	37	0	48	6	46	0	42	4	43	0	40	4
Silk, lb.	21	6	22	9	32	6	35	10	28	0	32	0	34	7	29	6
Sugar raw, cwt.	26	0	30	0	33	0	42	6	33	0	30	4	31	3	32	4
,, refined, cwt.	29	0	34	3	36	0	45	8	39	7	36	4	34	3	36	6
Tallow, cwt.	63	0	57	0	52	6	53	9	49	0	54	9	56	2	55	2
Tea ,,	145	0	140	0	135	0	164	0	154	0	173	0	173	0	155	0
Tobacco, ,,	51	0	58	0	82	0	88	0	70	0	61	0	58	0	67	0
Wheat ,,	16	6	15	0	15	3	12	10	10	7	10	7	13	8	13	6
Wine, gallon	12	4	13	4	14	9	12	4	10	4	8	6	6	1	11	2
Wood, load	76	0	73	0	62	0	60	9	54	0	58	4	63	0	64	0
,, staves, load	140	0	148	0	120	0	128	0	105	0	96	0	120	0	122	6
Wool, cwt.	168	0	172	0	196	0	210	0	191	0	192	0	205	0	191	0

British imports from 1861 to 1870:—

	1861		1862		1863		1864		1865		1866		1867		1868		1869		1870		1861–70	
	s.	d.	s.	d.	s.	d.	s.	d.	s.	d.	s.	d.	s.	d.	s.	d.	s.	d.	s.	d.	s.	d.
Bacon, cwt.	48	2	35	1	37	0	39	9	54	10	54	2	51	8	55	5	65	6	62	2	50	6
Barley, ,,	9	4	8	8	8	6	8	0	6	6	8	10	10	0	10	2	8	4	7	9	8	8
Beans, ,,	8	8	7	6	7	6	7	7	...		9	7	...		...		...		...		8	2
Beef, ,,	32	6	35	7	28	8	29	9	33	0	45	3	50	5	44	10	36	2	42	9	38	0
Brandy, gallon	9	1	9	1	7	6	7	6	6	3	5	5	5	1	5	8	6	4	5	5	6	6
Butter, cwt.	90	4	86	0	81	0	101	0	105	2	97	0	103	0	116	0	110	0	117	0	101	0
Cheese, ,,	45	10	42	1	48	3	52	0	58	6	66	8	56	0	59	0	63	0	63	0	55	6
Cigars, lb.	13	0	13	0	13	0	12	4	12	0	12	0	7	10	7	9	6	4	8	2	10	6
Cochineal, lb.	2	8	2	8	3	1	3	2	3	4	3	6	3	0	2	11	2	6	2	2	2	11
Cocoa, cwt.	58	0	54	0	46	8	46	0	42	6	60	6	65	0	55	0	55	0	56	6	54	0
Coffee, ,,	55	6	66	4	69	2	66	0	63	6	56	2	71	0	63	0	63	0	61	6	63	6
Copper ore, cwt.	17	8	17	2	16	8	16	8	18	2	16	6	11	9	12	6	11	5	11	10	15	0
Cotton, cwt.	72	5	141	0	206	0	255	0	176	0	151	0	92	0	93	0	104	0	90	0	138	0
Eggs (120)	6	5	6	1	6	1	6	0	6	1	6	0	6	0	6	4	6	2	6	2	6	2
Fish, cwt.	...		...		...		...		21	3	24	10	22	1	20	5	20	0	20	0	21	6
Flax, ,,	48	5	56	0	53	7	53	3	52	0	55	4	59	0	57	8	56	6	51	10	54	4
Flour, ,,	15	5	14	4	12	8	11	10	12	6	15	0	19	6	18	4	14	0	14	1	14	9
Glass, ,,	...		...		...		...		16	0	16	0	16	0	16	0	14	0	14	0	15	4
Guano, cwt.	12	0	12	7	12	4	12	0	12	0	12	0	11	0	11	2	12	6	12	5	12	0
Hams, ,,	47	0	35	5	33	2	43	5	51	4	57	4	51	4	59	7	68	9	66	7	51	6
Hemp, ,,	30	7	35	6	40	5	33	2	31	1	31	1	37	6	39	3	37	3	37	8	35	4
Hides, dry, cwt.	71	7	70	0	69	4	74	0	74	0	69	0	64	0	70	0	69	6	70	6	70	3
,, wet, ,,	60	4	58	4	51	4	54	4	48	3	48	9	...		...		...		...		53	9
Indigo, lb.	6	8	6	6	5	0	5	6	5	7	5	7	6	0	6	8	6	6	6	2	6	0
Jute, cwt.	...		...		25	0	...		16	9	18	2	17	9	17	8	17	4	19	6	19	0
Lard, ,,	53	0	42	1	38	3	44	6	63	4	69	0	51	0	64	0	72	7	66	9	56	6
Linseed, cwt.	13	2	14	0	15	0	13	2	13	6	15	0	15	0	13	6	13	4	13	6	14	0
Maize, ,,	7	10	7	0	6	9	7	2	6	11	6	9	9	0	8	5	6	9	6	11	7	5
Molasses, ,,	9	11	9	5	9	2	13	3	12	1	13	3	14	0	12	3	12	8	9	6	11	6
Nitre, ,,	13	0	13	7	14	3	15	3	13	0	11	6	11	0	13	0	15	6	15	6	13	8
Oats, ,,	8	1	8	2	6	10	6	6	7	2	8	2	9	2	9	6	8	4	8	0	8	0
Oil, olive, gallon	4	8	4	6	4	8	4	8	4	2	4	6	5	0	5	4	4	2	4	2	4	7
,, palm, cwt.	42	8	39	10	35	10	33	7	36	4	40	2	38	7	39	5	38	10	36	6	38	0
Oranges, bushel	11	3	13	3	12	6	12	1	12	1	12	1	10	2	9	7	9	6	6	8	10	10
Paper, cwt.	...		...		...		...		51	4	51	4	51	4	51	4	51	4	51	4	51	4
Pepper, cwt.	40	0	37	0	34	6	33	0	33	0	34	0	32	6	33	0	42	0	48	0	36	9
Petroleum, gallon	...		...		...		...		3	0	1	10	1	4	1	6	1	8	1	7	1	10
Pork, cwt.	45	3	33	0	31	5	39	3	41	6	50	0	46	8	50	6	60	4	62	3	46	0
Potatoes, cwt.	5	4	4	1	3	5	3	4	3	7	4	4	5	9	4	9	4	9	6	4	4	7
Rags, ,,	...		...		...		...		20	6	21	9	19	0	18	0	17	3	17	4	19	0
Raisins, ,,	28	6	25	0	27	3	30	0	32	4	28	2	28	9	32	10	35	8	32	6	30	0
Rice, ,,	12	8	11	10	11	11	11	2	12	4	13	1	14	8	12	4	10	8	10	7	12	1
Rum, gallon	2	7	2	2	2	0	2	3	2	8	2	6	2	0	2	3	2	4	2	4	2	4
Saltpetre, cwt.	32	6	34	8	36	9	32	6	24	9	20	6	18	6	20	5	22	1	26	0	26	9
Seeds, clover, cwt.	53	0	53	0	52	9	54	4	67	5	64	3	55	0	54	0	54	8	56	5	56	6
Sheep, each	45	0	42	7	35	0	36	8	50	0	50	0	35	0	31	0	34	0	34	0	39	6
Sheep-skins, each.	...		...		...		...		1	0	1	2	1	3	1	1	1	1	1	3	1	2
Silk, lb.	28	3	27	5	25	4	27	11	28	11	29	4	25	9	24	9	24	6	26	0	26	9
Sugar, raw, cwt.	30	10	28	0	26	2	33	1	27	1	27	3	21	10	22	7	24	6	22	6	26	4

	1861	1862	1863	1864	1865	1866	1867	1868	1869	1870	1861–70
	s. d.	s. d.	s. d.	s. d.	s. d.	s. d.	s. d.	s. d.	s. d.	s. d.	s. d.
Sugar refined, cwt.	35 0	34 0	34 5	35 9	31 4	31 1	31 6	31 8	33 3	32 0	33 0
Sulphur, cwt. . .	...	...	...	...	7 4	6 10	6 6	6 9	7 8	7 3	7 0
Tallow, ,, . .	50 9	45 9	42 4	41 0	48 3	44 9	44 0	48 0	45 4	43 4	45 3
Tea, ,, . .	159 0	190 0	172 0	168 0	196 0	196 0	176 0	180 0	166 0	160 0	176 0
Tobacco, ,, . .	108 0	140 0	142 0	132 0	126 0	88 0	70 0	80 0	80 0	82 0	105 0
Wheat, ,, . .	13 6	11 10	9 9	9 1	9 4	11 7	14 5	13 6	10 4	10 6	11 6
Wine, gallon . .	7 3	4 8	4 4	3 10	4 2	7 5	6 3	6 5	6 2	5 5	5 7
Wood, load . .	66 0	66 0	66 0	72 0	65 0	54 0	58 0	60 0	65 0	65 0	63 6
,, staves .	126 0	152 0	149 0	146 0	161 0	192 0	194 0	191 0	178 0	184 0	167 0
Wool, cwt. . .	180 0	180 0	174 0	201 0	180 0	193 0	152 0	133 0	127 0	134 0	165 0
Yeast, ,, . .	...	...	...	...	40 6	41 0	41 6	40 0	41 0	44 6	41 6

British imports from 1871 to 1880 :—

	1871	1872	1873	1874	1875	1876	1877	1878	1879	1880	1871–80
	s. d.	s. d.	s. d.	s. d.	s. d.	s. d.	s. d.	s. d.	s. d.	s. d.	s. d.
Bacon, cwt.. . .	49 3	41 0	40 10	45 9	52 4	53 5	47 10	38 7	34 4	40 0	44 6
Barley, ,, . . .	8 0	8 3	8 8	9 4	8 5	7 8	8 4	7 10	8 4	8 6	8 4
Beef, ,, . . .	42 1	36 9	40 0	40 0	42 2	45 8	49 9	48 5	47 9	47 8	44 0
Brandy, gallon .	7 3	7 6	7 4	8 8	7 9	6 7	8 6	8 0	8 6	8 10	7 11
Butter, cwt. . .	104 0	106 0	109 0	112 0	116 0	117 0	117 0	111 0	102 0	105 0	110 0
Cheese, ,, . .	55 0	57 0	60 0	60 6	58 0	55 6	58 0	50 4	43 0	57 0	55 6
Cigars, lb. . . .	13 0	14 2	13 9	13 9	13 9	14 3	12 3	12 9	12 0	13 9	13 4
Cochineal, lb.. .	2 4	2 4	2 4	2 2	2 2	2 0	2 3	2 1	2 4	2 8	2 3
Cocoa, cwt.. . .	51 0	70 0	70 0	67 0	61 0	62 0	73 0	86 0	93 6	82 0	71 6
Coffee, ,, . .	63 0	71 0	88 0	101 0	95 0	94 0	97 0	93 0	88 0	89 0	88 0
Copper ore, cwt. .	13 8	17 3	16 6	14 10	13 9	12 4	10 1	8 8	8 8	9 4	12 6
Cotton, cwt. . .	70 0	85 0	80 0	72 6	69 0	60 6	58 6	56 0	55 0	59 0	66 6
Eggs (120) . . .	7 7	8 0	8 7	8 7	8 4	8 4	8 0	7 8	7 2	7 2	8 0
Fish, cwt. . . .	23 6	25 7	28 0	29 8	30 2	30 3	30 7	31 0	28 6	24 10	28 3
Flax, ,, . . .	47 0	52 3	50 0	48 9	53 0	55 3	49 3	48 0	45 3	46 2	49 6
Flour, ,, . .	17 6	18 8	18 10	18 3	15 9	15 10	18 6	17 4	15 10	16 6	17 3
Glass, ,, . .	15 0	17 3	18 9	17 6	16 9	15 9	14 7	13 8	14 2	14 4	15 9
Guano, ,, . .	12 0	10 2	11 5	12 0	11 4	11 6	10 10	10 2	9 2	10 0	10 10
Hams, ,, . .	60 0	52 0	55 0	55 0	59 6	59 9	54 5	48 0	43 9	46 6	53 6
Hemp, ,, . .	36 5	37 9	37 1	35 5	33 6	33 4	33 3	30 9	28 0	28 6	33 6
Hides, ,, . .	70 0	80 0	83 0	73 0	70 0	63 0	62 0	59 0	58 0	62 0	68 0
Hops, ,, . .	80 0	100 0	98 0	127 0	93 0	91 0	94 0	75 0	93 0	92 0	94 4
Indigo, lb.. . .	5 0	5 1	5 0	4 6	4 10	4 3	4 10	4 4	4 2	5 3	4 9
Jute, cwt. . . .	21 8	19 6	15 8	16 8	15 0	14 8	16 0	15 3	13 8	17 4	16 6
Leather, cwt.. .	...	...	...	182 0	167 0	168 0	158 0	146 0	170 0	168 0	166 0
Lard, ,, . .	55 0	45 0	44 0	47 0	60 0	56 0	50 0	39 0	33 9	40 0	47 0
Linseed, ,, . .	14 0	15 0	14 3	14 0	13 0	12 5	13 3	12 4	12 4	13 0	13 4
Maize, ,, . .	7 8	7 1	7 6	8 6	8 0	6 4	6 6	6 1	5 5	6 0	7 0
Molasses, ,, . .	9 10	10 1	9 5	10 9	11 0	9 4	9 6	8 8	7 5	8 2	9 4
Nitre, ,, . .	15 6	15 4	14 8	12 0	12 0	11 6	13 6	14 10	14 0	15 4	14 0
Oats, ,, . .	7 8	7 3	8 0	9 0	8 9	8 3	7 9	7 2	6 8	7 2	7 10
Oil, olive, gallon .	3 10	4 0	3 6	3 6	3 6	3 7	3 9	4 0	3 7	3 7	3 7
,, palm, cwt. .	34 9	35 10	33 8	33 7	33 4	34 9	35 7	34 9	30 6	29 5	33 7
Opium, lb. . . .	...	...	...	22 1	21 0	19 8	19 3	15 6	15 2	17 10	18 9
Oranges, bushel .	8 5	9 8	9 9	9 8	9 4	8 5	8 9	8 3	7 8	8 0	8 6
Paper, cwt. . .	51 3	56 4	60 10	53 0	48 0	48 8	50 0	49 6	37 5	36 7	49 4
Pepper, ,, . .	50 6	61 0	70 0	65 0	50 6	40 0	40 0	34 5	34 8	42 0	46 9
Petroleum, gallon .	1 4	1 5	1 2	0 11	0 10	1 2	1 1	0 10	0 8	0 8	1 0
Pork, cwt. . . .	46 10	41 0	44 5	43 8	44 3	42 10	40 0	33 10	31 4	33 5	40 3
Potatoes, cwt. . .	5 4	5 5	5 8	5 3	4 6	5 9	5 10	5 6	5 9	5 10	5 6
Rags, cwt. . . .	16 6	16 9	17 8	17 0	17 4	16 6	15 0	15 2	15 4	15 3	16 4
Raisins, cwt. . .	33 2	37 3	35 3	36 3	37 9	36 3	34 3	31 8	34 4	36 10	35 3
Rice, ,, . .	10 2	10 0	9 10	10 4	9 0	9 0	10 6	10 6	10 2	9 6	9 11
Rum, gallon . .	2 0	2 0	2 2	2 3	2 4	2 1	2 0	1 10	1 8	1 9	2 0
Saltpetre, cwt. . .	25 5	26 1	26 4	22 10	20 4	18 3	22 3	21 0	19 0	22 2	22 5
Seeds, clover, cwt. .	54 6	51 4	47 9	46 0	47 0	51 9	51 10	47 6	43 9	43 3	48 6
Sheep, each . .	39 0	41 0	43 0	42 0	44 0	43 0	48 0	49 0	48 0	48 0	44 6
Sheep-skin, each .	2 2	2 10	3 2	2 9	2 10	2 7	2 6	2 6	2 6	2 10	2 8
Silk, lb.	21 7	21 5	21 0	16 9	15 4	19 2	20 0	17 8	17 5	17 0	18 9
Sugar, raw, cwt. .	25 1	26 2	24 0	22 5	21 2	21 0	25 9	21 6	20 3	21 9	22 9
,, refined, cwt.	36 2	36 4	33 10	30 9	30 4	29 6	33 9	29 3	27 4	29 3	31 8
Sulphur, cwt. . .	6 6	6 9	6 7	6 9	6 10	6 5	5 10	5 6	5 5	5 4	6 2
Tallow, ,, . .	42 0	42 10	41 3	40 4	42 4	42 9	42 0	39 4	35 10	35 2	40 5
Tea, ,, . .	152 0	155 0	154 0	157 0	155 0	152 0	148 0	142 0	135 0	125 0	147 6
Tobacco, ,, . .	75 0	77 0	72 0	77 0	80 0	77 0	75 0	62 0	67 0	65 0	72 9
Wheat, ,, . .	11 10	12 5	13 0	12 2	10 7	10 5	12 6	11 0	10 6	11 1	11 6
Wine, gallon . .	7 9	7 10	7 8	7 6	7 4	7 0	7 4	7 3	7 1	7 5	7 5
Wood, load . .	56 0	58 0	65 0	65 0	57 0	58 0	56 0	49 0	42 0	50 0	55 7
,, staves . .	144 0	188 0	199 0	149 0	133 0	133 0	133 0	98 0	97 0	91 0	136 6
Wool, cwt. . . .	124 0	135 0	137 0	137 0	144 0	134 0	133 0	129 0	125 0	126 0	132 6
Yeast, ,, . . .	50 0	50 0	51 0	52 0	49 0	49 0	49 0	52 0	52 0	52 0	50 6

British imports from 1881 to 1889 :—

	1881	1882	1883	1884	1885	1886	1887	1888	1889	1881–89
	s. d.	s. d.	s. d.	s. d.	s. d.	s. d.	s. d.	s. d.	s. d.	s. d.
Bacon, cwt.	45 10	53 0	53 0	49 3	40 6	37 9	42 2	44 9	41 6	45 8
Barley, „	8 4	7 2	7 0	6 6	5 10	5 9	5 3	5 8	5 8	6 5
Beef, „	49 10	51 7	52 10	51 4	49 0	43 8	41 5	42 8	41 2	47 0
Brandy, gallon	9 0	9 0	9 2	9 0	9 0	9 1	9 4	9 2	9 2	9 1
Butter, cwt.	106 0	105 0	101 0	101 0	110 0	105 0	106 0	107 0	106 0	105 0
Cheese, „	57 0	56 0	54 0	52 0	44 0	45 0	49 0	47 0	47 0	50 0
Chinchona, lb.	2 6	2 3	2 2	1 6	1 2	1 0	0 10	0 8	0 7	1 5
Cigars, „	14 0	14 3	12 5	11 0	12 3	11 0	10 5	9 9	11 5	11 9
Cochineal, „	2 1	1 9	1 3	1 0	1 1	1 2	1 1	1 2	1 1	1 4
Cocoa, cwt.	76 0	70 0	74 0	77 0	77 0	73 0	74 0	70 0	68 0	73 4
Coffee, „	78 0	76 0	70 0	66 0	64 0	65 0	81 0	75 0	83 0	73 3
Copper ore, cwt.	7 10	9 9	10 4	11 1	7 0	6 10	7 0	8 8	7 8	8 7
Cotton, cwt.	58 0	58 6	58 0	57 0	57 0	50 0	50 0	52 0	53 0	55 0
Eggs (120)	7 4	7 0	7 0	7 0	7 0	6 8	6 10	6 7	6 8	6 11
Fish, cwt.	30 6	33 7	35 6	30 8	26 3	25 9	25 4	24 4	26 0	28 6
Flax, „	41 0	39 0	40 0	40 9	41 7	41 6	36 4	34 0	36 0	39 0
Flour, „	16 3	16 4	15 2	13 6	12 2	11 2	11 1	11 3	11 8	13 4
Glass, „	14 7	15 9	15 8	13 10	13 8	12 6	12 2	12 0	11 6	13 6
Guano, cwt.	9 9	8 8	9 9	9 1	9 8	7 10	8 3	8 0	7 0	8 8
Hams, „	49 0	55 6	60 6	59 0	51 0	47 0	52 0	53 0	51 0	53 3
Hemp, „	30 0	32 8	33 6	31 3	30 8	28 5	29 3	31 0	35 0	31 6
Hides, „	64 0	63 0	64 0	64 0	63 0	59 0	54 0	52 0	50 0	59 0
Hops, „	94 0	185 0	168 0	126 0	75 0	58 0	59 0	74 0	72 0	101 0
Indigo, lb.	5 2	5 0	4 4	4 3	4 0	4 0	3 10	3 10	3 6	4 2
Jute, cwt.	16 2	14 6	12 3	15 0	11 4	11 3	11 3	12 5	14 2	13 2
Lard, lb.	51 0	56 0	53 0	44 0	37 0	34 6	35 4	42 0	36 6	43 0
Leather, cwt.	162 0	156 0	164 0	157 0	159 0	158 0	147 0	144 0	141 0	154 0
Linseed, „	12 0	10 8	10 3	10 6	10 7	10 2	9 2	9 5	10 0	10 4
Maize, „	6 3	7 2	6 6	5 10	5 4	4 10	4 10	5 5	4 9	5 7
Molasses, „	9 3	8 9	8 4	7 2	7 0	6 5	6 8	6 4	7 4	7 6
Nitre, „	14 8	13 3	11 5	9 8	9 6	10 0	9 7	9 7	9 5	10 10
Oats, „	7 4	6 9	6 8	6 6	6 6	6 6	5 10	4 9	4 10	6 1
Oil, olive, gallon	3 2	3 2	3 0	3 3	3 2	3 0	2 10	2 10	2 10	3 0
„ palm, cwt.	29 0	30 6	35 1	33 6	26 10	20 10	19 6	19 10	21 2	26 4
Opium, lb.	15 8	14 8	14 6	13 10	12 10	11 10	13 0	12 5	12 2	13 4
Oranges, bushel	7 8	7 10	7 8	7 2	6 10	6 9	6 5	6 0	5 11	6 10
Paper, cwt.	36 0	35 3	33 0	30 6	30 0	31 2	30 3	28 0	27 0	31 6
Pepper, „	51 0	53 0	60 0	66 0	68 0	68 0	76 0	72 0	65 0	64 3
Petroleum, gallon	0 8	0 7	0 7	0 8	0 7	0 7	0 7	0 7	0 6	0 7
Pork, cwt.	35 9	40 0	40 5	36 9	36 0	34 0	36 0	37 7	35 1	37 0
Potatoes, cwt.	5 5	6 8	6 2	6 9	6 4	5 10	7 0	6 9	8 0	6 7
Rags, „	14 10	14 4	14 0	13 6	13 2	12 6	12 2	11 4	10 0	13 0
Raisins, „	36 6	37 6	36 0	34 2	32 8	33 0	31 4	30 4	31 9	33 9
Rice, „	8 8	8 0	8 3	8 2	7 10	7 6	7 6	7 6	8 2	8 0
Rum, gallon	2 0	2 0	1 10	1 9	1 7	1 6	1 7	1 8	1 8	1 9
Saltpetre, cwt.	22 9	21 9	20 0	18 4	16 10	17 9	17 3	17 0	17 6	18 7
Seeds, clover, cwt.	44 3	42 8	47 6	45 3	46 8	40 10	41 2	41 3	41 0	43 2
Sheep, each,	47 0	46 0	45 0	45 0	43 0	39 0	34 0	36 0	35 0	41 0
Sheepskin, each	2 6	2 8	2 6	2 7	2 5	2 1	2 2	2 2	2 2	2 5
Silk, lb.	17 0	16 6	16 3	14 9	14 0	13 9	13 8	12 3	14 0	14 8
Sugar raw, cwt.	21 9	21 1	20 1	15 6	14 0	13 0	12 2	13 6	15 6	16 4
„ refined, cwt.	29 0	28 8	27 3	20 10	18 2	16 8	15 8	17 6	19 8	21 6
Sulphur, „	6 0	6 2	5 6	5 2	5 0	5 0	4 9	4 6	4 4	5 1
Tallow, „	35 3	40 4	40 6	37 9	31 4	25 8	24 0	25 0	26 6	31 10
Tea, „	120 0	118 0	117 0	110 0	112 0	110 0	98 0	102 0	101 0	110 0
Tobacco, „	63 1	72 0	72 0	74 0	74 0	68 0	68 0	70 0	65 0	69 6
Wheat, „	11 0	10 8	9 10	8 5	7 10	7 6	7 8	7 8	7 8	8 8
Wine, gallon	7 0	7 0	7 0	7 0	7 0	7 0	7 1	7 4	7 5	7 1
Wood, load	51 0	52 0	52 0	48 0	48 0	43 0	38 0	41 0	47 0	46 6
„ staves, load	99 0	104 0	91 0	82 0	86 0	81 0	82 0	82 0	82 0	88 0
Wool, cwt.	129 0	114 0	113 0	113 0	93 0	85 0	94 0	91 0	91 0	102 6
Yeast, „	52 0	53 0	56 0	55 0	56 0	55 0	54 0	55 0	55 0	54 6

Prices of British exports :—

	1854–60	1865	1866	1867	1868	1869	1870	1865–70
	£ s.	£ s.	£ s.	£ s.	£ s.	£ s.	£ s.	£ s.
Alkali, ton	9 14	8 15	10 15	10 5	8 11	7 17	7 14	9 0
Bags, gross	6 12	7 7	6 6	5 8	4 16	4 16	4 9	5 11
Beer, barrel	3 9	3 13	3 13	3 14	3 15	3 16	3 12	3 14
Books, cwt.	14 0	12 19	12 8	12 5	11 3	11 8	11 13	12 0
Boots, dozen pair	3 0	3 7	3 8	3 10	3 14	3 1	3 2	3 7
Brass, cwt.	6 0	5 5	5 9	4 13	4 17	4 14	4 6	4 18

	1854–60	1865	1866	1867	1868	1869	1870	1865–70
	£ s.	£ s.	£ s.	£ s.	£ s.	£ s.	£ s.	£ s.
Butter, cwt.	5 0	5 4	5 8	4 17	5 2	5 6	5 10	5 5
Candles, ,,	5 16	4 18	4 18	5 3	5 8	5 6	4 18	5 4
Carpet, 12 yards	1 11	1 16	1 18	2 0	1 16	1 16	1 16	1 17
Cement, ton	2 17	2 11	2 12	2 10	2 9	2 9	2 9	2 10
Cheese, cwt.	4 1	4 2	4 7	4 6	4 2	4 6	4 8	4 5
Cloth, 12 yards	1 7	1 18	1 19	2 1	1 17	1 16	1 15	1 17
Coal, ton	0 19	0 10	0 10	0 10	0 10	0 10	0 10	0 10
Copper, cwt.	5 10	4 9	4 10	4 1	4 1	4 0	3 15	4 3
Cordage, ,,	2 15	2 9	2 15	2 17	2 17	2 17	2 16	2 15
Cottons, plain, 100 yards	1 5	2 2	2 2	1 14	1 11	1 12	1 10	1 15
,, printed, ,,	1 14	2 8	2 9	2 4	2 0	2 1	2 0	2 4
Firearms, each	1 5	1 9	1 7	1 10	1 13	1 4	1 15	1 10
Flannel, 12 yards	0 16	1 0	0 19	0 19	0 18	0 18	0 17	0 18
Glass, flint, cwt.	3 4	3 1	2 15	2 14	2 12	2 13	2 14	2 15
,, bottles, ton	10 16	10 0	10 3	10 0	9 19	9 18	10 0	10 0
Gunpowder, cwt.	3 10	3 1	3 0	2 18	2 13	2 14	2 15	2 17
Hats, dozen	1 18	1 19	1 17	1 18	1 14	1 11	1 11	1 15
Herrings, barrel	1 5	1 8	1 8	1 8	1 8	1 9	1 5	1 8
Horses, each	58 0	42 0	41 0	43 0	49 0	61 0	35 0	45 0
Iron pig, ton	3 7	2 18	3 2	2 18	2 17	2 18	2 19	2 19
,, rails, ,,	8 6	8 4	8 8	8 7	8 0	8 3	8 5	8 4
,, hoops, ton	13 2	10 5	10 0	9 12	8 18	9 0	9 6	9 10
,, wire, ,,	20 0	19 12	20 11	19 14	19 7	18 16	18 15	19 9
Jute, 100 yards	2 4	2 0	1 17	1 14	1 13	1 10	1 10	1 14
Lead, ton	24 0	21 1	21 15	21 1	20 3	20 3	19 16	20 14
Leather, cwt.	8 16	9 12	11 5	9 11	9 0	8 8	8 4	9 7
Linens, plain, 100 yards	2 18	3 7	3 9	3 5	3 3	2 19	3 0	3 5
,, printed, ,,	3 3	3 17	4 2	4 1	3 18	3 15	3 8	3 18
Oil-seed, ton	30 5	30 5	34 16	34 9	31 5	28 0	28 12	31 5
Paper, cwt.	4 8	3 4	3 2	2 18	2 19	2 16	3 0	3 0
Sailcloth, 100 yards	5 0	5 6	5 6	5 7	5 12	5 18	5 5	5 8
Salt, ton	0 11	0 9	0 12	0 12	0 12	0 10	0 10	0 11
Soap, cwt.	1 6	1 6	1 7	1 6	1 6	1 8	1 8	1 7
Silks, 12 yards	1 18	2 6	2 8	2 9	2 7	2 7	2 6	2 7
Spirits, hhd.	11 16	7 12	8 3	8 0	7 16	8 0	8 0	7 18
Steel, ton	35 0	32 15	32 14	32 12	32 4	31 0	31 12	32 3
Sugar, cwt.	2 13	1 10	1 10	1 11	1 15	1 16	1 12	1 12
Tin, ,,	6 0	4 16	4 9	4 11	4 14	5 16	6 5	5 2
Wool, ,,	7 8	11 4	10 4	9 15	8 12	8 6	7 3	9 4
Worsted stuffs, 12 yards	0 10	0 14	0 14	0 14	0 14	0 15	0 14	0 14
Yarn, cotton, cwt.	5 12	11 4	11 1	9 16	9 8	9 6	8 17	9 19
,, linen, cwt.	6 1	7 12	7 18	8 0	7 17	7 10	6 14	7 12
,, woollen, ,,	14 0	18 12	19 1	17 4	16 5	16 13	15 12	17 5
Zinc, ton	28 0	21 4	24 0	22 0	21 16	20 10	19 5	21 9

British exports from 1871 to 1880 ;—

	1871	1872	1873	1874	1875	1876	1877	1878	1879	1880	1871–80
	£ s.	£ s.	£ s.	£ s.	£ s.	£ s.	£ s.	£ s.	£ s.	£ s.	£ s.
Alkali, ton	8 7	11 3	12 6	10 9	9 3	8 3	7 15	7 0	6 7	6 19	8 15
Bags, gross	5 0	5 6	5 3	4 9	4 2	3 12	3 14	3 12	3 8	3 9	4 4
Beer, barrel	3 17	4 0	4 3	4 8	4 3	3 19	4 3	4 6	4 5	4 5	4 3
Books, cwt.	11 11	10 17	10 18	10 15	10 14	10 15	10 13	10 7	10 0	10 0	10 11
Boots, dozen pair	3 0	2 18	3 5	3 7	3 6	3 3	3 1	3 1	3 1	3 1	3 2
Brass, cwt.	4 10	5 9	6 0	6 6	5 9	5 4	4 16	4 3	3 18	4 5	5 0
Butter, ,,	5 16	5 12	5 18	6 2	6 2	6 5	6 13	6 12	6 8	6 8	6 4
Candles, cwt.	3 13	3 14	3 15	3 17	3 15	3 12	3 11	3 11	3 3	3 3	3 11
Carpet, 12 yards	1 16	1 19	1 19	1 19	1 17	1 15	1 12	1 10	1 9	1 9	1 14
Cement, ton	2 9	2 9	3 0	3 0	2 12	2 11	2 12	2 11	2 10	2 10	2 12
Cheese, cwt.	4 6	4 5	4 6	4 7	4 3	4 1	4 3	4 0	3 17	4 5	4 3
Cloth, 12 yards	1 18	2 1	2 1	2 0	1 19	1 18	1 16	1 15	1 12	1 12	1 17
Coal, ton	0 10	0 16	1 1	0 17	0 13	0 11	0 10	0 9	0 9	0 9	0 12
Copper ingot, cwt.	3 16	4 16	4 14	4 8	4 8	4 3	3 16	3 10	3 3	3 8	4 0
Cordage, cwt.	2 16	2 18	3 0	2 16	2 15	2 15	2 15	2 13	2 6	2 10	2 14
Cottons, 100 yards	1 8	1 9	1 9	1 7	1 6	1 4	1 4	1 3	1 2	1 3	1 5
,, printed, 100 yards	1 19	2 1	2 0	1 19	2 0	1 17	1 16	1 15	1 13	1 11	1 17
Firearms, each	1 19	1 4	1 9	1 12	2 1	1 7	1 1	1 1	0 19	1 3	1 7
Flannel, 12 yards	0 18	0 18	0 18	1 0	0 18	0 18	0 18	0 17	0 17	0 16	0 18
Flour, ton	16 10	17 10	19 0	18 3	14 18	14 19	17 9	15 5	14 1	13 17	16 3
Glass, flint, cwt.	2 8	2 13	2 18	3 0	3 0	2 19	2 16	2 12	2 12	2 2	2 14
,, bottles, ton	9 14	9 16	10 4	10 8	11 2	11 3	11 0	10 14	10 4	10 2	10 9
Gunpowder, cwt.	2 14	2 15	2 19	3 2	2 19	2 16	2 14	2 14	2 17	2 16	2 17
Hats, dozen	1 10	1 9	1 9	1 10	1 8	1 6	1 5	1 4	1 3	1 2	1 6
Herrings, barrel	1 7	1 8	1 8	1 8	1 8	1 14	1 13	1 8	1 13	1 7	1 9
Horses, each	38 0	53 0	63 0	67 0	77 0	81 0	74 0	69 0	59 0	61 0	64 0
Iron, bar, ton	8 7	11 12	13 2	11 16	9 18	8 11	7 15	7 3	6 13	7 16	9 5

	1871	1872	1873	1874	1875	1876	1877	1878	1879	1880	1871–80
	£ s.	£ s.	£ s.	£ s.	£ s.	£ s.	£ s.	£ s.	£ s.	£ s.	£ s.
Iron, cast, ton	14 15	17 14	19 8	19 19	18 2	16 11	14 7	14 0	13 3	13 15	16 4
,, galvan., ton	20 12	26 2	26 19	25 11	24 9	22 16	20 7	18 18	16 16	18 7	22 2
,, hoop, ,,	9 8	13 0	14 12	13 6	11 3	9 12	8 11	7 17	7 4	8 9	10 7
,, old, ,,	4 16	6 2	6 12	5 14	4 15	4 5	4 6	3 17	3 8	4 16	4 17
,, plates, ,,	11 16	15 11	18 0	17 8	15 4	14 6	12 16	11 16	9 7	10 13	13 14
,, pig, ,,	3 1	5 1	6 5	4 15	3 13	3 2	2 17	2 14	2 12	3 4	3 14
,, rail, ,,	8 5	10 16	13 5	12 6	10 0	8 18	7 15	7 10	6 4	7 6	9 5
,, wire, ,,	17 0	20 1	23 10	21 0	18 10	16 8	14 14	14 9	13 8	13 18	17 6
Jute, 100 yards	1 13	1 15	1 13	1 10	1 8	1 6	1 7	1 6	1 4	1 5	1 9
Lead, ton	19 5	20 9	23 15	22 12	23 3	22 11	21 10	18 15	15 8	17 8	20 10
Leather, cwt.	8 3	8 16	9 0	8 18	8 18	8 2	8 2	7 6	6 17	7 17	8 4
Linens, 100 yards	3 2	3 2	3 3	3 5	3 3	3 0	2 18	3 0	2 19	3 2	3 1
,, printed, 100 yards	3 7	3 3	3 3	3 4	3 8	3 8	3 5	3 1	3 1	3 0	3 4
Oil-seed, ton	28 10	30 5	28 0	25 13	24 0	23 10	25 15	24 15	24 4	24 10	25 18
Paper, cwt.	2 19	2 18	3 1	3 2	2 19	3 0	2 16	2 13	2 9	2 7	2 17
Sailcloth, 100 yards	5 8	5 19	5 16	6 0	6 0	6 0	5 14	5 8	4 18	5 3	5 13
Salt, ton	0 10	0 14	0 19	0 16	0 15	0 12	0 11	0 12	0 12	0 11	0 13
Silk, 12 yards	2 0	1 18	2 2	2 0	1 17	1 19	1 18	2 0	2 1	1 19	1 19
Soap, cwt.	1 7	1 6	1 6	1 5	1 5	1 5	1 4	1 4	1 2	1 2	1 5
Spirits, hhd.	7 18	7 18	7 18	7 18	15 15	15 6	15 8	17 3	16 16	16 12	12 17
Steel bars, ton	30 12	32 18	37 2	38 6	36 6	34 3	33 11	31 19	27 18	28 5	33 2
Sugar, cwt.	1 12	1 12	1 10	1 7	1 4	1 3	1 8	1 4	1 2	1 3	1 7
Thread, 12 lbs.	...	...	...	2 2	2 4	2 4	1 19	1 18	1 18	1 18	2 0
Tin, cwt.	6 14	7 9	6 17	5 5	4 12	3 19	3 14	3 6	3 12	4 10	5 0
Tinplates, ton	24 5	32 5	32 15	30 4	26 13	21 16	19 16	17 12	17 16	20 10	24 7
Wheat, ,,	13 2	12 16	13 9	13 7	11 5	10 11	13 0	10 14	9 17	10 6	11 17
Wool, cwt.	7 14	9 6	9 17	10 4	9 16	8 12	8 5	9 6	6 13	7 12	8 15
Yarn, cotton, cwt.	8 14	8 16	8 6	7 8	6 16	6 3	5 19	5 18	5 15	6 3	7 0
,, jute, ,,	2 2	2 6	1 17	1 15	1 12	1 10	1 13	1 13	1 13	1 11	1 15
,, linen, ,,	6 15	8 12	8 13	7 1	7 8	7 5	7 9	7 6	6 18	6 12	7 8
,, woollen, ,,	15 10	17 5	17 7	17 13	17 17	15 17	14 16	14 0	12 10	14 0	15 13
Zinc, ton	17 18	20 3	24 18	24 18	23 16	23 0	20 14	18 0	15 3	16 15	20 10

British exports from 1881 to 1889 :—

	1881	1882	1883	1884	1885	1886	1887	1888	1889	1881–89
	£ s.	£ s.	£ s.	£ s.	£ s.	£ s.	£ s.	£ s.	£ s.	£ s.
Alkali, ton	6 3	6 3	6 2	6 7	5 18	5 15	5 13	5 3	5 5	5 16
Bags, gross	3 6	3 5	3 2	2 18	2 12	2 6	2 8	2 13	3 0	2 17
Beer, barrel	4 2	4 5	4 0	3 16	3 15	3 15	3 16	3 16	3 15	3 18
Books, cwt.	10 0	9 12	9 11	9 9	9 13	9 2	8 16	8 14	8 7	9 5
Boots, dozen pair	2 17	2 19	3 0	3 0	2 18	2 18	2 18	2 14	2 14	2 18
Brass, cwt.	4 3	4 9	4 9	4 5	4 0	3 15	3 15	4 18	4 10	4 5
Butter, ,,	6 4	6 19	7 0	7 0	6 2	5 13	5 13	5 14	5 15	6 5
Candles, ,,	3 1	3 1	3 2	3 2	2 17	2 10	2 3	2 1	2 1	2 13
Carpet, 12 yards	1 9	1 8	1 8	1 6	1 6	1 5	1 4	1 5	1 5	1 6
Cement, ton	2 7	2 7	2 6	2 5	2 4	2 0	1 19	1 18	1 19	2 3
Cheese, cwt.	4 3	4 1	4 4	4 4	4 2	3 19	3 19	3 19	3 17	4 1
Cloth, 12 yards	1 13	1 14	1 18	2 1	2 0	1 19	2 0	1 19	2 1	1 18
Coal, ton	0 9	0 9	0 9	0 9	0 9	0 8	0 8	0 8	0 10	0 9
Copper, ingot, cwt.	3 6	3 11	3 7	2 19	2 8	2 4	2 5	3 18	2 7	2 18
Cordage, cwt.	2 11	2 12	2 11	2 5	2 3	2 1	2 6	2 6	2 11	2 7
Cottons, 100 yards	1 2	1 3	1 2	1 0	1 0	0 18	0 19	0 19	0 19	1 0
,, printed, 100 yards	1 11	1 11	1 10	1 10	1 9	1 6	1 6	1 5	1 5	1 8
Firearms, each	1 5	1 8	1 7	1 6	1 10	1 17	1 15	1 12	1 8	1 10
Flannel, 12 yards	0 15	0 15	0 15	0 14	0 13	0 12	0 12	0 11	0 12	0 13
Flour, ton	14 1	14 15	13 10	12 5	10 8	10 5	10 8	10 5	10 16	11 17
Glass, flint, cwt.	2 2	2 7	2 5	2 7	2 3	2 8	2 9	2 4	2 5	2 6
,, bottles, ton	9 18	9 11	9 5	9 6	9 11	9 8	9 9	9 8	9 9	9 9
Gunpowder, cwt.	2 18	2 17	2 15	2 15	2 16	2 16	3 0	3 0	2 18	2 17
Hats, dozen	1 2	1 2	1 1	1 1	1 1	0 19	0 19	0 19	1 0	1 0
Herrings, barrel	1 15	1 10	1 10	1 5	1 5	1 4	1 1	1 3	1 2	1 6
Horses, ,,	62 0	63 0	56 0	58 0	60 0	56 0	58 0	66 0	69 0	61 0
Iron, bar, ton	6 17	7 7	7 1	6 11	6 3	5 13	5 10	5 11	6 9	6 6
,, cast, ,,	13 12	13 17	13 0	12 3	11 11	10 18	11 3	11 8	11 14	12 3
,, galvan., ,,	16 11	16 7	15 4	14 6	13 8	12 2	11 15	12 15	12 13	13 18
,, hoops, ,,	7 10	7 18	7 15	7 5	6 14	6 2	6 1	6 1	6 15	6 18
,, old, ,,	3 19	3 17	3 9	3 6	3 1	2 14	2 17	2 15	2 19	3 4
,, plates, ,,	9 15	10 5	10 2	9 8	8 3	10 6	9 1	8 13	9 4	9 8
,, pig, ,,	2 15	2 16	2 12	2 6	2 4	2 3	2 7	2 3	2 10	2 8
,, rail, ,,	6 18	6 16	6 4	5 14	5 9	5 0	4 11	4 12	4 18	5 10
,, wire, ,,	13 6	15 7	14 16	13 2	12 10	13 17	13 12	13 9	14 18	13 18
Jute, 100 yards	1 3	1 3	1 2	1 0	0 18	0 17	0 17	0 18	1 1	1 0
Lead, ton	15 14	15 9	14 1	12 12	12 5	13 17	13 15	15 0	14 11	14 3
Leather, cwt.	8 1	8 15	9 7	9 9	9 5	8 19	8 16	8 15	9 4	8 19

	1881	1882	1883	1884	1885	1886	1887	1888	1889	1881-89
	£ s.	£ s.	£ s.	£ s.	£ s.	£ s.	£ s.	£ s.	£ s.	£ s.
Linens, 100 yards . . .	2 18	2 17	2 18	2 18	2 15	2 13	2 10	2 11	2 6	2 6	2 12
,, printed, 100 yards .	2 18	3 8	3 5	2 14	2 17	2 12	2 11	2 9	2 13	2 17
Oil-seed, ton . . .	24 0	22 10	20 4	20 0	20 4	18 7	21 0	20 9	21 14	20 19
Paper, cwt. . . .	2 5	2 5	2 3	2 1	1 19	1 17	1 15	1 13	1 14	1 19
Sailcloth, 100 yards .	5 0	5 4	4 17	4 12	4 11	4 12	4 12	4 8	4 12	4 15
Salt, ton . . .	0 12	0 12	0 13	0 13	0 15	0 15	0 13	0 11	0 16	0 13
Silks, 12 yards . .	1 19	2 0	1 19	1 19	2 5	2 8	2 10	2 6	1 17	2 2
Soap, cwt. . . .	1 2	1 2	1 3	1 3	1 4	1 1	1 0	0 19	1 0	1 2
Spirits, hhd. . . .	17 14	18 11	18 14	19 3	19 12	21 3	21 3	21 10	22 0	19 19
Steel bars, ton . .	27 10	27 5	25 0	23 5	22 0	18 9	18 1	16 5	15 7	21 10
Sugar, cwt. . . .	1 4	1 3	1 1	0 18	0 15	0 14	0 13	0 15	0 16	0 18
Thread, 12 lbs. . .	1 16	1 17	1 19	2 0	1 18	1 16	1 15	1 15	1 17	1 17
Tin, cwt. . . .	4 16	5 5	4 19	4 5	4 9	5 0	5 10	5 16	4 16	5 0
Tinplates, ton . .	17 2	17 10	17 9	16 9	14 17	14 3	13 11	14 3	14 0	15 9
Wheat, ,, . .	10 4	10 1	10 14	8 11	8 6	7 15	8 6	8 15	7 17	8 18
Wool, cwt. . . .	7 3	7 3	5 18	5 1	4 9	4 13	5 5	4 16	5 0	5 10
Yarn, cotton, cwt. .	5 16	6 1	5 14	5 14	5 8	5 1	5 1	5 2	5 3	5 8
,, jute, ,, .	1 10	1 9	1 8	1 6	1 0	1 0	1 2	1 3	1 7	1 5
,, linen, ,, .	6 10	6 8	6 13	6 10	6 13	6 12	6 8	6 15	6 15	6 11
,, woollen, ,, .	12 2	11 18	10 19	11 2	11 6	10 16	11 2	10 12	10 14	11 4
Zinc, ton . . .	15 3	14 13	13 18	13 12	13 6	13 11	13 1	15 14	15 13	14 7

The prices of English grain per ton were :—

Year	Wheat	Barley	Oats	Year	Wheat	Barley	Oats
	£ s.	£ s.	£ s.		£ s.	£ s.	£ s.
1786	10 0	6 5	4 13	1839	17 14	9 18	6 10
1787	10 12	5 17	4 6	1840	16 12	9 2	6 9
1788	11 12	4 14	4 0	1841	16 2	8 5	5 12
1789	13 4	5 18	4 3	1842	14 6	6 18	4 16
1790	13 14	6 11	4 18	1843	12 10	7 8	4 12
1791	12 4	6 14	4 10	1844	12 16	8 9	5 3
1792	10 15	6 18	4 2	1845	12 15	7 19	5 13
1793	12 6	7 15	5 3	1846	13 14	8 4	5 19
1794	13 2	7 19	5 6	1847	17 9	11 1	7 4
1795	18 16	9 7	6 2	1848	12 13	7 18	5 3
1796	19 14	8 17	5 10	1849	11 1	7 0	4 8
1797	13 9	6 16	4 1	1850	10 1	5 18	4 2
1798	12 19	7 5	4 18	1851	9 13	6 4	4 13
1799	17 5	9 1	6 18	1852	10 4	7 3	4 15
1800	28 10	14 19	9 17	1853	13 1	8 6	5 5
1801	29 18	17 3	9 5	1854	18 2	9 0	7 0
1802	17 10	8 7	5 2	1855	18 14	8 14	6 17
1803	14 14	6 7	5 8	1856	17 6	10 5	6 6
1804	15 11	7 15	6 1	1857	14 2	10 10	6 5
1805	22 9	11 3	7 2	1858	11 1	8 14	6 3
1806	19 15	9 14	6 18	1859	11 0	8 8	5 16
1807	18 17	9 17	7 1	1860	13 6	9 3	6 2
1808	20 7	10 17	8 7	1861	13 17	9 0	5 19
1809	24 7	11 15	7 18	1862	13 17	8 15	5 13
1810	26 12	12 0	7 3	1863	11 4	8 9	5 6
1811	23 16	10 11	6 18	1864	10 1	7 10	5 0
1812	31 13	16 14	11 3	1865	10 5	7 9	5 10
1814	18 12	9 7	6 9	1866	11 0	9 7	6 3
1816	19 13	8 10	6 16	1867	16 2	9 0	6 10
1817	24 5	12 7	8 2	1868	16 0	10 15	7 0
1818	21 11	13 5	8 2	1869	12 1	9 17	6 10
1819	18 13	11 9	7 1	1870	11 15	8 13	5 15
1820	16 19	8 10	6 1	1871	14 4	9 1	6 6
1821	14 0	6 10	7 8	1872	14 4	9 6	5 16
1822	11 3	5 10	7 0	1873	14 14	10 2	6 12
1823	13 7	9 3	5 15	1874	14 9	11 5	7 5
1824	16 0	9 2	6 5	1875	11 5	9 12	7 4
1825	17 3	10 0	6 9	1876	11 11	8 16	6 11
1826	14 14	8 12	6 14	1877	14 4	9 19	6 10
1827	14 13	9 8	7 1	1878	11 12	10 1	6 2
1828	15 2	8 5	5 10	1879	11 0	8 10	5 9
1829	16 11	8 3	5 14	1880	11 2	8 5	5 15
1830	16 1	8 3	6 2	1881	11 7	8 0	5 9
1831	16 12	9 10	6 7	1882	11 5	7 16	5 10
1832	14 14	8 5	5 2	1883	10 8	8 0	5 7
1833	13 5	6 18	4 12	1884	8 19	7 14	5 1
1834	11 11	7 5	5 5	1885	8 5	7 10	5 3
1835	9 17	7 10	5 10	1886	7 15	6 13	4 15
1836	12 3	8 5	5 15	1887	8 3	6 7	4 2
1837	14 0	7 12	5 15	1888	9 0	4 14	4 14
1838	16 3	7 19	5 12	1889	7 14	4 17	4 17

The preceding table gives the following averages :—

Years	Wheat	Barley	Oats
	£ s.	£ s.	£ s.
1786-90 . . .	11 16	5 17	4 8
1791-1800 . . .	15 18	8 11	5 13
1801-10 . . .	21 0	10 10	7 0
1811-20 . . .	21 18	11 7	7 12
1821-30 . . .	14 18	8 6	6 8
1831-40 . . .	14 5	8 4	5 14
1841-50 . . .	13 7	7 18	5 5
1851-60 . . .	13 13	8 13	5 18
1861-70 . . .	12 15	9 0	5 18
1871-80 . . .	12 16	9 10	6 7
1881-89 . . .	9 5	6 17	5 0

The prices of meat at Smithfield Market, London, averaged as follows, per ton, from 1835 to date :—

Year.	£ s.	Year.	£ s.	Year.	£ s.
1835 . .	49 10	1853 . .	56 0	1871 . .	69 10
1836 . .	53 7	1854 . .	54 18	1872 . .	67 5
1837 . .	53 7	1855 . .	54 18	1873 . .	75 3
1838 . .	54 10	1856 . .	58 5	1874 . .	76 5
1839 . .	52 10	1857 . .	56 0	1875 . .	76 5
1840 . .	54 10	1858 . .	58 5	1876 . .	74 0
1841 . .	56 10	1859 . .	58 5	1877 . .	72 18
1842 . .	55 10	1860 . .	60 10	1878 . .	72 18
1843 . .	48 8	1861 . .	58 5	1879 . .	71 15
1844 . .	48 8	1862 . .	58 5	1880-81 . .	69 10
1845 . .	51 10	1863 . .	57 3	1882 . .	75 3
1846 . .	48 8	1864 . .	65 0	1883 . .	71 15
1847 . .	53 9	1865 . .	60 10	1884 . .	70 12
1848 . .	57 10	1866 . .	63 18	1885 . .	61 12
1849 . .	48 8	1867 . .	58 5	1886 . .	59 7
1850 . .	47 7	1868 . .	62 15	1887 . .	58 5
1851 . .	51 10	1869 . .	67 5	1888 . .	59 7
1852 . .	50 7	1870 . .	67 5	1889 . .	61 0

The prices at Christmas, per stone of 8 lbs. beef, averaged thus :—

Years	Pence	Years	Pence	Years	Pence
1841-42 . .	50	1857-58 .	49	1873-74 . .	70
1843-44 .	50	1859-60 .	53	1875-76 .	66
1845-46 .	54	1861-62 .	50	1877-78 .	63
1847-48 .	48	1863-64 .	54	1879-80 .	61
1849-50 .	44	1865-66 .	54	1881-82 .	64
1851-52 .	40	1867-68 .	57	1883-84 .	61
1853-54 .	51	1869-70 .	57	1885-86 .	52
1855-56 .	50	1871-72 .	60	1887-89 .	53

Tooke and Newmarch give the prices of hay and straw per ton in twenty-three years, thus :—

Year	Hay £ s.	Straw £ s.	Year	Hay £ s.	Straw £ s.
1834 . . .	5 0	1 13	1846 . . .	4 2	1 13
1835 . . .	4 19	1 18	1847 . . .	3 14	1 15
1836 . . .	4 6	1 19	1848 . . .	3 17	1 10
1837 . . .	5 2	2 4	1849 . . .	3 16	1 11
1838 . . .	5 7	2 0	1850 . . .	3 13	1 8
1839 . . .	5 0	2 1	1851 . . .	3 18	1 9
1840 . . .	5 0	2 0	1852 . . .	3 15	1 14
1841 . . .	4 17	2 2	1853 . . .	5 3	1 16
1842 . . .	4 11	2 1	1854 . . .	4 19	1 18
1843 . . .	4 6	2 5	1855 . . .	5 6	1 8
1844 . . .	4 12	1 11	1856 . . .	5 13	1 10
1845 . . .	5 12	2 1	Average 11 years . }	4 7	1 14
Average 12 years . }	4 18	2 0			

The prices of raw cotton, yarn, and calico from 1802 to 1888 averaged as follows :—

Period	Cotton, Pence per yd.	Yarn, Pence per yd.	Calico, Pence per yd.	Ratio of Price Cotton	Yarn	Calico
1802–10 .	22.2	39	20.5	100	100	100
1811–20 .	21.3	33	16.8	96	85	82
1821–30 .	8.3	17	8.2	37	43	40
1831–40 .	7.9	14	5.2	35	35	26
1841–50 .	5.3	13	3.4	24	33	17
1851–60 .	5.9	11	2.9	27	28	14
1861–70 .	12.8	20	4.2	57	51	21
1871–80 .	7.1	15	3.0	32	38	15
1881 . .	6.3	12	2.7	28	30	13
1888 . .	5.5	11	2.3	25	28	11

The medium prices in various years are taken from the *Economist* as follows :—

	1845–50 £ s.	1880 £ s.	1881 £ s.	1882 £ s.	1883 £ s.	1884 £ s.	1885 £ s.	1886 £ s.	1887 £ s.	1888 £ s.	1889 £ s.	1890 £ s.	1881–90 £ s.
Beef, ton . .	44 0	61 0	65 0	63 0	65 0	65 0	61 0	51 10	49 0	55 0	55 0	58 0	59 0
Butter, cwt. .	4 2	5 17	5 19	6 7	5 18	5 12	5 0	4 5	4 10	4 8	5 0	...	5 5
Calico, 100 yards .	1 4	1 1	1 4	1 2	1 0	1 0	1 0	1 0	1 0	1 0	1 1	1 1	1 1
Coal, ton . .	...	0 9	0 9	0 9	0 9	0 10	0 8	0 8	0 8	0 10	0 12	0 12	0 9
Coffee, cwt. .	2 9	3 14	3 0	2 9	2 0	2 12	2 6	2 2	3 15	3 14	4 3	4 11	3 2
Copper, ton .	88 0	71 5	66 5	75 10	70 10	62 5	53 0	44 0	43 0	78 0	62 0	56 5	61 0
Cotton, cwt. .	2 9	2 10	3 3	3 2	2 14	2 16	2 16	2 6	2 12	2 14	2 16	2 12	2 15
Flax, ton . .	44 0	33 0	29 0	30 0	27 10	27 0	30 0	29 10	30 5	27 0	26 0	23 0	28 0
Hemp, ton . .	32 0	25 10	23 15	26 5	23 10	29 0	29 10	28 5	28 5	20 0	24 0	26 0	26 0
Indigo, cwt. .	21 0	43 16	42 0	39 4	37 16	33 10	33 10	33 10	28 0	27 0	26 0	25 0	32 10
Iron bar, ton .	8 0	7 17	5 15	6 15	6 0	5 10	6 0	5 5	5 0	5 7	7 0	8 15	6 3
Lead, ton . .	17 10	19 12	15 5	15 7	14 10	12 5	11 5	12 12	12 10	14 10	13 7	14 6	13 12
Leather, cwt. .	8 8	11 14	11 14	11 14	11 14	11 14	12 2	11 14	11 10	11 4	11 3	11 3	11 12
Olive oil, tun .	44 0	46 0	42 0	40 0	36 10	40 10	40 15	40 10	36 15	36 12	34 10	37 5	38 10
Oil, palm . .	32 0	36 15	32 0	32 5	37 10	43 10	32 0	29 0	23 0	21 0	29 0	25 15	30 0
Petroleum, 40 gallons .	...	1 2	1 12	0 19	1 3	1 4	1 3	1 2	1 0	1 0	1 0	1 1	1 2
Pork, ton . .	50 0	58 0	73 10	58 0	58 0	54 0	44 0	38 0	42 0	38 0	45 10	46 0	49 14
Potatoes, ton .	...	7 5	4 5	4 5	6 0	4 0	3 10	4 10	4 10	4 10	4 15	3 0	4 10
Rum, 10 gallons .	1 10	1 14	1 7	1 18	1 10	1 8	1 6	1 8	1 7	1 3	1 4	1 7	1 9
Saltpetre, cwt. .	1 7	1 7	1 8	1 9	1 6	1 4	1 3	1 2	1 1	1 1	1 2	1 2	1 4
Silk, lb. . .	0 12	0 16	0 15	0 16	0 14	0 13	0 10	0 11	0 15	0 13	0 13	0 13	0 13
Steel rails, ton .	...	8 15	6 5	6 5	5 10	4 10	4 15	4 15	4 5	4 0	5 10	7 0	5 6
Sugar, cwt. . .	1 9	1 2	1 0	1 1	0 18	0 18	0 11	0 14	0 11	0 13	0 17	0 12	0 16
Tallow, ,, . .	2 4	2 5	1 19	2 3	2 9	2 12	2 2	1 15	1 11	1 14	1 19	1 13	2 0
Tea, ,, . .	4 6	6 1	4 4	3 14	3 5	3 18	3 6	3 18	3 5	3 14	3 1	2 13	3 10
Timber, load .	3 16	3 17	3 7	3 10	3 10	3 10	3 0	2 15	2 17	2 15	2 18	2 12	3 3
Tin, ton . .	85 10	94 0	94 0	114 10	98 0	88 10	77 5	97 0	105 0	120 0	99 0	103 0	99 10
Tobacco, cwt. .	2 1	3 14	3 7	4 18	5 2	4 9	4 4	4 4	4 3	4 18	4 5	4 4	4 8
Wheat, ton . .	13 5	11 15	10 17	11 1	10 5	9 18	8 0	7 10	8 15	7 15	7 8	7 9	8 18
Wool, cwt. . .	6 1	6 15	7 4	6 10	5 12	5 17	5 4	4 18	5 7	5 0	5 4	5 12	5 12
Yarn, cotton, cwt. .	4 11	5 0	5 0	5 0	4 11	4 10	4 11	3 15	3 18	4 0	4 6	4 4	4 8

FRANCE

Prices of cattle at various dates, according to weight of silver, were in English money of to-day as follows :—

Period	Horse £ s.	Ox £ s.	Cow £ s.	Sheep £ s.	Pig £ s.
1302–20 . . .	...	2 12	...	0 4	0 8
1321–70 . .	4 15	1 10	...	0 4	0 7
1371–1420 . .	...	...	0 19	0 4	0 10
1421–60 . .	1 14	2 3	0 11	0 5	0 6
1461–1550 . .	6 12	1 4	0 9	0 2	0 6
1551–80 . .	6 8	2 2	1 12	0 4	0 8
1581–1600 . .	...	2 12	2 8	0 7	...

Prices of grain and butter per ton were :—

Period	Peas £ s.	Oats £ s.	Rice £ s.	Butter £ s.
1341–80 . . .	6 8	...	22 0	...
1381–1440 . .	3 4	1 14	...	16 10
1441–1500 . .	5 4	1 6	20 0	...
1501–50 . .	3 12	1 12	...	16 0
1551–1600 . .	2 11	2 11	...	40 0

Professor Charles Guyot gives the following scale of prices and wages from the Middle Ages to date, reduced to English money :—

	Land, Acre £ s.	Calico, Yard s. d.	Cloth, Yard s. d.	Workman's Daily Food d.	Wages, Daily Man d.	Woman d.	Wages per Annum Man £ s.	Woman £ s.
1401–25 .	5 3	...	...	3	7	4	...	...
1520–50 .	7 10	...	...	3	7	4	...	...
1551–75 .	17 0	...	...	4	11	6	...	...
1576–1600 .	19 10	...	...				...	...
1601–50 .	9 0	0 10	7 6	5	9	7	2 15	1 16
1676–1700 .	11 0	0 9	5 0	6	11	8	2 16	1 16
1701–26 .	16 8	0 9	5 10	5	9	7	2 16	1 1
1751–75 .	19 0	0 8	5 10	5	8	6	2 8	2 6
1776–1800 .	38 0	0 11	4 9	6	9	6	3 16	2 4
1826–50 .	...	1 0	8 0	6	14	9	8 0	5 0
1851–71 .	84 0	1 0	6 6	7	20	14	12 0	6 0
1872–85 .	70 0	1 1	6 6	9	24	16	16 0	8 0

The prices of some other things were as follows :—

	Period	£	s.	d.		Period	£	s.	d.
Apples, 1000 .	1361	0	4	0	Onions, bush.	1372	0	5	0
Bacon, ton . .	1594	60	0	0	Oranges, 1000	1542	0	0	10
Brass, ,, .	1418	14	10	0	Paper, quire .	1431	0	1	8
Calico, yard .	1312	0	0	8	Partridge .	1563	0	0	6
Candles, lb. .	1499	0	0	3	Peaches, 1000	1435	0	0	6
,, ,,	1589	0	0	7	Pears, 100 .	1536	0	0	6
Cheese, ton .	1542	8	0	0	Pepper, lb. .	1450	0	1	0
Chicken . .	1563	0	0	3	Pheasant . .	1434	0	2	6
Copper, ton .	1542	32	0	0	Pigeons, pair	1440	0	0	5
Cotton, ,, .	1320	5	2	0	Rabbit . .	1563	0	0	8
Cowhide, tanned	1542	0	9	6	Salt, bush. .	1375	0	9	6
Eggs, 100 .	1376	0	1	8	,, ,, .	1589	0	18	0
,, ,, .	1598	0	2	6	Sheepskin .	1327	0	1	4
Fagots, 1000 .	1560	2	2	0	Shoes, pair .	1564	0	0	10
,, ,,	1600	1	10	0	Slates, 1000 .	1518	0	10	6
Fleece . . .	1341	0	2	0	Steel, ton .	1307	20	0	0
Gunpowder,cwt.	1594	13	8	0	,, ,, .	1542	8	0	0
Hay, ton . .	1567	1	7	0	Sugar, lb. .	1372	0	4	0
Herrings, 1000 .	1426	1	4	0	,, ,, .	1598	0	2	0
,, ,, .	1595	2	16	0	Thread, lb. .	1322	0	1	2
Horse-shoe .	1307	0	0	5	Tiles, 1000 .	1341	0	11	0
Iron, ton . .	1536	8	0	0	,, ,, .	1567	1	12	0
Lead, ,, . .	1312	20	0	0	Wax, lb. . .	1434	0	1	1
,, ,, . .	1518	8	0	0	Wine, gallon	1375	0	1	0
,, ,, . .	1542	4	16	0	,, ,,	1560	0	1	3
Oil, gallon . .	1375	0	5	0	,, Bur-gundy .	1577	0	2	6
,, ,, . .	1589	0	8	0					

The prices of some articles of food in French cities at various dates were :—

Year	Bread, Ton			Milk, 10 gallons			Eggs, 10 dozen		
	£	s.	d.	£	s.	d.	£	s.	d.
1830 . .	16	0	0	0	5	3	0	2	10
1840 . .	9	12	0	0	5	3	0	4	0
1850 . .	9	4	0	0	6	5	0	4	5
1860 . .	10	8	0	0	7	1	0	4	10
1870 . .	12	0	0	0	7	6	0	5	8
1880 . .	14	8	0	0	8	4	0	6	0
1886 . .	12	0	0	0	9	6	0	5	8

Prices of cattle and meat at Paris were :—

Year	Per Head			Per Ton	
	Oxen	Cows	Sheep	Beef	Mutton
	£ s.	£ s.	£ s.	£ s.	£ s.
1820 . . .	9 14	6 16	0 16	44 0	52 0
1830 . . .	14 4	7 12	1 0	49 0	54 0
1840 . . .	15 4	8 4	1 0	52 0	54 0

Prices of rural products in 1888–89 averaged thus :—

	Ton	Bushel			Ton	Bushel	
	£ s.	s.	d.		s. d.	s.	d.
Wheat .	10 10	5	3	Barley .	6 8	3	3
Oats . .	4 16	2	5	Potatoes .	2 2	1	1
Maize . .	6 14	3	5	Chestnuts .	3 8	1	8
Rye . .	6 12	3	4	Apples .	3 6	1	7

Prices of meat were as follows per ton :—

Year	Beef	Veal	Mutton	Pork	Average
	£ s.	£ s.	£ s.	£ s.	£ s.
1880 . . .	64 10	68 0	71 0	67 0	67 12
1884 . . .	67 0	71 0	76 0	65 0	69 15
1888 . . .	57 0	61 0	66 0	58 0	60 10

The prices of various kinds of grain, according to Broch, in twenty years ending 1883 were as follows per ton :—

				Wheat	Rye	Barley	Oats
				£ s.	£ s.	£ s.	£ s.
1864 .	.	.	.	10 5	7 8	6 15	4 18
1865 .		.	.	9 11	7 0	6 9	4 17
1866 .			.	11 9	7 8	7 9	5 5
1867 .			.	15 4	9 16	8 3	6 1
1868 .			.	15 8	10 14	8 18	6 9
1869 .			.	11 17	7 14	7 2	5 12
1870 .			.	11 18	9 6	7 7	5 17
1871 .			.	14 12	8 17	8 5	6 8
1872 .			.	13 10	7 18	6 8	4 17
1873 .			.	14 12	9 4	7 14	5 11
1874 .			.	14 7	10 1	8 15	6 12
1875 .			.	11 2	7 17	7 2	6 4
1876 .			.	12 3	8 3	7 6	6 8
1877 .			.	13 13	8 18	7 14	6 1
1878 .			.	13 9	8 10	7 17	5 16
1879 .			.	12 15	8 17	7 9	5 10
1880 .			.	13 7	9 6	7 11	5 16
1881 .			.	12 18	8 12	7 3	5 12
1882 .			.	12 11	8 2	7 6	5 14
1883 .			.	11 4	7 10	6 14	5 7

GERMANY

The average prices of grain at Königsberg, from 1815 to 1886, were as follows, per ton :—

Years	Wheat	Rye	Years	Wheat	Rye
	£ s.	£ s.		£ s.	£ s.
1815–16 . .	8 4	5 10	1851–52 . .	8 4	6 9
1817–18 . .	12 1	7 10	1853–54 . .	11 13	8 13
1819–20 . .	6 15	4 12	1855–56 . .	15 4	11 4
1821–22 . .	5 5	3 11	1857–58 . .	9 6	6 2
1823–24 . .	4 1	2 18	1859–60 . .	9 2	5 18
1825–26 . .	3 14	2 16	1861–62 . .	10 7	6 15
1827–28 . .	5 12	3 16	1863–64 . .	7 12	5 4
1829–30 . .	7 9	3 11	1865–66 . .	8 7	5 16
1831–32 . .	7 19	5 0	1867–68 . .	12 13	9 5
1833–34 . .	5 7	4 4	1869–70 . .	9 9	6 14
1835–36 . .	4 12	3 14	1871–72 . .	11 11	7 2
1837–38 . .	5 13	4 1	1873–74 . .	11 17	8 2
1839–40 . .	8 6	4 4	1875–76 . .	9 12	7 1
1841–42 . .	8 12	5 4	1877–78 . .	10 10	6 15
1843–44 . .	6 2	4 6	1879–80 . .	9 19	7 10
1845–46 . .	8 6	6 17	1881–82 . .	10 3	8 0
1847–48 . .	9 6	6 14	1883–84 . .	8 13	6 12
1849–50 . .	6 19	3 12	1885–86 . .	7 16	6 5

The prices of grain at Hamburg were as follows, per ton :—

Year	Wheat	Rye	Barley	Oats
	£ s.	£ s.	£ s.	£ s.
1826	4 19	3 3	2 8	1 10
1827	6 18	6 10	4 4	4 2
1828	6 8	5 11	3 6	2 2
1829	12 14	5 19	4 14	2 16
1830	7 14	4 16	3 3	2 9
1831	11 10	7 7	4 14	3 1
1832	9 2	7 0	4 4	2 9
1833	6 6	5 1	3 8	2 3
1834	5 14	4 13	2 17	1 18
1835	5 7	5 0	3 5	2 3
1836	5 6	4 12	3 8	1 18
1837	6 18	5 12	3 18	2 14
1838	6 14	5 4	3 2	2 3
1839	13 0	7 13	4 19	3 5
1840	10 6	6 0	4 17	3 2
1841	8 2	8 8	3 17	2 19
1842	11 3	7 0	3 16	2 11
1843	8 7	7 0	4 1	2 16

Year	Wheat		Rye		Barley		Oats	
	£	s.	£	s.	£	s.	£	s.
1844	8	15	6	2	4	1	3	0
1845	7	5	5	0	4	7	2	14
1846	10	10	7	14	4	9	3	6
1847	12	6	10	13	7	3	4	8
1848	10	17	6	19	4	16	3	5
1849	8	2	4	10	4	0	2	1
1850	8	2	4	10	3	12	2	3
1851	8	3	6	5	4	6	2	19
1852	8	15	8	8	5	4	3	0
1853	9	12	7	4	5	8	3	7
1854	14	18	12	8	7	13	4	18
1855	14	2	9	16	6	10	4	4
1856	16	18	13	13	8	3	5	1
1857	11	12	7	11	6	10	3	17
1858	9	10	7	0	5	2	4	10
1859	10	0	7	7	5	1	4	12
1860	10	17	8	2	7	0	4	13
1861	12	16	8	7	8	2	4	14
1862	14	0	9	17	6	5	4	13
1863	11	6	8	5	5	11	3	17
1864	9	0	6	8	5	17	3	19
1865	8	8	5	17	5	5	3	15
1866	11	10	7	15	8	0	5	7
1867	14	6	9	12	9	9	4	18
1868	16	0	13	7	9	1	5	12
1869	11	14	9	17	9	18	5	15
1870	10	5	7	9	7	12	4	6
1871	12	8	8	18	7	14	5	2
1872	13	16	9	10	9	10	4	18
1873	14	5	11	6	10	5	5	13
1874	10	14	9	8	9	8	6	5
1875	10	14	9	5	9	6	6	5
1876	11	7	9	3	7	15	5	14
1877	12	16	10	7	7	14	5	17
1878	12	5	9	1	9	7	5	11
1879	9	16	7	0	8	18	4	7
1880	12	19	9	16	9	5	4	16

The foregoing table is summed up as follows :—

Period	Wheat		Rye		Barley		Oats	
	£	s.	£	s.	£	s.	£	s.
1826–30 . . .	7	14	5	5	3	11	2	12
1831–40 . . .	8	0	5	16	3	17	2	10
1841–50 . . .	9	6	6	15	4	8	2	18
1851–60 . . .	15	17	8	15	6	4	4	3
1861–70 . . .	12	9	8	15	7	9	4	13
1871–80 . . .	12	2	9	9	9	3	5	8

The prices of twenty-one principal articles of consumption were as follows, per ton :—

	1880		1887			1880		1887	
	£	s.	£	s.		£	s.	£	s.
Barley . .	9	2	7	10	Pork . .	55	0	44	0
Beef . .	49	0	46	0	Potatoes .	1	16	1	8
Coal . .	0	5	0	4	Rice . .	13	0	10	0
Coffee . .	63	0	78	0	Rye . .	7	4	6	10
Copper .	63	0	47	0	Silk . .	136	0	108	0
Cotton .	55	0	52	0	Sugar . .	33	0	23	0
Herring .	12	0	7	0	Tin . .	79	0	120	0
Iron . .	2	12	2	10	Tobacco .	...		53	0
Mutton .	51	0	44	0	Wheat . .	11	14	8	10
Oats . .	6	14	5	12	Wool . .	167	0	140	0
Petroleum	8	0	6	0	Zinc . .	160	0	145	0

The prices of live stock in 1883 were as follows :—

	Horses		Oxen		Milch Cows	
	£	s.	£	s.	£	s.
Prussia . . .	23	6	13	16	11	6
Bavaria . . .	22	8	13	12	10	8
Saxony . . .	33	0	13	0	12	2
Wurtemburg . .	20	10	14	12	11	10·
All Germany . .	23	18	14	0	11	8

The prices of four principal articles in Germany in late years were as follows, per ton :—

Year	Cotton		Wool		Lead		Iron	
	£	s.	£	s.	£	s.	£	s.
1879 . . .	62	0	167	0	15	0	2	12
1885 . . .	55	0	134	0	11	0	2	8
1886 . . .	49	0	133	0	13	0	2	3
1887 . . .	52	0	116	0	12	10	2	10
1888 . . .	53	0	130	0	14	0	2	12

AUSTRIA

The prices of grain in fifteen years, taking the gulden at 20 pence, were as follows, per ton :—

	Wheat		Rye		Barley		Oats		Maize	
	£	s.	£	s.	£	s.	£	s.	£	s.
1874 . . .	11	14	9	9	9	0	7	2	7	2
1875 . . .	9	7	7	5	7	11	7	9	5	0
1876 . . .	9	16	8	0	7	15	7	2	5	3
1877 . . .	10	15	8	0	8	18	6	18	6	11
1878 . . .	9	14	6	9	8	0	5	15	5	18
1879 . . .	10	16	7	5	9	15	5	18	5	9
1880 . . .	11	14	9	0	8	5	6	2	6	11
1881 . . .	10	17	8	10	8	15	6	5	5	14
1882 . . .	9	18	7	7	8	10	6	5	6	14
1883 . . .	8	17	7	0	9	0	6	0	5	14
1884 . . .	8	0	6	10	8	17	6	0	5	18
1885 . . .	7	7	6	5	7	2	5	17	5	7
1886 . . .	7	14	6	0	7	18	5	11	5	5
1887 . . .	7	10	5	15	7	14	5	7	5	11
1888 . . .	6	17	5	7	7	10	5	0	5	3

The averages, in periods of five years, were as follows :—

Period	Wheat		Rye		Barley		Oats		Maize	
	£	s.	£	s.	£	s.	£	s.	£	s.
1874–78 . .	10	5	7	17	8	5	6	17	5	19
1879–83 . .	10	8	7	16	8	17	6	2	6	0
1884–88 . .	7	10	6	0	7	16	5	11	5	9
Gen. average	9	7	7	4	8	6	6	3	5	16

The prices of some other commodities were as follows :—

	1882		1887			1882		1887	
	£	s.	£	s.		£	s.	£	s.
Butter, ton . .	72	0	53	0	Rice, ton . .	13	15	16	0
Cheese, ,, .	54	0	55	0	Straw, ,, . .	...		1	18
Coffee, ,, .	80	0	102	0	Sugar, ref., ton	35	0	29	0
Hay, ,, .	...		2	16	Tea, ton . .	233	0	268	0
Potatoes, ton .	3	7	3	15	Tobacco, ton	90	0	90	0
Raisins, ,, .	17	10	17	10	Wine, 100 gal.	...		18	15

HUNGARY

The prices of rural products were as follows, per ton :—

	1884			1886		
	£	s.	d.	£	s.	d.
Barley	6	14	0	7	5	0
Beef .	...			42	0	0
Hemp	29	4	0	26	14	0
Maize . . .	5	4	0	5	0	0
Mutton . . .	...			31	10	0
Oats	5	12	0	5	2	0
Pork . . .	...			38	10	0
Potatoes . . .	3	7	0	2	10	0
Rye	6	14	0	5	8	0
Wheat . . .	8	0	0	6	14	0
Wool . . .	95	0	0	79	0	0
Wine, 40 gallons . .	...			2	14	0

ITALY

The prices of wheat per ton in the Udine market from 1606 to 1875 were as follows:—

Period	Highest	Lowest	Average	Year of Highest	Year of Lowest
	£ s.	£ s.	£ s.		
1606–10 ..	7 14	3 17	5 11	1601	1610
1611–20 ..	6 11	4 16	5 16	1618	1611
1621–30 ..	12 6	5 13	7 16	1628	1625
1631–40 ..	8 1	2 15	5 5	1631	1639
1641–50 ..	12 11	4 2	7 0	1649	1645
1651–60 ..	6 12	3 17	5 3	1656	1659
1661–70 ..	5 16	3 10	4 11	1664	1666
1671–80 ..	6 4	3 10	5 1	1677	1673
1681–90 ..	5 9	2 18	4 2	1685	1688
1691–1700 ..	7 6	4 5	5 15	1696	1691
1701–10 ..	8 4	3 16	5 8	1709	1702
1711–20 ..	6 10	4 10	5 9	1717	1720
1721–30 ..	5 7	3 10	4 7	1729	1727
1731–40 ..	7 0	3 16	5 13	1735	1731
1741–50 ..	7 10	4 14	6 3	1747	1745
1751–60 ..	8 1	5 0	6 5	1751	1754
1761–70 ..	9 14	4 15	6 18	1766	1762
1771–80 ..	10 17	6 8	8 5	1774	1776
1781–90 ..	10 13	7 7	8 16	1788	1781
1791–1800 ..	19 2	7 15	11 5	1800	1791
1801–10 ..	19 12	8 5	13 0	1801	1808
1811–20 ..	23 2	7 7	13 2	1816	1819
1821–30 ..	9 14	5 0	7 1	1828	1824
1831–40 ..	9 12	7 1	8 0	1839	1834
1841–50 ..	12 0	6 10	9 4	1846	1844
1851–60 ..	14 12	8 13	11 14	1855	1851
1861–70 ..	11 18	8 7	10 7	1867	1864
1871–75 . .	15 0	10 3	13 6	1873	1875

The prices of maize in the Udine market from 1626 to 1875 were per ton as follows:—

Period	Highest	Lowest	Average	Year of Highest	Year of Lowest
	£ s.	£ s.	£ s.		
1626–30 ..	9 5	3 6	5 10	1628	1626
1631–40 ..	3 6	1 12	2 8	1633	1639
1641–50 ..	8 10	1 18	3 18	1649	1645
1651–60 ..	3 16	2 0	2 11	1656	1659
1661–70 ..	3 11	1 10	2 2	1663	1669
1671–80 ..	4 10	1 18	2 12	1675	1678
1681–90 ..	4 1	1 10	2 4	1685	1682
1691–1700 ..	4 18	2 5	3 6	1695	1700
1701–10 ..	3 16	1 14	2 17	1709	1703
1711–20 ..	4 4	1 14	3 5	1717	1720
1721–30 ..	3 2	1 13	2 7	1724	1727
1731–40 ..	4 11	2 6	3 5	1739	1734
1741–50 ..	4 9	2 8	3 4	1750	1748
1751–60 ..	6 1	2 3	3 13	1751	1753
1761–70 ..	6 7	2 16	4 5	1763	1761
1771–80 ..	7 1	3 15	5 2	1772	1775
1781–90 ..	8 10	3 12	5 7	1782	1790
1791–1800 ..	16 2	4 19	7 17	1800	1791
1801–10 ..	15 4	5 9	8 15	1802	1808
1811–20 ..	16 18	3 5	8 14	1816	1819
1821–30 ..	8 0	3 13	5 8	1830	1823
1831–40 ..	8 4	3 19	5 10	1839	1831
1841–50 ..	8 7	4 18	5 18	1846	1844
1851–60 ..	10 11	5 14	7 4	1853	1858
1861–70 ..	8 3	5 0	6 4	1861	1868
1871–75 ..	9 12	6 5	8 0	1871	1875

Nothing is more surprising than the great difference of prices of grain in Italian cities. For instance, wheat in 1865 was £2 per ton dearer in Florence than in Genoa, and in 1877 it was £3 dearer in Genoa than in Florence, as shown in the following table:—

Year	Wheat		Maize	
	Genoa	Florence	Verona	Florence
	£ s.	£ s.	£ s.	£ s.
1862 . . .	13 0	14 16	9 8	7 16
1863 . . .	12 10	14 7	6 14	5 8
1864 . . .	12 0	13 19	6 15	6 8
1865 . . .	11 0	13 0	6 6	6 8
1866 . . .	12 10	12 15	7 2	6 5
1867 . . .	15 14	14 18	7 14	7 15
1868 . . .	16 0	15 16	6 17	7 11
1869 . . .	12 16	13 18	5 10	5 6
1870 . . .	13 18	13 10	6 14	5 19
1871 . . .	14 11	14 16	10 10	7 18
1872 . . .	14 6	15 9	10 13	9 1
1873 . . .	15 14	16 4	8 14	8 11
1874 . . .	14 0	15 15	11 5	9 6
1875 . . .	12 0	12 11	7 3	6 1
1876 . . .	12 14	13 6	7 4	5 14
1877 . . .	17 8	14 2	8 16	7 12
1878 . . .	14 8	13 4	8 15	8 8
1879 . . .	12 9	13 0	8 4	7 8
1880 . . .	13 12	13 4	9 12	8 15
1881 . . .	11 5	11 8	7 16	7 4
1882 . . .	11 4	11 4	9 2	7 8
1883 . . .	10 10	10 16	7 3	6 15
1884 . . .	9 7	10 6	6 10	6 6
1885 . . .	9 0	10 7	6 9	6 2

In the above tables the depreciated paper money of the years 1866 to 1882 is converted into gold at the average rates for each year, the premium on gold varying from 4 to 14 per cent.

The prices of rice, wine, and olive-oil were as follows:—

Year	Rice, Ton (Milan)	Wine, 100 Gallons (Rome)	Olive-Oil, 100 Gallons (Rome)
	£ s.	£ s.	£ s.
1862 . . .	13 0	9 16	22 0
1863 . . .	12 7	8 4	18 8
1864 . . .	13 7	8 2	17 12
1865 . . .	13 2	8 10	17 0
1866 . . .	13 8	6 8	18 0
1867 . . .	14 4	6 10	22 16
1868 . . .	13 12	8 5	21 12
1869 . . .	12 16	9 8	17 0
1870 . . .	10 14	8 13	16 4
1871 . . .	12 15	4 16	16 12
1872 . . .	14 12	5 12	18 8
1873 . . .	15 4	7 0	20 4
1874 . . .	15 0	6 16	...
1875 . . .	15 4	6 4	17 12
1876 . . .	15 12	5 8	16 12
1877 . . .	15 8	12 4	19 10
1878 . . .	13 4	12 6	23 4
1879 . . .	14 4	7 7	17 4
1880 . . .	14 0	5 17	22 0
1881 . . .	12 12	7 4	19 10
1882 . . .	13 0	9 6	17 0
1883 . . .	15 8	8 10	18 0
1884 . . .	14 4	8 5	20 4
1885 . . .	12 10	10 8	18 8
1862–65 . . .	12 19	8 13	18 15
1866–70 . . .	12 19	7 17	19 2
1871–75 . . .	14 11	6 2	18 4
1876–80 . . .	14 9	8 12	19 14
1881–85 . . .	13 11	8 15	18 12
General average .	13 18	8 0	18 17

Rice ranged from £10 14s. in 1870 to £15 12s. in 1876; wine from £4 16s. in 1871 to £12 6s. in 1878; and oil from £16 4s. in 1870 to £23 4s. in 1878. It would seem, therefore, that wine is subject to much more violent fluctuations of price than either rice or oil.

The prices of best beef per ton were as follows :—

Year	Milan	Naples	Florence
	£ s.	£ s.	£ s.
1862	42 10	52 8	50 0
1863	47 10	51 4	52 0
1864	45 12	61 4	53 4
1865	46 0	57 4	54 0
1866	43 0	53 5	52 0
1867	44 8	51 4	54 0
1868	45 0	60 8	54 0
1869	48 15	63 10	56 0
1870	50 8	63 12	54 0
1871	50 16	60 0	45 12
1872	52 15	63 4	48 2
1873	66 8	78 0	51 0
1874	60 4	82 0	61 0
1875	58 16	69 10	62 10
1876	55 4	69 5	63 6
1877	53 12	67 4	63 14
1878	53 16	62 16	69 0
1879	53 16	59 12	68 0
1880	53 12	67 0	68 5
1881	55 16	74 10	76 4
1882	51 4	76 0	80 0
1883	54 0	79 4	85 12
1884	56 0	82 8	91 10
1885	60 0	79 4	87 0

SWITZERLAND.

The price of meat per ton from 1845 to 1881 averages thus :—

Period	Beef	Mutton	Pork	Average
	£ s.	£ s.	£ s.	£ s.
1845–51	32 0	32 0	33 0	32 7
1852–61	39 0	41 0	42 0	40 13
1862–71	52 0	52 0	43 0	49 0
1872–81	62 0	64 0	54 0	60 0

The prices of other commodities were :—

	1885	1888		1885	1888
	£ s.	£ s.		£ s.	£ s.
Barley, ton	8 10	9 6	Spirits, 100 gall.	9 1	8 11
Butter, ,,	54 0	70 0	Sugar, ton	27 0	19 10
Cheese, ,,	74 0	70 0	Tea, ,,	204 0	204 0
Coffee, ,,	52 0	84 0	Tobacco,,	65 0	41 0
Oats, ,,	6 17	6 12	Wheat, ,,	8 10	9 1
Potatoes,,	2 0	3 2	Wine,100 gallons	8 3	5 11
Raisins ,,	18 0	18 10			
Rice, ,,	15 16	13 10			

Mr. Secretary Mühlemann, of Berne, gives the following table of prices per ton :—

Year	Wheat	Rye	Barley	Year	Wheat	Rye	Barley	Year	Wheat	Rye	Barley
	£ s.	£ s.	£ s.		£ s.	£ s.	£ s.		£ s.	£ s.	£ s.
1784	9 4	6 10	5 14	1812	18 7	12 3	9 16	1854	20 18	14 17	10 0
1785	13 8	8 2	6 16	1813	16 4	9 9	8 0	1855	18 8	11 13	8 14
1786	11 14	6 12	5 6	1814	12 2	7 13	6 10	1856	17 14	10 3	8 1
1787	11 8	6 12	5 6	1815	12 18	8 6	6 14	1857	15 6	10 11	8 15
1788	13 8	8 16	6 14	1816	23 17	15 10	12 5	1858	9 16	6 2	5 14
1789	14 0	10 0	8 2	1817	32 15	20 12	16 14	1859	10 12	6 7	5 17
1790	15 10	9 12	7 12	1832*	...	9 17	7 13	1860	14 18	10 12	8 7
1791	12 0	7 0	6 0	1833	...	7 1	6 10	1861	14 14	9 17	7 7
1792	12 0	7 0	6 0	1834	...	5 4	5 6	1862	12 17	7 14	6 18
1793	15 13	9 18	8 10	1835	...	5 4	5 7	1863	12 10	7 14	6 8
1794	20 12	14 12	12 2	1836	...	5 18	5 14	1864	...	6 14	6 17
1795	26 4	16 9	13 0	1837	...	5 19	5 5	1865	...	7 4	6 18
1796	16 8	10 1	8 11	1838	...	6 7	5 14	1866	...	7 17	7 6
1797	13 1	6 7	5 18	1839	...	7 11	6 7	1867	11 4	8 7	8 7
1798	14 18	5 12	5 16	1840	...	7 11	6 9	1868	...	9 17	8 6
1799	15 0	7 12	6 15	1841	...	6 7	5 0	1869	...	6 8	6 16
1800	17 2	11 2	9 1	1842	...	7 0	5 10	1870	...	7 2	7 8
1801	15 3	10 7	8 11	1843	...	9 12	7 5	1871	13 6	8 12	8 12
1802	19 6	11 12	8 15	1844	...	8 10	8 0	1872	13 14	8 3	8 5
1803	18 6	11 3	8 14	1845	...	8 3	6 17	1873	14 10	9 3	8 19
1804	12 6	7 6	6 16	1846	...	12 0	8 10	1874	14 0	9 17	9 19
1805	15 10	7 12	6 8	1847	22 0	16 10	11 17	1875	10 15	8 3	8 19
1806	17 15	10 10	8 14	1848	12 0	6 16	5 12	1876	11 8	8 15	9 5
1807	12 17	8 0	6 8	1849	10 2	6 10	5 0	1877	13 0	9 14	10 3
1808	11 16	6 16	6 1	1850	10 13	6 17	5 9	1878	11 18	8 16	9 10
1809	9 18	6 8	6 1	1851	11 8	7 16	6 4	1879	11 1	9 4	8 15
1810	10 18	6 14	5 17	1852	13 2	9 2	6 10	1880	12 8	9 4	9 4
1811	15 17	8 11	7 0	1853	15 4	10 1	6 10	1881	11 11	8 15	9 3

The price of common bread at Berne per 10 lbs. was as follows, in pence :—

Year	Pence	Year	Pence	Year	Pence	Year	Pence	Year	Pence	Year	Pence	Year	Pence	Year	Pence	Year	Pence	Year	Pence
1800	25	1808	16	1816	30	1824	16	1832	22	1847	28	1854	26	1861	20	1868	21	1875	20
1801	21	1809	16	1817	41	1825	15	1833	17	1848	16	1855	24	1862	18	1869	17	1876	20
1802	24	1810	16	1818	22	1826	13	1834	17	1849	15	1856	22	1863	17	1870	20	1877	22
1803	24	1811	21	1819	16	1827	13	1835	16	1850	16	1857	21	1864	17	1871	21	1878	20
1804	20	1812	25	1820	15	1828	16	1836	17	1851	17	1858	16	1865	17	1872	23	1879	20
1805	23	1813	23	1821	16	1829	17	1845†	17	1852	19	1859	17	1866	18	1873	21	1880	20
1806	24	1814	19	1822	15	1830	18	1846	20	1853	20	1860	20	1867	22	1874	23	1881	20
1807	19	1815	19	1823	14	1831	21												

* There is a gap in the table from 1817 till 1832.   † There is a gap from 1836 to 1845.

The preceding table may be summed up thus :—

Years	Average, Pence	Maximum Year
1800–10. . . .	20.1	1800
1811–20. . . .	23.1	1817
1821–30. . . .	15.3	1830
1831–50. . . .	18.7	1847
1851–60. . . .	20.2	1854
1861–70. . . .	18.7	1867
1871–81. . . .	21.0	1872

The price of the best potatoes per ton was as follows ;—

Year	£ s.	Year	£ s.	Year	£ s.
1846	5 10	1858	3 8	1870	4 4
1847	7 10	1859	4 2	1871	4 4
1848	4 2	1860	5 16	1872	6 0
1849	3 7	1861	5 19	1873	5 0
1850	3 12	1862	3 11	1874	3 12
1851	4 14	1863	4 1	1875	4 4
1852	5 4	1864	4 8	1876	5 0
1853	5 7	1865	4 12	1877	5 1
1854	7 0	1866	4 4	1878	5 8
1855	5 12	1867	5 13	1879	5 13
1856	4 18	1868	4 9	1880	4 11
1857	5 10	1869	3 14	1881	5 8

DENMARK.

Dr. Broch gives the following table of prices per ton at Copenhagen :—

Period	Rye	Barley	Oats	Period	Rye	Barley	Oats
	£ s.	£ s.	£ s.		£ s.	£ s.	£ s.
1601–10	3 8	2 18	...	1851–52	6 10	4 18	3 3
1611–20	3 9	3 3	...	1853–54	9 7	6 8	4 13
1621–30	5 16	4 1	...	1855–56	9 8	7 9	5 3
1631–40	4 8	3 12	2 1	1857	6 1	5 16	4 4
1641–50	4 16	3 17	2 1	1858	5 12	5 3	3 17
1651–60	4 1	3 9	1 15	1859	6 0	5 3	3 17
1661–70	4 7	3 9	2 1	1860	6 15	6 4	3 19
1671–80	4 1	3 3	2 4	1861	8 12	6 5	4 0
1681–90	3 18	3 0	1 17	1862	6 11	5 8	3 18
1691–1700	5 1	3 11	2 3	1863	5 10	4 11	3 3
1701–10	4 1	3 1	1 14	1864	6 10	5 6	4 7
1711–20	4 6	3 4	1 18	1865	7 14	6 1	4 15
1721–30	3 15	2 17	1 12	1866	7 7	7 3	4 11
1731–40	3 12	2 16	1 9	1867	11 4	7 19	5 10
1741–50	4 2	2 14	1 11	1868	8 17	8 11	6 6
1751–60	4 4	3 2	2 0	1869	6 8	5 8	3 17
1761–70	5 6	3 11	2 1	1870	7 6	6 8	4 9
1771–80	5 5	3 9	2 3	1871	8 3	6 19	4 11
1781–90	5 14	3 9	2 18	1872	7 16	7 10	4 12
1791–1800	6 10	4 11	3 3	1873	9 12	8 6	5 10
1801–10	9 18	5 14	3 17	1874	8 8	8 3	6 0
1819–30	3 18	2 16	2 0	1875	8 0	7 14	5 12
1831–40	4 15	3 9	2 9	1876	8 8	7 16	5 17
1841–50	5 9	4 3	2 18	1877	7 3	7 9	4 16
1851–60	7 5	6 0	4 4	1878	6 8	6 10	4 2
1861–70	7 13	6 6	4 9	1879	7 4	7 2	4 7
1871–80	8 1	7 10	5 0	1880	9 7	7 10	5 1

The prices from 1811 to 1818 cannot be given, owing to the fluctuations of paper money. All the above prices are reduced to silver.

The preceding table arranged in half centuries shows thus :—

Period	Rye	Barley	Oats
	£ s.	£ s.	£ s.
1601–50 . . .	4 8	3 11	2 1
1651–1700 . . .	4 6	3 8	2 0
1701–50 . . .	4 0	2 18	1 13
1751–1800 . . .	5 8	4 10	2 9
1801–50 . . .	4 13	3 9	2 9
1851–80 . . .	7 14	6 11	4 11

SWEDEN AND NORWAY

The following list of prices is official :—

	Sweden		Norway	
	1882	1888	1882	1888
	£ s.	£ s.	£ s.	£ s.
Bacon, ton	...	...	50 0	40 0
Barley, ,, ...	6 12	5 2	7 3	5 6
Butter, ,, ...	78 0	67 0	95 0	61 0
Cheese, ,, ...	52 0	56 0	64 0	63 0
Cocoa, ,, ...	81 0	85 0	84 0	79 0
Coffee, ,, ...	42 0	91 0	52 0	72 0
Fish, ,, ...	20 5	19 0	...	...
Flour, ,, ...	...	...	14 3	10 18
Lard, ,, ...	63 0	33 0	...	...
Maize, ,, ...	7 0	6 10	7 18	5 19
Oats, ,, ...	7 0	4 19	6 16	4 16
Pork, ,, ...	63 0	39 0	...	...
Potatoes, ton . . .	1 16	2 16	...	...
Raisins, ,, ...	31 0	33 0	31 0	21 0
Rice, ,, ...	9 17	11 10	12 8	11 0
Sugar, ref. ,, . . .	33 0	21 0	33 0	21 0
Tea, ,, ...	145 0	168 0	145 0	118 0
Tobacco, ,, ...	...	...	62 0	60 0
Wheat, ,, ...	14 14	8 4	10 3	7 18

HOLLAND

The prices paid per ton at the Meerenberg Hospital for supplies by tender were :—

	Wheat Bread	Rye Bread	Butter	Beef	Rice	Potatoes	Peas
	£ s.	£ s.	£ s.	£ s.	£ s.	£ s.	£ s.
1851	18 8	7 4	68 0	81 0	17 12	4 4	13 4
1852	18 10	8 0	68 0	29 0	14 8	3 12	12 0
1853	18 10	7 4	68 0	30 0	14 8	3 18	13 16
1854	24 0	10 16	70 0	40 0	16 12	3 6	12 6
1855	25 5	10 8	74 0	43 0	17 12	3 6	14 8
1856	21 0	8 16	84 0	44 0	17 4	4 4	13 5
1857	16 4	6 0	83 0	45 0	14 4	3 6	10 18
1858	14 8	4 16	96 0	46 0	13 4	2 18	10 14
1859	14 8	4 16	92 0	40 0	11 4	...	14 13
1860	14 16	...	91 0	50 0	11 16	4 16	12 16
1861	17 4	6 8	85 0	44 0	13 10	...	14 3
1862	17 5	7 0	83 0	43 0	14 16	4 16	14 18
1863	14 16	6 12	79 0	39 0	12 12	3 12	10 4
1864	13 15	5 8	78 0	37 0	12 0	2 18	9 14
1865	12 0	5 0	85 0	41 0	10 8	3 2	10 1
1866	13 16	5 12	93 0	46 0	12 16	4 10	12 7
1867	16 15	6 7	83 0	44 0	14 8	3 19	13 3
1868	18 8	8 0	75 0	43 0	14 16	3 5	13 8
1869	14 16	5 12	86 0	47 0	13 12	3 12	13 8
1870	12 0	5 8	85 0	45 0	11 4	3 11	11 16
1871	14 8	5 16	89 0	45 0	12 8	3 16	12 18
1872	16 0	5 12	89 0	48 0	12 8	3 16	10 16
1873	16 12	6 0	82 0	55 0	12 12	3 2	12 10
1874	17 12	7 12	85 0	55 0	12 10	2 18	14 0
1875	12 16	5 12	90 0	53 0	11 15	2 14	15 10
1876	13 12	6 8	90 0	49 0	11 12	3 5	16 4
1877	15 12	7 12	94 0	51 0	12 0	3 5	15 10
1878	16 8	7 4	83 0	54 0	12 15	4 16	14 4
1879	14 0	6 8	76 0	56 0	12 0	3 14	14 4
1880	14 16	7 4	76 0	45 0	13 4	4 14	19 14
1881	14 8	8 10	82 0	52 0	13 2	3 10	16 12
1882	14 16	8 0	77 0	52 0	11 4	3 5	15 16
1883	14 12	7 15	76 0	58 0	9 18	4 2	14 8
1884	14 0	7 4	76 0	58 0	10 4	3 2	13 15

	Highest	Lowest
Bread . . .	£25 5s. in 1885	£12 0s. in 1870
Butter . . .	96 0s. in 1858	68 0s. in 1851
Beef . . .	58 0s. in 1883	29 0s. in 1852
Rice . . .	17 12s. in 1851	9 18s. in 1883

BELGIUM

The following is an official statement of prices from 1840 to 1887 :—

	1840			1850			1860			1870			1880			1887		
	£	s.	d.	£	s.	d.	£	s.	d.	£	s.	d.	£	s.	d.	£	s.	d.
Barley, ton	8	8	0	6	0	0	9	8	0	9	0	0	8	12	0	6	6	0
Beef, ,,		...			...		50	0	0	63	0	0	65	0	0	50	0	0
Beer, 40 gallons		...		0	17	6	0	17	6	1	10	0	1	17	0	2	10	0
Butter, ton		...			...		85	0	0	119	0	0	129	0	0	104	0	0
Cheese, ,,	28	0	0	40	0	0	56	0	0	60	0	0	60	0	0	60	0	0
Coal, ,,		...		0	12	0	0	12	9	0	12	0	0	11	3	0	9	6
Coffee, ,,	56	0	0	52	0	0	68	0	0	56	0	0	84	0	0	88	0	0
Cotton, ,,	68	0	0	64	0	0	60	0	0	92	0	0	80	0	0	48	0	0
Cows		...			...			...		13	12	0	13	4	0	11	4	0
Flax, ton		...		64	0	0	60	0	0	52	0	0	68	0	0	40	0	0
Hay, ,,	2	14	0	2	6	0	2	12	0	4	4	0	4	10	0	3	8	0
Hemp, ton		...		40	0	0	32	0	0	44	0	0	48	0	0	32	0	0
Honey, ,,	35	0	0	28	0	0	28	0	0	40	0	0	36	0	0	20	0	0
Horses	14	8	0	14	8	0	17	4	0	30	0	0	30	0	0	30	0	0
Iron wares, ton	24	0	0	20	0	0	7	4	0	6	16	0	6	16	0	4	8	0
Lard, ton	40	0	0	40	0	0	48	0	0	44	0	0	36	0	0	28	0	0
Oats, ,,	7	4	0	5	8	0	8	4	0	8	10	0	7	10	0	5	14	0
Pigs	1	4	0	1	0	0	1	8	0	1	10	0	1	6	6	1	6	6
Potatoes, ton	2	14	0	2	16	0	3	8	0	3	8	0	4	2	0	3	10	0
Rye, ,,	7	14	0	5	16	0	8	12	0	8	8	0	8	18	0	5	10	0
Sheep		...			...			...		1	16	0	2	1	6	1	16	6
Silks, cwt.		...			...		600	0	0	600	0	0	260	0	0	312	0	0
Steel, ton	52	0	0	52	0	0	52	0	0	48	0	0	16	0	0	4	16	0
Straw, ,,	1	16	0	1	6	0	1	12	0	2	12	0	2	14	0	2	4	0
Sugar, ,,	28	0	0	26	0	0	29	0	0	24	10	0	22	0	0	11	12	0
Timber, cubic metre		...			...		3	4	0	1	16	0	2	4	0	2	4	0
Wheat, ton	11	10	0	8	8	0	12	10	0	11	14	0	11	8	0	7	16	0
Wool, ,,		...			...			...		84	0	0	152	0	0	72	0	0
Woollens, cwt.	64	0	0	40	0	0	40	0	0	36	0	0	46	0	0	28	0	0
Yarn, cotton, ton		...			...		128	0	0	252	0	0	180	0	0	112	0	0
,, linen, ,,		...			...			...		200	0	0	160	0	0	84	0	0
,, woollen, ton		...		320	0	0	360	0	0	260	0	0	400	0	0	260	0	0

UNITED STATES

The prices in Massachusetts from 1780 to 1880 were as follows :—

	1780–1800	1801–20	1821–30	1831–40	1841–50	1851–60	1861–80
Apples, bushel . pence	10	22	22	35	44	50	...
Beans, quart . ,,	2	4	4	4	3	4	4
Beef, lb. . . ,,	2	4	4	4	4	6	7
Boots, pair . shill.	25	22	20	15	10	9	...
Brandy, gallon . ,,	6	7	6	...	8	...	...
Butter, lb. . . pence	8	11	9	11	10	13	16
Calico, yard . ,,	25	19	15	12	8	5	...
Cambric, yard . ,,	63	40	18	13	11	10	...
Candles, lb. . . ,,	11	11	8	7	7	14	...
Cheese, ,, . ,,	5	6	4	5	5	6	7
Cider, gallon . ,,	3	9	10	7	8	5	...
Codfish, lb. . . ,,	2	2	2	2	2	3	4
Coffee, ,, . ,,	11	13	10	7	6	8	16
Cottons, yard . ,,	18	18	10	7	6	6	...
Eggs, dozen . ,,	4	11	8	10	10	11	14
Fish, lb. . . ,,	2	3	2	2	3	2	...
Flannel, yard . ,,	21	33	29	22	19	20	16
Flour . . . ,,	2	3	2	2	2	2	3
Gin . . . . ,,	62	58	60	65	...	...	...
Gloves . . . ,,	27	26	26	23	20	30	32
Ham . . . . ,,	11	..	5	5	5	6	7
Handkerchiefs, each ,,	33	28	22	22	25	21	26
Herrings, dozen . ,,	4	8	4	5	6	4	...
Hose, pair . . ,,	37	55	30	26	19	22	25
Lamb, lb. . . ,,	4	4	3	4	4	6	...
Lard, ,, . . ,,	...	8	5	6	5	7	7
Linen, yard . ,,	18	28	23	29	19	27	...
Maize, bushel . ,,	40	59	41	39	36	50	...
Milk, quart . . ,,	2	2	2	3	3	3	3
Molasses, gallon pence	24	36	19	22	15	22	34
Muslin, yard . ,,	26	37	29	27	18	13	11
Mutton, lb. . ,,	3	4	3	4	4	6	8
Oats, bushel . ,,	24	32	21	27	27	...	...
Pork, lb. . . ,,	5	6	4	5	5	6	5
Potatoes, bushel ,,	15	24	18	25	39	43	50
Raisins, lb. . ,,	8	9	7	5	5	7	...
Rice, lb. . . ,,	2	3	2	3	3	3	5
Rye, bushel . ,,	52	67	44	52	50	75	...
Rum, gallon . ,,	35	51	38	...	...	...	...
Salt, bushel . ,,	40	48	36	33	33	33	...
Shoes, pair . ,,	48	64	63	68	53	55	...
Silks, yard . ,,	46	65	40	33	42	49	50
Soap, lb. . . ,,	7	6	5	6	4	6	4
Starch, lb. . ,,	12	11	8	8	6	6	5
Sugar, ,, . ,,	7	8	7	7	5	4	5
Tallow, ,, . ,,	8	7	6	3	4	...	...
Tea, ,, . ,,	40	52	41	28	27	26	32
Veal, ,, . ,,	3	4	4	4	5	6	8
Vinegar, gallon ,,	8	13	9	10	8	8	...
Wine, ,, . ,,	75	83	66	...	63	...	...
Wood, foot . ,,	19	21	22	41	30	35	45

The prices of grain, cotton, and refined sugar per ton of 2240 lbs., at port of shipment, from 1817 to 1889 were, reduced to English gold, as follows :—

Year	Wheat		Maize		Cotton		Sugar	
	£	s.	£	s.	£	s.	£	s.
1817 . . .	17	6	12	10	122	0	117	0
1818 . . .	15	8	8	7	158	0	117	0
1819 . . .	9	12	6	5	112	0	102	0

Year	Wheat £	s.	Maize £	s.	Cotton £	s.	Sugar £	s.
1820	5	15	5	5	81	0	93	0
1821	6	3	3	14	74	0	71	0
1822	5	8	6	4	77	0	69	0
1823	10	6	5	0	55	0	56	0
1824	7	17	3	15	72	0	58	0
1825	7	19	4	3	98	0	65	0
1826	6	10	6	6	57	0	74	0
1827	5	3	5	0	47	0	66	0
1828	5	16	4	1	50	0	65	10
1829	12	6	4	9	47	0	50	0
1830	7	17	4	4	47	0	57	0
1831	10	4	5	16	43	10	49	10
1832	8	4	5	5	47	0	50	0
1833	7	1	5	16	52	0	45	10
1834	8	6	5	11	60	0	43	10
1835	8	8	6	9	78	0	37	0
1836	7	14	7	3	78	0	54	0
1837	12	3	8	4	66	0	55	0
1838	10	4	7	2	48	0	43	0
1839	11	13	7	11	68	0	51	0
1840	7	6	4	18	40	0	53	0
1841	7	6	4	18	48	0	47	0
1842	8	12	4	16	37	0	39	0
1843	6	11	3	9	28	10	36	0
1844	6	19	4	2	37	0	35	10
1845	6	12	4	2	27	10	38	0
1846	8	0	5	8	36	0	44	10
1847	10	13	7	7	47	0	37	0
1848	10	3	5	10	35	0	35	0
1849	8	16	5	0	30	0	31	0
1850	8	3	4	18	57	0	48	0
1851	7	14	4	5	56	10	38	0
1852	7	6	4	17	37	10	33	0
1853	8	12	5	1	46	0	33	0
1854	12	0	6	6	45	0	35	10
1855	12	17	7	9	40	0	35	0
1856	14	16	6	5	45	0	41	0
1857	11	14	5	16	59	0	54	10
1858	7	16	5	14	54	10	57	0
1859	7	6	6	8	54	10	45	0
1860	7	11	6	2	51	0	42	0
1861	9	12	5	8	52	0	41	0
1862	7	15	4	0	94	0	41	0
1863	7	0	3	15	186	0	37	0
1864	5	3	3	6	188	0	33	10
1865	9	10	7	7	233	0	60	0
1866	7	15	5	0	140	0	52	0
1867	7	0	5	18	102	0	32	0
1868	10	16	6	14	65	0	47	0
1869	8	2	5	18	84	0	52	0
1870	8	16	6	14	95	0	51	10
1871	9	3	5	16	60	0	56	0
1872	10	4	5	5	78	0	51	10
1873	8	16	5	8	74	0	47	0
1874	10	4	5	9	65	0	45	0
1875	7	12	6	5	60	0	45	0
1876	8	12	5	0	55	0	45	10
1877	8	13	4	10	53	0	53	0
1878	10	4	4	11	50	0	47	0
1879	8	4	3	18	47	0	39	0
1880	9	13	4	10	53	0	42	0

Year	Wheat £	s.	Maize £	s.	Cotton £	s.	Sugar £	s.
1881	8	11	4	11	53	0	43	0
1882	9	9	5	12	53	0	45	10
1883	8	12	5	14	51	0	43	0
1884	8	2	5	2	49	10	32	0
1885	6	13	4	10	50	0	30	0
1886	6	15	4	3	47	0	31	10
1887	6	17	4	0	45	0	28	0
1888	6	10	4	11	46	0	29	0
1889	6	19	4	0	46	10	35	0

The Iron and Steel Association publish the following prices (reduced to English gold) per English ton :—

Year	Pig Iron £	s.	Bar £	s.	Iron Rails £	s.	Steel Rails £	s.
1846	5	16	19	1	...		...	
1847	6	5	17	18	...		...	
1848	5	10	16	9	13	0	...	
1849	4	15	14	1	11	4	...	
1850	4	6	12	8	10	0	...	
1851	4	9	11	8	9	11	...	
1852	4	14	12	4	10	0	...	
1853	7	10	17	7	16	2	...	
1854	7	13	19	0	16	13	...	
1855	5	15	15	10	13	2	...	
1856	5	12	15	6	13	8	...	
1857	5	10	14	15	13	8	...	
1858	4	12	13	0	10	8	...	
1859	4	18	12	10	10	5	...	
1860	4	15	12	5	10	0	...	
1861	4	4	12	13	8	17	...	
1862	4	7	12	10	7	11	...	
1863	5	2	13	5	11	0	...	
1864	6	5	15	5	13	2	...	
1865	6	2	14	2	13	2	...	
1866	7	0	14	16	12	15	...	
1867	6	13	13	0	12	15	25	0
1868	5	1	12	15	12	2	24	0
1869	6	6	12	13	12	1	20	10
1870	6	1	14	8	13	0	18	10
1871	6	11	14	13	13	1	18	5
1872	8	15	17	18	15	14	20	10
1873	7	16	15	15	13	16	22	0
1874	5	13	12	15	11	0	14	14
1875	4	13	11	0	8	13	12	10
1876	4	3	9	14	7	14	11	2
1877	3	15	9	2	7	0	9	1
1878	3	11	9	0	6	17	8	13
1879	4	9	10	15	8	12	10	1
1880	5	18	12	10	10	5	14	1
1881	5	5	12	0	9	16	12	15
1882	5	7	12	14	9	8	10	2
1883	4	13	10	9	...		7	17
1884	4	3	9	3	...		6	8
1885	3	15	8	8	...		5	18
1886	3	18	9	0	...		7	3
1887	4	7	10	6	...		7	14
1888	3	19	9	15	...		6	1
1889	3	14	8	17	...		5	14

The *American Almanac* gives the following prices from 1825 to 1886 (reduced to English gold) :—

	1825-30 £	s.	1831-40 £	s.	1841-50 £	s.	1851-60 £	s.	1861-70 £	s.	1871-80 £	s.	1881-86 £	s.
Beef, ton	22	0	25	0	22	0	23	0	22	0	22	0	27	10
Butter, ton	70	0	80	0	61	10	89	0	106	0	104	0	102	0
Cheese, ,,	33	0	37	0	29	0	38	0	46	0	52	0	47	0
Coal, ,,	1	13	1	14	1	5	1	5	1	6	0	19	0	16
Coffee, ,,	65	0	55	0	36	0	49	0	71	0	77	0	50	0
Cotton, ,,	56	0	58	0	39	0	50	0	170	0	65	0	52	0
Fish, ,,	13	0	20	10	26	0	37	0	34	0	30	0	44	0
Flour, ,,	13	0	17	0	13	0	14	0	12	10	12	0	10	6
Hams, ,,	47	0	49	0	35	0	46	0	45	0	42	0	65	0
Iron, ,,	10	18	9	7	6	13	6	1	6	2	6	11	4	11

	1825–30		1831–40		1841–50		1851–60		1861–70		1871–80		1881–86	
	£	s.	£	s.	£	s.	£	s.	£	s.	£	s.	£	s.
Leather, ton . . .	98	0	89	0	73	0	102	0	104	0	116	0	107	0
Maize, ,, . . .	5	0	6	13	5	14	6	13	6	7	4	13	5	2
Pork, ,, . . .	30	0	39	0	25	0	39	0	40	0	34	0	34	0
Rice, ,, . . .	14	0	17	0	21	0	19	0	33	0	32	0	34	0
Sugar, ,, . . .	35	0	32	0	29	0	29	0	39	0	33	0	25	0
Tobacco, ,, . . .	19	0	33	0	27	0	42	0	58	0	40	0	37	0
Wheat, ,, . . .	8	10	10	10	9	0	12	3	11	13	10	0	8	2
Wool, ,, . . .	125	0	152	0	125	0	162	0	176	0	181	0	172	0

Prices at New York, reduced to English gold, from 1855 to 1889 :—

Year	Flour, barrel		Leather, cwt.		Bacon, cwt.		Lard, cwt.		Pork, cwt.		Beef, cwt.		Butter, cwt.		Cheese, cwt.		Tobacco, cwt.		Petroleum, 100 gallons		Eggs (120)	
	s.	d.	s.	d.	s.	d.	s.	d.	s.	d.	s.	d.	s.	d.	s.	d.	s.	d.	s.	d.	s.	d.
1855	38	0	90	0	39	0	48	0	34	0	41	0	84	0	50	0	...		...		...	
1856	35	0	121	0	43	0	48	0	41	0	35	0	92	0	48	0	...		...		...	
1857	29	0	130	0	48	0	60	0	47	0	35	6	88	0	47	0	...		...		...	
1858	23	0	113	0	44	0	53	0	41	0	40	6	83	0	42	0	...		...		...	
1859	25	0	113	0	49	0	53	0	37	0	33	0	76	0	42	6	...		...		...	
1860	25	0	107	0	41	0	52	0	35	0	30	0	70	0	47	6	...		...		...	
1861	24	0	95	0	45	0	46	6	40	0	30	6	71	0	48	6	...		...		...	
1862	20	0	84	0	30	0	35	0	27	0	30	0	64	0	33	0	...		95	0	...	
1863	19	0	93	0	28	0	33	0	22	0	24	0	62	0	33	0	...		53	0	...	
1864	15	0	80	0	26	0	27	0	22	0	20	0	68	0	28	0	...		108	0	...	
1865	28	0	120	0	70	0	60	0	49	0	36	0	100	0	66	0	...		198	0	...	
1866	24	0	95	0	56	0	65	0	54	0	47	0	114	0	56	0	52	0	165	0	9	0
1867	27	0	115	0	42	0	49	0	47	0	41	0	82	0	50	0	36	0	108	0	11	0
1868	31	0	80	0	42	0	49	0	38	0	41	0	94	0	47	0	38	0	87	0	9	0
1869	24	0	...		52	0	63	0	49	0	31	0	126	0	56	0	40	0	120	0	...	
1870	22	0	112	0	65	0	65	0	53	0	30	0	119	0	65	0	46	0	111	0	14	0
1871	24	0	107	0	47	0	54	0	46	0	37	0	92	0	58	0	38	0	95	0	10	0
1872	26	0	98	0	36	0	42	0	30	0	30	0	80	0	49	0	43	0	93	0	7	6
1873	27	0	102	0	36	0	37	0	32	0	32	0	90	0	52	0	44	0	90	0	9	0
1874	26	0	107	0	41	0	40	0	34	0	34	0	104	0	54	0	41	0	65	0	8	0
1875	22	0	106	0	46	0	57	0	41	0	35	0	98	0	56	0	46	0	51	0	9	0
1876	23	0	111	0	50	0	55	0	45	0	36	0	101	0	53	0	44	0	52	0	10	0
1877	26	0	108	0	49	0	49	0	40	0	34	0	92	0	53	0	46	0	84	0	9	6
1878	25	0	100	0	39	0	40	0	32	0	36	0	82	0	52	0	39	0	59	0	6	6
1879	22	0	95	0	32	0	33	0	27	0	29	0	65	0	41	0	36	0	45	0	6	6
1880	24	0	109	0	31	0	35	0	28	0	30	0	79	0	45	0	35	6	35	0	7	0
1881	23	0	105	0	38	0	44	0	35	0	30	0	92	0	52	0	39	0	43	0	7	0
1882	25	0	98	0	47	0	54	0	42	0	39	0	89	0	52	0	39	6	37	0	8	0
1883	25	0	99	0	53	0	56	0	46	0	41	0	87	0	53	0	40	0	36	0	8	6
1884	23	0	96	0	48	0	45	0	37	0	35	0	85	0	48	0	42	6	38	0	8	9
1885	20	0	93	0	44	0	37	0	34	0	35	0	78	0	45	0	47	0	36	0	8	9
1886	19	6	93	0	35	0	33	0	28	0	28	0	72	0	38	0	36	0	36	0	7	6
1887	18	6	88	0	37	0	34	0	31	0	25	0	73	0	45	0	40	0	32	0	6	9
1888	19	0	81	0	39	0	36	0	35	0	24	6	85	0	47	0	39	0	32	6	6	6
1889	20	0	77	0	39	0	39	0	35	0	25	6	76	0	45	0	41	0	32	0	5	9

Retail prices in 1870 were as follows :—

	New England		Middle States		Southern		Western		Union	
	s.	d.	s.	d.	s.	d.	s.	d.	s.	d.
Beef, lb. . . .	0	10	0	9	0	5	0	6	0	7
Butter, lb. . . .	1	10	1	8	1	5	1	3	1	7
Coal, ton . . .	46	0	31	0	40	0	32	0	44	0
Cheese, lb. . . .	0	10	1	0	1	1	1	0	1	0
Coffee, ,, . . .	1	4	1	3	1	2	1	2	1	3
Eggs, dozen . . .	1	5	1	2	1	0	0	11	1	2
Flour, barrel . . .	40	0	30	0	36	0	25	0	30	0
Lard, lb. . . .	1	0	0	10	1	0	0	11	0	11
Mutton, ,, . . .	0	8	0	7	0	5	0	5	0	7
Milk, gallon . . .	1	2	1	6	2	0	1	2	1	6
Molasses, gallon . .	4	2	4	0	4	2	4	4	4	2
Pork, lb. . . .	0	9	0	7	0	6	0	6	0	7
Potatoes, bushel . .	2	10	3	5	4	6	2	2	3	0
Petroleum, gallon . .	2	0	2	3	3	0	2	4	2	6
Rice, cwt. . . .	60	0	60	0	60	0	60	0	60	0
Soap, ,, . . .	56	0	47	0	51	0	47	0	50	0
Sugar, ,, . . .	65	0	70	0	78	0	74	0	70	0
Tea, lb. . . .	4	10	5	6	8	0	6	8	5	10

PRICE-LEVELS.

Mr. Jevons constructed several price-levels from 1782 to 1869, as follows :—

Table of Forty Classified Articles.

Years	Metals	Fibre	Grain	Colonial Products	General Average
1782	100	100	100	100	100
1783–90 . . .	95	102	109	88	91
1791–1800 . . .	116	119	135	86	112
1801–10 . . .	150	157	170	71	133
1811–20 . . .	124	134	166	72	115
1821–30 . . .	102	97	135	56	88
1831–40 . . .	91	96	134	53	83
1841–50 . . .	88	76	127	42	73
1851–60 . . .	97	84	132	39	79
1861–69 . . .	93	105	128	40	77

General Table at Intervals of Ten Years.

Year	Number	Year	Number	Year	Number
1789	100	1819	131	1849	75
1799	151	1829	93	1859	90
1809	184	1839	108	1869	89

Table of Price-Level from 1846 to 1869.

Year	Number	Year	Number	Year	Number
1846	100	1854	115	1862	108
1847	106	1855	112	1863	107
1848	89	1856	117	1864	106
1849	85	1857	123	1865	105
1850	87	1858	108	1866	111
1851	87	1859	110	1867	102
1852	89	1860	112	1868	104
1853	106	1861	110	1869	103

According to the prices given by Arthur Young, the following is a general price-level from A.D. 1301 down to his time, and continued to 1884:—

	1301-1400	1401-1500	1501-1600	1601-1700	1701-1800	1801-50	1880-84
Cattle	100	95	80	160	246	350	500
Beer	100	80	80	80	160	280	350
Butter	100	75	75	100	125	250	350
Grain	100	95	133	270	330	350	240
Horses	100	105	100	132	346	700	800
Wine	100	70	130	200	500	600	700
Eggs	100	100	70	70	135	160	270
Meat	100	85	65	200	300	400	550
Total	800	705	733	1212	2142	3090	3760

The following price-levels embrace a period of forty years to 1884:—

Years	Jevons	Economist	Hamburg	Soetbeer	Average
1845-50	100	100	100	100	100
1851-55	107	...	112	114	111
1856-60	120	127	121	125	123
1861-65	123	...	124	127	125
1866-70	121	140	124	125	127
1871-75	...	127	133	136	132
1876-80	...	115	123	127	122
1881-84	...	105	118	124	116

Sauerbeck's and other index-numbers for late years are as follows:—

Sauerbeck		Kral		Economist		Hamburg	
Year	No.	Year	No.	Year	No.	Year	No.
1867-77	100	1861-70	100	1845-50	100	1847-50	100
1873	111	1871	98	1871-77	124	1851-60	116
1878	87	1872	107	1878	115	1861-70	124
1879	83	1873	112	1879	100	1871-75	133
1880	88	1874	109	1880	115	1876-80	123
1881	85	1875	106	1881	108	1881	121
1882	84	1876	101	1882	111	1882	122
1883	82	1877	100	1883	106	1883	122
1884	76	1878	94	1884	101	1884	114
1885	72	1879	93	1885	94	1885	109
1886	69	1880	97	1886	92	1886	104
1887	68	1881	94	1887	95	1887	103
1888	70	1882	96	1888	99	...	...
1889	72	1883-84	90	1889	99	...	...

The *Economist* index-numbers for twenty principal articles of merchandise showed as follows:—

	1845-50	1857	1870	1880	1881	1882	1883	1884	1885	1886	1887	1888	1889	1890	1881-90
Calico	100	113	135	95	101	99	92	88	81	85	85	86	89	91	90
Coffee	100	151	134	151	122	100	82	106	89	84	153	199	166	186	129
Copper	100	133	83	81	75	86	80	71	57	49	48	88	71	64	69
Cotton	100	95	173	110	105	102	89	92	90	80	85	88	93	92	92
Flax	100	121	116	78	71	75	68	76	79	78	76	64	67	64	72
Indigo	100	121	151	205	197	195	190	151	145	141	131	129	126	120	153
Iron	100	121	88	92	79	86	78	69	72	67	62	67	70	109	76
Lead	100	143	109	112	87	88	83	70	68	75	72	82	74	82	78
Leather	100	150	128	144	144	139	139	139	143	141	135	132	130	130	137
Meat	100	105	123	119	146	125	145	123	127	113	110	114	108	123	123
Oil	100	141	126	106	95	94	100	110	89	83	75	74	78	82	88
Silk	100	204	174	135	130	139	126	117	88	98	129	113	110	114	116
Sugar	100	123	83	70	60	67	60	54	44	46	37	46	61	42	52
Tallow	100	147	105	102	89	103	111	113	85	68	64	77	87	75	87
Tea	100	162	102	141	100	89	76	92	80	93	77	81	64	62	81
Timber	100	103	99	105	106	110	108	100	97	92	89	85	110	115	101
Tin	100	166	138	109	110	134	114	104	100	118	122	140	115	120	118
Wheat	100	118	80	88	82	84	77	73	60	58	66	58	55	56	67
Wool	100	146	96	117	120	108	106	98	91	92	114	107	108	120	106
Total	2,000	2,563	2,243	2,160	2,019	2,023	1,924	1,846	1,685	1,661	1,730	1,830	1,782	1,847	1,835

Index-numbers according to Board of Trade prices for British imports were as follows:—

	1854-60	1861-70	1871-80	1881-88	1889
Bacon	100	96	88	91	81
Barley	100	102	98	76	66
Beef	100	95	110	120	102
Brandy	100	71	84	98	98
Butter	100	120	131	125	126
Cheese	100	108	108	99	92
Cigars	100	93	123	104	102
Cochineal	100	76	62	30	28
Cocoa	100	104	137	158	144

	1854-60	1861-70	1871-80	1881-88	1889
Coffee	100	131	181	149	169
Copper	100	73	61	43	35
Cotton	100	222	106	90	87
Currants	100	58	75	75	67
Eggs	100	109	142	124	120
Flax	100	115	105	83	76
Flour	100	83	94	72	64
Gloves	100	130	125	112	108
Guano	100	102	92	76	58
Hemp	100	96	92	84	95
Hides	100	94	90	80	75
Hops	100	87	88	98	67
Indigo	100	108	85	76	65

	1854–60	1861–70	1871–80	1881–88	1889
Jute	100	105	91	72	77
Lard	100	98	82	76	64
Maize	100	85	80	66	55
Molasses	100	88	70	58	57
Nitre	100	82	84	70	60
Oats	100	98	96	76	68
Oil	100	108	84	70	68
Oil-seeds	100	110	107	82	79
Oranges	100	92	73	61	50
Oxen	100	112	130	125	115
Pepper	100	80	104	142	142
Pork	100	104	91	84	80
Potatoes	100	128	157	180	228
Raisins	100	81	96	92	87
Rice	100	103	83	68	68
Rum	100	70	60	50	50
Saltpetre	100	75	63	53	50
Seeds	100	88	74	67	64
Sheep	100	98	110	104	85
Silk	100	90	62	50	48
Sugar	100	81	70	51	49
Tallow	100	81	74	59	48
Tea	100	113	95	71	66
Tobacco	100	157	109	105	98
Wheat	100	85	85	66	57
Wine	100	50	67	65	67
Wood	100	99	83	72	73
Wool	100	87	69	55	48
Total	5,000	4,921	4,727	4,252	4,026

Index-numbers of British exports :—

	1854–60	1861–70	1871–80	1881–88	1889
Alkali	100	90	92	61	54
Bags	100	91	64	43	45
Beer	100	106	120	113	110
Books	100	93	75	67	59
Boots	100	113	103	97	90
Brass	100	92	83	70	75
Butter	100	97	124	126	115
Candles	100	74	61	47	36
Carpets	100	113	110	84	80
Cement	100	93	91	75	68
Cheese	100	103	103	100	95
Cloth	100	133	137	140	151
Coal	100	104	133	95	111
Copper	100	80	73	55	43
Cordage	100	96	98	85	92
Cottons	100	140	103	80	76
,, printed	100	127	110	82	73
Firearms	100	136	112	120	112
Flannel	100	113	113	82	75
Glass	100	88	85	72	70
,, bottle	100	92	97	87	87
Gunpowder	100	85	81	81	83
Hats	100	92	68	52	52
Herrings	100	108	116	104	88
Horses	100	88	110	104	120
Iron, pig	100	85	111	72	75
,, rails	100	96	111	67	60
,, hoops	100	80	78	53	52
Jute	100	79	64	45	47
Lead	100	88	83	58	60
Leather	100	106	93	101	104
Linen	100	110	104	91	80
,, printed	100	118	101	91	83
Oilseed	100	106	88	69	70
Paper	100	71	65	45	39
Sailcloth	100	108	113	95	92
Salt	100	91	118	118	145
Soap	100	100	96	84	77
Silks	100	118	102	113	98
Spirits	100	67	108	173	188
Steel	100	91	94	65	44
Sugar	100	70	51	34	30
Tin	100	89	83	83	80

	1854–60	1861–70	1871–80	1881–88	1889
Wire	100	100	87	68	74
Wool	100	125	116	74	65
Worsted	100	140	110	92	88
Yarn, cotton	100	167	125	97	92
,, linen	100	123	123	108	112
,, woollen	100	123	112	82	77
Zinc	100	79	74	51	55
Total	5,000	5,077	4,872	4,151	4,047

The summary of import and export numbers is :—

	Imports	Exports	Total
1854–60	5,000	5,000	10,000
1861–70	4,921	5,077	9,998
1871–80	4,727	4,872	9,599
1881–88	4,252	4,151	8,403
1889	4,026	4,047	8,073

The foregoing method, however, has the disadvantage that all articles are treated as of equal importance, wheat the same as gunpowder in affecting the level of prices. The British Association appointed a committee under Professor Edgeworth to frame a more suitable method of price-level, and the committee adopted one similar to that of Mr. Jevons.

The following are the various scales that have been proposed :—

	Jevons	Edgeworth	Giffen	Sauerbeck	Soetbeer	Mulhall	Average
Butter*	35	75	75	30	45	80	57
Sugar	35	25	25	55	45	15	33
Wine	35	25	25	...	70	45	40
Wool	35	25	25	75	20	20	33
Silk	35	25	25	10	20	15	22
Tea and coffee	35	25	25	20	20	15	23
Wheat	35	65	50	110	45	100	67
Barley	35	65	50	55	45	35	47
Oats	35	65	50	60	20	50	47
Metals	70	50	50	15	40	80	51
Coal	...	...	100	...	...	40	70
Indigo	35	1	10	5	20	1	12
Flax	35	3	30	10	20	5	17
Palm-oil	35	1	10	...	20	1	13
Timber	70	30	30	20	70	60	47
Leather	70	25	25	20	70	40	62
Meat	110	100	100	155	90	120	113
Cotton	110	30	25	100	20	20	51
Sundries	150	365	370	260	320	258	195
Total	1000	1000	1000	1000	1000	1000	1000

* Butter includes also cheese and milk.

In the foregoing scales it will be observed that four writers took no account of coal, and one omitted wine. There seems to have been no good reason for inserting indigo and palm-oil, which are items of trifling value, while fish, lard, rice, potatoes, and other important articles, are omitted. Another feature that seems inexplicable is, that four of the above writers give barley the same relative importance as wheat, whereas the latter, (see page 12) ought to be three times greater than the former. A similar remark applies to oats, which should stand for only half the value of wheat.

A general price-level for the principal countries from 1860–62 to 1883 is taken as follows from my *History of Prices* (Longmans, 1885) :—

| Year | Ratio of Values | | | | | |
	United Kingdom	France	Italy	Belgium	United States	Average
1860–62	100	100	100	100	100	100
1863	121	103	101	94	90	109
1864	138	107	100	96	106	120
1865	126	102	107	92	104	113
1866	127	98	98	97	170	116
1867	115	86	107	90	99	102
1868	110	87	105	87	107	101
1869	109	87	106	81	125	101
1870	100	80	105	85	108	95
Average	118	94	104	90	114	107
1871	100	83	106	97	112	97
1872	106	87	118	105	125	102
1873	110	89	122	103	100	103
1874	104	83	107	99	102	97
1875	99	78	96	97	96	92
1876	93	80	109	93	85	89
1877	94	77	100	97	101	91
1878	87	76	92	92	83	84
1879	84	80	97	89	90	85
1880	86	81	90	96	96	88
Average	96	81	104	97	99	92
1881	85	78	87	95	94	86
1882	85	76	82	83	98	85
1883	84	71	77	78	91	81
Average	85	75	82	85	94	84

The manner in which the above price-levels were arrived at was this. The trade of each country, imports and exports, was set down for each year side by side with what the amount would have been (seeing the quantities imported and exported) if the prices of 1860–62 had been maintained. As regards Great Britain, the exports of foreign and colonial merchandise are not included.

Actual trade returns (millions £ sterling) :—

Year	United Kingdom	France	Italy	Belgium	United States	Aggregate
1860–62	346	180	54	41	101	722
1863	396	203	61	46	59	765
1864	435	218	62	51	46	812
1865	437	229	61	54	47	828
1866	484	239	59	56	82	920
1867	456	234	65	55	99	909
1868	475	244	67	61	92	939
1869	485	249	69	64	106	973
1870	503	227	66	64	144	1,004
Average	428	216	61	52	89	847
1871	554	258	81	87	175	1,155
1872	611	293	94	93	193	1,284
1873	626	294	96	103	207	1,326
1874	610	288	91	96	210	1,295
1875	598	296	89	96	184	1,263
1876	576	303	101	101	182	1,263
1877	593	284	83	100	206	1,266
1878	562	294	82	103	225	1,266
1879	555	313	93	109	236	1,306
1880	634	340	91	116	308	1,489
Average	592	296	90	100	213	1,291
1881	631	337	96	117	314	1,495
1882	655	336	95	117	300	1,503
1883	667	330	99	116	312	1,524

At prices of 1860–62 (millions £ sterling) :—

Year	United Kingdom	France	Italy	Belgium	United States	Aggregate
1863	328	197	60	49	65	699
1864	315	204	62	53	43	677
1865	347	225	57	58	45	732
1866	381	244	60	58	48	791
1867	396	273	61	61	100	891
1868	432	280	64	70	86	932
1869	445	286	65	79	85	960
1870	503	283	63	75	133	1,057
Average	393	249	61	63	76	842
1871	554	310	77	90	156	1,187
1872	599	338	80	88	154	1,259
1873	570	330	78	100	207	1,285
1874	586	348	85	97	206	1,322
1875	604	380	93	99	192	1,368
1876	618	379	93	103	214	1,413
1877	631	368	83	103	204	1,389
1878	648	387	89	112	271	1,507
1879	657	391	96	122	262	1,528
1880	737	420	101	121	321	1,700
Average	620	366	87	104	219	1,396
1881	742	431	110	123	334	1,740
1882	770	442	116	141	306	1,775
1883	794	463	129	149	343	1,883
Average	769	445	118	138	328	1,798

The following price-level for twelve principal items of international consumption is taken from the same work (to which the late Professor Neumann Spallart alludes in his *Uebersichten Ueber Production,* 1886) :—

Price-Levels of the World for 100 Years.

| Years | Agricultural | | | | | | |
	Grain	Meat	Dairy	Wool	Cotton	Sugar	Total
1782–90	100	100	100	100	100	100	100
1791–1800	133	141	131	121	110	170	132
1801–10	165	188	167	259	75	138	166
1811–20	175	208	190	206	75	165	172
1821–30	118	157	153	90	46	113	113
1831–40	110	173	144	75	41	110	109
1841–50	105	165	155	60	26	110	102
1851–60	128	184	175	54	28	104	118
1861–70	123	194	198	46	61	110	123
1871–80	115	220	218	36	34	88	119
1881–84	98	244	222	30	29	64	113

| Years | Industrial | | | | | | |
	Hardware	Timber	Coal	Cottons	Woollens	Leather	Total
1782–90	100	100	100	100	100	100	100
1791–1800	124	138	109	107	112	116	116
1801–10	159	263	85	82	199	173	138
1811–20	181	238	91	82	161	168	136
1821–30	144	108	91	58	92	90	95
1831–40	124	127	71	54	84	100	87
1841–50	82	182	57	42	73	111	75
1851–60	75	144	61	36	68	103	69
1861–70	72	144	61	52	78	108	75
1871–80	85	128	61	37	75	96	70
1881–84	55	116	48	32	62	94	57

It appears from the above that agricultural products have risen 13 per cent., manufactures fallen 43 per cent., in price-level since 1782–90.

Beginning from 1841, we have in the following table a retrospect of values for 44 years; that is to say, if the same quantity of merchandise produced and consumed yearly from 1881 to 1884 were bought and sold at prices ruling in the four preceding decades, the amounts would be approximately as follows :—

	Millions, £ Sterling				
	1841–50	1851–60	1861–70	1871–80	1881–84
Grain	1,419	1,724	1,658	1,547	1,326
Meat	560	628	661	747	830
Hardware . . .	576	525	504	593	384
Dairy products .	236	266	303	333	340
Cotton goods . .	386	335	484	346	302
Woollen goods .	263	245	280	268	223
Timber	428	338	338	301	273
Coal	224	241	241	241	189
Leather	218	202	212	188	184
Potatoes . . .	115	125	154	164	181
Wine	86	105	111	111	130
Raw cotton . .	76	85	183	101	87
Wool	160	145	125	97	83
Books	120	115	105	87	79
Silks	68	82	104	88	73
Linens, &c. . .	77	74	78	74	70
Sugar	106	100	106	84	61
Coffee	23	30	38	50	42
Tobacco . . .	29	44	53	38	37
Tea	16	20	24	21	16
Total . .	5,186	5,429	5,762	5,479	4,910

The above twenty items comprise 90 per cent. of all human industries as regards products or manufactures, and therefore enable us to arrive at the variations of price-level for the whole world—that is, the rise or fall in the purchasing power of gold since 1850. The result is as follows :—

Years						
1841–50 .	.	.	.	.	.	100.0
1851–60 .	.	.	.	.	.	104.7
1861–70 .	.	.	.	.	.	111.1
1871–80 .	.	.	.	.	.	105.7
1881–84 .	.	.	.	.	.	94.7

PROSTITUTION

				Prostitutes	Per 10,000 Inhab.
London	.	.	.	31,800	83
Paris .	.	.	.	26,990	122
Berlin .	.	.	.	27,300	248
Lyons .	.	.	.	5,520	145
Marseilles .	.	.	4,080	112
Bordeaux	.	.	.	2,610	125

The Paris police reports show that 89 per cent. are French, 11 per cent. foreign. According to the *Dict. des Sciences Méd.*, 100 prostitutes may be expected in their lives to give birth to 60 infants ; 100 married women to 480.

PROTECTION

In order to promote certain local products or manufactures, which in some cases could not be profitably cultivated otherwise, "protection" is given either by means of bounties or by heavy import dues on foreign goods.

UNITED KINGDOM.

Between the years 1690 and 1830 Great Britain paid the inhabitants of Belfast and Dundee 28 millions sterling to enable them to sell and export Irish and Scotch linen at less than cost. The export of linen has quadrupled since the bounties were abolished in 1830, the average bounty before that year having been £150,000 per annum.

Bounties on the exportation of grain in England averaged £160,000 per annum for some years, until their abolition in 1805.

FRANCE

In 1860, by virtue of the Cobden Treaty, it was stipulated that no duties on foreign imports should exceed 25 per cent. *ad valorem*. The treaty has since lapsed. In 1880 a system of shipping bounties was established as follows :—48 shillings per ton for building iron vessels, and 16 shillings for wooden ; 15 pence per ton per 1000 miles run on French-built vessels entering French ports ; 7½ pence per ton for French vessels not built in France. The amounts paid for these bounties were :—

Year	Building	Navigation	Total
1881 . . .	£38,000	£39,000	£77,000
1884 . . .	179,000	344,000	523,000
1886 . . .	120,000	303,000	423,000

There are also fishing bounties, which in some years reach £200,000, and sugar bounties, £600,000. The effect of the shipping bounties has certainly been to promote French shipping, viz. :—

Entries		1880	1887	Increase
French	. .	3,614,000	4,770,000	33 per cent.
Foreign	. .	8,750,000	8,710,000	...

In 1889 the duties were increased on imported food to protect the French farmers : cattle now pay 32 shillings, sheep 4 shillings per head, and wheat 50 shillings per ton. This causes bread to be at times so dear that municipal bakeries are established to sell cheap bread to the poor.

BELGIUM.

Sugar bounties average £170,000 a year in Belgium, and £150,000 in Holland.

UNITED STATES.

Protective duties in 1885 compelled San Francisco to pay £9 a ton for American made rails, when as good could be landed from England at £5 a ton. Iron ore at Pittsburg cost 40 shillings per ton, when Bilbao ores could be landed in New York at 12 shillings.

PUBLIC WORKS

There is no means of ascertaining the value or cost of these in the various countries. In France a sum of 402 millions sterling was expended in 80 years, down to 1880, on roads, bridges, harbours, and canals. In England about 200 millions have been spent on sanitary works and schools. The United States Government in 90 years, down to 1880, spent 93 millions sterling on public edifices, arsenals, lighthouses, &c. The system of dykes in Holland represents an outlay of 300 millions sterling. The following table shows the amount of loans for public works in the United Kingdom from 1817 to 1881 :—

		Advanced	Balance Due
Great Britain	. . .	£44,700,000	£26,020,000
Ireland .	. . .	31,800,000	6,100,000
Total .	. . .	£76,500,000	£32,120,000

The total account of public works loans from 1792 to 1890 for the whole United Kingdom showed thus :—

Sums advanced	.	.	.	£115,324,000
Repaid by borrowers	.	.	.	63,979,000
Bad debts, &c.	.	.	.	12,685,000
Balance due in 1890	.	.	.	38,660,000

Q.

QUAKERS

There are 18,000 in the United Kingdom. They have a longer span of life than the general population, their death-rate during twenty years averaging only 18 per thousand as compared with 22 per thousand, probably the result of temperate habits. They have, however, one-fifth more insane than the rest of the population, namely, 33 per 10,000 against 28, which perhaps arises from inter-marriage.

QUICKSILVER

The *Times* published the following estimate of production :—

Year	Tons		
	United States	Spain, &c.	Total
1880 . .	2005	1995	4000
1889 . .	880	2500	3380
Average ten } years . }	1360	2280	3640

The Almaden mines in Spain were worked by the Romans : they still employ 4000 miners, who suffer a tremendous death-rate. In 1888 the value exported from Spain was £500,000. A flask of quicksilver weighs 76 lbs. According to Kolb, the production in California was as follows :—

Year	Flasks	Tons	Value	Value per Flask
1859 . . .	3,400	113	£26,000	7.6
1860 . . .	9,450	315	66,000	7.0
1865 . . .	42,500	1,420	232,000	5.5
1870 . . .	13,800	460	96,000	7.0
1876 . . .	41,100	1,370	342,000	8.3

It appears that the production has now fallen to 26,000 flasks or 880 tons yearly, being about equal to one-third of what is produced annually in Spain.
The annual production and consumption average :—

Production	Tons	Consumption	Tons
California . .	900	Great Britain . .	1600
Spain . . .	1100	United States . .	600
Austria . . .	300	China . . .	500
Various . . .	1000	Various . . .	600
Total .	3300	Total . . .	3300

R.

RABBITS

The annual slaughter is supposed to reach 20 millions in Great Britain, 70 millions in France.* The annual exportation from Belgium averages 5 millions ; the importation into Great Britain, 3 millions. The consumption in Melbourne market is one million yearly. Rabbits were introduced into Australia a few years ago for food, but multiplied so rapidly as to become a pest. A single pair of rabbits can become multiplied in four years into 1,250,000. The Sydney Cabinet in the year 1887 destroyed 25,300,000 rabbits, having spent £700,000 in four years to mitigate the pest. Mr. Coghlan says that 100 million acres of land have been more or less injured by them. To check their onward march a fence of 290 miles between the Macquarie and Darling rivers was made at a cost of £24,000 ; another of 346 miles from the Murray River north ; another of 260 miles on the southern line of Queensland ; another of 340 miles from Albury to the Macquarie ; but the rabbits broke through. The number of rabbit-skins exported averages yearly :—

New South Wales	. . .	15,000,000
New Zealand	. . .	6,000,000
Victoria	. . .	3,000,000

besides 1000 bales yearly from South Australia. The Cabinet of Victoria spends £15,000 a year in killing rabbits.

RAILWAYS

The *Almanac de Gotha* gives the total mileage at various dates as follows :—

Year			Miles	Year			Miles
1830	.	.	210	1870	.	.	139,860
1840	.	.	5,420	1875	.	.	177,600
1850	.	.	23,960	1880	.	.	224,900
1860	.	.	67,350	1885	.	.	307,400

The Actual mileage, however, was as follows :—

	1840	1850	1860	1870	1880	1888
U. Kingdom	838	6,620	10,430	15,540	17,930	19,810
France . .	360	1,890	5,880	9,770	14,500	20,900
Germany .	341	3,640	6,980	11,730	20,690	24,270
Russia . .	16	310	990	7,100	14,020	17,700
Austria . .	90	960	2,810	5,950	11,500	15,610
Italy . .	13	270	1,120	3,830	5,340	7,830
Spain . .	...	80	1,190	3,200	4,550	5,930
Portugal . .	...	...	40	440	710	1,190
Sweden . .	...	...	375	1,090	3,650	4,670
Norway . .	...	...	40	170	690	970
Denmark . .	...	20	70	470	830	1,220
Holland . .	11	110	200	780	1,440	1,700
Belgium .	210	550	1,070	1,800	2,400	2,760
Switzerland .	...	15	650	890	1,600	1,870
Roumania .	...	...	...	150	860	1,530
Servia . .	...	...	...	...	100	340
Bulgaria . .	...	...	...	...	200	430
Greece . .	...	...	...	...	10	370
Turkey . .	...	...	40	390	700	900
Europe . .	1,679	14,465	31,885	63,300	101,720	130,000
U. States . .	2,820	9,020	30,630	53,400	93,670	156,080
Canada . .	16	70	2,090	2,500	6,890	12,700
Mexico . .	...	...	...	220	660	5,010
Peru . . .	...	...	50	250	1,180	1,630
Chili . . .	...	...	120	450	1,100	1,750
Brazil . .	...	...	135	505	2,175	5,580
Argentina .	...	...	15	640	1,540	5,550
Uruguay . .	...	...	...	60	270	450
Japan . . .	...	...	...	...	75	910
India . . .	...	...	840	4,830	9,310	15,250
Australia . .	...	...	250	1,230	5,390	10,140
South Africa .	...	...	...	...	1,010	2,010
Algeria . .	...	...	...	...	780	1,840
Egypt . . .	...	...	275	550	1,120	1,260
West Indies .	...	...	...	...	100	650	1,280
Various . .	...	...	...	200	900	2,870
The World .	4,515	23,555	66,290	128,235	228,440	354,310

* De Foville questions the number of rabbits in France.

The following table shows the condition of railways actually working, mostly for the years 1887-88 :—

	Miles	Cost, Millions £	Passengers, Millions	Goods, Tons, Millions	Receipts, £	Expenses, £	Net, £
England	13,980	714	720	239	62,000,000	32,400,000	29,600,000
Scotland	3,100	114	74	39	8,000,000	3,800,000	4,200,000
Ireland	2,730	37	22	4	2,900,000	1,500,000	1,400,000
United Kingdom . .	19,810	865	816	282	72,900,000	37,700,000	35,200,000
France	20,900	570	218	78	42,400,000	22,400,000	20,000,000
Germany	24,270	495	316	179	54,600,000	29,300,000	25,300,000
Russia	17,700	314	38	50	25,300,000	14,400,000	10,900,000
Austria	15,610	307	65	79	20,800,000	11,700,000	9,100,000
Italy	7,830	138	46	15	9,400,000	6,200,000	3,200,000
Spain	5,930	94	15	8	5,600,000	2,500,000	3,100,000
Portugal	1,190	19	3	1	900,000	400,000	500,000
Sweden	4,670	28	10	8	2,100,000	1,300,000	800,000
Norway	970	7	3	1	400,000	300,000	100,000
Denmark	1,220	10	9	3	800,000	680,000	120,000
Holland	1,700	35	18	8	2,300,000	1,300,000	1,000,000
Belgium	2,760	71	73	41	6,800,000	3,500,000	3,300,000
Switzerland . . .	1,870	37	27	9	3,300,000	1,800,000	1,500,000
Roumania . . .	1,530	29	2	2	1,100,000	650,000	450,000
Servia	340	6	1	...	200,000	100,000	100,000
Bulgaria . , . .	430	8	1	...	300,000	150,000	150,000
Greece	370	6	1	...	200,000	100,000	100,000
Turkey	900	16	1	1	600,000	300,000	300,000
Europe . . .	130,000	3,055	1,663	765	250,000,000	134,780,000	115,220,000
United States . . .	156,080	1,949	451	590	198,000,000	138,000,000	60,000,000
Canada	12,700	151	12	18	8,400,000	6,200,000	2,200,000
Mexico	5,010	62	13	1	1,000,000	700,000	300,000
Peru	1,630	41	...	...	...	...	...
Chili	1,750	14	...	...	2,000,000	1,200,000	800,000
Brazil	5,580	49	7	2	3,800,000	2,500,000	1,300,000
Argentina . . .	5,550	48	8	3	2,800,000	1,700,000	1,100,000
Uruguay	450	5	1	...	300,000	200,000	100,000
Japan	910	11	12	1	600,000	250,000	350,000
India	15,250	145	103	23	15,000,000	7,500,000	7,500,000
Australia	10,140	94	81	17	8,200,000	5,100,000	3,100,000
South Africa . . .	2,010	18	3	1	1,700,000	900,000	800,000
Algeria	1,840	26	4	2	1,400,000	900,000	500,000
Egypt	1,260	18	4	1	1,300,000	600,000	700,000
West Indies . . .	1,280	16	...	...	...	...	...
Java	790	7	...	...	...	...	...
Various	2,080	27	...	...	...	...	...
Total . . .	354,310	5,736	2,362	1,424	494,500,000	300,530,000	193,970,000

There are no particulars, except length of line, known as regards Servia, Bulgaria, Greece, and Turkey: it is assumed in the above table that the ratios per mile are the same as in Roumania. The cost of construction in Mexico, being unknown, is assumed to be the same as in the United States. In some cases the traffic is not for the same year as the mileage. Tables of traffic per mile are given farther on. In the preceding table there are blanks as regards traffic for 5780 miles, or 1½ per cent. of the total. Allowing for these blanks, the whole railway business of the world is summed up as follows :—

	Miles	Cost, Millions £	Passengers Millions	Goods, Tons Millions	Receipts Millions £	Expenses Millions £	Net Millions £	Interest on Cost
Europe .	130,000	3,055	1,663	765	250	135	115	3.8
America .	191,010	2,348	507	619	219	153	66	2.8
Africa .	5,530	67	12	5	5	3	2	3.0
Asia . .	17,630	172	121	25	17	9	8	4.6
Australia .	10,140	94	81	17	8	5	3	3.3
The World	354,310	5,736	2,384	1,431	499	305	194	3.4

The total mileage and cost of construction for Europe and the world at various dates were approximately as follows :—

Year	Europe			The World		
	Miles	Millions £	£ per Mile	Miles	Millions £	£ per Mile
1840	1,679	52	30,900	4,515	71	15,800
1850	14,465	404	27,800	23,555	465	19,800
1860	31,885	797	25,000	66,290	1,079	16,300
1870	63,300	1,476	23,300	128,235	2,097	16,400
1880	101,720	2,411	23,700	228,440	3,938	17,200
1888	130,000	3,055	23,300	354,310	5,736	16,100

A French scientific journal in 1890 summed up existing railways thus :—

	Miles
Europe	135,200
Asia	17,900
Africa	5,300
Australia	10,500
America	191,200
Total . .	360,100

The amount of capital invested in railways at various dates was as follows :—

	Millions £ Sterling					
	1840	1850	1860	1870	1880	1888
United Kingdom	28	240	348	530	728	865
France . . .	11	57	171	274	392	570
Germany. . .	6	61	116	204	431	495
Russia . . .	...	5	17	119	234	314
Austria . . .	2	20	57	120	255	307
Italy . . .	...	5	22	75	105	138
Spain	...	1	19	51	72	94
Portugal . . .	...	...	...	7	11	19
Sweden . . .	...	...	2	7	23	28
Norway . . .	...	...	...	2	4	7
Denmark. . .	...	...	1	4	7	10
Holland . . .	...	2	4	13	25	35
Belgium . . .	5	13	26	43	58	71
Switzerland . .	...	...	13	18	32	37
Roumania, &c. .	...	...	1	9	34	65
Europe . . .	52	404	797	1,476	2,411	3,055
United States .	19	60	239	497	1,171	1,949
Canada . . .	...	1	25	30	84	151
Spanish America	...	...	4	25	81	228
Japan. . . .	...	...	...	...	1	11
India	...	...	8	46	88	145
Australia. . .	...	...	2	12	51	94
South Africa .	...	...	...	...	9	18
Algeria . . .	...	...	...	...	11	26
Egypt . . .	...	...	4	8	16	18
West Indies . .	...	...	...	1	8	16
Various . . .	...	...	...	2	7	25
The World .	71	465	1,079	2,097	3,938	5,736

The progress of railway construction is shown as follows :—

	Miles Built Yearly		Capital Sunk Yearly, £	
	1841–70	1871–88	1841–70	1871–88
U. Kingdom .	490	240	16,700,000	18,400,000
France . . .	310	610	8,800,000	16,300,000
Germany . .	380	700	6,600,000	16,100,000
Russia . . .	235	600	4,000,000	10,900,000
Austria . . .	196	530	4,000,000	10,500,000
Italy	130	220	2,500,000	3,500,000
Spain . . .	105	150	1,700,000	2,400,000
Portugal . .	15	40	250,000	650,000
Sweden . . .	36	200	250,000	1,200,000
Norway. . .	6	45	70,000	270,000
Denmark . .	16	42	130,000	330,000
Holland . . .	26	52	430,000	1,200,000
Belgium . .	53	54	1,300,000	1,500,000
Switzerland .	30	55	600,000	1,000,000
Roumania, &c.	18	166	300,000	3,100,000
Europe . . .	2,046	3,704	47,630,000	86,350,000
United States .	2,690	5,640	15,900,000	80,700,000
Canada . . .	83	560	1,000,000	6,800,000
Spanish America	74	1,030	800,000	11,300,000
Japan . . .	...	50	...	600,000
India . . .	160	570	1,500,000	5,500,000
Australia . .	41	484	400,000	4,550,000
South Africa .	...	111	...	1,000,000
Algeria . . .	...	102	...	1,500,000
Egypt . . .	18	40	270,000	550,000
West Indies .	3	65	30,000	900,000
Various . . .	7	105	70,000	1,400,000
Total .	5,022	12,461	67,600,000	201,150,000

The following table shows the average cost of construction per mile, and also the latest traffic returns per mile (mostly for 1887–88) :—

	Construction, £	Receipts, £	Expenses, £	Net, £	Number of Passengers	Tons of Goods	Working Expenses, Percentage	Interest on Capital
United Kingdom .	43,600	3,680	1,910	1,770	41,200	14,200	52	4.1
France .	27,000	2,110	1,090	1,020	11,000	4,000	52	3.8
Germany .	20,400	2,250	1,210	1,040	13,000	7,400	54	5.1
Russia .	17,700	1,380	790	590	2,100	2,700	57	3.3
Austria .	19,700	1,390	780	610	4,600	5,100	56	3.1
Italy .	17,800	1,290	850	440	6,200	2,100	65	2.5
Spain .	15,800	1,220	540	680	3,300	1,800	44	4.4
Portugal .	15,800	900	390	510	2,700	1,000	43	3.3
Sweden .	6,100	470	290	180	2,200	1,700	62	2.9
Norway .	7,100	430	300	130	3,400	1,200	70	1.8
Denmark .	8,000	700	600	100	7,800	2,700	86	1.2
Holland .	20,600	1,350	750	600	10,900	4,800	54	2.9
Belgium .	25,800	2,450	1,280	1,170	26,700	14,800	52	4.6
Switzerland .	20,500	1,780	940	840	14,500	4,600	53	4.1
Roumania, &c. .	15,700	1,080	650	430	...	...	60	2.7
Europe .	23,400	1,940	1,050	890	12,800	5,900	54	3.7
United States .	12,500	1,290	900	390	2,900	3,800	70	3.1
Canada .	11,900	700	490	210	900	1,400	70	1.7
Spanish America .	10,900	510	340	170	1,800	400	67	1.6
Japan .	12,400	660	280	380	13,200	1,100	43	3.1
India .	9,500	1,050	525	525	7,100	1,500	50	5.2
Australia .	9,300	820	510	310	8,100	1,700	63	3.3
South Africa .	8,900	800	420	380	1,500	500	52	4.3
Algeria .	14,000	730	510	220	2,200	1,100	70	1.6
Egypt .	14,100	1,050	480	570	3,200	800	46	4.1
The World .	16,100	1,350	830	520	6,600	3,800	62	3.2

English lines are the most costly, Swedish the cheapest, the difference being as 7 to 1. Only India and Germany earn over 5 per cent. on capital, the average for the world being 3¼ per cent. There are 13 countries earning over the average, and 11 less than the average.

The passenger and goods traffic at various dates were approximately as follows :—

	Millions of Passengers				Goods, Millions Tons			
	1860	1870	1882	1888	1860	1870	1882	1888
U. Kingdom .	180	363	721	816	82	170	256	282
France . . .	57	103	180	218	22	52	90	78
Germany . .	48	136	210	316	24	98	157	179
Russia . . .	5	14	38	38	3	8	35	50
Austria . . .	12	21	44	65	7	25	57	79
Italy	6	24	34	46	1	6	10	15
Spain & Portugal	5	10	17	18	2	4	7	9
Scandinavia .	1	8	15	22	...	5	8	12
Holland . . .	2	6	18	18	1	2	4	8
Belgium . . .	17	41	56	73	7	27	37	41
Switzerland .	6	15	22	27	1	4	6	9
Roumania, &c.	...	1	4	6	...	...	2	3
Europe . . .	339	742	1,359	1,663	150	401	669	765
United States .	60	110	375	451	70	150	361	590
Canada . . .	2	3	8	12	2	4	11	18
Spanish America	1	4	14	36	...	1	5	9
India	4	20	64	103	...	3	12	23
Australia . .	6	18	44	81	...	2	9	17
Various . . .	1	3	10	38	...	1	3	8
The World. .	413	900	1,874	2,384	222	562	1,070	1,430

The rates for passengers and goods in 1883 in various countries, according to the *Jour. des Economistes*, were :—

	Pence per Ten Miles			Ton Goods, per 100 Miles
	1st Class	2nd Class	3rd Class	
U. Kingdom	21	16	10	140
France . .	20	15	10	110
Germany .	15	11	8	82
Russia . .	18	14	8	120
Austria . .	19	14	9	115
Italy . . .	18	13	9	125
Spain . . .	21	16	10	...
Portugal . .	18	14	10	...
Sweden . .	15	11	8	160
Norway . .	8	5	2½	120
Denmark . .	16	11	8	144
Holland . .	16	13	8	78
Belgium . .	12	9	6	80
Switzerland .	19	13	10	165
Greece . .	14	9	7	...
Roumania .	36	14	10	78
Turkey . .	29	26	14	...

In the United States in 1888 the average compared with the rates on the Canadian Pacific line thus :—

	Pence per 100 Miles	
	Passenger	Ton Goods
United States . . .	112	52
Canada	90	51

The passenger rates are those of first class, and are lower than in Europe.

The speed on some of the principal railways is :—

	Miles	Hours	Minutes	Miles per Hour
London to Grantham	105	1	57	54
Paris to Poitiers . .	209	5	20	39
Berlin to Minden . .	202	5	35	37
Vienna to Pilsen . .	220	6	45	33
Rome to Pisa . . .	211	7	...	30
Madrid to Saragossa.	214	9	26	23
Lisbon to Oporto . .	212	11	...	19
N. York to Washington	230	5	18	44

The distribution of passengers in 1884 was as follows :—

	Percentage of Passengers			
	First	Second	Third	Total
England . . .	6	10	84	100
Scotland . . .	7	6	87	100
Ireland . . .	7	16	77	100
United Kingdom .	6	10	84	100
France . . .	7	34	59	100
Germany . . .	1	13	86	100
Russia . . .	2	9	89	100
Austria . . .	1	13	86	100
Italy	6	28	66	100
Sweden . . .	4	10	86	100
Norway . . .	...	8	92	100
Denmark . . .	1	14	85	100
Holland . . .	9	25	66	100
Belgium . . .	5	14	81	100
Switzerland . .	2	17	81	100
Roumania . . .	5	22	73	100
India	1	2	97	100

In European countries the highest ratio of first-class passengers is in Holland, of second class in France, and of third class in Norway.

The following table shows the earnings and expenses per mile run by locomotives in various countries in 1887-88 :—

	Miles Run	Pence per Mile Run			Miles Run per Locomotive
		Receipts	Expenses	Net	
United States . .	688,800,000	69	48	21	24,000
Germany	171,400,000	77	41	36	14,000
France	158,800,000	64	33	31	18,000
Italy	46,600,000	48	32	16	24,000
Austria	66,100,000	76	42	34	16,000
Switzerland	13,100,000	61	33	28	22,000
Sweden	10,500,000	48	30	18	15,000
Holland	15,500,000	37	21	16	26,000
Belgium	32,700,000	50	26	24	14,000

The mileage run by locomotives in the United States far exceeds the aggregate mileage for the Continent of Europe. The cost of running in the United States is higher per mile than in Europe.

An ordinary locomotive has 300 horse-power, and burns one ton of coke for 40 miles of goods train, or 80 miles of passenger train. The life of a locomotive is usually fifteen years, during which it will run 240,000 miles, and earn £60,000. The price is usually £2000 ; and according to *Engineering*, Europe could turn out 6400 locomotives yearly, viz., Great Britain, 2200 ; Germany, 2000 ; France, 1000 ; Belgium, 500 ; Austria, 400 ; and other countries, 300. Boesig's factory at Berlin could make 300 yearly. Each locomotive has 5416 pieces. The first in use from Liverpool to Manchester in 1830 was of 8 tons, and had a speed of 20 miles an hour. In 1872 the largest in the United Kingdom were of 27 tons, rising in 1889 to 45 tons.

There are many 60-ton locomotives in the United States, and some in Canada of 70 tons. The weight of an empty passenger train in England is : locomotive, 35 ; tender, 25 ; two trucks, 12 ; eight carriages, 64 ; in all, 136 tons. If there be 60 passengers, their weight will be 3 tons, against 136 tons dead-weight. The engine of an express train consumes 10 gallons of water per mile ; some of the American locomotives have tenders with a capacity of 3000 gallons.

Jeans's table of rolling-stock in 1885 compares with mileage and traffic as follows :—

	Locomotives, Number	Carriages, Number	Waggons, Number	Locomotives, per 100 Miles	Carriages, per Million Passengers	Tons of Goods Carried per Waggon
U. Kingdom	15,200	33,700	464,000	76	41	610
France . .	8,800	19,700	223,000	44	90	340
Germany .	12,200	22,200	250,000	50	71	720
Russia . .	5,800	7,000	116,000	33	180	440
Austria . .	4,200	8,200	96,000	27	126	820
Italy . . .	1,900	5,600	32,000	25	122	460
Spain . .	1,200	3,700	22,000	20	245	360
Scandinavia	1,000	2,600	23,000	15	123	510
Holland .	600	1,600	8,000	35	90	1,000
Belgium .	2,300	5,000	56,000	84	68	740
Switzerland	600	1,800	9,000	33	67	1,000
Rouma-nia, &c. }	2,700	5,400	61,000	72	...	...
Europe . .	56,500	116,500	1,360,000	44	70	560
U. States .	28,600	18,000	804,000	18	40	740
Canada . .	1,500	1,300	38,000	12	105	480
Spanish America }	3,000	1,800	82,000	14	55	...
Australia .	2,300	2,100	69,000	23	26	250
India . .	3,000	1,900	82,000	20	18	270
Various . .	4,100	8,400	75,000	44	...	...
Total .	99,000	150,000	2,510,000	28	63	570

A French scientific journal in 1890 states that Europe has 61,000 locomotives, and the rest of the world 43,000, making a total of 104,000; it adds that England has 80 per 100 miles of railway, Germany 53, and France 47.

The increase of rolling-stock in ten years was very great :—

	Europe		The World	
	1875	1885	1875	1885
Locomotives	42,000	56,500	62,000	99,000
Carriages .	90,000	116,500	112,000	150,000
Waggons .	1,000,000	1,360,000	1,470,000	2,510,000

Jeans adds that the above rolling-stock in 1875 carried 1371 million passengers and 715 million tons of goods.

The following table shows the steepest gradients in some of the most difficult railways :—

		Per Cent.				Per Cent.
Mont Cenis	.	3.0	Oroya	.	.	6.0
Genoa-Turin	.	3.5	Utliberg	.	.	7.0
Darjeeling	.	4.0	Cantagallo	.	.	9.5
Tiflis	.	4.5	Righi	.	.	28.0
Einsiedlen	.	5.0	Vesuvius	.	.	63.0

The Righi is in one part as steep as a staircase, the Vesuvius as a ladder. Resistance increases with gradient, and if the normal figure be adopted of 8 lbs. per ton on level way, the resistance at various gradients will be :—

Gradient	Lbs. per Ton	Gradient	Lbs. per Ton
1 in 100 .	. 15	5 in 100 .	. 45
3 ,, .	. 30	10 ,, .	. 83

Resistance likewise increases with speed as follows, on level way :—

Miles per Hour	Lbs. per Ton	Miles per Hour	Lbs. per Ton
10	. . 8	40	. . 26
20	. . 14	50	. . 33
30	. . 17	60	. . 51

The resistance on a railway is only one-third of what it is on an ordinary highroad.

The standard gauge of the world may be said to be 4 ft. 8½ inches. In 1885 the lines were summed up thus :—

Gauge	Miles	Ratio
4 ft. 8½ in. . . .	224,000	74.0
Under 4 ft. 8½ in. . .	42,400	14.0
Over 4 ft. 8½ in. . .	36,600	12.0
Total .	303,000	100.0

Steel rails average 130 tons per mile of way, iron 145 tons. The consumption of iron and steel for railways has been approximately as follows :—

Period	Europe, Tons	The World, Tons
1825–40 . . .	400,000	800,000
1841–60 . . .	8,500,000	12,500,000
1861–70 . . .	10,100,000	14,000,000
1871–80 . . .	13,200,000	23,400,000
1881–88 . . .	12,800,000	32,300,000
Total .	45,000,000	83,000,000

The weight of rail in England varies from 28 to 76 lbs. per yard. In 1882 the tonnage of rails in various countries was as follows (an estimate for 1888 is added) :—

	Tons of Rails			Tons per Mile of Rail	Tons Estimate in 1888
	Iron	Steel	Total		
United Kingdom	1,980,000	2,410,000	4,390,000	240	4,750,000
France	1,570,000	1,715,000	3,285,000	202	4,000,000
Germany.	2,550,000	1,570,000	4,120,000	195	4,650,000
Russia	820,000	920,000	1,740,000	126	2,200,000
Austria	930,000	700,000	1,630,000	128	2,100,000
Belgium	265,000	255,000	520,000	210	600,000
Various	2,215,000	1,620,000	3,835,000	150	4,400,000
Europe	10,330,000	9,190,000	19,520,000	182	22,700,000
United States . . .	7,200,000	5,200,000	12,400,000	118	18,600,000
Colonies, &c. . .	3,200,000	3,100,000	6,300,000	110	7,800,000
Total . .	20,730,000	17,490,000	38,220,000	152	49,100,000

The railways of greatest elevation are the following :—

Line	Over the	Feet Over Sea-Level	Date of Construction
Semmering . . .	Alps	2,970	1854
Santos—San Paulo	Serra Cubaton .	3,500	1866
St. Gothard . . .	Alps	3,780	1882
Mont Cenis . . .	Alps	4,290	1871
Aarlberg	Alps	4,320	1884
Bremer	Alps	4,450	1867
Union Pacific . .	Rocky Mountns.	8,573	1869
Uspallata . . .	Andes	10,570	1890
Mollendo . . .	Andes	14,610	1878
Lima-Oroya . .	Andes	15,840	1874

All the above are working except Clark's line over the Uspallata Pass, which will establish direct transit from Buenos Ayres to Valparaiso, and approaches completion. The Union Pacific has a length of 1780 miles, of which 300 are through mountains. The cost was £38,800,000, including a subsidy of £11,000,000 from Congress : it was begun in 1862, and the first train ran from Chicago on May 1, 1869, for the terminus on the Pacific at San Francisco. The company received, moreover, a grant of 34,000 square miles of land, or 23 million acres, in alternate lots 20 miles deep on either side of the line. The cost of construction was £22,000 per mile, varying from £11,000 in level country to £36,000 a mile in the Rocky Mountains.

The saving which railways have effected for the public welfare in the matter of freight charges has been computed in different countries. In Prussia, in 1878, it was estimated at £6300 a mile for goods and passengers ; in Great Britain, in 1848, at £1500 for passengers only. It may be roughly estimated that railways as a rule have caused a saving to the public of each country equal to at least 10 per cent. per annum on the cost of construction.

The following table, according to latest returns, shows the number of persons killed or wounded by railways :—

	Killed			Wounded			Killed or Wounded	Per Million Passengers
	Passengers	Others	Total	Passengers	Others	Total		
United Kingdom	183	956	1,139	1,829	2,944	4,773	5,912	7.2
France	39	336	375	131	498	629	1,004	4.6
Germany	27	436	463	107	1,227	1,334	1,797	5.7
Russia	19	425	444	88	609	697	1,141	30.0
Austria	5	241	246	16	569	585	831	13.0
Italy	5	116	121	62	1,109	1,171	1,292	28.0
Spain	22	80	102	130	124	254	356	24.0
Portugal	1	7	8	7	16	23	31	10.3
Sweden	3	26	29	...	42	42	71	7.1
Norway	...	8	8	...	1	1	9	3.0
Denmark	...	...	11	...	...	56	67	7.4
Holland	4	37	41	4	31	35	76	4.2
Belgium	7	145	152	60	640	700	852	11.6
Switzerland . . .	8	34	42	6	194	200	242	9.0
Europe	323	2,847	3,181	2,440	8,004	10,500	13,681	8.2

The railways of the United Kingdom pay £1400 a day compensation, of which 60 per cent. for damage to passengers, 40 per cent. to goods. In other countries the amount is unknown.

UNITED KINGDOM

The first regular railway for carrying passengers was opened from Stockton to Darlington, 27th September 1825.

The following table shows the development of railways :—

Year	Miles Open	Cost, £	Receipts, £	Expenses, £	Passengers Carried
1843	1,950	65,500,000	4,540,000	...	...
1846	3,040	126,300,000	7,570,000	...	43,800,000
1850	6,620	240,300,000	13,200,000	...	72,900,000
1855	8,280	297,600,000	21,500,000	10,300,000	118,600,000
1860	10,430	348,100,000	27,800,000	13,200,000	163,500,000
1870	15,540	529,900,000	43,400,000	21,700,000	330,200,000
1880	17,930	728,300,000	63,000,000	33,600,000	603,900,000
1888	19,810	864,700,000	72,900,000	37,800,000	742,500,000

Holders of season-tickets are not counted ; add 10 per cent. for them.

The earnings and expenditure of thirty-four years are summed up thus :—

Period	Earnings, Millions £			Expenses, Millions £	Net Revenue, Millions £
	Passengers	Goods, &c.	Total		
1855–59 .	58	61	119	64	55
1860–69 .	159	185	344	169	175
1870–79 .	242	312	554	275	279
1880–88 .	265	336	601	302	299
34 years .	724	894	1618	810	808

In the first period, ending 1859, the passenger earnings were 49 per cent. of the total ; in the second, ending 1869, they fell to 46 per cent. ; in the third, ending 1879, to 44 per cent. ; and in the fourth, ending 1888, they were likewise 44 per cent.

The mileage and traffic of the three kingdoms showed as follows :—

	Miles		Cost, £		Receipts, £ per Mile		Expenses, £ per Mile	
	1860	1888	1860	1888	1860	1888	1860	1888
England	7,580	13,980	289,000,000	714,000,000	3,090	4,430	1,490	2,310
Scotland	1,490	3,100	39,000,000	114,100,000	1,990	2,580	905	1,240
Ireland	1,360	2,730	20,100,000	36,600,000	1,030	1,060	440	560
United Kingdom .	10,430	19,810	348,100,000	864,700,000	2,670	3,680	1,270	1,910

The following table (allowing mean average for missing years) shows the traffic during the same period, adding 10 per cent. for holders of season-tickets to the number of passengers :—

Period	Passengers, Millions	Goods, Millions Tons	Earnings, Pence Per Passenger	Earnings, Pence Per Ton
1855–59 . .	740	348	18	42
1860–69 . .	2,620	1,160	15	38
1870–79 . .	5,270	1,923	11	39
1880–88 . .	6,780	2,328	9	35
34 years . .	15,410	5,759	11	37

The aggregate traffic for ten years ending December 1888 showed the three kingdoms as follows :—

	Mean Capital, Millions £	Mean Miles	Passengers, Millions Carried	Goods, Millions Tons	Ten Years, Millions £ Earnings	Ten Years, Millions £ Expenses	Ten Years, Millions £ Profit
England . . .	660	13,300	6,580	2,165	588	308	280
Scotland . . .	101	3,000	601	344	75	38	37
Ireland . . .	35	2,500	205	37	27	15	12
U. Kingdom .	796	18,800	7,386	2,546	690	361	329

From the above we derive the following averages :—

	Cost per Mile, £	Yearly Traffic per Mile Passengers	Yearly Traffic per Mile Goods, Tons	Annual Mileage Earnings, £	Annual Mileage Expenses, £	Annual Mileage Profit, £	Interest on Capital per Cent.
England	49,600	49,400	16,200	4,410	2,310	2,100	4.2
Scotland	33,700	20,000	11,500	2,500	1,270	1,230	3.7
Ireland	14,000	8,200	1,500	1,080	600	480	3.4
United Kingdom .	42,200	39,300	13,500	3,670	1,920	1,750	4.1

The cost, traffic, and mileage earnings for the whole United Kingdom at various dates showed thus :—

Year	Cost, £	Passengers	Tons, Goods	Receipts, £	Expenses, £	Profit, £	Interest on Capital per Cent.
1855	35,900	15,700	...	2,590	1,240	1,350	3.7
1860	33,400	17,300	8,500	2,670	1,270	1,400	4.2
1870	34,200	23,400	10,300	2,800	1,400	1,400	4.1
1880	40,700	37,100	13,100	3,520	1,880	1,640	4.0
1888	43,600	41,200	14,200	3,680	1,910	1,770	4.1

The goods traffic returns for 1870 were lost : the above mileage is the medium between the preceding and succeeding years. The number of passengers killed or injured at various dates in the United Kingdom was as follows :—

Year	Passengers Carried	Killed or Injured	Per Million
1846 . . .	48,200,000	151	3.2
1855 . . .	130,400,000	321	2.5
1864 . . .	252,000,000	711	2.8
1873 . . .	501,000,000	1,542	3.1
1888 . . .	816,000,000	1,515	1.9

In the above table 10 per cent. for season-ticket holders is added. The number of killed or injured on railways, including servants and trespassers, is much greater than that given above, which applies only to passengers. The last four years show thus :—

Year	Killed	Injured	Total
1886	938	3,539	4,477
1887	919	3,590	4,509
1888	905	3,826	4,731
1889	1,076	4,836	5,912

The returns for 1889 were made up thus :—

	Killed	Injured	Total
Passengers . . .	183	1,829	2,012
Railway servants . .	435	2,769	3,204
Trespassers . . .	351	122	473
Various . . .	170	53	223
Total . .	1,139	4,773	5,912

The block system, which is considered a safeguard against collisions, is used as follows :—

	Miles	Ratio of Total
England	12,160	94 per cent.
Scotland	2,310	82 ,,
Ireland	570	21 ,,
United Kingdom . .	15,040	76 ,,

The number of passengers by the several classes in the United Kingdom were as follows in 1889 :—

Class	Number	Ratio
1st	30,100,000	3.9
2nd	62,700,000	8.1
3rd	682,400,000	88.0
Total .	775,200,000	100.0

The above, however, counts 1,271,000 season-ticket holders for only one journey each, whereas it is believed they should stand for 77,500,000, or 10 per cent. extra added to the traffic. Dividing them evenly between 1st and 2nd class (by which such subscribers usually travel) the result is as follows :—

Class	Number	Ratio
1st	69,000,000	8.1
2nd	101,500,000	11.9
3rd	682,500,000	80.0
Total .	853,000,000	100.0

The above estimate, as already stated, allows for holders of season-tickets sixty journeys yearly, which is, doubtless, below the reality.

FRANCE

The length of lines at various dates was as follows :—

	Miles					
	1841	1850	1860	1870	1880	1888
State	...	...	...	...	1,400	1,550
Companies	360	1,890	5,880	9,770	14,880	19,210
Total .	360	1,890	5,880	9,770	16,280	20,760

The first line was opened to traffic in 1828, the first Government line constructed in 1878. In the following returns of traffic since 1841 the number of miles working in 1880 appears to have been less than that of lines completed.

Year	Miles	Passengers	Goods, Tons	Average per Mile	
				Passengers	Goods
1841	360	6,400,000	1,100,000	17,500	3,000
1850	1,890	18,700,000	4.300,000	9,900	2,300
1860	5,880	56,500,000	23,000,000	9,600	4,000
1870	9,770	102,600,000	37,100,000	10,500	3,800
1880	14,500	165,000,000	80,800,000	11,400	5,500
1887	19,700	218,400,000	78,100,000	11,000	4,000

The mileage statistics were as follows :—

Year	Per Mile			Pence, per Mile		Per-centage of Ex-penses
	Earn-ings, £	Ex-penses, £	Profit, £	Pas-senger	Ton, Goods	
1843	1,810	970	840	1.08	1.71	53.6
1850	2,080	990	1,090	1.01	1.56	47.6
1860	2,890	1,300	1,590	0.90	1.10	45.0
1870	2,550	1,230	1,320	0.78	0.97	48.2
1880	2,830	1,410	1,420	0.80	0.95	49.8
1887	2,110	1,090	1,020	0.70	0.95	51.6

Counting the goods traffic by kilometric tons, that is, the number of tons carried one kilometer, and reducing it to English form by the number of tons carried 100 miles, we find as follows :—

Year	Millions of Kilometric Tons	Tons Carried 100 Miles
1843	59	378,000
1850	314	1,980,000
1860	3,119	19,700,000
1870	5,057	31,900,000
1880	10,350	65,200,000
1885	9,790	61,700,000

As the actual number of tons carried in 1885 was 75,200,000, it appears that the average haulage of each ton of goods was 83 miles, against 80 miles in 1880. Passenger traffic in 1885 showed as follows :—

Class	Number	Ratio
1st . . .	16,200,000	7.5
2nd . . .	73,000,000	34.0
3rd . . .	125,200,000	58.0
Total .	214,400,000	100.0

When railways were first made, in 1845, the cost of construction averaged thus per mile :—

	£	Ratio
Land . . .	2,540	8.0
Earthworks . .	11,430	36.0
Rails, engines, cars .	12,700	40.0
Stations, &c. . .	5,080	16.0
Total .	31,750	100.0

Subsequently, however, the cost diminished (being the reverse of what occurred in England), and the average

on 31st December 1885 for all railways then running in France was exactly £27,000 per mile. The number of railway servants at that date was 232,000. The following table shows approximately the number of passengers and that of tons of goods carried from 1841 to 1887 :—

Period	Millions	
	Passengers	Tons
1841–49	90	18
1850–59	320	110
1860–69	810	330
1870–79	1,320	560
1880–87	1,608	650
47 years . . .	4,148	1,668

The earnings and expenses in thirty-nine years were approximately as follows :—

Period	Earnings, Millions £	Expenses, Millions £	Profit, Millions £
1850–59 . .	97	45	52
1860–69 . .	211	98	113
1870–79 . .	327	161	166
1880–88 . .	374	194	180
39 years . .	1,009	498	511

GERMANY

The statistics for Prussia and other States show thus :—

Year	Miles Open						
	Prussia	Bavaria	Saxony	Wur-temberg	Baden	Various	Total
1840	106	42	79	...	16	98	341
1850	1,770	370	290	160	170	880	3,640
1860	3,450	1,130	470	210	220	1,500	6,980
1870	6,860	1,690	710	650	600	1,220	11,730
1880	12,640	3,000	1,300	840	820	2,090	20,690
1888	15,255	3,320	1,585	985	860	2,265	24,270

Hanoverian railways, which were included in the column "Various" down to 1860, were amalgamated with those of Prussia after the conquest in 1866. The returns for the whole German Empire show :—

Year	Miles Open	Cost, Mil-lions £	Receipts, £	Expenses, £	Profit, £	Interest on Capital, Per Cent.
1868	10,600	169	22,300,000	11,200,000	11,100,000	6.5
1870	11,730	204	25,300,000	12,800,000	12,500,000	6.1
1880	20,690	431	43,300,000	25,200,000	18,100,000	4.2
1888	24,270	495	54,600,000	29,300,000	25,300,000	5.1

The traffic and rolling-stock are shown below, kilo-metric passengers and tons being reduced to English form as passengers travelling 10 miles, goods 100 miles average.

Year	Kilometric, Millions		Millions of Passengers, 10 Miles	Millions of Tons, 100 Miles	Locomotives	Cars	Waggons
	Pas-sengers	Goods, Tons					
1868	3,213	5,042	203	32	4,640	8,920	98,440
1870	4,372	5,336	275	34	5,460	10,430	113,500
1875	5,994	10,392	378	66	9,940	17,520	206,000
1880	6,149	12,224	389	77	10,840	19,800	220,000
1887	8,385	16,516	527	104	12,750	23,440	256,000

The value of rolling-stock in 1887 was £75,800,000 ; it had a capacity for carrying 1,020,000 passengers, and 2,750,000 tons of merchandise.

Prussian railways showed as follows from 1844 to 1878 :—

Year	Kilometric Millions		Passengers, 10 Miles	Tons, 100 Miles
	Passengers	Goods, Tons		
1844. .	130	20	8,000,000	130,000
1850. .	420	190	26,000,000	1,200,000
1860. .	870	926	55,000,000	5,830,000
1870. .	3,020	4,044	196,000,000	25,700,000
1878. .	3,740	8,033	235,000,000	50,600,000

The total carried in thirty-five years was as follows :—

Period	Kilometric Millions		Millions of Passengers, 10 Miles	Millions of Tons, 100 Miles
	Passengers	Goods, Tons		
1844–50	1,730	611	109	4
1851–60	6,100	6,297	384	40
1861–70	16,530	24,412	1,040	153
1871–78	28,710	55,767	1,810	351
35 years	53,070	87,087	3,343	548

In 1879 the following statement was published, showing the saving of freight charges and passengers fares effected by the railways of Prussia in the above period, estimating the old charges at 27 silbergroschen for a ton of goods carried 10 kilometers, and a passenger at 40 silbergroschen the same distance :—

Period	Waggon Fares, Millions £			Railway Fares, Millions £			Saving, Millions £
	Goods	Passengers	Total	Goods	Passengers	Total	
1844–50	8	5	13	3	4	7	6
1851–60	84	16	100	25	14	39	61
1861–70	326	44	370	71	31	102	268
1871–78	744	77	821	136	52	188	633
35 years	1,162	142	1,304	235	101	336	968

Traffic returns for Russia showed as follows :—

Year	Miles	Passengers	Goods, Tons	Receipts, £	Expenses, £	Net, £
1870 . . .	7,100	14,400,000	7,700,000	...	...	...
1880 . . .	14,020	33,700,000	37,500,000	19,300,000	15,200,000	4,100,000
1887 . . .	18,380	38,200,000	50,400,000	25,300,000	14,400,000	10,900,000

	Per Mile		
	1870	1880	1887
Passengers . . .	2,030	2,400	2,080
Goods, tons . . .	1,090	2,690	2,740
Receipts, £ . . .	...	1,380	1,380
Expenses, £ . . .	...	1,090	790
Net, £	...	290	590

The total mileage in 1887 was made up thus :—

					Miles
European Russia	.	.	.	.	16,760
Finland	.	.	.	.	960
Central Asia	.	.	.	.	660
		Total	.	.	18,380

At that time (1878) the cost of construction had reached 240 millions sterling ; the saving which the railways effected to the benefit of the Prussian people was therefore four times what the lines had cost to make. If it be supposed that the traffic per mile on the other German lines was the same as on the Prussian, the business of all Germany since 1844 would be approximately as follows :—

Period	Millions of Passengers, 10 Miles	Millions of Tons Goods, 100 Miles	Receipts, Millions £	Expenses, Millions £	Net Earnings, Millions £
1844–50 . .	229	9	15	...	...
1851–60 . .	776	82	80	...	...
1861–70 . .	1,890	281	186	...	...
1871–80 . .	3,720	726	398	236	162
1881–87 . .	3,220	630	341	193	148
44 years . .	9,835	1,728	1,020	...	...

The distinction between State and Companies' lines is shown as follows in English miles :—

	State		Companies		Total	
	1875	1888	1875	1888	1875	1888
Prussia . .	4,280	14,120	5,590	1,135	9,870	15,255
Bavaria . .	1,580	2,890	880	430	2,460	3,320
Saxony . .	740	1,520	360	65	1,100	1,585
Wurtemberg	790	970	10	15	800	985
Baden . .	650	800	60	60	710	860
Hesse, &c. .	590	800	1,490	1,465	2,080	2,265
Total .	8,630	21,100	8,390	3,070	17,020	24,270

The total mileage in 1889 was 25,450, representing a cost of about 527 millions sterling. Railway employees numbered 343,000.

RUSSIA

The first line, 16 miles, was opened from St. Petersburg to Charsko-Selo in 1837, the second in 1844, the mileage increasing as follows :—

Year				Miles	Year				Miles
1840	.	.	.	16	1870	.	.	.	7,100
1850	.	.	.	310	1880	.	.	.	14,020
1860	.	.	.	990	1887	.	.	.	18,380

The respective mileages of Government lines and those belonging to companies are shown thus :—

				1870	1886
Government	.	.	.	730	2,250
Companies	.	.	.	6,370	14,000
		Total	.	7,100	16,250

All the companies' lines enjoy concessions or guarantees. The rolling-stock in 1884 comprised 5810 locomotives and 121,000 carriages and waggons. In the same year there were 420 persons killed and 654 injured, of whom passengers were 25 and 85 respectively.

AUSTRIA

Official tables give the following mileage :—

Year	Austria	Hungary	Total	State Lines	Companies' Lines
1840 . .	90	...	90	...	90
1850 . .	820	140	960	640	320
1860 . .	1,810	1,000	2,810	...	2,810
1870 . .	3,790	2,160	5,950	230	5,720
1880 . .	7,080	4,420	11,500	2,240	9,260
1888 . .	9,260	6,350	15,610	7,020	8,590

In the last-mentioned year 340 miles of Bosnian lines are counted as Austrian. The traffic for the whole Empire at various dates was as follows :—

Year	Passengers	Goods, Tons	Receipts, £	Per Mile Passengers	Tons
1863	15,000,000		7,400,000	4,700	...
1870	21,500,000	24,500,000	13,200,000	3,600	4,100
1880	40,500,000	54,400,000	21,100,000	3,500	4,700
1887	65,400,000	78,600,000	20,800,000	4,600	5,100

The receipts in 1889 rose to £23,300,000, being at the rate of £1500 a mile. Capital, earnings, and expenditure at various dates compare as follows :—

Year	Miles	Cost, Millions £	Per Mile, £ Cost	Earnings	Expense	Net
1870	5,950	120	20,200	2,220	1,280	940
1880	11,500	255	22,200	1,840	1,470	370
1887	15,050	298	19,800	1,390	780	610

Traffic returns on the railways of Italy at various dates compare as follows :—

Year	Miles	Passengers	Goods, Tons	Receipts, £	Expenses, £	Net, £
1875	4,770	28,000,000	7,200,000	5,800,000	3,900,000	1,900,000
1880	5,340	32,500,000	9,300,000	7,200,000	4,300,000	2,900,000
1887	7,330	45,500,000	15,400,000	9,400,000	6,200,000	3,200,000

Averages per mile were as follows :—

Year	Construction, £	Passengers	Goods, Tons	Receipts, £	Expenses, £	Net, £
1875	19,300	5,900	1,500	1,220	820	400
1880	19,600	6,100	1,700	1,350	800	550
1887	17,800	6,200	2,100	1,290	850	440

Returns on capital showed as follows :—

Year	Cost, Millions £	Net Earnings, £	Percentage
1875 . . .	92	1,900,000	2.1
1880 . . .	105	2,900,000	2.8
1887 . . .	122	3,200,000	2.6

Passenger and goods traffic showed the following earnings :—

Year	Passengers, £	Goods, £	Pence Per Passenger	Per Ton
1875 . . .	2,700,000	3,100,000	23	103
1880 . . .	3,000,000	4,200,000	22	108
1887 . . .	3,800,000	5,600,000	20	87

The net return on capital invested was as follows :—

Year	Cost, £	Net Earnings, £	Percentage
1870 . . .	120,000,000	5,600,000	4.7
1880 . . .	255,000,000	4,200,000	1.6
1887 . . .	298,000,000	9,100,000	3.1

Excluding 340 miles of Bosnian lines, the mileage in 1888 was made up thus :—

	Austria	Hungary	Total
State lines . . .	3,650	3,370	7,020
Company lines . .	5,270	2,980	8,250
Total . .	8,920	6,350	15,270

ITALY

The official returns of mileage show thus :—

Year	Miles	Year	Miles
1840 . . .	13	1870	3,830
1850 . . .	270	1880	5,340
1860 . . .	1,120	1889	8,130

The mileage of State lines and those of companies' lines were as follows :—

	1870	1880	1887
State	500	2,380	5,030
Companies . . .	3,330	2,960	2,300
Total . .	3,830	5,340	7,330

SPAIN

In 1848 the first railway was opened from Barcelona to Mataró, 18 miles. Progress is shown as follows :—

Year	Miles	Year	Miles
1848 . . .	18	1870 . . .	3,200
1855 . . .	300	1880 . . .	4,550
1860 . . .	1,190	1888 . . .	5,920

Traffic and earnings were as follows :—

Year	Miles	Passengers	Goods, Tons	Receipts, £	Expenses, £
1873	3,310	10,800,000	3,900,000	3,530,000	...
1880	4,550	14,800,000	8,100,000	5,570,000	2,450,000

Averages per mile were as follows :—

	Construction, £	Passengers	Goods, Tons	Receipts, £	Expenses, £
1873	...	3,300	1,200	1,070	...
1880	15,800	3,300	1,800	1,220	540

The cost of construction down to 1880 was officially stated thus :—

State subsidies	£28,000,000
Outlay by companies . .	44,000,000
Total . . .	£72,000,000

If the existing lines in 1888 be taken at the same mileage cost, they will represent an outlay of £98,700,000. The ratio of working expenses is the lowest in the world, only 43 per cent. of earnings. The net earnings in 1880 were about 4½ per cent. (4.4) on the cost of construction. Later information is wanting. All the lines in Spain are owned by companies.

PORTUGAL

The first line was in 1854, from Lisbon to Carregado, twenty-two miles. Official returns of mileage are as follows :—

Year	Miles	Year	Miles
1855	22	1875	640
1860	42	1880	710
1870	440	1888	1190

The official returns for 1881 and 1885 showed thus :—

Year	Miles	Passengers	Goods, Tons	Receipts, £	Expenses, £
1881	760	2,200,000	740,000	750,000	310,000
1885	950	2,600,000	960,000	860,000	370,000

Averages per mile were as follows :—

Year	Passengers	Goods, Tons	Receipts, £	Expenses, £	Net, £
1881	2,900	970	990	410	580
1885	2,700	1,010	900	390	510

If we suppose the cost of construction (which is unknown) to have been the same as in Spain, say £15,800 per mile, the cost and net percentage on capital of Portuguese lines will have been thus :—

Year	Cost, £	Net Earnings, £	Percentage
1881	12,600,000	440,000	3.5
1885	15,800,000	490,000	3.1

The receipts in 1885 were as follows :—

	£	Average Pence
Passengers	360,000	34 each
Goods	500,000	125 per ton
Total	860,000	...

The average fare for each passenger and ton of goods carried is much higher than in other countries. The lines belong to companies which receive State subsidies.

SWEDEN

Official statement of mileage is as follows :—

Year	State	Companies	Total
1860	187	188	375
1870	700	390	1,090
1880	1,210	2,440	3,650
1888	1,580	3,120	4,700

Traffic returns on the railways of Sweden were as follows :—

Year	Miles	Passengers	Goods, Tons	Receipts, £	Expenses, £	Net, £
1875	2,170	6,500,000	5,100,000	1,390,000	870,000	520,000
1880	3,650	7,000,000	5,900,000	1,800,000	1,000,000	800,000
1887	4,580	10,100,000	7,600,000	2,090,000	1,310,000	780,000

Averages per mile were as follows :—

Year	Construction, £	Passengers	Goods, Tons	Receipts, £	Expenses, £
1875	6,300	3,000	2,400	640	400
1880	6,400	1,900	1,600	500	270
1887	6,100	2,200	1,700	470	290

Earnings showed the following returns for capital :—

Year	Cost, £	Net Receipts, £	Percentage
1875	13,800,000	520,000	3.8
1880	23,300,000	800,000	3.4
1887	27,900,000	800,000	2.8

Mileage and traffic of Swedish railways in 1887 were made up thus :—

	Miles	Passengers	Goods, Tons	Receipts, £	Expenses, £	Net, £
State	1,550	4,000,000	2,500,000	1,030,000	730,000	300,000
Companies	3,030	6,100,000	5,100,000	1,060,000	580,000	480,000
Total	4,580	10,100,000	7,600,000	2,090,000	1,310,000	780,000

The average percentage which net earnings gave on capital during five years ending 1886 was as follows :—

State lines 3.3
Company lines 4.1

The average cost of construction down to 1886 was £8690 per mile on Government lines and £4700 on companies' lines.

NORWAY

The first line was opened in 1855, and the miles open since have been as follows :—

Year	State	Companies	Total
1860	...	42	42
1870	182	42	224
1880	650	42	692
1889	973	42	1015

Traffic returns in Norway showed as follows :—

Year	Miles	Passengers	Goods, Tons	Receipts, £	Expenses, £	Net, £
1872	256	840,000	540,000	130,000	85,000	45,000
1880	690	1,650,000	600,000	240,000	180,000	60,000
1888	970	3,300,000	1,200,000	420,000	290,000	130,000

Net returns compared with cost of construction as follows :—

Year	Cost, £	Net Earnings	Percentage
1872	2,000,000	45,000	2.3
1880	4,450,000	60,000	1.4
1888	7,100,000	130,000	1.8

Averages per mile in Norway were as follows :—

Year	Construc- tion, £	Passen- gers	Goods, Tons	Receipts, £	Expenses, £	Net, £
1872	7,800	3,300	2,100	510	340	170
1880	6,400	2,400	900	340	250	90
1888	7,100	3,400	1,200	430	300	130

All are State railways except a short line of forty-two miles.

DENMARK

The number of miles open was as follows :—

Year	State	Companies	Total
1850 . . .	...	20	20
1860 . . .	...	70	70
1870 . . .	300	170	470
1880 . . .	770	210	980
1888 . . .	970	250	1,220

Traffic returns were as follows :—

Year	Miles	Pas- sengers	Goods, Tons	Receipts, £	Ex- penses, £	Net, £
1875	780	5,600,000	1,800,000	560,000	340,000	220,000
1880	830	5,900,000	2,000,000	590,000	370,000	220,000
1888	1,220	8,800,000	2,900,000	780,000	680,000	100,000

The returns of traffic are exclusive of 100 miles of company's line in Jutland. The mileage traffic on Danish railways showed thus :—

Year	Per Mile				
	Pas- sengers	Goods, Tons	Receipts, £	Ex- penses, £	Net, £
1875 . . .	7,200	2,300	720	430	290
1880 . . .	7,100	2,400	710	445	265
1888 . . .	7,900	2,700	700	600	100

In 1889 the State lines had a length of 1000 miles, having cost exactly eight millions sterling. At this rate the total outlay on the existing 1210 miles would be £9,700,000. The net earnings in 1888 being £100 per mile, would represent only 1¼ per cent. on the cost of construction, against 3.7 in 1875 and 3.3 in 1880.

HOLLAND

The first line was opened in 1839. Government lines were not begun until 1863. The mileage grew thus :—

Year	State	Companies	Total
1840 . . .	...	11	11
1850 . . .	...	110	110
1860 . . .	...	200	200
1870 . . .	500	280	780
1880 . . .	670	770	1,440
1888 . . .	930	770	1,700

Traffic returns on railways in Holland were as follows :—

Year	Miles	Passengers	Goods, Tons	Receipts, £	Expenses, £	Net, £
1873 . . .	830	9,300,000	1,700,000	1,130,000	880,000	250,000
1880 . . .	1,440	16,000,000	4,400,000	1,860,000	930,000	930,000
1888 . . .	1,700	18,500,000	8,100,000	2,290,000	1,280,000	1,010,000

In 1888 the traffic was as follows :—

	Miles	Passengers	Goods, Tons	Receipts, £	Expenses, £	Net, £
State . . .	930	5,900,000	4,600,000	1,120,000	640,000	480,000
Companies . .	770	12,600,000	3,500,000	1,170,000	640,000	530,000
Total . .	1,700	18,500,000	8,100,000	2,290,000	1,280,000	1,010,000

The averages per mile were as follows :—

Year	Pas- sengers	Goods, Tons	Re- ceipts, £	Ex- penses, £	Net, £
1873 . . .	11,200	2,050	1,360	1,050	310
1880 . . .	11,100	3,050	1,300	650	650
1888 . . .	10,900	4,800	1,350	750	600

The return on capital was as follows in 1885 :—

	Construction, £	Net Earnings, £	Percentage
State . . .	15,900,000	390,000	2.5
Companies .	10,400,000	520,000	5.0

In four years ending 1886 the average was 36 persons killed and 35 injured, but of passengers only 1 killed and 4 injured per annum.

BELGIUM

A line from Brussels to Malines, opened in 1835, was the first of any importance on the European Continent, although the Lyons and St. Etienne preceded it by seven years. The growth of mileage is shown as follows :—

Year	State	Companies	Total
1840 . . .	210	...	210
1850 . . .	390	160	550
1860 . . .	460	610	1,070
1870 . . .	540	1,260	1,800
1880 . . .	1,730	670	2,400
1888 . . .	1,990	770	2,760

The balance-sheet of the State lines was :—

Period	Receipts, £	Expenses, £	Profit, £
1835–60 . . .	14,700,000	8,200,000	6,500,000
1861–70 . . .	15,400,000	8,200,000	7,200,000
1871–80 . . .	35,600,000	22,300,000	13,300,000
1881–87 . . .	33,400,000	19,800,000	13,600,000
53 years. . . .	99,100,000	58,500,000	40,600,000

The number of passengers on all lines carried, and that of those killed, were :—

	1835–87.		
Period	Number	Killed	One in
1835–50 . . .	45,000,000	15	3,000,000
1851–70 . . .	232,000,000	34	6,600,000
1871–80 . . .	465,000,000	77	6,100,000
1881–87 . . .	445,000,000	60	7,400,000

The return on capital of Belgian lines in 1888 was :—

	Cost, £	Net Product, £	Percentage
State . . .	55,300,000	2,460,000	4.5
Companies .	16,200,000	780,000	4.8
Total .	71,500,000	3,240,000	4.6

The traffic returns on all the railways of Belgium in 1888 were as follows :—

	Miles	Passengers	Goods, Tons	Receipts, £	Expenses, £	Net, £
State . . .	1,990	57,900,000	25,500,000	5,260,000	2,800,000	2,460,000
Companies . . .	770	15,500,000	15,300,000	1,520,000	740,000	780,000
Total .	2,760	73,400,000	40,800,000	6,780,000	3,540,000	3,240,000

Averages per mile were as follows :—

	Passengers	Goods, Tons	Receipts, £	Expenses, £	Net, £
State . . .	29,000	12,800	2,630	1,400	1,230
Companies .	20,100	19,900	1,980	960	1,020
Total . .	26,700	14,800	2,450	1,280	1,170

The average cost of construction was £25,800 per mile, the highest ratio on the Continent except France.

SWITZERLAND

Notwithstanding the mountainous character of the country, railways are general; the mileage was :—

Year	Miles	Year	Miles
1850	15	1870 . . .	890
1855 . . .	130	1880 . . .	1,600
1860 . . .	650	1889 . . .	1,950

Traffic returns were as follows :—

Year	Miles	Passengers	Goods, Tons	Receipts, £	Expenses, £
1875	1,260	21,300,000	5,100,000	2,300,000	...
1880	1,600	21,600,000	5,800,000	2,400,000	1,260,000
1888	1,870	27,100,000	8,600,000	3,300,000	1,760,000

Averages per mile were as follows :—

Year	Passengers	Goods, Tons	Receipts, £	Expenses, £	Net, £
1875 . .	17,100	4,100	1,840	...	...
1880 . .	13,500	3,600	1,500	790	710
1888 . .	14,500	4,600	1,780	940	840

All the lines belong to companies. The cost of construction down to the end of 1888 was £20,500 a mile.

ROUMANIA

Official statements show mileage thus :—

Year	Miles	Year	Miles
1870	150	1880 . . .	860
1875 . . .	770	1889 . .	1,530

GREECE

As late as 1880 there were but seven miles of railways, the length in 1889 being 360 miles, besides 240 miles actually under construction.

TURKEY

All the lines belong to companies; mileage as follows :—

Year	Miles	Year	Miles
1860	40	1880 . . .	730
1870 . . .	390	1888 . . .	1,260

In 1888 there were 900 miles of rail in European, and 360 in Asiatic, Turkey.

UNITED STATES

The first line was from Boston to Quincey, four miles, opened in 1827. All the lines belong to companies, and the returns of mileage show thus :—

Year	Miles	Year	Miles
1830 . . .	23	1870 . . .	53,400
1840 . . .	2,820	1880 . . .	93,670
1850 . . .	9,020	1885 . . .	123,320
1860 . . .	30,630	1889 . . .	161,250

The distribution of mileage, according to Poor's *Manual*, at various dates, was as follows :—

States	1850	1860	1870	1880	1889
New England .	2,510	3,660	4,490	5,980	6,730
Middle . . .	3,200	6,350	10,580	15,180	19,740
South	1,280	8,540	12,560	19,570	39,240
West	2,030	12,080	25,290	52,570	95,540
Total . .	9,020	30,630	52,920	93,300	161,250

The cost of construction per mile varied as follows :—

Year	Miles	Cost, £	Per Mile, £
1850	9,020	60,200,000	6,600
1860	30,640	239,000,000	7,800
1871	60,520	555,200,000	9,300
1881	101,730	1,274,100,000	12,500
1888	156,080	1,949,000,000	12,490

The cost of construction down to 1882 was approximately as follows, according to Census report, and in order to bring the general average up to that of Poor's *Manual*, a percentage must be added as below :—

	Census Report			Amended Average	
	Miles	Cost, £	Per Mile, £	Cost, £	Per Mile, £
New England	6,150	64,000,000	10,500	70,400,000	11,500
Middle	16,440	306,000,000	18,500	337,400,000	20,500
South	15,800	112,000,000	7,100	123,200,000	7,800
West	66,420	708,000,000	10,500	779,000,000	11,700
Total . . .	104,810	1,190,000,000	11,300	1,310,000,000	12,500

New railways had a marvellous effect in opening up the Western and some of the Southern States as follows :—

	Railways, Miles		Increase per Cent.	Farms, Acres		Increase per Cent.
	1871	1880		1871	1880	
Illinois	5,904	8,326	41	25,883,000	31,674,000	21
Ohio	3,740	6,664	78	21,713,000	24,529,000	13
Iowa	3,160	6,113	93	15,542,000	24,753,000	61
Texas	865	5,344	520	18,397,000	36,292,000	98
Indiana	3,529	4,765	36	18,120,000	31,674,000	74
Michigan	2,116	4,284	102	10,019,000	13,807,000	38
Missouri	2,580	4,211	62	21,707,000	27,879,000	27
Kansas	1,760	3,718	111	5,657,000	21,417,000	282
Wisconsin	1,725	3,442	99	11,715,000	15,353,000	31
Minnesota	1,612	3,391	110	6,484,000	13,403,000	106
Nebraska	943	2,310	146	2,074,000	9,945,000	380
Eleven States	27,934	52,568	88	157,311,000	250,726,000	60

It appears that in the above eleven States the construction of 26,600 miles of railway, at a cost of 280 millions sterling, was accompanied by a spread of farming to an extent of 93,500,000 acres; the value of the increased area amounting to 520 million dollars, or 108 millions sterling, that is, 39 per cent. of the total cost of the new railways.

The annual construction of railways has averaged :—

Period	Miles made Yearly				
	New England	Middle States	South	West	Total
1851–60 . .	115	315	726	1,005	2,161
1861–70 . .	83	423	402	1,321	2,229
1871–80 . .	149	460	701	2,728	4,038
1881–89 . .	75	456	1,967	4,297	6,795

Averages per mile, on the aggregate, of all railways in the United States were as follows :—

Year	Pas- sengers	Goods, Tons	Re- ceipts, £	Ex- penses, £	Net, £
1872 . . .	2,300	2,500	1,260	1,030	230
1875 . . .	2,600	2,700	1,400	880	520
1882 . . .	3,300	3,200	1,410	850	560
1888 . . .	2,900	3,800	1,290	900	390

Traffic returns for the whole Union show as follows :—

Year	Miles	Passengers	Goods, Tons	Receipts, £	Expenses, £
1872	66,200	150,000,000	170,000,000	84,200,000	68,800,000
1875	74,370	191,000,000	202,000,000	104,800,000	66,100,000
1882	113,330	375,400,000	360,500,000	160,500,000	95,800,000
1888	154,280	451,400,000	589,400,000	198,000,000	138,000,000

The receipts in 1888 were as follows :—

	Amount, £	Pence per Mile
Passengers . . .	52,200,000	1.12
Goods . . .	145,800,000	0.52
Total . .	198,000,000	...

The average for each passenger was a journey of 25 miles, for which he paid 28d., and for each ton of goods a haulage of 115 miles, for which the fare was 60d. The value of merchandise carried was estimated at 2950 millions sterling. The average price of locomotives was £1800, sleeping cars £3500. The railway of greatest passenger traffic was the New York Elevated, carrying 191 million passengers yearly. The construction of this line took 2200 tons of iron per mile, and cost £44 per yard, against £500 for the London Metropolitan. The return on capital is shown thus :—

Year	Cost, £	Net Product, £	Percentage
1872 . .	658,300,000	15,400,000	2.3
1875 . .	920,000,000	38,700,000	4.2
1882 . .	1,436,600,000	65,300,000	4.6
1888 . .	1,949,000,000	60,000,000	3.1

The following table for 1888 shows the traffic on the lines actually working in the principal States :—

	Miles Worked	Receipts, £			Expenses, £	Cost of Construction, £	Net Product, £	Per- centage
		Passengers	Goods	Total				
Illinois . .	18,055	5,200,000	15,900,000	21,100,000	14,600,000	155,000,000	6,500,000	4.2
Ohio . .	10,345	4,100,000	13,300,000	17,400,000	12,160,000	158,300,000	5,240,000	3.3
Minnesota . .	8,863	2,060,000	6,260,000	8,320,000	5,060,000	104,000,000	3,260,000	3.1
Missouri . .	8,801	2,200,000	7,300,000	9,500,000	6,540,000	79,000,000	2,960,000	3.7
Pennsylvania .	7,532	4,900,000	21,300,000	26,200,000	15,800,000	142,500,000	10,400,000	7.3
Wisconsin . .	7,482	1,600,000	5,100,000	6,700,000	4,620,000	56,000,000	2,080,000	3.7
New York . .	7,429	4,900,000	12,300,000	17,200,000	11,940,000	178,300,000	5,260,000	2.9
Kansas . .	7,233	1,390,000	3,510,000	4,900,000	3,800,000	52,800,000	1,100,000	2.1
California . .	6,940	2,980,000	7,580,000	10,560,000	7,030,000	78,300,000	3,530,000	4.5
Indiana . .	6,116	2,060,000	5,240,000	7,300,000	5,550,000	51,200,000	1,750,000	3.4
Michigan . .	5,486	1,940,000	4,160,000	6,100,000	4,360,000	47,500,000	1,740,000	3.7
Texas . .	5,019	850,000	3,050,000	3,900,000	3,160,000	61,800,000	740,000	1.2
Various . .	45,997	18,059,000	40,530,000	58,589,000	41,177,000	568,400,000	17,412,000	3.1
Total . .	145,298	52,239,000	145,530,000	197,769,000	135,797,000	1,733,100,000	61,972,000	3.6

CANADA

Traffic returns were as follows :—

Year	Miles	Passengers	Goods, Tons	Receipts, £	Expenses, £	Miles Run
1875	4,830	5,200,000	5,700,000	4,050,000	3,280,000	17,700,000
1880	6,890	6,500,000	9,900,000	4,900,000	3,500,000	22,400,000
1889	12,630	12,200,000	17,900,000	8,430,000	6,210,000	...

The first line was opened in 1836 to Laprairie, in the province of Quebec, sixteen miles. Mileage open to traffic has been as follows :—

Year	Miles	Year	Miles
1840 . . .	16	1870 . . .	2,500
1851 . . .	71	1880 . . .	6,890
1860 . . .	2,090	1890 . . .	13,330

Averages per mile were as follows :—

Year	Passengers	Tons	Receipts, £	Expenses, £	Net, £
1875 . .	1,100	1,200	830	660	170
1880 . .	940	1,440	710	500	210
1889 . .	970	1,440	670	490	180

The mileage cost of construction and traffic of the several lines in 1887 showed as follows :—

	Miles	Cost, £	Receipts, £	Expenses, £	Net, £	Interest on Cost
Pacific . . .	4,320	42,800,000	2,210,000	1,520,000	690,000	1.6
Grand Trunk . . .	2,600	60,300,000	3,330,000	2,290,000	1,040,000	1.7
Intercolonial . . .	900	9,200,000	540,000	580,000	...	...
Various . . .	3,870	30,200,000	2,000,000	1,310,000	690,000	2.3
Total . . .	11,690	142,500,000	8,080,000	5,700,000	2,380,000	1.6

	Passengers	Tons	Per Mile					Miles Run
			Passengers	Tons	Receipts, £	Expenses, £	Net, £	
Pacific . . .	1,950,000	2,120,000	450	490	510	350	160	6,900,000
Grand Trunk . . .	5,080,000	6,460,000	1,960	2,490	1,280	880	400	13,800,000
Various . . .	3,670,000	7,820,000	750	1,620	530	390	140	12,900,000
Total .	10,700,000	16,400,000	900	1,400	700	490	210	33,600,000

Some of the railways belong to the State, and to most of the others the Government has given subsidies. The mileage and traffic of all were made up in 1887 thus :—

	Miles	Passengers	Goods, Tons	Receipts, £	Expenses, £	Net, £	Miles Run
State . . .	1,200	1,100,000	1,200,000	580,000	600,000	...	4,800,000
Companies . . .	10,490	9,600,000	15,200,000	7,500,000	5,100,000	2,400,000	28,800,000
Total . .	11,690	10,700,000	16,400,000	8,080,000	5,700,000	2,380,000	33,600,000

The average cost of construction and earnings per train-mile run were as follows :—

	Cost, £	Cost £, per Mile	Per Train Mile, Pence		
			Receipts	Expenses	Net
Pacific . .	42,800,000	9,900	77	53	24
Grand Trunk	60,300,000	23,100	57	39	18
Various . .	39,400,000	8,200	47	35	12
Total .	142,500,000	12,200	58	41	17

The paid-up capital on all the lines in 1887 was made up as follows :—

	£
Shares	67,600,000
Debentures	40,600,000
Dominion Government . .	26,900,000
Provincial grants . . .	7,400,000
Total . . .	142,500,000

Latest returns to the end of 1889 showed 13,330 miles, made at a cost of £152,100,000, say £11,400 per mile.

MEXICO

Official returns of mileage show as follows :—

Year	Miles	Year	Miles
1865 . . .	20	1880 . . .	660
1870 . . .	220	1889 . . .	5,010

In 1889 the traffic was as follows :—

	No.	Receipts, £
Passengers	12,980,000	310,000
Goods, tons	880,000	720,000
Total . . .	...	1,030,000

There are no State railways in Mexico.

PERU

The number of miles working was as follows :—

Year	Miles	Year	Miles
1860 . . .	47	1880 . . .	1,180
1870 . . .	250	1889 . . .	1,630

In 1870–72 the Government borrowed in London 49 millions sterling, and proceeded to make railways up the Andes. In 1877 the lines then made had cost £35,990,000, of which £25,670,000 came from the State. The Oroya line, with many tunnels, cost £29,000 per mile, say £4,200,000; that from Tacua to Bolivia £34,000 a mile, say £3,700,000.

CHILI

Mr. Wheelwright began railways in 1851, making a line from Copiapo to Caldera. Mileage progressed as follows :—

Year	Miles	Year	Miles
1860	120	1880	1,100
1870	450	1889	1,750

Companies own 1000 miles, the State 750, the latter having cost £6,000,000, and the total about 14 millions sterling. The earnings of State lines in 1887 amounted to £800,000, and expenses £520,000, leaving a net gain of £280,000, say 4.7 per cent. on the cost.

BRAZIL

The first line was made by Baron Mauà to the Organ Mountains, near Rio Janeiro, in 1851. The progress of mileage was as follows :—

Year	Miles	Year	Miles
1860	135	1880	2,175
1870	505	1889	5,580

The Pedro Segundo is one of the finest in the New World, with a length of 520 miles, mostly through a difficult country, having sixteen great tunnels. It cost £12,200,000 and earns 5½ per cent. net on the outlay. Most of the railways are 5 feet 4 inch gauge, but there are 40-inch gauge in Rio Grande and some other parts.

The San Paulo line crosses the Serra Cubaton by four successive inclined planes, up which the train is drawn, till attaining a height of 3500 feet over sea-level. The total cost of railways down to 1888 was :—

	£	Miles	£ per Mile
State lines . . .	16,100,000	900	18,000
Companies . . .	32,700,000	4,400	7,400
Total . . .	48,800,000	5,300	9,200

Traffic returns in 1887 showed 7,300,000 passengers and 1,820,000 tons merchandise; receipts, £3,820,000; expenses, £2,540,000; net profit, £1,280,000, being a little over 2½ per cent. (2.6) on the total outlay of capital.

ARGENTINA

The first line from Buenos Ayres to Flores, six miles, was opened in 1857. Official records of mileage show thus :—

Year	Miles	Year	Miles
1860	15	1880	1,540
1870	540	1889	5,550

The mileage at various dates was composed thus :—

	1875	1884	1886	1889
State . . .	570	1,520	1,710	...
Companies .	600	1,520	2,070	5,550
Total . .	1,170	3,040	3,780	5,550

The total traffic returns on Argentine railways were as follows :—

Year	Miles	Cost, £	Passengers	Goods, Tons	Receipts, £	Expenses, £	Net, £	Interest on Cost
1872	600	5,300,000	2,300,000	330,000	680,000	400,000	280,000	5.3
1876	1,370	11,400,000	2,700,000	680,000	920,000	630,000	290,000	2.6
1886	3,780	32,700,000	...	...	3,060,000	1,740,000	1,320,000	4.1
1888	4,440	38,500,000	...	...	2,800,000	1,650,000	1,150,000	3.0

In 1889 there were 5550 miles, representing an outlay of about 48 millions sterling. All the lines now belong to companies, the State lines having been recently sold. The number of train-miles run in 1889 was 1,200,000, the Great Southern of Buenos Ayres occupying the first place. The rolling-stock on all the lines comprised 12,000 waggons, capable of carrying 2,400,000 tons yearly.

URUGUAY

Mileage progressed as follows :—

Year	Miles	Year	Miles
1870	60	1880	270
1875	190	1889	450

Traffic returns were as follows :—

Year	Miles	Passengers	Goods, Tons	Receipts, £	Receipts per Mile, £
1877	230	270,000	77,000	95,000	410
1883	300	290,000	160,000	170,000	570
1887	400	405,000	...	...	...

The system which Mr. Robert Crawford is pushing forward will, when completed, have a total length of 700 miles. There are no State railways.

JAPAN

Mileage records are as follows :—

Year	Miles	Year	Miles
1875	40	1885	260
1880	75	1889	910

Traffic receipts in Japan were as follows :—

Year	Miles	Passengers	Goods, Tons	Receipts, £	Expenses, £	Net, £
1886	360	4,100,000	320,000	240,000	130,000	110,000
1889	910	11,700,000	770,000	570,000	220,000	350,000

Averages per mile were as follows :—

Year	Passengers	Goods, Tons	Receipts, £	Expenses, £	Net, £
1886	11,200	900	670	350	320
1889	12,900	850	630	240	390

Two-thirds of the lines belong to the State, one-third to companies.

INDIA

In 1853 there was but one short line of 22 miles; at subsequent dates we find as follows :—

Year	Miles	Year	Miles
1860	840	1880	9,310
1870	4,830	1889	15,250

Traffic returns on Indian railways taking the rupee at 24 pence, were as follows :—

Year	Miles	Passengers	Goods, Tons	Receipts, £	Expenses, £	Net, £
1874	6,190	24,300,000	4,800,000	7,790,000	3,830,000	3,960,000
1888	14,380	103,200,000	22,400,000	19,700,000	9,870,000	9,890,000

Averages per mile were as follows :—*

Year	Passengers	Tons	Receipts, £	Expenses, £	Net, £
1874 .	3,900	800	1,250	620	630
1888 .	7,100	1,510	1,400	700	700

In 1889 there were 10,410 miles of State railways, the rest belonging to companies who had guarantees or subsidies. The total cost to end of 1888 was nominally £193,200,000, taking the rupee at 24 pence, but really about 145 millions sterling.

The receipts in 1888 were made up thus :—

	No.	Receipts, £	Each, Pence
Passengers . .	103,200,000	6,440,000	15
Goods, tons . .	22,400,000	13,320,000	14
Total . . .	...	19,760,000	...

The return on capital in 1888 was over 5 per cent., viz., 5.2, being the highest average in the World for any country.

* These returns being on the fictitious basis of 24 pence the rupee, it is necessary to take off at least one-fourth ; thus mile-earnings were really £1050, expenses £525.

AUSTRALIA

The first line was opened in 1854 from Melbourne to Hobson's Bay, and the growth of mileage has been as follows :—

	1861	1871	1881	1888
New South Wales .	73	358	1,041	2,206
Victoria	214	329	1,247	2,018
Queensland	...	218	800	1,931
South Australia . . .	56	134	832	1,518
New Zealand . . .	...	145	1,333	1,865
Tasmania	...	45	168	327
West Australia . . .	...	...	122	272
Total . . .	343	1,229	5,543	10,137

The gauge is 42 inches in all the Colonies except New South Wales, 56½, and Victoria, 63 inches.

The traffic returns in New South Wales showed thus :—

Year	Miles	Passengers	Goods, Tons	Per Mile Passengers	Per Mile Goods, Tons
1856	23	350,000	2,500	15,000	110
1888	2,206	15,900,000	3,200,000	7,300	1,450

The cost of construction down to 1888 and traffic in that year were as follows :—

	Cost, £	Cost, £ per Mile	Receipts, £	Expenses, £	Net, £	Interest on Capital
New South Wales	26,600,000	12,500	2,510,000	1,580,000	930,000	3.5
Victoria	27,500,000	13,600	2,750,000	1,750,000	1,000,000	3.6
Queensland	13,100,000	6,800	780,000	510,000	270,000	2.1
South Australia . . .	9,700,000	6,400	950,000	450,000	500,000	5.1
New Zealand	13,500,000	7,600	1,000,000	650,000	350,000	2.6
Tasmania	2,400,000	8,400	135,000	130,000	5,000	...
West Australia . . .	900,000	4,400	40,000	45,000	...	...
Total	93,700,000	9,500	8,165,000	5,115,000	3,050,000	3.2

The traffic returns for three of the Colonies in 1888 compare thus :—

	Miles	Passengers	Goods, Tons	Per Mile Passengers	Per Mile Tons	Per Mile Receipts, £	Per Mile Expenses, £
New South Wales . .	2,206	15,900,000	3,200,000	7,300	1,450	1,150	720
Victoria . . .	2,018	56,000,000	3,560,000	27,700	1,750	1,360	865
New Zealand . .	1,865	3,100,000	1,920,000	1,650	1,030	540	350

Mr. Coghlan shows that the saving of freight charges in New South Wales in twenty-five years down to 1888 by railways was £4,670,000. This is equal to £240 a mile per annum, and, applied to all Australia, would give the following result :—

Period	Saving in Freight Charges New South Wales	Victoria	Queensland	South Australia	New Zealand	Tasmania	Western Australia	Total
	£	£	£	£	£	£	£	£
1855–70 . . .	450,000	680,000	200,000	350,000	100,000	30,000	...	1,810,000
1871–80 . . .	1,220,000	1,390,000	850,000	800,000	1,200,000	240,000	60,000	5,760,000
1881–88 . . .	2,880,000	2,800,000	2,400,000	2,100,000	2,800,000	600,000	400,000	13,980,000
Total . .	4,550,000	4,870,000	3,450,000	3,250,000	4,100,000	870,000	460,000	21,550,000

The above estimate shows that, speaking approximately, the railways of Australia have already in saving of freight charges paid nearly one-fourth of the cost of construction ; also that they cause an annual saving to the people of £1,600,000 sterling.

SOUTH AFRICA

Mileage returns show as follows :—

Year	Cape Colony	Natal	Total
1874	64	...	64
1880	910	100	1,010
1888	1,780	230	2,010

The official returns are as follows :—

ALGERIA

Year	Miles	Cost, £	Passengers	Goods, Tons	Receipts, £	Expenses, £	Net, £
1877	410	7,700,000	1,020,000	260,000	270,000	230,000	40,000
1885	1,160	16,000,000	2,350,000	1,080,000	850,000	605,000	245,000
1887	1,580	...	...	...	840,000	...	...

Goods tons, as given above, averaged a haulage of 100 kilometres, or 63 miles : official returns give this item under the form of kilometric tons. Including the Tunis lines, 260 miles, the whole system in 1889 reached a length of 1840 miles, representing an approximate outlay of 26 millions sterling.

EGYPT

The first line was opened in 1856, from Alexandria to Cairo, 130 miles ; cost of construction, £8000 per mile. Records of mileage show thus :—

Year	Miles	Net Product, £
1860	275	...
1879	920	750,000
1885	950	930,000
1889	956	730,000

Details of receipts and expenditure showed thus :—

Year	Receipts, £	Expenses, £	Per Mile Receipts, £	Per Mile Expenses, £
1885	1,540,000	610,000	1,620	640
1889	1,330,000	600,000	1,400	630

In 1888 the lines carried 3,600,000 passengers. The actual length of railways is 1260 miles, but some are not working. The earnings on the total mileage would not exceed £1050, expenses £480 per mile.

Ismail Pachà, during his reign, expended a sum of £13,300,000 in the construction of railways, one line extending along the Nile valley to Siout, in Upper Egypt. Net earnings are 4 per cent. on cost.

All the lines belong to the State, except one of 180 miles in Cape Colony. Cape lines in 1880 carried 2,700,000 passengers and 420,000 tons goods, being 1500 passengers and 230 tons per mile. The average cost of construction was £8900. This would give a total outlay of 16 millions sterling. Receipts £1,450,000, expenses £760,000, leaving a net profit of £690,000, say 4.3 on the cost of construction.

The first line was from Cape Town to Wellington, 58 miles, opened in 1860 ; cost £500,000. The line to Kimberley diamond fields was opened in 1885. In 1888 there were three principal lines : the Western 720, the Midland 590, and the Eastern 290 miles.

WEST INDIES

The principal railways in this part of the world are :—

	Miles
Cuba	930
Jamaica, &c.	160
Santo Domingo	70
Martinique	120
	1,280

The traffic and earnings of these lines are unknown.

VARIOUS COUNTRIES

The latest returns of mileage in the following countries are :—

	Miles		Miles
Asia Minor . .	360	Mauritius . . .	90
Bourbon . .	70	Newfoundland . .	90
Central America .	570	Paraguay . .	90
Ceylon . .	180	Persia . . .	10
China . .	86	Sandwich Islands .	56
Cochin-China .	40	Senegal . . .	250
Malta . . .	10	Venezuela . . .	180

Making a total of 2082 miles for which we have no traffic returns.

RANSOM

In 1360 that of King John of France was fixed at £1,200,000 sterling. In 1521 that of Francis I. of France was fixed by Charles V. the Emperor at £800,000 sterling.

RELIGION

The following are the latest numbers as well as can be ascertained :—

	Roman Catholics	Protestants	Greeks	Jews	Mahometans	Total
England	1,066,000	24,858,000	...	44,000	...	25,968,000
Scotland	318,000	3,371,000	...	6,000	...	3,695,000
Ireland	3,952,000	1,169,000	...	1,000	...	5,122,000
United Kingdom . . .	5,336,000	29,398,000	...	51,000	...	34,785,000
France	29,202,000	693,000	...	53,000	...	29,948,000
Germany	16,789,000	29,370,000	...	563,000	...	46,722,000
Russia	8,300,000	2,950,000	65,549,000	3,000,000	2,600,000	82,399,000
Austria	20,227,000	400,000	493,000	1,005,000	...	22,125,000
Hungary	9,410,000	3,174,000	2,447,000	641,000	...	15,672,000
Italy	28,360,000	62,000	...	38,000	...	28,460,000
Spain	17,542,000	7,600	...	400	...	17,550,000

	Roman Catholics	Protestants	Greeks	Jews	Mahometans	Total
Portugal	4,707,500	500	...	...	...	4,708,000
Sweden	1,000	4,561,000	...	3,000	...	4,565,000
Norway	500	1,806,500	...	...	...	1,807,000
Denmark	3,000	1,973,000	...	4,000	...	1,980,000
Holland	1,440,000	2,491,000	...	82,000	...	4,013,000
Belgium	6,016,000	10,000	...	4,000	...	6,030,000
Switzerland	1,190,000	1,724,000	...	8,000	...	2,922,000
Greece	14,000	1,000	1,903,000	6,000	24,000	1,948,000
Roumania	114,000	14,000	4,529,000	400,000	2,000	5,059,000
Servia	8,000	1,000	1,874,000	4,000	15,000	1,902,000
Bulgaria	19,000	...	2,432,000	24,000	668,000	3,143,000
Turkey	280,000	45,000	788,000	51,000	3,626,000	4,790,000
Europe	148,959,000	78,681,600	80,015,000	5,937,400	6,935,000	320,528,000
United States . . .	9,000,000	50,890,000	...	110,000	...	60,000,000
Canada	1,792,000	2,440,000	...	...	...	4,232,000
Spanish America . . .	33,340,000	115,000	...	47,000	...	33,502,000
Australia	845,000	2,880,000	...	1,000	...	3,726,000
West Indies	2,480,000	1,030,000	...	...	...	3,510,000
Total . . .	196,416,000	136,036,600	80,015,000	6,095,400	6,935,000	425,498,000

The creeds of the world may be briefly stated thus :—

	Roman Catholics	Protestants	Greeks	Jews	Mahometans	Various	Total
Europe . . .	148,900,000	78,700,000	80,000,000	6,000,000	6,900,000	...	320,500,000
America . . .	44,100,000	55,300,000	...	100,000	...	...	91,500,000
Australia . . .	850,000	2,900,000	...	...	...	...	3,750,000
Asia and Africa .	6,600,000	3,100,000	...	670,000	194,000,000	440,000,000	644,370,000
Total .	200,450,000	140,000,000	80,000,000	6,770,000	200,900,000	440,000,000	1,060,120,000

The 440 millions of pagans in the above table marked "various" are made up, in almost equal proportions, of Buddhists, Brahmans, and followers of Confucius.

UNITED KINGDOM

In 1881 the classification was as follows :—

	Anglicans	Roman Catholics	Presbyterians	All Others	Total
England	18,798,000	1,066,000	114,000	5,990,000	25,968,000
Scotland	99,000	318,000	2,997,000	281,000	3,695,000
Ireland	636,000	3,952,000	486,000	48,000	5,122,000
United Kingdom	19,533,000	5,336,000	3,597,000	6,319,000	34,785,000

In 1871 the estimated numbers were :—

	Anglicans	Roman Catholics	Dissenters	Jews	Total
England	17,781,000	1,058,000	3,971,000	39,000	22,849,000
Scotland	73,000	320,000	2,959,000	6,000	3,358,000
Ireland .	683,000	4,142,000	577,000	1,000	5,403,000
U.Kingd.	18,537,000	5,520,000	7,507,000	46,000	31,610,000

No census as to religion is taken in England or Scotland. The above estimates are according to the ratios resulting from the marriages solemnised yearly in the different churches.

In 1882 a private census of people attending church on Sundays was taken, showing percentage to population as follows :—

Sheffield . . .	23	Southampton . .	38
Nottingham . .	24	Hull	41
Liverpool . . .	26	Portsmouth . .	41
Bristol . . .	31	Bath . . .	52

The above was, however, much in excess of the real percentage, many persons going to church twice. Only 37 per cent. of the total worshippers attended the Church of England, 8 per cent. being Roman Catholics and 55 per cent. Dissenters.

UNITED STATES.

The number of churches at various dates was :—

	1830	1840	1850	1860	1870	1885
Baptist .	4,384	7,900	9,600	12,100	13,900	31,350
Methodist	...	...	13,300	19,900	21,300	29,000
Presby- } terian }	2,253	2,800	4,800	6,400	7,100	10,940
R. Catholic	210	512	1,200	2,600	3,800	6,755
Various .	3,170	3,450	9,200	13,020	17,000	30,100
Total .	...	...	38,100	54,020	63,100	108,145

The value of church property was as follows :—

	1850	1870	Number of Believers	
	£	£	1835	1880
Methodists .	3,100,000	14,600,000	1,240,000	14,667,000
Baptists . .	2,300,000	8,700,000	2,929,000	10,464,000
Presbyterians	3,100,000	11,000,000	2,102,000	6,478,000
R. Catholics	1,900,000	12,700,000	555,000	6,143,000
Various . .	7,800,000	27,200,000	7,532,000	12,407,000
Total . .	18,200,000	74,200,000	14,358,000	50,159,000

In 1888 the Roman Catholics possessed 7424 churches, 650 colleges, 3100 schools, and 520 hospitals and asylums.

2 K

The *American Almanac* gives the following statistics for 1883–85 :—

	Churches	Clergy	Sittings
Baptists	31,350	16,190	2,572,000
Episcopal Methodists	17,935	11,676	1,660,000
Other Methodists . .	...	10,770	2,050,000
Presbyterians . . .	10,940	9,050	1,020,000
Roman Catholics . .	6,755	7,370	...
Various	30,240	29,100	3,650,000
Total . . .	97,220	84,156	...

In 1883 the number of Roman Catholics was 6,832,900, but the number of sittings was not known. In 1889 Cardinal Gibbon stated their number at 9,000,000.

GERMANY
The Census of 1885 compares with 1871 as follows :—

	1871	1885
Protestants . . .	25,582,000	29,370,000
Roman Catholics . .	14,868,000	16,789,000
Jews	512,000	563,000
Undefined . . .	99,000	137,000
Total . .	41,061,000	46,859,000

In 1885 the distribution was as follows :—

	Percentage				
	Prussia	Bavaria	Saxony	Wurtem-berg	All Germany
Protestants .	64.4	28.1	96.6	69.1	62.7
R. Catholics	34.0	70.8	2.8	30.0	35.8
Jews . . .	1.3	1.0	0.2	0.7	1.2
Undefined .	0.3	0.1	0.4	0.2	0.3
Total .	100.0	100.0	100.0	100.0	100.0

CANADA

	Number	Ratio
Roman Catholics . .	1,792,000	42.2
Anglicans	575,000	13.6
Presbyterians . . .	676,000	16.0
Methodists . . .	743,000	17.6
Various	446,000	10.6
Total .	4,232,000	100.0

Roman Catholics count 1,170,000 in Lower Canada, 320,000 in Ontario, and 302,000 in the other provinces, about 1,100,000 being French and 700,000 Irish.

AUSTRALIA
In 1889 the various congregations stood as follows :—

	Anglicans	R. Catholics	Presbyterians	Methodists	Various	Total
New South Wales . .	503,000	306,000	107,000	95,000	95,000	1,106,000
Victoria . . .	399,000	261,000	170,000	139,000	135,000	1,104,000
Queensland . . .	139,000	95,000	46,000	31,000	86,000	397,000
South Australia . .	85,000	48,000	20,000	59,000	103,000	315,000
New Zealand . . .	246,000	85,000	138,000	58,000	85,000	612,000
Tasmania . . .	60,000	38,000	19,000	16,000	15,000	148,000
Western Australia .	23,000	12,000	1,000	3,000	4,000	43,000
Total . .	1,455,000	845,000	501,000	401,000	523,000	3,725,000

INDIA
The Census of 1881 showed as follows :—

	Christians	Hindoos	Mahometans	Buddhists	Various	Total
Assam	7,000	3,062,000	1,317,000	6,000	489,000	4,881,000
Bengal	128,000	45,453,000	21,705,000	156,000	2,095,000	69,537,000
Bombay . . .	145,000	17,835,000	3,774,000	...	1,642,000	23,396,000
Burmah . . .	84,000	88,000	169,000	3,252,000	144,000	3,737,000
Madras . . .	711,000	28,498,000	1,934,000	2,000	26,000	31,171,000
Punjaub . . .	34,000	9,252,000	11,662,000	3,000	1,761,000	22,712,000
Travancore . . .	499,000	1,756,000	147,000	...	...	2,402,000
Various . . .	255,000	81,993,000	9,414,000	...	4,393,000	96,055,000
Total .	1,863,000	187,937,000	50,122,000	3,419,000	10,550,000	253,891,000

"Christians" included 963,000 Roman Catholics, 432,000 Protestants, and 568,000 Syrians, Greeks, &c.

RIBBONS
The value manufactured was estimated as follows :—

	1872	1881
	£	£
France . . .	4,920,000	5,016,000
Germany . . .	2,810,000	2,420,000
Switzerland . . .	2,590,000	2,230,000
Austria . . .	920,000	710,000
Great Britain . .	800,000	800,000
United States . .	100,000	3,430,000
Other countries . .	400,000	900,000
Total . .	12,540,000	15,506,000

RICE
The ordinary production is approximately as follows :—

	Acres	Crop, Tons	Consumption	Surplus
India . . .	22,600,000	16,800,000	15,400,000	1,400,000
Burmah . .	3,800,000	2,700,000	1,700,000	1,000,000
Japan . .	6,580,000	4,800,000	4,600,000	200,000
Manilla . .	3,140,000	1,800,000	1,750,000	50,000
Java . . .	5,000,000	3,000,000	2,500,000	500,000
Ceylon . .	600,000	400,000	350,000	50,000
Italy . .	500,000	400,000	360,000	40,000
Spain . .	50,000	40,000	40,000	...
U. States .	120,000	90,000	160,000	...

There are also 1,870,000 acres in Cochin-China, and 500,000 in Siam under this product ; no return as to crops.

The consumption in Europe has doubled since 1870, and now exceeds two million tons yearly. Consumption in the United Kingdom has been as follows :—

Year		Tons	Lbs. per Inhab.
1860	. . .	18,100	$1\frac{1}{2}$
1870	. . .	95,200	7
1880	. . .	221,000	14
1889	. . .	178,000	$10\frac{1}{2}$

It has been grown successfully in the Thames valley near Windsor.

RIVERS

The magnitude of rivers is best judged by their out-flow, which is as follows :—

	Cubic Feet per Second			Cubic Feet per Second
Amazon .	1,030,000	Dnieper .	.	120,000
La Plata .	850,000	Don .	.	115,000
Mississippi .	570,000	Euphrates .	.	110,000
St. Lawrence	470,000	Rhine .	.	65,000
Obi .	330,000	Rhone .	.	60,000
Volga .	310,000	Po .	.	60,000
Yang-tse-kiang .	300,000	Vistula .	.	45,000
Congo	250,000	Loire .	.	35,000
Danube	250,000	Elbe .	.	30,000
Ganges .	200,000	Seine .	.	20,000
Nile .	160,000	Thames .	.	10,000

The following table shows the length of the more important rivers :—*

		Miles				Miles
Amazon .	.	3,270	Mississippi	.	.	2,250
Amoor .	.	2,240	Murray .	.	.	1,703
Bramaputra .	.	1,560	Niger .	.	.	2,300
Columbia .	.	1,090	Nile .	.	.	2,750
Congo .	.	2,700	Norte .	.	.	1,250
Danube .	.	1,540	Obi .	.	.	2,800
Darling .	.	2,345	Orange .	.	.	1,000
Dnieper .	.	1,070	Orinoco .	.	.	1,150
Don .	.	985	Oxus .	.	.	1,300
Douro .	.	490	Plata .	.	.	2,130
Ebro .	.	470	Po .	.	.	356
Elbe .	.	615	Rhine .	.	.	715
Euphrates .	.	1,360	Rhone .	.	.	450
Ganges .	.	1,350	St. Lawrence	.	.	1,930
Garonne .	.	400	Seine .	.	.	429
Guadiana .	.	320	Senegal .	.	.	850
Hoang-ho .	.	2,400	Severn .	.	.	210
Hudson .	.	280	Shannon .	.	.	220
Indus .	.	1,720	Tagus .	.	.	570
Irrawaddy .	.	900	Thames .	.	.	204
Jenisei .	.	2,100	Tiber .	.	.	210
Kiang-ku .	.	1,050	Vistula .	.	.	601
Lena .	.	2,500	Volga .	.	.	1,990
Loire .	.	549	Yang-tse-kiang .	.	2,700
Mackenzie .	.	1,600	Zambesi .	.	.	950
Magdalena .	.	820				

The basins drained by the great rivers are as follows :—

		Sq. Miles			Sq. Miles
Amazon .	.	1,920,000	St. Lawrence	.	340,000
La Plata .	.	1,560,000	Danube .	.	310,000
Obi .	.	1,370,000	Euphrates .	.	240,000
Congo .	.	1,300,000	Don .	.	220,000
Mississippi .	.	1,170,000	Dnieper .	.	170,000
Yang-tse-kiang .	.	740,000	Rhine .	.	90,000
Nile .	.	710,000	Vistula .	.	75,000
Volga .	.	650,000	Elbe .	.	50,000
Ganges .	.	440,000	Rhone .	.	45,000

* The navigable length of rivers has been already given under the heading of *Canals*.

The outflow of European rivers is estimated as follows :—

Cubic Feet per Second

Into			Into	
North Sea .	336,000	Mediterranean .	310,000
Baltic .	273,000	Caspian .	365,000
Atlantic .	285,000	Black Sea .	603,000

Making a total of 2,172,000 cubic feet per second, or more than eight times the outflow of the Danube.

The current of certain rivers in ordinary times is as follows :—

		Feet per Minute			Feet per Minute
Seine .	.	135	Garonne .	.	230
Thames	.	180	Rhone .	.	390
Tiber .	.	200	Durance .	.	510
Danube	.	210	Rhine .	.	540
Loire .	.	220	Amazon .	.	780

The Amazon falls 2 ft., the Elbe 10 ft., the Paranà 22 ft. per 100 miles. The Danube falls 264 ft. from Vienna to Buda-Pesth, and 216 ft. from the latter place to the sea.

There have been some remarkable floods of the Seine at Paris and the Tiber at Rome, when the height over ordinary level was as follows :—

Date	River	Feet	Date	River	Feet
1658 . .	Seine . .	29	1530 . .	Tiber . .	45
1740 . .	Seine . .	26	1686 . .	Tiber . .	35
1802 . .	Seine . .	24	1742 . .	Tiber . .	31

The outflow of all Italian rivers is estimated thus, in cubic feet per second :—

		Cubic Feet	Basin, Sq. Miles
Po	. .	60,000	28,000
Tiber	. .	10,000	6,000
Other rivers	.	45,000	51,000
Total	.	115,000	85,000

The basin and outflow of French rivers are as follows :—

			Basin, Sq. Miles	Cubic Feet per Second
Rhone	. .	.	48,000	60,000
Gironde	. .	.	50,000	40,000
Loire	. .	.	54,000	35,000
Seine	. .	.	32,000	20,000
Various	. .	.	15,000	40,000
Total	.		199,000	195,000

The outflow of the Nile varies from 16,000 cubic feet per second in June to 400,000 in September, the yearly average being at the rate of 160,000 cubic feet per second; Sir John Fowler makes it only 120,000. The ordinary rise of the Nile is shown in the averages for thirteen years thus :—

						Ft.	In.
1866–70	.	.	.	.	.	25	2
1871–78	.	.	.	.	.	24	0

The ordinary discharge of the Nile is sixteen times that of the Thames.

ROADS

The following is a table of resistance for waggon-draughts per ton :—

Lbs. per Ton

Description		Level Road	Gradients of			
			1 per Cent.	3 per Cent.	5 per Cent.	8 per Cent.
Pavement .	. .	33	63	123	185	278
Macadam .	. .	46	87	170	255	382
Stone and clay .	.	65	123	245	368	552
Thick gravel .	. .	147	280	550	825	1,238

M'Neill's mail-coach dynamometer is as follows :—

Speed, Miles per Hour	Force Required			
	Level Road	2½ per Cent. Gradient	4 per Cent. Gradient	5 per Cent. Gradient
	Lbs.	Lbs.	Lbs.	Lbs.
6 . .	111	160	213	268
8 . .	120	166	219	296
10 . .	128	172	225	318

There are practically three kinds of roads—ordinary highways, railways, and rivers or canals. The total length is approximately as follows :—

	Miles				Miles of Way per 100 Sq. Miles
	Highways	Railways	Rivers	Total	
U. Kingdom	118,000	19,800	3,800	141,600	120
France . .	320,000	20,900	7,700	348,600	170
Germany .	265,000	24,300	17,100	306,400	150
Russia . .	65,000	17,700	33,900	116,600	5
Austria . .	81,000	15,600	7,200	103,800	37
Italy . . .	51,000	7,800	1,300	60,100	54
Spain. . .	14,000	5,900	1,100	21,000	11
Portugal .	2,000	1,200	500	3,700	10
Sweden . .	36,200	4,700	500	41,400	24
Norway . .	14,800	1,000	100	15,900	12
Denmark .	2,000	1,200	100	3,300	22
Holland . .	7,600	1,700	2,700	12,000	60
Belgium . .	5,700	2,800	1,200	9,700	85
Switzerland	...	1,900	500	2,400	16
Roumania, &c. }	...	3,600	1,100	4,700	3
Europe . .	982,300	130,100	78,800	1,191,200	35
U. States .	260,100	161,200	51,800	473,100	15
Canada . .	6,000	13,300	4,000	23,300	1
India . . .	58,000	15,300	5,000	78,300	6
Australia .	...	10,600	3,800	14,400	1
Argentina .	...	5,600	2,200	7,800	1
Brazil . .	700	5,600	24,300	30,700	1
Total .	1,307,100	341,600	169,900	1,818,700	10

In Switzerland, lake routes are counted as navigable rivers. The term "highways" includes also byways practicable for wheeled vehicles. The ordinary cost of making a road is £800 a mile in England, £1200 in France, £600 in Italy. The cost of maintenance is £18 a mile in England, £33 in France, £38 in Austria.

Macadamised roads are called after a Scotch engineer who began his labours in 1818.

UNITED KINGDOM

The mileage of roads in England and Wales increased until the introduction of railways, and then began to decline, viz. :—

Year	Miles		
	Main	Ordinary	Total
1813 . . .	19,700	95,100	114,800
1839 . . .	21,960	104,770	126,730
1870 . . .	15,125	102,615	117,740
1889 . . .	17,745	93,115	110,860

Expenditure in 1889 was as follows :—

	£	Average per Mile, £
Main	802,000	45
Ordinary . . .	1,222,000	13
Total . .	2,024,000	18

The Romans had roads from Brighton to York ; these were repaired by Edward I. and subsequent monarchs. In the 18th century Arthur Young wrote of the turnpike road from Preston to Wigan : "This infernal road has ruts four feet deep ; in 18 miles I counted three carts broken down." Scotland had no regular roads, at least in the northern parts, before 1745, when General Wade's soldiers made them. Telford resumed the work in 1800, and made 900 miles of road and 1200 bridges in twenty years. In 1887 Scotland had 2530 miles of main and ordinary highways. As for Ireland, it was customary in the 18th century to travel on horseback, Colonel Knox Gore stating recently in the House of Commons that he was the first man who travelled by coach from Connaught to Dublin.

FRANCE

Expenditure in 1885 was as follows :—

Roads	Miles	£	£ per Mile
National . . .	23,700	1,280,000	54
Departmental . .	18,900	880,000	47
Local	277,400	8,360,000	30
Total . .	320,000	10,520,000	33

In 1835 the mileage and value of routes was as follows :—

	Miles	£	£ per Mile
Canals	2,300	18,000,000	7,800
Highroads . . .	21,500	21,000,000	9,800
Byroads . . .	24,000	15,000,000	6,200
Bridges, No. . .	1,750	7,000,000	...
Total value . .	...	61,000,000	...

There are four classes of roads in France, viz. :—

Class	Width, Feet	Cost, £ per Mile
1st	50	1,900
2nd	40	1,200
3rd	33	800
4th	25	400

In fifty years ending 1880 France spent 180 millions sterling on highroads ; those now existing are worth about 240 millions sterling.

GERMANY

The main roads of the Empire in 1878 were as follows :—

	Miles
Prussia	25,300
Bavaria	6,200
Other States	33,700
Total	65,200

There were also 200,000 miles of byroads.

AUSTRIA

After the peace of 1815 the Government began to make roads, and in sixty years, down to 1875, no less than 60,000 miles of macadamised roads were laid down, besides sixty passes made over the Alps, with casemates for travellers. The grand trunk road from Verona (then Austrian Italy) to Bukowina was 1000 miles in length. Road-making is still carried on at the rate of 1000 miles yearly.

The returns of Austria proper, without Hungary, show as follows :—

	Mileage	
	1878	**1887**
Highroads . . .	9,700	9,800
Byroads . . .	42,300	52,300
Total . .	52,000	62,100

Highroads are kept in repair by the State at a cost of £38 per mile per annum, byroads by the local communes. Hungary had 18,800 miles of road in 1886, of which 4,400 were maintained by the State, and 14,400 of minor importance by the communes.

ITALY

In the last thirty years no less than 28,000 miles of road have been constructed, at an outlay of 17 millions sterling, being an average of £600 per mile. There are at present 5800 miles of main routes maintained by the State, and 45,000 of local roads by the communes.

SPAIN

The length of highroads at various dates was :—

Year		Miles	Year			Miles
1808	. .	1,860	1869	.	.	9,980
1827	. .	3,300	1880	.	.	13,970

In 1827 waggons paid a toll of twopence every 10 miles, and the State expended £91,000 on the maintenance of 3300 miles and thirty-five bridges. The rest of Spain had only mule-tracks. When Church properties were confiscated, a part of the spoil was devoted to making roads, and in this way £7,000,000 were expended between 1846 and 1858. In 1880 there were 12,420 miles of good carriage roads maintained by the State, and 1550 by the local authorities.

PORTUGAL

In 1840 there were neither roads nor mail-coaches; men travelled on mules, ladies in sedan-chairs borne by hand. At present there are about 2000 miles of road, including the great northern route, 300 miles, to Valenza on the Minho, and the great eastern to Badajoz.

BELGIUM

The mileage of roads has nearly trebled since 1830 :—

Year				Highroads	Byroads	Total
1830	.	.	.	1,620	430	2,050
1850	.	.	.	2,550	1,360	3,910
1870	.	.	.	3,360	1,280	4,640
1887	.	.	.	4,350	1,350	5,700

In 1879 the waggons used on the above roads had a carrying power of 470,000 tons.

UNITED STATES

The length of mail-coach roads at various dates was :—

Year						Miles
1800	.	.	.	.	.	20,820
1850	.	.	.	.	.	169,700
1889	.	.	.	.	.	260,100

At the period of independence there were not 1000 miles of highroad, the colonies of New England, Virginia, &c., having little other means of communication than by sea.

In 1834 the mail-coach roads of the principal States were as follows :—

		Miles			Miles
New York	.	12,300	North Carolina	.	6,500
Pennsylvania	.	9,800	Kentucky	.	5,600
Virginia	.	9,500	Tennessee	.	5,500
Ohio	.	8,100	Vermont	.	4,700

The other States having an aggregate of 42,500 miles, and thus making up a total of 104,500 for the Union.

CANADA

In 1826 there was such a want of roads that Major Strickland described a journey of fifty miles near Toronto, which took him three days to accomplish. In 1878 there were 5500 miles of regular mail-coach road.

BRAZIL

The interior is still destitute of good roads, but there are some admirable ones in the Maritime provinces. Those of Tijuca and Petropolis, near Rio Janeiro, are *chefs d'œuvre*, besides which those in the provinces of San Paulo and Rio Grande are worth mention. Waggontracks from Rio Janeiro to Matto Grosso and Goyaz, are in use for freight, the journey taking six months.

ARGENTINA

Except the routes over the Andes to Chili, roads are almost unknown. President Sarmiento bridged many of the rivers in 1868–74. Railways have meantime rendered roads superfluous. In 1860 the bullock-waggons between Tucuman and Rosario, 600 miles, usually took twelve months on the round trip, going ten miles a day, and making long halts. The distance is now done in one day by rail.

S.

SALT

The following table shows the percentage of salt in various seas :—

Sea	Percentage of Salt	Salt per Ton of Water, lbs.
Caspian	0.5	11
Black	1.2	26
Baltic . . .	1.3	28
English Channel . .	3.3	72
Red	4.3	93
Dead	8.5	187
Mediterranean . . .	3.9	85
Atlantic . . .	3.7	81
Salt Lake. . . .	20.0	440

In the Dead Sea the percentage of salt increases with depth, viz. :—

Depth, Feet					Salt	Water
1	.	.	.	.	93	907
66	.	.	.	.	204	796
400	.	.	.	.	263	737
1,000	.	.	.	.	278	722

The production of salt in Europe and the United States has been approximately as follows, in tons :—

			1830	1889
Great Britain	.	.	400,000	1,900,000
Continent	.	.	1,700,000	4,350,000
United States	.	.	100,000	1,050,000
Total	.		2,200,000	7,300,000

The following table shows approximately the present production and consumption yearly :—

	Tons		Lbs. Consumed per Inhabitant
	Production	Consumption	
United Kingdom .	1,950,000	1,050,000	62
France . . .	640,000	640,000	36
Germany . . .	910,000	755,000	35
Russia . . .	1,200,000	1,310,000	33
Austria . . .	340,000	340,000	18
Italy . . .	600,000	350,000	25
Spain and Portugal .	600,000	190,000	19
Scandinavia . .	...	190,000	44
United States .	1,050,000	1,360,000	48
Canada . . .	55,000	105,000	45
India	700,000	1,100,000	12
Various . . .	755,000	1,130,000	...
Total . .	8,800,000	8,520,000	...

Whenever the consumption falls below 20 lbs. per inhabitant, it is bad for public health. During the Paraguayan War of 1864–70, it was observed that the men who had been without salt for three months, when wounded, however slightly, died, as their wounds would not heal.

UNITED KINGDOM

Period	Average Production, Tons per Annum	Duty per Ton	Price per Ton	Lbs. Consumed per Inhabitant
1800–06 . .	203,000	£30	£32	16
1807–15 . .	230,000	30	32	16
1816–23 . .	257,000	30	32	16
1824–40 . .	410,000	...	1	19
1841–60 . .	880,000	...	16s.	32
1861–70 . .	1,540,000	...	14s.	58
1871–80 . .	2,020,000	...	12s.	72

The consumption in the United Kingdom averages 40 lbs. per inhabitant for cooking or condiment, the rest being used for chemicals, manure, &c. Reduced death-rate and higher efficiency of workmen are in some manner the result of increased consumption of salt.

The exportation at various dates has been as follows :—

Year	Tons	Value, £	Shillings per Ton
1830 . . .	220,000	...	...
1853 . . .	520,000	270,000	10.4
1860 . . .	700,000	360,000	10.3
1870 . . .	760,000	380,000	10.0
1880 . . .	1,050,000	600,000	11.4
1888 . . .	900,000	490,000	10.9

The number of saltpans in the United Kingdom rose from 752 in 1867 to 1311 in 1876, the production in the latter year including 1,780,000 tons of white salt made from brine, and 190,000 of rock-salt from Cheshire and Carrickfergus.

FRANCE

Production at various dates was approximately as follows :—

Year	Tons	Lbs. per Inhabitant
1830	300,000	20
1840	400,000	25
1850	600,000	36
1868	600,000	34
1886	640,000	36

The quantity made in 1886 was officially valued at £480,000, say 15 shillings a ton. The surplus for exportation is insignificant. The saltworks employ 4000 hands. The amount of salt which paid excise in 1885

was only 330,000 tons, being for cookery and table use ; what is used in manufactures is untaxed.

GERMANY

Official returns show as follows :—

Year	Tons		
	Production	Export	Consumption
1870 . .	430,000	40,000	390,000
1880 . .	660,000	100,000	560,000
1887 . .	910,000	155,000	755,000

Consumption compared with population showed :—

Year	Lbs. per Inhabitant		
	Table Use	Manufactures	Total
1870	17	8	25
1880	17	13	30
1887	17	18	35

In 1887 Prussia produced 470,000 tons, Wurtemberg 180,000, and the other states 260,000 tons.

RUSSIA

Production and consumption at various dates were :—

Year	Tons			Lbs. per Inhabitant
	Production	Imports	Consumption	
1840 .	440,000	...	440,000	18
1860 .	420,000	150,000	570,000	20
1870 .	450,000	180,000	630,000	20
1880 .	780,000	150,000	930,000	24
1888 .	1,200,000	110,000	1,310,000	33

AUSTRIA

The salt-mine of Wieliezka in Galizia, at the base of the Carpathians, is the greatest in the world, extending 600 miles, and seeming inexhaustible. For six centuries it has given prodigious quantities of salt, and it still occupies 9000 miners. The total tonnage production of the Empire for the years given was estimated thus :—

1834	260,000
1850	600,000
1887	340,000

If the estimate in 1850 was correct, this shows that the industry is declining apace, perhaps owing to the heavy salt-tax, the Government selling it at £1 per ton for exportation, but at £10 per ton for home use.

HOLLAND

In 1880–83 the average consumption was as follows :—

	Tons
For food	39,000
Manufactures	19,000
Total	58,000

The consumption for food averaged 20 lbs. per head. The salt-tax yields £300,000 per annum, say 18 pence per inhabitant.

SPAIN AND PORTUGAL

In 1850 Spain was estimated to produce 800,000 ; Portugal, 520,000 tons. An official report in 1863 gave the production in Spain as 3,800,000 tons, probably ten times the real quantity. Exports were as follows :—

Year	Tons			Total Value, £
	Spain	Portugal	Total	
1872 . . .	220,000	180,000	400,000	410,000
1880 . . .	320,000	190,000	510,000	320,000
1888 . . .	240,000	170,000	410,000	200,000

The production of the two countries is not thought to exceed 600,000 tons.

SCANDINAVIA

Imports of salt were as follows :—

Year	Tons			
	Sweden	Norway	Denmark	Total
1860 . . .	40,000	65,000	10,000	115,000
1870 . . .	60,000	100,000	20,000	180,000
1880 . . .	60,000	70,000	20,000	150,000
1888 . . .	70,000	90,000	30,000	190,000

The large consumption in Norway is explained by the fisheries.

UNITED STATES

Production and consumption at various dates were :—

Year	Tons			Lbs. per Inhabitant
	Production	Imports	Consumption	
1840	150,000	...	...	...
1870	400,000	...	...	...
1880	670,000	430,000	1,100,000	48
1888	1,050,000	310,000	1,360,000	48

Saltworks were established at Cape Charles, Virginia, in 1620, and the French began working salt-springs in Illinois in 1720. The principal works in 1850 were at Syracuse, New York, producing 250,000 tons yearly. The method of solar evaporation is by tanks six inches deep, with an area of 300 square feet, each tank producing one ton per annum, worth 8s. Boiling is also practised at Syracuse in kettles of 100 gallons ; the consumption of coal being one ton for each ton of salt. The production in 1870 and 1880 was as follows :—

	Saltworks		Tons Produced	
	1870	1880	1870	1880
Michigan . . .	65	86	90,000	280,000
New York . .	93	69	110,000	200,000
Virginia . . .	29	11	100,000	70,000
Ohio	40	25	65,000	60,000
Various . . .	55	73	35,000	60,000
Total . .	282	264	400,000	670,000

CANADA

The importation has been as follows :—

Year	Tons	Value, £
1874	60,000	90,000
1887	50,000	65,000

Salt-springs were discovered at Goderich, Ontario, in 1865, and a bore of 960 feet was sunk in 1876. The production in 1886 was 55,000 tons, valued at £45,000. The consumption is, therefore, 105,000 tons, equal to 45 lbs. per inhabitant yearly.

INDIA

About 500,000 tons are made yearly, besides which the importation has been as follows :—

Year	Tons	Value, £
1873	280,000	830,000
1880	350,000	760,000
1888	430,000	800,000

The salt-tax is enormous, and weighs heavily on the ryots. In 1876 it was six millions sterling, rising in 1890 to eight millions sterling. Consumption of salt barely averages 10 lbs. per inhabitant, which tends still further to debilitate the inhabitants.

SANITATION

In 1880 the amount of outstanding loans in Great Britain for sanitary purposes, such as water-supply, drainage, &c., exceeded 56 millions sterling. In 1888 it was stated that the total outlay on these works in the last thirty years reached 100 millions sterling. The following table of sewage was published in 1882 :—

	Sewers, Cost per Mile	Tons of Sewage discharged Weekly
Manchester . .	£1,240	770,000
Preston . . .	2,000	140,000
London . . .	5,550	5,500,000
Blackburn . .	4,700	150,000

The system of sewage-farms requires an acre for 500 inhabitants, say 1000 acres for a city like Manchester or Liverpool. Sewage is supposed to have a market value of 1d. per ton. In 1876 there were 65 towns in England with sewage-farms.

The length of drains or sewers in various cities in 1882 was as follows :—

	Miles		Miles
London . . .	2300	Bordeaux . . .	34
Paris . . .	440	Lille . . .	33
New York . .	200	Rheims . . .	14

The Romans understood the importance of sewers, and in the year 184 B.C. we find that the Senate spent 1000 talents, say £120,000 sterling, on enlarging the drains. Paris under Louis XIV. had nearly two miles of sewers, and under Bonaparte about sixteen miles. Dry refuse in English towns, which is thrown into dust-bins, is found to average 10 lbs. a week per inhabitant. The result of sanitation is shown in the reduced death-rate, by comparing the average for seven years before and seven years after the introduction of water-supply and drainage, viz. :—

	Deaths per 10,000 Pop.		Deaths from Typhoid	
	Before	After	Before	After
Cardiff . .	330	230	17	11
Croydon . .	240	190	15	5
Dover . .	230	210	14	9
Leicester .	260	250	15	8
Merthyr . .	260	180	21	9
Salisbury .	280	220	...	...
Warwick .	230	210	19	9

Deaths from typhoid in various towns showed a similar decline, both here and on the Continent, after the introduction of sanitary works :—

	Per 100,000 Inhabitants	
	Before	After
Brussels	22	15
Hamburg	48	22
Dantzig	99	27
Frankfort	63	24
Bristol	100	65
Cheltenham . . .	80	47

Buchanan shows that the annual death-rate for twenty-four towns in England fell from 24.7 per thousand inhabitants to 21.9 after the adoption of water-supply and sewers.

SCIENCE

The learned societies of the United Kingdom in 1880 were 118 in number and counted 66,200 members; but as many of these were repetitions, it is not likely that the cultivators of science were more than 44,000. The aggregate of 15 principal societies at various dates was :—

Year	Members
1830	2,201
1850	15,769
1880	29,061

In 1882 the principal societies showed as follows :—

Royal . . .	552	Pharmaceutical .	3,250
Statistical . .	807	Law . . .	1,530
Archæological . .	580	Arts	3,340
Geological . .	850	Agricultural . .	7,950
Antiquaries . .	640	Zoological . .	2,000
Geographical . .	3,430	British Association .	2,400
Botanical . . .	1,660	Social Science . .	1,550

In 1881 the United Kingdom had 1355 schools of science, with 66,600 pupils; annual cost £295,000, or 89 shillings per pupil. In the same year the number of visitors to the different museums was as follows :—

British Museum .	790,000	National Gallery	958,000
South Kensington	1,017,000	Kew Gardens .	612,000
Bethnal Green .	451,000	Edinburgh . .	350,000
Patent Office .	266,000	Dublin . .	192,000

SEAMEN

The number of seafaring men in all countries was in 1882 as follows :—

	Navy	Merchant	Coast, Fishing	Total	Ratio to Population, per Cent.
U. Kingdom	45,000	193,000	167,000	405,000	1.11
France . .	43,000	35,000	94 000	172,000	0.45
Germany. .	8,000	40,000	27,000	75,000	0.16
Russia . .	26,000	23,000	74,000	123,000	0.15
Austria . .	10,000	7,000	9,000	26,000	0.07
Italy . . .	15,000	52,000	74,000	141,000	0.50
Spain . .	7,000	23,000	44,000	74,000	0.45
Portugal . .	4,000	5,000	4,000	13,000	0.30
Holland . .	7,000	18,000	13,000	38,000	0.95
Denmark. .	1,000	7,000	5,000	13,000	0.70
Sweden and } Norway }	9,000	79,000	143,000	231,000	3.55
Greece .	1,000	11,000	15,000	27,000	1.52
Turkey . .	4,000	10,000	3,000	17,000	0.22
Europe . .	180,000	503,000	672,000	1,355,000	0.42
United States	8,000	120,000	54,000	182,000	0.35
Canada . .	...	50,000	65,000	115,000	2.54
Brazil . . .	2,000	6,000	8,000	16,000	0.18
Argentine } Republic }	1,000	2,000	8,000	11,000	0.55
Australia. .	...	11,000	3,000	14,000	0.48
Total . .	191,000	692,000	810,000	1,693,000	0.45

If marines and coastguards were added, the total would fall little short of two millions of men, or nearly 3 per cent. of the able-bodied men of the Christian world.

SEASONS

For medical purposes the seasons are supposed to begin on the following dates :—

	Northern Hemisphere	Southern Hemisphere
Spring. . .	March 1st	September 1st
Summer . .	June 1st	December 1st
Autumn . .	September 1st	March 1st
Winter . .	December 1st	June 1st

The mean temperature of the seasons in various countries is as follows, in degrees Fahrenheit :—

	Spring	Summer	Autumn	Winter
England . . .	47	61	51	40
France . . .	54	68	56	41
Germany . . .	48	65	48	33
Italy . . .	59	75	61	45
Spain . . .	61	79	67	51
Canada . . .	43	71	47	17
Jamaica . . .	77	81	79	76
New South Wales .	63	70	64	54
Cape Colony . .	61	69	63	56
Brazil . . .	73	79	75	69

SERVANTS

Of 1000 families at Berlin there were 194 which kept servants in 1864, and only 173 in 1871. Professor Leone Levi in 1883 computed 1,951,000 domestic servants in the United Kingdom, earning £68,500,000 per annum, say £35 each.

SHIPPING

The following is Mr. Kiaer's table of the shipping of the world, with a column added for carrying power, in which steamers are counted as four times the power of sailing-vessels :—

Year	Steam, Tons	Sail, Tons	Total, Tons	Carrying Power
1816 . .	1,500	3,420,000	3,421,500	3,426,000
1820 . .	6,200	3,160,000	3,166,200	3,185,000
1830 . .	30,200	3,020,000	3,050,200	3,140,000
1840 . .	97,000	4,560,000	4,657,000	4,950,000
1850 . .	217,000	6,380,000	6,597,000	7,250,000
1860 . .	764,000	10,710,000	11,474,000	13,770,000
1870 . .	1,710,000	12,350,000	14,060,000	19,190,000
1880 . .	4,650,000	13,270,000	17,920,000	31,870,000
1886 . .	7,400,000	12,000,000	19,400,000	41,600,000

Mr. Kiaer's figures doubtless apply only to vessels of "long cours," as they are less than the total shipping. For example, Lloyd's list in 1842 shows for Europe only, no fewer than 88,100 vessels of 6,547,000 tons.

The following is an approximate table of shipping at various dates, the British flag including colonial vessels :—

	1800	1820	1842	1860	1888
British	1,856,000	2,654,000	3,311,000	5,713,000	9,050,000
French	250,000	350,000	634,000	930,000	960,000
German	150,000	250,000	550,000	700,000	1,230,000
American . . .	970,000	1,280,000	2,180,000	5,350,000	4,310,000
Various	800,000	1,300,000	2,705,000	3,777,000	6,100,000
Total . .	4,026,000	5,834,000	9,380,000	16,470,000	21,650,000

The nominal tonnage of the various flags was approximately as follows (see *Lloyd's List for* 1842):—

	1842	1860	1888		
	All Vessels	All Vessels	Steam	Sail	Total
United Kingdom . . .	2,570,000	4,660,000	4,350,000	3,115,000	7,465,000
Colonies	741,000	1,053,000	265,000	1,320,000	1,585,000
British	3,311,000	5,713,000	4,615,000	4,435,000	9,050,000
French	634,000	1,010,000	510,000	450,000	960,000
German	550,000	700,000	500,000	730,000	1,230,000
Russian	240,000	400,000	140,000	610,000	750,000
Austrian	210,000	250,000	90,000	130,000	220,000
Italian	460,000	550,000	175,000	675,000	850,000
Spanish	280,000	470,000	395,000	205,000	600,000
Portuguese	80,000	90,000	15,000	63,000	78,000
Scandinavian	620,000	970,000	355,000	1,950,000	2,305,000
Dutch	270,000	300,000	105,000	140,000	245,000
Belgium	30,000	30,000	73,000	4,000	77,000
Turkish	182,000	180,000	64,000	153,000	217,000
Greek	186,000	200,000	31,000	227,000	258,000
United States	2,180,000	5,350,000	1,770,000	2,540,000	4,310,000
Various	147,000	387,000	202,000	330,000	532,000
Total . . .	9,380,000	16,600,000	9,040,000	12,642,000	21,682,000

The carrying power of the principal flags in 1888 was as follows:—

Flag	Carrying Power, Tons			Number of Vessels	Carrying Power per Vessel
	Steam	Sail	Total		
U. Kingdom	17,400,000	3,115,000	20,515,000	21,896	930
Colonies .	1,060,000	1,320,000	2,380,000	6,010	400
British . .	18,460,000	4,435,000	22,895,000	27,906	820
French . .	2,040,000	450,000	2,490,000	15,278	165
German .	2,000,000	730,000	2,730,000	3,635	750
Russian .	560,000	610,000	1,170,000	4,406	270
Austrian .	360,000	130,000	490,000	367	1,320
Italian . .	700,000	675,000	1,375,000	6,810	200
Spanish .	1,580,000	205,000	1,785,000	1,698	1,050
Portuguese	60,000	63,000	123,000	443	270
Swedish .	500,000	375,000	875,000	3,844	230
Norwegian	540,000	1,400,000	1,940,000	7,233	270
Danish . .	380,000	175,000	555,000	3,344	165
Dutch . .	420,000	140,000	560,000	609	920
Belgian . .	290,000	4,000	294,000	59	5,000
Turkish .	260,000	153,000	413,000	875	480
Greek . .	120,000	227,000	347,000	5,157	65
U. States .	7,080,000	2,540,000	9,620,000	22,623	425
Chili . .	80,000	58,000	138,000	166	820
Japan . .	290,000	60,000	350,000	1,284	270
Brazil . .	240,000	70,000	310,000	495	630
China * . .	100,000	10,000	110,000	135	810
Various .	100,000	132,000	232,000	770	300
The World	36,160,000	12,642,000	48,802,000	107,137	453

* Exclusive of junks and canal-boats.

Mr. Kiaer's table of vessels over 100 tons, in 1881, was as follows:—

Flag of	Number			Total Tonnage
	Steamers	Sailing	Total	
Great Britain .	2,869	11,893	14,762	7,010,000
France	335	2,772	3,107	840,000
Germany . . .	277	3,113	3,390	1,150,000
United States .	548	5,958	6,506	2,370,000
Norway . . .	148	4,160	4,308	1,460,000
Sweden . . .	258	1,979	2,237	470,000
Denmark . . .	109	1,172	1,281	230,000
Italy	103	2,936	3,039	1,070,000
Spain	226	1,578	1,804	450,000
Holland . . .	111	1,112	1,223	420,000
Greece	20	1,672	1,692	330,000
Canada . . .	918	6,459	7,377	1,140,000
Various . . .	470	3,780	4,250	1,385,000
The World . .	6,392	48,584	54,976	18,325,000

It would appear, therefore, that the whole shipping of the world may be summed up as follows, for 1888:—

	Number	Tons Register	Carrying Power	Carrying Power per Vessel
Steamers . .	19,740	9,040,000	36,160,000	1,820
Sailing-vessels	25,197	11,510,000	11,510,000	460
Small craft .	62,200	1,132,000	1,132,000	18
Total . .	107,137	21,682,000	48,802,000	453

Hence it may be said that, excluding 62,200 small craft, the commerce of the world is carried on by 45,000 vessels, of 20,500,000 tons register, with a carrying power of 48 million tons.

The relative amounts of carrying power that corresponded to steam and sail at various dates were as follows:—

Year	Nominal Tonnage			Carrying Power			Percentage	
	Steam	Sail	Total	Steam	Sail	Total	Steam	Sail
1820 . . .	20,000	5,814,000	5,834,000	80,000	5,814,000	5,894,000	1.4	98.6
1840 . . .	368,000	9,012,000	9,380,000	1,470,000	9,012,000	10,482,000	14.0	86.0
1860 . . .	1,710,000	14,890,000	16,600,000	6,840,000	14,890,000	21,730,000	31.5	68.5
1870 . . .	3,040,000	12,900,000	15,940,000	12,200,000	12,900,000	25,100,000	48.8	51.2
1880 . . .	5,880,000	14,400,000	20,280,000	23,500,000	14,400,000	37,900,000	61.5	38.5
1888 . . .	9,040,000	12,640,000	21,680,000	36,160,000	12,640,000	48,800,000	74.0	26.0

The following table shows approximately the merchant steam-navies of the world at various dates :—

	Nominal Tonnage of Steamers					
	1840	1850	1860	1870	1880	1888
British	95,000	188,000	502,000	1,203,000	3,105,000	4,355,000
American	198,000	481,000	870,000	1,075,000	1,211,000	1,765,000
French	10,000	27,000	84,000	170,000	278,000	510,000
German	10,000	20,000	50,000	82,000	216,000	503,000
Russian	10,000	20,000	40,000	70,000	100,000	142,000
Austrian	10,000	20,000	30,000	50,000	60,000	90,000
Italian	10,000	15,000	20,000	35,000	77,000	175,000
Spanish	5,000	10,000	13,000	45,000	230,000	395,000
Scandinavian . . .	5,000	10,000	25,000	88,000	190,000	355,000
Dutch	5,000	10,000	20,000	30,000	65,000	105,000
Various	10,000	20,000	60,000	190,000	350,000	645,000
Total . .	368,000	821,000	1,714,000	3,038,000	5,882,000	9,040,000

The carrying power of the principal flags at various dates was approximately as follows :—

Flag	Tons				
	1820	1840	1860	1880	1888
United Kingdom . . .	2,440,000	2,840,000	6,025,000	14,750,000	20,515,000
Colonies	210,000	756,000	1,194,000	2,060,000	2,380,000
British	2,650,000	3,596,000	7,219,000	16,810,000	22,895,000
American	1,340,000	2,780,000	7,960,000	7,700,000	9,620,000
French	450,000	664,000	1,265,000	1,753,000	2,491,000
German	300,000	580,000	850,000	1,830,000	2,743,000
Russian	150,000	270,000	520,000	1,040,000	1,170,000
Spanish	120,000	295,000	510,000	1,250,000	1,785,000
Italian	200,000	490,000	610,000	1,230,000	1,375,000
Norwegian	110,000	260,000	850,000	1,690,000	1,940,000
Dutch	140,000	275,000	400,000	525,000	560,000
Various	434,000	1,272,000	1,546,000	4,072,000	4,221,000
Total . . .	5,894,000	10,482,000	21,730,000	37,900,000	48,800,000

The increase of nominal tonnage and of effective carrying power in various periods was approximately as follows :—

	Annual Average of Increase			
	Tons Register		Tons Carrying Power	
	1841–60	1861–88	1841–60	1861–88
British	120,000	119,000	180,000	560,000
American	160,000	...	259,000	60,000
French	19,000	...	30,000	45,000
German	7,500	19,000	14,000	68,000
Italian	4,500	10,500	6,000	27,000
Spanish	9,500	5,000	11,000	45,000
Norwegian	29,000	25,000	29,000	40,000
Russian	8,000	12,200	12,500	23,000
Dutch	1,500	...	6,000	5,600
Various	1,000	...	14,500	94,400
Total . .	360,000	179,000	562,000	968,000

The net increase of nominal tonnage from 1861 to 1888 was 179,000 per annum; but this is not the sum of the above column, as several countries showed a decline.

Great as has been the growth of carrying power in the last 30 years it is much less than the increase in the tonnage of port entries, which has been 3½-fold, while the carrying power has little more than doubled, viz. :—

Year	Nom. Tonnage	Carrying Power	Port Entries
1860 . . .	16,600,000	21,730,000	64,100,000
1870 . . .	15,940,000	25,100,000	95,400,000
1880 . . .	20,280,000	37,900,000	166,300,000
1888 . . .	21,680,000	48,800,000	225,200,000

The tonnage of port entries of sea-going vessels at various dates was approximately as follows (the item marked "various" not being accurately known) :—

	1860	1870	1880	1888
U. Kingdom	12,350,000	18,120,000	29,360,000	33,950,000
France . .	4,230,000	6,800,000	12,370,000	14,030,000
Germany . .	3,730,000	6,200,000	6,530,000	9,440,000
Russia . .	2,110,000	3,520,000	5,020,000	7,410,000
Austria . .	2,600,000	3,430,000	4,820,000	7,540,000
Italy . . .	2,400,000	3,790,000	4,690,000	6,670,000
Spain . . .	1,350,000	2,500,000	5,700,000	11,440,000
Sweden and Norway	2,100,000	3,790,000	5,400,000	7,320,000
Denmark . .	600,000	710,000	2,230,000	3,380,000
Holland . .	1,660,000	2,310,000	3,450,000	5,110,000
Belgium . .	670,000	1,580,000	3,570,000	4,910,000
Greece . .	930,000	1,270,000	1,790,000	2,370,000
United States	5,005,000	6,270,000	15,250,000	15,390,000
British Colonies	10,880,000	15,200,000	28,260,000	41,300,000
Suez Canal .	...	440,000	4,350,000	9,440,000
Various . .	13,500,000	19,500,000	33,500,000	45,500,000
Total . .	64,115,000	95,430,000	166,290,000	225,200,000

Entries in ballast, which are included in the above table, showed tonnage and ratio to total entries thus :—

	1870	1880	1888	1870	1880	1888
	Tons	Tons	Tons	%	%	%
U. Kingdom	3,200,000	5,100,000	6,900,000	17	17	21
France . .	200,000	400,000	460,000	3	3	3
Germany .	810,000	370,000	700,000	13	6	8
Russia . .	1,820,000	1,860,000	4,800,000	52	36	64
Austria . .	840,000	820,000	700,000	25	17	9
Italy . . .	380,000	450,000	570,000	10	10	8
Spain . . .	600,000	1,900,000	3,800,000	24	33	33
Sweden . .	1,400,000	1,900,000	2,900,000	65	55	58
Norway . .	1,040,000	980,000	850,000	66	50	35
Denmark .	...	920,000	1,480,000	...	45	44
Holland . .	...	100,000	210,000	...	3	4
Belgium . .	40,000	110,000	700,000	2	3	14
U. States .	...	3,140,000	...	...	21	...

It would seem from the above that as regards European ports the aggregate of entries in ballast has not materially varied, in proportion, since 1870, the ratio being as 21 per cent. of all entries. The following table shows the ratio of entries in each country belonging to the flag of that country, and the ratio corresponding to other or foreign flags :—

	National			Foreign Flags		
	1870	1880	1887	1870	1880	1887
United Kingdom .	68.4	70.4	73.6	31.6	29.6	26.4
Russia . . .	11.2	11.4	7.9	88.8	88.6	92.1
Norway . . .	70.0	68.2	65.5	30.0	31.8	34.5
Sweden . . .	31.8	37.2	35.8	68.2	62.8	64.2
Germany . .	35.9	39.1	43.3	64.1	60.9	56.7
Holland . .	28.3	30.9	30.9	71.7	69.1	69.1
France . . .	31.5	30.0	36.2	68.5	70.0	63.8
Spain . . .	36.9	26.6	39.0	63.1	73.4	61.0
Italy . . .	36.5	34.8	23.6	63.5	65.2	76.4
United States .	38.2	18.9	21.0	61.8	81.1	79.0

The principal commercial ports of the world showed the tonnage of sea-going entries in 1888 as follows :—

	Tons		Tons
London . . .	7,470,000	Havre	1,810,000
New York . .	5,470,000	Buenos Ayres .	1,590,000
Liverpool . .	5,370,000	Alexandria . .	1,590,000
Hamburg . . .	4,410,000	Montevideo . .	1,620,000
Antwerp . . .	3,660,000	Athens	1,550,000
Marseilles . .	3,360,000	Genoa	1,480,000
Hong-Kong . .	3,330,000	Bremen . . .	1,180,000
Cardiff . . .	2,930,000	Boston	1,100,000
Rotterdam . .	2,530,000	San Francisco .	1,050,000
Sydney . . .	2,380,000	Bordeaux . . .	1,050,000
Melbourne . .	2,150,000	Stettin . . .	1,040,000
Newcastle . .	1,900,000	Philadelphia . .	1,030,000
Hull	1,900,000	Glasgow . . .	990,000

The above sums up a total of 64 million tons, which is nearly one-third of the commerce of the world, minor ports making up more than two-thirds.

If we compare the value of the imports of all nations with the tonnage of port entries (excluding ballast entries) at various dates, we find :—

Year	Imports, Millions £	Port Entries, Tons	Value, £ per Ton
1860 . . .	707	51,000,000	13.9
1870 . . .	1,040	76,000,000	13.8
1880 . . .	1,440	133,000,000	10.8
1888 . . .	1,502	180,000,000	8.3

This appears to show that coal, iron, and articles of less value, form every succeeding year a larger ratio of sea-borne merchandise.

The registered shipping belonging to the various ports in 1882 was as follows :—

	Sail	Steam	Total	Carrying Power
Liverpool . .	1,080,000	520,000	1,600,000	3,160,000
London . . .	620,000	570,000	1,190,000	2,900,000
Glasgow . . .	350,000	380,000	730,000	1,870,000
New York . .	530,000	210,000	740,000	1,370,000
Marseilles . .	60,000	160,000	220,000	700,000
Hull	40,000	150,000	190,000	640,000
Newcastle . .	60,000	140,000	200,000	620,000
Sunderland . .	110,000	110,000	220,000	550,000
Hamburg . .	140,000	70,000	210,000	420,000
Bremen . . .	160,000	60,000	220,000	400,000
Greenock . .	170,000	40,000	210,000	330,000
San Francisco .	110,000	50,000	160,000	310,000
Philadelphia .	110,000	50,000	160,000	310,000
Trieste . . .	30,000	60,000	90,000	270,000
Leith . . .	20,000	60,000	80,000	260,000
Havre	70,000	50,000	120,000	270,000
New Brunswick	270,000	10,000	280,000	310,000
Barcelona . .	100,000	40,000	140,000	260,000
Genoa . . .	120,000	30,000	150,000	240,000
Odessa . . .	20,000	50,000	70,000	220,000
Amsterdam . .	60,000	40,000	100,000	220,000
Copenhagen .	40,000	40,000	80,000	200,000
Southampton .	30,000	40,000	70,000	190,000
Antwerp . . .	10,000	40,000	50,000	170,000
Aberdeen . .	100,000	20,000	120,000	180,000
Bergen . . .	60,000	20,000	80,000	140,000
Yarmouth . .	160,000	...	160,000	160,000
Other ports . .	10,372,000	2,634,000	13,006,000	20,910,000
The world .	15,002,000	5,644,000	20,646,000	37,580,000

Italian vessels seem to be worked cheaper than others. The following statement was published in 1881 as the monthly average expense of a vessel of 1000 tons with a crew of twenty men :—

	£		£
Italian . . .	95	German . . .	135
Austrian . .	125	British . . .	145
French . . .	135	American . . .	200

The percentage of vessels lost yearly, and the average life of shipping of various flags, as shown by Mr. Kiaer, are :—

	Annual Loss		Years of a Ship's Life
	Steamer	Sailing	
American . . .	4.06	5.45	18
French	2.47	4.04	20
Dutch	3.84	4.49	22
German . . .	2.77	4.04	23
British	2.94	3.93	26
Italian	1.74	2.94	28
Scandinavian . .	1.96	3.20	30

The weight of anchors and chain-cables for vessels is as follows :—

Vessel, Tons	Anchors, Tons	Heaviest in Cwts.	Cable, Inches	Cable, Length in Fathoms
200	3	13	1.0	180
500	6	25	1.5	270
1,000	9½	42	1.9	300
2,000	18	77	2.1	300

It is usual for vessels to carry seven anchors, four of the maximum weight prescribed above.

The value of shipping and cargoes lost yearly at sea cannot be ascertained precisely. The *Annual Register* for 1881 published the following statement, but it seems very much exaggerated :—

	Vessels Lost		Value of Ships and Cargo, £	
	1879	1880	1879	1880
British . .	...	913	19,230,000	47,495,000
Foreign . .	...	767	6,270,000	20,832,000
Total .	1,688	1,680	25,500,000	68,327,000

Lloyd's Register gave the following summary of vessels lost in fifteen years, ending 1880 :—

	Number	Annual Average
Missing	1,403	94
Sunk by collision . .	2,753	183
Burnt	2,903	194
Stranded . . .	17,502	1,166
Waterlogged, &c. . .	8,026	535
Total . .	32,587	2,172

At Mr. Kiaer's rate of loss of shipping, the total annual loss by shipwreck would be as follows :—

	Shipping, Tons			Value of		
	Steam	Sail	Total	Vessels, £	Cargo, £	Total, £
British	135,000	175,000	310,000	5,600,000	3,000,000	8,600,000
French	12,000	18,000	30,000	500,000	300,000	800,000
German	14,000	29,000	43,000	650,000	400,000	1,050,000
Italian	3,000	20,000	23,000	300,000	200,000	500,000
Dutch	4,000	6,000	10,000	170,000	100,000	270,000
American. . . .	70,000	140,000	210,000	3,400,000	2,000,000	5,400,000
Scandinavian . .	7,000	60,000	67,000	700,000	400,000	1,100,000
Various . . .	25,000	62,000	87,000	1,300,000	800,000	2,100,000
Total . .	270,000	510,000	780,000	12,620,000	7,200,000	19,820,000

The loss of life among seamen is stated by Mr. Plimsoll, on various official returns, to average thus yearly :—

	Per 10,000		*Per* 10,000
Britain . . .	152	Norway . . .	36
Germany . . .	81	Italy . . .	22
Holland . . .	43	Average . . .	66

UNITED KINGDOM

British and Colonial shipping showed as follows :—

Year	Vessels	Tons	Sailors	Tons per Ship	Tons per Sailor	Reign
1588	470	37,400	...	80	...	Elizabeth
1610	910	83,000	...	90	...	James I.
1666	1,320	120,000	...	90	...	Charles II.
1688	2,620	210,000	...	80	...	James II.
1702	3,260	261,000	...	80	...	Anne
1760	5,730	487,000	...	85	...	George III.
1800	17,410	1,856,000	140,000	106	14	George III.
1810	23,703	2,426,000	162,000	102	15	George III.
1820	25,374	2,654,000	175,000	105	15	George IV.
1830	23,721	2,533,000	155,000	107	16	William IV.
1840	28,962	3,311,000	201,000	114	17	Victoria
1850	34,288	4,233,000	239,000	124	18	Victoria
1860	29,469	5,713,000	230,000	193	25	Victoria
1870	32,920	7,150,000	261,000	216	27	Victoria
1881	30,531	8,535,000	270,000	280	31	Victoria
1887	28,212	8,936,000	280,000	320	32	Victoria

The shipping of the United Kingdom, excluding colonial, has been as follows :—

Year	Vessels	Tons	Seamen	Tons per Vessel	Tons per Seaman
1810	20,253	2,211,000	145,000	105	15
1830	19,174	2,202,000	131,000	114	17
1850	25,984	3,565,000	148,000	138	24
1870	26,367	5,691,000	196,000	215	29
1881	24,830	6,490,000	193,000	260	33
1888	21,896	7,465,000	224,000	341	33

In 20 years succeeding the war with France our shipping declined in number and tonnage, and in number of men.

In 1808, at the outbreak of the Peninsular War, the merchant navy of the British Empire was composed thus :—

	Vessels	Tons	Sailors
England . . .	15,705	1,822,000	123,400
Scotland . . .	2,615	217,000	15,700
Ireland . . .	1,098	57,000	5,200
Colonies . . .	2,917	185,000	13,600
Total . .	22,335	2,281,000	157,900

If we discriminate steamers from sailing-vessels, allowing the former a carrying power of four to one, we find as follows :—

Year	United Kingdom			British Empire		
	Nominal Tonnage		Total Carrying Power	Nominal Tonnage		Total Carrying Power
	Sail	Steam		Sail	Steam	
1840 . . .	2,480,000	90,000	2,840,000	3,216,000	95,000	3,596,000
1850 . . .	2,990,000	110,000	3,430,000	4,045,000	188,000	4,797,000
1860 . . .	4,205,000	455,000	6,025,000	5,211,000	502,000	7,219,000
1870 . . .	4,580,000	1,110,000	9,020,000	5,947,000	1,203,000	10,759,000
1881 . . .	3,690,000	3,005,000	15,710,000	5,430,000	3,105,000	17,850,000
1887 . . .	3,250,000	4,090,000	19,610,000	4,581,000	4,355,000	22,000,000
1888 . . .	3,115,000	4,350,000	20,515,000	...	...	...

The Navigation Laws were repealed in 1849, and since that date our shipping traffic has increased seven times faster than population. The sea-going entries into ports of the United Kingdom were as follows :—

Year	Tons			British Per-centage
	British	Foreign	Total	
1840	3,245,000	1,475,000	4,720,000	69
1850	4,720,000	2,530,000	7,250,000	65
1860	6,960,000	5,390,000	12,350,000	56
1870	12,540,000	5,780,000	18,320,000	69
1880	20,670,000	8,690,000	29,360,000	70
1888	24,945,000	9,005,000	33,950,000	73

Coasting entries with cargoes only were as follows :—

Year	Tons		
	British	Foreign	Total
1854	15,320,000	50,000	15,370,000
1860	16,000,000	100,000	17,000,000
1870	18,210,000	90,000	18,300,000
1880	25,920,000	100,000	26,020,000
1888	29,000,000	80,000	29,080,000

The flags of foreign vessels entering British ports in 1878 and 1888 showed as follows :—

Flag	Tons	
	1878	1888
Norwegian	1,830,000	2,050,000
German	1,370,000	1,790,000
Dutch	530,000	1,040,000
French	740,000	990,000
Danish	620,000	770,000
Swedish	670,000	710,000
Spanish	230,000	505,000
Italian	630,000	280,000
Various	1,350,000	870,000
Total . . .	7,970,000	9,005,000

The sea-going tonnage entered and cleared at the principal ports in the United Kingdom was as follows :—

	Entered		Cleared	
	1878	1888	1878	1888
London . .	5,340,000	7,470,000	4,390,000	5,470,000
Liverpool .	4,400,000	5,370,000	4,390,000	4,940,000
Cardiff . .	1,480,000	2,930,000	2,800,000	5,150,000
Newcastle .	1,500,000	1,900,000	2,570,000	3,320,000
Hull . . .	1,470,000	1,900,000	1,310,000	1,500,000
Newport .	420,000	960,000	640,000	1,470,000
Shields . .	480,000	920,000	450,000	1,070,000
Southampton	905,000	870,000	750,000	790,000
Sunderland .	590,000	740,000	780,000	930,000
Middles-brough }	310,000	680,000	290,000	560,000
Grimsby . .	400,000	590,000	410,000	590,000
Bristol . .	440,000	580,000	230,000	180,000
Glasgow .	550,000	990,000	910,000	1,550,000
Greenock .	290,000	280,000	200,000	180,000
Dublin . .	330,000	210,000	190,000	80,000
Belfast . .	210,000	190,000	140,000	70,000
Various . .	6,175,000	7,370,000	5,850,000	6,720,000
Total . .	25,290,000	33,950,000	26,300,000	34,570,000

The tonnage of vessels entered at various dates was :—

Year	Sea-going	Coasting	Total
1801 . . .	1,720,000	6,000,000	7,720,000
1810 . . .	2,070,000	7,000,000	9,070,000
1820 . . .	2,110,000	8,000,000	10,110,000
1830 . . .	2,940,000	8,240,000	11,180,000
1840 . . .	4,720,000	12,600,000	17,320,000
1850 . . .	7,250,000	21,510,000	28,760,000
1860 . . .	12,340,000	24,400,000	36,740,000
1870 . . .	18,320,000	28,850,000	47,170,000
1880 . . .	29,070,000	36,140,000	65,210,000
1888 . . .	33,950,000	47,570,000	81,520,000

The service of pilot-boats in 1882 stood thus :—

	Boats	Pilots
England	692	2,066
Scotland	226	432
Ireland	132	395
United Kingdom . . .	1,050	2,893

Some of the merchant steamboat companies are equal in importance to the navies of some European Powers. The Cunard Co., for example, employs 10,000 men. The vessels, moreover, of the first-class companies are unsurpassed. At a recent meeting of the Society of Engineers the chairman said, " The *Teutonic*, 582 feet long, with a gross tonnage of 9680, can carry 1200 passengers, and in time of war twelve five-inch guns, with a range of five miles. The *City of Paris* runs twenty-four miles an hour, is 10,500 tons burthen, and has 18,000 horse-power. The Pacific and Oriental Steamers now use pressure at 160 lbs. with greater safety than they did fifty lbs. thirty years ago." As regards speed, British vessels beat all others. The *City of Paris* has run from Queenstown to New York in 5 days 20 hours, and from New York to Queenstown in 5 days 23 hours : on one day her run of 24 hours reached 511 miles, the highest on record. The *Roslyn Castle* has run from Cape Town to London in 17 days 13 hours. The *Stirling Castle* from Hankow (China) to London in 29 days 22 hours. The fastest steamer in the world appears to be the *Prince of Wales*, which averages twenty-four knots, or twenty-seven statute miles per hour (being three miles faster than the *City of Paris*), plying between Liverpool and Isle of Man. The greatest speed of sailing ships was as follows :— *James Baines*, 420 miles, *Flying Cloud*, 412 miles in 24 hours, being over seventeen miles an hour. The *Red Jacket* ran 2280 miles in seven days, averaging 325 miles a day.

Shipbuilding is carried on more extensively in the United Kingdom than elsewhere ; in fact, more than 80 per cent. of the world's shipping is built here. At a meeting in 1890 Mr. Palmer stated that " we were building in this country at the present time about a million tons of shipping, and the normal waste or loss was about 400,000 tons, leaving a surplus of 600,000 tons as an addition to mercantile marine."

The tonnage built in the United Kingdom was :—

Period	Sail	Steam	Total	Carrying Power
1801–10	520,000	...	520,000	520,000
1811–20	840,000	10,000	850,000	880,000
1821–30	800,000	40,000	840,000	960,000
1831–40	885,000	75,000	960,000	1,185,000
1841–50	990,000	160,000	1,150,000	1,630,000
1851–60	1,530,000	810,000	2,340,000	4,770,000
1861–70	2,100,000	1,490,000	3,590,000	8,100,000
1871–80	1,390,000	3,190,000	4,580,000	14,200,000
1881–89	1,265,000	4,555,000	5,820,000	19,500,000
89 years	10,320,000	10,330,000	20,650,000	51,745,000

From 1855 the distinction of vessels built for British from those for foreign flags was as follows :—

	Nominal Tonnage British			Nominal Tonnage Foreign		
	Steam	Sail	Total	Steam	Sail	Total
1855–59	283,000	930,000	1,213,000	144,000	8,000	152,000
1860–69	1,080,000	2,060,000	3,140,000	243,000	34,000	277,000
1870–79	2,590,000	1,390,000	3,980,000	474,000	40,000	514,000
1880–88	3,210,000	1,130,000	4,340,000	670,000	40,000	710,000
34 years	7,163,000	5,510,000	12,673,000	1,531,000	122,000	1,653,000

In ten years ending December 1889 there were built 5,932,000 tons of merchant shipping, of which 930,000 tons were for foreign flags, the rest for the British.

The Clyde is one of the principal seats of this industry :—

Year	Vessels Built, Tons		
	Clyde	Other Places	Total
1880 . . .	237,000	469,000	706,000
1882 . . .	389,000	391,000	780,000
1889 . . .	335,000	875,000	1,210,000

Vessels on the stocks on December 31, 1889, were :—

	Steam		Sail		Total	
	No.	Tons	No.	Tons	No.	Tons
Steel . . .	382	745,000	54	87,000	436	832,000
Iron . . .	57	21,000	8	6,000	65	27,000
Wood . .	7	1,000	35	3,000	42	4,000
Total .	446	767,000	97	96,000	543	863,000
Built for						
U. Kingdom	309	560,000	53	58,000	362	618,000
Colonies .	16	32,000	...	...	16	32,000
Germany .	16	46,000	4	7,000	20	53,000
Norway .	12	12,000	...	...	12	12,000
France . .	8	13,000	2	7,000	10	20,000
Various . .	85	104,000	38	24,000	123	128,000
Total .	446	767,000	97	96,000	543	863,000

The use of steel in shipbuilding was begun in 1879, when the tonnage of steamers built of it was 18,000 : at present, as shown above, 96 per cent. of all vessels built are of steel. It is found that a steel vessel can carry 20 per cent. more than an iron one. Improvements in machinery cause a great saving in coal, the average consumption now being 1½ lbs. per indicated horse-power hourly, as compared with 6 lbs. in the year 1837.

Lloyd's estimate of shipping value in 1882 was £30 a ton for steamers, including fittings and furniture, and £10 a ton for sailing vessels. The cost of building has, however, since fallen, and at present a fair valuation of our merchant navy would be as follows :—

	Tons	Value, £	£ per Ton
Sailing . . .	3,115,000	24,920,000	8
Steam . . .	4,350,000	108,750,000	25
Total .	7,465,000	133,670,000	18

The tonnage of British vessels lost or broken up in nine years (1880–88) was as follows :—

Period	Steam	Sail	Total	Carrying Power
1880–84 . .	810,000	1,338,000	2,148,000	4,578,000
1885–88 . .	580,000	854,000	1,434,000	3,174,000
9 years . .	1,390,000	2,192,000	3,582,000	7,752,000

The death-rate of vessels (that is, the percentage lost or broken up in the same nine years) was :—

Steam . . . . . 4.2 per annum
Sail . . . . . 7.0 per annum

According to Mr. Kiaer, the losses of British vessels on sea average 3 per cent. of steamers and 4 per cent. of sailing vessels : on this basis the decrease of shipping in 1880–89 would be made up thus :—

	Steam	Sail	Total, Tons
Lost at sea . .	990,000	1,224,000	2,214,000
Broken up . . .	400,000	968,000	1,368,000
Total decease .	1,390,000	2,192,000	3,582,000

The loss of life in British vessels was as follows :—

Year	Crews	Passengers	Total	Yearly Average
1871–75 . .	9,715	2,037	11,752	2,350
1876–80 . .	7,965	772	8,737	1,747
1881–83 . .	7,376	382	7,758	2,586
Total .	25,056	3,191	28,247	2,173

Lifeboats were established on the British coasts in 1824, which in sixty-three years down to 1887 were the means of saving 34,043 lives, an average of 550 yearly. There are at present 272, manned by 12,000 volunteer seamen, the coxswain alone being paid to mind the boat. They are supported by voluntary donations, which average £43,000 yearly.

FRANCE

In 1669 the merchant navy comprised 600 vessels, the number rising to 800 in 1720, of 150,000 tons aggregate, and to 1000 in 1788, with an aggregate of 250,000 tons.

French Shipping in	Number			Tons			Carrying Power
	Steam	Sail	Total	Steam	Sail	Total	
1840	94	14,354	14,448	10,000	624,000	634,000	664,000
1850	164	14,300	14,464	27,000	733,000	760,000	841,000
1860	346	14,823	15,169	84,000	929,000	1,013,000	1,265,000
1870	486	15,020	15,506	170,000	886,000	1,056,000	1,566,000
1880	652	14,406	15,058	278,000	641,000	919,000	1,753,000
1888	1,015	14,263	15,278	510,000	451,000	961,000	2,491,000

The total tonnage entered and cleared at French ports since 1837 showed the following averages :—

Period	Annual Average, Tons						Total Crew
	Steam	Sail	Total	In Ballast	French	Foreign	
1837–46	680,000	3,390,000	4,070,000	920,000	1,470,000	2,600,000	337,000
1847–56	1,270,000	4,370,000	5,640,000	1,260,000	2,230,000	3,410,000	443,000
1857–66	3,310,000	6,220,000	9,530,000	1,920,000	3,820,000	5,710,000	662,000
1867–76	8,050,000	6,850,000	14,900,000	3,080,000	4,950,000	9,950,000	868,000
1877–86	17,820,000	6,610,000	24,430,000	5,330,000	8,010,000	16,420,000	1,070,000
1886	22,480,000	4,270,000	26,750,000	5,030,000	9,600,000	17,150,000	1,096,000

Crew and tonnage are doubled in the above table, as it includes vessels both entered and cleared.

The following table shows the tonnage of entries only, that is, the annual average :—

Period	Vessels	Tons	Tons per Ship	Per Seaman
1837–46 . .	18,496	2,040,000	110	12
1847–56 . .	22,323	2,800,000	125	13
1857–66 . .	30,590	4,710,000	154	14
1867–76 . .	34,529	7,380,000	214	17
1877–86 . .	34,800	12,100,000	345	23
1886 . . .	30,463	13,100,000	430	24

The percentage of steam, sail, ballast, French and foreign vessels entered and cleared since 1837 was as follows :—

Period	In every 100 Tons of Shipping				
	French	Foreign	Steam	Sail	Ballast
1837–46 . .	36	64	17	83	23
1847–56 . .	40	60	22	78	22
1857–66 . .	40	60	35	65	20
1867–76 . .	33	67	54	46	21
1877–86 . .	33	67	73	27	21
1886 . . .	36	64	84	16	19

The *cabotage* or coasting trade of France since 1837 was as follows :—

Period	Annual Average			
	Vessels	Tonnage	Men	Tons Cargo
1837–46 . .	77,300	2,480,000	310,000	2,010,000
1847–56 . .	73,400	2,680,000	312,000	2,250,000
1857–66 . .	75,700	3,060,000	291,000	2,340,000
1867–76 . .	60,100	2,930,000	237,000	2,030,000
1877–86 . .	57,600	3,730,000	271,000	2,035,000

In 1886 the coasting trade was made up thus :—

	Vessels	Tonnage	Men	Tons Cargo
Ocean . . .	47,030	2,460,000	181,500	1,530,000
Mediterranean	8,870	1,980,000	112,800	700,000
Total . .	55,900	4,440,000	294,300	2,230,000

The following table shows the total sea-going and coasting tonnage entered and cleared at all ports in 1886 :—

	Tonnage	Tons Cargo
Marseilles . . .	8,300,000	1,190,000
Havre . . .	4,030,000	2,350,000
Bordeaux . . .	2,930,000	2,360,000
Dunkirk . . .	1,550,000	1,760,000
Various . . .	13,800,000	12,800,000
Total .	30,610,000	20,460,000

The great difference between tonnage of vessels at Marseilles and weight of cargo handled probably arises from the fact that the passenger traffic forms the principal share. The shipping registered at the various ports in 1885 was as follows :—

Port	Tonnage			Carrying Power
	Sail	Steam	Total	
Havre .	40,000	147,000	187,000	630,000
Bordeaux .	58,000	25,000	83,000	158,000
Marseilles .	29,000	245,000	274,000	1,009,000
Various .	365,000	84,000	449,000	701,000
Total .	492,000	501,000	993,000	2,498,000

The Empress Eugenie introduced lifeboat stations in 1866, of which in 1882 there were 37, at exposed points of the coast. The French merchant navy in 1886 had 93,800 seamen, viz. :—

Vessels of	Tonnage	Crew	Tons per Man
Under 100 tons . .	197,000	61,300	3
100–300 . . .	165,000	12,100	14
300–500 . . .	100,000	3,700	27
Over 500 . . .	531,000	16,700	32
Total .	993,000	93,800	11

The total tonnage entered and cleared at all ports in 1888 was as follows :—

	Tons		
	Entered	Cleared	Total
French .	10,980,000	11,260,000	22,240,000
Foreign .	7,150,000	9,300,000	16,450,000
Total .	18,130,000	20,560,000	38,690,000
Ballast .	1,470,000	6,080,000	7,550,000
Cargo . .	16,660,000	14,480,000	31,140,000
Total .	18,130,000	20,560,000	38,690,000

Most of the French merchant navy is of small tonnage, there being only 2475 vessels over 50 tons, and 12,803 below that standard.

GERMANY

The merchant navy in 1842 consisted of 8200 vessels, with an aggregate of 551,000 tons. Later statistics are as follow :—

Year	Vessels, Number			Tons		
	Steam	Sail	Total	Steam	Sail	Total
1871	147	4,372	4,519	82,000	900,000	982,000
1880	414	4,246	4,660	216,000	966,000	1,182,000
1888	750	2,885	3,635	503,000	731,000	1,234,000

The size and carrying power of the vessels have grown as follows :—

	Vessels	Tons	Carrying Power	Per Vessel	
				Tons	Carrying Power
1842	8,200	551,000	551,000	67	67
1871	4,519	982,000	1,228,000	218	270
1888	3,635	1,234,000	2,743,000	338	751

The carrying power compares with the number of seamen as follows :—

Year	Seamen	Carrying Power	Tons per Man
1871 . . .	39,500	1,228,000	31
1877 . . .	53,400	1,830,000	35
1889 . . .	36,300	2,743,000	75

The ratio of carrying power per seaman has more than doubled in twelve years. It is now 75 tons per man, against 91 in the British merchant-navy. But in spite of the increased efficiency of German seamen, the carrying trade of German ports is passing into the hands of other maritime nations, the ratio of German entries being less than it was thirty years ago.

The tonnage of entries into all German ports was as follows :—

Year	German	Foreign	Total	German Ratio per Cent.
1860 . . .	1,740,000	1,990,000	3,730,000	47
1870 . . .	2,705,000	3,500,000	6,205,000	43
1880 . . .	2,560,000	3,970,000	6,530,000	39
1888 . . .	3,910,000	5,530,000	9,440,000	42

Entries in the ports of the German Empire in 1886 were as follows :—

From	Vessels	Tons	Flag	Vessels	Tons
German ports . . .	28,320	1,520,000	German	6,967	3,740,000
Great Britain	7,042	3,420,000	British	4,193	2,710,000
Denmark	4,330	520,000	Danish	4,032	570,000
Sweden and Norway . .	3,238	560,000	Russian	457	120,000
United States	869	1,170,000	Sweden and Norway . .	3,054	800,000
Various . , . .	4,057	2,030,000	Various	29,203	1,280,000
Total . . .	47,856	9,220,000	Total . . .	47,856	9,220,000

Entries and clearances in 1888 were as follows :—

Ports	Entered, Tons	Cleared, Tons	Total
Hamburg . . .	4,410,000	4,440,000	8,850,000
Bremen . . .	1,180,000	1,190,000	2,370,000
Stettin	1,040,000	1,060,000	2,100,000
Dantzig . . .	630,000	640,000	1,270,000
Various . . .	2,180,000	2,105,000	4,285,000
Total . .	9,440,000	9,435,000	18,875,000

The trade of Hamburg has grown nearly tenfold since 1846, when the entries were 460,000 tons.

The coasting trade in 1885 showed the following entries :—

	Vessels	Tons
Hamburg	6,489	3,633,000
Bremen	2,426	976,000
Other ports . . .	52,270	5,615,000
Total . .	61,185	10,234,000

Vessels with cargo formed 92, in ballast 8 per cent. of the above tonnage.

RUSSIA AND FINLAND

In 1842 the merchant navy comprised 1000 vessels with 240,000 tons aggregate. In recent years the returns show :—

Year	Vessels			Tons			Carrying Power
	Steam	Sail	Total	Steam	Sail	Total	
1876	356	3,975	4,331	82,000	600,000	682,000	930,000
1880	529	5,776	6,305	100,000	640,000	740,000	1,040,000
1886	594	3,982	4,576	142,000	605,000	747,000	1,170,000

The tonnage of vessels entered into Russian ports was :—

Year	Russian	Foreign	Total
1837 . . .	47,000	888,000	935,000
1866 . . .	540,000	2,036,000	2,576,000
1871 . . .	595,000	3,400,000	3,995,000
1880 . . .	580,000	4,440,000	5,020,000
1888 . . .	510,000	6,900,000	7,410,000

The internal navigation in 1880 employed 385 steamers and 13,000 canal-boats. The sea-going and coast traffic in 1888 showed entries as follows :—

	Vessels	Tons
Sea-going	12,575	7,410,000
Coast	23,978	4,753,000
Total . .	36,553	12,163,000

Sea-going entries were distributed thus :—

	Vessels	Tons
Baltic	6,966	3,090,000
Black Sea . . .	4,921	3,730,000
Other seas . . .	688	590,000
Total . .	12,575	7,410,000

AUSTRIA

The first impulse given to Austrian shipping was the establishment of the Austrian Lloyd's Company to trade in the Levant in 1833 ; the second, the Danube Navigation Company, founded in 1850. The latter has steamers which carry 1,200,000 passengers and 1,400,000 tons of merchandise yearly. The merchant navy of the Empire in 1849 comprised 6083 vessels of 260,000 tons aggregate, manned by 27,000 seamen. In later years we find as follows :—

Year	Vessels			Tons			Carrying Power
	Steam	Sail	Total	Steam	Sail	Total	
1870	91	702	793	50,000	280,000	330,000	480,000
1880	80	526	606	60,000	230,000	290,000	470,000
1888	98	269	367	90,000	130,000	220,000	490,000

The tonnage of entries was as follows :—

Year	Austrian	Foreign	Total
1861 . . .	2,400,000	420,000	2,820,000
1870 . . .	2,840,000	590,000	3,430,000
1880 . . .	4,190,000	630,000	4,820,000
1888 . . .	6,740,000	805,000	7,545,000

In 1889 the tonnage of sea-going vessels that entered the Danube was as follows :—

	Tons
British	1,001,000
Greek	128,000
Various	285,000
Total . .	1,414,000

This table, however, applied only to that part of the Danube outside the Austrian dominions.

The total shipping of the Austrian Empire of all sizes in 1886 was as follows :—

	Vessels	Tons	Seamen
Sea-going . . .	393	250,000	5,400
Coasting . . .	8,975	62,000	23,400
Total .	9,368	312,000	28,800

The aggregate horse-power of merchant steamers was 23,000.

ITALY

In 1842 the merchant shipping of all the Italian States summed up 14,680 vessels, with an aggregate of 462,000 tons. In 1850 the marine of the three principal States was as follows :—

	Vessels	Tons
Naples	3,600	168,000
Sardinia	6,300	167,000
Tuscany	800	34,000
Total . .	10,700	369,000

In later years the returns of shipping of the kingdom of Italy show as follows :—

Year	Vessels			Tons			Carrying Power
	Steam	Sail	Total	Steam	Sail	Total	
1872 . . .	118	10,951	11,069	38,000	993,000	1,031,000	1,145,000
1880 . . .	158	7,822	7,980	77,000	922,000	999,000	1,230,000
1888 . . .	266	6,544	6,810	175,000	675,000	850,000	1,375,000

Port entries since 1861 have risen as follows in tonnage :—

Year	Italian	Foreign	Total Sea-going	Coasting	Total Entries
1861	820,000	1,700,000	2,520,000	...	...
1870	1,340,000	2,450,000	3,790,000	5,930,000	9,720,000
1880	1,700,000	2,990,000	4,690,000	8,400,000	13,090,000
1888	1,720,000	4,950,000	6,670,000	13,380,000	20,050,000

The above figures show that since 1870 the sea-going trade has risen 75 per cent., and coasting trade 125 per cent.

The total of entries and clearances in 1888 was as follows :—

	Entries, Tons	Cleared, Tons	Total
Sea-going . . .	6,670,000	6,400,000	13,070,000
Coasting . . .	13,380,000	12,790,000	26,170,000
Total . .	20,050,000	19,190,000	39,240,000

The aggregate of vessels' tonnage entered and cleared was as follows :—

Year	Sea-going	Coasting	Total
1861 . . .	5,080,000	8,000,000	13,080,000
1870 . . .	7,620,000	9,680,000	17,300,000
1888 . . .	11,070,000	26,170,000	39,240,000

This shows that the shipping business of Italy has more than doubled since 1870. The trade of the principal ports in 1888 was as follows :—

	Tons Entered	Tons Cleared	Total
Genoa	2,810,000	2,850,000	5,660,000
Naples	1,750,000	1,750,000	3,500,000
Palermo . . .	1,390,000	1,390,000	2,780,000
Leghorn . . .	1,300,000	1,290 000	2,590,000
Messina . . .	1,080,000	1,070,000	2,150,000
Venice . . .	890,000	890,000	1,780,000
Various . . .	10,830,000	9,950,000	20,780,000
Total . .	20,050,000	19,190,000	39,240,000

SPAIN

At the death of Charles II., in 1700, the merchant navy had an aggregate of 27,000 tons. In recent years the tonnage was :—

Year	Steam	Sail	Total	Carrying Power
1842	...	280,000	280,000	280,000
1859	13,000	460,000	473,000	512,000
1872	45,000	340,000	385,000	520,000
1880	230,000	330,000	560,000	1,250,000
1888	395,000	205,000	600,000	1,785,000

Port entries of sea-going vessels showed the following tonnage :—

Year	Spanish	Foreign	Total
1860 . . .	420,000	930,000	1,350,000
1872 . . .	890,000	1,960,000	2,850,000
1880 . . .	1,300,000	4,400,000	5,700,000
1888 . . .	4,600,000	6,850,000	11,450,000

The total port traffic in 1888 was as follows in tonnage :—

	Entered	Cleared	Total
Sea-going . . .	11,450,000	10,880,000	22,330,000
Coasting . . .	5,660,000	5,240,000	10,900,000
Total . .	17,110,000	16,120,000	33,230,000

The returns of coast traffic are for 1885; no later published.

PORTUGAL

In 1842 the merchant navy counted 798 vessels, with an aggregate of 81,000 tons; in 1889 it comprised only 443 vessels, with an aggregate of 78,000 tons. The tonnage of vessels entered and cleared was as follows :—

Flag	Entered		Cleared	
	1878	1888	1878	1888
Portuguese .	170,000	210,000	160,000	190,000
Foreign . .	2,330,000	3,750,000	2,250,000	3,730,000
Total . .	2,500,000	3,960,000	2,410,000	3,920,000

Of the foreign entries in 1888, British vessels stood for 2,140,000 tons, or considerably more than half the trade of Portugal.

SWEDEN

The merchant navy at various dates stood thus :—

Year	Steam	Sail	Total	Carrying Power
1800	...	64,000	64,000	64,000
1837	...	120,000	120,000	120,000
1872	48,000	340,000	388,000	530,000
1880	81,000	460,000	541,000	780,000
1888	125,000	375,000	500,000	875,000

The tonnage of port entries was as follows :—

Year	Swedish	Foreign	Total
1830 . . .	163,000	170,000	333,000
1866 . . .	495,000	1,135,000	1,630,000
1870 . . .	680,000	1,480,000	2,160,000
1880 . . .	1,270,000	2,170,000	3,440,000
1888 . . .	1,760,000	3,260,000	5,020,000

The entries in 1888 were as follows :—

	With Cargo	In Ballast	Total
Swedish . . .	1,060,000	700,000	1,760,000
Foreign . . .	1,010,000	2,250,000	3,260,000
Total . .	2,070,000	2,950,000	5,020,000

	Steamers	Sailing	Total
Swedish . . .	1,110,000	650,000	1,760,000
Foreign . . .	2,295,000	965,000	3,260,000
Total . .	3,405,000	1,615,000	5,020,000

NORWAY

In 1836 the merchant navy was one of the most considerable in the world, comprising 2430 vessels, with an aggregate of 212,000 tons, and 13,000 seamen. The tonnage at various dates was as follows :—

	Sail	Steam	Total	Carrying Power
1836 . . .	212,000	...	212,000	212,000
1872 . . .	1,090,000	30,000	1,120,000	1,210,000
1880 . . .	1,460,000	58,000	1,518,000	1,690,000
1888 . . .	1,400,000	135,000	1,535,000	1,940,000

Tonnage of port entries at various dates showed thus :—

Year	Norwegian	Foreign	Total
1860 . . .	700,000	260,000	960,000
1870 . . .	1,120,000	480,000	1,600,000
1880 . . .	1,340,000	630,000	1,970,000
1888 . . .	1,450,000	850,000	2,300,000

The sea-going trade in 1887 showed the ports thus :—

	Tons Entered	Tons Cleared
Christiania . . .	740,000	560,000
Bergen . . .	270,000	240,000
Drontheim . . .	110,000	120,000
Various . . .	1,210,000	1,500,000
Total . .	2,330,000	2,420,000

In 1876 the merchant navy of Norway had 56,200 seamen, of whom 43,700 in sea-going vessels, the rest in coasters.

DENMARK

In 1748 the Danish merchant navy counted 1800 vessels; in 1789 it exceeded 4000, declining in 1825 to 3870, and in 1835 to 3700. The tonnage at various dates showed :—

Year	Steam	Sail	Total	Carrying Power
1825 . . .	...	118,000	118,000	118,000
1835 . . .	...	144,000	144,000	144,000
1850 . . .	...	153,000	153,000	153,000
1872 . . .	15,000	175,000	190,000	235,000
1880 . . .	52,000	198,000	250,000	405,000
1888 . . .	95,000	175,000	270,000	555,000

Tonnage of port entries was as follows :—

Year	Danish	Foreign	Total
1860 . . .	260,000	340,000	600,000
1870 . . .	310,000	400,000	710,000
1880 . . .	1,200,000	1,030,000	2,230,000
1888 . . .	1,750,000	1,630,000	3,380,000

The shipping trade of 1888 was as follows in tonnage :—

	Steam	Sail	Total
Entered . . .	2,670,000	710,000	3,380,000
Cleared . . .	2,650,000	720,000	3,370,000
Total . .	5,320,000	1,430,000	6,750,000

The Sound dues during fourteen years down to 1799 averaged £150,000 a year from 10,000 vessels, that is, £15 each. In later years we find as follows :—

Year	Dues Paid by			Number of Vessels
	British	Other Vessels	Total, £	
1821 . .	67,000	100,000	167,000	9,200
1830 . .	51,000	110,000	161,000	13,300
1837 . .	54,000	160,000	214,000	13,100

The dues were 1 per cent. on the value of the cargo, and were abolished in 1857, when Great Britain paid Denmark £1,200,000 and other nations £2,400,000 as indemnity.

HOLLAND

The tonnage of merchant shipping of the Dutch flag was as follows :—

Year	Steam	Sail	Total	Carrying Power
1826 . . .	...	148,000	148,000	148,000
1842 . . .	...	275,000	275,000	275,000
1872 . . .	34,000	350,000	384,000	490,000
1880 . . .	65,000	265,000	330,000	525,000
1888 . . .	105,000	140,000	245,000	560,000

Tonnage of port entries was as follows :—

Year	Dutch	Foreign	Total
1828 . . .	284,000	439,000	723,000
1837 . . .	327,000	449,000	776,000
1860 . . .	650,000	1,005,000	1,655,000
1870 . . .	660,000	1,650,000	2,310,000
1880 . . .	1,055,000	2,390,000	3,445,000
1888 . . .	1,600,000	3,510,000	5,110,000

The trade of 1888 showed as follows :—

	With Cargo	In Ballast	Total
Entered . . .	4,900,000	210,000	5,110,000
Cleared . . .	2,960,000	2,080,000	5,040,000
Total . .	7,860,000	2,290,000	10,150,000

The principal ports showed as follows, cargo only :—

	Entered	Cleared	Total
Rotterdam . .	2,525,000	1,420,000	3,945,000
Amsterdam . .	940,000	570,000	1,510,000
Flushing . . .	630,000	650,000	1,280,000
Various . . .	805,000	320,000	1,125,000
Total . .	4,900,000	2,960,000	7,860,000

In 1670 Sir William Petty estimated that the Dutch possessed one-half the shipping of the world : at present they have less than 1½ per cent. of the total.

BELGIUM

The merchant navy was as follows, in tonnage :—

Year	Steam	Sail	Total	Carrying Power
1842 . . .	...	27,000	27,000	27,000
1870 . . .	10,000	20,000	30,000	60,000
1880 . . .	65,000	10,000	75,000	270,000
1888 . . .	73,000	4,000	77,000	295,000

Tonnage of port entries was as follows :—

Year	Steam	Sail	Total
1840 . . .	...	237,000	237,000
1850 . . .	...	315,000	315,000
1860 . . .	176,000	491,000	667,000
1870 . . .	839,000	736,000	1,575,000
1880 . . .	2,813,000	758,000	3,571,000
1887 . . .	4,080,000	492,000	4,572,000

The countries from which the tonnage came were :—

	1840	1860	1887
Great Britain . .	60,000	240,000	1,740,000
United States . .	30,000	40,000	620,000
Germany . . .	30,000	75,000	370,000
Russia	35,000	90,000	315,000
France	10,000	20,000	190,000
Argentina . . .	...	20,000	190,000
Various	72,000	182,000	1,147,000
Total . .	237,000	667,000	4,572,000

Antwerp stands for 80 per cent. of the shipping trade of the kingdom, viz. :—

	1840	1860	1887
Antwerp . . .	180,000	512,000	3,665,000
Other ports . .	57,000	155,000	907,000
Total . .	237,000	667,000	4,572,000

GREECE

The mercantile marine at various dates had the following tonnage :—

	Steam	Sail	Total	Carrying Power
1842 . . .	...	186,000	186,000	186,000
1872 . . .	6,000	234,000	240,000	258,000
1887 . . .	31,000	227,000	258,000	350,000

Tonnage of port entries was as follows :—

Year	Greek	Foreign	Total
1860 . . .	430,000	500,000	930,000
1870 . . .	420,000	850,000	1,270,000
1888 . . .	330,000	2,040,000	2,370,000

Piraeus (Athens) stood for 1,550,000 tons, or 66 per cent. of the total. The merchant navy of Greece in 1880 had 26,800 sailors.

TURKEY

The tonnage of the merchant navy at various dates was as follows :—

Year	Sail	Steam	Total	Carrying Power
1842 . . .	182,000	...	182,000	182,000
1875 . . .	170,000	10,000	180,000	210,000
1889 . . .	153,000	64,000	217,000	410,000

Port entries in 1888 were as follows :—

At	Tons	Flag	Tons
Constantinople . .	8,790,000	British . .	9,270,000
Levant and Black Sea	18,790,000	Turkish . .	4,810,000
Red Sea	540,000	Austrian . .	3,720,000
Persian Gulf . . .	160,000	Various . .	10,480,000
Total . .	28,280,000	Total .	28,280,000

In 1888 no fewer than 15,820 vessels entered the Dardanelles, with an aggregate of 10,460,000 tons, the share of British vessels being 7,030,000 tons.

EGYPT

The trade returns of the Suez Canal since 1870 will be found under the head of *Canals*, p. 102.

The tonnage of arrivals at Alexandria and that of vessels passing through the Suez Canal in 1888 showed thus :—

	Alexandria, Tons	Canal, Tons
British . . .	690,000	7,340,000
Turkish . . .	250,000	30,000
French . . .	250,000	580,000
Austrian . . .	160,000	170,000
Russian . . .	120,000	50,000
Italian . . .	60,000	400,000
Various . . .	60,000	870,000
Total . .	1,590,000	9,440,000

UNITED STATES

The merchant shipping of the Union at various dates was in tonnage as follows :—

Year	High Seas .	Coasting, &c.	Total	Sail	Steam	Carrying Power
1789	124,000	78,000	202,000	202,000	...	202,000
1795	530,000	218,000	748,000	748,000	...	748,000
1800	670,000	300,000	970,000	970,000	...	970,000
1810	980,000	440,000	1,420,000	1,420,000	...	1,420,000
1820	580,000	700,000	1,280,000	1,260,000	20,000	1,340,000
1830	540,000	650,000	1,190,000	1,125,000	65,000	1,385,000
1840	760,000	1,420,000	2,180,000	1,980,000	200,000	2,780,000
1850	1,440,000	2,095,000	3,535,000	3,010,000	525,000	5,110,000
1860	2,380,000	2,970,000	5,350,000	4,480,000	870,000	7,960,000
1870	1,450,000	2,800,000	4,250,000	3,175,000	1,075,000	7,475,000
1880	1,310,000	2,760,000	4,070,000	2,860,000	1,210,000	7,700,000
1889	1,000,000	3,310,000	4,310,000	2,540,000	1,770,000	9,620,000

American shipping differs from that of other nations, inasmuch as less than one-fourth is engaged on the high seas : coasting and internal traffic take 77 per cent. of the total merchant-navy. The carrying-power has risen only 20 in the last thirty years. It was less in 1880 than twenty years before, but has since recovered.

The tonnage of vessels built since 1812 was as follows :—

Period	Sail	Steam	Total	Carrying Power	Do. per Annum
1812-20	730,000	25,000	755,000	830,000	92,000
1821-30	830,000	65,000	895,000	1,090,000	109,000
1831-40	1,010,000	175,000	1,185,000	1,710,000	171,000
1841-50	1,480,000	370,000	1,850,000	2,960,000	296,000
1851-60	2,930,000	730,000	3,660,000	5,850,000	585,000
1861-70	2,110,000	910,000	3,020,000	5,750,000	575,000
1871-80	1,770,000	760,000	2,530,000	4,810,000	481,000
1881-89	930,000	970,000	1,900,000	4,810,000	534,000
78 years	11,790,000	4,005,000	15,795,000	27,810,000	356,000

If we suppose that the vessels which have disappeared from the register in the last nine years were either lost or broken up (since very few have been sold to other flags), we find the death-rate of American vessels as follows :—

	Lost, &c., Tons Yearly	Tonnage of Shipping	Annual Loss per Cent.
Sail . . .	140,000	2,700,000	5.2
Steam . . .	45,000	1,500,000	3.0
Total .	185,000	4,200,000	4.4

The principal maritime states showed tonnage of vessels belonging to citizens of same in 1850 and 1886 thus :—

State	Tons	
	1850	1886
New York . . .	944,000	1,220,000
Massachusetts . .	685,000	440,000
Maine . . .	501,000	490,000
Pennsylvania . .	258,000	280,000
Louisiana . . .	250,000	70,000
Maryland . . .	193,000	150,000
Various . . .	704,000	1,620,000
Total .	3,535,000	4,270,000

The proportions of trade—that is, of imports and exports combined—done on American and on foreign bottoms since 1821 are shown as follows :—

Year	Trade, £			Percentage	
	United States Flag	Foreign	Total	American	Foreign
1821	23,600,000	3,100,000	26,700,000	89	11
1830	27,300,000	3,100,000	30,400,000	90	10
1840	41,900,000	8,500,000	50,400,000	83	17
1850	50,000,000	19,000,000	69,000,000	72	28
1860	105,500,000	53,000,000	158,500,000	66	34
1870	62,000,000	132,000,000	194,000,000	32	68
1880	58,200,000	272,000,000	330,800,000	17	83
1889	54,000,000	253,000,000	307,000,000	17	83

The tonnage of entries into United States ports under various flags was :—

Flag	Tonnage			Ratio		
	1860	1870	1889	1860	1870	1889
American	3,302,000	2,452,000	3,130,000	66.0	39.2	23.5
British	1,263,000	2,792,000	6,820,000	25.2	44.4	51.3
German	231,000	679,000	1,130,000	4.6	10.9	8.5
Scandinavian . . .	32,000	108,000	725,000	0.6	1.7	5.4
Italian	32,000	48,000	290,000	0.6	0.8	2.2
French	24,000	81,000	320,000	0.5	1.3	2.4
Spanish	63,000	31,000	260,000	1.3	0.5	1.9
Various	56,000	79,000	635,000	1.2	1.2	4.8
Total . .	5,003,000	6,270,000	13,310,000	100.0	100.0	100.0

The tonnage entered and cleared at the principal ports was :—

State	Entered			Cleared		
	1865	1875	1889	1865	1875	1889
New York . . .	2,080,000	4,420,000	5,600,000	2,100,000	4,310,000	5,450,000
Boston . . .	660,000	770,000	1,400,000	670,000	630,000	1,220,000
Philadelphia . . .	160,000	580,000	1,100,000	140,000	620,000	870,000
San Francisco . . .	320,000	720,000	1,050,000	400,000	750,000	1,060,000
New Orleans . . .	50,000	450,000	770,000	70,000	520,000	770,000
Various . . .	560,000	2,200,000	3,390,000	780,000	2,510,000	4,300,000
Total . .	3,830,000	9,140,000	13,310,000	4,160,000	9,340,000	13,670,000

The following table of steamboat traffic was published in 1881 for the preceding year :—

	Steamers	Tonnage	Passengers	Goods, Tons	Earnings, £	Wages, £
Lakes	947	222,000	1,420,000	4,380,000	2,520,000	690,000
Mississippi	681	132,000	2,710,000	4,820,000	2,460,000	790,000
Ohio	473	107,000	4,030,000	2,410,000	1,580,000	585,000
New England . . .	463	119,000	15,470,000	2,630,000	1,620,000	560,000
Middle States . . .	1,459	433,000	135,720,000	7,190,000	6,660,000	1,830,000
Gulf	1,116	208,000	9,160,000	4,110,000	2,870,000	965,000
Total . .	5,139	1,221,000	168,510,000	25,540,000	17,710,000	5,420,000

The crews mustered 57,100 men, their wages averaging £85. The steamers carried merchandise 21 times their own tonnage, besides passengers. Each steamer carried in the year 33,000 passengers and 5000 tons of merchandise. One tug on the Mississippi can convey in six days, from St. Louis to New Orleans, boats carrying 10,000 tons of grain, which would require 70 railway trains of 15 waggons each.

The official return of wrecks and casualties shows :—

	Tonnage of Vessels			
	Lost		Damaged	
	1880	1889	1880	1889
Atlantic . . .	31,000	50,000	207,000	266,000
Lakes . . .	11,000	13,000	111,000	146,000
Various . . .	68,000	63,000	187,000	178,000
Total . .	110,000	126,000	505,000	590,000

	Loss, £ Sterling		Loss of Lives	
	1880	1889	1880	1889
Atlantic . . .	600,000	980,000	110	144
Lakes . . .	250,000	250,000	29	9
Various . . .	1,050,000	1,130,000	330	459
Total . .	1,900,000	2,360,000	469	612

CANADA

The merchant navy has grown in tonnage very rapidly, viz. :—

Year	Steam	Sail	Total	Carrying Power
1841	5,000	345,000	350,000	365,000
1866	28,000	727,000	755,000	840,000
1877	77,000	1,233,000	1,310,000	1,540,000
1888	207,000	880,000	1,087,000	1,710,000

Although there has been a decline of 220,000 nominal tonnage in the last eleven years, there is an actual increase of 170,000 tons in carrying power owing to steamers taking the place of sailing vessels. Port entries of the high seas show the following tonnage :—

Year	Tons	Year	Tons
1829 . . .	430,000	1880 . . .	3,690,000
1860 . . .	2,650,000	1885 . . .	3,840,000
1870 . . .	3,150,000	1888 . . .	4,620,000

Of the entries in 1888 there were 35 per cent. in ballast.

The provinces which owned the shipping of the Dominion in 1888 were :—

	Vessels	Tons
Nova Scotia . . .	2,851	486,000
New Brunswick .	1,009	240,000
Quebec . . .	1,498	180,000
Ontario	1,330	140,000
Various	454	44,000
Total . .	7,142	1,090,000

AUSTRALIA

The tonnage of entries at various dates was as follows :—

Year	Sydney	Melbourne	Various	Total
1822 . . .	57,000	...	17,000	74,000
1841 . . .	178,000	...	98,000	276,000
1851 . . .	146,000	120,000	278,000	544,000
1861 . . .	373,000	545,000	528,000	1,446,000
1871 . . .	750,000	678,000	770,000	2,198,000
1888 . . .	2,383,000	2,154,000	2,808,000	7,350,000

The average size of vessels has increased very notably, viz. :—

Year	Vessels	Tons	Tons per Vessel
1841 . . .	1,288	276,000	214
1851 . . .	2,670	544,000	204
1861 . . .	5,383	1,446,000	269
1871 . . .	6,866	2,198,000	320
1881 . . .	8,350	4,752,000	570
1888 . . .	9,306	7,345,000	790

The tonnage of port entries for the several Colonies was :—

	1860	1871	1888
New South Wales .	430,000	750,000	2,380,000
Victoria . .	590,000	680,000	2,150,000
South Australia . .	105,000	190,000	990,000
New Zealand . .	140,000	270,000	530,000
Queensland . .	40,000	140,000	500,000
Tasmania . .	115,000	110,000	390,000
Western Australia .	60,000	60,000	410,000
Total . .	1,480,000	2,200,000	7,350,000

OTHER COLONIES

Port entries at various dates showed tonnage approximately thus :—

	1860	1870	1880	1887
India . . .	1,470,000	2,005,000	2,850,000	3,580,000
Singapore .	680,000	820,000	2,400,000	4,180,000
Ceylon . .	400,000	710,000	1,450,000	2,070,000
Mauritius .	300,000	230,000	270,000	310,000
Hong-Kong .	780,000	1,320,000	3,040,000	4,580,000
South Africa .	290,000	210,000	1,005,000	1,070,000
West Indies .	540,000	770,000	1,785,000	3,130,000
Gibraltar .	980,000	1,480,000	3,220,000	5,250,000
Malta .	930,000	1,490,000	3,070,000	3,410,000
Various . .	410,000	920,000	1,190,000	1,760,000
Total .	6,780,000	9,955,000	20,280,000	29,340,000

CHILI

The merchant navy is made up thus :—

	Vessels	Tons
Steam	38	19,000
Sail	139	58,000
Total . .	177	77,000

Tonnage of entries was as follows :—

Year	Chilian	Foreign	Total
1878 . . .	150,000	1,070,000	1,220,000
1888 . . .	250,000	1,820,000	2,070,000

There is a very large coasting trade, the entries of which amount to 6,700,000 tons yearly.

ARGENTINA

Port entries showed tonnage as follows :—

Flag	1872	1882	1886
Argentine . . .	159,000	240,000	1,150,000
British	361,000	342,000	960,000
French	146,000	202,000	430,000
Italian	131,000	125,000	215,000
German . . .	57,000	90,000	240,000
Spanish . . .	9,000	40,000	30,000
Various	251,000	174,000	490,000
Total . .	1,114,000	1,213,000	3,515,000

The total sea-going and coast entries in 1886 had tonnage thus :—

At	Sea-Going	Coast	Total
Buenos Ayres . .	1,590,000	810,000	2,400,000
Rosario	410,000	580,000	990,000
Concordia . . .	220,000	25,000	245,000
Concepcion . .	180,000	65,000	245,000
Gualeguaychu .	170,000	10,000	180,000
Various . . .	945,000	620,000	1,565,000
Total . .	3,515,000	2,110,000	5,625,000

The high-seas entries in 1888 were as follows :—

	With Cargo	In Ballast	Total
Sail	1,160,000	40,000	1,200,000
Steam	2,640,000	1,040,000	3,680,000
Total . .	3,800,000	1,080,000	4,880,000

Tonnage of vessels cleared showed thus :—

	With Cargo	In Ballast	Total
Sail	270,000	730,000	1,000,000
Steam	2,280,000	1,030,000	3,310,000
Total . .	2,550,000	1,760,000	4,310,000

URUGUAY

Tonnage of port entries was as follows :—

Year	Uruguayan	Foreign	Total
1876 . . .	2,000	1,080,000	1,082,000
1888 . . .	1,000	1,620,000	1,621,000

In 1888 the returns of entries showed :—

At	Vessels	Tons
Montevideo . .	1,357	1,620,000
Other ports . .	3,540	1,550,000
Total . .	4,897	3,170,000

All the trade of the high seas was done at Montevideo ; the other ports had only coast traffic.

CHINA

Port entries had the following tonnage :—

Year	Chinese	Foreign	Total
1878 . . .	3,000	1,540,000	1,543,000
1888 . . .	93,000	2,737,000	2,830,000

The above was the traffic of the high seas : the total of tonnage entered and cleared, including coast trade, in 1888 was as follows :—

	Vessels	Tons
British . . .	15,115	14,070,000
Chinese . . .	9,054	5,740,000
German . . .	2,762	1,570,000
Various . . .	1,230	928,000
Total . .	28,161	22,308,000

Of the total tonnage, 95 per cent. was steam.
The tonnage of entries only in 1889 (sea-going and coast trade) showed as follows :—

British	7,500,000
Chinese	3,000,000
Various	1,300,000
Total .	11,800,000

JAPAN

The tonnage of the merchant navy was as follows :—

Year	Steam	Sail	Total	Carrying Power
1878	44,000	20,000	64,000	196,000
1887	72,000	61,000	133,000	350,000

Port entries showed tonnage as follows :—

Year	Japanese	Foreign	Total
1881 . . .	130,000	470,000	600,000
1888 . . .	230,000	1,100,000	1,330,000

Entries in 1888 were as follows :—

Port	Tons	Flag	Tons
Nagasaki . .	640,000	British . . .	590,000
Yokohama . .	420,000	German . . .	220,000
Kobè	260,000	American . .	130,000
Various . . .	10,000	Various . .	390,000
Total . .	1,330,000	Total . .	1,330,000

ALGERIA

In 1886 the port entries were as follows :—

Flag	Vessels	Tons	Crew
French	2,001	1,170,000	63,300
British	580	510,000	12,200
Spanish . . .	1,581	150,000	17,800
Various . . .	800	150,000	7,500
Total . .	4,962	1,980,000	100,800

In 1888 the entries reached 2,170,000 tons.

SICKNESS

Neison and Finlayson (contributions to *Vital Statistics*) find that two persons are constantly sick for one death during the year. The Board of Health of Massachusetts finds that each inhabitant loses 13 days yearly by sickness. According to Dr. Farr at the State Congress of 1860, you may expect to find 2 per cent. of people aged 30, and 10 per cent. of those aged 75 constantly sick any day of the year. Sir William Wilde found 2¼ per cent. of the people of Dublin confined to bed. International statistics of sickness are only to be found in the armies of the different powers. The following table, published in 1875, is for various years, showing the annual averages thus :—

	Loss of Days per Soldier	Men in Hospital per 1000	Invalided per 1000
British	18	50	36
French	18	47	7
German . . .	15	41	23
Austrian . . .	13	36	21
Italian	15	40	...
Portuguese . .	13	34	...
Belgian . . .	18	51	9
United States .	21	58	25
Do. coloured	19	53	...
Russian . . .	28	78	...

In the Crimean war the hospital entries of British and French were :—

Cause	Number		Ratio	
	British	French	British	French
Wounds . , .	18,300	116,000	11.3	26.7
Fever, &c. . .	144,400	320,000	88.7	73.3
Total . .	162,700	436,000	100.0	100.0

At the siege of Metz the French in hospital averaged 17,000 men, being more than 10 per cent., the garrison numbering 168,000. Towards the close of the siege, when the garrison was only 105,000, there were 21,000 in hospital.

In the American war of 1861-65, the Federal army enrolled 2,252,000 men, of whom 179,000 were coloured, and the average strength was 431,000 men : the average number in hospital was 37,000 or 9 per cent.

The following table shows the distribution of sickness according to months in various places as judged by hospital entries :—

	Paris	Rome	Algiers	Geneva
January . . .	101	99	65	116
February . . .	102	114	48	112
March . . .	132	85	49	121
April . . .	125	71	71	108
May . . .	114	60	70	110
June . . .	97	48	113	95
July . . .	85	81	170	93
August . . .	80	150	138	98
September . .	102	139	134	89
October . . .	91	121	164	83
November . .	86	128	107	88
December . .	85	104	71	87
Year . .	1,200	1,200	1,200	1,200

UNITED KINGDOM

Finlayson's tables as regards the sick ratios at various ages in England give the following results, that is, the percentage who become sick during the year, the duration of sickness, and the loss in days on the whole number of workpeople at each age :—

Age	Per Cent. Sick		Days of Illness		Loss of Days on Whole Number	
	Indoor	Outdoor	Indoor	Outdoor	Indoor	Outdoor
20	24.6	26.2	27	25	6.6	7.0
25	22.5	23.7	29	28	6.4	6.7
30	21.0	22.7	31	30	6.5	6.8
35	21.2	22.3	32	31	6.8	6.9
40	21.9	23.5	35	36	7.6	8.0
45	22.8	23.7	39	39	8.9	9.1
50	25.6	25.0	44	46	11.3	11.3
55	28.5	26.5	52	47	14.9	12.5
60	30.8	29.1	61	55	18.7	16.5
65	35.5	32.5	75	76	26.6	24.8

The ratio of sick has naturally declined with death-rate, the tables published in 1870 for England and Wales comparing with those of 1845 as follows :—

Days of Sickness per Inhabitant.

Age	Urban		Rural		All England		Scotland
	1845	1870	1845	1870	1845	1870	1845
21–30 . .	6.3	5.6	6.0	5.4	6.1	5.5	6.0
31–40 . .	11.4	7.1	6.4	7.1	8.9	7.1	6.2
41–50 . .	13.4	11.2	9.0	10.4	11.2	10.8	9.5
51–60 . .	23.2	20.3	17.8	20.1	20.5	20.2	19.9
40 years .	13.8	11.1	9.8	10.7	11.7	10.9	10.4

The Census returns taken of sickness in Ireland show thus :—

Diseases	Sick per 10,000 Inhabitants			
	1851	1861	1871	Medium
Zymotic . . .	53	17	9	26
Brain . . .	37	50	58	48
Respiratory . .	16	16	17	16
Various . . .	53	48	48	50
Total . .	159	131	132	140

FRANCE

A report was published in 1856 showing the working during three years of friendly societies among workmen, that is, the percentage falling sick during the year, the duration of illness, and the loss in days on the whole number of workers of each age, viz. :—

Age	Sick Percentage	Days of Illness	Loss of Days on Whole Number
16–35 . . .	29.0	17	4.9
36–55 . . .	30.0	21	6.2
56–75 . . .	33.0	27	9.2

Another report in 1886 for fifteen years gave the following averages, that is, the ratio falling sick during each year, and the average duration of illness :—

Period	Percentage Sick		Days of Illness	
	Men	Women	Men	Women
1871–80 . . .	26.0	29.0	20	14
1881–85 . . .	26.0	27.0	18	13
15 years . . .	26.0	28.3	19	13⅔

The number of convicts sent to hospital daily in ten years ending 1880, that is, the ratio per 100,000 of each class, was as follows :—

Year in Prison	Per 100,000	
	Male	Female
First	154	136
Second	170	154
Third	190	190
Fourth	220	172
Fifth	190	220
Over fifth	160	150

GERMANY

Mr. Heym's investigations during twenty years down to 1870 at Leipzig, resulted in the following percentage of persons sick during the year, the average length of illness, and the loss of days in each year from illness, to the whole population of each age :—

Age	Per Cent. Sick in Year		Days of Illness		Loss of Days in Whole Number	
	Men	Women	Men	Women	Men	Women
15–24	26.5	18.8	23	27	6.0	5.1
25–34	21.4	17.7	25	36	5.4	6.4
35–44	22.0	18.0	32	41	7.0	7.4
45–54	21.4	17.5	38	43	8.1	7.6
55–64	26.5	20.0	54	57	14.4	14.6
65–74	32.7	18.0	58	48	19.0	8.6
General average }	22.1	18.1	31	39	6.8	8.7

The associated clubs of workmen and others in Germany showed the number of sick during the year and other particulars as follows :—

	1885	1886
Associates	4,294,000	4,570,000
Sick in year . . .	1,805,000	1,713,000
Constantly sick . . .	69,400	71,400

The loss by sickness was less than six days on the whole number, namely, 5.9 in 1885, and 5.7 in 1886, which is much less than the average in Dr. Heym's table ; but his probably includes older people.

SILK

The consumption of silk and the approximate value of manufactures are shown as follows :—

	Annual Average, Lbs. Silk		Value of Manufactures, £	
	1861–70	1881–87	1861–70	1881–87
U. Kingdom	4,900,000	3,200,000	9,600,000	6,400,000
France . .	15,000,000	14,800,000	29,800,000	29,400,000
Germany .	2,100,000	6,800,000	4,100,000	14,500,000
Russia . .	300,000	900,000	600,000	1,800,000
Austria . .	1,100,000	1,800,000	2,000,000	3,700,000
Italy . . .	1,000,000	800,000	2,100,000	1,600,000
Spain. . .	300,000	600,000	600,000	1,200,000
Switzerland	1,600,000	3,100,000	3,300,000	6,000,000
Europe . .	26,300,000	32,000,000	52,100,000	64,600,000
U. States .	1,200,000	3,500,000	2,500,000	7,200,000
China . .	12,000,000	12,000,000	18,000,000	18,000,000
Japan . .	3,300,000	3,300,000	7,000,000	6,000,000
Other countries }	1,200,000	1,200,000	2,400,000	2,200,000
Total .	44,000,000	52,000,000	82,000,000	98,000,000

The annual production is estimated at 300,000 tons of cocoons or 52,000,000 lbs. raw silk, viz. :—

	Lbs.
China	21,000,000
Japan	6,800,000
Italy	10,600,000
France, Turkey, &c. . . .	13,600,000
Total . .	52,000,000

UNITED KINGDOM

Silk has been manufactured since the time of Edward III., the industry having been introduced by some French prisoners after the battle of Crecy. The consumption of raw silk since 1770 has been as follows :—

Period	Lbs. per Annum	Value of Manufactures, £
1770–90 . . .	790,000	3,400,000
1800–20 . . .	1,280,000	4,500,000
1836–50 . . .	5,500,000	10,800,000
1851–60 . . .	6,100,000	11,500,000
1861–70 . . .	4,900,000	9,600,000
1871–80 . . .	3,500,000	7,100,000
1881–88 . . .	3,200,000	6,400,000

The imports and exports of silk manufactures were as follows :—

Year	Imports, £	Exports, £	Surplus Imports, £
1854 . . .	2,280,000	1,440,000	840,000
1860 . . .	3,200,000	1,690,000	1,510,000
1870 . . .	15,250,000	1,700,000	13,550,000
1880 . . .	13,320,000	2,300,000	11,020,000
1888 . . .	10,470,000	3,400,000	7,070,000

The value of silk goods consumed in thirty-five years was as follows :—

Period	Millions £ Sterling Aggregate			Shillings Yearly per Inhabitant
	British	Foreign	Total	
1854–60	70	18	88	10
1861–70	79	91	170	11
1871–80	51	114	165	10
1881–88	32	88	120	8
35 years	232	311	543	...

The balance-sheet since 1840 shows the silk industry thus :—

Period	Millions £ Sterling		
	Raw Silk	Manufactures	Net Result
1841–50 . . .	65	108	43
1851–60 . . .	68	115	47
1861–70 . . .	55	96	41
1871–80 . . .	32	71	39
1881–88 . . .	18	50	32
48 years . . .	238	440	202

The silk-factories of the United Kingdom were as follows :—

Year	Factories	Operatives	Spindles	Looms
1838 . . .	268	34,000	...	...
1856 . . .	...	56,000	...	8,000
1870 . . .	696	48,000	1,130,000	12,400
1885 . . .	691	43,000	1,060,000	12,000

The Census returns show still more emphatically the decline of this industry, viz. :—

Silk Operatives in England and Wales

Year	Number	Year	Number
1841 . . .	54,000	1871 . . .	77,000
1851 . . .	117,000	1881 . . .	64,000

The use of silk decreases notwithstanding the increase of wealth.

FRANCE

The consumption of silk has been approximately as follows :—

Period	Raw Silk, Lbs. Yearly			Value of Manufactures, £
	French	Imported	Total	
1830–32	1,620,000	1,140,000	2,760,000	5,200,000
1842–46	2,770,000	4,070,000	6,840,000	12,700,000
1850–52	3,830,000	6,370,000	10,200,000	18,200,000
1868–73	1,200,000	15,400,000	16,600,000	34,600,000
1881–87	1,200,000	13,600,000	14,800,000	29,400,000

The output of the factories was approximately as follows :—

Period	Millions £ Sterling Aggregate		
	Exported	Home Use	Total
1831–40 . . .	33	47	80
1841–50 . . .	70	70	140
1851–60 . . .	110	90	200
1861–70 . . .	168	130	298
1871–80 . . .	138	150	288
1881–87 . . .	70	136	206
57 years . . .	589	623	1,212

The value of silk manufactures consumed in France was approximately as follows :—

Period	Millions £ Sterling Aggregate			Shillings Yearly per Inhabitant
	French	Imported	Total	
1831–40 . .	47	...	47	3
1841–50 . .	70	...	70	4
1851–60 . .	90	...	90	5
1861–70 . .	130	10	140	8
1871–80 . .	150	15	165	9
1881–87 . .	136	14	150	11
57 years . .	623	39	662	...

About the year 1620 the mulberry tree was first cultivated for the rearing of silkworms, and in 1780 the cocoons weighed 6600 tons, valued at £660,000 sterling. The farmers have recently been cutting down the mulberry trees for fuel, as the following table shows :—

Year	Mulberry Trees	Cocoons, Tons	Lbs. Silk Produced
1810 . . .	...	3,900	770,000
1820 . . .	9,632,000	5,230	1,010,000
1835 . . .	14,880,000	9,010	1,950,000
1853 . . .	...	26,100	4,300,000
1884 . . .	6,100,000	9,700	1,600,000

The price of cocoons was 1s. per lb. in the 18th century, and rose to 2s. about 1850. A few years later a disease carried off two-thirds of the silkworms, which were badly housed and overcrowded, causing the cocoons to rise to 4s. ; but the price fell owing to large importations, and is now hardly remunerative. In 1884 the total yield of cocoons sold for £1,500,000, and was divided among 141,400 cultivators, giving a little over £10 to each.

The balance-sheet of the silk industry since 1830 was approximately as follows :—

Period	Millions £ Sterling Aggregate		
	Raw Silk	Manufactures	Net Result
1831–40 . . .	48	80	32
1841–50 . . .	86	140	54
1851–60 . . .	120	200	80
1861–70 . . .	166	298	132
1871–80 . . .	125	288	163
1881–87 . . .	72	206	134
57 years . . .	617	1,212	595

In the 18th century Lyons counted 15,000 silk-factories, but the industry suffered so much during the Revolution that in 1800 there were only 3500 left. It revived in later years, Lyons consuming one-sixth of the silk crop of the world, or 50,000 tons of cocoons, one-half of which was imported from Italy until the recent rupture of commercial relations. In 1840 the silk-factories had 1790 steam-engines, of 36,000 aggregate horse-power. In 1866 France had 1172 mills, with 110,000 operatives, 1,080,000 spindles, and 50,000 power-looms, turning out silks to the value of 29 millions sterling.

GERMANY

In 1800 Oddy valued the silk manufactures of Prussia at £700,000 a year, and in 1840 the factories had 14,000 operatives with 12,000 looms, consuming 700,000 lbs. of raw silk per annum, the output being valued at £1,600,000 sterling. The consumption of raw silk in all Germany was approximately as follows :—

Period	Lbs. Yearly	Value of Manufactures, £
1841–50 . . .	1,100,000	2,200,000
1851–60 . . .	1,500,000	3,000,000
1861–70 . . .	2,100,000	4,100,000
1871–80 . . .	4,200,000	8,500,000
1881–87 . . .	6,800,000	14,500,000

The consumption and export were approximately thus :—

Period	Average per Annum		
	Home Use	Exported	Total Make
1873–80 . . .	£ 4,900,000	£ 3,600,000	£ 8,500,000
1881–87 . . .	5,800,000	8,700,000	14,500,000

The balance-sheet of the industry was approximately as follows :—

Period	Millions £ Sterling Aggregate		
	Raw Silk	Manufactures	Net Result
1841–50 . . .	13	22	9
1851–60 . . .	18	30	12
1861–70 . . .	23	41	18
1871–80 . . .	40	85	45
1881–87 . . .	38	102	64
47 years . . .	132	280	148

In 1884 the silk-factories counted 87,000 operatives, the chief seat of this industry being Crefeld, in Prussia.

RUSSIA

In 1828 Schubert found 184 silk-factories, the output of which he estimated much too high, at £800,000. In

1864 Buschen counted 326 factories, with 9000 operatives. The consumption of silk was as follows :—

Period	Lbs.	Value of Manufactures, £
1861–70	330,000	600,000
1871–80	580,000	1,200,000
1881–87	900,000	1,800,000

The consumption of silk manufactures was as follows :—

Period	Yearly Average			Pence per Inhabitant
	Russian	Imported	Total	
1861–70 . .	£ 600,000	£ 500,000	£ 1,100,000	4
1871–80 . .	1,200,000	400,000	1,600,000	5
1881–87 . .	1,800,000	200,000	2,000,000	6

The balance-sheet of the industry was approximately as follows :—

Period	Millions £ Sterling Aggregate		
	Raw Silk	Manufactures	Net Result
1861–70 . . .	4	6	2
1871–80 . . .	6	12	6
1881–87 . . .	5	13	8
27 years . . .	15	31	16

According to the *Bulletin Statistique* for 1884, Russia had 20,000 operatives engaged in silk-factories, turning out goods to the value of three millions sterling per annum ; but this estimate is too high ; probably paper roubles were mistaken for silver.

AUSTRIA

In 1834 the Empire counted 3990 silk-factories, with 160,000 operatives, producing manufactures worth £3,000,000 per annum ; but this included the Italian provinces. The consumption of silk since 1860 has been as follows :—

Period	Lbs. Yearly			Value of Manufactures, £
	Imported	Native	Total	
1861–70 . .	800,000	300,000	1,100,000	2,000,000
1871–80 . .	1,100,000	300,000	1,400,000	2,800,000
1881–87 . .	1,540,000	300,000	1,840,000	3,700,000

The consumption of silk manufactures was as follows :—

Period	Yearly Average, £			Pence per Inhabitant
	Austrian	Imported	Total	
1861–70 . .	2,000,000	300,000	2,300,000	17
1871–80 . .	2,800,000	1,100,000	3,900,000	26
1881–87 . .	3,700,000	300,000	4,000,000	25

The balance-sheet of the industry may be summed up thus :—

Period	Millions £ Aggregate		
	Raw Silk	Manufactures	Total
1861–70 . . .	11	20	9
1871–80 . . .	14	28	14
1881–87 . . .	10	26	16
27 years . . .	35	74	39

In 1884 the factories had 15,000 operatives engaged in this industry.

ITALY

Silk is one of the most valuable of Italian products, the exportation averaging 10 millions sterling per annum. Lombardy is the chief seat of silk-growing, and until recently 90 per cent. of the quantity was from Japanese eggs imported on cards from Japan. These cards are worth 7s. per ounce, or £12,000 a ton, about ten tons being now imported yearly. Formerly the eggs yielded 50 lbs. cocoons per ounce, but latterly only 35 lbs., representing a value of 50s., or seven times the original cost of the eggs. The province of Lombardy raises yearly 11,000 tons of cocoons, worth £200 a ton.

There are factories for throwing silk at Milan and Turin, and some of the fibre is consumed at home for velvets and damasks, but the greatest part is usually exported to France for the Lyons factories. The production and export of silk approximated yearly as follows :—

Period	Production, Lbs.	Export, Lbs.	Home Use, Lbs.
1861–70 . . .	5,600,000	4,600,000	1,000,000
1871–80 . . .	7,400,000	6,600,000	800,000
1881–87 . . .	10,600,000	9,800,000	800,000

The import and export of manufactured silks were as follows :—

Period	Yearly Average		
	Import, £	Export, £	Surplus Imports, £
1861–70 . . .	400,000	220,000	180,000
1871–80 . . .	880,000	600,000	280,000
1881–87 . . .	960,000	600,000	360,000

The consumption of silk manufactures was as follows :—

Period	Yearly Average			Pence per Inhabitant
	Italian	Imported	Total	
	£	£	£	
1861–70 . .	2,000,000	180,000	2,180,000	23
1871–80 . .	1,600,000	280,000	1,880,000	20
1881–87 . .	1,600,000	360,000	1,960,000	18

The value of silk industry to Italy may be summed up thus :—

Period	Cost of Japan Eggs	Silk Exported	Manufactures	Total Product	Deduct Eggs	Net Product
	Millions £ Sterling Aggregate					
1861–70 . . .	10	84	20	104	10	94
1871–80 . . .	8	122	16	138	8	130
1881–87 . . .	2	80	11	91	2	89
27 years . . .	20	286	47	333	20	313

In 1878 Italy had 2030 silk-factories, with 2,100,000 spindles, giving employment to 16,000 men ; there were also 120,000 women and 76,000 children engaged in attending to the silk-worms.

In 1840 the kingdom of Sardinia had several silk-factories, with an aggregate of 14,900 operatives. The cocoon crop of Italy for the years 1881–88 averaged 86 million pounds.

SPAIN

Silk manufacture flourished under the Moors for some centuries before the industry was known in France. It even survived their expulsion, for Seville had 16,000 silk-looms in 1550, but a hundred years later there were only sixty. Coming down to our own time, we find that in 1870 Spain had silk-factories with an aggregate of 3000 looms and 9000 operatives ; the number of the latter in 1884 was only 8000, and the output was valued at £1,000,000 in the *Bulletin Statistique*, although Spanish writers (prone to exaggerate) claim a value of £2,800,000 sterling. The silkworm thrives in the south, the production of native silk averaging 300,000 lbs. yearly.

The consumption in the factories averaged as follows :—

Period	Silk, Lbs. Yearly			Value of Manufactures, £
	Spanish	Imported	Total	
1861–70 . .	300,000	...	300,000	600,000
1871–80 . .	300,000	140,000	440,000	900,000
1881–87 . .	300,000	290,000	590,000	1,200,000

The consumption of silk manufactures was as follows :—

Period	Yearly Average			Pence per Inhabitant
	Spanish	Imported	Total	
	£	£	£	
1861–70 . .	600,000	300,000	900,000	15
1871–80 . .	900,000	200,000	1,100,000	17
1881–87 . .	1,200,000	400,000	1,600,000	22

The balance-sheet of the industry was approximately as follows :—

Period	Millions £ Aggregate		
	Raw Silk	Manufactures	Net Product
1861–70 . . .	3	6	3
1871–80 . . .	4	9	5
1881–87 . . .	3	8	5
27 years . . .	10	23	13

BELGIUM

Silk manufacture is declining, the average consumption since 1880 being only 400,000 lbs. raw silk yearly, and the output of the mills £800,000. Belgium, moreover, consumes imported silk goods to the value of £400,000 a year.

SWITZERLAND

Silk manufacture holds the foremost rank in Switzerland, the output averaging six millions sterling, nearly all of which is exported.

UNITED STATES

The Census returns show as follows :—

Year	Factories	Operatives	Capital, £	Manufactures, £
1850	67	2,000	200,000	400,000
1870	86	7,000	1,000,000	2,000,000
1880	382	31,000	4,000,000	7,300,000

The consumption of silk was as follows :—

Period	Lbs. Yearly	Value of Textures, £
1861–70 . . .	1,200,000	2,500,000
1871–80 . . .	1,400,000	3,000,000
1881–87 . . .	3,500,000	7,200,000

The value of all silk manufactures consumed was :—

Period	Yearly Average			Shillings per Inhabitant
	American, £	Imported, £	Total, £	
1861–70	2,500,000	3,100,000	5,600,000	3
1871–80	3,000,000	5,100,000	8,100,000	4
1881–87	7,200,000	6,800,000	14,000,000	5

The balance-sheet was approximately as follows :—

Period	Millions £ Aggregate		
	Raw Silk	Manufactures	Net Result
1861–70 . . .	14	25	11
1871–80 . . .	15	30	15
1881–87 . . .	20	50	30
27 years . . .	49	105	56

CHINA

Silk is known to have been cultivated for 3000 years, the best coming from the province of Kwantung. The ordinary crop is 21,000,000 lbs., of which 60 per cent. is consumed in China. The quantities exported have been :—

Period	Annual Average, Lbs.
1873–80	9,300,000
1881–87	8,100,000

The values of all silk exports have been as follows :—

Period	Raw Silk	Manufactures	Total
	£ Yearly	£ Yearly	£ Yearly
1873–80 . . .	3,900,000	700,000	4,600,000
1881–87 . . .	3,100,000	800,000	3,900,000

About 60 per cent. of the raw silk exported is from Shanghai, and 50 per cent. of manufactured silks from Canton.

JAPAN

Official returns for the years 1884–87 show an average production of 6,800,000 lbs. raw silk, disposed of in this manner :—

	Lbs.	Value, £
Home manufacture .	3,300,000	6,000,000
Exported raw . . .	3,500,000	2,400,000
Total . .	6,800,000	8,400,000

Of the silk goods manufactured in the country, about £250,000 worth is exported yearly, the rest consumed in Japan.

TURKEY

The annual production of silk averages about 1,200,000 lbs., of which five-sixths are exported.

The value of silk and cocoons exported in 1888 was £1,100,000 sterling. Local manufactures probably attain a value of £350,000 per annum.

INDIA

The imports and exports of raw silk have been :—

Period	Annual Average, Lbs.			
	Imports	Exports	Surplus Imports	Surplus Exports
1867–70 . .	1,800,000	2,300,000	...	500,000
1871–75 . .	2,100,000	2,200,000	...	100,000
1876–80 . .	2,000,000	1,600,000	400,000	...
1881–88 . .	2,100,000	1,600,000	500,000	...

The value of silk manufactures imported and exported was as follows :—

Period	Annual Average		
	Imports, £	Exports	Surplus Imports, £
1867–70 . . .	450,000	120,000	330,000
1871–80 . . .	660,000	210,000	450,000
1881–88 . . .	1,300,000	320,000	980,000

The value of Indian silk manufactures is unknown.

SLAVERY

In ancient Greece and Rome the ordinary wages of a slave and his market value were as follows :—

GREECE

	Day's Wage, Pence	Value, £
Labourer	6	56
Farmer	10	103
Cutler	8	77
Boatman	6	60

ROME

	Day's Wage, Pence	Value, £
Gardener	8	65
Carpenter	20	148
Blacksmith	20	145
Shepherd	6	51
Baker	19	140
Cook	...	430
Actress	...	820
Physician	...	1,100

Some of the wealthy Romans had 10,000 slaves. After great victories they could often be bought for a few shillings on the battle-field.

SLAVE-TRADE

The *Journal des Economistes* gives the following table of the number of slaves shipped from Africa in sixty years ending 1847 :—

Period	Shipped	Died	Landed in America
1788–98 . . .	100,000	14,000	86,000
1798–1805 . . .	85,000	12,000	73,000
1805–15 . . .	178,000	25,000	153,000
1815–30 . . .	441,000	110,000	331,000
1830–40 . . .	214,000	54,000	160,000
1840–47 . . .	444,000	112,000	332,000
60 years . . .	1,462,000	327,000	1,135,000

About 22 per cent. perished on the voyage.

There are no records of the number of slaves carried by English and other dealers in the 16th, 17th, and 18th centuries to America, but it is believed to exceed 3,000,000, the Treaty of Utrecht securing great advantages in 1713 to the British flag in this trade. The records for the year 1787 showed the number of African slaves landed alive in America as follows :—

Carried by	Number
British	38,000
French	31,000
Portuguese	25,000
Dutch, Danes, &c.	6,500
Total . .	100,500

The Danes were the first to abolish slavery in their West Indian islands. The emancipation of slaves in the

British West Indies and other colonies in 1834 gave liberty to 780,000, viz. :—

	Number	Indemnity, £	Per Head, £
Jamaica	311,700	6,152,000	20
Barbadoes . . .	83,000	1,721,000	21
Trinidad	22,300	1,039,000	50
Antigua, &c.. . .	172,093	3,421,000	20
Guiana	84,900	4,297,000	53
Mauritius	68,600	2,113,000	31
Cape of Good Hope	38,400	1,247,000	33
Total . .	780,993	20,000,000	26

The difference paid per head in the above colonies is very remarkable.

The French freed their West Indian slaves in 1848, the Dutch in 1863, the latter emancipating 46,000 at £32 per head paid to their masters.

Slavery was abolished in the United States in 1861, the number of slaves in that country having been as follows :—

Year			Number	Year			Number
1790	.	.	697,900	1830	.	.	2,009,030
1800	.	.	893,040	1840	.	.	2,487,500
1810	.	.	1,191,400	1850	.	.	3,204,300
1820	.	.	1,538,100	1860	.	.	3,979,700

The number of slaves in the several States was as follows :—

	1790	1820	1840
Virginia	293,000	425,000	449,000
South Carolina . .	107,000	258,000	327,000
North Carolina . .	101,000	205,000	246,000
Maryland	103,000	107,000	90,000
Georgia	29,000	150,000	281,000
Kentucky	11,000	127,000	182,000
Tennessee . . .	...	80,000	183,000
Louisiana	...	69,000	168,000
Alabama	...	47,000	254,000
Mississippi . . .	...	33,000	195,000
Various	54,000	37,000	111,000
Total . . .	698,000	1,538,000	2,486,000

The proportion of slaves in the total coloured population was as follows :—

Year	Coloured Population	Slaves	Slave Ratio per Cent.
1790 . . .	757,000	698,000	92
1820 . . .	1,772,000	1,538,000	86
1840 . . .	2,874,000	2,486,000	87
1850 . . .	3,639,000	3,204,000	88
1860 . . .	4,486,000	3,980,000	89

The slave ratio was steadily increasing for forty years until the war of emancipation in 1860, which (besides 655,000 men killed) cost an outlay of 555 millions sterling, equal to £140 per slave. In the French island of Guadaloupe slaves formed two-thirds of the population just before the emancipation in 1848, viz. :—

	1781	1833	1847
Free	14,800	23,800	38,800
Slaves	83,900	98,600	91,500
Total . .	98,700	122,400	130,300

From 1833 to 1847 the masters had voluntarily manumitted 18,600 slaves, being at the rate of 4 per cent. male, and 7 per cent. female slaves yearly. The annual

birth-rate and death-rate of slaves per 1000 compared with that of the French settlers thus :—

	French Settlers	Slaves
Birth-rate	33.2	24.9
Death-rate . . .	31.4	23.6
Increase of population .	1.8	1.3

Slavery was abolished in Cuba in 1880, in Brazil in 1889. In the latter country, by a previous enumeration, there were found to be 805,000 male and 706,000 female slaves, held by 41,000 owners, the average price being from £80 to £100.

Serfs

The condition of European serfs was a mild form of slavery. In the 18th century Danish noblemen gave their coachmen permission to flog women ; the peasants were bought and sold with the estates like cattle. As regards other countries, the conditions, &c., may be summed up thus :—

AUSTRIA

In 1840 the value of servitude to the nobility was estimated at £51,200,000 a year thus :—

		Value, £
Labour (two days per week)	. .	35,000,000
Tithe of crops, &c.	.	12,000,000
Male tribute, timber . . .	.	1,400,000
Female tribute, spun wool . .	.	1,800,000
Fowls, eggs, butter . . .	.	1,000,000
		51,200,000

There were 7,000,000 serfs. Some Bohemian nobles had as many as 10,000. The redemption was effected by giving the nobles 5 per cent. Government scrip, and land then rose 50 per cent. in value.

GERMANY

In 1848 the State took 60 million acres from the nobles, leaving them still 25 million acres, and gave the former among the serfs. Indemnity as follows :—

1. Government scrip, £180 for each serf family, to nobleman.
2. Land-tax, £3 per annum, transferred to peasant.
3. Interest, £7 per annum for forty-seven years, to be paid by peasant to the State, being 4 per cent. on cost of redemption.

FRANCE

The Corvée, which prevailed during the Middle Ages, was as follows :—

Each man gave one day's work with a waggon, or two days if he had no waggon, yearly, unpaid, to the State ; each woman one day. The man could commute by paying 2s., the woman 1s.

RUSSIA

Previous to the emancipation of 1861 the number of serfs was as follows :—

	Male	Female	Total
Crown serfs . .	11,168,000	11,683,000	22,851,000
Appanage . . .	1,624,000	1,702,000	3,326,000
Held by nobles .	10,674,000	11,081,000	21,755,000
Total . .	23,466,000	24,466,000	47,932,000

There were 103,000 noblemen holding 22 million serfs in this manner :—

Nobles			Serfs	Average
23,100	.	.	18,575,000	802
36,150	.	.	2,520,000	70
43,800	.	.	660,000	15
103,050	.	.	21,755,000	211

The cost of emancipating these serfs was 65 millions sterling, but as the nobles had already mortgaged them up to 30 millions sterling in the Imperial Bank, the Government deducted this sum. The account was made up thus :—

	£
Mortgages remitted . . .	30,400,000
Russian stock . . .	20,230,000
Paid by serfs . . .	10,470,000
Balance due . . .	3,900,000
Total . . .	65,000,000

The lands are mortgaged to the State until 1912 as security for the advances by Government, viz., £50,630,000 sterling. In 1879 the serfs were holders of 186 millions acres, viz. :—

Title	Holders	Acres
Crown-gift	6,117,000	84,200,000
Appanage	1,625,000	30,200,000
Purchase	10,137,000	65,500,000
Beggar-lots	1,840,000	6,440,000
Total . .	19,719,000	186,340,000

In return for crown-gift the holders have to pay 50 per cent. extra poll-tax till 1902. Beggar-lots are lands given gratis by the nobles to the peasants, rather than sell farm-lots at £1 per acre to them.

ROUMANIA

The emancipation law of 1870 compelled the Boyars either to give the peasant half his farm gratis or to sell the whole at 26s. per acre : 400 Boyars preferred the former. Previously the conditions of servitude were : to work twelve days in the year for the Boyar, to give him one-tenth of the crops, and to buy groceries at the Boyar's store.

EGYPT

Corvée, or compulsory labour, was imposed in 1883 on 202,000 Fellahs, who had to work 100 days unpaid, and in 1888 on 59,000 for the same term.

SMUGGLERS

In 1830 there were 100,000 contrabandistas in Spain, without counting their wives, &c., the total of persons living by smuggling being calculated at 300,000.

SOAP

The production and consumption in the United Kingdom were approximately as follows, the exact consumption not being known since 1853, when the duty was abolished :—

Year	Million Lbs.			Consumption per Inhabitant, Lbs.	Duty per Ton	Price per Ton
	Manufacture	Consumption	Export			
1791 . . .	48	46	2	3.1	£21	£76
1801 . . .	57	54	3	3.6	21	74
1811 . . .	76	73	3	4.2	21	73
1821 . . .	98	94	4	4.6	28	68
1831 . . .	123	107	16	4.5	28	52
1841 . . .	199	170	29	6.4	14	48
1851 . . .	217	195	22	7.0	14	40
1861 . . .	254	232	22	8.0	...	27
1871 . . .	...	...	17	...	...	27
1881 . . .	...	...	39	...	...	22

It is believed that the average consumption of soap per inhabitant has doubled since the duty was removed, and now reaches 14 lbs. The quantity manufactured yearly would, therefore, appear to be 260,000 tons, of which 235,000 are consumed in the United Kingdom, and 25,000 exported. The export of soap in recent years has been as follows :—

Year	Tons	Value, £	£ per Ton
1875 . .	12,500	310,000	25
1880 . .	19,500	440,000	22
1885 . .	20,100	470,000	23
1889 . .	25,000	505,000	20

In 1881 France manufactured 255 million lbs., the consumption in that country averaging 6 lbs. per inhabitant.

SOCIETIES

The following table shows approximately the principal features of friendly societies of all descriptions :—

	Societies	Members	Capital, £
Great Britain . .	22,000	7,000,000	58,000,000
France . . .	8,000	1,250,000	5,200,000
Germany . . .	24,000	7,400,000	23,000,000
Russia . . .	500	35,000	300,000
Austria . . .	1,900	870,000	17,000,000
Italy . . .	2,200	330,000	900,000
Switzerland . .	630	100,000	300,000
Belgium . . .	210	30,000	250,000
Denmark . . .	720	90,000	...
Canada . . .	40	80,000	5,100,000
Australia . . .	900	100,000	...

These societies may be said to have sprung up in the last thirty years, possessing at present a paid-up capital of nearly 120 millions sterling.

UNITED KINGDOM

The number of friendly societies registered in 92 years was as follows :—

Period	Number	Yearly Average
1793–1855	26,034	412
1856–73	20,058	1,114
1874–84	7,436	676
92 years	53,528	582

The above is exclusive of building societies and co-operative associations.

The advance of friendly societies in late years is shown thus :—

	1873	1880
Members	1,787,000	4,802,000
Assets, £ . . .	8,630,000	13,003,000

The progress of co-operative societies is shown thus :—

Year	Societies	Members	Capital, £	Sales, £
1861 . . .	66	38,000	365,000	1,100,000
1871 . . .	749	249,000	2,530,000	8,200,000
1880 . . .	1,182	604,000	6,200,000	23,200,000
1888 . . .	1,363	935,000	12,800,000	36,700,000

The above figures do not include 115 societies in 1888, which failed to publish particulars.

The returns published for 1888 were as follows :—

	Societies	Members	Capital, £	Sales, £	Profits, £
England	1,020	786,000	10,800,000	28,800,000	2,650,000
Scotland	323	148,000	1,800,000	7,100,000	640,000
Total . . .	1,343	934,000	12,600,000	35,900,000	3,290,000

There are twenty societies in Ireland, but the business done is small. The summary of transactions in Great Britain shows that in twenty-five years down to December 1888, the co-operative societies made sales exceeding 471 millions sterling, leaving a profit of £39,800,000, out of which the societies had made investments which amounted in December 1888 to a value of £5,300,000.

Building societies show the following progress in fourteen years :—

Year	Societies	Members	Receipts, £	Assets, £	Liabilities, £	Net Assets, £
1874	474	270,000	15,900,000	38,800,000	13,500,000	25,300,000
1888	2,545	604,000	20,400,000	53,200,000	15,200,000	38,000,000

The returns for 1888 show as follows :—

	Societies	Members	Receipts, £	Assets, £	Liabilities, £	Net Assets, £
England . . .	2,444	582,900	19,500,000	51,200,000	14,700,000	36,500,000
Scotland . . .	50	9,000	400,000	1,010,000	240,000	770,000
Ireland . . .	51	12,300	530,000	990,000	250,000	740,000
United Kingdom .	2,545	604,200	20,430,000	53,200,000	15,190,000	38,010,000

FRANCE

Official returns are to the following effect :—

Year	Societies	Members	Capital, £
1853	2,695	318,000	500,000
1860	4,252	358,000	1,000,000
1870	5,788	849,000	2,100,000
1880	6,777	1,066,000	3,800,000
1885	7,960	1,252,000	5,200,000

The above returns for 1885 include 182,000 honorary members. The sick ratio showed thus :—

	Members	Sick	Sick Ratio
Men	899,000	232,000	25.8
Women . . .	171,000	44,000	25.8
Total . .	1,070,000	276,000	25.8

The women who were sick showed an average duration of 13 days' illness, the men 18. The death-rate in 1885 was 13.5 per 1000. Receipts, £1,000,000; expenditure, £880,000; surplus, £120,000. Each sick person cost 36 shillings, or 25 pence per day.

GERMANY

Official returns for 1886 show as follows :—

	Societies	Members
Prussia	8,529	2,445,000
Bavaria	4,271	397,000
Saxony	2,188	571,000
Other States . .	4,250	1,157,000
Total . .	19,238	4,570,000

Some of the principal trades represented were :—

Textiles	.	.	543,000	Pottery .	.	.	223,000
Ironworks	.	.	345,000	Sugar .	.	.	127,000
Building	.	.	590,000	Carpentry	.	.	125,000

The total income of the above societies in 1885 was £3,300,000, and their expenditure £2,600,000.

Co-operative societies were begun about 1860, and received a great impulse from Mr. Schultz-Delitsch. Dr. Schenck published a report in 1888 which compares these societies with previous years :—

Year	Societies	Members	Paid Capital, £
1860 . . .	133	31,600	80,000
1870 . . .	740	314,700	2,200,000
1880 . . .	4,920	1,710,000	8,650,000
1888 . . .	5,000	2,000,000	15,000,000

The ratio of shareholders from the different classes of society in these companies, and in Schultz's popular banks, showed as follows :—

	Co-operative Companies	Popular Banks
Farmers	27.0	30.0
Artisans	29.0	34.0
Merchants . . .	44.0	36.0
Total . .	100.0	100.0

In December 1888 the Schultz-Delitsch companies comprised 2200 popular banks and 2620 co-operative societies. The progress of the popular banks appears as follows :—

Year	Shareholders	Capital, £	Advances, £
1859 . . .	18,700	370,000	620,000
1887 . . .	456,300	5,030,000	39,400,000

Deposits in 1887 amounted to £21,400,000 sterling. The Journeyman's Union, for the support of widows and orphans, had 270,000 members in 1882, with an income of £1,100,000 yearly.

AUSTRIA

In 1889 there were 1916 friendly societies, numbering 609,000 male and 262,000 female members. Only 1064 of these societies published statements, the aggregate of which showed :—

	£
Capital and reserve . . .	17,000,000
Deposits	37,100,000

ITALY

Official returns give the following particulars :—

Year	Societies	Members	Assets, £
1862 . . .	443	111,600	108,000
1873 . . .	1,447	217,900	396,000
1880 . . .	2,188	332,000	845,000

Days lost by sickness in the year average on the whole number of members 4.4, that is, 6.3 on women and 4.1 on men. Average duration of illness, 20 days.

BELGIUM

Official returns are to the following effect :—

Year	Societies	Members	Income, £
1860 . . .	36	6,300	17,000
1880 . . .	179	25,800	39,000
1886 . . .	211	31,700	44,000

There are seven building societies, which have built 1093 houses, containing 5400 rooms, accommodating 8430 persons, at an average rent of £2 yearly per head, or 63s. per room. Income £17,000, expenses £7600, net rental £9400.

AUSTRALIA

In 1873 Victoria had 682 societies with 50,000 members, whose death-rate reached 10 per 1000. Income £152,000, reserve £262,000.

SPIRITS

The consumption in the principal countries at previous dates was as follows :—

	Gallons per Inhabitant						
	1830	1840	1850	1860	1870	1881	1888
United Kingdom	0.95	0.80	0.88	0.95	1.01	1.06	0.96
France	0.26	0.33	0.39	0.51	0.60	0.90	1.10
Germany . . .	...	0.60	...	1.08	...	1.33	1.40
Russia . . .	5.00	...	3.70	4.80	...	2.20	1.10
Sweden . . .	8.80	8.00	8.40	6.00	4.60	4.25	4.20
Denmark . . .	...	7.20	...	5.80	...	4.20	4.30
Belgium . . .	0.96	...	1.26	...	1.90	...	2.40
United States .	5.55	3.10	2.50	2.10	1.62	1.50	1.20

The consumption in Russia in 1881 was estimated at 174 million gallons, but the official returns for 1886 only give 91 millions; perhaps illicit distilling may account for the difference.

The manufacture of spirits in England and Wales was as follows :—

Year	Gallons	Duty, Pence	Gallons per Inhabitant
1700 . . .	1,210,000	4	0.22
1720 . . .	2,530,000	4	0.42
1740 . . .	6,715,000	4	1.10
1760 . . .	2,320,000	30	0.33
1780 . . .	2,330,000	30	0.35
1800 . . .	4,410,000	60	0.50
1820 . . .	4,315,000	120	0.36
1830 . . .	7,680,000	90	0.55
1850 . . .	9,620,000	90	0.54
1860 . . .	12,910,000	90	0.65
1870 . . .	11,220,000	120	0.48
1881 . . .	16,930,000	120	0.65

The consumption in the three kingdoms of British and imported spirits was approximately as follows :—

Year	Gallons				Gallons per Inhabitant			
	England	Scotland	Ireland	United Kingdom	England	Scotland	Ireland	United Kingdom
1800 . .	4,350,000	1,280,000	1,330,000	6,960,000	0.51	0.74	0.26	0.45
1810 . .	4,790,000	1,750,000	4,730,000	11,260,000	0.48	0.97	0.80	0.62
1820 . .	4,280,000	1,860,000	3,300,000	9,450,000	0.35	0.92	0.49	0.45
1830 . .	7,730,000	6,010,000	9,005,000	22,745,000	0.55	2.60	1.15	0.95
1840 . .	8,280,000	6,180,000	7,402,000	21,862,000	0.52	2.40	0.90	0.80
1850 . .	9,330,000	7,120,000	7,410,000	23,860,000	0.52	2.43	1.12	0.88
1860 . .	12,910,000	7,890,000	6,400,000	27,200,000	0.65	2.62	1.10	0.95
1870 . .	14,630,000	8,580,000	8,300,000	31,510,000	0.67	2.56	1.55	1.01
1881 . .	21,600,000	8,800,000	6,610,000	37,010,000	0.84	2 35	1.29	1.06
1888 . .	22,400,000	8,400,000	6,300,000	37,100,000	0.77	2.10	1.33	0.96

The consumption of alcohol per head in French cities in 1885 was :—

	Gallons	Gallons per Inhabitant
Paris	3,100,000	1.40
Marseilles . .	440,000	1.40
Lyons . . .	440,000	1.10
Bordeaux . . .	220,000	1.00
Rouen . . .	300,000	2.70
Havre . . .	350,000	3.30

For further details see *Alcohol*, p. 58.

It is found that one bushel of grain will make 4½ gallons of spirits or 27 gallons of beer, and that 4 bushels of malt are equal to 5 bushels of grain. Thus, a ton of grain produces 180 gallons of spirits, a ton of malt 225 gallons.

SPONGES

On the coast of Syria 300 boats with 1500 divers pick up annually sponges worth £25,000; best worth 40s., inferior, 4s. per lb. Depth, 30 to 150 ft.

Simmonds states the sponge-fisheries as follows :—

	Value, £
West Indies	120,000
Mediterranean	150,000

The quantities imported into Great Britain were :—

	Lbs.
1840	78,000
1855	474,000
1870	840,000

No returns since 1870.

PLATE IX.

STEAM-POWER.

Aggregate horse-power of the world at various dates, in millions.

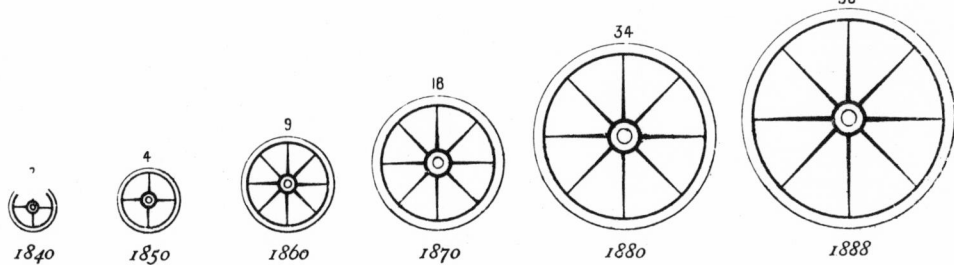

1840   1850   1860   1870   1880   1888

Horse-power of nations, in millions, in 1888.

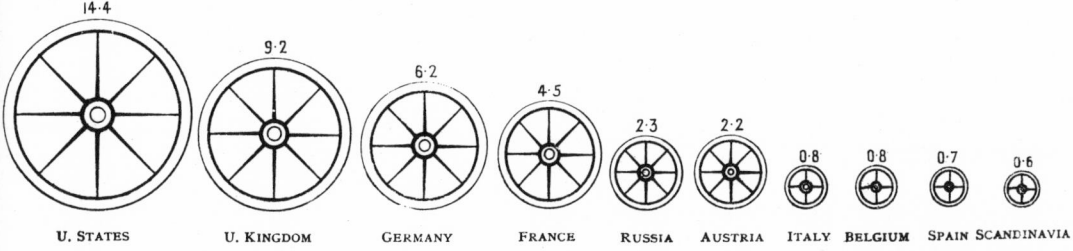

U. STATES   U. KINGDOM   GERMANY   FRANCE   RUSSIA   AUSTRIA   ITALY   BELGIUM   SPAIN   SCANDINAVIA

Horse-power per 1000 inhabitants.

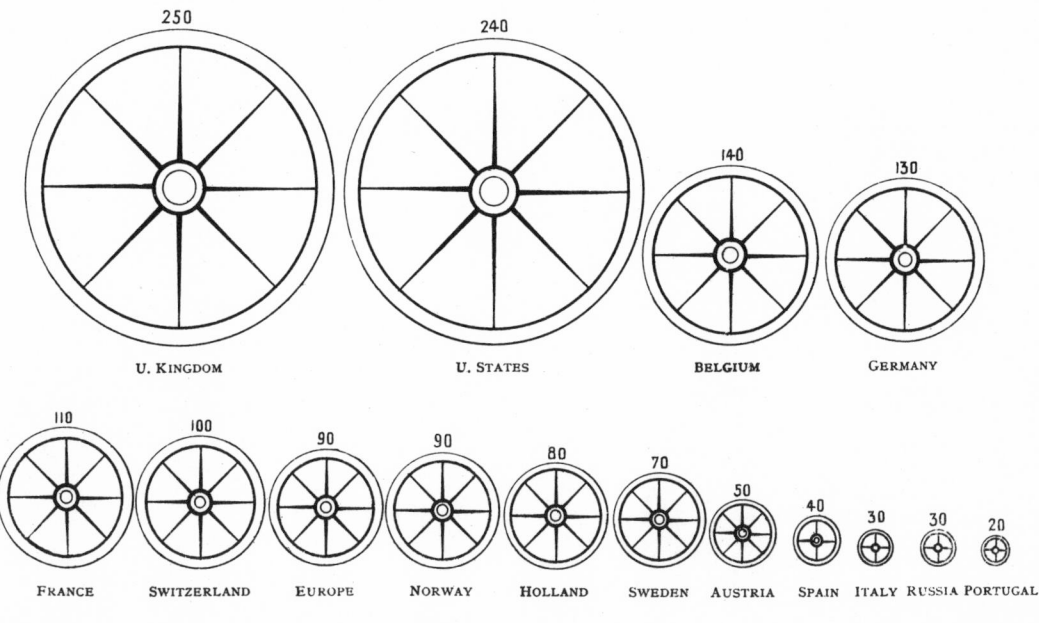

U. KINGDOM   U. STATES   BELGIUM   GERMANY

FRANCE   SWITZERLAND   EUROPE   NORWAY   HOLLAND   SWEDEN   AUSTRIA   SPAIN   ITALY   RUSSIA   PORTUGAL

Ballantyne, Hanson & Cº Edinburgh & London.

SQUARES

Name			City	Acres
Grosvenor	.	.	London	10
Parade	.	.	Vienna	15
Schloss	.	.	Berlin	16
Bellecour	.	.	Lyons	32
St. Stephen's	.	.	Dublin	40

STATISTICS.

The library of the Royal Statistical Society comprises 27,000 volumes, and is far from complete. There are at least 50,000 statistical works extant, and if a student were able to examine three of them daily he would require 50 years to get through them. More than 500 new works on statistics are published yearly.

STEAM

The following table shows approximately the steam-power of all nations at various dates :—

			Horse-Power						Per 100 In-habitants in 1888
			1840	1850	1860	1870	1880	1888	
United Kingdom	.	.	620,000	1,290,000	2,450,000	4,040,000	7,600,000	9,200,000	25
France	.	.	90,000	370,000	1,120,000	1,850,000	3,070,000	4,520,000	11
Germany	.	.	40,000	260,000	850,000	2,480,000	5,120,000	6,200,000	13
Russia	.	.	20,000	70,000	200,000	920,000	1,740,000	2,240,000	3
Austria	.	.	20,000	100,000	330,000	800,000	1,560,000	2,150,000	5
Italy	.	.	10,000	40,000	50,000	330,000	500,000	830,000	3
Spain	.	.	10,000	20,000	100,000	210,000	470,000	740,000	4
Portugal	.	.	...	...	10,000	30,000	60,000	80,000	2
Sweden	.	.	...	...	20,000	100,000	220,000	300,000	7
Norway	.	.	...	...	10,000	40,000	90,000	180,000	9
Denmark	.	.	...	...	10,000	30,000	90,000	150,000	8
Holland	.	.	...	10,000	30,000	130,000	250,000	340,000	8
Belgium	.	.	40,000	70,000	160,000	350,000	610,000	810,000	14
Switzerland	.	.	...	...	90,000	140,000	230,000	290,000	10
Various	.	.	10,000	10,000	80,000	120,000	390,000	600,000	6
Europe	.	.	860,000	2,240,000	5,540,000	11,570,000	22,000,000	28,630,000	9
United States	.	.	760,000	1,680,000	3,470,000	5,590,000	9,110,000	14,400,000	24
Colonies, &c.	.	.	30,000	70,000	400,000	1,300,000	3,040,000	7,120,000	...
Total	.	.	1,650,000	3,990,000	9,380,000	18,460,000	34,150,000	50,150,000	...

The distribution of fixed steam-power was approximately as follows :—

			1840	1850	1860	1870	1880	1888
United Kingdom	.	.	350,000	500,000	700,000	900,000	2,000,000	2,200,000
Continent	.	.	100,000	220,000	650,000	1,860,000	3,270,000	4,150,000
United States	.	.	360,000	600,000	800,000	1,220,000	2,200,000	3,300,000
Colonies, &c.	.	.	20,000	40,000	70,000	120,000	200,000	400,000
Total	.	.	830,000	1,360,000	2,220,000	4,100,000	7,670,000	10,050,000

The distribution of railway steam-power was approximately thus :—

			1840	1850	1860	1870	1880	1888
United Kingdom	.	.	200,000	700,000	1,400,000	2,140,000	3,200,000	3,500,000
Continent	.	.	90,000	630,000	2,210,000	5,200,000	9,640,000	12,780,000
United States	.	.	200,000	600,000	1,800,000	3,300,000	5,700,000	9,300,000
Colonies, &c.	.	.	...	10,000	300,000	1,100,000	2,700,000	6,400,000
Total	.	.	490,000	1,940,000	5,710,000	11,740,000	21,240,000	31,980,000

The distribution of shipping steam-power was approximately thus :—

			1840	1850	1860	1870	1880	1888
United Kingdom	.	.	70,000	90,000	350,000	1,000,000	2,400,000	3,500,000
Continent	.	.	50,000	100,000	200,000	470,000	1,490,000	2,670,000
United States	.	.	200,000	480,000	870,000	1,070,000	1,210,000	1,770,000
Colonies, &c.	.	.	10,000	20,000	30,000	80,000	140,000	180,000
Total	.	.	330,000	690,000	1,450,000	2,620,000	5,240,000	8,120,000

Summing up the table, we find as follows :—

	1840	1850	1860	1870	1880	1888
Fixed	830,000	1,360,000	2,220,000	4,100,000	7,670,000	10,050,000
Locomotives . . .	490,000	1,940,000	5,710,000	11,740,000	21,240,000	31,980,000
Shipping	330,000	690,000	1,450,000	2,620,000	5,240,000	8,120,000
Total . .	1,650,000	3,990,000	9,380,000	18,460,000	34,150,000	50,150,000

The following table shows approximately the number of fixed engines in 1880, and of locomotives and steamboats in 1888 :—

	Number		Steamers	
	Fixed Engines	Locomotives	Mercantile	War
U. Kingdom .	110,000	16,000	6,870	200
France . . .	37,800	9,600	1,020	200
Germany . .	55,100	13,000	750	60
Russia . . .	8,950	6,000	650	280
Austria . .	9,150	4,500	100	50
Italy . . .	4,450	2,000	270	150
Spain . . .	2,300	1,300	420	25
Portugal . .	140	250	40	30
Sweden . .	1,500	700	960	30
Norway . .	700	200	540	20
Denmark . .	800	200	290	20
Holland . .	5,750	650	110	30
Belgium . .	11,750	2,400	50	...
Switzerland .	1,500	650	30	...
Various . .	500	3,000	140	60
Europe . .	250,390	60,450	12,240	1,155
United States	60,300	31,000	5,920	70
Colonies, &c.	15,000	15,700	600	80
Total	325,690	107,150	18,760	1,305

Steam being measured by horse-power, it is well to bear in mind the following facts :—

One horse-power will raise 10 tons per minute a height of 12 inches, working 8 hours a day. This is about 5000 foot-tons daily, or 12 times a man's work.

(1.) Mail-coach horses: Four will draw a coach, say 2 tons, at the rate of 10 miles an hour, for 6 days every week, and last 5 years.

(2.) Canal horses: One will draw a barge of 25 tons, resistance 108 lbs., at 2½ miles per hour.

(3.) Waggoners' horses: One will easily draw a ton 30 miles in a day of 12 hours.

Sims mentions a Devonshire cart-horse, 15 hands, 1200 lbs., which gave an average of 8000 foot-tons daily.

The horse-power of Niagara is 3¼ millions effective, equal to 10 million horses effective, valued at £15,000,000 per annum, if conveyed by electricity to New York.

The measurement of horse-power, that is, of raising a certain weight 12 inches per minute during 8 hours daily, is variously given by the best authorities, viz. :—

	Lbs.		Lbs.
Smeaton . . .	22,000	Desaguliers . .	27,500
Sims . . .	23,400	Watt . . .	32,000
Tredgold . .	27,500	Saussure . . .	34,000

In 1880 Mr. Engel showed that the value of industries dependent on steam was 6275 millions sterling ; his table for 1880 may compare with one for 1888 as follows :—

	Millions £ Sterling		Increase
	1880	1888	
Railways . . .	4,000	5,700	1,700
Factories, &c. . .	2,000	2,600	600
Steamers . .	275	410	135
Total . .	6,275	8.710	2,435

This shows that in eight years about 300 millions sterling per annum of new capital went into industries worked by steam. Mr. Engel finds that the maintenance of a 300-horse locomotive costs £900 a year, or £3 per horse-power, whereas the food of a live horse costs £30 per annum. Stationary engines, he says, cost £15 per annum per horse-power. A water-wheel of 100 horse-power costs only £7 per annum, or less than 18d. per horse. He shows that during twelve years ending 1878 each locomotive in Prussia drew yearly 1710 tons a distance of 6 miles per horse-power; that is, a 300-horse engine drew nearly the above weight daily 10 kilometres or 6 miles. He shows further that a live horse draws about 92 tons in the year a distance of 6 miles, and that on comparing the cost of maintenance, the locomotive does its work at one halfpenny per ton, whereas the live horse costs 7s. for the same, that it, one ton for 6 miles. In other words, horse-draught costs 168 times as much as that done by locomotive. In simple form it may be stated thus :—

Locomotive draws daily 100 tons a length of 100 miles for 50s., say 6d. per ton per 100 miles.

Horse draws one ton two miles daily for 20d., being at the rate of 84s. per ton per 100 miles.

In 1880 the average power of locomotives was 250 horse in England, 290 in Germany, 350 in France, and 420 in Switzerland.

UNITED KINGDOM

In 1775 England had 20 steam-engines, with an aggregate of 300 horse-power. The use of steam in textile factories rose as follows :—

Year						Horse-Power
1835 .	.	.	.	.	.	41,000
1850 .	.	.	.	.	.	108,000
1860 .	.	.	.	.	.	375,000
1870 .	.	.	.	.	.	478,000

According to Fairbairn, in 1860 the steam-engines, fixed and movable, amounted to an aggregate of 3,650.000 horse-power. Engel made the aggregate in 1880 no less than 6,986,000. The following table shows approximately the growth of the various classes of steam-power :—

Year	Horse-Power			
	Fixed	Locomotives	Steamboats	Total
1840	350,000	180,000	70,000	600,000
1850	500,000	700,000	90,000	1,290,000
1860	700,000	1,350,000	350,000	2,400,000
1870	940,000	2,100,000	1,000,000	4,040,000
1880	2,000,000	3,200,000	2,400,000	7,600,000
1888	2,200,000	3,500,000	3,500,000	9,200,000

Engel seems to have under-estimated the horse-power of steamers, his estimate for the United Kingdom in 1880 being as follows :—

Fixed	2,000,000
Locomotives	3,240,000
Steamboats	1,746,000
	6,986,000

In the preceding table steamboats, of course, include both merchant vessels and the royal navy. Actual horse-power is double the nominal.

The power of locomotives in England is variously estimated at 220 to 250 horse-power. From the above table it appears that the steam force of the United King-dom has grown 15-fold in 48 years. In 1886 there were 134,000 factories in the United Kingdom, nearly all driven by steam.

FRANCE

Engel's tables down to 1878 are included in the following :—

Year	Engines, Number			Horse-Power			Total
	Fixed	Locomotives	Steamboats	Fixed	Locomotives	Steamboats	
1840 . . .	2,591	142	263	34,000	42,000	11,000	87,000
1850 . . .	5,322	973	537	67,000	291,000	22,000	380,000
1860 . . .	14,936	3,101	681	181,000	930,000	37,000	1,148,000
1870 . . .	27,958	4,835	973	341,000	1,452,000	60,000	1,853,000
1878 . . .	38,880	6,669	1,183	492,000	2,363,000	169,000	3,024,000
1885 . . .	50,980	9,155	4,290	695,000	3,290,000	530,000	4,515,000

The earliest record of steam-power is for 1835, when there were 1450 engines, with 19,000 horse-power. The distribution of steam, as officially reported, was in 1885 as follows :—

	Number	Horse-Power	Average
Mines . . .	4,140	102,000	25
Foundries . .	7,050	147,000	20
Textile factories .	6,470	147,000	22
Flour-mills . .	8,620	92,000	11
Farms . . .	11,940	66,000	6
Various . . .	12,760	141,000	11
Total fixed .	50,980	695,000	14
Locomotives . .	9,155	3,290,000	360
Steamboats .	937	530,000	560
Total .	61,072	4,515,000	74

In this table the number of steamboats is given; in the preceding that of engines.

GERMANY

The following contains Engel's table for Prussia down to 1878 :—

Year	Horse-Power			
	Fixed	Locomotives	Steamers	Total
1840	11,700	300	200	12,200
1852	43,000	40,200	9,200	92,400
1861	143,000	206,000	16,000	365,000
1878	958,000	2,033,000	50,000	3,041,000
1888	1,500,000	2,600,000	120,000	4,220,000

The number of engines in Prussia was as follows :—

	1840	1852	1861	1878
Fixed . .	615	2,124	7,000	35,430
Locomotives	13	607	1,450	6,990
Steamboats	6	102	198	623
Total .	634	2,833	8,648	43,043

Mr. Engel's locomotive steam-power for 1852 seems low, as Prussia had then 2000 miles of railway; it is only 20 horse-power per mile.

The distribution of steam-power of stationary engines in Prussia in 1878 was as follows :—

Class	Engines	Horse-Power
4-horse . . .	1,990	8,000
15-horse . . .	10,140	156,000
Various . . .	23,300	794,000
Total .	35,430	958,000

The total steam-power of Prussia in 1878 showed thus :—

	Engines	Horse-Power
Stationary . . .	35,430	958,000
Locomotives . .	6,990	2,033,000
Steamboats . .	623	50,000
Total .	43,043	3,041,000

The steam-power of Germany at various dates was approximately as follows :

	Horse-Power					
	1840	1850	1860	1870	1880	1888
Fixed	20,000	40,000	200,000	900,000	1,680,000	2,000,000
Locomotives . . .	20,000	200,000	600,000	1,500,000	3,020,000	3,700,000
Steamers	...	20,000	50,000	80,000	420,000	500,000
Total . .	40,000	260,000	850,000	2,480,000	5,120,000	6,200,000

According to the Census of 1880 the employment of steam in fixed engines was as follows :—

	Horse-Power
Factories	1,283,000
Mines	394,000
Total . . .	1,677,000

The increase of manufactures and mining since 1880 leads to the inference that the motive power of fixed engines in 1888 was 2,000,000 horse-power.

RUSSIA

Moscow had two steam-engines in 1820, and in ten years later the number had risen to 100.

In 1880 there were 8946 fixed engines, with an aggregate of 237,000 horse-power. The whole steam-power of the Empire may be estimated to have been approximately as follows :—

Year	Horse-Power			
	Fixed	Locomotives	Steamboats	Total
1840	10,000	10,000	10,000	30,000
1860	60,000	100,000	40,000	200,000
1880	237,000	1,400,000	100,000	1,737,000
1888	300,000	1,800,000	140,000	2,240,000

In 1888 the mining works alone had 100,000 horse-power, almost all steam.

AUSTRIA

Official returns for Austria proper give as follows :—

Year	Engines	Horse-Power
1841	312	7,100
1852	1,182	49,800
1863	4,416	336,000
1875	12,390	1,275,000

	Engines			Horse-Power		
	1852	1863	1875	1852	1863	1875
Fixed . .	671	2,882	9,160	9,000	47,000	157,000
Locomotives	405	1,244	2,786	27,800	249,000	990,000
Steamers .	106	290	462	13,000	40,000	128,000
Total .	1,182	4,416	12,390	49,800	336,000	1,275,000

SPAIN AND PORTUGAL

The amount of steam-power in the Peninsula in 1870 and 1888 is shown approximately thus :—

	1870			1888		
	Spain	Portugal	Total	Spain	Portugal	Total
Fixed .	20,000	1,000	21,000	48,000	3,000	51,000
Locomotives	150,000	20,000	170,000	300,000	60,000	360,000
Steamers .	45,000	5,000	50,000	390,000	15,000	405,000
Total . .	215,000	26,000	241,000	738,000	78,000	816,000

In 1873 the textile mills of Spain had 17,000 horse-power, the factories of Portugal 70 engines, with a total of 1200 horse ; in 1888 the latter had 2700 horse-power.

SWITZERLAND

In 1877 there were 1580 fixed engines, with an aggregate of 32,000 horse-power. In 1885 there were 600 locomotives, with an average power of 420 horse, being much above the European average. The total steam-power may be estimated thus :—

	Engines	Horse-Power
Fixed	2,000	38,000
Locomotives . . .	600	250,000
Steamers . . .	...	2,000
Total . .	...	290,000

In 1851 there were but 34 fixed engines, the number rising to 312 in 1860, and to 955 in 1870.

HOLLAND

In 1883 there were 6689 steam-engines against 4753 in 1877. The total in 1883 (exclusive of railway locomotives) showed as follows :—

	Engines	Horse-Power
On land	5,564	73,100
On water . . .	1,125	37,300

In 1887 the fixed engines of Austria without Hungary rose to 19,615, and the whole steam-power of the Empire in 1888 may be estimated thus :—

	Engines	Horse-Power
Fixed . . .	24,000	400,000
Locomotives . .	4,400	1,500,000
Steamers . . .	...	250,000
Total . .	...	2,150,000

ITALY

In 1877 there were 4459 fixed engines with 54,000 horse-power, and in 1888 the horse-power may be supposed to have reached 150,000, seeing that the consumption of coal has trebled in the interval.

The steam-power was approximately as follows :—

	Horse-Power	
	1877	1888
Fixed . . .	54,000	150,000
Locomotives . .	300,000	500,000
Steamers . .	60,000	180,000
Total . .	414,000	830,000

BELGIUM

In 1836 the total steam-power of the Kingdom was 20,000 horse.

Official returns are to the following effect :—

Year	Engines			Horse-Power		
	Factories	Locomotives, &c.	Total	Factories	Locomotives	Total
1845	1,501	172	1,673	39,000	9,000	48,000
1850	2,013	269	2,282	51,000	15,000	66,000
1860	4,346	651	4,997	99,000	63,000	162,000
1870	8,133	1,161	9,294	176,000	172,000	348,000
1880	11,758	2,302	14,060	275,000	332,000	607,000
1887	13,036	3,331	16,367	337,000	476,000	813,000

The steam-power in 1887 showed in detail thus :—

	Engines	Horse-Power	Average
Factories . . .	13,036	337,000	26
Locomotives . .	2,990	446,000	150
Steamers . .	341	30,000	88
Total . .	16,367	813,000	50

SCANDINAVIA

In 1888 the steam-power of the three northern king-doms was approximately as follows :—

	Horse-Power			
	Sweden	Norway	Denmark	Total
Fixed . .	28,000	10,000	10,000	48,000
Locomotives . .	140,000	30,000	40,000	210,000
Steamers . .	130,000	140,000	100,000	370,000
Total .	298,000	180,000	150,000	628,000

UNITED STATES

There is no record of fixed horse-power before 1870, but we can estimate by the number of hands engaged in manufactures at previous dates. The whole steam-power was approximately thus :—

Year	Horse-Power				Per 1000 Popu-lation
	Fixed	Loco-motives	Steam-boats	Total	
1840	360,000	200,000	200,000	760,000	44
1850	600,000	600,000	500,000	1,700,000	73
1860	800,000	1,800,000	900,000	3,500,000	111
1870	1,216,000	3,300,000	1,100,000	5,616,000	148
1880	2,186,000	5,700,000	1,200,000	9,086,000	180
1888	3,300,000	9,300,000	1,800,000	14,400,000	240

In the above table locomotives are taken at 300 horse each, and the horse-power of steamers as equivalent to their tonnage. The fixed horse-power for 1888 is not known, but as mining has increased 90 per cent. and manufactures over 30 per cent., it is likely motive-power has risen 50 per cent. since 1880.

STONE

The latest statistics as to stone-quarries show the annual yield thus :—

	Product, Tons	Value, £
Great Britain . .	11,000,000	8,700,000
France . , .	8,000,000	6,600,000
Belgium . . .	2,000,000	1,300,000
United States . .	7,000,000	5,300,000

The marble quarries of Italy have an output valued at one million sterling.

STREETS

Heavy traffic averages 100,000 tons, light 50,000 tons per yard per annum. The former wears wooden pave-ment an inch in five years. Some authorities estimate the first cost of paving per square yard as follows :—Stone 10s , wood 14s., asphalt 18s.

The cost of paving and keeping in order a street 10 yards wide and 1000 yards long in wood and stone is shown as follows :—

	Heavy Traffic, £		Light Traffic, £	
	Wood	Stone	Wood	Stone
First cost . . .	7,500	7,200	7,500	7,200
Maintenance, 30 years	15,000	3,600	7,500	2,400
Total .	22,500	10,800	15,000	9,600

The streets of Paris, taking a medium width of 50 feet, are as follows :—

	Square Metres	Miles Long	Mainte-nance, £
Cut stone . .	1,800,000	75	160,000
Rough . .	5,800,000	244	120,000
Asphalt . .	270,000	11	12,000
Total .	7,870,000	330	292,000

Side-walks made of granite cost 18s. per square yard for construction, and 1d. yearly for repairs. The sweep-ing of the streets employs 3100 men.

The streets of Berlin, at an average width of 50 feet, are :—

	Square Metres	Miles Long
Paved . . .	4,280,000	180
Asphalt . . .	125,000	5
Wood . . .	10,000	...
Total .	4,415,000	185

Sweeping costs £80,000 a year.

STRENGTH

Taking that of a man as 100, Byron's Gladiator is equal to 173, the Farnese Hercules 362, and a horse 750.

SUGAR

The following table shows the production approxi-mately :—

	Cane, Tons	Beet, Tons	Total
1840 . . .	1,100,000	50,000	1,150,000
1850 . . .	1,200,000	200,000	1,400,000
1860 . . .	1,800,000	400,000	2,200,000
1870 . . .	1,830,000	900,000	2,730,000
1880 . . .	1,860,000	1,810,000	3,670,000
1889 . . .	2,580,000	2,780,000	5,360,000

The production of beet-sugar according to the *Bulletin Statistique* was as follows in Europe :—

	Tons Yearly					
	1836–39	1840–49	1850–59	1860–69	1870–79	1880-84
France	43,000	34,000	93,000	188,000	370,000	406,000
Germany	6,000	14,000	87,000	169,000	297,000	667,000
Austria	1,000	3,000	28,000	70,000	205,000	478,000
Russia	...	...	26,000	118,000	260,000	284,000
Belgium	...	...	11,000	28,000	68,000	75,000
Holland, &c. . . .	...	...	...	1,000	18,000	30,000
Europe . .	50,000	51,000	245,000	574,000	1,218,000	1,940,000

According to the same writer, the United States produced in the last four years 337,000 tons of beet-sugar yearly.

Licht and Goerz compute the production of beet-sugar in 1887 and 1889 as follows in tons :—

	1887	1889
Germany	1,013,000	975,000
Austria	523,000	575,000
France	485,000	475,000
Russia	487,000	510,000
Belgium	132,000	137,000
Holland	36,000	45,000
Various	56,000	61,000
Total . .	2,732,000	2,778,000

This seems to exclude any beet-sugar raised in the United States. The *Economist* gives the following table :—

Year	Cane, Tons	Beet, Tons	Total
1882 . . .	2,107,000	2,147,000	4,254,000
1884 . . .	2,351,000	2,546,000	4,897,000
1886 . . .	2,346,000	2,729,000	5,074,000
1888 . . .	2,412,000	2,850,000	5,262,000

The following statistics refer to the manufacture of beet-sugar :—

	Factories		Tons Root Used		Sugar, Tons	
	1883	1887	1883	1887	1883	1887
Germany .	358	401	8,700,000	8,300,000	830,000	990,000
France .	496	391	7,200,000	4,900,000	410,000	415,000
Austria .	232	209	4,900,000	4,300,000	560,000	520,000
Belgium .	155	111	...	...	95,000	105,000

The production of cane-sugar, according to N. Spallart and others, was by latest accounts as follows :—

	Tons		Tons
Cuba . . .	530,000	Guadeloupe, &c. .	100,000
Java . . .	320,000	United States .	100,000
Brazil . . .	230,000	Porto Rico .	80,000
India . . .	220,000	Honolulu .	60,000
Jamaica, &c. .	210,000	Argentina . .	60,000
Manilla . .	180,000	Egypt . . .	40,000
Mauritius .	120,000	Peru . . .	30,000
Guiana . .	120,000	Mexico . . .	30,000
China . .	100,000	Australia . .	20,000

The *Ann. Stat.* for 1885 published the following table of average annual consumption during the four years immediately preceding, to which may be added a table published in Paris in 1868 :—

	1881–84		1868
	Tons	Lbs. per Inhabitant	Lbs. per Inhabitant
United Kingdom .	1,105,000	69	40
France . . .	386,000	23	18
Germany . . .	313,000	15	10
Austria . . .	231,000	13	4
Russia . . .	300,000	8	2
Sweden . . .	37,000	18	8
Norway . . .	10,000	11	10
Holland . . .	55,000	29	41
Belgium . . .	40,000	16	22
Denmark . . .	27,000	30	20
Switzerland . .	30,000	23	10
Italy	100,000	7	...
Spain and Portugal .	60,000	6	4
Total . .	2,694,000	...	...

In 1887 the total consumption of sugar was put down as follows :—

		Tons
United Kingdom		1,100,000
Continent		1,900,000
United States		1,500,000
Australia		100,000
Various		600,000
Total . .		5,200,000

It appears that the world consumes now twice as much sugar as in 1870, and four times as much as in 1850. The fall in price partly explains this prodigious increase of consumption.

UNITED KINGDOM

The consumption of sugar has been as follows :—

Year	Tons	Lbs. per Inhab.	Duty per Ton	Price per Ton
1705 . . .	12,000	3	£3	£70
1730 . . .	41,000	9	4	70
1750 . . .	53,000	11	5	70
1780 . . .	77,000	14	7	70
1801 . . .	165,000	22	20	85
1811 . . .	184,000	23	27	90
1820 . . .	143,000	15	27	63
1830 . . .	214,000	20	24	49
1840 . . .	188,000	15	24	48
1850 . . .	310,000	25	10	40
1860 . . .	420,000	32	13	35
1870 . . .	690,000	49	5	32
1881 . . .	1,050,000	68	...	22
1888 . . .	1,170,000	70	...	14

About 70,000 tons are annually consumed by brewers.

FRANCE

A table published in 1869 gives the consumption from 1817 till 1868 :—

Year	Tons	Lbs. per Inhabitant
1817	31,000	2
1825	55,000	4
1832	73,000	5
1840	109,000	6
1854	135,000	8
1862	200,000	12
1868	310,000	18
1887	410,000	23

The last item is not official, but the ratio already quoted for the years 1881–84. France has 439 sugar-factories, employing 68,400 men, moved by 48,000 horse-power of steam, and valued at £15,200,000. The production of beet-root averages 11 tons per acre.

GERMANY

The production of beet-root is officially stated thus :—

Period	Tons of Roots Yearly
1844–55	680,000
1856–65	1,710,000
1866–75	2,820,000
1876–80	4,680,000
1881–87	8,310,000

The quantity of sugar obtained from a ton of roots has risen in late years, viz. :—

Year	Tons Roots	Tons Sugar	Per Cent.
1872 . . .	2,250,000	185,000	8.3
1880 . . .	4,810,000	410,000	8.5
1887 . . .	8,310,000	990,000	11.9

The estimated consumption of roots in 400 beet-sugar factories during the year 1889 was 6,500,000 tons, which produced 992,000 tons of sugar, or more than 15 per cent.

The first mention of beet-sugar is in 1816, when 1400 tons were produced in Prussia. In 1836 it was found that 100,000 tons of beet did not yield quite 5000 tons of sugar.

RUSSIA

The sugar industry was begun at Tula in 1811, but was little heard of until 1850. The area under beet-root in 1864 was 290,000 acres, and the production close on a million tons of roots, an average of less than 3½ tons per acre. In 1883 there were 214 sugar-factories, consuming 4,000,000 tons of roots, from which they extracted 260,000 tons of sugar, say 6½ per cent., against 10 per cent. in Germany. In 1887 the mills turned out 405,000 tons of sugar. The millers buy the roots at 15s. a ton, and sell the sugar at £18 per ton, which leaves them a profit of 30s. per ton of sugar, after paying their 40,000 operatives and all expenses. The peasants who grow the beet-root count on an average crop of six tons per acre, which they sell for 90s., and their rent and taxes being 16s. an acre, they count on 74s. an acre for the support of their household.

SUICIDE

It is customary to compute the number per million inhabitants yearly, and under this heading whenever the term "million inhabitants" is used, it signifies more correctly one million persons of a given age or class. Partial records down to recent years will be found for the principal countries. The following is a general table :—

	Suicides Yearly per Million Population		
	1851–60	1871–77	1885–87
England	65	67	80
Scotland	...	40	...
Ireland	...	17	...
France	105	157	205
Germany	126	143	208
Russia	35	30	...
Austria	45	122	159
Italy	18	37	45
Spain	...	14	...
Portugal	14	18	...
Sweden	72	81	...
Norway	100	73	...
Denmark	274	258	...
Holland	...	36	...
Belgium	49	67	130
Switzerland	...	202	...
Massachusetts	...	82	...
Australia	...	86	115

City rates are usually much higher than the average for the corresponding countries.

The following table is not for a given term of years, but merely compares the latest rates recorded for various cities :—

Per Million Inhabitants

Berlin . . .	170	Naples . . .	60
Brussels . .	271	New York . .	144
Copenhagen .	302	Paris . . .	422
Dresden . .	240	Rio Janeiro . .	60
Florence . .	76	Rome . . .	53
Frankfort . .	344	St. Petersburg .	206
Genoa . . .	64	Stockholm . .	272
London . .	85	Turin . . .	110
Milan . . .	133	Vienna . . .	287

In all countries suicide is more frequent with men than

women, as the following table shows; as also the different rates per million for urban and for rural population :—

	Per Million		Percentage of Sexes	
	Urban	Rural	Males	Females
France . . .	217	118	79	21
Prussia . . .	162	97	81	19
Denmark . . .	307	271	77	23
Saxony . . .	317	219	81	19
Italy . . .	66	30	80	20
Belgium . . .	61	34	85	15
Sweden . . .	167	68	77	23
Norway . . .	103	65	76	24
Denmark . . .	236	238	77	23

In Holland, of 100 suicides 16 are by women; in Austria, 18; in England, 26; in Russia, 21; in Switzerland, 12; in Spain, 29; and in the United States, 28. The difference that prevails between married and single is pointed out by various writers. In Switzerland, during four years ending 1880, of 100 women under 30 years who committed suicide 80 were unmarried.

The following table shows approximately the ratios of adults, married and unmarried, in several countries, and the ratios of suicide according to Legoyt :—

	Inhabitants, Percentage		Suicides, Percentage	
	Married	Unmarried	Married	Unmarried
France . .	55	45	46	54
Germany . .	52	48	43	57
Italy . . .	53	47	44	56
Switzerland	47	53	43	57

In all countries the rate of suicide among unmarried is much higher than among married. In France, as shown later on, the value of domestic ties as a restraint against suicide is shown in the fact that persons with children are much less disposed to it than those who have none.

Suicide is much more frequent in Protestant than in Catholic countries. Legoyt and other writers show that in countries where both religions exist the tendency of Protestants to suicide is greater, as shown in the rates for the following countries per million inhabitants yearly :—

	Protestant	Catholic	General Rate
United Kingdom . .	63	17	56
Prussia	170	52	131
Bavaria	195	69	102
Austria-Hungary . . .	140	90	96
Switzerland	262	81	202

Legoyt says the Jews have even a lower rate of suicide than Catholics.

If we suppose 1200 suicides yearly in each of the following countries, the months in which they occur show as follows :—

	London	France	Austria	Italy	Sweden
January . .	88	86	74	71	74
February .	86	90	77	94	61
March . .	101	102	90	101	86
April . .	112	112	105	118	120
May . . .	120	117	132	136	137
June . . .	122	135	140	144	130
July . . .	108	119	132	122	125
August . .	107	102	104	104	120
September .	92	92	99	88	90
October . .	93	90	95	77	102
November .	87	79	82	73	82
December .	84	76	70	72	73
Total .	1,200	1,200	1,200	1,200	1,200

The causes of suicide vary with race and climate thus :—

Spain and Italy			North Europe		
Insanity . . .	29.0	Insanity . . .	34.0
Poverty . . .	22.0	Grief . . .	23.0
Sickness . . .	20.0	Drink . . .	15.0
Various . . .	29.0	Various . . .	28.0
Total .	100.0	Total .	100.0

The distribution according to seasons, from observations in 1861–77, was as follows :—

	Spring	Summer	Autumn	Winter	Total
U. Kingdom	336	372	264	228	1,200
France . .	331	356	261	252	1,200
Prussia . .	341	348	272	239	1,200
Saxony . .	332	353	270	245	1,200
Bavaria . .	348	364	254	234	1,200
Wurtemburg	335	373	252	240	1,200
Austria . .	357	375	235	233	1,200
Italy . . .	355	370	238	237	1,200
Sweden . .	343	375	274	208	1,200
Norway . .	383	366	273	178	1,200
Denmark .	350	370	264	216	1,200
Holland . .	384	356	220	240	1,200
Belgium . .	331	359	277	233	1,200
Switzerland	322	346	294	238	1,200
Spain . .	316	449	240	195	1,200

Suicide is most frequent in the summer months in all countries except Norway and Holland, where the spring months are most fatal.

The occurrence of suicide by day or night shows the following percentages in France and Switzerland :—

	France	Switzerland
Noon to 6 P.M. . .	22.8	22.0
6 P.M. to midnight . .	23.2	23.6
Midnight to 6 A.M. . .	18.3	18.0
6 A.M. to noon . .	35.7	36.4

The method of suicide varies with sex and country as follows, according to Ritti's observations in 1861–77 :—

Men

	Hanging	Drowning	Firearms	Knife	Poison	Various	Total
England . . .	407	155	66	218	70	84	1,000
France . . .	468	254	139	35	15	89	1,000
Prussia . . .	645	131	133	40	20	31	1,000
Saxony . .	701	134	104	20	16	25	1,000
Wurtemburg .	736	157	33	53	11	10	1,000
Austria . .	595	208	172	...	66	49	1,000
Italy . . .	166	350	163	63	53	205	1,000
Sweden . .	510	193	116	95	79	7	1,000
Norway . .	664	184	54	47	...	51	1,000
Denmark . .	727	142	37	18	60	16	1,000
Belgium . .	563	198	139	42	15	43	1,000
Switzerland .	458	228	186	70	25	33	1,000

Women

England . . .	281	324	1	115	155	124	1,000
France . . .	311	423	10	28	37	191	1,000
Prussia . . .	440	326	81	36	70	47	1,000
Saxony . .	461	440	5	25	45	24	1,000
Wurtemburg .	458	441	...	60	21	20	1,000
Austria . .	324	410	38	...	176	52	1,000
Italy . . .	175	491	31	54	79	170	1,000
Sweden . .	404	324	1	87	179	5	1,000
Norway . .	557	332	5	9	...	97	1,000
Denmark . .	583	359	1	26	31	...	1,000
Belgium . .	447	395	2	26	70	60	1,000
Switzerland .	228	516	45	45	91	75	1,000

According to Bulgarin, 73 per cent. of male suicides in Russia are by hanging. The Austrian classification does not distinguish those by the knife; hence the blanks. It is a painful fact that in all armies suicide is much more frequent than among civilians of same age. The rates per million in the several countries show thus, age 20 to 60 years, for the years 1869–73 :—

	Soldiers	Civilians
British	380	110
French	510	205
German	640	250
Austrian	860	120
Italian	300	80
Belgian	460	70
Swedish	450	120

In 1882 the rates in the British army were :—

Age	U. Kingdom	Colonies	India
20–25 . . .	200	210	130
25–30 . . .	390	330	390
30–35 . . .	510	450	840
35–40 . . .	710	810	1,030

The rates in the United Kingdom were 310 for infantry, 340 for artillery, and 500 for cavalry, per million.

UNITED KINGDOM

Dr. Ogle's paper for England and Wales shows 42,630 suicides in 26 years ending 1883. Some of these were of children under 10 years old, but not sufficient to adopt a rate. He therefore classifies age thus :—

	Rates per Million		
	Persons	Male	Female
10–15	4	4	3
15–20	28	26	30
20–25	47	62	34
25–35	69	99	42
35–45	116	175	62
45–55	184	271	103
55–65	251	396	119
65–75	243	394	113
75–85	183	306	85
Over 85 . . .	116	226	46
All ages . . .	72	104	41

It will be seen that suicide is much more frequent among males than females, the ratio being as follows :—

Age					Female	Male
10–15	100	133
25–35	100	236
55–65	100	333
Over 85	100	491

Suicides among males of 25–65 years of age were per million as follows :—

Miner . .	74	Painter . .	224	Baker . .	328
Clergyman .	139	Weaver . .	229	Clerk . .	329
Fisherman .	157	Miller . .	239	Broker . .	346
Gardener .	160	Tanner . .	249	Milkman .	353
Mason . .	175	Shoemaker .	252	Hairdresser .	364
Labourer .	177	Tailor . .	256	Butcher . .	407
Policeman .	201	Printer . .	262	Lawyer . .	408
Carpenter .	213	Farmer . .	270	Physician .	472
Carter .	214	Schoolmaster	290	Beer-seller .	474
Grocer . .	218	Cabman . .	303	Soldier . .	1,149
Smith . .	222	Watchmaker	315	Gen. average	222

The method of suicide is shown in the following table :—

Method	Persons	Males	Females
Hanging	365	417	240
Drowning	185	152	264
Cut or stab . . .	184	207	129
Poison	99	79	145
Gunshot	48	67	2
Jump from height . .	25	21	36
Railway train . . .	19	24	8
Otherwise . . .	75	33	176
All methods . .	1,000	1,000	1,000

The ratio of methods, however, varies with age, as shown thus :—

	Males		Females	
	25–35	55–65	25–35	55–65
Gun	101	45	2	1
Cut . . .	219	202	146	138
Poison . . .	111	58	206	83
Drowning . . .	185	132	295	200
Hanging . . .	282	500	184	305
Various . . .	102	63	167	273
Total .	1,000	1,000	1,000	1,000

The following table shows the suicide mortality at different ages in various occupations :—

	Per Million			Per Million	
	25–45	45–65		25–45	45–65
Lawyer. . .	324	562	Baker . . .	163	632
Physician . .	381	639	Hairdresser .	270	536
Schoolmaster .	156	536	Printer. . .	156	458
Broker . . .	271	485	Tailor . .	147	457
Clerk . . .	249	475	Shoemaker .	203	341
Farmer . . .	160	473	Mason . . .	90	330
Miller . . .	68	555	Carpenter . .	122	381
Gardener . .	98	274	Policeman . .	82	421
Beer-seller . .	402	606	Cabman . .	193	506
Druggist . .	380	563	Soldier. . .	506	2,336
Grocer . . .	160	326	Fisherman . .	43	367
Butcher . .	243	708	Labourer . .	114	292

There has been a steady decline of suicide in London compared with population, viz. :—

Period	Annual Average	
	Number	Per Million Inhabitants
1841–50 . . .	231	107
1851–60 . . .	257	100
1861–70 . . .	268	88
1871–80 . . .	305	85

This is contrary to the result in nearly all other cities. In Scotland the rates per million persons at various ages are stated as follows :—

Age	Per Million Persons		
	Male	Female	General Population
20–30 . . .	128	42	84
31–40 . . .	128	57	93
41–50 . . .	180	52	115
51–60 . . .	162	42	101
61–70 . . .	150	36	93
71–80 . . .	11	26	20

Scotland is the only country in the world where the rate of suicide in urban population is less than among the rural.

FRANCE

From whatever cause, the increase of suicide has been terrific ; the official returns show thus :—

Year	Number	Per Million Inhabitants
1830	1,756	51
1840	2,752	82
1850	3,596	103
1860	4,050	112
1870	4,957	133
1880	6,638	178
1885	7,902	205

Legoyt gives the annual average during fifty-three years as follows :—

Period	Number	Per Million Inhabitants
1827–30	1,739	50
1831–40	2,345	70
1841–50	3,200	90
1851–60	3,830	105
1861–70	4,935	130
1871–79	5,818	157

He shows the difference between persons with children and those without as follows :—

	Per Million	
	With Children	Without Children
Husband . . .	205	470
Widower . . .	526	1,004
Wife . . .	45	158
Widow . . .	104	238

He classes married and single persons as follows :—

	Per Million
Married	272
Unmarried	422
Widowed	737

Guerry classifies the ratios for days of the week, 100 being the average, as follows :—

Sunday . . . 96	Thursday . . . 110
Monday . . . 106	Friday . . . 96
Tuesday . . . 110	Saturday . . . 78
Wednesday. . . 104	

In five years ending 1880 no fewer than 238 children under fifteen years of age committed suicide.

GERMANY

In Prussia the official returns show the annual suicides per million inhabitants as follows :—

1816–20 . . . 70	1841–50 . . . 105
1821–30 . . . 86	1851–60 . . . 126
1831–40 . . . 99	1861–75 . . . 130

In Saxony and Frankfort the rates per million were :—

Saxony		Frankfort	
1836–50 . . . 191	1852–59 . . . 349
1851–70 . . . 264	1860–69 . . . 365
1871–77 . . . 299	1870–77 . . . 344

The rates for Bavaria, Wurtemburg, and Baden were as follows :—

	1841–45	1871–76
Bavaria	55	90
Wurtemburg	107	162
Baden	68	156

In Bavaria the lowest rates were from November to January inclusive, the highest in May and June. As regards condition, the rates per million in Bavaria were :—

Married	98
Unmarried	115
Widowed	197

These rates apply only to adults, the rate for all ages, as shown above, having been only 90.

As regards condition in Prussia, the annual average number of suicides in three years ending 1875 was as follows :—

	Men	Women	Total
Divorced . . .	43	8	51
Single	796	224	1,020
Married . . .	1,130	215	1,345
Widowed . . .	351	118	469
Total .	2,320	565	2,885

AUSTRIA

Official returns show that for Austria, without Hungary, the rates rose thus, per million inhabitants :—

1864–72	72
1873–77	122

The rate in Hungary for 1864–65 was only 52. The records of Vienna for 1876–78 showed yearly 110 suicides of children under 14.

ITALY

The following table is for all Italy from 1865, but previous rates are only for the kingdom of Sardinia :—

Period	Suicides Yearly	Per Million Inhabitants
1824	...	10
1838	...	15
1865–74	498	20
1874–77	990	37
1880	1,260	45

Those recorded in ten years ending 1874 were :—

Men	3,955
Women	1,028
Total . . .	4,983

Various cities and provinces had the following rates recorded at different dates, per million inhabitants :—

Naples		Milan	
1828	56	1821–25 . . .	52
1835	88	1831–35 . . .	58
1875	60	1876 . . .	133
Lombardy		Turin	
1817–27 . . .	20	1825–39 . . .	60
1865	50	1855–59 . . .	90
1874	44	1860–64 . . .	110

The rate of suicide per million inhabitants was five times higher in Piedmont and Lombardy than in Naples and Sicily, the ratio of persons able to read and write being twice as high in the former as in the latter provinces, from which Italian writers deduce (and Dr. Ogle favours the theory) that education is a predisposing cause. Perhaps climate or race has some effect, the northern Italians being a very different race from the southern.

The rates as to condition for all Italy in the years 1866–70 were as follows, per million :—

Men			
Married . . .	41	Firearms . . .	24.5
Unmarried . . .	44	Drowning . . .	19.0
Widowed . . .	15	Various . . .	56.5

Suicide was nearly three times more numerous in May than in October, as 280 to 100.

The occupations of those who committed suicide in 1874–75 were :—

	Number Yearly	Ratio
Farmers	252	26.0
Operatives . . .	206	21.2
Proprietors . . .	83	8.6
Merchants . . .	55	5.7
Soldiers	60	6.3
Various . . .	311	32.2
Total . .	967	100.0

SWEDEN

Official records are quoted by Morselli, which may be condensed as follows ; this table shows the rate of suicide yearly per million inhabitants :—

Sweden		Stockholm	
Period	Rate	Period	Rate
1749–80 . . .	12	1831–40 . . .	149
1781–1830 . . .	39	1841–50 . . .	177
1831–50 . . .	66	1851–60 . . .	210
1851–65 . . .	72	1861–70 . . .	363
1866–75 . . .	82	1871–75 . . .	272

The rates for all Sweden in the last fifteen years of Morselli's tables showed as follows :—

	1861–70	1871–75
Urban	205	167
Rural	63	68
All Sweden . .	80	81

The percentages as regarded sex showed this variation :—

	1861–70	1871–75
Males	78.1	76.3
Females . . .	21.9	23.7
Total . .	100.0	100.0

NORWAY AND DENMARK

These two countries peopled by the same race present as great a contrast as England and Ireland. The rates of suicide per million inhabitants were :—

Period	Norway	Denmark
1831–40	103	213
1841–50	108	245
1851–60	100	274
1861–70	81	282
1871–75	73	258

In Norway a law was passed in 1850 restricting the sale of liquor, which is supposed to have had some effect in diminishing suicide.

SWITZERLAND

Official returns for six years ending 1881 show the rates of suicide yearly per million inhabitants thus :—

Cantons	Catholics	Protestants	General Population
Catholics . . .	20	205	81
Protestant . . .	127	602	262
Mixed . . .	116	360	280

It would appear that in Catholic cantons the Protestants are much less prone to suicide than where their own religion is dominant. For like reason Catholics are much more liable to suicide in Protestant or mixed cantons than in their own.

BELGIUM

Official returns give the annual rate per million inhabitants as follows:—

1831–40	.	.	43	1866–75	. .	67
1841–50	.	.	61	1881–85	. .	105
1851–65	.	.	49	1887	. . .	130

The returns for the years 1881–85 showed the ratios of 1000 suicides as follows:—

Method	Men	Women	Total
Hanging . . .	425	53	478
Drowning . . .	205	72	277
Firearms . . .	118	3	121
Dagger . . .	32	3	35
Poison . . .	8	13	21
Various . . .	52	16	68
Total .	840	160	1,000

The returns for 1887 show age ratios as follows:—

Age	Men	Women	Total
0–16	19	5	24
16–25	98	35	133
25–40	197	38	235
40–50	180	32	212
50–60	179	24	203
60–70	113	19	132
Over 70 . . .	44	17	61
Total .	830	170	1,000

UNITED STATES

The *New York Chronicle* in 1888 published tables covering four years for the whole of the Union, but these cannot be regarded as complete. They summed up 6283 suicides, being less than 30 per million inhabitants yearly, whereas the actual rate will hardly fall short of 60. The tables meanwhile enable us to form averages as to age and other particulars:—

Age, Years				Annual Suicides	Ratio
0–15	.	.	.	12	0.8
15–20	.	.	.	88	5.7
21–30	.	.	.	205	13.3
31–40	.	.	.	213	13.9
41–50	.	.	.	231	15.1
51–60	.	.	.	175	11.5
Over 60	.	.	.	607	39.7
Total	.	.	1,531	100.0

The condition showed the following figures:—

	Men	Women	Total	Ratio
Married . .	513	150	663	53.3
Single . .	330	118	448	36.2
Widowed . .	72	32	104	8.4
Divorced .	16	10	26	2.1
Total .	931	310	1,241	100.0

The principal professions of suicides were:—

				Number	Ratio
Farmers .	.	.	.	195	15.8
Labourers	.	.	.	50	4.0
Courtesans	.	.	.	33	2.6
Innkeepers	.	.	.	30	2.4
Various .	.	.	.	933	75.2
Total	.	1,241	100.0

Some of those in the first table were not classified as to condition or profession.

AUSTRALIA

Coghlan's tables for thirteen years ending 1888 give the rates per million inhabitants yearly thus:—

Tasmania	.	.	51	New Zealand	. .	95
South Australia	.	87	Victoria	. .	113
New South Wales	.	88	Queensland	. .	135

General rate for Australia was as follows:—

1871	. . . . . .	86
1888	. . . . . .	115

SULPHUR

The quantities exported from Sicily and those imported into Great Britain were as follows:—

Year	Export from Sicily, Tons	Import into Great Britain, Tons	Value per Ton, £
1820 . . .	18,500	4,600	10
1830 . . .	38,100	12,100	8
1840 . . .	77,800	34,400	5
1850 . . .	85,000	33,500	8
1860 . . .	140,000	50,200	9
1870 . . .	173,000	53,300	6
1880 . . .	287,000	46,400	5
1888 . . .	324,000	40,000	4

There are 18,000 miners engaged at the sulphur deposits in Sicily.

SURGERY

The mortality after amputation in various hospitals was stated to be in 1880 thus:—

Deaths per 100

London	.	.	37.8	Edinburgh .	.	43.3
Paris .	.	.	60.0	Glasgow .	.	36.0
Zürich	.	.	46.0	English rural	.	17.8

In such German hospitals as have adopted the Listerian method, invented by Professor Lister of Glasgow, the death-rate after amputation has fallen to 4.7. Some English hospitals showed the following:—

Death-Rate per Cent.

London			*Rural*		
University . .	25.7	Tewkesbury	.	3.8
St. Bartholomew's	36.6	St. Leonard's	.	10.0
Guy's . .	38.2	St. Alban's .	.	14.2
St. George's	38.8	Ashford .	.	20.0
Whitechapel	47.3	Stockton .	.	25.0

Amputation	English Rural	Glasgow	Glasgow	Guy's	University College, London
	1859–78	1850–74	1795–1838	1854–61	1871
Arm . .	8.1	34.0	48.0	20.0	Fore-arm, 5.0
Leg . .	15.5	45.0	68.0	39.0	Leg, 22.6
Thigh . .	33.3	52.0	92.0	50.0	Shoulder, 37.4
General .	17.8	36.0	51.0	38.2	Hip, 40.0

The following tables refer to various campaigns:—

	Death-Rate per Cent.	
	Arm	Leg or Thigh
Peninsula . . .	12.9	20.8
Waterloo . . .	11.6	26.8
Crimea . . .	15.5	50.2
United States (1863) .	21.2	64.0

The amputation death-rates of the Crimean and American campaigns may be compared (Erichsen) thus :—

	Crimea	United States
Hand	...	1.6
Arm	19.0	21.2
Shoulder	35.0	39.2
Foot	16.0	9.2
Leg	37.0	26.0
Knee	57.0	55.0
Thigh	64.0	64.4
Hip	100.0	85.7

Schede compares the results of Lister's with other systems thus :—

	Percentage of Deaths		
	Old System	Kronlein's	Lister's
Arm	10	14	0
Leg	33	18	2
Thigh	41	36	7
Shoulder . . .	52	20	11
General . . .	30	20	4

Bugnot compares the general mortality of divers systems thus : Lister, 11 ; Kronlein, 17 ; Simpson, 33 ; Trelat, 46 ; old method, 53 per cent.

In previous records the average mortality of amputations was estimated per cent. thus: Lawrie, 37 ; Malgaigne, 39 ; Le Fort, 43 ; Trelat, 46 ; Churchill, 49. There were 790 cases at the Paris Hospital in 1841–46, of whom 320 died, say 40 per cent. The *Dict. Sci. Med.*

records 5000 amputations, of which 1900 proved fatal, say 38 per cent., the respective rates of mortality being :—

Fore-arm . . .	13.4	Leg	50.6
Arm . . .	51.5	Thigh . . .	84.8

Hall observed in the Crimea that the mortality after wounds and amputations was much greater in summer and autumn than in winter.

In the ligature of arteries, Philippe and Inman recognise a death-rate of 33 per cent. ; Norrit, 38 per cent. In cases of hernia : Textor, 43 ; Cooper, 47 ; London hospitals, 51 ; and Malgaigne, 60.

Sir Spencer Wells gives the age and death-rate of cases of ovariotomy thus :—

Age	Ratio of Cases	Deaths per 100
Under 30	27.6	25
30–40	26.4	27
40–50	24.6	23
Over 50	21.4	29
Total .	100.0	26

The above is the result of 500 cases. He shows also that in 1000 operations for this disease the death-rate has been diminishing thus :—

	Deaths		Deaths
1st hundred	34	6th hundred	28
2nd ,, ...	28	7th ,, ...	24
3rd ,, ...	23	8th ,, ...	24
4th ,, ...	22	9th ,, ...	17
5th ,, ...	20	10th ,, ...	11

T.

TALLOW

The production of tallow (including lard) averages 18 per cent. of that of meat, and is shown approximately as follows :—

	Tons		Consumption, Lbs. per Inhab.
	Production	Consumption	
United Kingdom .	200,000	290,000	18
France . . .	215,000	265,000	16
Germany . . .	250,000	270,000	12
Russia . . .	340,000	335,000	8
Austria . . .	200,000	190,000	11
Italy . . .	65,000	65,000	4
Spain . . .	95,000	95,000	22
Portugal . . .	15,000	15,000	8
Sweden . . .	25,000	27,000	12
Norway . . .	12,000	12,000	11
Denmark . . .	20,000	20,000	22
Holland . . .	20,000	90,000	48
Belgium . . .	20,000	25,000	9
Various . .	80,000	80,000	...
Europe . . .	1,557,000	1,779,000	12
United States . .	880,000	700,000	25
Canada . . .	40,000	40,000	18
Australia . . .	90,000	60,000	36
Argentina . . .	50,000	35,000	22
Total . .	2,617,000	2,614,000	...

The use of tallow candles has greatly declined since the introduction of gas, petroleum, and electric light, but the consumption of tallow has, nevertheless, steadily increased, as well as that of lard.

The countries with a surplus of tallow and lard exported thus :—

	Tons Exported				
	1830	1860	1870	1880	1888
Russia . .	66,400	40,300	21,100	10,400	3,000
U. States .	2,200	34,000	32,000	220,000	180,000
Argentina .	8,600	45,300	62,400	23,300	15,000
Australia .	...	6,200	25,300	32,100	30,500

The production and consumption of tallow and lard in the United Kingdom were approximately as follows :—

	Tons			Consumption, Lbs. per Inhab.
	Produced	Consumed	Imported	
1830 . . .	170,000	226,600	56,600	21
1840 . . .	175,000	231,300	56,300	21
1850 . . .	180,000	242,200	62,200	21
1860 . . .	185,000	265,100	80,100	22
1870 . . .	195,000	283,000	88,000	21
1880 . . .	200,000	299,000	99,000	19
1888 . . .	200,000	287,000	87,000	18

The production and consumption in the United States were approximately as follows :—

Year	Tons			Consumption, Lbs. per Inhab.
	Produced	Consumed	Exported	
1860 . . .	530,000	496,000	34,000	33
1870 . . .	460,000	428,000	32,000	24
1880 . . .	760,000	540,000	220,000	24
1888 . . .	880,000	700,000	180,000	25

TAXES

Omitting public services, such as the post-office and revenues from crown lands and forests, the amount levied by taxation yearly (1888–90) was about as follows:—*

	Amount, £			Shillings per Inhab.	Percentage of Earnings
	National	Local	Total		
U. Kingdom	73,440,000	45,780,000	119,220,000	63	9.3
France . .	102,000,000	40,800,000	142,800,000	74	13.6
Germany .	64,900,000	44,000,000	108,900,000	45	10.4
Russia . .	61,200,000	11,200,000	72,400,000	16	7.4
Austria . .	50,100,000	5,300,000	55,400,000	28	9.5
Italy . . .	53,800,000	27,200,000	81,000,000	54	22.0
Spain . . .	31,900,000	5,000,000	36,900,000	41	12.3
Portugal . .	6,600,000	1,000,000	7,600,000	33	14.0
Sweden . .	3,670,000	3,300,000	6,970,000	28	6.7
Norway . .	1,480,000	950,000	2,430,000	24	6.0
Denmark .	2,530,000	1,000,000	3,530,000	35	5.5
Holland . .	8,300,000	6,300,000	14,600,000	64	15.1
Belgium . .	6,800,000	3,900,000	10,700,000	36	6.0
Greece . .	2,400,000	...	2,400,000	24	...
Roumania .	4,200,000	...	4,200,000	17	...
Servia. . .	1,400,000	...	1,400,000	14	...
Europe . .	474,720,000	195,730,000	670,450,000	44	11.0

	Amount, £			Shillings per Inhab.	Percentage of Earnings
	National	Local	Total		
U. States .	73,800,000	52,200,000	126,000,000	40	5.4
Australia. .	10,700,000	...	10,700,000	60	7.2
Canada . .	6,000,000	...	6,000,000	24	4.6
Argentina .	9,700,000	...	9,700,000	54	11.2
India . . .	47,500,000	...	47,500,000	5	...
Total .	622,420,000	247,930,000	870,350,000		...

* The taxes of Prussia, Bavaria, &c., are included as national in Germany, but those of the States of New York, Pennsylvania, &c., are included among local in the United States. Local taxes of Canada and some other countries are in blank, because they cannot be ascertained.

Block's estimate of the percentage of direct taxes in the total amount raised by taxation in the several countries in 1872 compares with the percentage in 1889 as follows:—

Percentage of Direct Taxation

	1872	1889		1872	1889
U. Kingdom .	15	21	Sweden . .	24	17
France . . .	25	18	Norway . .	0	0
Germany . .	34	19	Denmark . .	28	20
Russia . . .	20	13	Holland . .	33	27
Austria . . .	46	24	Belgium . .	31	31
Italy . . .	51	30	Switzerland .	34	0
Spain . . .	44	39	Greece . . .	48	37
Portugal . .	30	15	U. States . .	0	0

Except in the countries of the United Kingdom and Belgium, the ratio of direct taxation has declined very notably.

The following table, by Professor Bochk in 1885, shows the sums levied on the principal articles of consumption :—

	Amount, £					Pence per Inhabitant				
	Liquor	Coffee, &c.	Sugar	Tobacco	Total	Liquor	Coffee, &c.	Sugar	Tobacco	Total
U. Kingdom .	19,000,000	4,400,000	...	8,600,000	32,000,000	130	30	...	60	220
France . . .	10,300,000	4,600,000	6,200,000	11,800,000	32,900,000	65	30	40	75	210
Germany . .	2,600,000	2,300,000	2,300,000	1,400,000	8,600,000	14	12	12	7	45
Russia . . .	22,800,000	1,800,000	1,200,000	1,600,000	27,400,000	10	9	7	50	76
Austria . . .	1,600,000	1,400,000	1,100,000	8,200,000	12,300,000	65	5	3	5	78
Italy	800,000	900,000	2,300,000	4,000,000	8,000,000	40	10	24	7	81
Spain . . .	300,000	300,000	200,000	3,200,000	4,000,000	27	20	28	15	90
Sweden . . .	800,000	200,000	500,000	100,000	1,600,000	112	2	...	2	116
Norway . . .	200,000	200,000	200,000	100,000	700,000	50	6	16	6	78
Denmark . .	200,000	100,000	300,000	...	600,000	20	10	35	5	70
Holland . . .	2,100,000	...	600,000	...	2,700,000	26	...	8	...	34
Belgium . . .	1,100,000	100,000	400,000	100,000	1,700,000	6	7	20	34	67
Switzerland .	300,000	..	100,000	...	400,000	4	5	3	48	60
Europe . . .	62,100,000	16,300,000	15,400,000	39,100,000	132,900,000	48	12	11	31	104

In some countries the salt-tax is not distinguished, and hence the blanks under that column in the following table, which shows as nearly as possible, by latest accounts, the sums paid as taxes on articles of consumption :—

	Sugar, £	Liquor, £	Salt, £	Tobacco, £	Sundries, £	Total, £	Shillings per Inhab.
United Kingdom . .	...	27,200,000	...	8,900,000	4,800,000	40,900,000	21
France	7,100,000	17,000,000	1,300,000	14,900,000	4,600,000	44,900,000	23
Germany	2,600,000	13,700,000	2,000,000	1,500,000	2,300,000	22,100,000	9
Russia	1,700,000	25,700,000	1,300,000	2,600,000	1,800,000	33,100,000	7
Austria	2,800,000	4,900,000	2,900,000	10,200,000	1,400,000	22,200,000	11
Italy	2,300,000	800,000	2,500,000	7,600,000	1,000,000	14,200,000	9
Spain	200,000	300,000	...	6,400,000	300,000	7,200,000	8
Portugal	...	200,000	...	900,000	100,000	1,200,000	5
Sweden	500,000	800,000	..	100,000	200,000	1,600,000	7
Norway	200,000	300,000	...	100,000	200,000	800,000	8
Denmark	300,000	200,000	...	...	100,000	600,000	6
Holland	600,000	2,100,000	300,000	...	600,000	3,600,000	16
Belgium	200,000	1,400,000	...	100,000	100,000	1,800,000	6
Europe . . .	18,500,000	94,600,000	10,300,000	53,300,000	17,500,000	194,200,000	13
United States . .	11,700,000	22,200,000	100,000	8,900,000	·1,400,000	44,300,000	14
Total . .	30,200,000	116,800,000	10,400,000	62,200,000	18,900,000	238,500,000	13

A simple classification of the national taxes in various countries is as follows ; customs, excise, stamps and death duties, property and income, viz. :—

	Customs	Excise	Stamps, &c.	Property	Sundries	Total
			£ Sterling			
United Kingdom . . .	20,000,000	25,500,000	12,700,000	15,300,000	...	73,500,000
France	15,000,000	39,000,000	26,000,000	14,300,000	7,700,000	102,000,000
Germany	13,500,000	22,100,000	9,000,000	12,500,000	7,800,000	64,900,000
Russia	12,100,000	30,000,000	3,300,000	8,200,000	7,600,000	61,200,000
Austria	3,900,000	22,200,000	6,600,000	11,700,000	5,700,000	50,100,000
Italy	10,600,000	13,400,000	7,900,000	16,200,000	5,700,000	53,800,000
Spain	6,900,000	7,200,000	3,600,000	6,600,000	7,600,000	31,900,000
Portugal	3,100,000	1,300,000	1,000,000	1,000,000	200,000	6,600,000
Sweden	2,100,000	800,000	200,000	600,000	...	3,700,000
Norway	1,100,000	300,000	100,000	...	...	1,500,000
Denmark	1,400,000	...	300,000	500,000	300,000	2,500,000
Holland	400,000	3,600,000	1,800,000	1,900,000	600,000	8,300,000
Belgium	1,100,000	1,400,000	2,000,000	1,800,000	500,000	6,800,000
Europe	91,200,000	166,800,000	74,500,000	90,600,000	43,700,000	466,800,000
United States . . .	46,600,000	27,200,000	...	...	...	73,800,000
Canada	4,500,000	1,300,000	...	...	...	5,800,000
Australia	8,200,000	2,500,000	...	...	...	10,700,000
India	1,200,000	17,500,000	3,300,000	19,500,000	6,000,000	47,500,000
Egypt	1,100,000	600.000	...	5,200,000	600,000	7,500,000
Total . .	152,800,000	215,900,000	77,800,000	115,300,000	50,300,000	612,100,000

Few articles of consumption are more generally or more heavily taxed than coffee. In 1889 the import duty on this article in various countries was as follows :—

Duty per Ton

	£			£
United Kingdom .	. 14	Sweden .	. . .	20
France .	. . . 62	Norway	. . .	22
Germany .	. . 20	Denmark	. . .	9
Russia .	. . . 15	Belgium	. . .	4
Austria .	. . . 40	Switzerland .	. .	2
Italy .	. . . 56	Greece .	. . .	19
Spain .	. . . 20	Roumania .	. .	8
Portugal	. . . 25	United States	. .	0

Holland is the only country of Europe which admits coffee free of duty.

British cotton manufactures are heavily taxed in many countries, the rates "ad valorem" according to tariffs in 1884 showing in the various countries thus :—

	Per Cent.		Per Cent.		Per Cent.
Argentina .	30	China . . .	5	S. Australia .	10
Austria . .	18	Greece . .	15	Tasmania . .	10
Belgium . .	15	Guiana . .	5	Turkey . .	7
Brazil . .	30	Holland . .	15	Uruguay . .	12
Canada . .	20	India . . .	5	Victoria . .	25
Cape . .	10	New Zealand	15	West Indies .	12
Chili . . .	25	Queensland .	5		

While the ratio of import dues is being reduced by Great Britain, it has increased in the rest of the world by more than one-fourth in the last ten years.

The customs dues of various nations compare with the value of merchandise imported (such dues being, as a rule, levied on imports, and not on exports) as follows :—

	Customs Dues, £		Imports, £		Duty, Percentage	
	Average 1871–80	1889	1871–80	1889	1871–80	1889
United Kingdom . . .	20,100,000	20,000,000	371,400,000	427,000,000	5.4	4.7
France	10,300,000	15,000,000	157,000,000	167,000,000	6.6	9.0
Germany	8,600,000	13,500,000	174,000,000	204,000,000	5.0	6.7
Russia	10,500,000	12,100,000	49,000,000	39,000,000	21.4	31.0
Austria	2,600,000	3,900,000	57,000,000	48,000,000	4.5	8.1
Italy	5,100,000	10,600,000	47,200,000	56,000,000	10.9	18.8
Spain	4,400,000	6,900,000	18,300,000	29,000,000	24.0	23.8
Portugal	1,800,000	3,100,000	7,000,000	11,000,000	25.7	28.2
Belgium	800,000	1,100,000	56,200,000	61,000,000	1.4	1.8
Holland	400,000	400,000	63,000,000	106,000,000	0.6	0.4
Denmark	900,000	1,400,000	13,000,000	15,000,000	7.0	9.3
Sweden	1,600,000	2,100,000	14,000,000	16,000,000	11.5	13.2
Norway	800,000	1,100,000	7,800,000	9,000,000	10.3	12.2
Europe	67,900,000	91,200,000	1,034,900,000	1,188,000,000	6.5	7.7
United States	26,050,000	46,600,000	98,800,000	154,000,000	26.3	30.3
Canada	2,700,000	4,500,000	17,900,000	23,000,000	15.0	19.6
Australia	4,300,000	8,200,000	40,200,000	68,000,000	10.7	12.1
India	2,000,000	1,200,000	36,800,000	54,000,000	5.5	2.2
Egypt	800,000	1,100,000	5,200,000	7,000,000	15.4	15.7
Total . . .	103,750,000	152,800,000	1,233,800,000	1,494,000,000	8.3	10.2

If the commerce of the United Kingdom be subtracted, the account will stand thus for the rest of the world :—

Period	Customs, £	Imports, £	Duty per Cent.
1871–80 . . .	83,600,000	863,000,000	9.8
1889	132,800,000	1,067,000,000	12.5

Property and income or personal taxes are approximately as follows :—

	Land-Tax	House-Tax	Income-Tax	Total
	£	£	£	£
U. Kingdom	1,020,000	1,940,000	12,700,000	15,660,000
France . .	4,800,000	4,500,000	5,000,000	14,300,000
Germany .	4,000,000	2,000,000	6,500,000	12,500,000
Russia . .	4,000,000	...	9,200,000	13,200,000
Austria . .	5,000,000	3,000,000	3,400,000	11,400,000
Italy . . .	4,300,000	2,700,000	9,200,000	16,200,000
Spain . .	6,600,000	...	...	6,600,000
Portugal .	700,000	100,000	200,000	1,000,000
Sweden . .	400,000	...	200,000	600,000
Denmark .	400,000	100,000	...	500,000
Holland . .	1,000,000	...	900,000	1,900,000
Belgium . .	1,000,000	...	800,000	1,800,000
Europe . .	33,220,000	14,340,000	48,100,000	95,660,000

The income-tax collected in the United Kingdom includes £1,200,000 from land and £2,500,000 from house property, for which reason the above items ought more correctly to read thus :—

	£
Land-tax	2,220,000
House-tax	4,440,000
Income-tax	9,000,000
Total . . .	15,660,000

Taxes on land in various countries are described at length under *Land-taxes.*

UNITED KINGDOM

The *Financial Reform Almanack* sums up from parliamentary blue-books the taxation and expenditure of the United Kingdom in eighty-nine years as follows :—

	Millions £ Sterling								
	Revenue				Expenditure				
Period	Customs	Excise	Sundries	Total	Debt	Army	Navy	Sundries	Total
1801–10	123	215	206	544	216	230	148	72	666
1811–20	150	272	252	674	292	290	152	91	825
1821–30	175	252	172	599	297	96	60	101	554
1831–40	204	163	146	513	290	83	48	103	524
1841–50	227	145	186	558	291	93	69	100	553
1851–60	237	181	244	662	290	151	107	124	672
1861–70	237	204	289	730	264	162	112	157	695
1871–80	217	271	313	801	276	176	106	212	770
1881–89	178	215	408	801	260	167	109	254	790
89 yrs.	1,748	1,918	2,216	5,882	2,476	1,448	911	1,214	6,049

The above table, however, includes not only taxes, but likewise public services, such as the Post-Office. The principal items of taxation have been in recent years as follows :—

	1853	1860	1870	1880	1889
	£	£	£	£	£
Customs	22,140,000	24,390,000	21,500,000	19,170,000	19,970,000
Excise	15,790,000	20,240,000	21,880,000	25,220,000	25,470,000
Income-tax	5,510,000	9,600,000	10,040,000	9,230,000	12,700,000
Stamps	6,920,000	8,040,000	9,290,000	11,310,000	12,340,000
Land-tax, &c. . .	3,380,000	3,230,000	4,500,000	2,670,000	2,960,000
Total . .	53,740,000	65,500,000	67,210,000	67,600,000	73,440,000

The following is a synopsis of the import tariff at four dates of distinct fiscal policy :—

	Duties Expressed in Shillings			
	1787	1819	1834	1890
Bacon, cwt. . .	47	56	28	...
Books, ,, . .	20	100	100	...
Butter, ,, . .	2½	20	20	...
Cheese, ,, . .	1½	10	10	...
Cocoa, ,, . .	240	280	19	2
Coffee, ,, . .	224	280	140	14
Cotton, ,, . .	9	9	3	...
Eggs, ,, . .	3	6	6	...
Paper, ,, . .	?	94	28	...
Potatoes, ,, . .	4	2	2	...
Rice, ,, . .	7	15	15	...
Soap, ,, . .	44	90	90	...
Spirits, gallon . .	6	22	22	10
Sugar, cwt. . .	27	63	63	...
Tallow, ,, . .	...	3	1	...
Tea, ,, . .	45	224	240	37
Tobacco, ,, . .	392	448	784	356
Wine, gallon . .	5	14	5½	1
Wool, cwt. . .	0	56	9	...

Blanks in the above table signify duty-free. Grain was subject to import dues on a sliding scale, according to market prices in Great Britain, down to 1846.

Customs dues are levied on fewer articles than formerly, the ratio of import duties to the value of all imported merchandise showing as follows :—

Year		Per Cent.	Year		Per Cent.	Year		Per Cent.
1580	. . .	1	1720	. . .	21	1844	. . .	40
1614	. . .	8	1800	. . .	20	1866	. . .	10
1684	. . .	13	1827	. . .	46	1889	. . .	5

The amount of customs dues per inhabitant at various dates was as follows :—

Year		Customs, £	Shillings per Inhabitant
1684	. . .	530,000	2.0
1720	. . .	1,555,000	5.1
1800	. . .	6,788,000	13.0
1844	. . .	24,277,000	18.0
1889	. . .	19,970,000	10.5

The amount per head is greater than in European countries (except Portugal, Denmark, and Norway), but less than in the United States, Canada, or Australia.

The principal items paying duty in recent years were :—

	1853	1860	1870	1880	1889
	£	£	£	£	£
Sugar	4,050,000	6,010,000	5,400,000	...	...
Tea	5,980,000	5,400,000	2,640,000	3,700,000	4,630,000
Coffee	440,000	440,000	350,000	210,000	180,000
Spirits	2,580,000	2,520,000	4,190,000	4,680,000	4,300,000
Wine	1,790,000	1,630,000	1,480,000	1,390,000	1,210,000
Tobacco	4,540,000	5,600,000	6,610,000	8,560,000	8,860,000
Grain	400,000	500,000	100,000	...	...
Sundries	2,360,000	2,290,000	730,000	630,000	790,000
Total . .	22,140,000	24,390,000	21,500,000	19,170,000	19,970,000

Excise is the tax which produces the largest sum to the exchequer. The articles on which this tax is levied were as follows :—

	1853	1860	1870	1880	1889
	£	£	£	£	£
Spirits	6,230,000	9,780,000	10,970,000	13,630,000	12,880,000
Malt	5,320,000	6,650,000	6,480,000	6,730,000	8,770,000
Licenses	1,180,000	1,460,000	3,700,000	3,500,000	3,510,000
Sundries	3,060,000	2,350,000	730,000	1,360,000	310,000
Total . .	15,790,000	20,240,000	21,880,000	25,220,000	25,470,000

If we sum up all the liquor-duties we find as follows :—

	1853	1860	1870	1880	1888
	£	£	£	£	£
British spirits	6,230,000	9,780,000	10,970,000	13,630,000	12,880,000
Imported spirits . . .	2,580,000	2,520,000	4,190,000	4,680,000	4,300,000
Wines	1,790,000	1,630,000	1,480,000	1,390,000	1,210,000
Malt	5,320,000	6,650,000	6,480,000	6,730,000	8,770,000
Total . .	15,920,000	20,580,000	23,120,000	26,430,000	27,160,000

Since 1881 the malt-tax is termed beer-tax.

The receipts from the excise at various dates have been :—

Year	Amount, £	Year	Amount, £
1744 . . .	3,750,000	1830 . . .	18,640,000
1786 . . .	5,540,000	1850 . . .	15,280,000
1808 . .	19,870,000	1889 . . .	25,470,000

Stamp-duties were invented by Charles II. ; the revenue derived from them showed as follows :—

Year	Amount, £	Year	Amount, £
1800 . . .	3,130,000	1850 . . .	6,560,000
1820 . . .	6,560,000	1870 . . .	9,290,000
1840 . . .	6,730,000	1889 . . .	12,340,000

Stamp-duties show as follows since 1853 :—

	1853	1860	1870	1880	1889
	£	£	£	£	£
Legacies	2,420,000	3,340,000	4,720,000	6,230,000	6,560,000
Insurance	1,350,000	1,760,000	520,000	120,000	170,000
Deeds	1,380,000	1,380,000	1,690,000	2,080,000	3,150,000
Bills	610,000	580,000	850,000	840,000	820,000
Receipts	180,000	390,000	580,000	810,000	1,040,000
Sundries	980,000	590,000	930,000	1,230,000	600,000
Total . .	6,920,000	8,040,000	9,290,000	11,310,000	12,340,000

Among the minor taxes included above under excise or stamp-duties, the product of some in 1889 was as follows :—

	Number	Amount, £		Amount, £
Dogs . . .	980,000	370,000	Medicines	200,000
Guns . . .	170,000	85,000	Plate . .	78,000
Game . .	62,000	160,000	Railways	310,000
Servants . .	184,000	138,000	Crests .	75,000
Carriages .	492,000	500,000	Cards .	17,000

Income-tax.—This was introduced by Pitt as a war-tax in 1798. The rate and product at various dates have been :—

Year	Pence per £	Product, £	Per Penny, £
1803	12	4,700,000	400,000
1808	24	16,500,000	700,000
1844	7	5,190,000	740,000
1856	16	15,070,000	960,000
1875	2	4,310,000	2,150,000
1889	6	12,700,000	2,100,000

The tax was repealed in 1816, revived in 1842, extended to Ireland in 1853. The principal features since 1842 were :—

Years	Average Rate (Pence)	Annual Product	Product per Penny	Product per Inhab.
		£	£	d.
1842–51	7.0	5,467,000	782,000	65
1852–61	9.8	10,224,000	1,041,000	89
1862–71	5.5	7,764,000	1,408,000	62
1872–81	3.8	7,062,000	1,868,000	52
40 years	6.0	7,625,000	1,275,000	66
1882–89	6.5	12,800,000	1,970,000	84
1889	6.0	12,700,000	2,100,000	80

The proportions of this tax collected in each of the three kingdoms were as follows :—

	1860	1870	1880	1888
England . . .	84.0	85.2	84.2	85.4
Scotland . . .	9.0	9.0	9.6	9.0
Ireland . . .	7.0	5.8	6.2	5.6
United Kingdom .	100.0	100.0	100.0	100.0

The various kinds of property or income which produced it were in the following ratio :—

	1860	1870	1880	1888
Houses . . .	18.3	17.3	20.0	21.2
Lands . . .	17.4	14.6	12.1	9.6
Professions, &c. .	64.3	68.1	67.9	69.2
Total .	100.0	100.0	100.0	100.0

Conscience-money.—Between the years 1870 and 1880, the average sum received yearly by the Chancellor of the Exchequer for unpaid taxes was £9100, in most cases for evasion of the income-tax.

Land-tax.—This tax is said to have produced £80,000 a year in the time of Edward the Confessor, which would be equivalent in weight of silver to £250,000 of present money, and in purchasing value to one million sterling. Under William III. in 1692 it produced £500,000, which was supposed to be equal to 20 per cent. or 4s. in the pound of the rental value. Pitt also fixed it at 4s. The following table shows the sum it has actually produced at various dates in this century, and what it ought to have produced at 4s. in the pound of assessed rental :—

	Product, £	Rental, £	Tax at 4s.
			£
1810 . . .	1,420,000	41,910,000	8,400,000
1840 . . .	1,300,000	47,700,000	9,500,000
1850 . . .	1,150,000	48,400,000	9,700,000
1876 . . .	1,090,000	57,700,000	11,500,000
1880 . . .	1,050,000	59,500,000	11,900,000
1889 . . .	1,020,000	51,300,000	10,300,000

House-tax.—This was originally a window-tax, but converted into a house-duty in 1851. Under either form the product is shown thus :—

Year	Amount, £
1850	1,749,000
1876	1,410,000
1889	1,940,000

The house-duty does not extend to Ireland. In 1887 the house-rental of Great Britain was £129,800,000, whence the actual product seems to be under 4d. in the pound, or about 1½ per cent. on the assessed rental, but it is in reality much more, as houses under £20 are exempted. The product in 1888 was :—

	Valuation, £	Tax, £
Houses . . .	44,100,000	1,650,000
Shops, &c. . . .	18,900,000	290,000
Total . .	63,000,000	1,940,000

This gives an average all round of 8d. in the pound, say 3½ per cent.

The window-tax was introduced by William III. in 1695, and increased by the Georges, but repealed in 1851. The number of windows taxed in 1801 and 1850 was as follows :—

Year	Houses	Windows	Windows per House
1801 . . .	1,781,000	10,300,000	5.8
1850 . . .	3,648,000	21,900,000	6.0

The returns of this tax in 1850 showed as follows :—

	Houses	Tax, £	Per House
			£ s. d.
Liverpool	11,500	33,000	2 18 0
Manchester . . .	7,900	22,000	2 15 0
Bath	3,800	22,000	5 18 0
Brighton . . .	3,600	18,000	5 1 0
Birmingham . . .	5,400	16,000	2 19 0
Bristol	4,700	15,000	3 4 0
Leeds	2,500	8,100	3 5 0

It was not extended to Ireland, and the proceeds from Great Britain in 1850 were as follows :—

Windows	Houses			Duty, £		
	England	Scotland	Great Britain	England	Scotland	Great Britain
8–10 . .	156,000	15,000	171,000	167,000	15,000	182,000
11–20 .	216,000	15,000	231,000	687,000	48,000	735,000
21–30 .	48,000	4,000	52,000	366,000	25,000	391,000
Over 30 .	30,000	1,600	31,600	404,000	37,000	441,000
Total .	450,000	35,600	485,600	1,624,000	125,000	1,749,000

The tax was graduated thus according to the number of windows :—

Windows	Tax			Windows	Tax		
	£ s. d.				£ s. d.		
8 . . .	0 16 0			20 . .	5 12 0		
10 . . .	1 8 0			50 . .	17 5 0		
15 . . .	3 10 0			100 . .	29 8 0		

Newspaper-duty was invented by Queen Anne, a penny on each sheet, which George III. raised ultimately to 4d. The tax was reduced to one penny per sheet in 1836, and abolished in 1855. The circulation of newspapers was as follows at various dates :—

Year	Tax, Pence	Circulation
1753	1	7,400,000
1790	2	14,100,000
1810	3½	20,200,000
1820	4	24,900,000
1843	1	56,400,000

Advertisement-duty.—This was another of Queen Anne's taxes, and was fixed for many years at 3s. 6d. per advertisement in England and 2s. 6d. in Ireland. It was reduced by one-half in 1833 and abolished in 1853. In 1851 the number of advertisements that paid duty was :—

England	1,770,000
Scotland	250,000
Ireland	240,000
United Kingdom	2,260,000

Soap-duty.—Another of Queen Anne's taxes, dating from 1711. It was at first £28 per ton, and produced approximately as follows :—

Year					Tons, Soap	Duty, £
1801	.	.	.	.	25,000	500,000
1811	.	.	.	.	34,000	700,000
1821	.	.	.	.	43,000	900,000
1831	.	.	.	.	55,000	1,200,000
1840	.	.	.	.	88,000	900,000
1852	.	.	.	.	97,000	1,130,000

Paper-duty.—Invented by William III. in 1694. It acted as an effectual check on knowledge, so much so that Charles Knight had to pay £20,000 on the paper consumed in his *Penny Cyclopædia* of 1830, which caused him to lose money in so useful a work. Porter gives the consumption of paper and amount of duty as follows :—

Year					Tons	Tax, £	£ per Ton
1803	.	.	.	.	14,000	400,000	28
1811	.	.	.	.	17,000	480,000	28
1821	.	.	.	.	22,000	580,000	28
1831	.	.	.	.	28,000	730,000	28
1841	.	.	.	.	44,000	640,000	14
1860	.	.	.	.	...	1,350,000	...

The duty was repealed by Mr. Gladstone in 1861.

Salt-duty.—Invented by Queen Anne in 1702. During the French war it was raised to £30 per ton, being fifteen times the value of the salt. The consumption then averaged 210,000 tons, or 16 lbs. per inhabitant, and when the tax was abolished in 1825 it rose very rapidly.

Carriage-duty.—The number of persons assessed to this tax at various dates was as follows :—

Year					Number	Per 10,000 Pop.
1812	.	.	.	.	63,100	52
1830	.	.	.	.	85,100	51
1860	.	.	.	.	245,000	112
1870	.	.	.	.	325,000	125
1880	.	.	.	.	463,000	154
1888	.	.	.	.	492,000	150

The carriages paying duty in 1888 were :—

Hackney carriages .	.	.	.	53,600
Private ,, one horse .	.	.	358,000
,, ,, two ,, .	.	.	80,600
Total	.	.	492,200

Servant-duty.—This was invented by George III. during the American war, and the number of servants taxed at various dates was as follows :—

Year		Number	Year		Number
1812	. .	86,100	1876	. .	220,000
1831	. .	101,800	1888	. .	184,000

This tax is only on male servants in Great Britain, that on female servants having been repealed in 1792.

Legacy Duties.—These began in 1796, and comprise legacy, succession, and probate duties ; they range from

1 to 11½ per cent. according to relationship. The amount of property on which these duties were paid was :—

	1840	1873	1888
	£	£	£
England . . .	47,100,000	106,800,000	170,500,000
Scotland . . .	3,100,000	14,200,000	19,000,000
Ireland . . .	4,500,000	8,400,000	12,100,000
United Kingdom	54,700,000	129,400,000	201,600,000

Excluding the property falling under succession-duty, that which came under probate-duty in the United Kingdom in 1888 was as follows :—

Estates of			Number	Value, £
Under £1000	.	.	31,079	10,600,000
£1000–£4000		.	8,343	17,200,000
£4000–£10,000	.	.	2,982	19,200,000
£10,000–£50,000	.	.	2,079	44,100,000
Over £50,000	.	.	432	67,000,000
Total	.	.	44,915	158,100,000

For local rates and taxes see *Local Taxation.*

FRANCE

Some of the principal taxes are shown as follows :—

	Amount, £		Shillings per Inhabitant	
	1880	1890	1880	1890
Customs . . .	12,400,000	15,000,000	6.6	8.0
Property . .	7,000,000	7,300,000	3.6	3.8
Sugar . . .	4,400,000	7,100,000	2.3	3.7
Windows . . .	1,700,000	2,000,000	0.9	1.1
Liquor . . .	17,300,000	17,000,000	9.2	9.2
Licenses . . .	4,000,000	4,200,000	2.1	2.2
Registration . .	19,500,000	20,400,000	10.4	11.0
Stamps . . .	5,600,000	6,400,000	3.0	3.5
Tobacco . . .	13,700,000	14,900,000	7.2	8.0
Sundries . . .	7,400,000	7,700,000	3.9	4.2
Total . .	93,000,000	102,000,000	49.2	54.7

The increase of taxation, national and local, has been very great in the past sixty years, viz. :—

Year	National, £	Local, £	Total, £	Shillings per Inhabitant
1830	37,600,000	7,100,000	44,700,000	28
1840	44,200,000	8,800,000	53,000,000	31
1850	52,200,000	11,700,000	63,900,000	35
1860	65,700,000	18,100,000	83,800,000	45
1870	68,500,000	21,300,000	89,800,000	48
1880	93,000,000	32,400,000	125,400,000	66
1890	102,000,000	40,800,000	142,800,000	75

Tobacco.—This is one of the principal taxes, and shows as follows :—

Year			Amount, £	Year			Amount, £
1815	.	.	2,000,000	1860	.	.	7,800,000
1830	.	.	2,700,000	1890	.	.	14,900,000

Registration.—This is mostly on transfer of property, and shows thus :—

Year			Amount, £	Year			Amount, £
1830	.	.	6,100,000	1871	.	.	15,000,000
1850	.	.	8,100,000	1880	.	.	19,500,000
1860	.	.	11,000,000	1890	.	.	20,400,000

Liquor-duties were as follows :—

Year	Amount, £	Year	Amount, £
1830	4,100,000	1870	9,100,000
1850	4,300,000	1886	17,000,000

The *octroi* and other local taxes are fully described under *Local Taxation*.

GERMANY

Apart from the taxes levied in each particular State, there are the following imperial ones :—

	Amount, £		Shillings per Inhabitant	
	1885	1890	1885	1890
Customs	10,400,000	13,500,000	4.7	5.6
Salt	1,900,000	2,000,000	0.9	0.8
Sugar	1,600,000	2,600,000	0.7	1.1
Tobacco	400,000	500,000	0.2	0.2
Liquor	2,900,000	7,700,000	1.3	3.3
Stamps	1,100,000	1,400,000	0.5	0.6
Total	18,300,000	27,700,000	8.3	11.6

In 1887 was published the following statement of the customs dues collected throughout Germany since 1835 :—

Year	Sum, £	Period	Average, £	Shillings per Inhab.
1835	2,400,000	1835-40	2,700,000	2.1
1850	3,400,000	1841-50	3,800,000	2.6
1860	3,500,000	1851-60	3,700,000	2.3
1870	4,300,000	1861-70	3,700,000	2.1
1880	7,100,000	1871-80	6,500,000	3.0
1887	12,700,000	1881-87	11,200,000	4.8

The duty on spirits was raised in 1887, and now produces £6,700,000.

The import dues collected on grain in 1889 were as follows :—

	Tons	Duty, £	Shillings per Ton
Wheat	370,000	930,000	50
Rye	750,000	1,870,000	50
Oats	260,000	520,000	40
Barley	630,000	710,000	23
Various	600,000	680,000	23
Total	2,610,000	4,710,000	38

The principal taxes (not local or municipal) levied in the several States of Germany may be summed up approximately thus :—

	Direct, £	Indirect, £	Total, £
Prussia	8,300,000	14,100,000	22,400,000
Bavaria	1,300,000	4,500,000	5,800,000
Saxony	1,100,000	400,000	1,500,000
Wurtemburg	600,000	600,000	1,200,000
Baden	600,000	600,000	1,200,000
Small States	1,800,000	3,300,000	5,100,000
Total	13,700,000	23,500,000	37,200,000

These, added to the imperial taxes before mentioned, sum up a total of £64,900,000.

Prussia has income-tax, land-tax, house-tax, and trade-tax, the aggregate of which has been as follows :—

Year	Amount, £	Shillings per Inhabitant
1880	7,600,000	5.5
1888	8,300,000	5.6

The assessments to income-tax in Prussia and Saxony will be found under the head of *Income*.

RUSSIA

The principal taxes are shown as follows :—

	Amount, £		Pence per Inhab.	
	1879	1889	1879	1889
Customs	9,200,000	12,100,000	27	32
Poll-tax	11,700,000	8,200,000	34	21
Liquor	22,800,000	25,700,000	66	68
Salt	1,300,000	...	4	...
Tobacco	1,300,000	2,600,000	4	7
Sugar	500,000	1,700,000	1	4
Stamps	1,400,000	2,000,000	4	5
Registration	900,000	1,000,000	2	2
Passports	300,000	300,000	1	1
Sundries	2,400,000	7,600,000	7	20
Total	51,800,000	61,200,000	150	160

The above does not include revenue from crown domains or departments of public service, such as post-office. The poll-tax in 1882 was as follows :—

	No. Taxed	Amount	Pence per Head
Proprietors	693,000	140,000	48
Cossacks, &c.	1,347,000	350,000	60
Serfs	21,502,000	5,203,000	57
Total	23,542,000	5,693,000	58

AUSTRIA

The principal taxes of Austria proper were as follows :—

	Amount, £		Shillings per Inhab.	
	1878	1887	1878	1887
Land-tax	3,700,000	2,900,000	3.3	2.5
House-tax	2,400,000	2,400,000	2.2	2.1
Income-tax	2,000,000	2,000,000	1.8	1.7
Licences	900,000	900,000	0.8	0.8
Customs	1,900,000	3,600,000	1.7	3.2
Salt	1,900,000	1,700,000	1.7	1.5
Sugar	1,400,000	2,800,000	1.3	2.4
Cattle	500,000	500,000	0.5	0.5
Tobacco	6,000,000	6,300,000	5.4	5.8
Liquor	2,600,000	3,200,000	2.3	2.8
Stamps	1,700,000	1,500,000	1.5	1.3
Lotteries, &c.	3,200,000	3,300,000	2.9	2.9
Total	28,200,000	31,100,000	25.4	27.5

In the above table florins are taken at 24d. for 1878, and 20d. for 1887. There are also some taxes common to the whole monarchy not included above,

In Hungary the principal taxes were :—

	Amount, £		Shillings per Inhab.	
	1882	1889	1882	1889
Land-tax	2,300,000	2,100,000	3.0	2.8
House-tax	500,000	600,000	0.7	0.8
Licences	1,000,000	1,100,000	1.3	1.4
Income-tax	800,000	1,400,000	1.0	1.8
Excise	1,500,000	3,300,000	2.0	4.4
Tobacco	3,200,000	3,900,000	4.2	5.2
Lotteries	2,500,000	2,100,000	3.3	2.8
Salt	1,200,000	1,200,000	1.6	1.6
Registration, &c.	2,300,000	3,300,000	3.1	4.4
Total	15,300,000	19,000,000	20.2	25.2

Incomes from crown domains and public services are not included.

ITALY

The principal taxes are shown as follows :—

	Amount, £		Shillings per Inhab.	
	1881	1890	1881	1890
Property-tax .	7,600,000	7,000,000	5.3	4.7
Income-tax .	7,400,000	9,200,000	5.2	6.2
Grist-tax . .	1,900,000	...	1.3	...
Registration .	2,400,000	2,800,000	1.7	1.8
Legacy dues .	1,200,000	1,500,000	0.8	1.0
Stamps . . .	1,700,000	2,900,000	1.1	1.9
Octroi . . .	3,300,000	3,300,000	2.2	2.2
Customs . .	6,200,000	10,600,000	4.2	7.2
Tobacco . .	4,200,000	7,600,000	2.8	5.1
Salt	3,300,000	2,500,000	2.2	1.7
Lotteries . .	2,900,000	3,100,000	2.0	2.1
Railway-tax .	600,000	700,000	0.4	0.5
Sundries . .	...	2,600,000	...	1.7
Total . .	42,700,000	53,800,000	29.2	36.1

The above is exclusive of state properties and public services. It is to be observed that octroi is here national, in other countries a provincial tax. The grist-tax was abolished in 1884. Property-tax was made up thus :—

Year	Land-Tax, £	House-Tax, £	Total, £	Shillings per Inhab.
1870 . . .	2,320,000	880,000	3,200,000	2.5
1876 . . .	2,840,000	1,220,000	4,060,000	3.0
1890 . . .	4,250,000	2,750,000	7,000,000	4.7

Local taxes in 1885 amounted to 27 millions sterling : see *Local Taxation.*

SPAIN

The principal taxes in 1887 were as follows :—

	£	Shillings per Inhabitant
Land-tax . . .	6,600,000	7.2
Tobacco . . .	6,400,000	7.0
Stamps, &c. . .	5,600,000	6.2
Customs . . .	6,900,000	7.6
Excise . . .	6,400,000	7.0
Total . . .	31,900,000	35.0

PORTUGAL

The principal taxes were as follows :—

	Amount, £		Shillings per Inhab.	
	1881	1890	1881	1890
Land-tax . .	700,000	700,000	3.1	3.0
House-tax . .	80,000	100,000	0.3	0.4
Licences . .	250,000	250,000	1.1	1.0
Tobacco . .	750,000	900,000	3.3	3.8
Customs . .	1,800,000	3,100,000	8.0	13.0
Octroi . . .	300,000	450,000	1.3	2.0
Income-tax .	180,000	200,000	0.8	0.9
Registration,&c.	950,000	900,000	4.2	4.0
Total . .	5,010,000	6,600,000	22.1	28.1

FINLAND

This is the least taxed country in Europe : total taxes £1,400,000, or 13s. per inhabitant.

SWEDEN

The principal taxes were as follows :—

	Amount, £		Shillings per Inhab.	
	1880	1890	1880	1890
Land-tax . .	250,000	440,000	1.1	1.8
Customs . .	1,350,000	2,060,000	6.0	8.4
Liquor . . .	830,000	750,000	3.7	3.0
Stamps . . .	170,000	200,000	0.8	0.8
Income-tax .	300,000	220,000	1.4	0.9
Total . .	2,900,000	3,670,000	13.0	14.9

NORWAY

The principal taxes were as follows :—

	Amount, £		Shillings per Inhab.	
	1879	1890	1879	1890
Customs . .	990,000	1,100,000	10.0	11.0
Liquor . .	320,000	280,000	3.2	2.8
Stamps, &c. .	100,000	100,000	1.0	1.0
Total .	1,410,000	1,480,000	14.2	14.8

DENMARK

The following were the principal taxes :—

	Amount, £		Shillings per Inhab.	
	1880	1889	1880	1889
Land-tax . .	370,000	370,000	3.7	3.5
House-tax .	110,000	140,000	1.1	1.3
Customs . .	1,100,000	1,400,000	11.0	13.3
Stamps, &c. .	480,000	620,000	4.8	5.9
Total .	2,060,000	2,530,000	20.6	24.0

HOLLAND

The principal taxes were the following :—

	Amount, £		Shillings per Inhab.	
	1879	1890	1879	1890
Land-tax . .	880,000	1,000,000	4.2	4.4
Poll-tax . .	810,000	900,000	3.9	4.0
Liquor . . .	1,900,000	2,200,000	9.0	9.7
Customs . .	380,000	400,000	1.8	1.8
Stamps, &c. .	1,960,000	1,800,000	9.3	8.0
Excise . . .	1,300,000	1,400,000	6.2	6.1
Sundries . .	400,000	600,000	1.9	2.6
Total .	7,630,000	8,300,000	36.3	36.6

Excise was made up in 1883 as follows (exclusive of the liquor-tax) :—

	Tons	Duty, £	£ per Ton
Sugar	120,000	520,000	4.4
Salt	40,000	300,000	7.5
Soap	18,000	150,000	8.3
Beef	...	250,000	...

The number of cattle killed for market was 280,000, say about 90,000 tons, and the tax averaged, therefore, nearly £3 per ton.

BELGIUM

The principal taxes were as follows :—

	Amount, £		Shillings per Inhab.	
	1879	1890	1879	1890
Land-tax . .	890,000	960,000	3.3	3.2
Income-tax .	620,000	800,000	2.4	2.7
Customs . .	740,000	1,090,000	2.8	3.6
Liquor . . .	1,100,000	1,400,000	4.2	4.7
Registration,&c.	2,500,000	2,560,000	9.0	8.5
Total .	5,850,000	6,810,000	21.7	22.7

GREECE

The principal taxes were as follows :—

	Amount, £		Shillings per Inhab.	
	1881	1890	1881	1890
Land-tax . .	220,000	380,000	2.5	4.2
Cattle-tax . .	70,000	90,000	0.8	1.0
House-tax . .	40,000	80,000	0.4	0.9
Licences . .	50,000	100,000	0.5	1.1
Customs . .	670,000	760,000	7.5	8.4
Stamps . . .	180,000	330,000	2.0	3.6
Sundries . .	...	650,000	...	7.1
Total .	1,230,000	2,390,000	13.7	26.3

Sundries include £70,000 from salt, £140,000 from the Government monopoly of petroleum, and £240,000 from tobacco.

ROUMANIA AND SERVIA

The principal taxes are as follows (1888) :—

	Amount, £		Shillings per Inhab.	
	Roumania	Servia	Roumania	Servia
Customs . .	900,000	200,000	3.6	2.0
Excise . . .	1,600,000	800,000	6.4	8.0
Sundries . .	1,700,000	400,000	6.8	4.0
Total .	4,200,000	1,400,000	16.8	14.0

TURKEY

The only taxes of which much is known are those on salt and tobacco (mortgaged to bondholders), which see under the section of *Finance*.

EGYPT

The taxes in this country are likewise set forth under the title of *Finance*.

UNITED STATES

The principal taxes have been as follows :—

Year	Amount, £			Shillings per Inhabitant		
	Customs	Internal	Total	Customs	Internal	Total
1790	900,000	...	900,000	4.5	...	4.5
1800	1,870,000	170,000	2,040,000	7.0	0.7	7.7
1810	1,780,000	2,000	1,782,000	5.0	...	5.0
1820	3,120,000	20,000	3,140,000	6.6	...	6.6
1830	4,590,000	3,000	4,593,000	7.0	...	7.0
1840	2,800,000	...	2,800,000	3.3	...	3.3
1850	8,300,000	...	8,300,000	7.2	...	7.2
1860	11,050,000	...	11,050,000	7.1	...	7.1
1870	34,500,000	32,500,000	67,000,000	17.8	16.8	34.6
1880	38,800,000	25,800,000	64,600,000	15.6	10.3	25.9
1889	46,600,000	27,200,000	73,800,000	15.0	8.7	23.7

Internal revenue was made up thus :—

	1865	1875	1889
	£	£	£
Spirits	2,600,000	9,600,000	15,400,000
Tobacco . . .	1,600,000	6,800,000	6,600,000
Beer	500,000	1,600,000	5,000,000
Sundries . . .	23,500,000	2,400,000	200,000
Total . .	28,200,000	20,400,000	27,200,000

The principal States producing internal revenue are :—

State	Amount, £	State	Amount, £
New York . .	3,200,000	Ohio	2,400,000
Illinois	6,400,000	Pennsylvania . .	1,800,000
Kentucky . . .	3,500,000	Missouri . . .	1,600,000

The above six States produce 70 per cent. of the total.

The items which composed customs revenue in the United States were as follows :—

	Value, £		Duty, £		Percentage	
	1880	1889	1880	1889	1880	1889
Sugar	16,100,000	17,400,000	8,800,000	11,700,000	55	67
Woollens	6,700,000	10,900,000	4,600,000	7,400,000	68	68
Silks	6,500,000	7,300,000	3,900,000	3,700,000	60	50
Cottons	5,300,000	5,600,000	2,100,000	2,200,000	40	40
Linens, &c. . . .	4,900,000	5,400,000	1,700,000	1,900,000	35	35
Iron	12,900,000	9,000,000	4,800,000	3,600,000	37	40
Tobacco	1,300,000	2,800,000	1,000,000	2,300,000	75	80
Liquor	1,700,000	2,300,000	1,200,000	1,600,000	72	70
Leather	2,400,000	2,300,000	700,000	700,000	30	30
Glass	1,100,000	1,600,000	600,000	900,000	55	55
China	1,200,000	1,300,000	500,000	700,000	42	52
Fruit	2,500,000	2,700,000	700,000	800,000	28	30
Drugs	2,800,000	2,700,000	800,000	1,000,000	28	36
Sundries	22,000,000	29,500,000	6,700,000	8,100,000	30	27
Total .	87,400,000	100,800,000	38,100,000	46,600,000	44	46

The aggregate of national and local taxation was approximately as follows:—

	Amount, £		Shillings per Inhabitant	
	1860	1889	1860	1889
National	11,050,000	73,800,000	7.0	23.7
Local	19,600,000	52,200,000	12.6	16.7
Total	30,650,000	126,000,000	19.6	40.4

State taxes are set forth at length under the title of *Local Taxation*.

CANADA

The principal taxes have been as follows :—

Year	Amount, £			Shillings per Inhabitant
	Customs	Excise	Total	
1868	1,700,000	600,000	2,300,000	14
1872	2,600,000	900,000	3,500,000	20
1876	2,600,000	1,200,000	3,800,000	20
1880	2,900,000	800,000	3,700,000	18
1884	4,100,000	1,100,000	5,200,000	23
1887	4,500,000	1,300,000	5,800,000	24

AUSTRALIA

The taxation in 1888 of the several colonies was :—

	Customs, £	Internal, £	Total, £	£ per Inhab.
N. S. Wales	2,140,000	540,000	2,680,000	2.5
Victoria	2,350,000	720,000	3,070,000	2.9
Queensland	1,350,000	230,000	1,580,000	4.2
S. Australia	530,000	210,000	740,000	2.4
W. Australia	180,000	...	180,000	4.3
Tasmania	300,000	110,000	410,000	2.8
New Zealand	1,390,000	640,000	2,030,000	3.4
Total	8,240,000	2,450,000	10,690,000	3.0

INDIA

The principal taxes show as follows :—

	1865	1875	1890	Pence per Inhabitant		
				1865	1875	1890
Land-tax	20,400,000	20,500,000	19,500,000	25	25	23
Opium	8,500,000	9,200,000	6,900,000	10	11	8
Salt	5,300,000	6,000,000	6,700,000	6	7	8
Customs	2,300,000	2,600,000	1,200,000	2	2	1
Excise	2,200,000	2,400,000	3,900,000	2	2	3
Stamps	2,000,000	2,500,000	3,300,000	2	2	3
Sundries	4,500,000	4,000,000	6,000,000	5	4	7
Total	45,200,000	47,200,000	47,500,000	52	53	53

In 1865 and 1875 the rupee is taken at 24d., in 1890 at 20d.

TEA

The consumption at present averages as follows:—

	Lbs.	Oz. per Inhab.
United Kingdom	184,500,000	80
United States	80,000,000	20
Russia	37,000,000	7
Australia	20,000,000	88
Canada	22,000,000	70
Various	106,500,000	...
Total	450,000,000	...

Tea is mostly grown in China, the plants being 4 feet apart, that is, 2700 to the acre. Plants seven years old will give 700 lbs. tea to the acre, or 4 oz. per plant. The average exportation from tea-growing countries is shown thus :—

	Millions of Lbs.		
	1880–83	1884–85	1887–88
China	284	290	290
India	53	66	90
Japan	37	35	40
Java	5	6	7
Paraguay	10	10	10
Ceylon	1	8	19
Total	390	415	456

The consumption in the United States, compared with population, has not varied in fifteen years, being about 20 oz. per inhabitant. In the United Kingdom it steadily increases, and Indian tea, which is said to contain much more body than Chinese (as 4 lbs. to 5 lbs.), is rapidly supplanting that of China.

In 1888 the consumption in the United Kingdom was as follows :—

	Lbs.
Chinese	78,500,000
Indian and Ceylon	105,800,000
Total	184,300,000

In 1878 India supplied only 17 per cent. of the tea consumed in Great Britain.

The following table shows the consumption since 1711 :—

Year	Lbs.	Oz. per Inhabitant	Duty per Lb., Pence	Price per Lb., Pence
1711	142,000	½	66	216
1725	370,000	1	66	200
1740	1,003,000	3	66	200
1750	2,568,000	6	40	150
1760	4,072,000	9	36	120
1770	7,149,000	14	30	100
1780	5,152,000	9	40	110
1790	14,693,000	24	7	65
1800	20,359,000	21	18	70
1810	19,093,000	17	46	80
1820	22,452,000	18	38	70
1830	30,047,000	20	30	60
1840	32,253,000	20	25	50
1850	49,572,000	29	26	48
1860	78,340,000	43	18	40
1870	118,200,000	61	6	30
1881	167,700,000	73	6	25
1888	184,300,000	80	6	20

In 1890 the duty was reduced to 4d., and as the price now averages 18d., it is probable the consumption will reach this year (1891) about 200 million pounds, or 5½ lbs. per inhabitant.

TELEPHONES

In 1876 there were 200 working in Europe, and 380 in the United States. In 1883 there were nearly 79,000 working in 303 towns, viz. :—

	Towns	Telephones
Europe	161	30,100
America	126	47,200
Asia	7	420
Africa	4	240
Australia	5	900
Total	303	78,800

The numbers in use in various countries in 1885 and 1888 were :—

	1885	1888		1885	1888
U. Kingdom .	12,000	20,400	Italy . . .	7,000	9,200
France . . .	10,000	10,000	Switzerland .	...	7,600
Germany . .	17,000	33,000	Spain . .	1,000	2,200
Russia . . .	3,000	7,600	Sweden . .	10,000	...
Denmark . .	...	1,900	Holland . .	4,000	...
Austria . . .	2,500	4,000	Belgium . .	4,000	5,200

In 1888 the numbers in various cities were :—

Berlin	. . .	8,600	St. Petersburg .	.	1,500
New York	. .	6,900	Milan .	. .	1,200
Paris	. . .	5,300	Manchester	. .	1,200
Stockholm	. .	3,800	Vienna .	. .	1,200
Buenos Ayres	. .	2,800	Liverpool .	. .	1,100
Montevideo	. .	2,200	Glasgow .	. .	1,100
Rome	. .	2,100	Zurich .	. .	1,100
Hamburg .	. .	1,900	Naples .	. .	1,000
Geneva	. .	1,500	Moscow .	. .	800

The total number of telephones in use in the United States in 1885 was 325,000, and in Canada 18,000. The number of messages transmitted daily averages 100,000 in Berlin, 90,000 in London, 26,000 in Belgium, 16,000 in Austria. The United Kingdom in 1887 had 30,000 miles of telephone wire in use, Belgium 7000, Austria 7000, Germany 51,000, and the whole of Europe 330,000 miles. The longest lines in Europe are Berlin-Hanover 225 miles, Vienna-Budapesth 150 miles.

THEATRES

The following table (1882) shows the number in each country, and how many have been burnt from 1880 to 1882 :—

	Number	Burnt	Period	Burnt
Great Britain .	152	68	1800–10	16
France	337	63	1811–20	14
Italy	348	45	1821–30	31
Spain	160	17	1831–40	33
Germany . . .	191	49	1841–50	44
Russia	44	25	1851–60	74
Austria . . .	152	26	1861–70	98
United States .	550	176	1871–82	159
Total . .	1,934	469	83 years	469

In 1882 the gross receipts of London theatres were £1,320,000, being an average of 7s. per inhabitant. The expenditure was :—

	£
Pay to actors	725,000
Pay to authors	79,000
Rent	119,000
Sundries and profits . . .	397,000
	1,320,000

The gross receipts of Paris theatres were as follows :—

Year	£	In 1889	£
1850 . . .	330,000	Opera . . .	160,000
1860 . . .	580,000	Hippodrome .	113,000
1867 . . .	840,000	Français .	94,000
1878 . . .	1,200,000	Comique .	77,000
1889 . . .	1,280,000	Various .	836,000

The sum paid to authors for plays in 1888 was £75,000 sterling. The number of actors employed was about 3200.

The loss of life by fires at theatres was as follows :—

Year	Theatre	Victims	Year	Theatre	Victims
1772	Amsterdam .	48	1847	Carlsruhe . .	63
1778	Saragossa . .	137	1857	Leghorn . .	102
1794	Capo d'Istria .	945	1867	Philadelphia .	13
1811	Richmond . .	78	1876	Brooklyn . .	283
1836	St. Petersburg	770	1880	Nice . . .	790
1845	Canton . . .	1,660	1881	Vienna . . .	1,460
1846	Quebec . . .	355	1883	Smolensk . .	380

THERMAL SPRINGS

The nature of some of the principal is thus shown :—

	Carbonates		Sulphates		Chlorides of Sodium	All Fixed
	Soda	Lime	Soda	Lime		
Aix-les-Bains .	...	148	096	016	008	430
Aix-la-Chapelle .	650	159	283	...	2.639	4.102
Baden-Baden .	...	166	...	300	1.600	2.314
Bath	...	126	274	1.143	180	2.060
Bigorre . . .	...	142	400	1.900	040	2.900
Bilin . . .	3.009	402	827	...	382	4.960
Bourboule . .	2.272	196	279	...	3.346	6.519
Bussang . . .	789	054	110	...	078	1.123
Buxton . . .	...	111	...	052	034	294
Castellamare . .	825	391	625	...	5.851	9.794
Cauterets . .	...	...	024	...	072	260
Cheltenham . .	125	...	1.678	146	3.081	5.520
Clifton	...	252	043	141	084	628
Dax	...	092	043	359	301	1.022
Eaux Chaudes .	035	...	042	105	115	309
Ems	1.979	216	034	...	983	3.519
Friedrichshal .	...	015	5.434	1.463	8.381	24.933
Gastein . . .	...	020	204	...	047	339
Harrogate . .	...	342	204	008	11.354	13.664
Huny. Janos . .	796	933	15.915	...	1.305	34.855
Lisbon . . .	...	571	...	485	15.428	20.507
Leamington . .	...	...	3.993	...	3.424	11.513
Malvern . . .	...	...	027	...	...	076
Neuenahr . . .	1.055	305	250	...	150	2.313
Ofen	029	122	21.196	7.066	2.753	56.816
Pfeffers . . .	...	142	009	007	052	291
Royat	349	1.000	183	...	1.728	5.586
St. Galmier . .	238	...	079	180	216	1.886
St. Moritz . .	191	726	272	...	039	1.446
Schwalbach . .	188	439	005	...	007	1.189
Seltzer	1.021	550	150	...	2.040	4.092
Spa	127	173	020	...	026	658
Tarasp . . .	3.545	1.619	2.155	...	3.828	12.251

The temperature, in Fahrenheit, of the principal springs, is shown thus :—

Bilin . . .	66	Thermopylæ	113	Ischia . . .	140
St. Didier . .	70	Vichy . . .	113	Ofen . . .	144
Mallow . .	72	Bath . . .	115	Arles . . .	145
Bristol . .	74	Gastein . .	117	Baden-Baden	147
Yverdun . .	76	Bigorre . .	119	Plombières .	147
Buxton . .	82	Töplitz . .	121	Viseu . . .	153
Kreuznach .	86	Lucca . .	124	Wisbaden . .	158
Patras . .	97	Cauterets .	130	Balkan . . .	163
Wildbad . .	98	Ems . . .	131	Acqui . . .	167
Pfeffers . .	101	Aachen . .	135	Carlsbad . .	167
Alicante . .	104	Guimaraens	138	Chaudes-Aigues	174
Pisa . . .	106	Luchon . .	140	Baths of Nero	182

In 1882 an official report of the result of some French springs was as follows :—

	Barèges	Amelie	Vichy	Bourbonne	General Average
Cured . .	12	9	22	16	15
Improved .	52	45	61	62	55
No effect .	33	36	14	17	25
Worse . .	3	10	3	5	5
Total .	100	100	100	100	100

TIDES

The height of ordinary tides at various places is :—

	Feet		Feet		Feet
Bantry . .	11	Granville . .	21	Penzance . .	16
Belfast. . .	8	Greenock. .	9	Portsmouth .	10
Bergen . .	4	Harwich . .	9	Queenstown .	9
Bordeaux . .	8	Havre . . .	13	Ramsgate .	15
Boulogne . .	13	Holyhead . .	12	St. Nazare .	9
Brest . . .	13	Hull . . .	15	St. Malo . .	19
Calais . . .	10	Isle of Man .	19	Scarborough .	12
Cherbourg .	9	Inverness .	12	Shields . .	9
Dieppe . . .	15	Jersey . . .	17	Sligo . . .	8
Dover . . .	14	Kingstown .	9	Sunderland .	10
Drontheim .	8	Kinsale . .	15	Thurso . .	9
Dundee . .	15	Leith . . .	12	Ushant . .	20
Dunkirk . .	9	Limerick . .	17	Waterford .	9
Fundy Bay .	66	Liverpool . .	19	Weston-S.-M.	27
Galway . .	10	London . .	16	Westport . .	13
Glasgow . .	9	Pembroke .	15	Whitehaven .	24

Toulon has a tide of 4 inches, which is about the average of the Mediterranean.

TIME

At London, Noon

Forenoon

Boston . .	7.15	Havanna .	6.30	Quebec . .	7.12
Buenos Ayres	8.06	Lima . .	6.52	Quito . .	6.45
Caracas. .	7.32	Lisbon . .	11.24	Rio Janeiro	9.07
Chicago .	6.26	Madeira .	10.48	San Francisco	3.52
Demerara .	8.06	Madrid . .	11.46	Sandwich }	
Dublin . .	11.35	Mexico .	5.24	Islands }	1.28
Edinburgh.	11.47	Montreal .	7.06	Sierra Leone	11.07
Falkland I.	8.04	New Orleans	6.00	Teneriffe .	10.52
Gibraltar .	11.38	New York .	7.05	Trinidad .	7.55
Glasgow .	11.44	Panama .	6.42	Valparaiso .	7.13
Halifax . .	7.44	Philadelphia	6.50	Washington	6.52

Afternoon *

Adelaide .	9.14	Copenhagen	12.50	Paris . .	12.10
Alexandria.	2.00	Dresden .	12.54	Pekin . .	7.46
Algiers . .	12.13	Florence .	12.45	Prague . .	12.58
Amsterdam	12.20	Geneva . .	12.25	Rome . .	12.50
Athens . .	1.35	Jerusalem .	2.21	St. Peters-}	
Berlin . .	12.54	Lyons . .	12.20	burg . }	2.04
Bombay .	4.51	Madras . .	5.21	Singapore .	6.55
Brussels .	12.17	Malta . .	12.58	Stockholm .	1.12
Buda-Pesth	1.16	Manilla . .	8.03	Suez . . .	2.10
Cairo . .	2.07	Mauritius .	3.48	Sydney . .	10.05
Calcutta .	5.54	Melbourne.	9.40	Tunis . .	12.40
Capetown .	1.12	Moscow . .	2.30	Venice . .	12.50
Constanti-} nople. }	1.56	Munich . .	12.46	Vienna . .	1.06
		Naples . .	12.57	Yokohama .	9.20

TIN

The average yearly consumption of tin metal in Great Britain was :—

Years	Tons, Tin Metal			Value per Ton, £
	British	Net Import	Total	
1800–20 average	2,510	...	2,510	76
1821–40 ,,	4,180	...	4,180	70
1841–60 ,,	5,910	450	6,360	107
1861 . . .	7,450	...	7,450	122
1871 . . .	10,900	810	11,710	136
1880 . . .	9,200	6,550	15,750	91
1888 . . .	9,200	22,000	31,200	117

* Dresden, for example, 12.54, signifies 54 minutes past noon.

The production in 1882 was as follows :—

	Tons		Value of Ore, £	Metal Ratio per Cent.
	Tin Ore	Tin Metal		
Great Britain .	13,700	9,200	670,000	66
Australia . . .	24,000	17,500	1,250,000	74
Java	15,000	9,000	700,000	60
Total . .	52,700	35,700	2,620,000	69

TOBACCO

In 1884 the production was as follows :—

	Acres	Tons
United States .	610,000	210,000
West Indies . .	50,000	22,000
Brazil . .	105,000	38,000
Japan . .	100,000	40,000
Java . .	110,000	46,000
India . .	580,000	170,000
Russia . .	110,000	75,000
Austria . .	140,000	65,000
Turkey . .	90,000	35,000
Germany .	52,000	32,000
France . .	26,000	15,000
Manilla, &c. .	54,000	20,000
Total .	2,029,000	768,000

The following table shows the consumption in 1883 approximately :—

	Tons	Oz. per Inhabitant
United Kingdom .	23,000	23
France . .	32,000	29
Germany. .	61,000	48
Russia . .	54,000	24
Austria . .	48,000	42
Italy . .	18,000	22
Spain and Portugal.	18,000	32
Belgium and Holland .	23,000	84
Scandinavia . .	10,000	40
Turkey . .	22,000	70
Switzerland . .	7,000	82
Europe . .	383,000	44
United States .	85,000	59
India . .	165,000	30
Japan . .	38,000	39
Brazil . .	20,000	70
Colonies, &c. .	77,000	...
The World . .	768,000	...

The consumption per inhabitant has increased much more rapidly in France than in the United Kingdom, viz. :—

	Million Lbs.		Oz. per Inhabitant		Duty, Pence per Lb.	
	United Kingdom	France	United Kingdom	France	United Kingdom	France
1801	17	...	16	...	20	...
1811	21	20	18	11	27	6
1821	16	22	12	12	48	6
1831	20	24	13	12	36	12
1841	22	36	13	17	36	12
1851	31	44	18	20	36	24
1861	35	56	19	24	36	30
1872	44	61	22	26	36	40
1881	51	70	23	29	42	40
1888	57	80	23	33	42	40

De Foville estimates the consumption as follows :—

	Oz. per Inhabitant		Oz. per Inhabitant
France . . .	28	Austria . . .	42
Belgium . . .	87	Norway . . .	35
Holland . . .	70	Denmark . . .	35
Germany . . .	53	Russia . . .	28

Professor Bochk estimates the annual consumption per head at two epochs as follows :—

	Oz. per Inhab.			Oz. per Inhab.	
	1870–74	1880–84		1870–74	1880–84
U. Kingdom	23	23	Norway .	40	37
France . .	29	33	Holland .	85	110
Germany .	67	48	Belgium .	45	51
Sweden . .	32	31	Italy. . .	29	21

Newmann Spallart's estimate (1885) is as follows :—

		Oz. per Inhabitant			Oz. per Inhabitant
France	. . .	33	Sweden	. .	41
Germany .	. .	69	Denmark .	. .	56
Russia	. . .	32	Norway .	. .	40
Austria	. . .	70	Holland .	. .	98
Italy	. . .	24	Belgium .	. .	88
Switzerland	. .	80	United States .	.	106

The market value of various kinds of tobacco in 1884 was as follows :—

		£ per Ton	Value of Crop, £
Cuba	. . .	400	4,800,000
Manilla	. .	90	1,800,000
Algeria	. .	45	300,000
United States	. .	50	10,000,000
Brazil .	. .	70	2,800,000
Java .	. .	63	1,200,000
Turkey	. .	63	2,200,000

The percentage of nicotine was as follows :—

Syria .	. . .	0.0	California	. .	4.0
Havana	. .	2.0	Kentucky	. .	6.1
Maryland	. .	2.3	Virginia	. .	6.9
Alsace .	. .	3.0	France .	. .	7.5

Snuff contains 2½ per cent., Brazilian tobacco 10 per cent. In most countries there are heavy taxes on tobacco, for which see *Taxes*.

FRANCE

The tobacco monopoly dates from 1816 ; the proceeds in 1889 amounted to £14,900,000, and it is believed that the Government makes a profit of 12 millions sterling per annum. The largest factory is that of Lille, which turns out 600,000 tons yearly. Not quite half the tobacco consumed is grown in France, the crop averaging 16,000 tons, imported tobacco 20,000 tons. About 20,000 persons are employed by Government in the manufacture or sale. Cigars and cigarettes form 13 per cent., tobacco for pipes 87 per cent. ; the sale of cigars has been as follows :—

Year				Tons	Ratio of Total
1839	.	.	.	226	1.5
1859	.	.	.	2,210	9.0
1883	.	.	.	4,800	13.0

Most of the imported tobacco comes from the United States. The tobacco grown in France covers 25,000 acres, the average number of plants being 10,000 to the acre.

GERMANY

The cultivation has been as follows :—

Year	Acres	Crop, Tons	Value, £	£ per Ton
1871 . . .	56,000	35,900	890,000	25.5
1877 . . .	54,000	31,700	580,000	20.5
1887 . . .	54,000	38,600	820,000	21.5

The production is short of requirements, imports averaging 25,000 tons yearly.

RUSSIA

The production according to N. Spallart has been :—

Year	Acres	Tons	Cwts. per Acre
1875 . . .	140,000	49,000	7.0
1885 . . .	130,000	51,000	7.8

Spallart estimates the consumption at 80,000 tons, which implies an importation of about 30,000 tons, but the trade returns show less than one-tenth of that quantity.

AUSTRIA

The production has been approximately as follows :—

Year	Tons		
	Austria	Hungary	Total
1835 . . .	7,000	15,000	22,000
1877 . . .	6,000	50,000	56,000
1885 . . .	4,000	60,000	64,000

Besides the above crop, Austria consumes yearly about 15,000 tons imported.

ITALY

The consumption according to Spallart was as follows :—

Year	Tons		
	Italian	Imported	Total
1879 . . .	4,300	12,100	16,400
1885 . . .	5,200	14,600	19,800

CUBA

The quantity of tobacco raised is comparatively small, exports seldom exceeding 8000 tons, including 500 tons of cigars. The quality, however, is so fine that the unmanufactured tobacco ranges from £200 to £800 a ton, and cigars from £1000 to £5000 a ton. Newmann Spallart gives the exportation as follows :—

Year	Tobacco, Tons	Cigars, Tons	Total
1875 . . .	7,100	700	7,800
1884 . . .	6,200	500	6,700

In 1888 Cuba exported 220 million cigars and 300,000 bales of tobacco. Porto Rico exports 2500 tons of tobacco.

MANILLA

The Compañia General, with a capital of three millions sterling, owns large estates, employs 10,000 hands, and turns out yearly 80 million cigars, 400 million cigarettes, and 2500 tons of cut tobacco. The island of Luzon has 60,000 acres under tobacco. In 1889 there were 112 million cigars exported, of which 26 millions went to Spain, 18 millions to England.

UNITED STATES

The United States exported the following quantities :—

			Tons	Value, £	£ per Ton
1800 .	.	.	40,000	1,100,000	27.5
1820 .	.	.	41,000	1,500,000	37.0
1840 .	.	.	62,000	1,900,000	32.0
1860 .	.	.	86,000	2,500,000	28.8
1870 .	.	.	84,000	4,300,000	51.5
1880 .	.	.	97,000	3,400,000	35.0
1889 .	.	.	100,000	4,700,000	47.0

Full details of the tobacco crop of the United States are given under the title of *Agriculture*.

TOYS

France exported the following in 1889 :—

To	Tons	Value, £
Great Britain . . .	1,325	500,000
Other countries . . .	6,335	2,300,000
Total . .	7,660	2,800,000

Berlin papers in 1890 give statistics of Christmas trees, viz. :—

Berlin takes	400,000
Dresden takes	200,000

Those of 3 feet sell for a shilling, 10 feet 2s., and 20 feet 10s. to 15s., including the flower-pot.

TRADE UNIONS

According to Mr. George Howell, there are about 8000 trade unions in Great Britain, counting 1,200,000 members, with an aggregate revenue of £2,000,000. He publishes the following balance-sheet for 30 years down to 1881 :—

Payments

Sick operatives	£1,004,000
Out of work operatives . .	1,979,000
On strike operatives . .	274,000
Pensions	330,000
Funerals	319,000
Accidents	120,000
Loans	67,000
Total . . .	£4,093,000

Forty-four principal unions showed as follows :—

	1871	1883
Members . . .	224,000	253,000
Income, £ . . .	240,000	293,000
Reserve, £ . . .	200,000	431,000

The following were the most important trade unions in the United Kingdom in 1887 :—

	Number	Funds, £		Number	Funds, £
Engineers	51,900	125,100	Ironfounders . . .	11,700	10,400
Carpenters	25,500	40,000	Printers . . .	8,100	20,200
Boiler-makers . . .	25,100	10,200	Bricklayers . . .	7,200	26,100
Cotton-spinners . .	15,400	51,700	Rail-porters . . .	10,800	62,200

Mr. Philips Bevan in 1880 compiled the following table of strikes in the United Kingdom in ten preceding years :—

Trades		Districts		Towns	
Builders .	598	Scotland . . .	473	London . .	56
Colliers .	339	York	338	Manchester .	44
Textile .	277	Lancashire . .	149	Leeds . .	73
Carpenters	187	Northumberland	138	Sheffield .	66
Masons .	151	South-West . .	135	Glasgow . .	85
Various .	800	Various . . .	1,119	Edinburgh .	65
				Newcastle .	63
Total .	2,352	Total . .	2,352		

ITALY

In five years ending 1876 there were 206 strikes :—

Masters gained	124
Operatives gained	82
Total . . .	206

There were 137 for higher wages, and 69 for other causes.

UNITED STATES

Commissioner Wadlin, chief of the Bureau of Statistics for Massachusetts, published in 1888 a report on strikes from 1825 to 1886 ; with a vast amount of detail on all the strikes by operatives and lockouts by employers during the six years ending December 1886. These latter may be summed up thus :—

	Strikes			Hands after Strike	Lockouts, Hands Involved
	Hands Employed	Hands on Strike			
Massachusetts	114,000	81,100		109,300	14,300
Illinois . .	214,000	191,900		213,300	21,400
New York .	376,600	329,900		374,100	71,200
Pennsylvania	361,600	283,400		358,100	16,700
Ohio . . .	132,700	109,700		130,200	7,500
Various . .	461,400	327,200		450,000	29,700
Total .	1,660,300	1,323,200		1,635,000	160,800

The trades in which the strikes in these States occurred were (1881–86) as follows :—

Trade	Hands on Strike						
	Massachusetts	Illinois	New York	Pennsylvania	Ohio	Various	Total
Mining	...	30,200	...	118,400	50,700	59,600	258,900
Metals	4,200	22,000	11,400	90,400	27,100	38,300	193,400
Transport . . .	2,500	17,900	51,200	2,700	3,500	50,100	127,900
Building . . .	7,600	9,700	57,100	4,200	1,900	19,400	99,900
Tobacco . . .	1,000	1,800	74,100	2,500	2,600	15,400	97,400
Clothing . . .	2,500	3,900	47,200	10,800	200	9,800	74,400
Cottons . . .	17,100	...	6,300	1,900	500	17,800	43,600
Shoes	22,900	900	3,500	1,200	4,500	7,800	40,800
Food	...	33,000	4,700	100	100	2,100	40,000
Timber	...	12,000	...	...	...	22,900	34,900
Furniture . . .	900	9,300	5,900	1,100	2,500	5,400	25,100
Machinery . . .	300	4,300	4,500	2,200	2,700	8,300	22,300
Brick	...	5,000	6,500	900	600	7,300	20,300
Various . . .	22,100	41,900	57,500	47,000	12,800	63,000	244,300
Total . .	81,100	191,900	329,900	283,400	109,700	327,200	1,323,200

The trades affected by lockouts by masters were (1881-86) as follows :—

	Hands Locked Out						
	Tobacco	Clothing	Shoes	Food	Metals	Various	Total
Massachusetts . . .	...	...	11,100	700	...	2,500	14,300
Illinois . . .	500	600	...	16,000	1,700	2,600	21,400
New York . . .	23,900	23,100	500	...	4,500	19,200	71,200
Pennsylvania . . .	800	1,400	4,000	...	5,900	4,600	16,700
Ohio . . .	1,700	...	2,000	...	1,000	2,800	7,500
Various . . .	3,600	1,900	300	...	3,500	20,400	29,700
Total . .	30,500	27,000	17,900	16,700	16,600	52,100	160,800

The following is a general summary of all strikes in the State of Massachusetts between 1825 and 1886 :—

Trade	Number	Locality	Number
Textiles . . .	59	Boston . . .	35
Shoemakers . .	34	Lynn . . .	14
Builders . . .	10	Lowell . . .	10
Various . . .	56	Various . . .	90
Total .	159	Total .	159

The causes and results were as follows :—

For		Result	
Better wages . .	118	Successful . . .	24
Shorter hours . .	24	Unsuccessful . .	109
Various causes . .	17	Compromised . .	26
Total .	159		159

The loss caused in Massachusetts by strikes to employers and operatives in the several trades during the said six years (1881–86) was as follows :—

Trade	To Employers	To Operatives	Total
	£	£	£
Shoes	100,000	330,000	430,000
Woollen-mills .	105,000	170,000	275,000
Cotton-mills . .	15,000	130,000	145,000
Building . . .	90,000	50,000	140,000
Indiarubber . .	30,000	30,000	60,000
Sundries . . .	70,000	160,000	230,000
Total . .	410,000	870,000	1,280,000

If the losses in Massachusetts be on a par with those of the other States according to the number of hands on strike and of those involved in lockouts, the total for the Union would be as follows :—

	Aggregate Loss in Strikes of Six Years			Loss in Lockouts
	To Employers	To Operatives	Total	
	£	£	£	£
Massachusetts	410,000	870,000	1,280,000	315,000
Illinois . . .	950,000	2,060,000	3,010,000	470,000
New York . .	1,650,000	3,560,000	5,210,000	1,580,000
Pennsylvania .	1,400,000	3,070,000	4,470,000	360,000
Ohio . . .	540,000	1,160,000	1,700,000	170,000
Other States .	1,630,000	3,530,000	5,160,000	650,000
Total .	6,580,000	14,250,000	20,830,000	3,545,000

This shows a total supposed loss of 24 millions sterling, or 4 millions a year, in disputes between employers and operatives.

The loss caused by lockouts in the same six years was :—

Trade	To Employers	To Operatives	Total
	£	£	£
Shoes	27,000	110,000	137,000
Building . . .	63,000	5,000	68,000
Leather . . .	12,000	75,000	87,000
Sundries . . .	13,000	10,000	23,000
Total . .	115,000	200,000	315,000

TRAMWAYS

Statistics are wanting as regards most countries.

UNITED KINGDOM

The mileage and cost have been as follows :—

	Miles		Cost, £		£ per Mile	
	1880	1889	1880	1889	1880	1889
England . .	269	758	4,200,000	11,200,000	15,550	14,700
Scotland . .	50	81	800,000	1,300,000	16,900	15,500
Ireland . .	48	110	700,000	1,200,000	13,500	11,000
U. Kingdom	367	949	5,700,000	13,700,000	15,400	14,400

Traffic returns in 1889 showed as follows :—

	Million Passengers	Passengers per Mile	Receipts, £	Net, £	Ratio to Capital
England .	380	501,000	2,370,000	543,000	4.9
Scotland .	71	871,000	400,000	119,000	9.3
Ireland . .	27	249,000	211,000	51,000	4.2
U. Kingdom	478	503,000	2,981,000	713,000	5.2

According to Scott Russell, the cost of working tramways by compressed air (as at Nantes) is 5d. per mile, by steam 39d., and by horse 56d. per mile. He also says that a tramcar drawn by two horses on the level will require the following number, according to gradients :—

Gradient	Horses
1 in 75	4
1 in 37	6
1 in 25	8

The above returns show that the average fare in pence is 1.5 in England, 1.3 in Scotland, and 1.8 in Ireland.

GERMANY

Berlin has 80 miles of tramway, which carried 52 million passengers in 1888.

FRANCE

In 1889 there were 455 miles of tramway in use. The cost of construction was £5,650,000, or £12,000 per mile, and the traffic in 1888 showed :—

	£
Earnings	1,430,000
Expenses	1,160,000
Net product . .	270,000

This was equal to 4¾ per cent. on the capital cost. The Omnibus Co. of Paris has 13,700 horses, of which 10,200 are used for busses and 3500 for tramcars, being 15 for each bus and 14 for each tramcar.

UNITED STATES

The United States and Canada showed tramways thus :—

	1882	1890
Lines	415	957
Miles	3,020	8,820

The lines running in 1882 employed 35,000 men and 100,000 horses, carrying 101 million passengers monthly. The horses drew 18,000 cars, and consumed yearly 150,000 tons hay and 300,000 tons grain: they last four years. The value of tramways in 1890 was :—

	£
Horse trams . . .	12,200,000
Steam and cable . . .	11,600,000
Electric . . .	10,200,000
Total . .	34,000,000

BELGIUM

In 1888 there were 42 miles of tramway; traffic of year, 14,800,000 passengers; receipts, £199,000; net earnings, £61,000; cost of construction, £1,030,000.

HOLLAND

In 1882 the returns were :—

	Miles	Passengers	Receipts, £
Amsterdam . .	38	8,400,000	85,000
Rotterdam . .	12	4,100,000	31,000
Hague . . .	20	2,350,000	27,000
Various . . .	190	4,050,000	57,000
Total .	260	18,900,000	210,000

Returns for later years show :—

	1884	1888
Miles . . .	380	555
Horses . . .	...	1,023
Locomotives . .	152	214
Passengers . .	20,100,000	30,900,000
Receipts, £ .	267,000	282,000

SWITZERLAND

In 1888 there were 22 miles of tramway, worked by 5 locomotives and 260 horses, carrying yearly 6,300,000 passengers; receipts, £37,000; net receipts, £8200; cost of construction, £169,000, or £7600 per mile.

TRANSPORT

The following table shows approximately the weight of sea-borne merchandise yearly :—

	Tons Yearly				Ratio in 1888
	1861–70	1871–80	1880	1888	
Grain	4,375,000	10,072,000	10,530,000	13,600,000	9.3
Cotton	486,000	995,000	1,170,000	1,450,000	1.0
Wool	121,000	252,000	301,000	440,000	0.3
Meat	125,000	380,000	660,000	730,000	0.5
Coal	14,200,000	22,100,000	30,400,000	38,200,000	26.2
Iron	1,920,000	3,490,000	4,588,000	4,700,000	3.2
Sugar	1,260,000	2,086,000	2,350,000	2,600,000	1.8
Clothing	1,410,000	2,520,000	2,815,000	3,100,000	2.1
Coffee	346,000	452,000	527,000	630,000	0.4
Timber	16,170,000	21,215,000	23,550,000	25,400,000	17.3
Sundries	13,807,000	26,778,000	35,875,000	55,550,000	37.9
Total * . . .	54,220,000	90,340,000	112,766,000	146,400,000	100.0

The weight and value of sea-borne merchandise at various dates were approximately as follows :—

Year	Tons, Millions	Value, Million £	Value per Ton
1830	10	193	£19
1840	15	287	19
1850	25	438	17
1860	41	701	17
1870	71	995	14
1880	117	1,360	12
1888	146	1,490	10

The weight borne on canals and rivers was approximately thus :—

	Tons			Tons
U. Kingdom .	34,300,000	Canada . .	3,400,000
France . .	24,500,000	United States .	51,000,000
Germany . .	8,000,000		
Russia . .	8,600,000	Total .	137,500,000
Belgium . .	7,700,000		

The foregoing is an estimate as regards the United States, based on the fact that in 1880 the steamboats alone carried 25,500,000 tons merchandise, without counting flat-boats drawn by tugs.

The weight of merchandise carried by railways was approximately as follows :—

	Millions of Tons			
	1860	1870	1880	1888
United Kingdom . .	82	170	256	282
Continent	68	231	413	483
United States . . .	70	150	361	590
Colonies, &c . . .	2	11	40	75
The World	222	562	1,070	1,430

* These totals are equal to 65 per cent. of the aggregate annual tonnage of the port-entries of the world at the various periods (see p. 522).

It appears, therefore, that the annual goods traffic of the world daily, counting 310 days to the year, is as follows :—

	Tons
By rail	4,610,000
On sea	470,000
By canal	440,000
Total . . .	5,520,000

But as each sea-voyage may be assumed to last ten days, during which the merchandise is being carried, the real goods traffic of the world (allowing three days for canal traffic) averages daily as follows :—

	Tons
By rail	4,610,000
By sea	4,700,000
By canal	1,320,000
Total . . .	10,630,000

As regards passenger traffic, the following table shows approximately the principal sea-routes and their number yearly :—

Between	Passengers
Europe and United States . .	900,000
England and France . . .	650,000
Mediterranean and South America .	450,000
France and Algeria	240,000
Danube ports	1,650,000
Adriatic and Levant	280,000

The traffic between England and the Continent has been as follows :—

Year		Passengers
1842		109,000
1848		124,000
1889		730,000

Dover and Calais boats carry 360,000; Newhaven and Dieppe, 190,000; Folkestone and Boulogne, 115,000; Dover and Ostend, 56,000.

As regards railway passengers, see *Railways*.

TRAVELLERS

In 1870 there were 398,000 in Russia, including 237,000 Germans and 123,000 Austrians.

In 1879 there were 947,000 persons who visited Switzerland, of whom 350,000 were Germans, 210,000 Americans, and 160,000 Russians. See *Passengers* and *Transport*.

TRUFFLES

Perigord produces 1500 tons per annum, worth £1000 per ton; 90 per cent. are consumed in France.

TULIPS

One root of the "Viceroy" sold at Amsterdam for £2600, and when a law was passed against paying over £500 for a root, a "Semper Augustus" fetched £460, with a carriage and pair of horses. Holland has 600 acres under tulips, and exports the value of £110,000 per annum.

TUNNELS

Herodotus mentions a tunnel 8 × 8 feet, with a length of 1100 yards, to supply Samos with water; remains discovered in 1882. The Schemnitz tunnel, completed in 1888, was begun in the 18th century, at a height of 3000 feet over sea-level: the original contract was for £7 a lineal yard, but the works were suspended from

1795 to 1825, and again from 1835 to 1855; the cost has been one million sterling. The Channel tunnel was first proposed by De Gramond in 1867, in the form of a metal telescope 30 × 24 feet, to cost 7 millions sterling, and be completed in seven years. Hawkshaw took up the project in 1869, Bateman and Revy being associated in the plans. A company was formed in 1874; estimated cost, 3 millions sterling; length, 30 miles; opening, 14 × 14 feet; trains to go 40 miles an hour, each having 12 carriages with 400 passengers, and 20 waggons with 100 tons goods; estimated yearly traffic, 6,000,000 passengers and 1,500,000 tons goods. Parliament opposed the project, and the works were suspended in 1883.

The most remarkable tunnels are the following :—

Date	Tunnel	Length, Yards	Cost per Yard, £	Maker	Years in Making	Aperture, Feet
1827	Harecastle .	2,926	...	Telford . .	3	14 × 16
1835	Kilsby . .	2,070	154	Stephenson	...	27 × 24
1843	Thames . .	560	1,100	Brunel . .	11	38 × 22
1870	Mont Cenis	13,540	201	Grattoni .	13	10 × 8
1879	Baltimore .	10,800	...	...		
1881	St. Gothard	16,390	152	Favre . .	8	9 × 8
1884	Aarlberg .	6,720	220	Favre . .	20	...
1884	Hudson .	1,833	1,100	Richardson	4	18 × 18
1885	Mersey .	2,700	200	Favre . .	4	27 × 20
1885	Severn . .	...	...	Richardson	12	...
1886	Hoosac . .	7,900	...	...	16	24 × 9
1888	Schemnitz .	19,400	52	...	106	9 × 7

The following engines have been used for tunnels :—

Date	Inventor	Strokes per Minute	Date	Inventor	Strokes per Minute
1813	Trevethick	...	1873	Darlington	500
1853	Bartlett . .	...	1873	Ferroux .	...
1857	Sommeiller	400	1873	Ingersoll .	400
1863	Sachs . .	400	1875	Barrow . .	...
1868	Dubois . .	300	1875	Ullathorne	...
1868	François .	300	1876	Beaumont .	...
1869	Burleigh .	400	1876	Geach . .	500
1869	Ostercamp	220	1877	Jordan . .	...
1872	M'Kean .	500	1877	Schramm .	500

Brunton's borer has been found in late years to make 49 inches of tunnel per hour, with 7 feet diameter. The following table shows various methods :—

Tunnel	Feet Opening	Engine	Pressure, Lbs. Sq. Inch	Tons Excavated	Tons Daily
Thames . .	800	Brunel . .	...	45,000	12
Mont Cenis	81	Sommeiller	90	240,000	60
Airolo . .	70	M'Kean .	90	...	...
Schemnitz .	60	Sachs . .	60	45,000	15
Comstock .	140	Burleigh .	70	...	155
Hudson . .	324	...	...	52,000	80
Ronchamps	52	Dubois . .	67	...	...
Belmore . .	27	Darlington	50	...	3
St. Gothard	72	Ferroux .	90	265,000	102

The Channel and Mersey tunnels employed Beaumont's compressed-air borer. The cost of excavation was £13 per ton of clay in the Thames tunnel, £11 per ton of rock in Mont Cenis, and £9 per ton in St. Gothard.

U. AND V.

UMBRELLAS

In France the value of those made yearly is known, and if four francs be taken as the average price, the account will stand thus :—

Year	Makers	Umbrellas	Value, £
1830 . . .	160	1,800,000	280,000
1847 . . .	303	2,500,000	405,000
1882 . . .	890	7,500,000	1,180,000

The value of British umbrellas exported from the United Kingdom was :—

Year	£
1875	360,000
1889	610,000

London imports about 3,000,000 umbrellas from the United Kingdom, and one million from other countries. China exports a large number of paper-covered umbrellas.

VITAL STATISTICS

The following is a conspectus of births, deaths, and marriages in various countries, showing the average for ten years ending 1888, or the latest available group of years :—

	Births	Deaths	Surplus of Births	Marriages
England . .	890,000	521,000	369,000	202,000
Scotland . .	125,000	74,000	51,000	26,000
Ireland . .	117,000	90,000	27,000	21,000
U. Kingdom	1,132,000	685,000	447,000	249,000
France . .	923,000	844,000	79,000	282,000
Germany . .	1,722,000	1,177,000	545,000	357,000
Russia . .	3,790,000	2,733,000	1,057,000	695,000
Austria . .	862,000	674,000	188,000	175,000
Hungary. .	713,000	556,000	157,000	159,000
Italy . . .	1,074,000	813,000	261,000	224,000
Spain . . .	575,000	514,000	61,000	118,000
Portugal . .	155,000	110,000	45,000	33,300
Sweden . .	137,000	79,000	58,000	29,500
Norway . .	60,000	32,000	28,000	12,700
Denmark . .	65,500	38,500	27,000	15,200
Holland . .	147,000	91,000	56,000	30,300
Belgium . .	175,000	119,000	56,000	39,800
Switzerland .	82,500	61,000	21,500	19,900
Roumania .	198,000	137,000	61,000	41,600
Servia . .	90,500	52,000	38,500	21,200
Greece . .	46,000	32,500	13,500	10,200
Europe . .	11,947,500	8,748,000	3,199,500	2,512,700
Australia . .	121,500	48,000	73,500	25,800
Uruguay . .	23,600	10,300	13,300	3,400
Japan . . .	981,000	739,000	242,000	305,000

Under the title of *Births, Deaths, and Marriages,* detailed statistics will be found, showing the birth-rate, death-rate, and other important considerations bearing on vital statistics. The above table shows that there are in Europe 33,000 births and 24,000 deaths daily, or 16 births and 12 deaths a minute. It shows also that the ordinary excess of births over deaths in Europe is 3,200,000 yearly; but the increase of population is not more than 2,400,000, as the ordinary emigration is 960,000, the number of emigrants returning to Europe being under 200,000.

UNITED KINGDOM

The number of births, deaths, and marriages was as follows :—

Births

Year	England	Scotland	Ireland	U. Kingdom
1870 . .	793,000	115,000	150,000	1,058,000
1871 . .	797,000	116,000	152,000	1,065,000
1872 . .	826,000	119,000	149,000	1,094,000
1873 . .	830,000	120,000	144,000	1,094,000
1874 . .	855,000	124,000	141,000	1,120,000
1875 . .	851,000	124,000	138,000	1,113,000
1876 . .	888,000	127,000	140,000	1,155,000
1877 . .	888,000	127,000	140,000	1,155,000
1878 . .	892,000	127,000	134,000	1,153,000
1879 . .	883,000	126,000	135,000	1,144,000
Average .	850,000	124,000	142,000	1,116,000
1880 . .	882,000	125,000	128,000	1,135,000
1881 . .	884,000	126,000	126,000	1,136,006
1882 . .	889,000	126,000	123,000	1,138,000
1883 . .	891,000	124,000	118,000	1,133,000
1884 . .	907,000	129,000	119,000	1,155,000
1885 . .	894,000	126,000	116,000	1,136,000
1886 . .	904,000	128,000	114,000	1,146,000
1887 . .	886,000	124,000	112,000	1,122,000
1888 . .	880,000	123,000	110,000	1,113,000
1889 . .	885,000	123,000	108,000	1,116,000
Average .	890,000	125,000	117,000	1,132,000

Deaths

Year	England	Scotland	Ireland	U. Kingdom
1870 . .	515,000	74,000	91,000	680,000
1871 . .	515,000	75,000	89,000	679,000
1872 . .	492,000	76,000	98,000	666,000
1873 . .	493,000	77,000	98,000	668,000
1874 . .	527,000	81,000	92,000	700,000
1875 . .	546,000	82,000	98,000	726,000
1876 . .	510,000	74,000	92,000	676,000
1877 . .	500,000	74,000	94,000	668,000
1878 . .	540,000	77,000	100,000	717,000
1879 . .	528,000	73,000	105,000	706,000
Average .	517,000	76,000	96,000	689,000
1880 . .	529,000	76,000	103,000	708,000
1881 . .	492,000	72,000	90,000	654,000
1882 . .	517,000	73,000	89,000	679,000
1883 . .	523,000	77,000	96,000	696,000
1884 . .	531,000	75,000	87,000	693,000
1885 . .	523,000	75,000	91,000	689,000
1886 . .	537,000	74,000	87,000	698,000
1887 . .	531,000	75,000	89,000	695,000
1888 . .	511,000	71,000	86,000	668,000
1889 . .	517,000	73,000	83,000	673,000
Average .	521,000	74,000	90,000	685,000

Surplus of Births over Deaths

Year	England	Scotland	Ireland	U. Kingdom
1870 . .	278,000	41,000	59,000	378,000
1871 . .	282,000	41,000	63,000	386,000
1872 . .	334,000	43,000	51,000	428,000
1873 . .	337,000	43,000	46,000	426,000
1874 . .	328,000	43,000	49,000	420,000
1875 . .	305,000	42,000	40,000	387,000
1876 . .	378,000	53,000	48,000	479,000
1877 . .	388,000	53,000	46,000	487,000
1878 . .	352,000	50,000	34,000	436,000
1879 . .	355,000	53,000	30,000	438,000
Average .	334,000	46,000	47,000	427,000

Surplus of Births over Deaths.

Year	England	Scotland	Ireland	U. Kingdom
1880 . .	353,000	49,000	25,000	427,000
1881 . .	392,000	54,000	36,000	482,000
1882 . .	372,000	53,000	34,000	459,000
1883 . .	368,000	47,000	22,000	437,000
1884 . .	376,000	54,000	32,000	462,000
1885 . .	371,000	51,000	25,000	451,000
1886 . .	367,000	54,000	27,000	448,000
1887 . .	355,000	49,000	23,000	427,000
1888 . .	369,000	52,000	24,000	445,000
1889 . .	368,000	50,000	25,000	443,000
Average .	369,000	51,000	27,000	447,000

Marriages

1870 . .	182,000	24,000	29,000	235,000
1871 . .	190,000	24,000	29,000	243,000
1872 . .	201,000	26,000	27,000	254,000
1873 . .	206,000	27,000	26,000	259,000
1874 . .	202,000	26,000	24,000	252,000
1875 . .	201,000	26,000	24,000	251,000
1876 . .	202,000	27,000	26,000	255,000
1877 . .	194,000	26,000	25,000	245,000
1878 . .	190,000	24,000	25,000	239,000
1879 . .	182,000	23,000	23,000	228,000
Average .	195,000	25,000	26,000	246,000
1880 . .	192,000	25,000	20,000	237,000
1881 . .	197,000	26,000	22,000	245,000
1882 . .	204,000	27,000	22,000	253,000
1883 . .	206,000	27,000	21,000	254,000
1884 . .	205,000	26,000	23,000	254,000
1885 . .	198,000	25,000	21,000	244,000
1886 . .	196,000	25,000	21,000	242,000
1887 . .	201,000	25,000	21,000	247,000
1888 . .	204,000	25,000	20,000	249,000
1889 . .	214,000	26,000	21,000	261,000
Average .	202,000	26,000	21,000	249,000

INDIA

In 1887 the birth-rates and death-rates per 1000 of population were :—

	Births	Deaths
Bengal	24.7	22.7
North-West and Oude .	41.2	32.0
Punjaub . . .	38.8	26.9
Central Provinces . .	45.4	34.2
Lower Burmah . .	25.5	19.9
Assam	28.0	27.9
Madras . . .	29.3	21.8
Bombay . . .	34.8	28.8
Mysore	24.1	15.9

FRANCE

Births

Year	Males	Females	Total
1810 . . .	481,000	451,000	932,000
1820 . . .	495,000	465,000	960,000
1830 . . .	497,000	471,000	968,000
1840 . . .	489,000	463,000	952,000
1850 . . .	490,000	464,000	954,000
1860 . . .	490,000	467,000	957,000
1870 . . .	483,000	461,000	944,000
1880 . . .	469,000	451,000	920,000
1885 . . .	474,000	450,000	924,000

Deaths

Year	Males	Females	Total
1810 . . .	379,000	351,000	730,000
1820 . . .	367,000	402,000	769,000
1830 . . .	407,000	401,000	808,000
1840 . . .	406,000	403,000	809,000
1850 . . .	381,000	381,000	762,000
1860 . . .	393,000	389,000	782,000
1870 . . .	553,000	494,000	1,047,000
1880 . . .	443,000	415,000	858,000
1885 . . .	435,000	402,000	837,000

Surplus of Births over Deaths

Year	Males	Females	Total
1810 . . .	102,000	100,000	202,000
1820 . . .	128,000	63,000	191,000
1830 . . .	90,000	70,000	160,000
1840 . . .	83,000	60,000	143,000
1850 . . .	109,000	83,000	192,000
1860 . . .	97,000	78,000	175,000
1870 . . .	...	...	...
1880 . . .	26,000	36,000	62,000
1885 . . .	39,000	48,000	87,000

In 1870 the deaths exceeded the births by 103,000. The sterility of the French people in late years is ominous, the surplus of births over deaths being much less than half what it was seventy years ago.

Marriages

Year	Number	Year	Number	Year	Number
1810 . .	233,000	1840 . .	283,000	1870 . .	224,000
1820 . .	209,000	1850 . .	298,000	1880 . .	279,000
1830 . .	270,000	1860 . .	289,000	1885 . .	283,000

The returns for the latest years were as follows :—

Year	Births	Deaths	Marriages	Still-births
1886 . . .	913,000	860,000	283,000	43,600
1887 . . .	899,000	843,000	277,000	42,900
1888 . . .	883,000	838,000	277,000	42,100
1879–88 . .	923,000	844,000	282,000	43,500

GERMANY

Official returns are as follow :—

Births

Year	Prussia	Bavaria	Saxony	Wurtemburg	Duchies, &c.	Empire
1879	1,052,000	208,000	125,000	81,000	270,000	1,736,000
1880	1,029,000	203,000	123,000	78,000	263,000	1,696,000
1881	1,013,000	204,000	125,000	77,000	263,000	1,682,000
1882	1,036,000	202,000	127,000	76,000	261,000	1,702,000
1883	1,029,000	197,000	127,000	73,000	258,000	1,684,000
1884	1,051,000	204,000	133,000	74,000	264,000	1,726,000
1885	1,065,000	200,000	133,000	72,000	260,000	1,730,000
1886	1,074,000	200,000	137,000	71,000	264,000	1,746,000
1887	1,085,000	200,000	137,000	70,000	265,000	1,757,000
1888	1,091,000	197,000	140,000	69,000	264,000	1,761,000
Average	1,052,000	202,000	131,000	74,000	263,000	1,722,000

Deaths

Year					Prussia	Bavaria	Saxony	Wurtemburg	Duchies, &c.	Empire
1879	.	.	.	.	667,000	155,000	81,000	58,000	183,000	1,144,000
1880	.	.	.	.	693,000	152,000	87,000	56,000	185,000	1,173,000
1881	.	.	.	.	682,000	152,000	83,000	54,000	185,000	1,156,000
1882	.	.	.	.	700,000	153,000	86,000	54,000	184,000	1,177,000
1883	.	.	.	.	711,000	155,000	90,000	51,000	183,000	1,190,000
1884	.	.	.	.	718,000	154,000	95,000	53,000	183,000	1,203,000
1885	.	.	.	.	717,000	153,000	91,000	53,000	186,000	1,200,000
1886	.	.	.	.	743,000	154,000	96,000	50,000	191,000	1,234,000
1887	.	.	.	.	686,000	151,000	88,000	46,000	181,000	1,152,000
1888	.	.	.	.	665,000	156,000	87,000	50,000	185,000	1,143,000
Average	.	.	.	.	698,000	154,000	88,000	53,000	184,000	1,177,000

Surplus of Births over Deaths

Year					Prussia	Bavaria	Saxony	Wurtemburg	Duchies, &c.	Empire
1879	.	.	.	.	385,000	53,000	44,000	23,000	87,000	592,000
1880	.	.	.	.	336,000	51,000	36,000	22,000	78,000	523,000
1881	.	.	.	.	331,000	52,000	42,000	23,000	78,000	526,000
1882	.	.	.	.	336,000	49,000	41,000	22,000	77,000	525,000
1883	.	.	.	.	318,000	42,000	37,000	22,000	75,000	494,000
1884	.	.	.	.	333,000	50,000	38,000	21,000	81,000	523,000
1885	.	.	.	.	348,000	47,000	42,000	19,000	74,000	530,000
1886	.	.	.	.	331,000	46,000	41,000	21,000	73,000	512,000
1887	.	.	.	.	399,000	49,000	49,000	24,000	84,000	605,000
1888	.	.	.	.	426,000	41,000	53,000	19,000	79,000	618,000
Average	.	.	.	.	354,000	48,000	43,000	21,000	79,000	545,000

Marriages

Year					Prussia	Bavaria	Saxony	Wurtemburg	Duchies, &c.	Empire
1879	.	.	.	.	207,000	35,000	25,000	13,000	55,000	335,000
1880	.	.	.	.	208,000	35,000	26,000	13,000	55,000	337,000
1881	.	.	.	.	210,000	36,000	26,000	12,000	55,000	339,000
1882	.	.	.	.	217,000	38,000	27,000	13,000	55,000	350,000
1883	.	.	.	.	221,000	36,000	27,000	12,000	57,000	353,000
1884	.	.	.	.	226,000	37,000	29,000	12,000	59,000	363,000
1885	.	.	.	.	231,000	35,000	29,000	13,000	60,000	369,000
1886	.	.	.	.	232,000	37,000	30,000	13,000	60,000	372,000
1887	.	.	.	.	230,000	37,000	30,000	14,000	60,000	371,000
1888	.	.	.	.	233,000	38,000	30,000	13,000	63,000	377,000
Average	.	.	.	.	221,000	37,000	28,000	13,000	58,000	357,000

Still-Births

Year					Prussia	Bavaria	Saxony	Wurtemburg	Duchies, &c.	Empire
1879	.	.	.	.	45,000	7,200	5,300	3,100	10,400	71,000
1880	.	.	.	.	43,000	7,000	5,100	3,100	9,800	68,000
1881	.	.	.	.	42,000	6,900	5,000	2,900	10,200	67,000
1882	.	.	.	.	43,000	7,000	5,000	2,800	9,200	67,000
1883	.	.	.	.	42,000	6,900	4,900	2,700	9,500	66,000
1884	.	.	.	.	43,000	7,200	5,100	2,900	9,800	68,000
1885	.	.	.	.	44,000	7,000	5,100	2,800	10,100	69,000
1886	.	.	.	.	44,000	6,800	5,300	2,800	9,100	68,000
1887	.	.	.	.	44,000	6,900	5,300	2,500	9,300	68,000
1888	.	.	.	.	43,000	6,600	5,500	2,500	9,400	67,000
Average	.	.	.	.	43,000	7,000	5,100	2,800	9,700	68,000

RUSSIA

Official returns are as follows :—

Year	Births	Deaths	Marriages	Surplus of Births
1856 . . .	2,706,900	2,146,900	557,100	560,000
1863 . . .	3,045,000	2,308,000	577,300	737,000
1876 . . .	3,549,000	2,443,000	590,000	1,106,000
1877 . . .	3,531,000	2,451,000	527,000	1,080,000
1878 . . .	3,418,000	2,760,000	665,000	658,000
1879 . . .	3,662,000	2,541,000	743,000	1,121,000
1880 . . .	3,669,000	2,658,000	702,000	1,011,000
1881 . . .	3,678,000	2,633,000	769,000	1,045,000
1882 . . .	3,906,000	3,034,000	716,000	872,000
1883 . . .	3,881,000	2,879,000	733,000	1,002,000
1884 . . .	4,336,000	2,857,000	754,000	1,479,000
1885 . . .	4,266,000	3,071,000	747,000	1,195,000
1876-85 . .	3,790,000	2,733,000	695,000	1,057,000

The above is only European Russia, exclusive of Poland, Finland, &c.

The following table shows the births and deaths of the whole Empire in 1887 :—

	Births	Deaths	Surplus of Births
Russia .	3,942,000	2,742,000	1,200,000
Poland .	329,000	202,000	127,000
Finland (1886) .	79,000	50,000	29,000
Siberia .	212,000	150,000	62,000
Caucasus .	268,000	172,000	96,000
Turkestan .	52,000	42,000	10,000
Total .	4,882,000	3,358,000	1,524,000

Exclusive of the Asiatic provinces, Russia has an increase of 1,300,000 souls yearly.

AUSTRIA

The official returns for ten years ending 1887 were :—

Births

Year	Austria	Hungary	Total
1878 . . .	855,000	665,000	1,520,000
1879 . . .	857,000	714,000	1,571,000
1880 . . .	829,000	672,000	1,501,000
1881 . . .	833,000	677,000	1,510,000
1882 . . .	874,000	697,000	1,571,000
1883 . . .	859,000	719,000	1,578,000
1884 . . .	878,000	741,000	1,619,000
1885 . . .	861,000	737,000	1,598,000
1886 . . .	876,000	760,000	1,636,000
1887 . . .	889,000	744,000	1,633,000
Average . .	862,000	713,000	1,575,000

Deaths

Year	Austria	Hungary	Total
1878 . . .	684,000	586,000	1,270,000
1879 . . .	652,000	566,000	1,218,000
1880 . . .	654,000	593,000	1,247,000
1881 . . .	677,000	553,000	1,230,000
1882 . . .	687,000	572,000	1,259,000
1883 . . .	677,000	527,000	1,204,000
1884 . . .	667,000	515,000	1,182,000
1885 . . .	689,000	536,000	1,225,000
1886 . . .	678,000	540,000	1,218,000
1887 . . .	672,000	569,000	1,241,000
Average . .	674,000	556,000	1,230,000

Surplus of Births over Deaths

Year	Austria	Hungary	Total
1878 . . .	171,000	79,000	250,000
1879 . . .	205,000	148,000	353,000
1880 . . .	175,000	79,000	254,000
1881 . . .	156,000	124,000	280,000
1882 . . .	187,000	125,000	312,000
1883 . . .	182,000	192,000	374,000
1884 . . .	211,000	226,000	437,000
1885 . . .	187,000	201,000	388,000
1886 . . .	198,000	220,000	418,000
1887 . . .	217,000	175,000	392,000
Average . .	188,000	157,000	345,000

Marriages

Year	Austria	Hungary	Total
1878 . . .	164,000	147,000	311,000
1879 . . .	169,000	162,000	331,000
1880 . . .	167,000	144,000	311,000
1881 . . .	177,000	158,000	335,000
1882 . . .	183,000	164,000	347,000
1883 . . .	176,000	168,000	344,000
1884 . . .	179,000	167,000	346,000
1885 . . .	175,000	165,000	340,000
1886 . . .	180,000	161,000	341,000
1887 . . .	182,000	152,000	334,000
Average . .	175,000	159,000	334,000

Still-Births

Year	Austria	Hungary	Total
1878 . . .	21,500	9,400	30,900
1879 . . .	22,500	10,800	33,300
1880 . . .	22,000	10,400	32,400
1881 . . .	22,500	10,900	33,400
1882 . . .	24,000	11,300	35,300
1883 . . .	23,800	12,300	36,100
1884 . . .	24,500	12,700	37,200
1885 . . .	24,500	13,100	37,600
1886 . . .	24,900	13,600	38,500
1887 . . .	26,100	13,800	39,900
Average . .	23,600	11,800	35,400

ITALY

Official returns come down to 1887, and show thus for ten years :—

Year	Births	Deaths	Surplus of Births	Marriages	Still-Births
1878 . .	1,012,000	814,000	198,000	200,000	31,300
1879 . .	1,064,000	837,000	227,000	213,000	33,600
1880 . .	958,000	870,000	88,000	197,000	30,400
1881 . .	1,081,000	784,000	297,000	230,000	35,300
1882 . .	1,061,000	787,000	274,000	224,000	35,400
1883 . .	1,071,000	794,000	277,000	232,000	37,200
1884 . .	1,131,000	780,000	351,000	240,000	38,300
1885 . .	1,126,000	787,000	339,000	234,000	39,300
1886 . .	1,087,000	845,000	242,000	233,000	39,200
1887 . .	1,153,000	829,000	324,000	236,000	42,500
Average .	1,074,000	813,000	261,000	224,000	36,300

SPAIN

Vital statistics are neglected and much in arrear :—

Year	Births	Deaths	Surplus of Births	Marriages
1868 . . .	580,000	549,000	31,000	112,000
1869 . . .	602,000	551,000	51,000	137,000
1870 . . .	600,000	510,000	90,000	106,000
1884 . . .	518,000	444,000	74,000	...
Average . .	575,000	514,000	61,000	118,000

PORTUGAL

According to the official returns we find :—

Year	Births	Deaths	Surplus of Births	Marriages
1873 . . .	148,000	116,000	32,000	32,100
1874 . . .	153,000	117,000	36,000	33,300
1875 . . .	154,000	107,000	47,000	33,100
1886 . . .	156,000	99,000	57,000	33,700
1887 . . .	166,000	109,000	57,000	34,300
Average . .	155,000	110,000	45,000	33,300

SWEDEN

Year	Births	Deaths	Surplus of Births	Marriages	Still-Births
1879 . .	139,000	77,000	62,000	28,600	4,200
1880 . .	134,000	83,000	51,000	28,900	4,000
1881 . .	133,000	81,000	52,000	28,300	3,900
1882 . .	134,000	79,000	55,000	29,000	3,800
1883 . .	133,000	79,000	54,000	29,400	3,700
1884 . .	139,000	81,000	58,000	30,200	3,800
1885 . .	137,000	83,000	54,000	30,900	4,000
1886 . .	140,000	78,000	62,000	30,100	4,000
1887 . .	140,000	76,000	64,000	29,500	3,900
1888 . .	136,000	76,000	60,000	28,100	3,800
Average .	137,000	79,000	58,000	29,500	3,900

NORWAY

Year	Births	Deaths	Surplus of Births	Marriages	Still-Births
1879 . .	61,000	29,000	32,000	12,900	2,200
1880 . .	59,000	31,000	28,000	12,800	2,100
1881 . .	58,000	32,000	26,000	12,300	2,000
1882 . .	59,000	35,000	24,000	12,900	1,900
1883 . .	59,000	33,000	26,000	12,700	1,800
1884 . .	60,000	32,000	28,000	13,300	1,800
1885 . .	61,000	32,000	29,000	13,000	1,800
1886 . .	61,000	32,000	29,000	12,800	1,800
1887 . .	61,000	32,000	29,000	12,500	1,700
1888 . .	61,000	34,000	27,000	12,200	1,800
Average .	60,000	32,000	28,000	12,700	1,900

DENMARK

Year	Births	Deaths	Surplus of Births	Marriages	Still-Births
1879 . .	62,000	39,000	23,000	14,300	1,900
1880 . .	63,000	40,000	23,000	15,000	1,900
1881 . .	64,000	36,000	28,000	15,500	2,000
1882 . .	65,000	39,000	26,000	15,500	1,900
1883 . .	64,000	37,000	27,000	15,600	1,900
1884 . .	68,000	38,000	30,000	16,000	1,900
1885 . .	67,000	37,000	30,000	15,600	2,100
1886 . .	68,000	38,000	30,000	14,800	2,100
1887 . .	67,000	39,000	28,000	14,700	2,000
1888 . .	67,000	42,000	25,000	15,100	1,800
Average .	65,500	38,500	27,000	15,200	1,940

HOLLAND

Year	Births	Deaths	Surplus of Births	Marriages	Still-Births
1879 . .	147,000	90,000	57,000	30,700	8,100
1880 . .	144,000	95,000	49,000	30,300	7,500
1881 . .	143,000	88,000	55,000	29,800	7,700
1882 . .	146,000	86,000	60,000	29,600	7,400
1883 . .	144,000	92,000	52,000	29,800	7,700
1884 . .	148,000	94,000	54,000	30,500	7,600
1885 . .	148,000	90,000	58,000	29,900	7,800
1886 . .	151,000	95,000	56,000	30,300	7,800
1887 . .	149,000	87,000	62,000	30,900	7,700
1888 . .	151,000	91,000	60,000	30,900	7,800
Average .	147,000	91,000	56,000	30,300	7,710

BELGIUM

Official returns from 1831 to 1887 show as follows:—

Period	Births	Deaths	Surplus of Births	Marriages
1831–40 . .	140,000	108,000	32,000	30,200
1841–50 . .	130,000	104,000	26,000	29,000
1851–60 . .	137,000	102,000	35,000	33,600
1861–70 . .	155,000	114,000	41,000	36,100
1871–80 . .	172,000	120,000	52,000	38,900
1881–87 . .	175,000	118,000	57,000	39,900

SWITZERLAND

Year	Births	Deaths	Surplus of Births	Marriages	Still-Births
1879 . .	86,000	64,000	22,000	19,500	3,500
1880 . .	84,000	62,000	22,000	19,400	3,200
1881 . .	85,000	64,000	21,000	19,400	3,400
1882 . .	83,000	63,000	20,000	19,400	3,300
1883 . .	82,000	59,000	23,000	19,700	3,200
1884 . .	82,000	58,000	24,000	19,800	3,200
1885 . .	80,000	62,000	18,000	20,100	3,200
1886 . .	81,000	60,000	21,000	20,100	3,400
1887 . .	81,000	59,000	22,000	20,600	3,400
1888 . .	81,000	58,000	23,000	20,700	3,300
Average .	82,500	61,000	21,500	19,900	3,300

ROUMANIA

Year	Births	Deaths	Surplus of Births	Marriages	Still-Births
1879 . .	168,000	132,000	36,000	46,000	1,900
1880 . .	171,000	163,000	8,000	40,000	2,300
1881 . .	192,000	123,000	69,000	42,000	1,900
1882 . .	189,000	132,000	57,000	44,000	2,200
1883 . .	204,000	124,000	80,000	47,000	2,000
1884 . .	201,000	124,000	77,000	41,000	2,300
1885 . .	214,000	124,000	90,000	40,000	2,300
1886 . .	213,000	135,000	78,000	39,000	2,400
1887 . .	210,000	156,000	54,000	39,000	2,500
1888 . .	220,000	159,000	61,000	38,000	2,500
Average .	198,000	137,000	61,000	41,600	2,200

SERVIA

Year	Births	Deaths	Surplus of Births	Marriages	Still-Births
1884 . .	90,000	48,000	42,000	20,400	1,100
1885 . .	91,000	52,000	39,000	17,100	1,300
1886 . .	83,000	59,000	24,000	23,300	1,400
1887 . .	94,000	50,000	44,000	22,600	1,400
1888 . .	95,000	51,000	44,000	22,800	1,500
Average .	90,500	52,000	38,500	21,200	1,340
1868–77 .	56,100	44,700	11,400	14,700	...

GREECE

Year	Births	Deaths	Surplus of Births	Marriages
1864–73 . .	41,000	30,700	10,300	8,900
1880 . . .	41,300	30,300	11,000	8,500
1881 . . .	41,700	32,200	9,500	7,800
1882 . . .	43,200	32,200	11,000	11,200
1884 . . .	58,000	35,900	22,100	13,700
1880–84 . .	46,000	32,500	13,500	10,200

URUGUAY

Year	Births	Deaths	Surplus of Births	Marriages
1882 . . .	21,700	9,100	12,600	3,300
1883 . . .	22,300	8,500	13,800	3,400
1884 . . .	21,800	9,700	12,100	3,500
1885 . . .	23,800	9,700	14,100	3,700
1886 . . .	24,700	11,100	13,600	3,100
1887 . . .	25,100	12,000	13,100	3,400
1888 . . .	25,800	11,600	14,200	4,000
Average . .	23,600	10,300	13,300	3,400

AUSTRALIA (1888)

	Births	Deaths	Surplus of Births	Marriages
New South Wales .	38,500	14,400	24,100	7,800
Victoria . . .	34,500	16,300	18,200	8,500
Queensland .	14,200	5,500	8,700	3,300
South Australia .	10,500	3,800	6,700	2,100
New Zealand . .	18,900	5,700	13,200	3,600
Tasmania . . .	4,800	2,000	2,800	950
Western Australia .	1,500	700	800	300
Total .	122,900	48,400	74,500	26,550
1861 . . .	52,300	21,200	31,100	10,900
1871 . . .	74,200	24,800	49,400	13,500
1881 . . .	98,700	38,800	59,900	20,500
1887 . . .	120,100	47,600	72,500	25,100

JAPAN

Year	Births	Deaths	Surplus of Births	Marriages
1879 . . .	877,000	721,000	156,000	...
1880 . . .	884,000	603,000	281,000	...
1881 . . .	941,000	686,000	255,000	...
1882 . . .	923,000	668,000	255,000	...
1883 . . .	1,005,000	676,000	329,000	...
1884 . . .	975,000	705,000	270,000	288,000
1885 . . .	1,025,000	887,000	138,000	259,000
1886 . . .	1,051,000	938,000	113,000	315,000
1887 . . .	1,058,000	753,000	303,000	334,000
1888 . . .	1,073,000	753,000	320,000	330,000
Average . .	981,000	739,000	242,000	305,000

W.

WAGES

The earliest scale of wages is that fixed by the Emperor Diocletian, A.D. 303, for the whole Roman Empire, viz. :—

Wages Daily without Food, Pence English

Shepherd . .	10	Labourer . .	10	Painter . . .	30
Ass-driver . .	10	Mason . . .	20	Smith . . .	20
Baker . . .	20	Carpenter . .	20	Stonecutter .	25

The pay to a brickmaker was 12d. per 100; to a sheep-shearer, 8od. per 100; to a common schoolmaster, 30d. per month; to one who taught Greek or geometry, 100d. per month for each pupil; and a lawyer's fee was 600d.

The following is a table of international wages at three periods of the present century, reduced to English money (see Embassy Reports, 1869) :—

	Day Labour, Pence			Indoor Labour, £ per Annum		Female Labour, £ per Annum	
	1835	1865	1880	1835	1880	1835	1880
England . . .	20	26	30	12	20	6	9
Scotland . . .	16	25	28	9	18	5	8
Ireland . . .	8	14	18	5	10	2	5
France. . . .	15	20	25	8	12	3	6
Germany . . .	8	16	18	4	10	2	5
Russia. . . .	6	12	12	3	8	2	4
Austria . . .	10	16	20	8	12	2	4
Italy	4	8	10	2	6	1	3
Holland . . .	9	15	20	6	10	3	5
Belgium . . .	9	18	20	6	10	3	5
Scandinavia . .	8	...	14	4	8	2	4
Spain & Portugal	8	10	16	...	8	...	5
United States .	42	74	66	28	40	...	...

Tradesmen's wages in 1880 in various countries were as follows :—

	Shillings per Week						
	Great Britain	France	Belgium	Germany	Italy	New York	Chicago
Printer . . .	32	20	19	20	16	54	62
Painter . . .	32	21	18	16	19	54	38
Plumber . . .	33	23	25	15	16	62	66
Tailor . . .	25	21	17	15	18	58	50
Shoemaker . .	31	20	14	13	18	62	56
Carpenter . .	33	23	23	16	17	44	42
Mason . . .	35	17	25	15	15	56	33
Smith . . .	31	23	18	15	16	50	44
Tinsmith . .	28	18	20	16	15	50	44
Baker. . . .	27	23	18	15	16	...	42
Collier . . .	24	15	14	16	...	...	...

The wages of farm labourers by the week in various countries were :—

	1850			1870			1880		
	£	s.	d.	£	s.	d.	£	s.	d.
England . .	0	9	6	0	15	0	0	17	6
France . .	0	9	0	0	12	6	0	14	0
Germany . .	0	8	6	0	10	6	0	12	6
United States .	0	16	0	1	0	0	1	5	0

Young's table of wages in Europe is as follows :—

	Pence per Day				
	1830–39	1840–49	1850–59	1860–65	1872
Boilermaker . .	13	15	17	21	31
Cabinetmaker . .	13	14	17	20	28
Carpenter . . .	14	15	18	25	31
Chemical operator	12	14	15	19	23
Cutler	14	16	20	22	26
Dyer	14	16	19	21	26
Jeweller . . .	20	24	25	32	50
Mason	14	16	19	26	32
Papermaker . .	12	14	17	19	26
Pianomaker . .	18	21	26	32	50
Printer	22	25	25	34	50
Painter	19	22	26	33	40
Sawyer	13	14	17	21	28
Shoemaker . . .	11	12	14	17	25
Smith	12	14	19	21	26
Stonecutter . . .	17	20	24	32	45
Spinner	14	15	19	22	27
Tailor	11	12	15	18	26
Tanner	14	15	18	21	27
Turner	12	13	16	18	27
Average	13	15	18	22	27

An Italian economist compares a bricklayer's wages at various dates in three countries thus :—

Year	Pence per Day		
	France	Switzerland	Italy
1850 . . .	21	17	15
1857 . . .	24	25	17
1874 . . .	31	38	35

White's memoir gives the following scale of wages in England, France, and United States in 1825 (an asterisk signifies "with food") :—

	England		France		U. States	
	s.	d.	s.	d.	s.	d.
Carpenter, by day . .	4	0	2	6	6	0
Mason, ,, . .	4	6	3	0	6	8
Machinist, ,, . .	4	6	3	6	5	6
Cotton-spinner, by day .	4	0	3	6	5	0
Woollen-spinner, ,, .	3	9	3	8	4	6
Weaver, ,, .	3	0	2	0	3	9
Farm labourer,* month .	27	0	20	0	38	0
Housemaid,* week . .	3	0		...	5	0

Tailors' wages in various countries in 1880 were as follows :—

Shillings Weekly

Great Britain . .	25	Belgium	17
France	21	Italy	18
Germany . . .	15	New York . . .	58

The pay in European armies in 1880 was as follows :—

	£ Sterling per Annum		
	English	French	Italian
General . . .	...	660	600
Colonel . . .	1,000	280	280
Lieutenant-colonel .	320	220	210
Major	292	180	170
Captain . . .	212	120	120
Lieutenant . . .	118	80	90
Ensign	100	52	...
Sergeant . . .	36	15	...
Private	18	5	...

The wages in woollen mills in various countries in 1880 were as follows :—

	Shillings per Week				
	England	France	Belgium	Germany	U. States
Sorter . .	24	22	10*	5*	44
Carder .	24	11*	8*	8*	25
Spinner .	12*	11*	...	12	26*
Dresser .	24	16	12	7*	54
Weaver .	30	24	18	12	35
Fireman .	26	19	15	...	35
Carpenter	33	27	15	...	52
Engineer .	40	27	18	16	75

(The asterisk signifies female hands).

In 1880 was published the following table of relation between wages and food in various countries :—

	Shillings per Week			Ratio		
	Wages	Food	Surplus	Wages	Food	Surplus
Great Britain .	31	14	19	100	45	55
France . . .	21	12	10	100	57	43
Germany . . .	16	10	6	100	62	38
Belgium . . .	20	12	8	100	60	40
Italy	15	9	6	100	60	40
Spain	16	10	6	100	62	38
United States .	48	16	32	100	33	67
Australia . . .	40	11	29	100	28	72

UNITED KINGDOM

Year	Nominal Wage				In Weight of Silver				In Purchasing Value			
	Shepherd	Labourer	Woman	Boy	Shepherd	Labourer	Woman	Boy	Shepherd	Labourer	Woman	Boy
	£ s. d.	£ s. d.	£ s. d.	£ s. d.	£ s. d.	£ s. d.	£ s. d.	£ s. d.	£ s. d.	£ s. d.	£ s. d.	£ s. d.
1400 . .	0 16 0	0 12 0	0 8 0	0 6 0	1 17 0	1 8 0	0 18 6	0 14 0	5 18 0	4 8 0	3 0 0	2 4 0
1450 . .	1 0 0	0 16 0	0 12 0	0 8 0	1 18 0	1 10 0	1 3 0	0 15 6	6 10 0	5 0 0	2 10 0
1500 . .	1 6 0	1 0 0	0 14 0	0 10 0	2 0 0	1 11 0	1 2 0	0 15 6	7 16 0	6 0 0	4 4 0	3 0 0
1550 . .	1 10 0	1 6 0	0 16 0	0 12 0	2 0 0	1 15 0	1 1 0	0 16 0	8 0 0	7 0 0	4 4 0	3 4 0
1600 . .	1 16 0	1 12 0	1 0 0	0 18 0	2 0 0	1 15 0	1 2 0	1 0 0	6 0 0	5 5 0	3 6 0	3 0 0
1650 . .	4 0 0	2 10 0	1 12 0	1 4 0	4 0 0	2 12 0	1 14 0	1 5 0	8 0 0	5 4 0	3 8 0	2 10 0
1700 . .	5 0 0	4 0 0	3 0 0	2 10 0	5 5 0	4 4 0	3 3 0	2 12 0	10 10 0	8 8 0	6 6 0	5 4 0
1750 . .	6 10 0	5 0 0	4 0 0	3 0 0	6 16 0	5 5 0	4 4 0	3 3 0	10 0 0	7 15 0	6 6 0	4 15 0
1800 . .	16 0 0	12 0 0	8 0 0	6 0 0	16 16 0	12 12 0	8 8 0	6 6 0	16 16 0	12 12 0	8 8 0	6 6 0
1850 . .	25 0 0	20 0 0	10 0 0	8 0 0	25 0 0	20 0 0	10 0 0	8 0 0	25 0 0	20 0 0	10 0 0	8 0 0
1880 . .	36 0 0	30 0 0	15 0 0	10 0 0	36 0 0	30 0 0	15 0 0	10 0 0	36 0 0	30 0 0	15 0 0	10 0 0

In the Middle Ages the pay of fighting men was :—

		Old Money, Groats	Present Value, £ s. d.
Count	.	40	2 2 0
Baron . . .	.	20	1 1 0
Knight . . .	.	12	0 13 0
Man-at-arms . .	.	3	0 3 0
Cross-bowman .	.	1	0 1 0
Archer . . .	.	½	0 0 6

Artisans' wages in England have been approximately as follows :—

Year	Shillings per Week				
	Black-smith	Mason	Carpenter	Plumber	Cotton-spinner
1740 . . .	16	16	15	18	12
1780 . . .	17	17	15	18	12
1820 . . .	24	25	20	25	16
1840 . . .	21	23	20	22	18
1860 . . .	28	30	25	30	20
1880 . . .	32	35	30	35	24

Wages in cotton-mills, according to Ellison, have been as follows :—

	1839	1849	1859	1887
	69 Hours	60 Hours		57 Hours
	s. d.	s. d.	s. d.	s. d.
Scutcher . . .	7 0	7 6	8 0	13 0
Stripper . . .	11 0	12 0	14 0	17 0
Overlooker . .	25 0	28 0	28 0	44 0
Mule-minder .	16 0	18 0	20 0	31 0
Piecer . . .	8 0	9 0	10 0	15 0
Spinner . . .	4 0	4 6	5 0	11 0
Winder . . .	9 0	9 6	9 6	15 0
Sizer	23 0	23 0	25 0	35 0
Weaver . . .	13 0	13 0	15 0	17 0

In 1886 Giffen gave the following factory averages :—

	Wages, Shillings Weekly		
	Cotton	Woollen	Linen
Men . . .	25.2	23.2	19.7
Women . .	15.2	13.2	8.9
Boys . . .	9.3	8.5	6.2
Girls . . .	6.8	7.4	4.9

Arthur Young found the weekly wages in 1768 thus:—

	£ s. d.		£ s. d.
Farm labourer . .	0 7 0	Cutler	0 14 0
Woman labourer .	0 3 0	Weaver	0 7 6
Collier	0 15 0	Woman do. . . .	0 4 7

Dr. Giffen gives the following table of agricultural wages in 1835 and 1885 per week :—

	1835	1885
	£ s. d.	£ s. d.
Surrey	0 10 6	0 16 0
Sussex	0 10 7	0 14 0
Essex	0 10 0	0 13 6
Dorset	0 7 6	0 12 6
Warwick . . .	0 10 0	0 16 0
Cheshire . . .	0 13 0	0 15 6
York	0 12 0	0 17 6
Wales	0 7 6	0 14 6
Scotland . . .	0 9 6	0 16 6
Ireland	0 4 6	0 8 0

In 1881 was published the following comparison between the wages of cotton-mill operatives in Great Britain and those in the United States :—

	Shillings per Week				
	England	United States		England	United States
Sizers . .	36	40	Cardboys .	14	10
Weavers .	30	35	Doffers . .	15	16
Pickers . .	15	28	Warpers . .	15	16
Strippers . .	17	28	Winders . .	15	16

In 1867 Leone Levi summed up the earnings of the working classes as follows :—

	Millions Sterling per Annum			
	England	Scotland	Ireland	United Kingdom
Agriculture . . .	44	8	23	75
Textiles	33	6	8	47
Building	35	4	4	43
Clothing	21	5	7	33
Metals	27	3	2	32
Ships and railways	25	2	1	28
Mines	13	2	...	15
Servants	47	5	8	60
Various	66	8	12	86
Total . .	311	43	65	419

In 1884 he published a second table in which he compared the earnings with 1867 thus :—

	Per Head, £		Total, Millions £	
	1867	1884	1867	1884
Males under 20 . .	19	18	23	29
Females ,, . .	20	23	27	30
Males over 20 . .	50	56	294	363
Females ,, . .	29	37	75	99
General average . .	38	43	419	521

The wages of able-bodied seamen, according to the *Year-Book of Commerce*, averaged as follows :—

Voyage	Shillings per Month					
	1860	1865	1870	1875	1880	1889
Mediterranean .	55	55	52	70	55	60
North America .	55	50	55	70	50	60
South America .	50	50	50	65	50	60
Africa	55	50	50	65	53	60
India	50	50	50	65	50	60
Australia . . .	50	50	50	65	50	60
Average . . .	53	51	51	67	51	60

The above were the rates in sailing vessels, the pay in steamers being usually 10s. a month higher.

From miscellaneous statistics published by the Board of Trade, the wages in 1880 appear as follows :—

Trade	Locality	Shillings Weekly	Hours per Week
Bookbinding . .	Edinburgh	24	54
Builders . . .	London	25	52
,, . . .	Portsmouth	21	56
,, . . .	Bristol	21	54
,, . . .	Liverpool	22	50
,, . . .	Sheffield	20	48
,, . . .	Edinburgh	20	48
,, . . .	Glasgow	18	48
Chandlery . . .	London	22	...
,, . . .	Bristol	21	64
,, . . .	Liverpool	21	54
Chemical . . .	Liverpool	18	54
,, . . .	Manchester	20	60
Coachbuilding . .	London	23	...
,, . . .	Liverpool	20	56
,, . . .	Dublin	16	58
Colliery	Stafford	20	54
,, . . .	Glasgow	18	57
Cotton-mills . .	Manchester	19	...

Trade	Locality	Shillings Weekly	Hours per Week
Cotton-mills . .	Glasgow	16	56
Foundry . . .	Birmingham	18	54
,, . . .	Wolverhampton	18	60
,, . . .	Nottingham	19	54
,, . . .	Manchester	18	54
,, . . .	Sheffield	19	54
,, . . .	Cleveland	19	60
Gasworks . . .	London	25	...
,, . . .	Bristol	21	70
,, . . .	Birmingham	20	54
,, . . .	Liverpool	21	56
,, . . .	Manchester	20	60
,, . . .	Edinburgh	20	...
,, . . .	Dublin	18	56
Hosiery . . .	Leicester	18	54
Jute	Dundee	15	56
Linen-mills . .	Dundee	19	56
Machinery . . .	Manchester	17	54
,, . . .	Glasgow	17	54
,, . . .	Birmingham	18	54
Paper-mills . .	London	21	60
,, . .	Manchester	19	60
,, . .	Edinburgh	15	60
Porcelain . . .	Stafford	15	...
Screws	Birmingham	24	54
Shipbuilding . .	Glasgow	16	54
,, . .	Liverpool	21	54
,, . .	Hull	19	54
,, . .	Dundee	16	54
Sugar	London	25	59
,, ...	Bristol	17	59
,, ...	Greenock	17	60
Twine	London	20	54
,, ...	Liverpool	20	60
,, ...	Greenock	18	56
,, ...	Dundee	18	56
Woollen-mills .	Stroud	15	56
,, .	Huddersfield	20	56

In 1882 the ordinary wages in piece-work for army-clothing were as follows :—

		Pence			Pence
Tunic		38	Dozen caps . .		30
Trousers . . .		14	,, towels . .		4
Frock		22	,, belts . .		12

A good worker earns 4s. daily.

The wages of a collier in 1884 averaged 49d. daily, being exactly the same as in 1870, but the output of coal rose in the interval from 230 to 318 tons per miner; thus the cost of extracting a ton of coal was 46d. in 1884, against 65d. in 1870.

FRANCE

Wages in the 13th and 14th centuries, reduced to the same weight of silver in English money of to-day, were as follows per month :—

	£ s. d.		£ s. d.
Archer	0 15 0	Field-marshal .	15 0 0
Baker	0 9 0	Footman . . .	0 5 0
Blacksmith . . .	0 8 0	Gardener . . .	0 18 0
Butler, king's . .	5 10 0	Knight	4 10 0
Carpenter . . .	1 5 0	Milliner . . .	1 2 0
Canon	4 0 0	Queen	800 0 0

In the 15th century they were as follows :—

	£ s. d.		£ s. d.
Archer	0 5 0	Physician . . .	15 0 0
Butler, king's . .	15 0 0	Secretary . . .	7 10 0
Chamberlain . .	20 0 0	Surgeon . . .	7 10 0
Chaplain . . .	15 0 0	Huntsman . .	30 0 0

De Foville gives the following wages in Paris from 1805 to 1875 :—

Trade	Pence per Day				
	1805	1810	1853	1866	1875
Bricklayer . . .	31	38	50	57	60
Carpenter . . .	29	31	48	57	57
Fitter	36	38	40	44	50
Glazier . . .	29	...	36	48	50
Joiner	33	30	38	43	48
Locksmith . . .	...	...	38	48	48
Labourer . . .	16	18	24	32	33
Mason	31	31	40	50	53
Navvy	21	21	28	38	38
Painter . . .	40	...	38	48	57
Plumber . . .	40	...	38	53	57
Slater	48	...	48	57	57
Smith	48	48	48	62	67
Stonemason . . .	32	33	48	53	53

The *Revue d'Economique* in 1887 published the following retrospect of wages :—

Year	Pence Daily	
	Rural	Operative
1768	6	9
1789	8	14
1825	12	17
1852	14	20
1872	19	29
1880	22	33

Another French economist gives the following table :—

	Average Daily Wages, Pence					
	1700	1750	1790	1810	1850	1880
Printer . . .	18	20	25	30	25	35
Painter . . .	15	18	20	35	22	33
Carpenter . .	15	18	20	35	22	35
Tailor	10	15	18	30	20	28
Blacksmith . .	15	18	20	30	25	35
Builder . . .	15	18	20	35	22	35
Bootmaker . .	10	15	18	30	21	28
Plumber . . .	15	18	20	35	22	33
Baker	10	15	18	30	20	33
Milliner . . .	6	8	9	10	13	20
Laundress . .	5	6	8	10	13	18
Farm-labourer .	8	10	12	18	20	25
Woman ,,	4	5	6	9	10	15
Boy ,, .	2	2	3	4	5	7

Wages of Women in France, Pence Daily

	1844	1853	1860	1872
Dressmakers . . .	12	17	19	19
Flowermakers . . .	15	24	22	28
Shirtmakers . . .	9	15	17	19
Staymakers . . .	10	15	19	19
Embroiderers . . .	15	19	19	28
Closers	15	24	19	28
Lacemakers . . .	15	22	24	28
Laundresses . . .	19	24	24	28

Wages of Miners Weekly

	s.	d.			s.	d.
1860 . . .	11	0	1875 . . .		16	6
1865 . . .	11	6	1880 . . .		16	0
1870 . . .	13	6	1886 . . .		15	6

Wages at Paris and in the departmental towns of France averaged as follows (without food) in 1885 :—

	Pence Daily			Pence Daily	
	Paris	Depart-ments		Paris	Depart-ments
Baker . . .	67	35	Hatter . .	62	35
Binder . .	53	30	Laundress .	38	18
Blacksmith .	67	37	Painter . .	72	36
Brewer . .	48	33	Plumber . .	57	36
Bricklayer .	77	35	Printer . .	62	37
Cabinetmaker	74	35	Saddler . .	43	33
Carpenter .	82	38	Sawyer . .	67	35
Confectioner	48	28	Shoemaker .	34	29
Cooper . .	48	33	Stonecutter .	82	38
Cutler . . .	57	31	Tailor . .	48	33
Dressmaker .	19	17	Tanner . .	48	32
Dyer . . .	43	31	Tinsmith . .	48	33
Fireman . .	57	34	Turner . .	48	34
Founder . .	67	37	Waggoner .	48	35
Glazier . .	53	31	Watchmaker .	57	40
Hairdresser .	29	27	Weaver . .	36	25

Other occupations showed the following yearly wages :—

	£ per Annum	
	Paris	Departments
Clerks	48	37
Lady-clerks . . .	32	25
Shop-girls . . .	20	20
Footmen . . .	24	18
Housemaids . . .	20	12

GERMANY

Yves Guyot gives the daily wages at Mulhouse in the spinning trade from 1835 to 1880 thus :—

	Pence Daily				
	1835	1845	1855	1865	1880
Overseers .	28	34	42	44	60
Enginemen .	18	22	30	27	34
Oilers . .	15	18	16	24	30
Scutchers .	9	10	10	13	17
Cardmenders	13	14	27	22	26
Throstlers .	15	15	16	17	23
Piecers . .	6	7	12	14	22
Doffers . .	...	...	9	10	16

The wages at Guebwiller silk-factory were as follows :—

	Pence Daily	
	1848	1880
Weavers	26	30
Warpers	19	23
Fluters	7	18
Winders	11	18
Folders	11	23

BELGIUM

Agricultural wages in Belgium at various dates were :—

Year	Pence Daily			
	Men		Women	
	With Food	Without	With Food	Without
1830 . . .	...	10	...	6
1840 . . .	...	11	...	7
1850 . . .	6	11	4	7
1874 . . .	11	19	6	12
1880 . . .	12	23	7	12

ITALY

Bodio's table of wages for certain trades, reduced to English money, gives the following :—

Trade	Shillings per Week			
	1817	1859	1866	1874
Iron mines . .	6	6	6	8
Marble mines . .	10	11	11	19
Chalk mines . .	6	6	9	10
Cotton-mill . .	7	7	8	10
Flax-mill . . .	8	10	10	12
Wool-mill . . .	6	7	7	8
Silk-mill . . .	6	8	8	10
Dyeing . . .	9	10	11	12
Tanning . . .	6	7	8	10
Stone-cutting . .	9	10	12	13
Foundry . . .	8	8	8	10
Masons . . .	7	8	10	14
Mechanics . .	7	9	11	17
Carpenters . .	10	13	16	19
Wheelwrights . .	8	8	9	11
Glass-blowers . .	18	18	22	22
Papermakers . .	5	5	6	6
Compositors . .	7	7	8	11
Tailors . . .	6	8	10	12
Brewers . . .	7	8	9	11

The aggregate weekly earnings of 20 operatives in the above occupations compared as follows :—

Year						Shillings	Average
1847	.	.	.	.	.	156	7.8
1859	.	.	.	.	.	174	8.7
1866	.	.	.	.	.	199	10.0
1874	.	.	.	.	.	245	12.3

Thus in 15 years, from 1859 to 1874, wages rose 41 per cent., but it would appear from the subjoined table that there has been hardly any perceptible rise since 1874.

Wages for a Working Day of 10½ Hours, in English Pence.

Year	Spinners	Weavers	Carpenters	Masons
1862 . . .	10.9	12.3	18.2	15.3
1863 . . .	11.4	12.7	18.2	15.3
1864 . . .	11.4	13.6	18.2	15.3
1865 . . .	11.8	14.5	18.2	15.3
1866 . . .	12.3	15.4	18.2	15.3
1867 . . .	12.7	15.4	18.2	15.3
1868 . . .	12.7	15.9	18.2	15.3
1869 . . .	13.2	16.4	18.2	15.3
1870 . . .	13.6	16.8	22.7	18.2
1871 . . .	14.5	17.3	22.7	18.2
1872 . . .	16.4	17.7	22.7	18.2
1873 . . .	18.2	19.1	22.7	20.5
1874 . . .	20.4	21.8	22.7	20.5
1875 . . .	20.4	21.8	22.7	20.5
1876 . . .	20.4	21.8	22.7	20.5
1877 . . .	20.4	21.8	22.7	20.5
1878 . . .	20.4	21.8	22.7	20.5
1879 . . .	20.4	21.8	22.7	22.7
1880 . . .	20.4	22.7	22.7	22.7
1881 . . .	20.9	22.7	22.7	22.7
1882 . . .	20.9	22.7	24.2	24.2
1883 . . .	20.9	22.7	24.2	24.2
1884 . . .	20.9	22.7	24.2	24.2

The ratio of increase is shown as follows :—

Year	Spinner	Weaver	Carpenter	Mason
1864 . . .	100	100	100	100
1874 . . .	180	160	125	134
1884 . . .	184	167	133	158

Professor Bodio's tables, comparing prices of wheat and maize with the average earnings of twenty-seven trades, and reducing these earnings to pounds of grain, may be summed up thus :—

Year	Day of Ten Hours			Days to Earn One Ton of Grain
	Wheat, Lbs.	Maize, Lbs.	Total, Lbs.	
1862 . . .	6.2	6.2	12.4	181
1863 . . .	7.5	7.5	15.0	148
1864 . . .	7.7	7.7	15.4	146
1865 . . .	8.0	8.0	16.0	140
1866 . . .	7.2	7.2	14.4	154
1867 . . .	6.2	6.2	12.4	181
1868 . . .	6.4	6.4	12.8	176
1869 . . .	8.6	8.6	17.2	130
1870 . . .	8.2	8.2	16.4	136
1871 . . .	7.0	7.0	14.0	158
1872 . . .	6.7	6.7	13.4	166
1873 . . .	6.8	6.8	13.6	163
1874 . . .	6.4	6.4	12.8	176
1875 . . .	9.6	9.6	19.2	116
1876 . . .	9.6	9.6	19.2	116
1877 . . .	8.2	8.2	16.4	136
1878 . . .	8.5	8.5	17.0	132
1879 . . .	8.8	8.8	17.6	127
1880 . . .	8.5	8.5	17.0	132
1881 . . .	10.5	10.5	21.0	106
1882 . . .	10.5	10.5	21.0	106
1883 . . .	12.1	12.1	24.2	93
1884 . . .	13.5	13.5	27.0	84
1885 . . .	13.7	13.7	27.4	82

UNITED STATES

Commissioner Carroll Wright, chief of the Washington Bureau of Statistics, has published a retrospect of wages, which may be condensed thus :—

Trade	Pence Daily					
	1770-1800	1801-20	1821-40	1841-60	1861-80	1881-83
Blacksmith . .	35	42	63	79	114	96
Bookbinder . .	...	...	46	72	96	75
Brewer . . .	...	...	...	101	107	122
Butcher . . .	17	31	46	...	101	68
Carpenter . .	30	55	74	85	121	120
Carriages . .	...	...	67	85	120	114
Clocks . . .	...	56	65	80	115	...
Clothing . . .	...	50	54	70	96	100
Cordage . . .	...	...	58	46	76	...
Cottons . . .	...	...	33	49	70	64
Glass	...	...	68	135	90	100
Harness . . .	...	44	60	77	...	...
Hats	...	...	...	115	98	84
Jewellery . . .	...	...	49	75	77	160
Labourers . .	24	43	42	46	74	66
Machinery . .	...	...	68	95	124	113
Masons . . .	42	73	65	72	140	107
Metals . . .	...	53	69	70	108	100
Millwrights . .	55	57	65	76	132	127
Nailers . . .	24	50	56	90	120	92
Painters . . .	...	62	64	83	116	98
Paper	...	54	35	50	85	85
Printers . . .	...	57	66	73	109	107
Shipbuilders .	45	63	68	125	125	162
Shoemakers . .	37	...	48	70	88	94
Stonecutters . .	...	...	65	71	117	100
Tanners . . .	...	50	65	70	104	93
Teachers . . .	70	95	...	...	115	...
Teamsters . .	...	...	58	68	72	88
Turners . . .	...	46	65	70	100	114
Woollens . .	...	...	53	44	66	62

Commissioner Carroll Wright compares the average wages in Massachusetts and Great Britain, from 1860 to 1883, in various trades as follows :—

Trade	Shillings Weekly		Trade	Shillings Weekly	
	Massachusetts	Great Britain		Massachusetts	Great Britain
Agricultural implements	43	37	Hats . . .	46	25
Boots . . .	48	21	Hosiery . .	28	20
Bricks . . .	36	17	Linen . . .	27	13
Building . .	62	32	Liquor. . .	53	80
Carpets . .	25	17	Machines . .	49	33
Carriages . .	57	35	Metals . . .	47	37
Clothing . .	42	30	Printing . .	48	28
Cottons . .	27	24	Printworks .	36	23
Food . . .	41	16	Stone . . .	60	42
Furniture . .	46	34	Woollens . .	29	23
Glass . . .	51	36	Worsted . .	30	18

He compares the wages of men only, as follows :—

Trade	Shillings Weekly		Trade	Shillings Weekly	
	Massachusetts	Great Britain		Massachusetts	Great Britain
Agricultural implements	44	37	Hats . . .	59	34
Boots . . .	57	30	Hosiery . .	38	27
Bricks . . .	36	23	Linen . . .	36	28
Building . .	62	33	Liquor . .	54	80
Carpets . .	33	25	Machines . .	50	33
Carriages . .	58	35	Metals . . .	51	44
Clothing . .	72	37	Printing . .	64	38
Cottons . .	40	31	Printworks .	42	33
Food . . .	46	23	Stone . . .	60	42
Furniture . .	46	34	Woollens . .	32	31
Glass . . .	62	40	Worsteds . .	36	25

The wages of women and children in 1860–83 are compared thus :—

Shillings Wages Weekly

	Women		Children	
	Massachusetts	Great Britain	Massachusetts	Great Britain
Boots . . .	36	15	19	11
Carpets . . .	23	15	17	12
Carriages . .	...	..	23	10
Clothing . . .	31	36	16	19
Cottons . . .	25	19	18	12
Food . . .	24	10	23	6
Furniture . .	25	...	23	...
Hats . . .	31	14	19	10
Hosiery . . .	25	16	23	9
Metals . . .	22	12	19	10
Printing . . .	26	12	19	10
Printworks . .	22	14	19	12
Woollens . . .	27	13	20	9
Linens . . .	21	11	16	6
Worsteds . . .	25	14	16	11

The average was for women 15½ shillings a week in Great Britain and 26 in the United States, and for children 10½ and 19 shillings respectively.

The following is a general average scale of wages at various dates :—

Wages Shillings Weekly

Trade	Massachusetts			Great Britain		
	1872	1878	1883	1872	1878	1883
Boots	61	50	48	23	19	18
Building . . .	64	52	62	27	23	30
Carriage . . .	70	58	57	27	30	20
Clothing . . .	51	40	42	24	15	26
Cottons . . .	33	32	27	22	20	19
Food	40	46	41	19	32	11
Glass	47	44	51	29	25	29
Linen	32	22	27	13	15	12
Machinery . .	56	42	48	28	20	29
Metals . . .	64	48	47	28	27	31
Printing . . .	53	56	47	28	27	23
Printworks . .	54	40	36	25	22	20
Shipbuilding .	66	49	84	28	25	33
Woollens . .	30	28	33	19	23	20

Atkinson gives the following wages for Massachusetts :—

	Shillings per Week				
	1840	1850	1860	1870	1880
Carder . . .	18	21	21	28	31
Dresser . . .	29	41	46	64	55
Dyer . . .	26	26	26	38	37
Labourer . . .	12	18	21	26	25
Mechanic . . .	25	31	38	38	40
Spinner . . .	21	28	31	42	40
Weaver . . .	18	21	18	27	31

The following table by Commissioner Wadlin, for Massachusetts in 1885, shows the percentage that wages stand for in cost of production in various articles :—

	Per Cent.			Per Cent.
Agricult. implements	38	Hosiery . . .	32
Arms . . .	30	Ink . . .	25
Boots . . .	25	Ivoryware . .	22
Bricks . . .	57	Leather . . .	14
Brooms . . .	33	Linen . . .	33
Building . . .	34	Liquor . . .	13
Buttons . . .	27	Lumber . . .	25
Carpets . . .	21	Machines . . .	47
Carriages . . .	46	Metals . . .	36
Cement . . .	32	Paints . . .	17
Chemicals . . .	9	Paper . . .	18
Clocks . . .	77	Printing . . .	39
Clothing . . .	23	Rubber . . .	25
Cordage . . .	14	Salt . . .	52
Cottons . . .	30	Silks . . .	30
Drugs . . .	23	Stone . . .	56
Dye-stuffs . . .	21	Tobacco . . .	35
Earthenware . .	66	Toys . . .	52
Electroplating . .	28	Trunks . . .	22
Furniture . . .	37	Woollens . . .	21
Glass . . .	62	Worsteds . .	21

Commissioner Wadlin's report gives in a classified form the wages of 248,000 operatives, which in English money show as follows :—

Weekly Shillings	Number			Ratio		
	Male	Female	Total	Male	Female	Total
Under 21	15,700	25,400	41,100	9.0	34.6	16.5
21–29 . .	20,300	28,200	48,500	11.6	38.3	19.5
29–37 . .	27,300	12,300	39,600	15.6	16.8	16.0
37–50 . .	43,600	5,500	49,100	25.0	7.5	19.8
Over 50 .	67,900	2,000	69,900	38.8	2.8	28.2
Total .	174,800	73,400	248,200	100.0	100.0	100.0

The following is a summary of the principal trades in 1875 and 1885 in Massachusetts; that is, the number of hands and the amount of wages (in gold) reduced to English money :—

	Hands		Wages Paid, £		Average, £ per Hand	
	1875	1885	1875	1885	1875	1885
Boots	48,000	64,900	3,700,000	5,600,000	77	86
Building	24,000	27,900	1,900,000	2,700,000	80	97
Clothing	13,700	18,300	1,000,000	1,200,000	73	66
Cottons	60,200	60,100	3,500,000	3,500,000	58	58
Food	4,700	11,500	500,000	1,000,000	106	86
Furniture	6,700	8,200	650,000	750,000	97	91
Leather	6,600	9,200	700,000	900,000	105	98
Machines	9,600	14,600	1,300,000	1,500,000	135	103
Metals	17,600	24,200	2,200,000	2,400,000	125	99
Paper	6,500	8,600	500,000	650,000	77	74
Printing	5,500	9,900	550,000	950,000	100	96
Printworks	3,200	8,600	40,000	600,000	125	70
Rubber	1,100	6,500	80,000	450,000	73	70
Woollens	19,000	19,000	1,200,000	1,200,000	63	63
Worsteds	1,500	8,000	100,000	500,000	67	62
Various	69,140	79,830	5,480,000	6,700,000	79	84
Total	297,040	379,330	23,400,000	30,600,000	80	81

The following table shows the average earnings per hour, and the number of hours of work, in the period 1860-83 :—

Trade	Pence per Hour		Hours Weekly	
	Massachusetts	Great Britain	Massachusetts	Great Britain
Agricultural implements	8.5	8.2	60	54
Boots	9.8	4.2	60	52
Bricks	6.7	...	64	...
Building	12.5	7.0	60	52
Carriages	11.5	4.5	60	54
Clothing	8.6	6.3	58	54
Cottons	5.4	4.2	60	56
Food	8.2	2.4	60	56
Furniture	9.3	7.6	60	52
Glass	10.2	...	60	...
Hats	9.2	5.1	60	54
Hosiery	5.4	4.3	60	54
Linen	5.4	2.6	60	54
Machinery	9.8	6.6	60	52
Metals	9.5	6.9	60	54
Printing	9.8	5.1	58	54
Printworks	7.2	4.6	60	54
Woollens	5.8	4.3	60	56
Worsteds	6.1	3.2	60	56

	Million Dollars				Per Operative, in £ Sterling			
	1850	1860	1870	1880	1850	1860	1870	1880
Virginia	5	9	9	11	35	50	49	41
Georgia	2	3	5	5	44	55	52	42
Kentucky	5	6	9	12	46	57	53	60
Tennessee	2	3	5	5	34	50	47	47
Louisiana	2	4	5	4	56	78	36	60
Various	4	9	12	15	44	52	48	50
South	20	34	45	52	50	57	45	47
Ohio	13	22	49	62	51	59	65	69
Illinois	3	8	31	57	50	53	69	75
Michigan	3	7	21	29	65	60	60	77
Wisconsin	2	4	14	19	65	55	56	67
Missouri	5	7	31	24	64	70	88	70
Indiana	4	6	18	22	58	60	57	70
Iowa	...	2	7	10	...	65	55	66
Minnesota	...	...	4	9	...	...	65	70
Various	8	38	35	38	58	60	63	70
West	38	94	210	270	58	60	64	70
The Union	235	382	785	951	51	58	69	73

We learn from the preceding table that the average wages for operatives have been increasing every decade. Three operatives in 1880 earned more than four did in 1850: they also produced more (see p. 379).

The ratio which wages bore to the value of goods manufactured was :—

States	1850	1860	1870	1880	Average per Cent.
New England	26	22	21	21	22
Middle	22	19	18	18	19
South	21	18	16	16	18
West	21	17	17	16	18
Union	24	19	18	18	20

The last four Census reports, down to 1880, give the following returns as to amount of wages paid (in gold) in all kinds of manufacturing industries :—

	Million Dollars				Per Operative, in £ Sterling			
	1850	1860	1870	1880	1850	1860	1870	1880
Maine	7	8	14	14	51	47	52	53
New Hampshire	6	8	14	15	46	50	60	65
Vermont	2	3	6	5	52	66	61	58
Rhode Island	5	9	19	21	50	57	66	67
Connecticut	12	19	39	44	51	60	75	78
Massachusetts	42	57	118	128	49	55	76	72
New England	74	104	210	227	49	55	72	70
New York	49	65	142	199	52	59	72	79
New Jersey	9	16	33	46	49	59	80	73
Pennsylvania	37	60	128	134	52	56	74	70
Delaware	1	2	4	4	50	60	70	62
Maryland	7	7	13	19	50	52	58	54
Middle	103	150	320	402	51	58	72	76

During the gold fever at San Francisco, daily wages were as follows :—

	s.	d.			s.	d.
Bricklayer	41	8	Tailor		16	8
Stonecutter	41	8	Hatter		29	2
Plasterer	37	6	Watchmaker		33	4
Glazier	25	0	Carpenter		41	0

Mr. Young published in 1870 the following scale of wages current in various States of the Union :—

	Maine	Massa-chusetts	New York	Pennsyl-vania	Texas	Louisiana	Illinois	California
	Wages Reduced to English Money, Shillings Weekly							
Blacksmith . . .	68	72	68	60	70	81	68	100
Bricklayer . . .	81	94	88	75	81	98	87	110
Cabinetmaker . .	66	68	68	50	68	68	65	95
Carpenter . . .	60	81	74	50	76	94	68	100
Cooper	63	78	65	63	75	75	63	93
Painter	67	70	75	63	75	82	68	100
Plasterer	81	92	90	78	80	94	80	114
Shoemaker . . .	61	65	60	63	64	70	60	95
Stonecutter . . .	84	98	94	81	105	100	87	110
Tailor	66	61	62	50	64	70	60	93
Tanner	66	68	68	50	68	75	65	98
Tinsmith	63	65	68	52	72	72	66	99
Wheelwright. . .	68	75	72	55	70	90	75	100
Farm labourer .	38	40	42	41	32	42	40	58

	New England	Middle	Southern	Western	General Average
	Wages Reduced to English Money, Shillings Weekly				
Blacksmith . . .	70	60	67	72	68
Bricklayer . . .	87	83	76	91	85
Cabinetmaker . .	72	61	65	69	67
Carpenter . . .	70	56	74	75	68
Cooper . . .	71	63	64	67	66
Painter . . .	72	66	70	74	71
Plasterer . . .	85	79	79	89	83
Shoemaker . . .	61	55	60	64	60
Stone-cutter . .	88	85	80	87	86
Tailor	65	58	61	65	62
Tanner	68	59	65	68	65
Tinsmith . . .	69	61	65	68	66
Wheelwright . .	72	63	72	75	71
Farm labourer .	42	37	29	41	37

Note.—The above wages were in paper money at 13 per cent. discount as compared with gold ; thus 80s. were in reality only 70s.

WARS

The wars of ninety years down to 1880 involved an expenditure of 3047 millions sterling, besides the loss of 4,470,000 lives, viz. :—

Date	Belligerents	Expendi-ture, Million £	Loss in Men
1793–1815 .	England and France .	1,250	1,900,000
1828 . .	Russia and Turkey . .	20	120,000
1830- 40 .	Spain and Portugal (civil)	50	160,000
1830–47 .	France and Algeria . .	38	110,000
1848 . .	Europe (civil) . . .	10	60,000
1854–56 .	England, France, Russia	305	485,000
1859 . .	France and Austria . .	45	63,000
1863–65 .	United States (civil) .	740	656,000
1866 . .	Prussia and Austria .	20	51,000
1866 . .	France and Mexico .	15	65,000
1864–70 .	Brazil and Paraguay .	48	330,000
1870–71 .	France and Germany .	316	290,000
1876–77 .	Russia and Turkey . .	190	180,000
		3,047	4,470,000

Period	Expendi-ture, Million £	Loss of Life	Per Annum	
			Million £	Loss of Life
1790–1820	1,250	1,900,000	42	63,000
1821–1850	118	450,000	4	15,000
1851–1860	350	548,000	35	55,000
1861–1880	1,329	1,572,000	66	79,000
	3,047	4,470,000		

British Wars.—In less than 300 years, Great Britain has expended 1359 millions sterling in war, viz. :—

Date	Locality	Expendi-ture, Million £	Commander
1599 . .	Ireland . . .	4	Essex
1642–48 .	England and Ireland	57	Cromwell
1688–97 .	Ireland and Holland	33	William III.
1702–63 .	Germany, Spain, &c.	182	Marlborough,&c.
1759 . .	Canada . . .	62	Wolfe
1775–80 .	United States . .	121	Cornwallis
1793–1815	France, &c. . .	831	Wellington
1854–56 .	Crimea . . .	69	Raglan
		1,359	

In the Crimean War, 97,860 men took the field, of whom 2755 were killed in action ; 18,280 were wounded, and of these 1847 died in hospital, and 17,580 died of disease ; total deaths 22,182, or 22½ per cent. of the total strength.

French Wars.—In 218 years France spent 993 millions sterling in war, viz. :—

Date	Reign	Locality	Expendi-ture, Million £	Commander
1654–1713	Louis XIV. .	Flanders,&c.	154	Turenne,&c.
1733–63	Louis XV. .	,,	82	Saxe
1778–83	Louis XVI. .	U. States .	22	Lafayette
1791–1815	Napoleon . .	Europe, &c.	255	Bonaparte
1830–47	Louis Philippe	Algeria . .	38	Bugeaud,&c.
1854–56	Napoleon III.	Crimea . .	93	Pellissier
1859	,,	Italy . . .	18	MacMahon
1866	,,	Mexico . .	15	Bazaine
1870–71	,,	Rhine . .	316	Lebeuf
			993	

In the Crimean war 309,400 men took the field, of whom 8490 were killed in action ; 39,870 were wounded, and of these 11,750 died in hospital, and 75,375 died of disease ; total deaths 95,615, or 31 per cent. of total strength. It is remarkable that 29 per cent. of the wounded died, and 30 per cent. of men admitted to hospital for disease, whereas the British lost only 10 per cent. of wounded and 12 per cent. of men admitted for disease. At the same time only 71 per cent. of the French army were admitted to hospital for disease, namely 225,000 ; whereas 147 per cent. of the British were so admitted, that is, the whole army nearly twice over during the campaign, such admission reaching 144,400, or 46,000 more than the total strength. The casualties of the

French compare with those of the other belligerents in the Crimea thus :—

	English	French	Turk	Russian	Total
Took field . .	98,100	309,400	165,000	888,000	1,460,500
Killed in battle	2,755	8,490	10,100	30,600	51,945
Died of wounds	1,847	11,750	10,800	42,000	66,397
Died of sickness	17,580	75,375	24,500	374,000	491,455
Total loss .	22,182	95,615	45,400	446,600	609,797

Shots Fired

By	Millions	Killed	Shots to Kill
English . .	15	21,000 Russians .	700
French . .	29	51,000 ,,	590
Russians . .	45	48,000 Allies . .	910
Total .	89	120,000 men . .	740

In the Franco-Italian war 128,000 French took the field, of whom 2536 were killed in action ; 17,054 were wounded, and of these 2962 died in hospital, besides 2040 who died of disease ; total deaths 7538, or 6 per cent.

In the Mexican war of 1862–66 there were 35,000 French landed in Mexico, of whom 1180 were killed in action ; 2559 were wounded, and of these 549 died ; deaths from disease were 4925, making a total of 6654, or 19 per cent. of total strength.

In the Franco-German war of 1870-71, 710,000 French took the field, and of these no fewer than 138,870 were killed in action or died in hospital, including 2977 officers. The death-roll of the French was, of men killed in action or died in hospital, as follows :—

In France	.	.	.	.	119,929
In Germany	.	.	.	.	17,240
In Switzerland	.	.	.	.	1,701
			Total	.	138,870

This includes 45,000 deaths from disease, but it is believed that many not recorded died of wounds, having gone to their homes. Deaths were at least 20 per cent.

German Wars.—The campaign of Sadowa, between Prussia and Austria, in 1866, showed as follows :—

	Prussians	Austrians	Total
Took field . . .	309,000	330,000	639,000
Killed	2,650	11,100	13,750
Wounded . . .	14,820	29,310	44,130
Missing . . .	3,304	43,750	47,054
Hors-de-combat .	20,774	84,160	104,934
Returned home .	288,226	245,840	534,066

The Prussians had one officer killed or wounded for 21 men, the Austrians one for 18 men.

In the Franco-German war of 1870-71 the casualties were as shown in the following table :—

	French	Germans	Total
Took field . . .	420,000	780,000	1,200,000
Reinforced . .	290,000	223,000	513,000
Total . .	710,000	1,003,000	1,713,000
Killed	41,000	19,782	60,782
Died of wounds .	36,000	10,710	46,710
Died of sickness .	45,000	14,259	59,259
Disabled . . .	116,000	89,000	205,000
Prisoners . . .	446,000	...	446,000
Hors-de-combat .	684,000	133,751	817,751

Killed and Wounded

	French	Germans	Total
Woerth . . .	32,000	11,000	43,000
Mars-le-Tour . .	26,000	16,200	42,200
Gravelotte . . .	28,500	20,100	48,600
Paris	30,000	13,300	43,300
Orleans, &c. . .	76,500	57,400	133,900
Total . .	193,000	118,000	311,000

The number of Germans killed includes 4010 missing, who are supposed to have been slain in action. The hospital records of the Germans showed that 127,870 wounded of their army were admitted, but only 10,710 died, say 8½ per cent. Deaths from disease included 6965 of typhoid fever. The minimum force in the field was 781,000 in August 1870, the maximum 937,000 in February 1871. The death-rate during the whole campaign in the different arms was :—

		Per 1000			Per 1000
Engineers .	.	17.6	Staff . . .	.	105.0
Cavalry .	.	27.1	Captains .	.	87.0
Artillery .	.	27.2	All officers .	.	76.0
Infantry .	.	52.8	Officers and men	.	45.9

The Germans fired off 30 million musket cartridges and 363,000 rounds of artillery, with which they killed or mortally wounded 77,000 French, being 400 shots to kill, as compared with 740 in the Crimean war (q.v.). See *Battles*.

Russian Wars.—The campaigns of the last sixty years cost 335 millions sterling and 664,000 men, viz. :—

Date	Reign	Locality	Expenditure, Million £	Loss in Men
1828 .	Nicholas . .	Balkans .	15	86,000
1854–56	Nicholas . .	Crimea .	142	447,000
1876–77	Alexander II.	Turkey .	133	110,000
1878–80	Alexander II.	Khiva, &c. .	45	21,000
52 years	...	...	335	664,000

American Wars.—According to Stedman, an officer under Lord Cornwallis, the strength of the British and American armies in the War of Independence was :—

Year		British	Americans
1776	. . . .	27,700	3,300
1777	. . . .	30,000	8,000
1781	. . . .	7,000	32,600

The British army consisted largely of Hessian and other soldiers bought in Germany by George III., and for whom the British Government paid the following sums to the German princes :—

	Men	Sum, £	£ per Man	Perished in the War
Hesse . . .	16,992	2,600,000	153	6,500
Brunswick . .	5,723	780,000	137	3,015
Anspach, &c. . .	6,451	1,747,000	275	2,328
Total . .	29,166	5,127,000	175	11,843

During the five years that the war lasted 288,200 Americans fought for their country, the States being represented by the following numbers :—

	Men		Men
Massachusetts . .	83,000	New Jersey . . .	17,000
Connecticut . .	40,000	New Hampshire .	15,000
Pennsylvania . .	33,000	Rhode Island . .	10,000
Virginia . . .	32,000	North Carolina .	7,300
New York . . .	21,000	South Carolina .	6,400
Maryland . . .	18,000	Georgia, &c. . . .	5,500

The American army, after the surrender of Lord Cornwallis, was found to number thus :—

49 regiments of foot	.	.	.	28,224
4	,,	horse .	.	1,536
4	,,	artillery	.	2,340
1	,,	pioneers	.	480
		Total	.	32,580

The total expenses of the war were 135 million dollars, say 28 millions sterling. In the second war with England (1812–15), the American army at one time counted 32,000 men under the colours. In the war with Mexico (1845), the Americans had 90,100 men, of whom 7780 died, including 6060 of disease, and the rest killed in action or who died of wounds received.

An official statement of the war for the Union in 1863–65 was as follows :—

Northern Army

	Officers	White Men	Coloured	Total	Ratio
Took field . .	84,000	2,073,000	179,000	2,336,000	100
Killed . . .	3,930	38,790	1,520	44,240	1.9
Died of wounds	2,070	30,890	1,046	34,006	1.5
,, sickness	1,720	121,110	26,200	149,030	6.4
Missing . .	1,600	60,910	4,614	67,124	2.9
Returned home	74,680	1,821,300	145,620	2,041,600	87.3

Kolb gives the following summary :—

	Killed	Wounded	Prisoners
Northerns . . .	43,573	132,265	87,481
Southerns . . .	26,720	101,843	78,731
Total . .	70,293	234,108	166,212

According to another account the Northern army lost:—

	Killed	Died of Sickness	Total
Officers . . .	5,221	2,321	7,542
Men . . .	90,868	182,329	273,197
Total . .	96,089	184,650	280,739

The Ordnance department served out 7892 cannon, 4,022,000 rifles, 2,360,000 equipments for infantry and cavalry, 12,000 tons powder, 42,000 tons lead, and 1022 million rounds of cartridge.

WATER

The weight of alluvial deposits to 1000 gallons of water is as follows :—

	Lbs.		Lbs.		Lbs.
Loch Katrine	¼	Danube . .	2	Wear . . .	16
Windermere .	½	Garonne . .	2	Ganges . .	22
Severn . . .	1	Rhine . . .	2	Cheltenham	134
Avon . . .	1	Mersey . .	3	Harrogate .	157
Tunbridge .	1½	Thames . .	4	Oxus . . .	250
Spree . . .	1½	Mississippi .	6	Seidlitz .	321
Geneva . .	2	Spa	14	Atlantic . .	448

A ton of water contains 224 gallons or 36 cubic feet, but sea-water is 2 per cent. heavier. An inch of rainfall gives 14,500,000 gallons of water to the square mile, or 22,500 gallons to the acre. Snow requires 8 cubic feet to produce one cubic foot of water. Current requires a minimum fall of one inch in 10 miles. The water-power of Niagara is 10,000,000 cubic feet per minute, equal to 3,000,000 horse-power. In 1880 the United States had 51,000 water-wheels with an aggregate of 1,500,000 horse-power.

Water supply has always been a matter of the highest importance. Rome, in the time of the Cæsars, had nine aqueducts, measuring 249 miles in the aggregate : they poured into the city 330 million gallons daily, or 160 gallons per inhabitant. The great aqueduct of Peru, built by the Incas, was 360 miles long. Among modern works the most famous are :—

Name	Miles	Million Gallons Daily	Cost of Work, £
Croton (New York) .	41	88	1,800,000
Madrid . . .	47	40	2,300,000
Marseilles . .	51	60	450,000
Glasgow . .	34	50	1,550,000
Washington . .	16	90	...

The supply of various cities is shown as follows :—

	Gallons Daily	Gallons per Inhabitant
Ancient Rome . . .	330,000,000	160
Modern Rome . . .	200,000,000	670
London . . .	145,000,000	38
Paris . . .	88,000,000	39
New York . . .	88,000,000	70
Chicago . . .	60,000,000	120
Sydney . . .	50,000,000	120
Glasgow . . .	26,000,000	48
St. Louis . . .	25,000,000	70
Marseilles . . .	18,000,000	50
Buffalo . . .	17,000,000	120
Manchester . . .	11,000,000	20
Liverpool . . .	11,000,000	20
Boston . . .	10,000,000	27
San Francisco . . .	10,000,000	42
Newark . . .	10,000,000	80
Edinburgh . . .	10,000,000	33
Dublin . . .	7,000,000	22
Melbourne . . .	7,000,000	25
Hamburg . . .	5,000,000	12

Artesian wells are of great antiquity ; they were known at Thebes 2000 years before the Christian era. In modern times that of Grenelle, near Paris, is the most famous, having taken eight years in boring, 1833–41 ; it gives 700,000 gallons daily, the water rising 32 feet above the surface, with a temperature of 81½° Fahr.

Well	Depth, Feet	Diameter, Inches	Gallons Water per Minute	Cost of Well, £
Grenelle . . .	1,798	3.74	484	14,550
Passy	1,923	27.60	1,980	40,000
Kissingen . .	1,880	4.00	600	7,000
St. Louis, U.S. .	2,200	...	...	2,000
Chicago . . .	700	...	820	...
Calais	1,138	...	...	3,560
Donchery . . .	1,215	...	...	3,045
Trafalgar Square	393	...	500	...
Lille	592	...	...	320
Algeria . . .	177	...	1,130	...
Elbeuf	492	2.95	66	...
St. Denis . . .	262	2.28	28	...

There are 78 of these wells in England, varying from 100 to 1000 feet. Several have been sunk in China more than 1000 feet, at a cost of only seven shillings per foot.

The water companies of London in 1880 showed : capital, £12,463,000 ; receipts, £1,460,000 ; expenses, £740,000 ; net profit, £720,000.

The water-supply of Paris in 1884 was as follows, daily :—

Aqueduct	55,000,000
Seine and wells . . .	33,000,000
Total . .	88,000,000

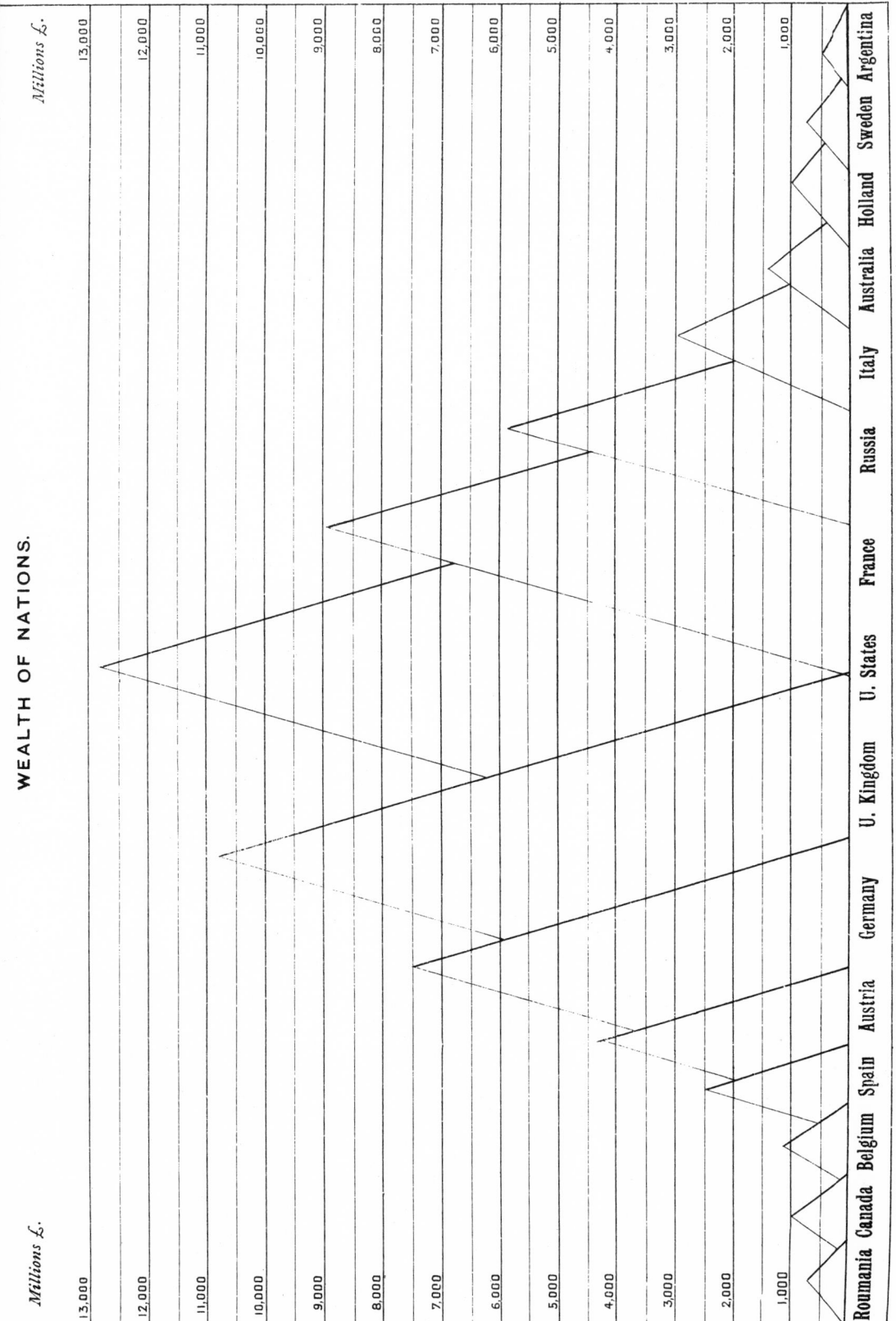

WEALTH OF NATIONS.

WEALTH

Various estimates have been made from time to time, by economists and others, as to the wealth of the principal countries and the ratio per inhabitant. Thus in a paper read at Bath in 1888, before the British Association, by the author of this Dictionary, the wealth of the United States was estimated at £212 per inhabitant, the census of 1890 afterwards showing that the real average was £216 per inhabitant, a difference of less than 2 per cent. The wealth of nations in 1888 was approximately thus :—

	Millions £ Sterling								£ per Inhab.
	Farms	Railways	Buildings	Furniture	Merchandise	Bullion	Sundries	Total	
United Kingdom .	2,287	865	2,420	1,210	690	120	3,208	10,800	300
France . . .	3,230	570	1,700	850	310	330	1,910	8,900	240
Germany . . .	2,500	495	1,560	780	360	170	1,635	7,500	160
Russia . . .	2,400	314	900	450	120	50	1,566	5,800	60
Austria . . .	1,730	307	640	320	100	30	1,073	4,200	105
Italy . . .	1,400	138	400	200	90	30	642	2,900	95
Spain . . .	1,200	94	340	170	60	40	596	2,500	150
Portugal . .	160	19	70	35	20	10	86	400	90
Sweden . . .	200	28	100	50	30	4	138	550	140
Norway . . .	80	7	30	15	16	2	50	200	100
Denmark . .	250	10	60	30	26	2	92	470	230
Holland . .	380	35	160	80	200	20	105	980	240
Belgium . .	445	71	160	80	110	20	124	1,010	170
Switzerland .	150	37	80	40	60	6	87	460	150
Greece . . .	133	6	30	15	7	3	46	240	90
Roumania . .	240	29	50	25	25	6	135	510	95
Servia . . .	105	6	20	10	4	3	32	180	85
Europe . .	16,890	3,031	8,720	4,360	2,228	846	11,525	47,600	180
United States .	3,600	1,950	3,200	1,600	320	235	1,915	12,820	210
Canada . . .	360	150	120	60	40	4	196	980	200
Australia . .	630	94	240	120	70	24	192	1,370	370
Argentina . .	190	45	100	50	42	1	92	530	140
Total . .	21,670	5,270	12,380	6,190	2,700	1,110	13,920	63,300	...

UNITED KINGDOM

The following table shows the estimates made at various dates :—

Date	Millions £	Comprising	Authority
1660	250	England and Wales	Petty
1703	490	,, ,,	Davenant
1774	1,100	,, ,,	Young
1800	1,740	Great Britain	Beeke, Eden
1812	2,190	United Kingdom	Colquhoun
1822	2,600	,, ,,	Lord Liverpool
1833	3,750	,, ,,	Pablo Pebrer
1840	4,100	,, ,,	Porter
1865	6,113	,, ,,	Giffen
1875	8,548	,, ,,	,,
1885	10,037	,, ,,	,,

Regarding Petty's valuation, we only know that land constituted 57 per cent. of the total, the selling price being then under £5 an acre. At the time of Davenant it had risen to £9, and of Young to £18. Towards the close of the 18th century Beeke, Pitt, and Eden made valuations of Great Britain, all previous ones being of England without Scotland. Dr. Beeke valued the real estate at 920 millions, viz. :—

	£
Land in England . . .	600,000,000
Land in Scotland . . .	120,000,000
Houses in Great Britain . .	200,000,000
Real estate . .	920,000,000

The most elaborate work of this kind was Colquhoun's in 1812, the first valuation of the United Kingdom : he made the total 2745 millions in the currency of the period, equal in gold to 2190 millions sterling. His table of values evidently formed the basis on which Lord Liverpool and Pablo Pebrer afterwards constructed theirs.

Pebrer's estimate of the value of the United Kingdom in 1833 was as follows :—

	Million £ Sterling			
	England	Scotland	Ireland	United Kingdom
Lands . . .	1,000	200	400	1,600
Cattle . . .	150	26	66	242
Grain . . .	40	7	13	60
Houses . . .	400	40	93	533
Furniture . .	173	20	53	246
Public buildings .	42	4	11	57
Mines and canals .	151	10	5	166
Merchandise . .	133	21	32	186
Jewellery and clothes	66	7	13	86
Sundries . .	316	38	64	418
Total . .	2,471	373	750	3,594

He furthermore estimated the earnings and capital of the United Kingdom and Colonies thus :—

	Earnings, £	Capital, Million £	Population	£ per Inhab.	
				Capital	Earnings
U. Kingdom	514,800,000	3,594	24,300,000	149	21.0
Canada . .	17,600,000	62	910,000	68	19.4
West Indies	22,500,000	89	730,000	121	31.0
Mauritius .	1,200,000	13	100,000	130	12.0
South Africa	1,100,000	6	55,000	109	20.0
Australia .	500,000	3	40,000	75	12.5
Total .	557,700,000	3,767	26,135,000	144	21.5

Porter's estimate in 1840 in a manner confirmed all those previously made, showing a progressive increase of wealth, and relied, moreover, on the legacy and succession returns. Dr. Giffen's tables for 1865-75-85 are *sui generis*, laying down a new method of valuation, namely, capitalising the various sources of income in the income-tax returns. His table for 1885 may be condensed thus :—

	Income, £	Capital Value, Mill. £	Years' Purchase
Lands . . .	65,090,000	1,691	28
Houses . . .	128,500,000	1,927	15
Farmers' profits .	65,223,000	522	8
Foreign loans . .	21,096,000	527	25
British railways . .	33,270,000	932	28
Foreign railways .	3,808,000	76	20
Trades and professions	38,096,000	541	15
Furniture, &c. . .	...	960	...
Various companies .	34,789,000	696	20
Mines and quarries .	8,536,000	34	4
Gasworks . . .	5,026,000	126	25
Waterworks . .	3,260,000	65	20
Ironworks . . .	2,265,000	9	4
Canals . . .	3,546,000	71	20
Investments abroad .	50,000,000	500	10
Public property . .	...	500	...
Sundries . . .	91,517,000	860	...
Total . .	554,022,000	10,037	...

If there be a weak point in Dr. Giffen's method, it is the capitalising of farmers' profits and income arising from trades and professions, together 1063 millions sterling; many people will question whether these items should be counted at all.

The following table shows approximately the principal items of national wealth at various dates :—

	Million £			
	1812	1840	1860	1888
Lands . . .	1,380	1,680	1,748	1,873
Cattle, &c. . .	240	280	350	414
Houses . . .	255	740	1,100	2,424
Railways . . .	...	21	348	865
Shipping . . .	15	23	44	134
Merchandise . .	70	110	370	690
Furniture . . .	130	370	550	1,212
Bullion . . .	23	61	105	124
Foreign loans, &c. .	105	330	420	1,660
Public properties .	266	485	925	1,404
Total . .	2,190	4,100	5,960	10,800

Land is still one of the great features of wealth. For the sake of comparison, we may capitalise the rental at thirty years' purchase since the middle of the 18th century. As regards 1888, it is admitted that the rental valuation is 20 per cent. more than the landlords actually receive, and hence in the following table the value for 1888 is doubtless too high :—

Year	Value of Land, Million £ Sterling			
	England	Scotland	Ireland	Total
1750 . .	381	24	93	498
1780 . .	507	36	159	702
1814 . .	1,112	145	213	1,470
1843 . .	1,264	167	246	1,677
1850 . .	1,286	167	252	1,704
1860 . .	1,289	189	270	1,748
1868 . .	1,433	216	276	1,925
1877 . .	1,548	231	298	2,077
1888 . .	1,365	207	301	1,873

The value of land in the three kingdoms rose 40 per cent. during the wars in Canada and United States, but the wars against Bonaparte caused a still greater rise owing to the enormous prices paid for grain. The upward movement continued until 1877, from which date there has been a steady, continuous decline.

Houses in the early part of the present century were little over 10 per cent. of the wealth of the nation; at present they exceed 25 per cent. of the total. I have capitalised the rental at 18 years, while Dr. Giffen thinks 15 years sufficient.

The increase of house property in the United Kingdom in a single lifetime, say 67 years, has been over 2000 millions sterling, viz. :—

Year	Number of Houses	Rental, £	Value, Million £	Annual Increase	
				Houses	Value, Million £
1821	3,572,000	20,300,000	366	...	...
1841	4,775,000	41,500,000	747	60,000	19
1861	5,131,000	61,200,000	1,102	18,000	18
1887	7,100,000	134,700,000	2,424	77,000	56

It must not, however, be supposed that 2000 millions sterling have been expended on new houses since 1821: the value of sites has risen very remarkably, which is included in the above table. The actual house property of the United Kingdom may be distinguished approximately thus :—

	Number	Value, Million £	£ per House
Built before 1840 . .	4,400,000	1,570	357
,, since 1840 . .	2,700,000	854	316
Total . . .	7,100,000	2,424	341

There is no country in the world in which the value of house property to population is so high as in England, nor any (except Russia) where it is lower than in Ireland. The houses and values in the three kingdoms stand thus :—

	Houses	Value, £	£ per House
England . .	5,206,000	2,131,000,000	408
Scotland . .	980,000	230,000,000	235
Ireland . . .	914,000	63,000,000	69
U. Kingdom . .	7,100,000	2,424,000,000	341

The growth of house property in each of the three kingdoms has been already set forth in detail under the title *Houses*.

Railways constitute an entirely new element of wealth that has sprung up in the last fifty years : they represent at present a value far in excess of the National Debt.

Year	Miles	Cost, £	Cost per Mile
1840 . . .	650	21,000,000	32,000
1860 . . .	10,430	348,100,000	33,400
1888 . . .	19,810	864,700,000	43,700

The increase of railway capital in twenty years, down to 1860, was £16,400,000 per annum, and £18,400,000 in the years from 1860 to 1888. Shipping has grown about nine-fold in value since Colquhoun's estimate in 1812, and at present represents a sum equal to the collective values of all the other merchant navies of the world; for this item, be it understood, does not include war-vessels, the latter being counted with dockyards, arsenals, and other public property.

The shipping of our merchant navy, including machinery and fittings, represents the following amount :—

	Tons	Value, £	£ per Ton
Sailing . . .	3,115,000	24,920,000	8
Steam . . .	4,350,000	108,750,000	25
Total . .	7,465,000	133,670,000	...

Merchandise in the above summary is put down at a sum equal to 12 months' imports and exports at the several dates.

Furniture is, at auctioneers' estimates, taken at 50 per cent. of the value of house property. Bullion and foreign loans have been estimated at various dates more or less at the figures stated. Foreign investments in 1888 were approximately as follows :—

	£
Colonial loans and railways . .	430,000,000
Australian mortgages . . .	330,000,000
Foreign loans and railways . .	900,000,000
Total . . .	1,660,000,000

Public properties in the United Kingdom were approximately thus :—

	£
180,000 miles of roads . . .	90,000,000
6000 miles of streets	60,000,000
Canals, docks, and royal navy .	115,000,000
Drains, waterworks, telegraphs .	178,000,000
Public buildings	400,000,000
Parks, crown forests, arsenals, &c.	561,000,000
Total	1,404,000,000

The total wealth of the three kingdoms in 1888 was, excluding public properties, thus :—

	Millions £ Sterling			
	England	Scotland	Ireland	Total
Lands . . .	1,365	207	301	1,873
Houses . . .	2,131	230	63	2,424
Cattle, &c. . .	267	53	94	414
Railways . . .	714	114	37	865
Furniture . . .	1,066	115	31	1,212
Other items * . .	2,271	229	112	2,612
Total . .	7,814	948	638	9,400

The distribution of wealth in the United Kingdom may be approximately arrived at if we multiply the number of estates that paid legacy-duty by fifty, which corresponds more or less to the number of inhabitants. The official returns showing the amount of property changing hands under probate or legacy in the years 1885–89 give the averages thus per annum :—

Estates	Number	Amount, £	Average, £
Over £500,000 . .	11	9,400,000	855,000
£100,000–£500,000	147	27,800,000	190,000
£10,000–£100,000 .	2,279	60,400,000	26,500
£1000–£10,000 . .	11,153	35,500,000	3,200
Under £1000 . .	30,660	10,100,000	330
Total . .	44,250	143,200,000	3,250

The above is exclusive of estates paying succession-duty, which amounted in the same years to an average of £44,800,000, equal to 31 per cent. of the former. In order, therefore, to estimate the total value of property

* As the amount under this heading that would correspond to each country cannot be ascertained, the sum is distributed *pro rata* according to the income-tax assessments of the three kingdoms.

changing hands, we may be permitted to add 31 per cent. to the number of each class as given above, and likewise to the amount. The account will then stand thus :—

Estates	Amount, £	Average, £
Over £500,000 . . .	12,000,000	855,000
£100,000–£500,000 . .	36,700,000	190,000
£10,000–£100,000 . .	78,500,000	26,500
£1000–£10,000 . .	46,800,000	3,200
Under £1000 . . .	14,000,000	340
Total . .	188,000,000	3,250

If we follow Porter's method, and multiply the above number of estates by fifty, as the number of living persons is about fifty times the annual number of deaths, we find the wealth of the kingdom is held as in the subjoined table. Moreover, as each estate proved may be taken to stand for a household averaging 5½ persons, we must distribute the amount in households, and not per individual :—

Class	Households	Average, £	Aggregate, Millions £
Millionaires . .	700	855,000	599
Very rich . . .	9,650	190,000	1,834
Rich	148,250	26,500	3,928
Middle	730,500	3,200	2,336
Struggling . . .	2,008,000	340	680
Poor . . .	3,916,900	...	...
Total . .	6,814,000	...	9,377

The above total is almost equal to the amount given in the conspectus as the wealth of the kingdom, if we deduct 1400 millions for public works, &c. It is, however, apparent that a portion (probably 10 per cent.) of the wealth on which probate duty is paid consists of fiduciary documents which cannot be considered in a nation's wealth, such as bills of exchange and stocks of the National Debt. This last, 700 millions sterling, is held in the United Kingdom, and consequently figures among testamentary estates, while adding nothing to the nation's wealth.

FRANCE

Numerous estimates have been made : those of Lavoisier, 1789, and Chaptal, in 1815, were as follows :—

	Millions £	
	1789	1815
Rural property . . .	840	1,040
Urban property . . .	280	320
Personal property . .	400	440
Total .	1,520	1,800

Those of Fournier de Flaix and Yves Guyot, from 1826 to date, are as follows :—

Flaix				*Guyot*			
Year	Million £			Year	Million £		
	Real	Personal	Total		Real	Personal	Total
1826	1,560	1,020	2,580	1826	1,720	1,120	2,840
1833	1,674	1,152	2,826	1833	1,840	1,280	3,120
1841	1,881	1,359	3,240	1841	2,080	1,520	3,600
1849	2,115	1,530	3,645	1855	2,280	1,560	3,840
1857	2,322	1,971	4,293	1860	2,480	1,880	4,360
1865	2,934	2,646	5,580	1865	2,640	2,200	4,840
1873	3,510	3,312	6,822	1875	3,560	3,240	6,800
1882	4,835	4,275	9,110	1885	4,480	4,080	8,560

The following is a summary of the most notable estimates :—

Year	Million £	Author
1789	1,520	Lavoisier
1815	1,800	Chaptal
1853	5,000	Girardin
1871	7,000	Wolowski
1872	7,600	Ayen
1879	8,000	Foville
1879	7,520	Leroy Beaulieu
1879	9,600	Amelin
1880	9,200	Vacher
1881	8,640	Mouey
1882	9,110	Flaix
1885	8,560	Guyot

The following table shows approximately the components of the wealth of France at various dates :—

	Value in Million £				
	1789	1826	1840	1873	1885
Land . . .	740	1,293	1,473	3,000	2,688
Cattle, &c. .	105	202	270	588	541
Houses . .	280	510	720	1,150	1,704
Furniture .	140	255	360	675	852
Railways .	...	...	10	270	532
Shipping .	4	7	7	12	15
Bullion . .	88	110	115	180	300
Merchandise	11	19	33	120	155
Public works	40	170	300	450	630
Sundries .	112	274	312	377	1,143
Total .	1,520	2,840	3,600	6,822	8,560

De Flaix and Vacher make the total 500 or 600 millions more than the above estimate for 1885, but perhaps they have not sufficiently allowed for the depreciation of land since 1880. The above total is that given by Yves Guyot for 1885. The increase of wealth since 1873 appears to have averaged 116 millions sterling per annum.

BELGIUM

Massalski, in his *Richesse de Belgique* (1880), sums up the national wealth at 29½ milliards of francs, or 1180 millions sterling, which is 17 per cent. over my estimate. It is to be observed that properties subject to legacy and succession duties from 1880 to 1885 averaged only 18 millions sterling, which at the current death-rate of 20 per thousand would give a total wealth of 900 millions sterling, exclusive of royal palaces, public works, &c. : these latter would hardly exceed 110 millions sterling.

GERMANY

It is remarkable that whereas the earnings of the German people, as set forth under the head of *Income*, are only 1 per cent. less than those of France, the wealth of Germany appears to be one-sixth less. This is, however, in great measure explained by the great difference in the value of land, Germany averaging £21, France £33 per cultivated acre. The imperial assessment for taxation is in the following ratio, and if we suppose wealth to be distributed in like manner, it will be as in the subjoined table :—

	Ratio	Millions £
Prussia	60.3	4,520
Bavaria	11.7	880
Saxony	6.6	500
Wurtemburg	4.3	320
Baden	3.4	250
Alsace	3.4	250
Hesse	2.1	150
Other States	8.2	630
Total . .	100.0	7,500

Soetbeer shows that the earnings of the Prussian people advanced 25 per cent. from 1872 to 1885, and if we suppose that wealth increased in like degree, this makes the accumulation of thirteen years amount to 1136 millions, or 88 millions sterling per annum—say 40s. per inhabitant, against 72s. in the United Kingdom.

AUSTRIA

In 1880 Beer estimated the total wealth of the monarchy at 40,000 million florins, or about 3800 millions sterling, being only 10 per cent. under my estimate. We have no means to arrive at the increase of wealth, but Roschmann in 1883 estimated the national earnings at 610 millions sterling, against 550 millions in 1874, an increase of 11 per cent. If wealth increased in the same ratio the accumulation must have been 380 millions sterling, or 42 millions per annum, say 23s. per inhabitant, against 40s. in Germany.

ITALY

Newmann Spallart valued the total wealth of the country thus :—

	Million £ Sterling
Lands	1,160
Houses	360
Furniture, railways, &c. . . .	404
Total . . .	1,924

This was too low a valuation, an Italian writer in 1868 having arrived at a total of 1934 millions.

Pantaleoni, following Porter's method, based on legacy returns, shows that (exclusive of public property) the wealth of the people exceeds 2100 millions ; he multiplies the amount of property subjected to legacy or succession by forty. The amount of such property in 1884 was £53,500,000, and hence the national wealth was 2140 millions sterling. This is exclusive of roads, public buildings, royal navy, arsenals, harbours &c., worth at least 300 millions, bringing up the total to 2440 millions sterling. This is 16 per cent. less than my estimate. Possibly some of the property subjected to legacy-duty was undervalued, in order to enable the heirs to evade a part of the duties. According to the *Archivio*, the value of lands and houses in 1880 was 1562 millions sterling ; in my table they stand for 1576 millions, a difference of less than 1 per cent.

SPAIN

The figures of the Junta de Medios in 1832 compare with mine for 1888 as follows :—

	Million £ Sterling		
	1832	1888	Increase
Lands	686	984	298
Houses	237	340	103
Railways . . .	...	94	94
Sundries . . .	186	1,098	912
Total . .	1,109	2,516	1,407

It is manifest that the item of sundries in 1832, which included everything in the kingdom except land and houses, was very much understated. Personal property alone would have been at least 25 per cent. of total. A proper valuation in 1832 would perhaps have shown a total of 1400 millions. In that case the accumulation of the 56 years down to 1888 would average 20 millions sterling per annum, or 27s. per inhabitant, as compared with 40s. in Germany, and 72s. in United Kingdom.

DENMARK

In 1885 Falbe estimated the total wealth at 372 millions sterling, or 20 per cent. less than my total for 1888. His figures were :—

	Million £
Houses and lands	257
Personal property	115
Total	372

He estimated that real estate had risen from 65 millions sterling in 1848, being an increase of 192 millions sterling in 37 years, say £5,200,000 per annum. This (irrespective of chattels or personal property) was equivalent to an accumulation of 60s. yearly per inhabitant. It was the direct result of breaking up the estates of the nobles, and facilitating their purchase by the peasantry.

HOLLAND

The value of testamentary and succession property which changed hands in the years 1879–83, latest that the *Résumé* publishes, averaged as follows :—

	£
Houses and lands	9,100,000
Dutch National Debt	1,200,000
Other personal assets	13,000,000
Total	23,300,000

Excluding the National Debt for reasons already given, we find a sum of £22,100,000, which, multiplied by 44 (as the living were in those years 44 times the number of deaths), gives approximately the wealth of Holland, say 972 millions sterling ; the figure in the conspectus is 980 millions.

UNITED STATES

The first Census of wealth was taken in 1790, which showed as follows :—

	$	£
Lands . . .	479,000,000 =	99,800,000
Houses, &c. .	141,000,000	29,400,000
Total .	620,000,000	129,200,000

The following table shows the results in English gold at each Census, and an estimate for 1888 as already given :*—

---

* The New York *Journal of Commerce* in 1887 estimated the wealth of the Union at 61,000 millions of dollars, or 12,700 millions sterling, showing, moreover, that the amount of insured property had risen as follows :—

Year					£
1870	.	.	.	.	735,000,000
1880	.	.	.	.	1,495,000,000
1885	.	.	.	.	2,184,000,000

Year	Wealth, Million £	£ Sterling per Inhabitant	Yearly Increase	
			Of Wealth, £	Per Inhabitant
				£ s. d.
1790 . .	129	33 .	...	...
1800 . .	222	42	9,300,000	2 1 0
1810 . .	312	43	9,000,000	1 9 0
1820 . .	392	41	8,000,000	0 19 0
1830 . .	552	43	16,000,000	1 9 0
1840 . .	782	46	23,000,000	1 11 0
1850 . .	1,484	64	70,200,000	3 10 0
1860 . .	3,361	107	187,700,000	6 16 0
1870 . .	5,413	140	205,200,000	5 17 0
1880 . .	9,077	180	366,400,000	8 4 0
1888 . .	12,824	210	468,400,000	8 10 0

The following table shows approximately the chief components of American wealth since 1850 :—

	Millions of Dollars, Gold				
	1850	1860	1870	1880	1888
Land . . .	3,310	6,910	8,320	10,197	12,300
Cattle . . .	550	1,080	1,415	1,630	2,405
Railways . .	290	1,140	2,047	4,897	9,340
Factories . .	520	1,010	1,902	2,790	3,500
Houses . . .	1,000	2,600	5,460	10,800	14,000
Furniture . .	500	1,300	2,730	5,400	7,000
Sundries . .	966	2,120	4,108	7,928	13,055
Total .	7,136	16,160	25,982	43,642	61,600

Comparing the Census returns of 1880 with those of 1850, it appears that the accumulations of thirty years amounted in the State of New York alone to 1360 millions sterling, and that the six States of New York, Pennsylvania, Illinois, Ohio, Massachusetts, and California stood for 60 per cent. of the total accumulations of the Union. If we suppose that each inhabitant contributed equally to the public wealth, and take the mean number of each nationality for the 30 years in question, we find the accumulations of 30 years ending 1880 were made up thus :—

State	Increase of Wealth, Million £ Sterling, by				
	Americans	Irish	Germans	Others	Total
New York . . .	1,027	156	87	90	1,360
Pennsylvania . .	831	63	41	37	972
Illinois . . .	494	27	47	43	611
Ohio	506	17	38	20	581
Massachusetts . .	355	66	4	37	462
California . . .	195	23	14	61	293
Other States . .	2,822	119	143	228	3,312
Total . .	6,230	471	374	516	7,591

The several Census returns from 1850 to 1880 show the wealth of each State in values reduced to English gold (allowing 14 per cent. discount for paper values in 1870) as follows :—

	Million £ Sterling				Increase of 30 Years	£ Sterling per Inhabitant			
	1850	1860	1870	1880		1850	1860	1870	1880
Maine	26	39	63	104	78	44	60	102	160
New Hampshire	22	32	46	68	46	70	96	144	196
Vermont	19	25	42	60	41	60	77	126	180
Rhode Island	17	28	53	87	70	112	160	240	320
Connecticut	32	92	140	177	145	85	201	256	283
Massachusetts	119	169	384	581	462	120	135	257	320
New England	235	385	728	1,077	842	86	122	208	270

	Million £ Sterling				Increase of 30 Years	£ Sterling per Inhabitant			
	1850	1860	1870	1880		1850	1860	1870	1880
New York	224	384	1,170	1,585	1,361	73	99	261	322
New Jersey	42	98	169	298	256	87	147	186	260
Pennsylvania	150	295	686	1,122	972	65	101	196	262
Delaware	4	9	17	29	25	44	80	136	200
Maryland	46	79	116	181	135	80	115	150	195
Middle States	466	865	2,158	3,215	2,749	70	105	220	257
Virginia	89	166	108	208	119	63	105	61	98
North Carolina	47	75	47	92	45	55	75	44	66
South Carolina	60	114	38	61	1	90	163	54	61
Georgia	70	134	48	115	45	77	126	32	77
Florida	5	15	8	20	15	15	105	43	74
Alabama	48	103	36	79	31	63	107	40	64
Mississippi	48	127	38	67	19	79	159	44	60
Louisiana	49	125	58	88	39	95	180	78	93
Texas	11	76	29	151	140	52	126	35	94
Arkansas	8	46	28	51	43	38	104	58	64
Kentucky	63	138	109	183	120	64	120	84	111
Tennessee	42	103	90	138	76	42	92	72	90
The South	540	1,222	637	1,253	713	66	119	57	82
Ohio	105	249	402	686	581	53	107	150	215
Illinois	32	181	382	643	611	38	105	151	210
Missouri	28	104	231	318	290	42	88	138	147
Indiana	42	110	229	312	270	42	82	138	156
Iowa	5	51	130	294	289	26	77	108	180
Michigan	12	53	130	285	273	30	70	108	177
Wisconsin	9	57	126	202	193	30	71	120	150
Minnesota	...	11	41	133	133	...	66	91	170
Kansas	...	6	34	120	120	...	55	93	120
Nebraska	...	2	13	60	60	...	70	104	132
Colorado	...	...	4	31	31	...	...	100	160
California	5	43	115	300	295	55	113	206	350
Oregon	1	6	9	26	25	75	120	100	150
Nevada	...	...	6	14	14	...	...	145	230
Territories	6	21	38	108	102	...	...	...	...
The West	245	894	1,890	3,532	3,287	43	92	136	187
The Union	1,486	3,366	5,413	9,077	7,591	64	107	140	180

The accumulations per inhabitant in thirty years average £205 sterling, or nearly £7 per annum, viz. :—

States	Increase Million £	Annual Average, £	Mean Population	Annual Accumulation per Head
				£ s. d.
New England	842	28,070,000	3,400,000	8 4 0
Middle	2,749	91,630,000	9,500,000	9 13 0
South	713	23,800,000	11,700,000	2 1 0
West	3,287	109,600,000	12,200,000	9 0 0
Union	7,591	253,100,000	36,800,000	6 17 0

This is a prodigious growth of wealth in thirty years, and without parallel in the history of the human race. Nevertheless the accumulation per head is less than in Australia.

AUSTRALIA

According to Mr. Coghlan the wealth of Australia was approximately as follows :—

	Millions £	Population	Per Head £
1838	26	200,000	130
1863	181	1,264,000	144
1888	1,136	3,680,000	307

This includes the five Colonies of the mainland, and also Tasmania and New Zealand. It is, however, incomplete, because it excludes public works, crown-lands, and other public properties.

The total wealth, as shown in the conspectus, appears to reach the sum of 1373 millions sterling, and to have grown in eighteen years as follows :—

	Million £ Sterling	
	1870	1888
Lands	89	533
Cattle	47	67
Railways	27	94
Houses	60	239
Furniture	30	120
Merchandise	29	65
Sundries	38	255
Total	320	1,373

At a meeting of one of the Australian banks in London in 1888, it was stated that the wealth of the seven Colonies was as follows :—

	Million £
Private wealth	1,015
Public works	175
Banks	148
Total	1,338

This was, however, irrespective of crown-lands, the value of which could not be easily stated.

Mr. Coghlan's distribution of the wealth of the several Colonies differs from my estimates as follows (1888) :—

	Millions Sterling	
	Coghlan	Mulhall
New South Wales . .	410	483
Victoria	386	370
Queensland . . .	106	132
South Australia . . .	57	131
Tasmania	26	36
New Zealand . . .	145	208
Western Australia . .	6	13
Total . .	1,136	1,373

Mr. Coghlan's figures, as already stated, exclude railways, crown-lands, &c. The principal components of wealth in 1888 may be estimated to have stood thus in million £ sterling :—

	Land	Cattle	Railways	Houses	Furniture	Merchandise	Sundries	Total	£ per Head
N. S. Wales	181	25	27	92	46	23	89	483	440
Victoria . .	107	12	28	91	46	18	68	370	337
Queensland .	58	12	13	12	6	6	25	132	330
S. Australia .	64	5	10	13	7	7	25	131	413
Tasmania .	16	1	2	5	3	2	7	36	240
New Zealand	100	11	13	25	12	8	39	208	345
W. Australia	7	1	1	1	...	1	2	13	310
Total .	533	67	94	239	120	65	255	1,373	377

The increase of wealth in Australia would therefore seem to have been as follows :—

Date	Wealth, Million £	Annual Increase, £	Mean Population	Annual Accumulation per Inhabitant
				£ s. d.
1838 . .	26	...	...	...
1863 . .	181	6,200,000	700,000	8 16 0
1870 . .	320	19,900,000	1,600,000	12 9 0
1888 . .	1,373	58,500,000	2,800,000	20 18 0

The average annual accumulation per inhabitant has been more than double that in the United States, where it has never exceeded £8 10s.

Respecting the Colony of New South Wales, Mr. Coghlan states that if public works, railways &c., were included, the total would reach 521 millions sterling, that is, 8 per cent. over my estimate. And as regards Victoria, one of the Melbourne papers (apparently quoting the official statistics of Mr. Hayter) says :—" In the statistics of the Colony for 1886, an estimate is made of the wealth of the population on the basis of the property left by deceased persons, it being supposed that the average amount left by each person dying is equivalent to the average amount possessed by each person living. On this basis the national wealth amounted to nearly 144 millions sterling, or £185 per head in the five years 1872 to 1876; to nearly 187 millions sterling, or £223 per head in the five years 1877 to 1881; and to nearly 286 millions sterling, or £305 per head in the five years 1882 to 1886."

The above is exclusive of railways, public works &c., which would doubtless bring up the total to my figure of 370 millions sterling in 1888. With respect to New Zealand, the official returns for 1886, exclusive of public

works, and crown-lands, amounted to 152 millions sterling, which was apparently equivalent to 200 millions, including the items omitted. It is right to observe that the public debt, which was 175 millions sterling in December 1889, is held almost wholly in England, and ought therefore to be deducted from the wealth. This would leave a balance of 1200 millions sterling, or £330 per inhabitant, against £247 in the United Kingdom, £210 in the United States, £230 in Denmark, £224 in France.

CANADA

The following table shows approximately the total wealth in 1861 and 1888 :—

	Million £ Sterling		
	1861	1888	Increase
Lands	102	282	180
Cattle, &c. . . .	38	80	42
Railways . . .	23	151	128
Houses	80	127	47
Furniture . . .	40	64	24
Merchandise . .	21	41	20
Sundries . . .	88	235	147
Total . .	392	980	588

This shows an annual accumulation of 22 millions sterling, with a mean population of 4,000,000 souls, say £5 10s. per head, against £8 10s. in the United States, and £17 10s. during the same period in Australia.

CAPE COLONY

In 1883 the value of lands and houses was assessed as follows :—

	£
Cape Town	4,979,000
Port Elizabeth . . .	1,950,000
Kimberley	1,711,000
Rural districts . . .	29,160,000
Total . .	37,800,000

WEIGHTS AND MEASURES

The following is a general table of weights and measures :—

Name	Locality	Equivalent
Acre	England	4,840 square yards
Almud	Turkey	7=8 gallons
,, . . .	Portugal	4=15 ,,
Amphora . . .	Rome	7 ,,
Ar	France	100=247 acres
Ardeb . . .	Egypt	300 lbs.
Arpent . . .	France	12=10 acres
Arroba . . .	Spain	25 lbs.
Aum	Germany	31 gallons
Bag, cocoa . .	England	112 lbs.
,, coffee . .	Brazil	160 ,,
,, rice . .	India	168 ,,
,, sugar . .	,,	168 ,,
Bale . . .	United States	485 ,,
,, . . .	Brazil	156 ,,
,, . . .	Egypt	600 ,,
,, . . .	India	376 ,,
Barrel, ale . .	England	36 gallons
,, apples .	United States	150 lbs.
,, flour . .	,,	200 ,,
,, fish . .	Norway	1,000 in number
Berkovetz . .	Russia	400 lbs.
Bonnier . . .	France	3 acres

Name	Locality	Equivalent	Name	Locality	Equivalent
Bushel, barley	England	54 lbs.	Mark	France	gold=£25
,, beans	,,	63 ,,	Maund	India	80 lbs.
,, hempseed	,,	44 ,,	Motre	France	100=328 feet
,, maize	,,	59 ,,	Mancus	England	2 ounces
,, malt	,,	38 ,,	Metzen	Germany	24=1 ton
,, oats	,,	40 ,,	Mile	England	1,760 yards
,, peas	,,	64 ,,	,,	Ireland	2,240 ,,
,, rye	,,	59 ,,	,,	Germany	8,140 ,,
,, salt	,,	56 ,,	,,	Turkey	1,870 ,,
,, wheat	,,	61 ,,	,,	Sweden	11,770 ,,
Bunder	Holland	2=1 acre	,,	Geographical	2,025 ,,
Butt	England	108 gallons	Millimetre	France	25=1 inch
Cable	,,	120 fathoms	Minute	,,	60=1 hour
Cantar	Egypt	100 lbs.	Morgen	Germany	5=3 acres
Cask, rice	United States	672 ,,	Mudden	Holland	14=1 ton
,, tallow	England	1,008 ,,	Muid	France	50 bushels
,, wine	,,	108 gallons	Oke	Greece	4=11 lbs.
Catty	China	3=4 lbs.	Ounce	England	16=1 lb.
Centner	Germany	110 lbs.	,,	Avoirdupois	12=1 lb.
,, metric	,,	220 ,,	Pack, wool	England	240 lbs.
Chain	England	66 feet	Palm	,,	4 inches
Chaldron, coal	,,	3=8 tons	Parasang	Persia	3½ miles
Chest, tea	China	82 lbs.	Peck	England	14 lbs.
Chetvert	Russia	310 ,,	Pennyweight	,,	20=1 ounce
Chittack	India	2 ounces	Perch	,,	5½ yards
Cord, wood	Germany	2½ tons	Picul	China	133 lbs.
Cuartillo	Spain	9=1 gallon	Piece, calico	England	24 yards
Cubit	Asia	18 inches	Pint	,,	8=1 gallon
Dessiatine	Russia	3=8 acres	Pipe	,,	126 gallons
Drachm	England	16=1 ounce	Poinçon	France	25 gallons
Eimer	Austria	12 gallons	Pocket, hops	England	168 lbs.
Ell	England	36 inches	Pole	,,	16½ feet
Fanega	Spain	4 bushels	Pond	Denmark	100=110 lbs.
Fanegado	,,	10=16 acres	Pood	Russia	36 lbs.
Fathom	England	6 feet	Pott	Norway	100=21 gallons
Feddan	Egypt	20=21 acres	Pound	England	16 ounces
Ferrado	Portugal	8=1 acre	,,	Rome	12 ,,
Firkin	England	68 lbs.	Puncheon	England	120 gallons
Flask, quicksilver	,,	76 ,,	Quarter	,,	8 bushels
Furlong	,,	220 yards	Queue, wine	France	54 gallons
Gallon	,,	4 quarts	Quintal	Spain	110 lbs.
Gill	,,	4=1 pint	,, metrical	Austria	220 ,,
Grain	,,	480=1 ounce	Rittergut	Germany	600 acres
Gramme	,,	453—1 lb.	Rood	England	4=1 acre
Hank	,,	840 yards	Sack, coal	,,	224 lbs.
Hectare	France	100=247 acres	,, flour	,,	280 ,,
Hectolitre	,,	22 gallons	Sågene	Russia	7 tons wood
,,	,,	150 lbs.	Second	,,	60=1 minute
Hide	England	100 acres	Salma	Spain	4½ acres
Hogshead	,,	63 gallons	Scheffel	Germany	100=145 bushels
Hundred, great, eggs	,,	10 dozen	Schekel	Asia	2=1 ounce
Inch	,,	12=1 foot	Septier	France	4=17 bushels
Jar, oil	Italy	25 gallons	Sextarius	Rome	6=1 gallon
Joch	Hungary	100=143 acres	Skalpund	Sweden	106=100 lbs.
Juchart	Switzerland	5=4 acres	Span	England	9 inches
Kanna	Sweden	100=58 gallons	Strema	Greece	4=1 acre
,,	Germany	100=44 ,,	Stadium	,,	120 yards
Kilderkin	England	18 ,,	Stère, wood	France	35 cubic feet
Kilogram	France	1,000=1 ton	Stone, fish	England	14 lbs.
Kilometre	,,	100=62 miles	,, meat	,,	8 ,,
Klafter, wood	Austria	2 tons	Stoup	,,	2=1 gallon
Knot	England	2,000 yards	Talent, gold	Asia	4 lbs.
Last	Norway	3½ tons	Tavola	Italy	40=1 acre
,,	Germany	2 ,,	Tierce, pork	England	320 lbs.
,, salt	England	18 barrels	Toise	France	6½ feet
League	Holland	6,380 yards	Ton	England	2,240 lbs.
,,	Spain	6,160 ,,	,,	United States	2,000 ,,
,,	Portugal	6,760 ,,	Tub	England	84 lbs.
,,	France	4,860 ,,	Truss, straw	,,	36 ,,
,, Marine	,,	6,075 ,,	,, hay	,,	56 ,,
Liño	Paraguay	50=1 acre	Tun, wine	,,	252 gallons
Litre	France	100=22 gallons	Tunna	Sweden	4 bushels
Load, bricks	England	500	Tunnland	,,	4=5 acres
,, corn	,,	40 bushels	Vara	Spain	34.1 inches
,, hay	,,	1 ton	Vedro	Russia	10=27 gallons
,, straw	,,	½ ton	Verst	,,	100=60 miles
,, wood	,,	50 cubic feet	Yard	England	36 inches
Mark	France	8 oz. silver			

Grain

	Cubic Feet	Bushel	Quarter	Hecto-litre	Scheffel	Metzen	Chetvert
Cubic metre	35.3	27.60	3.45	10.00	19.30	16.50	5.00
Bushel . .	1.3	1.00	0.12	0.36	0.70	0.60	0.18
Quarter .	10.4	8.00	1.00	2.90	5.60	4.80	1.44
Ton . . .	52.0	40.00	5.00	14.50	28.00	24.00	7.20
Hectolitre .	3.5	2.76	0.35	1.00	1.93	1.65	0.50
Scheffel .	1.9	1.45	0.18	0.53	1.00	0.86	0.26
Metzen . .	2.2	1.66	0.21	0.60	1.16	1.00	0.30
Chetvert .	7.0	5.55	0.70	2.00	3.90	3.30	1.00

Length

	Knot	Mile	Kilometre	Verst
Mile . . .	0.88	1.00	1.61	1.50
Knot . . .	1.00	1.14	1.83	1.71
Kilometre .	0.55	0.62	1.00	0.93
Verst . . .	0.58	0.66	1.07	1.00

Liquids

	Lbs.	Cubic Feet	Litre	Hecto-litre	Eimer	Barrel	Hogs-head
Gallon .	10.0	0.14	4.5	0.045	0.080	0.027	0.016
Litre . .	2.2	0.03	1.0	0.010	0.018	0.006	0.004
Hectolitre .	220.0	3.10	100.0	1.000	1.760	0.600	0.350
Eimer . .	124.0	1.75	56.0	0.560	1.000	0.340	0.200
Barrel . .	360.0	5.00	160.0	1.600	2.880	1.000	0.576
Hogshead	630.0	8.80	284.0	2.835	5.000	1.710	1.000

Sundries

	Lbs.	Cwt.	French Ton	American Ton	Kilogram	Pood	Picul
English ton	2,240	20.00	1.018	1.120	1,018	62.20	16.80
Cwt. . .	112	1.00	0.051	0.056	51	3.11	0.84
Quintal . .	110	0.98	0.050	0.055	50	3.05	0.82
French ton	2,204	19.64	1.000	1.100	1,000	61.00	16.50
American ton }	2,000	17.86	0.910	1.000	910	56.40	15.00
Kilogram .	2.20	00.02	0.001	0.001	1.0	0.06	0.016
Pood . .	36	0.32	0.017	0.018	16.3	1.00	0.27
Picul . .	133	1.20	0.061	0.067	60.0	3.67	1.00

Superficial

	Sq. Yards	Acre	Morgen	Hectare	Dessiatine	Square Kilometre	Square Mile
Acre . . .	4,840	1.00	1.56	0.405	0.367	0.0040	0.0016
Morgen . .	3,122	0.65	1.00	0.260	0.235	0.0026	0.0010
Joch . . .	6,914	1.43	2.23	0.576	0.520	0.0057	0.0022
Hectare. .	12,000	2.47	3.84	1.000	0.910	0.0100	0.0039
Dessiatine .	13,100	2.70	4.20	1.093	1.000	0.0091	0.0035
Sq. kilom. .	1,190,000	250	390	100	91	1.0000	0.3900
Sq. mile .	3,097,600	640	1,000	260	235	2.60	1.0

Old English Measures

Name	Date	Wine Gallon, Cub. In.	Beer Gallon, Cub. In.	Corn Gallon, Cub. In.	Bushel, Cub. In.
Magna Charta . .	1225	217	266	266	2,130
Edward III. . .	1353	219	268	268	2,148
Henry VII. . .	1496	224	280	280	2,240
Henry VIII. .	1531	231	282	282	2,256

WHEAT

It cannot be grown farther than 60° N. lat. The greatest elevation at which it is found is as follows:—

	Feet		Feet
Alps . . .	3,600	Sierra Nevada . .	8,200
Brazil . . .	5,000	Abyssinia . . .	10,000
Caucasus . .	8,000	Andes . . .	11,000

The yield in various countries for 100 lbs. of seed is:—

	Lbs.		Lbs.
Russia . . .	500	France . . .	750
Sweden . . .	500	Poland . . .	800
Denmark . .	600	Great Britain .	900
Prussia . . .	600	Holland . . .	900
Spain . . .	600	United States .	900
Austria . . .	700	Italy . . .	1,000

The cultivation in the United Kingdom was:—

Period	Annual Average			
	Acres	Million Bushels	Con-sumption	Deficit
1849-54 . . .	4,270,000	118	152	34
1855-66 . . .	3,740,000	107	161	54
1867-72 . . .	3,560,000	98	176	78
1873-78 . . .	3,310,000	80	184	104
1881-89 . . .	2,750,000	80	224	144

The average value of wheat crop per acre in United States was as follows in British money:—

Period	Shillings	Period	Shillings
1871-74 . . .	58	1880-83 . . .	49
1875-79 . . .	52	1884-87 . . .	34

See full statistics at page 8, *Agriculture*.

WINDMILLS

Holland has 10,100 windmills, representing a value of 20 millions sterling, with an aggregate force of 52,200 horse-power. Cost of drainage, 10d. per acre, with a lift of 3 feet; 20d. at 6 feet, and so on. The average area drained by each mill in Holland is 310 acres, each lifting 150,000 tons or 33 million gallons water daily.

WINE

*Vineyards, Area, and Production**

Country	Acres (1889)	Millions of Gallons per Annum			Gallons per Acre	Vintage Value, Million £
		1876-85	1880-88	Latest Estimate		
France . .	4,550,000	810	670	520	112	44
Italy . .	7,640,000	486	665	580	78	48
Spain . .	4,200,000	450	630	550	130	46
Austria . .	1,580,000	198	225	180	115	15
Portugal .	510,000	88	125	90	175	9
Germany .	335,000	45	75	70	210	6
Russia . .	300,000	40	75	40	130	4
Turkey . .	200,000	20	59	20	100	2
Greece . .	310,000	30	32	34	110	3
Servia . .	300,000	13	46	45	150	3
Roumania .	200,000	22	35	30	150	2
Switzerland .	70,000	13	15	15	210	1
Europe . .	20,195,000	2,215	2,652	2,174	108	183
U. States .	130,000	18	19	18	140	2
Chili . . .	200,000	20	20	20	100	2
Argentina	66,000	6	6	6	100	1
Cape Colony	18,000	4	4	4	220	...
Australia .	15,000	2	2	2	140	...
Algeria . .	132,000	15	18	40	300	3
Total .	20,756,000	2,280	2,731	2,264	109	191

* For consumption of wine see *Alcohol*, p. 58.

The figures for 1876–85 are by Newmann Spallart, those of 1880–88 from the *Moniteur Vinicole* (apparently too high), and the latest estimates are from numerous sources. An acre of vineyard has ordinarily 2400 vine plants.

Retrospect of Production

	Millions of Gallons		
	1810–20	1840–50	1880–88
France	455	820	670
Italy	310	360	665
Spain	170	250	630
Austria	590	500	225
Portugal . . .	75	100	125
Germany . . .	30	40	75
Other countries .	120	230	321
Total .	1,750	2,300	2,711

The vine flourishes between 35 and 50 degrees of N. lat., and 28 and 46 S.

The largest vine in the world is said to be one growing at Oys, Portugal, which has been in bearing since 1802. Its maximum yield was in 1864, in which year it produced a sufficient quantity of grapes to make 165 gallons of wine. In Portugal it is customary to plant 2500 vines to the acre, and the yield is often 240 gallons per acre, or a gallon from 10 vines. In South Africa a bushel of grapes gives a gallon of wine.

UNITED KINGDOM

The consumption has been as follows :—

Year	Gallons	Duty, Shillings per Gallon	Gallons per Inhabitant
1801 . . .	6,877,000	10	0.45
1811 . . .	5,630,000	14	0.32
1821 . . .	4,702,000	14	0.23
1831 . . .	6,220,000	6	0.26
1841 . . .	6,185,000	6	0.22
1851 . . .	6,282,000	6	0.23
1861 . . .	10,693,000	1	0.36
1871 . . .	16,145,000	1	0.53
1881 . . .	15,550,000	1	0.44
1888 . . .	13,500,000	1	0.36

GERMANY

The area and vintage in 1884 were as follows :—

	Acres	Gallons	Value, £
Alsace	80,000	21,000,000	4,200,000
Bavaria	60,000	9,000,000	1,800,000
Wurtemburg . .	60,000	9,000,000	1,800,000
Baden	55,000	8,000,000	1,600,000
Prussia	50,000	8,000,000	1,600,000
Other States . .	30,000	9,000,000	1,800,000
Total . .	335,000	64,000,000	12,800,000

ITALY

The vintage in the years 1883–85 averaged as follows :—

	Gallons	Value, £
Island of Sardinia . . .	9,000,000	700,000
Piedmont and Liguria . .	57,000,000	4,600,000
Lombardy and Venetia .	46,000,000	3,700,000
Tuscany	44,000,000	3,600,000
States of the Church . .	81,000,000	6,500,000
Naples	138,000,000	11,000,000
Sicily	106,000,000	8,500,000
Total . .	481,000,000	38,600,000

The area under vines increased rapidly in late years, from 4,800,000 acres in 1880 to 7,640,000 in 1888.

FRANCE

A table of French vintages since 1810 is given at page 19 (*Agriculture*).

The following statistics of Champagne are published at Rheims :—

Year	Millions of Bottles	
	Stock	Export
1850	20	5
1860	36	8
1870	39	14
1880	68	17
1886	83	15

The stock in 1886 was considered equal to four years' consumption, which comprises 3,000,000 bottles yearly in France, and 17,000,000 in other countries.

UNITED STATES

Official returns of the vintages since 1840 show thus :—

Year	Gallons	Year	Gallons
1840 . . .	120,000	1870 . . .	3,060,000
1850 . . .	220,000	1880 . . .	23,300,000
1860 . . .	1,860,000	1885 . . .	17,400,000

The Census of 1880 showed the vineyards thus :—

	Acres	Gallons Wine	Value, £ Stg.
California . .	32,000	13,600,000	850,000
New York . .	13,000	600,000	80,000
Ohio	10,000	1,600,000	330,000
Other States .	127,000	7,700,000	1,540,000
Total . .	182,000	23,500,000	2,800,000

GREECE

The area and vintage of grapes and currants were as follows :—

Year	Acres	Gallons
1860 . . .	162,000	15,000,000
1875 . . .	260,000	25,000,000
1879 . . .	310,000	30,000,000
1887 . . .	...	50,000,000

ALGERIA

Area and vintage have increased rapidly of late years, viz. :—

Year	Acres	Gallons
1880 . . .	55,000	9,000,000
1885 . . .	132,000	22,000,000
1888 . . .	238,000	40,000,000

In 1889 Algeria exported 34 million gallons to France.

WINE-EXPORTING COUNTRIES

The exportation was approximately (mill. galls.) :—

Year	France	Italy	Spain	Portugal	Greece	Total
1830 . . .	18	2	10	3	...	33
1840 . . .	24	3	15	4	...	46
1850 . . .	38	4	20	4	...	66
1860 . . .	48	5	24	5	1	83
1870 . . .	70	5	33	6	2	116
1880 . . .	55	48	134	7	3	247
1887 . . .	53	52	167	10	4	286

Rudesheimer is worth £20 a gallon. Prince Woronzoff sells his Tokay, 220 years old, at £9 a bottle. Champagne vintage averages 20 million bottles, of which France exports 17 millions. The Xeres vineyards, 15,000 acres, produce 4 million gallons yearly of sherry. Wine loses strength after 200 years.

WOOL

The production has been (unwashed) approximately as follows :—

			Millions of Lbs.		
	1820	**1840**	**1860**	**1880**	**1887**
United Kingdom .	100	121	155	176	160
France . . .	116	144	150	117	126
Germany . .	64	85	125	120	105
Russia . . .	102	126	164	203	240
Austria . .	60	72	81	80	70
Italy . . .	18	23	23	30	32
Spain . . .	40	42	58	70	70
Portugal . .	4	5	8	10	10
Scandinavia .	15	20	23	26	26
Various . .	7	8	8	17	16
Europe . .	526	646	795	849	855
United States .	20	65	75	233	320
River Plate .	4	15	56	280	360
Cape Colony .	2	10	28	52	82
Australia . .	2	14	70	390	420
Various . .	6	36	84	184	181
Total .	560	786	1,108	1,988	2,218

Europe in 1820 produced 94 per cent. of the wool of the world, whereas now it does not produce 40 per cent.

The principal features of the woollen industry in 1887–88 were approximately as follows :—

	Million Lbs. Wool		Million Lbs. Yarn Spun	Woollen Manufactures, £	
	Produced	Consumed		Produced	Consumed
U. Kingdom .	160	436	225	43,900,000	29,700,000
France . .	126	420	162	30,800,000	19,000,000
Germany .	105	340	133	25,100,000	15,700,000
Russia . .	240	154	100	17,700,000	18,000,000
Austria . .	70	100	65	11,400,000	11,100,000
Italy . . .	32	49	31	4,700,000	7,000,000
Spain . . .	70	56	35	6,000,000	7,400,000
Portugal .	10	14	10	1,600,000	1,900,000
Scandinavia	25	25	14	2,500,000	5,500,000
Belgium . .	2	101	35	6,000,000	3,000,000
Various . .	20	20	12	2,000,000	4,000,000
Europe . .	860	1,715	822	151,700,000	122,300,000
U. States .	320	434	213	34,400,000	42,400,000
Canada . .	15	14	8	1,500,000	4,000,000
River Plate .	360	10	...	500,000	2,000,000
Australia .	420	15	...	1,500,000	4,000,000
S. Africa .	82	5	...	100,000	400,000
India . . .	55	20	12	2,000,000	3,700,000
Various . .	106	5	...	100,000	13,000,000
Total .	2,218	2,218	1,055	191,800,000	191,800,000

The aggregate production of wool for sixty-seven years was approximately as follows :—

Tons Unwashed

Period	Europe	U. States	River Plate	Cape	Australia	Various	Total
1821–30	2,420,000	100,000	60,000	20,000	20,000	60,000	2,680,000
1831–40	2,650,000	150,000	100,000	30,000	60,000	80,000	3,070,000
1841–50	2,970,000	300,000	120,000	60,000	120,000	230,000	3,800,000
1851–60	3,275,000	320,000	190,000	100,000	250,000	320,000	4,455,000
1861–70	3,480,000	520,000	510,000	130,000	610,000	530,000	5,780,000
1871–80	3,490,000	880,000	1,020,000	185,000	1,330,000	990,000	7,895,000
1881–87	2,440,000	850,000	980,000	125,000	1,240,000	635,000	6,270,000
67 years	20,725,000	3,120,000	2,980,000	650,000	3,630,000	2,845,000	33,950,000

Equivalent in Washed, Tons

	Europe	U. States	River Plate	Cape	Australia	Various	Total
1821–30	1,820,000	60,000	20,000	10,000	10,000	40,000	1,960,000
1831–40	1,990,000	90,000	30,000	20,000	30,000	50,000	2,210,000
1841–50	2,230,000	180,000	40,000	40,000	60,000	140,000	2,690,000
1851–60	2,460,000	190,000	60,000	70,000	140,000	190,000	3,110,000
1861–70	2,610,000	310,000	170,000	90,000	330,000	320,000	3,830,000
1871–80	2,620,000	530,000	340,000	130,000	730,000	590,000	4,940,000
1881–87	1,830,000	510,000	330,000	90,000	680,000	380,000	3,820,000
67 years	15,560,000	1,870,000	990,000	450,000	1,980,000	1,710,000	22,560,000

Value, Millions £

	Europe	U. States	River Plate	Cape	Australia	Various	Total
1821–30	280	10	4	2	4	6	306
1831–40	307	15	6	3	10	8	349
1841–50	313	26	7	7	23	20	396
1851–60	348	28	10	12	45	30	473
1861–70	334	42	26	17	102	43	564
1871–80	297	64	46	25	184	47	663
1881–8	175	55	39	13	124	28	434
67 years	2,054	240	138	79	492	182	3,185

The movement of wool was approximately as follows :—

Period	Net Import, Tons							
	U. Kingdom	France	Germany	Austria	Belgium	Various	U. States	Total
1821–30 . .	100,000	50,000	20,000	...	20,000	10,000	...	200,000
1831–40 . .	170,000	60,000	30,000	...	30,000	20,000	20,000	330,000
1841–50 . .	240,000	200,000	50,000	...	60,000	30,000	40,000	620,000
1851–60 . .	380,000	300,000	70,000	...	90,000	40,000	100,000	980,000
1861–70 . .	580,000	650,000	150,000	...	300,000	80,000	170,000	1,930,000
1871–80 . .	820,000	1,010,000	420,000	60,000	490,000	130,000	370,000	3,300,000
1881–87 . .	680,000	880,000	600,000	90,000	310,000	120,000	360,000	3,040,000
67 years . .	2,970,000	3,150,000	1,340,000	150,000	1,300,000	430,000	1,060,000	10,400,000

Period	Net Export, Tons						
	Russia	Spain	River Plate	Cape	Australia	Various	Total
1821–30	30,000	10,000	60,000	20,000	20,000	60,000	200,000
1831–40	50,000	10,000	100,000	30,000	60,000	80,000	330,000
1841–50	70,000	20,000	120,000	60,000	120,000	230,000	620,000
1851–60	100,000	20,000	190,000	100,000	250,000	320,000	980,000
1861–70	130,000	30,000	510,000	130,000	610,000	530,000	1,940,000
1871–80	70,000	40,000	1,020,000	185,000	1,330,000	645,000	3,290,000
1881–87	110,000	40,000	980,000	125,000	1,240,000	545,000	3,040,000
67 years	560,000	170,000	2,980,000	650,000	3,630,000	2,410,000	10,400,000

The proportions of wool consumed in the country of its production, and of imported wool, were as follows :—

	1821–30	1831–40	1841–50	1851–60	1861–70	1871–80	1881–87
Not imported . . .	92.7	89.7	84.0	78.4	67.0	57.5	52.5
Imported . . .	7.3	10.3	16.0	21.6	33.0	42.5	47.5
Total .	100.0	100.0	100.0	100.0	100.0	100.0	100.0

The consumption in the several countries was approximately as follows :—

Tons Aggregate Wool Unwashed

	1821–30	1831–40	1841–50	1851–60	1861–70	1871–80	1881–87	Total
U. Kingdom	570,000	680,000	820,000	1,040,000	1,290,000	1,570,000	1,200,000	7,170,000
France . .	590,000	670,000	850,000	960,000	1,280,000	1,760,000	1,250,000	7,360,000
Germany .	330,000	380,000	470,000	580,000	690,000	950,000	950,000	4,350,000
Russia . .	420,000	430,000	470,000	490,000	520,000	720,000	480,000	3,530,000
Austria . .	270,000	290,000	310,000	320,000	320,000	380,000	310,000	2,200,000
Italy . . .	90,000	100,000	120,000	130,000	160,000	190,000	160,000	950,000
Spain . .	150,000	160,000	160,000	200,000	220,000	250,000	170,000	1,310,000
Portugal	20,000	25,000	30,000	40,000	50,000	55,000	45,000	265,000
Scandinavia	60,000	70,000	80,000	90,000	100,000	110,000	70,000	580,000
Belgium .	35,000	45,000	75,000	100,000	310,000	500,000	320,000	1,385,000
Various . .	45,000	50,000	75,000	85,000	150,000	160,000	105,000	670,000
Europe . .	2,580,000	2,900,000	3,460,000	4,035,000	5,090,000	6,645,000	5,060,000	29,770,000
U. States .	100,000	170,000	340,000	420,000	690,000	1,250,000	1,210,000	4,180,000
Total .	2,680,000	3,070,000	3,800,000	4,455,000	5,780,000	7,895,000	6,270,000	33,950,000

Equivalent in Yarn Spun, Tons

	1821–30	1831–40	1841–50	1851–60	1861–70	1871–80	1881–87	Total
U. Kingdom	380,000	440,000	520,000	650,000	790,000	930,000	700,000	4,410,000
France . .	370,000	430,000	490,000	530,000	620,000	670,000	510,000	3,620,000
Germany .	210,000	240,000	300,000	360,000	410,000	480,000	410,000	2,410,000
Russia . .	280,000	290,000	310,000	330,000	350,000	480,000	320,000	2,360,000
Austria . .	180,000	200,000	210,000	220,000	220,000	250,000	210,000	1,490,000
Italy . . .	60,000	65,000	75,000	80,000	95,000	115,000	95,000	585,000
Spain .	100,000	110,000	110,000	130,000	150,000	170,000	110,000	880,000
Portugal .	10,000	15,000	20,000	25,000	30,000	35,000	30,000	165,000
Scandinavia	40,000	45,000	50,000	60,000	65,000	70,000	45,000	375,000
Belgium . .	10,000	15,000	25,000	30,000	100,000	170,000	110,000	460,000
Various . .	20,000	25,000	40,000	45,000	75,000	80,000	60,000	345,000
Europe . .	1,660,000	1,875,000	2,150,000	2,460,000	2,905,000	3,450,000	2,600,000	17,100,000
U. States .	60,000	100,000	190,000	210,000	350,000	610,000	590,000	2,110,000
Total .	1,720,000	1,975,000	2,340,000	2,670,000	3,255,000	4,060,000	3,190,000	19,210,000

The value of wool consumed was approximately as follows:—

| | Millions £ Sterling | | | | | | | |
	1821-30	1831-40	1841-50	1851-60	1861-70	1871-80	1881-87	Total
U. Kingdom . .	70	81	91	119	140	156	97	754
France	68	79	86	96	111	113	72	625
Germany . . .	40	44	53	65	73	81	57	413
Russia	46	47	49	54	56	72	41	365
Austria . . .	30	33	33	35	34	36	25	226
Italy	11	12	13	15	17	20	12	100
Spain . . .	16	18	17	22	24	26	14	137
Portugal . . .	2	3	4	5	6	6	4	30
Scandinavia . .	7	7	8	10	10	10	6	58
Belgium . . .	2	3	5	6	18	29	15	78
Various . . .	4	5	7	8	13	13	8	58
Europe . . .	296	332	366	435	502	562	351	2,844
U. States . . .	10	17	30	38	62	101	83	341
Total . .	306	349	396	473	564	663	434	3,185

The value of woollen manufactures produced was approximately thus:—

| | Millions £ Sterling | | | | | | | |
	1821-30	1831-40	1841-50	1851-60	1861-70	1871-80	1881-87	Total
U. Kingdom	191	208	249	311	412	476	320	2,167
France . .	185	205	233	252	325	328	230	1,758
Germany .	105	114	142	171	215	235	185	1,167
Russia . .	126	124	132	141	166	211	130	1,030
Austria . .	81	85	90	93	107	110	84	650
Italy . .	27	27	32	34	46	49	34	249
Spain . . .	45	47	47	56	71	75	44	385
Portugal . .	5	7	8	11	14	15	12	72
Scandinavia .	18	19	22	25	31	30	18	163
Belgium . .	5	7	11	13	47	75	44	202
Various . .	9	11	17	19	37	35	24	152
Europe . .	797	854	983	1,126	1,471	1,639	1,125	7,995
U. States .	27	45	81	117	190	282	241	983
Total .	824	899	1,064	1,243	1,661	1,921	1,366	8,978

The consumption of woollen goods in various countries was approximately as follows:—

| | Millions £ Sterling | | | | | | | |
	1821-30	1831-40	1841-50	1851-60	1861-70	1871-80	1881-87	Total
U. Kingdom	140	158	179	207	242	281	190	1,397
France . .	170	184	193	187	235	191	117	1,277
Germany . .	100	104	117	131	155	167	110	884
Russia . .	126	124	135	145	172	220	135	1,057
Austria . .	81	85	90	93	109	105	78	641
Italy . . .	27	30	37	44	67	71	49	325
Spain . . .	45	47	52	62	79	83	52	420
Portugal . .	7	9	11	14	17	18	14	90
Scandinavia .	18	20	25	30	39	52	38	222
Belgium . .	10	12	15	20	32	46	21	156
Various . .	9	12	16	20	30	35	25	147
Europe . .	733	785	870	953	1,177	1,269	829	6,616
U. States .	35	57	103	173	242	369	297	1,276
Colonies, &c.	56	57	91	117	242	283	240	1,086
Total .	824	899	1,064	1,243	1,661	1,921	1,366	8,978

The annual average consumption per inhabitant was:—

| | Shillings per Inhabitant, Yearly | | | | | | |
	1821-30	1831-40	1841-50	1851-60	1861-70	1871-80	1881-87
United Kingdom . .	12	13	14	15	16	18	15
France	12	11	11	10	13	11	9
Germany	7	7	7	8	8	8	7
Russia	5	5	5	5	5	5	4
Austria	7	7	7	6	7	6	6
Italy	4	4	4	5	5	5	5
Spain	7	7	8	8	9	10	9
Scandinavia . . .	8	7	8	9	11	12	13
Belgium	6	6	7	8	12	18	11
Europe	8	8	8	8	9	9	8
United States . .	7	7	10	13	14	17	15

UNITED KINGDOM

The woollen industry dates its importance from the reign of Edward III., who introduced foreign workmen. Gregory King in 1690, estimated the value of woollen manufactures at eight millions sterling, of which one-fourth were exported; he valued the wool at two millions sterling. The woollen industry approximately was thus:—

| Year | Millions of Lbs. | | | | | | Value of Output, £ |
	British Wool	Imported	Total Wool	Yarn Spun	Exported	Yarn Consumed	
1780 . . .	80	3	83	58	...	58	16,600,000
1800 . . .	90	10	100	68	...	75	18,000,000
1820 . . .	100	10	110	75	...	80	18,700,000
1830 . . .	115	32	147	96	2	94	19,400,000
1840 . . .	120	48	168	108	4	104	22,100,000
1850 . . .	141	60	201	129	14	115	27,700,000
1860 . . .	144	104	248	153	28	125	34,600,000
1870 . . .	155	171	326	194	35	159	47,800,000
1880 . . .	159	226	385	224	26	198	47,500,000
1888 . . .	136	300	436	245	40	205	43,900,000

The output was composed as follows:—

| Year | Manufactures, £ | | | Exported Yarn, £ | Total Output, £ |
	Home Use	Export	Total		
1780	14,000,000	2,600,000	16,600,000	...	16,600,000
1800	11,100,000	6,900,000	18,000,000	...	18,000,000
1820	13,100,000	5,600,000	18,700,000	...	18,700,000
1830	14,500,000	4,700,000	19,200,000	200,000	19,400,000
1840	16,300,000	5,300,000	21,600,000	500,000	22,100,000
1850	17,600,000	8,600,000	26,200,000	1,500,000	27,700,000
1860	18,600,000	12,200,000	30,800,000	3,800,000	34,600,000
1870	21,100,000	21,700,000	42,800,000	5,000,000	47,800,000
1880	26,900,000	17,300,000	44,200,000	3,300,000	47,500,000
1888	19,800,000	20,000,000	39,800,000	4,100,000	43.900,000

The business of sixty-seven years may be stated thus:—

| Period | Tons | | Value, Millions £ | | |
	Wool	Yarn Spun	Wool	Manufactures	Net Result
1821-30 . .	570,000	380,000	70	191	121
1831-40 . .	680,000	440,000	81	208	127
1841-50 . .	820,000	520,000	91	244	153
1851-60 . .	1,040,000	650,000	119	311	192
1861-70 . .	1,290,000	790,000	140	412	272
1871-80 . .	1,570,000	930,000	156	476	320
1881-87 . .	1,200,000	700,000	97	320	223
67 years . .	7,170,000	4,410,000	754	2,162	1,408

The quantity of wool consumed was approximately as follows :—

Period	Tons Aggregate		
	British	Foreign	Total
1821–40 . . .	980,000	270,000	1,250,000
1841–60 . . .	1,180,000	680,000	1,860,000
1861–70 . . .	670,000	620,000	1,290,000
1871–80 . . .	690,000	880,000	1,570,000
1881–87 . . .	390,000	810,000	1,200,000
67 years . . .	3,910,000	3,260,000	7,170,000

In 1774 Campbell estimated woollen manufactures at 12 millions sterling, in 1815 Stevenson at 18 millions, and in 1837 M'Culloch at 22½ millions.

Notwithstanding the magnitude of this industry, Great Britain imports large quantities of foreign goods. The following table shows the value of the total consumption of woollen merchandise :—

Period	Annual Consumption		
	British, £	Imported, £	Total, £
1851–60 . . .	18,100,000	1,100,000	19,200,000
1861–70 . . .	21,300,000	2,050,000	23,350,000
1871–80 . . .	21,600,000	5,020,000	26,620,000
1881–88 . . .	22,600,000	7,100,000	29,700,000

The following table shows the surplus of exports since 1850 :—

Period	Millions £ Woollen Merchandise		
	Imports	Exports	Surplus Exports
1851–60 . . .	11	131	120
1861–70 . . .	21	237	116
1871–80 . . .	50	260	210
1881–88 . . .	57	185	128
38 years . . .	139	813	574

Since 1881 one-tenth of the imported woollen goods has been re-shipped to the Colonies or elsewhere.

This is meantime balanced by the importation of rags averaging £600,000 yearly value, not included in the above imports.

The imports and exports of woollen yarn were :—

Period	Millions of Lbs. Aggregate		
	Imported	Exported	Surplus Exports
1851–60 . . .	...	203	203
1861–70 . . .	63	333	270
1871–80 . . .	122	334	212
1881–88 . . .	118	306	188
38 years . . .	303	1,176	873

The statistics of woollen-factories are as follows :—

Year	Factories	Operatives	Spindles	Looms
1838 . . .	1,313	71,300	...	5,000
1850 . . .	1,998	154,000	2,500,000	42,000
1870 . . .	2,579	239,000	4,950,000	113,000
1878 . . .	2,410	271,000	6,310,000	146,000
1885 . .	2,751	282,000	6,140,000	140,000

The operatives were as follows :—

	1870	1878	1885
Men	96,000	101,000	113,000
Women . . .	119,000	139,000	145,000
Boys	12,000	15,000	12,000
Girls	12,000	16,000	12,000
Total . .	239,000	271,000	282,000

FRANCE

The first machinery for spinning wool was erected at Rheims in 1809, and that city now contains 330 factories. France has at present 2424 woollen factories, of which 740 are worked by steam ; spindles 3,100,000, power-looms 41,000. The industry since 1820 shows thus approximately :—

Year	Millions of Lbs.				Value of Output, £
	French Wool	Imported	Total Wool	Yarn Spun	
1820 . .	116	11	127	80	19,800,000
1830 . .	130	15	145	96	20,000,000
1840 . .	144	30	174	108	22,000,000
1860 . .	150	121	271	136	31,200,000
1870 . .	133	194	327	147	35,800,000
1880 . .	117	255	372	155	33,300,000
1887 . .	126	294	420	172	30,800,000

The value of goods exported, and of those kept for home consumption, were approximately as follows :—

Year	Home Use, £	Exported, £	Total, £
1820 . . .	18,100,000	1,700,000	19,800,000
1830 . . .	18,800,000	1,200,000	20,000,000
1840 . . .	19,000,000	3,000,000	22,000,000
1860 . . .	23,700,000	7,500,000	31,200,000
1870 . . .	25,200,000	10,600,000	35,800,000
1880 . . .	16,500,000	16,800,000	33,300,000
1887 . . .	15,200,000	15,600,000	30,800,000

The business of sixty-seven years may be stated thus :—

Period	Tons		Value, Millions £		
	Wool	Spun Yarn	Wool	Manu-factures	Net Results
1821–30	590,000	370,000	68	185	117
1831–40	670,000	430,000	79	205	126
1841–50	850,000	490,000	86	233	147
1851–60	960,000	530,000	96	252	156
1861–70	1,280,000	620,000	111	325	214
1871–80	1,760,000	670,000	113	328	215
1881–87	1,250,000	510,000	72	230	158
67 years	7,360,000	3,620,000	625	1,758	1,133

France, like Great Britain, consumes a considerable quantity of imported woollen goods. The total consumption since 1860 was :—

Period	Millions £ Sterling			Annual Average, £
	French	Imported	Total	
1861–70 . .	245	15	260	26,600,000
1871–80 . .	209	28	237	23,700,000
1881–87 . .	111	22	133	19,000,000
27 years . .	565	65	630	23,300,000

GERMANY

Woollen manufactures were of minor importance at the beginning of the century. Oddy valued the product of all Prussian woollen-mills in 1800 at £1,700,000 sterling.

The woollen industry of Germany since 1820 is summed up approximately as follows:—

Period	Tons		Value, Millions £		
	Wool	Yarn Spun	Wool	Manu-factures	Net
1821–30 . .	330,000	210,000	40	105	65
1831–40 . .	380,000	240,000	44	114	70
1841–50 . .	470,000	300,000	53	142	89
1851–60 . .	580,000	360,000	65	171	106
1861–70 . .	690,000	410,000	73	215	142
1871–80 . .	950,000	480,000	81	235	154
1881–87 . .	950,000	410,000	57	185	128
67 years . .	4,350,000	2,410,000	413	1,167	754

A statement published in 1878 showed that the woollen-mills of Germany counted 2,000,000 spindles, the annual output being estimated at 26 millions sterling. Germany consumes imported woollen goods to the value of £500,000 per annum. The output of German woollen-factories from 1871 to 1887 is accounted for thus, approximately:—

Period	Millions £			Average Home Use, £
	Home Use	Exported	Total Output	
1871–80 . .	167	68	235	16,700,000
1881–87 . .	110	75	185	15,700,000
17 years . .	277	143	420	16,300,000

RUSSIA

The business of sixty-seven years may be summed up thus:—

Period	Tons Wool Consumed	Tons Yarn Spun	Value, Millions £		
			Wool	Manu-factures	Net
1821–30 . .	420,000	280,000	46	126	80
1831–40 . .	430,000	290,000	47	124	77
1841–50 . .	470,000	310,000	49	132	83
1851–60 . .	490,000	330,000	54	141	87
1861–70 . .	520,000	350,000	56	166	110
1871–80 . .	720,000	480,000	72	211	139
1881–87 . .	480,000	320,000	41	130	89
67 years . .	3,530,000	2,360,000	365	1,030	665

Russia had a surplus of wool, and exported in the above period approximately the following quantity:—

Period	Tons	Lbs. Yearly
1821–40 .	60,000	6,600,000
1841–70 .	330,000	24,000,000
1871–87 .	260,000	35,000,000
67 years .	650,000	...

In 1824 there were 324 factories, and in 1866 the number had risen to 1831, with 105,000 operatives, who turned out goods valued at 18 millions sterling.

The importation of woollen manufactures from abroad was as follows, viz.:—

Year	£	Year	£	Year	£
1860 .	460,000	1870 .	970,000	1880 .	1,210,000
1865 .	400,000	1875 .	1,600,000	1887 .	270,000

It appears that Russia is now almost able to supply her own needs.

AUSTRIA

The business of sixty-seven years was approximately as follows:—

Period	Tons Wool Consumed	Tons Yarn Spun	Value, Millions £		
			Wool	Manu-facture	Net
1821–30 . .	270,000	180,000	30	81	51
1831–40 . .	290,000	200,000	33	85	52
1841–50 . .	310,000	210,000	33	90	57
1851–60 . .	320,000	220,000	35	93	58
1861–70 . .	320,000	220,000	34	107	73
1871–80 . .	380,000	250,000	36	110	74
1881–87 . .	310,000	210,000	25	84	59
67 years . .	2,200,000	1,490,000	226	650	424

In 1840 the woollen-mills of the Empire counted 100,000 operatives. Statistics for 1880 showed 657 mills, 62,000 operatives, 11,000 power-looms, 550,000 spindles, moved by 14,000 horse-power. Spallart valued the product at £12,300,000 in 1884. The disposal of the manufactures was as follows:—

	Yearly Average		
	Home Consumption, £	Export, £	Total, £
1841–60 . . .	9,100,000	...	9,100,000
1861–70 . . .	9,100,000	1,600,000	10,700,000
1871–80 . . .	8,800,000	2,200,000	11,000,000
1881–87 . . .	9,700,000	2,300,000	12,000,000

At the same time there has been a consumption of foreign imported goods.

The total value of woollen goods consumed since 1860 has been:—

Period	Millions £			Annual Average, £
	Austrian	Imported	Total	
1861–70 . .	91	18	109	10,900,000
1871–80 . .	88	17	105	10,500,000
1881–87 . .	68	10	78	11,100,000
27 years . .	247	45	292	...

ITALY

In 1860 the woollen-mills depended almost wholly on native wool, but now almost one-half is imported. The business of sixty-seven years may be estimated approximately thus:—

Period	Tons		Value, Millions £		
	Wool	Yarn Spun	Wool	Manu-facture	Net
1821–30 . .	90,000	60,000	11	27	16
1831–40 . .	100,000	65,000	12	27	15
1841–50 . .	120,000	75,000	13	32	19
1851–60 . .	130,000	80,000	15	34	19
1861–70 . .	160,000	95,000	17	46	29
1871–80 . .	190,000	115,000	20	49	29
1881–87 . .	160,000	95,000	12	34	22
67 years . .	950,000	585,000	100	249	149

The consumption of wool was approximately as follows :—

Period	Tons			Lbs. Yearly
	Italian	Foreign	Total	
1821–60 . .	370,000	70,000	440,000	24,000,000
1861–80 . .	230,000	120,000	350,000	39,000,000
1881–87 . .	90,000	70,000	160,000	52,000,000
67 years . .	690,000	260,000	950,000	...

Meantime the mills have been wholly insufficient to supply the needs of the country.

The total value of woollen goods consumed in Italy since 1860 was as follows :—

Period	Millions £ Sterling Aggregate			Annual Average, £
	Home-Made	Imported	Total	
1861–70 . .	46	21	67	6,700,000
1871–80 . .	49	22	71	7,100,000
1881–87 . .	34	15	49	7,000,000
27 years . .	129	58	187	6,900,000

It appears that not only 40 per cent. of the wool used in the country is of foreign growth, but also that one-third of the woollen goods is imported. In 1840 the kingdom of Sardinia had 62 woollen-mills, employing 5400 hands. In 1877 the kingdom of Italy counted in its woollen-factories 25,000 operatives, with 6600 looms and 305,000 spindles, the mills representing an aggregate of 7300 horse-power, of which 6200 water, the rest steam.

SPAIN

The business of sixty-seven years may be estimated approximately thus :—

Period	Tons Wool Consumed	Tons Yarn Spun	Value, Millions £		
			Wool	Manu-facture	Net
1821–30 . .	150,000	100,000	16	45	29
1831–40 . .	160,000	110,000	18	47	29
1841–50 . .	160,000	110,000	17	47	30
1851–60 . .	200,000	130,000	22	56	34
1861–70 . .	220,000	150,000	24	71	47
1871–80 . .	250,000	170,000	26	75	49
1881–87 . .	170,000	110,000	14	44	30
67 years . .	1,310,000	880,000	137	385	248

In spite of high protective duties, Spain is forced to obtain woollen manufactures in large quantities from abroad.

The consumption of Spanish and imported woollen goods since 1860 has been as follows :—

Period	Millions £ Sterling Aggregate			Annual Average, £
	Spanish	Imported	Total	
1861–70 . .	71	8	79	7,900,000
1871–80 . .	75	8	83	8,300,000
1881–87 . .	44	8	52	7,400,000
27 years . .	190	24	214	...

The export of Spanish wool has been as follows :—

						Tons
1861–80 .	.	.	.	.	.	70,000
1881–87 .	.	.	.	.	.	35,000
27 years .	.	.	.	.	.	105,000

The mills are unable to consume even the wool grown in Spain ; they contain 7000 looms and 25,000 operatives.

PORTUGAL

The business of sixty-seven years was approximately as follows :—

Period	Tons Wool Consumed	Tons Yarn Spun	Value, Millions £		
			Wool	Manu-facture	Net
1821–30 . .	20,000	10,000	2	5	3
1831–40 . .	25,000	15,000	3	7	4
1841–50 . .	30,000	20,000	4	8	4
1851–60 . .	40,000	25,000	5	11	6
1861–70 . .	50,000	30,000	6	14	8
1871–80 . .	55,000	35,000	6	15	9
1881–87 . .	45,000	30,000	4	12	8
67 years . .	265,000	165,000	30	72	42

Two-thirds of the wool used is native, one-third imported. Woollen goods are also imported to the value of £300,000, the total consumption of this class of goods being therefore nearly two millions sterling yearly.

SCANDINAVIA

The woollen industries of the three northern kingdoms collectively may be summed up approximately thus :—

Period	Tons Wool Consumed	Tons Yarn Spun	Value, Millions £		
			Wool	Manu-facture	Net
1821–30 . .	60,000	40,000	7	18	11
1831–40 . .	70,000	45,000	7	19	12
1841–50 . .	80,000	50,000	8	22	14
1851–60 . .	90,000	60,000	10	25	15
1861–70 . .	100,000	65,000	10	31	21
1871–80 . .	110,000	70,000	10	30	20
1881–87 . .	70,000	45,000	6	18	12
67 years . .	580,000	375,000	58	163	105

Denmark exports, and Sweden and Norway import wool. The consumption of home-made and imported goods was as follows :—

Period	Yearly Value, £ Sterling		
	Home-Made	Imported	Total
1861–70 . .	3,100,000	800,000	3,900,000
1871–80 . .	3,000,000	2,200,000	5,200,000
1881–87 . .	2,600,000	2,850,000	5,450,000

The importations of woollen goods into the three kingdoms were as follows :—

	Yearly Value, £		
	1861–70	1871–80	1881–87
Sweden . .	220,000	900,000	1,200,000
Norway . .	100,000	500,000	600,000
Denmark .	500,000	800,000	1,050,000
Total .	820,000	2,200,000	2,850,000

BELGIUM

The business of 67 years may be summed up approximately as follows :—

| Period | Tons Wool Consumed | Tons Yarn Spun | Value, Millions £ | | |
			Wool	Manu-factures	Net
1821–30 . .	35,000	10,000	2	5	3
1831–40 . .	45,000	15,000	3	7	4
1841–50 . .	75,000	25,000	5	11	6
1851–60 . .	100,000	30,000	6	13	7
1861–70 . .	310,000	100,000	18	47	29
1871–80 . .	500,000	170,000	29	75	46
1881–87 . .	320,000	110,000	15	44	29
67 years . .	1,385,000	460,000	78	202	124

The wool is almost all imported, only 2 per cent. being Belgian. It is not, however, all made into stuffs, about one-fifth being re-exported as woollen yarn. The imports and exports of woollen goods, including yarn, showed :—

| Period | Annual Average, £ | | |
	Imports	Exports	Surplus Exports
1861–70 . .	800,000	2,300,000	1,500,000
1871–80 . .	900,000	3,800,000	2,900,000
1881–87 . .	800,000	3,300,000	2,500,000

The output of the mills and the home consumption were :—

| Period | Annual Average, £ | | |
	Output	Net Export	Consumption
1861–70 . .	4,700,000	1,500,000	3,200,000
1871–80 . .	7,500,000	2,900,000	4,600,000
1881–87 . .	6,300,000	3,300,000	3,000,000

UNITED STATES

The wool consumed was approximately as follows :—

| Period | Tons | | |
	American	Imported	Total
1821–40 . .	250,000	20,000	270,000
1841–60 . .	620,000	140,000	760,000
1861–80 . .	1,400,000	540,000	1,9;0,000
1881–87 . .	850,000	360,000	1,210,000
67 years . .	3,120,000	1,060,000	4,180,000

In 1840 there were 1420 mills, with 21,000 operatives, the number of the latter reaching 39,000 in 1850. The Census of 1880 showed 2689 mills, with a capital of 33 millions sterling, which had 162,000 operatives and two million spindles.

The business of sixty-seven years was approximately as follows :—

| Period | Tons Wool Consumed | Tons Yarn Spun | Value, Millions £ | | |
			Wool	Manu-factures	Net
1821–30 . .	100,000	60,000	10	27	17
1831–40 . .	170,900	100,000	17	45	28
1841–50 . .	340,000	190,000	30	81	51
1851–60 . .	420,000	210,0c0	38	117	79
1861–70 . .	690,000	350,000	62	190	128
1871–80 . .	1,250,000	610,000	101	282	181
1881–87 . .	1,210,000	590,000	83	241	158
67 years . .	4,180,000	2,110,000	341	983	642

The consumption of woollen goods since 1840 has been approximately as follows :—

| Period | Value, Millions £ Aggregate | | | Yearly Average, £ | Shillings per Inhab. |
	American	Imported	Total		
1841–50	81	22	103	10,300,000	10.1
1851–60	117	56	173	17,300,000	12.5
1861–70	190	52	242	24,200,000	14.0
1871–80	282	87	369	36,900,000	16.6
1881–87	241	56	297	42,400,000	15.2
47 years	911	273	1,184	...	...

INDIA

In December 1889 there were four woollen mills, representing an aggregate capital of £1,200,000, with 7000 spindles and 300 looms. The consumption of wool is not stated, nor the value of products.

WORK

Foot-Tons of Energy

Walking 1 mile	17½
Walking 4 miles	70
Carrying 60 lbs. 1 mile	25
Carrying 60 lbs. 4 miles	100
Pedlar's day's work	303
Convict's day's work	310
Dock labourer's day's work . . .	325
Pile-driving	332
Pavior	352
Turning a winch	374
Man's ordinary work	300
Very hard ditto	400

Y.

YACHTS

The number in Great Britain has been as follows :—

Year	Clubs	Yachts	Year	Clubs	Yachts
1853 . .	18	1,046	1873 . .	40	2,805
1863 . .	18	1,348	1883 . .	55	4,030

France has 9370 yachts, averaging three tons, and £61 in value : of the whole number, only 103 are steamers.

Lord Brassey's *Sunbeam* circumnavigated the globe in eleven months, from July 1876 to May 1877, making 14,465 miles by steam and 20,312 under sail, in all 34,777 miles, averaging 105 miles a day, including time in port. She was 157 feet long, 531 tons, 70 horse-power, and consumed 4 tons of coal daily, steaming 10 knots an hour. Mr. Lambert's *Wanderer* was 23 months making the tour of the globe (1880–82), but only 280 days actually at sea, having made 48,490 miles between steam and sail.

YARN

Exports of British yarn were as follows :—

| Year | Million Lbs. | | | | Value, £ |
	Cotton	Woollen	Linen and Jute	Total	
1821	22	...	...	22	2,306,000
1831	64	2	1	67	4,270,000
1841	119	4	18	141	8,362,000
1851	144	14	19	177	9,071,000
1861	178	28	28	234	14,468,000
1871	194	44	50	298	23,641,000
1881	255	30	36	321	17,693,000
1889	252	45	48	345	17,300,000

The prices of yarn at various dates were in pence per pound :—

Year	Cotton	Woollen	Linen
1831	22	26	19
1841	14	29	12
1851	12	25	12
1861	13	30	14
1871	19	34	15
1881	13	26	14
1889	11	23	15

The consumption of imported yarn in various countries in 1888 was as follows :—

	Millions of Lbs.			
	Cotton	Woollen	Linen, &c.	Total
France . . .	20	...	...	20
Germany . .	34	27	...	61
Russia . . .	9	...	...	9
Austria . . .	22	9	...	31
Italy . . .	8	...	9	17
Spain . . .	1	...	8	9
Sweden . . .	3	3	...	6
Holland . . .	20	1	...	21
Roumania . .	9	...	...	9
Egypt . . .	3	...	...	3
China . . .	90	...	...	90
Japan . . .	64	...	...	64
Total .	283	40	17	340

Belgium and Switzerland produce more yarn than they require, the former exporting about 30 million lbs., the latter 16 million lbs. yearly.

Z.

ZINC

The production of zinc was as follows :—

	Tons	
	1880	1888
Great Britain . . .	22,000	27,000
Belgium . . .	99,000	133,000
Prussia . . .	64,000	83,000
United States . .	21,000	50,000
Spain, &c. . . .	22,000	24,000
Total . . .	228,000	317,000

The zinc industry of Great Britain is shown thus :—

Year	Tons					Value per Ton, £
	Production	Imported	Total	Exported	Home Use	
1831	700	3,800	4,500	3,100	1,400	14
1851	3,900	18,600	22,500	4,500	18,000	21
1871	4,960	20,930	25,890	8,060	17,830	18
1881	15,950	46,100	62,050	10,700	51,350	15
1889	9,400	56,400	65,800	7,700	58,100	15

In the previous table Great Britain is credited with a production of 27,000 tons, but this includes 18,000 tons extracted from foreign ores imported. Not all the zinc imported is metallic, a large portion being mineral ore. Belgian ore gives 18 per cent. of metal, German 16, British 28 per cent. The production of zinc in the world has trebled since 1870. See *Mining*.

DICTIONARY OF STATISTICS.

PART II.

A

AGES AND SEXES

THE ages of some nations have been seriously affected in the last half-century by wars, emigration, and other causes ; some have grown younger, others have lost severely in the age of 20 to 50, others show a lower percentage of children, as will appear in comparison further on. The census returns of all countries for 1890–91 (Spain 1887) show the relative proportions of age as follows :—

Age	England	Scotland	Ireland	France	Germany	Austria	Hungary	Switzerland	Spain	Scandinavia	Holland	Belgium	Bulgaria	Japan	Australia	U. States	Average
Under 10 . . .	239	243	208	175	242	239	262	217	230	239	245	224	305	228	265	243	238
10–20 . . .	213	216	234	174	207	197	191	198	186	195	202	202	192	204	208	217	202
20–30 . . .	172	168	162	163	162	162	156	161	160	146	156	165	116	153	197	183	161
30–40 . . .	131	126	108	138	127	131	137	125	132	124	121	126	122	135	132	135	129
40–50 . . .	99	96	98	123	104	109	108	114	114	101	101	103	108	115	85	94	104
50–60 . . .	71	72	85	101	78	83	78	91	86	84	83	83	65	78	64	64	79
60–70 . . .	47	48	60	76	52	52	46	64	65	68	59	60	45	57	33	39	54
Over 70 . . .	28	31	45	50	28	27	22	30	27	43	33	37	47	30	16	25	33
Total . .	1,000	1,000	1,000	1,000	1,000	1,000	1,000	1,000	1,000	1,000	1,000	1,000	1,000	1,000	1,000	1,000	1,000

The ratio of children, under 10, is so low in France and Ireland as to show that either the moral or the economic condition of those countries is unsatisfactory. The average of old persons, over 60, is highest in France and Scandinavia. The age of greatest physical strength being from 20 to 60, it is important to compare the ratios of this age in various countries as follows :—

Per 1000 Inhabitants

France	. .	525	Australia	.	478
Spain	. .	492	Belgium .	.	477
Switzerland .	.	491	U. States	.	476
Austria	. .	485	England	.	473
Japan	. .	481	Germany	.	471

Scotland	.	462
Holland	.	461
Scandinavia .		455
Ireland	. .	453
Bulgaria .	.	411

With the exception of Bulgaria there is no country where the able-bodied population stands so low as in Ireland, which in some manner accounts for the unfortunate condition of the island, and shows the direct result of emigration.

The relative smallness of the able-bodied population in Bulgaria seems to indicate that the country has not yet recovered from the effects of the massacres committed there by the Turks in 1876. The very high ratio in France is partly due to the fact that 400,000 Belgian, and 250,000 Italian, operatives have settled there.

As regard sexes, the number of females compared with males of corresponding age in the various countries is shown as follows :—

	Number of Females to 1000 Males																
Age	England	Scotland	Ireland	France	Germany	Austria	Hungary	Switzerland	Spain	Scandinavia	Holland	Belgium	Bulgaria	Japan	Australia	U. States	Average
Under 10 . . .	1,008	972	970	996	995	1,002	995	998	975	973	988	992	958	978	972	971	984
10–20 . . .	1,007	977	958	996	1,001	1,026	1,032	1,006	1,025	982	997	988	974	977	990	992	996
20–30 . . .	1,119	1,119	1,035	1,023	1,027	1,046	1,044	1,087	1,140	1,125	1,033	969	1,118	966	880	969	1,044
30–40 . . .	1,067	1,090	1,090	983	1,041	1,048	991	1,073	1,095	1,128	1,025	1,005	1,047	947	740	887	1,016
40–50 . . .	1,078	1,132	1,151	1,010	1,076	1,061	990	1,096	1,057	1,127	1,023	1,012	825	932	747	926	1,015
50–60 . . .	1,123	1,208	1,064	1,025	1,117	1,103	1,009	1,122	1,072	1,123	1,049	1,025	862	980	693	922	1,031
60–70 . . .	1,180	1,313	1,061	1,055	1,182	1,150	1,062	1,152	1,034	1,152	1,108	1,072	922	1,068	662	922	1,068
Over 70 . . .	1,308	1,653	1,077	1,137	1,223	1,094	1,042	1,137	1,128	1,311	1,239	1,194	973	1,310	700	932	1,153
General . . .	1,064	1,072	1,029	1,014	1,040	1,044	1,015	1,058	1,040	1,068	1,024	1,005	965	980	866	953	1,015

There is a dearth of females in Bulgaria, Japan, and Australia, but a large surplus in England, Scotland, Switzerland, and Scandinavia. If we take the usual marrying age for women, say from 20 to 40, we find as follows :—

MARRYING AGE

Females to 1000 Males

Scandinavia	1,127	Switzerland	1,080	Hungary .	1,017
Spain . .	1,118	Ireland .	1,063	France . .	1,003
Scotland .	1,105	Austria .	1,047	Belgium .	987
England .	1,083	Germany .	1,034	U. States .	928
Bulgaria .	1,083	Holland .	1,029	Australia .	810

It is worthy of notice that although Bulgaria has a deficit of females there is nevertheless in that country a surplus of women of marrying age, exceeding 8 per cent. It is also remarkable that, except in France and Germany, the excess of women of marrying age is greater in all countries than the average surplus of females of all ages.

As regards changes in the ratios of sex in the last decade * we find :—

Number of Females to 1000 Males

	1881	1891		1881	1891
England . .	1,053	1,064	Scandinavia .	1,051	1,068
Scotland . .	1,079	1,072	Holland . .	1,023	1,024
Ireland . .	1,041	1,029	Belgium . .	1,002	1,005
U. Kingdom .	1,053	1,062	Switzerland .	1,040	1,058
France . . .	1,005	1,014	Greece . .	901	921
Germany . . .	1,038	1,040	United States	966	953
Austria . . .	1,046	1,044	Canada . .	968	965
Hungary . .	1,031	1,015	Australia . .	849	866
Spain . . .	1,044	1,040	Average . .	1,013	1,016

It appears, therefore, that the surplus of females in general averages 3 per thousand more than was the case in 1881. And if we take only the 14 European countries we find the mean for 1891 was 1035, as against 1032 in 1881, showing in like manner an increase of 3 per thousand. Considering only the sexes of persons between 20 and 40 years of age, the surplus of females in European countries is as follows :—

England . . .	403,000	Austria	160,000
Scotland . . .	60,000	Hungary . . .	50,000
Ireland	35,000	Spain	196,000
United Kingdom	498,000	Scandinavia . .	144,000
France . . .	28,000	Holland . . .	19,000
Germany . . .	235,000	Bulgaria . . .	30,000
Switzerland . .	32,000	Total	1,392,000

On the other hand there is a deficit of women of that age (20–40) of 14,000 in Belgium, 127,000 in Australia, 49,000 in Canada, and 690,000 in the United States, in all 880,000. If this number were to emigrate from Europe it would reduce the surplus to 512,000.

ENGLAND AND WALES

Age	Number (000 omitted)			Ratio	Females to 1000 Males
	Males	Females	Total		
Under 10 . .	3,461	3,488	6,949	239	1,008
10–20 . . .	3,076	3,098	6,174	213	1,007
20–30 . . .	2,358	2,638	4,996	172	1,119
30–40 . . .	1,843	1,966	3,809	131	1,067
40–50 . . .	1,388	1,496	2,884	99	1,078
50–60 . . .	963	1,082	2,045	71	1,123
60–70 . . .	617	728	1,345	47	1,180
Over 70 . .	347	454	801	28	1,308
Total pop.	14,053	14,950	29,003	1,000	1,064

* In 1881 the ratio in Italy was 995 females to 1000 males : in Russia the new census gives 1028 females to 1000 males.

SCOTLAND

Age	Number (000 omitted)			Ratio	Females to 1000 Males
	Males	Females	Total		
Under 10 . .	497	483	980	243	972
10–20 . . .	440	430	870	216	977
20–30 . . .	319	357	676	168	1,119
30–40 . . .	243	265	508	126	1,090
40–50 . . .	182	206	388	96	1,132
50–60 . . .	130	157	287	72	1,208
60–70 . . .	83	110	193	48	1,313
Over 70 . .	49	75	124	31	1,653
Total pop.	1,943	2,083	4,026	1,000	1,072

IRELAND

Age	Males	Females	Total	Ratio	Females to 1000 Males
Under 10 . .	497	482	979	208	970
10–20 . . .	557	543	1,100	234	958
20–30 . . .	375	388	763	162	1,035
30–40 . . .	243	265	508	108	1,090
40–50 . . .	215	248	463	98	1,151
50–60 . . .	193	205	398	85	1,064
60–70 . . .	136	144	280	60	1,061
Over 70 . .	103	111	214	45	1,077
Total pop.	2,319	2,386	4,705	1,000	1,029

UNITED KINGDOM

Age	Males	Females	Total	Ratio	Females to 1000 Males
Under 10 . .	4,455	4,453	8,908	236	1,000
10–20 . . .	4,073	4,071	8,144	216	1,000
20–30 . . .	3,052	3,383	6,435	170	1,109
30–40 . . .	2,329	2,496	4,825	128	1,072
40–50 . . .	1,785	1,950	3,735	100	1,092
50–60 . . .	1,286	1,444	2,730	72	1,123
60–70 . . .	836	982	1,818	48	1,174
Over 70 . .	499	640	1,139	30	1,300
Total pop.	18,315	19,419	37,734	1,000	1,060

UNITED STATES

Age	Males	Females	Total	Ratio	Females to 1000 Males
Under 10 . .	7,715	7,494	15,209	243	971
10–20 . . .	6,824	6,768	13,592	217	992
20–30 . . .	5,803	5,621	11,424	183	969
30–40 . . .	4,476	3,968	8,444	135	887
40–50 . . .	3,073	2,845	5,918	94	926
50–60 . . .	2,081	1,918	3,999	64	922
60–70 . . .	1,285	1,184	2,469	39	922
Over 70 . .	811	756	1,567	25	932
Total pop.	32,068	30,554	62,622	1,000	953

Whites

Age	Males	Females	Total	Ratio	Females to 1000 Males
Under 10 . .	6,628	6,425	13,053	237	970
10–20 . . .	5,863	5,805	11,668	212	990
20–30 . . .	5,148	4,947	10,095	184	961
30–40 . . .	4,032	3,552	7,584	139	881
40–50 . . .	2,767	2,548	5,315	96	921
50–60 . . .	1,877	1,746	3,623	65	930
60–70 . . .	1,167	1,083	2,250	41	931
Over 70 . .	724	671	1,395	26	925
Total pop.	28,206	26,777	54,983	1,000	949

Coloured

Age	Males	Females	Total	Ratio	Females to 1000 Males
Under 10 . .	1,087	1,069	2,156	283	983
10–20 . . .	961	963	1,924	252	1,002
20–30 . . .	655	674	1,329	174	1,029
30–40 . . .	444	416	860	112	937
40–50 . . .	306	297	603	79	970
50–60 . . .	204	172	376	49	843
60–70 . . .	118	101	219	29	856
Over 70 . .	87	85	172	22	977
Total pop.	3,862	3,777	7,639	1,000	978

FRANCE

| Age | Number (000 omitted) | | | Ratio | Females to 1000 Males |
	Males	Females	Total		
Under 10 . .	3,345	3,331	6,676	175	996
10-20 . . .	3,339	3,325	6,664	174	996
20-30 . . .	3,064	3,136	6,200	163	1,023
30-40 . . .	2,652	2,608	5,260	138	983
40-50 . . .	2,337	2,361	4,698	123	1,010
50-60 . . .	1,899	1,947	3,846	101	1,025
60-70 . . .	1,401	1,478	2,879	76	1,055
Over 70 . .	895	1,015	1,910	50	1,137
Total pop.	18,932	19,201	38,133	1,000	1,014

GERMANY

Age	Males	Females	Total	Ratio	Females to 1000 Males
Under 10 . .	5,994	5,966	11,960	242	995
10-20 . . .	5,105	5,110	10,215	207	1,001
20-30 . . .	3,947	4,055	8,002	162	1,027
30-40 . . .	3,090	3,217	6,307	127	1,041
40-50 . . .	2,472	2,660	5,132	104	1,076
50-60 . . .	1,827	2,041	3,868	78	1,117
60-70 . . .	1,177	1,391	2,568	52	1,182
Over 70 . .	619	757	1,376	28	1,223
Total pop.	24,231	25,197	49,428	1,000	1,040

AUSTRIA

Age	Males	Females	Total	Ratio	Females to 1000 Males
Under 10 . .	2 849	2,856	5,705	239	1,002
10-20 . . .	2,332	2,393	4,725	197	1,026
20-30 . . .	1,896	1,983	3,879	162	1,046
30-40 . . .	1,531	1,604	3,135	131	1,048
40-50 . . .	1,258	1,335	2,593	109	1,061
50-60 . . .	939	1,036	1,975	83	1,103
60-70 . . .	580	667	1,247	52	1,150
Over 70 . .	304	333	637	27	1,094
Total pop.	11,689	12,207	23,896	1,000	1,044

HUNGARY

Age	Males	Females	Total	Ratio	Females to 1000 Males
Under 10 . .	2,293	2,289	4,582	262	995
10-20 . . .	1,641	1,694	3,335	191	1,032
20-30 . . .	1,328	1,388	2,716	156	1,044
30-40 . . .	1,197	1,187	2,384	137	991
40-50 . . .	943	933	1,876	108	990
50-60 . . .	682	688	1,370	78	1,009
60-70 . . .	389	413	802	46	1,062
Over 70 . .	195	204	399	22	1,042
Total pop.	8,668	8,796	17,464	1,000	1,015

AUSTRIA-HUNGARY

Age	Males	Females	Total	Ratio	Females to 1000 Males
Under 10 . .	5,142	5,145	10,287	248	1,001
10-20 . . .	3,973	4,087	8,060	195	1,029
20-30 . . .	3,224	3,371	6,595	160	1,045
30-40 . . .	2,728	2,791	5,519	134	1,023
40-50 . . .	2,201	2,268	4,469	108	1,031
50-60 . . .	1,621	1,724	3,345	81	1,064
60-70 . . .	969	1,080	2,049	49	1,112
Over 70 . .	499	537	1,036	25	1,076
Total pop.	20,357	21,003	41,360	1,000	1,032

ITALY (1881)

Age	Males	Females	Total	Ratio	Females to 1000 Males
Under 20 . .	5,967	5,827	11,794	416	976
20-30 . . .	2,263	2,312	4,575	162	1,022
30-40 . . .	1,901	1,932	3,833	135	1,016
40-50 . . .	2,847	2,861	5,708	201	1,005
Over 60 . .	1,288	1,262	2,550	86	980
Total pop.	14,266	14,194	28,460	1,000	995

SWITZERLAND

| Age | Number (000 omitted) | | | Ratio | Females to 1000 Males |
	Males	Females	Total		
Under 10 . .	317	316	633	217	998
10-20 . . .	288	290	578	198	1,006
20-30 . . .	225	244	469	161	1,087
30-40 . . .	176	189	365	125	1,073
40-50 . . .	159	174	333	114	1,096
50-60 . . .	125	140	265	91	1,122
60-70 . . .	86	100	186	64	1,152
Over 70 . .	41	47	88	30	1,137
Total pop.	1,417	1,500	2,917	1,000	1,058

SPAIN

Age	Males	Females	Total	Ratio	Females to 1000 Males
Under 10 . .	2,040	1,987	4,027	230	975
10-20 . . .	1,613	1,654	3,267	186	1,025
20-30 . . .	1,364	1,455	2,819	160	1,140
30-40 . . .	1,108	1,213	2,321	132	1,095
40-50 . . .	974	1,030	2,004	114	1,057
50-60 . . .	725	777	1,502	86	1,072
60-70 . . .	562	581	1,143	65	1,034
Over 70 . .	227	256	483	27	1,128
Total pop.	8,613	8,953	17,566	1,000	1,040

DENMARK

Age	Males	Females	Total	Ratio	Females to 1000 Males
Under 10 . .	269	264	533	243	981
10-20 . . .	214	210	424	194	984
20-30 . . .	153	173	326	149	1,129
30-40 . . .	135	146	281	129	1,085
40-50 . . .	106	114	220	101	1,068
50-60 . . .	85	92	177	81	1,077
60-70 . . .	64	71	135	62	1,114
Over 70 . .	39	50	89	41	1,282
Total pop.	1,065	1,120	2,185	1,000	1,051

SWEDEN

Age	Males	Females	Total	Ratio	Females to 1000 Males
Under 10 . .	560	546	1,106	231	973
10-20 . . .	466	454	920	192	976
20-30 . . .	336	360	696	146	1,071
30-40 . . .	281	314	595	124	1,121
40-50 . . .	232	263	495	104	1,134
50-60 . . .	198	227	425	89	1,146
60-70 . . .	156	185	341	71	1,186
Over 70 . .	88	119	207	43	1,340
Total pop.	2,317	2,468	4,785	1,000	1,065

NORWAY

Age	Males	Females	Total	Ratio	Females to 1000 Males
Under 10 . .	253	243	496	249	960
10-20 . . .	200	200	400	201	1,000
20-30 . . .	126	159	285	143	1,260
30-40 . . .	108	131	239	120	1,220
40-50 . . .	88	103	191	96	1,160
50-60 . . .	73	81	154	78	1,120
60-70 . . .	63	70	133	67	1,120
Over 70 . .	41	51	92	46	1,244
Total pop.	952	1,038	1,990	1,000	1,090

SCANDINAVIA

Age	Males	Females	Total	Ratio	Females to 1000 Males
Under 10 . .	1,082	1,053	2,135	239	973
10-20 . . .	880	864	1,744	195	982
20-30 . . .	615	692	1,307	146	1,125
30-40 . . .	524	591	1,115	124	1,128
40-50 . . .	426	480	906	101	1,127
50-60 . . .	356	400	756	84	1,123
60-70 . . .	283	326	609	68	1,152
Over 70 . .	168	220	388	43	1,311
Total pop.	4,334	4,626	8,960	1,000	1,068

HOLLAND

Age	Number (ooo omitted)			Ratio	Females to 1000 Males
	Males	Females	Total		
Under 10 .	555	548	1,103	245	988
10–20 . . .	456	455	911	202	997
20–30 . . .	347	359	706	156	1,033
30–40 . . .	270	277	547	121	1,025
40–50 . . .	225	230	455	101	1,023
50–60 . . .	182	191	373	83	1,049
60–70 . . .	126	139	265	59	1,108
Over 70 . .	67	84	151	33	1,239
Total pop.	2,228	2,283	4,511	1,000	1,024

BELGIUM

Age	Males	Females	Total	Ratio	Females to 1000 Males
Under 10 . .	683	678	1,361	224	992
10–20 . . .	617	609	1,226	202	988
20–30 . . .	510	494	1,004	165	969
30–40 . . .	380	382	762	126	1,005
40–50 . . .	310	314	624	103	1,012
50–60 . . .	249	255	504	83	1,025
60–70 . . .	175	187	362	60	1,072
Over 70 . .	103	123	226	37	1,194
Total pop.	3,027	3,042	6,069	1,000	1,005

FINLAND

Age	Males	Females	Total	Ratio	Females to 1000 Males
Under 10 . .	302	299	601	253	987
10–20 . . .	240	238	478	201	989
20–30 . . .	179	179	358	150	1,000
30–40 . . .	154	157	311	131	1,018
40–50 . . .	125	133	258	108	1,062
50–60 . . .	86	96	182	77	1,116
60–70 . . .	59	71	130	54	1,214
Over 70 . .	26	36	62	26	1,406
Total pop.	1,171	1,209	2,380	1,000	1,032

ROUMANIA

The official estimate of ages and population is as follows :—

	No.	Ratio
Under 20 . . .	2,450,000	430
20–40 . . .	1,730,000	304
40–60 . . .	1,190,000	208
Over 60 . . .	330,000	58
Total .	5,700,000	1,000

To every thousand males there are only 967 females.

BULGARIA

Age	Number (ooo omitted)			Ratio	Females to 1000 Males
	Males	Females	Total		
Under 10 . .	492	471	963	305	958
10–20 . . .	307	299	606	192	974
20–30 . . .	172	193	365	116	1,118
30–40 . . .	188	197	385	122	1,047
40–50 . . .	187	153	340	108	825
50–60 . . .	109	94	203	65	862
60–70 . . .	74	68	142	45	922
Over 70 . .	76	74	150	47	973
Total pop.	1,605	1,549	3,154	1,000	965

JAPAN

Age	Number (ooo omitted)			Ratio	Females to 1000 Males
	Males	Females	Total		
Under 10 . .	4,683	4,582	9,265	228	978
10–20 . . .	4,203	4,105	8,308	204	977
20–30 . . .	3,161	3,055	6,216	153	966
30–40 . . .	2,823	2,674	5,497	135	947
40–50 . . .	2,418	2,252	4,670	115	932
50–60 . . .	1,608	1,577	3,185	78	980
60–70 . . .	1,131	1,208	2,339	57	1,068
Over 70 . .	536	702	1,238	30	1,310
Total pop.	20,563	20,155	40,718	1,000	980

AUSTRALIA

Age	Males	Females	Total	Ratio	Females to 1000 Males
Under 10 . .	509	495	1,004	265	972
10–20 . . .	397	393	790	208	990
20–30 . . .	398	349	747	197	880
30–40 . . .	292	214	506	132	740
40–50 . . .	186	139	325	85	747
50–60 . . .	143	99	242	64	693
60–70 . . .	77	51	128	33	662
Over 70 . .	36	25	61	16	700
Total pop.	2,038	1,765	3,803	1,000	866

CAPE COLONY

Age	Whites	Coloured	Total	Ratio	Whites, per cent.
Under 10 . .	114	342	456	299	25.0
10–20 . . .	83	280	363	237	22.8
20–30 . . .	68	192	260	226	26.2
30–40 . . .	48	129	177	116	27.1
40–50 . . .	30	92	122	80	24.5
50–60 . . .	18	58	76	50	23.7
60–70 . . .	11	33	44	29	25.0
Over 70 . .	5	25	30	19	17.0
Total pop.	377	1,151	1,528	1,000	24.7

CANADA

The census of 1891 compares with 1881 as follows :—

Age	Number (ooo omitted)		Ratio	
	1881	1891	1881	1891
Under 5 . . .	579	604	134	125
5–15	1,061	1,136	245	235
15–20	476	512	110	105
20–30	761	860	176	178
30–50	865	1,018	200	211
Over 50 . . .	583	703	135	145
Total pop. .	4,325	4,833	1,000	1,000

UNITED KINGDOM

The census of 1891 shows that the proportions of age and sex in the three kingdoms have undergone the following changes since 1881 :—

ENGLAND AND WALES

Age	1881			1891		
	Males	Females	Total	Males	Females	Total
Under 15 .	182	183	365	175	176	351
15–45 . .	216	230	446	221	238	459
45–55 . .	40	44	84	41	46	87
Over 55 . .	49	56	105	47	56	103
Total .	487	513	1,000	484	516	1,000

SCOTLAND

Age	1881			1891		
	Males	Females	Total	Males	Females	Total
Under 15 .	185	181	366	180	176	356
15–45 . .	213	230	443	217	232	449
45–55 . .	37	45	82	39	41	80
Over 55 . .	46	63	109	47	68	115
Total .	481	519	1,000	483	517	1,000

IRELAND

Age	Males	Females	Total	Males	Females	Total
Under 15 .	178	172	350	165	160	325
15–45 . .	206	224	430	216	227	443
45–55 . .	41	45	86	46	51	97
Over 55 . .	65	69	134	66	69	135
Total .	490	510	1,000	493	507	1,000

UNITED KINGDOM

Age	Males	Females	Total	Males	Females	Total
Under 15 .	182	181	363	174	174	348
15–45 . .	214	229	443	220	236	456
45–55 . .	40	44	84	42	46	88
Over 55 . .	51	59	110	49	59	108
Total .	487	513	1,000	485	515	1,000

Comparing the last census with the preceding, we find that the ratio of young people under 15 has fallen very notably in the three kingdoms, especially in Ireland. As a necessary consequence the proportion of persons between 15 and 45 has risen: the ratio of this class has risen 3 per cent. in Ireland, the same in England, and 1½ per cent. in Scotland. Persons between 45 and 55 have risen in ratio both in England and Ireland, but fallen in Scotland. Finally, those over 55 show a relative decline in England, but a rise in the sister kingdoms. This last class is much greater in Ireland than in Great Britain. When we consider sexes we find the preponderance of females has increased in England, while it has declined in Scotland and Ireland. Taking the United Kingdom as a whole, the excess of the female population is now 62 per thousand, as compared with 53 per thousand in 1881. This cannot be the result of emigration, seeing that in Ireland the sexes are less unequal. If we limit our observation to persons between 15 and 45, we find the preponderance of females is 77 per thousand in England, 69 in Scotland, and 50 per thousand in Ireland. Altogether, the proportion of women between 15 and 45 in the United Kingdom is 3 per cent. higher now than in 1881, and yet the birth-rate has fallen remarkably.

FRANCE

The ratios of population by four censuses were :—

Age	1841	1861	1881	1891
Under 10 . .	185	186	183	175
10–20 . . .	176	169	170	174
20–30 . . .	163	164	158	163
30–40 . . .	148	144	137	138
40–50 . . .	125	125	123	123
50–60 . . .	102	101	103	101
Over 60 . . .	101	111	126	126
Total .	1,000	1,000	1,000	1,000

The ratio of persons between 30 and 40 is 4 per cent. less than it was in 1861, probably the result of the Franco-German war. The ratio of persons over 60 has risen 25 per cent.

GERMANY

The census of 1891 compares with that of 1871 as follows :—

Age	Number (000 omitted)			Ratio	
	1871	1891	Increase	1871	1891
Under 20 . .	17,850	22,175	4,325	435	449
20–40 . . .	12,220	14,309	2,089	298	289
40–60	7,790	9,000	1,210	190	182
Over 60 . . .	·3,160	3,944	784	77	80
Total pop.	41,020	49,428	8,408	1,000	1,000

The class which shows the greatest increase is that of persons under 20, which grew 24 per cent. in 20 years, while the rest of the population rose only 17 per cent. At present Germany has 449, France only 349, per thousand of her population under 20 years of age. The German census of 1891 compares with that of 1885 as follows :—

Age	Number (000 omitted)			
	Males		Females	
	1885	1891	1885	1891
Under 20	10,490	11,099	10,510	11,076
20–40	6,585	7,037	6,880	7,272
40–60	4,100	4,299	4,465	4,701
Over 60	1,760	1,796	2,065	2,148
Total pop. .	22,935	24,231	23,920	25,197

The changes which took place in the composition of the nation as regards sex were as follows :—

Age	Number of Females to 1000 Males	
	1885	1891
Under 20	1,002	998
20–40	1,045	1,033
40–60	1,089	1,093
Over 60	1,173	1,196
General	1,044	1,040

The surplus of females under 40 years of age has diminished, but over 40 it has increased, and on the whole it is 4 per thousand less than it was in 1885.

AUSTRIA

The census of Austria (without Hungary) in 1890 compares with that of 1880 as follows :—

Age	Number (000 omitted)			
	Males		Females	
	1880	1890	1880	1890
Under 20	4,770	5,181	4,845	5,249
20–40	3,190	3,427	3,365	3,587
40–60	2,045	2,197	2,245	2,371
Over 60	815	884	870	1,000
Total pop. .	10,820	11,689	11,325	12,207

The changes as regards sex are shown as follows :—

Age	Number of Females to 1000 Males	
	1880	1890
Under 20	1,016	1,013
20–40	1,055	1,047
40–60	1,098	1,079
Over 60	1,067	1,131
General	1,046	1,044

The surplus of females declined 2 per thousand in 10 years.

SWITZERLAND

The composition of the Swiss population was as follows :—

Age	1880			1888		
	Males	Females	Total	Males	Females	Total
Under 30 .	281	285	566	284	291	575
30–60 . .	167	179	346	158	172	330
Over 60 .	42	46	88	44	51	95
Total .	490	510	1,000	486	514	1,000

The surplus of females has gone up from 40 to 58 per thousand, and it is to be observed that the ratio of persons between 30 and 60 years has declined very seriously, while that of old people, over 60, shows a rise of 8 per cent.

SPAIN

The census of 1887 compares with previous ones thus :—

Age	1846	1860	1887
Under 20	442	420	416
20–40	322	343	292
40–60	179	179	200
Over 60	57	58	92
Total pop. . .	1,000	1,000	1,000

The classes under 40 show a startling decline, which may be the result of emigration or of civil wars, and is unfortunate.

SCANDINAVIA

The three northern kingdoms have undergone the following changes in 20 years :—

Age	Sweden		Norway		Denmark	
	1870	1890	1870	1890	1870	1890
Under 20 . .	431	423	434	450	422	437
20–40 . . .	312	270	310	263	310	278
40–60 . . .	179	193	166	174	184	182
Over 60 . . .	78	114	90	113	84	103
Total pop.	1,000	1,000	1,000	1,000	1,000	1,000

These kingdoms show a marked decline in the ratio of persons between 20 and 60 years of age, and a corresponding increase in that of old people.

HOLLAND

The census of 1889 compares with previous ones thus :—

Age	1849	1869	1889
Under 20	425	427	447
20–40	308	309	277
40–60	188	187	184
Over 60	79	77	92
Total pop. . .	1,000	1,000	1,000

Here, as in most countries, the ratio of old people has risen remarkably.

AUSTRALIA

The census of 1891 gave the following result :—

Age	Number (000 omitted)							
	N. S. Wales	Victoria	N. Zealand	Queensland	S. Australia	Tasmania	W. Australia	Total
Under 10 .	308	278	169	107	89	41	12	1,004
10–20 . . .	230	232	146	74	69	30	9	790
20–30 . . .	218	243	104	85	58	28	11	747
30–40 . . .	156	146	76	58	43	19	8	506
40–50 . . .	99	87	60	36	27	11	5	325
50–60 . . .	64	81	44	23	19	8	3	242
60–70 . . .	32	51	19	8	11	5	2	128
Over 70 . .	17	22	9	3	4	5	...	60
Total pop.	1,124	1,140	627	394	320	147	50	3,802
Ratio								
Under 20 .	142	135	83	48	41	19	5	473
20–40 . . .	98	102	47	37	27	13	5	329
40–60 . . .	43	44	27	16	12	5	2	149
Over 60 . .	12	19	8	3	4	2	1	49
Total .	295	300	165	104	84	39	13	1,000

The distribution of sexes in the colonies was as follows :—

	Males	Females	Females to 1000 Males
New South Wales	608,000	516,000	849
Victoria	598,000	542,000	907
New Zealand . .	333,000	294,000	883
Queensland . . .	224,000	170,000	760
South Australia .	167,000	154,000	922
Tasmania . . .	78,000	69,000	885
West Australia .	30,000	20,000	667
Total . .	2,038,000	1,765,000	866

BELGIUM

The census of 1890 compares with previous ones thus :—

Age	1846	1856	1880	1890
Under 10 . . .	225	206	235	224
10–20 . . .	188	191	192	202
20–30 . . .	166	165	154	165
30–40 . . .	135	140	127	126
40–50 . . .	118	116	107	103
50–60 . . .	78	94	86	83
60–70 . . .	55	55	59	60
Over 70 . . .	35	33	40	37
Total .	1,000	1,000	1,000	1,000

Persons between 20 and 40 stand in much lower ratio than they did 40 years ago, but this class has improved since 1880. It is probably affected by the large number of Belgian operatives who go into France, to avoid military service.

UNITED STATES

The census of 1890 compares with the preceding one thus :—

Age	Number (000 omitted)		Ratio	
	1880	1890	1880	1890
Under 10 . . .	13,394	15,209	267	243
10-20	10,727	13,592	214	217
20-30	9,168	11,424	183	183
30-40	6,309	8,444	126	135
40-50	4,558	5,918	91	94
50-60	3,111	3,999	62	64
60-70	1,830	2,469	36	39
Over 70 . . .	1,059	1,567	21	25
Total pop. .	50,156	62,622	1,000	1,000

The class of children under 10 shows a relative decline of 9 per cent., while all classes over 30 years of age show a notable rise.

AGRICULTURE

The productive area in 1895 was approximately as follows :—

	Millions of Acres			Acres per 100 Inhabitants
	Crops	Pasture	Total	
Great Britain .	16	17	33	91
Ireland . .	4	11	15	330
France . .	67	23	90	230
Germany .	65	22	87	170
Russia . .	255	335	590	560
Austria . .	52	33	85	205
Italy . . .	38	15	53	175
Spain & Portugal .	36	29	65	290
Other States .	47	42	89	240
Europe .	580	527	1,107	290
United States .	226	397	623	890

As a general rule two productive acres are required for the support of each inhabitant, and where this ratio does not exist food must be imported. It appears, thus, that Great Britain, Germany, and Italy are over-populated, while Russia, Spain, and Ireland have not sufficient inhabitants. The production of food in various countries may be compared by reducing all to a common denominator, that is considering 100 gallons of wine or 3 tons of potatoes as equal to a ton of grain, and one of meat equal to 8 of grain. In 1894-96 the production, on the said basis, averaged as follows :—

	Tons Yearly of Food			Tons per Farming-hand
	Grain	Sundries	Total	
U. Kingdom	7,500,000	10,900,000	18,400,000	7.2
France . .	18,100,000	22,700,000	40,800,000	5.7
Germany .	18,600,000	23,500,000	42,100,000	5.3
Russia . .	53,000,000	23,700,000	76,700,000	2.2
Austria . .	19,500,000	14,100,000	33,600,000	2.7
Italy . . .	6,700,000	10,600,000	17,300,000	2.2
Spain . .	5,800,000	9,900,000	15,700,000	3.8
Denmark .	2,100,000	1,200,000	3,300,000	8.2
Holland . .	1,100,000	1,700,000	2,800,000	6.1
Europe . .	145,200,000	132,000,000	277,200,000	3.2
U. States .	89,400,000	41,400,000	130,800,000	14.5

Considering merely the weight of food produced, it appears that one farming hand in the United States raises as much as two in the United Kingdom, three in Germany, five in Austria, or seven in Russia. There is, in fact, a prodigious waste of labour in most countries of Europe. The number of farmers and farm-labourers in Europe is just nine times that of the United States, while the weight of food raised is only double ; that is to say, it takes 4½ Europeans to raise as much food as an American. The production of grain in 1892-95 averaged as follows :—

	Millions of Bushels				Bushels per acre
	Wheat	Oats	Various	Total	
U. Kingdom .	49	167	85	301	34
France . . .	303	216	205	724	20
Germany . . .	122	176	384	682	18
Russia. . . .	322	590	1,208	2,120	12
Austria . . .	196	170	414	780	19
Italy	122	18	93	233	11
Spain & Port. .	96	13	153	262	11
Danub. States .	101	18	159	278	15
Other States. .	40	145	168	353	25
Europe . . .	1,351	1,513	2,869	5,733	16
United States .	467	824	2,284	3,575	24
Canada . . .	48	104	49	201	20
Australia . . .	38	17	11	66	12
Argentina . .	77	...	48	125	13
Total .	1,981	2,458	5,261	9,700	18

If the grain crops of India, Asia Minor, &c., were added to the above (say 600 million bushels), the total would be a little over 10 milliards of bushels or 250 million tons ; nearly double the quantity raised 40 years ago. This is, of course, exclusive of rice. The following table shows the approximate weight :—

	Millions of Bushels yearly		
	1851-60	1892-95	Increase
Europe	4,150	5,733	1,583
United States	1,050	3,575	2,525
Colonies	60	392	332
Total . .	5,260	9,700	4,440

Levasseur's table of wheat production in Europe shows :—

	Millions of Bushels yearly		
	1831-40	1876-82	1885-90
United Kingdom . .	119	91	77
France	188	279	304
Germany	50	102	108
Russia	110	276	268
Austria	64	138	171
Italy	36	141	121
Spain	58	168	86
Portugal	4	10	6
Scandinavia	4	8	10
Holland	...	6	6
Belgium	8	22	19
Switzerland	1	2	4
Roumania	15	34	39
Turkey, &c.	4	61	81
Europe	661	1,338	1,300

The *Bulletin des Halles* stated the wheat crop and consumption in 1894 thus :—

	Crop	Consumption		Crop	Consumption
	Million Bush.			Million Bush.	
U. Kingdom.	58	230	Europe. . .	1,360	1,520
France . . .	340	360	U. States . .	454	294
Germany . .	117	150	Canada . .	33	27
Russia . . .	300	200	S. America .	101	66
Austria . . .	180	170	Asia . . .	301	299
Italy . . .	117	143	Australia . .	40	29
Spain & Port.	100	110	Algeria . . .	37	29
Various . .	148	157	Egypt, &c. .	14	16
Europe . .	1,360	1,520	The World .	2,340	2,280

The area under wheat, and the crops, have increased in 20 years as follows :—

	Acres (000 omitted)		Million Bushels	
	1876	1896	1876	1896
U. Kingdom .	3,100	1,700	80	58
France . . .	17,100	17,100	280	310
Germany . . .	4,400	4,800	100	120
Russia	28,800	31,900	190	330
Austria . . .	8,800	10,900	120	200
Italy	11,700	11,300	140	120
Spain & Portugal	10,500	8,500	120	100
Scandinavia . .	300	300	8	9
Holland . . .	200	200	5	5
Belgium . . .	700	700	18	20
Switzerland . .	100	100	2	2
Roumania, &c. .	6,300	7,500	17	146
Europe . . .	92,000	95,000	1,170	1,420
United States .	27,600	34,600	290	430
Canada . . .	2,200	2,700	30	50
Australia . . .	1,800	4,500	24	30
Argentina . .	300	5,200	6	50
India	20,000	21,800	200	220
Various . . .	10,100	14,200	160	200
The World . .	154,000	178,000	1,880	2,400

The average product per acre at the two periods was as follows :—

	Bushels per Acre	
	1876	1896
United Kingdom . . .	26	33
European Continent . .	12	15
United States	11	$12\frac{1}{2}$
Other countries . . .	12	11
The World	12	$13\frac{1}{2}$

The average wheat crop of the world for 14 years (1880-93) was in millions of bushels as follows :— Europe, 1270; United States, 440; India, 260; other countries, 210; total, 2180. See report of United States Agricultural Department.

Wheat constitutes one-fourth of the grain crop of Europe, one-fifth of that of the world. Taking the average yield of all grain per acre, the heaviest ratio falls to Ireland.

The various countries show as follows :—

Bushels of Grain per Acre

Ireland . .	38	Sweden . .	27	Germany . .	18
Great Britain	33	U. States. .	24	Roumania .	15
Belgium . .	31	Canada . .	20	Russia . . .	12
Holland . .	31	France . .	20	Italy . . .	11
Denmark . .	28	Austria . .	19	Spain . . .	11

The percentage of area under grain in the various countries has a wide range, being influenced by climate, soil, population, and other circumstances, viz. :—

Acres under Grain in 100 of Area

Ireland . .	7	Spain . . .	17	Germany . .	29
U. States . .	8	Holland . .	18	Italy . . .	29
Great Britain	13	France . .	28	Denmark . .	32
Russia . . .	13	Austria . .	28	Belgium . .	33

The production of grain compared with population is as follows :—

Bushels per Inhabitant

Great Britain	7	Belgium . .	12	France . . .	19
Italy . . .	7	Germany . .	13	Russia . . .	20
Holland . .	9	Spain . . .	13	Denmark . .	42
Ireland . .	12	Austria . .	19	U. States . .	54

The area devoted to pasture in various parts of the world is :—

	Millions of Acres	Cattle,* Millions	Acres per Head
Europe	527	172	3.1
United States. . . .	397	76	5.2
Australia . . .	802	35	23.0
Argentina	238	41	5.8
Total . .	1,701	324	5.2

One hundred acres of pasture land will carry about 200 sheep or 33 horned cattle. An acre of artificial grasses or turnips will maintain 6 sheep or one head of cattle. In Australia, however, the pasture is usually so poor that 100 acres will carry only 100 sheep or 16 big cattle; in Argentina, on the other hand, the average is 300 sheep or 50 cattle per 100 acres.

The annual production of meat exceeds 15 million tons, and of this amount Europe stands for more than 60 per cent., viz. :—

	Tons			
	Beef	Mutton	Pork	Total
U. Kingdom	590,000	320,000	190,000	1,100,000
France . .	700,000	210,000	290,000	1,200,000
Germany .	880,000	150,000	490,000	1,520,000
Russia . .	1,380,000	480,000	430,000	2,290,000
Austria . .	710,000	140,000	360,000	1,210,000
Other States	1,045,000	608,000	407,000	2,060,000
Europe . .	5,305,000	1,908,000	2,167,000	9,380,000
U. States .	2,410,000	370,000	2,050,000	4,830,000
Colonies .	500,000	295,000	85,000	880,000
Total .	8,215,000	2,573,000	4,302,000	15,090,000

The live stock of Europe in 1896 compares with Moreau's tables for 1838 as follows :—

Year	Millions			
	Horses	Cattle	Sheep	Pigs
1838	26	71	185	43
1896	39	105	176	53

* The unit is a horse or a cow, and sheep are counted as six for one.

The live stock of the United States showed as follows :—

Year	Millions			
	Horses	Cattle	Sheep	Pigs
1840	4	15	19	26
1870	8	24	29	25
1897	17	47	37	41

The value of all farm products in the years 1891–95 averaged as follows :—

	Millions £			Shillings per Acre
	Tillage	Pasture	Total	
United Kingdom .	126	104	230	96
France	284	132	416	92
Germany	262	155	417	96
Russia	370	170	540	18
Austria	215	109	324	76
Other States . . .	417	226	643	61
Europe	1,674	896	2,570	47
United States . .	486	327	813	45

The value of farm products at four different periods in the nineteenth century is shown approximately in the following table :—

	Before 1840		1850–63		1874–84		1891–1895
	Year	Millions £	Year	Millions £	Year	Millions £	Millions £
Great Britain .	1836	158	1855	221	1878	196	175
Ireland . . .	1836	69	1855	72	1878	65	55
United Kingdom	1836	227	1855	293	1878	261	230
France . . .	1825	253	1862	440	1882	504	416
Germany . . .	1830	120	1856	231	1880	466	417
Russia . . .	1834	248	1850	295	1882	426	540
Austria . . .	1838	205	1863	281	1880	340	324
Italy	1838	114	1860	155	1874	180	204
Spain	1826	77	1852	112	1880	140	135
Portugal . . .	1826	13	1852	20	1880	31	26
Sweden and Nor.	1837	20	1857	30	1882	49	46
Denmark . . .	1827	7	1852	22	1882	35	35
Holland . . .	1830	21	1852	27	1882	39	36
Belgium . . .	1830	26	1852	38	1884	55	44
Switzerland . .	1830	12	1860	16	1884	22	20
Roumania, &c. .	1830	27	1860	50	1884	108	97
Europe		1,370		2,010		2,656	2,570
United States .	1830	140	1860	430	1880	703	772
Canada . . .	1836	9	1860	21	1880	46	57
Australia . . .	1836	3	1860	20	1880	56	70
Argentina . . .	1836	5	1860	15	1880	31	45
South Africa . .	1836	1	1860	2	1880	7	8
Uruguay . . .	1836	2	1860	5	1880	7	8
Total . .		1,530		2,503		3,506	3,530

In Europe there was a steady rise of agricultural values from 1820 till 1874–5, but a decline set in about 1878, since which year there has been a fall of about 200 millions, or 8 per cent. On the other hand the United States have had a rise of 10 per cent. since 1880.

The amount of agricultural capital in 1891–96 was approximately as follows :—

	Value, Millions £ Sterling			
	Land	Cattle	Sundries	Total
Great Britain . .	1,390	143	153	1,686
Ireland . . .	296	59	36	391
France . . .	2,580	232	281	3,093
Germany . . .	1,977	303	228	2,508
Russia . . .	2,113	350	247	2,710
Austria . . .	1,473	161	163	1,797
Italy . . .	1,180	92	127	1,399
Spain . . .	1,056	46	110	1,212
Portugal . . .	138	11	15	164
Sweden and Norway	212	41	25	278
Denmark . . .	205	26	23	254
Holland . . .	240	28	27	295
Belgium . . .	300	22	32	354
Switzerland . .	138	18	16	172
Danubian States .	420	42	46	508
Greece . . .	94	5	10	109
Europe	13,812	1,579	1,539	16,930
United States . .	3,314	451	377	4,142
Canada . . .	245	43	23	311
Australia . . .	236	120	36	392
Argentina . . .	129	51	18	198
Total .	17,736	2,245	1,992	21,973

Agricultural capital almost reaches 22 milliards sterling, and as the aggregate wealth of nations is a little over 70 milliards, the former may be said to represent one-third of the total. If we would compare the gross value of farm products yearly with the amount of capital, the result will be as follows :—

Percentage on Capital

U. Kingdom	11.1	Italy . . .	14.5	Switzerland	11.6
France . .	13.4	Spain . .	11.2	U. States .	19.6
Germany .	16.6	Denmark .	13.8	Canada . .	18.4
Russia . .	19.9	Holland .	12.4	Australia .	17.1
Austria . .	17.7	Belgium .	12.5	Argentina .	23.2

Agricultural capital divided among population gives the ratios per inhabitant thus :—

£ per Head

U. Kingdom .	53	Italy . . .	45	Belgium . .	56
France . . .	80	Spain . . .	68	U. States . .	58
Germany . .	48	Portugal . .	35	Canada . .	60
Russia . .	26	Denmark . .	115	Australia . .	92
Austria . .	41	Holland . .	61	Argentina . .	50

The relative importance of agriculture in the several countries is shown by the proportions of wealth, earnings, and population corresponding to this pursuit, viz. :—

	Percentage of Agricultural, in total		
	Population	Wealth	Earnings
Great Britain . .	10	15	8
Ireland . .	45	60	35
France . . .	42	32	21
Germany . . .	39	31	20
Russia . . .	70	43	32
Austria . . .	62	39	27
Italy . . .	52	45	28
Holland . . .	22	33	18
Belgium . . .	25	36	14
United States . .	35	25	16
Canada . . .	43	31	18
Australia . . .	25	36	20
Average . . .	40	31	20

Viewed simply as a money-making occupation, agriculture is by no means so profitable as other pursuits, for while it represents broadly about 40 per cent. of the population and 31 per cent. of the wealth, it stands for only 20 per cent. of the earnings of nations. Agricultural interests stand highest in Russia and Ireland, lowest in Great Britain and Holland.

UNITED KINGDOM

The returns of 1897 show the productive area to be nearly 48 million acres or 62 per cent. of the total, viz. :—

	Acres (000 omitted)			
	England	Scotland	Ireland	U. King.
Wheat . . .	1,840	50	50	1,940
Oats	2,090	970	1,170	4,230
Barley, &c. . .	2,280	250	190	2,720
All grain . . .	6,210	1,270	1,410	8,890
Potatoes . . .	390	120	680	1,190
Turnips . . .	1,360	480	310	2,150
Sundries . . .	4,650	1,630	1,440	7,720
All crops . . .	12,610	3,500	3,840	19,950
Pasture . . .	15,150	1,390	11,380	27,920
Total . .	27,760	4,890	15,220	47,870

The crops of the United Kingdom in the last 3 years were :—

	1895	1896	1897
Wheat, tons.	960,000	1,460,000	1,410,000
Oats, ,, .	4,360,000	4,070,000	4,090,000
Barley, &c., ,, .	2,120,000	2,220,000	2,110,000
All grain, ,, .	7,440,000	7,750,000	7,610,000
Potatoes, ,, .	7,060,000	6,250,000	4,110,000
Turnips, &c., ,, .	35,600,000	33,000,000	37,200,000
Hay, ,, .	12,200,000	11,400,000	14,100,000
Total . .	62,300,000	59,300,000	63,020,000

The crops of 1897 were 6 per cent. less in weight than those of 1894. The average yield per acre for the last three years was as follows :—

	Great Britain	Ireland	United Kingdom
Wheat, bushel . . .	30	30	30
Oats, ,, . . .	37	41	38
Barley, ,, . . .	33	37	34
Potatoes, ,, . . .	240	146	187
Turnips, cwt. . . .	262	288	266
Hay, ,, . . .	24	43	28

Irish crops are, as a rule, much heavier than those of Great Britain, the only exception being potatoes, which in Ireland rarely give 4 tons per acre, whereas in Great Britain the average is 6 tons. The most remarkable difference is as regards hay, the yield per acre in Ireland being always double what it is in Great Britain.

The crops of the last 10 years gave the following yield per acre for the United Kingdom.

Year	Bushels per Acre			
	Wheat	Barley	Oats	All Grain
1887 . . .	32	31	34	33
1888 . . .	28	33	38	34
1889 . . .	30	32	40	35
1890 . . .	31	35	42	37
1891 . . .	31	35	40	36
1892 . . .	26	35	40	35
1893 . . .	26	29	38	32
1894 . . .	31	35	42	38
1895 . . .	26	32	39	34
1896 . . .	34	34	38	36
1897 . . .	30	33	39	35

A comparison of the value of farm products at present with M'Culloch's estimates in 1846 and Caird's in 1878 results as follows :—

	1846 £	1878 £	1895 £
Grain	77,000,000	87,000,000	38,200,000
Hay and straw .	19,000,000	22,000,000	44,000,000
Potatoes, &c. .	41,600,000	16,700,000	43,800,000
Meat	46,500,000	87,000,000	55,200,000
Dairy	19,400,000	39,500,000	33,000,000
Sundries . . .	14,500,000	8,500,000	15,800,000
Total . .	218,000,000	260,700,000	230,000,000

M'Culloch's valuation for 1846 was made up for the three kingdoms as follows :—

	Millions £ Sterling			
	England	Scotland	Ireland	U. King.
Grain	51.8	9.7	15.5	77.0
Hay and straw .	13.0	2.4	3.6	19.0
Green crops . .	28.7	5.3	7.6	41.6
Meat	26.0	6.3	14.2	46.5
Dairy	13.4	2.4	3.6	19.4
Sundries	9.1	1.9	3.5	14.5
Total . .	142.0	28.0	48.0	218.0

The value of all farm products is now about the same as 60 years ago, viz. :—

Year	Millions £ Sterling			
	England	Scotland	Ireland	U. King.
1836	136.1	23.2	69.3	228.6
1846	142.0	28.0	48.0	218.0
1895	147.0	28.0	55.0	230.0

The estimate for 1836 was made by Moreau, that for 1846 by M'Culloch.

The mean value in the years 1893-95 was as follows :—

	Millions £ Sterling			
	England	Scotland	Ireland	U. King.
Grain	26.6	5.2	6.4	38.2
Straw	9.1	1.5	1.6	12.2
Potatoes	8.8	2.4	7.0	18.2
Hay	20.3	2.1	9.4	31.8
Sundries . . .	18.2	3.8	3.6	25.6
Tillage . . .	83.0	15.0	28.0	126.0
Meat	33.2	7.4	14.6	55.2
Dairy	21.0	3.6	8.4	33.0
Sundries . . .	9.8	2.0	4.0	15.8
Total . .	147.0	28.0	55.0	230.0

The value of products compared with the number of hands, according to last census, shows as follows :—

	Hands	£	£ per Hand
England	1,337,000	147,000,000	110
Scotland	249,000	28,000,000	112
Ireland	941,000	55,000,000	58
United Kingdom . .	2,527,000	230,000,000	91

There seems to be a great waste of labour in Ireland, since it takes two hands in that island to produce as much value as one in Great Britain. Moreover the value of yield per acre of productive area is comparatively low in Ireland, viz. :—

	Acres	£	Shillings per Acre
England	27,800,000	147,000,000	106
Scotland	4,900,000	28,000,000	114
Ireland	15,200,000	55,000,000	72
United Kingdom . .	47,900,000	230,000,000	96

Although the weight of crops per acre is heavier in Ireland, the gross value of product is less than in Great Britain, because the great markets of consumption are in the latter island. The gross product per acre of productive area in the United Kingdom is 4 shillings more than in France. Agricultural capital in the United Kingdom has declined about 450 millions sterling in 15 years, say 30 millions per annum, viz. :—

Year	Millions £			
	Land	Cattle	Sundries	Total
1880	2,086	209	230	2,525
1895	1,686	202	189	2,077

Agricultural capital in the three kingdoms stands approximately as follows :—

	Millions £			
	Land	Cattle	Sundries	Total
England . . .	1,202	118	132	1,452
Scotland . . .	188	25	21	234
Ireland . . .	296	59	36	391
United Kingdom .	1,686	202	189	2,077

The value of agricultural product after deducting rent and taxes in the three kingdoms is as follows :—

	England, £	Scotland, £	Ireland, £
Product . . .	147,000,000	28,000,000	55,000,000
Rent	40,100,000	6,300,000	10,800,000
Taxes	16,200,000	1,900,000	2,700,000
Balance . .	90,700,000	19,800,000	41,500,000

The balance gives the following averages as to productive area and hands :—

	Shillings per Acre	£ per Hand
England . . .	65	68
Scotland . . .	81	80
Ireland . . .	54	44
United Kingdom . .	64	60

Pastoral industry has increased as follows :—

	Great Britain		Ireland	
	1855	1897	1855	1897
Horses . .	1,490,000	1,540,000	550,000	530,000
Cattle . .	4,390,000	6,540,000	3,560,000	4,460,000
Sheep .	24,370,000	26,410,000	3,600,000	4,160,000
Pigs . . .	2,510,000	2,350,000	1,180,000	1,330,000
Total .	32,760,000	36,840,000	8,890,000	10,480,000

Thus the total live stock of the United Kingdom has risen from 41½ to 47 millions, an increase of 14 per cent. in 41 years, whereas population increased 40 per cent. in the same interval. Agricultural matters are also treated under the items of *Food Supply* and *Land*.

There has been little variation of agricultural area in the last 16 years, except as regards vineyards, which have suffered severely from phylloxera :—

	1880	1896
Wheat, acres . . .	16,990,000	16,970,000
Oats ,, . . .	8,580,000	9,670,000
Rye, &c. ,, . . .	11,440,000	9,320,000
All grain ,, . . .	37,010,000	35,960,000
Vineyards ,, . . .	5,450,000	4,360,000
Beetroot ,, . . .	1,110,000	1,630,000
Potatoes ,, . . .	3,220,000	3,810,000

While the area under grain is not much larger than it was 40 years ago, the system of agriculture has so much improved that the weight of crop is one-fourth heavier, viz. :—

	Crop, Tons		Bushels per Acre	
	1855	1896	1855	1896
Wheat . .	5,300,000	8,200,000	13.0	19.4
Oats, &c. .	9,800,000	10,800,000	19.6	22.8
All grain .	15,100,000	19,000,000	16.8	21.1

The area and crops of the last five years (1892-96) gave the following averages :—

	Acres	Bushels	Bush. per Ac.
Wheat	17,200,000	313,000,000	18.2
Oats	9,600,000	234,000,000	24.4
Rye	3,800,000	67,000,000	17.6
Barley	2,200,000	44,000,000	20.0
Various . . .	3,600,000	66,000,000	18.0
All grain . . .	36,400,000	723,000,000	19.9

The devastation caused by phylloxera resulted in the loss of 1,900,000 acres of vineyard :—

Year	Acres, Vines	Million Galls. Wine	Gallons per Acre
1871	6,040,000	1,300	215
1891	4,410,000	660	150
1895	4,150,000	590	142
1891-95 . . .	4,370,000	770	176

The average vintage during 40 years before the phylloxera was 140 gallons per acre, so that it may be said the present area of vineyards gives a fair crop (176 gallons per acre). Most of the destroyed vineyards have been laid down under potatoes or beetroot, the area of which has increased by one-fourth, viz. :—

	1880	1895	Increase, Ac.
Potatoes . . .	3,220,000	3,810,000	590,000
Beetroot . . .	1,110,000	1,630,000	520,000
	4,330,000	5,440,000	1,110,000

Pastoral industry is stationary, as official returns show :—

Year	Cattle	Sheep	Pigs
1885	13,100,000	24,100,000	5,880,000
1890	13,560,000	23,200 000	6,020,000
1896	13,330,000	21,200,000	6,400,000

The value of agricultural products has fallen heavily in recent years, notwithstanding protective tariffs and other futile measures, viz. :—

	Millions £ Sterling		1895
	1886	1890	
Grain	129	120	114
Wine	49	45	33
Other crops . . .	104	106	120
Meat	60	65	56
Dairy	59	46	46
Sundries . . .	59	56	47
Total . .	460	438	416

De Foville would include dung among agricultural products, and estimates the annual quantity at 100 million tons, worth about 40 millions sterling; it is, however, excluded by all statisticians. The loss of agricultural capital since 1880 has been even greater than in the United Kingdom, averaging 32 millions sterling per annum, viz. :—

Year	Millions £			
	Land	Cattle	Sundries	Total
1880 . . .	2,986	231	357	3,574
1895 . . .	2,580	232	281	3,093

Although agriculture occupies 44 per cent. of the population, France has to import both grain and meat. See *Food Supply.*

GERMANY

The cultivated area has almost doubled in 40 years, viz. :—

Year	Cultivated	Uncultivated	Total, Acres
1856	35,330,000	93,710,000	129,040,000
1896	65,200,000	68,300,000	133,500,000

The progress of agriculture in the last 15 years is shown thus :—

	Acres (000 omitted)		Crop, Tons (000 omitted)	
	1880-82	1894-96	1880-82	1894-96
Wheat . .	4,490	4,910	2,280	2,900
Rye . . .	14,620	14,800	5,500	6,950
Oats, &c. .	14,830	18,240	7,020	8,750
All grain .	33,940	37,950	14,800	18,600
Potatoes .	6,830	7,500	21,100	31,000
Beetroot . .	1,250	2,120	12,600	20,300
Hay . . .	14,600	14,600	18,200	17,200
Various . .	1,280	2,980	3,100	9,500
Total .	57,900	65,150	69,800	96,600

The area under crops has risen 12 per cent. since 1882. The average weight of crop per acre (excluding hay) was 31 cwt. (1.55 ton) in the last 3 years, as compared with 24 cwt. in 1880-82 ; that is to say, an improvement of 30 per cent. Nevertheless agriculture is backward : only 48 per cent. of the empire is under cultivation, although as many hands are employed as in the United States. The production of food is equivalent to 5 tons for each farming-hand, against 15 tons in the United States. Germany has to subsist on imported grain for two months every year. Notwithstanding the density of population, live stock (excepting sheep) is increasing in numbers :—

Year	Horses	Cattle	Sheep	Pigs
1873	3,350,000	15,780,000	25,200,000	7,120,000
1893	3,840,000	17,560,000	16,700,000	12,170,000

The value of farm products has almost doubled since the valuation by Block and Viebahn in 1856, and now reaches 417 millions sterling, viz. :—

	Millions £ *			
	Prussia	Bavaria	Other States	Germany
Grain . .	65.0	12.4	31.8	109.2
Potatoes .	41.8	8.6	13.2	63.6
Hay . . .	20.4	3.5	4.1	28.0
Roots, &c. .	38.0	8 3	14.9	61.2
Meat . . .	37.8	9.4	15.8	63.0
Dairy . .	35.9	8.9	15.2	60.0
Sundries .	19.1	4.9	8.0	32.0
Total .	258.0	56.0	103.0	417.0

Prussia is less productive than some of the other German states, and stands for only 60 per cent. of the value of farm products, while she has 65 per cent. of the productive area of the empire. The agricultural capital of Germany is nearly 600 millions sterling less than that of France, and is made up thus :—

	Millions £			
	Prussia	Bavaria	Other States	Germany
Land . . .	1,252	264	461	1,977
Cattle . .	187	46	70	303
Sundries .	144	31	53	228
Total .	1,583	341	584	2,508

Dividing the amount among the number of farms, we find a ratio of £840 to each farm in Germany, as compared with £880 in France, £3200 in England, and £760 in Ireland. The agricultural capital and products of Germany, France, and the United Kingdom may be compared thus :—

	Millions £ Sterling		£ per Inhabitant	
	Capital	Product	Capital	Product
Germany . . .	2,508	417	48	8
France	3,093	416	80	11
United Kingdom .	2,077	230	53	6

The quota of agricultural product to each farming hand is only £44 in Germany, against £58 in France and £91 in the United Kingdom.

* The table is read thus : 65.0 means £65,000,000, and 12.4 means £12,400,000.

RUSSIA

Official returns for 1892 show that the emancipation of the serfs has caused the farming area to be almost doubled in twenty years, viz. :—

	Millions of Acres	
	1872	1892
Farming area	305	589
Forests, &c.	939	752
Total . .	1,244	1,341

In the above table Poland is included, as also in the following statement of grain. The averages for 1893–1895 were :—

	Millions of Bushels		
	Crop	Export	Consumption
Wheat . . .	330	135	195
Rye	780	44	736
Oats	650	46	594
Various . . .	450	125	335
Total . .	2,210	350	1,860

The value of grain exported in the said three years averaged 34 millions sterling. The crops of Russia proper and Poland averaged separately as follows :—

	Millions of Bushels		
	Russia	Poland	Total
Wheat	314	16	330
Rye	728	52	780
Oats	605	45	650
Barley, &c. . .	427	23	450
Total . .	2,074	136	2,210

Later years show a great decline in Russian crops. The following table refers to Russia proper, exclusive of Poland :—

	Millions of Bushels			
	1895	1896	1897	Average
Wheat . . .	232	218	180	210
Rye	658	622	506	595
Oats . . .	545	506	405	485
Barley, &c. .	250	262	233	248
Total . .	1,685	1,608	1,324	1,541

Consumption is accounted for in this way : 360 million bushels kept for seed, 440 million given to cattle, and 900 million used for human food, an average of 8½ bushels per inhabitant : this last includes not only what is used for bread but also what is made into Vodka brandy and beer. The production of wine has increased so rapidly that the vintage reaches 55 million gallons, being 120 gallons to the acre. The production of meat is approximately 2,300,000 tons yearly, including 250,000 tons in Poland. The census of 1888 compared with that of 1877 showed a decline of 10 per cent. in cattle and 15 per cent. both in sheep and in pigs, which was perhaps owing to the rapid increase of population and conse-

quently greater consumption of meat. The census of 1888 showed as follows :—

	Russia	Poland	Total
Horses . .	19,700,000	1,200,000	20,900,000
Cattle . . .	24,600,000	3,000,000	27,600,000
Sheep . . .	44,500,000	3,700,000	48,200,000
Pigs . . .	9,200,000	1,500,000	10,700,000
Total . .	98,000,000	9,400,000	107,400,000

The area covered by the principal crops in 1895 was approximately :—

	Acres		
	Russia	Poland	Total
Grain . .	161,300,000	9,000,000	170,900,000
Potatoes . .	5,820,000	1,750,000	7,570,000
Flax and hemp .	4,680,000	...	4,680,000
Hay, &c. . .	116,200,000	2,250,000	118,450,000
Total . .	288,000,000	13,600,000	301,600,000

The value of agricultural products in 1894 was approximately :—

	Millions £ Sterling		
	Russia	Poland	Total
Grain	242	16	258
Potatoes . . .	16	5	21
Flax, &c. . . .	14	...	14
Hay	46	2	48
Sundries . . .	26	6	32
Meat	77	10	87
Dairy, &c. . . .	74	9	83
Total . . .	495	48	543

The above gives an average gross product per acre of 34 shillings in Russia and 70 in Poland. This, however, is exclusive of 290 million acres used for permanent pasture, and if these were brought into account the average yield on the whole farming area of Russia and Poland would be only 18 shillings per acre. The agricultural capital of the empire has more than doubled since the emancipation of the serfs, showing approximately as follows :—

Year	Millions £ Sterling			
	Land	Cattle	Sundries	Total
1870 . . .	798	320	112	1,230
1895 . . .	2,113	360	247	2,720

The capital in 1895 stood more or less as follows :—

	Millions £ Sterling			
	Land	Cattle	Sundries	Total
Russia . . .	1,957	325	228	2,510
Poland . . .	156	35	19	210
Total . .	2,113	360	247	2,720

See *Food, Land.*

AUSTRIA-HUNGARY

The area under crops in the whole monarchy showed the following averages :—

	Acres	
	1881-83	1893-95
Grain	35,400,000	41,200,000
Potatoes . . .	3,450,000	4,020,000
Beetroot . . .	710,000	1,600,000
Vines	1,440,000	1,300,000
Sundries . . .	2,200,000	4,180,000
Total .	43,200,000	53,300,000

The only branch of agriculture which shows a decline is vineyards, while the area of grain has increased at the rate of half a million acres yearly since 1883. The two portions of the monarchy stood in 1893-95 as follows :—

	Acres		
	Austria	Hungary	Monarchy
Grain . .	17,140,000	24,060,000	41,200,000
Vines . .	620,000	680,000	1,300,000
Roots, &c. .	6,740,000	4,060,000	10,800,000
Total . .	24,500,000	28,800,000	53,300,000

The average crops in the same three years were as follows :—

	Tons		
	Austria	Hungary	Total
Wheat . .	1,070,000	3,830,000	4,900,000
Oats . .	2,520,000	1,780,000	4,300,000
Rye, &c. .	4,110,000	6,090,000	10,200,000
All grain . .	7,700,000	11,700,000	19,400,000
Potatoes . .	9,100,000	3,300,000	12,400,000
Beetroot . .	7,500,000	4,500,000	12,000,000
Hay . .	10,800,000	8,200,000	19,000,000
Total . .	35,100,000	27,700,000	62,800,000

Nearly one-third of the monarchy is still under forest, viz., 24 million acres in Austria and 23 millions in Hungary. Austria does not raise enough food for her population, the deficit being met by the surplus in Hungary.

Pastoral industry seems to make no progress ; the latest returns give a total of 40 million head of live stock, as compared with 45 millions in 1870. At present the returns show as follows :—

	Austria	Hungary	Total
Horses . .	1,580,000	1,750,000	3,330,000
Cattle . .	8,640,000	4,880,000	13,520,000
Sheep . .	4,230,000	10,870,000	15,100,000
Pigs . .	3,550,000	4,800,000	8,350,000
Total . .	18,000,000	22,300,000	40,300,000

The gross value of farming products is approximately as follows :—

	Millions £ Sterling		
	Austria	Hungary	Total
Grain . . .	48	72	120
Green crops . .	59	36	95
Meat	26	25	51
Dairy, &c. . .	37	21	58
Total . .	170	154	324

The productive area of the whole monarchy, including 32 million acres of permanent pasture, is 85,400,000 acres, and the value of products averages 76 shillings per acre, as compared with 92 shillings in France. In half a century the agricultural capital has almost trebled, mainly owing to the emancipation of the serfs, viz. :—

Year	Millions £ Sterling			
	Land	Cattle	Sundries	Total
1840 . . .	543	50	59	652
1894 . . .	1,473	161	163	1,797

In 1894 the two kingdoms stood approximately as follows :—

	Austria	Hungary	Total
Land . . .	796	677	1,473
Cattle . . .	88	73	161
Sundries . .	88	75	163
Total . .	972	825	1,797

In 1885 the whole monarchy contained 6,150,000 farms. Each farm, therefore, represents a capital of £290, and a gross annual product of £52, the bulk of the peasants being poor, while the princely land-owners of Hungary and Bohemia possess enormous wealth.

ITALY

A great portion of the kingdom consists of mountains, forests, or waste lands, but so indefatigable is the Italian peasantry that in 15 years nearly 5 million acres have been reclaimed, the arable and the uncultivated areas showing as follows :—

	Acres		
	1880	1895	Increase
Grain	20,300,000	20,500,000	200,000
Vines	4,800,000	8,500,000	3,700,000
Olives	2,200,000	2,600,000	400,000
Sundries . . .	12,200,000	12,600,000	400,000
Tillage . . .	39,500,000	44,200,000	4,700,000
Pasture, &c. . .	31,300,000	26,600,000	...
Total . .	70,800,000	70,800,000	...

Grain crops are light, seldom exceeding 13 bushels per acre, the average for 3 years ending 1895 having been as follows :—

	Acres	Tons	Bushels per Acre
Wheat	11,300,000	3,030,000	10.7
Maize	4,750,000	1,720,000	14.5
Oats, &c.	4,380,000	1,050,000	9.5
All grain	20,430,000	5,800,000	11.3

The production of wine in the last 3 years has averaged 580 million gallons, or about 70 gallons per acre, against 176 in France, the Italian vintage rarely giving a higher average than 90 gallons per acre. Rice cultivation shows a remarkable falling off, the crop ranging from 350,000 to 400,000 tons, which is barely two-thirds of what it was 15 years ago, and this circumstance causes much satisfaction, as the growth of rice is a most unhealthy occupation. In order to convey a correct idea of the agricultural industry, it may be well to give here the old territorial divisions as they now stand in tillage area, approximately, thus :—

| | Acres (000 omitted) | | | |
	Grain	Wine	Sundries	Total
Venice	2,100	1,050	1,350	4,480
Lombardy . . .	2,050	500	1,420	3,970
Piedmont . . .	1,820	750	1,830	4,400
Duchies	2,400	1,650	2,150	6,200
Papal States . .	3,600	2,050	2,550	8,200
Naples	5,800	1,600	3,900	11,300
Sicily	2,200	720	1,580	4,500
Sardinia Island . .	530	180	240	950
Total . .	20,500	8,500	15,000	44,000

The acreage under grain is made up as follows (000 omitted) :—

	Wheat	Maize	Oats,&c.	Total
Venice	750	1,030	320	2,100
Lombardy	730	830	490	2,050
Piedmont	770	480	570	1,820
Duchies	1,480	530	390	2,400
Papal States . . .	2,180	930	490	3,600
Naples	3,340	960	1,500	5,800
Sicily	1,650	20	530	2,200
Sardinia Island . .	400	20	110	530
Total . .	11,300	4,800	4,400	20,500

Sundries include hay, green crops, olive groves, &c., as follows, in acres (000 omitted) :—

	Hay	Olives	Green Crops	Total
Venice	670	...	660	1,330
Lombardy	990	...	430	1,420
Piedmont	890	150	790	1,830
Duchies	870	300	980	2,150
Papal States . . .	1,190	330	1,030	2,550
Naples	510	1,440	1,950	3,900
Sicily	670	330	580	1,580
Sardinia Island . .	110	50	80	240
Total . .	5,900	2,600	6,500	15,000

The official valuation of farm products is only 176 millions sterling, but this is exclusive of hay. The total value appears to be 208 millions sterling, viz. :—

	Official, £	Real, £
Grain	53,400,000	53,400,000
Wine	33,500,000	33,500,000
Hay	...	26,700,000
Fruit, &c. . . .	9,600,090	15,200,000
Meat, dairy, &c. . .	79,000,000	79,200,000
Total . .	175,500,000	208,000,000

The productive area, including 9 million acres of permanent pasture, covers 53 million acres; the value of products therefore averages 77 shillings per acre, against 92 in France. The number of hands engaged in farming

is 7,800,000, which leaves the average product for each hand only £27, as compared with £58 in France.

Agricultural capital has trebled since 1840, viz. :—

| Year | Millions £ | | | |
	Land	Cattle	Sundries	Total
1840	377	30	41	448
1890	1,180	92	127	1,399

The agricultural resources of Italy are so insufficient for her population that the average importation of grain reaches 700,000 tons yearly. See *Food, Land*.

SPAIN

Official returns for 1888 show 41 million acres under grain, equivalent to a crop of at least 10 million tons, which would leave a surplus of 3 million tons for exportation. We find, however, that so far from any surplus there is an average deficit of 330,000 tons, which is covered by importation. This shows that the official return is a gross exaggeration. The *Uebersichten* of 1893 estimates the aggregate crop at 5 million tons, Spallart's estimate having been 8 millions, and the actual production appears to be under 6 million tons. Hence it will be evident that the statement of Spanish agriculture in Part I. of this volume is altogether too high. The area of the kingdom is 125,300,000 acres, of which 72,100,000 consist of mountain and forests, the rest being apparently as shown in the following table :—

	Area, Acres		Product, £
Grain . . .	20,800,000	Grain . . .	39,200,000
Vineyards . .	4,200,000	Wine . . .	33,600,000
Other crops .	7,200,000	Sundries . .	21,200,000
Pasture . .	21,000,000	Meat,dairy,&c.	41,200,000
Total . .	53,200,000	Total . .	135,200,000

This gives an average of 51 shillings per acre, against 77 shillings in Italy, but the product per hand is greater in Spain, namely £33, against £27 in Italy. As regards the production of wine, Spain holds third rank among nations, the vintage being usually one-fifth less than that of France, or about one-half that of France : in 1895 and 1896 the average was 420 million gallons. The growth of agricultural capital has been retarded by civil wars, the increase having been less than 50 per cent. in 60 years, viz. :—

| Year | Millions £ Sterling | | | |
	Land	Cattle	Sundries	Total
1832 . . .	724	34	76	834
1892 . . .	1,056	46	110	1,212

Dividing the above capital among the number of farms, it gives an average of £444 each, as compared with £880 in France. See *Cattle, Food, Land*.

PORTUGAL

The total area under crops is less than 4 million acres, or one-fifth of the kingdom, viz. :—

	Area, Acres	Product, £
Grain	2,600,000	5,500,000
Vineyards	500,000	6,700,000
Other crops	800,000	5,700,000
Pasture	7,700,000	8,100,000
Waste	9,200,000	...
Total . . .	20,800,000	26,000,000

Official returns give a total product estimated at £23,200,000, but this seems to omit dairy products. The productive area, tillage and pasture, being 11,600,000 acres, the average product is 45 shillings per acre, against 51 in Spain. Portuguese writers assert that the area under crops could be trebled but for the system of land tenure, which forces the people to emigrate. The vintage ranges from 50 to 80 million gallons, of which about one-fourth is exported. Agricultural capital reaches 164 millions sterling, of which 138 millions are represented by land. Peasant farms show an average value of £210 each. See *Cattle, Food, Land.*

SWEDEN AND NORWAY.

The climate of these countries is so adverse that agriculture has made little progress in recent years, the area under crops hardly reaching 9 million acres, or 5 per cent. of the total extent. Latest returns show :—

Area	Sweden	Norway	Total
Grain, acres . .	4,150,000	450,000	4,600,000
Sundries, acres .	4,250,000	150,000	4,400,000
Pasture, ,, .	3,900,000	2,200,000	6,100,000
Forest, &c. ,,	98,400,000	76,900,000	175,300,000
Total ,, .	110,700,000	79,700,000	190,400,000
Grain, tons . .	2,800,000	400,000	3,200,000
Potatoes, tons .	1,300,000	500,000	1,800,000

The hay crop of Sweden averages 2½ million tons, that of Norway may be estimated at 1 million. Live stock in Sweden shows an increase of 500,000 in 20 years, but in Norway has been stationary, latest returns being as follows :—

	Sweden	Norway	Total
Horses . .	500,000	150,000	650,000
Cattle . . .	2,520,000	1,010,000	2,530,000
Sheep . . .	1,400,000	1,700,000	3,100,000
Pigs . . .	770,000	120,000	890,000
Total . .	5,190,000	2,980,000	7,170,000

Farmers are not wholly dependent on agricultural products ; many of them devote themselves also to fishing or wood-cutting. The approximate value of agricultural industry is as follows :—

	Sweden, £	Norway, £	Total, £
Grain	13,000,000	2,000,000	15,000,000
Hay & sundries .	6,800,000	1,300,000	8,100,000
Meat . . .	8,000,000	2,800,000	10,800,000
Dairy, &c. . .	9,200,000	2,900,000	12,100,000
Total . .	37,000,000	9,000,000	46,000,000

Agricultural capital has quadrupled in 60 years, being now approximately as follows :—

	Millions £ Sterling			
	Land	Cattle	Sundries	Total
Sweden . . .	154	29	18	201
Norway . . .	58	12	7	77
Total . .	212	41	25	278

The average of capital to each farm is £730. See *Cattle, Food, Land.*

DENMARK.

This prosperous little kingdom shows an increase in the last 15 years of 400,000 acres under cultivation, 300,000 tons in average grain crop, and of 6 millions sterling in the value of exports of farm products. The average crops showed thus :—

	1879-82	1895-96
Oats, tons	750,000	950,000
Barley, tons	550,000	520,000
Rye, &c. tons	650,000	800,000
Total grain, tons . .	1,950,000	2,270,000
Potatoes, tons	240,000	520,000
Roots, tons	440,000	3,520,000
Total, tons . . .	2,630,000	6,310,000

Besides the above there are large crops of hay and clover, averaging together 1,400,000 tons yearly. Although the production of grain exceeds one ton per head of the population, there is none for export, a large quantity being kept for cattle. Pastoral industry thrives apace, the returns showing an increase of 10 per cent. in live stock since 1881. If we reduce all live stock to a common denominator equivalent to horned cattle, it will be found that Denmark carries a very high proportion to its area under grass, viz. :—

	Pasture, Acres	Cattle	Do. per 100 Acres
Denmark . . .	2,600,000	2,400,000	92
Holland . . .	2,800,000	2,100,000	75
Great Britain . .	16,600,000	12,300,000	75
Ireland	11,200,000	5,700,000	51

The productive area of Denmark, between tillage and pasture, is only 7,100,000 acres, yet the value of products reaches 35 millions sterling, equal to 99 shillings per acre, as compared with 92 shillings in France, and 73 in Ireland, which shows that in spite of an ungenial climate the Danes contrive to carry on agriculture with great success. They export meat, butter, and eggs to the value of 10 millions sterling per annum. The official value of crops is 15 millions sterling, apparently exclusive of market-garden products. The total value is approximately as follows : grain 12, other crops 7, meat 6, dairy 8, sundries 2 ; total 35 millions. The aggregate value of farms being 254 millions sterling, the product is equal to 14 per cent. on capital, against 13½ per cent. in France. The latest and best agricultural machinery is more used in Denmark than elsewhere. Agricultural exports are equal to £5 per head of the population, as compared with £2 in Canada, £2 in the United States, £3 in Ireland, and £8 in Australia. See *Cattle, Food, Land.*

HOLLAND

This little kingdom is so well irrigated that it has 420 yards of canal per acre of superficial extent. Hence we find that the yield of grain per acre is 7 per cent. higher even than in Denmark, and averages 30 bushels. Although the area under grain is 10 per cent. less than it was 15 years ago, the crops are heavier, the averages at two periods showing thus :—

	Tons		Bushels per Acre	
	1880-82	1893-95	1880-82	1893-95
Oats	310,000	370,000	42	45
Rye	230,000	270,000	19	23
Wheat, &c. . .	390,000	370,000	22	27
Total grain .	930,000	1,010,000	26	30
Potatoes . . .	1,200,000	1,830,000	138	200
Beetroot . . .	410,000	830,000	360	420

The yield per acre is heavier not only in grain but also in potatoes and beetroot. At the same time horned cattle have increased 2 per cent., pigs 92 per cent., and the export of dairy products risen to more than 100,000 tons yearly. Pastures are so rich that cattle for the market often weigh over a ton, and milch cows give an average product of 250 pounds of cheese and butter, a result unequalled in any part of the world. The following table shows the value of all products, and of what is exported :—

	Product, £		Export, £
Grain . . .	6,200,000	Butter . . .	1,150,000
Green crops .	11,700,000	Cheese . . .	950,000
Meat . . .	6,100,000	Flax . . .	300,000
Dairy . . .	9,800,000	Meat . . .	600,000
Sundries . .	2,200,000	Vegetables .	2,200,000
Total . .	36,000,000	Total . .	5,200,000

Agricultural capital has declined in the last 10 years, as shown thus :—

Year	Millions £			
	Land	Cattle	Sundries	Total
1886 . . .	314	28	38	380
1896 . . .	240	28	27	295

The value of products per acre is 142 shillings, against 92 in France and 96 in the United Kingdom. Dutch farmers are apparently the richest and most prosperous in the world, each farm representing a capital of £1800 and a gross output of £220, although the average area is no more than 34 acres. See *Cattle, Food, Land.*

BELGIUM

This is a country of kitchen gardens and spade cultivation, yielding a prodigious amount of agricultural products in ratio to extent, the average output showing 160 shillings per acre. The crops of 1893–96 compare with those of 1880 thus :—

	Tons		Bushels per Acre	
	1880	1893–96	1880	1893–96
Wheat . . .	440,000	440,000	24	26
Oats	660,000	650,000	43	43
Rye . . .	430,000	500,000	25	27
Barley, &c. . .	330,000	310,000	33	33
Total .	1,860,000	1,900,000	31	32
Potatoes . . .	2,820,000	3,650,000	115	...
Beetroot . . .	1,750,000	2,150,000	480	520

Notwithstanding the industry of the people, the country does not produce food for more than 60 per cent. of the population, whereas the waste of labour is so great that the number of hands engaged in agriculture ought to be sufficient, with proper machinery, to raise food for 11,000,000 persons, or nearly double the actual population of Belgium, if the area of the kingdom were larger. Thus it comes to pass that the maximum product of farming per acre, so far from being advantageous, must be regarded as deplorable in an economic sense. The old adage which says "the plough is silver but the spade is golden" contains as much nonsense as can be conveyed in so few words. Far better would it be if 500,000 Belgian farmers were located beyond the Mississippi.

The following table shows the value of agricultural products, and of similar imports :—

	Products, £		Imports, £
Grain . . .	12,100,000	Grain . . ,	7,800,000
Green crops .	16,800,000	Meat . . .	1,500,000
Meat . . .	5,000,000	Butter . . .	400,000
Dairy, &c. . .	10,100,000	Sundries . .	300,000
Total . .	44,000,000	Total . .	10,000,000

Agricultural capital has fallen heavily in 15 years, viz. :—

Year	Millions £ Sterling			
	Land	Cattle	Sundries	Total
1880 . . .	377	24	44	445
1895 . . .	300	22	32	354

The value of product compared with capital is the same as in Holland, 12 per cent. See *Cattle, Food, Land.*

SWITZERLAND

Agriculture is an industry of secondary importance, although it gives occupation to 40 per cent. of the Swiss people. There are 300,000 farms, with an average of 4 acres under tillage and 13 under pasture, the peasants in many cases adding to their income by cutting timber, or by receiving travellers into their houses in the summer season. The country hardly raises food for one-third of its population, the value of products and of imports showing thus :—

	Products, £		Imports, £
Grain . .	2,000,000	Grain . . .	3,300,000
Green crops .	7,000,000	Meat . . .	2,200,000
Meat . . .	4,000,000	Vegetables .	400,000
Dairy, &c. . .	7,000,000	Sundries . .	300,000
Total . .	20,000,000	Total . .	6,200,000

Dairy-farming is carried on with great success in various cantons, the export of cheese and condensed milk exceeding 40,000 tons yearly, worth 3 millions sterling. The total farming capital is 172 millions, of which land stands for 138 millions sterling, the average value of each farm being £490, against £880 in France.

THE DANUBIAN STATES

Although agriculture is the chief occupation, it is very backward in these countries, the number of hands engaged in farming being out of all proportion to the results obtained.

	Acres (000 omitted)			
	Roumania	Servia	Bulgaria	Total
Grain	10,600	2,400	4,900	17,900
Green crops. . .	2,600	2,500	1,600	6,700
Pasture	9,600	5,600	5,700	20,900
Forest, &c. . . .	9,600	1,700	11,400	22,700
Total . .	32,400	12,200	23,600	68,200

Crop, Million Bushels

	Roumania	Servia	Bulgaria	Total
Wheat	57	12	32	101
Maize	65	14	22	101
Barley, &c. . . .	46	10	20	76
Total . .	168	36	74	278

The aggregate area under vineyards in the three States is 1,100,000 acres, the vintage showing as follows:—

	Millions of Gallons		
	1895	1896	Average.
Roumania	68	164	116
Servia	17	25	21
Bulgaria	26	30	28
Total . .	111	219	165

Fruit is largely cultivated in Servia, orchards covering 180,000 acres, and producing the famous Slivovitz plum, of which 20,000 tons are exported yearly for making brandy. Cattle-farming is much attended to in all three States, live stock being approximately as follows:—

	Number (000 omitted)			
	Roumania	Servia	Bulgaria	Total
Horses . . .	600	150	250	900
Cattle	2,500	800	300	3,600
Sheep	5,200	3,500	8,500	17,200
Pigs	900	900	500	2,300
Total . .	9,200	5,300	9,500	24,000

These States export agricultural products to the value of 15 millions sterling yearly, for the most part grain; not more than two-thirds of the crops are kept for consumption, the surplus for export usually exceeding two million tons of grain. The value of farm products is approximately as follows:—

	Millions £ Sterling			
	Roumania	Servia	Bulgaria	Total
Grain	23	5	10	38
Green crops . .	9	4	6	19
Meat	8	4	4	16
Sundries . . .	6	2	2	10
Total . .	46	15	22	83

The total product gives only 38 shillings per acre, against 75 shillings in Austria-Hungary. The average coming to each hand employed in agriculture is no more than £21, as compared with £58 in France and the same in Ireland. Agricultural capital is shown approximately as follows:—

	Millions £ Sterling			
	Roumania	Servia	Bulgaria	Total
Land	200	90	130	420
Cattle	22	10	10	42
Sundries . . .	22	10	14	46
Total . .	244	110	154	508

There are altogether 1,300,000 farms; average value £384, average product £65. See *Food, Land*.

GREECE

The progress of agriculture has been slow, viz.:—

	Acres		
	1860	1889	1893
Cultivated . . .	810,000	2,090,000	2,340,000
Uncultivated . .	10,590,000	13,810,000	13,560,000
Total . .	11,400,000	15,900,000	15,900,000

The difference of area in the above table arises from the annexation of Thessaly in 1881. According to Greek writers, one-half of the uncultivated land could be brought under tillage, but agriculture is so backward that Greece has to import both grain and meat. Latest official returns showed 1,210,000 acres under grain, producing 200,000 tons of wheat and 200,000 of maize, barley, and rye; this was equivalent to an average crop of 13 bushels to the acre. Currant-growing was for some years most profitable, this fruit being worth £20 a ton in the decade ending 1890, but of late years it has fallen to £11, causing widespread agricultural depression. Currants have been grown chiefly for exportation, being much used in the manufacture of claret and other wines in France. Greece exported on an average 60,000 tons yearly before the phylloxera made great ravages (1876), and subsequently the demand for currants was such that the export reached 120,000 tons in 1893. The area under vineyards is 340,000 acres, and official returns put down the vintage at 66 million gallons, but this appears an exaggeration, the average for the last two years having been only 41 millions, that is, 120 gallons of wine per acre, as compared with 150 in the Danubian States. The value of agricultural products and the amount of capital are shown approximately as follows:—

	Products, £		Capital, £
Grain . . .	2,400,000	Land . . .	94,000,000
Other crops .	6,600,000	Cattle . . .	5,000,000
Meat, &c. . .	5,000,000	Sundries . .	10,000,000
Total . .	14,000,000	Total . .	109,000,000

The total productive area, between tillage and pasture, being 8,200,000 acres, the product is equal to 34 shillings per acre: it gives, moreover, £21 for each hand engaged in farming, being the same as in the Danubian States.

The progress made in Greek agriculture is seen by comparing Bickford's tables for 1889 with those of Bikelas for 1860, viz.:—

		1860	1889
Wheat, ...	acres	230,000	620,000
Other grain,	,,	330,000	590,000
Vines and currants,	,,	160,000	440,000
Sundries, ...	,,	90,000	440,000
Under crops, . .	,,	810,000	2,090,000
Fallow, ...	,,	630,000	1,010,000
Forest, ...	,,	1,350,000	1,500,000
Mountains, &c. .	,,	8,610,000	11,300,000
Total . .	,,	11,400,000	15,900,000

There are 60,000 acres under currant plantations, which give an ordinary yield of 3 tons per acre, the crop having quadrupled in 40 years, viz.:—

Year			Tons	Year			Tons
1851	.	.	41,000	1871	.	.	81,000
1861	.	.	43,000	1881	.	.	125,000
1866	.	.	56,000	1891	.	.	167,000

UNITED STATES

The position of agriculture may be taken in at a glance by considering the occupied and the unoccupied areas in the great divisions of the Union (exclusive of Alaska) according to the census of 1890, viz. :—

Division	Millions of Acres			
	Im-proved	Unim-proved	Unoccu-pied	Total
New England . . .	11	9	24	44
Middle	36	13	24	73
South	104	146	272	522
Prairie	184	73	271	528
Pacific	23	24	708	755
Total . .	358	265	1,299	1,922

The total area occupied by farms was 623 million acres, or nearly one-third of the Union. An official report for 1895 showed the area under other crops than hay to be 183 million acres, from which it would appear that 440 million acres are devoted to pasture. As a natural result of the Homestead Law of 1862, and of the new railways constructed in the West, we find that farming has made prodigious strides in the Prairie and the Pacific States. The improved area at the successive census dates was as follows :—

Divisions	Millions of Acres				
	1850	1860	1870	1880	1890
New England . . .	11	12	12	13	11
Middle	26	30	33	37	36
South	49	65	58	82	104
Prairie	27	52	78	137	184
Pacific	...	4	8	16	23
Union	113	163	189	285	358

If we compare the number of hands with the extent of farms at the above dates we find that, doubtless owing to improved machinery, each hand now cultivates 16 acres more than down to the year 1870, being an improvement of 50 per cent. in 20 years, viz. :—

Year	Hands	Acres	Acres per Hand
1850	3,120,000	113,100,000	36
1860	4,890,000	163,100,000	33
1870	5,668,000	188,800,000	33
1880	7,217,000	284,600,000	40
1890	8,323,000	357,600,000	49

Western and Southern farms are steadily growing larger, while those of New England and the Middle States become smaller, the latter being apparently the result of a great development of dairy-farming in recent years, viz. :—

Divisions	Hands		Acres per Hand	
	1870	1890	1870	1890
New England . . .	263,000	273,000	46	39
Middle	620,000	827,000	53	43
South	2,640,000	3,850,000	22	27
Prairie	1,950,000	3,060,000	40	60
Pacific	195,000	313,000	42	73
Union	5,668,000	8,323,000	33	49

The grain crops are on a colossal scale, summing up in the last 25 years almost 1600 million tons, being an average of 64 millions tons yearly, viz. :—

Period	Yearly Average, Tons (000 omitted)			
	Maize	Wheat	Oats,&c.	Total
1872–76	27,200	7,100	8,900	43,200
1877–81	36,400	10,100	11,500	58,000
1882–86	40,500	10,900	15,600	67,000
1887–91	43,600	11,100	18,700	73,400
1892–96	43,400	12,300	20,300	76,000
25 years	38,200	10,400	15,000	63,600

Less than one-twelfth of the grain produced has been exported, viz. :—

Period	Yearly Average, Tons		
	Crop	Export	Consumption
1872–76 . . .	43,200,000	2,700,000	40,500,000
1877–81 . . .	58,000,000	5,800,000	52,200,000
1882–86 . . .	67,000,000	4,500,000	62,500,000
1887–91 . . .	73,400,000	4,400,000	69,000,000
1892–96 . . .	76,000,000	6,500,000	69,500,000
25 years . . .	63,600,000	4,700,000	58,900,000

The weight of grain exported in 25 years was 118 million tons, of which 75 millions were wheat, 37 millions maize, and the rest oats and barley. The agricultural returns for the years 1893-95 give the following averages :—

	Acres	Tons	Crop Value, £ Sterling
Maize	72,200,000	41,500,000	119,000,000
Wheat	34,500,000	11,000,000	47,000,000
Oats	27,400,000	17,800,000	39,400,000
Rye, &c. . . .	6,000,000	2,700,000	10,100,000
All grain . . .	140,100,000	73,000,000	215,500,000

The following table shows for the same three years the average yield in bushels per acre, the value of crop per bushel, and the yield per acre of grain in money, American and English :—

	Bushels per Acre	Cents per Bushel	Produce per Acre	
			$	Shillings
Maize	23	36	8.00	33.3
Wheat . . .	13	51	6.60	27.5
Oats . . .	26	27	6.90	28.7
Rye, &c. . . .	19	43	8.10	33.7
General . . .	21	36	7.40	30.8

The crops of 1897, owing to the rise in wheat, gave a much better result, official returns showing as follows :—

	Tons	Value £	Cents per Bushel
Maize	47,600,000	104,000,000	26
Wheat	13,300,000	89,000,000	80
Oats	17,500,000	31,000,000	21
Rye, &c.	2,700,000	9,000,000	40
Total . .	81,100,000	233,000,000	34

An official return in 1894 estimated the cost of producing grain, per acre, as follows, in American dollars and cents :—

	New England $	Middle $	South $	Prairie $
Rent . . .	4.14	4.09	2.90	2.80
Manure . . .	4.55	5.58	1.99	1.74
Tillage . . .	3.77	2.87	1.62	1.70
Harvesting . .	3.52	2.05	0.87	1.27
Sundries . . .	8.14	5.26	4.00	3.47
Total . .	24.12	19.85	11.38	10.98

The cost of the two crops, wheat and maize, in 1894 was officially stated thus :—

	Wheat $	Maize $	Total $
Rent	98,300,000	189,700,000	288,000,000
Manure . . .	75,600,000	116,400,000	192,000,000
Tillage . . .	65,400,000	101,400,000	166,800,000
Harvesting. .	41,600,000	76,400,000	118,000,000
Sundries . .	128,100,000	249,100,000	377,200,000
Total . .	409,000,000	733,000,000	1,142,000,000

In the same year the value of the crops was, wheat 226 millions, maize 555 million dollars, showing a loss of 183 million dollars on wheat and 178 millions on maize. Such losses, however, are not in hard cash, as the farmer often holds his land free of rent, and not less frequently has manure and tillage free of actual outlay.

Cotton-growing during the last 30 years is shown as follows :—

Period	Tons Yearly		Value, Millions $	
	Crop	Exported	Crop	Export
1867–71 . . .	600,000	400,000	265	175
1872–76 . . .	810,000	550,000	275	188
1877–81 . . .	1,140,000	770,000	238	161
1882–86 . . .	1,310,000	880,000	268	179
1887–91 . . .	1,600,000	1,080,000	300	203
1892–96 . . .	1,810,000	1,200,000	275	183

The difference between the weight of crop and what was exported represents the home consumption in American factories. Cotton is grown solely in the Southern States.

Hay represents nearly double the value of the cotton crop, the average for the last three years being 478 million dollars, viz.:—

Divisions	Hay, Acres	Tons	Value, $
N. England . .	3,700,000	4,100,000	51,000,000
Middle	8,600,000	10,000,000	119,000,000
South	3,400,000	4,500,000	48,000,000
Prairie	23,900,000	27,300,000	185,000,000
Pacific	4,600,000	10,100,000	75,000,000
Union . .	44,200,000	56,000,000	478,000,000

Potatoes show the following average returns for the same three years, 1893–95 :—

	Acres	Tons	Value, $
N. England . .	180,000	550,000	10,600,000
Middle	710,000	1,440,000	23,800,000
South	240,000	420,000	9,700,000
Prairie	1,710,000	2,710,000	44,200,000
Pacific	110,000	290,000	4,800,000
Union . .	2,950,000	5,410,000	93,100,000

The Pacific States appear to give the heaviest hay crop in the world (except Ireland), their average being almost 2¼ tons per acre. New England gives a heavier yield of potatoes per acre than the rest of the Union, the average for the United States being under 3 tons per acre, as compared with 6 tons in Great Britain and 4 in Ireland.

The area, product, and value of crops in 1896 were :—

	Acres	Tons	Value, £	Shill. per Acre
Maize . . .	81,030,000	57,100,000	102,100,000	25
Wheat . . .	34,620,000	10,700,000	64,700,000	37
Oats . . .	27,570,000	17,700,000	27,400,000	20
Barley . .	2,950,000	1,750,000	4,600,000	31
Rye, &c. . .	2,580,000	950,000	3,300,000	26
All grain . .	148,750,000	88,200,000	202,100,000	27
Hay . . .	43,260,000	59,300,000	79,900,000	37
Cotton . .	23,450,000	1,840,000	59,200,000	51
Potatoes . .	2,770,000	6,300,000	15,100,000	108
Tobacco . .	590,000	180,000	5,100,000	173
Sugar, &c. .	3,580,000	290,000	19,700,000	110
Total . .	222,400,000	156,110,000	381,100,000	34

The average value of farm products in the last three years was approximately as follows, reduced to English money :—

	Millions £ Sterling							
	Grain	Hay	Cotton	Potatoes	Meat	Dairy	Sundries	Total
N. England .	2.1	10.5	...	2.2	3.1	6.7	5.4	30.0
Middle . .	19.9	24.8	...	4.8	12.0	26.8	17.7	106.0
South . .	56.2	10.0	51.0	2.0	44.0	19.4	26.4	209.0
Prairie . .	127.0	38.8	...	9.0	73.6	56.3	60.3	365.0
Pacific . .	10.8	15.9	...	1.0	23.3	0.8	10.2	62.0
Total . .	216.0	100.0	51.0	19.0	156.0	110.0	120.0	772.0

Cattle-farms, as already shown, cover an area of 400 million acres, with the following amount of stock in 1896 :—

	Live Stock (000 omitted)			
	Horses	Cattle	Sheep	Pigs
N. England . .	400	1,300	700	300
Middle . . .	1,600	4,100	2,600	2,100
South . . .	4,500	14,500	7,600	16,400
West . . .	10,900	28,300	27,400	24,000
Union . .	17,400	48,200	38,300	42,800

In the United States (as in Australia and Argentina) the flocks and herds are subject to great fluctuations. See *Cattle*, page 654.

The gross product per acre, counting only the improved area, comes out as follows in the various sections :—

States	Acres	£ Sterling	Shill. per Acre
N. England . .	10,750,000	30,000,000	56
Middle . . .	35,750,000	106,000,000	59
South . . .	103,800,000	209,000,000	40
Prairie . . .	184,300,000	365,000,000	40
Pacific . . .	23,000,000	62,000,000	54
Union . .	357,600,000	772,000,000	43

Comparing product with the number of hands engaged, we find as follows :—

States	Hands	£ Sterling	£ per Hand
Eastern . . .	1,100,000	136,000,000	124
South	3,850,000	209,000,000	54
Prairie	3,060,000	365,000,000	120
Pacific	310,000	62,000,000	200
Union . .	8,320,000	772,000,000	93

The United States consume about five-sixths, and export one-sixth, of their farm products, as measured by value, viz. :—

Year	Millions £ Sterling		
	Consumption	Exported	Total
1860	367	53	420
1880	556	143	699
1886	674	101	775
1893	685	128	813

The value of farm products consumed in 1893 was £10.3 per inhabitant, against £11.1 in 1880, the price level having fallen so much, that although the quantity was increased the value was less.

The following table shows the *official* value of farms at the census of 1890, and the *real* approximate value in 1895, compared with the number of agricultural hands:—

States	Millions £ Sterling		£ per Hand
	1890	1895	
N. England	122	142	523
Middle	548	646	780
South	610	713	185
West	2,050	2,641	784
Total . . .	3,330	4,142	497

Comparing the above amount of agricultural capital with the improved area, it gives an average of barely £12 per acre, which is lower than in most countries, viz. :—

	£ Capital			£ Capital	
	Per Acre	Per Hand		Per Acre	Per Hand
U. States . .	12	497	France . .	34	430
G. Britain . .	51	1,060	Ireland . .	16	415
Germany . .	29	270	Italy . . .	26	175

The contrast between the United States and Great Britain in the above table is very striking, and explains why agriculture progresses in the former, and languishes in the latter, country.

CANADA

The area under crops, by latest returns, was 20 million acres, equal to 4 acres per inhabitant, as compared with 3½ in the United States. In some respects Canada is more agricultural than the great Republic: the proportion of people living on farms is much higher, and the value of farm products is £11.5 per head of the whole population, whereas it is not quite £11 in the United States. The cultivated area stands thus :—

	Acres (000 omitted)			
	Grain	Hay	Sundries	Total
Ontario . . .	5,040	2,530	540	8,110
Quebec . . .	1,220	2,460	1,500	5,180
Manitoba . .	1,590	250	990	2,830
Acadia, &c. . .	1,900	970	910	3,780
Total . .	9,750	6,210	3,940	19,900

The latest estimates of grain crops was approximately as follows :—

	Tons		Tons
Ontario . . .	3,200,000	Wheat . . .	1,300,000
Quebec . . .	800,000	Oats	2,600,000
Manitoba . .	800,000	Barley . . .	400,000
Acadia, &c. . .	400,000	Maize, &c. . .	900,000
Total . .	5,200,000	Total . .	5,200,000

The production of grain averages 41 bushels per inhabitant, against 49 in the United States; this is the reverse of what we might expect, in view of the heavier crops obtained in Upper Canada, viz. :—

	Bushels per Acre		
	Wheat	Barley	Oats
Ontario . . .	18	26	35
U. States . . .	13	21	25

Tillage has not progressed so much as pastoral industry in late years. Dairy farms have multiplied, as well as grazing farms, and the value of exported food reaches 10 millions sterling per annum. In 1894 the value of all farm products was approximately :—

	Millions £ Sterling		
	Consumption	Export	Total
Grain	17	4	21
Meat	9	2	11
Dairy	5	4	9
Sundries . . .	16	...	16
Total . .	47	10	57

The improved or productive area increased 70 per cent. in a period of 10 years, down to 1891, viz. :—

Acres under	1881	1891
Tillage	15,100,000	19,900,000
Pasture . . .	6,400,000	15,300,000
Total . .	21,500,000	35,200,000

The total farming capital of the Dominion is approximately 311 millions sterling (which is equal to

£60 per inhabitant, against £59 in the United States), as follows:—

	Millions £ Sterling			
	Land	Cattle	Sundries	Total
Ontario . . .	155	21	10	186
Quebec . . .	50	11	6	67
Acadia . . .	23	6	3	32
West . . .	17	5	4	26
Total . .	245	43	23	311

Dividing the total among the number of farms, it gives an average of £517 to each, against £730 in the United States and £880 in France.

AUSTRALIA

Official returns show that the area under tillage has increased 400,000 acres per annum since 1891, viz.:—

	1891	1896
Victoria	2,120,000	2,660,000
S. Australia . . .	1,930,000	2,140,000
New S. Wales . . .	850,000	1,660,000
New Zealand . . .	1,420,000	1,600,000
Queensland, &c. . .	470,000	670,000
Total . .	6,790,000	8,730,000

The above returns, however, exclude 9,100,000 acres of sown grasses in New Zealand, which would bring up the total cultivated area to 17,800,000 acres, or two million acres less than in Canada. Compared with population the area is about equal, being 4 acres per inhabitant in both cases. The area under grain is almost six million acres, viz.:—

	Acres			Crop, Tons
	Wheat	Oats, &c.	All Grain	
Victoria . .	1,580,000	490,000	2,070,000	380,000
S. Australia	1,690,000	60,000	1,750,000	230,000
N. S. Wales	870,000	260,000	1,130,000	300,000
New Zealand	260,000	420,000	680,000	400,000
Queensland	35,000	115,000	150,000	70,000
Tasmania .	75,000	45,000	120,000	50,000
W. Australia	30,000	...	30,000	10,000
Total .	4,540,000	1,390,000	5,930,000	1,440,000

The aggregate grain crops of the seven colonies in the last three years were :—

	Tons			
	1894	1895	1896	Average
Wheat . .	790,000	630,000	670,000	700,000
Oats . . .	450,000	410,000	500,000	450,000
Maize, &c. .	300,000	270,000	300,000	290,000
Total .	1,540,000	1,310,000	1,470,000	1,440,000

Thus the average yield sums up only 58 million bushels yearly, which is less than 10 bushels per acre, against 21 in the United States. About 300,000 tons, or one-fifth

of the crop, are annually exported, home consumption (after deduction for seed) averaging .10 bushels per inhabitant. Vineyards cover an area of 60,000 acres, as compared with 22,000 acres in 1886 : the average vintage is over 4 million gallons, giving a yield of 72 gallons per acre, or about half the average in Europe. The average for five years shows :—

	Acres	Gallons	Gallons per Acre
Victoria	30,000	1,800,000	60
N. S. Wales	8,000	800,000	100
S. Australia . . .	17,000	1,400,000	85
W. Australia, &c. . .	4,000	300,000	75
Total . .	59,000	4,300,000	72

Potatoes are cultivated successfully in all seven colonies, sugar only in Queensland and New South Wales: the crops of last three years were :—

	Tons		Tons per Acre	
	Potatoes	Sugar-cane	Potatoes	Cane
1894	580,000	...	3.9	...
1895	450,000	...	3.5	...
1896	510,000	1,150,000	3.5	10.1

Pastoral interests greatly surpass those of tillage, wool alone standing for more than the total value of the crops, viz. :—

	Millions £ Sterling *			
	Crops	Wool	Sundries	Total
N. S. Wales . . .	4.0	9.6	7.2	20.8
Victoria	6.7	2.9	6.4	16.0
New Zealand . . .	4.8	4.8	4.5	14.1
Queensland . . .	1.4	3.3	5.0	9.7
S. Australia . . .	3.3	1.3	1.8	6.4
Tasmania . . .	1.0	0.3	0.8	2.1
W. Australia . . .	0.3	0.3	0.3	0.9
Total . .	21.5	22.5	26.0	70.0

Here, as well as in the United States and Argentina, the flocks are subject to violent fluctuations, viz. :—

	1881	1891	1896
Sheep	78,100,000	124,500,000	110,500,000
Cattle	8,700,000	11,900,000	12,700,000
Horses . . .	1,200,000	1,800,000	1,900,000
Total . .	88,000,000	138,200,000	125,100,000

The aggregate number of live stock rose 5 millions yearly between 1881 and 1891, but since the latter year we find an average fall of 2½ millions yearly. The wool-clip averages 320,000 tons, of which 300,000 are exported. The value of all farm products, as shown above, is 70 millions sterling per annum, equal to £17 per head of the population, against £11 in the United States and in Canada, the ratio in Denmark being the same as in

* This table is to be read thus: N. S. Wales 4.0 means £4,000,000.

Australia. Agricultural wealth stands approximately as follows :—

	Millions £ Sterling			
	Land	Cattle	Sundries	Total
N. S. Wales . . .	85	34	12	131
Victoria	49	21	7	77
New Zealand . . .	43	20	6	69
Queensland . . .	18	34	5	57
S. Australia . . .	28	7	3	38
Tasmania	9	2	1	12
W. Australia . . .	4	2	1	7
Total . .	236	120	35	391

Australian pasture lands are generally poor; they rarely carry more than 300 sheep to the square mile, whereas in the Pampas of Argentina it is usual to have from 1000 to 1500.

SOUTH AFRICA

Cape Colony and Natal are devoted rather to pasture than tillage. In 1893 the total area under crops between the two colonies was 1,540,000 acres, nine-tenths under grain. As population increases, the deficit of grain-supply diminishes, the importation having fallen from 50,000 tons in 1885 to 42,000 in 1895. The grain crop of Cape Colony in 1896 reached 200,000 tons, besides which the colonists raise 2000 tons of tobacco and 25,000 pipes of wine, including the well-known Constantia. The vineyards cover 30,000 acres, and contain 87 million vine-stocks, the average yield being 1 gallon of wine from 15 vine-stocks. Natal has 600,000 acres under tillage, a small portion of which is used for sugar-growing. How much sugar is produced cannot be ascertained, but the exportation has fallen 30 per cent. since 1885, and does not now exceed 7000 tons. The value of all farm products is approximately as follows :—

	Cape, £	Natal, £	Total, £
Wool . , . .	1,600,000	500,000	2,100,000
Grain	1,100,000	400,000	1,500,000
Sundries . .	3,300,000	1,100,000	4,400,000
Total . .	6,000,000	2,000,000	8,000,000

The breed of sheep has been much improved, the average fleece being now 5 lbs., or 40 per cent. heavier than in 1865. Nevertheless the exportation of wool fluctuates exceedingly, viz. :—

						Tons Shipped Yearly
1881–83	.	.	.	.	.	24,000
1891–93	.	.	.	.	.	42,000
1894–95	.	.	.	.	.	34,000

Angora hair and ostrich feathers likewise form valuable items of rural industry, the exportation showing as follows :—

Year	Lbs. Weight		Value, £ Sterling	
	Hair	Feathers	Hair	Feathers
1885 . .	5,700,000	250,000	220,000	350,000
1895 . .	11,500,000	590,000	730,000	530,000

Thus the aggregate value of these two items rose in ten years from £570,000 to £1,260,000, an increase of 120

per cent. The live stock of the two colonies stands thus approximately :—

	Cape	Natal	Total	
			1897	1889
Sheep . .	14,100,000	800,000	14,900,000	14,900,000
Cattle . .	2,230,000	740,000	2,970,000	2,120,000
Goats . .	5,030,000	370,000	5,400,000	5,450,000
Horses . .	400,000	50,000	450,000	350,000

Cape Colony has, moreover, 220,000 ostriches, and the average yield is nearly 3 pounds of feathers, worth 50 shillings, yearly per bird. The agricultural wealth of the two colonies is about 65 millions, of which 51 millions pertain to Cape Colony.

ARGENTINA

Tillage has made great strides in the last twenty years, owing to the enormous influx of Italians, the cultivated area showing as follows :—

	Acres	
	1874	1897
Wheat	270,000	5,200,000
Maize	250,000	2,700,000
Alfa, &c.	300,000	7,300,000
Total . .	820,000	15,200,000

The country, however, is less suited to tillage than grazing, the crops being light and, moreover, constantly exposed to drought and locusts. The wheat crop of the last four years showed as follows :—

Year	Tons		
	Crop	Consumption	Export
1892–93 . . .	1,400,000	550,000	850,000
1893–94 . . .	2,080,000	550,000	1,530,000
1894–95 . . .	1,550,000	560,000	990,000
1895–96 . . .	1,130,000	580,000	550,000
1896–97 . . .	750,000	600,000	150,000
Average . . .	1,380,000	570,000	810,000

The average for five years gave a mean crop of 9 bushels to the acre, as compared with 10 in Australia and 13 in the United States. The crop for (December) 1897 was expected to produce nearly the same as that for 1893, which would leave 1,400,000 tons for exportation. Maize covers one-third of the area under grain, and averages 30 bushels to the acre, but is a most uncertain crop, the surplus for exportation in 1896 having been only 180,000 tons, whereas in the preceding year it reached 800,000 tons. Alfa is an artificial grass, like clover, used for fattening sheep or cattle, within closed fences, called *Invernadas;* this crop covers about 3 million acres, chiefly in Buenos Ayres and Cordoba. Sugar-planting was begun on an enlarged scale in 1880, the production reaching 60,000 tons in 1892, and 120,000 in 1896 : two-thirds are used for home consumption, and 40,000 tons exported, the Government paying a bounty of £8 per ton on the latter. The production of wine has likewise progressed, under the favour of oppressive duties on foreign wines. Vineyards cover about 100,000 acres, and yield a vintage of 35 million gallons : an equal amount of artificial wines is manufactured at Buenos Ayres and Rosario from all manner of vegetable, and certain deleterious, ingredients, which (as physicians assert) increases the death-rate of those cities. The area under linseed varies exceedingly, the crop fluctuating between 100,000 and 300,000 tons, all of which is exported.

Pastoral farming has always constituted the real wealth of the republic, the Pampas offering plenty of room for countless flocks and herds : nevertheless this branch of industry shows little increase in the number of live stock, viz. :—

	1888	1895
Sheep	70,450,000	74,400,000
Cattle	22,870,000	21,700,000
Horses	4,400,000	4,450,000
Total . .	97,720,000	100,550,000

Although the number shows an increase of only 3 per cent. in seven years, the farmers have done much for improving breeds, by importing blood-stock of every kind from England and elsewhere. In this manner the average fleece has risen in twenty years from 3 lbs. to 5 lbs., and the weight of sheep in equal ratio. Many of the best sheep-farms belong to Irish or Scotch settlers, the area, stock, and gross income of which may be classed thus :—

Class	Acres	Sheep	Income, £ Sterling
Small	3,000	6,000	600
Medium . . .	15,000	30,000	3,000
Large	50,000	100,000	10,000

Consul Cowper (1872) stated that the progress of Buenos Ayres was mainly due to the Irish sheep-farmers ; they constitute three-fourths of all foreign settlers devoted to pastoral occupations. Cattle-farming is mostly in the hands of natives, an *estancia* being more or less as follows :—

Class	Acres	Cattle	Horses	Income, £
Small . . .	30,000	5,000	1,000	3,000
Medium . .	100,000	12,000	2,000	7,000
Large . .	400,000	50,000	6,000	25,000

The annual value of all farm products is about 48 millions sterling, viz. :—

	Product, £	Consumption, £	Export, £
Grain . . .	15,000,000	9,200,000	5,800,000
Wool . . .	8,000,000	100,000	7,900,000
Meat . . .	8,400,000	5,000,000	3,400,000
Hides, &c. . .	6,700,000	2,500,000	4,200,000
Sundries .	9,900,000	7,900,000	2,000,000
Total .	48,000,000	24,700,000	23,300,000

The farming product is equal to £12 per inhabitant, against £11 in the United States and £17 in Australia. The estimated value of lands, stock, &c., in 1890 was 198 millions sterling : the gross product, therefore, is about 25 per cent. on capital, against 18 per cent. in Australia and 19 in the United States.

The average weight and value of exports in three years ending 1896 were :—

	Quantity	Value, £
Wool, tons . . .	184,000	7,900,000
Sheepskins, tons . .	36,000	800,000
Hides, tons . . .	60,000	1,200,000
Meat, ,, . .	92,000	1,800,000
Cattle, number . .	320,000	1,200,000
Sheep, ,, . .	350,000	200,000
Horses, ,, . .	40,000	100,000
Tallow, &c. . . .	...	2,000,000
Wheat, tons . . .	1,100,000	4,300,000
Maize, ,, . .	800,000	1,600,000
Linseed, ,, . . .	210,000	1,300,000
Hay, ,, . . .	80,000	100,000
Total . .		22,500,000

Tillage estimates for 1897 were as follows :—

	Acres			
	Wheat	Maize	Sundries	Total
B. Ayres . .	1,020,000	1,860,000	860,000	3,740,000
Santa Fé . .	3,200,000	300,000	900,000	4,400,000
Entre Rios . .	600,000	100,000	200,000	900,000
Cordoba, &c. .	1,100,000	400,000	4,660,000	6,160,000
Total . .	5,920,000	2,660,000	6,620,000	15,200,000

URUGUAY

The area under tillage is supposed to reach 1,200,000 acres, of which two-thirds are under grain, the crops averaging 120,000 tons of wheat and 80,000 of maize, and leaving a small surplus for exportation. Pastoral interests are of superior importance, but the number of live stock does not increase (owing to civil wars), viz. :—

	1887	1895
Sheep	15,900,000	14,300,000
Cattle	6,120,000	5,250,000
Horses	410,000	400,000
Total . .	22,430,000	19,950,000
Value, £ . . .	16,800,000	15,400,000

The total value of farm products yearly is about 10 millions sterling, viz. :—

	Product, £	Consumption, £	Export, £
Wool	2,200,000	...	2,200,000
Meat	3,800,000	1,200,000	2,600,000
Hides, &c. . .	1,800,000	300,000	1,500,000
Grain, &c. . .	2,200,000	1,500,000	700,000
Total . .	10,000,000	3,000,000	7,000,000

The official value of land and stock is £38,500,000. and allowing for sundries this gives a total farming capital of 42 millions sterling : the gross product, therefore, is about 24 per cent. on capital, as compared with 25 in Argentina and 19 in the United States.

INDIA

The productive area is much too small for the actual population, viz. :—

	000 omitted			Acres per Inhab.
	Population	Area, Acres	Cultivated	
Bengal . . .	71,300	97,300	54,700	0.8
Bombay . .	18,900	80,100	30,100	1.6
Madras . . .	35,600	90,500	29,900	0.8
Assam . . .	5,500	31,400	2,900	c.5
Punjaub . .	20,900	70,400	27,000	1.3
Oude . . .	12,700	15,300	9,400	0.7
Burmah . .	7,600	106,100	11,100	1.5
N.W. Prov. .	34,300	50,500	27,400	0.8
Central, &c. .	14,400	76,400	34,500	2.4
Total . .	221,200	618,000	227,000	1.0

The cultivated area is only as one acre per inhabitant, but might be increased 60 per cent., there being, as shown in survey, 137 million acres available for cultivation, viz. :—

	Uncultivated	Available
Bengal	42,600,000	37,500,000
Madras . . .	60,600,000	6,700,000
Punjaub . . .	43,400,000	22,300,000
Burmah . . .	95,000,000	33,000,000
Assam, &c., &c. .	149,400,000	37,300,000
Total .	391,000,000	136,800,000

The principal areas of crops in 1895 were as follows :—

	Acres (000 omitted)			
	Rice	Grain	Cotton	Tea
Bengal . . .	39,000	13,100	200	4,200
Bombay . . .	1,800	18,400	2,700	1,800
Madras . . .	6,600	14,900	1,500	1,700
Punjaub . . .	900	19,700	1,000	1,100
N.W. Provinces .	5,100	21,100	1,200	900
Burmah . . .	6,400	1,100	200	400
Central, &c. .	9,500	24,000	2,900	3,800
Total . .	69,300	112,300	9,700	13,900

The total farming products are apparently of the annual value of nearly 400 millions sterling, of which one-seventh is exported, viz. :—

	Tons (000 omitted)		Value, Millions £	
	Crop	Export	Crop	Export
Grain . . .	32,400	400	130	2.2
Rice . . .	22,000	1,700	88	9.2
Cotton . .	800	240	20	7.5
Jute . . .	1,100	650	10	7.1
Oil-seeds . .	1,000	900	9	8.2
Opium . . .	60	50	7	6.1
Tea . . .	70	60	6	5.5
Coffee . . .	40	15	4	1.5
Sugar . . .	120	60	1	0.6
Sundries . .	...	...	115	8.1
Total . .	...	...	390	56.0

According to the census of 1891 the agricultural population amounted to 172 millions, from which it would appear that the farm products average 40 rupees or 46 shillings per head, say £10 a year for each adult male peasant.

CEYLON

One-eighth of the island is under crops, the whole area showing thus :—

	Acres
Rice	730,000
Tea, coffee, &c.	1,290,000
Pasture	910,000
Unproductive . . .	13,270,000
Total . .	16,200,000

Coffee-growing and chinchona have declined, and other products show a great increase, the exports having been as follows :—

	1873	1887	1895
Coffee, tons . .	49,000	9,000	3,000
Tea, ,, . .	...	6,000	44,000
Oil, ,, . .	6,000	16,000	21,000
Cocoa, ,, . .	...	800	1,400
Chinchona, £ . .	...	170,000	4,000

The aggregate value of the above exports was £4,400,000 in 1873, falling to £1,900,000 in 1887, and amounting to £3,500,000 in 1895. No less than 80 per cent. of the population is agricultural, the number of male adults so employed being 850,000.

JAVA

The *Statesman's Year-book* has the following official returns :—

	1890	1894
Rice, acres . . .	4,390,000	5,060,000
Maize, ,, . . .	1,880,000	1,930,000
Sundries, ,, . . .	2,070,000	2,380,000
Total, acres . .	8,340,000	9,370,000

The principal crops were as follows :—

	1891	1894
Sugar, tons . . .	420,000	480,000
Coffee, ,, . . .	51,000	58,000
Chinchona, ,, . .	3,100	3,200
Tea, ,, . . .	3,300	4,100
Tobacco, ,, . . .	8,200	10,300

Agricultural exports of Java average 12 millions sterling, and are mostly sold in Holland, the Dutch Government having a profit of about 25 per cent.

JAPAN

The area under crops is one-seventh of the total, viz. :—

	1891	1895
Rice, acres . . .	6,730,000	7,020,000
Grain, ,, . . .	4,170,000	4,340,000
Pasture, ,, . . .	33,600,000	33,600,000
Waste, ,, . . .	34,900,000	34,440,000
Total . .	79,400,000	79,400,000

The principal crops were :—

	1891	1895
Rice, tons . . .	5,300,000	5,000,000
Wheat, ,, . .	300,000	500,000
Barley, rye, ,, . .	1,020,000	1,900,000
Sugar, ,, . .	50,000	52,000

The value of tillage products sums up 45 millions sterling, or nearly £4 per acre. Live stock comprises 1,500,000 horses and 1,100,000 cattle. The production of raw silk averages 16 million lbs. yearly, worth 8 millions sterling.

BRAZIL

Although this country has the same area as the United States, the total extent of productive land does not exceed the area covered by the farms of the single State of Ohio, or about 18 million acres. The chief product is coffee, which has not declined since the emancipation of negroes (1888), as was expected, the crop showing thus :—

Year	Tons	Year	Tons
1880	333,000	1892	444,000
1885	389,000	1897	590,000

The value of the coffee-crop is about 36 millions sterling, most of it being exported to the United States. Sugar, cotton, tobacco, and Paraguayan tea are also largely exported, as well as maize and mandioca; these items making up about 14 millions sterling. Cattle-farming is almost confined to the southernmost State, Rio Grande do Sul, the *saladeros* of Pelotas killing 3000 head daily in the season. The sum total of tillage and pastoral industry in Brazil does not exceed 60 millions sterling, that is, about the same as Canada.

WEST INDIES, BRITISH

Sugar and bananas are the principal products, the cultivated area showing thus :—

	Acres		
	Sugar	Sundries	Total
Jamaica . . .	30,000	150,000	180,000
Trinidad . . .	60,000	140,000	200,000
Barbadoes . . .	30,000	70,000	100,000
Guiana	70,000	10,000	80,000
Antigua, &c. .	50,000	150,000	200,000
West Indies . .	240,000	520,000	760,000

The export of sugar has notably declined in quantity in the last fifteen years, and still more in value, viz. :—

Average	Tons	Value, £	£ per Ton
1881–85 . .	290,000	4,730,000	16.3
1891–95 . .	265,000	3,430,000	13.0

The quantities shipped gave the following yearly averages :—

	1881–83	1887–89	1893–95
Guiana, . tons .	111,000	120,000	104,000
Trinidad, ,, .	51,000	57,000	49,000
Barbadoes, ,, .	47,000	59,000	49,000
Jamaica, ,, .	27,000	21,000	20,000
Antigua, &c., ,, .	49,000	51,000	37,000
West Indies . .	285,000	308,000	259,000

The cultivation of fruit for the seaboard cities of the United States has increased very rapidly, the values exported from the single island of Jamaica showing :—

	1885–86	1895–96
Bananas, . . . £ sterling .	148,000	372,000
Oranges and nuts, ,, .	56,000	148,000
Total, £ . .	204,000	520,000

Not far from the West Indies are the Bermuda Islands, where small farms are very productive. The official report for 1897 shows that one farmer gets £100 an acre by growing lilies. Farms range from 5 to 25 acres, the gross product averaging £40 per acre.

FEEJEE ISLANDS

In this little group there are 3000 white settlers, who have 40,000 acres under cultivation, one-half under sugar, of which they export 25,000 tons yearly, the exportation having doubled since 1886. Live stock comprises 20,000 cattle, sheep, and Angora goats.

CHILI

This is essentially an agricultural country, with 7 million acres under crops, the production of grain ranging from 800,000 to 900,000 tons, of which one-fourth is exported. Live stock is insufficient, the deficit of meat-supply being met by the importation of cattle and sheep across the Andes from Argentina.

ALGERIA

Notwithstanding the great efforts and liberality of the French Government this colony makes slow progress in agriculture : the production of grain in 1895 compares with 1886 as follows :—

	Acres		Tons	
	1886	1895	1886	1895
Wheat . .	3,120,000	3,170,000	630,000	840,000
Barley . .	3,600,000	3,470,000	950,000	1,070,000
Oats, &c. .	240,000	290,000	80,000	110,000
Total . .	6,960,000	6,930,000	1,660,000	2,020,000
French . .	1,060,000	1,090,000	290,000	430,000
Native . .	5,900,000	5,840,000	1,370,000	1,590,000
Total . .	6,960,000	6,930,000	1,660,000	2,020,000

Although the area is less, the weight of crop has increased more than 20 per cent., probably owing to improved mode of agriculture. The average yield per acre shows as follows :—

	Bushels per Acre	
	1886	1895
Wheat	8.0	10.6
Barley	10.5	12.3
All grain	9.5	11.6
French farms . . .	11.0	15.8
Arab ,, ...	9.3	10.8

Vine-growing has progressed very satisfactorily, there being at present 30,000 vineyards, three-fifths belonging to French or other European settlers. The figures of this branch of industry in 1895 compare with 1886 as follows :—

	Acres	Gallons	Do. per Acre
1886 . . .	190,000	36,000,000	189
1895 . . .	300,000	79,000,000	263

On the other hand farm stock shows a decline, viz. :—

	Number (000 omitted)			
	Cattle	Sheep	Horses	Goats
1886 . . .	1,190	9,360	310	4,670
1895 . . .	1,130	7,700	350	3,370

Europeans own hardly 10, Arabs 90, per cent. of the live stock, which includes also 250,000 camels.

TUNIS

The territory covers nearly 29 million acres, of which only one-fourth is under cultivation, viz. :—

	Acres
Grain	2,300,000
Olives, &c.	4,500,000
Pasture, &c.	22,000,000
Total	28,800,000

Products average about 400,000 tons of grain, 4,000,000 gallons of wine, and 2,000,000 gallons of olive oil. The value of tillage and pastoral products exported (mostly to France) amounts to £1,300,000 per annum. Live stock is comparatively trifling, 1,200,000 sheep, 680,000 goats, 230,000 cattle, 120,000 camels ; the pasture lands could carry much more.

CENTRAL AMERICA

The little republics of Guatemala, Costa Rica, Nicaragua, Salvador, and Honduras, have an aggregate of about 900,000 acres under crops, mostly maize and other grain. There are 200,000 acres under coffee, average crop 50,000 tons, Guatemala standing for two-thirds of the total. The sugar crop of these republics is about 60,000 tons. See Part I.

CUBA

Before the revolution of 1896 there were 91,000 estates, covering altogether 2,800,000 acres, being an average of 30 acres each. The production of sugar, until the present revolution, was usually a million tons yearly, of which three-fourths went to the United States. The weight of tobacco and cigars exported averaged 120,000 tons. The total value of farm products ranged from 20 to 24 millions sterling, nine-tenths of the island being unpopulated and uncultivated, owing to the wretched system of government.

The adjacent island of Porto Rico has about 600,000 acres under cultivation, and exports coffee, sugar, and tobacco to the value of 3 millions sterling yearly.

CANARY ISLANDS

Free trade was introduced in 1890, and the result has been a marvellous improvement in the condition of these islands, which were previously subject to constant misery and periodical famines. The total cultivated area hardly exceeds 500,000 acres, but the climate and soil are so favourable for early fruits and vegetables that the African steamers which touch weekly at Teneriffe and Las Palmas convey cargoes of same to the London and other English markets. Farming is now so prosperous that land fetches high rents, and cannot be bought under £50 an acre.

EGYPT

The cultivated area shows a slight increase since the country was taken by the British forces in 1883. It was 4,960,000 acres in 1880, and the returns for 1891 show 5,170,000, that is, an increase of 4 per cent. There are 1,140,000 acres under double cultivation, which explains why the acreage of crops in the following table exceeds the total cultivated area, viz. :—

	1888	1891
Wheat	1,290,000	1,250,000
Other grain	3,205,000	2,960,000
Cotton	900,000	890,000
Clover, &c.	980,000	1,230,000
Total	6,375,000	6,330,000

The value of crops was estimated in 1884 at 30 millions sterling, but at present hardly reaches 25 millions. See *Land*, and Part I., page 39.

AGRICULTURAL COLLEGES

So much attention has been given of late years to agricultural science, that most nations have a number of institutions for the purpose.

France.—The Agronomic Institute of Paris, and 167 Agricultural Schools, receive from Government yearly grants amounting to £182,000 sterling.

Germany.—There are 31 Agricultural Colleges maintained by the State ; one of these is Hohenheim, near Stuttgart, which receives £6000 a year. There are Agricultural Schools in every district of Bavaria, the State defraying 50 per cent. of their cost. In other parts of Germany there are similar institutions, which receive on an average £300 a year each per annum.

Austria (proper).—There were 65 Agricultural Schools in 1880, and the number has now risen to 118, of which Bohemia has 45. The annual expenditure is £105,000, the State contributing £45,000, the local authorities £30,000, and students the rest. The State also gives £5000 a year to travelling lecturers.

Hungary.—At Magyar-Ovar is the great Academy of Agriculture. There are also 4 Agricultural Colleges and 35 Schools, of which 20 are maintained by the Hungarian Treasury at an annual cost of £43,000. These schools turn out 1100 agricultural graduates or licentiates yearly.

Switzerland.—There are 16 Agricultural Schools, maintained at a cost of £12,600, the Cantons giving two-thirds, the Federal Treasury one-third.

United States.—There are 65 Agricultural Colleges, with 1280 professors and 17,600 students. About 3000 graduate yearly, the course being one of four years. Income £840,000 sterling, of which Congress gives £300,000, the local authorities £240,000. The buildings represent an outlay of £3,700,000 sterling, including £750,000 for the libraries and apparatus.

ALCOHOL

The average production of liquors in five years ending 1895–96, and the equivalent of all in alcohol, were as follows :—

	Millions of Gallons			All Red. to Alcohol
	Wine	Beer	Spirits	
United Kingdom	...	1,180	47	78
France	840	194	99	143
Germany	70	1,230	136	130
Russia	40	90	154	85
Austria	115	376	102	80
Italy	605	2	8	65
Spain	460	21	...	47
Portugal	70	...	...	7
Scandinavia	...	86	16	12
Holland	...	50	15	10
Belgium	...	260	13	18
Switzerland	30	34	2	6
Various	190	2	2	20
Europe	2,420	3,525	594	701
United States	20	865	72	77
Total	2,440	4,390	666	778

Consumption during the same five years was approximately thus :—

	Million Gallons Yearly			All Red. to Alcohol
	Wine	Beer	Spirits	
United Kingdom .	15	1,160	39	73
France . . .	990	196	71	143
Germany . . .	60	1,230	99	111
Russia . . .	45	90	125	71
Austria . . .	130	376	97	78
Italy . . .	570	3	8	61
Spain . . .	330	21	...	34
Scandinavia . .	2	86	17	13
Portugal . . .	55	...	...	6
Holland . . .	2	50	9	7
Belgium . . .	6	260	13	19
Switzerland . .	45	34	4	8
Various . . .	150	4	5	18
Europe . . .	2,400	3,510	487	6,42
United States . .	20	870	73	78
Total . .	2,420	4,360	560	720

Consumption per inhabitant has been as follows :—

	Gallons per Head			All Red. to Alcohol
	Wine	Beer	Spirits	
United Kingdom .	0.4	30.0	1.0	1.90
France . . .	26.0	5.0	1.9	3.80
Germany . . .	1.2	24.0	1.9	2.20
Russia . . .	0.4	0.9	1.1	0.65
Austria . . .	3.1	9.0	2.3	1.80
Italy . . .	20.5	0.1	0.3	2.10
Spain . . .	18 0	1.4	...	1.86
Scandinavia . .	0.2	9.5	2.0	1.50
Holland . . .	0.4	10.5	2.0	1.50
Belgium . . .	0.9	41.5	2.1	3.10
Switzerland . .	15.0	11.5	1.3	2.60
United States . .	0.3	12.8	1.1	1.15

The above is exclusive of Temperance drinks, which according to Bannister, Government analyst, contain from 3 to 13 per cent. of alcohol.

BEER

Consumption in the principal countries has been approximately as follows :—

	Million Gallons		Gallons per Head	
	1885	1895	1885	1895
United Kingdom .	976	1,160	27.1	29.6
Germany . . .	908	1,216	19.8	23.5
Belgium . . .	209	271	35.6	42.2
Austria . . .	279	410	7.1	9.5
France . . .	183	197	4.6	5.1
Scandinavia . .	60	90	8.5	9.7
Russia, &c. . .	148	196	1.0	1.1
Europe . . .	2,763	3,540	7.5	9.0
United States . .	497	870	8.8	12.7
Total . .	3,260	4,410	7.8	9.8

A bushel of barley yields 15 gallons of beer in Great Britain, 25 in Germany. Five bushels of barley give 4 of malt.

SPIRITS

Consumption in the principal countries was approximately thus :—

	Million Gallons		Gallons per Head	
	1885	1895	1885	1895
United Kingdom .	35	39	0.96	1.00
Germany . . .	70	98	1.58	1.90
France . . .	64	68	1.69	1.78
Austria . . .	84	105	2.20	2.60
Russia . . .	137	132	1.46	1.03
Scandinavia . .	17	17	2.10	1.90
Belgium . . .	12	14	2.02	2.20
Holland . . .	9	9	2.02	1.91
Italy, &c. . .	16	18	0.25	0.25
Europe . . .	444	500	1.22	1.30
United States . .	59	65	1.05	0.93
Total . .	503	565	1.20	1.25

WINE

Production and consumption were approximately as follows :—

	Millions of Gallons			
	Production		Consumption	
	1885	1895	1885	1895
France . . .	690	590	810	940
Italy . . .	550	530	500	460
Spain . . .	510	470	330	350
Portugal . . .	110	70	60	55
Austria . . .	180	140	160	150
Germany . . .	82	44	80	80
Russia, &c. . .	238	276	270	305
Europe . . .	2,360	2,120	2,210	2,340

The *Moniteur Vinicole* gives the production of wine since 1885 as follows :—

	Millions of Gallons Yearly		
	1885-94	1895-97	Difference
France . . .	700	762	+ 62
Italy . . .	615	527	− 88
Spain . . .	564	420	− 144
Austria . . .	143	94	− 49
Roumania . . .	41	101	+ 60
Portugal . . .	79	62	− 17
Germany . . .	83	65	− 18
Turkey . . .	44	53	+ 9
Bulgaria . . .	56	26	− 30
Russia . . .	71	64	− 7
Servia . . .	61	21	− 40
Greece . . .	30	36	+ 6
Switzerland . .	27	29	+ 2
Europe . . .	2,514	2,260	− 254
Algeria . . .	70	90	+ 20
Argentina . . .	20	33	+ 13
Chile . . .	30	44	+ 14
South Africa . .	3	3	−
Brazil . . .	4	9	+ 5
Australia . . .	2	3	+ 1
United States . .	20	20	−
Total . .	2,663	2,462	− 201

The world produces at present 8 per cent. less wine than it did in the decade ending 1894. A vineyard has usually from 3000 to 5000 vine-stalks per acre, 20 vines producing as a rule one gallon of wine. In 1890 it was stated that 10,000 vines produced yearly the following quantity of wine :—

In	Galls.	In	Galls.
Australia	320	Germany	530
United States . . .	320	Switzerland . . .	930
France	400	Cape Colony . .	2800

Cape Colony has 20,000 acres of vineyards containing 60 million stalks. See *Wine*, p. 597.

UNITED KINGDOM

The quantity and value of liquor consumed in the United Kingdom in 1896 were :—

	Millions of Gallons			
	Beer	Spirits	Wines	Cider, &c.
England	1,044	27	13.4	14 0
Scotland	63	8	1.4	0.5
Ireland	99	5	1.0	0.5
United Kingdom .	1,206	40	15.8	15.0

Reducing all to alcohol, and taking the wholesale value (free of duty), the shares that correspond to the three kingdoms are as follows :—

	Gallons Alcohol	Value, £	Per Inhabitant	
			Gallons	Shillings
England .	62,500,000	67,000,000	2.0	43
Scotland .	7,100,000	6,700,000	1.7	32
Ireland . .	7,200,000	7,300,000	1.6	32
U. Kingdom	76,800,000	81,000,000	1.9	41

The quantities of alcohol and the money value of each kind of liquor were :—

	Gallons Alcohol	Value, £
Beer	54,300,000	60,300,000
Spirits	19,800,000	14,800,000
Wines, &c. . . .	2,700,000	5,900,000
Total . . .	76,800,000	81,000,000

The consumption of liquor in the United Kingdom has been as follows :—

	Millions of Gallons			
	1866	1876	1886	1896
Beer	890	990	977	1,206
Spirits	30	42	34	40
Wines	13	18	13	16

Gallons per Head

Beer	29.7	30.0	26.9	30.9
Spirits	1.0	1.3	0.9	1.0
Wine	0.4	0.5	0.4	0.4
Equivalent alcohol .	1.9	2.1	1.7	1.9

Reducing all to alcohol, the consumption per head is the same as it was 30 years ago.

GERMANY

In 1895 were produced 66 million gallons of alcohol, from 2,100,000 tons of potatoes and 350,000 tons of grain ; 54 million gallons were used for liquor, the rest for manufactures.

UNITED STATES

The production of spirits and beer, and the amount paid for Inland Revenue (which includes both liquor and tobacco dues) in 1897 were :—

	Spirits, Gallons	Beer, Barrels	In. Rev. £ Sterling
Illinois	22,700,000	3,300,000	6,600,000
New York . . .	3,800,000	9,500,000	3,800,000
Kentucky . . .	6,800,000	400,000	3,300,000
Ohio	7,500,000	2,600,000	2,600,000
Pennsylvania . .	1,200,000	3,900,000	2,400,000
Indiana . . .	8,700,000	600,000	1,800,000
Other States . .	13,600,000	14,200,000	10,000,000
Union	64,300,000	34,500,000	30,500,000

The amount levied on spirits and beer was £24,000,000 sterling, equal to a liquor tax of 80 pence per inhabitant.

TAXES ON ALCOHOL

In the United Kingdom these taxes have risen as follows :—

	Beer, £	Wine, Spirits, £	Total, £
1866	6,790,000	15,350,000	22,140,000
1876	8,590,000	23,040,000	31,630,000
1885	8,550,000	19,530,000	28,080,000
1896	10,900,000	21,630,000	32,530,000

The duties on British spirits and on beer in the three kingdoms were in 1897 as follows :—

	Spirits, £	Beer, £	Total, £	Shillings p. Inhab.
England .	6,450,000	9,790,000	16,240,000	11
Scotland .	6,130,000	600,000	6,730,000	32
Ireland . .	4,230,000	930,000	5,160,000	23
U. Kingdom	16,810,000	11,320,000	28,130,000	14

The above is exclusive of duties on wines and imported spirits, which if included would bring up the liquor duties of the United Kingdom to 16 shillings per inhabitant.

In France they were as follows :—

Year	Beer, £	Wine, £	Spirits, £	Total, £
1885	980,000	6,600,000	9,720,000	17,300,000
1896	1,000,000	8,800,000	10,700,000	20,500,000

In Holland they were :—

Year	Beer, £	Wine, £	Spirits, £	Total, £
1886	100,000	150,000	1,950,000	2,200,000
1896	100,000	150,000	2,250,000	2,500,000

In Belgium they were :—

Year	Beer, £	Wine, £	Spirits, £	Total, £
1885	600,000	200,000	1,400,000	2,200,000
1896	800,000	300,000	1,740,000	2,840,000

In the United States in 1897 the tax on spirits was £17,000,000 or 66 pence per gallon, that on beer was £7,000,000 or 48 pence per barrel.

The taxes on liquor were :—

Year	Beer, £	Wine, £	Spirits, £	Total, £
1888	5,000,000	800,000	15,000,000	20,800,000
1896	7,200,000	700,000	16,100,000	24,000,000

In Switzerland the tax on spirits produced :—

Year	Gallons	Tax, £
1891	1,500,000	240,000
1895	1,200,000	200,000

In Germany the liquor taxes in 1895 amounted to £11,900,000.

ANIMALS

Two dogs can draw a sleigh carrying 250 lbs. a distance of 20 miles in 5 hours; eight will draw a sleigh of 3 persons at the rate of 5 miles an hour, and travel 60 miles a day. A reindeer will draw a sleigh 5 feet long and 2 feet wide, carrying one passenger, 110 miles in a day.

The highest recorded price for a dog is £1500, paid by Mr. Reick of New York for a dog called Sir Belvidere. The highest price for a horse has been £25,000, paid by the Czar for an Irish horse called Galtee More. See *Animals*, page 161, and *Dogs*, page 691.

AQUEDUCTS

Since 1890 five great aqueducts have been constructed or enlarged, viz. :—

	Miles	Cost, £	Gallons Daily
New York . . .	40	5,200,000	...
Bombay . . .	65	..	...
Liverpool . . .	68	2,500,000	...
Manchester . . .	100	4,500,000	100,000,000
Glasgow . . .	35	3,000,000	50,000,000

See *Water*, page 588, and page 818.

ARMY

UNITED KINGDOM

The position of the British army in 1896, compared with 1888, showed thus :—

	1888	1896
England	83,000	76,000
Scotland	5,000	4,000
Ireland	30,000	26,000
United Kingdom . . .	118,000	106,000
India	72,000	78,000
Egypt	6,000	4,000
Colonies	25,000	34,000
Total .	221,000	222,000

The whole military force of the British empire shows thus :—

	1888	1896
Regular army	221,000	222,000
Militia and reserves . . .	174,000	210,000
Volunteers . . .	222,000	232,000
Indian troops	145,000	145,000
Colonial troops . . .	15,000	15,000
Total .	777,000	824,000

The different arms in 1896 stood as follows :—

	Regulars	Indians	Volunteers, &c.	Total
Infantry . .	126,000	113,000	341,000	580,000
Cavalry . .	18,000	23,000	19,000	60,000
Artillery . .	31,000	5,000	70,000	106,000
Engineers, &c.	47,000	4,000	27,000	78,000
Total .	222,000	145,000	457,000	824,000

There are 12,000 officers in the regular army : the nationality of the men, including petty officers, is :—

	Number in 1896	Percentage 1883	Percentage 1896
English . . .	163,000	70	78
Scotch . . .	16,000	8	8
Irish . . .	25,000	20	12
Colonial . .	5,000	2	2
Total . .	209,000	100	100

Compared with population we find that England produces 5 soldiers per thousand inhabitants, Scotland 4, and Ireland 6. Between regulars and irregulars the British army amounts to 679,000 men, equal to 17 per thousand, or nearly 2 per cent. of the population. The cost of the army in 1897 was :—

	£
Effective service	15,000,000
Sundries and extras . . .	6,000,000
Total .	21,000,000

The effective army represents an annual cost of £70 per man, a higher ratio than in other European countries.

The age of the regular infantry is now much younger than before, viz. :—

Years	1846	1870	1897
Under 20 . . .	17.7	16.0	23.1
20–30 . . .	62.0	52.5	71.0
30–40 . . .	18.2	30.4	5.6
Over 40 . . .	2.1	1.1	0.3
Total . .	100.0	100.0	100.0

FRANCE

The peace footing in 1897 stood as follows :—

	France	Colonies	Total
Infantry . . .	342,000	36,000	378,000
Cavalry . . .	70,000	7,000	77,000
Artillery . . .	81,000	7,000	88,000
Engineers, &c. . .	42,000	2,000	44,000
Total . .	535,000	52,000	587,000

If the gendarmerie were included, the total would reach 610,000 men. The first line of reserve counts 1,740,000 men, available in case of war. The second and third reserves, suitable for garrison duty, number two millions. Between the army and first reserve France is able to put nearly 2½ millions of men under arms, equal to 62 per thousand inhabitants, as compared with 17 per thousand in the United Kingdom. The cost of the War Office is £28,000,000, equal to £48 a man, against £70 for the British army.

GERMANY

There are 21 army-corps, of which 12 bear Prussian titles. The peace footing in 1897 showed thus :—

	Officers and Men	Horses
Infantry	396,000	...
Cavalry	69,000	64,000
Artillery	86,000	29,000
Engineers, &c. . . .	34,000	4,000
Total . .	585,000	97,000

Between the men under colours and the first line of reserve Germany can at any moment call out 3,000,000 effective combatants. The War Office expenditure in 1897 was £24,000,000, equal to £41 per man, against £48 in France.

RUSSIA

Peace footing stands thus :—

	Officers and Men			Number of Horses
	Europe	Siberia	Total	
Infantry . .	521,000	61,000	582,000	9,000
Cavalry . . .	115,000	9,000	124,000	106,000
Artillery . .	105,000	4,000	109,000	28,000
Engineers, &c.	51,000	3,000	54,000	12,000
Total .	792,000	77,000	869,000	155,000

War footing is shown as follows :—

	Regulars	Reserve	Total	Horses
Infantry . .	890,000	520,000	1,410,000	85,000
Cavalry . .	115,000	165,000	280,000	255,000
Artillery . .	150,000	110,000	260,000	210,000
Engineers, &c.	105,000	475,000	580,000	30,000
Total .	1,260,000	1,270,000	2,530,000	580,000

The artillery has 1800 field-guns on peace footing, and 5260 in time of war. It may be doubted whether the actual number of men under the colours is the same as above given. At the siege of Plevna the difficulties of the Russian army were apparent. Probably the effective army numbers 600,000 men, and this could be doubled in the event of war.

Army expenditure in 1897 reached £28,500,000, equal to £33 per man, peace footing, as compared with £41 in Germany.

AUSTRIA-HUNGARY

The army on peace and on war footing is shown thus :—

	Officers	Men	Horses	Guns
Peace . . .	25,000	335,000	47,000	1,050
War . . .	45,000	1,830,000	280,000	1,860

Peace footing in 1896 stood as follows :—

	Officers and Men	Horses
Infantry . . .	234,000	1,000
Cavalry . . .	54,000	43,000
Artillery . . .	38,000	2,000
Engineers, &c. .	34,000	1,000
Total . .	360,000	47,000

Army expenditure amounts to £15,000,000, equal to £41 per man, the same as in Germany. The War Office of Vienna spends £12,000,000 for the common defence of the monarchy, besides which the Austrian Diet spends £2,000,000, the Hungarian £1,000,000, for war purposes.

ITALY

There are 12 army-corps, in all 840,000 men ; but the number under the colours rarely exceeds 240,000.

	Regulars	Reserve	Militia	Total
Infantry . . .	160,000	450,000	340,000	950,000
Cavalry . . .	25,000	20,000	55,000	100,000
Artillery . . .	32,000	93,000	55,000	180,000
Engineers, &c. .	23,000	37,000	40,000	100,000
Total . .	240,000	600,000	490,000	1,330,000

This total is equal to 43 per thousand of the population. Army expenditure amounts to £10,800,000, equal to £45 per man, against £41 in Germany.

SPAIN

In normal times the peace and war footing are as follows :—

	Peace	War
Infantry	80,000	140,000
Cavalry	15,000	20,000
Artillery	10,000	12,000
Engineers, &c. . . .	5,000	12,000
Total . .	110,000	184,000

In 1897 Spain was said to have 150,000 men fighting the Cuban insurgents, besides 15,000 in the Philippine Islands, and a garrison in the Canaries, The expenditure on the army is usually £5,600,000, equal to £51 per man, against £41 in Germany.

PORTUGAL

The army consists of 35,000 men, including officers, besides 9000 colonials, mostly natives. It is supposed that in case of war the force could be raised to 150,000 men, 23,000 horses, and 260 guns. This would be equal to 32 men per thousand inhabitants. The army costs £1,100,000 per annum, or £32 per man.

SWEDEN AND NORWAY

The army of these kingdoms stands as follows :—

	Sweden	Norway	Total
Infantry . . .	28,000	15,000	43,000
Cavalry . . .	5,000	1,000	6,000
Artillery . . .	4,000	1,000	5,000
Engineers, &c. . .	2,000	1,000	3,000
Regulars . . .	39,000	18,000	57,000
Reserve . . .	100,000	12,000	112,000
War footing .	139,000	30,000	169,000

Expenditure in 1897 was £1,500,000 for Sweden and £500,000 for Norway; that is, £39 per man in the former, and £27 in the latter kingdom.
For other countries see Part I., page 72.

Military Expenditure.—The sums annually spent for military purposes compare with population and national earnings as follows :—

	Army	Navy	Total	Shillings per Inhab.
	£	£	£	
U. Kingdom .	18,500,000	22,700,000	41,200,000	21
France . . .	25,200,000	11,400,000	36,600,000	19
Germany . .	29,100,000	6,100,000	35,200,000	14
Russia . . .	30,600,000	8,000,000	38,600,000	7
Austria . . .	14,200,000	2,100,000	16,300,000	7
Italy	9,400,000	4,100,000	13,500,000	9
Spain . .	5,700,000	1,100,000	6,800,000	8
Portugal . .	1,300,000	500,000	1,800,000	8
Sweden . . .	1,500,000	400,000	1,900,000	8
Norway . . .	600,000	200,000	800,000	8
Denmark . .	600,000	300,000	900,000	8
Holland . . .	1,900,000	1,300,000	3,200,000	13
Belgium . . .	2,000,000	...	2,000,000	6
Switzerland . .	1,000,000	...	1,000,000	7
Roumania . .	1,800,000	...	1,800,000	6
Servia . . .	600,000	...	600,000	5
Bulgaria . . .	900,000	...	900,000	5
Turkey . . .	7,300,000	700,000	8,000,000	27
Greece . . .	600,000	300,000	900,000	8
Europe . . .	152,800,000	59,200,000	212,000,000	11
U. States . .	10,200,000	7,300,000	17,500,000	5
Japan . . .	5,000,000	1,600,000	6,600,000	3
Brazil . . .	1,300,000	700,000	2,000,000	3
Argentina . .	1,300,000	800,000	2,100,000	10
Chile	900,000	600,000	1,500,000	11
Mexico . . .	1,000,000	100,000	1,100,000	2
Total . .	172,500,000	70,300,000	242,800,000	10

ARTESIAN WELLS

Besides those given at page 588 are those made in the United States to December 1892.

	No. of Wells	Average Cost, &c.		
		Depth, feet	£ Sterling	Gallons per Minute
California . .	3,240	248	88	164
Utah . . .	2,524	146	16	26
Texas, &c. . .	2,333	250	56	34
Total . .	8,097	210	51	54

A well giving 50 gallons a minute suffices to irrigate 5 acres of land. The deepest wells known are, according to Chambers :—

Buda-Pesth	3,180 feet
St. Louis, U.S. . . .	3,840 ,,

The well at Buda gives water of the temperature of 165° Fahr., or 2 degrees less than Carlsbad (see p. 567).

ATHLETICS

There was a bicycle race at St. Albans, 16 entries, on October 13, 1894, which resulted as follows :—

Rider	Miles	Min.	Sec.	Rider	Miles	Min.	Sec.
Wright . .	5	13	32	King .	30	84	30
,, . .	20	55	26	,, . .	50	150	56

A race of 12 hours was won by Hunt, with the following results :—

Hours	Miles	Hours	Miles	Hours	Miles
2	47	6	134	10	217
4	91	8	176	12	260

He made 150 miles in 6 hours 44 minutes, and 200 miles in 9 hours 8 minutes. All the foregoing were the quickest runs on record, except King's run of 50 miles, this distance having been done by Knapp, in 1888, in 149 minutes 41 seconds.

On June 1, 1896, Stocks, at Hull, beat all previous records for short runs when he made the following :—

Miles	Min.	Sec.	Miles	Min.	Sec.
1	1	55	5	9	39
3	5	44	10	19	30

At Catford, England, on August 30, 1897, Walters rode 100 miles in 206 minutes, or 5 minutes less than the best run then on record.

In the last 10 years the record of jumps has been broken by the following :—

High running jump, 77.1 inches—M. Sweeny, New York, 1895.
High pole jump, 11 feet 9 inches—R. Dickenson, Kidderminster, 1891.
Standing broad jump, 12 feet 2 inches—J. Darby, Ashton, 1889.

The 20-mile foot race also has a new record, G. Crossland having done it in 1 hour 52 minutes, at London, 1894.

Cricket records show that the highest innings in England in 1896 fell to Dr. Grace, 301 runs. In the same year's record Prince Ranjitsinhgi had an average score of 53, which was the highest, the average for 10 best batters during the year having been 45. The 10 highest bowlers averaged 17. See *Athletics*, p. 74.

B

BANKS

In August 1896 the banks of the world stood as follows :—

Bank of	£ Sterling (ooo omitted)			
	Issue	Bullion	Deposits	Discounts
England	27,400	45,700	61,900	44,000
France	153,600	125,700	22,600	42,000
Germany	62,900	40,200	22,200	39,600
Russia	115,000	97,600	24,700	16,500
Austria Hungary .	55,400	36,000	900	18,000
Italy (3)	42,400	20,600	12,600	13,800
Spain	41,400	18,700	16,100	8,700
Portugal	13,000	3,000	500	3,900
Sweden	7,000	2,400	22,000	11,200
Norway	2,900	1,400	400	1,800
Denmark . . .	5,000	3,700	600	1,200
Holland	17,600	9,600	400	5,700
Belgium	18,900	4,000	2,200	17,100
Switzerland . . .	7,900	4,000	31,500	6,700
Roumania . . .	5,800	2,600	600	1,800
Servia	1,000	500	100	300
Greece	4,500	100	3,800	600
Ottoman	600	1,600	5,700	700
Europe	582,300	417,400	228,800	233,600
New York . . .	4,000	15,300	106,200	98,400
Total . .	586,300	432,700	335,000	332,000

The following table shows the issue of European banks, their bullion reserves, and the ratio of latter to former in March 1898 :—

	£ Sterling (ooo omitted)				Ratio of Bulln.
	Issue	Gold	Silver	Total	
England . .	27,600	32,600	...	32,600	118
Scotland . .	7,700	5,000	800	5,800	76
Ireland . . .	6,500	2,600	400	3,000	47
U. Kingdom .	41,800	40,200	1,200	41,400	99
France . . .	153,300	74,500	48,700	123,200	82
Germany . .	60,800	36,500	16,400	52,900	87
Russia . . .	91,800	120,900	4,600	125,500	136
Austria . . .	51,200	30,800	10,500	41,300	80
Italy	41,600	16,000	2,500	18,500	44
Spain . . .	50,200	9,600	10,900	20,500	41
Portugal . .	14,300	1,100	1,900	3,000	21
Sweden . . .	7,300	2,100	800	2,900	40
Norway . . .	3,100	1,800	...	1,800	58
Denmark . .	4,400	3,000	...	3,000	68
Holland . .	16,700	2,800	7,000	9,800	58
Belgium . .	19,000	3,600	600	4,200	22
Switzerland .	8,000	3,700	300	4,000	50
Greece . . .	5,400	100	...	100	2
Roumania . .	5,700	2,200	200	2,400	42
Servia . . .	900	200	300	500	56
Bulgaria . .	100	200	200	400	400
Total . .	575,600	349,300	106,100	455,400	79

In 1896 the nominal value of the Russian currency was reduced from 38 pence per rouble to 25 pence ; but if we suppose the rouble to have been always 25 pence, the currency of Europe and the bullion reserves of banks will show as follows for seven years :—

	£ Sterling (ooo omitted)				Ratio of Bullion
	Issue	Gold	Silver	Total	
1892 . . .	533.0	248.3	99.8	348.1	65.2
1893 . . .	551.0	244.6	99.7	344.3	62.5
1894 . . .	561.0	278.0	104.1	382.1	68.1
1895 . . .	583.0	314.5	100.2	414.7	71.1
1896 . . .	596.0	314.4	100.5	414.9	69.7
1897 . . .	563.1	327.9	106.4	434.3	77.1
1898 . . .	575.6	349.3	106.1	455.4	79.1

The amount of paper money in Europe in December of the last three years was :—

	Millions £ Sterling			Shillings per Inhabitant
	1895	1896	1897	
England . . .	26.3	26.7	28.3	18
Scotland . . .	7.3	7.8	8.0	36
Ireland . . .	6.5	6.8	6.8	30
United Kingdom .	40.1	41.3	43.1	22
France . . .	145.9	153.6	152.5	80
Germany . . .	69.7	68.9	76.0	30
Russia . . .	115.0	112.0	107.0	20
Austria . . .	52.0	55.4	58.8	28
Italy . . .	43.4	42.8	43.4	27
Spain . . .	39.6	41.1	48.2	54
Portugal . . .	12.5	13.2	14.6	60
Sweden . . .	6.6	7.2	7.9	32
Norway . . .	2.8	2.9	3.3	31
Finland . . .	2.2	2.6	2.9	25
Denmark . . .	3.9	5.1	5.1	46
Holland . . .	17.3	16.9	17.8	75
Belgium . . .	18.0	18.8	19.5	62
Switzerland . .	7.6	7.9	8.7	58
Roumania . .	5.2	5.8	5.8	20
Servia . . .	1.0	1.0	1.0	9
Greece . . .	4.5	4.5	5.4	48
Total . .	587.3	601.0	621.0	33

The bullion reserves of European banks at the close of the last four years were :—

	Millions £ Sterling			Ratio to Currency
	Gold	Silver	Total	
1894 . . .	279	104	383	68 per cent.
1895 . . .	304	89	393	67 ,, ,,
1896 . . .	314	100	414	69 ,, ,,
1897 . . .	350	102	452	73 ,, .

Gold reserve has risen 25 per cent. in three years, while silver reserve has declined 2 per cent. This shows that the world's supply of gold has been over-abundant.

The Bank of Russia has the largest issue in the world, and the largest bullion reserve except that of France. The latter holds 30 per cent. of the total amount of bullion or hard money held by the banks of Europe. If the reserves of the Banks of Germany and Austria were added to that of the Bank of England, the aggregate would still be less than the bullion held by the Bank of France. The only banks whose bullion reserve exceeds their issue are the Bank of England, the Ottoman, and the New York Associated Banks. The average of bullion reserve to issue, taken for all banks collectively, is as 67 to 100, but there are several where the reserve is less than 50 per cent. of issue, viz. Italy, Spain, Portugal, Sweden, Norway, Belgium, Roumania, and Greece.

The position of European banks in 1896 compares with the same in 1889 as follows :—

	1889	1896	Increase
Issue . . .	466,200,000	641,300,000	37 per cent.
Bullion . .	263,300,000	417,400,000	59 ,, ,,
Discounts .	229,100,000	233,600,000	2 ,, ,,

Discounts remained almost stationary, while the stock of bullion rose 59 per cent. Bullion reserves of European and New York banks in 1897 reached 450 millions sterling, that is 350 millions gold and 100 silver. The following table, comprising only seven of the European State banks (to the exclusion of those of Italy, Spain, Portugal, Sweden, Norway, Denmark, Switzerland, Roumania, Servia, Greece, and Turkey), besides the New York Associated Banks and the United States Treasury, shows the reserves of gold in December of the last three years :—

Bank of	Gold Reserve, £		
	1895	1896	1897
England . . .	45,000,000	34,600,000	31,800,000
France	78,000,000	76,600,000	78,500,000
Germany . . .	42,600,000	40,200,000	43,500,000
Russia	92,200,000	113,500,000	122,200,000
Austria	24,500,000	28,700,000	31,400,000
Belgium . . .	4,100,000	4,200,000	4,200,000
Holland . . .	3,500,000	2,600,000	2,600,000
New York . . .	13,800,000	15,300,000	20,800,000
Banks	303,700,000	315,700,000	335,000,000
U.S. Treasury .	19,900,000	35,000,000	38,800,000
Total . .	323,600,000	350,700,000	373,800,000

This shows that in two years the gold reserves rose 50 millions sterling, or 15 per cent.

Rates of interest in the last twelve years were as follows :—

Year	London	Paris	Berlin	Brussels	Amsterdam	St. Petersburg	Vienna	Rome	Average
1886 . . .	3.0	3.0	3.3	2.7	2.5	...	4.0	...	3.1
1887 . . .	3.3	3.0	3.4	3.1	2.5	5.1	4.1	5.5	3.7
1888 . . .	3.2	3.1	3.3	3.3	2.5	5.3	4.2	5.5	3.8
1889 . . .	3.5	3.1	3.7	3.5	2.5	5.8	4.2	5.2	3.9
1890 . . .	4.5	3.0	4.4	3.2	2.8	5.9	4.5	6.0	4.3
1891 . . .	3.3	3.0	3.8	3.0	3.1	4.9	4.4	5.8	3.9
1892 . . .	2.5	2.7	3.2	2.7	2.7	4.9	4.0	5.2	3.5
1893 . . .	3.0	2.5	4.1	2.8	3.8	4.7	4.2	5.2	3.8
1894 . . .	2.1	2.5	3.1	3.0	2.6	4.5	4.1	5.7	3.5
1895 . . .	2.0	2.2	3.2	2.6	2.5	5.0	4.3	5.0	3.4
1896 . . .	2.5	2.0	3.7	2.9	3.0	6.1	4.1	5.0	3.7
1897 . . .	2.8	2.0	3.8	3.0	3.1	5.9	4.0	5.0	3.7
Average . .	3.0	2.7	3.6	3.0	2.8	5.3	4.2	5.4	3.7

During the last three years the average rates were—at Madrid 4.8, at Lisbon 5.9, at Berne 3.7, and at Bucharest 5.1.

Exchange.—The rates of exchange were :—

Year	London on			N. York on London	Silver Pence per oz
	Paris	Hamburg	Calcutta		
1890 . .	25.47	20.66	18.6	4.82	47.7
1891 . .	25.48	20.60	17.4	4.83	45.1
1892 . .	25.34	20.51	15.5	4.85	39.7
1893 . .	25.39	20.60	15.1	4.84	35.6
1894 . .	25.34	20.55	13.8	4.86	28.9
1895 . .	25.35	20.58	13.2	4.88	29.8
1896 . .	25.27	20.59	14.6	4.85	30.7
1897 . .	25.31	20.57	15.2	4.84	27.0
Average .	25.37	20.58	15.4	4.85	35.6

The lowest price recorded for silver was on August 31, 1897, namely, 24 pence per ounce, being as 1 to 35 compared with the value of gold, or 60 per cent. below par.

UNITED KINGDOM

The statistics for 1897 compare with those of 1890 as follows :—

	Millions £ Sterling *			
	England		Scotland	
	1890	1897	1890	1897
Capital paid . .	53.8	59.3	9.1	9.3
Market value .	165.5	181.4	22.9	30.3
Reserve fund .	27.8	32.5	5.6	7.2
Note issue .	26.7	29.4	6.4	7.4
Deposits . .	387.7	565.0	88.3	95.8
Discounts .	289.8	376.2	58.0	64.8
Assets . .	517.1	707.9	113.4	124.9

	Ireland		U. Kingdom	
	1890	1897	1890	1897
Capital paid . .	7.0	7.1	69.9	75.7
Market value .	17.7	21.1	206.1	232.8
Reserve fund .	3.1	3.7	36.5	43.4
Note issue .	6.7	5.8	39.8	42.6
Deposits . .	37.8	45.6	513.8	706.4
Discounts .	27.6	35.0	375.4	476.0
Assets . .	54.8	62.7	685.3	895.5

	Colonial		Grand Total	
	1890	1897	1890	1897
Capital paid . .	43.0	33.8	112.9	109.5
Reserve fund . .	19.1	9.1	55.6	52.5
Deposits . .	240.7	156.3	754.5	862.7
Discounts .	303.1	164.4	678.5	640.4
Assets . .	387.0	238.5	1,072.3	1,134.0

If we take discounts as the gauge of banking business, England will stand for 78½ per cent., Scotland 14 per cent., Ireland 7½ per cent. of the total for the United Kingdom. The paid-up capital (excluding Colonial) rose 8 per cent. in 7 years, market value of stock 13 per cent., deposits 37 per cent., discounts 26 per cent., and

* *Note.*—This table reads thus: capital 53.8 signifies £53,800,000.

assets 30 per cent. The deposits in banks of the United Kingdom increased 108 millions in 7 years, being an average of 15½ millions yearly.

The note issue has been as follows :—

Year	£ Sterling (ooo omitted)			
	England	Scotland	Ireland	U. Kingdom
1890 . .	27,000	7,100	7,300	41,400
1892 . .	27,500	6,700	6,300	40,500
1894 . .	27,100	6,900	6,500	40,500
1896 . .	27,600	7,500	6,400	41,500

Bank of England returns at the close of each year showed as follows :—

Year	Issue, £	Bullion, £	Deposits, £
1890 . . .	24,700,000	21,800,000	35,400,000
1891 . . .	25,500,000	23,200,000	34,800,000
1892 . . .	26,000,000	25,000,000	34,400,000
1893 . . .	25,800,000	25,900,000	34,200,000
1894 . . .	25,500,000	35,300,000	41,600,000
1895 . . .	26,100,000	42,500,000	56,400,000
1896 . . .	26,700,000	35,900,000	50,600,000
1897 . . .	27,400,000	28,400,000	49,600,000

FRANCE

The progress of the Bank of France since 1880 is shown thus :—

	Millions £ Sterling		
	1880	1889	1897
Discount	348	340	415
Issue	92	115	151
Gold reserve	27	53	80
Silver reserve	54	51	48

The head-office at Paris does half the business of the bank, which has branches all over France (see page 179). The discounts at Paris in 1897 comprised 5,700,000 bills, of which 1,870,000 were for sums less than £4 sterling. The maximum of bills in portfolio was £42,400,000 in January, the minimum £21,400,000 in August. Expenses in 1897 amounted to £640,000. The bank is the property of 28,200 shareholders, who hold between them 182,500 shares of £40 each, the market value of each share being at present £142 sterling. Thus the paid-up capital is £7,300,000, and the value of the shares £26,000,000, the average of stock held by each shareholder being £920.

AUSTRALIA

The collective figures for the banks of the seven colonies sum up as follows :—

Year	£ Sterling (ooo omitted)			
	Issue	Bullion	Deposits	Assets
1890 . . .	5,500	20,200	111,100	168,500
1893 . . .	4,500	22,100	101,300	158,700
1895 . . .	3,700	25,200	99,200	146,500
1897 . . .	4,100	24,600	101,600	144,100
1890–97, av. .	4,400	22,600	104,700	157,000

The returns for June 1897 showed as follows (ooo omitted) :—

	Issue	Bullion	Deposits	Assets
N. S. Wales . .	1,200	6,500	30,300	45,500
Victoria	1,000	7,400	30,600	45,700
N. Zealand . . .	1,000	3,100	14,600	17,300
Queensland . . .	...	2,100	11,800	18,500
S. Australia . . .	400	2,300	7,200	7,800
W. Australia . .	400	2,400	4,100	6,100
Tasmania . . .	100	800	3,000	3,200
Total . .	4,100	24,600	101,600	144,100

CANADA

Aggregate returns for the several provinces show as follows :—

Year	£ Sterling (ooo omitted)			
	Issue	Bullion	Deposits	Assets
1890 . . .	6,600	1,300	28,100	52,400
1893 . . .	6,900	1,300	36,500	62,600
1896 . . .	6,400	1,600	39,200	65,400

The returns for 1896, distinguishing Old Canada (Quebec and Ontario) from the provinces added to the Dominion, show as follow (ooo omitted) :—

	Issue	Bullion	Deposits	Assets
Old Canada . .	5,100	1,300	33,100	55,100
Nova Scotia . .	800	200	4,400	7,400
Other Provinces .	500	100	1,700	2,900
Dominion . . .	6,400	1,600	39,200	65,400

Canadian banks have a paid-up capital of £13,000,000. Banking power is about 52 millions sterling, or £10 per inhabitant.

SOUTH AFRICA

Collectively, the returns for Cape Colony and Natal showed thus :—

	£ Sterling (ooo omitted).			
	Issue	Bullion	Deposits	Assets
1890	1,000	3,000	7,900	9,300
1893	700	2,000	7,100	9,500
1895	800	3,800	10,600	10,700
Average, '90–95 .	700	2,700	8,100	9,500

Banking power is about 12 millions sterling, equal to £5 per inhabitant.

INDIA

The amount of paper money in circulation, and its value in sterling, were :—

Year	Millions Rupees	£ Sterling	Year	Millions Rupees	£ Sterling
1891	257	19,300,000	1894	304	20,300,000
1892	241	16,100,000	1895	307	20,500,000
1893	264	17,600,000	1896	259	17,300,000

WEST INDIES

There are banks in Jamaica, Trinidad, and Barbadoes whose aggregate issue is about £800,000, and assets about 8 millions.

2 S

UNITED STATES

In October 1890 there were 3540 National Banks, and in October 1896 there were 3676. The principal features are shown as follows :—

	Millions $		Millions £	
	1890	1896	1890	1896
Issue	123	210	25.6	43.6
Capital	650	648	135.2	134.8
Deposits	1,759	1,799	366.0	374.4
Sundries	610	607	126.8	126.0
Liabilities , . . .	3,142	3,264	653.6	678.8
Bullion	196	201	40.8	41.8
U. S. notes . . .	87	142	18.0	29.6
Discounts	1,970	1,893	410.0	394.0
Sundries	889	1,028	184.8	213.4
Assets	3,142	3,264	653.6	678.8

The capital and dividends of the above banks showed thus :—

Year	Millions $		
	Capital	Dividend *	Rate
1891	660	50.8	7.7
1894	673	45.3	6.7
1896	653	45.5	7.0
Average . . .	668	48.0	7.2

The National Banks of New York city showed as follows :—

	Millions $		Millions £	
	1890	1896	1890	1896
Discounts	297	314	62.0	65.2
Deposits	333	373	69.2	77.6
Bullion	79	50	16.4	10.4

The returns for all National Banks of the United States were :—

	Millions $		
	Discounts	Deposits	Bullion, res.
1891	1,989	1,759	184
1894	2,007	2,019	237
1896	1,893	1,799	201
Average . . .	1,953	1,860	209

National Bank discounts in the principal States in October 1896 were as follows :—

	Millions $		
	City	Rural	Total
New York	314	112	426
Massachusetts . . .	141	104	245
Pennsylvania	87	156	243
Illinois	82	44	126
Other States . . .	176	677	853
Total . .	800	1,093	1,893

In the above table "city" counts only for the capital, such as New York, Boston, or Philadelphia, the banks of minor cities being classed under heading "rural."

* *Note.*—Dividends 50.8 signifies $50,800,000.

Clearing-houses.—The *monthly* returns in the United States for the principal cities during the years 1890-91 were as follows :—

	Millions £ Sterling		Millions £ Sterling
New York . .	621	Philadelphia .	62
Boston . . .	85	St. Louis . .	19
Chicago . . .	72	S. Francisco .	15

New York clearing-house returns since 1854 showed thus, in *monthly* averages :—

Year	Millions £ Sterling	Year	Millions £ Sterling
1854	100	1884	588
1864	416	1894	420
1874	395	1897	545

London clearing-house showed monthly averages thus :—

Year	Millions £	Year	Millions £
1839	82	1884	483
1869	302	1894	528
1875	474	1895	631

Provincial clearing-houses showed for 1896 and 1897 as follows :—

	Millions £ Monthly	
	1896	1897
Manchester	16.1	16.1
Liverpool	12.0	12.0
Newcastle	4.6	5.1
Birmingham	4.2	4.8
Bristol	2.0	2.1

The monthly average of the clearing-house of Paris rose from 88 millions sterling in 1876 to 157 millions in 1886, and 294 millions in 1896.

SAVINGS-BANKS

Those of the United Kingdom show as follows :—

Year	Amount held, £ (000 omitted)			
	England	Scotland	Ireland	U. Kingdom
1890 . . .	94,500	11,100	5,800	111,400
1892 . . .	100,200	11,800	6,200	118,200
1894 . . .	112,100	13,700	7,000	132,800
1897 . . .	136,600	18,800	9,000	164,400
	Number of Depositors (000 omitted)			
1890 . . .	5,570	540	250	6,360
1892 . . .	6,090	590	270	6,950
1894 . . .	6,650	620	310	7,580
1897 . . .	7,640	760	370	8,770

The average sum held by each depositor is £18 in England, £24 in Scotland, and £24 in Ireland. The number of depositors compares with population as follows :—In England, 246 ; in Scotland, 180, and in Ireland, 80 per thousand inhabitants.

The earliest statement of savings-banks on the European continent is that of Malchus, in 1837, viz. :—

	Banks	Deposits £		Banks	Deposits £
France . .	250	4,980,000	Belgium .	5	650,000
Prussia . .	80	950,000	Holland .	50	280,000
Austria . .	8	3,030,000	Switzerland	58	790,000
Bavaria, &c.	201	2,390,000	Italy . . .	2	150,000

Making a total of 654 banks, with deposits amounting to £13,220,000. Returns from 1840 to 1889 will be found at page 86.

The latest returns compare with those of 1889 as follows :—

	Amount, Millions £		Depositors in 1896	Do. per 100 Inhab.
	1889	1896		
U. Kingdom .	107.3	154.8	8,350,000	21
France . . .	111.8	165.8	9,120,000	24
Germany . .	144.6	212.5	7,222,000	14
Russia . . .	7.2	37.7	1,890,000	2
Austria . . .	122.6	178.4	4,670,000	11
Italy . . .	56.5	72.2	4,520,000	15
Spain . . .	2.0	3.2	70,000	...
Portugal . .	...	0.5	10,000	...
Scandinavia .	44.1	64.9	2,980,000	32
Finland . .	...	1.9	...	...
Holland . .	6.0	9.5	840,000	18
Belgium . .	10.4	18.1	1,150,000	19
Switzerland .	23.7	35.8	1,190,000	40
Europe. . .	636.2	955.3	42,010,000	13
U. States . .	284.0	446.0	5,065,000	7
Canada . .	10.7	12.2	240,000	5
Australia . .	15.5	26.1	890,000	22
India . . .	6.0	7.0	680,000	...
W. Indies, &c.	2.6	4.2	175,000	5
Japan . . .	...	3.0	1,220,000	3
Brazil . . .	...	4.2	...	...
The World .	955.0	1,458.0	50,280,000	...

From the above figures it would appear that people who use savings-banks, mostly the working classes, have added 503 millions sterling to their accumulations in 7 years, or about 72 millions per annum.

Australia.—During the last six years the number of depositors has risen 30 per cent., the amount of deposits 49 per cent., viz. :—

	Depositors		Amount, £	
	1891	1897	1891	1897
New S. Wales .	158,000	214,000	5,340,000	8,520,000
Victoria . . .	301,000	345,000	5,720,000	7,520,000
New Zealand .	127,000	175,000	3,410,000	5,070,000
South Australia .	79,000	105,000	2,220,000	3,020,000
Queensland . .	46,000	63,000	1,660,000	2,570,000
West Australia .	4,000	26,000	50,000	860,000
Tasmania . . .	27,000	33,000	550,000	700,000
Total . .	742,000	962,000	18,950,000	28,260,000

No less than 22 per cent. of the population are depositors in Savings-Banks, the ratio in Victoria rising to 30 per cent., and falling in Queensland to 13 per cent. The average amount held by each depositor is £30, the ratio being as much as £40 in N.S. Wales, and only £21 in Tasmania.

Canada.—In 1894 there were 673 Post-Office savings-banks, with 115,000 depositors, who held £4,800,000 sterling.

United States.—The returns for 1896 show 988 savings-banks, against 638 in 1886 :—

	Millions $		Millions £	
	1886	1896	1886	1896
Deposits . . .	1,142	1,907	237	397
Capital, &c. . .	119	236	25	49
Liabilities . .	1,261	2,143	262	446
Loans . . .	128	255	27	53
Mortgages . .	418	800	87	167
U.S. bonds . .	197	149	41	31
Railway ,, . .	64	135	13	28
State ,, . .	241	578	50	120
Sundries . . .	213	226	44	47
Assets . .	,261	2,143	262	446

The various sections of the Union in 1896 showed as follows :—

States	Depositors	Millions $	$ per Inhabitant
New England . .	2,210,000	803	150
Middle . . .	2,294,000	855	53
Southern . . .	52,000	9	...
Prairie . . .	322,000	104	4
Pacific . . .	187,000	136	31
Union . .	5,065,000	1,907	27

The average amount held by each depositor was $380, equal to £79 sterling. The principal states stood thus :—

States	Depositors	Millions $	$ per Inhabitant
New York . .	1,696,000	692	103
Massachusetts . .	1,302,000	439	176
Connecticut . .	347,000	143	180
California . .	160,000	132	88
Pennsylvania . .	283,000	74	12
Other states . .	1,277,000	427	8
Union . .	5,065,000	1,907	27

The increase in seven years is shown as follows :—

Year	Depositors	Millions $	$ per Inhabitant
1889 . . .	4,022,000	1,363	22
1896 . . .	5,065,000	1,907	27
Increase . . .	1,043,000	544	5

India.—The progress of savings-banks down to 1894 (latest returns) is shown thus :—

Year	Depositors	Rupees, Millions	Equivalent, £
1881 . . .	115,000	32.7	2,720,000
1890 . . .	475,000	80.6	6,040,000
1896 . . .	717,000	111.2	7,400,000

The average amount of each deposit has declined from £24 to £10.

Ceylon shows deposits amounting to 3,200,000 rupees, or £200,000.

Mauritius.—There has been an increase of depositors in the past ten years, but the amount is stationary, viz. :—

	1885	1895
Depositors	18,500	23,300
Amount, £	315,000	318,000

The average deposit has fallen from £17 to £14.

South Africa.—The progress made in ten years is shown as follows :—

	Depositors		Amount, £	
	1885	1895	1885	1895
Cape Colony. .	17,600	50,200	520,000	1,700,000
Natal	3,100	7,000	50,000	170,000
Total . .	20,700	57,200	570,000	1,870,000

The average amount to each depositor is £27, as compared with £30 in Australia.

Various British Colonies.

	Depositors		Amount, £	
	1885	1895	1885	1895
Malta	4,800	6,100	340,000	470,000
Gibraltar . . .	1,100	3,600	20,000	180,000
Newfoundland .	4,300	6,400	360,000	560,000
British Guiana .	13,000	19,900	190,000	260,000
W. India Islands	28,300	56,600	570,000	960,000
Total . .	51,500	92,600	1,480,000	2,430,000

The collective average for these colonies is £26 to each depositor, against £29 in 1885.

BANKRUPTCY

The returns for England and Wales show thus :—

Year	Number	Liabilities, £	Average, £	Assets, £
1885 . . .	4,354	9,060,000	2,100	3,100,000
1890 . . .	4,044	6,180,000	1,500	2,240,000
1897 . . .	4,098	5,770,000	1,400	2,800,000

The number of bankruptcies gazetted in England in ten years, 1885-94, was as follows :—

Trades	Number	Ratio
Grocers	3,202	7.0
Publicans	3,063	6.7
Farmers	2,519	5.4
Builders	2,449	5.3
Shoemakers	1,476	3.2
Bakers	1,146	2.5
Butchers	1,132	2.5
Various	30,845	67.4
Total . . .	45,832	100.0

In 1897 the number and amount of failures were :—

States	Number	Liabilities, £	Assets, £	Ratio of Assets
New England .	1,722	5,600,000	3,700,000	66 p.c.
Middle . .	3,723	10,500,000	5,800,000	55 ,,
Southern . . .	2,799	5,000,000	3,500,000	70 ,,
Prairie . . .	3,682	9,200,000	7,900,000	86 ,,
Pacific . . .	1,425	1,700,000	900,000	53 ,,
Union	13,351	32,000,000	21,800,000	68 ,,

The failures of recent years compare as follows :—

Year	Number	Liabilities, £	Assets, £	Ratio of Assets
1893 . . .	15,242	72,200,000	57,000,000	80 p.c.
1894 . . .	13,885	36,000,000	25,200,000	70 ,,
1895 . . .	13,197	36,000,000	25,200,000	70 ,,
1896 . . .	15,088	47,000,000	32,500,000	69 ,,
1897 . . .	13,351	32,000,000	21,800,000	68 ,,
Average. .	14,152	44,600,000	32,200,000	72 ,,

The figures for liabilities and assets in 1895 were the same as in the preceding year.

The number of failures and amount of liabilities were :—

Year	Number	Liabilities, £	Average, £
1870	3,987	5,550,000	1,400
1875	5,361	9,840,000	1,810
1880	6,295	9,500,000	1,510
1885	8,024	14,200,000	1,770
1890	14,004	26,900,000	1,920
1894	12,794	21,900,000	1,710

In 1893 and 1894 the ratios of assets to liabilities showed thus :—

Year	Liabilities, £	Assets, £	Ratio
1893	17,800,000	6,300,000	35 p.c.
1894	21,900,000	11,900,000	54 ,,

In the liquidation of 1894 there were 95 estates wound up whose assets sufficed to pay all creditors in full.

Official returns from 1880 to 1893 show as follows :—

Year	Bankruptcies	Liabilities, £	Average, £
1880 . . .	972	2,630,000	2,710
1885 . . .	1,083	1,550,000	1,430
1890 . . .	1,089	2,150,000	1,980
1892 . . .	1,073	1,540,000	1,440

Nothing is published further than the number of failures, viz. :—

Year	Number	Year	Number
1881 . . .	5,252	1890 . . .	5,936
1885 . . .	4,627	1894 . . .	7,411

AUSTRALIA

The returns of bankruptcy for 1894 show thus :—

	Number	Liabilities, £	Assets, £
New South Wales .	1,465	1,850,000	995,000
Victoria	1,067	5,240,000	2,100,000
New Zealand . . .	626	500,000	400,000
Queensland . . .	254	190,000	40,000
South Australia . .	80	120,000	100,000
Tasmania	168	50,000	25,000
West Australia . .	32	20,000	40,000
Total . .	3,692	7,970,000	3,700,000

Assets were estimated at 46 per cent. of liabilities, as compared with 72 per cent. in the United States.

CANADA

Liabilities of bankrupts in 1896 reached £3,250,000 against £2,250,000 in 1886. The estimates for 1896 were :—

	Number	Liabilities, £	Assets, £
Ontario	1,072	1,200,000	860,000
Quebec	718	1,720,000	1,250,000
Other Provinces . .	328	510,000	420,000
Total . .	2,118	3,430,000	2,530,000

BARLEY

The area and production of this grain are shown thus :—

	Acres	Tons	Bushels per Acre	Per Inhabitant
United Kingdom	2,200,000	1,800,000	33	1.8
France . . .	2,200,000	1,100,000	20	1.2
Germany . .	4,200,000	2,600,000	25	2.0
Russia . . .	16,800,000	5,900,000	14	2.2
Austria . . .	5,700,000	2,800,000	19	2.5
Spain	4,000,000	1,500,000	15	3.3
Danub. States .	3,200,000	1,200,000	15	4.4
Scandinavia . .	1,400,000	950,000	28	4.0
Italy, &c. . .	2,000,000	600,000	12	...
Europe . . .	41,700,000	18,450,000	18	2.0
United States .	3,000,000	2,200,000	29	1.2
Canada . . .	900,000	450,000	20	3.6
Total . .	45,600,000	21,100,000	19	1.9

BATTLES

Besides the list at page 89 there were the following :—

Date	Place	Won by	Force	Lost by	Force
B.C.					
334	Arbela . .	Alexander	35,000	Persians	950,000
31	Actium . .	Augustus	92,000	Anthony	112,000
A.D.					
1513	Flodden .	English	32,000	Scotch .	30,000
1704	Blenheim .	,,	52,000	French .	56,000
1745	Fontenoy .	French	60,000	English	60,000
1800	Hohenlinden	,,	70,000	Austrians	60,000

BEER

See *Alcohol*, page 533, also page 89.

BEES

Maraldi says that an ordinary hive has 18,000 bees, but forest hives in Russia range from 60,000 to 110,000. In France 1600 bees weigh a pound, but the wild bees of Russia are so light that 5000 go to a pound. Hives in Europe produce from 20 to 50 lb. of honey yearly. A bee sucks 219,000 flowers for every ounce of honey. See Part I., page 90.

BIRTHS

The following table shows the number of births in each country in 1896, the birth-rate to population, the ratio of illegitimate births in 1000, and the number of births to women of 15 to 50 years of age.

	No. of Births	Rate per 1000 Inhabitants	Illegitimate Per 1000	Births to 1000 Women (15–50)
England	917,000	29.9	42	121
Scotland	129,000	30.8	72	121
Ireland	108,000	23.7	26	92
U. Kingdom . .	1,154,000	29.2	44	117
France	866,000	22.7	88	89
Germany . . .	1,942,000	37.3	91	157
Russia	4,916,000	47.1	31	...
Austria	975,000	39.0	145	161
Hungary . . .	761,000	41.1	85	176
Italy	1,096,000	35.1	64	154
Sweden	135,000	27.5	107	117
Norway	63,000	30.0	71	131
Denmark . . .	70,000	30.4	101	131
Holland	160,000	32.0	29	148
Belgium	189,000	29.0	87	128
Switzerland . . .	92,000	30.7	45	123
Portugal	158,000	31.2	123	...
Roumania . . .	232,000	40.0	14	...
Servia	97,000	42.2	...	...
Bulgaria	128,000	38.4	...	...
Europe	13,034,000	35.2	55	...
U. States (1880) .	1,577,000	31.5 *		128
Canada	125,000	25.0	15	101
Australia	124,000	29.4	51	130

The birth-rates of Russia, Servia, and Hungary are the highest in Europe, those of France and Ireland the lowest. The ratio of illegitimacy is highest in Austria and Portugal, lowest in Roumania, Ireland, and Holland. The number of legitimate births, compared with the number of marriages, gives the following results :—

Births to 10 Marriages

France . .	27	Sweden . .	42	Norway . .	44
England .	36	Portugal .	42	Italy . . .	46
Belgium .	36	*Europe* .	43	Ireland . .	46
Switzerland .	37	Germany .	43	Hungary .	47
Denmark .	38	Holland .	43	Roumania .	49
Scotland .	40	Austria .	44	Russia . .	65

It may be that the early age of marrying in Russia accounts for such large families, although Dr. Ogle asserts

* The census report was evidently incomplete, as Dr. Billings shows : the birth-rate was really 35.0.

that a woman marrying at 25 is likely to have more children than one who marries at 20.

The number of illegitimate births in 1896, compared with that of women of 15 to 50 years of age in the various countries, is shown thus :—

	Women	Illeg. Births	Per 10,000 Women
England . . .	7,622,000	38,700	50
Scotland . . .	1,068,000	9,300	87
Ireland . . .	1,174,000	2,800	24
U. Kingdom . .	9,864,000	50,800	52
France . . .	9,701,000	76,300	79
Germany . . .	12,380,000	93,400	75
Austria . . .	6,071,000	141,600	239
Hungary . . .	4,321,000	65,400	151
Italy	7,160,000	70,300	98
Switzerland . .	746,000	4,000	53
Sweden . . .	1,155,000	14,400	125
Norway . . .	489,000	4,500	92
Denmark . . .	534,000	7,100	133
Holland . . .	1,084,000	4,600	42
Belgium . . .	1,483,000	16,500	111

The highest ratios are in Austria and Hungary, the lowest in Ireland.

The following table shows the numbers and ratios of still births :—

	Still Births		Per 1000 Births	
	1885	1895	1885	1895
France . . .	44,000	41,600	50	50
Germany . . .	68,700	64,400	41	33
Austria . . .	24,500	27,300	29	30
Hungary . . .	13,100	17,700	18	24
Italy . . .	39,300	45,900	36	43
Sweden . . .	4,010	3,460	31	26
Norway . . .	1,840	1,720	28	29
Denmark . . .	2,050	1,730	31	26
Holland . . .	7,790	7,610	52	49
Belgium . . .	8,520	8,630	50	45
Switzerland . .	3,230	3,210	40	40
Roumania . . .	2,200	2,640	...	...
Japan . . .	58,400	117,200	55	95

The above shows an ascending ratio in 5 countries, and a descending in 5 others, the former being especially noticeable in Japan.

The number and ratio of illegitimate births in 1890 and 1896 are shown thus :—

	Illegitimate Births		Per 1000 Births	
	1890	1896	1890	1896
U. Kingdom . .	50,400	50,800	46	44
France . . .	71,100	76,300	85	88
Germany . . .	165,700	176,300	94	91
Austria . . .	128,700	141,600	148	145
Hungary . . .	60,000	65,400	86	85
Italy . . .	78,800	70,300	73	64
Scandinavia . .	24,700	26,000	95	97
Switzerland . .	4,100	4,000	52	45
Holland . . .	4,760	4,600	32	29
Belgium . . .	15,250	16,500	86	87

There is a decline of illegitimacy in all countries except France, Belgium, and Scandinavia.

Illegitimate births are more numerous in cities than in rural districts ; returns for the following cities in 1888–89 showed :—

Illegitimates in 1000 Births

Rotterdam .	70	Berlin . .	154	Leipzig . .	211
Naples. . .	86	Christiania .	162	St. Petersburg	236
Hague. . .	99	Liege. . .	174	Paris . . .	268
Palermo . .	101	Bucharest .	175	Copenhagen .	279
Cologne . .	124	Breslau . .	186	Buda-Pesth .	299
Antwerp . .	129	Venice . .	189	Moscow . .	300
Frankfort . .	132	Rome. . .	194	Stockholm .	396
Turin . . .	132	Milan. . .	204	Prague. . .	439
Hamburg. .	138	Dresden . .	208	Munich . .	439
Ghent . . .	144	Trieste . .	211	Vienna. . .	449

The following table shows the rates of births and deaths per thousand inhabitants in the last 12 years as compared with 20 years down to 1880, in various countries :—

	Births		Deaths		Nat. Increase	
	1861-80	1885-96	1861-80	1885-96	1861-80	1885-96
England . . .	35.4	31.1	22.0	18.7	13.4	12.7
France . . .	25.8	22.8	24.0	22.0	1.8	0.8
Prussia . . .	39.1	37.4	27.1	23.6	12.0	13.8
Scandinavia. .	31.4	29.4	19.0	17.3	12.4	12.1
Austria . . .	38.9	37.7	30.8	28.3	8.1	9.4
Hungary . . .	42.6	42.7	39.4	31.8	3.2	10.9
Italy	37.2	37.0	29.9	26.4	7.3	10.6
Holland . . .	36.3	33.3	24.6	19.9	11.7	13.4
Belgium . . .	31.9	29.4	22.7	20.3	9.2	9.1
Mean	35.4	33.1	26.6	22.9	8.8	10.2

The mean birth-rate of Europe has declined 6 per cent. from what it was 30 years ago, but at the same time the death-rate has declined 14 per cent., so that it comes to pass that population is now increasing more rapidly. Thus the surplus of births over deaths 30 years ago was 8.8 per thousand inhabitants, and at present it is 10.2, equal to an improvement of 16 per cent. This decline of birth-rate and death-rate is progressive, as will be seen if we divide the last period into two of 6 years each, viz. :—

	Births		Deaths		Nat. Increase	
	1885-90	1891-96	1885-90	1891-96	1885-90	1891-96
England . . .	31.7	30.4	18.9	18.5	12.8	11.9
Scotland . . .	31.6	30.7	18.9	18.7	12.7	12.0
Ireland . . .	22.8	22.9	18.0	18.1	4.8	4.8
U. Kingdom . .	30.5	29.6	18.8	18.4	11.7	11.2
France . . .	23.3	22.4	21.9	22.1	1.4	0.3
Prussia . . .	37.5	37.3	24.3	22.9	13.2	14.4
Scandinavia . .	30.0	28.8	17.2	17.3	12.8	11.5
Austria . . .	37.7	37.7	29.0	27.6	8.7	10.1
Hungary . . .	43.8	41.6	32.2	31.4	11.6	10.2
Italy	37.8	36.2	27.3	25.5	10.5	10.7
Holland . . .	33.7	33.0	20.6	19.2	13.1	13 8
Belgium . . .	29.7	29.2	20.7	19.9	9.0	9.3
Mean	33.8	32.9	23.6	22.7	10.2	10.2

The natality or annual offspring to be expected from 100 husbands according to age is :—

Age	Nat. p. c.	Age	Nat. p. c.	Age	Nat. p. c.
23–25 . .	33	35–37 . .	23	47–49 . .	7
26–28 . .	35	38–40 . .	19	50–51 . .	5
29–31 . .	32	41–43 . .	15	52–54 . .	3
32–34 . .	28	44–46 . .	11	55–60 . .	2

The following table of natality by Körösi shows the ratio of births that may be expected yearly to 100 wives according to age :—

Mother's Age	Sweden	Norway	Alsace.	Brunswick	Berlin	Buda-Pesth	Edinburgh	Average
15–19 . . .	52	41	47	58	50	43	50	49
20–24 . . .	45	58	56	45	46	36	42	47
25–29 . . .	38	43	46	35	34	29	35	37
30–34 . . .	31	36	39	27	23	21	27	29
35–39 . . .	25	30	28	20	15	15	20	22
40–44 . . .	14	18	...	8	6	6	8	10
45–49 . . .	2	3	...	1	1	1	1	1

The most productive age for mothers is from 15 to 24, for fathers from 23 to 31 : of 100 mothers, 48 of the said age will have children yearly ; of 100 fathers, only 34. The reason that these numbers are not equal is because parents of those ages are not equal ; for example, the number of fathers over 40 is much greater than that of mothers. The reproductive age with men may be said to cease at 60, although at 65 the chance of paternity is 3 in 1000, and it is 2 in 1000 at 69. Bertillon shows that birth-rate is much higher among the poor than the rich, and that 1000 women between 15 and 50 years of age will have the following number of children yearly :—

Quarters	Births Yearly per 1000 Women				
	Paris	London	Berlin	Vienna	Average
Rich . . .	44	55	55	89	61
Comfortable .	68	107	105	154	108
Poor . . .	102	143	143	182	142
General rate .	80	109	102	153	111

The annals of Berlin from 1826 to 1896 record the following multiple births :—

147,000 births of twins.
7,733 ,, of 3 children.
106 ,, of 4 children.
3 ,, of 5 children.

(See page 93, where a case of 6 children at a birth is mentioned, in 1888.)

From the evidence of demographic tables it would appear that multiple births average as follows :—

Twins . . . 1,280 in 100,000 births.
Triplets . . 16 in ,, ,,
4 or more children . 2 in a million births.

Twins and triplets are most frequent in Bavaria. Twins are less frequent in Spain, triplets in England, than in other countries (see page 93).
In Paris the returns for 4 years ending December 1895 gave the ratios of twins as to sex thus :—

Sex	Mother's Age		
	18–25	26–35	Over 35
2 males	348	343	348
2 females	382	302	320
Mixed	270	355	332
	1,000	1,000	1,000

In St. Petersburg the number of twins to 1000 births was :—

Mother's Age		Mother's Age	
16–20 . . .	6	31–40 . . .	22
20–30 . . .	12	41–50 . . .	17

The general ratio all round was 14 twin births to 1000 births.
In Canada 100,000 births give 850 twin births and 29 births of triplets, twins being less, triplets more, frequent than in Europe.
The sexes of children born in 1895 were :—

	Number		Ratio	
	Males	Females	Males	Females
England	469,000	453,000	1,034	1,000
Scotland	64,900	61,600	1,054	1,000
Ireland	54,500	51,600	1,058	1,000
U. Kingdom . . .	588,400	566,200	1,039	1,000
Germany	999,000	943,000	1,064	1,000
Italy	561,000	531,000	1,060	1,000
Canada	64,000	61,000	1,050	1,000
Australia	63,400	60,200	1,054	1,000
U. States (1880) . .	807,000	770,000	1,048	1,000

UNITED KINGDOM

The following table shows the births and deaths and the natural increase from surplus of births in the United Kingdom in 1897 :—

	000 omitted			Per 1000 Pop.		
	Births	Deaths	Increase	Births	Deaths	Increase
England . .	921	541	380	29.7	17.5	12.2
Scotland . .	129	79	50	30.6	18.7	11.9
Ireland . . .	107	84	23	23.5	18.5	5.0
U. Kingdom .	1,157	704	453	29.0	17.7	11.3

The following table shows the population, birth and death rates of the largest cities in England :—

	Population (1897)	Per 1000 Inhabitants		
		Births	Deaths	Increase
London	4,463,000	30.7	19.0	11.7
Liverpool . . .	633,000	35.3	24.4	10.9
Manchester . .	534,000	33.3	23.1	10.2
Birmingham . .	506,000	33.3	21.6	11.7
Leeds	409,000	31.6	19.9	11.7
Sheffield	352,000	34.4	21.2	13.2
Bristol	232,000	27.8	17.2	10.6

A statement was published in 1891 on an average of five years, showing the birth-rates and death-rates of London and of the Peabody Buildings, to 31st December 1890, with the natural increase of population, as follows :—

	Per 10,000 Inhabitants		
	Births	Deaths	Increase
London . . .	308	191	117
Peabody . . .	402	188	214

The surplus of births over deaths in the Peabody Buildings was almost in twice the ratio of London.

France

Turquand shows that the fecundity of men and women in France (1892–95) is as follows, men being taken from 18 years of age, women from 15 years upwards :—

Age	Children Yearly to 1000		Number of	
	Husbands	Wives	Wives	Children
Under 24 .	318	299	705,000	210,500
25–34 . .	259	213	1,931,100	410,400
35–44 . .	247	81	1,864,000	152,000
45–50 . .	46	8	832,100	6,300
Over 50 . .	7	...	2,324,500	900
Of all ages .	102	102	7,656,700	780,100

The above regards only married persons, the ages of widows and unmarried girls having children being as follows :—

Age	Unmarried Women	Children	In 10,000 Women
0–20	1,928,900	14,592	75
20–24	1,066,000	27,370	257
25–34	854,500	24,980	292
35–44	612,000	5,596	91
Over 44 . . .	3,533,470	1,272	4
Total . .	7,994,870	73,810	92

Thus 10,000 married women of all ages will have 1020 children yearly, and the same number of unmarried will have 92. If we take only women under 44 years the yearly birth-rate will be as follows :—

	Women	Births	Per 10,000
Married . . .	4,500,000	773,000	172
Unmarried . .	4,462,000	73,800	17

Germany

Official returns for sixteen years (1875–90) show that birth-rate differs remarkably according to the religion of the parents, Roman Catholics being much above par, and mixed marriages no less below it. The table also gives the ratio of still births to each religion, viz. :—

Parents	Children to 100 Families	Still Births in 10,000 Births
Roman Catholic . .	524	356
Evangelical . . .	435	405
R. Cath. and Evangelical .	332	335
Jewish . . .	421	329
Jewish and Evangelical .	168	337

Hungary

Körösi shows that 1000 married couples will have the following number of children yearly :—

Children Yearly to 1000 *Wives*

Father's Age	Mother's Age		
	25–	30–	35–
25–29	356	250	212
30–34	312	236	199
35–39	275	218	194
40–50	275	153	125

Mother's Age	Father's Age		
	25–	35–	45–
20–24	430	313	160
25–29	308	273	185
30–34	335	237	144
35–39	...	189	118

The maximum age of fecundity is as follows :—

For Men		For Women	
Husband	Wife	Wife	Husband
25	19	18	25
35	21	25	28
40	24	30	30
45	29	35	29

Canada

The number of all births compared to marriages in 1895 was :—

	Marriages	Births	Ratio of Births
Ontario	13,990	41,630	3.0
Quebec . . .	10,170	58,650	5.8
Other Provinces .	3,910	13,160	3.4
Total . .	28,070	113,440	4.1

The above, however, does not include Nova Scotia or the North-West Territories, for which there are no returns. As illegitimate births constitute 1½ per cent., the ratio of lawful births to a marriage is found to be 4.0, the above table including bastards.

Australia

The following table shows the birth-rate of the colonies, the ratio of males born to 100 females, and the ratio of illegitimacy :—

	Births per 1000 Pop.	Male to 100 Fem. Births	Illegitimate per Cent.
New South Wales .	32.8	105	5.7
Victoria	31.0	106	5.0
New Zealand . .	27.7	105	3.2
Queensland . .	34.1	104	4.8
South Australia . .	31.5	106	2.5
Tasmania . . .	32.2	103	4.2
West Australia . .	31.2	101	4.3
Total . .	31.3	105	4.8

United States

The section on Births for the census of 1890 is not yet published. The figures for 1880 showed as follows, the column of Women indicating those between 15 and 50 years of age, to compare the number of births :—

	Number (000 omitted)				Births to 1000 Women
	Births			Number of Women	
	Male	Female	Total		
White . .	372	352	724	5,696	127
Coloured .	120	120	240	1,469	164
Doubtful .	315	298	613	5,208	118
Total .	807	770	1,577	12,373	127

The sexes of coloured children were equal, but those of white or doubtful classification showed male births 5½ per cent. in excess of female, as occurs also in Europe.

The birth-rate to the above three sections of population was as follows :—

	Population	Births	Per 1000
Whites . . .	22,599,000	724,000	32.0
Coloured . . .	6,233,000	240,000	38.6
Doubtful . . .	21,324,000	613,000	28.7
Total . .	50,156,000	1,577,000	31.4

The ratio of women of child-bearing age to the above classes was :—

	Population	Women	Per 1000
Whites . . .	22,599,000	5,696,000	252
Coloured . . .	6,233,000	1,469,000	236
Doubtful . . .	21,324,000	5,208,000	244
Total . .	50,156,000	12,373,000	247

The highest and lowest birth-rates were as follows :—

Highest

State	Per 1000 Pop.	Per 1000 Women
Arkansas . . .	42.7	190
Utah	41.9	199
Texas	41.3	187

Lowest

New Hampshire . .	19.1	72
Arizona . . .	19.3	114
Maine	20.9	81

BOUNTIES

See page 494.

BULLION

The following table shows the average annual imports and exports of bullion in ten years to December 1895 :—

	Imported, £ per An.		Exported, £	
	1886-90	1891-95	1886-90	1891-95
U. Kingdom	24,400,000	38,800,000	22,200,000	31,800,000
France . .	16,600,000	22,600,000	15,800,000	14,000,000
Germany .	5,600,000	11,200,000	5,600,000	7,200,000
Russia . .	2,600,000	12,000,000	3,800,000	1,000,000
Austria . .	2,000,000	6,200,000	500,000	1,600,000
Italy . . .	2,500,000	2,100,000	2,900,000	2,200,000
Spain . .	1,100,000	1,900,000	200,000	900,000
Portugal .	2,500,000	1,000,000	800,000	2,600,000
Scandinavia	600,000	400,000	200,000	100,000
Holland . .	1,700,000	3,600,000	1,400,000	2,200,000
Belgium . .	4,600,000	6,400,000	4,000,000	6,000,000
Switzerland	2,600,000	2,900,000	1,400,000	1,800,000
Europe . .	66,800,000	109,100,000	58,800,000	71,400,000
U. States .	9,200,000	12,200,000	12,600,000	24,200,000
Span. Amer.	5,200,000	2,400,000	12,800,000	11,800,000
China . .	4,000,000	4,500,000	4,000,000	3,800,000
Japan . .	1,400,000	2,100,000	1,500,000	1,900,000
Egypt . .	2,400,000	3,300,000	2,400,000	2,300,000
India . . .	17,200,000	17,000,000	4,200,000	8,000,000
Various . .	1,800,000	1,400,000	10,700,000	28,400,000
Total .	107,000,000	152,000,000	107,000,000	152,000,000

See *Gold and Silver*, pages 308 and 741.

C

CABS

The number of cabs and omnibuses in various cities in 1890 was :—

	Number		Per 10,000 Pop.	
	Cabs	Busses	Cabs	Busses
London . . .	11,300	2,210	27	5
Paris . . .	11,700	840	48	2
Berlin . . .	5,700	240	40	2
Vienna . . .	2,200	620	17	5
Buda-Pesth .	1,000	100	20	2
Bordeaux . .	1,200	140	48	5
Rome . . .	2,400	130	53	3
Naples . .	2,900	110	55	2
Genoa . . .	300	220	14	10
Florence . . .	900	70	45	3

The above 10 cities show an average of 37 cabs and 4 busses to every 10,000 souls. London is below the average in cabs, but above it in busses. See *Tramways*, page 814, also *Cabs*, page 100.

The Omnibus Company of Paris has 16,000 horses and 1,100 busses or tramcars, some of the latter being horse-cars, others drawn by locomotives (tramways 105 miles long), the development of this Company having been as follows :—

	Car-riages	Horses	Passengers, Millions	Tax Paid, £	Divdend, Francs
1865 .	732	8,230	107	88,000	60
1875 .	736	9,760	123	102,000	50
1885 .	896	12,980	191	148,000	55
1896 .	1,091	16,330	246	194,000	45

The statement for 1896 was as follows :—

	Cars	Horses	Passengers	Miles Run
Busses . .	670	10,550	135,400,000	14,400,000
Tramcars .	410	5,750	110,700,000	8,800,000
Total .	1,080	16,300	246,100,000	23,200,000

	Daily Average		Receipts, Pence per	
	Passengers	Miles	Mile	Passenger
Busses. . . .	370,000	40,000	16.7	1.78
Tramcars. . .	301,000	25,000	20.5	1.66
Total . .	671,000	65,000	18.2	1.73

Bus passengers were 57 per cent. inside, 43 out ; tramcars carried 55 per cent. inside, 45 out. Busses had 10 passengers, tramcars 12, per mile run. Each horse on active service ran 10 miles daily, carried 100 passengers, and earned 178 pence. Gross receipts, £1,760,000, say £4800 daily.

CANALS

Exclusive of the Manchester Ship Canal, those of the United Kingdom show the following traffic :—

	Worked by		
	Railways	Companies	Total
Tons carried . .	8,030,000	28,270,000	36,300,000
Receipts, £ . .	500,000	1,540,000	2,040,000
Expenses, £. .	370,000	950,000	1,320,000
Profit, £ . . .	130,000	590,000	720,000

	Miles in Traffic by		
	Railways	Companies	Total
England . . .	1,024	2,026	3,050
Scotland . . .	84	69	153
Ireland . . .	96	513	609
Total . .	1,204	2,608	3,812

The above includes 1070 miles of canals no longer used, but nominally belonging to Companies. The mileage traffic returns for canals owned by Railways and Companies show :—

	Railway Canals	Company Canals	Total
Tons per mile . . .	670	1,080	950
Receipts, £	420	600	535
Expenses, £	300	360	350
Profit, £	120	240	185

	England	Scotland	Ireland
Receipts, £ per mile .	625	460	160
Expenses	400	280	120
Profit	225	180	40

The Manchester Ship Canal, opened in 1894, is 36 miles long, 26 feet deep, and 120 wide, having cost £15,400,000, or £425,000 per mile ; traffic returns showed 2,100,000 tons in 1897, an increase of 13 per cent. over 1896, and 53 per cent. over 1895. This canal cost per mile more than twice as much as the Suez Canal.

Suez Canal.—Traffic returns for 1896 compare with those of previous years thus :—

Year	Ships	Tons	Average Tonnage	Fees, £
1886. . . .	3,100	8,180,000	2,640	2,260,000
1891. . . .	4,207	12,220,000	2,900	3,340,000
1897. . . .	2,986	11,120,000	3,720	2,840,000

Net profits in 1896 amounted to £1,690,000, equal to 7 per cent. on capital.

The various flags of vessels passing through in 1886 and in 1896 showed thus :—

	Tonnage		Percentage of Increase	Ratio in 1896
	1886	1896		
British . . .	6,260,000	8,060,000	29	67.0
German . . .	320,000	1,120,000	250	9.3
French . . .	700,000	820,000	17	6.8
Italian	190,000	590,000	210	4.9
Dutch	310,000	520,000	70	4.3
Various . . .	400,000	930,000	132	7.7
Total . .	8,180,000	12,040,000	47	100.0

The preponderance of British shipping in the Suez Canal traffic is declining, having fallen from 76½ per cent. of the total in 1886 to 67 per cent. in 1896. At the same time it will be observed that the increase of tonnage in the 10 years was 3,860,000, and of this the British increase amounted to 1,800,000 tons, or nearly half the total. The average size of ships (gross tonnage) passing through the canal in 1896 was :—

Flag	*Tons*	*Flag*	*Tons*
British	. . 3,730	Italian . .	. 2,600
German	. . 3,480	Dutch . .	. 2,600
French	. . 3,760	Various . .	. 3,340

For further particulars about this canal see page 102.

GERMANY

Germany.—According to statements published in 1878 and 1886, the navigable rivers had a length of 15,600 miles, canals 1320 miles, but the *Statesman's Year-Book* (1898) publishes an official statement as follows :—

Draft	Miles		
	Rivers	Canals	Total
Under 5 feet	6,170	1,304	7,474
Over ,, ...	1,030	150	1,180
Total . .	7,200	1,454	8,654

The Kiel Canal, from the German Ocean to the Baltic, is 61 miles long, 30 feet deep, and 213 wide ; it was opened, after eight years of work, in June 1895, having cost £7,800,000, equal to £128,000 per mile. Traffic returns for 1897 show that 16,960 vessels passed through in the year, paying £51,000, or an average of £3 each. Working expenses amounted to £100,000, or double the receipts. This canal shortens the route to the Baltic by 44 hours for vessels from Hamburg, and 32 from London.

FRANCE

Canal and river traffic in 1896 compare with previous years in tons carried 100 miles as follows :—

Year	Tons by		
	Canal	River	Total
1870 . . .	5,500,000	3,400,000	8,900,000
1880 . . .	6,800,000	5,500,000	12,300,000
1892 . . .	12,800,000	9,400,000	22,200,000
1896 . . .	15,200,000	10,600,000	25,800,000

The above, of course, does not express the actual number of tons carried, but the number which results from giving 100 miles to each ton. The tonnage carried one mile to each mile of canal and river at the above dates was :—

Year	Canal	River	Total
1870 . . .	192,000	81,000	273,000
1880 . . .	249,000	132,000	381,000
1892 . . .	423,000	214,000	637,000
1896 . . .	502,000	263,000	765,000

Traffic has doubled since 1880, and trebled since 1870. The length of canals and navigable rivers used for traffic varies every year. In 1896 it was :—

	In Use	Unused	Total
Canals, miles	3,030	50	3,080
Rivers, ,, ...	4,030	1,390	5,420
Total miles . .	7,060	1,440	8,500

It is proposed to make a ship canal from Bordeaux to the Mediterranean, 330 miles long and 70 feet wide : estimated cost £22,400,000, say £68,000 per mile. The canals are State property, and the traffic is carried on by 16,000 boats, which give employment to 41,000 men and women. In 1896 agricultural products formed 3,500,000 tons, and building materials 8,700,000 tons of merchandise carried.

AUSTRIA

The goods traffic on Danube and Elbe by steamer was as follows :—

On	Tons Carried		
	1891	1893	1895
Danube . . .	1,980,000	2,180,000	1,960,000
Elbe	650,000	550,000	640,000
Total . .	2,630,000	2,730,000	2,600,000

RUSSIA

There are 2200 steamboats and 345,000 vessels and rafts on the inland waters of Russia in Europe, carrying 24 million tons of merchandise, valued at 28 millions sterling. The length of navigable rivers and canals is 47,500 miles, and traffic returns show thus :—

	Tons	
	1890	1894
Timber	7,820,000	9,210,000
Grain	2,230,000	3,680,000
Naphtha	710,000	2,020,000
Sundries	5,900,000	8,420,000
Total . .	16,660,000	23,300,000

UNITED STATES

The coast and internal water traffic at last census were reported as follows for 1889 :—

Line	Vessels	Tonnage	Tons Carried	Passengers
Mississippi	7,453	3,390,000	29,400,000	10,900,000
Lakes. .	2,784	930,000	53,400,000	2,300,000
Pfc. coast	1,842	440,000	8,800,000	4,000,000
Atlantic .	13,466	2,860,000	80,700,000	152,700,000
Total .	25,545	7,620,000	172,300,000	169,900,000

The above is exclusive of canals, of which there are 2270 miles in active use :—

State	Miles	Cost, £	Tons Carried	Fees, £
New York. .	650	15,400,000	6,800,000	190,000
Pennsylvania.	465	6,600,000	1,400,000	500,000
Ohio . . .	660	3,000,000	1,100,000	20,000
New Jersey .	170	2,300,000	1,700,000	70,000
Various . .	325	4,100,000	2,200,000	120,000
Total . .	2,270	31,400,000	13,200,000	900,000

Besides the above there are 2200 miles of abandoned canals, which represent a sum of £13,000,000 spent in their construction. There is, moreover, a short canal made in 1855 to connect Lakes Huron and Superior, of which the traffic returns show as follows :—

	Tons	
	1885	1895
Grain	570,000	2,480,000
Coal	890,000	2,570,000
Iron ore	1,240,000	8,060,000
Sundries	560,000	1,950,000
Total . .	3,260,000	15,060,000

The value of merchandise in 1894 reached £30,100,000, an average of 45 shillings per ton.

CANADA

There is an unbroken length of 2260 miles of canalised river and canals from the Straits of Belleisle on the Atlantic to Port Arthur at the head of Lake Superior, which lake is 602 feet over sea-level. The whole system was originally intended for 9 feet draught, but is now available for vessels drawing 12 feet, and as high as Montreal for 27 feet draught, that is 980 miles from the sea. The canals have a total length of 70 miles, besides which there are forty miles of the St. Lawrence river between Montreal and Quebec dredged as a deep-water channel. These works have cost £13,400,000, of which £9,200,000 since the Dominion was established, in 1867. Traffic returns for 1885 and 1895 compare thus :—

	Welland Canal		All	
	1885	1895	1885	1895
Tonnage . .	680,000	1,070,000	3,230,000	3,870,000
Tons carried .	780,000	870,000	2,670,000	2,740,000
Passengers .	4,000	34,000	70,000	154,000
Tolls, £ . .	30,000	29,000	300,000	265,000

The goods carried in 1895 were of the following kinds :—

	Tons		
	Welland	Other Canals	Total
Timber	120,000	950,000	1,070,000
Farm products . .	490,000	350,000	840,000
Merchandise . .	260,000	570,000	830,000
Total . .	870,000	1,870,000	2,740,000

The net revenue which the Government receives from the canals averages £70,000 a year, which is about the half of 1 per cent., say £5 per thousand, on the cost of their construction.

GREECE

The Corinth Canal, 4 miles long, 72 feet wide, and 27 feet deep, was opened to traffic in 1893. It shortens the route from Marseilles to Constantinople by 95 miles, and from Trieste to Athens by 185 miles.

CAPITAL

New capital called up in 1897 in Europe was :—

	Millions £ Sterling *		
	Loans	Companies	Total
United Kingdom . .	21.8	114.2	136.0
France	0.6	15.2	15.8
Germany	18.3	76.0	94.3
Russia	4.8	25.2	30.0
Austria	6.7	4.2	10.9
Italy	0.1	1.9	2.0
Spain	7.4	1.6	9.0
Scandinavia . . .	4.0	0.3	4.3
Holland	0.6	5.6	6.2
Belgium	3.1	2.9	6.0
Switzerland. . . .	3.4	2.1	5.5
Turkey, &c. . . .	1.9	1.3	3.2
Europe	72.7	250.5	323.2
Average, 1881–85 . .	73.6	121.0	194.6
,, 1871–82 . .	157.0	206.0	363.0

For details before 1882 see Part I., page 106.

* *Note.*—The table reads thus: Loans 21.8 signifies £21,800,000.

GREAT BRITAIN

The amount of British capital invested abroad in 1893 was estimated (Dict. Polit. Econ.) as follows :—

Loans	Ml. £	Railways	Ml. £	Sundries	Ml. £
Foreign	525	U. States	120	Banks	50
Colonial	225	Colonial	140	Lands	100
Municipal do.	20	Various	128	Mines, &c.	390
Total	770	Total	388	Total	540

This makes a total of 1698 millions, which compares with previous estimates thus :—

Year	Millions £	
	Amount	Annual Increase
1862	144	...
1872	600	45.6
1882	875	27.5
1893	1,698	74.8

The amount of British capital invested abroad in 1893 was equal to 15 per cent. of the total wealth of the United Kingdom.

The registered paid-up capital of joint-stock companies in the United Kingdom was :—

	Millions £ Sterling		
	1884	1890	1896
England	428	706	1,036
Scotland	36	52	83
Ireland	12	17	27
United Kingdom .	476	775	1,146

The average amount of capital (paid-up) to each company was as follows :—

	1884	1890	1896
England, . £ .	56,000	61,000	56,000
Scotland, . ,, .	50,000	47,000	46,000
Ireland, . ,, .	31,000	28,000	31,000
United Kingdom, ,, .	54,600	58,100	54,000

The paid-up joint-stock capital of the three kingdoms has more than doubled in twelve years. The average to each company is unchanged, except a fall in Scotland.

The new capital actually called up in Great Britain was :—

Year	Millions Sterling	Per Annum
1879–85 . . .	581	83
1886–89 . . .	507	127
1890–97 . . .	643	80
19 years . .	1,731	91

In 1897 the new capital nominally created was £157,300,000, but the amount actually paid up was only £81,700,000, or 52 per cent. of the former sum. The nominal new capital may be summed up thus :—

	£		£
Foreign loans .	10,600,000	Breweries . .	18,000,000
Colonial ,, .	14,100,000	Factories . .	15,400,000
Foreign rails .	5,500,000	Municipal loans	7,700,000
Colonial ,, .	4,400,000	Railways . .	7,500,000
Foreign mines .	4,900,000	Cycle companies	7,200,000
Colonial ,, .	8,100,000	Stores ,,	9,000,000
For. companies	10,100,000	Hotels, gas, &c.	34,800,000
Foreign . .	57,700,000	British . .	99,600,000

The *Bankers' Magazine* (1898) gave the aggregate value of 325 descriptions of investments at the close of each year as follows :—

Year	Millions £
1891	2,777
1894	2,882
1896	3,198
1897	3,276

The par value of the above stocks was 2869 millions : the increase of value since 1894 was 394 millions, say 131 millions yearly.

FRANCE

In 1895 Neymarck set down the floating capital of France as follows :—

	Millions £	Holders	£ per Holder
French stock . . .	1,120	2,080,000	540
Bank of France . .	20	28,500	700
Railway shares . .	800	700,000	1,140
Credit Foncier . .	10	40,500	250
Bank deposits . . .	60	300,000	200
Savings banks . . .	155	8,600,000	18
Total . .	2,165	11,749,000	180

Another estimate makes the floating capital 2400 millions sterling; Government stocks 1040, municipal stocks 200, railway scrip 800, factories and companies 200, banks and insurance 200, millions sterling. The following table shows the number and amount of securities lodged with the Bank of France for collection of coupons :—

Year	Depositors, No.	Securities, Millions £	Govt. Stocks, Dividend, £
1860 . . .	15,360	32	400,000
1869 . . .	23,486	52	900,000
1880 . . .	21,567	63	1,200,000
1895 . . .	45,500	131	2,600,000

The average market value of Bank of France stock belonging to each shareholder, and the interest gained in dividends on such stock, was as follows :—

Period	Stock, £	Interest
1856-60	2,600	4.0
1876-80	2,550	3.7
1891-95	2,880	3.4

Notwithstanding the declining interest, the average stock to each holder is increasing.

According to Neymarck, the emissions of new capital in Europe in 22 years, ending December 1892, were as follows :—

	Millions £	France took
1871–85	4,020	824
1886–92	2,020	280
Total . .	6,040	1,104

French capital invested in foreign countries in 1893 was as follows :—

In	Millions £		
	Loans	Companies	Total
Russia	200	...	200
Spain	40	70	110
Austria	50	56	106
Italy	38	14	52
Total . .	328	140	468

French capitalists draw dividends amounting to 160 millions sterling per annum, of which, as Neymarck computes, about 31 per cent. comes from investments in foreign countries, 38 per cent. from joint-stock companies in France, and the rest from French State or municipal securities. In 1887 the joint-stock companies in France paid income-tax on a capital of 1360 millions : adding to this the amount of French Rentes or stock (1100 millions sterling), the floating capital would reach 2460 millions sterling.

ITALY

In 1897 the Italian Government paid coupons on Italian stock held in foreign countries representing the following capital value :—

In	Coupons, £	Capital, £
England	600,000	12,600,000
France	4,200,000	88,200,000
Germany	2,300,000	48,300,000
Total .	7,100,000	149,100,000

BELGIUM

The amount of floating capital in Belgium in March 1898 was as follows :—

	Millns. £		Millns. £
Belgian stocks . .	143.2	Railways	12.5
Foreign ,, . .	12.4	Tramways . . .	9.0
Debentures . .	40.8	Mines	27.2
Banks	21.0	Sundries	17.4

making a total of 284 millions sterling, which is an increase of 12 millions on 1897.

SUMMARY

In 1897 *L'Economiste* estimated the amounts held in stocks and shares in various countries as follows, between national and foreign :—

	Mlns. £		Mlns. £
United Kingdom .	2,922	Italy . .	281
France . . .	1,280	Holland . .	218
Germany . .	1,472	Belgium . .	99
Russia . . .	406	Denmark . .	43
Austria . .	392	Roumania . .	19

This makes a total for Europe alone of 7132 millions sterling, of which the United Kingdom holds 45 per cent.

M. Georges Martin, of the Paris Statistical Society, sums up the different kinds of investments, such as loans, railway stocks, banks, mines, and other joint-stock enterprises held in certain countries and belonging to other countries, as follows :—

Securities	Held in							
	France	G. Britain	Germany	Belgium	Holland	Switzerland	Various	Total
French . .	...	24	...	37	4	10	...	75
German . .	...	8	...	15	5	9	5	42
Spanish . .	44	29	4	25	5	12	...	119
Austrian . .	25	10	183	24	39	15	2	298
Russian . .	17	30	79	31	69	4	...	230
Brazilian . .	8	81	5	12	8	5	...	119
Argentine . .	14	123	9	37	3	7	...	193
Canadian . .	8	140	...	...	10	2	...	160
Australian . .	...	230	...	...	...	...	...	230
United States .	3	341	94	2	128	9	...	577
Turkish . .	14	26	15	4	7	4	8	78
Indian . . .	...	103	...	...	...	...	...	103
Italian . .	16	20	35	40	10	36	6	163
Egyptian . .	20	20	6	...	...	...	...	46
Mexican . .	4	26	...	...	...	...	4	34
Various . .	161	402	161	85	98	30	...	937
Total .	334	1,613	591	312	386	143	25	3,404
Public loans .	113	365	214	114	112	33	13	964
Companies .	221	1,248	377	198	274	110	12	2,440

Great Britain stands for nearly half the total, and as our investments abroad appear to exceed 1700 millions sterling, it may be roughly estimated that the above stocks represent altogether 3400 millions which the creditor countries have lent outside their own frontiers for investment.

CATTLE

The following table shows the number of live stock and value :—

	Horses	Cattle	Sheep	Pigs	Goats	Value, Millions £
United Kingdom . . .	2,070,000	11,000,000	30,570,000	3,680,000	600,000	202
France	3,030,000	13,300,000	21,200,000	6,400,000	1,500,000	232
Germany	3,800,000	17,600,000	13,600,000	12,200,000	3,100,000	303
Russia	21,700,000	27,600,000	48,200,000	10,700,000	1,300,000	350
Austria	3,600,000	14,200,000	14,400,000	9,100,000	1,400,000	161
Italy	1,200,000	5,000,000	6,900,000	1,800,000	1,800,000	92
Spain	900,000	2,100,000	16,500,000	1,900,000	2,800,000	46
Portugal . . .	150,000	600,000	3,000,000	1,000,000	900,000	11
Sweden and Norway .	650,000	3,500,000	2,700,000	800,000	400,000	41
Denmark . . .	400,000	1,700,000	1,330,000	800,000	...	26
Holland	300,000	1,500,000	700,000	1,100,000	200,000	28
Belgium	300,000	1,400,000	400,000	700,000	200,000	22
Switzerland . .	100,000	1,200,000	300,000	420,000	400,000	18
Danubian States . .	900,000	3,600,000	13,000,000	2,300,000	4,200,000	42
Greece	100,000	400,000	2,900,000	...	2,500,000	5
Europe	39,200,000	104,700,000	175,700,000	52,900,000	21,300,000	1,579
United States . .	16,600,000	46,500,000	36,800,000	40,600,000	...	344
Canada . . .	1,400,000	4,200,000	3,500,000	1,800,000	...	43
Australia . . .	1,900,000	12,700,000	110,500,000	1,000,000	...	120
Argentina . . .	4,400,000	22,900,000	80,200,000	300,000	...	51
South Africa . .	400,000	2,700,000	17,800,000	300,000	6,200,000	23
Algeria	400,000	1,100,000	7,900,000	...	3,500,000	21
Uruguay . . .	400,000	5,200,000	14,300,000	100,000	...	15
Total . .	64,700,000	200,000,000	446,700,000	97,000,000	31,000,000	2,196

The value of live stock in the United States fell from 451 millions sterling in 1894 to 344 millions in 1897, the number of head in the same interval (big and little) having declined from 162 millions to 140 millions, a fall of 13½ per cent. in 3 years.

The live stock of each country compared with population shows as follows :—

	Per 100 Inhabitants				Value, £ per Inhab.
	Horses	Cows	Sheep	Pigs	
U. Kingdom	5	27	78	10	5.1
France . .	8	33	55	15	6.0
Germany .	7	34	34	23	5.7
Russia . .	20	27	48	10	3.0
Austria . .	9	34	38	22	3.8
Italy . . .	4	16	28	6	3.0
Spain . .	5	12	105	11	2.7
Denmark .	20	85	65	40	11.5
Sweden . .	10	50	28	15	6.0
Holland . .	6	32	18	23	6.0
Belgium . .	5	24	10	11	3.4
Switzerland.	3	40	22	12	6.0
Europe . .	10	28	52	15	4.2
U. States .	23	65	51	56	4.8
Canada . .	28	84	70	34	8.6
Australia .	45	320	2,900	25	27.0
Argentina .	110	570	4,050	7	13.0

In the above table horses include mules, and goats are counted with sheep.

UNITED STATES

The live stock suffers frequent changes, being now less numerous than 10 years ago, viz. :—

Year	Number (000 omitted)			
	Horses	Cattle	Sheep	Pigs
1876 . . .	11,100	27,900	35,900	25,700
1880 . . .	12,900	33,200	40,800	34,100
1886 . . .	14,100	45,500	48,300	46,100
1890 . . .	16,500	52,800	44,300	51,600
1897 . . .	16,600	46,500	36,800	40,600

If we reduce all live stock to a common denominator as cattle (six sheep or pigs counting as one), the number compares with population at the above dates thus :—

	Cattle	Population	Cattle per 100 Inhabit.
1876 . . .	49,300,000	43,100,000	114
1880 . . .	58,600,000	50,200,000	117
1886 . . .	75,300,000	57,400,000	131
1890 . . .	85,300,000	62,600,000	136
1897 . . .	75,900,000	72,800,000	104

The ratio of cattle to population has fallen nearly 23 per cent. since 1890, but is not much below the level of 20 years ago, when population was 40 per cent. less than at present. The area devoted to pasture could easily carry 150 million head of cattle, that is double the actual amount of stock, and as we have already seen an increase of 30 per cent. in 6 years, from 1880 to 1886, it is quite possible that the number may rise to 100 million

head in the early years of the 20th century. In 1894 the richest States in live stock were :—

	Number (000 omitted)			
	Cattle	Horses	Sheep	Pigs
Texas . . .	7,400	1,440	3,810	2,560
Iowa . . .	4,010	1,410	780	6,000
Missouri . .	2,630	1,260	1,000	3,710
Kansas . .	2,650	1,050	320	2,250
Illinois . .	2,590	1,410	1,030	3,420
Nebraska . .	2,150	760	280	2,090
New York . .	2,280	710	1,390	660
Ohio . . .	1,580	880	3,770	2,350
Indiana . .	1,570	820	970	1,820
Pennsylvania .	1,680	690	1,470	1,030
Ten States . .	28,540	10,430	14,820	25,890

These ten States possessed 55 per cent. of the cattle, 56 of the horses, 33 of the sheep, and 60 per cent. of the pigs, of the Union ; that is to say, more than half the total live stock. Their farm area, tillage, and pasture covered 280 million acres, or 15 per cent. of the total area of the Union (excluding Alaska).

The following table shows the number of horses, cattle, sheep, and pigs to every thousand acres of farm area :—

	Horses	Cattle	Sheep	Pigs
New England . .	20	65	35	15
Middle . . .	33	84	53	43
South . . .	18	58	30	66
West . , .	36	93	90	80
Union . . .	28	78	62	69

In the foregoing tables no account is taken of the unoccupied area. Supposing that one-half of such area consists of mountains, deserts, or swamps, there is still a residue of 650 million acres available for pasture. Reducing all stock to horned cattle, and allowing 3 acres per head, the United States could carry as follows, on actual farms and unoccupied lands :—

	On Farms	Unoccupied	Total
New England .	5,400,000	4,000,000	9,400,000
Middle . .	11,300,000	4,000,000	15,300,000
South . .	62,700,000	46,000,000	108,700,000
West . .	67,600,000	163,000,000	230,600,000
Total .	147,000,000	217,000,000	364,000,000

It may, therefore, be reasonably anticipated that the United States will at no distant day possess three times the present amount of live stock, equivalent altogether to 228 million head of large cattle, and distributed approximately thus :—

	Number (000 omitted)			
	Horses	Cattle	Sheep	Pigs
New England . .	1,100	3,700	2,800	3,000
Middle . .	1,700	6,300	4,600	5,100
South . .	12,200	43,000	33,000	37,400
West . .	27,000	95,000	69,600	74,500
Union . .	42,000	148,000	110,000	120,000

AUSTRALIA

Live stock has been as follows :—

	Horses	Cattle	Sheep
1861 . . .	460,000	4,040,000	23,700,000
1871 . . .	780,000	4,710,000	49,800,000
1881 . . .	1,250,000	8,710,000	78,100,000
1891 . . .	1,790,000	11,860,000	124,500,000
1896 . . .	1,920,000	12,700,000	110,500,000

In 1896 the several colonies stood thus :—

	Horses	Cattle	Sheep
New South Wales	510,000	2,230,000	48,300,000
Queensland . .	450,000	6,510,000	19,600,000
New Zealand . .	250,000	1,140,000	19,100,000
Victoria . . .	430,000	1,830,000	13,200,000
South Australia .	190,000	640,000	6,400,000
West Australia .	60,000	200,000	2,300,000
Tasmania . . .	30,000	160,000	1,600,000
Total . .	1,920,000	12,710,000	110,500,000

For other countries see *Agriculture.*

CEMETERIES

The area of cemeteries attached to the principal cities of Europe compared with population gives the following results :—

Square Yards per 100 Inhabitants

London . .	71	Dresden . .	155	Turin . . .	75
Paris . . .	140	Bordeaux . .	125	Genoa . . .	90
Vienna . .	108	Brussels . .	270	Florence . .	90
Buda-Pesth .	360	Rome. . .	155	Venice. . .	130
Hamburg . .	206	Naples . .	47	Bologna . .	285
Leipzig . .	136	Milan. . .	95	Palermo . .	146

This gives an average of 150 sq. yards to 100 inhabitants, say 1½ yards each. London, Vienna, and some Italian cities are much below the average. See *Cemeteries* in Part I., p. 100.

CHARITIES

The number of charitable institutions in London rose from 1024 in 1889 to 1153 in 1897, expenditure showing as follows :—

		1889	1897	Increase, £
Hospitals, . £ .		650,000	830,000	180,000
Bible Missions, ,, .		1,980,000	2,490,000	510,000
Asylums, . ,, .		2,050,000	2,320,000	270,000
Total ,, .		4,680,000	5,640,000	960,000

The sum for Bible missions in 1897 included £1,430,000 for converting infidels, and £1,060,000 spent in the United Kingdom. Charitable bequests in the United Kingdom in 1894 amounted to £3,000,000, or three times as much as in 1889.

ITALY

There are 21,866 charitable institutions, holding endowments to the value of £75,900,000, with a gross income of £5,400,000, of which more than 50 per cent. goes in administration, the balance spent on the poor

amounting to £2,660,000. The endowments are held thus :—

	£
Italian consols	18,300,000
Landed estates	24,900,000
House property	10,700,000
Sundries	22,000,000
Total	75,900,000

For mode of distribution of charities see page 113. The legacies left for charitable purposes were :—

Years	No. of Legacies	Amount £ Sterling	Average Yearly Legacies	£
1881–85 . .	4,817	3,600,000	963	720,000
1886–90 . .	5,900	3,400,000	1,180	680,000
1891–97 . .	9,444	4,100,000	1,350	580,000
17 years .	20,251	11,100,000	1,190	660,000

FRANCE

The amount of charitable donations by legacy in France to religious institutions, hospitals, schools, &c., was as follows :—

Years	Religious £	Hospitals £	Schools, &c £	Total £
1836–55	880,000	3,320,000	1,360,000	5,560,000
1856–65	1,720,000	2,920,000	1,120,000	5,760,000
1871–80	3,560,000	4,640,000	2,440,000	10,640,000
1881–90	2,200,000	6,400,000	3,560,000	12,160,000
1891–93	800,000	2,040,000	1,240,000	4,080,000
53 yrs.	9,160,000	19,320,000	9,720,000	38,200,000

The records from 1866–70 have been lost. The average number of donors and the amounts given yearly were :—

Years	Annual Average Donors	Amount, £	Average, £	Pence per Inhab.
1856–65 . .	3,309	576,000	174	3.8
1871–80 . .	4,006	1,064,000	266	6.9
1881–90 . .	3,315	1,216,000	366	7.7
1891–93 . .	3,708	1,360,000	367	8.6

Donations were made in the following form :—

	1871–80 £	1881–90 £	20 Years £	Average £
Real estate .	3,560,000	2,560,000	6,120,000	306,000
Money . .	5,640,000	7,400,000	13,040,000	652,000
Stocks . .	1,080,000	1,440,000	2,520,000	126,000
Shares . .	360,000	760,000	1,120,000	56,000
Total .	10,640,000	12,160,000	22,800,000	1,140,000

BELGIUM

The amount of charitable legacies was :—

Year	£ Sterling	Pence per Inhab.
1887	105,000	4
1894	126,000	5

For particulars respecting other countries, see page 114.

CHEESE

See *Dairy*, page 683, also page 114.

CHURCHES

UNITED STATES

The census of 1890 gave the following :—

	Churches	Pews	Clergy	Communicants
R. Catholics . .	8,816	3,375,000	9,196	6,258,000
Methodists . .	46,138	12,863,000	30,000	4,590,000
Baptists . . .	36,671	11,568,000	25,646	3,712,000
Presbyterians .	12,469	4,040,000	10,448	1,278,000
Lutherans . .	6,701	2,206,000	4,591	1,231,000
Christ-Disciples	5,324	1,610,000	3,773	641,000
Episcopalians .	5,103	1,360,000	4,244	540,000
Congregationals.	4,736	1,553,000	5,058	512,000
Evangelicals .	2,737	760,000	1,960	357,000
Jews	301	139,000	200	130,000
Quakers . .	995	302,000	1,277	107,000
Various . . .	12,529	3,789,000	14,647	1,257,000
Total . .	142,520	43,565,000	111,040	20,613,000

The value of church property increased in 20 years as follows :—

	£ Sterling		
	1870	1890	Increase
Methodists . .	14,100,000	27,400,000	13,300,000
R. Catholics . .	12,200,000	24,600,000	12,400,000
Presbyterians .	10,600,000	19,700,000	9,100,000
Episcopalians .	7,200,000	17,200,000	10,000,000
Baptists . .	8,400,000	17,100,000	8,700,000
Congregationalists	5,100,000	9,000,000	3,900,000
Lutherans . . .	1,200,000	7,300,000	6,100,000
Christ-Disciples .	1,200,000	2,500,000	1,300,000
Evangelicals, &c.	10,800,000	16,600,000	5,800,000
Total . .	70,800,000	141,400,000	70,600,000

The value of church property compared with population thus :—

States	Amount, £	Population	£ per Head
N. England . .	18,200,000	4,690,000	3.9
Middle	58,300,000	14,110,000	4.2
South	18,100,000	18,280,000	1.0
West	46,800,000	25,540,000	1.8
Union	141,400,000	62,620,000	2.3

In 1870 the average to the whole population was only £1.8 (or 36 shillings) per inhabitant, the ratio in 1890 being 46 shillings.

CANADA

The number of churches and laity is shown thus :—

	Laity		Churches	
	1881	1891	1881	1891
R. Catholics . .	1,790,000	1,990,000	1,492	1,793
Methodists . .	740,000	850,000	3,038	3,360
Presbyterians .	675,000	755,000	1,356	1,767
Ch. of England .	575,000	645,000	1,259	1,674
Baptists . . .	295,000	305,000	936	1,260
Various . . .	145,000	195,000	571	626
Total . .	4,220,000	4,740,000	8,652	10,480

The laity are found to be distributed thus :—

	Quebec	Ontario	Other Provs.	Total
R. Catholics .	1,292,000	358,000	340,000	1,990,000
Methodists . .	40,000	655,000	155,000	850,000
Presbyterians .	52,000	453,000	250,000	755,000
Ch. of England .	75,000	385,000	185,000	645,000
Baptists . . .	8,000	106,000	191,000	305,000
Various . . .	14,000	104,000	77,000	195,000
Total . .	1,481,000	2,061,000	1,198,000	4,740,000

AUSTRALIA

The census of 1891 showed the increase of congregations since 1871 thus :—

	1871	1891	Increase
Church of England . .	752,000	1,485,000	733,000
Roman Catholics . .	444,000	801,000	357,000
Presbyterians	263,000	493,000	230,000
Methodists	203,000	434,000	231,000
Baptists	38,000	87,000	49,000
Congregationalists . .	45,000	79,000	34,000
Lutherans, &c. . . .	137,000	341,000	204,000
Total . .	1,882,000	3,720,000	1,838,000

See *Religion*, page 799, and page 513.

CITIES

See *Population*, page 788, and *Local Finance*, page 764.

COAL

Production has increased 70 per cent. since 1880 viz. :—

	Millions of Tons		
	1880	1889	1897
Great Britain	147	177	202
United States	70	142	176
Germany	59	85	120
Austria	16	24	34
France	19	25	29
Belgium	17	20	22
Various	11	13	27
Total .	340	485	610

The chief countries importing coal were as follows :—

	Tons	
	1885	1895
France	9,900,000	10,200,000
Holland	3,600,000	4,400,000
Italy	3,000,000	4,300,000
Scandinavia	2,900,000	4,200,000
Canada	2,100,000	3,400,000
Russia	1,800,000	2,200,000
Spain and Portugal . .	1,700,000	2,300,000
Switzerland	800,000	1,400,000
The East	1,200,000	2,600,000
Total . .	27,000,000	35,000,000

Factory engines usually consume 2 lbs. of coal per horse-power per hour ; that is, a 10-horse engine 30 tons yearly. Coke is produced from coal, three tons of the latter giving two of the former.

In 1897 Great Britain produced 202 millions tons, and exported 37 millions. Exports of coal from Great Britain were as follows :—

Year	Tons	Value, £	Shillings per Ton
1870	11,700,000	5,600,000	9.6
1880	18,700,000	8,400,000	9.0
1890	30,100,000	19,000,000	12.6
1896	34,300,000	15,200,000	9.0

According to a statement published in 1895, the output and number of miners during the previous year were as follows :—

	Tons Coal	Miners	Tons per Man
Great Britain .	188,000,000	666,000	282
United States .	152,000,000	363,000	420
Germany . . .	77,000,000	300,000	257
France . . .	27,000,000	132,000	205
Belgium . . .	21,000,000	117,000	180
Austria. . . .	10,000,000	50,000	200
Canada . . .	4,000,000	10,000	400
India	4,000,000	43,000	90
Japan	4,000,000	30,000	130
Total . .	487,000,000	1,711,000	283

It will be observed that this table omits Russia, Spain, and Australia, the aggregate of whose production would be 16 million tons, bringing up the total production in 1894 to 501 million tons. The above table takes no account of "brown coal," or lignite, in Germany and Austria, although it is usually counted as coal.

The annual consumption of coal is as follows :—

	Tons	Cwts. per Inhabitant
United Kingdom . .	165,000,000	82
United States . . .	177,000,000	48
Germany	104,000,000	40
Belgium	17,000,000	54
France	39,000,000	20
Holland	4,700,000	20
Canada	5,200,000	20
Australia	4,200,000	19
Italy	4,600,000	3
Scandinavia . . .	4,400,000	10
Austria	30,300,000	14
Russia	11,100,000	2
Spain and Portugal .	4,100,000	4
Switzerland . . .	1,400,000	9
Other nations . .	38,000,000	...
Total . .	610,000,000	...

Consumption in Europe in 1897 averaged 22 cwts. per inhabitant, against 18 in 1888 (see page 120).

GREAT BRITAIN
Production and export have been as follows :—

	Tons Raised	Value, £	Tons Exported	Value, £
1886 . . .	157,500,000	38,200,000	23,300,000	9,800,000
1890 . . .	181,600,000	74,900,000	30,100,000	19,000,000
1896 . . .	195,400,000	57,200,000	34,300,000	15,200,000

The average output per coal-miner in 1896 was 282 tons, being equal to 22 cwt. daily for each working day (256 days). The value at pit's mouth was 86 pence per ton, or 20 per cent. less than at port of shipment. England produces 76 per cent., Wales 13, Scotland 11 per cent. of the total. For Royalties, &c., see *Mining*, page 774.

UNITED STATES
Production has progressed as follows :—

	Tons Raised		
	1880	1890	1896
Pennsylvania .	46,700,000	79,300,000	92,800,000
Illinois . . .	6,100,000	13,700,000	17,700,000
Virginia . . .	1,800,000	7,300,000	12,600,000
Ohio	5,900,000	10,300,000	11,500,000
Alabama. . .	300,000	3,700,000	5,100,000
Maryland . .	2,200,000	3,000,000	3,700,000
Iowa	1,400,000	3,600,000	3,500,000
Indiana . . .	1,400,000	3,000,000	3,500,000
Kentucky . .	900,000	2,400,000	3,000,000
Other states . .	3,800,000	14,600,000	18,000,000
Total . .	70,500,000	140,900,000	171,400,000
Anthracite . .	28,600,000	41,500,000	48,600,000
Bituminous . .	41,900,000	99,400,000	122,800,000

Anthracite is found only in Pennsylvania. The value of the two kinds of coal is shown thus for 1896 :—

	Tons	£ Sterling	Shillings per Ton
Anthracite . .	48,600,000	17,000,000	7.0
Bituminous . .	122,800,000	23,900,000	3.9
Total . .	171,400,000	40,900,000	4.8

The increase in coal production has been much more rapid than in Great Britain, viz. :—

Year	Tons Raised		Value, £	
	G. Britain	U. States	G. Britain	U. States
1870 .	110,000,000	33,000,000	27,600,000	20,600,000
1896 .	195,400,000	171,400,000	57,200,000	40,800,000

Thus in 26 years British coal has increased 78 per cent., American 420 per cent. Moreover in 1870 American coal was 2½ times as dear as British, whereas now the latter is dearer than American, viz. :—

	Value, Pence per Ton	
	1870	1896
British	60	70
American	150	57

In 26 years British coal has risen 17 per cent. in price, American fallen 62 per cent.

The following table shows the production and value, as also the consumption per inhabitant, at various dates :—

Year	Tons Raised	Value, £	Pence per Ton	Cwts. per Inhab.
1870 .	32,900,000	20,600,000	150	17.5
1880 .	70,500,000	19,700,000	67	28.0
1890 .	140,900,000	30,200,000	51	45.0
1897 .	176,000,000	41,200,000	57	48.0

Improved machinery enables mine-owners to sell coal now at 38 per cent. of the price that ruled in 1870, and as a consequence the consumption per inhabitant has nearly trebled. The value of the coal (at pit's mouth) which is now consumed per inhabitant is 137 pence, as compared with 131 pence in 1870 for one-third of the quantity.

2 T

GERMANY

The production of coal and lignite, and the imports and exports, are shown as follows :—

	Tons		
	1876	1886	1890
Coal raised . .	38,500,000	58,100,000	85,700,000
Lignite raised .	11,100,000	15,600,000	26,800,000
Coal imported .	2,100,000	2,600,000	5,500,000
Total	51,700,000	76,300,000	118,000,000
Exported . . .	5,300,000	8,700,000	13,800,000
Consumption .	46,400,000	67,600,000	104,200,000

Germany consumes two tons per inhabitant. There are 341,000 coal-miners, who average 330 tons each. The value of coal and lignite raised was as follows :—

Year	Coal, £	Lignite, £	Total, £
1876 . . .	13,200,000	1,900,000	15,100,000
1886 . . .	15,000,000	2,000,000	17,000,000
1896 . . .	29,600,000	3,000,000	32,600,000

The production in 1895 was equal to £88 per miner

FRANCE

The product of the collieries was as follows :—

Year	Tons	Value, £	Pence per Ton
1880 . . .	19,400,000	9,860,000	122
1890 . . .	26,100,000	12,460,000	114
1896 . . .	29,200,000	12,600,000	103

France imports 10 million tons, bringing up consumption to 38 millions, or a ton per inhabitant.

RUSSIA

The consumption of coal has been as follows :—

Year	Tons		
	Native	Imported	Total
1876 . . .	2,050,000	1,450,000	3,500,000
1887 . . .	4,450,000	1,550,000	6,000,000
1896 . . .	9,100,000	2,300,000	11,400,000

The output of coal in Russia averages 140 tons yearly per miner.

AUSTRIA

The production and consumption of coal and lignite in 1895 were as follows :—

	Tons			Value, £
	Austria	Hungary	Total	
Coal . . .	9,700,000	1,100,000	10,800,000	3,300,000
Lignite . .	18,300,000	4,000,000	22,300,000	3,800,000
Coal imptd.	5,000,000	...	5,000,000	2,800,000
Total . .	33,000,000	5,100,000	38,100,000	9,900,000
Exported .	7,800,000	...	7,800,000	2,400,000
Consumption	25,200,000	5,100,000	30,300,000	7,500,000

Production and consumption in the Austrian Empire have been as follows :—

Year	Production Tons	Consumption Tons	Cwts. per Inhab.
1880 . . .	16,100,000	14,500,000	7.6
1889 . . .	24,000,000	22,000,000	10.6
1895 . . .	33,100,000	30,300,000	14.1

Austria-Hungary stands sixth among European nations in the consumption of coal per inhabitant.

ITALY

There are 28 coal-mines, employing 2360 miners, who raise 300,000 tons yearly, being an average of 127 tons each. Consumption has been as follows :—

Year	Tons			Cwts. per Inhab.
	Native	Imported	Total	
1875 . . .	120,000	1,060,000	1,180,000	0.9
1885 . . .	190,000	3,000,000	3,190,000	2.2
1895 . . .	300,000	4,300,000	4,600,000	3.0

The consumption per head is lower than in other countries, except Russia.

SPAIN

The coalfields are estimated by Zehden to contain 13,000 millions of tons, which is equal to 65 years' output of the coalfields of Great Britain ; they are, however, little worked, employing only 16,200 miners. Consumption has been as follows :—

	Tons			Cwts. per Inhabitant
	Native	Imported	Total	
1886 . . .	800,000	1,410,000	2,210,000	2.6
1892 . . .	1,460,000	1,870,000	3,330,000	3.6
1896 . . .	1,900,000	1,900,000	3,800,000	4.0

The output of the mines gives an average of 110,000 tons per miner.

SCANDINAVIA

The only coalfield is in Sweden, which gives usually 200,000 tons a year. Consumption in the three kingdoms is as follows :—

	Tons		Cwts. per Inhab.	
	1885	1895	1885	1895
Sweden . . .	1,650,000	2,200,000	7	9
Norway . . .	600,000	1,050,000	6	10
Denmark . . .	850,000	1,150,000	8	11
Total . .	3,100,000	4,400,000	7	10

HOLLAND

There is but one coalfield, which belongs to the State, producing 100,000 tons yearly, worth £30,000 sterling. Consumption depends chiefly on imports, viz. :—

	Tons Imported	Cwts. per Inhabitant
1875	2,150,000	11
1885	3,560,000	16
1896	4,700,000	20

The consumption per inhabitant is almost the same as in France.

BELGIUM

A report published in 1894 showed that in the preceding year the production was 19,400,000 tons, raised at a cost of £7,260,000, and sold for £7,550,000, which left a profit of £290,000, or 3½d. per ton. The weight and value were as follows :—

Year	Tons	Value, £	Pence per Ton
1880 . . .	16,900,000	6,800,000	96
1890 . . .	20,400,000	10,800,000	127
1896 . . .	21,300,000	8,100,000	90

There are 119,000 coal-miners, who averaged 172 tons each in 1895, being a product of £64 per miner.

CANADA

The production has quadrupled in twenty years, viz.:—

Year	Tons		
	Nova Scotia	Brit. Colum. &c.	Total
1876 . . .	710,000	120,000	830,000
1886 . . .	1,490,000	370,000	1,860,000
1896 . . .	2,230,000	1,100,000	3,330,000

Imports and exports were as follows :—

Year	Tons		
	Imported	Exported	Net Import
1876 . . .	710,000	250,000	460,000
1886 . . .	1,720,000	430,000	1,290,000
1896 . . .	2,770,000	910,000	1,860,000

Consumption compared with population gave as follows :—

Year	Tons	Cwts. per Inhab.
1876	1,290,000	6.5
1886	3,150,000	13.5
1896	5,190,000	20.0

The consumption per head is higher than in Australia.

AUSTRALIA

The monopoly was abolished in 1847, and the product from that time to December 1894 was as follows :—

	Tons Raised	Value, £	Pence per Ton
N. S. Wales . .	64,600,000	29,600,000	110
New Zealand .	9,200,000	4,900,000	128
Queensland . .	3,700,000	1,700,000	110
Tasmania . . .	500,000	300,000	144
Victoria, &c. .	400,000	200,000	120
Total . .	78,400,000	36,700,000	113

Production in 1888 and 1896 compares as follows :—

	Tons		Value, £	
	1888	1896	1888	1896
N. S. Wales . .	3,200,000	3,910,000	1,460,000	1,120,000
New Zealand .	610,000	800,000	340,000	430,000
Queensland,&c.	360,000	490,000	140,000	230,000
Total . .	4,170,000	5,200,000	1,940,000	1,780,000

Australia exports one million tons yearly ; consumption does not reach a ton per inhabitant.

COFFEE

Production has been as follows :—

	Tons		
	Brazil	Other Countries	Total
1880 . . .	330,000	280,000	610,000
1892 . . .	440,000	260,000	700,000
1897 . . .	590,000	250,000	840,000

Consumption has been as follows, "native" signifying what is used in the countries where coffee is grown :—

	Tons			
	Europe	U. States	Native	Total
1893 . . .	270,000	250,000	180,000	700,000
1897 . . .	310,000	320,000	210,000	840,000

Consumption in Europe is as follows :—

	Tons	Lbs. per Inhab.
United Kingdom .	12,000	0.7
France	77,000	4.5
Germany	136,000	5.8
Belgium	25,000	8.8
Austria	40,000	2.0
Italy	13,000	0.9

In the United States the average is 10 lbs. per inhabitant, a ratio which is surpassed only in Brazil. The consumption in Great Britain is now 25 per cent. less per head than it was in 1885.

COLONIES

Pebrer's estimate of the British Colonies in 1830 was as follows :—

	Population	Products, £	Commerce, £	Wealth, £
Canada .	910,000	17,600,000	3,200,000	62,000,000
W. Indies .	730,000	22,500,000	14,600,000	131,000,000
S. Africa .	154,000	1,100,000	1,400,000	6,000,000
Australia .	81,000	500,000	200,000	3,000,000
Total .	1,875,000	41,700,000	19,400,000	202,000,000

The same Colonies in 1896 showed as follows :—

	Population	Millions £ Sterling		
		Products, £	Commerce, £	Wealth, £
Canada . .	5,200,000	181	48	1,009
W. Indies .	1,470,000	21	14	110
S. Africa .	2,350,000	17	29	150
Australia .	4,280,000	174	76	1,076
Total .	13,300,000	393	167	2,339

It would appear that Pebrer's estimate of the wealth of the West Indies in 1830 was too high.
See *Colonies* of all nations, p. 123.

COMMERCE

The actual trade of the world compares with Juraschek's table of averages for five years ending 1890 thus:—

| | Millions £ Sterling | | | | | |
	Imports		Exports		Total	
	1886-90	1896	1886-90	1896	1886-90	1896
U. Kingdom .	398	442	241	240	639	682
France . . .	171	152	139	136	310	288
Germany . .	174	228	158	188	332	416
Russia . . .	40	59	62	69	102	128
Austria . . .	48	59	62	65	110	124
Italy	57	47	39	42	96	89
Spain	33	36	31	41	64	77
Portugal . . .	9	9	5	6	14	15
Scandinavia .	43	54	31	43	74	97
Holland . . .	101	136	88	112	189	248
Belgium . . .	61	71	53	59	114	130
Switzerland . .	34	42	28	30	62	72
Danub. States .	18	18	15	19	33	37
Greece . . .	5	5	4	3	9	8
Turkey . . .	18	15	12	17	30	32
Europe . . .	1,210	1,373	968	1,070	2,178	2,443
United States .	155	162	157	180	312	342
Canada . . .	25	22	20	25	45	47
Mexico . . .	7	8	8	11	15	19
Cent. America .	3	3	5	5	8	8
West Indies .	20	20	30	28	50	48
South America.	58	65	57	74	115	139
America . . .	268	280	277	323	545	603
India	52	48	70	65	122	113
Singapore . .	19	28	16	25	35	53
Ceylon . . .	4	6	3	6	7	12
Tonquin . . .	3	3	3	3	6	6
Siam	2	2	3	3	5	5
Java	11	13	16	19	27	32
Japan	9	19	10	13	19	32
China	28	34	22	22	50	56
Siberia . . .	4	6	5	9	9	15
Philippines . .	4	2	5	4	9	6
Persia . . .	2	3	2	3	4	6
Other states. .	10	10	8	8	18	18
Asia	148	174	163	180	311	354
Egypt . . .	8	10	12	13	20	23
Algeria & Tunis	11	13	10	11	21	24
Cape Colony .	7	17	8	17	15	34
Transvaal . .	5	14	2	9	7	23
Mauritius . .	2	2	2	2	4	4
Morocco . . .	2	2	1	2	3	4
East Africa . .	4	4	2	2	6	6
Senegal, &c. .	5	5	4	4	9	9
Africa . . .	44	67	41	60	85	127
Australia . . .	63	63	50	66	113	129
Hawaii . . .	1	1	2	3	3	4
Oceania . . .	64	64	52	69	116	133
The World . .	1,734	1,958	1,501	1,702	3,235	3,660

It will be observed that, notwithstanding the fall of prices since 1886, the trade of the world in 1896 showed an increase of value amounting to 13 per cent., or 425 millions sterling over the average given by Juraschek for five years ending 1890, viz. :—

| | Millions £ | | | Per Cent. |
	1886-90	1896	Increase	
Europe. . .	2,178	2,443	265	12.2
America . .	545	603	58	10.7
Asia . .	311	354	43	13.8
Africa . . .	85	127	42	49.0
Australia . .	116	133	17	14.7
The World .	3,235	3,660	425	13.0

Levasseur's table of European commerce shows :—

| | Millions £ Sterling | | |
	1830	1850	1894
United Kingdom . .	88	168	682
France	36	76	277
Germany . . .	32	104	346
Austria	16	28	124
Russia	20	32	124
Italy	12	24	85
Spain and Portugal .	12	16	73
Scandinavia . . .	8	20	89
Holland	16	48	214
Belgium . . .	12	36	115
Other states . . .	8	30	111
Europe . . .	260	582	2,240

Commerce increased 124 per cent. between 1830 and 1850, that is about 6 per cent. yearly ; and 286 per cent. between 1850 and 1894, or about 6½ per cent. yearly, say six times as fast as population. In the foregoing table the trade of the United Kingdom appears larger than it is, as it includes foreign and colonial merchandise imported to be forwarded to other countries (tea, wool, &c.). Juraschek gives the following table of imports and exports of all nations :—

| Year | Millions £ Sterling, Yearly | | | Excess of Imports |
	Imports	Exports	Total	
1875 80 . . .	1,547	1,356	2,903	14 p. c.
1881-85 . . .	1,732	1,510	3,242	15 ,,
1886-90 . . .	1,737	1,507	3,244	15 ,,
1891-94 . . .	1,876	1,619	3,495	16 ,,

UNITED KINGDOM

In the following table imports include not only merchandise for consumption but also goods that are afterwards exported as foreign (and colonial) produce. The gross trade exceeds the real trade by double the amount of such foreign produce. Thus the gross trade of 1888 would be 128 millions over the net figure, which would be 558 millions. The returns for 10 years stand thus :—

| Year | Millions £ | | | |
	Imports	British Exports	Foreign Exports	Total
1888 . . .	388	234	64	686
1889 . . .	428	249	67	744
1890 . . .	421	263	65	749
1891 . . .	435	247	62	744
1892 . . .	424	227	64	715
1893 . . .	405	218	59	682
1894 . . .	408	216	58	682
1895 . . .	417	226	60	703
1896 . . .	442	240	56	738
1897 . . .	451	234	60	745
Average . .	422	235	62	719

The principal items of imports were as follows :—

	Millions £		Shillings per Head	
	1888	1897	1888	1897
Food . . .	157	172	86	86
Fibres . . .	81	88	44	44
Manufactures . .	64	70	35	35
Metals . . .	22	18	12	9
Sundries . . .	64	103	35	52
Total . .	388	451	212	226

Exports

	1888	1897	1888	1897
Textiles . . .	109	100	58	50
Hardware . .	50	64	27	32
Sundries . . .	139	130	75	65
Total . .	298	294	160	147

The countries from which we received our imports were :—

	Millions £		Ratio	
	1887	1897	1887	1897
United States . .	83	113	23.0	25.0
France . . .	37	53	10.2	11.8
India . . .	31	25	8.5	5.6
Holland . . .	25	29	6.9	6.4
Germany . . .	25	26	6.9	5.8
Australia . . .	23	29	6.4	6.4
Russia . . .	16	22	4.4	4.9
Belgium . . .	15	21	4.1	4.7
Canada . . .	11	20	3.1	4.4
Various . . .	96	113	26.5	25.0
Total . .	362	451	100.0	100.0

The trade of the United Kingdom in 1897 showed an increase of 5 per cent. over the average of ten years ending 1896, and of 16 per cent. over 1887, as to value. The principal increase has been in imports, which rose 25 per cent. in ten years, while exports rose only 4 per cent. Taking imports and exports together our trade with other countries has increased since 1887 in the following ratios :—with Scandinavia 63 per cent., Russia 48 per cent., Canada 30 per cent., Egypt 27 per cent., France 26 per cent., United States 23 per cent., Argentina 22 per cent., Spain 21 per cent., Belgium 21 per cent., Australia 15 per cent., Germany 12 per cent., Holland 5 per cent.

The countries to which we sent our exports were :—

	Millions £		Ratio	
	1887	1897	1887	1897
United States . .	40	38	14.2	12.9
India . . .	32	28	11.4	9.5
Germany . . .	27	32	9.6	11.0
Australia . . .	22	24	7.8	8.2
France . . .	21	20	7.5	6.8
Holland . . .	15	13	5.4	4.4
Belgium . . .	13	13	4.6	4.4
Italy. . . .	9	6	3.2	2.0
Canada . . .	9	6	3.2	2.0
Various . . .	93	114	33.1	38.8
Total . .	281	294	100.0	100.0

Comparing 1897 with 1887, the nations with which trade is carried on show :—

	Millions £ Sterling		
	1887	1897	Increase
United States . . .	123	151	28
France	58	73	15
Germany . . .	52	58	6
India	63	53	...
Australia . . .	46	53	7
Holland	40	42	2
Russia	23	34	11
Belgium	28	34	6
Canada	20	26	6
Sweden and Norway .	15	22	7
Spain	14	17	3
Argentina . . .	9	11	2
Egypt	11	14	3
Denmark . . .	7	14	7
China	13	8	...
Various . . .	121	135	14
Total . .	643	745	102

FRANCE

Imports and exports of French trade for 1897 compare with 1886 thus :—

	Imports, £			Exports, £	
	1886	1897		1886	1897
Wool	15,400,000	13,800,000	Woollens . . .	15,000,000	10,600,000
Wine	20,700,000	11,200,000	Silks	9,700,000	10,800,000
Grain	6,400,000	9,900,000	Cottons . . .	4,300,000	4,800,000
Silk	11,700,000	10,600,000	Wine	10,400,000	9,200,000
Cotton	6,400,000	8,200,000	Leather goods . .	9,200,000	2,800,000
Timber	5,700,000	7,100,000	Dairy produce . .	4,700,000	3,400,000
Hides	7,000,000	5,700,000	Hardware . . .	3,600,000	3,200,000
Oil seed . . .	6,600,000	5,400,000	Skins	2,400,000	7,200,000
Coal	5,000,000	7,600,000	Spirits . . .	3,000,000	2,100,000
Textiles . . .	6,800,000	5,100,000	Sugar	2,100,000	5,400,000
Coffee	4,100,000	4,200,000	Chemicals . . .	1,900,000	3,000,000
Sundries . . .	72,500,000	69,400,000	Sundries . . .	63,700,000	81,400,000
Total . .	168,300,000	158,200,000	Total . .	130,000,000	143,900,000

The countries trading with France are shown in the following table :—

	Millions £ Sterling					
	1886			1897		
	Imports from*	Exports to	Total	Imports from	Exports to	Total
Great Britain .	21.0	34.2	55.2	19.4	45.4	64.8
Belgium . . .	16.8	17.9	34.7	11.5	20.5	32.0
Spain . . .	15.9	6.9	22.8	9.9	4.0	13.9
United States .	11.7	11.3	23.0	17.5	9.7	27.2
Germany . .	13.4	11.9	25.3	12.4	15.2	27.6
Switzerland .	4.3	8.4	12.7	3.2	7.6	10.8
Italy	12.4	7.7	20.1	5.2	6.1	11.3
India	7.7	0.3	8.0	5.6	0.6	6.2
Argentina . .	9.1	4.4	13.5	8.4	2.0	10.4
Algeria . . .	5.2	8.3	13.5	10.6	9.6	20.2
Russia . . .	6.8	0.4	7.2	9.4	1.0	10.4
Various . . .	44.0	18.3	62.3	45.1	22.2	67.3
Total . .	168.3	130.0	298.3	158.2	143.9	302.1

* *Note.*—This table reads thus : Imports from Great Britain 21.0, that is, £21,000,000.

While the trade of the world is rapidly increasing that of France is stationary, having risen only 1 per cent. in 11 years, as shown in the above table. Imports have declined 10 millions; while exports have risen 14 millions in the said interval.

The following table compares French trade in 1897 with the average for 5 years ending December 1892 :—

Trade with	Millions £ Sterling		Ratio	
	1888–92	1897	1888–92	1897
Great Britain . . .	62	65	19.6	21.5
Belgium	39	32	12.3	10.6
Germany	28	28	8.7	9.2
United States . . .	26	27	8.2	9.0
Spain	21	14	6.6	4.6
Other countries . .	140	136	44.6	45.1
Total . .	316	302	100.0	100.0

There is a visible increase of ratio in dealings with Great Britain and Germany, while trade with Belgium and Spain is declining.

GERMANY

Trade has increased very notably in recent years, viz. :—

Year	Value, Millions £			Weight, Tons, Millions		
	Imports	Exports	Total	Imports	Exports	Total
1887	159	160	319	19.4	19.5	38.9
1891	220	167	387	29.0	20.1	49.1
1897	232	183	415	40.2	28.0	68.2

The principal items of German trade (exclusive of Hamburg) for 1886 and 1897 were as follows :—

	Imports, £			Exports, £	
	1886	1897		1886	1897
Grain	10,300,000	21,100,000	Hardware . . .	10,500,000	23,000,000
Wool	10,900,000	10,700,000	Cottons . . .	5,900,000	8,900,000
Cotton	8,800,000	9,700,000	Sugar	7,100,000	11,600,000
Coffee	6,900,000	6,400,000	Woollens . . .	10,900,000	10,500,000
Cattle	8,200,000	6,100,000	Coal	4,400,000	8,700,000
Yarns	8,100,000	6,400,000	Leather goods .	7,600,000	8,100,000
Timber	3,700,000	10,200,000	Silks	9,000,000	5,800,000
Hides	4,600,000	7,400,000	Clothing . . .	4,800,000	4,900,000
Silk	7,500,000	4,800,000	Paper	2,500,000	4,800,000
Tobacco . . .	3,200,000	3,900,000	Cattle	5,000,000	1,100,000
Sundries . . .	72,200,000	145,500,000	Sundries . . .	81,600,000	95,700,000
Total .	144,400,000	232,200,000	Total . .	149,300,000	183,100,000

The countries with which Germany traded were :—

	Millions £ Sterling					
	1886			1896		
	Imports from	Exports to	Total	Imports from	Exports to	Total
Great Britain .	22.6	22.1	44.7	27.6	35.6	63.2
Austria . . .	20.2	14.3	34.5	27.3	20.0	47.3
United States .	5.3	10.6	15.9	26.4	19.2	45.6
Russia . . .	13.2	6.9	20.1	31.4	11.6	43.0
France . . .	11.1	12.5	23.6	11.5	10.1	21.6
Holland . . .	10.6	11.5	22.1	8.0	13.1	21.1
British colonies	1.6	1.1	2.7	15.6	6.6	22.2
Switzerland . .	7.8	7.6	15.4	7.0	11.9	18.9
Belgium . . .	13.9	7.7	21.6	8.7	8.4	17.1
Italy	4.5	4.2	8.7	6.6	4.2	10.8
Other countries	33.6	50.8	84.4	45.3	35.6	80.9
Total . .	144.4	149.3	293.7	215.4	176.3	391.7

The following table compares German trade in 1896 with the average of five years ending December 1892 :—

Trade with	Millions £ Stg.		Ratio	
	1888–92	1896	1888–92	1896
Great Britain . .	60	63	16.9	16.0
Austria . . .	43	47	12.1	12.0
United States . .	36	46	10.0	11.7
Russia . . .	32	43	8.9	11.0
Holland . . .	26	21	7.3	5.4
France . . .	23	22	6.6	5.6
Belgium . . .	22	17	6.3	4.3
Other countries .	114	133	31.9	34.0
Total . .	356	392	100.0	100.0

Trade relations with Belgium, France, and Holland have declined remarkably, while they have increased with Russia and United States.

In 10 years trade has increased 30 per cent. in value, and 75 per cent. in weight.

RUSSIA

Returns of imports and exports of Russia, including Poland, for 1886 and 1896 compare thus :—

	Imports, £			Exports, £	
	1886	1896		1886	1896
Cotton	7,300,000	7,600,000	Grain	23,300,000	32,200,000
Tea	6,500,000	4,200,000	Flax	5,400,000	7,900,000
Hardware . . .	4,100,000	8,300,000	Timber . . .	2,400,000	4,700,000
Yarns	3,300,000	2,100,000	Wool	2,200,000	800,000
Metals	2,500,000	4,800,000	Seeds	1,900,000	4,200,000
Chemicals . . .	1,300,000	1,400,000	Sugar	1,300,000	2,900,000
Coal	1,300,000	1,700,000	Petroleum . . .	1,300,000	2,900,000
Textiles . . .	1,100,000	1,400,000	Eggs	500,000	2,200,000
Sundries . . .	16,400,000	27,500,000	Sundries . . .	10,100,000	11,200,000
Total .	43,800,000	59,000,000	Total . .	48,400,000	69,000,000

The countries with which Russia traded in 1886 and 1896 were :—

	Millions £ Sterling					
	1886			1896		
	Imports from	Exports to	Total	Imports from	Exports to	Total
Great Britain .	11.0	14.4	25.4	11.2	16.1	27.3
Germany . .	13.5	11.9	25.4	19.0	18.6	37.6
France . . .	1.2	3.0	4.2	2.3	5.8	8.1
Austria . . .	1.7	2.5	4.2	2.3	3.0	5.3
Holland . . .	0.4	3.7	4.1	0.6	7.1	7.7
United States .	2.7	0.0	2.7	6.6	0.2	6.8
China	3.0	0.2	3.2	4.2	0.5	4.7
Italy	0.8	2.2	3.0	1.0	3.6	4.6
Other countries	9.5	10.5	20.0	11.8	14.1	25.9
Total . .	43.8	48.4	92.2	59.0	69.0	128.0

The trade of 1896 compares with that of five years ending 1892 as follows :—

Trade with	Millions £ Stg.		Ratio	
	1888–92	1896	1888–92	1896
Great Britain . .	29	27	30.2	21.3
Germany . . .	29	38	30.2	29.5
France . . .	6	8	6.2	6.4
Other countries .	32	55	33.4	42.8
Total . .	96	128	100.0	100.0

There has been a relative diminution of trade with Germany and Great Britain, which is accounted for by the rapid increase of dealings with China, Austria, and Italy. In the interval between 1886 and 1896 we find an increase of 34 per cent. in imports and 42 per cent. in exports. The shipments of eggs, petroleum, and sugar have increased prodigiously.

AUSTRIA-HUNGARY

Imports and exports of the whole empire for 1886 and 1897 compare thus :—

	Imports, £			Exports, £	
	1886	1897		1886	1897
Cotton	3,800,000	4,200,000	Sugar	4,000,000	5,100,000
Wool	2,600,000	3,200,000	Cattle	3,900,000	3,800,000
Yarns	2,400,000	2,500,000	Timber . . .	4,500,000	7,000,000
Textiles . . .	2,700,000	2,200,000	Grain	3,500,000	3,500,000
Coffee	2,600,000	2,200,000	Eggs	900,000	3,700,000
Coal	1,100,000	3,100,000	Leather goods . .	1,800,000	2,200,000
Hardware . . .	900,000	2,600,000	Coal	1,400,000	2,900,000
Tobacco . . .	2,700,000	2,200,000	Glass	1,600,000	1,900,000
Hides	1,900,000	1,900,000	Malt	1,200,000	2,000,000
Flax	1,500,000	800,000	Wool	2,000,000	900,000
Sundries . . .	22,800,000	38,100,000	Sundries . . .	33,400,000	31,000,000
Total . .	45,000,000	63,000,000	Total . .	58,200,000	64,000,000

Austria including Hungary has usually 500,000 tons of grain for exportation, but in 1897, on the contrary, she had to import 100,000 tons. Her exports of sugar and eggs have increased remarkably in ten years, viz. :—

	Sugar, Tons	Eggs, Millions
1887	220,000	880
1897	480,000	1,510

Trade with	Millions £ Stg.		Ratio	
	1891–94	1896	1891–94	1896
Germany . . .	55	55	46.3	44.8
Great Britain . .	10	12	8.4	9.7
Italy . . .	8	9	6.7	7.3
Other countries .	46	47	38.6	38.2
Total . .	119	123	100.0	100.0

The trade of 1896 compares with the average for 4 years ending 1894 thus :—

Trade with Germany is stationary, while it increases with Great Britain and Italy.

The countries trading with Austria were as follows :—

| | Millions £ Sterling | | | | | |
| | 1886 | | | 1896 | | |
	Imports from*	Exports to	Total	Imports from	Exports to	Total
Germany . .	15.7	19.2	34.9	21.5	33.5	55.0
Great Britain .	1.5	1.5	3.0	6.1	6.1	12.2
Italy	4.1	8.5	12.6	3.9	5.0	8.9
Russia . . .	2.8	1.6	4.4	3.7	2.3	6.0
United States .	4.4	1.3	5.7	3.5	1.4	4.9
Switzerland .	1.6	3.5	5.1	1.8	2.9	4.7
France . . .	0.6	4.1	4.7	2.1	2.5	4.6
India	2.2	0.6	2.8	3.6	0.6	4.2
Other countries	12.1	17.9	30.0	12.6	10.2	22.8
Total . .	45.0	58.2	103.2	58.8	64.5	123.3

The trade of the Austro-Hungarian monarchy shows an increase of 30 per cent. in imports, and 11 per cent. in exports between 1886 and 1896. There has been a great development of manufacturing industry, the value of imported coal having risen 135 per cent., and that of raw material (fibre) imported 25 per cent. At the same time certain exports show enormous increase, viz., eggs 260 per cent., sugar 60 per cent., leather goods 50 per cent.

ITALY

Imports and exports have been as follows :—

| Year | Millions £ Sterling | | | £ per Inhab. |
	Imports	Exports	Total	
1885 . . .	58.4	38.0	96.4	3.3
1890 . . .	52.8	35.8	88.6	2.9
1897 . . .	48.1	44.6	92.7	2.9

The principal items of the trade of Italy for 1886 and 1896 compare as follows :—

| | Imports, £ | | | | Exports, £ | |
	1886	1896			1886	1896
Cotton	3,000,000	4,500,000	Silk		12,600,000	11,500,000
Grain	7,600,000	4,400,000	Wine		3,500,000	2,100,000
Coal	2,700,000	3,600,000	Oil		3,200,000	2,200,000
Silk	2,600,000	2,100,000	Fruit		1,500,000	2,100,000
Hardware . . .	1,700,000	1,900,000	Flax		1,000,000	1,500,000
Timber . . .	2,400,000	1,300,000	Eggs		1,200,000	1,200,000
Wool	1,300,000	1,300,000	Coral		900,000	1,100,000
Hides	1,400,000	1,500,000	Sulphur . . .		1,000,000	1,100,000
Fish	1,300,000	1,200,000	Meat		1,200,000	1,200,000
Coffee	700,000	1,100,000	Ores		200,000	400,000
Sundries . . .	33,600,000	24,000,000	Sundries . . .		14,800,000	17,700,000
Total . .	58,300,000	46,900,000	Total . .		41,100,000	42,100,000

As regards imports, there has been on the whole a fall of 20 per cent. Nevertheless some items show a remarkable increase, for example, raw cotton 50 per cent., and coal 33 per cent., from which it is evident that textile and other manufactures have been developed considerably in the last ten years. As for exports, if we except wine and oil, the quantities show a marked increase, but this is somewhat counteracted as regards value by the fall in prices. Trade on the whole shows an upward tendency.

The quantities of principal exports were as follows :—

| Year | Gallons | | Millions Eggs | Tons Fruit |
	Wine	Oil		
1887 . . .	80,000,000	14,000,000	388	240,000
1897 . . .	52,000,000	12,000,000	592	290,000

The decline in wine and oil has been very serious.
The trade of 1896 compares with the average of 5 years ending 1892 thus :—

| Trade with | Millions £ Stg. | | Ratio | |
	1888–92	1896	1888–92	1896
Great Britain . .	16	14	17.6	16.2
France . . .	16	12	17.6	13.5
Germany . . .	11	12	12.0	13.5
Other countries .	48	51	52.8	56.8
Total . .	91	89	100.0	100.0

The countries trading with Italy in 1886 and 1896 were :—

| | Millions £ | | | | | |
| | 1886 | | | 1896 | | |
	Imports from	Exports to	Total	Imports from	Exports to	Total
Great Britain .	11.0	2.8	13.8	9.2	4.4	13.6
Germany . .	5.2	4.3	9.5	5.8	6.6	12.4
France . . .	12.4	17.8	30.2	5.5	6.3	11.8
Austria . . .	8.9	3.7	12.6	5.4	5.0	10.4
Switzerland .	3.2	3.5	6.7	1.8	6.9	8.7
United States .	2.2	2.1	4.3	4.8	3.4	8.2
Russia . . .	3.8	0.7	4.5	4.7	0.5	5.2
Other countries	11.6	6.2	17.8	9.7	9.0	18.7
Total . .	58.3	41.1	99.4	46.9	42.1	89.0

Trade with Germany is increasing, and with France is declining.

* To be read thus : Imports £15,700,000.

SPAIN

The foreign trade has risen 70 per cent. in 20 years, viz. :—

Year	Millions £ Sterling			£ per Inhab.
	Imports	Exports	Total	
1877 . . .	19.6	20.5	40.1	2.4
1887 . . .	32.4	28.9	61.3	3.5
1897 . . .	31.7	37.0	68.7	3.9

The trade of 1896 compares with the average for 5 years, down to 1892, thus :—

Trade with	Millions £ Stg.		Ratio	
	1888–92	1896	1888–92	1896
France . . .	21	20	36.8	26.0
Great Britain . .	11	15	19.4	19.5
Cuba . . .	4	14	7.0	18.2
Other countries .	21	28	36.8	36.3
Total . .	57	77	100.0	100.0

The principal imports and exports of Spain in 1886 and 1896 were as follows :—

	Imports, £				Exports, £	
	1886	1896			1886	1896
Cotton	2,400,000	2,800,000	Wine		13,400,000	5,800,000
Hardware . . .	2,300,000	2,600,000	Fruit		2,100,000	3,200,000
Coal	1,000,000	2,000,000	Minerals . . .		2,500,000	4,100,000
Timber . . .	1,500,000	1,500,000	Metals . . .		2,200,000	3,100,000
Tobacco . . .	1,700,000	1,300,000	Cottons . . .		500,000	2,100,000
Textiles . . .	2,200,000	1,100,000	Cattle . . .		900,000	1,100,000
Grain . . .	1,200,000	1,400,000	Cork . . .		700,000	1,300,000
Fish	1,100,000	1,000,000	Oil		600,000	1,000,000
Hides	1,000,000	900,000	Wool		600,000	700,000
Sugar	1,300,000	700,000	Quicksilver . . .		100,000	300,000
Sundries . . .	16,000,000	21,100,000	Sundries . . .		5,400,000	18,200,000
Total . .	31,700,000	36,400,000	Total . .		29,000,000	40,900,000

Spanish trade in the above interval of ten years showed a rise of 15 per cent. in imports, and 40 per cent. in exports. Wine has, indeed, fallen nearly 60 per cent., but minerals, metals, fruit, cotton manufactures, &c., have increased very remarkably.

The countries with which Spain traded were as follows :—

	Millions £ Sterling					
	1886			1896		
	Imports from*	Exports to	Total	Imports from	Exports to	Total
France . . .	9.8	13.5	23.3	8.7	11.3	20.0
Great Britain .	4.5	6.2	10.7	6.2	9.0	15.2
Cuba	1.6	2.8	4.4	3.3	10.2	13.5
United States .	3.8	0.8	4.6	2.9	0.4	3.3
Portugal . .	0.3	1.3	1.6	1.6	1.7	3.3
Other countries	11.7	4.4	16.1	13.7	8.3	22.0
Total . .	31.7	29.0	60.7	36.4	40.9	77.3

PORTUGAL

The countries trading with Portugal in 1886 and 1896 were :—

	1886		1896	
	Imports, £	Exports, £	Imports, £	Exports, £
Gt. Britain .	2,700,000	1,500,000	2,700,000	1,600,000
France . .	1,100,000	2,100,000	900,000	150,000
Brazil . .	400,000	1,000,000	400,000	1,450,000
Various . .	4,200,000	1,300,000	4,900,000	2,700,000
Total . .	8,400,000	5,900,000	8,900,000	5,900,000

Trade with France has declined very much, while it has increased with Brazil.

Trade returns for the kingdom of Portugal in 1886 and 1896 compare as follows :—

	Imports, £				Exports, £	
	1886	1896			1886	1896
Grain	990,000	890,000	Wine		3,800,000	2,500,000
Textiles . . .	1,320,000	980,000	Cork . . .		550,000	800,000
Cotton . . .	290,000	250,000	Cattle . . .		180,000	550,000
Sugar . . .	380,000	440,000	Copper . . .		160,000	250,000
Fish	400,000	510,000	Sardines . . .		220,000	220,000
Sundries . . .	5,020,000	5,830,000	Sundries . . .		990,000	1,580,000
Total . .	8,400,000	8,900,000	Total . .		5,900,000	5,900,000

* To be read thus : Imports from France £9,800,000.

SWEDEN

In the decade ending December 1896 imports rose 20 per cent., exports 50 per cent., viz. :—

	Imports, £			Exports, £	
	1886	1896		1886	1896
Coal	900,000	1,800,000	Timber . . .	4,200,000	7,300,000
Textiles . . .	1,900,000	1,500,000	Iron	1,900,000	2,800,000
Coffee	1,000,000	1,500,000	Butter . . .	1,100,000	2,500,000
Hardware . . .	1,200,000	1,800,000	Fish	200,000	400,000
Grain	1,600,000	1,300,000	Matches . . .	600,000	300,000
Sundries . . .	9,800,000	12,000,000	Sundries . . .	4,700,000	5,600,000
Total . .	16,400,000	19,900,000	Total . .	12,700,000	18,900,000

The countries trading with Sweden were :—

	Millions £					
	1886			1896		
	Imports from*	Exports to	Total	Imports from	Exports to	Total
Great Britain .	4.3	6.1	10.4	5.5	8.0	13.5
Germany . .	5.1	1.1	6.2	6.5	2.4	8.9
Denmark . .	2.4	1.4	3.8	2.5	2.3	4.8
Various . . .	4.6	4.1	8.7	5.4	6.2	11.6
Total . .	16.4	12 7	29.1	19.9	18.9	38.8

The principal Swedish exports which have risen (in value) are : timber 75 per cent., iron 48 per cent., butter 130 per cent., fish 100 per cent., over 1886. We see, moreover, that trade with Great Britain has risen 30 per cent.

NORWAY

It is probably in a great measure due to her merchant fleet that the trade of Norway has grown so much in ten years, viz. :—

Year	Imports, £	Exports, £	Total, £
1886	7,500,000	5,700,000	13,200,000
1896	13,300,000	8,200,000	21,500,000

The countries trading with Norway were :—

	Imports from, £		Exports to, £	
	1886	1896	1886	1896
G. Britain .	1,900,000	3,500,000	1,900,000	3,100,000
Germany .	2,100,000	3,500,000	700,000	1,000,000
Sweden . .	900,000	2,100,000	800,000	1,300,000
Various . .	2,600,000	4,200,000	2,300,000	2,800,000
Total .	7,500,000	13,300,000	5,700,000	8,200,000

The principal items of Norwegian trade in 1886 and 1896 were :—

	Imports, £			Exports, £	
	1886	1896		1886	1896
Grain	1,400,000	2,000,000	Fish	1,700,000	1,900,000
Textiles . . .	800,000	1,400,000	Timber . . .	1,600,000	1,900,000
Sundries . . .	5,300,000	9,900,000	Sundries . . .	2,400,000	4,400,000
Total . .	7,500,000	13,300,000	Total . .	5,700,000	8,200,000

DENMARK

The principal imports and exports of the trade of Denmark in 1886 and 1896 were :—

	Imports, £			Exports, £	
	1886	1896		1886	1896
Hardware . . .	1,000,000	2,400,000	Butter . . .	1,800,000	5,200,000
Grain	1,000,000	1,900,000	Meat	600,000	2,500,000
Textiles . . .	1,600,000	1,800,000	Cattle . . .	2,200,000	1,300,000
Coal	800,000	1,200,000	Eggs	200,000	600,000
Sundries . . .	7,400,000	14,000,000	Sundries . . .	4,300,000	6,200,000
Total . .	11,800,000	21,300,000	Total . .	9,100,000	15,800,000

* This table to read thus : Imports from Great Britain £4,300,000.

Trade has increased 80 per cent. in ten years, viz. :—

Year	Imports, £	Exports, £	Total, £
1886 . . .	11,800,000	9,100,000	20,900,000
1896 . . .	21,300,000	15,800,000	37,100,000

The principal trade is with Great Britain and Germany, viz. :—

	Imports from, Millions £		Exports to, Millions £		Total	
	1886	1896	1886	1896	1886	1896
Great Britain .	2.7	4.3	3.8	9.5	6.5	13.8
Germany . .	4.2	7.0	2.8	3.2	7.0	10.2
Sweden . . .	1.7	3.1	1.2	1.7	2.9	4.8
Various . . .	3.2	6.9	1.3	1.4	4.5	8.3
Total . .	11.8	21.3	9.1	15.8	20.9	37.1

Trade with Great Britain has more than doubled, while that with Germany has risen only 45 per cent. Thus in

1886 Germany stood ahead of Great Britain in the trade of Denmark, whereas now Great Britain is 36 per cent. ahead of Germany.

HOLLAND

Exclusive of trade in transit the commerce of Holland has advanced by leaps and bounds, viz. :—

	Imports, £	Exports, £	Total, £
1876 . . .	58,000,000	44,100,000	102,100,000
1886 . . .	91,900,000	79,100,000	171,000,000
1896 . . .	136,300,000	111,700,000	248,000,000

As Holland is the only free-trade country of Continental Europe, the growth of its trade offers an important lesson. In twenty years the imports have risen 135 per cent., exports 154 per cent. The increased importation of coal and metals, as well as of timber, points to a development of home manufactures, while the increase of exports shows a great activity in the colonial trade and in Dutch products generally.

The principal items of Dutch imports and exports in 1886 and 1896 were :—

	Imports, £			Exports, £	
	1886	1896		1886	1896
Grain	12,400,000	26,500,000	Drugs	9,800,000	16,300,000
Hardware . . .	8,800,000	8,100,000	Butter . . .	4,700,000	4,600,000
Metals	7,100,000	12,800,000	Sugar . . .	2,500,000	2,500,000
Cotton	3,800,000	3,900,000	Textiles . . .	2,400,000	3,400,000
Rice	3,000,000	3,300,000	Paper . . .	900,000	2,300,000
Coal	3,000,000	3,900,000	Fish . . .	1,000,000	1,200,000
Coffee	3,100,000	3,500,000	Hides . . .	1,000,000	1,300,000
Timber	1,400,000	3,000,000	Cheese . . .	900,000	1,000,000
Sundries . . .	49,300,000	71,300,000	Sundries . . .	55,900,000	79,100,000
Total . .	91,900,000	136,300,000	Total . .	79,100,000	111,700,000

The countries trading with Holland were as follow :—

	Imports from, Millions £		Exports to, Millions £		Total	
	1886	1896	1886	1896	1886	1896
Germany . .	26.3	25.0	34.5	58.3	60.8	83.3
Great Britain .	21.8	21.3	21.3	24.2	43.1	45.5
Belgium . . .	13.2	14.5	11.5	13.7	24.7	28.2
Java	7.5	20.0	3.8	4.4	11.3	24.4
Various . . .	20.6	55.5	7.9	11.1	28.5	66.6
Total . .	89.4	136.3	79.0	111.7	168.4	248.0

The following table compares Dutch trade in 1896 with the average for five years ending December 1892 :—

Trade with	Millions £		Ratio	
	1888-92	1896	1888 92	1896
Germany . . .	66	83	33.0	33.5
Great Britain . .	49	46	24.5	18.5
Belgium . . .	27	28	13.5	11.3
Java . . .	19	24	9.5	9.7
Various . . .	39	67	19.5	27.0
Total . .	200	248	100.0	100.0

There is a decline in trade with Great Britain.

BELGIUM

Reviewing the trade of the last two decades we find it was stationary in the first, but has greatly expanded in the second, viz. :—

	Imports, £	Exports, £	Total, £
1876 . . .	57,900,000	42,600,000	100,500,000
1886 . . .	53,400,000	47,300,000	100,700,000
1896 . . .	71,100,000	58,700,000	129,800,000

The countries trading with Belgium were as follow :—

	Millions £ Sterling					
	1886			1896		
	Imports from	Exports to	Total	Imports from	Exports to	Total
France . . .	10.1	13.2	23.3	12.4	11.5	23.9
Germany . .	6.1	7.8	13.9	8.6	13.1	21.7
Great Britain .	6.9	9.4	16.3	8.2	11.7	19.9
Holland . .	8.0	7.0	15.0	7.1	6.9	14.0
United States .	6.4	1.6	8.0	6.9	2.0	8.9
Various . . .	15.9	8.3	24.2	27.9	13.5	41.4
Total . .	53.4	47.3	100.7	71.1	58.7	129.8

The above is exclusive of transit trade, which exceeds 50 millions sterling. The chief items of imports and exports were :—

	Imports, £				Exports, £	
	1886	1896			1886	1896
Grain	8,200,000	11,600,000	Yarn		5,200,000	4,100,000
Fibre	6,400,000	6,600,000	Coal		2,800,000	3,500,000
Minerals	2,800,000	5,700,000	Hardware		2,500,000	5,200,000
Chemicals	2,700,000	4,400,000	Textiles		2,600,000	3,200,000
Timber	1,700,000	3,600,000	Glass		2,000,000	3,100,000
Cattle	2,900,000	2,200,000	Machinery		2,000,000	2,600,000
Coffee	1,300,000	2,100,000	Sugar		1,200,000	2,200,000
Sundries	27,400,000	34,900,000	Sundries		29,000,000	34,800,000
Total	53,400,000	71,100,000	Total		47,300,000	58,700,000

Comparing the trade of Belgium in 1896 with the average of 5 years ending December 1892, we find as follows :—

Trade with	Millions £ Stg.		Ratio	
	1888–92	1896	1888–92	1896
France	26	24	21.5	18.5
Germany	18	22	14.8	16.9
Great Britain	18	20	14 8	15.4
Holland	16	14	13.2	10.8
Various	43	50	35.7	38.4
Total	121	130	100.0	100.0

Germany and Great Britain are gaining ground, while France and Holland are receding.

SWITZERLAND

Comparing the trade of 1896 with the average of 5 years ending 1892 shows as follows :—

Trade with	Millions £ Stg.		Ratio	
	1888–92	1896	1888–92	1896
Germany	18	20	27.3	27.5
France	15	14	22.7	19.5
Great Britain	6	8	9.1	11.3
Italy	7	7	10.6	9.7
Various	20	23	30.3	32.0
Total	66	72	100.0	100.0

Great Britain and Germany are gaining ground, while France has lost heavily in the ratio of Swiss trade.

The principal items of imports and exports of Switzerland were as follow :—

	Imports, £				Exports, £	
	1886	1896			1886	1896
Silk	5,300,000	4,300,000	Textiles		10,200,000	10,200,000
Grain	3,400,000	4,400,000	Watches		3,200,000	3,900,000
Cattle	2,100,000	2,100,000	Cheese		1,500,000	1,500,000
Hardware	1,200,000	3,200,000	Yarn		1,200,000	1,100,000
Coal	700,000	2,900,000	Machinery		700,000	1,200,000
Cotton	1,400,000	1,400,000	Milk		500,000	800,000
Sundries	16,900,000	24,200,000	Sundries		9,500,000	10,900,000
Total	31,000,000	42,500,000	Total		26,800,000	29,600,000

Trade increased 25 per cent. in 10 years, viz. :—

Year	Imports, £	Exports, £	Total, £
1886	31,000,000	26,800,000	57,800,000
1896	42,500,000	29,600,000	72,100,000

The principal countries trading with Switzerland were :

	Millions £ Sterling					
	1886			1896		
	Imports from*	Exports to	Total	Imports from	Exports to	Tota
Germany	10.4	6.4	16.8	12.3	7.2	19.5
France	7.5	5.6	13.1	9.2	4.7	13.9
Great Britain	1.8	4.2	6.0	2.1	5.9	8.0
Italy	4.8	2.3	7.1	5.7	1.6	7.3
Austria	3.7	1.4	5.1	3.1	1.7	4.8
Various	2.8	6.9	9.7	10.1	8.5	18.6
Total	31.0	26.8	57.8	42.5	29.6	72.1

ROUMANIA

The nations trading with Roumania were as follow :—

	Millions £ Sterling					
	1886			1896		
	Imports from	Exports to	Total	Imports from	Exports to	Total
Great Britain	2.1	2.5	4.6	2.9	4.5	7.4
Austria	4.8	2.8	7.6	3.7	1.3	5.0
Belgium	0.2	0.1	0.3	0.4	4.6	5.0
Germany	1.7	0.3	2.0	3.8	0.7	4.5
Various	1.9	4.2	6.1	2.7	1.9	4.6
Total	10.7	9.9	20.6	13 5	13.0	26.5

The only country with which dealings have fallen off is Austria. It is to be observed that Great Britain, instead of second as in 1886, now holds the foremost place in Roumanian trade, beyond all competitors.

* To be read thus : Imports from Germany £10,400,000.

The country was impoverished in 1876, and hence exports exceeded imports. Since 1886 things are better, and imports are over exports. The principal items of trade were as follow :—

	Imports, £				Exports, £	
	1886	1896			1886	1896
Textiles . . .	3,200,000	6,000,000	Grain		6,200,000	11,100,000
Hardware . . .	600,000	2,500,000	Cattle		...	400,000
Sundries . . .	6,900,000	5,000,000	Sundries . . .		3,700,000	1,500,000
Total . .	10,700,000	13,500,000	Total . .		9,900,000	13,000,000

The trade of Roumania has risen 60 per cent. since 1876, viz. :—

Year	Imports, £	Exports, £	Total, £
1876 . . .	6,600,000	9,400,000	16,000,000
1886 . . .	10,700,000	9,900,000	20,600,000
1896 . . .	13,500,000	13,000,000	26,500,000

SERVIA

The trade of this kingdom has been as follows :—

Year	Imports, £	Exports, £	Total, £
1876 . . .	900,000	1,100,000	2,000,000
1886 . . .	2,200,000	1,900,000	4,100,000
1896 . . .	1,300,000	2,100,000	3,400,000

The trade of 1896 was as follows :—

Imports	£	Exports	£
Textiles . . .	400,000	Grain . . .	900,000
Hardware . .	100,000	Cattle . . .	900,000
Sundries . . .	800,000	Sundries . .	300,000
Total . .	1,300,000	Total . .	2,100,000

The countries trading with Servia are shown thus :—

	Imports from	Exports to	Total, £	Ratio
Austria . . .	780,000	1,900,000	2,680,000	78.8
Other countries .	520,000	200,000	720,000	21.2
Total . .	1,300,000	2,100,000	3,400,000	100.0

BULGARIA

The countries trading with Bulgaria in 1886 and 1896 showed thus :—

	Imports, £		Exports, £	
	1886	1896	1886	1896
G. Britain .	740,000	720,000	200,000	1,300,000
Austria . .	680,000	900,000	100,000	100,000
Turkey . .	450,000	400,000	1,200,000	900,000
Various . .	730,000	1,080,000	500,000	2,000,000
Total .	2,600,000	3,100,000	2,000,000	4,300,000

Trade with Great Britain has more than doubled in ten years, while it has notably declined with Turkey.

The principal imports and exports in 1887 and 1896 were :—

	Imports, £	
	1887	1896
Textiles . . .	800,000	800,000
Hardware . . .	200,000	200,000
Sundries . . .	1,600,000	2,100,000
Total .	2,600,000	3,100,000

	Exports, £	
	1887	1896
Grain	900,000	3,800,000
Cattle	200,000	150,000
Sundries . . .	700,000	350,000
Total .	1,800,000	4,300,000

The trade of the principality has grown thus in ten years :—

Year	Imports, £	Exports, £	Total, £
1886	2,600,000	2,000,000	4,600,000
1896	3,100,000	4,300,000	7,400,000

GREECE

Official returns for 1888 and 1896 compare as follows :—

Year	Imports, £	Exports, £	Total, £
1888	4,400,000	3,800,000	8,200,000
1896	4,700,000	2,900,000	7,600,000

The countries trading with Greece were :—

	Imports, £		Exports, £	
	1888	1896	1888	1896
G. Britain .	1,200,000	1,200,000	1,600,000	700,000
Russia . .	1,000,000	1,000,000	...	300,000
Turkey . .	500,000	600,000	200,000	300,000
Various . .	1,700,000	1,900,000	1,600,000	1,600,000
Total .	4,400,000	4,700,000	3,800,000	2,900,000

The fall in the price of currants, from £27 a ton in 1888 to £15 in 1896, has injuriously affected Greek commerce.

The principal items of imports and exports of Greece were :—

	Imports, £			Exports, £	
	1888	1896		1888	1896
Grain	1,400,000	1,200,000	Fruit	1,900,000	1,100,000
Textiles . . .	800,000	900,000	Oil	100,000	100,000
Sundries . . .	2,200,000	2,600,000	Sundries . . .	1,800,000	1,700,000
Total . .	4,400,000	4,700,000	Total . .	3,800,000	2,900,000

TURKEY

The chief items of Turkish imports and exports were the following :—

	Imports, £			Exports, £	
	1889	1894		1889	1894
Coal	200,000	2,300,000	Fruit	2,200,000	2,300,000
Sugar	1,400,000	1,600,000	Grain	2,000,000	1,500,000
Linens	1,600,000	1,400,000	Silk	1,400,000	1,500,000
Quilts	1,100,000	1,200,000	Mohair . . .	600,000	600,000
Coffee	700,000	800,060	Opium . . .	600,000	500,000
Woollens . . .	700,000	700,000	Oil	600,000	300,000
Sundries . . .	13,200,000	13,700,000	Sundries . . .	6,300,000	5,300,000
Total . .	18,900,000	21,700,000	Total . .	13,700,000	12,000,000

The returns for 1896 compare with 1882 as follows :—

Year	Imports, £	Exports, £	Total, £
1882	17,500,000	10,200,000	27,700,000
1896	15,400,000	16,600,000	32,000,000

The countries trading with Turkey were as follow :—

	Millions £ Sterling					
	1889			1894		
	Imports from*	Exports to	Total	Imports from	Exports to	Total
G. Britain . .	8.2	5.2	13.4	8.2	5.1	13.3
Austria . . .	3.7	1.2	4.9	4.7	1.2	5.9
France . . .	2.3	3.9	6.2	2.5	3.2	5.7
Russia . . .	1.6	0.3	1.9	1.3	0.3	1.6
Bulgaria . . .	1.0	0.3	1.3	1.1	0.3	1.4
Various . . .	2.1	2.8	4.9	3.9	1.9	5.8
Total . .	18.9	13.7	32.6	21.7	12.0	33.7

The only country that shows any remarkable increase in its dealings with Turkey is Austria.

UNITED STATES

The trade of 1897 compares with that of thirty years preceding as follows :—

Period	Annual Average, £ Sterling			£ per Inhab.
	Imports	Exports	Total	
1867-71 .	88,400,000	70,700,000	159,100,000	4.2
1872-81 .	114,000,000	132,000,000	246,000,000	5.4
1882-91 .	148,000,000	158,600,000	306,600,000	5.3
1892-96 .	160,600,000	185,600,000	346,200,000	5.1
1897 . .	159,000,000	214,800,000	373,800,000	5.1

It appears that since 1872 trade has not kept pace with population. Textile goods form a great part of imports, and show as follows :—

	Annual Average, £ Sterling			
	1867 76	1877-86	1887-96	1897
Cottons . .	4,800,000	5,800,000	5,900,000	7,200,000
Woollens .	8,500,000	7,100,000	8,900,000	10,200,000
Silks . . .	5,200,000	6,300,000	6,900,000	5,200,000
Linens, &c.	3,700,000	4,200,000	5,200,000	6,800,000
Total .	22,200,000	23,400,000	26,900,000	29,400,000

The importation of fibre is best understood by comparing its weight with that of native fibre, since 1867, thus :—

Period	Tons of Fibre Yearly		
	Imported	Native	Consumption
1867-71 . .	60,000	280,000	340,000
1872-81 . .	102,000	403,000	505,000
1882-91 . .	220,000	600,000	820,000
1892-96 . .	280,000	740,000	1,020,000
1897 . .	345,000	790,000	1,135,000

The value of imported fibres was as follows :—

	Annual Average £ Sterling		
	1867-81	1882-96	1897
Wool . .	2,300,000	3,400,000	11,000,000
Silk . .	1,200,000	4,200,000	4,000,000
Flax, &c. .	1,000,000	3,200,000	2,500,000
Total .	4,500,000	10,800,000	17,500,000

* *Note.*—To be read thus : Imports from Great Britain, £8,200,000.

As regards exports the increase has been much greater than that of imports, viz. :—

	Annual Average, £ Sterling			
	1867–76	1877–86	1887–96	1897
Food .	29,400,000	64,600,000	63,400,000	84,100,000
Cotton .	40,800,000	42,200,000	47,200,000	48,000,000
Sundries	19,400,000	48,800,000	63,000,000	82,700,000
Exports	89,600,000	155,600,000	173,600,000	214,800,000

The increase in weight of exports has been even greater than in value, taking for example four items, viz. :—

	Tons Yearly		
	1872–76	1892–96	1897
Meat . . .	190,000	590,000	650,000
Grain . . .	2,660,000	6,220,000	9,700,000
Cotton . .	560,000	1,210,000	1,410,000
Petroleum . .	910,000	3,850,000	4,410,000
Total . .	4,320,000	11,870,000	16,170,000

The trade of the United States with the several quarters of the globe was as follows :—

	Millions £ Sterling					
	1887			1897		
	Imports from	Exports to	Total	Imports from	Exports to	Total
Europe . . .	81	117	198	89	167	256
Asia	17	5	22	23	9	32
Australia . .	1	2	3	1	4	5
Africa . . .	1	1	2	2	3	5
America . . .	44	22	66	44	32	76
Total . .	144	147	291	159	215	374

Comparing the returns for 1897 with the average of 5 years to June 1894 we find the currents of trade, imports and exports together, as follows :—

Trade with	Millions £ Stg.		Ratio	
	1890–94	1897	1890–94	1897
Great Britain . .	128	134	36.2	35.8
Germany . . .	37	49	10.4	13.1
France . . .	27	26	7.6	7.0
Cuba . . .	18	6	5.1	1.6
Canada . . .	18	22	5.1	5.9
Various . . .	126	137	35.6	36.6
Total . .	354	374	100.0	100.0

There is a marked increase of trade with Germany and Canada, while the ratios of other countries are declining. Since 1894 transactions with Germany have risen 33, with Canada 22, per cent. The trade of the United States with South America in the years 1892–96 as compared with 1882–86 showed an advance of 48 per cent., while British trade with that part of the world increased 20 per cent. in the same interval. In regard to the British West Indies, their trade with the United States rose 50 per cent. in 10 years, while their dealings with Great Britain fell off 15 per cent.

CANADA

Trade since 1881 may be summed up thus, in yearly average :—

Period	Imports, £	Exports, £	Total, £
1881–90 . . .	23,100,000	20,100,000	43,200,000
1891–95 . . .	24,200,000	23,800,000	48,000,000
1897	23,000,000	25,800,000	48,800,000

The importation of fibre has multiplied five-fold in twenty years, viz. :—

	Tons		
	1876	1886	1896
Cotton	3,000	16,000	20,000
Hemp	2,000	5,000	10,000
Wool	2,000	6,000	4,000
Total . .	7,000	27,000	34,000

The trade of Canada may be said to be equally shared between the United States and Great Britain, the dealings with other countries being very small.

The returns for 1896 show thus, in comparison with 1886 :—

	Trade of 1896			1886
	Imp. from	Exp. to	Total, £	
G. Britain .	6,900,000	13,800,000	20,700,000	16,900,000
U. States .	12,200,000	7,600,000	19,800,000	16,700,000
Various . .	2,800,000	3,800,000	6,600,000	4,600,000
Total .	21,900,000	25,200,000	47,100,000	38,200,000

In ten years the trade with the United States has risen 18, with Great Britain 22, per cent.

The imports and exports of 1896 compare with 1886 as to value thus :—

	Imports, £	
	1886	1896
Textiles . . .	3,800,000	3,500,000
Hardware . . .	2,600,000	2,900,000
Coal . . .	1,400,000	1,900,000
Sugar . . .	900,000	1,200,000
Tea	900,000	700,000
Sundries . .	11,100,000	11,700,000
Total . .	20,700,000	21,900,000

	Exports, £	
	1886	1896
Timber . . .	3,900,000	5,100,000
Cheese, &c. . .	2,100,000	3,300,000
Meat . . .	1,600,000	3,000,000
Fish . . .	1,000,000	2,100,000
Grain . . .	3,800,000	2,000,000
Sundries . .	5,100,000	9,700,000
Total .	17,500,000	25,200,000

MEXICO

Imports are not classified. The trade returns of 1897 compare with previous dates thus :—

Year	Imports, £	Exports, £	Total, £
1880 . . .	5,000,000	6,800,000	11,800,000
1889 . . .	8,100,000	8,300,000	16,400,000
1897 . . .	8,400,000	11,100,000	19,500,000

Exports were as follows :—

Year	Silver, £	Sundries, £	Total, £
1889 . . .	5,800,000	6,700,000	12,500,000
1897 . . .	11,400,000	10,800,000	22,200,000

Import and export trade in 1897 stood thus :—

	Imp. from	Exp. to	Total, £	Ratio
United States .	4,500,000	8,700,000	13,200,000	67.6
Great Britain .	1,400,000	1,400,000	2,800,000	14.4
Various . . .	2,500,000	1,000,000	3,500,000	18.0
Total . .	8,400,000	11,100,000	19,500,000	100.0

CENTRAL AMERICA

This term embraces five small republics, Guatemala, Salvador, Nicaragua, Costa Rica, and Honduras, the trade in 1896 showing thus :—

	Imports, £	Exports, £	Total, £
Guatemala . .	2,200,000	1,900,000	4,100,000
Salvador . . .	1,900,000	1,700,000	3,600,000
Nicaragua, &c. .	2,500,000	2,800,000	5,300,000
Total . .	6,600,000	6,400,000	13,000,000

These states export 70,000 tons of coffee, valued at £4,700,000, besides a large quantity of bananas. Their trade with other nations stands thus :—

	Imp. from	Exp. to	Total, £	Ratio
United States .	1,400,000	2,200,000	3,600,000	27.7
Great Britain .	1,500,000	800,000	2,300,000	17.7
Various . . .	3,700,000	3,400,000	7,100,000	54.6
Total . .	6,600,000	6,400,000	13,000,000	100.0

SOUTH AMERICA

The commerce of these ten republics showed as follows :—

	Millions £ Sterling					
	1886			1896		
	Imports from*	Exports to	Total	Imports from	Exports to	Total
Colombia . .	2.8	1.6	4.4	2.0	3.0	5.0
Venezuela . .	2.5	3.3	5.8	3.3	4.4	7.7
Ecuador . .	2.2	2.0	4.2	1.2	1.7	2.9
Peru	1.8	1.3	3.1	1.7	2.5	4.2
Chile	6.6	7.5	14.1	11.7	11.7	23.4
Bolivia . . .	0.9	1.5	2.4	0.6	1.3	1.9
Paraguay . .	0.3	0.2	0.5	0.5	0.5	1.0
Argentina . .	19.1	14.0	33.1	22.4	23.0	45.4
Uruguay . .	4.2	5.0	9.2	5.5	6.5	12.0
Brazil . . .	13.7	15.3	29.0	16.0	19.0	35.0
Total . .	54.1	51.7	105.8	64.9	73.6	138.5

Venezuela exports yearly 1 ton of gold in bars, value £140,000, besides 70,000 tons of coffee, worth £3,500,000. Colombia also exports 20,000 tons of coffee. The trade of Peru, Bolivia, and Paraguay is insignificant.

CHILE

Imports are of a mixed character, and not precisely classified. Exports in 1890 and 1895 were as follows :—

	Value, £		Tons
	1890	1895	1895
Nitre	4,500,000	7,200,000	1,290,000
Minerals . . .	1,800,000	2,100,000	250,000
Grain	200,000	300,000	80,000
Sundries . . .	2,000,000	1,400,000	...
Total . .	8,500,000	11,000,000	...

The countries trading with Chile in 1890 and 1895 were :—

	Millions £		Ratio	
	1890	1895	1890	1895
Great Britain . .	9.1	12.8	53.5	58.2
Germany . . .	2.6	3.8	15.3	17.3
Various . . .	5.3	5.4	31.2	24.5
Total . .	17.0	22.0	100.0	100.0

ARGENTINA

The imports and exports of the Argentine Republic in 1890 and 1896 compared thus :—

	Imports, £				Exports, £	
	1890	1896			1890	1896
Textiles . . .	5,600,000	7,700,000	Wool		7,100,000	6,700,000
Hardware . . .	9,400,000	3,500,000	Grain		4,800,000	6,200,000
Comestibles . .	2,500,000	2,800,000	Hides		4,100,000	2,100,000
Wine	2,000,000	1,700,000	Meat		2,200,000	2,000,000
Coal	1,100,000	1,200,000	Linseed . . .		200,000	1,400,000
Sundries . . .	7,800,000	5,500,000	Sundries . . .		1,800,000	4,900,000
Total . .	28,400,000	22,400,000	Total . .		20,200,000	23,300,000

* To be read thus : Colombia, £2,800,000.

The countries trading with Argentina were :—

Trade with	Millions £ Sterling					
	1886			1896		
	Imports from	Exports to	Total	Imports from	Exports to	Total
Great Britain .	6.7	2.0	8.7	8.9	2.9	11.8
France . . .	3.4	4.5	7.9	2.4	4.7	7.1
Germany . .	1.6	1.4	3.0	2.8	2.7	5.5
Belgium . . .	1.5	2.2	3.7	1.7	2.4	4.1
Italy	0.9	0.5	1.4	2.3	0.8	3.1
Various . . .	5.0	3.4	8.4	4.3	9.5	13.8
Total . .	19.1	14.0	33.1	22.4	23.0	45.4

The ratios of trade corresponding to the various countries show thus :—

Trade with	Millions £		Ratio	
	1886	1896	1886	1896
Great Britain . .	8.7	11.8	26.3	26.0
France . . .	7.9	7.1	23.9	15.7
Germany . . .	3.0	5.5	9.1	12.1
Belgium . . .	3.7	4.1	11.2	9.0
Italy . . .	1.4	3.1	4.2	6.8
Various . . .	8.4	13.8	25.3	30.4
Total . .	33.1	45.4	100.0	100.0

France and Belgium have lost ground, while Germany and Italy have gained exceedingly, and Great Britain holds the same ratio as ten years ago.

The weight of the principal exports in the last three years was :—

	Tons Exported			
	1895	1896	1897	Average
Maize . .	770,000	1,570,000	360,000	900,000
Wheat . .	1,080,000	600,000	160,000	610,000
Linseed . .	220,000	240,000	160,000	210,000
Wool . .	201,000	188,000	203,000	197,000
Sheepskins .	34,000	37,000	35,000	35,000
Hides . .	48,000	52,000	56,000	52,000
Total . .	2,353,000	2,687,000	977,000	2,004,000

URUGUAY

The total trade, imports and exports, with the various nations in 1886 and 1896 was as follows :—

	£ Sterling		Ratio	
	1886	1896	1886	1896
G. Britain .	2,300,000	2,000,000	25.0	16.7
Brazil . .	1,300,000	1,900,000	14.1	15.8
Argentina .	400,000	1,800,000	4.4	15.0
France . .	1,300,000	1,600,000	14.1	13.3
Germany .	500,000	1,100,000	5.4	9.2
Various . .	3,400,000	3,600,000	37.0	30.0
Total .	9,200,000	12,000,000	100.0	100.0

There has been a great increase of trade with Germany, Brazil, and Argentina, while Great Britain has lost ground.

Trade returns of the republic of Uruguay for 1890 and 1896 compare as follows :—

	Imports, £				Exports, £	
	1890	1896			1890	1896
Comestibles . . .	2,400,000	1,500,000	Wool	1,700,000	2,200,000
Hardware . . .	1,800,000	1,400,000	Meat	1,300,000	1,700,000
Textiles . . .	1,200,000	1,300,000	Hides	2,000,000	1,500,000
Sundries . . .	1,600,000	1,300,000	Sundries . . .	1,200,000	1,100,000
Total . .	7,000,000	5,500,000	Total . .	6,200,000	6,500,000

BRAZIL

Imports are not properly classified. Exports in 1884 and 1896 were :—

	Value, £ Sterling	
	1884	1896
Coffee	6,500,000	12,200,000
Sugar . . .	2,000,000	1,900,000
Rubber . . .	800,000	2,400,000
Cotton . . .	500,000	200,000
Sundries . . .	2,800,000	2,400,000
Total . .	12,600,000	19,100,000

The countries trading with Brazil in 1890 were :—

	Imp. from	Exp. to	Total, £	Ratio
United States .	1,700,000	8,300,000	10,000,000	33.0
Great Britain .	5,800,000	2,900,000	8,700,000	28.5
France	2,600,000	1,000,000	3,600,000	11.8
Germany . . .	2,000,000	1,500,000	3,500,000	11.6
Various . . .	2,300,000	2,300,000	4,600,000	15.1
Total . .	14,400,000	16,000,000	30,400,000	100.0

EGYPT

Trade returns show an increase of 27 per cent. in ten years, viz. :—

Year	Imports, £	Exports, £	Total, £
1886 . . .	8,100,000	10,400,000	18,500,000
1896 . . .	10,100,000	13,500,000	23,600,000

Imports were as follows :—

Year	Textiles, £	Sundries, £	Total, £
1886 . . .	1,300,000	6,800,000	8,100,000
1896 . . .	2,700,000	7,400,000	10,100,000

Exports showed as follows :—

Year	Cotton, £	Sundries, £	Total, £
1886 . . .	7,100,000	3,300,000	10,400,000
1896 . . .	10,200,000	3,300,000	13,500,000

The nations trading with Egypt were :—

	Imports, £		Exports, £	
	1886	1896	1886	1896
G. Britain .	3,200,000	3,200,000	6,600,000	7,200,000
France . .	900,000	1,400,000	900,000	1,300,000
Turkey . .	1,300,000	2,100,000	400,000	400,000
Various . .	2,700,000	3,400,000	2,500,000	4,600,000
Total .	8,100,000	10,100,000	10,400,000	13,500,000

The ratios of trade for the principal countries were :—

	Millions £		Ratio	
	1886	1896	1886	1896
Great Britain . .	9.8	10.4	53.0	44.0
France . . .	1.8	2.7	9.7	11.5
Turkey . . .	1.7	2.5	9.2	10.6
Various . . .	5.2	8.0	28.1	33.9
Total . .	18.5	23.6	100.0	100.0

There is a relative decline in trade with Great Britain, and an increase with France and Turkey.

INDIA

The trade of India, excluding precious metals, shows thus :—

Year	Imports, £	Exports, £	Total, £
1877 . . .	33,700,000	55,000,000	88,700,000
1887 . . .	48,800,000	68,000,000	116,800,000
1897 . . .	47,500,000	65,000,000	112,500,000

The various countries trading with India were :—

	Imports, £		Exports, £	
	1887	1897	1887	1897
G. Britain .	41,900,000	31,500,000	26,300,000	19,800,000
China . .	600,000	1,400,000	2,000,000	8,500,000
Germany .	100,000	1,500,000	600,000	4,800,000
U. States .	1,400,000	1,000,000	2,500,000	3,000,000
Various .	4,800,000	12,100,000	36,600,000	28,900,000
Total .	48,800,000	47,500,000	68,000,000	65,000,000

The ratios of trade for the above countries are shown thus :—

	Millions £ Stg.		Ratio	
	1887	1897	1887	1897
Great Britain . .	68	51	58.2	45.5
China . . .	3	10	2.5	8.9
Germany . . .	1	6	0.8	5.4
United States . .	4	4	3.4	3.6
Various . . .	41	41	35.1	36.6
Total . .	117	112	100.0	100.0

Trade with Great Britain has declined remarkably, while there has been a prodigious increase in dealings with China and Germany.

The value of both imports and exports has declined in the last ten years, although the Board of Trade Report shows an enormous increase, by fictitiously valuing the rupee at 24, instead of 15, pence. The following table shows the imports and exports for 1887 and 1897 at their real value :—

	Imports, £			Exports, £	
	1887	1897		1887	1897
Textiles . . .	22,200,000	20,100,000	Jute	4,500,000	9,900,000
Hardware . . .	6,100,000	8,200,000	Cotton . . .	10,200,000	8,100,000
Sugar . . .	1,600,000	2,100,000	Rice	6,600,000	7,500,000
Petroleum . . .	900,000	2,100,000	Opium . . .	8,400,000	5,000,000
Silk . . .	600,000	1,400,000	Tea	3,600,000	5,000,000
Sundries . . .	17,400,000	13,600,000	Sundries . . .	34,700,000	29,500,000
Total .	48,800,000	47,500,000	Total .	68,000,000	65,000,000

CHINA

The principal items of Chinese trade are shown thus :—

	Imports, £			Exports, £	
	1886	1896		1886	1896
Cotton goods . .	7,300,000	13,200,000	Silk	7,200,000	7,000,000
Opium . . .	6,200,000	4,800,000	Tea	8,400,000	5,000,000
Sundries . . .	8,600,000	15,700,000	Sundries . . .	3,700,000	9,800,000
Total .	22,100,000	33,700,000	Total .	19,300,000	21,800,000

Official returns show as follows :—

Year	Imports, £	Exports, £	Total, £
1876	21,600,000	24,100,000	45,700,000
1886	22,100,000	19,300,000	41,400,000
1896	33,700,000	21,800,000	55,500,000

There has been no decline of trade with Great Britain, as most of the Hong-Kong trade is British : both together form 60 per cent. of the total, the same as ten years ago.

Adding together imports and exports, the countries trading with China show thus :—

Trade with	Millions £		Ratio	
	1886	1896	1886	1896
Hong-Kong . .	14.5	24.1	35.3	43.4
Great Britain . .	10.5	9.3	25.2	16.8
Japan . . .	1.8	4.8	4.3	8.6
India . . .	4.3	4.2	10.4	7.6
United States . .	3.5	3.8	8.4	6.8
Various . . .	6.8	9.3	16.4	16.8
Total . .	41.4	55.5	100.0	100.0

JAPAN

The principal items of trade of the Japanese empire were :—

	Imports, £				Exports, £	
	1886	1896			1886	1896
Textiles . . .	2,000,000	4,100,000	Silk . . .		3,300,000	3,500,000
Cotton, raw . .	100,000	3,600,000	Silk goods . .		100,000	1,400,000
Sugar . . .	900,000	1,500,000	Fancy goods . .		500,000	1,100,000
Hardware . . .	500,000	1,300,000	Coal		400,000	1,000,000
Sundries . . .	2,600,000	8,400,000	Sundries . . .		3,600,000	6,000,000
Total . .	6,100,000	18,900,000	Total . .		7,900,000	13,000,000

Trade has doubled in ten years, viz. :—

	Imports, £	Exports, £	Total, £
1886	6,100,000	7,900,000	14,000,000
1896	18,900,000	13,000,000	31,900,000
Increase . . .	12,800,000	5,100,000	17,900,000

The total trade between Japan and various countries stands thus :—

	£ Sterling		Ratio	
	1886	1896	1886	1896
Great Britain .	3,500,000	7,500,000	25.0	23.4
United States .	4,000,000	5,300,000	28.6	16.6
China	1,700,000	3,900,000	12.1	12.2
Hong-Kong . .	1,100,000	3,200,000	7.8	10.0
France . . .	1,900,000	3,000,000	13.6	9.4
India	600,000	2,900,000	4.3	9.1
Germany . . .	600,000	2,200,000	4.3	7.1
Various . . .	600,000	3,900,000	4.3	12.2
Total . .	14,000,000	31,900,000	100.0	100.0

Great Britain and Hong-Kong taken together represent one-third of the whole trade of Japan, the same as ten years ago.

AUSTRALIA

The nominal amount of trade has been as follows :—

Year	Imports, £	Exports, £	Total, £	£ per Inhab.
1871 .	31,100,000	38,400,000	69,500,000	35.9
1881 .	53,000,000	48,700,000	101,700,000	36.6
1891 .	72,100,000	72,700,000	144,800,000	37.7
1896 .	62,600,000	66,600,000	129,200,000	30.2

The above, however, includes local trade, such as between Sydney and Melbourne, and if this were excluded the real transmarine trade of Australia would stand thus :—

Year	Imports, £	Exports, £	Total, £	£ per Inhab.
1871 .	16,800,000	23,300,000	40,100,000	20.6
1881 .	33,800,000	31,100,000	64,900,000	23.2
1891 .	41,400,000	43,300,000	84,700,000	21.7
1896 .	34,200,000	40,100,000	74,300,000	17.5

The following table shows the ultramarine and intercolonial trade for 1896 thus :—

	Number (000 omitted)				
	Ultramarine			Inter-colonial, £	Total, £
	Imports, £	Exports, £	Total, £		
N. S. Wales	11,000	14,600	25,600	18,000	43,600
Victoria .	8,300	8,800	17,100	11,700	28,800
N. Zealand	6,000	8,100	14,100	2,400	16,500
Queensland	2,800	3,700	6,500	8,100	14,600
S. Australia	3,300	4,000	7,300	7,500	14,800
Tasmania .	400	200	600	2,100	2,700
W. Australia	2,400	700	3,100	5,100	8,200
Total .	34,200	40,100	74,300	54,900	129,200

The total foreign trade of 20 years ending December 1893 summed up 1336 millions sterling, the several colonies holding the following order :—

	Millions £ Sterling			Ratio
	Imports	Exports	Total	
Victoria . . .	233	201	434	32.5
N. S. Wales . .	220	191	411	30.8
New Zealand . .	112	116	228	17.1
S. Australia . .	67	76	143	10.7
Queensland . .	46	40	86	6.4
Tasmania . . .	11	8	19	1.4
W. Australia . .	7	8	15	1.1
Total . .	696	640	1,336	100.0

The total trade, imports and exports, between Australia and other countries was as follows :—

With	£ Sterling Yearly		Ratio	
	1881–85	1891–95	1881–85	1891–95
Great Britain .	56,800,000	54,800,000	79.4	77.1
British Colonies .	6,200,000	3,500,000	8.7	4.9
Other countries .	8,500,000	12,900,000	11.9	18.0
Total . .	71,500,000	71,200,000	100.0	100.0

The trade with foreign countries increases rapidly, while that with British colonies declines.

Imports cannot be classified, as they are mixed up with local or intercolonial trade. The principal exports are wool and gold, which averaged yearly as follows :—

Year	Wool, Million Lbs.	Value, £	Gold, Tons	£
1871–80 . .	282	14,900,000	52	·7,300,000
1881–90 . .	422	17,900,000	43	6,100,000
1891 95 . .	658	22,600,000	56	7,800,000
1896 . . .	678	20,600,000	63	8,800,000

SOUTH AFRICA

The aggregate trade, imports and exports, showed :—

With	£ Sterling		Ratio	
	1885	1895	1885	1895
Great Britain .	11,500,000	18,200,000	91.0	82.7
Other countries .	1,100,000	3,700,000	9.0	17.3
Total . .	12,600,000	21,900,000	100.0	100.0

Trade between South Africa and the United States has quadrupled in 10 years.

The nominal trade returns of Cape Colony and Natal show thus :—

	Cape, £	Natal, £	Total, £
Imports, 1876 .	5,500,000	1,000,000	6,500,000
,, 1886 .	3,800,000	1,300,000	5,100,000
,, 1896 .	16,900,000	5,400,000	22,300,000
Exports, 1876 .	3,500,000	700,000	4,200,000
,, 1886 .	3,600,000	800,000	4,400,000
,, 1896 .	16,700,000	1,800,000	18,500,000

Thus it would appear that the aggregate imports and exports of 1896 were 41 millions sterling, against 9½ in 1886. This is, however, a deception, which arises from the transit trade of the Transvaal or South African Republic being included. The real trade in 1895 was as follows :—

	Imports, £	Exports, £	Total, £
Cape	8,300,000	8,900,000	17,200,000
Natal	3,600,000	1,100,000	4,700,000
Total . .	11,900,000	10,000,000	21,900,000

Considering both these colonies as one, the principal items of South African trade may be summed up thus :—

	Imports, £				Exports, £	
	1885	1895			1885	1895
Textiles . . .	1,800,000	3,600,000	Diamonds . . .	2,500,000	4,800,000
Hardware . . .	500,000	2,800,000	Wool . . .	1,900,000	2,900,000
Sundries . . .	3,900,000	5,500,000	Sundries . . .	2,000,000	2,300,000
Total . .	6,200,000	11,900,000	Total . .	6,400,000	10,000,000

ALGERIA

Returns for 1896 compare with those of 1883 thus :—

Year	Imports, £	Exports, £	Total £
1883	9,400,000	6,400,000	15,800,000
1896	10,800,000	9,200,000	20,000,000

The trade of 1895 was as follows :—

Imports, £		Exports, £	
Textiles . .	2,500,000	Wine . . .	3,500,000
Hardware . .	700,000	Grain . . .	2,200,000
Coffee . . .	400,000	Meat . . .	2,100,000
Sundries . .	6,600,000	Sundries . .	3,600,000
Total . .	10,200,000	Total . .	11,400,000

The countries trading with Algeria in 1896 were :—

	Imports from	Exports to	Total, £	Ratio
France . . .	8,700,000	7,800,000	16,500,000	82.5
Great Britain .	200,000	500,000	700,000	3.5
Various . . .	1,900,000	900,000	2,800,000	14.0
Total . .	10,800,000	9,200,000	20,000,000	100.0

BRITISH WEST INDIES

This group of minor colonies includes British Guiana, Jamaica, Trinidad, Barbadoes and several small islands. The average trade of 5 years ending December 1895 compares with that of the period ending 1885 thus :—

	£ Sterling yearly		
	Imports	Exports	Total
1881–85 . . .	6,700,000	7,400,000	14,100,000
1891–95 . . .	6,900,000	6,900,000	13,800,000

A valuable trade has sprung up to supply American cities with tropical fruit, Jamaica alone exporting bananas and oranges worth £500,000 yearly to the United States. The countries trading with this group of colonies show thus :—

Trade with	£ Sterling		Ratio	
	1886	1896	1886	1896
Great Britain .	5,800,000	6,700,000	43.6	41.9
United States .	4,400,000	5,800,000	33.1	36.2
Various . . .	3,100,000	3,500,000	23.3	21.9
Total . .	13,300,000	16,000,000	100.0	100.0

The tendency is towards an increase of trade with the United States, and a decline in dealings with Great

Britain and the rest of the world. For the trade of other islands see *Colonies*.

The principal export is sugar, viz. :—

	Annual Average, £	
	1881–85	**1891–95**
Sugar . . .	4,730,000	3,430,000
Sundries . . .	2,670,000	3,470,000
Total . .	7,400,000	6,900,000

The decline as regards sugar is mainly owing to the fall in price, the average in the second term having been £13 per ton, against £16½ in the first. Shipments of sugar have been as follows :—

	Tons		
	1885	**1890**	**1895**
Guiana . . .	96,000	105,000	101,000
Trinidad . . .	64,000	51,000	55,000
Barbadoes . .	57,000	74,000	33,000
Jamaica . . .	25,000	19,000	19,000
Small islands .	48,000	49,000	29,000
Total . .	290,000	298,000	237,000

CONSOLS

Quotations since 1880 have been as follows :—

Year	Highest	Lowest	Average
1881–85 . . .	102.4	96.3	100.4
1886–90 . . .	103.2	94.6	99.6
1891 . . .	97.6	94.8	95.7
1892 . . .	97.5	95.7	96.7
1893 . . .	99.0	98.0	98.5
1894 . . .	103.1	98.8	101.1
1895 . . .	107.4	104.4	106.2
1896 . . .	113.5	107.0	110.7
1897 . . .	114.0	112.1	112.4

In 1889 the interest was reduced from 3 per cent. to 2¾ per cent., which caused quotations to fall from 101 to 98. Allowing for difference of interest, the quotations of 1897 would be equivalent to 122½ for the old Three per Cents.

For quotations from 1740 to 1881 see page 262.

CO-OPERATION

The number of co-operative societies in the United Kingdom rose from 1273 in 1885 to 1695 in 1895, and their figures compared thus :—

	1885	**1896**
Members	802,000	1,440,000
Capital, £ . . .	10,600,000	21,700,000
Sales, £	29,900,000	56,600,000

Building societies have declined in the same interval, viz. :—

	1885	**1896**
Shares, £	34,900,000	31,900,000
Deposits, £ . . .	17,800,000	13,100,000
Total . .	52,700,000	45,000,000

Horace Plunkett began co-operative dairies in Ireland in 1893 ; their number now reaches 243, with 27,000 members, and the sales of butter in 1897 amounted to a value of £346,000 sterling.

GERMANY

In May 1897 there were 14,842 societies, viz. : People's banks 9417, agricultural societies 3315, and supply associations 2110. This showed an increase of 1837 societies upon the preceding year. The Popular Banks had 1,430,000 members, of whom 950,000 belonged to Schultz-Delitzch and 480,000 to Raffeisen societies. Agricultural societies showed an increase of 360 on 1896.

FRANCE

In 1895 the mutual societies counted 1,540,000 members, with assets £8,700,000, investments £4,200,000, and cash £2,600,000. There were 280 Raffeisen banks.

ITALY

There are 720 Popular Banks, with 405,000 shareholders, capital £4,600,000, deposits £14,900,000, and discounts £39,700,000.

BELGIUM

In 1896 there were 417 rural co-operative societies, including 37 Raffeisen banks and 64 joint-stock dairies.

SWITZERLAND

There are 77 co-operative cattle associations, besides joint-stock dairies in every village.

AUSTRIA

There are 1250 Raffeisen banks between Austria and Hungary, and 3100 co-operative societies of other kinds, with 1,220,000 members.

UNITED STATES

In 1893 there were 5840 building societies, with 1,745,000 members, holding a capital of £93,600,000 sterling.

See *Friendly Societies*, p. 737, and *Societies*, p. 542.

COPPER

Production has more than trebled in 16 years :—

	Tons		
	1880	**1890**	**1896**
United States . .	20,300	104,000	210,000
Great Britain . .	40,000	76,000	100,000
Spain . . .	21,300	71,000	60,000
Chili . . .	20,000	20,000	20,000
Germany . .	10,100	15,000	25,000
France . . .	5,100	8,000	10,000
Russia, &c. . .	25,200	76,000	65,000
Total . .	142,000	370,000	490,000

Most of what is produced in Great Britain is from Chilian and other foreign ores or regulus, the quantity of native copper not exceeding 600 tons. The price of bar copper has been as follows per ton :—

1882	. . . .	£72	1888	. . .	£78	1893	. . . .	£48
1885	. . . .	48	1890	. . .	58	1896	. . . .	49

Great Britain exports 50,000 tons yearly. The copper mines of Spain give employment to 8600 men, who raise 2,700,000 tons of ore, valued at £560,000, being an average of 315 tons per miner, of the value of £65.

See *Metals*, page 773.

COTTON

Production has been approximately as follows :—

	Million Lbs.		
	U. States	India, &c.	The World
1881 . . .	3,200	900	4,100
1886 . . .	3,180	1,020	4,300
1891 . . .	4,310	1,290	5,600
1897 . . .	4,400	1,500	5,900

The United States crop was disposed of as follows :—

	Million Lbs.		
	Crop	Exported	Home Use
1881 . . .	3,200	2,190	1,010
1886 . . .	3,180	2,050	1,130
1891 . . .	4,310	2,880	1,430
1897 . . .	4,400	3,060	1,340

Since 1881 the crop has increased 37 per cent., home consumption 33 per cent.

The consumption by latest accounts was as follows :—

	Mil. Lbs.		*Mil. Lbs.*
Great Britain . .	1,570	Spain . . .	160
France . .	400	India . . .	480
Germany . .	620	Japan . . .	160
Russia . .	430	Brazil . . .	120
Austria . .	270	United States .	1,340
Italy . . .	240	Various . . .	110

Making a total of 5900 million lbs., or 2,650,000 tons, representing a value of 130 millions sterling. The value of cotton goods manufactured in 1896 reached 360 millions sterling.

GREAT BRITAIN

The consumption of cotton and the value of exported goods were :—

	Million Lbs. Yearly	Exports Yearly, £
1882-86 . . .	1,450	72,400,000
1887-91 . . .	1,600	71,800,000
1892-96 . . .	1,480	65,800,000
1897 . . .	1,570	64,000,000

The exports of cotton goods and yarn were as follows :—

Year	Yarn, Million Lbs.	Cotton Cloth, Million Yds.	Total Value, £ Sterling
1840 . . .	118	791	24,700,000
1860 . . .	197	2,776	52,000,000
1880 . . .	216	4,496	75,600,000
1890 . . .	258	5,125	74,300,000
1897 . . .	252	4,800	64,000,000

In 1894 the following estimate of consumption was published :—

		Million Lbs.		
		1880	1890-93	1894
Great Britain	. .	1,400	1,530	1,550
Continent	. .	1,150	1,890	2,010
United States	. .	830	1,340	1,110
India .	. .	120	460	480
Total	. .	3,500	5,220	5,150

Countries exporting cotton goods (and yarn) were :—

		Millions £ Sterling		
		1885	1890	1895
Great Britain	. .	67.0	74.4	63.8
France .	. .	4.1	4.4	4.7
Germany .	. .	4.9	9.4	10.0
Switzerland .	. .	6.4	6.3	5.2
Spain .	. .	0.3	1.0	1.7
Total	. .	82.7	95.5	85.4

Production and consumption of cotton goods were :—

		Output, Millions £	Consumption	
			Millions £	Shillings per Head
United Kingdom .	.	92.1	40.1	21
France .	.	22.4	19.8	10
Germany .	.	35.4	29.0	11
Russia .	.	20.4	20.5	4
Austria .	.	18.4	18.3	9
Italy .	.	12.9	13.5	9
Spain .	.	8.8	7.1	8
Other States .	.	19.6	20.7	9
Europe	.	230.0	169.0	9
United States	.	68.0	64.0	18
Total .	.	298.0	233.0	11

Cotton manufacture in the United Kingdom advanced as follows :—

Year	Spindles	Power-Looms	Operatives
1870 . . .	37,700,000	440,000	450,000
1890 . . .	44,500,000	620,000	530,000

There was an increase of 18 per cent. both in spindles and operatives. The consumption of raw cotton rose from 450,000 tons in 1870 to 710,000 tons in 1896.

The *Bremen Exchange* publishes the following on the growth of cotton manufacture in five European countries :—

	Spindles		Bales Cotton used	
	1887	1898	1887	1898
Germany .	5,060,000	7,880,000	1,010,000	1,580,000
Austria . .	2,070,000	3,140,000	500,000	600,000
Switzerland .	1,710,000	1,710,000	100,000	100,000
Poland . .	510,000	960,000	120,000	290,000
Belgium .	610,000	880,000	70,000	120,000
Total .	9,960,000	14,570,000	1,800,000	2,690,000

CRIME

Tables compiled by Rev. W. D. Morrison (1897) show the ratio of sexes among criminals in various countries thus :—

				Males	Females	Total
England	.	.	.	820	180	1,000
France	.	.	.	850	150	1,000
Germany	.	.	.	819	181	1,000
Austria	.	.	.	848	152	1,000
Spain	.	.	.	890	110	1,000
Sweden	.	.	.	864	136	1,000
Norway	.	.	.	791	209	1,000
Denmark	.	.	.	736	264	1,000
Mexico	.	.	.	858	142	1,000
Japan	.	.	.	913	87	1,000
Average	.	.	.	839	161	1,000

The number of persons in prison on a given day in various countries, compared with population, was as follows :—

					Prison Population	Per 100,000 Inhabitants
United Kingdom	.	.	.		17,800	46
Russia	.	.	.	.	155,020	155
Finland	.	.	.	.	2,120	85
Holland	.	.	.	.	4,010	84
Belgium	.	.	.	.	4,440	70
Switzerland	.	.	.	.	3,200	107
Italy	.	.	.	.	67,420	217
United States	.	.	.	.	82,330	132
Canada	.	.	.	.	4,034	85
Australia	.	.	.	.	6,001	150
India	.	.	.	.	101,180	44
Cape Colony	.	.	.	.	3,260	310
Jamaica	.	.	.	.	1,150	164

For France and some other countries there are no returns since 1888. See page 163.

UNITED KINGDOM

The annual average of committals has been as follows :—

	Number Yearly				Per Million Inhab.			
	England	Scotland	Ireland	U. Kingdom	England	Scotland	Ireland	U. Kingdom
1880-89	14,100	2,450	3,320	19,870	522	647	660	555
1890-94	12,070	2,330	2,190	16,590	410	574	470	435
1895-96	11,420	2,070	1,920	15,410	374	496	420	392

Convicted.

	England	Scotland	Ireland	U. Kingdom	England	Scotland	Ireland	U. Kingdom
1880-89	10,800	1,910	1,760	14,470	401	248	348	404
1890-94	9,470	1,860	1,300	12,630	322	460	280	331
1895-96	8,860	1,680	1,205	11,745	290	403	264	299

In 1895–96 the ratio of convictions to committals was 77 per cent. in England, 81 in Scotland, and 63 per cent. in Ireland.

The prison population of the three kingdoms has been as follows :—

			Number		Per 100,000 Pop.	
			1880	1893	1880	1893
England	.	.	19,835	13,178	76	44
Scotland	.	.	2,616	2,196	71	54
Ireland	.	.	2,620	2,428	50	53
United Kingdom	.		25,071	17,802	71	46

The diminution of crime is in great measure attributed to the action of reformatories (see page 799).

FRANCE

The number of convictions yearly, assize and correctional, was as follows :—

	Annual Average			Per 100,000 Inhab.
	Crimes	Offences	Total	
1871–80 . . .	3,650	128,850	132,500	358
1883–87 . . .	3,105	203,295	206,400	543
1889–94 . . .	2,916	218,854	221,770	576

The above does not include misdemeanours tried at the police courts, which averaged 440,200 convictions yearly in 1889–94. It is observed that professional criminals of the worst type, such as murderers and burglars, show an increasing ratio : they are termed " recidivistes," and their ratio in the records of crime has risen from 41 per cent. in 1870 to 48 in 1880, to 57 in 1880, and to 58 per cent. of all criminals tried at assize in 1893.

GERMANY

The returns for 1895 compare with those of 1886 as follows :—

	Convicted		Per 100,000 Inh.	
	1886	1895	1886	1895
Men	291,400	377,200	612	725
Women . . .	61,600	77,000	129	148
Total .	353,000	454,200	741	873

The number of recidivistes, or professional criminals, and of juvenile offenders (under 18) are shown thus :—

	Number		Per 1000 Convicts	
	1886	1895	1886	1895
Recidivistes . .	102,800	172,200	290	378
Juveniles . . .	31,510	44,380	89	98

Both these classes are rapidly increasing : the former have increased 70 per cent., the latter 40 per cent., in 9 years, while population has risen only 10 per cent.

RUSSIA

The prison population in 1893 compared with that of 1887 thus :—

		In Jail		Per 100,000 Pop.	
		1887	1893	1887	1893
In Russia	. .	75,350	116,380	84	116
,, Siberia	. .	33,490	38,640	37	39
Total	.	108,840	155,020	121	155

About 30,000 persons are exiled yearly to Siberia, some of whom are put in chain-gangs for working the gold mines, others are sent to the island of Saghalien, north of China, and established as farmers. Of the prisoners in Russia, 90 per cent. are males, 10 per cent. females ; 80 per cent. convicts, 20 per cent. untried.

AUSTRIA

The record for 1894 (Austria proper) compares with that of 1886 thus :—

	Convictions		Per 100,000 Pop.	
	1886	1894	1886	1894
Crimes . . .	29,710	30,130	129	123
Offences . . .	558,440	532,770	2,428	2,174
Total . .	588,150	562,900	2,557	2,297

The number of criminals undergoing penal servitude in 1894 was 10,270, or 420 per million of the population, against 490 in 1886. There are 4000 juvenile offenders in reformatories.

HUNGARY

The returns for 1886 and 1896 were as follows :—

Court	Convictions		Per 100,000 Pop.	
	1886	1896	1886	1896
Assize	20,210	10,580	125	57
Correctional . .	95,090	78,760	595	426
Total . .	115,300	89,340	720	483

This does not include cases tried at the police courts, which number about 250,000 per annum.

ITALY

The returns for 1885 and 1895 showed as follows :—

Court	Convictions		Per 100,000 Pop.	
	1885	1895	1885	1895
Assize	5,140	3,604	17	12
Correctional . .	53,100	78,030	177	252
Police	273,470	278,656	934	898
Total . .	331,710	360,290	1,128	1,162

The crimes on which convictions were obtained were :

	Number		Per 1000 Convicts	
	1885	1895	1885	1895
Homicide . .	2,445	2,286	8	6
Assault . . .	61,400	62,730	185	174
Robbery, &c. .	52,520	55,390	160	154
Minor offences .	215,345	239,884	647	666
Total . .	331,710	360,290	1,000	1,000

Prison population, including reformatories, showed :—

In	Number		Per 100,000 Pop.	
	1885	1895	1885	1895
Prison	30,130	34,790	102	112
Reformatories .	5,520	6,320	19	20
Penal servitude .	34,720	32,630	119	105
Total . .	70,370	73,740	240	237

Of the prison population 91 per cent. are males, and of those in penal servitude 95 per cent.

NORWAY

The returns for 1887 and 1894 compare thus :—

	Convictions		Per 100,000 Pop.	
	1887	1894	1887	1894
Crimes . . .	2,930	2,950	150	145
Offences . . .	22,660	28,820	1,155	1,415
Total . .	25,590	31,770	1,305	1,560

DENMARK

The returns for 1890 and 1885 compare as follows :—

Year	Convictions	Per 100,000 Pop.
1885	3,525	168
1890	3,897	177

In 1890 there were 73 per cent. of the convicts males, against 75 per cent. in 1885.

HOLLAND

The number of convictions was as follows :—

Court	Convictions		Per 100,000 Pop.	
	1885	1895	1885	1895
Assize	727	1,330	17	28
Correctional . .	15,080	16,070	351	338
Local	67,583	86,990	1,572	1,824
Total . .	83,390	104,390	1,940	2,190

The convictions showed 90 per cent. males. The prison population, including reformatories, in December 1896 was 4010, equal to 84 per 100,000 population, exclusive of asylums for drunkards and vagrants, which had 3600 inmates.

BELGIUM

Excluding police courts and reformatories, the records show :—

Year	Convictions	Per 100,000 Population	In Prison	Per 100,000 Population
1870 .	22,360	447	4,700	94
1880 .	34,245	623	3,705	67
1890 .	40,370	666	4,280	71
1894 .	44,910	713	4,440	70

SWITZERLAND

In 1895 the prison population was 3200, equal to 107 per 100,000 of the population, 85 per cent. being males.

SERVIA

The returns for 1894 compare with 1887 as follows :—

	Number		Per 100,000 Pop.	
	1887	1894	1887	1894
Accused . . .	7,540	12,590	360	550
Acquitted . .	1,840	9,010	88	392
Convicted . .	5,700	3,580	272	158

FINLAND

The records for 1892 show as follows :—

	Convictions	Per 100,000 Pop.
Crimes	2,710	113
Offences . . .	14,740	614
Total . .	17,450	727

The prison population in December 1894 was 2120, equal to 85 per 100,000 inhabitants.

UNITED STATES

The prison population was as follows :—

	Number	Per 100,000 Inhabitants
1870	32,900	88
1880 . . .	59,260	118
1890 . . .	82,330	132

The ratio of criminals and offenders is higher among foreigners than American whites, viz. :—

	Number		Per 100,000	
	1880	1890	1880	1890
Amer. Whites .	29,370	39,730	80	87
Coloured . . .	16,980	25,020	255	334
Foreigners . .	12,910	17,580	193	190
Total . .	59,260	82,330	118	132
Males	54,190	75,920	213	237
Females . . .	5,070	6,410	21	21

The increase of crime among the coloured population is remarkable. If we deduct from the population all children under 10, the comparison as regards criminals will stand thus for 1890 :—

	Pop. over 10	Criminals	Per 100,000
American Whites .	33,150,000	39,730	120
Coloured	5,480,000	25,020	455
Foreigners . . .	8,780,000	17,580	200
Total . . .	47,410,000	82,330	173

The prison population of the United States is higher than in most European countries. The number of prisoners charged with homicide was as follows :—

States	Number		Per Million Pop.	
	1880	1890	1880	1890
New England .	197	248	49	53
Middle . . .	636	939	54	66
South	2,023	3,532	132	193
Prairie . . .	1,269	1,796	73	80
Pacific	483	836	273	276
Union . .	4,608	7,351	92	117

Homicide, compared with population, is three times as frequent in the Southern, and four times as frequent in the Pacific, as in the Eastern States, which shows that Prof. Lombroso's theory of civilisation causing an increase of murder is unfounded.

JAVA

The returns for 1882 and 1894 compared as follows :—

Year	Convictions			Per 100,000 Pop.
	Crimes	Offences	Total	
1882 . . .	11,700	6,670	18,370	810
1894 . . .	11,170	8,470	19,640	780

AUSTRALIA

The records for 1894 show as follows :—

	Convictions			Per 10,000 Pop.
	Grave	Slight	Total	
N. S. Wales . .	10,120	36,090	46,210	361
Victoria	6,020	21,100	27,120	230
N. Zealand . .	3,910	8,700	12,610	180
Queensland . .	4,280	7,530	11,810	257
S. Australia . .	1,235	4,745	5,980	168
Tasmania . . .	1,275	2,465	3,740	234
W. Australia . .	1,540	2,860	4,400	440
Total . .	28,380	83,490	111,870	266

The number of crimes for which convictions were obtained before the Superior Courts were for all seven colonies in the aggregate thus :—

	Number	Per 100,000 Pop.
1871	1,622	86
1881	2,085	76
1894	2,110	50

This shows a progressive and healthy decline in the ratio of crime of a grave character.

CANADA

The returns of crimes and offences were as follows :—

Year	Convictions			Per 100,000 Pop.
	Crimes	Offences	Total	
1884 . . .	2,506	27,044	29,550	634
1888 . . .	3,747	33,903	37,650	800
1892 . . .	4,030	30,970	35,000	714
1896 . . .	5,204	32,076	37,280	730

The provinces showed as follows in 1886 and 1896 :—

	Convictions		Per 100,000 Souls	
	1886	1896	1886	1896
Ontario . . .	19,170	16,890	960	767
Quebec . . .	7,850	10,740	555	786
Nova Scotia . .	1,540	3,500	350	777
New Brunswick	2,180	2,300	680	720
Other provinces	3,130	3,850	870	710
Total . .	33,870	37,280	736	730

Convictions were for the following crimes and offences:

	Number		Ratio	
	1886	1895	1886	1895
Homicide . .	33	13	1	...
Assault . . .	704	1,105	21	29
Robbery . . .	281	527	8	14
Larceny, &c. .	2,238	3,460	66	92
Drunkenness .	11,160	11,160	330	297
Minor offences .	19,454	21,325	574	568
Total . .	33,870	37,590	1,000	1,000

The nationality of criminals and their proportion to the number of each nationality residing in Canada, during 12 years ending December 1895, averaged as follows :—

	Whole No.	Annual Average	Per 100,000 Souls
Canadians . . .	32,950	2,746	65
English . . .	4,210	350	160
Irish . . .	3,245	270	180
Americans . . .	2,655	221	276
Scotch . . .	1,010	84	80
Foreigners, &c. . .	4,340	363	...
Total . .	48,410	4,034	85

If children under 10 were excluded, the ratios would be approximately :—

	Pop. over 10	Criminals	Per 100,000
Canadians . . .	3,020,000	2,746	91
English . . .	210,000	350	167
Irish . . .	142,000	270	190
Americans . . .	77,000	221	287
Scotch . . .	102,000	84	82

The ratio for the whole population over 10 years of age would be 111 per 100,000 ; that for foreigners cannot be ascertained, as 2660 criminals were not classified in the whole period of 12 years. The high ratio of American criminals would indicate that many outlaws from the United States cross into Canada.

INDIA

The returns for 1881 and 1895 compare as follows :—

	Convictions			Per 100,000 Pop.
	Crimes	Offences	Total	
1881	177,000	468,000	645,000	323
1895	178,000	667,000	845,000	367

The prison population was as follows :—

	Males	Females	Total	Per 100,000 Pop.
1881	83,430	3,890	87,320	44
1890	86,730	3,050	89,780	41
1895	97,990	3,190	101,180	44

In 1895, of convicts for grave crimes, 14 per cent. were recidivistes or old offenders.

CAPE COLONY

The returns for 1888 and 1896 compared thus :—

	Convictions			Per 100,000 Pop.
	Crimes	Offences	Total	
1888	1,408	39,172	40,580	4,660
1896	2,400	48,810	51,210	4,860

The prison population was as follows :—

	Males	Females	Total	Per 100,000 Pop.
1888	2,032	200	2,232	260
1896	2,924	336	3,260	310

The ratio of persons in jail to population is remarkably high.

ALGERIA

The records for 1893 compare with 1886 as follows :—

	Convictions			Per 100,000 Pop.
	Crimes	Offences	Total	
1886	12,410	59,980	72,390	1,910
1893	22,750	60,660	83,410	1,980

Under the head of offences are included minor police-court cases.

JAMAICA

Returns for 1887 and 1897 were as follows :—

	Convictions			Per 100,000 Pop.
	Crimes	Offences	Total	
1887	2,410	8,120	10,530	1,720
1897	4,490	11,400	15,890	2,270

The prison population in March 1897 was 1150, equal to 164 per 100,000 inhabitants.

CURIOSITIES

A collection of Australian postage stamps, begun in 1872 by Mr. M. Castle, of London, was purchased by Stanley Gibbons in 1897 for £10,000, being £2000 more than the price of the Galliera collection (1880). At a sale in London in 1895, four Mauritius stamps were sold for £210, and one blue Mauritius twopenny stamp for £140. A sale of coins in London in June 1896 realised among others the following prices : farthing of Henry IV., £17 ; a silver groat, £28 ; a half-noble, £45 ; and a half-groat of Edward III., £23. Besides the 35 autographs recorded with their prices at page 172, the following have since been sold :—

The Pretender . £8 | Q. Elizabeth . £6 | Henry VII. . £18
Henry VIII. . 8 | Wesley . . . 3 | Paul Veronese 19

In March 1898 the bugle used for the Balaklava charge (1855) was sold in London for £750.

CURRENTS

The *Times* of December 8, 1896, mentions that on October 9, 1894, the s.s. *Hunter* threw overboard a box containing a letter in

S. lat. 45° 19′ 32″ ; E. long. 63° 59′ 15″,

which was picked up in July 1896 in

S. lat. 44° 0′ 0″ ; W. long. 176° 30′ 0″,

having drifted in a straight line 4791 miles in 20 months 26 days, being at the rate of 7½ miles per day.

In June 1881 was picked up in the Feejee Islands a bottle containing a letter which had been thrown overboard in March 1880 in 4° S. lat. and 119° W. long., having been carried 6700 miles in 455 days, that is, 15 miles a day.

CUSTOMS

See *Taxes*, page 811, and page 172.

D

DAIRY

The following table shows the production and consumption of butter and cheese, and the approximate number of milch cows :—

	Production, Tons	Consumption		Milch Cows
		Tons	Lbs. per Inhab.	
U. Kingdom	200,000	510,000	28	3,950,000
France . .	200,000	270,000	16	5,020,000
Germany .	300,000	440,000	17	8,950,000
Russia . .	350,000	345,000	7	10,000,000
Austria . .	170,000	170,000	9	6,000,000
Italy . . .	145,000	85,000	6	2,400,000
Spain & Port.	50,000	50,000	6	1,200,000
Swed. & Nor.	80,000	55,000	18	2,300,000
Denmark .	60,000	20,000	20	1,050,000
Holland. .	120,000	20,000	10	900,000
Belgium. .	60,000	65,000	23	800,000
Switzerland	70,000	30,000	22	500,000
Europe . .	1,805,000	2,060,000	13	43,070,000
U. States .	610,000	580,000	18	15,940,000
Canada . .	130,000	50,000	22	1,990,000
Australia .	55,000	50,000	24	1,100,000
Total .	2,600,000	2,740,000	15	62,100,000

The consumption in Holland is probably double what it appears to be, as margarine is largely mixed with what is exported as butter. For the same reason it appears in the above table that the consumption of butter and cheese in the world is 140,000 tons more than production, the difference being evidently ascribable to margarine.

Great Britain consumes more butter and cheese for population than any other country; the consumption (exclusive of Ireland) being over 30 pounds per inhabitant, or nearly twice as much as in France or Germany. See *Food*, page 715.

DEATHS

The death-rate of the principal countries, and the saving of life yearly by the reduction of mortality since 1880, owing to improved sanitation and other causes, are shown briefly thus :—

	Deaths per 1000 Pop. Yearly			Lives Saved Yearly
	1861–80	1885–90	1891–96	
England	22.0	18.9	18.5	103,000
Scotland. . . .	...	18.9	18.7	...
Ireland	...	18.0	18.1	...
United Kingdom .	...	18.8	18.4	...
France	24.0	21.9	22.1	73,000
Prussia	27.1	24.3	22.9	124,000
Scandinavia . .	19.0	17.2	17.3	16,000
Austria	30.8	29.0	27.6	79,000
Hungary . . .	39.4	32.2	31.4	145,000
Italy	29.9	27.3	25.5	131,000
Holland	24.6	20.6	19.2	26,000
Belgium	22.7	20.7	19.9	18,000
Bavaria	...	27.8	26.0	...
Wurtemburg . .	...	24.9	25.0	...
Saxony	...	27.7	25.2	...
Baden	...	23.5	23.0	...
Switzerland . . .	...	20.6	20.0	...
Bulgaria	...	18.5	28.7	...
Japan	...	21.1	21.1	...
Australia . . .	15.6	14.0	12.7	11,000

Thus in ten countries, of which we can compare death-rates in the last thirty-six years, the diminution of mortality yearly amounts to 726,000 lives; that is to say, the number of deaths in those countries is now 4,712,000, whereas at the rates prevalent down to 1880 they would have been 5,438,000. In other words, taking the ten countries collectively, the span of life has been lengthened 15 per cent.—say 6 years.

Bodio's tables for five years ending December 1891 give the annual average death-rate of various countries as follows :—

	Bronchitis, &c.	Diarrhœa, &c.	Consumption	Apoplexy	Diphtheria	Measles	Typhoid	Scarlatina	Small-pox	Whooping Cough	Various	Total
England	382	76	229	101	29	47	20	23	1	44	954	1,906
Scotland	363	71	252	108	42	47	23	20	0	64	930	1,920
Ireland	296	44	268	59	24	20	31	12	0	29	1,022	1,805
France	420	215	397	...	67	52	53	31	23	18	1,273	2,549
Prussia	...	109	290	103	142	32	23	25	0	50	1,552	2,326
Austria	303	139	372	67	132	54	54	56	44	98	1,513	2,832
Switzerland	...	113	211	86	35	15	15	12	1	20	1,838	2,346
Belgium	444	125	199	...	58	62	38	16	15	61	989	2,007
Holland	282	42	192	79	37	39	25	4	0	31	1,447	1,636
Sweden	...	38	...	...	52	23	22	37	0	17	1,214	2,675
Italy	509	334	196	107	71	62	78	30	39	35	1,125	2,185
Average	375	119	261	89	63	41	35	24	11	42		

The statistics for France refer to the urban population. In the above table Bronchitis includes Pneumonia and similar complaints, Consumption comprises all tubercular diseases, and Diarrhœa includes Cholera and Dysentery, while Diphtheria includes Croup.

The following table shows the number of deaths from certain diseases in 10,000 deaths from all causes :—

	England	Scotland	Ireland	France	Austria	Belgium	Holland	Italy	Average
Bronchitis . .	2,001	1,888	1,643	1,714	1,070	2,220	1,390	1,905	1,730
Diarrhœa . .	398	370	244	843	495	623	207	1,248	554
Consumption .	1,200	1,310	1,487	1,558	1,315	980	945	732	1,190
Diphtheria . .	152	218	133	265	464	290	180	265	246
Measles . .	247	247	111	204	190	310	190	232	216
Typhoid . . .	105	120	172	208	190	190	123	291	175
Scarlatina .	120	104	67	122	198	80	20	113	103
Whooping-cough .	230	332	160	70	345	303	153	132	216
Other diseases .	5,547	5,411	5,983	5,016	5,733	5,004	6,792	5,082	5,570
Total . .	10,000	10,000	10,000	10,000	10,000	10,000	10,000	10,000	10,000

The annual death-rate per million inhabitants from certain diseases in ten years, 1882–91, in various cities averaged as follows :—

	Per Million Inhabitants								
	Small-pox	Measles	Scarlatina	Diphtheria	Whooping Cough	Typhoid	Puerperal Fever	Phthisis	Total
London	60	610	290	280	710	180	80	2,940	5,150
Paris	110	550	90	1,050	180	600	100	4,510	7,190
Berlin	4	310	260	1,270	310	160	100	3,080	5,494
Vienna	270	370	200	540	130	100	120	5,340	7,070
Rome	400	690	60	500	100	430	50	3,490	5,720
Buda-Pesth	600	280	440	1,170	130	430	70	6,330	9,450
Hamburg	5	290	300	850	350	400	100	3,000	5,295
Leipzig	3	160	220	850	160	130	80	2,580	4,183
Dresden	...	210	260	1,380	260	120	110	3,240	5,580
Breslau	10	260	210	1,100	210	190	50	3,270	5,300
Naples	220	610	320	380	120	460	30	2,500	4,640
Milan	480	530	150	720	160	750	70	3,530	6,390
Turin	240	500	130	710	230	580	80	3,110	5,580
Genoa	450	390	40	350	110	460	50	2,520	4,370
Florence	250	270	120	470	130	880	60	3,880	6,060
Palermo	40	900	150	640	150	1,170	40	2,120	5,210
Venice	1,090	530	50	280	110	560	30	3,450	6,100
Bologna	300	290	240	540	150	590	60	3,220	5,390
Trieste	800	310	140	1,260	130	190	50	5,280	8,160
Brussels	320	320	70	470	280	260	180	3,450	5,350
Average	282	419	187	741	205	432	76	3,542	5,884

The following table shows the proportions which the above eight infectious diseases had in the total mortality during the said ten years :—

	Number of Deaths Yearly			Per 10,000 Inhabitants			Ratio of Infectious
	Infectious	Other	Total	Infectious	Other	Total	
London	20,800	61,500	82,300	52	152	204	25.5
Paris	16,800	38,700	55,500	72	166	238	30.2
Berlin	7,700	24,800	32,500	55	176	231	23.8
Vienna	7,300	14,900	22,200	71	144	215	33.0
Rome	2,500	6,900	9,400	57	199	256	22.4
Buda-Pesth	4,200	9,500	13,700	95	214	309	30.6
Hamburg	2,600	9,800	12,400	53	195	248	21.4
Leipzig	1,000	3,400	4,400	42	130	172	24.4
Dresden	1,500	4,300	5,800	56	163	219	25.5
Breslau	1,600	7,500	9,100	53	239	292	18.2
Naples	2,400	12,800	15,200	46	255	301	15.3
Milan	2,400	8,100	10,500	64	217	281	22.7
Turin	1,600	5,700	7,300	56	206	262	21.3
Genoa	800	4,200	5,000	44	212	256	17.2
Florence	1,100	3,800	4,900	61	204	265	23.0
Palermo	1,400	5,100	6,500	52	201	253	20.6
Venice	900	3,300	4,200	61	248	309	19.7
Bologna	700	3,000	3,700	54	226	280	19.3
Trieste	1,300	3,400	4,700	82	230	312	26.2
Brussels	900	3,200	4,100	52	192	244	21.3
Total . . .	79,500	233,900	313,400	Av. 59	198	257	23.0

It appears that during the said ten years Leipzig, London, and Vienna were the cities of lowest death-rate, while Trieste, Venice, Buda-Pesth, and Naples were the most unhealthy.

Friendly Societies

Bertillon's table of death-rates among Friendly Societies published in 1892 shows as follows :—

Age				England	France	Italy	Average
				Deaths Yearly per 1,000			
20–25	.	.	.	7.4	13.0	6.3	8.9
25–30	.	.	.	7.3	5.4	5.9	6.2
30–35	.	.	.	8.9	6.4	6.2	7.2
35–40	.	.	.	10.9	6.4	7.8	8.4
40–45	.	.	.	12.8	10.2	9.2	10.7
45–50	.	.	.	16.6	11.8	11.6	13.3
50–55	.	.	.	20.5	20.2	14.9	18.5
55–60	.	.	.	29.7	19.5	22.2	23.8
60–65	.	.	.	38.0	40.7	32.5	37.1
65–70	.	.	.	58.4	67.0	50.4	58.6
General	.	.	.	12.1	23.5	11.7	15.8

The table was compiled from observations by Neison, Bertillon, and Bodio, between 1871 and 1889.

Infant Mortality

The *Statistical Journal* of Paris gives a table of infant mortality in 1895, which compares with one for 1876–80 as follows :—

Percentage of Infants who Die under Twelve Months.

	1876–80	1895		1876–80	1895
Ireland .	...	10.0	Switzerland	18.9	19.0
Sweden .	12.6	10.0	Roumania .	...	20.0
Denmark	15.0	14.0	Holland .	21.1	20.0
Greece .	...	15.0	Prussia . .	20.5	21.0
G. Britain	14.5	15.0	Wurtemburg	30.2	25.0
France .	16.3	17.0	Austria . .	24.9	25.0
Belgium .	17.4	17.0	Bavaria . .	29.8	27.0
Italy . .	22.3	19.0	Russia . .	31.2	30.0

There is an increase of infant mortality in Great Britain, France, and Prussia, but a decline in most other countries. In Great Britain the death-rate of infants is 50 per cent. higher than in Ireland. Official returns in Prussia, for twelve years ending December 1888, show that infant mortality increases as we descend in the social scale; thus of 1000 children born in various classes we find :—

Class				Die First Year	Survive
Affluent	.	.	.	211	789
Labourers	.	.	.	251	749
Servants	.	.	.	332	668
Paupers	.	.	.	422	578

Drysdale (see page 178) gives the rates in England as 110 per thousand in the West-End of London, and 380 among the "slum" population.

The principal causes of death among infants showed the following averages in England and Wales during ten years to December 31, 1890 :—

				Deaths Yearly	Ratio
Inanition .	.	.	.	19,490	15.6
Convulsions	.	.	.	18,140	14.5
Bronchitis	.	.	.	16,160	13.0
Diarrhœa.	.	.	.	11,930	9.5
Pneumonia	.	.	.	5,950	4.7
Whooping-cough	.	.		5,340	4.3
Suffocation	.	.	.	1,490	1.2
Infanticide	.	.	.	103	0.1
Various	.	.	.	46,417	37.1
Total	.	.		125,020	100.0

As a rule the death-rate of infants under twelve months is eight times as much as that of the general public, in England, viz. :—

				Deaths Yearly per 1000 Living.	
				All Ages	Infants
Brighton .	.	.	.	17	149
Hull .	.	.	.	19	165
London .	.	.	.	20	158
Birmingham	.	.	.	20	176
Bristol	.	.	.	20	149
Leeds	.	.	.	21	172
Sheffield .	.	.	.	22	177
Liverpool .	.	.	.	24	186
Newcastle	.	.	.	25	174
Manchester	.	.	.	29	191
Average .	.	.	.	22	170

England

The following table shows the death-rate for males and females in England and Wales at various ages in 1891–95 as compared with 1881–85.

Ages	Deaths Yearly per 1000 Living			
	Males		Females	
	1881–85	1891–95	1881–85	1891–95
Under 5 .	61.3	62.1	51.9	52.0
5–10 . .	5.8	4.5	5.7	4.5
10–15 . .	3.2	2.5	3.3	2.7
15–20 . .	4.5	4.0	4.7	4.0
20–25 . .	6.0	5.3	5.9	4.8
25–35 . .	8.2	7.2	7.9	6.7
35–45 . .	12.8	12.2	11.0	10.3
45–55 . .	19.3	19.8	15.2	15.3
55–65 . .	34.2	36.3	28.1	29.8
65–75 . .	68.7	71.9	59.0	62.8
75–85 . .	145.0	150.0	129.0	136.0
All ages . .	20.5	19.8	18.3	17.7

As regards infants under 5 years there is not much change. The rates for ages between 5 and 45 show a notable decline, which accounts for the increased death-rates between 55 and 85. A woman's life is much better than a man's at all ages, except from 10 to 15. The death-rate both for males and females in 1891–95 was 3 per cent. less than in 1881–85.

Death-rates for age in English cities during 10 years ending December 1890, gave the following averages per 1000 living :—

Age	London		Liverpool		Bristol	
	Males	Females	Males	Females	Males	Females
Under 5 .	68.5	59.0	84.3	74.9	59.7	48.3
5–15 . .	4.3	4.2	6.1	5.8	3.9	3.8
15–25 .	4.6	3.9	6.0	5.2	4.8	4.3
25–35 .	8.2	6.5	10.9	9.8	7.7	6.2
35–45 .	14.0	10.8	17.9	15.8	12.4	10.3
45–55 .	22.2	16.3	28.5	24.0	19.6	15.1
55–65 .	39.1	29.4	50.8	42.5	34.7	26.9
65–75 .	74.4	60.7	94.3	80.0	72.3	57.6

Age	Birmingham		Leeds		Sheffield	
	Males	Females	Males	Females	Males	Females
Under 5 .	68.2	58.7	78.0	65.2	78.6	67.2
5–15 . .	3.7	3.7	5.3	5.5	5.3	5.3
15–25 .	4.2	4.0	5.8	5.2	5.3	5.1
25–35 .	7.7	7.0	7.7	8.1	8.4	7.7
35–45 .	13.7	11.4	13.2	11.5	14.7	11.7
45–55 .	21.7	17.4	23.3	18.5	25.0	17.4
55–65 .	40.9	32.0	45.5	37.0	46.8	34.8
65–75 .	81.6	67.2	94.0	77.0	94.9	74.1

The following table for England and Wales shows death-rate of males according to professions :—

	Deaths Yearly per 1,000 Living					Deaths Yearly per 1,000 Living			
	Age 25–45		Age 45–65			Age 25–45		Age 45–65	
	1860-71	1880-82	1860-71	1880-82		1860-71	1880-82	1860-71	1880-82
Clergyman	6.0	4.6	17.3	15.9	Printer	13.0	11.1	29.4	26.6
Farmer	7.7	6.1	17.3	16.5	Dyer	11.2	9.5	26.0	27.1
Grocer	9.5	8.0	17.2	19.2	Wool-spinner	9.4	9.7	23.3	27.5
Fisherman	11.3	8.3	15.8	19.7	Physician	13.8	11.6	24.6	28.0
Schoolmaster	9.8	6.4	23.6	19.8	Cooper	11.8	10.6	26.1	28.6
Bookseller	10.8	8.5	21.4	20.6	Butcher	13.2	12.2	28.4	29.1
Carpenter	9.4	7.8	21.4	21.7	Cotton-spinner	10.7	10.0	27.9	29.4
Watchmaker	10.8	9.3	24.9	22.6	Stone-cutter	10.9	10.0	28.7	31.0
Lawyer	9.9	7.5	23.0	23.1	Glass-blower	13.2	11.2	29.3	31.7
Shoemaker	10.4	9.3	22.3	23.4	Musician	18.9	13.8	34.8	32.4
Slater	10.7	9.0	30.8	24.9	Painter	12.5	11.1	34.7	32.5
Druggist	13.9	10.6	23.6	25.2	Hairdresser	15.1	13.6	30.1	33.3
Tanner	10.4	8.0	26.6	25.4	Publican	18.0	18.0	34.1	33.7
Mason	11.4	9.3	27.2	25.6	Cutler	11.9	11.7	32.7	34.4
Blacksmith	10.1	9.3	23.9	25.7	Cab-driver	15.9	15.4	35.3	36.8
Gasfitter	11.0	9.2	27.9	25.7	Chimney-sweep	17.5	13.7	42.9	41.5
Baker	10.7	8.7	26.4	26.1	File-maker	16.3	15.3	42.3	45.1
Chandler	11.8	7.7	27.2	26.2	Costermonger	20.1	20.3	37.8	45.3
Tailor	12.9	10.7	24.8	26.5	Potter	12.6	13.7	41.8	51.4
Coal-miner	11.3	7.8	30.5	26.5	General average	11.3	10.2	24.0	25.3

The tables of mortality of England and Wales for 20 years are summed up as follows :—

	Average Number of Deaths Yearly		Deaths per Million Inhabitants		Deaths Yearly, 1891–95	
	1876–80	1891–95	1876–80	1891–95	Male	Female
Accidents	15,789	16,765	630	562	11,772	4,993
Aneurism	810	823	32	28	632	191
Angina	469	672	19	23	426	246
Apoplexy	13,780	17,052	550	574	7,822	9,230
Asthma	2,564	2,605	102	88	1,430	1,175
Bladder	1,620	2,150	65	72	1,910	240
Brain *	18,414	13,710	736	462	6,664	7,046
Bright's	4,714	7,656	188	258	4,134	3,522
Bronchitis	59,632	61,645	2,378	2,076	30,508	31,137
Cancer *	12,383	21,194	494	712	7,891	13,303
Child-birth	1,998	2,700	79	90	...	2,700
Convulsions	24,322	20,475	972	688	11,558	8,917
Croup	3,864	2,073	154	70	1,118	955
Dentition	4,479	4,141	179	139	2,276	1,865
Diabetes	1,016	2,065	40	70	1,164	901
Diarrhœa	20,890	18,797	832	630	9,866	8,931
Diphtheria	3,049	7,545	122	253	3,644	3,901
Dropsy *	2,553	220	102	7	86	134
Enteritis *	2,758	7,202	110	241	3,780	3,422
Epilepsy	2,876	2,811	115	95	1,442	1,369
Erysipelas *	2,022	1,422	81	48	741	681
Gout	637	609	25	20	482	127
Hernia	1,119	1,295	45	43	626	669
Homicide	351	313	14	10	164	149
Hunger *	630	335	25	11	182	153
Influenza	208	12,320	8	416	6,102	6,218
Intemperance	1,052	2,018	42	68	1,248	770
Laryngitis	1,061	1,444	42	48	782	662
Liver *	9,977	7,498	398	252	3,942	3,556
Measles	9,659	12,117	385	408	6,232	5,885
Meningitis	8,112	6,738	324	226	3,692	3,046
Mesenterica	8,288	7,091	330	237	3,736	3,355
Nephritis	1,017	1,907	40	64	1,088	819
Old age	26,874	27,636	1,075	926	11,750	15,886
Peritonitis	2,017	2,346	80	79	1,092	1,254
Phthisis	51,092	43,520	2,043	1,458	23,538	19,982
Pleurisy	1,254	1,712	50	57	1,022	690
Pneumonia	25,058	37,226	1,002	1,247	21,520	15,706
Rheumatism	3,481	3,544	139	119	1,718	1,826
Scarlatina	17,042	5,424	682	182	2,684	2,740

* Those marked thus have undergone new classification since 1880.

	Average Number of Deaths Yearly		Deaths per Million Inhabitants		Deaths Yearly, 1891-95	
	1876-80	1891-95	1876-80	1891-95	Male	Female
Smallpox	1,946	596	78	20	352	244
Spinal *	695	2,112	28	71	1,234	878
Suicide	1,850	2,636	74	88	1,966	670
Syncope	2,032	1,910	81	64	1,002	908
Syphilis	2,120	2,036	84	68	1,106	930
Thrush	1,201	436	48	15	232	204
Tumour *	310	133	12	4	54	79
Typhoid	6,930	5,164	277	173	2,796	2,368
Typhus *	848	106	34	4	56	50
Whooping-cough	13,220	11,830	528	397	5,278	6,552
Various	121,029	141,303	4,818	4,777	70,894	70,409
Total . . .	521,112	557,078	20,791	18,738	285,434	271,644

* Those marked thus have undergone new classification since 1880.

The following table shows the annual number of deaths *per million inhabitants* from various diseases :—

	1886-89	1890-92	1893-95	1886-95
Zymotic . . .	2,492	2,677	2,748	2,625
Constitutional . .	3,243	3,294	3,131	3,225
Local . . .	9,736	10,324	9,132	9,731
Violent . . .	630	658	664	649
Sundry . . .	2,631	2,629	2,489	2,587
Total . .	18,732	19,582	18,164	18,817

ACCIDENTAL DEATHS

In England and Wales there are 16,800 persons killed by accident yearly, 70 per cent. being males, 30 females. Considering only males between 25 and 65 years of age, we find :—

Accidental Deaths of 1000 *Men who Die*

Shoemakers . 17	Cotton-spinrs. 30	Blacksmiths . 49
Tailors . . . 18	Ploughmen . 33	Costermongers 53
Bakers . . . 21	Butchers . . 35	Brewers . . 64
Printers. . . 24	C. travellers . 36	Painters . . 73
Gardeners . . 24	Carpenters . 38	Cab-drivers . 84
Potters . . . 24	Publicans. . 45	Fishermen . 152
Farmers . . 30	Bricklayers . 45	Miners . . . 190

The general average for all males between 25 and 65 is 67 per thousand, from which it appears that miners, fishermen, and cab-drivers have extra hazardous occupations. Accidental deaths in 1891-95 averaged yearly as follows (England and Wales) :—

By	Males	Females	Total	Per Million
Drowning . .	2,282	414	2,696	91
Fire . . .	1,078	1,324	2,402	81
Suffocation .	1,160	1,034	2,194	74
Vehicles . .	2,122	312	2,434	82
Mines . . .	1,023	1	1,024	34
Sundry . .	4,107	1,908	6,015	202
Total . .	11,772	4,993	16,765	564

Accidental deaths in Italy during ten years to end of 1896 averaged 10,140 per annum, or 13 per thousand.

As regards Germany and Austria see *Insurance,* page 755. For other countries see page 180.

IRELAND AND SCOTLAND

Some of the causes of death in Ireland during ten years ending 1895, and in Scotland for the year 1893, were :—

	Per 100,000 Inhabitants Yearly	
	Ireland	Scotland
Diphtheria . . .	8	24
Influenza . . .	25	30
Typhoid . . .	17	37
Whooping-cough . .	27	50
Diarrhœa . . .	32	65
Violent . . .	40	68
Cancer . . .	46	69
Measles . . .	19	90
Phthisis . . .	213	170
Bronchitis . . .	314	309

Under the last title is also included Pneumonia.

WORKMEN'S DWELLINGS

In 1891 was published a table comparing the death-rates of London with those of the Peabody and the Metropolitan Dwellings for Workmen, averaging two years previous, viz. :—

Disease	Deaths Yearly per 100,000 Persons		
	London	Peabody	Metropolitan
Scarlatina . .	23	34	22
Measles . .	55	104	59
Whooping-cough .	55	86	48
Diarrhœa . .	57	56	56
Diphtheria . .	34	54	37
Typhoid . .	14	7	7
Tubercular . .	254	263	236
Various . .	1,304	1,168	1,109
Total . .	1,796	1,772	1,574

Infant mortality under twelve months was 153 per 1000 births in London, 136 in Peabody Buildings, and 121 in the Metropolitan Dwellings, during five years to December 1890.

FRANCE

In the years 1890-93 the mortality in France was 40,000 more than in preceding years, apparently due to influenza. The returns were as follows :—

Period	Deaths Yearly	Per 1000 Pop.
1885-89 . . .	835,000	21.7
1890-93 . . .	875,000	22.8

In 1890 there were recorded 38,000 deaths from influenza.

The death-rate of the French army is as follows :—

Per 1000 *Men*

France . . . 7 | Senegal . . 74 | Tonkin . . 77
Algeria . . . 11 | Madagascar . 75 | Cayenne . . 237

Bertillon's table of male mortality (1892) is as follows for the city of Paris :—

	Deaths Yearly for 1000 Living			
	20–30	30–40	40–50	50–60
Grocers . . .	6.6	7.0	8.7	11.4
Druggists . .	7.8	9.2	11.1	15.7
Schoolmasters . .	7.0	8.5	5.8	17.0
Dairymen . .	5.7	9.9	11.8	17.4
Physicians . .	9.9	11.3	9.8	21.9
Lawyers . .	9.8	11.6	11.1	22.8
Watchmakers . .	9.7	14.0	14.9	24.7
Tanners . .	9.1	10.5	15.9	26.4
Butchers . .	10.6	14.0	22.2	27.5
Waggoners . .	17.6	21.5	26.7	30.4
Clergymen . .	5.0	8.2	9.0	30.5
Carpenters . .	10.5	18.8	24.3	30.7
Masons . .	9.5	16.0	23.7	31.4
Hairdressers . .	14.8	14.2	18.1	33.2
Shoemakers . .	13.4	19.2	20.4	35.3
Bakers . .	12.4	16.2	24.4	39.0
Tailors . . .	9.1	11.3	23.4	39.8
Printers . .	17.8	23.7	26.7	40.6
Painters . .	14.8	23.0	28.8	42.0
Cab-drivers . .	16.4	20.5	32.0	58.0
Average . . .	11.1	14.9	21.2	31.2

The heaviest death-rate falls to cab-drivers, painters, printers, tailors, and bakers, and of these classes only cab-drivers and painters are in the same position in the death-rate of England.

Switzerland

Tables for four years ending December 1882 show male death-rates thus :—

	Deaths Yearly per 1,000 Living			
	20–30	30–40	40–50	50–60
Farmers . . .	5.7	7.9	12.1	21.7
Clergymen . .	7.2	8.2	13.1	23.0
Schoolmasters . .	6.4	8.7	14.8	24.3
Cotton-spinners .	8.0	9.3	13.3	24.9
Printers . .	10.2	14.3	16.2	27.0
Bakers . .	6.8	11.4	15.9	28.9
Merchants . .	11.1	14.1	18.7	29.2
Butchers . .	5.3	17.9	21.5	29.9
Tailors . .	10.6	11.9	17.9	30.0
Shoemakers . .	7.7	10.0	14.2	30.0
Physicians . .	10.9	12.3	20.7	30.4
Carpenters . .	6.5	10.1	16.8	30.7
Blacksmiths . .	6.5	11.3	16.6	32.5
Innkeepers . .	7.8	16.9	24.2	32.8
Masons . .	9.5	13.1	18.9	34.9
Cab-drivers . .	10.8	18.3	26.0	51.0
General average	7.9	10.7	15.3	26.3

The most unhealthy occupations were cab-drivers, masons, innkeepers, and blacksmiths, and of these only cab-drivers stand in the same position in Bertillon's tables for Paris and in the official death-rates for England and Wales.

The following table shows the annual rate of mortality

of males from phthisis only, in Switzerland, according to occupation :—

	Deaths Yearly per 1,000 Living			
	20–30	30–40	40–50	50–60
Farmers . . .	1.5	2.0	2.0	2.4
Physicians . .	4.8	4.7	5.3	3.2
Clergymen . .	3.9	3.7	3.7	3.3
Schoolmasters . .	3.4	3.8	4.6	3.3
Cotton-spinners .	4.0	3.4	2.7	3.9
Innkeepers . .	4.4	6.9	6.1	4.0
Bakers . .	2.9	4.1	3.8	4.2
Merchants . .	5.8	6.6	4.8	4.4
Cab-drivers . .	2.7	4.8	5.8	4.5
Carpenters . .	1.9	3.8	3.4	4.8
Shoemakers . .	3.0	4.4	3.7	5.0
Blacksmiths . .	2.3	4.1	5.6	5.3
Tailors . .	4.9	5.6	5.5	5.5
Masons . .	2.8	3.5	4.1	5.6
Butchers . .	5.6	6.8	5.9	6.3
Printers . .	6.5	7.9	6.6	6.7
General average	3.1	4.0	3.5	3.7

The worst trades are printers, butchers, and masons, whose rates of death from phthisis are double those of farmers, clergymen, and schoolmasters.

Italy

Public health has improved in the last ten years, as shown by the diminished death-rate, viz. :—

	Deaths Yearly per 1,000 Population	
	1887	1896
Cities	28.9	23.7
All Italy	28.1	24.3

In 1896 the urban death-rate was lower than that of the nation. The causes of death in the kingdom were :—

	Per 100,000 Inhabitants	
	1887	1896
Bronchitis	217	233
Diarrhœa	316	346
Consumption	212	192
Diphtheria	84	21
Measles	81	37
Malaria	71	45
Various	1,829	1,556
Total . .	2,810	2,430

In the northern provinces the death-rate is 30 per cent. less than in the southern, viz. :—

Per 10,000 *Yearly*

Venetia . . . 198 | Umbria . . . 240
Piedmont . . . 202 | Sicily . . . 252
Tuscany . . . 229 | Romagna . . . 256
Lombardy . . . 236 | Naples . . . 288

Deaths from malaria and phthisis are as follows :—

Per 100,000 *Inhabitants*

Malaria | *Phthisis*
Romagna . . . 66 | Lombardy . . . 224
Sicily . . . 99 | Tuscany . . . 236
Sardinia . . . 171 | Liguria . . . 267
Basilicata . . . 199 | Romagna . . . 283

UNITED STATES

The census of 1890 showed the death-rate of certain cities thus :—

	Per 1000 Persons	
	White	Coloured
New York . . .	28.5	37.4
Chicago	21.0	23.3
Philadelphia . . .	22.3	32.4
St. Louis	18.2	34.6
Boston	24.6	33.3
Baltimore	22.6	36.4
San Francisco . .	23.6	24.1
Cincinnati	21.9	33.0
New Orleans . . .	25.4	36.6
Washington . . .	19.8	38.2
Average . . .	22.8	32.9

The death-rate of the Union being, as Dr. Billings shows, 15.0 per thousand, it appears that the whites in the above 10 cities collectively have a death-rate which is relatively 52 per cent. higher. Moreover, in the same cities the death-rate of coloured persons is 44 per cent. higher than that of whites. The total number of deaths recorded in 1890 was :—

	No.	Ratio	Per 100,000 Pop.
Consumption . .	102,199	11.6	164
Pneumonia . .	76,496	8.8	122
Diarrhœa . .	74,711	8.6	119
Diphtheria . .	41,677	4.7	67
Typhoid . .	27,058	3.1	43
Cancer . . .	20,984	2.4	33
Various . .	532,395	60.8	852
Total . .	875,520	100.0	1,400

The above would show an annual death-rate of 14 per 1000, but the returns are supposed to be incomplete, and Dr. Billings considers the real death-rate to be 15.1 per thousand. In his report already mentioned (1886) he states the death-rates, urban and rural, from certain diseases as follows :—

	Deaths Yearly per 100,000 Pop.		No. in 1000 Deaths	
	Rural	Cities	Rural	Cities
Consumption . .	163	286	124	138
Nervous affections .	146	257	111	124
Diarrhœa . . .	114	199	87	97
Pneumonia . .	123	143	93	69
Heart disease .	79	96	60	46
Accidents . .	65	85	50	41
Diphtheria . .	75	80	57	39
Apoplexy . .	45	51	34	25
Bronchitis . .	16	56	12	28
Croup . . .	35	41	26	20
Cancer . . .	23	40	17	20
Typhoid . . .	48	35	36	17
Malarial fever . .	43	25	32	12
Scarlatina . .	28	55	21	27
Whooping-cough .	22	20	16	10
Measles . . .	16	15	12	7
Various diseases .	279	576	212	280
Total . .	1,320	2,060	1,000	1,000

AUSTRALIA

The death-rates of the several colonies have been :—

	Per 1000 of Population Yearly.			
	1861–70	1871–80	1881–90	1891–95
New South Wales .	16.4	15.3	14.7	12.8
Victoria	16.9	15.5	15.3	14.1
New Zealand . .	13.0	12.2	10.4	10.2
Queensland . . .	19.4	17.3	17.0	12.5
South Australia . .	15.4	15.4	13.6	12.2
Tasmania	14.7	16.1	15.6	13.2
West Australia . .	16.3	15.2	16.6	16.1
General	16.2	14.9	14.4	12.7

In 1895 the ratio of sexes as to deaths showed as follows :—

	Deaths		Male Deaths to 1000 Female
	Males	Females	
New South Wales .	8,671	6,243	1,383
Victoria	8,891	6,758	1,314
New Zealand . . .	3,966	2,897	1,370
Queensland . . .	3,237	1,915	1,690
South Australia . .	2,203	1,760	1,252
Tasmania	1,047	764	1,373
West Australia . . .	1,201	403	2,980
Total . .	29,216	20,740	1,408

The census of 1891 showed the number of males to 1000 females was 1150, that is to say, the male surplus was 15 per cent. ; as the above table shows the mortality of males to be almost 41 per cent. over that of females, it is evident that the death-rate of males is excessive. If it were in the same ratio as that of females, the deaths of males in 1895 would have reached only 23,850.

For Canada see *Vital Statistics*, page 815.

DEATH-DUTIES

The total amount of property assessed for death-duties in the United Kingdom has been as follows :—

	Annual Averages, £		
	1883–87	1888–92	1893–97
England . . .	150,020,000	178,600,000	184,900,000
Scotland . . .	18,010,000	19,400,000	21,300,000
Ireland . . .	12,100,000	11,900,000	11,600,000
United Kingdom	180,130,000	209,900,000	217,800,000

Dividing the above amounts among the number of deaths, it would appear that the average fortune of each in the said periods was as follows :—

	£ per Decease		
	1883–87	1888–92	1893–97
England . . .	285	330	340
Scotland . . .	240	255	280
Ireland . . .	134	138	140
United Kingdom	261	298	310

The ratios of property assessed to death-dues were as follows :—

	No. of Estates		Value of Estates	
	1887	**1897**	**1887**	**1897**
Over £100,000 . .	3	5	221	273
£10,000 to £100,000	53	59	446	423
£1,000 to £10,000 .	256	246	261	227
Under £1,000 . . .	688	690	72	77
Total . . .	1,000	1,000	1,000	1,000

The value of estates in 1897 was as follows :—

	(000 omitted)			
	England £	Scotland £	Ireland £	U. King. £
Over £100,000 . .	53,000	5,100	2,200	60,300
£10,000 to £100,000	78,700	8,800	5,200	92,700
£1,000 to £10,000 .	41,800	5,600	3,200	50,600
Under £1,000 . . .	13,400	1,700	1,600	16,700
Total . . .	186,900	21,200	12,200	220,300

The deaths among the wealthy classes in the three kingdoms in 1896-97 were as follows :—

	Number	Amount, £	Average, £
England . . .	2,886	131,800,000	47,700
Scotland . . .	348	13,900,000	40,000
Ireland . . .	219	7,400,000	33,600
Total . .	3,453	153,100,000	44,400

Those among the middle classes were as follows :—

	Number	Amount, £	Average, £
England . . .	10,916	41,800,000	3,830
Scotland . . .	1,554	5,600,000	3,600
Ireland . . .	955	3,200,000	3,360
Total . .	13,425	50,600,000	3,770

Those among the artisan and tradesmen classes were as follows :—

	Number	Amount, £	Average, £
England . . .	11,463	8,900,000	77
Scotland . . .	1,530	1,100,000	72
Ireland . . .	1,440	900,000	63
United Kingdom	14,433	10,900,000	75

The rest of the wealth divided among the rest of the deaths of adults shows :—

	Number	Amount, £	Average, £
England . . .	270,415	4,500,000	17
Scotland . . .	38,928	610,000	15
Ireland . . .	53,406	720,000	14
United Kingdom	362,749	5,830,000	16

The total property which changed owners at death, divided among the number of adults who died in 1896, showed as follows :—

	Number	Amount, £	Average, £
England . . .	295,680	186,900,000	633
Scotland . . .	42,360	21,200,000	501
Ireland . . .	56,020	12,200,000	218
U. Kingdom .	394,060	220,300,000	558

The distribution of wealth in the three kingdoms shows the following ratios :—

Class	Population to Wealth							
	England		Scotland		Ireland		U. Kingdom	
	Pop.=	Wth.	Pop.=	Wth.	Pop.=	Wth.	Pop.=	Wth.
No. 1	1.0	70.5	0.8	65.6	0.4	60.5	0.9	69.4
,, 2	3.7	22.4	3.7	26.4	1.7	26.2	3.4	23.0
,, 3	3.9	4.7	3.6	5.2	2.5	7.4	3.6	5.0
,, 4	91.4	2.4	91.9	2.8	95.4	5.9	92.1	2.6
Total	100.0	100.0	100.0	100.0	100.0	100.0	100.0	100.0

The first and second classes in the United Kingdom combined form 4¼ per cent. of the population, and possess 92½ per cent. of the wealth ; the third and fourth classes combined represent 95¾ per cent. of population and 7½ per cent. of wealth. The distribution of wealth is much more uneven in Ireland than in Great Britain ; the second and third classes combined compare as follows :—

Percentage	England	Scotland	Ireland
In population . .	7.6	7.3	4.2
In wealth . . .	27.1	31.6	33.6

At the same time the percentage of people of the poorest class is much greater in Ireland than in the sister kingdoms.

DIET

See pages 190–192.

DISEASES

See pages 193–216.

DIVORCES

The average of divorces to 10,000 marriages shows increasing ratios, viz. :—

	Per 10,000 Marriages		
	1877–86	**1890–95**	**Increase**
England . . .	19	16	...
France . . .	121	229	108
Germany . . .	152	170	18
Austria . . .	10	48	38
Italy . . .	24	28	4
Belgium . . .	69	110	41
Holland . . .	91	120	29
Sweden . . .	73	106	33
Switzerland . .	468	400	...
Roumania . . .	106	200	94

In Germany the ratio is by no means even : it is 100 in Wurtemberg, 140 in Bavaria, and 180 in Prussia, to

10,000 marriages. In Russia the rates are : among Roman Catholics 2, Greeks 17, Protestants 67, to 10,000 marriages. In Switzerland, 7 among Catholic, 27 among Protestant, and 40 among mixed marriages, per 10,000.

The following table shows the number of divorced persons in various countries, and their ratio to adult population :—

	Men	Women	Total	Per 100,000
France . . .	16,680	19,920	36,600	131
Germany . . .	25,270	49,600	74,870	234
Austria . . .	7,590	9,730	17,320	110
Hungary . . .	4,870	7,620	12,490	113
Switzerland . .	4,010	7,600	11,610	586
Sweden . . .	1,300	2,590	3,890	122
Norway . . .	310	440	750	57
Denmark . . .	2,380	3,500	5,880	412
Holland . . .	2,130	3,400	5,530	188
Belgium . . .	1,550	2,140	3,690	90
Bulgaria . . .	1,190	1,320	2,510	130
11 countries . .	67,280	107,860	175,140	...

FRANCE

The number of divorces since 1887 compares with marriages thus :—

Period	Annual Average		Divorces in 10,000 Marriages
	Divorces	Marriages	
1887–90 . . .	4,647	274,000	170
1891–93 . . .	5,903	287,000	205
1894–96 . . .	6,740	286,500	235

The ratio of divorces has increased 40 per cent. in ten years.

See *Divorce*, pages 217–225.

DOCKS AND HARBOURS

See page 226.

DOGS

The number of dog-licences issued in 1897 was :—

England 1,270,000
Scotland 110,000

Sheep-dogs go free of tax, as also those belonging to blind persons.

The number of dogs which paid tax in France in 1895 was 3,005,000.

For dogs in other countries see *Animals*, page 61, also page 35.

DRAINAGE

The length of sewers in the principal cities is :—

	Length, Miles	Inches per Inhab.		Length, Miles	Inches per Inhab.
London . .	1,420	20	Buda-Pesth .	140	16
Paris . . .	570	16	Brussels . .	78	10
Vienna . .	490	24	Bordeaux .	46	11
Berlin . . .	395	15	Leipzig . .	60	10
Hamburg . .	190	20	Rome . . .	51	7
Breslau . .	156	26	Genoa . .	51	15
Dresden . .	100	19	Palermo . .	53	12

The above fourteen cities have an average of 16 inches of sewers per inhabitant. Rome, Brussels, and Leipzig have the lowest ratios.

DRUGS

The following table shows the weight and value of all drugs, chemicals, and spices imported into the United Kingdom at certain dates :—

	Tons Weight			Value £ (000 omitted)		
	1876	1886	1896	1876	1886	1896
Bones . . .	96,000	67,000	74,000	620	370	280
Caoutchouc .	7,900	9,700	21,600	1,540	2,220	4,990
Chinchona .	1,300	7,300	1,800	270	800	60
Cochineal .	1,500	700	300	340	100	40
Cutch . . .	26,000	28,000	27,000	610	650	550
Dye-woods .	89,000	78,000	91,000	590	420	590
Esparto . .	148,000	195,000	187,000	1,210	1,000	800
Guano . .	199,000	69,000	20,000	2,300	540	100
Gum . . .	13,000	16,000	24,000	1,030	1,050	1,590
Guttapercha .	1,100	2,000	2,200	160	270	400
Indigo . .	4,400	4,300	4,500	2,130	1,910	1,530
Nitre . . .	165,000	75,000	106,000	1,890	750	840
Opium . .	180	230	220	390	310	250
Paints . .	...	...	...	730	780	990
Pepper . .	12,000	12,000	12,000	460	870	300
Rosin . . .	49,000	58,000	83,000	310	290	420
Saltpetre . .	13,000	14,000	17,000	240	240	280
Sumach . .	13,000	13,000	15,000	220	180	150
Sulphur . .	44,000	32,000	23,000	280	160	90
Turpentine .	12,000	15,000	25,000	270	390	490
Valonia . .	35,000	34,000	33,000	630	480	330
Wood-pulp .	...	80,000	330,000	...	510	1,680
Yeast . . .	8,000	15,000	9,000	410	820	430
Sundries . .	65,000	127,000	74,000	1,690	1,780	1,570
Total . .	1,003,380	952,230	1,180,620	18,320	16,890	18,750

The average value of imported drugs and chemicals was £18.3 per ton in 1876, and £15.8 in 1896.

Exports of drugs and chemicals were as follow :—

	Tons Weight			Value £ (000 omitted)		
	1876	1886	1896	1876	1886	1896
Alkali . . .	270,000	310,000	240,000	2,220	1,790	1,240
Bleaching . .	47,000	78,000	59,000	330	500	410
Caoutchouc .	3,500	5,500	12,000	640	1,300	2,640
Chinchona . .	1,700	5,900	1,300	390	550	30
Cochineal .	850	550	200	190	80	20
Cutch . . .	6,700	10,200	6,500	160	260	160
Guano . . .	53,000	7,400	1,700	650	50	10
Gum . . .	6,300	9,600	10,700	480	630	750
Gunpowder . .	6,500	5,000	3,600	360	290	190
Indigo . . .	2,900	2,700	2,500	1,490	1,170	910
Manure . . .	150,000	300,000	350,000	890	1,610	1,810
Medicine . .	...	...	...	640	810	1,120
Opium . . .	100	160	110	220	220	120
Paints . . .	...	...	...	1,070	1,270	1,660
Pepper . . .	7,700	9,000	5,200	320	640	140
Sundries . . .	...	...	...	2,330	2,490	3,670
Total . .	556,250	744,610	692,810	13,030	13,710	14,880

DRUNKENNESS

The number of persons tried for drunkenness in England from 1874 to 1894 was as follows :—

Period	No. Yearly	Per 100,000 Inhabitants
1874–78	196,500	812
1879–83	181,800	698
1884–88	174,900	636
1889–94	176,400	604
21 years	182,100	683

In Scotland the Royal Commission of 1896 found that 72 per cent. of crime proceeded from drink.

Deaths from alcoholism of men between 25 and 65 years average 10 per thousand, or 1 per cent. of the total, in England and Wales, but vary exceedingly according to profession, viz. :—

Deaths from Drink of 1000 *Men who Die*

Ploughman .	. 1	Miner .	. . 4	Baker	. . .	15
Gardener	. . 2	Stonecutter .	5	Costermonger .		19
Printer .	. . 3	Farmer	. . 6	Butcher .	. .	23
Cotton-spinner .	3	Blacksmith .	8	Com. traveller		23
Cutler .	. . 3	Draper	. . 8	Brewer .	. .	25
Carpenter	. . 4	Grocer .	. . 10	Cab-driver .	.	33
Shoemaker	. . 4	Tailor .	. . 11	Publican	. .	55
Fisherman	. . 4	Painter	. . 12	Average .	. .	10

AUSTRALIA

The following table shows the arrests for drunkenness and the average consumption of alcohol in the several colonies :—

	Arrests for Drunkenness	Per 10,000 Pop.	Alcohol, Galls. per Head
New South Wales .	20,670	170	2.7
Victoria . .	15,890	140	3.2
New Zealand . .	5,350	80	1.8
Queensland .	4,915	120	2.5
South Australia .	2,715	75	2.5
Tasmania . .	920	60	2.0
Total . .	50,460	125	2.6

CANADA

Convictions for drunkenness in ten years ending 1894 averaged 12,026 yearly. In 1895 they were 11,558, that is 468 below the average, viz. :—

	Convictions	Per 10,000 Pop.
Quebec . . .	4,307	28
Ontario . . .	3,132	14
Acadia . . .	2,934	33
North-West . .	1,185	34
Total . .	11,558	24

From 1884 to 1890 the convictions for drunkenness rose 40 per cent. by a steady increase, but since 1890 there has been a continuous fall, and 1895 shows 17 per cent. less than 1890.

DUELS

A return of Italian duels for ten years down to 1890 shows that there were 2760, which resulted in 50 men killed, 1066 wounded, and 1644 unhurt. The percentage of combatants showed 30 military, 29 editors, 12 lawyers, and 29 per cent. various. The duels were influenced by the seasons in the following ratio :—

Par being 230			
Warm Months		Cold Months	
May . . .	273	November . . .	92
June . . .	319	December . . .	67
July . . .	330	January . . .	220
August . .	326	February . . .	263
September . .	271	March . . .	291
October . . .	121	April	187
Total . .	1,640	Total . .	1,120

E

EARTH

Ravenstein estimates the fertile and the unproductive areas as follows :—

	Square Miles		
	Fertile	Unproductive	Total
Europe . . .	2,888,000	667,000	3,555,000
Asia	9,280,000	5,430,000	14,710,000
Africa	5,760,000	5,754,000	11,514,000
Australia . . .	1,167,000	2,121,000	3,288,000
North America .	4,946,000	1,500,000	6,446,000
South America .	4,228,000	2,609,000	6,837,000
Total . .	28,269,000	18,081,000	46,350,000

The actual population is 1420 millions, equal to 50 persons per square mile of fertile area, or one-fourth of the number that can conveniently be supported, allowing 15 acres to each family.

EARTHQUAKES

Careful records are kept at Tokio, Japan, of the occurrence of earthquakes. In eleven years ending December 1886 there were 658, and the ratios, according to months, to barometer and thermometer showed thus :—

Months		Barometer		Fahrenheit	
January . .	96	29.9	13	0–32	88
February . .	94	30.0	21	32–37	129
March . .	128	30.1	23	37–42	124
April . . .	75	30.2	91	42–47	112
May . . .	94	30.3	144	47–52	85
June . . .	76	30.4	146	52–57	78
July . . .	53	30.5	155	57–62	114
August . .	58	30.6	181	62–67	53
September .	42	30.7	91	67–72	82
October . .	84	30.8	85	72–77	63
November .	79	30.9	40	77–82	42
December .	121	31.0	10	Over 82	30
Total .	1,000	Total .	1,000	Total .	1,000

The above shows that in Japan earthquakes are most frequent from December to March inclusive, that they occur mostly when the barometer stands between 30.2 and 30.7, and the thermometer between 32 and 47 Fahrenheit, the ordinary temperature at Tokio (Jeddo) being 58.

EDUCATION

The educational condition of nations in 1896 was approximately as follows :—

	Schools, No.	Pupils, No.	Percentage of Pop.	Expenditure, £	Pence per Inhab.	Percentage Adults can Write
England	19,850	4,420,000	14.4	10,500,000	82	96
Scotland	3,080	590,000	14.1	2,400,000	134	97
Ireland	8,610	540,000	11.7	1,300,000	70	85
United Kingdom . . .	31,540	5,550,000	14.0	14,200,000	86	94
France	89,110	6,250,000	16.0	8,000,000	50	95
Germany	56,560	7,930,000	15.5	12,100,000	54	99
Russia	66,040	3,130,000	3.0	5,000,000	11	22
Austria	37,510	5,910,000	14.5	3,000,000	17	69
Italy	64,200	2,720,000	8.8	4,900,000	36	56
Spain	30,100	1,840,000	10.5	1,200,000	16	42
Portugal	5,340	240,000	5.0	400,000	20	30
Holland	4,220	650,000	13.6	1,600,000	80	90
Scandinavia . . .	22,060	1,270,000	14.0	1,600,000	42	99
Belgium	5,670	620,000	10.0	1,100,000	42	83
Switzerland . . .	9,620	530,000	17.5	1,500,000	120	99
Danubian States . .	7,620	660,000	6.0	1,600,000	34	24
Greece	3,040	140,000	6.5	200,000	22	30
Europe . . .	432,630	37,440,000	9.5	56,400,000	34	60
United States . . .	252,000	9,750,000	13.7	38,500,000	130	83
Canada	17,270	630,000	12.5	2,100,000	98	90
Australia	8,040	540,000	13.0	2,300,000	132	90
India	152,600	4,300,000	1.5	2,200,000	2	6
South Africa . . .	2,810	100,000	4.5	300,000	33	...
Ceylon	3,870	180,000	5.5	100,000	13	...
Algeria	1,220	120,000	2.7	200,000	11	...
Argentina	3,750	260,000	6.5	700,000	42	...
Chile	1,660	100,000	3.6	400,000	35	...
Venezuela	1,570	100,000	4.4	100,000	11	...
Brazil	7,500	300,000	2.2	200,000	4	24
Egypt	9,000	190,000	2.0	100,000	2	7
Japan	28,170	3,770,000	9.0	300,000	2	...
Total . . .	922,090	57,780,000	7.5	103,900,000	30	...

UNITED KINGDOM

The progress of instruction in the three kingdoms is very satisfactory :—

	Schools		Pupils	
	1888	1897	1888	1897
England .	19,221	19,958	3,615,000	4,489,000
Scotland .	3,105	3,086	496,000	605,000
Ireland . .	8,196	8,631	494,000	521,000
Total .	30,522	31,675	4,605,000	5,615,000

The number of school-children on the registers is much greater than what is shown above, namely the average attendance, which is 82 per cent. of enrolled pupils in England, 84 per cent. in Scotland, and 66 per cent. in Ireland. The following table shows the percentage of school-children to population, and the percentage of adults who can write :—

	Pupils per 100 Pop.		Adults can Write	
	1888	1896	1888	1896
England . . .	12.7	14.4	91	96
Scotland . . .	12.3	14.1	94	97
Ireland . . .	10.4	11.7	77	85
U. Kingdom .	12.3	14.0	90	94

In England and Scotland the proportion of male adults who can write, as shown by signatures to the marriage register, is greater than that of females : in Ireland the reverse takes place, women being 2 per cent. better instructed than men. School expenditure compared with population in the above years shows as follows :—

	£ Sterling		Pence per Inhab.	
	1888	1896	1888	1896
England .	7,440,000	10,450,000	64	82
Scotland .	1,160,000	2,350,000	70	134
Ireland . .	1,090,000	1,330,000	54	70
Total .	9,690,000	14,130,000	63	86

In Great Britain, without Ireland, the schools can accommodate 6,900,000 pupils, or 38 per cent. more than the average attendance.

Statistics for England and Wales in 1896 and 1890 compare thus :—

	Average Attendance		
	1890	1896	Increase
Board schools . .	1,457,000	1,957,000	500,000
Anglican	1,681,000	1,872,000	191,000
Roman Catholic .	193,000	236,000	43,000
Wesleyan . . .	132,000	126,000	0
Various	255,000	233,000	0
Total . .	3,718,000	4,424,000	706,000

UNITED STATES

The returns for 1896 as regards average attendance at the schools compare with 1885 thus :—

	School-children		Per 100 Pop.	
	1885	1896	1885	1896
New England .	564,000	645,000	13.1	12.4
Middle States .	1,505,000	1,930,000	11.7	12.3
Southern ,, .	1,852,000	2,865,000	11.0	14.0
Western ,, .	3,099,000	4,310,000	13.9	14.5
The Union . .	7,020,000	9,750,000	12.5	13.7

The number of children on the rolls in the above years was as follows :—

	On Rolls		Per 100 Pop.	
	1885	1896	1885	1896
New England .	800,000	890,000	18.6	17.1
Middle States .	2,460,000	2,860,000	19.1	18.2
Southern ,, .	2,980,000	4,390,000	17.7	21.4
Western ,, .	4,930,000	6,240,000	22.1	21.0
The Union . .	11,170,000	14,380,000	19.8	20.2

Of the numbers on the rolls in 1896 the average attendance was 73 per cent. in New England, 68 in the Middle States, 65 in the Southern, and 69 per cent. in the Western States. The average for the whole Union was 68 per cent., against 63 in 1885. The expenditure, compared with population and the number of children on the rolls, was :—

	£ Sterling	Shillings per Inhabitant	Shillings per Child
New England .	4,100,000	16	91
Middle States .	10,700,000	14	75
Southern ,, .	4,300,000	4	20
Western ,, .	19,300,000	13	62
The Union . .	38,400,000	11	53

The United States spend the same amount yearly on education as all the nations of the European Continent collectively. The contribution for schools is equal to 11 shillings per inhabitant, against 7 shillings in the United Kingdom and a little over 2 shillings on the European Continent in the aggregate.

FRANCE

The expenditure on public schools is shown thus :—

	State, £	Local, £	Total, £	Pence per Inhab.
1860 . . .	200,000	1,200,000	1,400,000	9
1870 . . .	440,000	2,060,000	2,500,000	16
1880 . . .	800,000	2,500,000	3,300,000	21
1892 . . .	5,000,000	2,400,000	7,400,000	46

ITALY

The ratio of persons able to sign the marriage register in Italy in 1891 was as follows per 100 :—

Rome . . . 81.8 | Turin . . . 94.4 | Bologna . . 82.3
Naples . . 63.9 | Genoa . . 89.5 | Venice . . 70.8
Milan . . . 93.6 | Florence . . 88.1 | Palermo . . 63.4

The amount spent yearly on schools is £4,900,000, of which £1,700,000 is expended by the State, and £3,200,000 by local authorities.

INDIA

In 1893 the sum expended for education was as follows :—

	Amount, £		
	Grants	Fees, &c.	Total
University . .	100,000	100,000	200,000
High Schools .	280,000	520,000	800,000
Primary ,, . .	360,000	340,000	700,000
Staff, &c. . . .	320,000	100,000	420,000
Total . .	1,060,000	1,060,000	2,120,000

See *Education*, in Part I., pages 231–243.

EGGS

Production and consumption yearly in some countries are approximately as follows :—

	Millions		Consumption per Inhab.
	Production	Consumption	
United Kingdom .	2,120	3,810	95
France . . .	3,500	3,220	84
Germany . .	3,000	4,400	84
United States .	9,810	9,820	140

Importing and exporting countries show approximately as follows :—

Importers	Millions	Exporters	Millions
Great Britain . .	1,690	Russia	1,480
Germany . . .	1,400	Austria	1,150
Switzerland . . .	120	Italy	520
United States . .	10	France	280
Other countries .	450	Denmark . . .	160
		Canada	80
Total . .	3,670	Total . .	3,670

The value of eggs exported in the above table is about 7 millions sterling, say 10 million eggs daily, worth £20,000.

ELECTIONS

There have been sixteen in the United Kingdom since the Reform Law of 1832, which resulted as follows (Home-Rulers being counted as Liberals since 1886) :—

Year	Won by	Maj.	Year	Won by	Maj.
1832	Liberals	370	1865	Liberals	78
1835	,,	112	1868	,,	116
1837	,,	18	1874	Conservatives	98
1841	Conservatives	76	1880	Liberals	115
1847	Liberals	18	1885	,,	86
1852	Conservatives	20	1886	Conservatives	114
1857	Liberals	80	1892	Liberals	40
1859	,,	50	1895	Conservatives	152

The election of 1895 resulted as follows :—

	Conservatives	Liberals	Total
England . . .	349	116	465
Wales	8	22	30
Scotland . . .	33	39	72
Ireland . . .	21	82	103
Total . .	411	259	670
Boroughs . . .	200	84	284
Counties . . .	202	175	377
Universities . . .	9	...	9
Total . .	411	259	670

The number of electors and that of voters, and the ratios to population at the election of 1895, were as follows (England including also Wales) :—

	Electors, Number	Voters, Number	Per 100 Inhab. Electors	Per 100 Inhab. Voters
England . .	4,956,000	3,726,000	16	12
Scotland . .	638,000	466,000	16	11
Ireland . .	737,000	395,000	16	9
United Kingdom	6,331,000	4,587,000	16	11

Of the total number of electors on the roll only 72 per cent. voted.

The franchise in 1895 was held as follows :—

	Counties	Boroughs	Total
England . . .	2,820,000	2,136,000	4,956,000
Scotland . . .	352,000	286,000	638,000
Ireland . . .	623,000	114,000	737,000
United Kingdom . .	3,795,000	2,534,000	6,331,000

Of 1000 voters, in Scotland 9 were unable to write their names, in England 12, in Ireland 214, the ratio for the whole United Kingdom being 29 per 1000.

FRANCE

The number of names on the lists of franchise, and that of persons who voted at five general elections, were :—

Date	On Lists	Voted	Ratio
1877	9,948,000	8,013,000	80.5
1881	10,125,000	6,945,000	68.8
1885	10,181,000	7,896,000	77.4
1889	10,387,000	7,953,000	76.5
1893	10,446,000	7,427,000	71.0

GERMANY

The growth of the Socialist party is shown by the number of votes it polled, viz. :—

1881	550,000
1891	1,342,000
1893	1,734,000

Thus in twelve years this party trebled its strength.

UNITED STATES

The election of 1896 resulted thus :—

States	Voters M'Kinley	Voters Bryan	Electors M'Kinley	Electors Bryan
New England	613,000	235,000	39	...
Middle . . .	1,901,000	1,233,000	89	...
South . . .	1,127,000	1,740,000	18	113
West . . .	3,482,000	3,291,000	126	62
Union . . .	7,123,000	6,499,000	272	175

See *Electors*, page 243.

EMIGRATION

The following table shows the emigration that has taken place from 1890 to the end of 1896 : *—

	Destination U. States	Destination S. America	Destination Various	Destination Total
U. Kingdom	938,000	..	1,082,000	2,020,000
France . .	12,000	25,000	166,000	203,000
Germany . .	491,000	35,000	7,000	533,000
Austria . .	409,000	16,000	31,000	456,000
Russia . .	407,000	...	...	407,000
Italy . . .	308,000	737,000	762,000	1,807,000
Portugal .	10,000	163,000	14,000	187,000
Holland . .	17,000	...	...	17,000
Denmark . .	46,000	...	5,000	51,000
Sweden . .	169,000	...	26,000	195,000
Norway . .	78,000	...	...	78,000
Switzerland	39,000	2,000	...	41,000
Total .	2,924,000	978,000	2,093,000	5,995,000

There were also about 60,000 yearly from Spain (mostly to South America), that is 420,000 in the above period, which would bring up the total to 6,400,000, that is, an average of 910,000 yearly. Italian emigration to South America appears in the above table to have averaged 105,000 yearly, but in reality it reached double the figure given above, as the majority of those marked "various" proceeded to French or other ports to embark for Brazil, &c. In the above 7 years South America absorbed about 1,400,000 Italians, 400,000 Spaniards, and 350,000 Portuguese, Germans, &c.

Emigrants, as a rule, are of the age when their labour is likely to be most productive. Thus the returns of United States records during 31 years show that 53 per cent. of those who arrived were between 20 and 40, whereas the proportions of persons of that age in the United Kingdom, France, Germany, and Austria, averaged only 29½ per cent. Emigration, in a word, drew nearly double its proportion of persons in the prime of life.

Comparing the foreign element in each country with the whole population, we find the ratio stands thus :—

Foreigners per Thousand Inhabitants

England . . 8	Germany . . 9	Belgium . . 24
Scotland . . 4	Austria . . 5	Italy 2
Ireland . . . 3	Switzerland . 77	Russia . . . 1
France . . 30	Holland . . 10	Scandinavia . 3

* At pages 245-254 there are tables of European emigration during 70 years.

The following table shows the numbers of foreign settlers in various countries of Europe (Irish being included with British) :—

	U. Kingdom	France	Germany	Austria	Italy	Switzerland	Holland	Belgium	Various	Total
British	...	40,000	16,000	2,000	7,000	3,000	1,000	4,000	13,000	86,000
French	23,000	...	32,000	3,000	11,000	54,000	1,000	51,000	8,000	183,000
Germans	54,000	114,000	...	103,000	5,000	112,000	29,000	34,000	97,000	548,000
Russians	48,000	14,000	53,000	18,000	1,000	1,000	...	...	5,000	140,000
Austrians	6,000	12,000	206,000	...	16,000	14,000	...	...	47,000	301,000
Italians	19,000	296,000	15,000	53,000	...	42,000	...	...	46,000	471,000
Swiss	7,000	83,000	41,000	7,000	12,000	...	...	...	4,000	154,000
Spaniards	...	78,000	...	...	1,000	...	...	...	2,000	81,000
Scandinavians	17,000	...	38,000	...	...	...	...	...	7,000	62,000
Belgians	4,000	466,000	...	...	...	...	14,000	...	...	484,000
Greeks	...	...	...	...	1,000	...	...	...	105,000	106,000
Various	97,000	37,000	123,000	15,000	6,000	4,000	3,000	54,000	135,000	474,000
Total . . .	275,000	1,140,000	524,000	201,000	60,000	230,000	48,000	143,000	469,000	3,090,000

The following table shows approximately the number of persons living abroad in 1897 :—

From	Resident in					
	Europe	United States	S. America	Brit. Possess.	Various	Total
United Kingdom . . .	86,000	3,530,000	45,000	1,750,000	39,000	5,450,000
France	183,000	140,000	220,000	26,000	341,000	910,000
Germany	548,000	3,110,000	35,000	87,000	10,000	3,790,000
Russia	140,000	640,000	32,000	16,000	12,000	840,000
Austria	301,000	560,000	81,000	7,000	6,000	955,000
Italy	471,000	460,000	1,770,000	31,000	18,000	2,750,000
Spain	81,000	10,000	730,000	2,000	57,000	880,000
Portugal	10,000	20,000	240,000	...	20,000	290,000
Scandinavia	62,000	1,130,000	17,000	32,000	4,000	1,245,000
Holland	73,000	90,000	3,000	...	14,000	180,000
Belgium	484,000	30,000	7,000	...	4,000	525,000
Switzerland	154,000	110,000	53,000	...	13,000	330,000
Greece	106,000	10,000	12,000	38,000	44,000	210,000
Various	181,000	50,000	95,000	111,000	28,000	465,000
Europe	2,880,000	9,890,000	3,340,000	2,100,000	610,000	18,820,000
United States	72,000	...	12,000	115,000	11,000	210,000
Canada	2,000	980,000	1,000	5,000	2,000	990,000
Total . . .	2,954,000	10,870,000	3,353,000	2,220,000	623,000	20,020,000

The total number of foreign settlers in the various countries of Europe, as shown in the first table, is 3,090,000, of whom 2,880,000 are Europeans; the rest are Americans, Asiatics, &c.

It appears from the above table that there are (exclusive of Asiatics) no fewer than 20 million persons living out of their native country, made up thus :—

From	Number	Ratio
United Kingdom . .	5,450,000	27.2
Germany . . .	3,790,000	19.0
Italy	2,750,000	13.7
Scandinavia . . .	1,245,000	6.2
France	910,000	4.5
Spain	880,000	4.4
Various countries . .	4,995,000	25.0
Total . .	20,020,000	100.0

The foreign-born (including British) in the British possessions are :—

Born in	Canada	Australia	Egypt	India, &c.	Total
U. Kingdom	480,000	1,040,000	20,000	210,000	1,750,000
France . .	5,000	5,000	14,000	2,000	26,000
Germany .	28,000	50,000	1,000	8,000	87,000
Russia . .	10,000	3,000	3,000	...	16,000
Austria . .	...	...	7,000	...	7,000
Italy . . .	1,000	4,000	25,000	1,000	31,000
Scandinavia	8,000	21,000	...	3,000	32,000
Greece . .	...	...	38,000	...	38,000
U. States .	81,000	10,000	...	24,000	115,000
Canada . .	...	4,000	...	1,000	5,000
Various . .	27,000	73,000	5,000	8,000	113,000
Total . .	640,000	1,210,000	113,000	257,000	2,220,000

The purport of the foregoing tables may be summed up by saying that there are at present 16 million European settlers living beyond the seas, of whom the United States possess 10 millions, due in great measure to liberal land laws, especially the Homestead Law of 1862 (see page 347). On the other hand, the total number of emigrants from the European Continent now resident in British Colonies is barely 160,000, or if we include Egypt, 250,000. The failure of our colonies to attract European settlers is chiefly the result of Crown lands having been leased for long terms of years at nominal rents (one penny per acre) to squatters and other men of large fortunes. In Australia 2 per cent. of the population is made up of Germans and Scandinavians. In Canada only 1 per cent. of the inhabitants are natives of Continental Europe.

If we take each nationality, adding together those at home and abroad, we shall find the proportion that live abroad as in the following table :—

	At Home	Abroad	Total	Ratio Abroad
British . .	35,050,000	2,890,000	37,940,000	7.5
Irish . . .	4,540,000	2,560,000	7,100,000	36.0
Brit. Islands	39,590,000	5,450,000	45,040,000	12.0
French . .	37,400,000	910,000	38,310,000	2.4
Germans . .	51,970,000	3,790,000	55,760,000	6.8
Russians . .	106,000,000	810,000	106,810,000	0.8
Austrians .	41,400,000	955,000	42,355,000	2.3
Italians . .	31,200,000	2,750,000	33,950,000	8.0
Spaniards .	17,900,000	880,000	18,780,000	4.6
Portuguese .	5,000,000	290,000	5,290,000	5.5
Scandinavians	9,300,000	1,245,000	10,545,000	11.8
Hollanders .	4,880,000	180,000	5,060,000	3.6
Belgians . .	6,300,000	525,000	6,825,000	7.8
Swiss . . .	2,800,000	330,000	3,130,000	10.5
Various . .	13,460,000	705,000	14,165,000	5.0
Europe . .	367,200,000	18,820,000	386,020,000	4.7
United States	61,000,000	210,000	61,210,000	0.3
Canadians .	3,600,000	990,000	4,590,000	21.5
Total . .	431,800,000	20,020,000	451,820,000	4.3

The Canadians can hardly be considered living out of their own country, as they are mostly in the New England States, just over the border. The nations which have the largest proportion of their people abroad are the Irish, Scandinavians, and Swiss.

The returns for 1897 of emigrants sailing from the United Kingdom were :—

To	British	Irish	Foreign	Total
United States . .	52,000	33,000	47,000	132,000
Canada . . .	15,000	1,000	7,000	23,000
Cape Colony .	20,000	1,000	8,000	29,000
Australia . .	11,000	1,000	...	12,000
Other parts .	13,000	...	5,000	18,000
Total .	111,000	36,000	67,000	214,000

The aggregate returns for ten years (1888–97) show as follows :—

	Total Emigration		British and Irish
English . . .	1,290,000	To United States	1,388,000
Scotch . . .	216,000	,, Canada . .	321,000
Irish	534,000	., Australia . .	172,000
Foreign . . .	937,000	,, Cape, &c. .	259,000
Total . .	2,977,000	Total . .	2,040,000

For emigration from 1815–88 see page 248.

SOUTH AMERICA

The Argentine Republic shows as follows :—

	Immigrants	Per Annum
1873–82	493,000	49,300
1883–92	1,116,000	111,600
1893–97	343,000	68,600
25 years . . .	1,952,000	78,000

About one-third of the above returned to Europe. The last five years showed : immigrants, 343,000 ; returned to Europe, 117,000 ; net immigration, 226,000—say 45,000 per annum.

UNITED STATES

In the last seven years the arrivals of immigrants were :—

	Number	Annual Average	Ratio
British . . .	344,000	49,100	11.8
Irish . . .	270,000	38,600	9.4
Germans . .	491,000	70,100	17.4
Russians . .	407,000	58,200	14.3
Italians . .	419,000	59,800	14.7
Austrians . .	382,000	54,600	13.4
Scandinavians .	305,000	43,600	10.7
Various . .	237,000	33,800	8.3
Total . .	2,855,000	407,800	100.0

The increase of foreign population during the decade ending 1890 was equal to 60 per cent. of the number of immigrants ; as the current decade promises 4,000,000 immigrants, we may expect an increase of 2,400,000 in the number of foreign residents over last census, wherefore that of 1900 ought to show 11,650,000 foreigners in a population of 77,000,000 souls. This would give a ratio of 15 per cent. for the foreign population, the same as it was in 1890.

ITALY

An unofficial statement (1898) gives the number of Italian emigrants in 22 years, from 1875, as 625,000 to North America, and 1,350,000 to South America. The *Jornal do Commercio* of Rio Janeiro estimates the number of Italian settlers in Brazil at 1,374,000. The Argentine census of 1895 shows 610,000 Italians in Argentina ; there are also 70,000 in Uruguay, and 20,000 in Paraguay.

ALGERIA

The European population (including children born in the colony) has increased 80 per cent. in 10 years, viz. :—

	1886	1896	Increase
French . . .	220,000	318,000	98,000
Spaniards, &c. . .	206,000	446,000	240,000
Total . .	426,000	764,000	338,000

CANADA.

The census of 1891 compares the number of foreign settlers with the same in 1881 thus :—

	Number		Ratio	
	1881	1891	1881	1891
English . .	170,000	220,000	3.9	4.6
Scotch . .	115,000	108,000	2.7	2.2
Irish . . .	186,000	149,000	4.3	3.1
Germans .	25,000	28,000	0.6	0.6
Russians .	6,000	10,000	0.1	0.2
Scands . .	8,000	8,000	0.2	0.2
Various . .	99,000	124,000	2.3	2.5
Foreigners .	609,000	647,000	14.1	13.4
Natives . .	3,716,000	4,186,000	85.9	86.6
Total pop.	4,325,000	4,833,000	100.0	100.0

Except English, all foreign-born settlers have relatively lost ground : the foreign population is only 13½ per cent.

of the total, whereas it is 15 per cent. in the United States, and 29 per cent. in Australia. The foreign settlers in the several provinces showed as follows :—

	1881	1891	Increase
Quebec. . . .	77,000	82,000	5,000
Ontario . . .	430,000	406,000	...
Acadia. . . .	69,000	55,000	...
North-West . .	33,000	104,000	71,000
Total . . .	609,000	647,000	38,000

Taking the old provinces collectively, the foreign population has diminished by 33,000, but the new North-West, including Manitoba, British Columbia, &c., shows an increase of 71,000, so that, on the whole, the decade shows a gain of 38,000, or 6 per cent. on the foreign population of 1881.

AUSTRALIA.

In 25 years, ending December 1895, the net immigration into the colonies was as follows :—

	Number	Per Annum	Ratio
New S. Wales . .	309,000	12,300	38.4
Victoria . . .	49,000	2,000	6.2
New Zealand . .	157,000	6,300	19.8
Queensland . .	197,000	7,900	24.7
South Australia .	23,000	900	2.8
West Australia .	60,000	2,400	7.5
Tasmania . . .	5,000	200	0.6
Total . . .	800,000	32,000	100.0

The following table shows the number of foreign settlers (including British) according to census returns for 1881 and 1891, and an estimate of the existing number in 1896 :—

	1881	1891	1896
New S. Wales .	240,000	315,000	325,000
Victoria . . .	323,000	350,000	275,000
New Zealand .	311,000	244,000	240,000
Queensland . .	133,000	189,000	196,000
S. Australia . .	83,000	92,000	90,000
Tasmania. . .	32,000	32,000	31,000
W. Australia. .	6,000	19,000	68,000
Total . . .	1,128,000	1,241,000	1,225,000

Between 1891 and 1896 there was a net immigration of 77,000 persons, but a mean death-rate of 15 per 1000 in the same period would amount to 93,000, so that the foreign population in 1896 would not exceed 1,225,000. Comparing native and foreign born we find as follows :—

	Number		Ratio	
	1881	1896	1881	1896
Australian .	1,688,000	3,015,000	60.0	71.0
Foreign. .	1,128,000	1,225,000	40.0	29.0
Total pop.	2,816,000	4,240,000	100.0	100.0

The foreign element is diminishing rapidly, whereas in most new countries it is on the increase. The colony of Victoria lost 50,000 by emigration between 1891 and 1896.

ENERGY

The energy or working-power of a nation consists of : (1) human, which is computed at 300 foot-tons daily for a man between 15 and 60 years of age, 200 foot-tons for

a woman, and 100 foot-tons for a child of 10 to 15 years ; (2) the force of animals, that of a full-grown horse being 5000 foot-tons daily ; (3) steam-power of three kinds, fixed, railway, and steamboats ; (4) water-power ; (5) the force represented by wind-mills ; (6) the amount of power now exercised by electricity. The following table shows the first three powers, subject to these reservations : the power of women and children is not taken into account ; that of horses is estimated at 3000 foot-tons, because statistics of same include horses of all ages ; mules are counted as horses, but no account is taken of asses, oxen, or other animals. Water-power is added to steam whenever it can be ascertained ; wind-mills and electricity are omitted.

	Millions of Foot-Tons Daily			
	Hand	Horse	Steam	Total
United Kingdom .	3,200	6,330	54,800	64,330
France . . .	3,500	9,300	23,680	36,480
Germany . . .	4,200	11,500	32,320	48,020
Russia . . .	9,100	62,700	12,400	84,200
Austria . . .	3,530	10,700	10,080	24,310
Italy . . .	2,940	3,800	7,080	13,820
Spain . . .	1,590	2,640	4,720	8,950
Portugal . . .	350	420	680	1,450
Sweden . . .	420	1,500	2,040	3,960
Norway . . .	180	450	1,640	2,270
Denmark . . .	200	1,240	1,020	2,460
Holland . . .	420	810	2,400	3,630
Belgium . . .	560	810	4,720	6,090
Switzerland . .	270	300	2,320	2,890
Roumania, &c. .	1,620	3,500	2,280	7,400
Europe . . .	32,080	116,000	162,180	310,260
United States . .	6,400	54,600	72,240	133,240
Canada . . .	420	4,200	5,560	10,180
Australia . . .	340	5,700	3,360	9,400
Total . .	39,240	180,500	243,340	463,080

Energy may be classified as productive and distributive, the first including all that is human, all the power of fixed engines, and half that of horses. The account will then stand thus for 1896 :—

	Millions of Foot-Tons Daily			Foot-Tons per Inhab.
	Productive	Distributive	Total	
United Kingdom .	15,570	48,760	64,330	1,620
France . . .	12,670	23,810	36,480	950
Germany . . .	19,550	28,470	48,020	920
Russia . . .	42,170	42,030	84,200	750
Austria . . .	10,800	13,510	24,310	560
Italy . . .	5,560	8,260	13,820	440
Spain . . .	3,110	5,840	8,950	520
Portugal . . .	600	850	1,450	310
Sweden . . .	1,290	2,670	3,960	800
Norway . . .	450	1,820	2,270	1,130
Denmark . . .	860	1,600	2,460	1,100
Holland . . .	1,150	2,480	3,630	760
Belgium . . .	2,530	3,560	6,090	950
Switzerland . .	780	2,110	2,890	960
Roumania, &c. . .	4,170	3,230	7,400	450
Europe . . .	121,260	189,000	310,260	810
United States . .	49,460	83,780	133,240	1,880
Canada . . .	3,800	6,380	10,180	1,990
Australia . . .	4,230	5,170	9,400	2,240
Total . .	178,750	284,330	463,080	1,020

Productive energy stands for 38 per cent., distributive

62 per cent. of the total. The latter has increased much more rapidly than the former, viz. :—

		Millions of Foot-Tons Daily			Rate of Increase per Cent.
		1840	1896	Increase	
Productive	. .	73,700	178,750	105,050	142
Distributive	. .	50,300	284,330	234,030	465
Total	. .	124,000	463,080	339,080	273

See *Steam*, page 807.

ENGINEERING

Blackwall tunnel under the Thames, at London, was completed in May 1897, having occupied 800 men during 5 years : length 2100 yards, diameter 27 feet, with central road and foot-walk on each side. It is ventilated by 4 shafts of 48 feet diameter, and lit with 700 electric lights of 32-candle power. It comprises 3 sections :—

North side, 900 yards, incline 1 in 34.
Central, 400 yards, level.
South side, 800 yards, incline 1 in 36.

In mid-river the works are 5 feet below water ; the men were protected by a steel shield and progressed 4 feet daily. They excavated 500,000 tons, and the materials for the tunnel comprised 7,000,000 bricks, 1,000,000 tiles, 110,000 tons concrete, 20,000 tons cement, and 17,000 tons cast iron. Total cost £871,000, equal to £410 per lineal yard, whereas Brunel's tunnel cost £1300 per yard.

In Holland the pumping-out of Lake Haarlem, area 45,000 acres, depth 15 feet, was completed in 1852, after 11 years of labour : the land was sold at £17 per acre, and the work cost £1,080,000, that is £300,000. over the price of the land. In 1894 a project was laid before the Dutch Parliament to pump out the Zuyder Zee, area 480,000 acres, depth 12 feet, at an estimated cost of £26,000,000, or £54 for each acre of land reclaimed, the work to be finished in 33 years. The principal work would be a wall 25 miles long, 200 feet thick, and 18 feet over sea-level, to take 9 years in construction.

EXPLORATION

Nansen returned to Norway, after 3 years' absence, in August 1896, having reached 86.15 N. Lat., in 102 E. Long., in 1895, only 260 English miles from the North Pole. The furthest previous expedition was the United States schooner *Jeannette*, in September 1893, which reached Sanrikoff, 458 English miles from the Pole.

F

FAMINES

Besides those mentioned at page 256, an Indian blue-book states that in the famines of 1866-68-78 no fewer than 11,300,000 persons perished, viz. :—

Orissa	.	1,300,000	Madras	.	.	4,085,000
Punjaub	.	1,450,000	Oude, &c.	.	.	4,486,000

No returns are yet published as to the famine of 1896.

FINANCES

The finances of European States at four periods in the 19th century are shown as follows :—

	Revenue, Millions £				Debt, Millions £			
	1816	1830	1869	1898	1816	1830	1869	1898
U. Kingdom	61.3	63	72	116	9c2	838	803	638
France . .	35.2	41	84	134	140	191	504	1,244
Germany .	18.1	20	41	187	39	58	128	620
Russia . .	14.1	17	70	138	145	56	342	692
Austria . .	12.7	15	43	101	99	60	340	555
Italy . . .	7.2	9	33	67	25	50	333	516
Spain . . .	7.7	6	22	31	117	167	285	283
Portugal . .	1.9	2	4	11	7	14	59	134
Sweden . .	1.2	} 2	2	6	3	6	4	16
Norway . .	0.5		1	4	1	2	2	9
Denmark . .	1.1	2	3	4	4	11	13	11
Holland . .	6.4	7	9	11	110	157	76	92
Belgium . .	...	...	7	16	...	...	28	93
Switzerland .	0.4	1	2	4	...	...	2	13
Turkey . .	2.3	4	14	19	3	8	92	162
Roumania .	...	...	2	9	...	...	...	50
Servia . .	...	...	...	3	...	...	...	16
Bulgaria . .	...	...	...	3	...	...	...	7
Greece . .	...	...	1	1	4	...	18	37
Total .	170.1	190	410	868	1,595	1,618	3,029	5,188

In many of the above States a considerable portion of revenue arises from Government railways, and these also represent a great share of national debt. Deducting railways from both accounts, we find in 1898 as follows :—

	Revenue, Millions £	Debt, Millions £	£ per Inhab.	
			Revenue	Debt
United Kingdom	116	638	2.9	16.0
France . . .	134	1,214	3.5	31.8
Germany . .	124	115	2.4	2.3
Russia . . .	109	326	1.0	3.0
Austria . . .	83	324	1.9	8.0
Italy . . .	64	386	2.1	12.5
Spain . . .	31	283	1.8	15.5
Portugal . . .	11	120	2.3	28.0
Sweden & Norway	9	...	1.3	...
Denmark . . .	4	...	1.8	...
Holland . . .	11	70	2.3	14.5
Belgium . . .	9	36	1.5	5.7
Switzerland . .	4	13	2.3	4.3
Roumania . .	9	24	1.5	4.2
Servia	3	8	1.2	3.5
Bulgaria . . .	3	5.	1.0	1.5
Greece . . .	4	37	1.8	16.5
Turkey . . .	18	162	1.0	8.5
Total . .	746	3,775	2.0	10.1

See *Taxes*, page 810.

In the subjoined table are shown the amount raised by taxes, the income of State Railways, and the item of Sundries, which include postal service, crown lands, and the receipts from all Government properties or services, except lotteries and monopolies, which are put under taxes. It is to be observed that Germany and most countries count the gross receipts of State railways, while Holland and some others count only the net income from same. As regards France, there are 1700 miles of recently made State railways, but they seem to produce nothing.

	Revenue, £ (ooo omitted)			
	Taxes	Railways	Sundries	Total
United Kingdom .	98,000	...	18,000	116,000
France	117,800	...	16,700	134,500
Germany . . .	84,500	63,400	39,500	187,400
Russia	99,000	29,300	9,700	138,000
Austria	68,000	18,400	14,600	101,000
Italy	59,700	3,100	4,200	67,000
Spain	29,900	...	1,100	31,000
Portugal . . .	9,600	400	1,400	11,400
Sweden . . .	4,800	800	600	6,200
Norway . . .	2,500	500	800	3,800
Denmark . . .	2,800	300	700	3,800
Holland . . .	9,500	300	1,400	11,200
Belgium . . .	7,800	6,200	1,500	15,500
Switzerland . . .	2,100	...	1,500	3,600
Greece . . .	3,300	...	500	3,800
Roumania . . .	6,900	...	1,700	8,600
Servia	2,300	...	200	2,500
Bulgaria	3,100	...	200	3,300
Turkey	18,400	...	...	18,400
Europe	630,000	122,700	114,300	867,000
United States . .	71,800	...	17,600	89,400
Canada . . .	6,400	600	800	7,800
Australia . . .	11,700	10,600	8,400	30,700
India	42,800	12,900	4,200	59,900
Cape Colony . .	2,400	4,100	300	6,800
Egypt	8,400	1,800	300	10,500
Total . . .	773,500	152,700	145,900	1,072,100

DEBT.

Considering only national debt, that is, excluding communal, county, and municipal, and deducting the value of State railways, we can compare the same with the wealth of nations thus :—

	Millions £ Sterling		Ratio of Debt	£ Debt per Inhab.
	Wealth	Debt		
United Kingdom .	11,806	638	5.3	16.0
France	9,690	1,214	12.5	31.5
Germany . . .	8,052	115	1.4	2.2
Russia	6,425	326	5.0	3.0
Austria	4,512	324	7.2	7.5
Italy	3,160	386	12.2	12.2
Spain	2,380	283	11.9	16.1
Portugal . . .	411	120	29.0	24.0
Sweden	570	...	...	...
Norway	220	...	...	...
Denmark . . .	506	...	...	...
Holland	880	70	8.0	14.0
Belgium	988	36	3.6	5.7
Switzerland . . .	492	13	2.6	4.3
Roumania . . .	519	24	4.6	4.2
Servia	211	8	3.8	3.0
Bulgaria	296	5	1.7	1.5
Greece	222	37	16.5	17.0
Europe	51,340	3,613	7.0	10.0
United States . . .	16,350	378	2.3	5.3
Canada	1,003	57	5.7	11.5
Australia	1,076	96	8.9	23.0
Argentina	616	88	14.3	22.0
Total . . .	70,385	4,232	6.0	9.5

UNITED KINGDOM

The revenue of the United Kingdom for the year ending March 31, 1898, and the estimates for 1899, compare with the revenue of 1897 as follows :—

	£ Sterling		
	1897	1898	1899
Customs . . .	21,460,000	22,010,000	21,290,000
Excise	32,370,000	33,270,000	33,810,000
Income-tax . .	16,650,000	17,250,000	17,700,000
Stamps . . .	7,350,000	7,650,000	7,600,000
Duties	16,390,000	17,780,000	16,310,000
All taxes . . .	94,220,000	97,960,000	96,710,000
Post-Office . .	14,770,000	15,180,000	15,740,000
Sundries . . .	3,210,000	2,880,000	2,880,000
Total . .	112,200,000	116,020,000	115,330,000

A portion of the above was given in aid of Local Taxation accounts, viz. :—

	1897	1898
Local subsidies . . .	8,250,000	9,400,000
Imperial Treasury . . .	103,950,000	106,620,000
Total . .	112,200,000	116,020,000

The average revenue and expenditure for five years ending March 1896 were :—

Revenue	£	Expenditure	£
Customs . .	20,200,000	National Debt	25,100,000
Excise . .	29,300,000	Civil Service .	20,000,000
Income-tax .	14,800,000	Local grants .	7,400,000
Duties, &c. .	17,300,000	Army & Navy	34,800,000
Post-Office .	13,200,000	Post-Office .	10,000,000
Sundries . .	6,400,000	Sundries . .	4,300,000
Total . .	101,200,000	Total . .	101,600,000

Expenditure for 1896 and 1897 was as follows :—

	£ Sterling		
	1896	1897	Increase
National Debt .	25,000,000	25,000,000	...
Civil Service . .	21,250,000	21,470,000	220,000
Local grants . .	7,400,000	8,200,000	800,000
Army and Navy	38,330,000	41,460,000	3,130,000
Post-Office . .	10,480,000	10,830,000	350,000
Sundries . . .	4,790,000	4,540,000	...
Total . . .	107,250,000	111,500,000	4,250,000

While other nations, with few exceptions, have increased their debt in the last fifty years, ours has been reduced, viz. :—

Year	Debt, £	Interest, £	Per Inhabitant	
			Debt, £	Interest
1848 . . .	773,000,000	27,700,000	28.4	21s.
1857 . . .	808,100,000	28,500,000	28.8	20s.
1870 . . .	798,000,000	27,100,000	25.5	18s.
1889 . . .	694,400,000	24,800,000	18.2	13s.
1898 . . .	615,000,000	23,500,000	15.5	12s.

The nominal amount of debt on March 31st, 1898, was £638,300,000, from which deducting the value of Suez

Canal shares, the actual debt was as stated above. National debt is at present equal to 5¼ per cent. of the estimated wealth of the nation, whereas in the year of Queen Victoria's accession (1837) it was over 20 per cent. of wealth.

An official return of the imperial revenue, showing the portions furnished by Great Britain and Ireland, is as follows :—

Year	Millions £ Sterling		
	G. Britain	Ireland	U. Kingdom
1840 . . .	46.3*	5.4	51.7
1860 . . .	61.4	7.7	69.1
1880 . . .	69.8	7.3	77.1
1890 . . .	84.9	7.9	92.8
1897 . . .	101.9	8.2	110.1

The above, compared with population, shows per head as follows :—

Year	Shillings per Head		
	G. Britain	Ireland	U. Kingdom
1840 . . .	50	13	39
1860 . . .	53	27	48
1880 . . .	48	28	44
1890 . . .	51	34	49
1897 . . .	57	36	55

Comparing 1897 with 1840, we find that revenue in Great Britain has increased 7 shillings, in Ireland 23 shillings per head. The ratio of increase has been 14 per cent. in Great Britain, 177 per cent. in Ireland. The receipts from the three kingdoms in 1897 were as follows :—

	£ Sterling (000 omitted)			
	England	Scotland	Ireland	U. King.
Customs .	17,030	2,110	2,330	21,470
Excise . .	24,830	4,330	3,140	32,300
Taxes . .	34,690	3,690	1,700	40,080
Post-Office .	12,540	1,450	810	14,800
Sundries .	1,150	110	170	1,430
Total . .	90,240	11,690	8,150	110,080

See *Taxation*, page 810.

FRANCE

Revenue and expenditure accounts show as follows :—

Revenue	Millions £ Sterling			
	1880	1890	1894	1898
Direct tax . .	15.2	19.2	20.6	19.3
Customs . .	14.7	15.0	19.2	16.5
Stamp-duties .	27.9	28.5	28.4	29.9
Post-Office .	5.5	8.1	8.8	9.2
Excise . .	43.1	47.8	48.0	43 2
Sundries . .	30.8	34.7	13.4	16.4
Total .	137.2	153.3	138.4	134.5

* To read thus : 46.3 signifies £46,300,000.

Expenditure	Millions £ Sterling			
	1880	1890	1894	1898
Debt . . .	49.7	50.7	49.4	50.0
Army . . .	22.4	23.2	25.9	25.2
Navy . . .	7.8	8.0	14.2	10.3
Public works . .	26.2	14.4	13.0	7.8
Commerce . .	1.7	9.6	8.1	8.2
Instruction . .	4.4	7.6	8.2	8.5
Local grants . .	1.1	8.6	1.6	1.6
Sundries . .	37.1	27.7	18.8	22.1
Total . .	150.4	149.8	139.2	133.7

In 1890 the amount of revenue refunded to Communes was 7 millions sterling more than at present, which accounts in some measure for the reduction of expenditure. The ratio of revenue per head of population at various dates shows thus :—

Year	£	£ per Inhab.
1860	68,500,000	1.8
1880	135,700,000	3.5
1898	134,500,000	3.4

National debt has more than doubled since the year preceding the Franco-German war, as the following table shows :—

Year	Millions £			£ per Inhabitant
	Funded	Floating	Total	
1869 . . .	468	36	504	13.2
1887 . . .	828	118	946	24.8
1896 . . .	1,040	204	1,244	32.4

The floating debt properly so called is only 46 millions, but the " annuity " and other unfunded debts being added make a total of 204 millions. Interest on funded debt amounts to £32,500,000, being 3¼ per cent. on principal, and the other expenses, especially those of floating debt, bring up the annual burthen of this department to a total of 50 millions, equal to 26 shillings per inhabitant, against 12 shillings in the United Kingdom.

GERMANY

The revenue of the States composing the Empire has grown as follows :—

	1867 £	1890 £	1897 £
Prussia . . .	25,300,000	79,300,000	97,000,000
Bavaria . . .	5,900,000	12,200,000	17,200,000
Saxony . . .	2,200,000	3,900,000	7,500,000
Wurtemberg . .	1,300,000	2,800,000	3,700,000
Small States . .	5,800,000	9,500,000	18,000,000
Imperial tax . .	...	47,000,000	44,000,000
Total . .	40,500,000	154,700,000	187,400,000

The imperial revenue is in reality £65,000,000, but this includes £21,000,000 contributed by the various States as "matriculas" and already included in the revenues raised by those States. If we exclude railway receipts, and apportion imperial taxes according to population, the revenue shows thus :—

	£	£ per Inhab.
Prussia	74,400,000	2.4
Bavaria	16,100,000	2.7
Saxony	8,500,000	2.3
Wurtemberg	4,800,000	2.3
Other States	20,200,000	2.3
Total . . .	124,000,000	2.4

The average budget for the empire in five years ending 1897 showed thus :—

Revenue	Millions £	Expenses	Millions £
Customs . .	17.6	Debt . . .	3.5
Excise . .	13.6	Army . . .	29.0
Matriculas .	19.1	Navy . . .	4.2
Stamps . .	2.3	Civil Service .	18.8
Sundries .	9.8	Sundries .	7.9
Total . .	62.4	Total . .	63.4

Matriculas in the above table represent the contributions of the several States to defray imperial expenses, that of Prussia amounting to £12,800,000, of Bavaria to £2,600,000, and the other States making up between them £3,700,000 sterling.

National debt has grown as follows :—

	Millions £		
	1867	1890	1897
Prussia. . . .	49	230	325
Bavaria . . .	30	68	71
Other States. . .	49	105	118
Total . .	128	403	514
Imperial . . .	...	62	106
Grand total .	128	465	620

The increase of debt since 1867 has been caused by the purchase or construction of railways for the State, which have at present a length of 26,440 miles, representing a cost of 505 millions sterling. Deducting this from the above sum it will be seen that the real debt of Germany is only 115 millions sterling, or a fraction over £2 per inhabitant, against £16 in the United Kingdom and £32 in France.

RUSSIA

The growth of revenue and debt in late years has been as follows :—

	Millions £		Shillings per Inhab.	
	Revenue	Debt	Revenue	Debt
1875 . . .	74	370	18	90
1889 . . .	90	610	19	128
1898 . . .	138	692	27	133

Excluding State railways, the revenue and debt in 1896 were :—

	£ Sterling	Shillings per Inhabitant
Revenue . .	112,000,000	21
Debt . .	326,000,000	61

Revenue and expenditure during five years to December 1896 averaged as follows :—

Revenue	Millions £	Expenses	Millions £
Customs	15.8*	Debt	26.4
Excise	38.0	Army	27.0
Railways . . .	15.2	Navy . . .	5.4
Land-tax . . .	14.0	Public works . .	11.0
Stamps. . . .	7.1	Civil Service . .	8.3
Post Office . . .	3.7	Schools. . . .	2.2
Sundries. . . .	21.2	Sundries . . .	45.7
Total . .	115.0	Total . .	126.0

Excess of expenditure from 1892 to 1897 was caused by the purchase or construction of 9000 miles of railway for the State, at a cost of 135 millions sterling, which amount was obtained by loans: thus the national debt rose from 540 millions in 1885 to 700 millions sterling in 1895, an average increase of 16 millions per annum. The Government has expended 366 millions sterling on railways, of which 284 millions are represented by 17,000 miles of State Railways, and 82 millions by shares on lines built by companies. Deducting this from the imperial debt, the latter is reduced to 326 millions, say 61 shillings per inhabitant.

FINLAND

The finances of this duchy are kept distinct from those of Russia; the budget for 1896 was as follows :—

Revenue	£	Expenses	£
Customs, &c. .	1,200,000	Debt	240,000
Land-tax . . .	300,000	Army . . .	400,000
Sundries . . .	1,700,000	Government .	2,560,000
Total . .	3,200,000	Total . .	3,200,000

Public debt amounts to £4,400,000 sterling.

AUSTRIA-HUNGARY

The total revenue of the monarchy is shown as follows :—

	Millions £ Sterling		
	1893	1897	Average, 5 Years
Imperial customs . .	4.6	4.3	4.3
Austrian budget . .	55.0	57.5	54.4
Hungarian budget .	38.8	39.2	39.3
Total .	98.4	101.0	98.0

From the budgets of Austria and Hungary an annual quota is drawn, to defray the expenses common to the monarchy, the dual revenue showing thus :—

	Millions £ Sterling		
	1893	1897	Average, 5 Years
Imperial customs . .	4.6	4.3	4.3
Austrian quota . .	5.4	6.1	5.7
Hungarian quota . .	2.5	2.8	2.6
Total .	12.5	13.2	12.6

* To read thus : Customs, £15,800,000.

Joint expenditure for 1898 is estimated at £13,400,000, of which £11,700,000 for the army, £1,200,000 for the navy, and £400,000 for diplomatic agents.

The Austrian budgets for five years ending 1895 averaged as follows:—

Revenue	Millions £	Expenses	Millions £
Customs . .	3.7	Imperial quota .	5.7
Excise . . .	18.5	Debt . . .	12.8
Income-tax .	9.3	Public works .	9.4
Stamps . .	5.0	Agriculture .	1.5
Railways . .	6.7	Militia . .	1.6
Post-Office .	3.0	Worship . .	2.0
Sundries . .	6.3	Sundries .	18.6
Total .	52.5	Total .	51.6

Hungarian budgets for five years averaged as follows:—

Revenue	Millions £	Expenses	Millions £
Excise . . .	12.2	Imperial quota .	2.6
Income-tax .	8.2	Debt . . .	10.9
Stamps . .	2.8	Public works .	6.3
Railways . .	6.7	Agriculture .	1.2
Post-Office .	1.3	Militia . .	1.1
Sundries .	6.5	Sundries .	15.3
Total .	37.7	Total .	37.4

If we exclude railways, Post-Office, and other public services, in order to arrive at the precise amount of taxation, we find, for the whole monarchy :—

	£
Excise	30,700,000
Customs . . .	8,500,000
Income-tax . . .	17,500,000
Stamps, &c. . . .	11,300,000
Total .	68,000,000

National debt is as follows :—

	Millions of Florins			Millions £ Sterling
	Gold	Silver	Paper	
General . . .	500	400	2,170	264
Austrian . . .	...	1,000	270	106
Hungarian .	710	1,200	170	185
Total .	1,210	2,600	2,080	555

In apportioning the general debt Austria took 70, Hungary 30, per cent., which makes the total debt of the former 291, that of the latter 264 millions sterling. But if the value of State railways be deducted the net debt of Austria will be 184, that of Hungary 140, millions sterling. The total service of debt costs 24 millions sterling, or nearly 4½ per cent. on the capital sum : it averages not quite 12 shillings per inhabitant, against 26 shillings in France, and 12 in the United Kingdom.

Italy

The revenue and debt of the kingdom are shown as follows :—

	Millions £		£ per Head	
	Revenue	Debt	Revenue	Debt
1880 . . .	55	393	2.0	14.0
1891 . . .	64	489	2.1	16.3
1898 . . .	67	516	2.2	16.6

The budgets of revenue and expenditure for five years ending 1896 give the following averages :—

Revenue	Millions £	Expenses	Millions £
Customs	11.9	Debt . . . , .	23.6
Excise	10.3	Army . . . , .	11.1
Income-tax . . .	17.9	Navy . . . , .	4.2
Stamps . . .	7.4	Schools	1.7
Railways . . .	2.8	Public works . .	4.2
Post-Office . . .	2.6	Civil service . .	10.6
Sundries	12.3	Sundries . . .	18.1
Total . .	65.2	Total . .	73.5

There was a nominal deficit of 41 millions in the above five years, which was covered by 25 millions increase of debt, and 16 millions from sale of properties, &c.

If we deduct the cost of State railways (130 millions sterling), the national debt will amount to 386 millions sterling, equal to 12 per cent. of national wealth, being the same ratio as in France.

Spain

Revenue and national debt have been as follows :—

Year	Millions £		£ per Inhabitant	
	Revenue	Debt	Revenue	Debt
1878	30	550	1.8	32.0
1888	35	260	2.0	15.0
1898	31	283	1.8	16.2

The debt was repudiated in 1882, when bondholders were compelled to take new bonds of £40, for £100 old. Revenue and expenditure in the last five years averaged:—

Revenue	£29,200,000
Expenditure	31,200,000

The average deficit in the past ten years has been £2,300,000. The budget for 1898 shows as follows :—

Revenue	Millions £	Expenses	Millions £
Excise, &c. . . .	12.3	Debt	13.0
Property tax . .	11.9	Army	9.6
Monopolies, &c. .	6.8	Sundries . . .	12.4
Total . .	31.0	Total . .	35.0

In 1840 the debt was repudiated, bondholders receiving 30 per cent. in new scrip: this operation was repeated in 1882, bondholders being forced to accept 40 per cent. Thus the holder of a bond of £1000 in 1840 received new scrip for £300, and in 1882 this was again exchanged for £120 of newer scrip, so that 88 per cent. of the money due by Spain was thus wiped out, the actual debt representing only 12 per cent. of what should be the capital sum. This is exclusive of Cuban debt, amounting to 80 millions sterling, secured by revenues of that island.

Portugal

Revenue and national debt were as follows :—

Year	Millions £		£ per Inhabitant	
	Revenue	Debt	Revenue	Debt
1878	5.7	94.0	1.3	22.5
1888	8.4	113.0	1.8	25.0
1898	11.5	134.0	2.4	27.2

The budgets of five years ending 1896 gave the following average :—

Revenue	£10,100,000
Expenditure	11,200,000

The average deficit from 1888 to 1897 was 2 millions sterling per annum, and consequently the debt, as shown above, rose 21 millions in that interval.

The budget for 1898 showed as follows :—

Revenue	£	Expenses	£
Customs . . .	5,500,000	Debt	4,000,000
Income-tax . .	2,600,000	Army . . .	1,300,000
Stamps . . .	1,100,000	Public works .	1,300,000
Railways . . .	400,000	Civil Service .	1,400,000
Post-Office . .	300,000	Colonies. . .	900,000
Sundries . . .	1,600,000	Sundries . .	3,500,000
Total . .	11,500,000	Total . .	12,400,000

The amount raised by taxation is £9,600,000, equal to 40 shillings per inhabitant or 15 per cent. of national earnings. In 1893 the finances were so distracted that the Government compelled bondholders to accept a new arrangement whereby the interest on internal bonds was reduced to 70 per cent., that on the foreign or external debt to 33 per cent. of the interest previously paid. State railways stand for one-tenth of the national debt.

SWEDEN

Revenue and debt are shown as follows :—

Year	Revenue £	Debt £	£ per Head	
			Revenue	Debt
1878 . . .	4,100,000	9,800,000	1.0	2.4
1888 . . .	4,800,000	13,700,000	1.1	3.0
1897 . . .	6,200,000	16,100,000	1.2	3.2

Budgets for the last five years give the following averages :—

Revenue	£	Expenses	£
Customs . . .	2,100,000	Debt	600,000
Excise . . .	1,200,000	Army	1,600,000
Income-tax . .	600,000	Navy . . .	600,000
Railways . . .	800,000	Schools . . .	800,000
Post-Office . .	600,000	Civil Service .	1,400,000
Sundries . . .	1,200,000	Sundries . . .	1,200,000
Total . .	6,500,000	Total . .	6,200,000

The amount raised by taxation is £4,800,000. The national debt is represented by State railways, which give a net profit of £500,000, or 3 per cent. on their cost of construction.

NORWAY

Revenue and debt have been as follows :—

Year	Revenue £	Debt £	£ per Head	
			Revenue	Debt
1878 . . .	2,400,000	4,000,000	1.3	2.2
1888 . . .	2,400,000	5,900,000	1.2	3.0
1898 . . .	3,800,000	8,800,000	1.8	4.2

Budgets of the last five years give the following averages :—

Revenue	£	Expenses	£
Customs . . .	1,300,000	Debt	300,000
Excise	400,000	Army	500,000
Taxes	500,000	Navy	200,000
Railways . . .	400,000	Public works .	600,000
Post-Office . .	300,000	Schools . . .	300,000
Sundries . . .	300,000	Sundries . . .	1,400,000
Total . .	3,200,000	Total . .	3,300,000

The amount of revenue raised by taxation is £2,500,000. National debt is represented by a complete network of more than 1000 miles of railway, but the earnings do not suffice to pay the interest on the debt.

DENMARK

Notwithstanding the loss of Sleswig-Holstein in 1864, the Danish finances have improved in the last thirty years, viz. :—

Year	Revenue £	Debt £	£ per Head	
			Revenue	Debt
1866 . . .	2,000,000	14,800,000	1.2	8.4
1889 . . .	3,000,000	10,400,000	1.4	4.8
1898 . . .	3,800,000	10,900,000	1.7	4.9

Budgets of the last five years give the following averages :—

Revenue	£	Expenses	£
Customs . . .	1,400,000	Debt	400,000
Excise . . .	300,000	Army	800,000
Income-tax . .	500,000	Navy	400,000
Stamps . . .	400,000	Public works .	300,000
Sundries . . .	700,000	Sundries . . .	1,700,000
Total . .	3,300,000	Total . .	3,600,000

The debt is fully represented by the State railways, besides which the Treasury has always a reserve of 3½ millions sterling to provide against sudden emergency.

HOLLAND

Revenue and debt have progressed as follows :—

Year	Revenue £	Debt £	£ per Head	
			Revenue	Debt
1879 . . .	9,400,000	80,500,000	2.4	20.1
1888 . . .	10,000,000	89,200,000	2.2	19.8
1898 . . .	11,200,000	92,200,000	2.3	18.4

The budgets of the last five years gave the following averages :—

Revenue	£	Expenses	£
Customs . .	500,000	Debt . . .	3,200,000
Excise . . .	3,700,000	Army . . .	3,100,000
Direct tax . .	2,800,000	Public works	900,000
Sundries . .	4,000,000	Sundries . .	4,100,000
Total . .	11,000,000	Total . .	11,300,000

The revenue raised by taxation was £9,500,000. National debt is 92 millions, of which 22 millions stand for State railways, leaving a real debt of 70 millions sterling.

BELGIUM

Revenue and debt have grown as follows :—

	Millions £		£ per Head	
	Revenue	Debt	Revenue	Debt
1878 . . .	10.2	42.0	2.0	8.0
1890 . . .	12.9	77.4	2.1	12.8
1898 . . .	15.5	93.1	2.4	14.4

The budgets of five years ending December 1895 gave the following averages :—

Revenue	£	Expenses	£
Taxes . . .	6,900,000	Debt . . .	4,200,000
Railways .	6,600,000	Army . . .	2,100,000
Post-Office .	500,000	Railways . .	4,200,000
Sundries . .	200,000	Sundries . .	5,600,000
Total .	14,200,000	Total .	16,100,000

Surplus expenditure since 1890 has averaged two millions sterling per annum, caused by the construction of railways, which give a net profit of 4 per cent. on their cost. The State possesses 2050 miles of railway, which have cost 57 millions sterling, and if this be deducted the national debt will be reduced to 36 millions sterling.

SWITZERLAND

The Federal Government has an annual revenue of £3,400,000, and a public debt of £3,200,000, but if the finances of the 22 Cantons be taken into account the figures will stand thus—

	Revenue £	Debt, £
Federal . . .	3,600,000	3,200,000
Cantonal . . .	3,200,000	10,400,000
Total .	6,800,000	13,600,000

The federal budget for 1898 is made up thus :—

Revenue	£	Expenses	£
Customs . .	1,800,000	Army . . .	1,000,000
Post-Office .	1,500,000	Post-Office .	1,500,000
Sundries . .	300,000	Sundries . .	1,100,000
Total .	3,600,000	Total .	3,600,000

Between federal and local taxes the total is about 6 millions sterling, or 40 shillings per inhabitant, or 9 per cent. of national earnings. The total of federal and cantonal debts is hardly 3 per cent. of national wealth.

DANUBIAN STATES.

The finances of these States may be briefly summed up thus :—

			Revenue, £ (000 omitted).		
			Roumania	Servia	Bulgaria
Customs	.	.	2,500	200	900
Taxes .	.	.	1,500	1,100	1,700
Sundries	.	.	4,600	1,200	1,000
Total	.	.	8,600	2,500	3,600

			Expenditure, £ (000 omitted).		
			Roumania	Servia	Bulgaria
Debt .	.	.	3,200	700	800
Army .	.	.	1,800	600	900
Sundries	.	.	3,600	1,200	1,600
Total	.	.	8,600	2,500	3,300

The following shows public debt and how much of it is accounted for by State railways :—

			Millions £		
			Debt	Railways	Real Debt
Roumania	.	.	50	26	24
Servia .	.	.	16	8	8
Bulgaria	.	.	7	2	5
Total	.	.	73	36	37

GREECE

Revenue and debt have grown as follows :—

Year	Revenue, £	Debt, £	£ per Head	
			Revenue	Debt
1879 . . .	1,600,000	19,400,000	1.0	12.0
1889 . . .	3,400,000	22,700,000	1.5	10.3
1898 . . .	3,800,000	37,000,000	1.6	15.0

Expenditure exceeded revenue, the aggregate for the past ten years showing as follows :—

Revenues, 1888-97 . . . £34,800,000
Expenses, ,, . . . 43,600,000

The annual deficit has been close on a million sterling, and the debt now reaches 37 millions, this sum including the indemnity of 4 millions sterling payable to Turkey. Debt is equal to 17 per cent. of national wealth.

TURKEY

The financial position of the Ottoman empire is shown thus :—

Year	Revenue, £	Debt, £
1878	15,000,000	245,000,000
1887	16,200,000	180,000,000
1898	18,500,000	162,000,000

The budget of 1898 is made up as follows :—

Revenue	£	Expenses	£
Customs . . .	2,000,000	Debt . . .	6,500,000
Excise . . .	2,600,000	Army . . .	6,000,000
Rural taxes . .	8,600,000	Sultan . . .	900,000
Sundries . . .	5,300,000	Sundries . .	5,100,000
Total . .	18,500,000	Total . .	18,500,000

In five years down to 1896 the expenditure averaged one million sterling over revenue. No fewer than 26 loans have been issued since 1854, amounting as follows :—

Period			No. of Loans	Millions £
1854-64	.	. . .	6	31
1865-80	.	. . .	10	207
1881-96	.	. . .	10	40
Total	.	.	26	278

Fifteen of the above loans were converted by new

2 Y

issues in 1881-90-91-94. On the 8th December 1881, the empire was declared bankrupt, when loans and arrears of interest, amounting to 240 millions sterling, were reduced by 90 millions by an issue of new stock to foreign bondholders, leaving also an internal debt of 40 millions, besides 32 millions of war indemnity due to Russia, which made a total of 162 millions. Since then there have been loans and lottery bonds to the amount of 50 millions, and the funded debt in July 1897 amounted to £130,500,000, to which must be added £31,500,000 for Russian indemnity, making a total of 162 millions sterling.

EGYPT

The finances were rearranged in 1885: revenue and debt are shown thus :—

Year	Revenue, £	Debt, £
1878	7,400,000	85,000,000
1889	9,700,000	103,400,000
1897	10,500,000	104,600,000

The revenue of 1897 compares with that of 1889 as follows :—

	1889	1897
Customs . . .	1,000,000	800,000
Land tax . .	4,900,000	5,000,000
Railways . .	1,300,000	1,800,000
Sundries . .	2,500,000	2,900,000
Total .	9,700,000	10,500,000

The expenditure of the same years compares thus :—

	1889	1897
Debt . . .	4,100,000	4,200,000
Police . .	700,000	800,000
Government . .	4,600,000	4,900,000
Total .	9,400,000	9,900,000

The railways are State property, and give a net profit of £1,030,000 a year, equal to 6½ per cent. on their cost. The actual debt of £104,600,000 is accounted for thus: canals, £19,400,000; railways, £16,200,000; mills, harbours, &c., £13,500,000; discount on loans, £26,400,000; ballet-dancers, palaces, &c., £47,300,000. The actual sum realised by the loans was 78 millions sterling, and the service of the debt is nearly 5½ per cent. on same. It is impossible to say what were the profits of Messrs. Goschen, Oppenheim, Bischoffsheim, and Rothschild in the loans.

UNITED STATES

Finances compared with population at various dates show thus :—

Year	Millions £		£ per Inhabitant	
	Revenue	Debt	Revenue	Debt
1870 . .	71.5	490	1.9	12.6
1880 . .	69.2	441	1.4	8.8
1890 . .	96.5	323	1.5	5.1
1897 . .	89.4	378	1.2	5.4

The budgets of the last eight years give the following averages of revenue :—

	1890–93 Millions £	1894–97 Millions £	1890–97 Millions £
Customs . . .	43.2	32.2	37.7
Excise .	31.2	30.2	30.7
Post-Office . . .	14.1	16.5	15.3
Sundries . . .	5.5	4.3	4.9
Total . .	94.0	83.2	88.6

Expenditure averaged as follows :—

	1890–93	1894–97	1890–97
Debt	6.4	6.8	6.6
Army	10.4	11.0	10.7
Navy	5.6	6.4	6.0
Post-Office . . .	15.8	19.0	17.4
Interior . . .	31.2	33.2	32.2
Sundries . . .	16.6	15.0	15.8
Total . .	86.0	91.4	88.7

The first four years showed an average surplus of 8 millions sterling of revenue over expenditure, but the second four years showed the reverse, so that revenue and expenditure for the whole eight years were even. The budget of 1897 was as follows :—

Revenue	£	Expenses	£
Customs . .	36,700,000	Debt . . .	7,900,000
Excise . .	30,500,000	Army . . .	10,600,000
Post-Office . .	17,200,000	Navy . . .	7,300,000
Sundries . .	5,000,000	Government .	67,500,000
Total . .	89,400,000	Total . .	93,300,000

The national debt has varied between 1880 and 1897 as follows :—

Debt	Millions £ Sterling		
	1880	1890	1897
Bearing interest . . .	358	150	176
No interest . . .	82	172	202
Total . . .	440	322	378
Cash in Treasury . . .	41	137	172
Net debt . . .	399	185	206

Local taxation exceeds national: the former almost doubled between 1870 and 1890. See *Local Finance*.

CANADA

Revenue and debt have grown as follows :—

	Millions £		£ per Head	
	Revenue	Debt	Revenue	Debt
1880 . . .	5.1 *	32.1	1.1	7.0
1889 . . .	7.8	49.2	1.6	10.2
1897 . . .	7.8	69.0	1.5	13.8

* To read thus : Revenue, £5,100,000.

The budget for 1897 was as follows :—

Revenue	£	Expenses	£
Customs . . .	4,000,000	Debt	2,600,000
Excise	1,900,000	Subsidies . .	900,000
Post-Office . .	700,000	Militia . . .	400,000
Sundries . . .	1,200,000	Government .	4,000,000
Total . .	7,800,000	Total . .	7,900,000

The subsidies are grants to the several Provinces for local affairs, averaging 3 shillings per inhabitant. Each Province has also its own budget. See *Local Finance.*

Debt amounts to 69 millions, of which 59 have been expended on public works. The Intercolonial railway, belonging to Government, cost 12 millions sterling, deducting which the debt would be reduced to 57 millions. The Treasury is said to possess assets altogether worth 15 millions, and the real debt is officially put down at 54 millions sterling.

AUSTRALIA

Revenue has trebled since 1871, viz. :—

	£ Sterling (000 omitted)			
	1871	1881	1891	1897
N. S. Wales . . .	2,240	6,710	10,040	9,310
Victoria	3,730	5,190	8,340	6,630
New Zealand . . .	1,340	3,760	4,190	4,800
Queensland . . .	800	1,970	3,350	3,610
W. Australia . . .	110	210	500	2,840
S. Australia . . .	780	2,170	2,730	2,700
Tasmania	270	510	760	800
Total . . .	9,270	20,520	29,910	30,690

The above revenues gave the following averages per inhabitant :—

	Shillings per Head			
	1871	1881	1891	1897
N. S. Wales . . .	88	175	182	144
Victoria	101	119	147	113
New Zealand . . .	104	153	135	135
Queensland . . .	133	174	171	153
W. Australia . . .	84	140	215	412
S. Australia . . .	84	157	171	150
Tasmania	54	87	105	98
General	96	148	159	142

The revenue of 1897 was made up as follows :—

	£ Sterling (000 omitted)			
	Taxes	Railways	Sundries	Total
N. S. Wales . . .	2,460	3,370	3,480	9,310
Victoria	2,630	2,600	1,400	6,630
New Zealand . . .	2,520	1,290	990	4,800
Queensland . . .	1,500	1,140	970	3,610
W. Australia . . .	1,160	940	740	2,840
S. Australia . . .	940	1,040	720	2,700
Tasmania	470	160	170	800
Total . .	11,680	10,540	8,470	30,690

Expenditure in 1897 was made up as follows :—

	Debt	Railways	Sundries	Total
N. S. Wales . . .	2,310	1,830	5,180	9,320
Victoria	1,890	1,510	3,180	6,580
New Zealand . . .	1,710	780	2,020	4,510
Queensland . . .	1,260	680	1,660	3,600
W. Australia . . .	250	580	2,010	2,840
S. Australia . . .	970	640	1,150	2,760
Tasmania	310	120	320	750
Total . . .	8,700	6,140	15,520	30,360

The following table shows the sources of revenue in 1897 compared with population :—

	Shillings per Head					
	Taxes	Railways	Lands	P.-Office	Sundries	Total
N. S. Wales .	38	52	30	11	13	144
Victoria . . .	45	44	7	9	8	113
N. Zealand . .	71	36	8	12	8	135
Queensland . .	64	48	22	10	9	153
W. Australia .	169	136	27	30	50	412
S. Australia .	52	58	10	14	16	150
Tasmania . .	57	20	7	9	5	98
Australasia . .	54	49	17	11	11	142

Expenditure in 1897, compared with population, resulted as follows :—

	Shillings per Head					
	Debt	Railways	Schools	P.-Office	Sundries	Total
N. S. Wales .	36	28	11	11	58	144
Victoria . . .	32	26	10	10	34	112
New Zealand .	48	22	13	10	34	127
Queensland . .	54	29	10	13	47	153
W. Australia .	36	84	6	45	241	412
S. Australia .	54	35	9	11	44	153
Tasmania . .	38	15	5	8	26	92
Australasia . .	40	28	10	12	51	141

The following table shows the growth of public debt since 1871 :—

	£ Sterling (000 omitted)			
	1871	1881	1891	1897
N. S. Wales . . .	10,600	16,900	53,000	61,000
Victoria	12,000	22,400	43,600	47,500
New Zealand . . .	8,900	29,700	38,800	44,400
Queensland . . .	4,000	13,300	29,500	34,500
W. Australia . . .	...	500	1,600	7,300
S. Australia . . .	2,200	11,200	20,400	24,400
Tasmania	1,300	2,000	7,100	8,300
Total . . .	39,000	96,000	194,000	227,500

Public works represent 94 per cent. of the actual debt, namely, 213 millions sterling, including 156 millions spent on railways, telegraphs, water-supply, &c., which bring in a gross annual income of 12 millions sterling, or 40 per cent. of the total revenue. The remaining 57 millions were expended on roads, bridges, parks, public buildings, &c., which produce no income, though of equal utility. The expenditure has been as follows :—

	£ Sterling (000 omitted)			
	Railways	Water-works, &c.	Roads, &c.	Total
N. S. Wales . .	40,300	8,700	9,500	58,500
Victoria . . .	35,700	8,100	2,600	46,400
New Zealand .	15,300	1,400	24,900	41,600
Queensland . .	19,500	1,200	9,200	29,900
W. Australia .	4,500	300	1,800	6,600
S. Australia . .	12,800	4,900	4,700	22,400
Tasmania . .	3,700	100	3,800	7,600
Total . .	131,800	24,700	56,500	213,000

The following table shows the net profit yearly on railways, the net burthen of public debt after deducting the railway profits, and the ratio of the latter to population :—

	Railway Profits, £	Net Debt Charge, £	Shills. per Head of Interest
N. S. Wales . .	1,540,000	770,000	12
Victoria . . .	1,090,000	800,000	14
New Zealand . .	510,000	1,200,000	33
Queensland . .	460,000	800,000	34
W. Australia . .	360,000	...	...
S. Australia . .	400,000	570,000	32
Tasmania . . .	40,000	270,000	32
Total . .	4,400,000	4,300,000	20

This shows that the annual charge for public debt, after deducting the net profits of railways, is exactly 20 shillings per inhabitant; if we deduct from this the revenue received from public lands (17 shillings), it appears that the debt of Australasia imposes a burthen of only 3 shillings per inhabitant out of ordinary revenue.

SOUTH AFRICA

The revenue and debt of Cape Colony and Natal have been as follows :—

	Revenue, £		Debt, £	
	1887	1896	1887	1896
Cape Colony .	3,160,000	6,800,000	22,500,000	27,400,000
Natal	820,000	1,460,000	4,000,000	8,100,000
Total . .	3,980,000	8,260,000	26,500,000	35,500,000

The finances of Cape Colony in 1896 were as follows :—

Revenue	£	Expenses	£
Taxes	2,420,000	Debt	1,240,000
Railways . . .	4,080,000	Railways . .	1,920,000
Sundries . . .	300,000	Government .	3,200,000
Total . .	6,800,000	Total . .	6,360,000

The finances of Natal in 1896 showed thus :—

Revenue	£	Expenses	£
Railways . . .	750,000	Railways . .	400,000
Customs, &c. .	710,000	Government .	880,000
Total . .	1,460,000	Total . .	1,280,000

The aggregate debt of the two colonies is 35½ millions sterling, the whole expended on railways and other public works. The State railways cost 24½ millions, leaving the net debt only 11 millions sterling ; the railways give a net profit of £2,500,000 per annum, or 10 per cent. on capital.

INDIA

Revenue and debt have progressed as follows :—

Year	Millions of Rupees		Millions £ Sterling	
	Revenue	Debt	Revenue	Debt
1880 . . .	684	1,530	57.0	127.5
1890 . . .	857	2,185	64.3	163.8
1897 . . .	957	2,323	59.9	145.0

Rupees were worth 20 pence in 1880, 18 pence in 1890, and 15 pence in 1897. The budgets of 1890 and 1897, reduced to English money, compared thus :—

	Revenue, £	
	1890	1897
Land tax . . .	17,600,000	16,000,000
Railways . . .	12,600,000	12,900,000
Opium . . .	6,200,000	3,600,000
Salt tax . . .	6,000,000	5,500,000
Post-Office . .	1,700,000	1,900,000
Irrigation . .	1,400,000	2,000,000
Sundries . .	18,800,000	18,000,000
Total . .	64,300,000	59,900,000

	Expenditure, £	
	1890	1897
Debt . . .	4,400,000	3,600,000
Army . . .	16,600,000	15,200,000
Railways . .	14,100,000	14,700,000
Roads . . .	4,100,000	3,600,000
Canals . . .	1,900,000	2,000,000
Sundries . .	21,000,000	22,300,000
Total . .	62,100,000	61,400,000

Expenditure, counted in rupees, has risen 26 per cent. in ten years, viz. :—

Expended	Millions of Rupees		
	1886	1891	1896
In India . .	558	614	694
In Great Britain . .	184	206	275
Total . .	772	820	969

WEST INDIES, BRITISH

Revenue and debt have progressed as follows :—

Year	£ Sterling		Shillings per Inhab.	
	Revenue	Debt	Revenue	Debt
1881 . . .	1,850,000	2,020,000	24	27
1890 . . .	2,340,000	3,600,000	28	43
1896 . . .	2,440,000	4,900,000	30	58

The various islands and British Guiana showed in 1896 as follows :—

	Revenue, £	Debt, £	Shillings per Head	
			Revenue	Debt
Jamaica . . .	780,000	2,200,000	22	63
Trinidad . . .	580,000	600,000	50	52
Barbados. . .	180,000	400,000	19	42
Small Islands .	350,000	800,000	23	52
British Guiana .	550,000	900,000	40	66
West Indies . .	2,440,000	4,900,000	30	58

Although debt has risen 150 per cent. in fifteen years it is still light, being under £3 per inhabitant, against £12 in Canada.

ALGERIA

Revenue rose from £1,700,000 in 1885 to £2,100,000 in 1897, the budget for last year showing as follows :—

Revenue	£	Expenses	£
Customs . . .	520,000	Public works .	1,250,000
Land tax . . .	480,000	Gov. farms . .	620,000
Stamps . . .	550,000	Schools . . .	300,000
Sundries . . .	550,000	Sundries . .	630,000
Total . .	2,100,000	Total . .	2,800,000

Interest on debt, as well as army and navy expenses, are charged to the Colonial Department of the budget of France.

SPANISH WEST INDIES

In 1894 the revenue of these islands showed :—

	£	Shillings per Head
Cuba . . .	4,900,000	60
Porto Rico . .	800,000	20
Total .	5,700,000	47

The Cuban budget was made up thus :—

Revenue	£	Expenses	£
Customs . . .	2,300,000	Debt	2,500,000
Sundries . . .	2,600,000	Army, &c. . .	2,700,000
Total . .	4,900,000	Total . .	5,200,000

That of Porto Rico was as follows :—

Revenue	£	Expenses	£
Customs . . .	460,000	Garrison . .	200,000
Sundries . . .	340,000	Sundries . .	600,000
Total . .	800,000	Total . .	800,000

The debt of Cuba rose from 25 millions sterling in 1889 to 40 millions in 1894. Since the present revolution began Spain has piled up debt on Cuba, the amount in December 1897 reaching 91 millions sterling.

JAVA

Revenue and expenditure have been as follows :—

Year	Revenue, £	Expenditure, £
1870	10,300,000	9,600,000
1880	12,200,000	12,200,000
1890	11,500,000	10,600,000
1896	11,000,000	12,000,000

The following table shows the annual average revenues for six years :—

	£ Sterling		
	1892–93	1894–95	1896–97
Taxes	4,100,000	3,900,000	4,100,000
Products . . .	5,500,000	5,200,000	5,100,000
Sundries . .	1,500,000	1,700,000	1,900,000
Total . .	11,100,000	10,800,000	11,100,000

The revenue from products includes monopolies on opium and salt, as well as the profits from Government coffee-farms, &c.

CEYLON

Revenue and debt have progressed as follows :—

Year	Revenue, £	Debt, £	Shillings per Head	
			Revenue	Debt
1881 . . .	1,140,000	1,940,000	8	14
1890 . . .	1,220,000	2,520,000	8	17
1896 . . .	1,300,000	3,700,000	8	23

The budget for 1896 was made up as follows :—

Revenues	£	Expenses	£
Customs . . .	300,000	Debt	180,000
Railway . . .	400,000	Public works .	150,000
Excise	250,000	Garrison . .	100,000
Sundries . . .	350,000	Government .	870,000
Total . .	1,300,000	Total . .	1,300,000

The debt, amounting to £3,700,000, is represented by productive works, including piers, waterworks, and a railway of 300 miles.

ARGENTINA

Revenue and debt have grown as follows :—

Year	Millions £		£ per Head	
	Revenue	Debt	Revenue	Debt
1870 . . .	3.0	10.1	1.5	5.0
1880 . . .	3.9	23.0	1.3	8.0
1890 . . .	5.4	46.5	1.5	13.0
1897 . . .	9.4	88.0	2.3	22.0

The returns for five years, ending December 1896, gave the following averages :—

Revenue £7,700,000
Expenditure 10,200,000

The budget for 1898 showed as follows :—

Revenue	£	Expenses	£
Customs . . .	6,400,000	Debt	4,600,000
Excise	1,200,000	Army and navy	2,000,000
Sundries . . .	1,800,000	Sundries . .	4,200,000
Total . .	9,400,000	Total . .	10,800,000

Each of the 14 provinces has also its budget, the aggregate revenue amounting to £2,300,000. The total taxation amounts to £11,500,000, or £3 per inhabitant, as compared with £2 in Canada and £2½ in the United States.

Debt rose more than 40 millions between 1890 and

1897, because the Federal Government took over the debts of the provinces, amounting to 37 millions, besides redeeming the guarantees given to certain railway companies. There are still municipal debts to the sum of 5 millions sterling, bringing up the total to 93 millions sterling, or 15 per cent. of the wealth of the nation.

URUGUAY
Revenue and debt have grown as follows :—

Year	Revenue, £	Debt, £	£ per Inhabitant	
			Revenue	Debt
1870 . . .	900,000	8,000,000	2.2	20.0
1880 . . .	1,600,000	11,000,000	3.5	24.0
1890 . . .	2,400,000	15,000,000	3.2	20.0
1897 . . .	3,400,000	25,300,000	4.0	30.0

The budget of 1897 showed as follows :—

Revenue	£	Expenses	£
Customs . . .	1,900,000	Debt	1,100,000
Sundries . . .	1,500,000	Sundries . . .	2,300,000
Total . .	3,400,000	Total . .	3,400,000

Taxation, national and local, including £200,000 for the city of Monte Video, is about 4 millions sterling, or nearly £5 per inhabitant, against £3 in Argentina. Debt is equal to 21 per cent. of national wealth, against 15 per cent. in Argentina.

CHILE
The budgets of five years to December 1896 give the following averages :—

Revenue £5,800,000
Expenditure 5,500,000

The budget for 1897 was as follows :—

Revenue	£	Expenses	£
Customs . . .	1,700,000	Debt	900,000
Nitrate dues . .	2,900,000	Army and Navy	1,500,000
Sundries . . .	1,300,000	Government .	3,500,000
Total . .	5,900,000	Total . .	5,900,000

The debt of Chile amounts to £19,800,000, or £7 per inhabitant, against £13 in Argentina. The annual service of debt costs 7 shillings per inhabitant in Chile.

PERU
Revenue and expenditure during five years to end of 1896 averaged thus :—

Revenue £800,000
Expenditure 800,000

The budget for 1897 was as follows :—

Revenue	£	Expenses	£
Customs . . .	630,000	Army . . .	300,000
Taxes	250,000	Interior . . .	260,000
Sundries . . .	190,000	Sundries . .	570,000
Total . .	1,070,000	Total . .	1,130,000

Peru borrowed 32 millions sterling in England in 1870–72, and soon after became bankrupt ; in 1890 she handed over the State railways and mines to the bondholders, who agreed to cancel the debt. There is still an internal debt of 4 millions sterling.

VENEZUELA
The budget of 1896 shows as follows :—

Revenue	£	Expenses	£
Customs . . .	1,100,000	Debt	400,000
Sundries . . .	1,000,000	Government .	2,200,000
Total . .	2,100,000	Total . .	2,600,000

Debt amounts to 8 millions sterling, or £3½ per inhabitant.

MEXICO
Budgets of the last five years give the following averages :—

Revenue £5,200,000
Expenditure 4,900,000

The budget for 1898 was made up thus :—

Revenue	£	Expenses	£
Customs . . .	2,500,000	Debt	1,900,000
Excise	2,200,000	Army . . .	1,200,000
Sundries . . .	500,000	Government .	2,100,000
Total . .	5,200,000	Total . .	5,200,000

Public debt amounts to 30 millions sterling. There is local taxation, between States and municipalities, which sums up £3,000,000 per annum. Thus the total taxation is about 8 millions sterling, or 14 shillings per inhabitant.

BRAZIL
The budgets of five years to end of 1897 gave the following averages :—

Revenue £12,600,000
Expenditure 13,800,000

The budget for 1898 showed as follows :—

Revenue	£	Expenses	£
Customs . . .	6,800,000	Debt	3,500,000
Railways . . .	900,000	Army and Navy	2,200,000
Sundries . . .	1,800,000	Sundries . . .	3,200,000
Total . .	9,500,000	Total . .	8,900,000

The budget is unreliable as regards expenditure, which always exceeds revenue. The foreign debt amounts to 39 millions sterling, the internal to 1600 millions of milreis, nominally worth 176 millions sterling, but at the present rate of exchange, only 44 millions sterling. This includes 700 million milreis of paper-money, which bears no interest. The national debt, excluding this paper-money, may be set down at 63 millions sterling, besides local debts amounting to £2,500,000 sterling.

CHINA
The revenues of 1889 and 1893 showed as follows :—

	£ Sterling	
	1889	1893
Land tax . . .	4,800,000	7,500,000
Customs . . .	5,500,000	3,500,000
Salt tax . . .	2,300,000	2,200,000
Sundries . . .	6,400,000	1,800,000
Total . .	19,000,000	15,000,000

Foreign debt amounts to 55, internal to 5 millions, making altogether 60 millions sterling, the whole originating out of the war with Japan.

JAPAN

Budgets of the last five years give the following averages :—

Revenue	£16,200,000
Expenditure	15,600,000

Estimates for 1898 are as follows :—

Revenue	£	Expenses	£
Land Tax . .	5,800,000	Debt	4,400,000
Excise	6,300,000	Army . . .	4,400,000
Customs . .	1,000,000	Navy	1,500,000
Post-Office . .	1,800,000	Public works .	1,800,000
Sundries . . .	3,300,000	Sundries . . .	5,000,000
Total . .	18,200,000	Total . .	17,100,000

The above does not include an extraordinary expenditure of 20 millions sterling, probably a result of the late war. There are provincial taxes for local purposes, averaging 8 millions sterling per annum. Public debt 62 millions sterling.

TRANSVAAL

Revenue has quadrupled in five years, viz. :—

	£ Sterling	
	1892	1897
Revenue	1,260,000	4,900,000
Expenditure . . .	1,190,000	4,700,000

Public debt is £2,700,000, which is fully covered by the value of public lands.

FIRES

In 1891 the fires and fire-brigades showed as follows :—

	Fires	Firemen	Cost, £	Pence per Inhab.
London	2,427	820	123,000	7.0
Paris	2,708	1,750	104,000	10.0
Berlin	3,290	780	70,000	11.5
Vienna	540	270	12,000	2.5
Hamburg	240	180	40,000	16.0
Dresden	330	130	11,000	8.0
Leipzig	290	130	15,000	10.0
Buda-Pesth . . .	406	150	12,000	5.5
Breslau . . .	140	190	15,000	9.5
Brussels	120	170	11,000	5.2
Bordeaux	640	100	8,500	8.0
Rome	345	300	9,000	4.8
Naples	90	200	12,000	5.0
Milan	260	160	7,000	4.0
Genoa	120	120	6,000	6.6
Florence	150	130	3,000	4.0

The average cost of the fire-brigade in the above 16 cities is 7 pence per inhabitant yearly. Hamburg, Berlin, and Paris are much higher.

Fires in London since 1870 show thus :—

	Annual Average	Inhab. to a Fire
1870-80 . . .	1,795	2,150
1881-89 . . .	2,160	1,780
1893-97 . . .	3,444	1,320

The number of lives endangered, rescued, and lost, is shown as follows :—

Lives	Yearly Average	
	1888-92	1893-97
Endangered . . .	202	232
Rescued . . .	146	142
Lost . . .	56	90

Loss of life in the second period shows an increase of 60 per cent. over the quinquennium 1888-92, although the number of fires had risen only 15 per cent.

The following table shows the nature of the premises for an average of four years ending December 1897, and the causes as far as ascertained in the year 1897 :—

Premises	No.	Causes	No.
Private houses . .	926	Lamps	758
Lodgings . . .	712	Gas	268
Liquor shops . .	82	Candles . . .	253
Drug stores . . .	44	Children . . .	190
Shoemakers . .	41	Ovens	88
Cabinetmakers .	30	Hot ashes . . .	87
Bakers	27	Airing linen . .	72
Various	1,590	Various	1,784
Total . .	3,452	Total . .	3,500

The London fire brigade has 999 men, 67 engines, 115 hose-carts, 36 miles of hose, 235 fire-escapes, 159 horses, 8 steam-tugs, and 592 fire-alarm call points.

FRANCE

Fires in the city of Paris in 1890 destroyed property to the value of £360,000, being most numerous in December and January.

FISH

The fisheries of the world may be set down approximately as follows :—

	Fishermen	Tons Fish	Tons per Man
Great Britain . .	93,000	670,000	7.2
Ireland . .	27,000	30,000	1.1
United Kingdom . .	120,000	700,000	5.8
France . . .	85,000	150,000	1.8
Germany . . .	20,000	60,000	3.0
Russia	75,000	220,000	3.0
Italy . . .	70,000	100,000	1.5
Spain and Portugal .	50,000	90,000	1.8
Scandinavia . .	165,000	510,000	3.1
Holland . . .	18,000	120,000	6.6
Europe . . .	603,000	1,950,000	3.3
United States . .	192,000	880,000	4.6
Canada . . .	71,000	240,000	3.4
Total . .	866,000	3,070,000	3.5

FRANCE

France produced 1170 millions of oysters in 1890, of which 350 millions were exported and 820 millions retained for home consumption—that is, 43 per inhabitant.

Production multiplied twenty-fold in sixteen years, viz. :—

Year	Million Oysters	Value, £
1874	64	74,000
1876	259	...
1890	1,170	440,000

RUSSIA

Caviare is produced in large quantities, the export showing thus :—

Year	Tons	Value, £	£ per Ton
1874 . . .	1,800	180,000	100
1884 . . .	5,100	340,000	67
1894 . . .	2,400	180,000	75

A sturgeon weighing 200 lbs. will give 40 lbs. of caviare.

UNITED KINGDOM

Since 1888 the weight of fish taken has increased 25 per cent., the value 27 per cent., viz. :—

	Tons		Value, £	
	1888	1896	1888	1896
Herrings . .	230,000	280,000	1,090,000	1,090,000
Haddock. . .	120,000	180,000	940,000	1,660,000
Various . . .	230,000	270,000	3,490,000	4,250,000
Total . .	580,000	730,000	5,520,000	7,000,000

The above is exclusive of salmon and shell-fish worth £1,300,000, making a total value of £8,300,000.
In 1890 London consumed 50,000 tons of oysters.

UNITED STATES

The figures for 1892 compare with those of 1880 thus:—

	1880	1892	Increase
Fishermen . .	131,000	192,000	45 per cent.
Fish, value £ .	8,600,000	9,400,000	10 ,,

The average value of fish taken per man was £66 in 1880, and only £49 in 1892.

CANADA

The fisheries of 1895 show a value of £500,000 more than in 1885, viz. :—

	Value, £	
	1885	1895
Nova Scotia . . .	1,660,000	1,240,000
New Brunswick . .	800,000	880,000
British Columbia, &c. .	1,080,000	1,920,000
Total . .	3,540,000	4,040,000

The principal fish taken in 1895 were :—

	Tons	Value, £
Herring	60,000	560,000
Salmon	10,000	740,000
Sardines	12,000	80,000
Various	156,000	2,660,000
Total . .	238,000	4,040,000

FLAX AND LINEN

The production of flax has been approximately as follows :—

	Acres		Tons Flax	
	1885	1895	1835	1895
U. Kingdom .	111,000	97,000	21,000	13,000
France . . .	109,000	83,000	28,000	22,000
Germany . . .	270,000	270,000	44,000	44,000
Russia. . . .	3,250,000	5,480,000	330,000	670,000
Austria . . .	240,000	250,000	47,000	48,000
Italy	170,000	130,000	20,000	20,000
Belgium . . .	98,000	100,000	21,000	24,000
Other States . .	102,000	120,000	15,000	19,000
Europe . . .	4,350,000	6,530,000	526,000	860,000
United States .	400,000	1,320,000	40,000	80,000
Total . .	4,750,000	7,850,000	566,000	940,000

In the above interval of ten years the price of flax declined 15 per cent., that of linen 20 per cent. : the fall in price has naturally led to a great increase of consumption. The flax factories of Europe now consume nearly 3000 tons daily, or 50 per cent. more than they did ten years ago.

The production and consumption of linen goods show approximately thus :—

	Production, Millions £	Consumption	
		Millions £	Shillings per Head
United Kingdom . .	13.0	7.0	3.5
France . . .	10.5	10.0	5.2
Germany . . .	9.0	9.0	3.5
Russia . . .	20.0	20.0	3.5
Austria . . .	8.0	7.0	3.3
Italy . . .	5.0	5.0	3.2
Belgium . . .	5.5	2.0	6.0
Other States . .	4.0	8.0	3.0
Europe . . .	75.0	68.0	3.5
United States .	15.0	20.0	5.5
Total . .	90.0	88.0	4.0

This industry has declined as follows in the United Kingdom :—

Year	Spindles	Power-Looms	Operatives
1870 . .	1,550,000	35,000	125,000
1895 . .	1,200,000	49,000	108,000

The consumption of flax is about 100,000 tons, against 120,000 in 1870. Exports of linen goods from United Kingdom have been as follows :—

Year	Linen Exports, Millions of Yards	Value £ Exported		
		Linen	Yarns, &c.	Total
1860 . . .	144	4,800,000	1,800,000	6,600,000
1870 . . .	226	7,300,000	2,200,000	9,500,000
1880 . . .	165	5,800,000	1,000,000	6,800,000
1890 . . .	184	5,700,000	900,000	6,600,000
1897 . . .	165	4,800,000	1,000,000	5,800,000

Flax-mills in Ireland consume 46,000 tons of flax, and turn out 200 million yards of linen; that is, half the output of the United Kingdom.

FOOD

The principal items of food are grain, potatoes, and meat, which may be reduced to a common denominator if we consider one ton of meat equal to eight tons of grain, and three of potatoes to one of grain.

Year	Production, Millions Tons			Equiva-lent in Grain
	Grain	Meat	Potatoes	
1880 . . .	204	13.3	80	337
1895	232	15.2	96	386

In order to estimate the total food production of countries, we may adopt the following scale for arriving at a common denominator :—

Equivalents to a Ton of Grain

Meat, 280 lbs.	Sugar, ½ ton	Wine, 100 galls.
Butter, 224 lbs.	Fish, ½ ton	Potatoes, 3 tons

All kinds of food being reduced as above to a common denominator of grain, we find the production compared with population gives the following averages :—

Tons of Food produced per 100 Inhabitants

Great Britain	45	Spain . . .	83	Switzerland .	75
Ireland. . .	126	Portugal . .	54	Danub. States	110
France . . .	115	Sweden . .	112	Greece . . .	60
Germany . .	90	Norway . .	99	U. States. .	172
Russia . . .	80	Denmark .	180	Canada . .	190
Austria . .	86	Holland . .	94	Australia . .	178
Italy . .	58	Belgium . .	81	Argentina .	170

Denmark, Ireland, and France, among European nations, produce the highest ratios of food to population, while Great Britain, Portugal, Italy, and Switzerland occupy the lowest places in the above scale. The average for Europe is considerably less than one ton per inhabitant, whereas in the United States and the colonies above cited it is nearly two. The production and consumption of grain average as follows :—

	Wheat, Millions Bushels		All grain, Millions Bushels	
	Produc.	Consump.	Produc.	Consump.
Great Britain .	57	220	245	530
Ireland . . .	1	20	55	120
France . . .	304	340	725	760
Germany . . .	120	180	680	820
Russia . . .	330	210	2,210	1,880
Austria . . .	190	185	780	760
Italy	120	150	260	290
Spain	90	104	230	245
Portugal . . .	8	13	30	35
Sweden & Nor.	4	14	130	140
Denmark . . .	4	9	85	100
Holland . . .	5	27	40	70
Belgium . . .	18	30	75	140
Switzerland . .	2	18	10	30
Danub. States .	100	50	280	190
Greece . . .	7	10	15	20
Europe . . .	1,360	1,580	5,850	6,150
U. States. . .	470	330	3,050	2,850
Canada . . .	60	45	210	180
Australia . . .	30	20	60	50
Argentina . .	50	25	100	70
Total . .	1,970	2,000	9,270	9,300

There is a deficit of 30 million bushels in the above table, which is covered by imports from India, Chile, and other countries.

The following table shows the weight of each kind of food produced, and the equivalent of all in grain (butter and cheese are under the head of butter) :—

	Tons (000 omitted)						Wine, Millions Gallons	Equivalent in Tons of Grain
	Grain	Potatoes	Meat	Sugar	Butter	Fish		
Great Britain	6,200	3,400	760	...	140	670	...	16,150,000
Ireland	1,400	2,700	340	...	60	30	...	5,680,000
France	18,100	12,800	1,200	700	200	150	840	44,070,000
Germany	17,100	31,800	1,520	1,800	300	60	70	47,280,000
Russia	55,100	20,700	2,290	800	350	220	40	86,260,000
Austria	19,500	12,400	1,210	900	170	30	115	38,020,000
Italy	6,400	700	390	...	145	100	605	17,450,000
Spain	5,800	1,600	430	...	40	50	460	14,870,000
Portugal	800	300	100	...	10	40	70	2,580,000
Sweden	2,800	1,500	160	...	60	200	...	5,580,000
Norway	500	600	70	...	20	260	...	1,980,000
Denmark	2,100	400	130	...	60	50	...	3,970,000
Holland	1,000	2,200	130	200	120	120	...	4,610,000
Belgium	1,900	3,400	110	300	60	...	...	5,110,000
Switzerland	200	1,200	80	...	70	...	30	2,240,000
Danubian States	6,700	300	400	...	50	...	170	12,200,000
Greece	400	...	60	...	10	10	40	1,400,000
Europe	145,000	96,000	9,380	4,700	1,865	1,990	2,440	309,450,000
United States	74,000	6,300	4,500	400	610	880	25	121,010,000
Canada	5,000	1,200	300	...	130	240	...	9,580,000
Australia	1,500	500	600	80	55	20	3	7,260,000
Argentina	2,500	100	420	120	20	20	32	6,700,000
Total . .	229,000	104,100	15,200	5,300	2,680	3,150	2,500	454,000,000

It appears that the United States produce one-fourth of the food of Christendom. The total weight of food (for human beings) consumed yearly is 370 million tons, containing nutriment equal to 454 million tons of grain.

The grain crops of the world have increased 18 per cent. in 20 years, viz. : —

	Annual Average, Tons		
	1871–80	1883–88	1890–96
Wheat	48,600,000	54,500,000	56,400,000
Maize . . .	38,400,000	50,200,000	52,500,000
Rye	31,400,000	34,500,000	32,900,000
Oats	46,400,000	52,000,000	56,900,000
Barley	19,400,000	20,500,000	19,500,000
Total . .	184,400,000	211,700,000	218,200,000

Beerbohm's return of the world's wheat crop in the last four years was as follows :—

Year	Tons Produced		
	In Europe	Out of Europe	Total
1894	38,200,000	25,800,000	64,000,000
1895	37,300,000	25,300,000	62,600,000
1896	37,800,000	22,200,000	60,000,000
1897	30,000,000	26,000,000	56,000,000

The wheat crop of 1898 was the largest on record, reaching 62,800,000 tons. Exports of wheat from various countries in twenty years, ending 1895, were :—

From	Annual Export, Millions of Bushels			
	1876-80	1881–90	1891–95	Average
United States . . .	116	124	179	136
Russia	72	90	80	83
India	7	34	32	27
Roumania	17	21	29	22
Austria	15	15	6	13
Argentina	1	5	38	12
Canada	4	5	9	6
Uruguay	...	1	4	1
Total . . .	232	295	377	300

It appears from the foregoing that in the last period of five years, 1891–95, the annual weight of wheat carried from one to another country was 9½ million tons, to which adding maize, oats, &c., the total international grain trade will be found to exceed 12 million tons, or about 5 per cent. of the grain crops of the world. Thus, however enormous the grain trade between nations may seem, it is evident that 95 per cent. of grain is consumed in the country of its production. The wheat crop of Europe in the last two years showed as follows :—

	Millions Bushels		
	1896	1897	Average
United Kingdom . .	58	56	57
France	344	288	316
Germany	104	100	102
Russia	348	298	323
Austria	178	144	161
Italy	132	100	116
Spain and Portugal . .	92	100	96
Scandinavia	8	8	8
Belgium	20	20	20
Danubian States . . .	132	90	111
Holland, Greece, &c. .	56	44	50
Europe	1,472	1,248	1,360

The following table shows the world's "visible supply" of wheat on 1st December of each year, and the average price in England during the year :—

Year	Supply, Tons	Shillings per Ton
1894	5,000,000	103
1895	4,500,000	126
1896	3,800,000	167
1897	3,050,000	168
Average . . .	4,100,000	141

The production of meat is shown as follows :—

	Product, Tons (000 omitted)			
	Beef	Mutton	Pork	Total
Great Britain . . .	350	280	130	760
Ireland	240	40	60	340
France	700	210	290	1,200
Germany	880	150	490	1,520
Russia	1,380	480	430	2,290
Austria	710	140	360	1,210
Italy	250	70	70	390
Spain	100	260	70	430
Portugal	30	30	40	100
Sweden & Norway .	170	28	32	230
Denmark	85	10	35	130
Holland	80	10	40	130
Belgium	75	5	30	110
Switzerland	60	5	15	80
Danubian States . .	175	150	75	400
Greece	20	40	...	60
Europe	5,305	1,908	2,167	9,380
United States . . .	2,410	380	1,710	4,500
Canada	200	35	65	300
Australia	300	280	20	600
Argentina	205	207	8	420
Total . . .	8,420	2,810	3,970	15,200

The value of food consumed for human support is approximately as follows :—

	Millions £ Sterling							
	Grain	Meat	Liquor	Dairy	Sundries	Total	Native	Imported
Great Britain .	53	86	74	54	98	365	209	156
Ireland . .	5	4	7	3	6	25	20	5
U. Kingdom .	58	90	81	57	104	390	229	161
France . . .	77	62	46	45	95	325	309	16
Germany . .	80	68	55	62	122	387	340	47
Russia . . .	151	86	23	43	91	394	387	7
Austria . .	58	45	35	36	66	240	234	6
Italy . .	45	18	35	20	35	153	145	8
Spain . . .	27	20	25	12	23	107	101	6
Portugal . .	6	4	5	2	6	23	21	2
Swed. & Nor.	13	11	5	7	5	41	35	6
Denmark . .	6	3	2	3	2	16	14	2
Holland . .	12	5	4	6	11	38	23	15
Belgium . .	14	7	9	8	14	52	38	14
Switzerland .	5	5	2	4	4	20	12	8
Danub. States	18	16	6	6	7	53	52	1
Greece . . .	3	3	1	1	3	11	9	2
Europe . . .	573	443	334	312	588	2,250	1,949	301
United States	90	132	72	85	141	520	466	54
Canada . .	8	8	3	4	4	27	24	3
Australia . .	5	5	3	4	4	21	17	4
Argentina . .	6	5	3	4	4	22	18	4
Total .	682	593	415	409	741	2,840	2,474	366

The above countries contain a population of 455 millions, and the value of food consumed by them averages a little over £6 per head yearly, or fourpence a day. The ratio yearly per inhabitant is as follows :—

Shillings per Inhabitant

Great Britain	206	Spain . . .	120	Switzerland .	132
Ireland . .	110	Portugal . .	96	Danub. States	90
France . .	165	Sweden . .	120	Greece. . .	100
Germany . .	148	Norway . .	110	United States	150
Russia . . .	74	Denmark .	144	Canada . .	105
Austria . .	114	Holland . .	160	Australia . .	96
Italy . . .	99	Belgium . .	160	Argentina . .	110

Frankland says that a man requires any one of the following items to support life, daily :—

12 lbs. cabbage	3½ lbs. beef	1½ lbs. rice
10 lbs. carrots	2 lbs. bread	1 lb. cheese
6 lbs. fish	2 lbs. eggs	7 bottles stout

This subject is set forth at great length under *Diet*, p. 191.
The consumption of food is approximately as follows :—

	Tons (000 omitted)						Wine, Million Gallons	Equivalent in Tons of Grain
	Grain	Meat	Potatoes	Sugar	Butter, &c.	Fish		
United Kingdom . . .	16,100	1,880	6,200	1,500	510	700	16	42,900,000
France	19,300	1,250	12,800	500	270	150	970	47,300,000
Germany	20,600	1,720	31,700	650	440	200	100	52,000,000
Russia	47,000	2,270	20,100	700	220	350	80	77,000,000
Austria	19,000	1,160	10,000	350	240	30	100	35,700,000
Italy	7,200	370	800	100	90	150	560	17,400,000
Spain	6,100	430	1,500	60	40	100	450	15,300,000
Portugal	900	100	300	25	10	40	60	2,600,000
Sweden	2,800	160	1,500	40	50	100	2	5,400,000
Norway	700	70	600	20	20	120	1	1,950,000
Denmark	2,500	80	400	50	20	30	1	3,600,000
Holland	1,800	100	2,200	100	40	50	2	4,050,000
Belgium	3,500	160	3,600	130	70	50	6	7,100,000
Switzerland	800	120	1,200	50	20	10	40	2,900,000
Danubian States	4,500	380	100	40	50	10	190	10,100,000
Greece	500	70	200	15	10	10	32	1,600,000
Europe	153,300	10,320	93,200	4,330	2,100	2,100	2,610	326,900,000
United States	71,200	3,950	7,000	2,140	580	840	33	117,200,000
Canada	4,500	250	1,200	190	50	120	1	8,050,000
Australia	1,200	400	600	140	50	20	5	5,450,000
Argentina	1,800	280	...	100	20	20	31	4,800,000
Total . . .	232,000	15,200	102,000	6,900	2,800	3,100	2,680	462,400,000

UNITED KINGDOM

Production and consumption of wheat and of all grain, in terms of two years averaged as follows, in millions of bushels :—

	Wheat		All Grain	
	Produc.	Consum.	Produc.	Consum.
1887-88 . . .	75	235	302	591
1889-90 . . .	76	238	322	628
1891-92 . . .	68	253	314	627
1893-94 . . .	56	247	308	653
1895-96 . . .	48	255	293	668

The production of grain has not declined much in the last ten years, viz. :—

Year	Millions Bushels			
	Wheat	Barley	Oats	Total
1887 . . .	76	70	151	297
1888 . . .	74	75	158	307
1889 . . .	76	75	164	315
1890 . . .	76	81	171	328
1891 . . .	75	80	166	321
1892 . . .	61	77	168	306
1893 . . .	51	66	169	286
1894 . . .	61	79	191	331
1895 . . .	38	75	174	287
1896 . . .	58	78	163	299
1897 . . .	56	73	164	293

The quantities imported in the same period were :—

Year	Millions Bushels			
	Wheat	Barley	Oats, &c.	Total
1887 . . .	160	29	93	282
1888 . . .	161	43	91	295
1889 . . .	158	35	106	299
1890 . . .	165	34	114	313
1891 . . .	179	35	88	302
1892 . . .	191	29	103	323
1893 . . .	188	46	96	330
1894 . . .	194	63	103	360
1895 . . .	215	47	103	365
1896 . . .	199	45	141	385
1897 . . .	177	38	142	357

The importation of wheat from different parts of the world has been as follows :—

Year	Millions of Bushels from				
	U.States	Russia	India	Various	Total
1887 . . .	101	11	17	31	160
1888 . . .	64	44	16	37	161
1889 . . .	62	43	18	35	158
1890 . . .	68	40	18	39	165
1891 . . .	86	30	26	37	179
1892 . . .	122	9	25	35	191
1893 . . .	114	20	12	42	188
1894 . . .	94	34	11	55	194
1895 . . .	90	46	17	62	215
1896 . . .	106	34	4	55	199
1897 . . .	108	30	1	38	177

The importation of all grain was as follows, in millions of bushels, from the following countries :—

Year	U.States	Russia	Rou-mania	Various	Total
1887 . . .	124	56	28	74	282
1888 . . .	84	108	24	79	295
1889 . . .	108	93	22	76	299
1890 . . .	120	78	30	85	313
1891 . . .	104	74	30	94	302
1892 . . .	164	37	20	102	323
1893 . . .	138	70	34	88	330
1894 . . .	116	116	35	93	360
1895 . . .	123	107	17	118	365
1896 . . .	177	76	24	108	385
1897 . . .	211	59	19	68	357

If wheat had remained at the same price as in 1887, the cost to the nation would have been 479 millions sterling in the decade, viz. :—

	Tons	Cost, £ sterling
British	16,300,000	133,000,000
Imported	45,200,000	346,000,000
Total . . .	61,500,000	479,000,000

The actual cost has been only 438 millions, which shows a saving of 41 millions in the said period of ten years.

The total weight of grain consumed and value were as follows :—

Year	Tons (000 omitted) British	Im-ported	Total	Value, Millions £ British	Im-ported	Total
1887 . .	7,400	7,050	14,450	41.8	48.3	90.1
1888 . .	7,700	7,400	15,100	44.4	51.3	95.7
1889 . .	7,900	7,500	15,400	44.5	51.2	95.7
1890 . .	8,200	7,800	16,000	49.6	53.5	103.1
1891 . .	8,050	7,550	15,600	52.3	62.0	114.3
1892 . .	7,650	8,100	15,750	44.9	58.7	103.6
1893 . .	7,150	8,250	15,400	38.9	51.2	90.1
1894 . .	8,300	9,000	17,300	41.1	48.2	89.3
1895 . .	7,200	9,100	16,300	31.7	49.7	81.4
1896 . .	7,500	9,600	17,100	35.9	52.8	88.7
Average	7,700	8,150	15,850	42.5	52.7	95.2

The following table shows the weight and value of wheat consumed in the United Kingdom in ten years :—

Year	Tons (000 omitted) British	Imported	Total	Value, Millions £ British	Imported	Total	Price, Shillings per Ton British	Imported	General
1887	1,900	4,000	5,900	15.5	30.6	46.1	163	153	156
1888	1,850	4,030	5,880	14.7	31.1	45.8	159	154	156
1889	1,900	3,950	5,850	14.2	30.5	44.7	149	154	153
1890	1,900	4,130	6,030	15.2	32.2	47.4	160	156	157
1891	1,870	4,470	6,340	17.3	39.8	57.1	185	178	180
1892	1,530	4,780	6,310	11.6	36.5	48.1	151	153	152
1893	1,270	4,700	5,970	8.4	30.3	38.7	132	129	130
1894	1,530	4,850	6,380	8.7	26.0	34.7	114	107	109
1895	950	5,380	6,330	5.5	29.6	35.1	115	110	111
1896	1,450	4,970	6,420	9.5	30.8	40.3	131	124	126
Average . . .	1,630	4,520	6,150	12.1	31.7	43.8	148	140	142

The weight and value of other grain than wheat consumed were :—

Year	Tons (000 omitted) Barley British	Imported	Total	Oats, &c. British	Imported	Total	Collective Value, Millions £ British	Imported	Total
1887 . . .	1,750	710	2,460	3,750	2,340	6,090	26.3	17.7	44.0
1888 . . .	1,850	1,060	2,910	4,000	2,310	6,310	29.7	20.2	49.9
1889 . . .	1,850	870	2,720	4,150	2,680	6,830	30.3	20.7	51.0
1890 . . .	2,050	830	2,880	4,250	2,840	7,090	34.4	21.3	55.7
1891 . . .	2,000	870	2,870	4,180	2,210	6,390	35.0	22.2	57.2
1892 . . .	1,900	710	2,610	4,220	2,610	6,830	33.3	22.2	55.5
1893 . . .	1,650	1,140	2,790	4,230	2,410	6,640	30.5	20.9	51.4
1894 . . .	1,950	1,560	3,510	4,820	2,590	7,410	32.4	22.2	54.6
1895 . . .	1,900	1,180	3,080	4,350	2,540	6,890	26.2	20.1	46.3
1896 . . .	1,950	1,120	3,070	4,100	3,510	7,610	26.4	22.0	48.4
Average . .	1,890	1,010	2,900	4,210	2,600	6,810	30.5	20.9	51.4

The total weight of grain consumed in the United Kingdom in ten years was 158½ million tons, which cost 952 millions sterling.

	Tons (000 omitted) Wheat	Barley, &c.	Total	Cost, Millions £ Wheat	Barley, &c.	Total
British	16,300	61,000	77,300	121	305	426
Imported	45,200	36,100	81,300	317	209	526
Total	61,500	97,100	158,600	438	514	952

Not quite 60 per cent. of the above grain was used for human food, the rest being given to animals, the account standing approximately thus :—

Used for	Tons (000 omitted) British	Im-ported	Total	Value, Millions £ British	Im-ported	Total
Mankind .	35,200	55,300	90,500	242	373	615
Animals .	42,100	26,000	68,100	184	153	337
Total .	77,300	81,300	158,600	426	526	952

The total grain imports of thirty-six years were :—

	Wheat	Barley	Oats	Maize, &c.	Total
1861–70 . .	18,000	3,500	3,800	7,500	32,800
1871–80 . .	28,500	5,700	6,200	16,500	56,900
1881–90 . .	38,500	7,800	7,000	18,200	71,500
1891–96 .	29,000	6,600	4,700	12,700	53,000
36 years . .	114,000	23,600	21,700	54,900	214,200

Tons (000 omitted)

The production and consumption of grain and meat since 1861 was as follows :—

	Grain Produced	Grain Consumed	Meat Produced	Meat Consumed
1861–70 . .	9,700	13,000	1,040	1,170
1871–80 . .	8,500	14,200	1,050	1,340
1881–90 . .	7,820	14,970	1,080	1,650
1891–96 . .	7,650	16,500	1,100	1,800

Tons Yearly (000 omitted)

The production of meat has risen 6 per cent., consumption 54 per cent., since 1861, the former showing as follows :—

Tons Yearly — 1861–70	England	Scotland	Ireland	Total
Beef . . .	230,000	50,000	200,000	480,000
Mutton . .	265,000	65,000	40,000	370,000
Pork . . .	120,000	10,000	60,000	190,000
Total .	615,000	125,000	300,000	1,040,000

Tons Yearly — 1891–96	England	Scotland	Ireland	Total
Beef . . .	285,000	65,000	240,000	590,000
Mutton . .	200,000	80,000	40,000	320,000
Pork . . .	125,000	5,000	60,000	190,000
Total .	610,000	150,000	340,000	1,100,000

Production has increased 60,000 tons in 30 years, while imports of foreign meat rose from 100,000 tons in 1865 to 780,000 tons in 1895.

The consumption of meat in the United Kingdom, native and imported, showed as follows :—

	1875 Native	1875 Imported	1875 Total	1885 Native	1885 Imported	1885 Total	1895 Native	1895 Imported	1895 Total
Beef	490,000	100,000	590,000	570,000	180,000	750,000	590,000	260,000	850,000
Mutton	370,000	55,000	425,000	320,000	90,000	410,000	320,000	230,000	550,000
Pork	190,000	145,000	335,000	190,000	30,000	220,000	190,000	290,000	480,000
Total . .	1,050,000	300,000	1,350,000	1,080,000	490,000	1,570,000	1,100,000	780,000	1,880,000

The average consumption of meat was 108 pounds per inhabitant in 1895, as compared with 93 pounds in 1875. Meantime the average is much higher in Great Britain, considered apart from Ireland, the consumption in 1895 showing approximately as follows :—

	Beef	Mutton	Pork	Total
Native . . .	350	280	130	760
Irish . . .	220	30	30	280
Imported . . .	260	210	290	760
Total .	830	520	450	1,800

Tons (000 omitted)

This gives an average of 115 pounds per inhabitant, the above figures showing that Great Britain is fed during five months on native meat, two months on Irish, and five months on what is imported from foreign countries. As regards Ireland, the consumption is approximately 80,000 tons (one-fourth imported), being equal to no more than 40 pounds per inhabitant, the lowest ratio of all countries in Europe except Italy.

Importations of Irish and foreign live stock into Great Britain in 1896 were as follows :—

	Irish	Foreign	Total
Horses . .	40,000	40,000	80,000
Cows . . .	690,000	560,000	1,250,000
Sheep . . .	750,000	770,000	1,520,000
Pigs . . .	610,000	...	610,000

The imports of food for human use, retained for consumption, were as follows, per annum :—

	1861–70	1871–80	1881–90	1891–96
Wheat, tons	1,800,000	2,850,000	3,850,000	4,830,000
Meat ,,	130,000	290,000	570,000	700,000
Potatoes, ,,	60,000	330,000	150,000	150,000
Rice, ,,	90,000	170,000	180,000	140,000
Sugar, ,,	520,000	860,000	1,150,000	1,420,000
Butter, ,,	60,000	80,000	130,000	190,000
Cheese, ,,	45,000	75,000	90,000	105,000
Tea, ,,	45,000	65,000	80,000	95,000
Coffee, ,,	15,000	15,000	14,000	12,000
Cocoa ,,	2,000	4,000	7,000	10,000
Eggs, mill. .	360	690	910	1,420
Wine, gals.	12,500,000	16,500,000	14,200,000	14,600,000
Spirits, gals.	6,500,000	10,200,000	8,300,000	8,000,000

Compared with population, the imports were as follows, per inhabitant :—

	1861–70	1871–80	1881–90	1891–96
Wheat, lbs. . .	135	192	240	282
Meat, ,, .	10	19	36	40
Potatoes, ,, .	4	22	9	9
Rice, ,, .	6	11	11	8
Sugar, ,, .	39	58	72	82
Butter, ,, .	4	5	8	11
Cheese, ,, .	3	5	6	6
Tea, ozs. .	53	70	78	88
Coffee, ,, .	18	16	14	11
Cocoa, ,, .	3	5	7	10
Eggs, No. .	12	21	28	37
Wine, gals. .	0.42	0.51	0.39	0.38
Spirits, ,, .	0.23	0.31	0.23	0.21

Among the items of food consumed in 1896 were the following :—

	Native	Imported	Total
Butter, tons' .	90,000	200,000	290,000
Cheese, ,, .	110,000	110,000	220,000
Rice, ,, .	...	120,000	120,000
Potatoes, ,, .	6,260,000	110,000	6,370,000
Sugar, ,, .	...	1,510,000	1,510,000
Tea, ,, .	...	100,000	100,000
Coffee, ,, .	...	12,000	12,000
Cocoa, ,, .	...	11,000	11,000
Eggs, millions .	2,100	1,600	3,700

Food imports into the United Kingdom for the last three years (exclusive of wines, tea, &c.) were of the following value :—

	£ (000 omitted)			
	1895	1896	1897	Average
Wheat	30,200	30,900	32,900	31,300
Maize	7,800	9,400	9,200	8,800
Barley	5,500	5,700	4,700	5,300
Oats, &c.	5,500	5,900	5,600	5,700
All grain	49,000	51,900	52,400	51,100
Butter	16,800	17,800	18,400	17,700
Cheese	4,700	4,900	5,900	5,200
Lard	2,900	2,300	2,000	2,400
Milk	1,100	1,200	1,400	1,200
Meat, dead . . .	24,400	25,400	28,100	26,000
Cattle	9,000	10,400	11,400	10,300
Vegetables	4,100	4,500	4,600	4,400
Total . . .	112,000	118,400	124,200	118,300

Distinguishing what food was received from the British Colonies and from foreign countries (including sugar, tea, wines, &c.) the values in 1896 were :—

	£ Sterling		
	Colonies	Foreign Countries	Total
Grain	3,600,000	48,300,000	51,900,000
Meat	7,500,000	28,300,000	35,800,000
Butter, &c. . .	4,000,000	21,700,000	25,700,000
Sugar, ...	1,700,000	17,500,000	19,200,000
Vegetables, &c. . .	2,200,000	41,600,000	43,800,000
Total . .	19,000,000	157,400,000	176,400,000

Imports of butter, margarine, and cheese in the last five years were :—

Year	Tons			
	Butter	Marg.	Cheese	Total
1893 . . .	117,000	64,000	104,000	285,000
1894 . . .	129,000	55,000	114,000	298,000
1895 . . .	141,000	47,000	107,000	295,000
1896 . . .	152,000	46,000	112,000	310,000
1897 . . .	161,000	47,000	130,000	338,000
Average . .	140,000	52,000	113,000	305,000

Excluding margarine the importation of butter and cheese was together as follows :—

Tons from	1894	1895	1896	1897
Canada . . .	58,000	60,000	66,000	81,000
Denmark . . .	55,000	58,000	61,000	67,000
United States . .	35,000	29,000	36,000	40,000
Holland . . .	23,000	25,000	27,000	29,000
France . . .	24,000	26,000	25,000	24,000
Australia . . .	18,000	21,000	14,000	17,000
Various . . .	30,000	29,000	35,000	33,000
Total . .	243,000	248,000	264,000	291,000

The importation of cattle from Ireland into Great Britain has been as follows :—

Year	Number		
	Cattle	Sheep	Pigs
1893	689,000	1,108,000	457,000
1894	827,000	957,000	585,000
1895	781,000	650,000	550,000
1896	689,000	750,000	613,000
1897	745,000	811,000	684,000
Average . . .	746,000	855,000	580,000

The importation of poultry and eggs in 1896 was as follows :—

	Poultry, Tons	Eggs, Millions	Total Value, £
France	6,000	394	1,600,000
Denmark . . .	...	188	500,000
Canada . . .	3,000	63	300,000
Other countries .	14,000	945	2,900,000
Total . .	23,000	1,590	5,300,000

Importations of meat in 1896 were as follows (the equivalent being taken for live stock) :—

From	Tons			Value, £
	Dead	Live	Total	
United States .	340,000	130,000	470,000	19,500,000
British Colonies	170,000	40,000	210,000	7,300,000
Denmark . . .	70,000	...	70,000	3,000,000
Argentina . .	50,000	20,000	70,000	2,700,000
Various . . .	50,000	...	50,000	2,300,000
Total . .	680,000	190,000	870,000	34,800,000

The above is exclusive of 120,000 tons of lard and poultry, worth £3,400,000.

Imports of sugar in 1896 were as follows :—

From	Tons	Value, £	£ per Ton
Germany	760,000	9,300,000	12.2
W. Indies	160,000	1,700,000	10.6
France	140,000	1,800,000	12.8
Holland	110,000	1,500,000	13.6
Various	480,000	4,900,000	10.2
Total . . .	1,650,000	19,200,000	11.6

Imports of dairy products, &c., including butter,

margarine, cheese, condensed milk, eggs, and poultry, in the same year were :—

From	Tons	Value, £	£ per Ton
France	80,000	4,900,000	61
Holland	83,000	4,700,000	57
Denmark	76,000	6,800,000	90
Canada	86,000	3,700,000	42
United States . . .	36,000	1,800,000	50
Germany	35,000	1,400,000	40
Various	116,000	6,000,000	52
Total . . .	506,000	29,300,000	59

Food imports of all kinds from the principal countries in 1896 were :—

From	£	Ratio
United States	35,600,000	20.2
Russia	25,000,000	14.4
France	15,400,000	8.7
Germany	12,300,000	7.0
Canada	10,600,000	6.0
Denmark	10,300,000	5.8
Holland	8,600,000	4.8
Various	58,600,000	33.1
Total . .	176,400,000	100.0

This includes grain used for cattle.

The annual consumption of food per inhabitant has been approximately as follows :—

	1861–70	1871–80	1881–90	1891–96
Grain, lbs. . . .	358	380	385	390
Meat, ,, . . .	88	91	103	105
Potatoes, ,, . . .	530	460	385	360
Butter, ,, . . .	10	11	14	16
Cheese, ,, . . .	10	12	13	12
Eggs, No.	80	85	83	91
Beer, gallons . . .	31	32	29	30
Spirits, ,, . . .	0.9	1.2	1.0	1.0
Wine, ,, . . .	0.4	0.5	0.4	0.4

The above table shows that the people are now much better fed than they were 30 years ago, consumption per inhabitant having risen 20 per cent. for meat, 60 per cent. for butter, 20 per cent. for cheese, 14 per cent. for eggs. But this is not true of Ireland, and hence the increase of consumption, per head, in Great Britain is even higher than stated.

The quantity of each article consumed was approximately as follows, yearly :—

	1861–70	1871–80	1881–90	1891–96
Grain, tons	4,800,000	5,600,000	6,200,000	6,700,000
Meat, ,,	1,170,000	1,340,000	1,650,000	1,800,000
Potatoes, ,,	7,100,000	6,800,000	6,200,000	6,200,000
Butter, ,,	140,000	160,000	220,000	280,000
Cheese, ,,	140,000	180,000	200,000	215,000
Eggs, mill.	2,400	2,800	3,010	3,520
Beer, barrels	25,500,000	29,500,000	28,600,000	32,000,000
Wine, gall.	28,000,000	39,600,000	36,000,000	38,800,000
Spirits, ,,	12,600,000	16,800,000	14,100,000	14,600,000

As regards tea, coffee, sugar, rice, cocoa, and wine, see page 717.

In the above table the item of grain does not include what is used in breweries and distilleries, nor of course what is consumed by animals.

The value of food consumed (including the grain for breweries and distilleries, but excluding what was used by animals) during 1896 was approximately as follows :—

	Native, £	Imported, £	Total, £
Grain	21,700,000	36,400,000	58,100,000
Meat	55,000,000	35,400,000	90,400,000
Dairy	33,000,000	23,800,000	56,800,000
Potatoes . . .	25,100,000	900,000	26,000,000
Poultry and eggs	9,700,000	5,300,000	15,000,000
Veget. and fruit .	8,000,000	10,300,000	18,300,000
Sugar	...	19,000,000	19,200,000
Tea, coffee, &c. .	...	11,400,000	11,400,000
Fish.	7,500,000	3,200,000	10,700,000
Sundries . . .	7,000,000	6,800,000	13,800,000
Total . .	167,000,000	153,000,000	320,000,000

The above is exclusive of liquor, which stands approximately as follows :—

	Native, £	Imported, £	Total, £
Beer	72,000,000	...	72,000,000
Spirits	7,300,000	2,100,000	9,400,000
Wine	...	6,000,000	6,000,000
Cider	600,000	...	600,000
Total . .	79,900,000	8,100,000	88,000,000

Adding together food and liquor would give a total of 408 millions sterling, but the grain used for liquor having been counted in the first table there is a repetition, and if allowance be made accordingly, the total cost of food and liquor will be found to reach 390 millions sterling, viz. :—

	£	Population	Shillings per Head
Great Britain . .	365,000,000	34,900,000	210
Ireland	25,000,000	4,550,000	110
United Kingdom	390,000,000	39,450,000	198

There is no country in the world where the sum spent on food, per head of the population, is so high as in Great Britain, but on the other hand Ireland is among the lowest in the scale of nations in this respect.

Besides food imported for human use Great Britain receives large quantities of grain to feed cattle and horses, which causes the item of food to figure for a much larger sum in our imports than is shown above. The following table shows the total amount paid to foreign nations for food in recent years, exclusive of wines :—

	Millions £			
	1892	1894	1896	1897
Grain . . .	58.7	48.2	52.8	53.6
Meat . . .	32.1	32.3	35.9	39.5
Dairy . . .	22.0	23.1	23.9	25.7
Sundries . .	55.8	53.2	54.8	55.3
Total .	168.6	156.8	167.4	174.1

The value of imported food, compared with population, has been as follows :—

| Year | Millions £ | | | Shillings per Head |
	Grain	Meat, &c.	Total	
1854 . . .	23	25	48	35
1860 . . .	33	34	67	46
1870 . . .	37	53	90	58
1880 . . .	70	90	160	92
1889 . . .	54	91	145	78
1892 . . .	59	110	169	89
1894 . . .	48	109	157	81
1896 . . .	53	114	167	84
1897 . . .	54	120	174	87

If wines were included the total for 1897 would be 182 millions, that is, 91 shillings per inhabitant, equal to threepence a day per head, and as the earnings of the nation (*vide* "Wealth and Industries of Nations," p. 95) averaged £36 per head, it appears that one-eighth of the earnings of the people is expended on imported food which cannot be produced at so low a cost in Great Britain.

In case it were ever deemed expedient to produce within the British Isles all the grain required for consumption, it would be necessary to double the area under corn of all kinds. The following table shows the actual and the required areas :—

| | Acres | | | Required |
	G. Britain	Ireland	Total	
Wheat . .	1,690,000	40,000	1,730,000	8,200,000
Barley . .	2,160,000	180,000	2,340,000	3,400,000
Oats, &c. .	3,590,000	1,200,000	4,790,000	7,500,000
Total .	7,440,000	1,420,000	8,860,000	19,100,000

The actual yearly deficit of grain is 9,000,000 tons in Great Britain, 500,000 tons in Ireland, in all 9½ million tons, to produce which would need 10,200,000 acres, an area equal to the aggregate of Lincolnshire, Norfolk, Suffolk, Essex, and Devonshire.

The production and consumption of the principal items of food in Great Britain and Ireland, reduced to a grain denominator, show as follows :—

Production

| | Quantity, Tons | | | Grain Equivalent | | |
	Great Britain	Ireland	U. Kingdom	Great Britain	Ireland	U. Kingdom
Grain	6,200,000	1,400,000	7,600,000	6,200,000	1,400,000	7,600,000
Meat	760,000	340,000	1,100,000	6,100,000	2,700,000	8,800,000
Potatoes . . .	3,500,000	2,700,000	6,200,000	1,200,000	900,000	2,100,000
Butter and cheese .	140,000	60,000	200,000	1,400,000	600,000	2,000,000
Fish . . .	670,000	30,000	700,000	2,000,000	100,000	2,100,000
Total . .	11,070,000	4,530,000	15,600,000	16,900,000	5,700,000	22,600,000

Consumption

Grain	15,200,000	1,900,000	17,100,000	15,200,000	1,900,000	17,100,000
Meat	1,800,000	80,000	1,880,000	14,400,000	600,000	15,000,000
Potatoes . . .	3,600,000	2,700,000	6,300,000	1,200,000	900,000	2,100,000
Butter and cheese .	480,000	30,000	510,000	4,800,000	300,000	5,100,000
Fish	670,000	40,000	710,000	2,000,000	100,000	2,100,000
Total . .	21,750,000	4,750,000	26,500,000	37,600,000	3,800,000	41,400,000

Reducing all to a grain denominator, we find that Great Britain raises food for 45 per cent. of her population, while Ireland consumes only two-thirds of her production. Taking the whole United Kingdom collectively, the home production is equal to 55 per cent., imported food 45 per cent., of the total consumption.

FRANCE

The production and consumption of grain in four years ending 1895 were :—

| Year | Tons | | |
	Production	Consumption	Deficit
1892 . . .	17,700,000	19,300,000	1,600,000
1893 . . .	14,900,000	16,800,000	1,900,000
1894 . . .	19,400,000	20,600,000	1,200,000
1895 . . .	19,300,000	19,700,000	400,000
1896 . . .	19,000,000	19,100,000	100,000

Although the production averages almost half a ton per inhabitant, France has to import about 100,000 tons monthly. The crops of 1896 compared with those of four preceding years thus :—

		1892-93	1894-95	1896
Wheat,	tons .	7,100,000	8,300,000	8,200,000
Oats,	,, .	5,000,000	6,400,000	6,300,000
Rye,	,, .	1,600,000	1,800,000	1,700,000
Barley,	,, .	1,000,000	1,200,000	1,100,000
Maize, &c.	,, .	1,600,000	1,650,000	1,700,000
Total . .		16,300,000	19,350,000	19,000,000

The production and consumption of wheat in the last thirty-six years has been as follows :—

Period	Tons Yearly		Bushels per Inhab.
	Production	Consumption	
1861-64 . . .	6,900,000	7,200,000	7.7
1865-68 . . .	6,600,000	6,700,000	7.1
1869-72 . . .	6,400,000	6,700,000	7.3
1873-76 . . .	7,250,000	7,500,000	8.0
1877-80 . . .	6,500,000	7,900,000	8.5
1881-84 . . .	7,600,000	9,100,000	9.6
1885-88 . . .	7,350,000	8,100,000	8.5
1889-92 . . .	7,100,000	8,500,000	8.9
1893-96 . . .	7,900,000	8,700,000	9.0
Average . . .	7,100,000	7,800,000	8.3

In the last eight years the net imports of wheat averaged 1,100,000 tons yearly, from which it appears that (after deducting what is necessary for seed) the consumption in the form of food is 7,900,000 tons, equal to 8¼ bushels per inhabitant, and that France subsists on imported wheat almost two months in the year.

Although France is still the greatest wine-producing country in the world, she has had in this respect a constant deficit since 1880, the heaviest losses from Phylloxera having been felt in the preceding year. Production and consumption are shown as follows :—

Year	Millions of Gallons Yearly			
	Vintage	Imports	Exports	Consumption
1861-64 . . .	930	3	45	888
1865-68 . . .	1,230	4	64	1,170
1869-72 . . .	1,320	7	70	1,257
1873-76 . . .	1,250	13	78	1,185
1877-80 . . .	910	68	63	915
1881-84 . . .	880	178	56	1,002
1885-88 . . .	650	240	54	836
1889-92 . . .	610	235	45	800
1893-96 . . .	890	120	40	970
Average . . .	963	97	57	1,003

The consumption of meat is less than in the United Kingdom, amounting to no more than 1,300,000 tons, viz. :—

	Tons	Pounds per Head
Beef	700,000	40
Mutton	210,000	12
Pork	290,000	17
Imported meat . . .	100,000	6
Total . . .	1,300,000	75

France imports cheese, and exports butter. Net exports of dairy products compare with those of ten years ago thus :—

	Tons		Value, £	
	1885	1896	1885	1896
Butter	32,000	25,000	3,400,000	1,800,000
Eggs	22,000	17,500	1,200,000	900,000
Total . .	54,000	42,500	4,600,000	2,700,000

The value of food imports in last three years was :—

	£ Sterling		
	1895	1896	1897
Grain	3,100,000	1,500,000	9,900,000
Meat	5,800,000	3,200,000	4,000,000
Cheese. . . .	600,000	600,000	600,000
Fruit	1,000,000	1,000,000	1,400,000
Coffee	7,100,000	7,000,000	4,200,000
Total . .	17,600,000	13,300,000	20,100,000

The value of food consumed may be summed up approximately as follows :—

Millions £ Sterling

Grain	. . .	77.0		Coffee	. . .	7.1
Potatoes	. .	36.0		Sugar	. . .	6.5
Meat	. . .	62.0		Fish	. . .	4.8
Dairy	. . .	44.5		Wine, &c.	. .	46.1
Poultry	. . .	14.0		Sundries.	. .	15.0
Vegetables	. .	12.0		Total	. .	325.0

The value of imported food is only 5 per cent. of the total, whereas in the United Kingdom it is 45 per cent.

The production and consumption of sugar have been as follows :—

Year	Production, Tons	Consumption, Tons	Lbs. per Inhabitant
1885	460,000	390,000	23
1895	700,000	480,000	28

The annual expenditure on food averages 166 shillings per inhabitant.

The production of food, reduced to a grain denominator, shows as follows :—

		Quantity	Equivalent in Tons Grain
Grain,	tons . . .	17,800,000	17,800,000
Potatoes,	,, ...	12,600,000	4,200,000
Meat,	,, ...	1,200,000	9,600,000
Sugar,	,, ...	700,000	1,400,000
Butter, &c.	,, ...	200,000	2,000,000
Fish,	,, ...	150,000	300,000
Wine, gallons	. . . .	890,000	8,900,000
Total			44,200,000

This is equal to 23 cwt. per inhabitant, or 6 tons to each hand engaged in agriculture.

GERMANY

The weight of grain produced is far short of the requirements for the empire: the average crops for four years ending 1896 showed :—

	Tons			*Tons*
Wheat	. . . 3,090,000	Barley	. .	2,550,000
Rye	. . . 6,870,000	Oats	. .	4,620,000

making a total of 17,130,000 tons. Two-thirds of the population live on rye. If we deduct the grain used for seed or given to cattle, the balance left for human food is about 11 million tons, to which we must add 4 million tons imported, making a total of 15 millions. This includes about 3 million tons converted into liquor, leaving 12 million tons used in the form of bread. From this it would appear that Germany subsists during eight

2 Z

months of the year on native, during four months on imported, grain. The consumption of grain for bread has been approximately as follows :—

| Year | Tons per Annum | | | Bushels Per Head |
	Native	Imported	Total	
1885–87 . .	8,400,000	1,800,000	10,200,000	8.5
1890–92 . .	8,000,000	3,400,000	11,400,000	9.1
1894–96 . .	8,200,000	4,300,000	12,500,000	9.5

The deficit of grain increases rapidly with the growth of population, the weight imported having more than doubled in ten years. Germany has 250 inhabitants to the square mile, France only 188, and we find that one-third of the German population (as compared with one-sixth of the French) subsists on imported grain. There would be a greater deficit of grain in Germany but for the production of potatoes on a great scale, the crop rarely falling below 30 million tons, equivalent in sustenance to 10 million tons of grain. Germany grows one-third of all the potatoes produced in the world, the crop averaging 24 bushels per inhabitant, not all being used as food, but a large portion made into cheap brandy.

Meat production has increased, but not so fast as population :—

	1883	1895
Beef, tons . .	790,000	880,000
Mutton, ,, . .	200,000	150,000
Pork, ,, . .	370,000	490,000
Total . .	1,360,000	1,520,000

Down to the year 1888 no meat was imported, but the imports have grown so rapidly that they now exceed 200,000 tons yearly (mostly in the form of live cattle), the consumption reaching 74 lbs. per inhabitant, against 66 lbs. in 1883.

There is likewise a deficit as regards poultry and eggs : the imports of the latter show thus :—

Year	Eggs Yearly	Per Inhabitant
1885–86	510,000,000	11
1890–91	1,110,000,000	22
1894–96	1,630,000,000	32

Reducing grain, potatoes, and meat to a common denominator as grain, we find an increase of 6,900,000 tons, say 21 per cent., since 1882, viz. :—

| | Tons | | Grain Equivalent, Tons | |
	1880–82	1893–96	1880–82	1893–96
Grain . .	14,800,000	17,100,000	14,800,000	17,100,000
Potatoes .	21,100,000	31,000,000	7,000,000	10,300,000
Meat . .	1,360,000	1,520,000	10,900,000	12,200,000
Total .	37,260,000	49,620,000	32,700,000	39,600,000

The grain equivalent is now 15 cwt. per inhabitant, against 14 cwt. in 1880–82.

The number of milch cows is 500,000 less than that requisite (one to five inhabitants) in view of population. Nevertheless, about 8000 tons of butter are exported yearly, but there is, on the other hand, a considerable importation of margarine.

The production at present is as follows, in tons :—

	Grain	Potatoes	Meat
Prussia	9,700,000	20,000,000	920,000
Bavaria . . .	2,100,000	4,300,000	220,000
Other States . .	5,300,000	6,700,000	380,000
Total . .	17,100,000	31,000,000	1,520,000

More than half of the fish consumed is imported ; the annual take by German fishermen is about 100,000 tons : imports show as follows :—

Year	Barrels Yearly	Value, £
1885–86 . . .	1,070,000	1,500,000
1894–96 . . .	1,330,000	1,500,000

The consumption of coffee per inhabitant has declined, which is explained by the rise in price, viz. :—

Year	Tons Yearly	Value, £	Lbs. per Inhab.
1885–86 . . .	121,000	6,200,000	6.0
1894–95 . . .	122,000	10,100,000	5.2

Sugar is the only article of food of which there is a surplus, about 60 per cent. of the annual output being exported, viz. :—

| | Tons | | Lbs. per Inhab. | |
	1886	1896	1886	1896
Production . .	810,000	1,620,000	39	70
Consumption .	240,000	720,000	12	31
Export . . .	570,000	900,000	27	39

Germany does not grow enough wine for her requirements, the annual consumption showing thus :—

| | Gallons | | |
	Native	Imported	Total
1885–86 . . .	60,000,000	12,000,000	72,000,000
1894–96 . . .	65,000,000	15,000,000	80,000,000

Consumption averages 1½ gallon per inhabitant, wine being little in use, and beer the principal beverage of the people.

If we reduce food of all kinds to a grain denominator, the production will be found as follows :—

		Quantity	Equivalent in Grain Tons
Grain,	tons .	17,100,000	17,100,000
Potatoes,	,, .	31,800,000	10,600,000
Meat,	,, .	1,520,000	12,160,000
Sugar,	,, .	1,800,000	3,600,000
Butter and cheese,	,, .	300,000	3,000,000
Fish,	,, .	60,000	120,000
Wine, gallons		70,000,000	700,000
Total			47,280,000

This gives an average of 18 cwt. per inhabitant, or 5 tons to each hand engaged in agriculture.

The value of imported food shows as follows :—

	£ Sterling		
	1885	**1890**	**1897**
Grain	12,800,000	19,800,000	26,400,000
Coffee	5,600,000	11,000,000	8,100,000
Meat	...	6,100,000	7,600,000
Eggs	1,100,000	2,800,000	3,400,000
Wine	1,900,000	2,200,000	2,100,000
Fish	1,500,000	1,700,000	2,900,000
Sundries . . .	1,900,000	4,100,000	5,500,000
Total . .	24,800,000	47,700,000	56,000,000

The value of food consumed for human use is approximately as follows :—

	Millions £ Sterling		
	Native	Imported	Total
Grain	61	19	80
Meat	63	5	68
Potatoes, &c. .	73	...	73
Dairy and eggs .	74	4	78
Wine and beer .	53	2	55
Sugar, coffee, &c. .	10	11	21
Sundries . .	6	6	12
Total . .	340	47	387

The value of imported food is 12 per cent. of the total, against 5 per cent. in France. The average food expenditure is 148 shillings per inhabitant, against 166 in France.

RUSSIA

Although Russia has to feed a population of 103 millions, she has usually a large excess of grain for exportation, besides eggs and a varying quantity of butter, fish, and meat. Deducting the amount of grain required for seed, the home consumption and exportation during three years averaged :—

	Tons		
	Consumption	Export	Total
Wheat . . .	3,400,000	3,400,000	6,800,000
Rye	15,100,000	1,100,000	16,200,000
Oats	12,300,000	1,200,000	13,500,000
Various . .	6,400,000	3,100,000	9,500,000
Total . .	37,200,000	8,800,000	46,000,000

There is great fluctuation in the crops ; the wheat surplus for exportation in 1897 hardly reached 2,600,000 tons. The bulk of the population subsists on rye, and about 20 per cent. on wheat, the total weight of grain used as bread being about 20 million tons, equal to 8 bushels per head, exclusive of what is made into brandy. Potatoes were long viewed with such aversion that they are still little used, the crop averaging 20 million tons, or 8 bushels per inhabitant, against 24 bushels in Germany. The production of meat is approximately as follows :—

	Russia	Poland	Total, Tons
Beef	1,230,000	150,000	1,380,000
Mutton . . .	440,000	40,000	480,000
Pork	370,000	60,000	430,000
Total . . .	2,040,000	250,000	2,290,000

The above gives an average of 50 lbs. of meat per inhabitant in Russia Proper and 62 lbs. in Poland, and the consumption is about the same, the export of cattle being equivalent to no more than 10,000 tons of dead meat. The production of butter and cheese is not known, but cannot exceed 350,000 tons, of which 5000 tons are exported, leaving for home consumption nearly 8 lbs. per inhabitant, as compared with 14 lbs. in Germany. The export of eggs has increased prodigiously in 11 years, viz. :—

Year	Millions	Value, £
1885 . . .	235	340,000
1891 . . .	850	1,290,000
1896 . . .	1,480	2,200,000

Russia is now one of the largest exporters of eggs in the world, sending out 4 millions daily, for the most part to Germany. She also exports 10 million poultry per annum, and 3000 tons of caviare. Down to 1884 the production of sugar was hardly sufficient for the requirements of home consumption, but now there is a large surplus exported, viz. :—

	Tons	
	1886	**1896**
Production . . .	350,000	780,000
Consumption . . .	290,000	680,000
Exported	60,000	100,000

The consumption of sugar has risen in the above interval from 6 lbs. to 15 lbs. per inhabitant, but is still very low (as compared with 28 lbs. per head in Germany), owing to the extreme poverty of the rural population of Russia. Vodka brandy is the chief drink, of which 160 million gallons are consumed, according to official returns, but it is believed that the real consumption is double, illicit distilling being very common. The vintage varies from 40 to 70 million gallons, besides which 3 million gallons of wine are imported, the total consumption being less than three-quarters of a gallon per inhabitant. Fisheries yield 220,000 tons, besides which 150,000 tons of dried fish are imported, making a total of 370,000 tons, equal to 8 lbs. per inhabitant. About 70,000 tons of fruit are imported yearly, and 40,000 tons of rice. The consumption of coffee is declining, that of tea increasing, viz. :—

Year	Tons			Value, £
	Coffee	Tea	Total	
1885 . . .	8,000	29,000	37,000	6,300,000
1890 . . .	6,500	32,000	38,500	3,800,000
1896 . . .	6,400	41,000	47,400	4,500,000

Taking tea and coffee in the aggregate the consumption is now 17 oz. per inhabitant, against 14 oz. in 1885, the increase being the result of fall in price, the expenditure on these items being now 11 pence per inhabitant, as compared with 16 pence in 1885. The total imports and exports of food in the following years stood thus :—

Year	Imports, £	Exports, £	Surplus, £
1893	6,100,000	32,200,000	26,100,000
1894	6,900,000	44,100,000	37,200,000
1895	6,900,000	40,100,000	33,200,000
1896	6,600,000	38,800,000	32,200,000

The value of food consumed yearly for human use is approximately 394 millions sterling, or about ten times as much as that of food exported. Reducing all food to a grain denominator, we find the production as follows :—

	Quantity	Equivalent in Tons Grain
Grain, tons . . .	55,100,000	55,100,000
Potatoes, ,, . . .	20,700,000	6,900,000
Meat, ,, . . .	2,290,000	18,320,000
Sugar, ,, . . .	800,000	1,600,000
Butter, &c., ,, . . .	350,000	3,500,000
Fish, ,, . . .	220,000	440,000
Wine, gallons	60,000,000	600,000
Total		86,460,000

This is an average of only 16 cwt. per inhabitant, a very poor return, when we consider that two-thirds of the population are engaged in agriculture.

AUSTRIA-HUNGARY

The dual monarchy, like Russia, has always a surplus of food, which is not surprising, since 63 per cent. of the population is agricultural. The production is as follows :—

	Austria	Hungary	Total
Grain, tons .	7,900,000	11,600,000	19,500,000
Potatoes, ,, .	9,500,000	3,500,000	13,000,000
Meat, ,, .	600,000	610,000	1,210,000
Wine, gallons .	90,000,000	40,000,000	130,000,000

Hungary has usually a surplus of three million tons of grain, Austria a deficit of nearly 2½ million tons, whereby it comes to pass that the whole monarchy has a normal surplus of 550,000 tons for exportation. Hungary has, moreover, a surplus of 150,000 tons of meat, one-third of which goes to cover the deficit in Austria, leaving 100,000 tons for exportation in the form of live cattle. The ordinary grain crops are as follows :—

	Tons		
	Austria	Hungary	Total
Wheat	1,200,000	3,800,000	5,000,000
Rye	1,850,000	1,450,000	3,300,000
Oats	2,700,000	1,800,000	4,500,000
Barley	1,450,000	1,450,000	2,900,000
Maize, &c. . .	700,000	3,100,000	3,800,000
Total . .	7,900,000	11,600,000	19,500,000

The production of grain compared with population is equal to 13 bushels per inhabitant in Austria, 26 bushels in Hungary. The quantity used for bread in the whole monarchy is about 9 million tons, equal to 8 bushels per head, one half of the population subsisting on wheat, the other half on rye, maize, &c. The consumption of potatoes is equal to 16 bushels per head in Austria, 8 bushels in Hungary. The production of meat is as follows :—

	Tons		
	Austria	Hungary	Total
Beef	430,000	280,000	710,000
Mutton . . .	30,000	110,000	140,000
Pork	140,000	220,000	360,000
Total . .	600,000	610,000	1 210,000

More than half of the sugar produced is exported, viz. :—

	1886	1896
Production, tons . . .	430,000	830,000
Consumption, ,, . . .	190,000	320,000
Exported, ,, . . .	240,000	510,000

Consumption averages 17 lbs. sugar per inhabitant, against 11 lbs. in 1886. On the other hand coffee is declining, due to the rise in price, viz. :—

Year	Tons	Value, £	Oz. per Inhab.
1885	37,000	2,200,000	32
1895	38,000	3,100,000	30

The value of food imported is 6 millions sterling, of exported 20 millions, leaving a surplus of food exports worth 14 millions. Among the chief exports are eggs.

Year	Millions	Value, £
1885	760	730,000
1890	1,220	1,350,000
1896	1,780	3,300,000

About 140,000 tons of malt, valued at £1,500,000, are exported yearly.

Reducing all to a grain denominator, we find the production as follows :—

	Quantity	Equivalent in Grain Tons
Grain, tons . .	19,500,000	19,500,000
Potatoes, ,, . .	13,000,000	4,300,000
Meat, ,, . .	1,210,000	9,700,000
Sugar, ,, . .	900,000	1,800,000
Butter, &c., ,, . .	170,000	1,700,000
Wine, gallons . .	130,000,000	1,300,000
Total		38,300,000

This is equivalent to 18 cwt. per inhabitant, or 3 tons for each hand engaged in agriculture, the ratio of the latter being 6 tons in France.

The value of food consumed in Austria-Hungary for human use is approximately as follows :—

	£			£
Grain . . .	58,000,000	Liquor . . .		35,000,000
Meat . . .	45,000,000	Sugar . . .		4,000,000
Potatoes, &c. .	36,000,000	Sundries . .		15,000,000
Dairy, &c. . .	47,000,000	Total . .		240,000,000

This gives an average of 114 shillings yearly per inhabitant, against 166 in France and 148 in Germany.

ITALY

Although 60 per cent. of the population are engaged in agriculture, the production of food falls very much short. Reducing all to a grain denominator, we find :—

	Quantity	Equivalent in Tons Grain
Grain, tons . .	5,800,000	5,800,000
Rice, ,, . .	480,000	650,000
Potatoes, ,, . .	700,000	230,000
Meat, ,, . .	390,000	3,120,000
Butter, &c., ,, . .	145,000	1,450,000
Chestnuts, ,, . .	200,000	200,000
Fish, ,, . .	100,000	200,000
Oil, gallons . .	50,000,000	500,000
Wine, ,, . . .	605,000,000	6,050,000
Total		18,200,000

This gives an average of 12 cwt. per inhabitant, or 2 tons to each hand engaged in farming, the ratio of the latter in France being 6 tons. The ordinary grain crops are as follows :—

Provinces	Tons			
	Wheat	Maize	Oats, &c.	Total
Northern .	600,000	850,000	300,000	1,750,000
Middle . .	1,000,000	550,000	200,000	1,750,000
Southern .	1,400,000	350,000	550,000	2,300,000
Total .	3,000,000	1,750,000	1,050,000	5,800,000

Northern Italy comprises Venice, Lombardy, and Piedmont ; Southern includes Naples and Sicily ; all the rest is grouped under the Middle provinces. Deducting grain used for seed and cattle, the annual consumption averages 4,500,000 tons home-grown and 700,000 imported, to which adding rice the total will reach 5,700,000 tons, equal to 7 bushels per inhabitant.

Italy is so very poor as regards live stock that the supply of meat is the lowest in Europe, and yet the poverty of the people compels them to export some, viz. :—

	Tons		
	Supply	Export	Consumption
Beef	250,000	20,000	230,000
Mutton . . .	70,000	2,000	68,000
Pork	70,000	3,000	67,000
Total . .	390,000	25,000	365,000

A portion of what is exported is in the form of live animals. The consumption of meat is only 27 lbs. per inhabitant. In compensation for meat exported Italy imports 50,000 tons of dried fish. The consumption of wine is about 570 million gallons, which gives an average of 18 gallons per inhabitant, the same as in Spain.

Here, as in some other countries, the rise in the price of coffee has been attended with diminished consumption, viz. :—

Year	Tons, Coffee	Price, £ per Ton
1885–87	16,000	68
1893–95	12,000	100

Ten years ago the consumption of coffee averaged 20 ounces per inhabitant, whereas at present it does not exceed 14 ounces. The imports of sugar have likewise declined very notably, viz. :—

Year	Tons	Lbs. per Inhabitant
1885–87	116,000	9
1893–95	76,000	6

Dairy farming has progressed so favourably that whereas down to 1888 the imports of butter and cheese exceeded the exports, Italy now sends out yearly about 6000 tons more than she imports. In 1895 the output of the dairies was 29,000 tons of butter and 116,000 of cheese, together 145,000 tons, an average of 140 pounds per cow. The value of food imported and exported may be summed up thus :—

Imports	£	Exports	£
Grain . . .	4,000,000	Wine . . .	2,100,000
Fish . . .	1,300,000	Oil	2,000,000
Coffee . . .	1,200,000	Meat . . .	1,400,000
Sugar . . .	900,000	Eggs . . .	1,400,000
Sundries . .	600,000	Fruit . . .	1,900,000
		Sundries . .	1,800,000
Total . .	8,000,000	Total . .	10,600,000

The above shows that although Italy does not produce enough food for her population she is still an exporter rather than an importer.

Exports of fruit have increased 50 per cent. in ten years, viz. :—

Year	Tons	Value, £	£ per Ton
1885–86 . . .	141,000	1,600,000	11.3
1894–95 . . .	228,000	1,900,000	8.3

The fall in price has indirectly stimulated production, by extending the markets and increasing the demand in foreign countries for Italian fruit. Eggs are nearly stationary, exports showing as follows :—

Year	Millions	Value, £	Pence per Doz
1885–87 . . .	480	1,200,000	6.2
1893–95 . . .	520	1,360,000	6.5

The value of food consumed yearly is approximately as follows :—

	£		£
Grain . . .	45,000,000	Fruit, &c. . .	13,000,000
Meat . . .	18,000,000	Dairy, &c. . .	28,000,000
Wine . . .	35,000,000	Sundries . .	8,000,000
Fish, &c. . .	6,000,000	Total . .	153,000,000

This is an average of only 99 shillings per inhabitant, which is even lower than in Ireland.

SPAIN

Putting aside the unreliable official statements, the production and consumption of grain, meat, wine, &c., appear to be approximately as follows :—

		Production	Consumption
Grain, tons . .		5,800,000	6,100,000
Meat, ,, . .		430,000	430,000
Potatoes, ,, . .		1,500,000	1,500,000
Fish, ,, . .		50,000	100,000
Wine, gallons . .		420,000	310,000,000

Deducting what is used for seed and cattle, the consumption of grain by the inhabitants is about 3,600,000 tons, one-tenth imported, the average consumption being 8 bushels per head. Before the year 1880 there was always a surplus of grain for exportation,* and it is worthy of note that Neumann Spallart's estimate in 1876 of the grain crops was 60 per cent. higher than Jurascheck's in 1893. The following table compares what

* *Note.*—In fifteen years, down to 1878, Spain exported 1,350,000 tons of wheat, being an average of 90,000 tons per annum.

may be considered the actual production with Spallart's estimate in 1876 :—

			1876	1897
Wheat,	tons	. .	4,200,000	2,200,000
Barley,	,,	. .	1,900,000	1,500,000
Maize, &c.,	,,	. .	2,000,000	2,100,000
	Total	. .	8,100,000	5,800,000

Jurascheck's estimate (1893) is no higher than 5 million tons, but is perhaps too low.

Reducing all food to a grain denominator, the production is approximately as follows :—

			Quantity	Equivalent in Grain Tons
Grain,	tons .	.	5,800,000	5,800,000
Potatoes,	,,	.	1,500,000	500,000
Meat,	,,	.	430,000	3,400,000
Fish,	,,	.	50,000	100,000
Butter and ch.,	,,	.	40,000	400,000
Wine, gallons .		.	420,000,000	4,200,000
	Total	. . . .		14,400,000

The importation of wheat has almost doubled in ten years, viz. :—

			Tons Yearly	Lbs. per Inhab.
1885-86	.	. .	130,000	16
1890-91	.	. .	160,000	19
1893-96	.	. .	300,000	36

Two-thirds of the population subsist on wheat, the remainder on maize, rye, &c. The decline in the production of grain has been perhaps partly due to civil wars, but still more to the fact that Spanish peasants find it more profitable to devote their attention to fruit than to cereals.

Exports of fruit show thus :—

		Tons Yearly	Value, £	£ per Ton
1885-86	. . .	136,000	1,950,000	14.4
1890-91	. . .	160,000	2,350,000	14.7
1894-96	. . .	280,000	3,200,000	11.7

Fall of price has greatly stimulated production, by increased demand, the same as observed in Italy in the above period. At the same time there has been a decline in exports of wine, viz. :—

		Gallons Yearly	Value, £	Pence per Gallon
1885-86	. . .	160,000,000	13,000,000	20
1890-91	. . .	230,000,000	12,800,000	13
1894-96	. . .	120,000,000	4,700,000	9

In this case the fall of price (55 per cent.) has been tremendous, without any extension of markets or increase of demand. Hence vineyards are neglected, and the vintage, which had risen a few years ago to more than 600 million gallons, has now fallen to 420 millions. Home consumption is 310 millions, being an average of 18 gallons per inhabitant.

Imports and exports of food may be summed up thus :—

Imports	£	Exports	£
Wheat . . .	2,400,000	Wine. . . .	4,100,000
Fish	1,100,000	Fruit . . .	3,100,000
Sugar	800,000	Oil	600,000
Sundries . . .	1,200,000	Sundries . .	400,000
Total . .	5,500,000	Total . .	8,200,000

The value of food consumed for human use is approximately as follows :—

	£		£
Grain . . .	27,000,000	Fruit, &c. . .	8,000,000
Meat . . .	20,000,000	Dairy, &c. . .	17,000,000
Wine . . .	25,000,000	Sundries . .	5,000,000
Fish, &c. . .	5,000,000	Total . .	107,000,000

This gives an average of 120 shillings per inhabitant, as compared with 99 in Italy and 166 in France.

As regards colonial articles of food imports have not much varied, except sugar, viz. :—

		Coffee	Cocoa	Sugar	Fish
			Tons Yearly		
1885-86	. . .	5,100	7,000	55,000	46,000
1890-91	. . .	5,600	6,300	63,000	45,000
1894-95	. . .	5,500	6,600	45,000	45,000

The value of all imports and exports of food at various dates is shown thus :—

		Imports, £	Exports, £	Surplus Exports, £
			Yearly Average	
1885-86	. . .	4,200,000	16,500,000	12,300,000
1890-91	. . .	5,200,000	16,200,000	11,000,000
1894-95	. . .	5,500,000	8,200,000	2,700,000
Average	. . .	5,000,000	13,600,000	8,600,000

PORTUGAL

This kingdom, which is a little larger than Ireland, is for the most part fertile, and yet unable to produce enough food for its scanty population, having only 142 souls to the square mile. This miserable state of things is due to the nobles, who possess vast estates uncultivated, compelling the peasants to emigrate to Brazil. The production of food is declining, viz. :—

		1876	1896
Grain, tons	. .	930,000	750,000
Wine, gallons .	.	110,000,000	70,000,000

The grain crop comprises 350,000 tons of maize, 200,000 of wheat, and 200,000 of rye, barley, &c. Deducting what is used for seed and cattle, the consumption of grain is about 700,000 tons, or 7 bushels per inhabitant. Only 40 per cent. of the population subsist on wheat, the rest on maize and other grain. Small as is the consumption of wheat, no less than one-third of it is imported, the native crop being hardly equal to the requirements of eight months in the year. The items of imported food are :—

		Grain	Coffee	Sugar	Fish
			Tons Yearly		
1885-88	. . .	140,000	2,500	24,000	22,000
1892-95	. . .	140,000	2,000	25,000	22,000

Exports of food show as follows :—

	Annual Averages			
	Quantity		Value, £	
	1885-87	1893-96	1885-87	1893-96
Wine, galls.	37,000,000	15,000,000	3,100,000	2,400,000
Fruit, tons	27,000	30,000	200,000	230,000
Sardines, ,,	14,000	19,000	200,000	270,000
Sundries . .	...	...	100,000	100,000
Total			3,500,000	3,000,000

Home consumption of wine averages 55 million gallons, or 12 gallons per inhabitant, as compared with 18 gallons in Italy and in Spain. The total production of food, reduced to a grain denominator, is as follows :—

	Quantity	Equivalent in Grain Tons
Grain, tons .	750,000	750,000
Potatoes, ,, .	300,000	100,000
Meat, ,, .	100,000	800,000
Fish, ,, .	40,000	100,000
Butter and cheese, tons	10,000	100,000
Wine, gallons . .	70,000,000	700,000
Total		2,550,000

This is only 11 cwt. per inhabitant, a very low average for a nation essentially agricultural : the average in Spain is 16 cwt.

SWEDEN AND NORWAY

These kingdoms do not raise sufficient grain for their requirements. It is true that Sweden had a large surplus down to 1882, exporting usually 300,000 tons, but at present she has a yearly deficit of 200,000 tons, covered by importation. Norway has always been short of grain. The position stands thus :—

	Sweden	Norway	Total
Production, tons. . .	2,750,000	450,000	3,200,000
Imports, ,, . . .	200,000	370,000	570,000

Deducting what is used for seed and cattle, the consumption in the two kingdoms is about 2 million tons, or 11 bushels per inhabitant, including what is used for making liquor. The grain used for bread is approximately as follows :—

	Tons	Lbs. per Inhabitant
Wheat	300,000	96
Rye, &c., ...	1,200,000	384
Total . .	1,500,000	480

It appears that only one-fifth of the population subsist on wheat, the rest mostly on rye: two-thirds of the wheat is imported, and one-third of the rye. Net imports of grain have averaged as follows, yearly :—

Years	Tons			Value, £ Sterling
	Sweden	Norway	Total	
1885-87 . .	10,000	250,000	260,000	1,600,000
1890-92 . .	100,000	280,000	380,000	3,100,000
1894-96 . .	200,000	370,000	570,000	2,900,000

The production of meat is as follows :—

	Sweden	Norway	Total
Beef, tons . .	120,000	50,000	170,000
Mutton, ,, . .	15,000	15,000	30,000
Pork, ,, . .	25,000	5,000	30,000
Total . .	160,000	70,000	230,000

Sweden exports live cattle equivalent to 6000 tons of meat yearly, but imports a corresponding quantity of pork : the consumption of meat therefore averages 74 lbs. per inhabitant, and the same in Norway. There is a slight deficit of butter in the latter country, which imports yearly about 18 oz. per inhabitant, but Sweden has a surplus, exporting 25,000 tons, which is equal to 11 lbs. per inhabitant. Taking the two kingdoms collectively, the net imports and exports of food show as follows :—

Imports	£	Exports	£
Grain . . .	2,900,000	Fish . . .	3,300,000
Coffee . . .	2,300,000	Butter . .	2,300,000
Wine, &c. .	800,000	Sundries . .	400,000
Total . .	6,000,000	Total . .	6,000,000

Exports of fish have increased prodigiously. Ten years ago Sweden imported more than she exported, whereas now her net exports of fish average from 80,000 to 90,000 tons yearly. Net exports of both countries show :—

	Tons Fish Yearly		Value, £	
	1885-87	1894-96	1885-87	1894-96
Sweden . .	...	80,000	...	1,100,000
Norway . .	140,000	160,000	1,800,000	2,100,000
Total .	140,000	240,000	1,800,000	3,200,000

Exports of Swedish butter have exactly doubled since 1886.

Reducing all kinds of food to grain equivalent, the production is approximately :—

Tons	Quantity			Equiv. in Grain Tons
	Sweden	Norway	Total	
Grain . .	2,750,000	450,000	3,200,000	3,200,000
Potatoes .	1,500,000	600,000	2,100,000	700,000
Meat . .	160,000	70,000	230,000	1,840,000
Butter, &c.	60,000	20,000	80,000	800,000
Fish . . .	200,000	260,000	460,000	920,000
Total . .	4,670,000	1,400,000	6,070,000	7,460,000

This gives an average of more than one ton (22 cwt.) per inhabitant, being one of the highest ratios of food production in Europe, notwithstanding the disadvantages of climate and soil under which these northern kingdoms labour. The value of food consumed is approximately :—

	Sweden, £	Norway, £	Total
Grain	10,000,000	3,000,000	13,000,000
Meat	8,000,000	3,000,000	11,000,000
Dairy	5,000,000	2,000,000	7,000,000
Sundries . . .	7,000,000	3,000,000	10,000,000
Total . .	30,000,000	11,000,000	41,000,000

This gives an average of £6 per inhabitant in Sweden, 110 shillings in Norway, and 116 shillings for the two kingdoms collectively.

DENMARK

There is no country in Europe that produces so much food as Denmark in reference to population or to area. Reducing all to a grain denominator, we find :—

		Quantity	Equivalent in Grain Tons
Grain,	tons .	2,300,000	2,300,000
Potatoes,	,, .	450,000	150,000
Meat,	,, .	130,000	1,040,000
Butter and cheese,	,, .	60,000	600,000
Fish	,, .	50,000	100,000
	Total		4,190,000

This is equal to 2 tons per inhabitant, or 10 per cent. more than the ratio in the United States, and more than double the general European ratio. Down to 1884 Denmark used to export about 200,000 tons of grain, but so large is now the consumption in the fattening of cattle that there is a constant importation of grain, net imports showing :—

	Tons			
	1893	**1894**	**1895**	**1896**
Wheat . .	32,000	56,000	64,000	48,000
Rye . . .	49,000	115,000	140,000	96,000
Barley . .	8,000	155,000	160,000	6,000
Maize . .	84,000	60,000	50,000	220,000
Oats . . .	17,000	19,000	26,000	25,000
Total .	190,000	405,000	440,000	395,000

Deducting what is used for seed, the consumption of grain is as follows :—

		Home-grown	Imported	Total
Wheat,	tons .	100,000	50,000	150,000
Rye,	,, .	400,000	100,000	500,000
Barley,	,, .	500,000	50,000	550,000
Oats, &c.,	,, .	1,050,000	150,000	1,200,000
	Total . .	2,050,000	350,000	2,400,000

About one-fourth of the population subsists on wheat, the rest on rye. The value of imported grain is two millions sterling.

Exports of a pastoral character are shown thus :—

Years	Tons Yearly		Millions of Eggs	Total Value, £
	Meat	Butter		
1886–88 . .	50,000	20,000	102	4,500,000
1890–92 . .	70,000	35,000	145	7,100,000
1894–96 . .	80,000	40,000	166	7,900,000

Home consumption averages 65 lbs. of meat and 20 lbs. of butter and cheese per inhabitant.

Imports of colonial merchandise are as follows :—

Years	Sugar, Tons	Coffee, Tons
1886–88	15,000	5,000
1894–96	20,000	9,000

This gives an average yearly consumption of 20 lbs. of sugar and 9 lbs. of coffee per inhabitant.

The value of food consumed for human use is approximately :—

	£		£
Grain . . .	5,500,000	Coffee, &c. . .	1,500,000
Meat . . .	3,000,000	Liquor, &c. .	3,500,000
Dairy, &c. . .	2,500,000	Total . .	16,000,000

This gives an average of 144 shillings per inhabitant, against 120 in Sweden.

HOLLAND

Although Holland surpasses Denmark in productive area and has twice the population, the production of food, reduced to a grain denominator, is equal in the two countries. The ordinary production in Holland is :—

		Tons	Equivalent in Grain Tons
Grain	. . . .	1,000,000	1,000,000
Potatoes	. . . .	2,100,000	700,000
Meat	. . . .	130,000	1,040,000
Butter and cheese	. . .	120,000	1,200,000
Sugar	. . . .	200,000	400,000
Fish	. . . .	120,000	240,000
	Total		4,580,000

This gives an average of 1 ton per inhabitant, against 2 tons in Denmark.

The consumption of grain, after deducting for seed and exportation, averages as follows :—

		Home-grown	Imported	Total
Wheat,	tons .	120,000	430,000	550,000
Rye,	,, .	230,000	220,000	450,000
Barley,	,, .	100,000	350,000	450,000
Oats, &c.,	,, .	250,000	...	250,000
	Total . .	700,000	1,000,000	1,700,000

There is an ordinary exportation of 200,000 tons of oats, and if this be taken into account it may be said that Holland consumes 900,000 tons of native, and 800,000 of imported, grain. Rather more than half the population subsists on wheat, the rest on rye. The net value of grain imports was as follows :—

Year	Wheat, £	Rye, &c., £	Total, £
1893	5,400,000	4,600,000	10,000,000
1894	6,700,000	5,800,000	12,500,000
1895	6,500,000	5,200,000	11,700,000
1896	7,000,000	6,200,000	13,200,000

As regards colonial products, the net annual imports show as follows :—

Years	Tons			
	Rice	Margarine	Coffee	Tea
1885–87 . .	75,000	...	27,000	2,300
1893–96 . .	90,000	30,000	36,000	2,900

At present, consumption averages 40 lbs. rice, 15 lbs. coffee, and 21 oz. tea per inhabitant.

Exports of food show as follows :—

Years	Tons Yearly			
	Meat	Butter	Fish	Vegetables
1885–87 . .	25,000	103,000	70,000	68,000
1893–96 . .	20,000	98,000	90,000	83,000

In the above table, Butter includes also cheese and margarine. The rapid increase of population in Holland checks the exportation of meat and of dairy products. Home consumption averages 55 lbs. meat, 15 lbs. butter and cheese, 25 lbs. fish. The value of food imports and exports is as follows :—

Imports	£	Exports	£
Grain . . .	12,000,000	Butter, &c. .	5,300,000
Rice . . .	2,200,000	Vegetables .	2,200,000
Coffee . . .	2,200,000	Fish . . .	1,500,000
Tea, &c. . .	1,600,000	Meat, &c. .	1,000,000
Total . .	18,000,000	Total . .	10,000,000

Holland is debtor to foreign countries for food to the amount of 8 millions sterling, say 36 shillings per inhabitant, against 73 shillings in the United Kingdom and 18 in Germany. The value of food consumed for human use is approximately :—

	£		£
Grain	11,500,000	Sundries . . .	2,500,000
Meat	5,500,000	Rice, &c. . .	6,000,000
Dairy	6,000,000	Potatoes . . .	2,500,000
Liquor . . .	4,000,000	Total . .	38,000,000

This gives an average of 160 shillings per inhabitant, as compared with 148 in Germany.

BELGIUM

The production and consumption of the principal articles of food are :—

		Production	Consumption
Grain,	tons .	1,800,000	3,200,000
Meat,	,, .	110,000	140,000
Butter and cheese,	,, .	60,000	70,000

The population is so dense that there is a deficit in the above items. Deducting what is used for seed, the consumption is approximately as follows :—

	Home-grown	Imported	Total
Wheat, tons .	400,000	400,000	800,000
Rye, &c., ,, .	1,200,000	1,000,000	2,200,000
Total . .	1,600,000	1,400,000	3,000,000

About one-half of the grain is used in breweries and by cattle, the remainder giving an average of 9 bushels per inhabitant. Belgium may be said to depend on imported grain for six months in the year, and on foreign meat and butter for two months. The net value of imported food is shown thus :—

£ Sterling			
	1894	1895	1896
Grain	7,600,000	8,100,000	9,000,000
Meat	1,000,000	800,000	1,000,000
Butter	600,000	400,000	300,000
Fish	900,000	900,000	900,000
Coffee	2,200,000	2,200,000	2,100,000
Wine	1,100,000	1,300,000	1,200,000
Total . .	13,400,000	13,700,000	14,500,000

The people of Belgium pay 42 shillings per head for imported food, against which there is a set-off of 2 millions sterling yearly for exports of sugar, which brings down the net cost of imported food to 12½ millions sterling,

or 40 shillings per inhabitant. The production of beet-sugar has doubled in ten years, and now reaches 240,000 tons, of which 180,000 are exported, the balance sufficing to give each inhabitant 25 lbs. per annum. Reducing all food to a grain denominator, the production is as follows :—

	Tons	Equivalent in Tons Grain
Grain . . .	1,800,000	1,800,000
Potatoes . . .	3,600,000	1,200,000
Meat . . .	110,000	900,000
Butter . . .	60,000	600,000
Sugar . . .	240,000	500,000
Total . . .		5,000,000

This is no more than 16 cwt. per inhabitant, which is not surprising, as the agricultural population is only one-fourth of the total. The value of food consumed for human use is approximately as follows :—

	£		£
Grain	14,000,000	Coffee, &c. . .	5,000,000
Meat	7,000,000	Potatoes . .	7,000,000
Liquor . . .	9,000,000	Sundries . . .	2,000,000
Dairy, &c. . .	8,000,000	Total . .	52,000,000

This gives an average of 160 shillings per inhabitant, the same as in France and Holland.

SWITZERLAND

The productive area is so small that Switzerland subsists on imported grain during eight months, imported meat four months, of the year. Deducting what is used for seed, the consumption of grain is as follows :—

	Home-grown	Imported	Total
Wheat, tons .	50,000	390,000	440,000
Oats, ,, .	60,000	70,000	130,000
Barley, ,, .	50,000	20,000	70,000
Rye, &c., ,, .	60,000	30,000	90,000
Total . .	220,000	510,000	730,000

The amount used for human food is about 600,000 tons, equal to 8 bushels per inhabitant. Reducing all kinds of food to a grain equivalent, the production is as follows :—

	Quantity	Equivalent in Grain Tons
Grain, tons .	250,000	250,000
Potatoes, ,, .	1,200,000	400,000
Meat, ,, .	80,000	640,000
Butter and cheese, ,, .	70,000	700,000
Wine, gallons . .	30,000,000	300,000
Total		2,290,000

This is only 14 cwt. per inhabitant. The principal articles of imported food show as follows :—

	Quantity Yearly		Value, £	
	1886-88	1893-96	1886-88	1893-96
Grain, tons	370,000	540,000	3,400,000	3,700,000
Meat, ,,	25,000	30,000	1,000,000	1,400,000
Sugar, ,,	35,000	50,000	600,000	700,000
Coffee, ,,	8,000	9,000	600,000	700,000
Wine, galls.	15,000,000	20,000,000	1,000,000	1,100,000
Sundries .	...	...	800,000	1,100,000
Total			7,400,000	8,700,000

The average consumption per inhabitant is : meat, 75 lbs. ; sugar, 35 lbs. ; butter and cheese, 20 lbs. ; coffee, 6 lbs. ; wine, 13 gallons. There is a deficit of poultry, the importation of eggs averaging 120 millions yearly, or 40 per inhabitant. Exports of food are limited to cheese and condensed milk, viz. :—

	Tons Yearly		Value, £	
	1886-88	1893-96	1886-88	1893-96
Cheese . . .	27,000	22,000	1,500,000	1,500,000
Milk	13,000	18,000	500,000	700,000
Total . .	40,000	40,000	2,000,000	2,200,000

The net sum paid yearly for imported food, therefore, is £6,500,000, equal to 42 shillings per inhabitant, against 18 shillings in Germany and 40 in Belgium. The value of food consumed yearly is approximately as follows :—

	£ Sterling		
	Home-grown	Imported	Total
Grain	1,200,000	3,700,000	4,900,000
Meat	4,000,000	1,400,000	5,400,000
Wine	1,000,000	1,100,000	2,100,000
Dairy produce .	4,000,000	...	4,000,000
Sundries . . .	2,400,000	2,500,000	4,900,000
Total . .	12,600,000	8,700,000	21,300,000

This gives an average of 140 shillings per inhabitant, against 160 in France.

THE DANUBIAN STATES

These countries produce food much in excess of their requirements, and have always a considerable surplus for exportation. The production of grain, meat, and wine is approximately as follows :—

	Grain, Tons	Meat, Tons	Wine, Gallons
Roumania . .	4,200,000	200,000	100,000,000
Servia	900,000	100,000	35,000,000
Bulgaria . . .	1,800,000	100,000	35,000,000
Total . .	6,900,000	400,000	170,000,000

Wheat constitutes 40 per cent. of the total grain crop, maize 40 per cent., the remainder being made up of barley, rye, &c. The ordinary consumption and export are shown thus :—

	Tons		
	Crop	Consumption	Export
Wheat	2,500,000	1,300,000	1,200,000
Maize	2,500,000	1,700,000	800,000
Barley . . .	1,200,000	800,000	400,000
Rye, &c. . . .	700,000	500,000	200,000
Total . .	6,900,000	4,300,000	.2,600,000
Roumania . .	4,200,000	2,200,000	2,000,000
Bulgaria . . .	1,800,000	1,200,000	600,000
Servia	900,000	900,000	...
Total . .	6,900,000	4,300,000	2,600,000

Deducting what is used for seed and cattle, the consumption of grain is about 3 million tons, or 10 bushels per inhabitant. The average consumption of wine is 12 gallons per inhabitant, the surplus for exportation seldom reaching 25 million gallons. The production of meat may be stated thus : beef, 170,000 ; mutton, 150,000 ; pork, 80,000 ; total, 400,000 tons. Consumption averages 75 lbs. per inhabitant, leaving a small surplus for exportation, in the form of live cattle. Items of food imported average yearly as follows :—

		Value, £
Coffee, tons . . .	3,200	280,000
Sugar, ,, . . .	32,000	420,000
Olive oil, gallons . .	1,400,000	300,000
Total		1,000,000

On the other hand the value of exported food is very great, viz. :—

	1893	1894	1896
	£	£	£
Grain	15,400,000	12,200,000	10,000,000
Meat	200,000	200,000	200,000
Total . . .	15,600,000	12,400,000	10,200,000

The value of food consumed for human use is approximately as follows :—

	£ Sterling			
	Roumania	Servia	Bulgaria	Total
Grain . .	9,000,000	3,500,000	5,500,000	18,000,000
Meat . .	8,000,000	4,000,000	4,000,000	16,000,000
Wine, &c. .	3,500,000	1,000,000	1,500,000	6,000,000
Dairy . .	3,000,000	1,000,000	1,500,000	5,500,000
Sundries .	4,000,000	1,500,000	2,000,000	7,500,000
Total .	27,500,000	11,000,000	14,500,000	53,000,000

This gives an average of 90 shillings per head, against 114 in Austria.

GREECE

Even before the recent war the production of grain hardly sufficed for two-thirds of the population. Deducting what was used for seed, the normal consumption was as follows :—

	Home-grown	Imported	Total
Wheat, tons . .	150,000	100,000	250,000
Maize, &c., ,, . .	250,000	100,000	350,000
Total . . .	400,000	200,000	600,000

The production of meat is close on 60,000 tons, and about 3000 tons are imported yearly, the consumption averaging 64 lbs. per inhabitant.

The ordinary vintage is 36 million gallons, of which quantity one-tenth is exported, home consumption averaging 15 gallons per inhabitant. Reducing all food to a grain denominator, the production is approximately :—

	Quantity	Equiv. in Grain Tons
Grain, tons . . .	450,000	450,000
Meat, ,, . . .	60,000	480,000
Butter, ,, . . .	10,000	100,000
Fish, ,, . . .	10,000	20,000
Wine, gallons . . .	36,000,000	360,000
Total		1,410,000

This gives an average of only 12 cwt. per inhabitant, being even less than in Switzerland. Imports and exports of food show as follows :—

Imports	£	Exports	£
Grain	1,100,000	Currants . .	900,000
Fish	200,000	Wine . . .	200,000
Sundries . . .	400,000	Sundries . .	400,000
Total . .	1,700,000	Total . .	1,500,000

The net sum which Greece has to pay in ordinary years for imported food is, therefore, no more than £200,000, equal to two shillings per inhabitant. The value of food consumed for human use is approximately £11,000,000, equal to £5 per inhabitant.

UNITED STATES

This country produces food for more than 100 millions of people, or about 50 per cent. over its population. The normal production of the principal items, reduced to grain equivalent, is as follows :—

	Quantity	Equiv. in Grain
Grain, tons . . .	74,000,000	74,000,000
Potatoes, ,, . . .	6,300,000	2,100,000
Meat, ,, . . .	4,500,000	36,000,000
Sugar, ,, . . .	400,000	800,000
Butter, &c. ,, . . .	610,000	6,100,000
Fish, ,, . . .	900,000	1,800,000
Wine, gallons . . .	25,000,000	250,000
Total		121,050,000

This is equal to 35 cwt. per inhabitant. The average crops of the last six years, 1892–97, were as follows :—

	Tons	Value, £	Shillings per Ton
Maize	41,200,000	117,000,000	57
Wheat	12,500,000	54,000,000	86
Oats	17,600,000	38,000,000	43
Rye, &c.	2,700,000	10,000,000	74
Total . .	74,000,000	219,000,000	59

About 8 per cent. of the total grain crop is exported, the average of consumption and exports in five years ending December 1896 showing as follows :—

	Tons			Value Export. Millions £
	Produc.	Consump.	Export	
Wheat . .	12,300,000	7,800,000	4,500,000	30.2
Maize . .	43,400,000	41,800,000	1,600,000	6.2
Oats, &c. .	20,300,000	19,900,000	400,000	1.6
Total . .	76,000,000	69,500,000	6,500,000	38.0

Production and consumption in the various sections of the Union show thus :—

States	Tons		Surplus + Deficit −
	Production	Consumption	
New England .	500,000	2,400,000	− 1,900,000
Middle	5,500,000	8,200,000	− 2,700,000
South	15,000,000	19,700,000	− 4,700,000
Prairie	52,000,000	31,400,000	+ 20,600,000
Pacific	3,000,000	7,800,000	− 4,800,000
Total . .	76,000,000	69,500,000	+ 6,500,000

Consumption is accounted for approximately as follows :—

States	Tons		
	For People	Cattle & Seed	Total
New England .	1,300,000	1,100,000	2,400,000
Middle	4,000,000	4,200,000	8,200,000
South	5,000,000	14,700,000	19,700,000
Prairie	6,500,000	24,800,000	31,400,000
Pacific	1,100,000	6,700,000	7,800,000
Total . .	18,000,000	51,500,000	69,500,000

The Prairie States have a surplus of about 20 million tons, of which two-thirds go to meet the deficits in the rest of the Union, and one-third is exported.

Potatoes do not enter largely into American diet, the average consumption in the United States being only 3½ bushels per inhabitant, against 7 in the United Kingdom, 13 in France, and 24 in Germany. The crop compares with population as follows :—

States	Tons	Bushels per Inhab.
Eastern	2,400,000	4.5
Southern	400,000	1.0
Western	3,500,000	4.7
Union	6,300,000	3.5

The annual production of meat at various dates was approximately as follows :—

Year	Tons (000 omitted)			
	Beef	Mutton	Pork	Total
1876 . . .	1,340	360	1,030	2,730
1886 . . .	2,310	480	1,840	4,630
1890 . . .	2,690	440	2,060	5,190
1896 . . .	2,410	380	1,710	4,500

This gives an average at present of 142 pounds per inhabitant, against 180 pounds in 1886. The production is short in the Eastern States, but the South and West have a large surplus, viz. :—

States	Tons (000 omitted)			
	Beef	Mutton	Pork	Total
New England . .	60	10	10	80
Middle . . .	170	30	80	280
South . . .	760	80	650	1,490
West . . .	1,420	260	970	2,650
Union . . .	2,410	380	1,710	4,500

Consumption and production in the above divisions are approximately thus :—

States	Tons	
	Production	Consumption
New England . .	80,000	280,000
Middle . . .	280,000	1,010,000
South . . .	1,490,000	880,000
West . . .	2,650,000	1,780,000 *
Total . .	4,500,000	3,950,000

* *Note.*—Foremost in the production of food is the State of Iowa, which raises 500 pounds of meat and 5 tons of grain per inhabitant, being nearly five times as much grain and three times as much meat as the average for the whole Union.

There is usually a surplus of 550,000 tons for exportation, of which Great Britain takes 450,000 tons.

The available pasture lands are of sufficient extent (as already shown under *Cattle*, page 634) to carry almost three times the present number of live stock, and the production of meat may hereafter, without difficulty, be raised to the following quantity :—

States	Tons			
	Beef	Mutton	Pork	Total
N. England	100,000	20,000	20,000	140,000
Middle . .	230,000	40,000	100,000	370,000
South . .	1,250,000	140,000	1,050,000	2,440,000
West. . .	4,320,000	700,000	3,030,000	8,050,000
Total .	5,900,000	900,000	4,200,000	11,000,000

If this should come to pass the Eastern States (New England and Middle States) would have still only one-third of the meat necessary for their own population, while the South and West would have a surplus of 8 million tons over their present consumption.

Dairy-farming is so unevenly distributed that most parts of the Union have a deficit of butter and cheese. The following table shows the actual number of milch cows, and also the proper number required for the population :—

States	Milch Cows	Required Number	Surplus + Deficit −
New England .	820,000	1,040,000	220,000
Middle	2,880,000	3,200,000	− 320,000
Southern . .	4,000,000	4,100,000	− 100,000
Western . . .	8,500,000	6,060,000	+2,440,000
Total . .	16,200,000	14,400,000	+1,800,000

According to latest estimates the total output of butter and cheese reaches 610,000 tons yearly, of which 40,000 are exported. Home consumption therefore averages 18 lbs. per inhabitant, as compared with 22 lbs. in the United Kingdom.

The production of butter, honey, and eggs, according to census reports, was :—

Year	Butter, Tons	Honey, Tons	Eggs, Millions
1870 . • •	230,000	7,000	...
1880 . • •	345,000	12,000	5,484
1890 . • •	455,000	28,000	9,804

Poultry increased 130 per cent. in 10 years, viz. : from 126 millions in 1880 to 285 millions in 1890, the average production of eggs being 44 to each bird in the former and 35 in the latter year.

There is a deficit of poultry in some parts of the Union, the following table showing the yearly production of eggs in 1890 compared with population :—

States	Millions of Eggs	Eggs per Inhabitant
Eastern . • • • •	2,804	148
Southern . • • • •	2,090	114
Western . • • • •	4,910	195
Union . • • • •	9,804	157

In the year of the above census, and for many years preceding, the United States imported annually 180

million eggs; this would bring up the consumption to 160 per inhabitant. On this basis the Eastern States would appear to show a deficit of 220 millions, the South 840 millions, while the Western States had a surplus of 880 millions. In other words, the South and West balanced one another, and all the imported eggs were used in the Eastern States. But in 1891 a duty was imposed on foreign eggs, and since then the importation has rapidly declined, not exceeding 11 million eggs in 1896.

The consumption of sugar is five times greater than the production, as the following table shows :—

Year	Tons Consumed			Lbs. per Inhabitant
	Native	Imported	Total	
1875 . . .	60,000	820,000	880,000	44
1885 . . .	130,000	1,170,000	1,300,000	52
1890 . . .	170,000	1,310,000	1,480,000	53
1897 . . .	330,000	1,760,000	2,090,000	65

The increase of duties on foreign sugar in 1894 was followed by greater production in Louisiana and other States; nevertheless, the quantity imported is double what it was in 1875. Americans consume more sugar per head than any other nation except Great Britain.

United States fisheries stand for almost one-third of all the fish caught in the world, the latest returns showing 880,000 tons yearly. Imports and exports balance, being each about 50,000 tons. Consumption, therefore, averages 28 lbs. per inhabitant, whereas the average in Europe is only 11 lbs., but in the United Kingdom it is 40 lbs.

The consumption of wines and liquors of all descriptions may be set down as follows :—

	Gallons, Millions			Gals. per Inhab.
	Native	Imported	Total	
Beer . . .	865	5	870	12.0
Spirits . . .	72	1	73	1.0
Wine . . .	25	3	28	0.4
Total . .	962	9	971	13.4

Reducing the above to alcohol, the amount stands thus :—

	Gallons, Millions		Gallons per Head
	Quantity	In Alcohol	
Beer . . .	870	44	0.6
Spirits . . .	73	36	0.5
Wine . . .	28	6	0.1
Total . .	971	86	1.2

The following table shows the consumption per head of various articles :—

	1870	1880	1890	1896
Wheat, bushels . .	5.4	5.4	6.1	4.8
Sugar, lbs. . . .	33.0	43.0	53.0	63.0
Coffee, ,, . . .	6.0	8.8	7.8	8.0
Tea, ,, . . .	1.1	1.4	1.3	1.3
Beer, gallons . .	5.3	8.3	13.7	15.2
Spirits, ,, . .	2.1	1.3	1.4	1.0
Wine, ,, . .	0.3	0.6	0.5	0.3

The value of exported food is shown as follows :—

	£ Sterling Yearly			
	1887–90	1891–95	1896	1897
Cattle . .	3,800,000	6,800,000	7,900,000	9,000,000
Grain . .	29,800,000	37,400,000	29,400,000	41,200,000
Meat . .	18,900,000	25,000,000	24,400,000	25,000,000
Butter, &c.	3,300,000	4,000,000	3,100,000	3,200,000
Sundries .	3,800,000	4,000,000	3,700,000	3,600,000
Total .	59,600,000	77,200,000	68,500,000	82,000,000

The value of food imports in the same period was as follows :—

	£ Sterling Yearly			
	1887–90	1891–95	1896	1897
Coffee . .	14,000,000	20,400,000	17,700,000	17,000,000
Sugar . .	18,600,000	22,500,000	18,700,000	20,700,000
Fruit . . .	4,200,000	4,500,000	4,000,000	3,500,000
Tea . . .	2,900,000	2,900,000	2,600,000	3,100,000
Wines . .	2,300,000	2,500,000	2,300,000	2,300,000
Sundries .	7,300,000	6,200,000	5,300,000	5,400,000
Total .	49,300,000	59,000,000	50,600,000	52,000,000

The surplus value of exported food over imported during the last 10 years averaged 16 millions sterling, or less than 5 shillings per inhabitant.

The value of food consumed for human use is approximately as follows :—

	£			£
Grain . . .	90,000,000		Dairy and eggs	106,000,000
Meat . . .	132,000,000		Fruit, &c. . .	40,000,000
Liquor . .	72,000,000		Sundries . .	26,000,000
Imports . .	54,000,000		Total . .	520,000,000

This gives an average of 150 shillings per inhabitant, as compared with 166 in France and 206 in Great Britain.

CANADA

There is always a large surplus of grain, meat, cheese, and eggs, which items are exported chiefly to Great Britain. The ordinary production and net shipments of grain are :—

		Production	Consumption	Export
Wheat,*	tons	1,200,000	1,000,000	200,000
Oats,	,,	2,600,000	2,600,000	...
Maize,	,,	600,000	500,000	100,000
Barley, &c.,	,,	700,000	700,000	...
Total .		5,100,000	4,800,000	300,000

The production and consumption of meat are approximately as follows :—

		Production	Consumption	Export
Beef,	tons . .	210,000	180,000	30,000
Mutton,	,, . .	35,000	25,000	10,000
Pork	,, . .	65,000	45,000	20,000
Total . .		310,000	250,000	60,000

* The crops of 1896-97-98 averaged 1,320,000 tons : see *Wheat*, p. 820.

The net annual value of food exports, and their weight, have been as follows :—

		Tons Yearly		Value, £	
		1884–86	1897	1884–85	1897
Grain . .		300,000	560,000	1,800,000	2,600,000
Meat . .		50,000	90,000	1,500,000	3,100,000
Fish . . .		80,000	80,000	1,200,000	2,100,000
Butter, &c. .		40,000	80,000	1,900,000	3,400,000
Eggs, &c. . .		...	...	500,000	300,000
Total				6,900,000	11,500,000

Shipments of eggs have declined 40 per cent., namely, from 150 millions in 1886 to 90 millions at present. Potatoes have also fallen, exports being now 20,000 tons per annum.

Items of imported food show as follows :—

	Quantity Yearly		Value, £	
	1884–86	1894–97	1884–86	1894–97
Sugar, tons . .	110,000	190,000	1,200,000	1,900,000
Tea, ,, . .	8,000	9,000	700,000	600,000
Wine, gallons .	650,000	700,000	200,000	150,000
Total			2,100,000	2,650,000

Consumption averages 80 lbs. sugar, 4 lbs. tea, per inhabitant.

Reducing all food to a grain equivalent, the production is as follows :—

		Tons	Equivalent in Grain
Grain		5,100,000	5,100,000
Potatoes . . .		1,200,000	400,000
Meat		310,000	2,500,000
Fish		200,000	600,000
Butter and cheese . .		130,000	1,300,000
Total			9,900,000

This is equivalent to almost 2 tons per inhabitant, the ratio being 5 per cent. higher than in the United States. The value of food consumed for human use is approximately :—

		£			£
Grain . .		8,000,000		Imports .	2,700,000
Meat . .		8,000,000		Sundries .	4,300,000
Dairy . .		4,000,000		Total .	27,000,000

This is about 105 shillings per inhabitant.

AUSTRALIA

The production and consumption of grain in ordinary years are as follows :—

		Production	Consumption	Export
Wheat, tons .		700,000	400,000	300,000
Oats, &c., ,, .		740,000	740,000	...
Total . .		1,440,000	1,140,000	300,000

South Australia, Victoria, and New Zealand have collectively a surplus of 450,000 tons of grain yearly, but New South Wales, Queensland, and Western Australia have an aggregate deficit of 150,000, so that the surplus left for exportation to Europe is only 300,000 tons. As regards meat, the production is only one-third of what might be expected from the numbers of live stock, which is partly explained by the fact that sheep are bred not for the market but for growing wool : home consumption is estimated at 400,000 tons, equal to 208 lbs. per inhabitant, and the shipments of all kinds sum up 200,000 tons yearly. The time may come when Australian meat will be more in request. With the present numbers of stock the possible output of meat yearly would be :—

	Tons			
	Beef	Mutton	Pork	Total
N. S. Wales . .	90,000	470,000	10,000	570,000
Queensland . .	270,000	200,000	...	470,000
New Zealand .	40,000	200,000	10,000	250,000
Victoria . . .	70,000	135,000	15,000	220,000
S. Australia, &c.	40,000	105,000	5,000	150,000
Seven Colonies .	510,000	1,110,000	40,000	1,660,000

Reducing all food to a grain denominator, the production at present is :—

		Quantity	Equivalent in Grain
Grain,	tons .	1,500,000	1,500,000
Potatoes,	,, .	600,000	200,000
Meat,	,, .	600,000	4,800,000
Sugar,	,, .	80,000	160,000
Butter and cheese,	,, .	55,000	550,000
Wine, fish, &c.	. .	...	70,000
Total	. . . . .		7,280,000

This gives an average of 35 cwt. per inhabitant, the same as in the United States. The value of food imported and exported is shown as follows :—

Imports	£	Exports	£
Liquors . . .	1,600,000	Meat	3,800,000
Tea	1,200,000	Grain. . . .	1,500,000
Sundries . . .	1,200,000	Butter, &c. . .	1,700,000
Total . .	4,000,000	Total . . .	7,000,000

The value of food consumed for human use is approximately as follows :—

	£		£
Grain	5,000,000	Imports . . .	4,000,000
Meat	5,000,000	Sundries . . .	3,000,000
Dairy	4,000,000	Total . . .	21,000,000

This is equal to 96 shillings per inhabitant, as compared with 105 in Canada.

ARGENTINA

This country ought to have a large surplus of grain, meat, and dairy products for the European markets, seeing the vastness of its fertile Pampas, the millions of its sheep and cattle, and the mildness and salubrity of its climate. Tillage is, nevertheless, at a considerable disadvantage owing to the constant danger of drought and locusts. The area under grain is about 9 million acres, yielding in good years 4½ million tons, but in bad years the crop hardly reaches one-third of that quantity.

Thus the surplus available for exportation varies as follows :—

	Tons		Average
	1895	1896	1893–96
Wheat	990,000	550,000	1,050,000
Maize	770,000	180,000	270,000
Total . .	1,760,000	730,000	1,320,000

The production of meat (including cattle exported) is about 450,000 tons yearly, of which 200,000 are exported, the home consumption averaging 140 lbs. per inhabitant. The possible production would be as follows, if sheep-farmers were to grow less for wool than for meat :—

Provinces	Tons		
	Beef	Mutton	Total
Buenos Ayres .	380,000	640,000	1,020,000
Entre Rios . .	160,000	50,000	210,000
Santa Fé . . .	90,000	30,000	120,000
Cordoba . . .	80,000	30,000	110,000
Corrientes, &c. .	210,000	50,000	260,000
Total . .	920,000	800,000	1,720,000

Reducing all kinds of food to a grain denominator, the production is as follows :—

	Quantity	Equivalent in Grain
Grain, tons . . .	3,000,000	3,000,000
Meat, ,, . . .	450,000	3,600,000
Sugar, ,, . . .	130,000	400,000
Butter, ,, . . .	20,000	200,000
Wine, gallons . . .	35,000,000	350,000
Total		7,550,000

This is almost the same quantity of food as produced in Australia, and the average per inhabitant is 35 cwt., the same ratio as in the United States or Australia. The value of food produced, consumed, and exported, may be set down approximately thus :—

	Production £	Consumption £	Export £
Grain . . .	15,000,000	9,000,000	6,000,000
Meat . . .	8,400,000	5,000,000	3,400,000
Wine . . .	2,500,000	2,500,000	...
Dairy, &c. . .	5,500,000	4,700,000	800,000
Total . .	31,400,000	21,200,000	10,200,000

The value of imported food is 4 millions sterling : hence the sum total of food consumed reaches £25,000,000, but we must deduct 3 millions for grain used for cattle and seed, leaving a balance of 22 millions, equal to 110 shillings per inhabitant.

URUGUAY

Production and consumption of grain and meat are shown as follows :—

	Tons		
	Production	Consumption	Export
Grain . . .	200,000	160,000	40,000
Meat . . .	200,000	60,000	140,000

The actual amount of live stock is capable of producing from 300,000 to 350,000 tons of meat yearly. Climate and soil are, moreover, favourable to tillage, and as soon as a settled government be established, so as to admit a million of industrious European settlers, the Republic of Uruguay may easily produce five or six million tons of grain yearly.

FOREST

The Foreign Office Report of 1893 was as follows :—

	Acres of Forest			P.c. of Area
	Public	Private	Total	
U. Kingdom	...	2,700,000	2,700,000	4.0
France . .	7,400,000	16,000,000	23,400,000	17.9
Germany .	17,900,000	16,500,000	34,400,000	25.7
Russia . .	299,000,000	199,200,000	498,200,000	37.2
Austria Pr. .	5,900,000	18,300,000	24,200,000	32.6
Hungary .	9,400,000	9,400,000	18,800,000	23.5
Italy . . .	400,000	9,700,000	10,100,000	14.3
Spain. . .	16,400,000	...	16,400,000	13.0
Portugal. .	100,000	1,100,000	1,200,000	5.2
Sweden . .	14,300,000	30,200,000	44,500,000	40.7
Norway . .	2,900,000	16,400,000	19,300,000	24.5
Denmark . .	...	500,000	500,000	4.8
Holland . .	...	600,000	600,000	6.9
Belgium . .	500,000	700,000	1,200,000	17.1
Switzerland.	1,500,000	600,000	2,100,000	20.1
Roumania .	2,300,000	2,600,000	4,900,000	15.2
Servia . .	5,800,000	...	5,800,000	48.0
Bulgaria. .	1,100,000	...	1,100,000	4.6
Bosnia . .	...	6,700,000	6,700,000	45.0
Greece . .	1,600,000	400,000	2,000,000	12.6
Turkey . .	...	3,500,000	3,500,000	8.9
Europe . .	386,500,000	335,100,000	721,600,000	30.3
U. States .	...	450,000,000	450,000,000	23.3
India. . .	70,000,000	70,000,000	140,000,000	25.0
Algeria . .	5,100,000	700,000	5,800,000	5.5
N.S. Wales	5,400,000	13,800,000	19,200,000	10.0
Total .	467,000,000	869,600,000	1,336,600,000	

For Forests of Brazil, Canada, &c., see page 298.

The cutting of lumber is computed either by cubic foot or board measure, 8 feet of the latter being equal to 1 cubic foot, and 50 cubic feet to 1 ton.

GERMANY

Nearly half of the public forests belong to local authorities. The State forests in 1894 gave the following result :—

	Acres	Product £	Net do. £	Pence per Acre
Prussia . .	6,000,000	2,900,000	1,250,000	50
Bavaria . .	2,300,000	1,230,000	570,000	60
Baden, &c.	1,120,000	1,270,000	760,000	163
Germany .	9,420,000	5,400,000	2,580,000	66

In 14 years, from 1880, the felling of timber averaged 55 cubic feet per acre, including 15 cubic feet of lumber, the rest being firewood, &c. The cost of felling and conveying to the road is 17 pence per ton. In 1894 the Prussian Government paid £410,000 for the delivery of 6 million tons of lumber cut in Crown forests. There are 34½ million acres of forest in Germany, in which 380,000 wood-cutters earn a living, that is, one wood-cutter for 90 acres. The ordinary prices of timber per

ton and the stipend paid by the State to its wood-cutters are shown as follows :—

	Shills. per Ton.		Woodman's Fee.
Oak. . . .	25–29	1850 . .	80 pence, ton
Beech . .	15–17	1860 .	90 ,, ,,
Pine. . .	12–13	1870–80	110 ,, ,,
Firewood. . .	2	1890–95	110 ,, ,,

In the Harz Mountains timber fetches 25 shillings, poles, &c., 6 to 8 shillings a ton.

AUSTRIA

Export of timber exceeds 2 million tons yearly, value 5 millions sterling.

UNITED STATES

In 1894 the forest area was defined thus :—

State	Acres	Per Cent. of Area	Forest Acres per Inhab.
New England .	20,700,000	52.0	4.0
Middle	20,000,000	28.0	1.4
South	212,300,000	42.0	11.0
Prairie	89,500,000	18.0	3.5
Pacific	116,000,000	16.0	4.0
Union	458,500,000	25.0	6.6

Four States have nearly a quarter of all the forest area, viz. :—

State	Acres Forest	Do. per Inhab.
Texas	38,700,000	17.0
Washington . . .	23,500,000	60.0
Arkansas	20,400,000	18.0
Florida	20,300,000	52.0

On the other hand the Prairie States have less than 4 acres of forest per inhabitant, and the cutting is so excessive that Congress must take measures in the matter. The Prairie States, as shown in a previous table, have only 89½ million acres of forest, that is, one-fifth of the forest area of the Union, and yet the census of 1890 showed that they stood for 51 per cent. of the sawn timber produced in the United States. The States in which the forest area is relatively largest are :—

State	Acres Area	Acres Forest	Percentage
Maine	19,100,000	12,300,000	64
New Hampshire	5,800,000	3,600,000	62
Arkansas . . .	33,500,000	20,400,000	60
Florida	34,700,000	20,300,000	58
North Carolina .	31,100,000	16,800,000	54
Tennessee . .	26,700,000	14,700,000	55
Washington . .	42,800,000	23,500,000	55
Alabama . . .	32,700,000	17,400,000	53

The census report estimates the consumption yearly at 475 million tons, and the value of output at 215 millions sterling, which is about 9 shillings per acre of forest. This would be, however, more than a ton of timber per forest acre, which appears too high. The figures show :—

	Census		Better Estimate	
	Tons	Value, £	Tons	Value, £
Lumber . .	93,600,000	72,800,000	84,000,000	66,000,000
Firewood,&c.	360,000,000	93,600,000	240,000,000	62,400,000
Sundries .	21,400,000	48,600,000	16,000,000	11,600,000
Total . .	475,000,000	215,000,000	340,000,000	140,000,000

FREIGHT

The earnings of nations under this heading consist of : 1st, goods traffic by rail ; 2nd, by canal or river ; 3rd, by highroad ; 4th, by shipping : the first three taken collectively may be estimated at 6 per cent. on all products in countries not exceeding 100,000 sq. miles, and 10 per cent. in those of greater area.

The following table also includes passenger traffic by rail, so as to give the total transport earnings. Shipping is supposed to earn £2 a year per ton of carrying power.

	Millions £ Sterling						
	Internal Goods Traffic				Passenger Traffic	Shipping Earnings	Total
	Rail	River	Road	Total			
Great Britain	44.6	3.1	18.3	66.0	37.2	54.5	157.7
Ireland	1.6	0.2	3.8	5.6	1.9	1.3	8.8
United Kingdom	46.2	3.3	22.1	71.6	39.1	55.8	166.5
France	28.0	3.9	71.7	103.6	22.5	4.8	130.9
Germany	54.9	4.5	55.0	114.4	20.3	8.3	143.0
Russia	33.0	14.4	49.1	96.5	8.4	3.0	107.9
Austria	22.2	2.2	42.5	66.9	7.0	1.4	75.3
Italy	6.3	0.3	33.6	40.2	4.0	2.9	47.1
Spain	4.5	0.1	21.6	26.2	3.9	4.6	34.7
Portugal	0.7	...	2.7	3.4	0.6	0.4	4.4
Sweden	2.2	...	4.1	6.3	1.1	2.1	9.5
Norway	0.2	...	1.9	2.1	0.3	5.0	7.4
Denmark	0.5	...	2.8	3.3	0.6	1.5	5.4
Holland	1.5	1.0	2.7	5.2	1.5	1.7	8.4
Belgium	5.2	1.6	3.6	10.4	2.6	0.7	13.7
Switzerland	2.4	0.1	1.2	3.7	2.0	...	5.7
Danubian States	1.4	0.3	7.2	8.9	1.2	...	10.1
Greece	0.3	...	1.2	1.5	0.3	1.2	3.0
Europe	209.5	31.7	323.0	564.2	115.4	93.4	773.0
United States	179.0	16.6	103.4	299.0	55.0	3.2	357.2
Canada	7.0	1.2	9.9	18.1	3.5	3.4	25.0
Australia	5.4	...	12.1	17.5	5.5	1.8	24.8
Total . . .	400.9	49.5	448.4	898.8	179.4	101.8	1,180.0

UNITED KINGDOM

The number of persons employed in transport in 1891 was :—

	Rail	Highroad	Water	Total
England . . .	187,000	367,000	430,000	984,000
Scotland . . .	26,000	42,000	54,000	122,000
Ireland . . .	10,000	27,000	29,000	66,000
U. Kingdom .	223,000	436,000	513,000	1,172,000

The product of their labour, according to the preceding table, was 166½ millions sterling, equal to £140 per man ; of this sum wages would take about £80, while coal, fodder, and other raw material would stand for £20, leaving a balance of £40 per man or £47,000,000 for profit and dividends, on railways, shipping, express companies, and all other carrying enterprises. Secretary Morton, Minister of Agriculture in the United States, estimates charges in England for carts to or from shipping at 30 pence per ton, but this is too high : the estimate above given of £22,100,000 for the United Kingdom is only 10 pence a ton for cartage of 360 million tons carried by rail, and 150 millions to and from seaports.

UNITED STATES

In 1896 the railways had 874,000 employees, and the census of 1890 showed 488,000 waggoners, and 78,000 boatmen, in all 1,440,000. The product of their labour according to the preceding table would be equal to £247 per man. The railways average a net annual profit of 70 million pounds sterling, and the total transport service

yields probably 100 millions sterling net profit, that is £70 per man employed. The census of 1880 showed 419,000 railway employees, whose wages footed up £41,000,000, equal to £98 per man. See *Canals*, p. 649, and *Railways*, p. 795.

Rates of freight from Chicago for provisions per ton, to various European ports, by all rail to seaboard and thence by steamers, were as follows :—

To	Shillings per ton			
	1888	1891	1894	1897
Liverpool . . .	35	51	41	42
Glasgow . . .	43	55	43	49
London . . .	42	55	42	45
Antwerp . . .	42	49	38	48
Hamburg . . .	51	52	47	48
Copenhagen . .	52	60	52	54
Bordeaux . . .	55	70	59	60
Average . . .	46	56	46	49

Rates on wheat per ton from St. Louis down the Mississippi to New Orleans, and to Liverpool via New Orleans ; also from St. Louis by rail to New York and thence to Liverpool by steamer, were at various dates as follows :—

St. Louis to	Shillings per ton			
	1882	1890	1894	1897
New Orleans	10.8	11.0	9.9	8.1
Liverpool via New Orleans .	37.4	24.0	19.5	21.4
Liverpool via New York .	39.3	36.0	31.2	33.8

The distance from St. Louis to New Orleans is 1130 miles ; freight therefore per ton of grain 100 miles is less than 9 pence (8.55), which is about the same as the charge for water-carriage of wheat from Chicago to New York (haulage nearly 1000 miles) :—

Shillings per ton

| 1860 . . . 41 | 1880 . . . 20 | 1894 . . . 7 |
| 1870 . . . 28 | 1890 . . . 10 | 1897 . . . 7 |

On 13 lines which stood for one-third of the goods traffic of the United States, the charge for carrying a ton 100 miles averaged as follows :—

Year	Pence	Year	Pence	Year	Pence
1870	. . . 154	1880	. . . 51	1890 : . . 39
1875	. . . 66	1885	. . . 42	1895 . . . 36

FRICTION

Rennie's table is as follows :—

Steel on ice 014	Marble on marble . . 160
Ice on ice 028	Leather on iron . . 250
Brass on iron . . . 135	Granite on granite . 300
Steel on steel . . . 146	Iron on oak 620

FRIENDLY SOCIETIES

There are three kinds of societies — co-operative, building, and friendly societies—and the aggregate membership and funds in the United Kingdom show thus :—

	1886	1896	Societies	Funds, £
No. of Soc.	22,000	30,104	Co-Operative	20,040,000
Members	7,000,000	11,511,000	Friendly	26,100,000
Funds, £	79,000,000	107,470,000	Building, &c.	61,330,000

Excluding Co-operative and Building Societies, and considering only the Mutual Aid Societies of the working classes, their progress has been as follows :—

Year	Members	Funds, £
1873	1,787,000	8,630,000
1880	4,802,000	13,003,000
1897	8,320,000	26,100,000

There are 1333 of these societies, averaging 6300 members each, but 9 of the principal societies average 250,000 each, having increased 32 per cent. in 10 years, viz. :—

Societies	ooo omitted					
	Members		Income, £		Funds, £	
	1885	1895	1885	1895	1885	1895
Oddfellows .	676	906	1,060	1,320	5,780	8,500
Foresters . .	582	655	860	1,090	3,390	4,820
Hearts of Oak	109	205	250	460	770	1,610
Shepherds .	67	110	90	160	180	470
5 others . .	238	333	280	510	900	1,310
9 Societies .	1,672	2,210	2,540	3,540	11,020	16,710

See *Trade Unions*, page 570, and page 813. See also *Co-operation*, page 677, and *Societies*, page 542. For *Building Societies*, see *Co-operation*.

CANADA

Friendly and Building Societies showed as follows :—

	1874 £	1884 £	1894 £
Capital, paid . .	1,600,000	6,150,000	7,830,000
Reserve . . .	270,000	1,360,000	2,290,000
Deposits . . .	920,000	2,780,000	4,160,000
Debentures, &c. .	450,000	7,270,000	14,020,000
Liabilities . . .	3,240,000	17,560,000	28,300,000
Mortgages . .	3,100,000	14,800,000	23,400,000
Cash, &c. . . .	140,000	2,720,000	5,100,000
Assets	3,240,000	17,520,000	28,500,000

In 1894 the Provinces showed as follows :—

	Capital, £	Deposits, £	Mortgages, £
Ontario . . .	6,900,000	4,050,000	21,300,000
Quebec . . .	470,000	80,000	1,840,000
Nova Scotia, &c.	460,000	30,000	260,000
Total . . .	7,830,000	4,160,000	23,400,000

AUSTRALIA

In January 1895 there were 149 Friendly Societies with 242,000 members, and funds approaching 3 millions sterling, viz. :—

	Branches	Members	Funds, £
N. S. Wales . .	818	68,400	490,000
Victoria . . .	1,075	79,200	1,080,000
New Zealand . .	367	30,000	550,000
Queensland . .	243	17,100	150,000
South Australia .	422	35,900	420,000
Tasmania . . .	111	9,800	80,000
West Australia .	26	1,800	30,000
Total . . .	3,062	242,200	2,800,000

FRUIT

The apple crop of the United States averages 5,500,000 tons, valued at 20 millions sterling. One ton of apples yields 150 gallons of cider. See *Cider*.

Imports of fruit into the United Kingdom in 1896 were :

	Tons	Value, £
Almonds.	7,400	430,000
Apples	150,000	1,580,000
Currants	49,000	750,000
Raisins, &c. . . .	80,000	2,340,000
Oranges, &c. . . .	260,000	4,200,000
Total . . .	546,400	9,300,000

Consumption averages 30 lbs., worth 65 pence, per inhabitant.

The countries which exported fruit were as follows :—

	Tons		Value, £	
	1887	1895	1887	1895
Italy . . .	240,000	230,000	2,200,000	1,900,000
Spain . .	160,000	300,000	2,200,000	3,300,000
Portugal . .	17,000	20,000	140,000	130,000
Greece . .	107,000	140,000	1,900,000	1,100,000

The fruit crop of France in 1896 was valued at £7,500,000 sterling.

3 A

G

GAS

See *Light*, page 762, also page 304.

GLASS

The annual output of glass in certain countries is represented approximately by the following values :—

United Kingdom	£ 4,400,000	Belgium	.	.	£ 3,800,000
France	. 7,200,000	Russia	.	.	1,200,000
Austria	. 4,500,000	United States	.		9,800,000

The United States census showed the growth of this industry thus :—

Year	Capital, £	Operatives	Output, £
1880 . . .	4,400,000	26,000	4,900,000
1890 . . .	9,100,000	49,500	9,800,000

See *Glass* in Part II., page 305.

GOATS

See *Cattle*, page 635, also page 305.

GOLD

The production of gold in forty-seven years has been as follows :—

Year	Value, £ Sterling (000 omitted)					Weight, Tons				
	U. States	Australia	Russia	Various	Total	U. States	Australia	Russia	Various	Total
1851	11,600	1,400	3,600	2,200	18,800	83	10	26	15	134
1852	12,700	12,200	3,600	2,200	30,700	91	87	26	15	219
1853	13,700	13,000	3,400	2,200	32,300	98	93	25	15	231
1854	12,700	9,600	3,400	2,200	27,900	91	69	25	15	200
1855	11,600	12,000	3,500	2,200	29,300	83	86	25	15	209
1856	11,600	13,200	3,500	2,300	30,600	83	94	25	16	218
1857	11,500	11,600	3,900	2,300	29,300	82	83	28	16	209
1858	10,600	12,100	3,900	2,300	28,900	76	86	28	16	206
1859	10,500	12,200	3,600	2,300	28,600	75	87	26	16	204
1860	9,800	11,200	3,600	2,300	26,900	70	80	26	16	192
1861	9,000	11,000	3,500	2,400	25,900	64	79	25	17	185
1862	8,200	11,300	3,500	2,400	25,400	59	81	25	17	182
1863	8,400	11,400	3,300	2,400	25,500	60	82	23	17	182
1864	9,700	10,000	3,400	2,400	25,500	69	71	25	17	182
1865	11,200	10,300	3,400	2,400	27,300	80	73	25	17	195
1866	11,200	10,400	4,100	2,300	28,000	80	74	30	16	200
1867	10,900	9,900	4,100	2,300	27,200	78	70	30	16	194
1868	10,100	10,400	4,200	2,300	27,000	72	74	30	16	192
1869	10,400	9,700	4,300	2,300	26,700	74	69	31	16	190
1870	10,400	8,500	4,300	2,300	25,500	74	61	31	16	182
1871	9,700	9,900	4,400	2,500	26,500	69	70	31	18	188
1872	8,200	9,000	4,700	2,600	24,500	59	64	33	19	175
1873	8,200	8,400	4,800	2,700	24,100	59	60	34	19	172
1874	7,700	7,200	4,800	2,800	22,500	55	52	34	20	161
1875	7,700	6,900	4,800	3,000	22,400	55	49	34	22	160
1876	8,400	6,900	4,700	3,200	23,200	60	49	33	23	165
1877	9,900	6,300	5,700	3,200	25,100	70	45	41	23	179
1878	10,700	6,100	5,900	3,300	26,000	77	43	42	24	186
1879	8,200	6,100	5,900	3,200	23,400	59	43	42	23	167
1880	7,600	6,300	5,700	3,300	22,900	54	45	41	24	164
1881	7,300	6,400	4,700	4,000	22,400	52	46	33	29	160
1882	6,900	6,200	4,600	3,800	21,500	49	44	32	28	153
1883	6,300	5,600	4,600	4,300	20,800	45	40	32	31	148
1884	6,500	6,000	4,600	4,700	21,800	47	43	32	33	155
1885	6,700	5,800	4,200	5,100	21,800	48	41	30	36	155
1886	7,400	5,600	4,200	5,200	22,400	53	40	30	37	160
1887	7,000	5,800	4,200	5,100	22,100	50	41	30	36	157
1888	7,000	6,000	4,500	5,500	23,000	50	43	32	39	164
1889	6,900	7,000	4,900	5,800	24,600	49	50	35	41	175
1890	6,900	6,400	4,700	6,800	24,800	49	46	34	48	177
1891	6,600	6,600	4,700	7,500	25,400	47	47	34	54	182
1892	6,400	7,200	4,800	9,200	27,600	46	52	34	65	197
1893	7,100	7,500	4,800	11,900	31,300	51	54	34	85	224
1894	8,200	8,700	5,700	15,100	37,700	59	62	41	108	270
1895	9,700	8,800	5,400	16,600	40,500	69	63	39	119	290
1896	10,600	8,800	6,200	16,800	42,400	76	63	44	120	303
1897	11,100	10,200	6,500	20,500	48,300	79	73	46	147	345
Average	9,200	8,600	4,400	4,700	26,900	65	61	32	34	192

The value and weight of gold produced are summed up thus :—

Years	Millions £					Tons				
	U. States	Australia	Russia	Various	Total	U. States	Australia	Russsia	Various	Total
1851-60 . . .	116	109	36	22	283	834	775	260	155	2,024
1861-70 . . .	100	103	38	23	264	710	734	275	165	1,884
1871-80 . . .	86	73	52	30	241	617	520	365	215	1,717
1881-90 . . .	69	61	45	50	225	492	434	320	358	1,604
1891-97 . . .	60	58	38	97	253	427	414	272	698	1,811
47 years . . .	431	404	209	222	1,266	3,080	2,877	1,492	1,591	9,040

The production of gold during the last two years was :—

	£ Sterling (000 omitted)			Weight Tons
	1896	1897	Average	
United States . . .	10,580	11,100	10,840	77
Transvaal	8,370	11,090	9,730	70
Australia	8,740	10,180	9,460	68
Russia	6,200	6,500	6,350	46
India	1,160	1,430	1,300	9
China	1,330	1,330	1,330	9
Mexico	1,220	1,360	1,290	9
Canada	560	1,200	880	6
Colombia	620	780	700	5
Guiana	510	520	520	4
Brazil	500	500	500	4
Various	2,640	2,290	2,470	18
Total . . .	42,430	48,280	45,370	325

In Australia the yield of gold averages as follows per ton of quartz: Victoria, ½ oz.; New South Wales, 1 oz.; New Zealand, 1.1 oz.; Queensland and Tasmania, 1.7 oz. The Transvaal goldfields began working in 1888, and their yield has been as follows :—

Year	£	Year	£
1889 . . .	1,300,000	1894 . . .	8,500,000
1890 . . .	1,750,000	1895 . . .	8,400,000
1891 . . .	2,500,000	1896 . . .	8,400,000
1892 . . .	4,200,000	1897 . . .	11,100,000
1893 . . .	5,200,000	1888-97 . . .	52,100,000

These mines have averaged less than half-an-oz (0.4) of gold per ton of quartz : yield, 32 shillings ; expenses, 25 ; profit, 7 shillings per ton of quartz.

Klondyke, in Arctic America, produced £2,000,000 of gold in 1898, the world's production for this year reaching £58,100,000.

The stock of precious metals at various dates was :—

Year	Tons		Tons of Silver to 1 of Gold
	Gold	Silver	
1848 . . .	3,575	113,000	31½
1860 . . .	5,299	118,250	22½
1870 . . .	6,583	126,360	19
1880 . . .	7,400	142,960	19½
1890 . . .	8,054	168,650	21
1897 . . .	9,165	194,000	21

The world would require an increase of 97,000 tons in the present stock of silver, or exactly 50 per cent., in order to place it on the same footing as in 1848, with regard to the quantity of gold. If the relative stocks of the two metals determined the price of silver it would be now 90 pence per ounce ; it has, on the contrary, fallen 55 per cent. from the normal price of 1851-60, which shows that it simply follows the cost of production. The following table shows the amount (see *Money*, page 777) of gold and silver used for coinage from 1851-1897, tons gross representing the actual weight of metal issued by the mints of all nations, tons net the supposed weight of new metal after deducting what was reminted :—

Period	Tons Gold		Tons Silver	
	Gross	Net	Gross	Net
1851-80 . . .	7,500	3,900	65,000	33,000
1881-96 . . .	3,500	1,500	39,000	19,000
Total . . .	11,000	5,400	104,000	52,000

Coined and uncoined metals stood approximately :—

Date	Gold, Tons			Ratio Coined
	Coined	Uncoined	Total	
1848 . . .	1,125	2,450	3,575	31.5
1880 . . .	5,025	2,375	7,400	68.0
1897 . . .	6,525	2,640	9,165	71.3

Date	Silver, Tons			
1848 . . .	45,200	67,800	113,000	40.0
1880 . . .	78,200	64,760	142,960	54.7
1897 . . .	97,200	96,800	194,000	50.1

In 1885 Newmann Spallart estimated the weight of coined money in the world thus :—

Year	Tons Gold	Tons Silver	Silver Ratio
1848 . . .	1,125	45,200	40 to 1
1885 . . .	5,925	88,100	15 ,, 1

The total production of precious metals in 1894 was :—

	Weight, Tons		Value, £		Total, £
	Gold	Silver	Gold	Silver	
U. States .	59	1,540	8,200,000	6,400,000	14,600,000
Australia .	63	560	8,700,000	2,300,000	11,000,000
S. Africa . .	61	...	8,500,000	...	8,500,000
Mexico . .	7	1,460	1,000,000	6,100,000	7,100,000
Russia . .	42	10	5,800,000	50,000	5,850,000
Bolivia . .	...	680	...	2,800,000	2,800,000
China . .	9	...	1,200,000	...	1,200,000
Germany .	3	190	400,000	800,000	1,200,000
Guiana . .	6	...	800,000	...	800,000
India . . .	6	...	800,000	...	800,000
Colombia .	4	50	600,000	200,000	800,000
Austria . .	2	60	300,000	250,000	550,000
France . .	...	100	...	400,000	400,000
Brazil . .	3	...	400,000	...	400,000
Peru . . .	...	100	...	400,000	400,000
Chile . . .	...	90	...	350,000	350,000
Japan . . .	1	60	100,000	250,000	350,000
Canada . .	1½	7	200,000	30,000	230,000
Spain . .	...	60	...	250,000	250,000
Argentina .	...	40	...	150,000	150,000
Various . .	5½	153	700,000	670,000	1,370,000
The World .	273	5,160	37,700,000	21,400,000	59,100,000

The production of silver has been as follows :—

| Years | Tons | | | Value, Millions £ |
	U. States	Various	Total	
1851–60 . .	70	8,880	8,950	81.4
1861–70 . .	2,370	9,840	12,210	110.4
1871–80 . .	7,720	14,380	22,100	182.7
1881–90 . .	13,330	18,360	31,690	223.3
1891–94 . .	6,790	12,030	18,820	104.8
1895 . . .	1,640	3,500	5,140	21.8
1896 . . .	1,730	3,360	5,090	21.6
46 years . .	33,650	70,350	104,000	746.0

Spanish America has produced 47,000 tons of silver since 1850, that is, almost half the total supply of the world, Mexico taking the lead :—

| Years | Tons | | | Value, Millions £ |
	Mexico	Peru, &c.	Spanish America	
1851–70 . .	9,530	4,140	13,670	123.8
1871–90 . .	14,780	7,540	22,320	169.4
1891–96 . .	8,290	2,520	10,810	58.8
46 years . .	32,600	14,200	46,800	352.0

The price of silver per ounce, and its ratio to gold in thirty years, have been as follows :—

Year	Pence	Ratio	Year	Pence	Ratio
1868 . .	60.5	15.6	1883 . .	50.6	18.6
1869 . .	60.5	15.6	1884 . .	50.6	18.6
1870 . .	60.5	15.6	1885 . .	48.6	19.4
1871 . .	60.5	15.6	1886 . .	45.4	20.8
1872 . .	60.5	15.6	1887 . .	44.6	21.1
1873 . .	59.2	15.9	1888 . .	42.9	22.0
1874 . .	58.3	16.2	1889 . .	41.7	22.1
1875 . .	56.9	16.6	1890 . .	47.7	19.8
1876 . .	52.7	17.9	1891 . .	45.1	20.9
1877 . .	54.8	17.2	1892 . .	39.7	23.7
1878 . .	52.6	17.9	1893 . .	35.6	26.5
1879 . .	51.2	18.4	1894 . .	28.9	32.6
1880 . .	52.2	18.1	1895 . .	29.8	31.7
1881 . .	52.0	18.2	1896 . .	30.7	30.7
1882 . .	52.0	18.2	1897 . .	27.0	35.0

In 1897 the silver money in use was 15½ times the weight of gold money.

According to the best authorities, the consumption yearly of gold and silver for manufactures has trebled since 1850, when Spallart estimated it at 25 tons of gold and 250 of silver. In recent years the estimates have been :—

| | Tons of Gold | | | Value, £ |
| | Soetbeer | Kimball | Molinari | |
	1871–80	1887	1895	1895
U. States . .	13.5	18	15.7	2,200,000
G. Britain . .	17.0	16	17.0	2,400,000
France . . .	16.9	12	12.0	1,700,000
Germany . .	11.8	11	15.0	2,100,000
Switzerland .	11.3	9	6.0	850,000
Italy, &c. . .	...	14	9.8	1,350,000
Total . .	83.8	80	75.5	10,600,000

| | Tons of Silver | | | Value, £ |
| | Soetbeer | Kimball | Molinari | |
	1871–80	1887	1895	1895
U. States . .	102	115	185	770,000
G. Britain . .	72	72	80	330,000
France . . .	75	75	120	500,000
Germany . .	75	82	100	420,000
Switzerland .	24	24	50	210,000
Russia . . .	32	32	32	130,000
Austria . . .	32	32	30	120,000
Italy, &c. . .	59	83	66	280,000
Total . .	471	515	663	2,760,000

Moreover, the loss of money from wear-and-tear and shipwreck is 2 tons of gold, 100 of silver yearly. The following table, allowing for these deductions, shows the net increase of the world's stock of precious metals :—

| Years | Gold, Tons | | |
	Production	Consumption	Net Increase
1851–60 . .	2,024	300	1,724
1861–70 . .	1,884	600	1,284
1871–80 . .	1,717	900	817
1881–90 . .	1,604	950	654
1891–97 . .	1,811	700	1,111
47 years . .	9,040	3,450	5,590

| | Silver, Tons | | |
Years	Production	Consumption	Net Increase
1851–60 . .	8,950	3,700	5,250
1861–70 . .	12,210	4,100	8,110
1871–80 . .	22,100	5,500	16,600
1881–90 . .	31,690	6,000	25,690
1891–96 . .	29,050	3,700	25,350
46 years . .	104,000	23,000	81,000

The current of bullion to and from India, Straits, and Ceylon in thirty-six years was as follows :—

| Years | Millions £ Sterling | | |
	Imported	Exported	Retained
1861–70 . . .	195	26	169
1871–80 . . .	110	44	66
1881–90 . . .	171	39	132
1891–96 . . .	104	49	55
36 years . . .	580	158	422

The bullion current may be summed up thus :—

| | Gold Imported, Millions £ | | | |
	1861–80	1881–88	1889–96	36 Years
Great Britain . .	351	96	205	652
France . . .	340	63	107	510
United States . .	73	64	49	186
Various . . .	252	187	373	812
Total . .	1,016	410	734	2,160

| | Exported | | | |
	1861–80	1881–88	1889–96	36 Years
Great Britain . .	284	96	155	535
France . . .	209	67	69	345
United States . .	187	35	118	340
Various . . .	336	212	392	666
Total . .	1,016	410	734	2,160

	Silver Imported, Millions £			
	1861–80	1881–88	1889–96	36 Years
Great Britain . .	225	66	88	379
France . . .	203	62	49	314
United States . .	30	23	28	81
Various . . .	443	209	224	876
Total . .	901	360	389	1,650

	Exported			
Great Britain . .	210	68	99	377
France . . .	126	49	46	221
United States . .	95	41	65	201
Various . . .	470	202	179	851
Total . .	901	360	389	1,650

	Total Bullion Imports, Millions £			
	1861–80	1881–88	1889–96	36 Years
Great Britain . .	576	162	293	1,031
France . . .	543	125	156	824
United States . .	103	87	77	267
Various . . .	695	396	597	1,688
Total . .	1,917	770	1,123	3,810

	Exports			
Great Britain . .	494	164	254	912
France . . .	335	116	115	566
United States . .	282	76	183	541
Various . . .	806	414	571	1,791
Total . .	1,917	770	1,123	3,810

In the whole period of 36 years we find that Great Britain has had a net influx of precious metals averaging £3,300,000 per annum; France, 7,200,000; while the United States show an average outflow of £7,600,000 per annum over the same lapse of years.

The following table shows the net balance of imports and exports in 8 years down to end of 1896 :—

	Imports, Mill. £		Exports, Mill. £	
	Gold	Silver	Gold	Silver
Great Britain . .	50	...	...	11
France . . .	38	3	...	...
United States . .	...	...	69	37
Various . . .	...	45	19	...
The World . .	88	48	88	48

See *Bullion*, page 649.

The following table shows the production, net imports and exports of gold, as regards the United States :—

Years	Gold, Millions $			
	Product	Imports	Exports	Balance
1847–51 . . .	156	...	7	149
1852–56 . . .	295	...	196	99
1857–61 . . .	244	...	196	48
1862–66 . . .	232	...	282	...
1867–71 . . .	243	...	189	54
1872–76 . . .	179	...	168	11
1877–81 . . .	208	179	...	387
1882–86 . . .	160	...	14	146
1887–91 . . .	165	...	63	102
1892–96 . . .	207	...	202	5
50 years . .	2,089	179	1,317	951

It appears that 45 per cent. of the gold produced in the United States remained in the country. The production, imports and exports of silver, at the nominal value of 60 pence per ounce, were as follows :—

Years	Silver, Millions $			
	Product	Imports	Exports	Balance
1847–51 . . .	...	...	6	...
1852–56 . . .	...	6	...	6
1857–61 . . .	3	9	...	12
1862–66 . . .	45	...	18	27
1867–71 . . .	77	...	76	1
1872–76 . . .	172	...	111	61
1877–81 . . .	209	...	36	173
1882–86 . . .	245	...	59	186
1887–91 . . .	321	...	58	263
1892–96 . . .	372	...	136	236
50 years . .	1,444	15	500	959

This shows that 60 per cent. of the production of silver remained in the country. The total value of precious metal which the above balances represent, as surplus of production over exports in 50 years, is 198 millions sterling for gold, and 67 millions for silver at its present depreciated value (27 pence per ounce).

The current of bullion to and from the United States is shown in American money as follows :—

Years	Millions $ Gold			
	Imports	Exports	Net Imports	Net Exports
1851–60 . . .	37	465	...	428
1861–70 . . .	140	536	...	396
1871–80 . . .	191	337	...	146
1881–90 . . .	333	244	89	...
1891–96 . . .	230	501	...	271
46 years . . .	931	2,083	...	1,152

	Silver			
1851–60 . . .	40	31	9	...
1861–70 . . .	49	124	...	75
1871–80 . . .	114	273	...	159
1881–90 . . .	151	270	...	119
1891–96 . . .	113	254	...	141
46 years . . .	467	952	...	485

	Gold and Silver			
1851–60 . . .	77	496	...	419
1861–70 . . .	189	660	...	471
1971–80 . . .	305	610	...	305
1881–90 . . .	484	514	...	30
1891–96 . . .	343	755	...	412
46 years . . .	1,398	3,035	...	1,637

The account for 6 years ending Dec. 1896 showed :—

	Bullion, Millions $	
	Imports from	Exports to
Great Britain . . .	74	330
France . . .	45	116
Other countries . .	224	309
Total . . .	343	755

Imports and exports in 1897 were even; each 115 million dollars.

The outflow of gold caused anxiety in 1895: the minimum of "free gold balance" in the Treasury was touched on the 11th of February 1895 ($41,200,000).

The stock of gold in Great Britain was estimated in 1760 at £25,000,000; of gold and silver in 1799 at £44,000,000; and of gold alone in 1812 at £15,000,000. The stock of coined money in the United States was estimated at 7 million dollars in 1774, and at 17 millions (£3,500,000) in 1804. Humboldt calculated the coined money of the world in 1825 at 325 millions sterling; Jacob, a better authority, at 380 millions.

We have seen that the production of gold since 1850 has been as follows:—

Period	Millions £ Sterling	Per Annum
1851–70	547	27.4
1871–80	241	24.1
1881–90	225	22.5
1891–96	162	27.0
46 years	1,175	25.1

The countries which absorbed the above quantities * were as follows:—

	Millions £ Sterling				Tons of Gold
	1851–70	1871–80	1881–96	46 yrs.	
U. Kingdom .	103	15	49	167	1,190
France . . .	204	53	33	290	2,060
Germany . .	3	27	29	59	420
Russia . . .	31	23	94	148	1,050
Austria . . .	16	19	44	79	560
Spain . . .	8	4	3	15	107
Portugal . .	3	4	8	15	107
Holland . .	2	5	10	17	120
Belgium . .	7	3	8	18	128
Switzerland .	2	1	8	11	78
Europe . . .	379	154	286	819	5,820
United States .	49	49	76	174	1,235
Other countries	119	38	25	182	1,294
The World . .	547	241	387	1,175	8,350

The production of silver in the same period was as follows:—

Period	Value		Weight	
	Millions £	Per Annum	Tons	Per Annum
1851–70 . . .	192	9.6	21,160	1,058
1871–80 . . .	183	18.3	22,100	2,210
1881–90 . . .	223	22.3	31,690	3,169
1891–96 . . .	148	24.7	29,050	4,842
46 years . .	746	16.2	104,000	2,261

The countries which absorbed the above quantities were as follows:—

	Millions £ Sterling				Tons of Silver
	1851–70	1871–80	1881–96	46 yrs.	
U. Kingdom .	4.3	11.9	...	4.0	500
Germany . .	16.9	17.6	8.5	43.0	5,200
Russia . . .	7.8	7.8	13.5	29.1	3,600
Spain . . .	4.3	8.2	6.9	19.4	2,400
Holland . .	9.7	2.0	1.1	12.8	1,500
Belgium . .	0.9	8.2	6.6	15.7	1,900
Various . .	0.2	2.0	10.9	13.1	1,600
Europe . . .	44.1	57.7	35.3	137.1	16,700
U. States . .	8.2	31.3	81.3	120.8	18,500
India . . .	160.3	46.5	95.3	302.1	37,800
China . . .	12.6	13.5	23.8	49.9	7,100
Other countries	8.8	34.0	147.5	190.3	31,500
Total . .	234.0	183.0	383.2	800.2	111,600
Deduct . . .	42.0	...	12.2	54.2	7,600
Balance . . .	192.0	183.0	371.0	746.0	104,000

In the period ending 1870 France exported 42 millions of silver, and Great Britain 12 millions in that ending 1896.

GRAIN

See *Agriculture*, page 613; *Food*, page 713; also *Grain*, page 310.

H

HAY AND STRAW

See page 311.

HEMP

The production and consumption of this fibre in 1895 were:—

	Acres	Produc. Tons	Consum. Tons	Manufacture Value, £
Great Britain .	...	...	70,000	5,200,000
France . . .	90,000	27,000	50,000	3,500,000
Germany . .	30,000	10,000	30,000	2,100,000
Russia . . .	2,010,000	247,000	177,000	9,000,000
Austria . . .	290,000	70,000	70,000	5,000,000
Italy . . .	260,000	78,000	30,000	2,000,000
United States .	60,000	18,000	140,000	10,000,000
Manilla . .	260,000	50,000	...	...
Various . .	100,000	30,000	63,000	4,200,000
Total . .	3,100,000	530,000	530,000	41,000,000

Production has increased 20 per cent. since Neumann Spallart's estimate for 1885. See Part I., page 312.

Exports of hemp from Russia were as follows:—

Year	Tons	Value, £	£ per Ton
1885 . . .	50,000	1,300 000	26
1890 . . .	55,000	1,600,000	29
1896 . . .	70,000	1,600,000	23

Imports into the United Kingdom and the United States were:—

Year	Tons	
	U. Kingdom	U. States
1888	50,000	90,000
1892	50,000	120,000
1895	70,000	120,000

The hemp factories of the United Kingdom had

* See Atkinson's lecture to the Royal Statistical Society, in March 1898.

32,000 spindles in 1870, and 54,000 in 1890, being an increase of 70 per cent.

Exports of hemp from Italy rose from 32,000 tons in 1885 to 48,000 tons in 1895.

HORSES

The United Kingdom is no longer able to raise a sufficient number of horses for its own requirements, but has to import some thousands yearly, as the trade returns show :—

Year	Number		Value, £	
	Imported	Exported	Imported	Exported
1887 . . .	11,600	9,500	200,000	550,000
1892 . . .	21,000	11,200	400,000	560,000
1897 . . .	49,500	34,500	1,250,000	820,000

Respecting the losses of horses in war, Vet.-Capt. F. Smith in the *Journal of the United Service*, April 1894, gives 40 pages of statistics. The following table shows the records which exist as to losses in cavalry and artillery :—

Battle	Men, Loss	Horses, Loss	Observation
Dettingen . . .	313	483	9 regiments
Fontenoy . . .	301	635	8 ,,
Tournay . . .	143	229	9 ,,
Talavera . . .	244	288	2 ,,
Waterloo . . .	4,727	5,572	Allies
Moodkee . . .	254	298	Sikh war
Ferozeshah . .	335	582	,,
Aliwal . . .	265	351	,,
Balaklava . . .	383	476	Crimea
Gettysburg . .	1,255	1,629	Amer. war
Chickamauga .	303	406	,,
Koeniggratz . .	929	843	Prussians
,,	979	2,140	Austrians
Custozza . . .	464	566	,,
Worth	197	276	Germans
Vionville . . .	2,126	2,626	,,
Gravelotte . .	1,109	1,559	,,
Sedan	491	840	,,

In the war of 1812, Bonaparte crossed the Niemen in June with 187,000 horses, but on November 6 he had only 95,000 left; three days after the passage of the Beresina, on December 13, only 1600 horses came back from Russia.

At Corunna four British regiments landed with 2490 horses, and in two months lost 1210. In Massena's retreat from Portugal he had 8800 horses, of which he lost 1955 in ten days. In the Crimean war the British landed 7377 horses, and on April 1 only 3698 survived, showing a loss of 50 per cent. in six months, 2120 having died for want of food. At the siege of Plevna the Russians lost 22,000 horses out of 66,000, used only as draught, exclusive of horses killed in action.

See *Cattle.*

HOSPITALS

In 1891 London had 86 hospitals, with 8888 beds, but owing to want of funds 2510 beds were always kept vacant, the maximum never being allowed to exceed 6370 indoor patients, while outdoor patients in 1890 were 1,057,000. There are, meantime, 17,440 beds for the sick poor of London, in Poor-Law Infirmaries and Hospitals maintained by local authorities, which brings up the total accommodation to 23,800 beds, or 6 per thousand of the population of London. Dr. Steel's table (1891) shows the number of beds occupied and the cost

of 75 London hospitals, as well as the number of patients admitted, thus :—

Hospital	Beds	Expend. £	Per Bed £	Patients
London . . .	622	56,700	91	8,503
Guy's . . .	418	34,300	82	5,385
St. George's .	316	27,700	88	4,029
St. Mary's . .	251	21,200	84	3,451
University College .	179	19,700	110	3,007
Middlesex . .	254	26,400	104	2,948
Westminster . .	175	14,100	81	2,572
Seamen's . . .	186	11,700	63	2,401
Ophthalmic . .	96	6,200	64	2,337
King's College .	163	20,000	123	2,189
Royal Free . .	133	10,600	80	2,019
Charing Cross . .	143	14,300	100	1,948
Brompton . .	275	25,800	93	1,669
West London . .	87	5,600	64	1,283
Shadwell . . .	78	6,800	86	1,074
15 principal . .	3,376	301,100	90	44,815
60 others . .	2,274	208,900	92	23,585
Total . .	5,650	510,000	91	68,400

In the larger hospitals each bed averaged 13 patients, in the smaller only 10, yearly : the average cost for each patient was 133 shillings in the large, 177 in the small, hospitals. The Poor-Law Infirmaries of London had 12,300 beds, with an annual expenditure of £440,000, equal to £36 per bed.

In Paris there are 30 hospitals, besides various asylums for *aged* persons : the returns for the year 1894 showed :—

	Hospitals	Asylums	Total
No. on January 1 .	11,566	10,125	21,691
Admitted during year .	163,817	7,993	171,810
Left, cured . .	148,173	6,380	154,553
Died	15,667	1,508	17,175
No. on December 31 .	11,543	10,230	21,773

Death-rate was 9½ per cent. in the hospitals, 15 per cent. in the aged asylums. The days of sickness in the hospitals averaged 26 to each patient admitted.

Switzerland is the country best supplied with hospitals, having 17,800 beds, or 6 to every thousand of population. See *Charities,* page 655.

HOUSES

The following table gives an approximate statement of the number and value of houses in the principal countries.

	Number of Houses	Value, Millions £	Per House	
			Value, £	Inhab.
United Kingdom .	7,874,000	2,490	315	5.1
France	8,829,000	2,159	245	4.4
Germany . . .	5,791,000	1,755	303	9.0
Russia	11,436,000	1,019	89	9.3
Austria	4,996,000	719	144	8.7
Italy	4,470,000	503	113	7.0
Spain and Portugal	3,810,000	355	93	6.1
Scandinavia . .	1,200,000	221	184	7.7
Belgium	1,060,000	175	165	6.2
Holland	730,000	178	244	6.7
Europe	50,196,000	9,574	190	7.1
United States . .	12,690,000	3,889	306	4.9
Australia . . .	804,000	174	216	4.8

The above is irrespective of public buildings, which in some countries are estimated at one-fifth of the value of houses, but includes all houses, whether occupied or not.

The last census of the United Kingdom showed as follows :—

With Rooms	England	Scotland	Ireland	Total
One or two .	985,000	536,000	472,000	1,993,000
Three . .	757,000	143,000	361,000	1,261,000
Four or more	4,389,000	194,000	37,000	4,620,000
Total . .	6,131,000	873,000	870,000	7,874,000

The rateable annual value in 1896 was as follows :—

	Houses	Annual Value, £	Average, £
England . . .	6,170,000	135,930,000	22.1
Scotland . . .	930,000	14,600,000	15.7
Ireland . . .	870,000	4,010,000	4.6
U. Kingdom . .	7,970,000	154,540,000	19.3

The capital value of house property compares with population as follows :—

	Millions £	£ per Inhab.
England	2,266	74
Scotland	243	58
Ireland	67	15
United Kingdom . .	2,576	65

In the following table is shown the increase in value of house property in ten years :—

	Millions £ Sterling			£ per Inhab.
	1886	1896	Increase	
England . . .	1,924	2,266	342	11.8
Scotland . . .	209	243	34	8.5
Ireland . . .	57	67	10	2.1
United Kingdom .	2,190	2,576	386	10.2

The annual increase averaged £38,600,000, which is equal to about one-fourth of the ordinary accumulation of wealth in the United Kingdom.

There are 490,000 uninhabited houses in the United Kingdom, or 6 per cent. of the total, but in Ireland the ratio is 8 per cent.

The number and value of houses in Great Britain increased in twelve years as follows :—

	Number		Valuation, £	
	1884	1896	1884	1896
England . .	5,272,000	6,166,000	111,600,000	136,700,000
Scotland . .	816,000	930,000	12,100,000	14,700,000
Total . .	6,088,000	7,096,000	123,700,000	151,400,000

The number increased 17, the valuation rental 22, per cent. Those under £20 a year are exempt from house-duty. The total for Great Britain (there is no house-tax in Ireland) showed as follows :—

	Houses		
	1884	1896	Increase
Under £20 . .	4,424,000	5,181,000	757,000
Over £20 . . .	1,172,000	1,380,000	208,000
Pub. buildgs., &c.	492,000	535,000	43,000
Total . .	6,088,000	7,096,000	1,008,000

	Valuation, £		
	1884	1896	Increase
Under £20 . .	36,500,000	45,600,000	9,100,000
Over £20 . . .	60,800,000	70,200,000	9,400,000
Pub. buildgs., &c.	26,400,000	35,600,000	9,200,000
Total . .	123,700,000	151,400,000	27,700,000

The rental valuation of houses in the three kingdoms compares with population as follows :—

	£ Sterling		£ per Inhab.	
	1884	1896	1884	1896
England . . .	111,600,000	136,700,000	4.1	4.5
Scotland . . .	12,100,000	14,700,000	3.2	3.5
Ireland . . .	3,400,000	3,900,000	0.7	0.8
U. Kingdom .	127,100,000	155,300,000	3.6	3.9

On the usual basis of computation that the rateable value represents 6 per cent. of the selling price of house property, it appears that the values compared with population result as follows :—

England

	Assessed, £	Value, Millions £	£ per Inhab.
London . .	35,820,000	597	133
Manchester . .	3,670,000	61	84
Liverpool . .	3,630,000	61	95
Birmingham . .	2,080,000	35	70
Leeds . .	1,340,000	22	55
Sheffield . .	1,150,000	19	57
Bradford . .	1,070,000	18	82
Bristol . .	1,060,000	18	82
Newcastle . .	910,000	15	75
Cardiff . .	830,000	14	90
Hull . .	760,000	13	62
Brighton . .	710,000	12	101
Portsmouth . .	630,000	11	66
Croydon . .	600,000	10	90
Oldham . .	600,000	10	70
15 Cities . .	54,860,000	916	108

Scotland

Glasgow . .	3,730,000	62	90
Edinburgh . .	2,750,000	46	140
Dundee . .	700,000	12	80
Aberdeen . .	600,000	10	75
4 Cities . .	7,780,000	130	97

Ireland

	Assessed, £	Value, £	£ per Head
Dublin . . .	1,170,000	19,500,000	55
Belfast . . .	910,000	15,200,000	61
Cork . . .	165,000	2,700,000	36
Derry . . .	90,000	1,500,000	45
Limerick . . .	69,000	1,150,000	28
Waterford . . .	47,000	800,000	40
6 Cities . . .	2,451,000	40,850,000	52

The average value of house property to inhabitant is higher in Edinburgh than elsewhere, London taking the second, Brighton the third place. Building sites in London reach the highest price in the world, £2,000,000 per acre. In 1884 two sites were sold in Threadneedle Street and Cheapside at £30 and £44 respectively per square foot. In March 1898 an acre was sold in Edinburgh (for a new printing-office for the *Scotsman*) at the price of £120,000, or 53 shillings per square foot, which is perhaps the highest price recorded in that city. Outside of the large cities and in the rural districts the average of house property per inhabitant is much lower, viz. :—

England

	Millions £ House-prop.	Number of Inhabitants	£ per Head
15 Cities . .	916	8,500,000	108
Outside . .	1,350	22,200,000	61
Total . .	2,266	30,700,000	74

Scotland

4 Cities . .	130	1,330,000	97
Outside . .	113	2,850,000	40
Total . .	243	4,180,000	58

Ireland

6 Cities . .	41	780,000	52
Outside . .	26	3,780,000	7
Total . .	67	4,560,000	15

U. Kingdom

25 Cities . .	1,087	10,610,000	97
Outside . .	1,489	28,830,000	53
Total . .	2,576	39,440,000	65

The rural population of Ireland has almost the same ratio of house property per head as the Russian Moujiks. The ratio of house property to population is higher in Belfast than in Dublin, as already shown : Belfast built 49,000 new houses between 1862 and 1896.

There are five principal companies or trusts for the purpose of providing dwellings for the working-classes of London at a minimum rental, viz. :—

	Capital £	Occupants	Pence per Room Weekly
Artisans' Company .	2,250,000	6,600	18
Peabody . . .	1,150,000	25,100	26
Industrial . . .	600,000	6,300	26
Guinness . . .	260,000	7,300	26
County Council . .	390,000	6,600	...
Total . .	4,650,000	51,900	27

Miss Octavia Hill and Lord Rowton have also built blocks of workmen's dwellings to be let at 5 per cent. of cost. Lord Rowton's cost £50 per occupant, and the rent averages 1 shilling a week per head. The buildings of the County Council cost £60 per occupant. The Council cleared 15 acres, demolishing 20 streets and 730 houses, and erecting on the site blocks to admit 6600 persons, with rooms 12 × 8½ ft. The blocks are intersected by 7 avenues 60 ft. wide, and have a central garden 270 ft. diameter. The Artisans' Company have 5000 cottages in the suburbs of London : average cost £400. See page 413.

FRANCE

An official return by M. Boutin in 1890 shows the number and rental of houses thus :—

Year	Houses	Rental, £	£ per House
1851 . . .	7,325,000	38,300,000	5.2
1890 . . .	8,829,000	110,800,000	12.6

The value in 1890 was returned as 1942 millions sterling. Among the houses are 5650 castles, with an average rental of £160 each. The rental classification was :—

Rental	Number	Ratio
Under £10	1,150,000	13.1
£10 to £24	2,633,000	29.8
£24 to £48	2,140,000	24.2
£48 to £96	1,390,000	15.6
Over £96	1,516,000	17.3
Total . . .	8,829,000	100.0

Boutin further shows that France built 835,000 houses between 1871 and 1881, of the value of £640 millions sterling.

There are various philanthropic associations in the large cities for providing cheap houses for workmen. That of Lyons has expended £150,000 ; those of Paris, Marseilles, &c., £280,000, in erecting buildings on the Peabody system.

AUSTRIA

An official statement regarding the houses of Vienna shows the population to be lodged thus :—

In	Tenements	Population
1 room	23,920	64,620
2 rooms	103,430	411,310
3 rooms	86,600	426,520
Over 3 rooms	72,810	439,450
Total . .	286,760	1,341,900

Only the last class is properly housed, that is, one-third of the population. It appears that 902,000 persons live in 214,000 tenements, containing 490,000 rooms, being an average of 2 persons to each room.

UNITED STATES

The estimated value of buildings, according to census commissioners, includes public buildings worth 17, and houses worth 83, per cent. of the total, which in 1890 stood thus :—

States	Millions £ Sterling			Value of Houses. £ per Inhabitant
	Houses	Public Buildings	Total	
New England .	433	86	519	92
Middle . .	1,434	287	1,721	101
South . .	428	85	513	23
West . .	1,594	319	1,913	63
Union . .	3,889	777	4,666	62

In 1897 the assessed value of houses and buildings in New York city was 513 millions sterling, equal to £205 per inhabitant.

The total number of houses in the Union is shown by census thus (1890) :—

	Occupied by		
	Owner	Tenant	Total
Urban . .	1,074,000	2,625,000	3,699,000
Rural . .	4,992,000	3,999,000	8,991,000
Total . .	6,066,000	6,624,000	12,690,000

In the towns 30 per cent., and in the rural districts 55 per cent., of the people lived in their own houses.

Some of the largest cities showed as follows :—

	Occupied by			Inhab. per House
	Owner	Tenant	Total	
New York .	20,000	293,000	313,000	5.2
Philadelphia .	46,000	158,000	204,000	5.2
Chicago .	63,000	157,000	220,000	5.0
Brooklyn . .	32,000	139,000	171,000	4.7
St. Louis . .	19,000	73,000	92,000	4.9
Boston . . .	17,000	73,000	90,000	5.0
Baltimore . .	23,000	64,000	87,000	5.0
Cincinnati . .	12,000	51,000	63,000	4.8
San Francisco	11,000	41,000	52,000	5.8
New Orleans .	10,000	38,000	48,000	5.0
10 Cities . .	253,000	1,087,000	1,340,000	4.9

In three years ending December 1893, New York built new houses to the value of £24,300,000, say £8,100,000 per annum, as compared with £6,400,000 in 1888.

AUSTRALIA

The census of 1891 gave only the number of houses, but the approximate value will be as in the following table :—

	No. of Houses	Value, £	£ per House	Inhab. per House
N. S. Wales .	242,000	68,000,000	280	4.7
Victoria . .	242,000	53,000,000	218	4.7
N. Zealand .	134,000	25,000,000	187	4.7
Queensland .	81,000	8,000,000	90	4.8
S. Australia .	64,000	12,000,000	188	5.0
Tasmania . .	30,000	6,000,000	200	4.9
W. Australia .	11,000	2,000,000	180	4.5
Total . .	804,000	174,000,000	216	4.8

The material of the houses was as follows :—

	Number	Ratio
Brick or stone	232,000	29.0
Wood, &c.	572,000	71.0
Total	804,000	100.0

The two great cities have a high ratio of house-property per inhabitant, viz. :—

	Value, £	£ per Inhab.
Sydney	50,600,000	124
Melbourne	58,000,000	122

It would appear that the total value of house property in Australia is equal to £46 per inhabitant, against £62 in the United States, and £29 in Canada.

CANADA

Municipal assessments show an increase of 130 per cent. in house property in 20 years, viz :—

	£ Sterling		
	1873	1893	Increase
Quebec . . .	15,500,000	30,600,000	15,100,000
Ontario . . .	22,300,000	57,600,000	35,300,000
Acadia	9,600,000	12,100,000	2,500,000
North-West . .	1,200,000	11,700,000	10,500,000
Total . .	48,600,000	112,000,000	63,400,000

Bodio's tables of building sites and rents of houses in various cities (1888–91) may be condensed as follows : the rents shown are the average paid in those years for an unfurnished house or flat of 6 rooms :—

	Sites, Shillings per Sq. Foot	Rents, Shillings per Month
Paris	2–120	268
Berlin	4–10	60
Brussels . . .	16–75	36
Vienna	3–140	130
Dresden . . .	1–7	32
Rome	4–60	80
Genoa	3–9	53
Naples	4–20	80

In the above table the rent for Paris probably refers to the better quarters. As regards building sites, 53 shillings per sq. foot was recently paid in Edinburgh, £20 in London.

HOUSE-TAX

This tax in certain cities shows as follows :—

	£ Stg.	Pence per Inhab.		£ Stg.	Pence per Inhab.
Berlin .	590,000	95	Naples .	420,000	190
Breslau .	85,000	60	Milan .	420,000	230
Rome .	490,000	270	Genoa .	210,000	230

In London the Inhabited House-duty averages £400,000, or 20 pence per inhabitant yearly, whereas in Italy this tax is equivalent to 20 pence a month per inhabitant.

HUNTING

See page 319.

I

INCOME

The incomes or earnings of nations in 1895 were approximately as follows :—

	Agricul.	Manufac.	Trade	Transport	Mines, &c.	Domes-tics	House-Rent	Professions	Total
	Millions £ Sterling								
United Kingdom . .	138	438	161	167	87	100	150	180	1,421
France	250	298	120	131	35	79	118	174	1,205
Germany . . .	250	345	135	143	48	61	92	211	1,285
Russia	324	190	103	108	54	31	47	147	1,004
Austria	192	164	73	76	28	25	37	112	707
Italy	122	95	45	47	8	18	27	74	436
Spain	81	60	30	35	8	9	14	40	277
Portugal . . .	16	14	7	4	2	3	4	11	61
Scandinavia . . .	49	41	23	22	20	8	12	25	200
Holland	22	25	21	8	1	7	10	15	109
Belgium	26	59	24	14	11	5	8	22	169
Switzerland . . .	12	20	10	6	1	3	5	9	66
Danubian States . .	50	28	16	10	5	4	7	20	140
Greece	8	5	3	3	1	1	2	5	28
Europe	1,540	1,782	771	774	309	354	533	1,045	7,108
United States . .	488	976	313	357	250	178	267	349	3,178
Canada	34	49	20	25	25	5	7	21	186
Australia . . .	42	42	20	25	15	14	21	34	213
Argentina . . .	28	20	10	12	...	5	7	13	95
Total . . .	2,132	2,869	1,134	1,193	599	556	835	1,462	10,780

In the above table the column of Mines, &c., comprises the aggregate earnings from mines, forests, and fisheries ; that of Professions includes the income of army, navy, and civil service, and of all persons not engaged in any of the preceding employments.

UNITED KINGDOM

Baxter's table for 1867, compared with the apparent earnings of the people of the United Kingdom in 1895, stands thus :—

Class	1867			1895		
	Number	Millions £	Average, £	Number	Millions £	Average, £
Over £5000	8,500	126	14,800	27,000	216	8,200
£1000 to £5000	48,800	83	1,700	103,000	165	1,600
£300 to £1000	178,300	88	490	360,000	144	400
£100 to £300	1,026,400	111	108	1,600,000	240	150
Under £100	12,458,000	406	33	15,910,000	656	41
Total	13,720,000	814	59	18,000,000	1,421	79

The earnings of the people were certainly under-estimated by Baxter in 1867. They were approximately as follows in 1895 * :—

	Millions £			
	England	Scotland	Ireland	U. King.
Agricultural . .	88	17	33	138
Manufacturing .	351	68	19	438
Mines, forests, &c. .	74	13	...	87
Trade . . .	126	23	12	161
Transport . .	137	21	9	167
House-rent . .	132	14	4	150
Domestics . .	88	10	2	100
Public service . .	44	4	3	51
Professions . .	104	17	8	129
Total . .	1,144	187	90	1,421

The above gives an average income of £38 *per inhabi-* tant in England, £45 in Scotland, and £20 in Ireland. If the above were divided among the number of persons of gainful occupation, according to census of 1891, it would give to each person in England £89, in Scotland £105, in Ireland £42, and for the whole United Kingdom £84, which is only 32 shillings a week.

FRANCE

There were by last census 17,300,000 persons of gainful pursuits, and the gross earnings may be estimated to be apportioned thus :—

Class	Number	Millions £	Average, £
Rich . . .	700,000	440	630
Middle . . .	2,500,000	240	96
Working . . .	14,100,000	525	37
Total . .	17,300,000	1,205	70

* See "Industries and Wealth of Nations," Longmans, 1896.

The Société Statistique de Paris in 1891 estimated the earnings of the French people at 944 millions sterling.

Leroy Beaulieu says that there are in Paris 36,000 persons with incomes over £500 a year.

GERMANY

The principal States stand in the following order of earnings :—

	Millions £ Sterling					
	Prussia	Bavaria	Saxony	Wurtem-berg	Baden, &c.	Total
Agriculture. .	155	35	10	10	40	250
Manufacture .	197	34	38	16	60	345
Mines, &c. . .	36	3	3	1	5	48
Trade . . .	80	15	11	6	23	135
Transport . .	86	16	11	6	24	143
House-rent . .	55	10	6	4	17	92
Domestics . .	36	7	4	3	11	61
Professions . .	125	23	16	8	39	211
Total . .	770	143	99	54	219	1,285

The census of 1895 gave 22,910,000 persons earning a livelihood, and judging by income-tax returns the earnings may be apportioned thus :—

	Number	Millions £	Average, £
Over £1100 . . .	30,000	115	3,800
£240 to £1100 . .	144,000	70	480
£150 to £240 . . .	360,000	67	185
Under £150 . . .	22,376,000	1,033	46
Total . . .	22,910,000	1,285	56

SCANDINAVIA

The three northern kingdoms show thus :—

	Millions £			
	Sweden	Norway	Den-mark	Scandi-navia
Agriculture . .	22	6	21	49
Manufactures .	23	8	10	41
Trade .	12	4	7	23
Transport .	10	7	5	22
Forests, &c. .	13	6	1	20
Domestics .	4	1	3	8
House-rent .	6	2	4	12
Professions .	12	6	7	25
Total . .	102	40	58	200

DANUBIAN STATES

The earnings of these States are approximately as follows :—

	Millions £ Sterling			
	Roumania	Servia	Bulgaria	Total
Agriculture . . .	27	10	13	50
Manufactures, &c.	16	7	10	33
Trade, &c. . . .	15	5	6	26
Professions, &c. .	17	6	8	31
Total . .	75	28	37	140

AUSTRIA-HUNGARY

The earnings of Austrians and Hungarians seem to be:

	Millions £ Sterling		
	Austria	Hungary	Total
Agriculture . . .	99	93	192
Manufactures . .	90	74	164
Trade . . .	39	34	73
Transport . . .	41	35	76
Mines, forests . .	17	11	28
House-rent . .	28	9	37
Domestics . .	19	6	25
Professions . .	64	48	112
Total . .	397	310	707

The above, divided among the number of persons following gainful pursuits in 1890, gives :—

	Earners	Millions £	Average, £
Austria . . .	13,570,000	397	29
Hungary . . .	7,390,000	310	42
Total . .	20,960,000	707	34

UNITED STATES

The distribution of earnings is approximately :—

	Millions £ Sterling				
	N. Eng.	Middle	South	West	Union
Agriculture . . .	19	65	124	280	488
Manufactures . .	156	380	74	366	976
Mining . . .	4	32	8	57	101
Forestry, &c. . .	12	23	56	58	149
Trade	38	96	43	136	313
Transport . . .	44	109	49	155	357
House-rent . . .	30	98	30	109	267
Domestics . . .	20	65	20	73	178
Professions . . .	40	108	50	151	349
Total . .	363	976	454	1,385	3,178

If we allow an increase of 10 per cent. on the number of persons earning livelihoods by census of 1890, the division of earnings will be thus :—

States	No. of Earners	Millions £	Average, £
New England .	2,200,000	363	165
Middle . . .	6,080,000	976	160
South . . .	6,820,000	454	67
West . . .	9,900,000	1,385	140
Union . .	25,000,000	3,178	127

CANADA

The earnings of Canada are approximately :—

	£ Sterling (000 omitted)				
	Ontario	Quebec	Acadia	N. West	Dominion
Agriculture .	19,400	5,800	3,100	5,700	34,000
Manufac. .	24,700	15,600	5,600	3,100	49,000
Trade, &c. .	22,100	11,900	6,600	4,400	45,000
Sundries .	22,200	15,900	13,400	6,500	58,000
Total .	88,400	49,200	28,700	19,700	186,000

Acadia comprises Nova Scotia, New Brunswick, and the other maritime provinces. The number of persons earning a livelihood in 1890 was 1,611,000, giving an average of £115 each, against £127 in the United States.

AUSTRALIA

The earnings of the different colonies for 1895 may be distinguished thus :—

£ Sterling (ooo omitted)

	Farming	Mining	Manufactures	Trade	House-rent	Sundries	Total
New South Wales . .	12,400	4,900	13,000	14,000	6,800	15,400	66,500
Victoria	9,600	2,800	17,000	14,200	7,300	13,900	64,800
New Zealand . . .	8,500	1,700	6,700	7,800	2,300	7,200	34,200
Queensland . .	5,800	2,700	2,400	4,800	1,900	5,300	22,900
South Australia . .	3,900	400	1,900	3,000	1,300	3,400	13,900
Tasmania . . .	1,300	700	800	1,200	1,000	1,800	6,800
West Australia . .	500	800	300	700	400	1,200	3,900
Total . .	42,000	14,000	42,100	45,700	21,000	48,200	213,000

Dividing the above among the earners, we find :—

	Earners	£ Sterling	£ each
New South Wales .	465,000	66,500,000	143
Victoria	502,000	64,800,000	129
New Zealand . .	253,000	34,200,000	135
Queensland . . .	180,000	22,900,000	127
South Australia . .	134,000	13,900,000	104
Tasmania	61,000	6,800,000	111
West Australia . .	25,000	3,900,000	156
Total . .	1,620,000	213,000,000	132

The general average per worker is £132, against £127 in the United States, £115 in Canada, and £84 in the United Kingdom.

INCOME-TAX

The assessments have risen in twenty years as follows :

England, £

	1876	1886	1896	Increase in 20 Years
Land . . .	50,200,000	46,000,000	39,400,000	...
Houses . .	83,900,000	115,400,000	135,900,000	52,000,000
Railways .	24,200,000	31,800,000	43,500,000	19,300,000
Mines . .	13,200,000	6,500,000	11,500,000	...
Professions .	318,300,000	333,300,000	375,600,000	57,300,000
Total .	489,800,000	533,000,000	605,900,000	116,100,000

Scotland, £

	1876	1886	1896	
Land . . .	7,500,000	7,300,000	6,100,000	...
Houses . .	9,400,000	12,600,000	14,600,000	5,200,000
Railways .	2,700,000	3,900,000	4,300,000	1,600,000
Mines . .	1,400,000	1,000,000	1,500,000	100,000
Professions .	32,900,000	35,300,000	39,100,000	6,200,000
Total .	53,900,000	60,100,000	65,600,000	11,700,000

Ireland, £

	1876	1886	1896	
Land . . .	9,300,000	10,000,000	9,900,000	600,000
Houses . .	3,600,000	3,400,000	3,900,000	300,000
Railways .	1,100,000	1,300,000	1,600,000	500,000
Professions .	21,500,000	22,000,000	22,800,000	1,300,000
Total .	35,500,000	36,700,000	38,200,000	2,700,000

United Kingdom, £

	1876	1886	1896	
Land . . .	67,000,000	63,300,000	55,400,000	...
Houses . .	96,900,000	131,400,000	154,400,000	57,500,000
Railways .	28,000,000	37,000,000	49,400,000	21,400,000
Mines . .	14,600,000	7,500,000	13,000,000	...
Professions .	372,700,000	390,600,000	437,500,000	64,800,000
Total .	579,200,000	629,800,000	709,700,000	130,500,000

The average annual increase of income since 1876 has been £5,800,000 in England, £590,000 in Scotland, and £130,000 in Ireland.

The assessments of Schedule D (for trades and professions only) in 1896, compared with 1876, show as follows, excluding all under £300 :—

England

	1876	1896	Decrease
Over £10,000 . .	1,082	823	259
£2000 to £10,000 .	7,633	6,689	944
£800 to £2000 .	15,900	15,268	632
£300 to £800 .	68,406	65,799	2,607
Over £300 . . .	93,021	88,579	4,442

Scotland

	1876	1896	Increase
Over £10,000 . .	146	120	...
£2000 to £10,000 .	933	936	3
£800 to £2000 .	1,772	1,743	...
£300 to £800 .	6,519	7,322	803
Over £300 . . .	9,370	10,121	751

Ireland

	1876	1896	Decrease
Over £10,000 . .	38	11	27
£2000 to £10,000 .	321	172	149
£800 to £2000 .	884	565	319
£300 to £800 .	3,719	2,850	869
Over £300 . . .	4,962	3,598	1,364

United Kingdom

	1876	1896	Decrease
Over £10,000 . .	1,266	954	312
£2000 to £10,000 .	8,887	7,797	1,090
£800 to £2000 .	18,556	17,576	980
£300 to £800 .	78,644	75,971	2,673
Over £300 . . .	107,353	102,298	5,055

Although the number of assessed persons has diminished in twenty years, the profits under Schedule D have risen from 272 to 352 millions, that is, an increase of 80 millions, or 4 millions a year. This is partly explained by the fact that companies count only as one person, and small traders are diminishing, to make way for companies.

The assessments of Schedule D, for trades and professions only, were in 1896 as follows, excluding all under £300 :—

Income, £	Number of Persons			
	England	Scotland	Ireland	U. King.
Over 10,000 .	823	120	11	954
2000–10,000 .	6,689	936	172	7,797
800–2000 . .	15,268	1,743	565	17,576
300–800 . .	65,799	7,322	2,850	75,971
Total . .	88,579	10,121	3,598	102,298

The ratio of such persons to population is :—

	Population	Over £300	Ratio per 100,000
England . . .	30,720,000	88,579	289
Scotland . . .	4,190,000	10,121	241
Ireland	4,560,000	3,598	79

PRUSSIA

The assessments of income for 1897 compare with previous returns as follows :—

£ Sterling	Numbers Assessed			
	1881	1886	1893	1897
150 to 480 . .	150,700	172,000	260,100	272,800
Over 480 . . .	21,800	26,800	56,700	58,300
Total . .	172,500	198,800	316,800	331,100

The increase has been in the towns, while the rural districts show a decline in incomes over £480, viz. :—

£ Sterling	Urban		Increase per Cent.
	1893	1897	
150 to 480 . .	190,800	203,200	6.0
Over 480 . .	46,940	48,800	4.0
Total . .	237,740	252,000	5.5
	Rural		
150 to 480 . .	69,300	69,600	1.0
Over 480 . .	9,810	9,490	0
Total . .	79,110	79,090	0

It will be observed that since 1881 the number of persons with moderate incomes, between £150 and £480, increased 80 per cent., but it appears, moreover, that incomes over £480 increased 167 per cent., which shows that a congestion of wealth is taking place, just as in Great Britain.

INDIANS

The census of 1890 shows that the number of Indians in the United States was 248,000, against 332,000 in 1880, a decline of 25 per cent. They were classed as Civilised and Prairie, thus :—

States	Civilised	Prairie	Total
New England . .	1,400	...	1,400
Middle . . .	1,800	5,400	7,200
South . . .	6,800	64,900	71,700
Prairie . . .	16,800	46,200	63,000
Pacific . . .	32,000	72,900	104,900
Union . . .	58,800	189,400	248,200

The Cherokees numbered 29,600, the Creeks 14,600, the Choctaws 14,400, and the rest was made up of a variety of tribes. The total was 125,700 males and 122,500 females. See *Indians*, p. 123.

INDUSTRIES *

	Millions £ Sterling					£ per Inhabitant
	Agri-culture	Manu-factures	Mining, &c.	Trans-port	Total	
U. Kingdom	230	876	87	167	1,360	34
France . .	416	596	35	122	1,169	30
Germany . .	417	690	48	133	1,288	24
Russia . .	540	380	54	99	1,073	9
Austria . .	319	328	28	69	744	18
Italy . . .	204	190	8	31	433	14
Spain . . .	135	121	8	32	296	17
Portugal . .	26	29	2	4	61	12
Sweden . .	37	45	13	9	104	21
Norway . .	9	17	6	7	39	19
Denmark . .	35	19	1	5	60	27
Holland . .	36	49	1	8	94	20
Belgium . .	44	118	11	14	187	30
Switzerland .	20	41	1	6	68	23
Danub. States	83	56	5	10	154	14
Greece . .	14	10	1	3	28	13
Europe . .	2,565	3,565	309	719	7,158	20
U. States .	813	1,952	224	327	3,316	47
Canada . .	57	98	26	23	204	40
Australia . .	70	85	20	23	198	47
Total .	3,505	5,700	579	1,092	10,876	25

INFIRM

The proportions of insane, blind, and deaf mutes in the principal countries are as follows :—

				Per 100,000 of Population			
				Insane	Blind	Deaf Mutes	Total
England	.	.	.	291	81	49	421
Scotland	.	.	.	289	69	53	411
Ireland .	.	.	.	416	114	72	602
France .	.	.	.	250	84	55	389
Germany	.	.	.	240	88	92	420
Russia .	.	.	.	110	187	57	354
Austria .	.	.	.	217	81	129	427
Hungary	.	.	.	161	105	109	375
Italy .	.	.	.	170	93	66	329
Spain .	.	.	.	70	120	63	253
Sweden .	.	.	.	342	82	111	535
Norway .	.	.	.	387	128	107	622
Finland .	.	.	.	270	155	116	541
Belgium	.	.	.	187	81	41	309
Switzerland	.	.	.	110	75	230	415
Bulgaria	.	.	.	213	314	56	583
United States	.	.	.	323	81	65	469
Canada .	.	.	.	276	70	100	446
Australia	.	.	.	318	70	36	424
Average	.	.	.	244	109	85	438

It appears that 4½ persons per thousand, or one in 227 of all living, is mentally or bodily afflicted as in the above table. Meantime the average of 4.4 per thousand is exceeded in Norway, Ireland, Bulgaria, Finland, Sweden, and United States.

* See "Industries and Wealth of Nations," Longmans, 1896.

UNITED KINGDOM

The numbers of insane in 1895 were :—

	Male	Female	Total	Per 100,000 Inhab.
England . . .	42,796	51,285	94,081	310
Scotland . . .	5,426	6,234	11,660	280
Ireland . . .	9,121	8,534	17,655	390
United Kingdom .	57,343	66,053	123,396	316

Returns for 1896 are worse, viz. :—

	Insane	Per 100,000 Pop.
Great Britain . .	109,930	314
Ireland . .	18,966	416
United Kingdom .	128,896	328

The number of insane in the United Kingdom has increased as follows :—

Year	Number	Per 100,000 Inhab.
1862	55,525	181
1872	77,013	241
1882	98,871	294
1896	128,896	328

The ratio of age among lunatics in 1851 and 1881 was as follows :—

	Males		Females	
	1851	1881	1851	1881
Under 15 . . .	13	2	6	1
15–25 . . .	86	60	66	52
25–45 . . .	497	462	436	399
45–65 . . .	333	376	399	417
Over 65 . . .	71	100	93	131
Total . .	1,000	1,000	1,000	1,000

Dr. Humphreys maintains that the increased ratio of insane in England is due to kinder treatment, which of course diminishes the mortality. The death-rate yearly per thousand has been :—

Years	Males	Females	Total
1871–75 . . .	160	112	133
1876–80 . . .	105	67	83
1881–85 . . .	80	75	77
1886–88 . . .	78	71	74

Dr. Tuke shows the ratio of recoveries has been at Wakefield thus :—

Years		Per 1000
1849–58	.	451
1859–68	.	405
1879–87	.	407

Pauper lunatics in Ireland cost £22 per head yearly, the local rates contributing 60 per cent., the Government 40 per cent., of the cost (£330,000).

The number of blind in the United Kingdom was as follows :—

	Number		Per Million Pop.	
	1861	1891	1861	1891
England . . .	19,352	23,467	957	809
Scotland . . .	2,820	2,797	921	693
Ireland . . .	6,879	5,341	1,184	1,140
United Kingdom .	29,051	31,605	999	836

The number of deaf mutes in the same years was :—

	Number		Per Million Pop.	
	1861	1891	1861	1891
England . . .	12,323	14,192	610	489
Scotland . . .	2,335	2,125	762	527
Ireland . . .	4,930	3,365	850	720
United Kingdom .	19,588	19,682	675	520

It will be seen that the numbers of blind and of deaf mutes to population have declined remarkably since 1861, the blind 16 per cent., and deaf mutes 22 per cent.

There are 50 institutions in the United Kingdom, including 8 in Scotland and 4 in Ireland, for instructing deaf and dumb persons, and the number of inmates was as follows :—

	1861	1895
England . . .	1,001	2,755
Scotland . . .	240	525
Ireland . . .	399	555
United Kingdom .	1,640	3,835

The latest returns of schools for deaf mutes, in 1895, show thus :—

	Schools	Teachers	Pupils
United Kingdom . .	50	250	3,835
France	84	364	4,570
Germany . . .	97	595	6,280
Russia . . .	12	...	800
Austria . . .	31	...	1,820
Italy . . .	51	...	2,140
Switzerland . .	17	...	570
Scandinavia, &c. . .	30	...	2,010
Europe . .	372	...	22,025
United States . .	60	600	7,500
South America . .	43	...	2,700
Australia . . .	4	...	160
Asia, &c. . . .	10	...	270
Total . .	489	...	32,655

AUSTRIA

The census of Austria, without Hungary, for 1890 compares with that of 1880 as follows :—

	Number		Per Million Pop.	
	1880	1890	1880	1890
Insane . . .	45,140	51,880	2,050	2,170
Blind . . .	20,150	19,360	910	810
Deaf mutes . .	22,360	30,840	1,010	1,290
Total . .	87,650	102,080	3,970	4,270

The sexes in 1890 were as follows :—

	Number		Per Mill. Persons	
	Males	Females	Males	Females
Insane . . .	28,025	23,855	2,400	1,955
Blind . . .	10,100	9,260	863	760
Deaf mutes .	16,960	13,880	1,450	1,138
Total . .	55,085	46,995	4,713	3,853

HUNGARY

The census of 1890 showed as follows :—

	Number		Per Mill. Persons	
	Males	Females	Males	Females
Insane . . .	15,346	12,812	1,770	1,456
Blind .	9,174	9,189	1,058	1,044
Deaf mutes .	10,310	8,714	1,190	990
Total .	34,830	30,715	4,018	3,490

Compared with the whole population the number of afflicted persons is 3745 per million, against 4270 in Austria.

SWEDEN

According to the census of 1890 we find as follows :—

	Number		Per Mill. Persons	
	Males	Females	Males	Females
Insane . . .	8,595	7,727	3,708	3,132
Blind . .	1,880	2,068	812	838
Deaf mutes .	2,952	2,355	1,274	955
Total .	13,427	12,150	5,794	4,925

This gives an average for the whole Swedish people of 5330 afflicted persons per million, as compared with 4636 in the United Kingdom, and 4683 in the United States.

NORWAY

The census of 1890 gives the infirm as follows :—

	Number		Per Mill. Persons	
	Males	Females	Males	Females
Insane . . .	3,846	3,903	4,018	3,755
Blind . .	1,287	1,278	1,351	1,230
Deaf mutes .	1,176	963	1,235	927
Total .	6,309	6,144	6,604	5,912

The total number afflicted is equal to 6226 persons in a million of population, against 5330 in Sweden.

FINLAND

According to the census of 1890 we find as follows :—

	Number		Per Mill. Persons	
	Males	Females	Males	Females
Insane . . .	3,505	2,950	2,998	2,442
Blind . .	1,328	2,374	1,135	1,966
Deaf mutes .	1,537	1,230	1,313	1,018
Total .	6,370	6,554	5,446	5,426

The total number of afflicted persons is equal to 5432 in a million of population, which is a little higher than the ratio in Sweden.

BULGARIA

The census of 1890 gave the following results :—

	Number		Per Mill. Persons	
	Males	Females	Males	Females
Insane . . .	2,006	1,168	1,250	753
Blind .	5,520	4,411	3,440	2,846
Deaf mutes .	1,126	654	704	422
Total .	8,652	6,233	5,394	4,021

The total gives a ratio of 4715 afflicted persons per million inhabitants.

UNITED STATES

The census of 1890 compared with that of 1880 as follows :—

	Number		Per Million Pop.	
	1880	1890	1880	1890
Insane	168,854	202,094	3,366	3,227
Deaf mutes . .	33,878	40,592	675	648
Blind	48,928	50,568	976	808
Total . .	251,660	293,254	5,017	4,683

There is a decline in all three classes of infirmity, and it is to be observed that insanity and blindness are more frequent among foreign settlers than among the native-born population, the figures for 1890 showing these ratios :—

	Per Million Persons			
	Native	Foreign	Male	Female
Insane . . .	3,060	4,180	3,320	3,140
Deaf mutes . .	680	460	700	590
Blind . . .	780	990	880	740
Total .	4,520	5,630	4,900	4,470

	White	Coloured	Total Pop.
Insane . . .	3,360	2,290	3,227
Deaf mutes . .	680	420	648
Blind . . .	790	950	808
Total .	4,830	3,660	4,683

The coloured population suffers more from blindness, but less from other infirmities, than the white. The census further shows that the mothers of afflicted persons were born in the following countries :—

Mothers Born in	Insane	Blind	Dumb	Total
U. States * . .	145,557	37,842	30,013	213,412
England . . .	4,188	1,562	1,056	6,806
Scotland . .	1,115	370	254	1,739
Ireland . . .	22,118	4,290	2,229	28,637
France . . .	653	206	146	1,005
Germany . . .	15,408	3,509	3,833	22,750
Russia . . .	684	127	241	1,052
Austria . . .	837	152	218	1,207
Italy . . .	407	54	52	513
Scandinavia . .	4,001	566	665	5,232
Canada . . .	1,986	730	925	3,641
Various . . .	5,140	1,160	960	7,260
Total . .	202,094	50,568	40,592	293,254

* The census makes the items of this line less, and leaves 30,841 mothers unaccounted for, who should be counted as Americans, and are included in this table.

Comparing the parentage of afflicted persons with the population of each nationality in the United States in 1890, we find as follows :—

	In One Million Persons			
	Insane	Blind	Dumb	Total
Americans . .	2,726	709	562	3,997
English . . .	4,607	1,718	1,162	7,487
Scotch . . .	4,595	1,525	1,046	7,166
Irish . . .	11,830	2,294	1,192	15,316
Canadians . .	2,026	745	943	3,714
French . . .	5,760	1,817	1,288	8,865
Germans . . .	5,495	1,252	1,368	8,115
Russians . . .	3,762	698	1,325	5,785
Austrians . . .	3,482	632	905	5,020
Italians . . .	2,240	297	286	2,823
Scandinavians . .	4,280	606	712	5,598
Various . . .	6,120	1,380	1,143	8,643
General population .	3,227	808	648	4,683

Italians, Canadians, and Americans are much below the average as regards infirmities, while Irish, French, and Germans are greatly in excess. The ratio of insanity among Irish is extraordinary, and it is remarkable that in Ireland likewise the rate is higher than in any other nation of Europe. There is, of course, a difference between the rates of insane, &c., for persons native or foreign born, and for persons of native or foreign parentage (as regards the mother), as shown thus :—

	Number		Rate per Million	
	Natives	Foreigners	Natives	Foreigners
Insane . .	163,410	38,684	3,060	4,180
Blind . . .	41,652	8,916	780	990
Deaf mutes .	36,337	4,255	680	460
Total . .	241,399	51,855	4,520	5,630

	Of Mother		Rate per Million	
	American	Foreign	American	Foreign
Insane . .	145,557	56,537	2,726	6,106
Blind . . .	37,842	12,726	709	1,374
Deaf mutes .	30,013	10,579	562	1,142
Total . .	213,412	79,842	3,997	8,622

The census makes a distinction of two classes ; persons really insane, and those who are feeble-minded, viz. :—

	Number		Per Million Pop.	
	1880	1890	1880	1890
Insane . . .	91,959	106,485	1,833	1,700
Feeble-minded .	76,895	95,609	1,533	1,527
Total . .	168,854	202,094	3,366	3,227

As regards the former class, the following table shows the ratios according to age :—

	Male	Female	White	Col.	Total
0–20 . . .	21	18	17	53	19
21–30 . .	150	119	131	195	135
31–40 . .	260	226	242	258	243
41–50 . .	238	245	243	221	241
51–60 . .	166	193	182	134	180
61–70 . .	101	118	111	76	109
Over 70 . .	64	81	74	63	73
	1,000	1,000	1,000	1,000	1,000

Under 40 the rate of insanity is heavier among males than females, also among coloured people than whites, but after 40 the tables are reversed. Nevertheless, taken altogether, insanity prevails much more among males than females, and also among whites than coloured people, viz. :—

	Insane per Million		
	Males	Females	Total
Whites . .	3,450	3,260	3,360
Coloured . .	2,360	2,220	2,290
Total population	3,320	3,140	3,227

CANADA

The census of 1891 compares with that of 1881 thus :—

	Number		Per 100,000 Pop.	
	1881	1891	1881	1891
Insane . .	9,940	13,355	230	276
Blind . .	3,020	3,380	70	70
Deaf mutes .	5,180	4,840	120	100
Total .	18,140	21,575	420	446

In 1891 the statistics of insanity were as follows :—

	Number		Per 100,000 Persons	
	Males	Females	Males	Females
Married . .	1,239	1,576	156	199
Unmarried .	5,441	4,065	340	280
Widowed .	482	552	768	425
Total .	7,162	6,193	291	261

The nationality of the insane was as follows :—

	Number	Ratio
Canadians	6,906	51.7
Foreigners	3,044	22.8
Of foreign parentage . .	3,405	25.5
Total . . .	13,355	100.0

The rate of insanity among foreign (and British) settlers was 468 per 100,000 persons, whereas the native-born, including children of foreigners, had a rate of only 246 per 100,000. With regard to age the returns show :—

		Number	Per 100,000 Persons
Under 15		762	43
15–20		701	136
20–30		2,429	282
30–40		2,643	440
Over 40		6,820	575
Total . . .		13,355	276

The rate of insanity, 276 per 100,000, compares favourably with 323 in the United States and 303 in Australia.

3 B

AUSTRALIA

The census of 1891 gave the following results :—

	Insane	Blind	Mutes	Total	Per Mill. Pop.
N. S. Wales .	3,415	741	383	4,539	4,040
Victoria . . .	4,125	995	364	5,484	4,810
New Zealand .	1,926	274	166	2,366	3,777
Queensland . .	1,104	199	154	1,457	3,696
South Australia .	936	247	234	1,417	4,430
Tasmania . .	429	165	54	648	4,410
West Australia .	136	54	11	201	4,020
Total . .	12,071	2,675	1,366	16,112	4,240

Taking all the colonies in a group, the ratio of afflicted persons to population is 9 per cent. lower than in the United Kingdom, and nearly 10 per cent. lower than in the United States. In December 1894 the returns of lunatic asylums were as follows :—

	Inmates Number	Per Mill. Inhab.	Expense £	£ per Patient
New South Wales .	3,587	2,870	85,000	23.6
Victoria	4,116	3,480	89,000	21.6
New Zealand . . .	2,168	3,097	45,000	20.8
Queensland . . .	1,340	2,910	32,000	24.0
South Australia . .	893	2,502	23,000	25.8
Tasmania	367	2,290	11,000	30.0
West Australia . .	148	1,620	5,000	33.8
Total . .	12,619	3,030	290,000	23.0

The ratio of insane is 303 per 100,000 inhabitants, against 323 in the United States, 290 in Great Britain, and 416 in Ireland. It will be observed that although New Zealand has a higher rate of insanity than the Australian continent or Tasmania, its sum of afflicted persons of all kinds is only 378 per 100,000 of population, while the general average for Australasia is 424.

INSANE

See *Infirm*, page 750, also *Insane*, page 327.

INSURANCE

The number of Life Insurance Companies in the United Kingdom fell from 95 in 1886 to 82 in 1896, and the aggregate amount of business rose nearly 50 per cent., viz. :—

	1886	1896	Increase
Number of Policies	902,000	1,494,000	63 p. cent.
Amount, £ . . .	421,000,000	582,000,000	38 ,,
Premiums, £ . .	12,800,000	18,700,000	46 ,,
Assets, £ . . .	143,000,000	204,400,000	43 ,,
Paid-up Capital, £	11,300,000	12,300,000	9 ,,

Income and expenditure in 1896 were as follows :—

Income, £		*Expenditure*, £	
Premiums . .	18,700,000	Policies . . .	16,800,000
Investments . .	10,400,000	Sundries . . .	4,000,000
Total . .	29,100,000	Total . .	20,800,000

Assets in 1896 were made up as follows :—

	£
Mortgages	83,400,000
Debentures . . .	35,300,000
Stocks, &c. . . .	85,700,000
Total . . .	204,400,000

The business of 1882 compared with 1896 showed the relative progress in 14 years as follows :—

	1882	1896
Premiums	100	160
Claims	100	138
Assets	100	159

The investments which constituted the assets of the Companies gave a net return of 4¼ per cent. in 1882, and 3¾ in 1896.

The following table shows how much of the money received as premiums in Ordinary Companies goes back to insured persons under the head of claims, and how much goes for management, out of the total income :—

Year	Premiums £	Claims £	Per-centage
1885 . . .	12,850,000	11,350,000	88.3
1890 . . .	14,830,000	11,780,000	79.6
1895 . . .	18,660,000	13,610,000	73.0

	Income £	Management £	
1885 . . .	19,640,000	1,870,000	9.5
1890 . . .	22,870,000	2,120,000	9.3
1895 . . .	28,800,000	2,720,000	9.4

Turning to Industrial Companies the results to insured persons are less favourable :—

Year	Premiums £	Claims £	Per-centage
1885 . .	3,550,000	1,370,000	38.6
1890 . .	5,030,000	2,180,000	43.4
1895 . .	6,620,000	2,770,000	41.8

	Income £	Management £	
1885 . . .	3,690,000	1,500,000	40.5
1890 . . .	5,310,000	2,220,000	41.9
1895 . . .	7,100,000	2,920,000	41.1

It is evident that State insurances would be more beneficial to the public than the present system.

There are also industrial assurances for the working classes, viz. :—

	1887	1893	Increase
Policies . . .	9,146,000	13,214,000	4,068,000
Amount, £ . .	83,200,000	127,300,000	44,100,000
Premiums, £ .	5,040,000	5,930,000	890,000

The average amount of each policy is under £10, the object in most cases being to pay funeral expenses. Children are so often insured in this way that terrible abuses are at times reported in the police courts. Many eminent physicians regard these assurances as causes of child murder and wilful neglect or ill-treatment of the young.

The British Government issues insurances and annuities through the Post-Office and National Debt Office, the returns for 1896 comparing with 1887 thus :—

	Number		Amount, £	
	1887	1896	1887	1896
Post-Office	1,416	3,633	53,400	130,800
National Debt Office	1,000	514	60,000	34,900
Total . .	2,416	4,147	113,400	165,700

	Receipts, £		Payments, £	
	1886	1896	1886	1896
Post-Office	235,000	868,000	163,000	365,000
National Debt Office	688,000	475,000	...	...
Total . .	923,000	1,343,000	...	...

Annuities issued by the Post-Office in 1896 were for the average amount of £28 a year, say 11 shillings a week : the price paid by insurer averaged £375, so that the annuity averaged 7½ per cent. on the sum paid for it.

GERMANY

There are three kinds of compulsory insurance, showing in 1894 as follows :—

Against	No. Insured	Premiums £	Shillings per Head
Sickness . .	7,107,000	5,240,000	15.0
Accident . .	18,191,000	3,260,000	3.6
Old age . .	11,200,000	4,640,000	8.3

All the above persons were insured in two classes, the total numbers being only 18,200,000. The persons insured against sickness had 46,200,000 days of sickness in 1894, that is, 6½ days each. Those insured against accident had in the same year 6250 killed and 62,430 injured ; that is to say, one operative in 3000 was killed, and one in 300 injured or disabled. In a period of twelve years to December 1896, there were 349,000 operatives killed or disabled, which was equivalent to 48 per 10,000, the ratio being higher in manufactures than in agriculture, viz. :—

In agricultural labours	. .	38.4 per 10,000
In manufactures .	. . .	67.2 ,,

The number of killed or disabled during the last two years showed thus :—

Year	Insured	Injured	Per 10,000
1895	18,380,000	74,467	40.5
1896	17,620,000	85,272	48.4

Compensation paid for injuries in 1896 was as follows :—

	Insured	Injured	£	Average £
Agricultural . .	11,190,000	54,210	630,000	12
Manufacturing .	6,430,000	31,062	1,940,000	63
Total . .	17,620,000	85,272	2,570,000	30

The average paid for injuries to agricultural labourers was low, because they were mostly slight : of 10,000 such labourers only five were killed or permanently disabled ; 44 were slightly injured, the total number compensated being 49 per 10,000. The cost of management for both classes was £540,000, or sevenpence a year for each of the persons insured. Hospital and burial expenses amounted to £213,000. The number of widows and orphans receiving pensions was 86,000 : a widow's pension ceases if she re-marries. As regards the insurance for old age, there were in 1894 in enjoyment of pension 329,000 persons, being nearly 4 per cent. of the number insured. These pensions summed up £2,300,000, or £7 each, to which the Government adds £5, making in all £12 a year. The company charges for each operative

8 shillings a year, from the age of 20 until 50, 4 shillings from the master, and 4 from the man : the reserve fund on hand in 1894 amounted to £5,850,000 sterling. The cost of management for this section of insurance was £220,000, or sixpence per head yearly.

The premiums are made up as follows, yearly :—

Paid by	Sickness £	Accidents £	Old Age £	Total £
Masters . .	1,500,000	3,260,000	2,320,000	7,080,000
Operatives .	3,740,000	...	2,320,000	6,060,000
Total .	5,240,000	3,260,000	4,640,000	13,140,000

Of the total amount collected yearly the masters contribute almost 55 per cent., the men a little more than 45 per cent. The masters find that the burthen on them is £13 to every £1000 paid in wages, that is, about 3 pence to the pound sterling. From this it appears that the employers in Germany pay in wages 544 millions sterling, equal to £30 per head on the number of persons insured, say 12 shillings a week, wfth 2 pence a week added for insurance. The Companies have, moreover, a certain income from investments of accumulated reserves, the annual receipts and expenditure of all kinds summing up as follows :—

Class	Receipts, £	Outgoings, £	Reserve, £
Sickness . . .	6,600,000	6,200,000	5,500,000
Accident . . .	3,900,000	3,300,000	5,100,000
Old age . . .	5,000,000	2,500,000	5,900,000
Total . . .	15,500,000	12,000,000	16,500,000

The returns for the Insurance Companies of Miners in Germany during ten years ending December 31, 1894, show as follows :—

	Yearly Average		
	Collieries	Other Mines	Total
Men insured . .	238,000	124,000	362,000
Wages, £. . .	10,700,000	4,300,000	15,000,000
Killed	602	170	772
Disabled . . .	1,913	483	2,396
Widows left . .	380	117	497
Orphans left . .	1,063	304	1,367

The compensation paid, according to the actuaries' estimates, for capitalising pensions, and including cash payments, averaged as follows :—

	£		£
Person injured .	94	Orphan . . .	53.1
Widow . .	121.1	Relative . . .	90.8

The expenditure for such compensation averaged 26 shillings on each coal-miner, and 24 shillings on the number of miners all round. It amounted to 2.8 per cent. of the wages of all miners. The expenses were as follows, including capital of pensions :—

For	Yearly Average		
	Colliers, £	Others, £	All Miners, £
Sickness . .	72,000	17,000	89,000
Funeral . .	43,000	54,000	97,000
Pensions . .	125,000	27,000	152,000
Widows, &c. .	70,000	17,000	87,000
Total . .	310,000	115,000	425,000

FRANCE

The returns are incomplete, but 19 principal companies showed in 1896 as follows (amount of fire and maritime policies estimated from sums paid for premium):—

	Premiums, £	Policies, £	Do. Paid, £
Life . . .	...	139,000,000	2,100,000
Fire . . .	4,040,000	4,440,000,000	2,100,000
Maritime . .	800,000	200,000,000	740,000
Total . .	...	4,779,000,000	...

The death-rate of the life insurance offices, or rather the payments on policies of persons who died, compared with amount of policies running, was as follows:—

1886–90 . . . . 1.52 per cent.
1891–95 . . . . 1.57 ,, ,,

Payments on losses by fire compared with amount received as premium thus:—

1886 . . . . 56.8 per cent.
1890 . . . . 53.3 ,, ,,
1895 . . . . 51.8 ,, ,,

There is also insurance against hail-storms, premiums £130,000, payments for losses £120,000.

AUSTRIA

In 1894 the insurance of operatives showed thus:—

Against	Number Insured	Premiums £	Shillings per Head
Sickness . . .	1,940,000	1,200,000	12.4
Accident . . .	1,470,000	380,000	5.2
Total . .	3,410,000	1,580,000	9.3

The persons insured against sickness had 15,600,000 days of sickness, or 8 days each, as compared with 6½ in Germany. Those against accident had 10,900 killed or disabled, being 74 per 10,000, against 48 in Germany.

VARIOUS COUNTRIES

The amount of life insurance in various countries in 1890 compared with 1880 as follows, excluding the policies of workmen:—

	Millions £ Sterling			1890 Number of Policies
	1880	1890	Increase	
United States . .	312	636	324	2,410,000
United Kingdom .	422	442	20	1,150,000
Germany . . .	127	189	62	760,000
France	87	122	35	290,000
Austria	20	34	14	...
Various	22	27	5	...
Total . . .	990	1,450	460	...

This shows an increase of 46 per cent. in 10 years.

According to Bellour, in 1894 the life insurance business of the world stood thus:—

	Millions £ Sterling		Ratio of Assets
	Policies	Assets	
United States	980	182	18.6
Great Britain	573	115	20.1
Continent	498	140	28.1
Canada	31	5	16.0
Australia	68	20	29.5
Total . . .	2,150	462	21.5

Germany had 940,000 life policies, amounting to 205 millions sterling. The amount set down for Canada was only that of policies issued by native companies.

AUSTRALIA

The largest share of life assurance is done by the Australian Mutual Company, the business in 1895 showing:—

	Mutual	Various	Total
No. of Policies .	123,752	179,862	303,614
Amount, £ . .	39,940,000	47,840,000	87,780,000
Premiums, £ . .	1,310,000	1,620,000	2,930,000
Assets, £ . . .	13,710,000	10,700,000	24,410,000

The average amount of life assurance running was £287, against £336 in Canada.

UNITED STATES

Life insurance returns by census of 1890 compare with those of 1879 as follows:—

	£ Sterling (000 omitted)					
	Receipts		Liabilities		Assets	
	1879	1889	1879	1889	1879	1889
New York .	8,800	23,900	37,000	74,000	43,800	85,600
Connecticut .	3,800	3,500	18,700	21,300	21,600	24,000
Pennsylvania	1,900	700	3,100	9,300	3,800	10,800
Massachusetts	1,000	2,200	5,200	8,400	6,300	9,600
Various . .	1,800	7,400	14,000	22,200	16,500	24,000
The Union .	17,300	37,700	78,000	135,200	92,000	154,000

Fire and transport insurance showed as follows:—

States	Millions £ Sterling		
	1879	1889	Increase
New England . .	402	669	267
Middle . . .	1,044	1,738	694
South . . .	61	92	31
Prairie . . .	257	446	189
Pacific . . .	20	86	66
Union . . .	1,784	3,031	1,247
Foreign . . .	354	857	503
Total . .	2,138	3,888	1,750

The States that show largest amounts insured are:—

	Millions £		£ per Inhab.
	1879	1889	
New York . . .	628	1,116	186
Pennsylvania . .	297	491	93
Connecticut . .	173	301	401
Massachusetts . .	169	218	98
Illinois . . .	54	102	27
Rhode Island . .	41	97	276
Ohio . . .	87	83	23

The general average of property insured in 1889 was £48 per inhabitant of the whole Union.

CANADA

Fire insurance is done by native, British, and American companies, the aggregate of which shows as follows:—

	Premiums, £	Losses, £	Loss Ratio
1870 . . .	380,000	325,000	84.8
1880 . . .	700,000	330,000	47.9
1890 . . .	1,170,000	650,000	56.0
1896 . . .	1,410,000	830,000	58.7

The returns for 1896, compared with the average for 28 years, show thus :—

Companies	Premiums, £		Losses, £		Loss Ratio	
	1896	1869–96	1896	1869–96	1896	1869–96
Native .	210,000	230,000	140,000	160,000	67.0	71.5
British .	1,000,000	580,000	570,000	400,000	57.0	68.2
American .	200,000	90,000	120,000	60,000	60.0	66.7
Total .	1,410,000	900,000	830,000	620,000	58.7	69.0

Life insurance was as follows :—

Companies	Lives		Amount, £	
	1886	1896	1886	1896
Native . . .	52,601	121,817	17,600,000	38,500,000
British . . .	13,454	17,538	5,500,000	7,000,000
American . .	31,927	50,379	11,100,000	18,600,000
Total . .	97,982	189,734	34,200,000	64,100,000

The receipts as premiums for life insurance and the sums paid to policy holders showed as follows :—

Year	Premiums, £	Payments, £
1890	1,600,000	900,000
1892	1,800,000	1,100,000
1895	2,120,000	1,170,000

The increase of business is shown thus, as regards premiums :—

	1886 £	1896 £
Fire	980,000	1,410,000
Life	1,040,000	2,120,000
Marine, &c. . .	180,000	470,000
Total . .	2,200,000	4,000,000

Life insurance in 1895 showed 3078 deaths, out of 278,000 persons insured, being at the rate of 11 per thousand.

IRON

Production of pig iron increased 50 per cent. in 10 years, viz. :—

	Tons		
	1885	1895	Increase
United States .	4,040,000	9,450,000	5,410,000
Great Britain. .	7,420,000	8,020,000	600,000
Germany . . .	3,690,000	5,790,000	2,100,000
France	1,630,000	2,010,000	380,000
Austria. . . .	610,000	930,000	320,000
Russia	520,000	1,410,000	890,000
Belgium . . .	670,000	830,000	160,000
Sweden. . . .	430,000	500,000	70,000
Various . . .	330,000	360,000	30,000
The World . .	19,340,000	29,300,000	9,960,000

Production of iron in the United States has been as follows :—

	Tons		
	1885	1895	Increase
Pennsylvania. .	2,180,000	4,700,000	2,520,000
Southern States .	620,000	1,690,000	1,070,000
Western States .	1,240,000	3,060,000	1,820,000
Total . .	4,040,000	9,450,000	5,410,000

The production of steel increased 135 per cent. in the same interval, viz. :—

	Tons		
	1885	1895	Increase
United States .	1,710,000	6,110,000	4,400,000
Great Britain. .	1,920,000	3,880,000	1,960,000
Germany . . .	1,140,000	2,160,000	1,020,000
France	530,000	810,000	280,000
Austria. . . .	200,000	500,000	300,000
Russia	250,000	380,000	130,000
Belgium . . .	160,000	220,000	60,000
Sweden. . . .	40,000	170,000	130,000
Various . . .	250,000	370,000	120,000
The World . .	6,200,000	14,600,000	8,400,000

The production and consumption of iron in 1896 were in English tons as follows :—

	Production	Consumption
United Kingdom . .	8,660,000	5,010,000
France	2,340,000	2,330,000
Germany	6,370,000	5,900,000
Russia	1,550,000	1,950,000
Austria	1,000,000	1,120,000
Italy	200,000	300,000
Spain	200,000	300,000
Scandinavia . . .	500,000	450,000
Belgium	950,000	430,000
United States . .	9,450,000	9,500,000
Other Countries . .	380,000	4,310,000
Total . . .	31,600,000	31,600,000

GREAT BRITAIN

The output of pig iron, and the value of iron and steel manufactures at various dates, are shown thus :—

Year	Iron Tons	Value, Millions £		
		Manufac- tures	Home Use	Exported
1860 . . .	3,830,000	52	30	22
1870 . . .	5,960,000	82	45	37
1880 . . .	7,750,000	101	57	44
1890 . . .	7,900,000	116	59	57
1896 . . .	8,660,000	119	68	51

The average output for each blast-furnace was as follows :—

Year	Tons
1870	9,000
1885	18,000
1894	22,300

The details of the iron and steel industry in 1896 may be summed up thus : —

Used as	Tons	Destination	Tons
Steel . . .	4,130,000	Exported . .	3,650,000
Iron	4,530,000	Home use .	5,010,000
Total . .	8,660,000	Total . .	8,660,000

The value was approximately as follows :—

	£
Iron and steel exported . .	23,800,000
Machinery ,, . . .	16,100,000
Cutlery, arms, &c. . . .	11,300,000
Exports . . .	51,200,000
Home articles	67,500,000
Total output, value .	118,700,000

It needs 6 tons of pig iron to make 5 tons of steel, and 4 of iron to make 3 of railway bars. As a rule one mile of railway takes 270 tons of rails.

Although the weight of metal retained for British manufactures in 1896 was 5,010,000 tons, it appears that one-tenth of this quantity was subsequently exported as cutlery, machinery, &c., leaving for home use 4,500,000 tons. The goods manufactured herefrom, at an estimate of £15 per ton, would represent £67,500,000, or 56 per cent. of the total industry, and the home consumption of such goods is equal to 34 shillings per inhabitant. If we deduct the iron and steel exported in bars, &c., the remaining 5,000,000 tons are manufactured into goods of the approximate value of £93,000,000, or nearly £19 per ton. This shows that iron and steel goods are much cheaper here than in other countries. The official value per ton of such goods in 1892 was as follows :—

	£		£
Germany . . .	34	Austria	45
Holland . . .	36	Italy	45
Sweden . . .	45	Spain	57

Iron and steel exports from Great Britain were as follows :—

Year	In Bar £	Manufactures £	Total £
1860	12,200,000	9,900,000	22,100,000
1870	24,100,000	12,600,000	36,700,000
1880	28,400,000	15,400,000	43,800,000
1890	31,600,000	25,100,000	56,700,000
1896	23,800,000	27,400,000	51,200,000
1897	24,600,000	24,100,000	48,700,000

UNITED STATES

Production, imports, and consumption of pig iron show thus :—

Year	Tons		
	Product	Imported	Consumed
1877	2,070,000	50,000	2,120,000
1887	5,680,000	420,000	6,100,000
1892	8,280,000	70,000	8,350,000
1893	9,160,000	40,000	9,200,000
1894	7,120,000	...	7,120,000
1895	6,660,000	...	6,660,000
1896	9,450,000	50,000	9,500,000
1898	11,670,000	...	12,020,000

In 1898 consumption exceeded production, the stock remaining from previous years having been drawn upon.

VARIOUS COUNTRIES

The imports of iron in the following European countries were :—

	Tons	
	1885	1896
Russia	230,000	410,000
Austria	50,000	140,000
Italy	60,000	130,000
Denmark	50,000	110,000
Switzerland	40,000	190,000
Spain	70,000	60,000
Portugal	40,000	40,000
Norway	30,000	30,000
Total . . .	570,000	1,110,000

Exports of the principal countries were as follows :—

	1885	1896
Great Britain	3,130,000	3,650,000
Germany	320,000	510,000
Belgium	340,000	440,000
Sweden	40,000	80,000
Total . . .	3,830,000	4,680,000

So many improvements have taken place that a ton of iron is now produced with 1½ ton of coal, whereas it took 8 tons of coal in 1791. So rapid is the process in use that iron ore can be landed at Cardiff, and converted into steel-plates in 48 hours. Iron is now much used for building, as at Astor's Hotel, New York, 16 storeys, in which 10,000 tons are employed : the skeleton of an iron hotel of 13 storeys was run up at Chicago in 25 days. See *Iron*, pp. 332–37 ; also *Manufactures*, p. 767.

IRRIGATION.

The quantity of water ordinarily required per acre for irrigation is :—

Culture	Gallons per Minute	Hours each Time	Tons per Month
Meadow . . .	150	6	1,100
Grain	...	...	800
Garden	12	...	700

Meadow must be irrigated 4 days, grain 3 days, gardens 30 days, monthly. Irrigation for vineyards is estimated at 250 tons weekly per hectare, equal to 400 tons a month per acre. According to Messrs. Lawes and Gilbert, an acre of wheat evaporates 60 tons of water monthly.

Latest returns of irrigated areas and the annual cost per acre are as follows :—

	Acres	Shillings per Acre
India	25,000,000	8
Egypt	5,100,000	4
Italy	2,800,000	16
Spain	2,000,000	14
France	600,000	22
United States . . .	5,000,000	...
Australia	120,000	...

The charge for irrigation in Italy is measured by the "bocca," which is a supply of 480 gallons per minute.

The Cavour canal charges 36 shillings a year for a constant supply of 12 gallons a minute all the year round : a "bocca" would, therefore, cost £72 a year and suffice to irrigate 90 acres. Irrigated lands in France produce 25 per cent. heavier crops. Works are now in progress in Upper Egypt to extend the irrigated area of the Nile valley by 200,000 acres. Messrs. Aird signed a contract in January 1898 for constructing a breakwater at Assouan, 2000 yards long, which will hold 19 billion tons of water, and permit the discharge of Nile water in excessive flood at 14,000 tons per second : to be completed in 5 years, cost £2,000,000. The area to be irrigated will add £2,300,000 to the value of agricultural products, and £400,000 to revenue yearly.

For drainage and irrigation Holland has 1,900,000 miles of canals, big and little, being an average of 420 yards of canal for each acre of farm-lands.

See *Irrigation*, page 337.

ISLANDS

The area of the principal islands is as follows :—

	Sq. Miles			Sq. Miles
New Guinea . .	303,000	Formosa . .	.	15,000
Borneo . . .	284,000	Sicily . .	.	9,800
Madagascar . .	227,000	Jamaica. .	.	4,200
Sumatra . .	162,000	Cyprus . .	.	3,600
Great Britain .	83,700	Corsica . .	.	3,400
Celebes . .	68,800	Crete . .	.	2,900
Java . . .	48,400	Trinidad .	.	1,750
Cuba . . .	45,000	Teneriffe .	.	1,010
Newfoundland .	40,200	Mauritius .	.	710
Iceland . .	39,800	Madeira .	.	510
Ireland . .	32,600	Corfu . .	.	430
Hayti . . .	28,800	Man . .	.	230
Tasmania . .	26,200	Malta . .	.	100
Ceylon . . .	24,700	Jersey . .	.	45
Terra del Fuego .	18,500	Hong-Kong .	.	30

J

JEWS

See page 338 ; also *Religion*, page 799.

JEWELLERY

See page 338.

JUTE

Exports of raw jute from India have more than doubled in twenty years, viz. :—

Year	Tons	Value, £	£ per Ton
1876 . . .	260,000	2,500,000	9.6
1886 . . .	390,000	3,300,000	8.5
1896 . . .	610,000	5,500,000	9.0

The area under jute cultivation in 1896 was 2,250,000 acres, the ordinary crop being 900 lbs. per acre, and the product about 900,000 tons. There are in India 28 jute mills, employing 80,000 operatives, with 11,000 looms and 220,000 spindles, which consume 250,000 tons of jute per annum. Indian exports of jute manufactures rose from £800,000 in 1886 to £2,600,000 in 1896.

Jute manufacture in the United Kingdom shows :—

Year	Tons Jute	Output, £	Exported, £
1884 . . .	170,000	9,100,000	2,800,000
1890 . . .	260,000	13,000,000	3,000,000
1896 . . .	240,000	11,100,000	2,600,000

Dundee is the principal seat of this industry. The factories of jute in the United Kingdom have trebled their power since 1870, viz. :—

Year	Spindles	Power-Looms	Operatives
1870 . .	115,000	4,000	18,000
1890 . .	280,000	14,000	45,000

France consumes 55,000 tons of raw jute yearly, producing goods worth more than £2,000,000 ; Austria a like quantity. The imports of raw jute into the United States from 1888 to 1896 averaged 95,000 tons yearly. The world at present consumes nearly 900,000 tons, and the goods manufactured are approximately of the value of 35 millions sterling per annum. For details of earlier years see Part I., page 339.

K

KINGS

See Part I., page 340 ; also page 762.

L

LAND

The following is a record (*Times*, April 1889) of all landed estates over 30 acres sold *by auction* in London, situate in England and Wales, from 1781 to 1880 :—

Period	Acres	Rental, £	Price, £	£ per Acre
1781-1800 . .	72,000	76,000	2,430,000	33.8
1801-1820 . .	136,000	152,000	4,920,000	36.2
1821-1840 . .	246,000	221,000	5,830,000	23.7
1841-1860 . .	189,000	261,000	6,880,000	36.4
1861-1870 . .	122,000	153,000	5,250,000	43.0
1871-1880 . .	109,000	163,000	5,590,000	51.3
100 years . .	874,000	1,026,000	30,900,000	35.1

A similar record was published in 1897, for 3 years ending December 1896, showing 125,500 acres sold for £3,300,000, being at the rate of £26, 10s. per acre, a fall of 49 per cent. from the price of 1871-80.

According to a parliamentary report (1896) the productive area of the island of Great Britain was 32,580,000 acres, and the change of tenure since 1885 is shown thus :—

Acres	Number of Farms		Difference
	1885	1895	
1-5 . . .	135,000	118,000	− 17,000
5-50 . .	233,000	235,000	+ 2,000
50-100 . .	65,000	67,000	+ 2,000
100-500 . .	94,000	94,800	+ 800
Over 500 . .	6,000	5,200	− 800
Total . .	533,000	520,000	− 13,000

Farms	Area, Acres	
	1885	**1895**
Under 50 acres • •	4,800,000	4,900,000
50-100 acres • • •	4,600,000	4,900,000
Over 100 acres . • •	23,000,000	22,800,000
Total • •	32,400,000	32,600,000

For Ireland, see page 341.
Assessments of land in the three kingdoms compare :—

	1846 £	**1896** £
England . • • •	40,200,000	39,370,000
Scotland . • • •	5,600,000	6,150,000
Ireland . • • •	8,630,000	9,890,000
United Kingdom • •	54,430,000	55,410,000

In Ireland rents have been reduced by the Commissioners 20 per cent. since 1880, the rental in 1895 standing thus :—

	£ Sterling (000 omitted)			
	Old rent	Judicial	Un-reformed	Total
Ulster • • •	1,910	1,540	1,270	2,810
Leinster . • •	1,620	1,290	1,930	3,220
Connaught • •	760	600	680	1,280
Munster . • •	1,690	1,310	1,610	2,920
Total • •	5,980	4,740	5,490	10,230

In the United States the census of 1890 compared with that of 1860 thus :—

	1860	**1890**	Increase
Farmers • •	1,850,000	5,282,000	3,432,000
Labourers . •	1,509,000	3,038,000	1,529,000
Total • •	3,359,000	8,320,000	4,961,000

As to manner of holding land, the census of 1890 shows that the ratio of farms cultivated by the owner is declining, while that of tenants rapidly increases: there are two kinds of tenancy, that of a fixed money rental, and that of sharing profits on the system known in France as Metayer : the figures for 1880 and 1890 were :—

Worked by	Number of Farms		Ratio	
	1880	1890	1880	1890
Owner • • •	2,984,000	3,270,000	74.4	71.5
Tenant • • •	323,000	455,000	8.1	10.0
Metayer • • •	702,000	840,000	17.5	18.5
Total • •	4,009,000	4,565,000	100.0	100.0

The price of land in various sections of the Union shows as follows :—

States	$ per Acre		
	1850	1880	1890
New England • •	34	44	46
Middle . • • •	45	65	63
Southern • • •	20	21	23
Prairie . • • •	28	37	38
Pacific . • • •	...	25	48
Union, average • •	29	36	37

LAND-TENURE AND LAND-TAXES
See pages 341–352.

LANGUAGE
See page 352.

LAW COURTS

The total number of lawsuits in the superior and inferior courts of England and Wales, since 1859, is given by Dr. John MacDonell, Master, as follows :—

Period	Average Suits Yearly		
	Superior	Inferior	Total
1859–66 • •	113,000	837,000	950,000
1867–74 • •	83,000	959,000	1,042,000
1875–82 • •	94,000	1,065,000	1,159,000
1883–90 • •	83,000	1,064,000	1,147,000
1891–92 • •	82,000	1,115,000	1,197,000

Taking the number of barristers, solicitors, and law-clerks at each census of England and Wales, and comparing it with lawsuits, we find the amount of work to each was as follows :—

Period	Lawyers	Lawsuits	Per Lawyer
1859–66 . • •	34,990	950,000	27
1867–74 . • •	37,330	1,042,000	28
1875–82 . • •	43,640	1,159,000	27
1883–92 . • •	47,520	1,157,000	24

The supply of lawyers seems to exceed the demand, the average to each being now only 24 suits a year, which shows a relative fall of 11 per cent. since 30 years ago. Comparing the above figures with population, we find the number of suits and lawyers showed thus :—

Period	Per 100,000 Inhabitants	
	Lawsuits	Lawyers
1859–66 • • •	4,750	175
1867–82 • • •	4,580	170
1883–92 • • •	4,130	170

This shows that the spirit of litigation, as represented by the number of lawsuits, has declined 13 per cent. in the last 30 years.

For criminal cases, see *Crime*, pages 162 and 679.

LEAD

Production has increased 50 per cent. in eight years, viz. :—

	Tons		
	1888	1896	Increase
United States •	160,000	170,000	10,000
Spain . • •	84,000	170,000	86,000
Germany . • •	92,000	110,000	18,000
Great Britain •	38,000	30,000	...
Various • •	83,000	200,000	117,000
Total • •	457,000	680,000	223,000

In 1896 Australia produced 65,000, Mexico 50,000, tons.

The above is the weight of metallic lead produced, 100 tons of mineral giving usually 70 tons of metal. The price of pig lead has been as follows per ton :—

Year	£	Year	£	Year	£
1882 .	. 14.4	1888 .	. 13.9	1893 .	. 9.9
1885 .	. 11.2	1890 .	. 13.2	1896 .	. 11.1

Great Britain imports 150,000 tons yearly, and exports 60,000. The Spanish lead mines gave as follows :—

Year	Tons, Ore	Value, £
1892	310,000	1,050,000
1895	305,000	1,400,000

LEATHER

The production and consumption of all kinds of hides and skins (exclusive of furs), and the equivalent in leather, are approximately as follows :—

	Tons Hides		Tons Leather Consumed
	Production	Consumption	
U. Kingdom . .	102,000	196,000	118,000
France	105,000	150,000	90,000
Germany . . .	133,000	220,000	132,000
Russia	237,000	190,000	114,000
Austria	110,000	133,000	80,000
Italy	37,000	53,000	32,000
Other States . .	150,000	180,000	107,000
Europe	874,000	1,122,000	673,000
U. States . . .	420,000	510,000	306,000
Australia . . .	227,000	120,000	72,000
Argentina, &c. .	389,000	158,000	95,000
Total . .	1,910,000	1,910,000	1,146,000

Production and consumption of leather manufactures show approximately thus :—

	Output Millions £	Consumption	
		Millions £	Shillings per Head
United Kingdom . .	59	56	30
France	45	37	20
Germany . . .	65	60	12
Russia	57	57	10
Austria	40	39	18
Italy	16	16	10
Spain	14	13	15
Other States . .	39	39	16
Europe . . .	336	317	17
United States . .	106	108	30
Total . .	442	425	19

The estimate of British leather manufactures at page 354 is 10 per cent. too low as regards value.

LEGACY AND PROBATE

See page 354 ; also *Death-duties*, page 689.

LIBRARIES

See Part I., page 355.

LIFE

The value of life in persons devoted to science is shown by the returns of Fellows of the Royal Society from 1848 to 1891, viz. :—

Term	Average		Survivors in 1891	Average Age
	No. of Fellows	Age at Election		
1848–57 . . .	715	42	39	75
1858–67 . . .	614	43	67	67
1868–77 . . .	536	45	111	61
1878–87 . . .	481	45	138	53
1888–91 . . .	466	46	46	48
1848–91 . . .	575	44	401	59

FRANCE

According to Turquand, the span of life in France is now 7 years longer than it was 60 years ago :—

Period	Span of Life		Die under 20 per 1000 born
	Years	Months	
1821–40 . . .	33	0	394
1841–60 . . .	36	0	389
1861–76 . . .	36	10	376
1877–90 . . .	40	2	370

UNITED STATES

Dr. Billings's tables of the expectation of life in the city of Baltimore (1886), compiled from the census returns of 1880, show the difference between white and coloured people at all ages as follows :—

Age	Years to Live			
	White		Coloured	
	Male	Female	Male	Female
1 . .	44.7	47.4	32.2	38.4
5 . .	50.5	53.0	41.8	46.8
10 . .	48.5	50.8	40.1	44.8
15 . .	44.4	46.6	36.8	42.0
20 . .	40.4	42.7	33.8	39.5
25 . .	36.9	39.3	31.0	36.3
30 . .	33.5	36.0	27.8	33.5
40 . .	26.7	29.4	21.7	27.6
50 . .	20.0	22.6	16.3	21.6
60 . .	14.1	16.0	11.3	15.5
70 . .	10.1	10.4	7.8	9.9
80 . .	7.4	6.9	6.3	6.5
85 . .	6.2	5.8	5.9	5.6

Taking all inhabitants, without distinction of colour or sex, the expectation of life in other cities of the Union is :—

Age	Years to Live				
	New York	Philadelphia	Boston	Chicago	St. Louis
1 . .	43.7	49.5	46.7	47.3	51.3
5 . .	49.1	52.0	50.9	52.9	53.7
10 . .	45.9	48.6	48.0	51.1	50.0
15 . .	41.6	44.3	43.7	47.1	45.8
20 . .	37.6	40.4	40.1	43.2	41.7
30 . .	31.1	33.8	33.8	36.0	34.7
40 . .	25.1	27.5	27.4	29.1	28.1
50 . .	19.2	21.1	20.9	22.1	21.8
60 . .	13.8	15.1	15.0	15.7	16.1
70 . .	9.4	10.2	10.1	10.5	11.9
80 . .	6.7	6.9	7.1	7.3	9.3

For other countries see page 355.

The following table of survivals for Massachusetts and New Jersey shows the number of persons, out of 1000 born, who will survive to certain ages :—

Age	Massachusetts		New Jersey	
	Male	Female	Male	Female
0 . .	1,000	1,000	1,000	1,000
1 . .	858	880	868	892
5 . .	760	777	776	798
10 . .	729	742	748	769
15 . .	717	728	737	757
20 . .	700	707	723	740
30 . .	646	643	673	685
40 . .	588	580	615	627
50 . .	523	517	544	563
60 . .	434	440	444	481
70 . .	302	323	308	352
80 . .	135	163	141	167
90 . .	24	37	30	35

In New Jersey the woman's life throughout is better than the man's, but the reverse is true in Massachusetts between 30 and 50 years of age.

LIFE-BOATS

In 1897 those of the United Kingdom were launched 375 times, and saved 659 lives. Since 1824 they have saved 40,470 lives, or 550 yearly.

LIFE-SPAN

According to ten years' tables, 1881–90, those persons who safely complete their fifth year usually pass their sixtieth. The mean age at death (excluding infants under five) was :—

England	. . .	62.5	Sweden	. . .	67.8
Scotland	. . .	62.1	Norway	. . .	67.1
Ireland	. . .	62.8	Denmark	. . .	65.8
France	. . .	63.2	Holland	. . .	65.2
Russia	. . .	61.4	Belgium	. . .	64.3
Bavaria	. . .	62.2	Switzerland	. . .	61.8
Austria	. . .	58.1	Massachusetts	.	63.2
Italy .	. . .	63.8	Japan	. . .	60.8
Spain.	. . .	58.2	Average	. . .	63.0

LIVES OF MONARCHS

In 400 years, from 1498 to 1898, the average life of crowned heads has been as follows :—

Sovereigns	Number	Average Years	Sovereigns	Number	Average Years
Popes .	43	9.3	Denmark	13	30.8
Czars . .	27	15.0	Sweden .	24	16.6
Austria .	16	25.0	Portugal	22	18.2
Prussia .	16	25.0	Turkey .	27	15.0
Spain . .	16	25.0	England	17	24.0

The Popes, being usually elected at advanced age, may be omitted : the general average for the other 178 monarchs would be 20 years of reign ; but despotic rulers, Czars and Sultans, had short reigns, being sometimes assassinated.

LIGHT

The public lighting of the principal cities of Europe in 1891 was :—

	Number of Lamps			Cost	
	Electric	Gas	Oil	£ Sterling	Pence per Inh.
London . .	...	74,100	...	220,000	12
Paris . . .	380	58,400	400	230,000	21
Berlin . . .	70,400	20,300	1,200	110,000	16
Hamburg . .	70	21,600	...	...	...
Vienna. . .	...	17,200	300	50,000	9
Dresden . .	...	6,900	400	20,000	14
Buda-Pesth .	...	8,800	2,500	30,000	12
Brussels . .	...	5,600	...	...	...
Bordeaux . .	...	4,700	...	8,000	8
Rome . . .	45	6,700	1,600	48,000	25
Naples . . .	33	9,700	300	47,000	22
Milan . . .	264	3,800	...	23,000	12
Turin . . .	2,760	3,900	400	30,000	21
Palermo . .	...	3,000	1,100	18,000	16
Genoa . . .	73	3,300	...	15,000	16
Florence . .	29	3,500	400	18,000	22

The number of electric lights, public and private, in use in the above cities in 1891 was as follows :—

London .	10,000	Dresden .	10,000	Rome . .	13,000
Berlin .	115,000	Breslau .	8,000	Naples .	4,000
Vienna .	37,000	Venice . .	5,400	Milan . .	16,000
Hamburg .	42,000	Florence .	900	Turin . .	7,000
Leipzig .	22,000	Genoa . .	600	Palermo .	2,000

The annual consumption of gas, public and private, and the average cost per thousand feet, are shown in the following table :—

	Millions of Cubic Feet			Pence per 1000 feet
	Public	Private	Total	
London (inner) .	1,520	25,200	26,720	36
Paris . . .	950	9,450	10,400	60
Berlin . . .	500	4,300	4,800	45
Vienna . . .	250	...	...	48
Hamburg . .	240	1,200	1,440	50
Leipzig . .	80	550	630	50
Bordeaux . .	180	720	900	47
Brussels . .	160	800	960	28
Breslau . .	105	415	520	50
Dresden . .	140	600	740	48
Buda-Pesth .	170	590	760	47
Trieste . .	50	150	200	54
Rome . . .	130	390	520	64
Naples . . .	170	180	350	72
Milan . . .	60	480	540	55
Turin . . .	80	700	780	40
Palermo . .	60	70	130	100
Genoa . .	50	180	230	60
Florence . .	60	90	150	60
Venice . .	40	80	120	70

The average price in the above 20 cities is 54 pence per thousand feet, or 50 per cent. higher than in London. The annual consumption of gas per inhabitant is as follows :—

	Feet		Feet		Feet
London .	6,400	Brussels .	1,900	Naples . .	700
Paris . .	4,200	Breslau .	1,500	Milan . .	1,200
Berlin .	3,100	Dresden .	2,200	Turin . .	2,200
Hamburg .	2,400	Buda-Pesth	1,400	Genoa . .	1,100
Leipzig .	1,600	Trieste . .	1,200	Florence .	700
Bordeaux .	3,500	Rome . .	1,200	Palermo .	500

The average consumption in the above 18 cities is 2050 cubic feet per inhabitant yearly ; Paris is double, and London treble the average.

Those towns in England which are lit with gas by the municipal authorities had 192 establishments in 1894, against 148 in 1884, and showed statistics as follows :—

	Capital, £	Consumers	Street Lamps	Tons Coal Consumed
1884 . . .	17,300,000	917,000	137,000	2,350,000
1894 . . .	23,600,000	1,226,000	210,000	4,030,000

The total gas returns for England and Wales in 1897 were :—

Supply	Millions Cubic Feet	Tons Coal	Consumers
Municipal . . .	48,700	4,650,000	1,480,000
Companies . .	84,000	7,950,000	1,540,000
Total, 1897 .	132,700	12,600,000	3,020,000
Do. 1890 .	103,000	10,200,000	2,310,000

This gave an average of 4½ tons of coal per consumer in 1890, and 4¼ tons in 1897.
See *Gas*, page 304, and *Light*, page 357.

LIGHTHOUSES

See page 358.

LIVING, COST OF

The *Journal des Economistes*, 1895, estimates the annual expenditure for a workman's family in various countries thus :—

	Shillings per Annum				
	Great Britain	Belgium	Germany	Austria	Italy
Rent	188	99	74	62	61
Bread	136	360	214	354	504
Meat	180	75	74	52	0
Vegetables . . .	136	180	60	128	298
Dairy	90	180	472	60	72
Groceries . . .	676	316	134	188	210
Clothing . . .	175	256	120	79	112
Fuel, &c. . . .	115	65	130	79	35
Total .	1,696	1,531	1,278	1,002	1,292

Higgs's budgets of the working-classes in the United States show the average earnings and expenditure of 3000 families was as follows :—

	American £	English £	Scotch £	Irish £
Earnings . .	129	103	140	96
Rent . . .	15.5	10.4	10.5	9.4
Food . . .	50.7	46.8	68.7	44.7
Clothes . . .	23.7	17.2	21.4	14.0
Fuel . . .	6.3	5.7	4.3	5.7
Liquor, &c. . .	6.3	7.4	11.2	7.1
Sundries . .	13.1	8.5	8.9	8.1
Total . .	115.6	96.0	125.0	89.0
Surplus . .	13.4	7.0	15.0	7.0

The estimated ratios of expenditure for American working-classes, as given by the *Amer. Econ. Ass.*, compare with the above thus :—

	American	British	Continental
Rent . . .	18.6	11.1	5.8
Food . . .	45.3	65.4	73.0
Clothing . .	18.5	10.3	11.1
Fuel . . .	5.0	6.7	6.1
Sundries .	12.6	6.5	4.0
Total . .	100.0	100.0	100.0

The Statistical Society of Paris (1895) shows the yearly expenditure of a gentleman of £600 a year, residing in Paris, with wife, 5 children, and 2 servants, in all 9 persons, and how much goes in taxes :—

	Expenditure £	Tax Included £	Tax Ratio
House	125.0	36.6	29.5
Bread, flour . .	27.6	5.3	48.0
Meat and fish .	87.0	11.2	12.9
Dairy products .	37.2	2.7	7.3
Wines	35.6	17.6	49.5
Coffee, sugar, &c.	58.9	14.0	23.7
Clothing . . .	79.0	8.5	10.8
Fuel and light .	35.5	9.7	27.3
Sundries . . .	84.2	24.4	29.0
Total . .	570.0	130.0	22.8

It appears, therefore, that taxation, between national, communal, and municipal, is equal to 23 per cent. of the above gentleman's expenditure, and his family comprising 7 persons, the average incidence of taxation for them is almost £19 per head.
See *Living*, page 458.

LOCAL FINANCES

UNITED KINGDOM

Local expenditure in 1894 amounted to £88,500,000, as compared with £61,200,000 in 1880, viz. :—

	£ Sterling	
	1880	1894
Police and works .	34,500,000	46,500,000
Poor relief . .	9,900,000	11,800,000
Schools . . .	4,900,000	9,700,000
Harbours . . .	4,700,000	5,800,000
Rural affairs . .	7,200,000	14,700,000
Total .	61,200,000	88,500,000

In 1894 the expenditure was made up as follows :—

	£ (000 omitted)			
	England	Scotland	Ireland	United Kingdom
Urban . . .	40,220	4,930	1,410	46,560
Poor . . .	9,670	960	1,130	11,760
Schools . .	7,780	1,910	...	9,690
Harbours . .	4,030	1,170	580	5,780
Rural . . .	11,520	1,400	1,750	14,670
Total . .	73,220	10,370	4,870	88,460

Only 60 per cent. of the amount necessary to meet the above expenditure was raised by rates, tolls, and income from water and gas supply, viz. :—

	1880	1894
Rates and tolls . .	37,100,000	54,300,000
Imperial subsidy .	3,400,000	11,100,000
Loans . . .	15,100,000	16,100,000
Sundries . .	5,600,000	7,000,000
Total . .	61,200,000	88,500.000

Local revenue in 1894 was made up as follows :—

£ (000 omitted)				
	England	Scotland	Ireland	United Kingdom
Rates, tolls .	45,600	6,200	3,500	54,300
Imp. subsidy .	9,000	1,700	400	11,100
Loans . . .	13,400	2,100	600	16,100
Sundries . .	6,200	500	300	7,000
Total . .	73,200	10,500	4,800	88,500

Local debt has nearly doubled since 1880, amounting at present to nearly 262 millions sterling, viz. :—

	1880 £	1897 £
England	137,000,000	223,600,000
Scotland	16,300,000	30,900,000
Ireland	?	6,900,000
U. Kingdom . . .	...	261,400,000

The local debt of England showed as follows :—

	1880 £	1897 £
Urban	56,700,000	78,100,000
Docks	23,200,000	32,000,000
Schools, &c. . . .	57,100,000	113,500,000
Total .	137,000,000	223,600,000

Debt of London	£	Irish Debt	£
County Council .	19,100,000	Dublin . . .	1,840,000
School Board .	9,300,000	Belfast . . .	1,380,000
Vestries, &c. .	10,300,000	Harbours, &c. .	3,680,000
Total . .	38,700,000	Total . .	6,900,000

The debt of London is equal to £9 per inhabitant, with an annual burthen of £2,600,000, equal to 17 pence per pound of the valuation. The local debt of Ireland is equal to 32 shillings per inhabitant. The School Board debt of England is £20,200,000, equal to £10 per head of the children in Board schools.

In 1890, according to Sir John Lubbock, the taxation and debt of various cities gave the following averages per inhabitant :—

	Rates, £	Debt, £
London	2.4	9.2
Birmingham . . .	2.8	10.1
Paris	5.2	23.3
New York . . .	6.2	16.2
Boston	6.1	24.5

FRANCE

Local taxation and debt in 1895 were as follows :—

	Revenue, £	Debt, £
Paris	13,800,000	70,800,000
Other Cities . . .	17,500,000	69,800,000
Rural Departments . .	11,000,000	16,800,000
Total . . .	42,300,000	157,400,000

The debt of Paris exceeds £28 per inhabitant. The amount of Octroi (food tax) at the principal cities was :—

	£	Shillings per Inhabitant
Paris	6,010,000	50
Lyons	450,000	21
Marseilles . . .	450,000	22
Bordeaux	250,000	20
Lille	190,000	21
Rouen	150,000	27
6 Cities	7,500,000	38

GERMANY

Local taxation is about 48 millions sterling : see page 363.

RUSSIA

Local taxation is about 16 millions sterling, of which 40 per cent is municipal, 60 per cent. rural. Local debts sum up 7 millions.

ITALY

Local taxation, 31 millions sterling ; local debts, 54 millions. The Octroi of the principal cities is as follows :—

	£ Sterling	Shillings per Inhabitant
Rome	700,000	32
Naples	630,000	24
Milan	390,000	18
Turin	400,000	24
Genoa	380,000	35

Local taxation in 1897 was made up of £25,800,000 communal, and £5,200,000 provincial : of the former £2,100,000 went to the State.

SCANDINAVIA

Local taxes are £4,200,000 in Sweden, £1,300,000 in Norway, and £2,100,000 in Denmark. Sweden has a local debt of £11,000,000.

UNITED STATES

Local taxation consists of State, County, Municipal, and School taxes, and these have nearly doubled since 1870, the aggregate showing as follows :—

£ Sterling			
	1870	1890	Increase
New England .	8,000,000	11,000,000	3,000,000
Middle States .	16,000,000	28,700,000	12,700,000
Southern ,, . .	7,500,000	11,900,000	4,400,000
Western ,, . .	19,500,000	46,400,000	26,900,000
The Union . .	51,000,000	98,000,000	47,000,000

Local taxes are raised by a rate on property, varying from 1½ to 2¼ per cent., viz. :—

	Tax per $100 of Property	
	1870	1890
New England . . .	1.61	1.48
Middle	1.97	1.70
South	1.67	1.40
West	2.42	2.29
Union, average. . .	1.97	1.85

It will be seen that although local taxation has risen 92 per cent. since 1870, the increase of wealth has been such that the collective rates are lower per 100 dollars of property in every part of the Union, being 6 per cent. less all round. As regards the local taxation of 1890, if we distribute it over the whole population, it is as follows :—

Taxes	£ Sterling	Pence per Inhabitant
State	10,100,000	38
County	19,700,000	75
Municipal	42,200,000	161
Schools	26,000,000	100
Total . . .	98,000,000	374

Local debts in 1890 amounted to 237 millions sterling. The municipal debt of New York in 1897 was £47,300,000, equal to £19 per inhabitant.

Municipal Expenditure.—Körösi's and Bodio's latest reports show the following :—

	£		£
Paris	12,200,000	Naples . . .	690,000
Berlin	2,040,000	Milan	800,000
Vienna . . .	2,080,000	Turin	420,000
Rome	1,640,000	Genoa	700,000
St. Petersburg .	640,000	Florence . . .	440,000
Moscow . . .	500,000	Palermo . . .	330,000
Warsaw . . .	320,000	Venice . . .	180,000
Buda-Pesth . .	1,000,000	Dresden . . .	400,000
Stockholm . .	920,000	Amsterdam . .	1,080,000
Copenhagen. .	500,000	Bucharest . .	570,000
Prague . . .	920,000	Lyons	760,000
Washington. .	930,000	Munich . . .	1,400,000

Distributing the above sums according to population, we find as follows :—

Shillings per Inhabitant

Paris . . . 100	Bucharest . 49	Naples. . . 26
Prague. . . 100	Florence . . 45	Turin . . . 26
Washington . 80	Amsterdam . 44	Dresden . . 25
Rome . . . 78	Milan. . . 40	Berlin . . . 24
London . . 75	Buda-Pesth . 40	Venice . . . 24
Munich . . 70	Lyons . . 33	Palermo . . 24
Genoa . . . 68	Copenhagen 32	St. Petersburg 1c
Stockholm . 62	Vienna . . 30	Moscow . . 1c

M

MAIZE

The area and product are ordinarily as follows :—

	Acres	Tons	Bushels per Acre	Per Inhab.
United States .	72,200,000	43,500,000	24	24
Austria . . .	6,700,000	3,400,000	20	3
Russia . . .	6,800,000	2,600,000	15	1
Danub. States .	7,500,000	2,500,000	13	9
Italy	4,800,000	1,700,000	14	2
Spain	2,400,000	1,100,000	18	3
Argentina . .	2,700,000	1,100,000	16	11
France . . .	1,600,000	700,000	18	1
Portugal . . .	800,000	350,000	18	3
Australia . . .	300,000	200,000	26	2
Canada . . .	250,000	200,000	32	2
Greece . . .	200,000	100,000	20	2
Egypt	1,500,000	500,000	13	2
Java	1,900,000	600,000	13	1
Algeria . . .	100,000	30,000	13	...
Total . .	109,750,000	58,580,000	11	...

In France and some other countries millet is included with maize.

The production of maize has increased in recent times more rapidly than that of any other grain, having risen 50 per cent. in twenty-five years. Neumann Spallart estimated the world's crop to have averaged only 38,400,000 tons yearly in the decade ending 1880. The United States produce three-fourths of the total, and use the grain largely for fattening hogs.

See *Agriculture*, page 8, and *Food*, page 714 ; also *Maize*, p. 365

MANUFACTURES

The output of manufacturing industry has more than doubled since 1860, showing approximately as follows :—

	Millions £ Sterling		
	1860	1888	1896
Textiles . . .	420	684	904
Hardware . . .	243	563	604
Total .	663	1,247	1,508

The above are only two of the principal branches of manufactures, the various countries showing approximately the following value of output in 1896 :—

	Millions £ Sterling			
	Textiles	Hardware	Sundries	Total
United Kingdom .	191	142	543	876
France . . .	115	47	434	596
Germany . .	108	105	477	690
Russia . .	81	15	284	380
Austria . .	56	19	253	328
Italy . .	32	4	154	190
Spain . .	19	5	97	121
Belgium . .	17	19	82	118
Scandinavia .	9	8	64	81
Various . .	32	6	152	190
Europe .	660	370	2,540	3,570
United States	188	229	1,563	1,980
British Colonies	7	5	148	160
Total .	855	604	4,251	5,710

The above is exclusive of India, South America, &c.

The output of textile manufactures in 1840 was valued thus :—

	Value, £ (000 omitted)				
	Cottons	Woollens	Linens	Silks	Total
Great Britain .	48,000	24,000	12,000	9,500	93,500
France . . .	20,000	16,000	14,400	10,000	60,400
Germany . .	7,000	17,400	3,000	3,600	31,000
Austria . .	4,500	6,600	6,000	6,000	23,100
Belgium . .	3,400	1,000	1,000	...	5,400
Italy . . .	2,500	800	...	3,000	6,300
Russia . . .	2,800	4,200	800	800	8,600
Europe . .	88,200	70,000	37,200	32,900	228,300
United States	9,600	4,400	...	...	14,000
Total . .	97,800	74,400	37,200	32,900	242,300

In comparing the output of 1840 with that of 1896, we find the value in the various countries compares with population thus :—

	Millions £		£ per Inhabitant	
	1840	1896	1840	1896
United Kingdom .	94	191	3.6	5.0
France . . .	60	115	1.8	3.0
Germany . . .	31	108	1.0	2.1
Russia . . .	9	81	0.1	0.7
Austria . . .	23	56	0.7	1.3
Italy . . .	6	32	0.3	1.0
Spain . . .	6	19	0.5	1.1
Belgium . . .	5	17	1.2	2.7
Switzerland . .	2	12	1.0	4.0
Holland, &c. . .	2	29	0.2	1.3
Europe . . .	238	660	1.0	1.8
United States .	14	188	0.8	2.7
India, &c. . .	8	56	...	...
The World . .	260	904	...	...

The value of textile manufactures in 1896 was approximately as follows :—

	Millions £ Sterling			
	Cottons	Woollens	Linens, &c.	Total
United Kingdom .	92.1	61.7	37.4	191.2
France . . .	22.4	44.7	48.0	115.1
Germany . . .	35.4	42.2	30.6	108.2
Russia . . .	20.4	29.0	31.6	81.0
Austria . . .	18.4	14.5	22.8	55.7
Italy . . .	12.9	5.8	13.4	32.1
Spain . . .	8.8	6.6	4.0	19.4
Belgium . . .	5.2	5.3	6.4	16.9
Switzerland . .	3.2	1.6	7.0	11.8
Holland, &c. . .	11.2	8.6	8.8	28.6
Europe . . .	230.0	220.0	210.0	660.0
United States .	68.0	72.0	48.0	188.0
India . . .	24.0	2.0	10.0	36.0
Various . . .	8.0	7.0	5.0	20.0
The World . .	330.0	301.0	273.0	904.0

The progress of textile manufactures since 1888 is shown approximately thus :—

	Tons Fibre		Output Millions £	
	1888	1896	1888	1896
United Kingdom . .	1,240,000	1,360,000	192	191
France . . .	530,000	580,000	108	115
Germany . . .	430,000	590,000	82	108
Russia . . .	400,000	740,000	52	81
Austria . . .	260,000	360,000	36	56
Italy . . .	170,000	200,000	21	32
Spain . . .	100,000	110,000	16	19
Belgium . . .	130,000	110,000	16	17
Various . . .	60,000	150,000	15	41
Europe . . .	3,320,000	4,200,000	524	660
United States . .	840,000	1,210,000	112	188
India, &c. . .	360,000	690,000	48	56
The World . . .	4,520,000	6,100,000	684	904

The consumption of fibre and value of textile manufactures were approximately as follows :—

	Tons Fibre	Output Millions	£ per Ton Fibre
1820	950,000	158	166
1840	1,440,000	260	180
1860	2,380,000	420	175
1870	2,970,000	537	180
1888	4,520,000	684	152
1896	6,100,000	904	148

The weight of fibre consumed has doubled since 1870, but the value of manufactures produced has only risen 66 per cent.

See *Cotton*, page 678 ; *Flax*, page 712 ; *Hemp*, page 742 ; *Jute*, page 759 ; *Silk*, page 806 ; *Wool*, page 820.

The nations most largely exporting textiles show as follows :—

	Exported, Millions £ Sterling				
	1860	1870	1880	1890	1895
United Kingdom .	83	119	117	121	108
France . . .	28	37	37	39	36
Germany . . .	10	14	27	36	32
Switzerland . .	6	9	11	12	11
Belgium . . .	4	5	8	8	7
Austria . . .	3	4	4	4	4
Total . .	134	188	204	220	198

The export of British textile goods was as follows :—

	Millions £ Sterling				
	1860	1870	1880	1890	1896
Cottons . . .	42.1	56.7	63.7	62.1	59.3
Woollens . . .	12.2	21.7	17.3	20.4	18.3
Linens . . .	4.8	7.2	5.8	5.7	5.0
Silks . . .	1.6	1.5	2.0	2.2	1.4
Jutes . . .	...	0.8	2.3	2.6	2.3
Yarns . . .	15.8	23.2	17.1	19.4	18.7
Sundries . . .	6.8	8.3	8.9	8.2	7.6
Total .	83.3	119.4	117.1	120.6	112.6

The consumption of textile goods in various countries is shown thus :—

	Millions £ Sterling			
	Cottons	Woollens	Silks	Linens, &c.
United Kingdom .	40.1	45.0	19.0	17.4
France . . .	19.8	36.0	20.0	15.6
Germany . .	29.0	39.8	10.2	13.3
Russia . . .	20.5	29.4	3.5	27.6
Austria . . .	18.3	14.1	4.0	15.9
Italy . . .	13.5	7.1	3.0	7.4
Spain . . .	7.1	6.9	1.5	2.8
Belgium . .	5.0	5.5	1.4	1.3
Various . .	15.7	18.2	2.4	5.7
Europe . .	169.0	202.0	65.0	107.0
United States .	64.0	82.0	23.0	64.0
India . . .	54.0	4.0	?	10.0
Various . .	43.0	13.0	2.0	2.0
Total . .	330.0	301.0	90.0	183.0

The total value of textiles produced and consumed in various countries compares with population thus :—

	Millions £		Shillings per Head	
	Product.	Consump.	Product.	Consump.
U. Kingdom .	191	122	96	62
France . . .	115	92	60	48
Germany . . .	108	92	42	36
Russia . .	81	81	14	14
Austria . . .	56	52	27	25
Italy	32	31	21	20
Spain	19	18	22	21
Belgium . . .	17	13	54	41
Switzerland . .	12	5	80	51
Holland, &c. .	29	37	15	19
Europe . . .	660	543	36	30
United States .	188	233	52	66
India	36	68	3	5
Various . . .	20	60	...	...
The World . .	904	904	18	18

Textiles.—The annual consumption of fibre in the factories of the world is approximately as follows :—

	Tons			
	Cotton	Wool	Flax, Jute, &c.	Total
U. Kingdom	710,000	230,000	420,000	1,360,000
France . .	180,000	210,000	190,000	580,000
Germany .	280,000	200,000	110,000	590,000
Russia . .	190,000	110,000	440,000	740,000
Austria . .	120,000	60,000	180,000	360,000
Italy . . .	110,000	20,000	70,000	200,000
Spain . .	70,000	25,000	15,000	110,000
Belgium .	40,000	20,000	50,000	110,000
Various . .	100,000	25,000	25,000	150,000
Europe . .	1,800,000	900,000	1,500,000	4,200,000
U. States .	600,000	270,000	340,000	1,210,000
India . .	220,000	10,000	260,000	490,000
Various . .	80,000	20,000	100,000	200,000
The World .	2,700,000	1,200,000	2,200,000	6,100,000

The nominal consumption of wool is 1,200,000 tons, but the real does not exceed 1,100,000 tons (see *Wool*, page 820), the difference arising from the fact that woollen yarn is included in some countries as wool, having been already counted as wool in the countries which converted it from wool into yarn. In like manner the real consumption of cotton does not exceed 2,600,000 tons.

Hardware.—The production of steel, lead, copper, &c., is as follows :—

	Tons			
	Steel	Lead	Copper	Zinc
United States .	6,110,000	170,000	210,000	70,000
Great Britain .	3,880,000	30,000	100,000	70,000
Germany . . .	2,160,000	110,000	25,000	150,000
France . . .	810,000	30,000	10,000	25,000
Austria . . .	500,000	10,000	...	6,000
Russia	580,000	...	5,000	5,000
Spain	40,000	170,000	60,000	20,000
Belgium . . .	420,000	20,000	...	110,000
Various . . .	200,000	150,000	80,000	4,000
The World . .	14,700,000	690,000	490,000	460,000

The principal nations that export hardware are shown thus :—

	Exports, Millions £		
	1885	1895	Increase
Great Britain . .	43	55	12
Germany . . .	11	17	6
United States . .	5	11	6
Belgium . . .	6	9	3
France	4	5	1
Total . .	69	97	28

The hardware manufactures of nations sum up 604 millions sterling, and it appears that five-sixths are consumed in the countries where they are made, and one-sixth exported. Two of the largest factories in the world are Armstrong's at Newcastle, with 27,000, and Krupp's at Essen, with 24,000, workmen.

Birmingham is one of the centres of British hardware, turning out weekly 14 million pens, 10 tons of pins, 6000 bedsteads, 7000 guns, 4000 miles of wire, 500 tons of screw bolts, 300 million nails, 5 million coins, and 1 million buttons.

There are in Europe 45 million operatives and artisans, who produce goods worth 3570 millions sterling yearly, say £78 each ; and in the United States 6 million hands produce 1980 millions sterling, or £330 each.

MARKETS

The area of public markets compared with population in the principal cities of Europe gives the following :—

Square Yards per 1000 Inhabitants

Paris . . .	32	Leipzig . .	28	Rome . . .	204
Brussels . .	59	Bordeaux .	60	Naples . .	32
Hamburg .	490	Buda-Pesth	710	Florence . .	147

This gives an average of 196 square yards per 1000.

The meat markets of Paris in 1895 sold 166,000 tons of meat, 35,000 tons of fish, 23,000 tons of fowl and game, besides 34 million oysters, being an average of 150 lbs. meat, 33 lbs. fish, 22 lbs. fowl, and 14 oysters, per inhabitant. The meat consisted of :—

	Head	Tons Meat	Average, Lbs.
Cattle	477,000	105,000	496
Sheep	1,760,000	35,000	45
Pigs. . . .	286,000	22,000	162
Horses	16,000	4,000	550

Poultry and game included 6,700,000 chickens, 2,100,000 pigeons, 1,700,000 ducks, geese, and turkeys, 3,300,000 rabbits, besides deer, hares, wild boars, &c.

MARRIAGE

The following table shows, by latest census reports, the proportions of single, married, and widowed persons (divorced being included with widowed) in various countries :—

	Single	Married	Widowed	Total
England . . .	608	337	55	1,000
Scotland . . .	647	296	57	1,000
Ireland . . .	667	263	69	1,000
United Kingdom	619	323	58	1,000
France . . .	517	401	82	1,000
Germany . . .	600	340	60	1,000
Austria . . .	608	336	56	1,000
Hungary . . .	529	408	63	1,000
Switzerland . .	611	321	68	1,000
Italy	569	365	66	1,000
Spain	546	384	70	1,000
Sweden . . .	604	334	62	1,000
Norway . . .	617	322	61	1,000
Denmark . . .	594	345	61	1,000
Holland . . .	616	328	56	1,000
Belgium . . .	622	319	59	1,000
Finland . . .	607	337	56	1,000
Bulgaria . . .	535	420	45	1,000
Canada . . .	632	328	40	1,000
Australia . . .	665	296	39	1,000
Average . . .	599	342	59	1,000

The married ratio is highest in Bulgaria, Hungary, and France : it is lowest in Ireland, being 23 per cent. below the average of nations. The ratio of widowed persons is highest in France and Spain, lowest in Australia and Canada.

If we compare the proportion of adults, male and female, who are married in the various countries, we find thus :—

	Males, per Cent.		Females, per Cent.	
	Married	Un-married	Married	Un-married
England . . .	54.0	46.0	50.0	50.0
Scotland . . .	49.1	50.9	44.0	56.0
Ireland . . .	39.9	60.1	38.3	61.7
U. Kingdom .	51.5	48.5	47.7	52.3
France . . .	55.4	44.6	54.3	45.7
Germany . . .	54.0	46.0	51.0	49.0
Austria . . .	52.7	47.3	50.0	50.0
Hungary . . .	64.1	35.9	63.8	36.2
Switzerland .	49.3	50.7	45.6	54.4
Spain . . .	58.8	41.2	55.6	44.4
Sweden . . .	52.7	47.3	47.9	52.1
Norway . . .	53.2	46.8	47.4	52.6
Denmark . . .	55.0	45.0	50.5	49.5
Holland . . .	51.6	48.4	49.6	50.4
Belgium . . .	48.0	52.0	47.4	52.6
Finland . . .	54.2	45.8	51.3	48.7
Bulgaria . . .	69.7	30.3	72.6	27.4
Australia . . .	35.3	64.7	60.0	40.0
Average . . .	52.2	47.8	51.7	48.3

It would be a mistake to look for strict conformity between the ratio of married persons and the birth-rate of a country, which are often widely apart. Take for example the ratio of married women and the birth-rate of the following :—

	Married Women Percentage	Birth-rate per 1000 Pop.
France . . .	54.3	22.4
Scotland . . .	44.0	30.7
Australia . . .	60.0	27.5
Norway . . .	47.4	30.3

Nevertheless, in most cases a high married ratio indicates a high birth-rate.

The ratios of age at marrying in various countries stand thus :—

	Males				
	Under 20	20–30	30–40	Over 40	Total
England . . .	21	734	158	87	1,000
Scotland . . .	25	682	206	87	1,000
Ireland . . .	25	616	260	99	1,000
France . . .	19	669	223	89	1,000
Germany . . .	1	695	218	86	1,000
Russia . . .	320	519	98	63	1,000
Austria . . .	...	645	220	135	1,000
Hungary . . .	...	759	138	103	1,000
Italy	26	658	208	108	1,000
Switzerland . .	10	608	246	136	1,000
Sweden . . .	2	628	260	110	1,000
Norway . . .	18	606	259	117	1,000
Denmark . . .	...	642	261	97	1,000
Holland . . .	30	632	228	110	1,000
Belgium . . .	47	597	245	111	1,000
Europe . . .	36	646	215	103	1,000
Massachusetts .	19	687	201	93	1,000
Buenos Ayres .	28	647	248	77	1,000

	Females				
England . . .	111	722	113	54	1,000
Scotland . . .	116	708	131	45	1,000
Ireland . . .	118	737	112	33	1,000
France . . .	205	628	120	47	1,000
Germany . . .	81	736	136	47	1,000
Russia . . .	564	364	50	22	1,000
Austria . . .	173	606	149	72	1,000
Hungary . . .	368	493	80	59	1,000
Italy	234	606	107	53	1,000
Switzerland . .	72	687	166	75	1,000
Sweden . . .	64	675	201	60	1,000
Norway . . .	79	677	183	61	1,000
Denmark . . .	74	699	176	51	1,000
Holland . . .	124	652	157	67	1,000
Belgium . . .	182	570	176	72	1,000
Europe . . .	171	637	137	55	1,000
Massachusetts .	161	677	118	44	1,000
Buenos Ayres .	456	443	72	29	1,000

UNITED KINGDOM

The census of 1891 showed married and unmarried thus :—

England and Wales

	Number (000 omitted)			Ratio
	Males	Females	Total	
Single . . .	8,716	8,909	17,625	608
Married . . .	4,852	4,917	9,769	337
Widowed . . .	485	1,124	1,609	55
Total .	14,053	14,950	29,003	1,000

Scotland

	Number (ooo omitted)			Ratio
	Males	Females	Total	
Single . . .	1,289	1,315	2,604	647
Married . .	589	603	1,192	296
Widowed . .	64	164	228	57
Total .	1,942	2,082	4,024	1,000

Ireland

	Males	Females	Total	Ratio
Single . . .	1,614	1,528	3,142	667
Married . .	614	626	1,240	263
Widowed . .	92	232	324	69
Total .	2,320	2,386	4,706	1,000

U. Kingdom

	Males	Females	Total	Ratio
Single . . .	11,619	11,752	23,371	619
Married . .	6,055	6,146	12,201	323
Widowed . .	641	1,520	2,161	58
Total .	18,315	19,418	37,733	1,000

The ratio of married persons in Ireland is the lowest in Europe, being 11 per cent. less than in Scotland, and 22 per cent. less than in England.

If we compare the adult population (over 15) with the numbers married we find :—

England

	Population	Married	Per cent
Males	8,980,000	4,852,000	54.0
Females	9,849,000	4,917,000	50.0
Total . .	18,829,000	9,769,000	52.0

Scotland

	Population	Married	Per cent
Males	1,218,000	589,000	49.1
Females	1,376,000	603,000	44.0
Total . .	2,594,000	1,192,000	46.0

Ireland

	Population	Married	Per cent
Males	1,541,000	614,000	39.9
Females	1,635,000	626,000	38.3
Total . .	3,176,000	1,240,000	39.0

U. Kingdom

	Population	Married	Per cent
Males	11,739,000	6,055,000	51.5
Females	12,860,000	6,146,000	47.7
Total . .	24,599,000	12,201,000	49.6

The following table shows the number of women between 15 and 45 in the three kingdoms, and how many married :—

	Number	Married	Per cent.
England	6,892,000	3,244,000	47.1
Scotland	936,000	392,000	41.9
Ireland . . .	1,068,000	358,000	33.6
U. Kingdom . .	8,896,000	3,994,000	44.9

As the marriage ratio is so low in Ireland, the birth-rate is also extremely depressed, being 24 per cent. less than in England (see *Vital Statistics*, page 815).

The mean age of persons marrying in England and Wales showed as follows :—

	1885–88	1892–95
Bachelors	26.2	26.5
Widowers . . .	43.7	44.4
All men . . .	28.2	28.5
Spinsters . . .	24.7	25.0
Widows . . .	40.2	40.5
All women . .	25.9	26.2

The mean age in the second period is 1 per cent. higher than in the first. Marriages of minors are decreasing in ratio, viz. :—

	1871–80		1886–95	
	Men	Women	Men	Women
Under 21 . . .	80	220	60	191
Over 21 . . .	920	780	940	809
Total . .	1,000	1,000	1,000	1,000

The following table shows the probability of the husband's age in England for any given age of a woman at marriage :—

Wife Aged				*Husband's Average*
15–20	.	.	.	23.1
20–25	.	.	.	25.1
25–30	.	.	.	28.6
30–35	.	.	.	33.8
35–40	.	.	.	39.2

The religion of persons married, judging by the churches in which marriages took place, showed the following ratios, for England and Wales :—

	1856–65	1866–75	1876–85	1886–95
Church of England .	860	761	720	697
Roman Catholic . .	46	42	43	42
Various	94	197	237	261
Total . . .	1,000	1,000	1,000	1,000

GERMANY

The census of 1890 showed as follows :—

	Number (ooo omitted)			Ratio
	Males	Females	Total	
Single . .	15,058	14,592	29,650	60.0
Married . .	8,372	8,399	16,771	34.0
Widowed . .	775	2,158	2,933	5.9
Divorced . .	25	50	75	0.1
Total . .	24,230	25,199	49,429	100.0

A comparison of the adult population over 15 with the number married shows :—

	Population	Married	Per Cent.
Males . .	15,517,000	8,372,000	54.0
Females . .	16,511,000	8,399,000	51.0
Total . .	32,028,000	16,771,000	52.4

The married ratio is much higher than in the United Kingdom.

France

The census of 1891 gave the following results :—

| | Number (000 omitted) | | | Ratio |
	Males	Females	Total	
Single . . .	10,243	9,464	19,707	51.7
Married . . .	7,640	7,657	15,297	40.1
Widowed . . .	1,033	2,061	3,094	8.1
Divorced . . .	17	20	37	0.1
Total . .	18,933	19,202	38,135	100.0

Comparing the adult population over 15 with the number married, we find :—

	Population	Married	Per Cent.
Males . .	13,807,000	7,640,000	55.4
Females . .	14,101,000	7,657,000	54.3
Total . .	27,908,000	15,294,000	54.8

The married ratio is even higher here than in Germany, and yet the birth-rate is 40 per cent. less (see *Vital Statistics*, page 815).

Austria

The census of 1890 showed as follows :—

| | Number (000 omitted) | | | Ratio |
	Males	Females	Total	
Single . . .	7,342	7,180	14,522	60.8
Married . . .	4,004	4,034	8,038	33.6
Widowed . . .	336	982	1,318	5.5
Divorced . . .	7	10	17	0.1
Total . .	11,689	12,206	23,895	100.0

Comparing the adult population over 15, we find the married ratio thus :—

	Population	Married	Per Cent.
Males . .	7,594,000	4,004,000	52.7
Females . .	8,071,000	4,034,000	50.0
Total . .	15,665,000	8,038,000	51.3

The married ratio is lower than in France or Germany, but the birth-rate is higher.

Hungary

According to the census of 1890 we find as follows :—

| | Number (000 omitted) | | | Ratio |
	Males	Females	Total	
Single . . .	4,882	4,377	9,259	52.9
Married . . .	3,528	3,576	7,104	40.8
Widowed . . .	253	835	1,088	6.2
Divorced . . .	5	8	13	0.1
Total . .	8,668	8,796	17,464	100.0

Comparing the adult population with the married, we find :—

	Population	Married	Per Cent.
Males . .	5,502,000	3,528,000	64.1
Females . .	5,604,000	3,576,000	63.8
Total . .	11,106,000	7,104,000	64.0

The married ratio is 25 per cent. higher than in Austria, and is the highest in Europe except Bulgaria.

Italy

The census of 1880 showed as follows :—

| | Number (000 omitted) | | | Ratio |
	Males	Females	Total	
Single . . .	8,544	7,661	16,205	56.9
Married . . .	5,150	5,211	10,361	36.5
Widowed . . .	571	1,322	1,893	6.6
Total . .	14,265	14,194	28,459	100.0

Switzerland

The census of 1888 resulted as follows :—

| | Number (000 omitted) | | | Ratio |
	Males	Females	Total	
Single . . .	891	892	1,783	61.1
Married . . .	466	470	936	32.1
Widowed . . .	57	131	188	6.4
Divorced . . .	4	8	12	0.4
Total . .	1,418	1,501	2,919	100.0

Taking the adult population to compare with the married, we find :— .

	Population	Married	Per Cent.
Males . .	946,000	466,000	49.3
Females . .	1,029,000	470,000	45.6
Total . .	1,975,000	936,000	47.4

The married ratio is low, especially for women. Observations during fifteen years show that of 100 marriages, the husband dies first in 56, the wife in 44 cases.

Spain

According to the census of December 1887 we find :—

| | Number (000 omitted) | | | Ratio |
	Males	Females	Total	
Single . . .	4,864	4,725	9,589	54.6
Married . . .	3,357	3,387	6,744	38.4
Widowed . . .	391	842	1,233	7.0
Total . .	8,612	8,954	17,566	100.0

Comparing adult population with the number married, we find :—

	Population	Married	Per Cent.
Males . .	5,710,000	3,357,000	58.8
Females . .	6,085,000	3,387,000	55.6
Total . .	11,795,000	6,744,000	57.2

The married ratio is 10 per cent. higher than in Germany, and yet the birth-rate is less.

SWEDEN

The census of 1890 resulted as follows :—

	Number (000 omitted)			Ratio
	Males	Females	Total	
Single . . .	1,432	1,461	2,893	60.4
Married . . .	795	805	1,600	33.4
Widowed. . .	89	200	289	6.1
Divorced . . .	1	3	4	0.1
Total .	2,317	2,469	4,786	100.0

Comparing the adult population with the number married, we find :—

	Population	Married	Per Cent.
Males . .	1,508,000	795,000	52.7
Females . .	1,679,000	805,000	47.9
Total . .	3,187,000	1,600,000	50.2

The married ratio is lower than in Germany or England. It is ascertained in Sweden that 12 per cent. of marriages are barren.

NORWAY

According to the census of 1890 we find :—

	Number (000 omitted)			Ratio
	Males	Females	Total	
Single . . .	598	630	1,228	61.7
Married . . .	315	326	641	32.2
Widowed. . .	38	81	119	6.1
Total . .	951	1,037	1,988	100.0

The above number of married compares with adult population thus :—

	Population	Married	Per Cent.
Males . .	592,000	315,000	53.2
Females . .	688,000	326,000	47.4
Total . .	1,280,000	641,000	50.1

The married ratio is higher for males, but lower for females, than in Sweden.

DENMARK

The census of 1890 resulted as follows :—

	Number (000 omitted)			Ratio
	Males	Females	Total	
Single . . .	648	648	1,296	59.4
Married . . .	376	376	752	34.5
Widowed. . .	40	91	131	6.0
Divorced . . .	1	2	3	0.1
Total . .	1,065	1,117	2,182	100.0

Comparing adult population with the number married, we find :—

	Population	Married	Per Cent.
Males . .	682,000	376,000	55.0
Females . .	744,000	376,000	50.5
Total . .	1,426,000	752,000	52.8

The married ratio is almost the same as in Germany.

SCANDINAVIA

If we group together the three northern kingdoms we find :—

	Number (000 omitted)			Ratio
	Males	Females	Total	
Single . . .	2,678	2,739	5,417	60.5
Married . . .	1,486	1,507	2,993	33.4
Widowed. . .	167	372	539	6.0
Divorced . . .	2	5	7	0.1
Total . .	4,333	4,623	8,956	100.0

The adult population shows the married ratio thus :—

	Population	Married	Per Cent.
Males . .	2,782,000	1,486,000	53.4
Females . .	3,111,000	1,507,000	48.4
Total . .	5,893,000	2,993,000	50.7

The married rate of the three kingdoms collectively is 3 per cent. lower than in Germany, but the birth-rate is 20 per cent. lower.

HOLLAND

The census of 1889 resulted as follows :—

	Number (000 omitted)			Ratio
	Males	Females	Total	
Single . . .	1,407	1,375	2,782	61.6
Married . . .	738	739	1,477	32.8
Widowed . . .	81	166	247	5.5
Divorced . . .	2	2	4	0.1
Total . .	2,228	2,282	4,510	100.0

Comparing the adult population with the number married, we find :—

	Population	Married	Per Cent.
Males . .	1,429,000	738,000	51.6
Females . .	1,491,000	739,000	49.6
Total . .	2,920,000	1,477,000	50.6

This is just the same married rate as in Scandinavia, but the birth-rate is 14 per cent. higher in Holland than in the northern kingdoms.

BELGIUM

According to the census of December 1890 we find :—

	Number (000 omitted)			Ratio
	Males	Females	Total	
Single . . .	1,936	1,845	3,781	62.2
Married . . .	967	965	1,932	31.9
Widowed . .	122	230	352	5.8
Divorced . . .	2	2	4	0.1
Total . .	3,027	3,042	6,069	100.0

The adult population compares with the number married thus :—

	Population	Married	Per Cent.
Males . .	2,015,000	967,000	48.0
Females . .	2,039,000	965,000	47.4
Total . .	4,054,000	1,932,000	47.7

The married rate is almost the same as in Switzerland, and much below the average of European countries.

FINLAND

The census of 1890 showed as follows :—

	Number (000 omitted)			Ratio
	Males	Females	Total	
Single . . .	734	711	1,445	60.7
Married . . .	401	402	803	33.7
Widowed . .	36	96	132	5.6
Total . .	1,171	1,209	2,380	100.0

The adult population compares with the number married as follows :—

	Population	Married	Per Cent.
Males . .	741,000	401,000	54.2
Females . .	783,000	402,000	51.3
Total . .	1,524,000	803,000	52.6

The married ratio is almost the same as in Denmark, but the birth-rate is 6 per cent. higher than in that kingdom.

BULGARIA

According to the census of 1888 the results were :—

	Number (000 omitted)			Ratio
	Males	Females	Total	
Single . . .	897	792	1,689	53.5
Married . . .	664	660	1,324	42.0
Widowed . .	43	96	139	4.4
Divorced . .	1	1	2	0.1
Total . .	1,605	1,549	3,154	100.0

Comparing adult population with the number married, we find :—

	Population	Married	Per Cent.
Males . .	949,000	664,000	69.7
Females . .	913,000	660,000	72.6
Total . .	1,862,000	1,324,000	71.2

The ratio of married is 40 per cent. higher than in Austria, and yet the Austrian birth-rate is higher than the Bulgarian.

CANADA

The census of 1891 gave results as follows :—

	Number (000 omitted)			Ratio
	Males	Females	Total	
Single . . .	1,601	1,452	3,053	63.2
Married . . .	796	792	1,588	32.8
Widowed . .	63	129	192	4.0
Total . .	2,460	2,373	4,833	100.0

The adult population, male and female, over 15 years of age, was 3,093,000, from which it appears that the married ratio was 51½ per cent., as compared with 52 per cent. in England.

AUSTRALIA

According to the census of 1891 the results were :—

	Number (000 omitted)			Ratio
	Males	Females	Total	
Single . . .	1,417	1,109	2,526	66.5
Married . . .	565	564	1,129	29.6
Widowed . .	55	91	146	3.9
Total . .	2,037	1,764	3,801	100.0

The ratios of adult population married in the several colonies were :—

	Adult Pop.	Married	Per Cent.
N. S. Wales . .	701,000	332,000	47.4
Victoria .	745,000	345,000	46.3
N. Zealand . .	377,000	182,000	48.3
Queensland . .	247,000	115,000	46.6
S. Australia . .	194,000	97,000	50.0
Tasmania . .	90,000	44,000	48.9
W. Australia . .	33,000	14,000	42.4
Total . .	2,387,000	1,129,000	47.2

The ratio of married people is 5 per cent. less than in the United Kingdom, and the birth-rate is 7 per cent. lower.

MEDICINE

See Part I., page 387 ; also *Drugs*, page 691.

METALS

The production of metals at various dates was estimated as follows :—

Date	Tons						Total Value, £
	Iron	Steel	Lead	Copper	Zinc	Tin	
1806	550,000	10,000	24,000	6,000	2,000	3,000	7,400,000
1838	2,450,000	20,000	130,000	22,000	9,000	5,000	19,200,000
1850	4,420,000	70,000	170,000	52,000	58,000	6,000	38,500,000
1870	11,910,000	540,000	400,000	94,000	130,000	16,000	72,300,000
1885	19,340,000	6,200,000	420,000	230,000	280,000	35,000	96,700,000
1895	28,800,000	14,600,000	680,000	490,000	460,000	40,000	175,200,000

The prices of the above metals at the dates in question were as follows :—

Date	£ per Ton					
	Iron	Steel	Lead	Copper	Zinc	Tin
1806 . .	8.0	...	35	190	25	120
1838 . .	5.1	...	22	90	17	90
1850 . .	5.7	60.0	17	86	21	78
1870 . .	3.0	31.5	20	75	19	125
1885 . .	2.2	5.1	11	48	13	95
1895 . .	2.4	4.6	11	46	14	64

See *Iron, Lead, Copper,* &c., under their special headings. In the former table the item of steel reduplicates the value of the iron used in its production.

METEOROLOGY

Barometer.—The highest reading on record is 31.63 at Barnaul, in Siberia, on December 16, 1877. It was observed the same day that the thermometer stood at 54.4 below zero, Fahr. The lowest reading of the barometer is 27.33 at Perth, Scotland, on Jan. 26, 1884.

Thermometer.—Six experiments were made simultaneously in balloons on November 17, 1896, with the following results, at different places, viz. :—

Place	Height, Feet	Fahrenheit	Place	Height, Feet	Fahrenheit
Warsaw . .	6,600	− 4	Berlin . . .	19,700	− 14
Munich . .	11,500	+ 20	Strasburg .	25,300	− 22
St. Petersburg	16,400	− 11	Paris . . .	49,200	− 76

On September 16, 1898, Mr. Spencer ascended from the Crystal Palace to 27,000 feet, and found temperature minus 45 Fahr.

The greatest cold was until recently (see p. 397) believed to be a quotation at Yakutsk, Siberia, of minus 73 Fahr. in 1829, but Professor Hildebrandson, of Upsala, asserts that there has been a quotation of minus 68 Centigrade, equal to minus 90 Fahr., at Werchojansk in Siberia. The greatest cold records in Great Britain are :—

Year	Place	Fahrenheit
1796 . . .	London	16 below zero
1879 . . .	Blackadder, Berwick	18 ,, ,,
1895 . . .	Alford, Aberdeen	16 ,, ,,

The greatest heat recorded was 133 Fahr. in the shade at Mourzuk, India, but Professor Wrede's observation in Central Arabia is 57½ Centigrade, equal to 135½ Fahr. in the shade, while the heat in the sun was 194 Fahr.

At Liverpool in 1863 there was a hurricane which indicated 43 lbs. pressure per square foot, equal to 90 miles an hour.

See *Meteorology*, in Part I., pp. 388–398.

MINING

The progress of this industry since 1860 is shown approximately as follows :—

Year	Hands Employed	Millions Tons Raised	Value, Millions £	Tons per Miner
1860 . .	1,016,000	183	76	180
1876 . .	2,040,000	388	202	190
1896 . .	3,200,000	795	307	248

The condition of mining in 1876 and 1896 was approximately as follows :—

	Miners		Millions Tons Raised		Value, Millions £		Tons per Miner		£ per Miner	
	1876	1896	1876	1896	1876	1896	1876	1896	1876	1896
Great Britain . .	610,000	840,000	147	251	58	69	241	299	95	82
France	207,000	270,000	27	41	15	21	131	152	72	77
Germany . . .	223,000	404,000	56	130	15	39	250	322	67	96
Russia	300,000	460,000	28	44	10	14	95	95	33	30
Austria . . .	126,000	170,000	16	37	7	13	56	77	55	77
Italy	36,000	63,000	2	4	2	3	55	63	55	50
Spain	44,000	63,000	6	12	2	4	135	190	45	60
Sweden . . .	27,000	26,000	2	2	2	2	70	70	75	75
Belgium . . .	111,000	150,000	18	23	7	10	160	152	60	65
United States . .	230,000	526,000	77	233	70	101	330	444	300	190
Canada . . .	6,000	18,000	1	4	1	3	160	220	170	220
Australia . . .	90,000	110,000	8	10	11	14	90	90	120	127
South Africa . .	30,000	100,000	...	4	2	14	...	400	70	140
Total . .	2,040,000	3,200,000	388	795	202	307	190	248	99	96

Each miner on an average raises 5 tons of mineral weekly, worth about 36 shillings. Wages are usually three-fourths of the value of output.

UNITED KINGDOM

The weight of mineral has almost doubled since 1870, viz. :—

	Tons	
	1870	1896
Coal	110,400,000	195,400,000
Sundries	36,700,000	55,300,000
Total . . .	147,100,000	250,700,000

The value rose from £46,100,000 in 1870, to £69,100,000 in 1896, including not only minerals but also the product of quarries, the figures for 1896 showing thus :—

	Tons	£ Sterling
Coal	195,400,000	57,200,000
Ores	13,800,000	3,800,000
Stone, &c. . . .	41,500,000	8,100,000
Total . . .	250,700,000	69,100,000

Official returns in the *Statistical Abstract* give not the ores, but the metals obtained, and their value, while they exclude the product of quarries : thus they compare the figures for 1896 with 1886 as follows :—

	Tons		Value, £	
	1886	1896	1886	1896
Coal . . .	157,500,000	195,400,000	38,100,000	57,200,000
Iron . . .	7,010,000	8,660,000	15,900,000	20,700,000
Lead, &c. .	60,000	40,000	1,800,000	800,000
Total .	164,570,000	204,100,000	55,800,000	78,700,000

(This is a deceptive mode of estimating *mineral* products, since it even includes the value of pig iron produced from Spanish and Swedish ores.)

The real mining product and number of hands are shown thus :—

	Hands	Value, £	£ per Hand
Minerals . . .	726,000	61,000,000	84
Quarries . . .	113,000	8,100,000	72
Total . .	839,000	69,100,000	82

Royalties paid to the owners of coal and iron mines amount to £4,900,000 yearly, or 8 per cent. of the gross product. Loss of life averages one man killed for every million tons raised, whereas before 1870 the average was three killed per million tons. The total number of persons of this class was in 1896 as follows : under ground, 576,000 ; above ground, 150,000 ; in quarries, 114,000 ; total 840,000. Deaths of miners in the years 1851–55 averaged 43 per 10,000 yearly, and in 1891–95 the average had fallen to 15 per 10,000 ; this means a saving of 2000 lives yearly.

FRANCE

The weight of mineral increased nearly 50 per cent. in ten years, viz. :—

	Tons		Value, £	
	1885	1895	1885	1895
Coal . . .	19,500,000	28,000,000	9,200,000	12,300,000
Iron ore . .	2,300,000	3,700,000	360,000	470,000
Lead ,, . .	10,000	20,000	100,000	90,000
Zinc ,, . .	170,000	320,000	129,000	300,000
Salt . . .	640,000	870,000	460,000	480,000
Peat . . .	190,000	130,000	80,000	70,000
Total . .	22,810,000	33,040,000	10,320,000	13,710,000

The quarries, moreover, produce 8½ million tons of stone and slate, valued at £6,800,000, which, added to the foregoing, makes a total output of 20½ millions sterling. There are 160,000 miners and 110,000 hands employed in quarries : the product of the former averages £86, of the latter £62, each.

GERMANY

Since the formation of the Empire mining industry has more than trebled :—

	Tons	Value, £
1870	39,000,000	12,400,000
1880	68,000,000	17,700,000
1888	95,000,000	23,800,000
1896	131,000,000	39,300,000

This is exclusive of stone and other quarries, of which there are no returns, but of which the product may reach 10 million tons. The principal mining products were :—

	1876	1886	1896
Coal, tons .	49,500,000	73,700,000	112,400,000
Iron ore, ,, .	4,700,000	8,500,000	14,200,000
Zinc ,, ,, .	530,000	710,000	730,000
Copper ,, ,, .	310,000	500,000	720,000
Lead ,, ,, .	120,000	160,000	160,000
Salt, ,, .	750,000	1,390,000	2,540,000
Total . .	55,910,000	84,960,000	130,750,000

One-fourth of the coal is lignite or brown-coal. The best collieries are in Prussia, which produces 80 per cent. of the German total. About one-tenth of the coal raised is exported, home consumption reaching 100 million tons, or 2 tons per inhabitant. The ironstone of Silesia and Westphalia is inferior, giving only 36 per cent. of iron. The copper ore of Prussia and Saxony is likewise very poor, yielding only 3½ per cent. of bar copper, as compared with 18 per cent. obtained from American ore. The zinc mines of Prussia are very valuable, the ore giving 21 per cent. of metallic zinc, and producing 150,000 tons of metal, of which one-half is exported. The annual production of silver averages 400 tons, value £1,700,000, and of gold 3½ tons, value £500,000. In 1895 the total number of miners was 400,000, and the weight of mineral raised was 325 tons per man, against 180 tons in 1870. The number of miners killed or injured in ten years ending 1894 was in the ratio of 22 in 10,000 yearly.

RUSSIA

Mining is chiefly confined to Siberia, where convict labour is used. The ores are very poor, for it takes 600,000 tons of quartz to produce 1 ton of gold, each ton of quartz when crushed yielding only 5 shillings worth of gold. Production increases, viz. :—

	Tons Gold Yearly	Value, £
1871–80	38	5,300,000
1881–88	35	4,900,000
1890–95	42	5,900,000

The total weight of mineral raised shows as follows :—

	Tons		
	1888	1892	1895
Quartz . . .	23,000,000	25,800,000	24,700,000
Coal	4,500,000	6,800,000	8,900,000
Naphtha . . .	1,900,000	4,500,000	6,900,000
Salt	1,200,000	1,400,000	1,500,000
Ores	900,000	1,200,000	1,700,000
Total . .	31,500,000	39,700,000	43,700,000

The value of all mineral products rose from 10 millions sterling in 1888 to 14 millons in 1895, the latter sum being equal to £31 per man : but for convict labour, it would not be possible to carry on mining for so poor a return. The total number of miners, convicts and free, is 460,000, the largest number in any country of the world except Great Britain and the United States. The weight of mineral raised per miner is only 93 tons, as compared with 285 tons in Great Britain.

AUSTRIA

In 1860 the total mining industry of Austria-Hungary was 4 million tons, value £1,500,000. Since then it has grown ninefold, the output now exceeding 37 million tons, viz. :—

		1888	1895
Coal,	tons . .	23,700,000	33,200,000
Iron ore,	,, . .	2,200,000	2,400,000
Naphtha,	,, . .	400,000	900,000
Lead ores, &c.,	,, . .	300,000	300,000
Salt,	,, . .	400,000	500,000
Total	,, . .	27,000,000	37,300,000

The shares that correspond to Austria and Hungary are shown as follows :—

	Austria		Hungary	
	Tons	Value, £	Tons	Value, £
Coal . . .	28,100,000	5,700,000	5,100,000	1,400,000
Iron . . .	1,400,000	2,500,000	1,000,000	1,000,000
Sundries .	1,300,000	1,300,000	400,000	800,000
Total . .	30,800,000	9,500,000	6,500,000	3,200,000

Two-thirds of the coal is lignite, of which 8 million tons are exported yearly. The value of mineral products, excluding naphtha, has been as follows :—

Year	Austria, £	Hungary, £	Total, £
1880 . . .	4,700,000	1,500,000	6,200,000
1890 . . .	7,700,000	2,400,000	10,100,000
1895 . . .	8,800,000	3,200,000	12,000,000

There are 130,000 miners in Austria, and 40,000 in Hungary : the product averages £73 per hand in the former, £80 in the latter, country.

ITALY

Mining is not remunerative, the average product per man being the lowest in the world except Russia. In 1895 the industry showed as follows :—

	Hands	Tons	Value, £	£ per Man
Sulphur . .	22,000	2,400,000	600,000	27
Ores, &c. .	20,000	800,000	1,000,000	50
Quarries .	20,000	600,000	1,200,000	60
Total . .	62,000	3,800,000	2,800,000	45

SPAIN

This branch of industry has grown tenfold since 1863, viz. :—

		1863	1890	1896
Iron	ore, tons . .	170,000	5,700,000	6,800,000
Copper	,, ,, . .	140,000	2,500,000	2,800,000
Lead, &c.	,, ,, . .	200,000	680,000	700,000
Salt,	,, . .	400,000	...	350,000
Coal,	,, . .	320,000	1,280,000	1,830,000
Total	,, . .	1,230,000	10,160,000	12,480,000

There are 63,000 miners, and the output is valued at £4,000,000, which gives an average of £63 per miner.

BELGIUM

Mining has increased 50 per cent. since 1870, viz. :—

		1870	1895
Coal,	tons . . .	13,700,000	20,500,000
Sundries,	,, . . .	1,900,000	2,700,000
Total	,, . . .	15,600,000	23,200,000

The output of coal is valued at £7,700,000, and the total mineral product at £10,000,000, including quarries, which give occupation to 32,000 hands, and the product of which reaches £1,500,000 yearly. Mines and quarries have altogether 150,000 workmen, the product averaging £67 each.

SWEDEN

The returns of mining for 1895 compare with 1885 thus :—

		1885	1895
Iron ore,	tons . .	870,000	1,900,000
Other ores,	,, . .	90,000	100,000
Coal,	,, . .	170,000	220,000
Total	,, . .	1,130,000	2,220,000

The total output is valued at £1,800,000, equal to £70 for each hand employed.

CANADA

Mining products in 1896 compare with 1886 thus :—

	Tons (short)		Value, £	
	1886	1896	1886	1896
Coal . . .	2,400,000	3,700,000	1,060,000	1,450,000
Ores, &c. .	270,000	840,000	420,000	1,700,000
Naphtha .	130,000	160,000	120,000	250,000
Total . .	2,800,000	4,700,000	1,600,000	3,400,000

Official returns bring up the total value to £4,500,000. but this perhaps includes metals.

UNITED STATES

The weight of minerals raised in 1896 was four times as much as in 1870, viz. :—

	1870	1896
Coal, tons . .	33,000,000	171,400,000
Iron ore, ,, . .	3,200,000	11,000,000
Quartz, &c. ,, . .	20,200,000	50,600,000
Total ,, . .	56,400,000	233,000,000

The official value in 1870 was £66,600,000, and in 1896 rose to £129,000,000, an increase of 95 per cent., but the figures are not correct, silver being valued at 64 pence (instead of 28 pence) the ounce, and the value of pig iron substituted for that of iron ore. The real value of mineral products was as follows :—

	1870 £	1890 £	1896 £
Coal . . .	20,600,000	36,800,000	40,800,000
Iron ore. .	2,700,000	10,400,000	6,200,000
Copper ,, .	800,000	3,200,000	5,100,000
Lead ,, .	800,000	1,300,000	1,100,000
Petroleum .	10,000,000	7,300,000	12,200,000
Gold . .	10,200,000	6,900,000	11,000,000
Silver. . .	3,200,000	11,000,000	7,000,000
Sundries .	11,000,000	29,800,000	17,800,000
Total . .	59,300,000	106,700,000	101,200,000

The official value of mining products in 1896 was £129,200,000, or 28 per cent. over the real value, being made up thus :—

	Official, £	Real, £
Coal. . . .	40,800,000	40,800,000
Iron ore . . .	18,800,000	6,200,000
Other ores . .	14,000,000	7,400,000
Petroleum . .	12,200,000	12,200,000
Gold . . .	11,000,000	11,000,000
Silver . . .	15,800,000	7,000,000
Stone . . .	7,900,000	7,900,000
Sundries . . .	8,700,000	8,700,000
Total . .	129,200,000	101,200,000

The States which produce coal and iron are the following :—

	Tons	
	Coal	Pig Iron
Pennsylvania . . .	92,800,000	4,000,000
Illinois . . .	17,700,000	900,000
Ohio . . .	11,500,000	1,200,000
Virginia . . .	12,600,000	500,000
Alabama . . .	5,100,000	900,000
Various . . .	31,700,000	1,100,000
The Union . . .	171,400,000	8,600,000

The extraction of iron, copper, and lead ore has been as follows :—

	1870	1889	1896
Iron ore, tons.	3,200,000	13,300,000	11,000,000
Copper ,, ,, .	80,000	600,000	1,200,000
Lead ,, ,, .	100,000	250,000	250,000
Zinc ,, ,, .	...	250,000	400,000
Total ,, .	3,380,000	14,400,000	12,850,000

Iron ore gives 40 per cent., copper 17, lead 70, and zinc 20 per cent. of metal. The yield of petroleum increases year by year, at present reaching 61 million barrels, or a little over 12 million tons; about 60,000 wells have been sunk since 1859, of which 6000 are working, the annual yield in barrels of 42 gallons showing thus :—

Barrels	1860–80	1881–93	1896
Raised . .	7,800,000	33,800,000	61,000,000
Exported . .	3,600,000	13,200,000	23,000,000
Home use . .	4,200,000	20,600,000	38,000,000

Home consumption averages 23 gallons, or a little over half a barrel, per inhabitant.

The extraction of gold quartz and silver ore is estimated according to the yield of those metals, a ton of the former giving usually half an ounce, and of the latter 40 ounces, of pure metal. Thus the weight of ores may be set down as follows :—

Year	Tons		Ounces	
	Gold Quartz	Silver Ore	Gold	Silver
1850 . . .	4,800,000	...	2,400,000	...
1860 . . .	4,400,000	...	2,200,000	...
1870 . . .	4,800,000	300,000	2,400,000	13,000,000
1880 . . .	3,500,000	750,000	1,750,000	30,000,000
1890 . . .	3,200,000	1,400,000	1,590,000	55,000,000
1896 . . .	5,000,000	1,500,000	2,570,000	59,000,000

A detailed statement of the yield of precious metals since 1850 is given at page 738. The following table shows the auriferous and argentiferous States in 1890 and 1896 :—

	Gold, Ounces		Silver, Ounces	
	1890	1896	1890	1896
California .	630,000	650,000	900,000	600,000
Colorado .	210,000	740,000	18,700,000	22,500,000
Montana .	160,000	210,000	15,700,000	16,600,000
Dakota . .	160,000	250,000	100,000	200,000
Utah . . .	30,000	90,000	7,900,000	8,800,000
Idaho . .	90,000	110,000	3,600,000	5,100,000
Arizona . .	50,000	130,000	1,000,000	1,800,000
Nevada . .	140,000	120,000	4,300,000	1,000,000
Alaska . .	40,000	100,000	...	100,000
N. Mexico .	40,000	20,000	1,200,000	700,000
Washington	10,000	20,000	100,000	300,000
Various . .	30,000	130,000	1,000,000	1,100,000
The Union .	1,590,000	2,570,000	54,500,000	58,800,000

The mining for the precious metals from 1849 to 1897 may be summed up thus :—

	Tons Ore	Tons Metal	Value, £
Gold . . .	216,000,000	3,080	431,000,000
Silver . .	29,000,000	33,700	231,000,000
Total .	245,000,000	36,780	662,000,000

The number of persons engaged in mining rose from 234,000 in 1880 to 505,000 in 1890.

SOUTH AFRICA

The Kimberley diamond-fields were discovered in 1871, the Transvaal gold-fields in 1887, the quantities and value exported yearly showing as follows :—

Years	Diamonds		Gold	
	Carats	Value, £	Ounces	Value, £
1881–85 . .	...	3,240,000	10,000	40,000
1886–90 . .	3,200,000	4,060,000	250,000	920,000
1891–94 . .	2,900,000	3,750,000	1,450,000	5,050,000
1895 . . .	3,600,000	4,800,000	2,380,000	8,200,000

In 1897 the Transvaal gold-fields produced £11,100,000. The copper-mines of Cape Colony yield about £300,000 per annum. The total mining output of South Africa is about 16 millions sterling yearly. The Kimberley diamond-fields have produced in 27 years about 62 million carats of diamonds, worth 84 millions sterling : the Transvaal gold-fields in 10 years have yielded 15,500,000 ounces, worth 52 millions sterling.

AUSTRALIA

Official returns of mining products since 1850 are :—

	Yearly Product, £			Total, £
	1850–88	1889–95	1896	46 Years
Gold . . .	8,600,000	7,200,000	9,000,000	388,500,000
Silver . .	100,000	2,800,000	2,100,000	25,300,000
Copper . .	700,000	200,000	400,000	27,700,000
Tin, &c. . .	500,000	400,000	400,000	21,400,000
Coal . . .	700,000	1,800,000	1,800,000	40,300,000
Total .	10,600,000	12,400,000	13,700,000	503,200,000

The total value for forty-six years was made up thus :—

	Value, £ (ooo omitted)			
	Gold	Silver	Sundries	Total
New South Wales .	43,400	22,400	44,600	110,400
Victoria	244,100	800	1,700	246,600
New Zealand . .	52,400	200	5,900	58,500
Queensland . . .	39,200	700	8,500	48,400
South Australia . .	1,900	100	21,500	23,500
Tasmania	3,400	1,100	6,800	11,300
West Australia . .	4,100	...	400	4,500
Total . .	388,500	25,300	89,400	503,200

The value of mining products in 1896 was as follows :—

	£ Sterling (ooo omitted)				
	Gold	Silver	Coal	Sundries	Total
New South Wales	1,070	1,790	1,130	360	4,350
Victoria	3,220	10	110	...	3,340
New Zealand . .	1,040	10	430	...	1,480
Queensland .	2,240	30	150	110	2,530
South Australia .	100	...	...	220	320
Tasmania . . .	240	220	20	160	640
West Australia .	1,070	...	...	...	1,070
Total . .	8,980	2,060	1,840	850	13,730

In 1891 the number of miners was 94,000, at present it may be estimated at 110,000 ; the average product being £114 per annum for gold-miners, and £155 for colliers.

OTHER COUNTRIES

India and China produce each about 400,000 ounces of gold yearly ; Spanish America 800,000 ounces of gold and 2400 tons of silver. The aggregate value of these items is 14 millions sterling, which is not included in the general table of mining values already given at page 773.

MISSIONS

The Amer. Stat. Ass. (1893) publishes the following statement as to the number of Christians in Asia and Africa :—

	India	China	Siberia	Japan	Syria, &c.	Africa	Total
Roman Catholics . .	1,199,000	1,116,000	70,000	30,000	663,000	2,660,000	5,738,000
Protestants . .	534,000	88,000	20,000	...	20,000	1,740,000	2,402,000
Greeks, &c. . . .	...	...	7,000,000	...	3,660,000	3,000,000	13,660,000
Total . . .	1,733,000	1,204,000	7,090,000	30,000	4,343,000	7,400,000	21,800,000

The item Greeks, &c., includes Copts, who number 3 millions in Africa.

MONEY

The following table, from the United States Mint Report, shows the money now in use :—

	£ Sterling (ooo omitted)				Gold Ratio
	Gold	Silver	Un-covered Paper	Total	
G. Britain .	122,000	25,000	23,300	170,300	71.8
France . .	160,600	102,400	3,900	266,900	60.0
Germany .	140,400	43,000	26,200	209,600	66.8
Russia . .	101,600	9,000	97,000	207,600	49.0
Austria . .	34,800	13,500	42,500	90,800	38.3
Italy . . .	20,900	8,100	35,000	64,000	32.7
Spain . .	8,000	10,300	21,400	39,700	20.2
Portugal .	1,000	1,500	12,600	15,100	6.7
Scandinavia .	6,800	2,500	1,700	11,000	61.8
Holland .	5,600	11,700	6,700	24,000	23.3
Belgium .	10,400	11,900	15,100	37,400	27.7

	£ Sterling (ooo omitted)				Gold Ratio
	Gold	Silver	Un-covered Paper	Total	
Switzerland	3,300	400	3,000	6,700	49.0
Roumania .	8,000	2,200	2,400	12,600	63.6
Servia . .	300	300	600	1,200	25.0
Bulgaria .	200	1,400	...	1,600	12.5
Greece . .	100	300	3,000	3,400	3.0
Turkey . .	10,400	8,300	...	18,700	55.6
Europe . .	634,400	251,800	294,400	1,180,600	53.8
U. States .	139,800	131,300	88,300	359,400	38.8
Mexico . .	1,000	20,000	800	21,800	4.5
Canada . .	3,300	1,200	7,300	11,800	28.0
Australia .	27,000	1,400	...	28,400	95.0
The East .	54,700	423,200	8,000	487,200	11.5
Various . .	5,800	41,400	800	48,000	12.1
The World.	866,000	870,300	399,600	2,137,200	40.6

The following table shows, according to Mr. Fred. Atkinson, the increase of gold money during the period since 1851:—

	Millions £ Sterling			Weight, Mill. Oz.	
	1851	1896	Increase	1851	1896
U. Kingdom	41.5	122.0	80.5	10.8	31.9
France	3.0	160.6	157.6	0.8	41.8
Germany	3.0	140.4	137.4	0.8	36.5
Russia	30.8	101.6	70.8	8.0	26.4
Austria	2.0	34.8	32.8	0.5	9.0
Italy	2.0	20.9	18.9	0.5	5.4
Spain	18.0	8.0	...	4.7	2.1
Portugal	3.0	1.0	...	0.8	0.2
Scandinavia	2.0	6.8	4.8	0.5	1.8
Holland	14.0	5.6	...	3.6	1.4
Belgium	1.0	10.4	9.4	0.2	2.7
Switzerland	1.0	3.3	2.3	0.2	0.8
Turkey, &c.	4.5	19.0	14.5	1.2	5.0
Europe	125.8	634.4	508.6	32.6	165.0
United States	15.0	139.8	124.8	3.9	36.4
Japan	20.0	16.0	...	5.2	4.2
India, &c.	19.2	75.8	56.6	5.0	19.7
The World	180.0	866.0	686.0	46.7	225.3

The increase of silver money in the same interval was as follows:—

	Millions £ Sterling			Weight Millions Oz.	
	1851	1896	Increase	1851	1896
United Kingdom	14.0	25.4	11.4	52	85
France	100.0	102.5	2.5	362	371
Germany	35.0	43.1	8.1	127	140
Russia	21.2	9.1	...	78	28
Austria	7.0	13.5	6.5	26	46
Italy	5.0	8.1	3.1	18	28
Spain	6.0	10.3	4.3	22	35
Portugal	3.0	1.5	...	11	5
Scandinavia	9.0	2.6	...	33	9
Holland	12.0	11.7	...	44	43
Belgium	3.0	11.9	8.9	11	43
Switzerland	3.0	0.4	...	11	1
Turkey, &c.	6.0	12.6	6.6	22	46
Europe	224.2	252.7	28.5	817	880
United States	25.8	131.7	105.9	94	470
Japan	3.0	9.1	6.1	11	35
Other Countries	49.0	392.5	343.5	179	1,395
The World	302.0	786.0	484.0	1,101	2,780

The item of Other Countries for 1896 includes the following:—

	£ Sterling, Nom.	Ounces
India	232,300,000	799,000,000
China	70,000,000	264,000,000
Singapore	40,000,000	151,000,000
Ceylon	15,000,000	52,000,000
Mexico	20,200,000	76,000,000
South America	9,800,000	36,000,000
Cuba, &c.	5,200,000	17,000,000
Total	392,500,000	1,395,000,000

The following table compares the amount of money in various countries with the industries of same, and also with population:—

	Millions £		Money Ratio to Industries Per Cent.	Shillings per Head
	Industries	Money		
United Kingdom	1,360	170	12.5	85
France	1,169	267	22.8	140
Germany	1,288	210	16.3	80
Russia	1,073	208	19.4	38
Austria	744	91	12.2	44
Italy	433	64	14.8	42
Spain	296	40	13.4	46
Portugal	61	15	24.5	62
Scandinavia	203	11	5.4	24
Holland	94	24	25.5	100
Belgium	187	37	19.8	118
Switzerland	68	7	10.3	46
Danub. States	154	16	10.4	28
Greece	28	3	10.7	27
Europe	7,158	1,163	16.2	63
United States	3,316	359	10.8	102
Canada	204	12	5.9	48
Australia	198	28	14.2	132
Total	10,876	1,562	14.3	70

The above table comprises only gold, silver, and *uncovered* notes.

The coinage of all nations since 1851 has been as follows:—

	Gold, Mill. £			Weight Tons	Silver, Mill. £			Weight Tons
	1851–1880	1881–1896	Total		1851–1880	1881–1896	Total	
U. King.	166	74	240	1,710	16	17	33	3,630
France	292	16	308	2,200	51	1	52	5,720
Germany	87	63	150	1,070	22	3	25	2,750
Russia	110	52	162	1,160	28	6	34	3,740
Austria	17	34	51	360	45	12	57	6,270
Italy	10	7	17	120	23	3	26	2,860
Spain & P.	30	3	33	230	12	...	12	1,320
Belgium	23	...	23	163	18	...	18	1,980
Various	15	11	26	187	33	...	33	3,630
Europe	750	260	1,010	7,200	248	42	290	31,900
U. States	217	129	346	2,470	49	79	128	14,080
Australia	62	86	148	1,060	...	...	...	...
India, &c.	21	15	36	330	293	229	522	57,420
The World	1,050	490	1,540	11,060	590	350	940	103,400

It is supposed that the gold coin in use has been so far reminted that the actual amount used for coinage has been between 40 and 50 per cent. of the nominal weight, say 5400 tons, in the last fifty years. Thus in 1885 Spallart estimated the existing amount of gold coin in the world at 5925 tons, and since that date the amount minted by all nations has been 360 millions sterling, or 2600 tons. Assuming that 60 per cent. of this was new metal, the actual weight of gold coin now in use would be 6500 tons, as stated above, leaving 2660 tons uncoined. Allowing for recoinage, the amount of new silver minted since 1850 appears to be 52,000 tons, or half the nominal weight shown above. This would make the total weight of existing silver money in the world to be 97,000 tons. Spallart's estimate in 1885 was 88,100 tons, since which date the United States alone have coined 9000 tons, while other countries have done little more than remint old silver.

Gold and silver money were alike legal tender in England till 1664, when gold was demonetised, and silver only legal. In 1717 both were again made legal, till 1775, when gold was adopted, and only small debts, under £25, could be discharged in silver. Forced currency, Bank of England notes, prevailed from 1797 till 1816, when the gold standard was established, silver being legal only up to 40 shillings. In coining gold the British Government has a profit of a halfpenny in £10, or about £200 per million. In 1830 the shilling coin had nearly 11½ pence (11.3) of silver, the profit accruing to the Mint being 6 per cent., or £60,000 per million. In 1898 the shilling has only 5 pence of silver, and the profit to Government is £600,000 per million. The Mint price of gold is £3, 17s. 10½d., or 934½ pence per ounce, as fixed in 1717.

The total amount of hard money in the world, taking silver throughout at its nominal value, shows as follows :—

	Millions £ Stg.		Shills. per Inhab.	
	1851	1896	1851	1896
United Kingdom .	55.5	147.4	40	74
France . . .	103.0	263.1	57	138
Germany . . .	38.0	183.5	21	70
Russia . . .	52.0	110.7	17	20
Austria . . .	9.0	48.3	6	23
Italy . . .	7.0	29.0	7	19
Spain . . .	24.0	18.3	32	20
Portugal . .	6.0	2.5	35	10
Scandinavia . .	11.0	9.4	34	20
Holland . . .	26.0	17.3	170	72
Belgium . . .	4.0	22.3	20	70
Switzerland . .	4.0	3.7	34	25
Turkey, &c. . .	10.5	31.6	12	34
Europe . . .	350.0	887.1	26	49
United States .	40.8	271.5	35	76
Japan . . .	23.0	25.1	15	13
Other Countries .	68.2	468.3	...	...
The World .	482.0	1,652.0	...	...
Gold . . .	180.0	866.0	...	...
Silver . . .	302.0	786.0	...	...

The following table shows the amount of hard money coined by nations between 1851 and 1896, inclusive, and the actual increase of money in use, from which may be deduced the amount recoined or consumed :—

	Millions £ Sterling					
	Gold			Silver		
	Coined	Money Increase	Recoined, &c.	Coined	Money Increase	Recoined, &c.
U. Kingdom .	240	80	160	33	11	22
France . . .	308	158	150	52	3	49
Germany . .	150	137	13	25	8	17
Russia . . .	162	71	91	34	...	34
Austria . . .	51	33	18	57	7	50
Italy, &c. . .	99	29	70	89	...	89
Europe . . .	1,010	508	502	290	29	261
U. States . .	346	125	221	128	106	22
Australia . .	148	25	122	...	...	...
India, &c. . .	36	27	9	522	349	173
The World . .	1,540	686	854	940	484	456

The output of the British Mint since 1891 has been as follows :—

	£ Sterling (000 omitted)			
	Gold	Silver	Bronze	Total
1891 . . .	6,720	1,000	90	7,810
1892 . . .	13,910	850	60	14,820
1893 . . .	9,270	1,010	50	10,330
1894 . . .	5,670	940	30	6,640
1895 . . .	3,810	1,200	40	5,050
1896 . . .	4,810	1,230	120	6,160
1897 . . .	1,820	720	...	2,540
7 years . .	46,010	6,950	390	53,350

The Treasury report for 1898 shows that light gold coin withdrawn from circulation since 1891 amounted to £34,200,000 : the loss on 100 sovereigns was 246 pence, or 1.02 per cent., and on 100 half-sovereigns 216 pence, or 1.80 per cent. The loss to the Treasury in making the conversion was £540,000, being £16 per thousand, or 4 pence in the £. In the same period the Treasury withdrew from circulation old silver money to the value of £1,900,000. It appears that of the gold money withdrawn only £2,420,000 was pre-Victorian, while £31,800,000 was composed of sovereigns and half-sovereigns issued since 1837, and which had lost weight.

The activity of money, or rapidity of circulation, varies exceedingly in countries : in some it is found that money does its work over 100 times a year. Returns for five years ending December 1894 show that the number of payments effected yearly by the money employed in banks was as follows :—

Bank of

Germany . 167 | Belgium . . 133 | Portugal . . 25
France . . 127 | Italy . . . 30 | Spain . . . 14

The latest banking statement of the relative use of coin, notes, and cheques in the United Kingdom showed the following ratios :—

	London	Dublin	Edinburgh	Rural
Coin . . .	7	16	5	152
Notes . . .	21	85	127	119
Cheques . .	972	899	868	729
	1,000	1,000	1,000	1,000

The ratios in the Bank of France at various dates were :—

	1841	1861	1881	1895
Coin . . .	94	110	53	21
Notes . . .	373	342	293	238
Cheques . .	533	548	674	741
	1,000	1,000	1,000	1,000

In Belgium the banking census puts notes and cheques together, viz. :—

	1871	1881	1891	1895
Coin . . .	76	63	49	37
Paper . . .	924	937	951	963
	1,000	1,000	1,000	1,000

The money of the United States in 1897 compared with previous dates as follows :—

	Millions £ Sterling		
	1880	**1887**	**1897**
Gold *	73.2	136.1	144.8
Silver	29.8	73.4	131.4
Greenbacks . .	79.6	129.6	195.0
Bank-notes . .	71.8	58.1	47.8
Total . .	254.4	397.2	519.0

The money of 1897 was made up thus :—

	Millions £ Sterling		
	In Treasury	In Circulation	Total
Gold	37.1	107.7	144.8
Silver . . .	108.4	23.0	131.4
Certificates . . .	4.2	94.8	99.0
United States notes .	27.4	68.6	96.0
Bank-notes . .	1.0	46.8	47.8
Total . .	178.1	340.9	519.0

The following table compares the money of 1887 and 1897 thus :—

	Hard Money, Millions £					
	In Treasury		In Circulation		Total	
	1887	**1897**	**1887**	**1897**	**1887**	**1897**
Gold	57.8	37.1	78.3	107.7	136.1	144.8
Silver. . . .	51.8	108.4	21.6	23.0	73.4	131.4
Total . .	109.6	145.5	99.9	130.7	209.5	276.2

	Paper Money					
U. S. notes . .	6.0	27.4	66.2	68.6	72.2	96.0
Gold certificates	6.3	0.3	19.0	7.8	25.3	8.1
Silver do.	0.7	3.9	31.4	87.0	32.1	90.9
Bank-notes . .	0.5	1.0	57.6	46.8	58.1	47.8
Total paper .	13.5	32.6	174.2	210.2	187.7	242.8
Grand total .	123.1	178.1	274.1	340.9	397.2	519.0

The total reduced to ratios shows as follows :—

	1887			1897		
	In Treasury	In Circulation	Total	In Treasury	In Circulation	Total
Gold	14.5	19.7	34.2	7.1	20.8	27.9
Silver . . .	13.1	5.4	18.5	20.9	4.4	25.3
U. S. notes .	3.3	29.4	32.7	6.1	31.5	37.6
Bank-notes .	0.1	14.5	14.6	0.2	9.0	9.2
Total . .	31.0	69.0	100.0	34.3	65.7	100.0

* To be read thus : Gold, £73,200,000.

The amount of money compared with population was as follows :—

	Millions £ Sterling			£ per Inhab.
	Metal	Paper	Total	
1880 . . .	103	151	254	5.1
1887 . . .	209	188	397	6.7
1897 . . .	276	243	519	7.1

In the United States it is shown by Prof. Fisher that the amount of cheques used in 1891 reached 159 milliards of dollars, equal to 33,000 millions of pounds sterling, or 80 times the sum of all money (coin and notes) then existing in that country.

See *Clearing-Houses*, page 77, and page 642.

Gold and Silver Money.—Guthrie's table of the coins in use in 1774 was as follows :—

		Gold Coin	Value, Shillings	Silver Coin	Value, Pence
English . .		Guinea	21	Shilling	12
Scotch . .		,,	24½	...	...
Irish . . .		,,	22¼	Token	10
France . .		Louis	20	Livre	10
Poland . .		Ducat	9	Florin	14
Denmark . .		,,	8	Crown	36
Portugal .		Moidore	27	Cruzado	32
,, . .		Milree	6	Testoon	6
Spain . .		Ducat	5	Dollar	43
Germany .		Thaler	3½	Florin	14
Flanders .		Ducat	9¼	,,	18
Holland .		Dollar	4½	Guilder	21
Russia . .		Rouble	4½	10-kopeck	5
Italy . . .		Scudo	4½	Florin	9
Turkey . .		Sequin	7½	Piastre	48
India . .		Doubloon	63	Rupee	30

In France the livre contained the value of 20 sous, and there was also an ecu of 60 sous. In Holland the guilder was worth 21 copper stivers, each one penny, and in Flanders the florin had 18 stivers. In Germany the florin had 36 groschen, of which 2½ made one penny English. In Austria the thaler, as in Germany, was worth 42 pence, but there was also a gulden worth 30 pence or 60 kreutzers. In Denmark the crown had 60 skilligs, 20 of which were worth 12 pence. The Russian rouble had 100 kopecks or half-pence. The Spanish dollar had 8 reals, worth 5½ pence each.

MORTGAGES

ITALY

Rural mortgages rose from 198 millions sterling in 1880 to 250 millions in 1892, showing an average increase of £4,700,000 per annum.

PRUSSIA

The average increase of rural mortgages in 1886 to 1889 was £5,700,000 per annum : from 1887 to 1895 it was £8,800,000 per annum. The increase of mortgages in Prussia from 1886 to 1895 was 311 millions sterling, or 34½ millions per annum. Berlin had new mortgages in 1895 for £28,800,000.

SWEDEN

Rural mortgages in 1886 amounted to £51,000,000, or 25 per cent. of the value of farms in the kingdom : the average increase during 10 years was £1,400,000 per annum.

EGYPT

In 1894 rural mortgages amounted to £20,500,000.

RUSSIA

In 1895 there were mortgages amounting to £169,600,000 on 124 million acres, or 27 shillings per acre.

VARIOUS COUNTRIES

Rural mortgages in 1887, according to Sbrojavacca, were approximately as follows :—

	Millions £	Per Cent. of Property
France	402	13
Italy	196	14
Holland	60	20
Austria	450	25
Germany	750	30
Ireland	160	40

Mortgages registered in the United States from 1880 to 1890, were as follows :—

	Number	Millions £	Average, £
Urban	4,771,000	1,498	315
Rural	4,747,000	1,020	214
Total . .	9,518,000	2,518	265

The total amount of existing mortgages on January 1, 1890, was only half the foregoing, viz. :—

	Number	Millions £	Average, £
Urban	2,475,000	792	320
Rural	2,303,000	460	200
Total . .	4,778,000	1,252	262

The following table shows the amount of urban and rural mortgages, the value of city property and farms, and the ratio of mortgages to such property :—

States	Millions £ Sterling				Mortgage Ratio	
	Mortgages		Property			
	Urban	Rural	Urban	Rural	Urban	Rural
New England .	87	21	705	122	12.3	17.3
Middle . . .	448	90	1,962	549	22.8	16.4
Southern . .	29	55	597	610	4.8	9.0
Prairie . . .	183	249	1,675	1,770	11.0	14.1
Pacific . . .	45	45	615	272	7.3	16.6
The Union . .	792	460	5,554	3,323	7.1	13.8

States	Millions £ Stg.		Interest, £ Yearly	Average Rate	Interest Shills. per Inhab.
	Mortgages	Properties			
N. England .	108	827	6,100,000	5.6	26
Middle . . .	538	2,511	29,950,000	5.6	42
South . . .	84	1,207	6,700,000	8.0	7
Prairie . .	432	3,445	32,400,000	7.5	29
Pacific . .	90	887	7,500,000	8.3	50
The Union .	1,252	8,877	82,650,000	6.6	27

Rural mortgages covered 274 million acres, being an average of 119 to each mortgage : the amount was 460 millions sterling, an average of 33 shillings per acre mortgaged, and the annual interest was £33,800,000, equal to 30 pence per acre.

See *Mortgages*, in Part I., page 413.

N

NAMES

The following names occur among 1210 members in five Parliaments of the fourteenth, fifteenth, and sixteenth centuries :—

	Date			In Five Parliaments
	1314	1450	1529	
John . . .	50	77	76	338
William . .	34	52	47	188
Thomas . .	15	55	43	169
Robert . .	20	17	16	95
Richard . .	10	20	23	91
Henry . .	10	6	13	39
Walter . .	11	4	1	26
Roger . .	5	3	4	26
Edward . .	0	2	15	20
Nicholas . .	7	1	0	18
Ralph . .	2	1	1	15
Hugh . .	3	4	3	14
Various . .	40	24	61	171
Total . .	207	266	303	1,210

In the aggregate of the five Parliaments the following names occur the number of times expressed :—

	Times		Times		Times
Simon . .	12	George . .	10	Adam . . .	8
Milo . . .	10	Geoffrey . .	9	Peter . . .	8
Edmund . .	10	Gilbert . .	8	Reginald . .	7

	Times		Times		Times
Giles . . .	6	Elias . . .	4	Otto	2
James . . .	5	Philip . . .	4	Matthew . .	2
Alexander . .	5	Stephen . .	4	Ivo	2
Gerard . . .	5	Anthony . .	3	Francis . . .	2
Lawrence . .	5	Bartholomew .	3	Everard . .	2
Humfrey . .	5	Christopher .	3	Bernard . .	2
Andrew . . .	4	Vincent . . .	3	Charles . . .	1

There is no entry of two Christian names for one person except Thomas Maria Wingfield, for Huntingdon, in 1552. Joseph does not occur in any of the five Parliaments, nor Wilfred. The following names occur once : Michael, Paul, Maurice, Jaspar, Gervase, Cuthbert, Alan, Arnold ; and in the Parliament of 1554 we find once Arthur, Kenelm, Mark, Luke, Dominic, Ambrose, and a few others.

Clark's index of the Oxford Register from 1571 to 1622 contains 30,000 names, and the following Christian names occur, in this order :—

	Times		Times		Times
John . .	3,826	Nicholas .	326	Humphrey .	168
Thomas .	2,777	Edmund .	298	Charles . .	139
William .	2,546	Anthony .	262	Philip . .	137
Richard .	1,691	Hugh . .	257	David . .	129
Robert .	1,222	Christopher	243	Matthew .	116
Edward .	957	Samuel . .	227	Michael . .	103
Henry . .	908	Walter . .	207	Alexander .	98
George .	647	Roger . .	195	Arthur . .	98
Francis .	447	Ralph . .	182	Laurence .	90
James . .	424	Peter . .	175	Giles . . .	88

See *Names*, in Part I., page 414.

NAVY

A return of the British Admiralty in May 1898 gave the strength of the principal navies as follows :—

	Battle-ships	Cruisers	Torpedo-boats, &c.	Total
Great Britain .	64	161	247	472
France . .	35	75	287	397
Russia . .	22	22	244	288
Germany . .	22	41	137	200
Italy . . .	17	24	162	203
United States .	13	27	71	111
Japan . .	6	32	68	106

The steam power of the navies in 1898 was :—

British . 1,560,000 | Russian . 450,000 | Italian . 300,000
French . 730,000 | German . 300,000 | U. States 290,000

The British navy may be valued as follows :—

	Number	£
Battle-ships	64	35,200,000
Cruisers	161	24,200,000
Sundry	247	13,600,000
Armament	...	19,000,000
Total value		92,000,000

According to another classification there are 90 superior fighting ships, averaging 10,000 horse-power and a speed of 20 knots an hour, 180 second-class cruisers, 250 gunboats and transports, and 150 torpedo vessels, making a total of 670 vessels.

For naval expenditure in 1897, see *Military Expenditure*, page 638.

The age of men in the British navy (1897) is as follows :—

Age	Number	Ratio
15–25	44,010	60.6
25–35	20,610	28.4
Over 35	8,000	11.0
Total . .	72,620	100.0

The following statement of the navies of the world in 1890 is from *Chambers's Encyclopædia*.

	Battle-ships	Inferior	Total	Men	Guns	Do. over 12 Tons
Great Britain .	64	595	659	94,600	3,631	430
France . . .	53	404	457	70,600	1,735	252
Germany . .	34	183	217	16,500	608	135
Russia . . .	36	322	358	31,000	710	124
Austria . . .	15	153	168	9,000	309	49
Italy	22	245	267	23,000	611	78
Spain . . .	7	129	136	16,700	305	48
Portugal . . .	1	63	64	3,500	98	...
Sweden . . .	20	142	162	7,900	154	39
Denmark . .	9	67	76	1,400	202	22
Holland . . .	24	116	140	10,000	256	39
Greece . . .	5	70	75	1,100	82	8
Turkey . . .	18	387	405	23,000	382	54
Europe . . .	308	2,876	3,184	308,300	9,083	1,278
United States .	21	74	95	...	284	26
Brazil	10	56	66	...	134	28
Argentina . .	4	45	49	...	35	12
Chile . . .	4	34	38	...	95	18
Japan . . .	6	76	82	...	212	17
China . . .	6	83	89	...	133	25
Total . .	359	3,244	3,603	...	9,976	1,404

O

OATS

The area and product of this crop are shown as follows :—

	Acres	Tons	Bush. per Acre	Per Inhab.
U. Kingdom .	4,200,000	4,200,000	40	4
France . . .	9,700,000	5,400,000	23	6
Germany . . .	10,000,000	4,400,000	18	3
Russia	36,400,000	14,800,000	16	6
Austria . . .	7,500,000	4,300,000	23	4
Italy	1,170,000	450,000	15	...
Spain & Portugal	750,000	300,000	16	1
Danubian States	1,220,000	450,000	15	2
Swed. & Norway	2,300,000	1,800,000	32	10
Denmark . . .	1,050,000	880,000	34	16
Holland . . .	310,000	360,000	45	3
Belgium . . .	650,000	660,000	41	4
Europe . . .	75,250,000	38,000,000	20	4
United States .	27,400,000	17,800,000	26	10
Canada . . .	4,100,000	2,600,000	26	20
Australia . . .	700,000	450,000	25	4
Total . .	107,450,000	58,850,000	22	5

See *Agriculture*, page 613, and *Food*, page 714.

OCCUPATIONS

In most countries the number of persons following gainful occupations is 45 per cent. of total, or 60 per cent. of those over 10 years. The census returns of 1890–91 show :—

	Pop. over 10 years old	Number of Earners	Percentage	
			Agri-cultural	Various
England . . .	22,054,000	12,900,000	10.4	89.6
Scotland . . .	3,046,000	1,780,000	14.0	86.0
Ireland . . .	3,726,000	2,140,000	43.7	56.3
U. Kingdom .	28,826,000	16,820,000	15.0	85.0
France . . .	31,457,000	17,290,000	41.6	58.4
Germany . . .	40,290,000	22,910,000	35.6	64.4
Austria . . .	18,191,000	13,570,000	50.7	49.3
Hungary . . .	12,882,000	7,390,000	60.5	39.5
Italy	22,551,000	16,110,000	38.0	62.0
Spain	13,539,000	7,010,000	69.2	30.8
Sweden . . .	3,679,000	2,580,000	50.2	49.8
Norway . . .	1,494,000	1,210,000	27.3	72.7
Denmark . . .	1,652,000	680,000	32.0	68.0
Belgium . . .	4,708,000	2,070,000	31.4	68.6
Switzerland . .	2,284,000	1,360,000	36.8	63.2
Greece . . .	1,620,000	720,000	61.1	38.9
United States .	47,413,000	22,736,000	39.6	60.4
Australia . . .	2,800,000	1,620,000	23.6	76.4
Canada . . .	3,638,000	1,611,000	45.6	54.4

The total for Europe (excluding Russia and the Danubian States, for which there are no returns) will be found as follows :—

	Number	Ratio
Agriculture . . .	47,960,000	43.0
Manufactures . . .	36,430,000	33.0
Commerce, &c. . .	26,640,000	24.0
Total . . .	111,030,000	100.0

UNITED KINGDOM

The census of 1891 showed the three kingdoms as follows :—

	Number (000 omitted)					
	Eng.	Scot.	Ire.	U. King.	Males	Females
Agriculture	1,340	250	940	2,530	2,350	180
Manufact..	7,330	1,030	660	9,020	6,640	2,380
Commerce	1,400	180	80	1,660	1,615	45
Various .	2,830	315	465	3,610	1,000	2,610
Total . .	12,900	1,775	2,145	16,820	11,605	5,215

In the above table Agriculture includes fishing, and Manufactures mining. Details show thus :—

	Number (000 omitted)			
	England	Scotland	Ireland	U. King.
Civil Service . .	144	18	30	192
Army . . .	126	8	31	165
Teachers . . .	201	21	21	243
Students . . .	147	29	96	272
Professions . .	308	35	30	373
Professional class .	926	111	208	1,245
Farmers . . .	224	54	417	695
Labourers . .	1,088	166	513	1,767
Agricultural . .	1,312	220	930	2,462
Textile operatives .	1,128	207	103	1,465
Hardware ,, .	626	106	29	761
Carriers . . .	984	122	66	1,172
Builders . . .	681	87	47	815
Tailors . . .	1,100	123	153	1,376
Mines and quarries .	772	117	11	900
Domestics . .	1,900	203	238	2,341
Hucksters . .	416	59	29	504
Various . . .	3,055	425	309	3,789
Total . .	12,900	1,780	2,150	16,830

For previous dates see *Occupations*, page 423.

FRANCE

The number of workers by the census of 1891 compares with that of 1881 as follows :—

	Number		Ratio	
	1881	1891	1881	1891
Agriculture . .	6,460,000	7,220,000	40.2	41.8
Manufactures .	4,440,000	4,720,000	27.4	27.3
Commerce . .	1,160,000	1,980,000	7.2	11.4
Various . . .	4,050,000	3,370,000	25.2	19.5
Total . .	16,110,000	17,290,000	100.0	100.0

The census of 1891 gave the following classification :-

	Principals	Assistants	Total
Agriculture . .	3,570,000	3,650,000	7,220,000
Manufactures .	1,020,000	3,700,000	4,720,000
Commerce . .	880,000	1,100,000	1,980,000
Transport. . .	60,000	410,000	470,000
Professions . .	420,000	240,000	660,000
Various . . .	1,720,000	520,000	2,240,000
Total . .	7,670,000	9,620,000	17,290,000

GERMANY

The number of persons subsisting by various pursuits shows thus :—

	Number		Ratio	
	1882	1895	1882	1895
Agriculture . .	18,840,000	18,070,000	41.7	34.9
Manufactures .	16,060,000	20,250,000	35.5	39.1
Commerce . .	4,530,000	5,970,000	10.0	11.6
Professions, &c.	3,550,000	4,150 000	7.9	8.0
No occupation .	2,240,000	3,330,000	4.9	6.4
Total . .	45,220,000	51,770,000	100.0	100.0

The census of 1895 classifies pursuits in the principal States thus :—

	Number (000 omitted)			
	Agricul.	Manuf.	Various	Total
Prussia . . .	11,110	12,200	8,180	31,490
Bavaria . . .	2,600	1,790	1,390	5,780
Saxony . . .	540	2,180	1,030	3,750
Wurtemberg . .	920	720	430	2,070
Baden . . .	720	600	400	1,720
Alsace . . .	600	610	410	1,620
Hesse . . .	370	390	270	1,030
Brunswick . .	120	200	120	440
Oldenburg . .	170	120	80	370
Small States . .	920	1,440	1,140	3,500
Total . .	18,070	20,250	13,450	51,770

The census of 1895 shows that 45 per cent. of the population are workers, 55 per cent. dependents, including children, viz. :—

	Workers	Dependents	Total
Agriculture . .	8,160,000	9,910,000	18,070,000
Manufactures .	7,710,000	10,700,000	18,410,000
Mining. . . .	570,000	1,280,000	1,850,000
Commerce . .	1,210,000	1,730,000	2,940,000
Transport. . .	620,000	1,380,000	2,000,000
Professions, &c. .	4,640,000	3,860,000	8,500,000
Total . .	22,910,000	28,860,000	51,770,000

AUSTRIA

The census of Austria Proper for 1890 compares with 1880 thus :—

	Number		Ratio	
	1880	1890	1880	1890
Agriculture . .	6,490,000	6,890,000	57.0	50.7
Manufactures .	2,310,000	2,880,000	20.3	21.2
Commerce . .	510,000	810,000	4.4	6.0
Various . . .	2,090,000	2,990,000	18.3	22.1
Total . .	11,400,000	13,570,000	100.0	100.0

HUNGARY

The census of 1890 compares with that of 1880 thus :—

	Number		Ratio	
	1880	1890	1880	1890
Agriculture . .	4,520,000	4,480,000	62.0	60.5
Various . . .	2,770,000	2,910,000	38.0	39.5
Total . .	7,290,000	7,390,000	100.0	100.0

ITALY

The latest census is that of 1881, which see at page 430.

SPAIN

The census of 1887 compares with that of 1877 as follows :—

	Number		Ratio	
	1877	1887	1877	1887
Agriculture . .	2,720,000	4,850,000	47.3	69.2
Manufactures .	1,170,000	1,070,000	20.3	15.3
Commerce . .	210,000	310,000	3.7	4.4
Various . . .	1,640,000	780,000	28.7	11.1
Total . .	5,740,000	7,010,000	100.0	100.0

The mode of taking the census was changed ; the population increased only 5 per cent. from 1877 to 1887, while the number of persons occupied rose 22 per cent.

SWEDEN

The number subsisting by various pursuits was :—

	Number		Ratio	
	1880	1890	1880	1890
Agriculture . .	2,340,000	2,410,000	51.2	50.2
Manufactures .	580,000	850,000	12.8	17.7
Commerce . .	220,000	310,000	4.8	6.5
Various . . .	1,430,000	1,220,000	31.2	25.6
Total . .	4,570,000	4,790,000	100.0	100.0

NORWAY

The census of 1891 compares with that of 1875 thus :—

	Number		Ratio	
	1875	1891	1875	1891
Agriculture . .	380,000	330,000	35.4	27.3
Manufactures .	220,000	180,000	20.5	14.9
Commerce . .	160,000	110,000	15.0	9.1
Various . . .	310,000	590,000	29.1	48.7
Total . .	1,070,000	1,210,000	100.0	100.0

DENMARK

The number subsisting by various pursuits was :—

	Number		Ratio	
	1880	1890	1880	1890
Agriculture . .	930,000	880,000	47.0	40.5
Manufactures .	460,000	530,000	23.2	24.4
Commerce . .	130,000	190,000	6.6	8.8
Various . . .	460,000	570,000	23.2	26.3
Total . .	1,980,000	2,170,000	100.0	100.0

BELGIUM

The census of 1890 compares with that of 1880 thus :—

	Hands		Ratio	
	1880	1890	1880	1890
Agriculture . .	980,000	650,000	35.6	31.4
Manufactures .	950,000	770,000	34.6	37.2
Commerce . .	240,000	330,000	8.7	16.0
Various . . .	580,000	320,000	21.1	15.4
Total . .	2,750,000	2,070,000	100.0	100.0

The new classification in 1890 renders comparison fallacious.

SWITZERLAND

The census of 1888 compares with that of 1870 as follows :—

	Hands		Ratio	
	1870	1888	1870	1888
Agriculture . .	540,000	500,000	41.4	36.8
Manufactures .	490,000	560,000	37.4	41.2
Commerce . .	50,000	160,000	3.7	11.7
Various . . .	240,000	140,000	17.5	10.3
Total . .	1,320,000	1,360,000	100.0	100.0

GREECE

The census of 1889 compares with that of 1861 thus :—

	Number		Ratio	
	1861	1889	1861	1889
Agriculture . .	190,000	440,000	56.6	61.1
Manufactures .	50,000	90,000	15.8	12.5
Commerce, &c. .	90,000	190,000	27.6	26.4
Total . .	330,000	720,000	100.0	100.0

UNITED STATES

The census of 1890 showed that one-half of the population over 10 years of age had some gainful occupation, viz. :—

	Males	Females	Total
Employed . . .	18,821,000	3,915,000	22,736,000
Unemployed . .	5,532,000	19,146,000	24,678,000
Total . .	24,353,000	23,061,000	47,414,000

The occupations of the American people in 1880 and 1890 stood thus :—

	Number		Ratio	
	1880	1890	1880	1890
Agriculture . .	7,670,000	9,010,000	44.1	39.6
Manufactures	3,840,000	5,090,000	22.1	22.3
Commerce, &c. .	5,880,000	8,630,000	33.8	38.1
Total . .	17,390,000	22,730,000	100.0	100.0

In the above official classification Agriculture includes also fishing and mining. In the subjoined table for 1890 the same occurs, and Commerce includes also transport:—

	Males	Females	Total
Agriculture . .	8,330,000	680,000	9,010,000
Manufactures .	4,060,000	1,030,000	5,090,000
Commerce . .	3,100,000	230,000	3,330,000
Domestics . .	2,690,000	1,670,000	4,360,000
Professions . .	630,000	310,000	940,000
Total . .	18,810,000	3,920,000	22,730,000

Deducting fishermen and miners, the number of persons actually engaged in agriculture in 1890 was 8,320,000.

New England States

	Occupations		Ratios	
	1880	1890	1880	1890
Agriculture . .	301,000	328,000	19.2	16.4
Manufactures .	709,000	885,000	45.0	44.1
Trade, &c. . .	562,000	793,000	35.8	39.5
Total . .	1,572,000	2,006,000	100.0	100.0

Middle States

Agriculture . .	847,000	1,064,000	20.3	19.3
Manufactures .	1,425,000	1,824,000	34.0	33.0
Trade, &c. . .	1,912,000	2,637,000	45.7	47.7
Total . .	4,184,000	5,525,000	100.0	100.0

Southern States

Agriculture . .	3,626,000	3,935,000	69.0	63.5
Manufactures .	392,000	591,000	7.4	9.5
Trade, &c. . .	1,236,000	1,669,000	23.6	27.0
Total . .	5,254,000	6,195,000	100.0	100.0

Western States

Agriculture . .	2,897,000	3,686,000	45.4	41.0
Manufactures .	1,311,000	1,791,000	20.6	19.9
Trade, &c. . .	2,174,000	3,533,000	34.0	39.1
Total . .	6,382,000	9.010,000	100.0	100.0

The relative strength of the principal sections and occupations in 1890 was as follows:—

	N. Eng.	Middle	South	West	Total
Agriculture . .	14	47	173	162	396
Manufactures .	39	80	26	78	223
Various . . .	35	116	74	156	381
Total . .	88	243	273	396	1,000

Thus it appears that the Western States represented almost 40 per cent. of the working population of the Union, the Southern about 27, the Middle or Atlantic States 24, and New England 9 per cent.

CANADA

The number of earners by census returns were:—

	1880	1890	Increase
Agriculture . . .	655,000	735,000	80,000
Wood-cutters, &c. .	39,000	55,000	16,000
Manufactures . .	257,000	320,000	63,000
Trade and transport .	108,000	186,000	78,000
Domestics . . .	75,000	246,000	171,000
Professions . . .	53,000	69,000	16,000
Total . .	1,187,000	1,611,000	424,000

AUSTRALIA

The census of 1890 was not carried out in South Australia so as to specify occupations. The other colonies are shown as follows, it being premised that Agriculture includes both pastoral and tillage pursuits, and that persons unclassified are included in the column of Trade:—

	N. S. Wales	Victoria	New Zealand	Queensland	Tasmania	West Australia
Agriculture	101,000	101,000	69,000	54,000	18,000	7,000
Mining . .	31,000	25,000	17,000	12,000	4,000	1,000
Manufact.	71,000	96,000	43,000	22,000	7,000	4,000
Building .	38,000	34,000	13,000	11,000	5,000	1,000
Trade . .	111,000	133,000	57,000	41,000	14,000	5,000
Transport .	31,000	32,000	16,000	13,000	3,000	3,000
Professions	24,000	23,000	13,000	7,000	3,000	1,000
Domestics .	58,000	58,000	25,000	20,000	7,000	3,000
Total . .	465,000	502,000	253,000	180,000	61,000	25,000

The population of South Australia being one-twelfth of the total, we may allow a corresponding percentage for that colony in the several occupations: the total for Australasia will stand as follows:—

	Number	Ratio
Agriculture . . .	382,000	23.6
Mining	98,000	6.1
Manufactures . . .	265,000	16.4
Building . . .	111,000	6.9
Trade and transport .	501,000	30.8
Professions, &c. .	263,000	16.2
Total . . .	1,620,000	100.0

OIL

The production of petroleum in 1896 was as follows, in barrels of 42 gallons:—

	Raised	Exported	Home Use
United States .	61,000,000	23,000,000	38,000,000
Russia . .	36,000,000	5,500,000	30,500,000
Austria . .	4,700,000	...	4,700,000

The consumption of petroleum in the United Kingdom in 1885–87 averaged 74 million gallons yearly, and in 1895–97 no less than 184 million gallons, or 4½ per inhabitant yearly.

For further particulars see *Mining*, page 776.

With respect to olive-oil, big trees give 2 bushels of olives, which is equivalent to 3 gallons of oil. An ordinary olive-grove gives 25 gallons of oil per acre. France has 270,000 acres under olives, producing 105,000 tons of fruit, equal to 7 million gallons of oil, besides 150,000 acres under colza, producing 5 million gallons of oil. Italy in 1896 had 2,500,000 acres under olives, which produced 44 million gallons of oil, or 18 gallons per acre. See *Oil*, page 434.

ORDERS

Chambers's Encyclopædia states that 124,000 Franciscan friars perished in attending the sick during the great plague of 1346 (see *Plagues*, page 201).

Helyot says that in 1710 there were 7000 Franciscan convents with 120,000 friars, and 900 nunneries of the same Order, with 30,000 nuns. See *Orders*, page 434.

3 D

P

PAPER

The latest estimates of paper manufacture are :—

	Mills	Tons Paper
United Kingdom . .	300	400,000
France	490	350,000
Germany	1,080	180,000
Russia	50	110,000
Austria	740	80,000
Italy	230	50,000
Spain	100	20,000
Portugal	16	8,000
Scandinavia . . .	144	120,000
Holland	65	10,000
Belgium	40	25,000
Switzerland . . .	35	12,000
Europe	3,290	1,365,000
United States . .	1,005	1,200,000
Spanish America . .	85	55,000
Total . . .	4,380	2,620,000

In 1850 the total production was estimated at 220,000 tons, or one-twelfth of what it is at present. In that year the mills of the United Kingdom produced 62,000 tons. The output in the United States rose from 200,000 tons in 1872 to 1,200,000 tons in 1890, and is now probably 1,500,000 tons. Esparto grass is much used for making paper, the mills of Europe in 1889 consuming 300,000 tons, of which two-thirds were grown in Barbary, one-third in Spain. Wood pulp is also in great demand for this industry, the exports of same from Sweden and Norway showing as follows :—

From	Tons Exported	
	1885	1895
Sweden	16,000	152,000
Norway . . .	97,000	248,000
Total . . .	113,000	400,000

The value of paper turned out yearly by the mills of the world is about 80 millions sterling; the mills employ about 200,000 men and 400,000 women.

In 1897 Great Britain exported 46,000 tons of paper, valued at £1,350,000, against 38,000 tons in 1887, valued at £1,330,000.

PARKS

In the following table the parks of London include those of the suburbs, such as Richmond, Hampton Court, Epping Forest, &c. :—

	Park, Acres	Inhab. to an Acre of Park
London	19,000	230
Birmingham . . .	350	1,380
Liverpool . . .	1,060	580
Leeds . . .	600	610
Sheffield . . .	290	1,120
Hull	130	1,550
Brighton . . .	340	300
Nottingham . . .	290	710
York	800	90
Cheltenham . . .	1,590	30

For parks of Continental capitals, see page 438.

PASSENGERS

In 1897 there were 283,000 passengers from Europe landed at New York, of whom 91,000 were cabin, 192,000 steerage, by ten lines of transatlantic steamers. The largest number was carried by the North German Lloyd, namely, 55,600; the next on the list being the Cunard, with 32,400.

The passenger traffic of London by omnibus, rail, &c., rose from 82 million persons in 1864 to 407 millions in 1890.

The tramways of the United Kingdom in 1898 carried 858 million passengers, or almost 2½ millions daily. The steam ferry-boats on the Seine at Paris carried last year 25,400,000 persons, say 70,000 daily. The railways of the world carry yearly about 3380 million passengers, equal to 9 millions daily.

See *Passengers*, page 438; *Railways*, page 795; *Tramways*, page 814; and *Travellers*, page 573.

PAUPERS

The following table shows approximately the amount spent in various countries to relieve the indigent :—

	£ Yearly	Pence per Inhabitant
United Kingdom . .	11,800,000	73
France . . .	7,400,000	46
Austria Proper . .	710,000	8
Italy	2,600,000	20
Holland	500,000	25
United States . .	500,000	2
Australia . . .	800,000	48

UNITED KINGDOM

The numbers and ratios of paupers in the three kingdoms have been as follows :—

	Numbers			Per 1000 Pop.	
	1877	1887	1897	1877	1897
England . .	728,000	817,000	824,000	30	27
Scotland . .	96,000	100,000	101,000	27	24
Ireland . . .	78,000	113,000	99,000	15	22
U. Kingdom .	902,000	1,030,000	1,024,000	27	26

Expenditure for relief of paupers has been as follows :—

	Amount, £		£ per Pauper		Pence per Inhabitant	
	1884	1894	1884	1894	1884	1894
England .	8,400,000	9,700,000	10.8	11.8	75	78
Scotland .	870,000	960,000	9.0	10.1	55	56
Ireland .	1,220,000	1,130,000	11.2	10.9	59	61
U. King. .	10,490,000	11,790,000	10.7	11.7	70	73

Booth shows that 38 per cent. of all persons over 65 years of age in England are paupers: his scheme of State pensions of £13 a year for all persons over 65 would cost the Treasury £17,000,000 for England, or £23,500,000 for the United Kingdom, per annum.

FRANCE

Levasseur shows that pauperism is declining in Paris, viz. :—

Paupers per 1000 *Inhabitants*

1813	. . .	165	1847	. . .	79	1872 . . .	54
1829	. . .	79	1861	. . .	53	1887 . . .	41

The annual cost of maintenance of paupers in France, and the sources from which the necessary funds are derived, appear as follows :—

For	£	From	£
Ordinary poor .	5,350,000	Endowments .	3,020,000
Insane . . .	620,000	The State . .	300,000
Orphans . . .	680,000	City of Paris .	1,700,000
Asylums . . .	710,000	Local boards .	2,340,000
Total . .	7,360,000	Total . .	7,360,000

PINS

The manufacture is said to be declining, viz. :—

	Millions Weekly	
	1887	1897
Great Britain	280	310
France	120	180
Germany, &c.	180	72
Total . .	580	562

In 1897 Birmingham produced 220 millions weekly, against 180 millions in 1887.

POLICE

The police force in certain cities is as follows (1891):—

	Number	Per 10,000 Pop.		Number	Per 10,000 Pop.
London . .	16,000	30	Rome . .	520	12
Berlin . .	3,700	28	Naples .	670	13
Hamburg .	1,300	22	Turin . .	600	17
Bordeaux .	400	15	Genoa . .	420	19

The above eight cities show an average of 20 policemen per 10,000 inhabitants, or 2 per thousand.

The police force of the United Kingdom was as follows :—

	Number			Per 10,000 Inhab.		
	1876	1886	1896	1876	1886	1896
England .	29,720	36,450	41,560	12	13	14
Scotland .	3,170	3,820	4,600	9	10	11
Ireland .	12,370	13,960	13,140	23	28	29
U. King.	45,260	54,230	59,300	14	15	15

The ratio of police to population is now much higher than twenty years ago, having risen 17 per cent. in England, 22 per cent. in Scotland, 27 per cent. in Ireland.

For *Police* expenditure in European capitals see page 441.

POPULATION

The population of Europe has increased a little more than 10 per cent. in ten years, viz. :—

	1887	1897	Increase	Pop. per Sq. Mile
U. Kingdom .	36,600,000	39,830,000	3,230,000	330
France . . .	38,220,000	38,520,000	300,000	192
Germany . .	47,060,000	52,480,000	5,420,000	247
Russia . . .	88,350,060	106,190,000	17,840,000	47
Austria . . .	39,900,000	43,460,000	3,560,000	162
Italy	29,940,000	31,290,000	1,350,000	274
Spain . . .	17,560,000	17,970,000	410,000	98
Portugal . .	4,710,000	5,050,000	340,000	136
Sweden . . .	4,720,000	4,960,000	240,000	29
Norway . .	1,910,000	2,050,000	140,000	17
Denmark . .	2,090,000	2,310,000	220,000	154
Holland . .	4,390,000	4,930,000	540,000	234
Belgium . .	5,910,000	6,500,000	590,000	590
Switzerland .	2,920,000	3,040,000	120,000	190
Greece . . .	2,190,000	2,430,000	240,000	97
Roumania . .	5,380,000	5,570,000	190,000	116
Servia . . .	1,970,000	2,350,000	380,000	111
Bulgaria . .	3,150,000	3,310,000	160,000	85
Turkey . . .	6,100,000	7,650,000	1,550,000	115
Europe . . .	343,070,000	379,890,000	36,820,000	96

The population of Europe may be considered under two classes ; urban, including all cities and towns over 10,000 souls ; and rural, comprising all the rest, viz. :—

	Urban	Rural	Total	Urban Ratio per Cent.
U. Kingdom .	20,600,000	17,200,000	37,800,000	54
France . . .	9,200,000	29,200,000	38,400,000	24
Germany . .	15,600,000	36,600,000	52,200,000	30
Russia . . .	10,900,000	94,900,000	105,800,000	10
Austria . . .	5,600,000	35,800,000	41,400,000	13
Italy . . .	5,300,000	25,400,000	30,700,000	17
Spain . . .	2,900,000	14,700,000	17,600,000	17
Portugal . .	400,000	4,300,000	4,700,000	9
Scandinavia .	1,500,000	7,500,000	9,000,000	17
Holland . .	1,800,000	2,900,000	4,700,000	38
Belgium . .	1,700,000	4,600,000	6,300,000	27
Switzerland .	500,000	2,500,000	3,000,000	17
Danub. States	900,000	10,500,000	11,400,000	8
Greece . . .	300,000	1,900,000	2,200,000	14
Europe . . .	77,200,000	288,000,000	365,200,000	21

In 1861 Europe had 148 cities of more than 50,000 souls, and in 1891 the number had risen to 255. These cities had grown much more rapidly than the rest of the population, viz. :—

	1861	1891	Increase per Cent.
Cities over 50,000 .	22,600,000	44,800,000	99
Towns and rural .	200,200,000	308,600,000	54
Total pop. .	222,800,000	353,400,000	58

In 1860 the United States had 16 cities of more than 50,000 souls, and in 1890 they had 56, the increase of population having been as follows :—

	1860	1890	Increase per Cent.
Cities over 50,000 .	3,100,000	11,700,009	280
Towns and rural .	28,300,000	50,900,000	80
Total pop. .	31,400,000	62,600,000	99

The population of the principal cities of the world (except China) is as follows :—

City	Pop.	City	Pop.	City	Pop.	City	Pop.
Aberdeen	140,000	Christiania	150,000	Lille	220,000	Preston	110,000
Adelaide	140,000	Cincinnati	300,000	Lisbon	310,000	Providence	130,000
Agra	170,000	Cleveland	260,000	Liverpool	740,000	Rangoon	180,000
Aix-la-Chapelle	110,000	Cologne	320,000	London	4,460,000	Rheims	110,000
Aleppo	120,000	Colombo	130,000	Louisville	160,000	Riga	180,000
Alexandria	210,000	Constantinople	870,000	Lucknow	270,000	Rio de Janeiro	520,000
Allahabad	180,000	Copenhagen	310,000	Lyons	470,000	Rochester	130,000
Altona	150,000	Crefeld	110,000	Madras	450,000	Rome	460,000
Amsterdam	460,000	Damascus	200,000	Madrid	470,000	Rosario	110,000
Antwerp	260,000	Danzig	130,000	Magdeburg	210,000	Rotterdam	280,000
Astrakhan	110,000	Delhi	190,000	Malaga	130,000	Roubaix	120,000
Athens	110,000	Denver	110,000	Manchester	740,000	Rouen	110,000
Bagdad	180,000	Detroit	210,000	Mandalay	190,000	St. Etienne	140,000
Bahia	200,000	Dresden	330,000	Manilla	150,000	St. Louis	450,000
Baltimore	440,000	Dublin	360,000	Marseilles	440,000	St. Paul	130,000
Bangalore	180,000	Dundee	160,000	Meerut	120,000	St. Petersburg	1,040,000
Bangkok	200,000	Dusseldorf	180,000	Melbourne	450,000	Salonica	150,000
Barcelona	270,000	Edinburgh	280,000	Messina	150,000	San Francisco	300,000
Bareilly	120,000	Elberfeld	140,000	Mexico	350,000	San Paulo	110,000
Barmen	130,000	Fez	140,000	Milan	440,000	Santiago (Chile)	250,000
Baroda	120,000	Florence	200,000	Milwaukee	200,000	Saratoff	120,000
Baku	110,000	Frankfort	230,000	Minneapolis	160,000	Seville	140,000
Belfast	260,000	Genoa	220,000	Montevideo	250,000	Sheffield	350,000
Benares	220,000	Ghent	160,000	Montreal	250,000	Smyrna	200,000
Berlin	1,680,000	Glasgow	710,000	Moscow	830,000	Stettin	140,000
Birmingham	510,000	Gothenberg	110,000	Munich	410,000	Stockholm	270,000
Blackburn	130,000	Gratz	110,000	Nagpore	120,000	Strasburg	140,000
Bologna	150,000	Hague	190,000	Nantes	120,000	Stuttgart	160,000
Bolton	120,000	Halle	120,000	Naples	530,000	Sunderland	140,000
Bombay	820,000	Hamburg	630,000	Newark	180,000	Surat	110,000
Bordeaux	260,000	Hanover	210,000	Newcastle	210,000	Sydney	410,000
Boston	450,000	Havana	200,000	New Orleans	240,000	Tabriz	180,000
Bradford	230,000	Havre	120,000	New York	2,530,000	Tashkend	120,000
Bremen	140,000	Hull	220,000	Norwich	110,000	Teheran	210,000
Breslau	370,000	Hyderabad	420,000	Nottingham	230,000	Tiflis	150,000
Brighton	120,000	Karkoff	200,000	Nuremberg	160,000	Tokio	1,240,000
Bristol	230,000	Kazan	140,000	Odessa	330,000	Toronto	180,000
Brunswick	110,000	Kichineff	120,000	Oldham	140,000	Toulouse	150,000
Brussels	520,000	Kieff	190,000	Omaha	140,000	Trieste	160,000
Bucharest	230,000	Kioto	330,000	Oporto	140,000	Tunis	150,000
Buda-Pesth	590,000	Kobè	160,000	Osaka	490,000	Turin	350,000
Buenos Ayres	810,000	Konigsberg	170,000	Palermo	280,000	Valencia	170,000
Buffalo	260,000	Lahore	180,900	Paris	2,540,000	Valparaiso	150,000
Cairo	370,000	Leeds	410,000	Patna	170,000	Venice	150,000
Calcutta	980,000	Leghorn	110,000	Pernambuco	190,000	Vienna	1,360,000
Cardiff	160,000	Leicester	200,000	Philadelphia	1,050,000	Warsaw	530,000
Catania	120,000	Leipzig	400,000	Pittsburg	240,000	Washington	230,000
Cawnpore	190,000	Lemberg	130,000	Poona	160,000	Wilna	110,000
Chemnitz	160,000	Liège	160,000	Portsmouth	180,000	Yokohama	180,000
Chicago	1,090,000	Lima	110,000	Prague	180,000	Zurich	130,000

In the preceding table Liverpool includes Birkenhead, Manchester Salford, and the city of New York includes Brooklyn and suburbs. There are 28 of the above cities in the United Kingdom, 24 in India, 8 in the Colonies, making in all 60 for the British Empire ; there are 26 in Germany, 26 in the United States, 16 in Russia, 12 in France, 12 in Italy, and 58 in various countries.

The population of the British Colonies, exclusive of India, is shown as follows :—

	1881	1895	Increase
Canada . . .	4,500,000	5,300,000	800,000
Australia . . .	2,740,000	4,240,000	1,500,000
South Africa . .	1,120,000	2,350,000	1,230,000
West Indies . .	1,470,000	1,750,000	280,000
Ceylon	2,760,000	3,240,000	480,000
Various . . .	1,440,000	1,710,000	270,000
Total . . .	14,030,000	18,590,000	4,560,000

In this table Canada includes Newfoundland, and the West Indies Guiana. The gross increase of the Colonies in 14 years has been equal to 32 per cent. The population of India in 1891 was 221,200,000, showing an increase from 1881 of 23 millions, or 11½ per cent.

The population of Spanish America and Brazil was by latest dates as follows :—

	Pop.	Per Sq. Mile		Pop.	Per Sq. Mile
Mexico . .	12,570,000	16	Chile . .	2,960,000	10
Cent. Amer.	3,150,000	22	Bolivia . .	2,020,000	4
Colombia	3,880,000	8	Paraguay .	430,000	4
Venezuela .	2,320,000	4	Uruguay .	790,000	11
Ecuador . .	1,270,000	10	Argentina .	3,950,000	2
Peru . . .	2,620,000	6	Brazil . .	16,330,000	5

The continent of South America has 36,600,000 inhabitants, being at the rate of 5 to the square mile.

Urban population increased as follows between 1881 and 1891 : the column of Natural Increase shows the surplus of births over deaths, that of Immigration the net influx from rural districts or from abroad :—

	Natural Increase	Immigration	Total Increase	PerCent. on Pop. of 1881
London . . .	517,000	...	395,000	10.3
Paris . . .	62,000	123,000	185,000	8.3
Berlin . . .	139,000	318,000	457,000	40.8
Vienna . . .	67,000	45,000	112,000	16.0
Rome . . .	28,000	108,000	136,000	45.3
Buda-Pesth . .	18,000	117,000	135,000	36.5
Hamburg . .	50,000	108,000	158,000	38.7
Leipzig . .	19,000	123,000	142,000	95.2
Dresden . . .	25,000	31,000	56,000	25.5
Breslau . . .	18,000	44,000	62,000	22.7
Naples . . .	14,000	10,000	24,000	4.8
Milan . . .	13,000	85,000	98,000	30.7
Turin . . .	16,000	62,000	78,000	31.0
Genoa . . .	6,000	26,000	32,000	17.7
Florence . . .	15,000	14,000	29,000	17.2
Palermo . . .	26,000	1,000	27,000	11.0

While all other cities showed an influx of strangers during the decade ending 1891, London actually showed a loss of 122,000 persons by emigration.

The density of population of some principal cities is :—

	Acres	Per Acre		Acres	Per Acre
Berlin . .	15,800	94	Manchester	18,000	41
Brussels . .	2,200	240	Moscow .	26,000	32
Dresden . .	7,100	47	Naples . .	5,200	102
Dublin . .	5,100	70	New York .	46,400	55
Florence . .	6,800	30	Paris . . .	19,500	130
Genoa . .	2,200	100	Philadelphia	84,000	12
Glasgow . .	7,700	92	Rome . .	3,900	117
Hamburg . .	7,200	87	Turin . .	2,400	145
London . .	78,000	57	Vienna . .	13,800	99
Madrid . .	4,200	111	Washington	6,100	38

The above 20 cities show an average of 85 inhabitants per acre.

UNITED KINGDOM

The progress of population since 1871 has been thus :—

	Number		Per Sq. Mile	
	1871	1898	1871	1898
England . . .	22,857,000	31,400,000	391	536
Scotland . . .	3,360,000	4,250,000	113	143
Ireland . . .	5,412,000	4,540,000	166	139
U. Kingdom .	31,629,000	40,190,000	261	332

The population of the island of Great Britain has increased since 1871 at the rate of 350,000 yearly, or almost 1000 daily. In the same interval Ireland has lost 32,000 yearly, or 90 persons daily. The increase in Great Britain has been chiefly in urban population :—

Year	Urban Population		
	England	Scotland	G. Britain
1871	12,911,000	1,952,000	14,863,000
1881	15,445,000	2,307,000	17,752,000
1891	17,826,000	2,631,000	20,457,000
Increase from '71	4,915,000	679,000	5,594,000
	Rural Population		
	England	Scotland	G. Britain
1871	9,946,000	1,408,000	11,354,000
1881	10,664,000	1,429,000	12,093,000
1891	11,175,000	1,395,000	12,570,000
Increase from '71	1,229,000	...	1,216,000

The population of Ireland at census of 1891 comprised 3,860,000 rural and 845,000 urban, the latter being as 18 per cent. of the population. The several provinces showed thus :—

	1871	1891	Loss
Leinster	1,336,000	1,188,000	148,000
Ulster	1,840,000	1,620,000	220.000
Connaught . . .	846,000	725,000	121,000
Munster	1,390,000	1,172,000	218,000
Total . .	5,412,000	4,705,000	707,000

UNITED STATES

Dividing the population into four great classes, we find as follows :—

	1860	1890	Increase per Cent.
White Americans .	17,727,000	34,476,000	95
Coloured persons .	4,486,000	7,470,000	66
Foreigners . . .	4,139,000	9,250,000	123
Children of do. . .	5,091,000	11,426,000	124
Total . .	31,443,000	62,622,000	99

In the United States it is customary to count as urban population all towns that have more than 8000 souls, and the increase of such towns has been as follows :—

Year	Total Pop.	Urban	Urban Ratio
1860	31,440,000	5,070,000	16.1
1870	38,560,000	8,070,000	20.9
1880	50,155,000	11,320,000	22.6
1890	62,620,000	18,235,000	29.1

The increase of population in towns since 1860 has been 13,165,000, that is 260 per cent., while rural population has risen only 18,015,000, or 68 per cent.

Persons of working age, 15 to 60, according to the census of 1890 summed up nearly 36 millions, distributed thus :—

States	Number (000 omitted)			
	Americans	Ditto Coloured	Foreigners	Total
N. England .	1,887	21	952	2,860
Middle . .	5,755	265	2,396	8,416
South . .	6,205	3,125	336	9,666
West . . .	10,790	223	4,036	15,049
Union . .	24,637	3,634	7,720	35,991

The increase of population in the last ten years was 14,020,000, viz. :—

| 1887 | . | . | . | . | 58,680,000 |
| 1897 | . | . | . | . | 72,700,000 |

The increase was apparently made up of 10,740,000 surplus of births over deaths, being 18 per cent. on the population in 1887, and 3,280,000 net immigration, the total number of immigrants in the interval having been 4,390,000, of whom one-fourth are supposed to have gone away or died.

POST-OFFICE

The business has increased 60 per cent. in eight years, the following table showing the total number of letters, papers, &c., handled in the several countries :—

	Millions		Per Inhab.	
	1888	**1896**	**1888**	**1896**
United Kingdom .	2,363	3,142	63	80
France . . .	1,523	2,094	39	54
Germany . . .	2,488	4,025	53	76
Russia . . .	326	546	4	5
Austria . . .	960	1,220	24	28
Italy . . .	476	499	16	16
Spain . . .	124	173	7	10
Portugal . . .	40	55	9	11
Sweden . . .	106	170	22	34
Norway . . .	38	87	19	44
Denmark . . .	50	144	25	65
Holland . . .	180	268	40	55
Belgium . . .	290	369	49	58
Switzerland . .	221	257	74	86
Danubian States .	40	84	4	8
Greece . . .	12	17	5	7
Europe . . .	9,237	13,150	25	36
United States . .	7,028	11,688	110	170
Canada . . .	199	237	40	47
Spanish America .	230	455	5	8
India . . .	274	424	1	2
Japan . . .	137	506	4	12
Egypt . . .	17	24	2	2
Cape Colony . .	12	28	11	15
Australia . . .	294	414	82	99
Various . . .	42	71	...	...
The World . .	17,470	27,010	...	...

The postal service of the United Kingdom has 145,000 employees, of whom 30,000 are women : there are 21,000 post-offices and 29,000 pillar-boxes in the U. Kingdom.

The business may be summed up thus, post-cards counting as letters:—

	Millions		
	Letters	Papers, &c.	Total
England . . .	1,894	753	2,647
Scotland . . .	203	99	302
Ireland . . .	133	60	193
United Kingdom .	2,230	912	3,142
France . . .	1,006	1,088	2,094
Germany . . .	1,905	2,120	4,025
Russia . . .	311	235	546
Austria . . .	902	318	1,220
Italy . . .	247	252	499
Spain . . .	104	69	173
Portugal . . .	27	28	55
Sweden and Norway .	130	127	257
Denmark . . .	75	69	144
Holland . . .	128	140	268
Belgium . . .	176	193	369
Switzerland . .	124	133	257
Danubian States .	40	44	84
Greece . . .	9	8	17
Turkey . . .	11	3	14
Europe . . .	7,425	5,739	13,164
United States . .	3,044	8,644	11,688
Canada . . .	141	96	237
Spanish America .	180	275	455
India . . .	374	50	424
Japan . . .	404	102	506
Egypt . . .	15	9	24
Cape Colony . .	18	10	28
Australia . .	241	173	414
Various . . .	52	19	71
The World . . .	11,894	15,116	27,010

In 1896 there were 753 million money orders, &c., amounting in all to 3280 millions sterling.

Telegraphs.—The length of land-lines and number of messages sent yearly are :—

	Miles of Line	Messages Millions	Messages	
			Per 100 Pop.	Per Mile
United Kingdom .	41,400	79.4	198	1,913
France . . .	58,300	44.8	118	790
Germany . . .	84,400	38.4	74	455
Russia . . .	82,400	14.5	14	175
Austria . . .	46,100	20.7	48	450
Italy . . .	24,700	9.1	29	370
Spain . . .	23,600	6.0	34	255
Portugal . . .	4,000	1.4	30	350
Sweden . . .	8,300	2.2	45	265
Norway . . .	6,300	1.9	95	302
Denmark . . .	3,400	1.9	85	560
Holland . . .	3,600	4.6	95	1,280
Belgium . . .	4,000	8.7	140	2,175
Switzerland . .	4,400	3.7	120	840
Danubian States .	9,500	4.5	40	470
Greece . . .	5,100	1.5	63	295
Turkey . . .	21,800	...	...	...
Europe . . .	431,300	243.3	64	570
United States . .	210,000	58.8	84	280
Canada . . .	31,700	4.0	80	125
West Indies . .	5,400	1.0	24	185
Spanish America .	114,000	12.0	22	105
India . . .	46,400	4.7	2	101
Japan . . .	11,700	11.0	27	940
Egypt . . .	2,300	2.4	25	1,050
Algeria . . .	7,100	2.1	26	295
Cape Colony . .	6,400	2.2	140	344
Australia . . .	50,900	10.8	270	210
Various . . .	15,800	1.7	...	108
The World . .	933,000	354.0	30	380
Cables . . .	168,000	...	...	...
Total . .	1,101,000	...	...	...

There are 1480 submarine cables, in all 168,000 miles long, of which 18,000 are State property, the rest belonging to Companies. The average cost of land-lines was, according to Mr. Charles Bright, £94 a mile, and of ocean cables £300 a mile : the construction of existing lines and cables represents an outlay of £138,000,000, of which cables stand for £50,000,000. In 1897 the number of messages was just a million daily, of which 20,000 were by cable. There are at present 12 cables working between Europe and America, besides 3 that are dead : the charge between London and New York was £1 a word in 1866, and it is now only a shilling.

The progress of telegraphy in eight years is shown thus :—

	Miles of Line		Messages Millions	
	1888	**1896**	**1888**	**1896**
Europe . . .	368,000	431,300	170	243
America . . .	292,000	361,100	72	76
Asia . . .	50,200	68,900	8	17
Africa . . .	18,600	20,800	5	7
Australia . . .	39,200	50,900	11	11
The World . .	768,000	933,000	266	354

The Central Bureau at Berne controls the telegraphs of 47 countries, and reports the number of messages as almost 400 millions yearly.

The postal revenue of the principal States has been as follows :—

	£ Sterling		Pence per Inhab.	
	1888	1896	1888	1896
United Kingdom .	11,200,000	14,800,000	72	90
France . . .	6,500,000	9,000,000	42	57
Germany . .	11,400,000	17,000,000	54	78
Russia . . .	2,600,000	3,900,000	6	8
Austria . . .	4,000,000	6,100,000	23	34
Italy . . .	2,300,000	2,700,000	18	21
Scandinavia .	900,000	1,200,000	24	32
Holland . .	600,000	900,000	30	43
Belgium . . .	700,000	800,000	28	30
United States .	11,700,000	17,200,000	46	60
Canada . .	600,000	800,000	30	38
Australia . .	1,200,000	2,400,000	80	132
India . . .	1,200,000	2,000,000	1	2
Japan . .	400,000	1,800,000	2	11
Total . .	55,300,000	80,600,000	...	...

In 1892 various governments paid the following subsidies for carrying mails :—

	Miles Run	£ Sterling	Pence per Mile
Great Britain . .	4,700,000	1,000,000	52
France . . .	3,400,000	1,040,000	74
United States . .	1,500,000	620,000	100
Italy	1,600,000	360,000	54
Spain . . .	1,100,000	390,000	85
Germany . . .	1,100,000	240,000	52
Austria . . .	1,500,000	230,000	37
Holland . . .	1,100,000	210,000	46
Total . .	16,000,000	4,090,000	62

POTATOES

The area and production of this crop in 1897, compared with Spallart's average for 1880-84, are shown as follows :—

	1897		1880-84 Tons	Bush. per Head	
	Acres	Tons		1880-84	1897
G. Britain . .	505,000	3,400,000	3,300,000	4.4	4.0
Ireland . .	675,000	2,700,000	3,600,000	28.0	24.0
U. Kingdom .	1,180,000	6,100,000	6,900,000	8.0	6.0
France . . .	3,900,000	12,900,000	11,300,000	12.0	13.5
Germany . .	7,500,000	31,800,000	21,900,000	19.0	24.0
Russia . . .	7,600,000	20,700,000	12,100,000	5.0	7.0
Austria . .	4,100,000	12,400,000	9,600,000	10.0	11.5
Italy . . .	500,000	700,000	700,000	1.0	1.0
Spain & Port.	900,000	1,900,000	1,900,000	4.0	3.8
Scandinavia .	600,000	2,500,000	2,600,000	13.0	11.0
Holland . .	400,000	2,200,000	1,500,000	14.0	18.0
Belgium . .	500,000	3,400,000	2,500,000	18.0	22.0
Switzerland .	400,000	1,200,000	1,300,000	17.0	16.0
Roumania, &c.	120,000	300,000	300,000	1.0	1.0
Europe . .	27,700,000	96,100,000	72,600,000	9.0	10.5
U. States . .	2,800,000	6,300,000	4,600,000	3.7	3.5
Canada . .	400,000	1,200,000	1,200,000	10.5	9.5
Australia . .	150,000	500,000	400,000	5.5	4.8
The World .	31,050,000	104,100,000	78,800,000	...	...

Since 1884 the production of potatoes in Europe has increased 33 per cent., and almost every country on the Continent shows a greater consumption per inhabitant than fifteen years ago. On the other hand, the consumption in the United Kingdom is one-fourth less per head than it was in 1880-84, and a decline is likewise to be observed in the United States, as well as in Canada and Australia.

The United Kingdom pays more than a million sterling yearly for imported potatoes : in five years ending 1897 the average importation was 156,000 tons, value £1,040,000.

PRESS

UNITED KINGDOM

The average number of new books in the years 1896-97 compares with the same in 1888-89 as follows :—

	Yearly Average		Increase
	1888-89	1896-97	
Economy and trade .	111	389	278
History and travels .	557	774	217
Theology . . .	687	549	0
Medicine . . .	134	135	1
Poetry . . .	148	291	143
Fiction . . .	985	1,807	822
Sundries . . .	2,205	1,794	...
New books . . .	4,827	5,739	912

Works on economy and trade have trebled in eight years, those of poetry and fiction have doubled, while theology has declined, and medicine is stationary. This is exclusive of 1503 reprints yearly in the first period, and 1510 in the second. The aggregate of new books and reprints in the second period shows an increase of 919 works, equal to 19 per cent., which indicates great activity in literary labours.

Among the largest sales of books are noted : Webster's Spelling-book, 55 million copies ; "Uncle Tom's Cabin," 1,500,000 ; Longfellow's Poems, 520,000 ; "Pickwick Papers," 900,000. Moore's Almanac, down to 1820, had a yearly sale of 500,000 copies. Cassel says that Messrs. Routledge sell 6 million books yearly. The printing-houses of London and Edinburgh turn out more than 50 million volumes per annum, of which one-fifth are exported. Between 1842 and 1888 Messrs. Mudie bought 6 million books for their lending libraries.

In 1893 Professor Strahan estimated the issue of newspapers in the United Kingdom at 170 million copies monthly, as compared with 10 millions in 1854 (when Gladstone abolished the tax on newspapers), and at present the circulation may be estimated thus :—

	Papers Monthly
England	155,000,000
Scotland	17,000,000
Ireland	14,000,000
United Kingdom . . .	186,000,000

The newspapers have a gross income of £16,000,000, of which about 9 millions go in wages to printers, 3 millions for paper, and the rest in salaries to editors, writers, reporters, &c., and dividends. The number of writers and reporters at various dates shows thus :—

Year	Editors, &c.	Reporters	Total	Per Million Pop.
1861 . . .	1,528	636	2,164	74
1881 . . .	3,434	2,677	6,111	175
1891 . . .	5,111	2,374	7,485	199

According to Sell's Dictionary of Publications, London papers receive £4,000,000 a year from advertisements. Some of the London papers issue over 200,000 copies daily.

As regards the American Press there were 17,760 papers in the United States and Canada in 1890, with an ordinary impression of 41,524,000 copies, some daily, others weekly, the aggregate issue making up about 240 million copies monthly ; of which, according to Bromley, the press of New York stood for 57 millions. There were 132 newspapers whose daily issue exceeded, each, 50,000 copies.

See *Press*, in Part I., pages 464–467.

PRICES

United Kingdom

The prices of imported articles for the period from 1861 to 1897 have been as follows :—

	1861–70	1871–80	1881–90	1891	1892	1893	1894	1895	1896	1897
Bacon, ton, £	50.5	44.5	44.8	37.9	40.9	53.0	43.8	39.0	34.5	35.4
Barley, ,,	8.7	8.3	6.4	6.8	6.0	5.1	4.5	4.7	5.1	4.9
Beef, ,,	38.0	44.0	46.5	42.1	42.4	42.4	40.1	39.0	37.8	38.4
Brandy, gallon, s.	6.5	7.9	9.1	9.0	9.0	8.8	8.5	9.2	9.2	8.9
Butter, ton, £	101.0	110.0	105.0	109.0	110.0	110.0	105.0	101.0	101.0	99.0
Cheese, ,,	55.5	55.5	49.6	47.0	49.0	50.0	48.0	44.0	44.0	45.0
Chinchona, ,,	...	...	156.0	47.0	43.0	39.0	37.0	37.0	35.0	43.0
Cigars, lb., s.	10.5	13.3	11.7	10.2	9.2	6.8	6.2	8.0	10.1	10.0
Cochineal, cwt., £	16.2	12.6	7.4	6.0	6.2	6.1	5.9	6.6	6.4	6.2
Cocoa, ton, £	54.0	71.5	73.1	71.4	72.0	73.7	71.8	67.9	61.7	60.2
Coffee, ,,	63.5	88.0	75.2	94.6	93.0	96.4	96.4	97.6	99.8	94.8
Copper ore, ,,	15.0	12.5	8.5	8.2	6.4	6.0	6.0	5.8	6.5	5.8
Cotton, ,,	138.0	66.5	54.8	52.0	48.0	49.0	41.0	39.0	46.0	41.8
Eggs (100 doz.), s.	61.6	80.0	68.9	66.0	68.2	70.0	63.7	63.0	63.2	62.1
Fish, ton, £	21.5	28.3	27.9	25.9	23.9	24.3	23.2	24.3	25.3	26.6
Flax, ,,	54.3	49.5	38.5	35.0	34.3	37.3	37.1	34.1	36.5	35.6
Flour, ,,	14.7	17.3	13.1	12.2	11.1	9.6	8.4	8.4	8.7	10.3
Glass, ,,	15.3	15.7	13.3	11.5	11.4	10.7	10.3	10.3	10.0	9.9
Guano, ,,	12.0	10.5	8.4	5.9	6.8	5.2	5.1	7.9	5.2	5.4
Hams, ,,	51.5	53.5	52.7	46.3	47.3	58.5	49.1	45.0	43.0	42.7
Hemp, ,,	35.3	33.5	31.5	30.9	27.0	25.9	22.5	21.0	21.0	19.6
Hides, ,,	62.0	68.0	58.0	48.0	46.0	46.0	43.0	44.0	46.0	45.0
Indigo, cwt., £	33.6	26.6	22.8	20.5	19.0	20.7	19.2	16.8	17.1	17.8
Jute, ton, £	19.0	16.5	13.3	12.2	15.2	13.2	13.6	11.1	12.2	11.7
Lard, ,,	56.5	47.0	42.0	32.7	35.9	50.2	39.4	33.8	26.1	22.9
Leather, ,,	...	166.0	153.0	137.0	132.0	130.0	124.0	127.0	122.0	120.0
Linseed, ,,	14.0	13.4	10.3	10.4	9.8	10.2	9.5	8.5	7.8	7.8
Maize, ,,	7.4	7.0	5.5	6.3	5.3	4.8	4.5	4.6	3.6	3.4
Molasses, ,,	11.5	9.3	7.4	6.3	5.9	6.0	5.3	4.7	4.4	4.2
Nitre, ,,	13.7	14.0	10.6	8.6	8.5	9.3	9.3	8.1	7.9	7.7
Oats, ,,	8.0	7.8	6.1	6.6	6.4	6.2	5.2	4.8	4.8	5.0
Oil, olive, gallon, d.	55.0	43.0	36.0	38.5	35.3	36.0	32.8	33.4	30.9	31.8
,, palm, ton, £	38.0	33.6	26.0	23.3	22.1	24.9	21.8	20.9	21.0	20.6
Opium, cwt., £	...	105.0	74.5	61.0	52.0	56.0	56.0	56.6	57.1	53.2
Oranges, ton, £	21.7	17.0	13.5	12.3	12.1	12.0	11.2	11.2	10.7	10.4
Pepper, ,,	36.7	46.7	63.2	43.8	33.9	30.9	25.5	25.0	26.0	32.0
Petroleum, gallon, d.	22.0	12.0	6.8	4.9	4.5	3.9	3.7	4.6	4.7	4.3
Pork, ton, £	46.0	40.2	36.3	33.8	34.2	40.4	38.1	36.8	35.3	34.8
Potatoes, ton, s.	91.0	110.0	133.5	150.0	126.0	128.0	152.0	125.0	162.0	122.0
Rags, ton, £	19.0	16.3	12.7	9.7	9.3	9.6	9.2	9.2	9.8	9.9
Raisins, ,,	30.0	35.2	33.9	33.8	30.2	27.0	24.8	25.0	28.0	30.0
Rice, ,,	12.2	10.0	8.1	9.0	8.9	7.9	7.6	7.3	7.5	8.2
Rum, gallon, d.	28.0	24.0	21.0	22.6	20.8	17.3	16.8	15.7	15.5	16.0
Saltpetre, ton, £	26.7	22.4	18.6	18.0	17.4	17.6	18.4	18.7	16.4	15.0
Seed clover, ,,	56.5	48.5	42.9	43.1	42.7	47.5	47.8	43.2	38.9	38.6
Sheep, each, s.	39.5	44.5	40.8	38.5	31.8	28.3	33.2	33.5	29.5	30.1
Sheepskins, each, d.	14.0	32.0	28.6	26.0	27.1	25.4	24.2	22.4	22.0	21.6
Silk, lb., s.	26.7	18.7	14.7	13.5	13.1	12.9	13.1	12.6	12.5	12.3
Sugar, raw, ton, £	26.3	22.7	16.0	13.0	13.1	14.3	11.7	9.7	10.6	9.3
,, refined, ,,	33.0	31.7	21.1	17.4	18.0	19.4	17.0	14.5	14.8	13.4
Sulphur, ton, s.	140.0	123.0	101.0	121.0	113.0	97.0	88.0	80.0	83.0	91.0
Tallow, ton, £	45.2	40.5	31.1	25.9	25.4	27.7	25.5	23.7	21.3	19.2
Tea, ,,	176.0	147.5	109.0	100.0	94.0	91.0	89.0	90.0	88.5	87.4
Tobacco, ,,	105.0	72.7	69.8	79.8	76.0	69.7	64.4	64.4	64.5	65.0
Wheat, ,,	11.5	11.5	8.6	8.9	7.7	6.4	5.4	5.5	6.2	7.5
Wine, gallon, d.	67.0	89.0	85.0	85.0	84.0	87.0	84.0	82.0	85.0	88.0
Wood, load, s.	63.5	55.6	36.2	30.0	30.0	28.0	26.8	27.2	28.4	28.8
,, staves, s.	167.0	136.5	86.8	90.6	87.2	77.8	82.0	82.2	94.8	89.8
Wool, ton, £	165.0	132.5	102.0	87.4	81.5	81.4	79.3	75.6	78.4	74.4
Yeast, ,,	41.5	50.5	54.3	53.4	52.0	52.0	51.4	51.0	49.6	48.4

The prices of British exports from 1871 to 1897 were as follows :—

	1871-80	1881-90	1891	1892	1893	1894	1895	1896	1897
Alkali, ton, s.	175	118	150	144	127	109	100	103	103
Bags, gross, s.	84	57	54	54	54	49	48	48	50
Beer, barrel, s.	83	78	73	73	73	71	70	69	69
Books, ton, £	211	183	160	155	154	145	136	133	128
Boots, doz. pairs, s.	62	58	54	52	49	48	47	48	49
Brass, ton, £	100	86	91	84	80	75	78	82	87
Butter, ,,	124	124	116	117	117	115	110	110	104
Carpet, doz. yards, s.	34	26	25	24	25	24	25	25	25
Cement, ton, s.	52	43	40	37	34	33	32	33	33
Cheese, ton, £	83	81	78	78	81	78	73	72	74
Cloth, doz. yards, s.	37	38	40	39	40	39	36	36	30
Coal, ton, d.	144	112	146	132	119	126	112	106	108
Copper bar, ton, £	80	58	56	49	48	44	46	49	51
Cordage, ,,	54	47	46	42	42	39	37	38	37
Cottons, 100 yards, d.	304	237	218	199	198	186	177	191	185
,, printed, 100 yards, d.	446	334	288	275	277	263	253	258	260
Firearms, each, s.	27	30	29	35	30	31	37	49	45
Flannel, doz. yards, d.	220	151	102	101	100	98	93	93	96
Flour, ton, s.	324	234	242	218	181	157	154	165	198
Glass flint, ton, £	54	46	44	48	52	47	46	46	47
,, bottles, ton, s.	210	190	188	191	191	190	191	189	188
Gunpowder, ton, £	57	57	55	57	56	54	50	53	51
Hats, doz., s.	26	20	19	19	19	18	18	19	20
Herrings, barrel, s.	29	26	26	22	22	21	23	19	24
Horses, each, £	64	60	47	50	40	27	26	23	24
Iron bar, ton, s.	185	128	135	132	125	128	119	123	130
,, cast, ,,	324	243	251	263	262	252	252	249	250
,, galvanised, ,,	442	280	282	264	245	230	221	233	225
,, hoop, ,,	206	140	146	144	138	134	127	132	138
,, old, ,,	98	64	64	62	56	53	52	53	54
,, plates, ,,	274	188	168	203	194	183	171	149	165
,, pig, ,,	74	49	53	52	47	46	48	48	48
,, rail, ,,	185	110	101	88	83	79	77	89	92
,, wire, ,,	346	285	339	335	350	358	337	322	337
Jute, 100 yards, d.	348	239	214	231	213	211	204	212	216
Lead, ton, s.	410	284	283	244	226	220	237	254	267
Leather, ton, £	164	179	183	190	189	181	179	185	176
Linen, 100 yards, s.	61	52	45	44	45	43	39	42	41
,, printed, 100 yards, s.	64	57	51	50	43	45	39	44	42
Oil-seed, ton, s.	518	423	416	393	435	419	403	373	340
Paper, ton, £	57	38	34	33	31	31	31	30	30
Sailcloth, 100 yards, s.	113	94	89	92	89	90	86	84	86
Salt, ton, d.	156	162	213	198	190	188	177	171	168
Silks, doz. yards, s.	39	41	28	26	25	24	24	23	23
Soap, ton, s.	25	22	22	22	21	22	21	21	21
Spirits, gallon, d.	49	77	80	84	84	86	90	92	95
Steel bars, ton, s.	662	420	321	327	283	272	274	250	250
Sugar, ton, s.	540	353	288	303	322	281	238	240	218
Thread, doz. lbs., s.	40	37	43	43	42	41	32	30	30
Tin, ton, £	100	100	95	96	90	74	68	64	65
Tin plates, ton, s.	487	308	320	270	263	245	232	227	224
Wheat, ,,	237	176	188	167	139	139	151	165	165
Wool, ton, £	175	108	94	85	88	85	88	88	86
Yarn, cotton, ton, £	140	108	98	88	95	85	79	88	84
,, jute, ,,	35	25	23	25	23	24	23	23	23
,, linen, ,,	148	131	136	129	138	136	127	126	119
,, woollen, ,,	313	224	212	203	203	199	197	204	190
Zinc, ton, s.	410	298	421	365	326	276	264	284	314

ITALY

The prices of food were as follows :—

Period	Per Ton, Shillings			Per Ton,£	Per Gallon Pence	
	Wheat	Maize	Rice	Beef	Wine	Oil
1866-75	275	148	275	52	17	45
1876-85	244	159	280	55	21	46
1886-90	187	125	254	57	21	44
1891	208	139	295	60	23	44
1892	202	132	265	60	16	45
1893	176	112	229	60	14	45
1894	158	104	219	60	15	44
1895	170	143	226	64	17	44
1896	185	121	238	68	19	36

UNITED STATES

Prices have been as follows :—

	1874 to 1883	1884 to 1893	1894	1895	1896	1897
Bacon, ton, £	44	39	44	41	39	35
Barley, ton, s.	115	86	74	56	54	...
Beef, ton, £	36	28	27	27	26	24
Buckwht., ton, s.	118	96	92	75	65	...
Butter, ton, £	93	77	81	76	71	67
Cheese, ,,	53	43	45	42	39	42
Coal, ton, d.	178	128	112	100	114	90
Coffee, ton, £	73	69	77	73	57	46
Cotton, ,,	56	45	36	27	38	34
Cows, each, s.	110	103	91	92	94	96

	1874 to 1883	1884 to 1893	1894	1895	1896	1897
Eggs (120), d. .	105	90	84	84	74	69
Flax, ton, £ .	60	57	64	59	48	43
Flour, barrel, s.	25	20	17	14	15	16
Glass, ton, s. .	290	230	187	187	187	196
Hemp, ton, £ .	29	31	31	26	26	26
Horses, each, s.	255	291	200	151	138	131
Ind.-rub., ton, £	270	211	207	210	211	228
Iron bar, ton, s.	231	181	125	134	131	122
,, nails, ,,	296	192	102	137	217	137
,, pig, ,,	100	75	52	54	54	50
,, rails, ,,	183	129	100	101	116	81
Lard, ton, £ .	49	37	42	36	31	24
Leather, ,, .	107	82	70	72	84	80
Maize, ton, s. .	74	63	76	44	36	43
Mules, each, s. .	110	103	90	91	94	96
Oats, ton, s. .	61	50	54	33	31	...
Petrol., brl., d.	273	160	88	103	143	132
Pigs, each, s. .	22	20	25	21	18	17
Pork, ton, £ .	39	33	37	33	27	23
Rye, ton, s. . .	116	91	83	73	68	...
Sheep, each, d. .	120	113	99	79	85	91
Silk, lb., d. .	222	190	158	138	164	142
Steel, ton, s. .	239	129	100	101	116	81
Sugar,ref.,ton,£	47	29	21	22	23	22
Tallow, ,, .	34	23	22	20	16	16
Tea, ,, .	117	81	71	64	64	62
Tin, ,, .	93	98	73	66	63	60
Tobacco, ,, .	42	42	40	41	40	37
Wheat, ton, s. .	164	121	81	84	121	129
Wine, gallon, d.	30	35	35	35	34	47
Wool, ton, £ .	126	109	121	93	103	103

The price-level of the United States has been as follows:—

1874–83 .	.	.	.	.	1,000
1884–93 .	.	.	.	.	796
1894–95 .	.	.	.	.	650
1896–97 .	.	.	.	.	638

This shows a fall of 36 per cent. since the decade ending 1883.

PRICE-LEVEL

Sauerbeck's Index-numbers convey an accurate idea of the rise or fall of level of prices in England, viz.:—

Period	Food	Minerals	Textiles	Sundries	Gen. No.
1867–77 . .	100	100	100	100	100
1878–88 . .	83	73	71	80	79
1889 . . .	75	75	70	68	72
1890 . . .	73	80	66	69	72
1891 . . .	77	76	59	69	72
1892 . . .	73	71	57	67	68
1893 . . .	72	68	59	68	68
1894 . . .	66	64	53	64	63
1895 . . .	64	62	52	65	62
1896 . . .	62	63	54	63	61
1897 . . .	65	66	51	62	62

The above may be inverted by taking 1897 as par, thus:—

Period	Food	Minerals	Textiles	Sundries	Gen. No.
1897 . . .	100	100	100	100	100
1896 . . .	95	95	106	102	98
1895 . . .	98	94	102	105	100
1894 . . .	102	97	104	103	102
1893 . . .	111	103	116	110	110
1892 . . .	112	108	112	108	110
1891 . . .	118	115	116	111	116
1890 . . .	112	121	130	111	116
1889 . . .	115	114	138	110	116
1878–88 . .	128	110	140	129	127
1867–77 . .	154	151	196	161	161

It appears from the above that £100 now will buy as much merchandise as £127 in the period of eleven years ending 1888, or £161 in that ending 1877.

PUBLIC WORKS

The amount outstanding of loans by the Treasury for public works in the United Kingdom in 1897 was £38,400,000, against £37,200,000 in 1887. See page 494.

R

RAILWAYS

The mileage and cost of construction of existing lines (1897) are as follows:—

	Length, Miles	Cost, Millions £	£ per Mile	£ per Inhab.	Miles of Raily. to 1,000 Sq. Miles	Miles of Raily. to 100,000 Pop.
England . . .	14,710	843	57,300	27.2	253	47
Scotland . . .	3,390	147	43,300	34.2	113	80
Ireland . . .	3,180	40	12,600	8.8	99	71
U. Kingdom .	21,280	1,030	48,400	25.8	177	53
France . . .	26,020	661	27,600	17.2	130	67
Germany. . .	28,880	574	19,900	11.0	135	55
Russia . . .	27,270	403	14,800	3.6	12	25
Austria . . .	19,100	367	19,200	8.5	71	44
Italy . . .	9,580	201	20,800	6.4	84	32
Spain . . .	7,630	122	16,000	7.0	42	42
Portugal . . .	1,450	23	16,000	4.8	40	30
Sweden . . .	6,150	35	5,700	7.2	36	124
Norway . . .	1,090	8	7,000	4.0	9	50
Denmark . . .	1,430	15	10,500	7.0	95	65
Holland . . .	1,700	38	22,500	7.7	80	34
Belgium . . .	2,840	76	26,700	12.2	260	45
Switzerland . .	2,350	45	19,200	15.0	150	80
Roumania . .	1,830	30	16,000	5.2	38	33
Servia	350	4	12,500	1.6	16	16
Bulgaria . . .	600	7	12,000	2.2	15	18
Greece . . .	590	10	16,500	4.2	30	27
Turkey . . .	1,060	18	17,000	3.2	15	22
Europe . . .	161,200	3,667	22,800	9.7	40	44
United States .	182,600	2,355	12,900	33.6	61	250
Canada . . .	16,960	186	11,000	37.0	5	340
Mexico . . .	7,380	92	12,000	7.6	10	60
W. Indies . .	1,470	15	10,000	3.8	13	36
Cent. America .	600	6	10,000	2.4	4	20
Venezuela, &c. .	860	9	10,000	1.4	7	11
Peru . . .	920	37	40,000	13.0	2	31
Chile	2,500	23	9,200	8.5	10	83
Argentina . .	9,000	102	11,300	25.5	8	225
Brazil . . .	8,090	72	8,900	6.0	3	50
Uruguay, &c. .	1,680	17	10,000	4.0	3	55
America . . .	232,060	2,914	12,500	24.0	18	180

	Length, Miles	Cost, Millions £	£ per Mile	£ per Inhab.	Miles of Raily. to 1000 Sq. Miles	Miles of Raily. to 100,000 Pop.
E. Indies	22,170	223	10,100	7.0	22	10
Japan	2,500	30	12,000	7.5	16	6
Asia Minor	1,480	22	15,000	2.2	7	15
Asia	26,150	275	10,500	0.5	2	4
Egypt	1,220	18	15,700	2.0	2	12
Algeria, &c.	3,290	44	13,400	6.0	10	55
Transvaal	720	7	10,000	28.0	6	144
Cape Col., &c.	3,350	34	10,200	11.0	...	...
Africa	8,580	103	12,100	2.0	1	7
Australia	14,210	145	10,200	36.0	5	355
The World	442,200	7,104	16,100	6.0	10	32

	Averages Per Mile			
	Receipts £	Expen. £	Profit £	P. Cent. on Cap.
England	5,210	2,930	2,280	3.96
Scotland	2,960	1,510	1,450	3.36
Ireland	1,090	600	490	3.90
United Kingdom	4,230	2,360	1,870	3.87
France	2,245	1,215	1,030	3.50
Germany	2,600	1,480	1,120	5.64
Russia	1,520	960	560	3.72
Austria	1,570	900	670	3.42
Italy	1,240	870	370	1.80
Sweden	530	320	210	3.70
Norway	550	370	180	2.50
Denmark	840	630	210	2.00
Holland	1,760	1,470	290	1.30
Belgium	2,780	1,550	1,230	4.60
Switzerland	1,920	1,110	810	4.22
Europe	2,040	1,170	870	3.80
United States	1,280	904	376	2.91
Canada	620	430	190	1.72
Argentina	690	360	330	2.95
India	830	400	430	4.30
Japan	1,480	640	840	7.00
Egypt	1,575	700	875	5.50
Cape Colony	1,600	760	840	9.20
Australia	750	440	310	2.95
The World	1,430	890	540	3.35

In 1891, says the *Eisenbahnwesen*, 117,000 locomotives in the various countries ran 2325 millions of miles, or 25 times the distance of the earth from the sun, being an average of 6,600,000 miles daily.

The traffic, earnings, and expenses may be summed up thus:—

	Millions		Millions £ Sterling	
	Passengers	Goods Tons	Receipts	Expenses
England	860	300	76.6	43.2
Scotland	94	52	10.1	5.1
Ireland	26	5	3.5	1.9
U. Kingdom	980	357	90.2	50.2
France	349	101	50.5	27.4
Germany	592	248	75.2	42.8
Russia	52	91	41.4	26.2
Austria	202	118	29.2	16.7
Italy	49	17	10.3	7.2
Scandinavia	40	22	5.1	3.3
Holland	25	10	3.0	2.5
Belgium	100	55	7.9	4.4
Switzerland	43	12	4.5	2.6
Various	28	12	10.7	5.7
Europe	2,460	1,043	328.0	189.0
United States	535	774	234.2	165.0
Canada	15	24	10.4	7.1
Argentina	15	8	6.2	3.2
Brazil, &c.	45	14	10.2	6.7
America	610	820	261.0	182.0
India	161	32	16.9	8.1
Japan, &c.	65	6	5.1	2.9
Asia	226	38	22.0	11.0
Egypt	10	3	1.8	0.8
Cape Colony	9	2	4.1	1.9
Algeria, &c.	5	2	3.4	2.0
Africa	24	7	9.3	4.7
Australia	60	12	10.7	6.3
The World	3,380	1,920	631.0	393.0

Juraschek's summary of the railways of the world is as follows:—

	Miles		Cost Millions £		£ Per Mile	
	1880	1892	1880	1892	1880	1892
Europe	104,800	145,200	2,585	3,634	24,700	25,000
America	107,000	220,800	1,350	2,815	12,600	12,800
Asia	9,900	24,000	154	290	15,500	12,100
Africa	2,900	7,300	44	79	15,200	10,800
Australia	4,700	12,800	58	128	12,300	10,000
The World	229,300	410,100	4,191	6,936	18,200	16,900

The rolling-stock and traffic in 1892 were as follows:—

	Number of			Millions of	
	Engines	Carriages	Trucks	Passengers	Goods Tons
U. Kingdom	17,440	40,100	602,800	864	315
France	10,070	24,700	267,800	305	106
Germany	15,740	29,600	313,800	501	237
Russia	7,160	8,200	151,200	50	72
Austria	5,750	11,700	133,700	130	110
Italy	2,760	8,200	48,100	51	17
Spain	1,660	4,700	32,000	25	11
Portugal	390	1,100	7,500	53	17
Scandinavia	1,350	3,300	29,500	29	14
Holland	780	2,000	10,100	22	8
Belgium	2,650	4,400	57,500	88	37
Switzerland	870	2,300	10,600	37	10
Roumania, &c.	2,960	6,100	73,300	91	41
Europe	69,580	146,400	1,737,900	2,246	995
U. States	35,280	24,900	1,177,000	576	761
Canada	1,950	1,800	55,500	14	22
Argentina	880	1,300	24,900	10	2
Brazil	230	300	2,700	11	1
Chile, &c.	5,190	3,800	170,400	83	106
America	43,530	32,100	1,430,500	694	892

	Number of			Millions of	
	Engines	Carriages	Trucks	Passengers	Goods Tons
India . . .	3,760	10,600	71,900	127	27
Japan . . .	320	1,400	4,600	27	4
Java . . .	180	500	2,100	10	1
Various . .	910	2,700	16,800	25	5
Asia . . .	5,170	15,200	95,400	189	37
Egypt . . .	250	500	4,300	5	2
Algeria . .	300	700	6,300	3	2
S. Africa, &c.	830	1,800	15,800	12	5
Africa . . .	1,380	3,000	26,400	20	9
Australia . .	2,010	3,700	41,800	97	12
The World .	121,670	200,400	3,332,000	3,246	1,945

The following table shows the State lines, distinct from those held by Companies, in 1898 :—

	Miles		
	State	Companies	Total
United Kingdom . .	...	21,280	21,280
France . . .	1,700	24,320	26,020
Germany . . .	26,240	2,640	28,880
Russia . . .	19,180	8,090	27,270
Austria . . .	12,830	6,270	19,100
Italy * . . .	...	9,580	9,580
Spain . . .	...	7,630	7,630
Portugal . . .	910	540	1,450
Sweden . . .	2,280	3,870	6,150
Norway . . .	1,020	70	1,090
Denmark . . .	1,070	360	1,430
Holland . . .	900	800	1,700
Belgium . . .	2,040	800	2,840
Switzerland . .	2,350	...	2,350
Danubian States .	2,780	...	2,780
Greece . . .	...	590	590
Turkey . . .	...	1,060	1,060
Europe . . .	73,300	87,900	161,200
United States .	...	182,600	182,600
Canada . . .	1,350	15,610	16,960
Spanish America .	1,400	31,100	32,500
America . .	2,750	229,310	232,060
India * . . .	6,150	14,240	20,390
Japan . . .	630	1,870	2,500
Egypt . . .	1,150	70	1,220
Cape Colony . .	2,250	250	2,500
Natal . . .	400	...	400
Australia . .	13,570	640	14,210
Various . .	1,150	6,570	7,720
The World . .	101,350	340,850	442,200

Working expenses compared with earnings show the following percentages :—

England .	56.2	Germany. .	56.9	Sweden . .	60.4
Scotland .	51.0	Russia . .	63.2	Norway . .	67.3
Ireland .	55.0	Austria . .	57.3	Denmark .	75.0
France .	54.1	Italy . .	70.0	Holland .	83.5

* There are in Italy 5400 miles of railways built by the State, but leased to joint-stock companies for 60 years: also 11,130 miles of State lines in India leased to similar companies.

Belgium . .	55.8	Canada . .	69.4	Egypt . .	44.4
Switzerland .	57.8	Argentina .	52.2	Cape Colony	47.5
Europe . .	57.3	India . . .	48.2	Australia . .	58.7
United States	70.6	Japan . . .	43.2	The World .	62.0

The following table shows the proportion of passengers in each class, and the average number of miles to each traveller (in 1892).

	In 1000 Passengers			Miles per Traveller
	1st Class	2nd Class	3rd Class	
Great Britain . .	35	72	893	...
France . .	68	273	659	21
Germany. . .	5	102	893	15
Russia . . .	12	62	926	65
Austria . .	16	135	849	20
Italy . . .	42	249	709	28
Holland . .	52	207	741	16
Belgium . .	35	125	840	13
Switzerland . .	15	182	803	12
Roumania . .	39	156	805	42
Average . .	32	156	812	25

The fare by ordinary train for a run of 10 miles is as follows :—

	Pence per 10 Miles		
	1st Class	2nd Class	3rd Class
Great Britain	14.7	12.3	10.0
France	17.0	11.6	7.5
Germany	15.2	11.4	7.6
Russia	8.7	4.1	2.7
Austria	15.7	11.7	7.9
Hungary	18.2	13.7	9.1
Italy	17.1	12.0	7.7
Switzerland	15.8	11.0	7.9
Holland	16.1	12.9	8.0
Belgium	11.6	8.7	5.8
Average	15.0	11.0	7.5

Freight charge for carrying a ton 100 miles is as follows (1895) :—

Pence per 100 Miles

Great Britain	174	France. .	72	Belgium . .	68
Ireland .	232	Germany .	64	Holland . .	80
United States	41	Switzerland .	140	Italy . . .	160

The *Engineer* of January 1896 gives the maximum speed of trains as follows :—

Miles per Hour

United States	53	France. .	49	Italy . . .	42
Great Britain	51	Belgium . .	45	Austria . .	41
Germany . .	51	Holland . .	44		

The following are the quickest trains in Great Britain and United States :—

Run	Miles	Hrs. Min.	Miles per Hour
Perth to Forfar	32	0 32	60
Grantham to York. . . .	83	1 28	56
Swindon to London . . .	77	1 27	54
Carlisle to Aberdeen . . .	240	4 58	48
Philadelphia to Atlantic City	56	0 48	69
Syracuse to Rochester . .	80	1 20	60
New York to Buffalo . . .	440	8 15	52

Gross receipts per train mile run, and expenses, are shown thus :—

	Pence per Mile Run		
	Receipts	Expenses	Profit
United Kingdom . .	67	37	30
France	52	28	24
Germany	43	25	18
Russia	56	35	21
Austria	62	36	26
Italy	52	36	16
Belgium	34	19	15
Canada	57	40	17
Australia	77	45	32

UNITED KINGDOM

Traffic of passengers and merchandise increased in 10 years as follows :—

	Passengers, Mills.		Tons, Millions	
	1886	1896	1886	1896
England	642	860	216	300
Scotland . . .	65	94	35	52
Ireland	19	27	4	5
United Kingdom . .	726	981	255	357

Passenger traffic does not include season-ticket holders. Passengers showed an increase of 35 per cent., goods 40 per cent., in 10 years. Receipts, expenses, and profit in 1896 were as follows :—

	Receipts, £	Expenses, £	Profit, £	Interest on Cost
England . .	76,600,000	43,150,000	33,450,000	3.97
Scotland . .	10,050,000	5,120,000	4,930,000	3.35
Ireland . . .	3,470,000	1,920,000	1,550,000	3.92
U. Kingdom .	90,120,000	50,190,000	39,930,000	3.87

Earnings and expenses per mile showed as follows :—

	Earnings, £		Expenses, £	
	1886	1896	1886	1896
England	4,137	4,909	2,280	2,935
Scotland	2,407	2,853	1,248	1,510
Ireland	1,046	1,074	580	605
United Kingdom .	3,446	4,009	1,888	2,358

In the above table miscellaneous receipts are not included in earnings, which comprise only passenger and goods traffic; gross receipts would be 5½ per cent. higher than the above traffic earnings per mile.

Accidents on railways in the United Kingdom show the number of victims thus :—

	Killed		
	1876	1886	1896
Passengers . . .	38	8	50
Employees . . .	673	425	447
Total . .	711	433	497

	Injured		
	1876	1886	1896
Passengers . . .	1,279	615	388
Employees . . .	2,600	2,010	3,986
Total . .	3,879	2,625	4,374

	Total		
Passengers . . .	1,317	623	438
Employees . . .	3,273	2,435	4,433
Total . .	4,590	3,058	4,871

The number of killed and wounded, as compared with 1886, has increased by 1813, or about 60 per cent., whereas passenger traffic has risen only 21, and goods traffic 40, per cent. In fact 13 persons are killed or wounded on the railways of the United Kidgdom against 8 persons in 1886. At Clapham Junction 700 trains pass daily.

FRANCE

A statement published in 1895 showed passenger traffic thus :—

Class	Million Passengers		
	1866	1882	1894
First	8	15	19
Second	26	60	104
Third	52	106	197
Total . .	86	181	320

First-class passengers show a falling ratio, being now only 6 per cent. of the total.

UNITED STATES

Mileage and capital have been as follows :—

	Miles	Millions £	£ per Mile
1876 . . .	76,810	929	12,100
1886 . . .	133,560	1,682	12,600
1896 . . .	178,550	2,297	12,700

The length and cost of railways in the several parts of the Union in 1896 were as follows :—

States	Miles	Miles per 10,000 Pop.	Capital Mills. £	£ per Mile
New England .	7,130	14	97	13,600
Middle . .	21,500	14	545	25,300
South . .	45,650	22	403	8,830
Prairie . .	81,230	31	1,015	12,500
Pacific . .	23,040	53	237	10,300
Union . .	178,550	25	2,297	12,700

The number of passengers carried, and the equivalent carried 100 miles, were :—

Year	Passengers Millions	Miles Millions	Average Miles	Passengers Millions Carried 100 Miles
1882 . . .	375	10,484	28	105
1890 . . .	520	12,522	24	125
1896 . . .	535	13,055	25	131

With increase of population the average distance travelled by each passenger diminishes, being now 25 miles, against 28 miles in the year 1882.

Goods traffic shows as follows :—

Year	Million Tons	Miles Millions	Average Miles	Mill. Tons Carried 100 Miles
1882 . . .	360	39,302	109	393
1890 . . .	691	79,193	115	792
1896 . . .	774	93,886	121	939

The opening up of the Western States by new railways causes the average haulage of goods to increase, each ton being now carried 121 miles, against 109 miles in 1882. The average distance that merchandise was carried in 1882 was four times that of a passenger, and at present it is five times. The total mileage of passenger traffic rose 25 per cent. in 14 years, that of goods traffic 140 per cent. The latter is stimulated by the reduction of freight charges, viz. :—

1882	. . .	1$ 24 cents per ton 100 miles.
1890	. . .	93 ,, ,, ,,
1896	. . .	82 ,, ,, ,,

This charge is less than one-fourth of the charge in Great Britain, and little more than half what is customary on the Continent of Europe. It seems that American engines are heavier than British, going up to 400 tons : thus the Pennsylvanian lines carry 1600 tons coal in one train, whereas the Midland coal train of England rarely exceeds 400 tons.

Each passenger-engine draws 66,000 passengers, and each freight-engine 40,000 tons of goods, yearly. In 1893 there were 1890 different railway companies, employing 874,000 persons, of whom 2730 were killed and 31,730 injured, that is, 3 per thousand killed. Forty companies own half the railways of the Union.

The railways in 1896 compared with area and population thus :—

States	Miles of Railway to	
	1000 Square Miles	100,000 Inhabitants
New England . . .	105	145
Middle . . .	190	145
South . . .	56	230
Prairie . . .	108	325
Pacific . . .	19	540
The Union . . .	61	250

CANADA

The progress of Canadian lines is briefly shown thus :—

Year	Length Miles	Miles Run	No. of Passengers	Tons of Goods
1876 .	5,160	18,100,000	5,500,000	6,300,000
1886 .	10,700	30,500,000	9,900,000	15,700,000
1896 .	16,270	44,500,000	14,800,000	24,300,000

In twenty years passengers have almost trebled, goods quadrupled. The gross receipts and expenses were :—

Year	Receipts £	Expenses £	Profit £	Interest on Cost
1876 . . .	4,040,000	3,280,000	760,000	1.27
1886 . . .	6,950,000	5,040,000	1,910,000	1.54
1896 . . .	10,510,000	7,280,000	3,230,000	1.73

This shows a steady improvement in traffic, the average earnings and expenses per mile of rail showing thus :—

Year	Receipts £	Expenses £	Profit £	Pence Profit per Mile Run
1875 . . .	839	680	159	10
1886 . . .	646	470	176	15
1896 . . .	646	448	198	17

The length and cost of the principal lines are shown thus :—

	Miles	Cost, £	£ per Mile
Canadian Pacific . .	6,220	66,600,000	10,700
Grand Trunk . .	3,160	69,600,000	22,100
Intercolonial . .	1,360	12,300,000	9,050
Other lines . .	5,650	38,700,000	6,850
Total . .	16,390	187,200,000	11,400

The increase of railway capital in five years is shown thus :—

	1891 £ Sterling	1896 £ Sterling	Increase, £
Shares	71,100,000	77,000,000	5,900,000
Debentures . .	60,800,000	70,000,000	9,200,000
Subsidies . . .	38,100,000	40,200,000	2,100,000
Total . .	170,000,000	187,200,000	17,200,000

The subsidy by the Dominion Government amounts to £31,000,000, and those from local legislatures to £9,200,000.

The traffic on the principal lines in 1896 was as follows :—

	Passengers Number	Tons Goods	Per Mile	
			Passengers	Tons
Grand Trunk .	5,080,000	7,590,000	1,610	2,410
Can. Pacific .	3,040,000	4,580,000	488	738
Intercolonial .	1,590,000	1,430,000	1,170	1,050
Other lines .	5,100,000	10,670,000	903	1,880
Total . .	14,810,000	24,270,000	910	1,490

The goods traffic in 1896 compared with previous years as follows :—

	Tons Carried		
	1876	1886	1896
Grain . . .	1,120,000	3,640,000	5,040,000
Timber . .	840,000	2,800,000	4,680,000
Manufactures .	150,000	2,260,000	3,420,000
Sundries . .	4,220,000	6,970,000	11,130,000
Total . .	6,330,000	15,670,000	24,270,000

The Grand Trunk has 30 per cent., the Canadian Pacific 20 per cent., of the goods traffic.

RAINFALL

The rainfall of London in 1897, and the average for eighty-two years, as well as the average rainfall of Dublin for twenty-two years to 1896, are shown as follows :—

	London, Inches		Dublin
	1897	1816–97	1875–96
January . . .	1.6	1.9	2.1
February . . .	2.4	1.5	2.1
March . . .	3.4	1.6	1.9
1st Quarter . . .	7.4	5.0	6.1
April	1.6	1.7	2.1
May	1.3	2.0	2.2
June	1.9	1.9	2.0
2nd Quarter . .	4.8	5.6	6.3
July . . .	0.7	2.6	2.6
August . . .	2.9	2.4	3.0
September . . .	2.7	2.3	1.9
3rd Quarter . .	6.3	7.3	7.5
October . . .	0.5	2.8	3.0
November . . .	1.1	2.3	2.7
December . . .	2.1	2.0	2.4
4th Quarter . .	3.7	7.1	8.1
Year	22.2	25.0	28.0

Tables of rainfall yearly at 350 cities of the world will be found at pages 391, 392.

REFORMATORIES

The number of children in reformatories and industrial schools is shown thus :—

	G. Britain	Ireland	Total
1859 . . .	3,276	140	3,416
1866 . . .	7,364	163	7,527
1888 . . .	18,810	8,914	27,724
1897 . . .	24,380	8,220	32,600

There are 144 industrial schools and reformatories in England, 42 in Scotland, and 76 in Ireland, in all 262, of which 138 are for boys, 124 for girls ; 160 are for Protestant, 102 for Catholic, children. Since the establishment of these institutions the criminal records of England and Scotland show a great diminution of juvenile offenders (under sixteen years of age), viz. :—

	England	Scotland	G. Britain
1861 . . .	8,801	1,212	10,013
1870 . . .	9,998	1,204	11,202
1880 . . .	5,579	1,188	6,766
1893 . . .	4,036	741	4,777

The following table shows how many juveniles were in 1000 criminals :—

	England	Scotland
1861	79	65
1870	63	42
1880	34	23
1893	25	14

The sexes were distinguished in 1897 thus :—

Reformatories

	Males	Females	Total
England . . .	4,090	580	4,670
Scotland . . .	780	130	910
Ireland . . .	500	60	560
U. Kingdom . .	5,370	770	6,140

Industrial Schools

	Males	Females	Total
England . . .	10,770	3,180	13,950
Scotland . . .	3,480	1,370	4,850
Ireland . . .	3,440	4,220	7,660
U. Kingdom . .	17,690	8,770	26,460

Total

	Males	Females	Total
England . . .	14,860	3,760	18,620
Scotland . . .	4,260	1,500	5,760
Ireland . . .	3,940	4,280	8,220
U. Kingdom · . .	23,060	9,540	32,600

The number of children in reformatories per 100,000 inhabitants is 15 in England, 22 in Scotland, and 12 in Ireland.

For cost of maintenance, &c., see page 233.

RELIGION

Latest estimates and official returns show as follows :—

	Christians	Non-Christians	Total
Europe . . .	340,320,000	12,480,000	352,800,000
America . . .	124,740,000	170,000	124,910,000
Australia . . .	3,800,000	...	3,800,000
Asia and Africa .	7,240,000	641,550,000	648,790,000
The World . .	476,100,000	654,200,000	1,130,300,000

The creeds of Europe, America, and Australia sum up 481,500,000 souls, of which 468,800,000 are Christians, 6,300,000 Jews, and 6,400,000 Mahometans. The Christian population is made up as follows :—

	Number (000 omitted)			
	Roman Catholics	Protestants	Greeks	Total
United Kingdom .	5,410	34,430	...	39,840
France.	37,740	690	...	38,430
Germany	17,670	31,150	...	48,820
Russia	8,300	2,950	73,000	84,250
Austria	32,240	3,890	3,180	39,310
Italy	28,400	60	...	28,460
Spain and Portugal	22,690	10	...	22,700
Scandinavia . . .	10	9,280	...	9,290
Belg. and Holland .	7,990	2,710	...	10,700
Finland and Luxem.	210	2,390	50	2,650
Switzerland . . .	1,180	1,720	...	2,900
Danubian States .	180	20	9,730	9,930
Turkey and Greece .	290	50	2,700	3,040
Europe	162,310	89,350	88,660	340,320
United States . .	9,850	61,030	...	70,880
Canada	1,990	2,640	...	4,630
Spanish America .	45,610	120	...	45,730
West Indies . . .	2,480	1,030	...	3,510
Australia	850	2,880	...	3,730
Total . .	223,090	157,050	88,660	468,800

The American Statistical Society (1893) publishes the following :—

	Number (ooo omitted)					
	Europe	America	Asia	Africa	Oceania	Total
Roman Catholics	160,200	58,400	3,010	2,660	6,570	230,840
Protestants	80,800	57,300	660	1,740	2,720	143,220
Greeks	89,200	...	8,830	...	...	98,030
Mahometans	6,600	...	109,500	36,000	24,700	176,800
Jews	6,500	...	200	400	...	7,100
Pagans	...	1,300	667,800	91,000	4,400	764,500
Total	343,300	117,000	790,000	131,800	38,390	1,420,490

AMERICA

	Number (ooo omitted)			
	United States	Canada	Spanish America	Total
Roman Catholics .	8,800	1,800	47,800	58,400
Protestants . . .	50,300	3,000	4,000	57,300
Idolaters	280	...	1,020	1,300
Total . . .	59,080	4,800	52,620	117,000

ASIA

	Number (ooo omitted)				
	India	China	Japan	Siberia, &c.	Total
Christians . .	1,730	1,200	30	9,540	12,500
Mahometans .	51,600	21,000	...	36,900	109,500
Buddhists . .	5,400	84,000	24,900	33,600	147,900
Hindoos . . .	120,000	...	...	...	120,000
Confucians, &c.	46,000	256,000	14,070	84,030	400,100
Total . .	224,730	362,200	39,000	164,070	790,000

OCEANIA

	Number (ooo omitted)			
	Australia	Philippines	Java, &c.	Total
Roman Catholics .	850	5,500	220	6,570
Protestants . . .	2,500	...	220	2,720
Mahometans . . .	...	...	24,700	24,700
Pagans	...	...	4,400	4,400
Total . . .	3,350	5,500	29,540	38,390

See *Missions*, page 777, and *Churches*, page 656.

Roman Catholic authorities give the following particulars respecting English-speaking countries (1898) :—

	Bishops	Clergy	Churches	Souls
Ireland . .	28	3,440	2,760	3,550,000
England . .	17	2,700	1,480	1,500,000
Scotland . .	7	420	350	360,000
Canada . .	31	1,500	1,050	2,600,000
Australia . .	16	400	780	900,000
India, &c. . .	42	1,790	240	2,590,000
British Empire .	141	10,250	6,660	11,500,000
United States .	91	10,910	10,500	9,850,000
Total . .	232	21,160	17,160	21,350,000

In the United Kingdom there are 19 Privy Councillors, 31 Peers, and 73 Members of Parliament who are Roman Catholics. In the United States there are 927 Catholic colleges, besides a large number of schools, attended by 828,000 children. England, Ireland, Canada, United States, and Australia, have each a cardinal. In India there are 745 European and 655 native priests, the Roman Catholic laity numbering 1,870,000 souls.

As regards Protestants in the British Empire and the United States, they sum up 103 millions of all denominations; they have various missionary societies, with an aggregate income of £2,600,000, maintaining 11,660 male and female missionaries, say £225 for each missionary, including the cost of schools, &c. For further details see *Church*, p. 115 ; and *Religion*, p. 512.

According to the *Statesman's Year-Book* there are one million Roman Catholics in China and 50,000 Protestants, the former having 25 bishops and a numerous clergy.

The United States *Catholic Register* gives the numbers of Roman Catholics thus :—

Diocese	Number	Diocese	Number
New York . .	825,000	Baltimore .	240,000
Chicago . .	650,000	San Francisco .	225,000
Boston . .	600,000	St. Louis . .	220,000
Philadelphia .	450,000	St. Paul . .	212,000
New Orleans .	325,000	Various . .	5,860,000
Milwaukee . .	250,000	Total .	9,857,000

See *Religion*, page 513; also *Churches*, pages 115 and 656; and *Missions*, page 777.

ROADS

The value of existing streets, highways, railways, tramways, and canals in Europe is approximately :—

	Millions £ Sterling					£ per Inhab.
	Streets	Roads	Rails	Canals	Total	
U. Kingdom . .	31	125	1,044	35	1,235	31
France . .	14	240	670	31	955	25
Germany . .	23	210	580	23	836	16
Russia . .	16	19	405	10	450	4
Austria . .	8	73	370	17	468	11
Italy . .	8	30	205	7	250	8
Spain and Port. .	4	12	145	1	162	8
Scandinavia . .	2	10	60	2	74	8
Holland . .	3	7	40	20	70	15
Belgium . .	3	6	78	7	94	15
Switzerland, &c. .	3	11	115	1	130	6
Europe . .	115	743	3,712	154	4,724	13

See *Roads*, in Part I., pages 515–517.

RYE

The area and product of this crop are shown as follows :—

	Acres	Tons	Bushels per Acre	Per Inhab.
France . .	3,800,000	1,800,000	19	2.0
Germany .	14,800,000	7,100,000	19	5.5
Russia . .	67,100,000	19,500,000	12	7.0
Austria . .	7,500,000	3,300,000	18	3.1
Spain . .	2,000,000	900,000	18	2.0
Scandinavia .	1,700,000	1,100,000	27	4.6

	Acres	Tons	Bushels per Acre	Per Inhab.
Holland .	500,000	300,000	24	2.4
Belgium .	700,000	500,000	28	3.2
Italy . .	350,000	100,000	13	...
Roumania .	500,000	200,000	16	...
United States	1,850,000	600,000	13	...
Canada . .	300,000	100,000	13	...
Total .	101,100,000	35,500,000	14	3.2

See *Agriculture*, page 8, and *Food*, page 714

S

SALT

The production in various countries is as follows :—

	Tons	Lbs. per Inhab.
United Kingdom . .	1,950,000	110
Germany	2,540,000	109
France	870,000	52
Russia	1,500,000	30
Austria	500,000	25
Italy	480,000	36
Spain	350,000	45
United States . .	1,720,000	53

One-third of the salt produced in the United Kingdom is exported, but the exportation is declining, viz. :—

	Tons Yearly	Value, £
1883–87 . . .	890,000	610,000
1893–97 . . .	690,000	520,000

Consumption in the United Kingdom averages 72 lbs. per head, including what is used for manufactures.

For further particulars see page 517.

SHIPPING

The merchant shipping of the seventeenth and eighteenth centuries was as follows :—

Flag	Tons 1676	Tons 1774	Ratio 1676	Ratio 1774
Dutch . .	900,000	650,000	45.0	28.3
British . .	500,000	650,000	25.0	28.3
Scandinavian .	150,000	250,000	7.5	10.9
French . .	120,000	240,000	6.0	10.4
Spanish . .	110,000	180,000	5.5	7.8
German . .	100,000	120,000	5.0	5.2
Italian, &c. .	120,000	210,000	6.0	9.1
Total .	2,000,000	2,300,000	100.0	100.0

Shipping increased sevenfold between 1774 and 1860, amounting in the latter year to 16,600,000 tons. Since 1860 the increase has been 50 per cent., the total now exceeding 24,000,000 tons, viz. :—

Flag	Tonnage, Nominal Steam	Tonnage, Nominal Sail	Tonnage, Nominal Total
United Kingdom . .	6,280,000	2,740,000	9,020,000
United States . .	2,360,000	2,410,000	4,770,000
Scandinavia . . .	650,000	1,770,000	2,420,000
German . . .	880,000	620,000	1,500,000
Canadian . . .	250,000	680,000	930,000
French . . .	500,000	390,000	890,000
Russian and Finnish .	230,000	560,000	790,000
Italian . . .	220,000	560,000	780,000
Spanish . . .	530,000	190,000	720,000
Australian . . .	180,000	190,000	370,000
Greek	90,000	230,000	320,000
Japanese . . .	210,000	90,000	300,000
Dutch	190,000	100,000	290,000
Austrian . . .	150,000	120,000	270,000
Turkish . . .	40,000	150,000	190,000
Brazilian . . .	75,000	65,000	140,000
Chilian . . .	30,000	80,000	110,000
Belgian . . .	90,000	...	90,000
Portuguese . . .	40,000	50,000	90,000
Chinese . . .	30,000	20,000	50,000
Argentine . . .	20,000	30,000	50,000
The World . . .	13,045,000	11,045,000	24,090,000

In 1860 the United States merchant navy surpassed that of Great Britain both in nominal tonnage and carrying power, but in 1896 the positions were reversed, viz. :—

	Tonnage 1860	Tonnage 1896	Carrying Power 1860	Carrying Power 1896
G. Britain .	4,660,000	9,020,000	6,030,000	27,860,000
Colonies . .	1,050,000	1,380,000	1,190,000	2,740,000
British . .	5,710,000	10,400,000	7,220,000	30,600,000
U. States .	5,350,000	4,770,000	7,960,000	11,850,000
Scandinavian	970,000	2,420,000	1,050,000	4,370,000
German . .	700,000	1,500,000	850,000	4,140,000
French . .	1,010,000	890,000	1,270,000	2,390,000
Spanish . .	470,000	720,000	510,000	2,310,000
Russian . .	400,000	790,000	520,000	1,480,000
Italian . .	550,000	780,000	610,000	1,440,000
Dutch . .	300,000	290,000	400,000	860,000
Austrian . .	250,000	270,000	340,000	720,000
Greek . .	200,000	320,000	220,000	590,000
Turkish . .	180,000	190,000	200,000	310,000
Various . .	510,000	760,000	650,000	2,140,000
The World .	16,600,000	24,100,000	21,800,000	63,200,000

3 E

The proportions of the tonnage and **carrying power** of various flags is shown at the above dates thus :—

Flag	Tonnage		Carrying Power	
	1860	1896	1860	1896
United Kingdom .	28.0	37.5	27.7	44.1
Colonial . . .	6.3	5.7	5.5	4.4
British . . .	34.3	43.2	33.2	48.5
United States .	32.2	19.8	36.5	18.7
Scandinavian .	5.8	10.1	4.8	6.9
German . . .	4.2	6.3	3.9	6.6
French . . .	6.1	3.7	5.8	3.8
Spanish . . .	2.8	3.0	2.3	3.7
Russian . . .	2.4	3.3	2.4	2.3
Italian . . .	3.3	3.3	2.8	2.3
Dutch . . .	1.8	1.2	1.8	1.4
Various . . .	7.1	6.1	6.5	5.8
Total . .	100.0	100.0	100.0	100.0

The following table shows the average nominal tonnage of each steamer and sailing vessel of the various flags, as also the total number of merchant vessels, and the average carrying power in tons to each vessel, in 1896 :—

	Tons, Average		Number of Vessels	Average Carrying Power
	Steam	Sail		
United Kingdom .	740	220	20,800	1,340
United States .	360	150	22,630	520
Scandinavian .	320	150	13,620	320
German . .	820	240	3,590	1,150
French . .	410	28	15,600	150
Spanish . .	1,010	150	1,780	1,280
Canadian .	140	120	7,260	230
Russian . .	290	150	5,360	280
Italian . .	630	90	6,510	220
Japanese .	240	60	1,530	600
Dutch . .	1,160	250	570	1,510
Austrian .	1,030	420	300	2,400
Greek . .	510	40	6,160	90

The relative proportion of trade done by steamers is increasing so rapidly that it seems as if sailing ships must ultimately disappear, carrying power being shown as follows :—

	Steam		Sail	
	1888	1896	1888	1896
U. Kingdom	17,400,000	25,120,000	3,120,000	2,740,000
Colonial . .	1,060,000	1,720,000	1,320,000	870,000
British . .	18,460,000	26,840,000	4,440,000	3,610,000
U. States .	7,080,000	9,440,000	2,540,000	2,410,000
Scandinavian	1,420,000	2,600,000	1,950,000	1,770,000
German . .	2,000,000	3,520,000	730,000	620,000
French . .	2,040,000	2,000,000	450,000	390,000
Spanish . .	1,580,000	2,120,000	200,000	190,000
Russian . .	560,000	920,000	610,000	560,000
Italian . .	700,000	880,000	680,000	560,000
Various . .	2,360,000	3,880,000	1,000,000	940,000
The World .	36,200,000	52,200,000	12,600,000	11,050,000

In 1888 sailing vessels stood for one-fourth of the maritime carrying power ; at present they are only one-sixth. The increasing preponderance of the British flag (including Colonial) is also remarkable ; in 1888 it was under 47, and in 1896 it was over 48, per cent. of the

world's total. The relative increase of carrying power in the above interval of eight years was :—

	Per Cent.			Per Cent.
British . . .	33	Russian . . .		27
United States .	23	Italian . . .		5
Scandinavian .	30	Japanese . .		166
German . . .	52	Dutch . . .		54
Spanish . . .	30	The World . .		29

French carrying power declined 100,000 tons or 4 per cent. in the same interval, a proof of the absurdity of Navigation Bounties. France pays 150 francs or £6 per 100 tons for every French vessel per thousand miles' run during the year, if built in France, or half that premium if built abroad. These premiums averaged £300,000 per annum from 1881 to 1890.

SHIPBUILDING

The tonnage of vessels built in ten years in all countries has been as follows :—

Year	U. King.	U. States	Various	Total
1888 . . .	570,000	220,000	180,000	970,000
1889 . . .	850,000	230,000	180,000	1,260,000
1890 . . .	810,000	290,000	190,000	1,290,000
1891 . . .	810,000	370,000	190,000	1,370,000
1892 . . .	800,000	200,000	200,000	1,200,000
1893 . . .	590,000	210,000	200,000	1,000,000
1894 . . .	660,000	130,000	210,000	1,000,000
1895 . . .	650,000	110,000	210,000	970,000
1896 . . .	740,000	230,000	220,000	1,190,000
1897 . . .	700,000	230,000	290,000	1,220,000
Average . .	720,000	220,000	210,000	1,150,000

The total of vessels built in the United Kingdom (exclusive of British war vessels) in ten years was :—

	Tons			Tons
Steam . . .	5,950,000	British . .		5,930,000
Sail	1,250,000	Foreign . .		1,270,000
Total . .	7,200,000	Total . .		7,200,000

Vessels built in ten years in the United States were as follows :—

	Tons			Tons
Steam . . .	1,260,000	Sea-going .		1,220,000
Sail	940,000	Lakes . . .		980,000
Total . .	2,200,000	Total . .		2,200,000

The tonnage of vessels built in ten years (1881–90), including those built in British yards for foreigners, carried the following flags :—

Flag	Tons	Ratio
British	5,610,000	49.2
United States . . .	2,200,000	19.3
German	1,110,000	9.7
Scandinavian . . .	1,300,000	11.4
French	640,000	5.6
Italian	370,000	3.2
Dutch	190,000	1.6
Total . .	11,420,000	100.0

Notwithstanding the great activity in shipbuilding the nominal tonnage shows but a slow increase, owing to the number of sailing vessels and old steamers broken up or lost, as the following table shows :—

	Tons
Vessels afloat in 1880 . . .	22,540,000
New built, 1881-96 . . .	18,160,000
To be accounted for . . .	40,700,000
Afloat in 1896 . . .	24,100,000

It appears, therefore, that in 16 years the tonnage of vessels broken up or lost was 16,600,000, that is, over one million tons yearly. The loss by maritime disaster and wreck averages 3 per cent., say 700,000 tons, and hence the vessels broken up must have been 300,000 tons yearly. The difference between the tonnage of vessels afloat in 1888 and 1896 is shown as follows :—

	1888	1896
Steamer, tons	9,050,000	13,045,000
Sailing, ,, . . .	12,600,000	11,045,000
Total . . .	21,650,000	24,090,000

Thus steamers have had an increase of 4 million tons (equal to 16 million tons carrying power), while sailing vessels have declined more than 1½ million tons, in eight years.

The unofficial statement published yearly as to ship-building in various countries differs materially from that on preceding pages, which is net tonnage. The unofficial statement is as follows :—

Years	In United Kingdom	Other Countries	Total
1891 . . .	1,130,000	470,000	1,600,000
1892 . . .	1,110,000	557,000	1,667,000
1893 . . .	870,000	340,000	1,210,000
1894 . . .	1,050,000	274,000	1,324,000
1895 . . .	1,100,000	370,000	1,470,000
1896 . . .	1,450,000	450,000	1,900,000
1897 . . .	1,050,000	520,000	1,570,000
1898 . . .	1,370,000	520,000	1,890,000

The shipbuilding of the world in 1897 was :—

Built in	Steam	Sail	Total Tons
U. Kingdom. .	1,022,000	28,000	1,050,000
U. States . . .	106,000	126,000	232,000
Germany . . .	140,000	...	140,000
France, &c. . .	105,000	43,000	148,000
Total . .	1,373,000	197,000	1,570,000

In 1898 it was as follows :—

	British	Various	Total, Tons
Steam . . .	1,366,000	410,000	1,776,000
Sail . . .	4,000	110,000	114,000
Total .	1,370,000	520,000	1,890,000

In 1897 the French built three large sailing-ships, ranging from 3000 to 3500 tons.
The largest vessels launched in 1897 were :—

In U. Kingdom	Tons	In Germany	Tons
Briton . . .	10,200	Kaiser Fritz .	12,500
Brazilian . .	11,100	Pretoria .	14,000
Cymric. . .	12,300	Kaiser Wilhelm .	14,300

Of the steamers built in the year, as regards tonnage, 99 per cent. were of steel, 1 per cent. built of iron ; of the sailing vessels, 96 per cent. were of steel, and 4 per cent. were built of wood.

British and Irish shipyards in 1897 turned out 45 war vessels, 545 steamers, and 45 sailing vessels :—

Owners	Tons	Owners	Tons
British. . . .	848,000	Dutch . . .	19,000
Japanese . .	60,000	Russian . .	16,000
German . . .	30,000	French . . .	14,000
Colonial . . .	23,000	Spanish . . .	13,000
Scandinavian .	27,000	Total . .	1,050,000

Vessels built in our dockyards for foreign owners usually form 20 or 25 per cent. of the total.
The increase of shipping in 1897 in the world was :—

	Steam Tons	Sail Tons	Total	Carrying Power
Built . . .	1,373,000	197,000	1,570,000	5,690,000
Lost, &c. . .	316,000	396,000	712,000	1,660,000

This shows an increase of 860,000 tons nominal, but of 4,030,000 tons of carrying power, equal to 6½ per cent. of the carrying power of the world's shipping in 1896.
The largest merchant steamers under the British, German, and French flags are :—

Steamer	Feet Long	Tons	Horse-power	Speed Knots
Oceanic . . .	705	17,000	45,000	...
Kaiser Wilhelm .	645	14,000	30,000	25
Touraine . . .	...	9,000	12,000	22

The *Oceanic*, launched at Belfast in January 1899, is the largest vessel ever built.
The quickest trips by steamers in 1897 were :—

Steamer	Route	Days	Hrs.
Lucania . . .	Liverpool to New York .	5	7
Paris	,, ,,	5	13
Kaiser Wilhelm .	Southampton ,,	5	23
Lucania . . .	New York to Liverpool .	5	9
Kaiser Wilhelm .	,, Southampton	5	15
Scot	Southampton to Cape .	16	0
Dunottar . . .	,, ,,	15	20
Norman . . .	Cape to Southampton .	15	6
Dunottar . . .	,, ,, .	14	23

The *Lucania* and *Kaiser Wilhelm* averaged 22 knots an hour, the *City of Paris* 20, the *Dunottar* and *Norman* 17. The increased size and speed of vessels is shown thus :—

Year	Steamer	Horse Power	Knots per Hr.
1850	Asia . . .	1,500	11
1856	Persia . .	3,600	13
1879	Gallia . .	5,000	15
1883	Alaska . .	10,500	18
1889	Paris . .	17,300	20
1893	Campania .	30,000	21

In 1898 the *Britannic* had completed 500 ocean voyages in 23 years, in all 1,750,000 miles, carrying 222,000 passengers, and consuming 510,000 tons of coal in 114,000 hours of steaming, being 4½ tons per hour.

PORT ENTRIES

The tonnage of shipping from the high seas entered into the ports of various countries was :—

In	1885	1895	Increase
United Kingdom	31,860,000	40,000,000	8,140,000
France	12,790,000	13,780,000	990,000
Germany . . .	8,260,000	11,920,000	3,660,000
Russia	5,400,000	8,100,000	2,700,000
Austria	5,940,000	9,490,000	3,550,000
Italy.	5,900,000	8,260,000	2,360,000
Spain	7,470,000	13,000,000	5,530,000
Portugal . . .	3,550,000	5,950,000	2,400,000
Scandinavia . .	10,000,000	12,950,000	2,950,000
Holland . . .	4,140,000	6,770,000	2,630,000
Belgium . . .	4,070,000	6,860,000	2,790,000
Europe. . . .	99,380,000	137,080,000	37,700,000
United States .	12,290,000	16,730,000	4,440,000
Canada. . . .	8,240,000	11,760,000	3,520,000
Australia . . .	12,570,000	18,170,000	5,600,000
West Indies . .	6,300,000	8,670,000	2,370,000
East Indies . .	26,100,000	37,200,000	11,100,000
China and Japan	3,060,000	7,160,000	4,100,000
Africa	3,800,000	8,400,000	4,600,000
South America .	7,860,000	12,130,000	4,270,000
The World . .	179,600,000	257,300,000	77,700,000

Port entries in 1895, distinguished between native and foreign flags, were as follows :—

In	Native	Foreign	Total
United Kingdom	29,200,000	10,800,000	40,000,000
France	4,110,000	9,670,000	13,780,000
Germany . . .	5,010,000	6,910,000	11,920,000
Russia	610,000	7,490,000	8,100,000
Austria	8,440,000	1,050,000	9,490,000
Italy.	1,990,000	6,270,000	8,260,000
Spain	6,200,000	6,800,000	13,000,000
Portugal . . .	490,000	5,460,000	5,950,000
Scandinavia . .	6,070,000	6,880,000	12,950,000
Holland . . .	1,810,000	4,960,000	6,770,000
Belgium . . .	1,300,000	5,560,000	6,860,000
Europe	65,230,000	71,850,000	137,080,000
United States	3,680,000	13,050,000	16,730,000
Total . .	68,910,000	84,900,000	153,810,000

The percentage of native and foreign flags in port entries was as follows :—

In	1885		1895	
	Native	Foreign	Native	Foreign
United Kingdom .	72	28	73	27
France . . .	35	65	30	70
Germany . . .	42	58	42	58
Russia . . .	8	92	8	92
Italy . . .	25	75	24	76
Spain . . .	38	62	48	52
Portugal . . .	6	94	8	92
Scandinavia . .	48	52	47	53
Holland . . .	31	69	27	73
Belgium . . .	16	84	19	81
Continent . .	29	71	29	71
United States .	22	78	22	78

The proportion of trade done by the flag of the country has fallen considerably in France and Holland, while it has risen in Spain and Belgium, other countries showing but little change, and the ratio for the European continent collectively being the same now as in 1885, while the same is true of the United States. The increase of trade, as measured by port entries, has been much greater than that of tonnage of vessels afloat, viz. :—

	1885	1895	Increase
Vessels afloat, tons	21,100,000	23,700,000	8 per cent.
Port entries, ,,	180,000,000	257,000,000	43 ,, ,,

In 1885 each vessel made 9 voyages, in 1895 it made 11, which is explained by the substitution of steamers for sailing vessels, as appears when we compare carrying power, viz. :—

Years	Tons
1885	44,500,000
1895	62,400,000

The increase of carrying power in ten years was 40 per cent., which is nearly the same as the increase of port entries shown above.

UNITED KINGDOM

Port entries from the high seas and coastwise (the latter with cargoes only) were :—

	Millions of Tons		
	High Seas	Coastwise	Total
1870	18	18	36
1880	29	26	55
1890	37	29	66
1896	42	32	74

From this it appears that in 26 years the entries from the high seas rose 133 per cent., and coasting trade nearly 80 per cent., the whole trade of our ports having more than doubled.

Port entries for the United Kingdom in 1896 compare with 1886 thus :—

Flag	Tons		
	1886	1896	Increase
British . .	22,740,000	30,290,000	7,550,000
Foreign . .	8,300,000	12,190,000	3,890,000
Coasting . .	27,140,000	31,980,000	4,840,000
Total . .	58,180,000	74,460,000	16,280,000

Tonnage of entries into British and Irish ports rose 20 per cent. in 10 years, the ratio of increase with foreign vessels being 47 per cent., with British 25 per cent. Entries from the high seas, exclusive of coasting trade, were as follows :—

	1886	1896	Increase
London . .	6,810,000	8,990,000	2,180,000
Liverpool . .	5,020,000	5,640,000	620,000
Cardiff . .	2,390,000	3,960,000	1,570,000
Hull . . .	1,670,000	2,260,000	590,000
Shields . .	890,000	1,790,000	900,000
Newcastle . .	1,870,000	1,720,000	...
Southampton .	840,000	1,560,000	720,000
Glasgow . .	910,000	1,290,000	380,000
Middlesbro' .	560,000	1,010,000	450,000
Various . .	10,080,000	14,260,000	4,180,000
Total . .	31,040,000	42,480,000	11,440,000

Clearances from British ports, excluding coast trade, were as follows :—

Date	British	Foreign	Total Tons
1773	770,000	55,000	825,000
1803	1,440,000	570,000	2,010,000
1853	5,210,000	4,240,000	9,450,000
1873	15,110,000	7,470,000	22,580,000
1896	31,200,000	11,800,000	43,000,000

British vessels constituted 55 per cent. in 1853, and 72 per cent. in 1896, of the total.

UNITED STATES

Tonnage entries in American ports were as follows :—

Year	American	British	Various	Total
1870 . . .	2,450,000	2,790,000	1,030,000	6,270,000
1880 . . .	3,140,000	7,930,000	4,180,000	15,250,000
1890 . . .	3,400,000	8,110,000	3,850,000	15,360,000
1897 . . .	3,610,000	11,290,000	5,100,000	20,000,000

The proportions of American trade done by American and foreign flags were :—

Flag	1870	1880	1890	1897
British . . .	44.4	52.0	53.0	56.5
American . . .	39.0	20.6	22.2	18.0
Various . . .	16.6	27.4	24.8	25.5
Total . .	100.0	100.0	100.0	100.0

The relative decline of the share corresponding to the American flag is very remarkable, while the British stands for more than half the total. The growth of the principal ports in the last ten years is shown thus :—

	1887	1897	Increase
New York . . .	6,090,000	7,270,000	1,180,000
Boston	1,080,000	1,640,000	550,000
Philadelphia . .	1,290,000	1,530,000	240,000
New Orleans .	720,000	1,400,000	680,000
San Francisco .	970,000	1,260,000	290,000
Baltimore . . .	690,000	1,250,000	560,000
Other Ports . .	2,690,000	5,650,000	2,960,000
Union	13,530,000	20,000,000	6,470,000

Entries from the various countries were as follows :—

From	1887	1897	Increase
Great Britain . .	4,050,000	6,530,000	2,480,000
British Colonies .	2,230,000	3,330,000	1,100,000
Germany . . .	1,060,000	1,670,000	610,000
Cuba	1,020,000	1,040,000	20,000
Brazil	400,000	910,000	510,000
Belgium . . .	480,000	660,000	180,000
Italy	440,000	510,000	70,000
France	590,000	490,000	...
Various . . .	3,260,000	4,860,000	1,600,000
Total . .	13,530,000	20,000,000	6,470,000

SHIPWRECKS

The tonnage of vessels and number of lives lost by shipwreck or disaster to vessels of the United Kingdom showed yearly averages thus :—

Years	Tons	Lives
1881-83	273,000	2,600
1884-86	220,000	1,470
1887-89	187,000	1,620
1890-92	197,000	1,600
1893-95	180,000	1,890
General average	212,000	1,836

The loss of life in the last six years has been 15 per cent. less than in the years 1881–86, that of tonnage 23 per cent. less, although the merchant shipping of the United Kingdom has grown much in the interval.

SICKNESS

According to a report published at the **Turin** Exhibition in 1898, the ratios of sick and invalided men, as also the death-rate, in the principal armies and navies were as follows during twelve months :—

	Army			Navy		
	Sick	Inva-lided	Died	Sick	Inva-lided	Died
British . . .	922	30.4	8.5	1,056	37.5	9.9
French . . .	596	16.9	9.0	1,050	...	9.9
German . . .	825	28.0	6.5	1,010	28.5	5.2
Russian . . .	857	10.0	8.2	1,076	9.0	11.7
Austrian . . .	1,130	16.5	10.4	1,100	24.5	10.2
Italian . . .	902	15.8	9.2	525	7.2	7.2
Average . . .	872	19.6	8.6	970	21.4	9.0

This shows that, as a rule, 87 per cent. of soldiers and 97 per cent. of sailors are inscribed yearly on sick-list ; but, of course, this includes repetitions, where one man may be entered two or three times. About 2 per cent. of soldiers and sailors are invalided yearly. Death-rate is less than 1 per cent. in all but the Austrian armies, and in all navies except Russian and Austrian.

In 1892 Bertillon compiled tables of sickness among certain Mutual Aid Societies, including the labours of Bodio, Hubbard, Neison, Ratcliffe, Finlayson, Ansell, Oliphant, Behm, &c., viz. :—

Age	Number of Days of Sickness Yearly for Men					
	England	Scotland	France	Germany	Italy	Average
20-25	5.7	4.0	3.1	5.8	5.0	4.7
25-30	6.0	4.2	3.4	5.1	5.4	4.8
30-35	6.8	4.6	3.4	5.6	5.1	5.1
35-40	8.1	5.0	4.3	6.3	6.0	6.0
40-45	9.6	6.0	5.3	7.8	6.8	7.0
45-50	12.0	8.3	5.9	7.7	6.8	8.1
50-55	15.9	11.4	8.0	8.5	7.9	10.3
55-60	22.5	14.9	8.4	16.3	9.2	14.3
60-65	32.1	23.0	11.2	12.5	11.2	18.0
65-70	55.8	55.6	16.7	18.9	13.4	32.1
All ages . .	9.5	...	7.8	...	6.6	8.0

Bertillon's tables of sickness among operatives at Angers for thirty years down to 1894 show the proportions as regards age thus :—

Age	Cases		Days Sick, Ratio		No. of Days
	1864–79	1880–94	1864–79	1880–94	1880–94
17–24 . .	122	30	167	42	5.2
25–34 . .	393	330	305	278	3.6
35–44 . .	383	365	390	320	4.2
Over 44 . .	102	275	138	360	9.4
Total . .	1,000	1,000	1,000	1,000	4.4

Sickness prevails more among female than male operatives, viz. —

Age	Days of Sickness to each Person Yearly			
	France		Italy	
	Male	Female	Male	Female
20–30 . . .	3.2	6.9	5.2	7.9
30–40 . . .	3.8	7.6	5.5	8.3
40–50 . . .	5.6	7.9	6.5	8.8
50–60 . . .	8.2	10.3	8.6	9.5
60–70 . . .	13.9	16.5	11.8	9.1
General . . .	7.8	9.4	6.6	8.5

In 1895 the Friendly Societies of France, comprising 1,584,000 members, published returns of sickness for ten years to December 1894, showing the averages as follows :—

	Sick Days Yearly on No. of Hands	Days to Each Sick Person
Men . . .	5.1	17.3
Women . . .	3.8	12.5
General average .	5.0	16.6

Death-rate for all collectively averaged 16.4 per thousand yearly.

Sutton's report for Friendly Societies (England, 1896) is as follows :—

Period	Men, Yearly Average		
	Number	Days Sick	Per Man
1856–60 . . .	722,000	8,160,000	11.3
1861–70 . . .	1,790,000	22,400,000	12.4
1876–80 . . .	1,663,000	22,030,000	13.2
	Women		
1856–75 . . .	139,000	2,280,000	16.4

The following table shows death-rate per thousand yearly, and also average days of sickness in the year, to each worker according to age :—

Age	Death-rate	Sick Days
40	10.7	9.6
60	34.0	30.2
70	72.3	85.7

The above shows that each worker of 40 lost 9½ days through sickness, and a worker of 60 lost 30 days : the mean for all persons from 15 to 65 is supposed to be 13 days of sickness yearly.

In 1897 the sickness of the British navy averaged 2,838 men daily, or 4 per cent. of the force. Days of sickness during the year were 1,040,000, or 14 days to each man. The number invalided was 1987, or 27 per thousand.

Bodio's table as regards Italy (1881–85) is as follows :—

	Days of Sickness Yearly According to Age		
	15–30	30–45	45–60
Booksellers . . .	3.2	4.0	4.5
Clergy	2.9	3.6	5.0
Tailors	3.1	4.1	7.0
Butchers . . .	3.6	4.9	7.3
Shoemakers . . .	5.7	5.6	7.4
Carpenters . . .	5.6	5.8	8.0
Painters . . .	8.1	5.5	8.0
Bakers . . .	5.3	6.3	8.1
Blacksmiths . . .	6.1	6.2	8.2
Gardeners . . .	5.9	6.1	8.3
Servants . . .	5.1	5.6	8.5
Cab-drivers . . .	4.0	6.1	8.6
Chimney-sweeps . .	6.6	7.8	8.7
Masons . . .	4.8	6.2	8.9
Millers . . .	4.1	4.5	9.2
Street porters . .	6.9	9.4	9.3
General average . .	5.1	5.8	7.8

SILK

China and Japan produce about 28 million pounds, say 12,500 tons, yearly, but no less than 60 per cent. is retained for native manufacture, and hence it is usual in estimating the world's crop to count in the case of China and Japan only the surplus available for exportation. An estimate of silk production published in 1890 was as follows :—

Year	Crop, Tons	Crop of 1890	Tons
1886	11,554	China . . .	3,963
1887	11,888	Japan . . .	2,018
1888	11,588	Italy	3,443
1889	11,382	Various . . .	2,016
1890	11,440		
		Total . .	11,440

An ounce of eggs produced 39,000 silkworms, which consume yearly one ton of mulberry leaves, and give 132 pounds of cocoons or 13 pounds of silk, worth £8 sterling.

The countries which export silk manufactures are as follows :—

	Tons		Value, £	
	1885	1895	1885	1895
France . . .	6,000	7,000	8,900,000	10,800,000
Germany . . .	4,900	4,900	7,400,000	6,400,000
Switzerland . .	2,800	3,350	4,400,000	5,300,000
Italy	200	450	600,000	1,200,000
Total . . .	13,900	15,700	21,300,000	23,700,000

The production and consumption of silk manufactures in various countries is :—

	Output Millions £	Consumption	
		Millions £	Shillings per Head
United Kingdom .	6.0	19.0	10.0
France	28.2	20.0	10.5
Germany . . .	16.5	10.2	4.0
Switzerland . .	6.4	1.3	8.5
Italy	4.2	3.0	2.0
Austria . . .	4.5	4.0	2.0
Russia, &c. . .	5.2	7.5	1.0
Europe	71.0	65.0	3.5
United States .	19.0	23.0	6.5
Total . .	90.0	88.0	4.0

For further details see Part I., page 536.
Silk manufacture has declined in Great Britain since 1870, viz. :—

	Spindles	Power-Looms	Operatives
1870 . .	1,130,000	12,400	48,100
1890 . .	1,030,000	11,400	41,300

There is a fall of 9 per cent. in spindles and 14 per cent. in the number of hands.

SLAVES

Women slaves were sold at Cairo in September 1894 at prices averaging £18 per head.
For *Slave-trade* in various countries see page 540.

SOUND

The following instances of sound travelling great distances are recorded :—

Cannon at	Heard at	Miles	Date
Waterloo . .	Dover . . .	180	1815
Cepeda . . .	Buenos Ayres .	160	1859
Spithead . . .	Bridgwater . .	100	1897

Mr. Glaisher in a balloon two miles from the earth heard a musket-shot and a dog's bark, and at four miles a railway train.

SQUATTERS

There are 19,000 in Australia, who hold 690 million acres of Crown lands at one penny per acre, and 10,800 in South Africa, who hold 60 million acres : the former are sheep-farmers, whose average run is 36,000 acres, rent £150. African squatters' runs average 5500 acres.

STATUES

Those of Babylon were valued at £21,000,000 sterling, that of Belus being worth £3,500,000.

STEAM

The increase of steam-power * since 1870 has been

* The economic value of steam-power was thus set forth by the *Quarterly Review* in 1826 : "Steam-power now enables a man to do as much work as 120 could fifty years ago. One bushel of coal, value threepence, will raise 20,000 gallons of water from a depth of 350 feet in a few minutes, which would take 20 men 10 hours to raise with a pump, at a cost of 40 shillings. Steam does for £1 what would cost £160 by hand."

more than 250 per cent., the various nations showing approximately as follows :—

	Horse-Power		
	1870	1880	1896
U. Kingdom . .	4,040,000	7,600,000	13,700,000
France	1,850,000	3,340,000	5,920,000
Germany . . .	2,480,000	5,120,000	8,080,000
Russia	920,000	1,740,000	3,100,000
Austria	800,000	1,560,000	2,520,000
Italy	330,000	500,000	1,520,000
Spain	210,000	470,000	1,180,000
Portugal . . .	30,000	60,000	170,000
Sweden . . .	100,000	220,000	510,000
Norway . . .	40,000	90,000	410,000
Denmark . . .	30,000	90,000	260,000
Holland . . .	130,000	250,000	600,000
Belgium . . .	350,000	610,000	1,180,000
Switzerland . .	140,000	230,000	580,000
Roumania, &c. .	120,000	320,000	570,000
Europe	11,570,000	22,200,000	40,300,000
United States .	5,590,000	9,110,000	18,060,000
Colonies, &c. . .	1,300,000	3,040,000	7,740,000
The World . .	18,460,000	34,350,000	66,100,000

The respective shares of fixed, of railway, and of steamboat engines were :—

	1870	1880	1896
Fixed	4,100,000	7,670,000	12,470,000
Locomotive . .	11,740,000	21,440,000	40,420,000
Steamer . . .	2,620,000	5,240,000	13,210,000
Total . .	18,460,000	34,350,000	66,100,000

The steam-power of war-vessels is omitted as regards all nations. It will be found at page 782.
The total in 1896 was made up approximately as follows :—

	Horse-Power			Total
	Fixed	Locom.	Steamer	
U. Kingdom	2,300,000	5,100,000	6,300,000	13,700,000
France . .	1,130,000	4,200,000	590,000	5,920,000
Germany .	2,400,000	4,800,000	880,000	8,080,000
Russia . .	430,000	2,440,000	230,000	3,100,000
Austria . .	480,000	1,890,000	150,000	2,520,000
Italy . .	180,000	1,100,000	240,000	1,520,000
Spain . .	50,000	600,000	530,000	1,180,000
Portugal .	10,000	120,000	40,000	170,000
Sweden . .	30,000	300,000	180,000	510,000
Norway . .	10,000	80,000	320,000	410,000
Denmark .	10,000	100,000	150,000	260,000
Holland . .	80,000	330,000	190,000	600,000
Belgium . .	390,000	700,000	90,000	1,180,000
Switzerland	90,000	480,000	10,000	580,000
Rouma., &c.	20,000	400,000	150,000	570,000
Europe . .	7,610,000	22,640,000	10,050,000	40,300,000
U. States .	3,940,000	11,760,000	2,360,000	18,060,000
Canada . .	320,000	820,000	250,000	1,390,000
Australia .	260,000	400,000	180,000	840,000
Various . .	340,000	4,800,000	370,000	5,510,000
The World .	12,470,000	40,420,000	13,210,000	66,100,000

See *Steam*, page 545.

STREETS

The annual sum spent on maintenance and cleaning of streets in European cities is as follows :—

	Sum £	Pence per Sq. Yd.		Sum £	Pence per Sq. Yd.
Paris . . .	800,000	9.2	Dresden .	48,000	2.0
Berlin . .	123,000	1.7	Buda-Pesth	46,000	1.6
Rome . .	60,000	3.4	Naples . .	46,000	4.8
Vienna . .	85,000	2.2	Brussels .	24,000	1.1
Hamburg .	86,000	2.2	Milan . .	30,000	3.4

The mean expenditure for the ten cities was about 3½ pence (3.6) per square yard. Some of them, however, include only cleaning and watering expenses.

The street area, compared with population, is as follows :—

	Sq. Yds. (000 omitted)	Sq. Yds. per Inhab.		Sq. Yds. (000 omitted)	Sq. Yds. per Inhab.
London . .	52,000	12.0	Brussels .	5,200	10.0
Paris . . .	20,300	8.0	Breslau .	5,900	16.0
Berlin . .	17,300	10.5	Rome . .	4,200	9.2
Vienna . .	9,300	7.0	Naples . .	2,300	4.4
Hamburg .	9,500	15.0	Milan . .	2,200	5.0
Dresden . .	5,800	17.5	Genoa . .	900	4.0
Leipzig . .	3,000	7.5	Florence .	2,000	10.0
Bordeaux .	3,500	13.5	Turin . .	3,000	8.6

The above sixteen cities give an average of 10 yards of street per inhabitant. Paris has 4600 acres under streets and squares, or one-fourth of its area.

STRIKES

UNITED KINGDOM

The number of days lost in strikes and lock-outs has been :—

Year	No. of Days	Year	No. of Days
1893 . . .	30,800,000	1896 . . .	3,700,000
1894 . . .	9,100,000	1897 . . .	10,400,000
1895 . . .	5,500,000	Average . .	11,900,000

Thus the average for five years is the same as 119,000 men idle for 100 days. From 1890 to 1895 the number of strikes yearly averaged 878, with 392,000 hands on strike.

In 1897 there were 864 strikes in the United Kingdom, by 230,000 operatives, viz. :—

Cause		Numbers	
Wages . . .	106,300	Men	189,800
Shorter hours .	52,800	Women . . .	24,400
Various . . .	71,200	Children . .	16,100
Total . .	230,300	Total. . . .	230,300

The loss of labour amounted to 10,000,000 days, averaging 43 days per striker; whereas in 1893 the loss was 31,200,000 days, by 690,000 strikers, an average of 45 days each. The engineers' strike in 1897-98, by 47,500 men, caused a loss of 6,850,000 days, an average of 144 days each.

UNITED STATES

In fourteen years, ending 1894, there were 14,390 strikes, involving 3,714,000 operatives, and causing a loss of £59,300,000 sterling. In 44 per cent. of strikes the operatives succeeded, at a loss of £39,500,000 : the masters' loss was £19,800,000. The loss to each workman on strike averaged £10, 5s. : each strike cost £1,400 to masters.

In an interval of seven and a half years, ending June 1894, the aggregate of strikes and lock-outs in four principal cities was as follows :—

	Hands (000 omitted)			Loss, £ (000 omitted)		
	Strikes	Lock-outs	Total	To Hands	Masters	Total
N. York . . .	248	22	270	1,840	910	2,750
Chicago . . .	283	49	332	3,080	3,580	6,660
Pittsburg . .	101	12	113	2,810	720	3,530
Philadelphia .	60	9	69	560	300	860
4 Cities . . .	692	92	784	8,290	5,510	13,800

The annual average for the four cities collectively was 104,000 hands on strike, and a loss of £1,840,000 sterling.

FRANCE

The number of strikes and of operatives engaged in them were :—

Year	Strikes	Hands	Average
1874	22	2,730	124
1884	91	23,700	260
1890	313	118,900	380
1893	634	170,100	270
1894	391	54,600	140

The strikes of 1893 showed as follows :—

At	Number	Days Lost
Mines	22	1,510,000
Factories . . .	612	1,664,000
Total . . .	634	3,174,000

Each hand on strike (170,000) lost 18 days of work. The workmen gained their purpose in 57 per cent. of the strikes.

AUSTRIA

Dr. Juraschek's tables contain the following :—

Year	Strikes	Hands	Days lost
1891	104	14,030	247,000
1894	159	44,080	566,000

The average for four years was 134 strikes, with 25,000 hands on strike, and a loss of 370,000 days, equal to 15 days per hand.

ITALY

Official returns are as follows :—

Years	Annual Average			1896
	Strikes	Men		Men
1881-85 . .	67	17,100	Hatters . .	41,600
1886-90 . .	104	26,400	Miners . .	31,000
1891-95 . .	124	28,600	Various . .	23,500
1896 . . .	210	96,100		
			Total . .	96,100

The loss of days was as follows :—

Annual Average

1881–85 . . . . 124,000 | 1891–95 230,000
1886–90 . . . . 170,000 | 1896 1,150,000

See *Trade Unions*, p. 570.

SUBSIDIES

Annual subsidies are given yearly in various countries for agriculture and technical schools, viz. :—

	Agricul. £	Technical £	Total £	Pence per Inhab.
France. . . .	1,870,000	1,070,000	2,940,000	19
Prussia. . . .	680,000	560,000	1,240,000	9
Bavaria . . .	90,000	50,000	140,000	6
Wurtemberg. .	70,000	60,000	130,000	15
Denmark. . .	110,000	20,000	130,000	14
Holland . . .	60,000	50,000	110,000	6
Belgium . . .	110,000	40,000	150,000	6
Switzerland . .	150,000	1,570,000	1,720,000	135
Austria . . .	950,000	600,000	1,550,000	16
Hungary . . .	1,700,000	1,800,000	3,500,000	46
Italy	320,000	280,000	600,000	5
United States .	2,200,000	...	...	...

SUGAR

The world's crop of sugar has doubled since 1880, viz. :—

Year	Cane Tons	Beet Tons	Total	Beet Ratio per cent.
1880. . . .	1,860,000	1,810,000	3,670,000	49
1894. . . .	3,260,000	3,790,000	7,050,000	54
1895. . . .	3,140,000	4,690,000	7,830,000	60
1896. . . .	2,560,000	4,330,000	6,890,000	63
1897. . . .	2,430,000	4,780,000	7,210,000	66
1898. . . .	2,850,000	4,650,000	7,500,000	62

There are five principal countries that produce beet-sugar, viz. :—

	Tons		
	1876	1886	1897
Germany . . .	360,000	810,000	1,840,000
Austria. . . .	200,000	430,000	930,000
France. . . .	400,000	300,000	700,000
Russia	160,000	350,000	700,000
Belgium . . .	70,000	70,000	280,000
Various . . .	40,000	80,000	330,000
Total . .	1,230,000	2,040,000	4,780,000

Official returns for Germany show that a ton of roots gave the following percentage of beet-sugar at various dates :—

Year	Per cent.	Year	Per cent.
1850	. . . . 7.2	1880	. . . . 8.6
1860	. . . . 8.6	1890	. . . . 12.8
1870	. . . . 8.6	1896	. . . . 12.2

The average yield in Russia was 8 per cent. of sugar in 1885, and 11 per cent. in 1890–95. The production,

consumption, and export of beet-sugar in 1896 were estimated as follows :—

	Tons		
	Production	Consumption	Export
Germany . . .	1,620,000	720,000	900,000
Austria. . .	790,000	350,000	440,000
Russia . . .	780,000	680,000	100,000
France. . .	690,000	480,000	210,000
Belgium . .	230,000	80,000	150,000
Holland, &c. .	220,000	220,000	...
Total . .	4,330,000	2,530,000	1,800,000

The consumption of sugar of all kinds in various countries per inhabitant is :—

Pounds	*Pounds*	*Pounds*
U. Kingdom . 88	Austria . . . 17	Belgium . . 27
France . . . 28	Russia . . . 15	Canada . . 80
Germany . . 31	Denmark . . 20	U. States . . 63

Consumption has increased very notably in the United Kingdom and the United States, viz :—

Year	Tons		Pounds per head	
	United Kingdom	United States	United Kingdom	United States
1875 . . .	940,000	880,000	63	44
1885 . . .	1,200,000	1,300,000	75	52
1895 . . .	1,540,000	1,950,000	88	63

The exports of sugar from the British Colonies averaged :

	Tons Yearly			
	1881–85	1886–90	1891–94	1895
Mauritius	115,000	120,000	110,000	115,000
Guiana	110,000	115,000	110,000	100,000
W. Indian Islands .	175,000	165,000	160,000	135,000
Australia	20,000	40,000	55,000	75,000
India, &c.	70,000	70,000	55,000	55,000
Total . . .	490,000	510,000	490,000	480,000

See *Sugar*, page 549.

SUICIDE

Mayr's tables show an alarming increase of suicide in most countries during the last twenty years, viz. :—

	Suicides Yearly per Million Inhabitants			
	1871–77	1881–85	1886–93	Increase
England .	67	74	82	15
Scotland .	40	53	58	18
Ireland .	17	22	25	8
France .	157	195	224	67
Germany .	143	209	205	62
Russia .	30	31	29	...
Austria .	122	162	161	39
Hungary .	...	88	115	27
Italy .	37	49	52	15
Spain .	14	25	20	6
Sweden .	81	97	125	44
Norway .	73	69	65	...
Denmark .	258	249	256	...
Holland .	36	53	58	22
Belgium .	67	107	124	57
Finland .	..	39	43	4
Servia .	...	38	37	...
Switzerland .	202	234	220	18
Australia .	86	109	110	24

In all countries suicide is much more frequent among men than women, viz. :—

Female Suicides among 100.

England . .	26	Italy . . .	20	Holland . .	16
France . .	21	Spain . . .	29	Belgium . .	15
Germany .	20	Sweden . .	23	Switzerland .	12
Russia . .	21	Norway . .	24	United States	28
Austria . .	18	Denmark . .	23	Average . .	21

Bodio's tables for 1887–91 give the number of suicides yearly per million inhabitants for various countries as follows :—

England . .	80	Germany . .	246	Switzerland .	216
Scotland . .	56	Prussia. . .	197	Belgium . .	122
Ireland . .	24	Austria. . .	158	Holland . .	58
France . .	218	Italy . . .	52	Sweden . .	119

The above rate for Germany is for urban population.

In a period of ten years down to 1897, in Prussia, 407 children (under 15 years of age) committed suicide, 331 being boys and 76 girls.

UNITED KINGDOM

The rates of suicide in various professions of persons aged between 25 and 65 years are :—

Suicides Yearly of 1000 *Males who Die*

Miner . . .	5	Fisherman .	13	Carpenter .	17
Draper . .	5	Mason . . .	14	Painter . .	21
Printer . .	8	Cabdriver .	16	Butcher . .	23
Ploughman .	9	Tailor . . .	16	Baker . . .	26
Gardener . .	11	Farmer . .	17	Publican . .	26
Blacksmith .	11	Grocer. . .	17	Com. traveller	31
Stonecutter .	11	Shoemaker .	17	Costermonger	44

The average is 14 ; that is to say, of 1000 males who die between 25 and 65 years of age in England 14

commit suicide ; but the rate is two or three times as heavy as regards publicans, commercial travellers, and costermongers.

ITALY

In the years 1894–96 the average was 1870 suicides, equal to 60 per million inhabitants. In the old kingdom of Naples the ratio is only 31, in Sicily 41, in Venetia 58, per million, whereas in Genoa it is 101, and in Rome 108. The total number of suicides in 1896 gives the following ratios :—

	Males	Females	Total
Single	380	78	458
Married . . .	325	95	420
Widowed . . .	92	30	122
Total . .	797	203	1,000
Under 20 years . .	53	18	71
20–40	313	87	400
40–60	270	63	333
60–80	152	31	183
Over 80 . . .	9	4	13
Total . .	797	203	1,000

The seasons had the following ratios : spring 28, summer 31, autumn 20, and winter 21, per cent. of the total.

UNITED STATES

The ratios of age in suicides were :—

Under 15	66
15–30	1,995
31–50	3,740
51–60	1,984
Over 60	2,215
Total . .	10,000

T

TALLOW

In 1897 Great Britain imported 100,000 tons, value £1,900,000.

See *Tallow*, Part I., page 550.

TAXES

In the section of Finances it will be seen (page 700) that 71 per cent. of the revenue of nations is raised by taxes, 14 per cent. is produced by State railways, and 15 per cent. arises from post-office, crown lands, and other public properties. Local taxation has also to be considered, and the subjoined table shows both approximately, and the ratio per head :—

	National £	Local £	Total £	£ per Head
U. Kingdom .	98,000,000	61,300,000	159,300,000	4.0
France . . .	117,800,000	42,300,000	160,100,000	4.2
Germany . .	84,500,000	48,000,000	132,500,000	2.5
Russia . . .	98,000,000	16,400,000	114,400,000	1.0

	National £	Local £	Total £	£ per Head
Austria . . .	68,000,000	16,500,000	84,500,000	2.0
Italy . . .	59,700,000	29,000,000	88,700,000	2.9
Spain . . .	29,900,000	9,600,000	39,500,000	2.2
Portugal . .	9,600,000	3,200,000	12,800,000	2.5
Sweden. . .	4,800,000	4,200,000	9,000,000	1.8
Norway . .	2,500,000	1,300,000	3,800,000	1.9
Denmark . .	2,800,000	2,100,000	4,900,000	2.2
Holland . .	9,500,000	10,300,000	19,800,000	4.0
Belgium . .	7,800,000	5,400,000	13,200,000	2.1
Switzerland .	2,100,000	4,000,000	6,100,000	2.0
Greece . . .	3,300,000	700,000	4,000,000	1.6
Roumania,&c.	31,700,000	5,700,000	37,400,000	2.0
Europe . . .	630,000,000	260,000,000	890,000,000	2.3
United States	71,800,000	98,000,000	169,800,000	2.3
Canada . .	6,500,000	2,900,000	9,400,000	1.9
Australia . .	11,700,000	4,100,000	15,800,000	3.6
Total . .	720,000,000	365,000,000	1,085,000,000	2.3

See also *Taxes*, in Part I., pages 557 to 565.

National taxes are made up approximately as follows :—

£ (000 omitted)

	Customs	Excise	Property	Stamps	Sundries	Total
U. King. .	22,100	33,300	17,300	18,500	6,800	98,000
France . .	17,200	43,200	19,200	30,100	8,100	117,800
Germany .	17,800	29,500	22,600	5,100	9,500	84,500
Russia . .	16,900	37,200	19,100	7,100	17,700	98,000
Austria .	8,300	30,700	17,500	7,800	3,700	68,000
Italy . .	11,900	14,800	20,800	7,400	4,800	59,700
Spain . .	6,900	7,200	11,900	2,800	1,100	29,900
Portugal .	4,000	1,500	2,600	1,100	400	9,600
Sweden .	2,100	1,200	600	200	700	4,800
Norway .	1,300	400	...	200	600	2,500
Denmark .	1,400	300	500	400	200	2,800
Holland .	600	3,700	2,800	1,700	700	9,500
Belgium .	1,300	1,700	2,600	1,500	700	7,800
Switzerland	1,700	...	100	100	200	2,100
Turkey, &c.	6,500	6,300	13,400	4,000	4,800	35,000
Europe .	120,000	211,000	151,000	88,000	60,000	630,000
U. States .	36,700	30,500	...	...	4,600	71,800
Canada .	4,000	1,900	...	...	600	6,500
Australia .	8,300	2,600	...	...	800	11,700
Total .	169,000	246,000	151,000	88,000	66,000	720,000

In the above table Property-tax includes taxes on properties or individuals, whether in the form of income-tax, poll-tax, trade-licenses, or death-duties. See *Finances*, page 700, and *Taxes on Alcohol*, page 635.

The incidence of taxation compared with the earnings of nations gives the following result :—

	Millions £ Sterling		Tax per Cent.
	Earnings	Taxation	
United Kingdom . .	1,421	159	11.2
France . . .	1,205	160	13.3
Germany . . .	1,285	133	10.4
Russia . . .	1,004	114	11.4
Austria . . .	707	85	12.0
Italy . . .	436	89	20.4
Spain . . .	277	40	14.4
Portugal . .	61	13	21.0
Sweden . . .	102	9	9.8
Norway . . .	40	4	9.5
Denmark . . .	58	5	8.3
Holland . . .	109	20	18.0
Belgium . . .	169	13	7.7
Switzerland . .	66	6	9.1
Roumania . . .	75	9	11.5
Servia . . .	28	2	8.5
Bulgaria . . .	37	4	10.4
Greece . . .	28	4	14.5
Europe . . .	7,108	869	12.1
United States . .	3,178	170	5.4
Canada . . .	186	9	5.0
Australia . . .	213	16	7.4
Total . . .	10,685	1,062	10.0

It appears from the above that 10 per cent. of the earnings of mankind are necessary for taxation, but this ratio is surpassed in most European countries, especially in Portugal and Italy, where it is over 20 per cent. The average of taxation on 455 million inhabitants of the above countries is 44 shillings per head, as compared with 125 shillings for food (see *Food*, page 715): every inhabitant of Europe, big or little, pays on an average

1½ pence daily in taxes, but the ratio in the United Kingdom is almost 3 pence daily.

It is shown by M. Yves Guyot that indirect taxation presses more heavily on the poor than on the rich, and that, nevertheless, the tendency of the age is to augment this kind of taxation. The table of M. Block for 1872 compares with later dates as follows :—

	Percentage of Indirect Taxation		
	1872	1889	1898
United Kingdom . .	85	79	83
France	75	82	84
Germany . . .	66	81	73
Russia . . .	80	87	81
Austria . . .	54	76	74
Italy	49	70	66
Spain . . .	56	61	60
Portugal . . .	70	85	73
Sweden . . .	76	83	87
Denmark . . .	72	80	82
Holland . . .	67	73	70
Belgium . . .	69	69	67

The excuse that is made by financiers for the increase of indirect taxation is that it is levied much more easily than direct. It is, nevertheless, most unequal in its incidence, because falling mostly on articles of consumption viz. :—

	Ratios of Indirect Taxation		
	Articles of Consum.	Sundries	Total
United Kingdom . .	68.5	31.5	100.0
France	61.0	39.0	100.0
Germany . . .	76.3	23.7	100.0
Russia . . .	68.0	32.0	100.0
Austria . . .	67.5	32.5	100.0
Italy	62.0	38.0	100.0
Spain . . .	78.0	22.0	100.0
Portugal . . .	77.0	23.0	100.0
Sweden . . .	78.0	22.0	100.0

In order to have the burthen fairly adjusted between rich and poor, taxation should be 50 per cent. direct, 50 per cent. indirect.

UNITED KINGDOM

The amount of Government taxes levied in the United Kingdom, as already shown, is £98,000,000, but of this amount about 10 millions is handed over to the local authorities. The total burthen of national and local taxes stands approximately thus :—

	National, £	Local, £	Total, £
England . .	72,000,000	58,500,000	130,500,000
Scotland . .	9,000,000	8,400,000	17,400,000
Ireland . .	7,000,000	4,400,000	11,400,000
United Kingdom	88,000,000	71,300,000	159,300,000

Comparing taxation with earnings, we find as follows :—

	Millions £ Sterling		Ratio of Taxes
	Income	Taxes	
England . . .	1,144	130.5	11.4 p.c.
Scotland . . .	187	17.4	9.3 ,,
Ireland . . .	90	11.4	12.7 ,,
United Kingdom .	1,421	159.3	11.2 ,,

This shows that the incidence of taxation is 36 per cent. heavier in Ireland than in Scotland, and 12 per cent heavier than in England. If we compare taxation with wealth, the account stands thus :—

	Millions £ Sterling		Taxes on £1000 of Wealth
	Wealth	Taxation	
England . . .	10,062	130.5	26 shillings
Scotland . . .	1,094	17.4	32 ,,
Ireland . . .	650	11.4	35 ,,
United Kingdom . .	11,806	159.3	27 ,,

According to this basis the tax incidence in Ireland is 35 per cent. more than in England, 9 per cent. more than in Scotland.

UNITED STATES

The total of taxes, national and local, is 170 millions sterling, equal to 5½ per cent. of the earnings of the nation, the incidence being heaviest in the south, viz. :—

	Millions £		Tax Ratio
	Earnings	Taxation	
New England . .	363	17	4.7
Middle . . .	976	45	4.6
South	454	34	7.5
West	1,385	74	5.3
The Union . . .	3,178	170	5.4

TEA

The consumption in various countries was as follows :—

	Million Lbs. Yearly		Lbs. per Inhabitant	
	1880–84	1890–92	1880–84	1890–92
United Kingdom .	171	201	4.7	5.3
United States . .	71	85	1.4	1.3
Russia . . .	62	71	0.7	0.7
Australia . . .	23	28	8.0	7.0
Canada . . .	17	20	3.7	3.9
Holland . . .	5	6	1.2	1.3
Germany . . .	3	5	0.7	1.0
Other Countries .	8	9	...	...
Total .	360	425	...	...
British Indian .	53	171	...	...
Chinese . . .	307	254	...	...

TELEPHONES

The growth of telephones between 1883 and 1888 was as follows :—

	Towns		Telephones	
	1883	1888	1883	1888
Europe . . .	161	804	30,100	119,000
America . . .	126	739	47,200	...
Australia . . .	5	23	900	3,300
Asia, &c. . .	11	101	700	2,000
The World . .	303	1,667	78,900	...

In 1895 the United States had 397,000 miles of telephones, worked by 11,000 officials, and counting 244,000

subscribers. The number in use in Europe in 1891 was as follows :—

Berlin . .	15,300	Rome . .	2,800	Buda-Pesth	1,900
Paris . .	6,200	Leipzig .	2,100	Breslau . .	1,400
Hamburg .	5,000	Brussels .	2,000	Naples . .	1,000
Vienna . .	3,700	Dresden .	2,000	Genoa . .	1,000

The number in London is not known : the public generally make use of telephone stations belonging to companies, which charge threepence. In the Continental cities the annual charge for a telephone in a house ranges from £6 to £8 sterling.

CONTINENT

In 1895 the use of telephones was as follows :—

	Towns	Miles	Telephones	Messages
France . .	415	26,000	63,400	75,600,000
Germany .	397	97,000	184,400	425,000,000
Italy . . .	56	...	11,600	...
Switzerland	225	5,100	20,600	14,800,000

Receipts in France averaged one penny, and in Switzerland twopence, per message.

UNITED KINGDOM

In 1895 the National Telephone Company served the following number of towns and subscribers :—

	Towns	Subscribers
England . . .	537	57,400
Scotland . . .	17	12,700
Ireland . . .	5	3,300
United Kingdom . .	559	73,400

The number of messages conveyed was 280 millions, or about 9 millions daily (excluding Sundays) at an average cost of a halfpenny per dozen words. Average subscription, £9 a year.

TEMPLES

The following table shows the dimensions of the greatest Pagan temples of antiquity, and the number of persons they could hold :—

Dedicated to	At	Length Feet	Width Feet	Capacity Persons
Diana . . .	Ephesus . .	425	220	27,000
Jupiter . . .	Girgenti . .	369	182	20,000
Juno . . .	Samos . .	346	189	19,000
...	Selinus . .	330	160	16,000
Apollo . . .	Miletus . .	303	164	15,000
Sun	Baalbec . .	290	160	14,000
Venus . . .	Rome . . .	350	116	12,000
Jupiter . . .	Athens . .	259	96	7,500
Parthenon . .	Athens . .	228	100	7,000
Jupiter . . .	Olympia . .	230	95	7,000
Neptune . .	Paestum . .	195	79	4,600
Sun	Palmyra . .	180	95	5,000

The temple of Diana at Ephesus could hold 1000 persons more than St. Paul's of London, and covered exactly half the superficial area of St. Peter's at Rome. The temple of Jupiter at Girgenti had the same capacity as Notre Dame at Paris, and the Madeleine in the latter city has precisely the capacity of the great temple of the Sun at Baalbec.

TENACITY

The tenacity of materials in pounds on square inch is :

Pine .	.	.	13,000	Sheet copper .	.	30,000
Ash .	.	.	17,000	Bronze .	.	36,000
Oak .	.	.	18,000	Boiler plates .	.	50,000
Cast iron	.	.	17,000	Steel .	.	100,000

See also Part I., page 335.

THEATRES

The number of inhabitants to each theatre in the principal cities of Europe is as follows :—

London	.	.	115,000	Dresden	. .	74,000
Paris .	.	.	32,000	Hamburg	. .	115,000
Berlin .	.	.	81,000	Bordeaux	. .	84,000
Vienna	.	.	138,000	Naples	. .	37,000
Rome .	.	.	31,000	Genoa .	. .	26,000
Buda-Pesth .		.	86,000	Florence	. .	15,000

This gives an average of one theatre for 70,000 inhabitants, from which it appears that London, Vienna, and Hamburg, are ill supplied. London, in 1890, had 25 theatres, with 28,600 seats, that is, one seat for 150 inhabitants, the receipts nightly averaging £6000, that is, £1,860,000 a year, or 8 shillings per inhabitant. The receipts of the theatres in Paris were :—

Year				£ Sterling	Pence p. Inhab.
1850 .	.	.	.	330,000	80
1860 .	.	.	.	580,000	80
1866 .	.	.	.	680,000	95
1876 .	.	.	.	860,000	105
1886 .	.	.	.	1,000,000	103
1896 .	.	.	.	1,200,000	115

The receipts of 1896 were as follows :—

			£			£
Opera .	.	.	130,000	Opera Comique .		60,000
Français	.	.	80,000	Various .	.	930,000

The average expenditure in Paris per inhabitant, on theatres, is 20 per cent. more than in London.

TIN

The production of this metal has been approximately as follows :—

			Tons					*Tons*
1860	.	.	10,000	1882	.	.	.	35,000
1870	.	.	16,000	1892	.	.	.	40,000

The production in 1882 and 1892 was as follows :—

			Tons	
			1882	**1892**
Great Britain .	.	.	9,200	9,000
Australia .	.	.	14,500	9,000
Java .	.	.	9,000	11,000
Various .	.	.	2,300	11,000
Total	.	.	35,000	40,000

Great Britain imports 25,000 tons yearly.

TITHES

The value of tithe rent-charge is shown thus :—

		£				£				£
1836 .	.	100.0	1894 .	.	.	74.2	1898 .	.	.	68.7
1892 .	.	75.9	1896 .	.	.	71.5	1899 .	.	.	68.1

Showing a fall of 10½ per cent. since 1892.

TOBACCO

Production in 1884 and 1894 was estimated thus :—

					Tons	
					1884	**1894**
U. States	.	.	.	.	240,000	180,000
India .	.	.	.	.	150,000	280,000
Russia .	.	.	.	.	75,000	50,000
Austria .	.	.	.	.	65,000	60,000
Java .	.	.	.	.	46,000	28,000
Brazil .	.	.	.	.	38,000	40,000
Germany	.	.	.	.	32,000	40,000
France .	.	.	.	.	15,000	20,000
Japan .	.	.	.	.	40,000	20,000
Various .	.	.	.	.	69,000	62,000
The World	.	.	.	.	770,000	780,000

UNITED STATES

The crops during ten years averaged as follows :—

	Million Lbs.	Acres	Lbs. Per Acre
Kentucky . . .	180	250,000	720
Virginia . . .	100	120,000	830
N. Carolina . .	45	80,000	560
Tennessee . .	33	50,000	660
Maryland . . .	20	30,000	670
Other States . .	102	140,000	730
Union	480	670,000	720

Consumption is as follows (1896) :—

	Tons	Oz. Per Head
U. Kingdom . . .	30,500	28
France . . .	40,000	37
Germany . . .	85,000	56
Russia . . , .	90,000	32
Austria	55,000	45

Neumann Spallart estimated consumption (1885) in other countries thus: Italy 24, Scandinavia 45, Switzerland 80, Belgium 88, Holland 98, United States 106, ounces yearly per inhabitant.

TRACTION

The same force that moves 1 ton on a smooth high-road will move 8 tons on a railway or 32 tons on a canal. The force that moves 1 ton on a canal at the speed of 8 miles an hour will move :—

2½ tons at 5 miles per hour,
5 ,, ,, 3½ ,, ,, ,,
10 ,, ,, 2½ ,, ,, ,,

See *Resistance and Gradients* (under *Railways*), at page 499.

TRADE UNIONS

The progress of Trade Unions in the United Kingdom in thirty years may be seen by comparing the number of members whose deputies assisted at successive Trade Union Congresses, viz. :—

1868 .	.	.	118,000	1888 .	.	.	675,000
1873 .	.	.	256,000	1897 .	.	.	1,093,000

The principal guilds are the following :—

Members		Members	
Miners . . .	250,000	Carpenters . .	52,000
Engineers . .	94,000	Shoemakers . .	41,000
Weavers . . .	81,000	Ironfounders .	32,000
Railwaymen . .	66,000	Printers . . .	25,000
Shipbuilders . .	57,000	Tailors . . .	22,000

The numbers for 1887 will be found at page 570.
The ratios of hands employed and unemployed were :—

Year	Per Cent.	
	Employed	Unemployed
1893	92.5	7.5
1894	93.1	6.9
1895	94.2	5.8
1896	96.6	3.4

See *Friendly Societies*, page 737 ; *Strikes*, page 808.

FRANCE

The law permitting Trade Unions was passed in 1884 :
the associations increased as follows :—

Unions of	1884	1888	1891
Employers . . .	101	859	1,127
Workmen . . .	69	803	1,376
Farmers . . .	5	461	750
Total . .	175	2,123	3,253

See also *Trade Unions*, in Part I., page 570.

TRAMWAYS

In 1896 the length of lines in traffic was as follows :—

	Miles			
	Horse	Steam	Electric	Total
United Kingdom .	710	230	70	1,010
France	750	560	110	1,420
Germany	940	240	410	1,590
Russia	270	20	20	310
Austria	260	110	90	460
Italy	240	1,830	30	2,100
Spain	170	40	10	220
Portugal	80	10	10	100
Holland	450	330	10	790
Belgium	100	740	30	870
Switzerland . . .	20	160	30	210
Scandinavia . . .	80	...	10	90
Roumania, &c. . .	90	...	10	100
Europe	4,160	4,270	840	9,270
United States . . .	2,650	1,120	12,130	15,900
Total . . .	6,810	5,390	12,970	25,170

UNITED KINGDOM

Mileage and traffic have advanced in ten years :—

	Miles		Passengers Millions	
	1886	1896	1886	1896
England	706	792	303	585
Scotland	73	96	60	128
Ireland	86	122	22	46
United Kingdom .	865	1,010	385	759

At present the traffic averages yearly 800,000 passengers per mile, against 445,000 in 1886. Earnings and expenses in 1896 showed as follows :—

	Receipts £	Expenses £	Profit, £	Interest on Cost
England . .	3,320,000	2,490,000	830,000	7.4
Scotland . .	545,000	400,000	145,000	9.6
Ireland . . .	285,000	215,000	70,000	4.8
U. Kingdom .	4,150,000	3,105,000	1,045,000	7.4

The average receipts for every 100 passengers carried were : 102 pence in Scotland, 136 in England, and 149 in Ireland.

In 1898 the tramways of the United Kingdom had 1064 miles in length (450 miles municipal property), representing a capital cost of £15,900,000, or £15,000 per mile. They had 590 locomotives, 39,000 horses, 5300 cars, and carried 859 million passengers in the year. Receipts, £4,560,000 ; expenses, £3,510,000 ; net profit, £1,050,000, or 7 per cent. on capital.

FRANCE

The returns of French tramways in 1895 were :—

.	Paris	Provinces	Total
Miles . . .	210	1,100	1,310
Cost, £ . .	3,270,000	7,010,000	10,280,000
Receipts, £ .	1,020,000	1,064,000	2,084,000
Expenses, £ .	940,000	826,000	1,766,000
Profit, £ .	80,000	238,000	318,000

The tramway traffic of five cities in 1895 was as follows :—

	Million Passengers	Trips per Inhabitant
Paris	160	66
Marseilles	27	67
Lyons	24	54
Bordeaux	15	60
Lille	10	50
Total . . .	236	60

HOLLAND

In 1896 the trams carried 44 million passengers for £440,000, being at the rate of 2½ pence each.

ARGENTINA

Buenos Ayres trams carried 45 million passengers in 1898.

UNITED STATES

The following table shows the cost of construction :—

	£	Miles	£ per Mile
Horse	18,300,000	1,220	15,000
Cable	81,800,000	1,120	73,000
Electric . . .	186,100,000	12,130	15,300
Total . .	286,000,000	14,470	19,800

The rolling stock, cost of working, and average fare per passenger in 1896 were :—

	No. of Cars	Working Expenses Cts. p. Mile	Fare, Cents per Passenger
Horse . . .	5,380	18.2	3.7
Cable . . .	7,820	14.1	3.2
Electric . . .	35,000	13.2	3.8

The cost of working is highest on horse lines, but the average fare is highest on electric lines.

The census of 1890 showed that the tramway traffic in that year for the Union was equivalent to 350,000 passengers per mile yearly, or about 1000 daily. At this rate the traffic in 1896 must have been 14½ million passengers daily, or 100 millions a week, against 15 millions a week in the United Kingdom. Thus each inhabitant of the United States makes 70 trips yearly, and of the United Kingdom only 17 trips yearly.

V

VITAL STATISTICS

Mayr shows that the general rates for Europe were :—

Period	Per 10,000 Inhabitants Yearly		
	Births	Deaths	Surplus Births
1821–40	351	307	44
1841–60	334	304	30
1861–80	341	297	44
1881–90	330	277	53
70 years	340	299	41

The following table shows the average number of births, marriages, and deaths in the last five recorded years, and the rate per 1000 inhabitants :—

	Núm. (000 omitted)			Per 1000 Pop.		
	Births	Marriages	Deaths	Births	Marriages	Deaths
England . . .	908	228	545	30.3	7.6	18.2
Scotland . . .	126	28	76	30.5	6.8	18.4
Ireland . . .	106	23	83	23.0	4.9	18.0
U. Kingdom .	1,140	279	704	29.4	7.2	18.1
France . . .	857	286	858	22.4	7.4	22.1
Germany . .	1,844	404	1,184	36.2	7.9	23.2
Russia * . . .	4,079	705	3,022	55.9	9.7	41.4
Austria . . .	910	192	678	37.7	7.9	27.6
Hungary . .	743	160	568	41.6	9.0	31.4
Italy	1,113	229	787	36.2	7.5	25.5
Spain . . .	634	146	559	35.4	8.1	31.2
Portugal . .	164	35	112	32.8	7.0	22.4
Sweden . . .	133	28	82	27.5	5.8	17.0
Norway . . .	61	13	34	30.3	6.5	16.8
Denmark . .	68	16	42	30.3	6.9	18.5
Finland . . .	77	16	50	32.0	6.7	20.8
Holland . . .	155	34	92	33.0	7.2	19.2
Belgium . . .	181	47	126	29.2	7.6	19.9
Switzerland . .	84	22	60	28.2	7.4	20.2
Greece . . .	64	16	44	34.5	9.0	25.0
Roumania . .	226	45	171	39.0	7.8	29.5
Servia . . .	97	23	65	44.1	10.4	29.5
Bulgaria . . .	118	27	82	36.4	8.2	25.2
Europe . . .	12,748	2,723	9,320	38.2	8.1	28.0
Australia . .	126	26	51	31.4	6.5	12.7
Canada . .	125	31	64	25.0	6.2	12.8
Japan . . .	1,186	350	874	28.6	8.4	21.1

In the preceding table it will be seen that the rates for

* Returns for the Greek Church only, comprising 73 million inhabitants, or 70 per cent. of the population, including Poland, but not Finland and the Caucasus.

Russia are much higher than for other countries. If Russia be excluded, the rates for the rest of Europe are :

	Number	Per 1000 Pop.
Births	8,669,000	32.1
Marriages . . .	2,018,000	7.4
Deaths	6,298,000	23.3

The surplus of births over deaths yearly in Europe, exclusive of Russia, is 2,371,000, equal to 8.8 per 1000 of the population, but if Russia be included it is 3,428,000, or 10.2 per 1000 yearly.

AUSTRALIA

Returns for five years ending December 1895 give :—

	Births	Marriages	Deaths	Surplus Births
New South Wales .	39,600	8,000	15,400	24,200
Victoria	36,200	7,520	16,400	19,800
New Zealand . . .	18,300	4,040	6,700	11,600
Queensland . . .	14,600	2,700	5,300	9,300
S. Australia . . .	10,600	2,140	4,100	6,500
Tasmania	4,900	900	2,000	2,900
W. Australia . . .	2,100	470	1,100	1,000
Total . . .	126,300	25,770	51,000	75,300

Births and deaths compared with population gave :—

	Per 1000 Population		
	Births	Deaths	Natural Increase
New South Wales . . .	32.8	12.8	20.0
Victoria . . .	31.0	14.1	16.9
New Zealand . . .	27.7	10.2	17.5
Queensland .	34.1	12.5	21.6
South Australia . .	31.5	12.2	19.3
Tasmania . . .	32.2	13.2	19.0
West Australia . .	31.2	16.1	15.1
Average	31.3	12.7	18.6

CANADA

The census of 1891 gave the following rates :—

	Per 1000 Population		
	Births	Deaths	Surplus Births
Ontario	24.5	11.3	13.2
Quebec	36.9	18.9	18.0
Nova Scotia . . .	25.4	14.6	10.8
Prince Edward Island .	24.5	12.3	12.2
New Brunswick . .	27.7	13.4	14.3
Manitoba . . .	32.5	19.4	13.1
British Columbia . .	23.2	13.9	9.3
All Canada . . .	28.5	14.5	14.0

NATURAL INCREASE

The following table shows the natural increase, i.e. the surplus of births over deaths in various countries, and the number of years in which this would suffice to double a population if there were no emigration :—

	Natural Increase	Rate Per 1000 Pop.	Years to Double
England . . .	363,000	12.1	58
Scotland . . .	50,000	12.1	58
Ireland . . .	23,000	5.0	140
United Kingdom . .	436,000	11.3	62
France . . .	...	...	...
Germany . . .	660,000	13.0	54
Russia . . .	1,057,000	14.5	48
Austria . . .	232,000	9.7	72
Hungary . . .	175,000	9.7	72
Italy . . .	326,000	10.6	66
Spain . . .	75,000	4.2	167
Portugal . . .	52,000	10.4	67
Sweden . . .	51,000	10.5	67
Norway . . .	27,000	13.5	52
Denmark . . .	26,000	11.8	59
Finland . . .	27,000	11.2	62
Holland . . .	63,000	13.4	52
Belgium . . .	55,000	8.9	78
Switzerland . . .	24,000	8.0	88
Greece . . .	20,000	9.5	73
Roumania . . .	55,000	9.5	73
Servia . . .	32,000	14.6	48
Bulgaria . . .	36,000	11.2	62
Japan . . .	312,000	7.5	93
Australia . . .	75,000	18.5	38
United States . .	1,440,000	20.0	35
Canada . . .	61,000	12.2	57

The natural increase is highest in Servia and Russia. There is no increase in France, the deaths of the last five years having equalled the births.

The following table shows the average rates of birth and death, and the natural increase, in various cities for ten years ending December 1891 :—

	Per 1000 Inhabitants Yearly		
	Births	Deaths	Nat. Incr.
London . . .	33.0	20.4	9.6
Paris . . .	26.3	23.8	2.5
Berlin . . .	33.4	23.1	10.3
Vienna . . .	28.6	21.5	7.1
Rome . . .	29.5	25.6	3.9
Buda-Pesth . . .	36.0	30.9	5.1
Brussels . . .	31.0	24.4	6.6
Hamburg . . .	35.1	24.8	10.3
Leipzig . . .	27.0	17.2	9.8
Dresden . . .	31.1	21.9	9.2
Breslau . . .	35.2	29.2	6.0
Bordeaux . . .	22.8	24.0	...
Naples . . .	33.6	30.1	3.5
Milan . . .	32.7	28.1	4.6
Turin . . .	29.5	26.2	3.3
Genoa . . .	28.2	25.6	2.6
Florence . . .	26.1	26.5	...
Palermo . . .	35.2	25.3	9.9
Venice . . .	30.1	30.9	...
Trieste . . .	34.1	31.2	2.9
Average . . .	30.9	25.5	5.4

UNITED STATES

Deaths recorded in the census year 1890 were 875,520, being 14 per thousand inhabitants. Birth-rate is shown by Dr. Billings (1886), on the basis of the previous census, to be 34 per thousand, so that the natural increase on a population of 72 millions is 1,440,000 yearly.

MORTALITY

The following table (1881-90) shows the number of deaths yearly among 10,000 inhabitants :—

Age	England	France	Prussia	Italy	Sweden	Denmark	Holland	Belgium	Switzer.	Average
0-5 .	69	79	104	127	53	60	82	74	68	80
5-15 .	9	11	13	17	12	13	10	9	9	11
15-25 .	8	12	10	12	9	10	10	10	10	10
25-35 .	10	13	12	11	9	10	10	11	12	11
35-45 .	13	12	13	11	9	10	11	12	13	12
45-55 .	17	15	17	14	11	12	13	14	16	14
55-65 .	25	23	27	24	18	20	21	22	28	23
65-75 .	31	30	33	32	22	25	27	28	35	29
Over 75 .	28	26	31	34	25	23	27	29	32	28
Total .	210	221	260	282	168	183	211	209	223	218

Infant mortality, during ten years ending 1893, showed the number of deaths yearly per thousand of each age :—

	0-1	1-2	2-3	3-4
England . . .	146	54	22	14
Scotland . . .	122	53	24	15
Ireland . . .	96	36	19	12
France . . .	168	48	25	17
Prussia . . .	208	62	31	21
Russia . . .	269	98	59	40
Austria . . .	247	76	41	28
Hungary . . .	256	94	61	46
Italy . . .	190	96	47	29
Spain . . .	192	127	89	44
Sweden . . .	107	32	20	15
Norway . . .	96	33	20	15
Holland . . .	175	54	23	15
Belgium . . .	163	51	25	16
Roumania . . .	198	83	55	40
Japan . . .	132	45	29	20

Deaths from alcohol, in seven years ending 1893, averaged yearly per million inhabitants as follows :—

England	.	. 63	Prussia .	. .	23
Scotland	.	. 54	Belgium .	. .	53
Ireland .	.	. 30	Sweden .	. .	21

See *Births*, page 645, and *Deaths*, page 683.

Longevity.—The number of persons over 70 years of age in various countries is as follows :—.

	Number (000 omitted)			Per 1000 Pop.
	Males	Females	Total	
England . . .	347	454	801	28
Scotland . . .	49	75	124	31
Ireland . . .	103	111	214	45
France . . .	895	1,015	1,910	50
Germany . . .	619	757	1,376	28
Austria . . .	304	333	637	27
Hungary . . .	195	204	399	22
Switzerland . . .	41	47	88	30
Spain . . .	227	256	483	27
Scandinavia . . .	168	220	388	43
Holland . . .	67	84	151	33
Belgium . . .	103	123	226	37
United States . . .	811	756	1,567	25
Australia . . .	36	25	61	16

Longevity is most frequent in countries of low birth-rate, such as France and Ireland. The *Journal des Debats* (November 1898) published the following statement of centenarians living in Europe :—

Ireland	. . 578	France	. . 243	Germany	. . 75
Spain .	. . 401	England .	. 146	Scotland	. . 46

See tables of *Longevity*, pages 355-357.

W

WAGES

Tables of wages in various countries from 1836 to 1886 will be found in Part I., pages 579-586. The Board of Trade returns (by Giffen) in 1891 gave the summary for Great Britain thus :—

Working in	Wages, Shillings Weekly			
	Men	Women	Boys	Girls
Collieries . . .	22.9	8.2	10.7	5.6
Iron mines . .	16.5	5.8	7.0	4.7
Slate quarries . .	22.1	...	8.0	...
Cotton mills . .	25.3	15.3	9.3	6.8
Woollen ,, . .	23.2	13.3	8.5	7.4
Linen ,, . .	19.7	8.9	6.3	4.9
Hemp ,, . .	23.5	9.7	6.0	5.1
Silk ,, . .	22.3	10.1	7.2	5.7
Carpet ,, . .	26.6	11.1	8.3	6.9
Hosiery ,, . .	24.4	11.5	9.5	8.3
Hair ,, . .	25.0	9.8	7.4	5.9
Average . . .	21.0	9.4	7.3	5.5

In 1895 Mr. Bowley published a comparative table of wages since 1860 thus :—

Employed in	1860	1874	1880	1883	1886	1891
Agriculture . .	100	130	122	117	111	118
Building . . .	100	126	125	125	126	128
Cotton mills .	100	148	134	146	155	176
Woollen ,, .	100	121	126	120	115	115
Jute ,, .	100	140	120	142	120	140
Ironworks . .	100	143	112	110	100	124
Engineering .	100	124	120	127	126	126
Gasworks . .	100	125	128	130	130	149
Seamen . .	100	129	102	118	110	143
Mining . . .	100	150	100	115	100	150
Gen. average .	100	134	119	125	119	137

UNITED STATES

Mr. Carroll Wright, Director of Statistical Department, shows that wages rose 67 per cent. between 1860 and 1891, viz. :—

Employment	1860	1880	1891
Brewery . . .	100	176	225
Carpenter . . .	100	143	173
Leather . . .	100	131	138
Lumber . . .	100	173	178
Metals	100	134	149
Paper	100	159	182
Printer	100	141	149
Railroad . . .	100	144	146
Stone	100	129	165
Textiles . . .	100	140	165
Total . .	1,000	1,470	1,670

The census of 1890, compared with previous ones, showed wages thus :—

Year	Wages, £	Hands	£ per Hand
1850 . .	49,200,000	957,000	51
1860 . .	78,800,000	1,311,000	60
1870 . .	129,000,000	2,054,000	63
1880 . .	197,200,000	2,733,000	72
1890 . .	474,800,000	4,713,000	101

Comparing 1890 with 1860, we find the average earnings rose 67 per cent., precisely as Carroll Wright stated above. In 1897 he published a report on Wages, from which the following figures are taken :—

Weekly Earnings, Shillings

	Man	Woman		Man	Woman
Book-keeper	84	42	Salesman .	46	42
Carder . .	30	23	Shirtmaker	42	38
Cigar-maker	46	41	Shoemaker	30	21
Cook . . .	25	23	Spinner .	32	25
Paper-maker	56	21	Tailor . .	86	81
Printer . .	63	60	Weaver .	29	25

ITALY

Bodio's table, reduced to English money, is as follows :—

Employment	Pence Daily				
	1871	1881	1886	1891	1897
Dyer	17	21	21	20	20
Engineer . . .	33	42	32	28	30
Mason . . .	33	43	38	36	38
Miner	24	29	24	23	26
Papermaker .	13	17	19	24	25
,, woman	9	11	11	18	18
Spinner ,, .	8	9	10	12	12
Waggoner . .	19	21	24	24	20
Weaver . . .	27	47	47	40	40
,, woman .	14	16	17	15	15
Average . . .	20	26	24	24	24

The mean wages in seven branches of industry for a working day of 10½ hours, and the number of days' labour equal to a ton of wheat, were as follows :—

Year	Wage, Pence Daily	Wheat, Shill. per Ton	Day's Wage to a Ton
1871 . . .	17	250	15
1876 . . .	20	236	12
1881 . . .	22	218	10
1886 . . .	24	176	7
1891 . . .	25	202	8
1896 . . .	25	180	7

It appears that in 1896 an operative could earn the price of a ton of wheat in half the time necessary in 1871.

3 F

WAR

The campaigns against Bonaparte, 1793–1815, showed an annual death-rate in the British army of 57 per thousand, of whom only 7 per thousand were killed in action. Subsequent campaigns, being of shorter duration, show necessarily a higher annual death-rate, viz. :—

Date	War in	Army	Per 1000 Yearly
1855 . . .	Crimea . .	British . . .	120
,, . . .	,, . .	French . . .	103
1859 . . .	Italy . . .	Austrian . .	47
,, . . .	,, . . .	French . . .	56
,, . . .	,, . . .	Italian . . .	55
1864 . . .	Schleswig. .	Prussian . .	33
,, . . .	,, . . .	Austrian . .	40
1866 . . .	Germany . .	Prussian . .	34
,, . . .	,, . . .	Austrian . .	56
,, . . .	,, . . .	Bavarian . .	51
1870-71 . .	France . .	German . . .	50

In the Franco-German war the German army had a medium strength of 888,000 men in the field, of whom 44,750 died, including 26,900 killed in action : the mortality among officers was much higher than among men, viz. :—

	Killed	Died	Total per Thousand
Officers . . .	81	8	89
Men . . .	31	14	45

The British loss in the Crimea was very severe, the mortality in two years reaching one-fourth of the army in the field. For details see page 587.

WATER

According to latest information the daily supply of water to the principal cities and the average charge per gallon are as follows :—

	Gallons	Gall. per Inhab.	Pence Yearly
London . . .	183,000,000	40	2.5
Paris . . .	123,000,000	48	5.0
Vienna. . .	120,000,000	90	3.6
Buda-Pesth . .	176,000,000	300	2.0
Rome . . .	52,000,000	128	2.0
Genoa . . .	23,000,000	105	2.0
Hamburg . .	26,000,000	42	2.5
Berlin . . .	21,500,000	13	2.5
Bordeaux . .	12,300,000	48	2.4
Palermo . .	9,500,000	33	1.8
Naples. . .	6,400,000	12	1.8
Brussels . .	6,000,000	12	1.2

The volume of water discharged at Niagara is now computed at 1,500,000 tons, or 340 million gallons per minute, representing a force of 16 million horse power, which is equal to the energy contained in all the coal produced daily in the world, say 1,600,000 tons.

The water supply of London is provided by companies, whose shares and debentures sum up £22,300,000, but the market value in 1897 was £48,350,000, equal to a premium of 117 per cent. There is a project to bring a supply of 215 million gallons daily from Wales (162 miles) at a cost of £32,800,000.

See *Aqueducts*, page 636, and *Water*, page 588.

WEALTH

The methods for estimating the wealth of nations are laid down at length in my book on Industries and Wealth of Nations (Longmans, London, 1896), from which the following tables are taken :—

	Millions £ Sterling					
	Farms	Railways	Houses	Merchandise	Sundries	Total
England. . .	1,452	812	2,196	629	4,973	10,062
Scotland. . .	234	134	232	114	380	1,094
Ireland . . .	391	39	64	62	94	650
U. Kingdom .	2,077	985	2,492	805	5,447	11,806
France . . .	3,093	663	2,159	601	3,174	9,690
Germany . .	2,508	555	1,755	677	2,557	8,052
Russia . . .	2,710	349	1,019	515	1,832	6,425
Austria . . .	1,797	371	719	367	1,258	4,512
Italy	1,399	184	503	223	851	3,160
Spain	1,212	108	280	148	632	2,380
Portugal. . .	164	23	77	32	115	411
Scandinavia .	532	54	221	117	372	1,296
Holland . . .	295	46	178	104	257	880
Belgium . . .	354	75	175	118	266	988
Switzerland. .	172	44	91	49	136	492
Danub. States .	508	36	136	83	263	1,026
Greece . . .	109	6	31	15	61	222
Europe . . .	16,930	3,499	9,834	3,854	17,223	51,340
U. States . .	4,142	2,260	4,446	1,563	3,939	16,350
Canada . . .	311	186	145	103	264	1,009
Australia . .	392	139	174	88	283	1,076
Argentina . .	198	88	107	53	170	616
Total . .	21,973	6,172	14,706	5,661	21,879	70,391

The following table shows the distribution of wealth among the whole population of each country ; rural wealth, for example, is the ratio of same which would correspond not to the rural population but to all the inhabitants, and urban in like manner, viz. :—

	£ Sterling per Inhabitant				
	Rural	Urban	Total	Real	Personal
United Kingdom .	53	249	302	106	196
France . .	80	172	252	123	129
Germany . .	48	108	156	72	84
Russia . .	26	35	61	30	31
Austria . .	41	63	104	51	53
Italy . .	45	56	101	53	48
Spain . . .	69	66	135	76	59
Portugal . .	35	52	87	46	41
Sweden and Norway .	40	74	114	53	61
Denmark . .	115	115	230	124	106
Holland . .	61	122	183	87	96
Belgium . .	56	98	154	75	79
Switzerland. .	57	107	164	76	88
Danubian States .	44	46	90	49	41
Greece . .	50	51	101	57	44
Europe . .	45	94	139	64	75
United States .	59	175	234	111	123
Canada . .	60	136	196	73	123
Australia . .	93	163	256	97	159
Argentina . .	49	105	154	58	96
General average .	48	107	155	71	84

GERMANY

The wealth of the principal States stands thus :—

| | Millions £ Sterling | | | | | |
	Prussia	Bavaria	Saxony	Wurtemberg	Various	Total
Farms . . .	1,583	341	72	130	382	2,508
Railways . .	348	65	36	20	86	555
Houses . . .	1,048	179	132	77	319	1,755
Merchandise .	403	76	55	28	115	677
Sundries . .	1,558	288	161	115	435	2,557
Total . .	4,940	949	456	370	1,337	8,052

In two years (1896–98) *real* estate in Prussia increased 88 millions sterling. Molinari estimates that the wealth of Germany (real and personal) increased 600 millions sterling between 1893 and 1897, or 150 millions yearly.

AUSTRIA

The shares that correspond to the two nations of the monarchy are as follows :—

| | Millions £ Sterling | | |
	Austria	Hungary	Total
Farms	972	825	1,797
Railways . . .	217	154	371
Houses . . .	520	199	719
Merchandise . .	198	169	367
Sundries . .	799	459	1,258
Total . .	2,706	1,806	4,512

SCANDINAVIA

The wealth of the three northern kingdoms shows as follows :—

| | Millions £ Sterling | | | |
	Sweden	Norway	Den.	Total
Farms . . .	201	77	254	532
Railways . . .	33	7	14	54
Houses . . .	111	41	69	221
Merchandise . .	58	22	37	117
Sundries . . .	167	73	132	372
Total . .	570	220	506	1,296

DANUBIAN STATES

The wealth of these States stands thus :—

| | Millions £ Sterling | | | |
	Roumania	Servia	Bulgaria	Total
Farms . . .	244	110	154	508
Railways . .	26	4	6	36
Houses . . .	69	28	39	136
Merchandise .	46	15	22	83
Sundries . .	134	54	75	263
Total . .	519	211	296	1,026

UNITED STATES

The various parts of the Union are represented approximately as regards wealth in the manner shown in the following table (houses including also public buildings) :—

| States | Millions £ Sterling | | | | | |
	Farms	Railways	Houses	Merchandise	Sundries	Total
New England .	142	90	595	187	273	1,287
Middle . . .	646	310	1,967	480	994	4,397
Southern . .	713	556	591	214	396	2,470
Western . .	2,641	1,304	2,182	681	1,388	8,196
Union . . .	4,142	2,260	5,335	1,562	3,051	16,350

AUSTRALIA

The several colonies stand as regards wealth (public works including railways, waterworks, telegraphs, &c.) thus :—

| | Millions £ Sterling | | | | | |
	Farms	Public Works	Houses	Merchandise	Sundries	Total
N. S. Wales .	131	71	68	31	69	370
Victoria . . .	77	76	53	31	46	283
New Zealand .	69	29	25	18	25	166
Queensland .	57	22	8	11	16	114
S. Australia .	39	19	12	7	18	95
Tasmania . .	12	5	6	3	6	32
W. Australia .	7	3	2	2	2	16
Total . .	392	225	174	103	182	1,076

CANADA

The distribution of wealth is approximately as follows :—

| | Millions £ Sterling | | | | | |
	Farms	Railways	Houses	Merchandise	Sundries	Total
Ontario . . .	186	75	75	51	135	522
Quebec . . .	67	36	41	28	66	238
Acadia . . .	32	29	16	13	31	121
North-West .	26	46	13	11	32	128
Total . .	311	186	145	103	264	1,009

Acadia includes Nova Scotia and the other Atlantic provinces.

WEIGHTS AND MEASURES

See pages 595–597.

WHEAT

Canadian wheat crops were in tons as follows :—

	1896	1897	1898
Ontario . . .	460,000	720,000	800,000
Manitoba . . .	360,000	460,000	640,000
North-West .	40,000	40,000	60,000
Quebec . . .	100,000	130,000	150,000
Total . .	960,000	1,350,000	1,650,000

In 1898 Argentina had 5,800,000 acres under wheat, probable crop 1,200,000 tons, one-half for export. Buenos Ayres had 1,100,000 acres, Santa Fé 2,650,000, Cordoba 1,240,0c0, Entre Rios 600,000, other provinces 210,000.

See *Agriculture*, page 613 ; *Food*, page 713 ; *Wheat*, page 597.

WOOL

Production in 1894 was estimated as follows :—

Mil. Lbs.		*Mil. Lbs.*		*Mil. Lbs.*
Australia .	670	U. Kingdom	144	Germany . 55
River Plate .	380	France . .	104	Austria . . 52
United States	298	South Africa	90	India . . . 72
Russia . .	262	Spain . . .	66	Various . . 197

Making a total of 2390 million pounds, or 1,070,000 tons. Consumption in the factories of the United States was as follows :—

Year	Million Pounds		
	Native	Imported	Total
1840	36	10	46
1850	53	18	71
1860	60	25	85
1870	162	47	209
1880	233	124	357
1890	276	102	378
1897	259	342	601

Consumption in the United Kingdom has been as follows :—

Year	Million Pounds		
	British	Foreign	Total
1873	158	195	353
1883	109	219	328
1896	125	385	510

Sir J. Behrens, Bradford, summed up the consumption during twenty years thus :—

Year	Million Pounds Yearly		
	British	Imported	Total
1860–64 . . .	135	126	261
1865–74 . . .	144	181	325
1875–84 . . .	132	235	367
1884	114	280	394

He estimated the yearly output (1884) of woollen and worsted goods at £60,400,000, of which home consumption took £33,000,000, and exports were £27,400,000. The clip of British flocks averages 150 million lbs., of which one-fourth is exported.

The following table shows the average yearly production of wool from 1887 to 1894, and the equivalent in washed wool :—

	Million Pounds		Yield Per Cent.
	Unwashed	Washed	
Europe . . .	735	440	60
Australia . .	570	310	55
River Plate . .	345	120	35
United States . .	290	220	75
South Africa . .	95	70	75
Various . .	215	130	60
The World . . .	1,960	1,290	66

The countries which export woollen (and worsted) manufactures are :—

	Millions £ Sterling		
	1885	1890	1895
Great Britain . . .	24.4	25.7	26.9
France	14.6	15.8	14.2
Germany . . .	9.7	11.0	10.5
Total . . .	48.7	52.5	51.6

Production and consumption of woollen goods are as follows :—

	Output	Consumption	
	Millions £	Millions £	Shillings Per Head
United Kingdom . .	61.7	45.0	23
France . . .	44.7	36.0	19
Germany . . .	42.2	39.8	15
Russia . . .	29.0	29.4	6
Austria . . .	14.5	14.1	7
Italy . . .	5.8	7.1	5
Spain . . .	6.6	6.9	8
Scandinavia . .	4.2	6.2	14
Belgium . . .	5.3	5.5	17
Other Countries .	9.0	12.0	8
Europe . . .	223.0	202.0	11

Woollen manufacture in the United Kingdom has increased as follows :—

	Spindles	Power-looms	Operatives
1870 . . .	4,950,000	115,000	240,000
1890 . . .	6,580,000	132,000	302,000

See *Wool*, page 701.

Y

YACHTS

According to Lloyd's List there are nearly 7000 yachts, of which 60 per cent. are owned in Great Britain, 40 per cent. abroad, viz. :—

	No.	Tons	Average Tons
British	4,104	155,000	38
Foreign	2,643	110,000	42
Total . .	6,747	265,000	40
Steam	1,436	172,000	120
Sail	5,311	93,000	18
Built in Great Britain .	4,603	214,000	45
Built abroad . .	2,144	51,000	25

The yachts owned in the United Kingdom are as follows :—

	No.	Tons	Average
Steam. . . .	898	94,000	105
Sail	3,206	61,000	19
Total . .	4,104	155,000	38

YARN

Exports of British yarn were as follows :—

Year	Millions Lbs. Yarn				Value, £
	Cotton	Woollen	Linen, &c.	Total	
1889 . .	252	45	48	345	17,300,000
1893 . .	207	50	46	303	15,300,000
1897 . .	253	57	70	380	16,600,000

The prices of yarn were :—

	Pence Per Pound			
	Cotton	Woollen	Linen	Jute
1889 . . .	11	23	15	3.0
1893 . . .	10	22	15	2.5
1897 . . .	9	20	13	2.4

The consumption of imported yarn in various countries in 1888 and 1895 was as follows :—

	Millions Lbs.					
	1888			1895		
	Cotton	Woollen, &c.	Total	Cotton	Woollen, &c.	Total
China . .	92	...	92	151	...	151
Germany . .	35	27	62	34	35	69
Austria . .	22	12	34	31	18	49
India . . .	52	...	52	45	...	45
Holland. .	30	2	32	37	6	43
Japan . .	64	...	64	20	1	21
Russia . .	10	16	26	5	14	19
France . .	26	...	26	15	...	15
Italy . . .	8	11	19	3	12	15
Sweden . .	4	3	7	7	6	13
Spain and Port.	2	12	14	2	11	13
Roumania, &c.	13	...	13	17	...	17
Total . .	358	83	441	367	103	470

Austria exports 18 million lbs. of linen yarn, Belgium 62 million lbs. of linen and woollen yarns, Switzerland 20 million lbs. of all kinds.

Z

ZINC

Production of ores and of metal show approximately :—

	Ore, Tons		Zinc, Tons	
	1888	1896	1888	1896
Germany .	670,000	710,000	130,000	150,000
Belgium. .	20,000	20,000	90,000	110,000
Great Britain	40,000	30,000	30,000	70,000
United States	200,000	280,000	50,000	70,000
Sweden . .	50,000	30,000		
Spain . .	40,000	50,000	20,000	40,000
Austria . .	30,000	30,000		
Italy, &c. .	130,000	180,000		
France . .	20,000	70,000	10,000	20,000
Total . .	1,200,000	1,400,000	330,000	460,000

The production of metallic zinc has doubled since 1880. The richest mines are in Prussia, the ores giving 21 per cent. of metal. Large quantities of metallic zinc are produced in Belgium and Great Britain, mostly from imported ores.

The total production of metallic zinc in 1880 was only 230,000 tons.

The price of this metal has been as follows per ton :—

	£			£			£
1882 . . 14.7		1888 . . 15.7		1893 . . 16.3			
1885 . . 13.3		1890 . . 19.8		1897 . . 15.7			

In 1897 Great Britain imported 70,000 tons of crude zinc, in cakes, value £1,200,000, besides 20,000 tons of zinc manufactures, value £440,000. Exports of zinc were only 8000 tons.

BOOKS OF REFERENCE.

Achenwall, G., European Statistics, Berlin, 1808.
Actuaries' Journal of London, 1850–90.
Adolphus, The British Empire, London, 1818.
Agricultural Society's Journal, London, 1840–90.
Allard, A., Baisse des Prix, Brussels, 1885.
Allen, John, Wealth of Great Britain, London, 1840.
Almanac de Gotha, 1760–1890.
American Almanac, New York, 1831–90.
Annuaire d'Economie Politique, Paris, 1840–90.
Annuario Statistico Italiano, Rome, 1880–90.
Annual Register, London, 1758–1890.
Annales de Demographie, Paris, 1877–82.
Ansell, Charles, On Friendly Societies, 1834.
Ansell, Charles, jun., On Death-Rates, 1874.
Archer, W. H., Statistics of Australia, 1854.
Archivio di Statistica, Rome, 1876–83.
Argentine Statistics, by Latzina, 1885–90.
Arnold on Monts-de-Piété, Brussels, 1847.
Arrivabene, Count, Economie de Belgique, 1843.
Arts, Journal of Society of, London, 1853–90.
Asher, C. W., Statistics of Hamburg, 1865.
Aspland, A., On Reformatories and Prisons, 1868.
Atkinson, Edward, Labour and Capital, Boston, 1880.
Atkinson, William, Political Economy, London, 1840.
Aubanel, H., Statistics of Insanity, Paris, 1841.
Austria, Statistisches Jahrbuch, Vienna, 1869–90.
Avila, Marquis, Statistics of Portugal, 1865.
Axon, W., Statistics of Deaf and Dumb, 1875.
Bagehot, Walter, Economic Studies, London, 1880.
Baines, Edward, History of Cotton Industry, London, 1835.
Balbi, Adrien, Statistical Works Complete, Turin, 1841.
Balfour, Graham, Health of Soldiers, London, 1872.
Banfield, Thomas, Statistics of Prussia, 1848.
Banker's Magazine, London, 1844–89.
Banking Almanac, by Palgrave, 1875–90.
Barmeaud, Economie du Moyen Age, Paris, 1859.
Bascome, E., History of Epidemics, London, 1851.
Bastiat, Fred., Political Economy, Paris, 1853.
Baumhauer, M., Statistics of Holland, 1869.
Baxter, Dudley, Income and Taxation, London, 1871.
Bavaria, Statistics by Dr. Mayr, Munich, 1876.
Beaumont, G., Prisons and Penal Settlements, 1833.
Becher, S., Statistics of Austria, Stuttgart, 1841.
Becker, Lydia, Statistics of Female Schools, 1872.
Beddoe, John, Anthropometry and Health Statistics, 1879.
Beeke, H., Income of Great Britain, 1800.
Beer, Finances of Austria, Prague, 1877.
Behnn and Wagner, Population, 1880.
Belgium, Annuaire Statistique, 1871–90.
Bellini, Statistics of Italy, 1880.
Bengesco, Statistique de Roumanie, 1869.
Berg, Dr., Vital Statistics of Sweden, 1871.
Berthelot, S., Statistics of Cuba, 1843.
Bertillon, J., Statistics of Marriage, Paris, 1880.
Bertillon, L., Vital Statistics of Europe, 1877.
Besobrasoff, Russian Finances, St. Petersburg, 1886.
Bethlem Hospital, Insane Statistics, 1856.
Bevan, Phillips, Statistical Atlas, Edinburgh, 1882.
Bigelow, John, Resources of United States, 1863.

Bikelas, Statistics of Greece, 1868.
Black, M., Life Insurance, from 1706 to 1863.
Black, W., Mortality of Mankind at all ages, 1788.
Blanqui, Jerome, Political Economy, Paris, 1860.
Bloch, Maurice, International Statistics, Paris, 1860.
Boccardo, G., Dictionary of Economy, Milan, 1874.
Bodio, Professor, Vital Statistics of Italy, 1880.
Boeckh, Richard, Statistics of Large Cities, 1877.
Boetticher, J., Statistics of Europe, 1800.
Bosanquet, J. W., Paper-Money and Bullion, 1842.
Botly, W., Agricultural Statistics, 1870–88.
Bouchette, J., Statistical Description of Canada, 1832.
Boudard, A., Savings-Banks Statistics, 1858.
Bourgoing, J., Spanish Trade, Finances, &c., 1808.
Bourne, Stephen, Population and Food, 1880.
Brachelli, Statistics of Austria-Hungary, Leipzig, 1883.
Bradstreet's Weekly Journal, New York, 1890.
Brassey, Lord, Work and Wages, London, 1874.
Brazil at the Vienna Exhibition, 1873.
British Almanac, London, 1828–90.
British Association, Annual Reports, 1831–90.
British Trade Journal, London, 1880–90.
Browne, W., Money and Weights of all Nations, 1876.
Browning, G., European Finances, 1834.
Bryson, Dr., Manual of Medical Statistics, 1851.
Buckle, F., Hospital Statistics, London, 1865.
Bulgaria, Census Report, Sophia, 1881.
Bullion Committee of 1810 Report, 1810.
Burchard, Horatio, United States Mint Report, 1882.
Burdett, Henry, Stock Exchange Annual, London, 1891
Buschen, Arthur, L'Empire de Russie, Paris, 1867.
Caird, Sir James, British Agriculture, 1869.
Cairnes, John, Political Economy, London, 1874.
Caley, W., Statistics of Canada, 1855.
Camacho, Juan, Finances of Spain, Madrid, 1883.
Campbell, John, Political Survey of Britain, 1774.
Canada, Statistical Abstract, Ottawa, 1889.
Cape Colony, Statistical Register, Cape Town, 1889.
Capper, Ben., Statistics of United Kingdom, 1829.
Carey, H., On Wealth, Wages, &c., Philadelphia, 1835.
Carvalho, M., Statistics of Portugal, 1865.
Census of Great Britain, 1801–81 ; Ireland, 1831–81.
Cernuschi, Henry, Bi-Metallism, Paris, 1881.
Chadwick, Sir Edwin, Sanitary Report, London, 1847.
Chamber of Commerce Journal, London, 1890.
Chamberlayne, Condition of England, 1707.
Chambers's Encyclopædia, Edinburgh, 1891.
Chaptal, Count, L'Industrie Française, Paris, 1819.
Chateauvieux, L., Agriculture of Italy, 1819.
Chevalier, Michel, Political Economy, Paris, 1866.
Child, Sir Josiah, Trade and Manufactures, London, 1693.
Chile, Anuario Estadistico, published at Santiago.
China, Consular and Diplomatic Reports.
Cibrario, Chev., Economie du Moyen Age, Paris, 1859.
Clarke, Hyde, Statistics of Turkey, 1868.
Clarke, Thomas, Statistical View of Europe, 1791.
Cobden Club Essays, London, 1882.
Coghlan, Australian Statistics, Sydney, 1890.
Cohen, Bernard, Finances of Nations, London, 1822.

Colle, E., Colonies Françaises, Paris, 1878.
Collignon, Ed., Études sur la Russie, Paris, 1864.
Colonial Abstract, Board of Trade Annual.
Colquhoun, Pat., Wealth of British Empire, 1815.
Comber, W., Progress of Wealth, London, 1822.
Conferences Statistiques, Paris, 1880.
Congress, International, Reports, 1853-76.
Coni, Emile, Statistics of Buenos Ayres, 1879-89.
Cooke, L., British Husbandry, 1688-1827, London, 1828.
Coquelin, Ch., Economie Politique, Paris, 1854.
Cracroft, Bernard, British Funds, London, 1873.
Craik, G., History of Commerce, London, 1844.
Crump, Arthur, Banking and Currency, 1866.
Cucheval, Finances d'Italie, Paris, 1886.
Cunningham, W., Growth of British Commerce, 1882.
Cusani, Statistics of Greece, Milan, 1862.
Czoernig, Baron, Statistics of Austria, 1861.
Dawson, J., Maritime Insurance, 1873.
Daras, Abbé, Statistics of Deaf-Mutes, 1856.
Darwin, Geo., Marriages of Cousins, London, 1875.
Davenant, C., Statistical Works Re-edited, London, 1771.
Delmar, Alex., History of the Precious Metals, 1880.
Deloche, M., History of French Statistics, 1874.
Denmark, Résumé Statistique, 1878.
Deparcieux, Durèe de la Vie, Paris, 1746.
De Thünen, Prices and Wages, Paris, 1851.
Dictionnaire de Commerce, Brussels, 1849.
Dictionary of Commerce, M'Culloch, London, 1834.
Dieterici, C., Statistics of Prussia, Berlin, 1836.
Dodge, J., Agriculture of United States, 1876.
Doubleday, Thos., Financial History of England, 1847.
Dowell, Stephen, History of Taxes, London, 1876.
Dubois, Count, History of French Statistics, Paris, 1858.
Ducpetiaux, Ed., Crime Statistics, Brussels, 1835.
Du Mesnil, Political Economy of the Ancients, Paris, 1878.
Dun, John, British Banking, London, 1876.
Dupin, Ch., Industries of France, Paris, 1827.
Duval, Jules, History of Emigration, Paris, 1862.
Eaton, John, Statistics of Schools, New York, 1880.
Economic Journal, London, 1891.
Economist, The, London, 1843-90.
Economiste Français, Paris, 1873-90.
Eden, Sir Morton, History of the Poor, 1797.
Edmonds, I., Life-Tables, London, 1832.
Edwards, B., History of British Colonies, 1801.
Edwards, E., Public Libraries of Europe, London, 1849.
Edwards, H., Statistics of all Countries, 1872.
Egypt, Guide Annuaire, 1873.
Ellena, V., Statistics of Italian Industry, 1879.
Elliott, C. B., Statistics of United States, 1874.
Ellison, Thomas, Handbook of Cotton Trade, 1858.
Engel, Ernest, Steam, Food, &c., Berlin, 1878.
Espine, Marc, Swiss Death-Rates, 1843.
Esquirol, J., Statistics of Insane, Paris, 1835.
Evans, Morier, Facts and Figures, London, 1849.
Falbe, Statistics of Denmark, 1876.
Farr, Dr., Compendium of his Works, London, 1886.
Faucher, Leon, The Precious Metals, Paris, 1853.
Faure, F., Debts of Europe, Paris, 1887.
Fawcett, Henry, Political Economy, London, 1863.
Fawcett, W., Prices and Precious Metals, Chicago, 1877.
Fellows, Frank, The National Debt, London, 1873.
Fenn, Ch., On the Funds, London, 1838.
Ferraris, C., Gold Production since 1493, Rome, 1879.
Ferris, Finances of United States, 1867.
Ficker, A., Statistics of Austria, 1858.
Financial Reform Almanack, 1866-90.
Fleetwood, Bishop, Prices for Six Hundred Years, 1745.
Fletcher, Jos., Statistics of English Towns, 1842.
Fonblanque, A., Statistics of Great Britain, 1869.
Fordyce, W., History of Coal and Iron, 1860.
Forsell, C., Statistics of Sweden, Lubeck, 1835.
Fossick, W., Fifty Years of Iron Trade, 1883.
Foville, A., La France Actuelle, Paris, 1889.

France, Annuaire Statistique, 1878-90.
Franscini, S., Statistics of Switzerland, Geneva, 1855.
Fry, Danby, Local Taxes in England, 1846.
Fry, Joseph, History of Tithes, London, 1820.
Francis, John, History of Bank of England, 1847.
Garnier, Joseph, Economie Politique, Paris, 1848.
Garrido, F., Condition of Spain, Brussels, 1862.
Germany, Jahrbuch des Deutschen Reichs, Berlin.
Giffen, Dr., Essays on Finance, London, 1888.
Gilbart, James, Banking and Currency, London, 1866.
Gioja, M., Synopsis of Statistics, Turin, 1852.
Gladstone, W. E., Budgets of 1853-70, London, 1870.
Goschen, George, Theory of Foreign Exchanges, 1864.
Graunt, Capt., Vital Statistics, London, 1676.
Gray, Simon, Population since 1570, London, 1840.
Greece, Handbook at Paris Exhibition of 1878.
Guerry, A., Moral Statistics of France, Paris, 1833.
Guy, William, Public Health, London, 1874.
Guyot, Yves, Taxation in France, Paris, 1885.
Halliwell, Retrospect of Prices, London, 1852.
Hankey, Thomson, Principles of Banking, London, 1867.
Hassel, G., Statistique de l'Europe, Brussels, 1827.
Hawkins, F., Statistics of Diseases, London, 1829.
Haynes, John, British Textile Industries, London, 1715.
Hayter, H., Australian Statistics, Melbourne, 1890.
Health, Annual Report of Board of, 1858-89.
Hermann, F., Statistics of Bavaria, 1861.
Heuschling, X., Statistique de Belgique, 1838.
Hildebrand, B., Jahrbücher für Statistik, Jena, 1863.
Hoskyns, C., History of Agriculture, London, 1849.
Howard, F., Mineral Statistics of Great Britain, 1872.
Howell, Geo., Capital and Labour, London, 1878.
Hübner, Otto, Statistics of Nations, Leipzig, 1852.
Hull, Edward, Coal-Fields of Great Britain, London, 1881.
Hunt, Robert, Mineral Statistics of Great Britain, 1882.
Hunter, W., Statistics of India, 1877.
Hunt's Merchant's Magazine, New York, 1845-70.
Ignatius, C., Statistics of Finland, 1877.
India, Statistical Abstract, published yearly.
Ireland, Thom's Directory, Dublin, annual.
Italy, Annuario Statistico, Rome, 1878-90.
Ivernois, Sir Francis, Vital Statistics, Paris, 1836.
Jacob, Wm., The Precious Metals, London, 1831.
Jeans, J., Iron and Steel Trade Annual, 1879-89.
Jevons, Stanley, Money and Exchange, London, 1875.
Journal des Economistes, Paris, 1849-90.
Juraschek, Ubersichten, Vienna, 1890.
Kane, Sir R., Resources of Ireland, Dublin, 1844.
Kauffmann, R., French Divorces, Leipzig, 1882.
Keleti, C., Official Statistics of Hungary, 1869-85.
Kiaer, A., Statistics of Shipping, Christiania, 1881.
Körösi, Joseph, Statistics of Cities, Paris, 1876.
Kolb, G., Handbook of Nations, London, 1880.
Kummer, M., Statistics of Switzerland, 1879.
Laborde, A., Statistical View of Spain, Paris, 1809.
Lalor, John, Money and Morals, New York, 1852.
Lang, —, Statistics of Hungary, Buda-Pesth, 1885.
Laveleye, Emile, Le Marché Monetaire, Paris, 1865
Lavergne, Leonce, Economie Rurale, Paris, 1847.
Lavigne, Ger., Spain and Portugal, Paris, 1883.
Leber, C., Wealth in the Middle Ages, Paris, 1847.
Legoyt, Alf., On Suicide, Paris, 1881.
Leplay, F., Les Ouvriers Européens, Paris, 1855.
Leroy-Beaulieu, P., Science des Finances, Paris, 1879.
Leslie, Cliffe, Land Systems of Countries, London, 1870.
Levasseur, E., Tables of Population, Paris, 1881.
Levi, Leone, History of British Commerce, London, 1882.
Liverpool, Lord, On Currency, new edition, 1880.
Lloyd's Register of Shipping, London, 1890.
Local Taxation in United Kingdom, Annual Abstract.
Longstaff, Studies in Statistics, London, 1891.
Lorenz, S., Industries of Austria, Vienna, 1873.
Lowe, Joseph, Agriculture and Trade of England, 1823.
Loua, Toussaint, La France Sociale, Paris, 1888.

Lunacy, Annual Report of Commissioners, 1854–89.
Mabson, R., History of the British Funds, 1873.
M'Culloch, J. R., Statistical Account of Great Britain.
M'Gregor, John, Commerce of Nations, 1836.
M'Leod, Henry, Theory of Banking, London, 1866.
MacPherson, David, Annals of Commerce, London, 1805.
MacQueen, James, Statistics of British Empire, 1836.
Maestri, P., Statistique d'Italie, Rome, 1871.
Malchus, C., Staatenkunde von Europe, Stuttgart, 1826.
Malte-Brun, Geographical Dictionary, Venice, 1827.
Malthus, T. R., Principles of Population, London, 1817.
Mandello, Statistics of Hungary, Buda, 1890.
Marshall, Prof., Economics of Industry, London, 1879.
Mason, Shaw, Statistical Survey of Ireland, Dublin, 1819.
Mausolas, Alexander, Statistics of Greece, Athens, 1872.
Mayr, George, Statistical Studies, Munich, 1877.
Meidinger, H., Iron and Coal of Germany, Gotha, 1857.
Mensi, Finances of Austria, Vienna, 1890.
Messedaglia, A., Sistema Monetario, Rome, 1883.
Mill, James, Political Economy, London, 1824.
Mill, John S., Principles of Economy, London, 1848.
Molinari, J., Economy of Nineteenth Century, Paris, 1880.
Monnier, Al., History of Poor-Relief, Paris, 1856.
Moreau, César, Retrospects of Commerce, London, 1827.
Moreau de Jonnes, Statistics of Spain, Paris, 1834.
Morpurgo, E., Condition of Friendly Societies, Rome, 1878.
Morselli, E., Statistics of Suicide, Milan, 1879.
Neison, F., Vital Statistics, London, 1857.
Neumann Spallart, Ubersichten, Vienna, 1883.
Newmarch, William, Various Pamphlets, 1831–71.
Nicolai, Statistics of Belgium, Brussels, 1886.
Noble, John, Incidence of Taxation, London, 1870.
North, Dudley, Discourses on Trade, London, 1691.
Northcote, Stafford, British Finances, London, 1862.
Norway, Annuaire Statistique, 1879.
Oddy, Jepson, European Commerce, London, 1805.
Overstone, Lord, Economical Tracts, London, 1859.
Palgrave, R., Local Taxation, Statistical Society, 1871.
Pantaleoni, Richezza d'Italia, Rome, 1884.
Parieu, F., Histoire des Impôts, Paris, 1857.
Parnell, Henry, Financial Reform, London, 1831.
Patterson, R., Economy of Capital, London, 1865.
Pereire, Isaac, Système des Banques, Paris, 1866.
Perier, Casimir, Finances et Politique, Paris, 1863.
Pery, Gerard, Statistics of Portugal, Lisbon, 1875.
Petty, Sir W., Political Arithmetic, London, 1687.
Picot, J., Statistique de la Suisse, Geneva, 1819.
Playfair, W., Statistical Tables of Europe, 1800.
Poole, B., Commerce and Manufactures, London, 1852.
Poor, Henry, Manual of Railroads, New York, 1874–89.
Porter, G. R., Progress of the Nation, London, 1836.
Porter, Robert P., Census of United States, 1880–90.
Portugal, Tableaux Statistiques, Lisbon, 1878.
Postlethwayt, James, History of Revenue, London, 1759.
Pouget, L., Insurance Companies, Paris, 1855.
Price, Bonamy, Principles of Currency, Oxford, 1869.
Purdy, F., Reports on Poor-Relief, London, 1860–74.
Quetelet, Ad., Vital Statistics, Brussels, 1829–31.
Rau, Chas., National Economy, Brussels, 1839.
Rau, S., Fighting Forces of Europe, Paris, 1880.
Rawson, Sir R., Pamphlets on Vital Statistics.
Redgrave, A., Labour and Wages, London, 1873.
Registrar-General's Reports for England, Scotland, and Ireland.
Ricardo, David, Principles of Economy, London, 1821.
Ripalda, Count, Statistics of Spain, 1861.
Roberts, Chas., Anthropometry, London, 1878.
Rogers, Thorold, History of Agriculture, London, 1866–88.
Roscher, Wm., Principles of Economy, Paris, 1857.
Rossi, P., Political Economy, Paris, 1854.

Roswag, C., The Precious Metals, Paris, 1865.
Russia, Annuaire, by A. Vesselovsky, 1883.
Sargant, W., Taxation, London, 1874.
Say, J. B., Economie Politique, Paris, 1814.
Say, Léon, Principles of Taxation, Paris, 1886.
Schnabel, George, General Statistics, Vienna, 1833.
Schnitzler, J., L'Empire de Russie, Paris, 1829.
Schubert, Staatskunde von Europa, Königsberg, 1839.
Sémenow, P., Statistik von Russland, 1865.
Seneuil, J., Free Banking, Paris, 1867.
Senior, Nassau, Essays on Wealth, Oxford, 1854.
Serrestori, Count, Statistica dell' Italia, Florence, 1839.
Seyd, Ernest, Foreign Exchanges, London, 1868.
Seyd, Richard, Record of Bankruptcy, London, 1865–76.
Sinclair, Sir John, Statistics of Scotland, Edinburgh, 1799.
Smith, Adam, Wealth of Nations, Oxford, 1869.
Soetbeer, Precious Metals, Berlin, 1888.
Sommer, Johann, Statistics of Austria, 1839.
Sowray, John, Statistical Diagrams, 1600–1850.
Spackman, W., Statistical Tables of Great Britain, 1842.
Spallart, see Neumann Spallart.
Spain, Anuario Estadistico, Madrid, Official.
Statesman's Year-Book, London, 1864–90.
Statist, The, London, 1878–90.
Statistical Abstracts, British, Foreign, Colonial Annuals.
Statistical Society, Royal, Journal, 1834–90.
Stephanitz, Alex., Statistics of Russia, St. Petersburg, 1883
Stewart, Sir James, Trade and Industry, Dublin, 1770.
Stössel, J., Statistik von Schweiz, 1868.
Storch, Hen., Statistical Tables of Russia, Bâle, 1800.
Swank, J., Iron and Steel Statistics, New York, 1881–88.
Tait, Lawson, Hospital Death-Rates, London, 1877.
Tate's Modern Cambist, London, 1880.
Tayler, W., History of Taxation, 1853.
Tennant, Chas., The People's Blue Book, London, 1872.
Thorburn, Thomas, Scotch Statistics, Edinburgh, 1853.
Thurmann, Bibliotheca Statistica, 1701.
Thurnam, John, Statistics of Insanity, London, 1845.
Tooke, Thomas, History of Prices, London, 1824–56.
Townsend, Joseph, Condition of Spain, London, 1792.
Tozer, Wealth and Wages, Cambridge, 1838.
Tucker, G., Industries of United States, Philadelphia, 1837.
Tuckett, J. D., History of Working Classes, London, 1846.
United States, Statistical Abstract, published yearly.
Uruguay, Résumé Statistique, Paris, 1889.
Vesselovsky, A., Statistics of Russia, 1873–89.
Viebahn, Statistics of Germany, 1856.
Visschers, Caisses d'Epargne, 1861.
Vitu, Aug., Finances of Nations, Paris, 1864.
Waghorn, Railways and Canals, Manchester, 1890.
Wagner, H., Statistics of Population, Berlin, 1880.
Wakefield, Statistical Account of Ireland, Dublin, 1812.
Walford, Cornelius, Insurance Cyclopedia, London, 1878.
Walker, Francis, Statistical Atlas of United States, 1874.
Walras, Léon, Economie Politique, Lausanne, 1874.
Wappaeus, Dr., International Statistics, Hanover, 1865.
Warden, Statistics of United States, Edinburgh, 1819.
Waterston, W., Manual of Commerce, 1863.
Whittaker's Almanac, London, 1868–90.
Whitworth, Sir Chas., Retrospect of Prices, London, 1768.
Wilson, James, Capital and Banking, London, 1859.
Wirth, Max, Statistics of Switzerland, 1868.
Wolowski, Louis, Études de Statistique, Paris, 1848.
Worms, Emile, Histoire du Zollverein, Paris, 1874.
Wright, Carroll, Marriage and Divorce, Washington, 1889.
Young, Arthur, Travels in Ireland and France, 1779–89.
Young, E., Wages and Expenditure, Washington, 1873.
Yvernès, Em., Judicial Statistics, Paris, 1876.
Zedlitz, Statistics of Prussia, 1836.
Zimmermann, Edward, Political Survey of Europe, 1787.

SUPPLEMENTAL LIST OF BOOKS OF REFERENCE

Agriculture in Germany, Berlin, 1898.
   ,,   in Austria, Vienna, 1897.
American Economic Journal, New York, 1898.
Annuario Italiano, Rome, 1898.
Ayres, H., Finances of Nations, London, 1857.
Babbage, Ch., Economy of Machinery, London, 1832.
Baden-Powell, Industrial Ireland, London, 1898.
Bailly, Histoire Financière, Paris, 1830.
Bastable, Prof., Public Finance, London, 1895.
Besobrasoff, Economie de la Russie, St. Petersburg, 1886.
Bickford, Greece under King George, London, 1893.
Biedermann, Precious Metals, Berlin, 1898.
Block, Maurice, Science Economique, Paris, 1890.
Blunden, G., Local Taxation, London, 1895.
Bodio, Cav., Movimento Economico, Rome, 1891.
Booth, Charles, Life and Labour, London, 1897.
Bowley, Arthur, England's Trade, London, 1893.
Brabrook, E., Provident Societies, London, 1898.
Bremner, D., Industries of Scotland, Edinburgh, 1869.
British Economic Journal, London, 1898.
Burdett, Hospitals and Charities, London, 1898.
Canada, Year-Book, Ottawa, 1898.
Cannan, Ed., Production and Distribution, London, 1893.
Cantillon, Richard, Essays (new ed.), Boston, 1892.
Carnegie, A., Triumphant Democracy, London, 1886.
Census Compendium, United States, Washington, 1897.
Chisholm, George, Gazetteer of World, London, 1895.
Cobden's Works, by Mallet, London, 1878.
Cohen, F., Les Impôts de l'Europe, Paris, 1865.
Cohn, G., National Economy, Stuttgart, 1898.
Co-operative Societies of Europe, London, 1898.
Coste, A., Salaire des Travailleurs, Paris, 1890.
Cunningham, W., English Industry, London, 1896.
Daire, M, Les Grands Economistes, Paris, 1851.
Dawson, J. H., Stat. History of Scotland, Edin., 1853.
Delmar, Alex., Monetary Systems, London, 1895.
Dictionnaire de Commerce, Paris, 1898.
Dictionnaire d'Economie Politique, Paris, 1892.
Dodd, Geo., British Manufactures, London, 1845.
Economic Review, London, 1898.
Farrer, Lord, Studies in Currency, London, 1898.
Faucher, Leon, Mélanges d'Economie, 1856.
Fisher, Book of the World, New York, 1850.
Foreign Trade Competition, Blue-Book, London, 1898.
Gabaglio, Antonio, Teoria della Statistica, Milan, 1888.
Garcke, Emile, Electrical Manual, London, 1897.
Gorsse, H., edition of Fourier, Paris, 1846.
Goulichambaroff, Trade of World, St. Petersburg, 1898.
Griffith, S. H., British Iron Trade, London, 1873.
Guillard, A., Démographie Comparée, Paris, 1855.
Hall, H., Customs Revenues of England, London, 1892.
Hamilton, R., National Debt, London, 1814.
Haupt, Otto, Arbitrages, Paris, 1894.
Hazell's Annual, London, 1899.
Hirschberg, Dr., Condition of Working Classes, 1897.
Hole, James, National Railways, London, 1893.
Homan's Cyclopædia of Commerce, New York, 1858.
Horton, S. D., Currency, London, 1887.
Houghton, J., Trades and Husbandry, London, 1728.
Howell, George, Trade Unionism, London, 1892.
Hübner, Otto, Statistical Tables, Leipzig, 1893.
Huskisson, Currency Questions, London, 1831.
James, J., History of Manufactures, London, 1851.
Jeans, Stephen, Waterways and Transport, London, 1890.
Keltie, Dr., Partition of Africa, London, 1895.
Körösi, Joseph, Vital Statistics, Buda-Pesth, 1897.
Kowalewski, Russian Industries, Leipzig, 1898.
Latzina, Argentine Statistics, Buenos Ayres, 1898.
Lavergne, L., Les Economistes Français, Paris, 1870.
Lavollée, René, Classes Ouvrières, Paris, 1896.
Leroy, Beaulieu, Economie Politique, Paris, 1896.

Leroy, Beaulieu, Répartition des Richesses, Paris, 1881.
Levasseur, Em., France et ses Colonies, Paris, 1893.
Lichtenstern, Austrian Statistics, Vienna, 1805.
Lindsay, W., History of Commerce, London, 1874.
M'Arthur, J., Finances of 18th Century, London, 1801.
Macleod, Dunning, History of Economics, London, 1896.
   ,,   ,,   Indian Currency, London, 1898.
Madoz, P., España y Colonias, Madrid, 1850.
Marshall, Alfred, Principles of Economics, London, 1895.
Martin, Fred., History of Insurance, London, 1876.
Meusel, J., Manual of Statistics, Leipzig, 1782.
Milner, Alfred, England in Egypt, London, 1893.
Molinari, G., Mélanges d'Economie, Paris, 1848.
Mongredien, Aug., History of Free Trade, London, 1897.
Mortimer, Thos., Dictionary of Commerce, London, 1810.
Moxon, Thomas, English Banking, Manchester, 1897.
Necker, Finances de la France, Paris, 1784.
Neymarck, A., Valeurs Mobilières, Paris, 1897.
Nicholls, G., History of the Poor Law, London, 1856.
Nicholson, Shield, Political Economy, London, 1893.
Nimmo, J., Internal Commerce, Washington, 1891.
Noel, O., Histoire du Commerce, Paris, 1891.
O'Heguerty, Commerce and Navigation, Paris, 1757.
O'Meard, J., Municipal Taxation, London, 1894.
Ozenne, Statistical Atlas, Paris, 1878.
Palgrave, Inglis, Dic. of Polit. Economy, London, 1898.
Parr, Greswell, Growth of Brit. Colonies, London, 1898.
Pays Bas, Annuaire Statistique, Hague, 1898.
Peto, Morton, Incidence of Taxation, London, 1863.
Pittar, M., British Customs Tariffs, London, 1897.
Price, L. L., Hist. of Political Economy, London, 1891.
Probyn, Land Tenure, London, 1876.
Quarterly Journal of Economics, New York, 1898.
Quinn, M. J., Banking in England, London, 1833.
Rae, John, Contemporary Socialism, London, 1891.
Raffalovitch, A., Marché Financier, Paris, 1898.
Reid, Lloyd, Taxpayers' Rights, London, 1898.
Rogers, Thorold, Industrial History, London, 1892.
Ruding, R., Coinage of Great Britain, London, 1840.
Ruegg, Alfred, Employers' Liability, London, 1898.
Sandelin, A., Répertoire d'Economie, Hague, 1848.
Sargant, W. S., Essays on Manufactures, London, 1859.
Savary, J., Dictionary of Commerce, London, 1751.
Schloss, David, Industrial Remuneration, London, 1898.
Schoenberg, G., Handbook of Polit. Econ., Tubingen, 1891.
Scrivener, History of Iron Trade, London, 1841.
Scrope, J., Political Economy, London, 1833.
Seyd, Richard, Statistics of Failures, London, 1898.
Shaw, W., History of Currency, London, 1895.
Shaw-Lefevre, Agrarian Tenures, London, 1893.
Sinclair, Sir John, Revenues of Brit. Emp., London, 1804.
Simmonds, P. L., Science and Commerce, London, 1872.
   ,,   ,,   Handbook of Commerce, London, 1892.
Sismondi, S., Richesse Commerciale, Geneva, 1807.
   ,,   Economie Politique, Paris, 1837.
Sproule, Resources of Ireland, Dublin, 1853.
Stirling, Philosophy of Trade, Edinburgh, 1846.
Suisse, Annuaire Statistique, Berne, 1898.
Taylor, W. C., Modern Factory System, London, 1891.
Turgot's Works, edited by Daire, Paris, 1844.
Turquan, Victor, Statistique Pratique, Paris, 1891.
Ure's Dictionary of Arts, London, 1848.
Vidal, Répartition des Richesses, Paris, 1846.
Wade, J., England's Greatness, London, 1886.
Wagner, A., Science of Finance, Leipzig, 1890.
Walker, Francis, Wages Question, Boston, 1884.
Ward, J., Work and Wages, London, 1869.
Webb, Sydney, History of Trade Unions, London, 1894.
Williams, F. S., Our Iron Roads, London, 1888.
Willoughby, W. F., Working Men's Insur., N. York, 1898.
Wright, Carroll, Industrial Evolution, New York, 1895.

INDEX